Shakespeare
and the Classical Tradition

Shakespeare and the Classical Tradition

An Annotated Bibliography
1961–1991

compiled by
Lewis Walker

LONDON AND NEW YORK

Published 2002 by Routledge
2 Park Square, Milton Park, Abingdon, Oxon OX14 4RN
52 Vanderbilt Avenue, New York, NY 10017

First issued in paperback 2018

Routledge is an imprint of the Taylor & Francis Group, an informa business

Copyright © 2002 by Lewis Walker

All rights reserved. No part of this book may be reprinted or reproduced or utilised in any form or by any electronic, mechanical, or other means, now known or hereafter invented, including photocopying and recording, or in any information storage or retrieval system, without permission in writing from the publishers.

Notice:
Product or corporate names may be trademarks or registered trademarks, and are used only for identification and explanation without intent to infringe.

Library of Congress Cataloging-in-Publication Data

Shakespeare and the classical tradition / edited by Lewis Walker.
    p. cm.
    Includes bibliographical references (p.) and indexes.
    ISBN 0-8240-6697-9 (hardbound: alk. paper)
    1. Shakespeare, William, 1564-1616—Knowledge—Literature. 2. Shakespeare, William, 1564-1616—Knowledge—Greece. 3. Shakespeare, William, 1564-1616—Knowledge—Rome. 4. Classicism—England—History—16th century. 5. Classicism—England—History—17th century. 6. Classical literature—Appreciation—England. 7. English literature—Classical influences. 8. Civilization, Classical, in literature. 9. Greece—In literature. 10. Rome—In Literature. I. Walker, John Lewis. H. Title.

PR3037 .S55 2001
822.3'3—dc21   00-061043

Design and typography: Jack Donner

ISBN 13: 978-1-138-87954-6 (pbk)
ISBN 13: 978-0-8240-6697-0 (hbk)

To Julia Waite Walker
and
In Memory of
John Lewis Walker, Jr.

Contents

Introduction	ix
Abbreviations for Journals and Series	xxv
Editorial Abbreviations	xxx
Abbreviations for the Titles of Shakespeare's Works	xxxi
General Bibliographies, Surveys, and Reference Works (Items 0001—0066)	1
General Works (Items 0067–1154)	17
Individual Works	
All's Well That Ends Well (Items 1155–1158)	321
Antony and Cleopatra (Items 1159–1530)	322
As You Like It (Items 1531–1564)	410
The Comedy of Errors (Items 1565–1589)	417
Coriolanus (Items 1590–1752)	422
Cymbeline (Items 1753–1780)	461
Hamlet (Items 1781–1899)	467
Henry IV, Part 1 (Items 1900–1910)	493
Henry IV, Part 2 (Items 1911–1916)	495
Henry V (Items 1917–1933)	496
Henry VI, Part 1 (Items 1934–1935)	499
Henry VI, Part 2 (Items 1936–1937)	500
Henry VI, Part 3 (Items 1937a–1937b)	500
Henry VIII (Items 1938–1939)	500
Julius Caesar (Items 1939a–2136)	501
King John (Item 2137)	548
King Lear (Items 2138–2183)	549
A Lover's Complaint (Items 2184–2184a)	558

Love's Labor's Lost (Items 2185–2201)	558
Macbeth (Items 2202–2238)	562
Measure for Measure (Items 2239–2246)	570
The Merchant of Venice (Items 2247–2262)	571
The Merry Wives of Windsor (Items 2263–2268)	575
A Midsummer Night's Dream (Items 2268a–2318)	577
Much Ado About Nothing (Items 2319–2324)	588
Othello (Items 2325–2352)	589
The Passionate Pilgrim (Item 2353)	595
Pericles (Items 2354–2373)	595
The Phoenix and Turtle (Items 2374–2389)	599
The Rape of Lucrece (Items 2390–2440)	602
Richard II (Items 2440a–2452)	615
Richard III (Items 2453–2460)	617
Romeo and Juliet (Items 2461–2476)	619
Sonnets (Items 2477–2530)	624
The Taming of the Shrew (Items 2531–2543)	634
The Tempest (Items 2544–2609)	637
Timon of Athens (Items 2610–2708)	654
Titus Andronicus (Items 2709–2789a)	675
Troilus and Cressida (Items 2790–3074)	695
Twelfth Night (Items 3075–3087)	756
The Two Gentlemen of Verona (Items 3088–3090)	759
The Two Noble Kinsmen (Items 3090a–3104)	760
Venus and Adonis (Items 3105–3169)	764
The Winter's Tale (Items 3170–3210)	776
Index of the Names of Modern Scholars, Including Authors, Editors, and Compilers	787
Index of Names of Shakespeare's Works	811
Index of Subjects	820

Introduction

"The effect of Greek and Roman literature upon the modern literatures of Europe is no new theme," wrote James Hutton in 1935. "It is, in fact, a theme that must be endlessly worked out by those who profess to make the modern literatures the object of serious study" (ix). It is significant that Hutton, a distinguished classicist, prefaced these remarks to a study of the epigrams from the Greek Anthology as they had been transmitted by "middlemen" in Italy through the year 1800. It is further worth noting that Hutton regarded his study as the necessary prelude for an investigation of the Greek Anthology and English literature. His formulation, if adapted to the study of Shakespeare, is richly suggestive. The relationship of Shakespeare's works to the classical literatures is indeed no new theme; for the greater part of the past century, and especially during the period covered by this bibliography, it has been intensely studied. One of the key aspects of such endeavor, as Hutton's example illustrates for the Greek Anthology, has been to understand the nature of mediation: What, for example, were the literary sources that stimulated Shakespeare to treat Platonic themes? Or what political issues in Elizabethan society sent him to Greek myth for analogues? Most important is Hutton's idea of the process involved in this enterprise of studying adaptation; to use his language, we are faced with the endless working out of the relationship between Shakespeare and the classical cultures. Each new attempt to fix the nature of the transaction is focused through a different lens, which is both a burden and an opportunity. We will probably never settle all (or even a few) of the questions about Shakespeare's use of the classics, and new questions are constantly being raised. But the matter is too important to be ignored; in fact, we are compelled to treat it repeatedly.

For the bibliographer who would trace scholarly efforts in this area, its dynamism creates many difficulties. To raise only one of them: How far does one go in tracing classical influences through intermediaries? Is it appropriate, for example, to include scholarship on Chaucer's version of the classical world as it affects Shakespeare (see Donaldson, items 0325 and 2854), as I have done in many cases? Fortunately, anyone working in this field has an exemplary model, John Velz's *Shakespeare and the Classical Tradition: A Critical Guide to Commentary, 1660–1960* (item 0058), a ground-breaking work that admirably combines precision and flexibility. In his *Guide*, in two authoritative essays on modern views of Shakespeare's classicism (items 0057 and 0059), and in numerous critical articles, especially on *Julius Caesar* (for example, item 2128), Velz has done more than anyone else to define the subject. One need not follow him in all matters of organization or coverage to benefit from his remarkable achievement.

This bibliography attempts to provide a reasonably comprehensive view of scholarship on the subject of Shakespeare and the classics published in the period 1961–1991. I have confined myself to works in English and have included books, articles, chapters in books, essays in collections, dissertations (for which most of the the entries are based on the abstracts in *Dissertation Abstracts* or *Dissertation Abstracts International*), certain bibliographies and reference works, and some editions. In general, I have excluded theatrical criticism, materials primarily intended for students, introductions to collections of essays, reviews, correspondence (though there are a few exceptions in each of these categories), considerations of the authorship question, and works that I have not been able to see. There are three sections to the Bibliography: 1. General Bibliographies, Surveys, and Reference Works; 2. General Works; 3. Individual Works, with a subsection for each of Shakespeare's works. Within each section or, in the case of Individual Works, subsection, entries are arranged alphabetically by author. I have attempted to track, through cross-references, important articles published within the period of coverage that were reprinted or revised within the period. An example is John Bayley's 1964 article on *Troilus and Cressida* (item 2806), which is cross-referenced to its revision as part of another article in 1975 (item 2807), which is cross-referenced in turn to its inclusion in a 1976 book (item 0138). In the same way, I have tried to follow the course of dissertations that became articles and/or books. An instance of this is the 1967 dissertation of J. L. Simmons on Shakespeare's Roman Plays (item 0981), which is cross-referenced to three derivative articles (items 0977, 1459, and 2101) and to the 1973 book that grew from it (item 0980). The other cross-references, with a few exceptions, relate items that directly address each other, as in the case of the articles on Platonism in the *Sonnets* by James Devereux (item 2483) and Charles Forker (item 2486) or the extensive *Times Literary Supplement* (*TLS*) correspondence about *Troilus and Cressida* in 1967. Since any piece of scholarship on more than one work is included in the General section, readers should consult the Works index for commentary on individual works that is not found in the subsections on those works.

The period of coverage saw an explosion of new editions of Shakespeare. In order to represent the achievements of editors throughout, I have included, in the appropriate subsections of Individual Works, the relevant individual volumes from the Pelican, the Signet Classic, the New Penguin, the Arden, the New Cambridge, and the Oxford. In most cases, the annotation deals only with the editor's introduction, but in some instances, there is also comment on notes elsewhere in the volume (as with Harold Jenkins's 1982 *Hamlet*, item 1835) or on appendixes (as with Kenneth Palmer's 1981 *Troilus and Cressida*, item 2985). In the General Works section, there are separate

Introduction   xi

annotations for four collected editions: the Pelican (item 0496), the Signet Classic (item 0123), the Riverside (item 0362), and the third edition of Bevington (item 0159). Quotes from Shakespeare's works within annotations are to the act, scene, and line numbers given in Bevington's third edition of *The Complete Works*. When the title of an item includes act, scene, and line numbers that differ from those of Bevington, I have placed a citation to his edition in square brackets in the text of the annotation.

Classics, classical literature, classical culture, the classical tradition: All of these concepts have reference to an objective reality that we perceive in the ancient worlds of Greece and Rome up through the fifth or sixth century A.D. But so much depends on our way of seeing, and this was revolutionized during the period covered in the bibliography. St. Augustine, whose rejection of paganism might previously have disqualified him from inclusion in a bibliography such as this, plays a significant role in certain works whose purpose is to appraise Shakespeare's portrayal of Rome (Battenhouse, item 0133; Simmons, item 0980). I have noted M. C. Howatson's comment in the preface to *The Concise Oxford Companion to Classical Literature* that "from the third century A.D. there are entries for Christian writers who were important from a classical viewpoint" (v), and have been on the alert for modern scholars who refer to these writers with regard to Shakespeare. Examples can be seen in the discussions of Boethius in studies of Fortune and Elizabethan tragedy by Frederick Kiefer (item 0635) and of music in Shakespeare's tragedies by F. W. Sternfeld (item 1021). Formerly neglected areas in both classical and Shakespearean studies came to the fore during the period covered, resulting in new "topics" like the reclaiming of the feminine in Renaissance literature through consideration of humanist Neoplatonism and the Eleusinian mysteries (Davies, item 0307). The increasingly interdisciplinary nature of much Shakespearean criticism has given the classics a more substantial presence in certain types of studies, like those using the psychoanalytical approach (see Ebel's article on *Julius Caesar*, item 1988) and those concerned with art (Bowers, item 0179; Hunt, item 0576).

Among Shakespeare's individual works, I have given most comprehensive coverage to the following: *Titus Andronicus, Julius Caesar, Antony and Cleopatra, Coriolanus, Troilus and Cressida, Timon of Athens, Venus and Adonis*, and *The Rape of Lucrece*. Each of these works directly re-creates a classical whole; therefore, the eight relevant subsections attempt to include all important critical assessments, whether or not they directly address matters of classical influence. During the period of coverage, there are a number of efforts to extend or redefine the category of Shakespeare's Roman (Miola, item 0759a; Siegel, item 0973) and Greek (Hanna, item 0489) works. In view of these, and considering the intensified interest in the comedies and romances and their relationship to the late classical world (Dean, item 0311; Comito, item 0284; Gesner, item 0434; and Mowat, item 0769), I have been especially attentive to scholarship on the following quasi-, pseudo-, or semi-classical plays: *The Comedy of Errors, A Midsummer Night's Dream, Pericles*,

Cymbeline, The Winter's Tale, and *The Two Noble Kinsmen.* Although the classical imprint is less distinct in these works than in the first group of eight, their repeated inclusion by scholars in categories associated with the classics ensures that they are well-represented.

The period covered here is one of great energy and promise in the study of Shakespeare. The bibliography has been enriched by significant scholarship published in several journals established during this time, including *Classical and Modern Literature, Hamlet Studies, Res Publica Litterarum: Studies in the Classical Tradition, Shakespeare Studies* (Japan), *Shakespeare Studies* (U. S.), *Shakespeare Yearbook, Studies in English Literature, 1500–1900,* and *The Upstart Crow.* In addition, during the 1960s and 1970s Geoffrey Bullough completed his massive *Narrative and Dramatic Sources of Shakespeare* (items 0008, 0009, 0010, 0011, and 0012). Feminist studies like Jeanne Addison Roberts's *The Shakespearean Wild* (item 0901) and works of new historicism or cultural materialism like Jonathan Dollimore's *Radical Tragedy* (item 0324) depend, in different ways, on revisioning of Shakespeare's absorption or reflection of the classics.

The first section, General Bibliographies, Surveys, and Reference Works, describes the research tools that I have found most helpful in compiling this bibliography. Foremost among these is the annual bibliography published by *Shakespeare Quarterly* (item 0049), which has been a reliable guide in preliminary screening of potential entries. I have made up my list of abbreviations for journals and other sources and for the works of Shakespeare from the "Master List of Sources and Abbreviations" included in each issue of the *Shakespeare Quarterly* bibliography through 1991. Other important works include the annual "Bibliography of the Classical Tradition" in *Classical and Modern Literature* (item 0007), whose two parts juxtapose classical works with the post-classical works to which scholars have related them; Hanne Carlsen's bibliography on the classical tradition in English literature (item 0013), which has a section on Shakespeare; and Craig Kallendorf's bibliography of Latin influences on English literature (item 0028), also with a section on Shakespeare. There is broad consideration of scholarship on the intellectual context within which Shakespeare wrote in W. R. Elton's bibliography (item 0019); treatment of the study of Renaissance rhetoric in A. C. Hamilton's survey (item 0022) and Winifred Horner's bibliography (item 0025); and narrower focus on the influence of individual authors in Frederick Kiefer's bibliographies on Senecan influence (items 0030 and 0031) and Kallendorf's survey of Virgil scholarship (item 0029). Long essay reviews of yearly contributions to Shakespeare scholarship appear in *Shakespeare Survey* (item 0066), *Studies in English Literature* (item 0044), and *The Year's Work in English Study* (item 0053). As reference works, I have placed in this section the three-volume set on all aspects of Shakespeare edited by John Andrews (item 0002) and the last five volumes of Bullough's collection of Shakespeare's sources.

Introduction   xiii

The General Works section contains material on a great range of topics. There are, within the period, a number of biographies, most of which make some attempt to explain the classical content of Shakespeare's schooling and survey his works (Halliday, item 0483; Levi, item 0685; Quennell, item 0869; and Rowse, item 0914). Perhaps more concerned with critical appraisal of Shakespeare's art and its classical connections are Philip Edwards (item 0350) and Russell Fraser (item 0401). S. Schoenbaum's *Documentary Life* (item 0938) provides, among other things, a thorough and concise summary of the curriculum in the schools of Shakespeare's time.

Shakespeare's idea of Rome generates much discussion; the most comprehensive analysis comes from Robert Miola (item 0759a). Scholars put forth different positions about just which works should be admitted to the Roman canon. Fairly standard treatments of *Romanitas* (Thomas, item 1047; Weightman, item 1101) admit four Roman plays: *Titus Andronicus, Julius Caesar, Antony and Cleopatra,* and *Coriolanus*. David Bergeron (item 1754) would add *Cymbeline*, while Charles Martindale and Michelle Martindale (item 0721) would exclude *Titus* and *Cymbeline*. Clearly, the Roman plays and poems are central to any consideration of Shakespeare and politics (Kayser and Lettieri, item 0622; Leggatt, item 0679; Powell, item 0857), and the spiritual condition of Shakespeare's Romans attracts much study (Kranz, item 0656). Ernest Schanzer (item 0932) designates *Julius Caesar* and *Antony and Cleopatra* as problem plays evoking a divided response.

I have annotated some surveys of all or nearly all of Shakespeare's works to sample relatively brief commentary on classical works as part of a larger project. Examples are Marilyn French's feminist reading of the canon (item 0405), A. P. Rossiter's series of lectures (item 0909), and John Wain's guide for playgoers (item 1085). During the period of coverage, traditional groupings of the plays are connected with the classics in a variety of ways. The Greek qualities of the tragedies have been noted by Richard Sewall (item 0953), and T. McAlindon's notion of tragic contrariety (item 0729) is derived from classical sources. The comedies receive attention in terms of their indebtedness to Aelius Donatus (Snyder, item 1003), to the works of Plautus and Terence (Hosley, item 0556; Bruster, item 0214), and to the five-act structure of classical comedy (Mincoff, item 0759). In his book on Shakespeare and the traditions of comedy, Leo Salingar (item 0923) distinguishes between direct and indirect (through Italian comedy) influence of the classics on Shakespearean comedy. An article by Peter Davison (item 0309) draws parallels between Athenian Old Comedy and two works of Shakespeare. Investigations of the history plays often uncover classical roots. Robert Torrance (item 1056) examines Falstaff in the light of various classical manifestations of the comic hero. Parts 1 and 2 of *Henry IV* and *Henry V* can be seen as "an epic of education" like the *Cyropaedia* of Xenophon (Hawkins, item 0517), and David Riggs (item 0894) argues that Shakespeare, in composing the three parts of *Henry VI*, had classical examplars of heroic leadership in mind. Martin Mueller (item 0772) notes that Shakespeare, in the spirit of humanism, chooses for his English and Roman history plays subjects that are equivalent to those of Greek tragedy, following its pattern but not necessarily its story. The romances receive extensive treatment. In addition to works already mentioned, there is a book by Hallett Smith (item 0997) and an article by T. McAlindon tracing Greek romance through the Middle Ages to Shakespeare (item 0730). The narrative poems are often grouped with plays in discussions like Linda Woodbridge's article (item 1141) on the human body as an image of society in Elizabethan England. They do, however, receive book-length treatment in Clark Hulse's study of the Elizabethan minor epic (item 0571).

A number of other themes or topics are emphasized in the scholarship covered in the General Works section. Philosophy, especially Neoplatonism, is treated as both an influence on Shakespeare and his age (Shumaker, item 0968, and as a subject in the plays (Soellner, items 1005 and 1006). Rhetoric (Vickers, item 1073; Heninger, item 0529), vocabulary (Garner, item 0430), and proverb lore (Smith, item 0993) all receive attention. Music, with its background in Boethian and Neoplatonic thought, is the focus of several important studies, most notably two volumes on Shakespeare's use of music by John Long (items 0699 and 0700). The study of myth is taken up by Herbert Weisinger (item 1106) and others. Some individual myths or classical stories are considered as follows: Actaeon (Viswanathan, item 1077), Daedalus/Icarus (Rudd, item 0918), Dido (Roberts-Baytop, item 0902), Hecuba (Westney, item 1115), Hercules (Waith, item 1086), and Philomela (Thompson, item 1048). Shakespeare's use of the neoclassical idea of unity of time in drama is explored by David Riggs (item 0892) and Ernest Schanzer (item 0933). Much new work on issues of gender and sexuality is heavily dependent on examination of Shakespeare's interaction with the classical tradition, as evidenced in studies of androgyny (Whittier, item 1126), masculine identity (Kahn, item 0614), and homosexuality (Smith, item 0987). Classical matters have even managed to insinuate themselves into a debate between I. A. Shapiro (item 0958) and Frances Yates (item 1149) about what Shakespeare's theater(s) looked like; and Hal Smith (item 0994) has investigated the question of the authenticity of classical costumes on the Elizabethan stage. Several stimulating comparisons of Shakespeare's tragedy to Greek drama, with little or no suggestion of influence, have been annotated, including books by Gerhard Kaiser (item 0615) and Adrian Poole (item 0853).

As might be expected, Ovid receives significant attention during this period as an influence on Shakespeare (Marsh, item 0720; Martindale and Martindale, item 0721; Velz, item 1071). There is some debate about Seneca. On the one hand, G. K. Hunter (items 0582 and 0583) finds that he is not important as a source for Elizabethan or Shakespearean tragedy; on the other, Robert Welch (item 1108) argues that Seneca opened for the Renaissance and for Shakespeare a new sense of fear at the human capacity for cruelty, and Jeannette White (item 1124) finds that the themes of revenge and

Introduction xv

madness in Seneca were especially suitable for dramatizing the concerns of Shakespeare and his contemporaries. In a series of articles and a book (item 1052), J. J. M. Tobin has made a case for the strong influence on Shakespeare of Apuleius's *The Golden Ass*. The *Historia Apollonii Regis Tyri* has been translated and contextualized for Renaissance studies by Elizabeth Archibald (item 0092).

The section on Individual Works begins with *All's Well That Ends Well*, which inspires studies of the Mars and Venus myth (Bergeron, item 1156) and of the Hephaistan tradition (Lecercle, item 1157).

Antony and Cleopatra has the greatest number of entries among the individual works. A great deal of the commentary centers on whether or not the play is a tragedy and, if it is a tragedy, what kind. In the view of one scholar, it lacks terror (Caputi, item 1210); according to another, its humor undercuts its claims to gravity (French, item 1271); for a third, it is a heroic drama closely related to tragedy (Krook, item 1354); to a fourth, it is the tragedy of dual protagonists (Lezberg, item 1363). Critics have frequently relied on myth as the basis for their readings, usually connecting Antony in some way with Hercules (Coates, item 1218). Leeds Barroll devotes lengthy essays (items 1172 and 1174) to characterization. In addition to *The Lives of the Noble Grecians and Romans*, Plutarch's essay "Of Isis and Osiris" is invoked as a source (Coppedge, item 1222; Fisch, item 1261). Paul Dean (item 1236) senses Ovidian tragedy in the play, while James Greene (item 1287) cites the episode of Dido and Aeneas from the *Aeneid* as a key to its study of androgyny, and Donna Hamilton (item 1296) sees more pervasive parallels to Virgil's noble lovers. G. P. Jones (item 1336) has seen in references to cross-dressing the imprint of the episode of Hercules and Omphale. As far as the love of the principals is concerned, some view it as transcendent or at least potentially so (Foakes, item 1266), while others (Frost, item 1273; Labriola, item 1356) regard it as decidedly earthbound. Psychoanalytic criticism is also in evidence, as in Constance Kuriyama's use of the myth of Isis to read the play as a version of the incest fantasy (item 1355). Christian or quasi-Christian interpretation comes from Andrew Fichter, who views the play's imperfect tragedy as the result of a network of Christian allusions (item 1260), and John Cutts, whose note (item 1230) likens Charmian to John the Baptist. From a feminist perspective, L. T. Fitz (item 1264) takes male critics to task for mythification of Cleopatra. There is considerable interest in the play's and its characters' self-conscious theatricality (Bushman, item 1207; Holderness, item 1314). Other windows of interpretation include Elizabethan ideas of Roman history (Kalmey, item 1341); Platonism (Birkinshaw, item 1185); *Henry V* as a structural model (Emrys Jones, item 1334); medieval saints' legends (Higgins, item 1311); and language (Doran, item 1239; Hume, item 1323).

As You Like It attracts commentary on Jaques' speech on the seven ages of man as it parallels and diverges from Proclus's paradigm (Allen, item 1531) and as it recalls and distorts Ptolemy's version (Bradford, item 1535). As might be expected, Shakespeare's exploitation of the pastoral mode prompts a great deal of analysis: The play's pastoralism is seen as dialectical (Irot, item 1544), socially conciliatory (Kronenfeld, item 1549), and educative (Scoufos, item 1556). Criticism has been particularly concerned to examine emblematic, symbolic, and allegorical aspects (Bath, item 1532; Doebler, item 1538; Fortin, item 1541; Knowles, item 1547), which inevitably involve themselves in locating classical prototypes and in scrutinizing the ways in which they were transmitted to Shakespeare. Ovid is seen as an influence, mediated through Golding (Hankins, item 1543) or Lodge (Kaul, item 1545). The appearance of the New Variorum edition (ed. Knowles, item 1546) is also noteworthy.

The compositional elements of *The Comedy of Errors* receive exhaustive analysis by T. W. Baldwin (item 1567), who has several chapters on the influence of Plautus. Others deal with various aspects of the Plautine connection (Brooks, item 1571; Grivelet, item 1577; Long, item 1583). K. M. Briggs (item 1570) provides background, including much classical material, for ideas of witchcraft; Robert Heilman (item 1578) studies the play's transformation of the elements of farce; and Charles Garton (item 1576) is concerned with centaur-like ambiguity.

In discussing *Coriolanus*, critics have been attracted to pschoanalytical readings dealing with hunger and aggression (Adelman, item 1590) and the phallus fantasy of Volumnia (Stoller, item 1731). The fable of the belly, its classical antecedents, and its connection with the body politic are considered by Andrew Gurr (item 1649) and D. G. Hale (item 1650). There are several important examinations of language (Van Dyke, item 1740; Calderwood, item 1618; Fish, item 1637). The play encourages investigators to find parallels between its events and the social circumstances of Jacobean England (Fortescue, item 1638; Zeeveld, item 1751). We can regard the version of Roman civilization in the play as essentially authentic, though anachronistic in detail (see Nuttall in General Works, item 0811) or as purposefully altered from Plutarch to reflect an awareness of the new voice of the people in the Parliament of Shakespeare's own time (Tennenhouse, item 1736). Speculations about sources have connected the play with Titus Livius (Barton, item 1596), Plutarch's *Life* of *Marcus Cato* (Chappell, item 1624), and Socrates (Goldfarb, item 1646).

As one of Shakespeare's late romances, *Cymbeline* is discussed in terms of Greek romance (Gesner, item 1759; Hoeniger, item 1762). The possibilities of considering it as a more or less Roman play are explored by David Bergeron (item 1754), Patricia Parker (item 1774), and Hugh Richmond (item 1775). Joan Carr (item 1755) and Marjorie Garber (item 1757) are concerned with the ways in which it reflects the kinds of thinking that create myth.

Hamlet inspires a number of short studies that connect it with Quintilian (Alexander, item 1784), Plautus's *Pseudolus* (Bruster, item 1794), Seneca's *Epistles* (Draudt, item 1809; Honigmann and West, item 1833), Plutarch's *Moralia* (Gaunt, item 1823), Alexander (Reedy, item 1868), and other classical material. More detailed analyses treat Orpheus (Findlay, item 1816), Hercules (Economou, item 1812), Orestes (Eckert, item 1811; Kott, item

Introduction xvii

1844), and Aeneas (Miola, item 1859). Fredson Bowers (item 1790) provides a good example of adapting Aristotle's formulae for tragic plot to the analysis of Elizabethan drama; Julia Reinhard (item 1869) views the divided tradition of Senecan drama used by Shakespeare in *Hamlet* as a sort of parallel to Freud's ambivalence about Hamlet's psyche; and Bridget Lyons (item 1850) goes back to Ovid and Plutarch to understand the iconography of Ophelia. Several critics focus on the pattern of revenge, its classical sources, and the ways in which Hamlet responds to it (Guilfoyle, item 1828; Leech, item 1845). Louise Schleiner (item 1876) argues for the influence on Shakespeare of Latinized Greek tragedy. The Arden *Hamlet* (ed. Jenkins, item 1835) also makes its appearance during this period.

As might be expected, the history plays account for relatively few of the annotations. However, the period yields some interesting items. For *Henry IV, Part 1*, there are discussions that see Falstaff's behavior as a satiric thrust at Platonism (Crawford, item 1903), Falstaff himself as a centaur (Stewart, item 1910), and Hotspur as a version of Turnus (Mueller, item 1909). Norman Council (item 1902) rejects the idea that Hal exhibits a sense of honor that exemplifies the Aristotelian mean between two extremes. In *Henry IV, Part 2*, James Black (item 1912) notes that allusions to Greece and Rome are used to evoke the memory of Hotspur (a true hero) and to characterize counterfeit soldiership. Ronald Berman (item 1918) argues that the hero of *Henry V* is a reconstruction of Plutarch's Alexander, while Robert Merrix (item 1927) finds that the Alexandrian references in the play help to satirize the king. In addition, Virgil's *Georgics* is proposed as an influence (Betts, item 1920; Gurr, item 1925); and Gary Taylor, in a new edition (item 1933), argues for the significant influence of Chapman's translation of the *Iliad*. The New Cambridge edition of *Henry VI, Part 1*, edited by Michael Hattaway (item 1934) notes how classical allusions are used to fashion Pucelle into a false myth of Astraea. *Henry VI, Part 2* is compared with the *Aeneid* and *The Fairie Queene* in terms of how each work uses the episode of Nisus and Euryalus to construct a narrative that breaches linear time (Caldwell, item 1936); and the influence of Tacitus is discerned in *Henry VI, Part 3* (Womersley, item 1937b). Ronald Berman (item 1938) maintains that *Henry VIII* is informed in part by the myth of Ceres and Proserpina.

The considerable number of entries for *Julius Caesar* includes many on the treatment of philosophy. Analyses of Stoicism consider its petrifying effect (Anson, item 1942), its notion of destiny (Crawford, item 1980), and its relevance to Brutus (Sacharoff, item 2096; Vawter, item 2121). Jean Auffret (item 1943) and Julian Rice (item 2088) detect more than one ancient philosophy in the play. Several scholars investigate the awareness in the play of new approaches to history (Burt, item 1965; Chang, item 1973). Psychoanalytic criticism is represented by an unfavorable portrait of Portia (Faber, item 1992), among other works. The uncertainty of self-knowledge is found to be a key motif in the play (Fortin, item 1997; Scott, item 2100). Ritualism in the play–its failure (Hager, item 2009) and its Christian intimations (Kaula, item 2029)— is an important theme. Illustrating the rich possibilities for source study, this subsection annotates a detailed comparison of the play to Plutarch's *Lives* (Green, item 2005); an exploration of the three Greek lives that Plutarch paralleled to the lives of Brutus, Caesar, and Antony (Homan, item 2022); an examination of Lucan's *Pharsalia* (Ronan, items 2090 and 2091); and discovery of parallels, echoes, or imitations of Cicero (Vawter, item 2120), Seneca (Velz, item 2125), and Euripides (Bryant, item 1962). Appropriately in this context, Robert Miola (item 2058) takes *Julius Caesar* as his test case for discussion of new approaches to source study.

For *King John*, the commentary is negligible, with a single entry (Braunmuller, item 2137).

Studies of *King Lear* focus, among other things, on the myth of Ixion (Andrews, item 2139; Fraser, item 2157; Hardison, item 2159). Other interests are the identity of Lear's philosopher (Butler, item 2146; Cutts, item 2151), the association of Goneril with the Amazons, and the prayers offered to pagan gods by a variety of characters (Williams, item 2183). There are several discussions of how Aristotle's idea of tragedy applies to the play (Blisset, item 2142; Bowers, item 2144; Nagarajan, item 2170).

Aside from John Kerrigan's comments in the introduction to his anthology on the classical background of the female complaint poem (item 2184) and Richard Underwood's prolegomena to an edition (item 2184a), there is nothing on *A Lover's Complaint*.

In *Love's Labor's Lost*, commentators have explored Neoplatonism (Goldstien, item 2191), the importance of Mercury and Apollo (Hawkes, item 2193; Helton, item 2194), and the variety of mythological subjects (Montrose, item 2197).

Although the *Macbeth* subsection is of modest size, it illustrates admirably the range of approaches to the classical connections of an ostensibly nonclassical play. Direct influence of Seneca's *Medea* is posited by Inga-Stina Ewbank (item 2209), of Livy's *History* by William Godshalk (item 2210), and of Lucretius by Matti Rissanen (item 2228). Influence of Ovid through George Sandys's translation and commentary is suggested by John Cutts (item 2208) and of the tradition of the classical Furies by Arthur McGee (item 2221). The image of three-headed time, allegorized by Macrobius in the fourth century A.D., is viewed as crucial to the play's structure by Luisa Guj (item 2212). Finally, Rebecca Bushnell compares the oracular voices in *Oedipus the King* and *Macbeth* (item 2207), and Anne Paolucci (item 2225) observes that *Macbeth* is probably Shakespeare's most classical play.

Among the few items on *Measure for Measure*, there are a couple on Stoicism (Duncan-Jones, item 2241; Rosenheim, item 2245) and one on rhetoric (Kliman, item 2242a). *The Merchant of Venice* prompts essays on Aristotelian–Thomistic virtues and vices (Beauregard, item 2248), Neoplatonic ways of knowing (Hunt, item 2252), and allusions to Orpheus (Lewis, item 2254) and Medea (Palmer, item 2258) from Ovid's *Meta-*

Introduction xix

morphoses. For *The Merry Wives of Windsor*, we have articles on Falstaff's combining in himself two sorts of comic scapegoat (Hinely, item 2265) and Falstaff as Actaeon (Roberts, item 2267).

A Midsummer Night's Dream inspires much analysis of myth. Of course, Ovid's *Metamorphoses* receives attention as a source, directly (Rudd, item 2305) or through medieval and Renaissance alterations (Doran, item 2282; Scragg, item 2307). There is disagreement over whether, in the style of the Pyramus and Thisbe play, Shakespeare is parodying Golding's translation of Ovid (Willson, item 2315), imitating Ovid's humorous treatment of his own material (Crockett, item 2280), or mocking the playwright's alter ego, Peter Quince (Taylor, item 2312). There are treatments of the importance of the Minotaur legend (Ormerod, item 2301), of Theseus' unkindness (Pearson, item 2303), and of the Neoplatonic commonplace of the concord of discord (Guilhamet, item 2287).

For *Much Ado About Nothing*, we have articles on the centering metaphor of Hercules shaven (Crichton, item 2319), on Neoplatonism (Lewalski, item 2320), and on rhetorical figures (Pasicki, item 2323).

Othello stimulates a discussion about the extent of the play's affinities to Roman comedy between Douglas Stewart (item 2348) and Stephen Rogers (item 2341). Robert Miola (item 2339) puts forward Seneca's *Hercules Furens* as both a direct and an indirect source. Wallace Graves (item 2329) proposes Plutarch's *Life of Cato Utican* as a secondary source, and Madeleine Doran (item 2327) explains Othello's final speech in terms of Roman law. An Ovidian influence is suggested by C. S. Lim (item 2335), and Ruth Levitsky (item 2334) discovers in Iago's speech on reason and will a critique of ancient Roman notions of self-sufficiency.

In the only entry for *The Passionate Pilgrim*, C. H. Hobday (item 2353) argues for Shakespearean authorship of three Ovidian Venus and Adonis sonnets.

In the *Pericles* subsection, Thelma Greenfield argues (item 2361) that the hero of this play is modeled on Plutarch's Pericles, except that he is not patient like Plutarch's figure. According to MacD. Jackson (item 2364), the name Escanes is derived from Plutarch. Peggy Knapp (item 2365) explains the play's structure in terms of the Orpheus myth, while Cynthia Marshall (item 2367) says that it is based on Boethian cosmology. William McIntosh (item 2368) maintains that Boethius's concepts of music are especially relevant.

Sister Mary Bonaventure (item 2375) provides a survey of interpretations of *The Phoenix and Turtle*, noting classical influences. Other entries explore aspects of the poem's Neoplatonism (Ellrodt, item 2379; Matchett, item 2384; Petronella, item 2385).

Many discussions of *The Rape of Lucrece* during this period concern themselves with the *ecphrasis* of the wall-painting of Troy that Lucrece examines after her rape (Dundas, item 2402; Hulse, item 2411). Challenging those who see Lucrece as culpable, Robin Bowers (item 2395) contends that

Shakespeare, like most of his contemporaries, treats her sympathetically. In his examination of the myth of Lucretia, Ian Donaldson (item 2399) maintains that Shakespeare began to Christianize the story but then allowed the classical view of womanhood to control his conclusion. Heather Dubrow (item 2401) discovers that *Lucrece* is shaped by several issues in Renaissance historiography; Richard Hillman (item 2410) finds a source in Gower's *Confessio Amantis*; Coppélia Kahn (item 2414) reads the poem in terms of Roman ideas about marriage; Kenneth Muir (item 2422) looks at the consistency of Shakespeare's attitude toward the Trojan War; and Georgianna Ziegler (item 2440) investigates the question of female space.

On *Richard II*, we have studies of speaking styles (Hockey, item 2443); the influence of Lucan's *Pharsalia* on Daniel's *Civil Wars*, Shakespeare's chief source (Logan, item 2444); and Ovid's myth of Narcissus as an indirect influence (Nuttall, item 2448). *Richard III* attracts essays on Senecan echoes in the women's scenes (Brooks, item 2454) and on Shakespeare's omitting classical references from his source for Richmond's speech before the battle in act V (Hassel, item 2457).

For *Romeo and Juliet*, there are discussions of Prince Escalus's embodiment of the Ciceronian idea of prudence (Adams, item 2461), Mercutio's relationship to Mercury (Browne, item 2463), classical and Renaissance epithalamia as background for Juliet's soliloquy at the beginning of III.ii (McCown, item 2469), and Mercutio's background in classical and other sources (Porter, item 2473).

Among the contributions on the *Sonnets* there are several that mention Neoplatonism as an important influence (Devereux, item 2483; Koskimies, item 2497) and one that challenges this view (Forker, item 2486). Jerald Jahn (item 2493) pursues the influence of Aristotle's view of human perception, and A. W. Trueman (item 2527) argues for a specific echo of the *Aeneid*. Jonathan Bate (item 2480) analyzes Shakespeare's Ovidian sonnets to show how he conquered his anxiety about literary influence.

The Taming of the Shrew yields little, but there are articles on the influence of Plautus's *Mostellaria* (Harrold, item 2533) and the works of Ovid (Roberts, item 2540).

Work on *The Tempest* during this period gives a great deal of attention to the *Aeneid*. Jan Kott (item 2571) finds pervasive invocation of the epic throughout, though he believes that Virgilian myths are ultimately rejected by Shakespeare. Jacqueline Latham (item 2575) discovers that the *Aeneid* is a major source for the banquet scene. In defining the courtly aesthetic of Shakespeare's time, Gary Schmidgall (item 2593) cites the *Aeneid*'s influence. John Pitcher (item 2588) senses the presence of the Roman epic as a kind of spectral image in the background. Some critics cite Neoplatonic sources for the play's treatment of magic (K. Berger, item 2546; Rhoads, item 2590), though not everyone agrees (Pearson, item 2585). Harry Berger (item 2545) has an essay on Amphion's harp as a central emblem; Daniel Boughner (item

Introduction

2548) argues that Shakespeare employs the neoclassical four-part structure; Barbara Tovey (item 2599) regards *The Tempest* as Shakespeare's imitation of *The Republic*; and William Gruber (item 2563) claims that it is closer to Old Comedy that any other Shakespearean play.

During this period, *Timon of Athens* benefits from a plethora of serious attempts to define or redefine its genre. M. C. Bradbrook (item 2618) sees it as a dramatic show or pageant, while several other critics (Bergeron, item 2612; Lancashire, item 2658; Walker, item 2702) emphasize its indebtedness to the morality plays. William Slights (item 2693) detects a mixture of genres. On the matter of sources, scholars stress a greater presence of Plutarch than has been previously thought (Honigmann, item 2646), the importance of the old *Timon* comedy (Bulman, item 2622), and the influence of Renaissance references to Diogenes and Timon (Pauls, item 2673). Other areas of interest are the theme of friendship (Davidson, item 2633; Walker, item 2700), Shakespeare's expression of dismay about England's new economy of profit (Lombardo, item 2662) and Timon's imitation of Christ (Ramsey, item 2676). Rolf Soellner (item 2694) has a book-length study.

In analyses of *Titus Andronicus*, there is a lot of attention given to the sources: Seneca (Hansen, item 2735), Dionysius of Halicarnassus (Legouis, item 2755), and Golding's translation of the *Metamorphoses* (Taylor, item 2777). A dispute arises between Harold Metz (item 2760) on the one hand and Marco Mincoff (item 2761) and G. K. Hunter (item 2743) on the other over the status of *The History of Titus Andronicus* as a source. Ronald Broude (item 2717) reads Shakespeare's attitude toward the Romans as ambivalent and toward the Goths as neutral. Other contributions address the topic of false Latin learning in Tamora's sons (Enck, item 2730) and the idea of metamorphosis (taken from Ovid) at the end (Huffman, item 2740). David Willbern (item 2788) offers a psychoanalytical reading of rape and revenge.

Troilus and Cressida is one of the largest sites of scholarly activity during the period. The topic of genre has sparked especially keen interest. Sample opinions are that the play has a deliberately problematic plot (Fly, item 2874); that it is a history play (Dodd, item 2852); that it is a tragic satire (Hunter, item 2908); and that it presents inadequate formulae for tragedy, disposes of them, and thus clears the way for the great works to come (Kaufmann, item 2919). Peter Alexander's thesis that *Troilus* was composed for a private audience (item 2795) is responsible for extensive correspondence in the *Times Literary Supplement*. Much is said about the play's many ways of undermining norms: Harry Berger, for example, notes how the responsibility for determining value is assigned to observers who are not up to the task (item 2810); M. M. Burns (item 2828) shows that the ability to make judgments on individuals and groups is corrupted; and Gayle Greene (item 2889) explores the disorder that results when language is divorced from reality. More specific attacks on established values are perceived in Alice

Shalvi's article on honor (item 3015) and numerous pieces on chivalry (Potter, item 2988; Rose, item 2999). Feminist voices are strong in defense or explanation of Cressida (Harris, item 2898) and in proposing that Shakespeare's bitter appraisal of the Trojan War was derived in part from the voices of the Trojan women as they were mediated to him through a variety of texts (Helms, item 2900). New historicist/materialist critics find much of interest: See Bredbeck on sodomy (item 2823), Clarke on the class struggle (item 2836), and Dollimore on the inadequacy of Christian providentialism (item 2853).

Essays on *Twelfth Night* explore the imitation of classical and intermediate sources (Calkins, item 3077) the tradition of metamorphosis and Ovid's influence (Carroll, item 3079; Lamb, item 3082) and connections of the play with Hercules (McPherson, item 3083) and Echo and Narcissus (Palmer, item 3085). *The Two Gentlemen of Verona* is analyzed in terms of a variety of classical myths that unify it (Godshalk, item 3088) including those of Proteus and Vertumnus (Scott, item 3090). For *The Two Noble Kinsmen*, there are no fewer than four new editions; and D. A. Beecher (item 3092) analyzes the passion of the Jailer's Daughter for Palamon in terms of a subgenre of love story that can be traced back to Plutarch's *Life of Demetrius* and other classical sources.

Chronologically, the first treatment of *Venus and Adonis* in this period is, appropriately, a consideration by A. C. Hamilton of the Platonic meaning of the myth that is the poem's subject (item 3130). A somewhat later essay argues that the two figures unfold their meaning allegorically through their pictorial qualities (Hulse, item 3133). Coppélia Kahn (item 3137) sees the poem as a dramatization of narcissism; John Klause (item 3140) asserts that forgiveness is a key issue; James Lake (item 3141) discovers an early experiment in tragedy; and Wayne Rebhorn (item 3154) refers to the classical epic tradition in interpreting the poem as the temptation of Adonis to return to childhood. Tita Baumlin (item 3109) sees an analogy betweeen the development of Venus as rhetorician and Shakespeare's artistic growth within the poem.

There are some interesting discussions of form in *The Winter's Tale*, including C. D. Hardman's description of the two parts being hinged in the middle and thus revealing Shakespeare's familiarity with the theories of Evanthius and Donatus (item 3184). Louis Martz (item 3196) discerns three parts, beginning with the cyclical pagan world and ending in the present age of grace. It is noticed by Joanne Holland (item 3186) and S. R. Maveety (item 3197) that Shakespeare often altered his primary source, Robert Greene's *Pandosto*, by adding classical elements. Francis Lees (item 3192) suggests Plutarch's *Life of Dion* as a supplementary source, and Martin Mueller (item 3198) contends that the scene of Hermione's "resurrection" conflates the myths of Pygmalion and Alcestis.

This is a brief overview of what is contained in the several sections and subsections. I have been able only to suggest the richness of the materials

Introduction   xxiii

annotated. Many important themes and materials, especially in the larger sections, have not been mentioned in this introduction; these should be sampled through browsing or ruthlessly tracked down in the indexes.

I began this introduction with a quotation from James Hutton about the endlessness of working out the relationship between classical and modern literature. To this I would now like to add a statement about the interminability of reporting on the process as it relates to Shakespeare. Indeed, the word *endless* keeps coming up when Shakespeare bibliographers (Champion, item 2149) or critics (Lanham, item 0665) talk about their research. It has been a humbling but stimulating task. In addition to the vast production of Shakespearean scholarship, there is the constantly changing notion of what the classical tradition consists of. In the preface to the third edition of *The Oxford Classical Dictionary*, for example, Simon Hornblower and Antony Spawforth comment on "the increasingly interdisciplinary character of classical studies" and on areas of study that were "underrepresented" in previous editions (viii). I have tried to be sensitive to new conceptualizations of the classics as they are viewed in connection with Shakespeare. To claim, however, that I have found and classified everything worthy of inclusion would be foolish. I can only hope that I have provided an essentially complete picture of accomplishments in this dynamic field during an exciting third of a century.

Most of the work for this bibliography has been done in four libraries. To the staffs of the Alderman Library at the University of Virginia, the Davis Library at the University of North Carolina at Chapel Hill, and the Perry Library at Old Dominion University I am grateful for many courtesies. The staff of the Randall Library at the University of North Carolina at Wilmington has exhibited the highest degree of professionalism and patience; especially remarkable are the goodwill and efficiency of the interlibrary services department: Madeleine Bombeld, Mary Corcoran, and Sophie Williams.

It is a pleasure to acknowledge various kinds of institutional support. At the University of North Carolina at Wilmington, I have received a course release from the English Department, a summer initiative grant from the College of Arts and Sciences, a summer research grant, and a semester-long research reassignment. From the National Endowment for the Humanities, I have been awarded a travel-to-collections grant.

Colleagues and friends have been generous with their advice and time. Brooks Dodson and Michael Wentworth, master bibliographers both, have answered questions and made many useful suggestions. At different times, graduate students Virginia Ivanoff and Barry Wood volunteered their labors. In the early days of the project, Christie Prentice, with characteristic kindness, undertook to create a whole draft from my scraps; and more recently, Betty Levin has performed far above the call of duty in preparing the editing version. The final draft would not exist were it not for the heroic efforts of

Mary Stoughton, who some time ago offered to read through the manuscript with an editor's eye; much of what is coherent and felicitous in the style is due to her. Others who have supported me in important ways are Lloyd Cowling, Sandra Cowling, Christopher Gould, Kathleen Gould, Nancy Leavell, David Stoughton, Crimora Waite, Charles Walker, and Margaret Walker. In the final synthesis, I owe most to Catherine, whose fierce tuition of me in matters organizational is but one facet of her abiding love.

University of North Carolina at Wilmington
Wilmington, North Carolina

Works Cited

Howatson, M. C., and Ian Childers, eds. *The Concise Oxford Companion to Classical Literature*. Oxford: Oxford U. P., 1993.

Hornblower, Simon, and Antony Spawforth, eds. *The Oxford Classical Dictionary*. 3rd ed. Oxford: Oxford U. P., 1996.

Hutton, James. *The Greek Anthology in Italy to the Year 1800*. Ithaca, New York: Cornell U. P., 1935.

Abbreviations for Journals and Series

ACM	Aligarh Critical Miscellany
AI	American Imago
AJES	Aligarh Journal of English Studies
AN&Q	American Notes and Queries [superseded by ANQ]
Anglia	Zeitschrift für Englische Philologie
ANQ	A Quarterly Journal of Short Articles, Notes, and Reviews [formerly *American Notes & Queries*]
AR	Antioch Review
Archiv	Archiv für das Studium der Neueren Sprachen und Literaturen
ArielE	Ariel: A Review of International English Literature
AUMLA	Journal of the Australasian Universities Language & Literature Association
BJA	British Journal of Aesthetics
BNYSS	Shakespeare Bulletin [formerly *Bulletin of the New York Shakespeare Society*]
BSUF	Ball State University Forum
BuR	Bucknell Review
BWVACET	Bulletin of the West Virginia Association of College English Teachers
CahiersE	Cahiers Elisabéthains
C&L	Christianity & Literature
CCTE Studies	Conference of College Teachers of English of Texas Studies
CE	College English
CEA	CEA Critic
CentR	The Centennial Review
ChauR	Chaucer Review
CJ	Classical Journal
CL	Comparative Literature
CLAJ	College Language Association Journal
Classical Bull.	Classical Bulletin
CLS	Comparative Literature Studies
CML	Classical and Modern Literature
CollL	College Literature
CompD	Comparative Drama
CQ	Cambridge Quarterly
CR	Critical Review (Melbourne, Sydney)

CRCL	Canadian Review of Comparative Literature/Revue Canadienne de Littérature Comparée
CrSurv	Critical Survey
CritQ	Critical Quarterly
DA	Dissertation Abstracts
DAI	Dissertation Abstracts International
DR	Dalhousie Review
DUJ	Durham University Journal
EA	Études Anglaises
E&S	Essays and Studies by Members of the English Association
EDH	Essays by Divers Hands
EIC	Essays in Criticism (Oxford)
EIRC	Explorations in Renaissance Culture
EJ	English Journal
ELH	Journal of English Literary History
ELN	English Language Notes
ELR	English Literary Renaissance
EM	English Miscellany
ErasmusR	Erasmus Review: A Journal of the Humanities
ES	English Studies: A Journal of English Language and Literature
ESA	English Studies in Africa (Johannesburg)
ESC	English Studies in Canada
ETJ	Theatre Journal
Expl	Explicator
ForumH	Forum of Texas
GaR	Georgia Review
G&R	Greece and Rome
HAR	Humanities Association Review (Canada)
HamS	Hamlet Studies (U. of Delhi)
HLB	Harvard Library Bulletin
HLQ	Huntington Library Quarterly
HSL	Hartford Studies in Literature
HudR	Hudson Review
HUSL	Hebrew University Studies in Literature
IJES	Indian Journal of English Studies
IJP	International Journal of Psycho-Analysis
IQ	Italian Quarterly
IRPA	International Review of Psycho-Analysis
ITA	Index to Theses with Abstracts Accepted for Higher Degrees by the Universities of Great Britain and Ireland and the Council for National Academic Awards

Abbreviations for Journals and Series

JAAC	Journal of Aesthetics and Art Criticism
JAE	Journal of Aesthetic Education
JDS	Jacobean Drama Series
JEGP	Journal of English and Germanic Philology
JHI	Journal of the History of Ideas
JMRS	Journal of Medieval and Renaissance Studies
JRMMRA	Journal of the Rocky Mountain Medieval and Renaissance Association
JWCI	Journal of the Warburg and Courtauld Institutes
KN	Kwartalnik Neofilologiczny (Warsaw)
KR	Kenyon Review
L&P	Literature and Psychology
Lang&L	Language & Literature
Lang&S	Language and Style
LanM	Les Langues Modernes (Paris)
LC	Library Chronicle (University of Pennsylvania)
LCrit	Literary Criterion (University of Mysore)
LLC	Literary and Linguistic Computing
MLJ	Modern Language Journal
MichA	Michigan Academician
MLN	Modern Language Notes
MLQ	Modern Language Quarterly
MLR	Modern Language Review (London)
MLS	Modern Language Studies
MP	Modern Philology
MQ	Midwest Quarterly
MQR	Michigan Quarterly Review
MR	Massachusetts Review
MSE	Massachusetts Studies in English
N&Q	Notes and Queries (London)
Neophil	Neophilologus (Groningen)
NDQ	North Dakota Quarterly
NLH	New Literary History: A Journal of Theory and Interpretation
NM	Neuphilologische Mitteilungen
NTQ	New Theatre Quarterly [formerly *Theatre Quarterly*]
OL	Orbis Litterarum
PAPA	Publications of the Arkansas Philological Association
PBA	Proceedings of the British Academy
PCP	Pacific Coast Philology
PhoenixC	Phoenix: The Classical Association of Canada
PLL	Papers on Language and Literature

PMLA	Publications of the Modern Language Association	
PP	Philologica Pragensia (Praha)	
PQ	Philological Quarterly	
PsyQ	Psychoanalytic Quarterly	
PsyR	Psychoanalytic Review	
QJS	Quarterly Journal of Speech	
QQ	Queen's Quarterly	
RBPH	Revue Belge de Philologie et d'Histoire	
REAL	REAL: The Yearbook of Research in English and American Literature	
REL	Review of English Literature	
Ren&R	Renaissance and Reformation	
RenB	Renaissance Bulletin (Tokyo)	
RenD	Renaissance Drama (Northwestern University)	
RenP	Renaissance Papers	
RenQ	Renaissance Quarterly	
RES	Review of English Studies (London)	
RLMC	Rivista di Letterature Moderne e Comparate (Firenze)	
RLV	Revue des Langues Vivantes (Bruxelles)	
RMMLA	Rocky Mountain Modern Language Association Bulletin	
RMR	Rocky Mountain Review of Language & Literature	
RMS	Renaissance and Modern Studies (University of Nottingham)	
RN	Renaissance News	
RORD	Research Opportunities in Renaissance Drama	
RRWL	Renaissance and Renascences in Western Literature	
SAB	South Atlantic Review [formerly *South Atlantic Bulletin*]	
SAP	Studia Anglica Posnaniensia: An International Review of English Studies	
SAQ	South Atlantic Quarterly	
SCB	South Central Bulletin [now South Central Review]	
SEL	Studies in English Literature, 1500–1900	
SELit	Studies in English Literature (University of Tokyo)	
ShN	Shakespeare Newsletter	
ShakS	Shakespeare Studies	
ShS	Shakespeare Survey	
ShSoA	Shakespeare in Southern Africa: Journal of the Shakespeare Society of Southern Africa	
ShStud	Shakespeare Studies (Japan)	
ShY	Shakespeare Yearbook	
SixCJ	Sixteenth Century Journal	
SJ	Shakespeare-Jahrbuch	
SJH	Shakespeare-Jahrbuch (Bochum)	
SJW	Shakespeare-Jahrbuch (Weimar)	
SLitI	Studies in the Literary Imagination	

Abbreviations for Journals and Series

SN	Studia Neophilologica
SoQ	Southern Quarterly
SoR	Southern Review
SoRA	Southern Review: An Australian Journal of Literary Studies (University of Adelaide)
SP	Studies in Philology
SQ	Shakespeare Quarterly
SRASP	Shakespeare and Renaissance Association of West Virginia: Selected Papers
SRO	Shakespearean Research Opportunities
SSE	Sydney Studies in English
SUS	Susquehanna University Studies
Theoria	A Journal of Studies in the Arts, Humanities and Social Sciences
ThSw	Theatre Southwest: Journal of the Southwest Theatre Association (Texas A&M University)
TLS	Times (London) Literary Supplement
TP	Textual Practice
TriQ	Tri-Quarterly
TSE	Tulane Studies in English
TSLL	Texas Studies in Literature and Language
UC	The Upstart Crow
UCTSE	University of Cape Town Studies in English
UDR	University of Dayton Review
UES	Unisa English Studies
UMSE	University of Mississippi Studies in English
UTQ	University of Toronto Quarterly
VQR	Virginia Quarterly Review
WascanaR	Wascana Review
YES	Yearbook of English Studies
YJC	Yale Journal of Criticism
ZAA	Zeitschrift für Anglistik und Amerikanistik

Editorial Abbreviations

c.	century, centuries
comp(s).	compiler(s), compiled by
ed(s).	edition(s), edited by, editor(s)
introd.	introduction
no(s).	number(s)
N. S.	New Series
P.	Press
p(p).	page(s)
Sh	Shakespeare
tr.	translated (by), translator
trs.	translations, translators
U.	University, Universität, Université, Universidad
U. P.	University Press
vol(s).	volume(s)

Abbreviations for the Titles of Shakespeare's Works

Ado	Much Ado About Nothing	MM	Measure for Measure
Ant.	Antony and Cleopatra	MND	A Midsummer Night's Dream
AWW	All's Well That Ends Well	MV	The Merchant of Venice
AYL	As You Like It	Oth.	Othello
Cor.	Coriolanus	Per.	Pericles
Cym.	Cymbeline	PhT	The Phoenix and Turtle
Err.	The Comedy of Errors	PP	The Passionate Pilgrim
Ham.	Hamlet	R2	Richard II
1H4	Henry IV, Part 1	R3	Richard III
2H4	Henry IV, Part 2	Rom.	Romeo and Juliet
1&2H4	Henry IV, Parts 1 & 2	Shr.	The Taming of the Shrew
H5	Henry V	Son.	Sonnets
1H6	Henry VI, Part 1	TGV	The Two Gentlemen of Verona
2H6	Henry VI, Part 2	Tim.	Timon of Athens
3H6	Henry VI, Part 3	Tit.	Titus Andronicus
H6Triad	Henry VI Triad	TN	Twelfth Night
H8	Henry VIII	TNK	The Two Noble Kinsmen
JC	Julius Caesar	Tmp.	The Tempest
Jn.	King John	Tro.	Troilus and Cressida
LC	A Lover's Complaint	Ven.	Venus and Adonis
LLL	Love's Labor's Lost	Wiv.	The Merry Wives of Windsor
Lr.	King Lear	WT	The Winter's Tale
Luc.	The Rape of Lucrece		
Mac.	Macbeth		

General Bibliographies, Surveys, and Reference Works

0001 Accardi, Bernard, and others, comps. *Recent Studies in Myths and Literature, 1970–1990: An Annotated Bibliography.* New York: Greenwood P., 1991. ix + 251 pp.

Section 3, "English Literature to 1660," includes a subsection on Sh that has fifty-nine entries arranged alphabetically by author. Includes a significant number of entries having to do with classical myth. Provides substantial annotations.

0002 Andrews, John F., ed. *William Shakespeare: His World, His Work, His Influence.* 3 vols. New York: Charles Scribner's Sons, 1985. xvii + 954 pp.

Provides "a reference set that gathers into one convenient place a collection of essays on virtually every aspect of the phenomenon we refer to as Shakespeare." Includes essays on "Education and Apprenticeship" by Anthony Grafton (the classical grounding of Elizabethan grammar schools); "The Sense of History in Renaissance England" by J. G. A. Pocock (the importance of classical antiquity in formulating the sense of the past); "The Literate Culture of Shakespeare's Audience" by S. K. Heninger Jr. (Cicero as the most important influence on "civic humanism"); "Science, Magic, and Folklore" by Michael MacDonald (the ancient basis for Elizabethan cosmology and the Neoplatonic basis for magic); "The Life: A Survey" by S. Schoenbaum; "Thinking about Shakespeare's Thought" by J. Leeds Barroll; "Shakespeare's Professional Career: Poet and Playwright" by David Bevington (survey of the canon with key themes highlighted); "Shakespeare and His Contemporaries: Other Poets and Playwrights" by M. C. Bradbrook; "Shakespeare's Language" by Marvin Spevack; "Shakespeare's Poetic Techniques" by George T. Wright; "Shakespeare's Use of Prose" by Brian Vickers; "Shakespeare's Dramatic Methods" by Bernard Beckerman; "Music in Shakespeare's Work" by F. W. Sternfeld and C. R. Wilson (the idea of the ethos of music, inherited from classical sources); "The Visual Arts in Shakespeare's Work" by John Dixon Hunt (Sh's interest in using poetry as rival to painted imagery in *Tim.* and *Luc.*); "Locating and Dislocating the 'I' of Shakespeare's Sonnets" by Margreta De Grazia; "The Poems" by Hallett Smith (*Ven., Luc., LC, PhT*); "Shakespeare's Treatment of English History" by Peter Saccio; "Shakespeare's Treatment of Roman History" by J. L. Simmons (Sh sees Roman history as a Christian humanist); "Shakespeare as a Writer of Comedy" by David Young; "Shakespeare's Tragedies" by Arthur Kirsch; "Shakespeare's Tragicomedies and Romances" by John Russell Brown (*Tro.* as tragicomedy); "Shakespeare and His Audiences" by Ann Jennalie Cook; "Ethical and Theological Questions in Shakespeare's Dramatic Works" by John F. Andrews; and "Shakespeare's Psychology: Characterization in Shakespeare" by Meredith Skura.

0003 Barroll, J. Leeds. "Significant Articles, Monographs, and Reviews: August 1965–December 1966." *ShakS*, 2 (1966), 34–50.

Provides critical annotations of some forty-six articles and books; of these, five deal directly with works on classical themes. Section 2 lists books, with bibliographical information on reviews for each. Section 3 is headed "Ancillary Studies," defined as "those which may contain material of possible relevance to matters Shakespearean"; eighteen items are annotated here, including a reprint of the 1581 edition of *Seneca his Tenne Tragedies.*

0004   Barroll, J. Leeds. "Significant Articles, Monographs, and Reviews: January 1967–December 1967, *ShakS*, 3 (1967), 336–52."

Provides critical annotations of twenty-nine articles and books; of these, five deal directly with issues related to classical materials. Section 2 lists forty books with bibliographical information on reviews for each. Section 3, "Ancillary Studies," contains annotations of twenty-three items, including five that relate directly to the classics.

0005   Barroll, J. Leeds. "Significant Articles, Monographs, and Reviews: January 1968–December 1968." *ShakS*, 4 (1969), 11–24.

Provides critical annotations of twenty-four articles and books; of these, four deal directly with issues relating to classical materials. Section 2 lists thirty-four books with bibliographical information on reviews for each. Section 3, "Ancillary Studies," contains annotations of seven items, including a 1967 reissue of M. W. MacCallum's *Shakespeare's Roman Plays*, first published in 1910.

0006   Barroll, J. Leeds. "Some Articles and Monographs of Current Interest: July 1964–65." *ShakS*, 1 (1965), 310–14.

Provides critical annotations of twenty articles and books, including one article on *JC*.

0007   "Bibliography of the Classical Tradition," 1980–89. *CML*, 5–12 (1984–92).

Arranges the bibliography in two parts. Part 1 is ordered according to classical references, from Aeschylus to Xenophon. Lists, under each classical author or topic, entries in alphabetical order according to modern author. Provides brief annotations. Part 2 contains "post-classical cross-references." Includes the following rubrics: "English Literature, 16th Century," "English Literature, 16th/17th Centuries," "English Literature, 17th Century," and "Shakespeare." Lists entries under each of these rubrics in alphabetical order; each item is cross-listed with an item in part 1. The bibliography in each volume of *CML* covers a single year; usually there is a two to three-year gap. The bibliography in vol. 12 (1991–92), for example, deals primarily with items published in 1989.

0008   Bullough, Geoffrey, ed. *Narrative and Dramatic Sources of Shakespeare.* Vol. 4. *Later English History Plays: "King John," "Henry IV," "Henry V," "Henry VIII."* London: Routledge and Kegan Paul, 1962. xiv + 534 pp.

Prints selections from sources, possible sources, probable sources, and analogues for five plays. Introduces the sources for each play with a substantial essay discussing their relationship to the play. Provides a bibliography of modern historical works on the periods covered in the plays and of editions, sources and analogues, and source criticism for each play. Concludes with an index to the introductions. Includes a selection from Tacitus as a source of *H5*.

0009   Bullough, Geoffrey, ed. *Narrative and Dramatic Sources of Shakespeare.* Vol. 5. *The Roman Plays: "Julius Caesar," "Antony and Cleopatra," "Coriolanus."* London: Routledge and Kegan Paul, 1964, xiv + 577 pp.

Prints selections from sources, possible sources, probable sources, analogues, and summaries of possible sources and analogues for three Roman plays. Introduces the sources for each play with a substantial essay discussing their relationship to the play. Includes a bibliography of general critical works on Sh's sources and of editions, sources and analogues, and source criticism for each play. Concludes with an index to the introductions. Provides nearly complete reprintings of the lives of Julius Caesar, Marcus Brutus, Antonius, and Coriolanus from North's Plutarch, as well as versions of lesser-known works like Samuel Daniel's *The Tragedy of Cleopatra*, for which no modern edition exists.

0010 Bullough, Geoffrey, ed. *Narrative and Dramatic Sources of Shakespeare.* Vol. 6. *Other 'Classical' Plays:* "*Titus Andronicus,*" "*Troilus and Cressida,*" "*Timon of Athens,*" "*Pericles.*" London: Routledge and Kegan Paul, 1966. xiv + 578 pp.

Prints selections from sources, probable sources, possible sources, and analogues for four plays all based on themes that, though "not classical in any modern historical sense, were in the sixteenth century regarded as authentically of the ancient world." Introduces the sources for each play with a substantial essay discussing their relationship to the play. Considers as well the relationship between the verse passages in George Wilkins's novel *The Painful Adventures of Pericles, Prince of Tyre* and *Per.* Contains a bibliography of editions, sources and analogues, and source criticism for each play. Concludes with an index to the introductions.

0011 Bullough, Geoffrey, ed. *Narratives and Dramatic Sources of Shakespeare.* Vol. 7. *Major Tragedies:* "*Hamlet,*" "*Othello,*" "*King Lear,*" "*Macbeth.*" London: Routledge and Kegan Paul, 1973. xvi + 553 pp.

Prints selections from sources, possible sources, probable sources, and analogues for the four major tragedies. Introduces the sources for each play with a substantial essay discussing their relationship to the play. Provides a bibliography of general critical works on Sh and of editions, sources and analogues, source criticism, and other relevant critical works for each play. Concludes with an index to the introductions. Includes selections from a number of classical sources: for example, there are passages from Elizabethan translations of *The Romane Historie* of Titus Livius and two of Seneca's plays (for *Ham.*), and two plays of Seneca (for *Mac.*).

0012 Bullough, Geoffrey, ed. *Narrative and Dramatic Sources of Shakespeare.* Vol. 8. *Romances:* "*Cymbeline,*" "*The Winter's Tale,*" "*The Tempest.*" London: Routledge and Kegan Paul, 1975. xiv + 423 pp.

Prints selections from sources, possible sources, probable sources, and analogues for three romances. Introduces the sources for each play with a substantial essay discussing their relationship to the play. Offers a "General Conclusion" of some sixty pages to the entire eight-volume set, making summary observations about Sh's use of his sources. For example, "Greek and Roman history he took from Plutarch, Livy, and Tacitus; classical myths he knew mainly from Ovid; the Greek tragic themes from Seneca. He knew Latin fairly well, although he preferred to use translations." Uses *Tim.* as an illustration of how Sh could develop a play from sparse materials (in this case, hints about misanthropy from Plutarch, about prodigality from Lucian, and about ingratitude from a number of sources). Provides a bibliography of general critical works on Sh and of editions, sources, and analogues, and source criticism for each play. Concludes with an index to the introductions and to the general conclusion. Includes passages from Ovid's *Metamorphoses* as sources for *WT* and *Tmp.*

0012a Campbell, Oscar James, and Edward G. Quinn, eds. *The Reader's Encyclopedia of Shakespeare.* New York: Thomas Y. Crowell, 1966. xv + 1014 pp. Reprint. 1975.

Furnishes entries on various matters of Shakespearean interest, including characters in the plays, the plays and poems themselves, authors (like Ovid and Plutarch) who influenced Sh, and important topics (like "Classical Drama" and "Classical Myth in Shakespeare"). The first article under Sh's name surveys the known biographical facts, and another essay follows his development as poet and playwright throughout his career. For each of the works there is an entry that includes a brief essay on the source(s), a synopsis of the plot, a comment on the play by one of the encyclopedia's contributors, and a selection of comments from other critics.

0013 Carlsen, Hanne. *A Bibliography to the Classical Tradition in English Literature.* (Anglica et Americana 21.) Copenhagen: Dept. of English, U. of Copenhagen, 1985. 164 pp.

The section on Sh (pp. 49–59) lists alphabetically by author 132 items published between 1961 and 1982. Most items are not annotated, but in a few cases "where the subject of a particular work is not easily identifiable from the title," a brief explanatory note has been added.

0014 Coates, Richard, comp. "A Provincial Bibliography on Names in the Works of Shakespeare." *Names*, 35 (1987), 206–23.

Contains a brief introduction, followed by Sections A–E. Section C, "Specialized Works on Shakespeare's Names and Incidental Material," consists of 141 briefly-annotated items, with many from after 1960 and the most recent being 1986. Includes a number of entries on classical names or names with classical sources.

0014a Dees, Jerome S. "Recent Studies in the English Emblem." *ELR*, 16 (1986), 391–420.

Furnishes "a reasonably complete account of recent studies of English Emblem writers from 1569 to 1660 and a highly selective list of studies of the influence of emblems, both English and Continental, on English literature during the same period." Begins with a list of English emblem books published between 1569 and 1660. Section 1 covers general studies of the emblem, with subsectons on theory, historical and critical studies, and bibliographies. Section 2 covers work on individual emblem writers. Section 3 has one subsection covering general works and another devoted to individual authors, each of which is treated separately. Discusses a number of works on Sh, most of them devoted to a single play.

0015 Elton, W. R., comp. "Shakespeare and Renaissance Intellectual Contexts: A Selective, Annotated List, 1966–67." *SRO*, 3 (1967), 64–91.

Annotates books, articles, and dissertations that pertain to Sh's Renaissance intellectual context. Includes a large number of nonliterary studies. Classifies items under sixteen headings, including "Educational," "Ethical," "Historical," "Iconographical," "Musical," "Philosophical," "Political," "Psychological," and "Scientific." Most items do not refer directly to Sh. Revised as part of item 0019.

0016 Elton, W. R., comp. "Shakespeare and Renaissance Intellectual Contexts: A Selective, Annotated List, 1967–68." *SRO*, 4 (1968–69), 122–202.

Follows the rationale and format of item 0015, adding three headings: "Humanist-Classical"; "*Topoi*, Themes, Emblems, etc."; and "Research Tools" (in addition to those listed under other headings). Revised as part of item 0019.

0017 Elton, W. R., comp. "Shakespeare and Renaissance Intellectual Contexts: A Selective, Annotated Bibliography, 1968–1969." *SRO*, 5–6 (1970–71), 138–251.

Follows the rationale and format of items 0015 and 0016. Revised as part of item 0019.

0018 Elton, W. R., comp. "Shakespeare and Renaissance Intellectual Contexts: A Selective, Annotated List, 1970–71." *SRO*, 7–8, 1972/74 (1975), 122–98.

Follows the rationale and format of items 0015, 0016, and 0017. Revised as part of item 0019.

0019 Elton, W. R., comp. *Shakespeare's World: Renaissance Intellectual Contexts: A Selective, Annotated Guide, 1966–1971*. Assisted by Giselle Schlesinger. New York: Garland, 1979. xi + 464 pp.

Emphasizes the contexts within which Sh wrote by selecting and annotating some 2,835 items and organizing them into twenty categories. Although most of the items do not relate directly to Sh, a substantial minority mention him, and an important

General Bibliographies, Surveys, and Reference Works

handful say something significant about his relationship to the classics. The largest and most important category (119 pages; 1,031 items) is "*Topoi*, Themes, Emblems, etc.," which is presented as a dictionary, with entries like "Achilles," "Cleopatra," "Cosmos," and "Epyllion" arranged in alphabetical order with scholarly works on these subjects listed under them. Other categories of special interest are "Educational Contexts," "Humanist-Classical," "Linguistic–Rhetorical," "Philosophical," and "Research Tools." Includes unpublished dissertations. Revises and enlarges the compilations that originally appeared in *SRO*. See items 0015, 0016, 0017, and 0018.

0020   Enozawa, Kazuyoshi, and Miyo Takano, comps. *Bibliography of English Renaissance Studies in Japan: I, 1961–1970.* (Renaissance Monographs 6.) Tokyo: Renaissance Institute, Sophia U., 1979. v + 218 pp.

Provides a separate section for each year, listing Sh under "Individual Authors." Arranges Sh entries for each year under "General and Miscellaneous" and under titles of individual works. Includes a few items originally published in English. Does not annotate items.

0021   Enozawa, Kazuyoshi, and Miyo Takano, comps. "The 1971 Bibliography [of English Renaissance Studies in Japan]." *RenB*, 5 (1978), 41–62.

Includes Sh under "Individual Authors." Arranges Sh entries under "General and Miscellaneous" and under individual works. Covers a few items originally published in English. Does not annotate items.

0022   Hamilton, A. C. "The Modern Study of Renaissance English Literature: A Critical Survey." *MLQ*, 26 (1965), 150–83.

Singles out as revolutionary in Renaissance studies the relatively recent emphasis on rhetoric, with particular concern for decorum. Illustrates this concern by reference to *TGV*. Also mentions the variety of new historical perspectives, characterized by "extension of a poem's meaning into darkly learned, abstruse, and remote areas." Connected to this "extension of the poem's sources is the modern interest in iconography," and "the study of medieval and Renaissance mythological handbooks and the allegorical interpretation of classical myth."

0023   Hapgood, Robert. "Shakespeare and the Ritualists." *ShS*, 15 (1962), 111–24.

Surveys 20th-c. commentary on Sh's relationship to myth and ritual. Though most of the works discussed date from before 1960, the synthesis provided is useful as a basis for considering later contributions in this area.

0023a   Harner, James L., comp. *English Renaissance Prose Fiction, 1500–1660: An Annotated Bibliography of Criticism.* Boston: G. K. Hall, 1978. xxiv + 556 pp.

The introduction discusses the variety of works that can be considered under the rubric of prose fiction in the English Renaissance. States that most scholars agree that the main body of this kind of work "consists of imaginative narratives [that] may be classified as novelle, romances, jest books, anatomies, histories, or some combination of these types." Proposes to cover "editions and studies (published between 1800 and 1976) of prose fiction in English—both original works and translations—written or printed in England from 1500 to 1660." Classifies entries under four main headings: Bibliographies, Anthologies, General Studies, and Authors/Translators/Titles. Arranges entries in the first three sections in alphabetical order by author or editor. The last section follows one alphabetical sequence "by author, or translator, or title (for an anonymous work or translation)." Annotates a number of recent studies that discover links between Sh's works and prose fiction with classical origins. Provides an index that includes references to Sh's name but does not list his works. Supplemented by item 0023b.

0023b   Harner, James L., comp. *English Renaissance Prose Fiction, 1500–1660: An Annotated Bibliography of Criticism (1976–1983)*. Boston: G. K. Hall, 1985. xxi + 228 pp.

Supplements item 0023a, using the same principles of classification. The index, unlike that of item 0023a, lists references to Sh's works as well as to his name.

0023c   Hinchcliffe, Judith, comp. *"King Henry VI, Parts 1, 2, and 3": An Annotated Bibliography*. (Garland Shakespeare Bibliographies 5.) New York: Garland, 1984. xix + 368 pp.

Covers primarily works published between 1940 and 1981. Classifies entries under nine headings, including Criticism (427 items); Sources (54 items); Bibliographies (20 items); and Editions (117 items). Begins each section with the oldest entries and proceeds chronologically, except that within a given year items are arranged alphabetically by author. Concludes with a single index. Provides substantial and detailed annotations

0024   Hoeniger, F. David. "Shakespeare's Romances since 1958: A Retrospect." *ShS*, 29 (1976), 1–10.

Surveys selected critical works on the romances. Comments on the need to recognize classical as well as other elements in these plays.

0025   Horner, Winifred Bryan, ed. *Historical Rhetoric: An Annotated Bibliography of Selected Sources in English*. Boston: G. K. Hall, 1980. xii + 194 pp.

Comprises five sections, each devoted to a chronological period, and each provided with an introduction by a subeditor and divided into Primary Works and Secondary Works. Provides substantial annotations. The first three sections cover "The Classical Period," "The Middle Ages," and "The Renaissance," respectively. The third section, edited by Charles Stanford, includes a range of 16th-c. rhetorics in both Latin and English, both traditional and Ramist, among the primary works; and a few works with specific Shakespearean concerns among the secondary works. Within each subsection, entries are arranged alphabetically by author.

0026   Hulme, Hilda M. "Shakespeare's Language." *ShN*, 14 (1964), 43.

Surveys scholarship of the past 100 years that focuses on Sh's linguistic environment. Covers, among other things, researches into Sh's knowledge of Latin.

0027   Jayne, Sears. "Some Tools for Research in the Intellectual History of the English Renaissance." *SRO*, 5–6 (1970–71), 8- 29.

Suggests that, to find out what Elizabethans read, modern literary scholars should look at subject bibliographies, library catalogues, and commonplace books from the period. Uses some examples from Platonism.

0028   Kallendorf, Craig. *Latin Influences on English Literature from the Middle Ages to the Eighteenth Century. An Annotated Bibliography of Scholarship, 1945–1979*. New York: Garland, 1982. xvi + 157 pp.

Provides a guide to research on "the relationship of pre-Romantic English literature to its Latin models and sources." Section 1, "Basic Works on the Classical Tradition," has subsections entitled "General" (twenty items), "Generic Studies" (twenty-two items), "Myth and Legend" (sixteen items), and "Nachleben of Individual Latin Authors" (twenty-five items). Section 2, "Rhetoric and English Prose Style," is divided into "General" (fourteen items), "Middle Ages" (eight items), "Sixteenth Century" (fourteen items), and "Seventeenth Century" (ten items). Section 3 is on "Medieval Literature." Section 4, "Renaissance Literature," includes a subsection on "Ovid and the Epyllion" (nine items). Section 6, "Elizabethan, Jacobean, and Caroline Drama,"

General Bibliographies, Surveys, and Reference Works 7

includes subsections on "Senecan Influence" (twenty-one items) and "Shakespeare" (eighty-one items). The Sh subsection covers the years from 1961 to 1979 only.

0029   Kallendorf, Craig. "Nachleben." *Vergilius*, 36 (1990), 82–98.

Surveys Virgil scholarship since 1981–82. Remarks that Sh's use of Virgil becomes more adept as his style matures. Virgilian allusions in Sh's early works are awkward: The account of the fall of Rome in *Luc.* is long and unwieldy, and the rape of Lavinia in *Tit.* is a juvenile burlesque of the *Aeneid*. In later works, references to Virgil are more subtle: Cassius and Hamlet are types of Aeneas; the exaltation of the lovers in *Ant.* seems to oppose the values imparted in the *Aeneid*; and the theatricality of *Tmp.* seems influenced by the Roman poet.

0030   Kiefer, Frederick. "Seneca's Influence on Elizabethan Tragedy: An Annotated Bibliography." *RORD*, 21 (1978), 17–34.

Provides an introduction that charts trends in scholarship on Seneca and Elizabethan tragedy since 1875. Notes the movement away from attempting to prove influence by locating parallel passages and toward a broader consideration of common conventions and themes. Organizes scholarship by brief time periods, mostly decades, and introduces each section with a brief headnote. Covers fifteen items in the 1960–69 section and ten items in the 1970–79 section, all substantially annotated and many bearing directly on Sh. Concludes with a brief discussion of "Problems and Opportunities." Updated by item 0031.

0031   Kiefer, Frederick. "Senecan Influence: A Bibliographic Supplement." *RORD*, 28 (1985), 129–42.

Updates item 0030 to take into account the great variety of recent publications. Shows the range of current scholarship by commenting in the introduction on three representative specimens: a book, an article, and an edition. Includes forty-three items, substantially annotated, many of them focused on or significantly related to Sh. Concludes with a discussion of "Problems and Opportunities."

0032   Kolin, Philip C. *Shakespeare and Feminist Criticism: An Annotated Bibliography and Commentary.* (Garland Reference Library of the Humanities 1345.) New York: Garland, 1991. 420 pp.

Comprises 439 extensive annotations of English-language studies published 1975–88. Organizes items chronologically. Includes separate indexes for authors, poems and plays, and subjects. The introduction is divided into several sections, each addressing a key topic in feminist criticism and summarizing scholarship on that topic. Sections entitled "'In Defense of Cressida . . . ,'" "Dissolving Gender Boundaries," and "Genre and Gender" are especially relevant to the classics.

0033   Lever, J. W. "Shakespeare and the Ideas of His Time." *ShS*, 29 (1976), 79–91.

Surveys influential comments of the past 50 years on "Elizabethan ideas of nature and supernature, politics and society, psychology and ethics" and on how these ideas relate to Sh's mind and art. Concludes that many early studies, which insisted on schematic readings of Sh's politics, psychology, or religion, have been supplanted by works that emphasize Sh's willing embrace of the dualities and contrarieties of his age. Mentions some of the classical elements in Sh's thought (Seneca for example).

0034   McNamee, Lawrence F. *Dissertations in English and American Literature: Theses Accepted by American, British, and German Universities, 1865–1964.* New York: R. R. Bowker, 1968. xi + 1124 pp.

Comprises a bibliography listing all doctoral dissertations in English and American literature for the period covered. Chapter 6, devoted to Sh, classifies entries into categories like "Influences on Shakespeare," "Bibliographies of Shakespeare," and

"Rhetoric of Shakespeare"; genre groupings (like "Roman Plays"); and individual plays. Under each heading, entries are arranged chronologically, and each entry includes author's name, title, year of completion, and a code number for the university at which the work was done. Includes no annotations.

0035 McNamee, Lawrence F. *Dissertations in English and American Literature. Supplement One, 1964–1968.* New York: R. R. Bowker, 1969. x + 450 pp.

Follows the same format and has the same coverage as item 0034, except that dissertations from Canadian and Australian universities are included.

0036 McNamee, Lawrence F. *Dissertations in English and American Literature. Supplement Two: Theses Accepted by American, British, British Commonwealth, and German Universities,* 1969–73. New York: R. R. Bowker, 1974. ix + 690 pp.

Follows the same pattern as item 0035.

0037 McRoberts, J. Paul, comp. *Shakespeare and the Medieval Tradition: An Annotated Bibliography.* (Garland Reference Library of the Humanities 603.) New York: Garland, 1985. xxix + 256 pp.

Covers works published in English between 1900 and 1980. Classifies entries under three headings: General Works (362 items); Play Groups (subdivided into Comedies, Histories, Romances, and Tragedies; 97 items); and Particular Plays (subdivided into individual plays; 474 items). Within each section or subsection, entries are arranged alphabetically according to author. Concludes with four indexes: Author, Shakespearean Play, Medieval, and Subject. Provides, in most cases, substantial annotations. Treats a number of items that comment on medieval aspects of works by Sh about the classical world (the morality play's influence on *Tim.*, for example) or that investigate genres or subjects with both classical and medieval components (like the Greek romance).

0038 Motto, Anna Lydia, and John R. Clark. "Senecan Tragedy: A Critique of Scholarly Trends." *RenD,* N. S. 6 (1973), 219–35.

Reviews recent work done on Seneca. One section, "Seneca and the Elizabethans," makes the general point that current scholarship acknowledges Seneca's influence on Sh and his contemporaries but is wary of making excessive claims.

0039 Nejgebauer, A. "Twentieth-Century Studies in Shakespeare's Songs, Sonnets, and Poems: 2. The Sonnets." *ShS,* 15 (1962), 10–18.

Surveys 20th-c. scholarship in several areas, including "Sources," where questions of the relationship of *Son.* to Ovid and Platonic ideas are treated.

0040 Partridge, A. C. "Shakespeare's English: A Bibliographical Survey." *Poetica* (Tokyo), 11 (1979), 46–79.

Covers the period since 1920 and has fourteen sections, the first seven grouped under *Language* (Vocabulary, Meaning, Accidence, Syntax, Orthography, Punctuation, Pronunciation) and the last seven under *Stylistics* (Rhetoric, Poetic Style, Versification, Prose Style, Word Play, Proverbs, Miscellaneous). Each section begins by discussing a handful of key works, suggests possibilities for further scholarship, and then provides two lists, of books and articles, respectively, each list arranged alphabetically by author. Several sections cover works, especially articles, that use plays closely tied to the classical world to illustrate important linguistic points. For example, in the "Meaning" section there are three articles on *Tro.* and one on *Cor.,* and articles on *Tro.* and *JC* are cited in the list under "Rhetoric."

0041 Pechter, Edward. "Shakespeare's Roman Plays as History." *Res Publica Litterarum: Studies in the Classical Tradition,* 2 (1979), 233–41.

Discerns a new trend in recent criticism of Sh's Roman plays, especially in books by Huffman (item 1665), Simmons (item 0980), and Cantor (item 0239). That is, these books treat "the Roman plays themselves as works of the historical imagination." Raises questions about the validity of such historicizing, especially the reading of Sh with an Augustinian approach like that of Simmons. Suggests that Sh's real act of historical imagination in the Roman plays may involve us much more directly, and with less of a sense of ironic detachment, than these critics allow.

0042   Plutarch. *Selected Lives from the Lives of the Noble Grecians and Romans.* Tr. Sir Thomas North. Ed. Paul Turner. 2 vols. Fontwell, Sussex: Centaur P., 1963. xxxii + 338pp.; xlix + 231 pp.

Reprints sixteen of Plutarch's *Lives*, including the sources for *JC, Ant., Cor.*, and *Tim*. Has a brief introduction, with explanatory notes and glossary.

0043   Rajec, Elizabeth M. *The Study of Names in Literature: A Bibliography.* New York: K. G. Saur, 1978. xii + 261 pp.

Consists of an "Author Index," which lists 1346 items alphabetically by author, and a "Subject Index." Includes a small number of items, very briefly annotated, on classical connections of names in Sh's works.

0044   "Recent Studies in Elizabethan and Jacobean Drama." *SEL*, 1–31 (1961–91).

Consists of an essay featuring substantial explication and evaluation of selected recent books, including editions. Devotes most attention to Sh. Lists books reviewed either in a headnote or in a list of "Books Received" at the end.

0045   Rivers, Isabel. *Classical and Christian Ideas in English Renaissance Poetry: A Students' Guide.* London: George Allen & Unwin, 1979. vii + 231 pp.

Provides for the nonspecialist a grounding in the blend of classical and Christian thought to which the Renaissance was heir. Mentions Sh briefly (*Ven.*) when discussing the uses of myth. Chapters include "The Golden Age and the Garden of Eden," "The Pagan Gods," "Platonism and Neoplatonism," "Stoicism," "Humanism," "Theories of Poetry," and "Numerology." Includes an appendix on "Classical, Medieval, and Continental Renaissance Authors," which identifies each author and furnishes bibliographical information.

0046   Rouse, W. H. D., ed. *Shakespeare's Ovid, Being Arthur Golding's Translation of "The Metamorphoses."* New York: W. W. Norton, 1966. vi + 321 pp.

The introduction contains brief discussions on Sh and Ovid, early translations of Ovid, Golding's Ovid, and Sh and Golding. Reprints Golding's translation from the first edition (1567).

0047   Sabol, Andrew J. "Recent Studies in Music and English Renaissance Drama." *SRO*, 4 (1968–69), 1–15.

Essay review includes comment on a handful of works that consider music theory in the Renaissance, especially the classically-derived notion of universal harmony embodied in music.

0048   Satin, Joseph. *Shakespeare and His Sources.* Boston: Houghton Mifflin, 1966. xiii + 623 pp.

Brings together selections from the major sources for thirteen of Sh's plays, including *JC* and *Ant*. Introduces the selections for each play with a headnote outlining how Sh has handled them in this case. Keys the sources to relevant passages in the plays through footnotes that refer to act, scene, and line numbers.

0049 "Shakespeare: [An] Annotated [World] Bibliography," 1961–91. *SQ*, 13–43 (1962–1992).

Seeks "to record annually all important books, articles, reviews of books, dissertations and dissertation abstracts, theatrical productions, and significant reprints of works related to Shakespeare" published during a given year. Relies, in addition to the editor and (sometimes) an assistant or associate editor, on an international "Committee of Correspondents." The bibliography for items published in a certain year appears in the next year's volume of *SQ* . From 1961–1974, each year's bibliography is organized, with some slight variations, according to the following scheme: I. Annuals, Bibliographies, Surveys, and *Festschriften*; II. Editions, Translations, Adaptations, and Selections; III. Books; IV. Articles; V. Reviews of Current Stage and Screen Productions; VI. Reviews of Books Previously Recorded in *SQ* Bibliographies; VII. Selected Reprints. Through 1968, the section on articles includes notices of dissertations; beginning with 1969, a separate section on dissertations precedes the one on articles. Introduces significant changes with the 1975 bibliography. The new organization is as follows: I. General Shakespeareana, with a variety of subsections (expanded between 1975–1991) on such topics as Bibliographies, General Studies, Biography and Milieu Studies, and Editions and Texts; II. Studies of Particular Works: A. Play Groups (Apochrypha, Comedies, Histories, Romances, and Tragedies), B. Individual Works. The 1975 bibliography expands the number of indexes to four (Topics, Actors, Dramatists and Poets, and Modern Authors and Editors) from the three used from 1965–74 (Sh's Works, Topics, and General Names). From 1961–64, there is a single index. Beginning with the 1978 bibliography, there are subsections under individual works; under the broad heading of Scholarship and Criticism (which precedes another broad heading of Production and Staging), there are sections on Bibliographies, Editions and Texts, Sources and Influences (especially useful for information on classical materials), and Criticism. Before 1975, articles are nearly all annotated, but books are annotated lightly or not at all. Beginning with 1975, books are generally annotated, and all annotations are more thorough. Editors during this period are Robert W. Dent (1961–64), Rudolph E. Habenicht (1965–70), Bruce Nesbitt (1971–73), Thomas F. Grieve and Rudolph E. Habenicht (1974), Harrison T. Meserole (1975–77), Harrison T. Meserole and John B. Smith (1978–84), and Harrison T. Meserole (1985–91).

0050 "Shakespeare." "Literature of the Renaissance in (year): A Bibliography." *SP*, 58–66 (1961–69).

Section 4 under "English" of this annual bibliography, which ceased publication with the bibliography of 1968 (published in 1969), is devoted to Sh. During the 1961–68 period, the number of Sh entries ranges from a high of 508 to a low of 214. A few entries are lightly annotated; most are not.

0051 "Shakespeare." [1961–1968] *MLA International Bibliography. PMLA*, 77–84 (1962–69).

The Sh section for each of the 1961–68 bibliographies appears as a subsection of "English VI. Renaissance and Elizabethan" and is comprised of a miscellaneous subsection and subsections dealing with individual works. Does not annotate entries.

0052 "Shakespeare." [1969–1991] *MLA International Bibliography of Books and Articles on the Modern Languages and Literatures.* Vol. 1. New York: Modern Language Association of America, 1970–92.

The Sh section for each of the years 1969–80 appears as a subsection of "English Literature VI: Renaissance and Elizabethan" and is comprised of subsections on bibliography, general and miscellaneous, play groups (from 1971), and individual plays. For 1969, the Sh section appears alphabetically among other authors of the period; from 1970–80, it appears, out of alphabetical order, at the end of the Renaissance and Elizabethan section. Beginning with 1981, the Sh section appears under "English Literature/1500–1599" and is placed in alphabetical order among other authors of the period; and there is a general section (with no heading) followed by sections on bibliography (general), drama, drama/bibliography, comedy (general), comedy/comedy bibliography, comedy/[individual plays], history, history/bibliography, history/[individual plays], romance, romance/bibliography, romance/[individual plays], tragedy, tragedy/bibliography, tragedy/[individual plays], poetry (general), poetry/bibliography, poetry/*LC*, poetry/*PhT*, poetry/*Luc.*, poetry/*Son.*, and poetry/*Ven.* Also, beginning in 1981, descriptors used for indexing each item, but not included in the classification (author and title) are placed in a gloss following the citation. These descriptors, which can be found in the subject index, indicate key points in items that are otherwise not annotated. Includes a document author index and a subject index.

0053 "Shakespeare." *The Year's Work in English Studies*, 1961–91, vols. 42–72 (1964–94). Oxford: Blackwell. Published for The English Association.

The Sh chapter of each year's volume provides a "narrative bibliography" that attempts to record and evaluate "all significant contributions" in Sh studies. Through vol. 65 (for 1984), the chapter has between six and nine sections; a typical arrangement is as follows: 1. Editions; 2. Textual Matters; 3. Sources; 4. Biography; 5. General Criticism; 6. Shakespeare in the Theatre; 7. Individual Plays and Poems (with a separate subsection on each work). Beginning with vol. 66 (for 1985), the chapter concludes with one large section for criticism, subdivided as follows: (a) General; (b) Comedies and Romances; (c) Histories; (d) Tragedies; (e) Poems. There are no subsections on individual works. Through vol. 67 (for 1986), bibliographical information on books cited is given at the bottoms of pages in footnotes, and articles are cited parenthetically by journal title only in the text. Beginning with vol. 68 (for 1987), books reviewed are listed in alphabetical order by author or editor at the end of the chapter; and articles are cited parenthetically by journal title and page number in the text. Through volume 69 (for 1988), there are two indexes: one for critics and one for authors and subjects treated. Beginning with volume 70 (for 1989), the two kinds of entries are merged in a single index. Provides concise summaries and assessments of items covered.

0054 Smith, Eric. *A Dictionary of Classical Reference in English Poetry.* Cambridge, England: D. S. Brewer, 1984. xii + 308 pp.

Includes "virtually all the Classical references in some eighty English poets—subject to some qualification." The first part of the book lists classical topics (for example, Daedalus, Hector, Music of the Spheres, Ovid) in alphabetical order, usually providing a paragraph for each topic that explains or defines it and giving one or more classical sources. Appends to each paragraph a list of poets who have used the topic, with each poet's name followed by specific reference(s) to works in which the topic has appeared. The second part is an index of poets: Each poet's works are listed, and the specific places where classical topics have been used are noted for each work. Reveals substantial numbers of classical allusions throughout Sh's works, with the greatest quantity in *Ant.*, *Tit.*, and *Tro.*

0055 Spencer, T. J. B., ed. *Shakespeare's Plutarch: The Lives of Julius Caesar, Brutus, Marcus Antonius, and Coriolanus in the Translation of Sir Thomas North.* Harmondsworth: Penguin, 1964. 365 pp.

The introduction provides brief accounts of Plutarch as a biographer, of North as a translator, and of Sh as an adapter of Plutarch. Prints parallel passages from Sh's works at the bottoms of pages. Focuses on *JC*, *Ant.*, *Cor.*, and *Tim.*, though passages from other works (like *AYL* and *Cym.*) are also included.

0056 Trussler, Simon. *Shakespearean Concepts: A Dictionary of Terms and Conventions, Influences and Institutions, Themes, Ideas, and Genres in the Elizabethan and Jacobean Drama.* London: Methuen, 1989. 185 pp.

Emphasizes ideas "which shaped the world in which Shakespeare and his contemporaries lived." Includes entries for Aristotle, Epic, Greek, Latin, Ovid, Plutarch, Seneca, and Stoicism.

0057   Velz, John W. "The Ancient World in Shakespeare: Authenticity or Anachronism? A Retrospect." *ShS*, 31 (1978), 1–12.

Comments on recent scholarship. The question of accuracy in portraying the ancient world is an old one. In the 20th c., the argument has shifted from the issue of the absolute authenticity of character, thought, and style to the question of whether Sh and his audience believed them to be authentic. Most recent scholars have answered in the affirmative. T. J. B. Spencer, in a 1957 article, argued that Sh's view of Roman history as a succession of "garboyles" is essentially that of his contemporaries; it reveals a clear attempt to provide a coherent picture of Rome. Sh may have gotten the belief, operative in *Err.* and *MND*, that the Greek world was pervaded by harsh and rigorous, but vulnerable, laws from Pauline materials in the New Testament. In another article (1964), Spencer demonstrates that, to the Elizabethans, the Greeks were dissolute, deceitful, and treacherous. A couple of books (by Emerson Phillips and Howard B. White, respectively) have stressed the political nature of Sh's conception of Greece, but a tightly reasoned book has yet to be written on Sh's response to Greek political philosophy. Sh's Rome has still not been clearly defined, and modern scholarship has allowed its image to remain blurred failing to find generic links among the Roman plays and by applying the classical tradition to the entire canon (as in books by Milton Boone Kennedy and Reuben Brower). Two books that do attempt to distinguish Sh's Rome as a world apart are by J. L. Simmons (who argues that Rome is defined by its secularity) and Paul Cantor (who contrasts the public-spiritedness of Sh's Republic with the self-indulgence of his Empire). Other ways of understanding Sh's definition of Rome are through the distinctive styles of speaking in the plays (for example, the illeism of *JC*), attitudes and beliefs (antifeminism and Stoicism), institutions (see articles by G. K. Hunter and Coppélia Kahn on the importance of the family), and the sense of place (note the architectural terms in which Sh conceives of the city and his use of symbolic locations that contrast public and private life). A full study of Virgil that, among other things, deals with the wide range of symbolism in the plays is needed.

0058   Velz, John W. *Shakespeare and the Classical Tradition: A Critical Guide to Commentary, 1660–1960.* Minneapolis: U. of Minnesota P., 1968. xvii + 459 pp.

The preface explains the importance of the classical tradition to understanding Sh; sets the guidelines for inclusion of scholarship in the *Guide*; determines "the forward limit of classical culture" to be "the death of Boethius" (524 A.D.); notes that "tradition" is understood quite broadly to include, for example, Renaissance humanists like Erasmus who were steeped in the classics; and announces the organization of the *Guide*. The introduction surveys scholarly commentary on Sh and the classical tradition in three sections devoted, respectively, to the Restoration and 18th c., the 19th c., and the 20th c.; and ends by speculating about directions that the study of Sh and the classics might take. Classifies entries under nine headings: Bibliographies Consulted; General Works; The Comedies; The Histories; The Plays on Classical Themes (*Ant., JC, Cor., Tim., Tit., Tro.*); The Tragedies; The Last Plays; The Poems and Sonnets; and Shakespeare's Classics. Concludes with a single detailed index. Provides substantial annotations that both summarize and evaluate.

0059   Velz, John W. "Some Modern Views of Shakespeare's Classicism: A Bibliographical Sketch." *Anglia*, 81 (1963), 412–28.

Sums up pre-20th-c. views of Sh's knowledge of classical literature and culture. Notes that before 1900, the prevailing opinion was that he had very little acquaintance with the ancients. Surveys 20th-c. criticism on the subject, describing the various ways in which the majority of scholars have come to accept a considerable classical presence in Sh's works. An example of this altered consensus can be seen in "the restoration to the canon and to critical favor of the the three pseudo-classical tragedies" (*Tit., Tim., Tro.*). Scholars have gone much further than before in investigating Sh's direct and indirect indebtedness to classical literature and thought. Study of intermediate sources like translations, English rhetorical treatises, and mythological dictionaries has been especially significant.

0059a Verma, Rajiv. *Myth, Ritual, and Shakespeare: A Study of Critical Theory and Practice.* New Delhi: Spantech Publishers, 1990. xi + 227 pp.
Comprises five chapters, each one discussing "a theory or a group of theories about myth or ritual, then the application of these theories to literature and drama in general, and finally their application to the works of Shakespeare." Chapter 1, the longest, traces the allegorization of myth from the ancient Greeks through the Stoics and the Neoplatonists to the present. Divides Sh's works into five groups—comedies, tragedies, histories, romances, and poems—and treats them in chronological order within each group. Sums up, for each work, significant mythological/allegorical interpretation(s), many from after 1960. Chapter 2, which covers theories of ritual and "how ritual is related to myth, literature and drama," is organized in the same way as the previous chapter. Chapter 3 canvasses theories that "postulate a special 'mythical' mode of thought"; chapter 4 deals with structural analysis of myth; and chapter 5 considers "the relationship between myth and society." The last three chapters abandon the work-by-work organization of the first two, emphasizing general applications to Sh.

0059b Vickers, Brian, comp. "The Age of Shakespeare." *A Guide for Readers to The New Pelican Guide to English Literature.* Ed. Boris Ford. Harmondsworth: Penguin, 1984, pp. 101–91.
Consists of a series of bibliographies of scholarship on general topics as well as on individual authors. Includes "Classical Plays" (fourteen entries) as one heading under Sh. Does not annotate entries.

0059c Watson, George, ed. *The New Cambridge Bibliography of English Literature. Volume 1: 600–1600.* Cambridge: Cambridge U. P., 1974. xxxii + 2491 columns.
Classifies Sh items under eight major headings, including Bibliographies, Plays, Poems, and Criticism. Includes, under Plays and Poems, separate headings for most works. Lists criticism of each individual work in chronological order in a section designated "Studies" under that work. The Criticism section includes a subsection on Sources and Influences, which is further divided into Collections of Sources, Modern Studies, Classical Influences, Continental Influences, English Influences, Biblical Influences, and Miscellaneous Influences. Each subsection begins with the oldest item and proceeds chronologically. Does not number or annotate items.

0060 Webb, J. Barry. *Shakespeare's Animal (and Related) Imagery Chiefly in the Erotic Context: A Study of Word, Phrase, and Figure Arranged Alphabetically.* Hastings, England: Cornwallis P., 1988. 93 pp.
Includes entries that have Latin etymologies ("coney"), that refer to classical figures ("kite of Cressid's kind"), that have mythological origins ("Phoenix"), and that have special significance in one or more plays with classical settings ("serpent").

0061 Weisinger, Herbert. "Myth and Ritual Approaches." *ShN*, 14 (1964), 28–29.
Surveys the large number of critical works that can be said to use myth and ritual approaches to Sh. Includes discussion of Gilbert Murray, Colin Still, G. Wilson Knight, F. D. Hoeniger, Kenneth Muir, Roy Battenhouse, J. A. Bryant Jr., C. L. Barber, and Northrop Frye. Distinguishes five different approaches or emphases in myth studies: (1) "the use of myth and ritual as the source of the action in the drama"; (2) "the use of myth and ritual as the source of the *agon* ... of the protagonist"; (3) "the effort to link the plays to their medieval and folk sources as the intermediary between myth and drama"; (4) "the use of myth and ritual as the determinants of literary form"; (5) "the attempt to discriminate between the plays esthetically by showing how each

individual play reweighs and reassigns the importance of the elements which constitute the myth pattern for its own particular ends."

0062 Wells, Stanley, ed. *Shakespeare: Select Bibliographical Guides*. Oxford: Oxford U. P., 1973. ix + 300 pp. New ed. *Shakespeare: A Bibliographical Guide*. 1990. vi + 431 pp.

Offers a collection of essays, each appraising a selection of scholarly works on a single work or group of works or on a more general topic relating to Sh. The opening chapter, by the editor, discusses works of a general nature, including bibliographies, periodicals, biographies, handbooks, editions, and works on Sh's sources and influences. Chapter 4, by J. M. Nosworthy, covers *Son.* and other poems, including *Ven.* and *Luc.* Chapter 5, by D. J. Palmer, covers five early comedies: *Err., Shr., TGV, LLL,* and *MND.* Mentions works that discuss, for example, the influence of Plautus on *Err.* and that of Ovid on *MND.* Chapter 6, by Gāmini Salgādo, covers the middle comedies: *Ado, MV, Wiv., AYL,* and *TN.* Chapter 7, by John Wilders, covers the problem comedies: *Tro., AWW,* and *MM.* Calls attention to the general agreement that *Tro.* is intellectual and argumentative. Sums up the "opposing views" about "its characters, the quality of its achievement, the moral standpoint from which it was written, and its dramatic genre." Chapter 8, by Philip Edwards, covers the late comedies or romances: *Per., Cym., WT,* and *Tmp.* Chapter 9, by G. R. Hibbard, covers *Tit.* and *Rom.* Discusses considerations of *Tit.* that deal with justice, with the play's relationship to Sh's poems and early plays, and with the character of Aaron. Chapter 10, by John Jump, covers *Ham.*; chapter 11, by Robert Hapgood, covers *Oth.*; and chapter 12, by Kenneth Muir, covers *Lr.* Chapter 13, by R. A. Foakes, covers *Mac.*, giving consideration to some works that suggest the classical affinities of this play. Chapter 14, by T. J. B. Spencer, covers *JC* and *Ant.* Begins with a consideration of works on Sh's use of Plutarch's *Lives of the Noble Grecians and Romans* as translated by Sir Thomas North. Follows this with a section on each play. Discusses, for *JC*, the issue of who the hero is and the ways in which Brutus and Caesar are to be evaluated and, for *Ant.*, the morality of Cleopatra, the imagery, and the structure. Chapter 15, by Maurice Charney, covers *Cor.* and *Tim.* The section on *Cor.* surveys, among others, works on the morality and maturity of the hero, genre, the heroic tradition, politics (especially the nature of the mob), the classical background, and sources. The section on *Tim.* includes comments on works dealing with the play's unfinished state, its genre, and the character of its protagonist. Chapter 16, by A. R. Humphreys, covers the eight English history plays of the 1590s. Chapter 17, by G. R. Proudfoot, covers *H8, TNK,* and the apochryphal plays. Includes, at the end of each chapter, a list of references cited in that chapter. The new edition has most of the same chapters, mostly by different authors. Adds a chapter on critical developments by Jonathan Dollimore.

0063 Willbern, David. "A Bibliography of Psychoanalytic and Psychological Writings on Shakespeare: 1964–1978." *Representing Shakespeare: New Psychoanalytic Essays.* Eds. Murray M. Schwarz and Coppélia Kahn. Baltimore: Johns Hopkins U. P., 1980, pp. 264–86.

Comprises 461 entries. Includes a number of entries on plays with classical settings or connections. Concludes with a subject index. Does not annotate entries.

0064 "William Shakespeare." *Annual Bibliography of English Language and Literature*, 1961–91, vols. 36–66 (1964–94). London: Published for the Modern Humanities Research Association.

Includes, under Sixteenth Century, a section on Sh, with subsections on Editions and Textual Criticism, General Scholarship and Criticism, Productions, and Separate Works. Does not annotate items but references, in some entries on books, selected reviews. Recent volumes have two indexes: (1) Authors and Subjects and (2) Scholars. Each volume appears two or three years after the year it covers. The number of entries ranges from 271 in 1961, to 578 in 1971, to 560 in 1981, to 617 in 1991.

0065 Wright, Louis B., and Virginia A. LaMar. *The Folger Guide to Shakespeare.* New York: Washington Square P., 1969. xii + 463 pp.

Presents a brief discussion of critical issues and sources for each work, including those works (like *JC, Ant., Cor., Tro.,* and *Ven.*) most directly based on classical antecedents.

0066 "The Year's Contribution to Shakespear[e][ian] Studies." *ShS,* 14–44 (1961–91).

This section of each yearly volume is subdivided into three parts, each by a different scholar: 1. Critical Studies; 2. Shakespeare's Life, Times, and Stage; and 3. [Editions and] Textual Studies. Each part consists of an essay summarizing and appraising selected recent scholarship. In the most recent years, the essay on critical studies has been subdivided in a number of different ways, often including headings like "Freudians," "New Historicists," and "'Worlds' and Themes." Covers books and articles, giving bibliographical information usually in footnotes, though occasionally in the text.

General Works

0067 Adams, Martha Latimer. "The Greek Romance and William Shakespeare." *Studies in English*, 8 (1967), 43–52.

Examines three Greek romances of the 2nd or 3rd c. A.D.—*Aethiopica*, *Daphnis and Chloe*, and *Clitophon and Leucippe*—to highlight two important features of the genre that reappear "in disentangled clarity in Sh's dramas." The first feature—the theme of true love that "outlives time and even death"—is central to *Rom.* and *Ant.* The second feature—"the superior character of the heroine"—is found in *AWW*, *MM*, and *Ado*. Revised as part of item 0068.

0068 Adams, Martha Lou Latimer. "The Origins of the Concept of Romantic Love as It Appears in the Plays of William Shakespeare." Ph.D. dissertation, University of Mississippi, 1968. *DAI*, 29 (1968–69), 3968-A.

Finds the concept of romantic love first stabilized in its complete form in the Greek romances of the 2nd and 3rd c. A.D. The romances follow a rigid formula: Two noble young people of exceptional beauty meet, fall in love at first sight, suffer love-sickness, receive advice from a sympathetic counselor, face "apparently insurmountable obstacles to their love," make vows of loyalty to each other, are separated, and "endure harrowing trials as they struggle to achieve their goal of marriage." The romances always end happily in "an elaborate wedding." *Aethiopica* by Heliodorus, *Daphnis and Chloe* by Longus, and *Clitophon and Leucippe* by Tatius adhere to this pattern. English drama adapted this formula during the Renaissance. Parts of the formula are used in many plays, but in only two—*Rom.* and *Ant.*—are all of its requirements met. Sh transforms the conclusion of the pattern by having his lovers united in death, not marriage. Part is a revision of item 0067.

0069 Aggeler, Geoffrey Donovan. "The Ethical Problems of Revenge in English Renaissance Tragedy." Ph.D. dissertation, University of California, Davis, 1966. *DAI*, 27 (1966–67), 3830-A.

Devotes a great deal of attention to the influence of classical moral philosophy on the revenge theme in eight Renaissance plays. Treats themes, including "the Stoical response to oppressing evils" and the relationship of honor and revenge, that are also found in *Ham.*, to be given detailed consideration in a future study.

0070 Ahern, Matthew Joseph Jr. "The Roman History Play, 1585–1640: A Study Indicating How Plays Dealing with Roman History Reflect Political and Social Attitudes in England during This Period." Ph.D. dissertation, Tulane University, 1963. *DA*, 24 (1963–64), 3319.

Analyzes all the extant non-Shakespearean Roman history plays written in English between 1585 and 1640. The earlier plays are "didactic in emphasis," implying that "man can save himself by controlling his passions." In the later plays, the emphasis is on sensational actions, and man is treated as intellectually weak and morally corrupt. Roman history, no longer significant in itself, becomes in the late plays a "pseudo-authentic backdrop" for the depiction of "depraved middle-class fictional characters."

0070a Albright, Daniel. *Lyricality in English Literature*. Lincoln: U. of Nebraska P., 1985. x + 276 pp.

Chapter 1, "Lyricality as a Mode," adduces "the great ranting scene" of *Tim.* (IV.iii) as containing the purest example in Sh of a kind of lyricality "in which the energies of metamorphosis run wild; everything changes into everything else, and chaos swallows every finite change." In particular, Timon's speeches about cosmic thievery (IV.iii.441–447) and the counterfeiting of artists (V.i.78–80) announce that each image "violates what it is an image of" and that "metaphor is a kind of theft." Comments that T. S. Eliot appropriates from *Ant.* "a whole body of references to dissipating music, dislimning pictures, the undoing of Antony's reputation and even his physical presence."

0071 Alexander, Marguerite. *A Reader's Guide to Shakespeare and His Contemporaries*. (Reader's Guide Series.) London: Heinemann, 1979. 386 pp.

Covers most works in the Sh canon, providing for each a summary and then a critical commentary. Treats *JC*, *Ant.*, and *Cor.* under "Roman History," commenting that these plays are distinguished from Sh's tragedies in that "they lack a sense of evil." Treats *Tro.* as a dark comedy, a play about the operation of ideals "in a sordid world." Includes *Ven.*, *Luc.*, and *Son.* in a chapter on poetry. Maintains that the struggle of the speaker with the young man in *Son.* is reflected in Sh's understanding of the Trojan position in *Tro.*

0072 Alexander, Peter. "The Schoolmaster from the Country." *TLS*, Apr. 23, 1964, p. 327.

Reviews opinions about Sh's learning. Mentions Matthew Arnold, A. E. Housman, and J. W. Mackail as believing that he was vulgar and uneducated, with little or no knowledge of classical literature. Maintains, however, that Sh's grammar-school education, with its emphasis on Plautus and Seneca, prepared him for writing *Err.* and *Tit.* Accepts Aubrey's belief, based on information from William Beeston, that Sh in his youth was a schoolmaster with a good understanding of Latin.

0073 Alexander, Peter. *Shakespeare*. London: Oxford U. P., 1964. vii + 271 pp.

Provides a brief account of Sh's life and works. Entertains the possibility that Sh assisted the master at the Stratford Grammar School: *Tit.*, *Err.*, *Ven.*, and *Luc.* all show the sort of Latin learning that a schoolmaster would have had. Comments on every work in the canon. *Err.*, for example, is an adaptation of Plautus's *Menaechmi* and *Amphitruo*, which "transposes the asperities of the Plautine treatment into a more gracious key." *Shr.*, though not borrowed directly from Latin comedy, employs a subplot with Latin themes. For *Tit.*, Sh borrowed the banquet from the *Thyestes* of Seneca and embellished it "with motifs from Ovid." Sh wrote *Tit.* before he came under the influence of Plutarch and developed "a profounder and more human conception of the Roman scene." *JC* draws almost all of its material from North's Plutarch and shows Brutus as a virtuous but unwise leader. In *Ant.*, the battle of Actium "is at the center of the action" and makes the contradictory loyalties of the protagonist clear. *Cor.* is "the severest and most Roman of all Sh's tragedies." The "deliberately cynical treatment of classical material" in *Tro.* suggests that it was composed for an Inn of Court audience. *Tim.* has many similarities to *Lr.* in theme and style.

0074 Alexander, Peter. "Shakespeare, Marlowe's Tutor." *TLS*, Apr. 2, 1964, p. 280.

Presents evidence for Sh's extensive influence on Marlowe. Comments that Sh used his Latin learning in *Err.* and *Tit.* and owed nothing to Marlowe.

0075 Ali, Raza. "Satire and Shakespearean Tragedy." Ph.D. dissertation, Ohio University, 1975, *DAI*, 36 (1975–76), 6695-A.

Maintains that the satiric features of Shakespearean tragedy emphasize the hero's paradoxical nature, his potential as well as his limitations. Notes the Juvenalian origin of the malcontent persona, which was absorbed into drama in the 1590s by playwrights like Jonson and Marston and which made possible "the soul suffering of a Hamlet" on the one hand and the perverse nature of a Thersites on the other. In Sh's tragedies, the protagonist himself may be the voice of satire, or else he may be subjected to satiric commentary by others. Lear and Timon unleash powerful invective that indicates their psychological decline but at the same time reveals their adherence to ideals of beauty and goodness. Satiric commentators on the hero, like Thersites (*Tro.*), remind us by implication of the virtues of their targets even as they criticize them. In *Cor.* and *Ant.*, the heroes are the victims of considerable satiric devaluation, but our recognition of their greatness is not thereby canceled.

0076   Allen, M. J. B. "Toys, Prologues, and the Great Amiss: Shakespeare's Tragic Openings." *Shakespearian Tragedy*. Eds. Malcolm Bradbury and David Palmer. (Stratford-upon-Avon Studies 20.) London: Edward Arnold, 1984, pp. 3–30.

Finds that in the openings of most of Sh's tragedies there are, to differing degrees, intimations of their ends. An exception is *Tit.*, whose initial scene engages us at the simplest narrative and rhetorical levels and serves as an opening into the play and nothing more. In *Tim.*, the allegory of Fortune invoked at the beginning by the Poet and the Painter is so literal and so overwhelming that it defeats any potential for complexity. In the three Roman plays (*JC*, *Cor.*, *Ant.*), the openings are particularly concerned with rhetoric, "public language, the language of politics, of war, of altercation and debate." In *JC*, the opening is primarily interrogative, pointing to "conflict in the public and political world, the world that is always dominated by the rhetorical question." The opening of *Cor.* is savagely confrontational. This play asks fewer questions than *JC*; its "rhetorical norm" is the fierce antithesis used initially by the First Citizen. In *Ant.*, the opening introduces us to a wonder–producing dialectic between "rhetorical questions and their paradoxical answers," and this is how the play ends.

0077   Allman, Eileen Jorge. "Player–King and Adversary: The Two Faces of Play in Shakespeare." Ph.D. dissertation, Syracuse University, 1972. *DAI*, 34 (1973–74), 1231-A.

Maintains that Sh's plays reflect "a concept of the universe as metaphoric and sympathetic," with play as its "natural pattern of activity." However, play in Sh has "two faces," one creative (exemplified by the "Player–King" type of character) and one destructive (exemplified by "the Adversary"). Discusses the role of these two types of character on the genres of several works, including a middle comedy (*Tro.*) and a tragedy (*Cor.*). Revised as item 0078.

0078   Allman, Eileen Jorge. *Player–King and Adversary: Two Faces of Play in Shakespeare*. Baton Rouge: Louisiana State U. P., 1980. ix + 347 pp.

Remarks that Sh makes use of two character types—the Player–King and the Adversary—as "pattern-makers" within his plays. The first type, in his fullest embodiment, undergoes an educational process through which he comes to understand that any one role is an obstacle to dealing "justly and effectively with other people." He therefore lets go of his identity, assuming some sort of disguise and accepting anonymity in order to participate in communal life and to lead his society toward harmony. This pattern of the Player–King is followed, to a greater or lesser extent, in the careers of Richard II, Henry V, Duke Vincentio, Hamlet, Coriolanus, and Prospero. The Adversary, in contrast to the Player–King's flexibility, is absolutely single-minded in his desire to win and his sense of separateness from the community. Examples are Falstaff, Angelo, and Pandarus. In *Tro.*, the candidates for Player–King, Hector and Ulysses, isolate themselves from community, rejecting the wisdom of their own insights, and Pandarus, the Adversary, takes control of the play. *Cor.* portrays a potential Player–King, who is repeatedly presented with opportunities to change by accepting some degree of anonymity and thus contributing to social harmony. He is, however, unable to acknowledge his humanity, to assimilate "the principle of play." Revision of item 0077.

0079 Alvis, John. "The Coherence of Shakespeare's Roman Plays." *MLQ*, 40 (1979), 115–34.

Opposes most other critics by arguing that Sh's three Roman plays—*JC, Ant.,* and *Cor.*—have a common focus involving "marked similarities of tone, style, imaginative scope, and moral content." In contrast to the major tragedies, the Roman plays never involve the human cosmos in great, violent disruptions; "their conflicts are confined to politics and personalities." The Roman protagonists are not speculative men; instead, they are "completely absorbed in things of the city" and "never move far from their social identities." They are primarily concerned with their immortal souls; in their quest for glory, they are given to "prodigious self-dramatizing displays," tend to "estimate their conduct in terms of its impression on others," and "are ingenuously self-deceiving," never coming to terms with their ignorance. Sh seems to have adopted "the Machiavellian distinction between ancient and Christian paideia as the foundation for a sequence of dramatic inquiries into the consequence of living for a worldly glory within a regime that sanctions such a pursuit as the proper business of the noble spirit." The three Roman plays reach similar conclusions about "the tragic costs" of this endeavor. Revision of chapter 5 of item 0082. Part incorporated into chapter 1 of item 0080a.

0080 Alvis, John. "Introductory: Shakespearean Poetry and Politics." *Shakespeare as Political Thinker.* Eds. John Alvis and Thomas G. West. Durham, North Carolina: Carolina Academic P., 1981, pp. 3–26.

Finds politics to be a principal topic for Sh and notes that classical antiquity was one of the three chief sources for his political thought. Traces the classical tradition from Plutarch and Virgil back to Aristotle and Plato. Emphasizes that modern audiences, in order to come to terms with Sh, need to recover a sense of politics that is more concerned with education, morals, manners, religion, and ethics than it is with power. Notes that in the plays set in the ancient world "human lives take shape from individual propensities responding to the laws of cities," whereas in the plays with Christian settings the characters consult "not only their native inclinations and the laws of their state, but, concurrently, certain transcendent prescriptions decreed by the scriptural God." Holds that the variety of settings in Sh's plays indicates his "attempt to explore the alternative conceptions of the best civil life offered, respectively, by classical antiquity, Christianity, and modernity." The Grecian works—*Tro., Tim., Per., MND*—seem to recapitulate the range of possible forms found in "the Platonic–Aristotelian classifications of constitutions," while the Roman works consider imperial and republican versions of a regime driven by the notion that the best life is to be secured by the attainment of public honors. Distinguishes the types of the soul found in Sh's plays. The commoners are lively, unreflective, concerned primarily with physical comfort; the nobles are dominated by the desire for honor or public recognition; the prudential characters seem to exist for the sake of "guiding others to conduct consistent with an elevated understanding of human nature which only the guides themselves possess." There are other human dispositions exhibited in the plays—those of lover, misanthrope, and saint—that are essentially apolitical. Notes that there are no lovers in republican Rome and that two of the misanthropes (Thersites and Timon), whose souls seem unfit for life "in any human city," are in Greek plays. Points out that in Sh's pagan world religion is either "inertly nominal" (Rome) or simply one element in the political economy (Athens). The comic statesmen in Sh, of whom Theseus is one, exemplify political excellence in that they are superbly suited to "the task of harmonizing diverse human beings through the arts of speech, law, and deliberation." Comments that Sh's comedies, "at one remove from reality," provide us with a "distilled image of the political act" by which we can measure political actions and regimes in the non-comic plays. Neither Rome nor England finally produces a decent political life for Sh, and it is significant that none of his comedies is set in Rome. In the absence of prudential guides, the crucial political issue turns on the relationship between the many "bodily men" and the few but powerful "spirited men." Because in Rome manliness in war and in contention of any sort is prized as the key to nobility, the Roman republic in Sh's plays is constantly embroiled in disputes between plebeians and patricians. As poet, Sh makes it possible for us to understand how far politics is involved in determining human lives and thus helps us to assess the limitations of politics. Part incorporated into chapter 1 of item 0080a.

0080a Alvis, John. *Shakespeare's Understanding of Honor.* (Studies in Statesmanship.) Durham, North Carolina: Carolina Academic P., 1990. xv + 266 pp.

Proposes to discuss a number of Shakespearean works to analyze the playwright's depiction of "the varieties of excessive or deficient love of honor." Chapter 1, which incorporates material from items 0079 and 0080, suggests that Sh "was led to Roman subjects by Machiavelli, who had written his commentaries on Roman history in order to contrast the ways of Roman antiquity with Christian morality." Uses Aristotle and Cicero to explain the "judicious ambivalence" that characterizes the classical notion of honor: On the one hand, it is politically necessary to encourage ambition, while on the other "the most complete soul will ultimately require independence from a taste for honors." Regards this perspective as a major component in Sh's treatment of honor. Cites Sonnet 94 as "a compact view of the dilemma confronting every great-souled man."

Chapter 2 treats *Luc.* and *Tit.* In the latter work, Sh presents Romans who, educated by reading the degenerate poetry of Ovid and Seneca, behave with a kind of "pathetic desperation." In the former work, the conduct of Romans is shaped by "the more responsible temper of Virgilian heroism." In *Luc.*, political responsibility derives from a love of honor; in *Tit.*, the Romans, "having lost a steady sense of personal honor, have abandoned political responsibility."

Chapter 3, on *Ham.*, begins with a quotation from Machiavelli's *Discourses on Livy* on the political damage done by Christianity, which encourages men to be humble and patient, thus giving broad scope to tyrants. Notes that Machiavelli urges the revival of "the ancient Roman passion for worldly honors." Comments on Hamlet's inability to act on his "intermittently arising Roman impulses." Contrasts the prince's reaction to the Player's speech about the death of Priam at the hand of Pyrrhus (*Ham.*, II.ii.468–497) to Lucrece's response to the mural on the fall of Troy; unlike Hamlet, Lucrece is able to use art to turn a private injury into a public one and to inspire political action. In *Ham.*, Sh appears to go beyond Machiavelli by trying to strengthen Christian audiences; the play teaches "the dangers of passivity incident to a version of Christian education."

Chapters 4, 5, and 6 discuss honor as a tragic subject in the Roman plays. Chapter 4, "Coriolanus and Aristotelian Magnanimity," is a revision of item 1592; chapter 5, "Caesarian Honors, Brutus's Dilemma, and the Advent of Christianity," incorporates a revision of item 1940; and chapter 6, "*Antony and Cleopatra*: The Religion of Eros and the Limits of Personal Love," is a revision of item 1165. Chapter 7, "The Career of Henry Monmouth," analyzes *R2*, *1&2H4*, and *H5* to demonstrate that the greatness of Henry V lies "in his willingness and ability to share honor," while his chief flaw derives from "arousing men to admire spectacular displays" without inculcating a proper sense of justice. A postscript on *Tmp.* maintains that in Prospero Sh has created his most complete statesman, who through struggle comes to possess a truly balanced sense of honor.

0081 Alvis, John. "Unity of Subject in Shakespeare's Roman Plays." *PAPA*, 3, no. 3 (1977), 68–75.

Maintains that Sh's Roman plays (*JC*, *Ant.*, *Cor.*) are unified by intrinsic similarities in "tone, style, imaginative scope, and moral content." Compares these plays to the major tragedies (*Oth.*, *Mac.*, *Ham.*, *Lr.*) to show how distinctive Sh's Roman world is. In *JC*, *Ant.*, and *Cor.*, Sh eschews the emotional extremes, "the anguished tone, the emblematic moral contrasts, the metaphysical discord, the philosophical-minded protagonists, and much of the supernatural aura characteristic of the major tragedies." Sh's source, Plutarch's *Lives*, depicts the Romans as pious and accords divine providence a role in human affairs, but the playwright removes these emphases. In the three Roman plays, Sh explores the limitations of self-glorification; he seems to be testing "the secular humanist premises underlying Renaissance enthusiasm for Rome." As memorable as these ideas are, they are finally unsatisfactory as substitutes for "the Christian humanist moral norms embodied in the major tragedies." Revision of part of item 0082.

0082 Alvis, John Edward. "Shakespeare's Roman Tragedies: Self-Glorification and the Incomplete Polity." Ph.D. dissertation, University of Dallas, 1973. *DAI*, 35 (1974–75), 1034-A.

Attempts to demonstrate that Sh presents Rome as an "incomplete polity" in *JC, Ant.,* and *Cor*. The protagonists of these plays seek to stand out in their society by adhering to unsullied principle, but in each case the search is frustrated by a dependence on public acclaim. For Brutus, Antony, and Coriolanus, self-glorification results in a loss of authentic nobility. Sh modifies Plutarch's *Lives*, his source, to emphasize the themes of the incomplete polity and self-glorification. Parts revised as items 1592 and 0081. Chapter 5 revised as item 0079.

0083 Amiran, Minda Rae. "Some Thoughts on a Theory of Tragedy." *Studies in the Drama*. Ed. Arieh Sachs. (Scripta Hierosolymitana 19.) Jerusalem: Hebrew U., 1967, pp. 61–74.

Questions the validity of Dorothea Krook's definition of tragedy (see item 1354). Uses Aristotle's comments in the *Poetics* on the emotions tragedy evokes in the audience to argue that simply pointing out "elements" (as Krook does) is not sufficient to define tragedy as a whole. Uses a number of ancient and modern works (including *Mac., Rom., Lr., Ant., JC.* and *Ham.*) to suggest how a definition of tragedy might be approached.

0084 Amur, G. S. "The Comic Characters of Shakespeare." *Journal of Karnatak University—Humanities*, 9 (1967), 19–27.

Defines the comic character objectively as "an expression or embodiment of the Ridiculous in human nature" and subjectively as "a character which is an instrument of the perception of the objectively Ridiculous." Classifies Sh's comic characters into four groups: (1) "the clowns, the clownish rustics, and men drawn from the various professions"; (2) "a large dionysiac group who might conveniently be called the Falstaff family"; (3) "the professional Fools and wits"; and (4) "the Humour characters in the Jonsonian sense of the word Humour." The first group includes Patroclus from *Tro.*, Dromio from *Err.*, the Clown who brings Cleopatra the basket of figs in *Ant.*, the Clown in *Tit.* who is "put to death for just carrying an unpleasant letter," and Holofernes, "the Latin-loving schoolmaster of *LLL*." Thersites can be included in the second group. Feste is representative of the third, and Malvolio of the fourth.

0085 Anderson, Frances Elizabeth. "The Theme of the Exile and Fugitive in Shakespeare's Plays." Ph.D. dissertation, University of Denver, 1961. *DA*, 22 (1961–62), 3640.

Proposes to discover and define the significance of figures in exile in eight of Sh's plays, including the protagonists of *Tim.* and *Cor*. The circumstances of withdrawal as well as the place of exile are often important to meaning. Sh stresses "the responsibility of the withdrawal figure—whether his departure is forced or voluntary—to return to participation in the concerns of humanity."

0086 Anderson, Ruth L. "The Pattern of Behavior Culminating in *Macbeth*." *SEL*, 3 (1963), 151–73.

Calls attention to the Renaissance belief that men's behavior could be classified into patterns. The ambitious man, for example, could be expected to behave in certain ways to experience certain things, including fear and an all-consuming thirst for domination. Various handbooks gave the Elizabethans careful descriptions of the effects of ambitions, and the plays of Seneca dramatized for them the abuses of power. Sh's two chief studies of ambitious men are *R3* and *Mac.*

0087   Andreas, James R. "Remythologizing *The Knight's Tale*: *A Midsummer Night's Dream* and *The Two Noble Kinsmen*." *ShY*, 2 (1991), 49–67.

Detects in Sh's rehandling (*MND* and *TNK*) of Chaucer's Theban story (*The Knight's Tale*) the "progressive desacralization" of what was regarded "as an essentially religious fable." In *MND*, the deities have been humanized, Theseus's function as a mediator between the human and the divine is shared with the mischievous Puck, and there is no attempt "to moralize or allegorize the fable." In *TNK*, the stories of the gods, deprived of their supernatural standing, are viewed as studies in the effects of erotic passion and thus parallel to what happens to the human beings in the play.

0088   Ang, Gertrudes. "Shakespeare's Pygmy Lore." *Philippine Quarterly Journal of Culture and Society,* 5 (1977), 187–88.

Calls attention to brief references to the pygmies in three of Sh's plays: *Jn.*, *Lr.*, and *Ado*. The last of these has Benedict include "any embassage to the Pigmies" (II.i.257) as one of several exotic and impossible tasks he would gladly perform rather than talk to Beatrice. Although he does not specifically say so, Benedict may be thinking of the fight between the pygmies and the cranes, an account of which Sh would have known from the *Iliad*.

0089   Anikst, Alexander. "Shakespeare—A Writer of the People." *Shakespeare in the Soviet Union: A Collection of Articles.* Eds. Roman Samarin and Alexander Nikolyukin. Tr. Avril Pyman. Moscow: Progress Publishers, 1966, pp.113–39.

Denies that Sh's art was informed by the didacticism of the Middle Ages; his realism furnished a powerful picture of his times while it pointed the way toward a new freedom for humanity. Foregrounds *Tim.*, in a discussion of Sh's tragedies, as perhaps the clearest instance of the playwright's expression, through his protagonist, of rage at the degenerate social conditions that pervert the relationships between man and man. Calls attention to the role that Renaissance humanists' study of the classical writers played on the transformation of "the old medieval dramatic genres." Argues that the blend of the medieval and the Roman in the drama of Sh produced something entirely new.

0090   Aoki, Kazuo. "*The Praise of Folly* and Shakespeare's Early and Middle Comedies." *ShStud*, 18 (1979–80), 1–27.

Argues that Sh probably knew the works of Erasmus but that in any case there is a spiritual kinship between the world of *Praise of Folly* and that of Sh's early and middle comedies. *LLL* shares with *Praise of Folly* a sense of the vanity of learning, and *AYL* has a similar recognition of the need to live cheerfully even in the midst of melancholy experiences.

0091   Archer, M. "Shakespeare and the Ethics of Honour." Ph.D. thesis, Cambridge University, 1987. *ITA*, 36 (1988), 1386.

Attempts to show how Castiglione, Montaigne, Spenser, and Sh inherited and modified "an Aristotelian tradition of the virtues and an Aristotelian moral psychology." Through intermediary influences of his own time, Sh absorbed from Aristotle "an ideal of rational conduct and the concepts of a 'mean,' 'deficiency,' and 'excess' in the virtues that follow from it." Considers the ideas of grace and courtesy in *AYL*, the relationship of anger to friendship in *Ado*, and "the virtue of prudence" in *TN*.

0092   Archibald, Elizabeth. *Apollonius of Tyre: Medieval and Renaissance Themes and Variations*. Cambridge: D. S. Brewer, 1991. xiii + 250 pp.

Part 1 provides background on the *Historia Apollonii Regis Tyri*, "a 'novel' from late antiquity which was known and enjoyed throughout the Middle Ages and into the Renaissance, and maintained unbroken popularity and an almost unchanging plot from the fifth century to the seventeenth, and beyond." Notes that the earliest texts (in Latin) for the form of the story in which we now have it were probably composed in the late 5th or early 6th c. A.D., though there seems to have been an earlier text, in either Latin or Greek, from which this version derives. Gives a synopsis of the *Historia Apollonii*, discusses its style and structure, and outlines important themes (fathers and daughters, kingship, education and learning, and riddles). Finds sources and analogues for the *Historia* in epic (especially the *Odyssey*), drama (plays by Plautus descended from Greek comedies), romance, hagiography, and historical accounts. Attempts to explain the popularity of the *Historia* in the Middle Ages and the Renaissance. Refers frequently, though briefly, to the influence of the *Historia* on Sh: Barnabe Riche's *Apollonius and Silla*, a source for *TN*, is indebted to the *Historia*, as is the last act of *Err.*; and *Per.*, which is based on it, preserves "the traditional absence of rationale for the disasters which afflict Apollonius/Pericles and his family, as well as the pagan setting." Part 2 comprises a text of the *Historia* and an English translation.

0093   Ardolino, Frank A. "Severed and Brazen Heads: Headhunting in Elizabethan Drama." *Journal of Evolutionary Psychology*, 4 (1983), 169–81.

Provides a brief survey of the practice of "severing and displaying the heads of defeated antagonists or criminals" in a variety of cultures, including those of ancient Greece and Elizabethan England. Examines a number of Elizabethan plays that employ the motif of the severed head. Notes that in *R3* the decapitation of Hastings becomes a part of Richard's staging of political events in order to gain the throne. The imagery of decapitation is important throughout the rest of the play; in the final scene, the crown, "the royal extension of the head," is plucked off the head of Richard and delivered to Richmond. *Mac.* sums up the traditions associated with the head motif. The most important significance of the head in this play is as "the repository of diseased thoughts which when activated bring death into the country." At the end, when Macduff displays Macbeth's head, he emulates Perseus holding the Gorgon's head. In I.iii, Macbeth had called the murdered Duncan a new Gorgon; it is he himself, however, who has possessed the true Gorgon's head and who can no longer destroy men because his head is now separated from his body and exhibited by his conqueror.

0094   Armitage, David. "The Dismemberment of Orpheus: Mythic Elements in Shakespeare's Romances." *ShS*, 39 (1987), 123–33.

Argues that though Sh's detailed knowledge of Ovid's version of the Orpheus myth can be seen in his early plays, it is only in the late romances that he became truly Ovidian in his use of this myth and his approach to myth-making in general. In his late plays, Sh, like Ovid, moves beyond tragedy to romance, emphasizing "regeneration and transformation." More specific connections between the Orpheus story and the final plays can also be observed. Orpheus's association with the depths of the sea seems to inform Sh's plots, which use the sea as "an analogue to Hades in the Orpheus myth." Also, Ovid's belief in the ameliorative power of music is assimilated by Sh and given special prominence in the romance.

0095   Armstrong, John. *The Paradise Myth*. London: Oxford U. P., 1969. xi + 133 pp.

Chapter 3, "Themes in Renaissance Art and Literature," is chiefly devoted to an extended discussion of three of Sh's late plays as they treat "man's perpetual craving for the infinitely various and his need for the sure domicile of a continuing order." In *Ant.*, Cleopatra, compared with Venus in Enobarbus's famous account of her first meeting with Antony (II.ii), is like the goddess "a creature of the margin between sea and land," where boundaries are vague and things do not hold their visible shape. Sh greatly expanded the hint he got from Plutarch for associating Cleopatra with the snake; he had her identify the snake with the child and herself with both. Maintains that snake and child work to defeat form and boundary, and this impetus of the play is reinforced by pervasive images of "the continually shifting, the merging, and the indeterminate." Sh also took from Plutarch the idea of Antony as a ruined hero and expanded it into a study of the obsolescence of the heroic form itself. *WT* uses myth—especially that of Proserpina—to endorse the enrichment offered humanity by "the complex of living forces" that provides a settled order. Many things in the play—the pastoral idyll, the cycle of nature, the reconstitution of the broken society at the end—validate "inherited wisdom." Sh does provide glimpses of a world outside this cyclical stability, notably in Florizel's evocation of "the boundless versatility of the gods" in their metamorphoses, the poignant exclamation about age (influenced by Ovid) in Perdita's speech about Proserpina, and the boundary-breaking thief Autolycus (named after Mercury's son). This extra-cyclical element, however, is recessive in *WT*; essentially, the play "is a great many-tiered image of self-renewing organic strength and sure fulfilment." The opposite poetic themes of *Ant.* and *WT* are synthesized in *Tmp.*, in which Sh uses Prospero's two refractory servants (Caliban and Ariel), the masque of goddesses, the recollection of the Jason and Medea story from Ovid, and a host of other elements to embody the imagination in concrete form. The unifying force of the imagination is defined "through the structure of Prospero's power, his establishment of organization through complicity with the subversive, the collaboration between his inherited knowledge and beings at enmity with it, and the upholding of his charm by the very forces which require that it shall dissolve."

0096 Aronson, Alex. *Psyche and Symbol in Shakespeare.* Bloomington: Indiana U. P., 1972. viii + 352 pp.

The introduction explains Jungian theory and proposes its application to analyzing Sh's plays. Provides an overview of the book's three large sections. The first, "The Ego," sees the hero in terms of "his conscious mind only" and treats the symbols of the mask, of appetite, of the shadow, and of the inner voice. In the phase studied in this section, characters do not achieve a balance between conscious and unconscious, reason and instinct, spiritual and physical aspirations—in short, they do not attain individuation. The second section, "Anima," focuses on "the gradual domination of the ego by unconscious forces over which it has only partial control." It deals with "opposing psychic elements" in Sh's plays that appear as "archetypes of integration or division, as paternal or maternal figures which, whether actually present on the stage or not, promote or prevent individuation." The third section, "The Self," discusses the need for integration of the different elements of the human personality as it is seen in Sh: This section uses three figures from myth— Prometheus, Orpheus, and Asclepius—to provide "the symbolic equivalent for the psychological process" suggested in some of the plays.

Chapter 2, "Appetite," contains a discussion of *Tro.*, whose male protagonist declines to involve himself in adult life because of a divided ego. He is undone by a "mixture of unfulfilled sensuality and compulsive heroism, neither of which is provided with an adequate outlet." Cressida's divided personality—artless and cunning, simple and complex, wise and foolish—has given rise to much contradictory comment. Troilus is attracted to her because she seems to reflect his own dualism, but he fails to see that she accepts her divided self. Troilus finally disintegrates psychically: Defeated emotionally by Diomedes, he attempts to escape into heroism at the play's end.

Chapter 7, "Hecate," part of the section on Anima, collects passages from *Ham.*, *Mac.*, and *Lr.* that mention Hecate and from these passages reconstructs what the goddess must have meant for Sh. In these three plays, Hecate furnishes "an extreme instance of the maternal archetype in its most destructive aspect." Notes Sh's familiarity with the Hecate story in books 7 and 14 of the *Metamorphoses* and speculates that the playwright may have unconsciously appropriated certain passages from Ovid in these three nonclassical plays. In *Tmp.*, the Hecate myth is still present in the story of "Sycorax, the witch, her god Setebos, and her son Caliban."

Chapter 8, "Prometheus," associates the mythic figure with a "willingness to help others in distress." The Prometheus figure has an integrated self and is profoundly aware of "the destructiveness of uncontrolled impulses." Examples are Vincentio (*MM*), Friar Francis (*Ado*), Theseus (*MND*), and Prospero (*Tmp.*).

Chapter 9, "Orpheus," uses the mythical musician as a symbol of the integrative power of the healer. Though the Orpheus myth is mentioned in only three plays (*TGV*, *H8*, and *MM*), it informs many others, where the curing of divided minds through music is discussed or accomplished.

Chapter 10, "Asklepios," discusses healers and healings, both successful and unsuccessful, in the plays. Camillo (*WT*) and Helena (*AWW*) are examples.

0097 Aronson, Alex. "Shakespeare and the Ocular Proof." *SQ*, 21 (1970), 411–29.

Maintains that in Sh's early comedies, sight images are used to emphasize the lover's ability to perceive true beauty in the soul of his beloved. This kind of sight is available to the lover alone and is liable to neglect the presence of moral evil in the world around him. As Sh's art matured, he universalized the tension between sight and insight in his characters, emphasizing in the tragedies "the mythical nature of man's distorted vision that leads from spiritual to actual blindness." Through the metaphor of distorted vision, Sh expresses the evil attendant on "men's belief that what they see is manifestly impossible." Two characters who argue fallaciously that a man can see his true self reflected in the eyes of others are Achilles in *Tro.* and Cassius in *JC*. Cressida is one of several Shakespearean women who, being frail, blame their eyes for having misdirected their minds. The idea of wrongly using ocular demonstration to establish a "truth" that is not open to visual measurement is found in Greek tragedy (*Oedipus Rex*) and philosophy (*Phaedo*). Aristotle, however, suggests that sight helps us to know, to distinguish differences (*Metaphysics*). Othello allows Aristotelian ocular proof to cloud his vision of Desdemona's true self and to destroy the integrity of his character. Macbeth is "the most conscious of Sh's 'blind' heroes"; he is "only momentarily deceived by his wife's vision of ultimate success." Before and after the murder of Duncan, his eyes tell him the truth about what he is doing, prompting him to pray for darkness. In *Lr.*, Gloucester's blindness involves not having any moral consciousness about his own lust and the general presence of evil. Lear's madness is another form of this blindness. Leaving the realm of tragedy, Sh dramatizes in *Tmp.* "the victory of awareness over ocular proof," but Prospero does not escape without an uneasy consciousness that the ambiguities resulting "from too strong a reliance on the life of the senses remain intact."

0098 Arthos, John. *The Art of Shakespeare*. London: Bowes and Bowes, 1964. 198 pp.

A chapter on *Ant.* contends that throughout Sh's works and especially in this play, the gods of antiquity appear to enrich and beautify what is constantly presenting itself before us and then passing away. Throughout the play, the language, even in its irony and humor, enhances the sublimity of the protagonists in that "the words, the names, the imaginings of antiquity are the evidence of the greatness men acknowledge and emulate. The idea of eternity is granted the authority the imagination and the soul appear to require."

A chapter on *Tro.* suggests that it is derived from the medieval model of richly variegated comedy with a happy ending. Though contravening some of the conventions of this type of comedy, Sh preserves its essential spirit: The emphasis is still on "the valuing of love even when love is denied success." The drama lies in the composition, not the events: Interest is maintained by a pattern of contrasts that presents characters undergoing various experiences. Sh regards with a critical eye "everything in the play that compounds chaos," while he is "solicitous of what would resist it." Throughout, Troilus exhibits "truth, generosity, and love," and he preserves these qualities at the end. The comedy of the play invites us—at the end as well as the beginning—to contemplate "the charm of the romantic foolishness."

0099 Arthos, John. "The Forming of the Early Comedies." *SRO*, 3 (1967), 1–8.

Suggests that Sh's early comedies were influenced, through Lyly, by a conception of dramatic form, indebted to the Italian *Ballet Comique*, in which music and choreography are understood to be of the greatest importance in determining the structure of a work and its "manner of production and acting." A related idea is that Plautus's influence on Sh derives more from the musical structure of his plays, as interpreted in 16th-c. school productions, than from his plots or language. Song and motion are at the center of Plautus's plays, and the form of *Err.*, *LLL*, and *TGV* depends greatly on a "spatial conception in which display, spectacle, and dance-like movements entertain us in their own right," and with music and song, "determine the final delight."

0100 Arthos, John. "Shakespeare and the Ancient World." *MQR*, 10 (1971), 149–65.

Discusses *Err.* in some detail to show that its difference from Plautus's *Menaechmi* lies in "a magical power at work among men" that promises or gives intimations of a mysterious harmony. There is a metaphysical substance in *Err.* that is discernible throughout Sh's work: It informs even the tragedies, where isolation and destruction are never absolute. This is in sharp contrast to the beliefs of the ancient world, as exemplified in Homer, whose great characters accept as fact "the total abandonment of every mortal."

0101 Arthos, John. *Shakespeare's Use of Dream and Vision.* Totowa, New Jersey: Rowman and Littlefield, 1977. 208 pp.

The first chapter, on *PhT*, attempts to establish the value of metaphysical and philosophical considerations in interpreting Sh. Explains the part played by Platonism and Neoplatonism in such conceptions as the interchanging of the lovers' selves and the abolition of number. Notes that Platonism was mediated through Plotinus, the pseudo-Dionysius, Augustine, Aquinas, Pico della Mirandola, and Marsilio Ficino. Includes chapters on *MND*, *JC*, *Ham.*, and *Tmp.* In *JC*, Sh was able to probe more deeply than his sources, Plutarch and Appian, into the ironic tragedy of the events he was treating. Argues that Sh's imaginative sympathy with his characters allowed him to reconstruct events in the Roman world with an accuracy rivaling that of modern historians. Cites Plato's *Laws*, *Republic*, and *Timaeus*, as well as Plotinus and Longinus, as background for understanding the idea of necessity in *Ham.*

0102 Arthos, John. *Shakespeare: The Early Writings*. Totowa, New Jersey: Rowman and Littlefield, 1972. x + 264 pp.

Proposes to examine Sh's early works both "for their own sakes" and to see how they exemplify the rich engagement of the author's mind with whatever came to its attention. The first essay, "Plautus and *The Comedy of Errors*," foregrounds Plautus's exuberance of language and of contrivance, his interest in romantic elements (especially the sea, the excitement it provides, and a variety of wondrous events), his contrast between suffering and fun, his frequent subjection of characters to the blows of fortune, his stress on both the inevitability of deceit among men and on their good feeling and benevolent spirit, and his concern to exhibit decency and reconciliation among his characters. Sh's imagination played wonderfully with all of these attitudes and materials, being particularly attracted to Plautus's sense of nature's and humanity's extravagance and to the idea of hidden difficulties besetting our worldly existence. In *Err.*, Sh added to Plautus's world a sense of the holy, giving "the idyllic a Christian cast." Finds that Sh's conception of his play as a doubling of what he took from his original, with elaborate parallels and contrasts, was inspired by Plautus's use of analogous musical patterning in the *Menaechmi*.

The second essay, "Italian Contributions," investigates the ways in which Renaissance Italian playwrights and story-writers, especially Boccaccio, directed the imitation of classical drama into new channels. Notes that the Italian comedy is different from the works of Plautus and Terence in the following ways: It has different moral values, it is written in prose, it is realistic, it has greater variety of character and incident, and it makes a specific point. Discusses Machiavelli's *Mandragola* as a play that exhibits the tendency to make a point and names several of Sh's plays that do the same, the first two of which are *LLL* and *TGV*. Mentions Ariosto as a playwright who allowed "poetic and romantic interests" to qualify his realism; his gentleness and respect for honor make him like Sh.

The third essay, "*Love's Labour's Lost*," points out this play's debt to Plautus and Lyly, its exploitation of Platonic oppositions, and its mockery of Giordano Bruno's attempts to resolve "the conflicts between Platonism and naturalism."

The fourth essay, "*Two Gentlemen of Verona*," shows that in this play Sh explores the questions of constancy and inconstancy in lovers and friends through Neoplatonism. The failure of the ending suggests that this philosophy is insufficient to deal with the issues.

The sixth essay, "The Encounter with Rome," observes that in *Ven.* and *Luc.* Sh focuses on the external features of the dramatic action, exploiting the strangeness of an alien culture, a culture profoundly committed to maintaining decorum and more concerned with effects than with "processes and sensibility." This emphasis on the outer aspects of individuals in crisis is heightened in *Tit.*, where Sh feels free to exclude the "profoundly affecting" as he modifies the form of his earlier histories to concentrate on making a clear moral point about revenge and justice.

The afterword discovers in Sh's work the belief that "a sustaining power holds men together." Takes note of Sh's use, especially in the early works, of the Platonic doctrine of "the consultation of the principle of life and truth within the soul." In exploring this belief, Sh shows its inadequacy in the face of worldly evil. Distinguishes between the involvement in the "mesh of life" of Sh's characters and the relative isolation of the great figures of antiquity as portrayed in the Roman histories or in Petrarch's *Lives of Illustrious Men* (a sort of handbook for "the humanist appreciation of antiquity"). Cites *Cor.*, which Sh transported almost literally from ancient culture but which nevertheless subdues its hero to the bonds of kinship, as confirmation of the playwright's conviction that a man cannot exist totally on his own.

0103 Ashley, Leonard R. N., and Michael J. F. Hanifin. "Onomasticon of Roman Anthroponyms: Explication and Application." *Names*, 26 (1978), 297–401; 27 (1979), 1–45.

Provides a detailed explanation, along with illustrations, of the ancient Roman system of naming persons and its influence on the naming of things and places. Outlines the trinomial basis of this system, including the *nomen* (family name), *praenomen* (forename), and *cognomen* (added name comparable to a nickname). Includes a section on "Shakespeare's Handling of Roman Names," considering *JC, Ant., Cor., Tit.,* and *Cym.* Notes that Sh does not give evidence of a "clear and consistent understanding of the traditions of Roman nomenclature and, in fact, misses some useful dramatic points that strict and correct use of proper names might have made." Discusses Ben Jonson's use of Roman names for comparison.

0104 Asimov, Isaac. *Asimov's Guide to Shakespeare.* Vol. 1. *The Greek, Roman, and Italian Plays.* Vol. 2. *The English Plays.* Garden City: Doubleday, 1970. xiv + 723 pp.; xiv + 843 pp.

Proposes to "go over each of the thirty-eight plays and two narrative poems written by Sh in his quarter century of literary life, and explain, as I go along, the historical, legendary, and mythological background." Divides the works into "four broad groups: Greek, Roman, Italian, and English." The Greek works (*Ven., MND, TNK, Tro., Tim., WT,* and *Per.*) are those based on Greek legend or history or those set arbitrarily "in a time we recognize as Greek." The Roman works (*Luc., Cor., JC, Ant.,* and *Tit.*) are those based on actual history or on "utterly non–historical, but Rome-based, inventiveness."

0105 Astington, John H. "Eye and Hand on Shakespeare's Stage." *Ren&R*, 22 (1986), 109–21.

Discusses two of the Elizabethan arts of the actor, *vultus* (face, or more especially eyes as the center of the face) and *vita* (life, or more especially gesture of hands) and their significance in Sh. Explains that these physical arts were thought to reveal essential truth of character. Cites the account in *Luc.* of how, in the painting of the Trojan war, the faces and eyes of Ajax and Ulysses reveal their characters as an analogue to the way actors are to show forth the nature of those they impersonate. Discovers many references in Sh's plays to the "discourse of the eye." There are relatively few references to "manual gesture," the fullest description of its power being found in the passage on the Troy painting from *Luc.*, which speaks of Nestor's use of oratorical gesture to signify "in a manner different from that of speech." Notes that the Peacham drawing of characters from *Tit.* shows gesture used both as accompaniment to the specific demands of what is said and in an "abstract, non-specific sense." Makes the point that the eye and hand could sometimes be deliberately placed in a state of discord in order to figure "complex mental states." Examples of this can be seen in *R2*, *Cor.*, and especially *Mac.*

0106 Auchincloss, Louis. *Motiveless Malignity*. Boston: Houghton Mifflin, 1969. xi + 158 pp.

Comprises a series of essays on Sh's works, including separate pieces on *Ant.*, *Tro.*, *Cor.*, and *JC*. The tragedy of Antony is that he tries to glorify his obsession with a royal strumpet to compensate for his decaying powers as a leader of men. Despite what he says in the early part of the play, he does not really wish to abandon his worldly power. Observes that the ebb and flow of Antony's fortunes after the battle of Actium "prolongs the action unduly"; Sh here seems to rely too heavily on Plutarch. Comments on Antony's generosity in defeat, his dying wish to be remembered as a soldier, and Cleopatra's creation of a fascinating but ephemeral final image of her own royalty.

Tro. features the attractive Trojans fighting for a bad cause and the mostly contemptible Greeks pursuing a good one. Ulysses, the best of the Greeks, attempts to play the statesman in pointing out that Troy is doomed. Hector, the noblest of the Trojans, recognizes his brother Paris's fundamental violation of law but fails to act on his insight. Helen is clearly a loose woman, not worth a war, and Cressida is no better. Sh seems to be pointing to an inevitable connection between chivalry and the weakness of the cause it chooses to defend. Views Achilles' villainy (the worst in Sh) as linked to his homosexuality.

Cor. shows us more about the hero's childhood than we know about that of any other Shakespearean character. This is a clue that the play is a psychological study rather than a political one. Caught in a trap of "national gratitude" for his valor, the hero is tragically unfit for political office. We are able to see the reasons (chiefly Volumnia) why Coriolanus is so "hysterically isolated." At first unable to recognize how sick her son is, Volumnia later tries to help by counseling him to show restraint so that he can gain the consulship; however, it is too late. Raging against the people in a frenzy of invective—something he needs to do repeatedly—Coriolanus departs. Volumnia, the committed patriot, talks him out of his revenge on Rome and achieves heroic status at her son's expense. He dies in another frenzy of anger, having been manipulated by Aufidius as he was previously manipulated by the tribunes. Suggests that Coriolanus's disgust with popular rule might have been "a deliberate exaggeration of something that Shakespeare felt within himself."

JC is a play about the assassination of an essentially benevolent ruler who is about to become king. Finds no reason to see in Caesar the potential for tyranny. The anarchy and corruption that are unleashed after Caesar's murder can be blamed primarily on Brutus and the other conspirators. The play is the tragedy of an idealist (Brutus) who is persuaded to participate in the always-evil deed of assassination.

0107   Badawi, M. M. *Background to Shakespeare*. London: Macmillan, 1981. viii + 142 pp.

Presents an introduction to Sh "primarily for the overseas student of Shakespeare, especially for the Afro-Asian student with no classical and little or no Christian background." Chapter 2, "Shakespeare the Man," gives a brief account of the Latin authors Sh would have studied in school. Chapter 4, "Cosmology and Religion," describes the Elizabethan concept of the universe as Greek in origin, mentioning especially the Great Chain of Being, the four elements, and the humors. Chapter 5, "The Classical Background," describes the proliferation of translations from classical works in 16th-c. England; gives examples of the use of Greek myth in the plays; sums up several important myths as Sh would have encountered them in Ovid's *Metamorphoses* (for example, those of Diana, Apollo, Juno, Ceres, Venus, and Hercules); surveys other sources of mythological knowledge (handbooks on mythology and rhetoric, creative works of poetry and prose, tapestry, and pageants); and indicates the influence of Seneca and North's Plutarch on Sh.

0108   Bagchi, Jasodhara. "The Pastoral on the Elizabethan Stage and Shakespeare." *Shakespeare Commemoration Volume*. Ed. Taraknath Sen. Calcutta: Presidency College, 1966, pp. 197–213.

Indicates briefly the classical heritage of the Elizabethan pastoral. Discusses *AYL* and *WT*.

0109   Baines, Barbara J. "Shakespeare's Plays and the Erasmian Box." *RenP*, 1981 (1982), 33–44.

Describes the use of the Silenus box of Alcibiades, or the Socratic box, as a metaphor by Erasmus, who saw it as representing "the disparity between appearance and reality" and explicitly linked it to the world-as-theater trope. Suggests that Sh's concern with the dichotomy between the inside and outside of human beings and the *theatrum mundi* idea is significantly indebted to Erasmus. The Silenus box seems "most obviously relevant to *The Merchant of Venice* and to *Cymbeline*, for it is in these two plays that Shakespeare uses the box as both a concrete stage property and as an emblem of the inside-outside dichotomy pervasive in life in general and in human nature in particular."

0110   Baldwin, Leonora Leet. *Elizabethan Love Tragedy 1587–1625*. New York: New York U. P., 1971. xii + 404 pp.

Attempts to establish love tragedy as a distinctive genre in the Elizabethan drama. Discerns three types: the tragedy of courtly love, the tragedy of false romantic love, and the tragedy of worldly love. Explains the background of the tragedy of courtly love in the Platonic tradition: The lover seeks union, through his beloved, with the Absolute; is defeated by temporal difficulties, though "purified and ennobled through the intensification of obstruction"; and achieves union with the Absolute "through a paradoxical embrace of death." Though the courtly love tradition often portrayed its lovers as involved in adulterous relationships, the Elizabethan versions of courtly love tragedy almost all focus on young, innocent lovers. The tragedy of worldly love, with its background in Aristotle's theory of friendship as extended by Aquinas, emphasizes the attempt of two equal, independent lovers to achieve a relationship. The natural form for worldly love is marriage, but in the Elizabethan drama worldly lovers are usually involved in adulterous relationships. The false romantic lover may use the language of courtly love, but he has no depth of commitment to the relationship: He easily casts aside his love, finds to his horror that he has discarded something supremely good to which he can never return, and finally rises to a true affection for his lost beloved that redeems him as he falls. Includes analyses of *Rom.* as a tragedy of courtly love and of *Oth.* and *Ant.* as tragedies of wordly love.

0111 Balestri, Charles Angelo. "English Neoclassicism and Shakespeare: A Study in Conflicting Ideas of Dramatic Form." Ph.D. dissertation, Yale University, 1970. *DAI*, 31 (1970–71), 6537-A.

Analyzes *Ant.* and *WT* to show how Sh exploited the openness of time and space of the traditional English drama, thus rejecting the closed form advocated by reforming neoclassicists like Sidney.

0111a Bamber, Linda. *Comic Women, Tragic Men: A Study of Gender and Genre in Shakespeare.* Stanford: Stanford U. P., 1982. 211 pp.

Revision of item 0112.

0112 Bamber, Linda Vigderman. "Comic Women, Tragic Women: Genre and Sexuality in Shakespeare's Plays." Ph.D. dissertation, Tufts University, 1974. *DAI*, 36 (1975–76), 2212-A.

Maintains that in Sh's comedies women are the usual carriers of values, while in the tragedies men carry the primary values. Typically, a tragic hero must at some point confront the values his limited perspective leaves out; he is then forced to transcend both his own and the opposing sets of values, thus achieving a humanity that cannot be measured by either set. The new values are often represented by a woman. In *Ant.*, we see a tragedy whose hero is Antony as well as "a comparison of two modes of dealing with a shifting and decaying Nature." Antony's mode is male, Cleopatra's female: they "redeem each other." In *Cor.*, the main character is treated as a tragic figure in the last two acts, but his dilemma at the end is not really tragic. Committed to a sexless political life, Coriolanus is unable to engage with what is beyond him. His conflict with Volumnia does not place him in opposition to genuinely different values but rather compels him to accept his own values. Revised as item 0111a.

0113 Barber, Charles. *The Theme of Honour's Tongue: A Study of Social Attitudes in the English Drama from Shakespeare to Dryden.* (Gothenburg Studies in English 58.) Gothenburg, Sweden: University of Gothenburg, 1985. 171 pp.

Part 1 explains the definitions of *honor* as the term would have been understood in the late Elizabethan age. Notes that 16th- and 17th-c. writers of treatises on honor often cited ancient Greek and Roman authors, especially Aristotle, but that this stock material tells us little about the idea of honor as it was understood by contemporary gentlemen. The dramatists of the time also drew on earlier sources, but they often changed or supplemented what these sources said to more accurately reflect contemporary practice. In Sh's three Roman tragedies, for example, the key passages concerning honor have no parallels in Plutarch's *Lives*.

Part 2 consists of analyses of a variety of plays. Chapter 4 is on *Tro.*, which uses considerations of honor, especially in the Trojan council scene (II.ii), to reveal the inadequacy of traditional romantic ideas about love and war "in face of contemporary reality." Chapter 7 is on Sh's Roman plays (*JC*, *Ant.*, and *Cor.*). *JC* foregrounds the notion of honor as a virtue that is manifested in concern for the public welfare as well as for "individual dignity and independence." This helps us to understand the high-minded but disastrously impractical Brutus, the self-seeking and expediently political Cassius, and the prestige-conscious conspirators. *Ant.* investigates the competition between Roman honor and Egyptian Epicureanism. For the Romans, of whom Octavius Caesar is the quintessential representative, honor has to do with military achievement and reputation, public service, and government. Antony is caught between the Roman imperative to seek honor and the power of Cleopatra, temporarily escaping the latter and submitting to the former (II.ii) but quickly reversing himself and returning to Cleopatra's sphere of influence. He is tragically destroyed by this tension. Although Octavius's sense of honor allows for some political maneuvering and cynicism, his victory is not viewed as wholly negative because it inaugurates world peace and stability. *Cor.*, which depicts a Roman state torn by internal dissension and obsessed with predatory imperialism, treats honor almost exclusively as the possession of martial qualities, the renown achieved through such qualities, and the various rewards men garner for military achievement. The ruling class views honor in this sense as superior to love; war is indeed portrayed as a rarefied sort of sexual activity. Further, honor is the fuel for what the patricians conceive as the main activity of the Roman state: that of a war machine. Coriolanus takes the notion of honor to such an extreme that he pursues it for himself alone. It is left to his mother (V.iii) to introduce an aspect of honor, heretofore unrecognized in the play, that includes mercy, reconciliation, and peace. Coriolanus's acceptance of her expanded definition of honor helps to restore the natural order but results in his death.

0114 Barber, C. L., and Richard P. Wheeler. *The Whole Journey: Shakespeare's Power of Development.* Berkeley: U. of California P., 1986. xxix + 354 pp.

Follows Sh's development throughout his career, emphasizing among other things the role of the family, and in particular the feminine and the maternal. Chapter 5, "*Titus Andronicus:* Abortive Domestic Tragedy," notes that in this play Sh focuses so intensively on family matters that he fails to project a convincing image of the Roman state (despite abundant and highly self-conscious references to "Roman literature and its handlings of Greek myth"). Sh substitutes paternal for maternal parenting and sentimentalizes Titus so that his destructiveness within his own family is not acknowledged. Chapter 10, "'The masked Neptune and/The gentlest winds of heaven': *Pericles* and the Transition from Tragedy to Romance," discusses three plays with classical settings—*Ant., Cor.,* and *Tim.*—that are characterized by "the absence of the sacred in the human" and thus aid us in understanding "the need for the sort of visionary relationship to women dramatized in the reunions" of *Per.* and *WT*. The fulfillment proposed for the lovers in *Ant.* is a "radical alternative to the dominant patterns of social and familial relationships." In *Cor.*, the protagonist has no male role model; his identity is completely determined by his mother. Timon substitutes himself for the nurturing mother.

0115 Barfield, Rayford Elliott Jr. "Human Fecundity in Shakespearean Comedy with a Survey Chapter on the Histories and the Tragedies." Ph.D. dissertation, University of Tennessee, 1969. *DAI,* 31 (1970–71), 1749-A.

Studies "the concept of human fecundity" as treated by Sh. Explains how Sh draws on both classical and Judeo-Christian mythologies for parallels to this basic theme. Discusses "the relationship between human fecundity and the neo-Platonic doctrine of plenitude." Focuses on the comedies to show that the idea of fecundity gradually moved "toward the center of Shakespeare's interest." Finds, in a survey of the histories and tragedies, that fecundity provides a positive standard against which the events of the plot are to be judged.

0116 Barish, Jonas A. "Continuities and Discontinuities in Shakespearean Prose." *Shakespeare 1971: Proceedings of the World Shakespeare Congress.* Vancouver, August 1971. Eds. Clifford Leech and J. M. R. Margeson. Toronto: U. of Toronto P., 1972, pp. 59–75.

Argues that Henry W. Wells was essentially correct thirty years ago when he advanced the thesis that "Sh's prose matured early, but then changed relatively little over the course of the career, and that such change as can be perceived consists mainly in a widening of range, in the use of prose for increasingly serious and powerful effects." Proposes to annotate and correct Wells's argument. Provides an example of continuity by comparing the Clown's speech in *Tit.* (IV.iii.77–100) and the Clown's speech in *Ant.* (V.ii). An advance in Sh's prose may be seen by contrasting the sardonic quips of the tradesmen in *JC* (I.i) and the serious style of the mutinous citizens in *Cor.*

0117 Barish, Jonas A. "The Uniqueness of Elizabethan Drama." *CompD*, 11 (1977–78), 103–12. Reprint. *Drama in the Rennaissance: Comparative and Critical Essays*. Eds. Clifford Davidson, C. J. Gianakaris, and John H. Stroupe. (AMS Studies in the Renaissance 12.) New York: AMS P., 1986, pp. 1–10.

Argues that Elizabethan drama is unique in its "multiplicity or comprehensiveness." This can be shown by contrasting it with classical Greek drama, neoclassical French drama, and modern European drama. Elizabethan drama has a versatile stage, flexible time, large casts, social inclusiveness, multiple plots, and a variety of verbal styles. By contrast, the drama of the other three periods is severely limited in all these respects.

0118 Barkan, Leonard. "Diana and Actaeon: The Myth as Synthesis." *ELR*, 10 (1980), 317–59.

Begins by tracing the Actaeon–Diana myth from Ovid's *Metamorphoses* and other ancient sources through the medieval and Renaissance mythographers. Notes the "conflicting and yet interrelating significances" of the tale. From the ancient versions there is "the story of love carnal or visionary, the story of identity, self-consciousness, and transformation, the story of forbidden knowledge in all its glory and terror." To these possibilities, the mythographers added "moralistic alternatives: The norms of economic behavior, the norms of social and political behavior, and finally the recapitulation of the Christian story." Analyzes several creative works of the Middle Ages and the Renaissance to show how their authors synthesized some or all of these ideas by using Actaeon's story. Like other comic Actaeons of the Renaissance, Falstaff in *Wiv.* is transformed by persecuting women into a comically grotesque figure. Having attempted to play the satyr, he has the tables turned on him and becomes an emblem of cuckoldry, a jackass. Sh integrated all the associations of the Actaeon myth with the comic tradition of men who become first spiritual, and then physical, jackasses. From Apuleius's *The Golden Ass*, Sh took the notion that sexuality, beastliness, and other asinine qualities are no ultimate bar to a divine vision. The relationship of Bottom and Titania reenacts the Diana and Actaeon story in several important ways. Titania is the Diana of Renaissance Platonists, a stern divinity who is nevertheless surrounded by a natural lushness. Like the Actaeon of Ovid, Bottom goes to the forest with his comrades and is separated from them. Like later Actaeons, he is an inquisitive braggart. He possesses, moreover, a "metamorphic personality," wishing to play all roles in the tradesmen's performances. As a result of his experience of love (and in true Neoplatonic fashion), Bottom has a vision that allows him to bridge the gap between enraptured seer and fool. This "comic assertion of humanity" is "Shakespeare's most original contribution" to the Actaeon myth.

0119 Barkan, Leonard. *The Gods Made Flesh: Metamorphosis & the Pursuit of Paganism*. New Haven: Yale U. P., 1986. xvi + 398 pp.

Analyzes and provides a history of the metamorphic tradition, from pagan antiquity through the 17th c. Notes that the continued reimagination and reinterpretation of pagan myths of metamorphosis by postclassical (Christian) civilization comes to represent the essence of antiquity. Chapter 2, "Ovid and Metamorphosis," explains that the *Metamorphoses* is about changes of all sorts, none completely "real" or "scientific," none completely magical: The poem "proves the natural world magical and the magical world natural." Surveys the myths in the poem, classifying the different kinds of change they embody. Chapter 3 is on metamorphosis in the Middle Ages, chapter 4 on metamorphosis in Dante, and chapter 5 on metamorphosis and the Renaissance imagination.

Chapter 6, "Shakespeare & the Metamorphoses of Art and Life," investigates Ovid and Ovidianism in Sh's works. *Tit.* makes heavy and obvious use of Ovid. On a basic level, the play parallels the story of Tereus, but Sh is attracted to this story because its central concern is communication and competition between mediums of communication. In the *Metamorphoses*, Philomela, having had her tongue cut out, has to create a new medium, a tapestry which, in the Renaissance tradition of illustrated Ovid, is "a composite of words and pictures." Lavinia's multiple mutilations make it impossible for her to use tapestry (as does her Ovidian prototype); she is forced to point to a book, a copy of the *Metamorphoses*, which combines words and images, and then to draw in the earth. In the same way, Sh struggles with his source and competitor to find a new medium "by expanding and exploding other media"; he embodies "the whole fable in a drama: words, pictures, book, signs, and more." *Cym.* and *Luc.*, both of which contain narrative parallels to the Tereus myth, are concerned with "issues of image and word similar to those in *Titus Andronicus*." In *Cym.*, the ancient book of Ovid is the occasion of voyeurism and misreading, a reflection on pagan traditions themselves and the contemporary pursuit of them. *MND* is Sh's fullest translation of Ovidian materials into "his own mythic language." The progress of love in the play is attended by multiple transformations, at the center of which is the love-juice. In Oberon's account of this potion, for which there is no classical source, Sh creates "an original etiology in the Ovidian mode." Puck, who presides over much of the metamorphosis, is a translation of Cupid; the fairy world is a recasting of materials from Reginald Scot's hostile account of metamorphosis in his *Discoverie of Witchcraft*. Ovid's story of the Minyades, whose opposition to the metamorphic realm of erotic love prompts them to tell the cautionary tale of Pyramus and Thisbe, is turned upside down and assimilated; Bottom's transformation, though owing something to Ovid's account of Midas, is primarily "Shakespeare's own mythic invention." The only character who is literally transformed, Bottom as an ass "is not only moralized, amorous, and visionary"; he "helps to define the art of theater." In *Ven.* and *MV*, Sh looks at the ancient world through two different Ovidian lenses: *Ven.* depicts the power of "passionate and excessive love," while in *MV* the conversation of Lorenzo and Jessica (V.i) moves from consideration of the "accidents of love" to "the universals of cosmic harmony." Several Ovidian myths of transformation, as well as two non-Ovidian ones (those of Proteus and Circe), prompt "reflections on selfhood and love" and furnish a number of motifs that "become the metamorphic matter of Shakespearean romantic comedy." Issues of twinning and identity, for example, are crucial to *Err.* and *TGV*. Falstaff, in *Wiv.*, presents a different metamorphic paradigm; like Bottom, he salvages "visionary glory" from degradation. Sh, at the end of his career, seems interested in "the grand illusion of metamorphosis": In *WT*, he blends "the metamorphoses of art with the metamorphoses of life," while in *Tmp.* spectacular displays appear and dissolve before our eyes. In Prospero's speech of farewell to his art, as near as Sh ever comes to a lengthy quotation from Ovid, we are given a retrospective on all of the transformations of life and art. For the last time, Prospero enacts "the pagan mystery of universal change" and then closes his book: Ovid. Part of chapter 6 is a revision of item 3172.

0120   Barkan, Leonard. *Nature's Work of Art: The Human Body as Image of the World*. New Haven: Yale U. P., 1975. x + 291 pp.

Examines the treatment of the human body as microcosm, an analogue for society and the commonwealth, which began with Plato and Aristotle, developed through early Christian thought and the Middle Ages, and found a congenial climate in the poetry of the English Renaissance. Jonson's *Sejanus* makes use of the parallel between the human body and the state when the protagonist is literally dismembered by the people who are, at the same time, tearing apart the body politic. In *Cor.*, the basis for the body analogy is the fable of the belly, derived by Sh from Livy's *History of Rome* (translated in 1600 by Philemon Holland) and North's Plutarch. Sh uses the image of the body to make the multiple members of the commonwealth one thing (they form a body, part human, part monster) and to make single characters multiple: Menenius, Volumnia, Aufidius, and, above all, Coriolanus. Coriolanus's body, Sh suggests, is "an extension of the state," but Coriolanus cannot keep his vast multiplicity together. Neither can the common people hold together as one person. Sh uses the anthropomorphic analogy, though less extensively, in *Jn.*, *Mac.*, and the Lancastrian tetralogy.

Includes chapters on "Natural Philosophy: The Human Body and the Cosmos"; "The Human Body and the Commonwealth"; "The Human Body, Esthetics, and the Constructions of Man"; "*Astrophil and Stella*: The Human Body as Setting for the Petrarchan Drama"; and "*The Faerie Queene*: Allegory, Iconography, and the Human Body."

0121 Barnes, Arthur Dale. "Forms of the Master-Servant Relationship in Shakespeare's Plays." Ph.D. dissertation, Brandeis University, 1982. *DAI*, 42 (1981–82), 5125-A-5126-A.

Argues that Sh's plays present a society organized on the relation of master to servant. Begins by tracing the classical and biblical background of the idea that everyone is somebody's master and somebody's servant. Chapter 2 analyzes *MM* and *Mac.* to gain an understanding of the role of governors. Chapter 5 deals with the family in *Shr., Oth., Tro.*, and other plays. Chapter 6 examines *Lr.* as a "summary example."

0122 Barnet, Sylvan. *A Short Guide to Shakespeare.* New York: Harcourt Brace Jovanovich, 1974. xi + 206 pp.

The first two parts, "The Writer and His World," and "The Works," are revised from the general introduction of item 0123.

0123 Barnet, Sylvan, ed. *The Complete Signet Classic Shakespeare.* New York: Harcourt Brace Jovanovich, 1972. xvi + 1776 pp.

The editor's general introduction discusses the influence of the works of Plautus and Terence, themselves influenced by Greek New Comedy, on Sh's comedies, especially the early ones. Mentions the distant indebtedness of Sh's late romances to "Hellenistic romances." Comments on the ways in which the tragedies of Seneca, translated into English for the first time in 1559, prepared the way for Sh's tragedies: Seneca taught the Elizabethan dramatists about the twin themes of tyranny and revenge and about drawing on "history and legendary history" to show "the fall of tyrants and the suffering visited upon passionate heroes." Contrasts *Ant.* and *Cor.*, two tragedies based on Plutarch: The former depicts the glorious ambivalence of two extravagant lovers in the expansive world of the late Roman republic, while the latter focuses on the much narrower world of the early republic. Describes two plays set in classical Greece, *Tro.* and *Tim.*, as "satiric tragedies," ironically detached in their view of character. Notes the source of the narrative poems *Ven.* and *Luc.* in Ovid. Revision of the general introduction published as item 0122.

The volume includes the introductions, texts, and notes on sources from the individual volumes of the Signet Classic Shakespeare (items 0357, 1582, 1610, 1763, 2094, 2203, 2277, 2372, 2574, 2628, 2710, 3013, 3076, 3097, and 3188). Omits the selections from the sources and the critical commentaries that are included in the individual volumes.

0124 Entry deleted.

0125 Barroll, J. Leeds. "Structure in Shakespearean Tragedy." *ShakS*, 7 (1974), 345–78.

Challenges the belief that the structure of a Renaissance tragedy can be understood in terms of a fatalistic notion of Fortune and her wheel. Cites numerous Renaissance authorities who deny Fortune's power to control human actions. Suggests that the major Renaissance image for the operation of Fortune is to be found in the *Table of Cebes*, a visualization bearing the name of Cebes (a figure in Plato's dialogues) but now believed to have originated in Roman Stoic thought. In visual representations of this *Table*, there are three concentric rings (walls), each of which encloses a park. In the outer parks, false pleasures can be found, whereas truth resides in the central park. Fortune is to be found in one of the outer parks, standing on a round stone, giving "reputed goods" to some persons (portrayed as laughing fools) and taking them back from others, who are engaged in various forms of lamentation. One who escapes the blandishments of Fortune may approach another figure, Instruction (standing on a cubic stone), who will prepare him to enter the park of truth. This complex understanding of Fortune suggests that Renaissance dramatists were not interested so much in fatalism but in the relationship between "the classical idea of Fortune" and "the concept of the freedom of the will and the intellectual operations of the mind." Describes the rise and fall pattern imposed by many commentators on Sh's tragedies as inadequate, based as it is on the simplistic image of Fortune's wheel. Proposes two paradigms that better explain Sh's tragic process and better accord with the complex tradition of Fortune that helped form the context for the plays. According to one pattern, there are three phases of character-action: (1) The protagonist, under the influence of a tempting agent, plans to achieve a goal; (2) the protagonist attains his goal; and (3) the protagonist reacts to what he has done. *JC* and *Mac.* are examples of this structure. The other pattern, the dominant one for Sh, is primarily concerned with how the protagonist reacts to various stimulating agents; he does not decide to do anything. Examples are *R2, Cor., Lr.,* and *Tim. Ham.* partakes of both structures, as does *Tro.*

0126   Barroll, J. Leeds III. "Shakespeare's Other Ovid: A Reproduction of Commentary on *Metamorphoses* I–IV." *ShakS*, 3 (1967), 173–256.

The introduction notes that George Sandys's commentary is useful for a number of reasons. In naming his sources—classical, medieval, and "modern"—he gives some idea of the complex interweaving of traditions "characteristic of Renaissance intellectual endeavor," as well as the continuity between "Medieval" and "Renaissance." Sandys preserves "some traditional ways of understanding what it was that Golding translated." Examples of the relevance of Sandys's commentary to Sh's plays can be seen in what he says about the myths of Actaeon (alluded to in *TN*) and Ixion (important for *Lr.*). The reproduction is selective, including only the commentary on the first four books of the *Metamorphoses* (appropriate since these comprised the contents of the 1st ed. of Golding's translation) and omitting Sandys's verse translation of books 1–4 and his marginal notes. Uses the 1640 edition.

0127   Barroll, J. Leeds III. "Some Versions of Plato in the English Renaissance: Three Reproductions." *ShakS*, 2 (1966), 228–95.

The introduction points out that an examination of Platonism and/or Neoplatonism in English thought of the 16th and early 17th c. can be facilitated by considering three discussions about Plato "printed in England, and translated into English during the approximate period of Shakespeare's own life-time." Reproduces book 8 of St. Augustine's *City of God* with a commentary by Juan Luis Vives, translated by John Healey and printed in 1620 (1st ed. 1610); selections from Philemon Holland's 1603 translation of Plutarch's *Moralia* entitled "Platonique Questions" and "A Commentarie of the Creation of the Soule"; and *Epistle LVIII* from the *Workes* of Seneca, translated by Thomas Lodge and published in 1620 (1st ed. 1614).

0128   Barroll, J. Leeds III. "The Structure of a Shakespearean Tragedy." *ShakS*, 8 (1975), 1–27.

Contends that Aristotle, in the *Poetics*, does not adequately distinguish *mythos*, or "plot," from "character." Attempts to amend Aristotle to provide a more coherent theory for describing Shakespearean tragedy. *Mythos* and "character" are two of the key objects of imitation in Aristotle's theory of tragedy, but many things that he attempts to include in the concept of *mythos*—peripeteia and recognition, for example—seem more closely related to "character" than to what he means by *mythos*. Proposes the term "sequence," meaning the "sense of process" in a tragedy, as more satisfactory than *mythos*. Employs examples from *Ham., Oth.,* and *Mac.*

0129 Barton, Anne. "*Julius Caesar* and *Coriolanus*: Shakespeare's World of Words." *Shakespeare's Craft: Eight Lectures.* Ed. Philip H. Highfill Jr. (Tupper Lectures on Shakespeare.) Carbondale, Illinois: Southern Illinois U. P., 1982, pp. 24–47.

Investigates the importance Sh gives to oratory and its ethical stature in *JC* and *Cor.* Both plays open with scenes of persuasion, and in *JC* the presence of Cicero, antiquity's greatest orator, constantly reminds the audience that Rome is a city where rhetoric is cultivated. In *Cor.*, the protagonist fears and despises language because it inevitably transforms facts. His natural mode of speaking is not persuasive, and he is constantly being measured against more effective speakers. Once banished, Coriolanus becomes an orator and actor himself. For example, in the last scene, he tries to persuade the Volscians that he has not betrayed them; in this, of course, he fails because Aufidius, in an egregiously dishonest speech, goads him into boasting of his feats against those he is attempting to move. Though Sh allows rhetoric some credit in *Cor.*, set in the early days of the republic when debate and discussion were useful in establishing common goals, he depicts the persuasive arts as utterly corrupt in *JC*. The city of Rome is overrun by "professional persuaders," whose influence is uniformly malign: Caesar asserts his invulnerability to persuasion just after being persuaded to go to the Senate and thus to his death. Brutus uses oratory to blind himself and his friends to the ugliness of what they are doing, and Cassius, in persuading Brutus to initiate the conspiracy, takes advantage of what he perceives to be Brutus's jealousy of Caesar.

0130 Barton, Anne. *The Names of Comedy.* (Alexander Lectures.) Toronto: U. of Toronto P., 1990. x + 221 pp.

Focuses on the question, explored in Plato's dialogue *Cratylus*, of whether a name can "embody the truth of the thing named," can be "natural." Considers various questions of naming in "English comedy, and its classical antecedents." Discusses proper names throughout the Shakespearean canon.

0131 Barton, Anne. "Shakespeare: His Tragedies." *The New History of Literature.* Vol. 3. Ed. Christopher Ricks. New York: Peter Bedrick, 1987, pp. 197–233.

Points out that *Tro.* takes as its subject the last stages of the the Greek siege of Troy but deliberately subverts the tragic and heroic tone traditionally associated with its characters and events. *Tim.* is centrally concerned with moral questions but provides no reliable voice by which to assess them; its structure is eccentric, the disappearance of the hero violates tragic decorum, and the effort to restore order at the end cannot be taken seriously. *Cor.* has as its central character a man "whose consciousness is extremely limited." In *Ant.*, the ending suggests "an impatience with the false symmetries of tragic art." The play presents a world of ceaseless flux, and Cleopatra triumphs over it by establishing the imaginative preeminence of her vision in competition with that of others, especially those who would debase her relationship with Antony through comedy.

0132 Bate, Jonathan. "Ovid and the Mature Tragedies: Metamorphosis in *Othello* and *King Lear.*" *ShS*, 41 (1989), 133–44.

Maintains that Sh's indebtedness in midcareer to Ovid can be detected not so much through allusions as through broad affinities between the Roman poet's "pattern of physical metamorphoses brought on by 'extremity' of suffering or desire" and the "tragic pattern of similarly induced, but internal, metamorphoses" in *Oth.* and *Lr.* In *Oth.*, the relationship between Othello and Desdemona has similarities to those of Ceyx and Alcyone and Cephalus and Procris, and the final scene is illuminated by Ovid's account of the death of Myrrha in the *Metamorphoses* and the epistle of Phyllis to Demophon in the *Heroides*. The transformations in *Lr.*, indicating loss of identity and descent into brutishness, are almost certain to have been informed by the

Metamorphoses. Ovid's accounts of the Libyan god Ammon, the centaurs (to which Lear compares women), and Ixion are especially relevant.

0132a Bath, Michael. "The Serpent-Eating Stag in the Renaissance." *Épopée Animale, Fable, Fabliau*. Eds. Gabriel Bianciotto and Michel Salvat. Paris: Presses Universitaires de France, 1984, pp. 55–69.

Discusses the motifs of "the serpent-eating stag, the stag at the stream, the weeping stag, the bezoar stone, the stricken deer, the Ditanny-eating stag and the stag and reflection." Explores the points of contact between these motifs, their classical origins, their emblematic significance in the Renaissance, and their use in *AYL* and *Ham*.

0133 Battenhouse, Roy W. *Shakespearean Tragedy: Its Art and Its Christian Premises*. Bloomington: Indiana U. P., 1969. xii + 466 pp.

Proposes to discover the fundamental premises of Sh's tragic art in the Christian tradition. Chapter 1 engages in a close reading of *Luc.*, arguing that Sh reshaped his source materials from Ovid and Livy in accordance with Chaucer's ironic evaluation of the Lucrece story in *The Legend of Good Women*. Cites Augustine's *Confessions* and *City of God* to explain the two forms of covetousness displayed in the poem, one by Tarquin and one by Lucrece. Lucrece, driven by an inordinate desire for fame, is tragically flawed, as is the Roman civilization she represents. Her reasoning about the rape is flawed and self-contradictory, as her attempt to read and identify with the Troy story in the tapestry attests. Lucrece's suicide, a dark pagan substitute for "the Christian Passion story," corrupts those who witness it to seek revenge. The poem, which depicts a bankrupt Greco-Roman civilization consumed with moribund notions of reputation and honor, can be compared with *Lr.*, a play in which Sh brings the tragedy of the pagan world closer to an intimation of the Christian dispensation that is to replace it. See item 2766.

Chapter 3 attempts to clarify the term "Christian tragedy." Includes an analysis of *Ant.* (a revision of item 1177). The play is an imitation of pagan immorality that allows us to admire the grandeur of the protagonists and then, by witnessing the devastations wrought by their sin, to pity them. Chapter 4 adapts Aristotle's notion of *hamartia* to Christian doctrine and to an analysis of *Ham*. Chapter 6 provides a close reading of *Cor.* based on comparisons of the play with its source, Plutarch's *Lives*. Maintains that Sh has shaped his drama to reveal, in contrast to the insight of Christianity, "Plutarch's flawed vision as well as and alongside that of Coriolanus."

0134 Entry deleted.

0135 Baumbach, Lydia. "Shakespeare and the Classics." *Acta Classica*, 28 (1985), 77–86.

Reviews a number of questions about Sh's classical learning, including his ability to read Latin and the accuracy of his picture of the Roman world. Compares *JC*, *Ant.*, and *Cor.* with their chief source, Plutarch's *Lives*, to show how Sh made his Roman setting relevant to his own time and how he adapted, rearranged, and supplemented Plutarch. *JC*, *Ant.*, and *Cor.* are linked by a concern with careful character study and by a subtle analysis of Roman virtues like *virtus* and *pietas*. Suggests that Sh may have shaped significantly the way we think about the Roman world.

0136 Bayerl, Francis James. "The Characterization of the Tyrant in Elizabethan Drama." Ph.D. dissertation, University of Toronto, 1974. *DAI*, 36 (1975–76), 1516-A-1517-A.

Points to three especially important influences on the stage portrayals of the tyrant in Elizabethan drama: (1) the English mystery and morality plays; (2) Senecan drama; and (3) Machiavelli's writings and commentaries on tyrants. Mentions Sh's *Julius Caesar* (*JC*) as a variation of the Machiavellian type of tyrant, more conventionally represented by Richard III (*R3*) and Bolingbroke (*1H4*).

0137   Bayley, John. *Shakespeare and Tragedy.* London: Routledge & Kegan Paul, 1981. 228 pp.

Chapter 3 suggests that in *Tim.* Sh might have been inspired by Ben Jonson to attempt a "tough and thoroughgoing treatment both of classical themes and of social lessons that might be drawn from them." The play, however, is limited because it devotes so much self-conscious poetry to the expression of "the same obsessive and monotonous states of mind." There is no inwardness that gives the audience room to feel and think. Chapter 4, on *Tro.*, maintains that Sh transferred the death of Troilus, a postscript in Chaucer's *Troilus and Criseyde*, to Hector in order to give dramatic force to the sense of desolation with which the story ends. The play keeps apart "the fact of experience and the saving ability to cherish it, change it, build upon it." Chapter 5, focusing on *JC* and *Ant.*, treats these Roman plays as tragedies of construction, in which the characters passively accept the world they know "as the only world there is." In this, Sh is influenced by Plutarch, but his imagination takes him beyond his source to present the ancient world "as flat and bright as a painted board." Chapter 6, on *Cor.*, calls attention to the hero's "combination of rigidity and insecurity"; the climax, during which he agrees to show mercy to Rome and has a brief glimpse of the incongruity that makes him human; the hint, through the "gracious silence" of Virgilia, of softness and privacy in his life; the irony of Volumnia's having created in her son an integrity that "she does not possess herself"; and the terrible and callous process of comedy that sacrifices the "exceptional individual."

0138   Bayley, John. *The Uses of Division: Unity and Disharmony in Literature.* London: Chatto & Windus, 1976. 248 pp.

"Uses of Shakespeare," the third section, includes a discussion of *Tro.* (a revision of item 2807) and discussions of *Ant.* and *Cor.* Treats Coriolanus as "an exceptionally well-defined character," almost a case study. In *Ant.*, Sh "rightfully found himself content with a situation which his intelligence, in the imaginative working out, sensed to be all on the surface, in a way that could nonetheless be rendered with a felicitous bravura."

0139   Bean, John C. "Passion Versus Friendship in the Tudor Matrimonial Handbooks and Some Shakespearean Implications." *WascanaR*, 9 (1974), 231–40.

Argues that in the matrimonial handbooks written or translated by the Tudor humanists, marriage is rooted in classical and medieval concepts of friendship rather than in courtly love. Shows how humanists like Juan Luis Vives, in talking of marriage, transform Neoplatonism so that the heavenly Venus is no longer representative of "the soul's escape from matter"; rather, Vives uses the heavenly Venus to create a vision of love as "matrimonial friendship, non-idealistic, rational, sexually fertile," and attentive to individual human personality. Sh's idea of love in the romantic comedies is not exactly that of the marriage manuals. His characters, that is, are impulsive and suffer the woes of traditional romantic love; and he has a Neoplatonic idea of "a benign universe created and ordered by Love." Yet his comedies synthesize the animal and the spiritual in such a way as to achieve a vision of love that is compatible with that of the handbooks.

0140   Beck, Ervin. "Terence Improved: The Paradigm of the Prodigal Son in English Renaissance Comedy." *RenD*, N. S. 6 (1973), 107–22.

Defines prodigal-son comedy by contrasting it to the Roman New Comedy of Plautus and Terence. In the former, a young man departs "from the values of his forebears," causes disruption in his society, and eventually reforms. In the latter, a young man revolts against the society of his elders, which is then reconstituted around him. New Comedy assumes that characters are types—that is, youth and age will always be at odds. Prodigal-son comedy is redemptive, holding open the possibility for the reform of youth. Sh wrote six plays that follow this paradigm: *TGV, Shr., 1H4, 2H4, AWW,* and *Tmp.*

0141   Beckerman, Bernard. "Shakespeare and the Life of the Scene." *English Renaissance Drama: Essays in Honor of Madeleine Doran and Mark Eccles*. Eds. Standish Henning, Robert Kimbrough, and Richard Knowles. Carbondale: Southern Illinois U. P., 1976, pp. 36–45.

Discovers in Sh two chief types of scenes, exhibiting two ways of shaping energy. The first, exemplified by the scene in *Cor.* (V.iii) in which Volumnia persuades her son not to destroy Rome, is active; it looks forward to the moment when Coriolanus will either acquiesce to his mother's plea or reject it, and it follows the progress of his crumbling resistance. The other type of scene is reactive: A character is shown adjusting to a change that has already taken place. In *Ant.*, Sh offers a most skillful blend of "active and reactive patterns." Octavius Caesar, for example, is almost always shown "in an active state"; Antony, in the first half of the play, is primarily active, and in the second half oscillates rapidly between active and reactive.

0142   Beckwith, Marc Allan. "A Study of Palingenius' *Zodiacae Vitae* and Its Influence on English Renaissance Literature." Ph.D. dissertation, Ohio State University, 1983. *DAI*, 44 (1983–84), 2770-A.

Remarks on the widespread use of the *Zodiacae Vitae* as a grammar school textbook in Renaissance England. Summarizes the content of the book, analyzes its "organization and imagery," and "evaluates Barnabe Googe's translation." Chapter 4 considers the influence of the *Zodiacae Vitae* on Sh.

0142a Belsey, Catherine. The Subject of Tragedy: Identity and Difference in Renaissance Drama. London: Methuen, 1985. xi + 253 pp.

Uses Renaissance tragedy as a point of departure for an investigation of the construction of subjectivity in the 16th and 17th c., specifically what it means during this period to be a man or a woman. Discusses a number of Sh's plays. JC, for example, brings into collision "two distinct orders of sovereignty," without making a decisive choice between them. This play also shows that the allegiance of the Roman people is crucial in the violent struggle for supremacy but that the people are in no sense autonomous. Refers to the contrast between Coriolanus's silent wife and his voluble mother (*Cor.*) to make the point that, in this period, a woman who speaks may be thought "to adopt the voice of a man." In *Ant.*, the heroine is an unstable subject, "plural, contradictory, an emblem which can be read as justifying either patriarchy on the one hand or an emergent feminism on the other, or perhaps as an icon of the contest between the two."

0143   Bender, Daniel Robert. "Singing High and Low: Shakespearean Comedy and the Rhetoric of Variety." Ph.D. dissertation, University of California, Berkeley, 1989. *DAI*, 51 (1990–91), 1617-A–1618-A.

Argues that the stage characters in Sh's comedies involve the audience in what 16th-c. humanism would have seen as "the operations of deliberation and choice that lead to appropriate action." Notes that the training in deliberation about action was emphasized in 16th-c. textbooks like that of Erasmus, which was influenced by "Aristotle's notion of character." The comedies of Sh "emerge from the humanist emphasis on deliberation, choice, and the development of character."

0144   Bennett, Robert Beale. "The Figure of the Malcontent in Shakespeare." Ph.D. dissertation, Stanford University, 1970. *DAI*, 31 (1970–71), 6045-A.

Defines the Elizabethan malcontent as a "melancholy intellectual," with his origins in Aristotle's *Problems* and in the works of Marsilio Ficino. Elizabethan malcontents, however, were usually less philosophically introspective than Ficino's analysis of the wise man's melancholy would suggest; instead, they were likely to display their bitterness in Juvenalian tirades. Includes discussion of Cassius, Timon, and Coriolanus, all of whom discover more wrong in the world than really exists.

0145 Bensel-Meyers, Linda. "Empowering the Audience: The Rhetorical Poetics of Renaissance Drama." *Style*, 23 (1989), 70–86.

Discusses "high Renaissance drama" in England, that of the late 16th c. and early 17th c., as rhetorical in purpose. More particularly, the plays of Sh and his contemporaries are exercises in deliberative rhetoric, by which the audience is invited to make up its own mind on questions of morality. Cites Richard Rainolds's mid-16th-c. Oxford lectures on Aristotle's *Rhetoric*, which privilege "the probabilistic reasoning of rhetoric," as a key to the thinking of humanist playwrights later in the 16th c. Notes that the drama under consideration was written immediately before Aristotle's *Poetics* became widely accessible in England through translation. In light of Rainolds's lectures, we can explore how the elements of drama described in the *Poetics* (plot, diction, character), often anachronistically imposed by modern scholars on Renaissance drama, can be redistributed "as elements of a practical art of rhetoric." Uses *Oth.* as an example.

0146 Bentley, Gerald Eades. *Shakespeare: A Biographical Handbook.* New Haven: Yale U. P., 1961. 256 pp.

Attempts to present Sh's life and "methods of work" with the greatest possible objectivity. Mentions the Latin training Sh would have gotten in the Stratford grammar school. Quotes extensively from Francis Meres' *Palladis Tamia* to show how the author "sets off a large number of English writers against Greek, Roman, and Italian writers, regularly implying that the Englishmen are as good as the foreigners." Comments that these comparisons show Meres to be enthusiastic about Sh's work.

0147 Bentley, Greg W. *Shakespeare and the New Disease: The Dramatic Function of Syphilis in "Troilus and Cressida," "Measure for Measure," and "Timon of Athens."* (American University Studies Series 4: English Language and Literature 85.) New York: Peter Lang, 1989. 242 pp.

Argues that the imagery of syphilis is central to the theme, coherence, and genre of *Tro.* and *Tim.* The second chapter, on *Tro.*, asserts that this play satirizes the trade in human flesh heedlessly pursued by the society of Sh's day. Special scorn is directed at the agents and brokers of this commerce, represented by Pandarus, and at the unruly gentlemen of the Inns of Court, "the victims of such bawds." Sh also develops ideals of love and heroism and sets them in stark contrast to "the degeneration of love, marriage, and fidelity into lust and promiscuity." Finally, there is a clear focus on "the businesslike aspect of this decadent behavior." Chapter 4, on *Tim.*, contends that images of syphilis are employed to enact the broad theme of "human usury," the "appetite by which one person metaphorically devours another." Views both plays, on the basis of Sh's use of these images, as primarily satires. Revision of item 0148.

0148 Bentley, Gregory Wayne. "Shakespeare and the New Disease: The Dramatic Function of Syphilis in *Troilus and Cressida, Measure for Measure,* and *Timon of Athens.*" Ph.D. dissertation, University of California, Davis, 1985. *DAI*, 47 (1986–87), 534-A.

Discusses images of syphilis in three of Sh's plays, including *Tro.* and *Tim.*; suggests that the plays are primarily satires; and illustrates the ideas about syphilis that were current during Sh's age. Revised as item 0147.

0149 Bentley, Jonathan Scott. "The Hermetic Tradition in Three Shakespearean Romances: *Pericles, The Winter's Tale,* and *The Tempest.*" Ph.D. dissertation, University of Oregon, 1986. *DAI*, 47 (1986–87), 2591-A.

Explicates the ways in which Hermeticism, "the most popular synthesis of the pagan tradition" in the Renaissance, informs "the ethical assumptions and values" that underlie Sh's last plays. Notes how Renaissance Hermeticism drew on the philosophy of Plato and "its subsequent interpretations" by early Christian thinkers. Sh's assimilation of Christianity and Hermeticism is explicit in *Per., WT,* and *Tmp.*

0150 Bergeron, David M. *English Civic Pageantry 1558–1642.* Columbia: U. of South Carolina P., 1971. ix + 325 pp.

Refers briefly to several of Sh's plays (for example, *R2* and *Cym.*) to show how they share, with civic pageantry, in the emblematic use of classical mythology.

0151 Berggren, Paula S. "'From a God to a Bull': Shakespeare's Slumming Jove." *CML*, 5 (1984–85), 277–91.

Examines Sh's allusions to Jove's transformation into a bull, which, because they are never essential elements in the retelling of a larger story, allow the playwright some independence of treatment as he selectively recalls Ovid's *Metamorphoses*. These allusions to the bovine Jove, found primarily in the plays of the late 1590s, bespeak a deep disgust with condescension and exploitation. Prince Hal compares himself to a god diminished to a bull as he grows increasingly uneasy about his fellowship with Falstaff in *2H4*; Falstaff, in *Wiv.*, though identifying himself with Jove as seducer, knows he is ridiculous and ends up a victim; in *Ado*, the only play of the late 1590s without a metamorphosed character, a cluster of Jove–bull references at the conclusion registers the undercurrent of savagery that has torn apart a group of friends. Jove as bull is largely absent from the late romances, with their emphasis on miraculously benign metamorphoses. An exception is *WT*, in which Florizel does compare his disguise to Jove's assumption of the bull's shape; but he disavows any impure motives.

0152 Berman, Ronald S. "Fathers and Sons in the Henry VI Plays." *SQ*, 13 (1962), 487–97.

Argues that censure of the *H6Triad* for disunity can be mitigated if we recognize the historical awareness of all three plays. They "share the perceptiveness of Aeschylus and Sophocles, for whom the most significant tragic act was that emanating from guilt of the past, and affecting the family and the state." Sh thus explores "the relationship of fathers and sons within a history-making dynasty," with emphasis on increasing decadence as the trilogy proceeds. Classical references help mark the descent into cruelty apparently compelled by dynastic ambition and loyalty. In *2H6*, for example, Clifford juxtaposes the myths of Aeneas and Medea, thus condensing the mixtures of piety and cruelty that characterize the action. In *3H6*, York is tormented by Margaret, who hands him a napkin stained with Rutland's blood (I.iv), suggesting the feast of Thyestes, a feast of which she will eventually partake.

0153 Bermel, Albert. *Farce: A History from Aristophanes to Woody Allen.* New York: Simon and Schuster, 1982. 464 pp.

Chapter 2 identifies three "family traits" of farce: unreality, brutality, and objectivity. Chapter 3 summarizes and comments on the story of Dionysus, especially as found in *The Bacchae* of Euripides. Discusses several elements of farce that have close connections with this myth: (1) Women in farces are less bound by convention or tradition than are men; (2) farces are pervaded by a sense of "release from everyday behavior and reactions," akin to a spell or trance; (3) farces often include men in drag. Chapter 4, "The Shadowy Edges of Farce," discusses elements of farce as they enrich works that are not purely farcical. Analyzes the scene in the last act of *1H4* in which Falstaff, playing dead, is present for the fatal encounter of Prince Hal and Hotspur and subsequently stabs the dead Hotspur in the thigh as part of an attempt to take credit for killing him. Distinguishes four principal kinds of farce: "realism, fantasy, theatricalism, and the well-made play." Chapter 5, surveying the history of farce, begins with Aristophanes' *Lysistrata*, which incorporates all four types. Notes that Plautus's comedies have been repeatedly plundered for their stories (as by Sh in *Err.*) and their characters, especially the braggart soldier (Falstaff, for example). Describes the Italian commedia dell'arte of the 16th and 17th c. and suggests that its farcical routines and character types are derived from the farceurs of Greek and Roman antiquity. One of the stock types is a magician and ruler of a remote domain, of which Prospero in *Tmp.* is a reconstruction. Detects farcical episodes in most of Sh's plays, with *Wiv.* and *Err.* being most "heavily dosed."

0154   Berry, Francis. *The Shakespeare Inset: Word and Picture.* London: Routledge & Kegan Paul, 1965. x + 173 pp.

Proposes the term *inset* for the type of episode in a Shakespearean drama in which "the imagined spectacle is at odds with the actual spectacle." Such episodes occur when a character on stage speaks about something that diverges from the action in which he is immediately involved. Uses Mercutio's Queen Mab speech as an initial example of an inset. Discusses Sh's early poems, *Ven.* and *Luc.*, to make the point that these two narrative works, even though they comprise a high proportion of direct speech, do not contain dramatic insets; in neither case is there any true dialogue. Adduces Egeon's account of his wanderings in *Err.*, I.i, as an early example of an expository inset in a play. Enobarbus's account of the first meeting of Antony and Cleopatra (*Ant.*, I.i) is a more complex and skillful example of the same thing.

0155   Berry, Ralph. *The Shakespearean Metaphor: Studies in Language and Form.* London: Macmillan, 1978. xi + 128 pp.

Chapter 6, on *Tro.*, observes that the play's subject matter is love and war; that its business is "a sustained debate on values"; and that the debate is "largely corrosive of the values considered." Focuses on the images of food, eating, and tasting, which construct "a profound metaphor for human activity" and develop "an intellectual critique" of the actions recorded in the play. The tendency of the food and tasting imagery is to subvert human endeavor and its values. These images are associated with Time, and we see Time as the devourer, working to destabilize the characters' sense of self and finally to act as an accomplice in the play's consumption of itself. The final stages of *Tro.* force the audience to experience "surfeit and revulsion" and to witness its many genres "collapse inward upon themselves." Points to book 15 of Ovid's *Metamorphoses*, with its extended "meditation on Time as flux" and its use of the phrase *tempus edax rerum*, as a "stimulus to Sh's imagination."
    Chapter 7, on sexual imagery in *Cor.*, is a revision of item 1601.

0156   Bevington, David. *Action Is Eloquence: Shakespeare's Language of Gesture.* Cambridge: Harvard U. P., 1984. xii + 227 pp.

The introductory chapter proposes "to develop a contrastive vocabulary of visual signals in Shakespeare's plays and poems." On the one hand, there are the stable images of the hierarchical, familiar world of Sh's audience, as well as the easily interpreted emblems inherited from the medieval stage and the Neoplatonic assumption that visual manifestations correspond reliably to inner truth. On the other hand, there is in Sh's theatrical world a strong sense that order, sanity, wisdom, and meaning itself are constantly at risk of being subverted. In this world, human beings find themselves in a transitional or (as anthropologists like Arnold van Gennep and Victor Turner would say) "liminal" state, in between various kinds of social stability. Sh's visual language reflects both a longing for a settled meaning (as the Neoplatonists of his time would have it) and a radical skepticism about the possibility of achieving such a meaning. Cites Lucrece's attempt to read the Trojan tapestry in *Luc.*, the *paragone* argument about the relative merits of painting and poetry in *Tim.*, and the struggle of Titus and his family to find "a new language of action" in *Tit.* to reinforce the point that, in various ways, Sh interrogates the reliability of visual and gestural language. Chapter 2, "The Language of Costume and Hand Properties," observes that Sh was heir to a "mixed tradition" of costuming: (1) medieval moral symbolism and (2) neoclassical illusionism. He uses both of these in a complex blend. Chapter 3, "The Language of Gesture and Expression," mentions Brutus (*JC*) as an example of someone whose physical signs give evidence of distraction. Chapter 4, "The Language of Theatrical Space," includes consideration of the scene in *Tro.* (V.ii) in which Cressida's capitulation to Diomedes is observed by Troilus, Ulysses, and Thersites. Chapter 5, "The Language of Ceremony," refers to the triumphal entries in *JC*, *Ant.*, and *Cor.* Chapter 6 is entitled "'Maimed Rites': Violated Ceremony in *Hamlet.*" Draws illustrations from across the canon.

0156a Bevington, David. "Irony and Its Interrelatedness in Shakespeare." *Shakespeare's Craft: Eight Lectures.* Ed. Philip H. Highfill Jr. (Tupper Lectures on Shakespeare.) Carbondale, Illinois: Southern Illinois U. P., 1982, pp. 1–23.

Discusses the ways in which various kinds of irony in Sh are related to each other. Deals with three kinds of irony: "verbal irony, dramatic irony, and irony as both a criticism of life and a principle of dramatic structure." Includes an analysis of *JC* to explain the special kind of irony in Sh's classical tragedies. In *JC*, the basic irony is that the noble Brutus is incapable of carrying out a noble revolution: He is blind to his own resemblance to the man he would overthrow; he is prevented by his nobility from taking advantage of the opportunity that his ideals have created for him; and as a republican he clears the way for a period of one-man rule. In *JC*, and in other classical plays like *Tro.* and *Cor.*, characters often have ironic perceptions about fulfilling preordained purposes despite their best efforts. In *Ant.*, Sh may have achieved a synthesis in his use of irony in tragedy, since "it is at once a Roman play and yet one in which the final peripety brings with it an ambiguous sense that human blindness has not resulted only in tragic error and failure."

0157 Bevington, David. "Shakespeare vs. Jonson on Satire." *Shakespeare 1971: Proceedings of the World Shakespeare Congress.* Vancouver, August 1971. Eds. Clifford Leech and J. M. R. Margeson. Toronto: U. of Toronto P., 1972, pp. 107–22.

Compares Jonson's and Sh's attitudes toward satire. Concludes that "whereas Jonson lambasted all popular historical drama and romance, and thus limited himself to neoclassical forms albeit interpreted with some English latitude, Shakespeare debated the issues of satire and saw no reason why he should not try it out for himself." Shakespeare maintained a distance from satire, though he demonstrated a complex appreciation of its theory in *AYL* and experimented with the thing itself in *TN*.

0158 Bevington, David. "The Uses of Contemporary History in the Greek and Elizabethan Theatres." *Shakespeare's Art from a Comparative Perspective.* Ed. Wendell M. Aycock. (Proceedings: Comparative Literature Symposium, Texas Tech U., 12.) Lubbock: Texas Tech P., 1981, pp. 31–49.

Begins by surveying the evidence for Elizabethan exposure to ancient Greek drama. Notes that there were at least eight Greek tragedies translated into Latin or English in the 16th c. This list can be expanded to fifteen if we include the English translations of Senecan plays based or probably based on Greek originals. Although knowledge of Greek drama was not widespread, it must have been discernible in university circles and among the learned. Playwrights like John Lyly and Ben Jonson certainly had a good deal of such knowledge. Eschews any attempt to establish direct links between Greek and Elizabethan drama. Maintains instead that playwrights of the two eras took similar approaches to contemporary history because they were responding to similar situations: The audiences, the plays, and the political backgrounds were alike. Argues for a broad and flexible approach to topical meaning in the plays of both periods, using a narrow political reading of *MND* as one example (among many) of how not to interpret this drama.

0159 Bevington, David, ed. *The Complete Works of Shakespeare.* 3rd ed. Glenview, Illinois: Scott, Foresman, 1980. 1745 pp.

Includes texts for thirty-seven plays and six poems (including *Son.*). The general introduction includes information on classical influences in the sections on the intellectual background, the drama before Sh, and on Sh's life and work. More substantial discussion of Sh's use of the classics is found in the introductions to the individual plays and in appendix 2, which devotes an essay to the sources of each work. Provides the text for the citations in this bibliography.

General Works

0160 Bhattacherje, M. M. "Spenser and Shakespeare." *Visvabharati Quarterly*, 27 (1961), 106–21.

Surveys major similarities and differences between Spenser and Sh. One important likeness is the use by both poets of "the Ovidian strain," involving sex and lust as literary motifs (seen in *Ven.*, *Luc.*, and *The Faerie Queene*). Unlike Sh, Spenser was extensively exposed to classical culture and made a conscious effort to display his learning. Classical influences show up in Sh (as in the Platonism of some sonnets) but are not as obvious as they are in Spenser (note the elaboration of Platonic ideals of love and beauty in the *Fowre Hymnes*). Sh's plays avoid the kind of systematic exposition of the morality of the ancients that Spenser uses in the Aristotelian scheme of *The Fairie Queene*.

0160a Bieman, Elizabeth. *William Shakespeare: The Romances*. (Twayne's English Authors Series 478.) Boston: Twayne, 1990. xvii + 151 pp.

Chapter 1 traces the romance genre as popularized in the Renaissance to "the late Greek civilization of North Africa." Discusses the roots, in Neoplatonist thinkers like the 4th-c. A.D. Iamblichus, of the transformative power of magic and alchemy as they appear in Sh's romances. Devotes a chapter each to *Per.*, *Cym.*, *WT*, and *Tmp.*, adapting the psychological theories of Carl Jung to explain the pattern of the questing hero, the *puer–senex* conflict, and the transformations in these plays.

0160b Billington, Sandra. *Mock Kings in Medieval Society and Renaissance Drama*. Oxford: Clarendon P., 1991. xiii + 287 pp.

Part 1 examines "the evidence for calling men mock kings, or lords of misrule," in medieval sources and identifies the contexts to which such figures relate. Part 2 hypothesizes that most Renaissance drama "uses the festive impulse of saturnalian experience for the participants. They experience disorders under the auspices of a mock king who finally resigns (in comedy) or is otherwise disposed of." The conclusions of the plays are marked by "the restoration of order, the promise of such a restoration, or . . . the continuation of disorder through a further false king coming to power." Considers a number of Sh's plays, including *Tim.*, *Tro.*, and *Ant. Tim.*, partly authored by Thomas Middleton, follows "a strict summer king formula" to present an over-schematized satire of "the principle of court patronage." *Tro.* exhibits Pandarus as a lord of misrule and, using the imagery of armor, exposes the hollowness of the characters' idealistic pretenses. In *Ant.*, Sh designs a "festive tragedy," which ends by deifying the "misrule lord and his lady" through "their Christmas king pageantry."

0161 Bilton, Peter. *Commentary and Control in Shakespeare's Plays*. New York: Humanities P., 1974. 247 pp.

Advocates, as a critical strategy, submitting to the experience of a spectator, paying particular attention to characters within Sh's plays who act as intermediaries for the audience by commenting on the action and even controlling it. Treats the entire canon more or less chronologically, though five classical plays—*JC*, *Tro.*, *Tim.*, *Ant.*, and *Cor.*—are grouped together in chapter 9 under "Problem Tragedy." In *JC*, a certain degree of detachment is achieved because there is no emphatic verdict on the assassination and there is implicit ironic comment on much of the action. For *Tro.*, however, though the corrupt world of the play makes a strong impact on its own, Pandarus and Thersites provide guiding commentary. In *Tim.*, the commentary figures (Apemantus, Flavius, and Alcibiades) give significant help in developing the play. In *Ant.*, Enobarbus's critical yet sympathetic response to the lovers is ultimately compatible with what the audience feels. In *Cor.*, a variety of commentators maintain in the audience a tension between admiration for the idealist hero and regret that he cannot be moderate.

0162 Binns, J. W. "Shakespeare's Latin Citations: The Editorial Problem." *ShS*, 35 (1982), 119–28.

Surveys the 120 Latin passages cited in Sh's plays, classifying them into four principal groups: (1) original Latin composed by Sh; (2) quotations from classical Latin authors; (3) quotations from Renaissance Latin authors; and (4) proverbs, quotations from the Vulgate Bible, miscellaneous odd words, and grammatical tags. Comments on the effects of Latin in various play groups; for example, in the comedies, especially *LLL* and *Wiv.*, the misuse of Latin contributes to characterization and comic effect. Makes suggestions about how and to what extent editors should regularize or correct Sh's Latin.

0163 Birney, Alice Lotvin. *Satiric Catharsis in Shakespeare: A Theory of Dramatic Structure*. Berkeley: U. of California P., 1973. xi + 158 pp.

Propounds a theory of satiric catharsis based on Aristotle's ideas about tragedy. According to this theory, drama that includes a conspicuous satiric spokesman may purge the primary feelings—hatred and censure—he arouses. Applies the theory to five of Sh's plays, including *Tro.* and *Tim.* In *Tro.*, Thersites taints the characters and imagery with a jaundiced world view but does not suffer the rejection common to satirist figures. The play is a pure satiric drama, which blocks catharsis and forces the audience into a real confrontation with the problems enacted on the stage. In *Tim.*, Apemantus is the satirist who cures his society, but he does not achieve this goal by becoming an isolated and dismissed comic railer (like Jaques in *AYL*). Instead, he converts Timon into a "secondary satirist" who is purged as a tragic scapegoat. Revision of item 0164.

0164 Birney, Alice Lotvin. "A Theory of Satiric Catharsis with Illustrations from Shakespeare." Ph.D. dissertation, University of California, San Diego, 1968. *DA*, 29 (1968–69), 1899-A.

Revised as item 0163.

0164a Biswas, D. C. "Nature and Art in Shakespeare." *Journal of the Department of English* (Calcutta U.), 19, nos. 1–2 (1983–84), 45–65.

Seeks to understand Sh's attitude towards nature and art. Traces the orthodox Renaissance view that nature and art complement each other to classical writers, especially Horace. Notes that the opinion of Polixenes (*WT*, IV.iv) reflects this view. Surveys the relationship between the two terms as it is manifested in a variety of Sh's other works. Sh makes use of the traditional idea of nature as a principle of order as well as the revolutionary notion that nature is "wild and unchecked," "an amoral and disruptive force." Discusses Sh's use of "art" as meaning either "artifice" or "skill." Considers a number of "antithetical combinations" explored by Sh that relate to art and nature: fortune and nature, nature and nurture, and virtue and gentility.

0165 Biswas, Dinesh Chandra. *Shakespeare's Treatment of His Sources in the Comedies*. Calcutta: Jadavpur U., 1971. xii + 287 pp.

Accepts the sources for Sh's comedies identified by Geoffrey Bullough and other scholars. Attempts to discover the meaning of each comedy and to explain "the method Shakespeare has employed in building it up from the source materials." The introduction points out that in most plays Sh combines three forms of the comic, fuses elements from several sources, juxtaposes characters from different social levels, and links both character and plot to "a dominant idea." Includes a subchapter on each comedy, including the late romances. In *Err.*, Sh enriches the farcical materials borrowed from Plautus "by pun, parody, joke, discussion of topics, and new turns given to incidents." *MND* may have borrowed a number of hints from classical sources in constructing its "large-hearted and tolerant" vision. *Tro.* makes use of classical and medieval sources to convert exciting military adventures and chivalric romance "into a moral drama involving the eternal problems of value, which do not admit of any final solution."

0166   Black, Matthew W. "Aristotle's Mythos and the Tragedies of Shakespeare." *SJH*, 1968, 43–55.

Discusses Sh's ten nonhistorical tragedies in terms of Aristotle's analysis of plot in the *Poetics*, as translated and interpreted by Gerald F. Else (1957). Sh's tragedies conform rather closely to Aristotle's norms of seriousness and completeness. The notion of catharsis, as Else understands it, is also relevant: Catharsis is the purification of the hero from guilt "by course of events involving pity and fear." This describes what happens to Brutus, Hamlet, Lear, and Othello. Else's definition of *hamartia* as an error, not a moral flaw, allows the student of Sh to see that the two concepts can be distinguished. In some of Sh's plays (*Lr.*, *Ant.*, *Cor.*, and *Tim.*), the error and the tragic flaw are identical; in others (*JC*, *Mac.*, and *Oth.*), they are different.

0167   Black, Matthew W. "*Hamartia* in Shakespeare." *LC*, 30 (1964), 100–16.

Cites Gerald F. Else's redefinition of Aristotle's *catharsis* as "a process in which *the hero* undergoes purification by events, and which evokes various appropriate responses in the spectator." This leads to an understanding of *hamartia* not as a tragic flaw but as a tragic mistake, the *action* "which inaugurates the hero's fall from happiness to misery." Of Sh's chief tragic heroes, Antony, the slave of passion, and Hamlet, the victim of circumstances he did not create, have little to do with *hamartia* in this new sense. Several others, however, are guilty of mistakes that can be illuminated by the concept: Brutus joins the conspirators; the Macbeths murder Duncan; Othello marries Desdemona; and Lear divides his kingdom.

0168   Black, Matthew W. "Repeated Situations in Shakespeare's Plays." *Essays on Shakespeare and Elizabethan Drama in Honor of Hardin Craig.* Ed. Richard Hosley. Columbia: U. of Missouri P., 1962, pp. 247–59.

Suggests that Sh's development as an artist can be illustrated by examining the ways in which he repeats situations in several works. Discusses the "enumeration and ridicule of suitors" in *TGV* (I.ii), *MV* (I.ii), and *Tro.* (I.ii), and the use of twins in *Err.* and *TN*. In both cases, later renditions of the repeated situation show improvement.

0169   Blake, N. F. *Shakespeare's Language: An Introduction.* New York: St. Martin's, 1983. x + 154 pp.

Attempts to introduce modern readers to "the language of Shakespeare and his contemporaries." Chapter 1, "Language Environment," calls attention to the high status accorded to Latin language and literature by the humanists of Sh's day. Notes that the emphasis on Latin and its value was often coupled with an awareness that the linguistic resources of English needed to be enriched. Each chapter deals with an aspect of Sh's language. Chapter 3, on vocabulary, makes the point that the poet uses Latinate words because they are rhythmical and mellifluous. Cites examples from the entire canon.

0170   Blamires, Harry. *A Short History of English Literature.* London: Methuen, 1974. 536 pp. 2nd ed., 1984. viii + 484 pp.

Surveys Sh's plays in chapter 4, "Elizabethan Drama," pointing to the influence of Plautus on *Err.*, the antithesis between truth and falseness in *Tro.*, and the fusion between the features of Sh's history plays and his tragedies in the "three Roman plays" (*JC*, *Cor.*, and *Ant.*).

0171   Bliss, Lee. *The World's Perspective: John Webster and Jacobean Drama.* New Brunswick, New Jersey: Rutgers U. P., 1983. x + 246 pp.

Chapter 2 includes a discussion of how, in Sh's "late Roman tragedies," we are faced with a clash between the old morality of heroism and the new morality of flexible adaptation to the times. In *Ant.* and *Cor.*, Sh detaches us from the protagonist in a variety of ways, devaluing traditional heroism. There is, for example, a great deal of onstage commentary that encourages a comic response to the attempts of Antony and Coriolanus to assert their standard of heroic action. Nevertheless, in each case, the protagonist is seen as a great exemplar of "the heroic way of life," an embodiment of its values. The opponents of Antony and Coriolanus possess a new cynical view of human nature, and the defeat of these old-fashioned heroes seems to justify Octavius's and Aufidius's "possession of a value-less historical world."

0172 Bloom, Allan, with Harry V. Jaffa. *Shakespeare's Politics*. New York: Basic Books, 1964. 150 pp.

Chapter 1, "Political Philosophy and Poetry," asserts that Sh is "an eminently political author" who "devotes great care to establishing the political setting in almost all his plays." Chapter 4, "The Morality of the Pagan Hero," focuses on *JC* with some attention to *Cor*. Julius Caesar, as Sh portrays him, is the greatest of the pagan heroes because he is aware of the conditions under which glory and power must be sought in Rome and is willing to accept those conditions. The tragedy of Coriolanus is that he wants to maintain the independence of his virtue, but he is dependent (though he is unaware of this) on the people for recognition of his virtue. Caesar, by contrast, recognizes that his heroic deeds are not enough; he needs the support of the corrupt populace and will compromise to get it. In the sense that Caesar gains immortal glory through the survival of his spirit, he is politically successful. But his tragedy lies in his failure to gain the admiration of the best men of his time. The imperfect partnership of Brutus and Cassius reveals the political flaws of the conspiracy. Cassius, the instigator, has no scruples about achieving a rightful end by vicious means, but he lacks the respectability he needs to draw men to his cause. Brutus is a man of the strictest virtue, whose participation in a murder is a break with the absoluteness of his principles. He fails to recognize that once he has broken the rules by committing murder, he cannot simply return to business as usual under the same rules. Instead, he should take steps to ensure that the assassination achieves its desired goal. Brutus's insistence on his principles over Cassius's prudence is directly responsible for the failure of the plot.

0172a Bluestone, Max. From Story to Stage: The Dramatic Adaptation of Prose Fiction the Period of Shakespeare and His Contemporaries. (Studies in English Literature 70.) The Hague: Mouton, 1974. 341 pp.

Comments throughout on Sh. Chapter 2, on gestures, costumes, and properties, notes that the scene in which Coriolanus holds his mother's hand in silence (*Cor.*, V.iii) is adapted from Plutarch, who refers to both the handclasp and the silence but does not have the two occur simultaneously. Sh has taken what are two incidental narrative details in his source and imbued them with "tragic implications." Chapter 4, on language, points out that when Coriolanus goes to visit Aufidius at the latter's home (IV.v), Sh has him stand to emphasize his pride. Plutarch, however, shows him kneeling at Aufidius's hearth in the posture of a suppliant. The "kinetic exposition" with which Ulysses describes the mocking speeches and gestures of Patroclus when he impersonates the Greek leaders for Achilles (*Tro.*, I.iii.142–184) enables the audience to believe in the reality of Ulysses' character. Chapter 6, on time, contrasts the way in which a dramatic speech like Ulysses' "For time is like a fashionable host" (*Tro.*, III.iii.165–190) gives authenticity to the movement of time with the flat conventionality of Lucrece's complaint against Night, Opportunity, and Time (*Luc.*, 764–1036).

0173 Bonheim, Helmut. "Shakespeare and the Novel of His Time." *SJH*, 1982, pp. 133–45.

Discusses Sh's indebtedness to contemporary writers of prose fiction and mentions the debt of these novelists to the Greek romances. In matters of style, Sh was strongly influenced by the euphuistic prose of John Lyly.

General Works

0173a Bonjour, Adrien. "From Shakespeare's Venus to Cleopatra's Cupids." *ShS*, 15 (1962), 73–80.

Holds that the imagery and phraseology of *Ant.* are frequently anticipated in *Ven.* The paradoxical images that combine in one person the power to satisfy as well as to create hunger, that endow the same breeze with the powers to cool and kindle a flame are rooted in *Ven.*, though they are not as compact as in *Ant.* Reminiscences of the poem also suggested to Sh the equating of Venus with Cleopatra and of Mars with Antony.

0174 Boorman, S. C. *Human Conflicts in Shakespeare*. London: Routledge and Kegan Paul, 1987. xiii + 324 pp.

Asserts that the exploration of "conflicting impulses, purposes, and needs" within human beings is at the heart of drama. Part 1 outlines several "forms of human conflict as they existed in the consciousness of Elizabethans": soul–body, mortal–immortal, greatness–littleness, freedom–fate, reason–unreason, reason–love, reason–fantasy, private man–public man, order–disorder, justice–mercy. Points out that classical thought played a significant role in helping Sh's contemporaries formulate these oppositions; for example, the notion of the reason–unreason conflict was available in Cicero's *De Officiis* and Aristotle's *Nicomachean Ethics*, both of which were widely circulated in England during the 16th c.

Part 2 surveys human conflict in early English drama and the drama of Sh's contemporaries.

Part 3 covers human conflict in Sh and is divided into sections entitled "Comedies," "English History Plays," "Classical Plays," "Tragedies," "Retrospect," and "The Last Plays." The section on classical plays begins by alluding to *Tim.* as a rough portrayal, overly schematized, of the idea that man's nature could "swing him between an irrational faith in the goodness of his fellow men, and an equally irrational conviction that all Mankind is contemptible and worthless." Reads three other plays in the light of *Tim.*: *JC* is focused on the reason–unreason conflict, as is *Tro.*, though the latter play divides the conflict into reason–love and reason–fantasy; *Cor.* foregrounds the private–public conflict, though other oppositions are present as well. Discusses *Ant.* as one of the tragedies, arguing that its three worlds (political, heroic, and sexual) are connected with each other through a complex matrix of conflicts. Comments on the original story in Plutarch's *Lives*, how Sh altered it, and the resemblance of Antony to the Earl of Essex. Contends that the play represents an important point in Sh's development, "when a play based closely on the events of history has ended by rising above those events into the private and personal world of the two main characters."

0175 Borinski, Ludwig. "Shakespeare's Conception of History." *Bulletin de la Faculté des Lettres de Strasbourg* (Hommage à Shakespeare), 43, no. 8 (1965), 835–54.

Argues that Sh is the great realist in his depiction of history, which he sees as determined not only by politics but also by great individuals. Acute analysis of politics in the Roman plays is anticipated in the English history plays: For example, the demagogy of Richard III contains many of the tricks Antony uses in *JC*. Public opinion is studied acutely in *JC* and *Cor.*, and *Cor.* is "perhaps the best presentation of political life in the world's literature." Sh makes considerable use of the idea of the fickle multitude, inherited from antiquity, in both *JC* and *Cor.* Though he depicted political life in the Roman plays as similar to that in the English history plays, Sh was aware of differences because "the Roman historical scene is deliberately drawn in more heroic proportions than the English world." In writing *JC*, Sh grasped that the struggle being portrayed is between "two political ideas, republicanism and Caesarism." Sh's art of creating historical atmosphere reaches perhaps its highest expression in *Ant.*, where he describes "a decaying civilization" and "contrasts the Roman political and military environment with the oriental world of Cleopatra's court."

0176   Bose, Amalendu. "A Preface to Shakespearean Comedy." *Essays on Shakespeare*. Ed. Bhabatosh Chatterjee. Bombay: Orient Longmans, 1965, pp. 55–75.

Maintains that Sh's comedies cannot be fruitfully analyzed in terms of the Greco-Roman tradition, which maintains a sharp demarcation between genres. They are best read in light of the medieval dramatic tradition.

0177   Bose, Amalendu. "Shakespeare's Word-Music." *Studies in Elizabethan Literature: Festschrift to Professor G. C. Bannerjee*. Ed. P. S. Sastri. New Delhi: S. Chand, 1972, pp. 57–63.

Maintains that in no other Elizabethan playwright's works is word-music so completely unified "with dramatic character and action as in Shakespeare." Cites as illustrations an exchange between Antony and Cleopatra when Antony is dying (*Ant.*) and an angry series of speeches from *Cor.* between the tribunes, the protagonist, and others.

0178   Bosworth, Denise Mary. "'Fail Not Our Feast': The Dramatic Significance of Shakespeare's Repasts." Ph.D. dissertation, University of Oregon, 1981. *DAI*, 42 (1981–82), 710-A.

Analyzes scenes and images of feasting in many of Sh's works, including several classical plays. In *Tit.*, the banquet is the culmination of both ritual and horror, Coriolanus betrays Rome at a feast; and *Tim.* is organized around two contrasting banquet scenes. *Ant.* has many references to food and drink, emphasizing the vitality of the love relationship and preparing for the transmutation of lovers from water and earth to fire and air. In the romances, feasting reminds man of his mutability and prepares him to accept it.

0179   Bowers, A. Robin. "Emblem and Rape in Shakespeare's *Lucrece* and *Titus Andronicus*." *Studies in Iconography*, 10 (1984–86), 79–96.

Provides several Renaissance examples of pictorial representations of the rape of Lucrece and the rape of Philomela as background for an argument that Sh, in *Luc.* and *Tit.*, developed "the poetic and dramatic potential of the emblem." In these two works, as well as others, he often constructed "scenic units first by presenting a relatively static *pictura* (like those found in emblem books) in what I will call *emblemic* scenes; and second, by amplifying and mobilizing these *picturae* to produce what I will term *emblematic* scenes." The Trojan tapestry in *Luc.*, with its depiction of "rapacious destruction," is highly emblematic. Maintains that the rape scenes in *Luc.* and *Tit.* operate in similar emblemic and emblematic fashions to indicate both the ravaging of an individual and the consequent sociopolitical upheavals.

0180   Bowers, Fredson. "Climax and Protagonist in Shakespeare's Dramatic Structure." *SAB*, 47, no. 2 (1982), 22–52. Reprint. *Hamlet as Minister and Scourge and and Other Studies in Shakespeare and Milton*. Charlottesville: U. P. of Virginia, 1989, pp. 26–61.

Views the structure of Sh's tragedies as "pyramidal," with the climax being the point in the middle at which the protagonist's decision to allow passion to dominate reason becomes irrevocable. Comments that the climax of *Ant.* occurs when Antony agrees to fight at sea. Locates the climax of *Cor.* as coming when the protagonist loses control for the second time before the people and the tribunes and is consequently banished.

0181   Bowers, Fredson. "The Concept of Single or Dual Protagonsts in Shakespeare's Tragedies." *RenP*, 1982 (1983), 27–33.

Uses Aristotelian standards, especially as regards climax and catastrophe, to assess *Rom.* and *Ant.* In the former play, Romeo is the only character whose fault and

General Works

punishment satisfy the requirements for a tragic protagonist. In the latter, the title characters share in the faulty ethical decision to fight by sea at Actium (the climax), but Cleopatra is the only one who can be said to triumph in death by expiating her earlier mistakes. If we think in terms of tragedy rather than dramatized history, Cleopatra is thus the sole protagonist.

0182 Bowers, Fredson. "Death in Victory." *SAB*, 30, no. 2 (1965), 1–7. Reprinted as "Death in Victory: Shakespeare's Tragic Reconciliations." *Studies in Honor of DeWitt T. Starnes*. Eds. Thomas P. Harrison, Archibald A. Hill, Ernest C. Mossner, and James Sledd. Austin: U. of Texas P., 1967, pp. 53–71. Reprint. *Hamlet as Minister and Scourge and and Other Studies in Shakespeare and Milton*. Charlottesville: U. P. of Virginia, 1989, pp. 1–25.

Suggests that we can take Aristotle as a model in discovering how Sh's tragic effect is achieved, particularly how Sh uses the essential elements of tragedy in relation to each other. Hamlet's fifth soliloquy, beginning "'Tis now the very witching time of night," seems somewhat clumsy until it is recognized that Sh is carefully guiding our reactions and preparing us for the climax of the play in the next scene, roughly corresponding to Aristotle's reversal of situation. Finds that Aristotle's idea of catharsis neglects the role of "corrective justice," through which Sh brings the tragic protagonist to repentance. In a Greek tragedy, just before the catastrophe, the protagonist may be given a final chance to avoid the fatal consequences of his error; however, he rejects or does not recognize the opportunity. Sh, in contrast, leads his protagonist, best exemplified by Hamlet, to an understanding of his error and a rejection of irrational means to escape punishment. The hero is thus reconciled with God's plan, and this in turn "reconciles the audience to the tragic penalty that justice must exact." Also discusses *Lr., Oth., Mac., Cor.,* and *Ant*.

0183 Bowers, J. L. "The Romances." *Shakespeare at 400*. Ed. R. G. Howarth. Cape Town: Editorial Board of the U. of Cape Town, 1965, pp. 42–63.

Mentions, in an attempt to get at the essence of *Per., Cym., WT,* and *Tmp.,* some of the classical sources to which they may be indebted (the Greek romances, Greek myths, Menander). Comments that in these plays the Christian pattern of redemption "is somehow combined with that older version of the conflict between life and death, shadowed forth in the Eleusinian mysteries and in the rites of Dionysos."

0184 Boyle, Anthony Thomas. "The Epistemological Evolution of Renaissance Utopian Literature." Ph.D. dissertation, New York University, 1983. *DAI*, 44 (1983–84), 2138-A.

Chapter 1 identifies and analyzes several works by Plato as well as "other classical antecedents of the Renaissance utopia." Chapter 2 traces utopian thought in the works of more than a dozen Renaissance authors. Chapter 3 connects the altered ideas of utopianists like Sh to the decline "of classical idealism and the gradual dominance of the new philosophy."

0185 Bradbrook, M. C. *The Living Monument: Shakespeare and the Theatre of His Time*. Cambridge: Cambridge U. P., 1976. xv + 287 pp. Reprint. 1979.

Part 1 presents a sociology of the theater in which Sh developed his craft. Part 2, "Jacobean Shakespeare," discusses *Cor.* and *Ant.* in a chapter called "Love and War" and *TNK* in a chapter called "Shakespeare as Collaborator."

0185a Bradbrook, M. C. "Shakespeare's Recollections of Marlowe." *Shakespeare's Styles: Essays in Honour of Kenneth Muir*. Eds. Philip Edwards, Inga-Stina Ewbank, and G. K. Hunter. Cambridge: Cambridge U. P., 1980, pp. 191–204.

Maintains that *Tit.* is indebted to Christopher Marlowe's *The Jew of Malta*, especially in the relationship between Sh's villain Aaron and Marlowe's Barabas. Notes that *Ven.* is not significantly influenced by Marlowe's *Hero and Leander*; the two works seem to be parallel derivations from *Narcissus*, by John Clapham. Points out classical references that recall Marlowe in *H5* and *AYL*.

0186   Bradbrook, M. C. *Shakespeare the Craftsman*. (Clark Lectures 1968.) Cambridge: Cambridge U. P., 1969. iii + 187 pp. Reprint. 1979.

Chapter 6, "The Lives of the Noble Romans: *Julius Caesar* and the Other Roman Histories," views Sh's movement from English to Roman history in 1599 as breaking new ground. The Roman setting gave him the freedom to move away from court matters and to examine struggles within the city while at the same time giving him warrant to treat his story with the greatest dignity. Designates *JC*, *Cor.*, and *Tim.* as city tragedies. Notes that in *Tro.* Sh wrote a tragedy that mirrors the social confusion brought on by the shift in power away from the ancient hierarchical order toward the new commercial power centers. Argues that in *JC* Sh treats important public issues with clarity and simplicity. The style of the play has the effect of a learned tongue; even in its careful juxtaposition of the pithy style of Brutus to Antony's emotional rhetoric, it stands in stark contrast to the florid language of *Tro*. Calls attention to the masterful building of suspense, classical "in the deepest sense." Sh makes a "decisive break" with medieval tradition in (1) connecting the sin of pride with the Stoic doctrine of autarchy, which culminates in a justification of suicide and (2) demoting the goddess Fortune from her position as controller of experience to delineator of it. The play is primarily about Rome and two forms of social disorder—those caused by great men jockeying for position and by the instability of the plebeians—that show Sh recovering "the sense of the past in its contingency." Sees *Cor.* as a tragedy in which man is shown "at his most arrogant," maintaining "his inflexible nobility at the price of inflammable rage." In *Ant.*, man recovers "something of his godlike stature," Fortune is embodied "in the moods of a gipsy," and there is "a new sense of theatrical pageantry and triumph." Roman perspectives sharply deflate "the grandeur of the Egyptian scenes," but "they do not destroy it."

Chapter 8, "Blackfriars: The Pageant of *Timon of Athens*," is a revision of item 2618.

0187   Bradbrook, M. C. *Shakespeare: The Poet in His World*. New York: Columbia U. P., 1978. ix + 272 pp. Reprint. London: Methuen, 1980.

Traces Sh's career by examining the complex interrelations between his life, his art, and the social history of his time. Chapter 1 mentions the educational program of the grammar school that Sh would have attended, with its emphasis on grammar, rhetoric, and memorization of passages from Latin authors. Several plays, especially early ones, make obvious use of school learning. Chapter 2 comments on the Ovidian derivation of *Tit.* and on the ingeniously doubled Plautine action in *Err.* Chapter 4 calls attention to Ovidian elements of natural impulse in *Ven.*, as well as evidence of the poet's renewed contact with the countryside. In Sh's time, *Luc.* was regarded as a moral work, with everything given a symbolic value. It is also "a self-conscious study of the relation of art to life": In the painting of Troy, Lucrece sees powerful feelings related to her own experience "presented obliquely."

Chapter 11, "The Dream of Ancient Lands," treats *Tim.* as a dramatic production that hovers between "various possibilities." Its primary source, Plutarch's *Lives*, gives it a connection to the ancient past, but its satire on corruption of the city is thoroughly modern. Timon's combination of magnificent dream and sardonic observation was characteristic of the children's lofty vision and also connects him with the Roman heroes of later plays, Antony and Coriolanus. Coriolanus, like Timon, is misanthropic but not absolutely so. The family grouping of grandmother and grandchild in *Cor.* may owe something to the death of Sh's mother in 1608 and her burial in the Stratford churchyard near his dead son. In *Ant.*, the two lovers' visions of each other constitute a complex dream that subdues the world. Antony's last words are based on "the noble stoic phrases of Plutarch," though they are transmuted into the utterance of a great Protean character. The play's relationship to Plutarch reveals Sh's capacity to appropriate exactly what he needed and to reject what he did not.

0188 Bradbrook, M. C. "St. George for Spelling Reform! Social Implications of Orthography—Cheke to Whythorn; Mulcaster to Shakespeare's Holofernes." *SQ*, 15 (1964), 129–41.

Surveys attempts to reform English spelling in the later 16th c. and comments that in *LLL* and *Ado* "orthography" represents "hide-bound classical students of the previous generation at their most ill-tempered, or affected courtly students of the tongues at their most pretentious."

0189 Bradbrook, Muriel C. *English Dramatic Form: A History of Its Development.* London: Chatto and Windus, 1965. xii + [13]–205.

Includes, in a chapter entitled "Shakespeare and Tradition," discussions of *Tro.* and *Cym.* Comments on Sh's use of the sack of Troy, to the 16th c. "the greatest secular symbol" of disaster. Through compression and inversion, Sh ruthlessly deflates the romance and heroism of Chaucer's *Troilus and Criseyde.* There is no grandeur in *Tro.*, only the "meanness and triviality of betrayal." Notes the collocation of classical Rome, ancient Britain, and modern Italy in *Cym.* Sh seemed to return, in this play, to the form of the medley.

0190 Braden, Gordon. *The Classics and English Renaissance Poetry: Three Case Studies.* (Yale Studies in English 187.) New Haven: Yale U. P., 1978. xv + 303 pp.

Notes in the introduction that Renaissance authors were show-offs in their use of classical materials. They were also exceptionally fond of "tracing the very wording of classical texts more or less directly into their own works." Evidence of this habit gives us an unusually close look at what the author had in mind at a given moment in the composing process. Attempts to examine closely "the specific verbal interface between classical and Renaissance texts," to look at what certain Renaissance authors did with "the words of their predecessors," and to consider the larger aspects of the Renaissance works. The first chapter, "Golding's Ovid," points out Sh's interest in Golding's "mildly eccentric diction" and in the padding with which he often expanded the Latin text. Comments that Golding's simultaneous detachment from and fascination with the pagan world of his author produced in the translation a combination of "smirkiness and wonder" that contributed to Sh's evocation of enchantment and absurdity in portraying the fairy world of *MND*, for example, or in characterizing Jaques, "like Puck a joker in an enchanted world."

0191 Braden, Gordon. *Renaissance Tragedy and the Senecan Tradition: Anger's Privilege.* New Haven: Yale U. P., 1985. xii + 260 pp.

The introduction proposes to investigate "the rage that is the all-consuming subject of Senecan tragedy," the voice of "a style of autarchic selfhood distinctly characteristic of classical civilization." Notes that this style finds a paradoxical mirror in "the dispassionate philosophy that is the principal topic of Seneca's nondramatic writings." Seneca's "version of classical man, exaggerated and simplified to reveal something of his essence," is what the Renaissance writers responded to. Chapter 1, "Stoicism and Empire," analyzes the Stoicism set forth in Seneca's political and philosophical writings. Finds that in Seneca's time (1st c. A.D.), and in his plays, the ancient Greek notion of *thymos*, "the inner force that rouses Homeric warriors to action," has been interiorized as part of the new (sometimes pathological) imperial notion of power. The Stoicism set forth in Seneca's philosophical writings, with its precepts about control of anger, can be seen as a way "to clear space within which the thymos can be freed from all accountability." Stoic withdrawal and "imperial aggression" are both informed by the self's attempt to control its own boundaries. Stoicism is thus an inner form of imperialism.

Chapter 2 explains Senecan furor in detail by analysis of Seneca's tragedies, especially *Thyestes* and *Medea*. Notes that in contrast to the antecedents for this emotion in Greek tragedy, Seneca's version of it seeks to escape the normative in "dark privacies." Emphasizes the Senecan hero's pursuit of absolute autonomy and power. At the same time, however, the hero's unbounded desire to achieve, for example, perfect revenge has a curious irresolution because one is never certain when the point of perfection has been reached. There is a further qualification of the villain–hero's capacity to become omnipotent in his rage: The rhetoric of "psychic aggression" that he must use is inevitably dependent on an audience: his victim.

Chapter 3 attempts to clarify what is important for the Renaissance in the Stoic tradition of Seneca. Notes that the characteristic features of Senecan rhetoric are not simply a miscellaneous assemblage of effects but that they cohere in expressing "a particular style of selfhood." Comments on the text of Seneca's works, explaining that there was nothing like a complete edition in the Renaissance and that the two halves of the corpus (the tragedies and the philosophical works) have "largely separate editorial histories." Many of the Renaissance's ideas about Stoicism were indebted to this textual situation, but more influential were Western traditions that had absorbed Seneca's thought from earliest times. St. Paul, for example, is Stoic in his concern with control of the passions; Boethius is Stoic in his account of the heroic struggle between *virtus* and *fortuna*; Petrarch exhibits Stoicism in *De Remediis Utriusque Fortunae,* in which he assimilates classical philosophy to "Christian *contemptus mundi*"; Petrarch's *Africa*, the first Renaissance epic, is about "the coincidence of Stoic and military" virtue. This last connection was especially important to the aristocrats of the Renaissance, who found in it a way to supplement and modify "the ruling ethos of medieval feudalism." Cites Stoic elements in Montaigne, Rabelais, Guillaume du Vair, and Corneille, especially concern for "mastery of the self" and its expansion into mastery of the universe. Provides an account of "the main tradition of objection to Stoicism," which focuses on its "blanket suppression of the passions." This tradition, which gathered momentum during the 16th c., includes St. Augustine, Calvin, and Montaigne. The third of these develops from Stoicism "a concept of very private selfhood that nevertheless carries within it a sense of eccentric freedom from the will of its possessor."

Chapter 4 uses Albertino Mussato's *Ecerinis* (1315) as chief exhibit in a discussion of how the Renaissance, in the early phases of its revival of tragedy, began with formal imitation of Seneca. That the imitation tended to "replicate and exacerbate Seneca's flaws as a dramatist" did not cancel the underlying Senecan "fascination with the self's drive toward dominance and completeness" that contributed so much to Renaissance tragedy. Regards *Ecerinis* as the first Renaissance revenge tragedy and explains how important revenge as a theme is in portraying the recurrent crisis associated with "the indeterminate character of the aristocratic identity." Refers briefly to *3H6* and *R3*.

Chapter 6 analyzes Tristan l'Hermite's *Mariane* and Lodovico Dolce's *Marianna*, two plays that treat the Herod and Marianne story. Each of these plays presents a Renaissance version of the Senecan murderer (Herod); they differ in the extent to which "the murderer recoups his authority." Neither is entirely successful. Sh's version of the same story, *Oth.*, demonstrates that "fustian indulgence and moral rigor do not have to polarize, but can interact in intricate, unpredictable, and extraordinary ways." Includes as well a discussion of Thomas Kyd's *The Spanish Tragedy*, in which "England's unusually expansive version of Senecan selfhood" is brought into "the crucial arena of revenge tragedy, where Renaissance drama forces that selfhood into its most intimate dealings with the lives around it." Explains that in *Ham.* the hero transcends the limitations of Hieronimo in *The Spanish Tragedy*: Hamlet finally accepts his place in a larger order, achieves a kind of Christianized Stoicism, and surrenders to "the promptings and wisdom of occasion."

General Works

0192 Bradshaw, Graham. *Shakespeare's Scepticism.* Brighton: Harvester, 1987. xiv + 269 pp.

Uses Troilus's question "What's aught but as 'tis valued?" and Hector's confident reply that the value of things inheres in the things themselves and in those who value them (*Tro.*, II.ii.52–60) as a way to embark on a discussion of Sh's continuous preoccupation with "that difficult triad, *value, valuer* and *valued.*" This is a way to notice "the plays' imaginative integrity and creative continuity." Once we are focused on the act of valuing, we can make two further points: (1) Sh repeatedly discovers "a process of *disjunction*," whereby as soon as a thing or person has been "endowed with value" a separation occurs so that "the value *appears* to be inherent in the valued and detached from the valuer"; and (2) "different views of the nature of Nature yield different accounts of value." Notes the "radical scepticism" of *Ant.*, which forces us into the dilemma of judging between what we hear of nobleness (Antony) and imaginative power (Cleopatra) and what we see of physical clumsiness and debility and wish-fulfilling fantasy. Enobarbus may have been created by Sh to "*project* our judgmental dilemma" onto a man who dies because he cannot find his way out of it. Chapter 4, "The Genealogy of Ideals," is devoted to *Tro.* and includes sections entitled "Unpacking Motives," "Hector's *volte face*," "Rank and Degree," and "Unbodied Figures in Dumb Cradles." Concludes that the play swivels between "opposed perspectives": On the one hand, it fails to exhibit a *true* lover or hero, and implies that no such thing exists; on the other, it forces us to recognize how impoverishing and life-denying such a view is. Makes brief references to *Cor., Tim., JC, Luc.*, and *Ven.* Tends to avoid identifying Sh's skepticism with the thought of other authors or the temper of his age.

0193 Brenner, Myra. "Shakespeare and the Elizabethan Concepts of Envy." Ph.D. dissertation, Brandeis University, 1970. *DAI*, 31 (1970–71), 1263-A-1264-A.

Traces the Elizabethan concepts of envy from 16th-c. dictionaries, commonplace books, and moral treatises to sermons and penitential manuals of the 13th c. and "Aristotle's description of the passions." There seems to be a link between "a conceptual tradition and a dramatic tradition of envy"; the former provides "a moral and psychological model" that makes possible more precise interpretations of character. Discusses Sh's depictions of envy, especially in the early history plays and *Oth*.

0194 Breuer, Horst. "Theories of Generation in Shakespeare." *Journal of European Studies*, 20 (1990), 325–42.

Explains the two theories of sexual generation inherited by the Renaissance from Greek natural philosophy: (1) the Hippocratic two-seed theory, according to which both parents provide sperm to create the offspring, and (2) the one-seed Aristotelian theory, which held that the male semen is the only sperm involved. Generally speaking, Sh relied on the Aristotelian notion, tending to portray man as "active, expansive, inventive," and woman as "passive, submissive, fatalistic." This accounts for many features of *Lr., Cor., Ant., WT, Tim.*, and other plays. The plays are imbued with patriarchal ideas, "placing man distinctly above woman and justifying this anthropological hierarchy on biomedical grounds."

0195 Brewer, D. S. "Shakespearean Comedy: Structure and Character–Types." *Estudios sobre los géneros literarios, I (Grecia clásica e Inglateria).* (Acta Salmanticensia, Filosofía y Letras 89.) Salamanca: U. de Salamanca, 1975, pp. 119–29.

Observes that Sh's comedy is "less derisive" than other comedy. Acknowledges the general indebtedness of Sh to Latin New Comedy but asserts that the primary influence on his comedy was medieval romance. The open-ended plots and developing characters of romance were more congenial to Sh than the more limited, realistic plots, satiric tone, and conventional character types of neoclassical comedy.

0195a   Brewer, Derek. "The Place of Medieval Literature in English Studies." *Actes du Congrès de Poitiers* (Études Anglaises 90.) Paris: Didier, 1980, pp. 679-94.

Argues that Sh—with "his lack of naturalistic mimesis, his sketchy characterization, his indecorous mixture of levity and seriousness, his puns, wit and commonplaces, his adherence to traditional values–is "more medieval than he is [n]eoclassical."

0196   Brissenden, Alan. "Shakespeare and Dance." *Stratford Papers 1968-69*. Ed. B. A. W. Jackson. McMaster U. Library P., 1972, pp. 85-96.

Explains the connection of dance with Neoplatonic ideas of cosmic harmony and shows how these ideas are explored through dance in *Rom.*, *MND*, and *Mac.* In *Mac.*, the dancing of the witches is a travesty of the harmonious "ever-circling dance of the Graces." Revised as part of item 0197.

0197   Brissenden, Alan. *Shakespeare and the Dance*. Atlantic Highlands, New Jersey: Humanities P., 1981. xii + 145 pp.

The first chapter, "Dance and the Elizabethans," documents the currency in the 16th c. of the classical notion of the "cosmic dance, the rhythmic movement of all things in relation to one another." It was commonly employed as a "metaphor of order, a concept closely allied to the Pythagorean belief in the primacy of number." The notion that dance was the means by which primal chaos become order had been used by Plato in the *Laws* and the *Timaeus* and by Lucian in his dialogue on dancing. Sir John Davies' poem *Orchestra* (1594) makes graceful use of these ideas, as does Sir Thomas Elyot in *A Book Named the Governor* (1531). Sh's references to dance are also associated with ideas of order. In some plays, dance is a significant part of the dramatic action; in others, it furnishes important imagery. Succeeding chapters provide a survey of the entire canon, commenting on the use of the dance in each play. In *Ant.*, for example, the drunken revels on board Pompey's galley (II.vii) foreshadow the breakup of the triumvirate and the disorder that is to follow. In *Tim.*, the masque of the Amazons is an ironic device: At the conclusion, the performers dance with members of the audience, something that in most masques signifies harmony between the illusory world of the masque and the real world but here anticipates hatred and discord. The Amazons, seen in most Elizabethan texts as unnatural and depraved women, are forerunners of the whores in IV. The performance harmonizes with Apemantus's acerbic comments on Timon's way of life and presents a lively image of the luxury in which Timon still believes himself to be capable of living. Part is a revision of item 0196.

0198   Brittain, Kilbee Cormack. "The Sin of Despair in English Renaissance Literature." Ph.D. dissertation, University of California, Los Angeles, 1963. *DAI*, 24 (1963-64), 281.

Claims that "the Christian concern about despair grew principally from Biblical emphases on hope in Christ, and Greek and Roman counsels against grief and accidie." Sh makes full use of the traditions of despair: The Roman despair of *Ant.*, for example, is secular, but retains "theological colors."

0199   Broadbent, J. B. *Poetic Love*. London: Chatto and Windus, 1964. x + 310 pp.

Contrasts *Tro.* to Chaucer's *Troilus and Criseyde* and points out that Sh's play is not tragic or even sad because the love of Troilus and Cressida is "false all through." A chapter on Sh's plays characterizes *Tro.* as a problem comedy in which ideal love "trades with sensuality, but neither is redeemed by the other." *Ant.* is a problem tragedy: It fails "because the love celebrated in it is too public, too spectacular, too much like the other forces in the plot." This is probably due to Plutarch, who presented the story in such a "public, grave, and circumstantial" manner.

General Works 57

0200 Brockbank, J. P. "Myth and History in Shakespeare's Rome." *Mythe et histoire*. Ed. Marie-Thérèse Jones-Davies. Société Française Shakespeare, Actes du Congrès, 1983. Paris: Jean Touzot, 1984, pp. 95–111.

Discusses the relationship between myth and history in Sh's Roman plays based on Plutarch. Notes that each of these plays "opens three perspectives of significance—into antiquity, into Shakespeare's own time, and into our own state of awareness." The theatrical experience of the Roman plays offers "truths about human consciousness and community, and about the relationship between them," that can be expressed in no other way. *JC*, which was probably the first play performed at the new Globe theater in 1599, marks a crucial moment in Sh's art, in theatrical history, and in the development of "our consciousness of Rome." In both *JC* and *Cor.*, instabilities of the state can be related to "persisting, if not perennial instabilities of human consciousness." Reprinted as chapter 7 of item 0201.

0201 Brockbank, Philip. *On Shakespeare: Jesus, Shakespeare and Karl Marx, and Other Essays*. Oxford: Blackwell, 1989. xiii + 345 pp.

Comprises seventeen essays, eleven previously published and six new. Chapter 1, "Jesus, Shakespeare and Karl Marx—*Timon of Athens* and *The Merchant of Venice*: Parables for the City," discusses Jesus' story of the unjust steward (Luke 16) as preparation for studying *Tim.*: Each is a parable that "affords an elusive and paradoxical insight into the relationship between human values and what we have come to call market-values." *Tim.* prompts us, among other things, to examine the pre-Shakespearean history of the Timon story. In Aristotelian terms, Timon fails to observe the mean, mistaking prodigality for magnanimity or munificence. The play also assimilates, though it does not endorse, the Cynic tradition that "opposes the money-corrupted life of the city to the candid instinctual life of animals." In light of the Tudor interludes, *Tim.* seems to draw on both biblical parables and classical ethics. It also has certain links with the materialism of Roman comedy. Finally, *Tim.* is suspended between the tragedy of the protagonist's commitment to death, the purge Alcibiades proposes to Timon, and "the pragmatic solution finally agreed between Alcibiades and the senators."

Chapter 2, "*Troilus and Cressida*: Character and Value 1200 B.C. to A.D. 1985," discovers in *Tro.* "an immense imaginative effort to re-enact the experience and understanding of the remote past, and to bring it live into the present." Maintains that this play, more than any other by Sh, "scrutinizes the ideological, philosophical and metaphysical fields from which characters and their values are generated"; it also "invites fresh thought about the relationship between our private and public selves." Identifies three theaters of action in the play—those of war, government, and courtship—and remarks that in each theater we are offered "high and exquisite human values together with their gross desecration."

Chapter 6, "*Julius Caesar* and the Catastrophes of History," defines *catastrophe* in drama as a moment of crisis "when events or our consciousness of them could go either way." Notes that *JC* has an unusually large number of such moments: Caesar's refusal of the crown, Cassius's seduction of Brutus, the agreement among the conspirators to spare Antony, the attempt of Calpurnia to keep Caesar at home, the speeches in the forum after Caesar's death, the slaughter of Cinna, the quarrel between Cassius and Brutus, and the battle of Philippi. Though tragic patterns are active in the play, they are "subsumed in the catastrophic processes of Roman history."

Chapter 7, "Myth and History in Shakespeare's Rome," is a reprint of item 0200, and chapter 9, "Hamlet the Bonesetter," is a reprint of item 1793.

0202 Brockbank, Philip. "Shakespeare: His Histories, English and Roman." *English Drama to 1710*. Ed. Christopher Ricks. Vol. 3. *The New History of Literature*. New York: Peter Bedrick, 1987, pp. 148–81.

Finds that the English history plays enabled Sh to "meet the Roman past halfway." In *JC*, he emphasizes many Senecan elements he found in Plutarch, but the structure of the play is "less Senecal than historical and political." With the death of Brutus, there is also a tragic shape to the action. Plutarch's sense of the past is clearly present in *Ant.*, but it is confronted by a recognition of the transforming power of the imagination. In *Cor.*, Plutarch's "prudential judgements" on Coriolanus's brashness are given voice, but they are not unequivocally validated. Coriolanus has a tragic integrity that is both personal and political.

0203   Bromham, A. A., and Zara Bruzzi. *"The Changeling" and the Years of Crisis, 1619–1624: A Hieroglyph of Britain.* London: Pinter, 1990. xii + 207 pp.

The postscript discusses the myths of Lucrece and Troy as they appear in *Tit.* and *Luc.* Both works provide Roman settings for the Trojan story, Troy and Rome being symbolic links to Britain's origin; and both, especially *Luc.*, serve as political allegory for pre-Cromwellian England.

0204   Brook, G. L. *The Language of Shakespeare.* London: André Deutsch, 1976. 231 pp.

Attempts a systematic description of Sh's language, with illustrations from every work in the canon. Chapter 2, "Words and their Meanings," notes that Sh was not as fond of showing off learned loan words as many of his contemporaries, though he did use them occasionally. Points out that Sh often used words borrowed from Latin and other languages in a literal instead of a metaphorical modern sense. Provides a list of such words with explanations of their etymologies. Chapter 8, "Rhetoric," singles out and explains a few of the learned terms, borrowed from Greek, that the Elizabethans used for the figures of rhetoric, and shows how Sh employed these figures.

0205   Entry deleted.

0206   Brooke, Nicholas. "Marlowe as Provocative Agent in Shakespeare's Early Plays." *ShS*, 14 (1961), 34–44.

Investigates the deliberate echoing of Marlowe in certain early works of Sh. Suggests that Sh used Marlovian rhetoric in *Tit.* to create Aaron, a character whose villainy disturbs "the orthodox order of the play." Aaron is a character like Tamburlaine and Barabas but, unlike Marlowe's characters, is granted no sympathy. In *JC*, Caesar engages in Marlovian hyperbole as he approaches his death, and Brutus's jealous pride has him speak in the same vein toward the end of the play (IV.iii.45–46, 91–92). The intentional pastiche of Marlowe's style in these and other early works had the effect of forcing the audience to make critical judgments about the attitudes expressed in that style.

0207   Brooke, Nicholas. *Shakespeare's Early Tragedies.* London: Methuen, 1968. x + 214 pp.

Provides chapters on *Tit., R3, Rom., R2, JC,* and *Ham.* The chapter on *Tit.* explains the play's technique as emblematic: Sh adapts the nondramatic verse of *Luc.* and Spenser to present the theme of man's dignity being destroyed by vengeful bestiality. As an example, Marcus's speech when he sees the mutilated Lavinia is static, commenting on the action and making an emblem of Lavinia. Though this technique is partially successful, it does limit the actor's use of human personality (except in the case of Aaron). The chapter on *JC* points out the play's "questioning of values"; its juxtaposition of the heroic spirit of man with his grotesque, clumsy, and bloody physicality; and its tendency to view Roman nobility "as comically or farcically degraded." The heroic end of the play, the tragedy of Brutus's noble error, has not been clearly enough prepared for in the midst of all this ambivalence; the parts of the play "have not grown consistently into a whole."

0208 Brower, Reuben A. *Hero and Saint: Shakespeare and the Graeco-Roman Heroic Tradition.* New York: Oxford U. P., 1971. xvi + 424 pp.

The introduction, "The Noble Moor," finds elements of the classical hero as well as the Christian in Sh's Othello. Othello's heroic self, established early in the play, is ultimately undermined by his need to have his greatness imaged in his beloved. His "heroic simplicity" is also "heroic blindness," which results in his damnation in Christian terms.

Chapter 1, "Achilles Hero," begins with an analysis of the passion of Homer's Achilles involving his will to glory and his recognition of the limitations of "the heroic ethos." Next, in preparation for a consideration of Chapman's translation of Homer, there is a discussion of Renaissance views of epic, which covers Italian and Elizabethan commentators and shows how they espoused "a blend of medieval-romantic and classical elements," with the latter being derived primarily from Virgil. In this critical environment, Chapman developed a notion of the hero that incorporates a pursuit of classical greatness and glory through fortitude with an inner struggle to attain self-knowledge and control of the passions. This "mixed" vision of the hero— shared by Sh—tends to replace physical with moral courage and to view the heroic career as an exercise in humane learning or as "a tragic failure to achieve it."

Chapter 2, "Our Virgil," argues that through Aeneas the poet imbrues the heroic with a sense of the tragic, thus anticipating the complexity of Sh's tragic protagonists. The passage on the death of Priam from Book 4 of the *Aeneid* is helpful in understanding the effect of Virgilian tragedy on the heroic tragedy of the Elizabethans. For one thing, Virgil makes a sense of the past part of the heroic present. For another, Virgilian characters have inner concerns that are commented on by the narrator. In this passage, Virgil also introduces metaphorical language, reflecting "sensations and relations" that play a part in the imaginative pattern of the entire work, a step in the direction of Sh's "dramatic concentration." In addition, the tragedy of Dido—a woman in love—provided the Elizabethans with a closer look at Greek tragedy than they had in Seneca. None of the contemporary English translations of the *Aeneid* is fully satisfactory, but Surrey's version comes closest to rendering Virgil's heroic diction.

Chapter 3, "Metamorphoses of the Heroic," probes Sh's indebtedness to Ovid and Seneca. In the *Metamorphoses*, Sh was exposed to a world in which the transformations wrought as a consequence of humanity's errors are followed with utmost fidelity to their terrible conclusions. Ovid's "beautiful and monstrous changes" furnished the playwright with a central metaphor for his tragedies and comedies. Sh also learned from Ovid how to shape narrative "through metaphorical imagery to give unity and large meaning to moments of high drama." Two episodes in *Luc.*—Tarquin's attack and Lucrece's meditation on Troy—show Sh using Ovidian techniques in an early attempt at heroic tragedy. The characters of Seneca's dramas tend to strike exaggeratedly Stoic poses, either suffering death too readily or fearlessly pursuing criminal careers; but from them Sh and his contemporaries learned a language for expressing the state of the soul and its inner conflicts.

Chapter 4, "Most Lamentable Romaine Tragedie," focuses on the transitional character of *Tit.*, which makes heavy use of translation, imitation, and direct quotation of the Latin poets but lacks a fully integrated artistic vision. In *Tit.*, Sh created an apt style for Roman drama—the sort of "unforced dignity" found in the speeches of the councillors and generals in the first scene, containing many echoes of contemporary and ancient epic styles. Titus's "latest farewell" speech (I.i.151–58) reflects a mood both Senecan and Stoic and is in fact directly indebted to Seneca. As the play proceeds, Sh often moves beyond Seneca to show Titus alternating, like Lear, between hero-king and sufferer, and, like Hamlet, between avenger and antic. Throughout *Tit.*, there are heroic speeches and situations derived from Seneca, Virgil, and Ovid (for example, Titus's Ovidian glossing of "the tragic tale of Philomel," IV.i.53–60), which can be seen to anticipate *R2, Oth., Cor., Ham.,* and *Lr.* However, the play's moral world falls apart in a Senecan bloodbath, with Titus giving himself over to the happy criminality of characters like Clytemnestra and Medea. Although Lucius's final speeches hint at the kind of civilized order that will anchor Sh's mature work, the playwright has not yet harmonized the disparate elements of tragedy with much order.

Chapter 5, "The Discovery of Plutarch: *Julius Caesar*," views *JC* as the turning point between Sh's histories and his later tragedies. With his notion of the ancient heroic ideal enriched by reading or rereading Plutarch's *Lives*, Sh wrote a "noble" and "Roman" play that successfully dramatizes "the tragic strain between the 'personal' and 'general.'" Plutarch's perfect hero, Pericles, as modified in Amyot's French version and North's English one, is "the complete hero–prince," politically and martially supreme, able to control his base emotions, gentle, and merciful. Sh encountered various aspects of this ideal in the lives he read most carefully before composing *JC*: those of Caesar, Marcus Brutus, and Marcus Antonius. The word "noble" is applied by North to all three figures to indicate at different times, "virtuous," "of high birth," and "heroic." The glimpses of Brutus's inward passions and his war with himself show Sh's development of heroic ideas hinted at in Plutarch; but the playwright stops short of plunging Brutus into the tragic agony of Hamlet or Macbeth. In the portrait of Brutus there is maintained a balance between heroic and antiheroic, tragic and ironic. He finally stands before us as the perfect blend of ancient and Renaissance heroic elements. Stylistically, Sh is not so much following anyone as he is creating a mode of expression to distinguish noble Romans from others so they can act their part in history.

Chapter 6, "The Pensive Man: *Troilus and Cressida*," notes that in this play Sh showed himself thoroughly familiar with the ancient, medieval, and Renaissance versions of the Troy story. The eponymous lovers stand for the degeneracy of all love in the play. Troilus, though he possesses medieval knightly and heroic tendencies, suffers from an overly refined sensual imagination. Cressida is calculating, a shrewd knower of herself and others. In the two council scenes (I.iii and II.ii) and elsewhere, the play contains numerous subversions of the heroic. Agamemnon's pompous Latinity conceals mental vacuity; Ulysses, for the most part, speaks in the true heroic vein, though ironically most of what he says is never acted on; and Hector's character is an impossibly contradictory composite of all heroic features known to the Renaissance. The play is unified through its three major themes of degree, time, and value and through the skillful linking of the love sequence with the war sequence. In all of this, Sh relentlessly exposes "the corruption of order and all other values," including those associated with medieval chivalry and ancient heroism.

In Chapter 7, "Hamlet Hero," Sh is seen exploring the temperament of "the player–poet." Hamlet is acutely aware of all the heroic parts he must play, and he assumes each role with intense imaginative commitment. For this reason, although he is potentially the martial Achillean hero of Homer as well as "the moral hero of the Virgilian and Christian traditions," he cannot maintain a constant allegiance to any "ideal of noble action." He suffers from a "tragic disturbance of mind," being unable to progress "through the cycle of passion and action to a clarifying vision." His tragedy is incomplete.

Chapter 8, "Heroic Tragedy, Heroic Love: *Antony and Cleopatra*," asserts that nobility is the crucial quality in both protagonists. Sh, concentrating on the numerous references to Antony's nobility in North's translation of Plutarch's leisurely narrative, used a complex network of images to trace the loss and then the recuperation of his hero's greatness. In his final speech, Antony shows that he has regained control of his destiny. When he says that he is "A Roman by a Roman / Valiantly vanquished" (IV.xv.59–60), he becomes "the Roman of Shakespearean and Renaissance imagination," whose nobility derives from self-conquest. Cleopatra, in her dream of Antony and her death, raises their love to a cosmic, heroic level. A comparison of Plutarch's *Life of Marcus Antonius* with Sh's work reveals that the latter excels in sensitizing us to "the total tragic situation": There is pity for the destructiveness of heroic endeavor at the same time as there is admiration for its glory. In highlighting these two feelings, Sh's play becomes "an imaginative sequel" to the *Aeneid*'s "tragedy of two heroic lovers." Cleopatra, though she does experience some intimations of tragedy, never suffers, as Antony does, Dido's inner anguish over lost reputation. As a tragic figure in the ancient and Renaissance heroic tradition, Antony stands alone.

Chapter 9, "The Deeds of Coriolanus," is a revision of item 1610. See also item 1599.

Chapter 10, "Everything and Nothing," treats *Lr.* as a progress for its protagonist from heroic self-assertion in the antique pagan style to an acceptance of the need on his part for "pity and compassionate love."

"Epilogue: The Rarer Action," comments that the image of the Greco-Roman hero in Sh's tragic protagonists is "the source both of their grandeur and of their tragic conflicts and sense of failure." But the other way of confronting the worst in life, that of the saint, is also dramatized in Sh's plays. Though linked to Christianity, saintliness has its classical antecedents in Virgil, Ovid, Seneca, and Elizabethan translations of these Latin poets. With a heritage that included so much, Sh was able to sometimes vary his own emphases, as in *Oth.* and *Lr.*, to give both the heroic and the saintly nearly equal weight in the same tragedy. The saintly, in its purest form, eventuates in comedy, and the late romances of Sh demonstrate this, though they do retain traces of the ancient heroic.

0209 Brown, Arthur. "Shakespeare's Treatment of Comedy." *Shakespeare's World*. Eds. James Sutherland and Joel Hurstfield. London: Edward Arnold, 1964, pp. 79–95.

Points out that in composing *Err.* Sh drew on the classical models of Plautus and Terence, as well as various 16th-c. Italian adaptations of classical comedy. Likens the antiromantic treatment of classical material in Jonson's puppet-show version of the Hero and Leander story (*Bartholomew Fair*, V.iii-iv) to Sh's handling of Pyramus and Thisbe in *MND*.

0210 Brown, Elynor Pettus. "Shakespeare and Corneille: The Roman Patriot as Hero." Ph.D. dissertation, Emory University, 1972. *DAI*, 33 (1972–73), 2910-A.

Attempts to reveal the similar insights of Sh and Corneille about "societal tragedy as they found it so poignantly intimated in Roman history." In *Cor.* and *Horace*, the essence of the tragedy "consists of the painful confrontation between the State and its most representative citizen." *JC* and *Mort de Pompée* feature the most famous Roman of all, Julius Caesar, as hero. In both cases, Caesar is a "moot patriot," whose career gives rise to more intense but less competent patriots. Their attempts to eliminate him lead ironically to the destruction of the republic.

0211 Brown, James Neil. "Elizabethan Pastoralism and Renaissance Platonism." *AUMLA*, 44 (1975), 247–67.

Argues that the Neoplatonic "religion of Love ... underlies the pastoral use of nature as an image of man's inner state." Focuses on Spenser's and Sidney's pastorals and then comments briefly on Sh. A Neoplatonic exploration of the relationship between what man's mind is and "what it might become" served as the pattern for "Shakespeare's experiments in romantic comedies in the 1590s." Mentions *TGV, LLL, MND, AYL, MV, Wiv., Ado,* and *TN.* Sh was concerned with accommodating the Platonic idea of "the good interior life to the Renaissance literary myth of the courtier–lover–soldier."

0212 Browne, Marlene Consuela. "Shakespeare's Lady Macbeth and Cleopatra: Women in a Political Context." Ph.D. dissertation, Brown University, 1976. *DAI*, 38 (1977–78), 274-A.

Attempts to locate women in the political context of Sh's time as a way to understand Lady Macbeth and Cleopatra. Begins by examining major ideas from the *Republic* of Plato and the *Politics* of Aristotle and then discusses Renaissance adaptations of these ideas. In general, Western belief held that the rule of women was unnatural, and fear of such rule influences the depictions of Lady Macbeth and Cleopatra. In particular, Sh shows that their attempts to achieve power depend on "their manipulation of or repudiation of traditionally 'feminine' roles."

0213 Brucher, Richard Thomas. "Esthetic Violence in Elizabethan and Jacobean Tragedy." Ph.D. dissertation, Rutgers University, 1978. *DAI*, 39 (1978–79), 6772-A.

Analyzes stage violence in representative Elizabethan and Jacobean tragedies, with particular emphasis on "esthetic, or artfully plotted," violence. In *Tit.*, for example, "comic savagery" serves to reveal a degenerate world and a means of combating the degeneracy: That is "esthetics become a viable, if immoral, substitute for ethics." In his depiction of murder, Sh sometimes achieves maximum impact by "juxtaposing the intended artifice of the killing with its more immediate and shocking reality"— as in the case of Caesar's assassination in *JC*.

0214 Bruster, Douglas. "Comedy and Control: Shakespeare and the Plautine Poeta." *CompD*, 24 (1990–91), 217–31.

Investigates Sh's adaptation of Plautus's *poeta* figure, a slave whose low social status permits him a great deal of flexibility in bringing about the comic resolution of the play, which he achieves through an inspired manipulation of events and characters. Takes as a primary example Pseudolus, the crafty slave in Plautus's comedy of the same name. Drawing on plays like *Pseudolus*, Sh located his central control figure further up in the social register: His comedies are most often under the direction of aristocrats. Discusses the Oberon/Theseus dyad in *MND* and Prospero in *Tmp*. and notes that the servant figures who aid them in their plans are useful not so much for their ingenuity as for their geographical and social mobility. The Shakespearean *poeta* in many cases assumes the instrumental aspects of the servant in his own character; when this occurs, he must disguise himself as someone from a lower class, such as Hal/Henry in *1H4* and *H5*, Duke Vincentio in *MM*, or Lord Lysimachus in *Per*. In manipulating the outcome of the trial in *MV*, Portia is also a *poeta* figure. Sh's placement of the agency for comic resolution in the hands of characters from the upper class reveals "an essential conservatism."

0215 Bryant, J. A. Jr. *Hippolyta's View: Some Christian Aspects of Shakespeare's Plays*. Lexington: U. of Kentucky P., 1961. ix + 239 pp.

Argues that Sh did not use scriptural allusions simply as ornament or to point outward to some abstract value. He was a genuine typologist in that his scriptural references and analogies are inextricable parts of the context in which they are found and enlarge and extend its meaning.

Chapter 5 points out that several scriptural references in *Tro*. come from Matthew 23, where Jesus denounces the Pharisees for saying much but doing little, a defect shared by most of the characters in the play. Hector is Christlike in taking the responsibility for the folly of Troilus and Paris, and his death is sacrificial.

Chapter 7 attempts to make a distinction between ancient and Christian tragedy. In Sophoclean tragedy, man comes to know and accept the inevitable disorder in the cosmos and his participation in it. In Christian tragedy, man "discovers what remains of the divine image" in himself and "contrasts the original perfection of that image" with his present lapsed condition.

Chapter 11 maintains that in *Ant*., the Christian perspective, encouraged by Antony's reference to one of the Messianic Psalms (22), empowers us to see the tragedy of the play as one in which two people expend themselves selflessly and thus "achieve an image of humanity greater than themselves."

Chapter 12 suggests that *Cym*. requires acceptance of "certain Christian presuppositions" to make sense. Most obviously, the shape of the plot is Christian: The fortunate fault of the king brings about restoration and renewal. In the capricious art form of tragicomedy, Sh has discovered the forces of a mysterious Providence.

0216 Buck, William Stuart. "Shakespeare's Epic of Fathers and Sons." Ph.D. dissertation, University of California, Riverside, 1990. *DAI*, 51 (1990–91), 2383-A.

Emphasizes the relationship of fathers and sons in analyzing Sh's eight history plays on the Wars of the Roses. The first part examines the epics of Homer and Virgil, and the Renaissance Thirteenth Book of the *Aeneid* by Maphaeus Vegius, which disclose a pattern of warm devotion between fathers and sons, as well as presenting a number of "loving and domestic" father figures. Regards the history plays as parts of an epic that features variations on the classical father–son paradigm. In the *H6Triad* and *R3*, the "darkness and butchery" result from a lack of "old and good father figures." In the last plays, the focus narrows to Hal, who, like Aeneas, "wanders alone to seek his epic fortune as he carries around with him the complex inheritance his father left him."

0217 Bullough, Geoffrey. "The Defence of Paradox." *Shakespeare's Styles: Essays in Honour of Kenneth Muir.* Eds. Philip Edwards, Inga-Stina Ewbank, and G. K. Hunter. Cambridge: Cambridge U. P., 1980, pp. 163–82.

Notes the descent from classical times to the Elizabethan period of the "paradoxical encomium in which a person or subject not usually regarded as praiseworthy was praised for comic or ironic effect." Focuses on "the paradoxical encomium (and its reverse) and the use of paradoxical situations and characters in some of Sh's plays." One example is the disguised Duke's advice to Claudio to prepare cheerfully for death (*MM*, III.i), which is heavily indebted to pagan Epicurean and Stoic thought.

0218 Bullough, Geoffrey. *Mirror of Minds: Changing Psychological Beliefs in English Poetry.* U. of London: Athlone P., 1962. viii + 271 pp.

Proposes "to give some illustrations of the ways in which at various periods English poetry has reflected current views of the human mind and soul." Lists, in an introductory chapter, the chief features of the system of psychology and ethics "inherited by the Middle Ages and Renaissance from Aristotle and Galen" and "adapted by St. Augustine and St. Thomas Aquinas." The second chapter, "The Development of Shakespeare's Attitude to the Mind," surveys the canon. The early histories present a pageant of warring ambitions, with exaggerated Senecan expressions of passion; dreams and visions also "show Senecan influence." The early comedies emphasize traditional notions of marriage and give light sketches of young people under the spell of love; dreams in the comedies are often combined with the idea of enchantment. *MV* reveals a new emphasis on analyzing mood and temperament and a new interest in ethical problems. *Tro.* is preoccupied with "the baser side of human nature," a "pageant of souls at odds with themselves, driven by passions, their wills separated from their judgments." When he writes the tragedies, Sh's ethical concerns lead him to explore the "deep moral disturbance in the mind and environment of noble characters." Particularly important in the Roman plays is pressure from outside the protagonist's mind, from the public sphere of his relationships. In the final plays, "an initial state of moral and mental perturbation is transformed into one of rational balance."

0219 Bullough, Geoffrey. "The Uses of History." *Shakespeare's World.* Eds. James Sutherland and Joel Hurstfield. London: Edward Arnold, 1964, pp. 96–115.

Discusses *JC* and *Ant.*, along with the English history plays. After treating dissension in English history, Sh turned in *JC* to the discord that attended the end of the Roman republic. His reading of Plutarch had encouraged in him a distrust of politicians, and in writing of events from Roman history, he was free to treat his characters more realistically than he had treated his English heroes. He was also impressed by Plutarch's emphasis on the significance of small details in characterization. As a result, he came to see the fall of Caesar as a consequence of the interplay among the personalities of Brutus, Caesar, and Antony, and the groups they represented. Thus he composed *JC* with three heroes, each of whom has great strengths but is also seriously flawed. In *Ant.*, Sh decided to exalt his protagonists, and he accomplished this partly by ignoring or glossing over their more unsavory traits ("his cruelty in war and orgies in peace, her overriding ambition and mercenary nature") as recorded by Plutarch. In addition, the poetry of *Ant.* leads us to suspend our moral judgment and share joyfully in a passion of both flesh and spirit.

0220 Bulman, James C. *The Heroic Idiom of Shakespearean Tragedy.* Newark: U. of Delaware P., 1985. 254 pp.

Traces Sh's conception of tragic heroism from an early acceptance of "the conventions of the received heroic idiom" to a dramatization, in later works, of "the hero's inner life." Includes extensive treatment of *JC, Ham., Tro., Oth., Tim., Lr., Mac.,* and *Ant.* In *Ant.*, Sh took the opportunity to review the various ways in which he had previously re-created heroism and to raise the question of "whether the heroic idiom itself and the impact of its allusions are adequate to make us credit a character as heroic, even when the context encourages us to be skeptical." Parts of chapters 1 and 5 are revisions of items 1614 and 2621, parts of chapter 6 are a revision of item 2622, and the book as a whole is a revision of item 0222.

0221 Bulman, James C. "Shakespeare's Georgic Histories." *ShS*, 38 (1985), 37–47.

Maintains that Virgil's *Georgics* is a "deep source for Sh's conception of history as agricultural process" in the two English tetralogies. The four books of the *Georgics* focus, respectively, on "tilling, planting, animal husbandry, and bee-keeping"—all prominent images in the history plays. Though Virgil celebrates how strenuous husbandry can redeem a land torn by war, he is very much aware of the transitory nature of political life. The tension in the *Georgics* between "the enduring patterns of agriculture" and the tendency of nature to revert to chaos gives the poem a pessimistic edge. Sh would have encountered the *Georgics* in grammar school, and a number of passages in the histories seem to recall Virgil's poem: for example, Alexander Iden's praise of the retired life in *2H6*, IV.x; Carlisle's objection to crowning Bolingbroke in *R2*, IV.i; and Canterbury's analogy between the government of bees and the government of men in *H5*, I.ii. Like Virgil, Sh uses agricultural images to provide glimpses of the ideal state, but also like Virgil, he uses agriculture to suggest irresolution, unnatural behavior, and relapse.

0222 Bulman, James Cornelius Jr. "The Heroic Naif in Shakespearean Tragedy." Ph.D. dissertation, Yale University, 1976. *DAI*, 37 (1976–77), 4363-A.

Treats naiveté as "a mode of heroic perception: the hero's absolute image of himself and his projection of that image onto the world." Indicates, in a survey of Sh's early plays, that the playwright was at first satisfied with "conventional types of the naif"— the conqueror, the knight, the revenger—bequeathed to him by several heroic traditions. In the later history plays, *JC*, and *Ham.*, Sh employed the naif as a foil (Caesar) to a more complex *eiron* (Brutus) who is the tragic protagonist. Two central chapters discuss *Tro.* and *Tim.* as transitional plays that test the tragic potential of the naif. Critical difficulties with these plays may be partially removed by viewing them as "Sh's experiments with a heroic naif who fails to reach" a mature, perhaps ironic, self-awareness. In each case, the hero's naive idealism is contested by "a chorus of Greek cynics" who enable the audience to regard him with ironic detachment. Later plays allow for the full tragic development of the naif. An appendix presents evidence for "dating *Tim.* earlier than is customary," which lends credibility to the assumption, made in previous chapters, that like *Tro.*, *Tim.* is a midcareer work. The appendix is revised as item 2621, and the whole dissertation is revised as item 0220.

0223 Bunselmeyer, Josephine Elizabeth. "The Tragic Effects of Rhetoric: Shakespeare's Use of Rhetorical Schemes in the Tragedies." Ph.D. dissertation, Fordham University, 1973, *DAI*, 34 (1973–74), 5093-A.

Holds that rhetoric serves two chief purposes in Sh's tragedies—"it is a means of distinguishing public, politic speech from private tragic language, and it is the tool of men who would control others and who incite tragedy." Analyzes Sh's use of rhetorical schemes to show his awareness of how misuse of rhetoric can have tragic consequences. The first chapter studies ideas about the misuse of rhetoric from classical and Renaissance authorities. Subsequent chapters deal with a number of Sh's tragedies, discovering two basic linguistic patterns: Those characters who "incite the tragic action" (for example, Iago, Tamora, and Timon's false friends) are skilled public speakers whose words, though false, are "effective spurs to action"; the heroes, no matter how great their rhetorical skills, move away from rhetoric "as they experience tragedy."

0224 Burckhardt, Sigurd. "The King's Language: Shakespeare's Drama as Social Discovery." *AR*, 21 (1961–62), 369–87.

Examines seven of Sh's plays, concluding that they reveal the poet's "gradual, and painful, discovery of his medium": language. In the earlier plays, the social order is seen as "the ultimate guarantor of true human communion." As he becomes aware of "the order's impotences and then of its corruption, the poet himself is forced to act as surety." When this fails, he "tests two possibilities of direct truth: trust in the purity of language and reliance upon the automatic truth of creative speech." These "attempts to do without the third, the social term, are bound to end tragically." In *JC*, the body politic is destroyed with the assassination of Caesar, and "language, thus deprived of its support, acts strangely and destructively." Significantly, the two poets who appear in the play fail to communicate: Cinna is "killed by a pun," and the nameless versifier who tries to reconcile Brutus and Cassius is dismissed as a fool. *Ant.* offers one way "to gain sovereignty and truth": to give up absolutes, "to surrender with open eyes to falsehood."

0225 Burelbach, Frederick M. Jr. "Character Disintegration in the Early Shakespeare." *ShStud*, 6 (1967–68), 62–74.

Suggests that Sh, particularly in his early work, used "the metaphor of physical disintegration" to represent "the conflict between the one and the many, between ideality and actuality." Tragic disunity is symbolized in *Tit.* by "the fragmentation of the body," and comic disunity in *Err.* is seen in the rupture of the bond between husband and wife, parent and child, sister and sister, and master and servant.

0226 Burke, Mary Kathleen. "An Anthropological Perspective on Three Shakespearean Plays: *The Comedy of Errors, Two Gentlemen of Verona,* and *Measure for Measure.*" Ph.D. dissertation, University of Massachusetts, 1978. *DAI*, 39 (1978–79), 2949-A-2950-A.

Treats three of Sh's comedies as "initiation rituals which portray individual and societal conflicts, and present resolutions to these conflicts." An introductory chapter discusses several Greek and Roman comedies (by Menander, Terence, and Plautus), chosen because they lend themselves to "an anthropological analysis based on kinship relations and symbolism" and because they manifest a number of the same elements found in Sh's three comedies: the doubling of characters, the untangling of family relationships, the confusion of identities, and the problems inherent in arranging appropriate marriages.

0227 Burke, Peter. *The Renaissance Sense of the Past.* London: Edward Arnold, 1969. vii + 154 pp.

Chapter 2 highlights the increased awareness by men of the Renaissance that their age differed from the past and that things change over time. Describes Petrarch as an antiquarian deeply concerned with recovering the past. Claims that Sh communicates in his Roman plays "a sense of what it felt like to have values which were not English or Christian but Roman and Stoic; suicide as a noble act, for example." This sympathetic awareness of the past "owes a great deal, not only to Shakespeare's genius, but also to the Renaissance sense of the past."

0228 Burns, Edward. *Character: Acting and Being on the Pre-Modern Stage.* New York: St. Martin's P., 1990. ix + 238 pp.

Explains the pre-modern conception of character as rhetorical, an attempt to "establish ways of speaking and writing proper to particular kinds of people." This "transactional" model of character, originating with Aristotle and modified by other ancient writers and by Renaissance commentators like Julius Caesar Scaliger (in his *Poeticae* [1561]), was what Sh understood by the term. Chapter 1 discusses theories of character found in Aristotle's *Poetics* and "the development of an idea of character in post-Aristotelian rhetoric, and in the literary forms of biography, 'persona' and Theophrastean 'character.' " Chapter 2 includes a consideration of character and power in the Henry IV tetralogy. Chapter 3 focuses on character as political praxis in *Tro.*, *Ant.*, and *JC*. Chapter 4 approaches "the question of what acting and character are in English renaissance theatre, and through the use of the theatre as an analogy of life in the world." Explores acting and empathy in *Ham.*

0229   Bush, Douglas. "The Isolation of the Renaissance Hero." *Reason and Imagination: Studies in the History of Ideas 1600–1800.* Ed. Joseph A. Mazzeo. New York: Columbia U. P., 1962, pp. 57–69. Reprint. *Prefaces to Renaissance Literature.* Cambridge: Harvard U. P., 1965, pp. 91–96.

Claims that the Renaissance hero is far closer to the heroes of classical antiquity than to modern literary protagonists. Two reasons for this are the veneration Renaissance readers and authors felt for the ancients and the Renaissance sympathy with the ancients' belief in the didactic function of literature. Like the classical hero, the Renaissance hero is "eminent in worldly position"; his stature and personality were often "enlarged to something like superhuman dimensions," partly through the use of classical allusions. The Greek dramatists and Sh both assume a moral order. Their heroes do not appear "as helpless, unresisting victims of either fate or society; they make choices and are responsible for their acts."

0230   Bushnell, Rebecca Weld. "The Defiance of Augury: The Hero and Prophet in Sophoclean and Shakespearean Tragedy." Ph.D. dissertation, Princeton University, 1983. *DAI*, 43 (1982–83), 2988-A.

Shows, after a discussion of the hero's defiance of augury in Homer and in the plays of Sophocles, that Sh "reinvented the defiance of augury" in *JC*, *Mac.*, and *Ham.*

0231   Butler, Francelia. "The Relationship between Moral Competence and Old Age in *Richard II*, *2 Henry IV*, and *Henry V*." *SQ*, 16 (1965), 236–38.

Claims that the Renaissance, in its equation of physical and moral competence, returned to an essentially classical concept. *R2*, *2H4*, and *H5* are interesting in their application of "the physical–moral competence principle to old age." When a hero grows old, his physical strength can no longer match his moral strength. His son can then assume his role, as Bolingbroke does for Gaunt in *R2*. In the case of York, we see an old man who has lived on "until his moral competence shrivels to match his depleted physical competence."

0232   Cahn, Victor L. *The Heroes of Shakespeare's Tragedies.* (American University Studies. Series IV: English Language and Literature 56.) New York: Peter Lang, 1988. xi + 204 pp.

Provides analyses of the tragic heroes in ten of Sh's tragedies, focusing on how the qualities that define their greatness also lead to their downfall. Chapter 1, on *Tit.*, notes that Titus's power as a warrior is quickly perverted into a murderous savagery that engulfs the whole play. Calls attention to inconsistencies of tone, weaknesses in the portrayal of several characters, and other defects. The play does have a certain coherence of vision: Through animal imagery and other means, it does show that humanity is responsible for the evils it experiences.

Chapter 3, on *JC*, focuses on Brutus, whose destruction is the most moving exhibit in the play. Although an idealist with many admirable qualities, Brutus is "hopelessly out of touch with humanity." He is also susceptible to flattery. Views the Roman mob as the most formidable of all the characters, the motivation for the political mentality and the political oratory of everyone else. When men devote themselves to utterances that will please the majority, they inevitably resort to lies. This duplicity undermines the entire society portrayed in the play. *JC* is the first of Sh's tragedies in which the hero's decisions "directly influence the surrounding society."

Chapter 8, on *Ant.*, maintains that the play is built on a group of contradictions or seeming contradictions: those between Rome and Egypt, plot (which seems to suggest that Antony and Cleopatra are foolish) and poetry (which seems to vindicate their love), war and love, empowerment and insecurity in Cleopatra, and "public honor" and private desire in Antony. Discusses Octavius as a cold, hypocritical rationalist and Enobarbus as "a frustrated romantic." Admires the self-knowledge and purity of spirit that Cleopatra displays as she prepares for death. Remarks on Antony's inability to be moderate, concluding that he remains true to his own humanity, despite the cost.

Chapter 9, on *Cor.*, notes that the play is a bitter one, with a satiric mocking of the spirit of reconciliation at the end. Martius, it is clear, has been forced to play the role of supremely proud warrior by his mother. From a number of hints in the text (for example, his brief conversations with his wife, Virgilia), we can see that he would like to be more fully human, to relate to others more effectively; however, his mother's cruel domination has left him unable to do so. Although he has some keen political insights, Coriolanus is a failure as a leader of the feckless Roman people. Nor is anyone else in the play fit to rule. In the play's bleak, ironic ending, the hero dies as a boy, never having escaped his mother's control.

Chapter 10, on *Tim.*, points to the play's sketchy characterization, the tendency of its persons to represent exaggerated human traits in a kind of fable or allegory. Emphasizes the parallels between Timon and Alcibiades, both of whom err in regarding human behavior "with unqualified benevolence" and both of whom react with fits of temper when their rosy illusions are destroyed. Other characters who make an impression are Flavius, whose kindness undermines the justification for Timon's indiscriminate hatred of mankind, and Apemantus, whose criticism of society is vitiated because he "is smaller than those he satirizes." At the play's end, there is a shift in tone with Alcibiades' regeneration.

0233 Cairncross, Andrew S. "Shakespeare and the Golden Age." *SCB*, 30 (1970), 173–75.

Explains two meanings of "The Golden Age" to Sh: "the life of the pastoral tradition" and "the Age of Gold," where "money was the supreme or the only value." Sh admired the Golden Age of the first definition, but "he knew its practical limitations." The ideal visible in Sh's heroes, especially the tragic heroes, is that of "a liberally educated man living the life of a landed proprietor." Against the gentleman, Sh set "the new man of money." The excesses of these two types form the basis for the tragedies. The two excesses are brought together in *Tim.* and *Oth.*

0234 Cairncross, Andrew S. "Shakespeare and the Harp of Man." *ForumH*, 9, no. 1 (1971), 70–73.

Maintains that the "theme of the dependence and the independence and the interaction of man," a Renaissance theme derived directly from the classics, pervades Sh's plays. Independence from Fortune can be achieved by strength of character (the way of the magnanimous man), strength of judgment, and "the stoicism and cynicism developed in the Greek philosophies." The magnanimous man and the Stoic rise above Fortune, while the cynic "stays low and cannot fall." In the middle are two groups, the manipulators, or "harpers," and the manipulated, who have "little self-control or self-knowledge" and are thus natural victims. Examples of both types are seen in *JC*, which is largely devoted to persuasion; Antony is manipulated by Cleopatra in *Ant.*; Coriolanus is easily manipulated because of his hot temper; and several villains (Iago, Aaron, Richard III) are consummate manipulators.

0235 Cairns, Christopher. "Aretino's Comedies and the Italian 'Erasmian' Connection in Shakespeare and Jonson." *Theatre of the English and Italian Renaissance.* Eds. J. R. Mulryne and Margaret Shewring. (Warwick Studies in the European Humanities.) London: Macmillan, 1991, pp.113–37.

Argues that Aretino, in his comedies, followed the advice of Erasmus to adapt the plots of classical comedy "for morally improving purposes." In particular, Aretino developed opposing characters representing contrasting moral positions. Discusses the influence of Aretino on Jonson and Sh (*Err.*, *LLL*, and *TN*), suggesting that the theme of a "bewitched city" in *Err.* comes from Aretino's *L'Ipocrito*.

0236 Calder, Alexander Charles. "The Dramatic Language of Shakespeare's 'Henry VI': A Stylistic and Theatrical Study." Ph.D. dissertation, University of Aberdeen, 1989. *DAI*, 51 (1990–91), 3416-A.

Chapter 3 surveys the ideas about rhetoric familiar to Sh from classical and Renaissance sources. Places emphasis on "the persuasive modes of *logos, pathos, ethos* and their associated figures." Chapters 4, 5, and 6 engage in rhetorical analysis. Chapter 6 shows that King Henry's language exhibits "a remarkable blending of *logos, pathos, ethos*."

0237 Calderwood, James L. *Shakespeare and the Denial of Death*. Amherst, Massachusetts: U. of Massachusets P., 1987. xi + 233 pp.

Attempts "to suggest how often and how variously Shakespeare dramatizes the human desire for symbolic immortality." Discusses *Tim.* and *Cor.* in a chapter on cannibalism: Timon gives himself away and is symbolically fed upon by his pseudofriends, who consume him financially, while Coriolanus hoards himself and is finally torn apart and distributed to the hungry mob. Includes, in a chapter on disguise, a consideration of Coriolanus: His peculiar muffling when he visits Aufidius is significant because it makes clear that he has been more than usually undisguised throughout his life; his vulnerability is an exaggeration of the condition of the tragic hero. Mentions Adonis (*Ven.*) in a chapter on sex: The youthful hunter attempts to find his male identity by exorcising the female in himself, but he fails and is rendered feminine in death. A later chapter treats Coriolanus's devotion to death as "a substitute for sexuality, a flight from the dominating feminine world of his mother." Analyzes *JC* and *Ant.* in a section on immortality and art. In *JC*, we are forcefully reminded that we are watching a play that is at several removes from the events of ancient Roman history that are the ostensible subject of the play. The conspirators, in confidently asserting that the theater will memorialize their noble act of giving their country liberty, put their faith in something that is too changeable. Thus their noble purpose is lost through repeated performance. In *Ant.*, the same sense of theatricality induces us to lose sight of the historical lovers, but the play does not set itself up against a reality that cancels it out. Instead, reality is enveloped in Sh's imaginative vision, which thereby gains immortality.

0238 Canfield, J. Douglas. *Word as Bond in English Literature from the Middle Ages to the Restoration*. Philadelphia: U. of Pennsylvania P., 1989. xviii + 338 pp.

Explores "the chivalric code of the word as the bond of society, the mutual pledge of trust" through analyses of a variety of literary works, including *Tro.* and *Ant.* Includes *Tro.* in a chapter on corrective satire: Sh sets his play in "a world of broken words," denying us "the closure of tragedy" and leaving us "with a bleak satiric prospect." The only end we can envision is "the virtual destruction of civilization itself." Classifies *Ant.* as an absurdist satire in which the heroic speech of the principals is shown to be merely "the rhetoric of the desire for transcendence in a mutable world."

0239 Cantor, Paul A. *Shakespeare's Rome: Republic and Empire*. Ithaca: Cornell U. P., 1976. 228 pp.

Disputes the conventional view that Sh has little to say about Romanness in his Roman plays. Maintains that there is a distinctive conception of Rome as republic in *Cor.* and empire in *Ant.*, with *JC* representing a point in the evolution from one to the other. Focuses on *Cor.* and *Ant.*, deriving Sh's idea of Rome from the plays themselves rather than from Elizabethan commentators.

The three chapters of part 1 argue that the most highly prized quality in the republic is *spiritedness*, a complex combination of "austerity, pride, heroic virtue, and public service." *Eros*, the force that in *Ant.* takes the diverse forms of "hunger, thirst, sexual desire, and 'immortal longings,'" is present in the world of *Cor.* but is kept in check. The two parties—plebeians and patricians—need to stay in a state of tension for balance to be maintained in the city. Coriolanus cannot accept the divided world of the regime because it threatens to reduce the patricians to the level of the plebeians:

He wishes to conquer the plebeians once and for all and put an end to divided rule. His failure to assume the leadership of Rome can be laid to his unwillingness to see that peace and war require different sorts of leadership. He comes to hate the city because it forces him to compromise. In leaving Rome, Coriolanus is "pushing his heroism to new extremes," but ultimately he has to acknowledge his humanity—and bow to the force of *eros*—in caring about his family and what others will say about him. The weaknesses of the regime are clear: Rome needs a hero but will drop him when he becomes troublesome; however, "the hero is ready to rebel against the city ... whenever he feels ... he no longer needs it" or whenever it demands too many compromises.

The three chapters of part 2 deal with the nature of the early Roman empire as portrayed in *Ant*. In this world, public life holds few rewards, while the pursuit of private ends offers new satisfactions. There is almost no reference to the common good. All sorts of private longings arise, but it is difficult to find ways to satisfy them. Antony suffers acutely from spiritual emptiness and is perplexed about finding an object for his allegiance. In a departure from Plutarch, Sh excludes the supernatural from the republic of *Cor.*, presenting the gods as under the control of the city. In the empire of *Ant.*, the importance of the city gods is minimized as "characters turn to new sources of divine authority": *Ant.* is the only one of Sh's Roman plays in which personal deities are mentioned. As part of the emphasis on the private in the empire, fidelity between master and servant, leader and subordinate, and one lover and another replaces the republic's victory in battle as the chief value. But although the private is exalted in *Ant.*, the public is not utterly excluded: Antony and Cleopatra feel pride and ambition in their love, and they seek an audience for it. The political is not eliminated; it is simply assimilated into the erotic. Cleopatra, for example, cannot allow Antony any activity that is not in some way connected to his love for her. Thus the private needs of Antony and Cleopatra pervert their political judgment and cause them to behave tyrannically (for example, Cleopatra's treatment of the Messenger in II.v and Antony's beating of Thidias in III.xiii). In seeking a world elsewhere for their love, they have something in common with Coriolanus. The situation of Sh's Romans is tragic: They "chafe under the regime's restraints or even rebel against them, but if successful in breaking out of the city's control, they find they have difficulties without its guidance." The two plays are companion pieces in that "one helps to define what is lacking in the world of the other." See item 0041.

0240 Carducci, Jane Shook. "'Our hearts you see not': Shakespeare's Roman Men." Ph.D. dissertation, University of Nevada, Reno, 1985. *DAI*, 46 (1985–86), 1946-A.

Maintains that Sh's Roman men cannot express their emotional needs directly or make open requests for intimacy. Analyzes four plays. *Tit.* displays "the extremes of bombast and silence"; *JC* focuses on "ritual, plain speaking and public masks"; Antony, in *Ant.*, is a "perpetual adolescent," who veers between Roman plain style and Egyptian hyperbole; and Coriolanus is "isolated and uncompromising." Each play reveals that the manly ideal of Rome is inadequate because it is defined too narrowly in terms of "courage and martial skill." Parts revised as items 1970 and 1620.

0241 Carpenter, Nan Cooke. "Shakespeare and Music." *RenD*, N. S. 7 (1976), 243–55.

Cites the need for more studies on Sh and music. We need to know, for example, where Sh got his information on "the music of the spheres and its effects upon humans—ideas that go back at least to Pythagoras."

0242 Carroll, William C. *The Metamorphoses of Shakespearean Comedy*. Princeton: Princeton U. P., 1985. 292 pp.

Discusses metamorphosis as a significant concern of Renaissance drama. Notes that for Sh's time Ovid's *Metamorphoses* was the preeminent text on the subject and uses Ovid to examine metamorphosis with respect to questions of identity, love, language, and the structure of comedy in Sh. Part of chapter 3 is a revision of item 3079.

0243 Cartelli, Thomas. *Marlowe, Shakespeare, and the Economy of Theatrical Experience.* Philadelphia: U. of Pennsylvania P., 1991. xv + 241 pp.

Regards pleasure and engagement as the ends of Elizabethan playgoing and proposes an "audience-oriented theory of reading." Chapter 6, which includes a discussion of *Tro.*, is a revision of item 2832, and chapter 8, on *Tim.*, is a revision of item 2627.

0243a Casey, John. "The Noble." *Philosophy and Literature.* Ed. A. Phillips Griffiths. (Royal Institute of Philosophy Lecture Series 16.) Cambridge: Cambridge U. P., 1984, pp.135-53.

Devotes a section of the essay to Sh, noting that his plays "certainly express the ethic of the noble" and that in Sh's tragedies the noble is "a contested concept, probed and questioned as much as affirmed." Includes discussions of *Cor.* and *Ant.*

0244 Cavell, Stanley. *Disowning Knowledge in Six Plays of Shakespeare.* Cambridge: Cambridge U. P., 1987. x + 226 pp.

The introduction includes a substantial discussion of *Ant.*; the play addresses in the relationship of the protagonists the wish, born out of modern subjectivity and skepticism, for a new intimacy. Antony, experiencing the withdrawal of the world, himself withdraws from the world, unable to "represent the recession of heroism into the conduct of ordinary life." Cleopatra does manage such a representation, becoming "whatever constitutes the world" and inventing marriage for the two of them.
   Chapter 4, on *Cor.*, is a reprint of item 1623.

0245 Chaffee, Alan Jewell. "The Triple Eye: Paradigms of Time in Shakespeare's Plays." Ph.D. dissertation, Pennsylvania State University, 1970. *DAI*, 32 (1971-72), 381-A.

Attempts to "organize and articulate the many modes of time" in Sh's plays. One paradigm, myth, can be seen in the Kronos-Saturn myth, "which depicts the triple movement of procreation-preservation-destruction, a saturnian rhythm or mythos of the action" especially dominant in *Son.* and the later plays. Describes "external sources of the myth."

0246 Chakravorty, Jagannath. *The Idea of Revenge in Shakespeare: With Special Reference to "Hamlet."* Calcutta: Jadavpur U. P., 1969. xiv + 303 pp.

Studies the revenge motif in Sh's plays, with emphasis on *Ham.* Maintains that Sh transformed the revenge tradition in drama by imparting an ethical element to his characters. In *Tit.*, for example, the playwright goes beyond his Senecan and Ovidian source materials to create a complex protagonist, subject to the conflicting demands of justice, honor, and revenge. The complexity of Hamlet's nature is in part revealed by his reaction to the Player's Pyrrhus speech (*Ham.*, II.ii). *JC* presents Brutus as a public avenger and Mark Antony and Octavius as private ones. In addition, the revenge theme can be seen through the spirit of Pompey in the early part of the play and later through the spirit of Caesar.

0247 Chakravorty, Jagannath. "Shakespearian Transmutation of Revenge." *Shakespeare: A Book of Homage.* Calcutta: Jadavpur U., 1965, pp. 80-117.

Maintains that Sh transforms the revenge drama inherited from Seneca by giving an "ethical character" to his tragic personae. In *Tit.*, he endows the protagonist with a complex nature "caused by the conflicting demands of 'honor,' 'justice,' and 'revenge.'" Titus anticipates Brutus in his love of abstract principle and Coriolanus in his obstinacy. *JC* is a study of two opposite kinds of revenge—one public (Brutus's) and the other personal (Antony's). In *Ham.*, the two are portrayed in one person. Concludes by considering the revenge motif in *Oth.*, *Lr.*, and *Tmp.*

General Works

0248 Champion, Larry S. *The Evolution of Shakespeare's Comedy: A Study in Dramatic Perspective.* Cambridge: Harvard U. P., 1970. 241 pp.

Proceeds through Sh's career, discussing eleven comedies, classified into four groups: comedies of action, comedies of identity, problem comedies, and comedies of transformation. As his career progressed, Sh deepened his characterization to suit the types of plots he was using. The Italian tradition, represented by Plautus and Terence, is one of the strands Sh wove into the complex fabric of his comedy. Describes *The Knight's Tale* as a source of *MND*.

0249 Champion, Larry S. "Shakespeare's 'Nell.'" *Names,* 16 (1968), 357–61. Reprint. *Names and Their Varieties: A Collection of Essays in Onomastics.* Comp. Kelsie B. Harder. Lanham, Maryland: U. P. of America, 1986, pp. 203–207.

Points out that "Nell," the name given to Mistress Quickly in *1H4, 2H4,* and *H5,* is instrumental in the degrading of her character. Classical tradition (associating the name with Helen of Troy), usage by Sh's contemporaries, and Sh's other plays all testify to the name's connotation of a lower-class woman of questionable reputation.

0250 Champion, Larry S. *Shakespeare's Tragic Perspective: The Development of His Tragic Technique.* Athens: U. of Georgia P., 1976. viii + 279 pp.

Chapter 1, a revision of item 2720, treats *Tit.* as "an embryonic Elizabethan tragedy," a work of some power whose weaknesses keep the audience from responding to the tragic development of the hero. Chapter 3 includes a consideration of *JC,* a play which marks a significant advance in Sh's ability to give a view of the internal life of his characters. The first half of the play is more successful than the second in leading the spectators to simultaneous emotional involvement and ethical judgment of Brutus. Chapter 5, "The Social Dimensions of Tragedy," discusses *Tim., Cor.,* and *Ant.* as works that emphasize the societal as well as the personal nature of tragedy. In this, they differ from the earlier tragedies, which stress the internal struggle of the individual. *Tim.,* whose chief character is "too rigidly drawn," is not as successful as the other two public tragedies.

0251 Chang, Joseph, S. M. J. "'Of Mighty Opposites': Stoicism and Machiavellianism." *RenD,* 9 (1966), 37–57.

Focuses on Elizabethan tragedies in which a Stoic hero is opposed by a Machiavellian villain. The two philosophies are distinguished primarily by their respective views of Fortune. The Machiavellian sees Fortune as a collection of contingencies for which man has failed to make adequate provision: This Fortune can be controlled by more careful planning. The Stoic, however, rejects Fortune as "man's false understanding of the meaning of events arising from vain desires which have no basis in his rational nature." In causing the ruin of the hero, the villain preens himself with a false sense of independence, attempts to manipulate the world around him, and, though momentarily successful, eventually falls because his activities are in conflict with the power of the gods. The hero must struggle with his adversary, and he must preserve the integrity of his vision that "the world is rational and subject to the dominion of benevolent gods." Chapman's *The Revenge of Bussy D'Ambois* provides the clearest example of this type of tragedy, but it can also be seen in *Lr.* and *Ham.* Revision of part of item 0252.

0252 Chang, Joseph, S. M. J. "Shakespeare and Stoic Ethics." Ph.D. dissertation, University of Wisconsin, 1965. *DA,* 25 (1964–65), 5902–5903.

Argues that the extent of Stoicism in the Renaissance has not been fully recognized because it has been too closely identified with Senecan pessimism. With its basically optimistic belief in the individual's ability to transcend evil, Stoicism was ideally suited to "the new temper of the Renaissance." It could also be reconciled with Christian beliefs. Sh uses many Stoic commonplaces, including "all the world's a stage." More significantly, Sh's dramatic practice is indebted to "the Stoic's analysis of moral choice in terms of appearance and reality." In *JC*, Sh incorporates "the Stoic commonplaces of constancy and suicide" to establish the Roman tone. Brutus's growing involvement in the conspiracy prompts him to mask "the evil of assassination with the appearance of virtue." *Ham.*, "as perfect a Stoic play as one could expect to find," presents the hero with the problem of understanding how to submit to the will of Providence and at the same time retain his integrity. Part revised as item 0251.

0253   Charnes, Linda Anne. " 'So unsecret to ourselves': Notorious Identity in Shakespeare's *King Richard III, Troilus and Cressida,* and *Antony and Cleopatra.*" Ph.D. dissertation, University of California, Berkeley, 1990. *DAI,* 52 (1991–92), 1336-A.

Argues that Sh uses "the paradigm of notorious identity to interrogate the historical, ideological, and cultural forces that determine social, political, and gender identity." Sh's legendary characters are burdened by a fame that precedes them. Chapter 2 contends that the tale of Troilus and Cressida is used in *Tro.* "to represent the pathological forms and effects of cultural entrapment." Chapter 3 deals with the way in which *Ant.* enacts a contest between "the conflicting representational modes of narrative and spectacle, and the different kinds of politics and subjects—discursive and histrionic–they produce." The power of these works is due to the way in which Sh "builds his own representational difficulties into the plays themselves."

0254   Charney, Maurice. "The Persuasiveness of Violence in Elizabethan Plays." *RenD,* N. S. 2 (1969), 59–70.

Maintains that, although Elizabethan dramatists were influenced by Seneca, they differed from him in presenting violence directly on stage, thus powerfully evoking pity and fear. Discusses, among other examples, the blinding of Gloucester in *Lr.* and the murder of Macduff's children in *Mac.*

0255   Charney, Maurice. *Shakespeare's Roman Plays: The Function of Imagery in Drama.* Cambridge: Harvard U. P., 1961. 250 pp.

Offers readings of *JC, Ant.,* and *Cor.* based on a study of their imagery. Chapter 1, the introduction, explains two senses of the term "image": the "references to a significant subject matter," or theme, in a play and "the large body of images that is not part of the spoken words of the text but directly presented in the theater."

Chapter 2, "Style in the Roman Plays," makes general distinctions among the three plays. In *JC*, Sh seems to have deliberately limited his imaginative resources to produce a "Roman" style of order and control. In *Ant.,* the style is extended: The characteristic figure is hyperbole. The style of *Cor.* is closely linked to the character of the protagonist: It features precise, limited similes and can be described as "objective and public." It is also important to give weight to the nonverbal or presentational imagery of *Cor.*: The stage directions call for various kinds of public noise, which seems to emphasize Coriolanus's renunciation of eloquence.

Chapter 3, on *JC*, finds that the chief image themes "are the storm and its portents, blood and fire." The portents emphasize the disorder in Rome, which is further heightened by nonverbal images of sights and sounds in the stage directions. Brutus's tragedy is most forcefully presented through blood imagery: He persists in seeing Caesar's death as a noble sacrifice, a blood-letting for the health of the state, rather than the bloody murder it becomes. Blood imagery also shows Caesar at the height of his pride, just before the assassination (III.i). Fire is seen both as passion or emotional power and as a "destructive and purifying force." Both of these senses are united in Antony's funeral oration.

Chapter 4, on *Ant.*, argues that the hyperbolical style is expressed in a "repeated imagery of dimension and scope." There are three chief sets of imagery, involving cosmic reference, imperial grandeur, and mythological allusion. Prominent in the first are world images, through which Antony's career can be viewed in three stages: First, "before Actium, the world is the material domain of the Roman Empire," in which Antony plays a major role; second, "after his defeat there is only the memory of the world lost"; and third,"his death marks a devaluation of the world." Within the world theme, Sh presents a strong contrast between Rome and Egypt. The sense of Egypt is conveyed "in the themes of the Nile and its serpents, eating and drinking, hotness and indolence." Rome is characterized "partly in terms of stated opposites of Egypt, as in the themes of temperance, coldness, and business," and "partly in terms of implied opposites." In interpreting the play, we should hold both Egyptian and Roman themes together "as a tragic unity." The imagery enables us to do this—to see Cleopatra, for example, as both quean and queen.

Chapter 5, on *Cor.*, identifies food, disease, and animals as the major image themes. All of this imagery is organized around the conflict between the patricians and the plebeians. The images of food, for example, call attention to "the appetitive nature of the plebeians."

Chapter 6, "Concluding Remarks," justifies using imagery analysis. An appendix makes the case for considering *JC, Ant.*, and *Cor.*—and none of Sh's other works—as a distinctive "Roman" group. Three arguments support this classification: (1) the plays all use "Roman" costume; (2) they all treat suicide as "an act of moral courage and nobility"; and (3) they are all based on Plutarch.

0256 Charney, Maurice. "Shakespeare's Unpoetic Poetry." *SEL*, 13 (1973), 199–207.

Argues for "a more theatrical approach to Sh's poetry," one that recognizes the dramatic context of the words and does not insist on treating them as parts of lyrics. An example of "gestural poetry" can be seen in the stage direction "*holds her by the hand, silent*" (*Cor.*, V.iii.182). The language used in the quarrel scene of *JC* (IV.iii), though lacking figurative adornment, is perfectly adapted to the situation.

0257 Chatterjee, Sati. "A Note on Shakespeare's Poetics." *Shakespeare: A Book of Homage*. Calcutta: Jadavpur U., 1965, pp. 127–42.

Points out, in concluding, some similarities between Plato's ideas of mimesis and the properties of music, and "Shakespeares's mimetic concept with its gradations"—imitation of appearances and ideal imitation that represents "the truth of human life"—and Sh's view "that music reveals the inner harmony of the universe." It is best not to carry the parallels too far, however.

0258 Chaudhuri, Sujata. "Shakespeare and the Elizabethan Satire Tradition." *Shakespeare Commemoration Volume*. Ed. Taraknath Sen. Calcutta: Presidency College, 1966, pp. 170–96.

Cites the classical background for Elizabethan satire before analyzing Sh's use of certain common satiric images (for example, that of lancing a sore) and themes (for example, the vices of women). Sh "studies the objects of his ridicule or banter with a sympathetic eye." Aristotle's and Cicero's comments about how the comic arises from deformity that does not cause pain help explain Sh's treatment of characters like Falstaff and Dogberry.

0259 Chaudhuri, Sukanta. *Infirm Glory: Shakespeare and the Renaissance Image of Man*. Oxford: Clarendon P., 1981. xv + 231 pp.

Stresses the influence of Skepticism, absorbed by the Renaissance from classical sources and present even in the man-centered and generally optimistic thought of Neoplatonists, in forming the "intricate mingling of gloom and hope in a spirit of cautious and paradoxical enterprise" that characterizes the English Renaissance. Chapter 4, "Marlowe and Shakespeare," notices Skeptical elements, variously deployed and weighted, in *1&2H4, Ham., Tro., MM, Lr., Mac., Cor., Ant.*, and the last plays.

0260 Chaudhuri, Sukanta. "The Tragic Libertines: Self-Expression in the Tragedies of Shakespeare and His Contemporaries." *Shakespeare in India.* Delhi: Oxford U. P., 1987, pp. 98–118.

Argues that libertinism in the 16th and 17th c. is characterized by "the rejection of general laws and faith in private impulse." Notes that the most influential libertine writer of the age was Montaigne. Discusses the libertinism of the protagonists in *Cor.*, *Tim.*, and *Ant.* Explains that Sh's drama reveals "the tragic core of libertinism, the heroic potential of narcissism."

0261 Cheney, Donald. "Tarquin, Juliet and Other *Romei*," *Spenser Studies*, 3 (1982), 111–24.

Proposes to examine the imagery of *Luc.* and *Rom.* in light of "Sh's Roman sources and of his own later Roman plays, and to consider how his vision of Rome may have figured in the evolution of his language." In these two earlier works, Sh begins to develop the "microcosmic metaphor whereby an individual is seen as a besieged city or household, darkly sharing and conspiring with the enemy forces that seek to ravish and enthrall it." Sh's sources for Roman history contributed to this development. From Virgil, he took the theme of glory achieved at great cost; from Plutarch, he absorbed the habit of parallelism; and from Livy, he learned to think of Rome as a place of intrafamilial, even intrapersonal, conflict. In *Luc.*, Tarquin is self–destructively drawn from the siege of one city, Ardea, to a more active assault on another, Lucrece. In later Roman plays like *JC* and *Ant.*, the protagonists are often seized by a similar "hectic compulsiveness" reminiscent of "Livy's primitive Roman cityscape." As Sh adapts the story of *Rom.*, the significance of the feud to the fate of the lovers is minimized. What is important is the sense, developed through wordplay related to Rome, "that love represents a fatal attraction toward a perilous and forbidden enemy." *Rom.* contains a number of "complex involuted metaphors for self, time, or history which appear as more explicitly Roman in the later works."

0262 Cherry, Mary Jane. "A Classification and Analysis of Selected 'Sayings' in Shakespeare's Plays." Ph.D. dissertation, Catholic University of America, 1981. *DAI*, 42 (1981–82), 711-A-712-A.

Treats citations in Sh's plays from oral and written traditions, showing how these "announced sayings" appeal to the authority of Latin *sententiae*, proverbs, and other sources. Many of the sayings can be traced to the collections used in the 16th-c. English grammar schools. Chapter 3 discusses the sayings in the history plays, which are closely tied to Latin *sententiae* that stress fortitude and prudence. Chapter 4 considers the sayings—predominantly reflective—in the tragedies and romances. Chapter 5 deals with the comedies, in which the sayings are adapted in more sophisticated ways than they are by the characters in other genres.

0263 Chew, Audrey. *Stoicism in Renaissance English Literature: An Introduction.* (American University Studies Series 4: English Language and Literature 82.) New York: Peter Lang, 1988. 330 pp.

Surveys the classical background of Stoicism in writers like Cicero, Seneca, and Boethius and notes the similarities and differences between Stoicism and Epicureanism. There are Stoic elements in the concept of "the orderly process of nature," a benign plan that governs both the course of history and the lives of individuals and that can be temporarily disrupted but not permanently altered. Sh usually identifies "the law of nature with the current system" and tries to reveal some connection "between violation of the law and misfortune." To be virtuous is to conform to the laws of nature. Makes this point with respect to a number of the English history plays, as well as *Lr.*, *Rom.*, *JC*, *Tro.*, and *Cor.* Stoic virtue can be seen in characters like Horatio in *Ham.*, but its lack is frequently evident in characters like Claudio (*MM*) and Brabantio (*Oth.*) when they are advised to exhibit Stoic patience. Sh's treatment of suicide is adapted to dramatic situation; in Roman plays like *JC* and *Ant.*, it is presented as a way to end one's life with dignity.

0264 Chew, Samuel C. *The Pilgrimage of Life*. New Haven: Yale U. P., 1962. xxv + 449 + 75 pp. of plates.

Discusses the pilgrimage of human life and themes related to it in the English literature of the Renaissance, with analogues from the art of design. Makes frequent references to Sh. Cites the rivalry between Poet and Painter in *Tim.* to illustrate the claims of both poetry and painting to speak to the understanding, to convey a moral significance. Uses Sh's works to provide, among other things, examples of themes and images with classical roots: For instance, various aspects of Fortune are illustrated by *Tim., Lr., H5, JC,* and *Ant.*

0265 Choe, Jaisou. *Shakespeare's Art as Order of Life*. New York: Vantage P., 1965. 199 pp.

Begins by describing literature as "the way to organize interests and give order to feeling." Discusses Sh's plays in a series of six chapters, each of which considers a group of plays that are perceived to order "the empiric elements—sensation, conception, idea, thought, emotion, feeling, volition, instinct"—in a distinctive way. Devotes chapter 3, "Criticism of Life," to the problem plays, including *Tro*. In this play, a set of "complete men" (Agamemnon, Ulysses, Nestor, Hector) is juxtaposed with a set of "incomplete men" (Achilles, Ajax, Troilus) to effect a criticism of the latter. Chapter 5 treats the Roman plays as exemplars of transcendental order. Each of the three Roman plays stresses one aspect of the transcendental: *JC* is concerned with the ideal, *Cor.* with the absolute, and *Ant.* with the eternal. Notes that these plays, with their idea that "the transcendental order can be reached only through death," enlarge "the conception of Shakespearean tragedy."

0266 Christian, Lynda G. *Theatrum Mundi: The History of an Idea*. (Harvard Dissertations in Comparative Literature.) New York: Garland, 1987. xix + 294 pp.

Traces the *topos* of the world as stage to its earliest recorded appearances in the works of ancient Greek philosophers like Democritus, Pythagoras, Heraclitus, Plato, and Aristotle. Follows the *topos* through its uses in Hellenistic times (when it was often associated with "the capricious figure of Fortune"), in the Middle Ages (when it largely disappeared), and in the Renaissance (when it was revived by the Christian Neoplatonists and came eventually to express "the vanity of human life"). Chapter 5 discusses Sh's use of the metaphor in *AYL, MV, Mac., R2, Ham.,* and *Lr.*

0267 Clark, Sandra, ed. *The New Century Shakespeare Handbook*. Prepared by T. H. Long. Englewood Cliffs, New Jersey: Prentice-Hall, 1974. 291 pp.

Consists primarily of alphabetically arranged entries that cover the works, their characters and settings, and other relevant matters. Provides, in the entry for each play, an account of sources. Prefaces the alphabetical section with several articles, including one on "Shakespeare's Major Poetry," which discusses Ovidian elements in *Ven.* and *Luc.*

0268 Clark, Stephen Kay. "'A Place in the Story': The Perspective of Shakespeare's Common Soldier." DA dissertation, Middle Tennessee State University, 1985. *DAI*, 46 (1985–86), 987-A.

Chapters 3 and 4 consider "the waste surrounding martialism" in the tragedies of Sh, including Enobarbus's agony over having to follow a faulty leader in *Ant.* and "the suffering imposed by the supreme martialist, Coriolanus."

0269 Clarke, Joseph Kelly. "The 'Praeceptor Amoris' in English Renaissance Lyric Poetry: One Aspect of the Poet's Voice." Ph.D. dissertation, University of North Texas, 1985. *DAI*, 47 (1986–87), 187-A.

Concentrates on the "praeceptor amoris," or teacher of love, as he appears in English poetry between 1500 and 1660. Gives background for this figure in Ovid's *Art of Love*. Notes that in England the praeceptor is seen performing three functions:

"defining love, propounding a philosophy about it, and giving advice." Most of the poets cannot agree about whether love should be physically or spiritually oriented; their versions of the praeceptor have either one or the other emphasis. Sh attempts a reconciliation.

0270 Clemen, Wolfgang. *English Tragedy before Shakespeare: The Development of Dramatic Speech.* Tr. T. S. Dorsch. London: Methuen, 1961. 301 pp.

Provides background for study of Sh. Traces "the history of serious drama before Shakespeare" as it relates to the "development of the dramatic set speech." In early drama, the set speeches had to incorporate everything that in Sh and in realistic drama was made clear by other means. Cicero's *De Oratore* was one reason why rhetoric was held in such high regard in Renaissance England. Seneca's plays, which depend for their effects on the set speech, and which contain all three kinds of rhetoric as set down by Quintilian, provided the chief model for early English Renaissance tragedies. Chapter 5 discusses English plays written in the purely classical style of Seneca (for example, *Gismond of Salerne*, 1567–68). Chapter 14 follows one type of set speech, the dramatic lament, through various manifestations in ancient and Renaissance drama. It is used by Seneca and the Greek tragedians and shows up in *Rom.*, *1H6*, *Oth.*, *MND*, and *Ant.*

0271 Clemen, Wolfgang. *Shakespeare's Dramatic Art: Collected Essays.* London: Methuen, 1972. ix + 236 pp.

The first chapter, "Shakespeare's Art of Preparation," includes sections on *Tit.* and *JC*. Because of insufficient preparation for the many atrocities of *Tit.*, the audience remains largely unmoved. In *JC*, the first scene prepares us for the appearance of the hero as well as establishing the basic situation of the play. In the next two scenes, Caesar's brief appearances, along with the conversations other characters have about him, operate to produce a shifting, ambiguous impression of him. The numerous "omens, portents, prophecies, warning dreams and premonitions" also contribute to the dramatist's preparation. Sh uses great skill in grafting the play's first part (ending with Caesar's death) onto the second part. An important preparatory element in the first half of the play can be seen in the differing judgments passed on Antony by the conspirators.

0272 Clubb, Louise George. "Shakespeare's Comedy and Late Cinquecento Mixed Genres." *Shakespearean Comedy.* Ed. Maurice Charney. New York: New York Literary Forum, 1980, pp. 129–39.

Argues that Sh was thoroughly familiar with 16th-c. Italian dramatic practice and theory. In particular, by the time he wrote *Err.*, he had assimilated the principles developed by Italian humanists for mixing genres, derived from Terence's idea of *contaminatio* (mixing of two plots). Italian comedy of the 16th c. deliberately combined elements of greater and greater diversity to produce hybrids of different sorts that nevertheless still adhered in some way to neoclassical norms. Sh's comedies reflect a similar kind of experimentation, testing the limits of genre and creating a variety of dramatic effects. *TN* and *Err.* are good examples.

0273 Clubb, Louise George. "Theatregrams." *Comparative Critical Approaches to Renaissance Comedy.* Eds. Donald Beecher and Massimo Ciavolella. (Carleton Renaissance Plays in Translation Series 9.) Ottowa: Dovehouse Editions, 1986, pp. 15–33.

Acknowledges the indebtedness of Sh's comedy to Attic-Roman New Comedy. Suggests, however, that in England as well as in Italy comedy not only imitated classical models directly but produced "romantic comedy and mixed genres" by means of "a common process based on the principle of contamination of sources, of genres, and of accumulated stage-structures, or theatregrams." Discusses *TN*, *Oth.*, *Rom.*, and *Wiv.*

General Works

0274   Cody, Richard. *The Landscape of the Mind: Pastoralism and Platonic Theory in Tasso's "Aminta" and Shakespeare's Early Comedies.* Oxford: Clarendon P., 1969. [vi] + 191 pp.

Examines Tasso's *Aminta* to show that its pastoralism is based on the Platonic notion of reconciling "discords and contradictions in the medium of the work of art." The Renaissance pastoral poet used classical mythology to transform the sensible world into "a beatific version of divine perfection." Sh, imbued with this broadly allegorical way of understanding myth, and heir to Erasmus's serioludic use of language in *The Praise of Folly*, developed a "rich and unique variation on the Platonic sense of humour" in *TGV*, *LLL*, and *MND*. Revision of item 0275.

0275   Cody, Richard John. "The Pastoral Element in Shakespeare's Early Comedies." Ph.D. dissertation. University of Minnesota, 1961. *DA*, 23 (1962–63), 2902–2903.

Develops a model of pastoralism through "a close analysis of Tasso's *Aminta* in the light of Platonic as well as pastoral tradition." Discusses, with reference to the *Aminta*, "the implicit pastoralism of plot and character in *TGV*" and "the complex pastoral unity of theme in *LLL*." Revised as item 0274.

0276   Coggin, Bruce Wayne. "Studies in Shakespeare's Treatment of Old Age." Ph.D. dissertation, University of Texas at Austin, 1982. *DAI*, 43 (1982–83), 806-A.

Surveys the variety of opinions, both philosophical and medical, about old age in "the Western tradition from the Greeks to Shakespeare's own time." Reviews the history of the portrayal of old age in the theater. Concludes that Sh takes a sympathetic but clear-eyed view of old age.

0277   Coghill, Nevill. *Shakespeare's Professional Skills.* Cambridge: Cambridge U. P., 1964. xvi + 224 pp.

Attempts to show how well Sh used all the resources of the playwright. Mentions nearly every play in the canon. In *Ant.*, for example, Sh took the juxtaposed scenes of Eros's loving suicide and Antony's bungled attempt (IV.xiv) and Cleopatra's heaving the dying Antony aloft into her monument (IV.xv) from Plutarch, but he made alterations to suggest Cleopatra's deviousness. In *JC*, Sh shows great skill in handling Brutus's orchard soliloquy (II.i), which begins in the middle. Chapter 4 argues that *Tro.* was originally performed at the Globe theater without its prologue and epilogue; that it was conceived as a tragedy about Troy, "in line with the belief that the English were descended from the Trojans, that London was New Troy, and that the Greeks were the enemy"; and that it was "revived for performance at one of the Inns of Court," on which occasion the prologue and epilogue were added to protect it from an unfavorable reception by "rowdy young cynics." Chapter 5, "Morte Hector: A Map of Honour," analyzes *Tro.* structurally to show how it dramatizes a conflict between idealism and materialism by a series of "designed contrasts, balances, confrontations, and echoes." Sh's version of the Troy story is "a tragic contemplation" of the destruction of "a great tradition typified by two high secular ideals": faith and honor in war and love.

0278   Cole, Howard C. *A Quest of Inquirie: Some Contexts of Tudor Literature.* Indianapolis: Bobbs-Merrill, 1973. xiii + 582 pp.

Attempts to correct anachronistic modern assumptions about literature in order to foster a better understanding of Tudor writers. An Elizabethan poet, for example, is greatly concerned about "whether he has properly imitated the best ancient models." Points out the deftness with which Sh uses Ovid in *TN*: The mythological references and the literary sentiments of love call attention to the comic artificiality of romance in the play. Shows that classical ideas, mediated through the Renaissance Italian commentators, influenced "Elizabethan theories of tragedy." The example of *Ham.*, however, reveals that Sh either ignored or consciously rejected much of the theorists' "misinformation about the *Poetics*." Cites passages from *Mac.* and *Luc.* to stress that Sh's references to classical stories like the rape of Lucrece and the fall of Troy would not have been regarded as abstractions by contemporaries; rather, Tudor readers would have taken these in stride as "native wonders," perhaps made familiar by paintings and tapestries. Makes frequent reference to other works in the canon.

0278a Cole, Susan Letzler. *The Absent One: Mourning, Ritual, Tragedy, and the Performance of Ambivalence*. University Park: Pennsylvania State U. P., 1985. 183 pp.

Seeks to understand tragedy in terms of mourning ritual, which, like tragedy, "is a performance of ambivalence on behalf of an absent presence." Describes common elements of mourning and tragedy in three cultures, including that of the ancient Greeks. Chapter 2 presents an analysis of Aeschylus's *The Persians*. Chapter 3, on *Ham.*, notes that in this play we can find all of the elements that link tragedy and mourning: (1) a liminal status or space or journey linked to the protagonist; (2) the uncanny, connected with the dead; (3) "the beloved deceased, usually a father or father–figure; (4) "a mourner–inheritor, usually a son or son–surrogate"; (5) "the antithetical style and antiphonal exchange characteristic of ritual lament"; and (6) ambivalence. Chapter 6, "Examples and Counterexamples," includes discussion of *Lr.*, *Mac.*, and *Oth*.

0279 Coleman, Althea Mae. "The Observer Character in Shakespeare's Four Great Tragedies." Ph.D. dissertation, Fordham University, 1990. *DAI*, 51 (1990–91), 3417-A.

Comments, near the end, on the way in which the observer character functions in two late Roman tragedies, *Ant.* and *Cor.*

0280 Colie, Rosalie. *Paradoxia Epidemica: The Renaissance Tradition of Paradox*. Princeton: Princeton U. P., 1966. xx + 553 pp.

Proposes to investigate the epidemic of paradoxy during the Renaissance, chiefly in literature but also in a couple of other fields. The opening chapter, "Problems of Paradoxes," cites numerous classical examples (from Plato, Zeno, Isocrates, Lucian, Cicero, and Ovid) to show that there was a well-established tradition of paradox. Notes that paradox always involves dialectic, challenging orthodoxy and criticizing absolute judgment. Discusses Erasmus's *Praise of Folly* to illustrate many aspects of paradox, especially the topos of "learned ignorance," which goes back to Plato's *Parmenides*. Points out that the paradox became so popular during the Renaissance in part because it was easier to imitate than the other classical forms that the humanists were rediscovering. Proposes to deal with rhetorical, psychological, ontological, and epistemological paradoxes in a variety of authors. Chapter 7, "'Nothing is but what is not': Solutions to the Problem of Nothing," provides the classical background to the paradoxes of nothing and examines the significance of those paradoxes in *Mac., Ham.*, and *Oth.* Chapter 12, "'I am that I am': Problems of Self-reference," treats epistemological paradox in *Son.*, noting that "Platonic and human realities" are kept "in a precarious realist–idealist balance." Chapter 15, "'Reason in Madness,'" shows how, in *Lr.*, Sh blended several standard paradoxical topics into a remarkable whole that draws the audience into "the experience of contradiction."

0281 Colie, Rosalie L. *Shakespeare's Living Art*. Princeton: Princeton U. P., 1974. ix + 370 pp.

Explores some of the ways in which Sh "used, misused, criticized, recreated, and sometimes revolutionized the received topics and devices, large and small, of his artful craft." Assesses, in other words, "the range of Shakespeare's response to the conventions and devices available to him." Uses the term *forms* as a general designation for the kinds of things covered in the study. Each chapter focuses on a particular topic "dealing with some formal aspect of a play or plays." Chapter 2,

"*Mel* and *Sal*: Some Problems in Sonnet-Theory," calls attention to the incorporation of the epigram, either in its "sweet" mode (derived from Catullus) or its "sharp" mode (derived from Martial) into the discussions of Renaissance theorists on the sonnets. Argues that out of the paired and yet opposed styles of "epigram and amatory epigram," Sh fashioned a "triangle of active figures" in *Son.*, responding as poet to the demands of both friend and mistress and through them "coming to terms with love and with himself as lover." Chapter 4, "*Antony and Cleopatra*: The Significance of Style," maintains that in this play Sh used the "ancient antithesis," revived in the Renaissance by the debate over "Attic" and "Asiatic" styles, to scrutinize "the personal, psychological, and cultural meanings implicit" in that polemic. Chapter 6, "Perspectives on Pastoral: Romance, Comic, and Tragic," notes that Theocritus initiated the pastoral mode and that Virgil "made overt the *paragone* of city and country life." Discusses *AYL* and *WT*. Chapter 8, "Forms and Their Meanings: 'Monumental Mock'ry,'" provides an account of Sh's daring and puzzling derogation of a great variety of forms in *Tro*. In particular, the play subverts the much-admired Homeric story, offers "a low version of the Chaucerian narrative" at a time when Chaucer's reputation was high, and satirizes romance and epic just as these forms had achieved prominence in the works of Ariosto, Tasso, and Spenser. Sh exhibits here what it is like to live purely by forms. Comments that "the proud *epideixis* on which ancient civilization's memory is based is turned back on itself by self-referential, self-questioning, self-denying paradox, identical in technique with the rhetoric of praise it here destroys."

0282   Collier, Lewis Arlen. "The Redemptive Element of the Natural Setting in Shakespeare's Tragedies and Late Romances." Ph.D. dissertation, University of Washington, 1966. *DA*, 27 (1966–67), 1781-A.

Examines Sh's tragedies that make use of a natural setting and the redemptive potential of such a setting in "his tragedies and late romances." The earlier plays approximate "the archetypal movement from the corrupt court or city to the simple, natural countryside." By the time of *Lr.*, however, Sh saw no calm in the anticourt setting, nor does his hero "profit from the redemptive ritual." In *Tim.*, a kind of bridge between the tragedies and the late plays, the natural setting has no power to effect any changes whatsoever in the hero. Having ceased to endow the natural setting with redemptive power, Sh, in the late romances, uses it as "a vehicle for other thematic exposition."

0282a Collins, Stephen L. *From Divine Cosmos to Sovereign State: An Intellectual History of Consciousness and the Idea of Order in Renaissance England.* New York: Oxford U. P., 1989. x + 235 pp.

Analyzes a range of works from the 16th c. and early 17th c. to reveal the changes that took place during this period in the conception of the way in which society is structured and the way in which the individual's relationship to society is defined. Notes that the works of Sh "accentuate the culturally contestatory process of meaning redefinition." Chapter 2 focuses on the operation of this process in a number of plays. Examples are *JC* (Brutus and other characters resist looking for identity in their private selves); *Tro.* (the characters are obsessed by questions of "meaning and valuation," which, they discover, cannot be settled without negotiation); *Cor.* (the protagonist, more than any other in Sh's works, seeks meaning and definition "in a constant, private self"); and *Tmp.* (Prospero, in the spirit of the Hermetic/Neoplatonic movement of the late 16th c., self-consciously attempts "to provide his isolated self with an ordered existence").

0282b Collura, Jane Haney. "Guarini's Theory of Tragicomedy and Shakespeare's Last Three Plays." Ph.D. dissertation, Catholic University of America, 1979. *DAI*, 40 (1979–80), 5431-A-5432-A

Chapter 1 describes the background of Renaissance tragicomedy, calling attention "to the contributions of classical, medieval, and humanist periods to the form." Chapter 5 discusses the use of Giambattista Guarini's theory of tragicomedy by Sh in *Cym.*, *WT*, and *Tmp.*

0283 Colman, E. A. M. *The Dramatic Use of Bawdy in Shakespeare.* London: Longman, 1974. xi + 230 pp.

Outlines, in the opening chapter, the kinds of indecency to be found in Sh and warns against "assuming ribald significance" anywhere in the canon without careful examination of context. Chapter 2, which deals with "Bawdy as Simple Farce," points out that, in *Err.*, Sh eliminates much of the salacious potential he found in his sources, Plautus's *Menaechmi* and *Amphitryon.* What little bawdy he adds is mostly assigned to the two Dromios. Chapter 4 demonstrates how bawdy references are used for purposes of characterization in certain early plays. In *Tit.*, "the obvious criminals—Aaron, Tamora, Demetrius, Chiron"—strike a bawdy tone in reference to Lavinia's rape, while "the various motif-references" to the story of Philomela–Tereus–Procne avoid it. Notes that Tamora's blending of her lust for Aaron with gleeful anticipation of Lavinia's rape is a sign of Gothic bestiality. Aaron's ribaldry reveals his complexity; he can move suddenly from "the scabrous to the defiant" and just as suddenly from the defiant to the scabrous. The opposing strains of purity and vulgarity in Lavinia seen early in the play help to explain the "darker qualities" that emerge when she participates in "the ritualistic murders of V.ii." The small share that Titus has in the play's bawdy helps to establish that his madness is "in part genuine." Chapter 5 includes an analysis of the Latin lesson in *Wiv.*, IV.i., with Hugh Evans's unintentionally bawdy mispronunciations—and Mistress Quickly's ignorant misapprehensions—of grammatical terms. Chapter 7 includes analyses of *Tro.*, in which bawdy acts "as a belittling agent" to define the limits of idealistic love, and *Tim.*, in which the hero's fear and madness are exhibited in his diatribes of sexual revulsion in act IV. Chapter 8 shows that, in *Ant.*, ribaldry serves to balance the "transcendentalism of the love-affair and the all-too-apparent sensuality," to contrast Cleopatra's easy blending of levity and passion with Antony's inability to reconcile his impulses toward amatory and political greatness, and to affirm, in the end, the potential in mankind for "the illimitable and the ungovernable." Explains, also, that the masque of Ceres conjured up by Prospero in *Tmp.*, by rejecting Cupid and Venus, commends an "ordered fertility," a control of licence that is crucial for civilized society. Chapter 9 considers *Ven.* and *Luc. Ven.* uses bawdy to characterize the limited sensuality of Venus as well as the narrowness of Adonis's virtue. In *Luc.*, the indecent plays a small part in the description of Tarquin's excitement as he approaches Lucrece's bedroom and a more important role in providing motivation for her suicide.

0284 Comito, Terry. "Exile and Return in the Greek Romances." *Arion*, N. S. 2 (1975), 58–80.

Attempts to define "not so much the theme or conscious intention of the ancient romances as the peculiar sensibility that made them available to Shakespeare—and might make them more available to us as well." Draws examples from the story of Apollonius of Tyre, Heliodorus's *Aethiopian Romance*, and Achilles Tatius's *Clitophon and Leucippe*—all available in English translation at Sh's time—to show how these late classical works reflect the alienation from the world characteristic of their age. In this climate, the romances gave voice to a "particular experience of space, one that translates questions of how man should live into questions of where he should dwell." Thus the narrative of the romances exhibits a rhythm of exile and return. At first, the lovers are forced into wandering, withdrawing from society in the face of threats to their virginity and death; then, they recognize their true home, throw off their disguises, and allow love to "assume its completed form in marriage." Sh can be seen to adopt this pattern in his late plays, especially *Per.* and *Cym.*, where "the emphasis is put on wandering in space."

0285 Conrad, Peter. *The Everyman History of English Literature.* London: Dent, 1985. x + 740 pp.

Chapter 10, "Shakespeare: Tragedy, Comedy, Tragicomedy," adopts as its thesis that Sh's plays violate the boundaries between comedy and tragedy, thus renouncing classical precept. The drama of Sh "derives from and constantly returns to history,"

General Works

which is "generically impartial." Each of two early works that appear to be classically inspired, *Err.* and *Tit.*, operates to confound its generic prototype. The plays about Roman history—*JC*, *Cor.*, and *Ant.*—subvert classical ethics and aesthetics, which emphasize impersonal rectitude and attempt to subdue "sentient content" with "formal propriety."

0286 Conway, Daniel J. "Erotic Arguments: Rhetoric and Sexuality in Seventeenth Century English Stage Adaptations of Plutarch." Ph.D. dissertation, University of Minnesota, 1989. *DAI*, 50 (1989–90), 1139-A.

Contrasts four 17th-c. plays with their sources in Plutarch's *Lives* to demonstrate that stage adaptation can produce very different arguments from those of narrative rhetoric. Chapter 3 discusses "the role of Latin rhetorical tradition in Tudor pedagogy." The last three chapters include analyses of *Ant.* and *Cor. Ant.* focuses on sexuality, arguing on both sides of the question "the fundamental heroism of its central characters." *Cor.* is a coterie play, written for an audience of courtiers tolerant of homoeroticism; it involves sexual and political arguments in a debate about natural and unnatural behavior.

0287 Cook, Carol Jane. "Imagining the Other: Reading Gender Difference in Shakespeare." Ph.D. dissertation, Cornell University, 1986. *DAI*, 47 (1986–87), 2592-A.

Undertakes a feminist reading of Sh that locates gender "in language, in metaphor, in the shapes of plots." Examines ways in which "the plays align gender difference with the difference between subjects and objects of discourse, positioning men as the readers and manipulators of language and women as signs or texts to be read." Includes discussions of *Tro.* and *Ant.*

0288 Cope, Jackson I. *The Theater and the Dream: From Metaphor to Form in Renaissance Drama.* Baltimore: Johns Hopkins U. P., 1973. xi + 331 pp.

Explores the influence of 15th-c. Platonism on Renaissance drama. Shows how Nicolas of Cusa set up the logic "by which the artist becomes God's metaphoric equivalent in the world." Cusa, though he never uses the *theatrum mundi* metaphor, moves toward "the image of the shifting union of man and God as spectator and author in a theater." Marsilio Ficino revived the ancient metaphor of life as a dream. Discusses a number of Sh's plays. *MND*, for example, "develops a double dream world," where the dreamer "is a somnambulist who awakens into a transcendent dream of truth" and where we as spectators are not allowed to stand apart from the dream. In *Tmp.*, Prospero knows that, as punishment for his sin, he must "become the philosopher–prince who knows life is a dream, that in dreams begin responsibility," and that he must teach these lessons to "the other sleepwalkers in the dark cave." He performs his task through a masque that reveals how "the drama of this *theatrum mundi* is a mere shadow–play, a dream."

0289 Cornelia, Marie. *The Function of the Masque in Jacobean Tragedy and Tragicomedy.* (Jacobean Dramatic Studies 77.) Institut für Englische Sprache und Literatur: U. Salzburg, 1978. iv + 162 pp.

Revision of item 0290.

0290 Cornelia, Sister M. Bonaventure. "The Function of the Masque in Jacobean Tragedy and Tragicomedy." Ph.D. dissertation, Fordham University, 1968. *DA*, 29 (1968–69), 2705-A.

Explores the ways in which the masque inserted into a play served as a useful dramatic device for Jacobean playwrights. Chapter 4 discusses the masque in *Tim.* as a "mirror of the action," with the Amazons who dance before Timon serving as an extended metaphor for the perversion of natural order that is such a pervasive theme of the play. The scene on board Pompey's galley (*Ant.*, II.vii) serves as an antimasque that exhibits the tension between "Egyptian revelry and Roman mastery" and anticipates Antony's loss of control and fall. Chapter 5 mentions that the masque of goddesses orchestrated by Prospero in *Tmp.* and the masque-like vision of Jupiter experienced by Posthumus in *Cym.* foretell "the final harmony" to be achieved in these plays. Revised as item 0289.

0291 Council, Norman. *When Honour's at the Stake: Ideas of Honour in Shakespeare's Plays.* New York: Barnes & Noble, 1973. 165 pp.

Chapter 1, "Ideas of Honour in Shakespeare's England," explains that the orthodox concept of honor for the Elizabethans was derived from Aristotle and was set forth most systematically in Robert Ashley's *Of Honour*. Honor, in this formulation, involved publicly recognizable reward, both tangible and intangible, for virtuous action. Further, the virtuous man was expected to abstain from seeking more honor than he was entitled to or from seeking honor for the wrong reasons. The most significant of the unorthodox ideas about honor, that it is "an innate moral capacity" unrelated to an externally defined ethical system, was Stoic in origin and can be seen in Guillaume DuVair's *The Moral Philosophie of the Stoicks*, translated into English in 1598. Sh made considerable dramatic use of the various meanings of honor. Subsequent chapters deal with *1H4, JC, Tro., Ham., Oth.*, and *Lr.* Revision of item 0292.

0292 Council, Norman Briggs. "When Honour's at the Stake." Ph.D. Dissertation, Stanford University, 1967. *DA*, 28 (1967–68), 1047-A.

Distinguishes the various meanings of *honor* during the English Renaissance and explains how different traditions, including Stoicism, contributed to these meanings. Sh's Lancastrian history plays and *JC* emphasize "the pernicious effect of commitment to honor for its own sake." Both *Tro.* and *Ham.* treat honor, the former satirically and the latter tragically, as a subjective code that must be followed for its own sake. In *Oth.*, the protagonist is blinded by his rigid adherence to honor, and Macbeth knowingly commits wicked actions to acquire worldly honor. King Lear suffers at first from the delusion that honor demands certain things of him as king and father; he is eventually stripped of this delusion and accepts "positive moral values." Revised as item 0291.

0292a Coursen, Herbert R. "Agreeing with Dr. Johnson." *ArielE*, 10, no. 2 (1979), 35–42.

Uses a comparison between Macbeth's perception about the rebuke of his own genius next to that of Banquo and the erosion of Antony's fortune next to that of Caesar (*Mac.*, III.i.54–57) to discover similarities between *Mac.* and *Ant.* Suggests that Sh was influenced by a re-reading of North's translation of Plutarch's *Lives* while he was writing *Mac.* Despite significant differences, the two plays are alike in many ways: They both provide a heroic context from which a great warrior experiences a tragic fall; the two heroes possess a clearer knowledge than any of Sh's other tragic protagonists "of what is happening to them as their tragedies progress"; both plays resolve, "by a realistic politics," the disorder created by warrior–heroes who "defy the premises of the worlds they inhabit."

0293 Craig, D. H. "Plural Pronouns in Roman Plays by Shakespeare and Jonson." *LLC*, 6 (1991), 180–86.

Uses statistical analysis of thirteen plays by Sh and thirteen by Ben Jonson in a variety of genres to test the two-part hypothesis that Roman plays, defined as "plays set in Rome with a tragic outcome," (1) may be distinguished "from plays in other genres by the two authors on the basis of data from plural pronouns as a set" and (2) typically "employ more individual plural pronouns in a given stretch of text" than other plays by the two authors. Analyzes *JC, Ant.*, and *Cor.* The analysis confirms the hypothesis. Recognizes a greater emphasis "on issues of group conflict and opinion in the Roman plays."

0294 Craig, Hardin. "Man Successful." *SQ*, 15, no. 2 (1964), 11–15. Reprint. *Shakespeare 400: Essays by American Scholars on the Anniversary of the Poet's Birth*. Ed. James G. McManaway. New York: Holt, Rinehart and Winston, 1964, pp. 11–15.

Investigates the process of "concrescence," or sense perception with something added to it called "reflection," in the mind of Sh. Associational and reflective thought is habitual with Sh. Although he "does not often explain or generalize," Sh does abstract "freely and clearly" when he is working in the area of ancient rhetoric, "where argument and persuasion" are the object: Examples are Cassius's attack on Brutus in *JC*, I.ii, and the argument Ulysses addresses to Achilles in *Tro.*, III.iii. Even though Sh seldom states "general principles in general terms," he does make us indirectly aware of broad abstractions. Two of these are of special importance: The stoical principle of "bearing the ills of life" with fortitude (Brutus, Hamlet) and the idea of the masterful man (Henry V and Prospero).

0295 Craig, Hardin. "Shakespeare and the All-Inclusive Law of Nature." *Studies in Honor of DeWitt T. Starnes*. Eds. Thomas P. Harrison, Archibald A. Hill, Ernest C. Mossner, and James Sledd. Austin: U. of Texas, 1967, pp. 77–87.

Argues that Sh understood "nature" as the "vast compulsive force bending and sorting all things according to a hierarchical pattern." Makes brief reference to the classical origins of this doctrine before examining specific instances of it in Sh's plays.

0296 Craig, Hardin. "Shakespeare and the Trivium." *Shakespeare 1564–1964: A Collection of Modern Essays by Various Hands*. Ed. Edward A. Bloom. Providence, Rhode Island: Brown U. P., 1964, pp. 167–76.

Surveys the classical background of grammar school education in Sh's England. Focuses on the trivium, consisting of grammar, rhetoric, and logic, and incorporating Platonic principles that were first organized into a curriculum in Hellenistic times and then passed on to the Middle Ages through the *De Nuptiis Philologiae et Mercurii* of Martianus Capella. The grammar school curriculum was revived in 16th-c. England, and Sh would have had a thorough introduction to grammar through the study of Latin literature. Grammar is the basis for the generalizing activity of the higher brain, or "concrescence," and Sh's use of this power can be illustrated in Arthur's plea to Hubert from *Jn.* (IV.i).

0297 Cranfill, Thomas. "Shakespeare's Old Heroes." *TSLL*, 15 (1973–74), 215–30.

Touches on several figures with classical connections in a survey of older warriors in the canon. In some instances, Sh sets an older and a younger soldier together in order to contrast their qualities: When Brutus and Cassius quarrel in *JC* over strategy, Cassius cites his seniority; in *Cor.*, with no warrant from his source, Sh pairs Coriolanus with the elderly Cominius. Most of Sh's older warriors from the classical world exhibit a fierce spirit, even in the face of physical weakness: Titus Andronicus is certainly capable of being roused to violent action, Nestor (in *Tro.*) shows sparks of valor in his willingness to fight younger men, and Titus Lartius (in *Cor.*) says he will lean on one of his crutches and fight with the other. The Player's speech in *Ham.* about Priam's feeble attempts to defend himself is almost a parody of Sh's usual treatment of classical older warriors.

0298 Cruttwell, Patrick. "Shakespeare and the Baroque." *SJ*, 97 (1961), 100–108.

Admits that Sh evidences certain Baroque features but argues that he was primarily a poet who took "truth to Nature" as his central literary doctrine. That is, he followed the fundamental tenet of imitation as Aristotle had defined it. Baroque influence on Sh was limited by England's isolation, the English unease with highly emotional art, and the popular nature of Sh's drama.

0299 Curtis, M. H. "Education and Apprenticeship." *ShS*, 17 (1964), 53–72.

Calls attention to the Tudor humanists' belief that classical learning, once implanted in England, would "bring about the rise of a well-constituted commonwealth equal to those of the Greeks and Romans." The grammar schools that were founded during the 16th c. followed principles formulated by national authorities and thus adopted essentially the same curriculum. In brief, the purpose of such schools was "to teach a mastery of Latin grammar and to introduce a boy to the riches of learning and wisdom contained in Latin literature." In the 16th c., the medieval university curriculum was reformed in response to humanist criticism. Rhetoric was transferred "from the advanced part of the arts course to preparation for the B.A.," and work in grammar and rhetoric was expanded "to include readings from the *literae humaniores*," giving "the undergraduate curriculum more content," ending its "subservience to metaphysics and theology," and making it "into a self-justifying enterprise." In the universities, classical authors were used as the basis for studying grammar (Virgil, Horace, and Cicero), rhetoric (Aristotle and Cicero), logic (Aristotle), and arithmetic (Boethius).

0299a Cutts, John P. *Rich and Strange: A Study of Shakespeare's Last Plays.* Washington State U. P., 1968. 106 pp.

Includes, in discussion of *Per., Cym., WT,* and *Tmp.*, analyses of the classically inspired theophany scenes, noting that each theophany deserves careful study of its own application in its particular play. The chapter on *Cym.* comments on the Roman-British split in Cymbeline's character and the glimpse into the inner recesses of Imogen's mind offered by the mythological scenes found on the furnishings in her chamber.

0300 Daly, Peter. *Literature in the Light of the Emblem: Structural Parallels Between the Emblem and Literature in the Sixteenth and Seventeenth Centuries.* Toronto: U. of Toronto P., 1979. xiv + 245 pp.

Chapter 1 announces the book's concern with "the verbal art of literature which reveals those qualities associated with emblem books" and discusses some of the problems involved in defining the emblem. Describes "the first and most influential of all emblem books, Alciatus's *Emblematum liber.*" Includes, in a section on "Forerunners of the Emblem," the Greek epigram (Alciatus's foremost model), Renaissance commonplace books like Erasmus's *Adagia*, hieroglyphics (discovered by Renaissance humanists in a manuscript supposed to be written by an Egyptian priest named Horapollo and translated into Greek in the 4th or 5th c. A.D.), and classical mythology. Chapter 2, "The Word-Emblem," discusses the emblematic qualities of the scene in *WT* (III.iii) in which Antigonus is killed by a bear. Chapter 4, "Emblematic Drama," briefly considers *Wiv., R2, 1H4, 2H4, Lr., Tit.,* and *1H6.*

0301 D'Amico, Jack. "The Politics of Madness: Junius Brutus in Machiavelli and Shakespeare." *MQ*, 30 (1989), 405–22.

Examines Livy's *History* and Machiavelli's *Discourses*, both of which treat Junius Brutus's pretended madness, as background for Sh's portrayals of Brutus himself in *Luc.*; of Prince Hal in *1H4, 2 H4,* and *H5;* and of Hamlet. In composing *Luc.*, Sh could very well have picked up the image of Junius Brutus as court jester from Livy. Machiavelli approves the "feigned stupidity" of Brutus as exemplary for anyone who would reform the state but has no military resources. He also praises Brutus for staying near, even appearing to befriend, the prince he wishes to overthrow and for choosing the right moment to discard his foolishness and act. Prince Hal, with some modification, follows this course (in *H5*, II.iv.36–38, he is even compared to Junius Brutus by the Constable of France). Hamlet, who has some things in common with Brutus, never finds the right moment to act, nor does he seem ultimately to seek a political role.

0302 Danson, Lawrence. *Tragic Alphabet: Shakespeare's Drama of Language.* New Haven and London: Yale U. P., 1974. xi + 200 pp.

Contends that in his tragedies Sh involves us in observing men in the process of hammering out a language that answers "their expressive needs." There is a typical pattern of action: At first, a traditional "language" (of words and of gestures) disintegrates, and then a new, more satisfactory language is formulated. Chapter 1 (a revision of item 2725) acts as an introduction and explains how in *Tit.* Sh seeks a way to ritualize death and thus establish a sense of wonder. Chapter 3, on *JC*, argues that *sacrifice* is the gesture that leads to the play's new language: A series of false sacrifices marks the way to Brutus's acceptance of his fate at Philippi. Chapter 4 claims that language and gesture in *Tro.* are not only flawed at the beginning but become increasingly inadequate and are never repaired. The play parodies tragic structure. Chapter 7 (a revision of item 1629) finds that the figure of metonymy is especially important in producing the tragic effect of *Cor.* The book is a revision of item 0303.

0303 Danson, Lawrence Neil. "The Tragic Alphabet: Language, Ritual, and Action in Shakespeare's Tragedies." Ph.D. dissertation, Yale University, 1969. *DAI*, 30 (1969–70), 3427-A.

Identifies in Shakespearean tragedy a process by which language initially inadequate for tragic expression is reformed by play's end to convey an appropriate sense of wonder. The new language is "the completed play itself." Parts revised as items 2725 and 1629; the whole as item 0302.

0304 Dasgupta, Arun K. "The Interplay of Fortune and Freedom: A Shakespearian Theme." *Journal of the Department of English, Calcutta University*, 18 (1982), 1–32.

Discusses *Tit.*, *Tim.*, and *Lr.* to reveal some common ideas in these three plays and to show something about Sh's development as a dramatist. Notes that all the plays are ultimately concerned with "the problem of human freedom." Focuses on the theme of Fortune and its instability and on the images that are used in the plays to embody this theme.

0305 Datta, Amaresh. *Shakespeare's Tragic Vision and Art.* (Masters of English Literature Series 14.) Allahabad: Kitab Mahal, 1963. 192 pp.

Discusses *JC* as a prelude to Sh's four great tragedies. In this work, we have the first tragedy "that rises from a particular story to a universal theme and shows a mingling of political and cosmic issues." Brutus gives us "the first clear impression of Shakespeare's typical tragic hero with his divided mind," isolation, sense of chaos, sensitivity to human values, and "brooding on them." However, Brutus is not fully developed as a tragic figure. Notes that Sh "dissipates the bitterness" of his tragic mood through another Roman play, *Ant.*, which does not involve its persons in any great moral issues or any "conflict of ideas and ideals." Sh transforms conventions to make tragedy from "the human hope for the eternity of love." Regards the Antony of this play as continuous with the one in *JC*; Sh has disregarded certain elements of Plutarch's portrait to make his hero "less Roman and more universal." In act V, Cleopatra is converted from "an enchantress to a tragic heroine." *Cor.* is Sh's last tragedy, and it shows the playwright returning to Plutarch and foregrounding the political. Like *Ant.*, *Cor.* raises no issues of "universal importance." There is much bitterness, as in some of the earlier tragedies, but here it is concentrated in the outpourings of Coriolanus's angry mind. Sh kept close to "the Roman spirit" in *Cor.*, "partly because he wanted detachment from moral or spiritual problems and partly because, after his dramatic experiment on an unusually vast canvas in *Antony and Cleopatra*, he wanted to write a play that would suit the stage completely and meet all its conventional requirements." Suggests that Sh's digression from Plutarch in depicting the Roman crowd so unfavorably was in part due to his disenchantment with his audience.

0306 Datta, Pradip Kumar. "The Role of the Good Counselor in Selected Shakespearean Tragedies." Ph.D. dissertation, Howard U., 1990. *DAI*, 51 (1990–91), 3751-A.

Examines the "mediating role" of the good counselor in the audience's response to certain of Sh's great tragic heroes. The third chapter shows that, in *Ant.*, Enobarbus guides the audience by acting as counselor to both Antony and Cleopatra, and chapter 4 argues that, in *Cor.*, Menenius, combining pragmatism and sophistry, creates empathy for "an aggressive hero."

0307 Davies, Stevie. *The Idea of Woman in Renaissance Literature: The Feminine Reclaimed*. Brighton: Harvester P., 1986. xii + 273 pp. Reprinted as *The Feminine Reclaimed: The Idea of Woman in Spenser, Shakespeare and Milton*. Lexington: U. P. of Kentucky, 1986.

The introduction proposes to investigate the substantial influence of the idea of the feminine—reclaimed through "Platonism, humanism, alchemy, cabbala, Orphism and Hermeticism"—on Renaissance literature. The new philosophy of humanists like Pico della Mirandola and Marsilio Ficino emphasized "emanation, the coincidence of opposites, and the existence of the whole in the part and the part in the whole"— concepts readily compatible with the female principle. The mystic philosophies revived during the Renaissance were concerned to establish that "All is One" through "dynamic process" and thus used images of androgyny like the "double god" Isis and Osiris. Renaissance mythographers delighted in collecting images of pagan deities, especially goddesses, and mingling them in various ways with Christian beliefs. The Eleusinian mysteries—involving the goddess Ceres' loss of her daughter Proserpina, "her grief and reclamation"—was a natural female revision of the Christian story of sacrifice and redemption.

Chapter 3, on Sh, contends that, as the father of different-sex twins, the playwright was especially receptive to the new philosophy. *MND* and *TN* provide early versions of Sh's "tragi-comic vision of the antagonistic mother- and father-worlds." Both plays derive from "the Greek romances of the early Christian era," which moved Sh to explore a feminine world. In *TN*, we see the hermaphroditic experiment with Viola and Sebastian and the Hermes-like skill with which Viola "impersonates" Cesario as she mediates between the masculine court of Orsino and Olivia's female domain. In *MND*, there is a hint of the Ceres and Proserpina myth, but here Sh is inspired more by the Isis of Apuleius's *The Golden Ass*, who encourages him to imagine "a benign, teasing, all-inclusive mother goddess." The four last tragicomedies, with their sea-world and their exploration of the feminine, are "profoundly Greek." In *Per.*, the protagonist participates in a sequence of Eleusinian initiations. The Proserpina theme becomes more explicit as the play progresses; there is an Orphic resurrection of Thaisa; the male heroic code is renounced; and Pericles is drawn to the universe of compassion, that is, he comes to participate in the nature of woman. In *WT*, Hermione's name is one associated with Demeter, and the structure of the last part is Eleusinian. Sh was familiar with Hermetic tradition: Paulina is a female magus, and she and her art are connected with the female mythology of Eleusis. She mediates between male and female. In the tragicomedies, grace is Christian, but "it assimilates rather than denies the ancient Hellenic deities." Hecate's "dark presence" can be found in these plays, but she is not as sinister as she had become in more recent times; Sh's "new classicism reaches back to the purer image" which in Greece saw her "as an integral part of the cosmic adjustment of upper, middle and nether worlds."

0308 Davison, Mary Carol. "The Metamorphosis of Odysseus: A Study of Romance Iconography from the *Odyssey* to *The Tempest*." Ph.D. dissertation, Stanford University, 1971. *DAI*, 32 (1971–72), 1467-A.

Traces the romance form from Homeric epic through the *Aeneid* and the Greek and Latin prose romances to the Renaissance. Claims that romance became a separate narrative form "replacing the ancient theatre just as it declined as popular entertainment." Explains that the romance writers of the early Christian era developed certain iconographic symbols from the symbols of classical art, thus creating an "epiphanic" technique. Illustrates the romance genre's continuous appeal by following the development of the Apollonius of Tyre legend from its beginnings in the 2nd c. A.D. to its dramatization in *Per.* Cites *Tim.* as evidence that Sh was familiar with the debate over the relative merits of poetry and painting and then uses *Tmp.* to argue that the last plays were composed as "speaking pictures." Romance was thus allowed to "fulfill its inherently dramatic character."

0309 Davison, Peter. "Stabbed with Laughter: Resolution by Punishment in Two Comedies of Shakespeare." *Trivium*, 17 (1982), 1–20.

Suggests that Sh understood the nature of Aristophanic Old Comedy and that he employed its "didacticism and punishment, mockery and imposture, and the parting of those who might at the end of a New Comedy be joined in marriage" in resolving *LLL* and *MM*.

0310 Dawson, Anthony B. *Indirections: Shakespeare and the Art of Illusion.* Toronto: U. of Toronto P., 1978. xv + 194 pp.

Studies several of Sh's plays "from the point of view of their reflexivity, that is, their use of self-conscious techniques which radically affect the relation of the audience to the play." Focuses, then, on "the varied uses of illusion, deceit, disguise, and manipulation." Chapter 4 includes a discussion of *Tro.*, which employs a number of comic processes ("the multiple watching, the spying, tricks, and manipulations") that elsewhere in Sh lead to broader understanding but here result in fragmentation of the hero's consciousness and bewilderment for the audience. Chapter 7 includes a consideration of *Ant.*, emphasizing the characters' awareness that they are taking part in "a significant action," that they are performing for an audience "within the play and outside it as well." Analyzes the scenes in which Antony attempts suicide (IV.xiv) and Cleopatra dies (V.ii) to show that the theatrical self-awareness of the protagonists lifts the action out of a "purely tragic mode" and provides them and us with a sense of their mythic stature.

0310a Deal, Kenneth Lee. "Sybil's Voice: Speech, Action, and the Renaissance Idea of Conversation." Ph.D. dissertation, University of Iowa, 1980. *DAI*, 40 (1979–80), 4011-A-4012-A.

Suggests that 16th-c. men viewed the relationship between language and its referents in a variety of ways. Provides a survey of "the development of the juxtaposition of word (*logos*) and work (*ergon*) from the Homeric opposition of counsel and battle through the Athenian conjunction of eloquence and conduct." Illustrates "the Roman and medieval modifications of both these fundamental dichotomies." Examines "the Renaissance theory of civil conversation" and shows how it assimilates and qualifies "the traditonal approach to speech and action." Reads Sh's second tetralogy of English history plays as "a dramatization of the deterioration and redemption of political language."

0311 Dean, John. "Constant Wanderings and Longed-for Returns: Odyssean Themes in Shakespearean Romance." *Mosaic*, 12, no. 1 (1978–79), 47–60.

Investigates a number of similarities between Sh's four romances and the *Odyssey*. In both Sh and Homer, the protagonists are suffering wanderers: Both include in their tales an abundance of marvel, danger, and successful adventuring; and both employ a plot about an errant homeward journey with shipwreck and loss, a mixture of sorrows and blessings, and a conclusion involving familial and political reunion. All of these similarities center on the male–female relationships in both authors. As in the *Odyssey*, the protagonists of Sh's romances encounter two kinds of women: those who are beautiful and dangerous and those who are pure and virtuous. *Per.* and *Cym.* feature destructive women who at first seem to have the upper hand over the male heroes; in *WT* and *Tmp.*, the action is dominated by virtuous women from the beginning, and the dark, intemperate women exist in men's misimaginings or in the distant past. *Tmp.* is Sh's richest development of the experiences at "the core of Hellenistic romances and of all Classical Mediterrean romance." Both the *Odyssey* and *Tmp.* end with tensions unresolved; even though reunion of a sort has been achieved, neither Odysseus nor Prospero can find repose. The restlessness that has characterized the world as they have experienced it will continue. Revised as chapter 2 of item 0311a.

0311a Dean, John. *Restless Wanderers: Shakespeare and the Pattern of Romance.* Salzburg Studies in English Literature.) Salzburg: Institut für Anglistik und Amerikanistik, U. Salzburg, 1979. vii + 360 pp.

Chapter 1, "Classical Romance," considers the *Odyssey* as a romance and then discusses the influence of the Hellenistic romances (like the *Aethiopica* of Heliodorus) on the Elizabethan conception of the romance, noting that the earlier works invite dramatic adaptation. Chapter 2, "Odyssean Themes in Shakespearean Romance," is a revision of item 0311. Chapter 3 describes medieval and Renaissance romance, chapter 4 is entitled "The Nature of Romance," and chapter 5 analyzes some Pre-Shakespearean dramas based on romance. Chapter 6 examines Sh's four romances—*Per.*, *Cym.*, *WT*, and *Tmp.*—and explains how the playwright has adapted his sources in each case. Chapter 7 investigates Sh's use of the romance structure, and chapter 8 addresses the theme of love in Sh's romances.

0312 Dean, John. "Shakespeare's Romances and Herodotus's *Histories*." (Jacobean Drama Studies 74.) Salzburg: Institut für Englische Sprache und Literatur, 1977, pp. 95–100.

Argues that Sh's four last romances are likely to have been influenced by Herodotus's *Histories*, translated into English in 1584. In both the last romances and the *Histories*, we encounter "a vast world of impersonal forces and individual strivings," a threat that glory will perish in younger generations, an inclusion of love stories as a serious political theme, a rambling narrative that nevertheless always leads back to the author's major concern, a tightening of the narrative as it draws toward a conclusion, a reversal near the conclusion that is anticipated by the audience but unexpected by the characters involved, a keen interest in wondrous happenings, and a "disharmonious vision of life which is nevertheless ordered within artistic unity."

0313 Dean, Paul. "Shakespeare's True Tragedies." *CrSurv*, 3 (1991), 128–33.

Asserts that "Sh's tragedies are not true but they are explorations of what it means to be true." Includes brief discussions of *Ant.*, which dwells on "the power of images to enchant and enslave," and *JC*, which questions the knowability of oneself and others and yet hints at a kind of universal justice—"inscrutable, ironical, retributive."

0314 Dean, Paul. "Tudor Humanism and the Roman Past: A Background to Shakespeare." *RenQ*, 41 (1988), 84–111.

Traces English attitudes toward Roman history from the symbolic mentality of late medieval commentators to the recognition of unpredictability that enabled humanists like Erasmus and More to conceive of the tragic potential of events. Notes how, in Sh's immediate literary background (including the *Mirror for Magistrates* and various plays on Roman topics), British and Roman history were seen in terms of each other. This cross-fertilization reflects the new humanistic awareness that the dark uncertainties of Roman history were not sealed off from the present age by the new dispensation of Christianity but rather could be seen to mirror the confusion surrounding recent events in England. In Sh's first tetralogy about English history, the civil war prompts numerous Roman references; in *R3*, he owes many classical allusions to More's *Richard III*. Later, in moving from *H5* to *JC*, Sh can be observed, after rereading North's Plutarch, to reconsider the perils of civil war in a setting whose distance permitted him some objectivity.

0315   Denney, Constance Dorothy Baldwin. "The Dynamics of Shakespeare's Rhetoric: A Study of Judicial Debate in Four Plays." Ph.D. dissertation, Stanford University, 1973. *DAI,* 33 (1972–73), 6867-A-6868-A.

Argues that Sh used the full resources of the rhetorical tradition in his judicial scenes, most of which are based on the classical judicial oration. Analyzes key scenes and sequences of scenes in *1H4, MM, Oth.,* and *Lr.*

0316   De Rachewiltz, Siegfried Walter. "De Sirenibus: An Inquiry into Sirens from Homer to Shakespeare." Ph.D. dissertation, Harvard University, 1983. *DAI,* 44 (1983–84), 1782-A.

Provides an historical survey of "the motif of the Sirens," beginning with the *Odyssey.* Explains "the various literary and iconographic metamorphoses" undergone by the Sirens in "post–Homeric classical tradition," as well as in numerous Christian interpretations. Chapter 9 analyzes Sh's "image of the Siren/mermaid."

0317   Der, Don W. "Imitation and Imagery in Shakespeare: Factors of Originality in *Romeo and Juliet, As You Like It,* and *Twelfth Night.*" Ph.D. dissertation, University of Florida, 1968. *DAI,* 30 (1969–70), 1978-A.

Points to evidence that during Sh's lifetime imitation was widely recognized "as a method of composition." Analyzes the grammar school curriculum to establish Sh's knowledge of imitative composition. Surveys the views of several Greek and Roman writers on imitation and the importance of originality. Examines three of Sh's plays known "to be based on single contemporary English sources" to consider the originality of their imagery in an imitative context.

0318   Desai, S. K. "The Child in Shakespeare's Plays." *Journal of the Karnatak University,* 8 (1964), 113–23.

Discusses the dramatic significance of children in several of Sh's plays. In *Cor.,* young Marcius illuminates the nature of his father, who never escapes boyhood, and is present in the scene (V.iii) in which Coriolanus is persuaded to spare Rome. In *Tit.,* young Lucius (Titus's grandson) is used to humanize the play in III.ii and V.iii. Also, Aaron's son by Tamora has a softening effect on his father. In *JC,* the page boy Lucius is used to reveal Brutus's tender nature and to juxtapose "simple innocence" and "philosophic innocence," "calmness and restlessness," and "simple duty" and "complex duty."

0319   Desmet, Christy. "Rhetorical Selves: Shakespeare's Problem Characters and Their Critics." Ph.D. dissertation, University of California, Los Angeles, 1984. *DAI,* 48 (1987–88), 2342-A.

Uses Aristotle's ideas about the evolution of character through plot to suggest that dramatic characters do not have "essential selves"; rather, they develop from the roles they perform in the action. Generates an epideictic "rhetoric of character" from some of Sh's problematic works, including *Cym.* and *Ven.* Focuses on metaphor and hyperbole as the keys to this rhetoric.

0319a   Dessen, Alan C. "Interpreting Stage Directions: Elizabethan Clues and Modern Detectives." *The Elizabethan Theatre IX.* Papers Given at the Ninth International Conference on Elizabethan Theatre Held at the University of Waterloo in July 1981. Ed. G. R. Hibbard. Port Credit, Ontario: P. D. Meany, [1986], pp. 77–99.

Maintains that the significance of stage directions in the plays of Sh and his contemporaries can be more fully recovered if each stage direction is grouped with others like it. Discusses, for example, the appearance of female characters with dishevelled hair to indicate rape or madness (Cassandra in *Tro.,* II.ii; Lavinia in *Tit.,* II.iv) and the use of the nightgown to indicate sleeplessness and a troubled spirit (Caesar and Brutus in *JC,* II.i, II.ii, and IV.iii).

0319b Dessen, Alan C. *Shakespeare and the Late Moral Plays.* Lincoln: U. of Nebraska 1986. ix + 196 pp.

Chapter 7 gives attention to Sh's appropriation of the moral drama's technique of breaking entities into their component parts to exhibit on stage "the workings of the mind." The scene on board Pompey's galley (*Ant.*, II.vii) juxtaposes two figures (Lepidus and Pompey) engaged in emblematic activities that comment proleptically on Antony's fate. In *Tro.*, the Trojan council scene (II.ii) displays the mind of Troy at work, especially as it permits Reason to be undermined by "Will, Appetite, or the call to Honor."

0320 Dillon, Janette. *Shakespeare and the Solitary Man.* Totowa, New Jersey: Rowman and Littlefield, 1981. xvi + 183 pp.

Points out in the introduction that Sh wrote just in the middle of the period when the attitude toward solitude was changing from medieval condemnation to 17th-c. acceptance. In the plays, sympathy for the solitary reaches its height in *Ham.* and thereafter declines. The first chapter includes a survey of classical sources that influenced 16th–and 17th-c. England. Among these are Plato, Aristotle, and Cicero (all of whom insisted that the individual's first responsibility is to the state); Seneca; Plutarch; Virgil; and Horace. Aristotle and Cicero shared an abhorrence of solitude, and the former declared that a man who has neither need nor capacity to live in society "must be either a beast or a god." Seneca, through whom Stoic thought reached England, anticipated Elizabethan writers by separating duty to the state from the pleasure of solitude. The self-sufficiency of his heroes had a great influence on English tragedy. Mentions "the moral superiority of the retired life" as it is seen in Virgil and Horace. Classical pastoral and satire also influenced Renaissance attitudes about "the withdrawal from society." Finally, Greek and Roman epic, history, and drama—in their presentation of the hero as an uncommon man who stands apart—contributed to the Elizabethan notion of solitariness. In portraying Coriolanus, Sh began with a figure already guilty, in the eyes of Plutarch, of "solitariness." The play intensifies this singularity, showing Coriolanus as alone when Plutarch has him in company. His speeches are full of the word "alone" and the phrase "I am." In Aristotle's terms, he "aspires to be a god" but in effect becomes a beast. Timon enacts Aristotle's dictum literally, as he physically removes himself from the city and digs for roots. Unlike Coriolanus, Timon chooses solitude after an initial period of association, but he resembles the Roman hero in his self-destruction through isolation. Discusses, in addition to *Cor.* and *Tim., R3, R2, Son., AYL, Ham., Lr.,* and *Mac.* Part is a revision of item 0321.

0321 Dillon, Janette. "'Solitariness': Shakespeare and Plutarch." *JEGP,* 78 (1979), 325–44.

Considers three of Sh's tragic figures— Antony, Coriolanus, and Timon—as examples of "solitariness." Remarks on Sh's interest in such characters throughout his career and finds it significant that he chose three of them from Plutarch's *Lives* to treat as tragic heroes. Plutarch criticizes each of the three for his solitariness, following the classical philosophers, who generally condemn isolation from society. In the early 16th c., there was widespread agreement with the ancients, but by Sh's time the solitary life had gained advocates. There was, then, some disagreement about the matter, and Sh reflects this ambiguity in *Ant., Cor.,* and *Tim.* Plutarch stresses Antony's physical isolation, while Sh dramatizes his hero's spiritual loneliness: Antony is nearly always onstage with others, but he is never fully engaged with them. He is like an actor who plays many roles, never able to be himself and finally losing his identity. Sh followed Plutarch in making solitariness the defining quality of Coriolanus's nature, but he heightened Plutarch's emphasis, making his hero enter Corioli alone, for example, rather than with a handful of others. For Plutarch, as for Sh's contemporaries, Timon was "an archetype of the misanthropic solitary." Sh endowed Timon's solitude with a mythic quality, and Timon's self-conscious "progress towards isolation" makes him similar to Antony and Coriolanus. In depicting the unnatural qualities of all three characters, it is likely that Sh had in mind Aristotle's dictum that a solitary man is either a beast or a god. Revised as part of item 0320.

General Works

0322 Doebler, John. *Shakespeare's Speaking Pictures: Studies in Iconic Imagery*. Albuquerque: U. of New Mexico P., 1974. xiv + 236 pp.

Interprets six plays in the light of "an historical awareness of the conventions of Renaissance iconography, especially as those conventions affect our understanding of stage event." Chapter 1, "*As You Like It*: Herculean Virtue," is a revision of item 1538. Other chapters include discussion of images derived from classical sources, for example the goddess Fortune and the myth of Phaeton (in a chapter on *R2*).

0322a Doebler, John. "When Troy Fell: Shakespeare's Iconography of Sorrow and Survival." *CompD*, 19 (1985–86), 321–31.

Surveys the emblem books of the Renaissance as well as other works of Renaissance art to establish the commonplace treatment of the Aeneas/Anchises episode, originally described in book 2 of the *Aeneid*, as a wholly admirable example of filial loyalty. Other literary sources for this reading of the incident are Seneca's *De Officiis* and Ovid's *Fasti*. Sh's use of the image of the youthful Aeneas carrying his aged sire can be seen in Young Clifford's conveyance of his father's body (*2H6*, V.ii), in Cassius's scornful account of his rescue of Caesar from the Tiber (*JC*, I.ii), in Orlando's entrance with Adam on his back (*AYL*, II.vii), and perhaps in Edgar's care for the blinded Gloucester (*Lr.*, IV). Notes a negative tradition about Aeneas, based on his betrayal of Dido in book 4 of the *Aeneid*, that is alluded to in *MND* and *Cym*.

0323 Dollarhide, Louis E. "The Logic of Villainy: Shakespeare's Use of the Fallacies." *UMSE*, 10 (1969), 49–57.

Refers to the logical fallacies set down by Aristotle and repeated by logicians like Thomas Wilson (*The Rule of Reason*, 1552) as a hallmark of a group of Sh's villains: Richard III, Iago, Edmund, and Iachimo. There are 2 kinds of fallacies, *in re* (material) and *in dictione* (in the word). Richard III, for example, employs the material fallacy of "trying to prove a matter by a cause which is not able to prove it" when he argues that because he cannot prove a lover, he must prove a villain; he uses a fallacy of the word when he tells Clarence "that he will deliver him from prison or else 'lie' for him."

0324 Dollimore, Jonathan. *Radical Tragedy: Religion, Ideology and Power in the Drama of Shakespeare and His Contemporaries*. Chicago: U. of Chicago P., 1983. viii + 312 pp.

Argues that Jacobean tragedy provides a radical analysis of the crisis in early 17th-c. society. In reflecting this crisis, the drama undermines religious orthodoxy as well as questioning ideology, demystifying "political and power relations," and decentering the conception of "man." Chapter 2, on *Tro.*, is a revision of item 2853. Chapters 13 and 14, on *Ant.* and *Cor.*, respectively, maintain that the heroic *virtus* of Antony and Coriolanus, presented from one perspective as innate and the result of autonomous superiority, is revealed in each case to be "an ideological effect of powers antecedent to and independent" of the characters.

0325 Donaldson, E. Talbot. *The Swan at the Well: Shakespeare Reading Chaucer*. New Haven: Yale U. P., 1985. x + 165 pp.

Chapter 1 comments, in discussing the influence of Chaucer's story of Pyramus and Thisbe from *The Legend of Good Women* on *MND*, that Chaucer left the story "more open to ridicule than Ovid had." See item 2311. Chapter 2 examines the relationships between Chaucer's *The Knight's Tale* and *The Merchant's Tale* and *MND*. Points out in particular that the two poets share the theme of "the irresponsibility of romantic love." Notes that Sh's Theseus draws characteristics from both the Theseus of *The Knight's Tale* and Chaucer's Knight, who narrates the tale. Chapter 3 finds that "the heavy strain of pessimism underlying *The Knight's Tale*" appealed to Sh as he neared the end of his career and had significant influence on *TNK*. Sh attributes to people the horrors that in Chaucer are "mostly charged to the gods above." Chapter 4, in comparing Chaucer's Criseyde to Sh's Cressida, argues that it was because the former was "the prototypical unfaithful woman" that Sh chose to recreate her. That is, for Sh she conveniently serves to symbolize the inconsistency that is the hallmark of every character in the play who attempts to be idealistic. Chaucer's heroine is not as dissimilar to Sh's as has been claimed; she has evoked a more sympathetic reaction because of the narrator's fondness for her. Cressida has no such advocate. Chapter 5 further analyzes the love affair of Troilus and Cressida in light of their Chaucerian predecessors. Chapter 6 includes an investigation of the relationship between "the two greatest love *poems* in English," *Troilus and Criseyde* and *Rom.*, noting that the author of Sh's source, Arthur Brooke, knew Chaucer's poem. Contends that both works have the same "moral": "love at its most passionate and its most fulfilling does not last in the real world."

0326   Donawerth, Jane. *Shakespeare and the Sixteenth-Century Study of Language.* Urbana: U. of Illinois P., 1984. xi + 279 pp.

Includes discussion of classical ideas about language that influenced the Elizabethans and Sh. For example, Quintilian's notion that language is acquired under the sway of social custom may be reflected in the attitude of Prospero toward Caliban. Cicero's ideas about language as a civilizing force are also important, as are his pronouncements about the physical part of language (delivery), which can be seen underlying scenes in *JC, Ant., Cor.,* and *Tro*. Refers to most works in the canon; devotes a chapter each to *LLL, Jn, MV, AWW,* and *Ham*.

0327   Donoghue, Denis. *The Sovereign Ghost: Studies in Imagination.* Berkeley: U. of California P., 1977. x + 229 pp.

Chapter 1 discusses some lines from *Ven.* in a consideration of the imagination. Chapter 7, "Writing Against Time," in arguing that *H8* provides a reconciliation of history and romance, a movement "toward the grand rhythm of events," observes that Sh's first use of this kind of structure is found in *Tim.*, especially its last scene, where "expansive forces" are at work.

0328   Draper, John W. "Humoral Therapy in Shakespeare's Plays." *Bulletin of the History of Medicine,* 35 (1961), 317–25.

Mentions in passing the Galenic origin of the four humors upon which Sh often based the psychology of his characters. Focuses on characters in the plays (like Kate in *Shr.*) who undergo a change in humor as a result of "more or less deliberate therapy, usually on the part of a friend" who wishes to cure a malady or has an interest in changing it. Though Sh used humoral therapy less as his career progressed, he did not discard it entirely. In the tragedies, the failure of therapy is sometimes a theme. In *Tim.*, for example, the "somewhat bungling efforts of his steward and of Alcibiades to cure Timon and restore him to normal life amount to very little and are doomed from the start." In *Ant.*, the noble Roman is afflicted with a sort of schizophrenia, "but no one attempts a cure." *Cor.* presents "the fullest depiction of unrelieved choler" in Sh. In this case, "the cure, or at least the lessening, of his choler is the immediate cause of the catastrophe, though the ultimate cause was the original choler itself."

0329   Draper, John W. "Hybris in Shakespeare's Tragic Heroes." *EA,* 18 (1965), 228–34.

Measures the heroes of Sh's tragedies against a definition derived from Aristotle's *Poetics* and Sophocles' plays. The key features of tragedy, according to this definition, are pride and the tragic flaw. In most of the plays, even those with classical connections, there is little to link the heroes with either feature: *Tit.* focuses on revenge; *JC* portrays some pride in Caesar, though it is of minimal importance; Timon's ruin comes not from pride but "from a laudable excess of feudal liberality"; and Antony and Cleopatra are engaged in personal struggles that by and large exclude pride. Only in *Cor.* does Sh, altering his source in Plutarch to emphasize pride, come close to creating a Sophoclean protagonist and an Aristotelian tragedy.

0330 Draper, John W. "Shakespeare and the Problem of Evil." *West Virginia University Bulletin: Philological Papers*, 15 (1966), 3–21.

Discusses the sources of evil in Sh's villains and/or heroes. At first, as with Aaron of *Tit.*, these malefactors are chiefly influenced by social status or the stars; later, their wickedness arises from political misdoings; in the later tragedies, evil comes from their souls. Includes consideration of tragically flawed heroic characters like Antony and Coriolanus. Mentions the classical origin of the humors theory of psychology, which can help to explain some of the villainy in the plays. Comments on the unusual step the playwright took in *Tim.* of making a collective villain out of Athenian society.

0331 Draper, John W. *Stratford to Dogberry: Studies in Shakespeare's Earlier Plays*. Pittsburgh: U. of Pittsburgh P., 1961. viii + 320 pp.

Presents a series of essays, many previously published, on "a dozen of Sh's earlier plays." Makes brief comments on the classical roots of the rustic servant tradition as used in *Err.* and on how in *LLL* Sh outdoes his master Lyly in getting through the antecedent action to attempt a comedy that "concentrates on a single episode like classical tragedy." Chapter 8 describes Richard II as "mercurial" in terms of contemporary psychology; chapter 18 concludes that Kate (in *Shr.*) is "choleric" according to medical authority deriving from Galen; and chapter 21 argues that Falstaff, with his gluttony, flattery, buffoonery, impudence, and lechery, is descended as much from the parasite of Roman drama as from the *miles gloriosus*.

0332 Dubrow, Heather. *Captive Victors: Shakespeare's Narrative Poems and Sonnets*. Ithaca, New York: Cornell U. P., 1987. 277 pp.

Contends that *Ven.*, *Luc.* and *Son.* provide sophisticated explorations of human emotion and coherent analyses of human character, and that "these achievements are in fact produced, not precluded, by the formal strategies of the poems, especially by their interpretation of genre and mode and by their use of tropes." Investigates a number of connections between formal and psychological issues in the three works, including closure as an aesthetic and psychological problem and repetition as a reflection of character. Especially important are the ways in which each work approaches the question of whether the skilled rhetorician is "a victor over language and his listeners, a captive of his own words, or both."

Section 1, on *Ven.*, focuses on the portrait of Venus, especially her use of language. The goddess, for example, recasts the Petrarchan image of the hunt into the more passive, nourishing image of a park. Her habits, linguistic or psychological, are "a way of achieving and asserting domination." She names or renames the things around her; she attempts "to transform the material into the spiritual"; she tells or refashions stories (like that of her relationship with Mars) "to create a fictitious and factitious world"; she adapts the forms and modes of lyric poetry for her own ends (for example, she, rather than the narrator, makes use of the pathetic fallacy to attribute amatory intention to the boar); and she makes use of the epideictic mode of praise. Sh may have made Venus the aggressor as a way to encode "ambivalence about a brilliantly manipulative queen," but it is likely that he had a keen interest in such powerful women for other reasons, as can be seen in the plays. Notes also that Venus's most characteristic speech habit is the conditional mode, which stands for a complex range of oppositions (order/chaos, power/powerlessness, communication/subversion of meaning). Though Venus' deceptive use of rhetoric reminds us of the failures of speech and language and of isolation from people and the world around us, there are positive aspects to her use of language, as exemplified in the Wat episode, in which she reveals her ability to transcend her own interests. Cites the last four stanzas to show how Venus's final words, her poem to the flower that has sprung up, leave us with an ambivalent sense of her feeling for Adonis. The final stanza, which distances us from the goddess by describing her intention to immure herself, is a reminder that the poem's failure to achieve closure is analogous to Venus's inability to bring her experience to "a satisfactory conclusion." Adonis, though not as developed as Venus, can be analyzed in the same way. By changing his sources in Ovid's *Metamorphoses* and Golding's translation of that work, Sh emphasizes Adonis's role as a prisoner. In his neatly expressed pieties rejecting the erotic advances of Venus, Adonis enacts one generic potential for "Ovidian mythological poetry," while Venus enacts another: We are shown two ways of metamorphosizing the *Metamorphoses*. Adduces examples of several English Ovidian epyllia and observes that Sh differs from other poets in this genre by resisting the temptation "to distract attention from his principal characters"; by making his inset "digressive episodes" more closely related to his main story; by infusing his narratives with more drama and energy; by including both more farcical and more tragic elements; and by rendering landscape in much more precise and less ideal detail. Sh also uses a variety of strategies to evoke a complex mixture of reactions to a character at any given moment; but the larger, developing pattern that he utilizes steadily increases our sympathy. The poem educates readers by tempting them to impose facile generalizations, especially "moral axioms, on the complexities of human behavior." Such oversimplifications, like the Neoplatonic reading of the entire Venus and Adonis story and the "naturalistic moral" to be extracted from the episode of the horses, are shown to be inadequate. Sh seems to be employing many devices recommended by the classical rhetoricians, such as comparison and contrast and *sententiae*; but he is obviously examining them critically. Concludes with a discussion of how Sh resembles, and therefore is attracted to, Ovid: Both are fascinated by the power of language; both are concerned with the issue of power and control in love; both are interested in "deception, especially self-deception." For Sh, the Ovidian narrative is not an escape from "moral complexities," but rather an opportunity to explore them.

Section 2, on *Luc.*, emphasizes the importance in the poem of the rhetorical figure of *syneciosis*, when, according to Angel Day, "one contrary is attributed to another, or when two diverse things are in one put together." Unlike *antithesis*, *syneciosis* conjoins its two terms as well as opposing them. It serves many purposes, among them the exhibition of the divided nature and limited perception of the characters and the tensions in the Roman culture being evoked. Remarks on the importance of competition among the Romans and between abstract ideas and values promoted by their society. Other important impressions of this society include the necessity for its people to perform in public, their isolation, and their sexlessness. Key images include those of robbery and locks, protected treasure, and besieged cities; Lucrece becomes "the center of civilization that is threatened by barbarians." Rome, in a number of ways, "is divided against itself," as are its principal persons. Notes the self-divisions of Lucrece, Tarquin, and Brutus. Discusses the use of language, both successful and unsuccessful, and shows how the loss of speech represents a loss of power. Concludes with a subsection that describes the genre of *Luc.* as a particular kind of complaint (a revision of item 2400) and one that examines the poem's preoccupation with "the problems of reading and writing history" (a revision of item 2401).

Section 3, on *Son.*, includes an examination of the ways in which praise is metamorphosed into blame and vice versa. Connects the various kinds of equivocation and double meaning in *Son.* with what Renaissance logicians, drawing on Aristotle, call "sophistical fallacies." The speaker's use of these rhetorical devices expresses his psychological ambivalence. The readers are made to experience similar confusion; like him, we are unable to distinguish "the deception of others from the deception of oneself, manipulating language and emotions from being manipulated by them." The speaker is "captive and victor, and he is both at once." The "ugly beauty motif," famously explored in Sonnet 130, can be traced back to classical sources. Sh's participation in this tradition involves critical examination of both "conventional Petrarchism" and "anti-Petrarchism."

0333 Duncan, Charles F. Jr. "A Blackboard Model of Shakespearean Irony." *CE*, 34 (1972–73), 791–95.

Describes Sh's dramatic irony as "an exploitation of the distance between character and audience which allows the audience to regard as illusory appearance what the character takes for unassailable fact." In *Ant.*, the audience's task is to see "the pull of incompatible and incomplete absolutes, each the other's ironic mask," on Antony. In *JC*, there is virtually no distance between the audience and Cassius, and therefore, in contrast to Brutus, we do not regard him ironically.

General Works

0334 Duncan, Douglas. *Ben Jonson and the Lucianic Tradition.* Cambridge: Cambridge U. P., 1979, viii + 252 pp.

Argues that "the serio-comic balance and teasing rhetoric of Jonson's middle comedies mark a conscious adaptation to the stage of satiric techniques which are found in such works as *The Praise of Folly,* the *Colloquies,* and *Utopia,* and which Erasmus and More associated with their favorite Greek author, Lucian." Provides a survey of the Lucianic tradition as it was inherited and shaped by the Renaissance, emphasizing the ways in which Christian humanists adapted it for teaching by appropriating its characteristic use of detached skeptical intelligence. Sh created several characters (for example, Berowne in *LLL* and Jaques in *AYL*) who attempt a kind of Olympian, Lucianic stance. Inevitably, their posture of disengagement is a sign of weakness or pride. Timon is a typically Lucianic character, capable of only a simplified vision, unable to become involved in personal relationships, and finally amounting to no more than an "intellectual enigma." Suggests that *Tim.*, and perhaps other problematic plays like *MM* and *Tro.*, are Lucianic in the sense that they are intentionally designed to puzzle the audience and challenge its understanding.

0335 Dundas, Judith. "'Those Beautiful Characters of Sense': Classical Deities and the Court Masque." *CompD,* 16 (1982–83), 166–79.

Maintains that the English court masques of the Renaissance should not be seen exclusively as vehicles for political and ethical messages. In their use of classical mythology, they reveal a concern for beauty and delight that has been slighted in modern commentary. Mythology was viewed by poets, rhetoricians, and painters as "the subject matter of beauty." Examples from Jonson show that references to gods and goddesses served to create a pleasurable atmosphere in which the earthly exemplars of these mythological figures are molded into "an idealized art form." Of course, none of this art is incompatible with the moral goals of the masque, but the aesthetic pleasure to be found in it is at least as great as the instruction it offers. The pure delight to be derived by the leisured class from classical allusion may be glimpsed in Sh's catalogue of the pictures to be shown to Sly as the perquisites of a lord in *Shr.* (Induction ii), and in the teasing references to myth by Jessica and Lorenzo in *MV* (V.i).

0336 Dunn, Catherine M. "The Function of Music in Shakespeare's Romances." *SQ,* 20 (1969), 391–405.

Argues that Sh's romances rely heavily on "the complex musical ideology of his time," which was "derived from the Greek philosophers, notably Pythagoras and Plato, and later syncretized by Boethius and the Christian philosophers." Pythagoras was influential through his theories of perfect and imperfect consonance and the music of the spheres. Boethius's division of music into three branches (*musica mundana, musica humana,* and *musica instrumentalis*) was "accepted as canonical" well into the 16th c. *Musica mundana* denoted "the order and proportion of the heavens and the elements"; *musica humana* meant "the rapport existing between the parts of the body and the faculties of the soul, particularly the reason"; and *musica instrumentalis* included all the "practical" aspects of music as distinguished from the "speculative" qualities of the first two categories. An additional point about *musica humana,* tracing its origin to the Greek theory of *ethos,* was that music has curative powers. Though Sh alludes to speculative music elsewhere in the canon (for example, when Lorenzo mentions the music of the spheres in *MV,* V.i.60–65), he makes much more consistent use of it in the four romances. In *Per.*, references are primarily to *musica humana* (some are concerned with the idea of temperament and some with the iatric powers of music). At the end, there is one example of *musica mundana,* when Pericles hears the music of the spheres (V.i). There are fewer references to music in *Cym.*, and they are less central. In one example, Cloten suggests *musica humana* when he hopes that the song "Hark, hark, the lark" and the aubade in II.iii will "tune" Imogen to favor him. All but one of the allusions to music in *WT* are to practical music, but the *musica humana* at Hermione's resurrection (V.iii) "is given great emphasis because of its dramatic position as the climax of the play." In *Tmp.*, "music is woven into the very fabric of the play." Much of the music here is practical at the same time that it suggests a speculative purpose. Stephano's bawdy song (II.ii.42–55), an amusing example of *musica instrumentalis*, also reveals his gross nature and his inability to harmonize with himself and others. *Musica humana* is referred to frequently, for example by Ferdinand (I.ii.390–398), by Ariel (III.iii.53–58), and by Prospero (V.i. 50–60, 64–68, 79–82). *Musica mundana* is present during the entire play, with the tempest being heard as a disordered version of it. *Tmp.* marks Sh's most ambitious use of speculative music and can be interpreted as "one long concert, with Prospero as the director, in which the discordant elements of nature are gradually resolved into concord."

0337   Dusinberre, Juliet. *Shakespeare and the Nature of Women*. London: Macmillan, 1975. 329 pp. 2nd ed., 1996.

The introduction emphasizes the forces at work in Sh's culture that influenced him and other dramatists of his time to move in the direction of equal treatment for women: Puritanism and its ideal of married chastity, humanistic opposition to the corrupt idealization of war and love inherited from the Middle Ages, the rejection of both courtly and satiric stereotypes of women, and the stage conditions of the new commercial theater for adult actors. The book covers most of Sh's plays. Notes that in *JC* Portia, unlike her apologetic prototype in Plutarch, demands a full share of Brutus's confidence. In the spirit of both Puritanism and humanism, she rejects the role of plaything (referred to in the images of harlotry she uses). In Portia's agitation on the day of the assassination of Caesar (II.iv), we see how costly it is for women to free themselves from the stereotyped image they have in men's eyes. Explains how Sh has modified his Plutarchan source in *Ant.* to reveal the limitations imposed by Rome and its military culture on ideals of manhood and civilization. Cleopatra is given "her own moral law": As an artist, she is able to be "true to her own nature." Discusses Cressida (*Tro.*) as an artist who adopts the empty forms of chastity without its reality; in this case, Sh exposes an uncomfortable necessity for women in a society that allows them less freedom than men.

0338   Dutton, Richard. *William Shakespeare: A Literary Life*. (Literary Lives.) New York: St. Martin's P., 1989. xii + 180 pp.

Comments that *Ven.* and *Luc.* purvey "violence and eroticism discreetly handled within a classical framework." Calls attention to the Senecan qualities of *Tit.* and *R3*. Notes the kind of history Sh found in Plutarch's *Lives*: "biographical sketches heavily moralized, most of them arranged in Graeco-Roman pairings ... so as to facilitate a relative assessment of virtues and vices." Offers several speculations as to why Sh turned to this sort of history for a model: (1) He had exhausted the possibilities of English medieval history; (2) he wanted the challenge of analyzing "men and affairs outside the framework of Christian attitudes and assumptions"; and (3) because in 1599 the authorities became especially sensitive about the application of English history to contemporary affairs, he may have felt that classical history would be a safer area in which to work. Points out the anachronisms of *JC*, asserting at the same time that Sh's professionalism may be discerned in his inclusion of three comic scenes. Notes the "satirical venom" of *Tro.* and mentions the possibility that it was commissioned for a private performance. *Ant.* evinces "a fascination with imperial destinies, albeit not those of Britain; human weakness, folly and vice all contribute, by some perverse miracle, to the possibility of a more secure and splendid future." The tragedy of the lovers walks a fine line "between divine transfiguration and squalid comedy" and prepares the way for "the golden epoch of the Roman Empire." *Tim.* and *Cor.* are "smaller in conception," both dealing with "protagonists who in their different ways are misfits," neither having any softening touches of the comic, both notably bleak. Calls attention to Sh's distinctive power to juxtapose "a timeless generality" and "a most particular picture of his own age," exemplified in *Tmp.*, where we find an evocation of "the broad history of the European Old World" represented by one of its seminal books, the *Aeneid*, and "the immediate sensation of the exploration and exploitation of the New World."

General Works

0339 Dyson, H. V. D. "The Heroic and Unheroic in Shakespeare." *Listener*, Apr. 23, 1964, pp. 671, 673, 675.

Links *Tro.* with *H5* and *Wiv. Tro.* is an ironic echo of the heroic plot of *H5*, while *Wiv.* makes fun of the pandering element in *Tro.*

0340 Dyson, H. V. D. "This Mortal Coil—I: Shakespeare and Death." *Listener*, Apr. 9, 1964, pp. 586–88.

Traces the ways in which death appears in Sh's plays. In the early plays, it is almost a character, an "intrusive goblin." Then it becomes mere nonexistence, as in *JC*.

0341 Dyson, H. V. D. "This Mortal Coil—II: Shakespeare and Life in Death." *Listener*, Apr. 16, 1964, pp. 637, 639.

Emphasizes that in the later plays, death is "no longer a negative, a deprivation, but a positive, even an object for appropriate contemplation." *Ant.*, "the most entirely pagan of the plays," is "the only one to carry the full assurance of immortality."

0342 Eagleton, Terence. *Shakespeare and Society: Critical Studies in Shakespearean Drama.* New York: Schocken Books, 1967. 208 pp.

Attempts to show, in some of Sh's plays, the tension "between the self as it seems to a man in its personal depth, and as it seems in action, to others, as part of and responsible to a whole society." Chapter 1, on *Tro.*, discovers among the Greeks, and especially in the speeches of Ulysses, a sense that personal identity (and reality in general) is created contextually, in public, by a group that can change the reality as the values of the group change. Helen for the Greeks and Ajax for the Trojans serve as centers of value created by their respective groups. The Trojans, by and large, fashion their own values, each person acting as an individual without reference to the community. For both groups, the process of defining themselves is circular, and "the rhythm of circularity dominates the play." Among the Greeks, reason, which involves comparison and weighing of relative worth, obstructs rather than motivates action. The Trojans are devoted to spontaneity, which is socially irresponsible but achieves a kind of personal authenticity (as Troilus does in his love). Sh seems ultimately to side with reason and social responsibility, though he suggests that a fusion of the personal and the social would be desirable. The play, however, cannot find a way to accomplish this. Chapter 5 covers *Cor.* and *Ant.* The hero of the former is committed to personal fulfillment, truth to himself with no consideration of his social context. He can exist only outside society. The protagonists of the latter create their own reality in their love for each other; they refuse to tone down their authenticity in order to be socially responsible. Points out, in a note on *Tim.*, that the hero's generosity has an abstract circularity about it. Because Timon's giving ignores the concept of justice, which provides a social context for generosity and forgiveness, it degenerates into excess.

0343 Eagleton, Terry. *William Shakespeare.* (Rereading Literature.) Oxford: Basil Blackwell, 1986. x + 114 pp.

Discovers in *Tro.*, despite attempts by the characters to establish absolute standards for meaning, value, and personhood, that language, principles, reasoning, and history provide no certainties. Views Coriolanus as "a bourgeois individualist," who defines himself in disregard for outside opinion and is "a sort of blank tautology." Emphasizes the "gratuitous generosity" of the protagonist of *Tim.*, whose "abstract formalism" of giving is paralleled by the senate's legalistic condemnation of Alcibiades' friend (III.v). In *Ant.*, Sh makes a virtue of excess, showing how "the traditionalist social order flamboyantly burns itself out." Cleopatra, the figure in the play for desire, "deconstructs political order."

0344 Eastman, Arthur M. "Shakespeare's Heroes: They Died as They Lived." *SRASP*, 1, no. 2 (1977), 49–59.

Acknowledges that Sh's tragic figures achieve in death some higher awareness, some transcendent vision, but argues that their ends are also marked by further manifestation of their characteristic human weaknesses. Thus Cleopatra, though she has a magnificent dream of Antony and their love, is still posturing to gratify herself as she dies; and Coriolanus, having gained insight into his relationship with his mother, falls back into his old angry arrogance as the Volscians cut him to pieces.

0345 Eccles, C. M. "Shakespeare and Jacques Amyot: Sonnet LV and *Coriolanus*." *N&Q*, 12 (1965), 100–102.

Maintains that in Sonnet 55 Sh borrowed the theme of immortality through writing and some imagery from North's translation of Amyot's preface to his French translation of Plutarch's *Lives*. Also suggests that lines from Amyot's preface influenced two passages in *Cor*.

0346 Edgar, Irving I. *Shakespeare, Medicine and Psychiatry: An Historical Study in Criticism and Interpretation*. New York: Philosophical Library, 1970. xiv + 382 pp.

Proposes to evaluate the medical and psychiatric knowledge found in Sh's plays. Comments that medical learning was much more widely disseminated in the 16th c. than it is today. It consisted chiefly of teachings from Aristotle, Galen, and Hippocrates "brought into the limelight by the Renaissance": teachings Sh could have known either directly or through the variety of contemporary writings that incorporated medical materials. Discusses medical allusions in most of Sh's works. Emphasizes *Lr*. and *Ham*. in a section on psychopathology. Concludes that Sh's dramas reflect the medicine and psychiatry of his own day.

0347 Edmunds, John. "Shakespeare Breaks the Illusion." *CritQ*, 23 (1981), 3–18.

Surveys Sh's plays for instances of breaking the theatrical illusion. Suggests that the illusion is broken to discover a truth that turns out to be a more subtle illusion or to "take us into the sphere of myth" as it is shaped by the playwright. Examples include Brutus and Cassius's prediction, just after they have killed Caesar, that their "lofty scene" will be re-enacted in "states unborn" (*JC*, III.i); Troilus and Cressida's prophecy, as they swear their mutual love, that posterity "will look on them as paradigms of pure and constant love" (*Tro.*, III.ii); and Cleopatra's vision of how she will be impersonated in Rome as part of Caesar's triumph.

0347a Edwards, Philip. "The Brows of Grace." *ShStud*, 26 (1987–88), 1–19.

Explores, in several works of Sh, two intertwined themes: "the difficulty of distinguishing good from bad because of the chameleon power of the bad to assume the appearance of the good, and the instability of the good, which is liable to be infected by the contagion of evil, and to become corrupted while still maintaining its outward beauty." In *Luc.*, the protagonist is obsessed with both of these themes as she first contemplates the face of the traitor Sinon in the painting of the sack of Troy and then kills herself to prevent the infection caused by Tarquin's rape of her from spreading. The hero of *Tim.*, who at first takes the feigned friendship of his colleagues for the real thing, ends by calling for the infection he perceives throughout society to accelerate its growth until humankind is utterly destroyed.

0348 Edwards, Philip. "Person and Office in Shakespeare's Plays." *PBA*, 56 (1970), 93–109. (British Academy Shakespeare Lecture 1970.) Reprint. London: Oxford U. P., 1970. 20 pp.

Argues that Sh presents two views of man: In one, there is such a complete merging of "the person and his public activities" that who he is cannot be distinguished from what he does; according to the other, there is an infinitely adaptable self that always makes us "aware of the separateness of the person and his office." The first view can be fruitfully studied in *JC* and *Cor.*

0349   Edwards, Philip. *Shakespeare and the Confines of Art.* London: Methuen, 1968. 170 pp. Reprint. 1981.

Presents Sh as a restless experimenter, engaged throughout his career in a struggle against "his own skepticism about the value of his art as a model of human experience." Comments that *Tro.* is virtually alone among the plays because it subverts its own art: It demonstrates that the material of the play renders irrelevant or incongruous all efforts to make sense of its actions and all efforts to unify and control the actions. *Ant.* testifies to the "impossibility of single vision and simple judgment," making little attempt to explain the world. *Tim.* is unfinished, but instructive: In it we witness Sh's struggle with the problem of form, his skill at writing satirical city comedy, his attack on his own vocation (in the character of the Poet), and his development of a kind of symbolism that becomes a dominant feature of the romances.

0350   Edwards, Philip. *Shakespeare: A Writer's Progress.* Oxford: Oxford U. P., 1986. vii + 204 pp.

Opens with a brief account of Sh's life, noting that his Latin-based schooling would have placed emphasis "on the structure of language and the arts of language, on the analysis of expression, on the development of an argument, on logic, on debate and on oratory," and thus would have provided "a major foundation not only for the declamations of the history-plays but the wit-combats in the comedies and the passion or cunning in the arguments of Isabella or Iachimo." Notes that Sh would have been exposed to Roman comedy through the works of Plautus and Terence and that Ovid is the poet whose influence can be seen most clearly in the plays. Comments briefly on each work in the canon. Chapter 3, on the poems, covers *Ven.*, *Luc.*, *PhT*, and *Son.* Chapter 6 covers Sh's tragedies. Includes discussion of *Tit.* (exhibiting horror couched in elaborately rich poeticism), *Tro.* ("unnervingly anti-heroic"), and *Tim.* (seeking but failing to find tragic form) as plays that exist on "the outer edge" of Shakespearean tragedy. *JC* is a simpler tragedy than most, but it does incorporate "the balance of opposites which is the very stuff of tragedy." *Cor.* is a tragedy of violence, but it reduces "the violent liberating act" to "the passionate anger of a thwarted man." In *Ant.*, the heroine is extraordinarily complex, possessing "mysterious grace" and offering splendid love; the hero recognizes this partly, but not wholly.

0351   Edwards, Philip. *Tragic Partnership in Shakespeare's Plays.* (The W. D. Thomas Memorial Lecture.) Swansea: University College of Swansea, 1988. 15 pp.

Discusses several plays of Sh as "shared disasters, tragedies that befall two people because of the chemistry of their relationship." In *JC*, Cassius vehemently hates one-man rule, but his campaign against it is ruined by the political blunders of the man (Brutus) he recruits as leader. Other tragedies of partnership include *Ant.* (in which Antony cannot comprehend "the interdependence of partnership") and *Cor.* (in which the protagonist's identity dissolves without his mother).

0352   Efron, Arthur, and Robert Hapgood. "Shakespeare's Negated Myths?" *Paunch*, No. 27 (1966), 5–12.

Consists of a dialogue on myth criticism of Sh. Efron maintains that Sh raises the idea of ritual renewal through sacrifice in his plays only to negate or discredit it thoroughly. Hapgood responds that although there is much negation in Sh's treatment of myth (as in *JC*), there is some renewal, however qualified (as in *Rom.*). Also considers *R2*, *R3*, *Tit.*, and *Lr.*

0353 Eggers, Walter F. Jr. "'Bring Forth a Wonder': Presentation in Shakespeare's Romances." *TSLL*, 21 (1979), 455–77.

Explores the "presentational" quality of *Per.*, *Cym.*, *WT*, and *Tmp.*, by which the audience is invited, often by an on-stage presenter, to experience wonder at some person or event in the play. Surveys the history of the theory of wonder available to Sh, beginning with Aristotle and the Roman rhetoricians. Cites Quintilian as typical of the writers in this tradition, according to whom there are two phases of wonder: At first, an audience is astonished, transported, by what it beholds; then, having become detached, it wonders *about* what it has experienced.

0353a Elam, Keir. *Shakespeare's Universe of Discourse: Language-Games in the Comedies*. Cambridge: Cambridge U. P., 1984. xi + 339 pp.

Proposes, in the introduction, to elevate the language of Sh's comedies from the Aristotelian category of "mere diction" to which it has been consigned by many critics. Suggests that the principal mode of action in the comedies is "direct *acts* of language." Adapts Ludwig Wittgenstein's notion of "the language-game" to consider five kinds of language games in the comedies: theatrical games, world-creating games, semantic games, pragmatic games, and figural games. Considers, in a discussion of the self-reflection of Sh's baroque art, five ways in which "intertextual debts" are more or less overtly acknowledged: quotation, allusion, parody, hypertextual signals, and interdiscursive links. Makes reference throughout to "Renaissance theories of language and language-use." Devotes a chapter to each of the five language-games, with the following titles: "Performances," "Universes," "Signs," "Acts," and "Figures." Chapter 3, the first part of which is a revision of item 2188, analyzes Sh's treatment of Neoplatonic ideas of language. Chapter 5 scrutinizes the figures derived from classical rhetoric in Sh's comedies, as well as the notion of the figurality of theater itself. Gives most attention to *LLL*; also examines *AWW*, *AYL*, *Err.*, *MM*, *MV*, *Wiv.*, *MND*, *Ado*, *Shr.*, *TN*, and *TGV*.

0354 Ellis-Fermor, Una. *Shakespeare's Drama*. Ed. Kenneth Muir. London: Methuen, 1980. xiii + 169 pp.

Reprints the Shakespearean materials from two books by Ellis-Fermor, *Shakespeare the Dramatist* (1961; item 0355) and *The Frontiers of Drama* (1945). Makes some revisions in the original materials, combining a section on *Cor.* from the chapter on verbal music in *Shakespeare the Dramatist* with the chapter on *Cor.* from the same book.

0355 Ellis-Fermor, Una. *Shakespeare the Dramatist and Other Papers*. Ed. Kenneth Muir. London: Methuen, 1961. xvi + 188 pp.

Prints parts of a book left unfinished at the author's death, along with other papers, some previously unpublished. Chapter 4, on *Cor.*, argues that the original impression we gain of the protagonist—of a bold, haughty, heroic aristocrat—is transformed into that of "a vengeful soldier of fortune." In seeking to reconcile "these two contradictory phases of conduct," we need to notice hints throughout the play, "secret impressions" of elements in Coriolanus's nature that can explain his behavior. What we find is that from the beginning he longs "for the balancing silences, graces, and wisdom banished from the outer world but vital to wholeness of life." Chapter 5, "The Nature of Plot in Drama," treats the spatial aspect of plot by discussing the placing of characters in Aeschylus's *Agamemnon* and then in *Ant*. In Aeschylus, the characters are "spread across the foreground," but in *Ant*. there is a third dimension in that characters vary in their relative vividness. This helps create a sense of limitless extension in the play. Chapter 7, "Some Functions of Verbal Music in Drama," analyzes "the changes of mood and bearing" in Coriolanus in light of his "speech-music." Parts reprinted in item 0354.

General Works

0356 Elton, W. R. "Shakespeare and the Thought of His Age." *A New Companion to Shakespeare Studies*. Eds. Kenneth Muir and S. Schoenbaum. Cambridge: Cambridge U. P., 1971, pp. 180-98.

Points out that the Elizabethans "still held to the Aristotelian premises of teleology, or purposefulness, and causal action" and cites instances of this concern with causation from Sh's works. Sh also makes use of the language of Aristotelian formal logic.

0357 Empson, William, intro. *Narrative Poems*. (Signet Classic Shakespeare.) New York: New American Library, 1968. xlvii + [48]-223 pp.

Includes texts of *Ven.*, *Luc.*, *PhT*, *LC*, and selections from *PP*. The introduction emphasizes that both *Ven.* and *Luc.* recount myths of origin: The former explains why love is fraught with pain and difficulty and the latter "how Rome threw off her kings and thus acquired an almost superhuman virtue." The introduction and text are reprinted as part of item 0123.

0358 Erlich, Bruce. "Structure, Inversion, and Game in Shakespeare's Classical World." *ShS*, 31 (1978), 53-63.

Maintains that *Tro.*, with its self-canceling inclusion of competing texts, can be used to make a structural and thematic point about the canon as a whole and especially about "those dense and allusive plays set in the classical world": In reading or witnessing a performance of a play, we encounter "outside" aspects that paradoxically are "in" the text. The development of Sh's "political awareness as the Tudor Age becomes the Stuart" can be seen in his use of inversion and displacement "within a play, between plays, and between plays and the world." In the history plays up through *H5*, the king, a version of Elizabeth, is seen as a mediator who unites all factions of society. In the later plays, which signal the transition from Elizabethan to Jacobean, this type of ruler is replaced, in a series of inversions, by various manifestations of the Machiavellian figure. *JC* mediates between the later histories and the mature tragedies: Caesar, for example, is midway between Bolingbroke and Claudius. *Ant.* and *Cor.* are Sh's most challenging examples of inversion. In *Ant.*, the power axis of Rome is inverted by the pleasure axis of Egypt, and there is no chance of reconciling the opposites. In *Cor.*, the impossibility of mediation between inverted opposites is made more starkly obvious. These two plays thus reflect the tensions in the political makeup of Jacobean England. The classical plays, in their openness of reference, are experimental, turning outward from their verbal texts to the audience and to history and serving as the basis for a game of "inquiry, testing, and the formation of new perceptions."

0359 Erskine-Hill, Howard. *The Augustan Idea in English Literature*. London: Edward Arnold, 1983. xvi + 379 pp.

Chapter 6, "Shakespeare and the Emperors," begins by noting that Sh knew the Julian myth concerning "heroism, peace and justice," as embodied in the poems of Virgil. In *Tit.*, the Roman empire is "in a state of drastic decline" because it has been abandoned by Astraea, the Virgilian goddess of justice. In *Tit.*, *JC*, *Ant.*, and *Cym.*, Sh's "dialectical imagination" subjects the Augustan myth to a variety of complex revisions. Argues that in *JC* Cassius's comments to Brutus about Caesar (I.ii) incorporate republican sentiments analogous to those found in Machiavelli, which are set in dynamic opposition to Caesar's imperial ambitions. *Ant.* focuses on a dialectic between two kinds of ruler and between two worlds of experience. The character of Enobarbus—worldly and shrewd but not cynical—is an exemplar of the openness with which Sh wishes us to regard Antony. Plutarch led Sh to portray Antony as a victim of Spenserian intemperance; this defect, however, is more than counterbalanced by Antony's magnificence, his "inexhaustible vitality." *Cor.* provides another study in intemperance, but it is opposite to Antony's, the "nameless vice" that Aristotle had postulated in the *Ethics* that can be described as "a deficiency in pleasures, a too weak reaction to them." Speculates that

Plutarch's comparison of Alcibiades with Coriolanus in the *Lives* inspired Sh to conceive *Cor.* as an antithetical companion piece to *Ant.* Plutarch's Alcibiades, though similar to Coriolanus in many respects, is closer to Antony in the personal qualities that tend toward magnificence. Identifies Menenius in *Cor.* and Octavius Caesar in *Ant.* as the characters in those plays that come closest to expressing Aristotle's "mean." Sh may have relied on Jonson's *Poetaster* and on Simon Goulart's *Life of Caesar Augustus* (included in the 1603 edition of North's Plutarch) to construct in *Ant.* his complex image of the man who is about to become Caesar Augustus—a man characterized by youth, vulnerability, defensiveness, and determination. Calls attention to Sh's use of "extreme contrasts" to set up the reconciliation between a "primitive and aggressively independent Britain" and "the *pax Romana* of Augustus" in *Cym.* Here, near the end of his career, Sh presents a "distant yet positive view of the Augustan idea."

0360   Eskin, Stanley G. "Politics in Shakespeare's Plays." *BuR*, 15, no. 3 (1967), 47–64.

Comments that the Roman plays (*JC*, *Ant.*, and *Cor.*) are politically more pessimistic than the histories or the tragedies. In each of these plays, there is a "strong force pulling against the political order," and the politics are in continual flux, with no resolution in sight.

0361   Evans, Bertrand. *Shakespeare's Tragic Practice*. Oxford: Clarendon P., 1979. xi + 327 pp.

Proposes to interpret Sh's tragedies in terms of how the dramatist exploits the unequal, or discrepant, awarenesses of audience and tragic characters. Gives special attention to the "practices" of the villains, who do much to create the gaps between the protagonists' awareness and that of the audience. Includes chapters on *Tit.*, *JC*, *Ant.*, and *Tim.* and *Cor.* Notes that, in *Ant.*, we witness "a game of secret motives and marked cards dealt by high professionals," in which "all three of the competitors both win and lose." In *Tim.* and *Cor.*, there is less exploitation of discrepant awareness than in the earlier tragedies, and the protagonists have no guile, no "capacity for conceiving or executing practices."

0362   Evans, G. Blakemore, textual ed. *The Riverside Shakespeare*. Boston: Houghton Mifflin, 1974. xvi + 1927 pp.

The general introduction, by Harry Levin, mentions the influence of classical materials on Sh's education and provides a brief survey of the works. Another prefatory section, "Chronology and Sources," lists in tabular form the works with their dates and sources. Introductions to the individual plays include, where appropriate, information about classical sources. Introductions for the history plays are by Herschel Baker; for the tragedies by Frank Kermode; for the romances and poems by Hallett Smith; and for the comedies by Anne Barton.

0363   Evans, Gareth Lloyd. *Shakespeare I: 1564–1592*. Edinburgh: Oliver and Boyd, 1969. vi + 120 pp.

Proposes, as the first of five volumes on Sh's life and plays, to discuss his life and works for the period 1564–92. The first chapter, "The Making of the Man," includes an account of the education Sh was likely to have acquired in Stratford, with its heavily classical emphasis. First there would have been a thorough grounding in the rudiments of Latin grammar and memorization of tags from Latin authors; then consideration of important authors like Cicero, Virgil, Ovid, Terence, Plautus, and Seneca; then a study of logic and rhetoric; and finally the reading of historical texts like those of Julius Caesar, Sallust, and Livy. From this background, Sh's imagination was able to construct a living sense of the past. Includes chapters on Sh's early histories, including *Tit.*, and early comedies. Revised as part of item 0369.

0364   Evans, Gareth Lloyd. *Shakespeare II: 1587–1598.* Edinburgh: Oliver and Boyd, 1969. vi + 120 pp.

Observes the format of the first volume in this series (item 0363), with an initial chapter on Sh's life from 1587 to 1598 and succeeding chapters on plays written during this period. Chapter 2 is on history plays, chapter 3 on comedies, and chapter 4 on tragedy and tragicomedy. Revised as part of item 0369.

0365   Evans, Gareth Lloyd. *Shakespeare III: 1599–1604.* Edinburgh: Oliver and Boyd, 1971. viii + 119 pp.

Observes the format established in the first two volumes of this series (items 0363 and 0364), with an introductory chapter on Sh's life from 1599 to 1604 and succeeding chapters on plays written during this period. The first chapter describes the theatrical dispute called the War of the Theaters and shows how Sh was praised by some and deprecated by others as a writer who did not observe classical principles. Chapter 2 is on "The Mature Comedies," chapter 3 covers "The 'Problem' Plays" (including *Tro.*), and chapter 4 is devoted to "Rome and Julius Caesar." Revised as part of item 0369.

0366   Evans, Gareth Lloyd. *Shakespeare IV: 1601–1605.* Edinburgh: Oliver and Boyd, 1972. viii + 132 pp.

Observes the format of the first three volumes in this series (items 0363, 0364, and 0365), with an initial chapter on Sh's life from 1601 to 1605 and succeeding chapters on the plays written during this period. Chapter 2 covers the four major tragedies, and chapter 3 treats "A Problem Tragedy: *Timon of Athens.*" Revised as part of item 0369.

0367   Evans, Gareth Lloyd. *Shakespeare V: 1606–1616.* Edinburgh: Oliver and Boyd, 1973. viii + 120 pp.

Observes the format of the first four volumes in this series (items 0363, 0364, 0365, and 0366), with an initial chapter on Sh's life from 1606 to 1616 and succeeding chapters on the plays written during this period. Chapter 2 is on *Ant.*, chapter 4 on *Cor.*, and chapter 5 on *Cym.* Revised as part of item 0369.

0368   Evans, Gareth Lloyd. "Shakespeare, Seneca, and the Kingdom of Violence." *Roman Drama.* Eds. T. A. Dorey and Donald R. Dudley. New York: Basic Books, 1965, pp. 123–59.

Reviews the Senecan elements scholars have found in Elizabethan drama: "the stoical behavior and posturing of the tragic hero–villain, the rhetorical communication, the sensationalism of plot and incident, the implacable skeins of revenge, the demonstrations of cruelty, the descriptions of bloody acts, the reflectiveness of theme and tone in many speeches, the supernatural usages, the chorus, verbal devices, the five-act structure." Attempts to show how Sh transformed certain of these elements, "making tractable much that is dramatically and theatrically intractable." In the early plays *Tit.*, *H6Triad*, and *R3*, Senecan "themes and usages of blood, revenge, and cruelty" occupy much of Sh's attention. *Tit.* is the play of Sh most nearly comparable to Seneca. In some places (for example, in II.iv, where Marcus describes the mutilated Lavinia), Sh resembles Seneca in using undramatic rhetoric. Elsewhere, however (as in the short scene immediately before Marcus's speech where Chiron and Demetrius appear with Lavinia and describe what they have done to her), Sh makes Senecan materials dramatically credible. In *3H6* and *R3*, Richard of Gloucester shows traces of the Senecan revenger, but he differs from his prototype in having no precise reason for his villainy, in being malevolently playful, and in lacking a stoical attitude. In *R3*, other Senecan elements—the use of prophecy and oracle, images of physical repulsion, and the ritual curse—are endowed with greater theatrical and psychological depth than in Seneca. As Sh's career progressed, "the spectacular evocation of evil and violence" became secondary to an exploration of the "relation of mankind to the forces of evil in the world." This may be illustrated in *Ham.*, which for all its Senecan components is focused on the protagonist's inner questioning, a dimension undeveloped in the Senecan revenger.

0369   Evans, Gareth Lloyd. *The Upstart Crow: An Introduction to Shakespeare's Plays*. Ed. and revised Barbara Lloyd Evans. London: J. M. Dent, 1982. ix + 404 pp.

Covers all of Sh's plays. Consists of nine chapters, each of which treats a group of related plays, with a separate subchapter assigned to each play. Analyzes *Tit.* in chapter 1, "The Early Histories," as "a straightforward example of the influence of Renaissance classicism." Seneca's influence on *Tit.* can be seen in its claustrophobic atmosphere and its emphasis on "lust, greed, cruelty, ambition and above all revenge." Acknowledges the faults of *Tit.* but claims it offers promise of greatness. Chapter 2, "The Early Comedies," begins by noting that *Err.*, *Shr.*, and *LLL* are the result of Sh's exposure to Latin literature, his transformation of the form and content of Plautus and Terence, and his "susceptibility to the influence" of the University Wits. Chapter 3, "Years of Consolation," includes a discussion of *MND* that mentions Plutarch's *Lives*, Ovid's *Metamorphoses*, and Apuleius's *The Golden Ass* as possible sources. Chapter 5, "The Problem Plays," views *Tro.* as satiric. Sh seems to be subverting many themes, forms, and attitudes that "had created the life-blood of his earlier plays." In particular, the idea of order, which sustains both chivalric honor and romantic love, is "comprehensively annihilated." Chapter 6, "The Tragedies," includes an account of *JC*. This play resembles the great tragedies in its testing of Brutus's inner nature by outer circumstances, in its theme of "proliferating disorder," and in its use of "portents and supernatural occurrences" as "symbolic comments on the action." Yet *JC* does not delve into these matters as profoundly as the other tragedies. It does exhibit such an accurate "sense of politics" that it is always contemporary.

Chapter 7, "The Classical World," includes essays on *Tim.*, *Ant.*, *Per.*, and *Cor.* Notes, in an introduction, that though Sh's classical learning was confined to what he studied in grammar school (that is, it was almost exclusively Latin), his imagination was inevitably drawn "to classical history, politics, society, myth and legend"—especially in the period following the composition of his major tragedies. Points out that *Ant.* and *Cor.* draw on classical sources, using history to explore "the ironies of the political and the personal." *Tim.*, *Per.*, and *Cym.* (the last not treated extensively in this chapter) are romances that use classical settings and materials. *Tim.* is allegorical, employing personification to convey abstract ideas and evidencing "symmetry of construction." Its tone seems to be bitter and cynical, as it comments on the ambivalent nature of wealth in man's life and the corruption of the ruling class. *Ant.* is remarkable for its psychological accuracy, its subtle emotional shadings, its verbal richness, and its skillful construction. The matching of language to character is especially noteworthy. Speculates, on the evidence of *Ant.*, that Sh's "sense of naturalistic theatre" was more stimulated by Plutarch than by any other source. Discovers in *Per.* three distinctive theatrical merits: (1) its "spectacular visual effects," (2) the frequent power of its language, and (3) "the magnificent realism of the brothel scenes." Admires the effective portrayal of Marina's virtue and the power of the recognition scene between her and Pericles. Maintains that the protagonist of *Cor.* is presented as both "unattractive and sympathetic." Discusses several aspects of Coriolanus's pride. Considers Sh's penetrating study of the mother–son relationship; the carefully drawn portraits of Menenius, the tribunes, and Aufidius; the concern with order; and "the graphic quality of the play's communication" (reinforced by the precision of the stage directions). Includes revisions of items 0363, 0364, 0365, 0366, and 0367.

0370   Evans, Gareth Lloyd, and Barbara Lloyd Evans. *The Shakespeare Companion*. New York: Charles Scribner's Sons, 1978. xiv + 368 pp.

Includes, in the third section, entitled "The Works," plot summaries of all of the plays, with each summary preceded by a list of the source(s) for that play. Provides also a "Commentary of the Poems," which lists sources for, summarizes, and comments on *Ven.* and *Luc.*, among others. The fourth section, "Stratford upon Avon and Shakespeare," includes a very brief account of the classical authors that Sh would have studied in school.

0370a Evans, Maurice, ed. *The Narrative Poems.* (New Penguin Shakespeare.) London: Penguin, 1989. 263 pp.

The introduction points out that *Ven.* draws on two separate Ovidian traditions. The first, that of the *Metamorphoses*, is concerned with mythology and has a strong allegorical coloring, acquired during the Middle Ages. The second, that of the *Amores*, is erotic, chiefly comic, and deals with human behavior. Notes that the Elizabethans were more adept at appreciating Sh's combination of "myth with dramatic realism" than are modern readers. The poem exhibits a great consciousness of contemporary poetic styles, but it is characteristic of Sh that, imitating Ovid, he turns Petrarchan conventions upside down by portraying a sexually aggressive female. Sh follows the Renaissance theory of narrative poetry, derived from Aristotle and Horace, in emphasizing the pictorial. The poem sets up a variety of myths or allegories only to subvert them. It explores, in the context of recent idealizations of love evoked by Neoplatonism, the struggle between reason and passion, which Sh does not resolve; he does, however, offer consolation in the image of the flower with which *Ven.* ends.

Comments, in introducing *Luc.*, on Tarquin as Sh's most detailed study of lust and on Lucrece as a complex manifestation of "self-conscious grief." Suggests that Sh may be holding both of his major characacters in a double focus, Roman and Christian. Regards *Luc.* as a combination of two genres, tragedy and complaint. Notes that the poem is highly rhetorical, with the actions and speeches of the characters embedded in a matrix of "wise saws and moral instances." Through the episode in which Lucrece contemplates the painting of the fall of Troy, Sh is exploring the inevitable distortion that occurs when naturalistic art holds a mirror up to nature and the way in which our own experience colors our interpretation of such art.

Argues that *The PhT* presents the love of its protagonists as incapable of being realized in human terms. Sh provides no ladder of ascent by which the earthly can raise itself to the divine; it would seem that he is undercutting Neoplatonic idealism about love.

0371 Evans, T. M. "The Vernacular Labyrinth: Mazes and Amazement in Shakespeare and Peele." *SJH*, 1980, 165–73.

Discusses the classical as well as the Christian and native pagan elements in the concept of the maze, which seems to have been associated in Sh's time with a journey through the confusions of the world to a point of understanding and clarification. Sees the image of the maze—"a torturous path to a new spiritual awareness"—as central to the way *MND* and *Tmp.* function.

0372 Ewbank, Inga-Stina. "'More Pregnantly than Words': Some Uses and Limitations of Visual Symbolism." *ShS*, 24 (1971), 13–18.

Cites the Painter in *Tim.* (I.i.95–97) on the value of visual theater. Advocates seeing in individual Sh plays "a kind of purposeful dialectic between what is seen and what is said; between the power of words, on the one hand, and their impotence before a visually presented reality, on the other." Illustrates with the scene where Coriolanus is persuaded to spare Rome by his mother (*Cor.*, V.iii).

0372a Ewbank, Inga-Stina. "Shakespeare's Liars." *PBA*, 69 (1984), 137–68.

Proposes to examine Sh's liars–those characters who speak falsely, tell untruths–as an affirmation of "his interest in what people do to themselves and to each other through words." Cites a comment from Apemantus to the Poet in *Tim.* to show that Sh was aware that his art "was always open to charges of mendaciousness" from "strict Platonists." Observes, however, that the playwright "must have been grateful for the human inability, or unwillingness, to stick to truth." Identifies different kinds of lies and liars throughout Sh's works. In the histories and Roman plays, the dialogue repeatedly demonstrates the gap "between rhetoric and truth." When Troilus witnesses the faithlessness of Cressida (*Tro.*, V.ii), he first tries to prove in language that two "contradictory statements are equally true" and then struggles with a new truth that leads him to disillusionment. Dolabella's denial of Cleopatra's metaphoric vision of Antony (*Ant.*, V.ii) provokes her to "one of the most emphatic accusations of lying" in Sh's plays. Concludes that Sh gave to his greatest liars the power to make us see and know that what they say is real.

0373 Ewbank, Inga-Stina. "'These pretty devices': A Study of Masques in Plays."*A Book of Masques in Honour of Allardyce Nicoll*. Eds. T. J. B. Spencer and S. M. Wells. Cambridge: Cambridge U. P., 1967, pp. 407–48.

Sees in *Tim.* "perhaps the most far-reaching use of the masque as social symbol." The masque of Amazons, presented by Cupid (I.ii), symbolically represents "the excessive adulation" accorded to Timon as well as the "lavish expenditure, social grace, ceremony and ostentation" that characterize Timon's early life. Apemantus, who subverts the value of the masque while it is being performed, is literally "an antimasquer." The second banquet (III.vi), at which Timon acts as his own presenter, inverts the ritual of flattery when the guests are dismissed with abuse. In Sh's hands, the masque has here become "an important dramatic tool." In *Tmp.*, the masque works on many levels at once: (1) It celebrates the betrothal of Ferdinand and Miranda; (2) its mythological machinery, by stressing nature and fertility, reinforces an important theme of the play; and (3) its evanescence is "seized on for a comment on all reality."

0374 Ewing, Marilyn McKee. "Hydras of Discourse: The Uses of the Hydra in English Renaissance Literature." Ph.D. dissertation, University of Colorado at Boulder, 1982. *DAI*, 43 (1982–83), 1151-A.

Notes the frequency of the appearance of hydras in English Renaissance literature, in which they are used in various ways. Traces the development of the hydra motif from classical antiquity through the end of the Middle Ages. In the eyes of many classical writers, the hydra was a potent force of evil, but there were other ways to view it. Among Renaissance writers, Sh was the most skeptical of applying the hydra to political issues.

0375 Faas, Ekbert. *Shakespeare's Poetics*. Cambridge: Cambridge U. P., 1986. xxiv + 263 pp.

Deduces Sh's poetics from statements of his characters. Interprets each such statement "(1) within the context of the work in which it occurs, (2) within the context of Shakespeare's oeuvre in general, and (3) against the background of comparable non-Shakespearean writing of the period."

Chapter 1, "Shakespeare, Poet of Nature," notes that the playwright's comments on poetic creativity, the arts of language, poetic structure and genre, and major form and invention often reveal indifference to or variance from the theoretical pronouncements of his contemporaries. The Poet in *Tim.* is illuminating when he speaks of the fluidity of poetic composition. That is, for Sh, creativity is not sequential, "with invention preceding delivery"; rather, it is "a self-generative process of psychophysiological spontaneity, imagination, and composition occurring in near-simultaneous unison."

Chapter 2, "Acting and Drama," asserts that Hamlet's mimetic theory of drama, ultimately derived from Plato and Aristotle, stems more directly from a phrase attributed by Donatus to Cicero and frequently quoted in the Renaissance. Such a theory, congenial to Ben Jonson and many others, prizes well-made plays and didactic purpose, as well as emotional restraint in acting. It is clearly opposed by statements from Sh's other plays and is contradicted by the practice of Hamlet himself. The idea that drama should be pedagogical and/or satiric, a corollary of this theory, is presented and undermined in *Ham.*, *AYL*, and *Tim.*

Chapter 3, "Shakespeare and His Audience," describes the presentational theory of drama held by 16th-c. critics like Sir Philip Sidney, Ben Jonson, and Lodovico Castelvetro as showing little faith in the audience's intelligence and therefore requring exact verisimilitude. The representational elements in the theories advanced by Alessandro Piccolomini and Francesco Buonamici allow the playwright some latitude in appealing to the audience's recognition of artistic truth, however far it may be removed from real truth. Buonamici calls on Plato to explain that the audience is led to ideas or abstractions by experiencing particular stage actions. However, none of these neoclassical commentators shows the kind of flexibility in relationship to theatrical spectacle that Sh clearly favors. He satirizes both illusionism and "signifier-signified symbolism" (*LLL*, *MND*); on the one hand, he consistently disrupts "the illusion of the stage action," while, on the other, he attempts "to make the spectators lose themselves in the spectacle" (*H5*). The audience is thus engaged in a theater of multiple response. Examines potential classical influences on Sh, including Plutarch's treatise *On Listening*. Finds it more likely, though by no means certain, that Sh drew on statements made by Pliny and Philostratus about the fine arts, citing the passage in *Luc.* (lines 1422–1428) in which there is an "extensive discussion of imaginative spectator participation."

Chapter 4 treats Montaigne and Bacon, both of whom helped to dismantle "the traditional systems of essentialist metaphysics." They liberated poetry and the imagination from the control of reason. Bacon went beyond most of his contemporaries and challenged the Renaissance assumption that myths are created to express a meaning; instead, he maintained, myths come first, imaginatively created by poets. Notes that these ideas, which Sh shared, may serve as background for plays such as *MND* and *Tmp*.

Chapter 5 analyzes the collapse of essentialist discourse, or the undermining of the traditional assumption (Neoplatonic or Christian) that language is linked with ultimate realities, as it is depicted in Sh's works. Pays particular attention to *Son.* and *Tro.*, with some discussion of *Rom.* and *Ant.*

Chapter 6, "The Language of Poetry," argues that *LLL*, primarily through the character of Berowne, holds up for approval an approach to love that, while beginning in apparent Neoplatonism possibly inspired by Baldassare Castiglione's *Book of the Courtier*, ends by foregrounding an "empiricism of heightened sensory perception induced by love." In proposing an art that reenacts "this universal Eros," Berowne uses the image of "a lute strung with Apollo's own hair." Cites *Son.* as sharing with *LLL* an "inverted Platonism," whose most immediate expression is "a poetic language striving towards an utter immediacy of content."

Chapter 7, "The Poetic Imagination," cites Theseus's speech on the lunatic, the lover, and the poet (*MND*, V.i) as revealing Sh's tenet that the poetic imagination is to be understood in primarily psychological terms. Plato and his followers maintain that the *furor poeticus* is intellectual, a means to higher truths; Sh, by contrast, endorses the view that the poet is indeed a lunatic, fascinated by "the imagination's psychopathological bias." Observes that a number of characters in Sh's plays, especially Richard II, can be described as "poet lunatics," who translate the disordered promptings of their imagination "into some form of poetic language." Theseus's attempt to dismiss what he regards as the irrational power of poetry is doubly ironic because he himself comes from the realm of the antique fables (Greek myth) and because "he deprecates what is so clearly the outstanding achievement of the play in which he appears."

Chapter 8, "Mythopoetics," discusses Sh's portrayals of the supernatural, witchcraft, magic, and myth. Includes a treatment of *Tmp.*, Sh's "greatest mythopoeic creation," which illustrates his general approach to myth. For one thing, the classical material that forms the subject of Prospero's betrothal masque for Ferdinand and Miranda is revitalized by its association with traditions of magic and the demonic that Sh's contemporaries would have considered more authentic (this is also true of the classical elements in *MND*). For another, the masque encourages us to take a paradoxical view of mythopoeic creativity: The supernatural spectacle devised by "the mythmaker poet" is both fact and fantasy at the same time.

Chapter 9, "Time's Argument, or Art and Nature," concentrates on *WT*. Shows that the chorus, Time, at the beginning of act IV sets forth a view of time as cyclical, recalling Heraclitus, whom Sh may have known through Montaigne's "Apology for Raymond Sebond." Time as chorus helps to facilitate the transition from the teleogical pattern that dominates the first three acts to the cyclical rhythms of the last two. The latter part of the play also emphasizes classical figures who undergo metamorphosis. Especially important is Proserpine, who "symbolized the eternal rhythms of life and death to classical antiquity." Sh's notion of art is complex: Art is prompted by nature and "tries to enact the flux of nature" without subjecting it to preconceived ideas; however, there is at the same time a need for "conscious craftsmanship in the creative process." Like Bacon and Montaigne, Sh "dissolves the traditional dichotomy between art and nature."

0376 Faas, Ekbert. *Tragedy and After: Euripides, Shakespeare, Goethe.* Kingston, Ontario: McGill-Queen's U. P., 1984. ix + 223 pp.

Parallels Euripides and Sh as writers of traditional tragedy who "rebelled against and transcended" the genre. In each case, we can "trace the transition from tragedy via anti- towards post-tragedy." For Sh, *Rom.* is an example of traditional tragedy, conforming to the Aristotelian notion of characters being secondary to action. *Tro.* reveals Sh experimenting with "dislogistic rhetoric, having his characters argue two diametrically opposed points of view concerning the same issue with equally convincing effect." This practice derives ultimately from the Greek Sophists, who influenced Euripides, and Sh, if he had no direct knowledge of either, could have imbibed an even greater sense of relativism from Montaigne. Argues that *Tro.* is an anti-tragedy, questioning, negating, and inverting "the tragic patterns to which it alludes." Less parodically and more subtly, *Lr.* does the same thing. The anti-tragic vision also manifests itself in *Ham.* Subsequently, Sh, in his romances, exhibits at its most highly developed the post-tragic impulse, with its "metaphysical opportunism" in the face of "nature's duality of creation and destruction."

0377 Faber, M. D. "Freud and Shakespeare's Mobs." *L&P*, 15 (1965), 238–55.

Notes that according to Freud group behavior depends on an erotic bond (involving a desexualized version of the libido) between the group and its leader, a father figure. In *Cor.*, the protagonist hates the common people and prevents them from idealizing him as a unifying leader–hero. The tribunes Brutus and Sicinius make certain that no erotic ties are formed between Coriolanus and the people. Coriolanus's tragedy is that of a man who "cannot love beyond the narrow circle of those closest to him." In *JC*, the crowd forms an emotional tie to Brutus immediately following the assassination, but Antony, in his funeral speeches, subtly reminds the people of their former bond to Caesar, inducing in them feelings of deprivation and anger and thus making them susceptible to manipulation.

0377a Fabiny, Tibor. "'Ripeness is all': The Wheel of Time as a System of Imagery in Shakespeare's Dramas." *Papers in English and American Studies.*Vol. 2. Ed. Balint Rozsnyai. (Acta Universitatis Szegediensis de Attila József Nominatae.) Szeged: Department of English, Attila József U., 1982, pp. 153–93.

Argues that the dominant image of time in Sh's works is the wheel, analogous to the wheel of fortune. Cites, from the plays, four groups of images for time that imply, or depend upon, the idea of time's wheel: (1) the perfectness of time, or the image of its totality; (2) ripeness and rottenness, or nature imagery; (3) the powers of necessity and hope; and (4) discord and concord, or music imagery. Notes that Sh's wheel image is indebted to the classical notion of time as a cycle, as revived by Neoplatonists, although the plays preserve some traces of the idea of linear, one-way time, handed down through the Judeo-Christian tradition.

0377b Fabiny, Tibor. "*Theatrum mundi* and the Ages of Man." *Shakespeare and the Emblem: Studies in Renaissance Iconography and Iconology.* (Acta Universitatis de Attila József Nominatae: Papers in English and American Studies 3.) Szeged: Attila József U., 1984, pp. 273–336.

Begins by quoting Jaques's speech on the seven ages of man from *AYL* (II.vii. 138–165) and then cites several passages from *Tmp.*, *Son.*, *MV*, *R2*, and other works to demonstrate the importance to Sh of the *theatrum mundi* (world as theater) metaphor. Surveys the *theatrum mundi* image in Elizabethan literature and places it in the context of European literature. Points out the close connection between the images of *theatrum mundi* and *theatrum humanae vitae* (ages of man) and traces the latter to its roots in classical thought, mentioning also its Judaic and Christian versions. Reviews the iconographic tradition of these two interrelated images, beginning with *The Tablet of Cebes*. Offers a reading of *R3* that takes the *theatrum mundi* metaphor as "a structuring principle."

0377c Fabricius, Johannes. Shakespeare's Hidden World: A Study of His Unconscious. Copenhagen: Munksgaard, 1989. 274 pp.

Argues that Sh's career as an artist can be understood in terms of the development of the unconscious that Sigmund Freud and Carl Jung call the individuation process. Analyzes dreams, ghosts and spirits, symbolic imagery, recurrent imagery, errors, and symbolic objects to chart Sh's progress through *TN*. Emphasizes, for example, "the central symbolic object" of the bloody pit, associated with Tamora, the devouring female, in *Tit.* Treats *Ven.* and *Luc.*, along with *Tit.*, as products of a creative period in Sh's development "in which sex and aggression are mingled in ways that depth psychologists have unravelled in deep and early strata of the human mind."

0378 Farley-Hills, David. *Shakespeare and the Rival Playwrights 1600–1606.* London: Routledge, 1990. vi + 226 pp.

Analyzes seven of Sh's plays as responses to the works of contemporary playwrights and to the rapidly changing theatrical fashions of his time.

Chapter 2 argues that *Tro.* is an innovative attempt to treat a subject popular around 1600 in plays like the two parts of Thomas Heywood's *Iron Age*. Instead of focusing on action and on a logical sequence of events, as does Heywood, Sh breaks in at the middle of things and throughout emphasizes the unexpected. Speculates that *Tro.* was composed in a satirical manner derived to some extent from the comedies of John Marston; that it failed at the Globe; and that it was modified for private performance by increasing the satiric content and adding a comic ending. Though he employs various Marstonian techniques of dislocation and distancing that tend to expose "the vanity of a world dedicated to worldly glory and worldly lusts," Sh cannot entirely abjure "the brilliant character realism" characteristic of his earlier plays. We take the characters and their concerns seriously in a way that is foreign to Marston's grimly Calvinist world. Thus *Tro.* exhibits tonal ambiguity, a result of uncertainty of intention: It "has something both of the emotional dignity and commitment of tragedy and the multiplicity of focus and detachment of comedy."

Chapter 4 maintains that Ben Jonson's *Sejanus* stimulated Sh, in *Oth.*, to experiment with Aristotelian and Senecan requirements for tragedy.

Chapter 6 maintains that Thomas Middleton had a hand in *Tim.* and that Middleton's "sardonic Christianity" is an important presence. However, the play is successful neither as satire nor as tragedy.

0379 Farnham, Willard. *The Shakespearean Grotesque: Its Genesis and Transformations.* Oxford: Clarendon P., 1971. x + 175 pp.

Conceives of the grotesque, absorbed by Sh from the Middle Ages, as what is monstrous and low in art. It is often involved in conflict with itself and what is high or sacred, though at times it is skillfully incorporated into a unified whole. The grotesque produces laughter when the low presumes to be high in a "violation of all natural possibility." Cites two "serious" puns from *Tro.*, which are also used by Falstaff in comic contexts, to show how the grotesque coupling of incompatible words is a way of thinking with which Sh endows nongrotesque characters like Troilus and Helenus. Notes that the Pyramus and Thisbe interlude in *MND* provides a grotesque parallel to the lovers' story in *Rom.* In *JC*, the grotesque appears in Brutus's perception of the monstrous potential of Caesar as well as the monstrous nature of the conspiracy. Thersites, in *Tro.*, is a new type of grotesque figure in Sh: Unlike Falstaff and others, he is never complaisant about the nongrotesque high. Most especially, "he is inimical to all that mankind has set up as worthy of high regard within its ranks and within its codes of action."

0379a Farrell, Kirby. *Play, Death, and Heroism in Shakespeare.* Chapel Hill: U. of North Carolina P., 1989. xi + 235 pp.

Analyzes numerous Shakespearean variations on a "pattern of imaginative behavior" that involves "play-death and resurrection or heroic apotheosis." Situates Sh's works in their cultural context to show how art responded to the fear of death by construing death in such a way that it yielded heroic meaning. Chapter 3 argues that in *Ant.*, Cleopatra's death scene exhibits "some of the processes that generate symbolic immortality." Chapter 7, "Love, Death, and the Hunt in *Venus and Adonis*," maintains that Venus and Adonis enact "crucial fantasies of immortality that were in radical conflict in Shakespeare's England." Both heroic violence (Adonis) and love (Venus) are presented as visions of overcoming death, but they tend to subvert each other. The poet impersonates both hunter and goddess of love in offering an ambivalent artistic commodation between the two forces.

0380 Feinstein, Blossom Grayer. "Creation and Theories of Creativity in English Poetry of the Renaissance." Ph.D. dissertation, City University of New York, 1967. *DA*, 28 (1967–68), 1394-A.

Provides a detailed account of the two theories of creation in the Renaissance. The first, the orthodox Christian view of creation *ex nihilo*, "excludes the principle of chaos as an ongoing creative force equal in power to the Creator." A second view was widespread among certain English poets and theologians, who were fascinated by the idea of Creation *ex chaos* and drew on cosmogonies of the Near-East, "Plutarch's *Isis and Osiris*, the *Hermetica*, *Chaldean Oracles*, to some extent the classical accounts of Plato, Hesiod, Orpheus, Empedocles, Ovid, the writings of the heresiarchs, the alchemists, and Pico, Colonna, DuBartas, Marullo, and Bruno as well." Sh, among others, explored the conflict between the two beliefs about creation. In *Ant.*, *Tro.*, and *Tmp.*, the implications of creation *ex chaos* are in part affirmed.

0380a Felperin, Howard. "O'erdoing Termagant: An Approach to Shakespearean Mimesis." *Yale Review*, 63 (1974), 372–91.

Uses *Ham.* to illustrate the presence in Sh's work of two distinct notions of drama. The first connects drama with theology and philosophy, transcends "considerations of time and space," and is derived from medieval allegorical theater. The second conceives of the play "as lifelike illusion," is bound by time, and is identifiable with the theater "of classical Rome and renaissance Italy." Refers to several of Sh's other works (including *MND*, *Oth.*, *Lr.*, *R2*, and *1H4*) to show that Sh deliberately mediates theatrical change, "concentrating his archaism [the medieval element] at certain strategic points" and embedding it in a neoclassical drama of naturalism. The older forms raise questions of damnation and salvation, while the newer models, by repudiating the older ones, ensure that there will be no clear answers to the questions. Revised as part of item 0381.

0381 Felperin, Howard. *Shakespearean Representation: Mimesis and Modernity in Elizabethan Tragedy.* Princeton: Princeton U. P., 1977. 199 pp.

Advances a theory of literary history according to which there is a "restless dialectic between convention and the repudiation of convention, between imitation [of previous literary models] and innovation." Applies this conception to Shakespearean and

General Works   111

Jacobean tragedy: A given play by Sh or one of his successors therefore demands both
a conservative response to understand "the archaic sign-system" it is *re*-presenting
and a modernist awareness of its insistent difference from this older system, "its
departure from prior art in the direction of present life." Proposes "a series of
interpretations of the major tragedies of Shakespeare's age that is also a model for
reconstructing from within the genre a history of the genre." Chapter 2, on *Ham.*,
points out that Hamlet's advice to the players (III.ii) conflates two distinct notions of
drama: the universal allegorical vision identifiable with medieval and Tudor theater
and the timebound realistic illusion associated with "the more or less naturalistic
theater of classical Rome and renaissance Italy." Hamlet places greater emphasis on
the latter of these ideas, but he does recognize the value of the former, as does the
play *Ham.* itself. In the play–within–the–play (*The Murder of Gonzago*, III.iv), the
closet scene with his mother (III.iv), and elsewhere, Hamlet violates his own
neoclassical canons of decorum and attempts "to recast his experience into a morality
play" of revenge. However, Sh also borrows a great deal from the Senecan idea of
revenge in having Hamlet try out classical roles for himself and others, "but usually
in such a way as to reveal their inappropriateness to his situation and rule them out
as models for his own action." The play shows how Sh dramatizes, "with unfailing
control," the conflict between the protagonist's attempt to force his life to fit the
model of an old play and his ironic consciousness (informed by neoclassical theory)
that it cannot be done. Chapter 2 includes discussions of *Ant.* and *Cor.* In the former,
Sh has the principals attempt to impose on their world a morality structure, emptied
of its traditional Christian content. The Romans, by contrast, mythologize themselves
by adopting "the heroic model of renaissance epic." These two "rival constructs"
engage in dialectics of "mutual demystification" and "mutual remystification." The
severe atmosphere of *Cor.* results from its hero's insistence on modeling himself on
previous epic heroes. Much influenced by Virgil, especially by the portrait of Turnus
in the *Aeneid*, Sh exhibits an Achillean figure whose tragedy derives from his inability
to compromise by abandoning "an outmoded and inappropriate role." Part is a
revision of item 0380a.

0382   Felperin, Howard. *Shakespearean Romance*. Princeton: Princeton U. P.,
       1972. xi + 319 pp.

Part 1, consisting of one chapter, provides a substantial discussion of the background
and theory of romance. Views ancient Greece as the birthplace of romance (with the
Odyssey being the first romance) and singles out 3rd-c. A.D. Greek prose narratives
like *Daphnis and Chloe* as one of the three key influences on Sh. Another influence
was the miracle play, itself partly derived from Greek romance. Notes that the
presiding genius of Elizabethan dramatic romance is "Eros, or an Eros figure," who
sometimes appears as Orpheus, and is opposed by a figure representing Ate, "the
goddess of discord." Pre-Shakespearean romances often end in theophanies, and
Shakespearean traces of this convention can be found in the appearances of gods in
dreams (*Per., Cym.*), the oracle in *WT*, and the masque of *Tmp*. Points out that the
obstacles confronting the protagonists in classical and medieval romance were easily
adapted by Protestant poets to create a world of humanist romance, in which inward
virtue is put to the test. Sh, in his romances, takes older romance models and shows
that they are unable to comprehend the experiences he is treating; he reevaluates the
conventions he has inherited.
   Part 2, consisting of three chapters, discusses "the pervasive presence of romance"
in the Sh works written before the last plays. Notes, for example, that *Tro.* subjects
the romantic imagination to "unprecedented stresses and strains" but that Sh is not
unremittingly ironic toward romance in this play: He does allow romantic idealism
to shine through at certain moments. Embedded in *Tro.* are two romantic models,
that of the chivalric romance and that of the morality play, both of which are shown
to be inadequate to order the actions. In the major tragedies, Sh uses romance material
(for example, Hamlet's description of his encounter with the pirates [*Ham.*, IV.vi]) to
hint at optimistic outcomes but then repudiates the power of romance in order to
confirm the essential nature of the tragic experience. Treats *Cor., Tim.*, and *Ant.* as
works in which romance is moving into the foreground. Coriolanus has "a grand
opportunity for repentance and forgiveness," though he fails to take advantage of it;

the "inward logic" of *Tim.* is toward "a romantic reconciliation," though it is short-circuited by a tragic ending; and *Ant.* is "a tragedy and a romance at once," with both forms coexisting and being fully realized.

Part 3, consisting of four chapters, is devoted to *Per., Cym., H8, WT,* and *Tmp.* In *Per.,* Sh returns to miracle and morality play patterns, returning to "the inclusiveness of old tales." The design of *Cym.* is unified by the offstage action of the incarnation of Christ, which shapes the onstage actions, including the Roman demand for tribute, the British resistance to it, and the new relationship between the two polities established at the end. *WT* presents a world only nominally supervised by a god (Apollo); in it, men are fully responsible for their own lives. Sh's combination of "romantic design with mimetic fidelity" makes this play one of his greatest. Calls attention to the "neoclassical architecture" of *Tmp.* and to the play's remarkable self-containment. Notes that "the Bermuda pamphlets," often adduced as sources for *Tmp.*, can themselves be seen as based on ancient romance conventions: The Elizabethans "conceived of their voyages of exploration and colonization in terms of romance."

Concludes with a "Bibliographical Appendix," which summarizes major critical statements on Sh's romances, especially those of the 19th and earlier 20th c.

0383   Ferguson, Susan French. "Failure of the Warrior–Hero in Shakespeare's Political Plays." Ph.D. dissertation, North Texas State University, 1976. *DAI,* 37 (1976–77), 7141-A.

Contrasts the developing ideal of the kingship in the second tetralogy of Sh's English history plays with the failure of leadership in three Roman plays—*JC, Ant.,* and *Cor.* The ideal of the warrior–king, which reaches its fullest expression in Henry V, is presented in the Roman plays as outmoded. The code by which Henry thrives leads, in the Roman context, to "a radical insensibility" that deprives the hero of fulfillment and undermines public order.

0384   Fergusson, Francis. *Shakespeare: The Pattern in His Carpet.* New York: Delacorte, 1970. ix + 331 pp.

Reprints with minor changes the essays written as introductions to the plays in the Laurel Sh series. Arranges the essays chronologically "according to the four main parts of Shakespeare's career." Includes five new general essays, one on reading Sh and the others to introduce the four phases of his development. Notes that *Tit.* has "no relation to the specific facts of Roman history," though it does reflect the impression of Rome as "a city of incredible cruelty and corruption, such as one may get from a reading of the Latin historians of the decadence." The play is indebted to Ovid's *Metamorphoses* for some of its grisly details and to the morality plays for its two-dimensional style. *Err.* reveals the influence of Roman comedy not only in its plot but in its type characters. In his English history plays and elsewhere, Sh draws on a philosophy of monarchy based in part on the Greek theory of government (found in Aristotle's *Politics*). Behind the source of *AYL*, Thomas Lodge's *Rosalynde,* lie elements of Greek pastoral and romance. Discusses *JC, Cor.,* and *Ant.* in the introduction to part 3. These three plays show that Sh respects the authority of reason and common sense as found in Plutarch but that at the same time he "sees the ancient world with the insight of his own Christian or post-Christian Europe, and represents it, therefore, with richer resonance than Plutarch himself." Points out that Sh's treatment of his materials in *Tro.* is "Latin and medieval rather than Homeric." The view of humanity in this play is "almost unrelievedly sardonic." *Tim.* has a hero whose plight may be seen as both comic and pathetic. The first three acts seem to be inspired by the "ironic simplicity of classical comedy," specifically by Lucian's dialogue *Timon the Misanthrope.* In *Cym.*, the theme of the relationship between England and Rome is unique in Sh, who developed it from a hint in Raphael Holinshed's account of Cymbeline in his *Chronicles.* The reconciliation at the play's end may indicate the proper way for a new national culture to assimilate and reflect "the central tradition" from which it is derived.

General Works

0385 Fergusson, Francis. *Trope and Allegory: Themes Common to Dante and Shakespeare.* Athens: U. of Georgia P., 1977. 164 pp.

Sketches, in the first chapter, the "common heritage" of Dante and Sh, including "that classical–Christian vision of human nature and destiny which was composed of Aristotelian philosophy, Christian theology, and the heritage of pagan and biblical literature made relevant to their time by allegorical interpretation." In particular, both poets follow Aristotle's ideas that life "consists in action" and that poetry is "the imitation of action." Contains chapters on Paolo and Francesca and Romeo and Juliet (*Rom.*), Ugolino and Macbeth (*Mac.*), *Purgatorio* 16 and *MM*, "The Monarch as 'Figura'" (*R2* and *Lr.*), "Dante's Beatrice and Sh's Comedies and *WT*," and "Poetry as Evidence of Things Not Seen."

0385a Ferlo, Roger A. "The Language of Magic in Renaissance England." Ph.D. dissertation, Yale University, 1979. *DAI*, 40 (1979–80), 2693-A.

Outlines the tension in Renaissance England between two attitudes toward "the power of magical language." The first of these, descended from St. Augustine, rejects the notion that any verbal construct of man can usurp the role of "God's creating word"; the second, espoused by the Italian humanists and derived from Neoplatonic and Cabalistic writings, entertains the possibility that man can "remedy the linguistic effects of the Fall." Discusses four of Sh's plays–*Err.*, *MND*, *Oth.*, and *WT*–focusing on the ways in which the power of magic depends on "the inner disposition of its hearer."

0386 Fiedler, Leslie A. "Shakespeare's Commodity–Comedy: A Meditation on the Preface to the 1609 Quarto of *Troilus and Cressida*." *Shakespeare's "Rough Magic": Renaissance Essays in Honor of C. L. Barber.* Eds. Peter Erickson and Coppélia Kahn. Newark: U. of Delaware P., 1985, pp. 50–60.

Uses the advertisement to the 1609 quarto version of *Tro.* to classify most of Sh's comedies as popular or commodity comedies. Surveys the Sh canon to show how the playwright, eager to please his conventional urban audience, nearly always exploited the three most hackneyed sub-genres of comedy: New Comedy, Pastoral, and Romance. He was similarly subservient to popular taste in his use of stereotypical characters and verbal clichés. Nevertheless, there is evidence throughout his works that he was uncomfortable with the constraints imposed by his audience. As the preface to *Tro.* indicates, in this play Sh violated the canons of popular taste for comedy. Some time later, in *Tim.*, the playwright found himself back in "a world of generic ambiguity."

0386a Fields, Albert W. "*Nosce Teipsum*: The Study of a Commonplace in English Literature, 1500–1900." Ph.D. dissertation, University of Kentucky, 1967. *DAI*, 30 (1969–70), 1979-A-1980-A.

Begins by pointing out that Socrates' idea of a man's two selves—"one aspiring to divinity and another basely chained to the earth"—lies behind the tradition of self-examination. In Renaissance England, thoughtful men combined Erasmus's faculty psychology, his belief that self-knowledge is the beginning of wisdom, and Aristotle's idea that knowing men is the best way to self-knowledge. The literature of the age often deals with "faculties gone awry," especially, as in the tragedies of Sh, "the failures of great men to know themselves."

0387 Findlay, Heather. "Renaissance Pederasty and Pedagogy: The 'Case' of Falstaff." *YJC*, 3, no. 1 (1989), 229–38.

Points out that in *1&2H4* and *H5* Sh constitutes Falstaff's character "within a series of classical Greek paradigms, all of which recall homosexuality and/or a pedagogical relationship between men." Falstaff is surrounded by sodomitical references, and his relationship with Prince Hal is cast in terms of classical figures in a "great pedagogical, and often pederastic, chain" including Socrates, Alcibiades, and Alexander the Great.

In addition to all of this, Falstaff conceives of himself as the young king's Ganymede (2H4, V.v.46). Falstaff teaches Hal "the language of the marketplace, of truth and of desire." Notes that in Renaissance England acceptance of certain ideas about sodomy was unwittingly promoted by the increasingly secular schools, which, among other things, taught classical texts, especially their numerous homoerotic narratives, without resorting to medieval religious allegorizing. The dismissal of the fat knight by Henry V records the plays' participation in the suppression of an older, Greek way of approaching truth (the fondness of "an older male lover" [*erastes*] for a "young beloved" [*eromenos*]) and its replacement with a new homophobic paradigm (the desire of man for woman).

0388   Finkelstein, Sidney. *Who Needs Shakespeare?* New York: International Publishers, 1973. 261pp.

Focuses on Sh "the social thinker and the writer who dealt with politics in its deepest sense." Covers most of the canon. Views *JC* as a study of the relationship of the common people and the patricians. Brutus is honorable, but he mistakenly identifies the interests of the people with those of his own class. The theme of *Tro.* is "the decline of the medieval chivalry of the aristocracy." *Ant.* pits an old order, that of the great nobleman–warrior like Antony, who is a law to himself, against a new order of pragmatists like Octavius Caesar. In *Cor.*, the protagonist is a less attractive representative of the old order than Antony was, but he does have courage and honesty. The representatives of the new order, the tribunes Brutus and Sicinius, are especially contemptible because, like wealthy tradesmen of Sh's day, they scorn those whom they profess to lead. Though Sh bases his plot on materials from Plutarch, he ignores "Plutarch's picture of Roman politics and society" in order to anatomize the society of his own time. *Tim.* is a flawed play, though with many powerful passages, especially in Timon's curses toward the end; it concentrates on revealing the corruptive power of money.

0389   Fisch, Harold. "Shakespeare and 'The Theatre of the World.'" *The Morality of Art: Essays Presented to G. Wilson Knight by His Colleagues and Friends.* Ed. D. W. Jefferson. London: Routledge and Kegan Paul, 1969, pp. 76–86.

Points out that the world–as–stage metaphor had both a classical and a Christian force as Sh inherited it. In its Greek incarnation, "it suggests the cyclical, repetitive nature of time: it suggests the eternal sameness of things, their illusory quality, the emptiness of mere appearance." As a Hebraic image, it suggests that history is a covenant drama, "having room for both divine action and human freedom." Sh's plays (examples are *Ham.* and *Mac.*), through images like this, "evoke both the Hebraic and Hellenistic modes of existence," thereby allowing them "to confront one another in an unmitigated dialectic."

0390   Fischer, Sandra Kay. "'Who Steals My Purse': Economics and Value in Renaissance Drama." Ph.D. dissertation, University of Oregon, 1980. *DAI*, 41 (1980–81), 3590-A.

Examines the effects of the development of mercantilism on Renaissance drama. Some plays, while not principally focused on economics, concern themselves with the problems brought about by changing systems of value in which economics plays a major role. As materialistic concerns replace spiritual ones, the value of women, for example, is debated on economic grounds: *Tro.* investigates Helen's empirical worth as a basis for proper action. The structure and metaphors of certain plays (for example, *Tim.*) reflect the social disruption caused by the ambiguities of the new economic system.

0391   Fitch, Robert E. *Shakespeare: The Perspective of Value.* Philadelphia: Westminster P., 1969. 304 pp.

Asserts that Sh's plays are "saturated with the ideas and imagery of Christianity," though his use of religion is primarily concerned with human rather than divine significations. Argues that "the most compelling evidence of the power of the culture of Christendom over the mind of Shakespeare" lies in the number of Christian references in plays that are intended to have pagan settings. The largest body of such allusions concerns the prohibition against suicide, followed in number by those relating to "the fall of man and original sin." Includes frequent comments on the classical plays, noting, for example, that religious references help to convey the idea that Antony and Cleopatra's love is not spiritual. In *Tim.*, religion is used to create a mood of "savage cynicism," while in *Tro.* it suggests ribaldry.

0392 Fleissner, Robert F. "Falstaff's Green Sickness unto Death." *SQ*, 12 (1961), 47–55.

Argues that the Hostess's account of Falstaff's death (*H5*, II.iii) indicates that he died of "male green sickness" (*2H4*, IV.iii.92). Cites Hippocrates, Galen, and Renaissance psychological theory to show that Falstaff's lovesickness for the Prince can be understood as causing "iron deficiency anemia," which resulted in a greenish tinge in his complexion at the time of death.

0393 Fly, Richard. *Shakespeare's Mediated World*. Amherst: U. of Massachusetts P., 1976. xv + 164 pp.

Chapter 2, "Monumental Mockery: *Troilus and Cressida* and the Perversities of Medium," is a revision of item 2873.

Chapter 5, "Confounding Contraries: The Unmediated World of *Timon of Athens*," suggests that the protagonist of *Tim.*—in his rhetorical posture of "radical disengagement"—reflects the relationship between the poetic dramatist and "the expansive, though finally limited, capabilities of his medium." Everything about the play—its paratactic structure, its dialectical exchanges between characters, its protagonist's refusal to be moderate—has the effect of excluding any middle ground. There is no sense of mutuality in Athenian society, no means by which the individual can be beneficially related to the community; there is only a relentless competition, presided over by Fortune, which results in prosperity for some at the expense of others. Language in this environment becomes an instrument of competition, not a means of establishing contact; words seem static and lifeless. In this regard, Apemantus's snarls of hatred prefigure Timon's experiment with "sour words" in the last two acts. Having experienced the failure of language to act as a medium of social communication, Timon attempts to transform it into a vehicle for "the immediate articulation of a personally envisaged truth." In the play's last half, Sh as poet is engaged in a parallel experiment: He retreats from the dramatic into the lyric. This, of course, results in the temporary abandonment of genre. Like Timon, Sh is obsessed with self-destructive activity: His identification with the misanthrope allows him to explore his own revolt against the limitations of his medium. After Timon's death, however, the playwright returns to the world of social order, where there is mediation between the individual and society. In the last scene, with its focus on Alcibiades the mediator rather than on Timon the solipsist, we see Sh coming to terms with the requirements of his art.

0394 Foakes, R. A. "'Forms to His Conceit': Shakespeare and the Uses of Stage Illusion." *PBA*, 66 (1980), 103–19.

Begins by citing Renaissance formulations of the ancient doctrine that poetry, especially drama, is an imitation of life. Sir Philip Sidney finds the precept in Aristotle and Horace, and Thomas Heywood and others refer to one of its chief corollaries when they quote a remark, attributed to Cicero, that a play mirrors or reflects life. Sh clearly did not accept the naive equation of imitation and mirror reflection. In several works (*Ven.*, *Luc.*, *Tim.*, and *WT*), he uses a closely related idea—that painting is a mirror of nature—but he goes beyond this notion to credit the artist with the ability to surpass nature. Shows, through analyses of two plays (*MND* and *Ham.*) in which dramatic theory is discussed in the context of performances within the main action, that Sh plays complex variations on this neoclassical tenet about stage illusion. Argues that he exploits the audience's willingness to half-believe in the illusion before them at the same time that he exploits their awareness that they are in a theater. Thus he invites participation by the audience in the world of his plays.

0395 Foakes, R. A. "Shakespeare's Later Tragedies." *Shakespeare 1564–1964: A Collection of Modern Essays by Various Hands.* Ed. Edward A. Bloom. Providence, Rhode Island: Brown U. P., 1964, pp. 95–109.

Analyzes several Jacobean plays, including *Antonio's Revenge, The Changeling,* and *The Revenger's Tragedy,* to establish that the Christian humanist frame of reference is no longer operative in these works. In *Tim., Cor.,* and *Ant.,* Sh is following this trend: "the protagonists are distanced from us and presented critically"; there is no opposition between good and evil or between heroes and villains, and all values are relative.

0396 Foakes, Reginald A. *Shakespeare: The Dark Comedies to the Last Plays: From Satire to Celebration.* Charlottesville: U. P. of Virginia, 1971. vii + 186 pp.

Focuses on Sh's "development towards and achievement in his last plays." Chapter 1, the introduction, asserts that the argument will be conducted with the dramatic action as "the controlling perspective."

Chapter 2, "Shakespeare and Satirical Comedy," includes a discussion of *Tro.,* which shows the influence of Jonson's and Marston's new satirical techniques. Sh uses three strands in *Tro.:* the heroic, the romantic, and the satiric and comic. The discontinuity between word and action in both the war (Hector, Achilles) and love (Troilus) plots produces a sense of satiric detachment that is reinforced by the comic figures of Pandarus and Thersites (both of whom are voyeurs).

Chapter 3, "Shakespeare and Satirical Tragedy," includes comment on *Tim.* and *Cor.* In neither play is the protagonist trapped by or in conflict with evil (as Hamlet is, for example); rather, Timon and Coriolanus cannot adapt to a world in which one's capacity to be flexible is the key to survival. *Cor.* is a political tragedy in which the hero is admired, but within limits: We are distanced from him by his own comments and those of others about him. There is a new realism in the play's scrutiny of his psychological compulsion.

0397 Ford, P. Jeffrey. "Bloody Spectacle in Shakespeare's Roman Plays: The Politics and Aesthetics of Violence." *Iowa State Journal of Research,* 54 (1980), 481–89.

Argues that the spectacular violence found in *Tit.* has important thematic and dramatic links to Sh's other Roman plays. All of these works are concerned with the impact of bloody spectacles on those who witness them. Stage violence in the Roman plays also enables Sh to explore certain political and aesthetic issues of interest to his contemporaries. In *JC,* for example, the reaction of the characters to physical violence shows how the practical exercise of political power can "overwhelm judgment and obscure principles." In *Tit.,* the protagonist attempts to maintain old Stoic values but fails and is caught up in the primitive pursuit of justice through passion. *Cor.,* with its hero's exaltation of the harsh and the ugly, suggests that Roman virtue is founded on contempt for physical comfort and resistance to the pleasures offered by art.

0398 Foreman, Walter C. Jr. *The Music of the Close: The Final Scenes of Shakespeare's Tragedies.* Lexington: U. P. of Kentucky, 1978. xii + 228 pp.

Elucidates "the harmony of the tragic close" in thirteen of Sh's tragedies, including *Tit., JC, Tro., Tim., Ant.,* and *Cor.* Argues that a Shakespearean tragedy moves from an initial order that is challenged by a disorder or "a complex of disorders" and "issues in a disaster (one or more deaths) and a new order." Distinguishes plays in which the dynamic that leads to the new order "is directly opposed to the process generated by the energy of the tragic hero" (*JC, Ant.,* and *Cor.*) from plays in which "the process that eventually establishes the new order ironically moves in the same general direction as the process generated by the tragic energy" (*Tit.* and *Tim.*).

General Works

Considers the figures who, surviving at the ends of the several tragedies, are central to the values of the new order from which the tragic heroes are excluded. These include Lucius in *Tit.*, Antony and Octavius in *JC*, Alcibiades in *Tim.*, Octavius in *Ant.*, and Tullus Aufidius in *Cor. Tro.* may seem not to fit this pattern, since it has no real tragic figure and its energy is unfocused; however, that energy is destructive and therefore tragic. The new order of *Tro.* "is so ironic as to be nonexistent." Chapter 2, "The Art of Dying," includes a comparison between the endings of *Ant.* and *Tim.*, both plays based in part on the life of Antony in Plutarch's *Lives.* In *Tim.*, on the one hand, the protagonist leaves the stage to die, indicating a radical rejection of the world of drama. Cleopatra, on the other hand, concludes her life by embracing drama. Chapter 5 contains a detailed examination of the ending of *Ant.*

0398a Forker, Charles R. "The Green Underworld of Early Shakesperean Tragedy." *ShakS,* 17 (1985), 25–47.

Observes that in *Tit.* the struggle "between civilization and barbarism" is reflected in a division between the orderly and disorderly aspects of nature; that in *Luc.* the elaboration of conceits allows Sh to invoke nature "both as an earthly revelation of higher good and as a mirror of tragic defection from that good"; that in *Ven.* nature represents unresolved tensions between a number of polarities, including love and death and grief and regeneration; and that in *JC* what little reference to nature there is (the only green setting is Brutus's orchard) seems "almost wholly to echo the tragic disorders of men."

0399 Fortin, René E. "Desolation and the Better Life: The Two Voices of Shakespearean Tragedy." *SQ,* 32 (1981), 80–94.

Discerns within the tragic hero two voices: the heroic, confident, aspiring voice and the antiheroic, or kenotic, voice, which accepts limitations and acknowledges weakness. Although the presence of the kenotic voice in Sh may be interpreted in Christian terms, it is part of the primordial pattern of all tragedy and establishes a link between Sh and Athenian drama.

0400 Foy, Ted Cecil. "Shakespeare's Use of Time: A Study of Four Plays." Ph.D. dissertation, University of Delaware, 1974. *DAI,* 35 (1974–75), 2220-A-2221-A.

Examines Sh's use of time in four plays: *Err., Lr, Tro.,* and *Ant.* Surveys classical, medieval, and Renaissance ideas of time as background. Classical time is cyclical and negative, while medieval time is linear and providential. Both notions are important in Renaissance drama. In *Err.*, impatient behavior causes mistiming and is also a result of mistiming. Egeon's patience allows him, in contrast to most of the other characters, to work in accord with Providence. Time eventually reunites his family. *Lr.* contrasts characters who embody or learn patience (Cordelia, Edgar, Lear, Gloucester) with those who attempt to attain dominance over time. *Tro.* discloses a world in which characters put their faith in mutable and corrupt objects; no one is able to look beyond the transient. In *Ant.*, the exigencies of time dictate the ethically questionable proceedings of Octavius and (at times) Antony. Cleopatra at first attempts to discount time and then to transcend it. In the imagery surrounding the death scenes, there is a reconciliation of "spirit and flesh, eternal and temporal."

0401 Fraser, Russell. *Young Shakespeare.* New York: Columbia U. P., 1988. ix + 247 pp.

Chapter 3, "'I, Daedalus,'" describes the grammar school education Sh would have received, naming the Latin authors that were studied and commenting on how they affected his works. Sh not only used styles, materials, and structures absorbed from writers like Ovid, Plautus, and Terence, he also incorporated scenes (in plays like *1H4* and *Wiv.*) based on methods of Latin instruction and attitudes toward Latin learning that he would have observed during his time in school. Notes that Sh was a better scholar than his masters, penetrating beyond the superficial jauntiness of Ovid to understand him as "the great poet of renewals." Sh made some use of the Greek Anthology in writing his sonnets, but he had little knowledge of Greek, and none of Aristotle or Greek drama; however, his perception of human frailty as the basis of tragedy made him classical in spirit. Later chapters contain discussions of *Tit.*, *Ven.*, and *Luc.*

0402 Freehafer, John. "Leonard Digges, Ben Jonson, and the Beginning of Shakespeare Idolatry." *SQ*, 21 (1970), 61–75.

Leonard Digges (1588–1635), a minor poet, can be considered the first Sh idolator on the basis of the twenty-two lines of commendatory verse he contributed to the First Folio, in which he referred to "our bankrout Stage" since Sh's death, and on the basis of sixty-eight lines "that first appeared in the Benson edition of Shakespeare's *Poems* in 1640." In the latter, Digges mounted a prickly defense of Sh against two slurs he detected in Jonson's famous tribute of the First Folio and launched a savage attack on Jonson's works and aesthetic theory. The offending passages were those referring to Sh's "small Latine, and less Greeke" and to his use of Art as well as Nature. Digges rejects the Horatian notion, cited by Jonson, that "a good Poet's made, as well as borne," countering it with a translation of the Latin proverb "poeta nascitur non fit." Refusing to call Sh's plays "Workes" (as Jonson had called his) because they are productions of Nature only, not of laborious Art, Digges goes on to deal with the small Latin, less Greek charge by asserting that Sh "was an original writer, not an imitator of classical models or a plagiarist." Digges's poem was written for the Second Folio of 1632, but it was "so sweeping and sarcastic that it did not find its way into print on the occasion for which it was intended, and was not published until both Digges and Jonson had died."

0403 Freehafer, John. "Shakespeare, the Ancients, and Hales of Eton." *SQ*, 23 (1972), 63–68.

Cites anecdotes by Dryden, Tate, Gildon, and Rowe that record the opinion of John Hales of Eton (1584–1656) that Sh "had expressed the common subjects of poetry better than all other poets, including the ancients." Of these reports, Dryden's, written in 1665 or 1666, is the only one that probably "adds to our factual knowledge of the opinions of Sh's contemporaries." All of them, however, confirm the growing admiration for Sh in the later 17th c. by citing Hales, his contemporary and a man widely respected for his classical learning, as an authority for Sh's superiority over the ancients.

0404 Fregly, Marilyn S. S. *From Allegory to Realistic Illusion in Renaissance Drama: A Study of Mimetic and Logical–Rhetorical Devices in Dramatic Expression with Special Reference to Shakespeare's Plays.* [n.p., n.d.] vii + 192 pp.

Investigates the use of logical–rhetorical devices in Renaissance drama, especially Sh's works. Uses Aristotle's concepts of *ethos* and *dianoia* from the *Poetics* to analyze several works, including *Lr.*, *R3*, *1H4*, and *Ham*. The *Progymnasmata* of Aphthonius and Quintilian's *Institutes of Oratory* are of particular importance in the evaluation of *Ham*. Of special interest is Quintilian's distinction between *ethos* ("which concerns gentle and calm feelings") and *pathos* (which "includes the stronger, violent passions"). The final chapter attempts to identify the classical antecedents of logic and rhetoric as understood in the Renaissance.

0405 French, Marilyn. *Shakespeare's Division of Experience.* New York: Summit Books, 1981. 376 pp.

Interprets Sh's works in light of his struggle with the masculine and feminine "gender principles" into which, according to the traditional Christian notions he inherited, all experience is divided. Views the masculine principle as concerned with transcendence and permanence and the feminine principle as concerned with dynamic vitality, especially sexuality. Notes that Christianity dealt with the threat to transcendence posed by the feminine by dividing it into "inlaw" and "outlaw" principles. The inlaw side of the feminine nourishes masculine control of civilization; the outlaw side is sometimes a destructive force, sometimes a source of energy. These principles desperately need synthesis, but, because they inhabit two distinct conceptual realms, synthesis is virtually impossible. Sh struggled more than any other poet of his time with the problems involved in achieving such a wholeness, though he could not finally achieve it. To put the matter another way, the synthesis Sh did settle for is one in which the feminine principle is subordinated. Surveys the canon, with sections on most works (*Tit.* and *JC* are among the few not discussed). Argues that in *Tro.* we see an extreme version of the "failure of the inlaw feminine principle" and that "the masculine principle has become its own end"; that in *Ant.* constancy, having been separated from chastity, is redefined; that in *Cor.* and *Tim.* the heroes exhibit a dichotomy of the masculine principle that involves an attempt to transcend "the inlaw feminine principle"; and that in the romances a powerful male figure surrenders some control by incorporating "both gender principles into himself."

0405a French, Tita. "A Rhetoric of Comedy: Essays on Language as a Theme in Shakespeare's Comedies." Ph.D. dissertation, Texas Christian University, 1985. *DAI*, 46 (1985–86), 2699-A.

Uses "a historical analysis of the dialectical interplay of Platonic and Sophistic attitudes towards language" as background for tracing the development of Sh's view of language in his works. The Sophistic idea of language as capable of creating realities is dominant in the early comedies (*Shr.*). This gives way to an exploration of rigidly Platonic attempts to protect essences from change (*MV*), followed by a consideration of ambivalence towards language and a profound skepticism about its capacity to effect comic resolution (*AWW*). The tragedies are characterized by "linguistic nihilism," and *Tmp.* "offers a realistic resolution of this progression from comedic through tragic vision of language."

0406 Frey, Charles. "Shakespeare's Imperiled and Chastening Daughters of Romance." *SAB*, 43 (1978), 125–40.

Maintains that in his four romances (*Per., Cym., WT,* and *Tmp.*) Sh "solved" the problems of "over-controlling fathers and over-rebellious daughters" that had appeared in certain of the tragedies. In the romances, "patrilineal succession" is replaced by a process in which virginal daughters bid to improve the family stock by mating with outsiders. Argues that the debased mythologizing of Palamon and Arcite in *TNK* furthers Sh's critique of patriarchalism, creating a post-romance world in which the romantic imagination is simultaneously attacked and defended.

0407 Friedlander, Douglas Richard. "Shakespeare's Functional Characters." Ph.D. dissertation, State University of New York at Stony Brook, 1986. *DAI*, 47 (1986–87), 535-A.

Analyzes apparent discrepancies in certain secondary characters in four of Sh's tragedies to understand the function they perform. Includes discussion of Cassius's transformation from Machiavellian seducer to sympathetic character (*JC*) and of Aufidius's progression from hater to lover to hater of the protagonist in *Cor.*

0408 Friesner, Donald Neil. "William Shakespeare, Conservative." *SQ*, 20 (1969), 165–78.

Contends that Sh's political views can be characterized as consistently conservative. Among the influences on him were Aristotelian rhetoric and ethics, especially Aristotle's concept of political philosphy as "the ethics of civil society." *JC* and *Cor.* express their author's conservatism through unflattering portraits of the common people. In the latter play, Sh's tone is bitterly antidemocratic.

0409 Frost, David L. *The School of Shakespeare: The Influence of Shakespeare on English Drama 1600–1642.* Cambridge: Cambridge U. P., 1968. xi + 304 pp.

Recounts, in discussing Sh's reputation in his own time, the supposed dispute between Ben Jonson and John Hales of Eton over Sh's knowledge of and superiority to the ancient poets. Comments on most of Sh's works in the course of comparing them to those of his contemporaries. Chapter 4 insists on the clarity of *Ant.*, which begins with a complex and ambivalent attitude toward the two lovers but concludes with the clearly negative judgment that they are destroyed because of their irrational commitment to sensuality. Sh makes this point clear in the last scene through the image of the fig, associated with the phallus in Plutarch's *Moralia* and many other sources known to Sh, and most notably through the symbol of the serpent. Notes that this play "is remarkable for its imaginative re-creation of the pagan Roman ethos." Sh judges "the values of Rome and Egypt" from the standpoint of "the finest of Renaissance historians," reconstructing but also confidently evaluating the past. Chapter 5, "The Impact of *Hamlet* on the Revenge Tradition," attempts to explain how Sh transmuted the unpromisingly melodramatic form he had inherited from Seneca and early Elizabethan revenge writers like Thomas Kyd.

0410 Frye, Dean Carson. "Choral Commentary in Shakespearean Tragedy." Ph.D. dissertation, University of Wisconsin, 1961. *DA*, 22 (1961–62), 1997–1998.

Argues that choral commentary in a Shakespearean play can "represent a social view of the action, a practical and worldly response which stands for the judgment of society." This attitude, in the history plays and the comedies, "is largely shared by the audience, which identifies with collective ideas rather than with individuals." The later tragedies drive a wedge between the responses of chorus and audience, "heightening the hero's isolation and uniqueness." *Ant.* provides an illustration of how unreliable choral commentary is as a key to Sh's attitude toward his tragic characters. In the other Greek and Roman plays, factors that modify the tragic effect lead the audience to "identification with the choral point of view." *Tim.* and *Tro.*, for example, bring their heroes to a disillusionment that tends to validate the chorus's judgment.

0411 Frye, Northrop. *Fools of Time: Studies in Shakespearean Tragedy.* Toronto: U. of Toronto P., 1967. vii + 121 pp.

Argues that "the basis of the tragic vision is being in time," being subject to the conditions of man's contract with nature, which he fulfills by death. Also important in tragedy is the striving of heroic energy as a countermovement to the power of time. The heroic is generally destroyed. Classifies Sh's tragedies into three groups: tragedies of order (including *JC*), tragedies of passion (including *Ant.*, *Tro.*, and *Cor.*), and tragedies of isolation (including *Tim.*).

0412 Frye, Northrop. *The Myth of Deliverance: Reflections on Shakespeare's Problem Comedies.* Toronto: U. of Toronto P., 1983, viii + 90 pp.

Applies Aristotle's terms of recognition and reversal to the New Comedy of Sh. Suggests that this type of comedy illustrates a myth of deliverance, whereby the law, or Nomos, is defeated by Eros, thus insuring social survival. In *MM* and *AWW* there is a heavier emphasis than in most of Sh's other comedies on "the arbitrary whims and absurdities" that block the emergence of the new social order; nevertheless, the myth of deliverance does prevail. In *Tro.*, however, the blocking forces are too strong, and the play ends ironically. Notes the medievalization of the classical world by Sh in this play.

0413 Frye, Northrop. *A Natural Perspective: The Development of Shakespearean Comedy and Romance.* New York: Columbia U. P., 1963. ix + 159 pp.

Seeks, in four essays, to regard Sh's comedies and romances from "the middle distance," discovering their common structure and images. Connects Sh's typical comic structure with "the New Comedy pattern of Plautus and Terence." Supports many key generalizations with references to classical elements in the plays or to plays that have classical settings; for example, Sh's movement toward the mythic world of the old romances, and thus toward "primeval dramatic structure" to which any audience can respond, is indicated by the frequent appearance in his final plays of classical gods. Sh's use of anachronism is often indicative of a greater insight into history than might first appear; in *Cym.*, for example, the linking of Roman Britain and Italian Rome shows a concern with reconciliation between what Sh's contemporaries would have regarded as two "Trojan nations." Views *Tim.* as near to being a comedy, with a protagonist closely resembling the character who, within many comedies, is "the focus of the anticomic mood."

0414 Frye, Northrop. "Old and New Comedy." *ShS*, 22 (1969), 1–5.

Discusses Old and New Comedy as kinds of comedy that appear not only in Greek literature but in other contexts. New Comedy has a teleological plot, that is, characters who react predictably to whatever happens, and "Eros symbolism." Jaques, in *AYL*, is an example of the lonely figure who, by contrast, often helps define the general festivities at the end of a New Comedy. New Comedy has two chief forms, "the romantic form of Sh and the more realistic and displaced form of the Neo-Classical tradition." In Old Comedy, the structure is "dialectical rather than teleological, and its distinguishing feature is the *agon* or contest." Its form is sequential, and its development is in the direction of fantasy. In one play, *Tro.*, Sh experimented with Old Comedy.

0415 Frye, Northrop. *The Secular Scripture: A Study of the Structure of Romance.* Cambridge: Harvard U. P., 1976. viii + 199 pp.

Finds in romance a cyclical movement, beginning with a departure from identity and ending with a return to it, exhibiting "descent into a night world and a return to the idyllic world." Refers frequently to classical works, especially Greek romance and New Comedy. Makes a number of connections between these works and those of Sh. For example, *Err.*, in its use of Plautus's comedy of twins and its allusion to the recognition scene of the Apollonius romance at the end, with other references to Plautus's *Amphitryon* and to Apuleius's *The Golden Ass*, shows a profound insight into the structure of romance. Uses *Tro.*, Sh's "most ironic play," as an exemplar of the descending movement and disappearing identity that is part of the romance dynamic.

0416 Frye, Northrop. "Tragedies of Love and Fortune." *Stratford Papers on Shakespeare 1961*. Ed. B. W. Jackson. Toronto: W. J. Gage, 1962, pp. 38–55.

Discusses a number of plays but focuses on *Cor*. Sh modifies Plutarch to increase his hero's likability and thus "to make the dramatic conflict as sharp and as evenly balanced as possible." Coriolanus is "a man without a mask, or fully developed social personality." *Cor.* can be considered "the third of the four Plutarchan plays," an appropriate predecessor to *Tim.* and the misanthropy it portrays.

0417 Frye, Roland Mushat. *Shakespeare and Christian Doctrine.* Princeton: Princeton U. P., 1963. ix + 314 pp.

Insists on Sh's "theological literacy" and the skillful way in which he always makes theological matter serve dramatic purposes. Makes occasional references to classical authors in order to distinguish what is truly Christian from what is pagan. Comments on passages from nearly every work in the canon.

0418 Frye, Roland Mushat. *Shakespeare: The Art of the Dramatist.* New York: Houghton Mifflin, 1970. xii + 271 pp. Revised ed. Winchester, Massachusetts: Allen & Unwin, 1981.

Aims at helping "intelligent readers to study Sh with greater enjoyment, awareness, and profit." Begins with a section on "Life and Work." Approaches the canon topically, with sections entitled "Types of Plays," "Structure," "Style," and "Characterization." Includes, in the section on types, chapters on histories, comedies, tragedies, and tragicomedies. Mentions in these chapters the influence of Plautus on *Err.*; suggests that *Tro.* is the most problematic of the problem comedies; connects the extravagant rhetoric and violence of Seneca with *Tit., R3,* and even *Ham.*; judges *Tim.* to be flawed because it is difficult to write great tragedy "about an essentially ordinary man"; and describes the Greek romance as background for the tragicomedies.

0419   Frye, Roland Mushat. "Ways of Seeing in Shakespearean Drama and Elizabethan Painting." *SQ,* 31 (1980), 323–42.

Proposes to show that Sh shared with the English visual artists of his time a thematic and symbolic way of representing reality. His tendencies to move from place to place and cover many years in his plays (even "classical" works like *JC* and *Ant.*) show that he was largely unaffected by the Italian neoclassical theories of the dramatic unities—just as English painters of his time paid little heed to new Italian notions of unified perspective. Serious neoclassical experiments in drama and painting began in England during the reign of King James, and Sh may have observed the unities in *Tmp.* to demonstrate to his rival Ben Jonson that he could excel at the new game.

0420   Fulton, R. C. *Shakespeare and the Masque.* (Garland Publications in American and English Literature.) New York: Garland, 1988. 235 pp.

Deals with classical elements in masques of *AYL* (chapter 2), *Tim.* (chapter 3), and *Tmp.* (chapter 4). Chapter 3 is a revision of item 2638. The book is a revision of item 0421.

0421   Fulton, Robert Campbell. "Shakespeare and the Masque." Ph.D. dissertation, University of California, Berkeley, 1972.

Chapter 2, on the masque of Hymen in *AYL,* attempts to establish the significance of the marriage god as he is used here by Sh. Notes the extensive exposure of Elizabethans to classical authors like Ovid and Virgil and the general availability of classical dictionaries and handbooks. Surveys the masques produced in the years immediately following the death of Queen Elizabeth (whose virgin status inhibited marriage masques) and concludes that Hymen's appearance in *AYL* signifies the triumph of order over the potentially disintegrative forces of passion. Chapter 3, "*Timon of Athens* and the Masque of Cupid and Amazons," is revised as item 2638. Chapter 4, on *Tmp.,* maintains that here Sh demonstrates impressive sensitivity to classical myth and its symbolic interpretation, especially in the pre-nuptial masque of Iris, Ceres, and Juno that Prospero presents to Miranda and Ferdinand. Sh incorporates "verbal echoes and narrative recollections" that allow him to establish an analogy between the *Aeneid,* 1–4, and the play. This analogy, however, is "dramatically reversed": Unlike the unhappy Dido and Aeneas, whose union is consummated inauspiciously, the patient young couple in *Tmp.* is blessed and promised reward by the benevolent gods of the masque. The whole is revised as item 0420.

0422   Garber, Marjorie. *Coming of Age in Shakespeare.* London: Methuen, 1981. viii + 248 pp.

Applies the ideas of anthropologists Arnold van Gennep (on the passage of an individual through stages of growth and toward maturation) and Victor Turner (on the stage of "liminality" or "relatively undifferentiated" community in which individuals exist when they are in transition between two highly structured social domains) to the plays of Sh. Focuses on the ways in which Sh's characters respond to crisis at such "threshold" moments. Chapter 6, "Comparison and Distinction," includes among its examples the largely unsuccessful attempts of Troilus (*Tro.*) to differentiate himself as true lover from all other lovers; the movement of Brutus (*JC*) from seeing himself, in the distorting mirror offered by Cassius, as like and then unlike

Caesar, to understanding the deeper truth of their resemblance as he slays himself; and the growth of Octavius Caesar (*Ant.*) from a conviction that he is unlike his "heroic forebears," especially Antony, to a perception that he resembles them.

0423 Garber, Marjorie. *Shakespeare's Ghost Writers: Literature as Uncanny Causality.* New York: Methuen, 1987. xv + 203 pp.

Investigates "the ways in which Shakespeare has come to haunt our culture." Chapter 4, "A Rome of One's Own," discusses the ghostly presence of Julius Caesar (and the idea of Rome in general) in Sh's plays, especially *JC* and *Ham.* Chapter 5, "*Macbeth*: The Male Medusa," uses classical myth as revisioned by Renaissance mythographers, political discourse (especially that of James I), and archaeological evidence to connect Macbeth with the Medusa figure.

0424 Garber, Marjorie. "'What's Past Is Prologue': Temporality and Prophecy in Shakespeare's History Plays." *Renaissance Genres: Essays on Theory, History, and Interpretation.* Ed. Barbara Kiefer Lewalski. (Harvard English Studies 14.) Cambridge: Harvard U. P., 1986, pp. 301–31.

Discusses Sh's generation of paradox and irony through characters' use of prophecies that look to the future in their dramatic contexts, but whose truth or falsity the audience knows retrospectively. Focuses on the English history plays, but begins with three examples from classical plays: Cassius's prediction of what reenactments of the death of Caesar will mean for future spectators (*JC*, III.i); Cleopatra's fearful anticipation of how she and Antony will be mocked on the Roman stage (*Ant.*, V.ii); and the emblematic values that Troilus, Cressida, and Pandarus foresee for their own names (*Tro.*, III.ii).

0425 Garber, Marjorie B. *Dream in Shakespeare: From Metaphor to Metamorphosis.* New Haven: Yale U. P., 1974. x + 226 pp.

Includes discussions of *JC*, the last of Sh's plays "to use dreams and omens primarily as devices of plot," and of *Ant.*, in which dream is exchanged for reality and "translated back into a new form of reality." Revision of item 0426.

0426 Garber, Marjorie Beth. "The Size of Dreaming: Uses of Dream in Shakespeare." Ph.D. dissertation, Yale University, 1969. *DAI*, 31 (1970–71), 1227-A.

Argues that the use of dream and dreaming by Sh "develops and reflects" important themes in his plays. Dreams in the plays are influenced by Renaissance dream tradition, deriving from "Greek and Latin literature and philosophy," among other sources. In certain early plays, dreams are used primarily to advance the plot, but they gradually come to be associated with the imagination and "the creative irrational." For *MND*, the dream world is the setting and subject of the play, and is particularly linked to "the transforming power of the imagination." In the tragedies, the role of dream is extended to depict "the internal psychological consciousness" of the major characters. The last plays provide a synthesis of all earlier developments "as dream and reality flow into one another." Revised as item 0425.

0427 Gardner, C. O. "Themes of Manhood in Shakespeare's Tragedies." *Theoria*, 30 (1968), 19–43.

Points out that Antony is "colossally masculine." Throughout the play, two ideals of manhood, the Roman and Egyptian, compete within him, and he finally renounces the former in favor of the greater fulfillment offered by the latter, even though he is destroyed in the process. He triumphs in defeat, however, partly through Cleopatra's vision of him after his death. Like Antony, Coriolanus is "intensely virile"; his absolute fidelity to the warrior ideal is admirable, though narrow. At the end, in persuading him to question the virtues on which he has founded his integrity, Volumnia broadens his concept of manhood, though she assures his destruction. Concludes an article the first part of which was published in *Theoria*, 29 (1967), 1–24. See item 2000.

0428 Garner, Bryan A. "Latinate Past Participles as Metrical and Tonal Variants in Shakespeare." *Lang&S*, 18 (1985), 242–47.

Notes that in the early modern English of the Renaissance there were a fairly large number of adjectives formed from the past participle of the Latin verb. These words—for example *situate, exasperate,* and *confiscate*—could be used with the *t* ending they had from Latin or be augmented by the English past tense ending *ed*. Sh often chose between *t* and *ed* forms on metrical grounds, but he also considered stylistic effect. For an Elizabethan, the old-fashioned *t* form would have sounded appropriate in the mouth of a king or someone of the upper class. When used by a semi-educated person of lower class, however, it probably suggested pretension or social climbing.

0429 Garner, Bryan A. "Latin–Saxon Hybrids in Shakespeare." *Studies in the Humanities,* 10 (1983), 39–44.

Surveys the use of hybrid words—formed from a stem or word of one language and a suffix or prefix of another—in Renaissance England. Focuses on Latin–Saxon hybrids and shows that Sh was far more liberal in his use of such hybrids than most of the scholarly neologists of his day. Includes a list to demonstrate how many more Latin–Saxon hybrids there are in Sh's works than there are in the Authorized Version of the Bible.

0430 Garner, Bryan A. "Shakespeare's Latinate Neologisms." *ShakS*, 15 (1982), 149–170.

Uses a blend of philology and literary criticism to call attention to the need for a book on Sh's language. Presents evidence that Sh wrote during a time when more loanwords—most of them Latinate—entered the English language than at any other period. Counters the Saxonist bias of most Victorian and a few modern scholars on Sh's word-coining. Presents a tentative list of "Sh's Latinate Neologisms," that numbers more than 600 words.

0431 Gash, Anthony. "Shakespeare's Comedies of Shadow and Substance: Word and Image in *Henry IV* and *Twelfth Night*." *Word & Image,* 4 (1988), 626–62.

Attempts to explain the connection between Sh's theatrical practice and Neoplatonism by examining certain verbal and visual features of the two parts of *H4* and *TN*. Finds the Christian humanist Neoplatonism of Erasmus most analogous to the structure of Sh's comedy. Notes the "theatrical theme" of Plato's parable of the cave in the *Republic* and the Platonic links with the word "shadow," a crucial and complex term in "the Renaissance vocabulary of representation." The recognition scene in *TN*, with its sense of collapsing the many into one, its stage groupings of five and three, and its accent on androgyny, provides a Neoplatonic foreshadowing of resurrection.

0432 George, Kathleen. *Rhythm in Drama.* Pittsburgh: U. of Pittsburgh P., 1980. xi + 194 pp.

Explains how Troilus's repetition of words in his speech about Cressida's betrayal (*Tro.*, V.ii.141–164) reveals the inadequacy of his attempt to control the situation. Notes that the speech in which Antony shows himself to be a more effective orator than Brutus (*JC*, III.75–109) is organized through repetitions, slightly modified, of two lines dealing with Brutus's honor and Caesar's ambition. Adduces *Ant.* as "an excellent model of the rhythm of the changing scene." In this panoramic play, there is an alternation between the opposed worlds of Rome and Egypt that nevertheless allows for progression toward the resolution of the action.

0433 Gerstung, Estella Rose Baker. "*Oikonomia* and Dramatic Function of Seven Shakespearean Orations." Ph.D. dissertation, University of Kentucky, 1976. *DAI,* 38 (1977–78), 2805-A-2806-A.

Maintains that Sh organized many of the set speeches in his plays according to the pattern of the Ciceronian oration. Analyzes seven such speeches to demonstrate the variety of ways in which the playwright adapted the oration for his dramatic purposes. As examples, *Err.* opens with a judicial oration that accounts for the play's exposition, and Ulysses' deliberative speech on degree in *Tro.* furnishes a "proposed course of action." Examines the *oikonomia*, or disposition of parts, of all the Shakespearean orations, and finds that the sevenfold Ciceronian design (*exordium, narratio, propositio, divisio, confirmatio, refutatio,* and *peroratio*) is readily detectable in each. The most experimental of these speeches is Iachimo's confession in *Cym.*, which is interrupted for over 200 lines.

0434 Gesner, Carol. *Shakespeare and the Greek Romance: A Study of Origins.* Lexington: U. P. of Kentucky, 1970. x + 216 pp.

Argues in chapter 1 that the Greek romances of the early Christian era were important constituents of the Renaissance literary milieu. Describes several of the more prominent romances (for example, *Chaereas and Callirhoe* and the *Aethiopica*) and outlines their common features: the plot involving a quest that begins when two young lovers are separated; adventures that include shipwreck and tempest; a variety of narrow escapes from pirates, brigands, brothel keepers, poisoners, and kidnappers; a great crisis, frequently in the form of the heroine's falling into a trancelike state that is mistaken for death; and a final restoration scene that explains all mysteries and mistakes.

Chapter 2 describes the romance elements in "The Continental Tradition," focusing on Boccaccio and Cervantes.

Chapter 3 deals with several of Sh's plays that incorporate romance conventions from intermediate sources: *Err.* ("a Hellenistic separation plot"); *TN* (sea journey, shipwreck, disguise); *Rom.* (separation of secretly married lovers, sleeping potion, apparent death); *Ado* (false accusation of a lady); *Oth.* (slandered bride, tales of the marvelous); and *AYL* (stock pastoral plot). See item 0928.

Chapter 4 discusses *Per.* and *Cym. Per.* is directly based on *Apollonius of Tyre* as Sh found it in the versions of Twine and Gower. *Cym.*'s three plot strands—"the wager story and Imogen's travels, the loss and restoration of Cymbeline's heirs, and Cymbeline's war with Rome"—are all taken from exemplars of the romance genre.

Chapter 5 covers *WT* and *Tmp. WT* makes obvious use of a number of romance conventions (pastoral scene, shipwreck, Hermione's deathlike swoon) blended from various secondary sources. Longus's *Daphnis and Chloe* is an ultimate, possibly direct, source for *Tmp.* because of the clear parallels between the two works in using the pastoral plot. Sh employs the essential design of the Greek romances in his last plays to establish "a dramatic pattern of prosperity and well-being destroyed by evil, and finally re-created through forgiveness and reconciliation." An appendix provides a bibliography focused on Renaissance editions of the romances discussed in the text.

0435 Ghosh, Gauri Prasad. "*Antony and Cleopatra*: The First Recoil from the Tragic Impasse." *Journal of the Department of English, Calcutta University,* 20, no. 2 (1985–86), 1–20.

Explains that *Ant.* represents a transformation of Sh's tragic vision: It blends tragedy and romance; has will-less heroes; has no real evil; emphasizes the predominance of circumstance over character; creates an idealized vision of romantic love and woman's beauty; works toward a vision of flux; and recoils from the darkly realistic tragic world that had dominated the poet's imagination for several years. Comparison and contrast with *Cor.* reveals that the latter play, though similar in many ways to *Ant.*, has a "different tone and temper" because Sh was trying to write a tragedy in his former manner when he was no longer psychically engaged with the world for which that manner was appropriate. *Ant.* is the "the transitional link between the tragedies and the romances."

0435a Ghosh, P. C. *Shakespeare's Mingled Drama.* Calcutta: World P., 1966. viii + 143 pp.

Regards Sh's plays as "mingled drama," with each play blending tragedy, comedy, and other disparate elements. Provides detailed analyses of six plays, including *Tro.* ("a satiric thesis-tragedy") and *Tim.* (a satiric play, making use of the abstractions characteristic of medieval moralities: Sh's "boldest experiment").

0436   Gill, Roma. "Marlowe's Virgil: *Dido Queene of Carthage*." *RES*, 28 (1977), 141–55.

Finds that in adapting Virgil to the stage, Marlowe transforms his materials confidently, diminishing Aeneas to an average man concerned with the exigencies of everyday life, diversifying interest by enlarging the role of Dido's sister Anna, and presenting Dido successively as a "figure of fun," a "tyrant," and a "loving woman." Many critics have seen a close resemblance between Marlowe's play and *Ant.*, particularly between Dido and Cleopatra, but Sh's heroine is never sentimental or melodramatic in the mode of Marlowe's. *Dido* also reveals that Marlowe, early in his career, was primarily a "dramatic poet, not a poetic dramatist" like Sh.

0437   Gira, Catherine R. "Shakespeare's Venus Figures and Renaissance Tradition." *Studies in Iconography*, 4 (1978), 95–114.

Surveys the female figures in Sh's plays and poems who are "described as manifesting attributes of Venus." Provides background information on Renaissance use of the Venus motif in literature and art as a means of understanding Sh's complex vision of the goddess. Most popular sources for knowledge of Venus (dictionaries, *thesauri*, emblem books, translations of Ovid) present her in a negative light, as the emblem of destructive passion. Sh, however, endowed most of his Venus figures with an ambiguity that encompasses sensuality and modesty, often likening them to Diana as well. In *Ven.*, Adonis is both chaste and sensual, as is Lucrece in *Luc.* Imogen, the heroine of *Cym.*, is associated, through the objects in her room, with both Venus and Diana, and both Cloten and Posthumus suffer from distorted views of her sensuous chastity. Claudio's perception of Hero's Venus–Diana combination of qualities in *Ado* is similarly perverse and almost causes tragedy. In the case of Desdemona, tragic consequences do follow from Othello's inability to understand the balance between chastity and sensuality within her. Marina (in *Per.*) and Emilia (in *TNK*) are also explicitly described as partaking of the characteristics of both Venus and Diana. Some of Sh's Venus figures—Tamora (in *Tit.*), Helen and Cressida (in *Tro.*), and Cleopatra (in *Ant.*)—are more lustful than chaste. The third of these is the most Venus-like of all the dramatic heroines, and yet she is not the one-dimensional debauchee of much moral literature. Partly responsible for Cleopatra's infinite variety is her association with Isis, whose multiple connections with other goddesses give her a bewildering variety of attributes. To find analogues for Sh's Venus figures, we must look to Italian philosophers and painters of the Renaissance, who saw the two aspects of Venus's nature embodied in twin sisters: Venus Coelestis (representing "modesty, grace, and chastity") and Venus Naturalis (representing "sensuality, luxury, and fertility"). Titian's *Sacred and Profane Love* and Botticelli's *La Primavera* and *The Birth of Venus* all attempt to combine the complementary qualities of the two Venuses. Revision of part of item 0438.

0438   Gira, Catherine Russell. "Shakespeare's Venus Figures and Renaissance Tradition." Ph.D. dissertation, American University, 1975. *DAI*, 36 (1975–76), 1526-A.

Examines the figures in Sh's works who exhibit the attributes of Venus (seventeen female characters in the plays, Venus and Adonis in *Ven.*, and Lucrece). Analyzes these Venus references "in the context of the entire canon and in relation to traditional Renaissance views about the goddess." Part revised as item 0437.

0439   Girard, René. "Comedies of Errors: Plautus—Shakespeare—Moliere." *American Critics in the Poststructuralist Age.* Ed. Ira Konigsberg. (Michigan Studies in the Humanities.) Ann Arbor: U. of Michigan, 1981, pp. 66–86.

Considers the devices of the twins (borrowed from Plautus's *Menaechmi*) and of disguise (borrowed from the same playwright's *Amphutruo*) as they operate in *Err.*, arguing that their comic possibilities are essentially the same. Notes that the comic effects are generated by "the stubborn expectation of difference in the face of non difference." This derives, in turn, from the workings of "mimetic desire," according

General Works

to which antagonists who desire the same thing come to imitate and resemble each other. Comments on the fundamental importance of mimetic desire in *Tro.* (where the key word is "emulation") and in *MND* (where the activities of the craftsmen and the lovers "are all examples of the same desire to impersonate the most prestigious models and to be translated into someone else"). The device of the twins, then, is not a crude contrivance but a manifestation of the basic structure of all Sh's comedies (and, indeed, of all the plays in the canon).

0440   Girard, René. "Shakespeare's Theory of Mythology." *Classical Mythology in Twentieth-Century Thought and Literature*. (Comparative Literature Symposium Proceedings 11.) Eds. Wendell M. Aycock and Theodore M. Klein. Lubbock, Texas: Texas Tech P., 1980, pp. 107–24.

Maintains that *Tro.* is Sh's "interpretation of the Homeric mythology through mimetic desire." This play, along with *Err.* and *MND*, can be regarded as "an elaboration of the psycho–social disturbances that can upset any cultural pattern, then finally generate a new mythology through the arbitrary resolution of victimage, the ultimate source of Aristotelian catharsis."

0441   Girard, René. *A Theater of Envy: William Shakespeare*. New York: Oxford U. P., 1991. ix + 366 pp.

Explores Sh's portrayal of the desire to imitate, or "mimetic desire." Notes that for Sh mimetic desire is most often indicated by the word "envy" or by the adjective "envious" in combination with a word such as "desire" or "emulation." Includes chapters with the titles and topics of "Love Delights in Praises: Valentine and Proteus in *The Two Gentlemen of Verona*"; "Envy of So Rich a Thing: Collatine and Tarquin in *The Rape of Lucrece*" (a revision of item 2407); "All Their Minds Transfigured: Genesis of Myth in *A Midsummer Night's Dream*"; "A Woeful Cressid 'Mongst the Merry Greeks: The Love Affair in *Troilus and Cressida*"; "Lechery and War: The Subversion of the Medieval Troilus and Cressida"; "These Man's Looks: Power Games in *Troilus and Cressida*"; "O Pandarus! *Troilus and Cressida* and the Universal Go-Between"; "Pale and Bloodless Emulation: The Crisis of Degree in *Troilus and Cressida*"; "Confounding Contraries: The Crisis of Degree in *Timon of Athens* and Other Plays"; "O Conspiracy! Mimetic Seduction in *Julius Caesar*"; "Domestic Fury and Fierce Civil Strife: Violent Polarization in *Julius Caesar*"; "Great Rome Shall Suck Reviving Blood: The Founding Murder in *Julius Caesar*"; "Let's Be Sacrificers but Not Butchers, Caius: Sacrifice in *Julius Caesar*"; "Let's Carve Him as a Dish Fit for the Gods: Sacrificial Cycles in *Julius Caesar*"; "A Universal Wolf and a Universal Prey: The Founding Murder in *Troilus and Cressida*."

0442   Girard, René. *Violence and the Sacred*. Tr. Patrick Gregory. Baltimore: Johns Hopkins U. P., 1977. vii + 333 pp.

Maintains that sacrifice, the ritual killing of an animal or human victim, is a religious means developed by early societies to divert the spirit of revenge and its attendant violence into other channels, and thus preserve order. Ulysses' speech on degree in *Tro.* is an excellent exposition of the relationship of violence and "differences" found in primitive societies and Greek tragedy. The hierarchical structure Ulysses describes is based on distinctions, "the underlying principle of all order," and he gives an equally clear picture of the perpetual violence unleashed when such distinctions are lost. The surrogate victim, chosen in a primitive society because he or she lacks an essential social link to the community and thus can be sacrificed without fear of reprisal, can be well-illustrated in somewhat more modern embodiment by Sh's Richard II.

0443   Gleason, John B. "The Dutch Humanist Origins of the DeWitt Drawing of the Swan Theatre." *SQ*, 32 (1981), 324–38.

Attempts to explain certain peculiarities of the DeWitt drawing of the Swan Theater by reference to an engraving of the Colosseum at Rome in Justus Lipsius's treatise *De Amphitheatro*. Points out that both DeWitt and Aernout van Buchel, whose copy of DeWitt's drawing has come down to us, were familiar with Lipsius's works and shared his humanist enthusiasm for the monuments of antiquity. Moreover, DeWitt seems to have followed the engraving from Lipsius in showing the Swan in vertical half section, labeling its parts, and depicting a performance for a virtually empty theater. The actors on stage in the drawing need not represent merely a rehearsal, however; DeWitt's drawing, like the Colosseum engraving, is following the Renaissance convention of "simultaneous representation," according to which a print seeks to give the essence of its subject without concern for snapshot-like fidelity to a single moment. An audience, as an integral part of a public performance, is simply taken for granted.

0444   Glendinning, Charles Henry. "The Tragic Hero: A Re-evaluation." Ph.D. dissertation, Case Western Reserve University, 1972. *DAI*, 33 (1972–73), 1682-A.

Comments that "tragedy is a mirror of the society which produces it." Outlines the qualities that a tragic hero must possess and the place in society he must fill. Includes discussion of *JC* and *Cor*.

0445   Glickman, Susan. "'Seeing Unseen': Concealed Observation in Shakespeare's Plays." Ph.D. dissertation, University of Toronto, 1984. *DAI*, 45 (1984–85), 2884-A.

Considers, as part of the background for a study of the spying scene in Sh, "the influence of the classical drama and its Renaissance imitators upon the development of the convention."

0446   Godshalk, William Leigh. *Patterning in Shakespearean Drama: Essays in Criticism*. (De Proprietatibus Litterarum, Series Practica, 69.) The Hague: Mouton, 1973. 199 pp.

Proposes to uncover the "structural competence" Sh exhibits throughout his career, focusing on patterns of image, theme, action, characterization, and scenic layout. Places emphasis on contrastive or polar patterning. Chapter 1, on *Tit.*, points out that the first scene motivates the following action by introducing "a tripartite conflict between six brothers." Other patterns initiated in the first scene involve pleas, kneeling, and dismemberment. Contrasts within each of the patterns set up a series of ironies, reinforced by images of eating, heads, and hands. Remarks that Ovid's *Metamorphoses* provides for Lavinia's story "a mythic context of rape, mutilation, and finally cannibalism." After several carefully structured reversals, there is a reintegration of Rome and a resolution of the play, in which the patterns are neatly tied up. Chapter 2, on *TGV*, is a revision of item 3088. Chapter 9, on *Ant.*, analyzes the play's "pattern of instability," citing the frequency of references to fortune; images of the sea and the moon; and the impermanence of political and personal relationships.

0447   Goldman, Michael. *Acting and Action in Shakespearean Tragedy*. Princeton: Princeton U. P., 1985. x + 182 pp.

Investigates how "the different kinds of action are called together and made meaningful by dramatic texts," in this case by Sh's major tragedies.

Chapter 6, on *Ant.*, views the play as "centrally about greatness," defined as "a command over other people's imagination." Inventories the audiences for greatness: the onstage audience; "the entire known world" to whom the protagonists play; the "timeless, superhuman audience, the heroes of history and legend and the gods themselves"; and posterity, "of whom we in the theater are a part." Calls attention to the play's sense of constant renewal; its concern with display and reports; its focus on the charismatic presence of its two main actors and their attraction for each other; its insistence on ordinary or questionable things being transformed into or *becoming* "valuable and enduring entities"; its use of vertical imagery to show how the low is renewed and enriched so that it becomes high; its distinctive "mixture of glamor and demystification." Notes that here Sh "found a subject that richly indulged the ambiguity of the poet's position, a story that both challenged the claims of raw imaginative power and seductively breathed them forth."

Chapter 7, "Characterizing Coriolanus," is a revision of item 1647.

0448 Goldman, Michael. *Shakespeare and the Energies of Drama*. Princeton: Princeton U. P., 1972. ix + 176 pp.

Chapter 2 explores the treatment of the "unsounded self" in *Ven.*, *Luc.* and *Son.* In *Ven.*, Adonis is presented as a narcissistic, self-sufficient adolescent, resistant to the complications of experience. It is only under the stress of action that such complacency is challenged. In *Luc.*, the emphasis on crowds of people in the painting of Troy that Lucrece beholds suggests the multiplicity of personae within the individual. Lucrece, at the end, becomes another self, no longer simply a victim but now a motive to political action.

Chapter 8, "Coriolanus and the Crowd," argues that the rhythm of action in *Cor.* is driven by the relationship of the protagonist with the mob: Throughout the play, the crowd alternates swiftly and regularly from attacking Coriolanus to adoring him. This pattern gives the play its rough energy and prevents it from being monotonous.

0449 Goodale, Geoffrey Chartres. "Black Spirits and White: Shakespeare's Use of Goetic and Theurgic Tradition in *Macbeth* and *The Tempest*." Ph.D. dissertation, Boston University, 1975. *DAI*, 35 (1974–75), 7865-A.

Examines the Elizabethan and Jacobean notions of black and white magic (goety and theurgy) and provides interpretations of *Mac.* and *Tmp.* based on these occult systems. Especially important for an understanding of Sh's exploration of theurgy in *Tmp.* are the Neoplatonic and hermetic traditions.

0450 Goodman, Alice. "Falstaff and Socrates." *English* (London), 34 (1985), 97–112.

Maintains that in *1&2H4* and *H5* Falstaff's role is "essentially Socratic" and that the relationship between Falstaff and Prince Henry is derived from that of Socrates and Alcibiades. Notes that an account of Socrates' death, the model for Falstaff's, appeared in Earl Rivers's *Dictes and Sayings of the Philosophers* (1477). Falstaff's teaching of the young Prince is Socratic in that it inculcates "mastery of language" and "knowledge of the self." Discovers in Aristophanes' *Clouds* the source for the imprudent Socrates, whose acquaintance Sh would have made in Erasmus's *The Praise of Folly*. In his *Adages* (1515), Erasmus provided Sh with an image of the Aristophanic Socrates superimposed on that of Plato. Plutarch's *Life of Alcibiades* seems to have furnished Sh with much material that either confirmed or supplemented his English source (*The Famous Victories of Henry the Fifth*), including parallels to Prince Hal's changeability, his boxing of the Lord Chief Justice's ear and their reconciliation, and the usefulness of the friendship with Falstaff in realizing Hal's ambitions. Notes that the "conjunction of comedy, history, and tragedy" in Sir John Oldcastle's posthumous life is precisely congruent to the shape and composition of the posthumous life of Socrates." Emphasizes that the moral and rhetorical education to which Sh would have been exposed was "conceived of with reference to Socratic philosophy."

0451 Entry deleted.

0452 Gourlay, Patricia Southard. "Shakespeare's Use of North's Plutarch in the Roman Plays, with Special Reference to *Julius Caesar*." Ph.D. dissertation, Columbia University, 1969. *DAI*, 31 (1970–71), 1757-A.

Argues that in his Roman plays Sh explores the possibility of "Roman" values as he found them in Plutarch. To Plutarch, justice is the greatest virtue: It means selfless devotion to the state. He condemns personal ambition because it encourages flattery and envy. Plutarch's morality is heavily indebted to Stoicism, but though he admires Stoic principles, he perceives that the exercise of such principles can be untimely for the corrupt age in which they are practiced.

In *JC*, Sh changes his source material to reflect Plutarchan ambivalence. Brutus's sense of justice is heightened, but the gap between his virtue and reality is also widened. Images of role-playing convey the relationship between the ideal self-images of Caesar and Brutus and a destructive reality. Sh's two later Roman plays reveal greater opposition to Plutarchan idealism. In *Ant.*, Plutarch's ethic is distorted and fragmented in the Roman judgment of Antony; it is countered by Cleopatra's romantic idealization. Plutarch condemns Cleopatra's flattery of Antony, but Sh enables her to triumph in her final role-playing, the transforming vision of her lover. In *Cor.*, Sh presents the protagonist's severity as the performance of a diseased ideal for a diseased society. Though Sh, in the Roman plays, calls attention to "the self-delusion of Plutarchan idealism," he does remind us of the noble potential to which humanity lays claim.

0452a Grabes, Herbert. "'Glassy Essence': Shakespeare's Mirrors and Their Contextualization." *HUSL*, 9 (1981), 175–95.

Attempts to explain how Sh "handles the mirror in imagistic or metaphorical contexts." In one type of contextualization, the mirror undergoes an extension of meaning; an example occurs in *Ant.*, in which initially Mark Antony is a mirror for Caesar, and then the death of Mark Antony becomes a mirror of the fall of princes for Caesar. Another type of contextualization, seen in the lament of the ageing Lucretius for his daughter (*Luc.*, 1751–1764), is achieved by developing "the details of one mirror–convention that dominates an array of other conventions in such a way as to support the thematic tenor." Revised as a section of item 0452b.

0452b Grabes, Herbert. *The Mutable Glass: Mirror–Imagery in Titles and Texts of the Middle Ages and English Renaissance.* Revised and augmented ed. Tr. from the German by Gordon Collier. Cambridge: Cambridge U. P., 1982. xvi + 414 pp.

Proposes to study the central image or metaphor of the mirror in English literature from the 13th to the 17th c. Includes a bibliography of primary references that lists Sh's works and keys them to endnotes in the text. Covers Sh in a section of chapter 10, emphasizing his originality in using the conventional mirror image in new and individual contexts. This section is a revision of item 0452a.

0453 Grace, William J. *Approaching Shakespeare.* New York: Basic Books, 1964. 248 pp.

Seeks to introduce the reader to "the mind of Shakespeare" Chapter 2, "The Tragic Image," uses Aristotelian notions of pity, fear, and catharsis to analyze Sh's tragedies. Chapter 6, "Ideas in Sh," includes sections on "Sh and Renaissance Psychology" (on the elements and the humors); "Sh and the Preternatural" (on, among other things, the Pythagorean, Stoic, and Platonic elements in Elizabethan spirit lore); "The Humanist Ideal" (primarily on *The Book of the Courtier* and its influence); "Platonism in Sh" (on Sh's use and modification of the concepts of transcendent form, macrocosm, and microcosm); and "Sh's View of History" (Sh's "inclusiveness and impartiality" can be seen in *JC*).

0454 Graham, Kenneth John Emerson. "The Performance of Conviction: Anti-Rhetorical Plainness from Wyatt to Shakespeare." Ph.D. dissertation, U. of California, Berkeley, 1990. *DAI*, 51 (1990–91), 3082-A.

Treats the paradoxical nature of "rhetorical anti-rhetoricism" in Renaissance culture. This is a result of the essentialist desire to speak private truth publicly. Sh, in *Tim.* and *Cor.*, "portrays the anger and isolation of proud plainness as the self-consuming consequences of the desire to be absolute."

0455 Greaves, Margaret. *The Blazon of Honour: A Study in Renaissance Magnanimity.* London: Methuen, 1964. 142 pp.

Locates the origin of the concept of the Magnanimous Man in Aristotle's *Ethics* and, in an introductory chapter, shows how certain Christian accretions came to be added to the concept during the Middle Ages. Maintains that the idea is relevant to several of Sh's characters: Antony, Coriolanus, Brutus, Henry V, Armado, Hector, and Troilus.

0456 Green, David C. *Plutarch Revisited: A Study of Shakespeare's Last Roman Tragedies and Their Source.* (*JDS* 78.) Salzburg: Institut für Anglistik und Amerikanistik, U. Salzburg, 1979. iii + 280 pp.

Contends that Sh's last two Roman plays are superior to *JC* in their use of Plutarch. In *JC*, the best parts are those most completely Sh's (for example, Cassius's temptation of Brutus and Brutus's orchard soliloquy), while the weakest are those most directly drawn from the source. In *Ant.* and *Cor.*, Sh was more skillful at transforming Plutarch into great drama (memorable passages, like Enobarbus's Cydnus speech and Cominius's belly fable, have their originals in the source). Sh often altered Plutarch's sequence of events (both *Ant.* and *Cor.* begin in the middle of the source's account). Nevertheless, the source's digressive narrative style encouraged him to include details from the characters' lives before the action of the play takes place. In a study of this sort, one should read the source and then see what Sh does with it, instead of reading into the source an impression gained from the play.

0457 Green, Rosemary M. "The Treasure Chest of the Mind: Uses of Memory in Sidney, Shakespeare, and Renaissance Lyric Poetry." Ph.D. dissertation, Boston University, 1976. *DAI*, 37 (1976–77), 1563-A.

Points out that Renaissance poets regarded memory as "a treasure chest of images" that might serve three artistic purposes: (1) to idealize, (2) to moralize and teach, and (3) to "eternize." The idealizing notion was derived from Plato's theory that man retains vague memories of ideal forms; the eternizing idea came from Cicero's belief that history is "living memory." Sh, like the Neoplatonists, stresses the mind's capacity to control circumstances and to "replenish itself as nature does." Memory is used in his works as metaphor for intellectual and spiritual continuity. In the protagonist of *Ham.*, "memory dominates perception," but in other works (*Son.*, *H5*, and *WT*), memory is a way to seize and eternize "abstract values and ideal forms for the future."

0458 Greenberg, Robert David. "The Image of the Devouring Beast: Its Dramatic Use in Selected Works of Shakespeare." Ph.D. dissertation, University of California, Berkeley, 1968. *DA*, 29 (1968–69), 4487-A.

Views the image of the devouring beast in Sh's early works as a way to make dramatic statements about characters; in the later works, this sort of image helps form "symbolic actions that allusively run alongside literal plots." In *Ven.*, Venus argues for natural feeding, and the boar, "an aggressive feeder," slays Adonis. Tarquin, in *Luc.*, is characterized by this image. *Tro.* uses images of devouring beasts to show how men become separated from each other and themselves through pride. In *Cor.*, similar images indicate the hero's separation from his friends and enemies.

0459 Greene, James J. "A Contemporary Approach to Two Shakespearean Tragedies." *How to Read Shakespearean Tragedy.* Ed. Edward Quinn. New York: Harper & Row, 1978, pp. 355–85.

Devotes, in section 8 of the book, a chapter each to *JC* and *Cor.* Regards the first play as a critical examination and, finally, an indictment of the masculine world of Rome, which privileges patriarchal tradition, martial prowess, honor, and economy of speech, and is disgusted by physical weakness and sickness. Through the character of Portia and her emphasis on the conjugal bed from which Brutus has stolen so ungently, we see how the Roman world is to be judged. She attempts to give Brutus a chance to escape "the male cult of violence and death," but she fails, and they are both destroyed. *Cor.* is another devastating critique of the Roman "myth of masculinity." In this play, manhood is not seen as something one achieves permanently at a given time but rather as an unstable condition that must be continually reestablished by deeds of heroism. As a result, the protagonist never achieves manhood, but "remains a confused and enraged adolescent dominated by a grotesque mother." For Coriolanus, heterosexual love is subordinated to the murderous fellowship of soldiering. Notes that the play's disapproval of war is reinforced by the unintentionally ironic praise of military action by Aufidius's clownish servants in IV.v. The end of the play, with Coriolanus's death in the midst of yet another adolescent frenzy and Aufidius's hypocritical eulogy, provides us with "our final ironic glimpse of the heroic tradition."

0460   Greenfield, Thelma N. "Nonvocal Music: Added Dimension in Five Shakespeare Plays." *Pacific Coast Studies in Shakespeare*. Eds. Waldo F. McNeir and Thelma N. Greenfield. Eugene, Oregon: U. of Oregon Books, 1966, pp. 106–21.

Examines Sh's use of the varieties of nonvocal music. In certain "lyrical and meditative passages," Sh's nonvocal music "unites with both language and action and often relates to characters as well." In *R2* and *MV*, music comes late in the plot. As he meditates on his duty, the needs of his country, and his mistakes, Richard is prompted by music he actually hears (*R2*, V.v). Lorenzo's speeches on harmony in *MV* (V.i) belong to the *laudes musicae* tradition inherited from the ancients through Renaissance Neoplatonism. The music heard for forty-two lines is "an auditory symbol of the universal harmonies sensed by human beings in special moments when their perceptions are refined by the proper environment and mood." *Cor.* is full of music used for "signal and ceremonial effects": It depicts the "noise and progress" of battle, the formality of the proceedings for making Coriolanus a consul, and the short-lived hero-worship of the people. Treats music in *Ham.* and *Lr.* as well.

0461   Greenwood, John Philip Peter. "The Mannerist Shakespeare." Ph.D. dissertation, University of Toronto, 1983. *DAI*, 44 (1983–84), 2771-A.

Notes that "the art that mocks, conceals, and elaborates art is clearly realized in Shakespeare's Jacobean canon as a learned, self-conscious, and highly artificial new art form." Sh's mannerist display varies in intensity, being quite deliberate in *Tim.* and pronounced in *Ant.*

0462   Greer, Germaine. *Shakespeare*. (Past Masters.) Oxford: Oxford U. P., 1986. 136 pp.

Approaches Sh through chapters entitled "Life," "Poetics," "Ethics," "Politics," "Teleology," and "Sociology." The first chapter includes comments about the compliment paid to Sh by Francis Meres, who compares him favorably to Ovid and the Roman playwrights, and about *PhT*, "the most perfect statement of the Platonic ideal in English poetry." The chapter on poetics provides a classical genealogy for Hamlet's remarks to the players (*Ham.*, III.ii) and adduces *Tmp.* as "the nearest thing to a systematic exposition of Shakespeare's poetic." Chapter 4, on politics, calls *Tro.* Sh's "anti-history."

0463   Gregson, J. M. *Public and Private Man in Shakespeare*. London: Croom Helm, 1983. 255 pp.

Explores, in most of Sh's plays, the tension between the private and the public. Chapter 3 includes an analysis of *Tro.*, a problem play whose theme of conflict between private and public aspirations is pursued with "obscure diction," "passionate and intellectually demanding love poetry," "occasional legal jokes," and "obliquity of intentions." All of this suggests that it may have been intended for an Inns of Court audience. The play seems to be chiefly satiric in tone, though its "confusing mixture of styles" and lack of character development are serious weaknesses. Chapter 8 is devoted to "The Roman Plays." Notes that in *JC* Antony is the only man who is able to unite "private feeling with public action"; that in *Ant.* the protagonists' growing preoccupation with "the quality of their love" is paralleled by "a merciless commentary" on Antony's political collapse; and that in *Cor.* the conflict between the hero's adolescent private self and the tawdry political life of Rome is not as moving as the private–public oppositions in Sh's greatest tragedies.

0464 Grene, David. *The Actor in History: A Study in Shakespearean Stage Poetry*. University Park: Pennsylvania State U. P., 1988. ix + 158 pp.

Considers Sh's histrionicism—the tendency of a character's poetry "to substitute its independent or nearly independent values" for the "meaning" of the actor with regard to his role—in several history plays, including *Ant.*, *JC*, and *Cor.* Chooses to treat the three Plutarchan plays to contrast this histrionicism with "known historical deeds." Chapter 1, "*Antony and Cleopatra*: The Triumph of Fantasy," shows how the protagonists incorporate their sense of acting and staging into their lives and deaths: Through the mystery of their dramatic self-representation, they create a world that transcends history. Chapter 4, "English and Roman History: A Contrast," notes that "the pursuit of power is a much more convincing key to all the action and its consequences" in the Roman plays than in the English histories. When the Roman leader fails, it is usually because his broadly prescriptive role conflicts with "the definition of the actual political situation." Chapter 5, "Brutus and Coriolanus: Political Failures," notes that both men have private qualities that others seek to use for political purposes. Unable to sustain the political roles demanded of them, they are destroyed.

0464a Griffin, Jasper. The Mirror of Myth: Classical Themes and Variations. London: Faber and Faber, 1986. 144 pp.

Includes several references to Sh's works to illustrate variations on classical themes and genres. Chapter 2, "The Apotheosis of Pleasure," uses *Ant.* as a supreme example of godlike celebration of sensuous pleasure by humans who achieve mythic proportions. Lorenzo's speech on the music of the spheres (*MV*, V.i) shows mortal beings aspiring "to the pleasures of the gods of philosophy, sensuous and intellectual at once." Chapter 3, "The Endurance of Pain," describes "the spectacular suicide of defeated greatness" as part of Sh's inheritance from classical myth, though more Roman than Greek. Cites the suicides of Brutus and Cassius (*JC*), Antony and Cleopatra (*Ant.*), and Othello (*Oth.*); Horatio's desire to commit suicide (*Ham.*); and the death of Coriolanus (*Cor.*). Notes that the suicide for love, treated seriously in *Rom.* and burlesqued in *MND*, is also an important classical theme. Notes that the endings of many Shakespearean tragedies, in avoiding funerals, reflect an awareness of the problem posed for the tragic vision by Christianity. The passion and violence that characterize the Greek reaction to death is absent, but so are the resignation and hope offered by the Christian funeral. Finds that greatness of soul is shared by Greek figures like Oedipus and Antigone and Sh's Othello and Lear. The fourth chapter, "Heroism, Epic and Forgiveness," calls attention to the slight value placed on forgiveness and reconciliation in Greek literature. Refers to several of Sh's works in which forgiveness plays a major part, placing emphasis on *JC*, *Ant.*, and *Cor.*, all of which were modified to include reconciliations not in their source, Plutarch's *Lives*. As an intermediary between the Greeks and Sh, Virgil writes "in such a way that, while remaining within [the] heroic and unforgiving tradition, he draws attention repeatedly to an unsatisfied desire for forgiveness."

0465 Griffin, Robert J. "'These Contraries Such Unity Do Hold': Patterned Imagery in Shakespeare's Narrative Poems." *SEL*, 4 (1964), 43–55.

Begins by citing Coleridge's comments on poetic power in *Ven.* and *Luc.*, and extends some of these comments in analyzing the substructure of the poems. In both, there are several families of imagery that are manipulated so that their interrelationship "contributes significantly to both the complexity and the unity of the poems." The groups of images include red and white, hot and cold, warfare, birds, finance and commerce, weather, and day and night.

0465a Griffith, John William. "Shakespeare's Use of Dramatic Vows." Ph.D. dissertation, University of Pittsburgh, 1978. *DAI*, 40 (1979–80), 2353-A.

Notes the importance that Aristotle (*Rhetoric*) and Cicero (*De Officiis*) assign to vows and proposes to investigate the importance of vows "and the closely related oaths, pledges, and promises" in Sh's plays. Devotes a section to each of four genres: "comedy, tragedy, romance, and history." Observes of *Cor.*, for example, that the protagonist seals his fate by breaking "each of three promises." Comes to a number of conclusions about the rhetorical functions of vows in Sh: Vows "enhance credibility, they precipitate and motivate behavior, they rationalize actions previously taken, and they obligate to future course of action."

0466 Grivelet, Michel. "A Portrait of the Artist as Proteus." *PBA*, 61 (175), 153–70. Reprint. London: Oxford U. P., 1975. 20 pp.

Traces the influence of the myth of Proteus on Sh, beginning with Gloucester's comparison of himself to the classical Old Man of the Sea in *3H6*. The likely source of this idea of Proteus as fraud and seducer is the first book of Ovid's *Art of Love*. Notes Sh's "subtle involvement" with his character Proteus in *TGV*: In his role-playing, concern with constancy to himself, and addiction to soliloquizing, this Proteus is a man of the theater like Sh and a forerunner of many of the dramatist's major characters. *TGV* also presents in Julia the first of many Shakespearean women to get her man through disguise. Speculates that Sh knew the story of Proteus from the *Odyssey*, provides a detailed summary of this story, and explains its essence: "a myth of change confronted with the claims of identity and truth." Stresses the significance of Proteus for the metamorphoses that take place throughout the Shakespearean canon. Maintains that Sh's daring openness to change should make us all the more determined to wrestle with the protean dramatist for his identity and his meaning.

0467 Grossman, Allen. "Orpheus/Philomela: Subjection and Mastery in the Founding Stories of Poetic Production and in the Logic of Our Practice." *TriQ*, 77 (1989–90), 229–48.

Investigates the paradigm according to which "the subjection of Philomela becomes the mastery of disorder on behalf of general humanity (the audience of song) through the poem of which her metamorphosis is the sign." However, when original poets do not include "the pain of history, then history as representation is no longer within the paradigm of representation." This situation, in which the violence of history exceeds any violence exhibited by the logic of art, was addressed by Sh in his first analyses of the Philomela story. Comments on *MND*, *Rom.*, and especially *Tit.*, where Lavinia represents Sh's most profound use of the Philomela story. Like her prototype, Lavinia is raped, but her violators, familiar with the original myth, cut off her hands to prevent her from recapitulating it exactly. By "jostling" young Lucius's copy of Ovid, Lavinia uses Philomela to help reveal what has happened to her.

0468 Gruber, William E. "The Polarization of Tragedy and Comedy." *Genre*, 13 (1980), 259–74.

Contends that classification of comedy into separate types like Old and New is misleading, as is the assumption that comedy and tragedy are entirely distinct. Instead, the two genres should be seen as opposing representations of "the same fundamental reality." In Aeschylus, Sophocles, and Euripides, human action is shaped by the pressures of time. Sh returns to this conception: His tragic victims (Richard II, Antony, Hamlet, Lear, Macbeth, and Brutus) all misuse or misunderstand time. Comedy, on the other hand, is concerned with redeeming time, lessening its grip on audience and characters, either directly (as in Aristophanes) or indirectly (as in New Comedy). Sh's comedies also reflect this escape from time's constraints, most notably in the late romances. As one example, *WT* has the figure of Time, in a choral scene resembling the *parabasis* of Old Comedy, ask the audience's indulgence for omitting sixteen years of the story.

0469   Grudin, Robert. *Mighty Opposites: Shakespeare and Renaissance Contrariety*. Berkeley: U. of California P., 1979. vi + 217 pp.

Proposes to investigate the importance of contrariety—"the idea that experience derives from the interaction of opposing forces"—in Sh's works. Notes that "the interaction of contraries is one of the major issues of Renaissance thought" and that Sh made profound use of opposites in his language, his portrayal of human psychology, his vision of human experience, his structuring of drama, and his "treatment of theme and ideology." Chapter 2 discusses three 16th-c. thinkers—Castiglione, Paracelsus, and Bruno—who assimilated and promoted the principles of contrariety in especially significant ways. These advocates of dualism acknowledged Plato and Heraclitus as their intellectual progenitors. Succeeding chapters consider works throughout the canon. Chapter 4 includes a discussion of *Tro.*, in which Ulysses' celebrated speech on degree acknowledges contrariety and subverts rather than confirms the traditional notion of social order founded on natural law. Chapter 5 contains an analysis of *Ant.*, in which Sh combines "two schemes of contraries [tragedy and comedy]" to create "his closest approach to encompassing in art the dazzling miscellany of experience." Part of chapter 4 is a revision of item 2891.

0470   Grund, Gary R. "Rhetoric as Metaphor: Some Notes on Dramatic Method." *EA*, 33 (1980), 282-95.

Describes the two forms of classical rhetoric—the disputation and the declamation—and notes that the Elizabethan educational program incorporated both. Focuses on the disputation, a form of debate based on the classical *controversia* "and probably suggested by the widespread use of the colloquies of Erasmus and Vives." Of especial interest is *antipophora*, a rhetorical figure designated by Cicero, Quintilian, and Seneca as "an essential tool in disputation" and defined as "a reasoning with oneself by means of questions and answers or an answer to imaginary objections." Points to instances in which Sh uses *antipophora* (especially in *1H4* and *Ham.*) and shows how the figure enables the playwright to explore the problematic nature of language's capacity to represent truth. The appropriation of *antipophora* illustrates how an Elizabethan dramatist could "adapt the tradition of rhetoric to the demands of fiction."

0471   Gura, Timothy James. "The Function of the Hero in Shakespeare's Last Tragedies." Ph.D. dissertation, Northwestern University, 1974. *DAI*, 35 (1974-75), 3681-A.

Analyzes the heroes of *Tim.*, *Ant.*, and *Cor.* in light of Sh's earlier tragic heroes. Before Timon, the hero is an eminent man who is ruined because of a deliberate moral choice he makes in a world "whose ultimate order we approve." With Timon, we encounter the ambiguous hero who "asserts absolutes in an equivocal and finite world." Antony discovers all of himself, revealing a love that ennobles as it destroys; he makes no change in his world. Coriolanus attempts to be all of himself and is destroyed because he has to deny some of his principles. The flexible world in which he tries to operate is indifferent.

0472   Guthke, Karl S. *Modern Tragicomedy: An Investigation into the Nature of the Genre*. New York: Random House, 1966. xviii + 204 pp.

Presents modern tragicomic drama as a post-Enlightenment development. Chapter 1, however, does contain a section, "Historical Concepts," which provides information on the classical antecedents of tragicomedy in theory and practice (Plautus, Cicero, Horace, Aristotle) and their appropriation by Renaissance critics and dramatists.

Cites Sh frequently as a forerunner in exploring the mode of tragicomedy. For example, *Tro.* places a potentially tragic figure in a comic environment, and *Ant.* "combines two parallel plots of equal weight, one tragic, one comic."

0473   Guthrie, Tyrone. *In Different Directions: A View of Theatre.* New York: Macmillan, 1969. 221 pp.

Compares *Cor.* with its source in Plutarch's *Lives*: Plutarch's Coriolanus, for example, is more intractable than Sh's; and Sh makes Aufidius and the mother of Coriolanus more important than they are in Plutarch. Comments on the play's action, noting the different moods of the three meetings between Coriolanus and Aufidius and the domineering qualities of Volumnia as a mother. Points out that *JC* is about the death of Caesar and its aftermath and that the play's plot is distinguished from the theme. *JC* juxtaposes "political and military disintegration" with "the personal disintegration of Brutus."

0474   Hackett, Michael Joseph III. "*Cymbeline* and the Late Plays: Shakespeare's Use of Dramatic Structure." Ph.D. dissertation, Stanford University, 1981. *DAI*, 42 (1981–82), 2141-A.

Chapter 3 discusses the Neoplatonic philosophy of King James's court as it relates to "the early Baroque esthetics of action." Uses examples from *WT* and *Tmp.* to show how poetry and action are integrated in Sh's late plays.

0475   Hager, Alan. *Shakespeare's Political Animal: Schema and Schemata in the Canon.* Newark: U. of Delaware P., 1990. 164 pp.

Chapter 5, "'The Teeth of Emulation': Failed Sacrifice in Shakespeare's *Julius Caesar*," is a revision of item 2009. The epilogue, "Ulysses' Political Thoughts and Action in Reverse," argues that in *Tro.* Ulysses reverses the process of dissolution and decay among the Greeks and eventually reestablishes their identity. Sh thus "displaces all tragic elements in his Greek subplot and makes them comic."

0476   Hale, John K. "Can the *Poetics* of Aristotle Aid the Interpretation of Shakespeare's Comedies?" *Antichthon* (Sydney), 19 (1985), 16–31.

Begins by finding that two of Aristotle's chief concerns—his belief that plot (*mythos*) is more important than character (*ethos*) and "his preference for complex over simple plots"—are helpful in interpreting some of the the central features of *MV*. Proceeds to examine Sh's first ten comedies, ending with *TN*, in the light of Aristotle's observations on complex plots.

0477   Hale, John R. *The Art of War and Renaissance England.* Washington, D.C.: The Folger Shakespeare Library, 1961. 59 pp.

Reproduces a number of pages from various 16th-and 17th-c. works on war printed in England, with a one-page commentary on each. Includes the title page from John Bingham's translation of *The Tactics of Aelian* (1616). Explains that the examples of the ancients had considerable influence in the period and names other classical military writers whose works were translated into English at that time.

0478   Halio, Jay L. "The Metaphor of Conception and Elizabethan Theories of the Imagination." *Neophil*, 50 (1966), 454–61.

Traces the metaphor of conception back to Plato and explains its place in the faculty psychology of the Renaissance. Argues that Renaissance writers used the metaphor to express their understanding of "the shaping power of the imagination" for both good and evil. Sh relies on the metaphor to describe the operation of Ulysses' mind when dealing with Hector's challenge (*Tro.*, I.iii). In *Oth.*, the destructive force of the imagination is conveyed through the image of conception. See item 2896.

0479 Hall, Anne Drury. "Tudor Prose Style: English Humanists and the Problem of a Standard." *ELR*, 7 (1977), 267–96.

Points out that during the 16th c., English humanists were trying to develop a standard of speech that was sophisticated enough to assimilate the classical intellectual tradition. However, the rules of the classical rhetoricians Cicero and Quintilian, which many invoked during the Inkhorn controversy about importing strange foreign words into ordinary English contexts, emphasized the need for great caution in borrowing words from other languages and were thus largely inapplicable to the fast-changing vernacular. Latinate borrowings were not a serious problem when they were used for technical precision or in unusual figures of diction like Lear's "shake the superflux" and Macbeth's "multitudinous seas incarnadine." They caused difficulty when writers like Elyot tried to use them as proper words, that is, words suited to their context in urbane, unself-conscious discourse. Although Elyot was unable to prevent his Inkhorn terms from calling attention to themselves, he attempted to enfranchise them by including definitions in the text. In contrast to this cautious liberalism, the rhetoricians (Puttenham, Wilson) were generally opposed to borrowing. Sensitive discussions of borrowing are found not in the rule books (rhetorics), but in essays, prefaces, and commonplace books.

0480 Hall, Marie Boas. "Scientific Thought." *ShS*, 17 (1964), 138–51.

Explains that the basis for the widespread acceptance of astrology in Sh's day lay in the credence accorded to Aristotelian cosmology, Christianized and modernized. To Sh, as to others, "alchemy was a natural corollary to astrology." Cartography flourished in the 16th c., having been revived in the early 15th c. by the rediscovery of Ptolemy's geographical writings, and Sh shows an awareness of the new map-making. The theory and terminology of the four elements, ultimately derived from ancient Greek physiology, occur as commonplaces in Sh's work.

0481 Hall, Michael. *The Structure of Love: Representational Patterns and Shakespeare's Love Tragedies*. Charlottesville: U. P. of Virginia, 1989. xxi + 189 pp.

Assumes certain "standard readings" for several of Sh's works and proposes to explain "how the texts push us towards them." Chapter 6 discovers three distinctive "love types" in *Tro*. The first is the Ascetic type, whose spokesmen are Pandarus and Thersites, and which holds that all pretensions to love are merely attempts to put a gloss on animal lust. The second type is Petrarchan, whose premise is that "proper love results in increased honor." The presentation of this type in the play is ambiguous, with Troilus appearing alternatively as a true Petrarchan lover and as a parody of one. The combination and opposition of the Ascetic and Petrarchan types are used to view Cressida and Hector, as well as other characters. The third type of love is the Epic, whose chief spokesman is Ulysses. Discusses the Epic approach to life in terms of honor and, in this connection, analyzes Achilles, the Trojan council scene (II.ii), and Hector. Sh mercilessly undermines the two chief ways (the Petrarchan and the Epic) of "attaching honor to some human actions."

Chapter 7 considers *Ant*. in terms of four types of love: the Ascetic, the Etherealized, the Epic, and the Emasculating. Argues that the play "never conclusively discredits any of its four types, and thus never allows us a confident perspective from which to define the characters and actions before us."

0482 Halliday, F. E. "Reade Him, Therefore." *Stratford Papers on Shakespeare 1964*. Ed. B. W. Jackson. Toronto: W. J. Gage, 1965, pp. 90–134.

Surveys Sh's works with an emphasis on poetic style. Mentions the clarity and simplicity of *JC* and the obtrusive Latinisms in *Tro*. Jonson, when satirizing Marston in *The Poetaster*, may have been glancing at the style of *Tro*. as well: The words Crispinus is forced to vomit up are much the same as some of those in Sh's play. The sounds of the verse in *Ant*. create a sense of light, spaciousness, and grandeur.

0483 Halliday, F. E. *Shakespeare*. New York: Thomas Yoseloff, 1961. x + 248 pp.

Makes brief comments on Sh's works while filling in "the gaps between the beads of biographical fact." Describes the importance of Latin and Latin authors in the grammar school Sh would have attended and explains how Sh's experiences as a schoolboy may underlie various uses of Latin in *Wiv.*, *Shr.*, and *LLL*. Points out the influence of Ovid's *Metamorphoses* on *Luc.*, *Ven.*, *Tit.*, and *Tmp.*, and mentions the debt of *Tim.*, *JC*, *Cor.*, and *Ant.* to Plutarch's *Lives*.

0484 Hamilton, A. C. *The Early Shakespeare*. San Marino, California: Huntington Library, 1967. ix + 237 pp.

Views twleve of Sh's early works individually (with a chapter on each) and as a group (by constant reference to their relationships). Chapter 4 (a revision of item 2734) argues that Ovid's *Metamorphoses* gave Sh the pattern for his presentation of fallen nature. Chapter 5 analyzes Sh's modification of his Plautine original for *Err.* in terms of Aristotle's comments on dramatic plot in the *Poetics*. The play illustrates Aristotle's precepts that "the change in fortune that resolves the action —here the meeting of the two brothers—should involve recognition combined with peripety, and that both should result from the construction of the plot." Chapter 8 is a revision of item 3130. Chapter 9 maintains that Sh's treatment of the story of Lucrece is comprehensive and compares it to partial or abbreviated versions in Ovid's *Fasti*, Painter's translation of Livy, and Chaucer's *Legend of Good Women*. In developing the legend, Sh explores three moral states: "Tarquin's agony of lust as he contemplates his intent to rape Lucrece, the private guilt within Lucrece as she suffers for his sin, and the public shame that she seeks to avoid through her suicide."

0485 Hammer, Letha Ann Graves. "Shakespeare's Historical Epic." Ph.D. dissertation, Texas Tech University, 1987. *DAI*, 48 (1987–88), 1210-A.

Reviews the body of critical theory that shaped Renaissance thinking about the epic. Begins with a consideration of the ideas of Aristotle and Horace and then discusses the "improvements" on the classical model advanced by Cinthio, Trissino, Tasso, Castelvetro, and Minturno. The Italian theories were adapted to the English epic by Sir Philip Sidney and Edmund Spenser. Sh's two York–Lancaster tetralogies exhibit the qualities of the Elizabethan epic, including classical form.

0486 Hammersmith, James Philip. "Language and Theme in Shakespeare's Plays." Ph.D. dissertation, University of Wisconsin, Milwaukee, 1976. *DAI*, 37 (1976–77), 6497-A.

Investigates Sh's dramatic exploration of the relationship of language to reality, specifically the idea that "language creates reality in the process of defining it." *JC* is a transitional play, in which language is no longer an overt theme but rather helps develop the themes of knowledge and perception. In *Ant.*, Sh turns his attention toward "the specific artistic shape of language."

0487 Hammil, Carrie Esther. "The Celestial Journey and the Harmony of the Spheres in English Literature, 1300–1700." Ph.D. dissertation, Texas Christian University, 1972. *DAI*, 33 (1972–73), 2326-A.

Discusses the interrelationship between the notions of the celestial journey and the harmony of the spheres. The latter idea originated in the "theories of the geocentric cosmology and in the philosophy of the Platonists, Neoplatonists, and early Christian mystics." Fundamental to the articulation of the two notions "are the myths of Er, Pompey, and Scipio" as recounted by Plato, Lucan, and Cicero, respectively. In several plays, Sh made use of these two concepts, "especially with respect to harmony as order."

0488 Hankins, John Erskine. *Backgrounds of Shakespeare's Thought*. Hamden, Connecticut: Archon, 1978. 296 pp.

Attempts to elucidate the connections between Sh's works and his reading, focusing on the fields of science and philosophy. The introduction summarizes what Sh read in Latin, including translations he may also have used. Lists poets (for example, Ovid, Virgil, Lucretius, Palingenius); prose writers (Cicero, Seneca, Macrobius, Erasmus); Greek philosophers (Plato, Aristotle, Plutarch); and some works of Marsilio Ficino (including Ficino's translation of Plato). Comments on nearly every play in the canon in the course of chapters on "The Universal World," "Numbers," "The Psychology of Perception," "The Unsettled Humors," "The Human Condition," "The Ascent of Man," and "The Conduct of Man."

0489   Hanna, Sara. "Shakespeare's Greek Plays." Ph.D. dissertation, Indiana University, 1985. *DAI*, 46 (1985–86), 3040-A.

Proposes to study Sh's three Greek plays, *Tim.*, *Tro.*, and *Per.*, with the purpose of understanding the playwright's conception of Greek culture and of distinguishing his Greeks from his Romans. Surveys, in an introductory chapter, the sources of Sh's "knowledge of Greek language, literature, and history." Uses this background for interpreting *Ven.* and the three Greek plays. Comments also on "Greek features in the other plays with Greek settings": *Err.*, *MND*, *WT*, and *TNK*.

0490   Hansen, Abby Jane Dubman. "Shakespeare and the Lore of Precious Stones." *CollL*, 4 (1977), 210–19.

Mentions the role of classical and Hellenistic authors (like Pliny) in transmitting the complex lapidary tradition to the Renaissance and to Sh. Cites Duke Senior's reference to the toadstone (supposed to be an antidote to poison) in *AYL* and the name of Sir Topas (associated with the topaz, a moonstone) in *TN*. Discusses at greater length the diamond (thought to protect the worthy recipient from demons and to insure marital harmony) that Duncan sends to Lady Macbeth (*Mac.*, II.i), pointing out the irony of the gift. In *Oth.*, the protagonist, after murdering Desdemona, refers to the chrysolite, a gem described by Hellenistic lapidaries as conferring on its possessor most of the virtues that seemed to distinguish Othello before he was crippled by his suspicions. The chrysolite's powers to guarantee justice, to bestow intelligence, and to conquer devils are also pertinent in view of Othello's failures in precisely these areas. Ariel's song to Ferdinand in *Tmp.* (I.ii) about the apparent drowning of Alonso can be seen as "a song of magical comfort" if one recognizes the beneficent qualities traditionally associated with pearl and coral.

0491   Hanson, John Arthur. "The Glorious Military." *Roman Drama*. Eds. T. A. Dorey and Donald R. Dudley. New York: Basic Books, 1965, pp. 51–85.

Discusses the features of the *miles gloriosus* in Roman drama, especially in Plautus, and follows the development of the character in selected later works. Takes issue with critics who, following Maurice Morgann, deny that Falstaff is a representative of the type. This is an error based on misunderstanding of the Plautine *miles*, who resembles Falstaff, for example, in his extravagant lies. Falstaff is also like the *miles* of Plautus in being detached from the central action of the play. He concentrates in himself "the theme of the vanity of honor and military glory which is crucially relevant to the central action and reiterated in other characters." He has a wider range than that of any *miles* in Plautus, and in this resembles the Plautine slave. But he is a greater character than either braggart or slave, partly because he is not placed in a comic context.

0492   Hapgood, Robert. "Shakespeare's Maimed Rites." *CentR*, 9 (1965), 494–508.

Contends that in Sh's mature tragedies, the audience experiences hope that the sacrifice of life will achieve the purifying and regenerative effects of ritual. At the same time, Sh qualifies this hope by emphasizing "the unregenerate way things are." The early tragedies show the playwright experimenting with works in which total success for the sacrifice is claimed (for example, *Tit.*) and those in which its utter failure is recorded (*JC*). In *Tit.*, "the mythic dimensions" of the transformation said to be effected by the return of Lucius are extensively developed, but the characters are not well enough individualized for us to care. In *JC*, Sh creates a tragic community whose savior does not come. Caesar seems groomed to play the role of sacrificial redeemer, but then this role is undermined. Brutus sees himself as a savior performing a sacrifice but fails to recognize that he himself must be a scapegoat.

0493   Haponski, William Charles. "Shakespeare's Ambiguous Heroes: A Study of Shakespeare's Dramatic Method Which Provokes Ambivalent Response to his Mature Comedy and Tragedy." Ph.D. dissertation, Cornell University, 1967. *DA*, 28 (1967–68), 3670-A.

Defines the ambiguous Shakespearean hero as one who is placed in situations demanding our judgment, but to whom our response is finally ambivalent. Focuses on four such characters: Troilus, Bertram, Coriolanus, and Timon. In the first case, ambivalence is a proper response because the play in which he appears is itself perfectly and calculatedly ambiguous. Coriolanus is a man whose "chief vice, pride in personal accomplishment, is also his chief virtue." Timon's duality of character evokes an ambivalent response as well.

0494   Harbage, Alfred. "Intrigue in Elizabethan Tragedy." *Essays on Shakespeare and Elizabethan Drama in Honor of Hardin Craig*. Ed. Richard Hosley. Columbia: U. of Missouri P., 1962, pp. 37–44.

Points out that intrigue, one of the distinctive features of Elizabethan tragedy, was introduced to Elizabethan drama by Thomas Kyd in *The Spanish Tragedy*. The appearance of a trickster in tragedies of Sh's time seems to owe more to the comedies of Plautus and Terence than to classical tragedy. Sh's Roman plays (*JC*, *Cor.*, and *Ant.*) are classical in the sense that, unlike *Oth.* and *Ham.*, they do not contain intrigue.

0495   Harbage, Alfred. *William Shakespeare: A Reader's Guide*. New York: Farrar Straus, 1963. xiii + 498 pp.

Attempts to provide a precritical guide, "to encourage attentive reading." Chooses certain representative plays "for extended treatment." In each case, "objective description of the action of each scene" is followed by "a commentary on details in the order in which they appear." Makes brief mention of the way in which Sh appropriates classical mythology in *MND*. Analyzes *JC* as a representative of the Roman plays, calling attention to such things as the dictatorial potential of Caesar, the compromised virtue of Brutus, the malleability of the populace, and the passionate unscrupulousness of Antony. Comments briefly on three "tragedies or classical histories, deriving mainly from Plutarch": *Tim.* (which suffers from an incompatibility "between mood and material"), *Ant.* (which "succeeds in being both glamorous and astringent"), and *Cor.* (which is more intellectual than Sh's other Roman plays and exhibits an "unrelieved somberness of tone"). Notes that for *WT* "the frame of reference is Christian, despite the machinery of the Delphic oracle and the imagery drawn from pagan fertility myths." Mentions the role of classical myth in the masque created by Prospero in *Tmp.*, IV.i.

0496   Harbage, Alfred, general ed. *William Shakespeare: The Complete Works*. (Pelican Shakespeare.) Baltimore: Penguin, 1969. xxx + 1481 pp.

The general introduction includes a section on "The Intellectual and Political Background" by Ernest A. Strathmann that makes brief mention of classical influences on the Elizabethan notions of natural philosophy, cosmology, medicine, and history, and a section on "Shakespeare's Life" by Frank W. Wadsworth that comments on the emphasis on Latin language and literature in the grammar school the poet would have attended.

Includes the revised introductions and texts from the individual volumes of the Pelican Shakespeare, originally issued between 1956 and 1967. Volumes annotated in this bibliography are items 2535, 2643, 2722, 1129, and 1580.

0497   Harder, Helga Irene Kutz. "Right Self-Love as the Fulcrum of Balance in Shakespeare's Plays." Ph.D. dissertation, University of North Carolina at Chapel Hill, 1976. *DAI*, 38 (1977–78), 804-A.

Argues that in his plays Sh identifies proper self-love as "the fulcrum for balancing the antitheses in life." Analyzes four comedies and seven tragedies, including *Tit.* and *Ant.*, both of whose protagonists reject the self-love that would balance the oppositions in their lives.

0498 Harding, D. W. "Women's Fantasy of Manhood: A Shakespearean Theme." *SQ*, 20 (1969), 245–53.

Finds that in several plays, Sh explores the destructive consequences of women's fantasy of manhood for the men on which it is imposed. The most detailed development of this theme is in *Mac.*, but it is also important in *Ant.* and *Cor.* In the former, Cleopatra subverts Antony's authority in the masculine world and encourages his ruinous assumption that he can defeat Caesar while revelling in Egypt. In the latter, Volumnia forces her son to conform to a pattern of heroic arrogance and then unmans him.

0499 Harding, F. J. W. "Fantasy, Imagination and Shakespeare." *BJA*, 4 (1964), 305–20.

Lists various senses in which fantasy, fancy, and imagination are found in Sh. Shows that they are used more in the general sense of "the faculty and power of imagining and forming ideas" than in their other senses. Provides a historical survey of notions of the imagination, treating Plato, Aristotle, Stoic atomists like Lucretius, and Neoplatonists like Plotinus, Augustine, Aquinas, and Boethius. Boethius may have been a source, though not necessarily a direct one, of Sh's "notion of imagination as active rather than merely passive, of Prospero's picture of life here and now as a dream and possibly of Hamlet's intimations of ultimate felicity." But the Renaissance seems to have assimilated the notion of "the generative and shaping power of imagination" primarily through "psychological and medical knowledge," much of it derived ultimately from Galen. Sh appears to have shared with his age a belief that imagination is central to the poet's creative powers, though he did not confine himself to this one sense of the terms associated with it. In addition to the primary sense of "picture-making," he also connected Imagination with "the other traditional and Aristotelian senses" having to do with "motion, passion, mental disturbance, or dream."

0500 Hardison, O. B. "Three Types of Renaissance Catharsis." *RenD*, N. S. 2 (1969), 3–22.

Discovers three types of catharsis—moral, religious, and literal—"recognized by Elizabethan critics and embodied significantly in Elizabethan plays." Moral catharsis is achieved when a criminal sees his crime reenacted on the stage and is driven to confession through his guilt. In *Ham.*, Claudius is offered the opportunity for this type of catharsis but resists it. Religious catharsis involves poetic justice, with the audience given a dramatic imitation of divine justice. Though frequently discussed by Elizabethan critics, this type of catharsis has small relevance to major Elizabethan tragedies; it is most evident in comedies like *MV*, *TN*, *AYL*, and *Tmp*. Literal catharsis is best understood by reference to a recent analysis of Aristotle's term as meaning "clarification" rather than "purgation." The audience of *Ham.*, having witnessed "an almost perfect coherence of parts," experiences this type of catharsis.

0501 Hardison, O. B. Jr. *The Enduring Monument: A Study of the Idea of Praise in Renaissance Literary Theory and Practice.* Chapel Hill: U. of North Carolina P., 1962. xvi + 240 pp.

Proposes to examine the didactic theory, the dominant theory of poetry in the 16th c. Provides an account of the classical writers who transmitted this and other theories to the Renaissance. The didactic theory, "combined with the technical lore of epideictic rhetoric," became a systematic theory of praise. Chapters 4, 5, 6, and 7 treat several kinds of Renaissance literature in light of this theory. Chapter 4 includes a brief discussion of the use of *vituperatio*, a rhetorical technique of "reprehension," in *R3*. Chapter 8 measures the theory of praise against three important ideas of Aristotle—on imitation, universality of poetry, and formal unity—and concludes that it is "a reasonably comprehensive, consistent, and practical system."

0502 Hardison, O. B. Jr. "Logic versus the Slovenly World in Shakespearean Comedy." *SQ*, 31 (1980), 311–22.

Provides an account of classical commentary on comedy and its Renaissance revival. Notes the self-conscious prescriptiveness of neoclassical criticism and its inapplicability to much Shakespearean drama. Sh wrote more in the spirit of the medieval drama, which was untidy, sprawling, and irrational. Two plays that have superficially classical machinery, *Err.* and *MND*, are ultimately more indebted to the medieval tradition.

0503 Hardison, O. B. Jr. "Shakespeare's Political World." *Politics, Power, and Shakespeare.* Ed. Frances McNeely Leonard. Arlington, Texas: Texas Humanities Resource Center, U. of Texas at Arlington Library, 1981, pp. 3–26.

Examines a range of examples from Sh's plays that relate to the most explicit form of politics: the ruler's nature and the means by which he imposes order on the state. Cites Brutus in *JC* as an exemplar of moral confusion in politics and Antony in *Ant.* as a type of the political dropout. Remarks that "all of the Shakespearean plays in which the state appears as not only unredeemed but unredeemable have classical settings."

0504 Hardison, O. B. Jr. "Speaking the Speech." *SQ*, 34 (1983), 133–44.

Considers Sh's plays in the context of drama's purpose to move from text to performance. Notes that as Sh matured as an artist, the language of his plays became more natural in that it "is validated by its relation to action rather than to poetry." This development shows the playwright's acceptance of Aristotle's idea, set forth by Sir Philip Sidney and others, that a play is intended to express action rather than language.

0504a Hardy, Barbara. "Shakespeare's Narrative: Acts of Memory." *EIC*, 39 (1989), 93–115.

Looks at the ways in which Sh's imagination dwells on memorial, "an act and art of memory, in art and in life outside art." He plays with "the risk of imagining posterity's response" in *Tro.*, a play preoccupied with "rewriting and reimagining story, mythology and history, which have been worked over by other writers, like Virgil and Chaucer." Includes Octavius Caesar's comments about Antony's past and obituary praise for Antony and Cleopatra (*Ant.*) as examples of the political manipulation of memorialization. Discusse forgetting as "an act of memory," referring to Cleopatra's use of *occupatio*, hyperbole, and humor in her speech of farewell to Antony (*Ant.*, I.iii) in order to foreground her real or pretended lapse of recall. Cites a number of vivid figures for memory, several from *Ant.* and *Tro.*

0505 Hardy, Barbara. *Tellers and Listeners: The Narrative Imagination.* London: Athlone P., U. of London, 1975, xvi + 279 pp.

Chapter 4, "Abuses of Narrative," treats the fascination of great narrative artists with perversions of narrative. Notes that competing versions of the same story within an epic or a play often shape the action. Juxtaposes Virgil's concern with lying (Sinon) and rumor (*Fama*) in the *Aeneid* with Sh's interest in the tension between good and bad stories, truth and slander (especially in *Oth.* and *WT*)

0506 Harrison, Thomas P. "*Titus Andronicus* and *King Lear*: A Study in Continuity." *Shakespearean Essays.* Eds. Alwin Thaler and Norman Sanders. Knoxville: U. of Tennessee P., 1964, pp. 121–30.

Argues that there are numerous parallels between *Tit.* and *Lr.*, proving that the earlier play is a prototype for the later. Titus—aged, proud, stubborn, disillusioned, vengeful, mad—is very much like Lear. The two protagonists initiate similar sequences of events in similar ways. There are also echoes of imagery, situation, and language from *Tit.* in *Lr.*

0507 Hart, William Joel. "Shakespeare's Use of New Comedy in Three Love Tragedies: *Romeo and Juliet*, *Othello*, and *Hamlet*." Ph.D. dissertation, University of Southern California, 1985. *DAI*, 46 (1985–86), 1284-A.

Makes use of Northrop Frye's analysis of Sh's romantic comedy to develop a schema for understanding *Rom.*, *Oth.*, and *Ham.* as "comedies in reverse."

0508 Hartwig, Joan. *Shakespeare's Analogical Scene: Parody as Structural Device*. Lincoln: U. of Nebraska P., 1983. 244 pp.

Proposes to treat, in a number of Sh's plays, minor scenes that relate analogically rather than narratively to what precedes and/or follows them. Notes that two subspecies are parodic and emblematic scenes. In *Tro.*, Hector's pursuit and capture of the "goodly armor" (V.viii) is such a scene, emblematizing the play's precipitous movement toward the subversion of all of its idealisms. Includes, in chapter 2, a discussion of the Cinna-the-poet scene (III.iii) in *JC*, pointing out how Sh alters his sources, Plutarch's lives of Julius Caesar and Marcus Brutus, to set up a sequence that initially seems comic but then violently thwarts the audience's expectations. The plebeians parody the logic and rhetoric of Brutus and Antony in the previous scene, the murder of Cinna is a reduced imitation of Caesar's assassination, and the whole scene represents emblematically the chaos caused by such a murder.

0509 Harvey, John. "A Note on Shakespeare and Sophocles." *EIC*, 27 (1977), 259–70.

Makes a preliminary case for Sh's knowledge of Sophocles. By 1570, all of Sophocles had been translated into Latin, and there are a number of suggestive parallels in phraseology. More interesting is what Sh might have derived from Sophocles' plays as a whole, and there are some significant resemblances. In both dramatists, special emphasis is placed on the way the hero's personality aggravates his tragedy. Two important classes of protagonists appear in the works of both. The first is that of the "bereaved or displaced prince or princess" (Orestes, Antigone, and Electra can be compared with Hamlet). The second class is that of "the great aristocratic nature" who is "authoritative, impressive, generous, noble," but also "passionate" and "impetuous," so that he may be driven into "a furnace of destructive passion." Sophocles has Ajax, Heracles, Oedipus, Philoctetes, and Creon in this category, while Sh has Macbeth, Othello, and Lear. Sh, if he knew any Sophocles, would probably have been familiar with *Ajax*, the most frequently translated of Sophocles' tragedies in the 16th c. It would have been a particularly apt model for *Oth*. There are also striking similarities between *Lr.* and the Oedipus plays. Macbeth's "Tomorrow" speech is very close to a passage in *Ajax* where the hero, in disgrace for his slaughtering, thinks about the worthlessness of the life that lies ahead of him.

0510 Hassel, Rudolph Christopher Jr. "The Development of the Blocking Actions in Shakespeare's Comedies." Ph.D. dissertation, Emory University, 1968. *DA*, 29 (1968–69), 3577-A.

Offers an analysis of Sh's modification of the traditional blocking actions—or obstacles to happiness—in comedy. Sh's blocking comes to be focused increasingly on internal and psychological concerns, and leads to the education of the comic hero. Chapters on *Err.* and *TGV* show how "the superficialities of Roman comedy and romance discouraged a full development of character and theme."

0511 Haupt, G. E. "A Note on the Tragic Flaw and Causation in Shakespearean Tragedy." *Interpretations* (Memphis State University), 5 (1973), 20–32.

Cites a common modern misconception about what Aristotle meant by tragic flaw (*hamartia*)—that it is a serious moral defect in a character that causes his fall—and counters this error by rehearsing several more appropriate interpretations of Aristotle's term. Illustrates the need for flexibility and caution in applying the concept of *hamartia* to Sh by surveying the tragedies, commenting, for example, that in *JC*, *Ant.*, and *Cor.* the protagonists fall because they possess a kind of vulnerable excellence rather than a serious flaw.

0512 Hauser, Arnold. *Mannerism: The Crisis of the Renaissance and the Origin of Modern Art.* Trs. Arnold Hauser and Eric Mosbacher. Vol. 1. London: Routledge and Kegan Paul, 1965. xx + 425 pp.

Makes frequent reference to Sh as an exemplar of mannerism. Alienation, the key to mannerism, which prompts wondering about "the reality and identity of the self," can be seen throughout Sh's works; illustrations come from *Tro.*, where Troilus sees a double Cressida, and *Ant.*, where Antony feels that he cannot hold his visible shape. Mannerist tragedy is also closely linked to narcissism, the psychological counterpart of alienation. Cleopatra is a notable narcissistic heroine who achieves "real moral greatness." Coriolanus is another protagonist whose narcissism leads him to a lonely doom. Discusses *Ant.* as a mannerist masterpiece in its "overloaded metaphorism," its complexity of expression, its use of paradox, and its predilection for "the strange and the bizarre." The play juxtaposes the exotic and the mundane; foregrounds the narcissism of the self-centered lovers; and explores sexuality with great intensity. The structure is additive, free from classical concerns with time and space; and the principal characters are psychologically inconsistent.

0513 Hawkes, Terence. *Shakespeare and the Reason: A Study in the Tragedies and the Problem Plays.* London: Routledge and Kegan Paul, 1964. xiv + 207 pp.

Argues for the existence, in Sh's age, of concepts of two faculties of mind. The first, reason, works toward its conclusions through observation and experiment. The second, intuition, leaps to conclusions instantaneously. The roots of these concepts lie in Greek thought (especially Aristotle), St. Thomas Aquinas, and Neoplatonism. Analyzes several plays, with chapters on *Ham.*, the problem plays (*Tro.*, *AWW*, and *MM*), *Mac.*, and *Lr.* In *Tro.*, the two modes of perception are evident in the contrast between Troilus (intuition) and Ulysses (reason) and in the dichotomy between Troilus's two visions of Cressida. Troilus's tragedy is that he cannot harmonize the two ways of seeing. In the modern world, intuition and reason cannot work together as they did formerly; they are separate and opposed.

0514 Hawkins, Harriett. *Poetic Freedom and Poetic Truth: Chaucer, Shakespeare, Marlowe, Milton.* Oxford: Clarendon P., 1976. xv + 135 pp.

Chapter 1 cites the death of the poet Cinna in *JC*, III.iii, as an example of poetic injustice and of poetic truth. Points out, in a later chapter, that Cressida's betrayal of Troilus and his response to it (*Tro.*,V.ii) demonstrate that a person has a reality and value separate from "any and all convictions concerning them." Admires, in *Ant.*, the character of Cleopatra, who represents "a fusion of art with nature unprecedented" in Sh's tragedies.

0515 Hawkins, Harriett. "What Neoclassical Criticism Tells Us about What Shakespeare Does Not Do." *Shakespearean Comedy.* Ed. Maurice Charney. New York: New York Literary Forum, 1980, pp. 37–46.

Cites approvingly Dr. Johnson's *Preface to Shakespeare*, which, unable to explain Sh's plays in terms of neoclassical theory, uses the plays to discover the defects of the theory. Credits Plato with accuracy when he argues in *The Republic* that comedy depicts pleasurably subversive characters and actions. Challenges neoclassical critics like Sidney, who defend comedy by finding in it a scornful representation of common errors intended to reform the spectators. Cites numerous examples from Sh of characters whose morality could be questioned (Sir Toby, Olivia, Sir Andrew, Bottom, Holofernes) but who are instead portrayed with great sympathy. Comedy's chief virtue, then, is what Plato most strongly objects to and what the neoclassical critics take most pains to cover up: It creates a tolerance for human frailty.

General Works

0516 Hawkins, Harriett Bloker. "'All the World's a Stage': Some Illustrations of the *Theatrum Mundi*." *SQ*, 17 (1966), 174–78.

Analyzes three illustrations of the *theatrum mundi* from works contemporary with Sh. In one illustration, there is an amphitheater, and a "Herculean figure bearing the globe appears immediately above the arena." The commentary on this *impresa* does not mention the Herculean figure, but "the connection between the figure, the globe, and a theater is intriguing and suggests that it was an established one."

0517 Hawkins, Sherman. "Structural Pattern in Shakespeare's Histories." *SP*, 88 (1991), 16–45.

Proposes to view the two tetralogies of Sh's English history plays as related to each other by an elaborate structure of comparisons and contrasts, which can be properly designated as "chiasmic patterning." Uses Aristotle and Plato, the classical sources of a great deal of Renaissance political thought, to explain how, in the first tetralogy, the government degenerates from monarchy at the beginning to tyranny in the rule of Richard III at the end; and how, in the the second tetralogy, there is a rise from tyranny in the rule of Richard II to the just rule of Henry V. Sees the model for the "great diptych" formed by the two tetralogies as the classically-inspired school exercise of *comparatio*, which, on a large scale, is the method of Plutarch's *Lives*, with its parallels and antitheses of famous Greeks and Romans. Postulates that the three plays about Henry of Monmouth form "an epic of princely education, whose classical precedent is the *Cyropaedia* of Xenophon," while "the three parts of *Henry VI* form a negative epic of national collapse and civil war, whose classical model is the *Pharsalia* of Lucan."

0518 Hawkins, Sherman. "The Two Worlds of Shakespearean Comedy." *ShakS*, 3 (1967), 62–80. Reprint. *"Much Ado About Nothing" and "As You Like It": A Selection of Critical Essays*. Ed. John Russell Brown. (Casebook Series.) London: Macmillan, 1979, pp. 47–66.

Notes that several of Shakespeare's comedies (*TGV, MND, MV, AYL, WT*, and *Cym.*) follow the green world pattern described by Northrop Frye. In plays of this type, there are two clearly contrasting locales, the first of which is a court or a city subject to arbitrary constraints, from which the hero or heroine escapes into a green world, where losses are restored and sorrows end. Other Shakespearean comedies (*Err., LLL, Ado, TN*, and *Tmp.*) follow an alternate pattern: The characters remain in a single setting but are visited by disruptive intruders. *Wiv.* and *Shr.* exhibit a mixture of the two patterns. One way to link the two patterns is to see the closed world of the second group as corresponding to either the first or second phase of the green world comedies. The two may also be clarified by relating them to the archetypal narrative patterns of quest (green world) and siege (closed world) established in the *Odyssey* and the *Iliad*, respectively, and closely connected in the *Aeneid*. The green world pattern is present in the *R2-H5* tetralogy, though it is subordinated to Tudor myth. In four classical plays (*Tro., Tim., Cor.*, and *Ant.*), the green and closed world structures are subordinated to "the pattern of the double world," in which "complementary or contrasted settings are juxtaposed, but neither really satisfies." Of the four major tragedies, *Ham.* and *Mac.* follow the closed world pattern, while *Lr.* and *Oth.* follow that of the green world.

0519 Hawkins, Sherman. "Virtue and Kingship in Shakespeare's *Henry IV*." *ELR*, 5 (1975), 313–43.

Argues that *1&2H4* and *H5* constitute "an epic of education" for kingship, like the *Cyropaedia* of Xenophon, a work well-known during the Renaissance. *1H4* focuses on Prince Hal's acquisition of two of the cardinal virtues, temperance and fortitude. In *2H4*, he learns the other two, wisdom and justice. Analyzes the plays in terms of pronouncements on the virtues by Cicero, Plato, and Aristotle—the sources for most Renaissance handbooks on, or institutions of, princely education.

0519a Hayse, Joseph M. "Madness on Stage: The History of a Tradition in Drama." Ph.D. dissertation, University of Wisconsin, Madison, 1976. *DAI,* 37 (1976–77), 3602-A.

Surveys the use of stage madness "from Greek tragedy" to modern drama. Covers several cases of madness in Greek tragedy and notes that Seneca's *Hercules Furens* "is an important bridge between ancient drama and medieval and Renaissance plays." Shows that *Ham.* and *Lr.* "illustrate shifts in the perception of madness in the Renaissance."

0520 Hedrick, Carlyle Paff. "Shakespeare's Changing Use of Psychological Reference in His Comedies." Ph.D. dissertation, Stanford University, 1978. *DAI,* 39 (1978–79), 896-A-897-A.

Explains as background the Greek and Arabic origins of the physiological psychology that formed the basis for Renaissance faculty psychology. Focuses on Sh's use in his comedies of psychological reference—both to the descriptive features of faculty psychology and to the ethical and metaphysical interpretations given in the Middle Ages and Renaissance to that psychology. In the earlier, "golden" comedies, "descriptive" references predominate: the humors, the working of the affections, and the different kinds of judgment that reveal "different levels of cognition." Later comedies, like *Tro.*, begin to probe inner conflicts of judgment and conscience, and the psychological references in these works thus tend to emphasize the ethical implications of behavior and "the operation of free will."

0521 Heilman, Robert B. "From Mine Own Knowledge: A Theme in the Late Tragedies." *CentR,* 8 (1964), 17–38.

Focuses on three of Sh's later tragic heroes—Antony, Coriolanus, and Timon—whose natures seem to be defined by a lack of self-knowledge exceeding what is seen in any of the earlier tragic figures, even Macbeth. Although he experiences occasional "shocks of truth" about himself (as in the aftermath of Actium), Antony turns away from the conclusion that there is anything deeply flawed in himself. His basic mode of operating is to "drown consideration." Antony's strength is his charm, and the attractiveness that such a man must exude is incompatible with self-examination: All of his "psychic energy" flows outward. Coriolanus is exclusively a warrior, possessed of "an uncriticized sense of total rightness that justifies every instinctive act." His mother, far more complex and knowing, tries to teach him flexibility but fails. *Tim.* is a sort of practice run for *Cor.*, with a character who turns furiously on his fellow citizens and aids in a military campaign against his own city. Unlike *Cor.* and other later tragedies, however, the play fails to analyze Timon's "ignorance of human nature and of himself."

0522 Heilman, Robert B. "Manliness in the Tragedies: Dramatic Variations." *Shakespeare 1564–1964: A Collection of Modern Essays by Various Hands.* Ed. Edward A. Bloom. Providence, Rhode Island: Brown U. P., 1964, pp. 19–37.

Finds in Sh's tragedies "a remarkably full and varied account of man as he is understood to be, and can be, and ought to be." It is important, first, that he avoid being a woman, though sometimes shedding of womanish tears (as in the case of Timon's steward Flavius) may be a virtue. He has an obligation to be both reasonable and forthright, and Sh's characters combine these two qualities in many ways. Excellence in war and pursuit of honor are intensifications of man's forthright side which can develop into murderous self-indulgence (as in *Tit.* and *Cor.*). In the later tragedies, Sh presents an alternative to the manliness of violent self-assertion: "the manliness that yields, endures, even pities." Responding to Alcibiades' defense of his "hotheaded homicidal friend," the First Senator holds up an ideal of "self-controlled tolerance" (*Tim.*, III.v); and Volumnia, reversing her earlier faith in "blood-manliness," appeals to her son, "to yield and forgive" (*Cor.,* V.iii). Even in *Ant.*, Sh's treatment of manliness rarely concerns sexual potency, but his equal understanding of the "manliness of the militant self," and the "manliness of the pacific, forbearing self" is extraordinary.

0523 Heilman, Robert B. "Robespierre and Santa Claus: Men of Virtue in Drama." *SoR*, 14 (1978), 209–25.

Uses Robespierre and Santa Claus as metaphors for central human virtues (high-minded integrity and unqualified benevolence, respectively) that are often portrayed by dramatists as problematic. Among characters who exhibit a strenuous incorruptibility are Brutus and Coriolanus. Thersites, a "nonstop debunker," exemplifies the extreme development of one element in this type. Timon, in his "manic largesse," is a Santa Claus figure, trying to buy friendship. Interestingly, when his philanthropy fails, he turns into something close to the Robespierre model.

0524 Heilman, Robert B. "To Know Himself: An Aspect of Tragic Structure." *REL*, no. 2 (1964), 36–57.

Investigates the degree of "self-awareness and self-judgment" in the heroes of four tragedies from the first half of Sh's career, concluding with Hamlet, whose self-consciousness is significant but not that of the tragic hero, because it excludes guilt. In *Tit.*, *Rom.*, and *JC*, the actions "are rooted in feuds or civil likenesses of them," and there is almost no self-consciousness since all the conflicts involve fighting foes outside oneself.

0525 Heller, Agnes. *Renaissance Man*. Tr. from the Hungarian by Richard E. Allen. London: Routledge and Kegan Paul, 1978. vii + 481 pp.

Views the Renaissance as a revolution in the concept of man. Liberty, equality, and fraternity together (which were not linked in antiquity) became "an anthropological category." In antiquity, the concept of man was essentially static, whereas in the Renaissance it became dynamic, involving "freedom, work, many-sidedness, and boundlessness." Sh reflects this new dynamism in *JC*, where Stoic and Epicurean concepts applied, respectively, to Brutus and Cassius do not determine their behavior. The new sense of equality, applied to love and friendship, is found in the wide range of pairings in *AYL* and *MND*.

0526 Helsa, David H. "Greek and Christian Tragedy: Notes Toward a Theology of Literary History." *Art/Literature/Religion: Life on the Borders. (Journal of the American Academy of Religious Studies*, 49, no. 2.) Chico, California: Scholars P., 1983, pp. 71–87.

Begins by defining several terms, most used by Aristotle, that are significant for an understanding of Greek tragedy. Greek heroes pursue *arete*, or excellence, which involves discovering their *moira*, or destiny, whose place in the cosmic scheme is determined by *dike*, or justice. The danger is that one will violate the limits set on his own *moira* by *dike* and encroach on someone else's *moira*. Being circumscribed and ignorant, mortals cannot know in advance what these limits are and thus inevitably fail to observe them. Christian tragedy, using the concepts of the will (*voluntas*) and free choice (*liberum arbitrium*) absorbed from Roman law and Stoic philosophy, exhibits characters who know the law of God but whose will goes wrong through either defiance or weakness. Illustrates Christian tragedy by examples from *Oth.*, *Ham.*, *Mac.*, and *Lr.*

0527 Heninger, S. K. Jr. *The Cosmographical Glass: Renaissance Diagrams of the Universe*. San Marino, California: Huntington Library, 1977. xx + 209 pp.

Provides a clear definition of cosmography: "The study of the universe—the study of both the celestial and the terrestrial regions, and of the interaction between them." Notes that in 16th-c. England, cosmography was a fully developed and highly sophisticated science. Mentions numerous classical components of Renaissance cosmography. Plato's *Timaeus* is one of the seminal sources, especially in its idea that the created universe is *all*. The word *all* was frequently used in its cosmological sense by Sh and others, as was its antonym *nothing*, which indicates chaos, nonexistence, the void.

0528 Heninger, S. K. Jr. *Touches of Sweet Harmony: Pythagorean Cosmology and Renaissance Poetics*. San Marino, California: Huntington Library, 1974. xvii + 464 pp.

Seeks to reconstruct the doctrine of cosmology, the belief in a providentially ordered universe, that dominated Renaissance thought. This doctrine originated with Pythagoras and his followers, was absorbed by Plato and from him by the Church Fathers, and with various accretions and modifications was inherited by the Renaissance. Part 3 attempts to characterize the poetics inspired by Pythagoreanism in three chapters: "Poet as Maker," "Metaphor as Cosmic Correspondence," and "Poem as Literary Microcosm." Makes brief references to a number of Sh's works. Theseus, in *MND*, provides an apt description of the poet as maker; Menenius, with his fable of the belly in *Cor.*, and the Archbishop of Canterbury, with his speech about the beehive in *H5*, are mining the rich trove of metaphorical correspondences; and there is cosmic patterning in *LLL* and *MND*.

0529 Heninger, S. K. Jr. "A World of Figures: Enargeiac Speech in Shakespeare." *"Fanned and Winnowed Opinions": Shakespearean Essays Presented to Harold Jenkins*. Eds. John W. Mahon and Thomas A. Pendleton. London: Methuen, 1987, pp. 216–30.

Defines *enargeia* as the art by which the rhetorician, through vividness, creates images. Proposes to "reconstruct with some care the powers that Sh assigned to the imagination." Notes that Theseus, in *MND*, echoes a passage from Plato's *Phaedrus* about how the poet exercises his imagination when he is seized by a divine fury, a process about which Theseus is skeptical. For the most part, Sh relied on the Aristotelian conception of the imagination, which regarded it as "the faculty charged with producing images to correspond with actuality." This can be seen in passages from *AWW*, *Tmp.*, *Wiv.*, *Ham.*, and *R2*. Traces the rhetoricians' appropriation of the capacity of the imagination to produce images through Aristotle, Quintilian, and Cicero, noting that after Cicero it was common "to designate a quasi-sense faculty to receive the enargeiac images projected by the rhetor, what in English came to be called 'the mind's eye.'" Sh's familiarity with this concept is evident in a variety of works. In *R2*, the deposed king uses his imagination to fill his prison with "figures" (V.v); in *Ant.*, Cleopatra, after her lover's death, engages in an "enargeiac apotheosis" of him (V.ii); and in *1H4*, Worcester uses enargeiac speech to provoke Hotspur to rebellion (I.iii).

0530 Henn, T. R. *The Living Image: Shakespearean Essays*. London: Methuen, 1972. xi + 147 pp.

Probes Sh's use of technical images from nature, sport, and the military. The final chapter, an essay on *Ant.*, discusses several such images. For example, Antony's reference to Cleopatra as a "boggler" (III.xiii.111) likens her behavior to that of a hawk "that does not select and keep to one quarry."

0531 Henze, Richard Harold. "Shakespeare and the Golden World of the Pastoral." Ph.D. dissertation, University of Nebraska, 1965. *DA*, 26 (1965–66), 2752–2753.

Finds that Sh uses pastoralism differently in *AYL*, *WT*, and *Tmp*. In *AYL*, the pastoral is found within the "physical, identifiable world, possesses the power to cure malice brought into it from the city, serves as a refuge for sympathetic characters, and contains shepherds both idealized in the Arcadian manner and realistically characterized." In *WT*, refuge in the country is only temporary, the shepherds are all presented realistically, and the country is powerless to correct passion. In *Tmp.*, "the pastoral is a fantasy that man can imagine only as long as he is reasonable." These three kinds of pastoralism are paralleled in the works of Theocritus, Virgil, and Tasso, respectively.

0532   Herndl, George C. *The High Design: English Renaissance Tragedy and the Natural Law.* Lexington: U. P. of Kentucky, 1970. ix + 337 pp.

Makes brief mention of Platonic, Aristotelian, and other classical elements that were assimilated into medieval scholasticism to help form the conception of natural law, which achieved its "fullest imaginative realization" in the tragedies of Sh. Analyzes several of Sh's tragedies as the last great expressions of natural law and then goes on to detail the decline of the idea as evidenced in the works of other Jacobean dramatists.

0533   Herrick, Marvin T. "Hyrcanian Tigers in Renaissance Tragedy." *The Classical Tradition: Literary and Historical Studies in Honor of Harry Caplan.* Ed. Luitpold Wallach. Ithaca: Cornell U. P., 1966, pp. 559–71.

Discusses the use in Renaissance tragedy of a passage from the fourth book of Virgil's *Aeneid* in which Dido, venting her fury at Aeneas, refers to Hyrcanian tigers and the frightful Caucasus. Comments on Sh's adaptation of this passage and "its Senecan–Ovidian modifications" in *Tit., R3, 3H6, Rom., Ham., Mac.,* and *Lr.*

0534   Herrick, Marvin T. *Italian Tragedy in the Renaissance.* Urbana: U. of Illinois P., 1965. vi + 315 pp.

Surveys Italian tragedy of the Renaissance and emphasizes its imitation of classical models. During the 14th and 15th c., Latin tragedies drew their subject matter in part from Seneca's tragedies, Ovid's myths, and histories of ancient Greece and Rome. In the 16th c., when Greek texts of Euripides and Sophocles became available in Italy, a few learned poets like Giangiorgio Trissino began to imitate the Greeks when they composed Italian tragedies. Giraldo Cinthio, the leading tragic dramatist of the mid-16th c., drew eclectically on both Greek and Roman antecedents for his theory and practice (for example, he accepted "the Aristotelian doctrines that enjoined the three unities" and adapted the five acts of Terentian comedy to tragedy). Italian tragedy of the Renaissance, strongly influenced by classical precept and practice, made significant contributions to the theater of western Europe, including "a close-knit complex plot and, especially in England, an emphasis on revenge, blood and lust, ghosts and supernatural characters, prophetic dreams, elaborate laments, an attempt to out-Seneca Seneca, and a standard pattern of verse forms." Mentions Sh throughout, most notably in comparing *Ant.* to Cinthio's *Cleopatra,* in suggesting that Orlando Pescetti's *Il Caesare* may have been a direct influence on *JC,* and in pointing out that Elizabethan dramatists followed the Italians in respecting unity of action (as in *Lr.*).

0535   Heyartz, Irene. "The Endings of Shakespeare's Comedies." Ph.D. dissertation, Bryn Mawr College, 1963. *DA,* 25 (1964–65), 2490.

Proposes "to analyze the endings of Sh's comedies in a comparative manner from a structural viewpoint." Uses the term "catastrophe" for the reversal of fortune that usually takes place at the end of the fourth act. The actual resolution is the "unraveling" or "denouement." Treats a number of comic conventions (the wedding, the epilogue, the manipulator figure, the recognition, the reunion, and the reconciliation), relating them to plays Sh might have known from the classical tradition (Plautus and Terence) and elsewhere.

0536   Hibbard, G. R. "Adumbrations of *The Tempest* in *A Midsummer Night's Dream.*" *ShS,* 31 (1978), 77–83.

Maintains that the two plays constitute "a distinct sub-species of Shakespearean comedy, magical comedy." Among other ways in which *MND* foreshadows *Tmp.* are its frequent use of metamorphosis (often ironic translation of Ovidian myth) and its suggestion that the realm of magic is dark and not particularly reassuring. The latter idea is confirmed in *Tmp.* by the fact that Sh used material from Medea's invocation to "the sinister figure of Hecate" in the *Metamorphoses* as the basis for Prospero's speech abjuring his "rough magic."

0537 Hibbard, G. R. "*Henry IV* and *Hamlet*." *ShS*, 30 (1977), 1–12.

Investigates the relationship between *1&2H4* and *Ham.* to show how Sh's art "is constantly building on itself through a sort of reciprocal process." Shows, as one illustration of this process, how Sh moved from *H5* to *JC*. Fluellen's paralleling of Henry V and Alexander shows that Sh had Caesar in mind when writing *H5* because "in Plutarch the parallel life to that of Alexander is that of Julius Caesar." Furthermore, Sh probably was already planning a play about Caesar that would parallel him to Henry V, the English conqueror of France. In *JC*, Henry V splits into two: Hal, the wild prince, becomes Antony; while Henry V, "the efficient politician, becomes Octavius Caesar." Finally, in *H5* Sh had learned that success makes for less interesting drama than failure: Hence *JC* focuses on the defeated.

0538 Hibbard, G. R. "Sequestration 'into *Atlantick* and *Eutopian* polities': Milton on More." *Ren&R*, N. S. 14 (1980), 209–225.

Includes, in a comparison and contrast of More's *Utopia* and Milton's *Aereopagitica*, a discussion of how the idea of "community," as understood in the Elizabethan era, is portrayed positively in Ulysses' "degree" speech (*Tro.*, I.iii) and negatively in Timon's diatribes after he has left Athens (*Tim.*, IV.i, iii).

0539 Hibbard, G. R. "Words, Action, and Artistic Economy." *ShS*, 23 (1970), 49–58.

Follows Sh's use of the Renaissance commonplace of "the opposition between light and darkness, day and night," from *2H6* to *Mac*. In the course of this development, the commonplace becomes increasingly better assimilated to the contexts in which it is used. It appears in Lucrece's tirade against night (*Luc.*, lines 764–812) and in Brutus's soliloquy while the boy admits the conspirators to his house (*JC*, II.i.77–85). In Brutus's lines, "the association of conspiracy with a cavern and with night seems to have been caught up from the corresponding passage in *Luc.*"

0540 Hibbard, George R. "The Early Seventeenth Century and the Tragic View of Life." *RMS*, 5 (1961), 5–28.

Describes features of Jacobean tragedy that have to do with men's attitudes toward history and politics, including the view that history is the outcome of human actions and decisions, not providentially determined. Sh's transition from the "conception of tragedy as providential history to that of history as tragedy" was completed with *JC* and was probably facilitated by the fact that his source was Plutarch, "not a Christian writer of history."

0541 Hicks, Cora Eiland. "Suicide in English Tragedy, 1587–1622." Ph.D. dissertation, University of Texas, Austin, 1968. *DA*, 29 (1968–69), 1868-A–1869-A.

Analyzes twenty-two English tragedies that portray suicide. Nowhere is the tension between the medieval aversion to self-inflicted death and "the Renaissance" view of the matter so clearly defined. Sh links suicide with honor.

0542 Hilliard, Margret Wilson. "To Sacrifice a Child: The Development of a Theme in Medieval and Renaissance Drama." Ph.D. dissertation, University of Tennessee, 1989. *DAI*, 50 (1989–90), 1664-A.

Adduces the rediscovery of classical drama and philosophy as one of the factors contributing to the secularization of the treatment of child sacrifice in Renaissance drama. This motif, which had been given its prototypical form in the Abraham and Isaac episode of the medieval cycle plays, had originally been used to exemplify faith and obedience. Among plays that deal with a parent's literal or figurative sacrifice of a child are *Tit.*, *MV*, *1H4*, *Lr.*, *Cor.*, *Cym.*, and *WT*. None of the parents in these plays is responding to God's command, as in the medieval plays; instead, the plays are concerned with analyzing "the ethics of a parent's killing a child within the context of more secular motivations."

General Works

0543   Entry deleted.

0544   Hirsh, James E. *The Structure of Shakesperean Scenes*. New Haven: Yale U. P., 1981. ix + 230 pp.

The introduction sets forth criteria for dividing Sh's plays into scenes. The most important consideration is that a scene division occurs only when the stage is cleared of "all living characters." Considers examples of different types of scenes from across the canon. Chapter 2, "Solo Scenes," discusses the Prologue to *Tro*. Considers, in chapter 3, "Duets," the scene between a Roman who is working for the Volsces and a Volsce (*Cor.*, IV.iii). Chapter 4, "Unitary Group Scenes," analyzes scenes from *Cor.* and *Ant*. Chapter 5 is on "Two-Part Scenes" and chapter 6 on "Multipartite Scenes"; both make substantial reference to the Roman plays.

0545   Hobday, C. H. "Why the Sweets Melted: A Study in Shakespeare's Imagery." *SQ*, 16 (1965), 3–17.

Finds that in Sh's mind flattery was connected with four groups of images. Group A consists of *dream, sleep, sweet,* and *king* or *queen*; Group B of *glass, face, hair, eyes,* and *knee*; Group C of *sweet* or *candy, poison* or *venom, winter, ice* or *hail, cold, melt* or *thaw, sun, brook* or *stream, drop, tears,* and *stone*; and Group D of *dog, fawning, sweet* or *candy, melt,* and *knee* or *kneel*. The images of Group D all appear together for the first and last time in Caesar's response to the conspirators' kneeling to him (*JC*, III.i). In Caesar's speech here, as elsewhere in Sh, the image of *melting* seems to be derived from the melting of ice (or wax), not, as Caroline Spurgeon has suggested, from the melting of sweets licked by dogs. *Tim*. includes full examples of three of the four groups. Group B is represented in the opening dialogue between the Poet and the Painter, while Groups C and D are used in the slanging match between Timon and Apemantus in IV.iii. *Ant*. contains examples from Groups C and D, and *Cor*., in its preoccupation with flattery, makes references to a number of individual images from the four groups, but uses few clusters.

0546   Hobsbaum, Philip. *Tradition and Experiment in English Poetry*. London: Macmillan, 1979. xiii + 343 pp.

Chapter 4, "Shakespeare's Handling of His Sources," asserts that Sh's works provide the supreme example in English of the union between tradition and experiment. *TN* takes over a story originally found in the *Menaechmi* of Plautus and deepens the tone, for example, in the scene (II.iv) where Viola makes her Patience-on-a-monument speech to the Duke. *Tro.*, "a comedy of disillusion," debases all of the Homeric figures. In *Oth.*, some of the protagonists' "far-fetched and sonorous" language is quarried from Holland's 1601 translation of Pliny's *Natural Historie* "to show a figure caught in his own rhetorical toils." In *Ant.*, Antony's rhetorical mode derives from Seneca, and especially in the later scenes, he uses the grand style to conceal his waning fortunes from himself. Enobarbus's famous description of Cleopatra (II.ii), historically accurate in its closeness to Plutarch, is more important in its dramatic authenticity: It is an eyewitness report with no trace of "Antony-language." In *Cor.*, the chief commentator is Cominius, who, along with others, transforms the source material by sharpening details—in particular, by using imagery that represents the chief character as having "willed himself out of humanity." In the background of *Tmp*. lies the myth of Jason, who had to perform various labors to gain the Golden Fleece. The notion of Sh as a self-made genius must be discarded. He was "intelligently traditional," using "the best available sources" and "selecting, conflating, and developing material" as his themes demanded.

0547   Hochberg, Shifra. "Dramatic Definitions of Honor in Four Shakespeare Plays." Ph.D. dissertation, New York University, 1979. *DAI*, 40 (1979–80), 1481-A-1482-A.

Explores Sh's use of honor "as a theme closely related to the dynamics of drama itself and to the dramatic concern with role versus self—the essence of tragic and comic self-discovery and experience—in the spheres of public and private life." In *1H4, Tro.,*

Cor., and *Ham.*, the exploration of honor is involved with the exacting of revenge, and in this context a character's ability to modify his notions about honor is a "measure of his dramatic strength." Troilus is the only character in these plays who fails to meet this challenge of flexibility, though Martius meets it only temporarily. The four plays can also be studied to understand "how Sh relates his depiction of honor to genre."

0547a Hoeniger, F. D. "Musical Cures of Melancholy and Mania in Shakespeare." *Mirror up to Shakespeare: Essays in Honour of G. R. Hibbard.* Ed. J. C. Gray. Toronto: U. of Toronto P., 1984, pp. 55–67.

Traces the view that music can cure "acute mental illness" to Pythagoras and his followers. The most famous example in classical times of a physician employing musical therapy on madmen was Asclepiades, who practiced medicine during the 1st c. B.C. in Rome. This tradition was transmitted to Renaissance writers through Neoplatonists like Boethius and, later, Marsilio Ficino. A contrary tradition, that music could induce madness, derives from Hippocrates and Galen, and is memorably illustrated by Plutarch. Sh's evocation of the curative power of music can be seen in *Lr.* and *Per.*; his use of the opposing tradition is evident in *R2*.

0548 Holbrook, David. *Images of Woman in Literature.* New York: New York U. P., 1989. xi + 295 pp.

Chapter 8, "*Timon of Athens* and the Witch Archetype," argues that in *Tim.* Sh is imagining the world of the witch, in which all creatures, even the earth herself, are possessed by a voracious appetite, feeding on and deceiving each other. In this world, Timon is like an infant whose fear of "Bad Breast" renders him incapable of believing in benevolence. Only at the end, in his suicide and grave by the sea, is Timon able "to allow the possibility of redemption."

Chapter 12, on *Ant.*, asserts that, although Cleopatra has much of the witch's dark lustfulness, there is a "transcendent vitality" about the two lovers. We are no longer "revolted by humanness, passion, or woman," recognizing that through them we can "achieve meanings that are stronger than death."

0549 Holland, Norman N. *Psychoanalysis and Shakespeare.* New York: McGraw-Hill, 1966. xiv + 412 pp.

Chapters 1–5 attempt to provide an overview of the psychoanalytic theory of literature. Chapters 6–9 "survey, summarize, and evaluate piece by piece everything psychoanalysis has said about Sh and his works, from the beginnings up to 1964." Chapter 9, "Psychoanalysis and the Works," has a section (usually brief) on each work in the canon. *Ant.*, for example, shows a combination of Christian and pagan patterns, two different kinds of masculinity, and various characters mistiming their actions; *Cor.* is an Oedipal play stressing the relationship of mother and son; *Ham.*, among a great many other things, shows, through its protagonist's misrecall of the Pyrrhus speech, that Hamlet does not want to carry out the revenge his father has required; *JC* is seen primarily as a foil for *Ham.*; *Tim.* reveals a man motivated, in both benevolence and hatred, by vanity; *Tit.* is concerned with "the castration complex"; and *Tro.* exhibits in Cressida the narcissistic "woman of destructive beauty."

0550 Hollander, John. *The Untuning of the Sky: Ideas of Music in English Poetry, 1500–1700.* Princeton: Princeton U. P., 1961. xiii + 467 pp.

Studies change in the practice and philosophy of music during the period from 1500 to 1700 and the ways that change was reflected in "the poetic representation of musical subjects" in England. Proposes to show how, during the period in question, poetry's view of music was progressively demythologized.

Chapter 2 explains the musical theory and practice of the classical world and indicates how they were transmitted to the Renaissance. Boethius's *De Institutione Musica* was the primary authority on the division of music into parts for the Middle

Ages and Sh's age. In Boethius's scheme, the three branches of music were *musica mundana* (the harmony of the universe, whose typical model was the music of the spheres); *musica humana* ("that which unites the ... activity of the reason with the body"); and *musica instrumentalis* (music in the ordinary modern sense). Though not expressed by Boethius, an important distinction from classical writers that assumed immense importance in the Renaissance was the one between *musica speculativa* (the body of myths and abstract schemes about music) and practical music.

Chapter 3 includes a discussion of "Shakespeare's Many Sorts of Music." *Musica speculativa* is significant in Richard II's speech in Pomfret Castle (*R2*, V.v.41–66); in Brutus's response to Lucius's comment that the strings of his lyre are false (*JC*, IV.iii.290–291); in the talk about music at Belmont in *MV*; and in the concern of *TN* to show, through music, the "application of abstract order and proportion to human behavior."

Chapter 4 cites a song about Orpheus from *H8* (III.i.3–14) to illustrate a literary tradition about the fabulous powers of music to influence human behavior.

0551 Holloway, John. *The Story of the Night: Studies in Shakespeare's Major Tragedies*. London: Routledge and Kegan Paul, 1961. x + 187 pp.

Chapter 6, on *Ant.*, emphasizes the sense of the two protagonists that they must live up to a role of greatness in their love. They are also charged with exuberance and great physical energy. Their love, like the politics of the play, is characterized by flux. Notes that the play follows Plutarch in viewing Antony as exemplifying the vicissitudes of Fortune. Sees a change at the end for both lovers, from the greatness of public life to the simplicity of those whose inner lives have been touched. Chapter 7 discusses *Cor.* and *Tim.* as works in which a pattern underlying several of Sh's earlier tragedies becomes much more explicit: Instead of being gradually isolated, as, for example, Antony and Cleopatra are, the heroes of these two works are transformed into outcasts by ritual acts of expulsion.

0552 Homan, Sidney. *Shakespeare's Theater of Presence: Language, Spectacle, and the Audience*. Lewisburg: Bucknell U. P., 1986. 253 pp.

Aims to employ performance and metadramatic criticism in considering presence, language, spectacle, and audience in nine of Sh's plays. Chapter 2 finds that, in *Tro.*, the issue is how to effect a reconciliation between the facts of history and "the abstractions of language." Sh consciously drives a wedge between the metadramatics of language and spectacle; the play has a "metadramatic structure of failed enactment." Chapter 4 treats *JC* as an extreme example of stage spectacle; "the facts of Roman history are compounded by the presence of the supernatural, even as all philosophical systems prove inadequate to account for the cynical, cyclical history mirrored by the play." A succession of male would-be playwrights fail to order events; only when the supernatural, in the form of Caesar's ghost, intervenes near the end does vision become "sufficiently flexible to account" for the play's "larger world."

0553 Honigmann, E. A. J. *Shakespeare: Seven Tragedies: The Dramatist's Manipulation of Response*. London: Macmillan, 1976. viii + 215 pp.

Chapter 4, on *JC*, argues that Sh made Brutus both less and more attractive than he is in Plutarch's *Lives*. To create an impression of Brutus as a corrupted intellectual, Sh shows his mistakes as a conspirator, his confused thinking, and "his dangerously high conceit of himself." However, Brutus is also seen as gentle, trustworthy, a man in whose presence others can sleep. The audience is kept at a distance from this hero through his Stoical reserve, his preoccupation, and the play's generalized mood. We have similarly mixed responses to Cassius and Caesar. Chapter 9, on *Ant.*, notes that Sh removed virtually all enjoyment of joking from Plutarch's Antony in order to diminish the hero of his play. Sh's Antony also lacks high seriousness at times and seems to be stuck in the rigid posture of bidding farewell. By contrast, Cleopatra's sexual and physical mobility is stressed. In the middle of the play, however, Antony's "sense of shame" ennobles him, while Cleopatra's outbursts during the messenger scenes (II.v and III.iii) cause her to lose power. Notices a movement from comedy to tragedy through the progression of the five betrayal–reconciliation scenes in which the two principals participate. Regards Cleopatra's behavior during the final act as highly theatrical; the extent to which her death is triumphant is finally unclear. Chapter 10, on *Cor.*, uses the changes Sh made in Plutarch to create the poor host episode (I.ix) to argue for a problematic view of the hero, who is potentially noble and/or callous. Coriolanus is mysterious in himself as well as in his two most important relationships, with Volumnia and Virgilia. The former, whom Sh seems to have modelled on "Plutarch's Spartan mothers," exists "in a strange haze of motives"; she is "a man–woman and a wife–mother who loves and destroys." Menenius plays a variety of roles: He is a mixture of Pandarus, Nestor, and Ulysses in *Tro.* Analyzes the fable of the belly to show that it raises more questions than it resolves about "social roles and obligations." Comments on Coriolanus's rapid alternations between honor and pride; his gradual movement toward self-knowledge, culminating in the scene with his wife and mother (V.iii); and his relapse, just before his death, into his former self.

0553a Honigmann, Ernest A. J. "Shakespeare as a Reviser." *Textual Criticism and Literary Interpretation.* Ed. Jerome J. McGann. Chicago: U. of Chicago P., 1985, pp. 1–22.

Mentions the two contradictory couplets in the epitaph of Timon (*Tim.*, V.iv.70–73; one couplet was to be deleted upon revision), the ending of *Luc.* (the argument Sh prefixed to the poem envisages a larger role for Junius Brutus after Lucrece's death), and the ending of *Tro.* (which was originally intended to conclude with Troilus's death).

0554 Hoover, Sister Mary Frederic. "A Study of Imagery in Shakespeare's Sonnets, *Troilus and Cressida, Macbeth, Antony and Cleopatra,* and *The Winter's Tale.*" Ph.D. dissertation, Case Western Reserve University, 1973. *DAI,* 34 (1973–74), 5103-A-5104-A.

Analyzes several works in which the emotions of fear and love are reflected in images of space and time. Chapter 2 examines the destructive force of time in *Tro.* Cressida's falseness is due more to time than to depravity, and Troilus causes the collapse of their relationship through his misunderstanding of both time and love. Chapter 4 examines "the bounteous love relationship and the spacious political background of *Ant.*," showing how Antony "triumphs over time and attains heroic stature."

0555 Horowitz, David. *Shakespeare: An Existential View.* New York: Hill and Wang, 1965. x + 134 pp.

Finds that "a tension between imagination and reality" underlies the tragedy of the lovers in *Ant.* Traces the growing together of Antony and Cleopatra under "the main reaping movement of time and fortune." After Antony's loss at sea, he and Cleopatra share their mutual weakness (III.xi), and Antony recognizes that he does love her above all else. From this point on, their increasing awareness of the richness of their love accompanies the ebb of their fortunes. In the final "tragedy of errors," the two recognize that, despite their defeat by mutability, "they are born to each other and to themselves, even as they are dying to the world." Regards *Tro.* as a play without a resolution, which treats both love and honor as ideals that are divorced "first from 'reality' and then from their own meanings."

0556 Hosley, Richard. "The Formal Influence of Plautus and Terence." *Elizabethan Theatre.* (Stratford–upon–Avon Studies 9.) Eds. John Russell Brown and Bernard Harris. London: Edward Arnold, 1966, pp. 131–45.

Examines the evidence for the influence of Plautus and Terence on Elizabethan drama. Elizabethan plays borrowed general situations, specific scenes, and whole plots from both Roman dramatists, but more often from Plautus than from Terence. For example, in *Err.*, "Shakespeare adapts the *Menaechmi* and fuses it with part of the *Amphitruo.*" The tightly knit Terentian double plot (as found in the *Andria*), in part through the medium of the *commedia erudita* (as found, for example, in Ariosto's *Studenti*), became the basis for the more loosely constructed Elizabethan double-action play, as seen in *Shr., MV, Ado,* and *TN.* Roman comedy generally involves a stolen or lost child (usually female), her perilous wandering, the birth of her child, and a recognition that she is a citizen and therefore marriageable. Echoes of this structure can be found in *Per., WT,* and *H8.* Also indebted to Roman comedy is Elizabethan intrigue tragedy (for example, *Oth.*). Northrop Frye's ideas on the indebtedness of Elizabethan comedy to its Roman predecessor—especially the notion of the formation of a new society around the lovers—are helpful as well. In terms of character, Plautus and Terence provided the Elizabethans with a rich array of types, which were often modified or supplemented by the intermediary *commedia erudita* or by the Elizabethans themselves. Male characters are the *adulescens,* the *senex,* and the *servus;* female types consist of the *virgo,* the *meretrix,* and the *matrona;* and secondary types include the *miles gloriosus,* the *ancilla,* and the *leno.* Analyzes Gascoigne's *Supposes* to illustrate some of the formal influences of Roman comedy. Points out that Sh reworked this plot as the secondary action of *Shr.* In Sh's version of the story, one of the classical types (the parasite) is omitted, but two others (the servant and the old man) are retained. Though Sh used classical elements, he reorganized the plot. Instead of beginning, Roman-like, *in medias res,* he adhered to the English *ab ovo* practice.

0557 Houston, John Porter. *The Rhetoric of Poetry in the Renaissance and Seventeenth Century.* Baton Rouge: Louisiana State U. P., 1983. 317 pp.

Uses "rhetorical description," based on the concepts of ancient rhetoricians like Demetrius, Dionysius of Halicarnassus, Aristotle, Cicero, and Quintilian, to analyze 16th- and 17th-c. Italian, French, and English poetry in a variety of genres. Considers Renaissance criticism as an important extension of classical theory. Assumes that Renaissance poets had a fairly broad familiarity with this rhetorical tradition. Devotes a major part of chapter 5, "Tragic Poetry," to Sh. Argues that Demetrius, Dionysius of Halicarnassus, and Hermogenes are the ancient theorists most relevant to an understanding of Sh's tragic styles, chiefly because these writers, in attempting to account for the complexity of Greek poetry, advanced the notion that there is "a harsh, rough version of high style in sounds, vocabulary, and idiom." This *deinos* style is especially evident in major tragedies like *Mac., Ham., Oth.,* and *Lr.,* but it is present even in early works like *R2. Rom.* is unusual in that it is written chiefly in the middle style. As Sh developed, he enlarged his rhetorical range, for example extending the *deinos* style to express Othello's sexual jealousy, an application never imagined by the ancient authorities. Notes that Sh progressed from the relatively monolithic high style of *R2* to "an esthetic of language in which discordance plays a major role and whose unity is to be sought in a higher imaginative order than the ordinary rhetorical principles usually point to." Finds evidence of this harmonious discongruity in Sh's departure from normal idiom, "contrasting of double epithets," rapid changes of metaphor, "unusual metonymies," and juxtapositions of verse and prose. Related devices include "contrasts between Germanic and Romance terms, between Latinate and ordinary words, and between monosyllabic and polysyllabic terms." Finally, there are "the juxtaposition of abstract and concrete words, the use of catachresis, and the contrast of irony and serious hyperbole as in *Antony and Cleopatra.*"

0558 Houston, John Porter. *Shakespearean Sentences: A Study in Style and Syntax.* Baton Rouge: Louisiana State U. P., 1988. xi + 227 pp.

Attempts analyses of Sh's work based on "the stylistic values of sentence structure." Provides an introduction to "the problem of distinctive poetic word orders" and then considers a number of Sh's plays "in a roughly chronological order," treating new topics in syntax as they arise. Discusses the significance of inversions of the normal sentence order of subject–verb–direct object (SVO) like subject–object–verb (SOV) and object–subject–verb (OSV), as well as devices like *hypotaxis, syndeton,* and *asyndeton.* Notes, for example, that "the rhetorical notions underlying much of the peculiar grammar of *Hamlet* are those of *ordo naturalis* and *ordo artificiosus.*" The former signifies not only normal word order but also "the principle of arranging phrasal elements of the sentence or groups of independent clauses by increasing length." In this play, Sh brings together many kinds of unusual word order "to form a truly new stylistic medium." This includes "formal periods of a quite Latinate elegance." Points out that "the interplay of ways of speaking in *Troilus and Cressida* suggests ... a pronounced effort toward making abrupt contrasts between scenes." Finds the use of syndeton and asyndeton especially prominent in *Cor.*, where Sh "worked out one of his most elegant stylistic designs, one in which syntax plays an especially large role, since there is little place for golden words." Maintains that the style of *Ant.* "is marked by a notable use of sentence forms and grammatical devices that are associated with speech, as opposed to the written language, although some of them belong to both, an ambiguity that Shakespeare exploits in shifting tone and mood while maintaining a unified syntactic surface." Short sentences are prominent in this strategy. In *Ant.*, Sh abandoned "the density of highly developed sentences," so evident in his earlier works, in favor of "a more restrained distribution of lengthy hypotactic structures."

0559   Howarth, Herbert. "An Old Man Looking Life." *Stratford Papers on Shakespeare 1961.* Ed. B. W. Jackson. Toronto: W. J. Gage, 1962, pp. 178–94.

Remarks that Sh became a Socrates in his later works by having his characters talk about and experience self-knowledge. Self-knowledge is first mentioned in *MM* and is of great importance in *H8*.

0560   Howarth, Herbert. "Shakespeare's Gentleness." *ShS*, 14 (1961), 90–97.

Surveys "gentleness," both as a style and as a virtue, in the works of Sh. *Ven.*, "an English *Metamorphoses*," proved Sh a gentleman. Ovid's influence can also be seen in *MND*, which is "gentle in the courtier's sense." In *JC*, "the gentleness of Brutus" goes awry, and in *Tro.*, gentleness is perverted.

0561   Howarth, Herbert. *The Tiger's Heart: Eight Essays on Shakespeare.* New York: Oxford U. P., 1970. vii + 210 pp.

Notes that four chapters are reprints or partially so. Chapter 1, "Shakespeare's Gentleness," suggests that *Ven.* is "a deliberate first display of the gentle style" and that in *MND* Sh transformed "the art of the Latin *Metamorphoses* and the English *Venus and Adonis* into theatrical terms." Observes that gentleness is shown as "wrested awry" in Brutus (*JC*) and "gone awry" in Hector (*Tro.*). *Cor.* presents a study of aristocracy in which each aristocrat possesses some virtue, but none has a balance of all virtues. There is no gentleness in this play.

0562   Hoy, Cyrus. "Jacobean Tragedy and the Mannerist Style." *ShS*, 26 (1973), 49–67.

Attempts to explain mannerist features of Sh's late tragedies. Includes discussion of *Tim.*, *Cor.*, and *Ant.* Timon and Coriolanus are narcissistic figures who seek wholeness so relentlessly that their integrity becomes warped. In *Ant.*, we see the mannerist technique of "bringing together irreconcilable elements."

0563   Hoyle, James. "Some Emblems in Shakespeare's Henry IV Plays." *ELH*, 38 (1971), 512–27.

Finds that in *R2*, *1&2H4*, and *H5*, Sh uses "pictorial and proverbial emblems" in a "pervasive, self-conscious, and exuberant" way that he never employs again. Two emblems of fortune in these plays "have been overlooked by scholarship": "Fortune with her forelock and Fortune-and-the sea." Hotspur, for example, "is aware of the forelock attribute, but it is typical of him that he associates it not with Fortune, but with Honor." One of Falstaff's most important emblems is "the sea of Fortune." An emblematic climax to *1H4* is reached in Vernon's report of Hal's mounting his steed (IV.i.104–110): The Prince is presented in a rich mixture of images as Bellerophon (the tamer of the winged horse who therefore possesses the controlling power of a governor) and as Mercury (the patron of the arts and opposite of Fortune as mere luck).

0564 Hubler, Edward. "The Range of Shakespeare's Comedy." *SQ*, 15, no. 2 (1964), 55–65. Reprint. *Shakespeare 400: Essays by American Scholars on the Anniversary of the Poet's Birth*. Ed. James G. McNanaway. New York: Holt, Rinehart and Winston, 1964.

Maintains that Sh "explored the whole range of comic expression." At one end of his comic spectrum stands *Err.*, a farce; at the other, we find *Tro.*, which "shows us what happens when obligations demanding a measure of greatness are laid upon unheroic men."

0565 Hughes, Geoffrey. *Words in Time: A Social History of the English Vocabulary*. Oxford: Blackwell, 1988. x + 270 pp.

Notes Sh's skill at counterpoising Latinate and Saxon vocabulary. Suggests that in earlier plays like *R3* there is an air of artificial embellishment with Latinized terms, but in "mature tragedies" like *Mac.* the juxtaposition is "more daringly creative, profoundly revealing of character and psychology."

0566 Hughes, Geoffrey. "'A World Elsewhere': Romanitas and Its Limitations in Shakespeare." *ESA*, 28, no. 1 (1985), 1–19.

Discerns in Sh's Roman plays "how the intense, self-enclosed quality of Roman patriotism and stoicism led to certain life-denying impulses and attitudes which seem pointedly at variance with the life-enhancing and richer social identity shown in the plays concerned with other cultures, particularly English history." Discusses all four of these plays (*Cor.*, *JC*, *Ant.*, and *Tit.*) to establish that the concept of Rome is radically ambiguous: It is at one time "a social organism, a political entity, and a patriotic cypher." Traces "the ancient organic view" of society as a microcosmic hierarchy from Plato and Aristotle through Boethius to the Christian humanists of Sh's own time. Notes that as Sh observed contemporary liberalizing trends that seemed to undermine this traditional view, he found the distant pagan culture of Rome admirably adaptable for dramatizing these trends. Plutarch's *Lives* gave Sh a view of history that emphasized the power of individuals to affect the course of events, clearly compatible with the dramatist's ends. Notices that in the world of these plays, the Roman state is inevitably involved in "endless power-struggle," there is no "normal" standard by which things can be measured, there are no villains, and there is virtually no fraternization across class lines.

0566a Hughes, Vivienne. "Witchcraft and the Supernatural in Shakespeare." *En torno a Shakespeare: Homenaje a T. J. B. Spencer*. Ed. Manuel Angel Conejero. Valencia: Universidad de Valencia, Instituto Shakespeare, 1980, pp. 115–57.

Mentions the long history of witchcraft, going back to classical times, that lay behind the Elizabethan notions of the magic arts. Points to "the classical theophanies"in some of Sh's plays. The two appearances of Casesar's ghost to Brutus in *JC* (1) ensure that Brutus fights a battle at Philippi and (2) underline that Brutus's fate is sealed. Notes that the ghosts dramatized on the Elizabethan stage come from the Senecan tradition: They materialize in order to explain their deaths and to seek revenge. Discusses also *Ham.*, *MND*, and *Tmp.*

0567 Hulme, Hilda. "Shakespeare's Language." *Shakespeare's World*. Eds. James Sutherland and Joel Hurstfield. London: Edward Arnold; 1964, pp. 136–55.

Emphasizes, in a brief passage on Sh's learning, that lessons in the Elizabethan grammar school were committed to memory. The modern audience can better understand what Sh's contemporaries heard in the plays if we "become responsive to the Latin–English language patterns that were fixed for life in the average Elizabethan mind."

0568 Hulme, Hilda. *Yours That Read Him: An Introduction to Shakespeare's Language*. (Shakespeare Workshop.) London: Ginn, 1972. 96 pp.

Calls attention, in chapter 2, to the extensive grammar school training Sh would have had in Latin and to some of the ways this training is manifested in the works.

0569 Hulme, Hilda M. *Explorations in Shakespeare's Language: Some Problems of Lexical Meaning in the Dramatic Text*. London: Longmans, 1962. xii + 351 pp. Reprint. 1977.

Proposes to examine problems in the meaning of Sh's language by getting closer to "the language world in which Sh's plays were written and first performed." Explicates problematic passages selected from all of the plays, usually discarding editors' emendations. Chapter 3, "Proverb and Proverb–Idiom," concludes by considering five examples from *Tim*. Chapter 5, "'Latin' Reference in Shakespearean English," attempts to explain how "hearing" classical or schoolmaster's Latin as it would have been taught in the Elizabethan grammar school can shed light on a number of difficult passages. For example, knowledge of Latin enables us to see that Henry V's Folio line "commune up the blood" (*H5*, III.i.7) makes more dramatic sense than its usually emended form: "summon up the blood."

0570 Hulme, Hilda M. "*Malice* and *Malicious* in Shakespearean Usage." *ES*, 47 (1966), 190–99.

Points out that a word can be confusing when Sh uses it in several senses and its modern use is limited to one of those senses. Sh's chief use of *malice* (to mean "active ill-will or hatred") is close to the modern sense, but he also uses it to signify "power to harm" (*JC*, III.i.175) and "poison" (*Cor.*, IV.iv.43; *Tit.*, V.iii.13).

0571 Hulse, Clark. *Metamorphic Verse: The Elizabethan Minor Epic*. Princeton: Princeton U. P., 1981. xiv + 296 pp.

Chapter 1, "Minor Epic as Genre," is a revision of item 0572. Chapter 4, "Shakespeare, Poet and Painter," deals with *Ven.* and *Luc.* and combines revisions of items 3133 and 2411. The whole is a revision of item 0573.

0572 Hulse, S. Clark. "Elizabethan Minor Epic: Toward a Definition." *SP*, 73 (1976), 302–19.

Uses the *Poetics* of Aristotle to develop a loose definition of the Elizabethan minor epic. Finds that the minor epic is best understood in terms of the Renaissance theory of epic. Minor epic, like epic, leans toward the extravagant in its diction, verse forms, and mythological imagery. Its usual action is amorous, the minor counterpart to the epic's themes of public virtue. Minor epic is most closely related to the kind of epic embodied in Ovid's *Metamorphoses*, ostensibly organized as "a linear history," but characterized by sideways movement: "juxtapositions, recollections, and parallels among episodes." Ovidian narratives of the Renaissance commonly focus on a single incident detached from the *Metamorphoses*, but they also feature "digression and inset narration" in the manner of the *Metamorphoses* as a whole. Thus *Ven.* includes the episode of the jennet and the stallion to provide a debate on the value of passion parallel or analogous to what is going on in the main action. In addition to its combination of various materials and its mixture of "narrative, dramatic, and lyric movements," minor epic characteristically moves between "involvement and detachment." This can be seen in the frequent use of ecphrasis, "in which the poet describes a painting or tapestry" (*Luc.* is an example). Most minor epic also combines the emblematic and allusive narrative modes. Revision of part of item 0573. Revised as chapter 1 of item 0571.

0573 Hulse, Shirley Clark III. "Myth and Narrative in Elizabethan Poetry." Ph.D. dissertation, Claremont Graduate School, 1974. *DAI*, 35 (1974–75), 5408-A–5409-A.

Focuses on one form of the new poetry of Elizabethan England: "a highly conceited vein of narrative verse dealing with historical and mythological subjects." One crucial influence on this type of verse was Ovid's *Metamorphoses*, which provided a prototype for brief narratives—erotic, tragicomic, and wittily ironic. Much Elizabethan mythological verse features "a pattern of ironic wit in which the poem declares a serious subject and then evades it." This is true of *Ven.*, which begins as an allegory "of the decay of beauty" but turns aside from its theme to pursue "immediate sensuous effects." Parts revised as items 0572, 3133, and 2411; the whole as item 0571.

0574 Humphreys, A. R. "Shakespeare's Histories and 'The Emotion of Multitude.'" *PBA*, 54 (1968), 265–87. Reprint (British Academy Shakespeare Lecture 1968.) London: Oxford U. P., 1970. 25 pp.

Cites Aeschylus's *Agamemnon* and Aristotle's *Poetics* to help establish the idea that successful historical drama must spread "outward from the presented scene." Sh's English histories exhibit this quality.

0575 Humphreys, Arthur. "Shakespeare and the Tudor Perception of History." *Stratford Papers on Shakespeare 1964*. Ed. B. W. Jackson. Toronto: W. J. Gage, 1965, pp. 51–70.

Discusses the ways in which the Tudor study of history prepared the way for Sh's history plays. Ideas about history—that it should perpetuate fame, that it should provide a "theme or argument" instead of simply recording events, that it should be conducive to truth, memory, and virtue—articulated by Tudor writers and passed on to Sh were adapted from Cicero, Tacitus, and other ancients.

0576 Hunt, John Dixon. "The Visual Arts of Shakespeare's Day." *Shakespeare, Pattern of Excelling Nature*. Eds. David Bevington and Jay L. Halio. Newark: U. of Delaware P., 1978, pp. 210–21.

Explains that much of the visual art of Sh's time required that the spectators supply verbal elaborations from their own reading to complete the picture. This was especially true of mythological scenes such as those presented to Sly during the induction to *Shr*. The closest connection of image and text is to be found in emblem books. Ulysses' comment to Achilles, "Time hath, my lord, a wallet at his back" (*Tro.*), may allude to a visual emblem, or may be intended to exhibit its speaker's sententiousness by having him appropriate the *language* of the emblem book. Verbal–visual dialogues in the Renaissance were not concerned with copying or transcribing the devices of one medium by the other, but rather with translating ideas and images into another form. The two arts were often seen as rivals, as in *Tim*. Perspective painting seems to have provided one impetus for dramatists to present audiences with multiple viewpoints, as when Troilus, Ulysses, and Thersites watch Diomedes and Cressida in *Tro*.

0577 Hunt, Maurice. "Controlling Cupid in Shakespeare's Last Romances." *UC*, 9 (1989), 63–76.

Describes the attempt of Prospero in *Tmp.* to banish Cupid as sensual desire from the relationship of Miranda and Ferdinand. Notes that Prospero's need to deal with Caliban forces him to accept the place of erotic love in courtship and in general social intercourse. In *WT*, there is a pledge by the young lover Florizel that despite the classical gods' transformations for love, he will not allow lust to bestialize him (IV.iv). He does, however, admit that he burns for Perdita, whose yearning for "the flowers of spring" reveals her unconscious sensuality. In the dance of Perdita and Florizel, there is a blending of chastity and erotic love. The subduing of Cupid in *WT* gains force from the comic bawdiness of Autolycus, who acts as a foil for the young lovers. We also witness Leontes' perverse banishment of Cupid from his marriage in act I and the restoration to him of the power to feel erotic desire in act V.

0578 Hunter, G. K. "The Heroism of Hamlet." *"Hamlet."* Eds. John Russell Brown and Bernard Harris (Stratford–upon–Avon Studies 5.) London: Edward Arnold, 1963, pp. 90–109. Reprint. *Dramatic Identities and Cultural Traditions: Studies in Shakespeare and His Contempories. Critical Essays.* (Liverpool English Texts and Studies.) New York: Barnes & Noble, 1978, pp. 230–50.

Examines Sh's explorations of heroism during the years 1599–1602. Calls attention to three kinds of heroism: political (that of the king), ethical (that of the saint), and personal (that of the soldier). Sh may have been prompted to move away from his exclusive concern with the first of these in *H5* by his reading of Plutarch's *Lives*, which would have directed him to "the inner shape of greatness." In his next play, *JC*, Sh was probably inspired by Plutarch to portray the ethical heroism of Brutus and to contrast it with the political heroism of Julius Caesar. *Tro.*, another drama about antiquity from this period, considers all three types of heroism, analyzing them and setting them side by side rather than making any one of them central. In *Ham.*, the modes of heroism are collated and compared in the mind of the prince, whose feelings about them provide the focus lacking in *JC* and *Tro*.

0579 Hunter, G. K. "Italian Tragicomedy on the English Stage." *RenD*, N. S. 6 (1973), 123–48. Reprint. *Dramatic Identities and Cultural Tradition: Studies in Shakespeare and His Comporaries. Critical Essays.* (Liverpool English Texts and Studies.) New York: Barnes & Noble, 1978, pp. 13–56.

Argues that *AWW* and *MM* were in part stimulated by Sh's encounter with Italian pastoral tragicomedy, especially Guarini's *Il Pastor Fido*. Remarks that Guarini, in order to achieve his unknotting, employs the machinery of recognition he has taken from *Oedipus Rex*, but altered so that it moves the characters toward understanding and forgiveness. Sh's use of similar unknotting in *AWW* and *MM* provides the most interesting link in his work to Guarini.

0580 Hunter, G. K. *John Lyly: The Humanist as Courtier*. London: Routledge and Kegan Paul, 1962. ix + 376 pp.

Concludes with a chapter on Lyly and Sh that shows the latter transforming the court comedy of the former into "the comedy of courtliness." From Lyly, Sh takes the devices of groups of characters balanced against each other and witty verbal exchanges between lovers. The humanist learning deployed in *LLL* is particularly reminiscent of Lyly, but Sh is more concerned with the minds of the people who use it than his predecessor was. In adopting the elegance of Lyly, Sh makes use of classical *topoi*, but he characteristically complicates responses to them. For example, Lyly's inclusion in *Sapho and Phao* of advice on how a wooer can exploit the willfulness of his lady makes obvious its ultimate origin in Ovid. Sh uses the same idea in *TGV* but places it in "the ironic situation of Valentine advising the Duke and so betraying himself."

0581 Hunter, G. K. "The Last Tragic Heroes." *Later Shakespeare*. Eds. John Russell Brown and Bernard Harris. (Stratford–upon–Avon Studies 8.) London: Edward Arnold, 1966, pp. 11–28. Reprint. *Dramatic Identities and Cultural Tradition: Studies in Shakespeare and His Contemporaries.* New York: Barnes & Noble, 1978, pp. 251–69.

Suggests ways in which the last tragedies (*Tim.*, *Mac.*, *Cor.*, and *Ant.*) mediate between the great tragedies and the romances. The last tragedies are plays of exile: Timon and Coriolanus are physically exiled, while in *Mac.* and *Ant.* the heroes undergo a more complex psychological separation from their fellows (Antony is an exile from his glorious past). In *Tim.*, *Cor.*, and *Ant.*, the heroes live—and are finally forced to die—in pursuit of absolutes that dehumanize them. Exile continues to be a theme in the romances, except in *Tmp.*, where Prospero sacrifices his heroic aspirations to accept the world as it is.

0582   Hunter, G. K. "Seneca and English Tragedy." *Seneca*. Ed. C. D. N. Costa. London: Routledge and Kegan Paul, 1974, pp. 166–204. Reprint. *Dramatic Identities and Cultural Tradition: Studies in Shakespeare and His Contemporaries. Critical Essays.* (Liverpool English Texts and Studies.) New York: Barnes & Noble, 1978, pp. 174–213.

Refers to *Tit.* and *R3* in arguing that "below the level of cultural generality, the points of contact between Seneca and the public drama of the English Renaissance were small in number, distorted by great (though sometimes obscured) differences of outlook and expectation, and seldom wholly separable from other exemplars of similar taste." Seneca's ethic differs strongly from that of the Elizabethans in that his plays regularly leave the evil in "manic possession of what their wickedness has achieved," whereas in Sh, even in a play so devoid of explicit Christian reference as *Tit.*, there is a sense at the end that justice can be re-established with condign rewards and punishments all around.

0583   Hunter, G. K. "Seneca and the Elizabethans: A Case-Study in 'Influence.'" *ShS*, 20 (1967), 17–26. Reprint. *Dramatic Identities and Cultural Tradition: Studies in Shakespeare and His Contemporaries. Critical Essays.* (Liverpool English Texts and Studies.) New York: Barnes & Noble, 1978, pp. 159–73.

Disputes the notion that discovery of parallel passages in Senecan drama and various Elizabethan tragedies demonstrates the systematic influence of the former on the latter. Argues that the native Gothic tradition assimilated a variety of Senecan details but that these were nonessential. More important classical influences can be seen in the Ovidian "tenderness in the midst of horror" (*The Spanish Tragedy* and *Tit.*) and in the Terentian five-act structure.

0584   Hunter, G. K. "Shakespeare and the Traditions of Tragedy." *The Cambridge Companion to Shakespeare Studies*. Ed. Stanley Wells. Cambridge: Cambridge U. P., 1986, pp. 123–41.

Expresses skepticism about finding any significant link between classical and Shakespearean tragedy. Sees a greater connection between Sh and Ovid's *Metamorphoses*, which could be read as a collection of narrative tragedies along the lines of *The Mirror for Magistrates*. Ovid encouraged Sh in his tendency toward flamboyant exhibition of classical materials, most clearly seen in *Tit.* Views *Tro.* as a tragedy in which the facile collapse of idealism brings us very close to sardonic comedy. The pervasive concern of the Roman tragedies (*Tit., JC, Cor.*, and *Ant.*) with the practicalities of politics and history acts as a brake on the tragic hero's propensity to reshape the world to conform to his own desires.

0585   Hunter, G. K. "Shakespeare's Earliest Tragedies: *Titus Andronicus* and *Romeo and Juliet*." *ShS*, 27 (1974), 1–9. Reprint. *Dramatic Identities and Cultural Tradition: Studies in Shakespeare and His Contemporaries. Critical Essays.* (Liverpool English Texts and Studies.) New York: Barnes & Noble, 1978, pp. 319–34.

Mentions the "extreme polarities" represented by *Tit.* and *Rom.* and explains that later tragedies come close to one pole or another. (*Lr.*, for example, is in some ways a reworking of themes from *Tit.*, and *Ant.* has many resemblances to *Rom.*). Focuses, however, on the formal similarities and relationships that can be established between the two plays. In both works, the initial scenes establish "discord against rule"; both involve a conflict between two households; the setting for both plays is an appropriately chosen city whose walls "measure the limit of the ordered world"; and in each play a tomb is the primary focus of the action. The tomb in *Tit.* is particularly important as a reflection of Roman public ritual.

0586 Hunter, G. K. "Shakespeare's Reading." *A New Companion to Shakespeare Studies.* Eds. Kenneth Muir and S. Schoenbaum. Cambridge: Cambridge U. P., 1971, pp. 55–66.

Comments, in a brief section on "Shakespeare and the Classics," that the poet's deep consciousness of literary methods and conventions was instilled by grammar school study of the classics. Classical allusion in Sh is an integral part of his "whole mode of writing." His knowledge of Latin allows him to make sense of untranslated works or to recall passages from them. Classical authors, especially Ovid, are strong influences, but, more importantly, they act as catalysts to "release Shakespeare's own faculties."

0587 Hunter, George K. "A Roman Thought: Renaissance Attitudes to History Exemplified in Shakespeare and Jonson." *An English Miscellany Presented to W. S. Mackie.* Ed. Brian S. Lee. Cape Town: Oxford U. P., 1977, pp. 93–115.

Distinguishes two alternative ways of viewing Roman history in the 16th and early 17th c.: One emphasized "the *truth* of a historical sequence, seen as quite separate from the world in which we live," and the other emphasized "the *romance* of actions that are brought into an evaluative relationship with our own experience as models." From 1520 on, translation of and comment on the Roman historians were continuous, but only in the final years of Elizabeth's reign were the major historians, Tacitus and Livy, translated. The reason for this is that Tacitus and Livy see the defining virtues of Rome—*fides, pudicitia, libertas, concordia, disciplina*—as "essentially republican in their social context," which sets them "implacably against kingship, seen as the effeminizing degradation of Eastern tyrants, the state towards which all single rule naturally degenerates." Such a position was clearly at odds with the romantic one promoted by the Tudor monarchs and supported by many humanist scholars. What Tudor historians did was to fragment Roman history into brief, manageable ethical lessons that had relevance to 16th-c. life. Around the turn of the century, the view of Roman history as a process largely unaffected by ethics became available as an alternative to the older romantic view. In *JC*, Sh, "like earlier Tudor writers, offers us for our admiration the ethical splendors of *Romanitas* in his central figure of Brutus; but like the later 'political' writers he shows us the ethical standards of *pietas, fides, pudicitia,* which Brutus and Portia display, inside a framework which forces it to seek expression in the enlarged focus of political action and then undercuts it by revealing the total irrelevance of ethics to political and historical development." In *Ant.*, Sh includes a glimpse of the future of Rome (the empire) but does not allow it to dominate the play, which dramatizes certain ethical qualities "inside its present time." Sh's reticence about fully exposing the impact of present actions on the future distinguishes him from Jonson, who in *Sejanus* and *Catiline* sees the individual as caught up in the tragic sweep of history.

0588 Hussey, S. S. *The Literary Language of Shakespeare.* London: Longman, 1982. 214 pp.

Provides an introduction to Sh's literary language that ranges widely over the canon. Considers vocabulary, especially borrowings from Latin. Notes that Sh often calls attention to a single Latinate word by using it in a context whose language is otherwise unremarkable. There are also instances of Latinate doublets, and sometimes the Latin terms come in groups of synonyms, copiously expanded. The Latinate words are often used for comic effect, as when certain characters misunderstand them, or when, as in *LLL*, they caricature the fashion for coining inkhorn terms. Remarks on the unusual amount of Latinate diction in *Tro.*, especially for a play written in the middle of Sh's career. Discusses syntax as it was affected by rhetoric, particularly the branch of rhetoric covered in the Elizabethan textbooks under "ornaments of style." Sh's earlier plays and poems tend to rely more on the formal, schematic rhetorical devices; in later works, there is a loosening of these structures as the playwright adapts them to the needs of specific characterization. Distinguishes several "Shakespearean styles": the prose of the rational man (Brutus in *JC*), "the language of insult" (Thersites in

General Works 163

Tro.), the bombastic and often archaic language of the play within the play (*MND*, *Ham.*), the heightened discourse of affairs of state (the Prologue to *Tro.*), a soldierly language (prominent in the Roman plays, but also found in the English histories), the language of soliloquies and *Son.*, and the language of "absolute integrity."

0589   Ide, Richard S. *Possessed with Greatness: The Heroic Tragedies of Chapman and Shakespeare.* Chapel Hill: U. of North Carolina P., 1980. xvi + 253 pp.

Argues that in tragedies involving great military figures at odds with their societies, Sh and Chapman differ in identifying the causes of and assessing the conflict between "social consensus and heroic idealism." Chapman's translation of *The Iliad* provides a key to his later treatment of tragic heroism: He included a great deal of interpretative material that attempts to justify Achilles' isolation, to convert it into a virtuous stance according to Elizabethan norms. In his tragedies *Bussy D'Ambois* and *Byron*, he continued to present the displaced soldier as an ideal figure who undergoes very little change in his conflict with society. Sh, in *Tro.*, demythologizes the heroes of the Trojan War, rejecting the epic genre to the extent that it idolizes the egomania that accompanies heroic individualism. This prepares the way for his treatment of heroism in *Oth.*, *Cor.*, and *Ant.*, where the protagonists, to varying degrees, acknowledge human frailty and thus achieve "true human heroism" in suffering their tragic fates. Sh's devaluation of classical heroism may have led him, in his last years, to elevate pastoral and comedy in the hierarchy of genres. The last plays favor "a humble stance in the presence of a mysterious but beneficent Providence." Revision of item 0591.

0590   Ide, Richard S. "Shakespeare and the Pirates." *Iowa State Journal of Research*, 58 (1984), 311–18.

Attempts to demonstrate that Sh took the pirate attack, a conventional device of Greek romance, and transformed it into a vehicle of providential intervention in *Per.*, *Ham.*, *MM*, *TN*, and *WT*.

0591   Ide, Richard Smyth. "The Soldier Theme in Chapman and Shakespeare." Ph.D. dissertation, Johns Hopkins University, 1973. *DAI*, 34 (1973–74), 3345-A.

Explains that "the Elizabethan heroic soldier," his values outmoded at the end of the 17th c., was "transformed into a tragic hero on the Jacobean stage." Sh's distaste for the heroic tradition, revealed in *Tro.*, enabled him to view the great soldier and his deeds from an aesthetic distance in *Oth.*, *Mac.*, and *Cor.* In Sh's treatment, unlike Chapman's, the titan is humanized. Revised as item 0589.

0592   Ingram, Angela J. C. *In the Posture of a Whore: Changing Attitudes to "Bad" Women in Elizabethan and Jacobean Drama.* 2 vols. (Salzburg Studies in English Literature: JDS 93.) Salzburg: Institut für Anglistik und Amerikanistik, U. Salzburg, 1984. vi + 389 pp.

Defines a woman as "bad" when "her behaviour is both disruptive and disorderly, as well as more obviously destructive in terms of the 'norms' men have established." Chapter 6, "Seditious and Disorderly Women," includes comments on Tamora in *Tit.*, and Chapter 7, "The Helen-Image, or, War for a Whore," covers Helen and Cressida (*Tro.*) and Cleopatra (*Ant.*).

0593   Ingram, R. W. "Musical Pauses and the Vision Scenes in Shakespeare's Last Plays." *Pacific Coast Studies in Shakespeare.* Eds. Waldo F. McNeir and Thelma N. Greenfield. Eugene, Oregon: U. of Oregon Books, 1966, pp. 234–47.

Surveys Sh's uses of "the musical pause," a moment of "restful suspense" signaled by music before the resolution of the play. *JC* is the first play in which this device appears in its mature form: Music marks the suspension of action as Brutus seeks a moment of respite in his tent and is "disturbed by the ghost" (IV.iii). His rest is tinged with fearfulness, which hints at the closing scenes and their violence. A similar pause occurs when Coriolanus waits outside Aufidius's palace, pondering his decision to betray Rome while he listens to music from the festivities within (*Cor.*, IV.v). The musical pause is most richly developed in the vision scenes of the late romances.

0594 Ingram, R. W. "'Their noise be our instruction': Listening to *Titus Andronicus* and *Coriolanus*." *Mirror up to Shakespeare: Essays in Honour of G. R. Hibbard*. Ed. J. C. Gray. Toronto: U. of Toronto P., 1984, pp. 277–94.

Considers how the multitude of musical sounds (by which is meant all sounds) in *Tit.* and *Cor.* affect what appears on stage. The musical effects of the first act of *Tit.* are "energetic and melodramatic," though not shaped into a pattern. In *Cor.*, the stage directions and indications within the text show that Sh was extremely careful about how he wanted the noises and the action of the play to be related. The "prelude," with the furious citizens voicing their complaints and being opposed with equal stridency by the hero, and then "the quiet domestic interlude with Virgilia, Volumnia, and Valeria," announce the themes of the work. This is followed by the first "movement," during which Coriolanus's bravery is accompanied by "mounting crescendos of the instruments of war and the shouts of the soldiers." In the second movement, "Coriolanus in Rome," there are quiet moments, the acclamation bestowed on the hero for his triumph, his failed attempt to speak "mildly" to the people, and the citizens' raucous celebration of his banishment. The third movement, "Coriolanus in Exile," exhibits Coriolanus saying a quiet farewell to his intimates; waiting in muffled isolation outside of Aufidius's house, where festive music plays; standing silent as he capitulates to his mother; returning to Corioli with military pomp just before he is murdered; and, in death, being borne away to the sound of a death march.

0595 Ingram, R. W. "'The True Concord of Well-Tuned Sounds': Shakespeare and Music." *Review of National Literatures*, 3, no. 2 (1972), 138–62.

Provides a brief account of Boethius's threefold division of music, which provides background for Sh's use of musical metaphors in serious discourse. Especially important is Boethius's *musica mundana*, "the grand harmony of all creation."

0596 Iwasaki, Soji. *The Sword and the Word: Shakespeare's Tragic Sense of Time.* Tokyo: Shinozaki Shorin, 1973. xv + 264 pp.

Proposes an iconographical study of time in three plays: *R3*, *Mac.*, and *Lr.* In *R3*, Sh is imagining time as "the devourer of all things human and sublunary and also that aspect of 'history' which is the working out of God's providence." In *Mac.*, time is undergoing a transition between devourer and redeemer; and in *Lr.*, time, though still functioning as devourer, is primarily the revealer of truth. Chapter 1, "Time, Fortune, and Death," includes discussion of the classical elements associated with the complex idea of time inherited by the Renaissance. Notes the connection of the Greek idea for time, Chronos, with the god Kronos, who came to be identified with the Roman Saturn, a devourer. Saturn–Time also came to be associated with the Roman goddess Fortune, who was herself linked to Nemesis and Justice.

0597 Iyengar, K. R. Srinivasa. *Shakespeare: His World and His Art.* New York: Asia Publishing House, 1964. xvi + 711 pp.

Presents an introduction to Sh that gives "both an uncomplicated record of existing knowledge ... and a critical study of the poems and all the thirty-seven plays." Chapter 1 has a section, "Small Latin and Less Greek," that discusses Sh's grammar school education in the classics; it favors the notion that he was a country schoolmaster. This would have given him the background for *Err.*, *Tit.*, and *Ven.* Sh also showed that he had assimilated the spirit of the Greek tragedians. In introducing the early comedies, Chapter 5 sketches the "Classical Influence" of Plautus and Terence, which Sh blended with "the radiant spirit of Romance." Chapter 6, "Early Tragedy," begins with a discussion of Aeschylus, Sophocles, Euripides, and Seneca.

Chapter 9, on the poems, has a brief introductory section called "In the Wake of Ovid," which maintains that Sh liked the Roman poet because of his "propensity to make poetry out of everything." Sh's reputation as a love poet among his contemporaries made him "almost the English incarnation of Ovid."

0598 Jackson, MacDonald P. "A Non-Shakespearian Parallel to the Comic Mispronunciation of 'Ergo' in Hand D of *Sir Thomas More.*" *N&Q*, 19 (1971), 139.

Points out that the comic mispronunciation of "ergo" as "argo," which is found in the hand D part of *Sir Thomas More* and two other places in Sh, also occurs in Middleton's *The Phoenix*, IV.iii.16.

0598a Jacobs, Linda Lee. "Shakespeare and Euripides: The Androgynous Vision." Ph.D. dissertation, University of Kentucky, 1987. *DAI*, 49 (1988–89), 500-A-501-A.

Argues that in their late plays, both Euripides and Sh evidence similar androgynous visions. Uses three plays by each author (Euripides' *Ion, Iphigenia,* and *Helen* and Sh's *Cym., Per.,* and *WT*) to reach the conclusion that "both express a remarkable awareness of the female viewpoint; both associate women in a positive way with spiritual and irrational aspects of being; [and] both depict the world in terms of complementarity, using uniting symbols both mythic and dramatic."

0599 Jaffa, Harry V. "The Unity of Tragedy, Comedy, and History: An Interpretation of the Shakespearean Universe." *Shakespeare as Political Thinker.* Eds. John Alvis and Thomas G. West. Durham, North Carolina: Carolina Academic P., 1981, pp. 277–303.

Begins by noting that, though there is no direct evidence for Sh's acquaintance with Socratic writings, he seems to have deliberately set out to be the type of poet—capable of writing both tragedy and comedy—Socrates is talking about at the end of the *Symposium.* Accords *Tmp.* a special place as a comedy: Not only is this play explicitly about Sh's art, but it is Sh's version of the *Republic.* Explains that Sh wrote in a context created by "both Platonism and Christianity"; furthermore, the Machiavellian critique of Christianity meant that man's distress "was to be relieved not by salvation in the next world, but by security in this one." We see this "post-Christian modernity" in the lack of concern for honor in politically ambitious characters like Henry IV and Henry V and in the treatment of religious and racial prejudice in *MV* and *Oth.* Observes that the Roman plays and the English history plays are the center of Sh's treatment of things political. Discusses the suicide of the heroine in *Luc.* as defining the spirit of Roman matriotism, which is the basis for Roman patriotism. This is the spirit embodied by Volumnia in *Cor.,* a spirit with which she imbues her son. Such paganism, the source of the military power by which Rome conquered the world, prepared "the vehicle for Christianity." Coriolanus's obsession with his military virtue and honor keeps alive the hostility between the plebeians and the patricians that Sh, following Machiavelli, views as the driving force behind Rome's expansionism. In *JC,* we see the end of the republican tradition, with Mark Antony using "democratic rhetoric" to convince the people that they are Rome, not just one faction within it. In *Ant.,* Rome has become "the universal homogeneous state," in which politics proper has no place. The grounding of politics in loyalty to wife, family, and city is no longer possible for Antony, who has to find a new kind of "private love-making." Yet Antony and Cleopatra, in their tragedy, do achieve a transfiguration, a "final resurrection" that anticipates Christianity.

0600 Jagendorf, Zvi. *The Happy End of Comedy: Jonson, Molière, and Shakespeare.* Newark: U. of Delaware P., 1984. 177 pp.

Points to the device of discovery in the comedies of Plautus and Terence as the model for Renaissance playwrights. In Sh's romantic comedies, we see, through the playwright's experimentation with discovery, the clearest and most humane "modulation of riot and deadlock by recognition into change."

0601 Janakiram, Alur. *Reason and Love in Shakespeare: A Selective Study of Three Poems and Five Plays.* Machilipatnam: Triveni Publishers, 1977. xx + 228 pp.

Proposes to study the relationship of love and reason in three poems and five plays of Sh. Notes that Sh makes use of "the Neoplatonic equation of love with the higher intuitive reason." Chapter 1 describes the faculty psychology of the Renaissance, derived from ancient writers like Plato, Aristotle, and Galen, and outlined in contemporary works like Peter de la Primaudaye's *The French Academie,* Pierre Charron's *Of Wisdom,* Timothy Bright's *A Treatise of Melancholy,* and Robert Burton's *The Anatomy of Melancholy.* Chapter 2 presents various Renaissance perspectives on reason and love. Succeeding chapters examine the eight works of Sh. In *Ven.*, the goddess is "a paradoxical divinity who combines in herself the Renaissance Neoplatonic notions of love as a procreative principle and as a noble yearning." The paradoxical relationship of reason and love is also treated in *PhT*, and in *Luc.* there is a treatment of love as "an irrational descent to the lower level." *MND* exhibits the relation between reason and love "on the various levels of illusion and reality." In *LLL* and *Ado,* the principal characters learn that "love has its own compulsions which accord with those of reason." *Oth.* emphasizes that love and reason must support each other to ensure man's happiness. In *Tro.*, there is a separation between "love as it ought to be and love as a social posturing."

0602 Jardine, Lisa. *Still Harping on Daughters: Women and Drama in the Age of Shakespeare.* Totowa, New Jersey: Barnes & Noble, 1983. 202 pp.

Attempts to provide several ways to approach "the representations of women in the drama of theearly modern period." Comments on most of Sh's works. In *Tro.* and *Ant.*, women are in control, inverting the "natural hierarchy." Cleopatra's domination of Antony was well established by Plutarch, Sh's source for *Ant.* Notes in a chapter on Renaissance stereotypes of female heroism that the most powerful of these stereotypes involved the chastening of sexuality, even when, as in *Luc.* and *Tit.*, the female hero is a sexual victim. Lucrece's identification with Hecuba in the tapestry of Troy's fall unites the two figures in "a composite image" of radical guilt for the lust women passively arouse in men.

0603 Jenkins, Harold. *The Catastrophe in Shakespearean Tragedy.* (Inaugural Lecture Delivered on 3.XI. 1967.) Edinburgh: Edinburgh U. P., 1969. 22 pp.

Uses some Aristotelian terminology (catastrophe, peripeteia) in discussing the tragedies and focuses on *Ham., Mac., Oth.,* and *Lr.* Other plays also provide relevant examples. One tendency of Sh's tragedy is for the catastrophe to be indicated in some particular way by a previous scene. This may be seen in the appearance of Caesar's ghost to Brutus (*JC*, IV.iii). The foreshadowing of the protagonist's death by the death of someone close to him can also be illustrated from *JC* with the death of Portia, which Plutarch minimizes, and Sh could well have omitted. Sh's protagonists seem reconciled to dying: Timon and Cleopatra, for example, welcome death, "though for opposite reasons." Instances of the posthumous description of the hero "which governs our ultimate response to him" can be found in *JC, Ant.*, and *Cor.*, as well as elsewhere.

0604 Jenkins, Raymond. "The Tragic Hero of Shakespeare and Aristotle." *RenP,* 1958, 1959, 1960 (1961), 29–35.

Maintains that Sh so ennobles his tragic heroes that we sense that they are greater than the flawed protagonist Aristotle holds up in the *Poetics* as a model. In his tragic heroes, Sh most prizes a quality that closely resembles the greatness of soul that Aristotle describes in the *Ethics* as the essential virtue of the Magnanimous Man.

0605 Jensen, Ejner J. "A New Allusion to the Sign of the Globe Theater." *SQ,* 21 (1970), 95–97.

Discovers, in the induction to Marston's *Antonio and Mellida,* a slighting reference to two adult acting companies, the Admiral's Men and the Lord Chamberlain's Men.

General Works

A previously unrecognized allusion to the sign of the Globe is used to emphasize that the Admiral's Men are vulgar upstarts. They are so bold that they appear "to have appropriated the very symbol of their adult rivals," "as if Hercules / Or burly Atlas shoulder'd up their state."

0606 Jewett, Mike. "Shakespeare's Body Politic Imagery." Ph.D. dissertation, University of Missouri–Columbia, 1972. *DAI*, 33 (1972–73), 5180-A-5181-A.

Investigates the ways in which "anatomy and psychology assume political meanings in *Tro.* and in several of the histories and tragedies." Discusses *Tit., Tro., JC*, and *Ant.* at length.

0607 Jochum, Klaus Peter. *Discrepant Awareness: Studies in English Renaissance Drama.* (Neue Studien zur Anglistik und Amerikanistik, Band 13.) Frankfurt am Main: Peter Lang, 1979. 310 pp.

Proposes to investigate a group of Renaissance English dramas that make use of discrepant awareness, or the "uneven distribution of awareness and information" among different characters in a play and between the characters of a play and its audience. Chapter 3 traces the use of "informational strategies" in the revenge tragedy from its first appearance in the translations of Seneca's plays to its flowering in *Ham.* Chapter 6 covers Sh's tragedies. In *JC*, Caesar is unaware of the conspiracy that the audience has followed closely. After the assassination, the revengers and the conspirators compete quite openly; the retributive phase of this revenge play is unusual in that it is equal in length to the initial deception. In the end, the audience is not informed through any character of the motivations that lead to the deaths of Brutus and Cassius. The informational strategy offers no resolution, and as a result the play is morally ambiguous. In *Ant.*, informational discrepancies do not occur in extended form; it is as if Sh wastes many opportunities. There are some examples, however. Sh for a time keeps several characters in ignorance of Antony's decision to leave Egypt in act I, and he leaves Cleopatra partly in the dark about Antony's marriage and "subsequent behavior." Cleopatra's deceptions are effective and are treated effectively as parts of the drama. *Cor.* is a highly controlled play, using informational discrepancy with regard to geographical and personal isolation. Coriolanus is perfectly aware of the nature of the tribunes who oppose him, though he is tainted by underhandedness himself when he betrays Rome. He has no self-knowledge, and he fails to recognize the extent to which Aufidius is willing to go to destroy him. The audience is fully cognizant of the treacherous nature of both the tribunes and Aufidius and thus forms a relatively positive view of Coriolanus at the end. In order to preserve this sympathy, Sh withholds from us the reactions of a number of Romans to his hero's death. In *Tim.*, the Everyman figure of the morality plays has been split in two; the halves, Timon and his steward, make it possible for Sh to exploit discrepant awareness to exacerbate the outrage of the situation. Timon turns deceiver after he comprehends the unreliability of his friends, and the audience is partly surprised by his plan for a second banquet. Timon's visitors in the wilderness are all self-deceived; none can fathom the depths of his misanthropy. In this most pessimistic of plays, Sh does not furnish a perspective that could be used by both audience and characters to resolve the informational discrepancies that are so pervasive.

0608 Jones, David Edwards. "Shakespeare's Apprenticeship in Comedy." Ph.D. dissertation, University of Minnesota, 1963. *DA*, 25 (1964–65), 2491–2492.

Argues that Sh's apprenticeship in comedy consisted primarily of imitating the best models. Among classical writers, Terence modeled artistic integrity for him, and Plautus supplied him with "tricks for keeping audiences happy." In *Err.*, Sh increased the "farcical complexity" of classical comedy but altered the tone by the addition of pathos and romantic elements. In *Shr.*, he reworked classical motifs with help from Gascoigne's *Supposes*, and in the play's tone he approached "the heartlessness of Roman comedy." Sees Sh as "leaving his models behind" in *MND* and *MV*.

0609 Jones, Eldred. *Othello's Countrymen: The African in English Renaissance Drama.*. London: Oxford U. P., 1965. xii + 158 pp.

Chapter 1 provides a brief history of English perceptions of Africa and Africans. Notes that ancient writers like Pliny and Herodotus, whose fantastic tales of Africa were embedded in English writings, exerted a significant influence on the Elizabethans. From Pliny are ultimately derived, for example, some of the exotic details of Othello's career. More accurate information, however, was becoming available. Maintains that the most authoritative book on the interior of Africa available in the 16th c. was John Leo Africanus's *The History and Description of Africa*, originally published in 1550 and translated into English by John Pory in 1600. Sh seems to have drawn on this work for some details of Antony's description of Egypt (*Ant.*, II.vii). Chapter 2 includes discussions of Aaron (*Tit.*) and Othello (*Oth.*).

0610 Jones, Emrys. *The Origins of Shakespeare*. Oxford: Clarendon P., 1977. vii + 290 pp.

Attempts to explain in some detail how Sh emerged from the intellectual and cultural matrix of the mid-Tudor age to become a great dramatist. Chapter 1 describes the complex, pervasive influence of Christian humanism on 16th-c. England. Humanism's leading figure was Erasmus, who served as "a mediator of classical thought and experience" through his original works, editions, translations from Greek into Latin, and the compilations of idioms, sayings, proverbs, and anecdotes that constitute such works as his *Adagia* and *Apophthegmata*. The humanist educational program emphasized the study of classical Roman literature as well as a great deal of rote learning about linguistic matters. As a result of this system, many Elizabethan schoolboys became able classical scholars and "resourceful practitioners in English." Having memorized hundreds, perhaps thousands, of lines or fragments of lines from the Latin poets and having assimilated a multitude of phrases, rhythms, and constructions from the prose writers, these students would cast a classical coloring over everything they wrote. Sh's rhetorical training can be seen in his early plays: The presentation of several different points of view without clear identification with any one in a play like *1H6*, for example, derives from the schoolboy exercises known as *controversiae*, in which the student was required to present the best case he could make for an arbitrarily assigned side of an argument. Students were given innumerable exercises in imitation of classical models, and Sh seems to have become supremely adept at adapting casually and freely the vast store of materials he had memorized from ancient authors. The death of Falstaff, for example, appears to glance at the death of Socrates. At some level, Sh must have thought in quotations; it is likely that he kept copious notebooks. As an illustration, Hamlet's soliloquy beginning "O what a rogue" can be seen to have three sources: Quintilian, *R3*, and Seneca's *Thyestes*. It is impossible to trace all of Sh's sources, which are often of little importance, but in some instances knowledge of the raw materials can add to our understanding. In *Oth.*, it is helpful to recognize that Horace's oxymoron "splendide mendax" applies to Desdemona as a heroically faithful wife. In *Mac.*, the protagonist's desire to see Banquo at dinner after having him murdered shows him suffering from the same kind of inhuman forgetfulness that Suetonius remarks on in his *Life of Claudius*.

Chapter 2, "Shakespeare and the Mystery Cycles," finds several plays, including *Cor.* and *Tim.*, using the Passion paradigm from the cycle plays, which consists of four important elements: "the prominence given to the hero's adversaries and their malice; their conspiratorial method; their legalism; and the progressive isolation of the hero." All four of these are found in *Cor.*; *Tim.* includes all but the second. In *Cor.*, two successive scenes in which a Roman and a Volsce meet in the road and summarize the action (IV.iii) and Coriolanus appears "*in mean apparel*" as a mysterious stranger (IV.iv) are probably indebted to the episode from the cycles in which two travelers on the road to Emmaus meet a stranger (Christ). The most visually striking scene in *Cor.* is the visit of the three women to the hero to plead with him to spare Rome; this scene parallels the visit of the three Marys to the tomb. In IV.ii of *Tim.*, the final meeting of Flavius with Timon's other servants recalls the cycle plays' account of the meeting of the disciples after the Crucifixion.

Chapter 3, "Shakespeare and Euripides (I): Tragic Passion," proposes Euripides'

Hecuba as the chief dramatic model for *Tit. Hecuba* was popular in the 16th c. because it represented a supreme example of tragic grief. It appeared in a large number of translations (Latin) and editions; it was referred to by Scaliger, Minturno, and Sidney to illustrate their theories, especially with regard to structure; and it was translated into Latin by Erasmus, whose authority would have recommended it for educational use. The two parts of *Hecuba* are relevant to the structure of *Tit.*; in each case, a "heroically powerful character" moves swiftly from suffering and lamentation to "purposeful revenge." *Tit.* is more "Greek" in feeling (as the Elizabethans might have understood the term) than Sh's other Roman plays: That is, it tells a story of Thracian violence, with human sacrifice. The ritual lopping of Alarbus's limbs is particularly calculated to remove the action into a barbarous and alien world.

Chapter 4, "Shakespeare and Euripides (II): Tragic Sentiment," argues that the quarrel scene between Brutus and Cassius in *JC* (IV.iii) is indebted to the scene in *Iphigenia in Aulis* where Agamemnon and Menelaus quarrel and then suddenly drop their hostility and are reconciled. Both episodes exhibit not so much "passion" as "feelings." In each play, the humanity of the two principals, including their weakness, is given a sympathetic presentation. Sh is likely to have known *Iphigenia in Aulis* through the Latin translation of Erasmus.

Chapter 10, "*Richard III*: A Tudor Climax," points out that *R3* is a play of fortune, a favorite Tudor theme. Several parts of *R3* have classical sources. In composing Clarence's dream, Sh was prompted by part of the sixth book of the *Aeneid*, in which Aeneas visits the underworld and encounters his helmsman Palinurus, who had fallen off his ship and drowned. In his *History of King Richard III* (a source for both Sh and Holinshed), More incorporated details from the descriptions of Tiberius by Tacitus and Suetonius, in particular the hypocritical reluctance of Tiberius to assume the title of emperor. Other details may have come from Suetonius's life of Claudius, who was lame like Richard.

Appendix A, "Shakespeare and Seneca," surveys some of the major discussions of the past century on the subject and concludes that Sh had a subtle appreciation of Seneca's style as well as his substance. The word "hand," for example, a favorite of Seneca's, appears frequently in *Jn.* and *R3* in passages that seem intended to approximate the classical tragic manner. In *Jn.*, the tragic figure of Constance recalls Andromache in Seneca's *Troades* and Medea in *Medea*. In *WT*, the scene (II.iii) in which Paulina brings Leontes his newborn baby and is violently rebuffed may owe something to Cassandra's dismissal by Clytemnestra in Seneca's *Agamemnon*; and in *Ado*, Beatrice's sudden demand for Benedick to kill Claudio seems to echo a similar request by Medea to Jason.

Appendix B, "Shakespeare and Lucan," asserts that Sh's knowledge of Lucan's *Pharsalia* is manifested in several areas of his work. In *2H6*, some lines of Warwick describing battle (V.ii.3-4) conflate two of Lucan's typical effects: the sound of the trumpet and the cries of dying men. *1H6* seems to be influenced by Lucan's characteristic concern with fame, and *JC* makes effective use of the notion of a future audience observing and assessing present actions (which derives from Lucan's account of Pompey's assassination). In *Ham.*, the speech about the fall of Troy that Hamlet quotes and asks the Player to recite is a skillful imitation of Lucan's style.

Appendix C, "The Player King before Shakespeare," discusses Sh's use of "the idea of the actor who shares only his costumes and pomp with real kings." It is found in several classical texts, including Lucian's dialogue *Necromantia*, which was translated by More into Latin and therefore known to Erasmus. It would also have been familiar to Erasmus from two of Seneca's letters. Sh probably knew this concept from one of Erasmus's *Adages*. It is prominent in *3H6* (York on his molehill), *Mac.*, *R2*, *Lr.*, and *Ham.*

0611   Jones, William John. "Shakespeare the Rhetorician, Part III." *Essays in Foreign Languages and Literature* (Hokkaido U., Japan), 28 (1981), 197–223.

Begins by summarizing a "previous paper" that gives an account of what Aristotle and Quintilian have to say about two divisions of the art of rhetoric: disposition and invention. The classical model, especially as provided by Quintilian, would have been the basis for the curriculum in Sh's grammar school. This essay sketches classical and

Renaissance concepts of *elocution*, the subdivision of rhetoric that lists and defines the tropes and schemes (or figures). Lays the groundwork for an analysis, in future papers, of Sh's verse, which will attempt to demonstrate his "incomparable mastery of all these rhetorical devices."

0612 Jorgensen, Paul A. *Redeeming Shakespeare's Words.* Berkeley: U. of California P., 1962. x + 131 pp.

Discusses several plays in terms of Renaissance connotations of key words. Chapter 6, "*Noble* in *Coriolanus*," points out that *noble* was a word the Elizabethans thought of as especially applicable to the ancient Romans. Because of many debates about true nobility, the word almost always carried a connotation "testing the validity of its application." Gentlemen were exhorted to prove their nobility by virtuous actions. Coriolanus, like Sh's other Roman heroes, is proud of his ancestry and anxious to prove himself noble. He is noble in serving the state, in despising public acclaim, and in being guileless. But his nobility is imperfect because he is proud, reckless, and irrational.

0613 Jorgensen, Paul A. *William Shakespeare: The Tragedies.* (Twayne's English Authors Series 415.) Boston: Twayne, 1985. [x] + 164 pp.

Devotes a separate chapter to each of ten tragedies. Chapter 2, on *Tit.*, identifies sources in the revenge drama, especially Seneca's *Thyestes*, and in Ovid's *Metamorphoses*. Argues that Titus evokes some sympathy in his progression "from a man of rigorous honor to a man who can feel." Discusses the inhuman environment of Rome, the "wilderness of tigers" in which Titus and his family live, mentioning the fascinating qualities of Aaron, whose villainy is "meaninglessly evil." The unresponsiveness of the world to "pleas for justice or pity" is especially notable. The play has some sense of resolution, though it is not morally satisfying.

 Chapter 4, on *JC*, notes that one of the reasons for the play's success is that Sh used Thomas North's translation of Plutarch's *Lives of the Noble Grecians and Romans* as his source. Comments on Brutus as a hero who possesses a broad humanity but limits himself because he tries to conceal his emotions.

 Chapter 9, on *Tim.*, affirms that the play fulfills Sh's plan, which involves driving home "a dominating moral message." The opening scene, with its lessons about Timon exhibited by the Poet and the Painter, sets the tone for a formal structure with abstract characters conveying an unambiguous theme. The play studies the virtue of nobility, portraying Timon's flaw as deriving from motives that are "generous rather than meager-hearted." Timon's exercise of friendship is largely praiseworthy, distinguishing him as it does from the parasites that consume him. The last part of the play reveals that Timon's misanthropy, although powerfully expressed, is excessive. There is some sense of reconciliation and reordering of Athenian society at the end, but there is little sense that Timon has been enlarged sufficiently to be a tragic hero.

 Chapter 10, on *Ant.*, points out that Sh's adaptation of Plutarch stresses Antony's inner struggle and the choices that make him "responsible, sometimes heroically, for his own fate." Considers desertions and betrayals in the play, noting that the Romans are just as guilty of inconstancy as the Egyptians are. The protagonists are finally united, with Cleopatra's noble death answering that of Antony.

 Chapter 11, on *Cor.*, shows Sh, under the influence of Plutarch, "assessing the relative worth to Rome of the nobility and the commonalty." Calls attention to the raucousness and stupidity of the commoners, the great power of Volumnia in forming Coriolanus's idea of his own nobility, Coriolanus's flaw (his disdain for the citizens), the dangerous ambivalence of martial virtue (seen in the hero's self-banishment to the enemy camp), the greater nobility of feeling for other human beings induced in him by his family, and his final sacrifice.

 Includes a critically annotated bibliography of fifty-six major scholarly books on the tragedies.

General Works

0614 Kahn, Coppélia. *Man's Estate: Masculine Identity in Shakespeare.* Berkeley: U. of California P., 1981. xiii + 238 pp.

Proposes to examine "dilemmas of masculine selfhood" as they are revealed in Sh's works. Points out that Sh's men have two problems in defining their manhood. First, they must differentiate their masculinity from the femininity of their mothers to establish their sexual identity, but as adults they can fulfill their social roles only by reuniting with women in marriage. Second, in order to conform themselves to the requirements of the patriarchy that gives them control over their families, and, through a widely accepted analogy derived by Renaissance political theorists from Aristotle, over all social systems, men are paradoxically forced into an oblique dependence on women for the confirmation of their manhood. The chapters are arranged to follow "the ages of man." Chapter 2, a revision of item 3137, considers *Ven.* as a portrayal of adolescent masculinity in retreat from the sexual desire that would guide it into manhood. Chapter 6 includes a reading of *Cor.* that views its hero as an unfinished man, a boy who commits himself to violence because he has been convinced by a woman that it will make him manly. Volumnia's sexual identity is also confused as she attempts to transcend her femininity vicariously through a man.

0615 Kaiser, Gerhard W. *The Substance of Greek and Shakespearean Tragedy under Special Consideration of Shakespeare's "King Lear," "Macbeth," "Othello," and "Romeo and Juliet."* (Elizabethan and Renaissance Studies 67.) Salzburg: Institut für Englische Sprache und Literatur, 1977. 291 pp.

Examines works by Aeschylus, Sophocles, and Euripides in the first section to establish, inductively, the substance of Greek tragedy. Discusses, in the second section, *Lr.*, *Mac.*, *Oth.*, and *Rom.* to discover the substance of Sh's tragedy and provide a basis for comparing it to that of the Greeks. The primary difference lies in Sh's reliance on Christian assumptions (though these are seldom explicit in the plays). Sh does not insist as much as the Greeks on the determining power of fate. His heroes are not caused by outside forces to commit their fatal deeds; their wills, though free, are infected by a fatal flaw that makes them blind to reality. There are, however, important parallels between the two types of tragedy: The demonic force that possesses the Greek heroes is similar to the rash pursuit of illusion in the Shakespearean characters. Both types of protagonist become guilty and must endure intense suffering; for both, the depth of suffering brings them to a recognition of guilt and a clear perception of the truth, and in both cases, there is at the end a restoration of harmony and a sense of transcendent order.

0616 Kaiser, Walter. *Praisers of Folly: Erasmus, Rabelais, Shakespeare.* (Harvard Studies in Comparative Literature 25.) Cambridge: Harvard U. P., 1963. x + 318 pp.

Suggests that classical elements played a role in the Renaissance development of the paradoxical notion of the wise fool. With wisdom and folly confronting each other in the same person, "sustained irony becomes possible for the first time since the classical age, and in the language of fools the voice of wisdom is heard." Devotes a section to the character of Falstaff in *1H4* and *2H4*. Argues that Falstaff can be understood partly in terms of a contrast between the Epicurean philosophy, which he espouses, and Stoic regularity, which he seeks to overturn. His self-encomiastic remarks resemble those of Stultitia in Erasmus's *Praise of Folly*: Both are indebted to Aphthonius. Analyzes Falstaff's role as fool in terms of Aristotle's discussion of truthfulness in the *Ethics*. According to Aristotle, the moderate man (*alethes*) is truthful; the boaster (*alazon*) exaggerates; and the falsely modest man (*eiron*) understates. When Falstaff claims to be the butt of other men's wit, "he is wearing the mask of the *eiron*; when he boasts that he is the source of wit in himself, he is wearing the mask of the *alazon*."

0617 Kantas, Alexander Anastasios. "Enigmas of Justice: Marlowe to Ford." Ph.D. dissertation, University of Illinois at Urbana–Champaign, 1974. *DAI*, 35 (1974–75), 7257-A.

Chapter 1 explains how classical thought developed an idea of justice based on the capacity of the rational faculties to impose, by the use of analogy, a sense of order on an irrational universe. Combined with Judeo–Christian notions, this Greek idea of justice as reason was inherited by the Renaissance. Discusses a number of Elizabethan and Jacobean plays in which the inherited concepts of justice are challenged. Analyzes six of Sh's plays, in which "we see an intense insistence on a human justice that operates without the need of an ethical imperative to validate it."

0618 Karim, Md. Enamul. "The East in Shakespeare's Tragedies." *Homage to Shakespeare*. Ed. Syed Sajjad Husain. Dacca: Department of English, Dacca U., 1965, pp. 60–70.

Points out that Sh's knowledge of the Orient, "though not elaborate, is precise and deep." Conceptions of the East are significant in Sh's Moors (Aaron in *Tit.* and Othello) and in *Ant.*, which devotes more space to "the depiction of Eastern life" than any other play.

0619 Kastan, David Scott. *Shakespeare and the Shapes of Time*. Hanover, New Hampshire: U. P. of New England, 1982. viii + 197 pp.

Examines Sh's exploration of ways to give adequate dramatic form to "man's temporal experience." Explains two important "models of historical time" for Sh's age: The first was "providential and fundamentally linear" and was "derived from the patristic and medieval historical writings"; the second was exemplary and cyclical and was "derived from the traditions of late classical historiography." Shows, through an analysis of the Talbot episodes in *1H6*, that from the beginning of his career Sh was interested in scrutinizing both models. For example, the possibility of Talbot's acting as a heroic *exemplum*, a permanent reminder of virtue in the humanist/classical sense, is raised but then rejected. Consideration of the different kinds of plays in the canon reveals that Sh's "vision of man in time" is not confined to one perspective. Includes sections on the histories, the tragedies, and the romances. Likens Brutus in *JC* to Hotspur in *1H4*: Both men rigidly commit themselves to a standard of excellence that cuts them off from a rich interior life and prevents them from redeeming the time. Views *Ant.*, in its resistance to tragic closure, as an adumbration of Sh's romances. In *Cym.*, the marvelously constructed ending, revealing as it does the multiple manifestations of human love, is able to ransom history from its "irreversibility" if not from "its inflexible temporality."

0620 Kaufmann, R. J. "The Senecan Perspective and the Shakespearean Poetic." *CompD*, 1 (1967–68), 182–98.

Argues that Seneca offered Sh and other dramatists of the early 17th c. something beyond the reach of the other Roman poets. For one thing, he eagerly explored the effects of violent passion, especially in the degradation of the feminine character (note the rising control of powerful women in Sh's tragedies). He was alert to the movement of his own mind and tried to chart the course of the irrational in his characters. In creating atmosphere for his dramas, he used the pathetic fallacy. The Astraea myth, explained by Ovid as the withdrawal of divine order from the earth, and the consequent breaking of the bonds of humanity in the Iron Age, provides a useful insight into Sh's use of the Senecan perspective. Seneca's plays read like dramatizations of conditions in Ovid's Iron Age. Although not able to fully integrate his tragic vision, he thus gave Sh a way into the world of a play like *Lr*. It is as "a fabulist of cultural, psychological, and metaphysical crisis" that Seneca appealed most profoundly to the great dramatists of Sh's time.

0621 Kavros, Harry Emanuel. "Shakespeare and the Anti-Rhetorical Tradition." Ph.D. dissertation, University of California, Berkeley, 1981. *DAI*, 42 (1981–82), 3165-A.

Outlines the history of the art of rhetoric from 5th-c. Athens through the Renaissance and focuses on a small group of thinkers who, though not opposed to rhetorical training, were concerned about its "political, moral, and psychological ramifications" for their cultures. These commentators include Plato, Erasmus, Montaigne, and Francis Bacon. Sh, responding to some of the inadequacies of rhetoric pointed out by his predecessors, created "dramatic speech which is generated by personal wills and desires," and through which he could analyze "problems of discourse." *LLL* and *TN* focus on problems of discourse, but in these plays the problems generate laughter. In *JC* and *Tro.*, "failures of discourse" result in disasters.

0622 Kayser, John R., and Ronald J. Lettieri. "'The Last of All the Romans': Shakespeare's Commentary on Classical Republicanism." *Clio*, 9 (1979–80), 197–227.

Contends that to Sh, the essence of republican Rome lay in its mixed regime, combining, in an appropriate hierarchy, the courage or spiritedness of the nobility with the low *eros*, or instinct for self-preservation, of the plebeians. As Sh portrayed the republic in *Luc.* and *Cor.*, its formation and development were the result of historical accident, not, as would be the case ideally, through the conscious exercise of reason. In *JC*, Brutus fails to order the mixture of elements in his own soul by the use of reason and thus becomes a microcosm of Rome itself, which, lacking reason to sustain it as a republic, expires when custom or patriotism is no longer able to bind its disparate elements together.

0623 Kazarian, Albert I. "Shakespeare's Representations of Mourning in Seven Plays." Ph.D. dissertation, University of California, Davis, 1990. *DAI*, 52 (1991–92), 548-A.

Analyzes, in chronological order, seven plays that treat mourning over an extended period of time. Considers, among other issues, the way Sh explores the capacity of mourners "to benefit from classical and Christian teachings." Discusses *Ado*, *MM*, *JC*, *Ham.*, *Ant.*, *Per.*, and *WT*.

0624 Kearns, Terrance Brophy. "Prisoner to the Palsy: A Study of Old Age in Shakespeare's History Plays." Ph.D. dissertation, Indiana University, 1978. *DAI*, 39 (1978–79), 6777-A.

Traces the evolution of Sh's treatment of old age in his ten history plays. Begins by surveying the classical, medieval, and early Renaissance works that deal with the effects of aging. Two contradictory opinions on the subject emerge: The works of Cicero, Seneca, Roger Bacon, and Castiglione suggest that old age can be productive and fulfilling, while Horace's *Ars Poetica*, the plays of Euripides, and much medieval didactic literature emphasize its debilitating effects. Treats the histories in the order of their composition, remarking on Sh's increasing sympathy for the aged.

0625 Keeton, George W. *Shakespeare's Legal and Political Background*. London: Sir Isaac Pitman & Sons, 1967. viii + 417 pp.

Chapter 5 attempts to explain the classical background of certain concepts of law as Sh would have understood them. The law of nature, an idea first found in the Greek philosophers, was primarily a principle of order, founded on reason, by which the universe was governed. It could be contrasted with human laws, which were subject to frequent change. The Stoics gave the law of nature a secondary meaning: When man lives as directed by his reason, "he is in conformity with the Law of Nature." The Stoic concept influenced Roman law. Closely related to natural law was *jus gentium*, a special system, based on the common usages of other nations and developed by the Romans to apply to the foreign lands they ruled. St. Thomas Aquinas blended the legal doctrines of Aristotle, the Stoics, Cicero, the Roman imperial jurists, and St. Augustine, and passed them on to the Renaissance. Sh was familiar with the law of nature and *jus gentium*: For example, Hector uses the latter in his argument for the return of Helen (*Tro.*, II.ii.173–186).

Chapter 7, "The Law of Debt in Shakespeare," discusses, among other things, the problem of explaining Timon's indebtedness in terms of Greek, Roman, or English law.

Chapter 16, "Shakespeare and the Political Thought of the Sixteenth Century," points out the classical and medieval sources of the analogies used by Tudor writers to explain and reinforce the concept of a society based on a harmonious integration of all its parts. The notions of order and degree are important in *JC*, *Cor.*, and *Tro.*

Chapter 24, "The Politics of the Greek and Roman Plays," argues that Sh's political philosophy "was based on the conception of a natural order in which all classes, according to their degree, worked together for the common good." Thus, in *Cor.*, both the protagonist and the plebeians merit condemnation. In *JC* and *Ant.*, "divided authority leads directly to the destruction of civil order," and in *Tim.* and *Tro.*, the society portrayed is a corrupt one in which "all ranks have forgotten their obligations."

0626 Kelly, Lois. "Multiplicity and Meaning in Three Shakespearean Plays: *Titus Andronicus, Antony and Cleopatra,* and *Othello.*" Ph.D. dissertation, State University of New York at Buffalo, 1985. *DAI*, 46 (1985–86), 707-A-708-A.

Finds in metaphor "the structure which orders and gives meaning or universal significance" to the plays under consideration. Explains that in *Tit.* "two metaphors—each a binarism—convey a specific universal; one series of particulars points to the repetitive pattern of violent acts revenge tragedy spawns, while another series points to the nature of an initial act of violence." Eschews, in the spirit of Roland Barthes, a "'correct' or universal meaning" for *Ant.*, celebrating instead "the triumphant plural as it breaks away from any ideology of totality."

0626a Kermode, Frank. *The Patience of Shakespeare.* New York: Harcourt, Brace, & World, 1964. 19 pp. Reprint. *Encounter*, November, 1964, pp. 3–10. Reprint. *Shakespeare, Spenser, Donne: Renaissance Essays.* New York: Viking P., 1971, pp. 149–63.

Comments on Sh's learning, which after a "flourish of formal scholarship in the Ovidian imitations of his youth," consisted of raids on North's Plutarch and other works. The right way to comprehend his interest in the Roman Empire—and his portrayals of Caesar and Antony—is not to find out what others thought about them.

0627 Kermode, J. F. "The Banquet of Sense." *Bulletin of the John Rylands Library*, 44 (1961–62), 68–99. Reprint. *Shakespeare, Spenser, Donne: Renaissance Essays.* New York: Viking P., 1971, pp. 84–115.

Explains that the banquet of sense, which represents a descent into bestial gratification, has both Christian (St. Paul's reference to "the table of devils" in a discussion of the Eucharist in 1 Corinthians 10) and pagan (Xenophon's account of the myth of the choice of Hercules) sources. In the Renaissance, the choice of Hercules came to be associated with a banquet tempting him to give himself over to sensual pleasure, particularly to descend from the highest (sight and hearing) to the lowest (smell, taste, and touch) senses. The sensual banquet, associated by Ben Jonson and others with Ovid, was held up as a contrast to "the Banquet of Heavenly Love" (linked by Ficino to Plato's *Symposium*). Sh used the banquet of sense in Sonnet 141 (where the senses are introduced in order, from highest to lowest, and are connected with a "sensual feast"). In *Tim.*, where there are two banquets, the first of which features a masque of the senses, the motif is used to point out Timon's mistaken notions of honor and nobility. In *Ven.*, the goddess tempts Adonis by describing how he appeals to each of her senses, ending with the exclamation "what a banquet wert thou to the taste, / Being nurse and feeder of the other four!" (lines 445–446).

0628 Kermode, J. F. "On Shakespeare's Learning." *Bulletin of the John Rylands Library*, 48 (1965–66), 207–26. Reprint. *Shakespeare, Spenser, Donne: Renaissance Essays.* New York: Viking P., 1971, pp. 181–99.

Argues that Sh was learned in a special way: He was "capable of an intense interest—intense, yet sometimes at the same time wanton or even perverse—in the formulae of

General Works 175

learning: a strong-minded, willful, private, reading man." Illustrates this "habit of curious brooding upon ideas" by discussing the treatment of time in Sh's works, particularly *aevum*, the scholastic concept of "a third order between time and eternity." Sees *aevum* as related to the idea of continuity in human affairs: Sh seems to have applied this concept to the Roman Empire in *Ant.* and *Cym.* Focuses on *PhT*, which employs much learning (including materials from Lactantius, Ovid, and Catullus) to give metaphysical expression to *aevum* and related concepts.

0629   Entry deleted.

0630   Kernan, Alvin. "The Plays and Playwrights." *The Revels History of Drama in English.* Vol. 3. 1576–1613. Eds. Clifford Leech and T. W. Craik. London: Methuen, 1975, pp. 237–474.

Discerns in most important plays of the period a tension between a sense of freedom conferred by the imagination and a feeling of helplessness before the intractable reality of life. In *MND*, Theseus and Hippolyta, the representatives of order and reason in the sunlit world of Athens, are connected, by reference to their mythological past, with the primordial, disruptive powers of sexuality. The Ovidian and Senecan images of violence in *Tit.* are used to create a condition of complete tragic helplessness for Titus and his family, a condition from which they escape by taking bloody action. *JC* and *Tro.* both feature unsuccessful attempts by major characters to idealize everyday existence. In *JC*, the shaping power of the rational will is persistently challenged, while in *Tro.* the heroic fixity of myth is constantly undermined by history. The heroes of *Tim.* and *Cor.* are constricted by absolute, inflexible images of themselves and thus are led to meaningless deaths in a complex world where their visions make no sense. In *Ant.*, there is an intimation that at some level the imagination of man and the workings of nature corroborate each other.

0631   Kernan, Alvin B. *The Playwright as Magician: Shakespeare's Image of the Poet in the English Public Theater.* New Haven: Yale U. P., 1979. vii + 164 pp.

Discusses briefly, in a chapter on *Lr.* that examines Sh's reflections on "traditional theatrical form," the complex perspective set up in *Tro.* (V.ii) when Cressida transfers her allegiance to Diomedes. Comments that the limited perspective of Ulysses and Thersites, both of whom interpret the episode as a morality play, underlines Sh's reservations about the "old style" of the moralities. Argues, in a chapter on *Tmp.*, that this play figures the playwright's art as magic and affirms its central role in human affairs. Prospero's greatest play is the masque of Juno and Ceres in IV.i, which "makes visible the great gods themselves" to inform the young lovers of the bounty and fertility of the world.

0632   Keyes, Laura Catherine. "Silence in Shakespeare." Ph.D. dissertation, State University of New York at Buffalo, 1981. *DAI*, 42 (1981–82), 1647-A.

Includes a chapter on the Roman plays—*Tit., JC, Ant.,* and *Cor.*—which also treats *Luc.* and *Cym.* Examines the connection between "dumb stoicism and violence in the Roman ethic." Like the chronicle plays, the Roman works usually equate the ability to speak with power. Weakness in women, children, and other disenfranchised characters is often indicated by their being silenced.

0633   Khanna, Urmila. *The Tragic Hero in Shakespeare: The Dramatic Significance of His Isolation.* New Delhi: Orient Longman, 1974. 110 pp.

Chapter 5, on *Ant.*, traces Antony's gradual isolation from Rome, which takes place in three stages. Finally, he recognizes that he must give up all things Roman for Cleopatra, who, in her death, "becomes worthy of the isolation he had endured for her." Chapter 6, on *Cor.*, shows that from the beginning, and in contrast to Plutarch's version of the hero, Coriolanus is alone, priding himself on his self-sufficiency even when he fights for Rome. His tragedy arises from his attempt to acknowledge the bond of nature and thus save his native city at the same time that he "tries to be true to his pledge as a soldier."

0634 Kiefer, Frederick. "The Conflation of Fortuna and Occasio in Renaissance Thought and Iconography." *JMRS*, 9–10 (1979–80), 1–27.

Examines the "iconographic changes that Fortune underwent in the Renaissance and the conceptual transformation that shaped them." Analyzes 15th- and 16th-c. commentaries and visual representations to show that at this time Fortune's attributes (the sea, a sphere, a rudder, a wheel) were being combined with those of Occasion (a forelock, a sail) to indicate "the growing conviction" that man, through his own decisions, is largely responsible for what happens to him. Notes that classical writers had linked time with Occasion and shows that the attributes of Time were often transferred to Fortune in the Renaissance. Cites examples of the new conception of Fortune from *Luc.* and *Tmp.* However, the portrayal of Fortune on a hill by the Poet in *Tim.* is "distinctly medieval." Revised as chapter 7 of item 0635.

0635 Kiefer, Frederick. *Fortune and Elizabethan Tragedy.* San Marino, California: Huntington Library, 1983. xix + 354 pp.

Chapter 1 "explores the efforts of Christians to come to terms with a pagan symbol of change and contingency." Discusses Augustine, Boethius, Petrarch, Chaucer, and John Calvin. Chapter 7, "Fortune and Occasion," a revision of item 0634, shows how Fortune was significantly transformed in the late 15th and early 16th c. to assimilate attributes "that in antiquity had belonged to Occasio." Chapter 8 discusses *R2, JC,* and *Ham.* In the first of these, Richard is a victim of Fortune, descended from *de casibus* tragedy, whereas Bolingbroke, an aggressive opportunist, has little to do with the goddess. In *JC,* Brutus tries to balance "fatalism and self-determination," sensing that Occasio, or opportunity, is there for those who choose the right moment to act. Ironically, however, Brutus always mistimes his actions. In *Ham.,* the protagonist is tormented by Fortune until late in the play when he begins to feel that he is being guided by providence instead. See item 1860. Chapter 9 includes a discussion of *Lr.,* a play in whose world the power of Fortune "can no longer be checked." Chapter 10, on *Tim.* and *Ant.,* argues that the protagonist of the former tries unsuccessfully to protect himself from the vicissitudes of Fortune by cultivating friends and that the lovers in the latter, despite some intimations that opportunities to succeed might be seized, are unable to stand against the flux. In both plays, Fortune is seen as an opponent.

0636 Kiefer, Harry Christian. "Elizabethan Attitudes toward Music in Shakespeare's Plays." Ph.D. dissertation, Columbia University, 1961. *DA*, 22 (1961–62), 1177–1178.

Explores Elizabethan musical thought as it appears in Sh's plays. Focuses on "the multiple extensions of musical analogy by which the intricate design of the universe could be perceived." Mentions classical and other sources for this music lore, including Boethius's *De Institutione Musica.* Musical symbolism helps convey the romantic and social harmony with which Sh's comedies end, the political harmony of the state in the histories, and "the larger harmony of cosmic music" in the tragedies and romances. Furthermore, musical thought relates all the types of Sh's plays by articulating order in various ways. The idea of harmony in the state, for example, is crucial to the Roman plays as well as to *Ham.* and *Mac.,* and "the *musica humana* of the well-tempered self" is a concept essential to understanding Orsino, Lear, Prince Hal, and Hotspur.

0637 Kiernan, V. G. "Human Relationships in Shakespeare." *Shakespeare in a Changing World.* Ed. Arnold Kettle. New York: International Publishers, 1964, pp. 43–64.

Maintains that, writing at a time when the feudal order was being replaced by capitalism, Sh was particularly concerned with how men relate to each other. *JC* is especially rich in "positive relationships" among the characters: Brutus and Cassius; Brutus and Portia; Caesar and Antony; and Caesar and Brutus. Throughout the plays, Sh is particularly horrified by "the destruction of men's faith in one another."

0637a Kimbrough, Robert. "Androgyny Seen Through Shakespeare's Disguise." *SQ*, 33 (1982), 17–33.

Calls attention to the familiarity of medieval and Renaissance Europe with Plato's depiction of the "original wholeness of each human as Man, Woman, and Androgyne" in the *Symposium*. Notes the renewed interest in androgyny in the 15th- and 16th-c. study of the Kabbala, Gnosticism, Hermeticism, and alchemy. In this climate, many 16th-c. authors recognized that their humanistic aspirations could not be fulfilled until rigidly defined gender roles had been challenged. Uses this background to discuss *TGV*, *AYL*, *TN*, and *Ant*.

0638 Kimbrough, Robert. *Shakespeare and the Art of Humankindness: The Essay toward Androgyny*. Atlantic Highlands, New Jersey and London: Humanities P. International, 1990. xvi + 272 pp.

Treats *Ven*. as an androgynous myth of creation, with Adonis as "perfect androgyne beauty." In the comic mismatch between Venus and Adonis, Sh is experimenting, showing how the essay toward androgyny "de-classic-fies" myth. In *JC*, Portia makes a bid to transgress her prescribed gender role and participate in Brutus's world, and Brutus is momentarily moved to acknowledge her equal partnership. However, her attempt ultimately fails, there being no equal access to the Roman world for women.

0639 Kirschner, Teresa J. "The Mob in Shakespeare and Lope de Vega." *Parallel Lives: Spanish and English National Drama 1580–1680*. Eds. Louise and Peter Fothergill-Payne. Lewisburg: Bucknell U. P., 1991, pp. 140–51.

Cites examples from *JC* and *Cor*. to show that Sh is like Lope de Vega in amassing as many actors as possible in his crowd scenes and in employing an "all-encompassing character, usually called 'All,'" to represent the crowd's many voices. Sh is unlike de Vega, however, in that he always portrays the populace in negative terms, focusing on its fickleness and its stench.

0640 Kitto, H. D. F. "Tragic Drama and Intellectualism." *EDH*, N. S. 31 (1962), 95–113.

Finds parallels between the decline of tragedy after the great age of Athenian drama in the 5th c. B.C. and after Sh. In both ages there was a development of tragic drama from religious origins, a situation that produced plays having "constant and conscious reference to the whole cosmos." In each case, a relatively short period of great achievement was followed by drama that shirked tragic issues. What happened, for both the Athenians and the Elizabethans, was a new emphasis on individualism, intellectualism, and the study of character for its own sake. The result was a drama that avoided the broad realism of the earlier tragic vision (which had subordinated the study of individuals to a larger cosmic perspective) and became preoccupied with incidental details of characterization and poetic justice. In both instances, the succeeding, more "enlightened" age seemed to lose touch with the great tragic accomplishments of the past, as the comments of Aristotle and Dr. Johnson attest. Uses *Lr.*, *Ham.*, and two plays by Euripides as primary examples.

0641 Klein, David. *The Living Shakespeare*. New York: Twayne, 1970. 126 pp.

Considers Sh's plays in terms of political problems that still concern us today. Uses *Cor*. in defending Sh against the charge that he was hostile to the common man. The impassioned charges the protagonist makes against the people of Rome are not to be identified with the opinions of Sh himself. In bringing us to see the limitations of Coriolanus, Sh makes two important changes in Plutarch's account. In the source, "Coriolanus requests the liberation of a formerly rich well-descended friend of his in the captured city of Corioli, and the request is presumed granted." In Sh, the man is poor, and Coriolanus forgets his name. After Coriolanus is banished, Plutarch describes "great troubles and commotions at Rome," while Sh depicts a peace. Coriolanus, devoted to the old aristocratic order, is limited in his vision, while the tribunes, spokesmen for the people, are wise and statesmanlike. Chapter 3, "Four Types of Political Leader," analyzes four characters in *JC*: Caesar (the bombastic dictator), Mark Antony (the cunning demagogue), Brutus (the good man torn between two loyalties and flawed by self-consciousness about his own virtue), and Cassius (a noble man, willing to resort to political expedients to gain worthy goals, who has been unjustly maligned by commentators). Also treats *Ham.*, *Mac.*, and *MV*.

0642 Klene, Mary Jean. "Shakespeare's Use of the Renaissance Concepts of Honor." Ph.D. dissertation, University of Toronto, 1970. *DAI*, 32 (1971–72), 3256-A-3257-A.

Attempts to explain the relevance of the Renaissance concept of honor to Sh's plays. According to the courtesy literature of the time, a man's honor depends on his exercising two virtues—valor and justice—and on the chastity of his wife. Chapter 1 examines valor as it is prescribed for war or for duels by focusing on *Tro.* and *Ham.* In both of these plays, the distinction between honor and honesty is important. Chapter 2 deals with the assumption of female inferiority underlying the prescription that a woman's chastity is a constituent of her husband's honor. The heroines of *Ado*, *AWW*, and *MM* challenge this doctrine even when they repeat parts of it. Chapter 3 explores the idea of justice in Sh, which, as it is dramatized in *2H4*, *Lr.*, and *MM*, has little to do with a code of honor. Chapter 4 discusses *Oth.* as "the tragedy of a man of honor, one concerned about his reputation for valor and justice and keenly aware of dependence on female fidelity."

0643 Klink, Eileen Smith. "Quintilian's Legacy: Labeling Women in the Late Renaissance." Ph.D. dissertation, U. of Southern California, 1991. *DAI*, 52 (1991–92), 2151-A.

Focuses on the scurrilous epithet as applied to women in Renaissance English literature, including Sh's works. This sort of labeling was a rhetorical convention, derived in part from Quintilian.

0644 Knight, G. Wilson. *The Golden Labyrinth: A Study of British Drama.* New York: Norton, 1962. xiv + 402 pp.

Chapter 4 surveys Sh's plays with a series of polarities in mind: male and female, Apollonian and Dionysian, society (or king) and its or his antagonist. *JC* is a transitional piece between the histories, where the opposers of royalty, though strong, are of secondary interest, and the tragedies, where great individuals rebelling against order dominate the action. In *JC*, the interest is divided among four leading persons. In *Tim.*, the first three acts are Apollonian and the last two Dionysian. In *Ant.*, Sh celebrates a fusion of the two sexes, of two cultures, and of the Dionysian and Apollonian principles.

0645 Knight, G. Wilson. "Shakespeare and the English Language." *Shakespeare and Religion: Essays of Forty Years.* New York: Barnes & Noble, 1967, pp. 241–51.

Notes that during Sh's time new words from many sources, notably Latin and Greek, were being assimilated into English. In addition, through translation and other means, "the cultures of ancient Greece and Rome were becoming . . . common property." Points out the universality suggested by the many origins (several from Latin and Greek) of the names in *Ham.* Remarks on the simplicity of the style in *JC*, the comic sport at "the new love of Latin derivations" in *LLL*, and the "awkward and unnatural" Latinisms that are evidence of thought divorced from instinct in *Tro.*

0646 Knight, G. Wilson. *Shakespeare's Dramatic Challenge: On the Rise of Shakespeare's Tragic Heroes.* London: Croom Helm, 1977. 181 pp.

Part 1, consisting of seven chapters, surveys Sh's tragic heroes, emphasizing their poetry, especially how it accumulates power and rises toward the ends of long speeches and toward the ends of plays. Begins with *Tit.*, analyzing speeches by the protagonist and by Aaron. Chapter 3, "On Poetic Acting," gives the speech in which Antony, having heard of Cleopatra's supposed suicide, speaks to Eros about killing himself (*Ant.*, IV.xiv.34–54) as an especially fine example of "the build-up towards revelation" in Sh's tragic speeches. Continues the survey in chapter 4, observing that the attempt at creating a tragic hero in Brutus (*JC*) does not succeed because there is no growth in the character. Devotes chapter 6 to *Tim.* as the culmination of Sh's tragic sequence. This is Sh's last work of tragedy, an archetypal representative of the genre. Calls attention to the relationship between *Tim.* and other works of Sh (*Tit.*, *Son.*, late romances); the use of ingratitude, an important Shakespearean theme; the imperfection of the play; the unleashing of new power in the second half (characteristic of a Shakespearean tragedy, but taken to an extreme here); the importance of nakedness and gold; the "elemental simplicity" of Timon's experience; and the development of Timon into a kind of superman speaking in universal terms. No other Shakespearean tragic hero has "so nobly conceived and meaningful a conclusion." Includes suggestions for performance and rearrangement of some of the scenes in acts IV and V derived from the author's lecture–recitals. Chapter 7, "The Last Phase," comments briefly on the "two Roman dramas," *Ant.* and *Cor.*, which "return to a more or less normal treatment of heroism," and mentions the role of the tragedies, especially as represented by *Tim.*, as harbingers of the late romances. Notes that Sh "seems to have turned to the Greeks when searching for new adventure." Part 2 describes the performances given by the author in his lecture–recitals and provides the script for his commentary on and performance of excerpts from *Tim.*

0647   Knight, G. Wilson. *Vergil and Shakespeare.* (The Ninth Jackson Knight Memorial Lecture.) Exeter: U. of Exeter, 1977. 26 pp.

Compares Virgil and Sh, focusing on the similarities between their treatments of war and heroism. Both poets associate the pastoral with peace; both face the horrors of war unblinkingly; both view war with great pity, especially in their accounts of the slaughter of youthful warriors; both portray warriors (Turnus and Hotspur) whose single-minded devotion to fighting gives them emotional unity and credibility; and both create heroes (Hal and Aeneas) whose characters are "synthetic in the bad sense" because their instinct for peace is at odds with the necessity that they make war.

0648   Knight, George Wilson. "Shakespeare and Society." *Critical Dimensions: English, German and Comparative Literature Essays in Honour of Aurelio Zanco.* Eds. Mario Curreli and Alberto Martino. Cuneo, Italy: SASTE, 1978, pp. 93–105.

Asserts that Sh was essentially conformist in his social views but that more needs saying on the subject. Examines depictions of conformity and nonconformity, revolution and tradition, and order and disorder throughout the canon. *JC* represents "a well-intentioned revolution against a reasonably good order," with the plebeians being treated as unreliable. As in most other Sh plays, the significant action, good or bad, is taken by individuals. *Tro.* shows a profound concern with order, giving voice to two extremes: an individual's disgust with human insufficiency, and a universal "disrespect for authority"; and due acceptance of an order that derives its authority from a king. In *Tim.*, "Shakespeare's anti-social thinking" is concentrated and extended. *Cor.* exhibits a lively confrontation between plebeians and aristocrats.

0649   Knowles, Richard Paul. "'The More Delay'd, Delighted': Theophanies in the Last Plays." *ShakS*, 15 (1982), 269–80.

Senses a progression in the theophanies of Sh's romances from the "wish-fulfillment" of *Per.* and *Cym.* "through the more dramatically integrated use of Apollo in *The Winter's Tale*, to his most sophisticated application of the device in *The Tempest*, where the 'theophany' is supernatural, but is also an agent of human will." Explains the significance of the classical gods in the theophanies to this development.

0650   Kohler, Richard C. "Vitruvian Proportions in Theater Design in the Sixteenth and Early Seventeenth Centuries in Italy and England." *ShakS*, 16 (1983), 265–325.

Suggests that the designs for English theaters during Sh's time were to some degree indebted to a deliberate application of Vitruvian principles.

0650a   Koskenniemi, Inna. "On Some Physiological Terms Used for Characterization in English Renaissance Drama." *Five Hundred Years of Words and Sounds: A Festschrift for Eric Dobson.* Eds. E. G. Stanley and Douglas Gray. Cambridge, England: D. S. Brewer, 1983, pp. 92–99.

Describes the ways in which "four common physiological terms, *spleen*, *liver*, *gall*, and *blood*, are used" by Renaissance dramatists "for the delineation of character." Notes the connection of the physiological terms with "the psychological doctrines of the Elizabethan period" and the derivation of the whole system from "the humoral theory of Hippocrates and Galen." Cites examples from a number of Sh's plays.

0651   Kossick, S. G. "Musical Imagery in Shakespeare." *UES*, 20, no. 1 (1982), 6–9.

Notes the positive view of music that the Renaissance inherited from Pythagorean and Platonic theories, which stress "the power of music over the soul and the relationship of musical proportions to the perfection of the universe." In his plays, Sh gives ample evidence that he subscribes to these theories of speculative music (that music is a harmonizing principle reflecting the hierarchical order of the cosmos and possessing therapeutic power).

0652   Kott, Jan. *Shakespeare Our Contemporary.* Tr. Boleslaw Taborski. Preface by Martin Esslin. Garden City, New York: Doubleday, 1964. xx + 241 pp.

The third chapter, on *Tro.*, calls attention to this play's amazing modernity. Notes the play's *buffo* tone, its bitter philosophy, and its passionate poetry; the defense of an absurd war by both feudal mystics (the Trojans) and rationalists (the Greeks); the great profundity of the poisoned love relationship betweeen Troilus and Cressida; the two clowns, one sweet (Pandarus) and one bitter (Thersites); and the play's tragicomic nature.

The sixth chapter, on *Ant.*, emphasizes how concretely Sh realizes both space and time, adding scenes not in Plutarch. Sh makes history itself the drama. The choice of the two protagonists to commit suicide is inevitable; the struggle for power that is the matter of history will not allow either of them to hold on to the image of the other that he or she cherishes.

The seventh chapter, on *Cor.*, regards this play as informed by the class struggle between plebeians and patricians. Cites Plutarch's account of Coriolanus's character and the lesson to be learned from it to show how Sh, by contrast, has focused on historical forces. History is no longer royal or demonic (as in Sh's history plays and *Mac.*); it is merely "ironic and tragic." Coriolanus's death is tragic "according to his mad and absolute system of values" and "ironic in the real world."

0653   Kozikowski, Stanley John. "*Homo Fortunatus*: A Study of the Humanized Image of Fortune in Tudor Dramatic Literature." Ph.D. dissertation, University of Massachusetts, 1971. *DAI*, 32 (1971–72), 2059-A.

Attempts to explain the influence of "the anthropomorphic image of Fortune in Tudor dramatic literature." Notes that the impact of the image was intensified by its confinement to the court setting, its inclusion of characteristics that described human folly and vice, and its use in dramatic forms that emphasized "its contention with man." Studies "the contention between Man and Fortune" in *MV, Oth., Ant.*, and many other plays of Sh's time.

0654 Kranz, David L. "Shakespeare's New Idea of Rome." *Rome in the Renaissance: The City and the Myth*. (Medieval and Renaissance Texts and Studies 18.) Ed. Paul A. Ramsey. Binghamton, New York: Medieval and Renaissance Texts and Studies, 1982, pp. 371–80.

Argues that Sh's vision of Rome was constant from his first to his last Roman works and even in the scattered Roman references in plays like *Ham*. Notes the destructive turmoil reflected in the characteristic actions of the Roman plays: banishments, treasons, rapes, assassinations, and, most significantly, suicides. In all of this, there is tension between the nature of things or human nature and what it means to be Rome or a Roman. As the "quintessential Roman act in Shakespeare," suicide establishes "a certain and remembered point" in the midst of existential mutability and asserts the mind's Stoic dominance over the body. Characters in the plays talk continually about their Romanness, and the plebeians in their mutability are held up as the opposite of what a true Roman should be. As a Renaissance version of Rome, Sh's portrayal is unique in two ways. First, it is impartial, ambivalent, and paradoxical. Second, it goes farther than others in "discovering the psychological essence of Roman culture." Revision of part of item 0656.

0655 Kranz, David L. "'Too Great a Mind': The 'Mentis Integritas' of Shakespeare's Roman Heroes." *CML*, 4 (1983–84), 143–65.

Claims that greatness of mind (*mentis integritas*) is the essential quality Sh studies in his Roman heroes. Derived from Stoic thought, this quality was supposed to enable man, through reason, to mold his entire being into one. Metaphorically, the integrity of the city of Rome itself is associated by Sh with the integrity of its citizens' minds. In *Tit.*, for example, the protagonist's assertions of his constant virtue are closely linked to his attempts to "cement the city's political unity." Sh explores the notion of integrity in the heroes of all of his Roman works (*Luc.*, *Tit.*, *JC*, *Ant.*, and *Cor.*), ironically undercutting it. For example, the constant mind cannot, as the Stoics maintained, transcend the material world, and ultimate physical integrity (life) is often lost when a character tries to maintain mental integrity. Caesar's greatest claim of self-sufficiency (*JC*, III.i.58–73) comes just before his assassination. As Sh portrays it, the integrity of the Stoic mind is illusory. Brutus's conflicting ideas about his course of action if he is captured (suffer patiently/commit suicide [*JC*, V.i.100–112]) reveal how unaware he is of an illogical dichotomy in himself. Both Coriolanus's integrity and his aristocratic notion of the proper organization of the city are impossible. Finally, the suicides of a number of characters in these plays demonstrate that the ultimate expression of Stoic integrity of mind is achieved at too great a cost. Revision of part of item 0656.

0656 Kranz, David Lord. "Shakespeare's Roman Vision." Ph.D. dissertation, University of California, Berkeley, 1977. *DAI*, 38 (1977–78), 4846-A-4847-A.

Attempts to discover the common element in all of Sh's Roman plays. Argues that the organizing principle in Sh's presentation of Rome is the tension between art and nature. Rome embodies the operation of art: It holds out the possibility that man, by controlling his mutable nature, can attain moral perfection. The Roman leaders appear to emulate statues, thinking and speaking in the measured, artificial manner of public oratory to create for themselves "a god-like autonomy and immortality in history." However, these great sons of Rome—Brutus, Octavius, Coriolanus—cannot long endure their own attempts to stifle natural impulses and to shape an intractable reality to their purposes. Thus the ideals of the Roman state—reason, honor, integrity, and success—responsible for so much of her glory end by causing polarization, division, and destruction of her body politic. Parts revised as items 0654 and 0655.

0657 Kruegel, Sister Mary Flavia. "An Ideological Analysis of Honor in William Shakespeare's *Richard II, I* and *II Henry IV*, and *Henry V*." Ph.D. dissertation, St. Louis University, 1962. *DA*, 24 (1963–64), 4177–78.

Maintains that in *Tro.*, as well as in the second tetralogy of English history plays, Sh submits pagan concepts of honor, as formulated by Plato, Aristotle, and Cicero, to critical scrutiny from a Christian point of view. *Tro.* is "an overt satire on pagan concepts of honor," and its heroes are manifestly absurd. In the English plays, the playwright exhibits on a larger scale "the folly, hypocrisy, and danger of following pagan ideals." Even in *H5*, the honor of the supposedly Christian hero is "at least partially pagan."

0658 Krueger, Robert. "Politics and Politicians: Shakespeare's View and Ours." *Politics, Power, and Shakespeare*. Ed. Frances McNeely Leonard. Arlington, Texas: Texas Humanities Resource Center, U. of Texas at Arlington Library, 1981, pp. 76–104.

Cites Ulysses' speech on degree in *Tro.* (I.iii) as a key to Sh's notion of hierarchical order, which modern readers need to grasp to understand his treatment of politics. Discusses *JC* as Sh's most comprehensive and acute consideration of "the psychology of politics."

0659 Kujoory, Parvin. "The Development of Shakespeare Biography from 1592 through 1790." Ph.D. dissertation, Catholic University of America, 1967. *DA*, 28 (1967–68), 2212-A-2213-A.

Explains that the controversy over Sh's learning began in earnest during the 18th c., when the tradition of his "Small Latine" was established.

0660 Kushari, Ketaki. "A Note on Shakespeare's Language." *Shakespeare: A Book of Homage*. Jadavpur U., 1965, pp. 50–65.

Points out, among other things, that Sh's use of words newly imported into English from Latin emphasized the concrete Latin root meanings (for example, in "two pernicious daughters," *pernicious* has its radical sense of *death-bringing*). For Sh, the roots were still alive and their use came easily; for Milton, only a generation later, the task was more difficult because "most of the concrete meanings were already blurred and forgotten."

0661 LaBriola, Joseph Charles. "Dramatic Uses of Rhetorical Description in *Julius Caesar*, *Othello*, and *Coriolanus* with Reference to Other Shakespearean Tragedies." Ph.D. dissertation, University of Notre Dame, 1972. *DAI*, 33 (1972–73), 3589-A-3590-A.

Chapter 1 examines "the contents and forms of rhetorical description" and explains how they are derived from Aristotle's *The Art of Rhetoric* and Roman rhetoric. In this rhetorical system, as it developed in the 16th c., attributes of persons and actions were connected in many ways and had many functions. When the attributes of persons and actions are used to describe, they take one of the following forms: "a vivid, figured form; a schematic and formulaic form; or an expository form." Chapter 2 explains how the three forms of rhetorical description contribute to "the characterization and plotting of Shakespeare's tragedies." Chapter 3, a study of *JC*, shows that Brutus fails in his Forum oration (III.ii) because he makes only limited use of the many functions of rhetorical description, whereas Antony succeeds because he makes liberal use of them. Chapter 4, on *Oth.*, emphasizes the functions of rhetorical description in Iago's temptation of Othello. Chapter 5 discusses the role of rhetorical description in portraying the larger-than-life hero of *Cor*.

0662 LaCerva, Patricia. "The Paradoxical Humanism of Shakespeare's Villains." *The Humanist in His World: Essays in Honor of Fielding Dillard*. Eds. Barbara W. Bitter and Frederick K. Sanders. Greenwood, South Carolina: Attic P., 1976, pp. 46–56.

General Works

Argues that several of Sh's villains—notably Richard III, Aaron, and Edmund—violate or pervert the orthodox humanist faith in right reason, derived from classical sources. These paradoxical humanists use reason in the service of extreme egotism.

0663   Lanahan, William Francis. "Rhetorical Characterization in Elizabethan Drama." Ph.D. dissertation, Fordham University, 1971. *DAI*, 32 (1971–72), 922-A-923-A.

Points out that the Latin version of Aphthonius's *Progymnasmata*, the most widely used rhetorical handbook in the Renaissance, gave schoolboys a type of exercise in impersonating the lamentations of such ill-fated classical figures as Niobe and Hecuba. This exercise in self-characterization, called *ethopoeia*, was adapted by Renaissance dramatists in developing effective expression for their characters. Sh uses ethopoetic speeches in the *H6Triad*, *R3*, *R2*, and *Ham.*, giving characters in the latter two plays a heightened awareness that they are victims of grief.

0663a   Landis, Joan Hutton. "'To Arthur's Bosom': Locating Shakespeare's Elysium." *MLS*, 15, no. 4 (1985), 13–21.

Uses the terms *Elysium* and *paradise* to describe in Sh's plays a place or state of simplicity or true clarity viewed from a place or state of complexity or confusion. Discovers the location of Elysium "in all genres of Shakespearean drama" in the story. Most notably, the pointing toward Elysium occurs at the end of *Ham.*, when the protagonist requests that Horatio "tell my story" (V.ii.351). In the comedies, "where death is absent or peripheral," the story may be only a summary of the plot that promises to extend the ritual reconciliation of the ending and "to underline its coherence." Often in the tragedies and histories, the dying hero's only hope is that he will be properly reconstituted when his story is told. *Ant.* appears to be an exception because the hero, although he wishes "to be remembered and properly stellified," desires to survive only in Cleopatra's memory, not in any wider sense. Cleopatra, of course, offers him "the colossal memorial of her dream." Her potent imaginary landscape, which depicts so persuasively her union with Antony, "puts the category of the play into question."

0664   Landman, Sidney James. "The Tragic Mode of *Timon of Athens* and *Coriolanus*." Ph.D. dissertation, Vanderbilt University, 1967. *DA*, 27 (1966–67), 4223-A-4224-A.

Analyzes *Tim.* and *Cor.* in the context of the influences that shaped Sh's tragic vision. Chapter 1 discusses Aristotle's view of tragedy "as Renaissance commentators on the *Poetics* understood it," as well as the Senecan influence. Chapter 2 deals with "history as the subject matter for tragedy." The histories of Greece and Rome provided an excellent basis for a vision of divine providence operating through the rise and fall of nations; and a biographical study like Plutarch's *Lives* fused a number historical elements. Chapter 3 follows the development of medieval tragedy, "beginning with the Roman worship of the goddess Fortune." Chapters 4 and 5 focus on *Tim.* and *Cor.*, pointing out both classical and medieval elements. Noteworthy are Timon's nobility of character and his overreaching, based on pride, which causes his downfall. Many features of the morality play can be found in the pattern of damnation followed by Timon, as well as in the structure of *Cor.*

0665   Lanham, Richard A. *The Motives of Eloquence: Literary Rhetoric in the Renaissance*. New Haven: Yale U. P., 1976. xi + 234 pp.

Chapter 1, "The Rhetorical Ideal of Life," sets up a contrast between two views of reality: the "serious" view, which posits a "central self" committed to one way of seeing things, and the "rhetorical view," which sees reality as "dramatic" and approaches it playfully. Literary history needs to be rewritten as the relationship between the "central self" and the "social self" to acknowledge the fruitful collision between the serious and the rhetorical. Chapter 2, "The Fundamental Strategies: Plato and Ovid," proposes Plato and Ovid as respective champions in antiquity of the serious and rhetorical selves. Plato's Socrates embodies the serious self, while Ovid's lack of a central self directs attention to his style, his "diffuse authorial self." Comments that "the rhetorical stylist will inevitably, like Shakespeare, reincarnate Ovid." Chapter 4, "The Ovidian Shakespeare: *Venus and Adonis* and *Lucrece*," maintains that *Ven.* is about the relationship between the expectations of the serious reader and those of the rhetorical reader. This relationship is bound up in the juxtaposition of the principals, who are involved in two conflicting antitheses, one dramatic, one moral: "Adonis argues for virtue but symbolizes death; Venus speaks the lines of a literary temptress but symbolizes life, hope, the future." There is "a large Ovidian gap" between the two, a lack of the middle ground, which the reader is invited to supply by common sense. *Luc.* is a poem "about dramatic identity, an exploration of rhetorical life": Sh has both Tarquin and Lucrece play with feudal rhetoric so that he can anatomize "the feudal, aristocratic conception of identity." The appearance of Brutus, the kind of complex character who can use a role "without becoming it," is a warning that "naive feudal role-playing" is no longer sufficient; governors must be "self-aware and self-conscious about language." Chapter 5, "Superposed Poetics: The Sonnets," argues that *Son.* superpose "a rhetorical poetic on a serious one." Chapter 6, "Superposed Plays: *Hamlet*," maintains that in *Ham.* the protagonist's rhetorical revenge play coexists with Laertes' "straight" one. Chapter 9, "The Dramatic Present: Shakespeare's *Henriad*," views the four plays of the second English history sequence as representing both a fixed, "serious" past and a "rhetorical," dramatic present.

0666 Laroque, François. "Cannibalism in Shakespeare's Imagery." *CahiersE*, 19 (1981), 27–37.

Traces imagery associated with cannibalism in a number of Sh's works. In most cases, references to cannibalism, which are symptomatic of profound evil and disorder, are oblique. Notes that animal cannibalism, accounts of which could have been found in the works of ancient naturalists like Pliny the Elder, is often a portent of disaster in Sh (*Cor.* and *Mac.*). In the "black pastoral" of *Tim.*, the theme of universal greed leads back to cannibalism, and in *Ham.* there are many indirect references to the practice. Only in *Tit.* is cannibalism, derived from Seneca's *Thyestes* and from Greek myth, made explicit. Observes that Sh toned down the images and theme of cannibalism as his career progressed.

0667 Laroque, François. "Ovidian Transformations and Folk Festivities in *A Midsummer Night's Dream, The Merry Wives of Windsor* and *As You Like It.*" *CahiersE*, 25 (1984), 23–36.

Drawing on Ovid and on the nonliterary traditions of Warwickshire folklore, Sh provided, in *MND*, *Wiv.*, and *AYL*, three "successive variations" on the familiar theme of metamorphosis. In *MND*, Sh acts primarily as a translator, using hints from throughout the *Metamorphoses* to reinforce "the central motif of animal transformation." In *Wiv.*, direct references to the myth of Actaeon reveal that Sh is using it as "a burlesque emblem for the themes of cuckoldry, symbolical castration and charivari." Furthermore, the animal metaphors point to a deeper concern with the myth of Orpheus and an emphasis on the ritual dismemberment of "the sacrificial victim." *AYL* extends metamorphosis far beyond its earlier function as "a dramatic device and piece of stage business." The forest of Arden becomes a "distorting mirror" in which the animal and human worlds are interchangeable; Sh is thereby able to move beyond conventional pastoralism into "a satirical Pythagorean fable."

0668 Larson, Gale Kjelshus. "Bernard Shaw's *Caesar and Cleopatra* as History." Ph.D. dissertation, University of Nebraska, 1968. *DA*, 29 (1968–69), 4495-A.

Analyzes presentations of Caesar and Cleopatra by classical historians, Sh, and 19th-c. historians as background to Shaw's play. Early commentators on Caesar, like Lucan, Suetonius, and Plutarch, disparaged Caesar as an enemy of republican and Stoic principles and praised his assassins as supporters of those principles. Others, such as Appian of Alexandria and Dio Cassius, refused to idealize the conspirators. In the

General Works

Renaissance, the idealization of Brutus was revived: He was seen as having performed "an act of high political and moral duty." This was the view of Sh, who looked at Caesar through Brutus's eyes. Shaw, following 19th-c. historians, saw Caesar as "the great practical statesman." In the case of Cleopatra, writers like Lucan and Josephus had denounced her as corrupt and dangerous. A more tolerant view emerges in the works of Horace, Plutarch, and Sh, "who begin with moral censure but end in admiration of her suicide." Shaw neither censures nor exalts Cleopatra: He presents her as "a natural phenomenon in her Ptolemaic environment."

0669   Latif, Eva Leoni. "Ghosts on the English Renaissance Stage." Ph.D. dissertation, State University of Iowa, 1961. *DA*, 22 (1961–62), 1611.

Attempts to evaluate the contributions of religion, superstition, and literary tradition to "the development of the ghost on the English Renaissance stage," and to assess the importance of ghosts in the forty-four plays in which they appear from 1576 to 1642. Chapter 2 discusses, among other things, the influence of Greek and Senecan drama on the English stage ghost.

0670   Lawlor, John. "Continuity and Innovation in Shakespeare's Dramatic Career." *REL*, 5, no. 2 (1964), 11–23.

Asserts that the period of Sh's Greco-Roman plays (1599–1608) is the focal point of his development. Opening with *JC* and closing with *Cor.*, this period saw the playwright extend his concern with the themes of "exile and forcible dispossession," which had occupied him in earlier works, both tragic and comic. In the Greco-Roman works, Sh examines "a civilization which, once established, will not be overthrown; and this gives unrivalled insight into the individual who would seek fulfillment at the cost of separation from the society that nurtures him."

0671   Lawrence, Larry Lee. "Political Pointing as a Dramatic Technique in Shakespeare's Plays." Ph.D. dissertation, Stanford University, 1970. *DAI*, 31 (1970–71), 2349-A.

Argues that in Sh's plays, political ideas are used for dramaturgical purposes rather than for didactic or philosophical ones. At crucial moments in a play, familiar critical notions will be introduced to "work with calculated effect upon some aspect of the play." This technique of political pointing is important in the history plays and the tragedies, including *JC* and *Cor.*

0672   Lecercle, Ann. "The Letter that Killeth: The Desacralized and the Diabolic Body in Shakespeare." *Shakespeare et le corps à la Rénaissance*. Ed. M. T. Jones-Davies. Société Française Shakespeare Actes du Congrès 1990. Paris: Les Belles Lettres, 1991, pp. 137–52.

Traces "the dialectic of the Spirit and the Letter" from Plato's *Phaedrus* to the Renaissance and argues that it is "a conceptual keystone in the logic of representation" in plays of Sh in which its presence seems modest (as well as in works like *MV*, where it is explicit). Uses the Greek terms *nomos* (which can mean either *law* or *name*) and *petrus*, as well as an analysis of the Greek names Solinus (a diminutive of Solon, giver of laws) and Egeon to show that Sh begins *Err.* by calling attention to two "complementary and inverse errors": "1. the intextuation of the body by *nomos* as law, and conversely, 2. the migration of *nomos* as name from one body to another." Includes discussion of *1H4* and *Mac.* Notes that as the law becomes literalized at the expense of the spirit in the 16th c., it becomes demonized.

0673   Lee, Sung-Il. "Shakespeare as a Literary Critic." Ph.D. dissertation, Texas Tech University, 1980. *DAI*, 42 (1981–82), 1161-A-1162-A.

Examines Sh's works for passages of literary criticism and uses these as means of understanding and enjoying the works. Sh's critical comments also provide an indication of how he reacted to the critical notions of the ancients.

0674 Lee, Virgil Jackson Jr. "The Face in Shakespeare: A Study of Facial Gesture and Attitude as Aspects of Dramatic *Energeia*." Ph.D. dissertation, Columbia University, 1969. *DAI*, 30 (1969–70), 4416-A.

Traces the description of facial expressions, often used by Sh, to classical times. Aristotle considered it to be "a desirable rhetorical device and included it in his term *energeia*, i.e., the actions, gestures and facial expressions of men." It was also valued by Latin rhetoricians like Cicero and Quintilian and by Renaissance scholars like Erasmus. Focuses on Sh's "vocabulary of facial action," including words or phrases that refer to the *countenance*, the *eyes*, the *mouth*, and the *forehead*, as well as their movements. Also important are references to "facial coloration." Though Sh was thoroughly familiar with the Platonic notion that outward beauty signifies virtue, he also explored the ways in which evil masks itself in shows of righteousness. For example, in several of the great tragedies (*Ham.*, *Mac.*, *Oth.*, and *JC*), the prince's (or leader's) ability to "read" the faces of his people is a central motif. The *eye* is also important in Sh's works, especially in creating supernatural effects; and the *smile* is almost always a sign of "deceit, mockery, or death." In sum, Sh's use of facial *energeia* helps create strong dramatic effects, humanizes the world of the plays, and expands their poetic vision.

0675 Leech, Clifford. "Ephesus, Troy, Athens." *Stratford Papers on Shakespeare 1963*. Ed. B. W. Jackson. Toronto: W. J. Gage, 1964, pp. 151–69.

Points out that Sh had three ways of using locality: concentration, dispersal, and contrast. The first of these is illustrated by the setting of *Err.* in Ephesus, the second by the wide-ranging scene of the English history plays, and the third by *Tro.* (with alternation between two contrasting locations) and by *Tim.* (with the first half of the play set in one place and the second half set in another with clearly opposite features).

0676 Leech, Clifford. "Shakespeare's Greeks." *Stratford Papers on Shakespeare 1963*. Ed. B. W. Jackson. Toronto: W. J. Gage, 1964, pp. 1–20.

Maintains that in Sh's Roman plays, there is a uniform effect of dignity and awe but that the Greek plays—those that make prominent use of a Greek or Hellenistic setting—are much more varied. The Greek plays, which include *Err.*, *MND*, *Tro.*, *Tim.*, *Per.*, and *WT*, all have "something of an oddness about them." It seems that when Sh chose a Greek setting, he was encouraged to experiment. Cites T. J. B. Spencer's view that Sh shared the common Elizabethan opinion of Greeks as dissolute tricksters prone to wrath and violence but then analyzes *Tro.* and *Tim.* to show that this is too simplified a view: There is, for example, compassion in the world of *Tim.*

0677 Leech, Clifford. "Shakespeare's Tragic Fiction." *PBA*, 59 (1973), 159–74. Reprint. London: Oxford U. P., 1973. 16 pp.

Discusses "the co-existence of tragedy and history play in Shakespeare's theatre," associating the former with dream and the latter with memory. After his experiments with remembering English history and linking episodes from it in sequence in the 1590s, Sh turned to another kind of history in *JC*, a play hinting at a sequel (as the English history plays do) that, however, the author did not immediately provide. Instead, he escaped the bonds of history in the dream world of his four great tragedies. After the tragedies, he returned to Roman history in *Ant.* and *Cor.*, though he felt freer in dealing with this material (the story of Coriolanus was probably chosen because it was obscure) than he had felt in dramatizing English history. Observes that Sh's plays with "Greek or Hellenistic settings" are far more diverse than the Roman plays because the idea of Rome was thoroughly familiar to Elizabethans and permitted far less dreaming on the part of a playwright than the much vaguer idea of Greece.

0678 Leggatt, Alexander. *English Drama: Shakespeare to the Restoration 1590–1660*. (Longman Literature in English Series.) London: Longman, 1988. x + 298 pp.

Treats all of Sh's plays briefly in part 1. Notes that *Err.* combines the farce of Plautus's *Menaechmi* with various elements of romance to explore identity crises. In *LLL*, an important part of the comic irony is the "evocation of a lost world of heroism," which climaxes in the pageant of the Nine Worthies. *Tit.*, bookish in its references to classical works, ends with its tragic vision diminished into "revenge melodrama." *JC* presents "a republic that has lost faith in itself and its traditions, and has not yet found new ones." In *Tro.*, Sh experiments with radical instability of character: The ultimate reality is time. *Ant.* provides a "split reality," with the characters, especially the lovers, existing in the world of history, but also casting gigantic shadows in a heroic dream world. *Cor.* portrays a hero "at odds with the movement of history," a man whose extreme reliance on himself is ironically subverted by his dependence on his mother for identity, the name he is given by the state, and his collaboration with the enemies of Rome. *Tim.* focuses on the obsessed individual, a man who cannot stand sharing; it presents a "satiric caricature" of ancient Athens, where all social relationships are on "a cash basis."

0679   Leggatt, Alexander. *Shakespeare's Political Drama: The History Plays and the Roman Plays.* London: Routledge, 1988. xvi + 266 pp.

Includes three Roman plays—*JC*, *Ant.*, and *Cor.*—with the two English tetralogies in examining "the ordering and enforcing, the gaining and losing, of public power in the state." Considers two key issues: the relationship between myth and reality in political life and the impact on Sh's political thinking of the medium in which he works. In regard to the latter, the playwright views his characters as "role-players, at once freed and limited by their parts."

Chapter 6, on *JC*, argues that Rome has no defined political structure: Caesar's ambitions propel him toward something only vaguely like monarchy, and the conspirators' opposition is couched in terms of respect for individual integrity rather than a clear sense of republican tradition. In this Rome, everyone is an actor and everyone is audience; appearance is crucial, and individual actors need others to validate their images of themselves. Brutus constructs an "artificial world" in which he is the guardian of Roman values and other men are obliged to agree with him, to see him as he sees himself. In the face of intractable reality he never betrays any awareness of his own contradictions. His is "a genuinely fine nature," inextricably bound up with vanity and self-esteem. Cassius, by contrast, admits to some human inconsistencies. Although Caesar strikes poses of greatness that are devastingly undercut by events, Sh gains respect for his character in a variety of ways. By his performance during his own assassination, Caesar transforms himself into a legend and his death into a drama. Immediately, this drama becomes the site of competing interpretations, with Antony's being momentarily victorious. However, Antony's speeches after the assassination break open the play and ensure that history will move in unpredictable directions. The appearance to Brutus of Caesar's ghost is one final piece of evidence that "Caesar's spirit lives through others' invocations of it, changing shape to meet their different needs."

Chapter 7, on *Ant.*, argues that in this play, there is no feeling of "a fixed political state" or of "a fixed private self." The characters indulge themselves in a number of idealizing visions like Cleopatra's dream of Antony expressed to Dolabella (V.ii) and Enobarbus's artistic re-creation of Cleopatra's excursion on the Cydnus (II.ii). These are set against a realistic vision. Notes the "sharp, close observation" of the political scenes, both those dealing with the politics of state and those dealing with the politics of love. Antony's death is a combination of the base and the exalted, the comic and the heroic. The two identities cannot finally be reconciled: His greatness is secure only after his quotidian self is dead. Cleopatra, however, fuses the heroic and realistic in her death, not only achieving a triumph in her world of the imagination, but beating Caesar at his own game in the realm of the physical and practical.

Chapter 8, on *Cor.*, suggests that the contrast in this play is "not between imagination and reality, but between two areas of reality, war and civil life." The hero is capable of playing only one role satisfactorily, that of soldier, and his acceptance of another, that of family member, tears him apart. The result is one of Sh's darkest ironies.

0680 Lenson, David. *Achilles' Choice: Examples of Modern Tragedy*. Princeton: Princeton U. P., 1975. ix + 178 pp.

Argues that the dialectic in the ancient Greek theater between the actors on the stage and the chorus down below is expressive of the choice faced by every tragic character between active pursuit of one's destiny, clear definition, and brief existence and passive but enduring anonymity. In the Elizabethan theater, this prototypical Achilles' choice is articulated when Hamlet asks "whether 'tis nobler in the mind to suffer" or "to take arms." Lear and Macbeth have their versions of it as well.

0681 Lerner, Laurence. "Tragedy: Religious and Humanist." *REL*, 2, no. 4, (1961), 28–37.

Describes *Mac.* as a tragedy of disintegration and *Ant.* as a tragedy of triumph and asks for each one "if it can be Christian, if it can be humanist." If our view of the first type is Christian, the positives are found in divine justice; if our view is humanist, "in the compassionate spectator." It is easier to see *Mac.* as tragedy from the humanist perspective because, having witnessed Macbeth's destruction, we find the positives in ourselves. In a tragedy of triumph like *Ant.*, the humanist sees "man going down as well as he can," but the Christian must "place" the outcome: Cleopatra is "the best that man can do without grace, and her limitations are the limitations of the natural man."

0682 Lever, J. W. "Shakespeare and the Problem Play." *DUJ*, 56, N.S. 25 (1963–64), 86–88.

Challenges Ernest Schanzer's new definition of the term "problem play" (item 0932) and its application to any Shakespearean work, particularly *JC* and *Ant.*, which are acknowledged as tragedies.

0683 Lever, J. W. "Shakespeare's Narrative Poems." *A New Companion to Shakespeare Studies*. Eds. Kenneth Muir and S. Schoenbaum. Cambridge: Cambridge U. P., 1971, pp. 116–26.

Notes the Ovidian origins of *Ven.* and *Luc.* In *Ven.*, Sh reshaped his source materials, providing romance, comedy, fresh description of nature, intellectual debate, and an underlying sense of tragedy. Ovid's myth was given "a new breadth and universality." *Luc.* gave Sh the opportunity to show, through Tarquin's lust, "the workings of evil on a universal scale." For this, he chose the model of the Elizabethan "tragic morality," extending and modifying it.

0684 Lever, J. W. *The Tragedy of State*. London: Methuen, 1971. 100 pp. Reprint. 1987.

Chapter 4, "Roman Tragedy: *Sejanus, Caesar and Pompey*," discusses a number of non-Shakespearean Renaissance plays about Roman history, pointing out that, while, like Sh's Roman plays, these works use Plutarch as their source, they differ from Sh's treatments of the same events in being more concerned with "the political forces actuating individuals" than with "character as such." Examines Ben Jonson's *Sejanus* and George Chapman's *Caesar and Pompey* in some detail. Knowledge of these works helps us to contextualize Sh's plays.

0685 Levi, Peter. *The Life and Times of William Shakespeare*. London: Macmillan, 1988; New York: Henry Holt, 1989. xi + 392 pp.

Chapter 2, "Shakespeare's Youth," surveys the learning Sh would have acquired in school. Ovid's *Heroides* furnished him with a passionate rhetoric that he adapted in *Son.*; the rhetorical handbook of Aphthonius, used as a text, included the examples of Venus and Adonis and Pyramus and Thisbe, while the euphuistic style had its origins in schoolroom Latin.

Chapter 3, "Early Shakespeare," discusses *Tit.* as "a Senecan tragedy on a theme from Ovid," whose peculiar plot is due in part to the fact that it is driven by the momentum of poetry.

Chapter 4, "Comedy and Poetry," includes analyses of *Err.*, *Ven.*, *Luc.*, and *Son.* *Err.*, an adaptation of Plautus's *Menaechmi*, is more exotic in its setting than its model and concerned with courtship and marriage rather than prostitution. *Ven.*, unabashedly erotic, has multiple sources in Ovid's *Metamorphoses*, and is Ovidian in spirit as well: Like Ovid, it intensifies and then frustrates appetite, transforming the physical desires and sensations into a hunger for poetry, which its poetry then satisfies. *Luc.* is a serious, ambitious work about the defilement of beauty and innocence, social breakdown, and violation of honor and kinship. It is derived from Livy and Ovid, with "the set-piece about the picture of the fall of Troy" being indebted to "the temple paintings in Book I of the *Aeneid*, or perhaps to a Renaissance tapestry based on Virgil's description." The episode of Salmacis in the *Metamorphoses* lies behind Sonnet 20, and the last two sonnets (153 and 154) are translations "from a Greek original in the Palatine Anthology, perhaps by way of a Latin version."

Chapter 7, "Greatness," comments that *JC* is a new kind of drama, "almost but not quite a revenge tragedy, and almost but not quite a history play." It is dominated by the figure of Caesar, even though Brutus is more interesting psychologically. Sh was excited by the physical detail he discovered in Plutarch, though he seems to have been made uneasy by "the stiff verse of much of the play, with its overtone or subtone of Latin." Notes that in *Ham.* the recitations by Hamlet and the First Player are parodies of "speeches based on the *Aeneid*."

Chapter 8, "Transition," views *Tro.* as mocking, ambivalent, "irreducibly multiple." Speculates that Sh was commissioned by one of the Inns of Court to do "an *Iliad* play" and reacted by showing what the figures of the heroic world "might be like outside their static fictional frames." The play is full of deliberate incoherences, such as the incompatibility of "the medieval story and the classical Homeric setting"; Sh builds bitter and powerful ironies on these incoherences.

Chapter 9, "Tragedy," includes discussions of *Ant.*, *Cor.*, and *Tim.* In *Ant.*, Sh follows Plutarch fairly closely, relying on Horace and Philemon Holland's translation of Pliny for some details. Enobarbus's celebrated description of Cleopatra on the Cydnus is "more fully imagined and more erotic" than in Plutarch, revealing the Elizabethan notion of the ancient world as uninhibited, luxurious, and un-Christian. *Ant.* is "a love tragedy" but also "a triumph of love." Sh's last two tragedies, *Cor.* and *Tim.*, are violent and cruel, showing "the dark side of Plutarch, and of the ancient world," with a marked absence of Christianity.

0686 Levin, Harry. "Shakespeare and 'The Revolution of the Times.'" *TriQuarterly*, 23/24 (1972), 228–45. Reprint. *Literature in Revolution*. Eds. G. A. White and Charles Newman. New York: Holt, Rinehart and Winston, 1972, pp. 228–45. Reprint. *Shakespeare and the Revolution of the Times*. Oxford: Oxford U. P., 1976, pp. 29–50.

Cites Ulysses' speech on degree from *Tro.*(I.iii) as an example of an eloquent appeal to order that, when seen in context, dwindles into petty political maneuvering. The fable of the belly in *Cor.* (I.i), a similar attempt to affirm "the conservative norms of society," is placed in a scene where the citizens are given a strong counterargument. Suggests that Sh turned from English to Roman history partly because the setting in the distant past gave him more freedom to dramatize politics than did the difficult issues close to home.

0687 Levin, Harry. "Shakespeare's Nomenclature." *Essays on Shakespeare*. Ed. Gerald W. Chapman. Princeton: Princeton U. P., 1965, pp. 59–90.

Surveys Sh's plays, commenting briefly on a number of matters relating to naming. Calls attention, for example, to the importance of the virgin goddess Diana in *Per.* as well as to the significance of the name Diana in *AWW*. Notes that the name of Brutus's wife Portia *JC* is also used for the civic-minded heroine of *MV*. Discusses the role naming plays in the mob's murder of Cinna in *JC*, in Rosalind's disguise as Ganymede in *AYL*, in the celebration and destruction of Coriolanus, in the transformation of the private person into the embodiment of the state in *JC* and *Ant.*, in the creation of an exotic roll-call of great kings in *Ant.*, in the scatological punning on Ajax (*AYL* and *Tro.*), and in the mixed English/Greek ambiance of *MND*. Comments that the three women in *Cor.* share the same initial, which is an indication of their limitedness; that Latin names generally outnumber Greek names, even in *Tim.*; that the Roman name Caius is used in two primarily English plays; and that the fatalism of *Tro.* has much to do with the destiny that Troilus, Cressida, and Pandarus—given their names—must fulfill.

0688 Levine, Laura Ellen. "Men in Women's Clothing: Anti-Theatricality and Effeminization from 1579 to 1642." Ph.D. dissertation, Johns Hopkins University, 1987. *DAI*, 49 (1988–89), 511-A.

Begins by surveying the writings of anti-theatricalists from Sh's time to show that their theory of "signs" is defensive in purpose: The idea that clothing is a reliable indicator of gender "offers reassurance against the more disturbing idea" that there is nothing underneath the clothing. Sh problematizes anti-theatricality by suggesting, in *Tro.* and *Ant.*, that "anti-theatrical anxieties ultimately require theatrical expression, need to be 'acted out' or staged through others in order to be allayed."

0689 Levith, Murray J. "Juliet's Question and Shakespeare's Names." *Renaissance and Modern: Essays in Honor of Edwin M. Moseley.* Ed. Murray J. Levith. Saratoga Springs, New York: Skidmore College, 1976, pp. 21–32.

Provides a brief survey of names in Sh, including some derived from the classics. Notes that books explaining names in classical literature and the Bible began to appear in England near the end of the 15th c.

0690 Levith, Murray J. *What's in Shakespeare's Names.* Hamden, Connecticut: Archon, 1978. 147 pp.

Discusses the names in each play in terms of their sources, their etymology, and how they reveal character. *Tit.* takes half of its names from Plutarch's *Life of Scipio Africanus,* and most of them are derived from Latin or from the names of Roman gods. Nearly all of the names in *JC* come from Sh's source, Plutarch's *Lives.* In a notable episode (III.i), Antony names each of the conspirators as he shakes their bloody hands, thus identifying them as murderers. *Ham.* features names with origins in several languages, including Latin, to suggest universality. In *Ant.*, many names of both Romans and Egyptians have Greek etymologies, most interestingly Eros and Cleopatra. *Cor.* derives most of its names from Plutarch; it makes significant use of the naming process in its action. *Tim.*'s names are almost all from Plutarch. The chief characters (Timon, Apematnus, Alcibiades) have Greek names, and the large number of Roman names for other characters may be a way for Sh to indicate "the late Roman-like decadence of Timon's overly materialistic society." Takes account of various Latin and Greek names and names based on classical myth in the comedies, including Dromio in *Err.*, Proteus in *TGV*, Theseus and Hippolyta in *MND*, Hero in *Ado*, Celia in *AYL*, Caesario and Feste in *TN*, Helena in *AWW*, and Vincentio in *MM.* For *Per.*, Sh borrowed most of the Greek names from his principal source, John Gower's *Confessio Amantis,* but the hero's name probably comes from Plutarch. Many of the names in *Cym.* are Latinate, and some of these come from Holinshed. Although the source for *WT* is Robert Greene's *Pandosto,* the source for most of the names is North's translation of Plutarch's *Lives;* Autolycus, however, comes from Ovid's *Metamorphoses.* Places each name in the margin next to the text that discusses it.

0691 Lewis, Anthony J. "The Dog, Lion and Wolf in Shakespeare's Description of Night." *MLR*, 66 (1971), 1–10.

Discusses the connection of dog, lion, and wolf with future, present, and past, respectively, in Renaissance art and literature. Calls attention to Macrobius's *Saturnalia,* which had explained the significance of the three animals with respect to time. In Sh's work, and in that of other Renaissance dramatists, the three animals occur frequently in descriptions of nighttime, particularly "those nights during which death was either present or a distinct possibility." The animals appear in *2H6, 3H6,*

R3, and *Mac*. In *Tro.*, the death of Hector (V.viii) is accompanied by a description of night as a beast of prey, a dragon, and a sword that resembles a ravenous animal. Though dog, lion, and wolf are not mentioned, the association of night rapine with animals that suggest the sequence of time as Hector's death occurs indicates that they might lie behind the scene. Revision of part of item 0692.

0692 Lewis, Anthony Joseph. "Description of Time in Shakespeare." Ph.D. dissertation, University of Wisconsin, 1968. *DA*, 29 (1968–69), 2678-A.

Examines Sh's reactions to the problems of describing time. Describes *chronographia*, the formal method developed over the centuries by rhetoricians to describe time. In early plays, Sh is interested only in the figurative use of images from *chronographia*. In *MND* and *R3*, there is an interest in delineating actual time. Plays of Sh's middle period like *H5* use descriptions of time thematically as well as structurally. In the mature tragedies, the descriptions of time serve to universalize stage action and often have symbolic value. This happens, for example, in *Tro.*, when Hector is slain by Achilles and the Myrmidons as the sun sets. Part revised as item 0691.

0693 Lindenbaum, Peter Alan. "The Anti-Pastoral: The Education of Fallen Man in the Renaissance." Ph.D. dissertation, University of California, Berkeley, 1970. *DAI*, 32 (1971–72), 973-A-974-A.

Suggests that the anti-pastoral sentiment expressed in much English literature of the Renaissance arose from a suspicion that ideal realms like the Golden Age, which was associated with the pastoral, were escapist constructs. In *TGV*, *AYL*, and *WT*, the pastoral setting is used to bring characters from the courtly world to a recognition of their limited and fallen nature.

0694 Lings, Martin. *Shakespeare in the Light of Sacred Art*. New York: Humanities P., 1966. 132 pp. 2nd ed. Published as *The Secret of Shakespeare*. New York: Inner Traditions International, 1984.

Chapter 2, "Shakespeare's Outlook," remarks that the playwright's conception of Greece and Rome is "not typical of the Renaissance" because he does not merely appropriate the surface of classical antiquity; he "places himself at the very center of the ancient world" to portray the authenticity of the antique gods. Chapter 9, on *Ant.*, points out that the suicides of the protagonists are admirable, symbolic of the soul's ascent into the realm of the spirit. Chapter 10, on *Cym.*, notes that Sh's final romances are more medieval than his earlier plays, partly because they are infused with the presence of divine powers, necessarily veiled as pagan.

0695 Linn, Robert James. "The Fool in Renaissance Drama." Ph.D. dissertation, University of South Carolina, 1978. *DAI*, 39 (1978–79), 1592-A-1593-A.

Mentions Quintilian and the comedies of Plautus in discussing the fictional influences on the character of the fool in Renaissance drama. Considers Touchstone (*AYL*), Feste (*TN*), and the Fool in *Lr.*

0696 Little, Nancy Glass. "The Imagistic Feast: Feeding Imagery in Selected Plays of Shakespeare." DA dissertation, Middle Tennessee State University, 1984. *DAI*, 45 (1984–85), 3646-A.

Examines several imagistic strands linked to feeding imagery in eight of Sh's plays, arranged in four pairs. Includes treatments of *Tit.* and *Tim.*

0697 Livermore, Ann. "Shakespeare and St. Augustine." *Quarterly Review*, 303 (1965), 181–93.

Argues for the extensive influence of St. Augustine on Sh's works. For example, the operation of Fortune on Sh's Timon is similar to the effects of prosperity on a wealthy man described by Augustine, who also links anger with lust as Sh does in *Tro.* In *Ant.*, Sh may be relying on Augustine for notions of Egyptian magical powers. The fickleness of the Roman mobs in *JC* and *Cor.* may also owe something to him.

0698 Lloyd, Michael. "Antony and the Game of Chance." *JEGP*, 61 (1962), 548–54.

Discusses *JC* and *Ant.*, especially the latter, to show that in these two plays Sh focuses on "the Rome of sealike instability" that existed before Octavius Caesar established peace. Notes that Sh's emphasis differs from that of Plutarch, who in his essay "Of the Romans' Fortune" (*Moralia*) singles out Octavius as Fortune's chosen instrument in bringing permanence out of "dangerous flux." Sh's Fortune is not the controller of the flux, "but that element itself." In *JC* and *Ant.*, both Antony and the populace are subject to the motions of tide and wheel that are properties of Fortune. To live in this unpredictable world, one must be a gambler, knowing when to submit to the time and when to take advantage of the time. Sh's dominant image for such participation is the game of chance. As the character most temperamentally linked with Fortune, Antony is at the center of such imagery, although other characters are associated with it as well.

0699 Long, John H. *Shakespeare's Use of Music: The Final Comedies.* Gainesville: U. of Florida P., 1961. xiii + 159 pp.

Continues a study of Sh's use of music begun in a preceding book, *Shakespeare's Use of Music* (1955). Attempts to determine "the functions of the performed music in the comedies, the manner of performance, the original musical scores used (when possible), and the significance of these data to peripheral problems of interpretation, text, staging, stage history—in sum, Shakespeare's development as an artist." Covers *Shr., Wiv., AWW, MM, Per., Cym., WT,* and *Tmp.*

Chapter 3, "The Cosmic Gamut," serves to explain the cosmological symbolism of music for Sh and his contemporaries; it was "derived largely from Pythagoras, Plato, and Plotinus, as syncretized by later philosophers, notably Boethius and Polydore Virgil." Reproduces a table from M. Mersenne's *Traité de L'Harmonie Universelle* (1627) that illustrates how "the concept of order and degree" could be "symbolized by the musical scale." Mersenne's Neoplatonic system divides music into four categories, in "a descending order of spirituality." Mersenne, "with considerable debt to Aristotle's *Ethics,*" associates "the humane music of the soul with a harmony of the intellectual virtues and moral virtues." Joseph Barnes's *The Praise of Musicke* (1586) focuses on *musica mundana* (under which he discusses the music of the spheres) and *musica humana* (in the description of which he "draws from Plato and the Neo-Platonists to establish a relationship . . . between music and the human psyche"). Cites Lorenzo's speeches about music in *MV* (V.i.54–88) to show how Sh used these ideas.

Chapter 4 argues that there is a Christian and Platonic rationale for the music symbolism in *Per.* in that "performed music is associated with crucial steps in Pericles' ascent from the world of appearances to a perception of the divine."

Chapters 5, 6, and 7 on *Cym., WT,* and *Tmp.*, respectively, also emphasize the significance of Neoplatonic music symbolism. In *Tmp.*, love is equated with harmony, harmony with music, and music with divinity. See item 0700.

0700 Long, John H. *Shakespeare's Use of Music: The Histories and Tragedies.* Gainesville: U. of Florida P., 1971. xi + 306 pp.

Completes a study of Sh's use of music begun in *Shakespeare's Use of Music* (1955) and continued in *Shakespeare's Use of Music: The Final Comedies* (item 0699). Covers the two English history tetralogies, *Tit., Rom., JC, Ham., Tro., Oth., Lr., Mac., Ant., Cor., Tim.,* and *H8.*

Chapter 1 emphasizes the importance of music in the pageantry that the Elizabethan audience expected to find in histories and tragedies. Music in these types of plays can be described as military, ceremonious, or rhetorical.

Chapter 3, on *Tit.*, focuses on how music adds to the spectacle; for example, drums and trumpets announce Titus's triumphant entry into Rome (I.i).

Chapter 7, on *JC*, makes suggestions on how music is used to reflect on the political situation and on the characters of Caesar, Cassius, and Antony. Public, ceremonious music (such as the sennets in I.ii) accompanies Caesar and indicates his royal nature.

Dislike of music (such as Caesar notices in Cassius) and lack of music (during the conspiracy and when Caesar suffers from the falling sickness) indicate disharmony in the political order. Brutus's private nature is suggested by the song and lute music called for in IV.iii, just before he sees Caesar's ghost.

Chapter 9, on *Tro.*, comments that the music is associated with chivalry and courtly love rather than with classical heroism. For example, at the opening of I.iii, Agamemnon leads a group of kings onstage to the accompaniment of a sennet, normally employed for processional entrances, but there is no royal flourish, which might indicate that there are no truly royal figures in the council. When Aeneas comes to the Greek camp to deliver Hector's challenge, he is announced by a tucket that indicates his function as a herald instead of the royal flourish to which he is entitled. The most important performance of music is Pandarus's song in III.i, placed by Sh at the center of the play and used to express the decadent sensuality of the Trojan court. Music thus reinforces the play's bitter examination of chivalry and courtly love.

Chapter 13, on *Ant.*, argues that the character of Antony, around which the play is organized, is also the focal point for the music. The two episodes in which music is emphasized—the revels on Pompey's galley (II.vii) and Hercules' desertion of Antony (IV.iii)—are both related to the conflict that causes Antony's fall. In II.vii, loud music and dancing signify the intrusion of Egyptian sensuality into the austere Roman world. As the agent of this contamination, Antony is governed by Bacchus, one of his two geniuses. When his other genius, Hercules, leaves him in IV.iii, the music of hautboys, "probably grave," even funereal, is heard, foreshadowing his defeat and death. Plutarch gave no details of the drunken revelry on Pompey's galley, but Sh was able to compose his scene with information about Antony's riotous nature from other places in the *Life*. In Plutarch's account of the supernatural events Sh describes in IV.iii, the god who leaves Antony is Bacchus, and the music is festive. Having already highlighted Antony's bacchanalian propensities in II.vii, Sh altered the situation to a military one (Antony's soldiers leave him in response to the sounds they hear), the music to the somber strains on hautboys, and the departing god to Hercules.

Chapter 14 discusses the military or ceremonial nature of the music Sh included in *Cor*. Although the play calls for unusually full musical support (including a consort of cornets), Sh found no hint for any of this in Plutarch. There is little effort to characterize the protagonist through music.

Chapter 15, on *Tim.*, explores the ways in which music is used to link Timon and Alcibiades (as "protagonist and dramatic foil") in four important scenes: the masque of Amazons (I.ii), the mock banquet (III.vi), the military march of Alcibiades and his army when they encounter Timon in the woods (IV.iii), and "the military signals and drum march that accompany the triumph of Alcibiades" (V.iv).

0701 Long, Michael. *The Unnatural Scene: A Study in Shakespearean Tragedy.* London: Methuen, 1976. x + 266 pp.

Posits a tension in Sh's plays between the Law that human beings set up to structure their cultures and thus their social identities and "nature," or the "chaotic and dangerous 'other' world of raw kinesis." In the comedies, the Law is set up in temporary and absurd forms, while in the tragedies the nature of this Law and its delimiting effects are intensively examined. Presents, in the first chapter, a view of *JC* as a tentative, not entirely coherent study of the "civilized" Brutus, whose Stoicism cuts him off from "nature's volatility." Chapter 3, on *Cor.*, begins by calling attention to the emphasis in all of Sh's Roman plays on the primacy of codes. Rome thus becomes the model for "culture as Law reared in all its stubborn determination against the potencies of the kinetic world." Notices the way in which the Romans in *Cor.* transfer eroticism to the activities of war. Discusses the ruthless ethnocentrism of the patricians and the use of the hero as a god by his class. Ironically, Coriolanus, with all his vaunted integrity, ends as a near automaton. Chapter 5, on *Tro.*, regards this play as "high-spirited" and "exuberant," a work with roots in Sh's "general vision of the tragic world," which is profoundly involved in the world of comedy. Identifies five key ideas for *Tro.*: "The inflexibility of culture, the fury of kinesis, the vulnerable pride of attachment, and the twin energies of sexuality and violence." The play's tone is one of "cheerful derision." Chapter 8 foregrounds and contrasts two kinds of lyrical power: that of *Mac.* is Apollonian; that of *Ant.*, Dionysian.

0702 Longo, Joseph Anthony. "Shakespeare's 'Dark Period' Reviewed in the Light of Mid-Twentieth Century Criticism." Ph.D. dissertation, Rutgers—The State University, 1963. *DA*, 24 (1963–64), 2892–2893.

Analyzes several of Sh's plays written in the decade between 1600 and 1610 as mannerist works that reflect the central mannerist dichotomy between idealism and materialism. Among these "dark" works are *Tro.*, which "focuses on the quest and disillusionment of the protagonist"; *Ant.*, with its dual perspective on love; and *Cor.*, which portrays Rome as a city fallen into a disorder "which cannot be resolved because of the unusual nature of the hero."

0703 Loomba, Ania. *Gender, Race, Renaissance Drama*. (Cultural Politics.) Manchester: Manchester U. P., 1989. viii + 178 pp.

Discusses Tamora and Aaron (the unruly woman and black man) in *Tit.*, noting how they stand in opposition to the Roman patriarchy, which tries to locate them outside of its civilized masculinity. This stereotyping, however, is not entirely successful. Lists the ways in which the figure of Cleopatra (in *Ant.*) is constructed by various "male perspectives": (1) She exemplifies "the medieval notion of the sexual appetite of women as rampant and potentially criminal"; (2) her status as a queen is problematized by her gender; (3) her "dichotomous identity is elaborated in the images of her play-acting"; (4) her "play-acting specifically reverses gender roles"; (5) she is "the non-European, the outsider, the white man's ultimate 'other.'" Links the heterogeneity of the play's structure and content with a radical interrogation of "the imperial and sexual drama." In the first three acts, especially, "the issues of imperial expansion, political power and sexual domination are dramatically compressed into spatial and geographical shifts and metaphors." Antony, thinking he can control what he views as "the opposition between politics and pleasure," wavers between Cleopatra's space and Caesar's. As the play develops, he is unable to control this divide and, lacking space for exercise of his power, he disintegrates. At this point, the rapid movements of the play cease. The play ends with Cleopatra, closed within the narrow space of her monument, adopting a mode of performance more nearly allied to the Roman theater than to the volatile Egyptian one that has inspired her acting up to this point. Although "the narrative of masculinity and imperialism regains control," Cleopatra's final performance "not only cheats Caesar but denies any final and authoritative textual closure."

0704 Lordi, Robert J. "Brutus and Hotspur." *SQ*, 27 (1976), 177–85.

Considers *1H4* to be "a partial inspirational source for *JC*." In particular, Hotspur is parallel to Brutus in his desire for honor (though not in his impatience), Worcester anticipates Cassius in his role as tempter, Hotspur and Brutus have similar relationships with their wives, and each play associates the imagery of disease and disguise with a declining cause.

0705 Lyman, Stanford M., and Marvin B. Scott. *The Drama of Social Reality*. New York: Oxford U. P., 1975. 180 pp.

Argues that "the social world is inherently dramatic" and proposes to develop certain theoretical concepts of sociology through analysis of four Shakespearean plays. Chapter 3, on *Tro.*, cites the Greek council scene (I.iii) as a reflection of important concepts about the maintenance and subversion of hierarchy. Chapter 4, on *Ant.*, contends that in this play Sh has set up a contrast between the Apollonian principle of order and form (Rome) and the Dionysian principle of "unlimited expression" and sensuality. Antony is caught between the two ways of life and ultimately destroyed. With his death, he brings down the curtain on "the heroic and Herculean age" and leaves the stage to "the cold, unheroic administrative routine of Octavius and of modern men."

0706 Lynch, Barbara Furber. "Shakespeare's Comic Plots and the Nature of Man: A Study of the Relationship between the Romantic and the Low Life Plots in Light of Man's Unique Position in the Great Chain of Being." Ph.D. dissertation, University of Pennsylvania, 1971. *DAI*, 32 (1971–72), 4619-A.

General Works

Discusses Sh's comedies in light of their use of the two-plot form from romantic comedy. Conventionally, this form was employed to show the dual physical and spiritual nature of man. Elizabethan romantic comedies customarily link a main plot involving "idealized characters of noble birth" with a subplot involving "ridiculous characters of low birth." The function of the low plot is to parody the main one. Sh brings the two closer together by having sensual, earthy concerns intrude into the main plot. Each of Sh's double plots reflects the nature of man and helps him recognize his place in the scheme of things.

0707   Lynch, James Joseph. "The Mediating Figure in Shakespeare." Ph.D. dissertation, University of California, Davis, 1972. *DAI*, 33 (1972–73), 5684-A-5685-A.

Examines, in each of six tragedies of Sh, a key figure who acts as a mediator between the tragic protagonist and the audience. Includes analysis of the mediator in *Tit.* (Marcus), *Ant.* (Enobarbus), and *Cor.* (Menenius). Each mediator counsels patience and moderation and thus serves as a contrast, through his "ordinary nature," to the excesses of the great man with whom he is associated.

0708   Lyons, Charles R. *Shakespeare and the Ambiguity of Love's Triumph*. The Hague: Mouton, 1971. 213 pp.

Examines the typical actions of a group of Sh's plays that explore the complexities and ambiguities of the relationship between men and women.

Chapter 3 argues that in *Tro.* Sh depicts a world in which no permanence in human endeavors is possible. Natural law, as found in this world, teaches human beings that nothing outside the immediate deed exists. This accounts for the portrayal of the war as well as the love of Troilus and Cressida. It also accounts for the feeding imagery: The appetite must be continually satisfied. There is a persistent sense, however, that both the lover and the object of his love are being used up, consumed. Troilus, though trying to assert an idealized vision of constant love, fears love's finite nature. Because Cressida, however, has no illusions, she delays in surrendering to Troilus and shifts her allegiance to Diomede. There is no triumph of love in *Tro.* It is Sh's "strongest presentation of sexual love as a destructive energy."

Chapter 6, on *Ant.*, is a reprint of item 1368.

0709   MacDonald, Joyce Green. "The Political Family in Early Shakespeare." Ph.D. dissertation, Vanderbilt University, 1989. *DAI*, 51 (1990–91), 512-A.

Analyzes the parallels between "ideologies of family life and the organization of the sovereign state" as they are presented in five early plays of Sh, including *Luc.* and *Tit.* Sh explores the cost to families of their role "as seminaries of the commonwealth." These plays are especially sensitive to the kinds of events that can undermine "the clear lines of gender and generational authority, both inside private families and in the wider state."

0710   Magnusson, Augusta Lynne. "Studies in Shakespeare's Later Style." Ph.D. dissertation, University of Toronto, 1984. *DAI*, 45 (1984–85), 2887-A.

Examines "the tendencies in Shakespeare's syntax, diction, and prosody that emerge in *Antony and Cleopatra* and *Coriolanus* and become more pronounced in the plays from *Cymbeline* to *The Two Noble Kinsmen*."

0711   Mahon, John W. "'For now we sit to chat as well as eat': Conviviality and Conflict in Shakespeare's Meals." *"Fanned and Winnowed Opinions": Shakespearean Essays Presented to Harold Jenkins*. Eds. John W. Mahon and Thomas A. Pendleton. London: Methuen, 1987, pp. 231–48.

Notes that the Elizabethan playgoer, in witnessing a meal presented on stage, would have been aware not only of the implications of "fellowship, sharing, hospitality, common ritual," but also of the many scriptural references to meals, and especially the symbolism of Holy Communion. Includes discussion of two meals in *Tit.* (III.ii and V.iii) and two in *Tim.* (I.ii and III.vi). Sh uses meals to disappoint the audience's expectation, "to dramatize disunity by presenting it in a context associated with unity."

0712   Makaryk, Irena Rima. "'Let's make the best of it': The Late Tragedies of Shakespeare." *Ukrainsk'a Shekspiriiana na Zakhodi/Ukrainian Shakespeariana in the West.* Vol. 2. Ed. Yar Slavutych. Edmonton, Canada: Slavuta, 1990, pp. 27–39.

Finds that *Ant.*, *Tim.*, and *Cor.* have a number of features that distinguish them from Sh's earlier tragedies, most notably an emphasis on society and a tendency to induce the audience to side with society against the tragic hero. Points to the broad social panorama exhibited by each play, the strong links between each hero and his/her society, the unusual degree to which we see the heroes through the eyes of commentators, the critical view afforded of the protagonist(s) by each opening scene, other scenes (like those depicting the exile of Coriolanus and Timon in the wilderness) that increase our detachment from the heroes, the structural use of counterpoint, the significant integration of comedy, and the divided endings. The audience is made uneasy by the stress, in these plays, on the flux of human experience, on the humanity of the heroes, and on "the comic potential of man's behavior."

0713   Mandel, Oscar. *A Definition of Tragedy.* New York: New York U. P., 1961. viii + 178 pp.

Proposes an Aristotelian or nonmetaphysical definition of tragedy. For a work to be tragic, it must substantiate the following situation: A "protagonist who commands our earnest good will is impelled in a given world by a purpose, or undertakes an action, of a certain seriousness and magnitude; and by that very purpose or action, subject to that same given world, necessarily and inevitably meets with grave spiritual or physical suffering." Uses Sh for illustrations throughout. *Ant.*, which suits the definition, is tragic because the protagonist suffers as a result of his own action; Dryden's *All For Love* is not tragic because his hero "happens to be defeated" whether he leaves Cleopatra or not. *JC* is a paratragedy only because the fall of Brutus comes through a "dubious battle," not as a result of the central purpose of his action. *Lr.* and *Ham.* help us understand our response to pain in tragedy: We like "agitation within limits"; the form of a work of art makes detachment from pain easier, "but it does not insure detachment."

0714   Manlove, Colin N. *The Gap in Shakespeare: The Motif of Division from "Richard II" to "The Tempest."* (Critical Studies Series.) London: Vision, 1981. 200 pp.

Proposes to consider divisions and opposites in Sh that are largely unintentional and reveal a basic dividedness in the playwright himself. *Tro.* is more "directly philosophical" and "overtly conceptual" than other plays in disclosing "the split between mind and body"; *Ant.* is a striking portrait of the absence of "relationship and development in love," with the protagonists experiencing love only in "moments of ecstasy" and failing to react authentically to each others' betrayals; and *Tim.*, *Ant.*, and *Cor.* are focused on the unbridgeable gap between the individual and society. Among the last three plays, *Cor.* provides the most intense and sustained expression of "this motif of division" as well as Sh's most interesting struggle for impartiality.

0715   Marcotte, Paul J. *Priapus Unbound: Shakespeare's Concept of Love Inferred from Six Early Works.* Ottawa: U. of Ottawa P., 1971. xiii + 213 pp.

Treats each of six early works, including *Err.*, *Luc.*, and *Ven.* Proceeds analytically, with no reference to background materials. Concludes that in Sh's view man's love is neither wholly rational nor wholly carnal (shown most clearly in *Luc.*)

0716 Marder, Louis. "Folklore Stress in Shakespeare." *Mississippi Folklore Register*, 10 (1976), 115–37.

Mentions certain classical elements in the folklore of Sh's day and provides examples of Sh's use of folklore in most of his plays, including *Tit.*, *JC*, *Tro.*, *Cor.*, and *Ant.*

0717 Margeson, J. M. R. *The Origins of English Tragedy*. Oxford:Clarendon P., 1967. xiii + I + 196 pp.

Studies "the tragic potentialities of medieval and Tudor drama and of the organizing and shaping principles by which dramatists over a period of time began to give their work tragic form." Mentions Senecan violence as one component in tragedies of crime and revenge, including *Ham.* and *Tit.* In *Tit.*, interest is divided between the criminals and the victims, while in *Ham.* "the main dramatic attention has shifted to the revenger." Chapter 5, "A Realm Between Faith and Doubt," treats tragedies that were influenced by the chronicles and chronicle plays. What was important for tragedy in these earlier works was their attention to complex patterns of worldly intrigue and noble but imperfect characters. Plutarch's *Lives* provided ready examples of such characters, and Sh developed them in his Roman plays: *JC*, *Ant.*, and *Cor.* all "depict the failure in a worldly conflict of proud and passionate individuals."

0718 Markels, Julian. "Shakespeare's Confluence of Tragedy and Comedy: *Twelfth Night* and *King Lear*." *SQ*, 15, no. 2 (1964), 75–88. Reprint. *Shakespeare 400: Essays by American Scholars on the Anniversary of the Poet's Birth*. Ed. James G. McManaway. New York: Holt, Rinehart and Winston, 1964, pp. 75–88.

Sees three similarities between *TN* and *Lr.*: "Both give a prominent part to a domestic fool, and incorporate the familiar social philosophy of degree and custom that is implied by the institution of the domestic fool. Both plays seek to validate that philosophy by applying it to the wearing of clothes. And both plays seek to defend that philosophy against a belief in the disorderly caprice of Fortune." The differences involve their respective movements toward comedy and tragedy. In *Lr.*, for example, the plot insists on a "confrontation between the fool and Fortune, and is resolved when the fool of truth outfrowns false Fortune and thereby redeems the world." *TN*, on the other hand, never permits its characters to suffer the caprices of Fortune.

0719 Marsh, Derick R. C. *Passion Lends Them Power: A Study of Shakespeare's Love Tragedies*. Manchester: Manchester U. P., 1976. 240 pp.

Devotes a chapter to each of Sh's three love tragedies (*Rom.*, *Oth.*, and *Ant.*). An introductory chapter explores the tragic element in the comedies, especially as it relates to love. For example, in *Err.*, Sh moves beyond the Plautine convention of showing how ludicrous lovers are; he introduces the suggestion that "our notions of ourselves depend very largely on the reflections we receive back from those around us, and that is nowhere more crucial or potentially more wounding than in the sexual relationship." Another chapter deals with *Tro.*, which features a lover very much like the central character in the love tragedies in that he is blind to the truths he most needs to know and that it is his own desire, "swaying both will and judgment, that produces the blindness." Troilus never achieves self-knowledge, nor does he discover value and purpose in his love. In *Ant.*, the lovers have "an absolute importance" for each other, "which systematically strips all else away from their lives, and leaves them, at the end, glad to die, in the deepest sense for each other, rather than live on alone." The triumph of love is stressed, but it is clearly a momentary victory in the physical world, and when the two lovers die, their love dies as well. Concludes with a brief chapter on the romances, where time, "which so relentlessly drives on to the destruction of the main characters in the tragedies," seems to relax for a while, and "offer[s] another chance to those who have proved their capacity to use it."

0720 Marsh, George Reid Jr. "The Jerks of Invention: Ovid in Shakespeare's Early Comedies." Ph.D. dissertation, University of Michigan, 1972. *DAI*, 33 (1972–73), 6365-A-6366-A.

Contends that there are important similarities of spirit and theme, as well as verbal echoes, between Ovid's major works—the *Metamorphoses, Ars Amatoria, Heroides* and *Amores*—and *Err., Shr., TGV*, and *LLL*. In these plays, Sh makes verbal reference to Ovidian lines, directly borrows ideas on love or parodies them, adapts characters from the *Metamorphoses*, and shows a marked sympathy for Ovid's ambivalence toward all things, particularly love. Suggests that the most important idea Sh shares with Ovid is "the playfully serious hope of change through love."

0720a Marshall, Roderick. *Falstaff: The Archetypal Myth*. Longmead, England: Element Books, 1989. x + 233 pp.

Offers a history of the Falstaffian character type: "a grotesque, fat, feral, oversexed, crapulous, witty, profane, young-old creature who in times of trouble undertakes to misrule-rule a waste country and educate the heir of its sick and dying monarch in practices calculated to restore peace and prosperity." After learning his lessons, the prince wins two battles, the first with the help of his "tutor-buffoon" and a complement of rag-tag recruits, and the second, after the tutor's rejection and/or death, on his own to establish "joy and fertility in his kingdom." Assembles examples of the Falstaffian figure from various literatures and eras to show that it is "what Carl Jung calls an archetypal familiar of the psyche." Refers these examples to Sh's Henry plays (*R2, 1&2H4, H5*). Chapter 3 considers "Silenos of Greek mythology," who can be likened to Pan, Chiron, Marsyas, Priapus, and Kedalion. In these analogues of Falstaff, "the fat man's many animal traits and associations" are foregrounded.

0721 Martindale, Charles, and Michelle Martindale. *Shakespeare and the Uses of Antiquity*. London: Routledge, 1990. xii + 228 pp.

Proposes not so much to investigate sources but "in certain specific areas, to follow up the *critical* implications of our present knowledge of Sh's classicism." Chapter 1, "Introduction," examines "the extent of Sh's classical knowledge, the doctrine of imitation, and the influence of Seneca on English Renaissance drama." Sh was not a deeply learned writer; he made no systematic study of the ancients. But his grammar school education provided him with a basic competency in Latin (though little or none in Greek), and his imagination was inspired by the Greco-Roman mythology and history in which he was immersed by his culture. Sh's imitation of the classics takes many forms: imitation of plot (*Err.*: Plautus's *Menaechmi*); imitation of brief passages (Macbeth on sleep: passages from the *Metamorphoses* and Seneca's *Hercules Furens*); imitation of a speech from Ovid (Prospero's farewell to his art in *Tmp.*); and "theft" of a description from Plutarch (Enobarbus's account of Cleopatra on the Cydnus in *Ant.*). Sh never appropriated Seneca in as pure a form as some of his contemporaries (like Chapman) did, but passages of "outwardly turned introspection" in *Oth.* and *Mac.*, together with "the heated rhetoric, the brooding sense of evil, the preoccupation with power," and "the claustrophobic images of cosmic destruction" in *Mac.* are "strong evidence of Senecan influence."

Chapter 2, "Shakespeare's Ovid," notes that the fact that the Elizabethans mined Ovid for much more variety of matter and style than modern readers do accounts for his status as Sh's favorite poet. In *Tit.*, Ovid's influence works in two ways: The style of certain speeches is modeled on Ovid, and his version of the Philomela story underlies the play's action "and helps to characterize and control it." Modern readers often seek some sophisticated balance of horror and detachment in *Tit.*, but it is likely that Ovid's tale of Philomela appealed to Elizabethans because of its portrayal of "suffering, pathos, and vengeance," and that Sh's play was an attempt to depict just those qualities. When Sh again used the Philomela story, in the scene of *Cym.* (II.ii) in which Iachimo emerges from the trunk in Imogen's bedroom, it was more Ovidian (according to modern taste) in its "curious mixture of tones." *Ven.* represents an elaborate expansion of a story in the *Metamorphoses* and uses as its controlling image the Ovidian metaphor of "the opposition between love and hunting." Stylistically, the poem is weighed down with rhetorical ornament, which makes it less nimble than Ovid, though this might not have been apparent to its original audience. Sh seems to have prepared carefully for *Luc.* by consulting Livy and Ovid's *Fasti*, the two classical sources for the story. His effort, however, is marred by the mismatch of tragic content and Ovidian style. *MND* reveals Sh as getting further away from Ovid to become more like him. The play exhibits at least seven Ovidian features: (1) metamorphosis; (2) a fascination with its own art; (3) the Pyramus and Thisbe story; (4) the style of the lovers' couplets (this comes from the elegiacs of Ovid's love poetry); (5) the fairies, who can be seen as "a modernization of Ovid's gods"; (6) the use of etiological narrative (Oberon's account of the origin of love-in-idleness); and (7) several direct echoes of Ovid and Golding. In *WT*, Sh uses the Pygmalion story as a pattern "without attempting a recognizably Ovidian tone." Passages in five plays chosen from different phases of Sh's career show how different myths from Ovid could be used: *TGV*, III.ii.77-80 (Orpheus); *MV*, III.ii.53-60 (Hercules); *TN*, I.i.18-22 (Actaeon); *Tro.*, III.ii.7-12 (the underworld); *WT*, IV.iv.112-125 (Proserpina).

Chapter 3, "Shakespeare's Troy," regards *Tro.* as Sh's *Iliad*, inspired in part by the playwright's "only direct encounter with Homer," his reading of Chapman's *Seven Books* translated from the *Iliad* (1598). Chapman's dense, bombastic style seems to be what Sh thought of as authentically heroic and what he allows to predominate in *Tro.* Further, the Iliadic themes of debate, war, fame, value, and time, "covered with a medieval-chivalric wash," form the basis of the play. Cites the Player's speech in *Ham.* about Pyrrhus's slaughter of Priam as a serious attempt in the epic manner, not a parody. The case of *Tro.* is more complex because there are sardonic touches that question the high style; however, that style, self-conscious and nearly absurd as it sometimes is, must be granted its own "authentic grandeur."

Chapter 4, "Shakespeare's Rome," compares Sh with Ben Jonson to show that, even though the former employs both intentional and unintentional anachronism, and is not as aggressively "accurate" as the latter in his display of Roman details, nevertheless his portrayals of Rome seem more authentic because he has "the ability, on the basis of transmitted 'facts,' to imagine a believable past society that has its own coherence." To focus his vision, Sh probably made a conscious choice to base his Roman plays on one high-quality source—North's Plutarch. Only *JC*, *Ant.*, and *Cor.* should be considered as Roman plays; *Tit.* and *Cym.*, often included by scholars in this category, do not qualify, the former because it has no "precisely identifiable historical setting" and the latter because it is primarily a romance "with providentialist Christian overtones." In the Roman plays, Sh was interested in creating an alien world "and exploring political activities in a specific historical environment." A recognition of Sh's detached, secular vision in the Roman plays prevents reductive readings (for example, assuming that "local" Christian references warrant viewing an entire play as a demonstration of Christian truth or taking an exclusively pro- or anti-Caesar position, when there is evidence for both). Each of the Roman plays has its characteristic style: *JC*'s is "generally plain, oratorical, public"; *Ant.*'s is "rich and flexible"; *Cor.*'s is austere, but "dense, taut, and jagged."

Chapter 5, "Shakespeare's Stoicism," discusses the sources for the chief tenets of this philosophy and asserts that Sh was not hostile to it, as some modern critics have maintained, but rather that he mined it for raw material. Investigates one Stoic ideal, constancy, mentioning its treatment in the works of Seneca, Cicero, Marcus Aurelius, Diogenes Laertius, and Boethius. Justus Lipsius, through his treatise *De Constantia* (1584), was also influential. Comments on Sonnet 94 (self-containment is promoted); *Ham.* (Horatio's constancy acts as a contrast for the prince's more interesting instability); *Mac.* (several characters, except Old Siward, respond in unbalanced ways to deaths that closely concern them); *Cor.* (the protagonist's inflexibility is an overstrenuous attempt at constancy, undercut by the unsteadiness of his mind); and *Ant.* (Cleopatra's depiction as a paradoxical Stoic, whose constancy provides a foil for her fascinating mutability, might have been suggested by one of Horace's *Odes*).

0722 Matinuddin, Abu Rushd. "Shakespeare and the East." *Homage to Shakespeare.* Ed. Syed Sajjad Husain. Dacca: Department of English, Dacca U., 1965, pp. 29–39.

Identifies several elements in Sh's plays that are of particular interest to Eastern readers. Examples are the portrayals of Moors in *Tit.* and *Oth.* and of Cleopatra.

0723 Matthews, Honor. *Character and Symbol in Shakespeare's Plays: A Study of Certain Christian and Pre-Christian Elements.* Cambridge: Cambridge U. P., 1962. viii + 211 pp.

Offers a reading of Sh's works that depends on discerning a pattern formed by the Christian concepts of "sin, judgment and redemption." Treats *JC* in a chapter on attacking the throne, noting that the play's profound ambiguity has its seeds in North's translation of Plutarch's *Lives.* Sh must have perceived some connections between the role of Lucifer in Christian tradition and the characters of Caesar, Antony, Cassius, and Brutus in his Plutarchan material. However, none of these figures in the play can be adequately interpreted through exclusive reference to Lucifer: Each of them is created out of a mingled yarn, good and ill together. Comments briefly on the Machiavellianism practiced successfully by Octavius Caesar in *Ant.* Discusses, in a section on the conflict between justice and mercy, considerations of the law of nature and social justice in *Tro.*, diabolical obsession with revenge in *Cor.*, blindness to reality in *JC*, and despair in the face of a world devoid of justice or mercy in *Tim.* A final section includes a treatment of *Ant.* that views the lovers' death as a triumph of the private over the public. Maintains that suicide here, as in Sh's other Roman plays, is not a mortal sin but rather "a final achievement of personal integrity." The last chapter, which deals primarily with Sh's late romances, remarks that the Christian concept of mercy is still present; however, it is now conflated with the pagan notion of recurrent, cyclical natural life.

0724 Maxwell, J. C. "'Black Chaos': Shakespeare and Muretus." *N&Q*, 14 (1967), 138–39.

Points out a mistranslation by T. W. Baldwin of a line from Muretus. The line has to do with chaos and may be related to *Ven.*, line 1020 ("black chaos comes again") and *Oth.*, III.iii.94 ("Chaos is come again").

0725 Maxwell, J. C. "Shakespeare Criticism and Greek Tragedy: Two Corrections." *N&Q*, 16 (1969), 128.

Challenges R. W. Chambers, who said that there is a parallel between Sh's first tetralogy on current history and Aeschylus's trilogy of which the *Persians* is the surviving "fragment." The names of the other two plays in the trilogy are known, and they are not linked in subject like the plays of Sh's first tetralogy. Moreover, the *Persians* is not a fragment.

Corrects a mistranslation of a quotation from Keble about Oedipus as reprinted in Peter Alexander's *Hamlet Father: and Son* (1955).

0726 Maxwell, J. C., ed. *The Poems.* (New Shakespeare.) Cambridge: Cambridge U. P., 1966. xxxvi + 258 pp.

The introduction observes that in *Ven.* Sh has naturalized Ovid "in an English setting" and that the mythological figures in the poem permit us to contemplate beauty's vulnerability without having to discard "the comic reality" presented by the whole situation. Points to *Luc.*'s sources in Ovid, Livy, and various English writers; argues that it is a complaint poem; and maintains that, though the poem is not fully integrated, its study of Tarquin's psychological struggle makes it interesting to compare with Sh's tragedies. Notes Platonic echoes in *PhT*, but denies that the poem contains a full-fledged allegory, either Platonic or Christian.

General Works

0727 May, Robin. *Who Was Shakespeare? The Man—TheTimes—The Works.* New York: St. Martin's, 1974. 143 pp.

Comments briefly on Sh's grammar school education, which would have involved studying of Lilly's *Latin Grammar* and of Ovid. The influence of the *Metamorphoses* can be seen in *Ven.*, in the Pyramus and Thisbe scenes of *MND*, and in the statue scene of *WT*. Surveys the entire canon.

0728 McAlindon, T. *Shakespeare and Decorum.* New York: Barnes & Noble, 1973. viii + 227 pp.

The introduction explains the Renaissance concept of decorum, "variously referred to as comeliness, seemliness, fitness, decency, meetness, propriety, grace." Its roots can be found in Plato, Aristotle, and Stoic thought; but it was most immediately accessible to the Renaissance in the writings of Cicero and Quintilian. Decorum was both rhetorical and behavioral. In behavior, it had to do with considering the circumstances of an action. People must not confuse things fundamentally distinct in nature, must behave in accordance with their name or title, must adjust their behavior to other people's needs, must be aware of the importance of timeliness in actions and speech, must play their part on the world's stage with propriety, and must be constant to their own nature. For rhetorical decorum, the primary requirement was proper diction; in particular, this meant avoiding affectation and obscurity. Figurative language was held to be appropriate as long as it was discreetly used. Sh did not ignore decorum or cheerfully embrace indecorum, as is sometimes thought. Instead, he recognized the indecorum for what it was and treated it as his subject: "wherever in his plays the improper occurs, it is generally a means whereby he registers upon the esthetic sense of the judicious an intense visual or auditory perception of those defects, lapses or perversions of judgement [that] are the source of tragic or comic action." The book devotes a chapter each to *R2*, *Ham.*, *Oth.*, *Mac.*, and *Ant*. Stresses ceremony in *R2*, the notion of life as drama and form in *Ham.*, "the law that ripeness is all" in *Oth.* and *Mac.*, and the way in which the protagonists paradoxically achieve perfection through defect and excess in *Ant.*

0729 McAlindon, T. *Shakespeare's Tragic Cosmos.* Cambridge: Cambridge U. P., 1991. xvii + 306 pp.

The introduction argues that Sh made use of the traditional "synthesis of cosmological ideas derived from Aristotle, Plato, and the Presocratic thinkers Pythagoras, Heraclitus, and Empedocles, a system [that] had been reinforced over the centuries by Ptolmaic astronomy and Galenic medicine." From these sources, "two world models" emerged: One was hierarchical, reposing on stability, while the other regarded the universe "as a tense system of interacting, interdependent opposites." This "contrarious model" subverts philosophical certainty, encouraging dialectical, relativist, and paradoxical "modes of thought and expression." Throughout his career, Sh's tragedies were informed by the latter system, which, though predicated upon contradictions, is comprehensible in terms of a universal and essentialist idea of nature. The tragedies are enacted in a world where chaos is come again, time is calamitously out of joint, and the cost of putting things right is painfully great. There is in the endings of these plays, however, some "measure of reintegration and harmony." Important to the dialectical nature of the tragedies are their concerns with the different aspects of time and with the fragility of psychic unity in their heroes. Analyzes *Tit.* and *Tim.* to show that Sh deliberately "referred the contradictions [that] troubled him most to a transhistorical model of human and universal nature." Includes chapters on Chaucer's *The Knight's Tale* (to explain the literary background for Sh's cosmological model and to explore its relevance to *MND*); *Rom.*, *JC*, *Ham.*, *Oth.*, *Lr.*, *Mac.*, and *Ant.*

Chapter 4, a revision of item 2051, argues that *JC* is a supreme achievement of Sh's historical imagination. Movement toward harmony and disintegration into chaos are both presented in terms of the number four: there are four major characters, each of which represents one of the humoral types; four plebeians appear in several scenes; Brutus's forum speech can be analyzed into four parts; the weaknesses of two marriages are foregrounded; imagery of the four elements is pervasive. The central conflict is between love and honor, with the conspiracy a parody of marriage, a "dark bond." Brutus, like each of the other chief characters, contributes to the chaos by his impulse to lead. He invokes constancy, a noble Roman ideal, but is torn apart by the simultaneous requirements of constancy to his friend (Caesar) and to the conspiracy. The major theme is change, or metamorphosis (Ovid is a likely influence), a corollary of which is the uncertainty with which characters face events: There is great emphasis on interpretation and misconstruction. The motion of the play is circular: Its "central deed" (Caesar's murder) is a violation of time's order, and in the subsequent action time brings in its revenges. At the end, there is a temporary reconciliation of opposites, but there has been tragic loss of time, of friendship, and of peace.

Chapter 9 views *Ant.* as a tragedy of Fortune, with special emphasis given to warring opposites and to the notion of inevitable change. Important influences are Ovid's *Metamorphoses* and Plutarch's essay "Of Isis and Osiris." Two parallel myths, of Isis and Osiris and of Mars and Venus, reinforce the idea of duality and opposition in unity, which is also manifested in a variety of antitheses: reason and passion, comic and anti-comic, noble and base, nature and art, time and eternity, constancy and inconstancy. References to alchemy show that *Ant.* goes beyond the image of time "as an inflexible order" in the other tragedies: Here, time is "pattern as well as process, a reconciliation of flux and stasis." In the second half of the play, there are sharp distinctions and oppositions among Antony, Octavius, Octavia, and Cleopatra. Within Antony himself, the "contrariety of human nature is developed to a unique degree"; his "heroic identity," being "a union of martial valour and loving-kindness," is subject to radical instability. This is evident in the middle of the play, when his submission to Cleopatra causes him to lose his soldiership. Then, in act IV, he is reintegrated and harmonized with Cleopatra, winning a battle. The harmony is soon shattered, but in his suicide Antony regains the balance of valor and love that constitutes his heroic self. In death, each lover imitates the other: Cleopatra commits suicide for the same reasons as Antony, and their fortunes merge entirely. Each death is "a union of contraries."

0730   McAlindon, Thomas. "The Medieval Assimilation of Greek Romance: A Chapter in the History of a Narrative Type." *REAL*, 3 (1985), 23–56.

Inventories the significant features of the sophistic Greek romance of the 2nd and 3rd c.: "the separation of lovers, spouses, or a family; wanderings, shipwrecks, and much hardship; heroes and heroines of exalted rank reduced to or disguised as beggars and peasants; final reunion and recognition." Argues that these elements were absorbed into the "religious legends and chivalric romances" of the Middle Ages through "the virgin–martyr legends, and the legends of St. Clement and St. Thecla." More specific characteristics include the imperiled chastity of the heroine; recurrent marvels; concealed identity; the "resurrection" of a character; and a preoccupation with fortune, fate, and divine providence. Notes that Sh's romances draw heavily on this tradition.

0731   McCall, John. *William Shakespeare: Spacious in the Possession of Dirt.* Washington, D. C.: University P. of America, 1977. xxv + 348 pp.

Analyzes bawdiness in Sh's plays, arranging the plays in alphabetical order, listing and explaining the bawdy references in each play, and ranking the plays "from cleanest to bawdiest." The introduction lists "Reference to Mythological, Historical, Legendary Figures" as one of the "Typical Situations or Signals for Bawdy Talk" in the plays.

0732   McDonald, Russ. "Sceptical Visions: Shakespeare's Tragedies and Jonson's Comedies." *ShS*, 34 (1981), 131–47.

Suggests that Jonson's major comic characters and Sh's tragic protagonists share certain basic traits in that "they are imaginative, solipsistic, inflexible, larger than life." Each of these characters envisions an ideal way of life that collides with the imperfection of the actual world. Antony and Coriolanus possess particularly powerful visions of the world as it ought to be and thus resemble such Jonsonian characters as Mammon and Volpone.

0733 McElroy, Bernard. *Shakespeare's Mature Tragedies.* Princeton: Princeton U. P., 1973. ix + 256 pp.

Concentrates on the four "mature tragedies" (*Ham., Oth., Lr.,* and *Mac.*), which "isolate the protagonist in the cosmos, destroy his assumptions about it, and throw him on his own resources to cope with it as he can." Comments briefly in the conclusion on "the Roman tragedies" (*JC, Cor.,* and *Ant.*), which explore "the relationship between the individual and the state." The Roman heroes are not moved to "universalize their situations," nor do they feel compelled to conform to "a set of universal norms"; most important, none of them has "his private world undermined at the level of its most fundamental assumptions."

0734 McFarland, Ronald E. "The Rhodian Colossus in Renaissance Emblem and Poetry." *EM,* 25 (1975–76), 121–34.

Cites the *Natural History* of Pliny the Elder as the most familiar written source for the account of the Colossus of Rhodes in the Renaissance. By the 16th c., the Colossus was also a popular subject for engravings and tapestries, and probably through this visual tradition, it "came to be identified as a figure bestriding the harbor of the city of Rhodes between whose legs a ship might pass into the port." Sh's familiarity with the pictorial tradition of the Colossus can be seen in Prince Hal's speculation on what it would take to bestride Falstaff (*1H4*), Cassius's reference to Caesar (*JC*), Agamemnon's description of Margarelon's feats in battle (*Tro.*), and Cleopatra's imaginary figure of Antony (*Ant.*). In every case, Sh uses the Colossus to suggest "overwhelming size and power."

0735 McGrail, Mary Ann. "Shakespeare's Dramas of Tyranny: *Macbeth, Richard III, The Winter's Tale,* and *The Tempest.*" Ph.D. dissertation, Harvard University, 1988. *DAI,* 50 (1989–90), 450-A.

Attempts to recover Sh's conception of tyranny, which lies between Aristotle's belief (*Politics,* book 3) that it is always "the worst of all possible political regimes" and Machiavelli's contention that "every actual rule is a form of tyranny." For the playwright, "tyranny is an expression of underdeveloped excessive desires for love or honor." Discusses tyrants in four plays, noting that Sh exhibits and ponders "the potentially tyrannic power of the knower and shaper of human beings—the poet."

0736 McIntosh, William Alexander. "The Harmonic Muse: Musical Currents in Literature, 1450–1750." Ph.D. dissertation, University of Virginia, 1974. *DAI,* 35 (1974–75), 3692-A-3693-A.

Describes "the medieval vision of Boethius's *musicae instrumentalis, humana,* and *mundana* as emblems of an orderly and harmonic universe divinely created and preserved by a God of love." This metaphor has an influence on the creative processes of a number of poets, including Sh, and serves homiletic ends in *Per.* and *Tmp.*

0737 McKay, Margaret Rachel. "Shakespeare's Use of the Apostrophe, Popular Rhetorical Device of the Renaissance." Ph.D. dissertation, University of Colorado, 1969. *DAI,* 30 (1969–70), 4459-A-4460-A.

Notes the influence of the classical rhetorical tradition on Sh's use of the apostrophe, especially in his early works. Comments that Sh nearly always transcends the conventions of the apostrophe to reveal character and theme.

0738 McMahon, C. E. "Psychosomatic Concepts in the Works of Shakespeare." *Journal of the History of the Behavioral Sciences,* 12 (1976), 275–82.

Points out that the Renaissance saw the birth of a new theory of psychosomatics, based on "ancient medical tenets" and brought to light through renewed interest in classical languages and literature. Notes that this holistic, premodern, predualistic theory is thoroughly integrated into Sh's plays. Three important psychosomatic concepts occur throughout the canon: "cardiovascular involvement in emotion, experiential causation of psychosomatic disorders, and repression of emotion as psychogenic." The plays of Sh "reflect the medical wisdom of the ancients."

0739 McMillan, Douglas J. "The Phoenix in the Western World from Herodotus to Shakespeare." *D. H. Lawrence Review*, 5 (1972), 238–67.

Surveys the history of the Phoenix myth from classical antiquity to the Renaissance. Cites treatments of the Phoenix in Greek literature (Herodotus, Aelian, the Greek *Physiologus*), Roman literature (Ovid, Pliny the Elder, Tacitus, Solinus, Claudian, the Latin *Physiologus*), the Church Fathers, medieval literature, and early modern literature. Notes Sh's use of the myth in *PhT* and in six plays. Comments that Sh was able to assume his audience's familiarity with the story.

0740 McNamara, Robert Jeremy. "Shakespeare's Intellectual Villains." Ph.D. dissertation, Michigan State University, 1961. *DA*, 22 (1961–62), 2003–2004.

Contends that Sh's villains are primarily intellectual and hence unique. Part 3 provides "a brief survey of villains in Greek and Senecan tragedy" to show how distinct Sh's portraits of intellectual villainy are.

0741 McQuain, Jeffrey Hunter. "'The Authority of Her Merit': Virtue and Women in Chaucer and Shakespeare." Ph.D. dissertation, American University, 1983. *DAI*, 44 (1983–84), 761-A.

Begins with a brief conspectus of "the misogyny that permeates classical literature." Considers the works of Chaucer as vindication of "the words and deeds of women." Maintains that Sh's works extend Chaucer's arguments "in favor of women and marriage," going further than Chaucer in challenging classical ideas about male supremacy.

0742 Mehl, Dieter. *Shakespeare's Tragedies: An Introduction*. Cambridge: Cambridge U. P., 1986. x + 272 pp.

Treats *Tit.* in a chapter on the early tragedies, noting that this play is characterized by Sh's attempt to bring "sophisticated poetry" like that found in *Luc.* into closer contact with drama. Chapter 4, "Romans and Greeks in Shakespeare's Tragedies," begins by observing that three tragedies, *JC*, *Ant.*, and *Cor.*, provide a "consistent account of Republican Rome [that] has influenced the popular idea of classical Rome more deeply and more permanently than either the classical authors or modern historians." Singles out the declamatory style that is often characteristic of these plays as well as the rigorous patriotism they explore. Sh's two tragedies set in classical Greece, *Tim.* and *Tro.*, reveal their pagan world as considerably different from that of Sh's Romans: The Greek ambiance is one of magic, deceit, and libertinism. Key influences on Sh's (and the Elizabethans') ideas of Greece were Roman satire and St. Paul's epistles. Comments in detail on each of these five classical tragedies.

0743 Melchiori, Giorgio. "Questioning Shakespeare's Politics." *En torno a Shakespeare: Homenaje a T. J. B. Spencer*. Ed. Manuel Angel Conejero. Valencia: Universidad de Valencia, Instituto Shakespeare, 1980, pp. 7–27.

Comments that Sh's Roman plays are influenced by Plutarch's moralistic view of history. The Romans of Sh are "intellectual myths," governed by honor, even in *Cym.*, in which they are enemies of the Britons. The Roman plays are exempla, debates on the morality of exercising power and on "the responsibilities of government," but their world is one that allows little freedom, conditioned as it is by events already judged through the inexorable process of history.

General Works

0744 Mellers, Wilfrid. *Harmonious Meeting: A Study of the Relationship between English Music, Poetry and Theatre, c. 1600–1900.* London: Dennis Dobson, 1965. 317 pp.

Includes in a chapter of part 2, "Music in the Shakespearean Theatre," discussions of the music played during the dance of the Amazons in *Tim.*, I.ii, and of that played under the stage in *Ant.*, IV.ii.

0745 Mendilow, A. A., and Alice Shalvi. *The World and Art of Shakespeare.* New York: Daniel Davey, 1967. viii + 285 pp.

Surveys Sh's life and work, using materials developed teaching students in the Department of English at Hebrew University. Comments briefly on the Latin authors Sh probably studied in grammar school. Discusses, in a chapter on "The Dramatic Tradition," neoclassical influences on English drama of the 16th c. The example of Roman comedy caused "a tightening of structure and plot, the use of act and scene divisions," and the introduction of stock character types. *TGV* and *Err.* show these influences. Senecan elements of "revenge, murder, crime, ghosts and witches" can be seen in tragedies like *Ham.* Discusses *JC* as the tragedy of Brutus, a good, kind man who makes the error of believing that a crime can be justified when the aim is noble. *Tit.* is simply a revenge play, full of the bloodshed and spectacle Sh's audience wanted to see. *Tro.* is "a play of total disillusionment and utter despair, without a single ray of light or hope." In *Ant.*, there is an "awe-inspiring marriage-in-death of two great spirits" that reaffirms "the innate dignity of man." *Cor.* posits "national unity and personal moderation" as ideal qualities and shows how tragedy results from the violation of these ideals by both the hero and his opponents. *Tim.* contains some fine poetry and, in its first scenes, a few dramatic incidents, but is imperfect, probably a first draft.

0746 Mendl, R. W. S. *Revelation in Shakespeare: A Study of the Supernatural, Religious, and Spiritual Elements in His Art.* London: John Calder, 1964. 223 pp.

Discusses all of Sh's works in light of the assumption that they possess as their fundamental ingredient a spiritual quality, derived from and compatible with Christianity. Platonic and Neoplatonic elements help form the conception of order used in the history plays, while *Err.* distinguishes itself from its source in Plautus by emphasizing the supernatural. The focus on obsession in *Ven.* and *Luc.* is similar to the Christian insistence that the wages of sin is death; *Tit.* leaves an impression "entirely in accordance with Old Testament conceptions and even to some extent with Christianity." *Tro.*, unpleasant though it is, presents characters that are true to life; *JC, Ant.*, and *Cor.* portray, with varying degrees of spiritual exaltation, several kinds of divided loyalties; and, despite its pagan setting, a number of New Testament references and other softening touches in *Tim.* lead to perhaps the most serene ending among the tragedies.

0747 Merchant, W. Moelwyn. "The Harmony of Disenchantment." *Stratford Papers on Shakespeare 1963.* Ed. B. W. Jackson. Toronto: W. J. Gage, 1964, pp. 110–25.

Finds in *Tim.* and *Tro.* "a spiritual mode" that can be called "the harmony of disenchantment." It is useful to look at recent productions and "the visual history of the plays" to see to what extent such a spiritual condition "can be conveyed in visual terms."

0748 Michel, Laurence. "Shakespearean Tragedy: Critique of Humanism from the Inside." *MR*, 2 (1960–61), 633–50.

Argues that tragedy is about the destruction of humanism—i.e., "life-force, spirit, flesh, and all." The audience is reconciled to this defeat by art. Cites Aristotle as an example of how students of tragedy drift into considering "the audience, instead of the hero, or the theme, or the play, as recipient and beneficiary of the tragic action." In tragedy, we should focus on what happens, which is defeat for humanism. Aristotle himself, in commenting on Euripides, seems to accept the importance of human limitations and of the primacy of action in tragedy. *Oth.*, *Ham.*, and *Lr.* reveal tragedy as "the one form and attitude [that] copes with the powerful dynamics of humanism internally and integrally."

0749 Michel, Laurence. *The Thing Contained: Theory of the Tragic.* Bloomington: Indiana U. P., 1970. xiii + 177 pp.

Chapter 1 provides a "working formula": "Tragedy is consummated when the dream of innocence is confronted by the fact of guilt, and acquiesces therein." Chapter 2, "Some New Readings in Shakespeare," argues that the playwright remained loyal to "the hard tragic sense" throughout his career, and that this is manifested in his predilection for investigation and criticism. Adduces *Cor.* as a thoroughgoing critique of the concept of honor, which amounts to the glorification of bloodthirstiness. Romanism, as reflected in a number of Sh's plays, was a leading source of "Tudor self-congratulation." The Roman plays, on their surface, portray the mixture of "jingoism and complacent anachronism" that is "the mystique of Briticism," but "the mystique of Romanism itself, with its cult of honor and nobility," is critically examined in *JC*. Sh's tragic sense leads him to a continuing exploration of man's existence as an affair with unfeeling and capricious gods: We can see this in the Player's speech in *Ham.* about the gods' reaction to Hecuba's plight (II.ii). In *Tim.*, "the Spirit Ironical" seems to have been given free rein, and we are confronted with "a Blasphemy as well as a Misanthropy." *Ant.* is not devoid of the critical spirit, though it does present a version of triumph for the dream and thus opens the way "out of the tragic gods–men impasse to the sea–changes" of the four late romances.

0750 Miles, Gary B. "How Roman are Shakespeare's 'Romans'?" *SQ*, 40 (1989), 257–83.

Contends that modern scholars have not sufficiently examined ancient texts and contexts in order to answer the question of whether Sh's Romans are historically authentic. Cites a number of Roman *elogia* and reproduces several busts from the last centuries of the Roman republic to show that as the time of empire grew closer there was greater emphasis on competition among aristocrats for public honor. Points out that the translators of Plutarch, through whom Sh absorbed his information for this period of Roman history, concern themselves with "personal values and intentions" as the "measures of personal worth." Sh follows these sources in his focus on interiority and thus differs from the historic Romans, who were primarily concerned "with how personal motives bore directly upon public action." Illustrates by explaining how Sh uses the words "honorable" and "noble" and their cognates in *JC* to highlight, by contrast with Plutarch, the characters' "interior life."

0751 Miles, Thomas Geoffrey. "'Untir'd Spirits and Formal Constancy': Shakespeare's Roman Plays and the Stoic Tradition." D. Phil. thesis, University of Oxford, 1987. *DAI*, 50 (1989–90), 3238-A.

Considers the influence on Sh of two Stoic notions of constancy: Seneca's *constantia sapientis*, the godlike virtue of one unaffected by circumstance, and Cicero's *decorum*, the playing of a suitable role. Influenced by Montaigne, Sh viewed the balance required by these ideals as unattainable by inconstant man; more advantageous are adaptability and self-knowledge. *JC* portrays Roman constancy as social formality relying on pretense and deception. The hero of *Cor.* is an example of the destructive consequences of extreme self-containment. In *Ant.*, the protagonists strive for the Montaignesque ideal of "Stoic" flexibility; Antony falls short, but Cleopatra, in death, attains an equilibrium of constancy and mutability.

0752 Miller, Donald S., and Ethel H. Davis. "Shakespeare and Orthopedics." *Surgery, Gynecology & Obstetrics*, 28 (1969), 358–66.

Suggests that Sh read Hippocrates, Paracelsus, and Galen, as well as contemporary works, as the basis for his medical knowledge. Focuses on references in the plays to orthopedic concerns: "deformities, dismemberments, mutilations, defects, fractures, dislocations, all skeletal disablements." Mentions dismemberments in *Tit.*, figurative references to amputation in *Cor.*, references to the effects of syphilis on bones in *Tro.* and *Tim.*, and the skeletal defects of Thersites in *Tro.*

0753   Miller, William E. "*Periaktoi: Around Again.*" *SQ*, 15 (1964), 61–65.

Argues, from the evidence of a note "attached by Abraham Fleming to his translation of Virgil's *Georgics* (1589)," that there existed in the old Blackfriars Theater large movable pieces of stage machinery, called *periaktoi*. Fleming cites Vitruvius and Servius Grammaticus, who had described similar devices on the ancient stage.

0754   Milward, Peter. *An Introduction to Shakespeare's Plays*. Tokyo: Kenkyusha, 1964. x + 171 pp.

Chapter 2 includes a brief section on the sources of Sh's plays, mentioning the indebtedness to Latin literature, especially in translation. Refers to Ovid, Plautus, Terence, and Plutarch's *Lives*. Discusses *Ven.* and *Luc.*, both "calm and unemotional" treatments of classical subjects; the former deals with "female lust and youthful chastity," while the latter concerns "male lust and matronal chastity." Subsequent chapters survey the plays. Notes that Plautus furnished Sh with the subject matter for *Err.* and Terence provided the model for "the general structure of his comedies." Remarks that *Tit.* contains verbal echoes of *Luc.* and looks forward to the Roman plays as well as some of the major tragedies. Views Brutus, an ideal man who is tempted into committing a criminal act and is ultimately destroyed, as the central character of *JC*. Regards *Tro.* as a problem play that uses primarily medieval sources for the Troy story and that undermines both the ideals of chivalry and those of ancient heroism. Relates the later Roman plays, *Ant.* and *Cor.*, to *Tro.*: *Ant.* further develops *Tro.*'s criticism of "false idealism in romantic love," while *Cor.* intensifies *Tro.*'s criticism of "false idealism in romantic honor." *Tim.* is an imperfect, incomplete work whose protagonist unleashes forces of chaos so great that Sh is unable to contain them.

0755   Milward, Peter. "Shakespeare and Theology." *EIC*, 16 (1966), 118–22.

Argues that "an undercurrent of Christian meaning" exists in all of Sh's plays but that "the extent to which this undercurrent is evident" depends on the setting and subject matter of each play. Notes that the Roman plays avoid anachronistic Christian allusions, though they carry over certain Christian ideas and images from earlier history plays and tragedies. Sh uses Christian concepts because they arise from his religious faith; his employment of pagan myths and personages, however, is merely ornamental, "according to the literary fashion of the Renaissance."

0756   Milward, Peter. *Shakespeare's Religious Background*. Bloomington: Indiana U. P., 1973. 312 pp.

Examines the influence of various strains of Christian doctrine on Sh. Makes reference to every work in the canon, often in a variety of contexts. Discusses *Tro.* and *Cor.* in relation to Hooker's *Laws of Ecclesiastical Polity*, *Cor.* in terms of the limitations of honor, *Ant.* in terms of the limitations of romantic love, and the treatment of suicide in *Ant.* and *JC*. Chapter 10, "Elizabethan Atheism," includes comment on "the impact of classical paganism" on Sh and his contemporaries. Maintains that classical works were regarded only as literary models and that references to mythology were used primarily for ornamental purposes. Summarizes Sh's appropriation of classical materials throughout his career, noting the Ovidian sources of *Ven.* and *Luc.*, the Athenian setting and mythological references of *MND*, the importance of Roman history, the pagan setting and/or sentiment of the great tragedies, and the "pagan theophanies" of the last plays. These classical allusions, however, exist chiefly on the surface and have little or no religious significance. Rejects the notion that Epicureanism is the underlying philosophy of the comedies or that Stoicism dominates the tragedies. Suggests that Neoplatonism, as revived in Renaissance Florence and assimilated in England, was intimately connected with Christian theology. The "heterodox strain" of Neoplatonism found in the ideas of Giordano Bruno was not so much an influence on Sh as an object of satire in *LLL.*

0757 Mincoff, Marco. "Shakespeare and *Hamartia*." ES, 45 (1964), 130–36.

Discusses *hamartia* as it relates to tragedies of the Elizabethan period. Points out that the tragic flaw in the practice "both of the Greeks and the Elizabethans" is "a decision or trait of character that in the given circumstances makes the catastrophe seem inevitable, so that the hero carries the seeds of his own ruin within himself." Because "it seldom supplies the central tragic effect" in Sh, *hamartia* is sometimes overlooked in criticism of his plays. However, it is important because it is responsible for the realization that the hero has "brought his fate upon himself."

0758 Mincoff, Marco. "Shakespeare and Lyly." *ShS,* 14 (1961), 15–24.

Proposes that Lyly's court comedy has a constant theme: the way love thwarts our plans and makes fools of us. His comedies focus on the flirtations of courtiers but emphasize their ambivalence: They include Petrarchan worship of the lady but acknowledge the doctrine that sexual love is lowest on the Platonic scale. *LLL* is heavily indebted to Lyly's comedy but does not use Lylian mythology. *TGV* incorporates some elements of the comedy of love's foolishness. The classical background of *MND* is probably due to its being designed as a wedding entertainment for an audience used to Lylian comedy. In a direct challenge to Lyly, Sh replaced Cupid and other mythological machinery in *MND* with his own guardian spirits of love. Sh gradually distanced himself from Lylian comedy, but traces remain in the courtship of Beatrice and Benedick in *Ado,* the various love discussions in *AYL,* and the indirect way Viola has to woo the Duke in *TN.*

0759 Mincoff, Marco. "Shakespeare's Comedy and the Five–Act Structure." *Bulletin de la Faculté des Lettres de Strasbourg,* 43, no. 8 (1965), 919–34.

Argues that Sh learned very little from classical models with regard to the structure of his comedies. He seems to have followed something like the five–act structure inherited from Roman drama, but the unit of the act is less important in the movement of his plots than it is in Plautus and Terence. More important, Sh followed Elizabethan practice in trying "to present everything on stage as visible, concrete action, where the Romans had no hesitation about resorting to narrative, even narrative soliloquy, when it suited them." Sh also avoided the intrigue and dupery that were the heart of Roman drama and thus had no use for "what in Roman comedy was one of the basic means of securing a rising line of tension, the tangled net that the deceiver weaves as he is driven from one false position to another." Discusses *Err., Shr., MND, TGV, MV, LLL,* and *AYL.*

0759a Miola, Robert S. *Shakespeare's Rome.* Cambridge: Cambridge U. P., 1983. xii + 244 pp.

Chapter 1, "The Roads to Rome," notes the importance, for modern critics, of recognizing the Elizabethan and Jacobean context of Sh's classicism. Sh's contemporaries acquired their knowledge of the classics in a richly diverse, unsystematic way. Grammar school education involved readings from a variety of Roman authors, accompanied by collections of pithy Latin sayings. The growing number of English translations provided further access to classical learning, as did the variety of reference books (mythographies and encyclopedias), chronicles, and biographies. Imitation of the classical was pervasive. A chronological study of Sh's entire Roman canon reveals that he saw Rome as "a place apart" and that his idea of the city and its inhabitants underwent considerable change during his career.

Chapter 2, "*The Rape of Lucrece:* Rome and Romans," discovers in *Luc.* a number of the distinctive features Sh identifies with Rome in his later works: the image of a city under siege; a depiction of the Roman family with its values and its relationship to the city; the appearance of the image of Troy to enlarge character and define theme; and the account of a struggle between Roman and Rome, a city requiring nearly impossible fidelity and sacrifice to achieve fame and honor. The poem works toward a balance "between tragedy and history as it progresses through disorder, loss and sorrow to the costly expiation of evil and the chastened emergence of new order." Sh's chief source is "Ovid's *Fasti* with the commentary of Paulus Marsus."

Chapter 3, "*Titus Andronicus*: Rome and the Family," is a revision of item 2762.

Chapter 4, "*Julius Caesar*: Rome Divided," maintains that the places in and around Rome are more symbolically precise in *JC* than in Sh's previous Roman works. Specifically, the city is seen as "divided by civil war" as the action moves from a variety of locales within its walls to the vast battle fields where it ends. The Virgilian virtue of *pietas*—reverence for "gods, country, and family"—is featured prominently, though often ironically. An example is Cassius's comparison of his own saving of Caesar from drowning to Aeneas's rescue of his father Anchises from the burning ruins of Troy (*Aeneid* 2). Cassius appropriates this emblem of "filial piety" to emphasize "arrogant self-assertion and murderous betrayal." Brutus's marital relationship is perverted when Portia is forced to exhibit manlike constancy so that she may share her husband's secrets. Calpurnia, attempting to affirm family ideals crucial to the city, has her concerns brushed aside by Caesar's need to appear unshakable. Throughout the play, characters appeal to the Roman past in an attempt to align themselves with abstract ideals and to establish their heroic reputations for the future. In pursuing these ends, they participate in a variety of processions and often regard themselves as actors in the drama of history. Unaware that the past cannot be imposed on in this way—it repeats itself, unheroically—they are caught in its vast, indifferent sweep. Sh's imagery, involving storms and animals (especially the hunted deer and the serpent), helps to create the impression that Rome is a wilderness. Our response is ambivalent: We admire the struggles of Caesar, Brutus, and others to make this chaos conform to their own visions, but we recognize how destructive are their ignorance and errors of judgment. *JC* represents a new phase of Sh's interaction with classical authors, especially Plutarch and Virgil.

Chapter 5, "*Anthony and Cleopatra*: Rome and the World," points out that *Ant.* does have much in common with *JC*, like reliance on Plutarch's *Lives*, extensive use of other authors, especially Appian and Virgil, and increasingly critical probing of Rome and its traditional values. However, there are significant differences. In *Ant.*, the city of Rome is no longer the focus of attention; rather, it is Rome as empire, "a world unto itself," that occupies Sh's imagination. No longer is it possible to attain glory purely by military prowess; in the world of *Ant.*, it is often necessary to sully one's hands with political maneuvering. As the play opens, Roman *gravitas* seems to be contrasted with Egyptian *voluptas*, but the dichotomy is not precisely maintained; furthermore, the strengths and weaknesses of each place are exposed by the tension between them. Rome is set against itself, but more significantly "the Empire is in spiritual conflict with itself." Sh makes various use of classical allusions. The parting of the lovers early in the play, for example, draws on the leave–taking of Aeneas and Dido in Ovid's *Heroides* and in Virgil's *Aeneid*, though Sh reshaped the episode in a comic vein. The love affair is also seen as a reenactment of the liaison between Mars and Venus, and a series of associations between Antony's and Hercules calls attention to the sinister aspects of Antony's Egyptian dotage. Images from Virgil's *Georgics* help Sh stress female as well as male sexual desire, and simultaneously to deflate and exalt the passion of Antony and Cleopatra. Antony's suicide is unique because, though apparently a Roman act, it rejects Roman values. Cleopatra's final moments resonate with mythic tones: Her death scene much resembles Dido's; she appears as 'alma Venus,' the nurturing goddess of love and beauty"; and the serpent with which she kills herself is transformed from a traditional emblem of evil to an image of transcendence. The two lovers are paradoxical: Antony's attempts to maintain a heroic image of himself are completely noble and utterly preposterous by turns, and Cleopatra is at once the least, and most, Roman of Sh's women. No monolithic political or moral approach can lay claim to full comprehension of the play.

Chapter 6, "*Coriolanus*: Rome and the Self," notes that in this play Sh returns to a carefully detailed topography of Rome, rendering its citizens increasingly alien as they attempt to defend the city from others and from themselves. In the opening scene, in which Menenius tells the fable of the belly to the riotous plebs, Sh poses basic questions about the way the city is organized and the rights of its citizens. Caius Marcius, though he professes loyalty to the city, soon makes it clear that he is more loyal to himself. In scorning Virgilia's fear that her husband may be wounded, Volumnia compares Hecuba's "milk-filled breast to Hector's blood-spitting forehead," thus revealing how unnatural is her Roman ethos, exalting martial honor above home and family. At other points in the play, the natural erotic impulse is subordinated to and perverted by a sense of military duty. The siege of Corioli recalls sieges in Sh's other Roman works, and also seems descended from Hector's sortie into the Greek camp in *Iliad* 12 and Turnus's penetration of enemy walls to fight alone in *Aeneid* 9. Coriolanus does fight with epic energy, but his deeds are viewed ironically through references to Hector. Knowledge of the Roman rhetoricians (Cicero, Quintilian, and the author of *Ad Herennium*) provides a means of understanding the middle section of the play. Measured against the skillful eloquence of Menenius and Cominius, Coriolanus's disruptive speech discloses that he is "the antitype of the Ciceronian orator." However, his mother's attempt to enlist rhetoric in the service of deceit gains from us a measure of respect for his plainness. Coriolanus's departure from Rome is full of ambivalence: It signifies both "his virtues and vices and those of the city." Although Coriolanus dies in the marketplace rather than on a battlefield, his death resonates with epic overtones.

Chapter 7, "*Cymbeline*: Beyond Rome," a revision of item 1771, explains that though there is very little physical detail reminding us of the city, Rome is an important locality in the play. Britain's skirmishes with Rome supply a significant part of the action, and Sh incorporates numerous "scenes, characters, images, and allusions from previous Roman works." However, Roman features are constantly balanced and qualified by non-Roman elements. Iachimo's invasion of Imogen's bedchamber recalls Tarquin's assault on Lucrece, and Iachimo's hiding in the trunk is reminiscent of the Trojan horse; but these allusions are slyly turned to comic purposes. Roman qualities like military prowess and honor are found in Britons, but are tempered by love of family, humility, and spiritual growth. The Britons beat the Romans at their own game—war—and turn the characteristic Roman activities of siege and invasions into reconciliation. The pastoral world, so disordered and mutilated in Sh's previous Roman works, survives attempts to subvert it. Britain thus incorporates Roman virtues into a more flexible and comprehensive order.

Chapter 8,"Conclusion," compares each of the Roman works to a musical composition, noting that *Ant.*, with "its large scope, its sonorous majesty, and its variety of mood and emotion," is Sh's symphony. Much remains to be done in understanding the playwright's response to Rome, especially elucidation of the Roman allusions in other plays.

0759b Miola, Robert S. "Vergil in Shakespeare: From Allusion to Imitation."
Vergil at 2000: Commemorative Essays on the Poet and His Influence. Ed. John D. Bernard. New York: AMS P., 1986, pp. 241–58.

Insists on Sh's familiarity with Virgil and distinguishes three phases in his appropriation of the Roman poet. In early works, Virgilian references are labored and ostentatious. Titus (in *Tit.*) is rather clumsily viewed as a type of Aeneas, and the use of the name *Lavinia* (Aeneas's destined wife) for Titus's violated daughter seems inappropriate. Dido "appears incongruously in Tamora's seduction of Aaron" as well as elsewhere. In *Luc.*, Lucrece's meditation on Troy owes much to *Aeneid* 1 and 2 and enables Sh to depict "various vignettes from the epic tradition" and to express his heroine's violation through a "mythological perspective," although the heavy-handed *ekphrasis* "intrudes upon the narrative of the poem." In works of his "middle phase," Sh is in firm control of Virgilian allusion: Cassius's attempts (in *JC*) to imitate Aeneas expose his pretensions, and the account of Pyrrhus's revenge in *Ham.* represents the main character's internal struggle. In his third Virgilian phase, Sh transforms as he imitates, constantly recurring to the leave-taking of Dido and Aeneas (*Aeneid* 4) in *Ant.*, but reversing its tragic implications. He also incorporates the harpy episode (*Aeneid* 3) in *Tmp.*, III.iii, where Ariel, unlike Celaeno in Virgil, appears as an actor in Prospero's charade to show the way "to forgiveness and reconciliation."

0760   Miola, Robert Steven. "The Ancients Transformed: A Rhetorical Study of Political Conservatism in the Encyclopedias, Compilations, and Translations of the Renaissance." Ph.D. dissertation, University of Rochester, 1977. *DAI*, 38 (1977–78), 4848-A-4849-A.

Examines "ten popular volumes which were largely responsible for bringing classical learning to England" in the Renaissance, including the encyclopedia of Stephen Batman; the compilations of Bacon and Montaigne; and the translations of Plutarch, Aelianus, and Aristotle. Focuses on a group of images and conceptions from these popular volumes that are concerned with politics and government, attempts to describe the most frequently used rhetorical patterns in these works, and places them in the milieu of contemporary political thought. Contends that the popular works were "eclectic and ahistorical" in appropriating the past, being chiefly concerned with securing peace by enlarging "the power and responsibilities of the ruler" and by encouraging obedience and humility in the people. Notes the general influence of these works on a variety of "contemporary art forms," including the plays of Sh.

0761   Mitchell, Charles Edgar. "Shakespeare and the Politics of Honor." Ph.D. dissertation, University of Washington, 1964. *DA*, 25 (1964–65), 1196.

Argues that virtue and honor are paradoxically related: The two concepts are "both complementary and antithetical." The actions of a political man are not truly virtuous until submitted "to the judgments of others, who determine his motive." His "refusal to submit to a collective conscience might indicate a selfish feeling of superiority to public praise." He should, however, avoid seeking honor purely as a reward. This honor must be "simultaneously shunned and sought." In *JC*, Brutus seeks excessively after honor, while the protagonist of *Cor.* goes to extremes to avoid it. In each case, there is a private interest in honor that seems to taint the character's "professed idealism." Henry V, by contrast, succeeds as a leader because he accepts the paradoxical requirements of political honor.

0762   Monsarrat, Gilles D. *Light from the Porch: Stoicism and English Renaissance Literature.* (Études Anglaises 86.) Paris: Didier–Érudition, 1984. xiii + 301 pp.

Comments that Sh was familiar with key tenets of the Stoic philosophy, but contends that, believing the Stoic wise man to be extremely rare, he excluded him almost entirely from the plays. Considers various characters who have been identified with Stoicism in *Ham.*, *JC*, and *Lr.* and concludes that none is a true devotee of the philosophy. Uses Plutarch's *Lives*, the source of *JC*, to confirm Sh's portrayal of Marcus Brutus as a non-Stoic.

0763   Montano, Rocco. "From Italian Humanism to Shakespeare: Humanistic Positions." *IQ*, 13, no. 50 (1969), 3–31.

Disputes the view that humanistic study of classical literature in the 15th and 16th c. accompanied and helped advance a more secular vision of the world. This was the belief of Luther and other Protestants, who remained hostile to classical literature. But in fact humanism and its interest in the classics were incorporated by the Roman Church into a metaphysical system that emphasized confidence in man. Sh's tragedies should be interpreted in light of the "new, humanistic anti-medieval Christianity," which included a fusion of classical and sacred learning.

0764   Morris, Ivor. *Shakespeare's God: The Role of Religion in the Tragedies.* London: Allen & Unwin, 1972. 496 pp.

Focuses on *Mac.*, *Oth.*, *Lr.*, and *Ham.* but does use previous interpretations of *JC* and *Ant.* as examples of what the theological critic of Sh's play should and should not do. In *JC*, it is appropriate to point out that Caesar's invitation to those who will soon be his assassins to "taste some wine with me" (II.ii.127) calls up memories of the Last Supper, but it is important not to make the analogy the key to the play's interpretation. To assume that Sh "habitually imposes Christian principles on manifestly pre-Christian material" in a play like *Ant.* is to mince the limbs of tragedy.

0765 Morse, David. *England's Time of Crisis: From Shakespeare to Milton: A Cultural History.* New York: St. Martin's P., 1989. vii + 391 pp.

Chapter 8, "Shakespeare and the Crisis of Authority," contends that throughout the history plays and the tragedies "there is a recognition not simply of the fragility and arbitrariness of power, but also of the degree to which its exercise depends on the deliberate maintenance of appearances." Argues that Sh became increasingly aware of "the dilemma of authority" and that "his pessimism and his sense of the tragic" developed from his engagement with English history and was deepened by the sense of the ambivalent nature of human action that he found in Plutarch. Finds in *JC* many resonances with the uneasy temper of contemporary England, including a preoccupation with portents. Sh treats the chief characters with a great deal less kindness than does Sir Thomas North in his translation of Plutarch. In *JC*, the only man of unquestioned integrity is Brutus, whose status is troubling because he "offers to the modern age a pattern which it knows it cannot follow." Views *Tro.* as Sh's projection of his own anxiety about current events back into the classical tradition. He sees no difference between the evanescence and opportunism of the Trojan world and the same tendencies in his own. The play is an indictment of Western civilization for adorning "a sordid tale" to avoid having to come to terms with its vacancy. In *Ant.*, Sh progressively demystifies the traditional center (the city, Rome), whose values are reiterated with great tenacity even as they are being flouted. Antony, heavily criticized by Plutarch, is given the romantic role of living on the margins of the dominant culture. The play is a celebration of the forbidden and "a defiance of the public world." A contemporary audience would have seen parallels between Antony and Essex. In *Cor.*, the protagonist resembles King James I in his attempt to transcend divisions and unify the state. However, he does not understand that authority "can never rise above the social context that sustains it and gives it meaning."

0766 Morton, A. L. "Shakespeare's Historical Outlook." *SJW*, 100–101 (1964–65), 208–26.

Maintains that Sh's portrayal of society reflects the attitudes of all classes. The genuine, if critical, sympathy shown for the plebeians in *Cor.* is evidence that Sh gained insight into contemporary social ills during his career (his earlier portrait of Jack Cade is unsympathetic). Hector and Coriolanus are representatives of feudalism—magnificent but futile.

0767 Moseley, C. W. R. D. *Shakespeare's History Plays: The Making of a King.* (Penguin Critical Studies.) London: Penguin, 1988. x + 217 pp.

Mentions, in discussing the backgrounds of *R2*, *1H4*, *2H4*, and *H5*, the classical background for the cosmological view of the Elizabethans as well as for the ideas about genre and rhetoric that Sh would have absorbed.

0768 Moseley, Francis Sheeran. "The Mechanisms of Audience Response: A Study of Spectator Function from the Perspective of the Shakespearean Tragedy and Chronicle Play." Ph.D. dissertation, Fordham University, 1971. *DAI*, 32 (1971–72), 2063-A.

Uses the Shakespearean tragedy and chronicle play as the basis for examining the role of the theater audience "as it is actively involved in the totality of the performed play." Applies the Aristotelian–Thomistic view of entelechy to the play as "work-of-art in progress, a work to which the audience is seen as contributing in a way analogically creative."

0769 Mowat, Barbara. *The Dramaturgy of Shakespeare's Romances.* Athens: U. of Georgia P., 1976. ix + 163 pp.

Attempts to account for the special qualities of *Cym.*, *WT*, and *Tmp.* as romances. Assumes a close connection between these plays and the Greek romances of the 2nd–4th c. A.D., even though no direct influence of the works on Sh has yet been proved. *Cym.* resembles a Greek romance with its "multiple story lines, tales-within-tales, separate tracings of the adventures of the young lovers, pseudo-historical background, complex denouement." In *Tmp.*, Sh has caught the spirit of Greek romance in his intimate blend of narrative and drama. The mixed form of Greek romance becomes the open form of Sh's three plays. Appendix B, "Brief Notes on Greek Romance," points out the following: (1) the three romances that were translated into English by the 1580s, and therefore most accessible to Sh, are most like Sh's own romances; (2) the flaws that have been acknowledged in *Cym.* are the distinctive characteristics of the romances of Heliodorus and Achilles Tatius; and (3) the lament of Imogen over Cloten's headless corpse (*Cym.*, IV.ii) is very close to a passage in Tatius's *Clitophon and Leucippe*. Revision of item 0771.

0770 Mowat, Barbara. "Lavinia's Message: Shakespeare and Myth." *RenP*, 1982 (1983), 55–69.

Discusses Sh's use of mythologems—well-known tales that are susceptible to further reshaping—in *Tit.* and *MV*. In each case, a mythologem from Ovid is used to shape the drama. For *Tit.*, it is the story of Hecuba's revenge, while for *MV*, it is the story of Jason and Medea. At crucial moments in both plays, Sh calls attention to his shaping myth. In addition, other myths, also alluded to in the plays, are embedded in the primary mythologems (the story of Philomela is important in *Tit.*). Beyond this, Sh makes alterations in his structuring myths: Instead of "Ovid's frightening ritual of blood-spilling and magic brews," he substitutes the trial scene in *MV*.

0771 Mowat, Barbara Sue Adams. "Shakespeare's Last Plays: A Study of Late-Shakespearean Dramaturgy." Ph.D. dissertation, Auburn University, 1968. *DA*, 29 (1968–69), 4014-A–4015-A.

Reinforces the commonly held critical assumption that Sh's last plays as a group differ strikingly from his other works. The differences can be attributed to an "open" dramatic structure particularly appropriate for the Greek Romance stories told in *Cym.*, *WT*, and *Tmp.* Revised as item 0769.

0772 Mueller, Martin. *Children of Oedipus and Other Essays on the Imitation of Greek Tragedy 1550–1800*. Toronto: U. of Toronto P., 1980. xiv + 282 pp.

Purposes to study the responses of humanist and neoclassical playwrights to Greek tragedy, in particular to discover the means by which they adapted ancient works to their own times. Places greatest emphasis on analysis of "versions" of Greek tragedy (a version is a play "based on the plot pattern, though not necessarily on the story, of a particular pattern"). Draws examples chiefly from German and French literature but includes some brief comments on Sh. In attempting to restore the dignity of ancient tragedy, the humanists used a suitably lofty style, which influenced Sh's mature tragedies. Sh, however, never used the high style without a deflationary counter-style, provided in *Ham.*, for example, by the protagonist himself. The humanist sense of freedom in choosing "equivalent subjects" to Greek myth from Roman and local history underlies Sh's Roman and English history plays. As vernacular traditions of tragedy developed, many plays, while loosening their formal connection with classical models, still retained traces of them. *R3*, for example, exploits the ancient devices of stichomythia and a chorus of women to lament tragic events, and the wooing of Lady Anne is a transposition of a scene in *Hercules Furens*. *Ham.* is further removed from the Greek conventions but is based on a play (the *Ur-Hamlet*) that was probably chosen by its author as an equivalent of the Orestes myth. The Player's speech in *Ham.* derives from the type of work Sh's play has transcended. Though there is no longer any formal or thematic dependence on the classics, *Mac.* and *Lr.* invite comparison with *Oedipus Rex* and *Oedipus at Colonus*.

0773 Mueller, Martin. "Plutarch's 'Life of Brutus' and the Play of Its Repetitions in Shakespearean Drama." *RenD*, N. S. 22 (1991), 47–93.

Contends that Plutarch's *Life of Marcus Brutus* had "an extraordinary hold over Shakespeare's imagination." Throughout his career, Sh returned repeatedly to this *Life*, and especially to the part dealing with "the relationship of Brutus and Portia." Plutarch provides a lens through which the history of Holinshed is read in *1H4*, *2H4*, and *Mac*. Hotspur and Macbeth are modeled in part on Plutarch's Brutus; Lady Macbeth is "a full-length portrait of a demonic Portia"; Theseus's discourse on the imagination is indebted to Cassius's account of dreams in Plutarch; and the Portia of *MV* takes much more than her name from Brutus's wife. Other plays with echoes of the *Life* include *Ham.* and *Ant.* Points out that "we are likely to encounter traces of Brutus and Portia wherever Shakespeare submits a world that is vanishing or rapidly changing to a nostalgic critique that is also a critique of nostalgia."

0774 Muir, Kenneth. "Didacticism in Shakespearean Comedy: Renaissance Theory and Practice." *Review of National Literatures*, 3, no. 2 (1972), 39–53.

Cites Renaissance commentary on the plays of Plautus and Terence to show that in Sh's age the plays of these authors were viewed, often incorrectly, as morally instructive. Analyzes several of Sh's early comedies to show that, perhaps influenced by the commentators, he is more didactic than the two Roman playwrights.

0775 Muir, Kenneth. "Shakespeare and Politics." *Shakespeare in a Changing World*. Ed. Arnold Kettle. New York: International Publishers, 1964, pp. 65–83.

Maintains that though Sh is keenly interested in political issues, his political views are ambiguous. Examines some of the contexts in which the plays deal with "the connection between order in the state and the divine ordering of the universe." One important case is Ulysses' speech on order in *Tro.*, I.iii, which, eloquent as it is, cannot be taken to express Sh's opinion because it is carefully tailored to fit its dramatic situation. Inequalities in society are treated in *Cor.*, where Sh seems to "display more sympathy for the citizens' point of view than any previous writer" except Machiavelli. In *Tim.*, the supreme power of gold suggests that Sh sensed, at the dawn of the capitalist era, that power was shifting away from the old hierarchical order and toward "an authority animated entirely by self-interest." It is significant that the only sympathetic characters in *Tim.* are the servants.

0776 Muir, Kenneth. "Shakespeare's Open Secret." *ShS*, 34 (1981), 1–9. Reprint. *Shakespeare: Contrasts and Controversies*. Brighton, Sussex: Harvester P. 1985, pp. 1–16.

Points out that Sh gives his audience "conflicting impressions of a character," which convince us that the character is real—not a real person, "but startlingly natural." Previous dramas about Julius Caesar, for example, may have enabled him to "dally with conflicting views of the assassination: whether Brutus and Cassius were martyrs in the cause of freedom, or criminals who deserved to be relegated to the lowest circle of hell, alongside Judas." In *Cor.*, divergent views of the protagonist are expressed by different characters and, in the case of Aufidius, by the same character. The 20th-c. stage history of *Tro.* provides examples of how new productions and different actors can present radically opposing interpretations of the same role.

0777 Muir, Kenneth. "Shakespeare's Poets." *ShS*, 23 (1970), 91–100. Revised as chapter 2 of *Shakespeare the Professional and Related Studies*. London: Heinemann, 1973, pp. 22–40.

Surveys the treatments of poets and poetry in Sh's plays. In *JC*, there are two poets. The lynching of the poet Cinna by the enraged plebeians (III.iii) provides Sh with an opportunity to present the mob in action. In IV.iii, Sh has an unnamed Poet (rather than a philosopher, as in Plutarch) attempt to reconcile Brutus and Cassius, perhaps to "comment ironically on the position of the poet in his own society." Sh's fullest depiction of a poet is in *Tim.*, where we see the Poet present Timon with a work that closely reflects what happens in the play. The Poet's willingness to wait on the wealthy is a comment on Athenian society, in which "poetry and art are mere commodities." The poets of Sh are "never held up for our admiration."

0778 Muir, Kenneth. "Shakespeare's Roman World." *Literary Half-Yearly*, 15, no. 2 (1974), 45–63.

Finds that Sh's extensive knowledge of the Roman world and Roman literature, though evident in many plays, is clearest in *Luc., JC, Ant.,* and *Cor.* The poet used Ovid's *Fasti* and Livy for *Luc.* and followed earlier writers in making the heroine a martyr. In *JC,* he blended details from Plutarch's lives of Antony, Brutus, and Caesar and also drew on Appian's *Civil War* for many of Antony's most characteristic qualities. In *Ant.,* he relied heavily on Plutarch but nevertheless transformed the protagonists. For example, from a couple of hints in the source that Hercules was Antony's ancestor, Sh created the scene where the sentries report that the god is deserting him. *Cor.* also follows Plutarch closely, generating a great deal from the latter's statement that "in those days valiantness was honoured in Rome above all other virtues." Sh had a deep grasp of the different features of Rome at different times in its history. Despite some trivial anachronisms and a few possible contemporary allusions, he depicted the central situations of the Roman plays—the assassination of Caesar, the struggle between Antony and Octavius, and the class struggle in the early days of the republic—more sensitively than did many historians of greater learning.

0779 Muir, Kenneth. *Shakespeare's Tragic Sequence.* London: Hutchinson U. Library, 1972. 207 pp.

Chapter 4, on *JC*, emphasizes the delusion of the conspirators in thinking that they can avert autocratic rule by murdering Caesar and the "tragic error" of Brutus, who is led astray by his idealism and pride. Chapter 8, on *Ant.*, points out that Sh is very much concerned with preserving the unity of action in this play (as can be seen from the odd arrangement of scenes in acts II and III) and that Antony's tragedy comes primarily from his vacillation. Chapter 9, on *Cor.*, concludes that the protagonist's pride, though evil, is the foundation of his integrity; he is destroyed by his enemy Aufidius because his vice has been conquered by love. Chapter 10, on *Tim.*, points to the nobility of the protagonist in contrast to his surroundings and the commodification of everything, including love.

0780 Muir, Kenneth. *The Sources of Shakespeare's Plays.* New Haven: Yale U. P., 1978. viii + 320 pp.

Incorporates a revision of the author's *Shakespeare's Sources I* (1957) and new essays on the histories. Treats the plays individually in approximately chronological order. Attempts to determine the sources Sh used for his plays, discusses how he used them, and gives illustrations of "the way in which his general reading is woven into the texture of his work." The introduction considers the extent of Sh's classical learning, summing up and dismissing the argument that it was virtually nonexistent, while cautioning that many lists of classical parallels are unconvincing. Examples from *Lr., MV, H5,* and *Tmp.* show that Sh knew authors like Horace, Virgil, and Ovid both in the original and in translation; that he used Latin works when translations were unavailable; and that he was capable of improving on translations through superior insights into the originals. Sh's Latin enabled him to read Erasmus and, through him, to have access to Boethius and other ancient writers. His reliance on Ovid was heavy, especially in the early plays and especially for material drawn from mythology. He also seems to have read some of Seneca's plays in the original. Suggests that the absence of Latin quotations in the later plays is evidence of dramatic strategy rather than of ignorance. The same explanation applies to Sh's mistakes in classical mythology and his anachronisms. The strongest support for Sh's having had a fluent command of Latin comes from his coinages, which "compare favorably with those of Marston and Chapman." Indeed, the obsessive Latinisms of *Tro.* may grow out of an attempt to imitate "the style of Chapman's Homer."

0781   Muir, Kenneth. "Theophanies in the Last Plays." *Shakespeare's Late Plays: Essays in Honor of Charles Crow*. Eds. Richard C. Tobias and Paul G. Zolbrod. Athens: Ohio U. P., 1974, pp. 32–43. Reprint. *Shakespeare: Contrasts and Controversies*. Brighton, Sussex: Harvester P. 1985, pp. 67–77.

Comments that *Per.* marks a change in Sh use of references to the gods. Instead of aspiring to be demigods, human beings are, in the last plays, seen as being under divine control. Diana appears to Pericles, and her governing hand appears in the lives of Thaisa and Marina as well. In *Cym.*, Jupiter appears in the vision of Posthumus, while in *WT*, Perdita, often referred to as a goddess, is a substitute for theophany; the goddesses in *Tmp.* are impersonated by spirits under Prospero's providential direction; at the end of *TNK*, the kinsmen and Emilia offer prayers to Mars, Venus, and Diana, and Theseus speaks of men as playthings of the gods. Sh included the gods in these plays to indicate that even in a nominally pagan universe, things are providentially ordered.

0782   Mukherji, A. D. "Last Words in Shakespearean Tragedy." *Essays on Shakespeare*. Ed. Bhabatosh Chatterjee. Bombay: Orient Longmans, 1965, pp. 21–30.

Discusses the final speeches in most of Sh's tragedies, including *JC* (Octavius), *Ant.* (Octavius), *Cor.* (Aufidius), and *Tim.* (Alcibiades). These speeches suggest that each tragedy closes on a quiet note, that life continues, and that worldly success goes to those with "matter–of–fact prudence exercised with energy."

0783   Mullin, Donald C. "An Observation on the Origin of the Elizabethan Theatre." *ETJ*, 19 (1967), 322–26.

Urges the probability that the Shakespearean stage was "a conscious imitation of the antique amphitheatre," as seen in the illustrations to the works of Vitruvius printed in the 16th c., especially those of Cesare Cesariano.

0784   Murakami, Toshio. "Cleopatra and Volumnia." *ShStud*, 9 (1970–71), 28–55.

Discovers a pattern in Sh's later tragedies involving the hero and the influence of the heroine on him. Finds the basic elements of this pattern in *Mac.* and illustrates it by detailed analysis of *Ant.* and *Cor.*, in which the hero begins in a state of mental conflict, takes an irreversible step forward under the influence of the heroine, attempts to remain true to himself in the face of progressive isolation, is abandoned by the heroine, discovers too late that he has been deceived, and is left to face death alone. Perceives a progression from *Mac.* to *Ant.* to *Cor.* to *Tim.*: In each play, the force that works to counteract the tragic movement grows weaker. (In *Mac.*, it is loyalty to the king; in *Ant.*, duty to Rome; in *Cor.*, reluctance to descend to the level of common life; and in *Tim.*, almost no resistance.) Correspondingly, the importance of the heroine who influences the hero to act tragically diminishes during this sequence of plays, until, in *Tim.*, there is no need for a heroine at all. In the later tragedies, Sh employed heroines to enable his heroes to act and to change as "the inevitable result of their action." When it no longer became feasible to use such heroines, Sh stopped writing tragedies.

0785   Murerji, Ena. "A Shakespearean Theory of Poetry." *Shakespeare: A Book of Homage*. Calcutta: Jadavpur U., 1965, pp. 143–58.

Discusses the views of Plato, Aristotle, and Longinus on the value of poetry and on the ways in which it imitates life. Holds that Renaissance critics had a dualistic view of poetry, on the one hand committed to copying life (hence the concern for the unities) and preaching morality, and on the other intrigued with the Longinian idea of the poetic imagination, which "transforms and transcends the limitations of facts." Sh's works reflect this duality: The Poet in *Tim.* speaks of tutoring nature, while Hamlet speaks of holding the mirror up to nature. Sh's own practice, however, follows the Longinian concept, as can be seen in *MND* and *H5*.

0786 Murphy, Avon Jack. "The Critical Elegies of Earlier Seventeenth-Century England." *Genre*, 5 (1972), 75–105.

Proposes to "delineate the distinctive characteristics and evaluate the potential" of the early 17th-c. critical elegy, a subgenre of the funeral elegy. Describes the way in which schoolboys learned to write elegies, which was based on classical practice and models. Does not discuss anything by Sh, but does comment on elegies about him. Includes as an appendix "A Selective, Annotated Checklist of Critical Elegies Written in England Between 1600 and 1670."

0787 Murray, Patrick. *The Shakespearian Scene: Some Twentieth-Century Perspectives*. London: Longmans, 1969. x + 182 pp.

Examines "some of the major trends of Sh criticism during the past forty years or so" and tries "to indicate the place that the various modern approaches have in the great tradition of criticism that stretches from Dryden to Bradley and beyond." Covers four areas: character, dramatic imagery, religious interpretation, and historical criticism. Cites Aristotle as an authority used by some modern critics to argue that "plot, rather than character, was the playwright's main concern." It has been argued by W. H. Auden and others, however, that Aristotle's priorities should not be applied to Sh's plays because they are based on a very different kind of drama: The Greek tragic protagonist finds himself in a situation over which he has no control, while Macbeth's actions, for example, are his own responsibility. Language and imagery are frequently used for characterization in Sh's mature plays. In *JC*, for example, Brutus speaks in highly figurative, inflated language, "confirming our general impression of a rather unpractical, confused and divided mind." Hamlet's frequent classical allusions reflect the breadth and scope of his experience. In *Ant.*, the might and grandeur of the chief character are conveyed through images of enormous size and strength. Historical criticism can help the modern reader understand some of Sh's more confusing characters. For example, a knowledge of attitudes about Caesar inherited by the Elizabethans leads to the conclusion that in *JC* Sh presents him "with deliberate ambiguity."

0788 Namm, Milton. "Falstaff, Incongruity and the Comic: An Essay in Aesthetic Criticism." *Personalist*, 49 (1968), 289–321.

Discusses Falstaff as an example of how the artist transforms "non-aesthetic facts, among which are incongruities, into aesthetic values, among which are the tragic and the comic." Cites Plato (from *Symposium* and *Philebus*) to show that incongruity is an important consideration in the study of tragedy and comedy. We experience pains and pleasures from the tragedies of Aeschylus and the comedies of Aristophanes that are the same as those we experience in "the tragicomedy of life." Plato falls short, however, in failing to affirm that art and non-art cannot be judged on the same grounds. To correct this error, we can turn to Aristotle, who in the *Rhetoric* and the *Poetics* speaks of giving delight through an imitation of the incongruous or ugly, which is transformed by technique into comedy. If we add some principles from Kant's theory of laughter, we are prepared to appreciate Falstaff, "compact of incongruities," as "a creation to be judged in terms of aesthetic criticism."

0789 Nass, Barry Nathan. "The Troy Legend in Shakespearean Drama." Ph.D. dissertation, Princeton University, 1978. *DAI*, 39 (1978–79), 5530-A.

Examines the background of the Troy legend and analyzes its role in Sh's drama. The first chapter considers works from Homer to Henryson that were most influential in the evolution of the Troy myth. Certain themes and attitudes, such as discord and deceit of both Greeks and Trojans and medieval disapproval of the war, are especially significant for Sh's treatment of the legend. Distinctions between Troilus (who believes in the loyalty of Cressida and trusts in her promises) and Cressida and Pandarus (neither of whom is capable of such loyalty or faith in words) give Sh ways to illustrate in *Tro.* the flaws that characterize both love and war. The second chapter traces the Troy myth through the Sh canon. In the Henry VI trilogy, *Tit.*, *Luc.*, the Henry IV cycle, and *JC*, Troy represents "deception, dissension, and civil war." Characters in these works, as in *Ham.*, see the fall of Troy as an analogue to their own misfortunes. Trojan heroes and lovers also appear in the comic contexts of *Shr.*, *MV*, *AYL*, and *Ado*. In *AWW*, Helena is set in ironic contrast to Helen of Troy, thus affirming her virtues. *Ant.*, *Cym.*, and *Tmp.* are informed by the story of Dido and Aeneas, an indication that in Sh's late works his interest in the Troy myth becomes Virgilian. The third chapter analyzes the Player's speech in *Ham.*, explaining how the destruction of Ilium and the slaughter of Priam "raise serious questions about Hamlet's task as revenger." Chapter 4 shows how "problems in identification, perception, and value emphasize the folly of war and love in *Tro.*"

0790 Nathan, Norman. "Osric's Name and Oswald's." *Names*, 34 (1986), 234–35.

Finds that the most likely derivation of Osric's name in *Ham.* is from the Latin *rictus os*, meaning "mouth, mouth opened wide," the iteration emphasizing that the character is all speech and no substance. The name of Oswald in *Lr.* seems to come from *os, oris* and *validus* ("strong, stout, able"), indicating that all of his power is in his mouth.

0791 Neiditz, Minerva Helen. "Banishment: Separation and Loss in the Later Plays of Shakespeare." Ph.D. dissertation, University of Connecticut, 1974. *DAI*, 35 (1974–75), 2235-A.

Investigates "patterns of banishment" in Sh, attempting to show "the relationship of a structural theme to the inner world of infantile wishes and fears." Comments that because there is no growth from banishment–separation to banishment–individuation in the protagonist of *Cor.*, the audience does not identify with him. Argues that the structure of *Tim.* can be explained according to the "laws of primary process thought." Part revised as item 2668.

0792 Neill, Michael. "'Exeunt with a Dead March': Funeral Pageantry on the Shakespearean Stage." *Pageantry in the Shakespearean Theater*. Ed. David M. Bergeron. Athens: U. of Georgia P., 1985, pp. 153–93.

Comments on the way in which, in *Tit.*, the "black comedy of revenge" is carried out through a number of parodic funerals. At the end of *Tim.*, the hero's "self-interment" appears "designed to court an enigmatic oblivion." Alcibiades feels compelled, even without a body, "to contrive a funeral rite of sorts." Observes that in *Tit.* the action is framed by two funeral ceremonies, with the first anticipating much of what happens in between. The elaborate stage direction in I.i, with its insistence that the stage be filled by as many people as possible in the funeral procession for Titus's sons, imprints a key image on the audience's memory. The presence of the Andronicus tomb throughout the scene and the rites performed, including the sacrifice of Alarbus, in conjunction with the interment, give us a feel for the Roman ideals of order and piety to which Titus subscribes at the same time that they intimate the barbarity that will consume this civilization. The ancient tomb both acts as the repository for Roman honor and symbolizes the appetite for blood that inevitably accompanies that honor. In II.iii, the bloody pit into which the body of Bassianus is thrown and into which Martius and Quintus fall replaces the tomb as a receptacle of blood and death; these characters suffer "a kind of ghastly mock burial." At the end, Titus and most of his kin have been swallowed by the tomb as Tamora and hers have been swallowed by the earth. *JC* has two halves, each of which is concluded with a funeral; this comports with the play's double nature as the tragedy of Caesar and of Brutus. It should be noted that Antony's rousing of the mob to violence (III.ii) is a "wild travesty of civilized funeral custom" and makes his and Octavius's later pious epitaph and funeral instructions for Brutus ring hollow. The same can be said of Aufidius's ostentatious proclamation of mourning rites for Coriolanus, the man he has just butchered (*Cor.*, V.vi). At the end of *Ant.*, Caesar plans a funeral procession that will be a substitute for the triumph of which he has been balked. However, the most powerful image is of Cleopatra's monument, which emblematizes "a kind of transcendence, a triumph over the destructive agencies of Time and Death."

0793 Nelson, Conny Edwin. "The Tragedy of Power in Racine and Shakespeare." Ph.D. dissertation, University of Washington, 1964. *DA*, 25 (1964–65), 2985–2986.

Holds that in early modern tragedy, tragic man "is as much political, public man as he is private, individual man. His agony has to be articulated in the language of the public as well as the private solitude." Develops this observation by examining six tragedies of Sh and six of Racine. *Ant.* and *Cor.* are plays in which "power and politics are seen as essential determinants of character" and tragic structure.

0794 Nelson, Thomas Allen. "Shakespeare's Comic Tragedy: A Study of Symbolic Action and Character in the Dramatic Romances." Ph.D. dissertation, Tulane University, 1966. *DA*, 27 (1966), 1343-A.

Suggests that in his last four comedies, Sh articulates a particular concept of comedy. Using symbolic action and character, he dramatizes "the imaginative and transforming powers of comic art." Points out that in the so-called dramatic romances, Sh uses Greek romance (in *Per.*), history by Holinshed (in *Cym.*), and pastoralism (in *WT*)—all materials that are common to his earlier comedies. Thus there is unity of technique, purpose, and conception in Sh's comedy.

0795 Ness, Verna Marlene. "Some Aspects of Renaissance English Tragedy." Ph.D. dissertation, University of Washington, 1967. *DA*, 29 (1968–69), 235-A.

Presents four ideas about Renaissance tragedy that have been either neglected or treated unsatisfactorily. One of these is the tragic flaw, which is an integral part of many plays, including *Ham.*, *Cor.*, *Ant.*, and *JC*. Another is *anagnorisis*, or recognition, "a frequent though not omnipresent element in Elizabethan and Jacobean tragedy." This recognition does not have to be moral or even articulated. It can be, as it is with Brutus, "a silent acknowledgment."

0796 Neuville, H. Richmond Jr. "The Scepter and the Soul: The Nature and Education of a Prince in Renaissance Literature." Ph.D. dissertation, New York University, 1968. *DAI*, 30 (1969–70), 692-A.

Distinguishes two ideas of the ruler in the Renaissance: "the ideal Christian prince and the politically astute prince." Humanist writers like Erasmus, More, and Elyot set forth "the nature, virtues, and education of the ideal prince." In addition, the Renaissance did much to combine the Platonic notion of "a good and just state governed by a philosopher–king with the Aristotelian traditions of the virtuous mean and the ethical education of the citizen and ruler." Machiavelli emphasized the pragmatic necessities of rule, showing the prince to be a combination of ideal ruler and tyrant. This kind of dichotomy is also seen in the dramatic literature of the time (for example, *R3* and *1H4*). For the humanists, the ideal image of the individual in art and society was that of the courtier–gentleman (as presented, for example, by Castiglione).

0797 Nevo, Ruth. *Comic Transformations in Shakespeare*. London and New York: Methuen, 1980. vi + 242 pp.

Analyzes Sh's "ten early comedies" in light of the influence of New Comedy and its theoretical elaborations by neoclassical commentators. Chapter 1, "Shakespeare's New Comedy," describing the structure of this type of comedy and the figure of the trickster or fool who facilitates the action, is a revision of part of item 0798; and chapter 12, "Comic Remedies," which develops a theory of double catharsis for comedy, is a revision of another part of the same item. The intervening chapters treat, respectively, *Err., Shr., TGV, LLL, MND, MV, Wiv., Ado, AYL,* and *TN.*

0798   Nevo, Ruth. "Shakespeare's Comic Remedies." *Shakespearean Comedy.* Ed. Maurice Charney. New York: New York Literary Forum, 1980, pp. 3–15.

Argues that Sh developed his distinctive brand of comedy from the Terentian scheme for comic plots and from the variations he was able to play on the theme of romantic courtship. As elaborated by the neoclassical commentators, the formula of New Comedy included a five-act structure through which the characters recover what was lost at the beginning. They go through "a sequence of turbations" in the third act, the fourth makes clear how desperate their predicament is, and the fifth finds a remedy for all of their ills. The analogy, suggested in this description, between the development of a comic plot and the process of curing a disease had been recognized throughout the classical tradition, and Sh sophisticated the notion in his early comedies. Both the audience and the characters of these plays undergo a reordering of experience. For the characters, a particular, localized set of follies is cured, while for the audience the entire human condition is illuminated. This double catharsis is facilitated by the fools, whose many faces embody in various combinations the three types of comic characters, as analyzed by the ancient Greek *Tractatus Coislinianus*: the *bomolochos* (buffoon), the *eiron* (ironical man), and the *alazon* (impostor). A Shakespearean fool almost never stands alone as the representative of one comic type. He either pairs off with another fool in a complementary relationship (as Thersites and Pandarus do in *Tro.*) or incorporates within himself several aspects of fooling (as Falstaff does). Revised as parts of item 0797.

0799   Nevo, Ruth. *Tragic Form in Shakespeare.* Princeton: Princeton U. P., 1972. xi + 412 pp.

The first chapter, "The Tragic Progesss," explains that Sh inherited "a convention of dramatic form" and with it "a highly developed rationale," developed by Renaissance humanists from classical authors. Proposes to trace the progress of the protagonists in nine of Sh's plays by following them through a five-stage sequence: "predicament, psychomachia, peripeteia, perspectives of irony and pathos, and catastrophe." Chapter 4, *"Julius Caesar,"* identifies Brutus as the protagonist who goes through these stages but is deluded in the end: He gains no insight into his inner life. Chapter 9, "*Antony and Cleopatra,"* is a revision of item 1409. Chapter 10, *"Coriolanus,"* argues that this play follows Sh's "regular tragic structure," delaying the fatal mistake and the recognitions that it prompts until the last act. *Cor.* is marked by recurrences; repeatedly, the protagonist is pushed into action or diverted from his course of action. He is radically naive, the most deficient in self-awareness of all Sh's tragic heroes. His death at the hands of a Volscian mob provides perhaps Sh's bleakest tragic ending; the attempt to live heroically, to be true to one's self, is not to be tolerated by the world.

0800   Newkirk, Glen Alton. "The Public and Private Ideal of the Sixteenth-Century Gentleman: A Representative Analysis." Ph.D. dissertation, University of Denver, 1966. DA, 27 (1966–67), 1034-A.

Traces the "classical concept of the virtuous man trained to serve his state" from its origin to the 16th c. In 16th-c. England, the ideal of the perfect gentleman was formed by fusing many elements, including the "pattern of gentility" admired by humanist writers. In his plays, Sh shows how the abstract ideal needs modification when it comes into contact with the realities of everyday experience.

0801   Newman, Karen. *Shakespeare's Rhetoric of Comic Character: Dramatic Convention in Classical and Renaissance Comedy.* New York: Methuen, 1985. x + 153 pp.

Investigates the classical background for the conventions by which Sh reveals the inner life of comic characters, especially as these conventions are involved in mistaken identity. Begins with an analysis of the soliloquy in which Angelo first recognizes his desire for Isabella (*MM*, II.ii.167–192), a complex self-interrogation that makes use of the rhetorical devices described in Elizabethan handbooks and intended to help students in the making of fictions. Chapter 2 points out how Sh "creates complex comic characters within the confines of a mistaken identity plot" in *MM*. Chapters 3, 4, and 5 consider, respectively, the contributions of Menander, Plautus and Terence, and Renaissance Italian comedy to Sh's "rhetoric of consciousness" in comic plots of mistaken identity. Chapter 6 treats Sh's early comedies, Chapter 7 analyzes *AYL* and *TN*, Chapter 8 considers *Ado*, and Chapter 9 examines the rhetoric of consciousness as it is manifested in Hamlet's soliloquy after his first meeting with the players (*Ham.*, II.ii.549–606). Revision of item 0802.

0802   Newman, Karen Alison. "Mistaken Identity and the Structure of Comedy: A Comparative Study of Classical, Italian Renaissance and Shakespearean Comedy." Ph.D. dissertation, University of California, Berkeley, 1978. *DAI*, 40 (1979–80), 239-A.

Compares the deployment of mistaken identity in typical works from Menander, Plautus, Terence, *commedia erudita*, and Sh. This device "both develops comic plots and structures character development." With the earlier works as background, Sh extends the convention beyond character development to "pose certain epistemological questions about identity." Revised as item 0801.

0802a   Niculescu, Luminitsa. "Shakespeare and Alchemy: Let Us Not Admit Impediments." *REAL: The Yearbook of Research in English and American Literature*, 2 (1984), 165–98.

Finds common conceptual ground between alchemy and Renaissance poetics, especially in their sharing of the Neoplatonic notion that art (*Natura naturans*) improves nature (*Natura naturata*). Focuses on the sun–king analogy as it appears in the history plays, as well as the ways in which the language used by Sh's kings leads us to appraise, by its purity or corruption, the integrity of royal power. Concludes by considering how the Neoplatonic concept of the poet as God is expressed in alchemical imagery in *MND*, *Tmp.*, and especially *Son*. Revision of part of item 0803.

0803   Niculescu, Luminitsa Irene. "From Hermeticism to Hermeneutics: Alchemical Metaphors in Renaissance Literature." Ph.D. dissertation, University of California, Los Angeles, 1981. *DAI*, 42 (1981–82), 3590-A.

Proposes to illuminate "one area of Renaissance poetics by studying analogies between Renaissance Hermeticism and Neoplatonism." Discusses Sh in the context of an examination of "the role of the poet as re-creator." Part revised as item 0802a.

0803a   Norvell, Betty G. "Aristotle, Shakespeare, and the Experience of Wonder." *BWVACET*, 11 (1989), 53–58.

Argues that Sh, in his great tragedies and in *Tmp.*, brings us to experience the sense of wonder that Aristotle recognizes in the *Metaphysics*, the *Rhetoric*, and the *Poetics* as being one of the highest and most illuminating pleasures available to humankind. Finds the basis for wonder in the classical conception of the universe as "whole, vast, and beyond our limits, but numinous with integrity." Traces the transmission of this conception to Sh through Horace, Longinus, and "the Donatan tradition."

0804   Norvell, Betty Jeannine Groah. "'O Mother, Mother: What have you done?' Shakespeare's Mothers in Relation to Catastrophe." Ph.D. dissertation, West Virginia University, 1982. *DAI*, 43 (1982–83), 812-A.

Includes Plato and other classical Greek writers in an examination of the background of Renaissance thought, especially regarding order and chaos. Discusses strong mother figures in *Tit.*, *2H6*, *3H6*, *R3*, *Cor.*, *Ham.*, and *WT*. Concludes that aggressiveness by mothers results in catastrophe, while patience conduces to "order and peace."

0805 Nosworthy, J. M. *Shakespeare Puts the Clock Back.* An Inaugural Lecture Delivered at the University College of Wales, Aberystwyth, 4 May 1977. Cardiff: U. of Wales P., 1978. 25 pp.

Explores Sh's ways of recalling the past, noting that he was "a very nostalgic person." One vehicle for nostalgia is the noting of present misery and past happiness, something that first appears in the comedies and is already developing in the direction of the tragic sublime when Antony uses it to speak of the dead Caesar in *JC*. Sh imbues this theme with its greatest power in *Cor.*, in which it is subtly linked to "the whole process of humiliation" that anticipates the protagonist's downfall. Another device that Sh uses to create nostalgia is the *ubi sunt* formula, which was frequently applied by the Elizabethans to the heroes of classical antiquity (Hamlet employs it to speak of Alexander and Caesar in the graveyard scene). Disputes the notion that Sh's Roman tragedies recall the past in a similar way. *Ant.* and *JC* concern "the Julio-Claudian succession" and the establishment of "a vast, civilizing empire" that was not threatened by the mistakes of individuals. *Cor.*, however, takes us back almost to 500 B.C., focusing on a small, fragile city–state. Sh's other tragedies end with a note of hope, fostered by a regenerative agent. In *Cor.*, there is no such agent, for none was supplied by history. To mark this as his most extreme "retreat into the hinterland of history," Sh makes powerful use of "ancient" and its related adjectives. In probing history in this way, the playwright paradoxically brings us to understand that the conflicts in *Cor.* "are coterminous with human nature itself."

0806 Nosworthy, J. M. *Shakespeare's Occasional Plays: Their Origin and Transmission.* New York: Barnes & Noble, 1965. vii + 238 pp.

Contends that four plays—*Mac.*, *Tro.*, *Wiv.*, and *Ham.*—were first composed "for presentations before particular audiences on particular occasions." Chapter 1, which suggests that *Mac.* was hastily written in response to a royal command, argues for a date of 1606, partly on the basis of echoes from Plutarch's *Lives* shared by *Mac.* and *Ant.* Chapter 5 hypothesizes that the 1609 quarto of *Tro.* was based on a transcription (containing some revisions) of Sh's original draft by someone with a pronounced classical bias, perhaps Ben Jonson. The chapters on *Ham.* make the case that it was written for performance at the universities of Oxford and Cambridge while Sh's company was on tour. Evidence for this view includes Hamlet's status as a student, his entrance in II.ii while reading a book (possibly a copy of Juvenal), and the Pyrrhus speeches, which would have reminded the audience of academic drama on a familiar subject (in particular, Marlowe's *Dido, Queen of Carthage*). Appendix 1 proposes that *Tim.*, "with its generous provision for spectacle," was from the first conceived with both Globe and Blackfriars audiences in mind.

0807 Nosworthy, J. M. "Shakespeare's Pastoral Metamorphoses."*The Elizabethan Theatre VIII.* Papers Given at the Eighth International Conference on Elizabethan Theatre Held at the University of Waterloo, Ontario, in July 1979. Ed. G. R. Hibbard. Port Credit, Ontario: P. D. Meany, 1982, pp. 90–113.

Observes that Sh was fascinated with pastoral and that his powerful imagination led him to engage with the mode in ways completely unknown to his predecessors. Focuses on the five plays of Sh that can be categorized as pastoral—*LLL, MND, AYL, WT,* and *Tmp.*—for which the dramatist worked out a subtle and flexible formula for adaptation of the essentially classical model that he had inherited. In these five works, pastoral conventions are expanded to include a broad inventory of "normal country activities"; Greek and Roman legend and mythology are freely appropriated; metamorphosis becomes an important principle (with Ovid being an important influence in this respect); and North's translation of Plutarch's *Lives* and Adlington's translation of Apuleius's *Golden Asse* are important sources. Sees the "underlying conflict" in *LLL* as between Mercury and Apollo on the one hand and Cupid on the other and argues that the labors of Cupid are lost when "Mercury is metamorphosed into Marcade." Berowne's "Protean use of language" is allied to metamorphosis. The dream world of *MND* is exquisitely and often painfully metamorphic. *The Golden Asse* is a likely source for Titania's treatment of Bottom, and Plutarch's *Lives* furnishes many of the play's names. In *AYL*, we see metamorphoses of style (from prose to poetry and vice versa) and of character (Orlando's oscillation between lamb and lion). Several characters denounce the pastoral life in what seem to be variants of the same critical voice. Most notable of these is Jaques, whose intellectual eccentricity makes him "a walking metamorphosis" and whose speech about the seven ages of man reflects the play's preoccupation with time's changes. In *WT*, Sh's transposition of Sicilia and Bohemia, the two locales in his source (so that the setting of the early scenes is in Sicilia), signals an intention "to impose pastoralism from the outset." The playwright would have been aware of Sicily's association with pastoral poetry and with the Proserpina myth. Adumbrated in *AYL*, the pattern of *WT* is "that of a pastoral world [that] lapses into tragic chaos but is restored to its former state by the workings of Time." Leontes undergoes the ultimate mutation of character, and the sheep-shearing scene (IV.iv) accommodates a wide range of metamorphoses. As in *MND*, Sh draws on both Plutarch and Apuleius, the former for several names and the latter for the gruesome punishment that, according to Autolycus, awaits the Shepherd's son (IV.iv.787–808). Apollo is present in *WT*, primarily as a bringer of retribution in the early acts; in the second half, the dominant force is that of Mercury, represented by Autolycus, who heralds the play's final metamorphosis, the transformation of Hermione's statue.

0807a Novy, Marianne. Love's Argument: Gender Relations in Shakespeare. Chapel Hill: U. of North Carolina P., 1984. xi + 237 pp.

Suggests that Sh's plays "symbolically resolve in the comedies and the romances and act out in the tragedies two related but distinct conflicts—the conflict between mutuality and patriarchy and the conflict between emotion and control." Chapter 6 includes an analysis of *Tro*. as "one of the most devastating pictures in the Shakespeare canon or anywhere else of the gender relations consequent on the treatment of women primarily as property." Comments that *Ant*. has protagonists more open to mutuality, and hence possessing a more stable relationship, than those of *Tro*. and other plays.

0808 Nowottny, Winifred. "Shakespeare's Tragedies." *Shakespeare's World*. Eds. James Sutherland and Joel Hurstfield. London: Edward Arnold, 1964, pp. 48–78.

Comments that *JC* is a tragedy of action rather than of character: It involves a significant deed that cannot be managed by those concerned. Its language is more austere than that of the later tragedies. Illustrates the point that Sh powerfully dramatized much that had previously been treated in nondramatic literature by explaining the debt that Hamlet's speech,"What a piece of work is a man" (II.ii.304–311), owes to Platonic treatises like those of Ficino and Pico della Mirandola. Emphasizes the great power of the language in *Ant*., which transforms a tale about the fall of princes into an incomparable expression of Renaissance magnanimity.

0809 Nowottny, Winifred. "Some Features of Shakespeare's Poetic Language Considered in the Light of Quintilian and Thomas Wilson." *HUSL*, 4 (1976), 125–38.

Begins by suggesting that Wilson's *Arte of Rhetorique*, which borrowed extensively from Erasmus, who in turn borrowed from Cicero, foreshadows certain things in Sh's Sonnets 18, 19, and 20. Quintilian's *Institutio Oratoria* provides interesting parallels and is a possible source for the motif of the brainchild in Sonnet 77, the analogy between the sailing of a ship and style in Sonnets 80 and 86, the image of the actor overburdened by his part in Sonnet 23, and Macbeth's famous description of life as "a poor player" (*Mac*., V.v.24–28).

0810   Nugent, S. Georgia. "Ancient Theories of Comedy: The Treatises of Evanthius and Donatus." *Shakespearean Comedy.* Ed. Maurice Charney. New York: New York Literary Forum, 1980, pp. 259–80.

Provides an introduction to, translation of, and Latin texts for "Evanthius on Comedy" and "Donatus on Comedy," short treatises by two grammarians of the 4th-c. A.D. Calls attention to the great influence of these two texts, usually printed as one unit in commentaries on the comedies of Terence, on comic theory and practice in the 16th c.

0811   Nuttall, A. D. *A New Mimesis: Shakespeare and the Representation of Reality.* London: Methuen, 1983. viii + 209 pp.

Recognizes Sh as a great poet of realism, "so long as we remember that fictions involve mediated truth to probabilities rather than immediate truth to specific facts." Argues that Sh's imagination, though anachronistic in certain details, was easily able to discern the distinctive qualities of Roman civilization, especially in his depiction of Stoicism. The character of Brutus in *JC* is a complex and accurate portrayal of a Stoic in thought and action. Further, Sh is capable of distinguishing different periods in the development of Rome (the republican city of *Cor.* and the near-empire of *JC*) and different psychic stages within the same play (Brutus, the man of the past, and Antony, the man of the future, in *JC*). In *Cor.*, Sh has taken a hint from Plutarch in making his protagonist an embodiment of "virile heroism," while at the same time showing how Coriolanus owes his entire outlook to his mother. Parts revised as item 0815.

0812   Nuttall, A. D. "Some Shakespearean Openings." *The Arts of Performance in Elizabethan and Early Stuart Drama: Essays for G. K. Hunter.* Eds. Murray Biggs, Philip Edwards, and Inga-Stina Ewbank. Edinburgh: Edinburgh U. P., 1991, pp. 84–95.

Asserts that most Elizabethan playwrights, including Sh, were influenced by classical precepts when composing their opening scenes. Refers to Aristotle's comments about a play's recounting all the events that have occurred prior to its opening and Horace's notion of *in medias res. Ham.* opens after the Ghost has appeared twice, *TN* begins with Orsino's soliloquy but has a second opening with Viola's arrival in Illyria, and *Tmp.* thrusts us into the middle of a storm. Claims that Sh purposely uses the *in medias res* convention to draw in his audience and to plunge his nervous actors into performance.

0812a   Nuttall, A. D. "The Stoic in Love." *The Stoic in Love: Selected Essays on Literature and Ideas.* Savage, Maryland: Barnes & Noble, 1990, pp. 56–67.

Comments, in the context of an argument about the complexity of Stoicism in the *Aeneid*, that Sh's Coriolanus is an unreflective Stoic hero, whereas Brutus in *JC* is self-conscious about his Stoicism.

0813   Nuttall, A. D. *Two Concepts of Allegory: A Study of Shakespeare's "The Tempest" and the Logic of Allegorical Expression.* New York: Barnes & Noble, 1967. xiii + 175 pp.

Focuses on "a particular habit of thought—the practice of thinking about universals as though they were concrete things." Finds a strong affinity between allegory and metaphysics and attempts to weaken the division between them made by critics like C. S. Lewis. Of the "two concepts"—non-metaphysical and metaphysical allegory—the second is more useful. Mentions Plato frequently to show "such conceptual overlapping as can be found" between his philosophical practice and "the poetic practice of others." Chapter 5, "Shakespeare and the Idea of Love," deals with intuitionist ethics in *Tro.*, in which "sensation and evaluation are so interwoven in love" that "the defection of the beloved is at once painful to the sensibility and puzzling to the mind." Chapter 6, an analysis of *Tmp.*, argues that this play "gives us the heart-tearing intuitions of heavenly value, but in a radically empirical and undogmatic way."

0814 Nuttall, A. D. "Two Unassimilable Men." *Shakespearian Comedy*. Eds. David Palmer and Malcolm Bradbury. (Stratford–Upon–Avon Studies 14.) London: Edward Arnold, 1972, pp. 210–40. Reprint. *The Stoic in Love; Selected Essays on Literature and Ideas*. Savage, Maryland: Barnes & Noble, 1990, pp. 1–26.

Links Jaques and Caliban as two of Sh's prominent outsiders, opposed to the harmony of society. To establish a context for the two characters and in particular to gain an understanding of the atmosphere of Sh's late romances, we should note that Sh discerned the world of Greek myth through his immediately available Roman sources. Behind Plautus lay Menander and New Comedy, and behind that lay the late tragedies of Euripides. Sh never read Euripides, but he intuited the shape of the Greek myth of the Children Lost and Found through Plautus. In *Tmp.*, Sh seems to have used Virgil in the same way: The play is full of Virgilian allusions but is more essentially related to the *Odyssey* with its motif of "the journey home." In this case, Sh does seem to have been familiar with at least part of book 6 of the *Odyssey*. Another classical "channel of transmission" was the Greek erotic romance, especially *Apollonius of Tyre* with its sinister element of taboo sexuality, which goes back to the Oedipus myth. Prospero's relationship to Caliban is defined by the former's fierce possessiveness toward his daughter; Jaques is kept in spiritual subjection by Duke Senior because of his former libertinism and the threat he poses to the Duke's self-estimate. *AYL* and *Tmp.* explore, with Jaques, Caliban, and their masters, the paradox of pastoral—"civility sequestered but unchanged."

0815 Nuttall, A. D. "Virgil and Shakespeare." *Virgil and His Influence: Bimillennial Studies*. Ed. Charles Martindale. Bristol: Bristol Classical P., 1984, pp. 71–93.

Begins by surveying the passages in Sh's plays that betoken their author's familiarity with Virgil's *Aeneid* in the original Latin. Remarks that Sh is seldom less like Virgil than when he is citing him and turns to an investigation of the similar ways in which the two poets exercise historical imagination. In both the *Aeneid* and in the tetralogy beginning with *R2*, we sense an awareness of the changes wrought by war and politics as well as of "the subtler transformations of culture and consciousness." Finds analogy between the way Virgil treats Aeneas and the way Sh treats Prince Hal in *1H4*, *2H4*, and *H5*. Hotspur is parallel to Turnus, and Falstaff stands in for Dido. The effect of Falstaff is to provide a vision of historical process "at once larger and more skeptical" than anything in Virgil. Revision of parts of item 0811.

0816 O'Dea, Raymond. "The King of Men in Shakespeare's Early Works: Time." *Discourse*, 11 (1968), 141–44.

Argues that in Sh's early works, attempts to gain one's desires prematurely result in disappointment and destruction. This may be seen in *Ven.* and *Luc.*, among other works.

0816a Oliver, H. J. "Literary Allusion in Jacobean Drama." *Rice University Studies*, 60, no. 2 (1974), 131–40.

Points out, in the course of arguing that Sh borrows significantly from his own earlier work, a number of classical allusions in *Cym.* that may be derived from *R2*, *Ven.*, and *Ant.*

0817 Olson, David Bennett. "Cumulative Parallel Episodes in Four Shakespearean Plays: Essays on *Romeo and Juliet*, *Troilus and Cressida*, *Timon of Athens*, and *Coriolanus*." Ph.D. dissertation, University of Washington, 1971. *DAI*, 32 (1971–72), 1483-A-1484-A.

Investigates Sh's use of dramatic parallelism, which may be defined as the repetition of a scene, often with significant modification, several times in a given play. The parallel scenes in *Tro.* are I.i, I.ii, III.ii, IV.ii, and V.ii, in all of which the two lovers appear with a go-between. Each time, Troilus attempts to create imaginatively a love-rite that bears no resemblance to the reality of the match Pandarus has arranged. Sh constructs *Tim.* by linking together a series of episodes, each of which combines emblematic choric commentary and realistic action. Repeating this binary structure eleven times, Sh is able to develop the theme that different artistic representations stimulate "conflicting kinds of understanding." In *Cor.*, parallelism develops through a group of scenes in which characters plan to behave in certain ways for certain occasions. Through his attempts to perform roles, Coriolanus comes to comprehend the nature of dissembling more acutely than the other characters. He is unable, however, to act on what he has learned in this regard because it violates his deepest feelings.

0818   Olson, Elder. *The Theory of Comedy.* Bloomington: Indiana U. P., 1968. 145 pp.

Develops a theory based on Aristotle that defines comedy as "an imitation of valueless action, in language, performed and not narrated, effecting a catastasis of concern through the absurd." Chapter 5, on Sh and Molière, argues that only five plays by Sh qualify as comedies: *Wiv., Err., LLL, MND,* and *Shr.* There are two main types of comic plots—"plots of folly and plots of cleverness"—and all of these plays are dominated by folly plots except *Shr.* and *MND* (the enchantment of Titania by Oberon).

0819   Olson, Elder. *Tragedy and the Theory of Drama.* Detroit: Wayne State U. P., 1961. 269 pp.

Attempts to see tragedy from "the point of view of the working dramatist." Investigates "the problems of the dramatist, the technical means for their solution, the principles governing the different methods of solution." Makes use of Aristotelian concepts in several early chapters (for example, chapters 2, 3, and 4 are devoted to plot, incident and character, and representation and dialogue, respectively). Chapter 8 is devoted to an analysis of *Lr.* and suggests that the tragic mistakes here, as in several of Sh's tragedies, occur when "a character of conspicuous virtues and abilities, who has distinguished himself through them in one sphere, is thrown suddenly into a sphere of action in which to exercise them" is to invite catastrophe. Lear is a feudal lord who is trying to apply the laws of feudalism in a domestic sphere where they do not operate.

0820   O'Malley, Sister Judith Marie. *Justice in Shakespeare: Three English Kings in the Light of Thomistic Thought.* New York: Pageant P., 1964. vii + 57 pp.

Refers to the Aristotelian basis for St. Thomas's conception of justice, which is then used to judge the kings in three of Sh's plays: *R2, 1H4,* and *H5.*

0821   Orkin, M. R. "Modes of Speaking in Shakespeare's Tragedies." *Theoria,* 53 (1979), 59–69.

Points out that the humanists of Sh's time made certain that pupils of the grammar schools had all the devices of rhetoric by heart. These figures were used by writers of the time to indicate "emotional and psychological states of mind." Discusses the use of rhetorical figures, as well as ordinary colloquial speech, in *Oth., JC, Ant., Lr., Ham., Mac.,* and *3H6.*

0821a   Orme, Nicholas. *Education and Society in Medieval and Renaissance England.* London: Hambledon P., 1989. xiv + 297 pp.

The last chapter investigates what Sh has to say about education, focusing on works from before 1600 and from after 1608, in which the playwright is most concerned with the raising of the young. Notes that the plays are concerned primarily with aristocratic education. Discusses appearances of schoolmasters in *Ant., 3H6, Wiv.,* and other works. Calls attention to "satire on literary failings" (for example, the account of Sir Andrew Aguecheek's ignorance of Latin and other languages in *TN*) and to the relatively new Renaissance concern with education of women, depicted in *Shr.* The prescription of uniform grammars for every school in England in 1540–42 ensured a greater level of familiarity with Latin on the part of lay persons; this made it possible for listeners to understand the ways in which Latin quotations are used in a number of plays, including *TN*, *Tit.*, *Wiv.*, and *LLL*.

0822 Ornstein, Robert. *Shakespeare's Comedies: From Roman Farce to Romantic Mystery.* Newark: U. of Delaware P., 1986. 265 pp.

Discusses most of Sh's comedies in chronological order, devoting a chapter to each. Chapter 2, on *Err.*, points out that in this play Sh elevates the tone and humanizes the characterizations of his source, Plautus's *Menaechmi*. He retains Plautus's farcical plot, but he multiplies its comic confusions and joins to it the story of Egeon to infuse the farce with "some of the pathos of ancient romance." Chapter 14, on *Tmp.*, maintains that in this most romantic of Sh's comedies the playwright demonstrates a mastery of the sort of dramatic structure admired by Renaissance neoclassicists at the same time that he declines to exploit "the energies of plot" that customarily derive from that structure. *Tmp.*'s unity of action has less to do with its structure than with "Prospero's domination of all the other characters."

0823 Orr, David. *Italian Renaissance Drama in England before 1625: The Influence of Erudita Tragedy, Comedy, and Pastoral on Elizabethan and Jacobean Drama.* (University of North Carolina Studies in Comparative Literature 49.) Chapel Hill: U. of North Carolina P., 1970. ix + 141 pp.

Considers the question of how to distinguish between borrowing by English dramatists directly from Renaissance Italian drama and borrowing directly from classical sources that might have influenced the Italian drama. Notes that English use of the "new or almost new characters" (like the nurse, the Spanish braggart, the astrologer, and the innkeeper) created by the Italians is a good clue to the source of many borrowings. Also important is the appearance in Italian drama of romance between equals, something that is virtually absent from Latin drama but quite common in English comedy. Mentions several of Sh's plays briefly, with a detailed discussion of *MM*.

0824 Osborn, Neal J. "Kenneth Burke's Desdemona: A Courtship of Clio?" *HudR*, 19 (1966), 267–75.

Challenges Kenneth Burke's identification of Desdemona with the elements that make up Othello's occupation. Contends that the play calls for Desdemona, representing the erotic principle, to be seen as antithetical to the "principles of control, aspiration, honor, and duty." Discovers the same conflict in *Ant.*, in which Cleopatra actualizes both the noble and the unsavory sides of sexuality, thus lessening the necessity for a wicked interpreter like Iago. In both *Oth.* and *Ant.*, a conflict "pits the old comrade–in–arms against the intrusive power of the female."

0825 Ostwald, Barbara Lynne. "Fool and Malcontent: The Dramatic Function of the Licensed Commentator in Elizabethan Drama." Ph.D. dissertation, Indiana University, 1977. *DAI*, 39 (1978–77), 6746-A.

Discusses Apemantus in *Tim.* as an artificial malcontent, one who consciously controls his behavior to suit a defined role. In the character of Timon himself, we see the psychological imbalance resulting from a complete commitment to the role of malcontent. Maintains that fools and malcontents are most prominent in early 17th-c. drama as satiric spokesmen, though their presence in a variety of generic types of plays makes them adaptable to many purposes. Discusses the fools and malcontents in three Shakespearean plays, including Thersites in *Tro*.

0826 Pacheco, Anita. "Shakespeare and the Contradictions of Honour." D.Phil. thesis, U. of York, 1990. *DAI*, 52 (1991–92), 1342-A.

Studies the concept of honor in several of Sh's plays. Chapter 1 covers the chief classical and medieval notions of honor and their reception by the Renaissance. Identifies the pagan ideal of honor as "an unstable secular formation of virtue [that] defines the aristocratic public function." Chapter 4 considers Sh's interrogation of the chivalric tradition in *Tro.* Chapter 6 attempts to demonstrate that Sh depicts "the pagan concept of public service" in *JC* and *Cor.* as tragically flawed because it relies on "an aristocratic honour [that] makes individual excellence inseparable from self-assertion."

0827   Packert-Hall, James Michael. "The Structure of Love." Ph.D. dissertation, University of Illinois at Urbana–Champaign, 1979. *DAI*, 40 (1979–80), 5454-A.

Posits seven perspectives on love relationships in Renaissance literature: the Ascetic–Stoical, the Petrarchan, the Epic, the Emasculating, the New Comic, the Standard, and the Etherealized. Suggests that the tensions between two or more of these types of love generate the structures of three Shakespearean plays, including *Tro.* and *Ant.* In *Tro.*, the Ascetic–Stoical and the Petrarchan views of love are set in opposition, but both are made to seem worthless and unreliable. The audience is left with no choice but to accept the disjunctive, degenerate world of Pandarus and Thersites. *Ant.* attempts to show that four contradictory types of love are "all valid descriptions of the same relationship." We are forced to view the love of Antony and Cleopatra "as most dangerous and wrong for the same reasons that it is most attractive and right."

0828   Paglia, Camille. *Sexual Personae: Art and Decadence from Nefertiti to Emily Dickinson.* New Haven: Yale U. P., 1990. xiv + 718 pp.

Chapter 7, "Shakespeare and Dionysus," begins with a discussion of the importance of alchemy, which originated in Hellenistic Egypt, in the Renaissance. Alchemical ideas, especially those involving the synthesis of opposites, were crucial to the thinking of Sh's time. Uses "Mercurius," the name given by the alchemists to "an allegorical hermaphrodite constituting all or part" of the alchemical process, for "the androgynous spirit of impersonation, the living embodiment of multiplicity of persona." This spirit, invented by Sh, appears in "the transvestite Rosalind" in *AYL* and "the male-willed Cleopatra" in *Ant.* In the latter case, Sh gives us his most unrestrained Dionysian androgyne, who dissolves male into female and is herself "robustly half-masculine." True to her Dionysian self, Cleopatra is sadomasochistic, passionately active, and supremely theatrical. Sh contrasts her with Caesar and Octavia and their Apollonian world of order, dignity, and categorization. Despite her completeness (that is, she contains "all emotional modes and all powers of male and female"), she will not allow the play in which she exists to end hierarchically, as Renaissance art demands. Hence she cannot survive. Explains how Sh uses astrological metaphors to transform Plutarch without affecting historical accuracy. Thus Enobarbus's description of Cleopatra on her barge (II.ii) and the account of the battle of Actium in act III are more fully incorporated into the elemental pagan world. Views Sh's Dionysian fluidity in these plays as a response to the static (and Apollonian) pictorialism of Spenser.

0828a   Pal, József. "Some Iconological Aspects of the Poetic Sign in the Renaissance." *Shakespeare and the Emblem: Studies in Renaissance Iconography and Iconology.* Ed. Tibor Fabiny. (Acta Universitatis Szegediensis de Attila József Nominatae: Papers in English and American Studies 3.) Szeged: Department of English, Attila József U., 1984, pp. 57–109.

Uses the speculations of 15th- and 16th-c. philosophers, especially the Florentine Neoplatonists, to consider two views of pictures or emblems in Renaissance poetry. In discussing how to read classical poetry, the Renaissance developed two contrasting notions of the emblem: (1) "a holy sign, a mystical code in which the transcendental idea, or deity is directly revealed" and (2) "a unity of corresponding natural subjects organized by the artist's mind." Cites Theseus's statement about the poet (*MND*, V.i.12–20) as taking a middle position: "[T]he poet in a saintly state of madness glances at heaven and earth and he describes what he sees, embodying the heavenly idea in his imagination." Concludes with some reflections on the metaphor of the book, which in the 16th c. "signified itself less and less as the true revelation of *the* divine or *the* natural"; rather, "it came to reveal the general laws of Nature." Cites *Rom.*, *AYL*, and especially *Tmp.* (in which the artist, Prospero, becomes part of creative nature).

0829   Palmer, D. J. "Elizabethan Tragic Heroes." *Elizabethan Theatre.* (Stratford–upon–Avon Studies 9.) Eds. John Russell Brown and Bernard Harris. London: Edward Arnold, 1966, pp. 11–35.

Comments that Seneca's influence on 16th-c. tragedy is difficult to estimate because he was read in the light of contemporary beliefs. His vindictive and arbitrary deities, for example, were misrepresented "in order to reconcile his teaching with the Christian scheme of heavenly justice." To the Elizabethans, Seneca "showed wickedness bringing down destruction upon its own head," and he taught them to motivate this wickedness in their plays through passions like those that consume his characters. Seneca also provided the Elizabethans with rhetorical devices like "the pithy *sententiae* and the speeches of lamentation and suffering" that heighten the tragic effect. Mentions, among many other influences, the dignified high style of Virgil. Makes several brief comments on Sh. *Tit.*, for example, has a villain in the mold of Marlowe's Barabas; and the subtlety with which character is presented in *JC* reflects the psychological complexity of Sh's source.

0829a Palmer, D. J. "'We shall know by this fellow': Prologue and Chorus in Shakespeare." *Bulletin of the John Rylands Library*, 64 (1982), 501–21.

Points to the classical models for the prologues (Plautus and Terence) and choruses (Seneca) in Elizabethan drama. Comments on Sh's use of these two devices, observing that in his works, as in those of his fellow dramatists, prologues and choruses have an oblique or often ironic relationship to the plays they frame or introduce. In *Rom.*, the Senecan Chorus's preoccupation with vengeance and doom does not take us very far towards an understanding of the tragic romantic love of the protagonists. It does set up the audience for the fatal opposition of the feuding families, and its sonnet form hints at the play's critical examination of "the sonnet's conventional concern with love, suffering and metaphorical death." Notes that the character Rumor, who introduces *2H4*, is ultimately derived from the depiction of *Fama* in book 4 of the *Aeneid*. Argues that Sh's use of Rumor as Prologue is "wittily subversive of the trust we supposedly place in our official guide to the play" but that this figure is nevertheless an appropriate "tutelary spirit" for a play rife with false report and slander. The Prologue to *Tro.* is an ingenious pastiche of epic conventions calculated to ring hollow; it partly echoes—and partly parodies—the eloquence of the Chorus in *H5*.

0830   Pandit, Lalita. "Language in the Textual Unconscious: Shakespeare, Ovid, and Saxo Grammaticus." *Criticism and Lacan: Essays and Dialogue on Language, Structure, and the Unconscious.* Eds. Patrick Colm Hogan and Lalita Pandit. Athens: U. of Georgia P., 1990, pp. 248–67.

Discusses "the theme of authorial subjectivity in the context of *intersubjective mirroring* in the Shakespearean text." Includes a comparison of the flower speeches of Ophelia (*Ham.*) and Perdita (*WT*), with their connection to the Ovidian myth of Proserpina, to show that Sh, in the latter, is seeking a plausible antidote to tragedy. Ophelia, succumbing to the vituperation of Hamlet and the rhetoric of *Ham.*, which evidences "the underworld of a dense male fantasy," is "a sort of lost fertility goddess." Sh's "Ovidian double consciousness" is shown when he recycles the Proserpina myth in *WT* in search of "an authentic comic ending." Analyzes Hamlet's reaction to and manipulation of proverbial wisdom derived from classical *sententiae*, the authoritative sayings that would have been memorized by Elizabethan schoolboys. In the prince's imagination, these formulas are transformed as in a dream; they also represent to him "the privileged speech of the Other," a target for subversion.

0831 Paris, Bernard J. *Character as a Subversive Force in Shakespeare: The History and Roman Plays.* Rutherford, New Jersey: Fairleigh Dickinson U. P., 1991. 220 pp.

Attempts to rehabilitate currently-unfashionable character analysis by applying the Third Force psychology theories of Karen Horney to Sh's history and Roman plays. According to Horney, people defend themselves against a hostile environment by becoming "compliant, aggressive, or detached." Argues that viewing mimetic characters in this way allows us to contextualize them in their fictional worlds and also to regard them "as autonomous beings with an inner logic of their own." Chapter 6, on *JC*, is a revision of item 2072. Chapter 7, on *Ant.*, maintains that the characterization of the two protagonists is consistent throughout; their conflicts with each other and within themselves and their self-glorification in death are comprehensible in Horneyan terms. The triumphant rhetoric of the last two acts is, however, at odds with the self-destructive portrait that Sh draws of the lovers in the play's first half. That is, Sh is too close to his protagonists at the end to judge their self-deception. Chapter 8, on *Cor.*, analyzes the protagonist as a perfectionist whose hostility toward the plebeians is partly an effort to conceal his fear of being like them. After the psychological crisis provoked by his banishment, Coriolanus abandons his perfectionism to pursue revenge. When he accedes to his mother's plea to spare Rome, he is torn by inner conflict; he has violated his code to go over to the Volscian side, but if he shows mercy to Rome he will poison his honor. In this play, the rhetoric does not shift to obscure the tragedy of character, as it does in *Ant.* Of the characters discussed in the book, Coriolanus is "the least engaged in treason against his role in the play."

0832 Parker, Barbara L. "Shakespeare's Theory of Love." Ph.D. dissertation, New York University, 1982. *DAI*, 43 (1982–83), 2354-A.

Argues that Sh combines love and reason "in an ethic consistent with the humanist image of man." Chapter 1 clarifies "the concept of reason as perception" by following it from its classical origin "through its Renaissance reformulation." Chapter 2 analyzes the love tradition inherited by the Renaissance. Devotes chapters to *Ado*, *LLL*, *Tro.*, *Rom.*, and *H5*.

0832a Parker, Derek. *Familiar to All: William Lilly and Astrology in the Seventeenth Century.* London: Jonathan Cape, 1975. 272 pp.

Chapter 2, "Astrology and Society," surveys Sh's works to show that the playwright, as well as the average Elizabethan, regarded the influence of the planets on earthly affairs as natural and not open to serious question. Notes that the educated among Sh's contemporaries would be familiar with the ancient heritage of the astrological tradition, especially its influence in Greece and even greater influence in Rome. Cites, among many examples, Cassius's comment to Brutus about men being "at some time masters of their fates" (*JC*, I.ii.139), which refers to the commonly held idea that there are particular times when planetary influences make it propitious for men to seize opportunity. Exhibits Ulysses' speech on degree (*Tro.*, I.iii) as the most memorable expression of the Elizabethan's conception of the universe, with its palpable connection between the planetary system and earthly order.

0833 Parker, Patricia. "On the Tongue: Cross-Gendering, Effeminacy, and the Art of Words." *Style*, 23 (1989), 445–65.

Uses Erasmus's treatise *Lingua, sive de linguae usu ab abusu* (*On the Use and Abuse of the Tongue*, 1525) as a way to understand the Renaissance discussion of garrulity as a weakness associated with women. Though Erasmus, drawing on a multitude of classical sources, is overwhelmingly interested in accumulating evidence of male loquacity (from Homer's Thersites to the Sophists), it is clear that the vice is coded as feminine. Even in a series of contrasts between national and ethnic types (for example, Greeks are more talkative than Romans, Athenians than Spartans), there is an indication that brevity is linked to virility and copiousness to effeminacy. In regarding his own stylistic abundance, Erasmus raises the humanistic worry that male discourse is vulnerable to contamination by "female excesses." Discusses this concern as it relates to Thersites (*Tro.*), Falstaff and Hal (*1&2H4*), almost all of the characters in *Ham.*, the chief female characters in *Oth.*, and Rosalind in *AYL*.

0834 Parr, A. N. "'The Dance of Atoms': Lucretius and Renaissance Humanism." *UCTSE*, 9 (1979), 23–34.

Investigates the influence that "naturalist and materialist philosophies" had on Renaissance science and on the dramatization of scientific experiment in magician plays of the period like *Tmp*. Adduces Lucretius's *De Rerum Natura*, the clearest exposition of the doctrines of Epicurus, as a significant background source for materialism as it appears in works like *Ham.*, *Lr.*, and *Tmp*. Lucretius's importance is not as overt as that of some components of humanism, but if the definition of humanism is expanded to include the development of the higher liberal arts "into magical systems used to explore the hidden order of things," then his influence, transmitted through the works of Giordano Bruno and others, is pervasive.

0835 Partridge, A. C. *The Language of Renaissance Poetry: Spenser, Shakespeare, Donne, Milton.* London: Andre Deutsch, 1971. 348 pp.

Chapter 1 proposes to analyze Renaissance poetry in terms of (1) word choice, (2) movement, (3) grammatical structure, (4) meaning, and (5) rhetorical devices. Discusses as well the classical background of Renaissance rhetoric, mentioning Aristotle, Quintilian, and Cicero. Chapter 5 deals with Marlowe's *Hero and Leander*, *Ven.*, and selected sonnets For *Ven.*, Sh derived his material from Ovid (for example, the narrative detail of the early stanzas comes from the fourth book of the *Metamorphoses*), and the poem makes frequent use of classical rhetorical devices like antithesis and anadiplosis. In the best sonnets Sh abandons "the conventional Platonism of Spenser in favor of realism." Sh evolved, "through acquaintance with classical Latin poets and rhetoricians," a complex style, which can be illustrated by line 8 of Sonnet 64, in which four figures of rhetoric are combined. Chapter 6, "Shakespeare's Declamatory and Lyrical Dramas (to 1600)," shows how Sh gradually weaned himself from the trope of hyperbole (especially as found in Seneca). Passages from *R2*, *R3*, *Rom.*, and *MV* reveal this process. Chapter 7, "Shakespeare's Plays after 1600," argues that "Shakespeare's drama, in poetry or in verse, was written with an eye to performance." The Player's Senecan speech about Pyrrhus in *Ham.* (II.ii) is "Shakespeare's attempt to represent the characteristic best of classical drama, not a burlesque." Passages from *Oth.*, *Tim.*, *Lr.*, *Mac.*, *Ant.*, and *Tmp.* show Sh's progressive concern with "transforming the rhetoric of Kyd and Marlowe by the free association of ideas and feelings into speech that would be psychologically moving." Some rhetorical conventions persist in Sh's drama after 1600, but for the most part they are employed unconsciously.

0836 Paster, Gail Kern. *The Idea of the City in the Age of Shakespeare.* Athens: U. of Georgia P., 1985. xii + 249 pp.

Examines the ambivalence of the city for the Renaissance, encoded especially in ideas of Rome. Chapter 2 examines three ancient writers in and about the city: Horace and Juvenal furnish the two "most influential models for contrasting poetic responses to urban life"; and Plautus's comic city "provides essential background for the comic cities" of Sh and others. Chapter 3 is devoted to "Shakespeare's Idea of Rome" and discusses *Tit.*, *Cor.*, and *JC*. Each of these plays provides an ironic retrospective on the terrible cost of preserving whatever is valuable about the city. Chapter 4, which deals with *Tim.* and Ben Jonson's *Sejanus* and *Catiline*, notes that in these plays the city is so corrupt that tragic poise must give way, at least in part, to satire. Chapter 7, on three of Sh's city comedies (*Err.*, *MV*, and *MM*), shows how these plays present "urban environments faced with fundamental dilemmas."

0837 Patterson, Annabel. "Vergil's *Eclogues*: Images of Change." *Roman Images: Selected Papers from the English Institute, 1982*. Ed. Annabel Patterson. Baltimore: Johns Hopkins U. P., 1984, pp. 163–86.

Does not mention Sh, but provides background in four pages devoted to Renaissance readings of the *Eclogues*. Discusses Puttenham and Sidney and distinguishes "two voices of Elizabethan pastoral—the one idyllic, myth-making, or myth-supporting, the other ambiguous and sceptical."

0838 Paulson, Ronald. *The Fictions of Satire*. Baltimore: Johns Hopkins P., 1967. viii + 228 pp.

Includes, in chapter 2, a section entitled "The Satirist and the Satirist–Satirized," which includes a brief discussion of how authors have contained or tempered the raw brutality of the satirist's voice. That is, they include the persona of the satirist within a larger work of fiction and, while giving full play to the intensity of the satirist's denunciations, undercut them by fostering the recognition that the figure who utters them is a fool. Often the convention of the satirist's invective is not entirely absorbed by the fiction and thus causes some uncertainty of tone. Notes that "the misanthropic satirist, by a slight shift of tone or emphasis, can become the tragic hero" and cites Sh's progression of Thersites, Timon, Coriolanus, and Lear to make the point.

0839 Payne, Michael. *Irony in Shakespeare's Roman Plays*. (Elizabethan Studies 19.) Salzburg: Institut für Englische Sprache und Literatur, U. Salzburg, 1974. ix + 115 pp.
Revision of item 0840.

0840 Payne, Michael David. "Irony in Shakespeare's Roman Plays." Ph.D. dissertation, University of Oregon, 1969. *DAI*, 30 (1969–70), 4952-A.

Analyzes the relationship between the subjective and the ironic points of view in Sh's four Roman plays: *Tit.*, *JC*, *Ant.*, and *Cor*. The subjective view of a dramatic character forces him to cling to his own perspective as a response to the threat of an opposing perspective. The ironic view of the poet and audience enables them to see the conflict objectively as well as through the eyes of the characters participating in it. Chapter 1 explains how in *Tit*. Sh relies on "the Ovidian myth of the Four Ages of Man and the Elizabethan attitude toward Roman history" to develop the play's ironic perspective. Chapter 2 discovers two conflicting political myths in *JC* that are actually complementary but which the characters in the play, with their partial perspectives, see as wholly antithetical. Chapter 3 argues that in *Ant*. the ironic perspective is transformed into the central theme of the play itself. Chapter 4 describes Coriolanus as an "ironic rebel" who is destroyed because he is unable to see the world "with any ironic detachment whatsoever." Revised as item 0839.

0841 Payne, Robert. *By Me, William Shakespeare*. New York: Everest House, 1980. xvi + 469 pp.

Surveys Sh's life and works. A chapter on "The Schoolboy" describes the intensive instruction in Latin Sh would have received and names of some of the authors he would have read: Cicero, Virgil, Sallust, and Terence. From Horace and Ovid, he learned of a universe "peopled by gods, nymphs, and naiads, who rarely suffered and whose deaths were merely metamorphoses into other lives." A chapter entitled "The Armored Poet" comments on the "formidable knowledge" of the Greek and Roman classics possessed by the educated Elizabethan Englishman. Plutarch among the ancient historians and Ovid among the poets "impressed themselves deeply on the Elizabethan imagination." Sh seems to have become addicted to Ovid, whose *Metamorphoses* influenced *Ven*. and other works. Presents brief readings of all works in the canon. Hints that Queen Elizabeth prompted Sh's portrayal of Titus Andronicus, "a Roman general who possessed all the virtues and as a result plunged Rome into fratricidal struggle and horrors [that] can scarcely bear thinking about." In *Tro*., Sh "entertains himself with arguments on the mathematics of sexual love." *Tim.*, whose angry protagonist holds that "man deserves to die," was written "in a state of acute depression." *Cor.*, composed in the same mood, is a heavy, almost unactable play. *Ant.* marks a return to psychological health for Sh: Here he explores "the spiritual landscape" with "calm assurance" and in "a blazing light."

0842   Pearce, T. M. "Shakespeare's Classical Charactonyms." *ShN*, 13 (1963), 50.

Points out that Sh used Latin and Greek to create names for characters that reveal their dominant traits. "Holofernes" in *LLL* is a multiple-unit coinage that could mean either "Dr. Plumed Salad" or "altogether ancient and out-of-date." "Abhorson" in *MM* comes from *abhorre*, "to shrink from," and is an example of the personification of abstract qualities.

0843   Pearlman, E. "Shakespeare, Freud, and the Two Usuries, or, Money's a Meddler." *ELR*, 2 (1972), 217–36.

Mentions Aristotle's *Politics* and Roman law as background for a discussion of "the two usuries"—moneylending and "the generating of offspring construed as a payment made to nature in recompense for the use of the body"—in Sh's plays. Refers to *Tim.*, *WT*, *Cym.*, and *TN*, with detailed consideration of *MV* and *MM*.

0844   Pearson, Jacqueline. "Romans and Barbarians: The Structure of Irony in Shakespeare's Roman Tragedies." *Shakespearian Tragedy*. Eds. Malcolm Bradbury and D. J. Palmer. (Stratford–upon–Avon Studies 20.) London: Edward Arnold, 1984, pp. 159–82.

Argues that Sh's Roman tragedies—*Tit.*, *JC*, *Ant.*, *Cor.*—form a recognizable group, in which the playwright expresses "an ironic view of history." The focus is on presenting seriously flawed governments with radically imperfect political leaders and on examining the cost, in personal or political terms, of maintaining order in the state. The techniques used by the four plays are similar: "ironic juxtaposition, polarity, parallelism and repetition, ironic circularity, deflation and undercutting, and a tendency to begin with a hostile version of the central characters and to end with deliberate anticlimax."

0845   Pearson, Jacqueline. "Shakespeare and *Caesar's Revenge*." *SQ*, 32 (1981), 101–104.

Supports and extends Ernest Schanzer's hypothesis that *JC* was influenced by *Caesar and Pompey, or Caesar's Revenge*, an anonymous Senecan tragedy performed by the students at Trinity College, Oxford. Cites several passages from *R2* and one from *Tro.* that seem to be suggested by lines in *Caesar's Revenge*. Sh could have seen the academic play when he was in Oxford as part of a touring company in 1593.

0846   Pek, Giselle Mary. "A Study of the Beginnings and Endings in Later Shakespearean Tragedies." Ph.D. dissertation, University of Toronto, 1974. *DAI*, 36 (1975–76), 1533-A.

Uses Aristotle and his modern followers to develop definitions of "beginning" and "ending" and to establish "the general nature of the tragic ambiance in which the tragic hero" must operate. Discusses *Tim.* and *Cor.*

0847   Pellegrini, G. "Symbols and Significances." *ShS*, 17 (1964), 180–87.

Presents evidence for the considerable influence of symbols, "translated into diverse emblematical forms," on 16th- and 17th-c. life. Emblem books that appeared in England, for example *The Heroicall Devises of M. Claudius Paradin* (1591) and Henry Peacham's *Minerva Britanna or a Garden of Heroical Devises* (1612), were "rich in themes borrowed from the classical world." Sh clearly "shared the general dependence of his age upon the power of symbols" and was also "well acquainted with the emblem book literature." In *Per.*, II.ii, Thaisa's suitors display the devices and mottoes on their shields in a way "calculated to appeal directly to the emblematic culture of the spectators." Some of the devices and mottoes here are taken directly from the emblem books.

0848 Pendleton, Thomas A. "Shakespeare's Children." *Mid-Hudson Language Studies*, 3 (1980), 39–55.

Surveys the children in Sh's plays and finds that the dramatist created few child characters and did very little with the ones he did create. Approves of the character of young Marcius, the son of Coriolanus, "a delightfully pugnacious, hard-headed, self-directed, sullen and unhealthy" boy. Concludes with "A Roster of Shakespeare's Children," including Lucius in *JC*, young Lucius in *Tit.*, and the boy who impersonates Cupid, the presenter of Timon's banquet in *Tim*.

0848a Peterson, Richard S. Imitation and Praise in the Poems of Ben Jonson. New Haven: Yale U. P., 1981. xxi + 247 pp.

Chapter 4 presents Jonson's poem "To the Memory of My Beloved, The Author Mr. William Shakespeare: And What He Hath Left Us," a tribute published in the First Folio, as "a meditation on a coherent series of Horatian allusions" that is intended to assimilate Sh to the classical tradition. Jonson follows Horace in acting as a friend offering judicious praise to a fellow writer. From Horace, Jonson adapted the balance between images of blotting and filing and those of flowing; the dismissal of concern with tombs; the recognition that contemporary writing is more polished and thus more admirable than earlier writing; the belief in the cooperation of art and nature; the image of Sh "turning himself on the forge" to create polished art as well as to make himself a polished man; and the freedom from restraint that Horace admires in Pindar. In praising Sh, Jonson embodies the balance of "*exercitatio* and *imitatio*, labor and transformation," that he derived from "the Horatian tradition of writer judging writer." Refers to Horace's *Ars Poetica*, *Odes*, *Satires*, and *Epistles*.

0849 Piccolomini, Manfredi. *The Brutus Revival: Parricide and Tyrannicide During the Renaissance*. Carbondale, Illinois: Southern Illinois U. P., 1991. xiv + 142 pp.

Uses Brutus as the focus for an examination of "theories of parricide and tyrannicide from Dante to the High Renaissance." Argues that the rediscovery of Brutus as a historical figure for the Renaissance can be credited to Dante, who placed him once more in "the arena of moral and political debate" and transmitted his myth to the humanists. In the late Renaissance, Brutus came to be seen as a tragic figure. Cites numerous classical authors from whom the Renaissance learned about Brutus, various humanist writings that interpret his character, and several Florentine conspiracies of the 15th and 16th c. that involved dilemmas ("thought versus action, justice versus power, old values versus new ones") similar to those he faced. Concludes with discussions of *JC* (in which despite Brutus's Greek nobility and Stoic intellect, he experiences the tragedy of many failed Renaissance tyrannicides) and *Ham.* (in which the prince is "an evolution and transformation of the Brutus archetype").

0849a Pitt, Angela. *Shakespeare's Women*. London: David & Charles, 1981. 224 pp.

Seeks "to explore the attitudes towards women current in Shakespeare's time, and then to examine the various female roles in the plays, bearing these attitudes in mind." Analyzes *Ant.* to show that Cleopatra "has no fatal flaw," does not suffer degeneration in character as she approaches death, and thus cannot be considered "a true tragic heroine." Chapter 4, on women in the history plays, begins by commenting that Timandra and Phrynia (*Tim.*) are lightly-sketched reminders of the sex-nausea that is one component of Timon's misanthropy. In *Tro.*, Cressida's "libidinous and shrewdly calculating nature is revealed as her dominant trait." Shows how Volumnia (*Cor.*), in advising her son "from the highest possible motives" and with a suffocating affection, ironically causes his ignominious death.

0850 Platt, Michael. *Rome and Romans According to Shakespeare.* (JDS 51.) Salzburg: Institut für Englische Sprache und Literatur, U. Salzburg, 1976. v + 288 pp. Revised ed. Lanham, Maryland: University P. of America, 1983. iv + 331 pp.

Asserts that *Luc.* is Sh's account of the origin of the Roman republic, with the heroine representing the city and Tarquin the tyranny from which it must be delivered. In persuading her husband and her father to avenge her rape, Lucrece is entering the political sphere, in effect conferring on them the office of Consul, and setting the stage for the founding of the republic. In the painting of Troy in *Luc.*, Sh alters Virgil's account to show that Rome was founded by Romans alone, not by Trojans. Thus, Sh sees the city as autochthonous. *Cor.* presents Rome at a further stage in its development as a republic. The protagonist attempts to live outside the city, to be author of himself, but he is forced to acknowledge his bond to his origin: Volumnia, as his mother and as a representative of the body politic, exacts submission from him. But within Rome, there is no chance for felicity: The plebeians are constantly on the brink of becoming beasts, the patricians are full of contradictions, and Menenius compares the city to a chariot out of control. Rome has a collective origin with no divinity involved. Being devoted to nothing higher than itself, it has no immortal soul. Its life is thus a "continual emergency."

JC marks the end of Rome as a republic. Cassius exemplifies the defects of a polity devoted to honor: Envy is easily provoked when one who has been equal to others is raised above them by fortune. If Caesar were to become emperor, the competitive conditions under which honor is won would be eliminated. Under Caesar, friendship, which is based on equality, would also disappear. Caesar is the "mysterious victor" in the play; he probably knows what he is walking into on the Ides of March, but he wants to impose his spirit on Rome and succeeds in doing so by becoming a victim. Two fundamental weaknesses of the conspiracy involve the imperfect nature of Brutuss and Cassius's friendship and their flawed analysis of corruption in Rome (they believe Caesar is the sole cause).

In *Ant.*, Shakespeare depicts the fading of Roman virtue. Power is shown passing from Rome to the East, but even Cleopatra is ultimately sterile. Christianity will provide the new order. *Tit.* and *Cym.* are both set in the Roman empire. In each there is a comparison between the "central infamy" and the infamy that provoked the founding of the republic in *Luc.* There is a contrast between the "happy virtue" of *Cym.* and the "dark stupidity" of *Tit.* Only in the world of *Tmp.* could the aspirations of the Roman soul be fulfilled. For example, Lucrece could become a Miranda, Coriolanus a Ferdinand, and Caesar a Prospero. Part is a revision of item 2425; the whole is a revision of item 0851.

0850a Platt, Michael. "Tragical, Comical, Historical." The Existential Coordinates of the Human Condition: Poetic–Epic–Tragic: The Literary Genre. (Analecta Husserliana: The Yearbook of Phenomenological Research 18.) Dordrecht, Holland: D. Reidel, 1984, pp. 379–99.

Begins by noting that Sh is little interested in commenting on genre, except to make fun of neoclassic critics in the person of Polonius, whose comments on the forms of drama (*Ham.*, II.ii.390–402) proliferate absurdly, thus illustrating the fatuity of trying to contain plays within narrowly defined categories. Cites the comment of Socrates in Plato's *Symposium* about the ability of the skilled tragedian to write comedy as a starting-point for considering Sh's achievement in both of these genres and in historical drama as well. Mentions Sh's focus on women as the crucial difference between his comedy and tragedy and the comedy and tragedy of the ancients. Notes that Sh, in his history plays, excels in a genre never attempted by the ancients, one that foregrounds male virtue as female virtue is glorified in the comedies.

0851 Platt, Michael David. "Shakespeare's Rome." Ph.D. dissertation, Yale University, 1971. *DAI*, 32 (1971–72), 6999-A.

Focuses on Sh's account of the Roman republic. In *Luc.*, the playwright provides his version of the beginning of the republic; *Cor.* gives his most complete examination of the republic and its warriors; while *JC* presents the republic as threatened by Caesar and unsuccessfully defended by the conspiracy of Cassius and Brutus. *Ant.* transports "the active virtue of the Republic" to "the erotic East," but neither Rome nor Egypt takes notice of the new order of Christianity that lies just over the horizon. Part revised as item 2425; the whole as item 0850.

0852 Pohl, Frederick J. *William Shakespeare: A Biography.* Rochester, New York: Dupont P., 1983. iii + 256 pp.

Makes brief mention of the Latin authors Sh would have read in grammar school. Comments on all of the works in the canon, with *Ven.* and *Luc.* being treated at slightly greater length than the others. In the former, which Sh wrote in his early twenties, the poet, recalling his own experience, examines a youth who wishes to retain his virtue, who is "assailed by lust," and who to some extent feels compromised. In its exploration of love and its development of opposing characters, *Ven.* anticipates its author's career as a dramatist. *Luc.* makes use of "ancient Roman history," as transmitted by Livy in his *History*, Ovid in the *Fasti*, and Chaucer in *The Legend of Good Women.* To his sources Sh adds keen psychological analysis and drama "at every possible point." His description of the city of Troy in the tapestry viewed by Lucrece seems to be original; it anticipates *Tro.* Notes the contemporary London flavor of the crowd scenes in *JC*, the "thoughtful comedy" of *Tro.*, the pessimistic attempt to instruct society in "gentleness and decency" in *Tim.*, the tragedy of lust in *Ant.*, and the possible connection between attitudes expressed in *Cor.* and Sh's financial security and the death of his mother.

0853 Poole, Adrian. *Tragedy: Shakespeare and the Greek Example.* Oxford: Basil Blackwell, 1987. xi + 265 pp.

The introductory chapter contends that tragedy, by its very nature, provokes and interrogates, and that Greek tragedies have endured because they harbor "a stubborn power to ask difficult questions." They endue these inquiries with "flesh and blood and spirit, giving body and soul to questions about the meaning and value of pain." To compare them with Sh's works is to help us "recognize these questions." Chapter 2 focuses on the *Oresteia* of Aeschylus, comparing it to *Mac.*, Sh's "most Aeschylean tragedy," especially in terms of how the two playwrights deal with fear. Chapter 4 considers Sophocles' *Oedipus Tyrannus* and *Ham.*, in both of which the protagonist asks many questions and has many questions asked of him. Chapter 7, entitled "Last Things," considers the *Oedipus at Colonus* of Sophocles, the *Bacchae* of Euripides, and *Lr.*

0854 Pope, Maurice. "Shakespeare's Medical Imagination." *ShS*, 38 (1985), 175-86.

Claims that Sh's treatment of physiology, based on systems inherited by the Renaissance from Erasistratus (3rd c. B.C.) and Galen, is generally consonant with the medical opinion of his time and is self-consistent, though presenting some individual features. The richness of Sh's medical imagination can be illustrated through several passages in which his mastery of the various uses of "blood" is demonstrated.

0855 Popham, Elizabeth Anne. "The Concept of Arcadia in the English Literary Renaissance: Pastoral Societies in the Works of Sidney, Spenser, Shakespeare, and Milton." Ph.D. dissertation, Queen's University at Kingston, 1982. *DAI*, 43 (1982-83), 3326-A.

Comments on the origins of the poetic pastoral landscape in Theocritus and Virgil and notes that it could be deployed in the Renaissance to "reflect good or bad government." Treats Sh's pastoral plays as sites where "the pastoral convention is used to focus an anatomy of social and ethical behaviour" in the world surrounding "the shepherd society."

0856 Potter, Simeon. "The Language Gap." *TLS*, April 23, 1964, p. 342.

Attempts to explain the differences between Sh's language and contemporary usage. Comments that some knowledge of Latin is helpful in reading Sh: During his time, "one quarter of the whole Latin vocabulary was being incorporated into English." In this age of intense Latinization, however, "Sh used his Latin sparingly and with discretion."

0857 Powell, Henry Wesley. "Shakespeare's Rome: Major Themes in the Late Political Plays." Ph.D. dissertation, University of North Carolina, Chapel Hill, 1975. *DAI*, 37 (1976–77), 1568-A-1569-A.

Studies key themes in Sh's "late political plays," including *1H4, 2H4, JC, Ant.*, and *Cor*. In *JC*, role-playing is the chief "mode of behavior," and consequently the characters are unable to know each other or themselves. Language is unreliable, and history dissolves into flux. *Ant.* operates on both realistic and mythic levels. It assimilates the valueless political world of *JC* by insisting on the theatrical nature of all life. Cleopatra's theater, unlike the mundane vision of Octavius, attempts to incorporate "contrarieties and imaginative paradox": She achieves transcendence by embracing mythic drama. In *Cor.*, by contrast, the protagonist insists on a single version of the truth in a world of flux. This world undermines any affirmations that might have been suggested by *Ant.*: It provides "a pessimistic comment on the relation between public and personal life."

0858 Poynter, F. N. L. "Medicine and Public Health." *ShS*, 17 (1964), 152–66.

Maintains that in Sh's time medical knowledge was widespread and many "memorable phrases from the classics of medical literature had become a part of popular wisdom." For example, Sh's plays contain several direct translations of phrases from the *Aphorisms* of Hippocrates. The training of physicians was based on the Galenic system of four humors, four elements, and four complexions, and Sh refers frequently to medical practices that reflect this training. The most authoritative text of the time on medicinal plants was that of Dioscorides, "a Greek surgeon in the army of Nero."

0859 Prager, Carolyn. "Concepts of Slavery in the English Renaissance: With Illustrations from the Drama." Ph.D. dissertation, Fordham University, 1974. *DAI*, 35 (1974–75), 2951-A-2952-A.

Analyzes how slavery is treated in plays, including *Tit., Oth.*, and *Tmp*. Organizes the treatment of plays in which slavery is "thematic" into three chapters, "Slaves by Nature," "Slaves by Fortune," and "Slaves by Blackness." These three headings indicate the most common rationales for slavery, all of which were derived from Aristotelian theory and biblical commentary.

0860 Prater, Neal Byron. "The Origin of English Tragicomedy and Its Development before Shakespeare." Ph.D. dissertation, Vanderbilt University, 1967. *DA*, 28 (1967–68), 4141-A-4142-A.

Argues that the principal characteristics of English tragicomedy "were derived from native drama," especially the mystery cycles and morality plays. Continental and English dramatists of the Renaissance, however, did cite classical precedent for their mingling of comic and serious elements in the same plot: Plays like Euripides' *Iphigenia in Tauris* and *Ion* and Terence's *Andria* had done the same thing. Academic dramatists of the 16th c. contributed greatly to the development of tragicomedy by treating biblical subjects like the prodigal son in a Terentian framework. Lyly, Peele, and Greene contributed to tragicomedy by using mythology, among other things, to make the "sudden reversal of fortune on which the happy ending depends," acceptable. Sh and Fletcher inherited the fundamental tragicomic formula from these writers.

0861 Praz, Mario. "The Ambiguity of Shakespeare: A Review Article." *Shakespearean Essays*. (Tennessee Studies in Literature 2.) Eds. Alwin Thaler and Norman Sanders. Knoxville: U. of Tennessee P., 1964, pp. 181–85.

Points out that Sh's plays reflect the pagan–humanistic culture of his age: In them, we see a concern for social order, the "virtues of strength and constancy," "a thirst for honors and magnificence," a "desire for continuity," "glorification accepted as a poetic convention," admiration for loyalty and friendship, and "public ignominy" as "the worst disgrace that could befall a man." If we read *Ham.* in light of these concerns, we see that the protagonist's resentment against his mother grows out of the way she has "disgraced the memory of the dead sovereign" and thus undermined his chance for immortality through fame. Christian elements are present in Sh's plays, but they are muted, confined to the spirit of pardon, penitence, and unexpected compassion.

0862 Presson, Robert K. "Two Types of Dreams in the Elizabethan Drama, and Their Heritage: *Somnium Animale* and the Prick-of-Conscience." *SEL*, 7 (1967), 239–56.

Provides background for understanding the *somnium animale*, a dream in which the concerns of the waking mind persist in sleep (Mercutio's Queen Mab speech [*Rom.*, I.iv.53–95] presents the most outstanding example in Sh). This type of dream, with its list of illustrations, goes back to Lucretius's *De Rerum Natura*; it was probably transmitted to the Middle Ages by Claudian. Sh seems to have gotten some details from Chaucer's *Parliament of Fowls*. Sh also uses the topos in Lady Percy's complaining account of Hotspur's restless dreaming (*1H4*, II.iii) and in Lady Eleanor Cobham's ambitious dreaming (*2H6*, I.ii). Another type of dream in Sh—the prick-of-conscience—has a more exclusively medieval origin.

0863 Prince, F. T. *William Shakespeare: The Poems*. London: Longmans Green, 1963. 56 pp.

Has brief discussions of *Ven.*, *Luc.*, *Son.*, *LC*, and *PhT*. In *Ven.*, Sh bases his version of the myth on Ovid's, using material from two other Ovidian stories, those of Salmacis and Hermaphroditus and of Narcissus. *Luc.* is a tragedy in the same sense that *Tit.* is: "Crime and bloodshed, whether rape or murder, mutilation or suicide; the sufferings of the innocent, and a clash between violent evil and purest virtue: these are the ingredients of a form of tragedy associated with Seneca and classical myth, which in Sh's hands take on a lucid vitality." Comments on how the love expressed for Sh's friend in *Son.* "has the aspiration, the thirst for perfection, the worship of truth and beauty, of the Platonic tradition. But it is oddly lacking in the sense of the supernatural, the Christian hope, that was fundamental in Renaissance Platonism."

0864 Prior, Moody. *The Drama of Power: Studies in Shakespeare's History Plays*. Evanston, Illinois: Northwestern U. P., 1973. xvi + 410 pp.

Chapter 2, "Ideas of History," points out that Sh's chief sources for his English history plays—Edward Hall's *The Union of the Two Noble and Illustrate Famelies of Lancastre and Yorke* (1548) and Raphael Holinshed's *Chronicles of England, Scotland, and Ireland* (1577)—were guided largely by "the providential theory of history." However, they were also influenced, as was Sh, by "the new history," which was inspired by "classical, chiefly Roman, historians" and by "the philosophers and rhetoricians of antiquity." The new approach was characterized by "its concern for causes construed not in terms of cosmic history and divine justice but in terms of the characters of men and the nature of polity and war" and by "its bias in favor of instruction [that] was primarily political."

0865 Proser, Matthew N. "The Heroic Image in Five Shakespearean Tragedies." Ph.D. dissertation, University of Washington, 1963. *DA*, 24 (1963–64), 4683.

Examines the ways in which the hero's self-image precipitates his tragedy in each of five plays. In *JC*, Brutus's "self-image as a Roman patriot" suffers from the limitations imposed on him by the historical and political context in which he must operate. His failure is that of the moral man and questions "not only the nature of political action but the nature of all moral action." *Cor.*, which examines the warrior–hero from the outside, is a complement to *Oth.*, which examines this figure from the inside. In *Cor.*, we see a connection between "the self-dedicated 'constant Warrior,'" who causes division in his community, and the community, which is also divided and for which he becomes the symbol. In *Ant.*, Antony's attempts to reclaim his heroic image and Cleopatra's metamorphosis at the end "are pitted against realistic and satirical perspectives." Cleopatra succeeds in redeeming her heroic image and that of Antony through "poetry, theatrics, and ritual." Part revised as item 1711; the whole revised as item 0866.

0866 Proser, Matthew N. *The Heroic Image in Five Shakespearean Tragedies.* Princeton: Princeton U. P., 1965. v + 254 pp.

Treats *JC* and Brutus's self-image as a patriot in chapter 1; Othello and Coriolanus as they relate to the image of the warrior in chapter 3; and the heroic image as it is manifested in *Ant.* in chapter 4. Part is a revision of item 1711; the whole is a revision of item 0865.

0866a Pugh, Elaine Upton. "'The Art Itself Is Nature': The Fashioning of Shakespeare's Heroines." Ph.D. dissertation, Ohio State University, 1983. *DAI*, 44 (1983–84), 2775-A.

Discusses one aspect of the Renaissance concern with the relationship between art and nature as it appears in the ways in which female identity is constructed in Sh's plays. On the one hand, males like Prospero (*Tmp.*) and Othello (*Oth.*) use "a Pygmalion-like art to control or kill nature and fashion a woman into a statuesque or pictorial creation." On the other hand, several female characters in other plays (Hermione and Paulina in *WT*, Rosalind in *AYL*, and Cleopatra in *Ant.*) employ theatrical arts "to provide a unity of art and nature and to fashion unbounded selves."

0867 Purdom, C. B. *What Happens in Shakespeare: A New Interpretation.* London: John Baker, 1963. 192 pp.

Includes brief essays on all of Sh's plays. Notes that *Tit.* is a failure because the protagonist does not perform his function; that Brutus is the hero of *JC*; that *Tro.* fails as a tragedy because Troilus, the nearest thing to a tragic hero in the play, is unsatisfactory; that Antony is the sole hero of *Ant.*; that the central character of *Cor.* is destroyed by his refusal to meet the demands of politics; and that *Tim.* is "perfect drama" in its contrast between the hero's wealth and delight and his hatred, and in the "reconciliation and redemption" that is achieved at the end.

0868 Purdon, Noel. *The Words of Mercury: Shakespeare and English Mythography of the Renaissance.* (Elizabethan and Renaissance Studies 39.) Salzburg: Institut für Englische Sprache und Literatur, U. Salzburg, 1974. iv + 246 pp.

Chapter 1 points out that numerous kinds of mythographical sources were available during the Renaissance, including the classical poets, mythographers from the Hellenistic period through the Renaissance, emblem and icon books, rhetoric textbooks, and glosses to poems. These sources were used in different combinations and with various tones. An important step in the development of western mythography was the work of Martianus Capella and Macrobius in the early Middle Ages, and the line of transmission includes Boccaccio, Giraldi, and Comes, the last of whom had a particularly strong influence in England.

Chapters 2 and 3 illustrate the great variety of approaches in 16th-c. England to mythography by referring to Stephen Batman, Richard Lincke, and Thomas Underdowne. Batman's *The Golden Booke of the Leaden Goddes* (1577), with figures and glosses, falls into the category of iconographic myth-writing; Lincke's *The Fountaine of Ancient Fiction* (1599), a popular mythological manual, is discursive; and Underdowne's dictionary-like commentary on his translation of Ovid's invective against Ibis (1577) sums up the "vast verbal and rhetorical tradition of mythography."

Chapter 4 demonstrates that myth was embedded in the instructional materials and techniques used to teach Elizabethan students to write: (1) The epithets in dictionaries were frequently taken from classical myth; (2) the material of commonplace books invited searching out appropriate myths from classical writers and applying them in discourse and composition; (3) devices for composition like personification and metaphor, given in the speech manuals, encouraged symbolic and mythic writing; and (4) exercises in the rhetoric textbooks depended heavily on mythic illustrations.

Chapter 5 maintains that in analyzing Sh's use of myth, we need to know the kinds of material available to him and the paradigm of mythologizing he is following in any given play or at any one point in a play. Myth is an important part of Sh's writing, "sometimes as icon, sometimes as rhetoric, and sometimes as structure which depended on both."

Chapter 6 makes the point that in *MND*, the moon is an iconic point of reference for the events that unfold. The play's central argument is that marriage is preferable to virginity; there is a psychomachia between Cupid and Diana that links the moon and the argument about marriage and "forms a mythological substructure to the play." The play attempts to give new resonance to the Lylian drama of mythology by fully realizing myth as poetic.

0869   Quennell, Peter. *Shakespeare: The Poet and His Background*. London: Weidenfeld and Nicolson, 1963. xvi + 352 pp.

Attempts "to reach the poet at once through his work and through his times." Mentions the Latin instruction Sh would have received in grammar school. Discusses the fascination of the Elizabethan Age with ancient Greece and Rome. Ovid, in particular, was highly prized by the Elizabethans for his sweetness, and Sh fell under his spell just before writing *Ven.* Comments briefly on the reflection of Essex's tragedy in *JC, Tro.,* and *Cor.;* on the splenetic nature of *Tim.;* and on the true paganism of the protagonists in *Ant.*

0870   Quinones, Ricardo J. *The Renaissance Discovery of Time*. (Harvard Studies in Comparative Literature 31.) Cambridge: Harvard U. P., 1972. xvi + 549 pp.

Maintains that the new sense of time discovered by the Renaissance did much to energize the age. Triumph over time became a way to measure heroism of various sorts. Analyzes a number of Sh's plays, including, in chapter 9, *Tro.* and *Ant.,* as "Tragedies of Love." Troilus, unable to master the overwhelming present-ness of change, can only rage at a world inhospitable to his idealism. The defeat of Antony shows that heroic excesses in the effort to overcome time can no longer be taken entirely seriously in a new world devoted to precise schematization. The dream of man that "things will not come to an end" and his "quest for permanence" are doomed with Antony. Parts are revisions of items 0871 and 0872.

0871   Quinones, Ricardo J. "Views of Time in Shakespeare." *JHI,* 26 (1965), 327–52.

Discerns three distinct conceptions of time in Sh: (1) augmentative time, which governs the world of *Son.* and the English history plays; (2) contracted time, which helps us "to understand the experiences of the doomed lovers" in *Tro., Ant.,* and other tragedies; and (3) extended time, which is "the dominant perspective of Shakespeare's final romances." Revised as part of item 0870.

0872   Quinones, Richard Joseph. "Time in Dante and Shakespeare." *Symposium,* 22 (1968), 261–84.

Designates the process through which Sh sees change occur as *emulation,* found both in the natural world (Sonnet 60) and in "the society of man" (*Tro.*). In Sh, resistance to mutability is often involved with a concept called *augmentative time,* according to which one exercises "a virtuous control over experience" within time. If, however, like Troilus, one fails to grasp the "emulative nature of reality" he or she is doomed to be victimized by it. *Ant.* is the one exception to a tendency in Shakespearean drama: To find satisfactions and disappointments within time, the lovers abandon any attempt to manage experience and seek fulfillment and perpetuation outside of time. Revised as part of item 0870.

0873 Rabkin, Norman. *Shakespeare and the Common Understanding.* New York: Free P., 1967. ix + 267 pp.

Draws on the insight of modern physicist Niels Bohr to discover in Sh's works "a characteristic mode of vision" that is manifested in a "dialectical dramaturgy": Plays and poems are structured in terms of "a pair of polar opposites," which are "equally valid, equally desirable, and equally destructive." The power of Sh's art consists of suggesting that "reality when fully understood is more complicated than any simple, logical, and coherent reading of it, yet of such a nature that we find ourselves forced constantly to make, and to profit from, simple, logical, and coherent readings." Such a vision may be designated as one of complementarity. This quality makes Sh's works an unpromising quarry for those wishing to discover any "Renaissance orthodoxy."

Chapter 2, "Self against Self," includes an analysis of *Tro.* (a revision of item 2991). This play uses a modified version of the double plot to link the love story and the war story in an exhibition of the theme that time determines value. Points to the pervasiveness of this theme, especially in the debate scenes of I.iii and II.ii, the ironic prophecies that provide the climactic exposition of theme in the main (love) plot (III.ii), the contiguous exposition of theme in the war plot (III.iii), and the incessant personification of time. The last two acts are chiefly devoted to a working out of both plots' ironic prophecies.

Chapter 3, "The Polity," includes discussion of *JC* (a revision of item 2082) and *Cor.* (a revision of item 1715). In *JC*, Sh creates a symmetry between II.i and II.ii. These two scenes, because they focus, respectively, on Brutus and Caesar, might be expected to reveal only contrasts. However, they are also concerned to demonstrate the virtual identity of the two rivals. The first scene shows us Brutus at home with his servant, with the conspirators, and with his wife; in the second, Caesar is seen in a similar situation. Sh has altered his source, Plutarch's *Lives,* to give us "parallel scenes in the two homes." In each case, we see a noble Roman making admirably Stoic pronouncements which then degenerate into bluster as the speaker's vanity comes to the fore. Notes that once Brutus has committed the murder of Caesar, the play shifts from what might have been a historical tragedy to a revenge tragedy; that is, Sh uses Brutus's attempt to affect history by reason to create "a moral universe" in which, ironically, "events are brought about not according to man's idealistic intentions but deterministically by their own logic." In *Cor.,* Sh grapples most intensively with the question of honor. For the hero, the Roman state is the idea of honor, and paradoxically this idea leads him to renounce the state that is its avatar. There are alternatives to Coriolanus's abstract honor—the realpolitik of Aufidius and the temporizing of Cominius, Menenius, and Volumnia—but none is satisfactory. The most tempting, Volumnia's notion that honor, in order to preserve the polity, is justified in resorting to policy, is ultimately futile because its counsel of compromise results in disaster. Coriolanus's fate seems to be more inevitable, more confining than that of any other tragic hero in Sh; in a larger sense, however, he exemplifies a familiar Shakespearean pattern: The hero's virtue is also his vice.

Chapter 4, "Eros and Death," includes discussion of *Ven.* (a revision of item 3151) and *Ant. Ven.,* Sh's "unique excursion into the fashionable genre of allegorized mythological romance," attempts to create a myth that, in depicting the origin of love, "explains its tragicomic complementarity in the fallen world in which we live." *Ant.* is Sh's "fullest realization" of the theme of romantic love, basing its complementarity as much on the author's developed vision of "the political world and of tragedy as it does on his previous understanding of love." Rome is presented in two ways so as to make ambivalent the world that Antony throws away for love. Love is both ennobling and liberating, and yet wholly destructive; it appears in various other complementary terms throughout the play. In this "myth of the archetypical lovers," Sh discovers "the supreme model of the paradoxes of love."

Chapter 5, "The Great Globe Itself," deals with the last plays. Comments on *Tim.* (which lacks complementarity), and on *Per.* and *Cym.* (both of which call attention to the art of Sh's art without, however, connecting this emphasis to their thematic centers). *Cym.* picks up a number of stories and motifs from Sh's earlier tragedies, especially *Ant.* and *Tit.,* and shows how the tragic potency of these parallels can be deflated. Only in *WT* and *Tmp.* did Sh "contemplate art and life as mirrors of each other" with the full power of a new conception of both life and art.

0874 Rabkin, Norman. *Shakespeare and the Problem of Meaning.* Chicago: U. of Chicago P., 1981. x + 165 pp.

Chapter 3, "Tragic Meanings: The Redactor as Critic," attempts to get at the meanings of several Shakespearean tragedies by examining the simplifications of them in Restoration adaptations and imitations. From these comparisons, we can see, for example, how "full and satisfying" is the reality that Sh "gives to each of the poles between which the hero is drawn" in *Ant.*; how thoroughly, in *JC*, Sh "explores the contradictions" that undermine "attempts to redeem history through decisive action"; and how *Cor.* shows that "honor is a meaningless and destructive concept in politics without which the polity cannot survive."

0875 Race, William H. *Classical Genres and English Poetry.* London: Croom Helm, 1988. xix + 235 pp.

Devotes a chapter to each of seven genres of lyric poetry; each chapter begins with a definition and classical examples, followed by instances of the genre in English poetry. Chapter 2 considers the priamel, whose function is "to lead up to or introduce a subject." Classical priamels include works by Sappho, Horace, and Lucretius; Sh's Sonnet 91 is an English example. Cites Gertrude's speech to Hamlet (*Ham.*, I.ii.70–75) about accepting his father's death as an illustration of *consolatio*.

0876 Rackin, Phyllis. *Shakespeare's Tragedies.* (World Dramatists.) New York: Frederick Ungar, 1978. 184 pp.

Provides a brief chapter on each of Sh's tragedies. *Tit.* is defective because it is "all surface and sensationalism"; *JC* shows that pride is a particularly Roman quality, equally present in Caesar and Brutus, that keeps men from recognizing their own shortcomings; *Ant.*'s theatricalism is bolstered by the knowledge that Cleopatra would have been played by a boy on Sh's stage; *Cor.* presents a hero who, devoted to the "mindless and heartless principle of *virtus*," is destroyed when he momentarily allows his own feminine feeling to direct him and then tries to return to the hard Roman world; and *Tim.* possesses rich imagery and profound themes suggesting but not quite defining tragic nobility. Parts revised as item 1716.

0877 Radbill, April. "'All That's Spoke is Marred': Shakespeare and the Distrust of Language." Ph.D. dissertation, University of Connecticut, 1981. *DAI*, 42 (1981–82), 1650-A.

Chapter 1 explains that Sh's distrust of language reflects classical views (Plato's in the *Protogoras* and those of several Roman rhetoricians) as well as traditional religious beliefs. Chapter 2 locates the distrust of language in several 16th-c. writers, and Chapter 3 analyzes *LLL* in its demonstration of the unreliability of language. Chapter 4 discusses several plays to show that Sh's attitude toward language is implicitly moral. Chapter 5 deals in detail with *Cor.*, which depicts "a society built on hypocrisy and lies."

0878 Rao, O. M. Gopala. "The Missing 'Mother' in Shakespeare." *Triveni*, 56, nos. 3-4 (1987), 37–43.

Discusses the absence of the mother figure for most of Sh's important characters. Two apparent exceptions are Tamora in *Tit.* (who is primarily "an avenging monster") and Volumnia in *Cor.* (whose role is political rather than maternal).

0879 Rappoport, Rose, and Heather Boyd. "Shakespeare as a Critic of Language." *ESA*, 11 (1968), 135–50.

Surveys the canon to reveal Sh's self-conscious mastery of language. Cites several examples from *Tro.*: The Servant's ironic aloofness from the "verbose obliquity" of Pandarus (III.i) demonstrates the latter's lack of values and inability to communicate; and the proverbial wisdom of Cressida reveals her "shallow worldly wisdom." Comments on how Latinisms are used in *Lr.* to reinforce the hollowness of Regan's expression and her distance from her father.

General Works

0880   Reaske, Christopher R. "Shakespeare's Railers and Tragic Heroes." *MichA*, 2, no. 2 (1969), 99–103.

Maintains that the characters who rail in Sh's comedies—most notably Thersites and Jaques—begin with a kind of wisdom, or self-knowledge, that his tragic heroes arrive at only after completing a phase of railing. Coriolanus is a special case: He is "a blend of hero and railer from the very beginning."

0881   Reed, Robert Rentoul Jr. *The Occult on the Tudor and Stuart Stage*. Boston: Christopher Publishing House, 1965. 284 pp.

Emphasizes, in the first two chapters, the Greco–Roman origin of much of the supernatural material found in Tudor and Stuart drama. Through the works of Seneca, who had modeled his dramas on those of the principal three Greek tragedians, the English theater became acquainted with two of its favorite supernatural personae: the goddess of wrath and the revenge ghost. By 1600, the Senecan ghost had become "the product of a Christian underworld" (see *Ham.*). Greco–Roman tradition was also responsible for passing the following ideas on to the English: the incubus, night-riding Diana (or Hecate, as in *Mac.*), sympathetic magic (the use of waxen images to achieve a desired result), prophecy that uses consultation with demons or the dead, the sorcerer's power to transform himself or others into beasts, magical use of herbs, and the conjuration of tempests. Discusses Puck and Ariel as demons; the figure of the sorcerer in *Tmp.*, *2H6*, and *1H4*; and demonic possession in *Err.*, *Lr.*, and *TN*.

0882   Rees, Joan. *Shakespeare and the Story: Aspects of Creation*. London: Athlone P., 1978. 239 pp.

Analyzes Sh's handling of his narratives to better understand his "creative imagination." *Ven.* and *Luc.*, both dealing with the same situation (sexual attack) and both betraying a "courtly disdain of narrative," are not equally successful. *Ven.* fuses several episodes from Ovid's *Metamorphoses*, allowing for a "comic–ironic point of view" to sustain interest in very slight narrative materials. *Luc.*, however, is composed of a series of imperfectly integrated set pieces. In *Ant.*, Sh employs contrast to explore the differences between Rome and Alexandria and foregrounds Cleopatra's role-playing to emphasize the ease of "informal conversation," something he perfected in *1&2H4*. Treats *JC* and *Cor.* as works "more severely Roman" than *Ant.*, plays in which Sh is more constrained by his sources. From what his sources provide him, however, he chooses to emphasize "four areas of interest": a political struggle, the circumstance of a noble character surrounded by less noble figures, a sharply defined opposition between two men, and the conflict between a man's private life and his public role. Notes the predominance of the satiric dimension in the treatment of ancient history in *Tro.* and *Tim.* In *Tro.*, Sh binds together three strands (the Greek camp episodes, the Trojan camp episodes, and the love story) by means of abuse of language ("grandiose words," "trivial words," and "false words"), contrast, and emblematic scenes. *Tim.* presents starker satire than elsewhere in Sh, tracing "the satiric impulse" to its point of exhaustion in death. Sh works to get the most out of his sources, "especially in the Greek and Roman plays."

0883   Reese, Max Meredith. *The Cease of Majesty: A Study of Shakespeare's History Plays*. London: Edward Arnold, 1961. ix + 350 pp.

Discusses classical historians and their influence on Elizabethan thinking about history. Concentrates on the English histories but mentions other plays that are relevant to topics like order, politics, and power. Important examples of the plays on classical themes include *Tro.*, *Cor.*, *Tit.*, and *Tim.*

0884   Rhinehart, Raymond Patrick. "The Elizabethan Ovidian Epyllion: A Definition and Re-evaluation." Ph.D. dissertation, Princeton University, 1969. *DAI*, 30 (1969–70), 2040-A.

Attempts a detailed definition of the Ovidian epyllion in Elizabethan literature. Deals with poems that (1) focus on "an actual or attempted love affair between two central characters," (2) are derived mostly from the *Metamorphoses*, and (3) were written between the appearance of Lodge's *Scillaes Metamorphosis* and the death of Elizabeth I. Concludes that tradition played a significant role in the composition of these poems. They are similar to their medieval Ovidian predecessors in their comic irony; in their "type characters, icons, and formulaic action"; in their "orthodox moral allegory"; in their tight rhetorical construction; and in their exploration of "the bittersweet, tragicomic nature of romantic love." Another central theme is "the relationship between art and nature." Mentions Sh as one of the poets working in this genre.

0885   Ribner, Irving. *Jacobean Tragedy: The Quest for Moral Order*. London: Methuen, 1962. xii + 179 pp.

Sees Jacobean tragedy as reflecting the uncertainty of an age no longer able to believe in the old ideals and searching almost frantically for new ones to replace them. Does not treat Sh at length, but refers to *Ant.* and *Cor.* as revealing "a world in which man may be destroyed by evils [that] are the inevitable concomitants of those very virtues which make him great."

0886   Richmond, Hugh M. *Shakespeare's Political Plays*. (Random House Studies in Language and Literature 12.) New York: Random House, 1967. ix + 241 pp. Reprint. Gloucester, Massachusetts; Peter Smith, 1977.

Concludes with chapters on two of Sh's Roman plays. *JC* is constructed to include "the greatest possible number of revolutions of the wheel of political fortune." Detached from notions of providential order, the classical world gave Sh a chance to explore the responsibility of men for the difficulties they encounter. The dramatist modifies his source, Plutarch's *Lives*, to present Caesar as a decaying political genius; Brutus as an illogical, naive, self-ignorant idealist; Cassius as a ruthlessly precise pragmatist (and thus potentially Caesar's true successor); and Antony as an inspired nihilist. Undermining all claims to tragic heroism, the play ends by confirming that it is a study of political forces with the harsh message that sincerity is not enough. *Cor.*, through its presentation of a hero who resembles Aristotle's magnanimous man in the *Nicomachean Ethics*, explores the relationship between "individual excellence" and "political supremacy." Sh concludes in this play that personal virtue and "the dubious skills" by which one must maintain political authority are incompatible.

0887   Richmond, Hugh M. *Shakespeare's Sexual Comedy: A Mirror for Lovers*. Indianapolis: Bobbs–Merrill, 1971. 210 pp.

Chapter 3 includes a discussion of *Err.* that notes the importance of Plautus's *Amphitruo* in inspiring the sexual complexities in Sh's play and of Plautus's *Menaechmi* in providing Sh with some of his farcical material. Chapter 4 culminates with a consideration of *Ant.*, which assimilates Sh's sexual comedy into his tragic vision. Cleopatra's versatility in sexual role-playing includes, and is included by, her recognition of her sexual dependence on Antony. The play is a hybrid, "at once comedy, tragedy, and history."

0888   Richmond, Velma Bourgeois. "Shakespeare's Women." *MQ*, 19 (1978), 330–42.

Argues that the historical moment at which Sh wrote was auspicious for the celebration of the "intellectual and moral virtues" of women. Sh emphasizes the most positive attributes of women, usually in the context of marriage, though he does allow them to be villains (as in the case of Cressida). Discusses *Ven.* and *Luc.*, two early poems in which "conventional sex roles" are represented, and several plays, including *Ant.*, which validate the institution of marriage, though Cleopatra's recognition of its value comes too late.

0888a   Rico, Barbara Roche. "From 'Speechless Dialect' to 'Prosperous Art': Shakespeare's Recasting of the Pygmalion Image." *HLQ*, 48 (1985), 285–95.

Summarizes the story of Pygmalion as it appears in Ovid's *Metamorphoses*, book 10. Provides an account of the myth's deterioration during the Middle Ages and the Renaissance: It came to be associated with "seduction and idolatry" and the dangers of women and art. Analyzes *Shr.*, *MM*, and *WT* to show how Sh reflects Elizabethan distaste for the Pygmalion myth, "comes to terms with [the myth's] power and its unseemliness," and, in the "statue" scene of *WT*, restores its positive meaning.

0889 Ridley, M. L. *Studies in Three Literatures: English, Latin, Greek. Contrasts and Comparisons.* London: J. M. Dent, 1962. xi + 177 pp.

Discusses the rejection by English dramatists of the unities and adduces *Ant.* as an example of a play that must move through space and time on a vast scale in order to realize Antony "as a great historic figure." Also, points out two resemblances between Greek and Shakespearean tragedy: the choric commentary (divided by Sh between fools and "plain honest men") and the ending on a quiet note, where the "broken threads of affairs are knotted so that ordinary life can proceed."

0890 Ridlington, Sandra Schwartz. "A Survey of Mythological Burlesques in the English Renaissance." Ph.D. dissertation, Purdue University, 1979. *DAI*, 40 (1979–80), 5065-A-5066-A.

Surveys the jesting use of classical mythology in English Renaissance literature and notes that classical literature itself furnished precedents for such subversive treatment (for example, by Aristophanes, Lucian, and Ovid). English mythological burlesques deal satirically with a variety of subjects, most notably metamorphosis, erotic love, true love, the Trojan War, and Hades. In *MND*, the Bottom–Titania episode is used "to satirize the humanistic conception of metamorphosis as symbolic of man's dual nature." Comic versions of the Trojan myth, like *Tro.*, focus on war and love: They reduce heroism to "the dull realities of life" and expose the pettiness of the famous lovers associated with the war.

0891 Riehle, Wolfgang. *Shakespeare, Plautus and the Humanist Tradition.* Cambridge: D. S. Brewer, 1990. x + 309 pp.

Makes a case for significant influence on Sh of the New Comedy tradition, primarily as it was mediated through the works of the Roman playwright Plautus and of Renaissance humanists, especially Erasmus and Sir Thomas More. Concentrates on *Err.* Chapter 1, "The Elizabethan Reception of Plautus," notes that English dramatists were more attracted to Plautus than to Terence, that the universes of Sh and Plautus are similar, that Sh did not medievalize the plot of *Err.*, and that Plautus's *Amphitruo*, with its seriousness and its concern with identity, is an especially important source for *Err.* Chapter 2, "Characterization in Plautus and in *The Comedy of Errors*," discusses direct characterization (a character describes himself or is described by another character) as well as other modes like comparison and contrast and distinctive speech habits (especially in the case of the Dromios). Treats Sh's version of the *senex* figure (Egeon) and the variety of soliloquies. Plautus can be seen to have skillfully used many comic elements that Sh took over and used with even greater skill. Chapter 3, "The Structure of Plautine Comedy and Its Impact on Shakespeare," covers change of scene, creation of dramatic space offstage, parting and meeting of characters, soliloquies, and asides. Suggests that Sh, influenced by the editions of Plautus available to him, thought in terms of the five-act structure (though he did not adhere rigidly to it) and in terms of the four-part development of comic action that had been propounded by Evanthius and Donatus. *Err.* is further indebted to New Comedy by its focus on human error and irony. Chapter 4, "Game-Playing in the Theatre of Plautus and the Early Shakespeare," emphasizes "the metadramatic and theatrical element" in Plautus and Sh. Includes comment on the parody of tragic drama in both authors. Chapter 5, "Dramatic Language in Plautus and in *The Comedy of Errors*," considers the notion of *copia*, the dialogic situations involving persuasions and questions, and verbal games like punning. Chapter 6, "Metre in Plautus and Shakespeare's 'Classical' Play," shows that Sh's variations of meter may be purposeful, influenced by humanist comments on Plautus and Terence. Chapter 7, "Names and Their Meanings," argues that certain names used by Sh (such as Solinus for the Duke in *Err.*) reveal Sh's familiarity with humanist figures and that humanist values pervade *Err.* and other plays. Chapter 8, "Erasmus, Thomas More and the Lucianic Tradition," notes the importance in Lucian's works of the image of life as a play and of satire. Lucian, who influenced humanists like Erasmus and More, was influenced by classical comedy. Contends that Lucian's presence can be found not only in later Shakespearean works like *Ham.* (where the name Lucianus indicates a connection) but in earlier works like *Err.* Chapter 9, "The Significance of Shakespeare's 'Classical' *Comedy of Errors*," reasserts the importance of Plautus and New Comedy for Sh. Challenges or qualifies scholarly arguments that the primary influences on Sh were Christian, medieval, and romantic. Concludes that *Err.* reflects Sh's successful implementation of the humanist maxim that comedy should be educational. Chapter 10, "The Continuation of the New Comedy Tradition in the Shakespeare Canon," surveys all of Sh's comedies, noting, especially in the late romances, strong presence of New Comedy. Comments, for example, on satire in *Cym.*; the character of Autolycus and the mention of the playful and ironic imitator of the classics, Giulio Romano, in *WT*; and Plautus's *Rudens* as a likely source for *Tmp.*

0891a Riemer, A. P. Antic Fables: Patterns of Evasion in Shakespeare's Comedies. New York: St. Martin's P., 1980. ix + 228 pp.

Emphasizes the playfulness and the excessiveness of Sh's comedies. Explicates, in *Err.*, the "witty transformation of the conventions of Latin farce," partly by the solemn invocation by Aemilia at the end of "the benevolent magical medicine of Renaissance Platonism." Stresses the influence of Platonism on Sh's comic vision, especially in the discussion of *Tmp.* and *WT* in chapters 4 and 5.

0892 Riggs, David. "The Artificial Day and the Infinite Universe." *JMRS*, 5 (1975), 155–85.

Asserts that certain neoclassical critics of the 16th c., in developing the notion that the action of a drama should be confined to one day, were articulating a theory to suit a new perception of the individual's relationship to time. No longer was a chronology imposed on the dramatist as in the Middle Ages, when the "natural order" of sacred history had limited his autonomy. The new theory of the artificial day allowed the playwright to transcend the merely chronological and to reflect, in its fictional order, the shaping powers of the human mind. In most of his plays, Sh relied on the older concept of duration, even though the sacred history that had sustained it was no longer dominant. Thus the first scene of *Ham.* lasts several hours of fictional time; several days elapse in *MND*, and time is allowed to take its course in *TN*. In *WT*, an old-fashioned figure of Time ridicules the idea of trying to place oneself outside the natural flow of events. In *Tmp.*, however, Sh experiments with the new idea of the artificial day: The action is short because it reflects the operations of Prospero's mind.

0893 Riggs, David. "'Plot' and 'Episode' in Early Neoclassical Criticism." *RenD*, N. S. 6 (1973), 149–75.

Argues that Renaissance commentators rewrote classical literary theory to suit contemporary taste. Certain passages from Horace, Aristotle, and Donatus were at the center of a theory that analyzed fiction in the following way: "There is a linear, time-bound 'argument' (or main plot) localized at the beginning and at the end, and there is a congeries of additional material (retrospective, ornamental, or merely diverting) localized in the middle." The plot, or the main action, was said to have a beginning and an end. The middle is filled by a number of episodes meant to enlarge, enrich, or illuminate the plot, but their function is not to help its serial development. Suggests that many Renaissance plays conform to this paradigm. In several instances (for example, *MV, JC, MND*), a group of central characters is involved "in some situation that must come to an end within a limited period of time." These plays also include many episodes that are not necessary parts of the plot.

0894 Riggs, David. *Shakespeare's Heroical Histories: "Henry VI" and Its Literary Tradition.* Cambridge: Harvard U. P., 1971. viii + 194 pp.

Chapter 1 explains the development of the Elizabethan history play as a collaboration between literary and historical traditions. The humanist historians collected examples from antiquity of excellent behavior for the emulation of succeeding ages. In doing this, they gave poets a foundation for their portrayals of the warrior–prince. In the history plays of the time (especially those of Sh), the heroic leader attempts to exceed all limits and overcome all obstacles to personal honor, but there is a tension between his aspiration and the requirements of "the particular historical ethos within which the play is situated." Sh's history plays, beginning with *H6Triad*, subject the hero's individualism to a reappraisal in light of hierarchical notions of social order.

Chapter 2 describes how the "set topics" of classical rhetoric, used by historians like Tacitus to highlight characteristic features of a man's personality, were passed on to the 16th c. through school exercises in rhetoric and history and were adapted by the dramatists of the age.

Chapter 4 provides a reading of the three parts of *H6* that calls attention to Sh's reliance on "the conventional *topoi* and oratorical forms" to distribute praise and blame, especially to Talbot and Richard. Beyond this, Sh implies that the process by which heroic virtue is transmitted from one exemplar to another "loses some of its antique luster with every transfer."

Chapter 5 briefly analyzes *R3* and *1H4*. The former embodies Sh's most severe examination of the humanistic values that underlie "the quest for earthly fame." The latter presents a protagonist (Hal) who insists on being free from heroic tradition in order to reclaim it and reshape it in his own image.

0895 Righter, Anne. *Shakespeare and the Idea of the Play.* New York: Barnes & Noble, 1962. 224 pp.

Examines the idea of the world as a stage in the plays of Sh and his contemporaries. Chapter 2 argues that the Roman comedy of Plautus and Terence embodies "an attitude toward the audience that is essentially that of the self-contained play." In this kind of drama there is a clear separation between audience and actors, a separation that Sh and others were able to adapt in creating plays largely independent of audience involvement. Hints of the world-as-stage metaphor are also found in the Roman dramatists. Influenced by these classical traditions, as well as the medieval English drama, Sh was able to use the stage metaphor in a variety of ways. Aaron the Moor in *Tit.* and Richard III are notable players of numerous deceits, disguises, and illusions, and the histories and tragedies contain "Player Kings of the flawed rule" (for example, Henry IV and Macbeth). Certain of the plays based on classical themes show Sh exploring resemblances between the world and the stage that are negative and grim. In *Tro.* the theater image is used to express disorder; in *Tim.*, the idea of all imitative art is held up to scorn; in *Ant.*, Cleopatra focuses on the stage's "ability to cheapen and degrade"; and in *Cor.*, the protagonist, having refused to play one role, finds in the end that he has been playing another.

0896 Rizzolo, Patricia. "A Study of Shakespeare's Use of Speech Style in *Richard II, King Lear, Julius Caesar*, and *Troilus and Cressida*." Ph.D. dissertation, Temple University, 1978. *DAI*, 39 (1978–79), 902-A-903-A.

Attempts to use speech style in four Shakespearean plays as "the prime index of characterization, theme, and dramatic situation." Two of these plays are *JC* and *Tro*.

0897 Robbins, Martin Lewis. "Shakespeare's Sweet Music: A Glossary of Musical Terms in the Work of Shakespeare (with Additional Examples from the Plays of Lyly, Marston, and Jonson)." Ph.D. dissertation, Brandeis University, 1968. *DAI*, 30 (1969–70), 1534-A-1535-A.

Explores the full range of music in Sh's period, including the music itself, "the imagery of music," and "the philosophical ideas that underlie and unify these." Uses the form of a glossary, organized according to Boethius's "hierarchy of musical classifications: First, the Practical Music; then the Speculative Music comprised of the Human Music and the heavenly harmony of the World Music." Various instances of Practical Music in Sh's world include ceremonial and military music, ballads, and sacred music. Human Music involves "music as medicine (especially as a cure for madness), as an emblem of concord in souls, in marriage, and in government." World Music involves the music of the spheres and the metaphor of the Great String (Christ was viewed as "the single string [that] reharmonized the universe after the Fall"). Explains Sh's use of music and its imagery in both technical and philosophical terms. In Sh's plays, as in the Elizabethan Age generally, harmony indicates unity "in a character or a commonwealth." If this harmony is violated, chaos results.

0898   Roberts, G. J. "Shakespeare and 'Scratching.'" *N&Q*, 30 (1983), 111–14.

Calls attention to the belief common in 16th- and 17th-c. England that "to draw blood on a witch, especially from her face, was a way of removing her *maleficium*." This belief lies behind Antony's remark about Octavia's nails ploughing up Cleopatra's visage (*Ant.*, IV.xii.37–39) and passages in *Err.* and *WT*.

0899   Roberts, Jeanne Addison. "Animals as Agents of Revelation: The Horizontalizing of the Chain of Being in Shakespeare's Comedies." *Shakespearean Comedy*. Ed. Maurice Charney. New York: New York Literary Forum, 1980, pp. 79–96.

Traces Sh's use of animal figures, including metamorphoses, in the comedies. In early works like *MND* and *Wiv.*, human–animal links serve primarily as facilitators of comic vision. In Bottom and Falstaff, for example, the joining of man to animal is laughable because man's superiority to beasts makes such a connection absurdly incongruous. In these cases, Sh dallies with metamorphosis, but the two characters ultimately remain the same. Another use of animal signs in the early comedies can be seen in the association of sexual pursuit and cuckoldry with the deer. In *Wiv.* and *AYL*, deer images serve as reminders that sexual success is inextricably linked with concerns about betrayal. Because this suggests that humans resemble beasts in their sexual behavior, their superiority is threatened. In *Tmp.*, Sh uses animal signs to subvert hierarchy, as Prospero relinquishes his power and acknowledges his kinship with Caliban. Animals become, finally, agents through which new insights about humanity are revealed; they are no longer a source of laughter. This progress in Sh's deployment of animals was indebted to Ovid for the notion of "fluidity of forms" and a sense of nonhierarchical relationship between human and beast. Revised as part of chapter 2 of item 0901.

0900   Roberts, Jeanne Addison. "Shades of the Triple Hecate." *Proceedings of the PMR Conference*, 12–13 (1987–88), 47–66.

Contends that, in Sh's work, we can see traces of the triform Goddess (often called Hecate) who was worshipped in pre-Christian Europe. Shows that the patriarchal Christian tradition, which supplanted the matrilinear one nourished by the Goddess, evidenced a great deal of ambivalence about Hecate, who was demoted to "goddess of witchcraft." Of the three aspects of the triple Goddess—virgin, mother, crone—the Christian tradition had least trouble with the virgin. It tended to desexualize the mother, to depend on the category of whore to counteract aggressive female sexuality, and to demonize the crone. Mentions the three times Sh uses the classically derived name of Helen, pointing out that in each case the name is connected with unruly sexuality. Notes that in *The Golden Ass* of Apuleius, a possible source of *MND*, the Goddess appears to Lucius, and that in this play there is an evocation, even though only a temporary one, of "the more positive and powerful Triple Hecate of the matrilinear tradition." In *Mac.*, we see the devaluation of the crone to celebrate a world "where nature seems dead" and in *Tmp.* Prospero's great speech on his supernatural achievements (V.i.41–50), derived from Ovid's *Metamorphoses*, represents an appropriation of female power (in Ovid, it is spoken by Medea, who as priestess of Hecate is offering a prayer to the Goddess, to Night, to Earth, and to the Moon; Sh edits out all of these indications of female power). Revised as part of chapter 3 of item 0901.

0901 Roberts, Jeanne Addison. *The Shakespearean Wild: Geography, Genus, and Gender.* Lincoln and London: U. of Nebraska P., 1991. x + 214 pp.

Proposes to examine in the Sh canon the interaction at the border between male-defined Culture and the Wild (viewed by Sh as a mysterious, frightening, and fascinating territory inhabited by "strange and untamed creatures" and providing "resources for the maintenance of Culture"). Draws on a story told about Thales to investigate the relationship of Culture in Sh to three areas of the Wild: the female Wild, the animal Wild, and the barbarian Wild. Chapter 1 is concerned with natural landscapes and includes discussion of *Tit.* and *Ven.*, both of which enact the female association with the forest. Chapter 2 focuses on Sh's "use of animals," noting the breakdown of "man/animal, male/female, and male/barbarian boundaries through hybrid metaphors" in *Tro.* and *Tim.* Parts of this chapter are revisions of items 0899 and 2540. Chapter 3 probes Sh's portrayals of male problems in confronting the female Wild "embodied by female figures themselves." In *TNK*, for example, Theseus, Palamon, and Arcite exercise themselves in various aspects of the male struggle to master the female. Explores Sh's portrayals of "the imagined female," both as she is revealed in his characters and as the plays exhibit remnants of "the archaic memory of the Triple Hecate" (who embodies the three male clichés of virgin, mother, and crone about female identity). Analyzes *Err.*, *AWW*, and *WT* as attempts, with varying degrees of success, to reconcile these aspects of woman. Ancient memories of Hecate are especially noticeable in *MND* and *Mac.* Parts of this chapter are revisions of items 0900 and 3100a.

0902 Roberts-Baytop, Adrianne. *Dido, Queen of Infinite Literary Variety: The English Renaissance Borrowings and Influences.* (Elizabethan and Renaissance Studies 25.) Salzburg: Institut für Englische Sprache und Literatur, 1974. vii + 147 pp.

Surveys "the most notable Renaissance English and Neo-Latin works on and allusions to Dido"; makes available a representative extract from William Gager's Latin tragedy *Dido Tragoedia* (1583); and provides the text of Barton Booth's masque *The Death of Dido* (1716). One chapter, "Shakespeare's Dido Allusions," speculates that Sh did not write a play about Dido and Aeneas "either because the tale was already too commonplace, or because he felt that he could not eclipse those of his predecessors." Canvasses the nine overt Shakespearean references to Dido and Aeneas and proposes that Sh "did not depend only on literary sources" and that his "awareness of both the historical and the poetic Dido explains why the Dido of his nine allusions is almost of '*infinite variety*' and is more complex than the traditional literary Dido." Analyzes the Dido allusion in *Tmp.* to show how Sh combined the fickle abandoned figure of the *Aeneid* with the wholly admirable historical ruler to produce a sympathetic portrait. Virgil's Dido is similar in many respects to Miranda, and Hamlet's vow and duty bear strong resemblances to Dido's.

0903 Robertson, Hugh. "*Troilus and Cressida* and *Measure for Measure* in Their Age: Shakespeare's Thought in Its Context." *Self and Society in Shakespeare's "Troilus and Cressida" and "Measure for Measure."* Eds. J. A. Jowitt and R. K. S. Taylor. (Bradford Centre Occasional Papers 4.) Bradford: U. of Leeds Centre for Adult Education, 1982, pp. 3–26.

Asserts that *MM* and *Tro.* are both centrally concerned with "the loss of self-control, and with the destructive consequences." In both plays, Sh relies on a psychological and physiological system ultimately deriving from Plato and Aristotle but significantly expanded and somewhat confused by Elizabethan times. The problematic nature of this system, especially its ambiguous treatment of the concept of "will," made possible Sh's exploration of social and individual disorder in *MM* and *Tro.* *MM* is concerned with the administration of justice in a Christian state; it acknowledges human frailties but holds to the belief that self-control in the individual and order in society are possible. In *Tro.*, neither Christian nor pagan codes have any validity. Characters like Troilus and Hector speak as if they were rational, but no one's behavior is guided by reason or temperance. *Tro.* subverts the mythic reputations of its characters as well as questioning "rationalist and courtly accounts of how men behave in society."

0904 Robinson, Christopher. *Lucian and His Influence in Europe.* London: Duckworth, 1979. vii + 248 pp.

Contains chapters on "Lucian: the Man and the Work," "The Later Influence," and "Erasmus and Fielding." Suggests that because vernacular translations of Lucian came late, there was much less direct borrowing than from other classical writers. The English academic play of *Timon* (c. 1600) drew its plot and a number of other elements from the Lucianic dialogue of the same name. *Tim.* contains many details—the spendthrift images of act I and the Poet of acts I and V, for example—that derive from Lucian, but it is hard to determine how these reached Sh. The play is Lucianic "only in some secondhand and relatively insignificant way." The only dramatists to be significantly influenced by Lucian were Ben Jonson and Henry Fielding. *Volpone's* indebtedness, for example, can be seen in the plot of legacy-hunting and gulling of the hunters, patterned on *Dialogues of the Dead* 19.

0905 Robinson, Randal Fink. "Shakespeare's Orators: A Study of Shakespeare's Use of Oratory in Eleven Representative Plays." Ph.D. dissertation, University of North Carolina, Chapel Hill, 1966. *DA*, 27 (1966–67), 2508-A.

Provides background on the humanistic ideal of the citizen orator (indebted to such ancients as Isocrates, Cicero, and Quintilian) found in the Renaissance. This figure was thought of as "a champion of reason in a world of world of imperfect but nevertheless malleable societies." The appearance of oratory in Sh's drama is usually linked to the theory that "a life in public affairs can be illustrious, and that eloquence is essential to a good leader." This holds true when a hero succeeds in his speechmaking (for example, Henry of Monmouth in *1H4*, *2H4*, and *H5*); when a "comic character deviates from the oratorical norm" (for example, Armado in *LLL*); "when a serious, but unheroic character fails as a speaker simply because of his own flaws" (for example, the King in *Jn.*); and when a villain mimics the virtues of the orator–citizen for political reasons (for example, Richard III). By using oratory in some plays to establish sympathy for a "noble, but unsuccessful leader," Sh emphasizes the flaws in the society he tries to lead (Titus in *Tit.* and Brutus in *JC* are examples).

0905a Rolle, Dietrich. "The Concept of Tragedy in Plays and Theoretical Treatises of the Elizabethan Era." *Kunstgriffe: Auskunfte zur Reichweite von Literaturtheorie und Literaturkritik.* Eds. Ulrich Horstmann and Wolfgang Zach. Frankfurt am Main: Peter Lang, 1989, pp. 329–42.

Examines references to the concepts of *tragedy* and of *hamartia* in plays and theoretical treatises from 1564 to 1617. Finds that Sh used the terms *tragedy* and *tragic* chiefly for the *de casibus* plays he wrote before 1600. His mature tragedies depend on the notion of *hamartia*. Comments that the popularity of the revenge play prevented most of Sh's contemporaries from assimilating the ideas of Aristotle. Only the greatest masters (like Sh) were open to the subtleties made available by the concept of *hamartia*.

0906 Ronan, Clifford J. "The Onomastics of Shakespeare's Work with Classical Setting." *Literary Onomastics Studies*, 8 (1981), 47–69.

Presents a rough statistical analysis of classical names in Sh's twelve plays and two epyllia with classical settings to suggest directions that further scholarly investigations might take. The large number of Latin names in the Greek play *Tim.*, for example, is evidence that the play is unpolished, revealing "in fossil form" the author's habit of waiting until the last minute to assign final names to his minor characters. Another interesting possibility for investigation is offered by the fact that the classical works of Sh employ "national and locational names" with much greater frequency than any of his other plays except for the English histories. This is especially true of the four Roman tragedies (*Tit.*, *JC*, *Ant.*, and *Cor.*), perhaps because of the heightened Roman concern with patriotism. Sums up scholarship on *Tit.* and *Per.* and suggests how it might be extended. In *Tit.*, the few anachronistic names (such as the Greek Chiron) may be significant; and the name of the enemy Goths and their association with Scythia may be connected with Pentapolis, the city of Marina's grandfather in *Per.* In the latter play, Lysimachus, the name Sh invented for the ruler of Mytilene who delivers Marina from the brothel, is appropriate when its constituent Greek parts are analyzed (together they mean "dissolver of conflict").

0907   Rosand, David. "'Troyes Painted Woes': Shakespeare and the Pictorial Imagination." *HUSL*, 8 (1980), 77–97.

Cites examples from *H5*, *Shr.*, *Cym.*, *WT*, *Tim.*, *Lr.*, and especially *Luc.* to demonstrate Sh's "impressively complete pictorial vocabulary" (seen in his mastery of the *ecphrasis* "in its ambitious rhetorical function") and his familiarity with and ability to manipulate "the aesthetic *topoi* of Renaissance art theory" (such as the *paragone*, the comparison or competition of the arts or the senses). Notes Sh's witty allusions to "ancient art history," like the implied comparison in *WT* between the "artificial Hermione" and "the eclectic beauty of the celebrated image of Helen (or Venus) assembled by ancient Zeuxis from the selected particulars of the choicest maidens of Croton." Argues that Sh thoroughly assimilated "the new humanist esthetic" that assumed a close relationship between literature and painting, an esthetic that had been given theoretical voice in Leon Battista Alberti's *On Painting* (1435). Points out that Alberti drew on the ancient rhetorical tradition—including Cicero, Quintilian, Horace, and Pliny—to prove "the affective aims of pictorial imitation." Discusses *Luc.* in detail, suggesting that its expression of pathos "relates to certain traditions of empathetic response," originating in antiquity, then being thoroughly Christianized, and in the 16th c. finding "renewed secular expression."

0908   Rose, Mark. *Shakespearean Design.* Cambridge: Harvard U. P., 1972. xi + 190 pp.

Suggests that Sh's plays are constructed of scenic units, each of which is an individually designed composition, and that this fact was highlighted during performance by leaving the stage vacant for a few moments between scenes. Discusses scenes in a number of plays, including *Tit.* (I.i) and *Ant.* (I.i-II.i).

0909   Rossiter, A. P. *Angel with Horns and Other Shakespeare Lectures.* Ed. Graham Storey. London: Longmans, 1961. xi + 316 pp.

Prints fifteen lectures Rossiter gave at Stratford and Cambridge during the early 1950s. Chapter 6, "The Problem Plays," discusses *Tro.*, *MM*, and *AWW*, emphasizing that they share "the tragi-comic view of man." The chapter on *Tro.* stresses its intellectuality, its deflation of the medieval chivalric code and of classical heroes, and its lack of engagement with any of its characters. *Tro.* is best characterized as an inquisition: Its conclusion seems to be that "while the system of thought expounded by Ulysses and relied on by Hector *ought* to be the measure of human conduct . . . , it simply does not apply to realistically observed human conduct." Chapter 12, on *Cor.*, argues that the play is about political feeling: "the capacity to be not only intellectually, but emotionally and purposively, engaged by the management of public affairs; the businesses of groups of men in (ordered) communities; the contrivance or maintenance of agreement; the establishment of a will-in-common; and all the exercises of suasion, pressure, concession and compromise which achieve that *will* (a mind to *do*) in place of chaos of confused appetencies." *Cor.* is a political tragedy: "Marcius's unyieldingness and would-be-self-sufficiency" paradoxically make him "pliant to force of circumstance." Chapter 13, "Shakespearean Tragedy," rejects classical theory as a means of assessing Sh's tragedy, though it does acknowledge that some classical elements were incorporated by Sh in his works. For example, the influence of Seneca may be seen in Sh's conception of human greatness ("a complex ideal of self-sufficiency, pride and will"), which in the tragedies tends to clash with the conception of order. Chapter 14 argues that "comic relief" in Sh's tragedies is part of a complex artistic whole that raises questions about "the dignity and worth of man." Examples include the murder of Cinna the poet in *JC* and the scene on Pompey's galley in *Ant.*

0909a Roston, Murray. *Sixteenth-Century English Literature.* (History of Literature Series.) New York: Schocken Books, 1982. x + 235 pp.

The opening chapter describes the dual vision of the Renaissance: On the one hand, there was "a sober empirical insistence upon the provable fact or object and on the other a movement away from physical reality towards a concept of man unbounded in his abilities and reaching up to the universal ideals in heaven itself." Notes that the second part of this vision was significantly indebted to and involved with Neoplatonism. The revival of classical learning was a symptom of the movement toward this new way of looking at the world. Chapter 5, "Into the Playhouse," discusses the ways in which the works of Seneca, Plutarch, and Ovid helped to broaden the scope of English tragedy in the 16th c. Chapters 9 and 10 provide a selective survey of Sh's life and works, focusing on *Ant.*, "perhaps the most magnificent" of the major tragedies, which seems to disregard moral sanctions and emphasize "the blazing splendor of royal love."

0910 Rothenberg, Alan B. "Infantile Fantasies in Shakespearean Metaphor: I. The Fear of Being Smothered." *Psy. Rev.*, 60 (1973), 205–22.

Maintains that in order to incorporate the primitive pre-Oedipal fear of being smothered into *Tit.*, Sh has resorted to characters that are capable of extreme actions; that are, in fact, monsters. Metaphoric language in *Ven.* (like the image of enclosure and the portrayal of Venus as bird of prey) reveals Adonis's fear of being smothered or raped orally by a mother figure.

0910a Rouse, W. H. D., ed. *Shakespeare's Ovid, Being Arthur Golding's Translation of "The Metamorphoses."* New York: W. W. Norton, 1966. vi + 321 pp.

The introduction contains brief discussions on Sh and Ovid, early translations of Ovid, Golding's Ovid, and Sh and Golding. Reprints Golding's translation from the first edition (1567).

0911 Rovine, Harvey. *Silence in Shakespeare: Drama, Power, and Gender.* (Theater and Dramatic Studies 45.) Ann Arbor: UMI Research P., 1987. ix + 114 pp.

Investigates the occasions in Sh's plays "when a character's lack of speech has a particular meaning or effect on the audience's understanding." Notes the contrast between the silently observing Philo and Demetrius, severe Roman soldiers, and the elaborate display of indulgence by Antony and Cleopatra in *Ant.* (I.i.) In *Cor.*, Virgilia's silence is used to indicate her love for her husband and to contrast her with Volumnia. Later in the play (V.iii), Aufidius's silent witness to Coriolanus's interview with his family reminds us that the decision about saving Rome is a political one, and the stage direction that has Coriolanus hold his mother's hand silently reveals his resignation to the importunities of family and emotion. Brutus's silent presence next to Cassius as Caesar and his entourage return from the games in *JC* (I.ii), suggests that he may join the conspiracy.

0912 Rowse, A. L. *Discovering Shakespeare.* London: Weidenfield and Nicolson, 1989. xiii + 177 pp.

Comments briefly on all works in the canon, emphasizing the ways in which they reflect Sh's society. *Tro.*, with its bitter tone, responds to the factionalism of the last years of Elizabeth's reign and expresses disillusionment with chivalric figures (like the Earl of Essex) who squander their potential in foolish posturing. Argues that Sh's political instincts were conservative, as can be seen in the concern for order in works like *Tro.* and in the critical treatment of the masses in *JC* and *Cor.* Calls attention to the foreignness of Cleopatra as her "essential quality" in *Ant.* and notes that the play exhibits "both sides of sexual love." Points out that Sh's spirit was not drawn to "the classical ideal" but that he could write classical plays, like *JC* and *Cor.*, in which he abstained from his usual luxuriance. *Tim.* betrays a profound cynicism, though it is not Sh's usual or final mood. The play's unfinished state allows us a glimpse of how Sh composed: He wrote scenes "as he *saw* them." *Tim.* is also instructive as an anatomy of "the ostentatious extravagance" of the Jacobean age. Finds "the art-patter of the painter" and "the mutual flattery of painter and poet" to be "true enough to such exchanges at all times."

0913 Rowse, A. L. *Shakespeare's Globe: His Intellectual and Moral Outlook.* London: Weidenfeld and Nicolson, 1981. x + 210 pp.

Duplicates contents of item 0915 but uses a different title.

0914 Rowse, A. L. *Shakespeare the Man.* London: Macmillan, 1973. xi + 284 pp.

Proposes to place Sh's life and works in their Elizabethan context. Chapter 3, "Education," includes information on the classical basis of the curriculum to which the young Sh was exposed. Notes that Sh's early plays contain many quotations from and references to Lily's Latin grammar. Plautus and Terence, also studied in school, provided models for the first comedies. Emphasizes the supreme importance of Ovid for Sh's knowledge of mythology and poetic techniques. Calls attention to the playwright's exploitation of the rhetoric he learned as a schoolboy. Succeeding chapters provide brief comments on all of the works in the canon. *Tro.*, for example is an incisive, intellectual analysis of the problems of social order; *Ant.* a lush exploration of love as well as an insider's glimpse into the political maneuvering of factions in Sh's time; and *Cor.* "a severe and classic drama." In *JC, Ant., Cor.*, and *Tim.*, Sh developed all or much of his plot from North's translation of Plutarch's *Lives*; but he also exhibited a keen awareness of contemporary Elizabethan issues.

0915 Rowse, A. L. *What Shakespeare Read—and Thought.* New York: Coward, McCann & Geoghegan, 1981. x + 210 pp.

Chapter 1, "Shakespeare's Education," calls attention to the enormous emphasis on Latin learning in the grammar school Sh would have attended. Names the most frequently studied authors.

Chapter 2, "Shakespeare and the Classics," surveys the canon and comments on the ubiquitousness of Sh's classical knowledge. Provides illustrations of Latin words and phrases, mythical allusions, and direct influences from classical drama. Finds Senecan elements, for example, in English history plays like *H6Triad* and *R3*. Notes the parody of a Latin lesson in *LLL*. Judges *JC* to represent Sh's idea of classicism—severe in style, with little comedy. Even *Mac.* exhibits a number of classical features: compact form, little comic relief, and an off-stage murder. Duplicates contents of item 0913.

0916 Rowse, A. L. *William Shakespeare: A Biography.* New York: Harper & Row, 1963. xiv + 485 pp.

Discusses each of the poems and plays in some detail, emphasizing the importance of historical background in interpretation. For example, *Tro.* contains Sh's "maturest reflection on the problem of society and government," put forward in a mood of "utter disenchantment." It reflects the "shattering events of the past two or three years": the treason of Essex, the intrigues at court, and the endless war with Spain. Chapter 3 includes an account of Sh's education, stressing its basis in Latin grammar and literature. Latin phrase-books provided "moralizing tags" from authors like Aesop and Cato; Terence and Plautus would have given Sh his first taste of classical drama and provided inspiration for his early comedies; and Ovid, whom he would have studied in the upper school, made an overwhelming impression on him. Most of his classical mythology came from the *Metamorphoses*; he was most familiar with the first book, and after that the second: His mind was that of a poet, not a systematic scholar. Also in the upper school, Sh would have been trained in rhetoric according to the classical tradition; he would have studied classical historians like Sallust, Caesar, and Livy for their moral instruction (the idea of history as a moral tale is clearly discernible in the history plays).

0917 Rozett, Martha. "Aristotle, the Revenger, and the Elizabethan Audience." *SP*, 76 (1979), 239–61.

Argues that in late 16th-c. England, the popularity of revenge tragedy, ascribed to recent translations of Seneca, can be better explained by examining the Elizabethan audience's fascinated ambivalence about revenge. Conditioned by the combination of detachment and identification demanded by the Vice figure of the late morality plays, and exposed to numerous arguments in sermons and other writings of the time on the relative merits of justice and mercy in punishing crime, audiences were receptive to the revenger–protagonist, whose wrongs they could sympathize with at the same time that they detached themselves from his murderous retribution. Although it is unlikely that Sh and his contemporaries knew Aristotle's *Poetics*, the discussion of pity and fear in that work and the *Rhetoric* can be used to illuminate the effect of the revenge play as experienced by Sh's audience. According to Aristotle, fear is felt when the audience completely identifies with the protagonist, while pity is the result of a less complete identification, one that can be rationally analyzed. The tension between identification and detachment suggested by this reading of Aristotle can be found in *Ham.*, whose protagonist is simultaneously bonded to and distanced from the audience by a variety of techniques.

0918 Rudd, Niall. "Daedalus and Icarus, 2: From the Renaissance to the Present Day." *Ovid Renewed: Ovidian Influences on Literature and Art from the Middle Ages to the Twentieth Century*. Ed. Charles Martindale. Cambridge: Cambridge U. P., 1988, pp. 37–53.

Notes two evocations of the Daedalus–Icarus myth in *1H6*, in which it is modified to reflect the loyalty and bravery of Lord Talbot's son. In *3H6*, King Henry refers to himself as Daedalus. Suggests that in Sh, for the first time, Icarus's daring "is transferred from the sky to the battlefield."

0919 Rylands, G. H. W. "'What's Hecuba to him?' Shakespeare and the Classics." *Royal Institution of Great Britain Proceedings*, 39 (1963), 493–505.

Provides a partial text of a lecture given on 22 March 1963. Sh was inspired by the classics, particularly the story of Troy. In *Ham.* (II.ii) where Hamlet asks the players for a taste of their quality, he chooses the account of the slaughter of Priam by Pyrrhus, which Sh derived from Marlowe's *Dido, Queen of Carthage*. The Trojan War also inspired *Tro.*, in which Sh portrays a wide range of military types and anatomizes "the overthrow of the medieval by the modern world." Long before *Ham.* and *Tro.*, Sh showed how the tale of Troy had captured his imagination in *Luc.*, which devotes twenty-eight stanzas "to a minute delineation of a great painted battle-piece of Troy." In *Luc.*, there is the embryo of the drama to come: Both Hamlet and Lucrece, for example, turn to the image of Troy as they contemplate their betrayals. Summarizes, in italics, the lecturer's observations on the inspiration Sh might have gained from Seneca's tragedy of Troy and Ovid's *Metamorphoses* and on the Roman plays and their source in Plutarch's *Lives*.

0920 Saagpakk, Paul F. "A Survey of Psychopathology in British Literature from Shakespeare to Hardy." *L&P*, 18 (1968), 135–65.

Provides a brief explication of Renaissance psychological theory—derived from such classical authorities as Hippocrates, Plato, Aristotle, and Galen—upon which Elizabethan writers based their portraits of melancholic characters. Uses Robert Burton's *The Anatomy of Melancholy* as a main source in outlining the qualities and types of melancholy. Notes that melancholy had a wide range of meanings for the Elizabethans. One common melancholic literary type—the malcontent—appeared in many variations, including the cynic (Jaques in *AYL* and Timon and Apemantus in *Tim.*). Around 1600, the playwrights began to exhibit more detailed scientific knowledge in their dramatization of melancholy. Discusses Hamlet's life-weariness, thoughts of suicide, brooding on a single idea, outbursts of passion, satirical cynicism, moodiness, impulsiveness, erotic perturbations, and apathy as evidence of melancholy. Mentions the lethargy of Pericles; the love-longing of various characters in *AYL*, *TN*, and *AWW*; and the insanity of Lear, Ophelia, and Lady Macbeth.

0921   Sacks, Peter. "Where Words Prevail Not: Grief, Revenge, and Language in Kyd and Shakespeare." *ELH*, 49 (1982), 576–601.

Includes *Luc.* and *Tit.* in a discussion of Sh's exploration of characters' being cut off from means of consolation through language and, consequently, being frozen in attitudes of revenge or melancholy in response to loss.

0922   Salingar, L. G. "Time and Art in Shakespeare's Romances." *RenD*, 9 (1966), 3–35.

Argues that Sh drew on two traditions of non-chivalric romance—Euripidean and medieval Christian—in his late romances. He first made significant use of Euripidean conventions ("mistakes of identity" and "ironic reversals of a state of unhappiness and confusion") in *Err.*, along with the classical unities of time and place. In his late romances, he experimented with combining the "artificial" order of events (beginning in the middle of the story and providing exposition to account for antecedent action) characteristic of Euripidean romance and the "natural" order found in medieval romance. Sh's prolonged struggle to blend classical and medieval romance enabled him to achieve some remarkably subtle effects in "giving imaginative reality to the movement of time," especially in *WT* and *Tmp*.

0922a   Salingar, Leo. "Shakespeare and the Italian Concept of 'Art.'" *Renaissance Drama Newsletter*, Supplement 3 (1984), 23 pp. Reprint. *Dramatic Form in Shakespeare and the Jacobeans*. Cambridge: Cambridge U. P., 1986, pp. 1–18.

Outlines the new ideas of art that developed in Renaissance Italy, discussing classical influence, imitation, competition between arts, and the tendency to elevate what later came to be called the fine arts to a position to preeminence. Points out that Sh was clearly familiar with these themes of "humanistic art-criticism" but that he seems not to have followed the Italian view of art in the abstract. He tends to use the word *art* in "the common and miscellaneous Elizabethan way," and when he does consider the fine arts, he declines to associate them with normative rules or with the power of the visual arts to surpass nature. He gives emphasis to the arts of magic and medicine, which involve "wonder and illusion," and are concerned with "changing, not merely imitating, life." Provides a brief survey of references to art in Sh's earlier work, using a passage from to *Ven.* to illustrate that "some negative association" qualifies almost all the poet's "glowing images based on the Renaissance trope of art outgoing nature." Analyzes in more detail four late plays—*Ant.*, *Tim.*, *Cym.*, and *WT*—in which "passages about pictorial art stand out."

0923   Salingar, Leo. *Shakespeare and the Traditions of Comedy*. Cambridge: Cambridge U. P., 1974. x + 356 pp.

Attempts to discern the influences that certain classes of source material had on Sh and the kinds of things Sh did with them. Locates Sh's "points of departure": his choice of narrative and dramatic conventions from medieval stage romance, his use of classical and Renaissance ideas of comedy, and his innovations as Renaissance actor–dramatist.

Chapter 1, "The Unfaithful Mirror," points out how the humanist apology for comedy praised it as a mirror in one sense while limiting it in another. That is, it should be a reflection of the common errors of our life but only that, and it should avoid scornful matters as well as unhappy endings. From a modern point of view, the basic experience of comedy is not unlike that of the history play or the tragedy, but it is less accessible than either of these because it contains more conventions that need to be penetrated or mastered before it can be felt. In Sh's comedies, the fact that the characters and actions never carry the sense of comedy as performance is most obvious in episodes of clowning, dancing, and revelry. Sh clearly links comedy to celebration, usually with regard to marriage.

The third chapter, "'Errors' and Deceit in Classical Comedy," points to the classical tradition of "artificial order of a continuous plot unfolding causal connections," which meant beginning at the middle or end. *Err.* was the first play in English to adapt material from Plautus *and* to employ this artificial order. According to the late classical grammarians (like Donatus), comic plots are propelled by the complications of error, both innocent mistakes and guileful deceptions.

Chapter 4, "Fortune in Classical Comedy," explains the evolution of Fortune from a neutral or favorable goddess to one who represented an "unpredictable aspect of generalized divine power, whether helpful or harmful." The wheel of Fortune in Greek thought signifies "both regularity and fortuitousness," and human effort is required from time to time to renew the regular cycle of nature (as in Aristophanes). In New Comedy, there is no longer a schemer who causes the wheel to turn; the trickster now trusts to his luck and depends on Fortune for success. This process is often abetted by the self-deception of the serious characters. Donatus's notes emphasizing the "chain of errors" in Terence's *Andria* had a great influence on Renaissance comedy. The presentation of Fortune in dramatic plots and the role of the trickster working with Fortune gave Sh certain guidelines. In addition to individual episodes, he owed to the classical tradition some basic concepts of comedy as a kind of art "using logically connected plots to raise and satisfy expectations" and at the same time appealing to the spectators' sense of irony.

"Shakespeare and Italian Comedy" (Chapter 5) attempts to distinguish the playwright's debt to the classical dramatists from his debt to their Italian imitators, who reintroduced the methods of New Comedy. *Commedia erudita* originated in the early part of the 16th c. and combined Italian materials with externally classical form. Italian theorists preferred double plots to produce variety and surprise, which they saw as significant causes of laughter. Sh followed the Italians in employing double plots for *Shr., TN, Err.*, and other works. In addition, he used Gascoigne's *Supposes*, a translation of Ariosto's *Suppositi*, as his source for the Lucentio–Bianca plot in *Shr*.

The sixth chapter, "An Elizabethan Playwright," points out some of the things Sh did to modify the traditions he inherited. For one thing, he changed the Italian pattern of wit, which was based on a contrast between witty love and boorishness or dotage. Wit in Sh's comedies is primarily between lovers and is associated with free choice in love, particularly in regard to his female characters. Sh's comedies also enjoy a wider scope, geographically and socially, than earlier comedies. Unlike the Italian plays, which emphasize bourgeois characters, Sh usually includes a prince in the action and has him preside over the recognition scene. In several comedies, Sh included episodes of revelry or pastime, but in the four "problem comedies" such episodes are marginal (*MV* and *Ado*) or nonexistent (*MM* and *AWW*). These four, like others, employ trickery or disguise, with Fortune aiding the heroine, but there is a serious, deliberate opponent in each case, something not seen in other comedies. Trickery is not enough to carry the day, and recourse to the law is necessary.

0924 Salmon, Vivian. "Some Functions of Shakespearean Word-Formation." *ShS*, 23 (1970), 13–26.

Classifies the various types of Sh's neologisms and gives examples. The setting of *Tro.* may be responsible for what seems to be "a high proportion of neologisms and words of Latin origin" in the play. However, "a close analysis would be necessary to prove that the proportion of words of Latin origin, and of new formations from Latin elements, is higher here than in the non-classical tragedies." In creating compound epithets, "Shakespeare was imitating a style of diction most notably exploited by Spenser, but derived eventually from the practice of earlier English poets, the precepts of the Pleiade, and the Hellenistic influence on 16th-c. English culture."

0925 Saltzer, Nancy Kay Clark. "Masks and Roles: A Study of Women in Shakespeare's Drama." Ph.D. dissertation, University of Connecticut, 1975. *DAI*, 36 (1975–76), 1535-A.

Views Cressida and Cleopatra as self-aware actresses who empower themselves through continual gaming. Each qualifies our perception of the hero and helps to focus the values presented by the play in which she appears.

0926 Samsey, Patricia Jane Collins. "Contrariety, an English Renaissance Literary Principle: Instances and Origins." Ph.D. dissertation, University of Michigan, 1975. *DAI*, 36 (1975–76), 1536-A.

Investigates the aesthetic principle of contrariety, or "diametrical opposition," in English Renaissance literature, including some works of Sh. Suggests that English Renaissance writers gained their notions of contrariety from a classical source, the *De Mundo*, "a Greek treatise wrongly attributed to Aristotle, which in the course of a discussion of cosmological opposition comments upon the appearance of opposites in painting, in music, and in writing."

0927 Sanders, Wilbur, and Howard Jacobson. *Shakespeare's Magnanimity: Four Tragic Heroes, Their Friends, and Families*. New York: Oxford U. P., 1978. 188 pp.

Contains essays on four of Sh's plays, including *Ant.* and *Cor.* Chapter 4, on *Ant.*, begins by questioning the dichotomy between " a vital Alexandria and a desiccated Rome" that many critics see in the play. Romans, even when they seem to oppose the pleasures of Egypt, are fascinated by them. Argues that Sh's portrayal of the many Roman commentators on the lovers (Philo, Pompey, Octavius, the men who form the rapt audience for Enobarbus's account of Cleopatra's barge on the Cydnus) gives him an opportunity to enjoy "the ways men half-create the legend they are offering to judge." Enobarbus is the spokesman in the play for such enjoyment. Notes that Antony's stay in Rome is noteworthy for his passive submission to circumstance; even his return to Egypt is more of a reaction than the result of a careful decision. Once he is back in Egypt, Antony seems to exhibit a new solicitousness for Cleopatra, a new commitment; this destroys him as a soldier. His loving generosity to his followers in defeat, though moving, is also dangerous in its "splendid carelessness." Antony, having made himself too much a man of feeling, too much an object of pitiful love, evokes a sense of melancholy. His is a "torpid decline." Cleopatra, however, practically and cheerfully canvasses all the alternatives to self-sacrifice before she willingly embraces it; she is under no illusion about her circumstances but decides to construct one anyway and invites us to enjoy it.

Chapter 5, on *Cor.*, maintains that the hero of this play is admired by all, even those who oppose him; that he is not a simple bully or overgrown boy (being instead more thoughtful and sardonic than is usually granted); and that Sh gets much comic mileage out of the different versions of him constructed by others. Emphasizes the importance of recognizing the extent of Coriolanus's impossibility, the ultimately incompatible elements (like modesty and pride) that are nevertheless inextricably bound up in him. Analyzes the scene following the battle at Corioles (I.ix) to point out that Martius is unintrospective and naive and that, however uninstrospective and naive he is, he does have a certain limited sense of irony about himself and an ability to make satiric comments about others. Contends that the tribunes' action in banishing Coriolanus is necessary for the good of Rome but that at the same time Coriolanus's denunciation of the tribunes is justified. Coriolanus's banishment at first seems to open up the possibility for him of a world elsewhere, but his brief exhilaration modulates into hardship, then vagrancy, and finally treason. Aufidius, when he first receives the exiled Coriolanus, flirts with magnanimity, but he soon falls into division with himself and loses his integrity. Argues that Coriolanus, though significantly influenced by his mother, is not exclusively a product of her tutelage; he reveals his independence of her at crucial moments, even during the scene (V.iii) in which he seems to give in to her pleas. He is aware of the consequences of what he is doing while Volumnia and Virgilia are not. Sh's play is austere, but all the more supremely tragic in its "unmysterious humanity."

0928   Sandy, Gerald N. "Ancient Prose Fiction and Minor Early English Novels." *Antike und Abendland*, 25 (1979), 41–55.

The appendix challenges Carol Gesner's opinion (expressed in item 0434) that Sh derived Juliet's drinking of a sleeping potion and its consequences from the *Ephesiaca* of Xenophon of Ephesus. Suggests that more likely classical sources are certain works of Achilles Tatius, Apuleius, and Heliodorus, all of which were available in English translations during the Elizabethan period. Objects to Gesner's connection of the Ninus–romance by Longus with the Pyramus and Thisbe sketch in *MND*. It is much more likely that Sh's version is directly borrowed from Ovid's account in book 4 of the *Metamorphoses*.

0929   Saslaw, Naomi Ruth. "Shakespearean Humanism." Ph.D. dissertation, Case Western Reserve University, 1969. *DAI*, 30 (1969–70), 3919-A.

Depicts Sh's humanism as based on the principle that human greatness must grow out of an acceptance of the realities of life. In many versions of humanism from classical times and the Renaissance, there is a tendency to seek glory by denying the flesh. In Sh's plays, however, characters who try to glorify themselves by transcending the human condition are seen as unnatural. Discusses *Mac.*, *Ham.*, *Oth.*, *Rom.*, and *Tro*.

0930   Schanzer, Ernest. "Hercules and His Load." *RES*, 19, no. 73 (1968), 51–53.

Asserts that Edmund Malone got his information about the sign of the Globe Theater, depicting Hercules supporting the Globe with the motto *Totus mundus agit histrionem*, from George Steevens's 1778 edition. Steevens probably got the idea from the antiquary William Oldys.

0931   Schanzer, Ernest. "Plot–Echoes in Shakespeare's Plays." *SJH*, 1969, 102–21.

Discusses serious plot–echoes within several of Sh's plays. In *Ant.*, the scene between Antony and Caesar's Messenger (III.xiii) mirrors the scene between Cleopatra and the Messenger who informs her of Antony's marriage (II.v). In the last scene (V.ii), the deaths of Charmian and Iras parallel the death of Antony's companions Eros and Enobarbus. Both echoes convey a sense of unique resemblance between lovers. In *Tim.* and *Cor.*, plot–echoes have a more complex function: They heighten the irony of events and convince the audience that the protagonist is trapped and victimized by his own nature.

0932   Schanzer, Ernest. *The Problem Plays of Shakespeare: A Study of "Julius Caesar," "Measure for Measure," "Antony and Cleopatra."* London: Routledge & Kegan Paul, 1963. x + 196 pp.

JC and *Ant.*, along with *MM*, can be grouped together as Sh's problem plays, each of which deals with a central moral problem in such a way that "uncertain and divided responses to it in the minds of the audience are possible or even probable." In the background to *JC*, there was a long tradition of divided judgments on Caesar. Among educated men, beginning with ancient historians, some of whom Sh knew (for example, Plutarch and Appian), and extending to Montaigne, there was admiration for Caesar's personal qualities but condemnation for his ambition. Sh embeds this ambiguity in his play, never permitting a clear-cut assessment of Caesar or of the moral justifiability of his murder. Brutus, having set aside his personal love of Caesar, is tragically disillusioned when the republic with which he has thrown his lot becomes tainted. *Ant.* is Sh's problem play *par excellence*; it encourages constant changes of attitude in the audience toward the central question of whether Rome or Egypt should be preferred. Several classical analogues may have influenced Sh's presentation of Antony's choice. One of these is the story of Hercules choosing between Pleasure and

Virtue (in Xenophon's *Memorabilia*), which emphasizes his strength against voluptuous desires; another, in Plutarch and Ovid (*Fasti*), presents Hercules in "effeminate subjection" to Omphale, who steals his club and lion skin; and a third is Aeneas's choice between Dido and the fulfillment of his mission. See item 0682.

0933 Schanzer, Ernest. "Shakespeare and the Doctrine of the Unity of Time." *ShS*, 28 (1975), 57–61.

Argues that Sh, in the course of his career, "expressed his sense of the absurdity of the neo-classical demand for unity of time: through Berowne's explicit mockery; through associating it in the figure of Polonius with other forms of pedantic absurdity; through the device of making Father Time himself disparage it as a passing fashion; and finally, and most amusingly, through making Prospero enact before the audience's eyes the harassment of the plot–designer who is committed to its observation."

0934 Scheman, Lillian. "The Elizabethan Amorous Epyllion from 1589 to 1618." Ph.D. dissertation, St. John's University, 1978. *DAI*, 39 (1978–79), 4285-A-4286-A.

Traces the development of the epyllion, or minor epic, from 1589, when the publication of Thomas Lodge's *Scilla's Metamorphosis* marked its first appearance, to 1618. Attempts to show how Elizabethan poets "adapted classical material," using Ovid as their model, to produce tragedy (*Luc.*), comedy (*Ven.*), and satire in the epyllion. The Elizabethan epyllia freed Ovid from allegory and reversed the roles of male and female wooers. Sh, in *Ven.*, undermined the stereotype of Petrarchan love and established the paradigm for other epyllia.

0935 Schmidgall, Gary. *Shakespeare and the Poet's Life*. Lexington: U. of Kentucky P., 1990. x + 234 pp.

Chapter 1 begins with a reading of *Ven.* as "a parable of both the courtier's and the courting poet's experience 'in waiting,'" and chapter 3 includes an examination of *Tim.* as presenting an atmosphere of confusion, venality, and cynicism in which the transaction between poet and patron takes place. The epilogue speculates that in *Ant.* Sh anachronistically associates Rome with the structured world of the Renaissance courtier and court poet, and Alexandria with the fluid, excessive world of the theater. This is perhaps the last play in which he dramatized his renunciation of the former and his embracement of the latter.

0936 Schoenbaum, S. "Shakespeare and the Book." *Shakespeare's Art from a Comparative Perspective*. Ed. Wendell M. Aycock. (Proceedings: Comparative Literature Symposium, Texas Tech U., 12.) Lubbock: Texas Tech P., 1981, pp. 165–79.

Investigates the relationship of Sh with the book. Supports the assertion that the poet's birthplace was not "a bookless neighborhood" by citing some of the authors (Aesop, Cicero, Sallust, Virgil, Horace) whose books were in the library of John Bretchgirdle, the vicar who christened Sh. The rigors of the grammar school curriculum are reflected in passages from several of Sh's plays. Calls attention to the considerable amount of Latin literature Sh would have absorbed in the Stratford school. Notes that Ovid's *Metamorphoses* was Sh's favorite classical work, pointing out that it is both a source and a stage prop in *Tit.* and that it supplies a model for Prospero's speech of farewell to his art in *Tmp.* Mentions Thomas North's translation of Plutarch's *Lives* as the source for the Roman plays and *Tim.*

0936a Schoenbaum, S. *Shakespeare: His Life, His English, His Theater*. New York: Signet, 1990. 221 pp.

Includes, in the first chapter, a brief account of the Latin authors Sh would have read in grammar school. Chapter 2, "Shakespeare's English," notes among other things the playwright's frequent use of neologisms formed from Latin. Chapter 4, on the plays and playwrights that preceded Sh, comments on the neoclassical doctrine of the dramatic unities and Sh's usual (though not complete) disregard for it. Chapters 5–10 survey the works, touching, for example, on Sh's handling of the mattter of Troy in *Tro.* and his adaptation of Plutarch in *Cor.*

0937 Schoenbaum, S. "Shakespeare the Ignoramus." *The Drama of the Renaissance: Essays for Leicester Bradner.* Ed. Elmer M. Blistein. Providence: Brown U. P., 1970, pp. 154–64.

Surveys the history of the opinion that Sh lacked learning. Rowe, author of the first connected biography, was under the erroneous impression that Sh was one of ten children and therefore had to leave school early. In the 18th c., Richard Farmer, in his *Essay on the Learning of Shakespeare*, dismissed those who had tried to defend the poet's learning. More recently, T. W. Baldwin has provided an accurate picture of the grammar school curriculum in Sh's day and thus rehabilitated the idea that the poet could read many of his sources in their original languages. Another reason for assuming Sh's ignorance has been the uninspiring bust by Gheerart Janssen in Holy Trinity Church, which has reminded many scholars of a businessman rather than an artist or intellectual.

0938 Schoenbaum, S. *William Shakespeare: A Documentary Life.* NewYork: Oxford U. P., in association with Scolar P., 1975. xix + 273 pp.

Chapter 6, "Faith and Knowledge," sets forth in some detail and with a number of illustrations the curriculum Sh would have followed in school. In the lower school, Sh would have studied William Lily's *Shorte Introduction of Grammar*, the standard Latin grammar text; the *Sententiae Pueriles*, "a manual of brief sentences from Latin authors"; "Aesop latinized"; Plautus and Terence; "modern Latin moral poets" (like Palingenius [*Zodiacus Vitae*] and Baptista Spagnuoli ["Mantuanus"]); conversational colloquies like those of Corderius, Gallus, and Vives; and literary dialogues like those of Castalio and Erasmus. In the upper school, rhetoric would have been introduced through the works of Cicero, Susenbrotus, Erasmus, and Quintilian. The students would also have taken up poetry: Ovid, Virgil, and Horace. In some cases, Juvenal and Persius would also be added. Sallust and Caesar were read for history and Cicero's *De Officiis* for moral philosophy.

0939 Schwartz, Elias. *The Mortal Worm: Shakespeare's Master Theme.* (Kennikat P. National U. Publications: Literary Criticism Series.) Port Washington, New York: Kennikat P., 1977. 117 pp.

Chapter 2, on *JC*, views Brutus as a protagonist who evidences both "moral idealism and intellectual mediocrity" and who is tormented by personal feelings (of guilt, of tenderness) that he is never able to recognize fully. Chapter 3, on *Tro.*, is a revision of item 3011. Chapter 7, on *Ant.*, is a revision of item 1446. Appendix B, on *PhT*, is a revision of item 2386.

0940 Schwartz, Louis. "Old Love's Great Power: Mimesis, Imitation, and the Authority of Poetry in Petrarch, Wyatt, and Shakespeare." Ph.D. dissertation, Brandeis University, 1990. *DAI*, 51 (1990–91), 1242-A.

Concentrates on four poets and "the way in which each produced a self-validating didactic art in imitation of each other and in response to cultural pressures." Maintains that these poets used common Renaissance "tropes of transcendental access" with "an irony that derives from Plato's censure of poetry in the *Republic* and Augustine's later critique of Neoplatonic aesthetic idealism." In the works of Sh, poetry "begins to claim didactic authority precisely because it cannot claim transcendent authority."

0940a Scolnicov, Hanna. "Mimesis, Mirror, Double." *The Play Out of Context: Transferring Plays from Culture to Culture.* Eds. Hanna Scolnicov and Peter Holland. Cambridge: Cambridge U. P., 1989, pp. 89–98.

Begins with the proposition that the Renaissance inherited from Horace the idea that artistic *mimesis* is "an imitation of a classical writer." This concept of imitation is the basis for the complementary notions of the play as "a collective memory of the past" and the play as "mirror of present day society." Drama composed according to such notions can justly be called classical and has the power "to transcend geographical and cultural boundaries." Adduces as examples the ritualization and theatricalization of Caesar's murder by Cassius and Brutus (*JC*, III.i.111–116), the dramatization by Hamlet of his father's murder, and Hamlet's Ciceronian comment on playing as "a mirror of life."

0941   Scott, W. I. D. *Shakespeare's Melancholics.* London: Mills and Boon, 1962. 192 pp.

Explores eight examples of the melancholic character from Sh's plays. These eight are representative of "the various types of melancholy known both to Elizabeth and to modern psychology." Devotes chapter 8 to Timon, who is analyzed as a "general paralytic." Timon's sense of omnipotence both in his bounty and in his misanthropy is caused by syphilis. Such a diagnosis is supported by the prominence of prostitutes in the play to Alcibiades and Timon, and by Timon's use, in acts IV and V, of imagery drawn from "the classical symptomatology of syphilitic disease." (Sh ignores the homosexual relationship between Alcibiades and Timon found in his source, Plutarch's *Lives*, and develops in great detail the heterosexual corruption of Athens.) Describes, from hints in the speeches of other characters, a Timon once noble, prudent, and civic-minded. This admirable figure has been ruined by his disease. Timon may also be labeled "an inverted sensation type," with which these symptoms are consistent. In other plays, the character of Pericles exemplifies the schizophrenic, afflicted with "melancholy productive of prolonged stupor"; and Leontes' jealous melancholy (*WT*) reveals him as a type of the paranoid.

0942   Scott, William O. *The God of Arts: Ruling Ideas in Shakespeare's Comedies.* (U. of Kansas Publications, Humanistic Studies 48.) Lawrence: U. of Kansas Publications, 1977. 140 pp.

Refers in the title to Mercury, the god of arts, who was seen in the emblem literature of the Renaissance as a defense against the blind capriciousness of Fortune. Chapter 7, "Miracles and Fading Visions," discusses the suggestions in Sh's works that supernatural powers control events, suggestions that are especially powerful in the last plays. Notes that in *WT* the "enactment of myth and miracle" purposed by Apollo is abetted, albeit parodically, by Autolycus, the play's chief embodiment of Mercury. Camillo also serves as a representative of Mercury, working more directly than Autolycus to ensure good fortune.

0943   Scoufos, Alice Lyle. "The 'Martyrdom' of Falstaff." *ShakS*, 2 (1966), 174–91.

Contends that historical research can shed some light on the Elizabethan background for Sh's creation of the Falstaff plays. Despite his disclaimer in the epilogue to *2H4*, Sh did use the career of Sir John Oldcastle as the basis for some of the Falstaff material. In particular, Oldcastle's death by burning as a heretic and traitor during the reign of Henry V provided an analogue for the satiric martyrdom of Falstaff, who suffers a broken heart and a burning fever. It also seems likely that Sh, having been reprimanded for offending Oldcastle's descendants, added "a ludicrous inversion," changing heat to cold in Mistress Quickly's account of Falstaff's death. This is partly patterned on the description of Socrates' death in Plato's *Phaedo*; the parody is apt because of the parallels between Socrates' "crime" of preaching false religion and Oldcastle's heresy, and between the malice of comic poets against Socrates and the unflattering stage portraits of Oldcastle and his Elizabethan descendants. In addition, the remarks of the Hostess and the Page about Falstaff's handling of women are derived from the reputation of Socrates as a misogynist.

0944 Seamster, John Allan. "*If It Were Done*: Shakespeare's Deliberative Soliloquy." Ph.D. dissertation, University of California, Berkeley, 1980. *DAI*, 42 (1981–82), 230-A.

Discusses the deliberative soliloquy in *JC, Ham., Oth.*, and *Mac.* The discontinuities evident within the process of the protagonist's reasoning reveal hidden emotions and fantasies that cause him to act against his announced principles. Hypothesizes that in presenting deliberative soliloquies Sh was creating a psychological analogue of "the deterministic scheme he saw in Greek tragedy operative through the supernatural." The psychological configuration of each protagonist is indicated by the form taken by the discrepancies in his deliberation. Brutus, for example, reveals, through the discontinuity between "his major premise and his conclusion," a division between his conscious and covert attitudes toward Caesar.

0945 Sears, Lloyd C. *Shakespeare's Philosophy of Evil*. North Quincy, Massachusetts: Christopher Publishing, 1974. 363 pp.

Distinguishes two broad world views in the Renaissance: the "optimistic faith" of the humanists, with its background in Stoicism, Platonic idealism, and the thought of Aquinas, and the pessimism derived from Pyrrhonism, Cynicism, and Platonic disgust with the world. Interprets *Ham.* as "the beginning of Shakespeare's reflective study of evil" and concludes that this play profoundly questions the optimistic view (as, for example, expressed by Plutarch with his sentimentalized Stoicism). Reads *Tro.* as a penetrating study of the means by which we determine values and set standards, citing numerous philosophical sources to show that Sh projects in this play an immutable moral order that is interpreted in a wide variety of ways by individual human minds. Ulysses, the exemplar of a moderate skepticism, seems to be the character most capable of effectively dealing with the world of experience. Finds that Aristotle's notion of virtue as a mean between extremes informs the examination of justice linked with temperance in *MM* and the study of misanthropy in *Tim.* Discusses several works in terms of Elizabethan psychology, including *JC*, in which Brutus's moral struggle shows the difficulty that the reason and the will have in overcoming the passions. Emphasizes the philosophical background in discussing suffering and justice in *Lr.*, absolute evil in *Mac.*, and compassion and reconciliation in the late romances.

0946 Seko, Emmanuel Vincent. "The Shakespearean Tragic Movement." Ph.D. dissertation, University of Wisconsin, 1973. *DAI*, 34 (1973–74), 3357-A.

Uses Aristotelian terminology to describe the experience of Sh's tragic protagonists, which can be analyzed into three phases: (1) The protagonists's *arete* is portrayed; (2) the *arete* is transformed into the tragic flaw; (3) the *arete* is reasserted through the protagonist's *anagnorisis* and death.

0947 Semon, Kenneth Jeffrey. "Fantasy and Wonder: Shakespeare's Last Plays." Ph.D. dissertation, University of Washington, 1971. *DAI*, 32 (1971–72), 2653-A.

Mentions classical theories of *admiratio*, or wonder, as a response to tragic drama as background for exploring Renaissance Italian theories of the marvelous and then applying those theories to *Per., Cym., WT*, and *Tmp.*

0948 Sen, R. K. "Tragic Conflict in Shakespeare: Its Background in Christian Scholasticism." *Calcutta Essays on Shakespeare*. Ed. Amalendu Bose. Calcutta: Calcutta U., 1966, pp. 132–43.

Contrasts the nonmoral attitude toward tragic flaw in Aristotle with the morality of intention, derived from medieval Christian thought, that characterizes Shakespearean tragedy.

0949 Sen Gupta, S. C. *Aspects of Shakespearian Tragedy*. Calcutta: Oxford U. P., 1972. 176 pp. 2nd ed., 1977. vii + 234 pp.

Chapter 2 distinguishes two styles in *Ant.*: (1) the Roman, which is characterized by adequacy, clarity, and compression, and which is used for "the stirring incidents"; and (2) the Egyptian, which is opulent and mysterious. Caesar speaks almost entirely in the Roman style; Antony and Enobarbus employ mixed styles; and Cleopatra is extravagantly given to the Egyptian style. Mentions Plutarch frequently, especially in pursuing the point that Cleopatra's verbal artistry is seen as much in the incidents Sh borrows from his source as in those he creates. Concludes by considering the style in which each of the four principal characters comments on a single episode—Antony's message challenging Octavius to single combat. The second edition adds two chapters, 7 and 8. Chapter 7, "The Unity of *Julius Caesar*," maintains that there is no hero in this play; rather, Sh centers his attention on the Roman polity of the 1st c. B.C., which he "presents with complete ethical and political neutrality." Observes that the portrait of Caesar is a balanced one (he is at the same time valiant and timid, constant and wavering, autocratic and egalitarian). Sh evidences an equally fine impartiality in presenting the aristocrats who do not join the conspiracy, the tribunes, the conspirators, Antony, and Octavius. Cassius is depicted as a man of great intelligence, a "keen realist," who is nevertheless driven by envy and thwarted ambition to wishful thinking about Caesar. Forced at every turn to abandon his own superior insights, he is exhausted in both mind and body and dies in confusion. Brutus is a type of Plato's philosopher–statesman whose lofty idealism is ill-equipped to deal with the political exigencies he encounters. Notes the distinctive features of *JC*'s construction, especially its "wave-like flow in which there are crests and troughs, but no climax." Chapter 8 analyzes the character of the protagonist in *Cor.* to show that, though well- organized, the play is not a masterpiece. Coriolanus is limited by his egoism, which renders him incapable of being a patriot. The natural feeling for his family, which momentarily overcomes his egoism, is severely limited. Attempts a definition of the Shakespearean tragic hero, involving the conflict between good and evil and the character's assimilation and blending of many contradictory ideas and feelings. Finds Coriolanus a disappointment as hero because his emotions, shallow to begin with, are compartmentalized; his struggles have little to do with evil; and his general immaturity subverts any claims he may have to seriousness.

0950 Sen Gupta, S. C. *Shakespeare's Historical Plays*. Oxford U. P.,1964. ix + 172 pp.

Chapter 2, "Nature and Fortune," mentions the Roman origin of the goddess Fortuna, explains her link with Occasio, and describes Sh's use of Fortune in his history plays. In Sh's amoral vision of history, men and women are continually rising on Fortune's wheel, "ruling, falling, and being cast off." There is no regard for an individual's "efficiency or inadequacy."

0951 Sen Gupta, S. C. *The Whirligig of Time: The Problem of Duration in Shakespeare's Plays*. Bombay: Orient Longmans, 1961. ix + 201 pp.

Argues that Sh progressed, though not always in a strictly chronological way, from Time to Duration. In the history plays, Time reigns, with events being partitioned, producing a gap "between every two stages in the action." In the greatest plays, Duration takes over: There is a ceaseless flow of events, changes in situation are held together by character, and alterations in character occur as "part of a continuous spiritual process." Discusses, during application of this thesis to Sh's works, several classical plays. In *Tit.*, indications of Time's passage are prominent, but "it has not been attuned to growth of character." *Cor.* and *Tim.* are dominated by Time, but in *JC* and *Ant.* it is replaced by Duration. Surveys classical and Renaissance theory and practice with regard to the unities (chapter 4) and judges *Tmp.*, Sh's most temporally unified play, as lacking in passion because Prospero, in order to weld the diverse elements of the plot together, must be set "above the limitations of time and space."

0952 Sewall, Richard B. "Ahab's Quenchless Feud: The Tragic Vision in Shakespeare and Melville." *CompD*, 1 (1967–68), 207–18.

Uses parallels with Melville to stress the Greek quality of Sh's tragedies, particularly the idea that man learns by suffering. Each of Sh's great tragic figures looks into the abyss—"his own nature and the world's"—finds no exit, and is destroyed.

0953 Sewall, Richard B. "Shakespeare's Tragic Vision." *ShN*, 14 (1964), 80.

Places Sh's tragedies in "the tradition of the Greek tragic theater." Like the Greeks, Sh seems much concerned with "the public moral function of tragedy, its grappling with basic issues of survival in such a way as to suggest the deepest kind of involvement of author and spectators." Sh's last phase—*Cym.*, *WT*, and *Tmp.*—shows him following ancient tradition and moving into another mode. No author of tragedy (and no audience) can stand the relentless examination of destructive forces for long.

0954 Shaheen, Naseeb. *Biblical References in Shakespeare's Tragedies.* Newark: U. of Delaware P., 1987. 245 pp.

The introduction proposes to compare the plays under consideration with their literary sources in order to ascertain which biblical references Sh "borrowed from his plot sources and which he himself added from his own memory." In addition, a check of the sources can help to determine if "the many passages in Shakespeare that resemble Scripture but are not clear biblical references were actually taken from Scripture." Provides illustrations from *JC* (the invitation by Caesar to the conspirators to "taste some wine" [II.ii.127] may be an allusion to the Last Supper, but it may simply be Sh's dramatic realization of the liberality that Plutarch attributes to Caesar) and *Tim.* (the excuse-making of Timon's false friends when he invites them to a second banquet [III.vi], because it has no parallel in Sh's sources, is likely to have been modeled on Jesus' parable of the wedding invitation). Analyzes eleven plays, including *Tit.* (almost half of the biblical references within the play are to Job, Psalms, Ecclesiastes, and Lamentations), *JC*, *Tro.* (large number of references for a play with a classical setting), *Ant.* (remarkable use of Revelation), *Cor.*, and *Tim.* Part is a revision of item 1724.

0955 Shalvi, Alice. *The Relationship of Renaissance Concepts of Honour to Shakespeare's Problem Plays.* (JDS 7.) Salzburg: Institut für Englische Sprache und Literatur, U. Salzburg, 1972. 362 pp.

The first three chapters trace the development of the ideas of gentility, the gentleman, and honor in 16th- and early 17th-c. England. Notes the variety of opinions about what constitutes gentility, with three key attributes (birth, wealth, and virtue) being given different values by different writers. Calls attention to the importance of classical sources for Renaissance ideas about the gentleman and honor and argues that confusion about these matters in the 16th c. has a lot to do with conflict between the sources. Points out two models for the gentleman among Sh's contemporaries, Aristotle's Magnanimous Man and Seneca's Wise Man. Discusses several aspects of honor: external honor, the specific thing or deed for which one receives external honor, internal honor, and the code of honor. For each of these, there are classical commentaries; authors include Plato, Aristotle, Cicero, and Seneca. Elizabethan and Jacobean dramas seemed to develop a sense that the code of honor to which gentlemen must adhere was to be identified with an irascible obsession with reputation. In the dramas of the first two decades of the 17th c., this emphasis on strict maintenance of one's good name became increasingly less compatible with Christian virtue. Sees *Luc.* as a work in which Sh more or less accepts the conventions of the code of honor, validating Lucrece's suicide and the revenge intended by her family as appropriate responses to her ruined reputation. Devotes a chapter each to *Ham.*, *Tro.* (a revision of item 3015), *AWW*, and *MM*, contending that in these works Sh reveals an increasingly critical attitude toward the aristocratic virtue glorified by his contemporaries as honor. In *Tro.*, for example, the Trojans' concept of honor is "equated with sensual passion," while the whole chivalric code of warfare, with its concern for personal reputation, is indicted as irrational.

0956 Shanker, Sidney. *Shakespeare and the Uses of Ideology*. The Hague: Mouton, 1975. x + 224 pp.

Maintains that Sh began by accepting orthodox Tudor ideology and that this is reflected in his early plays. Around 1595, in response to various challenges to conventional thinking and under the influence of Stoicism, Sh started to change. Suggests that in developing his ideas about Stoicism, Sh read Seneca, Cicero, Plutarch, and Montaigne. In *JC* and more thoroughly in *Ham.*, the playwright subjected the ethical value of Stoicism to a searching critique. In *Tro.*, Sh's most densely philosophical play, there is a vision of "national disunity and dishonor" as Sh continues to respond to the decadence of his time. *Lr.* is the climax of Sh's career: It examines ideology, especially that of Stoicism, in the most radical and painful way, but it provides a glimpse of an alternative ethic of transcendence. Contends that *Cor.* is flawed: Because of Sh's "neutral ideological stance," he is unable to resolve the incompatibility between "the play as a political revenge melodrama and as a classic tragedy." When he reaches *Ant.*, Sh has moved away from concern with specific ideologies and toward transcendence, a movement that is completed in *Tmp.*

0957 Shapiro, Gloria Kaufman. "Death in the Shakespeare Comedies." Ph.D. dissertation, Brandeis University, 1961. *DA*, 22 (1961–62), 3650–3651.

Calls attention to the comic tradition inherited by the Elizabethans from Donatus and other 4th-c. grammarians. Though the Elizabethans were aware of this tradition, they violated it by mixing comic and tragic effects in their plays. In particular, death was included in many comedies. Sh deals with death in *MM, AWW, LLL, MV,* and *WT.*

0958 Shapiro, I. A. "Robert Fludd's Stage–Illustration." *ShakS*, 2 (1966), 192–209.

Asserts that to illustrate his system for memorizing, derived from classical practice, Robert Fludd included an engraving of a contemporary English theater in his *Ars Memoriae* (1619). The theater represented, however, is not the second Globe, as Frances Yates has argued (item 1149), but the Blackfriars, taken over by Sh and his company in 1608–09. See also items 1148 and 1150.

0959 Sharma, Ram Bilas. *Essays on Shakespearean Tragedy*. Agra, India: Shiva Lal Agarwala, 1965. 312 pp.

Introduces a discussion of Sh's tragedy by analyzing Aristotle's comments on pity and fear in the *Poetics*. Suggests that Aristotle designated these emotions as undesirable and emphasized their purgation as a way to answer Plato's "criticism of the expression of emotions in poetry and music." In fact, pity and fear are not necessarily undesirable, nor are they the only emotions aroused by tragedy. Tragedy is drama that "involves the contemplation of painful emotions," the chief of which is sadness. This feeling may be supported by "the allied feelings of anger, disgust, wonder, fear and heroism with a touch of the comic and the emotion of love." In tragedy, especially Sh's, "there is the awareness of the pull of contrary emotions." Devotes a chapter each to *Ham., Lr., Oth.,* and *Mac.*; has chapters on "Shakespearean Tragedy" and "Problems"; and concludes with a chapter on Sh's other tragedies, including *Ant., JC, Tim., Cor., Tit.,* and *Tro.*

0960 Shawcross, John T. *Intentionality and the New Traditionalism: Some Liminal Means to Literary Revisionism*. University Park: Pennsylvania State U. P., 1991. 236 pp.

Chapter 3, "Shakespeare and the Tragic," uses several plays to distinguish between tragedy as a genre and the tragic as a mode. Generically, tragedy has a closed ending because "the audience is concerned with the action to the point of the catastrophe" for the hero and no further. The tragic mode, however, is open-ended because "the questions on which the action exists are unsolved." Includes discussion of *Ant.*, in which the tragic mode implicates us in everything the lovers do, and *Cor.*, in which the tragic mode exhibits an individual who believes in his own superiority and insists that the outside world acknowledge that superiority.

0961 Shenk, Robert. *The Sinner's Progress: A Study of Madness in English Renaissance Drama.* (Elizabethan and Renaissance Studies 74.) Salzburg: Institut für Englische Sprache und Literatur, U. Salzburg, 1978. xi + 285 pp.

Examines a number of Renaissance dramas in light of the scholastic tradition, deriving from Aristotle through Thomas Aquinas. Focuses, in the introductory chapters, on such scholastic topics as right reason, natural law, and faculty psychology, noting that the philosophical underpinnings of these notions were still widely accepted in the England of the 16th and early 17th c. Sh's tragic heroes sin from what Aristotle calls intemperance. Chapter 6, on *Ham.*, argues that the vice of sloth lies at the root of the protagonist's behavior. At the very end, Hamlet achieves some degree of self-knowledge and frees himself from his vice to take action. His final act of vengeance on Claudius is a deliberate evocation of Aeneas's long-delayed decision to take vengeance on Turnus in the *Aeneid*. Chapter 7, on *Lr.*, concludes that Lear has been long addicted to "vanity and several kinds of intemperance" and that, with advancing age, this condition has corrupted his body chemistry, which in turn has made him mad. Chapter 8, on *MM*, treats Angelo as a reprobate, one who has given himself over completely to his passions. Chapter 9, "Radical Insanity," includes an analysis of *Mac.*, whose protagonist is afflicted with a hardened heart, which cannot feel compassion; a reprobate mind, which deprives him of all sense of what actions are good; and a "disorientation of the powers of the sense," which compels him to use these powers in a desperate way. Revision of item 0962.

0962 Shenk, Robert Edwards. "The Sinner's Progress: A Study of Madness in English Renaissance Drama." Ph.D. dissertation, University of Kansas, 1976. *DAI*, 38 (1977–78), 812-A-813-A.

Maintains that Sh's tragic heroes sin from what Aristotle, in the *Nicomachean Ethics*, calls intemperance, "a mode of action in which one believes in what he is doing, and sins by choice, not from passion." Vices of characters like Hamlet and Lear cloud their reason and in addition can bring about certain forms of madness. Moral viciousness can cause "willful," short-term insanity, "passionate," permanent insanity, and "radical" insanity (in which a man is so overwhelmed by vice that he forgets some of the chief precepts of natural law altogether). Characters like Iago, Macbeth, and Angelo suffer from the third of these conditions. Revised as item 0961.

0963 Shepherd, Simon. *Amazons and Warrior Women: Varieties of Feminism in Seventeenth-Century Drama.* New York: St. Martin's P., 1981. 234 pp.

Studies two manifestations of strong women in the drama of Sh's time. The warrior woman is one who combats men physically or verbally or who opposes men with "the strength of her moral views." The Amazon is connected to the Amazons of classical antiquity and was also viewed by Sh's contemporaries as "a woman who uses her strength for non-virtuous, specifically lustful ends." Both types have further classical associations. Comments on twenty-one of Sh's works. Treats Doll Tearsheet and Mistress Quickly of *2H4* in chapter 7, "Tavern Wenches"; the Princess of France and her ladies of *LLL*, Beatrice of *Ado*, Rosalind of *AYL*, Portia of *MV*, and Katherina of *Shr.* in chapter 11, "Witty Women"; Cleopatra of *Ant.* in chapter 12, "Revenge Goes Wrong"; and Lucrece of *Luc.* and Isabella of *MM* in chapter 13, "Virgin Martyrs."

0964 Shintri, Sarojini. *Woman in Shakespeare.* (Research Publication Series 32.) Dharwad: Karnatak University, 1977. xiv + 313 pp.

Classifies Sh's female characters as daughters, lovers, wives, mothers, secondary characters, low women, and other women. Treats Cressida, "for whom love is only a trade," and Cleopatra, a coquette whose love for Antony evokes some sympathy, as lovers. Considers Virgilia and Valeria (*Cor.*), Calpurnia and Portia (*JC*), Octavia (*Ant.*), and Andromache (*Tro.*) as gentle wives. Designates Tamora (*Tit.*) as a fierce mother, Volumnia (*Cor.*) as an idealistic mother, and Virgilia (*Cor.*) as a doting mother.

0965   Shirley, Frances A. *Shakespeare's Use of Off-Stage Sounds*. Lincoln: U. of Nebraska P., 1963. xv + 258 pp.

Includes brief discussions of most works in the canon. Discusses, for example, the sound of the hautboys in *Ant*. (IV.iii), which introduces a sense of foreboding, and the trumpets and cornets that are frequently heard in *Cor*. Provides detailed examinations of three plays, one of which is *JC*. This play uses sounds for a variety of purposes: to create "atmospheres of pageantry, of disturbed nature, and of war" and to reveal character, or the way a person thinks.

0966   Shirley, Frances A. *Swearing and Perjury in Shakespeare's Plays*. London: George Allen & Unwin, 1979. xiv + 174 pp.

Surveys the Shakespearean canon. *Tit*. features oaths that set the revenge mechanism in motion. In *Tro*., a blatantly satiric play, oaths place characters in positions in which they "display divided loyalties or waver." The Greeks are more deceitful in their swearing, but both sides change course so often that their vows seem empty. *Ant*. exhibits a great variety of oaths, ranging from "the satiric to the angry." References to Isis help to differentiate the Egyptian world from the Roman one. In *Tim*., there is a series of oaths that range from those that are "sincerely meant" to those that are "patently false." Oaths never seem to carry the importance that they do in a play like *Lr*. In *Cor*., oaths become more personal; are made almost exclusively to Roman gods; and are "used to show tension, to support other elements of characterisation, and to aid in establishing a cosmological background." Notes that the romances enjoy as background for their oaths a "non-Christian setting."

0967   Shulman, Jeff I. "Ovid among the Goths: The Ovidian Comedy of Eros in Lyly and Shakespeare." Ph.D. dissertation, University of Wisconsin–Madison, 1980. *DAI*, 41 (1980–81), 4405-A-4406-A.

Argues that Ovidian materials, as adapted for the stage by Lyly and then by Sh, enabled English comedy in the 1580s and 1590s to transform its approach to the conflict between Eros and chastity. Lyly employed the figures of Ovidian myth to articulate a notion of chastity that includes sensuality and rejects self-absorption. Sh assimilated this idea of chastity but concerned himself equally with another Ovidian motif: the danger of losing one's identity by fanatic devotion to love. In certain of his romantic comedies, Sh views single myths (for example, those of Hercules in *LLL* and of Pyramus and Thisbe in *MND*) from two opposing perspectives to suggest the limitations of being either too absorbed by love or too detached from it. Part revised as item 2200.

0968   Shumaker, Wayne. "Literary Hermeticism: Some Test Cases." *Hermeticism and the Renaissance: Intellectual History and the Occult in Early Modern Europe*. Eds. Ingrid Merkel and Allen G. Debus. Washington: Folger Shakespeare Library, 1988, pp. 293–301.

Defines *Hermeticism* as an "amorphous body of notions and attitudes deriving not merely from Hermes but also from the mystical side of Plato and his Neoplatonic successors and from such other esoteric systems as the numerology of Pythagoras and the Jewish cabala." Notes the traces of this occultism in Sh's plays, most notably in *Tmp*., but also in *1H4, MV, H6Triad, Mac., MND, Per., JC, Rom.*, and *R2*.

0969   Sider, John William. "The Serious Elements of Shakespeare's Comedies." *SQ*, 24 (1973), 1–11.

Maintains that Sh's comedies do not fit the Aristotelian paradigm, according to which comedy deals exclusively with the ridiculous in human nature and "appeals primarily to the intellect." Serious elements are commonly present in Sh's comedies, and they can be used to chart his development as a playwright. In four early works (*Err., LLL, Shr.*, and *Wiv*.), serious situations are discounted because the ridiculous dominates the action; in four others (*TGV, MND, AYL*, and *TN*), romance evokes a sentimental response to the serious. In *MV, Ado, AWW*, and *MM*, the pity and fear associated by

Aristotle with tragedy are evoked but are "not carried to a satisfactory conclusion"; in a final group (*Per., Cym., WT,* and *Tmp.*), Sh manages grave matters in such a way that "pity becomes 'congratulation' and fear becomes 'delight' as the observer identifies himself with the characters' final felicity."

0970   Siegel, Aaron Howard. "The Dramatic Function of Comic Elements in Three Shakespearean Love Tragedies." Ph.D. dissertation, University of Southern California, 1965. *DA,* 26 (1965–66), 2193–2194.

Argues that in *Rom.,* the structure is Plautine, including "blocking characters and apposition of the worlds of age and youth," as well as certain character types from Roman comedy. In *Ant.,* "Sh follows his source in presenting the lovers in a partially satirical light." Comedy helps develop the theme of duality: The lovers are "both heroic and foolish, dignified and comic."

0971   Siegel, Paul N. "Shakespeare and the Neo-Chivalric Cult of Honor." *CentR,* 8 (1964), 39–70.

Maintains that Renaissance humanism used classical philosophy to base its notion of honor on moral virtue. By contrast, the neo-chivalric cult of honor, which can be found in the dueling treatises of Sh's time, was inspired by a decadent medieval preoccupation with personal glory. In several works, Sh provides complex critiques of the neo-chivalric code. *Tro.* witnesses the despair of a splendid civilization fatally committed to the code. In *Cor.,* the protagonist is impelled to seek vengeance against his own country by a concept of chivalric honor. Alcibiades, in *Tim.,* is moved by his banishment to attack Athens, but, transformed at the end by humanistic virtue, he becomes capable of regenerating his city. Revised as part of item 0972.

0972   Siegel, Paul N. *Shakespeare in His Time and Ours.* Notre Dame, Indiana: U. of Notre Dame P., 1968. ix + 260 pp.

Claims that to be true to Sh, we must respond to him as an Elizabethan; in particular, we need to see his tragedies as expressions of "a Christian outlook on life." A chapter on "The Chief Controversy in Shakespearean Criticism Today" defends the identification of Timon as a Christ figure against antitheologizing critics. Chapter 5, "Shakespeare and the Neo-Chivalric Cult of Honor," is a revision of item 0971.

0973   Siegel, Paul N. *Shakespeare's English and Roman History Plays: A Marxist Approach.* Rutherford New Jersey: Farleigh Dickinson U. P., 1986. 168 pp.

Chapter 8, "Shakespeare's View of Roman History," sketches the idea of Rome that Sh assimilated from Roman historians like Tacitus, Livy, Appian, and Plutarch, and from their Christian successors like St. Augustine and Sir Thomas Elyot. All of these writers established "a tradition of ambivalence" regarding republic, empire, and the key event (the assassination of Julius Caesar) in the transition from the former to the latter. Designates *Cor., JC, Ant., Cym.,* and *Tit.* as Roman plays and treats them in the order given, "the order of the historical events they depict." There are a number of important themes in these plays: Providence can be seen (not always heavily emphasized) working through the deeds of men; ingratitude is frequent and is always the cause of disaster; from the earliest play (in historical time) to the latest, we encounter degeneration in the state of Roman society. Sh is historically accurate in depicting the spirit of Rome in each of the phases portrayed in the five plays, except that he portrays the mobs as lower-class Englishmen of his own time. The story of Rome is tragic, and the protagonists of the Roman plays participate in the tragic grandeur of the city.

0973a   Siemon, James R. *Shakespearean Iconoclasm.* Berkeley: U. of California P., 1985. xii + 307 pp.

Explains, in the first two chapters, the opposition that developed in the Renaissance, and especially in Elizabethan England, between belief in the medieval and Neoplatonic power of images and figurative language to reveal truth and the growing awareness that such symbolic and allegorical thinking fails to account for the complexities of reality. Argues that this tension between the unified pattern or meaning imposed by iconic imagining and "factual particulars" is more or less present throughout the Sh canon. Chapter 3 includes a consideration of *Luc.*, which suggests, especially in its treatment of Tarquin and Lucrece, that the poet is dallying with various kinds of iconoclasm. Chapter 4 sets Sir Philip Sidney's theory of the importance of patterning in literature in contrast to the idea that underlies Sh's achievement in *JC*. Notes that Sh's source for this play, Plutarch's *Lives*, evades the Sidneian requirement for unity by foregrounding "gaps and discrepancies, discord and disagreement" and by refusing to allow a fixed meaning for person, event, or thing. Sh's play presents a long series of attempts by characters to establish mythic meaning through imagery, but there are "strong counter thrusts" to this tendency "that work to disenchant, to alienate rather than to envelop us in satisfying participation." Revision of item 0974.

0974   Siemon, James Ralph. "Shakespearean Iconoclasm." Ph.D. dissertation, State University of New York at Buffalo, 1977. *DAI*, 38 (1977–78), 5502-A.

Detects in Sh's plays a tension between "a resistance to and an attraction to formal and thematic closure." This tension is felt in an uneasy attitude toward the image, as used by characters in metaphors that reduce the complexities of their situations and in emblematic staging that threatens to foreclose the ambiguities of the plays themselves. Among works that reflect these problems are *Luc.* and *JC*. Revised as item 0973a.

0974a   Sierz, Krystyna. "Some Medieval Concepts in Shakespeare's Plays." *SAP*, 17 (1984), 233–49.

Includes discussion of Aaron (*Tit.*) as bearing some of the characteristics of the Vice figure of the medieval morality plays. Suggests that certain incidents in *Cor.* may be derived from the mystery plays (the tribunes behave much as Christ's opponents do in tormenting and judging him, and the episode in act IV that features the meeting of a Roman and a Volsce is reminiscent of the meeting of Christ with two travellers on the road to Emmaus).

0975   Silber, Patricia. "The Unnatural Woman and the Disordered State in Shakespeare's Histories." *Proceedings of the PMR Conference*, 2 (1977), 87–96.

Analyzes Sh's two tetralogies about English history to show that in these plays women reflect "the fortunes of the realm and its ruler." Furthermore, women who behave unnaturally by usurping men's roles are "a certain indication of grave turmoil." In the first tetralogy, Joan and Margaret are examples of usurping women, whose characters are defined in part by comparisons with classical figures like Helen.

0976   Silver, Larry. "Step-Sister of the Muses: Painting as Liberal Art and Sister Art." *Articulate Images: The Sister Arts from Hogarth to Tennyson*. Ed. Richard Wendorf. Minneapolis: U. of Minnesota P., 1983, pp. 36–69.

Describes the struggle of Renaissance defenders of painting to have their art accepted as liberal and learned. Part of the process of legitimizing painting involved "the literal recreation of ancient works of art known only through literary description: *ekphrasis*." Notes that when Elizabethan authors began to describe works of art, they seem most frequently to have chosen "noble art works with suitable themes drawn from antiquity." Suggests that Sh, especially in *Luc.*, attempts to set up description as a rival to painting and to decide the *paragone*, or competition between painting and poetry, in favor of the latter. Cites the *paragone* debate in mentioning *Tim.* and *WT*; in the latter, things are settled so as to highlight the poet's "own creative manipulations."

0977 Simmons, J. L. "*Antony and Cleopatra* and *Coriolanus*, Shakespeare's Heroic Tragedies: A Jacobean Adjustment." *ShS*, 26 (1973), 95–101.

Links *Ant.* and *Cor.* to an awareness on Sh's part of a new kind of audience. Aware of a growing fragmentation within the Jacobean popular audience, an audience that could no longer be expected to respond corporately to visions of the heroic, Sh experimented with presenting, in *Ant.* and *Cor.*, "a theatrical relationship between aristocratic actors and popular audience." The audience of citizens on stage extends into the audience of citizens in the theater (Cleopatra imagines with loathing what it would be like to have her nobility dramatized for such an audience). These heroic tragedies treat "aristocratic appeals that are definitively and insistently exclusive." There are thus two images of Rome: "one idealistic and heroic, the other realistic and antiheroic." Revised section of item 0981. Revised as parts of chapters 2 and 4 of item 0980.

0978 Simmons, J. L. "Shakespeare and the Antique Romans." *Rome in the Renaissance: The City and the Myth.* Ed. Paul A. Ramsay. (Medieval and Renaissance Texts and Studies 18.) Binghamton, New York: Medieval and Renaissance Texts and Studies, 1982, pp. 77–92.

Discusses a number of Sh's tragedies with regard to their assimilation and transcendence of Senecan attitudes, especially in the constitution of the protagonist. According to the Stoic philosophy that informs Seneca's tragedies, a person who becomes passion's slave loses all awareness of the significance of what he or she is doing in its context and becomes the plaything of destiny. This is essentially the fate of the protagonist in *Tit.*, who is unable to assert his humanity in the face of suffering. Attempts to reconcile Stoicism and Christianity made new ways of experimenting with the tragic awareness of characters available to Sh. In *Rom.*, the plot moves toward "a providential clarification that good has come out of evil," and Romeo has occasional glimpses of providence, but in the end he falls back into fatalism. Brutus and Cassius, in *JC*, come to an awareness that their deaths occur as retribution for Caesar's murder, but they are blind to the providential pattern according to which Rome, the temporal city, is to be superseded by the Eternal City; both of them end their lives in confusion, failing to recognize their roles in this pattern. Hamlet is the first of Sh's tragic heroes to "rise above the plot and see that it, like providence divine, is both just and justifiable." Makes brief comments about *Cor., Lr., Mac.,* and *Ant.*

0979 Simmons, J. L. "Shakespearean Rhetoric and Realism." *GaR*, 24 (1970), 453–71.

Maintains that from the beginning of his career, Sh was struggling with "the limitations of language" and searching for "a reality of representation beyond artifice." Discusses, among other plays, *Tit.* (in which language fails to represent the horrors of tragedy) and *JC* (in which the rhetoric of Caesar shows him in the ambivalent position of a man playing a part).

0980 Simmons, J. L. *Shakespeare's Pagan World: The Roman Tragedies.* Charlottesville: U. P. of Virginia, 1973. ix + 202 pp.

The introduction, "Shakespeare's Pagan World," offers a rationale for treating "the Roman Tragedies" (*Cor., JC,* and *Ant.*) as a group. Cites the "Epistle Dedicatory" to North's translation of Plutarch's *Lives* to show that the Elizabethans were familiar with the Augustinian commonplace about Rome as the Earthly City. Sh makes use of this idea when he portrays Rome as a pagan world in which the idealism of heroes is tragically doomed by the lack of Christian revelation. The Roman heroes deserve a great deal of admiration and sympathy as they struggle to realize their "impossible absolute." In their quest for perfection, they are very much creatures of Rome, but paradoxically their absolutism brings them into conflict with Rome, which then must reject and destroy them. These heroes have little insight into their own tragedies. Chapter 2, "*Coriolanus*: The Graces of the Gods," discerns in this late play the clearest delineation of the pattern underlying the tragedy of all three Roman plays. The protagonist's moral vision can be identified with that of Rome: His single-minded pursuit of honor allows Sh to subject the supreme virtue of pagan Rome to ironic evaluation. Coriolanus's absolute integrity forces him into a violation of that integrity. This chapter contains revised material from item 0977. Chapter 3, "*Julius Caesar*: Our Roman Actors," is a revision of item 2101; chapter 4, "*Antony and Cleopatra*: New Heaven, New Earth," is a revision of item 1459 and contains revised material from item 0977; and chapter 5, "Conclusion," reinforces the evidence of Sh's preoccupation with the Christian historiography that made possible his view of Rome by referring to *Cym.* (a late romance) and *Tit.* (an early tragedy). The book as a whole is a revision of item 0981. See also item 0041.

0981 Simmons, Joseph Larry. "The Moral Environment in Shakespeare's Roman Plays." Ph.D dissertation, University of Virginia, 1967. *DA*, 28 (1967–68), 3157-A.

Proposes to treat *JC*, *Ant.*, and *Cor.* as sharing a "moral environment" that distinguishes them from Sh's major tragedies and his English history plays. In these Roman plays, the world is without the absolutes of good and evil that inform the tragedies. The Roman heroes refuse to accept the limitations of their secular context and attempt to impose an ideal vision that cannot be realized. From this conflict arises their tragedy. In *JC*, Brutus attempts to create the conditions for a perfect commonwealth, but he turns out to be imbued with "the spirit he wishes to destroy." In *Ant.*, there are intimations of love's Neoplatonic transcendence, but the lovers cannot free themselves from the trammels of their earthly existence. Reason and honor, denied Christian relevance, are expended entirely on the political world. Cleopatra is imaginatively successful in uniting the worlds of love and honor, but in the world of action the lovers "can end only in tragic defeat." Coriolanus believes that his idea of an eternal patrician Rome is the reality. Because of the inhuman requirements (destruction and death) of official Rome, the people's opposition to Coriolanus has some appeal. However, political innovation is "at best a tragic necessity": Compromise will ultimately be destructive. Parts revised as items 0977, 1459, and 2101; the whole revised as item 0980.

0982 Simonds, Peggy Muñoz. "'Killing care and grief of heart': Orpheus and Shakespeare." *RenP*, 1990 (1991), 79–90.

Suggests that the genre of Renaissance tragicomedy "may provide valuable clues to the meaning" of Sh's references to Orpheus. Notes that the harmonist theory of the period, derived from Plato through Boethius and Ficino, taught that to achieve concord within themselves, men must unite reason and the body, tune rational and corporal powers to each other. This tempering was to be accomplished by means of art, and the preeminent creative artist of classical antiquity was Orpheus, who could reshape "the elements of inner and outer nature into a temperate and harmonious unity" and exemplified both in his art and his career the regeneration after loss that lies at the heart of the tragicomic aesthetic. Discovers a number of Orphic allusions in *Cym.*, *Per.*, *WT*, and *Tmp.*; takes note of the musical imagery in these works; and concludes that Orpheus "haunts the final plays primarily to bring us consolation through art for all our losses."

0983 Singh, Jyotsna. "The Artist and His Inheritance: A Metadramatic Study of Shakespeare's *Troilus and Cressida* and *Antony and Cleopatra*." Ph.D. dissertation, Syracuse University, 1986. *DAI*, 48 (1987–88), 1212-A.

Examines Sh's "response to the tension within his culture between an impulse toward autonomy in any creative act and an awareness of existing cultural and social codes." In both *Tro.* and *Ant.*, "the characters attempt to stage themselves by emulating or rebelling against cultural models." *Tro.* shows the Trojans and Greeks striving unsuccessfully to renew their Homeric roles, just as the play itself struggles "to re-create an epic era." In *Ant.*, however, the artist (Cleopatra) appears in a positive role to transform "received models into distinctive self-representations." In a similar way, the play itself draws together a variety of traditions and blends them "into a unique form." *Tro.* "can only claim its genre through negation," but *Ant.* "moves beyond the conventional definitions of tragedy to embrace the expansiveness of the epic." Part revised as item 1460.

0983a Sircar, Bibhuti Bhusan. *An Appreciation of William Shakespeare: Ten Plays with Critical Estimates.* Calcutta: Sircar and South Calcutta P., 1975. iv + 777 + iii pp.

Chapter 6, on *JC*, provides a summary of the action, detailed commentary, and assessments of the major characters. Caesar is vainglorious and autocratic; Brutus has "a large heart and a noble mind"; Cassius is shrewd, selfish, and envious; and Antony is a calculating politician whose Machiavellian tactics can be forgiven because he restores order. Chapter 11, on *Ant.*, discusses sexual morality at length and concludes that Antony is a "mad enthusiast" in love, who abandons the dictates of reason, conscience, and propriety for a life of dissipation. Chapter 12, on *Tim.*, views the protagonist as a paradoxical character, idealistic but foolish, given to acts of apparent humanitarianism that actually reflect "the habitual prodigality of the aristocracy." Holds up Flavius as truly admirable.

0984 Sisson, C. J. *Shakespeare's Tragic Justice.* London: Methuen, 1962. vi + 106 pp.

Introduces discussions of justice in *Mac.*, *Oth.*, *Ham.*, and *Lr.* by rejecting the Aristotelian notion of tragic flaw, as elaborated by Bradley. Justice in Sh's major tragedies has little to do with such a flaw.

0985 Skemp, J. B. "Shakespeare and Greek Tragedy." *DUJ*, 56, N. S. 25 (1963–64), 89–90.

Chides classical scholars for rejecting the tendency to find universal meaning in Greek tragedy. Argues that "it would be wrong to abandon the search for real common ground between Sh in his histories and tragedies and the masters of Attic Tragedy."

0985a Skiffington, Lloyd A. *The History of the English Soliloquy: Aeschylus to Shakespeare.* Lanham, Maryland: U. P. of America, 1985. xi + 139 pp.

Chapter 1 provides a brief account of the soliloquy in Greek and Roman drama. Chapters 2 and 3 trace the rebirth of the soliloquy in the mystery and morality drama of the Middle Ages. Chapter 4 highlights three important kinds of content in Shakespearean soliloquies: plot exposition, homily, and character revelation. An example of the latter sort of soliloquy is that of Enobarbus, lamenting his defection from Antony (*Ant.*, IV.v). Chapter 5 focuses on two types of lesser-known Shakespearean soliloquies: the passion soliloquy and the lament. Chapter 6 discusses the evolution of the Shakespearean soliloquy. Traces a general development from primitiveness (characterized by "medieval types of set speech" and Senecan posturings and rhetoric) to sophistication (characterized by freedom from rhetorical and rhythmic rigidity and approximation of the features of natural speech). Includes analyses of Gloucester's "murderous Machiavel" speech, with its pervasive classical allusions (*3H6*, III.ii.124–195); Senecan speeches by Aaron (*Tit.*, I.i.1–24) and Henry VI (*3H6*, II.v.1–54); and three sophisticated soliloquies of Brutus at the beginning of act III in *JC*.

0986 Slater, Eliot. "Word Links between *Timon of Athens* and *King Lear.*" *N&Q*, 25 (1978), 147–48.

Reports the results of a statistical analysis linking *Tim.* to other plays by means of rare words. Concludes that *Tim.* is closely related to *Lr.* and that the two plays were written relatively late in Sh's career.

0986a Smidt, Kristian. *Unconformities in Shakespeare's Tragedies.* New York: St. Martin's P., 1990. xiv + 265 pp.

Analyzes Sh's plays by attending to their unconformities: "the kind of breaks in continuity that are occasionally found in the development of plot, or character, or in other elements of a play." Chapter 1, on *Tit.*, is a revision of item 2775a. Chapter 4, on *JC*, points to signs of "strong compression and rearrangement" in the storm scene (I.iii) and the orchard scene (II.i); in the part of the play occupied by these two scenes, it is likely that some significant matter "has been deleted or lost." Argues that Sh revised his original conception to create a diptych, so that the second part, beginning in III.ii, mirrors and reverses "the action in which Caesar is defeated by the conspirators." Discusses irregularities like absences among the conspirators and the double report of Portia's death (IV.iii) in connection with this hypothesis. Chapter 6, on *Tro.*, notes that the play's ironic procedure, which results in an almost continuous series of anticlimaxes, can help to explain many apparent unconformities. The epilogue of Pandarus, however, is "a gross irrelevance to the play as we have it." Chapter 10, on *Ant.*, views the play as tightly constructed with some ambivalence regarding Antony's motives for returning to Egypt and for committing suicide. Mentions some other irregularities but maintains that most of the problems involved in interpreting the protagonists can be explained by Sh's interest in observing "the unconformities of passionate minds." Chapter 11, on *Cor.*, acknowledges the great consistency of this play, which portrays the single tragedy of a man so devoted to pride that he fails to recognize the humanizing force of policy . Unconformity can be seen chiefly in I.iii, which creates impressions of Volumnia and Valeria that "have to be severely modified by their later appearances." Chapter 12, on *Tim.*, holds that this work is not fully realized. Points to a number of "major lacunae, interruptions and redundancies." Examples include insufficient development of Alcibiades, lack of explanation of Timon's great services to the state, and a number irregularities in the long interview between Timon and Apemantus in the woods (IV.iii).

0986b Smith, A. J. *Literary Love: The Role of Passion in English Poems and Plays of the Seventeenth Century.* London: Edward Arnold, 1983. viii + 184 pp.

Considers several literary explorations of sexual love in the 17th c. Notes in these works a longing for stability, for spiritual repose, that is set against a powerful awareness of the insufficiency of the sensible world to provide such permanent satisfaction. In this context, Sh dramatizes the sense of being imprisoned in time; he views love as "a dynamic process." Includes chapters on *Tro.* ("Time's Fools") and on *Ant.* ("Crowning the Present"). In the former play, we have an explicit "dramatic metaphor for the contrarieties of our being," and in the latter we witness two lovers whose intense apprehension of their mortality impels them to create a vision of human sublimity.

0986c Smith, Bruce R. Ancient Scripts and Modern Experience on the English Stage, *1500–1700.* Princeton: Princeton U. P., 1988. xii + 289 pp.

Describes three structures—"critical, spatial, and social"—that contextualized for Renaissance Englishmen the productions, including adaptations, of classical plays. Argues that though classical drama had increasingly significant influence on the drama of the Renaissance, classical plays themselves were transformed by contact with Renaissance culture. Thus *Err.*, an adaptation of Plautus's *Menaechmi*, bears the mark of its age in being more romantic than its source, though still retaining a satiric edge. In *Tit.*, Sh takes classical materials and aligns them with the philosophical viewpoint of Seneca, which provides the idea of an "inimical universe." In this, the playwright is truer to Seneca's thought than most academic adapters of his work, who set tragic characters in "the providential universe of medieval morality plays." Sh refuses to reduce man's relationship to the universe to a simple formula.

0987   Smith, Bruce R. *Homosexual Desire in Shakespeare's England: A Cultural Poetics.* Chicago: U. of Chicago P., 1991. xii + 329 pp.

Isolates six myths through which to investigate homosexual desire in the Renaissance. Notes that through such myths classical literature provided Renaissance writers with a variety of ways to articulate homosexual desire. Associates each of the myths with a particular classical text and then devotes a chapter to reading certain Renaissance texts in light of that myth.

Chapter 2, "Combatants and Comrades," begins by citing the story of Pirithous and Theseus from Plutarch's *Lives*, which illustrates the tendency of human males to compete aggressively against other males and yet to bond closely with them. In *Cor.*, the protagonist's relationship with his rival–ally Aufidius is expressed in sexual imagery that suggests a reenactment of the Pirithous–Theseus story. In *Tro.*, Achilles expresses "a woman's longing" (III.iii.237) to behold Hector, and his slaughter of Hector is "an act of sexual consummation, a homosexual gang rape."

Chapter 4, "The Shipwrecked Youth," uses *Clitophon and Leucippe*, a romance of the 3rd c. A.D. by Achilles Tatius, to discuss the love of men for adolescent boys. Includes an analysis of the wooing by Orlando of Rosalind in *MND*, which would have appeared on stage as the sexual pursuit of a boy (the actor playing Rosalind being a boy) by an older man.

Chapter 6, "Master and Minion," takes as starting point Ovid's account in book 10 of the *Metamorphoses* of the ravishing by gods, especially Jupiter, of "prettie boyes," especially Ganymede. Treats the relationship between Achilles and Patroclus in *Tro.* and Oberon's desire for the changeling boy in *MND*.

Chapter 7, "The Secret Sharer," begins with a selection from Horace's *Odes* and distinguishes these poems from any other love lyrics Renaissance readers might have encountered: (1) Horace writes as a jaded man of the world, one who has experienced all of Venus's delights; (2) he deals with sexual desire between males quite matter-of-factly; (3) he expresses great intensity of desire and intimacy. Maintains that all of these qualities are shared by *Son*.: Like Horace's poems, Sh's are focused "on what love is like after sexual consummation, not before; many of them ... are addressed, not to a woman, but to another man; and they are nondramatic, subjective, private."

0988   Smith, Bruce R. "Pageants into Play: Shakespeare's Three Perspectives on Idea and Image." *Pageantry in the Shakespearean Theater*. Ed. David M. Bergeron. Athens: U. of Georgia P., 1985, pp. 220–46.

Argues that Sh had three ways of handling the relationship between idea and image: (1) In the early plays, he inserted two-dimensional pageants in the middle of plays with fully-rounded characters; (2) in the middle plays, he incorporated "pageant moments" in "the human actors' plane of reference"; (3) in the late plays (the tragicomedies), he once again separated pageant elements from the human fable but gave them more complex functions than they had in the early plays. Cites *Ant.* and *Cor.* as examples of middle plays. Analyzes IV.iv of *Ant.* to show how smoothly Sh has integrated the pageants of the disarming of Mars by Eros and Venus and of Hercules at the Crossroads into the action. In *Cor.*, the protagonist's isolated heroism at Corioli (I.iv) shows that Sh is adapting an emblem that exhibits the excellencies of a military commander, though in this case Coriolanus's *virtus* is ironically seen as the very thing that causes his downfall. In both instances cited here, Sh is not only blending pageant moments with "the verisimilitude of the dramatic illusion"; he is also transforming the simplistic lessons of pageantry into something like the complexities of human experience. In the tragicomedies, the pageants, often involving classical deities, demand frequent and sometimes dizzying shifts of focus. All of these plays are imbued with a faith in the power of their pageants "not just to reflect human reality but to transform it."

0989   Smith, Bruce R. "Parolles's Recitations: Oral and Literate Structures in Shakespeare's Plays." *RenP*, 1989 (1990), 75–88.

Argues for the influence of oral tradition on the structure of Sh's plays. Notes that the literate idea of dramatic structure, absorbed by the Renaissance from Aristotle, Horace, and Donatus, is linear, while oral structure is spatial, with emphasis on the middle. Analyzes *Err.*, *1H4*, and *Cym.* to show that Sh gives us the story "both ways, as a spatial retreat toward the center and as a linear progression to the end." Notes that *Err.* is organized so that the central scene focuses on married love, "Sh's distinctively Renaissance addition to Plautus's bawdy Roman play."

0990   Smith, Bruce R. "Sermons in Stones: Shakespeare and Renaissance Sculpture." *ShakS*, 17 (1985), 1–23.

Attempts to discover what Sh's audience knew about statues in order to understand how they would have responded to sculptural references in the plays. Notes that, although there were "no classical statues to be seen in Sh's England," there were two collections of engravings of "ancient marbles and bronzes" published in the 16th c., which had made such works familiar. Renaissance Englishmen were likely to view statues from three vantage points. In the first place, they were prompted by Pliny and other classical writers to admire the lifelikeness of sculpture. A second approach to sculpture regarded a statue as embodying a moral or philosophical idea. Third, statues could be viewed as objects of devotion. Several plays contain important sculptural allusions or themes. Especially important are Pompey's statue, near which Caesar dies in *JC*; Cleopatra's monument, where she and Antony die in *Ant.*; and Hermione's statue, which comes to life in *WT*. In the tragedies, Sh presents "images of life transformed into marble constancy of art," while in the late romances he offers a variety of scenes in which "art is transformed into life." Hermione's revivification at the end of *WT* is the culmination of all statue references and statue scenes in Sh's earlier works: All three Renaissance perspectives on statues converge in this episode.

0991   Smith, Bruce R. "Sir Amorous Knight and the Indecorous Romans; or, Plautus and Terence Play Court in the Renaissance." *RenD*, N. S. 6 (1973), 3–27.

Uses *Err.* as one illustration of how Renaissance authors adapted Roman comedy. Sh heightened the love interest of his Plautine original, provided a more didactic plot, and gave his audience greater spectacle.

0992   Smith, Bruce R. "Toward the Rediscovery of Tragedy: Productions of Seneca's Plays on the English Renaissance Stage." *RenD*, N. S. 9 (1978), 3–37.

Attempts to demonstrate that three Senecan plays produced in England during the 16th c. show adjustments that were made to accommodate classical tragedy to contemporary audiences. First, the physical setting for performance became a hall, rather than the huge theater of ancient Rome. Second, the intimacy between 16th-c. actors and spectators prompted each adaptor to add a prologue to his Senecan text to introduce it. Finally, additions to the texts and explanations in the prologues reshaped them to provide the instruction that an audience nurtured on morality plays expected. The response evoked was a simple one: condemnation or approval of the protagonist.

0993   Smith, Charles G. *Shakespeare's Proverb Lore: His Use of the 'Sententiae' of Leonard Culman and Publius Syrus.* Cambridge: Harvard U. P., 1963. viii + 181 pp.

Presents 346 Latin proverbs—some from the *Sententiae Pueriles* of Leonard Culman (1497–1562), some from the *Sententiae* of Publius Syrus (1st c. B.C.), and some found in both collections—that have significant parallels in Sh's works. Cites each proverb in English, followed by its Shakespearean use(s) and then its Latin form. Cites other Latin authors who use the proverbs if these authors are likely to have been known to Sh. Suggests, on the basis of these parallels, that Sh most probably had "a comprehensive knowledge of classical proverbs."

0994   Smith, Hal H. "Some Principles of Elizabethan Stage Costume." *JWCI*, 25 (1962), 240–57.

Maintains that some Elizabethan plays, especially those of classical theme and setting, were costumed to re-create a distant historical setting. Emblematic dress, as seen in the Peacham drawing of *Tit.*, in which Aaron appears as a herald of death, was also used. Sh has Rumor (*2H4*) and Time (*WT*) "refer specifically to the emblematic properties they wear or carry." Records indicate that there was considerable concern for classical authenticity in costumes and properties like wigs and beards. A 1598 engraving by Titian shows "a simplified version of the Renaissance conception of classical costume": "a soldier dressed in a breastplate over a short, kilt-like garment with short sleeves, and with sandals on his feet." In the costumes for *Tro.*, the distinction between Trojan and Greek was probably indicated by "draping of cloaks and decoration of helmets." In addition, the luxuries of Priam's court would be reflected in the elaboration of costume, especially for civilian characters like Pandarus, which would be contrasted with the sober armor of the Greeks.

0995   Smith, Hallett. "Bare Ruined Choirs: Shakespearean Variations on the Theme of Old Age." *HLQ*, 39 (1976), 233–49.

Maintains that Sh's sonnets 62 through 74, concerned with metamorphosis "as one moves from one age to another," are based on the speech assigned to Pythagoras in book 15 of Ovid's *Metamorphoses*. This series of sonnets constitutes Sh's *De Senectute* and his mutability cantos. Cites Satire 10 of Juvenal (bitter) and Cicero's *De Senectute* (consolatory) as works that influenced Renaissance thinking on old age and that were probably known to Sh. Old Capulet in *Rom.* is the closest approximation in Sh to the *senex iratus* of Roman comedy. Includes discussion of old age in *MM*, *AYL*, *Err.*, *Ado*, and *Lr.* Examines commentaries on old age by Sh's contemporaries.

0996   Smith, Hallett. "The Nondramatic Poems." *Shakespeare: Aspects of Influence*. Ed. G. B. Evans. (Harvard English Studies 7.) Cambridge: Harvard U. P., 1976, pp. 43–54.

Begins by calling attention to the similarity of Titania's wooing of a reluctant mortal in *MND* to Venus's treatment of Adonis in *Ven.* and to references in *Mac.* and *Cym.* to Tarquin's performance of his evil deeds under cover of night. Comments that the most powerful influence of Sh's nondramatic poems "is upon Shakespeare himself."

0997   Smith, Hallett. *Shakespeare's Romances: A Study in Some Ways of the Imagination.* San Marino, California: Huntington Library, 1972. xiii + 244 pp.

Focuses on the ways Sh's imagination developed as he moved from the comedies and tragedies to the late romances (*Per., Cym., WT, Tmp.*). Considers the playwright's treatment of sources as a key element in this development.

Chapter 1, "The Romance Tradition as It Influenced Shakespeare," locates the ultimate sources of the romances (and romance elements in earlier plays) in the Greek romances of the 3rd c.: *Apollonius of Tyre*, Heliodorus's *Aethiopica*, Achilles Tatius's *Clitophon and Leucippe*, and Longus's *Daphnis and Chloe*. All of these works were translated into English during the last half of the 16th c. and were thus available to Sh. He also knew romance materials from Elizabethan fiction by Thomas Lodge, Robert Greene, Sir Philip Sidney, and others, and from popular tradition. He may also have known three romantic plays—*Common Conditions, Clyomon and Clamydes*, and *The Rare Triumphs of Love and Fortune*—that survive from the period just before he began to write.

Chapter 2, "Innocence and the Pastoral World," acknowledges the origin of the idea of pastoral innocence in Virgil; charts its development in Longus, Boccaccio, and Sidney; and discusses its exploration in the four romances.

Chapter 3, "From Comedy to Romance," compares Sh's use of the Apollonius of Tyre story in *Err.* with his use of the same story in *Per.* Notes some romance motifs (the conflict of age and youth, for example) that appear in the problem comedies (*Ado, MM,* and *AWW*) and again in the late romances.

Chapter 4, "From Tragedy to Romance," uses as its central exhibit the borrowing by Sh of the story of the Paphlagonian king from Sidney, who borrowed it in part from Heliodorus. The influence of romance on *Lr.* goes beyond plot, however: It extends to matters of "image, thought, and total meaning." *Lr.*'s concern with patience appears again in *Per.* and *Cym.*

Chapter 5 analyzes Sh's treatment of his source, Lodge's *Rosalynde*, in *AYL*, and chapter 6 analyzes his treatment of his source, Lodge's *Pandosto*, in *WT*. In *WT*, Sh reduced and naturalized Lodge's pastoral elements. He also added a happy ending, a spectacular scene at the conclusion, a dream vision, a shipwreck, and an attack by a wild beast—thus making the play more like a Greek romance than its source.

Chapter 7 compares *MND* and *Tmp.*, noting among other things their treatments

General Works 277

of classical myth. In *MND*, the fairy world is combined with myth. In *Tmp.*, this vision is enlarged: Classical figures (Iris, Ceres, and Juno) appear, but they are spirits who perform at Prospero's command.

0998 Smith, Jonathan Clark. "Destiny Reversed: A Study of Biblical and Classical Allusion Patterns in Shakespeare's *Henry VI*." Ph.D. dissertation, Indiana University, 1974. *DAI*, 35 (1974–75), 2242-A-2243-A.

Maintains that classical and biblical allusions in the H6Triad evoke the myth of Britain's "divine destiny" and act to discover the subversion of that myth in the age of Henry VI. The opening chapter includes a survey of Christian attitudes toward pagan mythology and emphasizes St. Augustine's influential (and ambivalent) view. Chapter 3 concentrates on allusions to Icarus, Phaethon, and the Phoenix, which throughout the three plays point to destructive individualism. The final chapter deals with allusions to Troy and Rome. Britain was usually seen as a third Troy, with Rome as a mediating link, and calamities such as Caesar's assassination and the civil wars were read as analogues for the fall of Troy. This network of references enables Sh to present English history up to Richard III as analogous to the fall of Troy.

0999 Smith, Marion. *Casque to Cushion: A Study of "Othello" and "Coriolanus."* Ottawa: Canadian Federation for the Humanities, 1979. ix + 176 pp.

Treats *Oth.* and *Cor.* as plays in which the protagonist falls because he accords "undue reverence" to "the military ethic." Notes that the concept of the noble military hero, as inherited by the Renaissance, is "touched with ambiguity" and that Sh's portrayal of such a figure in these two plays needs to be considered in terms of two traditions, that of the *miles gloriosus* and that of Aristotle's magnanimous man.

The first section, on *Oth.*, includes a consideration of Desdemona in the role of an "eclectic trinity," embodying in her person the Cyprian Aphrodite (the principle of bounty and fertility), "the higher love of the Renaissance Neoplatonists, and the Blessed Virgin Mary." Cites Ovid, Lucretius, and Apuleius to argue that there are also parallels between the story of Venus and Mars and the relationship of Desdemona and Othello.

The second section, on *Cor.*, begins with a detailed survey of recent criticism of the play. Proceeds with five chapters, each treating one act, that examine Sh's handling of his source, Plutarch's *Lives,* to argue that Coriolanus is Aristotle's magnanimous man brought down by a combination of excesses associated with his own virtues. Especially important is the hero's incapacity to transfer his military prowess to peacetime pursuits. Aristotle's *Politics* and *Ethics* make clear that Coriolanus's view of the polity and of his place in it are seriously flawed. Modifications of Plutarch nearly all have the effect of polarizing opposition between Coriolanus and others and thus of increasing his isolation. Three final chapters treat the play's harsh language (its epithets and its images of disease, animals, and blood); the destructive images connected with food and nourishment; and the notions of honor and honesty (the latter means, for Coriolanus, truth to himself, which comes to mean a denial of all outside loyalties, an impossible goal).

1000 Smith, Marion Bodwell. *Dualities in Shakespeare.* Toronto: U of Toronto P., 1966. vii + 252 pp.

Proposes to characterize and place in its context the "double vision" of Sh: "a lively awareness of contradictions accompanied by a particularly keen sensitivity to interdependent relationships." Chapter 1, "The Humanist Synthesis," points out the classical elements included in the Renaissance humanist attempt to harmonize differences. Notes humanist use of the Neoplatonist conceptions of celestial harmony and of the World Soul as well as of Aristotelian pragmatism and notions of virtue. Describes the extension and adaptation of traditional emblems of unity to absorb the increasing sense of diversity raised by the new philosophy at the end of the 16th c. Chapter 2, "Two Distincts, Division None: The Nature of Shakespeare's Dualities," surveys Sh's treatment of the themes through which dualities are expressed.

Comments, for example, on the doubleness in *Err.* and the divided nature of the hero in *JC*, *Ant.*, *Tro.*, *Tim.*, and *Cor.* Chapter 3, "The Poetry of Ambivalence," argues that Sh adapts Platonic concepts to achieve an uneasy truce between flesh and spirit in *Son.* Chapter 4 focuses on how imagery derived from the four elements is the key to Sh's realization of unity in diversity in *Rom.* Chapter 5 covers *TN.*

Chapter 6, on *MM*, explains the Aristotelian and Platonic elements that aid Sh in exploring "the laws of ethical polity" that are at the center of this play. Of the Aristotelian virtues, justice and temperance are emphasized, though prudence and fortitude are also treated. Aristotle's categories also influence the play's characterization. The reconciliation of opposites in the play is indebted to Platonism. Notes that Sh could have absorbed the thought of these authors from a variety of intermediary sources. Finds it likely that he would have known Boethius's *Consolation of Philosophy* and Cicero's *De Officiis*. Chapter 7 explicates the inverted world of *Mac.*

Chapter 8 treats *Ant.* as a play that deals with "the impossibility of maintaining the wholeness of life in the circumstances in which its characters are placed," torn as they are "between passion and public duty." The play's oppositions are incapable of being regarded as moral absolutes, which makes it irrevocably ambivalent. Maintains that there are three tragic figures—Antony, Cleopatra, and Caeser—who develop in parallel patterns, though not at the same time. The catastrophe involves not only these three but also many of the minor characters "in despicable or lamentable victory, however glorious, or in noble or magnanimous defeat, however ignominious." Antony possesses the qualities of greatness, but early in the play we see him as unbalanced, sometimes dominated by one part of himself, sometimes by another. Cleopatra is infinitely various through the early scenes, but her passion is projected in mainly negative terms. Caesar's virtues and vices complement Antony's; it is likely that, in *De Officiis*, Cicero modeled his contrasting sketches of two men unfit for public office on these two triumvirs, and Sh probably followed Cicero's lead. *Ant.* is unusual among Sh's tragedies in its double treatment of all of the major characters. Sh compensated for the lack of external dramatic conflict by "emphasizing all the other oppositions in theme, character, and situation, and, wherever possible, by universalizing them." Given the requirement that act V be devoted to Cleopatra and the historical importance of Caesar in the eyes of Sh's contemporaries, act IV places great emphasis on the internal struggle of Antony; he must not be allowed to lose the audience's "internal core of sympathy." Observes that several of the names Sh assigns to minor characters (Enobarbus, Philo, Demetrius, Dolabella) extend and support the various kinds of irony that pervade the play. Classical allusions (Mars, Venus, Hercules, Eros) have important functions, as do the ambivalent symbols of serpent and fig. Finally, Sh may have expressed in Cleopatra "his mixed feelings" about Queen Elizabeth.

Chapter 9 views *Tmp.* as giving the most complete expression to "the acceptance of oppositions as the basis of the natural, and therefore divinely appointed, pattern of being."

1001 Snyder, Susan. "*All's Well That Ends Well* and Shakespeare's Helens: Text and Subtext, Subject and Object." ELR, 18 (1988), 66–77.

Notes that the characters named Helen in *MND* and *AWW* are the only two women in Sh who actively pursue men. Their uniqueness as desiring subjects is underlined by their name, which "contradicts its prototype," Helen of Troy. The Helen of *MND*, denied her former comradeship with Hermia, is reassimilated by the patriarchy at the end. Helen of *AWW*, however, is reempowered by her association with the widow of Florence and her daughter and is thus more subversive.

1002 Snyder, Susan. "Ourselves Alone: The Challenge to Single Combat in Shakespeare." SEL, 20 (1980), 201–216.

Surveys Elizabethan criticism of modern machine warfare, commenting that tournaments were popular at the time because they were nostalgic reminders of the possibility of personal heroism in combat. Challenges to personal combat in Sh's plays present a similarly outmoded, though appealing, sense of chivalry in the midst of impersonal mass fighting. In *Ant.*, Sh emphasizes Antony's old-fashioned gallantry by showing his willingness to accept any personal dare and his fruitless attempt to get Caesar to fight him in single combat. In *Tro.*, Sh conflates the account of the duel between Hector and Ajax in book 7 of the *Iliad* with a similar account in Lydgate's *Troy Book* or Caxton's *Recuyell of the Historyes of Troye* to exhibit a trivial, pointless encounter. As Sh treats it, the abortive combat between the two cousins is emblematic of the play, in which noble enterprises (like the chivalric challenge by which Hector introduces the issue of the duel) dribble off into inconsequentiality. Hector and the Trojans are shown as being more bravely old-fashioned than the Greeks, who, by contrast, are efficient and modern; in this situation, as we might expect, the Trojans are at a disadvantage.

1003   Snyder, Susan. "Wise Saws and Modern Instances: The Relevance of Donatus." *Shakespearean Comedy*. Ed. Maurice Charney. New York: New York Literary Forum, 1980, pp. 29–35.

Explores the question of whether there was any theory informing the comedies of Elizabethan authors. Argues that the ideas of "Donatus" (the name given to an essay on tragedy and comedy by two 4th-c. grammarians, Donatus and Evanthius, and regularly included in school editions of Terence) provided a foundation on which the playwrights built. Donatus rehearses a succession of oppositions between tragedy and comedy. Comedy is about ordinary men, its dangers are small, and its outcome is joyous. In tragedy, the issues and persons are lofty, and the conclusions are lamentable. Comedy exhibits the embracing of life, whereas tragedy exhibits its rejection. Finally, tragedy often takes its plots from history, whereas comedy depends on feigned stories. Elizabethan practice infused this somewhat arid series of oppositions with considerable depth and consistency. Feigned plots in comedy, for example, were a means for Sh and his contemporaries to create new situations when old ones become intolerable, to reject mortality, and to soften or alter the constraints of law and time. Donatus's prescription for comedy can thus be seen as liberating: The writer is free to remake reality, to include ordinary folk, and to explore the quotidian. Comedy's interest in courtship, not discussed in Donatus, can be discerned in another early grammarian, Diomedes, who asserted that comic plots are about "love affairs and the stealing away of maidens." The principle that links all of these traditional formulas is *"the rejection of singleness."* This accounts for the multiple perspectives of Renaissance comedy, its happy endings, its puns, its double actions, its magician characters, its variety of fools and clowns, and its emphasis on community and the ongoing process of life. One of Donatus's precepts, *"vita capessenda est,* the imperative to take hold of life and fully engage it," accounts for a great deal more in the comedies of Sh's day than the didactic formula so frequently trotted out at the time: that comedy holds a corrective mirror up to life.

1004   Sochatoff, A. Fred. "The Tragedies." *"Starre of Poets": Discussions of Shakespeare*. (Carnegie Series in English 10.) Pittsburgh: Carnegie Institute of Technology, 1966, pp. 65–78.

Cites Ulysses' speech on degree in *Tro.* (I.iii) as evidence of Sh's devotion to the ancient Greek virtue of *sophrosyne*, or moderation. Argues that this concept, as discussed by Aristotle and other ancient writers, is a key to Sh's tragedies: The protagonists fall in large part because of unbalanced, immoderate behavior. Several kinds of immoderation appear in *Ham., Oth., Lr., Mac., Ant.,* and *Cor.*

1005   Soellner, Rolf. "'Hang up Philosophy!' Shakespeare and the Limits of Knowledge." *MLQ*, 23 (1962), 135–49.

Points out that in Sh's time, the humanists who were responsible for grammar school instruction included in the curriculum a heavy dose of moral sentences and passages from the ancients. Schoolboys also learned—chiefly from Cicero, Seneca, and Plutarch—various phrases and epithets on "the salutary effects of philosophy." A survey of Sh's uses of the word *philosophy* and his references to philosophers like Aristotle reveals that he was not hostile to philosophy, as is sometimes argued. Rather, he showed a keen interest in contemporary philosophical problems like "the methods of consolation, the limits of knowledge, and wisdom of folly." He also satirized excesses committed in the name of philosophy, like withdrawal from life, "overindulgence in pleasure, and pedantic dissection of the obvious."

1006 Soellner, Rolf. "Shakespeare, Aristotle, Plato, and the Soul." *SJH*, 1968, 56–71.

Maintains that Sh was familiar with ideas of the soul derived from Plato and Aristotle. Sh uses Platonic notions of the soul's quickness of flight (in Salerio's explanation of Antonio's melancholy [*MV*, I.i.8–14]) and of the identification of a man with his soul (in *Son.* and numerous plays). Aristotle and his medieval and Renaissance commentators supplied Sh with "most of the descriptions for the operations of the soul." In *LLL*, Nathaniel, the schoolmaster, analyzes Dull's psychological deficiencies in Aristotelian terms (IV.ii), and in *Err.* (II.i), Luciana's lecture to Adriana is based on the classical idea that men are distinguished from animals because they have souls, as well as more highly developed sense perceptions. Throughout *Lr.*, Sh uses both Platonic and Aristotelian ideas of the relationship of body and soul to bring the protagonist, through suffering, to some degree of self-discovery.

1007 Sorensen, Knud. "The Growth of Cataphoric Personal and Possessive Pronouns in English." *Current Topics in English Historical Linguistics*. Proceedings of the Second International Conference on English Historical Linguistics Held at Odense U., 13–15 April 1981. Eds. Michael Davenport, Erik Hansen, and Hans Freda Nielsen. (Odense U. Studies in English 4.) Odense: Odense U. P., 1983, pp. 225–38.

Concentrates on the history of a particular kind of cataphoric pronominal, "the complex sentence construction in which an adverbial subordinate clause precedes its main clause, where nominal and pronoun are coreferential, and there is alternation between anaphoric and cataphoric pronouns." Suggests that this kind of cataphora, of which there are several examples in Sh, was inspired in the Renaissance by "the corresponding Latin construction," transferred into English by translators.

1008 Spann, Philip. "Sertorius in Tragedy: or Shakespeare Manqué." *Within the Dramatic Spectrum*. U. of Florida Department of Classics, Comparative Drama Conference Papers. Lanham, Maryland: U. P. of America, 1986, pp. 187–98.

Sums up the career of Quintus Sertorius (1st century B.C.), a rebellious Roman general whose courage and shrewdness enabled him to achieve notable success in the civil war that followed Sulla's march on Rome in 88 B.C. Information about Sulla's life, including his devotion to his mother and his spectacular betrayal and assassination, was readily available in Plutarch's *Lives*, but Sh did not write a play about him, chosing Coriolanus instead. This is probably because the poet found few speeches in Plutarch's account, and no speech at all by Sertorius. Furthermore, Sertorius was too decent to be a tragic hero: He lacked the singlemindedness, the ruthlessness.

1009 Speaight, Robert. *Shakespeare: The Man and His Achievement*. London: J. M. Dent, 1977. vi + 384 pp.

Attempts to discuss Sh's art "in a biographical framework," covering all of the works in the canon. Chapter 1 describes briefly the classical foundations for the curriculum in Sh's school. Chapter 3 takes note of the Plautine sources for *Err.* and the pervasive classical allusions in *Tit.*

Chapter 4 comments on Ovid's *Metamorphoses* as the source for the playfully sensual *Ven.* and the *Fasti* as one influence on *Luc.* Chapter 6 mentions Sh's reliance on Plutarch's *Lives* and Chaucer's *The Knight's Tale* for the story of Theseus and Hippolyta in *MND*. Chapter 12 focuses on *JC*, explaining how Sh adapted his material (Plutarch, Appian, Tacitus, Sir Thomas Elyot) to depict political forces at work very much like those of Elizabethan society in the late 1590s. The play is about

Caesarism as well as conspiracy, intellectual idealism, and pragmatic politics. Chapter 14 maintains that, in *Tro.*, Sh created an anti-myth from materials furnished him by Homer and Chaucer, deliberately deflating both military and erotic romanticism. Chapter 18 includes an analysis of *Tim.*, noting that Plutarch was Sh's principal source and suggesting that the play is an incomplete attempt to deal with "the use or misuse of money, and the use or misuse of adversity."

Chapter 19 treats *Ant.* and *Cor.* For the former, Sh drew on Plutarch as well as more recent sources. The play is global in setting, with a relaxed rhythm and "sumptuous imagery" to depict the contrast between two cultures and the "the seduction of one by the other." *Cor.* is set in the period of Rome's adolescence and revolves around three conflicts: those "between the patricians and the plebs, between Rome and Antium, and between Coriolanus and his mother." Chapter 20 refers to classical Rome as one of four localities for *Cym.* Chapter 21 states that in *WT* Autolycus was created by Sh from hints in the *Metamorphoses* and wonders if Sh might somehow have known Euripides' *Alcestis*, so close is it to the story of Hermione.

1010 Spencer, T. J. B. "The Great Rival: Shakespeare and the Classical Dramatists." *Shakespeare 1564–1964: A Collection of Modern Essays by Various Hands.* Ed. Edward A. Bloom. Providence, Rhode Island: Brown U. P., 1964, pp. 177–93.

Surveys the history of commentary comparing Sh to the classical dramatists, from Francis Meres (1598) to H. D. F. Kitto (1959). Though by the time of Johnson's edition of his works (1762), Sh had achieved something of classic status, there were still many objections to that status from 17th- and 18th-c. men of letters. One of the strongest charges against Sh was that he marred tragic effect with "comic intrusions." From Sh's practice, we can infer that he believed his art to be superior to that characterized by the uniformity of tone prized by the classicizing critics. In his later plays, he moved more and more toward "a hybrid of tragedy and comedy," and Polonius's description of the kinds of entertainments the players are capable of providing (*Ham.*, II.ii.396–400) reads like a joke about the critical doctrine of generic purity. Gradually, it came to be recognized that the Greek tragedians had made use of comic scenes and, early in the 19th c., critics began to declare that Sh's comic scenes enhance the tragic feeling rather than inhibiting it. Sh was also judged inferior to the ancients because of his abundance of puns, a judgment that has been reversed only in the 20th c. In the 17th and 18th c., Sh's portrayals of women were deemed to be less serious than those of the Greek tragedians, but in the 19th c. it became "customary to compliment the women characters in Greek tragedy by comparing them with Shakespeare's." With the decline of Greek and Latin in 19th-c. British schools, Sh, particularly through his Roman plays, became a classic in the educational system. The 20th c. has seen an attempt to assert the similarity between Sh and the Greek tragedians.

1011 Spencer, T. J. B. "'Greeks' and 'Merrygreeks': A Background to *Timon of Athens* and *Troilus and Cressida*." *Essays in Shakespeare and Elizabethan Drama in Honor of Hardin Craig.* Ed. Richard Hosley. Columbia: U. of Missouri P., 1962, pp. 223–33.

Maintains that the unfavorable portrayals of the ancient Greeks and their society in *Tro.* and *Tim.* reflect the opinions of Sh's contemporaries. The 16th c. got its jaundiced view of Greeks from Latin writers like Cicero and Virgil and from St. Paul. Erasmus's disparaging comments reflect the tradition. There were two usages of the word *Greek* in the 16th c., both based on Roman tradition: Preceded by a term like "mad" or "merry," it meant "a person of loose and lively habits, a boon companion, a fast liver"; it also meant "a sharper, a cheat, a crook, any kind of confidence-trickster." One of Horace's well-known *Epistles* comments that the *Iliad* concerns wicked conduct, "including intrigue, double-crossing, lechery, and quarrelsomeness." This view was a common one in the Renaissance, and it informs *Tro.* as well as *Tim.*

1012   Spencer, T. J. B. "Social Assent and Dissent in Shakespeare's Plays." *Review of National Literatures*, 3, no. 2 (1972), 20–38.

Includes *JC* and *Cor.* in a discussion of Sh's expression of views critical of or sympathetic to established political order. Argues that these opinions are not necessarily Sh's; rather, he assigns them to characters as they are needed to fulfill his artistic requirements.

1013   Spencer, T. J. B. *William Shakespeare: The Roman Plays*. London: Longmans, Green, 1963. 56 pp. Reprint with additions to the bibliography, 1966. 2nd ed., 1973.

Includes an essay with brief sections on *Tit., JC, Ant., Cor.,* "Roman History in Elizabethan Literature," and "North's Translations of Plutarch's *Lives.*"

1013a   Spevack, Marvin. "The Art of Dying in Shakespeare." *SJH*, 1989, 169–73.

Inventories deaths in Sh's plays within "such larger interacting perspectives as genre, gender, social and moral attitudes." Notes that, although deaths in the tragedies tend to take place on stage, the especially fiendish men (like Aaron in *Tit.*) and sympathetic women (like Portia in *JC*) often die off stage. Notes that gender is often a consideration in whether or not women die on stage (most do not) and in women's manner of death (suicide is most common). Women prefer poison for suicide; Roman men, the sword. Madness is often connected with the deaths of women, while death by a broken heart seems to be reserved for men (like Enobarbus in *Ant.*). Remarks that the violence in tragedies is more intense than that in history plays because the relationships are more intimate and less politcal; *JC* and *Tit.* are examples.

1014   Spivak, Charlotte. "The Elizabethan Theatre: Circle and Center." *CentR*, 13 (1969), 424–43.

Describes the contributions of various traditions—primarily medieval, but also Stoic, Neoplatonist, and Vitruvian—to the Renaissance world-stage analogy and the conception of the symbolic circle. Shows how these images affected playhouse architecture and underlay the double *anagnorisis* of the protagonist in many of Sh's plays.

1015   Sprague, Arthur Colby. "Shakespeare's Unnecessary Characters." *ShS*, 20 (1967), 75–82.

Surveys minor characters who have been deemed "unnecessary" in Sh's plays by critics and directors. Comments on the Fool in *Tim.*; Luciana in *Err.*; Ventidius in *Ant.*; and Cinna the Poet, the Second Poet, and Cicero in *JC*.

1016   Stack, Robert Douglas. "The Intellectual Background of Dr. Johnson's Preface to Shakespeare." Ph.D. dissertation, Princeton University, 1967. *DA*, 28 (1967–68). 3649-A-3650-A.

Provides the intellectual context for Johnson's Preface, "the definitive Neo-classical evaluation of Sh." Chapter 1 examines Johnson's opening paragraphs: his attitude toward "the test of time, taste, the distinction between art and science, the existence of underlying philosophical principles." Chapter 2 is concerned with Johnson's praise of Sh "as a poet of nature." When Johnson speaks of Sh's characters, he uses nature in its ideal, Platonic sense; when he defends tragicomedy, he discards Platonism and invokes the "real state of sublunary nature." Chapter 3 focuses on "Johnson's attitude toward the three unities and dramatic illusion." Essentially, Johnson dismisses dramatic illusion and "hence can dispense with the unities as well." He is not primarily concerned with the audience's psychological involvement in the play, but rather "their reflective act of comparing the real with the imitation before them." His support of poetic justice is based not on its truth to life but on the opportunity it provides for moral reflection. Chapter 4 deals with Johnson's account of Sh's faults (in plot

General Works 283

construction, verisimilitude, and language); chapter 5 discusses Johnson's credentials as a historical critic; and Chapter 6 examines the Preface itself, describing the reviews it received and analyzing its literary qualities.

1017 Stampfer, Judah. *The Tragic Engagement: A Study of Shakespeare's Classical Tragedies*. New York: Funk & Wagnalls, 1968. 336 pp.

Proposes to investigate Sh's classical tragedies, placing particular emphasis on "those typologies that build the plot and shape the protagonist toward the central tragic engagement." Sees three types of hero in the classical tragedies: the ethical (Brutus), the willful (Antony), and the politic (Octavius). Distinguishes the Christian tragedies, which dramatize "the complex personal anguish of a man in torment," from the classical tragedies, whose heroes are more static and suffer more a loss of role than terrible pain. The "ruthless, secular modernity" of the classical tragedies makes them particularly relevant to our time. Devotes a chapter each to *Tit.*, *JC*, *Tro.*, *Tim.*, *Ant.*, and *Cor.*

1018 Steadman, John M. *The Lamb and the Elephant: Ideal Imitation and the Context of Renaissance Allegory*. San Marino, California: Huntington Library, 1974. xlvi + 254 pp.

Focuses on "the principle of 'ideal' presentation—the illustration of abstract universals or class concepts through concrete sensuous particulars—as seen against the background of changing poetic and rhetorical ideals, varying relationships to classical models and authorities, and altering conceptions of the literary genres and of the rules of poetic imitation."
Makes only two very brief references to Sh but provides a wealth of background material, especially in the first three chapters: "Innovation and Tradition: The Problem of the Renaissance"; "The Recovery of Antiquity"; and "Classical Tradition and Renaissance Epic."

1019 Steane, J. B. *Marlowe: A Critical Study*. Cambridge: Cambridge U. P., 1964. viii + 381 pp.

Chapter 2, on Marlowe's *The Tragedie of Dido*, calls attention to the parallels between that play and *Ant.*: Both plays concern pairs of heroic lovers whose relationships have cosmic implications. Given this similarity of subjects, Sh's imagery and verse music was probably influenced by passages from Marlowe at several points. Chapter 7 observes that "the vision of a whole world in confusion" projected in Marlowe's translation of the first book of Lucan's *Pharsalia* may have had an influence on Sh as he composed *Tro.*, especially the images of chaos in Ulysses' degree speech (I.iii).

1019a Steppat, Michael Payne. "Octavius 'cold and sickly.'" *N&Q*, 32 (1985), 53–54.

Cites passages from *JC* (V.ii.3–4) and *Ant.* (III.iv.6–8) to demonstrate that Sh uses images of coldness to describe Octavius Caesar. In addition to the accounts by Plutarch and other historians of Octavius's illness at Philippi, the playwright seems to have relied on Suetonius's depiction of the emperor's chronic suffering from cold temperature. Thus Sh suggests that Octavius is mentally and physically cold and that his coldness is a source of both strength and weakness.

1020 Sternfeld, F. W. "Music and Ballads." *Shakespeare in His Own Age*. *ShS*, 17 (1964), 214–22.

Discusses the philosophy of music in Elizabethan England as it descended from the medieval division of music into "*musica mundana*, the music of the spheres, *musica humana*, the well-ordered and harmonious commonwealth, and *musica instrumentalis*, the vocal and instrumental music performed by men." Music of the spheres is referred to directly in *Per.*, and references to divine or supernatural music occur in several of Sh's other plays (for example, *Ant.* and *Tmp.*). Closely related to the music of the spheres was the belief that music is "a means to influence the disposition of men," deriving from Pythagorean, Platonic, and Neoplatonic thought. Sh relies on this notion in several plays, notably *Oth.*, *Per.*, and *Tmp.*

1021   Sternfeld, F. W. *Music in Shakespearean Tragedy.* London: Routledge and Kegan Paul, 1963. xxii + 334 pp.

The first chapter attributes the relative paucity of songs in Elizabethan tragedy in part to the reliance of Sh and his contemporaries on "the Romans rather than the Greeks for their classical models." Instrumental music was more common than song in the tragedy of the day. Notes that Sh was more skillful than most of his contemporaries in weaving songs into his tragedies. Cites Pandarus's song in *Tro.*, which, though comic, is made a part of the tragic artistic design. Chapter 4 is devoted to "magic songs," that is, "songs to influence the disposition." Two Roman tragedies provide examples: the song Lucius performs for Brutus in *JC* and "Come thou monarch of the vine," sung by an unnamed boy on board Pompey's galley (*Ant.*, II.iv). Describes the ancient Greek theory of the ethos of music—as transmitted through Boethius, Cicero, Plutarch, and the Neoplatonists—as a significant influence on Sh. For example, the idea that Dorian music inspires courage in men and Lydian music makes them effeminate helped in the shaping of *Ant.* Chapter 6, on adult songs, analyzes the song of Pandarus, showing that it illustrates the ethos theory: The procurer of luxuries is "characterized by music that is luxurious beyond measure," a symbol of the depravity of the nobility. The first of two chapters on instrumental music describes Ulysses' famous speech on degree (*Tro.*, I.iii) as a comprehensive exposition of Sh's "beliefs concerning the interrelationship of the music of the spheres, the music of men's lives and the consort of strings." The second chapter on instrumental music shows how Sh, in the interest of greater economy, modified Plutarch's account of the music heard during two key scenes in the story of Antony and Cleopatra (the description of Cleopatra's barge [*Ant.*, II.ii] and the soldiers' perception that Antony is being deserted by the gods [*Ant.*, IV.iii]). Notes that some of the phrases about harmony of musical instruments and rhythmic movement from Plutarch's *Life of Marcus Antonius*, though not used in *Ant.*, emerge in later plays like *WT* and *Tmp.* The ancient rivalry between the Pipes of Pan (noisy and fleshly) and the lute of Apollo (spiritual), transmitted through the poems of Horace and others, lies behind scenes in a number of plays, including Cassio's serenade (*Oth.*, III.i) and Hamlet's praise of Horatio for not being a stop for Fortune's finger (*Ham.*, III.ii.75) and his criticism of Rosencrantz and Guildenstern for trying to play him (III.ii.354). Investigates Sh's use of the metaphor of sweet or harsh tuning to indicate the harmonious or discordant relationship between parts of a commonwealth, a marriage, or a soul. In several plays, there is reference to the healing power of stringed instruments. Examines several instances of the music of the spheres in the plays, including scenes from *Per.* and *Ant.*

1022   Stewart, Bain Tate. "Characterization through Dreams in the Drama of Shakespeare's Day." *Studies in Honor of John C. Hodges and Alwin Thaler.* Eds. Richard Beale Davis and John Leon Lievsay. Knoxville: U. of Tennessee P., 1961, pp. 27–34.

Points out that the Renaissance science of dreams is "an integral part of the faculty psychology inherited from the ancient and medieval worlds." Aristotle's authority was frequently cited by Renaissance writers, particularly concerning "the identification of dreams with imagination and sense experience." Examines Mercutio's Queen Mab speech in *Rom.*, Clarence's account of his dream of drowning in *R3*, and references to dreams in *1H4* and *Ham.* Concludes that in Renaissance drama "natural dreams arising primarily from thought and passion offer relatively little difficulty of interpretation to the modern reader, though some knowledge of faculty psychology is helpful."

1023 Stewart, Patricia Lou. "Renaissance Theories of Fortitude and Their Dramatic Use in Shakespeare's *King Lear, Timon of Athens*, and *Troilus and Cressida*." Ph.D. dissertation, University of North Carolina, Chapel Hill, 1967. *DA*, 28 (1967–68), 3649-A.

Discovers four concepts of "fortitude" current in the Renaissance that are relevant to Sh's works: Aristotle's "martial courage"; Cicero's "civic virtue"; Seneca's "courage of endurance"; and "Christian patience." Because he had available so many definitions of courage, Sh was able to use fortitude as a "kaleidoscopic norm" in all his plays: One character may view as rash or cowardly what another believes to be courageous. Sh sometimes portrays fortitude as unattainable. In *Lr.*, fortitude is established as both a virtue and "as a vanity and vexation of spirit." *Tro.* exposes the "lack of true courage" in all of its characters. *Tim.* "is structured on the principle of Ciceronian fortitude." In prosperity as well as adversity, the protagonist lacks civic virtue. Alcibiades, who in the middle of the play seems addicted to rashness, has matured by the last scene, in which he couples civic concern with his bravery and thus attains "the virtue of fortitude as it was defined by Cicero."

1024 Stimpson, Catharine R. "Shakespeare and the Soil of Rape." *The Woman's Part: Feminist Criticism of Shakespeare*. Eds. Carolyn Lenz, Gayle Greene, and Carol Neely. Urbana: U. of Illinois P., 1980, pp. 56–64. Reprint. *Where the Meanings Are*. New York: Methuen, 1988, pp. 77–83.

Discerns in Sh's work a sympathetic attitude toward women that makes for a remarkably clear-eyed view of rape. Cites *Luc., Tit.,* and *Cym.*, analyzing the vivid language in which rape is described, the competition between men that rape figures, and the comments of "moderate men" to expose the unfair punishments that women must undergo because they have suffered rape. Sh deplores the damage done to proper patriarchal patterns of authority by the outrage of rape, though he does not question the patterns themselves.

1025 Stock, R. D. *The Flutes of Dionysus: Daemonic Enthrallment in Literature*. Lincoln: U. of Nebraska P., 1989. xix + 438 pp.

Investigates the literary expression of "daemonic dread," connected chiefly with the Greek god Dionysus, but also embodied in a host of other "Dionysiac and chthonian deities." Chapter 5, "Dionysus Redivivus: The Renaissance," discusses *Ven.* as harking back to Euripides' *The Bacchae* in "its subject of daemonic assault on adolescence, its movement from pleasure to horror" and ruin; *Ant.* as full of destructive Bacchanalianism, with Cleopatra an embodiment of "the raging Amazonian sensibility"; Iago and Hamlet as Dionysiac types; the world of *Mac.* as polluted by the daemonic; and *Tmp.* as a fable in which the daemonic is "held rigorously in check."

1026 Stockholder, Katherine Sally. "In Depth and Breadth: Shakespeare's Fusion of Comedy and Tragedy." Ph.D. dissertation, University of Washington, 1964. *DA*, 25 (1964–65), 5263-A-5264-A.

Investigates Sh's mixture of comic and tragic techniques in *MM, Tro., Lr.,* and *Cor.* In *Tro.*, "comic perspective comments upon the tragic stance of the characters"; in *Cor.*, the hero, "trapped in the image reflected back at him by his surroundings," sometimes "resembles a Jonsonian humor figure." The protagonists in these plays "are comic victims of the meaningless world[s] they create." Parts revised as items 3038 and 1730.

1027 Streites, Aaron. "Against Discord: The Evolution of the Idea of Order in Certain Shakespearean Plays." Ph.D. dissertation, Brown University, 1968. *DA*, 30 (1969–70), 295-A.

Claims that the idea of order is at the intellectual center of Sh's mature plays. Notes the expression of this idea during the Elizabethan period in "Aristotelian rationalism" and other traditions. According to this notion, man is duty-bound to preserve order by subordinating his passions to reason. In a series of plays (*AYL, TN, AWW, Tro.,* and *Tmp.*), Sh traces the passion of love from charmingly innocent, to uncontrollably destructive, to reconstitutive and regenerative. In the first, as in the last, of the five plays, order prevails.

1028 Stříbrný, Zdeněk. "The Genesis of Double Time in Pre-Shakespearean and Shakespearean Drama." *Prague Studies in English* (Acta Universitatis Carolinae—Philologica 3), 13 (1969), 77–95.

Discusses "the essential features of the double time structure" in Elizabethan drama, especially that of Sh. One scheme of time in these plays "comprises references to a short duration of action and thus creates the impression that the whole plot does not take longer than a day or a few days at the most. The other scheme, usually termed *long time* or *psychological time*, or *historical time*, contains references and allusions to events which imply a much longer duration, sometimes of weeks, or years." Renaissance English playwrights inherited the long or elastic time scheme from various types of native drama, while they adopted short time from the classical and Italian traditions. Sh's immediate predecessors anticipated him in referring to "both a shorter and a longer duration of the action." In *MV*, Sh used short time for the Belmont plot and long time for the Venice plot. *R3*, while dramatizing the vicissitudes of the Wars of the Roses, is also heavily influenced by "the time concepts of the classical drama."

1029 Stroud, James Ronald. "Shakespeare's Unkind Selves: A Study of Self, Self-Knowledge and Decorum in Shakespearean Drama." Ph.D. dissertation, University of Texas at Austin, 1977. *DAI*, 38 (1977–78), 7351-A.

Investigates the concept of self in Shakespearean drama, which often presents a "dialectic between decorum and the indecorous individual," or, more specifically, a conflict between a dissident and a mentor. Two examples are Brutus–Cassius and Achilles–Ulysses. In some cases, Sh uses the dissident–mentor pattern to explore the problem of a person whose principles are so radically at odds with society's rules that adaptation for that person is psychologically destructive. Often this type of dissident (Cressida, for example) is endowed with deep insights about the society that requires deference. In Sh's later "unkind selves," including Coriolanus, there is a further intensification of the dissident–mentor tension through the introduction of a dissident of great integrity who is pressured to make an accommodation with a glaringly imperfect social order.

1030 Stroup, Thomas B. "'All Comes Clear at Last,' but 'the Readiness is All.'" *CompD*, 10 (1976), 61–77. Reprint. *The Humanist in His World: Essays in Honor of Fielding Dillard.* Eds. Barbara W. Bitter and Frederick K. Sanders. Greenwood, South Carolina: Attic P., 1976, pp. 25–45.

Uses Sh's works, especially *Ham., Lr.,* and *Mac.*, to demonstrate that while classical and Christian tragedies are similar in a number of respects, they differ in that the protagonist in a Christian tragedy has available a source of illumination outside himself.

1031 Stroup, Thomas B. *Microcosmos: The Shape of the Elizabethan Play.* Lexington: U. of Kentucky P., 1965. xi + 235 pp.

Argues that the metaphor of the world as stage, of life as cosmic drama, is crucial to the structure of Elizabethan plays. Although the Elizabethans absorbed the metaphor most directly from medieval drama, they were also aware, through the labors of humanists like Erasmus and More, that it was a commonplace of classical thought: It could be found in Lucian's *Dialogues*, in Epictetus, in Plotinus, in Renaissance Neoplatonists like Ficino, and even in Plato himself.

Chapter 1, "The World as Stage," observes that Sh's works make reference to the metaphor some fifteen times and gives examples from *Tmp.* and other plays.

Chapter 2, "Encompassing Actions," explains how the Elizabethan dramatists present the individual and private action at the center of the stage, "surround that action with the action belonging to the city or state, and that public action with an international action, and finally that whole earthly action (not always, but often) with an unearthly action or area for action." Examples from several Shakespearean plays include *Tit., JC, Tro.,* and *Tim.*

Chapter 3, "The Pageant Exits, the Ceremonies and Ceremonious Actions, and the Rituals," notes that these signify the connection of the play to the vast pageant of the world. Numerous examples can be found in *Tit.* and *Ant.*

Chapter 4, "The Places of Action," points out that localities were chosen to signify universality: In *Err.*, unlike its Plautine source, the action takes place in various parts of town.

Chapter 5, "The Characters," states that the characters in Elizabethan plays were chosen to represent all estates and degrees of humanity: *JC, Tit.,* and *Cor.* are examples.

1032 Stroup, Thomas B. "The Scenes in Shakespearean Plays." *All These to Teach: Essays in Honor of C. A. Robertson.* Eds. Robert A. Bryan, Alton C. Morris, A. A. Murphree, and Aubrey L. Williams. Gainesville: U. of Florida P., 1965, pp. 102-19.

Presents a brief analysis of the kinds of places represented in certain of Sh's plays "to reveal one aspect of the universalizing method" he employed. Exterior scenes placed "before" some interior allow for greater latitude in the action than similarly placed scenes from the classical drama. Cleopatra's monument in *Ant.*, for example, permits two levels of action. Interior scenes also provide variety, as in the case of the drinking party aboard Pompey's ship. In *Err.*, Sh's most Plautean comedy, there is "a variety of scenes altogether lacking in the *Menaechmi*, its source." The procession of scenes in *Ant.*—representing public and private places, interiors and exteriors, and combinations—helps "to create the magnitude of the action and the character of the protagonists."

1033 Strozier, Robert M. "Politics, Stoicism, and the Development of Elizabethan Tragedy." *Costerus* (Amsterdam), 9 (1973), 79-108.

Follows the change "in Elizabethan tragic conceptions" from 1559 through the 1590s. Notes that "the political and Senecan conceptions of life" become, in the 1590s, the means by which dramatists address "real rather than ideal views of the world, and the means by which they come to examine human nature as exposed in such a world." Discusses *R3, Tit.,* and *Rom.*

1034 Stugrin, Michael. "'But I must also feel it as a man': Pathos and Knowledge in Shakespearean Tragedy." *Iowa State Journal of Research*, 54 (1980), 469-79.

Identifies the classical tradition of "the rhetorical shaping of emotion," "the Ovidian pathos of erotic love with its attendant irony and wit," and "the *de casibus* tradition" (according to which a prominent figure falls from prosperity into misery through the operation of Fortune) as key influences on Sh's ability to present intense emotion. Comments on several of the mature tragedies, especially *Mac.*, to show how Sh draws us into and sustains our engagement with "the total emotional structure of dramatic action." To do this, he presents pathos in juxtapostion to "ironic comment, surface wit, or loud outrage." Cites three early works—*Rom., Ven.,* and *Luc.*—that refine the rhetoric of pathos. The intense emotion in these works, "rhetorically wrought," serves as a means to knowledge. The transformation of feeling and language allows us to feel and value the often profoundly sad "reality of human experience" without being overwhelmed by "its inevitable cost."

1034a Stukey, Johanna H. "Petronius the 'Ancient': His Reputation and Influence in Seventeenth Century England." *Rivista di Studi Crociani* (Naples), 20 (1972), 145–53.

Explains that during the 17th c. in England, Petronius, whatever else he may have been, was regarded as an "ancient," a classical authority. Points out that, despite the efforts of some scholars to discover numerous "Petronian allusions" in the works of Sh, the dramatist makes "no clear-cut reference" to Petronius. Reportedly, however, Sh did write "extempore verses on the alleged motto of the Globe Theatre," which is adapted from a line attributed to Petronius.

1035 Stump, Donald V. "Greek and Shakespearean Tragedy: Four Indirect Routes from Athens to London." *"Hamartia": The Concept of Error in the Western Tradition: Essays in Honor of John M. Crossett*. Eds. Donald V. Stump, James A. Arieti, Lloyd Gerson, and Eleonore Stump. (Texts & Studies in Religion 16.) New York: Edwin Mellen P., 1983, pp. 211–46.

Asserts that modern critics are perfectly justified in applying ancient Greek notions of tragedy, especially those of Aristotle, to Sh's plays because, though there is no evidence that Sh knew the *Poetics* or any Greek dramas directly, there are a number of intermediate vehicles through which he could have absorbed these ideas. Focuses on a group of ancient plays by Sophocles and Euripides (designated "*hamartia* plays") that are susceptible to Aristotelian analysis; lists, from the *Poetics*, the characteristics these plays have in common; and discusses four indirect ways by which Sh could have arrived at a knowledge of the genre. First, the Greek form could have been transmitted through certain tragedies of Seneca, for example *Hercules Furens*. Sh's grammar school education would have prepared him to assimilate crucial Greek elements from Seneca; he would have read the comedies of Terence, which follow plotting techniques derived from Greek tragedy; and he would have encountered the critical commentaries of Donatus, who clearly defines the structural points of the *hamartia* play and harmonizes them with the five-act structure. Second, the Greek romance, especially the *Aethiopica* of Heliodorus, had a likely influence. This work, which Sh probably knew in the translation of Thomas Underdowne, refers frequently to Euripides, structures many of its key episodes according to the pattern of Euripides' "romantic tragedies with happy endings," and uses theatrical terminology to describe its actions. Third, Sir Philip Sidney's *Arcadia*, a work Sh is known to have been familiar with, clearly reminds the reader that its action is being shaped "along the lines of a classical play." Fourth, in the plays and tales of Geraldo Cinthio and his imitator George Whetstone, Sh found "a secularized version of the Greek *hamartia* play, stripped entirely of Greek theology and myth."

1035a Stürzl, Erwin A. "Metamorphosis in Elizabethan Literature." *Jacobean Miscellany 3*. (JDS 95:3.) Salzburg: Institut für Anglistik und Amerikanistik, U. Salzburg, 1983, pp. 96–119.

Provides background for the motif of metamorphosis in Elizabethan literature, identifying Ovid's "Pythagorean exposition of the flux of the universe" in book 15 of the *Metamorphoses* as a key text. Surveys the drama of the period for instances of transformation. Calls attention to "the anagogical form of metamorphosis," which serves character transformation in Sh's comedies, especially *MND* and *Shr*.

1036 Styan, John Louis. *Shakespeare's Stagecraft*. Cambridge: Cambridge U. P., 1967. viii + 244 pp.

Uses examples from the entire Shakespearean canon. The classical plays furnish definitive illustrations of two key types of scenes treated in chapter 5: "Crowds" (*JC, Cor.*) and "Armies into Battle" (*JC, Tro., Ant.*). The final chapter cites *Ant., Cor., Tro.*, and *JC* to show how Sh alternates contrasting scenes.

1037   Sutherland, James. "The Moving Pattern of Shakespeare's Thought." *Papers, Mainly Shakespearean.* Ed. G. I. Duthie. Edinburgh: Oliver and Boyd, 1964, pp. 10–20.

Stresses Sh's exceptional capacity to sustain "a moving pattern," that is, "to shape long speeches, passages, and even whole scenes in a continuously developing movement." Includes discussion of the quarrel between Brutus and Cassius (*JC*, IV.iii), wherein we see "the two men exchanging verbal blows," and the scenes between Cleopatra and Dolabella (*Ant.*, V.ii) and between Antony and Eros (IV.iv), which illustrate the protagonists' absorption in a world of their own that cannot be entered by the ordinary man.

1038   Sutherland, Jean Murray. "Shakespeare and Seneca: A Symbolic Language for Tragedy." Ph.D. dissertation, University of Colorado, Boulder, 1985. *DAI*, 46 (1985–86), 3044-A.

Attempts to discover how Sh appropriated Senecan tragedy and its extended tradition "as a language for his own tragedy by creating recognizable and purposeful allusion through technique, motif, and symbol." Sh's use of "Senecan symbolic language and the Senecan–Ovidian intertext" is especially important because it allowed him to fashion "a meaningful Renaissance humanist synthesis along with a philosophic–symbolic base for dramatic action."

1039   Suzuki, Mihoko. "The Dismemberment of Hippolytus: Humanist Imitation, Shakespearean Translation." *CML*, 10 (1989–90), 103–12.

Explains that Renaissance humanists saw the "dismemberment of Hippolytus" as "a metaphor for the fragmentation and dispersal of classical learning," which they might restore to unity through imitation, much as Aesculapius healed Hippolytus. Suggests that the dismemberment figures Sh's concern with the "translation" of classical materials in various ways. In *Tit.*, for example, the untranslated Latin tags in the text, taken chiefly from Seneca's *Hippolytus*, emphasize the distance between the culture of Sh's England and that of ancient Rome. These broken phrases also highlight the fragmentation of classical learning, as well as reflect the various actual mutilations in the play. In *MND*, *Hippolytus* is also a source, but here Sh has suppressed and displaced "the violence and passion from the Senecan subtext" to produce civic order and a comic resolution. The Senecan elements are still present, as when Theseus and Hippolyta discuss their hounds (IV.i); this scene is transposed from the description of Hippolytus's hounds in Seneca, but there it foreshadows the death of the protagonist, whereas here it serves to set the stage for the comic conclusion.

1040   Svendsen, James T. "The Letter Device in Euripides and Shakespeare." *Legacy of Thespis.* (Drama Past and Present 4.) Ed. Karelisa V. Hartigan. Lanham, Maryland: University P. of America, 1984, pp. 75–88.

Parallels the use of the "letter device" in Euripides and Sh. Analyzes the use of letters in five plays of Euripides and two of Sh (*Ham.* and *TN*). Speculates that these two playwrights were prompted to endow this folkloric motif with new relevance because each lived in an era in which an oral culture was being revolutionized by "literacy and literary habits."

1041   Talbert, Ernest William. *Elizabethan Drama and Shakespeare's Early Plays: An Essay in Historical Criticism.* Chapel Hill: U. of North Carolina P., 1963. ix + 410 pp. Reprint. 1973.

Uses analyses of plays written by Sh from about 1590 to about 1596 to emphasize the ways in which the author catered to his audience's appetite for multiplicity. Maintains that the educated spectator would have noted how *Tit.* heightens both Senecan and Ovidian elements of horror. Even the unlearned spectators of *Tit.* "would have been reminded that they were hearing echoes of the current academic tradition." Notes that in *Err.*, with its use of Plautine models, we can see Sh adapting academic comedy to "the public acting of an adult company."

1042   Tanner, R. G. "Shakespeare and Greek Dramatic Techniques." *Nimrod*, 5, no. 1 (1967–68), 5–9.

Argues that Sh "saw passages of moralizing reflection inserted into soliloquy or dialogue as replacing and serving the function of the Senecan Chorus in his tragedies." Illustrates this point by assigning portions of dialogues and soliloquies in *Mac.* and *Ham.* to a Chorus or Chorus Leader.

1042a   Taylor, Anthony Brian. "The Non-existent Carbuncles: Shakespeare, Golding, and Raphael Regius." *N&Q*, 32 (1985), 54–55.

Adduces passages from *Ant.* and *Cym.* in which reference is made to the carbuncles that adorn Phoebus's chariot. The descriptions of this jewel-bedecked "car" derive from Ovid's *Metamorphoses*, which, however, contains no carbuncles. Sh got the idea of carbuncles decorating the Sun-god's palace from Arthur Golding's translation of *pyropus* (really meaning *bronze*) as *carbuncle*, under the influence of Raphael Regius's notes. The playwright then transferred the gems to the Sun-god's chariot,

1043   Taylor, Anthony Brian. "Shakespeare, Studley, and Golding." RES, 39 (1988), 522–27.

Discovers a source of Hamlet's phrase "peasant slave" (*Ham.*, II.ii.550) in John Studley's translation of Seneca's *Hercules Oetaeus*, in a speech in which Hercules reproaches Philoctetes for not acting "decisively and heroically" to aid a "beloved and admired figure." Finds that Golding's translation of the *Metamorphoses* influenced passages in *MV* and *WT* (related to Pythagorean doctrine) and in Sonnet 7, *Tit.*, and *TNK* (related to the myth of Phaethon).

1044   Taylor, Arvilla Kerns. "The Manège of Love and Authority: Studies in Sidney and Shakespeare." Ph.D. dissertation, University of Texas at Austin, 1969. *DAI*, 30 (1969–70), 3025-A–3026-A.

Considers imagery associated with the manège, or the art of horsemanship, in several of Sh's plays. Metaphorically, the rider (statesman, courtier, or knight) was seen in Sh's time as "the rational agent who attempted to control the rebellious passions of a furious animal." Points out the classical components of this symbolic imagery, especially the view inherited from Aristotle and Virgil that the horse represents "lust and procreation." In *LLL* and *Ado*, manège imagery indicates joyful surrender to erotic drives, and in several history plays (*R2*, *1&2H4*, and *H5*) it helps to reveal a contrast between the self-mastery required for effective rule and various kinds of intemperance that subvert one's power to govern.

1044a   Teague, Frances. *Shakespeare's Speaking Properties*. Lewisburg: Bucknell U. P., 1991. 222 pp.

Offers a systematic study of stage properties "specified in Shakespeare's plays either explicitly in stage directions or implicitly in speeches." Chapter 5 considers "spectacular scenes": "those in which the visual matters more than the verbal." Such scenes use more properties than "plainer scenes," in part because the properties identify social roles and symbolic characters. Examples of the latter are Revenge in *Tit.*, Cupid in *Tim.*, Jove and his eagle in *Cym.*, and the harpy in *Tmp.* Notes the purposeful multiplicity of meaning in spectacular scenes, especially those deriving from classical mythology, like Prospero's masque in *Tmp.* Chapter 6 includes discussions of the actor as property (as when, in *JC*, the actor who plays Caesar also plays his corpse), headgear (especially in *Cor.* [see item 1735]), and properties as "characterizing devices" (especially in act V of *Ant.*).

General Works

1045 Tennenhouse, Leonard. *Power on Display: The Politics of Shakespeare's Genres*. New York: Methuen, 1986. viii + 206 pp.

Regards the theater of the Elizabethans and Jacobeans as a platform for staging displays of power. For example, Sh modifies Livy's story of Virginius to equate rape with dismemberment and thus with disorder in the state. Instead of using Lavinia as an object of lust, Sh features her body "as the site for political rivalry among various families." The same thing is achieved in *Luc*. In *Ant*., Sh allows the audience to feel the seduction "of detaching sexuality from politics only to demonstrate the preprosterousness of thinking of the body this way." Cleopatra is endowed with "a body that incorporates the basest things" and consequently would have been seen by a Jacobean audience as subverting "the aristocratic community."

1046 Thaler, Alwin. *Shakespeare and Our World*. Knoxville: U. of Tennessee P., 1966. ix + 235 pp.

Attempts, in the first section, to show how Sh can teach mid-20th-c. people much about the problems they face. Chapter 1, for example, cites *Tim*. to show the importance of knowing the middle of humanity, of seeing both sides of vexed questions; *Tro*. to demonstrate the consequences of contempt for order; and *Cor*. to warn against extremism. The second section is concerned with dramatic technique. Chapter 5, which discusses mutes and off-stage characters, includes comment on Fulvia (*JC*). Chapter 6, on poetic scene-painting, provides detailed summaries of poetic scene-painting in seven representative plays, including *Tit*. and *Ant*.

1047 Thomas, Vivian. *Shakespeare's Roman Worlds*. London: Routledge, 1989. xi + 243 pp.

Provides a critical analysis of Sh's four Roman plays (*Tit*., *JC*, *Ant*., and *Cor*.), especially their value system, in the context of the relationship between their events and characters and the chief narrative sources on which they are based.

Chapter 1, "Shakespeare's Roman Worlds," serves as an introduction. More than any of Sh's other individual plays or groups of plays, the four Roman plays create "an intense sense of a social universe." Though the Roman world of each play has distinctive features, all four plays privilege the following values: "service to the state, constancy, fortitude, valour, friendship, love of family and respect for the gods." Gives special emphasis to Plutarch's *Lives of the Noble Grecians and Romans*, the principal source for *JC*, *Ant*., and *Cor*., noting the ways in which Sh departs from it: the conflation of events, the omission of prominent episodes, the alteration of important details, the development of characters or details, and the invention of certain features. It is important to give proper weight to the political and historical aspects of these plays and not simply to classify them as tragedies. Though lacking the historical basis of the other Roman plays, *Tit*. is clear about the kind of Rome it presents, a city that aspires to greatness but is confused about its values and "lacks an effective mechanism for choosing a leader." *Tit*. is set in a later time than the other Roman plays, but it "*feels* earlier," because of a contrast between the longing for "a truly civilized society" and "the immediate exhibition of a barbarous ritual." Despite its horrors, *Tit*. includes a "contemplation of the future and the relationship between the body politic and human values." This is what links it to the other Roman plays.

Chapter 2, "Images and Self-Images in *Julius Caesar*," notes that the most significant feature of Sh's handling of his source material in *JC* is his conflation of events and then proceeds to make a detailed comparison between the relevant passages of Plutarch's *Lives* and the play. Includes discussion of two "subsidiary sources," Suetonius's *The Historie of Twelve Caesars*, translated by Philemon Holland, and Appian's *The Civil Wars*. Argues that in this play Sh is concerned, as he is nowhere else, with "personal and political images and self-images." Cassius is a keenly observant politician who fails politically because he succumbs to personal feelings; Antony is capable of great personal warmth, but being a thoroughgoing political opportunist, he has no commitment to Roman values. Caesar has great stature as a statesman, military leader, and friend, but he becomes imprisoned in his image of invulnerability; and Brutus, though admirable in many ways, allows his self-perception as the altruistic servant of Rome to obscure his judgment. At the end of the play, a new, unstable world has come into being, and the dangerous potential of this world diminishes the personal tragedies of Brutus and Cassius.

Chapter 3, "Realities and Imaginings in *Antony and Cleopatra*," calls attention to the following departures from Plutarch in the characters of Sh's play: Antony is made more attractive by the removal of his viciousness; the significance of Octavia's relationship to Antony is suppressed and her character rendered colorless; the appealing qualities of Octavius are virtually eliminated; Cleopatra's "charm, vivacity and capriciousness" are accentuated; and Enobarbus, through whom our perception of many important events is filtered, is almost entirely Sh's creation. Considers changes Sh makes in Plutarch's account of Antony's "initial departure from Egypt," the events leading up to the battle of Actium, the festivities on the Isle of Samos, various omens, Antony's decision to fight at sea, Antony's suicide, Caesar's attempts to manipulate Cleopatra at the end, and other matters. Uses Octavius's comments on Antony's death to show that "Sh not only makes the audience aware that they are observing the re-creation of historical events, but conveys a sense of the participants in the original events being aware of their special location in the historical process and their sensitivity to the needs of the moment." There is thus a "duality of vision" throughout: The characters accept "historical reality," which consigns them to participation in "the tawdry and ignoble," but they also employ their imaginative powers in creating a "historical identity" or myth for themselves. For the audience, "these contrasting perceptions" are manifested in a variety of ways, one of which is the alternating positive and negative senses of several important clusters of images (for example, those of binding).

Chapter 4, "Sounds, Words, Gestures and Deeds in *Coriolanus*," begins with a detailed comparison between Sh's play and the accounts of Coriolanus in Plutarch's *Lives* and Livy's *Roman History*. Sh's differences from his sources (mainly Plutarch) include the following: Sh's hero is able to relate comfortably to his peers; Menenius is a patrician by birth; the citizen of Corioles whom Martius attempts to liberate is poor; Martius is more rigid and the citizens more generous; Rome is better off without Martius, except in time of war; Martius uses no guile in stirring up the Volsces against Rome; Martius is not insulted because the common people fail to honor him. Analyzes the play in some detail, emphasizing the dedication of Coriolanus to single-minded service to the state and his inability to act a role, to separate words and gestures from deeds. He is the perfect warrior, constructed by his mother and the other patricians to embody the quintessential Roman values. However, he is betrayed by his own class when they demand that he become a politician, a role fundamentally at odds with the one for which they have created him. His society is groping for a new definition of greatness at the very moment when he achieves greatness according to the old definition, and therein lies his tragedy. Concludes with a discussion of the "complex interplay between sounds, gestures, words and deeds, speech and action" in the play.

Chapter 5, "Conclusion," emphasizes the special social environment "laden with history and driven by a sense of mission" that is Sh's Rome. Notes that in Sh's Roman plays the common people are denigrated because of their inconstancy; that the chief characters attempt to live up to the ideals of the city as well as to realize personal ambitions; that the only character in tune with the changes taking place is Octavius; that the characters see themselves, and are frequently seen, as "part of the process of history"; and that Sh dramatized and enriched the ambiguities and complexities he discovered in Plutarch.

1048 Thompson, Ann. "Philomel in *Titus Andronicus* and *Cymbeline*." *ShS*, 31 (1978), 23–32.

Remarks that *Tit.* and *Cym.* make specific reference to the story of Philomel, which in its combination of rape and mutilation is suited to both plays. In *Tit.*, Lavinia is raped and mutilated; in *Cym.*, Cloten plans the rape of Imogen and the mutilation of her husband Posthumus but becomes a victim of mutilation himself when he is beheaded. *Tit.* uses images of mutilation in a localized way to intensify the sense of horror at the misfortunes of the Andronici. In *Cym.*, references to rape and mutilation are part of a wide and pervasive network of images (lopped hands, dismembered body politic) that have thematic significance. Both Marcus's speech (I.vi.11–57) when he meets the ravaged Lavinia in *Tit.* and Imogen's speech (IV.ii.292–333) over the headless body of Cloten in *Cym.* show Sh using narrative to slow down dramatic action and thus to achieve a dream-like effect, but Imogen's "fragmented and confused" speech leads back to the play's "general concern with dislocation and dismemberment." Sh seems to have sensed that the Philomel story was essentially narrative, not dramatic, material. On the stage, it would be best employed in melodrama like *Tit.* or, better yet, in tragicomedy.

1049 Thompson, Ann. *Shakespeare's Chaucer: A Study of Literary Origins*. New York: Barnes & Noble, 1978. xi + 239 pp.

Chapter 4 analyzes *Tro.* scene by scene, commenting on Chaucerian material where it is relevant. Concludes that *Troilus and Criseyde* was a significant influence on Sh's presentation of the love story and that Chaucer's poem furnished Sh with many suggestions about larger matters of structure and theme. Beyond this, Sh's tone in the play was inspired by Chaucer's self-conscious discussion of the problems of treating a familiar story that is "at once both tragic and sordid."

Chapter 5 provides a scene-by-scene analysis of *TNK*, making reference to Chaucer's *The Knight's Tale* where appropriate. In Sh's parts of the play, we see an attempt to extend the complex attitude and philosophy of Chaucer. Like Chaucer, Sh saw the story as absurd, and like Chaucer he sensed that its absurdity made it serious as well. Chaucer, through his narrator, provides a distancing from the tale, whereas Sh's approach is more melancholy.

1050 Thompson, Karl F. *Modesty and Cunning: Shakespeare's Use of Literary Tradition*. Ann Arbor: U. of Michigan P., 1971. 176 pp.

Views Sh as "a restorer and invigorator" of the literary conventions and traditions available to him. Focuses on four traditions (or sets of conventions): courtly romance, the plot and story of revenge tragedy, the didactic purpose of the drama, and "the doctrine of natural correspondences." Includes, in a chapter on the audience for which Sh wrote, a discussion of the classical emphasis in the grammar schools of the day. Discusses all of the plays in chronological order. Comments that North's translation of Plutarch's *Lives* was presented to the reading public as a book of instruction and that Sh would have understood it in that way when he wrote *JC*. In providing edification, *JC* makes use of conventions derived from the revenge play and the history play. *Ant.* provides "a full-scale romanticization of history," *Cor.*'s bleakness results from its narrow focus on "edificatory conventions of the history–play tradition," and *Tro.* attempts but fails to achieve a blending of traditions. Mentions, in discussing the last plays, that *Cym.* interweaves the message that Britain inherits and revives the greatness of Rome with romance.

1051 Tobin, J. J. M. "Shakespeare and Apuleius." *N&Q*, 25 (1978), 120–21.

Provides two notes on the influence on Sh of Apuleius's novel the *Metamorphoses*, translated by Adlington as *The Golden Asse*.

The first note sums up an episode from the novel in which Lucius, newly transformed into an ass, wanders into someone else's garden in search of food. Parallels in action and diction suggest that Sh had this passage in mind when he composed the scene of Jack Cade's hunger and death (*2H6*, IV.x).

The second note argues that the speech of Tyrrel describing the murder of the princes in *R3* (IV.iii.1–22) echoes Psyche's near-killing of Cupid in *The Golden Asse*. Revised as part of chapter 1 of item 1052.

1052 Tobin, J. J. M. *Shakespeare's Favorite Novel: A Study of "The Golden Asse" as Prime Source*. Lanham, Maryland: University P. of America. 1984. xxviii + 189 pp.

Identifies Apuleius as a Neoplatonic philosopher and rhetorician of the 2nd c. A.D., author of the Latin novel *Metamorphoses*, which was translated into English as *The*

Golden Asse by William Adlington in 1566. Proposes to demonstrate the pervasiveness of Apuleian elements throughout Sh's canon and to show what the significance of these elements is for our comprehension of Sh's "plots, characters, themes, and diction." Notes that Sh used both the original Latin and the translation. Chapter 1, "The Early Plays and *Venus and Adonis*," includes a revision of item 1051; chapter 2, "Romantic Plays of the Mid-1590s and Sonnets," covers *TGV*, *Rom.*, *LLL*, and *MND*; chapter 3, "The Falstaff Plays—and Dogberry," includes a revision of item 2324; chapter 4, "The Great Tragedies (1)," includes revisions of items 2116, 1053, 1884, 1885, 1886, and 2350. Chapter 5 covers "The Problem Plays." Part is a revision of item 2698. Chapter 6, "The Great Tragedies (2)," includes a revision of item 1490. Chapter 7, "The Romances," discusses *Cym.*, *Per.*, *WT*, and *Tmp.* Appendix A lists the 48 descriptive chapter headings for Adlington's translation of *The Golden Asse*, while appendix B, "*Othello* and the *Apologia* of Apuleius," consists of a revision of item 2351.

1053   Tobin, John J. M. "Apuleius and the Bradleian Tragedies." *ShS* 31 (1978), 33–43.

Contends that the *Metamorphoses* of Apuleius, translated by William Adlington as *The Golden Asse* in 1566, was a part of Sh's early reading and made a significant impact on him. He drew on it for important elements of plot, theme, and diction in the four central tragedies. A number of episodes in the plot of *Ham.* parallel episodes in the novel: For example, in book 2 of Apuleius, there is the murder of a husband for the purpose of adultery. Hamlet's calling Polonius a "fishmonger," a word that appears nowhere else in Sh, is likely to have been inspired by the corrupt elderly fishmonger in book 1. *Oth.* develops a theme strikingly similar to that of *The Golden Asse*, which has a man transformed into an ass for his "excessive curiosity about sexual appetite and magical practices." The central episode in Apuleius, the fairy tale of Cupid and Pscyhe, is likely to have influenced *Lr.*: It features two older, less favored sisters tormenting their younger sister. *Lr.* may also owe something to the account in the novel of a man disguised as a beggar with a naked belly, who describes himself as despising "pomp" and "delicacy," two words used in one of Lear's most important speeches (III.iv.12, 34). Thrasileon, the cornered thief of book 4, who disguises himself as a beggar, probably influenced the conception of Macbeth. There are also a number of words from the Thrasileon episode (for example, "thief," "seam," "porter," "compassed with," and "butcher") that came to Sh's mind when composing *Mac.* Revised as part of chapter 4 of item 1052.

1054   Toliver, Harold E. "Falstaff, the Prince, and the History Play." *SQ*, 16 (1965), 63–80.

Uses certain Aristotelian notions to explain the mixed structure of the history play as it is manifested in the *R2–H5* tetralogy. The concepts of *anagnorisis* and *catharsis* seem appropriate "in describing Falstaff's role as tragic victim," and, "as a rebel against history," Falstaff is "as guilty of *hubris* as he is of Saturnalian misrule." The central action of the history play is "the search for an effective adjustment between the inner self and the collective social organism," and Falstaff is a sort of mirror reflecting the various self-indulgences that threaten the adjustment. Prince Hal has the folk hero's ability to expel antitypes and absorb their strength: He thus disposes of threats like the wildness of Hotspur, the disease of his father, and the hedonism of Falstaff.

1055   Toliver, Harold E. "Shakespeare and the Abyss of Time." *JEGP*, 64 (1965), 234–54.

Argues that time, conceived as "continuous lapsing," is an important theme in Sh's sonnets and plays. In the middle plays, of which *Tro.* is an example, "the implications of the displacement of continuous order are explored in terms of the hero's inner life as well as in terms of social institutions." Incapable of "seeking gradual fulfillment in time," Troilus "cannot endure time at all." Unable to ground her love in any external reality, Cressida retreats into radical subjectivity, declaring that her love is the "center of the earth" (IV.ii.105). *Ant.* provides a view, through the creative imagination of Cleopatra, of a transcendent order beyond time, though it is still possible to see discontinuity as the destroyer of Antony.

1056   Torrance, Robert. *The Comic Hero.* Cambridge: Harvard U. P., 1978. xiv + 345 pp.

Has nine chapters on various manifestations of the comic hero in literature, who "repeatedly consents to encounter anew the unpredictable challenges and bewildering reversals of being alive." The first three chapters deal with figures from classical literature—Odysseus, the Aristophanic hero, and the Plautine slave and Lucius the ass—and these provide parallels, comparisons, and contrasts to Falstaff, who is treated in chapter 5. Chapter 5 begins with a discussion of the debt Sh's romantic comedies owe to classical New Comedy, primarily in their dependence on a final harmony brought about "through the restorative power of love." The history plays are quite different, containing as they do the clash between a responsible Christian king and "a flagrantly irresponsible Lord of Misrule." Though Prince Hal, through his use of stratagem, may seem to resemble "the classical comic hero" (for example, Odysseus), he makes clear that the part he is playing has nothing to do with who he really is. Falstaff, however, is true to all parts of his paradoxical nature. His comic heroism lies in his creation of his own preposterous vision of the world—a vision that is finally defeated by the moral authority of the king.

1057   Traschen, Isadore. "The Elements of Tragedy." *CentR,* 6 (1962), 215–29.

Argues that Shakespearean and Greek tragedy dramatize the relationship of three attitudes: the tragic, the orthodox, and the profane. The hallmark of the profane attitude is expediency: Characters who exemplify it can range from comfort-seeking time-servers like Osric in *Ham.* and the messenger in *Oedipus Rex* to villains like Iago in *Oth.* and Edmund in *Lr.* The orthodox attitude is represented by characters who espouse the prevailing moral and religious beliefs, like the chorus in Greek tragedy and Kent and Edgar in *Lr.* The tragic view comes into being in conflict with the other two: The hero experiences a breakdown of the orthodox order; he confronts and rejects both orthodox and profane attitudes; he arrives at self-knowledge (especially the conviction that the cosmos is inexplicable and he is born to suffering and death); and, by coming to terms with his limits, he achieves transcendence. The usefulness of this approach can be demonstrated by considering the graveyard scene in *Ham.*, in which the hero's alienation is defined by "recapitulating his encounters with the profane, the orthodox, and the tragic."

1058   Traversi, Derek. *Shakespeare: The Roman Plays.* Stanford: Stanford U. P., 1963. 288 pp.

Presents close readings of *JC, Ant.*, and *Cor.* and calls attention to the importance of Plutarch's *Lives of the Noble Greeks and Romans* in understanding these three plays. In several senses, Sh can be seen as collaborating with Plutarch. The unique combination of narrative clarity and poetic intensity in these plays owes much to the Greek historian. In addition, Sh profited greatly from Plutarch's "historical moralizing," with "its highly dramatic reading of history," especially its dramatization of great figures. In *JC,* Sh accepts the necessity of public order, and is willing to give Caesar some credit for establishing and maintaining this order; however, he refuses to ignore the potential for difficulties in Caesar's assumption of absolute power. There is ambivalence in the ways the play views both the dictator and the conspirators. The tragic structure of *JC* is divided between "two poles of interest," Caesar and Brutus. The latter, coming nearest to a tragic hero, is a man who, "rendered ineffective by the divisions in his own nature and by the contradiction between his own generous instinct and the spurious nature of the arguments which impel him to action, is finally brought to ruin." In *Ant.,* we have extraordinarily keen insights into complex and various private motives "wedded to a universal public theme." Order, in the form of Octavius's cold competence, prevails over the corrupt but "strangely vital" personal fulfillment represented by Egypt. Antony makes his tragic choice between these two outlooks as he surrenders to an emotion that, though potentially ennobling, is in this context "abstracted from the rest of life, pursued as a part at the expense of the whole." *Cor.* embodies "the most balanced and complete" of all Sh's political conceptions. The divisions in Rome, which are hinted at in Plutarch, are presented as operating "within a unity." The conflicts within the protagonist's own nature "stand in relation to a society divided against itself, tending fatally to its own ruin." Coriolanus's heroism is genuine but narrow, the product of class prejudice and impaired human relationships.

1059 Tribe, David H. *Free Thought and Humanism in Shakespeare*. London: Pioneer P., 1964. 17 pp.

Mentions, in the course of maintaining that Sh was a freethinker and a humanist, that throughout his plays respect is accorded "the Roman virtues of *gravitas* and *dignitas*, with *humanitas*," as well as "Aristotle's golden mean of conduct."

1060 Trnka, Bohumil. "Shakespeare's Ethics and Philosophy." *Charles University on Shakespeare*. Eds. Zdeněk Stříbrný and Jarmila Emmerová. Prague: Charles University, 1966, pp. 55–63.

Argues that Sh mastered the philosophical ideas of his time with ease and presented them in dramatic form as no one else was able to do. At the same time, his ethical realism raised him above the conventions of his time. In *Tro.*, as in other middle plays, a note of pessimism is heard. This may owe something to the essays of Montaigne. In his earlier plays, Sh emphasizes "the enjoyment of the pleasures of life," and the folly of theorizing. *LLL*, for example, is "an attack on the barren learning of Sh's time and particularly on the Platonizing English philosophers who had gathered round Giordano Bruno during his stay in England."

1061 Trousdale, Marion. *Shakespeare and the Rhetoricians*. Chapel Hill: U. of North Carolina P., 1982. xiii + 206 pp.

Draws on a variety of rhetoric texts from the 16th c., and on their classical forebears like Aristotle, Quintilian, and Cicero, to illuminate the idea—underlying Elizabethan poetic art—that language is artificial and can be distinguished from the fundamental reality of things. The pleasures of art derive from the copiousness (as defined by Erasmus) with which language, in its artificiality, represents reality. Discusses *R2*, *LLL*, *Ham.*, *JC*, *MM*, and *Oth*. In *JC* and *Ham.*, we see a structure determined by rhetorical elaboration of the significances of various actions. Analyzes *Oth*. in terms of Quintilian's comments about persuading judges. Notes that Iago is "the best student of Quintilian ever to appear on the Elizabethan stage."

1062 Truax, Elizabeth. "Venus, Lucrece, and Bess of Hardwick: Portraits to Please." *Shakespeare and the Arts: A Collection of Essays from the Ohio Shakespeare Conference, 1981*. Eds. Cecile Williamson Cary and Henry S. Limouze. Washington, D.C.: U. P. of America, 1982, pp. 35–56.

Uses Bess Talbot, Countess of Shrewsbury, and the art with which she adorned Hardwick Hall to illustrate the taste of the English upper classes in the late 16th c. for representations of classical myth that include amorous encounters uneasily framed by allegory and moralization. Sh had this audience in mind when he depicted Venus as both libidinous courtesan and grief-stricken goddess of generation (*Ven.*) and Lucrece as emblem of chastity, object of erotic desire, and devotee of her husband's honor (*Luc.*).

1063 Turner, Frederick. *Shakespeare and the Nature of Time: Moral and Philosophical Themes in Some Plays and Poems of William Shakespeare*. Oxford: Clarendon P., 1971. 193 pp.

Investigates "the arsenal of thoughts, feelings, and attitudes with which Shakespeare attacks the central problems of man's temporal nature and his relationship with his environment of time." Treats nine aspects of time: historical time, personal experience of time, time as agent, time as "realm or sphere" (the temporal as distinguished from the eternal), natural time ("cycles, rhythms, and periods" of the natural world), time as "the medium of cause and effect," "particular moments or periods of time," "time as revealer," and "time as rhythm." Includes chapters on *Son.*, *AYL*, *TN*, *Ham.*, "Tragedies of Love and Time" (including *Tro.*), *Mac.*, and *WT*. An appendix includes "some readings on time up to the Renaissance," with commentary on the readings. Notes that Sh could have absorbed the Greek philosophers (Heraclitus, Plato, and Aristotle) through such works as Pierre de la Primaudaye's *French Academie,* translated into English in 1594. Roman thought on time was directly available to Sh in translations. The *Meditations* of Marcus Aurelius Antonius are important in introducing a more directly ethical approach to time than that of the Greeks. Plotinus and St. Augustine also made significant contributions. Cites Sh's contemporaries, especially Fulke Greville, whose *Caelica* and *Treatie of Warres* include many notions about time derived from Greek and Roman sources.

1064   Turner, Robert Y. *Shakespeare's Apprenticeship*. Chicago: U. of Chicago P., 1974. 293 pp.

Classifies Sh's apprentice works (twleve plays and two poems) as either serious or comic and discerns a progression in both types from highly rhetorical speech to "increasingly flexible dialogue that depends as much upon tropes as upon verbal patterns." Chapter 6 cites Cicero, Quintilian, and Donatus, and their 16th-c. humanist followers, like Erasmus and Sir Thomas Elyot, to systematize the neoclassical "tradition of comic theory" into four topics: "meaning, plot, character, and emotion." The theory describes a "mirror comedy about social types" that is informed by certain ideas about plot variety and construction, decorum, and laughter. Considers the first five comedies of Sh: *Err.* and *Shr.* conform fairly closely to the neoclassical rules; *TGV*, in attempting to dramatize the difficulties of young love as "the central experience," can be viewed as "a transition to *LLL* and *MND*, two plays that solve the problem of encompassing the sentiments of love within the principles of neo-classical comedy."

1065   Ure, Peter. *Shakespeare: The Problem Plays*. London: Longmans, 1961. 59 pp.

Discusses *Tro.*, *AWW*, *MM*, and *Tim.* as problem plays, having the following features in common: the probing of characters in an ambiguous ethical situation, "an urgently satirical and disfiguring temper," "a willingness even in comedy to draw near to pain and death," an "interweaving of romantic and even fantastic takes with realistic characters," and an art that embodies the resistance of life to being translated into art. Points to the Duke's counsel to Claudio to be "absolute for death" (*MM*, III.i.5) as "the very roof and crown of the tradition of the classical consolation." Sees *Tro.* as a "sardonic rendering" of the stories of the Trojan War and of Troilus's love. Maintains that though Sh satirically diminishes much of what he treats, the character of Troilus achieves tragic stature by his hopeless adherence to his belief in Cressida's truth. Agrees with the view that Sh attempted to create in *Tim.* a tragic hero like Lear or Othello, but that "he failed to do so partly because he had not chosen a story and theme capable of sustaining him."

1066   van den Berg, Sara. "'The Paths I Meant unto Thy Praise': Jonson's Poem for Shakespeare." *ShakS*, 11 (1978), 207–18.

Analyzes Ben Jonson's eulogy for Sh printed in the First Folio to show that the poem's success depends on a contrast between the two men that "underlies the poem's large design of thematic oppositions and comparisons and lends special strength to the theoretical reconciliations that justify the final vision of Shakespeare's apotheosis." The poem summons up the classical playwrights as a way to remove Sh from "ephemeral history" by comparing him with dramatists whose works have been accorded the status of literature. The reference to Sh's small Latin and less Greek shifts the reader's attention to Jonson himself; as the leading exponent of classicism on the English stage, he has the authority to affirm that Sh is equal to the Greek playwrights. Like the ancients, Sh can "imitate Nature directly" and needs no models. After establishing Sh's parity with (and in some respects superiority to) the classical playwrights, Jonson refers to his subject as "my Shakespeare," an exemplar worthy of endorsement and imitation by a Jonsonian poet.

1067 Van Laan, Thomas S. *Role-playing in Shakespeare.* Toronto: U. of Toronto P., 1978. x + 267 pp.

Chapter 7 treats *JC* and *Tro.* as plays that dramatize history as an active force. The major characters in *JC* (except Octavius Caesar) engage in "discrepant role-playing," by means of which each of them projects an image of himself that is far superior to the reality. More important, Sh dramatizes "the opposition between their aspirations and what really happens to them." The "unsatisfactory reality" they experience is history. In *Tro.*, the celebrated legendary heroes are mocked through the radical contrast "between their real worth and the inflated conceptions of themselves they perform so badly." Instead of being merely based on history, then, both works are about history and about writing historical drama.

Chapter 8 includes consideration of *Cor.* and *Ant.* as tragedies that derive their action from the hero's "search for a setting in which he can perform his identity with greatest effectiveness."

1067a Van Norden, Linda. The Black Feet of the Peacock: The Color-Concept "Black" *from the Greeks Through the Renaissance.* Comp. and ed. John Pollock. Lanham, Maryland: U. P. of America, 1985. xii + 228 pp.

Chapter 1 comprises a brief survey of the definition and significance of the color black, beginning with the ancient Greek philosophers. Notes that in the Renaissance color symbolism was derived from a number of fields, including alchemy, astrology, cabalism, mythography, and heraldry. Chapter 2 studies the uses of the peacock emblem, going back to ancient writers like Epicurus, Lucretius, and Pliny, and concluding with the assertion that in the Renaissance the bird's colors came to have moral significance. Chapter 4 includes brief discussions of *Tit.*, *TGV*, and *Oth.*

1068 Vecchio, Monica Joan. "Sovereign Reality: Time and Necessity in the Political World of Shakespeare's Mature History Plays with Bibliographical Analysis." Ph.D. dissertation, Fordham University, 1985. *DAI,* 46 (1985–86), 2305-A.

Recognizes in Sh's second tetralogy of English history plays "a masterpiece of political theater." Studies these plays in the light of works by Plato and Augustine, and the Bible. Suggests that the quality of a ruler in these works can be evaluated by examining the extent to which he is obedient to time.

1069 Velz, John W. "Episodic Structure in Four Tudor Plays: A Virtue of Necessity." *CompD,* 6 (1972–73), 87–102.

Cites David Bevington's thesis that the episodic structure of much Tudor drama is traceable to the limited number of available actors, and discusses four instances in which such structure is perfectly harmonized with a play's theme. The *de casibus* pattern in *R3* is well-shown through episodic structure, as is the process of history that is Sh's overriding concern in *JC*.

1070 Velz, John W. "'Nothing Undervalued to Cato's Daughter': Plutarch's Porcia in the Shakespeare Canon." *CompD,* 11 (1977–78), 303–15. Reprint. *Drama in the Renaissance: Comparative and Critical Essays.* (AMS Studies in the Renaissance 12.) Eds. Clifford Davidson, C. J. Gianakaris, and John H. Stroupe. New York: AMS P., 1986, pp. 150–62.

Holds that the account of Porcia in Plutarch's *Life of Marcus Brutus* influenced Sh not only in *JC* but also in *MV, Luc., 1H4,* and *Mac.* The Portia of *MV* was created as a contrast to Porcia in Plutarch: The former is able to act in a world of men to assist her husband, while the latter, frustrated at her helplessness, commits suicide. When Sh came to write *JC*, though he followed Plutarch's account of Porcia closely, he borrowed important features from his own earlier portrayal in *MV*, particularly the idea of the wife as her husband's *alter ego*, merged with him in a metaphysical relationship. In *Luc.*, the heroine's viewing of the painting of Troy and her application of its story to her own case were probably conceived by another analogy with Plutarch's Porcia, who applies a painting of Andromache parting from Hector to her own separation from Brutus. Kate, in *1H4* II.iii, and Lady Macbeth, in *Mac.* III.ii, are two wives who, like Plutarch's Porcia (and of course Portia in *JC*), display curiosity about their husbands' public business.

1071   Velz, John W. "The Ovidian Soliloquy in Shakespeare." *ShakS*, 19 (1986), 1–24.

Finds a paradigm for several Shakespearean soliloquies in the speeches of self-analysis delivered by six young women in Ovid's *Metamorphoses* when they find themselves newly awakened to erotic passion. The first of these, Medea's, sets forth the elements of the *ethos* that Ovid is concerned with: "1) self-questioning in the face of entirely new emotion; 2) conflict between *amor* and *pudor* that takes a larger form as conflict between *amor* and another value; 3) tendency to universalize the moral position; 4) self-deceptive rationalization, including blaming the gods; 5) fearful reflection on the imagined consequences of the contemplated deed." Sh uses this pattern in Tarquin's contemplation of his rape of Lucrece (*Luc.*) and in Angelo's two meditations on his lust for Isabella (*MM*, II.ii and II.iv). More distant from the Ovidian archetype, but still related to it, are speeches by three invaders of bedrooms—Othello (*Oth.*, V.ii), Macbeth (*Mac.*, II.i), and Iachimo (*Cym.*, II.ii)—who have crime in their hearts.

1072   Vickers, Brian. *The Artistry of Shakespeare's Prose.* London: Methuen, 1968. ix + 452 pp.

Attempts to reveal "the artistry which has gone into the making of Sh's prose." Suggests that Sh placed prose in an inferior position to that of verse because he wanted to achieve "a great range of meaningful juxtapositions with verse." Finds three elements to be of greatest importance for the discussion of Sh's prose: imagery, linguistic structure, and rhetorical structure. Linguistic structure can be analyzed more fruitfully if one understands the classical training in rhetoric given to all schoolboys during Sh's time. For example, the four types of pun—*antanaclasis* ("repetition of words, shifting from one meaning to another"), *paronomasia* ("repetition of words nearly alike in sound"), *syllepsis* ("use of a word having simultaneously two different meanings, but not repeated"), and *asteismus* ("word returned by answer with unlooked-for meaning")—are all found frequently in Sh. Rhetorical structure refers to "the arrangement of prose into the patterns taught and practiced by traditional rhetoric, patterns of symmetry and balance." This involves the use of classical schemes like *anaphora* ("the same word beginning successive clauses or sentences"). Proceeds, after treating early plays in chapter 1 ("Shakespeare's Use of Prose") and chapter 2 ("A Critical Method"), to cover most of the canon. Chapter 3, "From Clown to Character," covers *LLL*, *Rom.*, *MND*, and *MV* and argues that in this group of plays there is a gradual movement by which the prose devices "become less the province of type–charactery such as the clown or of set–scenes, but are slowly integrated to more realistic personalities and to the dramatic texture." Chapter 4, "The World of Falstaff," deals with *1&2H4*, *H5*, and *Wiv.* as a group. Chapter 5, "Gay Comedy," points out that *Ado*, *TN*, and *AYL*—in keeping with their lightness of tone—have prose that is superior to their verse. Chapter 6, "Two Tragic Heroes," investigates the substantial amounts of prose given to Brutus and Hamlet. Chapter 7, "Serious Comedy," argues that in *Tro.*, *AWW*, and *MM*, the prose of the lower characters, normally used for lightly deflating commentary, is used here for concentrated abuse directed at the main action. Chapter 8, "Tragic Prose: Clowns, Villains, Madmen," points out that in six great tragedies—*Oth.*, *Lr.*, *Mac.*, *Tim.*, *Ant.*, and *Cor.*—"prose continues to be the medium for persons and states below the norm." Prose is used with ever-increasing effectiveness for madness and clown-scenes. Chapter 9, "The Return of Comedy," examines the four late romances, finding that "the prose under-plots are disappointing in themselves, and far less meaningfully related to the main action than in the mature comedies."

1073 Vickers, Brian. "'The Power of Persuasion': Images of the Orator, Elyot to Shakespeare." *Renaissance Eloquence: Studies in the Theory and Practice of Renaissance Rhetoric*. Ed. James J. Murphy. Berkeley: U. of California P., 1983, pp. 411–35.

Notes the classical origins of 16th-c. English praise for the beneficent powers of the orator and his rhetoric. Argues that Sh, like the theorists of his time, acknowledges the potential efficacy of rhetoric, but that he differs from them in emphasizing that the process of persuasion is often futile or unambiguously evil. Cites *Tro.* as an example of a highly rhetorical play in which language fails conspicuously to achieve anything. Persuasion used for evil ends is seen frequently in the history plays and tragedies, especially in *JC* (Cassius seducing Brutus), *Cor.* (the tribunes, as well as Volumnia, manipulating Coriolanus), *R3*, *Mac.*, *Oth.*, and *Lr.*

1074 Vickers, Brian. "Shakespeare's Use of Rhetoric." *A New Companion to Shakespeare Studies*. Eds. Kenneth Muir and S. Schoenbaum. Cambridge: Cambridge U. P., 1971, pp. 83–98.

Surveys the history of rhetoric and notes its classical origins and pervasiveness in Renaissance education. Comments that the rhetorical element of greatest interest to Sh was *elocutio*, or style, taught in the Renaissance handbooks through lists of schemes or figures. Discusses several of the more important figures, like *anaphora* and *anadiplosis*, as they appear in *R3*, and then cites later examples to show how these "structures of rhetoric" are assimilated into Sh's mature style.

1075 Vincent, Jeffrey S. "Jacobean Intrigue Comedy." Ph.D. dissertation, Rutgers University, 1974. *DAI*, 35 (1974–75), 6685-A-6686-A.

Discusses "the adaptations of the ancient conventions of comic intrigue in a variety of English plays," including *MM* and *Tmp*. Also considers "the intrigue comedies of Plautus and Terence." In all of these works, the figure of the intriguer is especially important; it is he who takes on the roles of actor and director to manipulate the plot and bring about the comic conclusion.

1076 Viswanathan, S. "'Illeism With a Difference' in Certain Middle Plays of Shakespeare." *SQ*, 20 (1969), 407–15.

Explains that "illeism with a difference" occurs when a character, speaking in the first person, refers to himself by name (not simply by a pronoun, which is illeism proper). Sh makes significant use of this device in only four "middle plays." It appears most frequently in *JC* (thirty times) and *Tro.* (fifteen times), and less often in *Ham.* (eight times) and *Oth.* (four times). This sort of illeism enriches the dramatic context by (1) showing "the relationship between the character using it . . . and his inner self"; (2) calling attention to the difference "between the public and the private selves of the characters"; (3) raising the question of how a character orders his behavior to accord with a "rightly or wrongly conceived idea of himself"; and (4) pointing toward "the search for identity of the human self" as it was portrayed on the Elizabethan stage by actors aware of their identities and yet at the same time conscious of the roles they were playing. Sh might have used the device in *JC* and *Tro.* because he wanted to explore the complex relationship between the grand images of Greek and Roman legend and history and the reality underlying them. Or he may have been influenced, through his reading of Plutarch, by the Greek idea that every man has "his guardian angel and his evil angel."

1077 Viswanathan, S. "Shakespeare's Metamorphoses of Actaeon." *Essays on Shakespeare in Honour of A. A. Ansari*. Ed. T. R. Sharma. Meerut, India: Shulabh Book House, 1986, pp. 46–57.

Surveys the various interpretations of the Actaeon myth, both learned and popular, available to Sh: the connection of the horned figure of Actaeon with the cuckold, the horn dance, or the figure exposed to public ridicule in the skimmington ride; the moral (emblematic) view that Actaeon's fate is the punishment for excessive physical passion; and the Neoplatonist reading that saw the myth as the figuring of the unification of the pursuer of love with his object. In *Tit., Wiv., AYL*, and *Ham*. Sh uses both moral and popular implications of the myth, while in *TN* he seems to emphasize the Neoplatonist idea. Sh outdoes Ovid in the transformations he works on the Actaeon story.

1078 Viswanathan, S. "Sleep and Death: The Twins in Shakespeare." *CompD*, 13 (1979–80), 49–64.

Explains the origins of "the conception of Sleep and Death as siblings" in Homer and Hesiod. The sleep–death conjunction, also used by Cicero and other classical authors, found a prominent place in Renaissance mythography and probably suggested a number of possibilities to Sh. For example, in *Luc.*, the description of Lucrece asleep at Tarquin's approach uses the device, thereby anticipating the heroine's death.

1079 Von Rosador, K. Tetzeli. "Plotting the Early Comedies: *The Comedy of Errors, Love's Labour's Lost, The Two Gentlemen of Verona*." *ShS*, 37 (1984), 13–22.

Adapts Aristotle's conception of plot as modified by Terentian theorists to discuss "the art of precipitation, of prefiguring within the *protasis* both the play's middle and its end" in *Err., LLL*, and *TGV*.

1080 Vosevich, Kathi Ann. "The Rhetoric of Shakespeare's Women: Figures, Sense, and Structure." Ph.D. dissertation, University of Denver, 1988. *DAI*, 49 (1988–89), 1812-A.

Explains that the 16th-c. rhetoricians emphasized the connection "among figures, sense, and structure" and that Sh makes use of this connection, especially in assigning dominant figures of rhetoric to the heroines of *Ado* (*copulatio*), *Rom.* (*interrogatio*), *H8* (*provocatio*), and *WT* (*negatio*).

1081 Vyvyan, John. *Shakespeare and Platonic Beauty*. New York: Barnes & Noble, 1961. 224 pp.

Argues that Sh possessed a clear philosophy of life that essentially coincides with the Christian Platonism of Marsilio Ficino. Whether or not Sh knew Plato's or Ficino's works, he could have absorbed the philosophy from works like Castiglione's *The Courtier* and Spenser's *Hymne in Honour of Beautie*. Sh's plays can be read as allegories or parables in which various aspects of this view of life are worked out. In Ficino's scheme, there are three worlds of creation: the Angelic Mind, the Soul of the Universe, and "the structure that our senses perceive." Each world begins in chaos but through the power of love is endowed with form by "the Ideas that originate in God." The absolute beauty of God draws to it all creation; hence love is seen as an ascent from the lower worlds toward the divine. In *The Courtier*, the ascent from the physical world to the heavenly is analyzed into seven steps, with the first involving the lover's being struck by the beauty of a woman. In *LLL, TGV*, and *Rom.*, the heroines are based on what Ficino calls "the Heavenly Venus," the power in the Angelic Mind that moves up "to contemplate the beauty of God." The heroes of these plays find themselves involved in a Platonic ascent, frequently described by Sh in the metaphor of pilgrimage, leaving behind the shadows of the physical world (represented, for example, by the unprofitable studies of the academy in Navarre [*LLL*]) and progressing toward real beauty (symbolized in *LLL* by the ladies). During the course of *MND*, the lovers move through a stage of confusion, rivalry, and discord, symbolic of the illusory outer world, toward the harmony of true love, which represents inner reality. The play follows the progress of several characters as they perfect their "love-sight," which enables them to see real beauty "behind the mask of mortality." *AYL* emphasizes the development of self-knowledge on the way to the apprehension of divine beauty. Rosalind, whom Orlando calls "heavenly," presides over the latter's movement through the first five of Castiglione's steps. Oliver and the usurping Duke repent of their initial wickedness through experiences that teach them self-knowledge through love. In *AWW*, Helena's pilgrimage is a symbolic ascent of love. Bertram at first turns his back on the ladder of Castiglione by rejecting the true beauty of Helena for false military glory and lust. He is eventually stripped of these shadows of the sensual world and rescued by Helena's work of love. *Tro.* reveals what happens when the link between earth and heaven, which draws men toward the divine and thus brings harmony to the world, is broken. Several characters, most notably Hector, have flashes of "self-insight" that allow them to proclaim the ideal standard, but they fail to maintain it. Troilus's vision of two Cressidas separates the higher from the lower and confirms the play's picture of dissolution.

1082 Waage, Frederick O. "Be Stone No More: Italian Cinquecento Art and Shakespeare's Last Plays." *Shakespeare: Contemporary Critical Approaches.* Ed. Harry R. Garvin. Special associate ed. Michael D. Payne. (*BuR*, 25, no. 1.) Lewisburg: Bucknell U. P., 1980, pp. 56–87.

Charts the growing sophistication with which Sh makes use, implicitly and explicitly, of the arts of painting and sculpture throughout his career. Cites the painting of Troy in *Luc.* as evidence that Sh in this early phase sees visual art as an imperfect means to imitate reality. In *Tim.*, cynicism about art underlies the satirical treatment of the Poet and the Painter. In *WT*, the references to Giulio Romano and the handling of the statue of Hermione reveal that the playwright has formulated his own version of the "newly discovered Italian art," combining elements of the Platonic and the sensually evocative to show how art can go beyond imitating nature to transforming it.

1083 Wagenknecht, Edward. *The Personality of Shakespeare.* Norman: U. of Oklahoma P., 1972. ix + 190 pp.

Comments briefly and frequently on most works in the canon. Surveys the few examples (Lavinia in *Tit.*, Brutus in *JC*, Imogen in *Cym.* are some) of characters who read or are described as reading on stage. Sh certainly read widely, absorbing, for example, more of Plutarch than he needed for the specific plots he was constructing. Suggests that the chief reason for Sh's antipathy to the lower classes was their foul smell, as indicated in *JC* and *Cor*. The "sex-obsessed imagination" is explored in *Tro.* In *Ant.*, the heroine is magnificent, though not good; Sh does not make her culpable, as does Plutarch, but he does not permit her allure to cloud his judgment. *Cor.* is one of Sh's two most military plays; the protagonist and his mother are exceptionally bloodthirsty, though she partly redeems herself by successfully pleading with her son to save Rome. Glances briefly at the suicides in Sh; the playwright recognizes the distinction between the ancient Roman and Christian attitudes. Describes key statements on order in *Tro.* and *Tim.*

1084 Wain, John. "Guides to Shakespeare." *Encounter.* March, 1964, 53–62.

Argues that Sh's great theme was order and harmony and that his imagination was rooted in "the world of dream, fairy-tale, and the collective unconscious." Like any folk artist, Sh did not create original material. Like his favorite poet, Ovid, he "used the myths that were familiar to everyone, and his art consisted in the imaginative skill with which he orchestrated story with story, and clothed narrative with words and images." Also like Ovid, he created an atmosphere of flowing, change, melting, and instability. An example occurs when Antony stops the action to discourse upon clouds (*Ant.*, IV.xiv.2). In fact, he is admitting that his Roman-ness cannot hold its shape against the lure of Cleopatra.

1085 Wain, John. *The Living World of Shakespeare: A Playgoer's Guide.* London: Macmillan, 1964. xii + 239 pp.

Addresses "the intelligent and informed person who doesn't happen to have formally studied English literature." Mentions Sh's attraction to Ovid, the "poet of melting, changing, flowing, other-seeming." Treats *Tro., Ant.,* and *Tim.* in some detail.

1085a Waith, Eugene M. "'Give Me Your Hands': Reflections on the Author's Agents in Comedy." *The Author in His Work: Essays on a Problem in Criticism.* Eds. Louis L. Martz and Aubrey Williams. New Haven: Yale U. P., 1978, pp. 197–211. Reprint. *Patterns and Perspectives in English Renaissance Drama.* Newark: U. of Delaware P., 1988, pp. 65–77.

Inventories Roman comedy for the ways in which an author can deputize an agent to ask for audience approval and "to tell us what to laugh at." Cites various instances of authorial intervention from the works of Plautus and Terence, and a comment on the practice from Horace's *Ars Poetica,* as background for consideration of Puck in *MND,* Rosalind in *AYL,* and Prospero in *Tmp.*

1086 Waith, Eugene M. *The Herculean Hero.* New York: Columbia U. P., 1962. 224 pp.

Anatomizes in chapter 1, "Demigod," Herculean heroism as it appears in classical myth and in Sophocles' *The Women of Trachis,* Euripides' *Heracles,* and Seneca's *Hercules Furens* and *Hercules Oetaeus.* Hercules emerges from these works as a warrior of extraordinary strength, valor, and fortitude. He is inordinately proud, subject to savage anger, capable of great loyalty, devoted to a heroic ideal, and regarded as a benefactor of mankind. Though raised far above the level of ordinary men, he is forced to endure great suffering. In his Stoic manifestation, both aspiration and endurance are given a value "which throws the final emphasis upon transcendence rather than limitation."

Chapter 2, "Heroic Man," sums up some of the Renaissance interpretations of the Hercules myth, including the allegorizing of Natalis Conti's *Mythologiae* (1551), Vincenzo Cartari's *Imagini de i Dei degli Antichi* (1556), and Cesare Ripa's *Iconologia* (1593). Here, Hercules was extolled as representative of careful self-control, though his association with magnificent excesses was not forgotten. The Florentine Neoplatonists praised Hercules as embodying man's capacity to aspire to the status of a god. Along with his "glorious individuality," the Renaissance often gave equal weight to Hercules' unselfishness.

Chapter 5, "Shakespeare," treats *Ant.* and *Cor. Ant.* incorporates a number of Herculean elements in its hero, but its tragedy—consisting in part of a final assertion of love—lies somewhat outside the Herculean pattern. Antony does resemble Hercules in his anger (which Cleopatra seems to admire), his valor, and the fortitude of his suicide. Cleopatra's visions of Antony do justice to his colossal stature, and the structure of the play is an apt analogue for his "Herculean magnitude." In *Cor.,* the hero is clearly based on the Herculean paradigm. He is compared to Hercules and described as a god. He is intemperate, scornful of the people, extraordinarily courageous, and generous. He rejects absolutely anything he does not believe in; he belongs to a different world from that of the plebeians and even that of his fellow patricians. Sh insists on his hero's powerful will and his "solitariness." Coriolanus has an intense loyalty to his personal honor and thus cannot be said to be inconstant when he joins the Volscians. In the final scene, the taunt that hurts him most is the word "boy," which strikes at the heart of his manhood, his heroic *virtus.* The play's conclusion affirms what the world is losing in the destruction of the hero.

1087 Waith, Eugene M. *Ideas of Greatness: Heroic Drama in England.* London: Routledge and Kegan Paul, 1971. xii + 292 pp.

Sketches the background of heroic drama—including the classical epic and its medieval mutations—in the first chapter. Considers "the concern with potentiality rather than limitation—with greatness rather than error—as a fundamental distinguishing characteristic of heroic drama." Chapter 2 includes a discussion of the heroic conception of character in *Ant.* and *Cor.* Antony, a protagonist more great than good, is portrayed as a colossus of generosity and power. Coriolanus's generosity is negative, and his godlike superiority eventually destroys itself.

1088 Waldo, Tommy Ruth Blackmon. "Musical Terms and the Complexity of Shakespeare's Style: An Illustration of the Style and Its Relationship to Rhetorical Precept." Ph.D. dissertation, University of Florida, 1961. *DAI*, 31 (1970–71), 371-A-372-A.

Argues that Sh's dramatic use of musical terms illustrates the complexity of his poetic control, which he seems to have achieved in part by absorbing classical rhetorical precepts. Enumerates four ways in which Sh's style manifests complexity in dealing with musical references. One of these occurs when the musical allusions in a play form a pattern, particularly one that evokes a concept like the music of the spheres.

1089 Walker, Ellen Louise. "The Varieties of Comedy: A Study of the Dramatic Comedies of Molière, Jonson and Shakespeare." Ph.D. dissertation, University of Connecticut, 1971. *DAI*, 32 (1971–72), 2655-A.

Points out that in Sh the supreme comic agent is a woman, who is related to "the myths of procreation, love, and earthly happiness." She helps give Sh's comedies their special festive quality. Man, released from society's rigidity and corruption, "creates a 'golden age' in which the demands of mortality and the chaotic nature of Eros lead to freedom rather than to fate."

1090 Waller, G. F. *The Strong Necessity of Time: The Philosophy of Time in Shakespeare and Elizabethan Literature.* (De Proprietatibus Litterarum: Series practica 90.) The Hague: Mouton, 1976. 176 pp.

The introduction, consisting of the first three chapters, sketches the notions of time (mainly cyclical) developed by the ancient Greeks and incorporated into Christian thought to form the basis of medieval belief. Includes a discussion of the Renaissance philosophy of Giordano Bruno, whose view of time, influenced by classical thinkers like Lucretius and Epicurus, rejects "the concept of an immutable divinity outside of time." Regards "infinity as coincident with the finite," and asserts that "every instant of time's passing contains eternity in itself." Speculates about Bruno's influence on Sh.

The third section, consisting of six chapters, surveys Sh's works with regard to their treatment of time. Chapter 9 covers *Tro.* and *Ant.* In the former, infinite ideals of love and heroism are defeated because their partisans attempt to embody them in time-bounded experience. In the latter, two arenas of human experience—public and private—in which "time can be fulfilled" are contrasted. The lovers choose the private world, which is an attractive one, but in doing so they must renounce so much that their fate is tragic. Chapter 12 examines *WT* and *Tmp.*, the latter of which—in its vision of "man's autonomy," his "inborn divinity," and his embracement of the potential for eternity in the moment—is strikingly close to the philosophy of Bruno.

1091 Walsh, Sister Mary Brian, O.S.B. "'Swift Eyesight Like a Flame': A Study of *Anagnorisis* in Shakespearean Tragedy." *Thoth*, 7 (1966), 35–52.

Applies the Aristotelian concept of *anagnorisis* (translated as both "recognition" and "discovery") to *Oth.*, *Lr.*, *Mac.*, and *Ham.* In all four plays, the hero comes to know both the "concrete realities of his situation" and "what his experience *means*," but in each case the discovery takes place in a different way. In *Mac.*, for example, there is a "suspenseful doling out of information to the protagonist," followed by "Macduff's fateful revelation" that he was untimely ripped from his mother's womb. In *Ham.*, however, the hero's physical recognition of his situation is of relatively little importance in the play.

1092 Warren, Roger. "Prospero's Renunciation and Coriolanus's Capitulation." *N&Q*, 21 (1974), 134–36.

Points out that while the major source for Prospero's renunciation speech in *Tmp.* is Ovid, Sh includes a number of details from the scene in which Coriolanus yields to his mother (*Cor.*, V.iii). Similar language is used because, in some sense, each character is "a would-be superman coming to terms with his own humanity." There are differences, however, because Prospero's response is dictated by his "nobler reason" (*Tmp.*, V.i.26), while that of Coriolanus comes from the heart.

1093 Washington, Edward T. "Beyond Cultural Stereotypes: The Dramatic Meanings of Shakespeare's Black Characters." Ph.D. dissertation, Boston University, 1990. *DAI*, 51 (1990–91), 1243-A.

Offers close readings of *Tit.* and *Luc.* to determine "the degree to which black roles in these works involve meanings that deflate, destroy, or invert stereotypical protrayals."

1093a Watson, Robert N. "Horsemanship in Shakespeare's Second Tetralogy." *ELR*, 13 (1983), 274–300.

Traces the origin of the references to horsemanship in *R2, 1&2H4*, and *H5* to the account by Plato in the *Phaedrus* of the human soul as a chariot "driven by reason and pulled by two horses, one noble and the other ignoble." By the time of the English Renaissance, this metaphor had been elaborated in such a way that good horsemanship could be used as a sign of self-control and bad horsemanship as an indication of inadequate self-control. Discusses images of horses and horsemanship, especially the Phaethon myth, in Sh's second tetralogy. Shows how, through horse imagery, Bolingbroke (Henry IV) and Prince Hal (Henry V) are portrayed as legitimate rulers, whereas Richard II, Hotspur, and Falstaff are seen as lacking the self-control to possess authority.

1094 Watterson, William Collins. "Elizabeth Pastoral Satire" Ph.D. dissertation, Brown University, 1976. *DAI*, 46 (1985–86), 2703-A.

Recognizes that from the age of classical antiquity, "the literary modes of pastoral and satire have enjoyed an affinity." Points out that Sh uses "the *topoi* of pastoral complaint" in the *H6Triad* to expose "moral ineptitude," while in *AYL* and the late romances he employs satire to attack "the excesses of primitivism" and sophistication.

1095 Watts, Cedric. "Shakespearian Themes: The Dying God and the Universal Wolf." *Critical Dimensions: English, German and Comparative Literature Essays in Honour of Aurelio Zanco*. Eds. Mario Curreli and Alberto Martino. Cuneo, Italy: SASTE, 1978, pp. 117–33.

Investigates a link "between Shakespeare's atheistic intuitions and his conception of appetite." In *Tit.*, possibility of a godless world is suggested by two episodes. The first is Titus's attempt to solicit the gods for justice by having arrows bearing letters shot toward the heavens (IV.iii). Instead of divine intervention, he gets the Clown, "a dimwitted buffoon." The second comes in the final act, when Titus's revenge is consummated through anthropophagy. Sh had precedents for this sort of revenge in Ovid's *Metamorphoses* and Seneca's *Thyestes*, but he added the ostentatious allegory of Revenge, Rapine, and Murder that helps to "dramatize evil as *appetitive*." In *Tro.*, Ulysses' "degree" speech (I.iii) emphasizes the destructive power of appetite, calling it "an universal wolf" (line 121); furthermore, the play's imagery associates food, disease, and sex in "this fallen, secular, appetitive world."

1096 Wayne, Don E. "Mediation and Contestation: English Classicism from Sidney to Jonson." *Criticism*, 25 (1983), 211–37.

Comments that Ben Jonson's "blending of Christian–humanism and Stoicism" is also evident in the later plays of Sh. Notes that Jonson, in contrast to Sh, insisted on "rigorous imitation of his classical sources," which suggests a "deep-felt need to find an authoritative basis for a revision of the Elizabethan courtiers' code of honor."

1097 Webber, Joan. "The Renewal of the King's Symbolic Role: From *Richard II* to *Henry V*." *TSLL*, 4 (1962–63), 530–38.

Maintains that in the tetralogy beginning with *R2* Sh is showing how the old, stylized rhetoric could be redirected to help accomplish the "revision and renewal of the king's symbolic role." Prince Hal, in the play-acting by which he educates himself to be king, may be following the advice of Quintilian, who urges that our daydreams or hallucinations be turned to some profit.

1098 Weidhorn, Manfred. *Dreams in Seventeenth-Century Literature.* The Hague: Mouton, 1970. 167 pp.

Chapter 1, "Major Theories of the Dream from Homer to Hobbes," sketches a background in classical authors like Aeschylus, Aristotle, Plato, and Democritus for ideas about supernatural objective dreams, self-generated heuristic and mantic dreams, naturalistic and skeptical theories about dreams, and dream interpretation. Chapter 5 discusses dreams in Sh's works, especially *Cym., JC, Rom., MND, R3* (Sh's "most dream-laden play"), *Mac.,* and *Ant.*

1099 Weidhorn, Manfred. "The Relation of Title and Name to Identity in Shakespearean Tragedy." SEL, 9 (1969), 303–19.

Contends that the tragic hero in Sh suffers a crisis of identity during which his title and name are lost. Near the end of his career, name and identity "are recovered, but not the title." Illustrations include Cleopatra, who fails to see herself as "Madam," "Royal Egypt," or "Empress" (*Ant.*, IV.xv.71–72) but rather the meanest milkmaid and finally wife. Antony and Timon both suffer crises of identity involving loss of name. The most detailed exploration of name-loss is in *Cor.*

1100 Weidhorn, Manfred. "The Rose and Its Name: On Denomination in *Othello, Romeo and Juliet, Julius Caesar.*" TSLL, 11 (1969–70), 671–86.

Discusses the significance of names in Sh, mentioning characters who lose their titles (Cleopatra), their names (Timon, Antony), or their identities (Coriolanus). Also mentions occasions on which a character postulates an exchange with another character (Cassius with Caesar and Antony with Brutus in *JC*). In *JC*, the power in an appellation is given its fullest scope: The name of Caesar is responsible for Caesar's death and Brutus's dilemma, and "denotes a spirit and a historical force [that] bridge the epochs of Republican and Imperial Rome."

1101 Weightman, Franklin Case. "Politics in Shakespeare's Roman Plays." Ph.D. dissertation, University of North Carolina at Chapel Hill, 1981. DAI, 42 (1981–82), 2692-A.

Examines *Tit., JC, Ant.,* and *Cor.* to arrive at an understanding of Sh's concept of Romanitas. Studies certain aspects of the Renaissance intellectual background and concludes that in these plays Sh dramatizes three motifs—those of the family, the soldier, and the private man—that develop from his view of history. Sh intended for his audience "to evaluate these three motifs" both separately and in the combinations by which they produce tragedy for the various protagonists. The conflicts between the family, the soldier, and the private man and the state underline two important Renaissance ideas: (1) Politics cannot be separated from other human endeavors and (2) a nation can prosper only if it comprehends "the lessons of judgment in the individual."

1102 Weil, Herbert S. Jr. "Comic Structure and Tonal Manipulation in Shakespeare and Some Modern Plays." ShS, 22 (1969), 27–33.

Maintains that most of Sh's comedies resemble modern works like Edward Albee's *The American Dream* and Jean Genet's *The Balcony* in that they "are *open* to different legitimate responses by different members of the same audience." *Tro.* and *Ant.* are not cynical contradictions to the "joyous romantic comedies"; rather, they emphasize an element that has been present through most of Sh's earlier comedies. The playwright's most complex use of multiple perspectives occurs in V.ii of *Tro.*, when Cressida commits herself to Diomedes.

1103 Weimann, Robert. "Society and the Individual in Shakespeare's Conception of Character." ShS, 34 (1981), 23–31. Reprint. SJW, 118 (1982), 91–99.

Cites Ulysses' comments to Achilles (*Tro.*, III.iii) as a way to explain the dialectical nature of Sh's conception of character. The would-be autonomous self (a very modern notion) works in a kind of creative tension with the socially defined self (the traditional notion). Sh's heroes have "meaningful and, sometimes, unpredictable dialogues with the image of the outside world," thus experiencing growth and change in a way that would be impossible for a medieval character. Also comments on *Cor.* and *Err.*

1104 Weimann, Robert. "The Soul of the Ages: Towards a Historical Approach to Shakespeare." *Shakespeare in a Changing World.* Ed. Arnold Kettle. New York: International Publishers, 1964, pp. 17–42.

Argues that Sh's plays, with their great range of subject matter, conventions, and values, reflect their author's success in discovering "how the issues of his time, its 'form and pressure,' could most significantly be turned into material for great art." One element in the cultural gallimaufry of the age was humanism, informed by classical learning and indebted to concepts like the Great Chain of Being, but at the same time able to question its own foundations and to form important ties with the popular tradition. Sh integrated such elements into his plays.

1105 Weinstock, Horst. "Loyal Service in Shakespeare's Mature Plays." *SN,* 43 (1971), 446–73.

Surveys examples of the relationship between master and servant in several plays. Comments that Sh's reading of "Plutarch and other Roman sources" might have influenced him to modify his notion of loyal service. Several of the Roman and Greek tragedies, for example, do not reveal the unwavering faithfulness between master and servant of earlier plays; but instead, they introduce the notion of a running account of "a master's or servant's deserts."

1106 Weisinger, Herbert. "The Proper Study of Myth." *CentR,* 12 (1968), 237–67.

Defends the "myth method" of interpretation in various fields but especially in literary studies. Attempts, in section 3, to show how myth study can be used to determine "the vision of life of an author" and illustrates by examining several key passages in Sh (including *JC,* I.ii.90–161 and I.iii.57–78) that "provide a detailed picture of the Renaissance in its most radical aspect." In these passages, Sh's "positive villains" present a world view "which intellectually justifies to them their relentless opposition to the traditional system of Christian–humanist values and urges them on in action." The failure of these villains does not validate the world view they oppose: They—and some of Sh's heroes (like Antony)—are largely self-defeating. Certain successful protagonists (like Octavius), who seem to support the traditional view, are ambiguous because they use methods that deny its values. As four passages from *Tro.* demonstrate, the point is that Sh's view of the world is somewhere between "the philosophical radicalism" of his villains and "the Christian–humanist tradition."

1107 Weiss, Theodore. *The Breath of Clowns and Kings: Shakespeare's Early Comedies and Histories.* London: Chatto and Windus, 1971. viii + 340 pp.

Notes the Ovidian mode of the pictures representing moments of transformation that the Lord and his servants promise to show Sly in *Shr.* In *MND,* the transformations in the woods and the tradesmen's play are also indebted to the *Metamorphoses.*

1108 Welch, Robert. "Seneca and the English Renaissance: The Old World and the New." *Literature and the Art of Creation.* Eds. Robert Welch and Suheil Badi Bushrui. Totowa, New Jersey: Barnes & Noble, 1988, pp. 204–18.

Attempts to answer the question of what Seneca "opened" for the Renaissance. Suggests that he prompted a new sense of fear at human beings' capacity for cruelty to each other, a feeling of panic, a view of the human body as grotesque and ludicrous, and a recognition that the coming together of people in cities is a radically precarious enterprise. Senecan despair, resulting from a conviction of man's inconsequentiality, opened the way for Sh and other Renaissance dramatists to discover a new kind of inclusiveness in human consciousness, a sense of life based on a Pauline interpretation of the Christian Gospel. Makes several references to Sh's works, especially *Son.*, *Ham.*, *MND*, and *WT*.

1109 Weller, Barry Leigh. "The Other Self: Aspects of the Classical Rhetoric of Friendship in the Renaissance." Ph.D. dissertation, Yale University, 1974. *DAI*, 35 (1974–75), 3959-A.

Begins with a discussion of the Aristotelian notion of friendship as "the mutual attraction of two virtuous and self-sufficient men, who recognize in one another their own highest qualities." A friend, then, is "an other self." Aristotle's idea of friendship was widely disseminated in later times through Cicero's *De Amicitia* and was revived for the Renaissance by Petrarch. The Aristotelian image of friendship also found its way into the Renaissance through fictions that dramatized the idea of a friend as another self. In the tale of Tito and Gisippo in the *Decameron*, Boccaccio examined the situation of two friends who fall in love with the same woman; Sh used this story in *TGV*. The conception of a friend as an other (male) self became, by the end of the 16th c., sufficiently modified to provide partial inspiration for plots containing doubles, like *Err.* and *TN*, and for the portrayal of sexual union as friendship.

1110 Weller, Philip James. "Politics in Shakespeare's Later Drama." Ph.D. dissertation, Kent State University, 1969. *DAI*, 30 (1969–70), 5423-A-5424-A.

Argues that in *JC*, *Cor.*, *Tro.*, and *Tmp.* we see reflections of Elizabethan political practice, not theory. Politics in Sh's time operated by means of institutionalized factionalism that belied the ideal of a political Great Chain of Being. In North's Plutarch, Sh would have found politics more accurately observed than in the works of many contemporary theorists. The *Lives* presents political arrangements as in a state of continual flux; harmony may be the ideal, but conflict is the reality. Political principle is subject to history, and "the movement of time dominates the action and destroys men." The view of politics in *JC* and *Cor.* is basically Plutarchan: Sh does not take sides in the disputes of either play. The only generalization that can be made is that "politics is a function of time as change." *Tro.* and *Tmp.* both present "explicit challenges to Elizabethan political orthodoxy."

1111 Wells, Charles. *The Northern Star: Shakespeare and the Theme of Constancy*. Upton-upon-Severn: Blackthorn P., 1989. 222 pp.

Proposes to investigate Sh's examination of the problem of seeking constancy in a world of mutability. Consists of four sections, each treating a broad area of constancy and each divided into several chapters. Discusses each work in the canon, with some works being mentioned in only one chapter but most being considered in several chapters and/or sections. Section 1, "Moral Constants," includes *Tro.* in chapter 1, on honor: Hector, to whom honor is the essence of being, can be contrasted with Thersites, to whom it is nothing. Chapter 2, "The Imperial Seat (Roman Values)," emphasizes the fascination with the Roman world—as an image of "permanence and supreme self-sufficiency"—found throughout Sh's works. Considers this image as it is presented in *JC*, *Luc.*, *Ant.*, and *Cor.* Notes the concern with "self-sacrificing courage" and suicide in the Roman (and some other) plays. Sh subjects Roman values to "the most rigorous questioning."

Section 2, "Relational Constants," devotes chapter 6 to various aspects of love. Foregrounds Platonic love as one type that influenced Sh. Analyzes numerous works under such headings as "Idealism," "Appetite," "Infidelity," "Love and Time," "Love and Energy," "Relativity," and "Perpetuation." Draws many examples from *Tro.* and *Ant.* Chapter 8, on friendship, has much to say about *Tim.*, citing Cicero's *De Amicitia* as one relevant background work.

General Works

Section 3, "Social Constants," refers to *Cor.* and *Ant.* in chapter 12, on custom and tradition. Chapter 13, on authority and rebellion, includes analyses of passages from *Cor.*, *JC*, and *Tim.*

Section 4, "Temporal Constants," begins with chapter 14, on time and process. Opens by discussing time in play groups and ends with separate sections on several plays, including *Tro.* (which depicts time as destroyer of all human values) and *Ant.* (which exalts the enjoyment of the present moment, while recognizing the reality of historical context). Chapter 15, on time, metaphor, and ambiguity, bases some of its conclusions on *Tim.*, *Cor.*, and *Ant.*

1112   Wells, Henry W., and H. H. Anniah Gowda. *Style and Structure in Shakespeare.* New Delhi: Vikas, 1979. xi + 253 pp.

Chapter 10, on *JC*, notes that Sh used Putarch to good effect, learning much from him about analysis of character and motive. The strength of this play lies in its "character delineation"; weaknesses include a "too insistent classicism." Chapter 11, on *Tro.*, stresses the alternating validity and hollowness of its rhetorical magnificence, which makes it "a conscious study in the various phases of the baroque." Chapter 18, on *Ant.*, finds passion to be "the dominant image." Chapter 19, on *Cor.*, discovers an archaic world devoted to "aggrandizement and physical force"; the play is closer in spirit to its source, Plutarch's *Lives*, than is any other work by Sh. Its severity distinguishes it from Sh's other Roman plays. Chapter 20, on *Tim.*, comments on the treatment of the main character, the satiric thrust of his later speeches, and the importance of Alcibiades in illuminating Timon's character.

1113   Wells, Stanley. "Shakespeare and Human Evil." *En Torno a Shakespeare: Homenaje a T. J. B. Spencer.* Ed. Manuel Angel Conejero. Valencia: Universidad de Valencia, Instituto Shakespeare, 1980, pp. 67–91.

Mentions Brutus as a character who seems to do evil deeds from good motives. We are forced to wonder if something so vile as murder can be justified "by the needs of the state." The situation is complicated by the fact that "Brutus stands to gain by the deed." Cites the proud boast of wicked deeds by Aaron in *Tit.*, V.i, as a description of the kinds of qualities that convey the mystery of evil in Sh.

1114   Wells, Stanley. "Shakespeare and Romance." *Later Shakespeare.* Eds. John Russell Brown and Bernard Harris. (Stratford–upon–Avon Studies 8.) London: Edward Arnold, 1966, pp. 49–79. Reprint. 1973.

Suggests that the important features of Shakespearean romance include "the separation and disruption of families, followed by their eventual reunion and reconciliation; scenes of apparent resurrection; the love of a virtuous young hero and heroine; and the recovery of lost royal children." Sketches the background of this sort of material in Greek New Comedy and especially in Greek romances like *Daphnis and Chloe*, *Aethiopica*, and *Clitophon and Leucippe*, all of which were available to Sh in recent translations. The romance of Apollonius of Tyre, on which Sh based *Per.*, was also available in a number of versions. Sh used romance conventions in different ways at different stages of his career. In *Err.*, he romanticized Plautus's *Menaechmi*, a primarily comic source, by emphasizing family relationships. *TN* recounts the separation by shipwreck of brother and sister and their reunion. *Pandosto*, the chief source of *WT*, was heavily influenced by Greek romance; and Sh readjusted the romance elements, sometimes intensifying them, sometimes qualifying them with "a modified realism," and "always investing them with a poetic rather than a mundane reality." Romance material pervades *Tmp.*, but the play's classical form forces the audience to experience most of the story by recalling the past rather than by moving through a present that becomes the past, as in most romances. Though chance plays a part as a causative agent, much of the plot is controlled by the art of Prospero, who "resembles the narrator of a romance story." With its moral seriousness, *Tmp.* is a romance that incorporates a criticism of both the glories and the limitations of the genre.

1115 Westney, Lizette I. "Hecuba in Sixteenth-Century English Literature." *CLAJ*, 27 (1984), 436–59.

Surveys accounts of Hecuba as grieving or avenging mother available in 16th-c. England: Euripides' *The Trojan Women* and *Hecuba*, Seneca's *Troades*, and Ovid's *Metamorphoses*. Hecuba was regarded by Elizabethan translators of these works as a mirror in which "others might see themselves." In *Luc.*, the heroine, in viewing a picture of the fall of Troy, launches into a lamentation like that of Hecuba just after she remarks on the face of the Trojan queen. In *Ham.*, the description of the "mobled queen" and the Player's reaction to her pitiable state reflect Hamlet's situation and seem to reproach him for inaction. Imogen, in *Cym.*, refers to Hecuba as the cursing revenger, and her madness and her thirst for revenge are both mentioned in *Tit.*

1116 Wheater, K. I. "Moral Theory and Shakespeare's Use of Normative Vocabulary." Ph.D. thesis, 1986, Oxford University. *ITA*, 37 (1988), 438–39.

Discovers through analysis of *MV*, *Tro.*, and *Tim.* that Sh's "normative vocabulary" is essential to "the presentation of moral problems and therefore articulates an argument [that] gives a play intellectual coherence." In deploying moral terms not only to characterize certain actions but also to comment on them, Sh betrays an indebtedness to Aristotle. Assesses the impact on Sh of the English Aristotelian revival of the last quarter of the 16th c.

1117 Wheeler, Richard P. *Shakespeare's Development and the Problem Comedies: Turn and Counter-Turn.* Berkeley: U. of California P., 1981. xiv + 229 pp.

The last chapter includes an account of Sh's tragedies that divides them into two groups: the trust-merger group (including *Ant.*), in which "the effort to establish power and autonomy is ultimately subordinated to what proves to be a stronger need for a lost or jeopardized bond to another" and in which "longing for merger shapes the action"; and the autonomy-isolation group (including *Tro.*, *Tim.*, and *Cor.*), in which "relations to the self and others that promise fulfillment instead prohibit the achievement of stable autonomy" and in which the action "moves through destructive merger toward isolation and emptiness."

1118 Whitaker, Virgil K. *The Mirror up to Nature: The Technique of Shakespeare's Tragedies.* San Marino: Huntington Library, 1965. ix + 332 pp.

Argues that Sh was "a more careful craftsman" than most of his contemporaries and that he was familiar with contemporary critical theory and built his tragedies "in terms of the best learning of his day as he understood it." Surveys, in the first chapter, extant tragedies written before the end of Sh's career, classifying them for the purpose of understanding "the Elizabethan notion of tragedy and comparing Shakespeare's dramatic practice with that of his contemporaries." Comments on the influence of Seneca. Chapter 2 surveys "Elizabethan critical theories," noting the general influence of Aristotle's *Poetics* and Horace's *Ars Poetica* and the more specific theories of drama deriving from Aelius Donatus, the Italian schematizations of Aristotle and Horace, and "the practice of Seneca and Terence." Concludes that Sh "exemplifies the ideas and assumptions of his age" but that he developed "a unique technique that allies him to Aristotle" and to thoughtful contemporaries. He deals in universals, but "as his special contribution to theory and practice, he will do so by making sure that the relevant universal principles find explicit statement even as the particular action unrolls." Chapter 3 discusses Sh's early tragedies, including *Tit.*, and concludes with an analysis of *JC*. There is an important breakthrough in this play: the attempt, not entirely successful, "to show Brutus actually making a tragic error." Chapter 4 discusses "the philosophic aspect" of the tragedies; chapter 5 *Ham.* and *Lr.*; chapter 6 *Oth.* and *Mac.*; and chapter 7 *Ant.* and *Cor.* These last two plays share several weaknesses, including episodic structure, failure to explore fundamental principles, and lack of complex character development. Both, of course, have brilliant scenes, and both are good stories.

1119 Whitaker, Virgil K. "Shakespeare the Elizabethan." *Rice University Studies*, 60, no. 2 (1974), 141–51.

Suggests that Sh's tragedies are very like those of his contemporaries. Maintains, for example, that the plot of *Ant.* is not well-articulated; though this play is infused with the magic of Sh's poetry, its action is just as diffuse as the plots of other plays that attempt to depict the Roman wars. In *JC*, there is unity of plot but no focus on a single tragic hero.

1120 Entry deleted.

1121 White, Gail Lana. "Pastoral Plays and Masques of Shakespeare, Jonson, Milton." Ph.D. dissertation, University of California, Irvine, 1973. *DAI*, 34 (1973–74), 7724-A-7725-A.

Investigates the connections between pastoral and masque conventions in *WT* and *Tmp*. The opening section uses examples from Theocritus and Virgil that summarize the conventions of pastoral poetry. This section also points out that "the didactic purposes of the masque ... enable the poet to treat pastoral problems through symbolic characters, including the shepherds and satyrs associated with Apollo and Dionysus in pastoral poetry." In *WT*, Sh considers the relative merits of mimetic and masque techniques for drama and shows that masque techniques allow the audience to set aside its usual notions of time. *Tmp.* uses masque techniques to ask "whether art can alter our political attitudes and our perceptions of reality."

1122 White, Howard B. *Antiquity Forgot: Essays on Shakespeare, Bacon, and Rembrandt*. (International Archives of the History of Ideas 90.) The Hague: Nijhoff, 1978. 160 pp.

Argues in chapter 1 that in Sh, Bacon, and Rembrandt, antiquity, though not forgotten, was "in some sense, over-passed." In Sh, whose frame of reference is "essentially Platonic," there was less forgetting of antiquity than in Bacon, who wanted to replace Aristotle.

Chapter 2 notes that Sh's plays make frequent reference to the shortcomings of the political life, but they also suggest a corrective process. Three means of correcting a monarchy, the predominant regime in Sh, are (1) modifying the king's power "by the rule of law"; (2) directing kingly power by wisdom; and (3) changing the regime to something other than a monarchy. In many plays, unseduced common opinion, praised by Plato and Aristotle as an intermediate step on the way to complete truth, is a reliable daily cure for political wrongs.

Chapter 3 is a revision of item 2232a.

Chapter 4 points out that *Jn.* deals with the two problems of legitimacy and the relation of church and state. John is an illegitimate king who is also associated with injustice. Faulconbridge, though his birth was illegitimate, has qualities of the natural ruler. In the spirit of Hellenism, he rises above the Christian wrangling in the play to advocate harmony and patriotism.

Chapter 5 maintains that Sh had to write *H8* as his final political statement about the English nation. Henry's divorce of Katherine should be read as the "triumph of the public over the private, of intellectual virtue over moral virtue." The play "fulfills what *King John* only suggests, freedom from civil strife."

1123 White, Howard B. *Copp'd Hills towards Heaven: Shakespeare and the Classical Polity*. (International Archives of the History of Ideas 32.) The Hague: Nijhoff, 1970. viii + 156 pp.

Argues in chapter 1 that Sh was a Platonic political philosopher. He is likely to have known some of the dialogues, and he certainly would have been exposed to Plato through Plutarch, Seneca, and Montaigne. The important thing is that his treatment of the polity is often Platonic in spirit.

Chapter 2 treats *Tim.*, in which the polity is shown in a decayed state. Timon's banquet lacks discourse, and Timon himself is unphilosophical in his largesse. There is flattery of Timon by others and flattery of others by Timon. Neither he nor the Senate commands loyalty, and the worship of private gain (usury) dominates the city. There are no women in the sense of mates—no wives, no families—and the gods are absent. The city is not wholly corrupt, because common people like the steward are generous. The Senators seem to recall a greater Athens in their plea to Alcibiades at the end, but there is no real hope.

Chapter 3 maintains that *MND* is about the founding of Athenian democracy. Theseus presides over a movement from arbitrary patriarchal rule like that of Egeus to law founded on justice, while Oberon acts as a mime of the powers of nature to educate the humans in establishing a polity, and the common folk are integrated into the society at the end. For most of the characters there is an ascent to "a greater purity of soul" as in a Platonic dialogue.

Chapter 4 contends that *Cym.* deals with the decline of pagan antiquity and the rise of Christian Europe. The process of Christianization in Britain is contrasted with "an established pagan regime" (Rome), which is more civilized. From a group of temporary exiles, Britain learns the lessons it needs to transform its obviously inadequate polity.

Chapter 5 analyzes *Per.* The hero's name recalls the great Athenian statesman, but Sh does not endow him with political understanding or show him ruling.

Chapter 6 sees *Tmp.* as about a philosopher–king on an island similar to the city of the *Republic*. On the island, Prospero has learned to rule, something he was unable to do before.

Chapter 7 continues discussion of *Tmp.* Wonder is perceived by Ferdinand as leading to wisdom. Reflection on passages from Aristotle and Plato shows that this sort of wonder comes from contemplating the mysteries of the everyday.

Chapter 8 suggests that for Sh, as for Plato, the highest art form was not tragedy or comedy, but the dramatic dialogue, of which *Tmp.* is the paradigm. In many plays, particularly the last ones, Sh's characters follow the Platonic ascent of the soul, gaining wisdom through inquiry.

1124 White, Jeannette Smith. "Seneca as Influence on Shakespeare: Classical Model or Elizabethan Malady?" Ph.D. dissertation, Brown University, 1989. *DAI*, 50 (1989–90), 2505-A.

Emphasizes that Renaissance playwrights recognized in Seneca's work themes appropriate to contemporary concerns. Chapter 3 explores the links between Seneca and Sh in the treatment of revenge. Chapter 4 examines the damaging effects of fanatical passion in the characters created by both writers and notes that both treat madness as central to tragedy.

1125 White, R. S. *Shakespeare and the Romance Ending.* Newcastle upon Tyne: Tyneside Free P., 1981. iii + 139 pp.

Comments briefly on the Greek romance as one source of the Elizabethan prose romance, itself a precursor of Sh's romances. Discusses the relevance of the "endless ending" of romance to several of Sh's plays, focusing on *Per., Cym., WT,* and *Tmp.*

1126 Whittier, Gayle. "The Sublime Androgyne Motif in Three Shakespearean Works." *JMRS*, 19 (1989), 185–210.

Discusses the three occasions in Sh's career—Sonnet 20, *Rom.*, and *Ant.*—when he engaged the theme of "sublime androgyny," the use of the hermaphrodite as symbolic of marriage, with marriage itself being symbolic of the union of opposites on which the welfare of the world and of individuals depends. Mentions Plato and Ovid as classical sources of the sublime androgyne motif. Sonnet 20 presents an image of sublime androgyny in the master–mistress who combines the virtues of both sexes into one form, so that he is "a source of art (the sonnet) but a perplexity in the world." Romeo and Juliet experience sexual role reversals, but their deaths prevent the consummation of "sublime completion." In *Ant.*, however, Sh poetically evokes the sublime androgyne as well as staging it; and he centers the action on the enterprise.

General Works

1127 Wickham, Glynne. "Neo-Classical Drama and the Reformation in England." *Classical Drama and Its Influence: Essays Presented to H. D. F. Kitto.* Ed. M. J. Anderson. London: Methuen, 1965, pp. 155–73.

Describes the struggle of the 16th-c. English humanists to renew interest in Greek and Roman drama. In adapting Latin plays "to meet conditions created by the Reformation," they "reinforced the didactic element of traditional religious plays inherited from the medieval past. In doing this they brought the refinement of their own style, grounded in the study of classical models, to bear upon historical narrative and ethical disputation." Abstract personifications inherited from the moralities were given distinctive personalities. *Ralph Roister Doister*, an interlude, thus anticipates Falstaff.

1128 Wickham, Glynne. "*The Winter's Tale*: A Comedy with Deaths." *Shakespeare's Dramatic Heritage: Collected Studies in Mediaeval, Tudor and Shakespearean Drama.* New York: Barnes & Noble, 1969, pp. 249–65.

Argues that Sh rejected the classical unities in constructing *WT*, "a parable set in two localities." Suggests that Sh was influenced by civic pageants of 1605 and 1609, which portrayed London as the New Troy and equated James I with "the second Brutus of ancient prophecy." The idea that ancient Troy is victorious and reunited in 16th-c. Britain has an effect not only on *WT* but on most of Sh's other plays written between 1603 and 1613. The Roman plays (*Cor., JC, Ant.*) are not directly related to Troy or to King James, but they could very well be Sh's response to England's new "national interest in an imperial future."

1129 Wilbur, Richard, ed. *The Poems*. (Pelican Shakespeare.) Baltimore: Penguin Books, 1966. 184 pp.

The introduction notes that most of Sh's material for *Ven.* is derived from Ovid's *Metamorphoses* and that the epigraph is from the *Amores*. Thus in some sense Sh was signaling his intention to imitate "a witty, charming, and delicately sensual Latin poet." The "high proportion of dialogue" makes *Ven.* unlike other Ovidian poems. Maintains that the characters do not have any psychological depth or consistency. Nor is it possible to defend a coherent allegorical or moral interpretation, though hints of allegory and morality can be discerned. Sh has used his Ovidian story as an occasion for "a concatenation of virtuoso descriptions, comparisons, apostrophes, essays, pleas, reproaches, digressions, laments, and what have you." For *Luc.*, the ultimate source was Ovid's *Fasti,* and the story is one that English writers had made familiar. Lucrece's extended lamentation shows that Sh was fashioning a hybrid genre from Ovidian narrative and the complaint. As in *Ven.*, the characters are inconsistent, undergoing abrupt shifts to provide opportunity for rhetorical exercises in antithesis. Praises the passage in which Lucrece contemplates the painting of Troy for its skillful exploration of the relationships between Lucrece's Rome and Troy. Calls attention to Sh's *ad hoc* revision of the myth of the phoenix in *PhT* and suggests that the two lovers in that poem owe "something of their wingedness" to the *Phaedrus* of Plato. Reprinted as part of item 0496.

1130 Wilders, John. *The Lost Garden: A View of Shakespeare's English and Roman History Plays.* London: Macmillan P., 1978. xi + 154 pp.

Notes the tendency of Sh to juxtapose public and private situations in his history plays and emphasizes the inseparability of the two. In this, the playwright was influenced by Plutarch. The history plays express a view of the human condition in which there are no permanent solutions to problems, only new problems, and in which men have choices forced on them "between various courses of action all more or less unsatisfactory." In the midst of a painful present, there is frequent allusion to an ideal past, calling attention to the ephemeral nature of the heroes' achievements. This longing for "the lost garden" is never satisfied. Covers *JC, Ant., Cor.*, and *Tro.* in each of the following chapters: "History and Tragedy," "Time and Change," "Fortune and Nature," "Prayer, Prophecy and Providence," "Knowledge and Judgement," "Dilemma and Discovery," and "The Lost Garden."

1131 Williams, George Walton. "Antique Romans and Modern Danes in *Julius Caesar* and *Hamlet*." *Literature and Nationalism*. Eds. Vincent Newey and Ann Thompson (Liverpool English Texts and Studies.) Liverpool: Liverpool U. P., 1991, pp. 41–55.

Discovers at significant points in the structure of *Ham.* the symbolic presence of a figure who exists outside the play. This referential structure was rehearsed by Sh in *JC*, which shares with *Ham.* the theme of the philosopher-hero's failure to carry out violent action to cleanse the state. In the first part of *JC*, the referential figure is Pompey, who seems to preside over the conspiracy against his great foe; in the latter part, Caesar himself appears to supervise the defeat of his assassins. In *Ham.*, the figure is Caesar, who appears three times, in acts I, III, and V, "at the structural nodes of the play." In each case, the emphasis is on death. The second reference to Caesar, Polonius's mention of his acting the role and being "killed i' the Capitol" (III.ii.101–102), prompts Hamlet's pun on Brutus (103–104), which links Hamlet with the murderer Brutus when shortly thereafter he stabs Polonius.

1132 Williams, Jimmy Lee. "*Titus Andronicus* and Shakespeare's Mature Tragedies: A Study in Continuity." Ph.D. dissertation, Indiana University, 1971. *DAI*, 32 (1971–72), 4584-A.

Finds that Sh derived many of the "ideas, themes, plot motifs, and fundamental concepts of character for his great tragedies, *King Lear*, *Macbeth*, *Hamlet*, and *Othello*," from *Tit*.

1133 Willis, Paul Jonathan. "The Forest in Shakespeare: Setting as Character." Ph.D. dissertation, Washington State University, 1985. *DAI*, 47 (1986–87), 918-A.

Canvasses Sh's plays with forest settings to show how the settings influence character. In the forest comedies, exposure of character is followed by change; in the forest tragedies (including *Tit.* and *Tim.*), exposure is followed by perception; in the forest romances (*Cym.*, *WT*, *Tmp.*, and *TNK*), exposure is followed by change and perception.

1134 Willson, Robert F. Jr. "The Plays within *A Midsummer Night's Dream* and *The Tempest*." *SJW*, 110 (1974), 101–11.

Suggests that the Pyramus and Thisbe play of the tradesmen in *MND* emphasizes the absurdity of the lovers during their adventure in the forest. It also reveals the sexual side of love. In *Tmp.*, the mythological figures of Prospero's wedding masque for Ferdinand and Miranda (IV.i) have a symbolic function. The succession of goddesses not only celebrates the nuptials of the lovers but also represents "the relinquishing of supernatural influence on human beings." For example, Miranda's progress from virgin to wife to mother is symbolized in the procession of Iris, Ceres, and Juno, and Prospero's recognition that the masque is an insubstantial dream prompts his decision to give up his magic and return to the society of men.

1135 Willson, Robert F. Jr. *Shakespeare's Opening Scenes*. (Salzburg Studies in English Literature: Elizabethan and Renaissance Studies 66.) Salzburg: Institut für Englische Sprache und Literatur, U. Salzburg, 1977. iv + 217 pp.

Chapter 1 covers *Err.* and *Tit*. The first of these has an opening scene that gives Egeon a past and creates "a framework of poignancy" that helps to play down the cynical and satiric tone of Plautine comedy, on which the rest of the play is based. *Tit.*'s opening scene makes up the entire first act; it is bristling with "action and powerful rhetoric." Composed of five segments, this scene uses the entire stage, beginning with a procession across it; the opening of the tomb and the positioning of certain characters in the space aloft indicate that Sh is establishing clearly "the range of places available for his monumental tragedy." This "hyperbolic staging" is fitting for the Senecan language. The movement from high to low and from orderly ceremony to fractious violence foreshadows what will happen to Rome and to Titus and his family. At the conclusion, Tamora's ascendance (in a literal sense) makes it clear that barbarism reigns. Chapter 6 treats three late Roman plays, *JC*, *Cor.*, and *Ant.*, all of which begin in the streets and reveal common people longing for values in leaders who seem preoccupied with private concerns. The first scene of *JC* serves to depict the Roman crowd, particularly its fickleness, and the tribunes' critical attitude toward it; it also gives the audience some idea of Caesar before he appears. In *Cor.*, the first scene shows Rome torn by internal and external revolt; the citizens rebellious but cowardly and fickle; the chief warrior and support of Rome himself in a state of revolt; and this same hero vulnerable to his own "basic instinct." The first scene of *Ant.* is a play within the larger play, dealing with Antony's character, and this play has a thoroughly Roman stage audience, which comments on Antony's behavior and draws the appropriate moral about his abandonment of Roman values. Within the scene Antony is presented in his private, Egyptian mode, though he does have some nagging thoughts about his past Roman image. Cleopatra's comments during the scene concur in some respects with those of Antony's Roman critics, perhaps to absolve both Egypt and Rome from responsibility for the hero's fall. This scene is "heavily symbolic," revealing "a fall in microcosm," but carefully qualifying the meaning of the fall that is suggested by "the morality play reading of the stage audience."

1136   Willson, Robert F. Jr. *Shakespeare's Reflexive Endings.* (Studies in Renaissance Literature 6.) Lewiston, New York: Edwin Mellen P., 1990. xiii + 127 pp.

Investigates the endings of six of Sh's tragedies. Finds that the features these plays have in common form a pattern suggesting the playwright's abiding interest in "what might be called character fate." In each play, the central figure creates the conditions under which he or she will be destroyed, even predicting such destruction; each displays the sudden turn of Fortune's Wheel; and each ending consciously recollects the play's beginning and is marked by strongly ironic elements. Chapter 5, on *Ant.*, is a revision of item 1527. Chapter 6, on *Cor.*, emphasizes the one-dimensional character of the protagonist; the foreshadowing throughout the play of Coriolanus's capitulation to his mother in V.iii and of his bloody death in V.vi; the ironic juxtaposition of the opening scene, in which Coriolanus is set in conflict with the Roman people, and the final scene, in which he enters Corioli at the head of an admiring throng; and the series of identities that he is forced to assume.

1137   Wilson, F. P. *Shakespearean and Other Studies.* Ed. Helen Gardner. Oxford: Clarendon P., 1969. x + 345 pp.

Surveys Sh's comedies, especially the early and middle works, in chapter 2. Comments on the indebtedness of *Err.* to Plautus's *Menaechmi*, both in terms of plot and Roman "flavor": the mercantile society, the slave-like status of servants, and the un-Shakespearean connection of Antipholus of Ephesus with a courtesan. The departures from Plautus are more interesting: the improbable doubling of the twins; the invention of Luciana, a "respectable unmarried girl"; and the reunion of Egeon with his sons and wife.

1138   Wilson, John Delane. "Some Uses of Physiognomy in the Plays of Shakespeare, Jonson, Marlowe, and Dekker." Ph.D. dissertation, Michigan State University, 1965. *DA*, 26 (1965-66), 4612.

Refers to the importance of physiognomy, which pretended "to reveal the secrets of a man's temperament, intelligence and character (and occasionally his future)," in the ancient world as well as in Renaissance Europe. By Sh's time, the claims of physiognomy were no longer accepted by all learned men. Thus it was treated ambiguously in the drama of the time. Sh seems to mock the pseudo-science in *Ant.* and to openly question it in *Mac.*, but in *R3* and *Ham.* he invokes its vocabulary and point of view "to explore the relationship of appearance and reality."

1139 Wilson, Robert Benjamin. "A Survey of Stoicism and Neostoicism in the Dramatic Works of Chapman, Marston, and Shakespeare." Ph.D. dissertation, Southern Illinois University, 1975. *DAI*, 36 (1975–76), 8038-A.

Argues that the philosophy used by Sh in his drama is "the Stoicism of Epictetus and Seneca, modified and made acceptable to Renaissance Christians by Boethius, Justus Lipsius, Guillaume du Vair, Louis le Roy, and others." The Renaissance retained Stoic asceticism but reshaped Stoic fatalism into a belief in the pervasive control of Providence. In Sh's plays, Providence is in control. The characters can be divided into those who espouse spiritual values and those who pursue Fortune. In this Neostoic world, "virtue represents being," and evil, non-being. Richard II develops into a Neostoic hero at the end; Macbeth falls into nonentity because of his devotion to worldliness; Antony, Cleopatra, and King Lear are raised above worldly vicissitudes through the Boethian concept of love. In *Ham.*, the prince takes on the role of a "Neostoic satirist." Providence rewards followers of Fortune (like Claudius) with death, while Hamlet enters the realm of the immutable as a reward for his virtue.

1140 Wilson, Rodney Earl. "The Influence of Stoicism on the Jacobean Drama." Ph.D. dissertation, North Texas State University, 1975. *DAI*, 36 (1975–76), 8038-A-8039-A.

Examines 16th-c. Neostoicism, the comments of modern critics, and plays from "the first four decades of the seventeenth century." Notes that in the period under consideration, the Stoic was perceived as one who is indifferent to externals. Also, the words "patience" and "constancy" often carry Stoic connotations. Chapter 4 treats Sh briefly.

1140a Witt, Robert W. "Prince Hal and Castiglione." *BSUF*, 24, no. 4 (1983), 73–79.

Maintains that Sh used Sir Thomas Hoby's translation of Baldassare Castiglione's *The Courtier* in shaping the character of Prince Hal as ideal man and king. Mentions the Platonic derivation of Castiglione's ideas in book 1 about the mean between "the cowardly and overzealous soldiers," which may lie behind Sh's characters of Falstaff, Hotspur, and Prince Hal. Another manifestation of Neoplatonism, perhaps suggested by the account of chaste love in book 4 of *The Courtier*, is the kiss Henry V requires of Katherine in *H5*.

1141 Woodbridge, Linda. "Palisading the Elizabethan Body Politic." *TSLL*, 33 (1991), 327–54.

Applies anthropological conceptions "of body and society, of pollution and dangerous margins" to *Luc.*, *Tit.*, and *Cym.*, which use women's bodies as metaphors for threatened societies. Each case involves Rome, a powerful symbol of invasion for Sh's England. In *Luc.* and *Tit.*, Rome is both invader and invaded. Like Lavinia's rape in *Tit.*, Lucrece's death frees Rome from tyranny; the endings of *Luc.* and *Tit.*, though politically redemptive, are bleak, and *Cym.*, which demonstrates a happier way to release power, envisions a society momentarily at peace with a Rome that no longer threatens invasion.

1142 Woodward, A. G. "The Roman Plays." *Shakespeare at 400*. Ed. R. G. Howarth. Cape Town: Editorial Board of the U. of Cape Town, 1965, pp. 25–41.

Discusses *JC* and *Cor.* as political plays (in their treatment of the relationship between rulers and the ruled and in their examination of "Governors"), then examines *Cor.* for the awesome portrait it paints of its hero, and finally focuses on the intimate glimpses of several people and groups of people that characterize *JC*.

1143 Worden, Blair. "Shakespeare and Politics." *ShS*, 44 (1992), 1–15.

Comments briefly on Sh's Roman plays, noting that they do not exhibit much of a sense of Rome's evolution "from a primitive to a sophisticated or corrupt society."

General Works

The playwright does, however, have a knack "for capturing, from the merest hints in his sources, the textures and the sentiments of the societies he re-creates on stage." His imaginative reconstruction of Rome is at least as persuasive as any effort by the historians of his time. Illustrates this point by comparing the language of Sh's Romans with that of his Englishmen. The former differ from the latter in speaking of liberty as an abstract ideal and by separating private from public life.

1144 Wright, Neil Hutchinson. "Shakespeare and Redemptive Illusion." Ph.D. dissertation, Forida State University, 1982. *DAI*, 43 (1982–83), 2356-A.

Regards the series of "redeemer–illusionists" in Sh's plays, who figure forth the playwright's "redemptive aesthetic," as constructed under the influence of Platonic ideas, descended originally from the *Ion* and mediated to Sh through *The Defence of Poesie* by Sir Philip Sidney. These figures, of whom the most fully developed is Prospero, share some of the qualities of Sidney's *vates*, but Sh has significantly altered the prototype.

1145 Wymer, Roland. *Suicide and Despair in the Jacobean Drama*. Brighton, Sussex: Harvester P., 1986. xiii + 193 pp.

Notes in chapter 1, "Suicide, Despair, and the Drama," that the Jacobean drama "was written at a time when suicide was reacquiring the dignity and honour of its Roman past, but had not lost its medieval connotations of shame and despair." With knowledge of the classical past becoming widespread, playwrights were interested in exploiting the theatrical potential of the typical Roman suicide, as well as self-inflicted deaths for love or chastity. Suicide, with its two faces of dignity and despair, can be said to embody, in part, the paradoxical effect of tragedy as well as the Renaissance view of man as proudly self-sufficient and yet wretched. *Ham.* explores the ambivalence of suicide in a fundamental way, seeming to endorse the protagonist's "middle course between extremes." Chapter 6, "Deaths for Love," concludes that the suicides of the protagonists in *Ant.* enable the various contraries foregrounded in the play to be balanced "in a precarious stasis." Chapter 7, "Stoicism and Roman Deaths," contends that the suicide of Brutus in *JC* is both noble and desperate, the defeat of a man "divided against himself," which makes him "the most tragic Roman of them all." Comments also on *Luc.*, *Lr.*, *Mac.*, *Oth.*, and *Rom.*

1146 Wyrick, Deborah Baker. "The Ass Motif in *The Comedy of Errors* and *A Midsummer Night's Dream*." *SQ*, 33 (1982), 432–48.

Contends that Sh "exploited the linguistic, thematic, and structural possibilities inherent in the word 'ass.'" Of the three symbolic meanings of the ass—the admirable ass, the licentious ass, and the foolish ass—found in *Err.* and *MND*, the foolish ass has the most obvious classical origins (in Aesop and Ovid).

1146a Yaffee, Glenn. "The Figure of the Parasite in Renaissance Comedy." Ph.D. dissertation, University of Toronto, 1983. *DAI*, 44 (1983–84), 2777-A.

Investigates the classical sources of the comic parasite in Aristophanes, Plautus, and Terence. This character is "a protagonist of superior mind but dependent social position who uses his intellectual capacity to create and resolve the comic *agon*." Tudor playwrights were drawn to the relationship between between an intelligent parasite and "a *gloriosus* type of patron." In *1&2H4*, Falstaff and Prince Hal, accomplished actors both, take turns playing the two roles. The serious implications of their enactments give the comic parasite "new depth as a very human, flawed protagonist."

1147 Yamada, Yumiko. "Shakespeare's Humour Plays." *ShStud*, 21 (1982–83), 35–64.

Refers to the ancient medical authorities Hippocrates and Galen, as well as Elizabethan medical tracts, to enlarge the sense of *humor* to mean (psychologically) "any peculiar quality or inclination, comical or tragical, leading to vice or folly," and (physiologically) a disorder or disease, especially of the body politic, that needs curing. Surveys Sh's plays up through the major tragedies, commenting on the senses in which they can be seen as possessing humors in any of these senses. *JC*, for example, concerns the humors of Cassius, Caesar, and Brutus, as well as the sickness of the state. In *Tro.*, both Greeks and Trojans are infected with "individual and cosmological humors." Speaks of the protagonist of *Cor.* as a disease that must be excised for Rome to be whole. Views *Tim.* in a similar way.

1148   Yates, Frances. *The Art of Memory.* Chicago: U. of Chicago P., 1966. xv + 400 pp.

Chapter 16, "Fludd's Memory System and the Globe Theater," is a revision of item 1149.

1149   Yates, Frances. "New Light on the Globe Theater." *New York Review of Books,* 6, no. 9 (May 26, 1966), 16–22.

Contends that certain illustrations in Robert Fludd's *Ars Memoriae* (1619) represent the second Globe Theater. In his attempt to keep alive the ancient art of memory, Fludd followed classical precept: He used a real building (in this case, a theater) to show how one can create a series of images, associate each image with an idea to be remembered, and then attach each image to a particular place within the building. If the theater in Fludd's illustration is based on the second Globe, it can provide key insights into the structure of the first Globe, which the second Globe strongly resembled. The evidence from Fludd strongly suggests that Sh's theater was an adaptation of the classical theater, assigning, for example, the five entrances of the latter (as described by Vitruvius) to upper and lower levels instead of to one level only. Revised as chapter 16 of item 1148. See item 0958.

1149a   Yates, Frances A. *The Occult Philosophy in the Elizabethan Age.* London: Routledge and Kegan Paul, 1979. x + 217 pp.

Includes discussion of Neoplatonism and other classical elements that helped to form the occult philosophy of the Elizabethans. Notes the importance of Henry Cornelius Agrippa's *De Occulta Philosophia* (1533) in combining the natural magic of Marsilio Ficino and the Cabalist magic of Giovanni Pico della Mirandola, and thus helping to spread "Renaissance Neoplatonism with its magical core." Remarks on the influence of the *Problemata Physica* of Pseudo-Aristotle in helping the Renaissance revalue melancholy from the lowest of the four humors distinguished by Galenic psychology to the highest, the temperament of genius. Connects Hamlet with this new conception of melancholy. Chapter 12 discovers the influence of Francesco Giorgi, an exponent of Christian Cabala, in *MV*. Chapter 13 examines "Renaissance Neoplatonism and its associated occultisms" in relation to the fairies, witches, and ideas of melancholy in *MND, LLL, Rom., Ham., Mac.,* and *Lr.* Chapter 14 argues that *Tmp.* exhibits a white magician modeled on John Dee, the Elizabethan magus, and that Prospero's magic is derived from *De Occulta Philosophia* of Agrippa.

1150   Yates, Frances A. "The Stage in Robert Fludd's Memory System." *ShakS,* 3 (1967), 138–66.

Reiterates and extends the author's argument, first advanced in *The Art of Memory* (item 1148), that the theater alluded to and used as illustration in the memory system developed in the second part of Robert Fludd's *Utriusque Cosmi Historia* (1619) is the second Globe. Notes the classical basis for Fludd's art of memory: the faculty psychology that is the foundation of memory, the distinction between natural and artificial memory, the emphasis first on "places" (usually five in number) and then on "images" to be used on the places, and the importance given to employing real places, not imagined ones, in a memory system. Fludd's *ars memoriae* features five memory places, corresponding to the five primary openings in the theater wall illustrated in his text, a wall based on that of the second Globe. Disputes Shapiro's claim (item 0958) that Fludd's illustration represents the Blackfriars theater.

General Works

1151   Young, David. *The Heart's Forest: A Study of Shakespeare's Pastoral Plays.* New Haven: Yale U. P., 1972. xi + 209 pp.

Focuses on the European and English context for Sh's treatment of the pastoral, with some brief references to the classical background. Discusses the mixture of the chivalric tradition with pastoral romance as an important step in preparing the way for pastoral drama. This made possible the concept of "the pastoral as sojourn" that Sh and others used in their plays. Offers a detailed discussion of *AYL, Lr., WT,* and *Tmp.*

1152   Zeeveld, W. Gordon. *The Temper of Shakespeare's Thought.* New Haven: Yale U. P., 1974. xv + 266 pp.

Explains how Sh's plays occupy themselves with the intellectual concerns of his day. Chapter 2 compares *JC* and *Cor.* as examinations of the idea of commonwealth, traditionally viewed in the Tudor period as a society controlled by an authority at the top with all other parts arranged beneath it in a carefully graduated hierarchy. Concerned with commonwealth in this traditional sense, *JC* presents two potential authority figures, Caesar and Brutus. Brutus is responsible for destroying Caesar for what he perceives to be the public good, but because he fails to assume the leadership himself, he unwittingly becomes the agent of dissolution in the commonwealth. Thus the cause of commonwealth, while given significant exposure, receives no advancement in the play. In *Cor.*, Sh modified the story as found in Plutarch and Livy, both of whom regard the rise of the people to political power as a positive development. Sh, writing with a new Jacobean awareness of the people's power, dramatized the defeat of commonwealth when both sides—the people and the controlling authority—are wrong because both set aside their traditional duties to contend about their rights. In *Ant.*, Sh explores the problems of empire as they had been raised by the recent union of England and Scotland and the extension of British dominion to the New World. The play's atmosphere of political expansion abandons the notion of the city-state bound together by the mutual obligations of its members and therefore subject to certain moral restraints. Instead, *Ant.* depicts a world in which political considerations alone control the characters' actions. It follows the decline of empire through Cleopatra's game-playing, Antony's idleness, and Octavius's ruthless pursuit of power. Chapter 4, "Civility," includes discussions of *Tit.* and *Tim.* In *Tit.*, Sh subverts the Elizabethan image of Rome as the exemplar of civility by showing how Titus and other Romans are capable of savagery to equal that of the most barbarous races. In *Tim.*, another city renowned for civility becomes a "forest of beasts."

1153   Zesmer, David M. *Guide to Shakespeare.* New York: Barnes & Noble, 1976. viii + 472 pp.

Provides background information, including a section on sources that discusses Plutarch's *Lives* as a source for *JC, Ant., Cor.,* and *Tim.* Surveys the Sh canon, summarizing and commenting on each work. Notes the influence of Ovid on *Ven., Luc., Tit.,* and *Tmp.*; of Seneca on tragedy, especially *Tit.*; of Virgil; and of Platonism on *Son.*

1154   Zukofsky, Louis. *Bottom: On Shakespeare.* Austin, Texas: Ark P., 1963. Revised ed. Berkeley: U. of California P., 1987. 470 pp.

Explores Sh's works as they embody "the definition of love as the tragic hero." Part 3, "An Alphabet of Subjects," includes headings like "Greeks," "*Iliad,*" and "Latine," in which passages from Sh are juxtaposed with passages from classical works like the *Iliad* or Lucretius's *De Rerum Natura* that have some bearing on the Shakespearean passages.

Individual Works

All's Well That Ends Well

1155 Bennett, Josephine Waters. "New Techniques of Comedy in *All's Well That Ends Well.*" *SQ*, 18 (1967), 337–62.

Contends that critics have misunderstood and devalued *AWW* because, preoccupied with the heroine's distresses, they have attempted to read it as a romantic play. With another purpose in mind, Sh used a variety of devices to prevent the destruction of comedy by sympathy. Chief among these is the point of view from which we see the young lovers: the wise and unsentimental perspective of the Countess and Lafew. To reinforce the audience's comic detachment, Sh calls attention to the myth of Venus and Adonis in the first half of the play and "the impossible tasks given to Psyche (in the Cupid and Psyche story)" in the second half.

1156 Bergeron, David M. "The Mythical Structure of *All's Well That Ends Well.*" *TSLL*, 14 (1973), 559–68.

Argues that the myth of Mars and Venus informs the structure of *AWW*. Bertram and Helena, though not exactly equivalent to Mars and Venus, approximate the pattern of their myth, thus effecting the peaceful union of opposites. Bertram is the chief representative of Mars, though Parolles presents an ironic version of him and serves to discredit his power. Helena's primary mythic role is that of Venus, but to earn her triumph over Bertram, she must also behave like Diana, the chaste huntress. Provides examples of other Renaissance and classical authors (Plutarch and Lucretius) who use the myth to symbolize the peaceful resolution of conflict.

1157 Lecercle, Ann. "An Elizabethan Configuration of Medicine, Magic, and Metaphysics: The Case of Helena as Hephaistan Helen in *All's Well That Ends Well.*" *L'Europe de la Renaissance: Cultures et civilisations: Mélanges offerts à Marie-Thérèse Jones-Davies*. Eds. Jean-Claude Margolin and Marie-Madeleine Martinet. Paris: Touzot, 1989, pp. 347–63.

Views Helena as a healer in the ancient tradition of Hephaistos, which means that her power is ambivalent. Like Hephaistos, Helena both looses and binds: She looses the hand of the French king in curing him, but she binds the foot (acts as a "clog") of Bertram. In other words, her healing of the monarch simultaneously undermines the potency of her husband. Notes that the three males with whom Helena is associated (the king, Bertram, and Parolles) represent the three images of Hephaistos (robust, club-footed, and phalloid and dwarfish). Sees a parallel "between loosing and binding on the one hand and *falling* and *rising* on the other," which produces a "phallic configuration" in the play. There are also Homeric echoes: "Helena's role *in* Paris" has much to do "with Helen's role *with* Paris in Greek myth." This reading of Helena's thaumaturgy accounts better for the play's pervasive "double-sidedness" than any morality play or Spenserian notion of her virtue.

1158 Walker, Alice. "Six Notes on *All's Well That Ends Well.*" *SQ*, 33 (1982), 339–42.

The fourth note, discussing Diana's statement that "men make rope" (*AWW*, IV.ii.38–39), traces the expression to Erasmus's *Adages*, which cites Horace's *Odes* and Persius's *Satires* as the source of the statement. The phrase is "a nautical metaphor for going back on one's word."

ANTONY AND CLEOPATRA

1159   Abraham, Lyndall. "Alchemical Reference in *Antony and Cleopatra*." *SSE*, 8 (1982–83), 100–104.

Explains Lepidus's comment in *Ant.* (II.vii.26–28), that "your serpent of Egypt" is bred of mud "by the operation of your sun: so is your crocodile" in terms of its alchemical images and references. Lepidus is employing the enigmatic terms of the alchemists to speak of "the generation of gold and the transforming 'serpent' or Stone from the 'mud' of the Nile or the *prima materia* by the heat of the 'sun.'" Notes that alchemical tradition recognized "Hermes Trismegistus or the Egyptian Thoth as its founder, and as the author of the *Emerald Table*, which contained the basic laws of alchemy." This speech, along with other alchemical allusions in the play, reinforces the notion that Cleopatra, Alexandria, and Egypt are "exotic and mysterious."

1160   Adams, Robert M. *Proteus, His Lies, His Truths*. New York: Norton, 1973. xii + 192 pp.

Considers the subject of literary translation. Includes a discussion of Sh's paraphrase of North's translation of Plutarch in Enobarbus's description of Cleopatra on the Cydnus (*Ant.*, II). Argues that Sh points to his source so directly in this case so that he can "enrich, deride, authenticate, and entangle the otherwise rather heavy-footed Roman business of the act." In making his appropriation of Plutarch so obvious, the playwright is asserting his superiority, demonstrating how someone else's prosaic historical material can be magically transformed through the power of imagination.

1161   Adelman, Janet. *The Common Liar: An Essay on "Antony and Cleopatra."* New Haven: Yale U. P., 1973. x + 235 pp.

Revision of item 1162.

1162   Adelman, Janet Ann. "Shakespeare's *Antony and Cleopatra*: A Study of Allegories on the Banks of the Nile." Ph.D. dissertation, Yale University, 1969. *DAI*, 31 (1970–71), 1256-A.

Argues that typical modes of three genres—tragedy, comedy, and romance—all operate in *Ant.* It is neither possible nor desirable to reconcile the various meanings suggested by these modes. Chapter 1 contends that in structure and in character presentation, *Ant.* is often closer to comedy than to tragedy. Chapter 2 explains the traditions that form the play's background, especially those of Dido and Aeneas and of Mars and Venus. Chapter 3 maintains that in the use of poetry and poetic symbol *Ant.* is similar in technique to the romances. Revised as item 1161.

1163   Adlard, John. "Cleopatra as Isis." *Archiv*, 212 (1975), 324–28.

Builds on (and corrects) an essay of the same title by Michael Lloyd (1959). Reinforces Lloyd's point that Sh derived his identification of Cleopatra with Isis from Philemon Holland's translation of Plutarch's *Moralia* (1603) by pointing out that in Caesar's account of how Cleopatra appeared "In th' habiliments of the goddess Isis" (*Ant.*, III.vi.17), the word "habiliments" is likely to have come from Plutarch's description of Isis. Suggests that Sh might have read of the many names of Isis (Minerva, Venus, Diana, Proserpina, Ceres, Juno, Bellona, and Hecate) in William Adlington's translation of *The Golden Asse* (1566). Cleopatra's association with Isis thus shows her versatility. The *Moralia* also connects Isis with the land of Egypt and with moisture, and Sh makes the same connections with Cleopatra. The *Moralia* helps us to understand how, in Sh's play, Cleopatra unites pleasure and wisdom and a host of other contraries.

1164 Altmann, Ruth. "Shakespeare's Craftsmanship: A Study of His Use of Plutarch in *Antony and Cleopatra*." Ph.D. dissertation, University of Washington, 1969. *DAI*, 30 (1969–70), 2474-A.

The introduction compares the sequence of events in *Ant.* with the sequence in Plutarch's *Life of Marcus Antonius*. Sh's changes in his source involve reducing the number of episodes to a minimum but making maximum use of what he chooses. He is interested in associative rather than chronological movement, focusing on the interplay of character and exploration of meaning. The action alternates between Rome and Egypt, but as the plot develops, the distance between them gets smaller.

Chapter 1 analyzes Enobarbus's well-known description of Cleopatra, which although quite close to Plutarch in language, has its context radically altered by Sh, who uses it satirically.

Chapters 2 and 3 deal with "the scenes of truce and celebration with Pompey at Misenum." In this case, Sh takes a brief account of a minor incident from his source and develops it into the chief political action of the first two acts. There is no relationship between the dispute of Antony and Caesar and Pompey's rebellion in Plutarch; Sh sees the two events as interconnected. The two scenes at Misenum epitomize the issues developed to this point and recapitulate the movement of the political action, from discord to harmony.

Chapters 4 and 5 examine the struggle between Caesar and Cleopatra in act V. Even though Sh seems to follow Plutarch closely here, he subtly alters sequence and detail in the concluding action. Cleopatra's scene with Dolabella, before her meeting with Caesar, is added to help frame the confrontation. Inside the frame Cleopatra performs several parts in her own drama. The confrontation scene, with its exploration of "value and estimation," serves to conclude the play thematically. It also creates an ambivalence about Sh's final judgment of Cleopatra.

1165 Alvis, John. "The Religion of Eros: A Re-Interpretation of *Antony and Cleopatra*." *Renascence*, 30 (1978), 185–98.

Calls attention to the two terms that, according to Plutarch's *Life of Marcus Antonius*, Antony and Cleopatra coined to designate "the successive stages of their union." The first, *amimetobion*, applied to their time of prosperity, means, in North's translation, "no life comparable and matchable with it." The second, *synapothanumenon*, invented in the wake of Actium, is translated "the order and agreement of those that will die together." Sh's play incorporates and evaluates these two ideas, diverging from Plutarch in depicting the lovers' choices "with tragic seriousness." Describes the love of Antony and Cleopatra as idolatrous, theatrically self-conscious, public, monotonous, aimless, and sterile. It achieves stability only through artful death. By contrast, Sh's comedies and sonnets portray sexual love as sacramental: In these works, love accords with "natural rhythms of harmony and fecundity," and it values courtesy. If we use the comedies as a standard, we can see that Sh's view of the two famous lovers is ironic. Revised as chapter 6 of item 0080a.

1166 Anderson, Donald K. Jr. "A New Glass for the 'Three Nook'd World' of *Antony and Cleopatra*." *ELN*, 17 (1979–80), 103–6.

Explains Octavius Caesar's phrase "three-nook'd world" (*Ant.*, IV.vi.6) by referring to the "T-in-O" maps that were plentiful in Sh's time and to a special meaning of "nook" (sector of a circle). The phrase, then, means "a circle divided into three sectors, each of them a continent."

1166a Andrews, Michael Cameron. "Cleopatra's 'Salad Days.'" *N&Q*, 31 (1984), 212–13.

Explains that Cleopatra's dismissal of her former life, when she praised Caesar, as her "salad days" (*Ant.*, I.v.76) is meant to characterize that life as one of emotional and sexual restraint.

1167   Ansari, A. A. "*Antony and Cleopatra*: An Image of Liquefaction." *AJES*, 8 (1983), 79–93.

Focuses on the images of liquefaction as a key to understanding Antony, Cleopatra, their love, and the dynamic of the play itself. Neither of the protagonists is able to hold a visible shape; they are psychically mutable. Cleopatra is composed of the four elements, which manifest themselves in different proportions at different times. In her association with Nilus's slime, she is both sterile and fecund; in her approach to death, she incorporates some Roman characteristics. Antony oscillates between Rome and Egypt, losing his heroic identification with Mars and Hercules as he is drawn closer to Cleopatra. As lovers, they are constantly engaged in trying to metamorphose the sexual into transcendent love. The rapid shifts of scene and of point of view in the play produce contrasting elements that interpenetrate and lose distinction.

1168   Aoyama, Seiko. "Magnificence and Folly: A Study of Value in *Antony and Cleopatra*." *Collected Essays by the Members of the Faculty* (Kyoritsu Women's Junior College), no. 13 (December 1969), 12–25.

Contends that with *Ant.*, "at the end of his tragic period," Sh came to be less interested in judging his protagonists or probing the mystery of evil than in revealing characters that are noble, although paradoxically flawed. In modifying Plutarch, Sh gave Cleopatra both good and bad qualities before as well as after Actium; in Plutarch's Antony, there was already a thoroughgoing conglomeration of good and bad, so Sh was able to adopt the character with minor changes.

1169   Ardinger, Barbara R. "Cleopatra on Stage: An Examination of the *Persona* of the Queen in English Drama." Ph.D. dissertation, Southern Illinois University, 1976. *DAI*, 37 (1976–77), 3634-A.

Examines eleven English plays, including *Ant.*, dealing with the career of Cleopatra. Notes that, historically, Cleopatra's goal was to rebuild the Ptolemaic Empire, but that her ambitions conflicted with those of Octavian, who defeated her in the battle of Actium and began a propaganda war against her that continues today. From the works of some two dozen Greek and Roman historians and poets, there developed a vicious image of Cleopatra with three parts: She is seen as divine figure, love figure, and political figure. This image, with all its components, is present in the plays under consideration.

1170   Aubrey, Brian. "Quantum Physics and the Experience of Shakespeare." *ACM*, 3 (1990), 111–31.

Comments that Sh's tragedy has "the ability to stimulate the mind to a more holistic level of functioning, to unify a fragmented consciousness." The last scene of *Ant.* provides a particularly clear example of this.

1171   Bache, William B. *Design and Closure in Shakespeare's Major Plays: The Nature of Recapitulation.* American University Studies, Series 4. (English Language and Literature 123.) New York: Peter Lang, 1991. xiii + 397 pp.

Includes a chapter on *Ant.* Analyzes the play's structure, emphasizing the ways in which scenes are framed and in which episodes anticipate and recapitulate each other. A key example is II.vii, the scene on board Pompey's galley. In this scene, the boy who sings the song about Bacchus is played by the same boy who plays Cleopatra, who is thus present to symbolize the Alexandrian revelry in which all of the Roman males are participating. The boy's symbolic power over the men here prefigures Cleopatra's successful manipulation of men in V.ii. The scene on the galley also prepares for the play's end in its discussions of the ebb and flow of the Nile and of serpents, while V.ii has Cleopatra planning to re-create her first meeting with Antony on the river Cydnus. Discusses the gathering of the forces of destruction in the last half of the play, the ways in which the "re-created Antony and Cleopatra" are presented in acts IV and V, the main characters' facing of themselves in those same acts, and the design of V.ii.

1171a Banerjee, Ron D. K. "Space: Form and Feeling in *Antony and Cleopatra*." *Shakespeare*. (Jadavpur U. Essays and Studies 5.) Ed. Debabrata Mukherjee. Calcutta: Jadavpur U., 1986, pp. 55–71.

Finds in *Ant.* confirmation of the view that Sh "attempted to synthesize the theories of the new science and the vitalistic and spiritual norms of the now passing medieval world." Analyzes the play's treatment of space as one manifestation of this synthesis. Sh seems deliberately to avoid examining the "inner space" of his characters. Even Antony's soliloquies in act IV eschew introspection, attempting instead to "look beyond himself and the moment" by paralleling his own death to that of Hercules and by changing the ending of the Dido–Aeneas story to announce "a new drama of union beyond the play's limits." The hero and heroine of *Ant.* stand for a view, similar to that of Giordano Bruno, that there is "an infinity of worlds in an infinity of space" (characteristic of the new science), but that "the universe is organic, animated by a vital principle [that] links man to it in the sphere of immanence" (characteristic of more traditional modes of thought).

1172 Barroll, J. Leeds. "The Characterization of Octavius." *ShakS*, 6 (1970), 231–88.

Attempts to discover the consistent features of Sh's characterization of Octavius Caesar in *Ant.* and to describe the techniques by which the playwright achieves this portrait. Octavius seems "removed" or "screened" from the audience in many ways: He has no asides or soliloquies and is always in a group. He does not "reflect" aloud, and his explanations for what he does are sparse and never personal. He has a utilitarian frame of mind and thinks of everything (even time) in terms of acquiring it. To create this impression, Sh presents him as efficient (his competence is significantly enhanced over that of his archetype in Plutarch), sparing in kindness, insistent on a calculus of "desert and retribution," preoccupied with information, and essentially humorless. In the first half of the play, Octavius is dominated by legalism, and this bespeaks a larger literalism that underlies both his single-mindedness and his limitations. To him, language is not a game (clearly seen in his reaction to Antony's humorous anatomy of the crocodile during the scene on Pompey's galley); rather, he understands words to have "real" referents in the world. Several scenes also serve to establish the hypocrisy of Octavius (for example, II.vi, in which he assumes the role of the affectionate brother), but his own literal-mindedness limits the success of his role-playing: He takes for granted that others accept his "personal word-symbols" and thus believe in his facade. His hypocrisy is made increasingly evident toward the end, as is its ineffectiveness. Most notably, his pretended kindness to Cleopatra fails to prevent her suicide. Although he has learned to control the material world, Octavius has not developed the ability to manipulate the minds of others. Finally, by several techniques (overlapping scenes, for example), Sh emphasizes that Octavius is often simply wrong. He is misinformed about certain events (in I.v, he spends much time complaining about Antony's idleness, which the audience knows to have ceased) and himself misjudges people (Enobarbus, Dollabella).

1173 Barroll, J. Leeds. "The Chronology of Shakespeare's Jacobean Plays and the Dating of *Antony and Cleopatra*." *Essays on Shakespeare*. Ed. Gordon Ross Smith. College Park: Pennsylvania State U. P., 1965, pp. 115–62.

Discusses, as part of a detailed argument about the date of *Ant.*, two figures from Plutarch that Sh combines in Eros. Before stabbing himself, Antony asks Eros to kill him, and Sh adds the detail (from Plutarch's description of another person earlier in the *Life* of Antony) that Eros is a freed slave. This same detail was borrowed from Sh by Samuel Daniel for his closet drama, *Cleopatra*, and helps establish a *terminus ad quem* for *Ant.*

1174 Barroll, J. Leeds. "Shakespeare and the Art of Character: A Study of Anthony." *ShakS*, 5 (1969), 159–235.

The first section begins an analysis of the characterization of Antony in *Ant.* with his response to the defeat at Actium. His shame is not so much "Roman" (public) as it is a private sense of self-abandonment. It is Antony's pride in soldierly bravery, indeed in physical preeminence of every sort, including voluptuosity, that is the key to his nature. He admires those (Fulvia and Pompey) who rival him in military reputation; he indulges in extreme self-condemnation when he senses he has failed in physical courage; and he exuberantly celebrates his martial successes.

Section 2 explains how some of Antony's limitations are exhibited. In the process of conquering the Parthians, Ventidius remarks that Antony, great soldier that he is, has always won more through his officers than by himself, a judgment that hints at Antony's inability to comprehend "the total requirements of war." Because he thinks like a foot soldier, he is inept as a strategist. Easily baited, he can be distracted from his purposes by challenges to his sense of military and physical supremacy (Cleopatra does this frequently). Significantly, Sh alters his source by having Antony decide to wage a naval battle at Actium because Caesar dares him to do it (in Plutarch, he fights by sea because Cleopatra desires it). Beyond his narrow outlook on military operations, Antony has a general blindness to reality.

The third section comments on the subjectivity that guides Antony in all of his relationships: He feels that others' responses derive from the same source as his. Antony sees his followers as becoming parts of himself and himself as dividing into followers. His bounty in giving gold to friends after Actium and treasure to Enobarbus after his desertion, and in bequeathing to Cleopatra a vision of himself in his former greatness, is more of a compensatory gesture for failing to live up to his self-image than true generosity.

The fourth section characterizes Antony's relationship with Cleopatra: It is not overwhelmingly physical (they are seldom together on stage). Antony thinks of Cleopatra the same way he thinks of Fulvia; that is, he admires in both women the qualities he admires in himself. Since he idealizes his own qualities in Cleopatra, he falls out with her whenever she "fails to share in that esteem which Antony has for himself."

Section 5 describes how Antony is portrayed in the second half of the play. In thinking of Caesar after Actium, he recognizes that he has been beaten by a younger man, and his sense of unworthiness prompts him to request leave to live privately. He then is presented with several challenges that threaten not only his life but "his very sense of existence." He seems to gain a temporary rebirth of confidence by challenging Caesar and asserting once again his physical prowess. He is soon reminded of his weakness, however, when Thidias arrives to "woo" Cleopatra away from him. The sexual threat represented by Thidias (Sh adds his kissing of Cleopatra's hand to Plutarch's account), his arrogance, and the tardiness of Antony's servants in this scene bring on an agonized struggle in the hero. In whipping Thidias, Antony attempts to reduce him—and his sender, Caesar—into whining boyishness. Antony now feels a need to assert his "essential manliness," to be completely worthy of his ideal (of Cleopatra, the token of this ideal). He flings himself into the search for a supreme gesture to lay the ghost of "physical inferiority." He fails to understand Caesar's rejection of his challenge to individual combat, appeals for love and support from his followers, exhibits happiness as he sets off for battle (IV.iv), and is ironically undermined because his attempts at "comradeliness" with his men stress his private orientation and ignore what they recognize as intelligent military options. When Antony does triumph in battle (IV.viii), he sees himself as recovering his youth and physical prowess.

Section 6 focuses on Antony's character as it is depicted at the end of IV. As Antony reports what happened at sea in act IV.xii, his sailors deserted him much more cheerfully than they do in Plutarch's account; but instead of branding them as traitors, he blames Cleopatra. Thus, through the most significant idealization of his nature, he turns against himself. As indicated in his speech about the shirt of Nessus (IV.xii.43–49), he is confused about Cleopatra's identity as well as his own. Antony is Herculean in his aspiration toward transcendent physical prowess but desperate in his contemplation of suicide. Cleopatra can be Antony's "worthiest self," the innocent messenger who brought the poisoned robe, or Deianira, the "witch" who poisoned it. With the false news of Cleopatra's death, Antony seems to recover a sense of "their meaningfulness together," but his botched suicide suggests how difficult it is for him to repudiate fleshly existence. Antony never attains self-knowledge, but at the end he has, or believes he has, regained his soldiers as well as his queen.

The last section maintains that Antony's advice to Cleopatra to trust Proculeius reveals the hero's final misjudgment. Antony believes that Proculeius shares his ideal of soldiership (which is centered on a private ideal of physical bravery) and will betray his master to further Cleopatra's interests. Proculeius, following the code of all professional soldiers, is politically attuned to his master's needs and thus captures Cleopatra for Caesar, though he does show some sympathy for her. Dolabella—a young gentleman, not a soldier—is the one who is willing to place a woman above his political duty. It is Dolabella, ironically, who is Antony's "spiritual heir," who more closely approximates Antony's notion of "soldiership" than the professional soldiers with whom he continually wishes to rank himself. Ultimately, however, Antony is neither Proculeius nor Dolabella; his identity suffers from a "tragic shapelessness."

1175 Barroll, J. Leeds. *Shakesperean Tragedy: Genre, Tradition, and Change in "Antony and Cleopatra."* Washington, D. C.: Folger Books, 1984. 309 pp.

Proposes to investigate Sh's idea of tragedy by providing historical and intellectual background about the tradition in which he was writing and then analyzing *Ant.* as an exemplary case. The first section, "The Nature of Tragic Drama," comprises two chapters. Chapter 1, "The Aesthetic Shape of Suffering," notes that Sh inherited the Western idea that "raging grief, madness, or despair comes not from the universe but from man himself." He was also heir to certain "ways of imagining and describing the human fallibilities" that are responsible for "these wreckings." Surveys the ideas of the ancients on faulty human choice and its consequences, noting that the Greek dramatists did not deal directly with "the psychic causes of human misery." Plato focused on "man's misperception of symbol," while Aristotle was interested in "logically fallacious reasoning." Argues that Stoicism, with its insistence that irrational behavior could be controlled, exerted a powerful influence on Western thinking through such works as Cicero's *De Officiis*. Mentions the Neoplatonic and Christian opposition to Stoicism. Emphasizes the importance of St. Augustine, who first constructed "an emotion-oriented theory of human psychology." Comments on Prudentius's reshaping of the classical epic device of personification to serve Christian purposes, a process that made certain classical notions of human impulse especially relevant to literature. Presents a brief summary of Boethius's *De Consolatione Philosophiae*, judging that this work distills "the best of classical and postclassical theory on the subject of mankind's own involvement in his calamities." Cites Seneca as making available to Renaissance dramatists a new subtlety in the depiction of anger, though he did not succeed in translating the tragic conception of human personality into drama. In the classical historians and biographers, Sh read accounts of the process by which men make choices and judgments about the quality of that process. This was particularly true in Plutarch, whose work was infused with the principles of Aristotle's *Nicomachean Ethics*. Plutarch also offered Sh a model for revealing the consistency of his hero's character through actions, anecdotes, and sayings. Maintains that Sh's use of material from Plutarch for the Roman plays (*JC, Ant.,* and *Cor.*) should not obscure his indebtedness to Plutarch's method in the great tragedies. Chapter 2, "The Human Figure on the Stage," adduces the suicides of Eros and Antony in *Ant.* to demonstrate that these two figures represent different kinds of artistic creations, requiring different responses. Eros is psychologically inscrutable, not complex as a personality; he takes his meaning from other aesthetic features in the play. Antony, however, is "fully developed," an "artificial person" whose motivations, within certain limits, we are invited to examine closely.

Part 2, "The Tragic Person," comprises two chapters. Chapter 3, "Mark Antony and the Tournament of Life," singles out "the strangeness of desire" as Sh's "basic framework" for bringing Antony to life. Antony is chiefly concerned to follow pleasure, but not in any narrow sense. He is not lured away from manly pursuits by the sensuality of Egypt; rather, his own inclination leads him to seek fleshly satisfactions in all things, be they feasting, women, or fighting. He has a need to believe in his own self-sufficiency, which governs his relationships with others and makes him a great fighter but also renders him naive about military strategy. In Plutarch's *Life of Marcus Antonius*, Antony decides to fight the battle of Actium by sea in order to please Cleopatra. Sh makes a crucial alteration of his source when he has Antony make this decision for the quite different reason that Caesar has dared him to do it. Antony's responses to Cleopatra are governed by the extent to which he feels, at any given moment, that she mirrors him and enhances his self-esteem. Discusses episodes involving Thidias, Scarus, Proculeius, and Dolabella. Chapter 4, "Cleopatra and the Size of Dreaming," proposes to set aside the view of Cleopatra as magnificently triumphant in order to see her as a fully tragic character. Her sense of death as "a floating to meet Mark Antony in a physical afterlife" is one that would have been denied her by most pagan thinkers, especially those Sh is likely to have known. An important clue to Sh's portrayal of Cleopatra is the way in which she tries to hold Antony. In Plutarch, she makes every effort to be kind and courteous to her lover, while in *Ant.* she employs the technique of "crossing," which ultimately fails. Cleopatra also conceives of her relationship with Antony in opposite images of control and worship, static symbolic pictures of Venus and Mars, which it is her mission to translate into action. Sh rejects Plutarch's restrained opinion of Cleopatra's appearance, insisting on her surpassing beauty and her competitive need to be prettier than all other women. Throughout the play, and especially in the scene with the Messenger (II.v), we observe her repudiating the symbolic. She presents us with a "cognitive kaleidoscope," and we must see her tragedy accordingly. As the play draws to a close, Cleopatra struggles to maintain a sense of decorum in the images she applies to herself and Antony. Unable to imagine anything greater than herself, she emphasizes, in her suicide, her own towering greatness. Her vision may be self-destructive, but it is unyielding.

Section 3, "The Tragic Ethic," comprises three chapters. Chapter 5, "Empire and Consequence," begins by noting that Sh went beyond the allegorical representation of ethical structure in the medieval drama. The ethical system of his tragedy is developed, among other things, by including vignettes of characters who comment on the tragic figures but who do not invite our analysis as "psychological constructs." Discusses Octavius Caesar as one such character, a man who judges Antony from the perspective of his own speed, efficiency, and ability to possess the time. Caesar is a hypocrite whose literal-mindedness puts him in a different category from the tragically represented protagonists. Points to a series of misjudgments by Caesar that derive from his inability to imagine that some men desire things that he does not understand. Considers, more briefly, a number of other characters who are like Octavius in not being developed fully as psychological entities and whose heterogeneous viewpoints ensure "an intellectually panoramic" ambiance for the play: Octavia, Lepidus, Pompey, Enobarbus. Chapter 6, "The View from out of Rome," explains *Ant.*'s ethical vision by investigating the ways in which the play incorporates the ancient motif of the vanity of human wishes. Techniques from the older English drama are utilized, though they are metaphorical and oblique instead of straightforwardly allegorical. Contends, for example, that the countryman who brings Cleopatra the asps in the basket of figs alludes both to the devil (in his connection with serpents) and to the biblical parable of the wise and foolish virgins (taken at Sh's time as a comment on readiness of souls for the Last Judgment). The conversation of Enobarbus and Menas in II.vi suggests that all soldiering in the service of empire is a form of thievery; this degradation of military conquest is very much like that which occurs in an anecdote about Alexander the Great found in St. Augustine's *City of God*. Sh embeds such an awareness in the play in order to set a characteristic Roman preoccupation in a traditional ethical framework. Another ethically suggestive scene that relies on a traditional idea comes in II.vii, in which the drunkenness of the triumvirs conveys the disharmony that is the essential condition of the Roman world. The supernatural, used elliptically, is nevertheless a reliable guide to the ethical standard of *Ant.* When the soldiers' comments in IV.iii note that the god Hercules is leaving Antony, we are invited to interpret our hero's behavior in terms of the ambivalent Renaissance view of this divinity: During the play, Antony progressively abandons the virtues of Hercules and associates himself with the excesses. As an enigmatic spokesman for the divine, the Soothsayer advises Antony well in telling him to return to Egypt (II.iii), but we should not equate this Egypt with the strident egoism and careless self-indulgence that he and Cleopatra seem to generate in Alexandria. What the Soothsayer points toward is ancient Egypt, a place of piety far removed from the politics of 1st-c. Rome and much revered among Sh's contemporaries. In this Egypt, Antony could truly exercise his great love, which manifests itself in an ability to cherish others, to draw them into community with himself. This love is his great truth, and his tragedy is that he relinquishes it for two lies: Rome and all that it stands for and "himself as hero and soldier." Chapter 7, "Shakespearean Tragedy," summarizes the key conclusions of previous chapters (for example, the idea that Sh's tragedy, following the traditions available to him, is optimistic in reinforcing principles of social order) and indicates briefly how they may be applied to major Shakespearean works other than *Ant*.

1176   Barton, Anne. *"Nature's piece 'gainst fancy": The Divided Catastrophe in "Antony and Cleopatra."* An Inaugural Lecture. London: Bedford College, 1973. 20 pp.

Argues that *Ant*. has a divided catastrophe, with the conclusion offered by Antony's death significantly qualified by Cleopatra's suicide in the last act. Throughout the play each of the protagonists oscillates between the glorious and the shabby, the sublime and the ridiculous. Antony's incompetent suicide does not resolve the ambiguity. Only Cleopatra's stage-managed death, which prevents the parodic enactment of the love affair Caesar intends in Rome and repels the comedic impulse of the Clown who brings the asps, can re-make the past and still the flux so that her great love with Antony can claim value.

1177   Battenhouse, Roy W. "Shakespearean Tragedy as Christian: Some Confusions in the Debate." *CentR*, 9 (1964), 77–99.

Argues that Christian tragedy possesses "a certain quality of insight into downfall" and that "any period in history can offer subject matter" for such tragedy. *Ant*., for example, depicts from a Christian perspective "the phantom bliss and actual perdition which consummate a self-deluded love." Revised as part of chapter three of item 0133.

1178   Beckerman, Bernard. "Past the Size of Dreaming." *Twentieth Century Interpretations of "Antony and Cleopatra": A Collection of Critical Essays*. Ed. Mark Rose. Englewood Cliffs, New Jersey: Prentice-Hall, 1977, pp. 99–112. Reprint. *Shakespeare: The Theatrical Dimension*. Eds. Philip C. McGuire and David A. Samuelson. New York: AMS P., 1979, pp. 209–23.

Contends that *Ant*. is not a vast, sprawling, imperial drama and should not be performed as if it were. Its focus is on the development of a fragile intimacy between the lovers. The opening scene, which frames the appearance of Antony and Cleopatra between two Roman commentators, suggests not that there are two worlds—Rome and Egypt— but that the Roman vision of Philo and Demetrius is transcended by what the audience comes to see as the movement of the love relationship. The pattern of this movement consists of Cleopatra's teasing and testing of Antony and his attempts to respond, and it has special power because it is "full of fruitful contradictions." To stimulate the structure, Sh employs a variety of messengers, whose purpose is to evoke responses in those to whom they deliver their messages. Our attention is thus directed to the steadiness of Caesar and especially to the impulsive, irregular course followed by Antony and Cleopatra. In the second half of the play, the lovers grow closer: Antony achieves a selflessness just before his death, and Cleopatra reaches a "complete state of spiritual identity" with him in the last scene.

1179   Bell, Arthur H. "Time and Convention in *Antony and Cleopatra*." *SQ*, 24 (1973), 253–64.

Notes that Sh, in *Ant*., frequently gives time a presence as the force that controls men's destinies. Suggests that the playwright was inspired by Plutarch, who describes Antony's wasting of time and emphasizes the rush of events in his life. In act I, Antony adopts, successively, four conventional attitudes, or world views, by which men have attempted to come to terms with time: those of the courtly lover, Homeric hero, man of policy, and Stoic sage. The rest of the play presents a dramatic assessment of these postures. Though by committing suicide Antony ends as a Stoic sage, none of the four world views succeeds for him. His restless quest for an accommodation with time is a measure of his humanness: No single approach can satisfy him.

1180 Benoit, Raymond. "The Prophecy in the Play: *Antony and Cleopatra*." *Greyfriar* (Siena College), 17 (1976), 3–7.

Discovers details throughout *Ant.* that supply the privileged audience with a perspective from which to judge "the action of Rome and Egypt just prior to Christian history." The various dualisms of the play are not resolved within it, but its prophetic hints at the Christian dispensation point the way to unity.

1181 Berek, Peter. "Doing and Undoing: The Value of Action in *Antony and Cleopatra*." *SQ*, 32 (1981), 295–304.

Uses of the verb "do" emphasize the paradoxical qualities of action in *Ant.* In the relationship of Antony and Cleopatra, there is never a definitive result from any one thing done; actions continually undo themselves. In the political/military world, success carries with it a loss of the popular acclaim that once seemed to be the reward for achievement. Antony, Cleopatra, and Caesar are all aware of the severe limits on the joy one can take in earthly accomplishments, but while Caesar accepts the dungy disappointments attendant on mastering the world, Antony and Cleopatra escape into their own imaginative space.

1182 Berggren, Paula S. "The Woman's Part: Female Sexuality as Power in Shakespeare's Plays." *The Woman's Part: Feminist Criticism of Shakespeare.* Eds. Carolyn Ruth Swift Lenz, Gayle Greene, and Carol Thomas Neely. Urbana: U. of Illinois P., 1980, pp. 17–34.

Includes an account of Sh's Cleopatra, who relaxes the rigidity of the masculine world of Sh's tragedies. This heroine is the first of Sh's characters to be liberated from the restraints of the physical world; she is "a forerunner of the openly magical conciliators led by Prospero."

1183 Berkeley, David S. "On Desentimentalizing Antony." *N&Q*, 11 (1964), 138–42.

Regards Antony's final attitude toward Cleopatra in *Ant.* as ambiguous, compounded of both love and hate. Cites five Shakespearean departures from Plutarch's *Life* of Antony as evidence for Antony's disenchantment. In these cases, Sh reveals Antony's anger and his desire for revenge. Especially intriguing is the recommendation for Cleopatra to trust Proculeius; it is entirely possible that Antony is aware of Proculeius's unswerving loyalty to Octavius and places Cleopatra in the hands of someone who is certain to betray her in order to take revenge.

1184 Bevington, David, ed. *Antony and Cleopatra.* (New Cambridge Shakespeare.) Cambridge: Cambridge U. P., 1990. xvii + 274 pp.

The introduction provides a variety of background materials. Sh used as his chief source *The Life of Marcus Antonius* in Plutarch's *Lives of the Noble Grecians and Romans.* Notes certain close verbal parallels between Plutarch and Sh, as well as the transformative power of Sh's changes. Discusses Sh's dramatic shaping of Plutarch's account, including the reordering of some events. In his characterization, Sh "goes beyond Plutarch in the direction of a multiplicity of points of view and a paradoxical complexity within the two protagonists." Takes account of contrasting traditions available to Sh about Augustus Caesar and about the lovers themselves. Sh may have derived his complex view of love in the play partly from mythology (Venus and Mars, Venus and Bacchus, Omphale and Hercules, Isis and Osiris). He was also influenced by Renaissance Neoplatonism. Samples the widely divergent critical responses to

Ant., reporting general agreement on one point: The words we hear the characters speak, especially vows, ideals, dreams, and images of greatness, are seldom matched by what we witness in their behavior. The two protagonists are indeed tragic in their suffering, but they win a kind of victory, with Antony daring to identify with Cleopatra and Cleopatra transcending death through art as she becomes like Antony, internalizing his Romanness. Comments on genre (a new kind of non-Aristotelian tragedy, based on medieval ideas of heroic love), style ("one of wholeness fashioned out of antithetical elements"), and stagecraft (the skillful juxtaposition of scenes, the realization on stage of image, and the use of messengers).

1185   Birkinshaw, Philip. "Heroic Frenzies: Neo-erotic Platonism in *Antony and Cleopatra*." *UCTSE*, 3 (1972), 37–44.

Describes Sh's treatment of Antony and Cleopatra's relationship as "a mystical celebration of love in an immense, baroque paradox." At certain points in *Ant.* the two moral extremes of Rome and Alexandria meet in brilliant paradoxes, most notably in two of Cleopatra's descriptions of Antony: "O heavenly mingle" (I.v.62) and "O infinite virtue" (IV.viii.17). In both cases, Antony is seen as embracing extremes and transcending their opposition. Argues that Sh derived this habit of dialectically resolving paradoxes from Renaissance Neoplatonism, or Neo-erotic Platonism, which had been worked out by Marsilio Ficino and Pico della Mirandola, spread by works like Hoby's translation of Castiglione, and assimilated by poets like Spenser and Donne. Instead of accepting the Aristotelian definition of virtue as a mean that shuns extremes (as the Romans in *Ant.* do), the Neo-erotic Platonists found a way to reconcile all contraries in the One. In particular, they allegorized the three Graces to represent the extremes of Beauty and Desire (or Sex) with Love in the center as a divine union of the other two. Other aspects of *Ant.* also make sense in terms of Neo-erotic Platonism: the implication that the protagonists are initiates in an elite religion of love; the paradoxes in Enobarbus's great description of Cleopatra on the Cydnus; the pervasive Mars–Venus comparisons; and the suggestions of transvestism. Though Sh dallies with the mystical belief that, through Love, all opposites can be reconciled in the One, his realism forbids him finally to endorse such a faith.

1186   Birringer, Johannes H. "Texts, Plays, and Instabilities." *South African Theatre Journal*, 1, no. 1 (1987), 4–16.

Makes a distinction between "the apparent language of the written text or script" of a play and "the language, or sign system, of performance." Cites the passage in which the dying Antony is heaved aloft to Cleopatra in her monument (*Ant.*, IV.xv.33–41): "The configuration of the scene is dense, a system of extreme variants with a complex verbal surface over the kinetic images." Contends that a performance-oriented interpretation must attend to instabilities that are incompatible with the attempts of modern scholars to establish authoritative texts, imagine the response of "the original audience," or provide an authentic reconstruction of Elizabethan theatrical conditions.

1187   Blakiston, J. M. G. "The Three-Nook'd World." *TLS*, Sept. 17, 1965, p. 868.

Letter to the editor speculates that Octavius's reference to "the three nook'd world" (*Ant.*, IV.vi.6) may derive from the T-in-O world maps found in certain medieval manuscripts. The "angled divisions" of these maps, which section the world into three parts labeled with the names of the three continents, would seem to satisfy several of the definitions of *nook*.

1188   Blissett, William. "Dramatic Irony in *Antony and Cleopatra*." *SQ*, 18 (1967), 151–66.

Discusses *Ant.*'s various manifestations of dramatic irony, in the sense of one character's knowing more than another or the audience's knowing more than anyone on stage. Some of the audience's superior knowledge comes from outside the play: Before it begins, they are aware of the broad outlines of a well-known story. As the play develops, the spectators are let in on things that constantly revise their perceptions. At first, Antony appears to face a conflict between pleasure and duty, with duty being of greater importance. However, when Pompey appears, we recognize that his threat is not credible; we thus can focus on a reappraisal of pleasure, which in the opening scene seemed an impediment to Antony's fulfillment of his Roman obligations. Shortly after the meeting of the triumvirs, during which Antony seems to be reduced to the mean-spirited level of Caesar, Enobarbus's magnificent description of Cleopatra prepares for Antony's return to the pleasure of Egypt and for Cleopatra's domination of the last scenes. It also firmly establishes the audience's sympathies on the side of Cleopatra and "makes ironic every speech and action before Antony's return." Audience awareness is sharpened by three parallels between Antony and the story of Hercules: at the beginning, Hercules at the crossroads, choosing between Virtue and Pleasure; later, Hercules and Omphale, showing Antony's subjection to effeminacy; finally, Hercules and the poison shirt of Nessus, emphasizing Antony's belief that Cleopatra has betrayed him. Cleopatra is associated with Circe as an enchantress of men, but this negative impression is neutralized by her links with the beneficent Isis. The chief means by which Sh prevents the audience from interpreting the play as a tale of Antony's destruction by a wanton is the character of Enobarbus, who frequently plays the deflating *eiron* to Antony's boastful *alazon*. Though Enobarbus uses irony in commenting on Antony's folly, he himself is subject to dramatic irony: The audience perceives that his judgment has been corrupted. Scriptural references (to a woman, a serpent, and death; to the imminent birth of Christ; and to the Book of Revelation), clear to the audience but unperceived by the characters in the play, are responsible for further dramatic irony.

1188a Blistein, Elmer M. *Comedy in Action*. Durham, North Carolina: Duke U. P., 1964. xvi + 146 pp.

Analyzes II.v of *Ant*. at the beginning of the first of two chapters devoted to comedy and cruelty. Describes Cleopatra's abuse of the Messenger who brings the news of Antony's marriage to Octavia as a kind of cruelty at which the audience laughs. Notes that comedy and cruelty, though they would seem "to have little in common," are related.

1189 Bloomfield, Morton W. "Personification–Metaphors." *ChauR*, 14 (1979–80), 287–97.

Uses Enobarbus's description of Cleopatra on her barge (*Ant*., II.ii.200–228) to illustrate personification–metaphors, in which the "metaphoric use of the verb or verb–phrase animates the noun or noun–phrase which governs the verb." Locates a number of these "subdued or modified personifications" in Enobarbus's account. Notes that classical rhetoricians like Quintilian were familiar with personification–metaphors, though they did not use the term "personification" to describe them.

1190 Blythe, David-Everette. "Shakespeare's *Antony and Cleopatra*." *Expl*, 49 (1991), 77–79.

Explains a scurrilous comment by Enobarbus about horses and mares serving together (*Ant*., III.vii.7–9) as referring to the instinct of stallions with riders to "serve" mounted mares. Comments briefly on other bestial/sexual imagery in *Ant*.

1191 Bonjour, Adrien. "Shakespeare and the Toil of Grace." *Shakespeare 1564–1964: A Collection of Modern Essays by Various Hands*. Ed. Edward A. Bloom. Providence, Rhode Island: Brown U. P., 1964, pp. 88–94.

Rejects the approach of critics who theologize *Ant*. to escape the incongruities caused by what they see as inconsistent characterization. There is nothing irreconcilable between Cleopatra's rich sensuality and her capacity for the highest sacrifice. From the play's beginning, Sh means to contrast the public image of his heroine with a more meaningful one, and she is true to this deeper character throughout. When Caesar pays tribute to her beauty by saying, after her death, that she looks as if she could "catch another Antony / In her strong toil of grace" (V.ii.346–347), he does not use "grace" in the theological sense. What he refers to is Cleopatra's great beauty, the exact counterpart to the rival power for Antony's attention that Cleopatra has referred to as "the world's great snare" (IV.viii.18).

1192 Bono, Barbara J. *Literary Transvaluation: From Vergilian Epic to Shakespearean Tragicomedy.* Berkeley: U. of California P., 1984. xii + 264 pp.

Investigates transvaluation, "an artistic act of historical self-consciousness that at once acknowledges the perceived values of the antecedent text and transforms them to serve the values of the present." Part 4 focuses on Sh's transvaluation of Virgil in *Ant.* Revision of item 1193.

1193 Bono, Barbara Jane. "'Sunt hic etiam ... mentem mortalia tangunt.' (*Aen.* I.161–162). Renaissance Transvaluations: From Vergilian Epic to Shakespearean Heroic Drama." Ph.D. dissertation, Brown University, 1978. *DAI*, 39 (1978–79), 5520-A.

Studies one example of the influence of classical texts on Renaissance literature: "the Renaissance vernacular dramatic transformations of the central tragic story of Dido from Vergil's epic, the *Aeneid*, and the topologically linked story of the downfall of the romantic and imperial ambitions of Egyptian Cleopatra and the Roman triumvir Marc Antony." This investigation sheds light on a number of topics: (1) the adaptation of works by late Greco-Roman historiographers like Dio Cassius and Plutarch to the formal concerns of Renaissance dramatists, (2) the evolution of "the problematic concept of universal empire," and (3) the relationship of tragedy to epic. Most important, it reveals how "Roman values of impersonal law, inflexible Fate, and Stoic self-restraint were strained, modified, and warmed by intervening concepts of the value of romantic love and the contiguity of other varieties of classical belief with the greater personalism of Christian providentialism." The fourth chapter analyzes *Ant.* by arguing that it represents a "generic inversion from the complex tensions of the *Aeneid.*" For Virgil, the story of Dido and Aeneas is a tragedy within an epic, contained by and sublimated to a harsh historical fate. In *Ant.*, Sh recognizes the necessity of historical realism, but "he ends with a hope for a greater heroism of the epic–erotic imagination." Revised as item 1192.

1194 Booth, Stephen. "Poetic Richness: A Preliminary Audit." *PCP*, 19 (1984), 68–78.

Presents a close analysis of *Ant.*, III.x, in which Enobarbus and two others discuss Cleopatra's disgraceful retreat during the sea battle, as a way of demonstrating that to talk about poetry in Sh's plays is to talk about insignificant details. Considers matters like simile, metaphor, sound, echoic and proleptic reference, and theme.

1195 Bose, Amalendu. "'The Barge She Sat In.'" *Calcutta Essays on Shakespeare.* Ed. Amalendu Bose. Calcutta: Calcutta U., 1966, pp. 81–97.

Maintains that Enobarbus's description of Antony's first meeting with Cleopatra (*Ant.*, II.ii) is an effective means of explaining Antony's subsequent behavior in leaving Octavia, whom he has just married. The speech is appropriately given to a third party, not to Antony himself. In the poetry he gives to Enobarbus, Sh creates an atmosphere of "more than human beauty" that could not be evoked if the Cydnus meeting were to be presented on stage with a boy actor as Cleopatra. This vision, which the audience experiences through Enobarbus, is the moment to which, at the play's end, Cleopatra looks back as she prepares to join Antony. The description of the Cydnus scene is a total "suspension of time and motion," "a vision of absolute entity, an immaculate essence." Nowhere else in Sh does anything like this occur.

1196 Bowers, Fredson. "Shakespeare's Art: The Point of View." *Literary Views: Critical and Historical Essays.* Ed. Carroll Camden. Chicago: U. of Chicago P., 1964, pp. 45–58.

Employs *Ant.* as a chief exhibit in an argument about how Sh manipulates his audience to accept his point of view. One means of doing this is through a touchstone character who can "illuminate another by word of mouth, or by the example of parallelism and contrast." Enobarbus is such a character, and Sh guides carefully the audience's initial agreement with Enobarbus's rational appraisal of Antony and its subsequent recognition that this appraisal is inadequate. Sh also guides audience response through the climax. In *Ant.*, this takes place in III.vii, in which, contrary to reason and what the Elizabethans would have viewed as the proper order of things, both principals make a choice that determines their tragic fates: Antony, subjecting himself to Cleopatra's control, decides to fight at sea against his better judgment; Cleopatra, usurping the male's role, insists on being part of an enterprise for which she has no competence. Reprint. *Hamlet as Minister and Scourge and Other Studies in Shakespeare and Milton.* Charlottesville: U.P. of Virginia, 1989, pp. 62–79.

1196a Bowers, Fredson. "Shakespeare's Dramatic Vagueness." *VQR*, 39 (1963), 475–84. Reprint. *Hamlet as Minister and Scourge and Other Studies in Shakespeare and Milton.* Charlottesville: U. P. of Virginia, 1989, pp. 80–89.

Makes the point that Sh's refusal to clarify the motivations of characters in certain complex situations is deliberate; he declines to oversimplify. One set of examples comes from *Ant.*, in which the reasons behind the exposure of Cleopatra's withheld treasure by Seleucis are not exhibited. Nor do we learn whether Antony's accusation about the surrender of the Egyptian ships to Caesar is true. In both of these cases, Sh follows Plutarch in not offering explanations. Elsewhere, however, he is perfectly willing to assign motives when Plutarch was silent (as in the episode of Ventidius's comment on not following up his victory over the Parthians) or to suppress motives "that Plutarch had assigned" (as in the case of the Soothsayer's warning Antony to leave Rome).

1197 Bowers, John M. "'I Am Marble-Constant': Cleopatra's Monumental End." *HLQ*, 46 (1983), 283–97.

Finds that Sh relied on funerary imagery derived from observation of monumental tombs in creating two episodes—"the interlude with the Clown and the suicide itself"—found at the end of *Ant.* (V.ii). Neither of these incidents has a source in Plutarch's *Lives.*

1198 Bowling, Lawrence Edward. "Antony's Internal Disunity." *SEL*, 4 (1964), 239–46.

Contends that in *Ant.* disunity occurs on three levels: "in the individual, in the family, and in the state." This disunity results from an individual's or organization's attempt to exist with two equally important centers of power or guiding principles. Throughout the play, Antony's love for Cleopatra contends with his ambition for honor as a soldier. He temporarily achieves personal unity by subordinating love to duty in his marriage to Octavia, but as the play progresses, he becomes "enmeshed in a complex of multiple dualities" involving Cleopatra. Only by choosing love over honor as he dies does Antony achieve unity.

1199 Brand, Alice Glarden. "Antony and Cleopatra and the Nature of Their Sexuality." *The Bard*, 1 (1976), 98–107.

Seeks to make the importance of the sexuality of both the protagonists in *Ant.* explicit. Antony's falling movement throughout, his connection with melting and mingling, his linking of carnal and military imagery, and his loss of potency in his sword all reveal his sexual diminution. Cleopatra's association with the Nile and with the serpents of Egypt exhibits her own eroticism. Structurally, the play "outlines a sustained metaphor for the love-act."

1200 Brandão, Nielson da Neves. "Defeat in *Antony and Cleopatra.*" *Signal* (Paraíba), 11 (1978), 101–16.

Finds the theme of *Ant.* in the defeat of a man who gradually surrenders his power to a woman. Notes that Plutarch, Sh's source, records that Antony was deceived by Cleopatra, whereas Sh emphasizes that Antony "knows her for what she is." Antony's defeat in politics and war is a consequence of his defeat in love. Antony and Cleopatra have contrasting personalities, but in the end they join, paradoxically, in triumphant death.

1201 Brennan, Anthony S. "Excellent Dissembling: Antony and Cleopatra Playing at Love." *MQ*, 19 (1978), 313–29.

Identifies the self-dramatizing tendencies of Sh's tragic heroes, especially in *Ant.* Discusses the competition between Antony and Cleopatra in the playing of roles. Cleopatra is a master performer, scene-stealer, and director. Her energy is focused on getting everyone else (Antony, the Messenger who brings news of Antony's marriage, Caesar) to play on her terms. Antony and Cleopatra, by submitting to the illusion of the roles they have created, achieve their own version of reality in death. Cleopatra's staging of the final scene preserves her tragedy and defeats Caesar's rival plan to parody her relationship with Antony in shows put on for the common people. Notes that Cleopatra, in her role as theatrical producer, is analogous to Sh as artist.

1202 Britton, Elizabeth Lindsey. "The Dido–Aeneas Story from Vergil to Dryden." Ph.D. dissertation, University of Virginia, 1984. *DAI*, 45 (1984–85), 3642-A.

Describes the two opposite interpretations to which the story of Dido and Aeneas has been subjected: The first, deriving from Virgil's *Aeneid*, is strongly moral and emphasizes duty; the second, originating in Ovid's *Heroides*, prizes love and personal commitment over "epic achievement." There is a similarly double attitude to the Antony–Cleopatra story, going back to the *Aeneid* and Horace's *Odes*. Devotes a chapter to "Shakespeare's *Antony and Cleopatra*: The Influence of the Historical Traditions."

1203 Brodwin, Leonora. *Elizabethan Love Tragedy: 1587–1625.* New York: New York U. P., 1971. xii + 416 pp.

Discuses *Ant.*, in chapter 9, as the greatest tragedy of worldly love ever written. In this type of tragedy, the lover accepts at the outset the all-important value of love and is willing to sacrifice the self-contained existence that he has pursued up until this time in order to establish full communion with his beloved. Society will not permit the relinquishing of his self-sovereignty in this way, however, and destroys the private life that lover and beloved attempt to create.

1204 Broussard, Mercedes. "Mother and Child: Cleopatra and the Asp." *CEA*, 37, no. 1 (1974), 25–26.

Describes the fertility of the Nile, conveyed in *Ant.* by the river's capacity to spawn serpents, as malignant. Cleopatra, seen as a serpent of the Nile, is thus characterized as evil; her evil is associated with her sexual powers, and the serpent (her "baby") that bites her on the breast provides condign punishment for her dalliance with Antony.

1205 Burke, Kenneth. "Shakespearean Persuasion." *AR*, 24 (1964–65), 19–36.

Discusses "the rhetoric of persuasion" as it is employed in *Ant.* The plot gave Sh the opportunity to perfect the theme of Love as an empire. He draws in his audience by translating the terms of love (which are relevant to everybody) into imperial ostentation. One way in which Sh makes his audience comfortable with this imperial version of love is through the references to eunuchs: Obviously, these help reinforce Antony's virility, but they also reassure the males in the audience who might not be as well-endowed sexually as the hero that with regard to one group of men they are in the same class as he is. At the end of the play, the grandeurs of love are swept aside as Cleopatra dies speaking of herself in the lowliest of images. Sh thus allows the audience to participate in building the imperial vision of love and then brings them back to "humble animality."

1206   Burton, Dolores M. *Shakespeare's Grammatical Style: A Computer-Assisted Analysis of "Richard II" and "Antony and Cleopatra."* Austin: U. of Texas P., 1973. xviii + 364 pp.

Proposes to "determine the role played by syntax in Shakespeare's stylistic development and to formulate a theory of style and a method for applying that theory to works of literature." Uses modern linguistic theory to analyze the "lyrical style" of *R2* and the "epic brilliance" of *Ant.* and to compare the two. Chapter 6, "From Stylistics to Poetics," considers the treatment of history, the theme of fortune, and different perspectives on the imagination in *Ant.* Notes that Cleopatra is the spokesman for the imagination, giving poetic immortality to Antony and herself. In the one instance when Antony is able to transcend history, imagining himself and Cleopatra stealing all the followers of Dido and Aeneas in Elysium (IV.xiv), we see Sh challenging Virgil: He chooses for his classical play a hero whose behavior is opposite to that of the pious Aeneas but expects to redeem him and Cleopatra through the verbal opulence of his art.

1207   Bushman, Mary Ann. "Representing Cleopatra." *In Another Country: Feminist Perspectives on Renaissance Drama.* Eds. Dorothea Kehler and Susan Baker. Metuchen, New Jersey: Scarecrow, 1991, pp. 36–49.

Points out that Cleopatra's characterization emerges from her awareness of being "an actor, a role-player," a self-consciousness denied to other women in Sh. However, she never attains the authoritative stasis that marks male tragic soliloquies in Sh; even when she adopts "a mode of speaking that might replace soliloquy" in revealing her character, her speech fails because of incompleteness and interruption. She uses her sense of acting style as part of her character to control the audience, revealing "a social model of selfhood that resists completion." Reflecting this uncertainty, *Ant.* occupies uneasily "the border between tragedy and tragicomedy."

1208   Cairncross, Andrew S. "*Antony and Cleopatra*, III.x.10." *N&Q*, 22 (1975), 173.

Suggests emending "ribaudred" (*Ant.*, III.x.10) to "ribaud," a standard contemporary spelling of "ribald," which would be highly appropriate in the context.

1209   Entry deleted.

1210   Caputi, Antony. "Shakespeare's *Antony and Cleopatra*: Tragedy without Terror." *SQ*, 16 (1965), 183–91.

Views Antony's movement in the play as a process of choosing "between distinctive kinds of experience." To keep us aware of the alternatives open to his protagonist, Sh in the first half of the play provides nearly equal representations of "the discipline and austerity of the Roman experience and of the self-indulgence and delight of the Egyptian experience." By devoting almost the last half of the play to the final days of the lovers, Sh signals his intention "to deepen and particularize our perception" of the commitment Antony finally makes. Antony's fault is that he senses more clearly than others "how delicious life can be." In loving life too much, he ruins himself. He is thus a tragic figure, but his fall evokes no terror. Sh validates the paradoxical experience of Antony and Cleopatra through the metaphysical qualities of the play's language, which conveys an appropriate sense of "strain and discord within harmony," of "diversity embraced and fused." The essential attribute of Cleopatra's world is "a density that insists on multiple angles of vision."

1211 Carducci, Jane. "Antony as Roman Soldier in Shakespeare's *Antony and Cleopatra*." *Lang&L*, 15 (1990), 79–107.

Contests the readings of Antony's character that view him either as ignominiously effeminized by obsession with Cleopatra or as successfully poised between the amour of Egypt and the armor of Rome. Afraid to accept responsibility, Antony engages in evasiveness, prevarication, histrionics, vacillation, scapegoating, and self-pity. Failing "to reconcile masculine and feminine values," he cannot escape, even in his "noble" death, the world of adolescent illusions. See item 2719.

1212 Cartwright, Kent. *Shakespearean Tragedy and Its Double: The Rhythms of Audience Response*. University Park: Pennsylvania State U. P., 1991. xi + 285 pp.

Uses a "phenomenological and modernist" approach to investigate how Sh's tragedy invites a rhythm of engagement and detachment from the audience. Deals with the ways in which the audience develops through the play's exploitation of "spectatorial distance." Chapter 5, devoted to *Ant.*, argues that in this play spectatorship, in a reciprocal relationship with acting, is a dominant activity, so much as "to constitute the paradigm of its tragic action." Discusses the various spectators within the play.

1212a Cavell, Stanley. "Introduction." *Disowning Knowledge in Six Plays of Shakespeare*. Cambridge: Cambridge U. P., 1987, pp. 1–37.

Includes discussion of *Ant.* as an exploration of a new kind of intimacy, or a desire for such intimacy, driven by the birth of skepticism. Another way to see this is that the play proposes "a more private, let us say Christian" view of both the political and the erotic realms. Places emphasis on the withdrawal of the world from Antony (for example, in the desertion of his soldiers and in the departure of Hercules as his guardian spirit) and from others (Antony himself withdraws from Cleopatra). The recurrence of this motif is "the play's interpretation of ... the truth of skepticism." Sees Antony as a figure shadowing that of Christ, partly as a speculation "that satisfaction is no longer imaginable within what we understand as religion" and partly as a result of the influence on Sh of Plutarch's paralleling of lives from different cultures (in Christendom, there is only one life to which our lives are to be paralleled, and the question then arises "whether we can any longer bear up under the parallel of Christ"). Regards one of the chief attacks of skepticism in literature to be directed against marriage and maintains that Cleopatra attempts to redefine marriage (and the world) by theatricalizing it.

1213 Charney, Maurice. "'This Mist, My Friend, Is Mystical': Place and Time in Elizabethan Plays." *The Rarer Action: Essays in Honor of Francis Fergusson*. Eds. Alan Cheuse and Richard Koffler. New Brunswick: Rutgers U. P., 1970, pp. 25–35.

Uses *Ant.* to demonstrate certain points about place and time. The two locales of Egypt and Rome help to generate the tragic conflict, and the successions of short scenes are used to create "a panoramic effect" or to compress time.

1214 Cheadle, Brian. "'His Legs Bestrid the Ocean' as a 'Form of Life.'" *Drama and Philosophy*. Ed. James Redmond. (Themes in Drama 12.) Cambridge: Cambridge U. P., 1990, pp.87–106.

Surveys critical response to Cleopatra's speeches, especially her description of Antony in *Ant.* (V.i.) Shows that Wittgenstein's notion of language usage as constituting "forms of life" accepted in a group can be employed to understand how the two lovers together construct a life whose imagery is richer than reality. For each lover, the death, presumed or real, of the other propels the survivor into language that reclaims the grandeur of their love. Though the reclamation is in some sense genuine, there is a sad awareness that when language "ceases to be spoken," we cannot be certain of knowing anything.

1215 Christopher, Georgia B. "The Private War and Peace in *Antony and Cleopatra.*" *A Festschrift for Professor Marguerite Roberts on the Occasion of Her Retirement from Westhampton College, University of Richmond, Virginia.* Ed. Frieda Elaine Penninger. Richmond: U. of Richmond, 1976, pp. 59–73.

Asserts that the lovers in *Ant.* inhabit a private emotional space of their own making and that the chief action of the play involves "defections from and returns to this charmed circle." Describes the pattern according to which first Antony betrays and then Cleopatra. Locates five "grand exits for love-making and revelry" that punctuate the betrayals, the final exit for each lover being entry through death into the poetic fantasy of mature love.

1216 Clayton, Thomas. "'Mysterious by This Love': The Unregenerate Resurrection of Antony and Cleopatra." *Essays and Studies* (Calcutta), 3 (1981), 95–116.

Focuses on the "dual protagonism" of *Ant.*, whereby the souls of Antony and Cleopatra live in each other's bodies. This interchangeability of the lovers is a function of the play's sensualized and paganized Neoplatonism. After Antony's death, Cleopatra is represented as "infused and inanimated with the transmigrated spirit of Antony while remaining very much herself." Sh's adaptation of materials from North's Plutarch for the Seleucus interlude (V.ii) creates an "ironical vignette" to emphasize the beguiling of Caesar, whose fatuous patronizing of Cleopatra as he departs leaves her free to pursue her amatory death and resurrection with Antony.

1217 Clemon-Karp, Sheila. "The Female Androgyne in Tragic Drama." Ph. D. dissertation, Brandeis University, 1980. *DAI*, 41 (1980–81), 2096-A-2097-A.

Discusses outstanding examples of the very few female protagonists in tragic drama who transcend "sex-role stereotypes" by committing themselves to "causes greater than themselves" and by dying in the pursuit of these goals. Calls these characters androgynes. Includes analysis of Sh's Cleopatra in *Ant.*

1217a Cluck, Nancy A. "Shakespearean Studies in Shame." *SQ*, 36 (1985), 141–51.

Employs recent psychological investigations to explicate the "complex of shame," which includes "exposure, a threat to identity, a fear of abandonment, [and] a sense of unlovability." Regards *Ant.* as Sh's "most perceptive and unrelenting exploration of shame." In the early part of the play, others try to shame Antony by recalling his past greatness, and Cleopatra uses shame to control him. Antony at first refuses to recognize that he has departed from his true self, but finally he takes responsibility for what he has done and transcends shame in his heroic suicide.

1218 Coates, John. "'The Choice of Hercules' in *Antony and Cleopatra.*" *ShS* (1978), 45–52.

Points out that a detailed consideration of Antony's connection with the Renaissance reading of the Hercules myth works against the view that Sh is engaged primarily in ironic debunking of the lovers. The esoteric meanings of the Choice of Hercules, as elaborated by the humanists, are most important in interpreting Antony's character. Rather than resting on a choice of virtue instead of pleasure, the Renaissance Hercules was presented as reconciling the two, with virtue firmly in control, and thus achieving a superiority to Fortune. In terms of Renaissance mythography, the desertion of Antony by Hercules could signal a descent into the self to control one's baser instincts. Indeed, following the god's departure, Antony's nobility is enhanced as he displays new courage, generosity, and capacity for mastering pleasure without rejecting it. Deserted by the Egyptian fleet, Antony explicitly links his feelings to the dying agony of Hercules ("The shirt of Nessus is upon me" [IV.xii.43]). This was interpreted in the Renaissance as a purificatory death, one that reconciles opposing elements, and

Antony's own death parallels it. He has attained a ripeness and completeness that raise him above fate.

1219 Cohen, Brent Martin. "Sexuality and Tragedy in *Othello* and *Antony and Cleopatra*." Ph.D dissertation, University of California, Berkeley, 1981. *DAI*, 42 (1981–82), 5127-A.

Uses a psychological and psychoanalytic approach to *Ant.*, which, "although a tragedy itself, regains the power of celebration felt unself-consciously in *Romeo and Juliet*." Maintains that the marked strain on the conventional assumptions and expectations of comedy in *Ant.* is a vehicle for Sh's growing concern with "the tragic consequences of sexual antagonisms."

1220 Colman, E. A. M. *The Structure of Shakespeare's "Antony and Cleopatra."* Sydney: The English Association, 1971. 24 pp.

Offers a reading of *Ant.* sympathetic to the "transcendental" as distinguished from the "realist" interpretation. At the beginning, the play presents a vision of idealized love and a "realistic" opposition to that love. In the second phase of the action, Sh shows Antony walking a tightrope between his "need for self-fulfillment as a statesman and his emotional tie to Cleopatra." In the third section, the protagonists are caught up in "periodic repetitions of the same essential sequence—love–hate, faith–disillusion, triumph–despair." Throughout these middle sections, there is significant evidence to support the "transcendental" view: For example, during the alternation of opposing feelings in the third part, Sh expands what is a minor skirmish in Plutarch to give Antony a military victory and show him living up to Cleopatra's image of him as "Lord of lords" (IV.viii.16). The suspense of the fourth part (coincident with act V) involves whether or not Cleopatra will remain true to her noble vision of Antony. In her suicide, she does remain true to a unified ideal of both lover and statesman. For herself, she achieves a calm fulfillment as the mate of "Emperor Antony" (V.ii.75).

1221 Cook, Elizabeth. *Seeing through Words: The Scope of Late Renaissance Poetry*. New Haven: Yale U. P., 1986. viii + 180 pp.

Chapter 4, on *Ant.*, maintains that the play explores erotic love as "a mode of thought, a way of seeing and organising experience." The play validates the child's, and the poet's, faith in the power of language to transform events according to "the way in which those events are described." The imaginative creativity of the lovers transcends the narrow, limited real world in which they live.

1221a Cooke, Michael G. *Acts of Inclusion: Studies Bearing on an Elementary Theory of Romanticism*. New Haven: Yale U. P., 1979. xx + 289 pp.

Includes, in chapter 2, a discussion of *Ant.* as a "drama of language," whose object is "to create and reside in its own authority." Notes that the play exhibits in miniature "the whole Elizabethan movement from revenge, an ambiance of rigid principle and action, to romance, a state founded on the transmuting word." Cites Cleopatra's encounter with Dolabella (V.ii.75–99) as the key example.

1222 Coppedge, Walter R. "The Joy of the Worm: Dying in *Antony and Cleopatra*." *RenP*, 1988 (1989), 41–50.

Examines the deaths of the principals in *Ant.* "to determine what, if any, attendant opportunities for 'new life' they bring." Cites Plutarch's *The Life of Marcus Antonius* to reinforce Antony's connection with Hercules and Mars; and Plutarch's essay "Of Isis and Osiris" to link him with Bacchus and that god's Egyptian manifestation, Osiris. Antony, mutilated like Osiris, is like that god "restored by the ministrations of his loving mate." Cleopatra, "radiant with love" at her death, becomes "a dish for the gods" through the "myriad images" that offer her as a kind of "marvellous food."

1223 Coppedge, Walter Raleigh. "Shakespeare's Oaths and Imprecations." Ph.D. dissertation, Indiana University, 1967. *DA*, 28 (1967–68), 2643-A-2644-A.

Analyzes oaths in Sh as affective language and examines their role in establishing the emotional intensity of scenes and providing a key to character. They also reveal dramatic themes. For example, oaths in *Ant.* associate Cleopatra with Isis and Antony with Hercules, thus highlighting the conflict between love and duty. Discusses twelve of Sh's plays, including *Ant.*

1224 Costa, Maria Gláucia de V. "The Moon and Cleopatra: A Case of Parallelism in *Antony and Cleopatra*." *Signal* (Paraíba), 1 (1978), 47–64.

Calls attention to Sh's pervasive use of moon imagery in *Ant.* Cleopatra is paralleled to the moon throughout, especially in her magnetic attraction for Antony, her changeableness, her duality, her embodiment of the goddess Isis, her power as enchantress, and her connection with Demeter. Like the course of the moon, Cleopatra's life can be divided into phases.

1225 Costa de Beauregard, Raphaelle. "*Antony and Cleopatra*: A Play to Suit the New Jacobean Taste." *Caliban*, 10 (1974), 105–11.

Points out that in *Ant.* the figure of Hercules, composed of conflicting elements of fury and serenity, provides a model for the hero, who wavers between Rome and Alexandria. Like Hercules in Elysium, Antony in Egypt enjoys bliss as he contemplates his past deeds of heroic beneficence. Also like Hercules, however, his anger, or untamed passion, is and has been the chief stimulus for his deeds. Cleopatra recalls his heroism in a vision of monumental muscularity (V.ii); here his passionate actions are exalted, but they are described as being in the past. His fury exhausts itself on unworthy objects like Thidias, thus reflecting weakness rather than strength. The myth of Hercules, with its potential to exhibit a character of superhuman proportions subject to unresolved contradictions, allowed Sh to create Antony to suit the new mannerist taste of the Jacobeans.

1226 Couchman, Gordon W. "*Antony and Cleopatra* and the Subjective Convention." *PMLA*, 76 (1961), 420–25.

Offers a critique of George Bernard Shaw's assault on *Ant.* for its romanticism. Emphasizes the realism in Sh's portrayal of Antony and of the Roman world in its moral decay.

1227 Cowser, Robert G. "The Use of 'Salad Days' in *Antony and Cleopatra*." *Word Study*, 38, no. 3 (1963), 8.

Points out that "salad days" (*Ant.*, I.v.76), referring to Cleopatra's youth and inexperience when she met Caesar, is reinforced by her references to herself as "green in judgment" and "cold in blood" (I.v.77), both suggesting qualities of salads.

1228 Cullum, Graham. "'Condemning Shadows Quite': *Antony and Cleopatra*." *Philosophy and Literature*, 5 (1981), 186–203.

Examines the dialectical relationship between public and private in *Ant.* Notes that in Sh's source, North's Plutarch, Antony is judged severely for his inability to control himself in a public world. This is the same judgment Sh's Caesar makes on Antony. The play, however, does not permit easy assessments based on dichotomies. Instead, it scrutinizes the various contraries—"Rome vs. Egypt; duty vs. pleasure; Caesar vs. Cleopatra; public vs. private"—and contestants, without offering definitive evaluations. Much about these competing contraries is paradoxical. For example, Caesar's need to exercise supreme public power commits him to an unceasing struggle against the unruly private aspects of life, which limits him (his activities and desires are frequently spoken of in terms of ordering and controlling); and Cleopatra's great dream of Antony (V.ii) is more than her vision of the facts of her experience (it is a validation of the imagination that hovers tentatively between public reality and private fancy).

1229 Cunningham, John E. "*Antony and Cleopatra*: The World Well Lost." *Critical Essays on "Antony and Cleopatra."* Eds. Linda Cookson and Bryan Loughrey. (Longman Literature Guides.) Harlow, Essex: Longman, 1990, pp. 105–14.

Notes that Sh presents Antony as a man caught between Stoic Rome and sensual Egypt. Cleopatra is politically astute, and her allure exceeds her physical beauty. Antony's irrational passion leads to his destruction.

1230 Cutts, John P. "Charmian's 'Excellent Fortune!'" *AN&Q*, 5 (1966–67), 148–49.

Argues that Charmian's wish to "have a child at fifty, to whom Herod of Jewry may do homage" (*Ant.*, I.ii.29–30) links her with John the Baptist (she is a forerunner of Cleopatra) and with the power of Christ. Sh uses Christian analogue to emphasize "the world-shattering significance of the events he describes."

1231 Daiches, David. "Imagery and Meaning in *Antony and Cleopatra*." *ES*, 43 (1962), 343–58.

Points out that Sh's chief focus in *Ant.* is on "the different roles that man can play on the various stages [that] human activity provides for him, and about the relation of these roles to the player's true identity." Seeking for the right identity, both protagonists play a variety of roles. In his death, for example, Antony finally unites his roles as lover and conqueror. Cleopatra's careful arrangement of her death allows her to conjoin a number of roles she has played. Through the emphasis on role-playing, Sh builds "a moral universe out of non-moral materials."

1232 Dash, Irene G. *Wooing, Wedding, and Power: Women in Shakespeare's Plays*. New York: Columbia U. P., 1981. xiii + 295 pp.

Chapter 8 argues that, in *Ant.*, Sh shows a woman of power combining her political and sexual selves, though she must struggle against a variety of male voices that seek to discount her political role.

1233 Davidson, Clifford. "*Antony and Cleopatra*: Circe, Venus, and the Whore of Babylon." *Shakespeare: Contemporary Critical Approaches*. Ed. Harry R. Garvin. Special associate ed. Michael D. Payne (*BuR*, 25, no. 1.) Lewisburg: Bucknell U. P., 1980, pp. 31–55.

Studies the "iconography and structure" of *Ant.* to show how Sh brings together many conflicting traditional elements to create magnificent theater. Notes that superficially the play presents a conflict between the philosophies of Stoicism and Epicureanism, the former of which was generally preferred by the Elizabethans. Antony's espousal of the latter is, however, not wholly condemned; his intemperance leads to glory as well as shame. Uses emblem books to argue that Antony's subservience to Cleopatra is rooted in idleness. Cleopatra is associated with Eve (especially through imagery of food) and the Whore of Babylon in the Apocalypse; with the "fatal female" Circe, who, according to Renaissance mythographers, has both negative (ensnaring enchantress) and positive (promoter of fertility) qualities; and with the divided image of Venus (earthly and heavenly), whose ambivalence allows Sh to explore both the effects of Luxury on a great soldier and the movement toward "universal peace" and "aesthetic redemption" as the play concludes.

1234 Davidson, Clifford. "Organic Unity and Shakespearean Tragedy." *JAAC*, 30 (1971–72), 171–76.

Cites Enobarbus's description of Cleopatra on her barge (*Ant.*, II.ii.201–215) as a "more poetic working up" of what Sh found in Plutarch, a "set piece which does in no way grow out of the character of the speaker." Uses this as part of an argument against the validity of Samuel Taylor Coleridge's notion of organic unity in interpreting Sh's tragedies.

1235   Davis, Timothy C. "Shakespeare's *Antony and Cleopatra*." *Expl*, 48 (1990), 176–78.

Claims that Antony's crocodile speech (II.vii), though its immediate target is Lepidus, contains mockery of Caesar's ostensible love for Octavia. The metaphor of "crocodile tears" provides a clue to understanding Caesar's hypocritical display of sorrow when he parts from his sister (III.ii).

1235a Dawson, R. MacG. "But Why Enobarbus?" *N&Q*, 34 (1987), 216–17.

Maintains that Sh, in developing his character Enobarbus in *Ant.* from the few hints provided by Plutarch, gave him that name instead of Domitius (the name used in the *Lives*) because it describes his red hair and beard. The connection of the red beard with Judas in the English stage tradition would have further reminded the audience of Enobarbus's ultimate untrustworthiness.

1236   Dean, Paul. "*Antony and Cleopatra*: An Ovidian Tragedy?" *CahiersE*, 40 (1991), 73–77.

Maintains that Ovid's influence is pervasive in *Ant.* There are a few verbal parallels to Ovid's work in act IV, but more significant Ovidian debts are *Ant.*'s use of "multiple perspectives," its "skepticism about heroic tragedy," its combination of sympathy and detachment, and its preoccupation with the theme of metamorphosis. Sh shared Ovid's critical attitude toward "the militaristic and moralistic values" of the Augustan establishment.

1237   deBrito, João Batista Barbosa. "Duality in *Antony and Cleopatra*." *Signal* (Paraíba), 1 (1978), 32–46.

Interprets *Ant.* in terms of number symbolism. Finds the number two to be especially significant, especially as it is manifested in antithesis. Classifies the play's antitheses into three groups: exterior, psychological, and philosophical. Distinguishes a leitmotif for each act (imminent change in I, false harmony in II, antagonism and belligerence in III, decay in IV, and transcendence in V) and explains the extent to which the three types of antitheses contribute to the development of each leitmotif.

1238   Dias, Walter. *Shakespeare: His Tragic World: Psychological Explorations.* New Delhi: S. Chand, 1972. xxiii + 532 pp.

Interprets six Shakespearean tragedies according to "the play of sex," according to which "the closer the relationship between persons of the opposite sexes, with their essential characteristics interchanged—predominance of reason in man and emotion in woman—the more poignant the resultant tragedy of their lives." Chapter 6 treats *Ant.*, noting that "the mechanization of the sexual response" in Antony, which is the basis for the spiritual oneness of the lovers, is attributed by Sh to their long relationship, not, as Plutarch would have it, to Fulvia. Discusses two other major "corrections" of Plutarch by Sh to make clear how the playwright insists on emphasizing that the play of sex lies at the heart of the tragedy: (1) Sh assigns responsibility for Antony's choice to fight by sea at Actium and for his subsequent flight from the battle entirely to Antony; and (2) Sh lifts the encounter between Cleopatra and Octavius in the last scene from one of "undignified animal passion" to "a sober but lively display of the masculine–feminine battle of wits." Antony chooses sexual love instead of worldly affairs or realism, and so is rewarded with sexual love's highest joys. For this, however, he must suffer "tragic consequences in the material world."

1239 Doran, Madeleine. "'High Events as These': The Language of Hyperbole in *Antony and Cleopatra*." *QQ*, 72 (1965–66), 26–51. Revision. *Shakespeare's Dramatic Language: Essays by Madeleine Doran*. Madison: U. of Wisconsin P., 1976, pp. 154–81.

Suggests that in *Ant*. Sh employs hyperbole, often qualified by plain speech or literal statement, "to give us a sense of pleasurable participation in a credible, but rare experience." In describing Rome and its power, and Antony's part in these, Sh uses "a whole set of images that magnifies the power by reducing the objects of its control." We assent both to the largeness of Antony's character and to the comments others make in reproof of him.

1240 Dorius, R. J. "*Antony and Cleopatra*." *How to Read Shakespearean Tragedy*. Ed. Edward Quinn. New York: Harper & Row, 1978, pp. 293–354.

Consists of four chapters, comprising part 7 of the book. Seeks to convey the complexity of *Ant*., noting that the tragic, heroic, satiric, and romantic modes "form a unity" in the play. Includes generous citations from a variety of critics. Points out that Sh derived his conception of the heroic, which involves an excess of virtue, from classical writers like Plutarch; *Ant*. is Sh's chief portrait of "the heroic man in love." Considers the first two acts by analyzing the characters of Antony, Cleopatra, and Caesar as they are there presented. Views the events of acts III and IV in terms of Antony's two defeats in battle and his death. In act V, we witness the transformation of Cleopatra, through the power of her imagination, into an icon, a work of art.

1241 Dorius, R. J. "Shakespeare's Dramatic Modes and *Antony and Cleopatra*." *Literatur als Kritik des Lebens: Festschrift zum 65. Geburtstag von Ludwig Borinski*. Eds. Rudolf Haas, Heinz-Joachim Müllenbrock, and Claus Uhlig. Heidelberg: Quelle & Meyer, 1975, pp. 83–96.

Makes distinctions between the modes characteristic of Sh's comedies and romances and those characteristic of the histories and tragedies. In the former two groups, the powers of time, nature, and women work toward regeneration. In the histories, these agents are pushed to the perimeters of the action, and in the tragedies they are often destructive. The tragedies take love from the comedies and power from the histories to form their polar themes. Maintains that *1&2H4* and *H5*, which are "balanced between comedy or comic epic" and "near-tragedy," help us to understand what happens in *Ant*. Whereas in the history plays the hero (Prince Henry) is finally directed away from the world of love and pleasure (represented by Falstaff) toward the world of public affairs, in *Ant*. the hero is led to accept the somewhat Falstaffian world of Cleopatra. Although *Ant*. is a tragedy in the sense that its protagonists are destroyed, it is unusual in that its hero dies before the end and is "posthumously transfigured" by the woman who has led to his political failure. Cleopatra, in many ways similar to the malign women of the other tragedies, gains in stature during the last act as she transforms both her lover and herself and gains a triumph of the imagination. The play, then, is "balanced between the emphasis of the tragedies on time and death and that of the romances on nature and eternity."

1242 Downer, Alan S. "Heavenly Mingle: *Antony and Cleopatra* as a Dramatic Experience." *The Triple Bond: Plays, Mainly Shakespearean, in Performance*. Ed. Joseph G. Price. University Park: Pennsylvania State U. P., 1975, pp. 240–54.

Asserts that Enobarbus's mixed role as a loyal follower, deserter, fool, and cynic is crucial for the full demonstration of Cleopatra's power. Compares Enobarbus's speech about Cleopatra on the Cydnus (*Ant*., II.ii) with the passage from North's Plutarch that Sh embroidered to create it: In the mouth of the cynical soldier, the phrases describing the queen's exquisite beauty have a mocking effect. Yet shortly afterwards (in the same scene), when contemplating the picture of her he is painting, Enobarbus loses his instinct for mockery and is overcome with wonder. Sets a conventional view of Antony and Cleopatra (as "paradigmatic sinners") from a moralizing treatise by

Thomas Beard (1597) beside Sh's presentation of the pair. Responding to the ambivalent pressures of his time, Sh overthrew traditional expectations about his protagonists, portraying them as somewhat ennobled, though with a residue of their well-known flaws. Analyzes the first three scenes, as well as several others, to show how carefully Sh organized the play through juxtapositions. The play recalls many of the common features of Renaissance tragedy, though it creates ambivalence about its genre through its variations on convention. There are, for example, three movements: The first ends with the atonement of Octavius, and Antony and Cleopatra's anguish at the news; the second with "the revival of Antony's determination"; and the third with the victory of Octavius over both of the lovers. Within each movement, there is an evocation of chaos and a restoration of order. Most tragedies use this pattern, but they use it only once. The conventional figure used to restore order at the end of a tragedy (here, Octavius) is far more ambivalent than usual. Antony is caught between the world ideas represented by Cleopatra and Octavius, respectively; finds that neither idea is clear-cut; and is nevertheless forced to choose one idea, even though the choice of either will lead to his destruction. The panoramic action, combined with a complex of ambiguities, produces a marvelously constructed nontragedy.

1243   Draper, John W. "Shattered Personality in Shakespeare's Antony." *Psychiatric Quarterly*, 39 (1965), 448–56.

Points out that, in constructing *Ant.*, Sh followed his source, Plutarch's *Life of Marcus Antonius*, quite closely for the external action. For this reason, the playwright could not furnish motives for his hero from the humoral theory of psychology, derived from Galen, which was familiar to the Elizabethans. Plutarch obliged Sh to "depict advancing years as turning the soldier into the sybarite," to invent for Antony a disorder that modern psychiatry calls the "shattered personality."

1244   Dronke, Peter. "Shakespeare and Joseph of Exeter." *N&Q*, 27 (1980), 172–74.

Finds evidence that some details of Enobarbus's description of Cleopatra on the Cydnus (*Ant.*, II.ii.200–236) not found in Plutarch were suggested to Sh by a passage in Joseph of Exeter's late-12th-c. Trojan epic that describes "the ship in which Paris set out to make his conquest of Helen." The most striking detail found in both *Ant.* and Joseph (but not in Plutarch) is "the conceit of the rivalling winds."

1245   Dunbar, Georgia. "The Verse Rhythms of *Antony and Cleopatra*." *Style*, 5 (1971), 231–45.

Analyzes the prosody of *Ant.*, considering end-pauses, internal pauses, masculine line-ends, and syntax to account for various degrees of formality. Prosodic features help to develop, for example, the contrast between Antony's self-assurance and Cleopatra's playful vitality early in the play; they also register the change in Cleopatra as she asserts her final resolution to join Antony in death.

1246   Dunn, T. A. "The Imperial Bawd." *Literature and the Art of Creation*. Eds. Robert Welch and Suheil Badi Bushrui. Totowa, New Jersey: Barnes & Noble, 1988, pp. 26–32.

Describes Cleopatra as "an Imperial bawd." The relationship between Antony and Cleopatra is not ethereal or other-worldly; it is the love of a soldier and general, a man of the world, a member of the triumvirate, for "a woman of the world and a queen, a royal courtesan." *Ant.* is a very Roman love story, with the real theme of honor. Even Cleopatra dies a Roman death. The play does not achieve the distinction of some of Sh's greatest tragedies, chiefly because it is unable to move from the specific world of history "into the world of myth."

1247 Ellis, Mark Spencer. "A Cloud That's Dragonish." *Critical Essays on "Antony and Cleopatra."* Eds. Linda Cookson and Bryan Loughrey. (Longman Literature Guides.) Harlow, Essex: Longman, 1990, pp. 93–103.

Comments that in *Ant.* Sh has created characters whose participation in a struggle for political power is attended by paradoxes. Antony seeks to identify with his image as "prince o' the world" but, separated from the world of Rome, finally recognizes that his legend no longer defines him. Cleopatra is the one character who, despite her mutability, remains constant in her knowledge of self.

1248 Erickson, Peter. *Patriarchal Structures in Shakespeare's Drama*. Berkeley: U. of California P., 1985. xii + 209 pp.

Traces the development of male characters' capacity "to imagine and engage in constructive relations with women" in Sh's drama. Analyzes seven plays to show how male bonding becomes less important later in the playwright's career. Chapter 4, "Identification with the Maternal in *Antony and Cleopatra*," argues that this play marks a definitive break "with the convention of male bonding": Antony is much less interested in the loss of reputation than earlier Shakespearean heroes; he is much more interested in the new realms that a woman has revealed to him; his relationship with Enobarbus is relegated to a secondary status; and he relinquishes all claims to being a military hero. Cites Plutarch's account of Antony's father's potentially dangerous generosity as background for discussing Antony's liberality and its modulation into reckless giving. Antony seems bent on stripping himself of everything that reinforces his heroic status. The claims of conventional manliness are "reasserted at the end of the play through the military success of Octavius." By showing how the suicides of Antony and Cleopatra evade the reality embodied in Octavius, Sh is able to criticize the protagonists as escapist at the same time that he admires them.

1249 Erlich, Richard Dee. "Wise Men and Fools: Values and Competing Theories of Wisdom in a Selection of Tragedies by Tourneur, Marlowe, Chapman, and Shakespeare." Ph.D. dissertation, University of Illinois at Urbana–Champaign, 1971. *DAI*, 32 (1971–72), 5735-A.

Focuses on the question of "self-sufficiency as opposed to a man's dependence upon God, the State, society, family, or friends." Includes a discussion of *Ant.*

1250 Erskine-Hill, Howard. "Antony and Octavius: The Theme of Temperance in Shakespeare's *Antony and Cleopatra*." *RMS*, 14 (1970), 26–47.

Suggests that Sh may have had Spenserian and Aristotelian ideas of Temperance in mind when writing *Ant.*: The hero can be seen as failing in Temperance through extreme indulgence in pleasure. It is instructive to compare him with Coriolanus, who is intemperate in the opposite direction of having too weak a reaction to pleasure. *Cor.* and *Ant.* were probably "conceived in conscious antithesis to each other." In Octavius, Sh presents the exemplar of Temperance but reduces the attractiveness of the quality. Finally, Antony's deficiency in Temperance can be seen as "part of his richness in another Aristotelian virtue: Magnificence."

1250a Estrin, Barbara L. "Becoming the Other/The Other Becoming in Wyatt's Poetry." *ELH*, 51 (1984), 431–45.

Mentions, in a discussion of the lover/speaker's recollection of the past in Sir Thomas Wyatt's "They flee from me," a similar speech in which Cleopatra recalls wearing Antony's sword (*Ant.*, II.v.18–23); this took place at a special time during which sex became an interchange, "a crossing of borders into the other."

1251 Estrin, Barbara L. "'Behind a dream': Cleopatra and Sonnet 129." *Women's Studies*, 9 (1982), 177–88.

Begins by describing the male speaker's complaint about the sexual experience in Sonnet 129: Once consummated, the sexual act is a source of insecurity, a "dream."

In *Ant.*, the female heroine, Cleopatra, begins with a recognition "that love jeopardizes security," suffers the loss of her past and future with Antony, and finally recreates Antony in a dream that abolishes the "before" and "behind" of Sonnet 129 in favor of "an abiding presence of desire, eternally renewed and, hence, constantly renewable."

1252   Everett, Barbara, ed. *Antony and Cleopatra*. (Signet Classic Shakespeare.) New York: New American Library, 1964. xxxvii + [38]-276 pp.

The introduction distinguishes *Ant.* from Sh's other tragedies by noting that in it the tragic and the comic experiences coexist, among others. Notes that the political contest in the play is between two men sharply differentiated in character for "the rule of the whole civilized world some forty years before the birth of Christ." Argues that the tragedy of the principals in the play consists chiefly of the destruction of pride that accompanies the loss of their world and their deaths. The tragic development is presented by the play in a series of juxtapositions: The small and great, the insignificant and significant are set beside each other in a leisurely fashion that displays the variety of the world. The characters are presented in an equally fluid manner. Insists that *Ant.* creates "a physical rather than a metaphysical world." Maintains that two different attitudes toward time, that of living intensely in the present moment (Cleopatra's) and that of establishing "universal power and universal peace" (Caesar's), are inextricably bound up in the play and are responsible for its deep interfusion of comedy and tragedy. The note on the source, Plutarch's *Life of Marcus Antonius*, calls attention to Sh's borrowings and how he modified them. Sh's account of the events following Actium, for example, rearranges and abbreviates details from Plutarch to accentuate the importance and finality of Antony's defeat and Cleopatra's responsibility for it. Even passages that seem very close to their Plutarchan original, like Enobarbus's famous description of Cleopatra at Cydnus, show Sh using small changes to bring alive "the conflicting values of the play." The introduction, text, and note on the source are reprinted as part of item 0123.

1252a   Ewbank, Inga-Stina. "*Hamlet* and the Power of Words." *ShS*, 30 (1977), 85-102.

Refers to *Ant.* in a discussion of Hamlet's use of language. Like Hamlet in her language, Cleopatra "combines intense self-preoccupation with strong awareness of others." Plutarch emphasizes her ability to speak many foreign languages, and Sh may have translated this into "an intralingual flexibility."

1253   Faber, M. D. "*Antony and Cleopatra*: The Empire of the Self." *PsyR*, 72 (1985), 71-104.

Begins by positing that Western tragedy presents us with a hero who undergoes "a traumatic reactivation of infantile feelings." His most profound urge is to "resolve the mystery of maternal ambivalence." In *Ant.*, the hero's attraction to the queen is described in terms of dissolving one thing into another, of feasting, of incorporation: These are all images that stress Cleopatra's engagement of pregenital, oral aims. Antony's desire for empire is associated with this hunger, and the Roman patriarchy, epitomized by Octavius, is vehemently resistant to the Egyptian way of life because the latter has the potential to undermine the Roman defenses and "to awaken the Roman longing for the Mother" or for matriarchy. Notes the puritanical disapproval Octavius expresses during the feasting scene on Pompey's galley, the Roman counterpart to the scene in which Enobarbus describes Cleopatra on the Cydnus. In order to preserve patriarchal Roman order, Caesar must keep Rome and Egypt apart: Witness his implacable drive to eliminate Antony. With Cleopatra's betrayal and his loss of empire, Antony loses his self, indulging in the self-destructiveness of "a profoundly *dependent* person." In his final moments, the "aggressive side of his oral fixation" on Cleopatra disappears, and he evinces a "protective attitude toward the mother–substitute." Cleopatra's ambivalence, her sense of being lost, derives from her anxiety, her insecurity, and her "fear of abandonment." As she approaches her death, Cleopatra undergoes a partial transformation in response to Antony's demonstration that he trusts her. This play reveals Sh's understanding of "the enigmatic female"; he shifts the focus away from the *femme fatale* to "the diseased social order which produces the deleterious object relation that eventually vitiates the love between man and woman."

1254 Farmer, Harold. "'I'll Give Thee Leave to Play': Theatre Symbolism in *Antony and Cleopatra*." *ESA*, 20 (1977), 107–19.

Argues that Plutarch, in his *Life* of Antony, explains how Antony changed his style of expression to suit his audience. Sh develops this idea in *Ant.* to include styles of acting. From the beginning, the lovers relate to each other and those around them in terms of role-playing. Antony is torn between the roles of business-like Roman and ornate, self-indulgent Asiatic. Only after his failed suicide does he transcend ambiguity by finally playing the role of Cleopatra's lover. As Cleopatra enacts her death for the dead Antony, their relationship "consciously reflects the kind of actor–audience relationship [that] seems to have existed in Shakespeare's theatre."

1255 Fawkner, H. W. "The Concept of Taste in the Post-Modernist Era." *Criticism in the Twilight Zone: Postmodern Perspectives on Literature and Politics*. Eds. Danuta Zedworna-Fjellestad and Lennart Björk. Stockholm: Almqvist & Wiksell, 1990, pp. 101–12.

Critiques Immanuel Kant's distinction between "conceptual truth" and "esthetic experience." According to Kant, criticism of a work of artistic genius proceeds without reference to a prior set of rules by which the work is to be evaluated; the work itself, though imitating no model, must be recognized as furnishing an example for others to *follow*, not *imitate*. Advances *Ant.* as a work that stages "exemplariness" as well as "the difference between following and imitation." Calls attention to the scenes in which Cleopatra and Antony argue over his joining her in retreat from the battle of Actium (III.xi) and in which the dying Antony is hoisted into Cleopatra's monument (IV.xv) as evidence of Sh's "solicitation of following." The episodes involving the false example of Cleopatra's pretended suicide, Eros's killing of himself rather than Antony, Antony's botched suicide, and Cleopatra's suicide show how Sh is problematizing exemplariness. Finds that Sh, with his "conceptual gaiety," evades the polarity of the esthetic and the conceptual that Kant and some of his postmodernist followers would like to apply to art.

1256 Fawkner, H. W. *Shakespeare's Hyperontology: "Antony and Cleopatra."* Rutherford, New Jersey: Farleigh Dickinson U. P., 1990. 199 pp.

Proposes to lay bare "various self-deconstructing features of Shakespeare's text," using a hyperontological approach, which goes beyond the tendency of ontology "to prematurely appropriate meaning and furnish interpretative closure." Argues that *Ant.* "consistently traces a crucial (non)structure, that this (non)structure is hyperontological, and that the hyperontological trace engages the polar opposites 'following' and 'leaving.'" The concepts of following and leaving are hyperontological in that they do not work, they do not establish a conceptual order; rather, they play. Devotes a chapter to each of the play's five acts. Chapter 1, "Presence and Oblivion," shows how Sh's language "stitches opposed concepts into each other" in the first act; when Cleopatra says that her oblivion is an Antony, she is negating the surface notion that Antony is a "fickle deserter." Chapter 2, "To Follow Faster," considers transmigration, which in the play involves no destination; rather, the transmigratory process "migrates toward nothing but its own possibility." Chapter 3, "The Remains of Leaving," explains that in act III we encounter more straightforwardly than anywhere else the conventional morality that framed the story of the lovers for the Renaissance. Unlike his English predecessors, Sh "deconstructs the binary systems that inhere in the tradition he starts off with." Chapter 4, "Exemplariness," maintains that Antony's death prompts no sudden, great outpouring of emotion because it is another form of the leaving that pervades the play. Chapter 5, "Cadaverous Space," contends that in the final act there is a struggle for absolute triumph between Caesar and Cleopatra. Cleopatra wins by evading the reductive performance to which Caesar would confine her; instead, she implements a different staging that will "secure the success of the play/legend itself." She undergoes a liquefication that is both a dissolution and a rarefaction; in this, she joins Antony, whose "absolute spending" is also characterized by liquidness. Chapter 6, "Trace," suggests that, "hyperontologically speaking," leaving becomes staying. *Ant.* provides us with a mythic movement that is circular rather than ascendental; we receive from it a sense of "recyclable nontranscendence."

1257   Fegan, James. "Philo's Sonnet in *Antony and Cleopatra*: The Fact, Features and Possible Interpretative Implications." *ILT News*, 70 (1980), 90–112.

Maintains that, except for rhyme, Philo's opening speech of thirteen lines in *Ant.* possesses all the features of a sonnet. Hears the voice of Philo in this speech as echoing that of the "I" in *Son.*; that is, Sh has invested Philo's comments with greater authority than those of an ordinary character in a play. Two key feelings found in both *Son.* and in Philo's speech are (1) regret for the failure of beauty to perpetuate itself through legitimate increase and (2) dismay at the loss of a noble young friend, debauched by an unworthy woman. Points out that the sexual connotations of Philo's language allow for readings that range from bitter indignation at Antony's excesses to amusement at the farcical figure he presents. The weight given in Philo's utterance to religious references gives warrant for paying close attention to allusions elsewhere in the play to Judas, the Last Supper, and the Apocalypse.

1258   Fergusson, Francis. "Poetry and Drama." *Symbolism and Modern Literature: Studies in Honor of Wallace Fowlie*. Ed. Marcel Tetel. Durham: Duke U. P., 1978, pp. 13–25.

Uses Aristotle's belief that "the arts are imitations of action" to comment on Antony's meditation about his failure to hold a visible shape, like clouds (*Ant.*, IV.xiv). He is the persona of his poem, and his action is "to see through the cloudy shapes before him to himself, as he really is."

1259   Fernandez, Maria Luisa Dañobeitia. "Cleopatra's Role Taking: A Study of *Antony and Cleopatra*." *Revista Canaria De Estudios Ingleses*, 12 (1986), 55–73.

Sees Cleopatra's game-playing as forced on her by the political power struggle in which she is involved. Follows her games throughout the play and comments that her final game conquers Octavius and the audience, and "transforms poetry and drama into an impressive literary game."

1260   Fichter, Andrew. "*Antony and Cleopatra*: 'The Time of Universal Peace.'" *ShS*, 33 (1980), 99–111.

Maintains that in *Ant.*, the imperfection with which tragedy is realized is due to the presence of a network of Christian allusions (for example, Antony's Christ-like experiences of a Last Supper, suffering, and betrayal; Cleopatra's Nativity vision at her death; and Octavius's reference to "the time of universal peace") that suggests the inadequacy of the tragic view of life. Antony, in his partial renunciation of the Roman view of heroism and his romantic attempt to give all for love, and Cleopatra, in her concluding vision of death as a kind of fulfillment, intimate for the audience the Christian idea that "propitiatory self-sacrifice" reverses "fatalistic Stoic self-conquest." Finally, the characters are not able to see the Christian parallels. The audience, perceiving them, is suspended between the Roman view of history as tragedy and the Christian sense that tragedy has been transcended. The generically problematic nature of the play is made more acute by the urgency with which it anticipates the historical event that will undermine the basis for tragic consciousness.

1261 Fisch, Harold. "*Antony and Cleopatra*: The Limits of Mythology." *ShS*, 23 (1970), 59–67.

Sees myth-ritual as the actual subject of *Ant*. The protagonists appear both as Mars and Venus and as Isis and Osiris (for details about the second pair, Sh may have drawn on Plutarch's "Of Isis and Osiris" or on Apuleius's *The Golden Ass*). Sh, however, provides an ironic framework for viewing the mythic status of Antony and Cleopatra: There are deflating comments about Mars and Venus at several points; the Clown's appearance with the serpents reminds us of the Old Testament idea of death and suggests Cleopatra's kinship with Eve; and the Roman drama of universal history diminishes the significance of ritual enactments. There is a sense that Cleopatra's final vision of herself as Antony's wife transcends both "the world-conquering inhuman conception of time and history" of the Romans and "the Egyptians' myth-world."

1262 Fiskin, A. M. J. "*Antony and Cleopatra*: Tangled Skeins of Love and Power." *University of Denver Quarterly*, 10, no. 2 (1975), 93–105.

Examines several aspects of *Ant*. with reference to Sh's use of Plutarch. The use of *fortune* as a motif (the word is used more than in any other Shakespearean play) was possibly suggested by Plutarch's soothsayer, who warns Antony that Caesar's fortune will always dominate his. Emphasis on the love affair is achieved by Sh's omission of nearly everything in Plutarch that does not refer to Antony and Cleopatra. At the end of the play, acting on hints in Plutarch, Sh ennobled the lovers to give them tragic dignity.

1263 Fitch, Robert E. "No Greater Crack?" *SQ*, 19 (1968), 3–17.

Poses the question of whether or not nature should have convulsions at the tragedy of *Ant*., as Octavius seems to believe. Answers in the negative for three reasons: (1) The conflicting values of the play are pleasure and power, which exclude higher values; (2) the love affair is devious, destructive, selfish, faithless, and soulless; and (3) Sh, at this point in his career, is allowing his imagination "to move beyond the stage," is letting the poet in his nature predominate over the playwright, and is turning from time to eternity.

1264 Fitz, L. T. "Egyptian Queens and Male Reviewers: Sexist Attitudes in *Antony and Cleopatra* Criticism." *SQ*, 28 (1977), 297–316.

Contends that sexism pervades critical commentary on *Ant*. In the commonly practiced game of comparing Shakespearean characters, Cleopatra is always likened to or placed in the same category with other female characters, with whom she has little in common, instead of the major tragic protagonists, whom she resembles more closely. Some critics see her as quintessential Woman, a beguiling practitioner of feminine wiles, an attitude at odds with Sh's probable disapproval of this tactic. It seems more likely that Sh has her resort to this questionable maneuver as evidence of her desperation at losing her youth, not out of an effort to display the eternally feminine. Many denigrate Cleopatra as deceptive and manipulative and approve the virtuous but wronged Octavia; but against this view there is the fact that Sh reduces the importance of Octavia and has Antony treat her better than he does in Plutarch. There has been much objection to the play's bawdry, not per se, but because so much of it comes from the mouth of Cleopatra (a woman). Another sexist assumption is that what is laudable in Antony (public duty) is reprehensible in Cleopatra. For example, Cleopatra's political overtures to Caesar in the Thidias scene are condemned, while Antony's desertion of Cleopatra for Roman duty and his political marriage to Octavia are praised. The most flagrant sexist assumption is that Antony is the protagonist, but this neglects the fact that Antony dies in act IV and Cleopatra is the focus of the rest of the action. An examination of changes Sh made in Plutarch reveals that he wanted to augment Cleopatra's presence in the story and diminish her culpability. (In Plutarch, Cleopatra forces Antony to fight the battle of Actium by sea; in Sh, Antony makes the decision because of Caesar's dare.) Cleopatra, because she is sympathetic yet flawed, because her inner life is explored, and because she grows as Antony does not, can be seen as the tragic protagonist. Arguments that she is incomprehensible are founded on sexist biases about the inscrutability of women; actually, her motives, even those for her "unpredictability," are quite clearly explained. She needs to be "demythologized."

1265 Flint, Kate. "Significant Otherness: Sex, Silence and Cleopatra." *Critical Essays on "Antony and Cleopatra."* Eds. Linda Cookson and Bryan Loughrey. (Longman Literature Guides.) Harlow, Essex: Longman, 1990, pp. 9–16.

Notes how the stage portrayal of Cleopatra's sexuality, aggressiveness, and political power in any given age is determined by that age's cultural assumptions. This is because Sh never looks into Cleopatra's private mind: She speaks no soliloquies, so she almost always appears in the public mode.

1266 Foakes, R. A. "Vision and Reality in *Antony and Cleopatra*." *DUJ*, 56, N. S. 25 (1963–64), 66–76.

Identifies three points of view expressed toward the love of Antony and Cleopatra in the play: "that Antony is an adulterer, Cleopatra a whore; that their love in its vastness outweighs all else; and that, at the same time, it is itself paradoxically outweighed by practical concerns of empire." One way to reconcile these perspectives and those of critics who have responded to them is to prize the two lovers for their transcendent extravagance, which has almost nothing to do with morality or virtue. Their emotional intensity transforms them for each other "into god and goddess, Mars and Venus, Hercules and Isis." Beside them, the virtuous, dutiful, and temperate Octavia and Octavius seem insipid.

1267 Foreman, Walter C. Jr. *The Music of the Close: The Final Scenes of Shakespeare's Tragedies.* Lexington: U. P. of Kentucky, 1978. xii + 228 pp.

Treats thirteen of Sh's plays, including *Tit.*, *JC*, *Tro.*, *Tim.*, *Ant.*, and *Cor.* Examines the ways in which "the tragic process separates the tragic characters from the characters who survive to form a new order." Explains how the movement toward death of the tragic heroes involves them in a creative effort to control their lives that is analogous to the tragic dramatist's attempt to control his materials. Chapter 5 includes a lengthy discussion of *Ant.* that discovers a great and self-conscious artistry in Cleopatra's blending of tragic and comic values in the final scenes. As Cleopatra's creator and critic, Sh has fashioned in the play and in himself an even more comprehensive image of "the union of art and life." Revision of item 1268.

1268 Foreman, Walter Cyril Jr. "The Music of the Close: The Final Scenes of Shakespeare's Tragedies." Ph.D. dissertation, University of Washington, 1974. *DAI*, 36 (1975–76), 3729-A.

Comments that in the final scene of *Ant.* Sh exploits the interplay of tragic and comic forms and values, thus creating a world in which the two protagonists can be said to have lived better as well as greater lives. Revised as item 1267.

1269 Fox, Jan. "'Something rich and strange. . . .'" *Viewpoints on Shakespeare.* Ed. Brian McFarlane. Melbourne: Longman Cheshire, 1990, pp. 210–20.

Defends *Ant.* from various charges that have been levelled against it. Argues for attention to its complexity and ambiguity. Notes that Sh transformed the clear moral theme (the great man ruined by a wicked woman) of his source, Plutarch's *Lives*, to create a complex drama about the variability of the world and the constancy of love.

1270 Frantz, David Oswin. "Concepts of Concupiscence in English Renaissance Literature." Ph.D. dissertation, University of Pennsylvania, 1968. *DAI*, 30 (1969–70), 1133-A.

Explores the passion of concupiscence—defined as "excessive sexual appetite"—as it appears in the English literature of the Renaissance. Examines a variety of writings. Concludes with a chapter on *Ant.*

1271 French, A. L. *Shakespeare and the Critics.* Cambridge: Cambridge U. P., 1972. ix + 239 pp.

Deems it unfortunate that we usually assume Shakespeare's plays to be perfect and that the job of the critic is thus to explain why this perfection exists. While background study is not to be ignored, neither should it be allowed to reduce the plays to Elizabethan artifacts or, worse yet, gibberish.

Chapter 5, on *Ant.*, argues that critics' assumption of relentless seriousness in the play has led them to ignore its humor. The hero is given to using "Antony-language," "an idiom in which sense counts for little and grandiosity for much." Enobarbus and others are held prisoner by this rhetoric (in the sense that they accept it as a genuine representation of the man Antony now is), while Cleopatra consciously and skillfully parodies it. There is even comedy in Antony's death scene (IV.ii), in which Shakespeare modifies Plutarch to give us a preoccupied Cleopatra, interrupting her expiring lover, refusing to accept his suggestions, and forcing him to plead for attention.

1272 Friedman, Stanley. "*Antony and Cleopatra* and Drayton's *Mortimeriados.*" *SQ*, 20 (1969), 481–84.

Points out that a poem by William Harbert, published in 1604, compared the lovers in *Ant.* with Queen Isabella and Mortimer, the deposers of Edward II. This comparison leads to the consideration of *Ant.* in the light of Michael Drayton's *Mortimeriados* (1596), which offers the fullest of all the medieval and Elizabethan accounts of the affair between Isabella and Mortimer. There are numerous parallels between the pairs of lovers in that "each work presents an adulterous relationship involving a powerful warrior and a queen, a pair no longer young, the story being set against a background of civil strife." *Mortimeriados* should not be regarded as a source of *Ant.* but rather as an "independent use of similar themes and *topoi.*" Drayton's work is of value in understanding the morality of *Ant.*: It provided "a contemporary precedent . . . for extremely eulogistic treatment of historical characters known to have participated in a morally questionable love affair."

1273 Frost, David L. "*Antony and Cleopatra*—All for Love; or the World Ill-Lost?" *Topic*, 7 (1964), 33–44.

Challenges D. A. Traversi, who has discerned a double viewpoint in *Ant.*, both prizing the transcendent nature of the lovers' passion and recognizing the triviality and lack of decency to which their sensuality reduces them. Argues that the experience of the play is wholly on the side of the latter view. Evidence of this can be seen throughout, where even the magnificent speeches about love are undercut by reminders of the debased nature of sexuality. Cleopatra's final speech, often regarded as an exaltation of her love because of its high poetic imagery, is properly understood as self-deception when considered in light of the Clown's precedent comments about the worm, symbolic of sensuality.

1273a Frye, Northrop. "The Stage is All the World." *Northrop Frye: Myth and Metaphor. Selected Essays, 1974–1988.* Ed. Robert Denham. Charlottesville: U. P. of Virginia, 1990, pp. 196–211.

Speculates that "the central Shakespeare play" for the 21st c. will be *Ant.*, in which there is only one world (with two aspects) depicted; the focus is on a public love affair; the motivation of the characters is dramatic, "to put on a show"; and human existence is "what the stage is: a place where illusion is reality, with a procession of actors waiting to be applauded."

1274 Frye, Roland Mushat. "Theological and Non-theological Structures in Tragedy." *ShakS*, 4 (1968), 132–48.

Illustrates "the differences between theological and non-theological structures in tragedy" by comparing *Samson Agonistes* and *Ant*. Although the two male protagonists are similar in many ways and although the plays resemble each other thematically, the two authors differ considerably in their use of theology. Milton builds the structure of *Samson* on the relationship of man's behavior to the divine, whereas Sh's play makes only casual and rhetorical use of the gods. At the end of *Samson*, there is *pax dei*; at the end of *Ant.*, *pax Romana*.

1275 Fujita, Minoru. "The Concept of the Royal in Shakespeare." *ShStud*, 7 (1968–69), 1–32. Reprint. *English Criticism in Japan: Essays by Younger Japanese Scholars on English and American Literature.* Ed. Earl Miner. Tokyo: Tokyo U. P., 1972, pp. 30–48.

Analyzes the connotations of the word "royal" in Sh; discusses the idea of the royal as it was known in Sh's time from the tradition of pageantry; and examines the stage tableau of the final scene in *Ant.* in light of the foregoing discussion. In Cleopatra's death scene, she is called "royal," and the images Sh uses bring to mind "the traditional idea of beauty cultivated in the history of royal pageantry." Revised as part of chapter five of item 1276.

1276 Fujita, Minoru. *Pageantry and Spectacle in Shakespeare.* (Renaissance Monographs 8.) Tokyo: Renaissance Institute, Sophia U., 1982. v + 161 pp.

Chapter 5, "New 'Cydnus' in *Antony and Cleopatra*," interprets the play in light of the "royal or princely processions on pageant occasions" to which the Elizabethan audience was accustomed. The opening scene presents Antony and Cleopatra in a procession, with all characters richly costumed (magnificence, not historical accuracy, would be emphasized). Enobarbus's description of Cleopatra on a barge in the Cydnus (II.ii), based on Plutarch's description in the *Lives* as translated by Sir Thomas North, is meant to evoke the sumptuous visual power of contemporary Elizabethan water pageants. "Cydnus," representing the visionary aesthetic splendor of Egypt, is the chief metaphor of the play, a metaphor that is emblematically realized in Cleopatra's death scene, a pageant-like presentation of the new Cydnus. Part is a revision of item 1275.

1277 Fuzier, Jean. "*Antony and Cleopatra*'s Three-Stage Structure: A Study in Development." *CahiersE*, 13 (1978), 69–74.

Suggests a progression in Sh's development of a three-part tragic structure in plays involving couples. Early experiments of this kind occur in the Pyramus and Thisbe playlet within *MND* and in *Rom*. The three elements in both cases are (1) the ostensible death of the beloved woman, (2) the subsequent suicide of "the disconsolate lover," and (3) the suicide of the woman. Sh then employed a simplified two-stage structure for three plays about tragic couples (*Ham.*, *Oth.*, and *Mac.*) before giving the three-phase structure its most elaborate and successful treatment in *Ant*. Acknowledges that Sh might have been influenced to add the third part (the Cleopatra coda) to his play by the postscript about Cleopatra in Plutarch's *Life of Marcus Antonius* but speculates that this augmentation might just as well be the culmination of Sh's experiments with structure.

1278 Gajowski, Evelyn Jacqueline. "The Art of Loving: An Inquiry into the Nature of Love in Shakespeare's Tragedies." Ph.D. dissertation, Case Western Reserve University, 1987. *DAI*, 48 (1987–88), 1774-A.

Points out that Sh prizes "personal relationships among family, friends, and lovers" as superior to all other human achievement. The most valuable quality in Sh's protagonists is "the capacity for love." The playwright both "exploits and criticizes conventional notions of love in tragedy as in comedy, representing romantic and antiromantic attitudes only to expose their inadequacy and to frame a concept of love rooted in psychological reality." In *Ant.*, Sh departs from literary tradition by depicting Cleopatra as "a woman devoted to Antony." Like Desdemona and Juliet, she has a total commitment to her lover and "a comprehensive concept of love that includes but is not confined to the sexual." Unlike Desdemona but like Juliet, she instructs her beloved, enabling his transformation from soldier to lover.

1279   Gallwey, Kay. "Shakespeare's Cleopatra: Strumpet or Good Angel?" *Crux*, 22, no. 4 (1986), 47–59.

Surveys critical opinion on the character of Cleopatra and cites passages from *Ant.*, concluding that, for Sh, she is neither strumpet nor angel.

1280   Gardiner, Alan. "Leadership in *Antony and Cleopatra*." *Critical Essays on "Antony and Cleopatra."* Eds. Linda Cookson and Bryan Loughrey. (Longman Literature Guides.) Harlow, Essex: Longman, 1990, pp. 18–27.

Attempts a political appraisal of four chief male characters in *Ant.* Lepidus is too conciliatory and lacks the personal magnetism that would enable him to succeed in a Rome infected with self-interest and constantly changing allegiances. Pompey appears confident and insightful, but in reality he lacks courage and quickly backs down when confronted with the united triumvirs. Antony has great personal magnetism that derives from his kindness and military prowess, but his followers lose respect for him when he acts impulsively. Only Octavius has the traits needed to survive in Rome's contentious climate: He is calculating, deceitful, ambitious, and passionless. However, he lacks humanity.

1281   Gearin-Tosh, Michael. "Love in *Antony and Cleopatra*." *Critical Essays on "Antony and Cleopatra."* Eds. Linda Cookson and Bryan Loughrey. (Longman Literature Guides.) Harlow, Essex: Longman, 1990, pp. 53–59.

Analyzes Sh's alterations in the story of Antony and Cleopatra, which transform an account of a soldier and his mistress to a tale of obsessive love. Octavia's long union with Antony is reduced to a marriage of political convenience lasting only a few months. Cleopatra is presented as a woman of paradoxes; with her, love is an intoxicating experience. As the play develops, the lovers' speech grows more opulent, underlining the escapism of their suicide and contrasting their world with the mundane aspects of historical reality.

1282   Givan, Christopher Forrest. "Thematic Doubling in Shakespeare's Plays." Ph.D. dissertation, Stanford University, 1970. *DAI*, 31 (1970–71), 6010-A.

Points out that thematic doubling in the plays Sh wrote before *Ant.* is used for a variety of purposes, especially to sharpen the audience's capacity to make careful judgments. In *Ant.*, in which the theme of the play is moral ambiguity, Sh deliberately downplays the technique of doubling.

1283   Godshalk, W. L. "Dolabella as Agent Provocateur." *RenP*, 1977 (1977), 69–74.

Suggests that Dolabella's confidential advice to Cleopatra, hinting that she could commit suicide before Caesar sends her to Rome (*Ant.*, V.ii), is not a betrayal of Caesar's orders but a fulfillment of them. Sh alters his source, Plutarch's *Lives*, making Dolabella Cleopatra's guard rather than Epaphroditus; and he also has Dolabella dismiss Proculeius from his charge of guarding the queen. In Plutarch, Dolabella is the name given to one of Antony's inveterate political enemies, and Sh appropriates this for the man who serves his master well by subtly inducing Cleopatra to get rid of herself.

1284 Goldberg, S. L. "The Tragedy of the Imagination: A Reading of *Antony and Cleopatra*." *Melbourne Critical Review*, 4 (1961), 41–64.

Analyzes the means by which Sh's art depicts in *Ant.* a world of discord, where "each element, desire, force, and choice seems to struggle ceaselessly with its opposite." For example, in tracing Antony's attempt to participate in "every impulse, every paradox, of life," and then collapsing, the art of the play stands "as a living symbol of what Antony fails to achieve in living." The success of Sh's art in reflecting the "manifold shifting possibilities of life" and holding them in balance, however, involves also "the loss of power to direct events." As poised and disciplined as it is, Sh's art cannot provide definitive answers to the problems raised in *Ant.*

1285. Grant, Michael. *Cleopatra*. London: Weidenfield and Nicolson, 1972. xviii + 301 pp.

Presents the historical Cleopatra. Makes several references to Sh, calling attention to passages in which *Ant.* confirms the historical record and to passages that show the two at odds. An example of the former is Sh's reference to Cleopatra as a "gipsy" (accurately describing her dark complexion); one of the latter is Cleopatra's constant nagging of Antony about Fulvia.

1286 Green, J. T. "Shakespearean Women Contrasts: Cleopatra, Cordelia, and Isabella." *Fort Hare Papers*, 3, no. 5 (1966), 17–23.

Argues that Sh's Cleopatra is full of vitality and charm at the same time that she is "the incarnation of passion, part Siren, part Fury." In *Ant.*, she is a consummate actress whose artifice never fails her. Though she leads Antony to his destruction, her character "gains tragic unity and grandeur as the play proceeds."

1287 Greene, James J. "*Antony and Cleopatra*: The Birth and Death of Androgyny." *HSL*, 19, nos. 2–3 (1988), 24–44.

Defines *androgyny* as "an ideal of human conduct [that] rejects as restrictive those traditionally assigned, arbitrary gender roles in favor of a new view of human experience which combines the best and richest of both kinds of sexual traits." Argues that the protagonists of *Ant.* engage in an admirable and daring, though tragic, struggle to achieve an androgynous relationship. In particular, throughout the play Antony strives to escape the domination of the exclusively masculine Roman world. Central to the conflict is the interpretation of the exchange of clothes between Antony and Cleopatra, which Plutarch and others view as "the nadir of Antony's fall from manhood" but which Sh opens up to the possibility of a positive reading. One of the authoritative texts for the conception of woman as inconstant is the account of Aeneas's rejection of Dido in the *Aeneid*. Sh has Antony, as he prepares for death (IV.xiv), assert the superiority of his choice to remain with Cleopatra by imagining how much more he and Cleopatra will be admired in the afterlife than Dido and Aeneas.

1288 Greenwood, Kathy Lynn. "The Transforming Eye: The Poetic Fictions of Falstaff and Cleopatra." Ph.D. dissertation, Ohio State University, 1981. *DAI*, 42 (1981–82), 4458-A.

Observes that Falstaff and Cleopatra are unique among Shakespearean transformers of reality in that they work solely in "the province of the imagination." The "innocent" transformations of these two characters "engage us even as we recognize them to be 'fictive' versions of reality." In *Ant.*, Cleopatra is the wholly successful poetic transformer, releasing the audience into a world of "'fictive truth' [that] takes precedence over reality."

1289 Grene, W. D. "Antony and Cleopatra." *Hermathena*, 118 (1974), 33–47.

Notices that *Ant.* mimes the greatness of a past world of military and political glory, a world that has become, by and large, sordid and ugly. The clumsiness with which the two protagonists play the roles of great queen and preeminent warrior, respectively, opens the way for the creation of a new reality of the imagination. The play's power resides in its ability to register, at moments when its heroes are acutely aware of worldly failure, a transcendent sense of human potential. There is little concern with what or how the lovers choose or with their moral perception; instead, the focus is on their fatedness to fail and the stimulation this provides for them to reflect on their condition. Their new poetic vision redeems their lives from the squalor in which they are enmeshed. That Sh is calling attention to how the ungainliness of living in the world leads to, indeed is necessary for, notable achievements of the individual imagination is confirmed by his "audacious readiness to play with the difficulties of stage presentation and the absurdities it can create for the passionate representation of depth of meaning."

1290   Gruber, William E. "The Actor in the Script: Affective Strategies in Shakespeare's *Antony and Cleopatra*." *CompD*, 19 (1985), 30–48.

Examines the introductory scenes of *Ant.* to illuminate the "affective strategies" Sh uses. Focuses on the importance attached to Antony's location and his comings and goings (concern with "mechanisms of expectation and fulfillment") and to the questions of identification raised by the fact that Cleopatra would have been played by a boy.

1291   Hall, Joan Lord. *The Dynamics of Role-Playing in Jacobean Tragedy.* New York: St. Martin's P., 1991. viii + 241 pp.

Chapter 6, "Double-edged Theatrics: *Antony and Cleopatra*," shows that this play presents its protagonists as "energetic chameleons" while it examines the ambiguity "at the heart of the histrionic impulse: the way that the self may be transformed creatively, and not necessarily diminished, through playing roles." Even Octavius and the Romans are attracted to the theatricalization of self, albeit in a somewhat limited way. Antony's attempt at playing simultaneously the two roles of lover and warrior, though temporarily successful in acts III and IV, ultimately fails because of the demands of his Roman ego. He acknowledges the disintegration of his psyche just before his death. Cleopatra's role-playing is, on one level, a testimony to her resourcefulness and calculation; on another level, however, it leads us to interpret her "as an immensely complex, realistically presented character whose mystery, arising in part from her very mixture of artifice and naturalness, strongly evokes the quality of actual life." In her death, she goes a long way toward vindicating "the histrionic mode as a vehicle for affirming and consolidating a complex identity." Other chapters make brief comments on Coriolanus (whose distrust of role-playing is extreme), Titus Andronicus (whose role as revenger engulfs him in bizarre savagery), and Cressida (who fulfills the role of "faithless woman," determined to a large extent for her by Ulysses).

1292   Hall, Joan Lord. "'To the very heart of loss': Rival Constructs of 'Heart' in *Antony and Cleopatra*." *CollL*, 18, no. 1 (1991), 64–76.

Discusses the uses of "heart" in *Ant.*, showing that the Romans mean manly, martial courage by it, while the Egyptians understand it to signify the center of love or affection and sometimes pair it with "affection" to connote "passion as well as emotional warmth." The play examines "the dissonances both within 'heart' and between 'heart' and 'affection.'" Sometimes the disparate meanings of "heart" are briefly combined (as in IV.iv-viii, when Antony feels an exuberant sense of wholeness as lover and soldier), but more often the meanings "remain polarized and eventually undermine one another—in keeping with the fundamentally divided sensibilities of Rome and Egypt." Antony most fully exhibits the ambivalence of "heart," mirroring the crippling division at the center of Roman culture in his own failure to synthesize valor with "the feminine principle."

1293 Halle, Louis J. *The Search for an Eternal Norm: As Represented by Three Classics.* Washington, D. C.: University Press of America, 1981. 213 pp.

Treats *Ant.*, in a final chapter, as an eloquent story of mature love. Antony is torn "between pleasure and the opposing demands of a political self-interest upon which his survival depends." His deterioration manifests itself in "an increasingly wild capriciousness." Cleopatra is just the opposite, behaving in a childlike manner until near the end, when she rises to a great and solemn dignity in death. Antony represents the quintessentially masculine, and Cleopatra the eternally feminine. Neither protagonist is endowed with moral stature, but they, and the entire play, are redeemed by the magnificent and somehow believable hyperbole of the language.

1294 Hallett, Charles. "Change, Fortune, and Time: Aspects of the Sublunar World in *Antony and Cleopatra*." *JEGP*, 75 (1976), 75–89.

Maintains that in *Ant.* Sh created a world subject to Fortune and Time in order to emphasize instability. Unlike most of his other plays, *Ant.* lacks reference to a spiritual world "against which decisions can be weighed." If Sh had wanted to furnish his classical setting with Christian values, he would have done so. Instead, he endowed Plutarch's pagan world not with a reconciling and stabilizing heaven but "with all those unstable attributes traditionally associated in Christian–Humanist thought with the mundane world": Time, Fortune, Change. Clearly, he wanted to use the setting as a metaphor for the sublunary world. The play provides evidence of impermanence on all levels—the personal, the social, the natural. Politics involves constantly shifting loyalties, and individuals are incapable of making final judgments. Forms of the word *fortune* are more frequent in *Ant.* than in Sh's other Roman plays, and much of the action mimics the turning of Fortune's wheel. In this play there is "an almost clinical analysis of eros, its power and glory, but also its ultimate inability to sustain itself and those who venture all in its cause."

1295 Hamer, Mary. "Cleopatra: Housewife." *TP*, 2 (1988), 159–79.

Studies descriptions of Cleopatra as transgressive Other in classical literature and in Boccaccio's *De Claris Mulieribus* and the woodcuts illustrating its 1473 edition. Analyzes 16th- and early 17th-c. depictions and accounts of Cleopatra to suggest that Reformation reconceptualization of the male–female relationship in marriage enlisted the formerly threatening energies of the Egyptian queen in the service of domesticity. Among 17th-c. representations of Cleopatra, only that in *Ant.* is "intensely conflicted," preserving her threatening ambiguities and precluding a "unitary interpretation."

1296. Hamilton, Donna B. "*Antony and Cleopatra* and the Tradition of Noble Lovers." *SQ*, 24 (1973), 245–51.

Shows that in writing *Ant.*, Sh had available a strong tradition of the protagonists as noble lovers, which he juxtaposed with a moral perspective to provide complex characterizations. The early parts of the play suggest the noble lovers idea, but it is not allowed to dominate. Antony's preparation to leave (I.ii) parallels Aeneas's action in book 4 of the *Aeneid*, while Cleopatra's behavior at hearing the news is reminiscent of Dido's manner as described in Ovid's *Heroides*. The emphasis here is on Antony's moral choice, not on the nobility of their love. In the last half of the play, however, the tradition of the noble lovers is moved to the forefront. For example, act IV has no reference to Antony as "lustful, careless, and ambitious"; he still possesses greatness. Before his death, he makes an explicit reference to Dido and Aeneas by maintaining that he and Cleopatra will attract even more admiration in Elysium than their celebrated predecessors. The tradition of noble lovers enables Sh to temper the moral emphasis of his story with "a dimension of unsurpassable glory."

1297. Hapgood, Robert. "Hearing Shakespeare: Sound and Meaning in *Antony and Cleopatra.*" *ShS*, 24 (1971), 1–12.

Tries to get at the sound of *Ant.* by analyzing the text with the help of two recordings. Sees the play as a kind of drawing-room tragedy, with its numerous interior scenes featuring "accusations of infidelity, vows of loyalty, pleas for pardon, and words of reconciliation." Puts emphasis on "hearing" the opening scene, Antony's first encounter with Caesar (II.ii), and Cleopatra's final speech (V.ii).

1298 Hargreaves, George Brooks. "Love and Identity in Eight Plays of Shakespeare." Ph.D. dissertation, University of Toronto, 1977. *DAI*, 39 (1978–79), 4272-A.

Studies the developing "relationship of human love and identity" in a series of eight plays by Sh. Love "increasingly approximates the substance of human identity from play to play in the chronological sequence." In *Ant.*, the penultimate play considered, love and identity are closely related. If love is viewed as "a principle of permanence within change," then it is the foundation of the identities of the two protagonists.

1299. Harrier, Richard C. "Cleopatra's End." *SQ*, 13 (1962), 63–65.

Points out that between Antony's death and the end of *Ant.*, Cleopatra is in a state of double-mindedness: She "wishes to seal in death a lover's bond with Antony, yet she desires more deeply—out of her essential being—to go on with life and power." In discovering from Dolabella "what Caesar means to do with her," Cleopatra, though she has "indulged her will to live to the last ounce," now knows that "life without Antony is meaningless." Sh's dramatic point is that only through Antony's rashness "could so strong an earthly force as Cleopatra be brought to a high Roman sacrifice."

1300 Harris, Duncan S. "'Again for Cydnus': The Dramaturgical Resolution of *Antony and Cleopatra.*" *SEL*, 17 (1977), 219–31.

Argues that the final scene of *Ant.* validates, for the audience that has attended to the poetry, the heroism of the lovers. From the beginning, there has been a tension between telling and showing: The lovers have been presented, and described by some characters, as irresponsible and foolish, though their own language had suggested something more. Enobarbus's speech about their meeting on the Cydnus provides an image of Cleopatra's attractive power that is at odds with her behavior in the scenes immediately surrounding it. Only in Cleopatra's death scene do we finally witness the full confirmation of the lovers' vision: Cleopatra's compelling charm and the unique qualities of their relationship. The visual presentation on stage realizes what the poetry has suggested.

1301. Hartsock, Mildred E. "Major Scenes in Minor Key." *SQ*, 21 (1979), 55–62.

Shows that three short Shakespearean scenes—the garden scene in *R2*, the mad scenes of Ophelia in *Ham.*, and the music-under-the-ground scene in *Ant.*—are crucial because they "provide an emotional experience for the audience [that] defines a major character who might, without the scene, be wrongly interpreted." The music in *Ant.* (IV.iii), through its sad harmonies, reverses the optimistic mood of the soldiers who hear it, who are thereby convinced that Antony is doomed. Sh omits Plutarch's comment that the music involved a sound of people singing "as they use in Bacchus feasts," probably because he does not want "to suggest the irresponsible revelry of earlier scenes." He is interested in conveying "the sad fact that Antony cannot have both love and leadership." The music is heard underground and also in the air; and its earth and air "are later echoed in Cleopatra's great dying speech." The scene thus points toward the "happier fact that love is the triumphant value [that] the play affirms."

1302 Hawkes, Terence. *Shakespeare's Talking Animals: Language and Drama in Society.* London: Edward Arnold, 1973. viii + 247 pp.

Includes, in chapter 10, a discussion of *Ant.* In this play, Egypt is a realm of body language where womanly powers prevail, and Rome is a place of words and manly prowess.

1303 Hawkes, Terence, and Michael Quinn. "Two Points of View on *Antony and Cleopatra.*" *Anglo–Welsh Review,* 13, (1963), 7–18.

Hawkes maintains that *Ant.* is "a work of high complexity, of deep ambiguity, in which the values that we often talk about so glibly are probed and tested in a variety of ways to reach, perhaps not one conclusion, but at least a more subtle view of the world we live in." Quinn responds that the play is complex but not ambiguous. The protagonists are morally deficient, but their nobler images, of which we catch glimpses, "stand as assertions of the potential glory of fallen man, who, in spite of his moral delinquency, can find honor, nobility, redemption."

1303a Hawkins, Peter S. "The Truth of Metaphor: The Fine Art of Lying." *MSE,* 8, no. 4 (1982), 1–14.

Discusses metaphor as "the factual lie that tells another level of truth." Includes an analysis of the metaphor of the boat that Enobarbus uses to describe the way in which Cleopatra came to Antony when they first met (*Ant.,* II.ii). Comments that Cleopatra's barge is also her jewel box, displaying herself as "the kingdom's pearl of greatest price," and her throne. The metaphoric burning of the barge on the water suggests the contradictory nature of Cleopatra's influence, which is both creative and destructive.

1304 Hedayet, A. A. El. A. "Cleopatra in English Literature from Chaucer to Thomas King." Ph.D. thesis, University of Wales, Bangor, 1984. *ITA,* 35 (1987), 43.

Chapter 1 provides a historical sketch of Cleopatra's life. Chapter 2 explores the heroic and romantic vision of her story, including a discussion of *Ant.* Chapter 3 sums up the moral and didactic adaptations of Cleopatra's history from the Middle Ages onward. Chapter 4 considers her death, commenting on Sh's indebtedness to "the Stoic belief in death as a liberator." Chapter 5 concentrates on *Ant.,* pointing out the importance of its use of mythology, pageant, and emblem.

1305 Heffner, Ray L. Jr. "The Messengers in Shakespeare's *Antony and Cleopatra.*" *ELH,* 43 (1976), 154–62.

Focuses on the great number and variety of messengers in *Ant.,* necessary because of Sh's need to keep the dramatic tension between widely scattered characters constantly in view. Several scenes achieve great intensity through presenting the treatment of messengers by the principal characters. In many cases, the messengers are extensions of the personalities of those sending the messages, and loyal subordinates of the main characters often perform messenger-like functions. During acts II and III, messengers help Sh create the impression that Antony is "almost simultaneously present" in many places.

1306 Heinemann, Margot. "'Drama for Cannibals?' Notes on Brecht and Shakespearean Characterization." *SJW,* 126 (1990), 135–39.

Offers a Brechtian commentary on *Ant.,* a play about which Brecht said little. Acknowledges that we cannot ignore the charismatic fascination of the two chief figures but insists that we should also recognize the fragility of their "self-fashioned identities as godlike rulers and lovers." Theirs is perhaps the most public love affair in Sh; they are never alone together, and everything they do is entangled "with political and historical events." The play is also about "the splitting of an empire and the disintegration of a world, with the dissolution of the old republican Rome into military rat-race, hard-faced ambition, ruthless scheming, destructive warlordism." Stresses the importance of the minor characters, who are fully integrated into the action and who "set the heroic example" in the face of death.

1307 Hendricks-Wenck, Aileen Alana. "Sexual Politics in *Antony and Cleopatra.*" *ThSw*, 15, no. 2 (1988), 18–22.

Argues that from the beginning of *Ant.* the protagonists strive to free themselves from the sexual politics of patriarchy that Sh found in his source, Plutarch's *Lives*, and in Elizabethan society. Antony and Cleopatra do triumph over patriarchy, but tragically they do so in death.

1308 Henry, Graeme. "The Mythmakers." *Viewpoints on Shakespeare*. Ed. Brian McFarlane. Melbourne: Longman Chesire, 1990, pp. 192–209.

Recounts the paradoxical, multi-dimensional behavior of the lovers in *Ant.* and argues that, as they move toward their death, they, having gone beyond the limits of normal human experience, half-consciously strive to "enter the world of myth." Calls attention to the humanity, even the comedy, of their relationship.

1309 Herbert, T. Walter. "A Study of Meaning in *Antony and Cleopatra.*" *All These to Teach: Essays in Honor of C. A. Robertson*. Eds. Robert A. Bryan, Alton C. Morris, A. A. Murphree, and Aubrey L. Williams. Gainesville: U. of Florida P., 1965, pp. 47–66.

Examines "four dramatic constituents" in *Ant.*: setting, action, poetry, and characters. Setting is not just location but involves, for example, "the Roman mode of life," to which Antony belongs and which "never leaves off demanding his allegiance." The Egyptian way of life, found only where Cleopatra is physically present, is more localized. The characteristic rapturous music of Cleopatra can be distinguished from "the sturdy sounds of the Romans." While the imagery associated with Antony emphasizes separation and division, Cleopatra's characteristic imagery is concerned with "putting things harmoniously together." In the action, Antony is continually called on "to master irreconcilable opposites," while Cleopatra possesses "a constant though variously expressive character." Antony's character "develops away from oneness and dominance," toward disintegration, while Cleopatra's personality "never suffers any loss."

1310 Hibbard, G. R. "*Feliciter audax: Antony and Cleopatra*, I.i.1-24." *Shakespeare's Styles: Essays in Honour of Kenneth Muir*. Eds. Philip Edwards, Inga-Stina Ewbank, and G. K. Hunter. Cambridge: Cambridge U. P., 1980, pp. 95–109.

Maintains that the first twenty-four lines of *Ant.* provide a model in miniature for the stylistic program of the play. In Philo's strictures against his captain and in the exchange between Antony and Cleopatra, we hear the mingling of the hyperbolical and the simple that marks the style of nearly every character. This uniform style, which blends the sublime and the mundane, the amorous and the heroic, suggests that Sh intended for *Ant.* to be his version of Renaissance epic, whose themes were war and love. Philo's measuring of Antony's present effeminacy against his past greatness, a bold critique of his protagonist that Sh does not allow in any other tragedy, appears to be an ingenious variation on the epic *topos* employed by Virgil when he has the mutilated ghost of Hector appear to Aeneas. The point of view Philo expresses is reiterated throughout the play by numerous speakers, notably by Antony himself, and is not finally confuted until the close. The immediate appearance of the lovers, however, does qualify Philo's reductive scorn: It is obvious that their relationship is greater than the sordid affair he has described, yet there is also a clear indication of Cleopatra's constant manipulation of Antony.

1311 Higgins, Anne. "Shakespeare's Saint Cleopatra." *DR*, 70 (1990–91), 5–19.

Maintains that Sh absorbed several details in his presentation of Cleopatra's suicide (*Ant.*, V.ii) from the account of the death of Saint Christina in the medieval *South English Legendary*. Both versions introduce snakes by means of "an ambiguous male character"; both employ the English word *worm*; both assert that the nature of worms, "their *kind*, is to cause people to die of their bites"; both "pun on the word *joy* as a euphemism for sexual intercourse"; both at first stress "erotic imagery in the woman's confrontation with the snakes"; and both "shift from erotic to positively presented maternal imagery as the suicide scene ends." The idea of Christina, as presented in the *Legendary* and Chaucer's sympathetic portrayal of Cleopatra in *The Legend of Good Women*, may have influenced Sh to exhibit the queen of Egypt as a saintly martyr to "transcendent human love in a pagan world."

1312 Hill, James L. "The Marriage of True Bodies: Myth and Metamorphosis in *Antony and Cleopatra*." *REAL: The Yearbook of Research in English and American Literature*, 2 (1984), 211–37.

Traces the path of change in *Ant.*, noting that none of the mythological allusions exercises a controlling influence on our perception of the characters or action. Antony is to some degree linked with Bacchus, Mars, Hercules, Jove, Osiris, Ajax, and Aeneas, while Cleopatra is associated with Isis, Dido, Io, Venus, and *Voluptas*. No matter how close the lovers come to identification with these figures, "some point in the presentation refuses to allow the human and the mythical to coalesce" or distorts the mythical materials. In a similar fashion, the three major pagan philosophies of Stoicism, Epicureanism, and Neoplatonism "each of them slightly out of focus," are present in the last scenes, but they fail to merge into a definitive account of the mutable world of the play. Neither pagan myth nor philosophy is able to rescue the love of Antony and Cleopatra from the control of Fortune and the prison of the flesh.

1313 Hillman, Richard. "Antony, Hercules, and Cleopatra: 'the bidding of the gods' and 'the subtlest maze of all.'" *SQ*, 38 (1987), 442–51.

Focuses on the scene in which the god Hercules abandons Antony (*Ant.*, IV.iii) to show how Sh altered his source, Plutarch's *Lives*: The identity of the departing god is changed from Bacchus to Hercules; the scene immediately following, in which Cleopatra helps to arm Antony in an atmosphere of harmony, is invented; the harmony is sustained in the reunion of the lovers after the battle (IV.viii); and the departure scene is placed earlier so that it heralds victory, not defeat. Sums up Neoplatonic ideas about the myths of Hercules and of Venus and Mars to argue that Sh is demonstrating how "a myth of choice" yields "to one of creative union." The audience is encouraged to reinterpret the classical model.

1314 Holderness, Graham. "'Some Squeaking Cleopatra': Theatricality in *Antony and Cleopatra*." *Critical Essays on "Antony and Cleopatra.*" Eds. Linda Cookson and Bryan Loughrey. (Longman Literature Guides.) Harlow, Essex: Longman, 1990, pp. 42–51.

Highlights the irony of Cleopatra's speech from *Ant.* (V.ii), in which she describes her prospective humiliation at the hands of Octavius. The unappealing scene she describes is an accurate reflection of the audience, actors, and conditions in the theater during Sh's time. The illusion she (the boy actor) portrays is not shattered by her accurate revelation; instead, the audience is included in the creation of the illusion. The actors and the audiences in the Elizabethan and Jacobean eras were viewed with contempt, and contemporary plays are full of references to this baseness. Sh, at the end of *Ant.*, permits Cleopatra to reclaim the full force of theatrical performance with her staged suicide. By her eloquence, she is restored to her former glory while simultaneously transforming the "squeaking boy" into the regal Cleopatra.

1315 Hollindale, Peter. "Music under the Earth: The Suicide Marriage in *Antony and Cleopatra*." *Critical Essays on "Antony and Cleopatra*." Eds. Linda Cookson and Bryan Loughrey. (Longman Literature Guides.) Harlow, Essex: Longman, 1990, pp. 28–40.

Investigates the ways in which Sh uses language, symbol, and scene in *Ant.* to underscore the union in death of the protagonists. This linkage begins in act IV, with Hercules' departure from Antony. The language shared by the lovers speaks of evaporation and instability. Each looks to suicide as a means of escaping dishonor at the hands of Octavius, a vehicle to control fate, and the ultimate self-mastery. The greatest motivation for suicide in each is despair over the death of the other. For Antony and Cleopatra, suicide is their marriage ceremony, a transformative act permitting the union of two domains that are incompatible on earth.

1316 Homan, Sidney. "When the Theater Turns to Itself." *NLH*, 2 (1970–71), 407–17.

Explores "certain moments" in which the theater "turns to itself, to metaphors taking their source not directly from life but from art—acting, the imagination, the stage itself, the pleasure in illusion which is at the very heart of the drama." Cites Cleopatra's death scene (*Ant.*, V.ii), and especially her encounter with the asps, as one such moment: Working with "bad material," she triumphs imaginatively in a way that parallels Sh's own accomplishment in portraying "highly sensual femininity" with a boy actor. Revised as part of the preface of item 1317.

1317 Homan, Sidney. *When the Theater Turns to Itself: The Aesthetic Metaphor in Shakespeare*. Lewisburg, Pennsylvania: Bucknell U. P., 1981. 238 pp.

Part of the preface is a revision of item 1316. Chapter 7, "Love and the Imagination in *Antony and Cleopatra*," is a revision of item 1318.

1318 Homan, Sidney R. "Divided Response and the Imagination in *Antony and Cleopatra*." *PQ*, 49 (1970), 460–68.

Focuses on the paradoxical aesthetic statement of *Ant.* The Egyptian way of life, as exemplified by Cleopatra, is associated with sexuality, acting, and the artist's power to transform; the Roman world, dominated by Octavius, is strong, dignified, and successful. Cleopatra's creative achievements are finally illusory, while the Romans suffer from unimaginative dullness. Revised as chapter 7 of item 1317.

1318a Honigmann, E. A. J. "Past, Present and Future in *Macbeth* and *Antony and Cleopatra*." *Myraid-Minded Shakespeare: Essays, Chiefly on the Tragedies and Problem Comedies*. New York: St. Martin's P., 1989, pp. 93–111.

Points out that *Ant.*, in contrast to *Mac.*, assumes a knowledge of the history that lies behind it and makes pervasive use of looking backward. In *Ant.*, Sh shows how the present is constantly being destabilized, chiefly by means of excessive drinking and Cleopatra's "cultivated unpredictability." Predicting the future is of great significance in the play: There is great emphasis on prophecy and soothsaying; Enobarbus and Cleopatra are accurate in their forecasting; and Antony habitually misreads signs of what is to come. The use of "prophecy and the supernatural" makes clear that Sh's model was *JC*.

1319 Hooks, Roberta M. "Shakespeare's *Antony and Cleopatra*: Power and Submission." *AI*, 44 (1987), 37–49.

Focuses on "the mother–child boundary dilemma" as the key to "the complications and unreseoved tensions of adult sexuality" in *Ant.* Antony's furious claims to autonomy can be attributed to "the child's claim to omnipotence that arises in the context of total dependency upon a maternal figure whose constancy allows for the dissolution and rearrangement of boundaries." Frustrated by his inability to possess the ambivalent Cleopatra, Antony conceives of death "as an extension of the transcendence and stability" he had sought with her.

1320 Hope, Alec Derwent. *The Cave and the Spring: Essays on Poetry.* Adelaide: Rigby, 1965. Reprint. Chicago: U. of Chicago P., 1970. ix + 173 pp.

Devotes a chapter to John Dryden's *All for Love,* commenting that this play, in contrast to its model, *Ant.,* is not tragic at all. In attempting to write a moral tragedy in which virtue is rewarded and vice punished, Dryden has missed the tragic altogether. What he has written can be regarded as "pathetic comedy." Sh, however, presents things as they are, leaving the audience to draw its own moral conclusions. Notes that *Ant.* is "based on a genuinely tragic opposition of values to be decided by a choice having the seriousness of a public action of the utmost moment."

1321 Howarth, R. G. *A Pot of Gillyflowers: Studies and Notes.* Cape Town: R. G. Howarth, 1964. 110 pp.

Describes, in a brief note, the enigmatic qualities of Cleopatra in *Ant.* that are so irresistible to Antony. The relationship between the two lovers will always be a mystery.

1322 Hughes-Hallett, Lucy. *Cleopatra: Histories, Dreams and Distortions.* London: Bloomsbury, 1990. 338 pp.

Surveys the various "dream-Cleopatras" that have been fashioned by different cultures and in different historical contexts. Includes comments on Sh's version of Cleopatra throughout. Devotes chapter five to *Ant.,* noting that Sh is dramatizing "the conflict between reason, the wise person's prop and guide, and its adversary, sexual love." The play re-creates the story of "manly effort [Rome] and womanly self-indulgence [Egypt]" that Sh found in Plutarch, though with greater subtlety and less censoriousness. Antony abandons his reason and his maleness, reappearing in "his submerged character of Dionysus, master of holy mania, androgynous lord among women." Sh allows us to feel the attraction of this "self-abandonment," but he cannot approve it. Cleopatra, in the grip of such passion, is shown to be mean-spirited and foolish, as when, in a scene Sh invented, she questions a Messenger about Octavia's appearance. Remarks that Sh's great poetry allows the love affair to speak for itself but that the "bathetic reality" in which the lovers are embedded undermines their idealistic claim. Claims that "the writers of the Renaissance" were "intellectually closer to the newly rediscovered ancient world," with its "cool and reductive view" of sexual passion, than they are to the modern age.

1323 Hume, Robert D. "Individuation and Development of Character through Language in *Antony and Cleopatra.*" *SQ,* 24 (1973), 281–300.

Notes that in *Ant.,* the characters are clearly differentiated by "language, rhythm, and rhetorical habit." Lepidus's timidity and obsequiousness are emphasized by terms of solicitude and begging; Pompey's ineffectual propriety is suggested by his use of words related to justice and honor. Antony and Cleopatra employ a duality in their imagery, setting the exalted against the degraded, and thus indicating their ambiguous nature. Caesar's Roman qualities are shown in his lack of imagery, regular verse, and logical progression of thought; and the bluntness of Enobarbus comes through in his concrete vocabulary. Throughout acts III and IV, Antony's language shows him vacillating between Caesar and Cleopatra, but just before his death he speaks with a "firmness and clarity of purpose." Cleopatra, who early in the play has exhibited her infinite variety in irregular rhythms, repetitions, and parallelism, settles down at the end to longer, smoother rhetorical units that indicate free, growing commitment to Antony.

1324 Hunter, Robert G. "Cleopatra and the 'Oestre Junonicque.'" *ShakS*, 5 (1970), 236–39.

Points out that in III.x of *Ant.*, Scarus describes Cleopatra's flight from the battle of Actium with the disgusted comment that she, with "The breeze upon her, like a cow in June, / Hoists sail and flies" (lines 14–15). The image of a breeze (gadfly) stinging a cow in June is paralleled by a passage in Rabelais, who refers to "un oestre Junonicque," a gadfly "of the type that Juno in her jealousy had torment poor Io." Both Sh and Rabelais may have drawn on Virgil's *Georgics* for the gadfly image, and Sh would also have encountered the story of Io transformed into a heifer in Golding's Ovid, *Metamorphoses* 2. Like Io, Cleopatra is being persecuted for her lover's betrayal of his wife. In Cooper's *Thesaurus linguae Romanae & Britanicae*, Sh could have found that Io was identified with Isis, Cleopatra's goddess. A case can be made that Scarus's speech contains an emergent allusion to the Io myth, which goes as far as the syllable "June" and stops, perhaps because its full elaboration would be inappropriate for a blunt soldier.

1325 Huzar, Eleanor G. "Mark Antony: Marriages vs. Careers." *CJ*, 81 (1985–86), 97–111.

Provides a biographical account of Mark Antony, with emphasis on the influence of his five wives. Cites three passages from *Ant.*, one about Fulvia, one about Octavia, and one about Cleopatra. Depends otherwise on ancient sources.

1326 Hyman, Stanley Edgar. *Poetry and Criticism: Four Revolutions in Literary Taste*. New York: Atheneum, 1961. 178 pp.

Chapter 2, "English Neo-Classicism," compares *Ant.* with Dryden's *All for Love*. *Ant.*'s significant action consists of a number of overcomings or transcendences: "spiritual value embodied in true love over the material things of the world"; "loyalty over betrayal"; and Egyptian values over those of Rome. The characters "show depths of complex humanity richer than anything in Greek drama," and "the language and metaphor of the play, fitting its action and character, [are] indescribably splendid."

1326a Hymel, Cynthia D. "Shakespeare's *Antony and Cleopatra*, V.ii.243–78." *Expl*, 37, no. 4 (1978–79), 2–4.

Regards Cleopatra's conversation with the Clown who is bringing her "the pretty worm of Nilus" [*Ant.*, V.ii.243–279] as a compression and contrasting of "several of the chief conflicts presented earlier in the play." A number of puns suggest that the worm is to viewed as a symbol of sexual relations. Cleopatra is raising the issues of the value of sexuality and the motivation for her suicide.

1327 Jackson, Russell. "The Triumphs of *Antony and Cleopatra*." *SJH*, 1984, 128–48.

Defines the Roman Triumph as "a procession in which the *triumphator* displayed the spoils and captives—especially important ones—he had brought back to Rome, gave thanks to the gods and achieved something near to immortality." Examines *Ant.*'s references to the triumph and analyzes their part in Sh's "general strategy of paradox and contrast." The play is full of triumphs in its action and its imagery, the two most completely realized being Cleopatra's appearance on her barge (described by Enobarbus) and Ventidius's victorious entry in III.i. The first of these serves as Cleopatra's triumph in Rome, an indication of her power over the official virtues celebrated in the usual triumph. The second is a reminder of what a real triumph is (scores have been settled, the body of a distinguished foe is borne before the army), but the concept must be qualified because Ventidius is afraid to take too much credit. The implication is that Antony's dereliction of duty has affected his subordinates. The reference to kings and kingdoms in the play—suggesting aspects of the triumph—signify "the crescent and waning power of Antony and Cleopatra." Both protagonists use the imagery of the triumph—normally applied to public occasions—increasingly to refer to their personal triumph as the play draws to a close. *Ant.* is thus poised between public and private: It reminds the audience of public glory by pervasive references to the triumph, but it challenges conventional notions of decorous behavior for public people by appropriating triumph imagery to celebrate acts of intimacy.

1328 James, Max H. "'The Noble Ruin': *Antony and Cleopatra*." *CollL*, 8 (1981), 127–43.

Takes Scarus's description of Antony as a "noble ruin" (*Ant.*, III.x.19) after the sea battle at Actium as a key to the play as a whole. Insists that *Ant.* is about decay, that it is pervaded by images of dissipation, decay, and ruin. The protagonists lay claim to nobility of status, of action, and of authority; and ruin overtakes them in all of these realms. Their world is a postlapsarian one, and they themselves are experienced, mature, and nonvirginal. Their fall is thus not a loss of innocence; it is a violation of experience. Antony loses his manhood, his honor, and his soldierly ambition. It is primarily his tragedy that is acted out, as he is destroyed in the competition between the rational Caesar and the pleasure-loving Cleopatra. The play possesses a remarkable realism: In both the Egyptian and the Roman views of life, the admirable and the blameworthy are "almost inseparably intermingled." Out of the ruins of nobility arises, phoenixlike, a new nobility.

1329 Jamieson, Michael. "Shakespeare's Celibate Stage: The Problem of Accommodation to the Boy-Actress in *As You Like It*, *Antony and Cleopatra* and *The Winter's Tale*." *Papers, Mainly Shakespearean*. Ed. G. I. Duthie. Edinburgh: Oliver and Boyd, 1964, pp. 21–39.

Emphasizes the skill of the boys in Sh's company who played female roles. In *Ant.*, Sh shows great tact in suffusing speeches throughout the play with indications derived from Plutarch of Cleopatra's legendary power of enticement. Thus the boy who took the part of the heroine was not given the impossible task of generating her imaginative appeal on his own; he would have been able to complement the rich image built up in the text with his considerable ability.

1330 Jankowski, Theodora A. "'As I am Egypt's Queen': Cleopatra, Elizabeth I, and the Female Body Politic." *Assays: Critical Approaches to Medieval and Renaissance Texts*. Vol. 5. Ed. Peggy A. Knapp. Pittsburgh: U. of Pittsburgh P., 1989, pp. 91–110.

Essays a feminist–historicist interpretation of *Ant.*, reading the character of Cleopatra "through the text of Queen Elizabeth I's strategies for rule." As a woman ruler in an age that was hostile to female power in any form, Elizabeth challenged and subverted patriarchal hegemony. Recognizing the danger of her situation, she contained her subversion by allowing her sexuality to be contained within the paradigm of virginity. She was thus able to enhance her political power by removing herself from the sexual life that consigned women to powerlessness in the eyes of the dominant ideology of her day. Sh's Cleopatra resembles Elizabeth in challenging patriarchal assumptions about female power. However, the Egyptian queen goes much further: She unites "her body natural and her body politic" by taking advantage of her sexuality to consolidate her royal power. Sh shows her success in maintaining power by contrasting her with two women—Fulvia and Octavia—who are "silenced or dismembered." At the end of the play, Cleopatra, having given her heart to Antony, is deprived of her chief strategy for rule—her use of sexuality for political purposes—in her negotiations with Octavius. Views *Ant.* as "a text of female political theory" and suggests that Sh had Elizabeth in mind when he created Cleopatra. Revision of part of item 1330a.

1330a Jankowski, Theodora Ann. "Women in Power in the Jacobean Drama: Shakespeare's *Antony and Cleopatra* and Webster's *The Duchess of Malfi*." Ph.D. dissertation, Syracuse University, 1987. *DAI*, 49 (1988–89), 258-A.

Argues that Sh's presentation of Cleopatra "as a powerful female ruler who insists upon the wholeness of both her natural and political bodies is iconoclastic because it subverts traditional Renaissance ideologies regarding the powerlessness of women." Part revised as item 1330.

1331 Jensen, Paul A. "Antony and the Protesting Soldiers: A Renaissance Tradition for the Structure of *Antony and Cleopatra*." *Essays on Shakespeare*. Ed. Gordon Ross Smith. College Park: Pennsylvania State U. P., 1965, pp. 163–81.

Focuses on the first two acts of *Ant.*, in which Sh diverges most from Plutarch, and seeks secondary sources as structural influences. Sh uses a familiar Elizabethan tragic pattern of the noble warrior "diverted from his proper business by amorous dotage," and in the first half of the play through the comments of military men he repeatedly stresses this question: Will Antony "renounce his idleness" and "regain his lost soldiership"? Lyly's *Compaspe* provided Sh with ideas for "grouping of characters into patterns of conflict," and *Caesar's Revenge* offered "a compelling woman, an internal struggle, the poignancy of recollected soldiership, and a scene constructed so as to highlight the strain in Antony's breaking away from Egypt." Venus, a symbol in Elizabethan literature of "the folly of soldiers dallying in love," gave Sh some hints for the Cleopatra of the first two acts.

1332 Johnson, Anthony L. *Readings in "Antony and Cleopatra" and "King Lear."* Pisa: ETS, 1979. 174 pp.

Part 1 essays a structural–semiotic analysis of *Ant.*, viewing Cleopatra and Octavius as actors who embody two controlling paradigms (the private principle and the public principle, respectively) that are polar opposites. This pair of superparadigms is subtended by a number of other pairs; examples are Egypt/Rome, East/West, pleasure/duty, excess/measure, water/land, bodily mobility/bodily stability, political immobility/political mobility, curved spatiality/straight spatiality, horizontality/verticality, microcosm–made macrocosm/macrocosm–made–microcosm, and liberality/parsimony. Notes that Antony is unique among Sh's characters in that he exhibits a divided self, split between enacting one or the other of the ideals indicated in each pair of paradigms. Designates *Ant.* as a "tragedy of the hubris of love" in refusing to accept its "private locus" and to coexist with public life.

1333 Johnson, Anthony L. "Semiotic Systems and Lexical Clues." *Shakespeare: la nostalgia dell'essere*. Ed. Alessandro Serpieri. Parma: Pratiche Editrice, 1985, pp. 125–57.

Notes that in the first scene of *Ant.* Sh orients his audience by giving it the role of spectator at Cleopatra's court, especially through the eyes of the two Roman soldiers, who provide "an extra semantic, discursive and deictic frame within that of the staging itself." The soldiers, who work within the Roman semiotic system, associate Antony's dotage with excess, which in turn is indicated by water imagery (much that happens later in the play has to do with the four elements). Further, from the Roman point of view, Antony's eyes (visual attention) and his heart (emotional energy) have been diverted from their proper objects. We see here the split in Antony's character that later is manifested in the tension between Rome and Egypt. The first scene also reveals, in the conversation between the protagonists, the alternating pull of public power and private pleasure, which "are seen to call for radically different forms of action and verbal interaction." Other important lexical clues in the early part of the play point to ideas of linking and separation; Cleopatra's "visual attractiveness in all her moods"; "Cleopatra as simultaneity of opposites"; fancy and nature in the protagonists; and self-conscious display in the interests of love and power. The play encourages us to recognize that "there is no fixed dividing line between power and love, taking and giving, public and private, or even between art and nature, drama and life."

1334   Jones, Emrys. *Scenic Form in Shakespeare.* Oxford: Clarendon P., 1971. 269 pp.

Treats Sh as a scenic poet, whose concern is to present visible, concrete actions on the stage and, more important, to create patterns that will induce in the audience a sense of excitement or concern. Chapter 7 analyzes *Ant.*, which, like many of Sh's other histories and tragedies, has two parts, the first ending at III.vi. Of all dramatists to deal with Antony's story, Sh is the only one to give it a rich development in the spirit of Plutarch. Sh's two halves correspond to two large sections of Plutarch's narrative, but in the *Lives* they are separated by an account of the Parthian campaign, which Sh omitted. For a structural model, Sh seems to have relied on *H5*, which, like *Ant.*, has a first movement involving preliminaries to an important battle and a second movement covering the battle and its consequences. The "expressive poetic style" of *Ant.* engages the audience's attention in a way analogous to the operation of the Chorus in *H5*. The rapid succession of short scenes, especially in the first half, stimulates the audience but does not allow it to become emotionally involved: A sense of irony is generated. In the second half, there are also a number of short scenes, but the development is more continuous. Irony is still present, but it is deeper and more serious. The play balances intimacy and detachment in the manner appropriate to a historical poet.

1335   Jones, Emrys, ed. *Antony and Cleopatra.* (New Penguin Shakespeare.) Harmondsworth: Penguin, 1977. 299 pp.

The introduction points out that *Ant.* is full of conflicting opinions and judgments, none of which can be taken as definitive. The variety of human assertions about value is matched by the geographical diversity of the world depicted: It lacks unity. In revealing his characters and their milieu in the process of becoming, Sh created a "fluid and intimate history play" that transferred to the stage, as no one had been able to do before him, the "small-scale anecdotal progression" that was the essence of Plutarch's narrative structure in the *Life* of Antony. Plutarch's influence may also be sensed in the "drifting movement" of *Ant.*, which allows the dramatist to convey ethical information about his characters in seemingly inconsequential actions. Sh divided his play into two movements, the first ending in III.vi, which correspond to two large sections of the *Life.* Omitting most of the details of the Parthian campaign, which Plutarch uses to connect the two sections, Sh used many short scenes. In the first part especially, these scenes preclude the audience's deep emotional involvement; they encourage a certain ironic detachment. Furthermore, they furnish an "illusion of intimacy" and a feeling that life is a matter of intense, moment-to-moment sensations. In the second movement, the short scenes are more focused, especially as they record Antony's decline. One of Sh's goals seems to have been "to imitate disorder and formlessness" as they manifest themselves in life. Accepting the traditional view that Antony was a great man ruined by love as a starting point, Sh complicated it by having the lovers call up a private, almost religious vision of their relationship and by endowing Antony with largeness of soul, generosity, and courtesy. In the last act, Cleopatra takes over as the initiator of the action and is able to use art to move toward an end, a stopping point in the process that has been so relentless throughout. The play's elegant lyricism, which is shared by all the characters, may be Sh's attempt to ornament this play about imperialism by recalling the style of Augustan Rome's "greatest lyric poet, Horace."

1336   Jones, Gordon P. "The 'Strumpet's Fool' in *Antony and Cleopatra.*" *SQ*, 34 (1983), 62–68.

Calls attention to a stage direction indicating Cleopatra's entrance (*Ant.*, I.ii.80), after which Enobarbus mistakenly comments, "Here comes Antony," and is corrected by Charmian: "Not he; the queen" (line 81). Enobarbus's misidentification may be caused by the dressing of Antony and Cleopatra in each other's clothes in the play's first scene. That Sh might have used such cross-dressing to symbolize the unmanning of his hero by the power of love is suggested by a well-known episode in the life of Hercules, a figure with whom Antony is identified in the play. Forced to sell himself into slavery, Hercules was purchased by Omphale, Queen of Lydia, who assigned him to perform women's tasks in women's clothes while herself wielding his club and wearing his lionskin. Plutarch, in his *Lives*, refers to this incident and compares the disarming of Antony by Cleopatra to that of Hercules by Omphale. Although cross-dressing would have been a plausible way to convey Antony's enslavement to love on Sh's stage, it should be avoided in modern productions because it would suggest homosexuality, something entirely foreign to *Ant.* and to the Hercules–Omphale story. See item 1438.

1337 Jones, William M. "Protestant Zeal in the Personality of Mark Antony." *McNeese Review*, 18 (1967), 73–85.

Argues that the key to Antony's personality in *Ant.* is his zeal, a tendency to conduct his life on the basis of strong emotional attachments formed on an ad hoc basis. Antony's zeal is responsible for his violent pleasure-seeking, the warmth of his friendship, and his vacillation. It makes possible both his good and bad qualities and distinguishes him from Cleopatra, who throughout the play manages to balance zeal with reason.

1338 Jorgensen, Paul A. "Antony and the Protesting Soldiers: A Renaissance Tradition for the Structure of *Antony and Cleopatra*." *Essays on Shakespeare*. Ed. Gordon Ross Smith. University Park: Pennsylvania State U. P., 1965, pp. 163–81.

Analyzes *Ant.* to show how, in constructing most of his scenes in the first two acts, Sh drew on a Renaissance dramatic tradition, exemplified in John Lyly's *Campaspe*, that shows a great military conqueror in danger of being diverted from heroic exploits by "amorous dotage" and has either the conqueror himself or his soldiers registering their concern about the situation. Dramatic representations of Venus may have contributed to Sh's portrayal of Cleopatra. This hypothesis accounts for structural elements in the first half of the play that are not found in Plutarch's *Lives*, Sh's primary source.

1339 Jose, Nicholas. "*Antony and Cleopatra*: Face and Heart." *PQ*, 62 (1983), 487–505.

Argues that *Ant.* is "a complex manifestation of the abiding needs and desires of the personalities involved." For this reason, there is continuous probing of how one's face and one's facing of others relates to the truth that is in one's heart. We see Cleopatra, for example, coming up with some penetrating observations about Caesar's relationship with Antony and about Octavia, but she frequently fails to read what she sees in Antony. We see Antony as a consummate politician who nevertheless makes some serious blunders. Beginning in III.vii, he "rages through a dizzying variety of moods and shapes," seeking stability in each one, failing every time, and finally clinging to his invalidated self-image as a Roman. In all of this, he is holding on to life, being human, and Cleopatra pays fine tribute to his being "simply the thing he is." Cleopatra recognizes that without Antony she is deprived of her "distinguishing sense of life." Her dream of Antony in V.ii is true to her heart's knowledge, countering Caesar's brittle vision of "universal peace," and making inevitable her tragic death.

1340 Josephs, Lois. "Shakespeare and a Coleridgean Synthesis: Cleopatra, Leontes, and Falstaff." *SQ*, 18 (1967), 17–21.

Attempts to extend Samuel Taylor Coleridge's fragmentary comments on three characters by reference to his critical method. He notes a contradiction between Cleopatra's superficially sensual passion for Antony in *Ant.* and the depth and energy of that passion. Perhaps he would derive an answer from his definition of love as "a desire of the whole being to be united to some thing or being that will complete it." In such an interpretation, Cleopatra needs Antony's love to fulfill herself, and in struggling to do so, she may become involved in contradictions. But her movement is always in the direction of self-completion. Hence her attempt to undermine Antony militarily: If he wins, he controls Rome, and his interests remain divided. If he loses, he will be entirely devoted to her.

1341 Kalmey, Robert P. "Shakespeare's Octavius and Elizabethan Roman History." *SEL*, 18 (1978), 275–87.

Argues that Cleopatra's contemptuous appraisal of Octavius Caesar's character at the end of *Ant.* should be credited against those modern critics who wish to see him as a temperate, benevolent statesman. Cleopatra's opinion is supported by Elizabethan historians of Rome, who made a sharp distinction between Octavius's unprincipled lust for power *before* he became emperor and his exemplary behavior as prince *after* being crowned. Sh's examination of him, confined as it is to the earlier period, is consonant with contemporary learned consensus.

1342 Kastan, David Scott. "'More than History Can Pattern': Notes Towards an Understanding of Shakespeare's Romances." *Cithara*, 17, no. 1 (1977), 29–44.

Argues that Sh's romances achieve their special effect by including tragic action, death, and loss at the same time that they refuse to recognize the completeness or finality of tragedy. *Ant.* points the way to the romances in that its protagonists imaginatively resist tragic closure, even though the play does not entirely ratify their vision. In the romances, the resistance to tragedy comes to dominate the playwright's imagination.

1343 Kaula, David. "The Time Sense of *Antony and Cleopatra*." *SQ*, 15 (1964), 211–23. Reprint. *Essays in Shakespearean Criticism*. Eds. James L. Calderwood and Harold E. Toliver. Englewood Cliffs, New Jersey: Prentice Hall, 1970, pp. 576–89.

Claims that the treatment of time is of special importance in *Ant.* The play creates a sense of rapid, continuous movement, with time progressing at different velocities at different locations and at different points in the action. Among the major characters, there are "sharply differing responses" to this "heightened sense of temporal change." Caesar, who strives to present himself as the "just, conscientious ruler," focuses on the future. Antony, whose self is divided between what he is in the present and what he was in the past, spends a good deal of time trying to recover his past glory. For Cleopatra, time consists of "a flexible, continuous present." At the end, the forward-looking Caesar achieves a sort of victory over "directionless time," but Cleopatra's free acceptance of the present gives her a greater triumph in her ceremoniously fashioned death.

1344 Kelly, William Joseph. "The Comic Perspective in Shakespeare's *Henry V, Hamlet,* and *Antony and Cleopatra*." Ph.D. dissertation, University of Oregon, 1972. *DAI*, 33 (1972–73), 6874-A.

Distinguishes two perspectives in *Ant.*: a "near" (interior) one and a "far" (exterior) one. According to the latter, Time and Fortune make fools of everyone in a vast "comedy of accidents." To defy Time and Fortune, as the lovers do, is heroic, even though their efforts are comic in many ways. They are noble fools, while Caesar, who acquiesces to Time and Fortune, is a paltry fool.

1345 Kennedy, William J. "Audiences and Rhetorical Strategies in Jodelle, Shakespeare, and Lohenstein." *Assays: Critical Approaches to Medieval and Renaissance Texts*. Vol. 1. Eds. Peggy A. Knapp and Michael A. Stugrin. Pittsburgh: U. of Pittsburgh P., 1981, pp. 99–116.

Investigates the interaction of "tradition, text, and audience" in three plays about Antony and Cleopatra that appeared within a little more than a century of each other. Surveys the complex background of the story, which reaches back to the single text of Plutarch's *Life of Marcus Antonius*. Notes other accounts by Dio Cassius and Appian and "literary analogues of Cleopatra" in Horace's *Odes* (1.37), Virgil's *Aeneid*, and Ovid's *Heroides*. Mentions, in later literature, the innumerable references to the topos of "Cleopatra's improper subordination of honor to lust or femininity." The playwrights concretized "these texts and others" by allowing them "to grow together." Characterizes Sh's audience in the public theater to help explain the rhetorical strategies used in *Ant*. Analyzes the play's eight soliloquies to reveal the variety of roles played by the characters. Antony's first soliloquy, for example, in which he resolves to break off from Cleopatra (I.ii), is "Roman, laconic"; his second, in which he decides to return to Cleopatra (II.iii), is "rich, luxuriant."

1346   Kerrigan, William. "The Personal Shakespeare: Three Clues."
        Shakespeare's Personality. Eds. Norman N Holland, Sidney Homan, and Bernard J. Paris. Berkeley: U. of California P., 1989, pp. 175–90.

Offers three clues to Sh's personality: "a deep attunement to acting, a fascination with improbable couples, and an easy vulnerability to a peculiarly sexual or genital form of misogyny." In *Ant.*, Sh finally wrote a tragedy in which "acting and improbable love triumph over sexual disillusionment." The play is a kind of counterepic, with Antony as "an Aeneas who stays in Africa with Dido." It "absorbs and subordinates the imperial drives" of Sh's age.

1347   Kimura, Teruhira. "Observations upon Some Textual and Annotatory Problems in *Antony and Cleopatra*." *ShStud*, 20 (1981–82), 91–107.

Makes observations about four problematic passages or groups of passages in *Ant*. (1) In view of the accounts in Plutarch of the extravagant life of Antony and Cleopatra, the Folio reading "pleasure now" (I.i.48) should be emended to "pleasure new." (2) The apparent discrepancy between Caesar's explanation of his deposition of Lepidus (III.vi) and Eros's explanation to Enobarbus (III.v) can be accounted for by noting Sh's use of Plutarch's *Life of Octavius Augustus Caesar*. Sh appears to have manipulated his source to make Caesar seem cold and calculating. (3) When Cleopatra, having made peace with Antony, mentions her birthday and then says, "I had thought t' have held it poor" (III.xiii.187), she may well mean Antony's birthday by "it." (4) Historically, Cleopatra's affair with Cneius Pompey would have come earlier than her affair with Julius Caesar, though the reverse order is implied by both Antony (III.xiii.117–119) and Cleopatra herself (I.v.30–33).

1348   Kindred, Jerome Clayton. "Unity and Disunity in *Antony and Cleopatra*."
        Ph.D. dissertation, University of Texas at Austin, 1972. *DAI*, 33 (1972–73), 3588-A-3589-A.

Claims that in *Ant*. Sh uses characters and dramatic devices (messengers, minor characters like Enobarbus and Octavius, Cleopatra's desire to become a "Roman," the imagery of "splitting and alienation") that can be perceived as "potential unifiers" to suggest, paradoxically, the "disruption and disorder" of the play's world.

1349   Kinney, Clare. "The Queen's Two Bodies and the Divided Emperor: Some Problems of Identity in *Antony and Cleopatra*." *The Renaissance Englishwoman in Print: Counterbalancing the Canon*. Eds. Anne M. Haselkorn and Betty S. Travitsky. Amherst: U. of Massachusettss P., 1990, pp. 177–86.

Compares the female/male union, duplicity, and mutability of Cleopatra as Queen of Egypt to the static, competitive homocentricism of the Roman world as reflected in the relationship between Antony and Octavius. Cleopatra acquires many labels, ranging from "whore" to "Great Egypt." In the fluidity of her nature, she can take any negative identifier and transform it into a positive statement. Cleopatra, no matter what she is called, is Egypt and is inseparable from it. She has the ability to embrace maleness and violate male space on the battlefield. Antony is a divided entity, torn between Cleopatra and his Roman virtue. Minus his Roman identity, he cannot assume any other role. Cut off from Rome, Antony loses his self–definition. Only suicide, death at a Roman's hand, can reclaim his identity. Cleopatra's final "becoming" is her suicide, a transformation of the Roman expedient into a mystic

Egyptian rite. The union of the lovers, and, through their deaths, of the male/female, prevails over Roman male rivalry.

1350 Kinsley, Dominic Alfonso. "The Voice of the Interloper: Essays on Three Shakespearean Characters." Ph.D. dissertation, Yale University, 1980. *DAI*, 41 (1980–81), 2614-A.

Analyzes Enobarbus, who plays a significant role in *Ant*. On the evidence of Plutarch and from his behavior in *Ant.*, Enobarbus can be interpreted as a sensualist whose way of life is set in contrast to "the complex love relationship of Antony and Cleopatra."

1351 Kozikowski, Stanley J. "Shakespeare's *Antony and Cleopatra* V.ii.309–11." *Expl*, 35, no. 4 (1976–77), 7–8.

Argues that Cleopatra's wish to hear the asp "call great Caesar ass / Unpolicied" [V.ii.306–308] is a mocking reference to the brass image of an ass that, according to Plutarch's *Lives*, Caesar adopted as a sign of his victory at Actium. Thus Cleopatra imagines that her emblem, the asp, will subvert Caesar's.

1352 Kranz, David L. "'Too Slow a Messenger': The Certainty of Speed in *Antony and Cleopatra*." *CEA*, 47, nos. 1 and 2 (1984–85), 90–98.

Contends that *Ant*. presents what is perhaps Sh's culminating treatment of "the problems of rational certainty," explored in this case through the motif of speed. Though the play maintains, for the most part, a fine ambivalence between Egypt's idleness and Rome's efficiency, in the last act Cleopatra appropriates the speed that has been the special property of Octavius Caesar throughout and defeats him at his own game. In a defeat for rational certainty, Caesar, who seems elsewhere to materialize at will, comes too late at the end to claim his prize.

1352a Krause, David Harold. "Gods of Power: Poetry, Politics, and Language in Shakespeare's Plays." Ph.D. dissertation, Yale University, 1979. *DAI*, 40 (1979- 80), 5848-A.

Chapter 5 interprets *Ant*. "as tragedy through an analysis of of various ways in which its language pushes towards the limits of poetry, politics, and language—limits [that] keep us from ever becoming real gods of power, but [that] simultaneously keep us human."

1353 Krohn, Janis. "The Dangers of Love in *Antony and Cleopatra*." *IRPA*, 13 (1986), 89–96.

Notes that only in *Ant*. does Sh portray a couple, past the stage of wooing, in love over an extended period of time. Through imagery and action, we come to understand that the tragedy of the protagonists lies not so much in the external obstacles they face but in their incapacity to overcome "the internal conflicts and fears posed in their relationship." Cleopatra desires Antony because she wishes to possess a paragon of virility, to obtain phallic power. Antony's self-esteem depends on the image his beloved woman holds of him, yet his devotion to her removes him from the arena of manly competition, the only place where he can replenish that power for which she admires him. No viable solution is offered for the difficulties raised by Antony's unconscious fantasy of emasculation: We are left with a sense of "resignation and futility."

1354 Krook, Dorothea. "Tragic and Heroic in Shakespeare's *Antony and Cleopatra*." *Studies in the Drama*. Ed. Arieh Sachs. (Scripta Hierosolymitana 19.) Jerusalem: Hebrew U., 1967, pp. 231–61.

Investigates the perception by many readers that *Ant*. transcends tragedy. Suggests that in *Ant*., the four fundamental elements of tragedy—the initial "act of shame or horror," the spectacle of suffering, the knowledge that issues from the suffering, and the affirmation that springs from the knowledge—are presented ambiguously. This helps to explain why the play seems in some ways to defeat the ends of tragedy. Uses

Aristotle's concepts of "propriety" and "consistency" from the discussion of character portrayal in the *Poetics* to maintain that Cleopatra is equal to Antony in tragic stature. *Ant.* may be more precisely described as a heroic drama, closely related to tragedy in its quality of high seriousness. The defining virtues of the heroic view of life can be subsumed under what Aristotle calls Magnanimity in the *Nicomachean Ethics*. Antony and Cleopatra are in love with each other's greatness. In portraying their love, Sh presents a non-Christian or anti-Christian world. However, there is a Christian sensibility hovering over this world and exploring the limits of its glory. See item 0083.

1354a Kujawinska-Courtney, Krystyna. "Derrida's *The Truth in Painting*." *Expl*, 50 (1991–92), 124–25.

Relates Cleopatra's "cosmic fantasy" of Antony (*Ant.*, V.ii.75–91) and Octavius's recollection of Antony's capacity to consume disgusting food and drink (I.iv.56–72) to J. Derrida's concept of the colossal in art: a concept that is almost too large, "almost unpresentable," and therefore "obscene."

1355 Kuriyama, Constance Brown. "The Mother of the World: A Psychoanalytic Interpretation of Shakespeare's *Antony and Cleopatra*." *ELR*, 7 (1971), 324–51.

Maintains that some of the apparent difficulties of *Ant.* can be removed if it is read, psychoanalytically, as a dramatization of "a basic human sexual fantasy, *liebestod* (a classic version of incest fantasy), and also as an exploration of the conflicts attending the central fantasy." Cleopatra, associated with Isis, is a mother–goddess figure who also possesses male attributes and threatens men with emasculation. Antony reverts toward infancy during the play until, convinced of Cleopatra's loyalty, he envisions their reunion in death. At the end, Cleopatra, whose ambivalence has throughout seemed threatening, artfully ensures the triumph of the lovers by portraying herself in death as a faithful wife, a mother, and a noble queen.

1356. Labriola, Albert. "Renaissance Neoplatonism and Shakespeare's Characterization of Cleopatra." *HUSL*, 3(1975), 20–35.

Maintains that in *Ant.* allusions to certain Neoplatonic concepts (the World Soul, the Stair of Love, the soul-uniting kiss) in Cleopatra's later speeches show that she aspires to a spiritual reunion with Antony, but constant reminders of the physical (the desire to dress in ornate clothes, the rivalry with Iras for Antony's first kiss after death) that pervade those same speeches reduce her imagined consummation to one of the flesh.

1357 Labriola, Albert Christy. "An Organization and Analysis of the Post-Variorum Criticism of *Antony and Cleopatra*." Ph.D. dissertation, University of Virginia, 1966. *DA*, 27 (1966–67), 3430-A.

Organizes criticism of *Ant.* into "moralistic criticism, character criticism, impressionistic criticism, historical criticism, thematic criticism, a study of the play within the context of Elizabethan stagecraft, image study, and a study of the play's mythical analogues."

1358 Larson, Marilyn. "The Fallen World of Shakespeare's *Antony and Cleopatra*." *Encyclia*, 66 (1989), 79–86.

Rehearses the reasons for considering *Ant.* as tragedy, comedy, or psychodrama and finds none of these classifications satisfactory. Compares Plutarch's account of Cleopatra's suicide to Sh's to show that the latter makes unequivocal the manner of the suicide—by a serpent's bite—to create "an echo of Eden." This does not evoke a Christian ethos, but it does emphasize nostalgia for a heroic world, now fallen away from its greatness. The tragedy is that of the entire world, not just of two people.

1359 Laub, Martin. "Love's Violence in Shakespeare." Ph.D. dissertation, Loyola University of Chicago, 1989. *DAI*, 50 (1989–90), 2065-A.

Provides a detailed discussion of Sh's dualistic vision of love in three plays, including *Ant*. Love is spiritual and ecstatic, and also impulsive and self-deceiving. Sh never resolves the paradox because doing so would vitiate dramatic tension.

1360 Leavenworth, Russell E. *Daniel's "Cleopatra": A Critical Study*. (Salzburg Studies in English Literature: Elizabethan & Renaissance Studies 3.) Salzburg: Institut für Englische Sprache und Literatur, Universität Salzburg, 1974. 137 pp.

Argues, in a section entitled "The Influence," that Sh's borrowing in *Ant*. from Samuel Daniel's *Cleopatra* is significant. Cites several instances of Daniel's influence. Notes tendencies in Sh's treatment of Daniel: He provides immediate and concrete illustrations of Daniel's moral generalizations; he condenses; he sharpens imagery; and he changes emphases. Only rarely does he attempt to improve Daniel's "thought content." Discusses the scene in which Cleopatra kneels to Caesar (V.ii); a couple of scenes that contrast Antony's guilelessness and Cleopatra's cunning (I.ii, iii); and a number of comments throughout the play on the weakness of women, the fickleness of courtiers, the humiliation of being exhibited in Caesar's triumph, and the uses princes make of treachery. Disputes the claim that Daniel's 1607 revision of *Cleopatra* was a response to the popularity of Sh's play and was influenced by the latter.

1361 Lerner, Laurence. "Love and Gossip: Or, How Moral is Literature?" *EIC*, 14 (1964), 126–47.

Imagines a dialogue of three critics: A is an advocate of pluralism; B is a Christian; C is a romantic. B denies the nobility of Cleopatra's death in *Ant*., and C asserts that her death demonstrates the heights to which sexuality can rise.

1362 Levin, Harry. "Two Monumental Death Scenes: *Antony and Cleopatra*," 4.15; 5.2. *Shakespeare: Text, Language, Criticism: Essays in Honour of Marvin Spevack*. Eds. Bernhard Fabian and Kurt Tetzeli Von Rosador. Hildesheim: Olms-Weidmann, 1987, pp. 147–63.

Describes the structure of *Ant*., with thirty-seven expansive scenes leading to a climax at the battle of Actium in act III and then five scenes of contraction, in which the focus of the action is the upper stage, representing Cleopatra's monument. Explains how this ending movement displays the dynamic complementarity of Antony and Cleopatra, revealing both their likenesses and differences. To some extent Antony ends his life as a Roman, attempting suicide on the Stoic model, and Cleopatra's view of Caesar as Fortune's fool is "pure Stoicism." However, Antony's vitality survives his attempt to die, at least for the moment, and Cleopatra is seen as the Egyptian goddess Isis (Plutarch had located her tomb adjoining the temple of Isis). Cleopatra's death by the worm (developed by Sh from a slight hint in Plutarch) dissolves the hard Roman paradigm Octavius wishes to impose on her, focusing attention on the power of the serpentine Nile, which outlasts that of equestrian Rome (Antony had envisioned the last stage in the dissolution of his identity as equine). The Nile's own dynamic of alternating fertility and sterility is incorporated in the love of Antony and Cleopatra, whose tragic deaths are softened because at the end they are brought together "in the ripeness of fulfillment." The serpent suggests a further connection: The lovers at the end are like Adam and Eve, the archetypal man and woman, after the fall but before their expulsion from the garden.

1363 Lezberg, Amy Kirle. "The Jacobean Tragedy of Dual Protagonists." Ph.D. dissertation, Boston University, 1980. *DAI*, 40 (1979–80), 6292-A.

Discusses four Jacobean tragedies that have two heroes, deuteragonists whose relationships violate the moral conventions of their societies and thus make them outcasts. One of these plays, *Ant*., features lovers who attempt to cement their union while clinging to political power. Ultimately they fail, but "in their death and apotheosis they finally achieve a mythic reality greater than that possible in the temporal world which they abandon to Caesar."

1364   Lindsay, Jack. *Cleopatra.* New York: Coward McCann & Geoghegan, 1971. xvi + 560 pp.

Makes one important reference to Sh, describing his imaginative grasp of the essential conflict between Antony and Cleopatra and Octavian in *Ant.*: "Stirred by the Plutarchian narrative, Sh, however ignorant of the full bearings of the events, was able to penetrate to the essence of the conflict and to produce a play [that] is true in its value-judgements of the epoch."

1365   Logan, Robert A. "The Sexual Attitudes of Marlowe and Shakespeare." *HSL*, 19, nos. 2 and 3 (1987), 1–23.

Uses *Ant.* to show that Sh's concept of love is more inclusive than Marlowe's, moving beyond sexuality to a wide range of psychological considerations.

1366   Long, John H. "*Antony and Cleopatra*: A Double Critical Reversal," *RenP*, 1964 (1965), 28–34.

Argues that, contrary to most scholarly opinion, Sh is heavily indebted to Plutarch for the musical parts of the drinking party on Pompey's galley (II.vii) and that the music under the stage, accompanying the desertion of Antony by his genius Hercules (III.iii), is almost wholly Sh's invention. Sh conflates in II.vii two passages of revelry from Plutarch to show Antony under the spell of Bacchus; in III.iii, he substitutes the more severe music of hautboys for Plutarch's wild singing, dancing, and music to mark the departure of the demigod Hercules.

1367   Longo, Joseph A. "Cleopatra and Octavia: Archetypal Imagery in *Antony and Cleopatra.*" *UDR*, 10, no. 3 (1974), 29–38.

Employs Nietzschean terms to analyze a major element of *Ant.*: the conflict between the Apollonian rationalism of Octavia and the Dionysian energy of Cleopatra. The battleground for these two states of being is Sh's Antony, who resolves the struggle in favor of the Dionysian.

1368   Lyons, Charles R. "The Serpent, the Sun and 'Nilus Slime': A Focal Point of Shakespeare's *Antony and Cleopatra.*" *RLMC*, 21 (1968), 13–34.

Suggests that *Ant.* is Sh's first complete response to "the tension between the creative and destructive sexuality of human love." The ambiguity of this tension is conveyed in a series of images dealing with earth, the fertile slime of the Nile, melting, and decay. The serpent in Nilus's slime is impregnated by the sun, creating new life, and the earth, which serves as the matrix for this action, is enriched by the decay and melting of living things. In a similar fashion, the heroic Antony, who exists only as a dream, is dissolved by the reality of the world around him but then re-created in Cleopatra's dream. In the end, *Ant.* "accommodates the concept of the total realization of identity in the communion of lovers simultaneously with the recognition that the process of creation is the regeneration of life within the decay, the decomposed substance of previous life." Reprinted as chapter 6 of item 0708.

1369   Lyons, Clifford. "The Dramatic Structure of Shakespeare's *Antony and Cleopatra.*" *RenP*, 1983 (1984), 63–77.

Maintains that *Ant.* has two main sections, each of which has two divisions. The first begins with an "Overture" (I.i), which announces the theme of boundless love, followed by part 1 (I.ii-III.vi); the second begins with part 2 (III.vii), which is followed by a "Coda" (V). Antony's statement of love without bounds for Cleopatra is confirmed in part 1 by the separation and reunion of the lovers and reiterated three times in part 2. The tragedy is driven by the ruinous ethical choice Antony makes to follow Cleopatra despite the dictates of reason.

In V, we see Cleopatra wavering on the brink of disloyalty to Antony (as she has in the first two parts) as a prelude to her reunion with him in death. The theme can be stated in the words Scarus applies to Antony after the shameful defeat at Actium: "The noble ruin of her magic" (III.x.19).

1370 Lyons, Clifford. "Stage Imagery in Shakespeare's Plays." *Essays on Shakespeare and Elizabethan Drama in Honor of Hardin Craig.* Ed. Richard Hosley. Columbia: U. of Missouri P., 1962, pp. 261–74.

Defines stage imagery as "all that the spectators see on the stage, together with all that they hear other than the spoken lines—music and sound effects." Analyzes several instances of "the interplay of the imagery–discourse with the stage imagery" in Sh's plays. Discusses the image of Antony's blood-stained sword, brought on stage by Dercetas in V.i, as a key to the proper editorial emendation of the punctuation in the First Folio for Caesar's speech reacting to Antony's death. Suggests that in *Ant.* there is a cumulative effect created by Cleopatra's assumption of "a submissively ingratiating posture" at various points when she is trying to charm Antony and Caesar. Shows how "the stage picture and action" of the opening scene—with Antony's scornful soldiers on one side, the scorned messengers from Rome on the other side, and the lovers in the middle—reveal Antony's contempt for Caesar.

1370a MacDonald, Ronald R. "Playing Till Doomsday: Interpreting *Antony and Cleopatra.*" *ELH,* 15 (1985), 78–99.

Argues that in all his plays, and especially in *Ant.,* Sh self-consciously challenged the authoritative status of classical assumptions about history, "stability and order," and the role of language in establishing what is so often taken as fact. As Sh uses it, language cannot fully and easily represent the complexities of either inner or outer worlds in *Ant.* Dramatic conventions like that of the messenger reporting offstage action are playfully questioned. The uncertain ebb and flow of events and feelings in the play convinces us that no "hard truths" are to be had. In the handling of historical and literary "facts," Sh manipulates his materials so that "the histrionic control of imagination and language assumes primary importance." This explains Antony's apparent solecism (IV.xiv) in imagining Dido and Aeneas united in death, something patently contrary to Virgil's testimony. Antony's (and Sh's) "mistake," however, may arise from a refusal to accept one interpretation of the story as conclusive and an insistence that other interpretations are equally valid.

1371 Mack, Maynard. "*Antony and Cleopatra*: The Stillness and the Dance." *Shakespeare's Art: Seven Essays.* Ed. Milton Crane. (Tupper Lectures on Shakespeare.) Chicago: U. of Chicago P., 1973, pp. 79–113.

Takes account of the doubleness of *Ant.*: its joy in paradox, its "defiant plurality." On the one hand, for example, there is a strong tendency toward moral *exemplum* and allegory. On the other, there are individualizing, psychologically powerful touches adapted from lyric poetry, especially the sonnet. Both of these tendencies appear in the analogies of Antony to Hercules at the crossroads and of the lovers to Hercules and Omphale, Aeneas and Dido, and Mars and Venus. The world of flux is given full play through changes of place, movement of people, an exceptionally large number of entrances and exits, and the use of the optative mood. But there are also intimations of love's potential triumph over change. At the end, movement surrounds the stillness of Cleopatra's body. The "pressures of mobility" that remind us of historical forces at work "are countered, to a degree, by the traditions of ideal devotion, and of escape from mutability through love, that are implied in the Petrarchan and romance idiom in which both lovers have been immersed by their creator."

1372 MacKenzie, Clayton G. "*Antony and Cleopatra*: A Mythological Perspective." *OL,* 45 (1990), 309–29.

Disputes the idea that *Ant.* is an unambiguous reflection of certain classical mythological motifs and characters. Considers the play's comparison of Antony to

Hercules, of Antony's devotion to Cleopatra to Hercules' bondage to Omphale, of Cleopatra to Juno, of Antony to Mars, and of Cleopatra to Venus. In every case, the possibility of interpreting the persons and actions in terms of the stern Roman "mythology of military heroism" is raised and then undermined. Cleopatra's references to Juno, for example, come at moments when she (unlike the goddess) is helpless; and her conception of Antony as Mars (II.v) has reference to a comprehensive range of "human excellences" that is vastly richer than the narrow soldierly virtues to which Philo's Mars comparison would confine his captain in I.i. *Ant.* moves from the subversion of classical mythologizing in its early acts to a new way of seeing human greatness in act V (which has no overt mythological references). In her final visions of Antony, Cleopatra exemplifies this new mythology, created by the Egyptian imagination and emphasizing "the worth of the human bond and interpersonal obligations." Antony, who dies at the end of act IV, never becomes fully attuned to the new way of thinking.

1373   MacMullan, Katherine Vance. "Death Imagery in *Antony and Cleopatra*." *SQ*, 14 (1963), 399–410.

Maintains that *Ant.* "is the last Shakespearean play in which the theme of love and death is employed as an integral part of the dramatic situation." Death imagery depicts both plot and character in *Ant.*, linking it, in this regard, with *Rom.* and *Oth.* Images of love and death are used throughout the play to portray the character of Cleopatra and to indicate "Antony's tragic passion and decline, demonstrating with forceful irony the strengthening of his attachment to Cleopatra and the weakening of his judgment in the command of practical affairs."

1374   Mallery, Mary Aileen. "The Changing Face of Fortune in Six English Versions of the Tragedy of Antony and Cleopatra." Ph.D. dissertation, City University of New York, 1990. *DAI*, 51 (1990–91), 865-A.

Notes that the concepts relating to the goddess Fortune "change with the idea of the individual's ability to shape his own destiny." Discusses six versions of the tragedy of Antony and Cleopatra, including *Ant.*, written between 1592 and 1678.

1375   Marchant, Robert. *A Picture of Shakespeare's Tragedies*. Doncaster, South Yorkshire: Brynmill P., 1984. 180 pp.

Proposes to interpret Shakespearean tragedy according to an idea of action derived from Aristotle's *Poetics*. Argues that the protagonist of a tragedy creates his destiny through the actions he performs, not because of his psychic makeup. Provides close readings of *Ham.*, *Oth.*, *Mac.*, *Lr.*, and *Ant.* Chapter 6, on *Ant.*, points to Cleopatra's indifference, in the earlier parts of the play, to the threats to her control of Antony and finds tragedy in her "sublime sacrifice," her "voluptuous triumph" at the end. Follows Antony in his various twistings and turnings while he remains Cleopatra's man; his attempts to be heroic; his manly encounters with Octavius and Pompey; his attempts to revive the camaraderie with his men that has defined him in the past; and his courageous yet foolish death.

1376   Markels, Julian. *The Pillar of the World: "Antony and Cleopatra" in Shakespeare's Development*. Columbus: Ohio State U. P. 1968. 191 pp.

Argues that the key to Sh's development is the opposition between public and private values, which can be seen throughout the canon and reaches its culmination in *Ant.* In this play, Antony is tempted either to choose between the contrary values of Cleopatra and Octavius or not to choose between them. Instead, "he resolves the conflict by striving equally toward both values and rhythmically making each one a measure of the other." To this end, Sh enhances Antony's moral stature, negating the "effeminacy" to which he is subject in Plutarch. Traces the tension between public and private from the Henriad and *JC*, through *Ham.* and *Lr.*, to the transcendence of both sets of values in *Ant.*

1377 Marsh, Derick R. C. "Lords and Owners of Their Faces: A Study of Octavius Caesar and Prince Hal." Eds. G. A. Wilkes and A. P. Riemer. (Sydney Studies in English.) Sydney: Department of English, U. of Sydney, 1985, pp. 19–28.

Compares Octavius Caesar (*Ant.*) with Prince Hal (*1&2H4*): Both are examples of the kind of character who is able to control his emotions, thereby exerting power over those less capable of doing so. In each case, Sh is exploring the question of what sort of man makes a good ruler. Octavius is the less complex of the two: He wants sole possession of authority and cares little about the values of order and stability or the affection of his followers. As the antitheses of Octavius and Hal, respectively, Antony and Falstaff, despite their enormous differences, have in common the attitude that life is to be enjoyed "in a variety of ways."

1378 Martín, María Jesús Pérez. "A Brief Reflection on the Apotheosis in the Final Act of Shakespeare's *Antony and Cleopatra.*" *Anglo-American Studies*, 7, no. 2 (1987), 149–52.

Compares the panegyrics of Octavius (*Ant.*, V.i) and Cleopatra (V.ii) for Antony. Cites North's translation of Plutarch's *Lives* to show that Octavius's eulogy is subtly designed to glorify the speaker rather than the subject. There is no equivalent in Plutarch for Cleopatra's "dream" of Antony: She forgets about herself and creates an awe-inspiring, colossal image of her lover.

1379 Mason, H. A. "*Anthony and Cleopatra*: Angelic Strength—Organic Weakness?" *CQ*, 1 (1966), 209–236.

Challenges the belief that *Ant.* is a fully realized dramatic poem. Singles out the opening scene and the two scenes between Cleopatra and the Messenger as superior in their staging of reality. However, much of the play, especially what takes place between the first act and III.vii, fails to gratify our expectations; Sh often resorts to to "magnificent subterfuge," poetry that "merely conditions or colours the sense of fact arising from the dramatic fiction," instead of providing dramatically effective poetry. Contends that the speech in which Enobarbus describes the appearance of Cleopatra on the Cydnus takes us out of the material world and that the scene in which the speech occurs is "abrupt, shapeless and anti-climactic." Continued in item 1380. Revised as the first chapter of the last section of item 1381.

1380 Mason, H. A. "*Anthony and Cleopatra*: Telling versus Showing." *CQ*, 1 (1966), 330–54. Reprint. *Shakespeare: "Antony and Cleopatra." A Selection of Critical Essays.* Ed. John Russell Brown. London: Macmillan, 1968, pp. 201–14.

Maintains that Sh, through heightened language, *tells* us about the glories of Antony, but never *shows* us these glories in the drama. For example, the numerous comparisons of Antony with classical figures—both by himself and by others—remove him from "the earth we know" and deliver him over "to hyperbole and bombast." Similarly, the appeal of Cleopatra's final scene is to the imagination; we are not given "an embodied dramatic creation." The play fails as a tragedy because Sh did not attempt to dramatize the heroic suggestions he introduced. Conclusion of item 1379. Revised as the second chapter of the last section of item 1381.

1381 Mason, H. A. *Shakespeare's Tragedies of Love: An Examination of the Possibility of Common Readings of "Romeo and Juliet," "Othello," "King Lear" and "Antony and Cleopatra."* London: Chatto and Windus. xi + 290 pp.

The last section, on *Ant.*, has two chapters, the first a revision of item 1379 and the second a revision of item 1380.

1382 Matchett, William H. "Reversing the Field: *Antony and Cleopatra* in the Wake of *King Lear*." *MLQ*, 45 (1984), 327–37.

Regards *Ant.* as the play that most directly follows from *Lr.* That is, in *Ant.*, Sh "begins with, and then proceeds to test, the final value Lear asserted." Comments on several direct links in the first scene of *Ant.* to *Lr.*

1383 Matthews, Roger. "*Antony and Cleopatra*: Enter the Imagest: A Work in Progress." *SELit*, English Number (1981), 3–23.

Analyzes *Ant.* to present the operations of the imagest (image + gesture), in which we experience "the image of poetry" working in unison with "the gesture of drama." Suggests that the crucial imagest of the raising of Antony to Cleopatra's monument at the end of the play (IV.xv), which is anticipated in Cleopatra's musing that she will be pulling up an Antony every time she catches a fish (II.v), has its genesis in the image of "the courser's hair" (I.ii.197). The intersection of male and female is conveyed in various images throughout the play, the two most important having to do with *sword* (Roman, hard) and *snake* (Egyptian, soft). Analyzes the scene on Pompey's galley (II.vii) to show how the process of blurring things Roman and Egyptian takes place in both word and gesture. Notes the significance of the "reed/partisan/cable" cluster of images/gestures for the idea of "the penetration of water," itself an imagest for creativity. Other important imagests are "the unarming of Antony" and the knot that ties him to Cleopatra.

1384 Maxwell-Mahon, W. D. "Character and Conflict in *Antony and Cleopatra*." *Crux*, 9, no. 3 (1975), 39–44.

Notes that *Ant.* is a sequel to *JC* and comments that we can benefit from understanding that some of the characters, especially Antony, are fundamentally the same as they were in the earlier play. Antony and Cleopatra are morally ambiguous, but they attract us by "the integrity of their love and the courage with which they face its tragic conclusion."

1385 McManaway, James G. "Notes on Act V of *Antony and Cleopatra*." *ShStud*, 1 (1962), 1–5.

Adduces the ending of Anouilh's *The Lark*, in which Joan of Arc is brought back from death to have a final triumphant scene, as similar to Sh's giving the last act of *Ant.* to Cleopatra. Before act V, she seems of questionable worth, but after Antony's death she increases in stature so that we understand why Antony was willing to count the world well lost for her.

1386 Meltzer, Gary Stephen. "The Comic Side of the Tragic Mask: The Role of Comic Perspectives in Shaping Tragic Vision." Ph.D. dissertation, Yale University, 1987. *DAI*, 49 (1988–89), 812-A.

Exhibits *Ant.* as one of five tragic works in which comic intervention plays a significant role. In this play, "the comic element pervades the text, even disrupting the tragic catastrophe." The "psychic and spiritual disintegration" suffered by Antony makes him "susceptible to an array of techniques of comic subversion." As a consequence, his tragic predicament appears at times to be "absurd, melodramatic, or grotesque." Comedy reveals in Antony "unconscious conflicts and blockages that threaten to paralyze him." Through this use of comic perspective, Sh includes the audience in "a dialogue about the meaning and possibility of tragedy itself."

1387 Meredith, Peter. "'That Pannelled Me At Heeles': *Antony and Cleopatra* IV.x.34." *ES*, 55 (1974), 118–26.

Challenges various emendations of the Folio reading *pannelled* (*Ant.*, IV.xii.21) and proposes *pantled*, which conveys the "scorn-in-grief" that Antony feels for his deserting followers. Suggests that this word came to Sh through "a complex association of hearts, dogs and food."

1387a Miller, Milton. "A Contrary Blast: Milton's Dalila." *Drama, Sex and Politics.* Ed. James Redmond. (Themes in Drama 7.) Cambridge: Cambridge U. P., 1985, pp. 93–108.

Includes a comparison of Dalila with Sh's Cleopatra (*Ant.*). Both portraits are versions of "the *Venus armata* or the *Venus victrix* who in Renaissance paintings is seen as restraining or pacifying Mars, and sometimes wearing his armor." This is an equivocal figure, meant to be "various, inclusive, and shifting."

1388 Mills, Laurens J. *The Tragedies of Antony and Cleopatra.* (Indiana University Humanities Series 55.) Bloomington: Indiana U. P., 1964. v + 66 pp.

Treats the tragedies of the two protagonists separately. Antony's virtues are primarily his Roman qualities, which are seen to some extent in the first part of the play, especially the reconciliation scene with Caesar (*Ant.*, II.ii). After Actium, Antony gives himself over to emotion, losing his resolve in the face of Cleopatra's challenge. It is through Enobarbus's speeches that Antony's decline is chronicled, and Enobarbus becomes a victim of his master's failure to control his passion. Cleopatra's tragedy is not a fall, since she has nowhere from which to fall. She changes slightly in that she comes to recognize Antony's greatness, albeit after his death, but she never recognizes her guilt or shows any sign of penitence.

1389 Mitchell, Bruce. "The Language of Shakespeare." *Spicilegio Moderno*, 12 (1981), 3–17.

Notes that sometimes characters in Sh's plays speak in a manner that is not strictly appropriate to their role. Cites Enobarbus's description of Cleopatra's appearance on the Cydnus (*Ant.*, II.ii) as an example, juxtaposing it with the passsage in Plutarch from which Sh created it. Quotes other passages from *Ant.* to illustrate the developing functionality and richness of Sh's imagery in his mature plays.

1390 Mitchell, Dennis S. "Shakespeare's *Antony and Cleopatra* II.ii.811–813." *Expl*, 35, no. 1 (1976–77), 22–24.

Maintains that the First Folio punctuation of part of Caesar's speech to Antony (II.ii.121–123) expressing a wish for atonement is superior to subsequent emendations. The Folio punctuation allows the phrase "from edge to edge" to describe the tightness with which Antony and Caesar would be bound if Caesar had his way. This is compatible with the imagery of unity and division that pervades the play.

1391 Mitchell, Robin Norman. "Tragic Identity: Studies in Euripides and Shakespeare." Ph.D. dissertation, Brown University, 1988. *DAI*, 49 (1988–89), 2211-A.

Uses the theories of René Girard about mimetic desire to read *Ant.* as a "tragedy of mimesis," in which "Antony engages in mimetic rivalries with Cleopatra and Octavius, creating a political crisis" that results in "the scapegoating of Antony." The mythification of Antony by Cleopatra and Octavius in an attempt to remove blame from themselves resembles what happens at the end of Euripides' *Hippolytus*.

1392 Miyauchi, Bunshichi. *Immortal Longings: The Structure of Shakespeare's "Antony and Cleopatra."* Tokyo: Shinozaki Shorin, 1978. iv + 369 pp.

Proposes a structuralist analysis of *Ant.*, examining its dramatic dialogue as "a dispersal field of performance interminably actualized between the opposing parties, in which they will merge their ideas with each other, as well as reduce them to properties at the deep level of design." Regards *Ant.* as "the acme of Shakespeare's tragic grandeur" because it focuses on "international politics" and because the protagonists are aware from the beginning of their paradoxical combination of strengths and weaknesses, of their responsibility for their fate. Coming finally to a recognition that love beyond "mundane morality" is their last resort, the undaunted lovers reach and cross the frontier of tragedy. Discusses Sh's reliance on and departures from Plutarch throughout. Focuses on Plutarch and other possible sources and analogues in a chapter entitled "The Literary Background," pointing out Sh's enhancement of Cleopatra's nobleness and his skillful handling of Fulvia and Enobarbus. Notes that Sh shapes the story so that from the beginning Antony and Cleopatra are forced to live with a keen awareness of death.

1393 Mooney, Michael E. *Shakespeare's Dramatic Transactions*. Durham, North Carolina: Duke U. P., 1990. xiv + 226 pp.

Attempts interpretations of seven of Sh's plays "by bringing to bear the theatrical and histrionic conventions Shakespeare inherited when he began to write for the stage." Uses the theories of Robert Weimann to discuss how "information, in the forms of language, gesture, and action," crosses the boundary between actors and audience in an aesthetic transaction. Chapter 8, on *Ant.*, counters arguments that the play's ultimate impression is one of ambiguity. Acknowledges that the lovers evoke varying responses in the earlier parts of the play but maintains that we are guided to a sure sense of their constancy of purpose at the end. One reason for this is Enobarbus, a character Sh invented, who enjoys "a privileged relationship with the audience" and who shapes their reactions, first through his cynical aloofness and then by his increasing involvement. Enobarbus's "crisis of confidence in Antony," brought home by his developing status as choric commentator (he frames actions through soliloquies and asides) in acts III and IV, is shared with the spectators. What he discovers, in league with the audience, is that the critical Roman attitude toward Antony is deeply flawed because it fails to comprehend the hero's bounty of spirit. Another guide for the audience is the "mythological substructure" of the play, through which Sh pictures the lovers dramatizing episodes taken from the stories of Venus and Mars. Notes that Cleopatra is enigmatic and inconstant up until the moment of Antony's death in her monument in IV.xv. From this point on, she is marble–constant in her resolution to exalt her relationship with Antony in a "timeless, dreamlike state" and to reject "the epic Roman world of history and action."

1394 Moore, John Rees. "The Enemies of Love: The Example of Antony and Cleopatra." *KR*, 31 (1969), 646–74.

Argues that Sh's protagonists in *Ant.* are enemies of love in that they are not young: "They have not the excuse of youth, they defy the decrees of religion and morality, they act absurdly in terms of self-interest, and they are too worldly-wise to fall victim to idealism." Throughout the play, they refuse to give up public status or worldly power for the sake of love. Eventually they learn "the higher sophistication of love" and choose to leave worldly entanglements for the eternity of the poetic realm.

1395 Morgan, Margery. "'Your Crown's Awry': *Antony and Cleopatra* in the Comic Tradition." *Komos*, 1 (1968), 128–39.

Contends that from the beginning *Ant.* cultivates a critical perspective "that interferes with total empathy and prepares a resistance to the seductive rhetoric in store." The dramatist makes the audience self-conscious about what they are witnessing; and the characters deliberately create impressions by "play-acting" and "by their willful, self-amused shifts from mode to mode." *Ant.* "reveals the secondary character of artistic creation and guards it from false valuation," producing in the process a wide range of comic effects, among them farce, bawdry, "parody to the point of burlesque," mixture of incompatible metaphors, mock-death, and quibbles. The play celebrates "a creative joy in the risible lie."

1396 Morris, Helen. "Queen Elizabeth 'Shadowed' in Cleopatra." *HLQ*, 32 (1968–69), 271–78.

Suggests that Sh's portrait of Cleopatra was influenced in some respects by Elizabeth's behavior. Cites, among other sources, the *Memoirs* of Sir James Melville, who came to London in 1564 "as emissary from Mary, Queen of Scots." Melville's account of

Elizabeth's "anxious inquiries about the appearance and accomplishments of her dreaded rival" bears a remarkable resemblance to two scenes, invented by Sh, in which Cleopatra asks the Messenger about Octavia (*Ant.*, II.v and III.iii).

1397 Morris, Helen. "Shakespeare and Dürer's Apocalypse." *ShakS*, 4 (1968), 252–62.

Comments that Sh, in writing *Ant.*, drew frequently on the Apocalypse for imagery and thematic material. Argues that Albrecht Dürer's series of prints on this theme (1498 and 1511) and later illustrations that imitated Dürer also influenced Sh. Dürer's woodcuts seem to have contributed to the images of Antony as a falling star, of Cleopatra on the river Cydnus, of Antony's eyes as a sun and a moon, and of Antony's delights as "dolphin-like."

1398 Morrison, Mary. "Some Aspects of the Treatment of the Theme of Antony and Cleopatra in Tragedies of the Sixteenth Century." *Journal of European Studies*, 4 (1974), 113–25.

Argues that sympathetic interest in Cleopatra, sparked in part by the discovery at Rome of a statue thought to represent her in death, was responsible for the publication of nine tragedies about her in the last half of the 16th c., three each in France, Italy, and England. These "Senecan" tragedies are strikingly similar: The action is restricted to the last day of the life of Antony and Cleopatra; there is little dramatic action; there are no scenes of reciprocated love; the emotions of the lovers are poured out in monologues; and debates and moral discussions are common. The authors all treat the story of the lovers as a moral *exemplum*; they all show detailed knowledge of Plutarch, their source; and, though generally faithful to history, they all change Cleopatra considerably to make her noble and virtuous, despite harsh censure of her lust and ambition in the choral odes. Many of these features appear in Sh's *Ant.*, in particular the idealization of Cleopatra and the tension between condemnation of and sympathy for the lovers's passion.

1399 Moseley, C. W. R. D. "Cleopatra's Prudence: Three Notes on the Use of Emblems in *Antony and Cleopatra*." *SJH*, 1986, 119–37.

Refers to 16th- and 17th-c. emblem books to elucidate three emblematic scenes/passages in *Ant.* that invite consideration and redefinition of the concepts of prudence and wisdom. The first of these is Antony's likeness to a Colossus, which can be read as an indication that he might possess the wisdom appropriate to a just ruler. Second, there is the image of Antony engaging in the Choice of Hercules, which resonates in the rapid alternation between contrasting locales and the counterposition of Cleopatra and Octavia. As in the Colossus emblem, wisdom is a key consideration. Finally, Cleopatra's appearance with snakes in her death scene associates her with prudence. Thus the play may suggest that "there is a higher wisdom, a higher prudence," beyond the reach of "the conventional ideas of empire."

1400 Moseley, Charles. "Speaking Pictures: Visual Symbol in *Antony and Cleopatra*." *Critical Essays on "Antony and Cleopatra."* (Longman Literature Guides.) Eds. Linda Cookson and Bryan Loughrey. Harlow, Essex: Longman, 1990, pp. 85–91.

Explores the connection of symbols from the emblem books of Sh's day and the imagery presented in *Ant.*: Antony/Colossus, Antony/Hercules, and Cleopatra/Prudence or Wisdom. Focuses on the organization of the play's early scenes and Cleopatra's staging of her suicide.

1401 Muir, Kenneth. "*Antony and Cleopatra*, III.xiii.73–78." *N&Q*, 8 (1961), 142.

Argues that the "rhythm and sense would be improved" if lines 76–78 were emended to "there to kneel, / Till, from his all-obeying breath I hear / the doom of Egypt."

1402 Muir, Kenneth. "Elizabeth I, Jodelle, and Cleopatra." *RenD*, N. S. 2 (1969), 197–206.

Suggests that Sh's portrait of Cleopatra is more sympathetic than many have allowed. Cleopatra has been stigmatized as unqueenly in her questioning of the messenger about Octavia (III.iii), but an account of Elizabeth I's questioning of James Melville about Mary, Queen of Scots, shows that this sort of behavior was characteristic of at least one queen. Dramatic treatments of Cleopatra before Sh's play, especially that of E. Jodelle, contained a good deal of sympathy for the queen. Sh may have known Jodelle's play, but even if he did not, Jodelle's sympathetic treatment of Cleopatra means that there was precedent for a favorable depiction of her.

1403 Muir, Kenneth. "The Imagery of *Antony and Cleopatra*." *KN*, 8, no. 3 (1961), 249–64. Revised as "The High Roman Fashion," chapter 9 of *Shakespeare the Professional and Related Studies*. London: Heinemann, 1973, pp. 158–70.

Argues that the imagery of *Ant.* reinforces the view that the protagonists are many-sided, contradictory, and ambiguous during the earlier parts of the play but that they are transformed by love at the end. Analyzes four main groups of images: "the world and heavenly bodies; eating; bodily movement; and melting." These "are supported by the iteration of words relating to nobility, the Gods, serpents' poison, kingship, and fortune." The cosmic imagery, for example, has a twofold effect: First, "it underlines the stakes for which Antony and Cleopatra are playing and the power which Antony is sacrificing by his passion for Cleopatra"; and, second, toward the end of Antony's life, "it stresses his superhuman qualities."

1404 Mulryne, J. R. "The Paradox on the Stage: *Antony and Cleopatra*." *Le Paradox au temps de la Renaissance*. Ed. Marie-Thérèse Jones-Davies. (Université de Paris—Sorbonne, Institut de Recherches sur les Civilisations de l'Occident Moderne, Centre de Recherches sur la Renaissance 7.) Paris: Jean Touzot, 1982, pp. 155–68.

Maintains that in *Ant.* Sh presents the paradoxical story of the lovers by insisting both on their poetic appeal and on the strenuous and/or awkward physicality involved in staging certain scenes, most notably Antony's being hoisted into Cleopatra's monument to die (IV.xv). Sh emphasizes the messiness and pain of Antony's ascent to death, eloquently described in Plutarch, by ostentatiously taxing the resources of his theater. In a similar manner, Cleopatra's attempt to repose in artful permanence is betrayed by her crown's refusal to stay in place and other disruptions of her ritual suicide.

1405 Murr, Priscilla. *Shakespeare's "Antony and Cleopatra": A Jungian Interpretation*. (European University Studies, Series 14: Anglo-Saxon Language and Literature 187.) Berne: Peter Lang, 1988. xii + 196 pp.

Chapter 1 considers the setting of *Ant.*, establishing the pattern of opposition that is the foundation of its structure. Sh presents the Roman view of things first, and the Egyptian way of life is then defined against it. The play's duality "unfolds in a triadic world." Chapter 2, which concentrates on II.ii, in which Antony arrives in Rome and immediately becomes subject to Caesar's manipulation, explains how the tragedy is "sealed" in this scene. Chapter 3 describes how Antony, caught in a conflict between the persona (Rome: the outer world) and the anima (Egypt: the inner life), fails to individuate himself and is destroyed. Chapter 4 argues that Cleopatra, having manipulated Antony throughout the play, comes at last to recognize and accept "her own inner masculine" and is transformed in death to a true queen and a wife. Chapter 6 treats Cleopatra as participating in the archetype of the Great Mother. Chapter 7 provides an account of Octavius Caesar as a masterful rhetorician and historian with little inner life. Chapter 8 argues that in writing *Ant.* Sh was influenced by what Jung called "the archetype of the individuation process," the "inner urge to become what we were born to become." The Roman world, given a chance by Cleopatra and Egypt to escape its bondage to duty and social reality, fails to do so. Antony and Cleopatra, though they achieve some new perceptions, cannot deal with their inner problems and are destroyed. Octavius, the representative of the persona, is finally triumphant.

1406 Nandy, Dipak. "The Realism of *Antony and Cleopatra*." *Shakespeare in a Changing World*. Ed. Arnold Kettle. New York: International Publishers, 1964, pp. 172–94.

Maintains that Sh presents in *Ant*. a clash "of different ways of looking at the world." The Roman view, often associated with realism, is characterized by corruption, cynicism, and stasis. The Egyptian view, exemplified in Cleopatra, affirms that love is "the model of genuine human relationships"; it involves acceptance of a cyclical, health-giving motion. Interestingly, Cleopatra is just as realistic as Caesar in pursuing her ends: She uses politic deception, for example, to hold Antony. Antony's struggle to define himself is resolved when, with the news of Cleopatra's death, he senses that his relationship with her is "the very ground of his being." Enobarbus's experience as a realistic observer who dies of a broken heart after distancing himself from Antony's way of life tips the balance of the play in the Egyptian direction and validates the relationship of the protagonists. Sh offers a dialectical vision of Antony and Cleopatra: They share in the corruption of the world (and to that extent they are portrayed with realism), but they also transcend it.

1407 Neely, Carol Thomas. *Broken Nuptials in Shakespeare's Plays*. New Haven: Yale U. P., 1985. xi + 261 pp.

Chapter 4, "Gender and Genre in *Antony and Cleopatra*," attempts to show that, in this play, gender roles "are not exchanged or transcended, but are played out in more variety than in the other tragedies." As a result, the play's generic boundaries are extended to comprehend "motifs, roles, and themes" found in Sh's histories, comedies, problem plays, and romances.

1408 Nelson, C. E. "*Antony and Cleopatra* and the Triumph of Rome." *University Review*, 32 (1965–66), 199–203.

Maintains that the love story in *Ant*. "does not contain the seeds of its own destruction"; the public world of power, represented by Rome, determines the love story's tragic structure. More than any of Sh's other tragedies, *Ant*. "ends in a devastatingly neutral sense of peace and rightness."

1409 Nevo, Ruth. "The Masque of Greatness." *ShakS*, 3 (1967), 111–28.

Views act V of *Ant*. as a dramatic realization of Cleopatra's resolve to triumph, with Antony, over the world of Caesar. A crucial element in this progress is the imagery of pageantry and masquing, used to exhibit Cleopatra's visions of both herself and Antony, and the Roman triumph she imagines Caesar to be planning, in which she will be forced to play a humiliating part. As act V develops, Caesar's triumphal pageant becomes, in Cleopatra's imagination, an antimasque, a grotesque, ignoble spectacle acting as a prelude to the true magnificence of her own triumph. Cleopatra is "consistently Roman" in directing her attention entirely to suicide as a means of achieving her imaginative goal; she disdains common humanity in setting forth a "manifest demonstration of an unvanquished spirit." The play's ambiguity can be traced to its depiction of a man trying to serve two contradictory masters—*virtus* and *voluptas*—each of which makes heroic claims on him. Cleopatra's recognition of Antony's greatness in paradox and her affirmation of his magnanimity are, like the masques that seem to have exercised such a great influence on this play, both superlative spectacles and insubstantial pageants. Such ambivalence, shared by Sh's other Roman plays, seems to have been "inherent in a representation of Rome in the mind of a Renaissance Christian." Revised as chapter 9 of item 0799.

1410 Nicol, Bernard de Bear, ed. *Varieties of Dramatic Experience: Discussions on Dramatic Forms and Themes between Stanley Evernden, Roger Hubank, Thora Burnley Jones and Bernard de Bear Nicol.* London: U. of London P., 1969. vii + 291 pp.

Chapter 5 includes a discussion of *Ant.* Hubank finds that the play calls attention to the "ambiguity of judgment," "the difficulty of perceiving rightly," that is a central fact of the human condition. Contends that the love affair is "by its very nature tragic," demanding as it does "a total commitment of the personality" in circumstances of ignorance. Rome is the world of expediency, of political reality, embodied by Octavius. Antony aspires to be master of this world as well as that of Egypt; he also attempts, through his magnanimity and loyalty, to be the ideal man that Cleopatra fantasizes about after his death. His tragedy is that he fails in these aspirations. Jones insists that Antony's tragedy is shared with Cleopatra, while Nicol believes that the last act is a "tragic farce," a mockery of the Roman world that makes such grand love affairs as that of Antony and Cleopatra impossible to sustain.

1411 Nochimson, Richard L. "The End Crowns All: Shakespeare's Deflation of Tragic Possibility in *Antony and Cleopatra.*" *English*, 26 (1977), 99–132.

Argues that Antony and Cleopatra, like Troilus and Cressida, are diminished to the extent that their deaths do not "evoke a tragic response." Antony is irresolute, blind to his own defects, and self-centered; and Sh makes alterations in his source to stress these traits. For example, Plutarch has him return to Egypt out of love of Cleopatra, but in the play he is motivated primarily by the feeling that he cannot flourish near Caesar. Also, Ventidius's revelation (III.i) that Sosius fell into disfavor with Antony because he won too much is not found in Plutarch. Although Cleopatra is portrayed positively in a couple of scenes, her irresponsibility, mood changes, and distrust of Antony make it equally impossible to accord her tragic stature. Tragic possibilities exist in the story, or myth, of the two lovers, but not in the characters as presented in this play.

1412 Novy, Marianne. "Shakespeare's Female Characters as Actors and Audience." *Shakespearean Metadrama.* Ed. John W. Blanpied. MLA Special Session 711, 1977. Rochester: U. of Rochester Department of English, 1977, pp. 17–40.

Notes that while women as actors are often central to Sh's comedies, in the tragedies the men are the chief actors and find women's assuming of roles to be suspect. *Ant.* is something of an exception because the lovers' playing of roles is essential to their acceptance of the ambiguities in their relationship. Cleopatra has a larger scope for being artist, actor, and audience than any other woman in Sh's tragedies.

1413 Nowottny, Winifred. *The Language Poets Use.* New York: Oxford U. P., 1962. 225 pp.

Refers to *Ant.*, V.ii.85–87, in making a point about "the power of the metaphorical term to bring associations and suggestions with it."

1414 Nunes, Herta Maria F. de Queiroz. "Enobarbus: 'He is of note.'" *Signal* (Paraíba), 1 (1978), 10–31.

Proposes to analyze the character of Enobarbus in *Ant.*, finding a parallel between him and his master. In the early part of the play, when Antony is at the height of his power, Enobarbus is a loyal observer, balancing his sharp observations with admiration. However, as Antony's inner conflict comes to dominate the play, Enobarbus's rationality asserts itself in progressively harsher criticism, which is a sign that he has lost faith in himself as well as in Antony. Enobarbus dies of a broken heart, unable to face the consequences of his decision to desert. His death contrasts interestingly with that of Eros, who would "rather kill himself than his master."

1415 Ornstein, Robert. "The Ethic of the Imagination: Love and Art in *Antony and Cleopatra*." *Later Shakespeare*. Eds. John Russell Brown and Bernard Harris. (Stratford-upon-Avon Studies 8.) London: Edward Arnold, 1966, pp. 31–46. Reprint. 1973. Reprint. *Twentieth-Century Interpretations of "Antony and Cleopatra": A Collection of Critical Essays*. Ed. Mark Rose. Englewood Cliffs, New Jersey: Prentice-Hall, 1977, pp. 82–98.

Emphasizes the imaginative honesty of *Ant.*, which is based primarily on Sh's infusion of paradoxes into Plutarch's account. One of these involves the dichotomy between "the hard masculine world of Rome" and "the soft yielding world of Egypt." This apparently absolute distinction, suggested by the imagery, is qualified by the action. For example, according to Roman standards, Antony loses his manhood, but the play tests the standards and finds them wanting. Egypt seems to be a land where sensual indulgence leads to neglect of duty, but it is Cleopatra who insists on accompanying Antony into battle and who speaks the play's "finest Roman words." Antony is "warm and generous as well as callous." And Cleopatra, the world's most notorious courtesan, longs to be Antony's wife; she dies a sensual Egyptian death but fashions it into a vehicle of immortality for her and Antony. The play itself exemplifies "the paradox of tragic art, which depicts immeasurable loss and yet preserves forever that which the artist supremely values."

1416 Pandurangan, Prema. "Shakespeare's Enobarbus." *Aryan Path*, 39 (1968), 227–30.

Points out that although Enobarbus is only a shadowy figure in Plutarch, in *Ant.* Sh endows him with substance as a soldier, chorus, humorist, and, primarily, poet.

1417 Patrick, J. Max. "The Cleopatra Theme in World Literature up to 1970." *The Undoing of Babel: Watson Kirkconnel: The Man and His Work*. Ed. J. R. C. Perkin. Toronto: McClelland and Stewart, 1975, pp. 64–76.

Surveys treatments of Cleopatra by Horace, Virgil, Propertius, and other Roman writers, who "crystallized the Cleopatra legend, translating her and her mates into symbols that could be freely manipulated in easy formulae." Plutarch, a Greek, integrated the legend, transforming her from "a mere symbol of shame into a unified, credible *femme fatale*" who bewitched Antony. Later handlings of the Cleopatra story include those by Dante, Boccaccio, Chaucer, Gower, the Countess of Pembroke, and Samuel Daniel. *Ant.* is clearly superior to other versions in its copiousness of treatment, complex characterization, and rich poetry. Sh endows his two protagonists with a dualism that has them living on two levels, "the legendary and the actual."

1418 Payne, Michael. "Erotic Irony and Polarity in *Antony and Cleopatra*." *SQ*, 24 (1973), 265–79.

Detects in *Ant.* "a series of interrelated polarities—Rome–Egypt, masculinity–femininity, space/time boundary–space/time transcendence, death–love—which at first appear to be mutually exclusive or dualistic concepts but which are shown to be polar concepts instead." "Polar concepts," as used here, are opposites within a single whole and hence inseparable. In the first act, Roman perception of the world (characterized by measurement, authority, setting of boundaries, and uniformity) is established and then ironically undermined by Egyptian freedom and fluidity. Act II at first suggests that masculinity and femininity are "exclusive, opposite psychophysical designations" but then shows them as "complementary in the personalities of Antony and Cleopatra." In acts III and IV, the technique of montage (twenty-eight short scenes shift rapidly from one place or time to another) helps achieve the transcendence of space/time boundaries. Cleopatra's death in act V paradoxically transcends the limitations "of the existential sphere." The generic structure of the play, like its thematic polarities, "is neither tragic nor comic, but both."

1419 Pelling, C. B. R., ed. *Plutarch: "Life of Antony."* (Cambridge Greek and Latin Classics.) Cambridge: Cambridge U. P., 1988. xiii + 338 pp.

Section 5 of the introduction compares Plutarch's *Life* with *Ant.*, noting that Sh knew Plutarch in North's translation, not in the original Greek. The ambiguities of North and his French source Amyot, and those translators' choice of texts, are sometimes significant for Sh's treatment, especially in "inspiring the entire episode of Enobarbus's repentance." Notes that in *Ant.* the verbal echoes of North are "more restricted" than in *Cor.*, *JC*, or *Tim.* but that the "borrowings of material, emphasis, and characterisation are much closer." Lists notes in the commentary in which "Shakespeare's adaptation is discussed in detail." Describes the visual and theatrical qualities of Plutarch's *Life of Marcus Antonius* that made it more readily susceptible to dramatic adaptation than any of the other *Lives*. Mentions the parts of Plutarch that Sh ignored or chose not to develop, especially the first third (with its "catalogue of excesses, its relative absence of dramatic confrontation, and its complicated plot"). Sh takes the polarity between the gravity of Rome and the "languor and informality" of Alexandria from Plutarch and sharpens it, leaving out the "distinctive atmosphere" that Plutarch develops for Greece. Sh also follows Plutarch in sometimes blurring the distinction between Rome and Egypt, though he does this more completely than his source. While the events covered in *Ant.* span a decade, Sh does not create "much sense of time." He does, however, convey—through messengers and through Antony's showy journey to Rome—a sense of great spaciousness. Sh adapted Plutarch's technique of characterizing a principal by "reconstructing how observers of the time would have responded." The comments of Antony's troops, particularly Enobarbus, are especially important in this regard. Sh's emphasis on Hercules (where Plutarch stresses Dionysus) shows the playwright grappling with the need to provide a sense of "Antony's soldierly greatness" without staging battle scenes. Points out that Sh introduces Antony's complex mental struggle over the attractions of Cleopatra at a much earlier stage than does Plutarch but that he does not develop the struggle. Sh is more concerned with the inevitability of Antony's abandonment of Octavia and his return to Cleopatra. Like his Antony, Plutarch's Cleopatra deepens as the *Life* goes on. In dramatizing her transformation from crude erotic gamester to woman in love, Sh is more bewildering than he has to be. Her enigmatic qualities, however, are what make her a match for Antony. Observes that Sh, in composing his play, often chooses to elaborate "the *distinctive* Plutarchan touches."

1420 Perret, Marion. "Shakespeare's Use of Messengers in *Antony and Cleopatra*." *Drama Survey*, 5 (1966–67), 67–72.

Investigates the importance of messengers in *Ant.* They link the worlds of Rome and Egypt; "create an impression of time's passage"; call attention, by their abundance or scarcity, to the degree of power wielded by their masters; and, by the treatment they receive, illuminate the heights and depths of character in Antony (calm control when he hears of Fulvia's death, but jealous anger when he sees Thidias kissing Cleopatra's hand) and Cleopatra (femininity as well as an unwillingness to accept unpleasant facts).

1421 Piper, H. W. "Shakespeare's *Antony and Cleopatra*, V.ii.279–281." *Expl*, 26, no. 1 (1967), no. 10.

Suggests that Cleopatra's robe and crown are Christian symbols for "the immortality gained through the suffering and the blood of Christ," translated into terms of the pagan world. In a similar way, her comment that "the juice of Egypt's Grape" will no longer "moist this lip" is derived from a comment of Christ's at the Last Supper.

1422 Quinones, Ricardo J. *The Changes of Cain: Violence and the Lost Brother in Cain and Abel Literature*. Princeton: Princeton U. P., 1991. viii + 284 pp.

Introduces the conflict of Octavius and Antony in *Ant.* as an example of the Cain–Abel story. Octavius, the Cain figure, is admirably suited for rule, but his power must be purchased by the sacrifice of "the other, the mysterious brother, who here represents vital qualities and energies." In some versions of the Cain–Abel story, the sacrificed brother is "brought back into a greater fullness of being." This does not happen in *Ant.*, in which instead there is a constriction of being.

1423 Quinney, Laura. "Enter a Messenger." *William Shakespeare's "Antony and Cleopatra."* Ed. Harold Bloom. (Modern Critical Interpretations.) New York: Chelsea House, 1988, pp. 151–67.

Examines several characters in *Ant.*, especially the protagonists, to reveal how language affirms itself in the absence of its subject's "empirical authority." Cleopatra's sense of theatricalism, of self-dramatization, isolates her throughout from political or imperial power and gives her language this "alterity that makes it at once distant and free." Antony, however, gains verbal power only as his worldly authority slips away. His isolation is dramatized not only in his changed relationship to language, but in "his changed relationship to the play's messengers and messenger-figures," who occupy a "liminal position," exemplifying "the quasi-human, but impersonal and anonymous traits of the alterity of language—its generosity, intimacy, and distance."

1424 Ray, Robert H. "The 'Ribaudred Nagge' of *Antony and Cleopatra*, III.x.10: A Suggested Emendation." *ELN*, 14 (1976–77), 21–25.

Proposes to emend "ribaudred nag" (*Ant.*, III.x.10) to "ribaud red nag." This phrase, uttered by Scarus as a description of Cleopatra in her desertion of Antony, makes sense in light of Scarus's mention of the "tokened pestilence" in the previous line. The image of redness is one Sh often associates with plague; and in the following line, Scarus curses Cleopatra with "leprosy," thus providing a white disease to contrast with the red one he has just described.

1425 Reynolds, Peter. "The Divided Self: The Public and Private Loves of Antony and Cleopatra." *Critical Essays on "Antony and Cleopatra."* Eds. Linda Cookson and Bryan Loughrey. (Longman Literature Guides.) Harlow, Essex: Longman, 1990, pp. 73–82.

Discusses the conflict between the private lives and public images of four main characters: Pompey, Octavius, Antony, and Cleopatra. The lovers are of primary importance: Cleopatra must repair Antony's heroic image after his botched suicide by comparing him to a Colossus. She stages her own suicide to preserve their myth.

1426 Rhodes, Ernest L. "Cleopatra's 'Monument' and the Gallery in Fludd's *Theatrum Orbi*." *RenP*, 1971 (1972), 41–48.

Maintains that "a gallery with a penthouse, a bay window-like structure similar to the one shown above the double doors" in Robert Fludd's stage-illustration *Theatrum Orbi*, "was used in the original production of *Ant.* to represent the 'monument' in which the Queen locks herself (IV.xv) and is later tricked and captured (V.ii)." The movements of the actors in these two scenes, traced by reference to the First Folio and Plutarch, support this hypothesis.

1427 Rice, Julian C. "The Allegorical Dolabella." *CLAJ* 13 (1970), 402–7.

Argues that Sh makes Dolabella in *Ant.* into an incarnation of his name: "beautiful grief." In V.ii, he expresses "empathetic grief" at Cleopatra's vision of Antony and then reveals that Caesar intends to lead her in triumph. Caesar's last words in the play mention Dolabella, as if, despite the triumph of passionless rationality, "the human capacity for feeling and nobility" still exists.

1428 Rice, Julian Carl. "Renaissance Perspectives on *Antony and Cleopatra*: A Study of Themes, Sources, and Elizabethan Skepticism." Ph.D. dissertation, University of California, Los Angeles, 1968. *DA*, 29 (1968–69), 1877-A-1878-A.

Contends that not all members of the original audience for *Ant.* would have condemned the sexual passion of Antony and Cleopatra. Identifies strains of "religious skepticism and sexual naturalism" in the Renaissance and explains their background in Lucretius and Ovid. Discusses these influences in "Marlowe's translation of Ovid's *Amores* and *Hero and Leander*, and Shakespeare's sonnets," as well as *Ven.* and *Luc.* Analyzes *Ant.* as a mature dramatic treatment of the skepticism and naturalism implicit in his own earlier poetry. One chapter is devoted to the hunt motif in works like the *Bacchae* of Euripides, the plays of Seneca, and *JC*, *Ham.*, and *Ant.* Trapped, as in the hunt, man is viewed as having little or no free will in Sh's tragedy, and hence his dignity resides in "his capacity for passion." This idea can be related to Renaissance anti-Stoicism, which grows out of Epicurean doctrine, and is relevant to considerations of Roman plays by Sh and others. *Ant.* also features Sh's tragic adaptation of Pyrrhonism: Antony's "agonizing self-doubts" are universalized to explore the question of man's identity. Finally, the play's structure builds sympathy for Antony, Cleopatra, and "Egypt," while increasing the audience's detachment from Octavius and "Rome."

1429 Riemer, A. P. *A Reading of Shakespeare's "Antony and Cleopatra."* Sydney: Sydney U. P., 1968. 119 pp.

Chapter 1 discusses the play's background and suggests that North's Plutarch "liberated Sh from the mass of moralistic traditions which had formed around the protagonists" and enabled him to present them as complex and ambiguous. Chapter 2 is a close reading of the play and emphasizes its unique dialectical manner. The first scene, for example, has Philo presenting one view of Antony while Cleopatra presents the opposite view: It is a "microcosmic image of the whole play." Chapter 3 reviews the conflicting critical opinions about *Ant.* and concludes that Sh has removed from the play "all those metaphysical and even moral considerations [that] tragedies (and other versions of this story) possess, and he has, instead, made these tragic possibilities parts of the play's dialectic." The process of the protagonists' relationship on a human level, that is, the state of flux they experience, "provides the central vision of the play."

1430 Riemer, Seth Daniel. *National Biases in French and English Drama.* (Garland Studies in Comparative Literature.) New York: Garland, 1990. 172 pp.

Emphasizes, in a comparison of *Ant.* with Pierre Corneille's *Cinna*, the former play's insistence on affirming the public standards of morality from which its characters are deviating even as they are in the process of violating those standards. Analyzes Antony, Cleopatra, Octavius, Lepidus, and Enobarbus to show that Sh keeps the principle of virtue intact even when he is pointing out the bankruptcy or perversion of good intentions in specific situations. Revision of item 1431.

1431 Riemer, Seth Daniel. "National Biases in French and English Drama." Ph.D. dissertation, Cornell University, 1985. *DAI*, 46 (1985–86), 2686-A.

Distinguishes between the English and French theatrical traditions by noting that the intellectual and moral attitudes of the former exhibit "a propensity for integration," while those of the latter tend toward "a dynamic of conflict." The first section includes a comparison of Pierre Corneille's *Cinna* and *Ant.* Revised as item 1430.

1432 Rinehart, Keith. "Shakespeare's Cleopatra and England's Elizabeth." *SQ*, 23 (1972), 81–86.

Maintains that Sh may have used Queen Elizabeth as a model for Cleopatra in *Ant.* Even though much of Cleopatra's character "has specific warrant from Plutarch," many details were "equally true of Elizabeth," including skill with languages, rough treatment of subordinates, and a taste for gorgeous apparel. Sh's audience "was sufficiently acquainted with Elizabeth's court" and her demeanor "to appreciate many aspects of Cleopatra's behavior." To be politic, Sh avoided making the resemblances too close, but the outline of Elizabeth is there. In one scene (III.iii) the English queen is clearly the model. According to an account given by Sir James Melville, who in 1564 was sent from Mary, Queen of Scots, as ambassador to England, Elizabeth showed an almost obsessive interest in Mary's appearance. Just as Cleopatra does with the Messenger from Rome, Elizabeth went to great lengths to extract from Melville comparisons with Mary that were flattering to herself. Although the political situations of the two queens are manifestly different, they are close to each other in temperament.

1433 Robertson, Patricia R. "'This Herculean Roman': Shakespeare's Antony and the Hercules Myth." *PAPA*, 10 (1984), 65–75.

Assesses the importance of the Hercules myth in *Ant.*, noting that Sh derived his knowledge of this myth from both classical and Renaissance sources. The play's references to the myth help to focus attention on Antony's Herculean choice between honor and love. Like Hercules, Antony has great physical strength, deep personal insecurity (especially with women), a tendency toward quixotic behavior, courtesy, gentleness, and a need "to expiate his wrongs." Antony's paradoxical, excessive tragic heroism is better understood if the allusions to his mythic forebear are explicated.

1434 Roerecke, Edith M. "Baroque Aspects of *Antony and Cleopatra*." *Essays on Shakespeare*. Ed. Gordon Ross Smith. University Park, Pennsylvania: Pennsylvania State U. P., 1965, pp. 182–95.

Argues that the extravagant theatricality of *Ant.*—its "mass, energy, spectacle and paradox"—show that it is wholly baroque in style; and the magnificent passion, which seems to assert itself so confidently, and compel our approval, reveals it as baroque in theme.

1435 Ronan, Clifford J. "*Caesar's Revenge* and the Roman Thoughts in *Antony and Cleopatra*." *ShakS*, 19 (1987), 171–82.

Supports the view that the anonymous *Caesar's Revenge* (printed 1606) predated and provided some material for *Ant.* Sh's language is very close to that of *Caesar's Revenge* in references to the unpeopling of Egypt; "the royal tears of a victorious Triumvir over his dead rival; the concept of imperialism as legalized land piracy; and the way Egyptian mirth contrasts with busy, sober Roman thought."

1436 Rose, Paul Lawrence. "The Politics of *Antony and Cleopatra*." *SQ*, 20 (1969), 379–89.

Argues that the political impact of *Ant.* needs to be clarified for a modern audience. Sh's audience would recognize the political attitudes of Caesar, Cleopatra, and Antony as representative of "conflicting sixteenth-century views on kingship." Like most of the Tudor monarchs, Caesar is rational, calculating, and pragmatic—politically the ideal ruler. He engages in war to pursue certain policy goals, and he delegates important responsibilities to his subordinates. Like Bloody Mary, Cleopatra is a hereditary despot: She uses her power to satisfy her romantic whims. Antony's actions serve to increase the honor of his name. He fights to display his prowess and allows little opportunity for his lieutenants to acquire glory. Antony and Cleopatra are alike in that both have "an emotional view of the purpose of power." In *Ant.*, Sh draws a complex picture of the conflict between reason and impulse. It is clear that impulse will always fail if it tries to compete with reason in the alien world of politics. But Sh's play goes deeper than that to explore and represent, without resolving, this conflict in human nature that is the dynamic of history.

1437 Ross, Gordon N. "Enobarbus on Horses: *Antony and Cleopatra*, III.vii.7–9." *SQ*, 31 (1980), 386–87.

Glosses Enobarbus's comment as meaning that if horses and mares serve together in battle, the horses will mount the mares and thus fail to carry out their intended function. The adverb "merely," describing the activity of the horses, would have been pronounced as "marely," giving reinforcement to the sense of their distraction. Sh's imagery may have been suggested by Plutarch's statement about the influence of Plato's "horse of the mind," or concupiscence, on Antony.

1438   Rossky, William. "*Antony and Cleopatra*, I.ii.79: Enobarbus's 'Mistake.'"
       SQ, 35 (1984), 324–25.

Agrees with Gordon P. Jones (item 1336) that the Folio stage direction for Cleopatra's entrance just before Enobarbus remarks, "Hush, here comes Antony" [I.ii.81], is not an error, but offers a different explanation from Jones's: Enobarbus is not deceived because Antony often dresses in Cleopatra's clothes; rather, his remark is ironic, recognizing Antony's "unmanly subservience."

1439   Rothschild, Herbert B. Jr. "The Oblique Encounter: Shakespeare's
       Confrontation of Plutarch with Special Reference to *Antony and
       Cleopatra*." *ELR*, 6 (1976), 404–29.

Contends that, beginning with *Ant.*, Sh incorporated the relationship—or contest—between historiographer and dramatist as a critical element in the conflicts of his plays. In *Ant.* he did not simply develop the tensions implicit in Plutarch and alter emphases, as he had done in *JC*; rather, he included the historian's mode of perception as part of his dramatic design and demonstrated his independence as a dramatist by revealing the limitations of the historical way of thinking. An example can be seen in the presentation of the opening scene, in which Philo and Demetrius comment on the love affair, viewing it with a Roman, or historical, consciousness that attempts to impose a moral interpretation like Plutarch's. As a challenge to this view, Sh presents events that it cannot contain or account for. Cleopatra, for Sh, has a life of her own; she is not present merely to help us understand Antony's life, as Plutarch would have it. Antony himself is pulled in different directions and strives to remain whole. He is denied comprehension of what is happening; maintaining his integrity in the here and now will not allow him the historian's perspective. Caesar has that perspective, and it is of some value: It provides a businesslike interpretation against which the poetic truth of *Ant.* can be measured. It is, however, incapable of giving final shape to the wondrous events of the play. Although Sh's drama is true to history, it refuses to be confined to history's truth.

1440   Royle, Nicholas. "Some Thoughts on *Antony and Cleopatra* by
       Moonlight." *Telepathy and Literature: Essays on the Reading Mind*. Ed.
       Nicholas Royle. Oxford: Blackwell, 1990, pp. 142–79.

Muses over the conscious and subconscious links among love, death, life, and passion that exist between the title characters. The moon is one of the primary symbols in the play and represents emotionality, the progression of events, and the movement of time. The dialogue is rife with reference to death, literal and sexual. References to poison and serpents underscore the telepathic nature of the lovers. Sh creates characters who blur the distinction between life and death. They are psychically symbiotic; for each, life without the other is impossible.

1441   Rozett, Martha Tuck. "The Comic Structures of Tragic Endings: The
       Suicide Scenes in *Romeo and Juliet* and *Antony and Cleopatra*." *SQ*, 36
       (1985), 152–64.

Calls attention to the drawn-out process of the suicides of the protagonists in *Ant.*, during which, in his adaptation of North's Plutarch, Sh lays stress on a number of comic or potentially comic elements. Speculates that Sh might have been thinking of *Rom.* and its double suicide when he was composing *Ant.*; this time, he decided to exhibit a pair of lovers whose comic potential resides in their unconventional natures and who enjoy a sense of triumph even in their tragedy.

1442   Sahel, Pierre. "Some Versions of Coup d'État, Rebellion and Revolution."
       ShS, 44 (1992), 25–32.

Begins by discussing the potential coup d'état proposed by Menas to Pompey in II.vii of *Ant.*

1443 Saner, Reginald. "*Antony and Cleopatra*: How Pompey's Honor Struck a Contemporary." *SQ*, 20 (1969), 117–20.

Shows how *Bloudy Murther*, an anonymous pamphlet of 1614, contrasts the villainous behavior of servants who had recently murdered their master as he slept with the honorable restraint exercised by Pompey in refusing to allow Menas to cut the throats of Caesar and Antony aboard his galley. Because of his obvious ignorance of Roman history and because he echoes certain phrases from Sh's dialogue, the pamphlet's author was recalling *Ant.*, not Plutarch. The pamphlet preserves an instance of a London playgoer passing off knowledge gained in the theater as Roman history.

1444 Schulman, Norma M. "A 'Motive for Metaphor': Shakespeare's *Antony and Cleopatra*." *HUSL*, 4 (1976), 154–74.

Maintains that, in *Ant.*, Cleopatra's creative imagination refuses to conform to the facts of external reality; she insists, rather, on continually reshaping this reality to suit her autonomous vision. Her intransigence in the face of circumstance can be seen in her treatment of messengers, her consideration of many possible unrealities before favoring a particular fantasy, and her delight in fluidity. In using the world as raw material for the fancy to refashion, Cleopatra is acting out "the process of metaphor." Antony, although he sometimes makes figurative statements of some power, is finally subject to the dominion of fact, as his reception of messengers and his statements about the crocodile witness. When he does use his imagination, he tends, in contrast to Cleopatra, to negate reality rather than transform it metaphorically.

1445 Schwartz, Elias. "The Idea of the Person and Shakespearian Tragedy." *SQ*, 16 (1965), 39–47.

Maintains that Sh's tragic characters are distinguished by the Christian idea of the person; that is, they are "unique selves which transcend their individual natures, worlds in themselves, capable of knowledge and love, infinitely precious images of God." Applies this idea to *Ant.*, [that] "is about human love and human persons, and the supreme good in such a context is the personal realization that the lovers achieve in bestowing their all on each other." Antony and Cleopatra, along with other Shakespearean tragic figures, have a claim on our attention based on our perception of them as persons: We feel their destruction "to be not only pitiful and terrible, but a waste of the most precious substance in our experience."

1446 Schwartz, Elias. "The Shackling of Accidents: *Antony and Cleopatra*." *CE*, 23 (1962), 550–58.

Regards *Ant.* as embodying a new form, perhaps more of "a secular mystery play" than a tragedy, created by Sh to register the triumph of heterosexual human love over self-love and rationality. Traces Antony's movement from Roman preoccupation with power and reason to acceptance of the instinctual dream–world in which he and Cleopatra live for each other. Cleopatra's approach to death validates this world by imaginatively blurring the distinction between mortality and immortality. *Ant.* allows flesh and spirit to meet in "a harmonious and mystical union." Revised as chapter 7 of item 0939.

1447 Schwartz, Murray M. "Shakespeare through Contemporary Psychoanalysis." *HUSL*, 5 (1977), 182–98.

Discovers in most of Sh's tragedies a degradation of the feminine that coincides with the violation of "ceremonial order" by men. In *Ant.*, however, there is an attempt on Antony's part to accommodate both "masculine hardness" and "feminine fluidity." The "interpenetration of opposites" in this play proclaims a new and larger vision.

1448 Seng, Peter J. "Shakespearean Hymn-Parody?" *RN*, 18 (1965), 4–6.

Argues that the song in *Ant.* (II.vii.112–117) "Come, thou monarch of the vine," may be a parody of a Pentecost hymn, *Veni sancte spiritus*. The meter and rhyme scheme of the hymn exactly duplicate those of the song, and the ominous atmosphere in which the song occurs would make a parody appropriate.

1449 Sen Gupta, S. C. "Shakespeare and His Sources." *Essays on Shakespeare*. Ed. Bhabatosh Chatterjee. Bombay: Orient Longmans, 1965, pp. 31–54.

Argues, by citing a number of plays, that Sh transforms his sources to make them more improbable, more fabulous. Notes that these transformations may be best observed where he follows a source most closely. Cites several examples from *Ant.*, including the speech of Enobarbus describing Cleopatra sailing down the Cydnus to meet Antony (II.ii); the two brief scenes in which Cleopatra discusses with a Messenger the appearance of Octavia (II.v, III.iii); and Cleopatra's flight from the sea battle (III.x).

1450 Shapiro, Michael. "Boying her Greatness: Shakespeare's Use of Coterie Drama in *Antony and Cleopatra*." *MLR*, 77 (1982), 1–15.

Attempts to demonstrate the influence of "the long tradition of children's plays about Cleopatra and other pathetic heroines" on *Ant.* Observes that Sh had access to this tradition through "relatively pure" neoclassical plays like Samuel Daniel's *Cleopatra* and through children's plays of the London private theater like Marlowe's and Nashe's *Dido, Queen of Carthage*. From the neoclassical drama, Sh assimilated a more sympathetic attitude toward Cleopatra than he found in Plutarch's *Lives*, his chief source; in particular, he learned to heighten sympathy for his heroine by dramatizing the death of her servants. The private theater taught him that "this essentially sympathetic treatment of a pathetic heroine could be successfully and harmoniously combined with irony, perhaps even with a self-conscious playfulness." Of course, Sh surpassed his models both in "evoking sympathy for Cleopatra" and in presenting a sophisticated theatrical self-consciousness.

1451 Shapiro, Stephen A. "The Varying Shore of the World: Ambivalence in *Antony and Cleopatra*." *MLQ*, 27 (1966), 18–32.

Explains that *Ant.* is best interpreted as "meaning in motion." Instead of reading the play as a moral condemnation of lust or as a rhapsody to love, we need to see it as rapidly shifting the audience's perspectives throughout, "sustaining a controlled ambivalence." Sh never allows us to grasp a static, single meaning from character, situation, or imagery. For example, Antony's "insistence that messengers are sacred, no matter what their message (I.ii.94–96), is reversed by Cleopatra's behavior and Antony's own treatment of Thidias." Paradox is pervasive: There is a strong element of hate in the love of the protagonists, as can be seen in Cleopatra's sometimes sadistic attempts to master Antony; and in Cleopatra's death "mortality and immortality become indistinct."

1452 Shapiro, Susan C. "Paradox, Analogy, and the Imitation of an Action in Shakespearean Tragedy." Ph.D. dissertation, Bryn Mawr College, 1969. *DAI*, 30 (1969–70), 5420-A.

Suggests that at the center of each of four major tragedies lies a paradoxical action. Discusses how a key paradox underlies structure, characterization, and diction in each play. For *Ant.*, the paradox is "to 'o'er flow the measure' and create by destroying." Part revised as item 1453.

1453 Shapiro, Susan C. "To 'O'erflow the Measure': The Paradox of the Nile in *Antony and Cleopatra*." *Studies in the Humanities* (Indiana U. of Pennsylvania), 4, No. 2 (1975), 36–42.

Maintains that Antony, Cleopatra, and Caesar all embody the central paradox upon which *Ant.* is constructed: "The destruction [that] comes about through excess necessarily precedes and is an integral part of the process of creation." The Nile, agent of both destruction and fertility, is the emblem of this paradox. The lovers, through their excess, destroy themselves and each other; yet in death they undergo an imaginative rebirth. Caesar's overflowing ambition, which may be said to destroy everyone in his way, also restores world order. Revision of part of item 1452.

1454 Shaw, John. "Cleopatra and Seleucus." *REL*, 7, no. 4 (1966), 79–86.

Discusses new evidence for the view that Cleopatra is play-acting to deceive Caesar during the scene in which she is "betrayed" by Seleucus (*Ant.*, V.ii.133–179). In order to guide the audience, Sh gives her response to Seleucus's perfidy "an artificiality of sentiment, language, and rhythm" that stands out when compared to the more natural and direct quality of those passages elsewhere in the play in which she expresses true anger.

1455 Shaw, John. "'In Every Corner of the Stage': *Antony and Cleopatra*, IV.iii." *ShakS*, 7 (1974), 227–32.

Investigates the staging of *Ant.*, IV.iii, in which soldiers stand "in every corner of the Stage," after which the music of hautboys signals, according to one of the soldiers, that the god Hercules is now leaving Antony. This arrangement is clearly inspired by the emblematic stage of the Middle Ages, with the platform representing the entire earth. Sh thus abstracts his stage to stress that the imminent demise of Antony means the departure of strength and greatness from the world. Two changes he makes in Plutarch reinforce this idea: Instead of Bacchus, Sh has Hercules (a Renaissance exemplar of heroic virtue) desert Antony, and instead of departing for Caesar's camp (as does Plutarch's Bacchus), Hercules is leaving earth altogether. In this scene, Sh's imagination seems to have been working with Revelation 7, in which four angels are described as standing on the four corners of the earth holding the four winds, and a fifth angel ascends bearing the seal of God. Another influence may have been an illustration of this passage by Albrecht Dürer.

1456 Shaw-Smith, R. "*Antony and Cleopatra*, II.ii.204." *SQ*, 24 (1973), 92–93.

Cites the famous description of Cleopatra in which Enobarbus claims that she outdid "that Venus where we see / The fancy out-work nature" [*Ant.*, II.ii.210–211]. The picture of Venus referred to is probably like one described by Captain John Saris as hanging in his cabin during a voyage to Japan (1611–1613), in which Venus was "verye lasiviously sett out."

1457 Siemon, James Edward. "'The Strong Necessity of Time': Dilemma in *Antony and Cleopatra*." *English Studies*, 54 (1973), 316–25.

Classifies Antony as "the hero of a tragedy" rather than "a tragic hero." That is, he exemplifies a conception of tragic dilemma that is experienced by the audience in response to the vision of the world enacted by *Ant*. Caesar, according to this vision, is the irresistible force of history and yet an ass; Cleopatra is a goddess who triumphs "over time and mortality," though also a whore. Subject to both of these forces, and incongruously responsive to each of them in turn, Antony has little power to affect outcomes by any choice he makes. The pervasive motif of Antony's failing to be himself reinforces the impression of his passiveness. He has little responsibility for the events in which he becomes enmeshed, nor does he understand them. The play, carefully designed to exploit this kind of role, is a new achievement for English Renaissance tragedy: It fully embodies a world "irremediably flawed, and yet one whose like we shall never see again."

1458 Simard, Rodney. "Source and *Antony and Cleopatra*: Shakespeare's Adaptation of Plutarch's Octavia." *SJW*, 122 (1986), 65–74.

Regards the character of Octavia as the key to what Sh was doing when he adapted Plutarchan materials to compose *Ant*. Since the play is intended to chronicle a Roman/Egyptian love affair, it is appropriate that Octavia's character was much diminished by Sh. Though reduced in dramatic stature, Sh's Octavia does perform three important functions: "to intensify the lovers' relationship and to contrast what love and marriage can be on a grand scale; to underscore Cleopatra's nobility and Antony's impetuosity; and, perhaps most important, to subtly expose the ruthlessness of Caesar's political ambition." Changes Sh made in the other characters accord with these purposes: Cleopatra, instead of being a "royal whore," is a complex woman who finally becomes a noble lover; much of Antony's dubious past is omitted by Sh to transform him into a "noble and honorable man torn between love and duty"; and Caesar is no longer Plutarch's "goodly prince," but a "Machiavellian tyrant."

1459 Simmons, J. L. "The Comic Pattern and Vision in *Antony and Cleopatra*." *ELH*, 36 (1969), 493–510.

Contends that "the pattern and thematic concerns of *Antony and Cleopatra* . . . support the many facets of Shakespearean comedy." Egypt fosters the "pure holiday spirit"; the conflict of Rome and Egypt generates critical comedy; and, most important, the protagonists' tragedy is based on the comedy of love. In *Ant.*, the audience's comic expectations are fulfilled by Cleopatra, who arranges her death to reconcile the contradictions that have precluded the fulfillment of her life in the world. Her dream of Antony and his capacity to unite contraries is a triumph for her as a creative artist, a consummation of the lovers' aspiration. Antony seeks to realize such a universal vision but is torn apart by his attempt to maintain absolute commitments to both honor and love. Revision of part of item 0981. Revised as chapter 4 of item 0980.

1460 Singh, Jyotsna. "Renaissance Antitheatricality, Antifeminism, and Shakespeare's *Antony and Cleopatra*." *RenD*, N. S. 20 (1989), 99–121.

Cites antitheatrical tracts from 16th- and 17th-c. England to establish that the opponents of plays objected to the threat dramatic performances posed to a stable sense of gender identity. In particular, the influence on the audience (viewed primarily as male) of acting roles was associated with the irrational attractions of the senses, and hence of women, who subvert masculinity. This fear of the mutable, histrionic female personality is incorporated by Sh in the Roman attitude toward Cleopatra in *Ant.*, but the Roman view is dialectically opposed by Cleopatra's improvisatory playfulness. Through Cleopatra, Sh makes a positive connection between theatricality and femininity. Revision of part of item 0983.

1460a Smith, Gerald A. "'Good Brother' in *King Lear* and *Antony and Cleopatra*." *SQ*, 25 (1974), 28.

Notes that when "good-brother" appears as a hyphenated word in Elizabethan English, "it means brother-in-law." Suggests that "Good brother," as used by Octavius Caesar when he requests Antony to leave the drunken revels aboard Pompey's galley (*Ant.*, II.vii.118–120), carries this meaning.

1461 Smith, Gordon Ross. "The Melting of Authority in *Antony and Cleopatra*." *CollL*, 1, no. 1 (1974), 1–18.

Analyzes the political behavior of several characters in *Ant.*, frequently focusing on the changes Sh made in Plutarch. Octavius's rigorous self-control is attended with so many faults that we may question whether it is a merit: He ruthlessly pursues power, even to the extent that he willingly sells his sister to entrap and destroy Antony. Sh further debases Caesar's morality by having him offer provocations to Antony that cause the latter to return to Rome; in Plutarch, the provocations take place after Octavia has returned to Rome and Antony to Egypt. Antony, by contrast, has been improved from Plutarch. For example, his cruel confiscation of other people's property is transformed into private riot and excess. He is more irresponsible, but less vicious. Like Octavius, Cleopatra is lowered by Sh. An example can be seen when she disowns Antony (to Thidias) before his death, whereas in Plutarch this takes place after he dies. Her character is "capricious, despotic, amoral, licentious." Finally, Pompey, an aspiring leader, is hindered by idealism and imprudence; and Lepidus is merely foolish.

1462 Smith, J. Oates. "The Alchemy of *Antony and Cleopatra*." *BuR*, 12, no. 1 (1964), 37–50.

Points out that *Ant.*, unlike most tragedies, does not dispel illusion. Antony cannot free himself from his obsession with Cleopatra, nor can Cleopatra free herself from the earthbound, comic elements of her own mortality. For both protagonists, and for the Romans, "faith in appearances supersedes faith in reality." Antony, continually changing, declines various opportunities to see reality and dies with a restored commitment to love. The play's poetic language enables it to translate mundane reality into "something rich and strange."

1463 Smith, Maria Selma A. "Last Farewells in *Antony and Cleopatra*." *Signal* (Paraíba), 1 (1978), 65–77.

Considers the love of Antony and Cleopatra in terms of their last farewells to each other. When Antony dies in IV.xv, his last thoughts are of his former glory as a soldier. Cleopatra's words at this death display an egoism almost equal to his. When Cleopatra dies in V.ii, her last words show she is thinking only of Antony. There are similarities between the farewells: (1) They both achieve nobility, (2) they both seek "to escape public humiliation," and (3) they both see their death as a sort of marriage.

1464 Smith, Michael Harold. "Men of Ice: The Dehumanizing Effects of Ambition in Shakespeare's *Antony and Cleopatra*." *Signal* (Paraíba), 1 (1978), 117–26.

Describes how the vice of ambition, pervasive in the Roman world, suppresses the potential warmth of Octavius Caesar. Mentions the effects of ambition on Lepidus, Pompey, Agrippa, and Menas.

1465 Smith, Sheila M. "'This great Solemnity': A Study of the Presentation of Death in *Antony and Cleopatra*." *ES*, 45 (1964), 163–76.

Argues that the three main conflicts in *Ant.*—between Caesar and Antony, between Antony and Cleopatra, and within Antony himself—"all look to their resolution in death." As death is presented throughout the play (for example, in the cases of Enobarbus and Eros), it is a calm, peaceful event. Furthermore, with Antony and Cleopatra, it is also "splendid and dignified." Sh does not ignore the disasters that befall the lovers; rather, he shows that they are controlled and transcended by the "solemn representation of death" in the final scenes. For this reason, *Ant.* is the most optimistic of Sh's tragedies.

1466 Smith, Stella T. "Imagery of Union, Division, and Disintegration in *Antony and Cleopatra*." *Claflin College Review*, 1, no. 2 (1977), 15–28.

Maintains that *Ant.* is marked by a pattern of union, division, disintegration, and reunion that shows Antony at first turned toward Egypt and away from his responsibilities as soldier and ruler, then pulled away from the bonds of Egypt toward Rome, then bound to Rome and Caesar, then attracted back to Egypt for reunion with Cleopatra. The imagery that supports this pattern also develops a contrast between Antony's present ruin and his former glory.

1467 Snyder, Susan. "Patterns of Motion in *Antony and Cleopatra*." *ShS*, 33 (1980), 113–22.

Holds that the essence of drama is action, and that Sh, as a dramatic poet, relies to an extent that has not been adequately recognized on patterns of "kinetically linked images." In *Ant.*, "images of solid fixity or speedy directness" set in contrast to "images of flux and of motion unpurposive but beautiful" are used to express "the opposition of Rome and Egypt and, through their incompatibility, the nature of

Antony's tragic dilemma." The opposition is made particularly clear in the play's first scene and during the feast aboard Pompey's galley (II.vii).

1468   Spevack, Marvin, ed. Michael Steppat and Marga Munkelt, associate eds. *Antony and Cleopatra.* (New Variorum Edition of Shakespeare.) New York: Modern Language Association, 1990. xxxvii + 885 pp.

The appendix includes a section on "Sources, Influences, and Analogues." Reprints the following "Major Sources and Influences," each preceded by a sampling of critical opinion about its relationship to the play: *The Life of Marcus Antonius* and *The Comparison of Demetrius with Antonius* from Plutarch's *Lives of the Noble Grecians and Romans* (1579); Simon Goulart's *Life of Octavius Caesar Augustus* (1602); Appian's *The Romanes Warres* (1578); the Countess of Pembroke's translation of Robert Garnier's *Antonius* (1592); and Samuel Daniel's *The Tragedie of Cleopatra* (1594) and *A Letter from Octavia to Marcus Antonius* (1599). Another section of the appendix, "Other Sources, Influences, and Analogues," is subdivided into four parts, each of which samples scholarship without reprinting any of the sources commented on. The first part, "Dramatic Versions," discusses works by Giraldo Cinthio, Etienne Jodelle, Hans Sachs, Samuel Branden, and the anonymous author of *Caesar's Revenge*. The second part, "Classical Works," considers possible borrowings from Virgil, Ovid, Horace, Apuleius, Heliodorus, Homer, Seneca, Juvenal, Plato, Boethius, Lucretius, Longinus, Pliny, Dio Cassius, Appian, Cicero, and Lucan. The third part focuses on "Medieval Works and the Bible" and the fourth on "Renaissance Works." The "Criticism" section of the appendix is subdivided into the following parts: "General Assessments," "Genre," "Themes and Significance," "Technique," "Characters," and "*Antony and Cleopatra* on the Stage." As in the sections on sources, the criticism summarized and quoted ranges in date from the 17th c. to recent decades. Concludes with a substantial bibliography.

1469   Song, Nina. "Death in the Tragedies of William Shakespeare and Eugene O'Neill." D.A. dissertation, State University of New York at Albany, 1988. *DAI*, 49 (1988–89), 1139-A.

Concentrates on three themes in Sh: the wish for death, the idea of love as death, and "the emphasis on life-in-death." In *Ant.* and other Shakespearean tragedies, "the characters die to achieve perception and nobility." For Sh, tragedy is "a tale of suffering ending in death, followed by the Christian concept of regeneration."

1470   Sprengnether, Madelon. "The Boy Actor and Femininity in *Antony and Cleopatra.*" *Shakespeare's Personality*. Eds. Norman N. Holland, Sidney Homan, and Bernard J. Paris. Berkeley: U. of California P., 1989, pp. 191–205.

Views the use of the boy actor by Sh for female roles as "the locus of conflicting attitudes" about gender. In *Ant.*, by making explicit in the text that Cleopatra is played by a male, Sh diminishes the threat of female otherness, especially its perceived tendency toward infidelity. The boy actor thus makes possible "an ease and range of imaginative expression in the end of the play" unusual even for Sh; and, paradoxically, permits the playwright "to represent female sexuality with less rigidity and greater tolerance" than in other plays.

1471   Stallings, Alden Page. "'When I Perceive Your Grace': Patterns of Vision in Shakespeare." Ph.D. dissertation, University of Virginia, 1980. *DAI*, 41 (1980–81), 4048-A-4049-A.

Finds three essential patterns of vision in Renaissance literature. Hierarchically arranged, these are (1) an enslavement to false sense impressions; (2) the intermediate stage of recognizing an underlying reality, linked to a "genuine resolve to transform one's moral condition"; and (3) a direct apprehension of God. Applies this hierarchy to four of Sh's plays, including *Ant.*, whose protagonist is torn between "the claims of love and the world" and who finally achieves in his defeat "a luminous apprehension of love's transcendent value."

1472 Steppat, Michael. "Shakespeare's Response to Dramatic Tradition in *Antony and Cleopatra*." *Shakespeare: Text, Language, Criticism: Essays in Honour of Marvin Spevack*. Eds. Bernhard Fabian and Kurt Tetzeli Von Rosador. Hildesheim: Olms-Weidmann, 1987, pp. 254–79.

Maintains that in creating *Ant.* Sh was indebted to the Countess of Pembroke's translation of Robert Garnier's *Marc Antoine*, especially for its "extended dramatic focus on Antony's inner suffering and soul-searching," and to Samuel Daniel's *Tragedie of Cleopatra*, especially for its depiction of the process by which Cleopatra's pleasure-seeking develops into a noble, proud, and triumphant love. Sh was stimulated by both Pembroke and Daniel in structure, characterization, and verbal detail.

1473 Stirling, Brents. "Cleopatra's Scene with Seleucus: Plutarch, Daniel, and Shakespeare." *SQ*, 15, no. 2 (1964), 299–311. Reprint. *Shakespeare 400: Essays by American Scholars on the Anniversary of the Poet's Birth*. Ed. James G. McManaway. New York: Holt, Rinehart and Winston, 1964, pp. 299–311.

Argues that the episode in which Seleucus exposes Cleopatra (*Ant.*, V.ii.123–196) has been misread: There is no clear indication in Plutarch that Cleopatra and Seleucus conspire to deceive Caesar, and Sh exploits the uncertainties deriving from this. Sh goes beyond Plutarch in keeping Cleopatra's behavior ambiguous. Plutarch explains her motive (to pretend that she is eager to live and thus put Caesar off his guard) at the same moment he describes her behavior (her excuses for concealing part of her fortune). Daniel, in his *Tragedie of Cleopatra*, presents the queen's inventory as the last in a series of impostures. Sh, by contrast, keeps the audience guessing as to the intention behind the imposture, or indeed as to whether it is an imposture at all. Only after Caesar has departed does Cleopatra admit to playing for time. This scene should be read as the climactic episode in a series that begins in IV.xiv. Each episode "presents the old Cleopatra of whim and contradiction" and ends with a strong resolution on her part that moves her closer to tragic stature. Among the changes Sh made in Plutarch is Cleopatra's interpretation of her betrayal by Seleucus as a *de casibus* tragedy.

1474 Stockholder, Kay. *Dream Works: Lovers and Families in Shakespeare's Plays*. Toronto: U. of Toronto P., 1987. x + 281 pp.

Proposes to investigate several of Sh's plays in terms of the conflict between the playwright's "sense of the necessity for romantic love integrated into a harmonious family to transform a world contaminated by hatred and violence, and his sense of the depth and intransigence of the dark forces embedded in the family." Addresses these concerns with an interpretative method "based on dream theory, which assumes the protagonist to be the dreamer of the work in which he or she appears." Includes a discussion of *Tro.*, in which Troilus as protagonist experiences a world in which all relationships are "drained of significance." The two key issues of love and authority are so intermingled in language and action that "the debasement of one necessarily implies the debasement of the other." Devotes chapter 8 to *Ant.*, whose protagonist, Antony, has at least a partial awareness of the chief conflicts that "structure its action." Considers Cleopatra as "the protagonist–dreamer" for the last act in order to summarize "the configurations Antony has generated" in her, then subsumes her structuring of the last act in Antony's dream. Part is a revision of item 1474a.

1474a Stockholder, Kay. "Worlds in Dream and Drama: A Psychoanalytic Theory of Literary Representation." *DR*, 62 (1982–83), 374–96.

Proposes "a mode of literary analysis [that] involves assuming the protagonist to be the dreamer of the work in which he or she appears." Refers to several of Sh's works. In a work like *Ant.*, with two protagonists almost equally compelling, we should follow the dreaming of both. Finally, however, we gain greater immediacy from taking

Antony as the protagonist; and it is generally true that one figure "will function most strongly to organize the configurations of a work." Revised as part of item 1474.

1475 Stroup, Thomas B. "The Structure of *Antony and Cleopatra*." *SQ*, 15, no. 2 (1964), 289–98. Reprint. *Shakespeare 400: Essays by American Scholars on the Anniversary of the Poet's Birth.* Ed. James G. McManaway. New York: Holt, Rinehart and Winston, 1964, pp. 289–98.

Points out that the structure of *Ant.* was heavily influenced by the morality play. If this is recognized, we can perceive unity in its Gothic diversity. Among the morality conventions visible in *Ant.* are the ideas of the world as a stage, life as a play, man as a microcosm, the psychomachia, the pageant of humanity, and the representation of all ranks and degrees of society.

1476 Sugnet, Charles J. "Exaltation at the Close: A Model for Shakespearean Tragedy." *MLQ*, 38 (1977), 323–35.

Rejects the presence of a beneficent world order in Shakespearean tragedy. The hero, at the end, reaffirms his initial image but does so without the faith that he used to have in external authority. In *Ant.*, Cleopatra's detailed stage management of her own death is an example of this defiance of fate.

1477 Summers, Joseph H. *Dreams of Love and Power: On Shakespeare's Plays.* Oxford: Clarendon P., 1984. xi + 161 pp.

Chapter 6, "A Definition of Love: *Antony and Cleopatra*," insists that the audience of this play is virtually compelled to revise its judgments of the lovers in response to the profound changes they undergo at various points in the action. Analyzes the ways in which Sh follows these changes in the context of "the tradition and the realities of the heterosexual wars." Provides evidence that in the early phases of the play, Antony is indeed "dazed and subservient" and Cleopatra "termagant, emasculating, and potentially faithless." Cleopatra's dalliance with Thidias in (III.xiii), suggesting that she may very well abandon Antony for the protection of Caesar, should be taken at face value—as a response to Antony's pathetically foolish behavior at that moment. Later in the same scene, when Antony returns in a fury, "conscious of who he is and was and insisting on a relation between the two," her love and loyalty are rekindled. Notes that Octavius's oracular speech about "The time of universal peace" (V.vi), possibly influenced by a passage in North's Plutarch, coupled with the soliloquy of Enobarbus that mentions the alliance of Caesar and Herod of Jewry in the same scene, gives the audience a perspective from which it can view "the ensuing action with more detachment—as something inevitable and, however painful in part, at some distance from both our ordinary and our most sacred experience." Antony exhibits a significant transformation as he prepares to die (IV.xiv): He first recognizes that he can no longer perform his role in time and that he must end his present visible shape in order to reassert his past invisible one. As he lies dying, he utters no word of reproach for Cleopatra's "fatal deception"; instead, he reveals himself as a heroic lover in his concern for Cleopatra's welfare. Cleopatra's death scene, which differs from Plutarch's account in its "transcendent image of beauty and nobility," rehabilitates her "as queen and goddess of love."

1478 Swander, Homer. "Menas and the Editors: A Folio Script Unscripted." *SQ*, 36 (1985), 165–87.

Analyzes the passages in the Folio text of *Ant.* in which Menas appears and sets these beside what modern editors have done with the character. Argues that the play's theatricality has been damaged by the editors' transformations.

1479 Takei, Naoe. "Dreams as Metaphysical Visions—A Study of Shakespeare's Major Tragedies." *ShStud*, 8 (1969–70), 18–47.

Discusses the "inner visions" that seem to overwhelm the protagonists in Sh's major tragedies. Tragedy often results from the clash between the visions and their material surroundings. Cites, among other examples, *Ant.*, in which the romantic dream of the lovers is set off against the hard reality of the Roman world. Antony and Cleopatra have a magnificent vision of themselves as "the gods of love, for which hubris they have to be punished."

1480   Tanaka, Susumu. "*Antony and Cleopatra*: A General Approach." *Studies in English Literature and Language* (Kyushu U.), 21 (1971), 15–42.

Discovers the theme of *Ant.* in the conflict between "the two opposites of Rome and Egypt, Caesar and Antony," politics and love. Antony is the slave of love from the beginning; Caesar is totally absorbed in politics. Cleopatra "possesses both Caesar's powers of intrigue and Antony's passion in one person." She never wavers between politics and love until the very end. By dramatizing Plutarch, Sh, in this play, commits himself to history, to the physical (as distinguished from the metaphysical) world of the earlier tragedies. The conflict between "the timeless lust for power" and "the timeless passion of love" is both tragedy and history when Sh expresses it "in terms of the macrocosm."

1481   Tanner, Jeri. "The Power of Names in Shakespeare's *Antony and Cleopatra*." *Names*, 35 (1987), 164–74.

Focuses on the names of the protagonists. Discusses especially Antony's *praenomen* (forename), Mark, which relates him to the god of war, and indicates the ways in which it is used to indicate his fall and rise in his own estimation and in the opinion of others. The name Antony and the variety of epithets that other characters apply to him also register his disgrace as well as his subsequent rehabilitation. The name Cleopatra can be found in at least three Greek myths and was one of the favorites among Ptolemaic queens and princesses. The Egyptian queen is likewise referred to by many epithets, covering a range of attitudes "from disdain to idolatry." *Ant.* uses names "to characterize, to reveal cultural attitudes, prejudices, and superstitions, to show conflict or concord, to enhance themes, and to add humorous and serious dimensions" to the dramatic narrative.

1482   Tanner, John S. "'Here is my space': The Private Mode in Donne's Poetry and Shakespeare's *Antony and Cleopatra*." *Iowa State Journal of Research*, 60, no. 3 (1986), 417–30.

Speculates that there might have been "mutual knowledge between Donne and Shakespeare of each other's work," though such a connection remains conjectural. Maintains that among Sh's plays *Ant.* is "uniquely comparable" to Donne's poetry because of its pervasive use of paradox, its dialectical perspective on love as "a conflict between a private and public world," and its inscription of the tension between private and public in "the language of empire." Sh's view of his lovers, in its mixture of skepticism and belief, is similar to the posture of Donne's speakers of dramatic soliloquies. Through the play's action and its multivocality, Sh is able to offer a greater challenge than does Donne to the notion that "love's private sphere" is self-sufficient.

1483   Tanner, Tony. "*Antony and Cleopatra*: Boundaries and Excess." *HUSL*, 15 (1987), 78–104.

Maintains that the contrast between Rome and Egypt in *Ant.* is conveyed by a fundamental opposition of measure ("control, constraint, containment") and excess ("overflow"). Antony and Cleopatra constantly seek to transcend the limitations of language, to "mark out new lexical space to define their situation." Cites three instances of Antony's exceeding Roman "boundaries" through his "bounty." Notes that what the Romans define as "waste" is "feast" to the Egyptians. Sh radically complicates Plutarch's simple ethical judgment of Antony, concentrating on his protagonist's relationship to Hercules, the model for wondrously excessive heroism. Finally, Cleopatra's "Oriental" imagination, her "self-validating poetry," triumphs over the "alphabetic" pragmatism of Caesar. Writing against "the recorded inexorable movements of history," Sh forces a revaluation of what was lost in Caesar's victory.

1484   Taylor, Marion A. "'Not Know Me Yet?'" *BSUF*, 5, no. 3 (1964), 63–66.

Discusses Cleopatra in *Ant*. as a "representative of all women, high or low, who ever fell in love with a married man." This explains her lies, her sensuality, her jealousy, her lack of control, and her final nobility of behavior.

1484a   Thomas, Helen A. "'Breeze' and 'Bees,' 'Sailes' and 'Tailes': *A&C*, III.x.17–22." *CEA*, 37, no. 1 (1974), 23–24.

Quotes Scarus's outraged comment that Cleopatra, during the sea battle, "like a cow in June, / Hoists sail and flies" [III.x.11–15]. Defends the First Folio reading of *sail* by citing a passage from *Gammer Gurton's Needle* that refers to a cow's *tail* as her *sail*.

1485   Thomas, Mary Olive. "Cleopatra and the 'Mortal Wretch.'" *SJ*, 99 (1963), 174–83.

Points out that in *Ant*. Cleopatra's death from the bites of two asps, one of which is at her breast, rather than a single one on her arm, as in Plutarch, is especially appropriate for Sh's dramatic purposes. Cleopatra's use of two asps indicates her impatience to be with Antony, her imperiousness (she commands the asps to strike), her pleasure in frustrating Caesar's aims, and her maternal tenderness. Sh was interested in showing here that "human love, paradoxically compounded of *concupiscentia* and *caritas*, is the source both of life and its value," and he chose for this purpose the symbol of the serpent at the breast.

1486   Thomas, Mary Olive. "The Opening Scenes of *Antony and Cleopatra*." *SAQ*, 11 (1972), 565–72.

Provides a corrective to those critics who have emphasized the extent to which the opening scenes of *Ant*. depart from Plutarch's *Life* of Antony. If Sh's ways with his source were better understood, these early scenes would be seen as more heavily indebted to Plutarch than has been acknowledged. Philo and Demetrius reflect the censorious attitude toward Antony of Plutarch himself; the processional entry in the first scene may owe something to Plutarch's later description of Cleopatra on her barge; the treatment of messengers is an amalgam of passages about messengers from other points in the *Life*; and the fortune-telling scene (I.ii), though Sh's invention, owes something to Plutarch's references to Charmian and Iras dying with Cleopatra.

1487   Thomas, Shirley Forbes. "'One that's dead is quick': A Study of Counterfeit Death and Resurrection in Relation to Plot, Character, and Theme in the Plays of William Shakespeare." Ph.D. dissertation, University of Arkansas, 1988. *DAI*, 49 (1988–89), 1812-A.

Studies Sh's use of "supposed, feigned, and staged death and resurrection in relation to overall structure, characterization, and theme." Chapter 4 includes a discussion of *Ant*.

1488   Thomson, Leslie. "*Antony and Cleopatra*, Act 4, Scene 16: 'A Heavy Sight.'" *ShS*, 41 (1989), 77–90.

Proposes a staging of *Ant*., IV.xvi, in which the dying Antony is heaved aloft to Cleopatra in her monument. Suggests that this action should be presented as difficult and cumbersome to emblematize the ambiguity of Antony's love for Cleopatra: It is both tragic and comic; it elevates him and it weighs him down. It is romantically admirable but militarily reprehensible.

1489 Thorssen, Marilyn. "Varieties of Amorous Experience: Homosexual and Heterosexual Relationships in Marlowe and Shakespeare." *Human Sexuality in the Middle Ages and Renaissance*. (U. of Pittsburgh Publications on the Middle Ages and Renaissance 4.) Ed. Douglas Radcliffe-Umstead. Pittsburgh: Center for Medieval and Renaissance Studies, U. of Pittsburgh, 1978, pp. 135–52.

Cites *Ant.* to show that for Sh, as for Marlowe, the perfect love relationship is virtually impossible to attain in the real world. The Roman Antony exemplifies "those Apollonian virtues typically associated with the masculine principle, while the Egyptian Cleopatra embodies the sensuality and the fertility typically associated with the feminine principle." Their union, like that of the two lovers in *PhT*, is possible only in death.

1490 Tobin, J. J. M. "Apuleius and *Antony and Cleopatra* Once More." *SN*, 51 (1979), 225–28.

Observes that three passages from *The Golden Asse* by Apuleius shed light on Antony's line "Alack, our terrene moon / Is now eclips'd" (III.xiii.156–157). "Terrene" is used in Apuleius to suggest the indignation of Venus at being neglected, the luxuriousness of Cupid, and the subservience of male followers of Isis. Since all of these descriptions fit Antony in his relationship with Cleopatra, it is likely that he is referring to himself as "terrene moon," not to Cleopatra. Revised as part of chapter 6 of item 1052.

1491 Toliver, Harold. *Transported Styles in Shakespeare and Milton*. University Park: Pennsylvania State U. P., 1989. vii + 276 pp.

Chapter 4, "Cleopatra's Phantom Marriage," focuses on *Ant.*'s participation in the elegiac mode through its numerous retrospections and recollections. The play is remarkable for "its prolonged partings and recasting." By removing Antony early, Sh gives the play's "off-going a twofold rhythm"—first Antony's departure, "recollected by Cleopatra, and then hers, as eventually recollected by Plutarch and Shakespeare."

1492 Tolmie, L. W. "'Least cause' / 'All cause': Roman Infinite Variety: An Essay on *Antony and Cleopatra*." *SoRA*, 11 (1978), 113–31.

Observes that the Roman world of the play is marked by relativism, easy movement from one phase of experience to another, with no awareness of contradictions in behavior. The Romans measure life in materialist terms, but they make absolute verbal claims to commitment and stability. Antony is the most egregious exemplar of these traits, which help him to avoid self-examination. He is always Roman in his view of Cleopatra. His retreat at Actium, for example, has nothing to do with Cleopatra; it is a characteristically Roman vacillation. Enobarbus, in the absolute terms (for example, "infinite variety") he uses to describe Cleopatra, and Caesar, with his materialist assessment of Cleopatra's value, are also typically Roman. Cleopatra, by contrast, "always relates absolutely to the person before her."

1493 Tomlinson, Maggie. "Making Defect Perfection." *Viewpoints on Shakespeare*. Ed. Brian McFarlane. Melbourne: Longman Chesire, 1990, pp. 180–91.

Discovers the essence of *Ant.* in its fluid complexity, indicated through both imagery and characterization. Concentrates on the richness of the Egyptian scenes, remarking briefly on "the radical instability and corruption" of Roman power politics. Antony seems at times to be simply reacting to experience, though he does remain constant in his love for Cleopatra. Cleopatra, though finally defeated by death, adapts so brilliantly to change that she often seems to anticipate it.

1494   Traci, Philip J. *The Love Play of "Antony and Cleopatra": A Critical Study of Shakespeare's Play.* The Hague: Mouton, 1970. 171 pp.

Chapter 1 sketches the difficulties critics have had in coming to terms with *Ant.*: They feel constrained to qualify their admiration in a vague way, or they neglect the text, or they overemphasize the Elizabethan background. Chapter 2 argues that the two protagonists cannot be viewed exclusively as characters or as symbols, but should be considered as both. Furthermore, symbol and character exist only as parts of the unified play. Chapter 3 critiques the tendency to isolate one cluster of images and derive a dominant tone from those images. This can be illustrated by analyzing the one-sided readings critics have given to the play's "world" or "colossal" imagery. Comic and bawdy elements need to be recognized, as they "function in the interactions of tone, characterization, imagery, structure, and theme." Chapter 4 reviews critical commentaries on love in Sh and especially in *Ant.*, and concludes that *Ant.* is "as full and deep a treatment of the nature and paradoxes of love as any ever written," distinctive in the extent to which it successfully dramatizes its theme. Chapter 5 describes the movement of the play as "a sustained metaphor of the love-act," including love in its broadest sense. Chapter 6 sums up the findings of previous chapters and adds that *Ant.* is chiefly "about the nature of the many varieties of love and creation." Revision of item 1495.

1495   Traci, Philip Joseph. "The Love Play of *Antony and Cleopatra*: A Critical Study." Ph.D. dissertation, Duke University, 1965. *DA*, 26 (1965–66), 1030.

Contends that *Ant.* dramatizes many of the paradoxical questions of love and that the movement of the play "imitates the love-act." Revised as item 1494.

1495a   Traversi, Derek. "The Imaginative and the Real in *Antony and Cleopatra*." *The Literary Imagination: Studies in Dante, Chaucer, and Shakespeare.* Newark: U. of Delaware P., 1982, pp. 197–227.

Argues that the theme of *Ant.* is "the relationship of the imaginatively *creative* to the obstinately *real*."

1496   Tucker, Kenneth. "Psychetypes and Shakespeare's *Antony and Cleopatra*." *Journal of Evolutionary Psychology*, 5 (1984), 176–81.

Avers that Carl Jung's theory of psychetypes is a valuable tool for literary analysis. According to Jung, each person experiences the world primarily in terms of one of four functions: thinking, feeling, sensation, and intuition. This theory can aid in an understanding of conflict between fictional personalities. In *Ant.*, the lovers are feeling types, whose involvement with each other is crucial to their existence. Octavius, their antagonist, is a thinking type. Enobarbus, an almost obsessive rationalist, is also a thinker. This is one of the earliest literary works to treat "differences between psychological types as the modern world has come to know them"; it suggests that tragedy is to some extent the result of our inability to view things from the perspective of another type.

1497   Uéno, Yoshiko Y. "*Antony and Cleopatra*: The Last Phase of Shakespearean Tragedy." *ShStud*, 6 (1967–68), 1–36.

Argues that in *Ant.* the tragic impact "is weaker than that of the preceding four great tragedies." One reason is that the play is "less metaphysically and more politically and historically conceived," which creates a distance between audience and hero. The heroine, who is essentially comic, is "on a plane above the hero."

1498   Uphaus, Robert W. "Shakespearean Tragedy and the Intimations of Romance." *CentR*, 22 (1978), 299–318.

Explains that *Ant.*, though a tragedy, exhibits strong intimations of Sh's romances. By presenting concepts of eternal time to which all are subject, by insisting on the importance of private values, and by undermining the impetus toward an absolute close of the action, Sh makes available an alternative to the Roman tragic view of events—the view of Alexandrian romance.

1499   Vaish, Y. V. "*Antony and Cleopatra.*" *The Modern Review*, 120, no. 3 (1967), 183–90.

Finds that the chief aim of Sh in *Ant.* is to show that a man of high political rank should not indulge in the weaknesses of common men. By doing this, the great man encourages disregard for order among the people.

1500   Van Woensel, Maurice J. F. "Revelry and Carousing in Shakespeare's *Antony and Cleopatra.*" *Signal* (Paraíba), 1 (1978), 78–100.

Locates and analyzes terms related to revelry and carousing in *Ant.* Divides the semantic field occupied by such terms into (1) social drinking, (2) vulgar drinking, (3) ritual drinking, (4) revelry, and (5) poor drinking. Relates revelry and carousing to the opposition between Rome and Egypt and to the notion that the play is "almost a joyful tragedy," closer to the Rome of Horace than to that of Virgil. Examines II.vii, the drinking scene on board Pompey's galley, which lays bare the unprincipled nature of the Roman world that is about to destroy Antony and Cleopatra.

1501   Verma, Rajiva. "Winners and Losers: A Study of *Macbeth* and *Antony and Cleopatra.*" *MLR*, 81 (1986), 838–52.

Regards these two plays as polar opposites in the ways their protagonists deal with time, in the ideal of manhood they present, and in their images of feeding and motherhood. All of this amounts to a "radical psychological opposition between the two plays," a contrast "between trust and mistrust" that is reflected in both plays' style and structure.

1502   Vincent, Barbara C. "Shakespeare's *Antony and Cleopatra* and the Rise of Comedy." *ELR*, 12 (1982), 53–86.

Reads *Ant.* as a contest between the genres of tragedy and comedy: Sh dramatizes, in the opposition of Rome and Egypt, a progress from the classical heroic tradition to "Renaissance Christianized romance literature." The contrast between the traditions begins in the first scene, with the Roman attempt of Philo and Demetrius to trivialize the Egyptian comedy of the lovers and thus to subordinate it to the heroic, martial ideal. Enobarbus is interesting as an intermediary: He resists the heroic ethos that Rome would impose on Antony. Although appreciative of the attractions of Egypt, he takes a kind of detached, Ovidian stance toward matters amatory; and, in his death, recognizing fully the claims of love, he speaks in the manner of an incipient Petrarchan. Classical decorum insists on the superiority of the tragic–heroic mode to the comic–romantic mode, as well as their separation. By the end of *Ant.*, the comic mode has achieved dominance, but not by excluding the tragic. Antony is both the great soldier and the heroic lover; and Cleopatra, in the final scene, encompasses the tragic in the heroic vision of love that she enacts. Revision of part of item 1503.

1503   Vincent, Barbara Cutts. "The Anatomy of Antony: A Study of the Literary Worlds in Shakespeare's *Antony and Cleopatra.*" Ph.D. dissertation, Rutgers University, 1978. *DAI*, 39 (1978–79), 904-A-905-A.

Depicts *Ant.* as a climactic work in Sh's development, a work that juxtaposes tragedy and comedy in Antony's experiences of the worlds of Rome and Egypt, respectively. The Roman literary world, under whose influence the play begins, maintains a strict separation of genres, with tragedy the dominant mode. Antony first attempts to exclude Roman business from Egypt and later tries to suppress comic propensities when he is in Rome. However, the genres cannot be kept apart: The Roman world of tragedy turns into an anti-comic movement within a larger comic structure. Comedy, which under the Roman dispensation should be kept separate from and subordinate to tragedy, overflows its boundaries and appears in new and elevated forms (romantic epic and intimations of Christianity) toward the end of the play. Much expanded and now dominant, the comic vision, like Antony at his death, has become at once heavier and more exalted. Part revised as item 1502.

1504 Waddington, Raymond B. "*Antony and Cleopatra*: 'What Venus did with Mars.'" *ShakS*, 2 (1966), 210–27.

Maintains that in *Ant.* the protagonists are associated primarily with "the mythical and cosmological affair of Mars and Venus, rather than the unrelated characters of Hercules and Isis—though the latter are subsumed typologically by Mars and Venus." As a hero made effeminate by his love for a woman, Antony is connected with Hercules. But Sh is far more interested in him as a Mars figure disarmed by Venus. This relationship of the warrior god and the queen of love was interpreted in the Renaissance as a *concordia discors* that creates harmony. By describing and alluding to the disarming of Mars during the first three acts, Sh prepares for the suicides of Antony and Cleopatra, which emphasize the productive reconciliation of Roman sternness and Egyptian love.

1505 Walter, J. H. "Four Notes on *Antony and Cleopatra*." *N&Q*, 16 (1969), 137–39.

1. Suggests that "Her infinite variety" (II.ii.246) may be derived from Plutarch's essay "Isis and Osiris" in his *Moralia*, in which Isis is described as having "an infinite number of names."
2. Holds that "shards" (III.ii.20) means "patches of dung" between which the beetle rolls a ball containing its seed. Plutarch's "Isis and Osiris" contains a description of this.
3. Notes that Cleopatra's answer to Antony's accusation of cold-heartedness (III.xiii.159–168) is "skillfully evocative" of the divine threats preceding the plagues that befall the Egyptians in the book of Exodus.
4. Argues that Cleopatra's statement that she is dominated by a "poor passion" (IV.xv.73–75) refers to what Elizabethan medical authorities would call "*hysterica passio*, or the Mother."

1506 Waterhouse, Ruth. "Shakespeare's *Antony and Cleopatra* I.iv.12–13 and 44–47." *Expl*, 33 (1974–75), item 17.

Observes that in the first passage Lepidus speaks of Antony in a confused image that equates light with evil and goodness with darkness. It is indicative of Antony's greatness—and tragedy—that Lepidus should use "a cosmic simile in reverse about him, and so stress that polarity of qualities which hovers about him." In the second passage, Caesar's expression of contempt for the fickleness of the masses is conveyed through the simile of "the flag iris floating on the moving water," an image most people would find beautiful. The simile reveals Caesar's "blindness to natural beauty" and to anything that might be of worth in the relationship of the two lovers.

1507 Watson, Gilbert. "The Death of Cleopatra." *N&Q*, 25 (1978), 409–14.

Surveys ancient accounts of Cleopatra's death, pointing out that none of them speaks of more than one asp, while in *Ant.* Sh uses at least two. Sh also departs from Plutarch and other classical writers in having Cleopatra bitten on the breast. The only ancient writer to mention the breast story is Paul of Aegina, who lived in the 7th c. Sh may have drawn on Paul as well as on Galen's *Theriake,* which mentions the asp as a means of mercifully executing condemned men by having them bitten on the chest. Other Renaissance dramatists who treat Cleopatra's death refer to asp bites on either the breast or the arm, but Sh is the only one who has both. Conclusion is item 1508.

1508 Watson, Gilbert. "The Death of Cleopatra." *N&Q*, 26 (1979), 133–37.

Attempts to establish what type of serpent Cleopatra's asp was. Notes that Galen mentions three kinds of asps, of which the chersea is the likeliest candidate. The chersea is described by Philumenus, a physician slightly later than Galen, as being five or more feet long and as having venom that kills within two or three hours and does not cause excessive pain. In terms of modern herpetology, the chersea can be identified with the hooded cobra, whose religious significance for the Egyptians is emphasized by recent experts. Plutarch says more than any other ancient writer about Cleopatra's death, giving two accounts that assign responsibility to the asp and one where poison is the cause. He is careful to state, however, that no one knows the truth of the matter. Concludes the argument of item 1507.

1509 Watts, Cedric. "*Antony and Cleopatra*: The Moral and the Ontological." *Critical Essays on "Antony and Cleopatra."* Eds. Linda Cookson and Bryan Loughrey. (Longman Literature Guides.) Harlow, Essex: Longman, 1990, pp. 61–71.

Contends that the thematic center of *Ant.* lies in the conflict between the moral and sensual worlds, a conflict Sh presents in terms of cultures, characters, locations, and philosophies. According to history, the moral wins: Virtuous Rome triumphs over hedonistic Egypt. However, Sh's display of the lovers' magnificence and their abundant energy enables them to steal the victory from Octavius.

1510 Weil, Herbert S. Jr. "On Expectation and Surprise: Shakespeare's Construction of Character." *ShS*, 34 (1981), 39–50.

Discusses "the beholder's share" in Sh's creation of character, in particular the audience's shared expectations and the ways in which those expectations are violated. Finds that in *Ant.*, for example, the cynical Roman view of the lovers expressed at the beginning is continually shown to be inadequate. Another source of surprise is the notion accepted by Antony and Cleopatra that their own characters are "essences that can be gained and lost."

1511 Weis, René J. A. "*Antony and Cleopatra*: The Challenge of Fiction." *English* (London), 32 (1983), 1–14.

Analyzes Cleopatra's exchange with Dolabella about her dream vision of Antony (*Ant.*, V.ii.92–99), Enobarbus's description of Cleopatra on the Cydnus (II.ii.200–236), Cleopatra's horrified anticipation of how her relationship with Antony will be travestied in Rome (V.ii.216–221), and Cleopatra's dying moments, with the asp at her breast (V.ii.308–313), to support the position that Sh is drawing on Neoplatonism like that of Sidney in *An Apology for Poetry* to plead, through his heroine, "for an imagination that can create independently of nature and beyond its scope." Cleopatra presents a paradoxical but effective integration of "the Platonic sanction against art, and its intrinsic prestige, in her defence of a truly creative imagination." She is unique among Sh's tragic figures in that she "consciously tries to transcend the limits of fiction through affirming, in the face of death, valid, but ultimately impossible, alternate fictions." One the one hand, the tragedy demands a death, but on the other "a love-death becomes a part" of the lovers' relationship in the fiction, "leaving us with a sense of wonder and fulfillment."

1512 Weis, René J. A. "*Caesar's Revenge*: A Neglected Elizabethan Source of *Antony and Cleopatra*." *SJH*, 1983, 178–86.

Maintains that the anonymous play *Caesar's Revenge* (c. 1592) was a stylistic and thematic source for *Ant.* Like *Ant.*, *Caesar's Revenge* is concerned with Antony's emasculation, caused by doting on Cleopatra. Most striking is the analogy between Antony and Cleopatra and Dido and Aeneas, which occurs in both plays.

1513 Weitz, Morris. "Literature Without Philosophy: *Antony and Cleopatra*." *ShS*, 28 (1975), 29–36.

Discovers that in *Ant.* there are a number of philosophical themes, but no philosophical thesis, or universal claim. A largely unexplored theme is that "of generation and corruption, of coming into being and passing away," and it is so prominent that *Ant.* may be called Sh's "pre-Socratic" tragedy. The imagery of transformations, of one thing bringing forth its opposite, is found throughout the play. In many instances (for example, the description of the Nile's destructive flooding that begets fertility), the transformations of this type are natural and can be anticipated. In other cases, there is no natural connection between what is transformed and its opposite. Transformations of this sort apply primarily to Antony and Cleopatra, leading to the conclusion that one theme of the play is a love that destroys in its own perfection. This theme, however, is not universal; it holds only for "such a mutual pair."

1514   Wertime, Richard Allen. "Excellent Falsehood: Theme and Characterization in *Antony and Cleopatra*." Ph.D. dissertation, University of Pennsylvania, 1969. *DAI*, 30 (1969–70), 2983-A.

Employs close analysis to discover what Sh is trying to accomplish in *Ant*. Focuses on explication of Antony's character. In revealing that character, the most important verbal and structural pattern is the relationship between Egypt and Rome. Though each place provides "a different perspective on the nature of truth and reality," their relationship is dynamic: At the end of the play, there is an intermingling of their respective values. Antony can be seen as a man who plays a series of roles, taking each one seriously, but failing to coordinate them successfully. He falls short of tragic grandeur, but his expansive effort to attain it makes him a great man nevertheless. The downfall of Enobarbus exemplifies the limitations of rationalism in judging a man like Antony, whose involvement with Cleopatra is not simply a holiday but a way of life. Cleopatra finally comes closest to embodying "the relationship of art to nature": She approaches truth "through the self-conscious exploration of make-believe."

1515   Whallon, William. *Problem and Spectacle: Studies in the Oresteia*. Heidelberg: Winter, 1980. 159 pp.

Chapter 4 includes a discussion of how the use of males to play female roles led Sh, especially in *Ant.*, and Aeschylus in the *Oresteia* to depictions of algolagnia. The *Oresteia* and *Ant*. have the following features in common: "(1) a problem of female impersonation, (2) a solution in sadomasochism, (3) the suckling of a serpent (4) by a woman who is somehow a serpent herself."

1516   Whitaker, Juanita Josephine. "*Antony and Cleopatra*: Cosmological Contexts and the Dramatic Achievement." Ph.D. dissertation, University of Wisconsin, 1972. *DAI*, 33 (1972–73), 736-A.

Maintains that *Ant*. "is patterned after the microcosm–macrocosm analogy, and that within the structure of that analogy the play moves from finitude to infinity." The play's transcendence is successful "because of the rich element of theatrics, histrionics, and illusion, especially as culminated in Cleopatra's death scene."

1517   Whitney, Cynthia Kolb. "The War in *Antony and Cleopatra*." *L&P*, 13 (1963), 63–66.

Presents the conflicts in *Ant*. as between opposing elements within individual characters. Especially is this true for Antony, whose "Roman honor" is at war with his "Egyptian sexuality." Rome is associated with fathers and harshness while Egypt is clearly a realm of women's influence. The tragedy results from ill timing, and this can be seen as related to every man's separation from the nurturing mother by his own life span.

1518   Wigginton, Waller B. "'One way like a Gorgon': An Explication of *Antony and Cleopatra*, 2.5.116–117." *PLL*, 16 (1980), 366–375.

Attempts to explain Cleopatra's comment about Antony, "Though he be painted one way like a Gorgon, / The other way's a Mars." The metaphor is that of a perspective painting, which viewed from one side appears to depict one thing, but which viewed from the other side appears to represent its opposite. The point is to understand the identity of the two contraries, "to look for the general class beneath the opposed subclass." To identify Cleopatra's Gorgon with the conventional classical figure, a frightening female monster who transforms all she looks upon into stone, is to obscure Cleopatra's perception of Antony. Instead, the Gorgon in this passage should be seen as a masculine figure, representing bestial fury in an otherwise noble man. Cleopatra is thus contrasting the dehumanizing aspects of Antony's wrath with its potentially ennobling qualities (associated with Mars). Cites as evidence *The Governor*, in which Elyot modifies a passage from Ovid's *Ars Amatoria* to make a reference to Gorgon illustrate the masculine vice of wrath. The image of Gorgon, rightly interpreted, constitutes an important element in one of the central patterns of *Ant.*: People and things remain the same, though their appearances change.

1519 Williams, George Walton. "*Antony and Cleopatra*, III.xiii.26." *Expl*, 20, no. 9 (1962), item 79.

Supports Alexander Pope's emendation of the First Folio's "gay comparisons" to "gay caparisons" because Sh "invariably uses 'gay' to modify nouns of clothing ... or to suggest brave finery that may be worn."

1520 Williamson, Marilyn. "Antony and Cleopatra in the Late Middle Ages and Early Renaissance." *MichA*, 5 (1972), 145–51.

Surveys different versions of the Antony and Cleopatra story in the Middle Ages and early Renaissance to explain "the state of the tradition [that] helped shape the reception and interpretation" of Plutarch's account when his *Lives* was translated into the vernacular languages in the 16th c. Points out that Antony and Cleopatra are frequently used as *exempla* in Dante, Petrarch, Boccaccio, Lydgate, Gower, and Chaucer, but that the morals of these *exempla* may vary, often in quite contradictory ways, from author to author, within the works of a single author, or even within a single work. Cleopatra, for example, is at times a model of constancy but can also be an egregious instance of lust, greed, and fickleness. Revised as part of item 1524.

1521 Williamson, Marilyn. "The Political Context in *Antony and Cleopatra*." *SQ*, 21 (1970), 241–51.

Contends that Sh modifies Plutarch to shape the political elements in *Ant.* into patterns that guide our interpretation of the narrative, action, and characters. The two principals are characterized as much by their political as by their romantic behavior. Their relations with inferiors define their roles as rulers: For example, Antony's generous treatment of the Messenger who brings bad news (I.ii) establishes the true self from which he is divided at other points in the play, particularly in III.xiii, where he flies into a rage and has Thidias beaten. Sh also relies heavily on the Renaissance notion that a ruler's character is mirrored in the behavior of his people. The scenes in Cleopatra's court show her followers to be sensual and frivolous like their mistress, and the scene aboard Pompey's galley (II.vii) reveals the Romans, except for Caesar, to be "drunken, divided, and careless" like Antony himself. The "wavering loyalties and affections" of the two lovers are paralleled throughout the play by the political actions and attitudes of lesser people. Sh invented the resolve of Menas to desert Pompey for refusing to take advantage of his offer to kill the triumvirs, and this initiates the pattern of betrayal that is most clearly manifested in the various desertions by Antony's followers. Enobarbus, whose character Sh developed from hints in Plutarch, epitomizes the ambivalent state of the follower of a prince divided from himself in a divided world. Cleopatra, also a ruler in a divided world, betrays others and is herself betrayed to complete the pattern established earlier. The relationship between rulers and subjects is used to present a *de casibus* interpretation of the story. Antony, for example, constantly emphasizes the contrast between his former greatness and present weakness. Finally, Sh "greatly expands from Plutarch" the political motive for Cleopatra's suicide. Revised as part of item 1524.

1522 Williamson, Marilyn L. "Did Shakespeare Use Dio's *Roman History?*" *SJH*, 1971, 180–90.

Suggests that Sh might have used Dio Cassius's *Roman History*, originally written in Greek and available in several Latin and vernacular translations (though not in English), as a source for certain elements in *Ant*. Dio's accounts of Agrippa fighting as Octavius Caesar's lieutenant and of Ventidius fighting for Antony seem to lie behind Ventidius's comment on his Parthian victory (III.i. 11–27). In treating the desertion of Antony's most trusted follower, Sh emphasizes that Enobarbus disapproves of the actions of Antony and Cleopatra, that he has a grievance against Cleopatra, and that his action is the culmination of a series of betrayals by Antony's subordinates. None of these things is found in Plutarch; all are present in Dio. Revised as part of item 1524.

1523 Williamson, Marilyn L. "Fortune in *Antony and Cleopatra*." *JEGP*, 67 (1968), 423–29.

Urges the importance of the goddess Fortune in *Ant*. Various forms of the word *fortune* occur more frequently in *Ant*. than in any other Shakespearean play, and there is pervasive use of images associated with Fortune: those related to games of chance, the sea, the winds, and the moon. Though Fortune is to be found in Plutarch's *Lives*, Sh's source for *Ant.*, she is there a beneficent goddess, disposed favorably to Rome. Sh made her "the blind, fickle personification of chance and change." Fortune is "an appropriate figure to preside over *Ant.*, not only because the play involves love and war, two of her special provinces, but also because both of the principals have many qualities in common with her." An interpretation of the play that sees it purely as a tragedy of character will find it less satisfactory than one that views its outcome as being strongly influenced by Fortune. Revised as part of item 1524.

1524 Williamson, Marilyn L. *Infinite Variety: Antony and Cleopatra in Renaissance Drama and Earlier Tradition*. Mystic, Conn.: Lawrence Verry, 1974. viii + 254 pp.

The preface sets forth certain guidelines for the study of individual literary works pertaining to a given traditional subject matter. Essentially, the tradition cannot be allowed to do the work of the critic, who must deal with the individual artistic whole and then consider relationships among works in the tradition. Chapter 1 challenges the notion that all pre-Renaissance versions of the Antony and Cleopatra story condemned the lovers. In fact, there was great variety of treatment in ancient, medieval, and Renaissance accounts.

Chapter 2 analyzes the story as it is found in ancient sources. In several Roman poets, including Virgil, Propertius, and Horace, and in some historians, the focus is on empire, power, and ambition. In other writers, notably Appian and Dio Cassius, the love affair assumes a greater prominence. Plutarch, in his *Life of Marcus Antonius*, puts a great deal of emphasis on his protagonist's domination by women and his emotions and personal relationships. Though not neglecting the public or Roman perspective on Antony's life, Plutarch gives more private details than any other ancient writer. In the Renaissance, Plutarch's version inspired some ten plays, but only two of these (*Ant*. being one) accept the structure of the biography as the basis for drama. The other eight employ the Senecan model, which focuses on the end of an action, in this case the final phase of the power struggle between Caesar and Cleopatra, and Cleopatra's death. *Ant*. is the only Renaissance version that truly assimilates Plutarch's structure, achieving a synthesis of personal and public, love story and power struggle, and the life of Antony and the death of Cleopatra.

Chapter 3 deals with the Antony and Cleopatra story in the late Middle Ages, pointing out that no single medieval version is told for its own sake. Since each account is subordinated to other purposes, authenticity or historicity is of little moment, and more variety is possible. There is great diversity of treatment not only between authors, but among different accounts by the same author. The imperial issue, so important to the ancients, diminishes, and there is more interest in the love relationship (the English writers, for example, all agree that Cleopatra killed herself for love of Antony).

Chapter 4 explains the impact of the recovery of the classical past, through Plutarch's *Lives*, on the story of Antony and Cleopatra as it was told in the Renaissance. Inspired by Plutarch, Renaissance writers recounted the story more frequently and in more detail than ever before, inviting sympathetic involvement in the drama of the lovers. During a sixty-five-year period beginning in the mid-16th c., ten plays on the Continent and in England focused on this subject.

Chapter 5 describes and comments on the eight Renaissance Antony and Cleopatra plays classified as "Senecan." Chapter 6 treats the two "panoramic" Antony and Cleopatra dramas of the Renaissance and discusses *Ant.* in some detail. Sh took up and developed a variety of elements in the subject that his predecessors had used in simpler forms. Egypt and Rome, for example, are not simply conflicting opposites: Each contains elements of the other. Likewise, neither Antony nor Cleopatra is self-sacrificing about the other: Each wants to possess the other and the world too. The world they seek is presided over by Fortune: Its corrupt nature tempts the onlooker to think he can possess it, but it disappoints all would-be masters by relentless change. Caught up in this world, the two protagonists exhibit contradictory and fluctuating attitudes, acting impulsively in crucial situations. Unable to control the literal world, Antony and Cleopatra turn to mastery of themselves and create new worlds of imagination to inhabit: Antony creates an old-fashioned world of spectacular chivalry in which he reigns supreme; and Cleopatra stages her suicide in such a way that her version of the story triumphs, in imagination, over that of Caesar. Yet the triumph of the lovers is a narrow one: Their tragedy is that they cannot master the alien world of flux; they can only impose a glorious imaginative order on the past and the dead. Includes revisions of items 1520, 1521, 1522, 1523, and 1525.

1525   Williamson, Marilyn L. "Patterns of Development in *Antony and Cleopatra*." *TSL*, 14 (1969), 129–39. Reprint. *Cleopatra*. Ed. Harold Bloom. (Major Literary Characters.) New York: Chelsea House, 1990, pp. 108–17.

Argues that the character of Cleopatra progresses through "perceptible stages" that serve to unify her infinite variety. Sh achieves this effect by careful placement, in the earlier part of *Ant.*, of materials in his own devising that anticipate structurally "the later parts of the play where he is following Plutarch closely." In I.iii, Cleopatra sends Alexas to lie about her condition, anticipating the more consequential lie she sends Mardian to tell about her death in IV.xiv; in I.iii, her chiding of Antony for his leaving modulates into a dignified farewell, a sort of rehearsal for her departure from life in V; several early scenes remind us of Cleopatra's temptation (often yielded to) to violate queenly decorum and thus prepare us for the temptation (after Actium) to betray Antony and compound with Caesar to retain her throne. Attention to the motif of hands allows us to follow the stages of Cleopatra's development. Notes that other characters (Antony, Enobarbus) undergo similar development and that the scene on Pompey's barge (II.vii) is "a symbolic analogue to the general action of the play." Revised as part of item 1524.

1526   Willson, Robert F. Jr. "A Note on Symbolic Names in *Macbeth* and *Antony and Cleopatra*." *CEA*, May, 1969, 7.

Suggests that Eros, symbolizing Love, teaches Antony a way of death that fulfills the requirements of both "Roman honor and earthly love."

1527   Willson, Robert F. Jr. "'With News the Time's With Labour': Messenger Scenes and the Ending of *Antony and Cleopatra*." *Midwest Review*, 3 (1978), 71–83.

Points out that involvement with messengers reveals significant character traits in Antony, Cleopatra, and Octavius Caesar. Cleopatra's reaction to and use of messengers discloses her insecurity and her blindness to the political dimension of Antony's life.

Antony uses messengers unwisely, and he is unable to accept and interpret accurately the news they bring. When Caesar hears news, he usually reacts coolly, using reporters and reports for his own ends. Sh also uses messenger scenes to foreshadow the ending of *Ant.*, which can be better understood if it is read as "a messenger scene in which Cleopatra greets Death." Another messenger, the Clown who banters with Cleopatra as she prepares to die, helps to insure the paradoxical, comic-tragic tone of the ending. Revised as chapter 5 of item 1136.

1528   Wolf, William D. "'New Heaven, New Earth': The Escape from Mutability in *Antony and Cleopatra*." *SQ*, 33 (1982), 328–35.

Maintains that though much has been made of the distinctiveness of the worlds of Rome and Egypt, both are subject to "the principle of fluctuation." In Egypt, this is seen in emotional terms: Cleopatra's adopting of various roles to control Antony and Antony's violent swings between love and valor. In Rome, fluctuation takes political forms: the formation and immediate dissolution of alliances and the swift transfer of loyalty by soldiers eager to gain the favor of a more powerful captain. As in other Shakespearean plays, this underlying emphasis on mutability is presented in terms of "the material versus the non-material." At the end, both Antony and Cleopatra perceive themselves as no longer part of the material world against which they have been struggling. Their suicides put them beyond the reach of mutability but leave ambivalent the extent to which they achieve transcendence, which is only hinted at in Cleopatra's visions.

1528a   Worthen, W. B. "The Weight of Antony: Staging 'Character' in *Antony and Cleopatra*." *SEL*, 26 (1986), 195–308.

Notes that a central concern of *Ant.* is "how events are written into narrative, transformed into history, literature, and myth." Investigates the ways in which the "contest between narrative and drama, text and performance, animates the characterization of the play's major roles." During the play, Sh calls attention to the difficulty the actors have in fulfilling the text's demand that they play certain roles. Their struggle to do this, as, for example, in the scene when the dying Antony is heaved aloft into Cleopatra's monument (IV.xv), is one source of the play's fascination.

1529   Yachnin, Paul. "'Courtiers of Beauteous Freedom': *Antony and Cleopatra* in Its Time." *Ren&R*, 15 (1991), 1–20.

Attempts to re-create the Jacobean *Ant.*, to contextualize the play, to reveal the "politicized resonances" of its "language, characterization, and handling of sources." In the play's overall design, the protagonists represent the chivalric, aristocratic, magnificent past, while Caesar is a man of the political, mercantile, pragmatic present. When the triumvirs visit Pompey aboard his galley (II.vi), he delivers a speech (lines 8–23) in which he is cast as the agent of "the heroic past," attempting to revive aristocratic Roman values, and in which his guests are viewed as factors for the utilitarian new order. The play's political subtext appropriates this contrast between Roman present and Roman past to its treatment of the relationship between Jacobean present and Elizabethan past.

1530   Yoshioka, Fumio. "A Passage to 'New Heaven, New Earth': A Study of Identity in *Antony and Cleopatra*." *SELit*, 60, no. 2 (1983), 275–91.

Traces the process by which the hero and heroine of *Ant.* lose their inner selves "through their difficulty in self- and mutual identification." The lovers' identities are caught up in "the mutability that is the natural state of being in this play." For both of them, dualism in time, space, and sexuality is dissolved "by a third factor of ethereal nature and melts down into an obscured framework of triplex structure."

As You Like It

1531 Allen, Michael J. B. "Jaques against the Seven Ages of the Proclan Man." *MLQ*, 42 (1981), 341–46.

Describes at some length the seven ages of man paradigm as presented in Marsilio Ficino's Latin translation of Proclus's commentary on Plato's *First Alcibiades*. In this Neoplatonic progression, man is influenced at each stage of his development by a different planet, ending under Saturn, when he reaches his goal of contemplation, freed from worldly, physical concerns. At the center of man's movement through this sequence is the sun, under whose aegis he acquires the power of discursive reasoning. Up until this point, he has been more or less controlled by the planets; in his subsequent development, he is no longer subject to them. Jaques's version of the seven ages in *AYL* perverts or inverts the chief characteristics of each age. Significantly, it omits the solar middle stage, which in the Neoplatonic progression signals the arrival of what makes man fully human. It also transforms Saturn into a baleful influence and extends his dominion to the last two stages. The Proclan paradigm—which was widely known at Sh's time—is thus a valuable measure of Jaques's divergence from the norm. What Jaques offers is a radically pessimistic view of man, derived from the deterministic philosophy of contemporary astrologers.

1532 Bath, Michael. "Weeping Stags and Melancholy Lovers: The Iconography of *As you Like It*, II, i." *Emblematica*, 1, no. 1 (1986), 13–52.

Investigates the problematic way in which Sh uses the description of the weeping stag in *AYL*. Although this is one of "the most strictly emblematic images" in Sh, it is handled with a skepticism about "the truth value of received iconographic and linguistic conventions" that makes its meaning in this context far from settled. Notes the association of the weeping/stricken stag at a stream with melancholy lovers and traces it back to Ovid's account of Actaeon's metamorphosis into a stag; to writers on natural history like Pliny, Aelian, and Oppian; to commentary of the early church fathers like Augustine on the opening verses of Psalm 41; and to Virgil's "description of the love-sick Dido." Cites emblem books of the Renaissance to show how the image shifted its meaning from a love emblem to a moral emblem and, in the 17th c., to a spiritual emblem. In presenting the image of the stag, the play makes use of many elements from its rich heritage, some of them contradictory. Its concerns with the untrustworthiness of love and the instability of language are thus echoed by its questioning of definite meanings for "received iconographic topoi."

1533 Beckman, Margaret Boerner. "The Figure of Rosalind in *As You Like It*." *SQ*, 29 (1978), 44–51.

Contends that in *AYL* Sh invites us to entertain the notion of "two opposites existing simultaneously, truly contrary and mutually exclusive, but bound together in a creative, if paradoxical, union—like man and wife." Rosalind, most clearly the exemplar of this *concordia discors*, may be related to "the Renaissance prototype of all combinations of male and female, the union of Mars and Venus."

1534 Blythe, David-Everett. "Ox-eyed Phebe." *SQ*, 33 (1982), 101–2.

Maintains that the "bugle eyeballs" (*AYL*, III.v.47) with which Phebe is endowed should be imagined as "large expressive eyes." Explains that "bugle" is derived from the Latin word for ox and that classical poets (Homer and Ovid, for example), as well as others, have a notion of "pretty bovinity," which they express in the description of large eyes.

1535. Bradford, Alan Taylor. "Jaques' Distortion of the Seven–Ages Paradigm." *SQ*, 27 (1976), 171–76.

Cites Ptolemy's account of the seven-ages-of-man scheme: Each of the stages in human life corresponds to one of the planetary spheres. In later accounts, such as that in

As You Like It 411

Raleigh's *History of the World*, the astrological traits assigned to each age are set forth in great detail. In keeping with his bitter nature, Jaques in *AYL* distorts the paradigm to heighten the sense of meaninglessness in human life. He eliminates the fourth age, traditionally the climax of human life under the beneficent influence of the sun, and he allows the melancholy influence of Saturn to dominate the last two ages (instead of just the seventh, as customary).

1536 Burns, Margie. "Odd and Even in *As You Like It*." *Allegorica*, 5, no. 1 (1980), 119–40.

Proposes to explain how, in *AYL*, Sh celebrates "the possibility of harmony and continuity in human relationships." One feature that pulls the play together and thus helps it to image unity is "its multiplicity of classical allusions." References to Ovidian myth throughout elevate the play's style, and "the multiple changes of role and of disguise" are derived from Ovid. Traces ideas of the Golden Age in *AYL* to show how "myth and experience interact." During the play, the myth itself "undergoes Ovidian metamorphoses," finally merging with Christian elements to form a new myth of origin. When Hymen appears to lend the highest sanction to the marriages at the end, "myth becomes reality and classical topoi become sacrament." The rejuvenation of the myth allows Sh to harmonize disparate elements.

1537. Crupi, Charles William. "Pastoral Elements in Plays from the Elizabethan Public Theaters of the 1590's." Ph.D. dissertation, Princeton University, 1967. *DA*, 28 (1968), 3175-A-3176-A.

Argues that the pastoral dramas written for the English public stage during the 1590s employ a variety of pastoralism also seen in Elizabethan prose romance. This "popular pastoralism" is "best defined not by the use of shepherds or a sense of leisure, but by the presence of conventional moral implications in environments explicitly isolated from the world of Fortune," a world that "implies a measure of stoical resignation." Chapter 8 places *AYL* in this context.

1538. Doebler, John. "Orlando: Athlete of Virtue." *SQ*, 26 (1973), 111–17.

Suggests that Orlando in *AYL* is partly patterned on Hercules, who in innumerable Renaissance "emblems, epigrams, and allusions" represents "all that is manly and virtuous." Orlando's encounter with Charles is reminiscent of Hercules' victory over Antaeus, and his rescue of his brother recalls the great hero's slaying of the Nemean Lion. In Orlando can be seen "the conflation of the athlete and the Arcadian, both drawn from the Golden Ages of classical civilization." Revised as chapter 1 of item 0322.

1539 Doran, Madeline. "'Yet am I inland bred.'" *SQ*, 15, no. 2 (1964), 98–114. Reprint. *Shakespeare 400: Essays by American Scholars on the Anniversary of the Poet's Birth*. Ed. James G. McManaway. New York: Holt, Rinehart and Winston, 1964, pp. 98–114.

Explores Sh's conception of civility, originally a Greek and Roman ideal, involving orderly, responsible social behavior, self-control, and respect for others. Provides background on the myth of the Golden Age (as found in Ovid and Virgil), which lay behind the Renaissance suspicions about overcivilization; and on various other myths (like those of Prometheus, Amphion, and Orpheus) that furnished the Renaissance with an account of man's praiseworthy advances from earlier states of barbarism. Focuses on Sh's complex use of these attitudes toward civilization and primitivism in *AYL*, though other plays are mentioned.

1540 Elam, Keir. "'As they did in the Golden World': Romantic Rapture and Semantic Rupture in *As You Like It*." *Shakespeare: La nostalgia dell'essere*. Ed. Alessandro Serpieri. Parma: Pratiche Editrice, 1985, pp. 39–56. Revision. *CRCL*, 18 (1991), 217–32.

Distinguishes between pastoral and romantic literary modes, noting that the former is an exercise in nostalgia while the latter "narrates a world of fantastic happenings, governed by the autonomous logic of the marvellous." In *AYL*, Sh liberates his inherited pastoralism from "all its accumulated earnestness through strategic and ironic semantic play." The play also adopts the narrative conventions of romance "to bring the comedy back into contact with the mythical, magical and above all the ludic roots of pastoral itself." The conclusion of *AYL* is a gesture in the direction of recovering the "mythical Orphic magic" that underlies "the romance and pastoral modes."

1541 Fortin, René E. "'Tongues in Trees': Symbolic Patterns in *As You Like It*." *TSLL*, 14 (1972–73), 568–82.

Attempts to establish a crucial connection between II.i and IV.iii by explicating key symbols in the two scenes. Discusses the myth of the Golden Age, the oak tree, the serpent, and the lion (the last two associated with Hercules) to show that Sh is using a symbolic system combining classical and Christian images to enrich his audience's response to this drama of atonement.

1542 Halio, Jay L., and Barbara C. Millard, comps. *"As You Like It": An Annotated Bibliography, 1940–1980*. (Garland Shakespeare Bibliographies 8.) New York: Garland, 1985. viii + 744 pp.

Covers primarily works published between 1940 and 1980, though some works published before and reprinted later than 1940 are included. Classifies entries under nine headings, including Criticism (628 items), Sources and Background (199 items), Texts and Editions (142 items), and Bibliographies (33 items). Begins each section with the oldest entries and proceeds chronologically. Concludes with a substantial general index and a brief index of actors according to roles. Provides substantial and detailed annotations.

1543 Hankins, John E. "The Penalty of Adam—*As You Like It*, II.i.5." *Shakespearean Essays*. Eds. Alwin Thaler and Norman Sanders. Knoxville: U. of Tennessee P., 1964, pp. 41–43.

Argues that the Duke's association of "the penalty of Adam" with "the seasons' difference" comes from Golding's prefatory *Epistle* to his translation of the *Metamorphoses*. According to Golding, Ovid's Golden Age corresponded to Adam's life in Paradise, and the loss of the Golden Age paralleled Adam's expulsion from Paradise. Thus Golding associates the effects of the loss of the Golden Age (one of which was the change of seasons) with the loss of Paradise.

1543a Harley, Maria Power. "Rosalind, the Hare, and the Hyena in Shakespeare's *As You Like It*." *SQ*, 36 (1985), 335–37.

Investigates the ways in which Rosalind employs animal lore to allude to "her role as sexual chameleon." In having her identify with the hyena, Sh may have been influenced by book 15 of Ovid's *Metamorphoses*, in which this animal is described as capable of changing from female to male.

1543b Hieatt, Charles W. "The Quality of Pastoral in *As You Like It*." *Genre*, 7 (1974), 164–82.

Notices that *AYL* is a dramatized pastoral romance, a hybrid form developed in the Renaissance that involves the importation of an aristocratic character into the static world of shepherds inherited from Virgil and other classical writers. While the aristocratic character sojourns in the pastoral landscape, he or she adopts the role of a shepherd in order to explore the complexities of love; later, instructed in love, he departs from this world. This dynamic allows for the pastoral to retain the authentic shepherds (both serious and comic) of classical tradition while showing development in the imported character(s). Sh also superimposes a comic world on the romantic one, providing "a nice monitoring" of pastoral conventions like the shepherd's Stoicism and melancholia. The hybrid work that results furnishes a definition of love that is "admirably richer in humor and more forgiving of human limitations than that in the uniform pastoral vision."

1543c Hunt, Maurice. "*Kairos* and the Ripeness of Time in *As You Like It*." *MLQ*, 52 (1991), 113–35.

Explicates the notion of *kairos* (a moment or epoch in time propitious for action that will lead to spiritual fulfillment) in its classical and Christian manifestations. Urges that a proper understanding of *kairos* is important for analysis of *AYL*, a play that examines whether its "characters' acts of seizing opportune moments coincide with a time of most significant personal ripeness: that of fulfilled spiritual or intellectual growth." Orlando reenacts several heroic moments from the Golden Age: Hercules' defeat of Antaeus, interpreted by Renaissance humanists as the overthrow of the passions by reason (in the wrestling match with Charles); Aeneas's carrying of his father Anchises from the ruins of Troy (in carrying Adam through the forest); and "Hercules' slaying of the Nemean lion" (in rescuing his brother Oliver). Rosalind, in recovering a moment from classical antiquity by having the marriage god Hymen appear at the end of the play, also works in accord with Christian *kairos*. Time, having re-created redemptive moments from the classical age, has, as the play concludes, "reached the age of Genesis and the Garden of Eden." From a Christian perspective, a new age of innocence has been instituted.

1544 Irot, M. Kristina Faber. "The Pastoral Inquiry: Dialectical Form in Renaissance Pastoral Literature." Ph.D. dissertation, Claremont Graduate School, 1978. *DAI*, 38 (1977–78), 6742-A-6743-A.

Uses the term "dialectical" to describe those pastorals that involve "serious inquiry into complex philosophical and psychological questions." This term is appropriate because pastoral literature may have originated in or been influenced by "Socratic or pre-Socratic philosophical prose" and because the form of certain Renaissance pastorals strongly resembles Platonic dialectic. Discusses *AYL*.

1545 Kaul, R. K. "Lodge, Shakespeare and the Olde Daunce." *LCrit*, 6, no. 1 (1963–65), 19–28.

Argues that in writing *AYL*, Sh modified his source, Thomas Lodge's *Rosalynde*, by eliminating Ovidian levity and cynicism about the game of love. He retained Ovid's common–sense attitude as a corrective to the excessive abasement of the lover inherited from the Middle Ages.

1546 Knowles, Richard. "Myth and Type in *As You Like It*." *ELH*, 33 (1966), 1–22.

Proposes that in *AYL* mythological and biblical allusions are playfully combined to provide hints of the heroic and divine in the midst of other, primarily comic, matters. Orlando, in his wrestling match with Charles and his slaying of the lion, is reminiscent of Hercules, whose deeds were moralized by Renaissance commentators as triumphs of virtue over vice. In his refusal to take vengeance on his sinful brother, Orlando is also Christ-like. The descriptions of Arden contain explicit echoes of the golden age of Saturn's reign, commonly taken by Renaissance writers as a gentile corruption of the story of paradise in Genesis. The Masque of Hymen that concludes the play uses a classical framework to suggest the providential Christian atoning of earthly and heavenly things. These double classical–Christian allusions are not pervasive enough to warrant an allegorical or symbolic interpretation of the play, but they do enrich its texture and widen the perspective of the modern reader.

1547 Knowles, Richard, ed., with a survey of criticism by Evelyn Joseph Mattern. *As You Like It*. (A New Variorum Edition of Shakespeare.) New York: Modern Language Association, 1977. xxviii + 737 pp.

The appendix includes several sections on sources, each of which samples critical commentary. The sections on "The Pastoral" and "Classical and Continental Sources" provide opinions on classical background. Notes 1118 and 1122 discuss classical analogues for Jaques's "All the world's a stage" speech and the seven ages of man described therein.

1548 Kronenfeld, Judy Z. "Shakespeare's Jaques and the Pastoral Cult of Solitude." *TSLL*, 18 (1976–77), 451–73.

Discusses Jaques's cultivation of the solitary life in *AYL* in light of Renaissance ideas about the appropriateness of the *vita solitaria*. Summarizes Petrarch's defense of the *vita solitaria* and notes classical wariness on the matter (Seneca's highly qualified approval and Cicero's distrust of introspection). In the works of the Italian Neoplatonists, there was much admiration for the solitary melancholic; but other commentators found in such withdrawal an unhealthy idleness, an unwillingness to make significant decisions, and an absorption in one's own emotional state. Jaques is vulnerable to all of these criticisms, but he does change during the course of the play from a posturing melancholic to someone who will in the future attempt to put his solitude to proper use. Revision of part of item 1550.

1549 Kronenfeld, Judy Z. "Social Rank and the Pastoral Ideals of *As You Like It*." *SQ*, 29 (1978), 333–48.

Argues that in *AYL* Sh explores the potential of pastoral ideals to reconcile the different ranks of society and their respective values. He submits the "pastoral idealizations" of social relationships to a gentle, corrective pressure that finally revitalizes "the pastoral vision of charitable relations among humans." Cites various Renaissance versions of the pastoral theme, including Sidney's *Arcadia* and Angel Day's adaptation of Longus's *Daphnis and Chloe*, as contrasts to Sh's achievement. Revision of part of item 1550.

1550 Kronenfeld, Judy Zahler. "The Treatment of Pastoral Ideals in *As You Like It*: A Study in Convention and Traditional Renaissance Dichotomies." Ph.D. dissertation, Stanford University, 1971. *DAI*, 32 (1971–72), 921-A.

Provides background on the pastoral vision in Sh's time and explicates the ways in which that vision is judged in *AYL*. Uses the notion of the *vita triplex* (active, contemplative, amorous) to focus on a core of important themes. There is also the matter of social rank: Pastoral activities are confined to noblemen. Sh's presentation in *AYL* of the shepherd as amorous man burlesques the Neoplatonic mode of wooing by aristocrats. Parts revised as items 1548 and 1549.

1551 Lerner, Laurence. "The *Eclogues* and the Pastoral Tradition." *Virgil and His Influence: Bimillennial Studies*. Ed. Charles Martindale. Bristol: Bristol Classical P., 1984, pp. 193–213.

Distinguishes two forms of self-consciousness fostered by Virgil's *Eclogues*, which result in two types of rural poetry: "that of direct response to nature, and that of escape." Cites Duke Senior's speech in praise of nature in *AYL* (II.i.1–17) as an example of the latter.

1551a Marx, Steven. "'Fortunate Senex': The Pastoral of Old Age." *SEL*, 25 1985), 21–44.

Cites classical precedent, especially Virgil's *Eclogues*, to show that the pastoral world has always had a substantial complement of senior inhabitants. These aged rustics tend to emphasize "hard pastoral," that which teaches lessons about how to conduct onself in a world of seasonal and human change. Notes that often age and youth are seen engaged in partnership in a pastoral world that is "remote from the center" of worldly affairs, though the "satiric and moral strain" of pastoral is primarily associated with old age. Several examples come from *AYL*, which locates aged shepherds and courtiers in the forest and features a satiric commentator (Jaques) who allies himself with seniority.

1552   Miller, William E. "All the World's a Stage." *N&Q*, 10 (1963), 99–101.

Calls attention to several previously unnoticed versions of the notion that the world is a stage, including one from Abraham Fleming's translation of a letter of Cicero to Lucceius in *A Panoplie of Epistles* (1576). Any or all of these uses of the stage image could have influenced Sh in composing Jaques's speech in *AYL*.

1553   Morris, Harry. "*As You Like It*: *Et in Arcadia Ego.*" *SQ*, 26 (1975), 269–75.

Maintains that the Forest of Arden in *AYL* suggests Arcadia as it is portrayed in Poussin's famous painting, in which shepherds in a pastoral landscape come upon a tomb with the motto "*et in Arcadia ego.*" Suggests that within Arden, Sh has included pervasive reminders of mortality and death.

1554   Priest, Dale G. "*Oratio* and *Negotium*: Manipulative Modes in *As You Like It*." *SEL*, 28 (1988), 273–86.

Identifies one group of characters in *AYL* as manipulators and focuses on two of them, Touchstone and Rosalind. Touchstone exhibits a mastery of "the ancient art of *oratio*—the purposeful use of mannered prose—and so illustrates a pervasive Renaissance interest in this use of a manipulative rhetoric employed to disarm or otherwise persuade an audience." Deriving from Socrates and Cicero, this sort of discourse reached its Renaissance culmination in Erasmus's *Encomium Moriae* (1509). However, the detachment of the *oratio* weakens Touchstone's authority. Rosalind, whose position as the negotiator of the play has her balancing the Horatian ideal of *otium* (the various manifestations of the pastoral ideal, including fulfilled romantic love) and the Ciceronian ideal of *negotium* ("non-leisure" or business), engineers a number of benign manipulations that obviously have Sh's blessing.

1555   Rickey, Mary Ellen. "Rosalind's Gentle Jupiter." *SQ*, 13 (1962), 365–66.

Argues that Rosalind's exclamation, "O most gentle Jupiter" (*AYL*, III.ii.153) needs no emendation. In the first act, Rosalind takes the name of Ganymede, and the motif of Jupiter and Ganymede is used throughout acts II and III. It is appropriate that Rosalind, having identified herself with Ganymede, refers to her lover as Jupiter; this "gives important perspectives to her supposedly mock love scene with Orlando."

1556   Scoufos, Alice-Lyle. "The *Paradiso Terrestre* and the Testing of Love in *As You Like It*." *ShakS*, 14 (1981), 215–27.

Examines two important pastoral conventions—the *paradiso terrestre* setting and "the idea of the testing of various levels of love"—used by Sh in *AYL*, including the classical elements in these conventions. Of particular importance is the education of Orlando, a Herculean hero whose initial propensities to violence are refined through a series of tests until he becomes a "true Renaissance image of Christ." The Herculean struggle with the Nemean Lion becomes "a symbol of the subjective struggle with a Satanic impulse to evil." At the play's end, Sh has the cave in book 7 of the *Republic* in mind: Jaques is preoccupied with the same false images that the majority of mankind in Plato regard as the source of their information about the meaning of reality.

1557 Shulman, Jeff. "'The Recuyell of the Historyes of Troye' and the Tongue-tied Orlando." *SQ*, 31 (1980), 390.

Finds a source for Orlando's abashed inability to speak to Rosalind in Caxton's translation of Raoul LeFevre's *Le Recueil des histories de Troye*. In LeFevre's account, Hercules, after wrestling for four hours, finds himself dancing with Megara, the king's daughter, before whom he is tongue-tied.

1558 Stanton, Kay. "Shakespeare's Use of Marlowe in *As You Like It*." *"A Poet and a Filthy Play-Maker": New Essays on Christopher Marlowe*. Eds. Kenneth Friedenreich, Roma Gill, and Constance B. Kuriyama. New York: AMS P., 1988, pp. 23–35.

Argues that in *AYL* Sh offers a criticism not only of "the specific poetic efforts of his characters, but also [of] poetry itself." Through references to Ovid, Chaucer, and Marlowe, the playwright both mocks and pays tribute to his own art. Touchstone self-consciously puts himself in the tradition of Ovid and Marlowe when he raises the crucial issue of poetry's feigning. Rosalind's references to those like Leander and Troilus who purportedly died for love, but did so only by "attorney" (that is, in the persons created for them by "foolish chroniclers" like Marlowe and Chaucer), further undermine the "truth" of poetry. All three of these great poets (and Sh himself) are tested to reveal that their art "involves a complex layering of literal and figurative truth."

1559 Taylor, Donn Ervin. "Time and Occasion in *As You Like It*." *TSLL*, 24 (1982), 121–36.

Maintains that in *AYL* time, which exists independently of the characters' perception of it, is a means of measuring each character's growth. Suggests that the challenges posed by time to the characters, and their response to it, are conveyed emblematically through the merged images of Fortune and Occasio, both of which have classical origins.

1560 Thron, Edward Michael. "*As You Like It*: Jaques and Touchstone." Ph.D. dissertation, University of Nebraska, 1968. *DA*, 29 (1968), 1881-A-1882-A.

Claims that Jaques and Touchstone are "dramatic amplifications" of Rosalind's inner struggle: whether she should accept Orlando or reject him as too much of this world. Following "the Renaissance theory of *De Copia* or rhetorical amplification," Sh develops two extreme characters to represent Rosalind's dilemma: Jaques rejects the world entirely, while Touchstone accepts it all too readily.

1561 Trautvetter, Christine, and Ernst Leisi. "Some New Readings in *As You Like It*." *SJH*, 1969, 142–51.

Attempts to discover what is meant by "Atalanta's better part" (*AYL*, III.ii.) in Orlando's poem about the ideal woman. The attributes of the mythological Atalanta do not seem to be relevant; it is more productive to investigate what "better part" means elsewhere in Sh's work. The most appropriate gloss on "Atalanta's better part" would seem to be "mind" or "spirit."

1562 Waddington, Raymond B. "Moralizing the Spectacle: Dramatic Emblems in *As You Like It*." *SQ*, 33 (1982), 155–63.

Provides a reading of *AYL* based on a number of emblems, illustrated from emblem books of Sh's time. The play, because of its characters' tendency to moralize, is particularly susceptible to this approach. Points out classical myths (for example, those of Hercules and Aeneas) that inform many of the emblems.

1563 Walter, J. H. "'In a Little Room': Shakespeare and Chapman." *N&Q*, 12 (1965), 95–96.

Suggests that Touchstone's words "strikes a man more dead than a great reckoning in a little room" (*AYL*, III.iii.12–13) echo lines in Chapman's *Ovid's Banquet of Sense* (1595).

1564 Williamson, Marilyn. "The Masque of Hymen in *As You Like It*." *CompD*, 2 (1968–69), 248–57.

Mentions, in defending the aesthetic appropriateness of the concluding masque in *AYL*, the preoccupation of pastorals from classical times through the Renaissance with romantic love. Pastoral dramas of Sh's time, in keeping with this tradition, often end with reference to or evocation of Hymen, the god of marriage. After individualizing the lovers earlier in the play, Sh merges them into the generalized pattern provided by the masque. Permanence is thus achieved within mutability.

THE COMEDY OF ERRORS

1565 Altman, Joel B. *The Tudor Play of Mind: Rhetorical Inquiry and the Development of Elizabethan Drama*. Berkeley: U. of California P., 1978. ix + 406 pp.

Proposes to examine the origins of Tudor dramatic structure in rhetorical theory, in particular the theory of wonder derived from Aristotle, its rhetorical instrumentation in Cicero and the sophists, and its assimilation into the 16th-c. school curriculum. Rhetorical exercises gave the budding dramatists of the Tudor period the habit of exploring intellectual and emotional questions from several different perspectives to enlarge their understanding. In the plays they later came to write, these former schoolboys used a similar play of mind to attempt such explorations: The plays themselves are questions. Chapter 5 shows that studying Terence in the grammar schools taught the playwrights to think of a comic action as containing "specific problems to be examined and resolved by the human wit." Section 3 of chapter 6 contains an analysis of *Err.* as an inquiry into "the moral significance of error." Most of the characters attempt to answer questions about who they are and what is happening from within themselves. It is only when they turn to others for help in these quests that they gain understanding.

1566 Arthos, John. "Shakespeare's Transformation of Plautus." *CompD*, 1 (1967–68), 239–53.

Argues that Sh, in *Err.*, owed much to the imaginative conception of Plautus. Sh heightened or enriched elements suggested by his source. In *Err.*, for example, there is a sense of stable social life; there is also a feel for the invaluable and, when that is lost, for the irretrievable. Most important is a sense of common humanity, which Sh added to Plautus's acceptance of mankind's tendency to deceit and vulnerability to Fortune's blows. Plautus gave Sh warrant for outrageous defiance of verisimilitude, as well as construction of *Err.* on musical principles.

1567 Baldwin, T. W. *On the Compositional Genetics of "The Comedy of Errors."* Urbana: U. of Illinois P., 1965. xi + 422 pp.

Attempts to explain how some of the larger elements of *Err.* were put together "and how these threads of composition tie the play in with the body of Shakespeare's work, even to his last play." Includes a number of chapters on Sh's use of Plautus's *Menaechmi*, which provided him with the witchcraft theme, the five-act structure, the twin masters, the confused statements of age, Egeon's helplessness before fate, and the waterdrop image. Sh also drew on Plautus's *Amphitruo* for the details of the doubled servants and the shut-out husband, on the *Aeneid* for Egeon's description of the shipwreck, and on Ovid for the important image of the ragged rock. The composition of *Err.* follows essentially the Erasmian method of imitation: The *Menaechmi* "has been analyzed and relevant materials have been synthesized into a similar but different structure." Sh seems to have used D. Lambinus's Latin edition of *Menaechmi* (1576), not the translation by William Warner (1595). The tone has been Christianized by the setting in Ephesus (rather than Plautus's Epidamnus) and the modification of fate to providence. See item 1585.

1568 Bonazza, Blaze Odell. *Shakespeare's Early Comedies: A Structural Analysis.* The Hague: Mouton, 1966. 125 pp.

Provides a detailed summary of Plautus's *Menaechmi* as a background for *Err.* and argues that Sh "attempts to shift the emphasis from situation to character by setting the mechanical elements of farce within a larger, more humane framework and by trying to create more subtle characters."

1569 Boulukos, Athanasios. "Twinship in *Menaechmi, Amphitruo* and *The Comedy of Errors.*" Ph.D. dissertation, Boston University, 1975. *DAI*, 35 (1974–75), 7860-A-7861-A.

Examines three aspects of twinship stressed by ancient literature: "twin rivalry and its relation to Oedipal conflict, twin sacrifice and the lost self, and a connection between twinship and a pre-conscious fusion of parents and children which is evidenced in a number of creation myths." These are all useful in interpreting *Err.*, whose recognition scene is an epitome of "the entire drama of friendship." *Err.* combines a farcical strand from *Menaechmi* and a romantic strand from *Amphitruo*.

1570 Briggs, K. M. *Pale Hecate's Team: An Examination of the Beliefs on Witchcraft and Magic among Shakespeare's Contemporaries and His Immediate Successors.* London: Routledge and Kegan Paul, 1962. viii + 291 pp.

Attempts to uncover the folk beliefs that underlay the references to witchcraft in "the writings of Shakespeare, his contemporaries and successors." Mentions, among other influences on the witchcraft lore of Sh's time, the works of Ovid, Plutarch's *Roman Questions*, Cicero's *De Divinatione*, Tacitus's *Germania*, Pomponius Mela's *De Situ Orbis*, and Apuleius's *Golden Ass*. Discusses several of Sh's plays, including *Err.*, in which Antipholus of Syracuse comments on witchcraft in Ephesus (I.ii.97–102) in a manner reminiscent of the opening of the *Golden Ass*, "when Lucius arrives in Witch-haunted Thessaly."

1571 Brooks, Harold. "Theme and Structure in *The Comedy of Errors.*" *Early Shakespeare*. (Stratford-upon-Avon Studies 3.) Eds. John Russell Brown and Bernard Harris. London: Edward Arnold, 1961, pp. 55–71. Reprint. 1967.

Analyzes the plot and themes of *Err.*, focusing on Sh's use of Plautine intrigue, which is based on elements from the *Menaechmi* and *Amphitruo*. Notes such Plautine or Terentian features as the adherence to the unities of time and place and "the setting, with its three houses." Sh outdoes Plautus and Terence not only in their intrigue but in their supposed romantic qualities. The first scene functions like a classical prologue,

The Comedy of Errors 419

being descended from both Plautus and Seneca, and the influence of the Terentian five-act structure is also in evidence.

1572   Candido, Joseph. "Dining out in Ephesus: Food in *The Comedy of Errors*." *SEL*, 30 (1990), 217–41.

Compares Sh's approach to food and lodging in *Err.* to that of his source, Plautus's *Menaechmi*. Suggests that Sh had access to William Warner's 1595 translation of Plautus. Argues that Sh foregrounds what is only implicit in Plautus: the social and psychological significance of the rituals of dining.

1573   Clubb, Louise George. "Italian Comedy and *The Comedy of Errors*." *CL*, 19 (1967), 240–51.

Argues that, in reworking materials from Plautus to compose *Err.*, Sh was influenced by Renaissance Italian comedy, which had already complicated and refined its Plautine models.

1573a   Cooper, David Jay. "A Waterdrop's Revenge: A Study of William Shakespeare's *The Comedy of Errors*." Ph.D. dissertation, State University of New York, Buffalo, 1981. *DAI*, 42 (1981–82), 222-A.

Chapter 2 provides a critical summary of scholarship on *Err.* Chapter 3 attempts "a detailed reading of the images and structure of the play, on its own terms." Chapter 4 explains how "intentional dis-orientation seems to be an important factor in Shakespeare's selection of material from the discourse of the 'real' world." The play intersects six "boundary lines in the world of Elizabethan England," including "England and the Classical learning of the ancient world."

1574   Dorsch, T. S., ed. *The Comedy of Errors*. (New Cambridge Shakespeare.) Cambridge: Cambridge U. P., 1988. xiv + 115 pp.

The introduction includes among the sources of *Err.* two or three plays of Plautus (the most popular of the ancient playwrights in Renaissance Europe). From the *Menaechmi*, which he read in Latin, Sh took the essential elements of his account of twins; and he "contaminated" this plot with episodes taken from the *Amphitruo*. For the romantic side of the play (Egeon's adventures and his reunion with his long-lost wife), Sh seems to have turned to Gower's version of the tale of Apollonius of Tyre in *Confessio Amantis*. For other details of "the story of loss and recovery," Sh may have used Plautus's *Rudens*.

1575   Foakes, R. A., ed. *The Comedy of Errors*. (Arden Shakespeare.) London: Methuen, 1962. lv + 117 pp.

The introduction shows how Sh "multiplied the turns and possibilities of error" in Plautus's *Menaechmi*, his chief source for *Err.*, and argues that *Err.* is more than just a skillful farce because it explores the loss of identity and the disruption of relationships. Comments on various changes Sh made, including the marginalization of the courtesan, the enhancement of the wife of Antipholus of Ephesus, the creation of a sister for the wife, the transfer of the courtesan's maid and cook to the wife, the multiplication of the twins, the greater prominence given to the visiting Antipholus, and the greater humanity of all of the characters. Sh could have read the Latin original, though there is only slight evidence of verbal borrowing from it; he also might have used William Warner's translation. Plautus's *Amphitruo* is a source for the scene (III.i) in which Antipholus of Syracuse is feasted by Adriana in the belief that he is her husband. Appendix 1 furnishes summaries of *Menaechmi* and *Amphitruo*, "drawing attention, in the passages in square brackets, to the most significant connections between the Latin texts, Warner's translation of *Menaechmi*," and Sh's play.

1576 Garton, Charles. "Centaurs, the Sea, and *The Comedy of Errors.*" *Arethusa*, 12 (1979), 233–54.

Suggests that the name Antipholus in *Err.* is compounded of *anti-* and *Pholus*, the name of a centaur Sh would have encountered in Ovid. It means both "counterpart to a centaur" and "reciprocal to a centaur," descriptions appropriate to each of the twins in his relationship to the other. Acting as a mythopoeic shorthand, "Antipholus" encodes the centaur-like ambiguity of identity that bedevils the twins, as well as their animal-like vitality. The name of the inn—the Centaur—where Antipholus of Syracuse lodges also reinforces the connection. In mythology, centaurs were associated with the sea through their protector Poseidon, and thus the setting of the play in a seascape is appropriate, as is the naming of the twins' father after Aegeus, the son of Neptune.

1577 Grivelet, Michel. "Shakespeare, Molière, and the Comedy of Ambiguity." *ShS*, 22 (1969), 15–26.

Suggests, as part of an analysis of ambiguity in *Err.* and Molière's *Amphitryon*, that Sh's sources, *Menaechmi* and *Amphitruo*, both treat "man's doubtfulness about being one or two, identical with himself or not."

1578 Heilman, Robert B. "Farce Transformed: Plautus, Shakespeare, and Unamuno." *CL*, 31 (1979), 113–23.

Uses the relationship between *Err.* and Plautus's *Menaechmi* as an example of how elements of farce, which are primarily physical, can lead into the tone or structure of other genres when augmented or modified by the dramatist. On the one hand, Sh multiplies the farcical confusions and beatings and adds the kitchen wench who lays claim to Dromio of Syracuse; on the other, he moves sharply away from farce by introducing elements from melodrama and romance (the story of Egeon) and by transforming essentially farcical materials into something else (Adriana's concern with ideas and feelings transcends the farcical ranting of the stereotypical jealous wife).

1579 Henze, Richard. "*The Comedy of Errors*: A Freely Binding Chain." *SQ*, 22 (1971), 35–41.

The golden chain, substituted in *Err.* for the cloak found by Sh in his source, Plautus's *Menaechmi*, is "a complex symbol of the recommended norm in the play, the bridling of headstrong freedom and wandering individuality." In Plautus, "the husband gives his wife's mantle to a prostitute, and his wife then locks him out so as to recover it"; it then passes through several hands and ends up at an auction. It is never invested with the symbolic value of Sh's chain, which is an emblem of marital harmony and "the bonds of society."

1580 Jorgensen, Paul A., ed. *The Comedy of Errors*. (Pelican Shakespeare.) Baltimore: Penguin, 1964. 98 pp.

The introduction notes changes Sh made in his chief source, the *Menaechmi* of Plautus, including the discarding of "the explanatory prologue" (thus letting the play speak for itself), the softening of Roman cynicism, the "tragic overcast," and the addition of a pair of twin servants (inspired in this last instance by 16th-c. Italian versions of Plautus as well as Plautus's own *Amphitruo*). For the sadness introduced by Egeon's story, as well as the loss by shipwreck and eventual reunion, Sh was indebted to the romance of Apollonius of Tyre. Revised as part of item 0496.

1581 Levin, Harry. "Two Comedies of Errors." *Stratford Papers on Shakespeare 1963*. Ed. B. W. Jackson. Toronto: W. J. Gage, 1964, pp. 35–57. Reprint. *Refractions: Essays in Comparative Literature*. New York: Oxford U. P., 1966, pp. 128–50.

Points out that Sh probably chose Plautus's *Menaechmi* as a model for his one direct imitation of Roman comedy because, untypically, it depends almost entirely on chance, not scheming. Sh added another pair of twins, amplified the wife's role and reduced

The Comedy of Errors

that of the courtesan, gave the wife a sister for one of the twins to court, and arranged for us to see things from the viewpoint of the alien (rather than from that of the resident, as in Plautus). The most important thing about *Err.*, in contrast to *Menaechmi*, is that there are no "supposes," or tricks—no contrivances by anyone but Sh himself. Reprinted as the introduction to item 1582.

1582 Levin, Harry, ed. *The Comedy of Errors.* (Signet Classic Shakespeare.) New York: New American Library, 1965. 176 pp.

The introduction, which explores the relationship between *Err.* and Plautus's *Menaechmi*, is a reprint of item 1581. The introduction, text, and note on sources are reprinted as part of item 0123.

1583 Long, Timothy. "The Calculus of Confusion: Cognitive and Associative Errors in Plautus's *Menaechmi* and Shakespeare's *Comedy of Errors.*" *Classical Bull.*, 53 (1976–77), 20–23.

Maintains that in comedies like these, involving doubles, characters may mistake the identity of someone (an error of cognition) or incorrectly assign actions to someone they identify correctly (an error of association). Though Plautus and Sh both combine the two types of error, Sh does so in a more complex way.

1584 Marathe, Sudhakar. "From Father to Sister: Luciana in *The Comedy of Errors.*" *Dibruyarh University Journal of English Studies*, 5 (1986), 17–22.

Argues that in *Err.* Sh based the character of Luciana on that of Menechmus Citizen's father-in-law (Senex) in Plautus's *Menaechmi*. Senex tells his daughter that her husband stays away from home because she nags him and advises her to accept her subordinate role in marriage. Luciana offers similar advice to Adriana. Later in the play, Luciana is forced to take Adriana's part, just as Senex eventually takes his daughter's side. The Abbess in *Err.* also performs some of the father-in-law's function. Luciana is unlike Senex in that she acts as "confidante, friend, and guide to Adriana" and that she does not play a significant role in directing the action. Thus Sh used Senex as a model for Luciana and gave Luciana a number of interesting new functions without allowing her to detract from the focus on Egeon's near-tragedy and the main comic action.

1585 Maxwell, J. C. "*The Comedy of Errors* and *Menaechmi*." *N&Q*, 16 (1969), 128–29.

Points out that T. W. Baldwin (item 1567) missed an echo of Plautus's *Menaechmi*, 258–262, in *Err.* Baldwin was interested in comparing the Plautine passage with its exactly corresponding passage in Err. (I.ii); Sh omits a line of Plautus there but uses it later in the lines about "a gentle nation" (IV.iv.151–156).

1585a Roberts, Gareth. "*The Comedy of Errors*, II.ii.190: 'Owls' or 'Elves'?" *N&Q*, 34 (1987), 202–4.

Cites a passage in which Dromio of Syracuse expresses fear that "owls," among other creatures, will "suck our breath" [*Err.*, II.ii.189–191]. Accepts the Folio reading of "owls," instead of "elves," to which it has often been emended, on the grounds that the screech owl is often regarded in classical sources like Ovid's *Fasti* as a bird that sucks blood from children.

1586 Salgādo, Gāmini. "'Time's Deformed Hand': Sequence, Consequence, and Inconsequence in *The Comedy of Errors.*" *ShS*, 25 (1972), 81–91.

Finds in *Err.* that characters sense that their identities are threatened by "the dislocation of the time sequence." Sh's combination of Plautus's *Menaechmi* and *Amphitruo* does more than "multiply the possibilities of confusion"; it introduces a new dimension of time gone awry, and family, social, and personal relationships are disrupted.

1587 Shaw, Catherine M. "The Conscious Art of *The Comedy of Errors.*" *Shakespearean Comedy.* Ed. Maurice Charney. New York: New York Literary Forum, 1980, pp. 17–28.

Assumes that *Err.* was originally presented for a specific audience, at Gray's Inn, in 1594. Explains that this occasion stimulated Sh to show his virtuosity by deliberately borrowing and then improving on elements from various sources, especially Plautus and Terence. In Sh, the bawdy farce of Plautine comedy is reduced and relegated largely to the servants. In addition to the low comedy of the Dromios and Nell, there is a middle level (with Adriana and her concerns about marriage) and a high, romantic level (the realm of Egeon, Emilia, and Luciana). Sh begins with a plot from Plautus's *Menaechmi* and introduces into it material from another of Plautus's plays (the identical twins, from *Amphitruo*); he then develops a Terentian double plot by separating the two Antipholi into distinct character types and includes a Terentian debate on marriage that comes down on the side of moderation, represented by Adriana. Finally, he gives the plot a surprising twist with the appearance of Emilia. The abrupt conclusion to *Err.*, with the two Dromios leaving the stage in a "series of burlesque gestures," suggests an antic dance that might have led into the masque dances on the occasion of the first performance at Gray's Inn.

1588 Wells, Stanley, ed. *The Comedy of Errors.* (New Penguin Shakespeare.) New York: Penguin, 1972. 190 pp.

The introduction notes that Sh's chief source for *Err.* was Plautus's *Menaechmi*, which the playwright is likely to have read in Latin. Provides a detailed summary of *Menaechmi*, pointing out that in inventing the twin Dromios Sh seems also to have been influenced by Plautus's *Amphitruo*. This additional doubling allowed for and encouraged "the increased intellectual complications of the action." Plautus's prologue to *Menaechmi* probably gave Sh the seed for his serious framing story. *Err.* is one of only two plays in which Sh was concerned with observing the neoclassical unities of time, place, and action.

1589 Williams, Gwyn. "*The Comedy of Errors* Rescued from Tragedy." *REL*, 5, no. 4 (1964), 63–71.

Argues that Sh was interested in the predicament of Antipholus of Syracuse, which might have led in the direction of tragedy. However, the play was saved as a comedy by the "addition of the two Dromios to the material" taken from Plautus. That Sh did not pursue the tragic implications of Antipholus's threatened loss of identity might have resulted from his unwillingness to flout a classical model at a time when he was competing openly with university wits.

CORIOLANUS

1590 Adelman, Janet. "'Anger's My Meat': Feeding, Dependency, and Aggression in *Coriolanus.*" *Shakespeare, Pattern of Excelling Nature.* Eds. David Bevington and Jay L. Halio. Newark: U. of Delaware P., 1978, pp. 108–24. Reprint. *Representing Shakespeare: New Psychoanalytic Essays.* Eds. Murray M. Schwartz and Coppélia Kahn. Baltimore: Johns Hopkins U. P., 1980, pp. 129–49.

Discovers that "the transformation of hunger into phallic aggression" is central both to the mutiny of the crowd in *Cor.* and to the character of the protagonist. Coriolanus's mother has taught him to disdain food: To take in nourishment is a sign of dependency. To feed is to make oneself vulnerable, to suffer a wound. In accord with Volumnia's instruction, Coriolanus combats his vulnerability by converting it into "an instrument of attack." That is, he refuses to eat, or to suffer wounds passively; rather than incorporate or accept, he spits forth. Feeding solely on his own anger, he struggles constantly to see himself as an autonomous creature. For this reason, he finds it impossible to show his wounds and request the approval of the plebeians. In such a scenario, the wounds would become begging mouths, and his flattery of the people would be the verbal equivalent of eating, of dependency on an outside source. Coriolanus has been conditioned to stand alone, in phallic independence from the mob. He is unable, however, to maintain his posture of self-sufficiency because he has adopted it under the tutelage of his mother and needs her to script his actions. When she forces him to question his role by identifying herself with Rome (thus making clear that his desire to destroy Rome is a mutiny against her as well), he cannot face the consequences of being truly alone, and his personality collapses.

1591 Allen, Guy Pierce. "Seven English Versions of the Coriolanus Story." Ph.D. dissertation, University of Toronto, 1978. *DAI*, 40 (1979–80), 864-A-865-A.

Provides a "comparative analysis of seven versions of the Coriolanus story that appeared in England between 1600 and 1850." Discusses *Cor.* first, pointing out that it has two protagonists, Coriolanus himself and "the body politic, Rome." The tragedy of Coriolanus follows a familiar pattern of rise and fall, but the hero's unusual relationship with his mother restricts its universality. The tragedy of Rome is a story of "destruction and waste" that "offers no climax or purgation, but a depressingly static vision of men in society." Underlying the pessimistic tone of *Cor.* is a strong sense of "positive values," but the play expresses a skeptical view about how effective these values can be in public life.

1592 Alvis, John. "Coriolanus and Aristotle's 'Magnanimous Man,' Reconsidered." *A Journal of Political Philosophy*, 7, no. 3 (1978), 4–28.

Argues that the character of Coriolanus in *Cor.* an be understood in both its grandeur and its limitations by measuring it against the standard of Aristotle's magnanimous man. Coriolanus approximates the magnanimous man in many ways: his willingness to face great danger, his disdain for material possessions, and his frankness in expressing his hate and love. He also seems to follow Aristotle's ideal in seeking honor, the greatest of external goods according to the *Ethics*. However, the most important feature of magnanimity for Aristotle is self- sufficiency, and Coriolanus, always dependent for his renown on the opinion of others, never achieves it. He exemplifies a defective Roman version of magnanimity, which tragically confuses noble autonomy and vainglory. Revision of part of item 0082. Revised as chapter 4 of item 0080a.

1593 Ansari, A. A. "*Coriolanus*—The Roots of Alienation." *AJES*, 6 (1981), 14–34.

Seeks the roots of Coriolanus's alienation. Takes note of the factionalism in Rome and the competition between the Romans and the Volsces. More to the point are Coriolanus's epic military stature; the control exerted over him by his mother; his peculiar mixture of paradoxical attitudes; his monolithic integrity; and his betrayal by Brutus and Sicinius, by the Romans in general, and by Aufidius.

1594 Azar, Inés. "Self, Responsibility, Discourse: An Introduction to Speech Act Theory." *Things Done with Words: Speech Acts in Hispanic Drama*. Ed. Elias L. Rivers. Proceedings of the 1984 Stony Brook Seminar. (Hispanic Monographs.) Newark, Delaware: Juan de la Cuesta, 1986, pp. 1–13.

Sums up, in the course of analyzing *La Celestina* by Rojas, Stanley Fish's treatment of *Cor.* in terms of speech act theory (item 1637), according to which the tragedy is propelled by "the unfolding of Coriolanus's linguistic behavior." The hero constantly asserts "his independence from the shared system of conventional speech acts" but dies because his individual transgression of established conventions is ultimately not able to stand on its own. By explicitly rejecting these conventions, Coriolanus "acknowledges their existence and their binding force."

1595   Barron, David B. "*Coriolanus*: Portrait of the Artist as Infant." *AI*, 19 (1962), 171–93.

Provides a psychoanalytic reading of *Cor.* Sh made important modifications of the source materials he found in Plutarch to emphasize Volumnia's influence on the hero (she has diverted his appetite for herself to the enemy). The theme of hunger and cannibalism was also intensified by Sh to highlight the mob's lack of discipline and to contrast them with Coriolanus, who appears as a rigid parent figure. There is also Coriolanus's homoerotic relationship to the enemy, not found in Plutarch. This play reveals Sh struggling to resolve "the tensions induced by a capricious mother" and overcome "the fickleness of time."

1596   Barton, Anne. "Livy, Machiavelli, and Shakespeare's *Coriolanus*." *ShS*, 38 (1985), 115–29.

Maintains that the essentially positive view of the plebeians and of the mixed state (involving aristocrats and plebeians in an evolving partnership) in *Cor.* owes its general conception to Sh's familiarity with Titus Livius's *Roman History* and with Machiavelli's commentary on that history in his *Discourses*. Livy, who was read in the upper forms of grammar school during Sh's time, emphasizes the evolution of the Roman state, especially the need to cultivate the arts of peace as well as those of war. He notes how, in the days of the republic, the Roman patricians used war to unify the people and to distract them from domestic difficulties. Significantly, Coriolanus is the only character in the play who sees war in this way, failing to recognize that a new stage in the relationship between commons and nobles has been reached. Machiavelli views the struggle between Roman patricians and plebeians as positive, maintaining that the resultant sharing of power gave the state more flexibility in responding to emergencies. In the play, this principle is illustrated ironically when the simple warrior society of the Volscians accords Coriolanus the uncritical admiration denied him at home and then, with equal unreflectiveness, tears him to pieces. The successful embassy of the women to Coriolanus is celebrated in Rome as a victory of the mixed state.

1597   Barton, Anne. "Shakespeare and the Limits of Language." *ShS*, 24 (1971), 19–30.

Explains that Coriolanus's tragedy in *Cor.* is worked out largely in terms of his hatred of words: To him, they "violate the integrity of events."

1598   Bayley, John. "The Shakespearian Freedom in Literature." *EDH*, 37 (1972), 1–16.

Attempts to demonstrate how Sh empowers his characters to act in contradictory, fully human ways. This includes liberation of these characters from the prescriptions of the sources from which they are quarried. Uses as a key example the figure of Coriolanus, whose domination by his mother in *Cor.* is incongruously offset by his happy marriage to Virgilia.

1599   Bell, Arthur H. "*Coriolanus* III.ii.72–80: 'Cryptic' and 'Corrupt'?" *ELN*, 9 (1971–72), 18–20.

Disagrees with Reuben Brower's comment (item 0208) that Volumnia's instructions to her son about handling the common people [III.ii.74–82] are cryptic and probably represent a corruption of the text. If "stretched" (line 74) is properly understood, "business" (line 75) is taken as "stage business," "humble" (line 79) is read as a verb, and the passage is judiciously punctuated, it makes perfect sense.

Coriolanus

1600 Berry, Francis. "Stage Perspective and Elevation in *Coriolanus and Sejanus*." *Jonson and Shakespeare*. Ed. Ian Donaldson. Atlantic Highlands, New Jersey: Humanities P., 1983, pp. 163–78.

Includes an analysis of *Cor.*, I.iv, set before the city of Corioli, in which the Volsces sally out of their gates and beat the Romans back to their trenches. Then Marcius pursues the Volsces to the gates, is shut in, and comes back through the gates, bleeding. Argues that this is a bold and powerful use of "the physical geometry of the stages of the theatre" (involving the platform, the inner stage, and the gallery) to convey the message that Coriolanus is alone. That is, his isolation is vividly depicted when he is "'shut in' within the most spatially remote playing area."

1601 Berry, Ralph. "Sexual Imagery in *Coriolanus*." *SEL*, 13 (1973), 301–16.

Notes that the subject matter for this play is "politics and war" but that the imagery reveals that "the underlying statement of the play" is the close interdependence of war and sex. Shows that Volumnia views war as "a quasi-sexual activity" and that she has raised her son to feel a powerful link between the erotic and the martial. Explains the connection between the sexual imagery and that of acting a part and suggests that the simplifications provided by the part of a warrior give Coriolanus a way to suppress his "inner uncertainty." Volumnia, who controls her son and ultimately destroys him, makes herself the focus of all of Coriolanus's sexuality, excluding all other "sexually-related figures in his life." Cites the statements of Aufidius's servants to underline the ideas that sex is an alternative to war and that war is a substitute for sexual activity, a communal therapy and bond. Discusses the possibility of a homosexual relationship between Coriolanus and Aufidius, which is hinted at in the latter part of the play and is involved in the power struggle of the 2 men. Revised as chapter 7 of item 0155.

1602 Blackwood, Robert J. Jr. "Coriolanus: In Shakespeare and the Historians." Ph.D. dissertation, Loyola University of Chicago, 1973. *DAI*, 34 (1973–74), 267-A.

Includes a study of seventeen historians, most of them ancient, who dealt with the Coriolanus story. Uses the attitudes of the historians toward various characters in the story to establish the expectations with which Sh's audience would have gone to see *Cor.*, as well as to analyze how Sh handled his materials. Chapter 1 shows that Sh relied primarily on Plutarch in portraying his protagonist, emphasizing Coriolanus's anger and intransigence. Chapter 2 examines the character of Menenius Agrippa, praised by the historians for his political skill. Sh invented his relationship with Coriolanus. Chapter 3 confirms the historians' view of the tribunes as "self-seeking demagogues" and shows that Sh added cowardice to their vices. Chapter 4 asserts that Sh is more sympathetic than any of the historians to the cause of the plebeians, though his viewpoint is still aristocratic. Chapter 5 points out that Aufidius is more treacherous in Sh than in the historians. Chapter 6 explains that Coriolanus's mother, who goes under a variety of names in the historians, was commonly portrayed as "a weak woman who appeared in tears before her son." Sh modified this character considerably, emphasizing her sternness and authority. Chapter 7 contrasts *Cor.* with Alexandre Hardy's *Coriolan* (c. 1600), revealing how Sh transformed "a historical personage into a tragic protagonist who learns magnanimity too late and compels the audience's pity and admiration for his self-sacrifice."

1603 Bligh, John. "The Mind of Coriolanus." *ESC*, 13 (1987), 256–70.

Finds the key to Marcius's behavior in his "inner vision of an ideal city of Rome," ruled by aristocratic consuls "who are also generals." His Rome is very much like Plato's republic. He is misunderstood by everyone around him: his mother, Menenius, Cominius, Aufidius. Coriolanus's extremism is based on his awareness that the ruling elite must constantly demonstrate their superiority to those they govern. This is why war is so important to him. From the outset, his idealism is subject to inner contradiction: Though he claims to be rigidly truthful, he is unable to confront the truth about either the plebeians (who have some good in them) or the patricians (who are not up to his exacting standards). Coriolanus is forced by his mother to abandon his ideals and becomes something of a Machiavellian. When he leaves Rome and joins the Volscians, however, his extremism asserts itself again, only to collapse when he is persuaded to spare Rome. He recognizes that the final capitulation to his mother spells his doom, and the spiritual suffering he undergoes at this moment is "transformed into great beauty." He allows love to drive out revenge and thus in his death affirms his nobility.

1604 Blissettt, William. "Coriolanus and the Helms of State." *Familiar Colloquy: Essays Presented to Arthur Edward Barker.* Ed. Patricia Bruckmann. Ottawa: Oberon P., 1978, pp. 144–62.

Analyzes the opening scene of *Cor.* and the hero's final speech (V.vi) to show that the play is a tragedy of "the solitary achiever, whatever is unsocial and not to be educated, alone and raging." Maintains that Sh accepts Plutarch's evaluation of Coriolanus. Explicates this evaluation by comparing it with what Plutarch says in the *Lives* about a number of other patricians, soldiers, and statesmen.

1605 Bock, Philip K. *Shakespeare and Elizabethan Culture: An Anthropological View.* New York: Schocken Books, 1984. xv + 204 pp.

Chapter 4, "A View of Nobility: *Coriolanus*," suggests that the play encodes a skepticism about the pretensions of royalist and aristocrats to power. Calls attention to the special bond between the hero and his mother, the justifiability of the citizens' complaints against the patricians, and Coriolanus's lack of political skills and tendency toward self-destruction.

1606 Bolton, W. F. "Menenius's 'Scale't': A New Defense." *ELN*, 10 (1972–73), 110–11.

Argues that Menenius's use of "scale't" (*Cor.*, I.i.90), which is found in all of the Folios, should not be altered to "stale't," as most editors have done. "Scale" should be taken to mean "to split off scales or flakes from a coin for the purpose of fraud." If language is seen here as coin (a metaphor that goes back at least to Quintilian), then Menenius's meaning is "eke out the value of the tale by scaling it as though it were a coin." This reading accounts for the response of the Second Citizen.

1607 Bowden, William R. "The 'Unco Guid' and Shakespeare's Coriolanus." *SQ*, 13 (1962), 41–48.

Surveys Sh's virtuous characters and discusses the protagonist of *Cor.* as an example of the virtuous but unamiable person, the "unco guid." Coriolanus is self-righteous, rude, and tactless, but he is essentially justified in what he says. He is "a tragic hero, not a satiric butt," though today historical circumstances have made us less able to admire his aristocratic martial virtues and more likely to censure his faults.

1608 Bristol, Michael. "Lenten Butchery: Legitimation Crisis in *Coriolanus*." *Shakespeare Reproduced: The Text in History and Ideology.* Eds. Jean E. Howard and Marion F. O'Connor. London: Methuen, 1987, pp. 207–24.

Asserts that the most fundamental opposition between Coriolanus and his enemies is in "the goal-value of social life." For the hero, the fundamental activity of social life is war; for the plebeians, social health is subsistence and is figured in the images of a living organism or "the grotesque body." Connects the contest between Coriolanus and the plebeians with the battle between Lent and Carnival in early modern Europe. Coriolanus's "self-cancellation" averts the subjection of the body politic to "charismatic authority and rationally administered violence." A class compromise then ensues, which enables the patricians "to reestablish dominance over the popular element."

1609 Brockbank, Philip, ed. *Coriolanus*. (Arden Shakespeare.) London: Methuen, 1976. xii + 370 pp.

The introduction is divided into two large sections on "The Text" and "The Play," respectively. Each of these is subdivided, with the "Play" section treating "Date of Composition," "Sources," "The Tragedy of Coriolanus," "The Language of the Play," "The Play on Shakespeare's Stage," and "Coriolanus in the Theater." The play's date can be tentatively set as 1608, thus making it the last of Sh's tragedies. It represents a late phase of Sh's engagement with Plutarch, a process whereby the germ of one "classical" play is found in the previous one, with each succeeding protagonist running to greater extremes. For a source, *Cor.* depends almost exclusively on Plutarch's *Life of Caius Martius Coriolanus*, as translated by Thomas North. In one passage, the fable of the belly (I.i.154–162), it can be demonstrated that Sh echoes "not only North's version but also Holland's Livy, Camden's *Remaines*, and William Averell's *A Marvailous Combat of Contrarieties* (1588)." There are few other direct traces of Sh's reading, but the play itself bears witness to his interest in Roman manners and values. Sh used various strategies to shape the Plutarchan material. For example, he gave characters like Menenius, Aufidius, and Volumnia, who appear briefly or intermittently in the source, a significant presence in the play. In reordering the events in Plutarch, Sh combined two riots (about usury and corn, respectively) into one. Other changes include giving Coriolanus a popular welcome on his return to Rome and having him object on principle to showing his wounds from the very beginning (in Plutarch, he willingly exhibits his scars). Coriolanus's tragedy develops from two coincident crises, one political and one personal. Pride, particularly in the soldierly virtue of valiantness, is what defines the protagonist's nature. It is both his vice and his great strength, at once enlisting and alienating the audience's sympathies. Great stress is placed on physicality: Menenius's fable establishes a connection between the state and the body, and there is a strong emphasis, especially in Coriolanus, on the unity of body and mind. Menenius can be characterized as a demagogue who disingenuously deploys a great political parable and ends by finding himself in accord with a couple of demagogues (the tribunes) from the opposing side; Volumnia is a purveyor of inflexible heroic precepts who nevertheless counsels her son to be politic, thereby ensuring his destruction; and Aufidius is a soldier whose virtue in the service of his profession is compromised and tainted by the ways of expediency he shares with Volumnia and the tribunes. Having lost himself by giving way to humanity early in act V, Coriolanus recovers his old self as he faces the murderous mob of Volscians at the end. But the recovery of this self is also a farewell to it: He surrenders himself to death. The language of *Cor.*, reflecting its theme, issues in "invective, exhortation, suasion," and "amplification of a fame won by deeds of violence." Sh is attuned to the quotidian rhythms of the marketplace as well as to "heroical resonances of an English in touch with Plutarch and the Roman annals." He also displays—in his use of words like *noble, gentle, virtue, name, fame, deed*, and *honor*—a mastery of the patrician vocabulary of ancient Rome as it was assimilated into English. Includes detailed textual and critical notes, which among other things comment on the relationship of certain passages to the sources. For example, the commentary on Menenius's fable of the body includes indications of where Sh follows Camden's *Remaines* rather than Plutarch. An appendix prints *The Life of Caius Martius Coriolanus* from North's Plutarch (1579) and an extract from Camden's *Remaines of a Greater Worke, Concerning Britaine* (1605).

1610 Brower, Reuben A., ed. *Coriolanus*. (Signet Classic Shakespeare.) New York: New American Library, 1966. l + [51]-304 pp.

The introduction to the play argues that Sh, by emphasizing Coriolanus's aloneness—or at least his illusion of aloneness—was setting down in the Roman forum an Achilles figure whose importance to the life of the city he had learned from Plutarch's *Lives* and the Roman historians. Taking hints from Plutarch, the playwright developed a central theme of conflicting ideas of "nature" in his protagonist, as well as a connection between Coriolanus's "heroic energy and his love of his mother." The note on the source, Plutarch's *Life of Caius Martius Coriolanus*, maintains that the play's attribution of civil disorder in republican Rome to famine rather than usury (as in Plutarch) was almost certainly influenced by the social unrest in contemporary England caused by the enclosure of farm lands. Sh's reshaping of Plutarchan material includes the following: All references to Coriolanus's political maneuvering are omitted; all scenes involving Menenius, except the first one, in which he tells the fable of the belly, are Sh's invention; except for the women's embassy (V.iii), all scenes in which Volumnia appears are added; and Sh constructs the ambivalent relationship between Aufidius and Coriolanus from one reference in Plutarch. The introduction and the introduction to the source are combined to form chapter 9 of item 0208. The introduction, text, and note on the source are reprinted as part of item 0123.

1611   Entry deleted.

1612   Bryan, Margaret B. "Volumnia—Roman Matron or Elizabethan Huswife." *RenP*, 1972 (1973), 43–58.

Maintains that *Cor.* is an *exemplum* about chaos in the commonwealth, reinforced by the presence in Volumnia of traits opposite to those considered ideal for an Elizabethan woman. Volumnia's unwomanly qualities, often brought out through contrast with Virgilia, include fierceness, garrulity, eagerness to go abroad, scorn of tears and tenderness, and a domineering attitude toward men. In addition, she raised Coriolanus poorly by encouraging him to concentrate on military skills to the neglect of more humane qualities, and during the play she encourages him to flatter and lie. Sh often modifies his source in Plutarch to emphasize these tendencies. In the background lie a number of precepts about women and motherhood, perhaps assimilated from the 1598 English translation of Aristotle's *Politics*.

1613   Buechmann, Claus-Peter. "Shakespeare's Coriolanus: The Icon of Mars." Ph.D. dissertation, University of New Mexico, 1972. *DAI*, 33 (1972–73), 3633-A-3634-A.

Argues that in creating his protagonist for *Cor.*, Sh relied on the well-established Coriolanus tradition, which in turn was based on Plutarch's account and reflected his moral judgment of the character. Sh also made consistent use of the Renaissance "icon of Mars" in developing his hero. Suggests that the audience's interest in Coriolanus is maintained by setting him off from "almost uniformly unheroic friends and enemies in Rome and Antium." When he confronts his family, he comes to a recognition that he is merely a mortal and a reversal of intention, which makes this play Sh's most classical tragedy.

1614   Bulman, James C. "*Coriolanus* and the Matter of Troy." *Mirror Up to Shakespeare: Essays in Honour of G. R. Hibbard*. Ed. J. L. Gray. Toronto: U. of Toronto P., 1984, pp. 242–60.

Argues that Sh's treatment of heroism in *Cor.* is significantly indebted to *Tro*. Hector's relationship to Achilles is the model for that of Coriolanus to Aufidius, allowing Sh to establish the legendary story of the Trojan hero's life and death as a point of reference for the tragedy of the historic figure Coriolanus. This counterpointing emphasizes the greater naturalism of Coriolanus's tragedy, while at the same time it makes clear the conflicting forces that cause his downfall, invests them with legendary meaning, and finally elevates the action to near-mythic status. Revised as parts of chapters 1 and 5 of item 0220.

1615   Burke, Kenneth. "*Coriolanus*—and the Delights of Faction." *HudR*, 19 (1966), 185–202. Reprint. *Essays in Shakespearean Criticism*. Eds. James L. Calderwood and Harold E. Toliver. Englewood Cliffs, New Jersey: Prentice Hall, 1970, pp. 530–47.

Uses *Cor.* to illustrate a formula for tragic catharsis. The hero of this "grotesque tragedy" is placed in the middle of a conflict between the privileged and the underprivileged and calls attention to the conflict in an excessive way. Unlike the "typical sacrificial victims of Greek tragedy," Coriolanus is a scurrilous railer. His invective, however, has a curative value. He arrives at an end proper to his nature, but this is paradoxically dependent on a "conspiracy" of other persons and events. For these reasons, the audience finds pleasure in Coriolanus's role as a scapegoat. Mentions *Tim.*

1616 Burton, Dolores M. "Odds beyond Arithmetic: Comparative Clauses in *Coriolanus.*" *Style*, 14 (1980), 299–317.

Notes that comparative clauses are more frequent in *Cor.* than in any other serious Shakespearean play except *Tro.* Analyzes comparative clauses in *Cor.*, demonstrating that Volumnia employs them more than any other character and that they contribute to the tragic action by making "statements about similarity and difference, differences of kind and degree, of equality and inequality."

1617 Butler, F. G. "Vestures and Gestures of Humility: *Coriolanus* Acts II and III." *ESA*, 25, no. 2 (1982), 79–108.

Points out that in act II of *Cor.* Sh deviates from his source, Plutarch, by emphasizing the symbolic significance of the gown Coriolanus is required to wear to stand for consul and Coriolanus's extreme reluctance to wear it. The white gown would have had a contemporary resonance for Sh and his audience, who would have associated it with the common people and their power to assent to the assumption of power by a king, as well as with the virtue of humility that a king must possess. Act III focuses on "an act of public penitence" that is not in Plutarch but that ironically parallels the "initial stages of an English coronation." Sh thus submits his pagans "to Christian scrutiny" at the same time that he converts his Roman tale into "a contemporary parable about the proper relationship between sovereign and people."

1618 Calderwood, James L. "*Coriolanus*: Wordless Meanings and Meaningless Words." *SEL*, 6 (1966), 211–24. Reprint. *Essays in Shakespearean Criticism.* Eds. James L. Calderwood and Harold E. Toliver. Englewood Cliffs, New Jersey: Prentice Hall, 1970, pp. 548–59.

Describes the world of Rome in *Cor.* as one in which there is a divorce between public use of words and their referents. The plebeians, in their bondage to "opinion," attach no fixed meaning to any word. Coriolanus, on the other hand, is obsessed with imposing a consistently private meaning on language. Not given to wordplay or metaphorical embellishment, Coriolanus is as insensitive to distinctions among words as he is to subtleties in human affairs. Because there is no public standard of linguistic exchange, no verbal transaction between the plebeians and Coriolanus is possible. Since the hero's self-worth cannot be validated in the public consciousness, he withdraws into his private world. But in having Coriolanus forget the name of his poor host and in other episodes, Sh illustrates the futility of clinging to private meanings that cannot be expressed publicly. In the end, the strain of maintaining a consistent private meaning in his language proves too much for Coriolanus: He loses his "name" when he joins the Volscians, is unable to keep his word to them, and dies trying to reassert a sense of solitary grandeur.

1619 Calderwood, James Lee. "Shakespeare and the Theme of Honour: Essays on *1 Henry IV, King John, All's Well*, and *Coriolanus.*" Ph.D. dissertation, University of Washington, 1963. *DA*, 24 (1963–64), 4677.

Shows how Sh, in the plays analyzed, increasingly subjects honor to critical scrutiny. The playwright moves from a melodramatic portrayal of honor as a pure virtue combating various evils to a more mature examination that emphasizes honor's "internal division and conflicting valuations."

1620 Carducci, Jane S. "Shakespeare's Coriolanus: 'Could I find out / The Woman's part in me.'" *L&P*, 33, no. 2 (1988), 11–20.

Maintains that in the protagonist of *Cor.* Sh embodied and finally rejected the Roman ideal of manliness, much admired by his own culture, that he had explored in *Tit., JC*, and *Ant.* This ideal—characterized by independence, bravery, stoicism, pride, and competitiveness—results in Coriolanus's denial of his feminine side, his failure to admit vulnerability, and his inability to communicate. The play emphasizes his isolation through rhetoric, stage directions, stage groupings, and costumes and disguises. Revision of part of item 0240.

1621   Carey, Anna Kirwan Steck. "'Less Than a Man': The Child Actors and Tragic Satire." Ph.D. dissertation, University of Cincinnati, 1986. *DAI*, 47 (1986–87), 908-A.

Maintains that in Sh's era the writers for child actors shaped dramatic conventions to call attention to the performers' immaturity. The heroes of tragic satire cry a good deal for their mothers, find themselves unable to promote significant action, and are often referred to as "boy" and "child." Adapting these conventions to adult drama, Sh created in *Cor.* an ambivalent hero who shares the intractability and ineffectiveness of the child heroes of Chapman, Marlowe, and Marston.

1622   Carr, W. I. "'Gracious Silence'—A Selective Reading of *Coriolanus*." *ES*, 46 (1965), 221–34.

Argues that Coriolanus "is incomplete, but alive enough to suffer and to make us sympathetic witnesses of his suffering." He is the scapegoat for the failure of his class and his world.

1623   Cavell, Stanley. "*Coriolanus* and Interpretations of Politics ('Who does the wolf love?')." *Representations*, 1, no. 3 (1983), 1–20. Reprint. *Themes Out of School: Effects and Causes*. San Francisco: North Point P., 1984, pp. 60–96. Reprint. *Disowning Knowledge in Six Plays of Shakespeare*. Cambridge: Cambridge U. P., 1987, pp. 143–77.

Focuses on images of "food and hunger, of cannibalism and disgust" to investigate the "paradox and reciprocity of hungering," whereby Volumnia and Coriolanus are both starvers and hungerers: For them, desire has "a structure of endlessness," and what they hunger for is "not to hunger, not to desire, that is, not to be mortal." This situation is registered in the ambivalent question Menenius asks the tribunes, "who does the wolf love?" (II.i.7), which can mean either "who is the object of the wolf's affection?" or "who loves the wolf?" Sicinius's answer, "The lamb," preserves the ambiguity and allows the speculation that Coriolanus longs to be a god and that his fate is an inflection of Christ's: his sacrifice, unlike Christ's, is not redemptive; his tragedy is that he cannot achieve tragedy. Notes the parallels between *Cor.* and Euripides' *Bacchae*, especially the similarity of Coriolanus's final plea to his mother to the plea of Pentheus to his mother. Sh did not necessarily know the *Bacchae*; he could have read the story of Pentheus in Ovid. See item 1747.

1624   Chappell, Fred. "Shakespeare's *Coriolanus* and Plutarch's Life of Cato." *RenP,* 1962, (1963) 9–16.

Suggests that Sh used Plutarch's *Life* of Marcus Cato as an "ideological source" for *Cor.* Like Cato, Coriolanus is modest, is a famous soldier, and refuses "to gain office by flattering the plebeians." Certain images—of the body and body politic, of poison, of the herd—that are prominent in *Cor.* are also found in Plutarch's *Life* of Cato but not in his *Life* of Coriolanus.

1624a   Coleman, William S. E. "The Peculiar Artisitic Quality of Shakespeare's *Coriolanus.*" *On-Stage Studies*, 7 (1983), 73–84.

Proposes to review scholarship on *Cor.* that deals with its theatrical side, to understand how it works on the stage. Breaks the play down into "five major elements": plot, imagery, word usage, sound and music effects, and visual theatrical effects. Notes that the stage directions recognize with unusual explicitness that this is a play intended for the theater rather than the printed page." Notices the "lavish use of extras," the frequent appearance on stage of the lower classes, the prominence given to Marcius's wounds, the bluntness of the language, and the frequent references to sounds. Finds the play to be well-constructed and interesting; it is not, however, especially successful in the theater because it unappealingly exposes "the spiritual nudity of the human race."

1625 Colman, E. A. M. "The End of *Coriolanus*." *ELH*, 34 (1967), 1–20.

Disputes critics who find the end of *Cor*. faulty. In this play, Sh employs a technique different from that found in the other tragedies: He establishes many things through dramatic action rather than through speech. Coriolanus is repeatedly faced with situations that challenge his integrity, and he alternates between complying with others and asserting himself. The same issues keep confronting him, but each time they are presented with increasing complexity. As the play progresses, and especially in the crises of act III, Coriolanus becomes more aware of the threats to his integrity and more capable of caring for other people. The cyclic pattern of "defiance–compliance–defiance" established early in the play leads us to expect one further gesture of self-assertion from the hero after his surrender to his mother in V.iii, and this is what we get with his explosive rage in the face of the Volscian murderers. His last words are few, but they are sufficient to provide a reaffirmation of his "aspiration to personal integrity." Together with Coriolanus's last interview with Volumnia, his death scene constitutes a tragic conclusion that draws together the important concerns of the play in a delicate balance between good and evil.

1626 Craig, Hardin. "*Coriolanus*: Interpretation." *Pacific Coast Studies in Shakespeare*. Eds. Waldo F. McNeir and Thelma N. Greenfield. Eugene: U. of Oregon Books, 1966, pp. 199–209.

Argues that *Cor*. has been misinterpreted both in terms of "the philosophy of nature that underlies the action and the nature of the tragedy that results." Coriolanus is not proud; he simply stands for the hierarchical order almost universally approved in Sh's age. Many excesses for which he is blamed cannot be documented: There is no evidence, for example, that as leader of the Volsces he intends to burn Rome. "A superior member of a superior class," Coriolanus makes the play a great tragedy by his "success in failure."

1626a Crookes, David Z. "'Small as a Eunuch': A Problem in *Coriolanus*, Act III, Scene 2." *Music and Letters*, 67 (1986), 159–61.

Analyzes a key speech in which, after the riot (*Cor.*, III.i), Coriolanus expresses his unwillingness to seek the approval of the rabble, whom he detests. When he comments that in order to perform such a dishonorable action, he must be possessed by "[s]ome harlot's spirit" and his "throat of war" must "be turn'd ... into a pipe / Small as a eunuch" (III.ii.114–116), he is referring to a musical instrument called a eunuch. This instrument consists of a hollow tube "open at one end and closed at the other by a piece of thin parchment, which is stretched like the head of a drum and protected by a perforated cap." To make the instrument sound, one vocalizes through "a hole in the pipe body." Alone of musical instruments, the eunuch–flute can generate no sound of its own. What Sh is having Coriolanus say in this powerful image is that in trying to win the love of the people, he "will be a host instrument for breath not his own, and his cheeks, eyes and lips will be taken over."

1627 Crowley, Richard C. "*Coriolanus* and the Epic Genre." *Shakespeare's Late Plays: Essays in Honor of Charles Crow*. Eds. Richard C. Tobias and Paul G. Zolbrod. Athens: Ohio U. P., 1974, pp. 114–30.

Contends that *Cor*. can be better understood if it is seen as a work whose protagonist is in the epic, as well as the tragic, mode. Its relationship to the epic can be explored in three ways: (1) The imagery invites frequent comparisons between Coriolanus and legendary heroes like Hector, Ulysses, and Achilles; (2) the plot and the character of the hero highlight the magnificent, the marvelous, and the unusual qualities derived from the epic that 16th-c. Italian critics identified as highly desirable in tragedy; (3) as in epic tradition, Coriolanus's *agon* centers on the conflict between love and honor. Revision of part of item 1628.

1628 Crowley, Richard Charles. "*Coriolanus* and the Epic Tradition." Ph.D. dissertation, University of Pittsburgh, 1971. *DAI*, 32 (1971–72), 3245-A–3246-A.

Considers *Cor*. as an example of epic drama, with a soldier–warrior for a hero. There are several reasons for this classification. First, the play seems to follow Renaissance prescriptions for investing the dramatic protagonist with qualities found in the epic hero: love of battle and great reputation among his peers, contempt for the less courageous, and rash hot-headedness. Second, we are invited throughout the text to make comparisons between Martius and the great mythic warriors—Odysseus, Achilles, Hector, and Mars. Third, the hero of the play is faced with the classic conflict between love and valor. Sh can be seen to treat the ideas of nobility, devotion to duty, and loyalty to the state with considerable irony. Part revised as item 1627.

1629 Danson, Lawrence N. "Metonymy and *Coriolanus*." *PQ*, 52 (1973), 30–42.

Maintains that the figure of metonymy—in which the parts stand for the whole and the whole absorbs its parts—is unusually prominent in *Cor*. This is appropriate for a play that is about "the relationship of the individual to the community, of the community to its constituent members, of the association of man with man, and of man with the elements that compound him." Menenius's fable of the belly is a metonymy that defines the macrocosm of Rome in its fragmentary reality. Once this way of seeing Rome is established, microcosmic metonymies inevitably follow. In the midst of fragmentation, Coriolanus stands alone, refusing—though in vain—"any division of his essence." His distrust of language and his reluctance to exhibit his wounds rise from a hatred of allowing parts to speak for his whole. But his quest "to be heroically self-constituted" is doomed because, in being true to himself by joining the Volscians, he is false to another self—one that is "a son, a husband, a father, a Roman." The prominence of metonymy in *Cor*. helps account for "the peculiarly narrow effect of the play." Metonymy is a figure of contiguity, which works only "within a single world of discourse," rather than linking different worlds, like metaphor and simile. In most cases, Sh relies more on metaphor. *Cor*., because of its theme, is an exception. Revision of part of item 0303. Revised as chapter 7 of item 0302.

1630 Davidson, Clifford. "*Coriolanus*: A Study in Political Dislocation." *ShakS*, 4 (1968), 263–74.

Maintains that *Cor*. investigates the question of the proper relationship between the individual and the state. In the play, Coriolanus and the patricians fail to provide the leadership appropriate for their class; for example, the fable of the belly associates them with greed. Contemporary English commentary, including the glosses of the translator in a 1598 version of Aristotle's *Politics*, emphasized that dislocation in the state results from the irresponsibility of the nobles, that love binds together the parts of the commonwealth, that the whole takes priority over the parts, and that a primary obligation of leaders is to exercise self-control. Coriolanus, who represents and defends the nobles, loves not Rome but his family and himself, views political order in terms of a class struggle, and lacks all of the cardinal virtues, including temperance. The audience should not choose sides between the patricians and the plebeians; both fall short. Along with *Tro*. and *Tim*., *Cor*. is a tragedy of political and moral chaos.

1631 Dean, Paul. "*Coriolanus*: A Tragedy of Love." *English*, 40 (1991), 117–34.

Views *Cor*. primarily as "a story of frustrated love and betrayal," in which the hero, identifying his mother with Rome and unable to disentangle love and civic duty, recognizes that he no longer has a place in the Rome that his mother and Menenius have colluded with the tribunes to establish.

Coriolanus

1632 DeGrazia, Margreta. "Shakespeare's View of Language: An Historical Perspective." *SQ*, 29 (1978), 374–88.

Maintains that Sh's view of language was a traditional Christian one, according to which communication can be corrupted by moral defects in a speaker. For example, Coriolanus's pride prevents him from talking to the populace. In interpreting works like *Cor.*, we should avoid imposing modern skepticism about the capacity of language itself to communicate on Sh.

1632a Dessen, Alan. "The Logic of Elizabethan Stage Violence: Some Alarums and Excursions for Modern Critics, Editors, and Directors." *RenD*, N. S. 9 (1978 [1979]), 39–69.

Includes discussion of the only scene in *Cor.* (I.iv) in which the hero is shown as living up to his claim that he can stand alone as author of himself. Notes that the rest of the play emphasizes "the failure of Coriolanus either to be self-sufficient or to find a place in any city."

1632b Donno, Elizabeth Story. "*Coriolanus* and a Shakespearean Motif." *Shakespeare and Dramatic Tradition: Essays in Honor of S. F. Johnson.* Eds. William R. Elton and William B. Long. Newark: U. of Delaware P., 1989, pp. 47–68.

Surveys the use in Sh's plays of the "antirhetorical" motif that the tongue should speak only what the heart believes, associating it with a range of characters, "good, mixed, or evil." Focuses on *Cor.*, in which this motif becomes thematic. The protagonist's political failure under the conditions of a primitive, warring Rome and his tragedy are defined by his "inability to tolerate the disjunction between what the heart prompts and what is required by expediency."

1633 Doran, Madeleine. "'All's in anger': The Language of Contention in *Coriolanus.*" *Shakespeare's Dramatic Language: Essays by Madeleine Doran.* Madison: U. of Wisconsin P., 1976, pp. 182–217.

Explores the ways in which the language of *Cor.* gives life to Sh's contentious plot. Sh uses rhetorical figures of opposition like *antithesis, synoeciosis, paradox,* and *dilemma,* though he modifies them freely. He also employs other modes of contrast (like comparison) that are not antithetical figures in the strict sense. In the first three scenes of *Cor.*, three separate strands of the plot are presented through stylistic devices of contrariety: the conflict between the patricians and the plebeians, the war against the Volscians, and the domination of Coriolanus by his mother. In two later scenes, those of Martius's victory after Corioli and the formal celebration at Rome, the intensity of the action is increased by a brilliant combination of "hyperbole and meiosis, of fulsome praise" on the part of Coriolanus's admirers and "surly reticence" on his part. The episodes leading to the banishment and those just before the catastrophe are also fraught with stylistic devices indicating opposition. In particular, we see in these scenes the various challenges to Coriolanus's integrity that will eventually bring him down.

1634 Draper, John W. "'Hybris' in Shakespeare's Tragic Heroes." *EA*, 18 (1965), 228–34.

Explains that hubris, as described in Aristotle's *Poetics*, is the chief element in the makeup of the Sophoclean tragic hero. Surveys Sh's chief tragic heroes and finds all of them, except Coriolanus, lacking in hubris. Only in his last tragedy *Cor.*, and without the direct knowledge of Sophocles or Aristotle, did Sh create a classical tragic protagonist.

1635 duBois, Page. "A Disturbance of Syntax at the Gates of Rome." *Stanford Literary Review*, 2, no. 2 (1985), 185–208.

Argues that *Cor.* is about "breaks in lines," "the failure to follow," and "sequences [that] are broken." The play reads the world through the relationship of mother to son, and Rome exemplifies a matriarchal universe that malfunctions. Trapped by his mother, Coriolanus sacrifices himself rather than cause her dishonor or death.

1636 Fields, Albert W. "The Shakespearean Self-Author." *South Central Bulletin*, 34 (1974), 150–56.

Includes the hero of *Cor.* in a group of Shakespearean characters who, defying what the Elizabethans would have seen as natural order, attempt to create themselves according to their own desires. Among these characters, Coriolanus is most like Macbeth in his initial nobility, his great military prowess, and his subscription to a notion of self that "has been largely designed by a strong-willed woman." Unable to practice hypocrisy like the other self-authors, Coriolanus nevertheless resembles them in his self-deception, which leads him to fulfill his notion of self in a "destructively aggressive" fashion, to attempt the manipulation of others, to privilege his baser instincts, and to violate the ethical and ontological concepts of his society.

1637 Fish, Stanley E. "How to Do Things with Austin and Searle: Speech Act Theory and Literary Criticism." *MLN*, 91 (1976), 983–1025. Reprint *Is There a Text in This Class?* Cambridge: Harvard U. P., 1980, pp. 197–245.

Argues that *Cor.* is a "Speech Act" play; that is, it concerns "the conventions" or "discourse agreements" that allow the audience to determine the "felicity" of the particular speeches of the hero. Comments on the way that language functions for Coriolanus: It is "the servant of essences he alone can recognize because he alone embodies them." He seeks "a world where essences are immediately recognized and do not require for their validation the mediation of public procedures." See items 1594, 1707, and 1747.

1638 Fortescue, Jonathan. "The Folds in the Belly: A Parable of Taking Up Representation in *The Tragedy of Coriolanus*." *SJW*, 127 (1991), 106–19.

Analyzes the first scene of *Cor.*, noting that the plebeians who storm onto the stage are both part of the linguistic fiction of the drama and an approximation of "the space at the margin of London where the theatrical voice could register, even foreground the divisive tension between a representable authority and the artisans who 'show forth' significant roles which are contiguous with the vulnerable mechanisms of theatre." This bifold perspective can also be applied to Menenius, who was played by Robert Armin, recognizable to the audience as a clown with the ability to demonstrate the varied qualities of the platform stage. Menenius's fable of the belly can thus be read both as a "response to the political turmoil of Rome" and "a way to accommodate the impatient desires of the audience for entertainment." As the fable proceeds, Menenius asks for patience from the plebeians so that they can "digest" what he has to say; similarly, the audience is asked to be patient with "representational strategy." Armin, in his role of Menenius, belches several times during the recounting of his parable, comically implicating the citizens and the audience in this strategy. Coriolanus's isolation, however, compels him to use a diction that sequesters him from the turbulence of "the Roman streets and the barren stage."

1639 Frye, Dean. "Commentary in Shakespeare: The Case of *Coriolanus*." *ShakS*, 1 (1965), 105–17.

Shows how commentary within a play has much to do with the ways in which "the sympathies of the audience are allotted." At the beginning of *Cor.*, the citizens portray the protagonist as proud and contemptuous, but subsequent scenes show these attitudes on his part to be largely justified. Once they come under the control of the tribunes, the citizens lose their standing as reliable commentators. Sicinius and Brutus are "self-serving Machiavellians," and hence the authority of their comments on

Coriolanus, even when true, is compromised in the eyes of the audience. Menenius's choric statements work to discredit both the tribunes and the citizens. The patricians, as well as the two officers of II.ii, are critical of Coriolanus but finally see more to praise than to blame. Other characters come to share this view and thus give it considerable weight for the audience.

1640 Frye, Roland M. "Shakespeare's Mirror Image of Failure: *Richard II* and *Coriolanus.*" *Forum H*, 11, nos. 2 and 3 (1973–74), 11–20.

Points out that Coriolanus, unlike Richard II, has no flexibility; though he is encouraged to develop a repertory of roles that will ensure his success as a peacetime leader, he stubbornly refuses to compromise his rigid integrity.

1641 Gajdusek, R. E. "Death, Incest, and the Triple Bond in the Later Plays of Shakespeare." *AI*, 31 (1974), 109–58.

Regards the three women who visit Coriolanus to save Rome (*Cor.*, V.iii) as a mythic trinity. Like the Fates, they draw Coriolanus toward the realm of life and death (in his triple role of husband, son and father). His capitulation signifies his understanding that he is relinquishing honor and greatness, overthrowing his masculine self, and entering the realm of nature, where the feminine instructs man to accept mortality. Suggests that in Coriolanus's acquiescence can be seen the aging Sh's "recognition of his human limits."

1642 Gaudet, Paul. "Gesture in *Coriolanus*: Textual Cues for Actor and Audience." *UC*, 8 (1988), 77–92.

Examines two scenes from *Cor.* (II.i and V.iii) in which Sh uses "internal performance cues" simultaneously "as response cues" for the audience. In the first of these scenes, Volumnia's haste to greet her triumphant son is dramatized; her exit is delayed three times while she talks with maternal pride of her son's martial achievements. The fact that her narration momentarily takes precedence over the action of meeting with Coriolanus indicates the extent to which she regards her son's character as her own creation, and the scene's conclusion, with Coriolanus coming to her rather than the reverse, confirms her dominance. The second scene, in which Coriolanus capitulates to his mother, is the culmination of a carefully arranged sequence. From the perspective of the characters in the play, the series of appeals to save Rome, denied by Coriolanus through various gestures of dismissal and turning away, seems doomed to failure. To the audience, however, "the climactic structure of appeals and textual indications of Coriolanus's inner turmoil subtly redefine his gestures as defensive poses" and prepare for his holding his mother's hand in an "unexpected" action of silent surrender.

1643 Giese, Loreen Lee. "Denied Identities: Social Rituals in Selected Shakespearean Drama." Ph.D. dissertation, Emory University, 1991. *DAI*, 52 (1991–92), 1338-A.

Adduces *Cor.* as one example of the dramatization of a conflict "between a person's definition of identity and a socially agreed-upon one," a conflict that ends by denying the person's "self-contrived identity."

1644 Gillham, E. G. "*Coriolanus.*" *ESA*, 20 (1977), 43–52.

Refers to a speech by Aufidius in IV.vii that details the hero's faults and suggests that they are also his merits. Emphasizes Coriolanus's unshakable integrity, which makes him impossible to live with. Examines the protagonist's speeches in III.i to show that his three-part indictment of Rome's weakness is essentially accurate: (1) The senate has foolishly relinquished power to the people; (2) the commons, who have taken over this power, are unfit to rule; and (3) the aristocrats have rendered themselves incapable of governing. Coriolanus, being intuitive rather than rational, does not entirely understand the implications of what he is saying. His "Roman ideal of service to the state" is rigid and narrow, but unlike the people who taught it to him, he takes it seriously and serves it honorably and consistently.

1645 Givan, Christopher. "Shakespeare's *Coriolanus*: The Premature Epitaph and the Butterfly." *ShakS*, 12 (1979), 143–58.

Claims that Coriolanus loathes the mob because it exemplifies everything he hates and fears in himself. His use of various kinds of dehumanizing imagery (especially animal and inanimate) finds a parallel in the tendency of the other characters to dehumanize him as an animal or a thing in order to praise him. This tendency is particularly noticeable in a "premature epitaph" for Coriolanus voiced by Lartius in act I. Coriolanus struggles constantly to define himself, but society's renaming of him and its compulsion to reckon his value in mathematical terms wrest control of his identity from him. The thrice-recurring motif of the butterfly provides insight into Coriolanus's role as both aggressor and victim and into the obsessive pattern of winning and losing from which he cannot free himself.

1646 Goldfarb, Barry. "The Socratic Paradigm in Shakespeare's *Coriolanus*." *Text and Presentation: The Journal of the Comparative Drama Conference*, 11 (1991), 39–48.

Suggests that *Cor.* is "informed by the example of Socrates," who resembles Coriolanus in excelling his fellow-citizens, in being connected with an alter-ego who seeks to destroy his homeland, and in being condemned to death by his countrymen. There is an important difference, however, "with Coriolanus betraying his city" and Socrates dying under the jurisdiction of his. Two things help to explain this: Coriolanus is finally governed by his relationship with his family, while Socrates has no such relationship; and Socrates, though wary of the improper use of language, approves it for philosophical purposes, while Coriolanus regards all language with suspicion, preferring the purity of action. In very different ways, both men are victims of rhetoric.

1647 Goldman, Michael. "Characterizing Coriolanus." *ShS*, 34 (1981), 73–84.

Rejects discursive analysis (suitable for the novel and modern psychology) as the appropriate means for understanding character in drama; instead, we should accept a more problematic approach. In *Cor.*, Sh presents a hero whose inner life cannot be consistently explained from any one point of view. Throughout the play, Coriolanus's friends and enemies attempt unsuccessfully to characterize him psychologically. Coriolanus repeatedly rejects the authority of the audience on the stage and even the audience in the theater as he essays to author his own character. The project is self-deluding, however, because his character depends to a great extent on these audiences. Coriolanus as an authentic individual seems to be situated somewhere between himself and his fellows, not wholly identified with either. To emphasize "the problematics of characterization," Sh took Plutarch's clear image of "a great warrior" who is "intemperately angry and hence given over to solitariness" and introduced several complexities that make him less susceptible to analysis. Revised as chapter 7 of item 0447.

1648 Gordon, D. J. "Name and Fame: Shakespeare's *Coriolanus*." *Papers, Mainly Shakespearean*. Ed. G. I. Duthie. Edinburgh: Oliver and Boyd, 1964, pp. 40–57. Reprint. *The Renaissance Imagination: Essays and Lectures by D. J. Gordon*. Ed. Stephen Orgel. Berkeley: U. of California P., 1976, pp. 203–19.

Maintains that *Cor.*, like *1H4* and *Tro.*, is centrally concerned with a critique of honor. Working with a set of words (*glory, fame, report, praise, opinion, voice, honor,* and *name*) derived from classical writers, Sh explores the relationships between Coriolanus and the members of his community. He presents the civil life "in terms of empty, perverted, destructive relationships between speaker and utterance, word and subject, which is between man and man and man and himself." The absoluteness of the self Coriolanus seeks cannot be maintained; he must finally turn toward relationship. But within the city, "the words that identify and bind become words that debase and destroy." The language that gives name or honor to the self is unstable: Words are separated from what they signify and turn into their opposites. Coriolanus is destroyed in the act of asserting his identity.

1649 Gurr, Andrew. "*Coriolanus* and the Body Politic." *ShS*, 28 (1975), 63–69.

Contends that through his presentation of the belly fable in *Cor.* Sh exposed the basic anomalies in the concept of the body politic. This Aristotelian notion, which had been promoted by the Tudors, envisioned the state as "a corporate organism, symbolised in parliament with the king as head and lords and commons as 'members.'" It became important "to be able to say that the actions of government went forward with the consent of the whole nation." James I challenged this idea by asserting that authority resides solely "in the person of the king." Edward Forset's *Comparative Discourse of the Bodies Natural and Politique* (1606) reflects this new emphasis in its retelling of the belly fable. Forset unwittingly reveals the difficulties with the body politic image by linking it with the belly fable and by indicating that the rebelling commons saw the aristocrats as the belly, not (as in previous versions) the head. Sh's version of the belly fable, which connects it with the body politic, shows the possible influence of Forset. *Cor.* stresses the anomalies of the body politic image in other ways. Instead of two riots, one about usury and one about food, as in Plutarch and other sources, Sh chooses to depict only the food riot, probably as a parallel to the Midlands food riots of 1607; also, he transfers the belly fable from the usury riot in the sources to the food riot and suppresses the point, found in the episode of the belly fable in Livy and Plutarch, that Menenius "was popular with the citizens because he was a former pleb himself." All of this underlines the civil strife most Elizabethan commentators saw as characteristic of the Roman republic. Through his alterations of the belly fable, Sh seems to have registered an awareness of the strains being put on the organic analogy for the state in the early 17th c.

1650 Hale, D. G. *The Body Politic: A Political Metaphor in Renaissance English Literature*. The Hague: Mouton, 1971. 150 pp.

Studies the use of the human body as an analogy to express the unity of the state in England during the Renaissance. Chapter 2 surveys classical antecedents for the analogy, including passages from the *Areopagitica* of Isocrates, the *Republic* and *Laws* of Plato, the *Politics* of Aristotle, the *Antigone* of Sophocles, the *Wasps* of Aristophanes, the *De Officiis* of Cicero, and the *Moral Essays* of Seneca. The fable of the belly occurs in Aseop; the Roman historian Livy; the Greek historians Dio Cocceianus, and Dionysius of Halicarnassus; and Plutarch. The organic analogy of society passed into the Christian tradition from the late Stoics. Chapter 4 includes an analysis of the body politic metaphor in *Cor.*, in which Sh uses it to discuss and judge political acts. The tragedy of *Cor.* arises from the breach between the ideal of the common weal and "the imperfect men who live on this imperfect earth." Parts are revisions of items 1651 and 1652; the whole is a revision of item 1653.

1651 Hale, D. G. "*Coriolanus*: The Death of a Political Metaphor." *SQ*, 22 (1971), 197–202.

Maintains that during the first three acts of *Cor.*, there is "a sustained attempt to impose the analogy of the body politic on a political situation." In I.i, Menenius's fable of the belly is undermined by the Second Citizen's suggestion of an alternative hierarchy controlled by the head. The scene is inconclusive; the fable does not completely satisfy the mutineers. In III.i, the body analogy is used by both the tribunes and Coriolanus to accuse each other of poisoning the state. The people join in and employ the analogy to emphasize their independence of the body politic. The fable of the belly is not applicable to Coriolanus, whose aristocratic nature never permits him to see himself as a member of the state. It is not only Coriolanus to whom the body analogy for the city is irrelevant; many other characters are "selfish or self-righteous" and are uncomfortable with being part of anything. They are so flawed that the analogy fails. Revision of part of item 1653. Revised as part of item 1650.

1652   Hale, David G. "Intestine Sedition: The Fable of the Belly." *CLS*, 5 (1968), 377–88.

Traces the fable of the belly from its earliest appearances in Greek and Roman authors through Milton. In its simplest form, attributed to Aesop, it first appears in a Greek prose collection of the 3rd c. A.D. or earlier. In Livy's version, Menenius Agrippa applies the fable to the plebeian recession. Throughout its history, the fable is usually nonpolitical when it is included in a collection; when it appears alone, however, it commonly has a political purpose. In *Cor.*, Menenius's attempt to maintain political stability with the fable fails: The analogy cannot account for or contain the protagonist. Revision of part of item 1653. Revised as part of item 1650.

1653   Hale, David George. "The Body Politic: A Political Metaphor in Renaissance English Literature." Ph.D dissertation, Duke University, 1965. *DA*, 26 (1965–66), 4658–4659.

Traces the analogy between the human body and society from its classical origins through the 17th c. Notes that "the fable of the belly and the rebellious members" is an important aspect of this tradition. Includes a discussion of the analogy as it is used in *Cor.* Parts revised as items 1651 and 1652 and the whole as item 1650.

1654   Halio, Jay L. "*Coriolanus*: Shakespeare's 'Drama of Reconciliation.'" *ShakS*, 6 (1970), 289–303.

Treats *Cor.* as a tragedy of reconciliation, a harbinger of Sh's romances. The hero, even from the beginning, is not without humanity or compassion. He is persuaded by his mother and friends to prostitute himself by seeking the consulship. The central action of the play consists of the conspiracy by the tribunes that results in his rejection of all ties with Rome and his family. But in reversing his decision to destroy Rome, Coriolanus makes the right choice: Instead of trying to be godly in the pagan sense (knowing no other kin), he emulates Christian godliness (recognizing his own kinship with other frail human beings and showing mercy). It is noteworthy that Sh eliminated numerous supernatural events in Plutarch, his source, probably because he wanted to signify that the ending of *Cor.* is not as disastrous as those of certain other tragedies. A number of other things soften the tragic conclusion: Volumnia's appeal to her son to save the city is not ignoble; Aufidius, operating under a pagan code of revenge, is clearly intended as a foil to Coriolanus; Coriolanus, though making himself vulnerable by showing mercy, is restored to his family; and Rome rejoices at its rescue.

1655   Helphinstine, Frances. "Volumnia: The Life of Rome." *SRASP*, 4 (Spring 1979), 55–63.

Explains that in *Cor.* Volumnia controls Coriolanus by using a variety of appeals. She values some ancient Roman ideals (endurance, courage, and self-reliance), distorts or misuses others (a sense of the importance of things at hand, parental respect, and honor), and employs effective rhetorical skills to divide her son against himself. Her preoccupation with her son's reputation results in an unfeminine delight in violence and bloodshed. She does, however, achieve fame for herself as Rome's savior by creating a hero to defend the city and then destroying him when he turns his strength against it.

1656.   Henderson, Archibald. "*Coriolanus* and the Grief of Shakespeare." *Shakespeare in the Southwest: Some New Directions.* Ed. T. J. Stafford. El Paso: Texas Western P., 1969, pp. 71–79.

Argues that *Cor.*, "written in 1608 or 1609, both demonstrates the relationship of Shakespeare to his mother and records his sorrow at her death." Many of the family relationships in Sh's life—domination by the mother, rejection by the father, sibling rivalry—are reflected in the play.

1657 Hibbard, G. R., ed. *Coriolanus*. (New Penguin Shakespeare.)
Harmondsworth: Penguin, 1967. 264 pp.

The introduction discusses the five strands of action in *Cor.* that are woven together to form the plot; the tight structure (the most symmetrical of all Sh's tragedies); the conflict between the Roman virtues of *virtus* and *pietas*; the paradoxical fact that *Cor.* is Sh's most Roman play at the same time that it is thoroughly Jacobean; the appropriateness of Sh's writing *Cor.* as the last of a cluster of three late works (the other two are *Tim.* and *Ant.*) based on Plutarch's *Lives*; the three movements (after the overture of the first three scenes) that occupy the entire action; the ambivalence (which is to say the judiciousness) of Sh's handling of the class struggle and of the protagonist himself; the Aristotelian ideas of the city and of the natural association of men by which Sh seems to measure the world of the play; and Coriolanus's incomplete integrity (based only on individual honesty, not on a sense of organic community), his vulnerability to words, his lack of self-knowledge, and his tragic final acceptance of the natural in the capitulation to his mother.

1658 Hill, R. F. "*Coriolanus*: Violentest Contrariety." *E&S*, 17 (1964), 12–23.

Canvasses "the syntactical and rhetorical ordering" in *Cor.* Antithesis is used pervasively to characterize Coriolanus, the patricians, and the plebeians. Through this device the principal figures can all be seen as flawed by crudeness, immoderation, and intransigence. Antithesis thus contributes to the sense that *Cor.* is intensely narrow in its moral reference, a tragedy involving "a blank facing of entrenched positions."

1659 Holbrook, Peter James. "The Social Symbolism of Literary Modes in the English Renaissance: Social Interplay in Shakespeare, Nashe, and Bourgeois Tragedy." Ph.D. dissertation, Yale University, 1990. *DAI*, 51 (1990–91), 2753-A.

Studies "the social meaning and status of literary modes in the Elizabethan period." Includes a discussion of *Cor.* as a play that achieves a certain detachment toward a tragic ethos, "which is isolated, and to some extent criticized, as a specifically aristocratic ideology."

1660 Holstun, James. "Tragic Superfluity in *Coriolanus*." *ELH*, 50 (1983), 485–507.

Explains that, in the revolt of the plebeians with which he begins *Cor.*, Sh conflates two rebellions in his principal source, Plutarch's *The Life of Caius Martius Coriolanus*, one prompted by usury and the other by famine. This combination seriously compromises the fable of the belly through which Menenius attempts to attribute organic unity to the body politic (I.i). The play eschews "the monarchical model of the body politic," which is allied with "the tragedy of kingly transition." Instead, it can be more accurately described as "aristocratic satire," allied with "property and strategy." Both the protagonist and the conventions of tragedy itself are the butts of satire. At the end, for example, Aufidius "invokes tragedy with comic abruptness" to dispose quickly of Coriolanus and the threat he has posed to the nonorganic aristocratic orders of both the Romans and the Volscians.

1661 Holt, Douglas Leigh Jr. "From Man to Dragon: A Study of Shakespeare's *Coriolanus*." Ph.D. dissertation, Yale University, 1973. *DAI*, 34 (1973–74), 2563-A.

Points out that the focus of *Cor.* on the public and the ordinary distinguishes it from Sh's other tragedies. The protagonist's view of political integrity involves a fierce devotion to "Roman" consistency in the self, which figures the necessity for coherence among all parts of the state. Coriolanus's complete self is available in the public arena, but this same availability makes him a "lonely dragon," surrounded by men who do not express themselves so freely. He maintains his integrity through "pure play," which issues in "action itself," not in action for ulterior purposes. His concept of self is undermined by his mother, who counsels play-acting for political gain, and he "becomes his own antithesis" when he commits himself to the objective of destroying Rome. Forced to deal with ambiguity, he cannot retain his unified sense of self. Revised as item 1662.

1662 Holt, Leigh. *From Man to Dragon: A Study of Shakespeare's "Coriolanus."* (JDS 61.) Salzburg: Institut für Englische Sprache und Literatur, U. Salzburg, 1976. 241 pp.
Revision of item 1661.

1663 Huffman, Clifford Chalmers. "Coriolanus and His Poor Host: A Note." *EA*, 35, no. 2 (1982), 173–76.
Points out that in Sh's source for *Cor.*, Plutarch's *Life of Caius Martius Coriolanus*, Coriolanus asks that an unnamed "olde friende and hoste" be spared from slavery. This request is met with unqualified approval, and there is no suggestion that it is not carried out. By having Coriolanus forget the host's name (I.ix.81–91), Sh makes the scene equivocal. Other versions of the poor host theme, in essays by Plutarch and Montaigne that display a fascination with the unpredictable response of conquerors to the noble behavior of their prisoners, may have influenced Sh. The Plutarch essay also suggested the name "Lotus" for Aufidius's servant (IV.v).

1664 Huffman, Clifford Chalmers. "*Coriolanus* and Jacobean Attitudes toward the Mixed State." Ph.D. dissertation, Columbia University, 1969. *DAI*, 33 (1972–73), 3650-A.
Studies the history of English political commentary on the Roman republic, or "mixed state," and notes that many writers favored it. Based on "works of classical political philosophy," especially those of Plutarch and Polybius, these views encouraged Sh to treat the republic positively in works like *Luc.*, *Tit.*, and *JC*. In *Cor.*, however, Sh reflects "the anti-democratic bias of the Jacobean court" by depicting the republic in an ironic, ambivalent way. Revised as item 1665.

1665 Huffman, Clifford Chalmers. "*Coriolanus" in Context.* Lewisburg: Bucknell U. P., 1971. 260 pp.
Provides a thorough background for *Cor.*, particularly in giving detailed information about attitudes toward mixed government in classical, Italian, and English sources. Mixed government involved a sharing of power among the monarch, the aristocracy, and the people, usually with one of these components possessing somewhat more authority than the others. Sh wrote *Cor.* at a time of crisis and deliberately avoided endorsing either aristocracy or popular government (there is no monarch in the play). We see only two opposing extremes and are exposed to the potential tyranny of each. Sh presents a moral ideal of temperance, but "the ironic mode of *Cor.* prevents its implementation." Revision of item 1664. See also item 0041.

1666 Hunt, Maurice. "Shakespeare's Tragic Homeopathy." *Shakespeare: Text, Subtext, and Context.* Ed. Ronald Dotterer. (Susquehanna University Studies.) Selinsgrove: Susquehanna U. P., 1989, pp. 77–84.
Traces in the views of Italian neoclassical critics like Castelvetro and Minturno the combination of the classical principle of homeopathy (rediscovered by Paracelsus in the 16th c.) with Aristotelian tragic catharsis. Argues that in Edgar's reaction to Lear's suffering in *Lr.*, homeopathic cartharsis refines pity and fear, making them bearable for him, though this effect does not apply to the play as a whole. The primary catastrophe of *Cor.*, however, does operate through homeopathic cartharsis.

Coriolanus

1667 Hunt, Maurice. "'Violent'st' Complementarity": The Double Warriors of *Coriolanus*." *SEL*, 31 (1991), 309–25.

Cites Plato's *Symposium*, with its account of how men were originally creatures with four arms and four legs and were split into the men of today, as background for the study of the complementarity that Sh explores in *Cor*. Maintains that the relationship between Othello and Iago, which Sh had recently created, was influential in his development of Coriolanus and Aufidius, whose complementarity of two separate selves is modulated at times into "a symbolic union of selves." In these two figures, we see the qualities of "absolutism and policy tragically unassimilated in the composite classical aristocrat."

1668 Hutchings, W. "Beast or God: The *Coriolanus* Controversy." *CritQ*, 24, no. 2 (1982), 35–50. Reprint. *Shakespeare's Wide and Universal Stage*. Eds. C. B. Cox and D. J. Palmer. Manchester: Manchester U. P., 1984, pp. 218–33.

Surveys some twenty critical essays on *Cor.*, twelve published after 1960, focusing on the question of whether the play is primarily political (about Roman society) or humanistic (about the tragedy of one great man who stands out from his society). Favors the view that there is a "coherent relationship between character and state." At the heart of *Cor.* is a "conjunction of its concern with social cohesion and its stress on appropriate language"; in the end, both the hero and the Roman and Volscian states are isolated by reduction of the language they use to "bestial noise," though Coriolanus momentarily reasserts his identity as a Roman just before his death.

1669 Jagendorf, Zvi. "*Coriolanus*: Body Politic and Private Parts." *SQ*, 41 (1990), 455–69.

Analyzes *Cor.* as political discourse embracing the opposing notions of wholeness (man in nature) and fragmentation (man as part of society). Rome and its citizens, described in language grotesquely physical, are absorbed in a class struggle for food and power. The separate pieces refuse to join and unify. Any attempt at appeasement, such as Menenius's retelling of the belly fable, fails and causes further division. Coriolanus is the pre- political man: one who is defined and sustained solely by his own being. He attempts to avoid being valued in terms of his parts (battle scars being equal to political currency). His exile from fragmentation, from Rome and his center/mother, leads paradoxically to nonexistence. He fails to be a self-authored man, for his very definition of "self" derives from service to the body politic he rejects. Unwilling to become part of that body, he is forced into fragmentation. Coriolanus can be seen as part of a ritual sacrifice in which a torn victim represents food, either actual or spiritual, to sustain society. The tragedy in this play rests on the fact that no such nourishment is provided by his death. Hunger becomes the "unifying" motif: The people's unquenched hunger for bread and political voice incites Coriolanus's unappeased hunger for revenge, which in turn evolves into his desire for his own fragmentation and death.

1670 Johnson, Robert C. "Silence and Speech in *Coriolanus*." *AJES*, 5 (1980), 190–210.

Uses the scene in which Coriolanus acquiesces to his mother's request that he cancel his purposed invasion of Rome (*Cor.*, V.iii) as the key text in a discussion of language and silence in the play. The stage direction (*"holds her by the hand, silent,"* line 182) signals the moment at which Volumnia has succeeded in imposing her own interpretation on the situation, allowing her to sacrifice her son for the sake of Rome. Coriolanus, at this moment, recognizes that he cannot sever the ties that bind him to family and country. Notes Coriolanus's complete honesty in the use of language during the first part of the play. In the last part, he comes to understand the significance of naming, of describing instead of simply doing. At the end, when Coriolanus attempts to justify his reconciliation with Rome, he tries for the first time to use language for persuasion. His attempt fails, and he is killed

1670a Johnson, Vernon E. "Shakespeare's *Coriolanus*, IV.vii.27–57." *Expl*, 33 (1974–75), item 21.

Argues that the speech with which Aufidius ends act IV of *Cor.* [vii.28–57] reveals the cynical, pragmatic nature of the speaker and the "devouring world" in which the whole play is set, a world in which power defines value and "history is always written by the winners."

1671 Kim, Kwang-Ho. "Shakespeare's Treatment of the Source in *Coriolanus*." *English Studies* (Seoul, Korea), 7 (1984), 49–62.

Compares *Cor.* with its source, North's translation of Plutarch's *Lives*. Notes that Sh follows North most closely in diction and cites several "great declamatory speeches" as examples. Several characters, notably Volumnia, Menenius, Virgilia, and Aufidius, are significantly expanded from Plutarch. Sh also "simplifies and condenses" the source's narrative.

1671a King, Bruce. "*Coriolanus*." (Critics Debate.) Atlantic Highlands, New Jersey: Humanities P. International, 1989. 113 pp.

Part 1 appraises various critical approaches to *Cor.* under the headings of contextual approaches; textual and formal approaches; religious, sociological and anthropological approaches; interdisciplinary approaches (including Marxist, materialist, and psychoanalytical); and theater approaches.

Part 2 offers a postmodernist interpretation of *Cor.* based on the insight that the play is a "house of mirrors with no clearly articulated central theme and the idea of the equality of the plot, character and imagery." Foregrounded themes include "virtue and pride, self-hood versus community, language and persuasion, planning and deceit, role-playing and directing others, the influence of sexual attraction and of emotional dependency on individual and communal conduct, the necessity and futility of politics (and perhaps all relations)."

1672 Kishlansky, Mark A. *Parliamentary Selection: Social and Political Choice in Early Modern England*. Cambridge: Cambridge U. P., 1988. xiii + 258 pp.

Notes that in *Cor.*, a play that seldom departs from its sources in Plutarch and Livy, the episode of Coriolanus's quest for the consulship is completely invented by Sh. Suggests that Sh's portrayal of the incident reflects his intimate knowledge of the selection of officeholders in the early 17th c. and that the clash of values in the play is indicative of the tensions in a society that was moving from a participatory mode of choosing officeholders to one of choice and election.

1673 Kitto, H. D. F. *Poiesis: Structure and Thought*. (Sather Classical Lectures 36.) Berkeley: U. of California P., 1966. x + 407 pp.

The concluding chapter contains a discussion of *Cor.* to illustrate how 20th-c. readers have misunderstood Sh's work much as they have the works of Aeschylus, Sophocles, Euripides, and Thucydides. Argues that Sh's *poiesis* leads him to modify his source for *Cor.* (Plutarch) in many respects so that he can explore the operations of hatred, pride, and envy in virtually all of the characters. The play is about people giving in to passions that disrupt the harmony of nature; it is thus political in the broadest sense. Finds parallels between *Cor.* and the *Ajax* of Sophocles.

1674 Kitto, H. D. F. "Why Blame Aristotle?" *Shakespeare 1971: Proceedings of the World Shakespeare Congress*. Vancouver, August 1971. Eds. Clifford Leech and J. M. R. Margeson. Toronto: U. of Toronto P., 1972, pp. 133–43.

Compares two of Sophocles' plays, the *Trachiniae* and *Ajax*, with *Cor.* In each of these plays, the author introduces a conception familiar to the audience and intended as a background to the action. This is done in *Cor.* with the parable of the belly. In each case, the playwright is emphasizing the natural order of things and the way all of the characters relate to that order. Aristotle's theory of tragedy, the product of the enlightened 4th c., is not particularly helpful in interpreting the classical tragedy of the 5th c. Instead of focusing on the tragic hero as a one-man show whose fate must be logical, as Aristotle did, we need to respond to the amplitude of classical Greek and English plays. Then works like *Cor.* can make their proper impact.

1675 Kowalski, Carl Francis. "*Coriolanus* and the Tragic Vision: The Limitations of Time." Ph.D. dissertation, Lehigh University, 1977. *DAI*, 38 (1977–78), 2142-A.

Considers the limitations of *Cor.* as a tragedy. Though the plot possesses many of the qualities of tragedy—for example, a heroic figure whose human frailty makes him subject to the destructive power of time and space—it ultimately fails to escape from human history and thus to provide the cathartic experience upon which tragedy depends.

1676 Kytzler, Bernhard. "Classical Names in Shakespeare's *Coriolanus*." *Archiv*, 119 (1967), 133–37.

Suggests origins for certain names in *Cor.* Cotus (IV.v.3) probably came from Caesar's *Commentaries*, and Nicanor and Adrian (IV.iii) were derived from Plutarch, but not from his *Life* of Coriolanus. In Plutarch, the order of the hero's names is Caius Martius Coriolanus, while three times in Sh's play we have Martius Caius Coriolanus. Sh's transposition of Martius to first place in the sequence was deliberate, emphasizing the connection between the war god (Mars) and the war hero.

1677 Langman, F. H. "'Atmosphere' and Repeated Action in *Coriolanus*." *SoRA*, 3 (1969), 324–33.

Argues that the world of *Cor.* is one of harsh realism, affording no escape for the characters into a realm of mystical indefinability. *Tim.* resembles *Cor.* in this, as well as in showing how "a man's rage against humanity models itself on the pattern of a divine judgment." In *Cor.*, "the idea of the doomed city reverberates all through the play." In the structure, Sh achieves a sense of complexity and intricacy by the repeated action, thus producing "perfect imaginative possession" of his subject.

1678 Langman, F. H. "*Coriolanus*: The Poetry and the Critics." *CR*, 9 (1966), 92–105.

Disagrees with critics who have argued that *Cor.* is an achievement of a narrower or lower kind than Sh's other great tragedies because the poetic style is austere. A better way to experience the play's poetry is to dwell on its vitality, its unusual capacity to render intensity of feeling. The emotions conveyed by the language are often negative, and the images are harsh or repulsive (for example, the continual concern with the grossness of the human body). But the style is "precise, dense, fluent, masculine, full of nervous force." There is "peculiarly tight relation in this play between poetry and action."

1679 Lechay, Daniel T. "The Escape from the Lonely Dell: Studies in Spenser, Shakespeare, Wordsworth and Blake." Ph.D. dissertation, University of Iowa, 1975. *DAI*, 36 (1975–76), 2220-A.

Argues that *Cor.* presents an allegory involving "the image of a *changeling*," which stands for Coriolanus's obsessive attempts at self-authorship. The image is finally revealed as a dream of treason "to state, family, and self," and is relinquished at the climax.

1680 Leggatt, Alexander, and Lois Norem, comps. *"Coriolanus": An Annotated Bibliography.* (Garland Shakespeare Bibliographies 17.) New York: Garland, 1989. xxviii + 738 pp.

Covers primarily works published between 1940 and 1986. Includes significant works published before 1940 and some items from 1987 and 1988. Classifies entries under seven headings, including criticism (631 items), sources and background (55 items), and editions (37 items). Begins each section with the oldest entries and proceeds chronologically. Concludes with a single index. Provides substantial and detailed annotations.

1680a Lepley, Jean. "Should Rome Burn? The Morality of Vengeance in *Coriolanus* (and Beyond)." *Soundings,* 66 (1983), 404–21.

Contends that Sh presents the hero of *Cor.* in such a way that, despite our misgivings about the childishness of his fantasies of autonomy and omnipotence, we admire his *virtus,* share at some level his sense of wrongness, and see a certain kind of justice in his desire for vengeance. Notes that Coriolanus is similar in his wrath and desire for pure vengeance to Aristotle's heroic man, Homer's Achilles, and the God of the Old Testament. Points out changes Sh made in his source, Plutarch's *Lives,* to render his hero's quest for vengeance more sympathetic: For example, the play shines a wholly unfavorable light on the common people.

1681 Littlewood, J. C. F. "*Coriolanus* [I]." *CQ,* 2 (1967), 339–57.

Disputes the prevailing critical judgment that *Cor.* is a success of a lower order. Argues that although it does not "achieve itself" with precision, the play is a more important experiment than its critics are willing to recognize. The chief character, despite his shortcomings, has true greatness: He exemplifies the aristocracy at its best. He calls his fellow aristocrats to be true to the living ideal of Rome. Their failure to come up to the mark can be indicated by a comparison of Menenius's sophisticated equivocations to Coriolanus's uprightness. The tribunes are also foils to Coriolanus: Their inferior natures are envious of what he is, not just what he does. Part II is item 1682.

1682 Littlewood, J. C. F. "*Coriolanus* [II]." *CQ,* 3 (1968), 28–50.

Begins with act III, suggesting that Coriolanus's aggressiveness is not just battlefield greatness, but an assertion of the "aristocratic sense of what a self-respecting member of his community—one who believes in it—can or cannot permit to take place in it." In a sense, he *is* Rome, and this is the source of his greatness. At this point we might anticipate that this is going to be the tragedy of a Roman "in whom this passionate strength, this ability to invoke and in a sense embody the national Idea at a crisis, is inseparable from a blind passion to destroy both the nation and himself." Yet in acts IV and V his vital power is "allowed to fade away and fall quite out of the reckoning." We receive "no vivid conception of whatever it is that's been wasted, and cannot therefore care very much about it." We are given, for example, no intimation of the effect Coriolanus's exile has had on him. It seems clear that in acts IV and V, Sh's inspiration dried up and his "imagination was no longer at work on the hero." Part I is item 1681.

1683 Longo, Joseph A. "Dynamic Equilibrium in *Coriolanus*." *BSUF,* 10, no. 3 (1969), 53–56.

Argues that in *Cor.* Sh maintains "a condition of dynamic equilibrium" between the opposing forces of aristocrats and plebeians and of Romans and Volscians. Within Coriolanus himself there is tension between sensitivity and brutality, maturity and adolescence. These irreconcilable opposites point to disease in Roman society and in the protagonist. The play discloses "a world of unrest and harsh contradictions which cannot be resolved."

1684 Lowe, Lisa. "'Say I play the man I am': Gender and Politics in *Coriolanus*." *KR*, 8, no. 4 (1986), 86–95.

Proposes a feminist reading of *Cor.* that rejects the familiar notion that Volumnia as a domineering mother is to blame for her son's obsession with martial prowess. It is the civic patriarchy, not maternal authority, that is responsible for Coriolanus's rigid personality and for other forms of oppression in Roman society. Coriolanus's rebellion is not against his mother, but rather against "the Roman patriarchal city and its system of conferring civic manhood and attributing gender through the naming of wounds." The play directs us to analyze political conflicts in the family and to understand "the ways in which gender is not restricted to psychological interrelationships but is inscribed in civic activities as well."

1685 Luckyj, Christina. "Volumnia's Silence." *SEL*, 31 (1991), 327–42.

Concentrates on Volumnia's appearances in *Cor.* to support the belief that she is not frozen throughout in a condition of destructive, domineering motherliness, but rather goes through a series of changes that testifies to her full humanity: She starts by mirroring her heroic son and by speaking in his heroic voice, "then passes into a comic, anti-heroic phase in the second and third acts, only to return to her former strength in a different way."

1686 Lynch, Robert E. "Popular Insurrection in Elizabethan and Jacobean Drama." Ph.D. dissertation, New York University, 1971. *DAI*, 32 (1971–72), 5744-A.

Surveys ten plays of the period that treat insurrections, violent clashes between "the ruling class and an armed populace." Detects a weakening of the orthodox condemnation of insurrection in plays that were written around the beginning of the 17th c. In *Cor.*, for example, Sh took advantage of the play's remote setting to express a far more ambivalent view of insurrection than he had shown in his early history plays.

1687 MacIntyre, Jean. "Words, Acts, and Things: Visual Language in *Coriolanus*." *ESC*, 10, no. 1 (1984), 1–10.

Calls attention to the heavy reliance in *Cor.* on specific costumes, stage properties, and movements. Headgear (helmet, cap, oaken garland) is especially important, revealing a character's status or value. The "gown of humility" Coriolanus has to wear is mentioned by Plutarch, and Sh no doubt intended for this to be a garment that a Jacobean audience would recognize as inappropriate for an aristocrat. Cushions are also important because they go with the "seated posture appropriate for counsel and judgment," and they help to emphasize that Coriolanus sits very little (rather, he is "maniacally active"). In *Cor.*, Sh carried experimentation with visual language to an extreme. Other late plays in the canon use similar effects, but they accompany things with a full range of verbal language. *Cor.* often lets the things stand alone.

1688 Magnusson, A. Lynne. "'I paint him in the character': Prose Portraits in *Coriolanus*." *ELN*, 25, no. 2 (1987), 33–36.

Maintains that in the prose portraits that Menenius provides of Coriolanus, the two tribunes, and himself, Sh is experimenting with the fashionable Jacobean "character," a description in the Senecan style—curt, disjunctive, atomistic. Such a style seems well-adapted to the world of *Cor.*, where "irreconcilable forces collide."

1689 Màrcus, Leah. *Puzzling Shakespeare: Local Reading and Its Discontents.* (The New Historicism: Studies in Cultural Poetics 6.) Berkeley: U. of California P., 1988. xiii + 267 pp.

A section of chapter 4 discovers in *Cor.* a reflection of early Jacobean London's concern with the expansion of civic "liberties and franchises." The protagonist's banishment and subsequent death constitute a symbolic purging of "royal and aristocratic privilege" from a city whose political composition makes it "readily comparable to London." The citizens of London in 1608—the date of *Cor.*—would have been able to see their "weaknesses as a group," especially factionalism, in their Roman counterparts and thus would have been lessoned in achieving political unity.

1690 McCanles, Michael. "The Dialectic of Transcendence in Shakespeare's *Coriolanus.*" *PMLA*, 82 (1967), 44–53.

Maintains that the action of *Cor.* is rigorously governed by the movement of the hero through a series of dialectical love–hate relationships, the most important of which are those with Rome, with Tullus Aufidius, and with Volumnia. Coriolanus needs the people (person) he hates so that he can have something against which to define what he admires; but he cannot get along with those he loves. The play's ultimate irony is that the two amount to the same thing. Coriolanus is bound to the Roman people, the tribunes, and others by a drive toward transcendence that denies the connection in order to achieve transcendence. Images that are used to reinforce the sense of dialectic have to do with master/slave and petitioner/petitioned. The process moves toward isolating the hero, with a significant change being made by Sh in his source, Plutarch's *Lives*, to show Martius entering Corioli alone. At the conclusion, the hero's death results from "a power play to which his own drive to power on the scale of transcendence has left him particularly vulnerable." The two sides of the dialectic cancel each other as Coriolanus is nullified in asserting most strenuously the claims of his ego.

1691 McFarland, Thomas. "Individual and Society in Shakespeare's *Coriolanus.*" *The Scope of Words: In Honor of Albert S. Cook.* Eds. Peter Baker, Sarah Webster Goodwin, and Gary Handwerk. New York: Peter Lang, 1991, pp. 111–34.

Maintains that *Cor.* is exclusively devoted to realizing the insight (articulated in the 20th c. by Freud) that, though the individual depends on society to define his existence, he is "necessarily in conflict with society." Coriolanus's assertion of radical individualism through his valor is undermined by his love for his mother, which makes him vulnerable to the will of society. His military prowess seems to make him acceptable in both Rome and Antium, but the societies of both cities harbor murderous hatred toward him. Coriolanus's struggle to triumph over society is doomed to failure. Sh modifies his source in Plutarch's *Lives* to foreground that struggle.

1692 McKenzie, Stanley D. "'Unshout the noise that banish'd Martius': Structural Paradox and Dissembling in *Coriolanus.*" *ShakS*, 18 (1986), 189–204.

Maintains that in *Cor.* Sh employs "vocabulary, rhetorical figures, ironic foreshadowing, thematic development, and characterization to create an all-pervasive sense of uncertainty and paradox surrounding the events of the play." There are no absolutely correct ways to respond to this world: Coriolanus, the only absolutist, is destroyed. The skeptics Aufidius and Volumnia survive only through dissembling.

1693 Meszaros, Patricia K. "'There is a world elsewhere': Tragedy and History in *Coriolanus.*" *SEL*, 16 (1976), 273–85.

Treats *Cor.* as the tragedy of a great individual adhering to what he believes are absolute values, who is destroyed by "the larger, ironic movement of history." Sh shapes his classical materials to dramatize a historical change that was being felt for the first time in the Jacobean age. The hierarchical, organic idea of the medieval commonwealth was receding, and the notion of the "state," a mechanistic assemblage of competing interests, was taking its place. Coriolanus is more isolated than any of Sh's other tragic figures: He has no confidante, he understands no one, and no one understands him. He lives by an outmoded aristocratic ideal. Every other character—Menenius, the tribunes, Volumnia, Aufidius—is "political" in the modern sense of maneuvering to gain one's private ends, to stay in power. Though defeated by the ironic forces of history, Coriolanus triumphs as a tragic figure.

1694 Michael, Nancy Carolyn. "Shakespeare's *Coriolanus*: His Metamorphosis from Man to Monster." *BSUF*, 19, no. 2 (1978), 12–19.

Maintains that the protagonist of *Cor.* is not primarily a partisan for the patrician cause against the plebeians of Rome. Sh's chief concern is to portray his hero as isolated from all others, those of his class as well as those of the lower class. Stage placement of characters and stage directions make obvious Coriolanus's separateness. Further, three images—those of god, machine, and dragon—are applied incrementally to Coriolanus throughout the play to exhibit his transformation from man to monster. Even his capitulation to his mother at the end, being the act of a child, fails to restore his manhood.

1695 Miller, Anthony. "*Coriolanus*: The Tragedy of *Virtus*." *SSE*, 9 (1983–84), 37–60.

Maintains that in *Cor.* Sh engaged in "a remarkable exercise of historical imagination" to anatomize the power and "internal politics" of the early Roman republic. Cites Plutarch's discussion of *virtus*, or valiantness, the ideal to which Coriolanus commits himself, as a basis for understanding his tragedy. Notes that Sh would have absorbed the political emphasis of this play from Renaissance accounts of Roman history and from the Roman historians themselves. Works Sh would have studied in school that stress a kind of dialectic between Rome's military successes abroad and its internal dissension include Livy's *Roman History*, Florus's epitomes, and Plutarch. Points out a number of ways in which Sh modified Plutarch's *Life* of Coriolanus to bring this conflict into the foreground. For one thing, Sh begins the play by plunging us into a political atmosphere of mutual distrust and scorn, leaving the particulars of the dispute about corn more obscure than they are in Plutarch and virtually ignoring Plutarch's concern with usury. To stress the Roman state's tendency to produce a certain kind of machine-like warrior who will carry out its military missions, Sh invents the episode of young Martius's destruction of the butterfly (I.iii). Coriolanus's loneliness, a condition enforced by his military prowess, is figured in his solitary entry into Corioli (in Plutarch, he is accompanied by others). The matrix of political forces in which Coriolanus must operate, and which his devotion to *virtus* renders him incapable of comprehending, is given greater power through two scenes of public ceremony (II.i, ii) invented by Sh, in which the Romans offer formal praise for his exploits. In a series of juxtapositions, the play conveys just how tenuous Rome's political unity is. Coriolanus, though he does not recognize it, is a product of the Roman state; the patricians need him, as they do the common people and the tribunes, to perform a certain function so that they can remain in power. Parallel to the tribunes in performing a certain service, he is different from them in his lack of calculation. He is manipulated by the patricians when they try to institutionalize him, just as the commoners are manipulated by the tribunes. He and the people enact political roles that others script for them. Despite the violence on which he seems to thrive, Coriolanus is a curiously passive character in many ways, being finally discarded and destroyed by the city that has made use of him. His mother's appeal to him to save Rome, though couched in the language of family loyalty, is essentially political; she deploys her maternal power "to win a victory for her city." Her son, whose acquiescence to her plea forces him to violate his ideal of *virtus*, becomes for the first time a politician and dies as "the submissive product of his compromised but triumphant Rome."

1696 Mitchell, Charles. "*Coriolanus*: Power as Honor." *ShakS*, 1 (1965), 199–226.

Discovers that a drama of honor is played out within the hero of *Cor.* During most of the play, Coriolanus conceals his motives from himself and consequently suffers from an inner conflict between his own unrecognized private interest (pursuit of honor) and his "publicly avowed purpose" (service to his country). Wishing to achieve self-definition, he struggles to escape from all forms of dependency. When he is forced to concede that he wants a reward (the consulship) that depends on others to grant, he revolts against the plebeians, who have brought him to this awareness. For Coriolanus, public power means personal honor. In his last interview with his mother, however, and even in his death at the hands of Aufidius, he acknowledges finally that his honor is dependent on others.

1697 Mitra, P. K. "The Relevance of Volscian Servingmen to *Coriolanus*." *Journal of the Department of English, University of Calcutta*, 20, no. 2 (1985–86), 21–39.

Argues that the servingmen's comments provide us with the common people's view of Coriolanus, an approximate summing-up of his character. Further, they provide key evidence for assessing the hero's relationship to other Romans, especially the Roman nobles; his welcome by Aufidius; and the alteration he seems to have undergone when he appears outside Aufidius's residence. Through the servingmen and Coriolanus's reaction to them, we see the popularity of the hero among the common people and his consistent contempt for them; his intention to spare the nobles of Rome when he invades; and the people's love of war and their willingness to be drawn into war by their aristocratic leaders. The account by one of the servingmen of the banquet at which Aufidius receives Coriolanus, in its images of harlotry, shows how temporary the alliance between the two leaders is and how likely the former is to betray the latter. Comments on Sh's treatment of his source in Plutarch's *Lives*.

1698 Murray, Patrick. "Shakespeare's *Coriolanus*: A Play for Our Time." *Studies* (Dublin), 61 (1972), 253–66.

Argues that *Cor.* is "very much a play of our time" by explaining how it deals with class struggle, democracy, and patriotism. Its hero, however, is closer to the Homeric world, with its warrior culture, than any other; and he fails because he is placed in a society "whose norms and procedures are fundamentally non-heroic."

1699 Nemoianu, Virgil. "Coriolanus, or the Secondary as Hero." *Alphonse Juilland: D'une passion l'autre*. Eds. Brigitte Cazelles and René Girard. (Stanford French and Italian Studies 53.) Saratoga, California: ANMA Libri, 1987, pp. 63–83.

Views the hero of *Cor.* as "ambiguously tragic" because he represents the historical and philosophical secondary: That is, he stands against the irresistible movement toward progress and normality that enlists all of his opponents. These antagonists—the tribunes, the patricians, Volumnia, and Aufidius—lack stature and are unappealing. Coriolanus, however, is made more admirable than his prototype in Plutarch. Thus, while we recognize that Coriolanus's elitism, and especially his disdain for language, must ultimately fail to provide a center for civic life, we regret the loss of human completeness when he is gone. Progress is significant only when its costs are sympathetically understood. Revised as chapter 2 of item 1700.

1700 Nemoianu, Virgil. *A Theory of the Secondary: Literature, Progress, and Reaction*. Baltimore: Johns Hopkins U. P., 1989. xvii + 242 pp.

Chapter 2, on *Cor.*, is a revision of item 1699.

1701 Neumeyer, Peter F. "Ingratitude Is Monstrous: An Approach to *Coriolanus*." CE, 26 (1964–65), 192–98.

Presents ingratitude as the theme of *Cor*. The people of Rome are ungrateful to the senators and to Coriolanus, who is ungrateful in forgetting the name of his host in Corioli and in refusing all reward for his victory. Menenius and Volumnia stress Rome's ingratitude to Coriolanus when he is banished, and Coriolanus shows further ingratitude, this time to his mother, Menenius, and Cominius, when he turns against

Rome. Volumnia reproaches Coriolanus with ingratitude when she persuades him to spare Rome, and Aufidius uses the charge of ingratitude as an excuse for murdering Coriolanus.

1702 Neumeyer, Peter F. "Not Local Habitation nor a Name: Coriolanus." *University Review*, 32 (1965–66), 195–98.

Points out that the isolation of the hero in *Cor.* is accompanied by lack of a name. Throughout the play, Coriolanus lives with a name borrowed from his enemies, and this signifies his failure to be loyal to anything, even himself. His mother gets him to abandon his plan to attack Rome by taunting him with his borrowed name; and by calling him a boy at the end, Aufidius strips all names from him. Without a name, he is nothing.

1703 Parker, R. B. "*Coriolanus* and 'th'interpretation of the time.'" *Mirror Up to Shakespeare: Essays in Honour of G. R. Hibbard*. Ed. J. C. Gray. Toronto: U. of Toronto P., 1984, pp. 261–76.

Discusses the idea of politics in *Cor.*, beginning with the entirely relativistic view announced in Aufidius's statement that "our virtues / Lie in th'interpretation of the time" (IV.vii.49–50). Surveys earlier plays in the canon to show that Sh's notion of politics broadened over time to include the interaction between the individual, "his institutions" (the most basic of which is the family), and the whole of society. One important political issue in the play is the class struggle between the patricians and the plebeians, which is connected to the external conflict with the Volscians and the question of "right government." Menenius's parable of the belly attempts to suggest an "organic body politic" but is given the lie by the various power struggles exhibited in the play. Coriolanus operates with an acute awareness of the competitiveness that alone drives Roman politics, and he is the only character to insist publicly that this is the true state of things. The tragedy of Coriolanus, however, arises from Sh's perception that rootedness in the family is the political foundation of a society, the power that resists "the constant flux of history." Coriolanus's choice to give in to his mother, though providing no permanent solution, affirms the importance of the family link. Sh thus can be seen as sharing the Neoplatonic view that society is and should be "rationally dynamic" based on "the reciprocities of family life."

1704 Paster, Gail Kern. "To Starve with Feeding: The City in *Coriolanus*." *ShakS*, 11 (1978), 123–44.

Studies the idea of community in *Cor.* The city of Rome is a repository of aristocratic ideals of individual aspiration and makes possible the achievement of these ideals. At the same time, however, it compulsively and savagely destroys the hero who exhibits the very qualities it holds up for admiration. Sh portrays Rome through contrasts, in particular by setting concretely realized locations against the abstract idea of the city. The process begins in the first scene, where Menenius's fable of the belly develops the notion of mutuality between plebeians and patricians; this ideal is immediately belied by the disruptive entrance of Coriolanus. Throughout the play, the patricians are driven by an extreme civic consciousness: There is no private dimension to people's lives. As a way to demonstrate the suffocating intimacy of civic life, Sh associates personal emotion with public, usually military, action. Ceremony is a key structural element, leaving little room for Coriolanus as a public figure. Character and setting are closely identified, with Coriolanus increasingly referred to in architectural terms. Anatomical imagery, first used in Menenius's fable, finally comes to mean fragmentation. Other imagery patterns—of animals and eating—stress the predatory and appetitive nature of life in Rome. In Volumnia, the various images coalesce to guide our response to the death of Coriolanus: She, like Rome, is the unnatural mother devouring her child in order to survive. For Volumnia and for Rome, the play is comic: It celebrates the continuity of the city's ideals. For Coriolanus, there is tragedy in the city's need to regenerate itself by feeding on its heroes.

1705 Patrides, C. A. "'The Beast with Many Heads': Renaissance Views on the Multitude." *SQ*, 16 (1965), 241–46.

Cites a number of Renaissance sources on the untrustworthiness of the common people to show that the protagonist's attitude in *Cor.* was shared by many of Sh's contemporaries. Sh himself, however, may have had a more tolerant view.

1706 Patterson, Annabel. *Fables of Power: Aesopian Writing and Political History.* (Post-Contemporary Interventions.) Durham, North Carolina: Duke U. P., 1991. vi + 178 pp.

Proposes to recover the Aesopian tradition, especially as it encodes the social commentary of those without power and especially as it is manifested in the Renaissance. Chapter 1 argues that "the legendary *Life* of Aesop" prefixed to Renaissance collections of the fables encouraged readings of his works as subversive. Chapter 4, "Body Fables," includes a reading of Sh's treatment of *The Belly and the Members* in *Cor.* Inspired by the Midlands Rising of 1607, the opening scene of the play is organized to show the intelligent skepticism of the plebeians toward Menenius's fable.

1707 Petrey, Sandy. *Speech Acts and Literary Theory.* New York: Routledge, 1990. 175 pp.

Includes a discussion of Stanley Fish's application of speech–act theory to *Cor.* (item 1637). Coriolanus ignores the power of social discourse and relies on deeds alone for his definition. He fails to gain power because collective society neither accepts nor enacts his assertions. His banishment does not lead him to a world where he can function independently, but rather into another speech–act community.

1708 Poisson, Rodney. "*Coriolanus* I.vi.21–24." *SQ*, 15 (1964), 449–50.

Suggests that Cominius's description of "the wounded Martius mantled in blood like a man flayed may have come from Ovid's description of the wretched satyr Marsyas, flayed by Apollo for his presumption" (*Metamorphoses*, 6.494 in Golding's translation).

1709 Poisson, Rodney. "Coriolanus as Aristotle's Magnanimous Man." *Pacific Coast Studies in Shakespeare.* Eds. Waldo F. McNeir and Thelma N. Greenfield. Eugene: U. of Oregon Books, 1966, pp. 210–25.

Argues that Sh's Coriolanus is best understood as Aristotle's Magnanimous Man, though Sh may have known the *Ethics* only indirectly. From Aristotle and his commentators, the following qualities of the Magnanimous Man, all of which fit Coriolanus, can be listed: willingness to take great risks for a great cause; self-esteem; distaste for praise, especially from the undiscriminating; modesty; reluctance to give flattery; openness in expressing hate and love; and a readiness to display righteous anger. *Cor.* is "conceived in the classical ethic," and its mature irony should be appreciated: "The shoddy and the second-rate are seen to inherit the earth—precisely because the magnanimous man cannot be shifty or ruthless, and noble anger is helpless against the calculation of the base."

1710 Poole, Adrian. "*Coriolanus*." (Twayne's New Critical Introductions to Shakespeare.) Boston: Twayne, 1988. xx + 140 pp.

Brief introductory sections contain accounts of the play's stage history and its critical reception. Chapter 1 discusses the ambiguous effect of Menenius's fable of the belly; the instant volubility of Martius and his derisive wit; the heightened importance Sh gives to Aufidius and Volumnia (beyond their significance in Plutarch); the two kinds of confrontation (between Martius and the masses and between Martius and Aufidius); the tension between Volumnia and Virgilia, especially regarding Martius's departing and returning; and the way in which Martius's feat at Corioli turns him into a legend.

Chapter 2 notes the potential for absurdity in Lartius's premature obituary for Martius in I.iv, while at the same time viewing this speech as the prelude to three scenes in which the legend of Coriolanus is established: the naming on the battlefield (I.ix), the victorious entry into Rome (II.i), and the formal oration of Cominius before the Senate (II.ii). Discusses issues involving Martius's relationship to sound in general and speech in particular. Sh places the incident of the Volscian prisoner whose name Martius forgets after he has received the name of Coriolanus; this departure from Plutarch suggests that Martius is uncomfortable with the obligation he has been placed under to Rome and that he may be projecting his desire not to be named, not to be subject to language, onto someone else. Martius is uneasily and unwillingly placed at the center of Rome; Aufidius, whose enmity to Martius is abetted by a dangerously strong memory, is able to live on the periphery of things. Remarks on the political maneuvering of Menenius and the tribunes, the meeting of Coriolanus with his family, and Cominius's progressively horrifying speech praising Coriolanus in II.ii. Coriolanus is both a professional soldier and an aristocrat.

Chapter 3 points out Martius's inability to accept the idea of an audience, literal or figurative; his difficulty in standing *for* things (in both senses); his unwillingness to play a part; his sense of being under siege in the marketplace; his ambiguity about custom in his soliloquy (II.iii); his belief in an ideal state in which action and language are identical; and his outrage at the people's claims to speech and food. Discusses also the question of whether personality precedes principle in the play. Comments on the powerful and terrifying figures of speech that Martius uses in his confrontation with the people as well as the patricians' attempt to limit the damage he is doing. Remarks on the way the play adapts Roman history to view all of the sides in the political dispute with a critical eye. Brings out the harsh comedy of the scene (III.ii) in which Volumnia excites a loathing in her son by advising him to counterfeit a mildness that she has from his childhood taught him to scorn. In the climactic banishment scene (III.iii), the tribunes show themselves to have schooled the commoners much more skillfully than the patricians have rehearsed Martius. There is a semblance of a legal process orchestrated by the tribunes. Martius's speech renouncing Rome and its people (III.iii.124–139) is "a magnificent repudiation of reality" in which he is exhilaratingly free of the hypocrisies under which he has been forced to operate.

Chapter 4 begins by painting the mood of Martius and his family and friends as he prepares to go into exile; in IV.i, we catch a hint that, though he is accustomed to being away from Rome, this absence will be different (the word "lonely" [line 30] that he uses to describe himself occurs here for the first time in English). In IV.ii, in Volumnia's cursing of the tribunes and their coolness under pressure, we witness the bitter skirmishing that marks everyday life in Rome. The next scene, the meeting between two secret agents, one being the Roman traitor Nicanor, shows in a minor way the importance of naming and recognition, so important for Martius and Aufidius elsewhere in the play. Analyzes Martius's soliloquy outside Aufidius's house (IV.iv.13–27) to reveal that the exile's visit to his sworn enemy is based on a complex mix of feelings, including a fascination with that enemy (not, as in Plutarch, simply on the desire for revenge). Compares the scene in which Martius enters Aufidius's house (IV.v) to the scene in which he was at home with the three women (I.iii): These are the only scenes in which there is an attempt to establish a sense of "domestic space." Aufidius's house is different; it is a "bustling, festive household," something Sh created (the feast is not in Plutarch), perhaps to suggest a more feudal atmosphere than obtains in Rome. Martius's appearance in Antium is fraught with the ambivalence surrounding "the alien stranger" awaiting admission to an established group; he can be murderously disposed of or he can be deified. Aufidius decides to deify his guest, abandoning for the moment his former vow to destroy him. However, Martius must surrender his name before he is allowed in. Sh dwells much more than does Plutarch on the awkwardness of Aufidius's initial failure to recognize his old enemy. Observes that Aufidius is dazzled by Martius's appearance and that Aufidius's servants furnish a perspective that shows this new alliance for "the grotesque thing that it is." Act IV concludes with a view of the unreal harmony in Rome now that Martius is gone and with a candid speech by Aufidius that attempts to explain his adversary/ally in several ways, falls back on proverbial wisdom, and ends by dismissing logic and frankly admitting that he must destroy Martius.

Chapter 5, covering act V, follows the humiliation of Menenius, whose attempt to save Rome is subverted by his "son," Martius, and by the women who succeed where he has failed; the passion with which Martius greets the women, especially his mother; the isolation of Martius from Volumnia, "the double source of his being in nature and custom"; the irresistible appeal Volumnia makes to "the sense of *history*, both personal and public"; the painful ceremony of the women's kneeling and the postponement on Sh's part of the moment of Martius's yielding to them; the Christian echoes prompted by the women's visit; the way in which Aufidius stage-manages Martius's death; and the shocking and precipitate nature of that death.

1711 Proser, Matthew. "Coriolanus: The Constant Warrior and the State." CE, 24 (1962–63), 507–12.

Argues that in *Cor.*, the hero is constant in the sense that he is always a potential killer, a destroyer. In his relationships with war, with the community, and with his mother, he remains true to his image of the warrior, but, blind to his own human nature, he fails to understand how this constancy is a threat to the city he professes to serve and to himself. His image thus contains the seeds of his own destruction. Revision of part of item 0865. Revised as part of chapter 3 of item 0866.

1712 Pujante, A. Luis. "'No Sense nor Feeling': A Note on *Coriolanus*, 4.1." SQ, 41 (1990), 489–90.

Comments on the variety of critical analyses of Coriolanus's lack of anger immediately before his exile. Supports Una Ellis-Fermor's explanation that the protagonist is in such a state of shock that he does not fully feel his grief. Finds textual justification for this position in North's translation of Plutarch.

1713 Putney, Rufus. "Coriolanus and His Mother." PsyQ, 31 (1962), 364–81.

Maintains that the tragedy in *Cor.* arises from the conflict between a man whose superego enforces on him an "iron rigidity" and the mother who trained him to be so inflexible. Volumnia destroys her son by demanding that he sacrifice the principles she taught him "to the demands of reality."

1714 Quinn, Michael. "Caius Marcius Coriolanus: The Self as Art." BNYSS, 5, no. 6–6, no. 1 (1987–88), 5–8.

Urges that appreciation of the protagonist in *Cor.* involves an understanding that he consciously models himself on the ideal image of the ancient Greek hero. In following this "Greek aesthetic of the self," Mar[t]ius attains heroic stature "through martial—not political—service." When he is called upon to enter the political arena, he undermines his authenticity and thus loses his heroic image. His recognition of this loss permits us to see him as a tragic figure in the Aristotelian mold.

1715. Rabkin, Norman. "*Coriolanus:* The Tragedy of Politics." SQ, 17 (1966), 196–212.

Indicates through detailed analysis that the first act of *Cor.* sets up the problem that will "generate the entire play"—that is, the nature of honor. For Coriolanus, honor means "absolute allegiance to his ideals." When he accepts the name "Coriolanus" from the city of Rome, he seems to acknowledge that honor is conferred by the recognition of others. His loyalty to himself, however, will not let him rest easy with the compromise. He is ultimately destroyed when his mother calls on him to conform to public honor (putting Rome above all), and he is consequently forced to violate his personal honor. The society, the people who surround Coriolanus, offers no alternatives to his self-destructive behavior. *Ant.* deals with the same sort of world as *Cor.*—there is no hope for "heroism and self-fulfillment." But in *Ant.*, Sh endows the hero with a passion, "self-destructive as it is," that "leads him to a better world than political reality can provide." Revised as part of chapter 3 of item 0873.

1716 Rackin, Phyllis. "*Coriolanus*: Shakespeare's Anatomy of *Virtus*." MLS, 13, no. 2 (1983), 68–79.

Contends that the fable of the belly told by Menenius to calm the rebellious plebeians at the beginning of *Cor.* is indicative of the disorderly state of Rome: Just as the belly and the members in the fable have no head, Rome lacks a king to exercise rational control over its constituent parts. In such a world, what Plutarch calls *virtus*, or, as Sir Thomas North translates it, *valiantness*, is the supreme value. Like Plutarch, Sh recounts the story of Coriolanus to exhibit "the nature and limitations" of *virtus*, testing the proposition that this ideal includes in itself "all the other virtues." Points out that in a world dominated by *virtus*, manhood is equated with military valor; further, *virtus* opposes and excludes womanliness. Throughout the play, images of food, nurture, and harvest—womanly concerns—are opposed to or perverted by the predominant political and martial concerns. At several points, we see characters perversely substituting slaughter for feeding and passionate competition between warriors in killing for loving procreation. Volumnia has instilled in her son a single-minded desire to pursue *virtus*, a life-denying and narrow idea of manliness, and although she possesses rational qualities herself, she has failed to pass them on to him. Ironically, his mother has taught him a morbid distrust of all things associated with the maternal. Notes that Sh follows Plutarch in emphasizing Coriolanus's fatherless upbringing, suggesting that in the playwright's view this has much to do with his hero's lack of rational control. Even though Coriolanus momentarily relents, his consecration to *virtus* finally makes it impossible for him to love his country, his people, or his family. Like Sh's other Roman plays, but more paradigmatically, *Cor.* illustrates the inadequacy of *virtus*. Revision of parts of item 0876.

1717 Reed, Regina Balla. "Rebellion, Prophecy and Power in Four Works of the English Renaissance." Ph.D. dissertation, State University of New York at Buffalo, 1970. *DAI*, 31 (1970–71), 4731-A.

Examines the struggle for power in *Cor.* and three other works. Finds similarities in the works, including enactment of the paradox that power is dependent on weakness. Each work is allegorical in mode, with a hero who, having begun arrogantly, finds through prophecy that he is actually a servant. Chapter 4 is entitled "Coriolanus, the Functionary as Daemonic Hero."

1718 Relihan, Constance C. "Appropriation of the 'Thing of Blood': Absence of Self and the Struggle for Ownership in *Coriolanus*." *Iowa State Journal of Research*, 62 (1987–88), 407–20.

Contends that the identity of Coriolanus was constructed by his mother to suit the needs of a martial Rome that no longer exists. Coriolanus has no private self, and his public identity is dysfunctional in the modern Machiavellian state of *Cor.* The play studies the attempts of various partisans (Volumnia, Menenius, the tribunes, Aufidius) to reshape his character and appropriate it for their own political ends.

1719 Rothschild, Herbert B. Jr. "The Conqueror–Hero, the Besieged City, and the Development of an Elizabethan Protagonist." *South Central Review*, 3, no. 4 (1986), 54–77.

Includes Coriolanus (*Cor.*) in a study of military conquerors as protagonists in Elizabethan drama. When this type of figure threatens the annihilation of a besieged city, he becomes transparently willful, and the play becomes a study of "the tension between the ways of God and the ways of men." Coriolanus exists, for most of the play, "in a state of being, not of becoming," a condition suitable only for a god. He identifies himself totally with Rome, as her warrior, and in a negative sense he asserts his integrity through his constant vituperation of the plebeians. Underlying his scorn for the people is a fear of them as "an interpreting community" susceptible to instability. Yet finally Coriolanus is unable to preserve his identity apart from the polity. He illustrates the tragic paradox that "we can fully realize ourselves neither as moral beings nor as gods."

1720 Rouda, F. H. "*Coriolanus*—A Tragedy of Youth." *SQ*, 12 (1961), 103–06.

Argues that *Cor.* is "a tragedy of youth." Its hero is idealistic—he is innocent, not mercenary, chivalrous, and faithful to his wife. His tragedy is that he is an untried youth who insists on "asking more of the world than it has to offer."

1721 Schlösser, Anselm. "Reflections Upon Shakespeare's *Coriolanus*." *PP*, 6 (1963), 11–21.

Analyzes *Cor.* in terms of how it presents a class conflict that leads the spectator to take sides according to his own class affiliation. Although neither side in the conflict is portrayed in an entirely favorable light, "Shakespeare's sympathies are with the common people." Sh does not crudely attempt to set events of his own time in the classical past, but he is "clearly concerned with the problem of absolutism and its imminent clash with the demands of the bourgeois class." Brecht's version of *Cor.* is on the whole to be approved: It allows us to see the Senate's reaction to Coriolanus's death. Proposals for erecting a monument to the hero and mourning for him in public are turned down, thus making the point that he has been annihilated by history. The social and historical processes emphasized by Brecht are "all inherent in the action as Shakespeare shaped it," but Sh remains ambiguous about them, while Brecht is "boldly partisan."

1722 Seidenberg, Robert. "For This Woman's Sake: Notes on the 'Mother' Superego with Reflections on Shakespeare's *Coriolanus* and Sophocles' *Ajax*." *IJP*, 44 (1963), 74–82.

Contends that Coriolanus exhibits a kind of hypermasculinity that, when reformed under feminine influence, can disintegrate with disastrous results.

1723 Selzler, Bernard John. "The Design of *Coriolanus*." Ed.D. dissertation, East Texas State University, 1974. *DAI*, 35 (1974–75), 7880-A.

Provides a scene-by-scene analysis of *Cor.* according to "the principles of dramatic structure laid down by Aristotle and Freytag." Concludes that in *Cor.* Sh combined 2 types of tragedy: (1) the Macbeth type, in which the action is initiated by the hero and (2) the Othello type, in which the action is initiated by forces opposed to the hero.

1724 Shaheen, Naseeb. "Shakespeare and the Rheims New Testament." *AN&Q*, 22 (1983–84), 70–72.

Disputes the belief that Coriolanus's use of the word *cockle* in the phrase "cockle of rebellion" (*Cor.*, III.i) is derived from the Rheims version of the New Testament. Sh got this word from North's translation of Plutarch's *Life of Caius Martius Coriolanus*. Revised as part of item 0954.

1725 Sicherman, Carol M. "*Coriolanus*: The Failure of Words." *ELH*, 39 (1972), 189–207.

Argues that in *Cor.*, Sh dissects "verbal inadequacy," the disjunction of word and meaning. Sh modifies Plutarch's Coriolanus to deny his hero eloquence. Coriolanus is incapable of soliciting votes, is baffled by names, and is addicted to using proverbs and cursing—all indications of verbal insufficiency. He is also afflicted with logorrhea, unable to stop talking or to control his syntax. Failing to grasp the larger point of another's speech, he often seizes on a single word or phrase and repeats it obsessively. His own speech is either "rampantly uncontrolled or else uncommonly rigid," and he is thereby isolated.

1726 Simonds, Peggy Muñoz. "*Coriolanus* and the Myth of Juno and Mars." *Mosaic*, 18, no. 2 (1985), 33–50.

Claims that the underlying myth of *Cor.* involves the relationship between Juno, "patroness of Rome," and "her chthonic son Mars, protective god of the city's outermost boundaries." Cites the account of "Juno's conception of Mars by parthenogenesis" in Ovid's *Fasti*, a text Sh is likely to have read in grammar school. Volumnia is bloodthirsty and angry like Juno; she is linked with two other women in saving Rome and is thus, like Juno, associated with "the Indo-European Triple Goddess who presides over the human extremities of birth and death"; and, like Juno, the protectress of the city, she symbolizes Rome itself. Coriolanus personifies Mars in his "dragon-like nature," his "tremendous noise," his "sexual popularity," his inability to alter his rigid devotion to war, and the ease with which he changes allegiance to his native city. Several important scenes ultimately derive from ancient rituals honoring Juno and Mars. Examples are Coriolanus's being conceived of as a sword (I.vi), his being cut to pieces by the Volscians (V.vi), and the ceremony of strewing flowers before Volumnia when she returns from the Volscian camp (V.v).

1727. Skretkowicz, Victor. "*Coriolanus* (I.iii.44): An Alternative Emendation." *N&Q*, 25 (1978), 153–54.

Proposes an emendation for the Folio's "Contenning" in a speech by Volumnia to a gentlewoman [I.iii.43]. Suggests that this should be a stage direction, "*Continuing.*"

1728 Sorge, Thomas. "The Failure of Orthodoxy in *Coriolanus.*" *Shakespeare Reproduced: The Text in History and Ideology.* Eds. Jean E. Howard and Marion F. O'Connor. London: Methuen, 1987, pp. 225–41.

Notices that the fable of the belly, which the ruling class in *Cor.* uses in an attempt to make the plebeians obedient, fails in its rhetorical purpose because it has potentials for meaning that undermine or even contradict its official application. The failure of the belly metaphor is analogous to the failure of the oligarchy's chief representative "to make himself palatable to the people." However, the body analogy is apt for a new, "fairly self-contained" social organization, centered in the citizens, that emerges in the play.

1729 Sprengnether, Madelon. "Annihilating Intimacy in *Coriolanus.*" *Women in the Middle Ages and the Renaissance: Literary and Historical Perspectives.* Ed. Mary Beth Rose. Syracuse: Syracuse U. P., 1986, pp. 89–111.

Proposes to interpret *Cor.* in terms of pre-Oedipal "object–relations theory," according to which "the infant must undergo a process of separation and individuation from its mother with whom its first experience is one of union." According to this theory, femininity is "primary, while masculine identity is something achieved rather than given and always at risk of becoming lost or diffused back into the original feminine matrix." Surveys Sh's tragedies in light of the male hero's ambivalence toward "that which he considers feminine." In one group of plays, which includes *Ant.*, the hero attempts to escape the feminizing influence of a woman, and "that in turn creates the condition of union in destruction that comprises both the conclusion of the play and the actualization of a basic fantasy about heterosexual relations." The other significant group of tragedies, including *JC*, features a hero who recoils from heterosexual passion as he pursues "heroic masculinity through the defeat of one or more rivals." Despite his attempt to avoid the submissive feminine posture, this hero is forced ultimately to embrace it. *Cor.* combines "the structures of relationship" that control the two groups previously described "in a particularly excruciating way": While its hero "dies as a soldier," the way in which he dies "involves submission to a woman." Suggests that the obstacles to intimacy in Sh's tragedies derive from "the hero's anxieties regarding the figure of a mother/lover who threatens the annihilation of his identity, a condition he both desires and fears."

1730 Stockholder, Katherine. "The Other Coriolanus." *PMLA*, 85 (1970), 228–36.

Regards the protagonist of *Cor.* as engaged in "image making": creating and then identifying the self with a particular image, in this case one of "extreme virile masculinity." Paradoxically, though his image is one of manly martial independence, he relies for its maintenance on others, who reflect it back to him. Because he must remain true to type, he frequently comes very close to the parodic opposite of his image; that is, he often resembles a Jonsonian humors character or a *miles gloriosus*. The weeping figure of his wife, Virgilia, hints at qualities of tenderness and compassion in him, but he denies these indications of inward life because they are at odds with his self-image. Sh compresses three issues from Plutarch into one in order to make "the outcome of the play spring directly from Coriolanus's behaviour," not from "a general political position." Referred to many times as a god, Coriolanus is ironically and easily manipulated by nearly everyone else: the tribunes, his mother, Aufidius. Lacking the self-recognition that helps the tragic figure defeat absurdity, he is "tragically ridiculous." Revision of part of item 1026.

1731 Stoller, Robert J. "Shakespearean Tragedy: *Coriolanus*." *PsyQ*, 35 (1965), 263–74.

Argues that *Cor.* studies the relationship between the hero and his mother. Coriolanus acts out his mother's phallus fantasy "as her surrogate until his repressed (feminine) identification with her—and his guilt about his repressed hatred of her—lead him to contrive his destruction."

1732 Story, Elizabeth. "*Coriolanus* and a Shakespearean Motif." *Shakespeare and Dramatic Tradition: Essays in Honor of S. F. Johnson.* Eds. W. R. Elton and William B. Long. Newark: U. of Delaware P., 1989, pp. 47–68.

Surveys the use in Sh's plays of the "antirhetorical" motif that the tongue should speak only what the heart believes and associates it with a range of characters, "good, mixed, or evil." Focuses on *Cor.*, in which this motif becomes thematic. The protagonist's political failure under the conditions of a primitive, warring Rome and his tragedy are defined by his "inability to tolerate the disjunction between what the heart prompts and what is required by expediency."

1733 Tanselle, G. Thomas, and Florence W. Dunbar. "Legal Language in *Coriolanus*." *SQ*, 13 (1962), 231–38.

Points to the great importance of legal language in the play. Words associated with several branches of the law abound, with the greatest number coming from procedural law, which concerns "the process, hearing and judgment of a case." When Menenius remonstrates with the tribunes in II.i, he uses eight procedural phrases. The third scene of act III contains a great deal of criminal and procedural terminology. There are also a number of words and phrases associated with "the rules of evidence and pleading," "the law merchant," and "inheritance, execution, and seals." Some words, like "malice," normally taken in a nonlegal sense, take on legal meaning from the context of the play. If the tendency to use words with legal overtones is recognized, light can be shed on a famous crux: The words "an overture" (I.ix.46) can be emended to "in coverture," and the line can be read metaphorically as comparing the parasitical courtier's position during wartime to that of a wife under the legal disability of coverture (which rendered her powerless).

1734 Taylor, Michael. "The Modernity of *Coriolanus*." *SAP*, 16 (1983), 273–89.

Maintains that *Cor.* is "an acute presentation of the eternal tragic conflict between the possible and the necessary, between ideals and realities, between ethics and politics." Sketches what happens in the play and then explains how Sh transforms this "factual record" into "a study of tragic inevitability," offering a masterful analysis of "an incomplete man, whom psychological, ethical and political forces all combine to destroy." Psychologically and spiritually, Coriolanus is innocent and pure. His mother's suffocating tutelage has rendered him incapable of dealing with the larger world outside of himself. The key quality attributed to Coriolanus is *pride*, which has different meanings for the tribunes (arrogance), the politicians plotting to have him elected (nobility and virtue), and Coriolanus himself ("an urge toward self-deification"). Observes that Coriolanus is required to leap from the realm of radical individualism straight into the arena of political competition, without passing through the intermediate dimension of "ethical interaction." Finally, he is not so much proud as he is indignant, frustrated, and furious about the incomprehensible ways of the world. *Cor.* has several modern features: Its ethical concerns can be better formulated in Christian than in Roman terms; its psychological preoccupations are meaningful only in democratic societies; it opens the possibility that militarism could be substituted for "political idealism"; and it articulates a dark, hopeless vision of history.

1734a   Taylor, Michael. "Playing the Man He Is: Role-Playing in Shakespeare's *Coriolanus*." *ArielE*, 15 (1984), 19–28.

Compares and contrasts the hero of *Cor.* with a number of other characters in Sh's plays who have trouble playing a part and with some (like Prince Hal) who are consummate actors. Discusses failed attempts by others in the play to persuade Coriolanus to play a role. Notes that the "authentic self" of this character is "the extreme expression of the mores of the Roman patrician warrior caste," which depends on "the existence of a valued mode of social conduct for him to be truly what he is." He is most untrue to his nature when he tries "to redefine himself" as someone who is separate from his Roman identity.

1735   Teague, Frances. "Headgear in *Coriolanus*." *BNYSS*, 4, no. 4 (1986), 5–7.

Analyzes the significance of headgear in *Cor.*, especially in light of the social customs of Sh's time. Notes twenty references in speeches and three in stage directions to some form of hat. Argues that Coriolanus's bareheadedness before the citizens means, in their eyes, that he submits to them. When the citizens cast their caps in the air to cheer Coriolanus's exile, they recognize him as one of them. Once he has removed his hat, Coriolanus cannot resume his role of patrician; nor can the citizens, once they have acknowledged an equivalence between themselves and him, collaborate in his banishment without inviting retribution. The opposition that many critics have discovered between Coriolanus and the citizens is thus no opposition at all. Revised as part of item 1044a.

1736   Tennenhouse, Leonard. "*Coriolanus*: History and the Crisis of Semantic Order." *CompD*, 10 (1976), 328–46. Reprint. *Drama in the Renaissance: Comparative and Critical Essays.* (AMS Studies in the Renaissance 12.) Eds. Clifford Davidson, C. J. Gianakaris, and John H. Stroupe. New York: AMS P., 1986, pp. 217–35.

Argues that *Cor.* begins by depicting a Rome which has just undergone a significant change because the plebeians have gained a voice in the affairs of the city. The tribunes, who represent this voice, are given a much greater part than they are in Sh's sources. That Sh's contemporaries associated the tribunes with a new and often disturbing voice of the people can be surmised from the comments of some 16th-c. writers and Jacobean references to the self-conscious oratory of Parliament members in their conflict with King James. As explored in the play, the establishment of a "public tongue" for the mob signals the end of the old patrician order, which had used action as its expression of power. The new order, as the play proves, will use language, the thing Coriolanus most distrusts, as its weapon. As the formative influence on Coriolanus's character, Volumnia has taught him to use the language of public service but to attach private meaning to it. Thus he cannot speak effectively in public: His "linguistic solipsism" makes him invincible as a soldier but incompetent as a political man. Finally, Volumnia unknowingly betrays her son by forcing him into the role of mediator. Words now have different meanings—honor, for example, now equates to mercy—and he cannot square this change with his private code. *Cor.* is the only one of Sh's history plays that does not center on a period of transition at the end of which a new stable order emerges as the hero is destroyed. At the end of *Cor.*, the mob has gained political power, the hero is dead, and "language turns to violence in a crisis of meaning."

1737 Trousdale, Marion. "*Coriolanus* and the Playgoer in 1609." *The Arts of Performance: Essays for G. K. Hunter.* Eds. Murray Biggs, Philip Edwards, and Inga-Stina Ewbank. Edinburgh: Edinburgh U. P., 1991, pp. 124–34.

Speculates that the first audience's disapproval of *Cor.* might have been prompted by attempts to suggest social identity (of soldiers, upper class Romans, and common citizens) by the dress of the actors.

1738 Ure, Peter. *Shakespeare and the Inward Self of the Tragic Hero.* Durham: U. of Durham P., 1961. 22 pp. Reprint. *Elizabethan and Jacobean Drama: Critical Essays by Peter Ure.* Ed. J. C. Maxwell. (Liverpool English Texts and Studies.) Liverpool: Liverpool U. P., 1974, pp. 1–21.

Discusses the theme, in Sh's tragedies, of "the hero's devotion of himself to a role in society, to the burden of an office such as kingship, or of a relationship such as fatherhood, or of an occupation such as soldiering. It is the character's awareness of himself as playing one or other of those parts, playing them rightly or wrongly, joyfully or in pain, that helps to make him come alive in our imaginations." Coriolanus, for example, seems absolutely committed to his role as a proud, self-sufficient soldier, but his surrender to his mother at the end of *Cor.* forces him to recognize that she has all along been the "ultimate source of the approval without which he cannot live." After Rome has been spared, his attempts to play the peacemaker are ironically pathetic.

1739 Van Dyke, Joyce. "The Decomposition of Tragic Character in Shakespeare." Ph.D. dissertation, University of Virginia, 1980. *DAI*, 41 (1980–81), 1620-A.

Analyzes the composite nature of the tragic hero in Sh and explains how his character undergoes decomposition through the tragic action. Chapter 4, on *Cor.*, regards this protagonist's character as "more elemental, less 'composite,'" than Lear or Macbeth. He is a tragic figure "because he is paradoxically both an essential part of Rome who cannot survive separation from the state, and a singular wholly integral being who cannot survive the self-division necessary to remain there."

1740 Van Dyke, Joyce. "Making a Scene: Language and Gesture in *Coriolanus*." *ShS*, 30 (1977), 135–46.

Maintains that for Coriolanus words have "virtually a material existence." His habits of response are gestural: For example, he always tends "to convert verbal altercations into physical ones." Further testimony about his mode of communication comes from the other characters, who discuss him in terms of his physical features. Because of his physical sense of language, Coriolanus is a poor actor, ill at ease when trying to use words to disguise himself or his feelings.

1740a Vickers, Brian. " Teaching *Coriolanus*: The Importance of Perspective." *Teaching Shakespeare.* Eds. Walter Edens, Christopher Durer, Walter Eggers, Duncan Harris, and Keith Hull. Princeton: Princeton U. P., 1977, pp. 228–70.

Points out that in *Cor.* Sh adjusts his source, Plutarch's *Lives*, to present equally negative views of the Roman people and the patricians. Outlines the four chief images of the play's hero within the play; these are held by (1) the patricians, (2) the people, (3) Volumnia, and (4) Aufidius. Argues for the validity of the following view of Coriolanus: "He is violent, intolerant, unreasonable, and unfeeling in his attitude toward the people"; he is full of youthful energy and innocence; he is a supremely gifted soldier; and he is one of only two people (Virgilia is the other) who lives "according to ideals of humanity and love."

1741 Wakeman, Carolyn Grant. "Action and Interpretation: The Impact of *Coriolanus* in the Theater." Ph.D. dissertation, Washington University, 1980. *DAI*, 41 (1980–81), 1068-A.

Approaches *Cor.* as "a text conceived for theater" in an attempt to explain its peculiarly unsympathetic hero. Chapter 1 explains how the play uses metaphors drawn from theater and play-like incidents to encourage the audience to see their own lives as play-like and to make them bear the play's tragic burden. Chapter 2 shows how Coriolanus's strengths are subverted by the deflationary ways in which they are presented. Chapter 3 maintains that the play's chief concern is the destiny of Rome rather than the destiny of Coriolanus. Political compromise is shown to be necessary for the survival of civilization. Chapter 4 examines five adaptations of *Cor.* during the 150 years following Sh's death.

1741a Watson, Robert N. *Shakespeare and the Hazards of Ambition.* Cambridge, Massachusetts: Harvard U. P., 1984. 330 pp.

Revision of item 1742. Chapter 3, "Martial Ambition and the Family Romance in *Coriolanus*," shows how the protagonist of this play, aspiring to "an identity based on a classical model of manly virtue," defies his "merely human father," represented by the citizens of Rome, and acts in the name of a father more responsive to his needs, the god Mars. He is finally forced to accept "the limitations imposed by his natural context."

1742 Watson, Robert Nathaniel. "The Hazards of Adopted Identity in *Coriolanus, Macbeth*, and *The Winter's Tale*." Ph.D. dissertation, Stanford University, 1979. *DAI*, 40 (1979–80), 5066-A.

Analyzes the fates of three Shakespearean protagonists who attempt to substitute "ideal adopted identities" for "their limited hereditary identities." Seeking to be an ideal martial hero, Coriolanus attempts to escape the constraining contexts of family and Roman citizenship. Despite his efforts, however, he is fatally reincorporated into the natural order. Revised as item 1741a.

1743 Weckermann, Hans-Jurgen. "*Coriolanus*: The Failure of the Autonomous Individual." *Text, Language, Criticism: Essays in Honour of Marvin Spevack*. Eds. Bernhard Fabian and Kurt Tetzeli Von Rosador. Hildesheim: Olms-Weidmann, 1987, pp. 334–50.

Points out that the chief conflict in *Cor.* is between the protagonist's "self-reliant individualism and the demands of the commonweal." Coriolanus's reluctance to have his deeds praised grows out of a fear that they will then become common property, beyond his control. He rejects the reciprocity that underlies all social relations, distrusting even language itself. Because it is based on the unreconcilable antagonism between "individual nature and natural social ties," his tragedy is similar to that of certain heroes of ancient Greek drama.

1744 Weixlmann, Joseph. "How the Romans Were Beat Back to Their Trenches: An Historical Note on *Coriolanus*, I.iv." *N&Q*, 21 (1974), 133–34.

Proposes stage action to make sense of the stage direction in *Cor.*, I.iv.30: "*The Romans are beat back to their trenches.*" Suggests that "the Roman soldiers, but not their leaders, were driven off the platform into the yard-alley, whereas Marcius and Lartius, pursued by a small party of Volsces, must have made an embattled, temporary exit through the outer stage door nearer the alley since both are later required to enter."

1745 Weixlmann, Joseph. "Some Key Presentational Images in Shakespeare's *Coriolanus*." *ForumH*, 12, no. 2 (1974), 9–13.

Observes that "the ironic pattern of the action" in *Cor.* is reinforced by "presentational images" of "a bloodied man" and of a character's entrance to or exit from gates.

Both of these images first occur in I.iv, when they are associated with the protagonist's triumphant courage. Later, when Coriolanus leaves Rome after his banishment, his passage through gates represents the city's rejection of him. The image of a man covered in blood is powerful confirmation of Coriolanus's failure in the play's final scene, when he is slaughtered by the Volsces. Comparisons between the bloodied Coriolanus and various unbloodied characters (the most significant of whom is Aufidius) are also important.

1746 Whitt, Nancy Marie. "The Structural Placement and Function of the Choric Scenes in Three Plays by William Shakespeare." Ph.D. dissertation, University of Alabama, 1977. *DAI*, 39 (1978–79), 302-A.

Defines choric scenes as "entire scenes, beginning and ending with a cleared stage, in which there is no development of the temporal plot." In *Cor.*, the key choric scene is the Roman soldier's betrayal (IV.iii), which serves to mark the end of the first movement of the plot and the turning point in the hero's career.

1747 Wihl, Gary. "Why the Interpretive Community Has Banished Literary Theory." *Philosophy and Literature*, 11 (1987), 272–81.

Analyzes Stanley Fish's reading of *Cor.* (item 1637) to show that Fish, in interpreting the play, is guilty of applying too narrowly "certain speech–act conventions." In particular, Fish's effort to theorize Coriolanus's use of the verb "banish" (III.iii.127) into "constitutive stability" refuses to acknowledge the ambiguities that the more satisfactory interpretation of Stanley Cavell (item 1623) takes into account.

1748 Williamson, Marilyn L. "Violence and Gender Ideology in *Coriolanus* and *Macbeth*." *Shakespeare Left and Right*. Ed. Ivo Kamps. New York: Routledge, 1991, pp. 147–66.

Notes that *Cor.* never settles on one political perspective. The play does rely on a specific notion of gender: that only males should be violent. Sh portrays Volumnia as transgressing the boundaries of the woman's role by her personal violence and her sponsorship of violence in her son; however, by dissuading Coriolanus from attacking Rome, she relinquishes her ambition and anger to the patriarchal city. Coriolanus, by capitulating to her, sacrifices his "warrior's anger and violence to his mother and the patriarchal family." Points out that the manipulations of family rituals by Volumnia to ensure Coriolanus's acquiescence in V.iii are invented by Sh; they are not in Plutarch's account of the scene.

1749 Wilson, Emmett Jr. "Coriolanus: The Anxious Bridegroom." *AI*, 25 (1968), 224–41.

Discusses "unconscious fantasies [that] may have determined the handling of the narrative material from which Sh worked." In particular, Coriolanus's reference to his wedding night in connection with the battle at Corioli (*Cor.*, I.v.29–32) warrants an analysis that symbolically parallels the penetration of the city to defloration. In addition, the award of the name "Coriolanus" as recognition for wounds received in battle is similar to a compensatory maneuver to avoid castration or to alleviate castration anxiety. During the play, Coriolanus has two surrogate fathers: Menenius and Aufidius. At first, the strong mother figure (Volumnia) dominates both Coriolanus and Menenius, but then Coriolanus rejects his mother "and all her symbolic representatives to seek out the strong, masculine father"—Aufidius.

1750 Wilson, Richard. "Against the Grain: Representing the Market in *Coriolanus*." *The Seventeenth Century*, 6 (1991), 111–48.

Contextualizes Sh within "the economic and power relations" of his day, which were causing a shift from "collective values based on shared consumption to exchange values and private enterprise." It is this movement that drives the plot of *Cor.* The hero's inability to act is "a metonym for the crisis of representation at the onset of market society."

Cymbeline

1751 Zeeveld, W. Gordon. "Coriolanus and Jacobean Politics." *MLR*, 57 (1962), 321–34.

Argues that *Cor.* reflects the political climate developing in the first decade of the 16th c. as a result of the increasingly vocal complaints to the crown from the House of Commons. In the debate over purveyance ("the supply of the royal household at values assessed by the purveyors"), the public recognized a parallel between those arguing against the crown and Roman tribunes. For the first time, the concept of the body politic had been seriously challenged. Sh responded to this critical situation by writing a tragedy about the "dismemberment of commonwealth."

1752 Zolbrod, Paul G. "Coriolanus and Alceste: A Study in Misanthropy." *SQ*, 23 (1972), 51–62.

Finds that taking note of the similarities between Sh's *Cor.* and *Le Misanthrope* of Molière enriches our understanding of both plays. Each work emphasizes almost continual conflict. Moreover, the protagonists, Coriolanus and Alceste, are strikingly alike: Both scorn the common people, both are quick to insult others, both see things as either black or white, both want to stand alone, both are paralyzed by their aggressiveness when called on to be benign, and both are heroic in despising vices but mistaken in hating the people who practice them. Alceste's proposal to Eliante to take revenge on Célimène is like Coriolanus's betrayal of his city out of spite. They are most alike in failing to carry out their intended revenge, which results in ruin for both.

CYMBELINE

1753 Abartis, Caesarea. *The Tragicomic Construction of "Cymbeline" and "The Winter's Tale."* (Jacobean Dramatic Studies 73.) Salzburg: Institut für Englische Sprache und Literatur, U. Salzburg, 1977. 128 pp.

Provides background for analysis of tragicomedy by reference to G. B. Guarini's *Il Pastor Fido* and the plays of Beaumont and Fletcher. Regards *Cym.* as a failure, in part because the happy ending for the British required by the tragicomic formula is not entirely compatible with the ascendancy of the Romans, which is necessary in order to validate the Tudor myth tracing the origins of the the British race back through Rome to Troy.

1754 Bergeron, David M. "*Cymbeline*: Shakespeare's Last Roman Play." *SQ*, 31 (1980), 31–41.

Discerns a knowledge of Roman history in Sh's composition of *Cym*. The play, unlike any of Sh's other romances, is focused on military affairs, something the Elizabethans associated with Rome. Sh had available to him several recent translations of Roman historical writing about the age of Augustus: *The Annales of Cornelius Tacitus* (1598); Suetonius's *Historie of Twelve Caesars, Emperours of Rome* (1606); and Plutarch's *Lives* (the 1603 edition included an anonymous *Life of Octavius Caesar Augustus*). He would also have been able to draw on two plays: Jonson's *Sejanus* (1603) and the anonymous *The Statelie Tragedie of Claudius Tiberius Nero* (1607). Underscoring the Roman atmosphere in *Cym.* is the emphasis given to Jupiter. In addition, several characters seem to have been developed from hints in works treating Roman history. Cymbeline is connected to Augustus; Posthumus resembles Germanicus, the nephew and adopted son of Tiberius; Cloten is like Tiberius himself; and the Queen, in her ambition and use of poison, bears a strong likeness to Livia, Augustus's wife.

1755 Carr, Joan. "*Cymbeline* and the Validity of Myth." *SP*, 75 (1978), 316–30.

Argues that in *Cym.* Sh is dramatizing the childlike satisfactions that human beings take in the benevolent, regenerative power of myth. At the same time, the playwright questions the absolute nature of the answers myth provides for human problems. For example, Cloten, his head severed and thrown in the creek, is clearly linked to Orpheus; he is also closely associated with Posthumus, whose clothes he is wearing. Thus Cloten's Orphic death presages a resurrection for Posthumus. Though Imogen, a victim of Posthumus's brutishness through most of the play, is readily and lovingly reconciled with him, the mythical pattern by which redemption is achieved is somewhat too self-consciously invoked by Sh to allow us to have complete faith in it.

1756 Davies, Rowena. "'Alone th'Arabian Bird'—Imogen as Elizabeth I?" *N&Q*, 26 (1979), 137–40.

Notes that Sh was fascinated with the image of the Phoenix and used it several times. Iachimo's association of Imogen with "th'Arabian bird," in *Cym.*, however, is the first such reference to a female character in Sh's plays. Given the Phoenix symbolism that had been applied to Elizabeth during her reign and the fact that Sh later referred to her as a Phoenix (in *H8*), it is likely that Imogen is intended as a nostalgic reminiscence of the great queen.

1757 Garber, Marjorie. "*Cymbeline* and the Languages of Myth." *Mosaic* 10, no. 3 (1976–77), 105–15.

Discovers that in the deep structure of the play, the ability to decipher "seeming," to read the truth behind appearance, is important; this is linked to providence, the belief that all will be well in the end. Examined in the light of these two concerns, several apparently disparate themes can be seen as congruent. Boxes, chests, and trunks—in the cases of Imogen and the Queen—appear to contain precious things but, like Pandora's box, once opened, prove baneful. The cave in which the sons of the king are raised also seems other than it is: In this case, it contains something better than appearances warrant. During the play, characters are educated to penetrate these seemings. Pandora's connection with Prometheus leads to a consideration of the latter's role as a "unifying presence" behind the play. As giver of "fire, civilization, and ceremonial sacrifice," Prometheus illuminates a number of things. The king's two sons, for example, have "the sparks of nature," while Cloten becomes a sacrificial victim "because he denies civilization." Cloten's sacrifice is purgational, but Cymbeline orders another type of sacrifice—sweet-smelling and representing gratitude. Recalling that Cymbeline ruled Britain when Christ was born and that, for Renaissance mythographers, Prometheus was a pagan anticipation of Christ, we can see how these seemingly unconnected details grow to something of great constancy.

1758 Geller, Lila. "*Cymbeline* and the Imagery of Covenant Theology." *SEL*, 20 (1980), 241–55.

Locates a precise center of meaning and imagery for *Cym.* in covenant–contract theology. Remarks that Sh was following contemporary chroniclers, who were in turn following Eusebius, in viewing Roman history, and especially the Pax Augustus, as an essential part of the providential plan for the Incarnation.

1759 Gesner, Carol. "*Cymbeline* and the Greek Romance: A Study in Genre." *Studies in English Renaissance Literature*. Ed. Waldo F. McNeir. Baton Rouge: Louisiana State U. P., 1962, pp. 105–31, 226–31.

Points out that Sh's four romances share elements derived from Greek romance that give them a common bond. Argues that *Cym.* has three plot threads characteristic of Greek romance: "the wager story and Imogen's travels, the loss and restoration of Cymbeline's heirs, and Cymbeline's war with Rome." Several romances have resemblances to *Cym.* (for example, Chariton's *Chaereas and Callirrhoe* has a similar

Cymbeline

wager plot), and the pervasive parallels with the *Aethiopica* of Heliodorus make it likely that Sh modeled his play on that work.

1760   Haffenreffer, Karl. "Jan Kott's 'Lucian in *Cymbeline*.'" *YES*, 6 (1976), 38–40.

Declares that Jan Kott's contention (item 1766) that two lines in *Cym*. ("Thersites' body is as good as Ajax' / When neither are alive" [IV.ii.252–53]) are directly based on Lucian's *Charon* seems to break "six rules of Shakespearian source study." The connection between *Cym*. and *Charon* is unproved.

1761   Hieatt, A. Kent. "*Cymbeline* and the Intrusion of Lyric into Romance Narrative: *Sonnets*, 'A Lover's Complaint,' Spenser's *Ruins of Rome*." *Unfolded Tales: Essays on Renaissance Romance*. Eds. George M. Logan and Gordon Teskey. Ithaca: Cornell U. P., 1989, pp. 98–118.

Connects Spenser's *Ruins* with the theme of Rome's self-destruction in Sh's earlier works. Detects a renewed interest in Spenser's (and Sh's own) lyrical descriptions of Rome's ruin in *Cym*. (involving images of birds, giants, trees, and ruined buildings). Sh's modifications of the image of ruined Rome allow him to discredit Cloten's isolationist idea of Britain, to present the British as maintaining their honor, and to affirm the Roman ideas of internationalism and peace by reconciling the English and the Romans. *Cym*., then, is a romance that has strong historical elements.

1762   Hoeniger, F. D. "Irony and Romance in *Cymbeline*." *SEL*, 2 (1962), 219–28.

Focuses on the highly ironic perspective brought to bear on the characters until near the play's end. Mentions in passing that Sh had precedent for the marriage of romance and irony in prose epics by Heliodorus, Achilles Tatius, and Sir Philip Sidney.

1763   Hosley, Richard, ed. *Cymbeline*. (Signet Classic Shakespeare.) New York: New American Library, 1968. xxxvii + [38]–239 pp.

The introduction analyzes the plot of *Cym*. into three stories: (1) that of a wife "who is separated from and eventually reunited with her husband" (sources: a tale from Boccaccio's *Decameron*, a dramatic romance entitled *The Rare Triumphs of Love and Fortune*, and the Greek romance tradition [especially the *Aethiopica* of Heliodorus]); (2) that of two sons "who have been separated from their father in infancy and who are eventually reunited with him"; and (3) that of a king who "successfully defends his country against invasion." Notes that the death of Cloten is a "mock–mythic or mock–epic" allusion to the death of Orpheus and that the vision of Jupiter that apears to Posthumus (V.iv) is part of a literary tradition that derives from classical epic. Calls attention to Holinshed's *Chronicles of England, Scotland, and Ireland* as the chief source of the Cymbeline story with its account of the denial of the Roman demand for tribute. Other details about the denial of tribute were contributed by Edmund Spenser's *The Fairie Queene* and *The Mirror for Magistrates*. The note on the sources indicates the standard editions for the works discussed in the introduction. The introduction, text, and note on the sources are reprinted as part of item 0123.

1764   Jacobs, Henry E., comp. "*Cymbeline*." (Garland Shakespeare Bibliographies 3.) New York: Garland, 1982. xlviii + 591 pp.

Covers primarily works published between 1940 and 1980, with some coverage of significant work done before 1940. Classifies entries under eight major headings, including Criticism (801 items), Sources (66 items), Bibliographies (33 items), and Editions (105 items). The section on Sources contains a number of items on classical influences. Subdivides the Criticism section into (a) Authorship, (b) Characters, (c) Genre and Mode, (d) Language and Music, (e) Structure and Staging, (f) Thematic Approaches, and (g) Surveys and Collections of Criticism. Begins each section or subsection with the oldest entries and proceeds chronologically. Includes extensive cross-references. Concludes with a single index that "lists authors, plays, texts, historical figures, characters, and subjects." Provides substantial and detailed annotations.

1765   Jones, Emrys. "Stuart *Cymbeline*." *EIC*, 11 (1961), 84–99.

Notes that Cymbeline reigned in Britain at the time of Christ's birth as Augustus did in Rome. Suggests that Sh set his play in that time of peace partly because his sovereign, James I, was seen (and saw himself) as a peacemaker and figure of Augustus.

1766   Kott, Jan. "Lucian in *Cymbeline*." *MLR*, 67 (1972), 742–44. Reprint. *The Eating of the Gods: An Interpretation of Greek Tradgedy*. Trs. Boleslaw Taborski and Edward J. Czerwinski. New York: Random House, 1973, pp. 268–73.

Makes a case for Sh's use of Lucian's dialogue *Charon* in *Cym*. (IV.ii.255–256), where Guiderius comments on what he thinks is the dead body of Imogen: "Thersites' body is as good as Ajax' / When neither are alive." Lucian's version is quite close to this, except that Achilles is mentioned instead of Ajax. Sh may have gotten the reference to Ajax from Sophocles' play of that name, and he could have read both Lucian and Sophocles in Latin translation. See item 1760.

1767   Lawrence, Judiana. "Natural Bonds and Artistic Coherence in the Ending of *Cymbeline*." *SQ*, 35 (1984), 440–60.

Includes a discussion of the *Aethiopica* of Heliodorus as a source of *Cym*. and an influence on the self-consciousness of the play. Sh's ending "fosters both assent to the aims of ethical romance and a critical analysis of its means."

1768   Marsh, D. R. C. *The Recurring Miracle: A Study of "Cymbeline" and the Last Plays*. Pietermaritzburg: Natal U. P., 1962. ix + 197 pp. Reprint. Lincoln: U. of Nebraska P., 1969. Reprint. Sydney: Sydney U. P., 1980.

Comments, during an analysis of *Cym.*, that the Romans in the play are anachronistically distinguished from the Italians. The Roman ideals of *virtus* and *pietas* are meant to be admired, as they indicate "a readiness to subordinate the desires and ambitions of the self to some higher ideal."

1769   Middleton, David Loren. "Shakespeare's *Cymbeline* and British Mythical History." Ph.D. dissertation, University of Wisconsin, 1969. *DAI*, 30 (1969–70), 5415-A-5416-A.

Places *Cym*. in a historical context, focusing on its nonromance aspects. Surveys the nondramatic treatments of British mythical history (chief among these being Geoffrey of Monmouth's *Historia*) before Sh. Points out that this subject matter became the basis for a group of English plays whose purpose was to explain "Britain's secular dogma." Sh's play captures two outstanding features of the reign of the historical Cymbeline: It was "a time of peace in Britain corresponding to a period of world peace" and, "because it spanned Christ's birth and life, it marked the realization of a new ethic of forgiveness superseding old notions of law." In a larger sense, *Cym*. is an example of "authentic" British history "from the Roman period of Britain's past."

1770   Miklachki, Jody Beth. "Taking the Measure of England: The Poetics of Antiquarianism in the English Renaissance." Ph.D. dissertation, Yale University, 1990. *DAI*, 52 (1991–92), 170-A.

Investigates the power of antiquarianism to construct and change national identity "in early modern England." Anxious about the savage origins of their society, antiquarians sought the foundations of the modern state in "the civilized period of Roman Britain." Anxieties about the past persisted, however, especially with reference to "the disturbing presence of powerful women in Britain's ancient past." In *Cym.*, "the crisis of the nation's relation with its past" is gendered; that is, we see a contrast between Roman *virtus* and "the native savagery of the wicked British queen." This play shows a new "masculine model of the state" displacing the chorographical (topographical), feminine construction.

1771 Miola, Robert S. "*Cymbeline*: Shakespeare's Valediction to Rome." *Roman Images*. Ed. Annabel Patterson. (Selected Papers from the English Institute, 1982. N. S., no. 8.) Baltimore: Johns Hopkins U. P., 1984, pp. 51–62.

Contends that *Cym.* is Sh's final Roman play and that it contains a wealth of allusions to Rome and especially to his earlier Roman works. In *Cym.*, however, Roman pride, high seriousness, and savagery are transformed or supplanted by more humane British values. Revised as chapter 7 of item 0759a.

1772 Moffet, Robin. "*Cymbeline* and the Nativity." *SQ*, 13 (1962), 207–18.

Investigates the ways in which the occurrence of the Nativity of Jesus Christ during Cymbeline's reign is "reflected in the form and details of the play." Various aspects of paganism (for example, the famous lament emphasizing the ills of "nature, fortune, and human malice" sung by Guiderius and Arviragus over the "body" of Imogen [IV.ii.259–270]) are exhibited but are shown to be insufficient to portray the whole truth. During Posthumus's vision (V.iv) of the ghosts of the Leonati and Jupiter, "allegorical paganism is made most explicit" precisely when "we are expected to think most unmistakably of the Christian God." This is because of a reverence that does not wish to "behave too familiarly in the presence of a sacred object" and an "acknowledgment of limitation which will not attempt to find expression for the ineffable but is content with a sign or a gesture which will carry part, but only part, of the way."

1773 Moseley, C. W. R. D. "Innogen's Bedroom." *N&Q*, 37 (1990), 196–98.

Points out that Iachimo's account of the items in Imogen's bedchamber (especially the two blind Cupids guarding the fire), which he uses to convince Posthumus of his wife's infidelity, operates on a mythic level, in ways Iachimo cannot understand, to enlighten the audience about the chaste love of Imogen and Posthumus.

1774 Parker, Patricia. "Romance and Empire: Anachronistic *Cymbeline*." *Unfolded Tales: Essays on Renaissance Romance*. Eds. George M. Logan and Gordon Teskey. Ithaca: Cornell U. P., 1989, pp. 189–207.

Claims that Sh's mixing of modern (Renaissance) Italy with ancient Rome and Britain is deliberate anachronism, designed to chart the westward translation of empire. Echoes of and parallels to the *Aeneid*, most notably in the similarities between the careers of Posthumus and Aeneas, remind us of empire's progress from Troy to Rome and then from Rome to Britain. *Cym.* combines "folktale and imperial elements," exploiting the "romance resources of delay" inherited from the *Aeneid*. The double submission at the play's end—Cymbeline's agreement to pay tribute after he has bested the Romans in battle and Iachimo's humbling of himself to Posthumus—is a chiastic recognition that Britain, purged of the narrow nationalism represented by the Queen and Cloten, has superseded Rome as the proper locus of imperial power.

1775 Richmond, Hugh M. "Shakespeare's Roman Trilogy: The Climax in *Cymbeline*." *SLitI*, 5, no. 1 (1972), 129–39.

Points out that *Cym.* is set historically just at the beginning of Christ's life and attempts to explain its apparent eccentricities in this light. The play offers a critique of Roman law and the attitudes associated with it, especially obsessive faith in formal reason and propriety. Like Brutus in *JC* and Octavius in *Ant.*, the characters in *Cym.*, even the Britons, are addicted to judging themselves and others by the shallow standard of outward plausibility and to meting out punishment with "specious severity." It is only when characters like Posthumus and Cymbeline are constrained to relinquish their egotistical, aristocratic, pagan pretensions that they can be truly creative and heroic. Sh hints at a "humane politics," unattainable by the Romans and based on the Christian notion of "white Machiavellianism," but he cannot fully externalize this concept without anachronism.

1776 Schork, R. J. "Allusion, Theme, and Characterization in *Cymbeline*." *SP*, 69 (1972), 210–16.

Shows that two characters in *Cym.*—Iachimo and Imogen—use allusion to ancient Roman legend, mythology, and history to describe present action. Iachimo's allusions, primarily to Ovid's *Metamorphoses*, which he usually misunderstands, serve to characterize him as a villain and to point to the ultimate futility of his machinations. Imogen's references to Rome show her to be free of the jingoism that characterizes many other Britons, and her allusions to Aeneas and Sinon demonstrate that she is unwilling to condemn a group because of the unworthy behavior of one of its members.

1777 Simonds, Peggy Muñoz. "'No More . . . Offend Our Hearing': Aural Imagery in *Cymbeline*." *TSLL*, 24 (1982), 137–54.

Cites the scene in which Jupiter descends to deliver his prophecy (V.iv) to highlight the importance of correctly judging what one hears. The three princely characters (the king, Posthumus, and Imogen) are seduced aurally and must be redeemed through sound. Points to an emblem book by Hadrianus Junius that interprets Jupiter descending as a model for princes because he does not lend "a slavish ear to anyone." Junius, in turn, cites Plutarch as a source.

1778 Simonds, Peggy Muñoz. "Some Emblematic Courtier *Topoi* in *Cymbeline*." *RenP*, 1981 (1982), 97–112.

Points out three "courtier *topoi*"—the caged bird, the ravished tree, and the empty head—used in *Cym*. and attempts to explain them by reference to their background in Renaissance emblem books and classical literature.

1779 Tylus, Jane Cecilia. "The Myth of Enclosure: Renaissance Pastoral from Sannazaro to Shakespeare." Ph.D. dissertation, Johns Hopkins University, 1985. *DAI*, 46 (1985–86), 1619-A.

Begins by describing Battista Guarini's *Il Pastor Fido*, which sought to make pastoral as inclusive a genre as possible, and its opponents, who wanted to keep pastoral as "a model of limitation, constraint, and understatement." Guarini and his followers were both undermining "the traditional Aristotelian hierarchy of literary kinds" and reinterpreting antiquity as "a moment of incompleteness rather than a perfect and irretrievable past." Further, the new way of looking at pastoral placed trespassing at the center of "a supposedly unambitious genre" and "blurred the distinctions" between civilized society and the unenlightened pastoral world. Includes consideration of "the relationship of Renaissance writers to the classical world they had lost." Notes the importance of Ovid for Renaissance ideas of pastoral. Devotes chapter 5 to *Cym.*, which dramatizes invasions into the enclosed, insular domain of England.

1780 Wickham, Glynne. "Riddle and Emblem: A Study in the Dramatic Structure of *Cymbeline*." *English Renaissance Studies Presented to Dame Helen Gardner in Honour of Her Seventieth Birthday*. Ed. John Carey. Oxford: Clarendon P., 1980, pp. 94–113.

Explains that the structure of *Cym*. can be best understood in terms of the riddles propounded by the soothsayer and Jove and "the emblems they contain" (eagle, cedar, tribute, and Jove [IV.ii, iv]). The riddles and the relationship between Rome and Britain in the play can be seen as responding to the contemporary views of King James as pacifier and unifier.

HAMLET

1781 Abel, Lionel. *Metatheatre: A New View of Dramatic Form.* New York: Hill and Wang, 1963. xi + 146 pp.

Claims, in a chapter on *Ham.*, that this play is not a tragedy. It cannot be explained as a ritualistic tragedy like Sophocles' *Oedipus the King*, in which the protagonist is faced with the duty of purifying Denmark. Instead, it is a form of metatheater: "For the first time in the history of drama, the problem of the protagonist is that he has a playwright's consciousness."

1782 Ahrens, Rüdiger. "The Poetics of the Renaissance and the System of Literary Genres." *Functions of Literature: Essays Presented to Erwin Wolff on His Sixtieth Birthday.* Eds. Ulrich Broich, Theo Stemmler, and Gerd Stratmann. Tübingen: Max Niemeyer Verlag, 1984, pp. 101–17.

Cites Polonius's rehearsal of the types of plays the visiting actors are able to perform and Hamlet's advice to the players (*Ham.*, II.ii) as evidence that Sh was thoroughly familiar with contemporary genre theory, especially Sir Philip Sidney's *An Apology for Poetry*. Analyzes the *Apology*, showing that Sidney draws on "the classical intellectual tradition" to reposition poetry, considered in its various genres, so that it fills a social need: to teach people about "new secular ideals."

1783 Aldus, P. J. *Mousetrap: Structure and Meaning in "Hamlet."* Toronto: U. of Toronto P., 1977. xiii + 235 pp.

Discovers in *Ham.* "the most sophisticated of all literary myths." Uses Plato and Aristotle as guides for analysis of the play. Plato, especially in the account of invention in the *Phaedrus*, helps to explain the combination of the intuitive and the literary that "creates literary myth." Aristotle's *Poetics* provides structural principles, especially the idea that "the end is everywhere the chief thing."

1784 Alexander, Nigel. "Hamlet and the Art of Memory." *N&Q*, 15 (1968), 137–39.

Suggests that, in *Ham.*, Hamlet's lines at I.v.111–113 may be explained by reference to Quintilian's *Institutio Oratoria*, in which the student is advised to learn a passage by heart by visualizing it on the tablets where he has written it. The technical device Hamlet plans to use for remembering what the ghost has said (his "word") is "Adieu, adieu! Remember me." Hamlet's art of memory is important throughout the play and is opposed to Claudius's "rhetoric of oblivion."

1785 Bagchi, Josodhara. "Hamlet and the Problem of Love." *Essays on Shakespeare.* Ed. Bhabatosh Chatterjee. University of Burdwan Shakespeare Memorial Volume. Bombay: Orient Longmans, 1965, pp. 145–59.

Distinguishes "two important aspects of the European traditions of love" in English Renaissance literature: idealized love, deriving from Plato, and debased love, "quite often drawing upon the actual experience of love," but linked in humanist analyses with Ovid. The tension between these two types of love is present in Sh's work from the beginning, and his growing interest in the seamier aspect can be followed from *Ven.*, through *Son.*, to *Ham.* He is groping in all of these works toward a satisfactory dramatization "of a complexity in love that was a product of the age itself."

1786 Battenhouse, Roy W. "Apocatastasis of *Hamlet*'s Ghost." *AN&Q*, 9 (1970), 57–58.

Argues that the ghost of Hamlet's father has the outlook of "a Christian soul recrudescently pagan," lost in the illusion (held by many Renaissance and earlier Platonists, and by the Christian Origen of Alexandria) "that *all* suffering is purgative" and that the torments of hell are only temporary. This heretical doctrine of *apocatastasis* is given by Sh to the ghost to reveal old Hamlet's error and his misleading of his son.

1787 Battenhouse, Roy W. "The Significance of Hamlet's Advice to the Players." *The Drama of the Renaissance: Essays for Leicester Bradner*. Ed. Elmer M. Blistein. Providence: Brown U. P., 1970, pp. 3–26.

Sees Hamlet's advice to the players (*Ham.*, II.ii) as evidence of his belief in a neoclassical, Senecan view of drama. His reference to self-controlled action on the part of the players, his belief in drama mirroring nature, and his apparent commitment to the didactic–satiric purpose of playing put him in Ben Jonson's camp. However, Hamlet's neoclassicism is evidence of his misjudgment; he believes that by turning dramatist he can justify an irrational vision of life and discover a course of action. Sh's play, as distinguished from Hamlet's dramatic theory, uses Aristotelian principles, according to which the hero of a tragedy is brought down by an error in judgment. Part of Hamlet's error is his attempt to apply a faulty notion of drama to his circumstances.

1788 Beardsley, Theodore S. Jr. "Isocrates, Shakespeare, and Calderón: Advice to a Young Man." *Hispanic Review*, 42 (1974), 185–98.

Contends that Polonius's advice to Laertes (*Ham.*, I.iii) is derived from Isocrates' *Oratio ad Demonicum*, which was available in the 16th c. in Erasmus' Latin translation. There are clear parallels for most of Isocrates' maxims in Polonius's speech, but Sh modified the advice about money (Isocrates says to be generous in aiding a friend) and replaced Isocrates' exhortation to cultivate the intellect with an injunction to be true to oneself. Throughout Isocrates' speech, the emphasis is on "moderation and reputation." The former idea is hardened by Polonius into "an explicit juxtaposition of opposites," and the latter is largely ignored.

1789 Boitani, Piero. "Anagnorisis and Reasoning: Electra and Hamlet." *REAL: Yearbook of Research in English and American Literature*, 7 (1990), 99–136.

Uses Aristotle's discussion of anagnorisis in the *Poetics* to compare the treatment of "the shift from ignorance to knowledge" in Electra (with regard to the identity of her brother, Orestes) by the three great ancient Greek tragedians to the treatment of the same shift in *Ham*. Notes that these accounts of anagnorisis in tragedy show different attitudes to a question that is basically epistemological: "What is the value of signs, clues, reasoning?" In *Ham.*, the recognition scenes profoundly explore this question without answering it.

1789a Borthwick, E. Kerr. "'So Capital a Calf': The Pun in *Hamlet*, III.ii.105." *SQ*, 35 (1984), 203–4.

Suggests that, in a passage that contains a number of other puns at Polonius's expense [*Ham.*, III.ii.96–104], the word *calf* embodies yet another play on words. Since the Latin word *calvus*, "bald," was often applied to Caesar (as, for example, in Suetonius's *Life of Caesar*), and since Hamlet is teasing Polonius about the elderly courtier's youthful performance as the Roman dictator, this further pun would be a way of calling attention to Polonius's agedness.

1790 Bowers, Fredson. "Dramatic Structure and Criticism: Plot in *Hamlet*." *SQ*, 15, no. 2 (1964), 207–18. Reprint. *Shakespeare 400: Essays by American Scholars on the Anniversary of the Poet's Birth*. Ed. James G. McManaway. New York: Holt, Rinehart and Winston, 1964, pp. 207–18. Reprint. *Hamlet as Minister and Scourge and Other Studies in Shakespeare and Milton*. Charlottesville: U. P. of Virginia, 1989, pp. 137–54.

Uses Aristotelian notions of plot to analyze *Ham*. Locates the climax, or "incident in which the fate of the protagonist is irrevocably decided," in Hamlet's slaying of

Polonius during the closet scene. Hamlet's tragic error here, in Aristotelian and Christian terms, is that he breaks his inaction, casting off heavenly guidance in a rash attempt at vengeance. Proper attention to plot saves the critic from finding Hamlet's error in his delay. Hamlet does come to recognize his error, and in his defiance of augury, reconciles himself and the audience to the justice of the catastrophe. See items 1791 and 0182.

1791 Bowers, Fredson. "The Moment of Final Suspense in *Hamlet*: 'We Defy Augury.'" *Shakespeare 1564–1964: A Collection of Modern Essays by Various Hands.* Ed. Edward A. Bloom. Providence: Brown U. P., 1964, pp. 50–55. Reprint. *Hamlet as Minister and Scourge and Other Studies in Shakespeare and Milton.* Charlottesville: U. P. of Virginia, 1989, pp. 114–22.

Explains the moment of final suspense in classical tragedy as the point at which the protagonist is given a final chance "to escape the fatal consequences of the tragic act." Showing the same lack of self-knowledge that led to his original error, the protagonist dismisses an omen or a prophetic warning and thus goes to meet his doom. In *Ham.*, the moment of final suspense comes when the hero is presented with a challenge to the fatal fencing match. He agrees to the match because he does not think Claudius has had time to instigate a new plot against him and because his "generous nature cannot conceive that Laertes will turn villain." Further, he sets aside his own foreboding of evil and Horatio's advice. Hamlet's actions here amount to a Christianization of the classical moment of final suspense. His rejection of pagan augury is not a confirmation of his original tragic blindness. Rather, it is an acceptance of Providence, a recognition that he must pay the penalty for his error. See items 1790 and 0182.

1792 Breuer, Horst. "Three Notes on *Hamlet*." *ES*, 56 (1975), 20–28.

The first note discusses the comment by Hamlet that Claudius is "no more like my father / Than I to Hercules" (I.ii.152–153). Suggests that the image of Hercules in the literature of the Tudor period was one of a furious, bombastic giant. Hamlet, the aristocratic courtier, is quite right in stating that he cannot be compared with so crude a figure. The fact that Hamlet is not huge and brawny in no way detracts from his manliness and athleticism.

1793 Brockbank, J. Philip. "Hamlet the Bonesetter." *ShS*, 30 (1977), 103–15.

Argues for "the lines of continuity between the tragic play [*Ham.*] and its primordial spectre, the sacrifice ritual." Cites Gilbert Murray's *Five Stages of Greek Religion* to establish that St. Paul "assimilated the insights of Greek tragedy" about sacrificial renewal "into an experience of the significance of Christ." This makes it possible to claim that *Ham.* is a sacrificial tragedy in a tradition "reaching back to Aeschylus." Cites parallels between *Ham.* and *Oedipus Rex* to illuminate the tragic effects of the former. Reprinted as chapter 9 of item 0201.

1794 Bruster, Douglas S. "'Nor Plautus too light': *Hamlet* 1.2.184–85 and Plautus's *Pseudolus*." *ANQ*, 4 (1991), 118–19.

Suggests that a situation in Plautus's *Pseudolus*—in which Pseudolus claims to see his young master's girlfriend, the master takes the comment literally, and Pseudolus then jokingly explains that he sees her in wax tablets—provided Sh with a model for the exchange in which Hamlet explains to a too-literal Horatio that he sees his father "in my mind's eye."

1795 Burelbach, Frederick M. "Names of Supporting Characters in *Hamlet, King Lear*, and *Macbeth*." *Names*, 35 (1987), 127–38.

Comments that Sh named some characters on the basis of historical allusion. Illustrations from *Ham.* include Claudius, who resembles the cruel emperor Claudius, the second husband of Nero's mother, and Horatio, whose loyalty and courage in the face of tyranny link him with several Romans of that name.

1796 Burton, J. Anthony. "Hamlet, Osric, and the Duel." *BNYSS*, July/August 1984, 5–7, 22–25.

Discovers four crucial references in the last two acts of *Ham.*, by Claudius, Laertes, Hamlet, and Osric, respectively, to "the classical myth of the giants' rebellion against Jupiter" and their effort to pile Mount Ossa on Mount Pelion so as to overthrow "the divine order of the Olympian gods." Argues that this series of allusions helps to explain how Claudius modifies his original plan (announced to Laertes in IV.vii) for drawing Hamlet into a fatal duel. Once Hamlet experiences the open hostility of Laertes in the graveyard scene (V.i), he can scarcely be expected to consent to an "innocent" fencing match. Claudius provokes him into accepting the challenge by sending Osric (V.ii) to describe the arrogant wager that Laertes has made on himself. In Osric's terms, Laertes has "impon'd" or "piled" an additonal stake of "six French rapiers" on top of the king's prize of six Barbary horses. In addition, Laertes has increased the odds against himself. "Impon'd" is a Latinism derived from the word Virgil had used in his account (*Georgics* 1) of the giants' attempt "to pile up Mount Ossa on Mount Pelion." It is Hamlet's imprudent desire to chastise Laertes for this seeming presumption that overcomes his reluctance. Hamlet is guided neither by providence nor by reason, but solely by his feelings about Laertes. Claudius's improved plan works brilliantly.

1797 Camden, Carroll. "On Ophelia's Madness." *SQ*, 15, no. 2 (1964), 247–55. Reprint. *Shakespeare 400: Essays by American Scholars on the Anniversary of the Poet's Birth*. Ed. James G. McManaway. New York: Holt, Rinehart and Winston, 1964, pp. 247–55.

Surveys 16th- and 17th-c. medical literature to support the conclusion that Ophelia in *Ham.* suffers "physically and mentally the pangs of despised love." Hints at the classical background of this medical knowledge.

1798 Cantor, Paul A. *Shakespeare. "Hamlet."* (Landmarks of World Literature.) Cambridge: Cambridge U. P., 1989. xv + 106 pp.

Emphasizes that *Ham.* enacts the incompatibility between classical and Christian notions of heroism available during the Renaissance. The protagonist recalls with some admiration the classical tradition, which drives him toward revenge, but he is deflected from pagan remedies, most obviously suicide, by his awareness of living in a Christian world.

1798a Carson, Ricks. "Shakespeare's *Hamlet*." *Expl*, 49 (1990–91), 76.

Examines the soliloquy that begins at IV.iv.32 of *Ham.*, in which the protagonist criticizes himself for delaying his revenge. Shows that the word *precisely* in "thinking too precisely in the event" (Latin *prae* + *caedere*, "briefly cut") is the key to a submerged metaphor involving other words of Latin derivation in the passage. All of these words together suggest that Hamlet's mind dissects his action in advance and fragments "his revenge into shards."

1799 Charney, Maurice. "The 'Now Could I Drink Hot Blood' Soliloquy and the Middle of *Hamlet*." *Mosaic*, 10, no. 3 (1977), 77–86.

Discerns a "middle movement" in *Ham.*, beginning with the soliloquy at the end of III.ii and ending with the soliloquy at the end of IV.iv. During this part of the action, Hamlet is close to the savage revenger Pyrrhus, the subject of the First Player's speech in II.ii. At the end, Hamlet achieves a more metaphysical understanding of what he must do as Christianity and Stoicism merge.

1800 Claro, Sílvia Mussi da Silva. "The Dramatic Function of 'Aeneas' Tale to Dido' in *Hamlet*." *Estudos anglo-americanos* (São Paulo), 1 (1977), 95–112.

Remarks that Aeneas's tale to Dido, begun by Hamlet and continued by the First Player (II.ii), bears unmistakable features of the set speech, a staple of pre-

Shakespearean drama. As Sh uses it here, however, the set speech has been transformed into a piece that is organically related to the whole play. The circumstances described by the player mirror Hamlet's plight, and the ordering of the speech itself is mirrored in the soliloquy that Hamlet delivers just after it. Further, the dramatization of Aeneas's tale incites Hamlet to take action in the form of another dramatization—*The Murder of Gonzago*. The imagery of the Player's account "shapes paradoxical aspects" of Hamlet's predicament. Finally, Hecuba, who appears at the climax of the Pyrrhus episode, "represents the essence of Hamlet's conflict."

1801 Clubb, Louise George. "The Arts of Genre: *Torrismondo* and *Hamlet*." *ELH*, 47 (1980), 657–69.

Contends that in *Ham.* Sh used subject matter from a recent, medieval past and arranged it so as to make oblique references to the myths of Oedipus and Orestes. This resonance of Greek myths leads to a critical exploitation of genre in the play, with a variety of conventions being introduced and dismissed. Sh here works toward a hybrid tragic structure.

1802 Cohen, Eileen Z. "*Hamlet* and *The Murder of Gonzago*: Two Perspectives." *RBPH*, 61 (1983), 543–56.

Suggests that Sh manipulates theatrical conventions in *Ham.* "to help define the subtleties" of his hero's conflict. Hamlet's choice of the Pyrrhus speech for the Player to recite and his sponsorship of *The Murder of Gonzago* indicate that he would like for life and his role in life to be simple. He resists the ambiguities of the actual world through the kinds of theatrical theory and practice he favors. Near the end of Sh's play, Hamlet comes to recognize that he cannot play roles for which he is temperamentally unsuited; he accepts life as it is.

1803 Cooke, William. "Shakespeare's *Hamlet*." *Expl*, 36, no. 4 (1977–78), 10–11.

Comments on the exchange between Hamlet and Polonius concerning the latter's acting the part of Julius Caesar (*Ham.*, III.ii.96–104). Hamlet's observation that it was "a brute part" of Brutus to kill Polonius plays on the Latin meaning of "brutus" ("dull," "stupid"), which is consonant with the "antic disposition" adopted by the prince. A more important meaning of "brutus" here is the Middle English one ("knight," "hero," "worthy"), which was probably suggested to Sh by a passage from North's Plutarch describing how the people of Rome considered the tribunes Marullus and Flavius to be "Brutes" for disrobing the images of Caesar and thus following in the path of the Brutus who "in old time" drove the kings out of Rome. If the chivalric connotations of the word are present, then the cruelty of Hamlet's retort to Polonius is greater and his warning to Claudius sharper.

1804 Cooperman, Stanley. "Shakespeare's Anti-Hero: Hamlet and the Underground Man." *ShakS*, 1 (1965), 37–63.

Comments briefly on Aeneas's tale to Dido, part of which Hamlet speaks to prompt the First Player (*Ham.*, II.ii). The repulsive image of revenge presented in the figure of Pyrrhus reveals the ambivalence Hamlet feels about proceeding against Claudius.

1805 Des Jardins, Gregory. "The Hyrcanian Beast." *N&Q*, 30 (1983), 124–25.

Points out that Hamlet's sample of a passionate speech to the players, beginning "'The rugged Pyrrhus, like the Hyrcanian beast'" (*Ham.*, II.ii.450), is spoken in the person of Aeneas. In its Virgilian context (*Aeneid* 2), the speech describes Pyrrhus's revenge on Priam and then goes on to reflect Aeneas's desire for retribution and his final decision to forgo it. Hamlet's association of the Hyrcanian beast (used in the *Aeneid* to describe Aeneas) with Pyrrhus suggests his own inability to pattern himself after the nonvengeful Aeneas.

1806 Dessen, Alan C. "Hamlet's Poisoned Sword: A Study in Dramatic Imagery." *ShakS*, 5 (1969), 53–69.

Asserts that in drama "presentational or stage imagery" is equal in value to "verbal or poetic imagery." Analyzing the role of Hamlet's sword illustrates the advantages of this enlarged notion of dramatic imagery. In *Ham.*, the "bleeding sword" of Pyrrhus (II.ii.491), referred to in the First Player's speech, can be crucial in presenting an image of "the revenger in action." If the Player mimes the ferocious slaughter of Priam with a sword (perhaps borrowed from Hamlet), the stage audience will be able to see what it means to be consumed with the desire for revenge. Further, the bloody weapon of Pyrrhus becomes an image by which to gauge Hamlet's subsequent behavior. For example, as Pyrrhus stands with his sword over the helpless Priam, so Hamlet stands over the praying Claudius (III.iii). In this case, Hamlet declines to kill Claudius, thus momentarily distinguishing himself from the violent revenger. The next scene (III.iv), however, reveals the Prince in a very different light, as he stands over the body of Polonius with a bloody sword, lecturing his mother on how to avoid letting her blood overwhelm her judgment.

1807 Dillon, Andrew. "The Prince, the Lion, and Hercules: Another Strand of Tragic Destiny in *Hamlet*." *NDQ*, 58, no. 3 (1990), 152–58.

Calls attention to the powerful and burdensome mythological references with which the protagonist is surrounded in act I of *Ham.* The prince builds up his father through comparisons with Hyperion and Hercules and diminishes himself and Claudius by suggesting that they are opposites to Hercules (I.ii). In I.iv, when Hamlet is preparing to meet his father's ghost, he compares himself with the Nemean lion. Because of the lion's fierceness, this seems to enhance the prince's stature, but when one recalls that Hercules' first labor was to kill the Nemean lion by strangling it, Hamlet's comparison shows that he is already unwittingly accepting the role of victim. Much later, when Hamlet says, "Let Hercules himself do what he may / The cat will mew and dog will have his day" (V.i.291–292), he has gained a measure of maturity and is perhaps declaring his independence of his father's "once dominating power."

1808 Doran, Madeleine. "The Language of *Hamlet*." *HLQ*, 27 (1964), 259–78. Revised as "'No art at all': Language in *Hamlet*." *Shakespeare's Dramatic Language: Essays by Madeleine Doran*. Madison: U. of Wisconsin P., 1976, pp. 33–62.

Accounts for the impression that the world of *Ham.* is natural, with living human beings, by pointing out how Sh highlights the artificiality of certain speeches outside the main action to conceal the art of the play itself. In a couple of instances, these speeches purport to be from literary works outside the play. One example is Aeneas's narration to Dido of the slaughter of Priam, supposedly from a play Hamlet admires, which Hamlet begins and the First Player continues (II.ii). The turgid, highly rhetorical Senecan style of this speech disposes the audience to accept Hamlet's own utterances as being in "the very language of men."

1809 Draudt, Manfred. "Another Senecan Echo in *Hamlet*." *SQ*, 34 (1983), 216–17.

Discovers a borrowing from Seneca's *Epistles* (24), "On Despising Death," in *Ham.* (V.ii.217–220). This background helps to explain Hamlet's state of mind in the last act and shows Sh's "fusion of Christian and Stoic concepts."

1810 Eaton, Sara. "The Rhetoric of (Dis)praise and Hamlet's Mother." *Iowa State Journal of Research*, 62 (1987–88), 377–86.

Contends that in *Ham.* the protagonist uses epideixis, or the type of classical rhetoric connected with praise and dispraise, to attack his mother. Since, as Aristotle points out in his *Rhetoric*, epideixis directs the audience's attention to the speaker and his performance rather than to his subject, Gertrude's character exists primarily as Hamlet shapes it. Fashioned by her son's rhetoric, she "does not achieve full tragic stature." Cites Quintilian and Renaissance rhetorician Rudolf Agricola.

1811   Eckert, Charles W. "The Festival Structure of the Orestes–Hamlet Tradition." *CL*, 15 (1963), 321–37.

Argues that attempts like Gilbert Murray's to seek the origin of the Hamlet–Orestes tradition in a single ritual of "slaying a sacred king" are too narrow. Examines a "large unified body of rituals which provide an orderly sequence of analogues" to a number of motifs common to the Hamlet and Orestes myths. Four pre-Shakespearean versions of the Hamlet story (the accounts of "Amleth" as related by Belleforest in *Histoires tragiques* and by Saxo Grammaticus in the *Gesta Danorum*; the saga of "Ambales"; and the story of Lucius Junius Brutus as found in Saxo and earlier sources) share certain characteristics: (1) The hero's father has been murdered by an uncle, who then succeeds to the throne, and the hero feigns madness to protect himself; (2) except in the Brutus version, the hero is a thoroughgoing misogynist; (3) except in the Brutus version, the hero kills an eavesdropping councilor of the king; (4) except in the Brutus version, "the slaying of the councilor is followed by the exile of the hero to a friendly court in the company of two servants of the king who bear a letter instructing the foreign monarch to put the hero to death"; and (5) except in the Brutus version, the hero returns home during a celebration, fires the hall, and kills the king. All of these elements are "the mythic corollaries of two of the oldest and most universal bodies of ritual activities—purgative or apotropaic ceremonies . . . and initiatory rites." The rituals in question, and the heroes being discussed, all have something to do with New Year's.

1812   Economou, George D. "Hercules in the Mind: Mythographic Tradition and the References in *Hamlet*." *The Mythographic Art: Classical Fable and the Rise of the Vernacular in Early France and England*. Ed. Jane Chance. Gainesville: U. of Florida P., 1990, pp. 246–56.

Explains the tradition of "the sham Hercules," the portrayal of Hercules engaging in some unflattering act or of someone imitating Hercules in an unworthy manner. Argues that the four references to Hercules in *Ham.* show that Hamlet makes a "private identification" of his usurping uncle Claudius with the sham Hercules.

1813   Eden, Kathy Hannah. "The Influence of Legal Procedure on the Development of Tragic Structure." Ph. D. dissertation, Stanford University, 1980. *DAI*, 41 (1980–81), 2097-A.

Describes the theoretical connection "between tragedy and law as originally formulated by Aristotle," who defends "poetic fiction, like its legal counterpart, equity, as an instrument of knowledge designed, by negotiating between universal propositions and particular instances, to discover the truth (cause, intention) in the context of ethical action." Notes that subsequent supporters of poetry rely on this concept of fiction, especially its "fundamentally legal formulation of intention" that "distinguishes between voluntary and involuntary action." Observes that these ideas were transmitted through classical Rome to the Renaissance in various ideas of the image, including those of Quintilian, St. Augustine, and Philip Sidney. Distinguishes two kinds of legal procedure, the accusatorial or adversarial (characteristic of 5th-c. Athens and Elizabethan England) and the inquisitorial (characteristic of Senecan Rome and Renaissance Continental Europe), and shows how these models of procedure influenced tragic structure. Notes that Elizabethan tragedy, including *Ham.*, developed a structure in many ways comparable to Attic tragedy, despite the fact that its dramatic conventions were "avowedly Senecan."

1814 Edwards, Philip, ed. *Hamlet, Prince of Denmark*. (New Cambridge Shakespeare.) Cambridge: Cambridge U. P., 1985. xi + 245 pp.

The introduction stresses that *Ham.* is in some sense a reworking of the theme of *JC*.

1814a Evans, G. Blakemore. "Two Notes on *Hamlet*: II.2.357–58; III.1.121–31." *MLR*, 81 (1986), 34–36.

The first note cites an anonymous elegy on the death of the actor Richard Burbage (1618) as contemporary evidence for the suggestion that Rosencrantz is referring to the sign as well as the flag of the Globe playhouse when he tells Hamlet that the boy actors carry away "Hercules and his load too" [II.ii.361–362].

1815 Falk, Doris V. "Proverbs and the Polonius Destiny." *SQ*, 18 (1967), 23–36.

Points out that proverbs are important in the characterization of the Polonius family in *Ham*. Calls attention to the classical origin of many of the proverbs that would have been known to Sh through collections like those of Erasmus and Richard Taverner (who translated Erasmus). For example, Erasmus's version of Isocrates' *Letter to Demonicus* is one source for the conventional fatherly advice Polonius gives Laertes.

1816 Findlay, L. M. "Enriching Echoes: Hamlet and Orpheus." *MLN*, 93 (1978), 982–89.

Finds an affinity between the "pattern of events in Orphic legend and *Hamlet*." Suggests that more specific echoes of the Orphic legend in Sh's play enrich our understanding. Hamlet and Orpheus, for example, both look behind themselves at the moment they lose their beloved; both are linked with "the mysterious power of art"; and both suffer their greatest losses at a significant threshold. (Orpheus loses Eurydice at the mouth of hell, while Hamlet loses Ophelia at the entrance of her closet and later gives vent to his sorrow at the mouth of her grave.) It is likely that Sh derived his knowledge of Orpheus from Ovid's *Metamorphoses*, either in the original or in Golding's translation.

1816a Fleissner, R. F. "*Princeps Arte Ambulandi*: The Pace of Hamlet." *HamS*, 6, nos. 1–2 (1984), 23–29.

Investigates *Ham.* in terms of the motif of walking about, finding that one source of the image of perambulation may be *JC*, a play that also makes prominent use of it.

1817 Foakes, R. A. "The Art of Cruelty: Hamlet and Vindice." *ShS*, 26 (1973), 21–31. Reprint. *Aspects of "Hamlet": Articles Reprinted from "Shakespeare Survey."* Eds. Kenneth Muir and Stanley Wells. Cambridge: Cambridge U.P., 1979, pp. 64–74.

Perceives Hamlet as able to identify imaginatively with action of extreme cruelty but unable to perform it himself. Uses the First Player's speech about Pyrrhus's slaughter of Priam to demonstrate this.

1818 Fortin, René E. "*Hamlet* and the Mythic Hypothesis." *TSL*, 18(1973), 49–61.

Maintains that the mythic patterns we can discern in *Ham.*—like those of Oedipus and Orestes—are used ironically by Sh. Hamlet tests several kinds of heroism, among them "the mythic roles of water-king, scapegoat, and fool-prophet." However, he fails to fulfill any of these roles; his "frustrated quest for heroic identity" is reflected in the play's structure.

1819   Freeman, James A. "Hamlet, Hecuba, and Plutarch." *ShakS*, 7 (1974), 197–201.

Notes that the anonymous *A Warning For Fair Women* (1599) has been suggested as a source for Hamlet's catching the guilty conscience of the king by staging the murder of his father. A far more likely source, however, is "an episode told in Plutarch's *Pelopidas* about Alexander of Pherae." Alexander, who is characterized as utterly vicious, is holding Pelopidas prisoner. Though sadistic, murderous, and licentious, Alexander is moved to tears by a performance of Euripides' *Troades* in which the miseries of Hecuba and Andromache are portrayed. Hamlet, of course, is moved to plan his mousetrap by the First Player's tears at the griefs of Hecuba. Claudius is not as inhuman as Alexander, but in Hamlet's eyes he is guilty of two atrocities that parallel those of Plutarch's tyrant: unbridled sexuality and murder of a close male relative. *Pelopidas*, like *Ham.*, concerns intrigues at court, with a noble character unjustly detained by a monster. Alexander, his guilty conscience awakened by the performance, frees Pelopidas, while Hamlet, stimulated to action, frees himself.

1820   Frye, Roland Mushat. *The Renaissance "Hamlet": Issues and Responses in 1600*. Princeton: Princeton U. P., 1984. xvi + 398 pp.

Examines *Ham.* with "rigorous historical scholarship" to see it as it would have been seen in 1600. Discusses Fortune as it was understood by Sh's contemporaries. Mentions Stoicism and its expression in the works of Seneca in connection with the passionate nature that prevents Hamlet from being stoical.

1821   Garvin, Katharine. "Slings and Arrows." *REL*, 8, no. 3 (1967), 96–98.

Argues that Hamlet's sequences of metaphor when he speaks of suffering "slings and arrows" or taking "arms against a sea of troubles" (*Ham.*, III.i.58–60) may be derived from Arthur Golding's translation of Caesar's *Gallic War* (1565). Caesar uses the terms "slings" and "arrows" to describe weapons he used to attack the Britons; this passage is followed closely by an account of British attacks on his soldiers while they were "troubled in the water."

1822   Gatti, Hilary. *The Renaissance Drama of Knowledge: Giordano Bruno in England*. London: Routledge, 1989. xvi + 228 pp.

Argues for the influence of Bruno's new theory of knowledge in early modern England. Bruno, like Erasmus in the *Adagia*, used the image of the Silenus box which, when opened, contained nothing, to exhibit the emptiness of the traditional way of saying things. Discovers clear Brunian elements in *Ham.*: Claudius is a Silenus figure, accepting the tired and meaningless formulas of the past, while in Hamlet we see Bruno's "heroic intellect" attempting to develop a new system of signs, words, and gestures that penetrates to the truth. Horatio bears a strong resemblance to the Calm Spirit of Bruno (a conception related to Stoic moral philosophy), while Polonius upholds "the Aristotelian, hierarchical cosmos centred on earth."

1823   Gaunt, D. M. "Hamlet and Hecuba." *N&Q*, 16 (1969), 136–37.

Argues that in having Hamlet reflect on the contrast between "the player's ability to conjure up emotion at will" and "his own ineffectiveness" (*Ham.*, II.ii), Sh had in mind Plutarch's anecdote about the tyrant Alexander of Pherae, not, as has been previously suggested, from the version in the *Life of Pelopidas*, but from that in the *Moralia*.

1824   Gellert, Bridget. "The Iconography of Melancholy in the Graveyard Scene of *Hamlet*." *SP*, 67 (1970), 57–66.

Maintains that the graveyard scene in *Ham.* (V.i) represents the subject of melancholy, important throughout the play, "in a highly condensed verbal and pictorial form." The Renaissance concept of melancholy included the Galenic tradition that it was the most difficult of the temperaments and the Aristotelian idea that it was the temperament of "people exceptionally gifted in politics and the arts." It was also associated with Saturn, whose "children" were both blessed and cursed, holding either exalted positions of authority or menial jobs like that of gravedigger. In *Ham.*, the clowns "discuss and represent the lower Saturnian professions," while Hamlet talks of the higher ones. Saturn's close connection with time is also reflected in the scene. The emblematic treatment of melancholy, associated both with "disordered behavior" and with "contemplative thought," confirms Hamlet's character.

1825 Goldstein, Philip. "Hamlet: Not a World of His Own." *ShakS*, 13 (1980), 71–83.

Views Hamlet as imbued with Neoplatonic idealism, a mark of the humanistic courtier as well as the Puritan. In Neoplatonic fashion, Hamlet assumes that reason prevails in earthly life. His failure is not that of the melancholy, indecisive scholar; rather, his reason is incapable of reforming the "corrupt, Machiavellian aristocracy" with which he has to deal.

1826 Gourlay, Patricia S. "Guilty Creatures Sitting at a Play: A Note on *Hamlet*, Act II, Scene 2." *RenQ*, 24 (1971), 221–25.

Points to a passage in Plutarch as an influence on the choice of subjects for Hamlet's mousetrap play. In the *Life of Pelopidas,* Plutarch tells the story of the cruel tyrant Alexander, who was unable to attend a performance of the *Troades* of Euripides because he did not want to be seen weeping at the representation of the woes of Hecuba and Andromache. In this anecdote, Sh found many elements he could use dramatically: the "guilty spectator at a play"; Hecuba, "the grieving tragic queen"; and "the fall of Troy as symbol of a general falling off."

1827 Grivelet, Michel. "Racine's 'Dream of Passion.'" *Shakespeare 1971: Proceedings of the World Shakespeare Congress: Vancouver, August 1971.* Eds. Clifford Leech and J. M. R. Margeson. Toronto: U. of Toronto P., 1972, pp. 144–55.

Compares the treatments of classical Greece in Racine and Sh. Focuses on the First Player's speech about the sack of Troy in *Ham.* because this play "is one in which the vision of figures from the heroic past of Greece, brief and puzzling as it is, or rather because it is brief and puzzling, raises the problem of its function in modern tragedy." Sh presents "a brief fragment of the archetypical tragedy" of Troy as a foil in that "the play does its utmost to move away from the threat and example of tragedy." Concludes that "for both Racine and Sh, Greece is the dwelling-place not so much of reason and good sense as of much darker powers of the mind. But while Sh seems always to yearn for 'good things of Day,'" Racine seems to be "in constant need of a refuge from the glare of daylight."

1828 Guilfoyle, Cherrell. "A Kind of Vengeance: Images of Classical and of Divine Vengeance in *Hamlet.*" *Parergon*, N. S. 5 (1987), 127–34.

Maintains that the ghost of Hamlet's father and Hamlet's responses to the ghost are made considerably more complex than they are in Sh's sources for *Ham.* Locates classical prototypes for Hamlet's situation in the stories of Orestes and Alcmaeon, the latter of which was available throughout the 16th c. in several editions of Statius's *Thebiad.* In handling these materials, Sh "introduced certain subtleties in his use of classical imagery, and then with the use of Christian imagery indicated the course of divine vengeance outstripping the conventions of classical usage."

1829   Guilfoyle, Cherrell. "'Ower Swete Sokor': The Role of Ophelia in *Hamlet*." *CompD*, 14 (1980–81), 3–17. Reprint. *Drama in the Renaissance: Comparative and Critical Essays*. (AMS Studies in the Renaissance 12.) Eds. Clifford Davidson, C. J. Gianakaris, and John H. Stroupe. New York: AMS P., 1986, pp. 163–77.

Points to a fragment of Euripides, possibly known by Sh, that refers to woman as man's greatest succor and greatest harm. The word for "succor"—*ophelian*—may have suggested Ophelia's name.

1830   Hathorn, Richmond Y. *Tragedy, Myth and Mystery*. Bloomington: Indiana U. P., 1962. 282 pp.

Defines myth as a story that symbolizes "man's mysterious position in the universe." Points out, in a chapter on *Ham.*, that Sh uses mythic materials of "ancient and pagan provenience" as appropriate "symbols for mystery." The play contains parallels with the Orestes, Oedipus, and Hippolytus myths. The First Player's speech (II.ii) containing the account of Pyrrhus's bloody murder of Priam is central to the mythic symbolism. Pyrrhus shares qualities with Fortinbras, Claudius, and Laertes, but, above all, he is the Hamlet of the final scene: "destroyer of the state, murderer of a ruler, unscrupulous avenger." Guilty of the sin of Sloth, or "indifference to one's good," Hamlet attempts to thwart Fortune "by withdrawing from the game of life." The play's conclusion is a triumph for the strumpet goddess.

1831   Hedrick, Donald Keith. "The Elizabethan Satiric–Heroic Mode: Jonson, Shakespeare, and Marston." Ph.D. dissertation, Cornell University, 1974. *DAI*, 35 (1974–75), 1101-A-1102- A.

Examines the combination of satiric and heroic elements in drama to provide insight into the Elizabethan "satiric hero." This "good" satirist can be of noble mind and rank. Finds a paradigm for the magnanimous jesting of the satiric–heroic mode in the relationship between the Cynic Diogenes and Alexander the Great (explored in *Campaspe* and other Elizabethan works). *Ham.* participates in this kind of satire.

1832   Helgerson, Richard. "What Hamlet Remembers." *ShakS*, 10 (1977), 67–97.

Seeks to demonstrate that Hamlet's encounter with the Ghost stimulates for us and for Hamlet "three distinct patterns of memory and expectations, and that the tensions between these three patterns and their final reconciliation constitute the essential action of the play." The first pattern, most vividly represented in the speech Hamlet recalls from the *Aeneid* about the bloody revenger Pyrrhus (*Ham.*, II.ii), is that of the revenge play.

1833   Honigmann, E. A. J., and D. A. West. "With a Bare Bodkin." *N&Q*, 28 (1981), 129–30.

Locates in Seneca's *Moral Epistles* a reference to suicide by means of a *scalpellum*, which Sh might have translated as "bodkin" to include in Hamlet's most famous soliloquy (*Ham.*, II.i),. The term "bodkin" might also have been suggested by an account of the death of Caesar in Chaucer's *The Monk's Tale* and an account of Cleopatra's suicide in R. Robinson's *A Golden Mirrour* (1589). In any case, the soliloquy is a "fascinatingly Senecan speech."

1834   Horálek, Karel. "The Folk Sources of *Hamlet*." *Charles University on Shakespeare*. Eds. Zdeněk Stříbrný and Jarmila Emmerová. Prague: Praha Universita Karlova, 1966, pp. 115–25.

Points out that there are considerable elements of folklore in *Ham.* and suggests that folk parallels to the whole Hamlet story are particularly valuable for the interpretation of Sh's play. Sh's ultimate source, Saxo Grammaticus's account of Amleth, incorporates several folk tales but was probably also influenced by Livy's literary account of Brutus, who avenged "the murder of his father on his uncle Tarquinius."

1834a Hubert, Judd D. "Hamlet: Student Prince and Actor." *The Dialectic of Discovery: Essays on the Teaching and Interpretation of Literature Presented to Lawrence E. Harvey*. Eds. John D. Lyons and Nancy J. Vickers. (French Forum Studies 50.) Lexington, Kentucky: French Forum, 1984, pp. 132–44.

Points out the pervasive intellectuality of *Ham.*, with its many student characters; its protagonist who prefers knowledge to power; and its frequent recourse to "lectures, lessons, and books." Hamlet, as the perfectly prepared scholar, is constantly transforming "a given situation into its bookish equivalent"; his dependence on other texts, many of them classical, "repeats and comments on the theater's own subordination to textuality." In creating his character, Sh seems to have rewritten a variety of precursor texts, including those of Seneca, Cicero, Virgil, and Horace; and these works "interfere with and misdirect the hero's assigned role as avenger." Comments on Hamlet's "theatrical situation," allied to his textual situation, which is based on "a fundamental ambiguity—the character's awareness of belonging both to the fable and to the stage." Describes the characters' and the play's elusive and illusive pursuit of truth. Views Claudius as "an extension of the dramatist."

1835 Jenkins, Harold, ed. *Hamlet*. (Arden Shakespeare). London: Methuen, 1982. xvii + 574 pp.

Several of the "Longer Notes" following the text address matters of classical influence and allusion (for example, in Polonius's advice to Laertes [I.iii], the First Player's speech about the death of Priam [II.ii], and Hamlet's "To be, or not to be" soliloquy [III.i]).

1836 Johnson, W. R. "The Figure of Laertes: Reflections on the Character of Aeneas." *Vergil at 2000: Commemorative Essays on the Poet and His Influence*. Ed. John D. Bernard. New York: AMS P., 1986, pp. 85–105.

Illuminates the relationship between Aeneas and Turnus in the *Aeneid* by reference to that between Hamlet and Laertes in *Ham.* Turnus and Laertes are both foils, extroverts who exhibit "singleness of will," especially in pursuing revenge; by contrast, Aeneas and Hamlet suffer the introvert's inwardness and isolation.

1837 Johnston, Arthur. "The Player's Speech in *Hamlet*." *SQ*, 13 (1962), 21–30.

Attempts to explain the function of the First Player's speech in II.ii. by setting it in context. The references to Jephtha and to Dido and Aeneas just before the speech "are suggested by the elements they have in common with the situation of Ophelia." The second of these references reveals a parallel between Hamlet, who must abandon his beloved in the interest of a greater mission, and Aeneas. His mission is revenge on his father's murderer, and the First Player's speech, dealing with the vengeful murder of a king, follows naturally. There are other links between the Hamlet story and that of Troy. Sh had used Troy as a backdrop for the rape of Lucrece, who in *Luc.* sees herself, like Troy and like Hecuba, as the innocent victim of another's crime. The Troy–Lucrece–Hamlet parallels stress the significance of lust as the original crime. In the First Player's speech, traditional details of Priam's death are altered to focus on the "slaughter of a king by a remorseless revenger." The purpose of this speech is to demonstrate to the audience the problematic nature of revenge and thus to prepare them for Hamlet's questioning of the Ghost's honesty.

1838 Jones-Davies, Margaret. "'Dull substance' and Buzzing Words: A Study of the Function of Language in Shakespeare's *Hamlet*." *Verité et illusion dans le théâtre au temps de la Renaissance*. Ed. Marie-Thérèse Jones-Davies. (U. de Paris-Sorbonne, Institut de Recherches sur les Civilisations de l'Occident moderne, Centre de Recherches sur la Renaissance 8.) Paris: Jean Touzot, 1983, pp. 153–59.

Argues that in *Ham.* Sh modernizes the medieval scholastic conception of the dichotomy between the material and immaterial components of man's nature. Possibly inspired by the account of Pythagoras's speech in book 15 of Ovid's *Metamorphoses*, Sh links various ways of considering the soul–body opposition with "the function of language." He avoids a strict dichotomy through language emphasizing the metamorphosis from one state to another, from substance to spirit. Further, immortality is achieved not by the union of body and soul but through the equivocating instrument of language as it is shaped by the actor. *Ham.* seems to draw on a "Pythagorean image of man as a continuum undergoing the infinite transformations of substance, like the characters in the play."

1839 Joseph, B. L. "*The Spanish Tragedy* and *Hamlet*: Two Exercises in English Seneca." *Classical Drama and Its Influence: Essays Presented to H. D. F. Kitto*. Ed. M. J. Anderson. London: Methuen, 1965, pp. 119–34.

Points out that Seneca was a model for the Elizabethan dramatists both in his use of violent revenge plots and as a stylist. Thomas Kyd's *The Spanish Tragedy* and *Ham.* are both indebted to Seneca, but Sh's play is better because it is written out of the belief that evil in the world is ultimately controlled by Providence. Kyd, however, intends his play to be a "contrived demonstration of the thesis that Revenge rules the world," a thesis in which he does not believe.

1840 Kastan, David Scott. "'His semblable is his mirror': *Hamlet* and the Imitation of Revenge." *ShakS*, 19 (1987), 111–24.

Argues that Sh's Hamlet seeks a model for his role of revenger whom he can transcend. He considers the classical example of Pyrrhus but recognizes that a commitment to revenge consigns him to endless imitation. He therefore relinquishes his pursuit of revenge. Sh, by creating a protagonist who does not take revenge, absorbs and transforms the revenge play.

1841 Kernan, Alvin. "Politics and Theatre in *Hamlet*." *HamS*, 1 (1979), 1–12.

Discusses the plays within the play in *Ham.* to show that in this work Sh is making far larger claims for his art than the conventional moral function with which Sir Philip Sidney and Hamlet himself invest the theater. Maintains that the lines shared between Hamlet and the First Player relating to the death of Priam (II.ii) have a complex and ambiguous application to the events and the onstage audience of *Ham.* The situation in Troy at the time of Priam's murder both resembles and does not resemble the situation in Elsinore; the dramatization of the episode simultaneously encourages and discourages revenge. This play, *The Murder of Gonzago*, and all of the internal plays of *Ham.* reveal "the very structure of life itself prior to any particular form it may take or any particular moral it may illustrate."

1841a Kernan, Alvin B. "Courtly Servants and Public Players: Shakespeare's Image of Theatre in the Court of Elsinore and Whitehall." *Poetic Traditions of the English Renaissance*. Eds. Maynard Mack and George deForest Lord. New Haven: Yale U. P., 1982, pp.102–21.

Takes *The Murder of Gonzago*, the old-fashioned play performed at the court of Elsinore in *Ham.*, to be the closest thing in Sh to the experience the playwright and his company would have had in performing at Whitehall for the King. Notes that the players, those who visit Elsinore and those in Sh's company, have a different notion of the theater from that of the courtiers. Polonius and Hamlet himself, with their neoclassical, humanistic ideal can be said to stand for the latter. Sh, however, deals with the difference in a complex and subtle way. Despite its crude, melodramatic style derived from the public theater, *The Murder of Gonzago* exhibits "the essential voice of the theater," informing the court of the theatrical nature of life, a message that the sophisticated courtiers understand not at all.

1842   Kilpatrick, Ross. "Hamlet the Scholar." *Mélanges Offerts en hommage au Révérend Père Étienne Gareau.* Ed. Pierre Brind'Amour. Ottawa: Éditions de l'Université d'Ottawa, 1982, pp. 247–61.

Argues that *Ham.* is imbued with classical knowledge, predominantly in its satiric emphasis. The two university men, Hamlet and Horatio, are in a variety of ways representatives, respectively, of the Roman satirists Juvenal and Horace. Surveys the influences uncovered by previous scholarship on this subject and adduces many other allusions and parallels. Hamlet's "cankered view of the world" is presented in themes and images that can be found throughout Juvenal's *Satires*: melting flesh, fortune, nobility, sufferings of long life, dreams, conscience, revenge, "vanity of military ambition," Stoic "readiness," poison, incest, adultery, misogyny, pirates, and voyaging. The works of Horace, especially the *Odes,* can provide keys to Horatio's character, including his learning, objectivity, skepticism, aesthetic and philosophical bent, taste, and loyalty.

1842a   Klein, H. M. "'Rightly to be great': *Hamlet,* IV.iv.53–6." *N&Q,* 33 (1986), 357–58.

Suggests that Hamlet's observation in his last great soliloquy about what it is "Rightly to be great" can be illuminated by a passage from Aristotle's *Nicomachean Ethics* about the reasons that prompt (and those that do not prompt) the great-souled man to face danger.

1843   Klein, Joan Larsen. "*Hamlet,* IV.ii.12–21 and Whitney's *A Choice of Emblemes.*" N&Q, 23 (1976), 158–61.

Argues that Hamlet's reference to Rosencrantz and Guildenstern as sponges [IV.ii.12–22] owes more to an emblem in Whitney's *A Choice of Emblemes* than to Suetonius, the source suggested by previous scholarship.

1844   Kott, Jan. "Hamlet and Orestes." *PMLA,* 82 (1967), 303–13. Revised as an appendix in *The Eating of the Gods: An Interpretation of Greek Tragedy.* Trs. Boleslaw Taborski and Edward J. Czerwinski. New York: Random House, 1973, pp. 240–67.

Attempts a structural analysis of the Orestes myth to "extract the elements that do not change in various versions" and that can also be found in *Ham.*: the series of three deaths; the division between past and present; the presence of the past that predicts the choice of the revenger to kill; and the presence of the father. Calls attention to the particular ways in which Sh modifies this tragic pattern. Notes the exact point at which "the real action of Orestes" enters *Ham.*: the moment at the end of V.i when Hamlet jumps into Ophelia's grave. From this point to the end, as in Greek tragedy, Sh "maintains the unity of time and place." This scene acts as a forecast of Hamlet's death, which we now know will occur.

1844a   Lampson, Robin. "Should It Have Been Called Shakespeare's Hoist with His Own Petard?" *CEA,* 36, no. 3 (1974), 12–13.

Speculates that Sh, in having Hamlet say of Claudius that the engineer will be "Hoist with his own petard" (*Ham.*, III.iv.214), is engaging in a word play involving (1) the meanings of the word *petard* that have to do with various kinds of explosives and (2) the Latin word *pedere,* meaning "to break wind," from which *petard* is derived.

Inventories the ways in which several characters, especially Claudius, are "blasted or lifted" by their own farts and suggests that *Hoist with His Own Petard* would make an admirable title for the play.

1845   Leech, Clifford. "The Hesitation of Pyrrhus." *The Morality of Art: Essays Presented to G. Wilson Knight by His Colleagues and Friends*. Ed. D. W. Jefferson. New York: Barnes & Noble, 1969, pp. 41–49.

Contends that in composing the scene of the First Player's speech in *Ham*. (II.ii), Sh had the account of Priam's death from Marlowe's *Dido Queen of Carthage* in mind. By having Hamlet begin the speech, Sh associates the prince with Pyrrhus. Unlike Marlowe, Sh brings the episode to a climax before the killing of the king. Thus Hamlet is further linked to Pyrrhus as a revenger who pauses.

1846   Levin, M. H. "Tragic Figure, Tragic Form." *Renascence*, 31 (1979), 215–28.

Analyzes *Ham*. and *Oedipus Tyrannus* in order to "isolate a single dramatic shape and some accompanying values within the larger tragic tradition." Several things account for the great stature of the central tragic figures: the intervention of the superhuman in their lives; imagery and dialogue that point to supernatural powers; the fact that each fulfills the supernatural request and yet is destroyed in the process; the personal traits of pride, harshness, and over-reaching; suffering; and learning. Each tragic figure experiences a series of confrontations with intermediaries, which progressively embody the forces arrayed against him and are successively disposed of, leaving him finally free to face his opposition in its purest form. Both plays are "metaphysical and deeply religious quests for the essence beneath appearance which affirm the self's reality."

1847   Levine, Richard A. "The Tragedy of Hamlet's World View." *CE*, 23 (1961–62), 539–46.

Emphasizes that the prince undergoes a negative purgation during the course of the play. In the earlier parts, he wavers between traditional Christian belief in Providence and Stoic acceptance of a meaningless world. In act V, by contrast with the Christian view expressed by the gravedigger, he has relinquished the notion that he can restore Denmark as God's minister. His intellectual struggle is thus similar to that of modern man, who is faced with a meaningless universe.

1848   Levitsky, Ruth M. "Rightly to be Great." *ShakS*, 1 (1965), 142–67.

Examines Hamlet's dilemma, which is "how to be rightly great" in a situation in which Christian, Stoic, and Aristotelian ethical principles provide frequently conflicting guidelines. In debating the relative merits of these various principles in his mind, Hamlet finds the issues clarified for him by characters who represent them. Claudius and Polonius, for example, deliver precepts about the Aristotelian Golden Mean; Horatio exemplifies Stoic control of the emotions and indifference to the goddess Fortuna; and Fortinbras's quest for honor in battle marks him as a model of Aristotelian greatness. In working out his destiny, Hamlet renounces dispassionateness and suicide, which are basic to Stoicism; Aristotelian honor; and in general the conduct of life by bookish rules. At the end of *Ham*., he is prepared to act in the faith that Divine Providence can be relied upon to take care of the consequences. His final attitude, marked by satisfaction at the death of Claudius, is not, however, purely Christian. He has transcended the traditions he received to develop his own sense of greatness.

1849   Lorant, André. "*Hamlet* and Mythical Thought." *Diogenes*, 118 (1982), 49–76.

Finds traces of mythical thought underlying the situation and action of *Ham*. Mythic elements, some of which can be associated with classical antiquity, include the adulterous incest, the murder of the king, the unnatural marriage, and the usurpation of the throne. All of these things contribute to a sense of "cosmic catastrophe." Notes that Horatio connects the ghost's appearance with the various omens that preceded the death of Julius Caesar and cites references to these omens in *JC*.

1850 Lyons, Bridget Gellert. "The Iconography of Ophelia." *ELH*, 44(1977), 60–74.

Suggests that the ambivalence with which we regard Ophelia may be traced in part to her embodiment of two contradictory myths of Flora. In one of these, found originally in Ovid's *Fasti*, the flower goddess symbolizes the bounty of nature and the harmony between man and nature. In the other, mentioned by Plutarch in his *Roman Questions*, Flora Meretrix was a Roman prostitute whom Heracles rewarded for her favors with a wealthy husband. Ophelia's discourse of flowers in her madness and Gertrude's description of her death (*Ham.*, IV) evoke both the pastoral scene of natural harmony and the court environment of political intrigue and sexual danger.

1851 Malagi, R. A. "From Irreligion to Religion: The Metaphysic of Revenge in the *Oresteia* and *Hamlet*." *Journal of the Karnatak University*, Special No. 20 (1976), 265–78.

Shows how Aeschylus's probing of divine justice in the *Oresteia* is comparable to Sh's exploration of Providence in *Ham*. Each poet features a hero who begins as an avenger, learns the limitations of pursuing revenge for its own sake, and becomes aware of his harmonization with the divine.

1852 Manley, Frank. "The Cock Crowing in *Hamlet*." *PQ*, 45 (1966), 442–47.

Points to several traditions behind Marcellus's speech about the crowing of the cock all night long at Christ's nativity (I.i.157–164). Some ancient sources (for example, Pliny in his *Natural History*) describe the crowing of cocks as "an augury of victory and joy," but in his *De Divinatione*, Cicero, citing Democritus, comments that cocks are not to be relied upon as "messengers of the gods." Though the crowing of cocks was still associated in the popular mind of Sh's time with favorable events, most learned men of the Renaissance sided with Cicero in attributing it to the birds' digestion. Sh's Horatio shares this skepticism.

1853 Marker, Lise-Lone. "Nature and Decorum in the Theory of Elizabethan Acting." *The Elizabethan Theatre II*. Ed. David Galloway. Hamden: Archon Books, 1970, pp. 87–107.

Uses Hamlet's advice to the players (*Ham.*, III.ii) as the key to understanding the Elizabethan theory of acting. Hamlet's speech is permeated with views of acting derived from classical sources like Cicero and Quintilian. Foremost among these is the belief that there is an ideal, universal truth that can be imitated. According to Cicero in *De Oratore*, every emotion "has from nature its own peculiar look, tone, and gesture," and these can be given an appropriate outward form by the actor. Rules or guidelines for acting, gleaned from manuals of rhetoric and other sources, confirm the classical basis for the Elizabethan idea of theatrical performance, an attitude that "hinged on the belief in the vivid imitation of absolutes through the medium of formalized emotions, reactions, and expressions."

1854 Marlowe, Christopher. *"Dido Queen of Carthage"* and *"The Massacre at Paris."* Ed. H. J. Oliver. (Revels Edition of the Works of Christopher Marlowe.) London: Methuen, 1968. lxxvi + 187 pp.

The introduction suggests that the First Player's speech of "old-fashioned bombast" describing the murder of Priam by Pyrrhus (*Ham.*, II.ii), includes three lines (472–474) that comprise "a good-natured parody" of Marlowe's *Dido* (II.i.253–254). A note to line 254 of Marlowe's text maintains that "Sh was not quoting Marlowe but half-affectionately pushing over the verge of absurdity what was only trembling on the brink of it."

1855 McCombie, Frank. "*Hamlet* and the *Moriae Encomium*." *ShS*, 27 (1974), 59–70.

Suggests that Sh relied on the *Moriae Encomium* of Erasmus to give Hamlet "a humanist's turn of mind, even of phrase." For example, Hamlet's view of Fortune as luck for the foolhardy is an Erasmian conception that excludes the pagan notion of Fortune as strumpet.

1856 McDonald, Charles O. "*Decorum, Ethos,* and *Pathos* in the Heroes of Elizabethan Tragedy, with Particular Reference to *Hamlet*." *JEGP*, 61 (1962), 330–48.

Defends English Renaissance tragedy against charges of inconsistent characterization by arguing that playwrights were following the principles derived from their rhetorical training. One of the most influential textbooks of the Renaissance was the *Progymnasmata* of Aphthonius, a Greek sophist of the 4th c. A.D. A Latin translation of this book, edited by Reinhard Lorich, and containing supplementary material from Cicero, Quintilian, and other sources, was used as a composition handbook by many Elizabethan schoolboys. One of Aphthonius's exercises, on *ethopoeia*, the art of characterization, points out the distinction between the habitual psychology of a fictive person and the irregular emotions that might be expressed, for example, by Hecuba after the destruction of Troy. Quintilian, in the *Institutio Oratoria*, makes the distinction clearer and uses the term *ethos* for "a consistent habit of mind" and *pathos* for "a transient, passionate compulsion." Renaissance characterization in comedy is based on *ethos*, or typical behavior; tragic character, however, "is controlled by *pathos*, a more intense but shifting, inconsistent, apsychological thing, or group of things (emotions), motivating now this, now that, and subject only fitfully to the behests of the individual's *ethos*, or characteristic modes of thought." Hamlet's soliloquy after he meets the players (*Ham.*, II.ii.549–606), with its reference to Hecuba, seems to recall "the Aphthonian exercise *ethopoeia*, in which she is the prototypical exemplar of *pathos*; and Hamlet's remarks on the [First] Player's ease in assuming emotion are clearly derived from Quintilian, as is the forensic imagery of the whole passage." Throughout the play Hamlet has extreme difficulty with the art of rhetoric; he is acutely aware of his own—and others'—inadequacies about suiting words to feelings and actions to words. Hamlet's delay is caused by his *ethos* soothing or overriding his *pathos* until Fortinbras's expedition into Poland rouses his emotions irrevocably. In the final scene, Hamlet is resolute, passionate, inconsistent, apsychological—and "in complete mastery of everyone and everything around him." Revised as chapter 4 of item 1857.

1857 McDonald, Charles Osborne. *The Rhetoric of Tragedy: Form in Stuart Drama*. U. of Massachusetts P., 1966. vii + 360 pp.

Examines "the influences of the modes of rhetorical instruction used in 5th-century B.C. Greece, 1st-century A.D. Rome, and 16th- and 17th-century A.D. England upon the form of tragic drama in these three times and places." Finds "a continuum of rhetorical teaching that influences dramatic creativity in each of the three ages." Chapter 4, "The Rhetoric of *Hamlet*" (a revision of item 1856), analyzes the apparently inconsistent character of Sh's protagonist as a result of the *ethos–pathos* antilogy in rhetoric, which was derived from Quintilian and familiar to Sh through Aphthonius. According to this distinction, a man's *ethos* is his characteristic frame of mind, what makes him consistent, while his *pathos* consists of his passions, the intermittent, irrational emotions that master him at times of crisis. Hamlet's *ethos* is composed of a number of elements pointed out by critics: melancholy, sexual neurosis, introspective bent. One of his habits of mind, however, has not received sufficient notice: the antilogistic tendency "common to all students of rhetoric, a habit of contrasting words with deeds, appearance with reality." Until act V, Hamlet cannot find sufficient *illustrationes* ("exhortations to action," according to Quintilian) to rouse his *pathos* and incite himself to action. In the final act, Hamlet is almost all *pathos*. Renaissance tragic characters are distinguished by such outbursts of *pathos*, whereas their comic brethren are explored through *ethos*.

1858   McLean, Susan Kay. "'A little more than kin': Incest in English Renaissance Drama." Ph.D. dissertation, Rutgers University, 1990. *DAI*, 52 (1991–92), 928-A.

Regards the topic of incest in English Renaissance drama as a focus for anxieties about breakdown of order within the family and for "debates about natural law." Notes that works by Seneca, Ovid, and Plautus furnished "precedents for the literary treatment of incest and contributed several conventions and plot devices" used in the Renaissance. Mentions *Ham.* as one of over eighty plays that concern incest in some way.

1859   Miola, Robert S. "Aeneas and Hamlet." *CML*, 8 (1987–88), 275–90.

Contends that Sh made significant use of the *Aeneid* in *Ham.*, in which, in addition to many direct allusions to and verbal borrowings from Virgil, the protagonist's career is developed by a series of parallels and contrasts to the story of Aeneas. Like Aeneas, Hamlet has a special relationship with his father that extends beyond the grave; experiences, with a loyal friend, exile, loss, and despair; suffers through an impossible love affair and is tormented by the conflict between love and fate; descends to the underworld to question divine justice and confront human mortality; struggles to conform to "a heroic code of honor despite its terrible costs"; seeks and finally achieves revenge. Paradoxically, both Hamlet and Aeneas can satisfy the requirements of piety only by giving themselves over to impious rage. Parts of the Virgilian paradigm provide revealing counterpoints to Hamlet's experience, especially the encounter with the Ghost and the descent to the underworld: Hamlet, unlike Aeneas, is left confused by these episodes.

1860   Monitto, Gary V. "Shakespeare's *Hamlet*." *Expl*, 46, no. 2 (1988), 6.

Challenges the view held by Frederick Kiefer (item 0635) that at the end of *Ham.* the power of the irrational goddess Fortune has been "expunged" and has been replaced by Divine Providence. Notes that in the final scene, Hamlet (as he lies dying), Horatio, and Fortinbras all describe what has happened in terms that suggest Fortune's continued sway.

1861   Muir, Kenneth. "Four Notes on *Hamlet*." *AJES*, 6 (1981), 115–21.

The first note uses evidence from *Ham.* and *Ant.* to suggest that Sh's references to the Dido story, while partly indebted to Marlowe's *Dido*, probably show the author's first-hand knowledge of Virgil's *Aeneid*. The second note argues that a reading from one of the Dido speeches in the first quarto of *Ham.* is preferable to the reading in the second quarto or the First Folio.

1862   Nuttall, A. D. "*Hamlet*: Conversations with the Dead." *PBA*, 74 (1988), 53–69. Reprint. *The Stoic in Love: Selected Essays on Literature and Ideas*. Savage, Maryland: Barnes & Noble, 1990, pp. 27–40.

Attempts to understand *Ham.* as a conversation with a dead person: Hamlet's father, the devil, or "negation itself." The prince is "made party to the dark world, is changed utterly, cut off from marriage and friendship, made an agent of death." Hamlet's paralysis is caused more by his involvement in this realm of nonbeing than by any Oedipal conflicts. Because his apprehension of the living world is seriously impaired, his attempt at histrionic deception begins to unravel almost as soon as he has resolved to assume an antic disposition. Cites Virgil's use of the Questioning of the Dead (the *nekuia* of Homeric epic) in *Aeneid* 6, where "the dispossessed leader of his people rejects the woman who loves him, visits his father in the world of the dead and returns, strangely dehumanized, with a mission," as an illuminating analogue for *Ham.* Even more relevant is the story of Orestes from Greek tragedy; it helps to confirm that "behind the revenge story of *Hamlet*, blood for blood, lies a metaphysical drama of substance and unbeing."

1863 Otten, Charlotte F. "Ophelia's 'Long Purples' or 'Dead Men's Fingers.'" *SQ*, 30 (1979), 397–402.

Counters Karl P. Wentersdorf's argument (item 1890) that Ophelia's "fingers" (*Ham.*, IV.vii.168–171) are to be identified as the wild arum or cuckoo-pint. Argues instead for an identification with the orchid, whose Greek and Latin names refer to the generative organs and which from "early Greek medical treatises down into Renaissance continental and English botany and medicine ... had more gross names than Arum had." Thus it is more dramatically fitting that the virgin Ophelia in her madness adorn herself with orchids than with wild arum.

1864 Pal, R. M. "*Hamlet*: The Culmination of a Tradition." *Quest*, no. 44 (1965), 60–66.

Finds in *Ham.* the last great revenge tragedy. Sh rejects the traditional idea, going back to the Greeks, that external conflict, involving "every conceivable barbarity," is the key to heroic tragedy. Instead, Sh probes the soul of the avenger by focusing on "the ethical basis of revenge as a motive for human action."

1865 Pollin, Burton R. "Hamlet, A Successful Suicide." *ShakS*, 1 (1965), 240–60.

Contends that throughout *Ham.* the protagonist courts death at the hands of Claudius: His efforts to end his own life form the dominant theme in the play. Surveys the references to suicide in Sh's other plays, noting that the practice is especially associated with the Roman spirit's noble refusal to "yield to ignominy." Sh also seems to invoke the spirit of Roman Stoicism and of Greek ritualistic drama in having Hamlet accept death as a sort of inevitable justice. Classical Stoicism is central to the discussions of suicide in the works of Montaigne and Girolamo Cardanus, both of whom probably influenced Sh.

1866 Proser, Matthew N. "Hamlet and the Name of Action." *Essays on Shakespeare*. Ed. Gordon Ross Smith. University Park: Pennsylvania State U. P., 1965, pp. 84–114.

Introduces, in an analysis of Hamlet's delay, a discussion of the ancient mythic hero, who acts to purge his corrupt society after going through a process of initiation that includes a number of rituals. Examples are madness, misogyny, sacrifice, travel, and symbolic death. These can all be seen in "translation" in *Ham.* The mythic hero finds it easy to fulfill his role as purger and regenerator because "the traits he proves by his personal initiation are automatically transformed into public virtues." For Hamlet, the process is difficult, because "to assume his public role means the loss of his private identity."

1867 Qazi, Javaid. "The Madness of Hamlet." Ph.D. dissertation, Arizona State University, 1978. *DAI*, 39 (1978–79), 902-A.

Analyzes *Ham.* to gain an understanding of its protagonist's mental state. Compares Hamlet with tragic figures in other, earlier works, among them Seneca's *Hercules Furens*. Concludes that Hamlet is never truly insane.

1868 Reedy, Gerard, S. J. "'Alexander Died': *Hamlet*, V.i.216–40." *SQ*, 24 (1973), 128–34.

Suggests that in the graveyard scene of *Ham.* the prince's references to Alexander and Caesar [V.i.194–217] indicate an important change in his outlook. Plutarch parallels the life of Alexander with that of Caesar and relates an episode in which Caesar, when reading the history of Alexander, weeps because he has accomplished so little at an age when Alexander had conquered many nations. Two soliloquies earlier in the play show Hamlet's "self-recrimination" paralleling "Caesar's grief over a lack of accomplishment." The first comes after Hamlet hears the First Player's speech on the death of Priam and implicitly approves the vengeance taken by Pyrrhus for his father's death (II.ii); the second is a response to the warlike achievements of young Fortinbras (IV.iv). If, in the graveyard scene, Alexander stands in Hamlet's mind for Pyrrhus and Fortinbras, the prince's laughter at the conqueror's mortality indicates that he now accepts his own "lack of Alexandrian heroism."

1869 Reinhard, Julia. "Shakespeare and Freud: Studies in Narrative and Genre." Ph.D. dissertation, Yale University, 1989. *DAI*, 50 (1989–90), 3579-A.

Examines "productive relationships between Shakespeare and Freud." Section 1 discerns a tension in Freud's writing between "an Oedipal and a melancholic Hamlet" and then restages this ambiguity in terms of the interaction of *Ham.* with Senecan drama, "a post-classical and 'post-Oedipal' tradition divided—like Freud's writings on *Hamlet*—between ghostly fathers and violent mothers in mourning."

1869a Richards, Bernard. "Hamlet and the Theatre of Memory." *N&Q*, 35 (1988), 53.

Suggests that Hamlet's "this distracted globe" (*Ham.*, I.v.98) refers, in addition to his own head and the whole world, to the Globe Theater. Points out that this passage, in which Hamlet asserts his resolve to remember the Ghost, is likely to be glancing at "artificial and self-conscious memory systems," imposed by Renaissance commentators on images of the classical theater. Since the sign of the Globe Theater was Hercules supporting the globe, the play's two references to Hercules (I.ii.153 and II.ii.361–362) could have been accompanied by gestures towards this "ready-made and readily available emblem."

1869b Ronan, Clifford J. "Sallust, Beasts That 'Sleep and Feed,' and *Hamlet*." *HamS*, 7, nos. 1–2 (1985), 72–80.

Acknowledges Cicero's *De Officiis* as a source for Hamlet's condemnation of "Bestial oblivion" (*Ham.*, IV.iv.33–44) and offers Sallust's *Bellum Catilinae* as another source. Sallust not only comments on eating but also links it, as does Sh ("sleep and feed" [line 35]), "with sleep alone." Furthermore, the *Bellum Catilinae* has a number of previously unnoticed analogues to *Ham.* that relate to Sh's "themes of sloth, deliberation, and action, and of fame and story telling."

1870 Rose, Mark. "*Hamlet* and the Shape of Revenge." *ELR*, 1(1971), 132–43.

Maintains that Hamlet's heroism lies in the way he has taken the vulgar role of Senecan revenger and "reformed it so that it no longer offends the modesty of nature or the dignity of man."

1871 Rozett, Martha. "Aristotle, the Revenger, and the Elizabethan Audience." *SP*, 76 (1979), 239–61.

Argues that Aristotle's discussion of pity and fear in the *Poetics*, supplemented by definitions from the *Rhetoric*, can provide a key to understanding the complex audience appeal of the revenger in Elizabethan tragedy, especially his simultaneous evocation of sympathy and detachment. Analyzes *Ham.*

1872 Rudat, Wolfgang E. H. "Ernest Jones' *Hamlet* Interpretation and Nevile's Translation of Seneca's *Oedipus*." *AI*, 38 (1981), 369–87.

Supports Ernest Jones's Oedipal reading of *Ham.* by arguing that Sh alludes to passages from Alexander Nevile's 1581 translation of Seneca's *Oedipus*. Adduces the final lines of *Oedipus* as a possible source for Hamlet's self-pity and self-accusation. Cites Creon's account of the speech in which Laius's ghost revealed the repulsive truth about Oedipus and his mother as "allusively operative" in *Ham.* This confirms that Hamlet feels unconscious guilt for wanting to destroy and replace his father as well as Claudius, his father's successor. Old Hamlet's ghost is thus himself an avenger, with his subconsciously incestuous son as his target. Notes that the underworld exchange between Aeneas and his father Anchises in *Aeneid* 6 may also shed light on Hamlet's death wish and on the purgatory in which his father's ghost is confined.

1873 Ruoff, James. *Shakespeare's Elegy in a Country Churchyard: Stoic or Christian?* (University Studies 62.) Wichita: Wichita State U., 1965. 10 pp.

Contends that the world of *Ham.* is imbued with "deep anxiety" and that the "philosophical basis" of the play more closely resembles modern existentialism than it does Christian thought or Stoicism, though Claudius is an "archetypal Stoic."

1874 Sachs, Arieh. "'To Be or Not to Be': Christianity vs. Stoicism." *Studies in the Drama*. Ed. Arieh Sachs. (Scripta Hierosolymitana 19.) Jerusalem: Hebrew U., 1967, pp. 291–305.

Argues that Hamlet's second soliloquy (*Ham.*, III.i) is a "debate between two opposing points of view that in themselves are perfectly lucid." To understand the debate, we need to attune our minds to "the rhetoric of the period in which the speech was written." What needs to be recognized is that Hamlet is applying the criterion of nobility "to both patient suffering *and* to suicide." Stoic doctrine, as exemplified by Epictetus and Marcus Aurelius, holds that "suicide is an assertion of liberty, hence of nobility." This Greco–Roman view is opposed in Hamlet's soliloquy to the medieval Christian belief that suicide is sinful. Sh's ambiguous portrayal of suicide "reflects an age of transition in which classical humanism and medieval Christianity join to form a particularly rich and paradoxical mixture of ideas."

1875 Schell, E. T. "Who Said That—Hamlet or *Hamlet?*" *SQ*, 24 (1973), 135–46.

Begins by acknowledging that most speeches in *Ham.* are clearly motivated in the emotional and intellectual makeup of the characters who deliver them. In some cases, however, the sources are not so much in the character as they are in "the mind of the play." When Hamlet calls Polonius a "fishmonger" (II.ii.174) and later refers to him as "Jepthah" (II.ii.403, 410), he is accusing him of "misusing his daughter." There is, however, no explanation in the play of how Hamlet came to the knowledge on which he bases these accusations. It is inappropriate to construct some kind of inner life for Hamlet by which he can be supposed to have acquired such knowledge; instead, we should regard him as speaking "not from his mind but from the mind of the play." Hamlet's knowledge of Polonius's mistreatment of Ophelia is the kind of element in a play that reflects dramatic or poetic necessity as Aristotle discusses it in the *Poetics*, not "the rational necessity of cause and effect." Hamlet's voice provides the moral perspective of the play, which focuses on "the moral grossness of the Danish Court." To set up the logic by which we see the corrupt Polonius's responsibility for his daughter's death, Hamlet, serving dramatic probability, speaks things that he cannot rationally be expected to know.

1876 Schleiner, Louise. "Latinized Greek Drama in Shakespeare's Writing of *Hamlet*." *SQ*, 41 (1990), 29–48.

Explores the possible influence of available Latin translations of Aeschylus's *Oresteia* and Euripides' *Orestes* on *Ham*. Sh worked primarily from English translations, but these volumes, as well as two English plays, *Agamemnon* and *Orestes' Furies*, were accessible in 1599. These titles are identical to the titles of Latin translations of the aforementioned Greek works by Jean de Saint-Ravy and Adrien Turnèbe. Sh probably had access to the translations in 1598–99, while Jonson, whose library contained them, worked with the Chamberlain's men. Influences of these works can be noted in the churchyard scene and the matricide theme in *Ham*. The churchyard scene, in which Hamlet and Horatio, after a meditation on death, take cover to eavesdrop on a party of mourners, corresponds to one between Orestes and Pylades in Saint-Ravy's

Agamemnon. Another strong parallel exists between the characters of Horatio and Pylades. Horatio's character, traditionally viewed as inconsistent, was originally drawn as that of a foreigner who is yet an old familiar of Hamlet: a relationship similar to that of Pylades and Orestes. As Sh worked from scene to scene, Horatio may have evolved to assume an insider's role. *Ham.* is a reworking of the Orestes and Oedipus legends wherein Sh displaces Gertrude as the target of revenge. Hamlet is to redeem his mother by removing the source of her contamination: the brother–rival.

1877 Segal, Charles P. "Tragic Heroism and Sacral Kingship in Five Oedipus Plays and *Hamlet*." *Helios*, N. S. 5, no. 1 (1977), 1–10.

Explores, in *Oedipus Rex* and *Ham.*, "how the spatial parameters and the ritual dimensions of the hero's suffering and action help to define his position both at the center of and beyond civilized values." As is the case with every tragic hero, Oedipus and Hamlet are located at the point of intersection between cosmic order and chaos. They both "lose security amid stable values, confront the potential meaninglessness of existence, and oscillate violently between the extremes of order and chaos, quasi-divinity and bestiality, humane sensitivity and savage cruelty."

1878 Sinfield, Alan. "Hamlet's Special Providence." *ShS*, 33 (1980), 89–97.

Cites extensively from Seneca and Calvin to show that *Ham.* reflects the deep unease that many writers of revenge tragedies felt with Protestant ideas of Providence. On the one hand, the play undermines humanistic Stoicism and posits a controlling deity; on the other, the providence of this deity appears "so arbitrary and overwhelming" that "Senecan resignation seems a reasonable response."

1879 Sjögren, Gunnar. "'Take this from this': Polonius and Ulysses." *N&Q*, 15 (1968), 139.

Supports the usual interpretation of Polonius's "Take this from this" (*Ham.*, II.ii.156) as a reference to taking his head from his shoulders. The same idea is found in a speech of Ulysses from the second book of the *Iliad*, which Sh could have read in Chapman's translation.

1879a Skulsky, Harold. "'I Know My Course': Hamlet's Confidence." *PMLA*, 89 (1974), 477–86.

Explains the classical rhetorical device of *notatio*—"the description of a person's inward nature (or state) by means of outward signs that somehow unequivocally 'denote' it"—and its Renaissance manifestations. Discusses "the Neoplatonic doctrine of the cosmic soul" and Aristotle's and Cicero's comments on friendship to show how difficult it is to know the essence of others. Contends that in *Ham.* the prince, although initially denying that it is possible to penetrate to his true feelings by contemplating his outward appearance, puts just as much faith in *notatio* as his foils, Polonius and Claudius. Hamlet's attempts to spy by means of an antic disposition are not especially novel, being paralleled by classical and biblical examples; and his mask fails to have its desired effect on either Claudius or his mother. His belief that he can pluck out the heart of others' mysteries is belied by his inconsistent standard for interpreting external evidence.

1880 Spencer, T. J. B., and Anne Barton, eds. *Hamlet*. (New Penguin Shakespeare.) Harmondsworth: Penguin, 1980. 384 pp.

The introduction notes, without claiming any direct influence, the strong resemblance of *Ham.*, especially in handling of the revenge theme, to the *Oresteia* of Aeschylus. Sh did know the revenge plays of Seneca and English works derived from them. Comments that the familiar speech of Aeneas to Dido recounting Pyrrhus's vengeance on Priam is suddenly seen in a new light by Hamlet as he recognizes that the speech is "an uncanny gloss on his own situation."

1881 Sprott, S. E. *The English Debate on Suicide from Donne to Hume.* LaSalle, Illinois: Open Court, 1961. viii + 168 pp.

Details classical contributions to the debate on suicide at the time Sh had his protagonist in *Ham.* frame the question of "to be or not to be." Plato, Cicero, and Aristotle were cited against self-slaughter, while Stoic and Epicurean beliefs that the practice was honorable were rejected by the orthodox.

1882 Taylor, Marion A. *A New Look at the Old Sources of "Hamlet."* The Hague: Mouton, 1968. 79 pp.

Maintains that the *Historia Danica* of Saxo Grammaticus, the ultimate source of *Ham.*, reflects, among other things, classical Greek and Roman stories (such as that of Junius Brutus, founder of the Roman republic), brought back from the Near East by the Varangians, a group of Scandinavian Vikings.

1883 Taylor, Michael. "A Note on the 'Pyrrhus Episode' in *Hamlet*." *SQ*, 21 (1970), 99–103.

Points out that the extract from Aeneas's tale to Dido recited by Hamlet and the First Player in II.ii of *Ham.* is ironically appropriate because it presents simple images of villainy (Pyrrhus), reverend age (Priam), and "wronged innocence" (Hecuba) in contrast to the complex realities of the world in which Hamlet lives. Hamlet's enthusiasm for the "ritualistic world of the epic," where things are what they seem to be, is of a piece with his admiration for Fortinbras and Horatio. That the former's penchant for unreflective action and the latter's commonsense rationalism are attractive to Hamlet reveals a flaw in his perception of reality, which is further displayed in his response to the Virgilian passage.

1884 Tobin, J. J. M. "Apuleius and Ophelia." *Classical Bull.*, 56 (1979–80), 69–71.

Argues that hints from William Adlington's *Golden Asse* and its Latin original, Apuleius's *Metamorphoses*, helped Sh to form the character of Ophelia in *Ham*. In particular, Apuleius's account of Psyche's career provided details about suicidal drowning, premarital pregnancy, and morganatic marriage. Among the words echoing or suggested by Apuleius are "unpolluted," "dalliance," "thorny way," and "pastors." Revised as part of chapter 4 of item 1052.

1885 Tobin, J. J. M. "'Bawds' Not 'Bonds.'" *HamS*, 4 (1982), 94–95.

Supports Lewis Theobald's emendation of Polonius's "pious bonds" to "pious bawds" (*Ham.*, I.iii.130). Maintains that "bawds" was suggested to Sh by the word "bawd" in Adlington's translation of Apuleius's *The Golden Asse*. In writing of Polonius–Hamlet–Ophelia, Sh was influenced by the Venus–Cupid–Psyche tensions from Apuleius, and many terms from the translation found their way into the lines of the three characters in the play. Revised as part of chapter 4 of item 1052.

1886 Tobin, J. J. M. "The Unique 'Flaxen' in Ophelia's Mad Song." *HamS*, 3 (1981), 110–11.

Suggests that the word "flaxen," used by Ophelia in her last Song (*Ham.*, IV.v) to describe, ambiguously, both her father and Hamlet, derives from Adlington's translation of Apuleius's *The Golden Asse*, in which Psyche uses the word in a similarly ambiguous fashion. Revised as part of chapter 4 of item 1052.

1887 Tracy, Robert. "The Owl and the Baker's Daughter: A Note on *Hamlet* IV.v. 42–43." *SQ*, 17 (1966), 83–86.

Suggests that Ophelia's comment in her madness that "the owl was a baker's daughter" (*Ham.*, IV.v. 42–43) leads naturally into her song "To-morrow is St.

Valentine's Day" (line 48), about the loss of virginity. The owl, "probably because of its association with the virgin goddess, Athena–Minerva," was a common Renaissance symbol for virginity and was also connected (in Ovid and other sources) with the loss of virginity. To the Elizabethans, bakers' daughters represented "sensuality and harlotry." Bakers in ancient Rome kept prostitutes in their shops, and Sh may have known of this connection from Plautus's *Poenulus*. Once we understand the reference to the owl and the baker's daughter, we can see that Ophelia is commenting on appearance and reality, especially in regard to female sexuality.

1888   Weitz, Morris. "*Hamlet*" *and the Philosophy of LiteraryCriticism*. Chicago: U. of Chicago P., 1964. xvi + 335 pp.

Investigates "the major philosophical problems of criticism" by focusing on the criticism of *Ham*. Part 1 describes the approaches of several major critics and "schools." Part 2 analyzes the four major types of questions raised by *Ham*. critics, that is, questions of description, explanation, evaluation, and poetic theory. Of these four, only the first, questions of description, can have true or false answers. Concludes that criticism of *Ham*. "incorporates a multiplicity of properties, none of which is necessary and sufficient." Makes several references to Plato and Aristotle, particularly in establishing the wide range of opinion among critics about concepts like *hamartia* and their relevance to *Ham*.

1889   Wentersdorf, Karl P. "Hamlet and the Players: The 'Magnificent Irrelevancies.'" *SJH*, 1978–79, 73–88.

Disputes G. B. Harrison's remark that the episodes showing Hamlet with the players (*Ham*., II.ii and III.ii) are irrelevant to the main action. These scenes provide a carefully constructed, psychologically convincing development of a rationale for the presentation of the "mouse-trap" to ensnare Claudius. Part of this build-up comes in the First Player's speech about Pyrrhus's slaughter of Priam, which reminds Hamlet of the murder of his helpless father. In hearing the account of Hecuba's spectacular mourning, Hamlet is forced to contemplate his own mother's perfunctory demonstration of grief.

1890   Wentersdorf, Karl P. "*Hamlet*: Ophelia's Long Purples." *SQ*, 29 (1978), 413–17.

Argues that the "long purples" or "dead men's fingers" that Gertrude describes Ophelia as including in her "fantastic garlands" (*Ham*., IV.vii.168–171) are more likely to refer to the *Arum maculatum* (wild arum or cuckoo-pint) than to the *Orchis mascula* (the wild orchid), with which some scholars have identified them. The arum's purple spadix has the right color and for Ophelia in her madness is appropriately phallic in shape. The spadix is enclosed in a white sheath, whose shroud-like appearance helps produce the image of a dead man's finger. Finally, the many phallic names for arum seem to be in Gertrude's mind when she says that the "long purples" are given a "grosser name" by shepherds. See item 1863.

1891   West, Gilian. "*Hamlet*: The Pearl in the Cup." *N&Q*, 38 (1991), 479.

Describes the tradition of placing pearls in cups of wine as one of genuine generosity and argues that Sh's original audience would have recognized Claudius's placing of a pearl in a poisoned cup from which he urges Hamlet to drink (*Ham*., V.ii) as a perversion of that tradition. Sh's source for this episode seems to be the account by Pliny in his *Natural History* of a wealthy actor's son named Clodius, who, enjoying the taste of pearls, gave each of his guests a pearl to swallow.

1892   Westlund, Joseph. "Ambivalence in the Player's Speech in *Hamlet*." *SEL*, 18 (1978), 245–56.

Maintains that the speech Hamlet requests the First Player to recite (part of Aeneas's tale to Dido from the *Aeneid*) mirrors Hamlet's ambivalence. Hamlet himself begins the speech, which appropriately describes Pyrrhus, an avenger who might seem to be a role model for the prince. Yet Sh modifies the Virgilian original of the lines to eliminate any suggestion that Pyrrhus is heroic: He is dark and evil, an appalling murderer. Hamlet hands the speech over to the Player at precisely the moment when Pyrrhus is about to commit the murder of Priam, a break suggesting Hamlet's own tendency to stop just short of vengeance. As the speech continues, "Hamlet's model becomes Aeneas, the son who can only lament the murder of his king." The speech is both rehearsal for the act of vengeance against Claudius and a retrospective of Old Hamlet's murder, and because in the second instance Hamlet would play a role like that of Claudius in the first, he is further distanced from action. He is incapable of imitating Pyrrhus, of becoming a Claudius. Instead of Pyrrhus, Hamlet comes to identify with the passion of Priam, Hecuba, and "the Player in his response to their suffering."

1893 White, Beatrice. "Two Notes on *Hamlet*." NM, 65 (1964), 92–96.

Makes the suggestion, in the first note, that Sh's debt to Juvenal for *Ham.* has not been sufficiently recognized. Hamlet's attitude toward Ophelia and his mother, for example, may owe something to Satire 6 "on the repulsive ways of women."

1893a Willson, Robert F. Jr. "Hamlet's Bellerophontic Letters." HamS, 7, nos. 1–2 (1985), 69–71

Explains the mythological background of two letters in *Ham.* In Greek legend, Bellerophon was sent by Proteus to Iobates, king of Lycia, with a letter asking that the bearer be put to death. This story provided Sh with the outline of Claudius's attempt to dispose of Hamlet by similar means. Hamlet's discovery of the plot and his ingenious redirection of the first bellerophontic letter are counteracted by his writing, in anger, a second such letter, which ironically condemns him to death.

1894 Wilson, Luke. "*Hamlet*: Equity, Intention, Performance." SLitI, 24, no. 2 (1991), 91–113.

Claims that "the intention that a playscript be performed (or the intention to produce something that is performed) both involves and invokes the same sort of supplementary hypothesizing that generates fictions in the Aristotelian account of the operation of Greek tragedy and law." Makes an analogy between "juridical performance" in cases of equity, where the author of a law is imagined to be present "to fill in the gaps revealed in its application to particular cases," and theatrical performance, where the author is supposed to be present and the authority to modify his intention, or supply what particulars are wanting, is thus delegated to his representatives, the actors. Notes that the Elizabethan notion of equity derives from Aristotle's *Ethics* and *Politics*. Employs these conceptions of intention, equity, and performance in an analysis of *Ham.*

1895 Wilson, Robert Rawdon. "Narrative Boundaries in Shakespeare's Plays." CRCL, 18 (1991), 233–61.

Focuses on *Ham.* in a discussion of embedded narrative in Sh's plays. Offers a detailed analysis of "Aeneas' Tale to Dido," a narrative shared between Hamlet and the First Player (II.ii.445–497), which "exemplifies a wide range of specific narrative techniques" and "raises, in great depth and with considerable power, the problem of narrative's inherently distinct effects within drama." Notes the greatness of the distance (in time, space, and character) that must be traversed to gain access to the fictional world of Troy in the Player's speech. Another example of embedded classical narrative in *Ham.* is Horatio's reference to the "last moments of the Roman Republic" (I.i.113–116), which, like the later allusion to the fall of Troy, evokes a fictional world that is at a great distance from the world of the play.

1896   Wimsatt, James I. "The Player King on Friendship." *MLR*, 65 (1970), 1–6.

Adduces Cicero's *De Amicitia*, Ovid's *Tristia*, Boethius's *Consolation of Philosophy*, and Jean de Meun's *Roman de la Rose* to help explain the relevance of the Player King's lines on the changeableness of friends, *Ham.* (III.ii.196–207) to an important theme of the play. These four works furnish a background for the idea that bad luck is the test of friendship, that one's true friends are not friends of Fortune. Rosencrantz and Guildenstern (friends of Claudius, Fortune's surrogate) are clearly contrasted with Horatio, whose friendship is constant.

1897   Woodhead, M. R. "Hamlet's 'Hyrcanian Beast' Reconsidered." *N&Q*, 25 (1978), 139.

Suggests that the phrase "Hyrcanian beast," which Hamlet uses to describe Pyrrhus in his speech to the players (*Ham.*, II.ii.450), refers not only to the tigers of Hyrcania (as described in the *Aeneid*) but also to certain dogs described by Montaigne. In the *Apology for Raymond Sebond*, Montaigne notes the extreme loyalty of a dog named Hircanus to his master Lysimachus. He then recounts how King Pyrrhus was able to apprehend a murderer who was identified and attacked by the murdered man's dog. The loyalty and will to revenge in these dogs, coupled with the name Pyrrhus, show how even beasts are providing models for what Hamlet should do.

1898   Wray, William R. "You, Claudius: An Anatomy of a Name." *PAPA*, 6, no. 1 (1980), 78–94.

Connects Claudius's name, which derives from the Latin verb *claudere*, "to close, shut up, keep secret, suppress," with "the idea of secrecy and concealment" in *Ham*. Claudius never unambiguously confesses his crime (except in soliloquy); he declines to warn Gertrude that what she is about to drink is poisoned (V.ii); his crime, murder, carried the connotation of a secret slaying in the Middle Ages and Renaissance; he is associated with Cain, one who attempts to conceal his brother's murder from God; he is not named in the dialogue (a witty omission by the playwright). Two other characters who attempt to play the game of concealment, Polonius and Hamlet, may be contrasted with Claudius. Polonius is obsessed with secrecy but is too foolish to be effective, while Hamlet's free and open nature dooms his plan to put on an antic disposition.

1899   Zitner, S. P. "*Hamlet* and *Hamartia*." *"Hamartia": The Concept in the Western Tradition: Essays in Honor of John M. Crossett*. Eds. Donald V. Stump, James A. Arieti, Lloyd Gerson, and Eleonore Stump. (Texts & Studies in Religion 16.) New York: Edwin Mellen P., 1983, pp. 193–210.

Speculates on the possibility that Sh knew Aristotle's *Poetics* and concludes that there is no way to know. Notes, however, that *hamartia* is "an inevitable concern" of the tragic dramatist, involving the annexation of guilt to the protagonist's defect in order to make him more sympathetic. The protagonist can be in some senses "shielded" from his tragic deeds through "ignorance, the displacement of guilt from intent to behavioral style, and plot-perspective." In *Ham.*, the hero is presented both as "skeptical empiricist" and "intuitive moralist," but his striving for "the incontrovertible" impairs observation. This absolutism is the *hamartia* of the tragedy.

HENRY IV, PART I

1900 Bevington, David, ed. *Henry IV, Part I.* (Oxford Shakespeare.) New York: Oxford U. P., 1986. 300 pp.

The introduction discusses the classical "braggart cowardly knight," or *miles gloriosus,* in considering Falstaff as a soldier.

1901 Bolger, Stephen G. "A Logical Note on 'Barbary.'" *SQ,* 22 (1971), 79–80.

Points out that in his teasing of Francis, Prince Hal includes as a cap to one of his nonsensical speeches, about the sullying of a "young white canvas doublet," the following: "In Barbary, sir, it cannot come to so much" (*1H4,* II.iv.75–76). "Barbary" probably is a corruption of "Barbara," a name used as part of a memory system in the schools to facilitate recall of syllogisms. The Prince is using a nonsense syllogism to complete Francis's confusion.

1902 Council, Norman. "Prince Hal: Mirror of Success." *ShakS,* 7 (1974), 125–46.

Rejects the idea that Falstaff, Hotspur, and Hal are arranged in an Aristotelian paradigm of honor in *1H4.* Writers on honor in Sh's time agree that it is a positive good that man has an ethical responsibility to pursue and that his pursuit of this good is to be judged excessive or defective according to his deserts. Hotspur is not aiming at honor beyond his deserving. He is the essence of the honorable man. Falstaff is not unambitious for honor, nor does he reject reward. Thus he is not defective in the Aristotelian sense. Nor is Hal the mean between these two in the Aristotelian sense. He is practical in wanting to gain Hotspur's honor, but he avoids committing himself about honorable behavior until late in the play. He exploits rather than serves the code of honor. Hotspur's irascibility is a trait said by Sh's contemporaries to be characteristic of men of honor.

1903 Crawford, John W. "Shakespeare's Falstaff: A Thrust at Platonism." *North Carolina Journal of Speech and Drama,* 10, no. 1 (1976), 15–21.

Cites Marsilio Ficino's *Platonic Theology* as representative of Renaissance Platonism, which advocates detachment from the outside world and ascent through contemplation to a vision of God. In various episodes of *1H4* presenting Falstaff's remorse for his sinful life and his vows to reform—both of which are always immediately forgotten—Sh is satirizing the contemplative ideal of the Platonists. Prince Hal, by contrast, exemplifies the ideal of active moral virtue, which is more compatible with Renaissance Aristotelian thought.

1904 Emmett, V. J. Jr. "*1 Henry IV*: Structure, Platonic Psychology, and Politics." *MQ,* 19 (1978), 355–69.

Proposes a Platonic system of psychology, similar to that described in Sir Thomas Elyot's *Of The Knowledge Which Maketh a Wise Man: A disputation Platonike* (1533), to explain the structure of *1H4* and the two plays that follow it. In this analysis, Falstaff represents the appetites, Hotspur represents the will directed by perverse reason, and Hal represents the reason. By the end of *1H4,* Hal has "achieved a kind of synthesis in which the attributes of Hotspur have been assimilated and those of Falstaff subordinated." But Hal needs to move beyond this point of balance and become a supremely "rational calculator of national interests" in *H5,* which is why he needs to reject Falstaff in *2H4.*

1905 Gillett, Peter J. "Vernon and the Metamorphosis of Hal." *SQ,* 28 (1977), 351–53.

Claims that Vernon's speech (*1H4,* IV.i.97–110) that describes first Prince Hal and his comrades and then Hal alone marks a crucial stage in the transformation of the prince from wastrel to mirror of Christian kings. The first part of the speech, beginning with "All furnish'd, all in arms" (line 97) and ending with "wild as young bulls" (line 103) is ambivalent and allows for an ironic view of Hal as well as his friends. The second half of the speech, beginning with "I saw young Harry, with his beaver on" (line 104) and concluding with "And witch the world with noble horsemanship" (line 110), has the primary effect of glorifying the Prince and suggests, in part through the references to Mercury and Pegasus, that Hal's noble qualities "partake of something magical or supernatural." The name Pegasus makes a subtle distinction between the "earthbound Hotspur" and the ascendant Prince.

1906 Harlow, C. G. "Shakespeare, Nashe, and the Ostrich Crux in 1 Henry IV," SQ, 17 (1966), 171-74.

Suggests that when Vernon describes Prince Hal and his men as "All plum'd like estridges" (1H4, IV.i.98), he has in mind a belief going back to classical writers like Aelian, and found by Sh in Thomas Nashe's *The Unfortunate Traveller*, that the ostrich spreads its wings and sails before the wind.

1907 Jorgensen, Paul. "Valor's Better Parts: Backgrounds and Meanings of Shakespeare's Most Difficult Proverb." ShakS, 9 (1976), 141-58.

Provides background for Falstaff's "The better part of valor is discretion" (1H4,V.iv.119-120). The phrase is not a proverb that Sh is repeating; it represents Sh's version of a *topos* involving the relationship between courage and wisdom. The Renaissance discovered this *topos* in Isocrates, Plato, Aristotle, Cicero, Plutarch, and Lactantius. Sh, "with much folk wisdom behind him," seems to have created the maxim that he is often said to be quoting. During the Renaissance, English writers on military affairs, drawing on classical sources, began to urge greater attention to policy and less reliance on courage; they also began to express this new preference in short, epigrammatic form. The use of "discretion" as a contrast to "will" (which means prideful indulgence in valor) in matters military was used for the first time in North's translation of Plutarch's account of Alexander the Great (1579). "Discretion" and "valor" were first used as opposites in Sidney's 1590 *Arcadia*. By this time there was an ironic humor in the opposition that faintly disparaged valor. Sh added to this already rich combination "the better part," which has multiple meanings—logical, theatrical, and sexual.

1908 Levin, Lawrence L. "Hotspur, Falstaff, and the Emblem of Wrath." ShakS, 10 (1977), 43-65.

Explains how Falstaff's role as an emblem of wrath helps define Hotspur's character by parody. Traces the notions of anger and of the wrathful man, as the Renaissance would have known them, to Aristotle's *Rhetoric*.

1909 Mueller, Martin. "Turnus and Hotspur: The Political Adversary in the Aeneid and Henry IV." PhoenixC, 23 (1969), 278-90.

Compares Sh's treatment of Hotspur in *1H4* with Virgil's treatment of Turnus. Virgil had two conflicting notions of Turnus: (1) "a great but imperfect human being" with an impressive tragic fate and (2) a rash, cowardly fool, guilty of war crimes, who suffers an ignominious death. Virgil's task in the *Aeneid* was to provide "an apology for the Empire and its ideology," and thus he could not finally be generous toward the proud opponent. Sh's problem in dealing with Hotspur was similar, but he found a way to dispose of an admirable adversary without humiliating him. In his invitation to duel Hotspur and his magnanimous epitaph, Prince Hal grants the heroic qualities of his rival without detracting from his own.

1910 Stewart, Douglas J. "Falstaff the Centaur." *SQ*, 28 (1977), 5–21.

Argues that in *1H4* Sh wanted to create a hero "in the timeless sense of the heroes of ancient legend." In portraying Hal, he thus, at some subconscious level, sensed the importance of following "the patterns of the ancient myths." Because the classical Greek hero's father is usually weak or absent, the son is turned over to a second father figure, Chiron the centaur, for his upbringing. In *1H4*, Falstaff acts as Hal's Chiron, teaching him about ordinary life as his real father, who is made "unhistorically old and weak," cannot.

HENRY IV, PART 2

1911 Aston, Margaret E. "The Fiery Trigon Conjunction: An Elizabethan Astrological Prediction." *Isis*, 61 (1970), 159–87.

Explicates the humor of an exchange between Prince Hal and Poins (*2H4*, II.iv.262–266) that involves a conjunction of Saturn and Venus and an appearance of "fiery Trigon." The connection of these three figures—here representing Falstaff, Doll Tearsheet, and Bardolph, respectively—would have reminded many in Sh's audience of a notable controversy of the 1580s that had left astrologically-based predictions open to ridicule.

1912 Black, James. "Counterfeits of Soldiership in *Henry IV*." *SQ*, 24 (1973), 372–82.

Argues that in *1&2H4*, an "ideal of soldiership is established, broken, and then re-established." Concentrates on *2H4*, in which most of the antiheroic breaking action takes place. Sh uses references to ancient Greece and Rome in evoking the memory of Hotspur (the pattern of heroism) and in characterizing Falstaff, Pistol, and Shallow (types of the counterfeit soldier).

1913 Corballis, R. P. "'Buzz, Buzz': Bee-Lore in *2 Henry IV*." *N&Q*, 28 (1981), 127–28.

Proposes Virgil's *Georgics* as the source for two uses of bee lore (IV.v.74–78 and IV.iv.79–80) in *2H4*.

1914 Humphreys, A. R. "Two Notes on *2 Henry IV*." *MLR*, 59 (1964), 171–72.

The second note deals with IV.iii.40–41, where Folio omits quarto's "their cosin." Shows how the quarto compositor might have misread "in three wdes [wordes]" as "their cosin," and this can be supported by references to Plutarch's *Life of Caesar*, which twice mentions Caesar writing "three words" to signify a victory.

1915 Isler, Alan D. "Falstaff's Heroic Sherris." *SQ*, 22 (1971), 186–88.

Maintains that Falstaff's praise of sherris-sack in *2H4* alludes to the heroic *topos sapientia et fortitudo*, which has been traced "from classical sources through the Middle Ages to the Renaissance" by Ernst Robert Curtius. For Falstaff, sherris-sack produces heroes, giving them both wisdom and courage. This mock-encomium serves to contrast the cold ruthlessness of Prince John with the true heroism of Hal, though we may doubt Falstaff's explanation of the latter's source.

1916 Shaaber, M. A., comp. "*Henry the Fourth, Part Two*": *A Bibliography to Supplement the New Variorum Edition of 1940.* New York: Modern Language Association, 1977. ix + 18 pp.

Covers the period from 1938–1972. Comprises 398 items, classified into eight sections, and an index of authors and editors. Includes sections on editions, criticism, sources, and commentary. Lists entries alphabetically within each section, except in the section on editions, which is arranged chronologically. Does not annotate entries, except for bracketed references to act, scene and line numbers of passages discussed by items in the commentary section.

Henry V

1917 Battenhouse, Roy. "*Henry V* in the Light of Erasmus." *ShakS*, 17 (1985), 77–88.

Cites passages from Erasmus's *Praise of Folly* and *Education of a Christian Prince* as background for the argument that Sh views Henry V ironically, as violating the norms that should govern the actions of a Christian prince. The play's Chorus sees the king uncritically, celebrating his achievements according to a "Roman sense of values." Suggests that Erasmus provided Sh with insights into "the comedy of pagan values masquerading as Christian."

1918 Berman, Ronald S. "Shakespeare's Alexander: Henry V." *CE*, 23, (1961–1962), 532–39.

Claims that in *H5* the protagonist is, "in certain ways, a reconstruction of Plutarch's Alexander." *JC*, written the same year (1599) as *H5*, is based on Plutarch's account of Caesar, who is paired with Alexander in the *Lives*. Plutarch's *Life of Alexander* begins with a sort of apology and introduces, as does the play's prologue, the question of mimesis. Both Plutarch and Sh raise the possibility of combining intellect and action in the hero. Each hero has an "intellectual hardness" by which he disciplines himself and orders the world around him. In each case, a supreme exertion of will can turn the hero into a figure of rage and terror. Finally, both Alexander and Henry represent "the failure of nature" to master human limitations.

1919 Berry, Edward I. "'True Things and Mock'ries': Epic and History in *Henry V*." *JEGP*, 78 (1979), 1–16.

Recalls the Elizabethan oversimplification—exemplified by Sir Philip Sidney—of the classical notion of epic and uses this in an analysis of *H5*. In Sidney's mind, the salient feature of the epic was its presentation of an ideal: a hero who establishes a pattern of behavior worthy of emulation. Sh was aware of this perspective and included it in *H5*, but he tempers it with a naturalistic sense of history: The ideal is something we can imagine, but the king can never achieve it.

1920 Betts, John H. "Classical Allusions in Shakespeare's *Henry V* with Special Reference to Virgil." *G&R*, Series 2, no. 15 (1968), 147–63.

Discovers a number of classical echoes in *H5*. For example, Fluellen and Pistol, in their discussion of Fortune (III.vi), both seem familiar with "a fragment of Pacuvius preserved in the *ad Herennium*," and Quintilian's discussion of the salutary effect of the teacher's authoritative voice on his pupils is probably the basis for the Chorus's description of Henry's comforting of his troops at the beginning of act IV. Sh uses classical allusions with a due regard to their original context, something that can be seen in the two passages he appears to have derived from Virgil's *Georgics*: the Archbishop of Canterbury's account of the kingdom of the bees (I.ii) and the plea of the Duke of Burgundy for peace (V.ii). The decay of agriculture brought about by civil war was what prompted Virgil to write the *Georgics*, and Sh, in having Burgundy reflect on the corrupted garden of France, is suggesting that France has been in rebellion against proper English husbandry.

1921 Betts, John H. "Shakespeare's *Henry V* and Virgil's *Georgics*." *N&Q*, 25 (1978), 134–35.

Suggests that in composing *H5*, Sh seems to have drawn on the *Georgics* "in at least two specific passages: the Archbishop of Canterbury's explanation of how the activities of bees 'teach the act of order to a peopled kingdom'; and the Duke of Burgundy's lament for France's husbandry neglected in the pursuit of war."

1922 Candido, Joseph, and Charles R. Forker, comps. *"Henry V": An Annotated Bibliography*. (Garland Shakespeare Bibliographies 4.) New York: Garland, 1983. xxiv + 815 pp.

Covers primarily works published between 1940 and 1979, with a few items before and after that period. Classifies entries under eleven headings, including Criticism (630+ items); Individual Editions (137 items); Complete and Collected Editions (26 items); Language, Vocabulary, Prosody (77+ items); and Sources, Historical and Intellectual Background, Topicality, Influences on the Play (230+ items). Begins each section with the oldest entry and proceeds chronologically. Concludes with a name index and a subject index. Provides substantial and detailed annotations.

1923 Erickson, Peter B. "'The Fault / My Father Made': The Anxious Pursuit of Heroic Fame in Shakespeare's *Henry V.*" *MLS*, 10 (Winter 1979–80), 10–25.

Argues that the character of Henry in *H5* is problematic. That is, he is presented as divided between rage and humility, aggression and compassion. Cites Tacitus's account of Germanicus's wandering disguised among his men the night before battle as a contrast to Henry's similar activity before Agincourt. Germanicus overhears nothing but praise for himself, while Henry is immediately put on the defensive by Williams. All of this helps Sh to examine critically "the stereotype of successful king."

1924 Fleissner, R. F. "Putting Falstaff to Rest: 'Tabulating' the Facts." *ShakS*, 16 (1983), 57–74.

Supports the authenticity of the Folio reading for the Hostess's description "as sharp as a Pen, and a Table of greene fields," *(H5,* II.iii.16–17) by contending that in depicting Falstaff's demise, Sh had recourse to Galen's translation of Hippocrates' *Prognostica*, which lists six symptoms of a dying man. Falstaff unquestionably exhibits five of these, including a sharp nose, and the sixth, a pale green face, validates the Folio reading "a Table of greene fields," if "Table" is taken to mean "picture."

1925 Gurr, Andrew. "*Henry V* and the Bees' Commonwealth." *ShS*, 30 (1977), 61–72.

Points out that the Archbishop's use of the fable of the bees as a model for the organization of Henry's commonwealth in time of war shows Sh was probably drawing on Erasmus's *Institutio principis Christiani*. Earlier uses of the parallel between human society and the beehive are to be found in Virgil's *Georgics* 4 and Seneca's *De Clementia*, both of which were available to Sh. Erasmus uses the fable to emphasize that a good prince should remain in his own realm and cultivate a reputation for clemency. Henry does follow some of Erasmus's advice for a Christian prince, but he contravenes or modifies it in several ways (for example, by invading France and by killing his prisoners). All of his actions, however, can be seen to have some basis in the precepts laid down by military or other authorities of his time. *H5* "studies kingship under pressure," where, for example, leniency toward one's enemies is generally desirable but cannot be practiced in certain situations.

1926   Humphreys, A. R., ed. *Henry V.* (New Penguin Shakespeare.) Harmondsworth: Penguin, 1968. 239 pp.

The introduction notes that the Archbishop's "parable of the ordered hive" (I.ii), derived ultimately from Pliny and Virgil, came to Sh through Sir Thomas Elyot's *The boke named the Governour* (1531) and other works. The visit of Henry to his camp the night before the battle may have come from the *Annals* of Tacitus, translated by Richard Grenewey in 1598; and Fluellen's antiquarian obsession with "the Roman disciplines" was probably suggested by the *Stratioticos* of Thomas Digges (1579).

1927   Merrix, Robert P. "The Alexandrian Allusion in Shakespeare's *Henry V.*" *ELR*, 2 (1972), 321–33.

Discusses Fluellen's humorous comparison of Henry to Alexander the Great (IV.vii). Henry is thus symbolically connected with rashness and ambition. The reference comes at a climactic moment in the play and shows that Sh was following a common pattern in late Elizabethan drama: A crucial action occurs (in this case, the cutting of the prisoners' throats); there is a classical reference relating to the action; and then a contemporary figure, to whom the allusion is relevant, appears. In this case, the allusion to Alexander also satirizes Henry by linking him with Pistol, who is an ironic parody of the king throughout the play.

1928   Price, George R. "Henry V and Germanicus." *SQ*, 12 (1961), 57–60.

Points out that Sh may have taken a hint for the episode in *H5* when the King visits his troops in disguise (IV.i) from Richard Grenewey's translation of Tacitus's *Annales* (1598), in which the Roman general Germanicus covers himself with a wild beast's hide and passes among his men the night before a great victory over the Germans.

1929   Quint, David. "'Alexander the Pig': Shakespeare on History and Poetry." *Boundary 2*, 10 (1982), 49–67.

Cites the discussion in *H5*, IV.vii, which involves Fluellen's struggle to discover a parallel between King Henry and Alexander the Great, to show that "in Shakespeare's poetic treatment, history ceases to be the didactic instrument of classical humanism and becomes instead an occasion for historicist self-reflection." Cites a number of Renaissance humanist writers on Alexander traditions.

1930   Renault, Mary. "Shakespeare and Xenophon." *TLS*, July 12, 1974, 749.

Argues that Sh derived Fluellen's comparison of the rivers in Macedon and Monmouth (*H5*, IV.vii) from Xenophon's digression in the *Anabasis* about his estate near Olympia. To have picked up this kind of detail, Sh must have read Xenophon in either Greek or Latin. Moreover, the episode of Xenophon cheering up the disconsolate Ten Thousand in the *Anabasis* probably suggested to Sh the incognito nocturnal patrol of the king.

1931   Spencer, Janet Marie. "The Politics of Mixed-Genre Drama: The Comic Treatment of Punishment Spectacles in Shakespeare." Ph.D. dissertation, University of Pennsylvania, 1990. *DAI*, 51 (1990–91), 4134-A.

Explores "the use of gallows humor to voice dissent during an age of extensive repression and censorship." Chapter 4 analyzes *H5* as "an anamorphic portrait depicting Henry as both Christian prince and tyrant." The ambiguity is generated by the comic scenes and references to anecdotes relating to Alexander the Great.

1931a Taylor, Anthony Brian. "The Case for Pistol's 'Base *Tike.*'" *N&Q*, 36 (1989), 24–25.

Notes that the Oxford edition of *H5* (1984) has Pistol call Nm "base *tick*" (II.i.29). Argues for the reinstatement of *tike* on the grounds that Pistol makes several references to Nm as a dog in the scene and that, in a passage known to Sh from John Studley's translation of Seneca's *Hercules Oetaeus*, the "hellish hound" Cerberus is referred to as a *tike*.

1932 Taylor, Gary. "Shakespeare's Leno: *Henry V*, IV.v.14." *N&Q*, 26 (1979), 117–18.

Cites the speech of Bourbon during the French rout at Agincourt, in which the soldier who will not return to battle is compared to "a base pandar" (*H5*, IV.v.14). The 1600 quarto reads "Leno" for "pandar." "Leno," a Latin word for "pander" should replace "pandar," as the authentic reading.

1933 Taylor, Gary, ed. *Henry V*. (Oxford Shakespeare.) Oxford: Clarendon P., 1982. ix + 330 pp.

The introduction includes a section on "Chapman, Epic, and the Chorus," which proposes classical ideas of epic and mythology in general, and in particular George Chapman's translation of *Seven Books of the Iliads of Homer* (1598), as significant influences on *H5*. Beyond the comparisons of Henry with his "classical counterparts" (especially Alexander the Great), Fluellen's fixation on "classical military history," Pistol's propensity for classical allusion, and the "serious use of classical mythology from the very first lines" of the Chorus, there are some half a dozen parallels with Chapman throughout the play. Most important are the similarities between "the night-scene at Agincourt and that before Troy in books nine and ten of the *Iliad*."

HENRY VI, PART 1

1934 Hattaway, Michael, ed. *The First Part of King Henry VI*. (New Cambridge Shakespeare.) Cambridge: Cambridge U. P., 1990. xvii + 210 pp.

The introduction remarks that Charles the Dauphin's references to Joan as daughter of Astraea and to her promises as the gardens of Adonis (*1H6*, I.vi) act, in view of the background of these allusions in Plato's *Phaedrus*, Ovid's *Metamorphoses*, and Virgil's Eclogue 4, to turn Pucelle into a myth, "but it is a myth of a false Astraea, the antitype of the order represented by Talbot." Notes also that Suffolk, in the play's epilogue, likens his expedition to secure Margaret for Henry's bride to Paris's trip to Greece; this speech "ironically invokes the romantic archetypes of antiquity."

1935 Jackson, Gabriele Bernhard. "Topical Ideology: Witches, Amazons, and Shakespeare's Joan of Arc." *ELR*, 18 (1988), 40–65. Reprint. *Women in the Renaissance: Selections from "English Literary Renaissance."* Eds. Kirby Farrell, Elizabeth H. Hageman, and Arthur F. Kinney. Amherst: U. of Massachusetts P., 1990, pp. 88–117.

Argues that *1H6* presents Joan of Arc disjunctively, "first as numinous, then as practically and subversively powerful, and finally as feminized and demonized." In characterizing Joan, Sh makes use of the ambiguity surrounding Elizabethan ideas of the strong woman, as seen in Penthesilea and other Amazons inherited from classical tradition.

Henry VI, Part 2

1936 Caldwell, Ellen Cashwell. "The Breach of Time: History and Violence in the *Aeneid*, *The Faerie Queene*, and *2 Henry VI*." Ph.D. dissertation, University of North Carolina at Chapel Hill, 1986. *DAI*, 47 (1986–87), 1719-A.

Discusses the *Aeneid*, *The Faerie Queene*, and *2H6* as narratives of purportedly historical events that use metaphors to present these events, and, in turn, create a sense of "time and history as asequential." The three works are similar in several ways: They are all epics; they all concern the reigns of kings or patriarchal leaders; they all focus on civil wars; they all exhibit excessive violence; and they all "use the human body as a major metaphor." Analyzes the Nisus and Euryalus episode as it is treated in the three works to show that they all provide "poetic versions of what is usually considered a linear process." Shows that "the corporate analogy, especially its most violent images," is essential to constructing "poetic narratives of the discontinuous, fragmented events and the shifting perspectives of history."

1937 Maxwell, J. C. "Three Notes on *2 Henry VI*." *N&Q*, 20 (1973), 133–34.

The first note proposes to emend *Pine* in the Latin quote in IV.i.117 to *Prae te* so that the Latin is closely paraphrased by the English that follows it.

Henry VI, Part 3

1937a Sanders, Norman, ed. *Henry VI, Part Three*. (New Penguin Shakespeare.) Harmondsworth: Penguin, 1981. 297 pp.

The introduction, in commenting on Richard of Gloucester's first proclamation of his evil nature (*3H6*, III.ii.124–195), observes that "[t]he classical learning proper to a Renaissance prince is to provide [Richard] with the qualities necessary to pluck the crown from the hands of its owners."

1937b Womersley, D. J. "*3 Henry VI*: Shakespeare, Tacitus, and Parricide." *N&Q*, 32 (1985), 468–73.

Expresses doubts about the 16th-c. texts that have been proposed as sources for the appearance in *3H6*, II.v, of a son who has killed his father. Proposes instead a passage from Tacitus's *Histories* (3.25), which Sh probably read in the 1591 translation of Sir Henry Savile.

Henry VIII

1938 Berman, Ronald. "*King Henry the Eighth*: History and Romance." *ES*, 48 (1967), 112–21.

Draws a contrast between the dark chaos that constantly threatens to destroy the "historical world" of *H8* and the play's mythical content, which seeks to redeem this world. Anne Bullen and her daughter, in their evocation of Ceres and Proserpina, provide reassurance that life will be renewed. The mythic power that they share with Henry infuses the play to some extent with the spirit of the mysteriously wonderful found in Sh's late romances.

1939 Micheli, Linda McJ., comp. *"Henry VIII": An Annotated Bibliography.* (Garland Shakespeare Bibliographies 15.) New York: Garland, 1988. xxxii + 444 pp.

Covers primarily works published between 1940 and 1984, with a significant number of items from before 1940. Classifies entries under ten headings, including Criticism (185 items); Sources and Backgrounds (60 items); Editions and Adaptations (117 items); and Bibliographies (54 items). Begins each section with the oldest entry and proceeds chronologically. Concludes with a single index. Provides substantial and detailed annotations.

JULIUS CAESAR

1939a Adams, Robert P. "Transformations in the Late Elizabethan Tragic Sense of Life: New Critical Approaches." MLQ, 35 (1974), 352–63.

Calls attention to the shortcomings of traditional criticism to account for the tendency of several great English dramatists writing between about 1596 and 1603 to transform the sense of the tragic by creating "dramatic explorations of corruption and tyranny in the great state." Cites JC as "a radical inquiry into tragedies of state" during this period.

1940 Alvis, John. "A Probable Platonic Allusion and Its Significance in *Julius Caesar.*" UC, 2 (1979), 64–73.

Points out that in the second scene of *JC*, as Cassius and Brutus discuss Caesar, references to eyes are prominent. The image of the eyes of others as mirrors in which people can see themselves may be borrowed from Plato's *First Alcibiades*, in which Socrates begins by persuading Alcibiades that self-knowledge can be gained "by viewing one's reflection in the eye of another." However, Socrates goes on to insist that to achieve the truest self-knowledge one must practice a kind of introspection, looking into that part of his soul that resembles God. Brutus, having begun to know himself in the manner first recommended to Alcibiades, fails to follow Socrates' subsequent advice: Throughout the play he accepts the common eye, or public opinion, as the true mirror of the self. By emphasizing Brutus's departure from Socratic teaching in this respect, Sh provides a key to his tragedy. Revised as part of chapter 5 of item 0080a.

1941 Anderson, Peter S. "Shakespeare's *Caesar*: The Language of Sacrifice." CompD, 3 (1969–70), 3–26.

Views *JC* as embodying a "mythic pattern of sacrifice in which Caesar is sacralized and victimized by his 'sons' as they seek contiguity with the divine Pompey." Pompey is the divinity to whom the sacrifice is made, his statue is the place of sacrifice, Brutus is the prophet of the sacrifice, and Cassius is its high priest. Sacrifice takes place as an exchange between men and gods, a means of communication. Throughout the play, "signs" of "the mythic language of sacrifice" can be found in abundance (statues, portents, genuflection, blood). In sharing the pulpit with Antony and in his own funeral oration, Brutus is resisting the "*privacy* which the special and separate discourse of sacrifice creates." But the sacrificial pattern continues, with Antony exacting death as an exchange for Caesar's death. See item 2028.

1941a Ansari, A. A. "Marcus Brutus: The Divided Self." *AJES*, 10 (1985), 17–34.

Analyzes several passages from *JC* to stress the point that Marcus Brutus is "a divided being": He is incapable of disentangling the variety of "discordant impulses" in himself and comes to be burdened with the realization that the great project of liberation for which he committed himself to the conspiracy has come to nothing. He feels, at the end, only "desolation and emptiness."

1942 Anson, John. "*Julius Caesar*: The Politics of the Hardened Heart." *ShakS*, 2 (1966), 11–33.

Explains that in the Elizabethan mind, the "self-sufficient impassivity" of the Stoics was associated particularly with Seneca and the Romans. *JC* re-creates the world of Rome by exploring "the moral petrification of Senecal man." As exhibited in the play, Stoic attempts to control the body and other externals by an inner spiritual fire causes a moral hardening in the individual and the body politic, expressed through the separation of hand from heart. Caesar, the heart of Rome, isolates himself from other men and from his own physical nature by insisting on his constancy. The conspirators, who represent the members of the Roman state, or hands, turn against Caesar and try to regain the life-giving spirit from which he has separated them. They, however, are also hardened: Cassius is a "leveling detractor," and Brutus is forced to hide his envy of Caesar under a love of Rome. In their suicides, Cassius and Brutus turn their hands against their own hearts. The Roman–Stoic ethic is finally indicted as a commitment to self-mutilation.

1943 Auffret, Jean. "The Philosophic Background of *Julius Caesar*." *CahiersE*, 5 (1974), 66–92.

Cites copious examples from classical writers to show that Sh made a conscious effort to portray the characters in *JC* in the light of ancient philosophical doctrines. Casca, with his outspokenness and coarse jocularity, is clearly a Cynic. His style is "a convincing recreation of the diatribe of the Empire, as practiced by Persius, Juvenal, ... and Epictetus." Starting with Plutarch's Cassius, a choleric Epicurean, Sh, probably under the influence of Lucretius, made the character into a melancholy Epicurean who lapses from orthodoxy in his hatred of tyrants and his intermittent fear of omens. Antony and Caesar cannot be classified by any school of philosophy. The former is a "life-force and has not found himself yet"; the latter is all too human in his emotions, with a magical, not a philosophical, outlook (which sets him apart from Stoic and Epicurean alike). The last three sections address the "Stoical Problems" of suicide, reason and passion, and providence, with special reference to Brutus. Though Sh enriched his character with some faults and inconsistencies, Brutus remains the exemplar of Stoic virtue in the play.

1944 Baines, Barbara J. "Political and Poetic Revisionism in *Julius Caesar*." *UC*, 10 (1990), 42–54.

Contends that various politicians in *JC* "attempt to displace the poet by appropriating his art," each revisioning through language the scenes constructed by others. Caesar, Brutus, Cassius, and Antony all refashion the script to suit their own purposes. As these revisionings succeed each other, we become aware of the disparity between language and reality. Through the play, Sh "demystifies political power" by paralleling it to this verbal revisioning, thus reasserting "the authority of the poet."

1945 Barnes, Richard. "Shakespeare New: Shakespeare Now." *Claremont Quarterly*, (1964), 33–51.

Notes recent productions of *H5*, *JC*, and *TN*. Discusses "the interaction between the plays and their audiences when the plays were new." The original audience would have been excited by the many parallels between characters and incidents in *JC* and the Essex rebellion, which was in the air when the play was first performed in 1599. Essex himself, who had written, "What, cannot princes err?" resembled Brutus, while the aged Queen—imperious, capricious, contradictory—was like Caesar in many ways. Intellectually, the Renaissance had brought about an important change in attitude toward the Romans by the time of *JC*. They "had ceased to be ancestors" and were becoming "the Ancients as they were for Milton, Classics, models for humanist Imitatio"; "the Renaissance myth of the Roman Republic was superseding the outworn medieval reality of the Holy Roman Empire." With this notion reinforced by Amyot's and North's translations of Plutarch, Sh's audience would have had a heightened awareness of the issues presented in *JC*.

1946 Basu, Kajal. "*Julius Caesar* and *Henry V.*" *Shakespeare Commemoration Volume*. Ed. Taraknath Sen. Calcutta: Presidency College, 1966, pp. 89–124.

Argues that *JC* and *H5* were both written in 1599 and that the plays can be fruitfully compared. The two protagonists, Henry and Brutus, provide an interesting contrast: Henry is "cold, ruthless, passionless," while Brutus, facing the same conflict as Henry ("individual morality versus collective morality"), is "more emotional than intellectual." Brutus fails as a leader, but his sensitivity gives him a nobility Henry cannot attain. Antony's temperament is basically the same as Henry's.

1947 Bate, A. Jonathan. "The Cobbler's Awl: *Julius Caesar*, I.i.21–24." *SQ*, 35 (1984), 461–62.

Detects a reference to male genitals in the cobbler's word play on "awl" in *JC*.

1948 Bellringer, A. W. "*Julius Caesar*: Room Enough." *CritQ*, 12 (1970), 31–48. Reprint. *Shakespeare's Wide and Universal Stage*. Eds. C. B. Cox and D. J. Palmer. Manchester: Manchester U. P., 1984, pp. 146–63.

Explains that in *JC* Sh was interested in "analyzing a transfer of power" and the errors that were committed during its course. He was also concerned with portraying the old Roman aristocratic ideals, balancing sympathy with a distaste for their sterility. These ideals harken back to an earlier age, when "honor," "the general good," and "Rome" were narrowly defined. Brutus and Cassius fail to recognize that the widespread Roman dominions make their parochial notion of identifying the public good with a code peculiar to a small group of aristocrats in the city irrelevant. Sh's style is appropriate for this: It is "dignified and clear, rarely persuasive, capable of giving away the speaker without satire, and yet suggesting a certain hollowness." The play "mourns the supersession of a political tradition by armed force." There is no individual tragic focus.

1949 Berman, Ronald. "A Note on the Motives of Marcus Brutus." *SQ*, 23 (1972), 197–200.

Points out that in *JC*, Cassius mentions Lucius Junius Brutus, who drove Tarquin from Rome, as a model for Marcus Brutus, who is contemplating the assassination of Caesar. The story of Lucius Junius Brutus, found in Titus Livy's *History of Rome*, was well-known to Sh, and he makes Marcus Brutus familiar with it as well. As translated in William Painter's *Palace of Pleasure* (1566), Livy's account of Lucius Junius Brutus's reaction to the rape of Lucrece emphasizes his transformation, his "determination to save Rome from monarchy, and his natural assumption of leadership in the battle to establish the Republic." Each of these themes has a parallel in *JC*: Marcus Brutus seems to have in mind an account of "how a great man had once before undertaken a task essentially like the one before him." As a "modern man," however, Marcus Brutus fails to equal the "legendary" qualities of Lucius Junius Brutus: He suffers from "ambiguity, hesitation, and a rather fragile combination of moralism with idealism."

1950 Berry, Ralph. "*Julius Caesar*: A Roman Tragedy." *DR* 61 (1981–82), 325–36.

Maintains that *JC* emphasizes the subordination of the individual to the city, which is manifested in the frequent references to "Rome," "Roman," and "Romans." The characters display an intense ancestor worship, a keen interest in statues, and a marked tendency to refer to their own names as externalized selves. Both the conspirators and Caesar constantly strive to live up to the roles they have imposed on themselves, readjusting them when they slip, as Caesar does when he momentarily forgets to be "Caesar" before going to the Senate. The numerous references to actors and acting take on special significance here: The characters perform a sort of ritual sacrifice of themselves to the Roman past. Revised as chapter 6 of item 1951.

1951 Berry, Ralph. *Shakespeare and the Awareness of the Audience.* New York: St. Martin's P., 1985. xi + 157 pp.

Chapter 6, "Communal Identity and the Rituals of *Julius Ceaser*," is a revision of item 1950.

1951a Bevington, David. *Tudor Drama and Politics: A Critical Approach to Topical Meaning.* Cambridge: Harvard U. P., 1968. 360 pp.

Includes, in chapter 16, a reading of *JC* that confirms Sh's conservative view of monarchy and the political actions that would, on the one hand, overthrow it or, on the other, effectively maintain it. Caesar, as Sh sees him, is a tyrant, but this does not justify the attempt to supplant him. Brutus, however commendable his desire to set things right, is stained by the "flaw of rebellion," which destroys the institutions "it had hoped to preserve."

1952 Bizley, W. H. "To Catch the Ear of Rome: The Interrelation of Language and History in Shakespeare's *Julius Caesar*." UCTSE, no. 5 (1973), 49–53.

Aims to characterize the "cultural texture" or "sensibility" of Rome as it is presented in *JC*. Maintains that the procession of great leaders (Pompey and Caesar being the two most recent) whose achievements lie outside the walls of the city has focused the people's attention on that space beyond the city where "Roman honors can still be won." In this context, heroes on whom the people can project their desire for grandeur tend to provide the city's continuity, replacing the more individual, inward focus on civic cohesion characteristic of the Republic. The staging of Roman history as a pageant of heroes like Caesar quite understandably disturbs a republican like Brutus, who speaks not as an awestruck admirer of the great but as a thoughtful, deliberate, and balanced analyst of the problems faced by the city. What Brutus attempts is to ritualize the conspiracy and assassination, to restore a kind of "republican decorum" to Roman life. His speech to the citizens is an effort to contain Caesar's death as part of "an assured civic process" that diminishes the great man's stature and locates the center of Rome inside the city once again. Antony, however, subverts Brutus's initiative and regains center-stage for the dead Caesar; he is able to catch the ear of the crowd by inviting them to identify with their fallen hero, one who, like them, has been dispossessed.

1953 Bligh, John. "Cicero's Choric Comment in *Julius Caesar*." ESC, 8 (1982), 391–408.

Discovers in the exchange between Cicero and Casca in *JC*, I.iii, and especially in Cicero's choric comment that men may construe things "Clean from the purpose of the things themselves" (line 35), a key to the tragedy of the play. Cites several examples of misconstruction on the part of the characters, especially Brutus. Cicero's comment is "an epistemological thesis" that helps us to understand how "a good man like Brutus" came to do what he did. Maintains that Sh is in agreement with Plutarch, his source, in his moral and political condemnation of the assassination. Unlike Plutarch, however, Sh discourages us from attempting a metaphysical explanation for "the events depicted." No providential superstructure is needed for Brutus's tragedy, which results from his very human failure to understand the times.

1954 Blits, Jan H. *The End of the Ancient Republic: Essays on "Julius Caesar."* Durham, North Carolina: Carolina Academic P., 1982. 95 pp.

Argues that the vice of Caesarism, as portrayed by Sh in *JC*, is an important factor in the corruption of political life that destroyed republican Rome. Chapter 1, "Manliness and Friendship in *Julius Caesar*," is a revision of item 1955. Discusses the virtues and limitations of the kinds of men who built the Republic. Manliness, the quality admired most, is a contentious virtue, not conducive to cooperation, and subject to various tensions and contradictions. Cassius, the character most concerned with being manly, is nevertheless heavily influenced by the womanly qualities in his nature. Portia's attempt to draw closer to Brutus is actually an effort to be manly, which separates her from him. In his suicide, Brutus seeks a fame unrivalled by any other Roman, and by doing so he sets himself apart from the city in whose name he has been claiming to act. Chapter 2, "Caesarism and the End of Republican Rome: Act I, scene i," analyzes the play's first scene as indicative of the decline of republican consensus. The two tribunes, ostensibly advocates for republicanism, attack Caesar on Caesarian grounds: They chide the people not for worshiping any hero but for worshiping the wrong hero. The scene provides evidence that republican traditions (for example, the feast of the Lupercal) are being neglected and that political oratory, a traditional prop of republican freedom, is no longer a viable force in Rome. Chapter 3, "Politics, and the Ethics of Intention: Brutus's Glorious Failure," analyzes the three decisions Brutus makes during the meeting of the conspirators at his house (II.i). In each instance, Brutus seeks to rise above attachments to "his own" but ends by sacrificing the welfare of those he "seems selflessly to serve." Chapter 4, "Caesar's Ambiguous End," concentrates on two scenes (I.i and II.ii) to show that what appear to be failures in Caesar's attempt to become a king are actually successes in his effort to become a god. Caesar anticipates the assassination, and in submitting to his death as a man acts out his role as a god. He does not aspire to be a king; rather, he wants future kings to aspire to the rank of "Caesar." Caesar's triumph in this regard, however, diminishes the possibilities for those Romans who succeed him and confirms the demise of republican Rome. It is finally a hollow victory.

1955 Blits, Jan H. "Manliness and Friendship in Shakespeare's *Julius Caesar*." *Interpretation*, 9, nos. 2–3 (1981), 155–67.

Revised as chapter 1 of item 1954.

1956 Blits, Jan Harold. "All the Sway of Earth: The Politics of Shakespeare's *Julius Caesar*." Ph.D. dissertation, New School for Social Research, 1975. *DAI*, 36 (1975–76), 1057- A.

Suggests that Sh's treatment of Roman political life is grounded in "human concerns" that are not themselves political: They revolve around the tension between "human self-love and love of beauty." Three related characteristics of *JC* are based in this tension. First, Caesar's proud love impels him to make several claims to divinity, which conflict with each other and make him incapable of transcending political life. Second, Sh emphasizes that the conspiracy against Caesar is led by two political philosophers, one a Stoic and the other an Epicurean. Neither Brutus nor Cassius, however, adheres to his principles when his own happiness hangs in the balance. Third, the gods or the heavenly powers "seem to take a direct interest in honor- loving pride." By conventionalizing eros, the gods "make the things men can love as their own appear worthy of their highest love of beauty."

1957 Bowden, William R. "The Mind of Brutus." *SQ*, 17 (1966), 57–67.

Argues against the view of Brutus in *JC* as a "sensitive, introspective intellectual." Brutus's intelligence is not respected by others in the play. Furthermore, Sh alters his source in two important ways. In Plutarch, the letters Brutus finds urging him to action are genuine ones from his fellow citizens; in *JC*, they are planted by Cassius. Sh also diminishes Brutus's studiousness from what it is in Plutarch, and his character is limited by a lack of inner conflict and a failure to recognize error. This analysis offers a better characterization of Brutus: a man who is "completely well-meaning, completely upright, and not very perspicuous."

1958 Bradford, William Clark Jr. "Julius Caesar as a Literary Device: English Plays 1594–1663." Ph.D. dissertation, Duke University, 1970. *DAI*, 32 (1971–72), 908-A-909-A.

Surveys attitudes toward the figures of Caesar in ancient times and the medieval period as preparation for a discussion of his appearance in English Renaissance drama. In the mid-16th c., the secularization of Caesar began to take place, and the development of popular drama encouraged new ways to use him as a character. The classical ambivalence toward Caesar, which included much admiration, was recovered. In *JC*, Sh considers the tragedies consequent on wrong moral choices by both Caesar and Brutus.

1959 Brittin, Norman A. "Shakespeare and the Conflict between Tyranny and Liberty." *Estudios Generales* (San Juan, Puerto Rico), 6, no. 12 (1964), 75–90.

Argues that Cassius and Brutus fail to perceive, in plotting to assassinate Caesar, that liberty means little to the masses in *JC*. As a result, their idealistic overthrow of the existing order creates chaos and leads to their deaths and those of other Romans.

1960 Bromley, John C. *The Shakespearean Kings*. Boulder: Colorado Associated U. P., 1971. xiii + 138 pp.

Includes a brief discussion of *JC* in chapter 7. Views Brutus as Sh's "first great lesson in that ethical failure which proceeds from the distortion or abandonment of thought."

1961 Brown, John Russell. *Shakespeare's Dramatic Style*. New York: Barnes & Noble, 1972. x + 191 pp.

Aims to "increase the range and sensitivity of the language of theatrical response" and "to encourage individual dialogues with Shakespeare's works." Analyzes five plays, including *JC*, which has three or four roles that give opportunity for significant personal drama, as well as large ensemble scenes. In I.ii, Sh explores personal aspects of Caesar's relationships with Calpurnia and Antony but makes subtle changes in Plutarch's account of the same episode (where Caesar commands that Antony touch Calpurnia in his "chase," to cure her barrenness) to heighten the inexplicability of the scene. In III.i, after several scenes of argument, verbal statements, and obscure motivation, Sh places action—the killing of Caesar—at "the center of the dramatic illusion."

1962 Bryant, J. A. Jr. "*Julius Caesar* from a Euripidean Perspective." *CompD*, 16 (1982–1983), 97–111.

Attempts to show that *JC*, Sh's first mature work of tragedy, is "not so much another sophisticated metamorphosis of the Senecan play as a continuation of Greek drama in its own right—in particular, of the drama and vision of Euripides." Sh and his contemporaries shared the admiration of the 16th c. for at least two plays of Euripides, *Hecuba* and *Phoenissae*, and probably knew his *Iphigenia in Aulis*. Both *Hecuba* and *Iphigenia* deal with bloody sacrifices that "place the perpetrators of those sacrifices in the position of having sought to appease cosmic forces with a gesture that is almost certain to outrage human ones. Both plays leave us uncertain about the reaction of the gods to the blood that has been offered them; both, in fact, in keeping with Euripides' normal practice, are equivocal about whether there are any gods at all." Brutus's "misdirected motive" and its "bloody consequence" suggest the rational Euripidean protagonist (like Pentheus in the *Bacchae*) who brings about the debacle of classical tragedy "without achieving the compensatory epiphany that should accompany it." *JC* is also Euripidean in the fragmentation of the hero into several opposed antagonists.

1963 Burckhardt, Sigurd. "How Not to Murder Caesar." *CentR*, 11 (1967), 141–56. Reprint. *Shakespearean Meanings*. Princeton: Princeton U.P., 1968, pp. 3–21.

Argues that Sh intended to commit an anachronism when he had a clock strike in *JC*, II.i.192. Several references to telling time in the play indicate uncertainty about the hour, the month, and the year. The conspiracy, in other words, is surrounded by confusion. In the orchard scene, Brutus tries to impose a pure classicism on the assassination of Caesar by rejecting three proposals made by others. He is a tragic poet attempting to force an unruly, confusing reality to fit a preconceived formula. The clock strikes just at the moment when Brutus has persuaded the conspirators to follow him in performing the play of Caesar's murder as an almost Aristotelian tragedy. The sound of a timepiece reminds us that what the conspirators are doing is not taking the form of "the time and temper of the people." In most of his tragedies, Sh was alert to the pressure of the times, and this made it impossible for him (except in the case of *Oth*.) to write a "perfect" tragedy.

1964 Burnet, R. A. L. "Some Echoes of the Genevan Bible in Shakespeare and Milton." *N&Q*, 27 (1980), 179–81.

Suggests a marginal note in the Geneva Bible as a source for *JC*, I.i.35: "You blocks, you stones, you worse than senseless things!"

1965 Burt, Richard A. "'A Dangerous Rome': Shakespeare's *Julius Caesar* and the Discursive Determinism of Cultural Politics." *Contending Kingdoms: Historical, Pyschological, and Feminist Approaches to the Literature of Sixteenth-Century England and France.* Eds. Marie-Rose Logan and Peter L. Rudnytsky. Detroit: Wayne State U. P., 1991, pp. 109–27.

Uses *JC* to clarify a way of interpretation called "application" in the Renaissance, "a process that links the past to the Renaissance present." Sh's play thematizes that process by showing that control of representation (assumed by the conspirators when they confidently predict how future generations will reenact their liberation drama) does not ensure political success. To rewrite Rome, as was often done in Sh's time, puts "Elizabethan and Jacobean political assumptions at risk precisely because the past and the present never entirely conform to one another."

1966 Bushnell, Rebecca W. *Tragedies of Tyrants: Political Thought and Theater in the English Renaissance.* Ithaca, New York: Cornell U. P., 1990. xv + 195 pp.

Chapter 4, a revision of item 1967, includes a discussion of the language and imagery that define a tyrant, as used in *JC*. Although Caesar avoids the title *king*, synonymous in the Roman mind with *tyrant*, he adopts all of the other names and symbols associated with royalty. His public image as a powerful ruler is contradicted by private scenes that show him as wavering and weak. The conspirators utilize an antityrannical language that presents Caesar in monster or animal images. In claiming divinity and adopting the name *Caesar* as a title, Caesar reveals the tyrant's desire for absolute power. After his death, he becomes an abstraction, a symbol that continues to control the fates of the conspirators.

1967 Bushnell, Rebecca Weld. "Stage Tyrants: The Cases of Creon and Caesar." *CML*, 7 (1987), 71–86.

Discusses the character of Caesar in *JC* and its relationship to antiquity's definitions of tyranny, especially those of Herodotus and Plato. Explores the question of whether Caesar is truly a tyrant. Revised as chapter 4 of item 1966.

1968 Cairncross, Andrew S. "A Source for Antony." *ELN*, 13 (1975–76), 4–6.

Argues that *The Hystorie of Hamlet*, Sh's chief source for *Ham.*, was also a source for *JC*. It is especially clear that Antony's oration over Caesar's body parallels

"Hamlet's speech to the people concerning his father Horvendile, and his actions taken to avenge him."

1969 Cantrell, John Bruce. "A Commentary on Shakespeare's *Julius Caesar*." Ph.D. dissertation, University of South Carolina, 1975. DAI, 36 (1975–76), 7432-A.

Attempts to provide "a full explanation of 1) all vocabulary items whose meanings are not accessible through a modern dictionary (other than the *Oxford English Dictionary*), 2) all obscure phrasing, and 3) all obscure place- or name-references and references to historical events." Deals with the "problem area" of classical allusions.

1970 Carducci, Jane. "Brutus, Cassius, and Caesar in Shakespeare's *Julius Caesar*: Language and the Roman Male." *Lang&L*, 13 (1988), 1–19.

Argues that, under the influence of Seneca, the Elizabethans viewed the male culture of ancient Rome as Stoic, exalting "manly prowess and heroic spirit." In JC, Sh critically examines this narrow ideal by severely limiting the language of his characters. The laconic speech of Brutus, Cassius, and Caesar does not necessarily indicate openness or honesty; in fact, these three characters' use of the languages of persuasion and ceremony works to distance them from the audience and to conceal their self-deception. The inadequacy of their Senecan posture of invulnerability and self-sufficiency is demonstrated when, unable to express their feelings in words, they are constrained to fall back on gestures, especially the gesture of death. Revision of part of item 0240.

1971 Carson, David L. "The Dramatic Importance of Prodigies in *Julius Caesar*, Act II, Scene i." *ELN*, 2 (1964–65), 177–80.

Points out that while Brutus and Cassius whisper privately about the conspiracy, and Decius and Cinna mistake the evil exhalations in the heavens for the approach of dawn, Casca corrects them (II.i.101–111). Sh uses this exchange to increase suspense: As Brutus makes his decision to join the conspiracy, the evil omens in the sky reach their greatest intensity, so bright as to be taken for the sun. See item 2105.

1972 Cath, Stanley H. "Caesar and His Barren Relationship with Rome." *Psychohistory Review*, 16 (1988), 259–82.

Reviews the history of Caesar's relationship with Rome to support the hypothesis that his tragic flaw was "narcissistic in nature." Adduces his defiance of taboos, his appetite for honor and power, his "distorted sense of his place in history," and "his tendency to over-idealize himself and certain others" as factors in his assassination. Argues that Caesar made himself vulnerable to the assassins by "living out certain narcissistic fantasies that radically disturbed the psychological and therefore the political equilibrium of Rome." Claims that Sh's portrayal of Caesar in JC is informed by these ideas, as can be seen in Calpurnia's dream and its interpretation (II.ii).

1973 Chang, Joseph S. M. J. "*Julius Caesar* in the Light of Renaissance Historiography." *JEGP*, 69 (1970), 63–71.

Explores the new awareness among Renaissance historians that coherence cannot be imposed on the past; that the actions of a man at different times spring from entirely different motives; and that responsibility for events cannot be conveniently assigned to heroes or villains. Montaigne and Jean Bodin were among those who followed the new way of thinking about history. It was exploited by Sh in JC, in which Caesar behaves differently about death in varying circumstances and Brutus commits "acts of unavoidable moral significance" without a full awareness of what he is doing. The rush of events, clearly not under Brutus's control, allows him his nobility "even when his actions are deplored."

1974 Clarke, M. L. *The Noblest Roman: Marcus Brutus and His Reputation.* Ithaca, New York: Cornell U. P., 1981. 157 pp.

Includes, in chapter 3, "Brutus in Literature," a discussion of how, for *JC*, Sh shaped his source material from Plutarch. Notes, for example, the following changes or modifications: the creation of Casca from a mere name in Plutarch; the emphasis on the kindness Brutus exhibits toward his slave Lucius and his wife Portia; the dramatic arrangement of the two funeral speeches; the motivation for the quarrel between Brutus and Cassius in the condemnation of Lucius Pella; the decline in Brutus's self-confidence toward the end; and the mismanagement of the final interview between Brutus and Cassius and their discussion of suicide. Declares that Brutus, an idealist who cannot cope with the world around him, is the hero.

1975 Clemen, Wolfgang. *Shakespeare's Soliloquies.* Tr. Charity Scott Stokes. London: Methuen, 1987. x + 211 pp.

Includes an analysis of Brutus's meditation in his orchard, interrupted three times by Lucius (*JC*, II.i). Shows that these soliloquies reveal Brutus as inconsistent; as tormented by his decision to murder Caesar; and as ambivalent about having to advance what he regards as a noble cause by what he believes are tainted means.

1976 Colman, E. A. M. *"Julius Caesar": A Lecture before the Sydney Branch of the English Association.* Sydney: The English Association, 1965. 21 pp.

Observes that in *JC* Sh undermined the vague notion of the heroic with which his audience would have come to a play about classical Rome by emphasizing the contradictions in Caesar's character and by viewing the characters of Brutus, Antony, and Cassius in light of these contradictions. Brutus begins as an idealist, but his rigidity shows him to be very much like the man he kills as a potential tyrant. He is out of touch with reality. Antony—young, brave, and eloquent—also turns out to be ruthlessly indifferent to the social chaos he unleashes. Cassius, at first the choleric man reacting only to Caesar's flaws, gains in stature as his shrewd judgment and indomitable spirit are progressively revealed. The impression of tragedy at the conclusion is only superficial; what we have is an ironic picture of "human beings muddling through, some to victory, some to death."

1977 Cook, W. A. "Shakespeare's Cinna—Tribune Not Poet." *SQ*, 14(1963), 97.

Points out that all ancient sources except Plutarch identify the Cinna killed by the mob after the death of Caesar as Helvius Cinna, a tribune friendly to Caesar. Plutarch is the only ancient writer to call him a poet, and Sh follows Plutarch in this error (*JC*, III.iii).

1978 Coursen, Herbert R. Jr. "The Fall and Decline of *Julius Caesar*." *TSLL*, 4 (1962–63), 241–51.

Contends that *JC* fails because "it lies in the shadow of the greatest works towards which it points." The play collapses with the death of Caesar, in large measure because its structure, successful until that point, has been sustained by a set of highness–lowness images. With Caesar gone, half of this contrast disappears, and the play is impoverished.

1979 Craig, Hardin. "The Shadow of Pompey the Great." *Topic*, 7 (1964), 5–11.

Points out that "the number and intimacy of Sh's references to the story of Pompey the Great may suggest something more than casual recollections of Plutarch." As a "proponent of ancient liberty," Brutus in *JC* speaks in the political voice of Plutarch's Pompey. Sh's company might have possessed a Pompey play, possibly Chapman's *Caesar and Pompey*, that influenced *JC*.

1980 Crawford, John W. "The Religious Question in *Julius Caesar*." *SoQ*, 15 (1976–77), 297–302.

Asserts that the Stoic belief that the gods control the world through Destiny and reveal their purposes by omens is opposed in *JC* by the Epicurean view that there is no divine direction. The Stoic notion is validated by the play, however. Caesar dies because he accepts the misinterpretation of an omen; Cassius, though he converts during the play from an Epicurean to a Stoic, has already, in contempt of Destiny, set in motion the conspiracy that will be his downfall; and Brutus, a faithful Stoic throughout, nevertheless attempts to alter Destiny and fails.

1981 Crewe, J. V. "Shakespeare's *Julius Caesar*." *Theoria*, 37 (1971), 31–43.

Accepts George Bernard Shaw's designation of *JC* as a "political melodrama." In reading it, we see Sh indulging the impulse to "re-examine myths of heroic greatness." Caesar, though imperfect, is about as great as a successful public figure can be. Brutus, Cassius, and Antony should be seen as three representative political types: "Brutus stands for principle, Cassius for its absence, and Antony for its negation."

1982 Dachslager, E. L. "'The Most Unkindest Cut': A Note on *Julius Caesar* III.ii.187." *ELN*, 11 (1973–74), 258–59.

Suggests that Antony's "unkindest cut" refers to the wound Plutarch says Brutus gave Caesar "about his privities." If true, this would emphasize the degeneracy of Brutus's role in the murder, since he was reputed to be Caesar's illegitimate son.

1983 D'Ardenne, S. "Shakespeare, a West Midland Man." *RLV*, 31 (1965), 547–54.

Draws attention to the resemblance between Cassius's account of his swimming match with Caesar (*JC*, I.ii) and the taunting of Beowulf by Unferth about a swimming contest between Beowulf and Breca. Notes that the historians Plutarch and Suetonius emphasize Caesar's prowess in swimming and speculates that Sh was influenced indirectly (through hearsay) by the Beowulf legend.

1983a Davidson, Clifford. "Renaissance Dramatic Forms, Cosmic Perspective, and Alienation." *CahiersE*, 27 (1985), 1–16.

Uses *JC* as one example of how important it is to understand the emblematic nature of many episodes in Renaissance drama. Argues that the emphasis on the sacrificial nature of Caesar's death connects it with the first murder, that of Abel by Cain, of which it is in some sense a repetition. It is also linked to the sacrifice of Christ, of which it is a failed imitation.

1983b de Gerenday, Lynn. "Play, Ritualization, and Ambivalence in *Julius Caesar*." *L&P*, 24 (1974), 24–33.

Uses Brutus's orchard soliloquy about killing Caesar and his conversation with the conspirators (*JC*, II.i) as key texts in arguing that Brutus is driven to create a private reality, isolated from the external world, through ritualization and play-acting. The theme of double interpretation is recurrent in the play: Cicero (I.iii) comments on how men may construe things eccentrically, missing their real meaning; Antony undercuts Brutus's attempts to ritualize; Caesar gathers in himself various themes of doubleness. Brutus's tragedy is one of "failed ritual": His "potentially integrative" ego is "prevented from realization through the use of ritualistic elements as defense against ambivalence."

1984 Doran, Madeleine. "'What should be in that "Caesar"?' Proper Names in *Julius Caesar*." *Shakespeare's Dramatic Language: Essays by Madeleine Doran*. Madison: U. of Wisconsin P., 1976, pp. 120–53.

Points out that Sh chose to give the names "Brutus" and "Caesar" unusual emphasis in *JC*. Analyzes the dramatic function of these names. References to Caesar when he is not present—all negative before his death and all positive after it—are intended to control the audience's response to the action. At first, there is sympathy for the conspirators and their fear of Caesar's power, and then there is recollection of his greatness. When Caesar is present, the interactions between second and third persons and between direct and indirect address skillfully move our attention back and forth between "Caesar the man and Caesar the public figure." Caesar's habit of referring to himself in the third person always concerns his constancy, his immovability. It gives the audience various chances to sense both his hubris and his greatness. The uses of Brutus's name are more varied and provide a fuller, more intimate portrait than the uses of Caesar's. "Brutus" is often paired with "Caesar" to indicate the former's importance as antagonist. When Brutus is addressed directly, it is usually by an equal like Cassius or Portia. Brutus is also referred to in the third person, as when Portia remarks on his present separation from his usual self. Like Caesar, Brutus speaks of himself in the third person but less insistently. One important third-person role in which Brutus sees himself is that of Roman republican and patriot. Throughout the play, "Rome" and "Roman" are positive, and the suicides near the end are praised for their Roman virtue. In his epitaph for Brutus, Antony brings together the three names, thus ending the disjunction between "Brutus" and "Caesar" and paying tribute to the noblest Roman of all.

1985   Drakakis, John. "'Fashion it thus': *Julius Caesar* and the Politics of Theatrical Representation." *ShS*, 44 (1992), 65–73.

Regards *JC* as "not so much a celebration of theatre as an unmasking of the politics of representation per se." In its reading of Roman history, the play produces rather than expresses meaning. It shuttles between "the generic requirements of *de casibus* tragedy" and Senecan revenge tragedy, thus simultaneously disclosing and withdrawing "historical possibilities." Maintains that the play, in vacillating between "'fate' and human agency as the origins of action, and hence of history itself, enacts the precarious position of the Globe itself."

1986   Draper, John W. "Hero and Theme in *Julius Caesar*." *RLMC*, 20 (1967), 30–34.

Argues that *JC* has no hero: The theme is that Rome needs a "Divine Right monarch," but no character appears as "God-Anointed" to act as the state's "personal savior." The tragic hero may be Rome itself.

1987   Driscoll, James P. *Identity in Shakespearean Drama*. Lewisburg, Pennsylvania: Bucknell U. P., 1983. 202 pp.

Includes, in the opening chapter, a discussion of *JC* that regards this play as a transitional work in which the character of Brutus hints at "an inner complexity" that is fully realized only in Sh's later tragic figures. Following Plutarch, Sh made Brutus superficially "noble and pure." He failed, however, to make Brutus "either realistic or self-critical." The audience cannot be allowed to see the passions that lie behind the sham logic of Brutus's orchard soliloquy (II.i) or the intimacy between Brutus and Portia because these things would threaten Brutus's noble image. Brutus, Cassius, and Caesar are all destroyed by the demands of their personae.

1987a   Durham, Mildred O. "Drama of the Dying God in *Julius Caesar*." *HSL*, 11 1979), 49–57.

Contends that Caesar is the central character in *JC*. He is godlike, and his death can be paralleled to "the drama of the dying god of the Hellenistic Mystery religions," which acted as an initiation ritual for the worshipers to insure their own resurrections. It is through the ritual nature of Caesar's death that Rome is reborn. He invites the conspirators into his house for wine, a kind of communion, before going to his death at the Senate; and the conspirators kneel ceremoniously to Caesar as they prepare to murder him. His spirit survives to witness the destruction of his murderers and the renewal of the city.

1988 Ebel, Henry. "Caesar's Wounds: A Study of William Shakespeare." *PsyR*, 62 (1975), 107–30.

Begins by describing Rome as "the theater of the Western unconscious" and proceeds to argue that in *JC* Sh surpassed the classical historians themselves in penetrating to the core of the Roman drama. Describes Sh as "the last and greatest of the Roman historians." Discusses several changes Sh made in his source material from Plutarch's *Lives* to expunge or qualify heterosexual or familial relationships and focus on the drama of Oedipal rebellion. The world of Rome is severely masculine, but the sublimated feminine principle appears in the homoerotic relationships in the play. Caesar himself is ambisexual—masculine in his fatherlike power and feminine in his fallibility and wounds. He thus has deeper roots in "the cosmos of the human psyche" than any other character. Brutus is the most masculine of the characters, obsessed with self-control; he is also the most neurotic. Sh's play portrays self-suppressive Stoicism as seriously flawed.

1989 Edelman, Edward. "Shakespeare's Tragedy of Definition." Ph.D. dissertation, Columbia University, 1969. *DAI*, 30 (1969–70), 1979-A.

Suggests a theory about mature Shakespearean tragedy: It is an attempt "to define the nature of 'reality'; the poet's main concern is rather with the intellectual shape of the world than with men, although a brilliant succession of men are his agents of discovery." Finds in *JC* a hero who is "a norm both of human excellence and of the nature of things for man."

1990 Edinborough, Arnold. "*Julius Caesar.*" *Manner and Meaning in Shakespeare.* (Stratford Papers, 1965–67.) Ed. B. A. W. Jackson. Hamilton, Ontario: McMaster U. Library P., 1969, pp. 129–44.

Argues that, having finished *H5*, Sh felt the need to probe more deeply into the "nature of politics, of government and monarchy." He chose Rome as his setting because to the Elizabethan mind "Roman history was the great place in which to interpret political motives and movements" and because Rome represented a pattern of "fictions, tumults and massacres" from which something might be learned. Sh breaks new ground in *JC* by looking beneath the surface of politics. Caesar is a proper ruler, but we see him "through the eyes of the conspirators": Brutus is the arch-conservative who is goaded into revolutionary action but is not able to take control of the revolution he has started; the people can be individually sharp-witted but are unruly in the mass and require a strong hand to govern them.

1991 Eriksen, Roy T. "Extant and in Choice Italian: Possible Italian Echoes in *Julius Caesar* and Sonnet 78." *ES*, 69 (1988), 224–37.

Suggests that Marullus's speech at the beginning of *JC* (I.i.37–55), which attempts to conjure up the image of a nobler heroic past featuring the conquests of Pompey, may be indebted to Tasso's *La Gerusalemme liberata*, especially with regard to the word "replication" (line 46).

1992 Faber, M. D. "Lord Brutus's Wife: A Modern View." *PsyR*, 52, no. 4 (1965–66), 109–15.

Rejects the generally favorable picture of Portia in *JC* drawn by recent critics. Argues that both in Plutarch and in Sh's play there is conclusive evidence that Brutus's wife is unstable, impulsive, dependent, deficient in self-knowledge, and prone to self-mutilation. Denies that a Tudor audience would have found anything praiseworthy in her behavior.

1993 Finkelstein, Sidney. "On Updating Shakespeare: Part I."*Mainstream*, 14, no. 7 (1961), 21–32.

Sees two main themes in *JC*. The first is "social" and involves the contradiction between "the ruling figures or those seeking rule" on the one hand, and the commoners

1994 Fleissner, R. F. "That Philosophy in *Julius Caesar* Again." *Archiv*, 222 (1985), 344–45.

Challenges and attempts to correct the opinion of Mark Sacharoff (item 2096) that, by "that philosophy" (*JC*, V.i.100), Brutus means Platonism. Maintains that Brutus anachronistically espouses Renaissance Stoicism in referring to "the philosophy of a prominent Roman Stoic (Cato), whom he had once admired and followed but whose cause he had to reject, in part, when he returned to Caesar." Finds it useful to consider *JC* in the light of the opposition to dramatic suicide expressed in *The Meditations of Marcus Aurelius*, although it is unlikely that Sh knew this work directly.

1995 Fleissner, Robert F. "'Non sanz droict': Law and 'Heraldry' in *Julius Caesar*." *HSL*, 9 (1977), 196–212.

Investigates the significance of the legal term *iusta causa*, "just cause," with regard to *JC*, Ben Jonson's comment on *JC*, and Sh's coat of arms. Suggests that Sh learned the phrase from Cicero or perhaps from a copy of *Archaionomia*, a law book that might have been in his possession. Notes that Jonson imputed the line "Caesar did never wrong, but with just cause" to Sh and considered it "ridiculous." Argues that the line was probably in *JC* originally and meant that Caesar believed he never did wrong, except, that is, "when he thought that he had legal justification for so doing." Jonson missed Sh's point, which was to reveal Caesar's willingness to cover up questionable activity by legal quibbling. Sh, however, revised the line anyway, perhaps because Jonson's needling also had reference to "his fuss about a coat of arms."

1996 Forrest, James P. "'Blocks' and 'Stones' in *Julius Caesar*." *N&Q*, 20 (1973), 134–35.

Suggests that Marullus's comment to the commoners (*JC*, I.i.35) is an echo of Golding's "To the Reader," prefatory to his translation of the *Metamorphoses*. In discussing metamorphosis, Golding says that when we lose ourselves to beastly lusts, we become "a block or stone."

1997 Fortin, René E. "*Julius Caesar*: An Experiment in Point of View." *SQ*, 19 (1968), 341–47.

Maintains that in *JC* Sh is primarily concerned with "the limitations of human knowledge." The play's structure can be seen as "a series of subject–object relationships," with Caesar as the primary "object of knowledge" and Brutus as the "principal subject." Through Brutus, Sh illustrates how subjectivity frustrates self-knowledge, which in turn impairs one's ability to know what is outside the self. The notion of misconstruing things, introduced in the play by Cicero, is the crucial point of a great many scenes involving most of the characters. Sh also draws the audience into the misconstruing by encouraging it to see things through the fallible eyes of first one and then another of the characters. The epistemological problem Sh explores in *JC* can be understood in terms of Stoic doctrine (passions cloud men's reason) or in terms of Montaigne's more modern skepticism about man's capacity for certitude. Revision of part of item 1998.

1998 Fortin, René Ernest. "The Dialectic of Point of View: An Approach to Meaning in *Richard II*, *Julius Caesar*, and *Hamlet*." Ph.D. dissertation, Brown University, 1964. *DA*, 25 (1964–65), 4686.

Argues that in three plays Sh carefully manipulates point of view to control meaning. In *JC*, the characters are subjected to limited points of view that "dramatize the limitations of human judgment, the source of errors which lead to their downfall." Part revised as item 1997.

1999 Fuzier, Jean. "Rhetoric versus Rhetoric: A Study of Shakespeare's *Julius Caesar*, Act III, Scene 2." *CahiersE*, 5 (1974), 25–65.

Calls attention to the considerable interest in rhetoric in 16th-c. England, the number of rhetorical handbooks produced during this period (twelve), and the compatibility of Elizabethan rhetorical theory with the classical precepts of Aristotle, Cicero, and Quintilian. Uses this background as a justification for a detailed rhetorical analysis and comparison of the two public speeches (by Brutus and Antony, respectively) in the wake of Caesar's assassination in *JC*. Each speech consists of an *exordium*, a three-part *oratio*, and a *peroratio*; each uses an abundance of figures derived from classical rhetoric; and each employs the three traditional appeals of *pathos*, *ethos*, and *logos*. In his prose oration, Brutus incorporates a higher proportion of figures than does Antony, and, being a Stoic, depends much more heavily on *logos* than on the other appeals. In several cases, Brutus is betrayed by his own artfulness. Antony, not being a Stoic, relies almost exclusively on *pathos*, and Sh further distinguishes him from Brutus by giving him vivid figures, which are more effective with the plebeian audience than Brutus's geometrically precise figures of symmetry, parallelism, and opposition. Especially effective weapons in Antony's arsenal are *irony* and *negatio* (calling attention to something by pretending not to mention it). Cites Plutarch's *Lives* to show that Sh had a great deal of freedom in fashioning Brutus's speech: Plutarch mentions that Brutus gave two speeches, which Sh conflates into one; and the source says little about the content of Brutus's orations, leaving the way open for Sh to assign him a highly abstract, artificial address. Interestingly, one might expect that, of the three types of public discourse distinguished by the ancient rhetoricians—political, forensic, and epideictic—Brutus, in this situation, would deliver a political speech, while Antony would attempt an epideictic (panegyric) oration. Instead, they both engage in forensic discourse, which attempts "to defend or condemn someone's actions"; and Antony, though he starts at a disadvantage, emerges as the winner of the competition. Concludes with two appendices: The first diagrams the structure of Brutus's oration; and the second lists the figures used by Brutus alone, by Brutus and Antony, and by Antony alone.

2000 Gardner, C. O. "Shakespeare: Some Recent Critical Approaches." *Theoria*, 56 (1981), 15–24.

Describes the main tendencies of recent structuralist, Marxist, and post-structuralist criticism, especially the challenges of these schools to traditional or liberal criticism. Considers a "liberal" article written by the author eleven years ago on how we should judge Brutus in *JC* (item 0427) in light of the newer approaches and calls for a partnership of new and old criticism, beginning with "a language in which the the *productiveness* of literature (and indeed of reality) and their *producedness* are properly and subtly intertwined."

2001 Gill, Roma. "The Craft of Shakespeare's Art." *AJES*, 10 (1985), 9–16.

Discusses the changes Sh made in his source, Plutarch's *Lives*, in crafting the first three acts of *JC*. Focuses on the alterations in sequencing and pacing. For example, in the first act, the feast of Lupercal is superimposed on Caesar's Triumph after the Battle of Munda. In I.iii, it should be noticed that a "multiple time-scheme" is in operation. From the beginning of act II, things slow down: Time now passes "from hour to hour" instead of "from month to month" (as in act I).

2002 Girard, René. "Collective Violence and Sacrifice in Shakespeare's *Julius Caesar*." *Salmagundi*, 88–89 (1990–91), 399–419.

Views *JC* as a tragedy of "mimetic desire." Brutus loves Caesar, wants to be like Caesar, wants to have what Caesar has (Rome). This leads to rivalry and then hatred. Follows the "logic of mimetic rivalry and mimetic contagion" through the play, showing how the conspiracy is "a mimetic association of murderers." As the process continues, the rivals become doubles of each other until "the entire community" is divided into two opposing armies that can do nothing but go to war with each other. The real subjects of the play are "collective violence and sacrifice."

2002a Gless, Darryl J. "*Julius Caesar*, Allan Bloom, and the Value of Pedagogical Pluralism." *Shakespeare Left and Right*. Ed. Ivo Kamps. New York: Routledge, 1991, pp. 185–203.

Counters Allan Bloom's narrow and anti-demoncratic reading of *JC* by emphasizing a more inclusive interpretation. Challenges, for example, the views that the commoners in the play are insolent and that all is well in the marriage of Brutus and Portia. More in accord with the complexities of the text is a recognition that characters like Brutus have no settled bearings and are in the process of constructing their own meaning and indeed their very identities as the play proceeds.

2003 Goy-Blanquet, Dominique. "'Death or Liberty': The Fashion in Shrouds." *CahiersE*, 38 (1990), 25–40.

Discusses opinion on suicide in the Roman Republic and early Empire as background for Brutus's suicide in *JC*. Contrasts the suicide of Cato, who killed himself to show his rejection of tyranny, with that of Brutus, who, in Sh's play, perverts "the Republican ideal of man's freedom" into a terrorist's contempt for human life.

2004 Green, André. "Moral Narcissism." *International Journal of Psychoanalytical Psychotherapy*, 8 (1980–81), 243–69.

Cites Brutus, who in *JC* "assassinates for virtue," as a heroic figure of moral narcissism.

2005 Green, David C. "*Julius Caesar*" and Its Sources. (JDS 86.) Salzburg: Institut für Anglistik und Amerikanistik, U. of Salzburg, 1979. 129 pp.

Compares in detail *JC* and Plutarch's *Lives*, the source of the play. Sh, who is sympathetic to Caesar as a representative of monarchy, enhances him politically (Plutarch points out a number of his misdeeds) and belittles him personally (his deafness and boasting are Sh's additions). Sh improvises a good deal in his ambiguous portrait of Antony, and his characters of Cicero and Octavius are inadequate and sketchy. Brutus remains essentially the admirable figure he is in Plutarch: Sh simply makes him more admirable by omitting the one fault—paying his unruly soldiers 2000 drachmas apiece—ascribed to him by Plutarch. Properly understood, Brutus does not have the flaws usually attributed to him. He is not an impractical idealist, for example: His objections to including Cicero in the conspiracy and to killing Antony are practical ones he is not given in Plutarch. Nor is Brutus self-deluded. His speech at Caesar's funeral is, in the circumstances, a shrewd one. During the quarrel with Cassius, Brutus is under complete control of himself, while Cassius, by contrast, behaves like a spoiled child. In *JC*, "Sh has created a tragic hero without a flaw."

2006 Greene, Gayle. "The Language of Brutus's Soliloquy: Similitude and Self-Deception in Shakespeare's *Julius Caesar*." *Humanitas: Essays in Honor of Ralph Ross*. Ed. Quincy Howe Jr. Claremont, California: Scripps College, 1977, pp. 74–86.

Analyzes the soliloquy (*JC*, II.i) in which Brutus decides to become part of the conspiracy to murder Caesar. Brutus's language reveals him to be reasoning by analogy or similitude, a procedure that rhetoricians of Sh's day warned against. This faulty decision and others (to risk everything at Philippi and not to kill Antony) are made by Brutus when he obscures the particulars of each situation by thinking in metaphors. In *JC*, Sh is engaged, among other things, in a sophisticated exploration of Rome's fascination with rhetoric: The play is structured "on a series of persuasion scenes"; there are victims (Brutus) and clever manipulators (Antony) of words; and there is an implicit skepticism about knowledge and language. Revision of part of item 2008.

2007 Greene, Gayle. "'The Power of Speech / To Stir Men's Blood': The Language of Tragedy in Shakespeare's *Julius Caesar*." *RenD*, N. S. 11 (1980), 67–93.

Maintains that in *JC* Sh emphasizes the negative potentials of language. Rome is a city of expert speakers whose adroit manipulation of words obscures truth. In four crucial scenes involving persuasion—Cassius's seduction of Brutus, Brutus's talking himself into the assassination, Brutus's funeral oration, and Antony's funeral oration—we see language working to mask political and moral reality. Cassius wins Brutus over by appealing obliquely to his vanity and pride; Brutus's dialogue with himself moves between apothegmatic pronouncements on human behavior and metaphors to illustrate the pronouncements, without consideration of the specific case of Caesar. Brutus's speech to the people is brilliantly contrived to create the illusion of a reasonable man in control when the reality is quite different, and Antony's oration is effective because it makes skillful use of irony and *pathos*, with no regard to truth. Sh's various criticisms of language are integrated into "an epistemological focus which is central to the play's tragic vision." Revision of part of item 2008.

2008 Greene, Gayle Jacoba. "'Contract of Error': The Thematic Function of Language in Shakespeare's *Julius Caesar*." Ph.D. dissertation, Columbia University, 1974. *DAI*, 37 (1976–77), 4367-A.

Argues that Sh depicts in *JC* a culture "in terms of its language." The values of Roman society are closely allied with the "notion of honor as name, fame, or reputation," and the way the characters speak and think of themselves is determined by this notion. In this context, language is habitually used as "an instrument of appearance, in the presentation of self and manipulation of others." Analyzes three crucial scenes (I.ii, Cassius's "seduction" of Brutus; II.ii, Brutus's soliloquy, in which he convinces himself of the need to murder Caesar; and III.ii, in which Brutus and Antony persuade the populace to accept their differing views of Caesar's death) in which language is used "to construe things . . . clean from the purpose of the things themselves" (I.ii.34–35). Thus *JC* abounds in implied criticisms of language, suggesting that there is great danger "inherent in man's verbal medium." Parts revised as items 2006 and 2007.

2009 Hager, Alan. "'The Teeth of Emulation': Failed Sacrifice in Shakespeare's *Julius Caesar*." *UC*, 8 (1988), 54–68.

Argues that in *JC* Sh dramatizes the reversion of man to a savage state by foregrounding the motif of failed sacrifice. The play opens with the tribunes disrupting an observation of "Rome's primeval sacrificial rite"; the conspirators attempt a ritual sacrifice of Caesar that fails "because it lacks 'general' sanction"; the plebeians echo Brutus's irrational prosecution of Caesar when they murder Cinna for arbitrary reasons; and the assassination of Caesar is linked to that of Pompey and to other group murders that failed to contain violence. Led by Cassius, Brutus emulates Caesar (though unconsciously) in a variety of ways, most notably in several flaws that mark "a disability of rule," thereby making his brief replacement of Caesar as the "model for emulation in a society sick with turmoil" no cure for that society's ills. Revised as chapter 5 of item 0475.

2010 Halio, Jay L. "*Hamartia*, Brutus, and the Failure of Personal Confrontation." *Personalist*, 48 (1967), 42–55.

Discusses the nature of *hamartia*, or tragic error, in *JC*, a "tragedy of dilemma," where it is not immediately clear what choice the protagonist should make. Brutus's problem is that although he loves Caesar well, he would not have him made king. An abstractionist, Brutus is unable to confront Caesar as a friend and seek a resolution to the problem. The play makes clear that Brutus does have alternatives: He could see Caesar's ambition as another personal infirmity to be cured rather than an illness of the state requiring purgation. Brutus never achieves full awareness of his basic error, and thus the play "lacks the power" of Sh's later tragedies. It is important, though, that Brutus does change toward the end by responding to Cassius's friendship in a personal way that was not possible for him with Caesar.

2011 Hampton, Timothy. *Writing from History: The Rhetoric of Exemplarity in Renaissance Literature*. Ithaca, New York: Cornell U. P., 1990. xiii + 309 pp.

Chapter 5 stresses that *JC* is a study of the difficulties involved in transferring nobility or virtue through time. In examining two virtuously exemplary figures (Caesar and Brutus) and setting them in contrast to each other, Sh alters the procedure of his source, Plutarch's *Lives*, which had compared each to another, similar figure. Sh's treatment makes each a divided, ambiguous character, embodying "the tension between public virtue and private virtue." The phrase "noble Roman," which occurs frequently in the play, is an indication that the portrayed conflicts grow out of aristocratic attempts to control the meaning of Roman history, indeed to define *Romanitas*. Discusses the slipperiness of language, the effectiveness of Antony's funeral oration in its use of both oral and written (Caesar's will) discourse, and the connection between "artistic performance and political action." Notes that in the world of *JC* "the excellence of ancient heroism" is undermined, while at the same time the value of heroic action is questioned because it is linked to theatrical performance.

2012 Hapgood, Robert. "Shakespeare's Delayed Reactions." *EIC*, 13 (1963), 9–16.

Maintains that *JC* is one of three plays in which Sh leads the audience to one view of a central event and then attempts a reversal of that view by a "delayed reaction." Initially, we favor the conspirators and oppose Caesar, but after the assassination, we shift our sympathies because of Antony's oration and the civil disorder caused by Caesar's death. Things that earlier counted against Caesar (such as his scenes with Calpurnia) now reflect favorably on him, and things that earlier counted for the conspirators (such as Brutus's concern with honor) now count against them.

2013 Hapgood, Robert. "Speak Hands for Me: Gesture as Language in *Julius Caesar*." *Drama Survey*, 5 (1966–67), 162–70. Reprint. *Essays in Shakespearean Criticism*. Eds. James L. Calderwood and Harold E. Toliver. Englewood Cliffs, New Jersey: Prentice Hall, 1970, pp. 415–22.

Analyzes the gestures in *JC*, which include "stabbing; rising; falling; leading; following; gathering; dispersing; shaking hands, weeping, and other 'shows of love.'" All of these gestures occur in patterns, the most prominent one being that of reversal, best illustrated by the way in which "the stabs by Caesar's assassins return to their own proper entrails." In the course of the play, gestures are "twisted from their normal significance," and then at the end "return to norm." Brutus participates in the reversal pattern, but "his characteristic pattern is one of emergence, in which a gesture is first restrained and then progressively released." Sh's use of gestural patterns in *JC* implies a critique of the Roman world, where "spontaneous, direct expression of natural impulses is regarded as a weakness."

2013a Hartsock, Mildred E. "The Complexity of *Julius Caesar*." *PMLA*, 81 (1966), 56–62.

Rehearses the conflicting critical views of *JC* as preparation for arguing the point that the ambiguities of the play cannot be resolved. Examines Plutarch's *Lives*, Sh's source, to show that the playwright intended to leave us in a state of suspended judgment about the key issues. For example, Plutarch's Caesar is clearly "a potential tyrant," while Sh makes him "a doubtful figure"; in Plutarch, Antony appears "in a consistently bad light," while in Sh he is both a genuinely compassionate figure and a "shrewd contriver"; for Plutarch, Brutus is a true patriot, but Sh complicates his character with pride, intellectual confusion, and flawed judgment; in Sh, the Roman people are markedly more volatile than they are in Plutarch. Through *JC*, we come to understand that history is a construct.

2014 Hatlen, Burton. "A World Without Absolutes: Dialectic in Shakespeare's *Julius Caesar*." *Proceedings of the PMR Conference: Annual Publication of the International Patristic, Mediaeval, and Renaissance Conference*, 3 (1978), 167–82.

Observes a dialectical process at work in *JC*. Each of four major characters attempts to name and thereby define Rome, and each generates different or opposite meanings from what he intends. Brutus sets himself up as the guardian of what he sees as the supreme Roman virtue, *pietas*, the reverence for public good and household gods; he is obsessed with purity. In contrast to the self-effacement of Brutus, Caesar's egotism prompts him to regard Rome as an extension of himself. Unlike Brutus and Caesar, Cassius is a nihilist, refusing to affirm any idea of Rome. Antony tends to see Rome as a theater in which various historical personages act their parts. His conception is more comprehensive than any of the others, but, being subject to the dialectical process itself, it cannot provide an ultimate definition of the city. Other dialectics in the play include those between "what we hear" and what we see on stage, what readers and audiences of the Christian era know and what "the characters in the play know," the political situation of Sh's time and the political situation of Rome, and "the structures we create to contain history" (like *JC*) and "history itself." Though he dallies with the possibility that the creation of a play world might transcend this dialectical process, Sh finally acknowledges that all such endeavors "become actions in history."

2015 Hawkins, Harriett. "Likeness with Difference: Patterns of Action in *Romeo and Juliet, Julius Caesar*, and *Macbeth*." *Maryland English Journal*, 6, no. 2 (1968), 1–13.

Considers Sh's juxtaposition of "actions that parallel, and simultaneously, contrast with each other" as a major organizing principle in *Rom.*, *JC*, and *Mac*. Sh's contemporaries had ambivalent views on the assassination of Caesar, some abhorring the murder of a man in authority and some applauding the destruction of a tyrant. Sh exploits a similar ambivalence in *JC*, balancing "scenes [that] present various characters in an unfavorable light" with "scenes [that] present them in a favorable light." The cause of tragedy in *JC* is the misconstruction of men and events by several characters. This emphasis on misconstruction can be illustrated by the series of parallel death scenes: those of Caesar, Cinna, and Cassius.

2016 Hawkins, Harriett. *Likenesses of Truth in Elizabethan and Restoration Drama*. Oxford: Clarendon P., 1972. xi + 174 pp.

Challenges modern moralistic critics, who make severe judgments about characters in 17th-c. drama according to a standardized world picture. This kind of approach fails to come to terms with either the literal or emotional truth that the plays express. The final chapter explores *JC* as a political tragedy of misconstruction: A series of misunderstandings on the part of the major characters creates the tragic pattern. For example, Caesar errs in trusting Brutus, Brutus in trusting Antony; Caesar, Brutus, and Cassius all err in assessing their own abilities as well as the motives of others. No easy judgment is possible on the characters, and Sh drives this point home by suggesting that the audience may be susceptible to misconstruing things as well.

2017 Henry, Karen S. "The Shattering of Resemblance: The Mirror in Shakespeare." Ph.D. dissertation, Tufts University, 1989. *DAI*, 50 (1989–90), 1664-A.

Analyzes Sh's use of the mirror metaphor as indicative of his (and his characters') increasing awareness of "the split between words and things," a split that occurred near the end of the 16th c. in Western culture. Includes discussion of *JC*.

2018 Henze, Richard. "Power and Spirit in *Julius Caesar.*" *University Review*, 36 (1970), 307–14.

Maintains that the primary conflict in the play is "not between Caesar and Brutus but between the two sides of the force of power." One side is that every man wants power over others, and the other is that each man has the need to "surrender to some force greater than himself." Marullus and Flavius fail to gain power over Caesarism in the opening scene because the commoners insist on giving power to someone. After Caesar's death, the commoners empower Brutus and then Antony. Brutus, despite his republican intentions, assumes power at Caesar's death; he never understands that the assassination, far from destroying Caesar's spirit, has released it to range freely.

2019 Herbert, Edward T. "Myth and Archetype in *Julius Caesar.*" *PsyR*, 57 (1970), 303–08.

Interprets *JC* mythically, as the "dramatization of an archetypal situation such as that discussed by Freud in *Totem and Taboo.*" In the play, we can see the attitude of the primal horde, who worship their clan leader as a god one day and on the next slay him as a criminal. In *JC*, as in primitive tribal contexts, hostility toward the ruler is disguised as a ceremonial. Other resemblances between *JC* and primitive clan sacrifices are that the slaying is communal and that the victim becomes "a kind of archetypal father."

2020 Item deleted.

2021 Hoey, M. P., and E. O. Winter. "'Believe Me for Mine Honour.'" *Lang&S*, 14 (1981), 315–39.

Provides a stylistic analysis of the speeches by Brutus and Antony at Caesar's funeral (*JC*, III.ii). Pays particular attention to clause construction in showing that Brutus uses a highly rhetorical technique that is at first successful in persuading the plebeians but which has serious weaknesses that Antony then exploits to change their minds. Brutus employs matching contrast and repetition to remove himself from responsibility for Caesar's murder and indeed to reduce the harshness of the deed itself. He then launches a series of rhetorical questions whose inevitably negative answers appear to clear him from having committed any offense. The two weaknesses in Brutus's argument are that he produces no evidence for his assertion that Caesar was ambitious and that he makes belief in his assertion "solely dependent on belief in his own honor." Antony mentions these two claims as being consistent with each other but shows that they are at odds with his own claim about Caesar. He then uses several "situation-evaluation" clauses that question the existence of ambition in Caesar. Finally, he gives evidence that Caesar was not ambitious.

2022 Homan, Sidney. "Dion, Alexander and Demetrius—Plutarch's Forgotten *Parallel Lives*—as Mirrors for Shakespeare's *Julius Caesar.*" *ShakS*, 8 (1975), 195–210.

Recommends study of the three Greek lives—those of Dion, Alexander, and Demetrius—that Plutarch paralleled to the three Roman lives of Brutus, Caesar, and Antony, respectively, to gain a better understanding of the three Romans as they appear in *JC* and to appreciate more fully Sh's use of his source material. Some of Brutus's flaws—his moral righteousness, his inflexibility, his harsh personal code, and his snobbishness—can be found in the parallel *Life of Dion*. Both Dion and Brutus are students of philosophy, both murder their best friend, both are liberators, and both are rebels against established order. Plutarch's brief "Comparison" of Brutus and Dion presents a Brutus much like the one Sh gives us in the last two acts of *JC*: a weary man whose idealism has been compromised by war. Alexander's *Life*, which Plutarch parallels to Caesar's, has the effect of making Caesar seem more temperate, which is in harmony with the impression one receives from *JC*. Finally, the *Life of Demetrius* emphasizes Demetrius's sense of theater and of acting a role, which may have influenced Sh's treatment of Antony.

2022a Honigmann, E. A. J. "Politics, Rhetoric and Will-Power in Julius Caesar." *Myriad-Minded Shakespeare: Essays, Chiefly on the Tragedies and Problem Comedies.* New York: St. Martin's P., 1989, pp. 21–42.

Notes, in attempting to account for the complexity of *JC*, that it was Sh's "first mature play with a consciously non-Christian background." Refers to the ways in which Sh's portrayals of his Roman characters surprise those familiar with the Caesar story; for example, most of Caesar's weaknesses are added by the playwright, and Antony, instead of the powerful politician he is in Plutarch, is "something close to a lackey." Contends that Sh, in competition with playwrights who had a university education, decided to exhibit for his audience a new rhetoric "loosely based on Latin models in its self-conscious artistry, its sheer professionalism." Suggests that the "classical" flavor of *JC* is due to the "high concentration" of Roman allusions and, even more, to the great skill with which most of the characters are able to deploy the traditional Roman arts of persuasion. Given this situation, it is noteworthy when characters fail to speak well. Sh includes "a full rhetorical range, from formal orations and other long set speeches that set out to persuade down to mumbled excuses and near-helpless echoing of what another has said." Argues that strength of spirit, or will, is set in contrast to rhetoric and is finally the force that determines the course of events. That is, characters such as Brutus and Caesar often impose their wills despite the power of rhetoric or even reason that may be arrayed against them. Concludes with an explanation why act V, which on one level is a stitching-together of the last, confused events in "the lives of the principal conspirators," seems to represent a loss of power: Just beneath the surface "it retraverses the ground of the first four acts, and suggests that history keeps on repeating itself."

2023 Humphreys, Arthur. "The Death of Portia: To Cut or Not to Cut?" *KM 80: A Birthday Album for Kenneth Muir, Tuesday, 5 May 1987.* Liverpool: Liverpool U. P. for Private Circulation, [1987], pp. 74–75.

Surveys the conflicting scholarly opinions about the dual accounts of Portia's death in *JC*, IV.iii, one given privately by Brutus to Cassius and the other given publicly by Messala. Concludes that both accounts should stand as they are, with the first showing Brutus's deep personal emotion and the second presenting "the self-controlled leader making no public demonstration of distress."

2024 Humphreys, Arthur, ed. *Julius Caesar.* (Oxford Shakespeare.) Oxford: Clarendon P., 1984. ix + 253 pp.

The introduction includes a consideration of what Sh found in his primary source, Plutarch's *Lives*: "Good narrative and biographies vividly set within their times, their subjects shrewdly analysed as to qualities and motives, and seen to be controlled by a shaping destiny." Notes that from the first three quarters of Plutarch's *Life* of Caesar Sh took a few details but that the fourth quarter furnished the playwright with the essential events of the play. Provides a "consecutive discussion" of Sh's shaping of Plutarch, noting the use of the lives of Caesar, Brutus, and Antonius. A particularly masterful instance of remodeling is the combination of three incidents from the *Life* of Brutus in the construction of the scene of the quarrel and reconciliation of Brutus and Cassius (IV.ii). Sh condenses and rearranges, "to create a plot comprising the conspiracy's rise and fall, and Caesar's bodily defeat and spiritual triumph." Mentions other possible sources, like Appian's *Chronicle of the Romans' Wars,* the anonymous *Tragedy of Caesar and Pompey,* R. Grenewey's translation of Tacitus's *Annals,* and Kyd's *Cornelia.* There are parallels for some of the portents of Caesar's death in Ovid's *Metamorphoses,* Lucan's *Pharsalia,* and Virgil's *Georgics.* Maintains that Sh conveys a genuine sense of the characteristic greatness of Rome in the context of the Renaissance's reading of history as presenting "Roman arms triumphant abroad, and the Roman state stormily evolving at home." Sh explores the Roman struggle to achieve nobility, to live up to the code of honor through public service. Surveys the variety of views from antiquity through the Renaissance on two key questions, that of the relative worth of "republican virtue" and "imperial tyranny" and that of private morality under "political pressure." Explains that the style of *JC* is "lucid and

Julius Caesar

vigorous" (in accord with its *romanitas*), primarily public, expository, and disciplined, but also picturesque.

2025 Isler, Alan D. "Sidney, Shakespeare, and the 'Slain–notslain.'" *UTQ*, 37 (1967–68), 175–85.

Contends that Sir Philip Sidney's treatment of the slaughter of rioting rebels by aristocrats in the *Arcadia* is intended to be humorous: The rebels are cardboard figures who should not engage our sympathy. In Sh, comic riot in serious circumstances is portrayed in the Jack Cade episode of *2H6* and in the murder of Cinna the poet in *JC*. In Cinna's case, the comic aspect of the death reestablishes aesthetic distance for the audience after so much bloodshed.

2026 Jump, John. "Shakespeare and History." *CritQ*, 17 (1975), 233–44.

Argues that *JC* is the culmination of Sh's "progress through the long line of English history plays." In this play, Sh depicts a society moving from "a republican to a monarchist political system." Monarchy is in favor. In these circumstances, Sh explores various types of political behavior. Henry V's qualities are here distributed among several characters.

2027 Kanzer, Mark. "Shakespeare's Dog Images—Hidden Keys to *Julius Caesar*." *AI*, 36 (1979), 2–31.

Traces two dog images in *JC*, "the candy-licking dog" and "the hunter," discovering images of "the heart" and "blood" that are frequently associated with them. Uses these images to develop certain interpretations of the play: Caesar's rise and fall seem to be based on "traditional battles between the Winter King and the Summer King"; the relationship between Brutus and Cassius is characterized by "latent homosexuality and misogyny"; and the conspirators can be seen as "sons" relating to a "primal father." The dog images also provide an insight into Sh's "inner reality," a paranoid world where "familiar friends" are transformed into fiendish enemies.

2028 Kaufmann, R. J., and Clifford J. Ronan. "Shakespeare's *Julius Caesar*: An Apollonian and Comparative Reading." *CompD*, 4 (1970), 18–51.

Proposes an Apollonian reading of *JC* as a complement to Peter S. Anderson's Dionysian approach (item 1941). In the late 16th c., English dramatists were influenced by Plutarch, Montaigne, Seneca, and Lipsius to make "a four-way identification between stoic, constant, heroic, and Roman behavior." Sh fully assimilates this identification in *JC* and provides "a painstaking and powerful narrative investigation of the psychological and moral implications of living under the twin Roman ideals so frequently discussed in the Renaissance: stony constancy and fiery spirit." The quarrel scene (IV.ii and iii), for example, is "an emblem-in-action of Roman strivings after the appearance and reality of fiery constancy." Portia's suicide, reported in IV.iii, exposes the "self-exhausting nature of Stoic composure," and provides a link between "the two archetypal Republican suicides who so interested the Renaissance": those of her father and her husband. The suicide of Brutus "shows him to be a viable model of conventional Roman manliness and at the same time a weak and inconsistent—which is to say a deeply human—person." Elsewhere in the play (as in the final speeches of Caesar) Roman constancy is also subjected to ironic questioning. The more active, aggressive side of Roman manhood is shown through characters other than Brutus (for example, Titinius). In *JC*, Sh shows that "true Roman manhood" is nearly impossible for the individual, no matter what form of government he lives under. Brutus seems to be the only one to have managed it.

2029 Kaula, David. "'Let Us Be Sacrificers': Religious Motifs in *Julius Caesar*." *ShakS*, 14 (1971), 197–214.

Discovers in *JC* a typological mode of expression that casts many of the characters and events in religious terms. Sh adds several portents to those found in Plutarch, apparently drawing on biblical accounts of Doomsday, and has Brutus think of the assassination as a "dignified ritual." One effect of all this is to enhance Caesar's importance as a "quasi-divine" figure who is both a mortal man and a god. In stripping the images of ceremonial decorations, the tribunes (I.i) are behaving like 16th-c. Protestant reformers, as is Cassius in his objections to Caesar's assumption of godlike powers. Cassius's Puritan qualities are emphasized: Unlike Antony, he dislikes plays. Caesar is given "pontifical" tendencies, and Antony provides a "Catholic" appreciation of Caesar, speaking of him as a bleeding victim and referring to his blood as a source of relics. Brutus also resorts to religious ideas and imagery: He wishes to shape the murder of Caesar into an impersonal sacrifice, exhorting the conspirators, in terms reminiscent of the Anglican homily on preparation for taking the Sacrament, to be worthy of the ritual in which they are about to participate. Of course, significant ironies are involved: Brutus and his colleagues treat Caesar hypocritically, betraying their principles and producing a "disastrous imitation of true redemptive action." Religious ideas and language allow glimpses of the ideals of mystical union in marriage, among brothers, and throughout society, but such glimpses operate ironically, to show how far the ideal is from being realized.

2030   Kearney, Colbert. "The Nature of an Insurrection." *Studies*, 63 (1974), 141–52.

Suggests that *JC* follows what Jan Kott calls the Grand Mechanism, a pattern according to which the end of a history play returns to the point from which it began. In this case, "Caesarism," the unbridled rule of one man, is just as much a concern in the last act as it is in the first. Sh explores Brutus's development of Caesarism through his family pride, his domination of the conspiracy, and his quarreling with Cassius. In his encounter with the Ghost and his suicide, Brutus glimpses that he both exemplifies and is victimized by Caesarism. In Plutarch, the ghost is simply Brutus's evil spirit, and Brutus is unafraid. Sh, in order to represent the connection in Brutus's mind between himself and Caesar, between his own autocratic tendencies and those of the man he murdered, has the Ghost unsettle him as his "evil spirit" in the form of Caesar.

2031   Kennedy, George. "Antony's Speech at Caesar's Funeral." *QJS*, 54 (1968), 99–106.

Contends that the historical Antony did not deliver the speech Sh composed for him in *JC* or "a traditional Roman funeral laudation either." Surveys ancient sources, including Cicero, Appian, Plutarch, and Dio Cassius, to reach a "probable conclusion" about what happened at Caesar's funeral. Antony first read, or had a herald read, "decrees of the senate granting honors to Caesar, and he commented briefly on each." When he sensed that "he had the crowd's sympathy, he continued with a *miseratio* for Caesar," which included "reference to Caesar's favors to those who killed him." As the speech became increasingly dramatic, "a voice or voices cried out from Caesar's corpse, a wax image of his wounded body was revealed, and Antony showed the tunic [that] Caesar was wearing when he died." This last portion, called by Cicero the *cohortatio*, or emotional appeal, caused a riot.

2032   Kinney, Joseph A. Jr. "Dramatization of Fear in Elizabethan Political Plays, 1580–1600." Ph.D. dissertation, Bryn Mawr College, 1967. *DA*, 29 (1969), 2265-A-2266-A.

Describes certain techniques of structure, character, language, and the supernatural used to dramatize fear in Elizabethan political plays. The final chapter is devoted to *JC*, the last political play of the 16th c., and shows that Sh employs, at various points, most of the ways of dramatizing fear in earlier plays.

2033   Knight, W. Nicholas. "Brutus' Motivation and Melancholy." *UC*, 5 (1984), 108–24.

Argues that in *JC* Brutus is a type of the Elizabethan revenger, driven to a state of distraction by melancholy. Plutarch is the source for Brutus's melancholia, but he offers an analysis of this condition through a speech by Cassius just before Philippi, whereas Sh dramatizes a good deal of the evidence for Brutus's mental disturbance before the assassination. This evidence includes sleeplessness, the use of "figures and phantasmas to cover reality," the opinion of Portia that her husband is ill, overmuch concern with books and study, disordered clothing, careless exposure of himself to the elements, contemplation of suicide, and the driving of his wife to suicide. With his madness, Brutus deceives himself and thus fulfills the atavistic role of his ancestor Junius Brutus. Revision of part of item 2036.

2034 Knight, W. Nicholas. "*Julius Caesar*: A Case of Pre- and Post-Christian Story." *C&L*, 28, no. 4 (1979), 27–35.

Contends that *JC* contains clear analogues to the events leading up to the Crucifixion and the Crucifixion itself (feasting, betrayal, sacrifice). Furthermore, Antony's speech over Caesar's body, along with the ritual elements suggested by the action, parallel aspects of the Mass but work against its intents. Sh is darkly hinting at the power of Christian salvation but deliberately frustrates Christian expectations for the pagan world of Caesar.

2035 Knight, W. Nicholas. "*Julius Caesar* and Shakespearean Revenge Tragedy." *ErasmusR*, 1 (1971), 19–34.

Connects *JC* to the Kydian school of revenge tragedy by examining it in relation to *The Spanish Tragedy, Tit.*, and *Ham.* Elements that *JC* shares with other revenge tragedies include the return of the conquering hero, feasting, references to the spoils of war, and the establishment of peace. In the revenge play tradition, as in *JC*, the hero's "prior outrage to a victim is crucial to the opening action." If Brutus, Caesar's instrument, is seen as the revenge hero throughout the play and as the victim in the second half, then *JC* does not change genres in the middle or fall into two halves. It has a structure unified by the revenge conventions. Revision of part of item 2036.

2036 Knight, William Nicholas. "*Julius Caesar* and Revenge Structures." Ph.D. dissertation, Indiana University, 1968. *DA*, 29 (1968–69), 1513-A.

Contends that the structure of *JC* follows the pattern of Elizabethan revenge tragedies. The pattern is initiated through a military triumph by the tragic hero; the object of outrages previously committed by the hero appears, and a conspiracy against the hero that includes characters who are related to each other and to the victim then evolves. There is mental disorder in some of the characters, and the play ends with "words of fate and fatalism on the part of those who will complete the final revenge." Parts revised as items 2033 and 2035.

2036a Knights, L. C. "Personality and Politics in *Julius Caesar*." *Anglica*, April, 1964, 1–24.

Suggests that *JC* focuses on the attempt by several characters "to make public action and public appearances something separate and remote from personal action."

2037 Kraemer, Don J. Jr. "'Alas, thou hast misconstrued everything': Amplifying Words and Things in *Julius Caesar*." *Rhetorica*, 9 (1991), 165–78.

Analyzes the forum speeches of Brutus and Antony in *JC* (III.ii) to exhibit "two ways of seizing and controlling situations." Brutus employs what Quintilian had called the ethical appeal, which depends on "propriety and good manners" to invoke the audience's friendship. In making the ethical argument that Caesar was dangerously ambitious, Brutus amplifies his point by using figures of speech like *enumeratio*, anaphoric isocolon, antithesis, *taxis*, rhetorical questions, and *sententia*. Antony, on the other hand, depends on Quintilian's pathetic appeal, which invokes the audience's love. Antony's use of figures of thought like *interruptio* (pausing in a speech as if unable to proceed) and *praeteritio* (emphasizing something by pretending to pass over it) compels the plebeians "to make their own inferences" from what he shows them and to act on the basis of these inferences. In this instance, Antony is victorious, but he is denied ultimate victory. Thus the play interrogates "the nature of persuasion itself": The prescriptions of rhetoric, as understood by the Renaissance humanists, operate to destabilize political situations.

2038   Kurland, Stuart M. "'No Innocence Is Safe, When Power Contests': The Factional Worlds of *Caesar* and *Sejanus*." *CompD*, 22 (1988), 56–67.

Analyzes the two plays in light of contemporary English history, especially the rivalry between the Earl of Essex and Robert Cecil. Sh's treatment of two matters, power and how it is transferred and dynastic issues, seems not to have occasioned official concern, unlike the handling of these matters in *Sejanus*. Sh, while aware of dynastic concerns, does not stress them.

2039   Levang, Lewis D. "$Cinna_1$ is not $Cinna_2$." *ETC: A Review of General Semantics*, 23 (1966), 76–77.

Points to a clear illustration of Sh's handling of semantic ambiguity in *JC*, III.iii, when the mob tears Cinna the poet to pieces despite his protestations that he is not Cinna the conspirator. Here one symbol (the name Cinna) has two references (the poet and the conspirator). The mob refuses to deal with referents and chooses instead to consider only the symbol.

2040   Liebler, Naomi Conn. "'Thou Bleeding Piece of Earth': The Ritual Ground of *Julius Caesar*." *ShakS*, 14 (1981), 175–96.

Points out that the significance of the opening of *JC* during the Lupercalia has not been properly appreciated. The Lupercalia—"Rome's most ancient ritual of purgation and fertility"—provides a background for understanding the political and religious changes going on in Rome and sets a context for Brutus's attempt to ritualize Caesar's assassination and the ultimate failure of his plan. Sh could have found particulars about the Lupercalia in Plutarch's *Life of Romulus*, which identifies the festival as an important ceremony for holding society together. With the contention between the tribunes and the tradesmen about the nature of Lupercalian celebrations, Sh reveals the ambivalence over ritual in a changing Rome. Marullus prefigures Brutus's conservatism when he attempts to restore traditional significance to the festival, while the commoners want to focus their rejoicing on Caesar himself. Brutus's effort to cast the assassination into the form of a ritual sacrifice is an attempt to assert traditional values, not, as some have argued, a way to demonstrate how bloodthirsty he is. Antony also espouses a sacramental system, but it is the "new" one invented by Caesar, which results in chaos and destruction. Brutus fails because he is unable to see where the tide of history is taking him. Sh's references to the Lupercalia would have struck sympathetic chords in Elizabethan audiences, since they were surrounded by analogous folk festivals.

2041   Low, J. T. "*Julius Caesar*: A Note on Its Stage Rhythms and Patterns." *LanM*, 62, no. 2, (1968), 88–93.

Suggests that *JC* is composed of two large movements, the first extending through act III and the second covering acts IV and V. To understand how the play should be presented, we need to visualize the pattern of each movement (for example, the first sequence is initiated and concluded by crowd scenes). In both movements, the play's oscillation between public and private scenes reflects its thematic concerns.

2042   Lowenthal, David. "Shakespeare's Caesar's Plan." *Interpretation*, 10, nos. 2–3 (1982), 223–50.

Highlights apparent inconsistencies in Sh's portrayal of Caesar in *JC* as prelude to the argument that Sh constructed Caesar, changing a number of details from Plutarch to present a leader who is so ambitious to create a new form of government in Rome bearing his stamp that he colludes in his own assassination. Taking a hint from Plutarch that Caesar was always driven to outdo his past achievements by future ones, Sh has him arrange for his own deification. The dramatist's view of the events

Julius Caesar 525

he treats is extraordinarily complex. On the one hand, he seems to favor republican Rome, though not without awareness of its flaws; on the other, he modifies Plutarch by omitting "the whole ugly undercarriage of Caesar's career." Caesar is set before us as "the perfection of political or honor-seeking man," but this ideal is subjected to critical scrutiny through the philosophical perspectives that Sh introduces into the play. Epicureanism (Cassius) and Stoicism (Brutus) are viewed as defective, partly because they are both apolitical. The philosophy of the Peripatetics, as presented and embodied in the play by Cicero, is preferable because it "regards the citizen as essential to the man." Cites Cicero's discussion of these three philosophies in his *De Finibus Bonorum et Malorum* to show how the judgment of Sh is similar to that of the Roman statesman. The ultimate philosophical conflict in the play is between Cicero (who represents Plato and Aristotle, "the greatest philosophers of antiquity") and Caesar, "the greatest political man of antiquity." As Sh sees him, Caesar bases human happiness on ambition and thus lacks interest in the truth, in friendship, in justice, and in the common good.

2043   Ludowyk, E. F. C. *Understanding Shakespeare*. Cambridge: Cambridge U. P., 1962. x + 266 pp.

Attempts to provide "a general introduction to Sh." Part 1, "The Background," contains six general chapters while part two has detailed discussions of six plays, including *JC*. Points out that *JC* treats two Elizabethan notions of ancient Roman virtues: *gravitas* (philosophical strength) and *virtus* (zeal for the public good). Sh's choice of source materials from Plutarch's lives of Brutus, Antony, and Caesar was determined in part by his interest in studying subversion and conspiracy, 2 matters of great concern to Elizabethans. The play is complex, involving a conspiracy, the fall of a great man, and the entanglement of an essentially good hero in murder.

2044   Lyons, M., and H. C. Montgomery. "'Friends, Romans, Countrymen.'" *Classical Bull.*, 44 (1968), 37–39 and 41.

Compares Sh's account of the aftermath of Caesar's death (*JC*, III.ii) with those of Plutarch (the lives of Caesar, Antonius, and Brutus), Suetonius, Appian (*Bella Civilia*), and Dio Cassius (*Historia Romana*). Of the ancient writers, only Appian and Dio Cassius furnish prototypes of Antony's funeral oration. Plutarch, Dio Cassius, and Appian are all historians, loyal to a heroic image of Caesar. Sh, not bound by the constraints of such an image (and indeed probably ignorant of Appian's and Dio's versions), makes his Caesar more flawed, and thus more successfully exploits the dramatic potential of the oration he creates for Antony.

2045   Maguin, Jean-Marie. "Play Structure and Dramatic Technique in Shakespeare's *Julius Caesar*." *CahiersE*, 5 (1974), 93–106.

Views *JC* as divided into two halves by the death of Caesar. The second half resembles a revenge tragedy, with all of the characters looking back to Caesar's assassination. Finds symmetry between the two parts; for example, act III is "framed by two murders," that of Caesar at the beginning and that of Cinna at the end. Notes that the differing lengths of the acts reveal Sh's adaptation of the received five-act structure for his purposes. A key structural device is parallel situations: examples include the "psychological evolution of characters destined to die or be stricken in their family"; the suicides; the portrayals of man and wife; the variations on things mentioned in Calpurnia's dream; and "an ironic verbal chain that is unwittingly and prophetically forged by the characters to run parallel with the sequence of events over which their control is obviously partial."

2046   Maguin, Jean-Marie. "Preface to a Critical Approach to *Julius Caesar*." *CahiersE*, 4 (1973), 15–49.

Sums up the accounts of Julius Caesar in ancient literature, emphasizing the uniquely balanced treatment in Plutarch's *Lives*. In the Middle Ages, Caesar was sometimes viewed as an enemy of virtue (for example, by Anselm and Thomas Aquinas) and sometimes as a worthy leader (for example, by Dante and Petrarch). Those who admired Caesar (Dante and Chaucer) usually dwelt on the wickedness of Brutus and Cassius. With this background, there were two main points of view about Caesar in the Renaissance: the moral and the political. The moral point of view reminds princes that, no matter what their personal merit, Fortune is fickle and may destroy them at any moment. The political point of view can take the observer in either of two directions, depending on whether he sides with Caesar or with Brutus; and "the lesson intended is either imperial–monarchical or republican." Critics have tended to emphasize Renaissance interest in the monarchical view and to neglect the republican one. Thirteen British and Continental plays written between 1553 and 1616 attest to Renaissance interest in the Caesar story and to the variety of approaches that could be taken with it. The balanced, dramatic presentation of *JC* reflects Sh's careful blending of materials from Plutarch's lives of Brutus, Caesar, and Mark Antony. Examines the four great moments of *JC* to show which life or lives Sh used for each of them. The first moment, Cassius's seduction of Brutus and the night scenes with the conspirators and Portia, comes from the *Life* of Brutus, while the second, the omens and Caesar's assassination, is taken from the *Life* of Caesar. In the third, the oratory of Brutus and Antony in the Forum, Brutus's speech comes from the *Life* of Brutus and Antony's from the *Life* of Antony. The fourth, the deaths of Cassius and Brutus, closely follows the *Life* of Brutus. Analyzes several points on which *JC* diverges from Plutarch to show how Sh adapts "prose narratives for dramatic action," incorporating "constant shifts of sympathy." Plutarch, for example, directly presents Antony's offering of the crown to Caesar, while Sh provides an impression of the same episode through off-stage sound and the report of Casca. Brutus is thus seen to make up his mind about Caesar's ambition without firsthand evidence. Set against this rashness are Brutus's gentleness toward Lucius and his love of music (the first invented by Sh and the second transferred from Plutarch's description of Antony). In addition, Sh omits Plutarch's suggestion that Brutus was Caesar's bastard son and the detail of Brutus's castrating thrust against Caesar during the assassination. Concludes with a "Chronological Catalogue of Facts and Events, Features of Characterization and Psychology, and Elements of Speech Derived from North's Translation of Plutarch's 'Lives' of Julius Caesar, Marcus Brutus, and Marcus Antonius and Incorporated in Shakespeare's *Julius Caesar*."

2047 Manzalaoui, M. A. "'Noght in the Registre of Venus': Gower's English Mirror for Princes." *Medieval Studies for J. A. W. Bennett*. Ed. P. L. Heyworth. Oxford: Clarendon P., 1981, pp. 159–83.

Identifies Brunetto Latini's *Livres dou Tresor* as the source for Gower's illustration of the power of rhetoric in Book 7 of *Confessio Amantis*. This *exemplum*, ultimately derived from Sallust, compares two types of funeral orations: One type is "rational and plain," the other "emotive and embellished"; the first is limited in its appeal, the second engenders in its audience enthusiastic support for the speaker; the former attacks the reputation of a defeated man, the latter enhances it. Speculates that Sh might have been influenced by Gower's example to pair the contrasting orations by Brutus and Antony following the assassination of Caesar in *JC*.

2048 Marshall, Cynthia. "Totem, Taboo, and *Julius Caesar*." *L&P*, 37, nos. 1–2 (1991), 11–33.

Discovers in *JC* the historicization of the parricidal drive that Freud posited for primitive societies. Brutus's struggle against the patriarchal figure of Caesar is both an individual Oedipal struggle and "the necessary accommodation of personal desires to group requirements." The play "dramatizes a foundational story for Western culture."

2048a Martland, T. R. "The Arts Do, What? for Whom?" *JAAC*, 41 (1982), 188–94.

Considers Julius Caesar's comment about being comfortable with fat men and fearing "lean and hungry" men such as Cassius (*JC*, I.ii.192–195), as well as the source of

2049   Maxwell, J. C. "Brutus's Philosophy." N&Q, 17 (1970), 128.

Takes issue with those scholars who have commented that Brutus's opposition to suicide expressed in *JC*, V.i.100–107, is an indication of his Stoic philosophy. Actually, Stoicism was favorably disposed toward suicide. Brutus is more properly described as one of "Plato's sect."

2050   Maxwell, J. C. "The Name of Brutus." N&Q, 14 (1967), 136.

Cites Cooper's *Thesaurus* to show that the Latin adjective *brutus* could mean "Dull: grosse witted: brutish: without reason." Sh seems to be playing on this sense in Antony's lines, "O judgment! Thou art fled to brutish beasts, / And men have lost their reason" (*JC*, III.ii.106–107).

2051   McAlindon, Thomas. "The Numbering of Men and Days: Symbolic Design in *The Tragedy of Julius Caesar*." SP, 81 (1984), 372–93.

Maintains that number symbolism is used by Sh in *JC* to involve his audience in "a conscious search for meaning." The numbers in the play "stand for a changeless and significant pattern which patient historical hindsight can discover behind the turbulent flux in which the living struggle to understand and control their destiny." Such symbolism is consistent with the Pythagorean–Platonic idea of "number as a hidden system of cosmic signs, existing beyond mutability and error." In the play, however, the numbers function ironically, indicating the blindness of tragic characters. The number four was associated with the humors, the elements, the ages of man, the seasons, and the cardinal points of the compass; it was also the number of unity and opposites reconciled, and of amity. Sh has frequent references to four, sometimes in puns ("forth," "quarter"), sometimes more directly (as when Cassius says that he has won over "three parts" of Brutus and will achieve "the man entire" on the next encounter). There are four chief characters (each one corresponding roughly to one of the "humoral types which comprise humanity"), four citizens hear the speeches of Brutus and Antony in the Forum, and there are several other groupings of four. Eight, the other important number in the play, was traditionally the number of justice and regeneration. We see this in the number of conspirators and the name of Octavius. The symbolism leads to a recognition that the assassination is "a violation of Time's order" and that the untimely deaths that follow are "the fulfilment of Time's design." Revised as chapter 4 of item 0729.

2051a McClelland, John. "Text, Rhetoric, Meaning." *TEXT: Transactions of the Society for Textual Scholarship*, 3 (1987), 11–26.

Provides a rhetorical analysis of Antony's forum speech (*JC*, III.iii) in arguing for the importance of interpretation that takes into account a physical text and the context within which one experiences it. Notes the First Folio's italicization of all proper names and capitalization of certain key words (for example, Ambition and Honorable). Also present are certain rhetorical commonplaces: repetition and contrast, irony, the association of honor with truth-telling, and ad hominem argument. Antony's rhetoric refutes the commonplaces of the tragedy up to the point his speech is delivered; it forces us to re-evaluate our preconceptions of the characters.

2052   McConnel, Frances Hunt Ruhlen. "Tragic Irony in Shakespeare: A Study of Brutus, Macbeth, and Leontes." Ph.D. dissertation, University of Washington, 1972. *DAI*, 33 (1972), 2335-A.

Describes several kinds of irony in order to clarify what is meant by tragic irony. *Verbal irony* is the term used to designate a technique employed by "a knowing and self-conscious speaker who takes an ironic stance toward something outside himself." A character who is the vehicle of *tragic irony* tries to achieve the dominance of the verbal ironist, but the authoritative tone of his words discloses to the audience the extent to which he is "not masterful, not in control." In *JC*, Brutus attempts to justify the assassination of Caesar in a speech that subjects him to tragic irony: He believes that he is reasoning carefully, but his rhetoric is shaped to conceal his own thoughts from himself.

2053   McNeir, Waldo F. *Shakespeare's "Julius Caesar": A Tragedy without a Hero.* Akademie der Wissenschaften und der Literatur. *Jahrgang 1971*, 2, 37–52. Reprint. Wiesbaden: Franz Steiner, 1971. 18 pp.

Analyzes the action of the play in terms of the five principal characters. Caesar, the protagonist, is vain and vacillating before his death and a relentless, vengeful shade afterward. Brutus, the chief antagonist, is fragmented by his love–hate attitude toward Caesar; he is inconsistent in being devoted to republican ideals while at the same time maintaining an aristocratic sense of superiority. He is also inflexibly wrong-headed. Antony is shrewd but shallow, Cassius is envious and pragmatically manipulative, and Octavius "shows symptoms of hard-headed realism" but "remains secondary to Antony as an avenger of Caesar's murder." The play is carefully constructed, but "no hero emerges from the dynamics of the two groups aligned against each other."

2054   Melrose, Susan. "Theatre, Linguistics, and Two Productions of *No Man's Land.*" *NTQ*, 1 (1985), 213–24.

Suggests that contemporary linguistics offers key insights into staging the first scene of *JC*. Calls attention to the social split indicated by the dependence of Marullus and Flavius on interrogatives and commands and the indirect, playful, and delaying responses of the Cobbler.

2055   Midgaard, Anne. "The Women in *Julius Caesar.*" *Miscellenea: Essays by Present and Former Students in the English Department of the University of Oslo.* Oslo: Norwegian Universities P., 1966, pp. 28–33.

Argues that the brief appearances of Calpurnia and Portia in the man's world of *JC* reveal "their strengths and weaknesses as women" and highlight "the qualities of the men that surround them." Cites Plutarch's *Lives*, Sh's source, to confirm that the playwright is bringing out "the genuine anxiety" of Calpurnia about her husband's safety and Portia's "sense of her own worth."

2056   Miller, Anthony. "The Roman State in *Julius Caesar* and *Sejanus.*" *Jonson and Shakespeare.* Ed. Ian Donaldson. Atlantic Highlands, New Jersey: Humanities P., 1983, pp. 179–201.

Reads *JC* as an expression of Renaissance "orthodoxy" on Roman history, which, as set forth by commentators like William Fulbecke and Jean Bodin, views the Republic, especially in the years leading up to the rule of Augustus Caesar, as a "framework for civil dissension and its consequent evils." The empire, however, is seen as "the seat of monarchical rule and the blessings of peace." Such an understanding of Republic and Empire is also that of Sh's immediate source, Plutarch's *Lives*, which traces the operation of providence in Rome's movement toward monarchy. Following this notion, *JC* emphasizes the factionalism fostered by republican conditions. Personal antagonisms abound, and the conspirators in their blindness promote rioting, interfering momentarily with the people's sound instinct that a strong leader is required. Jonson, in contrast to Sh, follows Tacitus in making *Sejanus* a depiction of divisions under a corrupt monarchical system, which must nevertheless be patiently accepted because the ancient republican order, however admirable, cannot be restored.

2057   Miola, Robert S. "*Julius Caesar* and the Tyrannicide Debate." *RenQ*, 38 (1985), 271–89.

Testifies to the vitality of the debate about tyrannicide in Sh's England, summing up opinion from various sources on the key questions treated in *JC*: how to distinguish a tyrant from a rightful king; how to distinguish "envious murderers from heroic republicans; how and when to justify assassination." Guided by the debate, Sh shaped his Plutarchan source material into "taut, balanced, and supremely ambivalent drama." Cites classical definitions of *tyrant*, noting that the term came "to describe an evil ruler, any one who governed by whim for personal gain instead of by law for the general welfare." Medieval and Renaissance commentators noted that a man could be a tyrant "in entrance, *ex defectu tituli*, or in execution, *ex parte exercitii*." Sh teases us with suggestions that Caesar is a tyrant on both counts but then qualifies his tyrannical characteristics by legitimizing his rise to power and having him display love and trust for his fellow Romans. Similarly, the playwright portrays the conspirators in an ambiguous manner: They are justified in that they seem to act "on public authority" according to the will of the people, but they are disturbingly susceptible to petty personal emotions (and the public in whose name they act is shown to be "dangerously unstable"). There is no reliable basis for sovereignty in *JC*; there is only a confusing competition for power. With regard to the tyrannicide debate, Sh dramatizes how difficult it is to fit the unpredictable movements of history and of life into neat political formulations.

2058   Miola, Robert S. "Shakespeare and His Sources: Observations on the Critical History of *Julius Caesar*." *ShS*, 40 (1988), 69–76.

Discusses the concept of literary "source," explaining possible alternatives to the idea of a book consciously consulted by an author and directly and visibly present in his text. Surveys other terms—for example, tradition, background, influence, origin, echo, subtext, and analogue—now in use that suggest modifications of the notion of source as verbal iteration. New thinking about sources has had four effects on the study of *JC*: "1) the revaluation of North's Plutarch as source; 2) the consideration of source as background or influence; 3) the discovery of source as subtext; 4) the introduction of new texts as sources."

2059   Mise, Raymond S. "Motivation and Ritual Again in *Julius Caesar*." *Paunch*, no. 23 (1965), 45–57.

Focuses on Brutus's need to turn the assassination of Caesar into a ritual. To avoid painful reality, Brutus has to transpose the murder of a father figure (Sh would have known from Plutarch the father-like role Caesar played in Brutus's life) into "a slaying of the aging king for the good of the social unit." The political theme of the play, which involves rendering "specific acts within a stated period of time," is linked in Brutus to the ritual theme, which relates these acts "to the human situation, both past and present, unbounded by time."

2060   Molan, Ann. "*Julius Caesar*: The General Good and the Singular Case." *CR*, 26 (1984), 84–100.

Faults *JC* for setting up a central concern with the fate of characters like Caesar, Brutus, and Cassius but failing to probe this matter to its center. Notes that Sh's chief focus in the earlier part of the play seems to be on the relationship between the singularity of certain men (like Caesar and Brutus) and the social and moral standards ("the general good") by which ordinary men can be judged. In the last two acts, Sh seems to lose this focus, transferring his interest to characters who "represent no more than competing versions of the general good."

2061   Mooney, Michael E. "'Passion, I See, Is Catching': The Rhetoric of *Julius Caesar*." *JEGP*, 90 (1991), 31–50.

Investigates the way in which Sh manipulates his audience in *JC*, first drawing them into the republican Roman world by identifying them with the plebeians and then distancing them "from their onstage counterparts." Up through Caesar's assassination, the spectators have been let in on "a series of manipulations in which, repeatedly, reasons justify emotional decisions." However, those same spectators are then shown how Antony manipulates their onstage representatives to commit acts of indiscriminate violence with which no one could identify. As the play draws to its conclusion, its rhetoric forces constant questioning, shifting, and revising of the audience's judgments about the chief characters. *JC* brings ancient Rome to life by modulating audience response between extremes, by declining to maintain "a definite viewpoint."

2062 Moore, Nancy. "The Stoicism of Brutus and the Structure of *Julius Caesar.*" *SRASP*, 8 (1983), 29–37.

Maintains that Brutus exhibits in himself the shortcomings that all of the Romans in *JC* share: lack of insight, fondness for devices of rhetoric (especially the use of proper names to stand for individual reputations and the words *Rome* and *Roman* to "evoke a collective reputation," the reference to oneself in the third person, and the addressing of other characters through names instead of directly), and commitment to the self-mutilating and divisive doctrine of Stoicism.

2063 Motohashi, Edward Tetsuya. "'The Suburbs of Your Good Pleasure': Theatre and Liberties in *Julius Caesar.*" *ShStud*, 26 (1988), 41–75.

Uses a discussion of the "liberties" and "suburbs," places where there was energetic interaction between marginalized people and activities and various impulses for control and censorship in Elizabethan England and where the Elizabethan theaters were located, to argue that *JC* reproduces this interaction in a multitude of ways. These include the "holiday" mood of the plebeians as opposed to the authoritarian suppression of celebration by the tribunes in the first scene; the conflict between Caesar's status as an aristocrat and his populist appeal; the skill of several aristocrats at theatricalizing politics (Brutus has initial success in this, but Antony ultimately triumphs primarily because he is the most adroit appropriator of Caesar's physical remains); Casca's aristocratic parody of the inversionary popular rite of seeming to crown Caesar; the mastery by the effective manipulators of the signs of discourse (Antony and Octavius) so that they are able to distinguish "the surface theatricality from the base context."

2064 Moynihan, Robert D. "Stars, Portents, and Order in *Julius Caesar.*" *MLS*, 7, no. 2 (1977), 26–31.

Maintains that "the portents and the references to the heavenly bodies" in *JC* signify the disruption of civil life attendant on the ill-conceived assassination plot. Emphasizes the inability of Brutus and the other conspirators to understand or interpret manifestations of disorder and confusion in their own lives or in the heavens.

2065 Mukherji, Asoke Kumar. "Shakespeare's Temptation Scenes: A Study of Some of the Lesser Ones." *Shakespeare Commemoration Volume*. Ed. Taraknath Sen. Calcutta: Presidency College, 1966, pp. 138–58.

Highlights temptation scenes in a number of plays, including *JC*, in which Cassius appeals to Brutus's "sensibilities as a private person" and associates the prospective coup against Caesar with honorable action. Discusses also Cassius's seduction of Casca (*JC*, I.iii) and Menas's suggestion to Pompey that the latter have the throats of the triumvirs cut (*Ant.* II.vii).

2066 Mulryne, J. R. "'Speak hands for me': Image and Action in *Julius Caesar.*" *Shakespeare et le corps à la Renaissance*. Ed. M. T. Jones-Davies. Société Française Shakespeare Actes du Congrès 1990. Paris: Les Belles Lettres, 1991, pp. 101–12.

Calls attention to the ways in which the language of the body is emphasized in *JC*. Notes how eloquence of language and of gesture are often denied, as in Caesar's *"Et tu, Brute?"* (III.i.77), whose Latin has the contradictory effects of distancing us from Caesar's death and bringing it closer. The scene in which Caesar is assassinated is remarkable for its juxtaposition of "action and inarticulacy: hands, not words, speak." Points out that Caesar's mangled body remains on stage for some 400 lines and that Antony more than once refers to Caesar's wounds as mouths that will assist him in speaking. Mentions the failure of Brutus's attempt to ritualize, through words, the slaughter of Caesar; "the realities of political action resist the mind's elevation of them." The dichotomy between word and body is also reflected in the juxtaposition of statue and bloody corpse in Calpurnia's dream (II.ii) and in the fact of Caesar's body lying at the foot of Pompey's statue (III.i, ii).

2067   Murty, G. Srirama. "A Note on *Julius Caesar.*" *Triveni*, 42, no.1 (1973), 46–51.

Focuses on Caesar's passivity in *JC*, arguing that Caesar is a Christ figure. Notes several parallels between Caesar and Christ: Both are of royal families, the followers of each attempt to make him a king, both are born in supernatural ways, and the circumstances of their deaths are similar.

2068   Nathan, Norman. "Brutus's Oratory." *San Jose Studies*, 8, no. 1 (1982), 82–90.

Argues that Brutus's funeral oration in *JC*, III.ii, is beautifully crafted to appeal to an educated patrician audience. The qualities of the speech depend on four elements: "balance, type of sentence structure, important words used in harmony, and important words used in opposition to a harmonious group." The utterance is characteristic of Brutus in that it displays an extreme dependence on form and reason with little concern for "facts and evidence." Contrasts Brutus's speech over the dead Caesar with Antony's, which relies heavily on emotion.

2068a   Orkin, Martin R. "A Cluster of Proverb Allusions in *Julius Caesar.*" *N&Q*, 31 (1984), 195–96.

Notices that Brutus alludes to three proverbial phrases when he is feeling his way toward joining the conspiracy in a conversation with Cassius (*JC*, I.ii.167–175). Brutus tends to rely on "proverbial authority."

2069   Owen, Trevor Allen. "Julius Caesar in English Literature from Chaucer through the Renaissance." Ph.D. dissertation, University of Minnesota, 1966. *DA*, 27 (1966–67), 3847-A.

Judges the medieval attitude toward Julius Caesar to be overwhelmingly favorable: Caesar was a hero whose fall was brought about by his malevolent enemies and the capricious goddess Fortune. In the 16th c., Caesar became a more ambiguous figure: Praise for his abilities is balanced by disapproval of his illegal seizure of power. Several Caesar dramas of the period develop the theme of Caesar as a tyrant, though most of these are continental. Sh's image of Julius Caesar in *JC* does not include the tyrant theme but does incorporate many other characteristics associated with Caesar in contemporary thought.

2070   Oz, Avraham. "Julius Caeasar [sic] and the Prophetic Mind." *Assaph, Section C: Studies in the Theatre*, 1 (1984), 28–39.

Interprets Sh's use of prophecy in light of the increasing tendency in the Renaissance to discover new levels of self-consciousness and to disengage the individual's destiny from the sacred notion of history inherited from the Middle Ages. Prophecy, which simultaneously involves "a reflection of eternal truth and a constant regard for temporal events," operates in Sh to reflect this ambivalent new view of experience in complex ways. Caesar's refusal to listen to the Soothsayer's warning to "beware the Ides of March" (*JC*, I.ii.18) reveals his unwillingness to recognize that his human existence is fragile and endangered by the world. Instead, he insists on identifying his own fate with the world's destiny. This first encounter with the Soothsayer is an important dramatic image for what becomes Caesar's growing blindness "to the evidence of his own experience."

2071 Palmer, D. J. "Tragic Error in *Julius Caesar*." SQ, 21 (1970), 399–409.

Maintains that in *JC*, Sh relies on the commonplaces of Elizabethan psychology in a detailed, precise way to impose a tragic pattern on episodic material from Plutarch. The play's tragedy results from the overthrow of reason and judgment by passion. Caesar's assassination "is presented as the disastrous consequence of a series of misjudgments and misinterpretations." As chief conspirator, Brutus exemplifies the general confusion. His first orchard soliloquy (II.i) alternates between rational, nonmetaphorical descriptions of what Caesar is and figurative fantasies of the danger he might become. Brutus's melancholy, according to the psychological conceptions with which Sh was working, would make him particularly vulnerable to these flights of imagination. The pattern of misjudgments brought on by passion or fantasy is evident in other characters throughout the play. Caesar's shrewd appraisal of Cassius's character is rendered useless by his pride, which prevents him from "acting on the evidence"; different assessments of Cicero, Caesar, and Antony by the conspirators call attention to how flawed the process of interpretation can be; and the conflicting responses to various portents emphasize that characters read omens "according to their hopes and fears."

2072 Paris, Bernard J. "Brutus, Cassius, and Caesar: An Interdestructive Triangle." *Psychoanalytic Approaches to Literature and Film*. Eds. Maurice Charney and Joseph Reppen. Rutherford, New Jersey: Farleigh Dickinson U. P., 1987, pp. 139–55.

Notes that Caesar in *JC* wishes "to actualize an idealized image of himself as a fearless, all-conquering hero." In order to do this, he makes irrational demands of both himself and others. Competitive like Caesar, Cassius is threatened by Caesar's success and needs to appear invulnerable. Cassius succeeds in seducing Brutus not because he is a skillful tempter but because he discovers Brutus's "hidden envy, competitiveness, and aggression." The interaction of the inner conflicts of Cassius and Brutus both energizes and destroys the conspiracy. Because of his need for love, Cassius sheds his arrogance and becomes more sympathetic toward the end, whereas Brutus persists in his haughty self-delusion. Revised as chapter 6 of item 0831.

2073 Parker, Barbara L. "'This Monstrous Apparition': The Role of Perception in *Julius Caesar*." BSUF, 16, no. 3 (1975), 70–77.

Emphasizes the importance of the perception motif in *JC*. The motif is established in the first scene through the unreasoning mentality of the mob. Caesar and Brutus are similar in being easily deceived by surface appearances, while Cassius and Antony resemble each other in their shrewd perception of others. The play has two parts, both closely related to the motif of perception: The first part comprises "Brutus's seduction by Cassius, Caesar's consequent downfall, and the rise of the conspirators"; the second comprises "the mob's seduction by Antony, Brutus's consequent downfall, and the rise of the counterconspirators."

2074 Paster, Gail Kern. "'In the spirit of men there is no blood': Blood as Trope of Gender in *Julius Caesar*." SQ, 40 (1989), 284–98.

Connects Caesar's death to the meaning of blood and bleeding in the early modern period. That his body bleeds uncontrollably, something associated with women, calls into question his maleness; and his failure to control bodily functions is used by the conspirators to justify his murder. Caesar's shedding of blood for his people links him with Christ, whose body was likened to the nurturing female flesh. The outbreak of civil unrest in Rome results not so much from the reading of Caesar's will (his maleness) as from the revelation of his wounds (his femaleness).

2075 Payne, Michael. "Political Myth and Rhetoric in *Julius Caesar*." BuR, 19, no. 2 (1971), 85–106.

Contends that in *JC* Sh "dramatizes the relationship between two political myths": the primal father exercising his authority over his sons, and the sons overthrowing the father and attempting to establish equal rights for all. In the first three acts, the conflict between father and son is predominant, and in the last two it is replaced by "a series of conflicts between brothers." Sh does not endorse either paternalism or fraternalism; rather, "the rhetoric of the play argues indirectly and ironically for the dialectic of paternity and fraternity in the state."

2076 Pechter, Edward. "*Julius Caesar* and *Sejanus*: Roman Politics, Inner Selves, and the Powers of the Theatre." *Shakespeare and His Contemporaries: Essays in Comparison.* (Revels Plays Companion Library.) Eds. E. A. J. Honigmann, J. R. Mulryne, and R. L. Smallwood. Manchester: Manchester U. P., 1986, pp. 60–78.

Presents *JC* as an exploration of the tensions between the impulse to public action and the alternative need to retreat into a private inner self. Further, though we are moved to believe in the need for such a refuge, we are made skeptical about "whether this autonomous inner self is a reality, or at least whether there is any access to it by theatrical means." Argues that three climactic moments in the middle of the play—the assassination of Caesar, Antony's oration, and the murder of Cinna—reverse the flow of our feeling twice, "from Brutus to Antony and back again." Thus our sympathy with the inner kindness and gentleness of Brutus is broken and then reestablished. We become conscious of the contradictions between Antony and Brutus, the first an extrovert for whom all feelings have a political significance, and the second an introvert, whose imperfect attempts to withdraw from action can nevertheless be acknowledged as real and granted a measure of admiration.

2077 Peterson, Douglas L. "'Wisdom Consumed in Confidence': An Examination of *Julius Caesar.*" *SQ*, 16 (1965), 19–28.

Argues that the character of Caesar can be better understood if certain of Sh's departures from Plutarch are freshly examined. To begin with, Caesar's reference to his deafness does not indicate a physical infirmity. When Caesar tells Antony to "Come on my right hand, for this ear is deaf" (I.ii.213), he is using a proverbial expression that means he is deaf to Antony's opinion that Cassius is not dangerous. Unlike Plutarch, Sh avoids any suggestion that Caesar is guilty of past political crimes. In Sh, the omens are warnings from a sympathetic Providence. If Caesar heeds them, the conspiracy will be discovered and history will proceed on its normal course; if he ignores them, the city will be plunged into chaos. This makes Caesar a tragic hero: He is responsible for his own death. Caesar's flaw is a "belief in his own invulnerability" or "wisdom–consuming confidence." This is accompanied by a susceptibility to flattery. Sh's departure from Plutarch in having Caesar refuse the letter from Artemidorus is not to ennoble him but again to emphasize his flaw.

2078 Petronella, Vincent F. "Dramatic Conjuring in Shakespeare's *Julius Caesar.*" *DR*, 57 (1977), 130–40.

Discovers pervasive references to conjuring in *JC*. Near the beginning of the play, Cassius talks of conjuring with Brutus's name, but Brutus, tragically, turns out to be a reluctant and ineffectual conjuror. He wishes to head a conspiracy without conjuring (in the old-fashioned sense of swearing a common oath), and he accidentally conjures up the spirit of Caesarism in his speech to the people following the assassination. In contrast to the reasonable Brutus, Antony, the man of passion, is adept at "the art of figurative conjuring," as can be seen when he descends from the pulpit to the level of the people, asks them to form a circle around the body of Caesar, and calls forth the spirit of Caesar in "animated rhetorical terms." It is noteworthy that Plutarch, the primary source for *JC*, does not identify the ghost that appears to Brutus, nor is there anything in Plutarch about conjuring. The feeble attempts at conjuring that link the deaths of Cassius and Brutus show that "the name of Caesar *is* a more powerful conjuring name than any other in the play." Conjuring in *JC*, then, "helps to clarify scenic relationships, dramatic emblems, character relationships and the personal tragedy of Brutus."

2079 Pinciss, G. M. "Rhetoric as Character: The Forum Speeches in *Julius Caesar*." UC, 4 (1982), 113–21.

Explains that the Forum speeches of Brutus and Mark Antony in III.ii of *JC* are modeled on entirely different rhetorical principles, each disclosing fundamental qualities of its speaker. Brutus's prose defense of the assassination is based on three devices characteristic of euphuistic writing: "Isocolon (successive phrases or clauses of about the same length); parison (successive members of the same form, so that word corresponds to word); and paramoion (similarity of sound between words and syllables)." His speech is divided into four sections: "1) an invocation or call for attention; 2) a statement of the argument or cause; 3) a summing-up of the consequences of the argument explaining Brutus's actions; and 4) a challenge suggesting the irrefutability of his claims." Brutus's performance is impressive, though old-fashioned: He is confident in his rectitude and mentions his co-conspirators only briefly. Antony's speech operates on principles very close to those set down in Thomas Wilson's *The Arte of Rhetorique*, the most psychologically oriented of all the contemporary handbooks. In accord with Wilson's advice, Antony begins by gaining favor with the audience, quickly presents specific examples (of Caesar's good qualities), defers direct attack on his opponents, gains attention by promising his audience something profitable to them (Caesar's will), and affects artlessness and modesty. Brutus, a man of sophisticated taste, believes in logic, argument, and refined style; Antony, a demagogue, relies on emotional appeal.

2080 Prior, Moody E. "The Search for a Hero in *Julius Caesar*." RenD, N. S., 2 (1969), 81–101.

Challenges the notion that Brutus is the tragic hero of *JC*, and stresses the play's affinity with the histories, "specifically in maintaining a strong line of action and achieving unity while dividing the interest among several characters." *JC* is a tragedy and does anticipate some characteristics of Sh's later tragedies, but we should not attempt to "find the source of its unity and to identify its special powers through the centripetal effect of a dominating protagonist analogous to Othello or Lear or Hamlet."

2081 Pughe, Thomas. "'What Should the Wars Do with These Jigging Fools?': The Poets in Shakespeare's *Julius Caesar*." ES, 69 (1988), 313–22.

Contends that the fate of the two poets in *JC* represents a conflict between the dominant discourse of "power politics, which declares itself to be reasonable, and the suppressed discourse of imagination, emotion, and intuition." Both poets are "victims of their trade." Other "men of the word" (Cicero and the punning Cobbler of the first scene) are also marginalized.

2082 Rabkin, Norman. "Structure, Convention, and Meaning in *Julius Caesar*." JEGP, 63 (1964), 240–254.

Points out that Sh made significant alterations in his source, Plutarch's *Lives*, to create, in two successive scenes (II.i and II.ii), clear parallels between Brutus and Caesar. We see that both "are great men who put country before self"; both possess Stoic nobility; both are vain and susceptible to flattery; and both exhibit a mixture of "perception and self-righteous blindness." Sh also directs our response by calling up the world of revenge tragedy in the moments following Caesar's murder. Because Brutus commits an act that "makes possible the dialectic of the revenge play," he removes from history "the feasibility of that high-minded governance to which he dedicates his life." Revised as part of chapter 3 of item 0873.

2083 Rackin, Phyllis. "The Pride of Shakespeare's Brutus." LC, 32 (1966), 18–30.

Points out that in *JC* Sh made "a conscious effort to evoke a sense of the classical world" but that he did so from a critical 16th-c. perspective. In particular, Brutus's

Stoicism is presented as inadequate for the conduct of his personal and political life. Brutus's pride in his own reason, and in that of mankind, leads him to misread Antony and the plebeians. For Brutus, Stoicism leads to desperation and inconsistency: He violates his own ideal when he commits suicide, never having acknowledged the existence of sin and evil in human nature.

2084   Rao, Kolar Surya Narayana. "A Note on Dr. Gordon R. Smith's Article, 'Brutus, Virtue, and Will.'" *SQ*, 12 (1961), 474–75.

Points out that, ironically, Brutus is the real dictator in the play. Smith's article, in stating that Brutus is "clothed" in virtue, implies that Brutus's virtue is superficial and detachable. On the contrary, his sense of honor is essential to his nature. (For Smith's reply, see item 2104.)

2085   Rebhorn, Wayne A. "The Crisis of the Aristocracy in *Julius Caesar*." *RenQ*, 43 (1990), 75–111.

Investigates the contradictory implications of "emulation" among the leading figures in *JC* and among Elizabeth I's courtiers (especially the Essex and Cecil factions), who are mirrored in the play. Brutus, Cassius, and the others, regarding Caesar as their peer, kill him to maintain their equality with him. Like Elizabeth's courtiers, these Romans are always rivals, and their competitive spirit leads them to self-destruction, the ultimate emulation of Caesar. Sh's Romans are unable to see the ruinous potential of their emulation because it also has positive aspects: love, loyalty, and brotherhood. Having destroyed their class, they clear the way for a political strong man; in a similar manner, the Elizabethan aristocrats made possible the rise of Cromwell and the Puritans.

2085a   Reinsdorf, Walter. "Brutus, Self and Society." *NDQ*, 50 (1982), 83–92.

Regards Brutus's participation in the conspiracy to kill Caesar as motivated by a need to preserve his own power and privilege as an aristocrat in republican Rome. In resorting to force to defend his position, Brutus is a Machiavellian rather than an idealist. Unable to recognize his moral error, he is not a tragic hero.

2086   Reynolds, Robert C. "Ironic Epithet in *Julius Caesar*." *SQ*, 24 (1973), 329–33.

Asserts that *JC* is an ambiguous play, and its ambiguity is presented in terms of antinomies: Every dramatic element contains opposites. The ironic epithet, contained in a single word, is a case in point. Casca's mention of the "alchemy" of Brutus's countenance (I.iii.159) suggests a priestly function as well as fraud. When Ligarius compares Brutus to an "exorcist" (II.i.323), his intended praise is undercut by associations with sorcery and trafficking with evil spirits. Cassius's ironic comparison of Caesar to a "Colossus" (I.ii.136) can be seen as more sharply derogatory in light of a passage from Castiglione's *Courtier* that speaks of figures of Colossus whose grand appearance belied the fact that they were stuffed with rags. But in the sense that Caesar's spirit ultimately triumphs, he is a Colossus.

2087   Reynolds, Robert Charles. "The Operation of Destiny in *Julius Caesar*." Ph.D. dissertation, University of Florida, 1965. *DA*, 29 (1968–69), 877-A.

Argues that in *JC* Caesar embodies an irresistible amoral force, indifferent to the values represented by Brutus. The Renaissance idea of Rome—based on "moral ambiguity and inevitability"—supports this interpretation. Sh creates sympathy for Brutus but also taints him with blindness, thus causing us to question Brutus's claim for moral victory. Ultimately Brutus's values, admirable as they are, have no effect on the course of Roman history. Caesar's spirit, which promises only barrenness and death, triumphs, affording no hope for the future.

2088 Rice, Julian C. "*Julius Caesar* and the Judgment of the Senses." *SEL*, 13 (1973), 238–56.

Analyzes three important Roman philosophies— Epicureanism, Stoicism, and Pyrrhonism—as they are employed in *JC*. Cassius, the representative of Epicureanism, finds his belief in "the complete autonomy and effectiveness of the individual will" inadequate for life as he encounters it. At one point, he is even forced to recant (partly) his previous rejection of portents. Brutus's Stoicism fails in precisely those circumstances in which an adherent would expect it to be most efficacious: Neither Brutus nor Portia can bear pain patiently, and Brutus has a tendency toward intemperance. Though Brutus kills himself in what appears to be the Stoic fashion, he does so "as a last resort out of despair." The play seems to be imbued with Pyrrhonism, which views human knowledge and beliefs as "determined more by fear and hope than by reason." The ideas of Renaissance Pyrrhonists like Montaigne about the untrustworthiness of the senses as a basis for knowledge help explain the numerous misjudgments in *JC*, some of them resulting in comic incongruities. An antiheroic reading is thus eminently plausible.

2088a Rish, Shirley. "Shakespeare's and Plutarch's Brutus: Shakespeare's Dramatic Strategy to Undercut the Noble Image." *JRMMRA*, 3 (1982), 191–97.

Argues, by citing a number of key episodes in *JC* (the notes urging Brutus to liberate Rome from tyranny, the formation of the conspiracy, the quarrel with Cassius), and comparing them with the presentation of the same material in Plutarch's *Lives*, that Sh has subtly altered his source to show Brutus as vain, manipulative, willful, humorless, and inconsistent.

2089 Robinson, Marsha Studebaker. "Shakespeare and the Rhetoric of History." Ph.D. dissertation, University of Pennsylvania, 1987. *DAI*, 48 (1987–88), 2069-A.

Explicates the relationship between "the rhetorical and literary strategies of Shakespeare's second tetralogy and *Julius Caesar* and the strategies of historical representation [that] characterize the historical texts from which the poet–historian drew his material." Comments that in these works Sh both obliquely and directly concerns himself with the problems of writing history.

2090 Ronan, Clifford J. "Lucan and the Self-Incised Voids of *Julius Caesar*." *CompD*, 22 (1988), 215–26.

Argues that Sh imitated Lucan's *Pharsalia* in *JC*, particularly in his "use of motifs of self-mutilation and parricide to describe civil war." The most significant of the resemblances between *JC* and the *Pharsalia* is the motif of "incised entrails," which is associated both with the deep wounds of war and with the exposure of hollowness or "the releasing of some embarrassing or intractile inner reality."

2091 Ronan, Clifford J. "Lucanic Omens in *Julius Caesar*." *CompD*, 22 (1988), 138–44.

Surveys two echoes from Lucan previously noted in *JC* by scholars and discovers two more: one in Cassius's "walk during the portentous thunderstorm" (I.iii) and the second "in Calpurnia's ominous dream of Caesar as a fountain running blood" (II.ii). Because there was no English translation available for the parts of the *Pharsalia* from which these two parallels come, it is likely that Sh read at least some of Lucan in Latin.

2091a Rose, Mark. "Conjuring Caesar: Ceremony, History, and Authority in 1599." *ELR*, 19 (1989), 291–304.

Argues that in *JC*, Sh dramatizes the opposition in his own time between the antiritualism of the Puritans and "a more conservative belief in the efficacy of ceremony."

The mystifications of the play serve to advance its tautological design whereby Caesar the fleshly man becomes Caesar the historical figure, and the past becomes "the completed past that we know." Sees *JC* as a kind of political mass, presenting a sacrificial death that begins a new era in history; it could also be called "an originary myth." It is possible to see a parallel situation in the emergence of the "Imperial Tudor State."

2092 Rose, Remington Edward II. "Julius Caesar and the Late Roman Republic in the Literature of the Late 16th Century, with Especial Reference to Shakespeare's *Julius Caesar*." Ph.D. dissertation, Princeton University, 1964. *DA*, 25 (1964), 3558.

Attempts to clarify the meaning Sh's *JC* would have had for its original audience. Examines the primary Elizabethan sources of information on Caesarian Rome, including "popular tradition, classical and English histories, military manuals, political tracts, and classical and Renaissance works of literature." The evidence makes plain that Sh was not trying to "subvert the traditional beliefs of his time." Sh focuses on Caesar as governor rather than general and omits all evidence of Caesar's crimes. The narrative is politically conventional in that "the murder of a monarch brings chaos and civil war." With this understanding, we can appreciate "the power and subtlety with which the figures of fire, blood, seeing, names, omens, and so forth harry the conspirators to an ignoble end."

2093 Rosen, William, and Barbara Rosen. "*Julius Caesar*: 'The Specialty of Rule.'" *Twentieth Century Interpretations of Julius Caesar*. Ed. Leonard F. Dean. Englewood Cliffs: Prentice-Hall, 1968, pp. 109–15.

Argues that Sh might have been influenced to write *JC* by fears of what could happen to his own country when Elizabeth died. Fortune seems to be the presiding authority in the play and to operate with pervasive capriciousness. *JC*'s emotional ambivalence may owe something to Plutarch's habit of contrasting the favorable and unfavorable traits of a character. With most of the main characters—Caesar, Brutus, Cassius, and Antony—there is some kind of dichotomy that prevents them from assuming and maintaining power. Octavius is the only one whose impersonal lack of entanglement promises success in the role of ruler.

2094 Rosen, William, and Barbara Rosen, eds. *Julius Caesar*. (Signet Classic Shakespeare.) New York: New American Library, 1963. xxix + [30]–240 pp.

The introduction begins by pointing out that in *JC* Sh gained perspective on "the drama of power politics and personal conscience" that he had explored in the English history plays by shifting his setting to the ancient past. Suggests that the politics of his own time and hints in Plutarch's *Lives*, the source of *JC*, prompted Sh to explore the idea that the private virtues and defects of a man have little bearing on his fitness for public rule. In order to make clear what sort of ruler can "wield power in the spirit of Caesar," Sh alters Plutarch's conception of Octavius, making him more soldierly and businesslike and less charming. The note on the source calls attention to Sh's freedom in employing material from a number of Plutarch's Lives. The technique of treating all of the characters in an ambivalent manner may be derived from Plutarch. The introduction, text, and note on the source are reprinted as part of item 0123.

2095 Entry deleted.

2096 Sacharoff, Mark. "Suicide and Brutus's Philosophy in *Julius Caesar*." *JHI*, 33 (1972), 115–22.

Comments on Brutus's disapproval of Cato's suicide (*JC*, V.i.100–107), which shows that Brutus is not a Stoic. Stoics (for example, Seneca, Epictetus, and Marcus Aurelius) generally approved of suicide, while Plato, Aristotle, and St. Augustine opposed it. However, there is probably more to Brutus's criticism of Cato than opposition to suicide. North's Plutarch would have given Sh the history of Brutus's shifting relationship with his uncle Cato. Brutus fought with Cato against Caesar, but after Caesar defeated Pompey at Pharsalia, Brutus switched sides. Cato remained firm in his opposition to Caesar and ended by committing suicide in 46 B.C. Sh may have deduced from these events a sense of guilt in Brutus and a need "to justify his own moral compromise by casting doubts upon the justifiability of Cato's act." In addition, Sh probably needed to present Cato in an unfavorable light because he was "the leading symbol of the anti-monarchic forces of antiquity," and to glorify him would be to court accusations of sedition. See item 1994.

2097   Sanders, Norman. "The Shift of Power in *Julius Caesar*." REL, 5, no. 2 (1964), 24–35.

Claims that in *JC*, Sh focuses on "a moment in history when the power inherent in a great civilization is released by a shift of control, and there ensues the basic political pattern of chaos sandwiched between two effective alternatives." When the play opens, power is in the hands of Caesar. The first scene, with the dismissal of the citizens by Marullus and Flavius, hints at the fickleness of the mob, illustrates how it can be controlled, and suggests one source of opposition to Caesar. In his appearances during the play, Caesar is shown as conscious of his position as the repository of power, though Sh also emphasizes his human weaknesses. After the assassination, Brutus does not attempt to appropriate the power seized from Caesar; instead, he indulges in extended self-excusing. Antony's oration removes power from the conspirators and delivers it to the people of Rome. For one scene, when the poet Cinna is torn to pieces by the mob, Roman power is seen in its uncontrolled state. After that, power moves into the hands of Octavius, who is eventually identified with Caesar.

2098   Sanders, Norman, ed. *Julius Caesar*. (Penguin Shakespeare.) Harmondsworth: Penguin, 1967. 251 pp.

The introduction begins by commenting on Sh's use of three of Plutarch's Lives—those of Brutus, Caesar, and Antony—as sources. The spare style of North's translation of Plutarch was especially congenial to Sh, who took over some passages with very little change. Sh created from his source materials a complex, well-proportioned drama that explores a number of political issues familiar from his history plays. Points out the tensions within the characters of Caesar (between greatness and weakness) and Brutus (between gentle integrity and rigid, egoistic idealism). Describes the play—one of Sh's "most profound explorations of political action"—the men who engage in it, and its relationship to the larger subject of morality. Analyzes the formation of the conspiracy, focusing on Cassius as both republican and hate-filled detractor and on Brutus as man of principle who struggles to ascribe the unsavory actions he contemplates to "exalted motives." With the assassination and Caesar's funeral, the initiative passes from the conspirators to Antony, whose character is given a duality like those of the other major figures. Antony's Machiavellian side begins to dominate his actions, and divisions are seen between him and the other members of the triumvirate. Sh also calls attention to the strains that develop between Cassius and Brutus. Mentions some of the image patterns that pervade the play (blood and fire, for example) and discusses three of the labels that have been applied to it (tragedy, history, problem play) without accepting any of them.

2099   Sargent, Seymour H. "*Julius Caesar* and the Historical Film." EJ, 61 (1972), 230–33, 245.

Suggests that *JC* anticipates the kind of re-creation of history that film has made possible in recent times. Sh provides a cinema-like depiction of the urban environment of Rome, of masses of people in action, and of political maneuvering with public significance. As in successful history films, there is a balanced portrayal of "the historical scope as well as the inner human meaning of events."

2100 Scott, William O. "The Speculative Eye: Problematic Self-Knowledge in *Julius Caesar.*" *ShS*, 40 (1988), 77–89.

Adduces passages from several Renaissance authors to show that there was considerable skepticism about the possibility of self-knowledge in Sh's day. In *JC*, the characters know themselves only by the ways they perceive that others respond to them, but these responses constantly challenge the self-image they would like to project. This is also true of the interaction between the characters on stage and the audience. The play thus frustrates and puzzles both characters and audience but paradoxically teaches both a great deal.

2101 Simmons, J. L. "Shakespeare's *Julius Caesar*: The Roman Actor and the Man." *TSE*, 16 (1968), 1–28.

Contends that neither Caesar nor Brutus knows himself. In attempting to act the part of an immutable spirit, Caesar fails to recognize his humanity. His fall "implies a personal tragedy, but Shakespeare develops the personal tragedy only in Brutus." Brutus makes a claim to perfect reasonableness: He tries to dissociate the spirit of Caesar from human nature (as Caesar does), he disregards the importance of passion, and he holds to an ideal of self requiring for its validation that all men agree with him. By making Brutus waver from his ideal of pure rationality (in his love for Portia, Cassius, and Lucius), Sh shows that, on a private level, Brutus does have an ideal nature. Brutus's tragedy is that he recognizes the "potentiality for evil in the spirit of Caesar" but cannot destroy that spirit "because he is infused with it himself." Sh modifies the Brutus of Plutarch to make him more idealistic. Revision of part of item 0981. Revised as chapter 3 of item 0980.

2102 Slights, Camille. "Murder, Suicide and Conscience: The Cases of Brutus and Hamlet." *Familiar Colloquy: Essays Presented to Arthur Edward Barker.* Ed. Patricia Bruckmann. Ottawa: Oberon P., 1978, pp. 113-31.

Interprets Brutus's tragedy in *JC* in terms of probabilism, the doctrine "that in cases of moral doubt one has the freedom to act when there is some real probability that the action is lawful, even when its unlawfulness is more probable." Brutus settles for this justification, the doctrine of the Counter-Reformation church, instead of probabiliorism, the belief that "moral doubts can be resolved only when the lawfulness of the proposed action is the most probable conclusion." Brutus is lax in passing judgment on Caesar "without full intellectual assent," but he then assumes a rigid posture of moral authority. Both *JC* and *Ham.* are tragedies of moral choice in the midst of uncertainty, but in the former the hero retreats into ignorant pride while in the latter he accepts "the limitations of human knowledge." Incorporated into chapter 3 of item 2102a.

2102a Slights, Camille Wells. *The Casuistical Tradition in Shakespeare, Donne, Herbert, and Milton.* Princeton: Princeton U. P., 1981. xix + 307 pp.

Examines the casuistical tradition—according to which moral and theological principles were applied to the activities of daily living—in several of Sh's plays, including *JC*, which "presents assassination and suicide not as clear-cut examples of treachery or heroism but as perplexing moral problems" and which "finds tragedy not in the hidden corruption of men's motives but in the mistaken application of general principles to particular situations." Chapter 3, on Sh's tragedies, incorporates materials from item 2102.

2103   Smith, Alan R. "Shakespeare's *Julius Caesar*". *Expl*, 42, no. 4 (1983–84), 9–10.

Suggests that when Antony, in his Forum speech, says of Caesar's death, "Then burst his mighty heart" (III.ii), his use of the verb "burst" constitutes a panegyric. Medical authorities of Sh's time believed that grief caused the blood to rush to the heart from the extremities, sometimes in such quantities that it would break. The fact that Caesar, despite having lost blood from numerous wounds, still had enough to "burst his mighty heart" over grief at the ingratitude of Brutus is a tribute to his greatness.

2104   Smith, Gordon Ross. "The Character of Brutus: An Answer to Mr. Rao." *SQ*, 12 (1961), 475–78.

Argues that Rao (item 2084) has made the mistake of taking Brutus in *JC* at face value, believing that his virtue is what he says it is and that it is consistent with his actions. Several changes made by Sh in adapting his source (for example, in Brutus's reason for sparing Antony and in the quarrel scene with Cassius) show Brutus as considerably less virtuous than he is in Plutarch. Ultimately, though, the interpretation of Brutus (and of any other Shakespearean character) should be based on the pattern of his behavior in the play and the way that behavior can be read in the light of "modern psychiatric observation."

2105   Southwell, Michael G. "Dawn in Brutus's Orchard." *ELN*, 5 (1967), 91–98.

Maintains that David Carson (item 1971) is wrong to associate the luminescence over Brutus's orchard in *JC* with the conspiracy. The argument that the three conspirators have about what the brightness represents (II.i.101–111) reflects on another level the difficulty Brutus has in deciding whether it is right to join the conspiracy.

2106   Spakowski, R. E. "Deification and Myth-Making in the Play *Julius Caesar*." *University Review*, 36 (1969–70), 135–40.

Contends that *JC*, viewed from a certain perspective, furnishes a number of parallels between Caesar and Christ. Most significantly, Caesar sees himself as a man–god, comparing himself in constancy to the North Star, a metaphor derived from Aristotle's concept of the unmoved mover. Along with this process of self-deification, Sh "also embodies the process of myth-making within the play." There is the growing legend of Caesar's greatness, and there is also the objective perspective, embodied in Cassius, by which myths or legends are rejected.

2107   Spencer, Lois. "The Antony Perspective." *London Review*, 2 (1967), 20–29.

Argues that Plutarch's presentation of Antony in the *Lives of the Noble Grecians and Romans* gave Sh a figure of "extreme and unresolved duality" that the playwright was able to shape in such a way as to give him "a consistent inconsistency" and to endow him with the potential to "be taken up again and shown in markedly different contexts, capacities and treatments and yet still be the Antony of *Julius Caesar*." Shows that in *JC* Sh eliminates or reduces the most reprehensible features of Plutarch's Antony (such as his scheming and ruthless cruelty) while at the same time retaining the perspective that hints at these features. Distinguishes three versions of the character: the "initial" Antony (generous and patriotic), whom we encounter as we first see the play; the "hindsight" Antony (calculating and somewhat sinister); and "Antony Plus," who comes into view when the dramatic figure in *JC* is compared to the historical one and we becomes aware of what Sh has included, omitted, and adjusted. Sh's handling of Antony in *JC* allows him to use the same enigmatic character in *Ant.*, though with somewhat different emphases.

2108 Spevack, Marvin, ed. *Julius Caesar*. (New Cambridge Shakespeare.) Cambridge: Cambridge U. P., 1988. xv + 184 pp.

The introduction includes a section on sources (primarily Plutarch's *Lives of the Noble Grecians and Romans*) that credits Sh's "concentration, combined with repetition" as giving "the real contours of the plot." Discusses several other topics, including "The Frame" (the inextricability of private and public), "Structure" (two parts, connecting with time and with the characters' "self-conscious historicity"), "Theme" (the tension between "the prevalence of change and the desire for constancy"), and "Persons and Politics" (the play's chief technical achievement is a striking sense of individual character and "the interaction of characters," with Brutus at the center). The appendix supplies substantial excerpts from Plutarch's lives of Julius Caesar and Marcus Brutus.

2109 Spriet, Pierre. "Narrative Structures in *Julius Caesar*." *Essays and Studies* (Calcutta), 3 (1981), 117–27.

Argues that *JC* is deliberately ambiguous in the manner of Sh's great tragedies. It has a double structure: there is a quest, with Caesar as the subject and "the acquisition of the imperial crown as the *object*," and there is an anti-quest, in which a group of nobles have as their object "the denial of the imperial crown to Caesar." The two sequences are strictly parallel in their deep structures and are linked by the assassination scene. The play is organized around the role of Caesar.

2110 Starr, G. A. "Caesar's Just Cause." *SQ*, 17 (1966), 77–79.

Maintains that the line in *JC* recalled by Ben Jonson as "Caesar did never wrong, but with just cause" is what Sh wrote rather than the line that replaced it in the First Folio (III.i.47). Sh's source is probably Cicero's *De Officiis*, in which Caesar is quoted as saying that if it is ever right to do wrong, it is most right to do wrong for the sake of a throne. Sh could have read the *De Officiis* either in the original or in English translation.

2111 Stewart, J. I. M. "Shakespeare's Lofty Scene." (Annual Shakespeare Lecture of the British Academy 1971.) *PBA*, 57 (1971), 181–95. Reprint London: Oxford U. P., 1971. 17 pp.

Uses an analysis of the *theatrum mundi* metaphor and the imagery of blood in *JC* to show that Sh presents history ironically and sometimes with disillusionment. However, private moments (like Brutus's interactions with Portia and Lucius and the quarrel between Brutus and Cassius) are evidence that Sh did not subscribe to a narrowly pessimistic philosophy of history, as the critic Jan Kott would have us believe.

2112 Stirling, Brents. "*Julius Caesar* in Revision." *SQ*, 13 (1962), 187–205.

Cites patterns in speech prefix variations as evidence of postproduction literary revision in II.i (the night-time meeting of the conspirators with Brutus) and IV.iii (particularly the double disclosure of Portia's death) of the First Folio text of *JC*. In both cases, Sh complicates what was originally simpler and neater. In II.i, two original scenes have been merged, one in which Brutus, Cassius, and Casca meet at Brutus's house, and a second in which the massed conspirators meet at Pompey's Theater. Sh's revision suggests in one scene "a complex of idealism and opportunism, candor and furtiveness, cohesion and incompatibility." In IV.iii, Sh added a number of details, including the farcical intrusion of the Poet, who provokes the would-be Stoic Brutus to new rage (shortly after his outburst at Cassius) and Brutus's first account of his grief over Portia's death. In the original version, Messala's news about Portia was the first Brutus had heard, but in the revision Brutus already knows and tries to keep Messala from announcing it and adding to the lugubriousness of the occasion. The departures from the original scene represent a "shift from 'logical' motivation and action toward a logic of the emotions and a feast of cross-purposes."

2112a Syme, Ronald. "Caesar: Drama, Legend, History." *The New York Review of Books*, Feb. 28, 1985, pp. 12–14.

Cites details from *JC* emphasizing Caesar's weaknesses and his tendency to exaggerate his own power and constancy. These flaws are not in Plutarch's *Lives*, and Sh's invention of them has the effect of downplaying Caesar's tragedy. Notes that even the biographies by Plutarch and Suetonius fail to take into account the way in which Caesar "fitted in with his contemporaries, how far he is different from them." Argues that as a member of the ruling class, Caesar was more or less suited to the competition among aristocrats that characterized the politics of the late Republic. Having eliminated his rivals, he was forced, probably unwillingly, to become a monarchist and to seek absolute power. He seems almost to have courted assassination, something Sh seems to have understood in assigning him lines about the inevitability of death.

2113 Takada, Shigeki. "Calls and Silence: Style and Distance in *Julius Caesar*." *ShStud*, 23 (1984–85), 1–37.

Posits a tension between the call of *JC* to the audience to invest the events being shown on the stage with universal significance as symbolic acts of "human liberation" and the distance felt by the audience from these events that hinders its sympathetic response. The sense of distance is felt chiefly through observing the character of Brutus, who is attempting to protect a "style of human relationship" that he sees as peculiar to the Roman military republic. Caesar's attempt to impose his imperial style threatens the freedom and autonomy of men like Brutus, who like to maintain a measured distance between themselves and others. Recognizes also that the distance of ancient Rome from Elizabethan culture and the paradigmatic status of Rome for the Elizabethans direct the audience's attention to the fulfillment of "established necessity" and prevent the audience from "sympathizing with anyone or responding emotionally to any events." Notes the difficulty in reconciling the autonomous mode of relationship prized by Brutus and the "passionate union of the people" that Antony relies upon. Both of these modes are present in the Republic, and Brutus makes use of the evocative power of language, characteristic of Antony's style, without recognizing it. Brutus does achieve heroic status because he makes an "unrelenting effort to transcend his human limitations and conform to the traditional Roman warrior and civilized citizen to the very best of his ability." Maintains that "the eternal Rome," as the unreachable goal at which Brutus and the audience aim, becomes "something like a metaphor for the omnipresent aspiration of men toward the transcendent."

2113a Tarlinskaja, Marina. "Rhythmical Differentiation of Shakespeare's Dramatis Personae." *Lang&S*, 17 (1984), 287–301.

Observes that Sh consistently juxtaposes "high and low personages, heroes and villains," making the verse text of the former "more symmetrical, more canonized" than that of the latter. Suggests that in *JC* such rhythmic patterns distinguish the heroic Brutus from the low, passionate Cassius. A study of Plutarch's treatment of these two figures confirms that Sh intended to differentiate them much more sharply than does his source.

2113b Taylor, Gary. *Moment by Moment by Shakespeare*. London: Macmillan, 1985. viii+ 263 pp.

Chapter 2 is devoted to an analysis of the assassination scene in *JC* (III.i) in terms of audience awareness, economy, and the relation between "speech and action, or text and performance." Comments, for example, on how Sh modifies the account of the exhange between the Soothsayer and Caesar in his sources to produce maximum economy. See item 2113d.

Julius Caesar

2113c Taylor, Gary. "*Musophilus, Nosce Teipsum,* and *Julius Caesar.*" *N&Q*, 31 (1984), 191–95.

Identifies several parallels between *JC* and both Samuel Daniel's *Musophilus* and Sir John Davies' *Nosce Teipsum*, showing that Sh read both works before or while he was composing his play in 1599.

2113d Taylor, Gary. *To Analyze Delight: A Hedonist Criticism of Shakespeare.* Cranbury, New Jersey: Associated U. Presses, 1985. viii + 263 pp.

Published in Great Britain as item 2113b.

2114 Taylor, Myron. "Shakespeare's *Julius Caesar* and the Irony of History." *SQ*, 24 (1973), 301–8.

Argues that in *JC* Sh reinforces an important lesson of the English history plays: that men are not masters of their fates. Their actions often have consequences very different from those they intend. Cassius's philosophical naturalism leads him to believe that Caesar is only a man, whose death will destroy tyranny. Instead, Cassius and Brutus succeed only in making possible the worse tyranny of the triumvirate. Sh shows a clear preference for supernaturalism because it indicates an acceptance of fate. When Caesar permits himself to trust omens and dreams, he is right; when he tries to rise above his superstitiousness, he is destroyed. The play validates Caesar's supernaturalism by showing how the materialism of the conspirators ironically produces effects opposite from what they intended. Antony is more successful than the others because he is willing to accept the importance of destiny in determining the events of history.

2115 Tice, Terrence N. "Calphurnia's Dream and Communication with the Audience in Shakespeare's *Julius Caesar.*" *ShY*, 1 (1990), 37–49.

Comments on the importance of Calpurnia's dream in *JC*, noting that it is used "to deepen the integration of the play." Suggests "an underlying depressive theme in the work."

2116 Tobin, J. J. M. "Apuleius and the Proscription Scene in *Julius Caesar.*" *Archiv*, 216 (1979), 348–50.

Contends that although the proscription scene in *JC* (IV.i) derives in the main from Plutarch, the images of horse and ass applied to Lepidus and the notion of him as "odd-man-out" are likely to have been suggested by the account of Lucius's bestial transformation in William Adlington's translation of *The Golden Asse* by Apuleius. Revised as part of chapter 4 of item 1052.

2116a Tobin, J. J. M. "Nashe and *Julius Caesar.*" *N&Q*, 32 (1985), 473–74.

Finds an additional source—Thomas Nashe's *The Terrors of the Night*—for certain elements of conspiracy and dream interpretation, especially the "contrary analysis" of dreams, in *JC*.

2117 Toole, William B. "The Cobbler, the Disrobed Image and the Motif of Movement in *Julius Caesar.*" *UC*, 4 (1982), 41–55.

Finds that the thematic focus of *JC* is on mental misconstruction, which is seen most prominently in the interrelationship of Caesar, Cassius, and Brutus. In the opening scene, through the movement, both physical and mental, of the crowd, the disrobing of images, and the comments of the Cobbler, Sh directs attention to the central ironies of misconstruction in which these three characters are involved. As the play begins, the tribunes move the crowd to give up their celebration and comment on how easily common men can be induced to change their minds. Caesar claims to be unmoved by the feelings of common men but ironically changes his mind to go to the Senate, where he is murdered just after describing himself as Colossus-like. The tribunes change the mood of the mob by reminding them of Pompey's blood; they then disrobe the images of Caesar. Antony, in III.ii, disrobes the body of Caesar, revealing that his blood could be moved like any other man's, in particular like that of Pompey, at the base of whose statue he lies. The movement of Brutus's mind by Cassius misfires: Cassius believes that Brutus's name will conjure up a spirit, and it does. The spirit, however, is one of revenge raised by Antony and ironically associated with Caesar. The Cobbler, whose name means "botcher" or "bungler," foreshadows Brutus and his mismanagement of the conspiracy in an attempt to "mend" the state.

2118 Toole, William B. "The Metaphor of Alchemy in *Julius Caesar*." *Costerus*, 5 (1972), 135–51.

Asserts that the "material side of alchemy derives from Aristotle's view on the constitution of matter." Sums up the key beliefs of alchemy in the latter half of the 16th c. in the following way: "Through the creation of a philosopher's stone or elixir, a substance made up of purified, perfectly proportioned elements, base metals could be transformed into precious metals and sickness turned into health; the process by which such transformations took place was symbolic of or made possible in part by the spiritual purification of the alchemist himself." Describes Renaissance English writings on alchemy to draw attention to the great "importance of analogy in alchemical thought." Discovers that Sh used alchemical allusion in *JC* in order to shed light on the story of Caesar's assassination. Cassius draws Brutus into the conspiracy with the intention of spiritualizing a base action, but he misinterprets the effect that Brutus will have. Brutus turns out to be an unsuccessful alchemist; his failure to keep the assassination pure leads to the unnatural magic unleashed by Antony when he stirs up the spirit of revenge in the Roman mob. Indirect alchemical references also play a part in the quarrel scene between Brutus and Cassius (IV.iii).

2119 Ure, Peter. "Character and Role from Richard III to Hamlet." "*Hamlet.*" Eds. John Russell Brown and Bernard Harris. (Stratford-upon-Avon Studies 5.) London: Edward Arnold, 1963, pp. 9–28.

Considers *JC* in a discussion of how Sh exploits the gap between who a character is and the role or roles he feels called upon to play in society. Brutus is shown struggling to reinterpret the role of conspirator to suit his idea of himself, and Caesar puts great effort into living up to his notion of his own constancy.

2120 Vawter, Marvin L. "'After Their Fashion': Cicero and Brutus in *Julius Caesar*." *ShakS*, 9 (1976), 205–19.

Avers that Sh knew Cicero's *De Divinatione* and echoed its detailed refutation of Stoic epistemology in *JC*. In *De Divinatione*, Cicero is particularly concerned with attacking the validity of portents, so revered by the Stoics. Sh, appropriately, has Cicero speak only when omens are being discussed and has him comment skeptically about the power of men to "construe" what they see. Again and again in the play, characters relying on their reason (as Cicero says the Stoics do) misconstrue things, shaping portents to mean what they wish. Caesar, of course, does this with Calpurnia's dream. Brutus reshapes many people he touches into imitations of himself. Portia, for example, becomes a parody of his Stoicism. Unable to fit the Caesar he knows into the scheme he has in mind, Brutus refashions the real Caesar into someone whose assassination can be justified. Brutus's reasoning here—involving the construction of a false argument—is precisely the kind of verbal high-handedness that Cicero criticizes in the Stoics. Revision of part of item 2122.

2121 Vawter, Marvin L. "'Division 'tween Our Souls': Shakespeare's Stoic Brutus." *ShakS*, 7 (1974), 174–95.

Explains that Cicero's philosophical essays provided the Renaissance with both a detailed outline of Stoic principles and an acute refutation of them. Possibly influenced by Cicero's *De Finibus* (which is addressed to Brutus), Sh in *JC* seems to have identified

Brutus as a Stoic Wise Man who attempts to separate his mind from his body and to enforce a narrow tyranny of his rational over his sensitive being. Brutus fails in his attempt to apply Stoic doctrine. He becomes physically ill (unable to eat, sleep, or love); he believes he is the physician for the state's sickness but is ironically incapable of diagnosing his own; his efforts at constancy suppress his love for Caesar, Portia, and Cassius; and he can neither acknowledge his own faults nor accept those of his friends. Brutus's "disembodied mind brings chaos to an entire social order." Revision of part of item 2122.

2122 Vawter, Marvin Lee. "Shakespeare and Jonson: Stoic Ethics and Political Crisis." Ph.D. dissertation, University of Wisconsin, 1970. *DAI*, 31 (1970–71), 2358-A.

Summarizes the evidence for the presence of Stoic ideas in English Renaissance literature and then provides a detailed description of an anti-Stoic tradition that influenced much of the same literature. Anti-Stoicism began with Cicero and continued in the works of Horace, St. Paul, Plutarch, Augustine, Lactantius, and Erasmus. It satirized the Stoic Wise Man and his presumptuous claim to live by reason alone. Sh in *JC* and Jonson in *Sejanus* and *Catiline* both test Stoicism as it responds to political crisis. Each author finds the philosophy inadequate, even destructive. Parts revised as items 2120 and 2121.

2123 Velz, John W. "Caesar's Deafness." *SQ*, 22 (1971), 400–01.

Suggests that since there is no mention of Caesar's deafness in any ancient biography, Sh may have gotten the idea from Plutarch's *Life of Alexander the Great*. Alexander is there described as holding a hand over one of his ears while hearing an accusation so that he might listen without prejudice to the justification of the accused. If Sh had this passage in mind, then Caesar's response to "Antony's naive opinion" that Cassius is harmless—"Come on my right hand, for this ear is deaf" (*JC* I.ii.213)—is an "invitation to Antony to bring an indictment against Cassius."

2124 Velz, John W. "Cassius as a 'Great Observer.'" *MLR*, 68 (1973), 256–59.

Points out that several characters in *JC* are marked by "radical inconsistency." Cassius not only changes morally; he is "*physically* different in Act V from what he has been shown to be in Act I." As he is presented by Plutarch, Cassius has bad eyesight. Sh portrays him at first as possessing acute vision, along with keen moral perception. Toward the end, he tells Pindarus that his sight "was ever thick" (V.iii.21). The failure of his physical vision parallels his misunderstanding of the events going on around him. It is a sad irony that Cassius, whose pessimistic insights into men and events have frequently proven so accurate, is destroyed because he literally cannot see the events of the battle and misconstrues what is reported to him.

2125 Velz, John W. "Clemency, Will, and Just Cause in *Julius Caesar*." *ShS*, 22 (1969), 109–18.

Suggests that a passage in Seneca's *De Clementia* helps resolve the "just cause" crux in *JC*. In discussing clemency for political offenders, Seneca says that kings are cruel only out of necessity, while the harshness of tyrants feeds the pleasure of their own will. If Caesar's speech about his banishment of Publius Cimber, as it appears in the Folio, is emended to read, "know, Caesar doth not wrong but with just cause" (III.i.47), his pretensions to kingly virtue become clear. However, his willfulness shows that, in Senecan terms, he is really a tyrant and that his "appeal to the doctrine of just cause is . . . a tragic self-delusion."

2126 Velz, John W. "'If I Were Brutus Now': Role-Playing in *Julius Caesar*." *ShakS*, 4 (1969), 149–59.

Asserts that role-playing dominates *JC*. Characters frequently assume—or consider assuming—roles that have been played by others (for example, Cassius, Antony, and

Portia all speak of "playing" Brutus). Three republican heroes who do not appear (Pompey, Marcus Cato, and Lucius Junius Brutus) survive in the reenactment of their attitudes by Cassius, Portia, young Cato, and Brutus. Other characters (Antony and Octavius), committed to "the decadent present," take on the role of Caesar. Caesar, in the early part of the play, emphasizes his role by speaking of himself as Caesar, and this practice is unconsciously imitated by both his friends and enemies. Thus conscious playing of roles differentiates the conflicting forces in the play, while unconscious imitation of Caesar provides thematic and structural unity.

2127   Velz, John W. "*Orator* and *Imperator* in *Julius Caesar*: Style and the Process of History." ShakS, 15 (1982), 55–75.

Finds that in JC Sh uses oratory as a means of energizing the process of Roman history. Throughout the play a variety of characters assume the role of the *orator*, and we follow the course of events through the effects of their speeches. The chiefly deliberative discourses of the first half, which promote change, give way in act V to epideictic oratory, an indication that a new stasis has been reached. Instead of adopting the *orator*'s persuasive style, Caesar speaks as an *imperator*, declaratively. His mistake is in adopting the imperial voice "before he has the *Imperium* in his grasp." Caesar's imperiousness is briefly echoed by others, notably when they are delighting in their power.

2128   Velz, John W. "Undular Structure in *Julius Caesar*." MLR, 66 (1971), 21–30.

Sees the structure of JC as "a sequence of rises to prominence and of declines from it." Although the play concentrates on the death of Caesar, "it implicitly covers Roman history from a time before Pharsalus to the peace that follows Actium." Thus the series of rises and falls is part of a pattern that is larger than the play: Pompey is succeeded by Caesar, Caesar by Brutus, Brutus by Antony, and Antony by Octavius. The image of a succession, of waves, a "tide in the affairs of men" (IV.iii.217), possibly adapted from Plutarch's essay "De Fortuna Romanorum," is used frequently to indicate the operation of Fortune in history. Similarities between the various waves confirm the undular structure. For example, Antony, at the height of his power, three times reminds us of interpretations or prophecies made by the conspirators.

2129   Velz, John W., comp. "*The Tragedy of Julius Caesar*": A Bibliography to Supplement the New Variorum Edition of 1913. New York: Modern Language Association, 1977. x + 58 pp.

Covers the period from 1913–1972, with some earlier items. Comprises 1256 items, classified into seven sections, and an index of authors and editors. Includes sections on editions, commentary, sources, and criticism. Lists entries alphabetically within each section, except in the section on editions, which is arranged chronologically. Includes brief annotations in brackets to indicate specific passages being discussed in the commentary and source sections and to convey special emphases of items in the criticism section that cannot readily be discerned from their titles.

2130   Velz, John W., and Sarah C. Velz. "Publius, Mark Antony's Sister's Son." SQ, 26 (1975), 69–74.

Points out that in Plutarch's *Life of Antonius*, Antony consents to the proscription of his uncle Lucius Caesar while in Sh the proscribed relative is Publius, Antony's sister's son (JC, IV.i.4–5). Suggests that Sh got the name "Publius" from Plutarch's account of the events immediately preceding the proscription in the *Life of Marcus Brutus*, where Publius Silicius is described as weeping at the sentence condemning Brutus and Cassius.

2130a Venugopal, C. V. "*Julius Caesar* and 'The Common Understanding.'"
Journal of the Karnatak University, 27 (1983), 48–52.

Rejects the notion that Brutus is the hero of *JC*, highlighting the "extraordinary resemblance" between II.i (in which Brutus is visited by the conspirators and Portia begs to share his secret) and II.ii (in which Caesar hears of Calpurnia's dream and rejects her plea that he not go to the Senate) to argue that both Brutus and Caesar are composed of "equally desirable and equally destructive opposed elements" and that neither is hero or villain of the play.

2131 Wilkinson, Andrew M. "A Psychological Approach to *Julius Caesar*." *REL*, 7, no. 4 (1966), 65–78.

Argues that descriptions of Shakespearean "character" in terms of function tend to dismember the characters so that their unity disappears. An approach founded on modern clinical psychiatry may supply this unity. Such an approach is particularly helpful in explaining Julius Caesar, who exhibits strong paranoid tendencies. Like the paranoiac, Caesar conceives of himself as possessing great power and is characterized by repressed homosexuality, avoidance of blame, and sentimental benevolence. In him, "the super-ego has become dissociated from the ego or reality principle," so that he pays no attention to "the real conditions of human life and to his own safety."

2132 Williams, George Walton. "Pompey the Great in *Julius Caesar*." *RenP*, 1976 (1977), 31–36.

Maintains that Pompey's spirit, as well as Caesar's, presides over the play. It is most prominently invoked at the center of the play (III.i,ii), when Caesar's body is at the base of Pompey's statue. At this point, the spirit of republicanism, exemplified by Pompey, seems to triumph. References to Pompey at two other crucial points (I.i and V.i), however, alert us to the ultimate defeat of republicanism by the spirit of Caesar. The name of Pompey is also associated, in the speeches of the tribunes, with three major image patterns: aspiration or climbing, "desecration of ceremonial," and sickness. Pompey's spirit, unlike Caesar's, is primarily a sign of defeat.

2133 Willson, Robert F. Jr. "*Julius Caesar*: The Forum Scene as Historic Play-within." *ShY*, 1 (1990), 14–27.

Analyzes Sh's use of theatrical analogues for interpreting the assassination and Forum scenes in *JC*. Notes, for example, Brutus's inadequacies as actor and stage manager and both Antony's skill as an actor and his distortion of "the end of art."

2134 Wilson, Richard. "'Is This a Holiday?': Shakespeare's Roman Carnival." *ELH*, 54 (1987), 31–44.

Contends that *JC* recapitulates the ways in which the socially powerful construct their dominant discourse by appropriating the radically subversive language of carnival. From the opening scene, when the Puritanical tribunes interrupt the artisans' holiday, through the conspirators' failed attempt to rationalize rebellion, to the apparent triumph of Caesarism, various discourses of power are advanced and then displaced. Sh seems to be consciously exploring the continuous struggle in the Renaissance to control the meaning of carnival.

2134a Womersley, David. *Julius Caesar* and Caesar's *Commentaries*." *N&Q*, 34 (1987), 215–16.

Cites Decius Brutus's comment that Caesar likes to hear about unicorns being "betrayed with trees" (*JC*, II.i.203–205) and suggests that the source is a passage in Caesar's *Commenatries* on the practice of capturing unicorns by cutting trees below the ground so that, although weak, they appear sturdy. The unicorn, leaning against a tree to rest, falls to the ground with it and is unable to get up.

2135 Wood, James O. "Intimations of Actaeon in *Julius Caesar*." *SQ*, 24 (1973), 85–88.

Suggests that when Antony, looking down at Caesar's body in the presence of the assassins, calls him "brave heart" (*JC*, III.i.205), he is probably alluding to the Ovidian myth of Actaeon, often used by Sh as an emblem (for example, in *Tit.*, *TN*, *MWW*, *Mac.*, and *Lr.*), "whether of a heart acutely distressed or of a man suddenly turned upon by subjects or supposed friends." If Caesar is an Actaeon figure, his thirty-three wounds (not twenty-three, as in Plutarch) can be explained as Sh's recollection of the thiry-three hounds named in the *Metamorphoses* that comprise Actaeon's main pack.

2136 Yoder, R. A. "History and the Histories in *Julius Caesar*." *SQ*, 24 (1973), 309–27.

Sees *JC* as "the turning point in Sh's career," telescoping the drama of "continuous disintegration and the inevitable progress of power" found in the second English tetralogy and pointing ahead to the great tragedies. In the Roman world, the historical process is "circular and absurd," with the chief characters, although sharply differentiated, mirroring each other's actions and taking on each other's roles. Brutus, in the last scenes, parallels Caesar when he is "emotionally crowned with his own righteousness." Cassius also resembles Caesar in growing superstitious and crediting omens before the battle of Philippi. Antony assumes Caesar's part, and at the end Octavius takes on the "title and tone of Caesar." Role-playing indicates a lack of vitality in the Romans, who are driven by external forces. The poetry reinforces this impression, revealing "ceremony," "honor," and "courtesy" as empty forms. *JC* thus recapitulates the treatment of ceremony in the *R2-H5* tetralogy, in which Richard trusts in barren ritual, and Bolingbroke and Prince John follow traditional courtesies only to manipulate their adversaries. (Henry V briefly revitalizes ceremony, something for which there is no counterpart in *JC*.) In *JC*, Rome is clearly suffering from a "crisis of disunity": Public rituals and private "ceremonies of love and friendship" are hollow, and images of animals (predatory) and metals (hard, impenetrable) dehumanize men. The narrow, meaningless posturing of the Romans allows history to triumph over them.

KING JOHN

2137 Braunmuller, A. R. "Plautus, Abraham Fleming, and *King John*." *KM 80: A Birthday Album for Kenneth Muir, Tuesday, 5 May 1987*. Liverpool: Liverpool U. P. for Private Circulation, [1987], pp. 18–19.

Suggests that a source for the last lines of *Jn.* (V.vii.112–118) may be a Latin passage slightly misquoted from Plautus's *Persa* and added by John Fleming to the account of the reign of King John in the second edition of Holinshed's *Chronicles*. The Plautine passage asserts that the virtues of a people are their best defense, and their vices their worst enemy.

KING LEAR

2138 Andresen, Martha. "'Ripeness is all': Sententiae and Commonplaces in *King Lear*." *Some Facets of "King Lear": Essays in Prismatic Criticism*. Eds. Rosalie L. Colie and F. T. Flahiff. Toronto: U. of Toronto P., 1974, pp. 145–68.

Focuses on "the aphoristic expression of commonplaces" in *Lr.*, a device that encourages us to respond both to the play's "psychological realism" and to its emblematic meaning. Notes the derivation of many aphorisms from the ancients, "as well as theories for their use."

2139 Andrews, Michael. "Lear's Wheel of Fire and Centaur Daughters." *RenP*, 1965 (1966), 21–24.

Supports R. B. Heilman's idea that Lear is struggling to recognize the relationship between his inner evil and the outer evil (Goneril and Regan) he has authored. Lear's reference to himself as being on Ixion's wheel and to Goneril and Regan as Centaurs (IV.vi) show him making this connection: Ixion, according to widely available accounts, attempted to seduce Hera, "but was deluded into embracing a cloud-image of her," thus fathering the race of Centaurs. These creatures were known for their sexual rapacity and for violence, particularly in the context of the host–guest relationship.

2140 Bauer, Robert J. "Despite of Mine Own Nature: Edmund and the Orders, Cosmic and Moral." *TSLL*, 10 (1968–69), 359–66.

Explains that the concept of nature held by Edmund in *Lr.* is "nature as vital force," or *physis*, to be distinguished from "nature as law," or *nomos*. The distinction, implicit in Renaissance discussions of nature, can be traced back to the pre-Socratics. Edmund's individualistic celebration of *physis* throughout the play severely shakes the cosmic order, but his dying attempt to do some good shows that he has rejected *physis* and now accepts his place in that order.

2141 Bieman, Elizabeth. "The Alienation of Lear: *King Lear*: Act Two, Scene Four." *Mosaic*, 2, no. 1 (1968), 110–22.

Examines *Lr.*, II.iv, in which "the alienation of Lear is accomplished." The Fool's lines about the great wheel that "runs down a hill" and "the great one that goes upward" (lines 70–72) suggest a paradigm for the play: "an inversion of the Aristotelian metaphors of rising and falling action." Lear, through his own folly and his elder daughters' wickedness, is pulled down until he is bound upon a fiery wheel in the pit, "rolling neither down nor up." Once Cordelia arrives (IV.vii), "the motion is upward."

2142 Blisset, W. F. "Recognition in *King Lear*." *Some Facets of "King Lear": Essays in Prismatic Criticism*. Eds. Rosalie L. Colie and F. T. Flahiff. Toronto: U. of Toronto P., 1974, pp. 103–16.

Attempts an Aristotelian analysis of *Lr.* by extending the definition of *recognition* (or *anagnorisis*) to mean "the realization of any relevant truth, most especially the realization by the protagonist of the erroneous basis of his conduct," and by tracing "the pace and process of recognition in the play."

2143 Blythe, David Everett. "Lear's Soiled Horse." *SQ*, 31 (1980), 86–88.

Explains that Lear's reference to "the soiled horse" (*Lr.*, IV.iv.121) derives from the agricultural term "soiling," which refers to "the practice of keeping horses or cattle confined and fed primarily with fresh pasture cuttings." "Soiled" comes from the Latin word *satullare*, "to fill, glut, cloy, satiate." Virgil recommends soiling in the *Georgics* as a means of strengthening bulls and stallions and thus bringing them into a state of "aroused sexuality." Variations on this image occur in *Cym.*, *Ant.*, and *Ham.*

2144 Bowers, Fredson. "The Structure of *King Lear.*" *SQ*, 31 (1980), 7–20. Reprint. *Hamlet as Minister and Scourge and Other Studies in Shakespeare and Milton.* Charlottesville: U. P. of Virginia, 1989, pp. 163–80.

Attempts to account for the uniqueness of *Lr.*'s structure. Unlike other Renaissance tragedies, *Lr.* seems to locate its climax—the moment at which the protagonist makes his fatal decision—in the first scene, with Lear's division of his kingdom and banishment of Cordelia. Normally, Renaissance tragedies place the climax in the third act, but Sh uses a modified classical structure in *Lr.* The classical dramatists, thinking in terms of the whole tragic action, conceived of the climax as taking place at some time anterior to the stage action and included an anticlimax, in which the protagonist confirms his original error. In *Lr.*, Sh moved the climax of the whole action up into his opening scene and, in the storm scene, provided an anticlimax that confirms the destructive powers unleashed by Lear's decision. But in an appropriately Christian modulation, it also witnesses the restoration of Lear's reason, which makes possible his reconciliation with Cordelia and alters the significance of his death.

2145 Bridges, Phyllis. "The Western Heritage of Wisdom from the Greeks through Shakespeare's *King Lear.*" Ph.D. dissertation, Texas Tech University, 1972. *DAI*, 33 (1972–73), 3575-A.

Derives the Renaissance idea of wisdom from the Greeks through Augustine, Boethius, and Aquinas. Various Renaissance writers reflect this "synthesis of Hellenic and Judeo–Christian philosophy." In *Lr.*, we see the culmination of the philosophical tradition of wisdom, as Sh develops a tragedy that results from "deficiency of knowledge."

2145a Butler, F. G. "The Barbarous Scythian in *King Lear.*" *ESA*, 28, no. 2 (1985), 73–79.

Cites ancient sources like Plutarch and Strabo, as well as medieval and Renaissance authorities, to suggest the range of meanings evoked by Lear's comparison of Cordelia to "The barbarous Scythian" (*Lr.*, I.i.116). On the one hand, the phrase could "be shorthand for an inarticulate, poor, barely clad, sexually promiscuous cannibal, wandering through a vast wilderness." On the other hand, there was a positive way of looking at the Scythians; they were often regarded as exemplars of integrity and frugality. Their reputation for communalizing both private ownership and the family is also relevant to the play.

2146 Butler, F. G. "Who Are King Lear's Philosophers? An Answer, with Some Help from Erasmus." *ES*, 67 (1986), 511–24.

Identifies the "good Athenian" (*Lr.*, III.iv.179) Lear imagines Tom (Edgar) to be as Diogenes the Cynic and the "learned Theban" (III.iv.155) as Crates, Diogenes' chief disciple. Argues that in portrayng Lear's revolutionary pilgrimage, Sh drew heavily upon "the political speculations of the ancient philosophers, and chiefly the Cynics; in particular, the Cynics as presented by Erasmus in the *Apophthegmes.*" These concerns can be seen in the debate about need; the transformation of the beggar Tom into a philosopher, Lear's brief re-creation of himself as a Scythian king, and the triumph at the end of Cynical renunciation of the world.

2146a Butler, Guy. "King Lear and Ancient Britain." *Theoria*, 65 (1985), 27–33.

Rejects the notion that *Lr.* has a primitive setting. Argues that for Sh's contemporaries Lear was a member of a dynasty descended from Brutus, the Trojan founder of Britain. Cites the work of the chronicler John Stow, Sh's contemporary, to show that Lear's father, who had studied in Athens, brought with him four philosophers to help found a university. Notes a number of references in the play that suggest a highly developed civilization. Concludes that *Lr.* "presents the corruption and collapse of an advanced culture, saturated in western, hellenic and judaic thought."

2147 Calarco, N. Joseph. *Tragic Being: Apollo and Dionysus in Western Drama.* Minneapolis: U. of Minnesota P., 1969. 202 pp.

Explores "the hidden order behind tragedy's visible circle of action and suffering" by focusing on "a set of plays central to the history of Western drama." Employs Nietzsche's concepts of the Apollonian and the Dionysiac to illuminate "the complex and unstable balance" of tragedy. In tragedy, the dissolution of boundaries between men and the annihilation of individuation characteristic of the Dionysian illusion combine with the Apollonian illusion of order. Both Apollonian and Dionysian illusions are derived from a need "to overcome the terrors of quotidian reality." The ways in which this need is addressed in Western drama reveal a "shifting relation between historicist and anhistorical elements, between a valorization of man's existence mediated by time and one mediated by some version of eternity." Chapter 4, "The Tragic Universe of *King Lear,*" uses a number of comparisons between Sh's play and Greek tragedy to focus the argument. For example, the Fool is similar to the Greek chorus in speaking "bitter truths from a privileged vantage point" and in acting as a "repository of traditional wisdom." Unlike the Greek chorus, he provides his commentary in a comic vein. Dionysiac elements are seen in Lear's experience during the storm, but these are mediated by the "Apollonian harmony of Cordelia." Lear as a character "affirms the archaic ontology which the Middle Ages held in common with Hellenic Greece." However, much of the play "affirms the historicism which the Middle Ages holds in common with the modern world." Sh declines to make a choice between these two views of man's being; he seems to embrace both. Revision of item 2148.

2148 Calarco, N. Joseph. "Tragic Being: Apollo and Dionysus in Western Drama." Ph.D. dissertation, University of Minnesota, 1968. *DA,* 28 (1967–68), 3805-A-3806-A.

Revised as item 2147.

2149 Champion, Larry S., comp. *"King Lear": An Annotated Bibliography.* 2 vols. (Garland Shakespeare Bibliographies 1.) New York: Garland, 1980. Vol. 1, xxx + 484 pp.; Vol. 2, 425 pp.

Covers primarily materials published between 1940 and 1978, with some items from before 1940 and some from 1979. Classifies entries under eight headings, including Criticism (1236 items), Sources (109 items), Bibliographies (10 items), and Editions (262 items). Begins each section with the oldest entries and proceeds chronologically. Concludes with an index that lists items both by author and by subject. Includes, in the sections on criticism and sources, a number of items that consider classical influences on *Lr.* Provides substantial and detailed annotations.

2150 Charney, Maurice. "The Persuasiveness of Violence in Elizabethan Plays." *RenD,* N. S., 2 (1969), 59–70.

Points out that although Elizabethan dramatists were influenced by Seneca in their emphasis on violence, they presented violent actions directly, not through the words of a messenger as Seneca did. This was partly in response to the audience's taste for violence, but it was also a powerful way to evoke pity and fear. Analyzes the effects of Gloucester's blinding in *Lr.*

2151 Cutts, John P. "Lear's 'Learned Theban.'" *SQ,* 14 (1963), 477–81.

Suggests that in calling Poor Tom a "learned Theban" (*Lr.,* III.iv.155), Lear is referring to Oedipus, whose answer to the riddle of the Sphinx provides an insight into the nature of man similar to that which Lear has just gained from Tom.

2152 Doloff, Steven. "'Let me talk with this philosopher': The Alexander/Diogenes Paradigm in *King Lear.*" *HLQ,* 54 (1991), 253–55.

Suggests that Lear's meeting with the disguised Edgar (whom Lear calls a "philosopher" [*Lr.,* III.iv.152, 171, 175]) is an ironic version of the meeting of

Alexander the Great and "the beggar philosopher, Diogenes." Notes classical and medieval sources for popular Renaissance accounts of the two men and their encounter. In Edgar, Sh seems to mock the "proud naturalism" of Diogenes, while Lear is the antithesis of the youthful, omnipotent, wealthy, and generous Alexander.

2153 Donawerth, Jane. "Diogenes the Cynic and Lear's Definition of Man, *King Lear*, III.iv.101–109." *ELN*, 15 (1977–78), 10–14.

Claims that Lear's definition of man as a "poor, bare, forked animal" [III.iv.101–108] is derived from Plato through Diogenes Laertus' life of Diogenes the Cynic. Sh might also have encountered the definition in Erasmus's *Apophthegmata*. Lear's response to Edgar in the guise of Poor Tom is that of the Cynic.

2154 Elton, W. R. *"King Lear" and the Gods.* San Marino, California: Huntington Library, 1966. xii + 369 pp.

Rehearses, in an opening chapter, the optimistic Christian reading of *Lr.* that has been adopted by so many modern critics. Proposes to challenge this view. Chapter 3, on Sir Philip Sidney's *Arcadia*, one of Sh's acknowledged sources, finds in this work four attitudes to providence that are connected with Calvinist thought and that would, in Elizabethan eyes, be appropriate for the pagan world of *Lr.* Discerns, in later chapters, that these attitudes are embodied in Sh's characters: (1) The *prisca theologia*, or virtuous–heathen view, is that of Cordelia and Edgar; (2) the atheistic pagan view is adumbrated in Edmund, Goneril, and Regan; (3) superstition dominates the beliefs of Gloucester; and (4) Lear is a representative of heroic pagan society who cannot perceive any purpose in providence and never frees himself of the the belief that "death ends all." Analyzes the double plot and minor characters. Refers copiously to classical authors as background. Concludes that *Lr.* is "a syncretically pagan tragedy," which, by its portrayal of a pagan coming to doubt his gods, secured the approval of "the less speculative devout," and which, by its image of the unstable world of the late Renaissance, gained the interest of the "more troubled and sophisticated."

2155 Fleissner, Robert F. "King Lear's Love-Test: A Latin Derivation." *N&Q*, 15 (1968), 143–44.

Proposes adopting the Folio readings of "nothing" in several lines of *Lr.*, I.i, rather than the quarto readings, which omit a number of the nothings. Cites repetition of *nihil* in Corderius's *Dialogues*—a possible source of *Lr.*—as support.

2156 Fleissner, Robert F. "Lear's 'Learnèd Theban' and 'Justice[r]': A Resonance of Tiresias." *ShY*, 2 (1991), 182–86.

Argues that Lear's designation of Edgar, who is disguised as Poor Tom, as "learnèd Theban," "Noble philosopher," and "good Athenian" (*Lr.*, III.iv.155, 171, 179) is a reference to Tiresias in the Oedipus legend.

2157 Fraser, Russell A. *Shakespeare's Poetics in Relation to "King Lear."* London: Routledge & Kegan Paul, 1962. xi + 184 pp.

Approaches Sh's poetics by examining the iconology of *Lr.* Discusses "crystallizing images" in *Lr.* for the following central motifs: "the idea of Providence; of Kind; of Fortune; of Anarchy and Order; and Reason and Will; and Show against Substance; and Redemption." Cites classical images from the emblem literature of the 16th c. as illustrations. For example, in the chapter on anarchy and order, Lear, bound to a wheel of fire, is likened to Ixion, for the Renaissance one of the four chief "archetypes of usurpation and its issue."

2158 Godshalk, W. L. "'Ripeness is All.'" *N&Q*, 14 (1967), 145.

Suggests that E. K.'s comment on the emblem to "November" in *The Shepherds' Calendar* is a more illuminating gloss on Sh's "Ripeness is all" than the passage from Cicero mentioned as a source by H. Rossiter-Smith (item 2175).

2159 Hardison, O. B. Jr. "Myth and History in *King Lear*." *SQ*, 26 (1975), 227–42.

Supports the view that Sh used the myth of Ixion to give significance to the historical materials in *Lr*. Recapitulates the myth as it was interpreted "by mythographers who influenced 16th-century thought" and then applies it to *Lr*. The Ixion myth symbolizes "the desire for pomp without responsibilities"; the failure to gain real power (represented by Juno, whom Ixion attempted to seduce; failing this, he became infatuated with a cloud woman); the disillusionment with vain action (represented by Jove's thunderbolt, which sent Ixion to hell); divine punishment (represented by the wheel to which Ixion was bound); the effects of lust (represented by the 100 centaurs Ixion begot on the cloud woman and kept as retainers); ingratitude; and redemption (represented by Chiron, the one good centaur). These elements are all found in *Lr*. For example, the storm is Lear's thunderbolt, his unruly retainers (and his two bad daughters) are his centaurs, and Cordelia is his Chiron.

2160 Hebert, Catherine A. "Shakespeare's *King Lear*, III.iv.161." *Expl*, 34 (1975–76), item 72.

Finds it likely that Lear's use of the phrase "learned Theban" [III.iv.155] to describe Edgar in the guise of Poor Tom refers to "Oedipus, solver of riddles." Sh might have known of Oedipus from the *Oedipus* of Seneca, a staple of the school curriculum of the time and a play that was translated by Alexander Nevile in 1560 and included in *Seneca, His Tenne Tragedies* by Thomas Newton in 1581.

2161 Hiatt, Ann Carolyn. "Madness in *King Lear*: Division Within." Ph.D. dissertation, Southern Illinois University at Carbondale, 1979. *DAI*, 40 (1979–80), 4606-A.

Explores the shattering of the self in Lear's madness. He loses his sense of himself as father and king and takes on a number of other, often mutually contradictory roles. In a deeper sense, Lear's mind is divided between increasing madness and intensifyingly clear sanity. Appendix A discusses madness in Greek and Senecan tragedy and maintains that the mad characters of Seneca are basically static, whereas numerous characters in the Greek tragedies manifest a division into opposing personalities and a variety of mad voices that make them similar to Lear.

2161a Hoover, Claudette. "Goneril and Regan: 'So Horrid as in Woman.'" *San Jose Studies*, 10, no. 3 (1984), 49–65.

Examines *The True Chronicle History of King Leir*, the chief source of Lr., to show that the medieval assumptions that women are controlled by jealousy, vanity, rivalry, and avarice—which clearly govern the behavior of Leir's evil daughters in the older play—are conspicuously absent in Sh's portrayal of Goneril and Regan. Sh does seem to glance at the qualities of "the masculine woman" of classical drama in Lear's two older daughters, but he does not allow them to achieve the heroic stature of figures like Clytemnestra and Medea. He introduces another vice traditionally assigned to women—sexual insatiability—late in the play to account for the falls of Goneril and Regan. Sh teases the audience by declining to use the most conventional motivations for feminine evil and by hinting at—but then undercutting—other possible motivations.

2162 Iwasaki, Soji. "Time and Truth in *King Lear*." *ShStud*, 5 (1966–67), 1–42.

Uses illustrations from Renaissance emblematists to make the case that Sh is employing the idea of *Veritas filia temporis* as "a formative principle" in *Lr*. Sees Cordelia as Truth and Lear, finally, as Time. Lear's suffering, through which he assumes the role of Time, is partly conveyed by the images of a vulture tearing out Prometheus's heart and of Ixion's being bound on a wheel of fire.

2163 Jenkins, Raymond. "The Socratic Imperative and King Lear." *RenP*, 1963 (1964), 85–93.

Argues that in *Lr*. the king begins in a state of self-ignorance and goes through a process of self-education. In accord with the Socratic precept that knowing oneself is the key to moral insight, Sh shows Lear finally achieving self-knowledge in "his awe before the mystery of Cordelia's self-effacing love."

2164 King, T. J. "'Darnel' in *King Lear*, IV.iv.5." *N&Q*, 15 (1968), 141.

Points out that Cordelia's reference to darnel may "reinforce the themes of madness and blindness found elsewhere in the play." Cooper's *Thesaurus* (1565) says darnel makes the head giddy, and in Plautus's *Miles Gloriosus* there is a reference to its causing impaired vision.

2165 Kinney, Arthur F. "Some Conjectures on the Composition of *King Lear*." *ShS*, 33 (1980), 13–25.

Proposes *Six Bookes of Politickes or Civil Doctrine, Written in Latine by Iustus Lipsius*, translated into English by William Jones (1594), as a source for *Lr*. This work was "the chief book of political philosophy by one of three or four of the most renowned humanist scholars of Sh's day, and the period's greatest Roman historian." A "storehouse of ideas from Tacitus and Cicero," as well as other classical writers, Lipsius's neo-Stoic compendium directs us to consider carefully the "rich and pervasive strain of neo-Stoicism" in the play.

2166 Lindheim, Nancy R. "*King Lear* as Pastoral Tragedy." *Some Facets of "King Lear": Essays in Prismatic Criticism*. Eds. Rosalie L. Colie and F. T. Flahiff. Toronto: U. of Toronto P., 1974, pp. 169–84.

Contends that though *Lr*. is not finally pastoral, it makes use of pastoral–romance structure and one of the key ideas of the pastoral—the highly civilized notion that to be human requires one to respond with sympathy to the suffering of another or to any offense to one's human values. Compares *Lr*. with *AYL*, in which this idea is developed through reference to Aeneas's entrance into the temple of Carthage (*Aeneid* 1).

2167 MacIntyre, Jean. "Shakespeare's *King Lear*, III.vi.8." *Expl*, 21, no. 3 (1962), 24.

Suggests that when Edgar, after hearing Lear rage about the unnatural behavior of his daughters, says that "Nero is an angler in the lake of darkness," he is aptly recalling Nero's incest with and murder of his mother, as recorded by Tacitus and Suetonius.

2168 Martin, William Franklin. "The Indissoluble Knot: An Analysis of the Comic and Tragic Strands in the Fabric of *King Lear*." Ph.D. dissertation, Texas Tech University, 1971. *DAI*, 32 (1971–72), 2061-A.

Contends that Sh deliberately violated the classical precepts of tragedy in *Lr*. to create a blend of tragedy and comedy and present life "in its ironic reality." In Aristotelian terms, much of the action is too trivial and the two major characters—Gloucester and Lear—are too ordinary for tragic treatment. Sh was able, however, to transcend the narrow categories of comedy and tragedy and achieve a vision of life beyond either one.

2169 McCullen, J. T. Jr. "Edgar: The Wise Bedlam." *Shakespeare in the Southwest: Some New Directions.* Ed. T. J. Stafford. U. of Texas at El Paso: Texas Western P., 1969, pp. 43–55.

Cites Plato's *Phaedrus* as background for Renaissance commentary on the distinction between opinion and knowledge. Also quotes an account of the Pandora legend used by Girolamo Cardano (1563) to illustrate "man's struggle with opinion versus knowledge" and to provide "a controlling idea for a masterful treatise on relativistic philosophy." Edgar, in *Lr.*, lives by this philosophy, thus furthering the process by which Lear and Gloucester are weaned from false opinion and learn to accept "life and death for what they are."

2170 Nagarajan, M. S. "Chicago Critics and *King Lear*." *IJES*, 13 (1972), 161–72.

Considers the New Critical approach to *Lr.* (as exemplified in Robert Heilman's *This Great Stage: Image and Structure in King Lear*) in relation to the Aristotelian approach of the Chicago critics. Cites W. R. Keast's criticism of Heilman's emphasis on recurrent image patterns, which, according to Keast, arbitrarily forces all interpretation of the play to serve the notion that it is a metaphor. Sums up the analysis of another Chicago critic, Elder Olson, which studies *Lr.* by examining the plot, character, and thought in the manner of Aristotle. Shows how Norman Maclean, another Aristotelian, "discusses the madness of Lear—the order, completeness, vividness, probability and 'emotional unity' in it." The Chicago Aristotelians thus provide "a salutary corrective to the approach of the New Critics" by taking into account "the structure of the play as an artistic whole and not just a collection of the systems of language."

2171 Oyama, Toshikazu. "*King Lear* and Its Tragic Pattern." *ShStud*, 5 (1966–67), 43–71.

Points to Lear's swearing by Hecate when he disinherits Cordelia as a key to the tragic pattern of *Lr.* The use of Hecate in this way suggests that "demonological thinking" is deeply embedded in Lear's consciousness. During the play, Lear comes to terms with his partially submerged perception that the world is not a harmonious whole but exists in a state of tension between positive and negative. The play reveals, and Lear is forced to accept, that the dominant pattern of life is "to be *and* not to be."

2172 Parotti, Philip. "A New Dimension to Goneril's Depravity: Shakespeare's Amazonian Allusion in *King Lear*." *PAPA*, 8, no. 1 (1982), 33–41.

Adduces Goneril's speech to Edmund about her husband, Albany (*Lr.*, IV.ii.11–24), as evidence that Sh enhances her unnatural depravity by "casting her in the role of an Amazon." Points out that classical sources were virtually unanimous in portraying the Amazons as "grossly repellent" but that Virgil's favorable treatment of Camilla in the *Aeneid* gave rise to a misleadingly positive portrait of other Amazons by a number of later writers like Dante and Boccaccio. Some Elizabethan writers continued this idealization, but Ariosto, Spenser, and Sh accepted the authentic classical conception of the Amazons as "malignant symbols of disorder."

2173 Pratt, Norman. "From Oedipus to Lear." *CJ*, 61 (1965–66), 49–57.

Contrasts *Oedipus the King* and *Lr.* to show that the difference lies in the treatment of nature. In the former, nature is imperfect, or imperfectible; in the latter, only a part of nature, the human dimension, is defective. The transition between these two types of drama can be located in Seneca, whose Stoicism directed him to write tragedy of moral order. *Lr.* evidences strong elements of Stoicism.

2173a Pratt, Norman T. *Seneca's Drama.* Chapel Hill: U. of North Carolina P., 1983. ix + 229 pp.

Chapter 1, a revision of item 2173, offers a contrast between Sophocles' *Oedipus the King* and *Lr.* to demonstrate that the two works are based on two radically different conceptions of the human condition. In Sophocles, the catastrophe grows out of a confrontation of the human and the divine; in Sh, the conflict is a moral one. Argues that this difference can be explained by the fact that Sh wrote after Seneca had established a new kind of drama. Proposes to give due attention to three major elements in Seneca's work: "the hypertensive mode of rhetoric as a form of expression, feeling, and thought; the Stoic, and specifically Neo-Stoic, conception of a rational moral order threatened by the human passions; and the personal experience of a statesman whose ideals were tortured by the moral savagery of Rome."

2174 Presson, Robert K. "Boethius, King Lear, and 'Maystresse Philosophie.'" *JEGP*, 64 (1965), 406–24.

Argues that there is a pronounced Boethian emphasis in *Lr.*, noting that Sh could have read *De Consolatio* in Chaucer's translation. In both works, we find strongly contrasted good and evil; a sense that experiencing reality involves suffering great pain and turbulence; tempest imagery to convey the restless nature of life; the concept of Fortune; and the glimpse of another world in which "men and natural phenomena" are held together "by the bond of love." In *Lr.*, Sh raises the same issues that troubled Boethius, but the optimistic answers that Philosophy gives and that satisfy Boethius are not able to dispel the pessimism evoked by the dramatist.

2175 Rossiter-Smith, H. "'Ripeness is all.'" *N&Q*, 12 (1965), 97.

Points out a possible use of Cicero's *De Senectute* in *Lr.* (V.ii.9–11), in which Edgar says, "Ripeness is all." Thomas Newton's translation of *De Senectute* (1569) uses the word "ripeness" in describing how old men die. See item 2158.

2176 Rusche, Harry. "Edmund's Conception and Nativity in *King Lear*." *SQ*, 20 (1969), 161–64.

Contends that Ptolemy's *Tetrabiblos* can help to explain the full significance of the astrological details Edmund gives in *Lr.*, I.ii, about his conception ("under the dragon's tail") and his birth ("under Ursa Major"). According to Ptolemy, the astrological influences at the time of conception are essentially the same as those at the time of birth. That Edmund was conceived under the dragon's tail, a maleficent influence, confirms that his birth was indeed ill-omened. This could not be determined from the single fact that he was born under Ursa Major, which by itself might be either favorable or unfavorable, depending on other circumstances. The kind of astrological knowledge necessary to understand these references could be casually acquired in Sh's time; it was available to the educated layman through such works as translations of Ptolemy, handbooks, almanacs, and treatises for and against astrology.

2177 Salingar, Leo. "Romance in *King Lear*." *English* (London), 27 (1978), 5–21.

Comments, while pursuing the argument that in *Lr.* Sh sets up "a dialectic between expectations belonging to romance and those attached to tragedy," that the playwright reinforces the tragic force of the old legend about Lear by importing elements from "Seneca's two plays about Oedipus."

2178 Skulsky, Harold. "*King Lear* and the Meaning of Chaos." *SQ*, 17 (1966), 3–17.

Begins a discussion of the relationship between suffering and Providence in *Lr.* with a reference to *Tro.*, in which Ulysses' doctrine of the good as the natural, derived from the scholastic–Aristotelian tradition, is useless because it offers no answer to a character like Troilus, who professes to find value in idiosyncrasy, and because it "makes distinctions of value merely *de facto* and extrinsic." In *Lr.*, Sh "calmly searches the chaos that Ulysses has glanced at with a shudder." As it turns out, Sh achieves "an empirical test of the simplicity and irreducibility of the experience of value against the negations of moral relativism."

2179 Smithers, G. V. "Guide-Lines for Interpreting the Uses of the Suffix '-ed' in Shakespeare's English." *ShS*, 23 (1979), 27–37.

Discusses *-ed* as an adjective–forming suffix in Sh's works. Explains the word *stelled* (*Lr.*, III.vii.62) as created by the replacement of the Latin adjective–forming suffix *-ate* on *stell-* with the native suffix *-ed*. *Stelled* thus means "consisting of stars" or "of the stars."

2179a Soellner, Rolf. "*King Lear* and the Magic of the Wheel." *SQ*, 35 (1984), 274–89.

Explains that the circular images in *Lr.* are primarily vertical and are thus associated with the wheel of Fortune. Notes that the conception of life as "a rotating wheel or circle" was held by the Greek tragedians and that this notion was transmitted through Seneca's tragedies to the Middle Ages and the Renaissance, "where it merged with the wheel turned by the goddess Fortuna, an image which derived from Boethius, Dante, and Boccaccio." Argues that Sh's most pervasive and complex use of the wheel image occurs in *Lr.*, probably because the playwright sensed that such a commonplace is "the best means of expressing a world in which elemental upheavals in man and nature become heartbreakingly common."

2180 Stanley, E. G. "'Ripeness is All.'" *N&Q*, 14 (1967), 228.

Cites examples of the Ciceronian idea of ripeness for death in 17th-c. English literature that have relevance for a discussion of *Lr.*, V.ii.10.

2181 Stockholder, Katherine. "The Multiple Genres of *King Lear*: Breaking the Archetypes." *BuR*, 16, no. 1 (1968), 40–63.

Argues that the play's ambiguous vibration "results from Shakespeare's deliberate intermingling of the devices of and the vision inherent in comedy, fairy tale, and farce on the one hand and tragedy on the other" and that "the continuously shifting balance of emotional response evoked by these genres contains the play's meaning." Contributing to this ambiguity, Lear becomes, for part of the play, a fool, a *senex*, a comic *alazon*, who "confers power on the forces of absolute evil to exploit the folly he thereby demonstrates."

2181a Viswanathan, S. "'This same learned Theban': *King Lear*, III.iv.161." *N&Q*, 33 (1986), 362–63.

Maintains that the "learned Theban" [*Lr.*, III.iv.155] alludes to the Greek philosopher Cebes of Thebes, whose *Tabulae Vitae*, explicating "the education and progress of man through the stages of life" and often accompanied by an illustrative woodcut, was a familiar school text of Sh's time.

2182 Weidhorn, Manfred. "Lear's Schoolmasters." *SQ*, 13 (1962), 305–16.

Cites the spiritual education of Achilles in the *Iliad* as a parallel to Lear's tragic probing of "every ramification of his experience."

2183 Williams, George Walton. "Petitionary Prayer in *King Lear*." *SAQ*, 85 (1986), 360–73.

Identifies twenty-two prayers in *Lr.* and maintains that they are directed to the gods of the classical tradition: Apollo, Jupiter, Phoebus, Juno, Cupid, Nature, and Fortune, and "the heavens." There are eight petitioners, one bad (Edmund) and seven good. All prayers are answered, though not necessarily at the time or in the exact manner requested. We see that the gods are just, though their way is not easy: The first and last prayers in the play are for Cordelia, whose death is a form of protection by the gods (they take her to their dear shelter). The tragedy leaves us with a sense of "pagan optimism."

A Lover's Complaint

2184   Kerrigan, John, ed. *Motives of Woe: Shakespeare and "Female Complaint." A Critical Anthology.* Oxford: Clarendon P., 1991. xiv + 310 pp.

Collects examples of "female complaint" from c. 1300 to 1729, with *LC* as the central text. The introduction emphasizes the importance of Ovid's works, especially the *Heroides*, both through their absorption into medieval tradition and through their use as stylistic models in the upper forms of Elizabethan grammar schools. Notes prototypes for "the literature of echoes" (Sh's speaker overhears a maiden complaining with "double voice" [line 3]) in Virgil and Ovid. Comments that the maid, in presenting her "cause" in disarray, is "almost a parody of the Ciceronian orator."

2184a   Underwood, Richard Allan. Shakespeare on Love: The Poems and the Plays. *Prolegomena to a Variorum Edition of "A Lover's Complaint."* (Elizabethan and Renaissance Studies 91.) Salzburg: Institut für Anglistik und Amerikanistik, U. Salzburg, 1985. xv +189 pp.

Presents the text of *LC*. Traces the complaint, especially the love lament by women (of which *LC* is a specimen), to book 4 of Virgil's *Aeneid* and to Ovid's *Heroides*. Discusses a number of other works by Sh and others related to the complaint, including *Luc*. Includes chapters that discuss *LC* generally (chapter 2) and the poem's style (chapter 3).

Love's Labor's Lost

2185   Agnew, Gates Kennedy. "An Approach to *"Love's Labour's Lost."* Ph.D. dissertation, Stanford University, 1964. *DA*, 25 (1964–65), 4122.

Approaches *LLL* as "a play about simplicity." Surveys appeals to simplicity of style in the 16th c., including those made by didactic writers, religious controversialists, and humanistic and courtly writers. Polite authors like Sir Philip Sidney were aware of the classical precedents for simplicity of style. The low plot of *LLL* can be illuminated by reference to "the ideal of simplicity among didactic and utilitarian writers," while Sidney's *Astrophil and Stella* is an instructive point of reference for the high plot.

2185a   Carroll, William C. *The Great Feast of Language in "Love's Labour's Lost."* Princeton: Princeton U. P., 1976. xii + 279 pp.

Reads *LLL* as "a debate on the right uses of rhetoric, poetry, and the imagination." Chapter 1 focuses on "the language and prose styles in the play," especially the styles of the six low characters. Throughout the play, the notion that the names of things have an essential connection to the things themselves, recognized in the Renaissance as being partly derived from Plato's *Cratylus*, works in dialogue with the theory that language is arbitrary. Notes the pervasive use of rhetorical figures, especially synonymy and paronomasia. What the characters and the audience are taught by the play is the principle of decorum, the flexible use of language in a variety of contexts. Chapter 2 considers three scenes that foreground the play's preoccupation with its own theatricality, including that of the Nine Worthies (V.ii). Chapter 3 analyzes several explicit examples of "poetry" composed by the characters. Holofernes' critique of Berowne's sonnet (IV.ii) in the light of Ovid's achievement is particularly revealing. The pedant possesses a narrow understanding of the Roman poet and of the concept of imitation; he points out, correctly, that Berowne's poem is only a barren aping of the flowers of rhetoric, but he does not understand the transformative power of the imagination for which Ovid stands and which permeates the play. Chapter 4 pursues transformations among the different groups of characters, including those with "spectacularly warped imaginations." At play's end, the noblemen "are moving in the right direction," but the metamorphosis is incomplete. Chapter 5 discusses the structure of the play in order to address its treatment of "the traditional Art–Nature dualism," and chapter 6 argues that the songs of Spring and Winter at the end blend art and nature in a kind of resolution. Appendix B inventories some of the ideas the Renaissance attached to Hercules, whose appearance as one of the Nine Worthies and frequent mention give him significance in the play. Explains Hercules' association with both the active and the intellectual life and shows how the references to his labors in *LLL* have both comic and serious resonances.

2186   Crawley, Thomas Francis. "*Love's Labour's Lost* and the Pageant of the Nine Worthies: A Thematic and Structural Analysis." Ph.D. dissertation, University of Nebraska, 1969. *DAI*, 30 (1969–70), 1522-A.

Maintains that the burlesque pageant of the Nine Worthies concentrates in itself three thematic patterns of *LLL*: the affected learning of the courtiers, pretentiousness in love, and "frivolous conduct in a moral universe." In the Middle Ages and the Renaissance, the Nine Worthies were associated with the *De casibus* and *Ubi sunt* themes, and thus their use by Sh helps prepare for Mercade's sobering news and the chastening of the perjured courtiers.

2187   Draudt, Manfred. "Shakespeare's Unpretentious Ending to *Love's Labor's Lost.*" *SJH*, 1982, pp. 162–68.

Claims that "The words of Mercury," a line spoken by Armado at the end of *LLL*, refers to a line spoken by Moth (who as a swift messenger would possess the attributes Sh usually associated with Mercury) and would have been either an ironic comment on the songs just heard or a reminder that "the ladies are about to take their leave."

2188   Elam, Keir. "The Words of Mercury and the Songs of Apollo: The Status of the Linguistic Sign in *Love's Labour's Lost* and Other Shakespearean Comedies. Part I." *Annali. Instituto universitario orientale. Anglistica*, 24, no. 3 (1981), 7–43.

Attempts a semiotic analysis of *LLL* and comments more briefly on some of Sh's other comedies. Explains that "semantic naturalism"—the belief that language is composed of "names," each having a "one-to-one relationship" with the "slice of reality denoted"—was given authority in the Renaissance by a misreading of Plato's *Cratylus*. Neoplatonists like Marsilio Ficino and Pico della Mirandola promoted this belief because it allowed them to affirm a mystical union (perceptible only to the initiate) between the spoken or written word and the inner reality it expresses. In *LLL*, Sh engages in a critical examination of Neoplatonism, and more especially the Neoplatonic doctrine of language. The aristocratic academicians of Navarre are possessed by "a faith in the phenomenal and numinal fullness of the linguistic sign." Even after they have been converted from scholars to "pseudo-Platonic lovers," Navarre and his bookmen still direct their ardor toward the name. Their social inferiors are also entangled in the problems of linguistic naturalism. The French princess and her ladies, however, adopt a metalinguistic strategy to expose the men's credulity. Other comedies of Sh provide "more occasional glimpses of apparent linguistic superstition." Revised as the first part of chapter 3 of item 0353a.

2189   Evans, Malcolm. "Mercury Versus Apollo: A Reading of *Love's Labor's Lost.*" *SQ*, 26 (1975), 113–27.

Draws on Renaissance encyclopedic handbooks of mythology to explain the importance of Mercury and Apollo in *LLL*. Mercury is associated with "book-learning, the quest for fame, and the desire for immortality." The influence of Mercury isolates individuals and is socially divisive. In the play, this tendency is represented on its most general level by concern with the written word. Apollo, however, presides over spoken language and all that it entails: communication, reciprocation, self-knowledge, and society. In this play, Sh was clearly expressing his preference for the "oral medium of drama." The quarto's speakerless line, "The words of Mercury are harsh after the songs of Apollo," may thus be considered a footnote in which Sh registered somewhat grudgingly that he had revised the play for its 1598 printing, adding much that was not in the acted version.

2190 Fisher, S. T. "The Song of the Seasons in *Love's Labor's Lost.*" *N&Q*, 29 (1982), 110–11.

Argues that careful attention to two Greek legends about the origin of winter—the absence of Apollo from Delphi and a Persephone's rape by Hades—clears up confusion about the song at the end of *LLL* and Armado's final lines. The first two verses, headed "*Ver*" and sung by the cuckoo, are "the songs of Apollo"; the last two, headed "*Hiems*" and sung by the owl, are "the words of Mercury" (V.i.926–927).

2191 Goldstien, Neal L. "*Love's Labor's Lost* and the Renaissance Vision of Love." *SQ*, 25 (1974), 335–50.

Argues that *LLL* presents a satirical view of the Renaissance conception of ideal love, with its combination of Petrarchanism and Neoplatonism. Instead of celebrating the Platonic ascent from the lowest of the senses to the apprehension of divine beauty, the play, through character and situation, mocks both the conventions of ideal love and the spirituality on which they are based. Berowne's speeches often contain lines that are superficially Platonic, but he always falls back on the sensual; other characters—even the ladies—betray an intractable sensuality as well. In the two songs at the end, the life of the senses is itself subjected to cynical questioning, but it dominates the rest of the play.

2192 Harvey, Nancy Lenz, and Anna Kirwan Carey, comps. *"Love's Labor's Lost": An Annotated Bibliography.* (Garland Shakespeare Bibliographies 6.) New York: Garland, 1984. xiv + 220 pp.

Covers primarily works published between 1940 and 1980, with some items from before 1940 included. Classifies entries under eight headings, including Criticism (210 items); Sources (38 items); Bibliographies, Concordances, Dictionaries, and Listings (16 items); and Editions (87 items). Begins each section with the oldest entry and proceeds chronologically. Concludes with a single index that treats each entry according to author, subject, and motif. Provides substantial and detailed annotations.

2193 Hawkes, Terence. "Shakespeare's Talking Animals." *ShS*, 24 (1971), 47–54.

Cites Plato's distrust of writing in the *Phaedrus* as an entry into *LLL*, in which "the oral world of speech is comically opposed to the silent world of books." Explains the line at the end about "the words of Mercury" and "the songs of Apollo" as referring to the written version of the play and the words heard in its actual performance, respectively.

2194 Helton, Tinsley. "Shakespeare's *Love's Labor's Lost*, V.ii.940–941." *Expl*, 22 (1963–64), no. 25.

Suggests that the sentence "The words of Mercury are harsh after the songs of Apollo" at the end of *LLL* [lines 926–927] refers to Apollo in the "comprehensive sense of god of the arts" and to Mercury in his dual role of messenger of the gods and patron of travelers. Mercade acts as a sort of Mercury by bringing news that causes the princess and her ladies to travel; and this puts an end to the Apollonian "feast of the arts" that has constituted the play's action.

2195 Hibbard, G. R., ed. *Love's Labour's Lost.* (Oxford Shakespeare.) Oxford: Clarendon P., 1990. viii + 263 pp.

The introduction points out that *LLL* is "the dramatization of a whole collection of closely interrelated oppositions," including "Plato versus Ovid." The images of the relationship between the sexes as a kind of war, of women as the enemy, and of the lover as soldier—all prominent in the play—can be traced back to Ovid.

2196 Montrose, Louis Adrian. "'Curious-Knotted Garden': The Form, Themes, and Contexts of Shakespeare's *Love's Labour's Lost*." Ph.D. dissertation, University of California, San Diego, 1974. *DAI*, 35 (1974–75), 5418-A.

Attempts to present "a comprehensive critical reading of the play" by interpreting it as "a fundamentally thematic and satiric comedy." Sh uses mythological subjects like the Choice of Hercules, the Hard and Soft Hunts, and the Judgment of Paris as "projections of the characters' fantasies," which are exposed as "confused and self-deceiving parodies of mythic models." Part revised as item 2197.

2197 Montrose, Louis Adrian. "'Folly in wisdom hatch'd': The Exemplary Comedy of *Love's Labor's Lost*." *CompD*, 11 (1977–78), 147–70.

Points out that Navarre perverts the *ars vivendi* of classical Stoicism as understood by the Renaissance. It was "associated with the active, not the contemplative life," but the King and his courtiers attempt to master the world without participating in it. The play relies heavily on allusions to heroic models, particularly Hercules, who was recognized in the Renaissance as an exemplar of active virtue. During the play, the language of heroic virtue is used ironically to image forth the aristocrats' self-absorbed efforts at contemplation. Not only do they fail to realize their goal, but, according to "the humanistic side of Renaissance Neoplatonism," their goal is a false one: Instead of pursuing one narrow pattern, they should seek integration of active virtue, pleasure, and wisdom. Sh playfully exposes "the limitations of exemplary images of the heroic" and "the problems [that] are created by the attempt to apply inadequate models to the complexities of actual existence." Revision of part of item 2196.

2198 Murphy, Georgeann. "The Nature of Language and Genre in *Love's Labour's Lost*." Ph.D. dissertation, Tulane University, 1984. *DAI*, 45 (1984–85), 3647-A.

Notes that the notion of genre was closely tied to rhetorical tradition in Sh's time. Chapter 2 traces the skeptical view of language exhibited in *LLL* back to Plato. Notes that "the abusers of language" in *LLL* are ranked in a hierarchy. The women in the play prevent the language abuse from having tragic consequences, but they cannot prevent it from "obscuring the comic genre of the play."

2199 Nosworthy, J. M. "The Importance of Being Marcade." *ShS*, 32 (1979), 105–14.

Argues that Apollo presides over *LLL* until the last act, in which control passes to Mercury. The sun god makes possible the outdoor setting; as Apollo Musagetes, he receives offerings of song, sonnet, dance, and pageant; as god of institutions, he oversees the establishment of academe; and as agent of sudden death, he brings the revelry to an abrupt end. In addition, the Delphic precepts—"Know thyself" and "Nothing in excess"—shape the play's moral pattern. With the appearance of Marcade (V.ii), Mercury becomes predominant. Marcade's name could be pronounced "Markedy," which is the form used for Mercury's name in Robert Wilson's *The Cobbler's Prophecy* (1594). Marcade also fulfills two of the god's functions: messenger and psychopomp (he is responsible for sending both Navarre and Berowne to underworlds). Thus the words of Armado at the end of the Folio text, "The words of Mercury are harsh after the songs of Apollo" (V.ii.926–927), are precisely appropriate. *WT*, with its first half under the aegis of Apollo and its second half imbued with the spirit of Autolycus, who is named for Mercury's son, helps corroborate this reading of *LLL*.

2199a Perryman, Judith C. "A Tradition Transformed in *Love's Labour's Lost*." *EA*, 37 (1984), 156–62.

Maintains that Sh's choice of Worthies for Armado's pageant (*LLL*, V.i) and the manner in which the Worthies are presented are calculated to make a satirical comment on the court of Navarre. Pompey, the first Worthy to appear, lends his name to word play that calls attention to and deflates pomp. In addition, he is an ironic substitute for his conqueror Julius Caesar, a more usual member of the group of Nine.

North's translation of Plutarch makes clear that much of Pompey's career involved defeat and shame. The second Worthy, Alexander, recalls the king's description of the members of his academe as "brave conquerors" (I.i.9), and his silent retreat before the taunts of his audience to be replaced by Ajax suggests the failure of the lords to conquer either their desires or the ladies. The next Worthy, Hercules, played by the diminutive Moth, is ridiculous in his lack of heroic stature; his appearance makes a succinct point about "the failure of extravagant language" and "the insignificance of love." The final Worthy, Hector, who comes first in the more traditional order, is brought on stage with ironic cheering as a victim instead of a conqueror. The commoners who play the Worthies are mocked, but at the end they become disengaged from their roles. The lords, however, remain blind to their vices, shown by the pageant "to have the essence of discord, defeat, and death."

2199b Perryman, Judith. "'The words of Mercury': Alchemical Imagery in *Love's Labour's Lost*." *The Spirit of the Court*. Selected Proceedings of the Fourth Congress of the International Courtly Literature Society (Toronto 1983). Eds. Glyn S. Burgess and Robert A. Taylor. Cambridge, England: D. S. Brewer, 1985, pp. 246–53.

Contends that the major of theme of *LLL* is "the matter of oath-breaking" and that this theme is explored through group of symbolic images related to the alchemical process as it was understood in the 16th and 17th c. Apollo and Mercury, mentioned at the end of the play, make more sense as alchemical symbols than they do as the gods of classical myth.

2200 Shulman, Jeff. "At the Crossroads of Myth: The Hermeneutics of Hercules from Ovid to Shakespeare." *ELH*, 50 (1983), 83–105.

Points out that Ovidian mythmaking often involved a juxtaposition of incompatible elements. Consequently, most recapitulations of tales from the *Metamorphoses* "rend asunder what Ovid joined." Follows the Hercules legend from Ovid. Claims that the tale's original complexity is not found in a retelling until *LLL*. Revision of part of item 0967.

2201 Thorne, Barry. "*Love's Labor's Lost*: The Lyly Gilded." *HAB*, 21, no. 3 (1970), 32–37.

Suggests that in *LLL* Sh was, among other things, mocking and humanizing the Platonic philosophy of Lyly's *Endymion*.

MACBETH

2202 Andrews, Michael Cameron. "Erasmus and *Macbeth*: 'Making the Green One Red.'" *ErasmusR*, 15 (1987–88), 30–31.

Suggests that Sh recalled the Latin of Erasmus's colloquy *Amicitia* when he composed Macbeth's lines about "Making the green one red" (*Mac.*, II.ii.65–67). In the colloquy, there is a description of a green lizard seriously wounded in the side by a snake, which makes the green one red.

2203 Barnet, Sylvan, ed. *Macbeth*. (Signet Classic Shakespeare.) New York: New American Library, 1963. xxxiii + [34]–247 pp.

The note on the sources suggests that Sh might have been helped by Seneca's *Agamemnon* in drawing his portrait of Lady Macbeth and that the account of

Macbeth's nighttime murder of Duncan is indebted to Tarquin's rape of the heroine in *Luc*. The introduction, text, and note on the sources are reprinted as part of item 0123.

2204 Belsey, Catherine. "Senecan Vacillation and Elizabethan Deliberation: Influence or Confluence?" *RenD*, N. S. 6 (1973), 65–88.

Suggests that the Senecan soliloquy, concerned with expressing a character's vacillation between competing passions, is different from the more deliberative soliloquy of the English tragic hero in the Renaissance. The main source for the substance of the English soliloquy was the native morality tradition, but Seneca did provide the concept of the soliloquy itself. Uses *Mac.* as an example.

2205 Belsey, Catherine. "Shakespeare's 'Vaulting Ambition.'" *ELN*, 10 (1972–73), 198–201.

Discusses the origins of the image of "vaulting ambition" in *Mac*. The idea of Pride falling from a horse comes originally from Prudentius's *Psychomachia*, while the notion that the disastrous fall is "caused by leaping upwards" seems to have been borrowed directly from Thomas Preston's *Cambises*.

2206 Brooke, Nicholas, ed. *The Tragedy of Macbeth.* (Oxford Shakespeare.) Oxford: Clarendon P., 1990. xii + 249 pp.

The introduction notes the influence of Seneca's works on *Mac.*, especially in Sh's modeling of Lady Macbeth on the characters of Medea (from *Medea*) and Clytemnestra (from *Agamemnon*).

2207 Bushnell, Rebecca Weld. "Oracular Silence in *Oedipus the King* and *Macbeth*." *CML*, 2 (1981–82), 195–204.

Compares the supernatural oracular voices in *Oedipus the King* and *Mac*. The oracular voice "does not compel the hero; rather, it tempts, and it frustrates him, for when the important questions are asked, the supernatural voice is always silent." In *Mac.*, the Weird Sisters resemble the Delphic Oracle, though they lack "the Oracle's conventional authority." Also unlike the Delphic Oracle, the witches become increasingly duplicitous in their pronouncements. At the end, Macbeth escapes the prison of silence in which the witches attempt to confine him. Like Oedipus, he finds his own language and gains a measure of triumph over the oracular voice.

2208 Cutts, John P. "'Till Birnam Forest Come to Dunsinane.'" *SQ*, 21 (1970), 497–99.

Adduces a passage from George Sandys's prose commentary to his *Ovid's Metamorphoses Englished, Mythologiz'd, and Represented in Figures* (1632) as a key to understanding the symbolism of the moving wood in *Mac*. Orpheus's ability to make trees move (*Metamorphoses* 10) is seen by Sandys as a restoration of order to "lawless elements." Apparently the invading forces must "calm their disorderly rage for mere vengeance" and proceed in a measured, controlled manner to reestablish harmony in Scotland.

2208a Eade, J. C. *The Forgotten Sky: A Guide to Astrology in English Literature.* Oxford: Clarendon P., 1984. xiii + 230 pp.

Offers a handbook of the essential elements of "pre-Newtonian astrology" that will enable the layperson to assess particular literary references to this system. Acknowledges the importance of Claudius Ptolmaeus (Ptolemy) in codifying the system in the 2nd c. A.D. Includes an explication of the Captain's reference to the sun in *Mac*. (I.ii.25–28), which means that "just when the sun, having reached its furthest point of travel away from the northern hemisphere, is turning round to come back and so promises a seasonal up-turn—what you get, instead, is a down-turn in the weather."

2209 Ewbank, Inga-Stina. "The Fiend-Like Queen: A Note on *Macbeth* and Seneca's *Medea*." *ShS*, 19 (1966), 82–94.

Proposes Seneca's *Medea* as one source of *Mac*. Sh "has seized on a few emotional key-moments in the *Medea*, linked them with other themes and images in the play, and built them into his own moral structure." Two particular moments that seem to echo the *Medea* come when Lady Macbeth asks to be unsexed (I.v.40–54) and when she whets Macbeth's purpose by indicating her willingness to murder her own children (I.vii.55–60). In using the *Medea* as a source, however, Sh also turns away from it; Seneca's character "finds her heroic self *through* evil," while Lady Macbeth loses herself. The vision of evil in *Mac*. contains an awareness of its own destruction.

2209a Ghosh, Gouri Prasad. "Macbeth: Struggle and Defeat of the Moral Will." *Journal of the Department of English* (Calcutta U.), 19, nos. 1–2 (1983–84), 1–20.

Argues that *Mac*. records Sh's profoundly objective and profoundly puzzled witness to the dark and bizarre evil that seems to be part of "civilized human life." Finds a similarity in this regard between Sh and Sophocles.

2210 Godshalk, William Leigh. "Livy's Tullia: A Classical Prototype of Lady Macbeth." *SQ*, 16 (1965), 240–41.

Suggests that Sh supplemented the material he found in Holinshed about Lady Macbeth with the account of Tullia in the first book of Livy's *History*. There are several obvious parallels between Lady Macbeth and Tullia: Each is ambitious for her husband to be king, each incites her husband to murder the reigning monarch, each is directly involved in the murder, and each subsequently goes mad (Holinshed does not foreshadow Lady Macbeth's degeneration). Sh is likely to have read Livy's story of Tullia; it immediately precedes the account of Lucretia, which he used for *Luc*. See item 2234.

2211 Grenander, M. E. "*Macbeth* as Diaphthorody: Notes Toward the Definition of a Form." *Literary Criticism and Philosophy*. Ed. Joseph P. Strelka. (Yearbook of Comparative Criticism 10.) University Park: Pennsylvania State U. P., 1983, pp. 224–48.

Challenges several critics who have inaccurately or incompletely applied Aristotle's *Poetics* to *Mac*. Draws on the *Ethics* as well as the *Poetics* to offer a more satisfactory interpretation of the play. Proposes to designate *Mac*. a *diaphthorody*: "a non-didactic drama or novel [that] imitates a serious and complete action of appropriate magnitude, in either dramatic or narrative form, with incidents revealing morally repellent character deterioration that arouses horrified fascination, anguished concern, and grievous regret at human waste on a grand scale; and release of tension when it has worked itself out." The plot is one of character and shows a "continent good man" becoming an "incontinent bad man."

2212 Guj, Luisa. "*Macbeth* and the Seeds of Time." *ShakS*, 18 (1986), 175–88.

Points out that "the iconographic motif of three-headed time," originally allegorized by Macrobius in the 4th c. A.D. and widely used by Renaissance scholars, is central to the theme and structure of *Mac*.

2213 Hammond, Paul. "Macbeth and the Ages of Man." *N&Q*, 36 (1989), 332–33.

Analyzes Macbeth's meditation on the features of old age (*Mac*., V.iii.22–26) in terms of the accounts of the ages of man in Aristotle's *Rhetoric* and Horace's *Art of Poetry*. Macbeth seems to attribute to old age what was traditionally thought of as characteristic of middle age. He has thus confounded the ages of man, and his life "has fallen outside the regular path of human development."

2214 Hunter, William B. Jr. "A Decorous Macbeth." *ELN*, 8 (1970–71), 169–73.

Maintains that Sh conceived *Mac.* "so that it could be played two different ways. In both of them Duncan and Lady Macbeth die offstage. But the deaths of Banquo, the Macduffs, Seyward, and Macbeth himself all occur in such a way that the victim can be killed either in full view or hidden." The staging, in other words, can be done "in accordance with the classical principle of decorum, or it can be acted with sufficient blood and guts to satisfy an average Jacobean playgoer."

2215 Jacobson, Howard. "*Macbeth*, I.vii.7–10." *SQ*, 35 (1984), 321–22.

Suggests that these lines, in which Macbeth meditates on "Bloody instructions," which "return To plague th' inventor," are derived from Seneca's *Thyestes*, which Sh could have read either in the original Latin or in Jasper Haywood's 1560 translation.

2216 Jorgensen, Paul A. *Our Naked Frailties: Sensational Art and Meaning in "Macbeth."* Berkeley: U. of California P., 1971. viii + 234 pp.

Attempts a careful analysis of the sensational in *Mac.*, taking *sensational* in its "deeper interior meaning of causing sensation." Because the play is so "violently vivid, tactile, and generally sensory," it can benefit from such an approach. Includes, in chapter 2, an outline of the qualities the Elizabethans prized in the writings of Seneca. Though superficially Seneca may have contributed to the taste for "blood, revenge, and cruelty," he is more notable for the "decorous power" of his style. Most important, he was valued for "his potent moral lesson," especially the way in which vices are properly punished at the ends of his tragedies. The vividly sensational punishment for evil is the most Senecan quality of *Mac.* Points out classical examples of "condign punishment" (like that of Ixion) for "evil imagination and ambition" that, along with those from other sources, were available to Sh. Examines, in chapter 4, the artistry with which Sh depicts the murder of Duncan and the preparation for it. Playing a significant role in this episode is a stylized, ritualistic language previously used by Sh in the declamation about Priam's slaughter in *Ham.*, II.ii, deriving immediately from Christopher Marlowe and more fundamentally from Seneca. Chapter 5 discusses the imagery of blood in *Mac.*, showing how Sh drew on Seneca and on "the English classical dramatists" who imitated him. Chapter 6 focuses on the idea of "Innocence as victim" in the play, most powerfully conveyed in imagery connecting innocence with babies. For this idea, Sh probably found models in Seneca's tragedies (*Troas* and *Medea*, for example), especially as they were augmented by their Elizabethan translators. Chapter 7 analyzes the strangeness of the play's atmosphere, in part by speculating that Banquo's "enigmatic and frightening ghost" is modeled on the appearance of the ghost of Laius to Creon in Seneca's *Oedipus*.

2217 La Belle, Jenijoy. "'A Strange Infirmity': Lady Macbeth's Amenorrhea." *SQ*, 31 (1980), 381–86.

Analyzes the biological dimension of Lady Macbeth's aberrant desire for amenorrhea in her opening soliloquy (*Mac.*, I.v.40–54). Notes that her language recalls the opening speech of Seneca's *Medea* (in Studley's translation of 1581), in which Medea wishes to "exile all follysh Female feare and pity" from her nature as she prepares to murder her children.

2218 Lyle, E. B. "Two Parallels in *Macbeth* to Seneca's *Hercules Oetaeus*." *ES*, 53 (1972), 109–13.

Suggests that Sh borrowed from *Hercules Oetaeus* for Macbeth's challenge to Banquo's ghost (*Mac.*, III.iv.101–107) and for Macbeth's recognition that the only beneficiaries of his crime of murder may be Banquo's descendants (III.i.63–67). It would appear that Sh referred to Seneca in the original Latin in these cases.

2219 Markels, Julian. "The Spectacle of Deterioration: *Macbeth* and the 'Manner' of Tragic Imitation." *SQ*, 12 (1961), 293–303.

Analyzes *Mac.* in the light of Aristotle's conception in the *Poetics* of the "manner" of tragic imitation. In speaking of "manner," Aristotle commonly means spectacle, which he treats pejoratively as visual embellishment. He does, however, occasionally suggest that "manner" has to do with the playwright's choice of whether to narrate or render a particular episode, thus revealing thought, character, and action; arousing the tragic emotions; and intensifying a sense of probability. Sh's presentation of Macbeth as a tragic hero is intimately connected with his choice of incidents "to render rather than narrate, and of the sequence in which to render them." For example, the audience's outrage at Macbeth's crimes is qualified because Macbeth is not seen committing the three great acts of violence in the play. Sh manipulates what is presented to emphasize his protagonist's suffering and mask his depravity. *Mac.* is also rich in "the visual trappings and machinery" that Aristotle refers to slightingly as spectacle, but Sh skillfully uses these to exhibit the degeneration of his hero. The example of *Mac.* demonstrates that Aristotle is not sufficiently detailed in his treatment of the two senses of "manner."

2220 McCanles, Michael. "Mythos and Dianoia: A Dialectical Methodology of Literary Form." *Literary Monographs: Volume 4*. Ed. Eric Rothstein. Madison: U. of Wisconsin P., 1971, pp. 1–88.

Proposes an Aristotelian method of analyzing literary form, according to which plot "is generated out of the attempt on the part of the agent of the plot to avoid and deny plot." Includes a discussion of *Mac.*

2221 McGee, Arthur R. "*Macbeth* and the Furies." *ShS*, 19 (1966), 55–67.

Focuses on the role of the witches in the damnation of Macbeth. Points out that Sh, like his contemporaries, associated witches with the Furies of classical tradition as well as with biblical demons and fairies. In acting as "agents of remorse and despair," the Weird Sisters are especially close to their classical prototypes.

2222 Merchant, W. Moelwyn. "'His Fiend-like Queen.'" *ShS*, 19 (1966), 75–81.

Contrasts Lady Macbeth's willful submission to demonic powers with her husband's "painful, casuistic deliberations." As the Infernal Goddess to whom the Weird Sisters owe direct allegiance, Hecate is the presiding spirit of the play.

2223 Naito, Kenji. "Macbeth: A Thief or Dwarf?" *ShStud*, 16 (1977–78), 29–39.

Elucidates from a metaphysical perspective Angus's comment toward the end of *Mac.* that the protagonist has become a "dwarfish thief." Locates the notion of good as it is productive of being in Plato, from whom Plotinus developed the idea of evil as nonbeing. The Renaissance borrowed the idea indirectly through Boethius, St. Augustine, and St. Thomas, and directly through Ficino. According to Augustine, evil actions diminish man's being though they do not annihilate it. It is this kind of contracted, eroded being that Angus accurately perceives in Macbeth.

2224 Palmer, D. J. "'A new Gorgon': Visual Effects in *Macbeth*." *Focus on "Macbeth."* Ed. John Russell Brown. London: Routledge & Kegan Paul, 1982, pp. 54–69.

Emphasizes the special importance that the "faculty of sight" has in *Mac.* Especially significant are visible appearances of things usually unseen, bloody spectacles, the strong appeal of the language to "the visual imagination," Macbeth's inner vision, and the striking images reported from the offstage world by "the play's many messengers." Facial expressions, entrances and exits, and physical gestures make profound impressions. Particularly noteworthy are the description of the murdered Duncan by

Macduff as "a new Gorgon" and the appearance of Macbeth's head as an appropriate end to the play's horrors.

2225 Paolucci, Anne. "*Macbeth* and *Oedipus Rex*: A Study in Paradox." *Shakespeare Encomium*. Ed. Anne Paolucci. New York: City College, 1964, pp. 44–70.

Maintains that *Mac.* is in many ways the most classical of Sh's plays and "invites serious comparison with *Oedipus Rex*." The two plays are similar in their use of prophecy and in the hero's response to it. Macbeth and Oedipus both waver between accepting and rejecting what is foretold, thus reflecting the paradox of "human freedom and divine necessity or fate"; both take the initiative in seeking out the agent of prophecy; and realizing that "freedom is insight into necessity," both accept responsibility for their deeds. Jocasta and Lady Macbeth both experience a reversal from complete confidence in human reason to despair in the face of oracles, and both commit suicide. In *Oedipus Rex* and *Mac.*, there is skillful management of dramatic juxtaposition as well as verbal irony, which is intensified in both plays by references to "light and sight, night and blindness."

2226 Pearlman, E. "Malcolm and Macduff." *Studies in the Humanities* (Indiana, Pennsylvania), 9, no. 1 (1981), 5–10.

Remarks that in composing *Mac.* Sh might very well have consolidated the opposition to the tyrant king in one character, but instead he filled out the character of Macduff from a few hints in Holinshed so that Macduff and Malcolm can be seen as different alternatives to Macbeth. This deliberate splitting of the hero allows Sh to handle the juxtaposition of Christian and pagan. The early parts of the play are largely pre-Christian in mood and ethic, emphasizing revenge and perhaps Stoicism. Macduff is a counterweight to Macbeth in pagan terms, but he offers no spiritual advance over the latter. Malcolm—who differs from Macduff in his youth, sexual innocence, status as a son, and different figuring of masculinity—provides an opportunity to transcend Macbeth's old unforgiving world with a new Christian dispensation.

2227 Rexroth, Kenneth. "Classics Revisited—XXX: *Macbeth*." *Saturday Review*, June 25, 1966, p. 17.

Considers the extent to which *Mac.* can be viewed as a classical tragedy. Notes that it is "the greatest of the Senecan tragedies" written during Sh's age by dramatists who believed they were imitating "classic tragedy." Macbeth opens his soul to the frivolous force of the irrational, which makes for "a triumph of the absurd." The "illusory time and space" of the play seem to observe "the dramatic unities attributed to Aristotle," and there is "plenty of Aristotle's pity and terror." However, *Mac.* is finally not a classical tragedy because the feelings aroused are not for the protagonist, who, in Sh's view, has "exhausted infinite pity."

2228 Rissanen, Matti. "'Nature's Copy,' 'Great Bond,' and 'Lease of Nature' in *Macbeth*." *NM*, 70 (1969), 714–23.

Maintains that "nature's copy" (III.ii.41), "great bond" (III.ii.52), and "lease of nature" (IV.i.99) in *Mac.* are "specimens of a recurrent image which could be called 'the lease of life' pattern." Man and nature have a "bond" by which man "has his life from nature by lease." Man holds this lease for the extent of his natural life, being forced to relinquish it only at death. The pattern is related to the image that describes death as "paying the debt of nature," a sample of which occurs in *Mac.*, V.viii.39. The lease of nature image is found in book 3 of Lucretius's *De Rerum Naturae*, and it seems probable that Sh was drawn to this work around 1600.

2229 Robertson, Jean. "Macbeth on Sleep: 'Sore Labour's Bath' and Sidney's *Astrophil and Stella*, XXXIX." *N&Q*, 14 (1967), 139–41.

Discusses the possible influence of Seneca's *Hercules Furens* and Ovid's *Metamorphoses*, as well as Sidney's *Astrophil and Stella*, on Macbeth's thoughts on sleep (*Mac.*, II.ii.35–38).

2230 Smith, Grover. "The Naked New-Born Babe in *Macbeth*: Some Iconographical Evidence." *RenP*, 1964 (1965), 21–27.

Attempts to connect the image of the new-born babe and that of the cherub in Macbeth's summary of why he should not murder Duncan (*Mac.*, I.vii) in order "to justify the whole simile in terms of pictorial conventions normal to renaissance allegory." Cites the figures of the winds in classical epic, mad beings mounted on equally lawless steeds. Argues that Sh has replaced these fierce personifications with two kinds of "air-borne" infants, who act as "winds of pity," curbing "the lawless winds of antiquity."

2231 Truax, Elizabeth. "Macbeth and Hercules: The Hero Bewitched." *CompD*, 23 (1989), 359–76.

Argues that in *Mac.* Sh uses the myth of Hercules "as a vehicle to express the concept of history as a complex process involving the interaction between nature and human behavior." Men of great stature like Macbeth interrupt natural cycles of "birth, maturation, and death," either through rational and wise conduct or through rash actions. All men, even the demigod Hercules, are susceptible to temptations, and most succumb in some way. Macbeth's experiences parallel those of the hero in Seneca's *Hercules Furens* in many ways, though there are important differences. Macbeth, like Hercules, aspires to manly virtue; Macbeth's witches are similar to the furies who offer the lure of vice to Hercules; Macbeth and Hercules both journey to homes that become a kind of hell, driving them toward self-destruction; both protagonists are called upon to kill, but Hercules victim is a tyrant and seducer, whereas Macbeth plans to murder a good king; Lady Macbeth mirrors several Senecan women (Megara, Deianara, Juno) in her attempts to dominate her husband; both Macbeth and Hercules are transformed into corrupt madmen, but Hercules is rehabilitated, while Macbeth is inexorably led to his destruction.

2231a Vickers, Michael. "A Source in Plutarch's *Life of Pelopidas* for Lady Macbeth." *N&Q*, 33 (1986), 365–67.

Argues that the character of Lady Macbeth, her plan for Duncan's murder, and her goading of her husband to commit the deed are indebted to the account of the murder of Alexander of Pherae by his wife and her three brothers in Plutarch's *Life of Pelopidas*.

2232 Wheeler, Thomas P., comp. *"Macbeth": An Annotated Bibliography*. (Garland Shakespeare Bibliographies 22.) New York: Garland, 1990. xix + 1099 pp.

Covers materials published primarily between 1940 and 1987. Classifies entries under fourteen headings, including Criticism (1245 items), Sources and Background (153 items), Bibliographies (26 items), and Editions (169 items). Begins each section with the oldest entry and proceeds chronologically. Concludes with a single index. Provides substantial annotations. Includes, in the sections on criticism, sources, and bibliographies, a number of items that discuss the relationship of *Mac.* to the classics.

2232a White, Howard B. "Macbeth and the Tyrannical Man." *Interpretation*, 2, no. 2 (1970), 143–55.

Likens Macbeth to the tyrannical man described in the ninth book of the *Republic* in that he is seized by madness. Plato's tyrant, however, is subject to many passions, while the modern tyrant like Macbeth is controlled by one: the lust for power. Revised as chapter 3 of item 1122.

2233 Wickham, Glynne. "To Fly or Not to Fly? The Problem of Hecate in Shakespeare's *Macbeth*." *Essays on Drama and Theater: Liber Amicorum Benjamin Hunningher Presented to Professor B. Hunningher on the Occasion of His Retirement from the Chair of Drama and Theatre Arts in the University of Amsterdam*. Ed. Erica Hunningher-Schilling. Amsterdam: Moussault's Uitgeverij, 1973, pp. 171–82.

Cites several of Ben Jonson's notes to *The Masque of Queens* (1609) that draw on Homer to explain the figure of Ate as Mischief, and that connect Hecate, the supervisor of all witchcraft, with her description in the *Aeneid*. Speculates that the actor who originally played Ate in Jonson's *Masque* graduated, because of Ate's association with Mischief, to the part of Hecate in Thomas Middleton's *The Witch* and then persuaded Sh or Burbage to rearrange the scenes in *Mac.*, initially performed without Hecate or any flying witches, "to incorporate new ones for himself as Hecate." This revised text of the play was the one used in the First Folio.

2234 Williams, Edith Whitehurst. "In Defense of Lady Macbeth." *SQ*, 24 (1973), 221–23.

Disputes William Godshalk's suggestion that Livy's Tullia is a prototype for Lady Macbeth (item 2210) on two counts: Tullia shows no compunction over the murder of her father, while Lady Macbeth recoils from murdering Duncan because he resembles hers; and Lady Macbeth's remorse over the bloodshed she has shared in is quite different from the "maniacal bloodlust" of Tullia, who has her chariot driven over her father's corpse.

2235 Wood, James O. "'Fillet of a Fenny Snake.'" *N&Q*, 12 (1965), 332–33.

Points out that the "fillet" referred to as an ingredient of the witches' brew in *Mac.* (IV.i.12) can be identified by reference to a passage in Golding's Ovid (4.616ff.) as the cast skin of the snake. Golding also helps us to understand that the snake is "'fenny' because fen-bred."

2236 Wood, James O. "Hecate's 'Vap'rous Drop, Profound.'" *N&Q*, 11 (1964), 262–64.

Argues that Hecate's speech in *Mac.* containing the phrase "vap'rous drop profound" (III.v.2–35) is by Sh because it contains echoes from known Shakespearean sources by Reginald Scot and John Leslie.

2237 Wood, James O. "Lady Macbeth's Suckling." *N&Q*, 13 (1966), 138.

Suggests that Lady Macbeth's lines about dashing out her child's brains are adapted from a passage in Ovid's *Metamorphoses* 4, which describes how Athamas snatches his infant son from his wife, Ino, and shatters the boy's head against a rock.

2238 Zeong, Yun-Shig. "Shakespeare and Milton: A Poetic Approach through Aristotle's *Poetics* and Longinus' *The Sublime*: *Macbeth* and *Paradise Lost*." Ph.D. dissertation, University of Arkansas, 1984. *DAI*, 46 (1985–86), 3729-A.

Uses Aristotle and Longinus to derive criteria for "the definition, cause, device, effect, and purpose of tragedy." Applies these criteria to *Mac.*

Measure for Measure

2239 Bennett, J. A. W. "*Nosce te ipsum*: Some Medieval Interpretations." *J. R. R. Tolkien, Scholar and Storyteller: Essays in Memoriam*. Eds. Mary Salu and Robert T. Farrell. Ithaca: Cornell U. P., 1979, pp. 138–58.

Traces the evolving meanings of the precept *nosce te ipsum*, "know yourself," from classical times to Sh, noting that Isabella in *MM*, II.ii, provides its "supreme formulation." As she states it, man's inability to recognize his sin is the fundamental lack of self-awareness. Self-knowledge is peculiar to the deity.

2240 Dickinson, John W. "Renaissance Equity and *Measure for Measure*." *SQ*, 13 (1962), 287–97.

Maintains that in *MM* Sh makes use of the principle of equity, which Renaissance theorists derived from Aristotle's *Nicomachean Ethics*. As defined by Aristotle, equity is "a correction of the law where it is defective owing to its universality." Through Escalus, Sh shows equity to be an appropriate corrective to Angelo's strict application of the law. The primary lesson of the play, however, is "one of Christian mercy," which is superior to equity.

2241 Duncan-Jones, Katherine. "Stoicism in *Measure for Measure*: A New Source." *RES*, N. S. 28 (1977), 441–46.

Suggests that the Countess of Pembroke's translation from the French of *A Discourse of Life and Death* by the Huguenot theologian Philippe du Plessis-Mornay was an immediate source for "the Duke's great philosophical speech against the fear of death" in *MM* (III.i). Through this translation (1592), Sh may have received some of his early impressions of "the Senecan tradition of stoicism."

2242 Gibbons, Brian, ed. *Measure for Measure*. (New Cambridge Shakespeare.) Cambridge: Cambridge U. P., 1991. xvi + 213 pp.

The introduction mentions the possibility that Ben Jonson's *Sejanus* might have influenced *MM*, especially in the way that the Duke's use of letters to confuse Angelo resembles a similar stratagem by Tiberius. Notes the ultimate indebtedness of the kind of tragicomic double plot used in *MM* to Terence, who had defended this principle of *contaminatio*.

2242a Kliman, Bernice W. "Isabella in *Measure for Measure*." *ShakS*, 15 (1982), 137–48.

Cites the pseudo-Ciceronian *ad Herennium* and Aristotle's *Rhetoric* to show that Sh cast Isabella as an inept rhetorician in order to turn attention to the Duke, the only character who can provide a resolution.

2243 Lever, J. W., ed. *Measure for Measure*. (Arden Shakespeare.) London: Methuen, 1965. xcviii + 203 pp.

The introduction notes that the example of the Roman emperor Alexander Severus, much cited in the 16th c. as a ruler who disguised himself to uncover wrongdoing, probably helped Sh to construct the character of the Duke. Points out that, in discussing the proper role of magistrates, 16th-c. commentators like Sir Thomas Elyot found guidance in "the classical *via media* of equity grounded on reason." The Duke's temperate wisdom is founded on this notion.

2244 Rosenheim, Judith. "Philosophical and Religious Backgrounds to the Dramatic Oppositions of Shakespeare's *Measure for Measure*." Ph.D. dissertation, City University of New York, 1976. *DAI*, 37 (1976–77), 1569-A.

Views the three major characters of *MM*—the Duke, Angelo, and Isabella—as exponents of Stoicism, Calvinism, and Neoplatonism, respectively. In addition, *MM* incorporates ideas of "Machiavellian and Calvinist politics as the politics of reason and will, and includes as well aspects of Cynicism and Epicureanism" (in the characters of Barnardine and Lucio) as humanistic philosophies "derived from reason and will." If the play is allowed an allegorical dimension in which the conflicts among the various characters can be seen in part as explorations of "the paradoxical relationships between the philosophical values that they represent," then some of the ambiguities can be cleared up. Part revised as item 2245.

2245   Rosenheim, Judith. "The Stoic Meaning of the Friar in *Measure for Measure.*" *ShakS*, 15 (1982), 171–215.

Argues that in his disguise as Friar, the Duke of *MM* sets forth Stoic doctrine, which Sh intends to reveal as inadequate. Uses passages from Cicero, Seneca, and Plutarch's *Moralia* to define Stoic beliefs about providence and other matters and to demonstrate their insufficiencies. The Friar's Stoic view of providence leads him to failure in ordering the world of the play, but this failure forces him, in resuming his identity as Duke, to take on a more successful Christian providential role. He acknowledges both the heavenly and the natural elements in his makeup and in his world. Revision of part of item 2244.

2245a   Sokol, B. J. "Figures of Repetition in Sidney's *Astrophil and Stella* and the Scenic Form of *Measure for Measure.*" *Rhetorica*, 9 (1991), 131–46.

Emphasizes the classical derivation of the rhetorical figure of *gradatio*, known to Renaissance readers through the *Rhetorica ad Herennium*, erroneously thought to be by Cicero, and other handbooks of rhetoric. *Gradatio* involves advancing through an utterance by a careful series of steps, each step consisting of a term that prepares for a related one that follows it. Discerns a connection between Sir Philip Sidney's use of *gradatio* in *Astrophil and Stella* and "the dynamics of scenic form" in parts of *MM*. Duke Vincentio predicts in act IV that he intends to proceed with "cold gradation" (iii.100–101) in judging Angelo, and act V comprises "a graduated series of illusory falsifications" that reveals not only "the multiple shortcomings of others" but also "Vincentio's own crippling misapprehensions and vanities." The last act thus enacts "a gradual process capable of thawing frozen barriers to the ability to love."

2246   Sweeney, Mary Clare. "A Candle of the Lord: The Renaissance Ideal of Virtue as Imaged in Shakespeare's *Measure for Measure.*" Ph.D. dissertation, Arizona State University, 1980. *DAI*, 41 (1980–81), 3121-A-3122-A.

Analyzes "the Renaissance concept of virtue for women as it is presented in *MM*." Includes a discussion of chastity from both classical and Christian perspectives.

THE MERCHANT OF VENICE

2247   Barrett, D. S. "Plautus, *Mostellaria* 630–32 and *The Merchant of Venice.*" *Classical Bull.*, 59 (1983), 60–62.

Challenges critics who claim that Portia's maneuver in extricating Antonio from Shylock's bond is derived from a passage in *Mostellaria* in which a slave wishes that his master's creditor ask for one penny more than what he is owed. Contends that the provision of Roman law commentators profess to find in this Plautus passage and by extension in *MV* does not apply to the kind of debt Antonio owes to Shylock. Speculates that Shylock's bond may derive from a literal reading of Table 3 of the Twelve Tables and that Portia's defense may be based on ideas like those set forth by

Justinian and Gaius regarding the kind and manner of debt repayment. Because Sh's sources for *MV* remain obscure, however, there is no way to determine the extent to which he relied on Roman law. The passage cited from *Mostellaria* does not involve a significant point of law and should not be adduced as a source for Sh's play.

2248 Beauregard, David N. "Sidney, Aristotle, and *The Merchant of Venice*: Shakespeare's Triadic Images of Liberality and Justice." *ShakS*, 20 (1988), 33–51.

Claims that the characters in *MV* represent "certain Aristotelian–Thomistic virtues and vices." In the earlier scenes, we see the virtue of liberality (Antonio) and its extremes of prodigality (Bassanio) and avarice (Shylock); in later scenes, there is "the virtue of justice (Portia), and its extremes of 'unjust action' (Shylock) and 'unjust treatment' (Antonio)."

2249 Cosgrove, Mark Francis, O.S.B. "Biblical, Liturgical, and Classical Allusions in *The Merchant of Venice*." Ph.D. dissertation, University of Florida, 1970. *DAI*, 31 (1970–71), 3498-A.

Contends that classical allusions in *MV* are inextricably intertwined with patterns of Biblical and liturgical allusions. The classical allusions are reinforced by the Biblical and liturgical patterns. Discusses in detail the references to Troilus and Cressida, Pyramus and Thisbe, Ariadne and Dido, and Medea and Jason.

2250 Daalder, Joost. "Senecan Influence on Shylock's 'Hath Not a Jew Eyes?' Speech." *ES*, 65 (1984), 405–8.

Attempts to reestablish Seneca as a powerful influence on Sh. Asserts that Shylock's speech (*MV*, III.i.55–69) is deeply indebted to the Senecan notion that one who teaches evil must expect that evil to be turned against him by his pupil. Finds this idea in *Thyestes* and in one of Seneca's epistles.

2251 Hamill, Monica J. "Poetry, Law, and the Pursuit of Perfection: Portia's Role in *The Merchant of Venice*." *SEL*, 18 (1978), 229–43.

Emphasizes the importance of Portia as a "poet–lawmaker": In the lottery episodes, the trial scene, and the ring game, she uses "poetic language and fictions" in close association with the upholding and interpreting of law. In arguing that poets act as legislators for mankind, Elizabethan commentators often cited ancient bards like Orpheus and Amphion as the original civilizing force in primitive society. Taking on this role in *MV*, Portia acts to draw others closer to perfection. For example, when Bassanio is deliberating over which casket to choose, she refers to him as Hercules, thus staging his quest as a heroic action.

2252 Hunt, Maurice. "Ways of Knowing in *The Merchant of Venice*." *SQ*, 30 (1979), 89–93.

Suggests that Sh exploits the tensions between Christian and Neoplatonic ways of knowing in *MV*. In the Neoplatonic thought of Baldassare Castiglione and others, man is deemed capable of intuiting divine beauty; Christian belief, however, views man's infected will as a barrier to this perfect knowledge. In V.i, Lorenzo refers to both the music of the spheres and the inability of imperfect mortals to hear it. Given human limitations, the best way of achieving knowledge (exemplified by Bassanio) is to use reason to avoid dependence on ornament or the outward "shows" of things that deceive the eye and ear. Bassanio's skillful coordination of reason and music also brings him closer to true knowledge than the other suitors because it approximates the experience of hearing the music of the spheres.

2253 Kozikowski, Stanley J. "The Allegory of Love and Fortune: The Lottery in *The Merchant of Venice*." *Renascence*, 22, no. 2 (1979–80), 105–15.

Suggests that Sh draws on Tudor moralities that feature contentions of Love and Fortune and lotteries of Fortune to present, in the casket scenes, an allegory that includes both motifs. When confronted with the two unworthy suitors who woo her for gain, as Fortune is traditionally wooed, Portia plays the role of the capricious goddess; but she lays aside this role and appears as a maid in love when Bassanio exhibits humility, the Christian remedy against Fortune. The allegory of the caskets is connected to the major theme of the play, Fortune being associated with Justice and humility with Mercy.

2253a Lecercle, Ann. "Tubal: The Resurrection and Fall of a/the Cipher." "*Le Marchand de Venise*" *et* "*Le Juif de Malte*": *Texte et Représentations*. Eds. Michèle Willems, Jean-Pierre Maquerlot, and Raymond Willems. (Publications de l'Université de Rouen 100.) Rouen: Publications de l'Université de Rouen, 1985, pp. 133–40.

Traces the figure of Tubal in *MV* to the Tubal who is mentioned in Genesis 4 as the archetypal metal-worker and to Tubal's half-brother Jabal, the father of musicians. The two biblical characters were seen by some later commentators as joint forebears of the single figure of Pythagoras, whose musical theory is celebrated in act 5 of Sh's play. However, the Tubal of *MV*—through his links with music, strings, time, weights, and scales—symbolizes "a grotesque distortion of Pythagorean harmonics and cosmology."

2254 Lewis, Anthony. "An Allusion to Orpheus in *The Merchant of Venice*, III.ii. 43–47." *N&Q*, 25 (1978), 126–27.

Proposes that Portia's description of Bassanio's potential death is an allusion to the death of Orpheus, which echoes Golding's translation of the *Metamorphoses*. This is appropriate as a way to imagine the consequences of Bassanio's failure to choose the right casket. Since he is successful, Portia properly moves on to compare him to Hercules, a live conqueror.

2255 Mahood, M. M., ed. *The Merchant of Venice*. (New Cambridge Shakespeare.) Cambridge: Cambridge U. P., 1987. xv +190 pp.

Mentions as background for the depiction in *MV* of idealized friendship the *Phaedrus* of Plato and Castiglione's *The Courtier*, a Renaissance Platonic dialogue.

2256 McMahon, Robert. "'Some there be that shadows kiss': A Note on *The Merchant of Venice*, II.ix.65." *SQ*, 37 (1986), 371–73.

Suggests that the lines about kissing shadows that Aragon reads from the scroll in the silver casket refer to a passage in Ovid's *Metamorphoses* 3 that describes Narcissus. Cites a passage from *Ven.* and one from Arthur Golding to show that Narcissus was commonly associated with self-love, pride, and sterility. Thus the allusion sheds light on Aragon and his choice.

2257 Merchant, W. Moelwyn, ed. *The Merchant of Venice*. (New Penguin Shakespeare.) Harmondsworth: Penguin, 1967. 214 pp.

The introduction points out that, to the Elizabethan, "Venice was probably the most evocative name in Europe," in part because of its association with the revival of classical learning. In particular, Sh was indebted to the 16th-c. Italian academies established in a number of cities to discuss and propagate Neoplatonic doctrine, which underlies the discussion between Jessica and Lorenzo about heavenly harmony and the limits placed on the immortal soul by the body that clothes it (*MV*, V.i). Notes that the complex ideas behind the play's setting, especially "the delicate relationship between Venice and Belmont," have much to do with "the classical rhythms" of some of the poetry. Emphasizes Portia's ambiguity, due in large measure to the parallel drawn between her and Portia the daughter of Cato and wife of Brutus, and between her and two figures from mythology, Medea and Hesione. The opening of the last act—with Lorenzo and Jessica mentioning Ovidian love martyrs (Cressida, Thisbe, Dido, and Medea) whose affairs were marked by "duplicity, misconception, even treachery"—darkens the tone just when we might expect a movement toward a "radiant conclusion." Medea's name brings to an ominous conclusion "the theme of Jason's quest which traverses the play."

2258   Palmer, D. J. "*The Merchant of Venice*, or the Importance of Being Earnest." *Shakespearian Comedy*. Eds. David Palmer and Malcolm Bradbury. (Stratford-upon-Avon Studies 14.) London: Edward Arnold, 1972, pp. 97–120.

Argues that Sh's allusions to the Medea legend help establish the sad and serious tone of most of the play. Medea, in love with Jason against her will (*Metamorphoses* 7), suffers from an "uncouth maladie," as do Antonio (at the beginning of *MV*) and Portia (I.ii). In addition, Sh appropriated from Ovid the importance of "'blood' as the physical basis of passion and of friendship." The parallels between Medea and Portia are substantial; in particular, each woman is torn between loyalty to her father and the desire to choose her own mate. Finally, though, Portia is contrasted with Medea, because she refuses to violate her father's will or to perform unlawful practices. Points out that the references to tragic mythological lovers by Lorenzo and Jessica (V.i) mark a shift in mood: With the bitterness of the trial scene in the past, the two happy lovers recollect tranquilly the griefs of their predecessors. Lorenzo reinforces the sense of serenity when he mentions the Platonic doctrine of the music of the spheres and the harmony between souls that it signifies. The music of Orpheus, also alluded to by Lorenzo, is associated with the poet's power of moving the passions to virtuous ends. Portia, whose art is analogous to that of Sh, is a benevolent Medea with the magic of Jacob (described by Shylock in his story of Laban's sheep) and Orpheus.

2259   Reed, James Kennedy. "Perspectives on a Comic Shylock." Ph.D. dissertation, University of Colorado, 1968. *DA*, 29 (1968–69), 3107-A.

Attempts to replace the conventional romantic image of Shylock in *MV* with a more Elizabethan conception. Argues that Shylock would have been perceived by the play's original audience as a usurer and a miser whose comic genealogy can be traced back to Plautus. In fact, Shylock should be seen as a "full-blown, Aristophanic-sized caricature, a clown of savagely heroic proportions."

2260   Sklar, Elizabeth S. "Bassanio's Golden Fleece." *TSLL*, 18 (1976–77), 500–509.

Finds an analogy between Bassanio's activities in *MV* and the story of Jason's search for the Golden Fleece. Bassanio's quest is metaphorically compared to Jason's in two crucial passages, and he is like Jason in his opportunism. Sh seems to have modeled Bassanio in part on Jason as he appears in book 5 of Gower's *Confessio Amantis*, in which we also find the casket motif. Gower's main theme is covetousness in love, which applies to Bassanio as well as to Jason. In addition, Jason's perjury finds its way into the oath-breaking of Bassanio. These two Jasonian flaws—confusion of love and money and perjury—are also found in a number of other characters in the play; they appear to be the inevitable consequence of being bred in Venice.

2261   Waddington, Raymond B. "Fortune, Justice and Cupid in *The Merchant of Venice*." *ELH*, 44 (1977), 458–77.

Distinguishes between the Prince of Morocco's pagan notion of blind Fortune and that of Bassanio, who chooses to trust completely in Christian providence. The most important mythological referent for Bassanio is Hercules, whose choice of Virtue over Pleasure enabled him to conquer Fortune.

2262 Wheeler, Thomas, comp. *"The Merchant of Venice": An Annotated Bibliography.* (Garland Shakespeare Bibliographies 9.) New York: Garland, 1985. xxii + 386 pp.

Covers primarily works published between 1940 and 1979, though some items that appeared earlier and later than this period have also been included. Classifies entries under nine headings, including Criticism (622 items); Sources (36 items); Bibliographies (15 items); and Editions (100 items). Begins each section with the oldest entries and proceeds chronologically. Concludes with a single index. Provides substantial and detailed annotations.

THE MERRY WIVES OF WINDSOR

2263 Frantz, David O. *"Festum Voluptatis": A Study of Renaissance Erotica.* Columbus: Ohio State U. P., 1989. xiii + 275 pp.

Includes discussion of the Italian Renaissance tradition of learned erotica, including the adaptation of classical myth to erotic purposes. Chapter 8 incorporates an analysis of the erotic context of *Wiv.*, noting the background of merry tales and jestbooks with which Sh's audience would have been familiar. Calls attention in particular to Falstaff's enrolling himself in the catalogue of classical gods transformed by lust (V.v) and to Mistress Quickly's comic misapprehension of the Latin lesson administered by Hugh Evans to young William (IV.i).

2264 Gianakaris, C. J. "Folk Ritual as Comic Catharsis and *The Merry Wives of Windsor.*" *Mississippi Folklore Register*, 10 (1976), 138–53.

Blends Aristotelian and psychoanalytic elements to develop a theory of comic catharsis for analyzing *Wiv.* Notes the classical derivation of some of the humors characters whose folly is purged.

2265 Hinely, Jan Lawson. "Comic Scapegoats and the Falstaff of *The Merry Wives of Windsor.*" *ShakS* 15 (1982), 37–54.

Interprets Falstaff of *Wiv.* as combining the roles of two traditional comic scapegoats: (1) the *alazon*, or "boasting impostor, who lays claim to society's traditional rewards for heroic achievement—sexual prerogatives, feasting, and wealth—on the basis of personal virtues he does not really possess" and (2) the *pharmakos*, "whose 'guilty' nature is a reflection of the vanities and pretensions [that] afflict the society punishing him." Shows a connection between Falstaff's three punishments and well-known rituals performed over an unworthy knight to signify the loss of knightly status. If *Wiv.* was performed in 1597 at the installation of Lord Hunsdon as a Knight of the Garter, a courtly audience would have recognized Falstaff as a representative of its own vices and follies and thus he would have served as an *alazon*. In the middle-class world of the play, Falstaff is a *pharmakos*, who mirrors the flaws of Windsor's citizens, primarily an egocentricity that drives them to abuse sexuality "for mercenary or selfish purposes." Falstaff's wooing of the wives to fill his purse is thus a reflection of the mercenary motivation of all the parties (except Fenton) to the wooing of Anne Page. Falstaff's exposure in the final scene is related to the defeat of egocentricity and sterility and the triumph (as in Aristophanic comedy) of "true knighthood, fertility, and mutuality." Other comic scapegoats in Sh—Malvolio, Parolles, and Shylock—are all to some extent *alazon/pharmakos* combinations, and the plays in which they appear show the strains involved in both (1) differentiating a scapegoat from society and (2) assimilating him back into society after his exposure. Of all Shakespearean comedies that use the *alazon/pharmakos* figure, *Wiv.* is most successful at achieving this balance because Falstaff and the citizens of Windsor both acknowledge their faults, with the result that he casts off his role as a scapegoat and they accept their part in his human follies.

2266   Huebert, Ronald. "Levels of Parody in *The Merry Wives of Windsor*." *ESC*, 3 (1977), 136–52.

Points out that *Wiv.* is to some extent "a pastiche of quotations from and allusions to literary forms and fashions" that had become outmoded by the time Sh wrote his play. These targets of parody include the Latin lesson (with Mistress Quickly's comments reducing it to a burlesque), Ovidian myth (in Falstaff's scene as Herne the Hunter), and *Doctor Faustus* (whose protagonist's appeal to the Pythagorean doctrine of *metempsychosis* is travestied in Falstaff's address to Jove at the beginning of the Herne scene).

2266a   Parten, Anne. "Falstaff's Horns: Masculine Inadequacy and Feminine Mirth in *The Merry Wives of Windsor*." *SP*, 82 (1985), 184–99.

Suggests a "thematic affinity" between the traditional folk ritual known as the skimmington, in which a community bands together to mock a male whose ineffectuality with respect to women has threatened the social order, and the treatment of Falstaff at the end of *Wiv.* Argues that the identification of Falstaff with Actaeon is compatible with this interpretation. In the popular mind of Sh's time, Actaeon was associated with both the excessive sexuality of the adulterer and the impotence of the cuckold.

2267   Roberts, Jeanne Addison. "Falstaff in Windsor Forest: Villain or Victim?" *SQ*, 26 (1975), 8–15.

Maintains that Falstaff is an ambiguous figure at the conclusion of *Wiv.* His association of himself with love and his appearance under the oak tree—in classical times, sacred to Jove—suggest superhuman sexual prowess. Yet the tree is described as blasted, suggesting "virility diminished by age." His horns connect him with Actaeon, both aggressor and victim. The final reconciliation can take place only when, after being chastened, "Falstaff is recognized as an essential element of, and possibly even a savior of, that very society he threatens."

2268   Steadman, John M. "Falstaff as Actaeon: A Dramatic Emblem." *SQ*, 14 (1963), 231–44. Reprint. *Nature into Myth: Medieval and Renaissance Moral Symbols*. (Language and Literature Series 1.) Pittsburgh: Duquesne U. P., 1979, pp. 117–30.

Relates Falstaff's disguise as Herne the Hunter in the last act of *Wiv.* to Renaissance emblematic portrayals of the Actaeon myth. Like Actaeon in the emblem literature, and unlike Ovid's presentation of him, Falstaff appears with his head transformed into that of a stag but otherwise retaining his human shape. Sh also incorporates the common moral significance of the myth: that Actaeon's fate represents lust and its punishment. Further, Falstaff's two earlier transformations may be indebted to traditional images of lust and its chastisement as well. In the buck-basket episode, Falstaff resembles the poet Virgil, who in *The Lyfe of Virgilius* (c. 1518) is tricked into entering a basket and humiliated by a woman with whom he has made an assignation. As the woman of Brainford, Falstaff is reminiscent of Hercules, whose service to Omphale in woman's clothes was a standard emblem of bondage to lust.

A Midsummer Night's Dream

2268a Andrews, Michael Cameron. "Titania on 'enforced chastity.'" N&Q, 31 (1984), 188.

Cites Ovid's *Amores* in arguing that Titania's phrase "enforced chastity" (*MND*, III.i.195) refers to the would-be lover's restraint from consummation.

2269 Ansari, A. A. "Shakespeare's Allegory of Love." *AJES*, 3 (1978), 44–62.

Views *MND* as an exploration of "the various manifestations of the irrationality of love, governed by chaotic, subconscious impulses and drives." Through the Pyramus and Thisbe playlet, the threat of certain dark elements, especially death, encountered in the dream world of the lovers is contained and dismissed.

2270 Baldwin, T. W. "The Pedigree of Theseus's Pups: *Midsummer Night's Dream*, IV.i.123-130." *SJH*, 1968, 109–20.

Points out that Theseus's discussion of his hounds [IV.i.118–125] is partly derived from the account of Actaeon's hounds in Golding's translation of Ovid's *Metamorphoses*. Sh's use of Ovid shows the pervasive influence of the classics during his age. The physical features of the hounds, however, come from experience, not literary sources.

2271 Brooks, Harold, ed. *A Midsummer Night's Dream*. (Arden Shakespeare.) London: Methuen, 1979.

Part 1, section 3, of the introduction identifies and discusses sources, including North's Plutarch for the names of Theseus's loves; Ovid's *Metamorphoses*, both in Golding's translation and in the original Latin, for "Pyramus and Thisbe"; *The Golden Ass* of Apuleius for the transformation of Bottom; and several of Seneca's plays. Appendix 1 reprints selections from Plutarch, Golding's Ovid, and Seneca's *Oedipus*, *Medea*, and *Hippolytus*.

2272 Brown, Jane K. "Discordia Concors: On the Order of *A Midsummer Night's Dream*." *MLQ*, 48 (1987), 20–41.

Discovers in *MND* an articulation of the Neoplatonic doctrine of the "harmony of opposites in which higher truth was understood to be veiled." The play presents the dynamic opposite of higher and lower forms of love as leading to an understanding of love's "mystery." *MND* locates the truth both "in the mind of the Neoplatonist God" and "simultaneously in the mind of the spectator"; there is a universal order embodied in the play, "the concord of all discord."

2273 Calderwood, James L. "*A Midsummer Night's Dream*: The Illusion of Drama." *MLQ*, 26 (1965), 506–22.

Cites Theseus's past sexual infidelities and his wooing of Hippolyta as evidence of "the evolution of order between the sexes" in *MND*. The other lovers go through a similar process, as the dream of chaos in the forest is subjected to "the objective clarity of dramatic form."

2274 Carlsen, Hanne. "'What fools these mortals be!': Ovid in *A Midsummer Night's Dream*." *Literary Miscellany Presented to Eric Jacobsen*. Eds. Graham D. Caie and Holger Norgaard. (Publications of the Department of English, U. of Copenhagen, 16.) Copenhagen: Department of English, U. of Copenhagen, 1988, pp. 94–107.

Maintains that Sh assimilated Ovid's attitude toward love more thoroughly than any of his contemporaries. In many of his plays, but especially *MND*, Sh follows Ovid in treating love with ironic detachment and in hinting at the cruelty and danger associated with it. Points out the Ovidian treatment of the four groups of characters in *MND*. Notes that most of the tales in the *Metamorphoses* are obvious in their emphasis on lust and on the danger and cruelty of love. Even episodes in Ovid that seem to celebrate "ideal love"—those of Ceyx and Alcyone, Pyramus and Thisbe, and Philemon and Baucis—are viewed ironically by the poet. Sh caught this spirit from his master as well as the more general insistence on proudly asserting "the role of the artist."

2275 Carroll, D. Allen, and Gary Jay Williams, comps. *"A Midsummer Night's Dream": An Annotated Bibliography.* (Garland Shakespeare Bibliographies 12.) New York: Garland, 1986. xxxvii + 641 pp.

Covers primarily works published between 1940 and 1984. Classifies entries under seven headings, including Criticism (566+ items); Sources, Background, Date (120 items); and Editions and Translations (234+ items). Begins each section with the oldest entries and proceeds chronologically. Concludes with a single index. Provides substantial and detailed annotations.

2276 Clayton, F. W. *The Hole in the Wall: A New Look at Shakespeare's Latin Base for "A Midsummer Night's Dream."* (Tenth Jackson Knight Memorial Lecture.) Exeter: U. of Exeter, 1979. 32 pp.

Shows how words, names, and themes in *MND* may have been derived from a complex series of associations Sh made among classical works. Discusses Ovid, Juvenal, Martial, Apuleius, Quintilian, and others. Notes that the minds of the Elizabethans "moved easily between the ancients. Echoes inside antiquity, links of word and theme, operate on later memories and imaginations at various levels of consciousness. There's a sort of creative circle which may be entered at any point."

2277 Clemen, Wolfgang, ed. *A Midsummer Night's Dream.* (Signet Classic Shakespeare.) New York: New American Library, 1963. xxxvii + [38]–186 pp.

The introduction points out the possible indebtedness of *MND* to "the mythological dream plays of John Lyly" and the ways in which the tradesmen's play of Pyramus and Thisbe parodies both "the torments of love" and "the Senecan style of Elizabethan tragedy." The note on the source comments that the story of Theseus and Hippolyta comes in part from Chaucer's *The Knight's Tale*, that hints for the character of Theseus may have been derived from Plutarch's *Lives*, and that Ovid's *Metamorphoses* may have furnished Titania's name. The tale of Pyramus and Thisbe was available to Sh in a number of Elizabethan versions. The introduction, text, and note on the sources are reprinted as part of item 0123.

2278 Cohen, Marion. "'Dian's Bud' in *A Midsummer Night's Dream*." *N&Q*, 30 (1983), 118–20.

Proposes a blend of two plants—"Euphrasia or Eye-bright" and "Spurge, a species of Euphorbia"—as the key to the identity of Dian's Bud, the antidote to Cupid's Flower in *MND*.

2279 Cox, Richard H. "Shakespeare: Poetic Understanding and Comic Action." *The Artist and Political Vision.* Eds. Benjamin R. Barber and Michael J. Gargas McGrath. New Brunswick: Transaction Books, 1982, pp. 165–92.

Calls attention to the sobriety of two classical treatments of Theseus—those of Plutarch and Plato—as hero and lawgiver in relation to the common people and notes that Sh's comic account of this relationship in *MND* is at odds with the conception of most educated people of his day. By placing the hilarious deeds and speeches of the artisans at the center of the play's structure, Sh mitigates the seriousness with which the audience regards Hermia's and Lysander's violation of the ancient law of Athens, the madness with which Hermia is punished (her dream), and Theseus's peremptory overturning of that law. Discusses at some length the artisans' attempt to exercise their talents on the imitative rather than the productive arts. Claims that through their misadventures Sh demonstrates that "there is a tension between the natural and the poetic solutions to the problem of bringing in moonlight, and that his own practice of the poetic art is the ultimate cause of making the poetic solution prevail over the natural one." Argues that when Bottom enters into the fairy world, he saves Athens from a progeny of evils like those described by Titania in her speech about the effects of her quarrel with Oberon. Cites Thucydides's account of the plague in 430 B.C. that reduced Athens to lawlessness and impiety on a grand scale, Lucretius's adaptation of that account in *On the Nature of Things*, and Spenser's transformation of part of Lucretius' poem in *The Fairie Queene* as background for the contention that Sh, through the rude mechanicals, offers a fragile, foolish, and poetic solution to the "fundamental political problem of joining essentially different natures into a well-ordered whole." By means of his ludicrous depiction of Athens "at its founding phase," Sh seems to be teaching his audience about the radiant potentialities as well as the limitations of "life in the city as such."

2280 Crockett, Bryan. "'The wittiest partition': Pyramus and Thisbe in Ovid and Shakespeare." *CML*, 12 (1991–92), 49–58.

Reviews modern scholarship on the inspiration for Sh's parodic treatment of Pyramus and Thisbe in *MND*. Although most critics believe that Sh was parodying overly sentimental Elizabethan versions of the *Metamorphoses*, his burlesque is to a great extent implicit in Ovid's Latin. One indication of this is that Ovid puts the story of Pyramus and Thisbe into the mouth of one of the daughters of Minyas, who, refusing to participate in Dionysiac revelries, amuse themselves with tales illustrating the perils and follies of sexual excess. Because of their exaggerated restraint, the Minyeides are turned by Bacchus into bats, ironically undermining the seriousness with which we are allowed to approach their cautionary tales. The Babylonian setting of the story, as well as its excessive language, also suggest that humor is a crucial element in Ovid's account.

2281 Cutts, John P. "'The Fierce Vexation of a [Midsummer Night's] Dreame.'" *SQ*, 14 (1963), 183–85.

Maintains that the Pyramus and Thisbe episode in *MND* is a satirical comment on the exaggerated love of the two pairs of lovers. It also "acts as a satirical contrast with the Theseus–Hippolyta relationship" and with "the Oberon–Titania relationship." Oberon, as King of Faery, is to some extent detached from the love folly of the others, but his pursuit of the Indian boy (like Jove's desire for Ganymede) leaves him open to criticism as well. All of this is given a richer significance by Sh's use of the flower "love-in-idleness" to induce the "vexation of a dream" and of "Dian's bud" to dispel it. Sh substituted "love-in-idleness" for the mulberry tree found in the source, Ovid's *Metamorphoses* (4.125–127). Golding's translation explains that the moral has to do with frantic love that ends in pain. But Gerarde's *Herball* (1597) describes love-in-idleness as a *cure* for "the French disease." Sh may thus have deliberately conflated the cure and the cause as a way of underlining the paradoxical humor of the situation. "Dian's bud," according to Gerarde, enables people to live chastely, but at the play's end Demetrius is still subject to love-in-idleness, and Oberon, who prescribes chastity for others, has his Indian boy.

2282 Doran, Madeleine. "Pyramus and Thisbe Once More." *Essays on Shakespeare and Elizabethan Drama in Honor of Hardin Craig*. Ed. Richard Hosley. Columbia: U. of Missouri P., 1962, pp. 149–61.

Begins by summarizing the essential features of the Pyramus and Thisbe story as set down by Ovid and then details the modifications introduced in an anonymous 12th-c. Norman *lai* and in Giovanni Andrea dell' Anguillara's translation of the *Metamorphoses* (1561). The *lai* emphasizes the anguish of love, while Anguillara is interested in increased verisimilitude and psychological credibility. Sh's parody of the story in *MND* catches both the Ovidian features and those that were added in later works like the *lai* and Anguillara's translation.

283   Doran, Madeleine. "Titania's Wood." *Rice University Studies*, 60, no. 2 (1974), 55–70.

Focuses on "the woodland setting" in acts II–IV of *MND*, especially on how the flowers and the moonlight help to endow the woods with meaning. Mentions the literary (primarily classical) and emblematic associations of the flowers described by Oberon (II.i) as well as those in Titania's bower. References to the moon in "the woodland scenes," accompanied by classical epithets, recapitulate many things said by the poets and allow Sh to create the delicate artifice of the fairy world. Cites the triple valence (Phoebe, Diana, and Proserpina) given by classical poets like Ovid and Virgil to the moon goddess and finds that Titania, through her connection with growing things, can be linked with Proserpina.

2284   Duffy, Maureen. *The Erotic World of Faery.* London: Hodder and Stoughton, 1972. 352 pp.

Investigates the background of fairy lore in the British Isles. Remarks that the attempts of the early Christian church to repress sexuality caused, on the one hand, the educated to yearn for the looser mythology of the classical writers and, on the other, the folk artists to turn to the fairy world, often itself incorporating classical elements. Considers *MND* in chapter 8, discovering a historical layer in which Queen Elizabeth, Essex, and Raleigh can be identified. Views Lyly's *Endymion* and the first three books of *The Faerie Queene* as significant influences on *MND*. Spenser's poem was especially important in spurring Sh to combine classical myth with native fairy traditions. Comments on the extensive use in *MND* of Ovid's *Metamorphoses,* especially the story of Diana and Actaeon in book 3.

2285   Foakes, R. A., ed. *A Midsummer Night's Dream.* (New Cambridge Shakespeare.) Cambridge: Cambridge U. P., 1984. xii + 148 pp.

The introduction suggests that John Lyly's Ovidian comedies *Gallathea, Sapho and Phao,* and *Midas* furnished Sh with hints about myth and the process of transformation. The framing device for *MND*, the wedding of Theseus, came from Chaucer's *The Knight's Tale,* and Sh took the names of Theseus's former loves from Plutarch's *Life of Theseus.* The idea of a king and queen of fairies who quarrel with each other and interfere in mortal affairs is probably derived from Chaucer's *The Merchant's Tale,* in which the king and queen are named Pluto and Proserpine. Titania's name comes from Ovid's *Metamorphoses,* and the general theme of transformation, especially as it is manifested in Bottom's change into an ass, owes much to Ovid and to Apuleius's *The Golden Asse,* as translated by William Adlington. Golding's *Metamorphoses* is also the source of the Pyramus and Thisbe story, used by Sh as the basis for the mechanicals' play.

2286   Green, Roger Lancelyn. "Shakespeare and the Fairies." *Folk Lore,* 73 (1962), 89–103.

Investigates the background for Sh's fairy knowledge, including literary sources like Chaucer and Ovid that would account for the association of fairies with the kingdom of Pluto and Proserpina. Explains that Titania's name has a perfect balance of classical and medieval flavors to provide a context for Theseus's court.

2287   Guilhamet, Leon. "*A Midsummer Night's Dream* as the Imitation of an Action." *SEL,* 15 (1975), 257–71.

Defines "action" in drama by drawing on modern critical explications of Aristotle's *Poetics,* as "psychic movement." Explains that in *MND* the action is to discover "the concord of discord," which reflects Sh's awareness and use of this great Neoplatonic commonplace. Sh could have absorbed the concept from Renaissance commentators like Pico della Mirandola and from classical sources (Ovid's myth of creation in book 1 of the *Metamorphoses,* Plutarch's *Moralia,* Horace, Seneca, and Plotinus). Different groups of characters—Theseus and Hippolyta, the young lovers, the mechanicals, and the fairies—are all involved in a search for harmony, which is interrupted in some way but is finally crowned with success. Crucial for Sh's strategy is Bottom's dream, which, incomprehensible as it is to Bottom, suggests heavenly perfection. This relates to the dramatist's conception of the play, a consciously "inadequate mirroring of divine order." In light of this, Theseus's famous comments about lovers, madmen, and poets are more sympathetic than most critics have acknowledged: For example, he correctly identifies the characteristic activity of poets as a search for concord in discord. On all levels, then, the play is about "poetry and its role in the discovery of concord."

2288   Henning, Standish. "The Fairies of *A Midsummer Night's Dream.*" *SQ*, 20 (1969), 484–86.

Points out that Sh is commonly credited, in *MND*, with first reducing the size of the fairies from their traditional dwarfishness to diminutiveness. He was probably influenced by Reginald Scot's *Discoverie of Witchcraft* (1584), which attributes many powers like those of the fairies in *MND* to witches of extremely small size. In describing the influence of witches on the weather, Scot includes a marginal note referring to book 7 of the *Metamorphoses*, an indication that the *Discovery* "might have sent Shakespeare to refresh his memory of Ovid."

2288a Henze, Richard. "*A Midsummer Night's Dream*: Analogous Image." *ShakS*, 7 (1974), 115–23.

Sums up Sir Philip Sidney's account of the poet's art, with its blend of Platonic ideas about the golden world and "Aristotelian ideal imitation" of the actual world, a combination characteristic of Renaissance theory of the imagination. Maintains that in *MND* Sh frees himself from this hybrid theory. He assigns to Theseus a Platonic rationalism that views the poet's creation as an insubstantial pageant, but it is clear that this view is not endorsed by the play. Instead, Sh invests the poet with imaginative power that creates not in its divine madness, but in "its very workmanlike ability to deliver an image analogous to the images of most men yet unique as an artistic expression of that image." The poet's art is emphasized instead of his inspiration (as in the Platonic model) and "imitation of common images instead of ideal imitation of the truth" (as in the Aristotelian model).

2289   Herbert, T. Walter. "Invitations to Cosmic Laughter in *A Midsummer Night's Dream.*" *Shakespearean Essays*. Eds. Alwin Thaler and Norman Sanders. Knoxville: U. of Tennessee P., 1964, pp. 29–39.

Argues that in *MND*, Sh invites his audience to laugh at "self-assertive persons and hot actions gently reduced to size." He achieves this by giving the lovers names that remind those educated in the classics of epic characters (Helena, over whom two young men fight, is a vastly scaled-down version of Helen of Troy). Posits a young scholar as a member of Sh's original audience and explains how in being led to laugh at Lysander he would be laughing at his own smug faith in reason.

2290   Holland, Peter. "Dreaming the *Dream*." "*Le songe d'une nuit d'été*" et "*La Duchesse de Malfi*" (texte et réprésentation). Actes du colloque Shakespeare–Webster, Limoges, 9–10–11 décembre 1988. (TRAMES: Travaux et memoires de l'Université de Limoges, Faculté des lettres et des sciences humaines.) Limoges: Centre d'études et de recherches sur la Renaissance européene, U. of Limoges, 1989, pp. 9–27.

Uses the *Oneirocritica* by Artemidorus of Daldis (2nd c. A.D.) and its elaboration in Macrobius's commentary on Cicero's account of Scipio's dream (400 A.D.) to discuss *MND*. Artemidorus distinguishes two kinds of dreams, *oneiros* (predictive) and *enhypnion* (non-predictive, resulting from anxiety or desire). Classifies Hermia's (II.ii) and Bottom's (IV.i) dreams as oneiric. For the lovers, the experience of the play is that of an *enhypnion*, but Puck's epilogue gives the audience the option of treating *MND* "as a benevolent *oneiros*."

2291 Holleran, James V. "The Pyramus–Thisbe Theme in *A Midsummer Night's Dream.*" *California English Journal*, 3, no. 1 (1967), 20–26.

Contends that the mechanics' choice of the love tragedy of Pyramus and Thisbe to celebrate a wedding "serves to enlarge and conclude Sh's commentary on the most important subject in the play—love and marriage." Ironically, the love of Pyramus and Thisbe is the most idealistic in *MND*; other loves, in descending order of perfection, are those between Lysander and Hermia, Oberon and Titania, Demetrius and Helena, and Theseus and Hippolyta.

2292 Kott, Jan. "The Bottom Translation." *Assays: Critical Approaches to Medieval and Renaissance Texts.* Vol. 1. Eds. Peggy A. Knapp and Michael A. Stugrin. Pittsburgh: U. of Pittsburgh P., 1981, pp. 117–49.

Explores the complex evocations of St. Paul's first letter to the Corinthians and *The Golden Ass* of Apuleius in Sh's portrayal of the transformation of Bottom in *MND*. Relies on the idea that, in the 16th c., both of these texts were read "in two distinctly separate intellectual traditions": Neoplatonism and the carnivalesque.

2293 Lamb, M. E. "*A Midsummer Night's Dream*: The Myth of Theseus and the Minotaur." *TSLL*, 21 (1979), 478–91.

Argues that the myth of Theseus and the Minotaur is a significant influence in *MND*. The young lovers are lost in a kind of labyrinth at the center of which is a comic Minotaur, half man and half ass. In the Renaissance allegorical interpretation of the myth, the labyrinth represented excesses of sensuality and irrationality into which people could fall and from which they could not escape without external aid (the fairies provide such help in the play). Bottom is both a monster representing the dangers of love and a way out of this labyrinth because he never succumbs to love and because he, after all, is a weaver like Ariadne, who aided Theseus in his escape, and his name can mean "thread." In the Renaissance, Theseus was regarded as a sinister figure, a deserter of women, but in the play he is portrayed as having reformed: He has been lost in the labyrinth where the lovers now wander but has found his way. The myth also helps make sense of the play's treatment of art: The particularity with which the tradesmen's crafts are identified connects them with Daedalus the artificer and focuses attention on the playwright (Sh) as craftsman. The mechanicals' concern over the response of the audience to their play can be illuminated by viewing the labyrinth as a metaphor for a work of art. In this context, Theseus's famous speech about lunatics, lovers, and poets is finally about the experience of the artist, who must accept the risks of losing himself in the labyrinth of his work. Ultimately, the myth would have reminded an Elizabethan audience of Theseus's future: his abandonment of Hippolyta and his murder of his son. It is hinted, then, that there is a dangerous side to the irrational, which, though it plays a primary role in generating the comedy of *MND*, can produce tragedy out of the same materials.

2294 Langford, Larry. "The Story Shall Be Changed: The Senecan Sources of *A Midsummer Night's Dream.*" *CahiersE*, 25 (1984), 37–51.

Finds that Sh's treatment of "the possession and domination of one sexual partner by the other" in *MND* owes a great deal to the plays of Seneca (*Medea, Hippolytus, Oedipus, Hercules Furens*, and *Thyestes*), which explore this theme intensively.

2295 Lecercle, Ann. "Of Mazes, Merry-Go-Rounds and Immaculate Conceptions: The Dream Logic of *A Midsummer Night's Dream.*" "*Le songe d'une nuit d'été*" *et "La Duchesse de Malfi" (texte et représentation).* Actes du colloque Shakespeare–Webster, Limoges, 9–10–11 décembre 1988. (TRAMES: Travaux et mémoires de l'Université de Limoges, Faculté des lettres et des sciences humaines.) Limoges: Centre d'études et de recherches sur la Renaissance européenne, U. de Limoges, 1989, pp. 141–53.

Hypothesizes that the structure of *MND* is based on "a dialectic of two major types" of Renaissance labyrinth: The first, placed under the sign of the eye, is the mannerist maze; the second, under the sign of the verb, is the symbolic, Cnossan one. Asserts that this dialectic is paralleled in the play by a counterpoint of deficiency and excess. Identifies Bottom as the onocentaur or English minotaur of Celtic legend; he is at the heart of the verbal labyrinth as the object of desire, the desiring subject, and the paradigm of desire itself. Indeed, he occupies all of the places in this maze. The pneumatic spirit that seeks out the secrets of God, associated with Bottom and the other tradesmen, passes to the fairies at the end of the play. Finally, we sense the triumph of spirit over letter.

2296 Lee, G. M. "Plotinus and Shakespeare." *N&Q*, 14 (1967), 134.

Draws attention to a remark of Tudor Vianu that Plotinus's conception of "internal form" influenced Sh when he wrote some of Theseus's lines on the imagination (*MND*, V.i.14–18).

2297 Longo, Joseph A. "Myth in *A Midsummer Night's Dream*." *CahiersE*, 18 (1980), 17–27.

Contends that Sh consciously invokes the world of myth in *MND* by including the story of Pyramus and Thisbe. On a mythic level, the play progresses from Apollonian reason through "Dionysian release of frenzied energy to an Orphic re-creation." In his handling of the dispute at the beginning and in his general attitude, Theseus is Apollonian; the woods are the setting for the pre-rational impulses released in a number of the characters; and Puck, in his epilogue, gathers "the mythic materials of the play into a final true Orphic statement about the creative experience and the role of the artist."

2298 McPeek, James A. S. "The Psyche Myth and *A Midsummer Night's Dream*." *SQ*, 23 (1972), 69–79.

Points out that Sh probably knew Apuleius's *Golden Asse* both in the original Latin and in William Adlington's translation (1566). In *MND*, he reshaped the Psyche myth as recounted by Apuleius. Helena and Hermia resemble Psyche as women who remain true to their loves in adversity. Hermia, at the beginning of the play, is in a situation similar to that of Psyche, whose father seemingly wishes her to marry a serpent, and both Hermia and Helena use serpent imagery extensively. The "unseen servitors who wait on Psyche" are counterparts to the play's fairies. Oberon and Puck share aspects of the Cupid figure in the myth, and Titania resembles Venus as well as Psyche herself. When Titania awakens, she loves "a mock figure of the Golden Ass." Bottom's "rare vision" parallels the dream of Lucius. The main action of the drama concludes with "an extensive dreamlike correspondence" to the end of the Psyche myth. Psyche returns from Hades and falls into "a dense fog of sleep." She is awakened by Cupid, who arranges for their marriage with Jupiter. Sh may have been influenced by Adlington's preface to his translation, which justifies what might seem to be a trivial work by insisting that it shows how men can transform themselves into their "right and perfect shapes." Hippolyta's defense of the transforming power of the imagination may be derived from this. The moral tone of the preface may also be responsible for Sh's refinement of certain aspects of *The Golden Asse*. Bottom, for example, shows no traces of the lust with which Lucius is infected.

2299 Mowat, Barbara A. "'A Local Habitation and a Name': Shakespeare's Text as Construct." *Style*, 23 (1989), 335–51.

Cites Theseus's pronouncement that poets, seized by a "fine frenzy," create their work *ex nihilo* (*MND*, V.i). Argues that this idea is subverted by Sh's deliberate construction in *MND* of a complex Theseus from several texts. Examines Plutarch's *Life of Theseus*, Chaucer's *The Knight's Tale*, and Ovid's *Metamorphoses* as works that contributed to Sh's systematically self-contradictory, "language-shaped," and "book-based" character. Theseus's speech about lovers, lunatics, and poets weaves together the wonder of Theseus and the scoffing of Pirithous at marvelous tales in *Metamorphoses* 8, the skepticism about such tales in Reginald Scot's *The Discoverie* of *Witchcraft*, and the admiration for the divine madness of the poet that is part of a discourse stretching back to Plato's *Phaedrus*. Sh's Theseus can be viewed as a "re-representation of a late-Renaissance prince, dependent for his role on the stuff of the past but skeptical even of that which has made him." There are numerous other examples of Sh's construction of characters from a vast field of texts.

2300 Murphy, Georgeann. "'The Story Shall be Changed': When Chastity is Not a Virtue." *Kentucky Philological Review*, 3 (1988), 27–35.

Calls attention to the importance of transformation in *MND*. Focuses on the ways in which Sh links Titania and the goddess Diana and then distinguishes sharply between the two in order to show how Sh transforms chastity from a positive to a negative quality. The moon, a traditional emblem of chastity, is also transformed—into an image of fecundity, which the play exalts. Other images of chastity undergo similar transformations. The play also places a high value on the transforming power of the imagination.

2301 Ormerod, David. "*A Midsummer Night's Dream*: The Monster in the Labyrinth." *ShakS*, 11 (1978), 39–52.

Develops an interpretation of *MND* based on the opposition between the orderly world of Theseus and the fairy world. Examines the play's exploitation of Theseus's legendary feats. In the Renaissance, Theseus was associated with the control of irregular passions through his defeat of Hippolyta and his slaying of the Minotaur. The youthful lovers of *MND*, driven by disordered emotions into the woods, are counterparts to the tribute Athens paid to Minos; their wanderings are reminiscent of the Minotaur's labyrinth; and Bottom, half man and half ass, replaces the legendary monster. Several well-known stories (those of Midas, Circe, and especially Lucius in Apuleius's *The Golden Asse*) are relevant to Bottom's dalliance with Titania. Adlington's translation of Apuleius (1566) describes how Lucius, transformed into an ass, copulates with a rich noblewoman. In this light, Titania becomes an icon for the degradation that results when passionate love judges by appearance and not by inner reality. But two episodes in Apuleius indicate the opposite of bestial debasement: the story of Cupid and Psyche and the appearance to Lucius of the goddess Isis, who raises him from bestial form and initiates him into her worship. Lucius thus becomes the *asinus portans mysteria*, a means of achieving a state of higher spiritual consciousness. The ass's head in the woods, then, can be seen as an image of "moral mischoice" that contains the potential for ultimate enlightenment. Renaissance commentators on the labyrinth viewed it as an emblem of the ease with which one could fall into an immoral life and the difficulty in extricating oneself. This is one way to understand the confusion into which the lovers are plunged in *MND*. However, they can also be seen as engaged in the game of Troy-town, a rural turf maze derived from the Troy Game described by Virgil in book 5 of the *Aeneid*. The idea of this maze was to move from initial bewilderment to the beginning of understanding. The lovers, having wandered in a maze of wrongheaded passion, are by the end of the play starting to see the light: They are on the first rung of the ladder of Platonic enlightenment.

2302 Parker, Douglas H. "'Limander' and 'Helen' in *A Midsummer Night's Dream*." *SQ*, 33 (1982), 99–101.

Calls attention to three possible ways of understanding the references by Pyramus (Bottom) to Limander and by Thisbe (Quince) to Helen in the tradesmen's play in *MND*: as bungling attempts to recall Hero and Leander, as an obvious reference to Leander and an ironically mistaken allusion to the inconstant Helen of Troy, and as unwitting references to the undependable Lysander and the loyal Helena.

2303 Pearson, D'Orsay W. "'Unkinde' Theseus: A Study in Renaissance Mythography." *ELR*, 4 (1974), 276–98.

Rejects modern attempts to view Theseus in *MND* as a benevolent, rational prince. Points out that the usual conception of Theseus in the Renaissance emphasized his unkind (unnatural) behavior. That Sh meant to present an obviously pagan world—as his age understood it—can be seen, for example, in the specific references made to classical costume. These reinforce the notion that the playwright provided a portrait of his protagonist that is in accord with contemporary opinion of him. From medieval writers like Chaucer and Gower and from classical sources like Ovid's *Metamorphoses* and *Heroides*, Seneca's *Hippolytus*, Virgil's *Aeneid*, and Plutarch's *Lives*, it is clear that Sh inherited a portrait of Theseus that stressed his womanizing, his injustice, and his responsibility for his son's death. In *MND*, Theseus follows this pattern. It is noteworthy that Sh gives his Amazonian wife the name Hippolyta rather than the more usual Antiopa; this is probably to remind the audience of what is to happen to his son Hippolytus. It is particularly ironic that, given his reputation as a deserter of women, Theseus is given a role as a sort of marriage sponsor.

2304   Robinson, James E. "The Ritual and Rhetoric of *A Midsummer Night's Dream*." *PMLA*, 83 (1968), 380–91.

Postulates that *MND* contains and combines two kinds of comedy: (1) the celebration of man's union with nature through symbolic, magical, and ritualistic means and (2) the exhibition of folly through argument and rhetoric. Notes that the Elizabethans absorbed the ritualistic idea of comedy in many ways, one of which was a recollection that comedy originated "in ancient Greek times." The social, rhetorical model of comedy had taken shape for the Renaissance under the influence of a comment of Cicero's in the oration *Pro Sexto Roscio Amerino*; an expansion of Cicero by Aelius Donatus, a 4th-c. A.D. commentator on Terence's comedies; classical notions about the power of rhetoric "to give persuasive force to the truths of civilized life"; and a whole body of Terentian commentary that saw comedy as "an imitation of life" as well as "a set of principles" that guided that imitation "as an eloquent and dramatic argument about the problems of finite experience." Shows how Sh relates and assimilates the two "contexts of nature and society" by, for example, making it possible to read the play's movement in terms of the protasis–epitasis–catastrophe structure that Renaissance commentators derived from Roman comedy or in terms of a magical, ritualistic pattern for the unfolding of young love. Throughout the play, even in the figures of speech that move from debate to incantation, Sh moves between one reality and the other; and in the Pyramus and Thisbe play he displays "amusement at the artist's power through style to comprehend and relate the worlds of nature and experience."

2305   Rudd, Niall. "Pyramis and Thisbe in Shakespeare and Ovid: *A Midsummer Night's Dream* and *Metamorphoses* 4.1–166." *Creative Imitation and Latin Literature*. Eds. David West and Tony Woodman. Cambridge: Cambridge U. P., 1979, pp. 173–93.

Observes that the influence of Ovid, both in Golding's translation of the *Metamorphoses* and in the Latin, is pervasive in *MND*. The Ovidian ambiance is created by such details from the *Metamorphoses* as Hippolyta's account of hunting on Crete with Cadmus (IV.i), Helena's reference to Apollo's pursuit of Daphne (II.i), and Puck's resemblance to Mercury as both messenger and prankster. Most important is Ovid's story of Pyramus and Thisbe, from which the wall, moonlight, tomb, forest, and shedding of blood are borrowed by Sh and transformed into farce. As performed by the mechanicals, the Pyramus and Thisbe story parallels and parodies a number of other romances in the play. It can be said that Sh, inspired by Ovid, composed in this play his own *Metamorphoses*.

2306   Schalkwyk, David. "The Role of Imagination in *A Midsummer Night's Dream*." *Theoria*, 66 (1986), 51–65.

Surveys Elizabethan psychological writings, acknowledging their indebtedness to "a Greek epistemological framework devised to provide an *ethics* of perception" in terms of which problems of truth and knowledge are understood according to "the Platonic struggle between the senses and the understanding, imagination and reason." Contends that *MND* rejects the dichotomy by which reason was seen as the only means to overcome the delusions and inconsistencies of the imagination. In this play,

Sh recognizes imagination as a paradoxical force that is aligned with emotion and illusion but that can "lead to stability, harmony and a greater grasp of reality through the liberating power of illusion and fiction."

2307 Scragg, Leah. "Shakespeare, Lyly and Ovid: The Influence of 'Gallathea' on *A Midsummer Night's Dream.*" *ShS*, 30 (1977), 125–34.

Argues that the influence of Ovid on *MND* is both direct (in the borrowing of the Pyramus and Thisbe story from the *Metamorphoses* and in the "pervasive concern with 'translation'") and indirect (through conscious use of elements of location, plot, character, and theme from Lyly's *Gallathea*).

2308 Sillars, Stuart. "Phoebe and Phoebus: Bottom's Verbal Slip." *N&Q*, 25 (1978), 125–26.

Maintains that the "Phibbus" referred to by Bottom in *MND* (I.ii.30) is "a comic malapropism which provides a parody of the more serious role of the moon in the play." It refers, in other words, to Phoebe, not, as many critics have argued, to Phoebus.

2309 Spisak, James W. "Pyramus and Thisbe in Chaucer and Shakespeare." *Chaucerian Shakespeare: Adaptation and Transformation.* Eds. E. Talbot Donaldson and Judith J. Kollmann. (Medieval and Renaissance Monograph Series 2.) Detroit: Michigan Consortium for Medieval and Modern Studies, 1983, pp. 81–95.

Contends that Chaucer, in his treatment of the Pyramus and Thisbe story in *The Legend of Good Women*, uses his narrator to offer ironic praise of the young lovers and allows their excessive speeches to render them slightly ridiculous. Sh, responding to this irony, transforms "the mildly excessive young lovers" into utterly ludicrous types who "parody other types of love" that appear in *MND*. He also seems to mock the courtly poet Chaucer (or at least the persona of the courtly poet Chaucer presents) and "his courtly little poem."

2310 Staton, Walter F. Jr. "Ovidian Elements in *A Midsummer Night's Dream.*" *HLQ*, 26 (1962–63), 165–78.

Notes the Elizabethan habit of drawing indiscriminately on classical myth and native tradition and explores, in this context, the Ovidian character of the fairies in *MND*. The relationship of Oberon, Titania, and Robin Goodfellow is similar to that of Jupiter, Juno, and Mercury in Ovid. Other elements of Ovidian derivation include the changeling boy (Ganymede), the "effects of divine bickering," and the story of Titania's votaress (Callisto). In the Titania–Bottom episode, Sh parodies the Ovidian theme of "a nymph wooing a reluctant boy" found in many contemporary poems, including his own *Ven*.

2311 Taylor, Anthony Brian. "Chaucer's Non-Involvement in 'Pyramus and Thisbe.'" *N&Q*, 36 (1989), 317–20.

Asserts that the source of Pyramus's "O wicked wall" (*MND*, V.i.179) is not Chaucer's *The Legend of Thisbe*, as maintained by Kenneth Muir, but rather the anonymous "History of Pyramus and Thisbe" in *A Ggorgeous Gallery of Gallant Inventions* (1598). Further, E. Talbot Donaldson (item 0325) is wrong to attribute Pyramus's seemingly effeminate features, including his "pap," to Sh's borrowing from *Sir Thopas*. The sources of these details are Ovid's *Metamorphoses* and Sh's Ovidian poem *Ven*.

2312 Taylor, Anthony Brian. "Golding's Ovid, Shakespeare's 'Small Latin,' and the Real Object of Mockery in 'Pyramus and Thisbe.'" *ShS*, 42 (1990), 53–64.

Counters the assumption that Sh's satiric target when he has the tradesmen in *MND* present a clumsy dramatic version of the Pyramus and Thisbe story is Golding's translation of Ovid's *Metamorphoses*. Presents evidence that the Elizabethans admired Golding. Analysis of "Pyramus and Thisbe" reveals that much of its verbal ineptness derives from incompetent translation of Ovid's Latin. The mockery, then, is directed at Sh's alter ego, Peter Quince, the versatile writer–actor–playwright with small Latin.

2312a Taylor, Anthony Brian. "Thomas Phaer and Nick Bottom's 'Hopping Heart.'" *N&Q*, 34 (1987), 207–8.

Suggests that in Bottom's ludicrously inappropriate description of his left pap "Where heart doth hop" (*MND*, V.i.294–295), Sh is mocking the clumsy translation of Virgil by Thomas Phaer.

2313 Weiner, Andrew D. "'Multiformitie Uniforme': *A Midsummer Night's Dream*." *ELH*, 38 (1971), 329–49.

Views *MND* as Sh's defense of poetry. Theseus's "antic fables" speech (V.i.2–17) is an adaptation of the Platonic attack on poetry as a distortion of reality. Hippolyta's correction of Theseus (V.i.23–27) should be understood in the context of defenses like Sir Philip Sidney's, in which the poet is said to have a particularly clear perception of the Platonic Idea as well as the inspiration of the Holy Spirit. In *MND*, the poet's imagination moves the audience to apprehend, through a variety of emotional responses, the new thing he has created out of a "multiplicity of incident, allusion, characterization, and comment."

2313a Weller, Barry. "Identity Dis-figured: *A Midsummer Night's Dream*." *KR*, 7, no. 3 (1985), 66–78.

Mentions Ovid's *Metamorphoses* and Aupleius's *The Golden Ass* as sources for *MND*. Sketches an approach the play that combines ideas about metamorphosis, "metaphor, the physicality of the theater, and the way in which *A Midsummer Night's Dream* conceives and represents identity."

2314 Wells, Stanley, ed. *A Midsummer Night's Dream*. (New Penguin Shakespeare.) Harmondsworth: Penguin, 1967. 171 pp.

The introduction acknowledges that *MND* has no narrative source but suggests that Sh might have been influenced by Plutarch's *Lives* and Chaucer's *The Knight's Tale*. The parodic treatment of the Pyramus and Thisbe tale might have been prompted by Arthur Golding's translation of the same story from Ovid's *Metamorphoses*. Although there are a few hints of Theseus's origin in classical legend, Sh portrays him primarily as an Elizabethan nobleman. Oberon and Titania are, among other things, "strongly reminiscent of classical deities." In general, classical elements are muted as they mingle with native English material.

2315 Willson, Robert F. "Golding's *Metamorphoses* and Shakespeare's Burlesque Method in *A Midsummer Night's Dream*." *ELN*, 7 (1969), 18–25.

Questions Kenneth Muir's belief that the Pyramus and Thisbe play is a conscious parody of Thomas Mouffet's poem, *Of the Silkwormes and Their Flies*. Contends that Sh is parodying the regular rhythm, alliteration, and apostrophes found in the rendition of the episode given by Golding in his translation of the *Metamorphoses*. In addition, Sh omitted Ovid's account of how Pyramus's blood turned the mulberries purple to "illustrate the lack of romantic imagination on the part of the actors." He also left out the moral of Ovid's tale—that the lovers are sacrificed to effect a reconciliation between their families—to show that the workmen "overlook the moral implications of art."

2316 Wood, James O. "'Finde Out Moone-Shine, Finde Out Moone-Shine.'" *N&Q*, 13 (1966), 128–30.

Contends that the exchange between Theseus and Hippolyta in the first eleven lines of *MND* refers to a fulling moon rather than a new moon, a view that receives support from a passage in Golding's Ovid about Medea's magic. The passage, used by Sh elsewhere in *MND* and in *Tmp.*, establishes that the image of a drawn bow, to which Hippolyta compares the moon, is quite appropriate for "a moon approaching the full."

2317 Young, David P. *Something of Great Constancy: The Art of "A Midsummer Night's Dream."* (Yale Studies in English 164.) New Haven: Yale U. P., 1966. xii + 190 pp.

Treats *MND* as "the earliest dramatic handling of Sh's vision of his art." Discusses the complexity with which Sh handles sources in the first chapter. Myth and folklore complement each other in various ways: A reasonably literate spectator "would have seen in Bottom's transformation the parallels in the stories of Midas, Circe, and Apuleius," while the less educated would see parallels in "folklore stories of human–animal metamorphosis." The moon is both classical (associated with Phoebe and Hecate–Diana–Proserpina) and English, and the same is true of the fairies. Revision of item 2318.

2318 Young, David Pollock. "Something of Great Constancy: A Study of *A Midsummer Night's Dream*." Ph.D. dissertation, Yale University, 1965. *DA*, 27 (1966–67), 491-A–492-A.

Chapter 1 includes a discussion of the play's dual focus on "classical mythology and native folklore." Revised as item 2317.

Much Ado About Nothing

2319 Crichton, Andrew B. "Hercules Shaven: A Centering Mythic Metaphor in *Much Ado About Nothing*." *TSLL*, 16 (1974–75), 619–26.

Discovers two parallel chains of references, to beards and to Hercules, respectively, that are eventually linked in *Ado* when Benedick shaves off his beard. Much of the play's action is organized around this "centering metaphor of the shaven Hercules." In the early scenes, Benedick expresses his resistance to strong women in terms of Hercules' difficulties with Omphale Iole. Under Beatrice's civilizing influence, he comes to recognize that tonsorial fashion is of little importance in signifying authentic heroism or virility.

2320 Lewalski, B. K. "Love, Appearance and Reality: Much Ado About Something." *SEL*, 8 (1968), 235–51.

Maintains that *Ado* sets forth "a complex theme concerning the various levels of knowledge and love in relation to the confusions of appearance and reality." The theme is rooted in Neoplatonism, fused with Christian concepts. Life in Messina is marked by an inability to distinguish between illusion and truth, which is highlighted by "four central masque or play-acting sequences." Since "the conditions of perceiving and knowing" in *Ado* are strongly linked to conditions of loving, several of the ideas found "in Bembo's classic discourse on love in the fourth book of *The Courtier* provide surprisingly apt categories for analyzing the various levels of action." Benedick and Beatrice act out "the pattern of Bembo's rational lovers, attracted by physical beauty but regarding the inner qualities of the soul more highly, basing love on genuine knowledge, and accepting it not in terms of mad passion but by conscious choice." Claudio, at first entirely dependent on the senses in his love, must be educated to direct his attention to Hero's inner qualities and to accept the veiled Hero completely on faith, "with no sensory confirmation or prudential inquiry into the truth of Leonato's promises."

2321 Lewalski, Barbara K. "Hero's Name—and Namesake—in *Much Ado About Nothing.*" *ELN*, 7 (1969–70), 175–79.

Argues that the source of the word-play on Hero's name in the denunciation scene of *Ado* (IV.i) is "George Chapman's four-canto continuation, published in 1598," of Marlowe's *Hero and Leander*. Only in Chapman's continuation does Hero become an emblem for dissimulation of chastity; she is denounced by Venus "in terms suggestive for Claudio's denunciation of that later Hero."

2322 Ormerod, David. "Faith and Fashion in *Much Ado About Nothing.*" *ShS*, 25 (1972), 93–105.

Argues that *Ado* explores the contention between faith and fashion. Messina is largely governed by the latter, which encourages "shallowness, triviality, pettiness, volatility, and wrong choice." Beatrice, however, values faith, which implies the ability to make the right choice. There are frequent allusions to Hercules and Blind Cupid, representing faith and fashion, respectively. Ultimately, the play's scheme suggests a kind of Platonic reunion of base love (prompted by fashion) and higher love (prompted by faith).

2323 Pasicki, Adam. "Some Rhetorical Figures in *Much Ado About Nothing.*" *KN*, 15 (1968), 147–54.

Reviews several instances of two rhetorical figures of repetition—*anaphora* and *antimetabole*—in *Ado*.

2324 Tobin, J. J. M. "On the Asininity of Dogberry." *ES*, 59 (1978), 199–201.

Suggests that the Dogberry episodes in *Ado* were influenced by the Adlington translation of Apuleius's *The Golden Asse*, where Lucius the protagonist, soon to be transformed into an ass, is "brought before the bar of justice as a homicide by the captain of the watch." Revised as part of chapter 3 of item 1052.

OTHELLO

2325 Altman, Joel B. "'Preposterous Conclusions': Eros, *Enargeia*, and the Composition of *Othello.*" *Representations*, 18 (1987), 129–57.

Argues that the Renaissance revival of classical rhetoric was deeply influential in the aesthetic, intellectual, and political enterprises of the 16th and 17th c.; the modes of rhetoric "frequently provided the paradigms on which the imagination focused and the means by which the mind reasoned its way to understanding." In *Oth.*, Sh consciously interrogates this way of understanding through "a rhetorical poetics" that explores improbabilities at the same time that it is implicated in them. Finds that the rhetorical figure of *hysteron proteron*, which means setting the cart before the horse or putting ends before means or effects before causes, "figures *Oth*. at large and also in several particulars." The psychology of the play's composition, which can be glimpsed in the first three scenes, operates in its major action: "the decomposition and recomposition of Othello." The protagonist's life, founded in rhetorical discourse, is seen as matter for tragedy. Iago's exploitation of "the eros of knowing, the drive to come to conclusions," has an effect on Othello similar to the effect on the audience of the play's use of disorienting foreshadowings.

2326 Boose, Lynda E. "Othello's 'Chrysolite' and the Song of Songs Tradition." *PQ*, 60 (1981), 427–37.

Challenges the acceptance by most scholars of Pliny's *Naturall Historie* as Sh's source for the word "chrysolite" in *Oth*.(V.ii.143–146). A more likely source is the Song of Solomon in the Geneva Bible.

2327 Doran, Madeleine. "Good Name in *Othello*." *SEL*, 7 (1967), 195–217.

Argues that Othello's final speech can be illuminated by certain concepts of Roman law. *Existimatio* or *fama* was a man's good name, "a condition of uninjured dignity," which he possessed by virtue of being a man. There were two ways a man could lose his *fama*, either under law (*infama juris*) or outside law (*infama facti*). Infamy of fact was most commonly the result of *mala fama*, "rumor or suspicion of criminal behavior whether or not that rumor was true." Othello, in his final speech and in his suicide, acknowledges the *infama juris* that he has incurred but seeks to clear this name of *mala fama*.

2328 Fleissner, Robert F. "The Moor's Nomenclature." *N&Q*, 25 (1978), 143.

Suggests that Sh was influenced in creating Othello's name by the name of Otho, the Roman emperor who died in 69 A.D. Both men were figures of authority from Italy. Both died by stabbing themselves, and both had problems with their wives.

2328a Gouws, John. "Shakespeare, Webster and the Moriturus Lyric." *ShSoA*, 3 (1989), 45–57.

Discovers the origin of the *moriturus* lyric—a song or poem by a person who is about to die—in the *Phaedo* of Plato, in which Socrates, awaiting execution, compares his own recent poetic composition with the songs of swans, who sing best when "they feel that they are to die." Cicero probably transmitted this idea to the Renaissance. The emperor Hadrian perhaps contributed to the broadening of the *moriturus* genre from its exclusive concern with someone under threat of execution to a concern with anyone whose death is imminent. Comments on the Christian elements that also became part of the genre. Discusses the episode in which Desdemona sings the "Willow Song" (*Oth.*, V.ii), noting that in this context Sh has put the *moriturus* conventions "to extensive dramatic use."

2329 Graves, Wallace. "Plutarch's *Life of Cato Utican* as a Major Source of *Othello*." *SQ*, 24 (1973), 181–87.

Notes that the *Life of Cato Utican* is an important secondary source for *Oth.*; it helps explain a number of details not found in G. B. Giraldi Cinthio's *Hecatommithi*, the primary source. Iago's resentment at being passed over for promotion parallels the similar feeling of one Munatius, who is angered because his old friend Cato, a general, places more trust in Canidius than in him. In act I of *Oth.*, Iago is presented as the general's oldest friend and Cassio as the newcomer, but thereafter Cassio becomes Othello's longtime confidant. This inconsistency may derive from Sh's use of Munatius's situation to give Iago his initial motivation. *Cato Utican* may also be responsible for Othello's calling Cassio a "Roman" and for the presence of a Senate in Venice.

2330 Hansen, Abby Jane Dubman. "Shakespeare's Othello." *Expl*, 35, no. 4 (1976–77), 4–6.

Comments that "Sagittary" (*Oth.*, I.i.160), the name of the inn where Othello is staying, constitutes a "concentrated symbolic allusion to a tradition of violent legends." Cites Polybius and Livy to establish that the first *Sagittarii* were foreign bowmen sent to fight for Rome in the Second Punic War. Typically, the ancient representation of the constellation Sagittarius shows a creature, "half man, half horse, wielding a bow." In medieval romance, "sagittary" can also refer to a centaur, especially the monster in the Trojan army who fought against the Greeks. References to centaurs in Sh's other plays (for example, *Lr.* and *Tit.*) emphasize their association with lust. Othello's address is thus richly suggestive of his foreignness and his "susceptibility to bestial behavior."

2331 Holloway, Julia B. "Strawberries and Mulberries: *Ulysses* and *Othello*." *Hypatia: Essays in Classics, Comparative Literature, and Philosophy Presented to Hazel E. Barnes on Her Seventieth Birthday*. Eds. William M. Calder III, Ulrich K. Goldsmith, and Phyllis B. Kenevan. Boulder: Colorado Associated U. P., 1985, pp. 125–36.

Uses feminist, anthropological, and psychoanalytic perspectives in making the case that Sh based the marriage of Othello and Desdemona on the relationship of Pyramus and Thisbe as he found it in Ovid's *Metamorphoses*. Neither marriage is consummated except in death, and in both cases the tragic outcome is caused by "a piece of white cloth sprinkled with red." Sh seems to link women "with bloodshed and death."

2332 Holmer, Joan Ozark. "Othello's Threnos: 'Arabian Trees' and 'Indian' Versus 'Judean.'" *ShakS*, 13 (1980), 145–67.

Asserts that two problematic allusions in Othello's death speech (*Oth.*, V.ii.348–366), if properly understood, can be related to each other and used to shed light on the speaker's tragic experience. The first, "Arabian trees," is probably a reference to the myrrh, located by Pliny (in Holland's translation of *The Historie of the World*, 1601) in Arabia. Sh values the myrrh image most for the analogy of weeping it furnishes Othello. In the tenth book of the *Metamorphoses*, Ovid recounts the story of Myrrha, the mother of Adonis, who, tearfully repentant for crimes of passion, is transformed by the gods into the weeping myrrh. Allegorical readings of Ovid in the Middle Ages and the Renaissance had made Myrrha a figure of the great sinner who truly repents. Othello, though he weeps like Myrrha, is unable to repent. He is more like Judas Iscariot in that he feels remorse but remains desperate and commits suicide. Thus the "base Judean" (line 357) reading of the Folio is preferable to the quarto's "base Indian."

2333 Jeffrey, David L., and Patrick Grant. "Reputation in *Othello*." *ShakS*, 6 (1970), 197–208.

Traces the concept of *fama* to classical sources, especially Virgil's *Aeneid* 4 and Ovid's *Metamorphoses* 12. Notes that Augustine synthesized the pagan personification of fame and Christian theology in *The City of God*. According to Augustine, there are two cities, Jerusalem and Babylon, that symbolize, respectively, two types of love, *caritas* and *cupiditas*. Arising from these two loves are two kinds of glory, one based on love of God and one on love of fame among men and desire for their praise. This distinction between good and bad fame became linked to Lady Fortune in Boethius's *Consolation of Philosophy*: Bad fame is, of course, associated with Fortune and the acclaim one enjoys under her sponsorship. Sh could have learned of good and bad fame from Erasmus's *Enchiridion Militis Christiani* or another of the school texts used at the time. In *Oth.*, the protagonist's love of his wife is from the beginning based on an attitude toward fame that is sure to ruin him. Othello places his concern for worldly reputation above all else: This is what he describes as having won Desdemona, this is what he relies on to keep her, and this is what he believes he is losing when he thinks she is unfaithful. In his final speech, Othello, though recognizing that he is Fortune's fool, maintains his mistaken loyalty to bad fame.

2334 Levitsky, Ruth. "All-in-All Sufficiency in Othello." *ShakS*, 6 (1970), 209–21.

Acknowledges that Iago's speech on reason and will can be read in terms of the contemporary theological debates about grace and free will but insists that Sh, in putting these terms in the mouth of his villain, is calling attention primarily to the inadequacy of ancient Roman notions of self-sufficiency. An examination of 16th- and 17th-c. writings on the subject reveals that there was much hostility toward what was perceived to be the ancient philosophical idea of achieving autonomy through reason and will. Othello, from the beginning, exhibits a certain Stoic harshness and attempts to conduct his affairs according to the principles of reason. He is destroyed because he does not possess an infallible reason to discover the truth and a will sufficient to execute what the reason dictates.

2335 Lim, C. S. "An Ovidian Source for Othello's Success in Love." *N&Q*, 30 (1983), 127.

Points out that Sh might have been indebted to the description of Ulysses in Ovid's *Ars Amatoria* 2 for the idea in *Oth*. that success in love may come from skillful storytelling.

2336 Macey, Samuel L. "The Naming of the Protagonists in Shakespeare's *Othello*." *N&Q*, (1978), 143–45.

Notes that Cassio's name can be easily related to Cassius, the Latin name of a famous Roman; it is thus appropriate for a character of whom Othello says, "Do you triumph, Roman?" (IV.i.119).

2337 Melchiori, Giorgio. "The Rhetoric of Character Construction: *Othello*." *ShS*, 34 (1981), 61–72.

Includes an analysis of the *dispositio* of Othello's last speech (V.ii), commenting that it is a small-scale replica of his speech to the Venetian Senate in I.iii: Each opens with a *captatio*, proceeds to an *excusatio*, and concludes with an *ornatus*. Before the Senate, Othello focuses on his relationship with Desdemona; in V.ii, he focuses on "his relationship to the Venetian State." The rhetorical parallelism of the two speeches suggests that at the end he has recovered his true self.

2338 Mikesell, Margaret Lael, and Virginia Mason Vaughan, comps. *"Othello": An Annotated Bibliography.* (Garland Shakespeare Bibliographies 20.) New York: Garland, 1990 xxxv + 941 pp.

Covers materials published between 1940 and 1985. Classifies entries under seventeen headings, including Criticism (1402 items), Sources (87 items), Single Editions (45 items), and Bibliographies (7 items). Begins each section with the oldest entries and proceeds chronologically. Concludes with subject and name indexes. Provides substantial annotations. Includes, in the sections on criticism and sources, a number of items that discuss classical influences on *Oth*.

2339 Miola, Robert S. "Othello *Furens*." *SQ*, 41 (1990), 49–64.

Offers Seneca's *Hercules Furens* as a source, both direct and indirect, for *Oth*. Section 1 discusses the correlation between these two works and their protagonists: reputations based on battles, enemies that are "dispatched" offstage. Tales of Hercules provided a mythical archetype that Sh used to build great tragedy. The madness/murder sequence in Seneca's play furnishes the blueprint for act V of *Oth*. Section 2 explains how Seneca's play supplies the model of Othello's tragic furor: "transforming madness, uncontrollable rage and self-destructive passion." Neither Hercules nor Othello is capable of following the right path because each is blinded by madness. For both heroes, their rage destroys those nearest them and eventually themselves.

2340 Nass, Barry. "'Of One That Loved Not Wisely, But Too Well': *Othello* and the *Heroides*." *ELN*, 19 (1981–82), 102–4.

Observes that Sh seems to have used the second epistle of Ovid's *Heroides* as a source for "Othello's penultimate speech," in which he asks his auditors to tell of his "unlucky deeds" in letters (V.ii.349–365). In Ovid, Phyllis speaks of having loved unwisely, but, unlike Othello, she is the injured party, having been abandoned by Demophon after a promise of marriage. Othello thus uses the language of Phyllis, but Desdemona is her true counterpart.

2340a Parker, Patricia. "Shakespeare and Rhetoric: 'dilation' and 'delation' in *Othello*." *Shakespeare and the Question of Theory*. Eds. Patricia Parker and Geoffrey Hartman. New York: Methuen, 1985, pp. 54–74.

Calls attention to the classical linking of judicial delation (accusation) and rhetorical dilation (amplification), suggests that Sh uses "dilation" in both senses throughout

Oth., and connects both with yet another sense of "dilation": delay. The multiple structure of "dilation," with its nexus of "rhetorical, judicial, and temporal," has much to do with determining the play's structure, which makes insistent demand for narrative, for the provision of circumstances.

2341   Rogers, Stephen. "*Othello*: Comedy in Reverse." *SQ*, 24 (1973), 210–220.

Notes that critics have found important resemblances between the characters of *Oth*. and "perennial comic types." More particularly, Douglas Stewart (item 2348) has demonstrated "analogies with Roman comedy, not only in the characters but in significant sections of the plot." Stewart, though perceptive, is wrong in believing that *Oth*. is "not properly a tragedy at all." In fact, the play "achieves much of its tragic power through the adaptation, often the rearrangement or inversion, of techniques, devices, and other materials traditionally belonging to comedy." Othello, for example, though he is not so at first, becomes under Iago's tutelage, "the *miles gloriosus*, the false soldier and cruel lover." Iago is "the serious and terrible embodiment" of the Vice and the *fallax servus* of Roman comedy.

2342   Ross, Lawrence J. "Shakespeare's 'Dull Clown' and Symbolic Music." *SQ*, 17 (1966), 107–28.

Views the scene at the beginning of act III in *Oth*., often discounted as superfluous, as an induction to the main action of the play. Read in the light of the rich tradition of symbolic music inherited by the Renaissance, this episode, in which the Clown orders Cassio's musicians to stop playing, provides an emblem for the tragic discord to come. Cites Boethius's synthesis of classical thought on music as "a comprehensive theory of harmony" according to which music "becomes an image of all concord, proportion and unity in a universe of parallel worlds instrumenting the harmoniousness of the divine creator." In III.i, the music is that of bagpipes, which convey the sense of carnality and error associated with all wind instruments since classical antiquity (stringed instruments, by contrast, were linked to virtue and order). The pipers, when asked if they "have any music that cannot be heard," concede that they do not. What they are admitting is that they are out of touch with the principle of harmony found in the unheard music of the spheres and supposed to be recollected in *musica humana* ("the ordering of human harmony analogous to the music of the spheres") and in *musica instrumentalis*, or "practical" music. The symbolism of the incident extends to Cassio, who is using devious means to court Othello's favor, and to Othello, whose wish for silence has nothing to do with a perception of harmony but enables him to enjoy the carnal delights of his wedding night. Thus the passage offers "an oblique and generalizing comic image of the human insufficiency from which the substance of the tragedy is to grow."

2343   Sanders, Norman, ed. *Othello*. (New Cambridge Shakespeare.) Cambridge: Cambridge U. P., 1984. xiii + 209 pp.

The introduction, in discussing sources, briefly rehearses the arguments that Sh borrowed details from Pluatrch's *Life of Cato Utican*, Philemon Holland's translation of Pliny's *Naturalis Historia* (1601), and Apuleius's *Golden Ass*.

2344   Smith, John Hazel, comp. *Shakespeare's "Othello": A Bibliography*. New York: AMS P., 1988. xii + 337 pp.

Presents the bibliography compiled as groundwork for the New Variorum edition of *Oth*. Covers works published through 1984, with some from 1985. Classifies entries under nine headings, including Editions (not numbered), Sources (264 items), Textual Commentary (966 items), and Criticism (2049 items). Arranges entries in the section on editions in chronological order. Arranges the entries in other sections alphabetically by author. Supplies, in about one-fifth of the entries, line numbers for passages discussed. Includes an index to the commentary on individual lines and a general index. Contains, especially in the sections on sources and criticism, many entries relating *Oth*. to the classical tradition. Does not annotate entries.

2345   Soellner, Rolf. "Baroque Passion in Shakespeare and His Contemporaries." *ShakS*, 1 (1965), 294–302.

Analyzes *Oth*. as one of three examples of the baroque in drama, featuring "impetuous movement" of action and the exhibition of "gigantic passions" in its hero. In depicting Othello's breakdown, Sh used the stage convention of *Hercules Furens*, which involved violent acting as a way to represent "temporary, blinding madness of passion."

2346   Sorelius, Gunnar. "Comic and Tragic Metamorphosis in *Othello*." *The Tragedie of Othello, the Moore of Venice: Atti del Convegno*. Gargnano, 25–30 marzo 1984. Milano: Edizioni Unicopli, 1985, pp. 23–39. Reprint. *Universita Degli Studi di Milano*, 42 (1985), 23–39.

Provides background on the Renaissance habit of thinking in mythological terms, more specifically, of using the language of metamorphosis to dramatize change. Two classical sources that were particularly influential in this regard are Ovid's *Metamorphoses* and Apuleius's *The Golden Ass*. Traces two metamorphoses in Othello. The first is comic, owes a great deal to Neoplatonism, is analogous to the uniting of Mars and Venus by Cupid, and involves his transformation from soldier to heroic lover. The second is tragic and involves his descent from a godlike being (he speaks of himself in cosmological terms before his fall) to a monster of revenge. Othello does regain some of his godlike stature before the play's end, speaking in mythological and Neoplatonic terms at the end. His language also suggests that he can be seen as "the giant Tityus tormented by the green-eyed monster."

2347   Sorelius, Gunnar. "Othello and the Language of Cosmos." *SN*, 55 (1983), 11–17.

Foregrounds the mythological and cosmological language used by Othello, especially when he equates the loss of his love for Desdemona with the dissolution of the world into elemental chaos, to argue that Sh used such language, which links the play, through Renaissance Platonism, with the mythological imagination of ancient Greece, to enhance the tragic potential of his protagonist.

2348   Stewart, Douglas J. "*Othello*: Roman Comedy as Nightmare." *Emory University Quarterly*, 22 (1966–67), 252–76.

Makes the case that *Oth*. "reproduces great chunks of plot enginery and many of the techniques of role portraiture that are native to Roman or 'New' comedy." The characters of *Oth*. frequently seem to have immigrated more or less directly from Roman comedy: Othello is the *miles gloriosus*; Iago is the conniving slave; Desdemona resembles the "typical comic heroine"; Roderigo is the "stupidly authentic post-adolescent mooncalf"; and Brabantio is "the obvious heavy father." *Oth*. "is a very comic tragedy, if it is a tragedy at all, and the kind of plot it has lays down certain laws for the roles of its characters." See item 2341.

2349   Teague, Frances. "*Othello* and New Comedy." *CompD*, 20 (1986–87), 54–64.

Entertains the possibility that Roman New Comedy influenced *Oth*. in its urban setting, its use of double time, and its exploitation of a situation in which a soldier's mistaken feelings of sexual jealousy are manipulated by a clever servant. In a comedy, these unrealistic and exaggerated elements are amusing, but their appearance in tragedy suggests anarchy. In particular, the figures of the soldier and the servant are remodeled: Othello is not a braggart, Iago serves his own malicious nature, and "the lovers are destroyed."

2350   Tobin, J. J. M. "Apuleius and *Othello*." *N&Q*, 24 (1977), 112.

Argues that Othello's address to the light (*Oth*., V.ii.1–22) is indebted to "Psyche's would-be slaying of Cupid and her address to the lamp in Book 5, Chapters 22 and 23 of Apuleius's *The Golden Ass*." Revised as part of chapter 4 of item 1052.

2351   Tobin, J. J. M. "*Othello* and the *Apologia* of Apuleius." *CahiersE*, 21 (1982), 27–33.

Argues that in the composition of *Oth.*, Sh was influenced by the *Apologia* of Apuleius, either in the original Latin or in a now-lost English translation. Points out the following common elements in the two works: "1) the charge of witchcraft made for the purpose of annulling a marriage. . . .; 2) the central concern with reputation; 3) a magical handkerchief; 4) a marriage of persons disproportionate in age and country; 5) a marriage which begins as a kind of elopement. . . .; 6) the presence of an epileptic and a drunkard; 7) the theme of subornation; and finally, 8) diction unique in the Shakespearian canon, derived from words present in the *Apologia*." Revised as appendix B of item 1052.

2352   Zitner, S. P. "Iago as Melampus." *SQ*, 23 (1972), 263–64.

Asserts that Lodovico's reference to Iago as a "Spartan dog" (*Oth.*, V.ii.370) was probably inspired by the story of Actaeon and Diana as recalled by Sh from Golding's translation of Ovid's *Metamorphoses*. Melampus, the first of Actaeon's dogs to run down his master, is described by Ovid as being of the Spartan breed. Like Melampus, Iago "changes from servant to destroyer."

THE PASSIONATE PILGRIM

2353   Hobday, C. H. "Shakespeare's Venus and Adonis Sonnets." *ShS*, 26 (1973), 103–9.

Argues for Shakespearean authorship of three Venus and Adonis sonnets included in William Jaggard's anthology *PP*. All three sonnets are Ovidian, with the first clearly indebted to Ovid's story of Salmacis and Hermaphroditus. Sh used this story in writing *Ven.*, and there are similarities in imagery between the sonnet and some of the plays.

PERICLES

2354   Barker, G. A. "Themes and Variations in *Pericles*." *ES*, 44 (1963), 401–14.

Posits that a lost play on the Apollonius legend was the source for both George Wilkins's novel *The Painfull Adventures of Pericles, Prince of Tyre* and *Per*. Points out that the Apollonius story is derived from Greek romance and that Sh's modifications of the traditional version can be studied by comparing *Per*. with the hypothetical source play. Sh seems to follow the author of the source play in grafting the theme of kingship on to the Apollonius story, but he goes beyond his source in making *Per*. "a drama of faith."

2355   Barrett, Debbie L. "*Pericles*, Social Redemption, and the Iconography of 'Veritas Temporis Filia.'" *ShY*, 2 (1991), 77–94.

Discerns in the dramaturgy of *Per*. a reliance on the emblematic tradition, and in particular the allegory derived from the classical motto, "*Veritas temporis filia*" (truth is the daughter of time). Sh's protagonist, through time, rescues his daughter, truth, from "the persecutors Envy, Strife, and Slander."

2356 Bishop, Thomas Geoffrey. "The Uses of Recognition from Aristotle to Shakespeare: 'A notable passion of wonder.'" Ph.D. dissertation, Yale University, 1988. *DAI*, 50 (1989–90), 3597-A.

Applies a framework "derived from comparing Aristotle's treatment of wonder and recognition in the *Poetics* with other classical testimony" to certain plays from the medieval English cycles, to "the Elizabethan romantic plays," and to *Per.* Argues that the recognition scene in *Per.* serves as "an analogue for Shakespeare's dramatic practice as it subsumes the received tradition of romantic drama."

2357 Cutts, John P. "Pericles and the Vision of Diana." *AN&Q*, 2 (1963–64), 21–22.

Corrects F. D. Hoeniger's Arden note to *Per.* V.i.242. Hoeniger is right to seek a description of Diana in Samuel Daniel's *The Vision of the Twelve Goddesses* (1604), but he seems to conflate Daniel's Proserpina and Diana by giving the latter gold flames embroidered on her mantle rather than the silver half moons Daniel gives her.

2358 Easson, Angus. "Marina's Maidenhead." *SQ*, 24 (1973), 328–29.

Interprets Boult's remark that Marina's maidenhead might have to be executed by "the common hangman" (*Per.*, IV.vi.129–130) in the light of Tacitus's account of the fall of Sejanus, whose young daughter was violated by the hangman before being executed. Having acted in Jonson's *Sejanus*, in which this event is described, Sh would have been familiar with the episode. In Boult's remark, he intended a grim threat that Marina might be broken by a professional, the hangman.

2359 Edwards, Philip, ed. *Pericles, Prince of Tyre.* (New Penguin Shakespeare.) Harmondsworth: Penguin, 1976. 208 pp.

The introduction notes that the story derives ultimately from Greek romance. Calls attention to Hellenistic settings in *Per.* that contrast with the play's medievalism, creating a "feeling of all-time and no-time." Many pagan gods are mentioned in *Per.*, most significantly Neptune and Diana; they help to create and reinforce the sense that the happy outcome for all of the characters is due to divine providence.

2360 Gearin-Tosh, Michael. "*Pericles*: The Death of Antiochus." *N&Q*, 18 (1971), 149–50.

Suggests that the account of the deaths of Antiochus and his daughter (*Per.*, II.iv.9–12), in which they are described as having been "shriveled up" by "A fire from heaven" and left unburied because of their stench, is indebted to Plutarch's *Moralia*, which calls attention to the "piercing scent" of the corpses of those struck by lightning and a general reluctance to bury them.

2361 Greenfield, Thelma N. "A Re-Examination of the 'Patient' Pericles." *ShakS*, 3 (1967), 51–61.

Rejects the image of the long-suffering, patient Pericles seen by some critics. Instead, Sh's hero is "the Renaissance descendant of the wily Greek traveler, a solver of riddles, a master of escape and incognito, skilled in the arts, and in his accomplishments and understanding a born ruler of men." The play emphasizes Pericles' escape from misfortune rather than his patient endurance of it. Sh's choice of the name of his hero may have been influenced by Plutarch's portrayal of Pericles as knowledgeable in rhetoric, music, and natural philosophy and possessed of superior native intelligence: One element Sh did not borrow from the *Lives* is the patience there attributed to Pericles. Pericles may also be associated with the characters of Odysseus and Oedipus, who among other things resemble him in living by their wits.

2362 Helms, Lorraine. "The Saint in the Brothel: Or, Eloquence Rewarded." *SQ*, 41 (1990), 319–32.

Provides background on Roman schools of debate and rhetoric, as described by Seneca the Elder, focusing on the *controversia* of the Prostitute Priestess, the virtuous woman brought by force into the brothel who must strive to save her chastity through eloquence. Traces the various manifestations of the Prostitute Priestess's dilemma through literary history. In most cases, both medieval saints' biographies and pagan legend, the woman, even if she is not physically defiled, ends by committing suicide. This is so because the arguments about what constitutes rape, defilement, salvation, and purity are controlled by male-oriented rhetoric. In *Per.*, Sh gives Marina a one-sided presentation of the case that returns to the original story and allows her to use eloquence to ward off ravishers, escape the brothel, and live to be rewarded for her virtue. Through the power of her rhetoric, she is able to convince Boult and her "owner" that she is more valuable for the skills she learned as a princess. To appease the patriarchy, she is married to a noble. Thus Sh attempts closure on the debate without radical disruption of the Senecan tradition.

2363 Hoeniger, F. D., ed. *Pericles*. (Arden Shakespeare.) London: Methuen, 1963. xci + 188 pp.

The introduction calls attention to the "ultimate source" of *Per.* in the romance of Apollonius of Tyre, a well-known story during the Middle Ages and Renaissance, which descended from "a Hellenistic novel somewhat like those by Xenophon, Heliodorus, and Achilles Tatius." Notes how Sh modified the story as he found it in his two immediate sources, John Gower's *Confessio Amantis* and Lawrence Twine's *The Patterne of Painefull Adventures*, to emphasize the importance of patient suffering as the way to redemption. Argues that not only the framework but also the thought, structure, and form of the play draw heavily on the medieval past. Points especially to the connection of *Per.* to the miracle play.

2364 Jackson, MacD. P. "North's Plutarch and the Name 'Escanes' in Shakespeare's *Pericles*." *N&Q*, 22 (1975), 173–74.

Argues that Escanes, a character in *Per.*, derives his name from Aeschines, an Athenian orator mentioned three times in Plutarch's *Life of Pericles*. This provides a link between Plutarch's *Life* and *Per.* and suggests that Sh named his protagonist with the Athenian statesman in mind.

2365 Knapp, Peggy Ann. "The Orphic Vision of *Pericles*." *TSLL*, 15 (1973–74), 615–26.

Challenges readings of *Per.* based on ideas of moral causality. The structure of the play is more easily explained by reference to the Orpheus myth, which is a natural manifestation of the tension between the disruption and restoration of harmony characteristic of romance. Of the three parts of the myth—Orpheus's control of nature, the loss and recovery of Eurydice, and the dismemberment—the first two are most congenial to romance, and it is these two parts that provide a paradigm for *Per*. A comparison of Sh's play with the medieval *Sir Orfeo* reveals how clearly Sh follows the shape of the Orpheus story and its tone: The heroes of both works are musicians; they both suffer loss through deep, inexplicable evil; both renounce their kingships; both rely on faithful regents in their absence; both are transformed almost beyond recognition by their suffering; both become passive in the face of their loss; and both are restored to happiness through music.

2366 Lawrence, Harold Whitney. "'To Sing a Song That Old Was Sung': *Pericles* and *Apollonius of Tyre*, the Play and the Tradition." Ph.D. dissertation, Texas Christian University, 1970. *DAI*, 31 (1970–71), 6062-A-6063-A.

Attempts to clarify the tradition that informed a contemporary audience's understanding of *Per*. That tradition was dominated by the Apollonius of Tyre story, which was taken to exemplify chaste love and disciplined virtue.

2367 Marshall, Cynthia. "The Seven Ages of *Pericles.*" *JRMMRA*, 8 (1987), 147–62.

Maintains that the structure of *Per.* is based on the medieval notion of the Seven Ages of Man, which itself depends on the Boethian view of time. This dual perspective on human life, neatly reconciling fortune and providence, allows Sh to incorporate "the symbolic history of the human race into the history of one man."

2368 McIntosh, William A. "Musical Design in *Pericles.*" *ELN*, 11 (1973–74), 100–106.

Contends that the "Boethian concepts of *musicae instrumentalis, humana,* and *mundana*" are particularly important in *Per.* Sh uses *musica instrumentalis* both for negative characterization (Antiochus and his daughter) and positive suggestion (Pericles wins Thaisa by his skill in dancing). Cerimon's actions "are intended to be a manifestation of *musica humana,*" and Pericles alone hears *musica mundana,* which prepares him for seeing the vision of Diana.

2369 Michael, Nancy C., comp. *"Pericles": An Annotated Bibliography.* (Garland Shakespeare Bibliographies 13.) New York: Garland, 1987. xxii + 289 pp.

Covers primarily works published between 1940 and 1985. Classifies entries under eight headings, including Criticism (334 items); Sources, Analogues, and Background (52 items); and Editions (81 items). Begins each section with the oldest entries and proceeds chronologically. Concludes with a single index. Provides substantial and detailed annotations.

2370 Pickford, T. E. "*Apollonius of Tyre* as Greek Myth and Christian Mystery." *Neophil,* 59 (1975), 599–609.

States that because it could easily be read in Christian terms as well as those of Greek mythology, *Apollonius of Tyre* was one of the most popular Hellenistic romances of the Middle Ages. In the broadest terms, the story of Apollonius—involving exile, destitution, purification, and eventual return—could be seen as parallel to the experience of Israel as a whole or to the lives of individuals like Joseph and Jesus.

2371 Schanzer, Ernest, ed. *Pericles.* (Signet Classic Shakespeare.) New York: New American Library, 1965. xlii + [43]-208 pp.

The introduction points out that the story of Pericles, known as Apollonius of Tyre in accounts previous to Sh's treatment of him, was one of the most popular tales of the Middle Ages and Renaissance and derived ultimately from Hellenistic romance (as attested by the place names in *Per.* as well as its variety of "marvelous adventures"). Asserts that the medieval miracle play, which has strong affinities to the Greek romance, was a significant influence on Sh. Discounts the suggestion that Sh named his hero after the Athenian statesman Pericles, who is said by Plutarch to be an exemplar of patience. Sh's character is not remarkable for his patience; he is modeled instead on Pyrocles, a pattern of princely virtues in Sir Philip Sidney's *Arcadia.* Views *Per.,* whose presiding goddess is Fortune, as a play about the undeserved misfortunes of the hero. Mentions the vision of Diana to Pericles (V.i) as a means of bringing about the final reunion of father and daughter but maintains that Diana's influence is limited to this one part of the play. Argues that *The Painfull Adventures of Pericles Prince of Tyre* (1608), a prose novel by George Wilkins, is partly based on *Per.* and can be used to reconstruct Shakespearean parts of the text omitted or obscured by the corruption of the 1608 quarto, the only text for the play. The note on the sources contends that the chief "literary influence" in *Per.* is Sidney's *Arcadia,* though the two "main sources" are book 8 of John Gower's *Confessio Amantis* (from which most of the characters' names come) and Laurence Twine's *The Patterne of Painefull Adventures,* both 16th-c. redactions of the Apollonius story. The introduction, text, and note on the sources are reprinted as part of item 0123.

2372 Schrickx, Willem. "*Pericles* in a Book-List of 1619 from the English Jesuit Mission and Some of the Play's Special Problems." *ShS*, 29 (1976), 21–32.

Argues that the first two acts of *Per.* were written by George Wilkins, who was attracted to the Antiochus theme because "this ruler was for him the embodiment of sinfulness." The Antiochus who inspired the character in *Per.* was Antiochus IV Epiphanes, the pagan tyrant who had been opposed by Judas Maccabeus in the 2nd c. B.C. and who had become, by the 16th c., a symbol of oppression against true religion.

2373 Welsh, Andrew. "Heritage in *Pericles*." *Shakespeare's Late Plays: Essays in Honor of Charles Crow*. Eds. Richard C. Tobias and Paul G. Zolbrod. Athens: Ohio U. P., 1974, pp. 89–113.

Discovers four heritages in *Per.*, each put to a new use by Sh: (1) the tale itself, an old story that carries the flavor of being transmitted from one generation to another (Sh used Gower to maintain contact with the narrative original); (2) ten riddles, not in the original Greek romance of Apollonius of Tyre, that were composed by Symphosius in the 4th or 5th c. A.D. and included in the Latin version of the story around that time (Marina asks these riddles on board ship in the harbor of Mytilene); (3) the seven capital sins, from the Middle Ages; and (4) Renaissance emblem books, for the devices of the knights in II.ii. In the epilogue, the first and last of these heritages are brought together when Gower, the teller of an old tale, emblematizes the entire play.

THE PHOENIX AND TURTLE

2374 Axton, Marie. *The Queen's Two Bodies: Drama and the Elizabethan Succession*. (Royal Historical Society Studies in History.) London: Royal Historical Society, 1977. xiv + 174 pp.

Focuses on one kind of Elizabethan political drama: "the plays that wrestle with the problem of the succession and with the very principles by which government and authority are perpetuated." Includes a discussion of Robert Chester's collection of poems by several authors called *Love's Martyr* (1601), which uses the Phoenix myth to look forward to the miraculous process through which the virgin queen will beget a successor. Comments that Sh's contribution to this collection, *PhT*, as well as being prophetic, also looks elegiacally at Elizabeth's union with her people.

2375 Bonaventure, Sister Mary, O. S. F. "The Phoenix Renewed." *BSUF*, 5, no. 3 (1964), 72–76.

Sums up and categorizes the interpretations of *PhT* during the past decade. Mentions, among many other things, the classical influences on the poem, including Ovid's *Amores* and Pliny. Supplements previous criticism by claiming that the unity of the Phoenix and the Turtle goes beyond the Neoplatonic conception of love and draws the reader's attention to transcendent Christian values.

2376 Buxton, John. "Two Dead Birds: A Note on *The Phoenix and the Turtle*." *English Renaissance Studies Presented to Dame Helen Gardner in Honour of Her Seventieth Birthday*. Ed. John Carey. Oxford: Clarendon P., 1980, pp. 44–55.

Argues that *PhT*, though part of a collection of occasional poems added to Robert Chester's *Love's Martyr* (1601), is not occasional. The poem celebrates love and constancy, using birds that, according to Greek authors like Herodotus and Pliny, symbolize these qualities. In the anthem praising the two lovers, Sh employs philosophical language that fuses Platonic and scholastic terms.

2377 Copland, Murray. "The Dead Phoenix." *EIC*, 15 (1965), 279–87.

Reads *PhT* as Sh's contribution to the late Elizabethan Platonizing fashion in metaphysical poetry. In Platonic terms, the Phoenix represents "the 'idea' of female beauty and the Turtle the 'idea' of fidelity"; mated, they become a third 'idea': "human love in its barely imaginable perfection." The most original stroke in Sh's poem is the assertion that "the unique, peerlessly beautiful bird is fully and finally *dead*." *PhT* is "genuinely a poem of mourning, a meditation on the hard fact of mortality."

2378 Dronke, Peter. "*The Phoenix and the Turtle*." *OL*, 23 (1968), 199–220.

Relates *PhT* to Robert Chester's *Love's Martyr* (1601), on which it was a variation. *Love's Martyr* is a development of the *Planctus Naturae* pattern, first found in a poem of Parmenides and then in many medieval and Renaissance versions. In these poems, Nature or another character ascends to heaven, is supernaturally endowed with an "idea" or revelation, and returns with it to earth. Sh uses this basis, along with Neoplatonic ideas of "Reason transcending herself in Love," to present the Phoenix and Turtle as a pattern of perfection in love for the world they leave behind. The poem's genre is the bird-mass, which medieval and Renaissance tradition absorbed in part from two classical elegies: Ovid's poem on the death of Corinna's parrot (*Amores*) and Statius's imitation of Ovid (*Silvae*).

2379 Ellrodt, Robert. "An Anatomy of *The Phoenix and the Turtle*." *ShS*, 15 (1962), 99–110.

Reexamines the bird imagery and "Platonic" assumptions in *PhT* in order to assess Sh's originality in treating the Phoenix theme. The mating of the amorous Turtle and the virginal Phoenix brings together two extremes of love, constancy and chastity. This paradoxical combination is Platonic in the sense that it is concerned with the two-in-one union of the lovers' souls. It does not, however, invite an ascent to the contemplation of Heavenly Beauty. Sh was original in substituting "an immediate apprehension of unity for the Neoplatonic argument based on the assumption that each lover died in his own person to live in the beloved." The theme "is not the rational intuition of Platonism: it is the triumph of Love over Reason."

2380 Eriksen, Roy T. "'Un certo amoroso martire': Shakespeare's *The Phoenix and the Turtle* and Giordano Bruno's *De gli eroici furori*." *Spenser Studies*, 2 (1981), 193–215.

Discusses *PhT* in terms of its *topoi* and their arrangement, its use of distinctive mood and/or tense in each of its three sections, its imagery conducing to the union of opposites (flaming, burning, seeing, dissolution of self, androgyny, funeral ritual, kissing of crows), its tone (oracular), and its form (roundel) to demonstrate that Sh was directly influenced by the Neoplatonic allegory of Bruno's *Eroici furori*. The connection of Sh's poem with Bruno's reveals the former as "a poetic riddle or emblem of eternity unraveled."

2381 Green, Brian. "Shakespeare's Heroic Elixir: A New Context for *The Phoenix and Turtle*." *SN*, 51 (1979), 215–23.

Provides an alchemical reading of *PhT*, making reference to the background of alchemy in Hermetic philosophy and Theophrastus.

2382 Green, Brian. "'Single Natures double name': An Exegesis of *The Phoenix and Turtle*." *Generous Converse: English Essays in Memory of Edward Davis*. Ed. Brian Green. Cape Town: Oxford U. P., 1980, pp. 44–54.

Notes that in the summons of the birds that begins *PhT* there are "two incompatible responses to death" that "dramatize a conflict similar to the Neoplatonic idea of a noble and a vulgar love." The poem's ideal is chaste love, which Reason fails to understand. Refers briefly to *Ant.* in arguing that the interaction between "the vulgar, the sublime, and the chaste" attitudes to sexual love creates Shakespearean love–tragedy.

2383   Kaplan, Marion. "The Phoenix in Elizabethan Poetry." Ph.D. dissertation, University of California, Los Angeles, 1964. *DA*, 25 (1964–65), 5258–5259.

Surveys symbolic values assigned to the phoenix myth in the Renaissance. The phoenix symbolized incomparability, the union of unexcelled qualities, rarity, preciousness, matchless beauty, and chastity. In Sh's *PhT*, the Phoenix and Turtle are dead, their union having been destroyed by reason.

2384   Matchett, William H. *"The Phoenix and the Turtle": Shakespeare's Poem and Chester's "Loves Martyr."* The Hague: Mouton, 1965. 214 pp.

Uses both "historical scholarship and close textual analysis" to explicate *PhT*. Argues that Sh, by using Platonic imagery in the poem, "first establishes a triumph worthy of praise, but ultimately undercuts that triumph by asserting Reason's reluctant rejection of it."

2385   Petronella, Vincent F. "Shakespeare's *The Phoenix and the Turtle* and the Defunctive Music of Ecstasy." *ShakS*, 8 (1975), 311–31.

Explicates *PhT* by calling attention to its chronicling of the death of mystic ecstasy. Explains the four Neoplatonic *furores* as described by Marsilio Ficino (the madnesses of poetry, of the mysteries, of prophecy, and of love) and notes that they are all reflected in the poem, though it ultimately denies the kinds of ecstasy to which they supposedly lead. The structure of *PhT* can be analyzed in terms of the tripartite Orphic pastoral of the Neoplatonists: "*Emanatio* (procession), *Raptio* (rapture or ecstasy), and *Remeatio* (return or recession)." The middle part of the poem has the Phoenix and Turtle in a state of ecstasy, but this movement recedes and at the end (the Threnos) Reason pronounces grimly that truth and beauty have been extinguished.

2386   Schwartz, Elias. "Shakespeare's Dead Phoenix." *ELN*, 7 (1969), 25–32.

Argues that *PhT* is not a philosophical poem, "though it makes use of philosophical terms and concepts." It is primarily a funeral elegy about two dead lovers. Unlike the Phoenix myth, the poem does not allow immortality in the world. From a Platonic point of view, the deaths of the two lovers remove Truth and Beauty and perfect love from the world because these things were embodied in them, and they have left no posterity. The poem should be associated with the disillusionment and pessimism of such plays as *Ham.*, *Tro.*, and *Oth.*, not with later plays like *Ant.*, which allow greater possibilities for human love. Revised as appendix B of item 0939.

2387   Seltzer, Daniel. "'Their Tragic Scene': *The Phoenix and Turtle* and Shakespeare's Love Tragedies." *SQ*, 12 (1961), 91–101.

Calls attention to the scholastic vocabulary in *PhT*, which relates lover and beloved in the same way the Persons of the Trinity are related. That is, the poem's lovers are paradoxically distinct in their union. *PhT* "carefully states the nature of love to remain always itself, with a power stronger than the power of two identifiable ('propertied') individuals to remain separate and discrete quantities." In this, the poem resembles Sh's love tragedies, especially *Rom.*, *Oth.*, and *Ant.* Examination of book 15 of the *Metamorphoses*, in Golding's translation, suggests that Sh may have been drawn to the Phoenix legend as a vehicle for describing the events of a love tragedy.

2388 Underwood, Richard Allan. "Shakespeare's *The Phoenix and the Turtle*: A Survey of Scholarship." Ph.D. dissertation, University of Michigan, 1970. *DAI*, 31 (1970-71), 2357-A.

Surveys modern scholarship on *PhT*. Chapter 1 deals with texts, authenticity, and date; chapter 2 with allegorical readings; chapter 3 with literary sources; and chapter 4 with "the modal nature of the piece," as well as its "ideal and platonic overtones." Chapter 5 provides a "critical afterword." Revised as item 2389.

2389 Underwood, Richard Allan. *Shakespeare's "The Phoenix and the Turtle": A Survey of Scholarship*. (Elizabethan Studies 15.) Salzburg: Institut für Englische Sprache und Literatur, U. Salzburg, 1974. iii + 366 pp.

Surveys modern publications on *PhT* through the 1960s. Organizes each of the five chapters and the two appendices around lengthy extracts from scholarly works. Chapter 3 is on "Classical and Source Studies"; chapter 4, "Critical and 'Dramatic' Interpretations," includes studies that relate the poem to the intellectual climate of its time, particularly the various forms of Platonism; and appendix A recounts the history of the Phoenix legend, especially in classical writers like Hesiod, Herodotus, Pliny, Ovid, and Plutarch. Revision of item 2388.

THE RAPE OF LUCRECE

2390 Allen, D. C. "Some Observations on *The Rape of Lucrece*." *ShS*, 15 (1962), 89-98. Reprint. *Image and Meaning: Metaphoric Traditions in Renaissance Poetry*. New enlarged ed. Baltimore: Johns Hopkins P., 1968, pp. 58-76.

Points out that to the 16th-c. reader, as to St. Augustine, Lucrece would have appeared as spiritually unredeemed. Lucrece's study of the painting of the Trojan War gives her the opportunity to compare her ruined body to the sack of the city. In allegorical readings of the Troy story, Aeneas's decision to leave his ruined city is prompted by a longing for divine wisdom. By contrast, Lucrece's departure from her "city" (her suicide) is motivated only by her desire to preserve pagan honor.

2391 Andrew, Malcolm. "Christian Ideas about Sin and the First Stanza of *Lucrece*." *RES*, N. S. 24 (1973), 179-82.

Explains the phrase "lightless fire" (*Luc.*, lines 1-5) as indicative of hell-fire, which, according to Christian commentators, "burns but gives no light." In describing Tarquin, then, the phrase means that "he comes in sin and brings with him hell on earth."

2392 Bal, Mieke. "Visual Poetics: Reading with the Other Art." *Theory between the Disciplines: Authority/Vision/Politics*. Eds. Martin Kreiswirth and Mark A. Cheetham. Ann Arbor: U. of Michigan P., 1990, pp. 135-50.

Focuses on Rembrandt's two paintings of Lucretia but comments briefly on *Luc*. Sh's Tarquin is stimulated to plan his rape by the intensity of the visual image Collatine presents of his wife. After the rape, Lucrece seeks solace in visual imagery: the painting of the Trojan War. She allies herself with Hecuba yet laments that the artist has given Hecuba eyes to see but no tongue with which to speak. In this sense, the pictorial cannot replace the verbal.

2393 Berry, J. Wilkes. "The Conclusion of *Lucrece*: Shakespeare Solves a Problem." *McNeese Review*, 20 (1971–72), 65–69.

Supports the contention that Sh sensed a problem as he came to the end of *Luc.*: He needed to enliven the material found in his sources, Ovid's *Fasti* and Livy's *Roman History*. He therefore gave Lucrece a "histrionic flair" by having her withhold the name of her assailant until the very last moment and use melodramatic terms in describing the rape. He also added the mourning competition between Lucrece's husband and father and made much more dramatic than did his sources the transformation of Brutus from an ostensible fool to a magnificent man of action.

2394 Berry, Philippa. "Woman, Language, and History in *The Rape of Lucrece*." *ShS*, 44 (1992), 33–39.

Proposes to examine the long central section of *Luc.* in which the protagonist laments the loss of her virtue as an indication that she, "through her private use of language," becomes the agent of "republican political ideals." Finds that in her apostrophes to Night, Time, and Opportunity, Lucrece is associated with the thought of Orpheus, regarded by Renaissance Platonists not only as "the inspired poet par excellence" but also as a great magician whose secret powers could effect radical change. Lucrece's language allows her figuratively to seize control of history instead of "remaining its passive victim." Although Lucrece, in the first part of her lament, seems to exemplify "a new, feminine model of *virtu*," with the capacity, "through the language of grief and mourning," to overturn the order of "time and its processes," her meditation on the painting of Troy's fall shows that she is now in the world of Virgil's *Aeneid*, where the Greeks' linguistic powers are seen as treacherous. She is profoundly enmeshed in the hierarchical system of her society, but at the same time she is in some sense a traitor to that system because she has unleashed powers of language that can (and will) result in radical change. She never fully recognizes her contradictory position.

2395 Bowers, A. Robin. "Iconography and Rhetoric in Shakespeare's *Lucrece*." *ShakS*, 14 (1981), 1–21.

Challenges critics who see Sh's Lucrece as morally wayward and rhetorically excessive. Sh followed most of his contemporaries in presenting Lucrece sympathetically. Both artists and writers of the Renaissance emphasized her chastity, fidelity, and constancy and depicted as tragic the violence of Tarquin's rape and its ruinous effect of making her resort to suicide. Sh employs two debates—internal monologues by Tarquin and Lucrece, respectively—to organize his materials. First, Tarquin allows his will to overcome his reason as he decides to commit the rape. The rape then follows as a consequence of his decision. Finally, Lucrece's interior debate reveals the chaotic state of desperation to which she has been reduced by Tarquin's act. Throughout, Sh's narrator is present to insist on this chain of causes and effects and to maintain sympathy for Lucrece as victim. *Luc.* should be approached through "Renaissance psychic and literary theory which depended largely on traditional, medieval ways of explaining the corruption of the mind and the ensuing vicious actions in this world."

2395a Bromley, Laura G. "The Lost Lucrece: Middleton's *The Ghost of Lucrece*." *PLL*, 21 (1985), 258–74.

Notes that Thomas Middleton's poem *The Ghost of Lucrece*, unlike its source, *Luc.*, is bitterly ironic. Sh's heroine lives in an historical context, the beginning of Rome's "Golden Age," in which action "can root out corruption and restore order." In Middleton's poem, there is no hope for society, no way in which its "rampant disorder" can be counterbalanced.

2396 Bromley, Laura G. "Lucrece's Re-Creation." *SQ*, 34 (1983), 200–211.

Argues that Sh's Lucrece, having been defiled by Tarquin, is indeed tainted. According to her narrow view of chastity, which we must accept, she is infected with Tarquin's evil and must seek a way to counterbalance it. In the meditations leading up to her suicide, and especially in the recognition of the public repercussions of private evil forced upon her by the painting of Troy, she struggles to re-create her self. At the end, her suicide is "a positive, constructive, and self-creative act."

2397 Crewe, Jonathan. *Trials of Authorship: Anterior Forms and Poetic Reconstruction from Wyatt to Shakespeare*. (The New Historicism: Studies in Cultural Poetics 9.) Berkeley: U. of California P., 1990. vii + 196 pp.

Chapter 6, "Shakespeare's Figure of Lucrece: Writing Rape," argues that the frequent retelling of the Lucrece legend by writers like Livy, Ovid, Augustine, Chaucer, and Machiavelli suggests a correspondence between its "textual repetition" and "the sociohistorical recurrence of rape," indicating an endless, inevitable cycle of rape. Sh's portrayal of the episode in *Luc.*, while partly implicated in this repetition, attempts to create a reflective attitude toward the social and political significance of rape. Rape is more than physical penetration; the poem explores the emotional reactions of the victim as well as the public response.

2398 DiGiovanni, Robert Bernard. "Shakespeare's 'Lucrece': A Topical Evaluation of and Supplement to the Scholarship and Criticism Since 1936." Ph.D. dissertation, University of Michigan, 1971. *DAI*, 32 (1971–72), 6371-A-6372-A.

Surveys and categorizes into chapters the scholarship and criticism done on *Luc.* since the compilation by Hyder E. Rollins in 1936. Supplements what has been done in certain areas with original investigations. Among the findings not yet offered by other scholarship are that *Luc.* is clearly related both to the complaint poem and to dramatic poetry, that its most significant sources are the accounts of the Lucrece legend in Ovid's *Fasti* and Chaucer's *Legend of Good Women*, and that it plays an important part in Sh's artistic development as he moves toward the great tragedies.

2398a Donahue, Patricia Ann. "Circe's Potion: The Language of Passion in English Renaissance Poetry." Ph.D. dissertation, University of California, Irvine, 1981 *DAI*, 42 (1981–82), 157-A.

Analyzes several poems in which the Renaissance humanist's opinion that "rhetoric promotes rationality" is challenged. Chapter 2 maintains that in *Luc.* passion "threatens norms and revokes rhetorical and psychological guarantees."

2399 Donaldson, Ian. *The Rapes of Lucretia: A Myth and Its Transformations*. Oxford: Clarendon P., 1982. xii + 203 pp.

Chapter 3, "'A Theme for Disputation': Shakespeare's Lucrece," discusses *Luc.*'s concern with the psychological "waverings to and fro" of the two chief characters. Sh gives full play to two conflicting ethical systems, the Roman and the Christian, but wavers with regard to solving the problems raised by this tension. He seems to have begun to Christianize the classical story of Lucrece, endowing his heroine with a Christian sensibility, but then he allows the older view of what a dishonored woman should do to dictate his conclusion.

2400 Dubrow, Heather. "A Mirror for Complaints: Shakespeare's *Lucrece* and Generic Tradition." *Renaissance Genres: Essays on Theory, History, and Interpretation*. (Harvard English Studies 14.) Ed. Barbara Kiefer Lewalski. Cambridge: Harvard U. P., 1986, pp. 399–417.

Designates *Luc.* as a type of complaint in which a heroine's chastity is threatened: In some examples of this type, her chastity is preserved, while in others it is surrendered. Sh's critical approach to this subgenre distinguishes his poem from others in its category: He explores the obsession of his characters with their reputations and the consequent need they have to perform in public. He renders problematical the notion of guilt; he calls attention to the ambivalence of several ideas, like those of competition and chastity, associated with sexuality; and he embeds the complaint proper, assigned to Lucrece, in a context where other voices suggest other responses to the protagonist's misfortune. Revised as part of section 2 of item 0332.

2401 Dubrow, Heather. "The Rape of Clio: Attitudes to History in Shakespeare's *Lucrece*." *ELR*, 16 (1986), 425–41.

Notes that *Luc.* is shaped by several issues in Renaissance historiography: the difficulty of recovering the past, the nature of causality, the difference between poetry and history, and the question of style. Sh was also influenced by his own experiences in writing history; in the case of Lucrece, he was familiar with the different, even contradictory, attempts by others to tell the story. Livy, for example, locates Lucrece's tragedy "in the broader historical context of the previous misdeeds of Tarquin's father and the subsequent political changes in Rome, while Ovid focuses more on Lucrece herself." In Sh's poem, the view of Lucrece herself is more like that of Ovid and of the complaint: That is, she laments the past, dwells on her sufferings, and declines to consider the broader implications of her experience for her culture. The epic idea of history involves the assumption that suffering serves some larger purpose and that one can and should aggressively shape historical events. In *Luc.*, this view is taken by Brutus and, even more important, by Aeneas, whose implicit presence in the poem reminds us that he is not simply a shaper of history through glorious deeds but also one who reads and recounts events so that "they conform to the epic pattern." Sh plays off the prose Argument prefaced to *Luc.* against the poem itself. The former, with its apparently detached tone and its providential view of history, takes the approach of Livy, while the latter is more Ovidian. The effect of this contest between perspectives is to undermine the reader's confidence in the trustworthiness of historical accounts. Further vitiating the claim of providential history to objectivity is Sh's reminder through the Argument that this form of writing does have a style as distinctive as that of poetry. There is also in the poem a broader concern with the character of language itself, that is, the difficulty of reading and interpreting it. *Luc.*, however, does not leave its readers in confusion and despair: It does attempt to write a more accurate kind of history than any of the accounts within it and to teach its readers to evaluate sources better than any of its characters are able to do. Revised as part of section 2 of item 0332.

2402 Dundas, Judith. "Mocking the Mind: The Role of Art in Shakespeare's *Rape of Lucrece*." *SixCJ*, 14 (1983), 13–22.

Suggests that the *ecphrasis* in *Luc.*, which describes the wall painting of Troy that Lucrece studies after her rape, gives Sh's most explicit account of the way in which art works. As she examines the painting, Lucrece is at first taken in by the illusion of art, dallying with the notion of Sinon's innocent appearance. Then she recalls that Tarquin came to her with just such a plausible show of honesty. As she gazes at the painting, then, Lucrece comes to understand herself and what has happened to her, and she prepares for her tragic end. By educating the spirit in this way, "the mural fulfills its role as art." The poem itself acts as if it were an *ecphrasis* for a Renaissance painting of Lucrece's story.

2403 El-Gabalwy, Saad. "The Ethical Question of Lucrece: A Case of Rape." *Mosaic*, 11, no. 4 (1979), 75–86.

Points out that the legend of the rape of Lucrece seems to have taken its final form in Livy's *History of Rome* and Ovid's *Fasti*. Explores three distinct approaches to the legend: "Christian attitudes towards Lucrece's rape and suicide in writings of Tertullian, Augustine and Tyndale; the use of her model as an *exemplum* to incarnate concepts of fidelity, chastity and self-sacrifice in works of Gower, Chaucer and Shakespeare; the trend of naturalism in cynical libertine speculation about her moral conduct in allusions by Pietro Aretino" and others. Notes that Sh's Lucrece is "the perfect patriarchal woman"; she understands the importance, in the Roman social system, of a wife's role in maintaining her husband's honor in a world of male rivals. Her tragedy is that only by dying can she regain "her social identity as a chaste wife."

2404 Fineman, Joel. "Shakespeare's *Will*: The Temporality of Rape." *Representations*, 20 (1987), 25–76. Reprint. *Misogyny, Misandry, and Misanthropy*. Eds. R. Howard Bloch and Frances Ferguson. Berkeley: U. of California P., 1989, pp. 25–76.

Discovers in *Luc.* three characteristically Shakespearean features: "(1) the evocation of a fallen language opposed to a clear vision, (2) a stressedly chiastic figurality, (3) the imagination of a material phenomenality folded over on itself." These features help to explain why the literary characters of Sh, when they give an effect of strong subjectivity, "both evidence and are conditioned by a particular Shakespearean erotics and a particular Shakespearean sense of space and time." Discusses the description in *Luc.* of the painting of scenes from Troy, which raises the issue of the "displacement of ideal vision by language."

2405 French, Tita. "A 'badge of fame': Shakespeare's Rhetorical Lucrece." *EIRC*, 10 (1984), 97–106.

Notes that Sh developed his eloquent and loquacious heroine in *Luc.* from a largely silent figure in his sources, Livy's *History of Rome* and Ovid's *Fasti*. In medieval and Renaissance literature, the moral ideal for man was basically pagan, emphasizing honor and reputation, and that for woman was basically Christian, emphasizing chastity. Lucrece's verbosity is a reflection of her struggle to give proper weight to the contradictory demands of each of these codes. Sh uses the painting of Troy, which was probably suggested by Virgil's *Aeneid*, as an occasion for Lucrece's meditations upon "the nature of suffering, honor and fame." In her inner debate, Lucrece prefigures Sh's great tragic protagonists; and her self-conscious concern with fame reflects the poet's preoccupation with achieving immortality through his art.

2406 Frye, Roland Mushat. "Shakespeare's Composition of *Lucrece*: New Evidence." *SQ*, 16 (1965), 289–96.

Calls attention to four stanzas quoted from *Luc.* in a miscellany volume of 1633, entitled *The Philosophers Banquet*. These, as well as a passage from the same poem quoted by Sir John Suckling, are all written in the sesta rima stanza of *Ven.*, rather than the rhyme royal stanza found in the final version of *Luc.*, as published in 1594. Suggests that Sh wrote part of the original version of *Luc.* in sesta rima and part in rhyme royal and that the compiler of *The Philosophers Banquet* used a manuscript containing both forms. The compiler, in introducing one of the passages from *Luc.*, refers to the author as "a learned writer," the first clear evidence that Sh "was regarded as learned by at least one person in his own age."

2407 Girard, René. "Envy of So Rich a Thing: *The Rape of Lucrece*." *The Scope of Words: In Honor of Albert S. Cook*. Eds. Peter Baker, Sarah Webster, and Gary Handwerk. New York: Peter Lang, 1991, pp. 135–44.

Describes Tarquin's desire for Lucrece as mimetic or imitative, that is, inspired by Collatine's boasting about his wife's beauty and chastity before Tarquin has seen her. Speculates that Sh altered his source, Livy's *History of Rome*, in which Collatine first sees Lucrece and is then inflamed by her beauty, in order "to distribute the violence equally between the rapist and the husband." By not differentiating his protagonists, Sh "brings us closer to the violent matrix of mythical themes." Revised as part of item 0441.

2408 Goldman, Rachel Margaret. "The Lucretia Legend from Livy to Rojas Zorilla." Ph.D. dissertation, City University of New York, 1976. *DAI*, 37 (1976–77), 1531-A.

Traces the Lucretia legend to Livy and considers the debate about her yielding to Tarquin and her decision to commit suicide as it appears in six Renaissance works, including *Luc.*

2409 Hawkins, Harriett. *The Devil's Party: Critical Counter-Interpretations of Shakespearian Drama.* Oxford: Clarendon P., 1985. xii + 196 pp.

Proposes to discuss key modern critical approaches to Sh and to specific works of Sh, especially approaches that are one-sided, to present counterarguments to them, and to show that such a dialectical process is largely beneficial. Discusses Plato and his strictures on poetry in *The Republic* as a way to raise issues about mimesis and morality that Shakespearean critics still need to confront. The last chapter includes a discussion of *Luc.* questioning the contention of St. Augustine and his successors that Lucrece shares the blame for her rape.

2410 Hillman, Richard. "Gower's Lucrece: A New Old Source for *The Rape of Lucrece.*" *ChauR*, 24 (1990), 263–70.

Contends that Gower's tale of Lucrece in *Confessio Amantis* was a significant influence on Sh. Certain plot elements, such as Lucrece's entertaining Tarquin and the latter's subsequent praising of Collatine, exist only in *Luc.* and Gower; and, like Gower, Sh presents a balanced rendering of characters and events. Both writers focus on the immorality of Tarquin's motives, and both explore in depth Lucrece's shame, loss of self, and suicide. The apparent awkwardness of Sh's poem can be attributed to his mixture of sources: The nondramatic accounts of Ovid, Livy, and Chaucer are combined with Gower's version, which emphasizes character development.

2411 Hulse, S. Clark III. "'A Piece of Skilful Painting' in Shakespeare's *Lucrece.*" *ShS*, 31 (1978), 13–22.

Asserts that Sh, in describing the tapestry or painting of Troy in *Luc.*, "draws on Virgil and Classical art theorists to create for his poem a proper epic *ecphrasis*," or "extended description of something, such as a person, place, battle, or work of art." Sh begins his *ecphrasis* with praise for the work that uses the same criteria employed by Pliny to judge painting. There seems to be direct borrowing from Philostratus in Sh's description of Nestor addressing the troops, with its emphasis on the artist's "imaginary work," suggesting a whole figure by showing only a hand, a foot, or a face. The rest of the passage, which is based on two *ecphrases* in the *Aeneid*, portrays the fall of Troy. The Virgilian model violates the temporal limits of the visual arts to make the events described more vivid. Sh is doing this when, in the last scene of his Troy painting, he depicts Sinon, so that Lucrece can move from a contemplation of the fall of Troy to a recognition of how, betrayed by a smooth face, she has suffered a similar fate. Being a woman, Lucrece is unable to control her body, and this "limits the actions of her heroic self." She can finally respond to her dilemma only as an artist: Her suicide reveals the inner truth that, though her body is stained, her mind is pure. As an emblem of this, her blood divides into two streams, one red and "the other black and foul." Thus are combined the characteristic excellencies of poetry (to penetrate to the reality beneath the surface) and painting (to render vividly). Revised as part of chapter 4 of item 0571.

2412 Janakiram, Alur. "Chastity and Unreason in Shakespeare's *The Rape of Lucrece.*" *Triveni*, 49, no. 2 (1980), 21–30.

Uses Renaissance faculty psychology to interpret *Luc.*, which contrasts two views of love. In Tarquin, we see love debased into lust by "the alliance of will and appetitive affections against reason's hegemony." In Lucrece, we see "love as a rational concern for chastity and fidelity in marriage." Resists the idea that Lucrece's suicide, because it is unchristian, diminishes her tragic stature. Argues that the Elizabethans were sympathetic to the "pagan–humanist attitude towards suicide as a means of vindicating one's honour."

2413 Kahn, Coppélia. "*Lucrece*: The Sexual Politics of Subjectivity." *Rape and Representation*. Eds. Lynn A. Higgins and Brenda R. Silver. (Gender and Culture.) New York: Columbia U. P., 1991, PP. 141–59.

Maintains that Sh attempts to create in Lucrece a subject not totally dominated by Roman views of chastity and patriarchal marriage and to distance himself as poet from those values. His failure reveals "how narrowly the rhetorical traditions within which he works are bounded by an ideology of gender in which women speak with the voices of men." Notes that Tarquin's discourse is that of agonistic competition, the language of the heroic tradition. His gaze is dominating, penetrating, while Lucrece's "innocence is figured as a passive, superficial looking." Lucrece is "unified" because she is modeled "on the Vesta principle," while Tarquin, because he is divided, can be seen as heroically tragic. Lucrece's only resistance to Tarquin comes in a speech she makes before the rape, but this cancels itself out "because it is inscribed within the same structures of power as the rape is." She is left with only the victim's voice; Sh seems unable to allow her to lament her rape in terms that would subvert patriarchal power. Notes classical antecedents for the story and observes that the continuity between the *Iliad*, the *Aeneid*, and Sh's brief epic makes it virtually impossible to see the violation of Lucrece by Tarquin as "a departure from the heroic norm."

2414 Kahn, Coppélia. "The Rape in Shakespeare's *Lucrece*." *ShakS*, 9 (1976), 45–72.

Analyzes the rape of Lucrece in the light of Roman ideas about marriage, according to which a woman's technical chastity was essential in maintaining her husband's honor. For a wife to remain physically chaste was to guarantee that the patriarchally controlled family to which she belonged would not be compromised in its line of descent. A chaste wife was thus one of the proudest possessions a man could boast of: She ensured his social status. It is Collatine's boasting about his wife that arouses Tarquin's interest in her, and Tarquin's violation of Lucrece is more a political, colonializing action than it is an erotic conquest. For Tarquin, the rape is an ambitious, competitive act in a world of men. Lucrece accepts and embodies the Roman ideal of the materially chaste wife, which is why she must commit suicide. Sh, however, through his narrator, includes a perspective of which Lucrece herself is not aware: the Christian view that chastity is spiritual and cannot be lost through mere physical violation. Sh's portrayal of Lucrece is informed by a sympathetic understanding of her duty as a perfect Roman wife, but he also laments the tragically destructive behavior imposed on her by the male-dominated society in which she lives.

2415 Kramer, Jerome A., and Judith Kaminsky. "'These Contraries Such Unity Do Hold': Structure in *The Rape of Lucrece*." *Mosaic*, 10, no. 4 (1977), 143–55.

Contends that *Luc.* is structurally unified by a "pattern of oppositions": "action–reaction, point–counterpoint, the ruthless pursuit of antitheses, paradoxes, and ironically similar action and utterance." Tarquin, for example, causes the ruin of a tyranny by "his tyrannous personal act," while Lucrece helps to create a republic by her virtuous death and "her recognition of the need for public virtue"; Tarquin forsakes everything that preserves public honor, while Lucrece chooses, by her death, to preserve "those very concerns" that Tarquin neglects; Tarquin wills an action and then attempts to rationalize it, while Lucrece "reasons and then activates will"; Tarquin becomes divided, indeed another self, to satisfy his lust, while Lucrece does not change her moral status; Tarquin and Lucrece respond in different ways to "external phenomena," though the motif that is used to organize the actions of both characters is that of a journey.

2416 Lanham, Richard A. "The Politics of *Lucrece*." *HUSL*, 8 (1980), 66–76.

Observes that in *Luc.* Sh takes two elements from Livy, the famous of story of Lucrece's rape and suicide and "the Roman change, in 509 B.C., from a monarchical to a consular form of government." Analyzes the motives of Tarquin and Lucrece to explain the changes Sh made in his source. As Sh presents him, Tarquin is an exemplum or allegory of "chivalric, rather than Roman, political power." In Livy, Tarquin comes to desire Lucrece when he sees her, but Sh, in order to emphasize that the rape is solely about power, has Tarquin seized with lust before he meets her. In the chivalric world, the only available roles are victimizer and victim. After her rape, Lucrece, seeking a new role, decides to play the sacked city of Troy. Her experience comes to represent "the change from a naive sense of self, role and society to a different *kind* of self and society, a radically dramatic one." Tarquin's—and Lucrece's—chivalric world corresponds to the divinely ordained external reality that supports monarchy, while the consular authority established at the end of the poem acknowledges that political power is "an agreed-upon theatrical effect."

2417 Lever, J. W., ed. *The Rape of Lucrece*. (Penguin Shakespeare.) Harmondsworth: Penguin, 1971. 151 pp.

The introduction discusses the two halves into which *Luc.* Is divided (the execution of Tarquin's raging lust and Lucrece's lament); previous versions of the story (Livy's *History of Rome*, Ovid's *Fasti*, Chaucer's *Legend of Good Women*); and Sh's reliance on the narrative mode of *A Mirror for Magistrates* (didactic tragedy for Tarquin, pathetic tragedy for Lucrece). Compares *Ven.* with *Luc.*, noting Sh's movement from the golden world of myth in the former to the fallen world of history in the latter. Notices how the images and matter of the poem draw us into a world of contradictions and discord that is characteristic of many of Sh's later works. The passage in which Lucrece contemplates the painting of Troy resembles a "preliminary sketch" for *Tro.*, with its "coincidence of contraries." Despite its flaws (chiefly Lucrece's overlong lament), *Luc.* is valuable for its exploration of Tarquin's desire and guilt and for its skillful elaboration of Lucrece's story into "an epitome of the multiple contradictions of the universe."

2418 Levin, Richard. "The Ironic Reading of *The Rape of Lucrece* and the Problem of External Evidence." *ShS*, 34 (1981), 85–2.

Points out that ironic readings of Sh's works, which purport to show apparently sympathetic characters as actually "ridiculous or reprehensible," depend heavily on "moral and religious authorities" to establish what their authors claim to be a historical or contemporary perspective. However, none of the ironic critics cites contemporary responses to the works themselves, which often contradict their conclusions. *Luc.* is a case in point. A number of external sources, "including Petrarch, Landino, Fabrini, Tyndale, several books of the Bible, and above all St. Augustine" have been adduced as evidence that Lucrece, instead of being a "model of chastity and fidelity," is actually "one of the guilty parties." A study of twelve allusions to *Luc.* or to the Lucrece legend (collected for the modern reader in *The Shakespeare Allusion Book* and E. K. Chambers's *William Shakespeare*) reveals a consistently positive response to the heroine. Of Sh's nine references to Lucrece in his other works, two are neutral and the other seven are "entirely favorable." Thus two kinds of crucial external evidence refute the ironic critics' reading of the poem.

2419 Majors, G. W. "Shakespeare's First Brutus: His Role in *Lucrece*." *MLQ*, 35 (1974), 339–51.

Focuses on the introduction of L. Junius Brutus in the last seven stanzas of *Luc.* Cites Sh's classical sources, Ovid and Livy, to show that the poet intensified the sense of ambiguity in Brutus's character. Brutus's behavior—throwing off his pretended foolishness, plucking the bloody knife from Lucrece's wound, kissing the knife, and stepping forward to persuade Collatine to revenge—suggests a Machiavellian character who can operate effectively in the real world. By contrast, Lucrece proved incapable of manipulating her public image to reflect her inner innocence, and Tarquin, though able to disguise his true feelings, was motivated by "mindless passion," not wit. Brutus's odd ambivalence—which complicates a narrative that has been until this point morally clear-cut—provides a way to understand "this sentimental, moral tale on a basis unsentimental and unmoral."

2420 Maus, Katharine Eisaman. "Taking Tropes Seriously: Language and Violence in Shakespeare's *Rape of Lucrece*." *SQ*, 37 (1986), 66–82.

Perceives that in *Luc.* the two chief figures seem to be prisoners of the tropes they employ. Tarquin views love as a military campaign, and Lucrece thinks of her body in terms of, among other things, a house, a fortress, and a temple. That is, once her fortress is battered or sacked, she will suffer regardless of her innocence or guilt. The picture of Troy reinforces this lesson. Both she and Tarquin attempt to organize experience and unify their moral thinking through metaphor, unable to avail themselves of other ways of interpreting things. The narrative voice has the same tendency as the protagonists. Shows, for example, that the poem suggests two alternative forms of representation that might at first seem more reliable: the "nonfigural prose of the 'Argument,' and naturalisitic visual depiction as exemplified by the painting of Troy." Neither of these, however, is long allowed to claim "superior certainty." The unreliability and occlusiveness of language in the poem is evidence "of an acute and profoundly uneasy self-consciousness about poetic techniques and resources."

2421 Montgomery, Robert L. Jr. "Shakespeare's Gaudy: The Method of *The Rape of Lucrece*." *Studies in Honor of DeWitt T. Starnes*. Eds. Thomas P. Harrison, Archibald A. Hill, Ernest C. Mossner, and James Sledd. Austin: U. of Texas P., 1967, pp. 77–87.

Examines the "formal, patterned, extravagant rhetoric" of *Luc.*, especially as it appears in three passages: "The first begins at line 281 where Tarquin, having yielded to lust against his better judgment, moves towards Lucrece's chamber, and ends, approximately, with her awakening; the second deals with Tarquin's reactions after the rape (lines 694–742); the third is the well-known description of the painting of burning Troy (lines 1366–1568)." In these passages, Sh used rhetorical figures in an attempt "to do several things nearly at once, to shift perspective, create mood, explore psychology, moralize, and suggest a broad philosophical atmosphere." At the very least, he took a legend with "conventional and obvious limits of meaning" and made it "reach out in many directions," thus enlarging "the capacities of the kind of narrative poem he had to work with."

2422 Muir, Kenneth. "*The Rape of Lucrece*." *Anglica*, Apr. 1964, 25–40. Revised as chapter 11 of *Shakespeare the Professional and Related Studies*. London: Heinemann, 1973, pp. 187–203.

Stresses "the importance of Tarquin as a forerunner" of Sh's later dramatization of sin. Points out that the thirty-one stanzas of *Luc.* that describe the painting of the destruction of Troy are based in part on the first two books of the *Aeneid* but that the account "is amplified by details derived from the 13th book of the *Metamorphoses*." In these stanzas, the crafty Sinon is likened to Tarquin, and Lucrece also "inveighs against Helen and Paris, whose lust was the cause of the war." Sh's attitude to the Trojan War is essentially the same in these stanzas, in the Dido play in *Ham.*, and in *Tro*. Lucrece's duty after she is raped is not as clear as many commentators suggest: Her suicide should not be so readily deplored.

2423 Patton, Jon Franklin. "Essays in the Elizabethan She-Tragedies of Female-Complaints." Ph.D. dissertation, Ohio University, 1969. *DAI*, 30 (1969–70), 1534-A.

Surveys the female–complaint poems of the Elizabethan period, provides information on the origin of the genre, and analyzes in detail the three most significant works of this kind published in the second half of the 16th c. Points out that the female–complaint poems, or she-tragedies, differ significantly from the De Casibus poems of the *Mirror for Magistrates*, with which most critics have grouped them. Specifically, the she-tragedies are distinguished by a sympathetic heroine–narrator; the thematic importance of love; emphasis on private rather than public morality;

The Rape of Lucrece

and stress on the personal aspects of tragic experience as well as "the conditions, causes, and meanings of tragic action." The final essay examines *Luc.*, which exhibits the basic features of the she-tragedies and confirms "the classical and medieval origins of the genre outside the *De Casibus* tradition."

2424 Percy, LeRoy Pratt Jr. "Shakespeare's *Lucrece* and Its Literary Traditions." Ph.D. dissertation, University of Virginia, 1975. *DAI*, 36 (1975–76), 2853-A.

Focuses on the "unique characterization of Lucrece," which reveals Sh's developing interest in the "psychological reality of his characters." Sh transforms a variety of literary conventions to explore Lucrece's unbearable grief and her inability to express it.

2425 Platt, Michael. "*The Rape of Lucrece* and the Republic for which It Stands." *CentR*, 19 (1975), 59–79.

Argues that *Luc.* furnishes Sh's version of the beginning of the Roman republic. Revision of part of item 0851. Revised as part of item 0850.

2426 Schmitz, Götz. *The Fall of Women in Early English Narrative Verse.* (European Studies in English Literature.) Cambridge: Cambridge U. P., 1990. xi + 300 pp.

Includes *Luc.* in a study of the female–complaint poem. Concentrates on "the poem's position between the epic and the elegiac traditions and the light that questions of genre can shed on Shakespeare's treatment of the central themes of innocence and experience, public and private virtues." Analyzes the poem's three-part structure, which devotes sections to Tarquin, Lucrece and her lamentations, and Lucrece with her family. Notes that on the ethical question of Lucrece's suicide, Sh wavers "between Christian and Roman ethics." Lucrece and her attacker, Tarquin, represent extremes of angel–devil and prey–predator that meet in the middle of the story, "in the rape"; the attraction of these opposite poles to each other can be expressed only in paradox, which is a key figure in the poem. After the middle of the poem, Sh tries to lift his heroine from elegiac status (indicated by her writing of a letter to her husband in the Ovidian tradition of the *Heroides*) to epic heroism (indicated by her viewing of and sympathy with the picture of events surrounding the fall of Troy). Seeking to give Lucrece's story universal appeal, "Shakespeare drives his characters almost beyond the confines of humanity and develops them into types of obedience and brutality."

2427 Simone, R. Thomas. *Shakespeare and "Lucrece": A Study of the Poem and Its Relation to the Plays.* (Elizabethan and Renaissance Studies 38.) Salzburg: Institut für Englische Sprache und Literatur, U. of Salzburg, 1974. iv + 228 pp.

Revision of item 2428.

2428 Simone, Reno Thomas Jr. "Shakespeare and *Lucrece*: A Study of the Poem and Its Relation to the Plays." Ph.D. dissertation, Claremont Graduate School, 1973. *DAI*, 33 (1972–73), 5142- A.

Contends that in *Luc.* Sh transformed his source materials to focus on the inner tragic experiences of Tarquin (damnation) and of Lucrece (violation of innocence). The poem also provides evidence of Sh's developing mastery of emblematic method, the climactic example of which is the lengthy account of the painting of Troy. In its deepening of tragic themes and its skillful deployment of emblems, *Luc.* represents a significant advance over Sh's earlier serious works and anticipates his mature tragedies and romances. Revised as item 2427.

2429   Soellner, Rolf. "Shakespeare's *Lucrece* and the Garnier–Pembroke Connection." *ShakS*, 15 (1982), 1–20.

Speculates that in composing *Luc.* Sh was influenced by three neoclassical closet tragedies, two of them, *Antonie* and *Cornelia*, translations of French plays by Robert Garnier, and the third, Samuel Daniel's *The Tragedy of Cleopatra*, an original drama in the Garnier mold. Points to the neoclassical features of *Luc.*, including its emphasis on the pathetic rather than the dramatic, its limited number of actors, and its observance of the unities. *Luc.* also resembles these feminist tragedies in presenting a suffering heroine who, though victimized by a male-dominated society, maintains loyalty to the man she loves. Sh may also have borrowed the Ciceronian metaphor of suicide for the soul's release from the body from *Cornelia* and Daniel's *Cleopatra*. Like the neoclassical tragedies, *Luc.* attempts to provide a sympathetic treatment of suicide without approving it.

2430   Starnes, D. T. "Geoffrey Fenton, Seneca and Shakespeare's *Lucrece*." *PQ*, 43 (1964), 280–83.

Points out that *Luc.*, lines 1478–1484, reflects the idea of a sin or crime recoiling on the perpetrator. Geoffrey Fenton refers to this idea in his *Tragicall Discourses* (1567) when discussing the case of a woman who drowned herself after being raped; and Octavius Mirandula's *Illustrium Poetarum Flores* gives three quotations from the works of Seneca that not only express the idea but use phrasing like Lucrece's. *Lr.* and *Mac.* also make use of the notion.

2431   Sylvester, Bickford. "Natural Mutability and Human Responsibility: Form in Shakespeare's *Lucrece*." *CE*, 26 (1964–65), 505–11.

Attempts to demonstrate that patterns in the imagery and structure of *Luc.* "emphasize man's responsibility to control the forces of selfishness and violence which, within himself and in external nature, are constantly straining to overwhelm beauty and gentleness." Tarquin loses control of himself to "masculine pride and sensuality." Lucrece, physically defeated, triumphs spiritually in her suicide. Though her self-destruction is tragic, through it she can "at once reaffirm the system of orderly absolutes necessary to man, and exemplify the human responsibility upon which it depends."

2432   Truax, Elizabeth. "Lucrece! What Hath Your Conceited Painter Wrought?" *Shakespeare: Contemporary Critical Approaches*. Ed. Harry R. Garvin. Special associate ed. Michael D. Payne (*BuR*, 25, no. 1.) Lewisburg: Bucknell U. P., 1980, pp. 13–30.

Speculates on Sh's inspiration for the painting of the Trojan War in *Luc.* (lines 1366–1568). Finds it likely that Sh was acquainted with the Mannerist style of the artists trained and/or influenced by Julio Romano (praised in *WT* for his lifelike sculpture of Hermione) to decorate Francis I's palace at Fontainebleau. These artists often drew on Greek and Roman myths, investing them with great energy, tension, and allegorical significance. Analyzes a series of six etchings executed by Jean Mignon, a Fontainebleau artist, that treat the Troy story in a manner remarkably similar to that of the painter in *Luc.* It is possible that Sh saw these etchings, or similar ones. In any case, his handling of art here and elsewhere shows that he is working "in the mode of Renaissance artists."

2433   Vickers, Nancy. "'The blazon of sweet beauty's best': Shakespeare's *Lucrece*." *Shakespeare and the Question of Theory*. Eds. Patricia Parker and Geoffrey H. Hartman. New York: Methuen, 1985, pp. 95–115.

Defines *blazon* in the English poetic tradition as a description listing praiseworthy parts of the female body whose sum constitutes a beautiful but disturbing totality. Argues that certain of Sh's sonnets suggest inadequacies and dangers of this traditional rhetoric of description. Examines *Luc.* as a demonstration of the damage wrought when men compete by blazoning women. Sh departs from his sources, Ovid's *Fasti* and Livy's *From the Founding of the City*, and from his own prose "Argument," in making Collatine's boastful speech about Lucrece the catalyst that inflames Tarquin to commit the rape (in the sources, Tarquin's lust is provoked by the sight of Lucrece). Lucrece's body becomes a battleground between two men, a tainted heraldic device (another meaning of *blazon*), and, at the end of the poem, a sign of Tarquin's dishonor. Sh's artful construction of *Luc.* "calls into question description fashion while amply demonstrating that he controls it." Like Collatine, the poet enters a contest of skill and publishes the poem as his heraldic shield, the sign of his identity, and the proof of his excellence. Connects Lucrece with Medusa, who in classical sources is a victim of rape associated with eloquence. Lucrece's face, viewed as a shield at one point in Sh's poem, resembles Medusa's face on the shields of Perseus, Athena, and others: In these cases, the male rhetorician places the shield of eloquence between himself and the world of dangers that surrounds him.

2434 Vickers, Nancy J. "'This Heraldry in Lucrece's Face.'" *Poetics Today* (Tel Aviv), 6, nos. 1–2 (1985), 171–84.

Argues that throughout *Luc.* the heroine's face is metaphorized as a shield and that this warlike (as well as heraldic) device is the key to understanding the male competition in describing a woman that instigates the rape. Sh modifies his classical sources (Ovid and Livy) to place emphasis on how the words of Collatine boasting of his wife's chastity inspire Tarquin to commit the crime. Indeed, when Tarquin sees Lucrece for the first time, his thoughts return to the paradoxical contest between beauty and virtue that was part of Collatine's boast at the beginning of the poem. Collatine's boast may also be seen as a blazon (a description in proper heraldic language of a shield as well as "a codified poetic description of an object praised or blamed by a rhetorician–poet"), which transforms Lucrece's face into a field for "gentlemanly combat." Tarquin's use of the word "colors" to mean the colors of Lucrece's face, the colors of heraldry, and the colors of rhetoric shows how woman's body, shield, and verbal description become one. Sh's poem is itself a blazon, a shield, a rhetorical display piece in competition with other male poets.

2435 Walley, Harold R. "*The Rape of Lucrece* and Shakespearean Tragedy." *PMLA*, 76 (1961), 480–87.

Notices that *Luc.* deals with a situation that permitted Sh to lay the foundation for "his subsequent treatment of tragedy." *Luc.* contains numerous details echoed in later tragedies: For example, the picture of Hecuba as an emblem of sorrowing devotion (lines 1448–1449) "supplies the theme for the player's declamation in *Ham.*" (II.ii). More important than such details, however, is that in *Luc.* Sh for the first time explicitly posed the essential problems of tragedy, revealed his thinking about them, and worked out the conclusions concerning their significance that he was to follow from then on. The first section of the poem explores the reason for the commission of an act like Tarquin's. As in later tragedies, susceptibility to evil comes from the overthrow of "rational order by the anarchy of unleashed impulse." The second section assesses the impact of the fatal deed on those involved. As with all of Sh's tragedies, the evil done is irreversible and forces the protagonist into "a dilemma with no possible resolution in satisfactory human terms." *Luc.* is "a key document in the record of Sh's coming of age as an artist."

2436 Winny, James. *The Player King: A Theme of Shakespeare's Histories*. New York: Barnes & Noble, 1968. 219 pp.

Cites in the introduction a passage from *Luc.* that provides a view of art similar to that underlying Sh's achievement in the history plays. In the passage, Lucrece contemplates a picture that displays a variety of incidents and characters from the Trojan War, with no strict observance of narrative order. Since Lucrece examines only one scene at a time, the chronological incoherence is not evident; rather, there is "an effect of dramatic profusion and vitality." The picture is full of vigorous action and violent emotion, often using fragmentary forms to suggest whole figures. There is an emphasis on how well the painter has depicted human nature in the description of his heroic subjects. In this picture, we see Sh's sense of history realized: The destruction of Troy is to be seen as a great event, but it does not result from the action of impersonal forces. The figures are portrayed as driven by their passions, and this is what determines their destiny.

2436 Widdicombe, Karen Elizabeth. "'The worth of my untutored lines': A Study of *Lucrece* and the Erotic Narrative Verse of the 1590s." Ph.D. dissertation, University of Toronto, 1986. *DAI*, 47 (1986–87), 2172-A.

Examines the conventions in contemporary narrative verse for "comic erotic courtship" and then shows how Sh transforms these conventions in Tarquin's violent "wooing." Discusses other narrative poems to gain insight into "the poetic options" available to Sh; surveys critical literature on *Luc.*; and offers, in the last chapter, a reading of Sh's poem.

2437 Willbern, David. "Rape, Writing, Hyperbole: Shakespeare's *Lucrece*." *Compromise Formations: Current Directions in Psychoanalytic Criticism.* Ed. Vera J. Camden. Kent, Ohio: Kent State U. P., 1989, pp. 182–98. Revision. "Hyperbolic Desire: Shakespeare's *Lucrece*." *Contending Kingdoms: Historical, Psychological, and Feminist Approaches to the Literature of Sixteenth-Century England and France.* Eds. Marie Rose Logan and Peter L. Rudnytsky. Detroit: Wayne State U.P., 1991, pp. 202–24.

Maintains that *Luc.* is more than simply a treatment of rape or the intervals between wish, deed, and response, but is also about the writing process. Lucrece's corpse is an emblem of "innocence re-marked by lust." The personae of Lucrece are rhetorical and psychological constructs rather than mere characters. The poem is a dramatic narrative of self-division, and collapsing it allows the act of rape to be seen as an idealization of imagination.

2438 Wilson, E. Rawdon. "Shakespearean Narrative: *The Rape of Lucrece* Reconsidered." *SEL*, 28 (1988), 39–59.

Identifies four kinds of attempts to "recuperate" *Luc.* as a significant part of the Shakespearean canon and argues that the best method for doing so is narrative analysis. The poem is a compendium of "the conventions that constitute the embedded narratives, many and frequent, of the plays." These conventions include augmentation and culmination (the piling up of details and the movement toward a climactic moment or "inward turn"), characterization through an Ovidian "split awareness," and "textual playfulness" (manifested through recursiveness and reflexivity).

2439 Winny, James. *The Player King: A Theme of Shakespeare's Histories.* New York: Barnes & Noble, 1968. 219 pp.

Cites in the introduction a passage from *Luc.* that provides a view of art similar to that underlying Sh's achievement in the history plays. In the passage, Lucrece contemplates a picture that displays a variety of incidents and characters from the Trojan War, with no strict observance of narrative order. Since Lucrece examines only one scene at a time, the chronological incoherence is not evident; rather, there is "an effect of dramatic profusion and vitality." The picture is full of vigorous action and violent emotion, often using fragmentary forms to suggest whole figures. There is an emphasis on how well the painter has depicted human nature in the description of his heroic subjects. In this picture, we see Sh's sense of history realized: The destruction of Troy is to be seen as a great event, but it does not result from the action of impersonal forces. The figures are portrayed as driven by their passions, and this is what determines their destiny.

2440 Ziegler, Georgianna. "My Lady's Chamber: Female Space, Female Chastity in Shakespeare." *Textual Practice*, 4, no. 1 (1990), 73–90.

Parallels a woman's body with her bedchamber and contends that a male's forced or clandestine violation of this space constitutes a "rape." The idea of private space was strikingly new in Elizabethan times, very much in line with the newly developing conception of the individual. A woman's role was seen as that of "house person," one who guards her husband's possessions, especially herself. Sh explores the consequences of the "violation" of female space in *Luc.* and other works. Sh's language prefigures Lucrece's rape. Collatine's adulation of his wife leads to Tarquin's desire to "storm" his rival's "fortress," and the rape is described in a soldier's vernacular. Lucrece's honor can be redeemed only through self-violation, her suicide.

RICHARD II

2440a Bashier, Kathleen Ryniker. "Rhetoric as an Art of Self-Defense: An Analysis of Trial Scenes in the Works of Peele, Shakespeare, Webster, and Massinger." Ph.D. dissertation, New York University, 1979. DAI, 40 (1979–80), 1476-A-1477-A.

Analyzes "the forensic oration as it is applied in the trial scenes of four plays," including R2. Outlines, as background, the rhetorical theory of Aristotle and Cicero as well as medieval and Renaissance adaptations of these classical authors.

2441 Fleissner, Robert F. "Richard's Phaëthon Image." *AN&Q*, 10 (1971–72), 52.

Argues that the Phaëthon image Richard uses to describe himself (*R2*, III.iii.178) has as its direct source Thomas Lodge's *Rosalynde*.

2442 Freeman, Arthur. "*Richard II*, I.iii.294–295." *SQ*, 14 (1963), 89–90.

Suggests that scholars have overlooked an obvious combination of fire and the Caucasus that is probably the source of Sh's connection of the two in these lines. In classical mythology, the Caucasus was known as the place where Prometheus, the archetypical exile who brought fire from heaven to earth in his hand, was chained.

2443 Hockey, Dorothy C. "A World of Rhetoric in *Richard II*." *SQ*, 15 (1964), 179–91.

Dissents from the view that in *R2* there are two speaking styles, one ceremonial (used to characterize Richard and his party) and the other plain (assigned to Bolingbroke and his adherents). Analyzes the play's style in terms of Renaissance rhetoric to show that in all of the characters Sh is striving for the high style: Everyone uses complex figures of speech. For example, *antimetabole*, "repetition in transposed order," occurs in the speech of Gaunt, Carlisle, Bolingbroke, York, and Richard. It is thus hard to maintain that *R2* "is written in two styles to suggest two warring worlds." Richard, it is true, is distinguished from other characters by his power of poetic visualization, but they are all masters of the "elaborate language patterns described by Tudor rhetoricians" and derived from classical sources.

2444 Logan, George M. "Lucan—Daniel—Shakespeare: New Light on the Relation between *The Civil Wars* and *Richard II*." *ShakS*, 9 (1976), 121–40.

Maintains that Sh's *R2* is indebted to the first edition of Samuel Daniel's *Civil Wars* (1595) and challenges the opinion of some scholars that Daniel borrowed from Sh. Daniel was heavily influenced by Lucan's *Pharsalia*, an account of the civil wars between Caesar and Pompey, and Sh is often closest to Daniel where Daniel is closest to Lucan. Sh seems to have absorbed, through Daniel, the contrast between Caesar and Pompey, who are models for Bolingbroke and Richard, respectively. The closest link between Sh and Daniel is in the parting scene of Richard and Queen Isabel (V.i), which is not to be found in Sh's chronicle sources. It is, however, in Daniel, who was inspired by Lucan's description of Pompey's reunion with his wife Cornelia after being defeated at Pharsalia. It is also likely that Carlisle's prophecy (IV.i) is derived from the opening thematic stanzas of Daniel, which are virtually paraphrased from the beginning of the *Pharsalia*.

2445 MacKenzie, Clayton G. "Paradise and Paradise Lost in *Richard II*." *SQ*, 37 (1986), 318–39.

Points out that John of Gaunt's reference to Neptune suggests an ambivalence—the god, as in the Troy story, is both protective and threatening—that Sh adapts to his idea of England as a paradise under attack from within. In V.i.11–15, Queen Isabel's comparison of Richard himself to Troy provides the image of an outer wall enclosing inner desolation: The king's individual spirit has been laid waste, as has England's heroic character.

2446 Maxwell, J. C. "Two Notes on *Richard II*." *N&Q*, 25 (1978), 124–25.

The first note lends support to George Steevens's suggestion that *Tusculan Disputations* is the source for the "frosty Caucasus" passage in *R2* (I.iii. 293-299) by pointing out that a few pages later in the same work the Caucasus is referred to in a context recalling Sh's "hold a fire in his hand" and "wallow naked in December snow."

2447 Merrix, Robert P. "The Phaëton Allusion in *Richard II*: The Search for Identity." *ELR*, 17 (1987), 277–87.

Maintains that Sh was influenced by Arthur Golding's translation of Ovid's *Metamorphoses* when he had Richard II compare his descent to the base court at Flint Castle (*R2*, III.iii.178–179) to the fall of Phaëton, the son of Helios. Ovid's myth, because it "incorporated such themes as the search for identity, pride and its fall, and the physical and social chaos that results from ambivalent leadership," was especially appropriate for Sh to use as a parallel to Richard's career.

2448 Nuttall, A. D. "Ovid's Narcissus and Shakespeare's Richard II: The Reflected Self." *Ovid Renewed: Ovidian Influences on Literature and Art from the Middle Ages to the Twentieth Century*. Ed. Charles Martindale. Cambridge: Cambridge U. P., 1988, pp. 137–50.

Compares the treatments of self-love or self-knowledge in Ovid's account of Narcissus and Sh's history of Richard II. Though not necessarily a direct source for *R2*, Ovid's myth of the youth who unsuccessfully longs for his reflection in the water lies at the heart of Sh's story of the self-regarding king who fails to find the fictive image(s) he has constructed for himself in the mirror brought to him as he is being deposed. With Narcissus in the background, Sh is attempting something new in English literature: an exploration of the problematic nature of achieving self-knowledge. To know oneself requires some distancing from oneself, but the distancing changes that which is to be known.

2449 Roberts, Josephine A., comp. *"Richard II": An Annotated Bibliography.* 2 volumes. (Garland Shakespeare Bibliographies 14.) New York: Garland, 1988. xxxviii + 593; 656 pp.

Covers primarily materials published 1940–1982. Classifies entries under eleven headings, including Criticism (1177 items), Sources and Historical Background (303 items), Individual Editions (111 items), and Bibliographies (32 items). Begins each section with the oldest entries and proceeds chronologically. Concludes with a name and subject index. Includes, in the sections on criticism and sources, a number of items that discuss classical influences on *R2*. Provides substantial annotations.

2450 Shady, Raymond C. "The Goddess Fortuna in Shakespeare's *Richard II.*" *Greyfriar: Siena Studies in Literature*, 20 (1979), 5–13.

Associates the alternate rising and falling of the king in *R2* with the turning of Fortune's wheel. Traces one of Fortune's attributes—her fickleness—to classical authors like Horace and Boethius. To this quality was added in the early Renaissance, the notion of Fortune as an agent of divine retribution for the sins of men, especially men of high rank. In Sh's play Richard remains in the top position on Fortune's wheel until well into act III, after which he falls. His perception is that he is merely a victim of Fortune's mutability; he never acknowledges that he is suffering divine retribution for his misgovernance. Sh exploits the difference between Richard's simplistic, self-serving ideal of Fortune and the more complex conception of her dual personality to illustrate the king's incapacity to recognize the truth about himself.

2451 Smith, Robert A. H. "Three Notes on *Richard II.*" *N&Q*, 30 (1983), 116–17.

Note 2 proposes *Dido Queen of Carthage*, V.i.26, as the source for references to Troy, a map, and a plan in *R2*, V.i.

2452 Talbert, Ernest W. "Mythological Allusion and Mythological Moral." *RenP*, 1964 (1965), 3–11.

Makes the point that a Renaissance poet might refer to a myth because of the current moral meaning given to it "rather than because of the narrative or the figures of that myth." This can be illustrated when Sh has Richard II liken himself to Phaëthon. In this instance, the part of Apollo in the myth is forgotten because Phaëthon is all that is necessary for the poet's immediate purpose: to point out "censurable ambition" in Bolingbroke and "censurable lack of skill" in Richard.

RICHARD III

2453 Brooks, Harold F. "*Richard III*: Antecedents of Clarence's Dream." *ShS*, 32 (1979), 145–150.

Observes that Clarence's dream belongs to the tradition of the dream vision of Hell. Among many works that may have contributed suggestions that coalesced in Sh's imagination as he composed this scene are the Senecan tragedies (with "twenty-five descriptions of Hades, or significant allusions to it"), Virgil's *Aeneid* (book 6), and Golding's Ovid.

2454 Brooks, Harold F. "*Richard III*, Unhistorical Amplifications: The Women's Scenes and Seneca." *MLR*, 75 (1980), 721–37.

Supports the idea that in *R3* Sh drew on Seneca, particularly the *Troades*. Each of Sh's four women corresponds to one from Seneca's play: the Duchess of York is like Hecuba; Elizabeth is like Andromache; Anne is like Polyxena; and Margaret is like Helen. In addition, Richard's courtship of Anne is indebted to Seneca's *Hercules Furens* and *Hippolytus*. *R3* exhibits many other Senecan features, which it combines with elements of the native dramatic tradition.

2455 Burton, Dolores M. "Discourse and Decorum in the First Act of *Richard III*." *ShakS*, 14 (1981), 55–84.

Argues that in the four scenes of act I of *R3* a theory of "decorum according to the forms of speech" is operating to produce a variety of styles. Derived from Hermogenes of Tarsus, this notion of decorum was propagated in the Renaissance by such influential critics as Antonio Minturno. Gloucester's opening speech is inspired by deliberative discourse; his wooing of Lady Anne is an exercise in forensic or judicial discourse; and he employs epideictic or ceremonial discourse in the third scene to build himself up at the expense of the Woodvilles. Within each scene, numerous figures and other rhetorical devices are used to achieve Gloucester's desired effects.

2455a Grubb, Shirley Carr. "Women, Rhetoric, and Power: The Women of Shakespeare's *Richard III* as Collective Antagonist." Ph.D. dissertation, University of Colorado, Boulder, 1987, *DAI*, 48 (1987–88), 1058-A.

Examines *R3* as "a rhetorical document, which, in the tradition of Terence and Seneca, explores the *Quaestiones* of resistance to tyranny and the rule of women." Employs the classical divisions of *inventio*, *dispositio*, *elocutio*, and *pronuntiatio*, as well as the concept of the three types of appeal (*logos*, *pathos*, and *ethos*), to analyze the rhetoric of the women's scenes. The women confront Richard in series, "in order of increasing success," until the role of antagonist is assumed in act V by Henry Richmond.

2456 Hammond, Antony, ed. *King Richard III*. (Arden Shakespeare.) London: Methuen, 1981. xvi + 382 pp.

The introduction discusses possible sources for Clarence's dream (I.iv) in Golding's Ovid and Seneca's plays. Mentions Senecan influences for the wooing of Lady Anne (I.ii) and the scenes of the wailing queens (II.ii and IV.iv especially). Notes also the indebtedness of the play's "highly organized and formal" structure to "its Senecan models."

2457 Hassel, Chris R. Jr. "Richard Versus Richmond: Aesthetic Warfare in *Richard III*." *SJH*, 1983, 106–16.

Contends that in act V of *R3*, Sh modifies his source, Edward Hall's *Union of the Two Noble and Illustre Famelies of Lancastre and Yorke*, in order to show Richard as less vigorous and attractive and Richmond as more heroic and less vainglorious. One significant alteration is in Richmond's speech before the battle: Sh omits the comparisons between Richard and the classical tyrants Tarquin and Nero, to tone down the stuffiness of Hall's Richmond.

2458 Higdon, David Leon. "Shakespeare's *King Richard III*, V.ii.7–11." *Expl*, 33 (1973–74), item 2.

Notes that the pre-battle speech of Richmond "fuses references to heraldry, theology, and classical myth and compresses three of the play's major motifs into the space of five lines." The references to Richard as the "wretched, bloody, and usurping boar" links him with the Calydonian boar, sent by Diana to ravage the crops of Oeneus, King of Calydon, who had angered her (Ovid, *Metamorphoses* 8). This myth reinforces the Christian idea of Richard as the chastizing instrument of divine providence.

2459 Honigmann, E. A. J., ed. *King Richard III*. (New Penguin Shakespeare.) Harmondsworth: Penguin, 1968. 256 pp.

The introduction mentions the influence of Seneca—whose *Ten Tragedies* were translated, collected, and published in 1581—on the rhetoric and sensationalism of *R3*.

2460 Moore, James A., comp. *"Richard III": An Annotated Bibliography*. (Garland Reference Library of the Humanities: Garland Shakespeare Bibliographies 11.) New York: Garland, 1986. li + 867 pp.

Classifies entries under eight headings, including Criticism (577 entries), Editions (177 entries), Bibliographies (29 entries), and Sources and Background (297 entries). Begins each section with the oldest entries and proceeds chronologically through 1983. Includes, in the sections on criticism and sources and background, a number of items that discuss classical influences on *R3*. Provides substantial annotations. Concludes with subject and name indexes.

ROMEO AND JULIET

2461 Adams, Barry M. "The Prudence of Prince Escalus." *ELH*, 35 (1968), 32–50.

Maintains that the prince's three appearances in *Rom*. reveal him to be a man of prudence, as the Renaissance understood that virtue. In Cicero's *De Inventione*, likely to have been the ultimate source of Sh's ideas on the subject, prudence is said to consist of three "parts"—memory, intelligence, and providence— "corresponding to the division of time into past, present, and future." Escalus, by looking back to the past (especially in his first appearance) and forward to the future (especially in his last appearance), shows himself to be a rational man exercising prudence. In his bifrontality, he is also an emblem of Fortune, representing good and bad fortune and suggesting the rapidity with which the former is likely to be succeeded by the latter. His second appearance, appropriately, comes at the center of the play and separates two parallel units of action, one comic and the other tragic. Sh unites in Escalus these "antithetical concepts of prudence and fortune," thus suggesting that the tragedy cannot be completely attributed either to a character flaw or to fate. There is also the insistence that prudence and fortune cannot always be distinguished from each other; though logically opposite, the two sometimes produce remarkably similar results. It is from "such a conflation of the rational and the irrational" that *Rom*. derives its tragic irony.

2462 Andrews, John F. "The Catharsis of *Romeo and Juliet*." *Contributi dell'Instituto di filologia moderna*. Ed. Sergio Rossi. (Serie inglese 1.) Milan: Università Cattolica del Sacro Cuore, 1974, pp. 142–75.

Proposes to interpret *Rom*. using the Aristotelian concept of *catharsis*, which can be elaborated as *clarification*. Introduces the Boethian notions of Providence, Fate, and Fortune to show that the protagonists, though to some extent admirable for the intensity and fidelity of their passion, are fools of Fortune because they idolize each other. The catharsis experienced by the audience involves a perception (or clarification) of what it means to be a slave of passion.

2463   Browne, Thomas. "Mercutio as Mercury: Trickster and Shadow." *UC*, 9 (1989), 40–51.

Maintains that in creating Mercutio in *Rom.*, Sh was influenced by the figure of Mercury as a "youthful trickster." Cites other plays of the time and mythological and astrological treatises as evidence for the availability of this conception of the god. Connects the trickster figure with C. J. Jung's notion of the "shadow," a puerile and inferior version of the self. Mercutio, then, is not older than Romeo but younger; his irresponsible adolescence is what Romeo is in the process of escaping. To see Mercutio in this way is to understand *Rom.* as "a tragedy of character" in which Romeo struggles unsuccessfully but nobly to maintain a balance between his youthful shadow and the maturity to which he is called by his love for Juliet.

2464   Cribb, T. J. "The Unity of *Romeo and Juliet*." *ShS*, 34 (1981), 93–104.

Argues that the structure, imagery, and characterization of *Rom.* are informed by Renaissance Platonism. Cites Marsilio Ficino's commentary on the *Symposium* to provide background for Romeo's soliloquy in the Capulet orchard (II.ii): "The master image of light, the peculiarly ideal nature of the description, and the climactic ideal of beauty as a theophany" are all consistent with Ficinan thought. As a result of the revaluation of *eros* by the Florentine Academy, the quest for beauty becomes heroic, and a lover like Romeo, who casts aside reason in his all-consuming desire to be united with beauty, can claim heroic status. Other characters also fit into this Platonic reading. Tybalt, representing hate, is joined with Romeo in a "metaphysic of opposites." Mercutio and the Nurse must both disappear from the world of the play, the former because he is skeptical about love in any form and the latter because she cannot see beyond the initial physical impulse toward ideal love.

2465   Diverres, A. H. "The Pyramus and Thisbe Story and Its Contribution to the Romeo and Juliet Legend." *The Classical Tradition in French Literature: Essays Presented to R. C. Knight by Colleagues, Pupils, and Friends.* Eds. H. T. Barnwell et al. Edinburgh: Authors, 1977, pp. 9–12.

States that an unknown Norman poet of the 12th c. expanded the story of Pyramus and Thisbe to approximately four times its length in Ovid. Unlike Ovid, who is most interested in the climax, the French adaptor emphasizes the growth of the couple's love and "the inner conflicts it causes." Luigi Da Porto's *La Giulietta* seems to owe a number of details to direct knowledge of a medieval French version based on the 12th-c. adaptation. Matteo Bandello, who next retold the story, and Pierre Boaistuau, whose French version brought it to England, also appear to have introduced changes based on a medieval French account. As Sh inherited it, the tale of the two lovers owed much more to the early French adaptation than to Ovid.

2466   Evans, Robert O. *The Osier Cage: Rhetorical Devices in "Romeo and Juliet."* Lexington: U. of Kentucky P., 1966. vii + 108 pp.

Proposes to analyze the rhetorical figures in *Rom.* These figures were derived from classical authors and would have been familiar to Elizabethans through handbooks like those by Henry Peacham. Argues that an emphasis on the figures will reveal something about the characters of the two protagonists, who, according to the Platonic psychology of Sh's time, lay claim to high rationality through their skillful use of rhetoric. Chapter 2, "Oxymoron as Key to Structure," stresses the importance of this figure, especially by Romeo and Juliet, because it forces together the "disparate elements" (for example, Mars and Venus) that make up the play. Chapter 3, "The Osier Cage," focuses on the ambivalent role of Friar Laurence. Chapter 4, "Mercutio's Apostrophe to Queen Mab," shows how the brilliant use of figures in the Queen Mab speech (I.iv) reveals Sh's themes and hints at "the outcome of the action." Chapter 5, "The Play's the Thing," concludes that the tragedy depends on the protagonists' retaining "to a great extent their rationality even in the throes of the greatest passion in English literature" and that the rhetorical devices help us to understand that they do this.

2467 Evans, Robert O. "*Romeo and Juliet*, II.i.13: Further Commentary." NM, 64 (1963), 390–400.

Accepts John Upton's 1746 emendation of "Young Abraham Cupid" to "Young Adam: Cupid" in Mercutio's speech [II.i.14]. The effect produced is oxymoronic (young–old Cupid) and mirrors the contradictory structure of the first part of Mercutio's speech. The oxymoron may also suggest something about the nature of love in the play: "the oldest of passions given to the youngest of adults."

2468 Gray, J. C. "*Romeo and Juliet* and Some Renaissance Notions of Love, Time, and Death." DR, 48 (1968), 58–69.

Finds that *Rom.* dramatizes a type of love that appealed to the Renaissance poet's imagination—"erotic, heterosexual love that is intense, mutual, and short-lived." Romeo and Juliet were associated with such famous classical pairs as Hero and Leander, Pyramus and Thisbe, and Venus and Adonis. Perhaps taking his cue from Golding's portrayal of Pyramus and Thisbe in the *Metamorphoses*, Sh made the love of Romeo and Juliet a paradox: It is both constant and rash.

2468a Kilinski, Janusz. "Elements of Neo-Platonism in *Romeo and Juliet*." SAP, 17 (1984), 271–77.

Maintains that Sh was familiar with the basic assumptions of Neoplatonism, perhaps through Baldassare Castiglione's *The Book of the Courtier*. Notes that *Rom.* makes distinctions, as does Neoplatonism, "between the divine and the earthly, between the spiritual and the material, the pure and the vulgar." Other Neoplatonic elements in the play include the reconciliation between "the idealistic concept of love and the Christian doctrine of love," the portrayal of Juliet as *Venus Coelestis*, the use of the image of blind Cupid to indicate a distinction between divine and illicit passion, the presence of lust and lechery representing "bestial love," and the idea that love and beauty are forces capable of "restoring the natural order."

2469 McCown, Gary M. "'Runaway's Eyes' and Juliet's Epithalamium." SQ, 27 (1976), 150–70.

Provides a survey of classical and Renaissance epithalamia as background for considering Juliet's soliloquy beginning "Gallop apace, you fiery footed steeds" (*Rom.*, III.ii.1–31) as a special representative of the genre. Catullus's epithalamia and others model many of the conventions Juliet seems to be following: the twilight setting, the optative mode, the references to a night setting, and the refrain. There was also ample precedent, classical and Renaissance, for Cupid's presence in epithalamia; and Juliet has him in mind when she refers to "runaway's eyes" that "may wink" (line 6), emphasizing haste and secrecy in the consummation of her nuptials. Juliet's speech, however, contains a number of radical alterations of epithalamic conventions: Congratulation is provided by the bride herself, not the priest–poet; the bride is eager for consummation, not fearful; there is no social setting; Juliet asks for light to be banished; and the matron of honor who will deck the bride is Night. Sh has given Juliet an ironic epithalamium—appropriate as a recognition of "the beauty and pathos of young love smothered by a dark world." Revision of part of item 2470.

2470 McCown, Gary Mason. "The Epithalamium in the English Renaissance." Ph.D. dissertation, University of North Carolina, Chapel Hill, 1968. DA, 29 (1969), 2220-A-2221-A.

Provides a detailed discussion of the classical epithalamium before treating the revival of the genre by Renaissance English poets. Analyzes Catullus's three Latin epithalamia as well as narrative versions by Statius and Claudian. The genre suffered an eclipse in the Middle Ages but was revived in the Renaissance. Sidney brought it to England by including an epithalamium in the *Arcadia*. Thereafter, the poem became a vehicle for the promotion of Christian humanist views about marriage. Juliet's soliloquy in *Rom.* (III.ii) is an "ironic epithalamium" analogous to Musaeus's *Hero and Leander*. Part revised as item 2469.

2471 Pearce, T. M. "*Romeo and Juliet* as Situation Ethics." *Shakespeare in the Southwest: Some New Directions.* Ed. T. J. Stafford. U. of Texas at El Paso: Texas Western P., 1969, pp. 1–15.

Rejects interpretations of *Rom.* that, drawing on Aristotle's *Poetics*, locate its tragedy in the personal flaws of the protagonists. Romeo's character, in fact, can be defended as moderate in terms of Aristotle's *Ethics*, which maintains that "an action must judged by the situation in which it happens." The play emphasizes the narrow constraints imposed on Romeo and Juliet by family, church, and community. Their responses to these constraints are situationally justified, and their deaths throw the spotlight on society's failure, not their own flaws.

2472 Peterson, Douglas L. "*Romeo and Juliet* and the Art of Moral Navigation." *Pacific Coast Studies in Shakespeare.* Eds. Waldo F. McNeir and Thelma N. Greenfield. Eugene, Oregon: U. of Oregon Books, 1966, pp. 33–46.

Suggests that the protagonists of *Rom.* fall because they reject providential guidance and follow passion as their blind pilot (in the case of Romeo, blind Cupid).

2473 Porter, Joseph A. *Shakespeare's Mercutio: His History and Drama.* Chapel Hill: U. of North Carolina P., 1988. xi + 281 pp.

The introduction raises the question of why Sh developed the character of Mercutio (in *Rom.*) from the few hints he found in his source, Arthur Brooke's *The Tragicall Historye of Romeus and Juliet*. The introduction to part 1, "Shakespeare's Mercury," surveys the references to the god in Sh's plays. Chapter 1 provides a brief history of Mercury up to the Renaissance, including Greek (Homer, Hesiod, "Hymn to Hermes"), Latin (Plautus, Horace, Virgil, Ovid, and Apuleius), and medieval (Martianus; various forms of Hermeticism, astrology, and alchemy; Chaucer; Henryson). Chapter 2 discusses Mercury in Renaissance "pictorial representations, especially those associated with text or commentary, particularly in Cartari and in emblem books." Chapter 3 covers Elizabethan texts that refer to Mercury up to 1595. Uses John Eliot's *Ortho-epia: Eliots Fruits for the French* (1593), a work known to Sh, to demonstrate the various meanings with which the god's name could be associated and which might have inspired the playwright to connect his character Mercutio with "a complex of ideas of magic, mystery, and transformation." Includes sections on "The Heraldic and Hierophantic Mercury" and "The Erotic Mercury." Suggests that Sh's Mercury about 1595 is "a figure weighted with complex significances that have evolved through his history and that are implicated in such new cultural factors as mercantile capitalism and the celebration of mind and body." Chapter 4, "Eloquence and Liminality," uses speech-act theory to analyze Mercutio's verbal performances. Chapter 5, "The Thief and Marlowe," maintains that the character of Mercutio and the foregrounding of economics in *Rom.* are delayed aesthetic responses by Sh to the issue of thievery raised in Robert Greene's famous attack on him as "an upstart crow." Chapter 6 is concerned with friendship and love; in Mercutio's "phallicity and even his physicality," Sh appears to process some of the most disturbing elements in Marlowe.

2474 Siegel, Paul N. "Christianity and the Religion of Love in *Romeo and Juliet*." *SQ*, 12 (1961), 371–92.

Refers to the classical–Christian doctrine that "sexual love is a manifestation of the all-pervading love of God, through which the universe is governed." This helps further a sense at the end of *Rom.* that the tragic fate of the lovers "serves the end of providence."

2475 Smith, Gordon Ross. "The Balance of Themes in *Romeo and Juliet*." *Essays on Shakespeare.* Ed. Gordon Ross Smith. University Park: Pennsylvania State U. P., 1965, pp. 15–66.

Uses the classical and Renaissance motto, *festina lente*, "make haste slowly," as a key element in the argument that *Rom.* is about the conflict between grace and rude will.

This proposition rehabilitates some previous critics (G. G. Gervinus) and confutes others (Edward Dowden). On another level, the play is organized "in terms of the Platonic tripartite division of the mind into the reasonable, the irascible, and the concupiscible," which can be "approximately equated with Freud's tripartite division" of ego, id, and super-ego.

2475a Smith, James C. "Ptolemy and Shakespeare: The Astrological Influences on *Romeo and Juliet.*" *SRASP*, 7, no. 2 (1982), 66–70.

Investigates the background of *Rom.* in the astrological thought of classical authorities like Manilius (1st c. B.C.). Points out that Sh has changed the season of the year from spring (in his source, Arthur Brooke's poem) to late summer, a time that is subject to the malign influence of Dogstar. Notes the dog–cat imagery that pervades the play. Views Juliet as a symbolic Dogstar, under whose power Romeo engages in increasingly mad behavior. The disastrous result of Friar Laurence's experiment with the sleeping potion can be linked to the idea that certain drugs used "during the reign of Dogstar" have a "deleterious effect."

2475b Taylor, Anthony Brian. "The Elizabethan Seneca and Two Notes on Shakespeare and Spenser." *N&Q*, 34 (1987), 193–95.

The first note argues that Juliet's reference to the "fiery-footed steeds" of the Sun-god (*Rom.*, III.ii.1–2) echoes a passage in John Studley's translation of Seneca's *Medea* (1581). This is a more likely source than a reference in Ovid's *Metamorphoses* that has been previously suggested. In the passage from *Medea*, unlike that from Ovid, the heroine is in a position similar to that of Juliet, and the image of *lodging* the horses, also found in Sh, is used.

2475c Taylor, Anthony Brian. "'Wash they his wounds with tears?': Shakespeare's Discriminate Reading of Golding." *N&Q*, 35 (1988), 52.

Finds that the passage from Ovid in which Thisbe embraces the body of Pyramus and fills his wounds with tears (*Metamorphoses* 4), translated by Arthur Golding to have Thisbe "wash his [Pyramus's] wounds with tears," is recalled in *Rom.* when Juliet, hearing of Tybalt's death, asks the Nurse about her parents' reaction: "Wash they his wounds with tears?" (III.ii.130).

2476 Thompson, Ann. "*Troilus and Criseyde* and *Romeo and Juliet.*" *YES*, 6 (1976), 26–37.

Compares Chaucer's poem with Sh's play to reveal important similarities that illuminate both works. Both authors attempt to reconcile the religions of Christ and Cupid; both rely heavily on Fortune and chance; both feature a strong association between love and death; both are able to maintain a positive tone much of the time; both prevent their lovers from becoming farcical or melodramatic in large part by deflecting laughter onto Pandarus and the Nurse, respectively; and both significantly enhance the role of the heroine. Sh may have borrowed directly from Chaucer's poem at several points; he was certainly familiar with *Troilus* and the legend of Troy. More important than source study, however, is the critical insight that may be gained by juxtaposing the two works.

SONNETS

2477 Aiken, Ralph. "A Note on Shakespeare's Sonnet 30." *SQ*, 14 (1963), 93–94.

Suggests that Sh borrowed the phrase "remembrance of things past" in Sonnet 30 from Sir Thomas North's translation of "the essay Jacques Amyot prefaced to his French version of Plutarch's *Lives* in 1559."

2477a Bagg, Robert. "Some Versions of Lyric Impasse in Shakespeare and Catullus." *Arion*, 4 (1965), 64–95.

Proposes to consider the *Carmina* of Catullus and *Son.* to distinguish between the ways the two poets respond when each is faced with "an emotional disaster" involving "a shattering sexual betrayal." Sets up a series of contrasts: Catullus is unable to transcend his feelings, while Sh attempts to escape his misery "through shifting values distilled from pun, paradox, steep changes in context and meaning"; Catullus tries to express his emotions "through physical actions and sensations," but Sh, because of "his superior verbal and emotional flexibility," is not limited in this way; Sh's personality is "more volatile, less nakedly vulnerable" than that of Catullus; and Sh lives more in the poetic event itself than does Catullus. Both poets write from "a deep knowledge of impasse," and Sh "arrives through grace and ambiguity not far from where Catullus is driven by frank ferocity."

2478 Baldi, Sergio. "Shakespeare's Sonnets as Literature." *Shakespeare Celebrated: Anniversary Lectures Delivered at the Folger Library*. Ed. Louis B. Wright. Ithaca, New York: Published for The Folger Shakespeare Library by Cornell U. P., 1966, pp. 133–54.

Argues that *Son.* are Platonic in that they deal with love as an absolute. Sonnet 144 suggests Plato's dichotomy between sensual and chaste love, and the tutorial attitude displayed to the young friend follows "the behavior of the followers of Apollo as represented by Socrates." Other Platonic ideas in *Son.* include natural and heavenly immortality and ideal beauty. Discusses manneristic and baroque conventions in *Son.* as well.

2479 Bannerjee, Srikumar. "The Sonnets of Shakespeare." *Shakespeare Commemoration Volume*. Ed. Taraknath Sen. Calcutta: Presidency College, 1966, pp. 1–10.

Contends that in *Son.* Sh is writing in extravagant praise of his patron but also in celebration of their Platonic friendship.

2480 Bate, Jonathan. "Ovid and the Sonnets; or, Did Shakespeare Feel the Anxiety of Influence?" *ShS*, 42 (1989), 65–76.

Examines the relationship between Ovid and *Son.* "in the light of sixteenth-century imitation theory and late twentieth-century influence theory." Discovers, in a discussion of imitation from Erasmus's *Dialogus Ciceronianus*, concern for something like Harold Bloom's "anxiety of influence." Suggests that Elizabethan sonneteers encouraged their readers to ponder "imitation and paradigm," the weak poets being "obsessive imitators" and the strong ones departing from their paradigm at "the very point where they are like him." In *Son.*, numerous references to ancient books, especially in Sonnet 59, reveal Sh's anxiety about literary influence, but in most of his Ovidian sonnets, especially Sonnet 60, he conquers that anxiety through "a process of reiteration and variation that corresponds to both Pythagorean metempsychosis and Bloomian 'revision.'"

2481 Bates, Paul A. "Shakespeare's Sonnets and Pastoral Poetry." *SJW*, 103 (1967), 81–96.

Points out that Sh's framework for *Son.* derives from two developments of the 1580s in England: "interest in the Second Eclogue of Virgil" and "the tendency to fuse elements of pastoral with the sonnet tradition." Richard Barnfield's *Affectionate Shepherd* (1594), an expanded imitation of the Second Eclogue, incorporates "classical and Christian elements of pastoral." Sh probably used Barnfield as a source for the triangle of Poet, Youth, and Dark Lady in sonnets 126–152, while going back to Virgil for the relationship of Poet, Youth, and Rival.

2482 Booth, Stephen, ed. *Shakespeare's Sonnets*. New Haven: Yale U. P., 1977. xx + 583 pp.

Reprints in appendix 2 selections from Pythagoras's speech in Ovid's *Metamorphoses*, book 15, in Golding's translation. Comments that Ovid's concern with metempsychosis in this passage stimulated Sh's imagination and that "the assertion of the paradox of constancy and constant change provides a good description of a prime stylistic characteristic of the first fourteen books of *Metamorphoses* . . . and of Shakespeare in the individual sonnets" and "in their interrelation." Makes frequent reference to Ovid in the commentary on individual sonnets. Also discusses the rhetorical figures derived from classical authors and their use in *Son.*

2483 Devereux, James A., S. J. "Shakespeare's Sonnets of Participation." *UC*, 2 (1979), 18–25.

Remarks that in several sonnets, the poet conceives of himself as participating in the ideal love and beauty of his friend. In these poems (for example, 37, 53, 67, and 98), Sh uses the Platonic notion whereby sensible things relate to ideal forms by participating in their perfection. In another group of sonnets (for example, 76 and 108), there is a distinction between the ideal of love itself and the beloved. Marsilio Ficino's concept of the *primum* may help remove the apparent contradiction between the two groups. According to Ficino, a *primum* is the individual "within every genus in the universal hierarchy of beings" that "embodies in itself the whole content of that quality or perfection found in the genus and common to its members. The *primum* communicates that quality to the other members, which are therefore related to the universal ideal only through their participation in the *primum*." This representative Renaissance philosopher "provided his age with a conceptual pattern which made it possible for a poet to speak at one moment of a Platonic idea of love, and in the next of that idea's complete realization in a single person." See item 2486.

2484 Donow, Herbert S., comp. *The Sonnet in England and America: A Bibliography of Criticism*. Westport, Connecticut: Greenwood P., 1982. xxii + 477 pp.

Devotes a section to Sh (items 1428–3325). Covers scholarship published through mid-1981. Provides brief annotations for most, though not all, items. Concludes with three indexes, for contributors, poets, and subjects, respectively.

2485 Fiedler, Leslie A. "Some Contexts of Shakespeare's Sonnets." *The Riddle of Shakespeare's Sonnets*. New York: Basic Books, 1962, pp. 55–90.

Cites four Venus and Adonis sonnets from *The Passionate Pilgrim*, *Ven.*, and various sections of the *Metamorphoses* to argue that Sh, in *Son.* and elsewhere, longs for an "epicene beauty," a "pure and rational love of males" free from the evil element of lust represented by the female. Sh is not able to realize this ideal in *Son.* or in plays like *JC* and *MV*, falling back instead on "the Christian doctrine that there is no rebirth of beauty except in God."

2486 Forker, Charles R. "A Response to James Devereux." *UC*, 2 (1979), 26–33.

Contends that although *Son.* contain much Neoplatonic vocabulary, as Devereux argues (item 2483), it is a mistake to suggest that Sh defined his friend or his relationship to the friend in precise Marsilian terms. Instead of placing his friend exactly on the Neoplatonic ladder of perfection, the poet conveys to his readers the sense that, even though flawed, the friend is "a unique incarnation of all that is valuable."

2487 Fowler, Alastair. *Triumphal Forms: Structural Patterns in Elizabethan Poetry*. Cambridge: Cambridge U. P., 1970. xiii + 234 pp.

Provides an introduction to numerological analysis of Elizabethan poetry. Explains the widespread use of numerology in Sh's time as an inheritance from the Greco–Roman tradition, mediated through medieval and humanist writers. Chapter 8, "Sonnet Sequences," discovers a Pythagorean triangular structure in *Son.*, when they are considered together with *A Lover's Complaint*, which was included in the 1609 quarto.

2488 Frye, Northrop. "How True a Twain." *The Riddle of Shakespeare's Sonnets*. New York: Basic Books, 1962, pp. 23–53.

Divides "the scale of themes in courtly love poetry" into "high" and "low" phases, pointing out the Platonic influence on the former. The middle ground is occupied by the Petrarchan norm, influenced strongly by Ovid. In *Son.*, "the beautiful-youth group tells a 'high' story of devotion," while "the dark-lady group is 'low' and revolves around the theme of *odi et amo*." *Son.* "are a poetic realization of the whole range of love in the Western world."

2488a Gianetti, Robert Michael. "Amor Razionale and Amor Sensuale: An Approach to Shakespeare's Sonnets." Ph.D. dissertation, Duquesne University, 1979. *DAI*, 40 (1979–80), 6271-A.

Attempts to establish an appropriate historic context for interpreting *Son.* Chapter 2 offers a detailed discussion of "the philosophical texts in which the literary modes of Petrarchism and anti-Petrarchism are rooted." Discusses Plato's *Symposium* and *Phaedrus*, along with a number of Neoplatonic authors. Chapter 3 maintains that Sh's sequence is "basically an anti-Petrarchist statement seeking to carry the literary possibilities of the Platonizing impulse to their utmost limits." Sh's speaker, however, deludes himself in the undertaking, and "the sequence finds its ultimate repose in reaffirmation of the medieval wisdom of *contemptus mundi*."

2489 Gilbert, A. J. *Literary Language from Chaucer to Johnson*. London: Macmillan, 1979. ix + 224 pp.

Proposes to describe and analyze literary language during the period covered in terms of three styles or "registers" derived from classical rhetoric: high, middle, and low or plain. Chapter 2 includes discussion of several of Sh's sonnets. Notes that the typical register for the sonnet is the middle style and observes that Sh "develops a new realism in the sonnet tradition" by incorporating a wider range of "low style imagery" than do Spenser and other sonneteers. Points out that Sh uses all three registers, often in the same sonnet. For example, in 107, the first two lines are in the middle style, the next two in the plain style, and the next four, suggesting ancient Rome by their archaic diction, in the high style. In 130, "high style diction" is juxtaposed with "a reality that is more complex and paradoxical."

2490 Gilbert, A. J. "Philosophical Conceits in Shakespeare and Chapman." *ES*, 54 (1973), 118–21.

Notes several "remarkable and illuminating" parallels between Sonnet 24 and George Chapman's *Ovid's Banquet of Sense* (1595). The sonnet depends for its complete understanding on Chapman's "philosophical conceits," including some borrowed from Aristotle.

2491 Hieatt, A. Kent. "The Genesis of Shakespeare's *Sonnets*: Spenser's *Ruines of Rome: by Bellay.*" PMLA, 98 (1983), 800–814.

Contends that in creating *Son.* Sh was transmuting the image of "the ancient exemplary city," ruined by time but preserved in its excellence through literary artifacts, that he had assimilated from Spenser's nonamatory sonnet sequence, itself a translation of Joachim Du Bellay's *Les Antiquez de Rome*. Verbal echoes of Spenser's sequence, many of which involve forms of the word "antique," as well as thematic parallels, make it virtually certain that Sh was translating Spenser's Rome into an image of the beloved young man, whose excellence is subject to physical and moral decay but "who inspires the *Sonnets* and thus gains eternity."

2492 Ingram, W. G., and Theodore Redpath, eds. *Shakespeare's Sonnets*. London: U. of London P., 1964. xxxiv + 382 pp. Reprint. London: Hodder and Stoughton, 1978.

Notes to individual sonnets give some brief explanations of classical background. The "General Note" on Sonnet 55, for example, cites Ovid (*Metamorphoses* 4) and Horace (*Odes* 3) as exemplars of the "defusing of time, and the boast of immortality verse alone can confer."

2493 Jahn, Jerald D. "Shakespeare's Aristotelian Memory." SRASP, 2, no. 3 (1978), 51–59.

Contends that Sh's style in *Son.* reflects an Aristotelian understanding of human perception. In particular, Sh operates on the principle that knowledge is derived from sensation: Information from the senses is recorded by the perceptual soul, which provides images for the mind to work on. The mind then abstracts universals from the images (sonnets 46 and 47 exploit the Aristotelian view of perception by presenting a dispute between the poet's eye [the senses] and his heart [the mind] "over which of them properly possesses the image of the friend"). Similarly, the memory "receives and records sensory perceptions as wax takes the impression of a seal." Memory—the ability of the "heart" to record sense impressions accurately—can be disrupted by strong emotions (as in Sonnet 113). Sonnets that concern the operation of images "within the mind itself" include 53 (a poem "about thinking in mental images" that inverts Platonic ideas), 27, 43, and 61. Sonnets 122, 77, 100, and 101 focus specifically on memory. In his treatment of the "eternizing theme," Sh thinks of poetry as a kind of "mnemonic token" in that "the image of the young friend stands in the same relationship to the minds of Sh's readers as the images of memory do to the poet's intellective soul: both are 'living records' which preserve vividly the original object of perception." *Son.* follow the fluctuations of the world closely, which is not surprising in view of a poetic based on "observed experience."

2494 Kaula, David. "In War With Time: Temporal Perspectives in Shakespeare's Sonnets." SEL, 3 (1963), 45–57.

Divides the sonnets addressed to the friend into two groups, according to "the conceptions of time they embody." Sonnet 60, for example, unlike the sonnets of procreation, explores the changing nature of the relationship between the poet and his friend. Sh intensifies time's power in this sonnet by speeding up the process through which man's physical integrity is destroyed. Although he got much of his time imagery from Ovid, Sh transformed Ovid's portrayal of gradual change.

2495 Kerrigan, John, ed. *"The Sonnets" and "A Lover's Complaint."* (New Penguin Shakespeare.) Harmondsworth: Penguin, 1986. 458 pp.

The introduction comments that in *Son.* Sh thinks of his young friend in "violently reversed metaphors, subduing the nature of things for the sake of his beloved's particularity and being." A crucial example is 53, in which Adonis and Helen are made to "resemble the youth rather than he them." Explains that the invention of mechanical clockwork to record time in the Renaissance caused "a complete reordering of sensibility," an anxiety about time. The symbols of time from classical literature did not create this concern; they were borrowed by Elizabethans like Sh to express their new hopes and fears. Discusses the question of homosexuality in *Son.* by citing a passage from Marsilio Ficino's commentary on Plato's *Symposium*, which exalts the love between man and youth without any "imputation of unchastity." Although this passage might have some points of contact with *Son.*, it is clear that Sh was not a Neoplatonist, being aware of how easily "ideals like Ficino's are corrupted in practice." What we see in *Son.* is "profound homosexual attachment of a scarcely sensual, almost unrealized kind." Argues that 153 and 154, "about Cupid and his brand," make apparent the erotic principle at work in the dark–lady sonnets.

2496   Kobayashi, Minoru. "A Note on the 'Inverted Platonism' of Shakespeare's Sonnets." *ShStud*, 2 (1963), 31–48.

Challenges the concept of "inverted Platonism" as it has been applied to *Son.* by George Wyndham and J. B. Leishman (item 2501). Sh's references to pattern, substance, shadows, and other possibly Platonic concepts do not reveal a systematic concept of inversion. As reflected in Renaissance poetry, and particularly *Son.*, Platonism "is a more or less vague and indefinable mixture," not exact enough to be inverted.

2497   Koskimies, Rafael. "The Question of Platonism in Shakespeare's Sonnets." *NM*, 71 (1970), 260–70.

Argues that Platonism, as mediated through the Italian humanists and as found in the *Symposium*, had a decisive influence on Sh in writing *Son*. In the *Symposium*, Diotima discusses procreation as the object of rational love, and this shows up in the sonnets to the young man. The sonnets dealing with the dark lady treat what Platonists would call "sensual love."

2498   Landry, Hilton. "In Defense of Shakespeare's Sonnets." *New Essays on Shakespeare's Sonnets*. Ed. Hilton Landry. New York: AMS P., 1976, pp. 129–55.

Begins a defense of *Son.* against the attack of John Crowe Ransom, a linguistic rationalist, by summing up "what an educated man of the Renaissance might be expected to know of the imagination." Influenced by Aristotle, people in the Renaissance believed that the imagination is not simply "dangerous and fallible," but also "versatile and indispensable."

2499   Landry, Hilton. *Interpretations in Shakespeare's Sonnets*. (Perspectives in Criticism 14.) Berkeley: U. of California P., 1963. x + 185 pp.

Mentions some classical works briefly. Aristotle's comments in the *Rhetoric* on the insolence of the wealthy help elucidate Sonnet 66, and Platonic ideas on shadow and substance are found in 53. *Tro.*, because of its preoccupation with time, is relevant to 123.

2500   Latham, Jacqueline E. M. "Shakespeare's Sonnet 21." *N&Q*, 25 (1978), 110–12.

Argues that Sh had Sidney's *Astrophil and Stella* in mind when he wrote Sonnet 21. Line 9, for example, points to a characteristic theme of Sidney, "the conflict between Neoplatonic theory and personal desire."

2501   Leishman, J. B. *Themes and Variations in Shakespeare's Sonnets*. London: Hutchinson, 1961. 254 pp. 2nd ed., 1963.

Proposes to analyze selected sonnets of Sh on certain themes and to compare and contrast "his treatment of those themes and their treatment by other poets." Section 1, "Poetry as Immortalisation from Pindar to Shakespeare," contains a chapter on "Shakespeare and the Roman Poets" that suggests several links between *Son.* and Horace and Ovid. The relationship between Horace's ode *Diffugere nives* (4.7), which insists that we all end as *pulvis et umbra*, and the Censorinus and Lollius odes (4.8,9), which proclaim the immortalizing power of poetry, is nearly the same as that between two pairs of Sh's sonnets, 64 and 65 and 73 and 74. Finds it likely that Sh was familiar with Horace's *Odes*: They are the two European poets who have written best on poetry as the defier of time. Notes also Sh's appropriation of Ovid's comments on the same theme, especially at the end of the *Metamorphoses*. Chapter 2, "Shakespeare and Petrarch," contains the observation that, in considering the theme of poetry's power to eternize, Sh stands in a "uniquely mediatorial position between the ancient and the modern" worlds because, while Ovid and Horace celebrate poetry in itself, Sh and Petrarch always subordinate it to the person they profess to honor. The inwardness of his sonnets distinguishes Sh from his pagan forebears.

Section 2, "Devouring Time and Fading Beauty from the Greek Anthology to Shakespeare," speculates in chapter 1 on why the themes of *carpe diem* and *carpe florem* are totally absent from *Son.*: Unlike the ancients, Sh refuses to collaborate with Time. Chapter 4, "Personifications of Time, Age and Youth by Ovid, Horace and Shakespeare," notes passages in *Son.*, especially 60, that might have been suggested by Ovid, especially the Pythagorean passage in *Metamorphoses* 15. Lists several personifications of Age and Time from Horace's *Odes* and then several from *Son.*

Section 3, "Hyperbole and Religiousness in Shakespeare's Expressions of His Love," explains in chapter 1, "Shakespeare's un-Platonic Hyperbole," that what in *Son.* has been taken as Platonism is actually a kind of inverted Platonism. See item 2496.

2502 Lerner, Laurence. "Ovid and the Elizabethans." *Ovid Renewed: Ovidian Influences on Literature and Art from the Middle Ages to the Twentieth Century*. Ed. Charles Martindale. Cambridge: Cambridge U. P., 1988, pp. 121–35.

Cites Ovid's *Amores* as background for Sh's Sonnet 140, which advises the poet's mistress to pretend virtue even if she is not virtuous. Shows that in *Ven.*, Sh, like Ovid before him, used digressions both to mock and to celebrate his subject.

2503 Levi, Peter. *The Art of Poetry: The Oxford Lectures, 1984–1989*. New Haven: Yale U. P., 1991. viii + 331 pp.

The lecture on "Shakespeare's Sonnets" discusses the classical connections of a number of sonnets. The sonnet to John Florio, signed Phaethon, expresses the same "soaring ambition" as the passage from Ovid the poet put on the title page of *Ven*. The slow pace of *Son.*, which is not that of dramatic poetry, may come from the "pondering of foreign or of Latin poetry as one translates it." Sh adapted two Venus and Cupid sonnets from the Palatine Anthology; his concern with what the lover might say in a given situation arose from Ovid's *Heroides*; and his notions about the immortality of poetry came from Horace and Ovid.

2504 Maxwell, J. C. "'Rebel Powers': Shakespeare and Daniel." *N&Q*, 14 (1967), 139.

Points out that Sh may have taken the phrase "rebel powers" in Sonnet 146 from Daniel's *Cleopatra* (1594).

2505 McKernan, John J. "The Influence of Erasmus on Shakespeare's Sonnets." *SRASP*, 11 (1986), 72–91.

Refers briefly to Cicero and Seneca, the classical models for Erasmus's letters and his theories about letter writing, in the course of arguing that Sh used images and themes from Eragmus's *De Conscribendis Epistolis*, especially chapter 47, containing an exhortation to marriage, in composing Sonnets 1–20. Revision of part of item 2506.

2506 McKernan, John Joseph. "An Investigation of the Epistolary Nature of Shakespeare's Sonnets 1–126." Ph.D. dissertation, Boston University, 1980. *DAI*, 41 (1980–81), 2125-A.

Detects four modes of epistolary verse in the Renaissance, two inspired by Horace and two by Ovid. A direct influence on *Son.* was Erasmus, whose textbook *De*

Conscribendis Epistolis (1522) was widely used in English schools. One chapter in this work, translated by Thomas Wilson as "An Epistle to Persuade a Young Gentleman to Marriage" and included in his *The Arte of Rhetorique* (1553), was used by Sh in Sonnets 1–20. Ovid's *Heroides, Tristia,* and *Epistulae Ex Ponto* also influenced Sh. The Pontic epistles, with their *topoi* of distance and absence, are particularly significant for Sonnets 1–126. Part revised as item 2505.

2507 Muir, Kenneth. "Blundeville, Wyatt and Shakespeare." *N&Q,* 8 (1961), 293–94.

Thomas Blundeville, in a translation of an essay from Plutarch's *Moralia* on contentment of mind (1561), used the phrase "pleasant remembrance of things past." Wyatt used the same phrase in his translation of the essay, and Blundeville may have borrowed it from him. It was later used in one of Sh's sonnets.

2508 Muir, Kenneth. *Shakespeare's Sonnets.* (Unwin Critical Library.) London: George Allen & Unwin, 1979. xi + 179 pp.

Notes the connections of *Son.*, particularly 55, with the works of Horace and Ovid, especially in the treatment of time and in the poet's boast of his work's immortality and his ability to confer immortality on those he celebrates.

2509 Nowottny, Winifred. "Some Features of Form and Style in Sonnets 97–126." *New Essays on Shakespeare's Sonnets.* Ed. Hilton Landry. New York: AMS P., 1976, pp. 65–107.

Notes "a quality of poise" that is especially evident in Sonnets 97–126. Comments on a reference in Sonnets 113 and 114 to the same passage in Ovid's *Metamorphoses* (1.7) describing chaos before the creation. Regards the repetition of this allusion as evidence that 114 is "a recasting of 113, worked up into a closer and wittier texture."

2510 Ong, W. J. "Commonplace Rhapsody: Textor, Zwingli and Shakespeare." *Classical Influences on European Culture a.d. 1500–1700.* Ed. R. R. Bolgar. Cambridge: Cambridge U.P., 1976, pp. 91–126. Reprint. *Interfaces of the Word: Studies in the Evolution of Consciousness and Culture.* Ithaca: Cornell U. P., 1977, pp. 147–88.

Studies the commonplace tradition in the Renaissance. Calls attention to the way in which knowledge of the past—mostly from classical antiquity—was made available to Renaissance readers in systematic collections by humanists like Ravisius Textor (c. 1470–1524). One of Textor's works, *Epitheta,* is "a collection of standard qualifiers and substitutes for nouns [that] a writer of Latin poetry imitating the classics might use." In writing Sonnet 129, which is "almost entirely a piling up of epithets," Sh seems to have used the *Epitheta*: Under *luxuria* (for "lust in action") and *libido* (for lustful appetite), Textor has "striking equivalents for every epithet in this sonnet."

2511 Oshio, Toshiko. "*The Sonnets*: From the Poems to the Poet." *ShakSt,* 12 (1972–73), 46–71.

Analyzes several groups of *Son.* Cites Lucretius, Ovid, and Horace as forming the background for Sh's treatment of transitoriness in Sonnets 1–17. Recalls the Ovidian and Horatian origins of the poet's claim to immortality for his verse in contrast to the mutability of worldly things.

2512 Patterson, Annabel M. *Hermogenes and the Renaissance: Seven Ideas of Style.* Princeton: Princeton U. P., 1970. xv + 240 pp.

Proposes to investigate the influence of Hermogenes of Tarsus, a rhetorician of the 2nd c. A.D., in the Renaissance. Describes Hermogenes' Seven Ideas of style as found in his book *Concerning Ideas*; links them with the concept of decorum; and treats them in relation to "the major nondramatic genres of poetry" in the Renaissance. *Son.* make use of the two Ideas of Truth and Beauty, exploring their opposition and the ways in which they can be made interchangeable. Throughout *Son.*, Sh uses rhetorical figures associated with the Ideas of Truth and Beauty. For example, in connection with the Idea of Truth, there is "a whole group of sonnets which all take their impetus and structure from the figures of doubt, hesitation, and self-blame."

2513 Peterson, Douglas L. *The English Lyric from Wyatt to Donne: A History of the Plain and Eloquent Styles.* Princeton: Princeton U. P., 1967. viii + 391 pp.

Chapter 6, on *Son.*, calls attention to Sh's familiarity with the handbooks of rhetoric. This is especially evident in the use of "the grammatical trope of antithesis" and other rhetorical devices in Sonnet 129, which may in fact be based on passages from Thomas Wilson's *Arte of Rhetorique.* Comments that though *Son.* sometimes make use of the plain style and criticize courtly literary practice, they are chiefly representative of the eloquent style.

2514 Pirkhofer, Anton M. "The Beauty of Truth: The Dramatic Character of Shakespeare's Sonnets." *Essays on Shakespeare's Sonnets.* Ed. Hilton Landry. New York: AMS P., 1976, pp. 109–28.

Discerns "a public function" assumed by the speaker in *Son.*, which distinguishes him from the speakers of most contemporary sonnets. The speaker resembles "the chorus leader in Greek tragedy" warning the protagonist about "impending evil." Certain sonnets also seem to include an analogue to "the chorus proper" of the Greeks. This "formal affinity" is not surprising in view of "the fact that in Sonnet 7 Shakespeare traces the mythic career of Helios or Phoebus, which seems to be the classical prototype underlying the demythologized stories of *De Casibus Virorum Illustrium.*" Another classical affinity is the parallel between two types of sonnets (those of fate and of character) and the same two types of tragedy.

2515 Platt, Michael. "Shakespearean Wisdom?" *Shakespeare as Political Thinker.* Eds. John Alvis and Thomas G. West. Durham, N. C.: Carolina Academic P., 1981, pp. 257–76.

Uses Aristotle's ideas about "the great-souled man" in the *Ethics* to understand who the "they" of Sonnet 94 refers to. Discovers that, though there are similarities between the type of being Sh is describing and the great-souled man, Sh's conception goes beyond Aristotle: Sonnet 94's subject seems to be one who is "a unification of what is high in antique philosophy and what is high in Christianity." Concludes that "they" are dramatists.

2516 Poisson, Rodney. "Unequal Friendship: Shakespeare's Sonnets 18–126." *New Essays on Shakespeare's Sonnets.* Ed. Hilton Landry. New York: AMS P., 1976, pp. 1–19.

Examines Sonnets 18–126 in the light of "the friendship material of classical philosophy" as it was known to the Renaissance through works like Cicero's *De Amicitia,* Montaigne's "Of Friendship," and Marsilio Ficino's *Commentary on Plato's Symposium.* Sh begins with idealized friendship between youth and older friend, but, with the instinct of the dramatist, he injects this classic pattern with a "social disparity which puts strain on it."

2517 Roche, Thomas P. Jr. "How Petrarchan is Shakespeare?" *Shakespeare's Art from a Comparative Perspective.* Ed. Wendell M. Aycock. (Proceedings: Comparative Literature Symposium, Texas Tech U., 12.) Lubbock: Texas Tech P., 1981, pp. 147–64.

Begins by arguing that Petrarch, in his sonnets, is concerned with undercutting the cupidinous love of the flesh and with measuring its shortcomings against the sacrificial love of Christianity. Finds that *Son.* are Petrarchan in this way. Sonnets 153 and 154 borrow Cupid, assorted nymphs, and a pastoral setting from the poems of Anacreon, recently rediscovered, and use these Greek trappings "to generalize and distance the issues that have been at stake in the first 152 sonnets." It is possible to understand 153 and 154 as offering a Christian cure for "naturalistic" love, but Will, the speaker, is too enmeshed in worldly things to take advantage of it.

2518 Schaar, Claes. "'Qui me alit me extinguit.'" *ES*, 49 (1968), 326–27.

Suggests that lines 9–12 of Sonnet 73 refer to a well-known emblem, an extinguished torch turned upside down, with the motto, *Qui me alit, me extinguit*, as found, for example, in Geoffrey Whitney's *A Choice of Emblemes* (1586). "Consum'd with that which it was nourish'd by" (line 12) thus describes "the approach of death (life that creates also destroys)."

2519 Schwartz, Jerome. "Aspects of Androgyny in the Renaissance." *Human Sexuality in the Middle Ages and Renaissance*. (U. of Pittsburgh Publications on the Middle Ages and the Renaissance 4.) Ed. Douglas Radcliffe-Umstead. Pittsburgh: Center for Medieval and Renaissance Studies, U. of Pittsburgh, 1978, pp. 121–31.

Traces the Renaissance idea of the androgyne as a symbol of union and balance of opposites (masculine and feminine, pagan and Christian) back to the fable told by Aristophanes in Plato's *Symposium*. Notes the optimistic view of Marsilio Ficino, whose *Commentary* on the *Symposium* reads the myth of the androgyne as representative of the perfect state of the soul. By the second half of the 16th c., there was skepticism about the potential for harmony in matters of love, and the image of the hermaphrodite became correspondingly ambivalent. In *Son.*, the poet's exploration of his "bisexual sensibility" draws on the notion of the Neoplatonic androgyne but recognizes the earlier Renaissance dream of "bipolarity and conflict" as "overoptimistic illusion."

2520 Sen Gupta, Satya Prasad. *Some Aspects of Shakespeare's Sonnets*. Calcutta: Vidyodaya Library, 1966. 118 pp.

Chapter 4, "Platonism in Shakespeare's Sonnets," argues that Sh absorbed Platonic thought indirectly, through Castiglione and "the entire Petrarchan tradition," but not from the Italian Neoplatonic philosophers. Cites the *Phaedrus* and the *Symposium* to foreground several Platonic beliefs—"the love of the youth, the love of beauty, and the reproduction of beauty"—that Sh incorporates in *Son*. Chapter 8, on the impersonality of *Son.*, briefly mentions classical echoes.

2521 Simonds, Peggy Muñoz. "Eros and Anteros in Shakespeare's Sonnets 153 and 154: An Iconographical Study." *Spenser Studies*, 7 (1986), 261–85, 311–22.

Argues that Sonnets 153 and 154, both of which derive from an epigram in *The Greek Anthology* by Marianus Scholasticus, are companion pieces partly inspired by "a popular humanist tradition of two opposing Cupids—namely the Renaissance topos of Eros and Anteros." The basic myth with which Sh is working is the account of the theft of the sleeping Cupid's torch by one of Diana's nymphs. The story of Eros and Anteros, Venus's two sons, was first reported by Pausanias in the 2nd c. A.D.; in classical times, it was held to represent "reciprocal or mutual love." In the Renaissance, the emblem of Venus's two sons competing could represent marital love or the mutual love "between God and the human soul." Under the influence of philosophers like Marsilio Ficino, Renaissance humanists like Andrea Alciati altered the Eros–Anteros myth to represent a Platonic opposition between earthly and heavenly, sensual and rational, vicious and virtuous. Detects throughout *Son.* a series of "wild gyrations" between sensual love and awareness of virtue that sets up the two final poems in the sequence. Sonnet 153 expresses "the hopeless paradox of physical love" and the frustration of the poet–lover, who burns for metaphysical truth but is in thrall to "the slippery inadequacies of words and to images drawn from the material world." Sh seems to have conflated two classical traditions about love's bath to suggest in 154 a Neoplatonic cure for the problems summed up in 153.

2522 Singh, Satyanarain. "The Theme of Immortality in Shakespeare's Sonnets." *Osmania Journal of English Studies*, 4 (1964), 125–40.

Argues that *Son.* are neither Christian nor Platonic but ultimately advocate "discipline and control of the senses as being conducive to realization of the power inherent in man."

2523 Smith, Hallett. *The Tension of the Lyre: Poetry in Shakespeare's Sonnets.* San Marino, California: Huntington Library, 1981. xii + 172 pp.

The introduction comments that Sh's concern in *Son.* with "the passage of time—whether there had been deterioration, progress, or neither"—was stimulated by his reading of Ovid's *Metamorphoses*, especially the long speech of Pythagoras near the end.

2524 Stanivukovic, Goran. "The Erasmian Echo in Shakespeare's Sonnet 60." *N&Q*, 37 (1990), 173–74.

Suggests that Erasmus's *Parabolae sive milia* (1514), a compendium of wise sayings adapted from Seneca and Plutarch, lies behind the subtlety with which Sh treats the "devouring time" theme in Sonnet 60.

2525 Strachan, Peter. "The Linguistic Contexts of the Elizabethan Love Sonnet." D.Phil. thesis, University of Oxford, 1987. *DAI*, 51 (1990–91), 172-A.

Maintains that the love sonnet sequence flourished in the 1590s because it was able "to engage major issues concerning the vernacular, by means of emphasizing the linguistic surface over the predictable conventions of content." Argues for "an affective approach to criticism." Considers classical texts on rhetoric in chapter 2 and major 16th-c. English texts "on logic, rhetoric, and poetics" in chapter 3. Other chapters deal with "the response of poetry between 1557 and 1600 to these contexts." Includes a reading of *Son.* in view of this background and commentary.

2526 Thomson, Patricia. "The Date Clue in Shakespeare's Sonnet 98." *Neophil*, 50 (1966), 262–69.

Makes a case for dating Sonnet 98 in the 1580s, when Saturn and the sun were in conjunction four times. Refers to Sh's knowledge of traditional astrology.

2527 Trueman, A. W. "Sonnet 130 and *The Aeneid*." *SQ*, 25 (1974), 129–30.

Proposes that the last two lines of Sonnet 130 echo the final clause of a passage in the *Aeneid*, 1.402–405.

2527a Vickers, Brian. *Classical Rhetoric in English Poetry.* New York: St. Martin's P., 1970. Reprint. Carbondale: Southern Illinois U. P., 1989. iii + 186 pp.

Chapter 1 provides a concise history of rhetoric, beginning with Greece and Rome and including the Middle Ages and the English Renaissance. Chapter 2 is entitled "The Processes of Rhetoric," and includes discussion of the parts of an oration and the three types of oratory. Chapter 3 classifies and discusses the functions of the figures of rhetoric. Chapter 4 lists several of the figures (for example, *asyndeton* and *gradatio*). Defines each figure and then gives one or more examples from classical literature followed by examples from English literature, including many from *Son.* Chapter 5, The Rhetorical Analysis of English Poetry," includes a reading of Sonnet 129 that foregrounds the poet's use of figures.

2528 Waddington, Raymond B. "Shakespeare's Sonnet 15 and the Art of Memory." *The Rhetoric of Renaissance Poetry from Wyatt to Milton.* Eds. Thomas O. Sloan and Raymond B. Waddington. Berkeley: U. of California P., 1974, pp. 96–122.

Maintains that Sonnet 15 makes use of the tradition of Prudence, whose most prominent source in the Renaissance was Cicero's *De Inventione*. Cicero assigns three parts to Prudence: memory, intelligence, and foresight. It is this notion of Prudence and its connection with time—derived from Cicero, influenced by Platonic thought, and Christianized by St. Augustine—that informs the structure of Sonnet 15. Such a view of the sonnet makes it possible to read the three dominant metaphors of the first quatrain (*grows*, *stage*, and *stars*) as "constituent members of one figurative construct."

2529 West, Michael. "The Internal Dialogue of Shakespeare's Sonnet 146." *SQ*, 25 (1974), 109–22.

Finds a Platonic element in "the radical Pauline dichotomy between the flesh and the spirit," one of the two Christian traditions that Sh struggles to balance in Sonnet 146.

2530 Wilson, John Dover, ed. *The Sonnets*. (New Shakespeare.) Cambridge: Cambridge U. P., 1966. cxxvi + 267 pp. 2nd ed., 1967.

Section 5 of the introduction, "Themes and Sources," asserts that the main source for the sonnets on Time the devourer (like Sonnet 55) was Golding's version of Ovid's *Metamorphoses*. The motion of the sea waves in Sonnet 60 and the constant "encroachment of land on sea and sea on land" in Sonnet 64 echo specific passages in Ovid.

The Taming of the Shrew

2531 Barnett, Louise. "Ovid and *The Taming of the Shrew*." *BSUF*, 20, no. 3 (1979), 16–22.

Insists that Ovidian ideas inform *Shr.* and enable Sh to transmute his sources into a new and coherent whole. The induction, which presents the Lord's superficial transformation of Sly, makes several allusions to the *Metamorphoses*. Sly, however, is like many of the other minor characters in that his change is "neither permanent nor genuinely reflective of his real self." The metamorphoses of Katharina by Petruchio and of Petruchio by love are more authentically Ovidian because they reveal the characters' inner selves. Petruchio's wooing of Katharina is an ironic or parodic deployment of the exaggerated compliance Ovid recommends to lovers in the *Ars Amatoria*.

2532 Farley-Hills, David. *The Comic in Renaissance Comedy*. Totowa, New Jersey: Barnes & Noble, 1981. x + 189 pp.

Notes, in a chapter on *Shr.*, that classical allusion "is unusually intrusive" in this play. Lucentio, burning with love at first sight, views himself as Dido to his servant Tranio's Anna; Tranio responds with advice from Terence that his master had better escape from his bondage of love with as little harm as possible. In the scene of the first Latin lesson, Lucentio, disguised as Cambio the schoolmaster, chooses as his text the letter in Ovid's *Heroides* in which Penelope complains that her husband has not yet returned, while she fears that he may have abandoned her. Proposes that Lucentio, who has seen himself as Dido, may be seeing himself here as "the imploring Penelope." The added idea in this letter of love as a disruptive force would have made it an appropriate choice for Sh's purpose. Tranio indicates that Bianca is a source of trouble when he compares her to "Leda's daughter"; Lucentio similarly compares her to Europa. Jupiter appears in the role of "unnatural seducer" in the pictures Sly is offered in the induction. In another Latin lesson, Lucentio is reading Ovid's *Ars Amatoria*. Petruchio ironically wishes the classical roles of Diana and Lucrece on Kate, in both cases projecting on her "an alluringness she does not have, but the Lucrece comparison suggests the tragic results of love and reflects the kind of ambivalence to love" that is implied in the other classical references.

2532a Garner, Bryan A. "Shakespeare's *The Taming of the Shrew*, V.ii.54." *Expl*, 41 (Spring 1983), 16–17.

Points out an instance of *hypallage*, by means of which Petruchio's use of "currish" (*Shr.*, V.ii.54) applies both to Tranio as creater (in the previous two lines) of a simile comparing himself to a greyhound and to the greyhound that is the subject of this simile. In addition, "currish" puns on the Latin root *cur-* "to run," which refers back to Tranio's use of two verbs for runnin ("runs" and "catches").

2533 Harrold, William E. "Shakespeare's Use of *Mostellaria* in *The Taming of the Shrew*." *SJH*, 1970, 188–94.

Begins by summarizing the evidence to date that Sh used Plautus's *Mostellaria* in composing *Shr.* Supports this theory with additional points: For example, the roughhousing of Grumio and Tranio in *Shr.* (I.i) may have been suggested by the servants beating each other in *Mostellaria*; and the banquet motif in Plautus may have found its way into *Shr.* (V.ii). Provides a chart showing the relationship among *Mostellaria*, *Shr.*, and *The Taming of A Shrew*. Concludes that *Shr.* and *A Shrew* derive from a common source by Sh and that Sh consulted *Mostellaria* twice, "once in writing the common source" and once in writing *Shr.*

2534 Homan, Sidney. "Induction to the Theater." *Shakespearean Metadrama*. Ed. John W. Blanpied. MLA Special Session 206, 1978. Rochester: U. of Rochester Department of English, 1978, pp. 2–27.

Sees in *Shr.* a concern with two changes "necessary for perpetuating the illusions of the stage": The spectator is drawn from the real world into the fictive world within the theater, and the playwright and the director convert an individual actor into a character. Notes that this focus on transformation is strengthened by the presence of Ovid throughout the play, beginning with the descriptions in the induction by the Lord and his servants of the mythological pictures they will show to Christopher Sly.

2535 Hosley, Richard, ed. *The Taming of the Shrew*. (Pelican Shakespeare.) Baltimore: Penguin, 1964. 138 pp.

The introduction observes that the subplot is based on George Gascoigne's *I Supposes* (1566), which in turn is based on Ludovico Ariosto's *I Suppositi* (1509), an early example of "Italian Renaissance comedy in the classical tradition represented by Menander, Plautus, and Terence." The introduction and text are revised as part of item 0496.

2536 Ibrahim, Gamal Abdel-Nasser T. "Patterns and Themes in Shakespeare's Early Comedies." Ph.D. dissertation, University of Glasgow, 1983. *DAI*, 49 (1988–89), 3369-A.

Chapter 2 examines classical allusions in *Shr.*

2537 Martin, Randall. "Kates for the Table and Kates of the Mind: A Social Metaphor in *The Taming of the Shrew*." *ESC*, 17 (1991), 1–20.

Attempts to understand *Shr.* by placing it in historical context; the play reflects genuinely contradictory Elizabethan attitudes about women. Notes the influence of Neoplatonic theory, most notably propounded by Marsilio Ficino (*In Convivium Platonis De Amore Commentarius*, 1475) and by such polemical writers as Cornelius Agrippa (*Of the Nobilitie and Excellencie of Womankynde*, 1542), which discounts the physical differences between men and women and argues for intellectual and moral equality. Neoplatonic ideas about love were encoded in the familiar metaphor of the banquet of senses, in which each course focuses on one sense and there is a movement from lower to higher senses. The metaphor can be inverted to signify a descent into pure sensuality, in which case the banquet is called "Ovidian." Sh uses this metaphor to show that the identity-altering joke on Christopher Sly and the wooing of Bianca move in an Ovidian direction, downward toward sensuality and materialism. Though Petruchio's ideas about love and marriage reflect some of the enlightened Neoplatonic views, he does not reform his society. The sense of intellectual equality that he and Katharina come to share remains at the end a purely private arrangement, embedded in and dominated by a patriarchal dramatic and social structure. Notes that the classical allusions in the early part of the play help to distinguish the various characters' attitudes toward sexual relationships.

2538   Oliver, H. J., ed. *The Taming of the Shrew.* (Oxford Shakespeare.) Oxford: Clarendon P., 1982. 248 pp.

The introduction mentions, in discussing *Shr.*'s style, that there is in the play a tendency toward exaggerated "literariness," often involving classical allusions. The classical allusions in the second part of the induction represent deliberate overwriting, indicating "the pleasure taken by the intriguers in their intrigue, and their awareness of the glorious inappropriateness of references to Adonis, Cytherea, Io, and Daphne when addressing Christopher Sly."

2539   Perret, Marion. "'A Hair of the Shrew....'" *HSL*, 11 (1979), 36–40.

Calls attention to Petruchio's homeopathic treatment of Kate's shrewishness in *Shr.* Cites ancient authorities—Dioscorides, Hippocrates, and Pliny, for example—who suggest that to treat a shrew bite, one should use a shrew "as or in medicine applied to the wound." Sh could have known of this cure from many sources, and his audience would have readily seen the analogy between such a procedure and what Petruchio is doing with Kate.

2540   Roberts, Jeanne Addison. "Horses and Hermaphrodites: Metamorphoses in *The Taming of the Shrew*." *SQ*, 34 (1983), 159–171.

Maintains that acknowledgment of the Ovidian resonances of *Shr.* can lead to an appreciation of the significant romance elements embedded in its main action of realistic farce. The play's Ovidian connections are clearly established by two lines from *Heroides* in Bianca's first Latin lesson (III.i.28–29) and a reference to the *Ars Amatoria* in the second Latin lesson (IV.ii.7). Allusions to Adonis and Cytherea, Daphne and Apollo, and Io are among a large number that probably come from the *Metamorphoses*. As employed by Sh, images of metamorphosis usually signal characters' transformation for the better, a key feature of romance. Sly improves from a bestial drunkard to a husband and a lord. Kate and Petruchio, after attempting to dehumanize each other with animal epithets, experience a positive transformation on the road to Padua. In this scene (IV.v), Kate echoes a speech from the *Metamorphoses* by Salmacis, a young woman, to Hermaphroditus, the young man with whom she will merge to become a hermaphrodite. A common Elizabethan symbol for the miracle of marriage, the hermaphrodite here replaces images of disorder, in particular the unruly horses that earlier had thrown both Kate and Petruchio. At this point, having established a cooperative relationship that makes the consummation of their marriage possible, Kate and Petruchio mount their horses and ride to Padua together. Revised as part of chapter 2 of item 0901.

2541   Rudd, Niall. "*The Taming of the Shrew*: Notes on Some Classical Allusions." *Hermathena*, 129 (1980), 23–28.

Cites Ovid's *Metamorphoses* in the original Latin and in Golding's translation to establish connections between Ovid and *Shr.* and to show how Sh treats Ovid similarly in *Shr.* and in several other works (*PP, MND, Ven., Luc.*). Observes further, regarding I.i, that Tranio's witty remark about Ovid means the Roman poet is to be considered "an outcast from the Augustan world"; that Lucentio's comparison of himself to Dido is appropriate, given the parallel between his situation of falling in love suddenly and against all expectation and that of the Carthaginian queen in the *Aeneid*; and that Lucentio's exchange with Tranio about burning, pining, and perishing is a recollection not only of certain language but also of a comic situation in *The Eunuch* of Terence.

2542 Thompson, Ann, ed. *The Taming of the Shrew.* (New Cambridge Shakespeare.) Cambridge: Cambridge U. P., 1984. xiii + 190 pp.

The introduction notes that, while the taming plot has its origin in oral tradition, the subplot of *Shr.* can be "traced back beyond its immediate Renaissance sources in Gascoigne's *Supposes* and Ariosto's *I Suppositi* to Roman comedy."

2543 Tillyard, E. M. W. "Some Consequences of a Lacuna in *The Taming of the Shrew*." *ES*, 43 (1962), 330–35.

Suggests an emendation for Hortensio's assertion that "this is / The patroness of heavenly harmony" (*Shr.*, III.i.4–5). It seems likely that "this" refers to something mentioned just before Bianca's two tutors enter, and Urania, as established in Pythagorean lore, was "the soul of the fixed stars" who presided over the music of the spheres. In its emended form, the passage would read, "this Urania is / The patroness of heavenly harmony."

THE TEMPEST

2544 Barber, Lester E. "*The Tempest* and New Comedy." *SQ*, 21 (1970), 207–11.

Cites an article published in 1955 by Bernard Knox suggesting that "the design of *The Tempest* is founded on certain of the stock patterns of Greek and Latin New Comedy." Although essentially sound, Knox's argument distorts the tradition of classical comedy in some respects and oversimplifies "the situations of Shakespeare's play." According to Knox, Ariel and Caliban are, "respectively, the clever and the disgruntled slaves of Roman comedy." It is true that there are two slave types in Roman comedy, but they are not distinguished in the way Knox contends. Knox also accepts the traditional assumption that New Comedy slaves are motivated by a strong desire for liberty, but in only a few plays is this true. Ariel, whose activities are planned by Prospero, is not "a good example of the clever Roman slave" who invents his own intrigues. Caliban is more a "New World savage" than a Roman slave, who by contrast is always civilized. The similarities between *Tmp.* and New Comedy warrant using the term "analogue" but nothing more.

2545 Berger, Harry Jr. "Miraculous Harp: A Reading of Shakespeare's *Tempest*." *ShakS*, 5 (1969), 253–83. Reprint. *Second World and Green World: Studies in Renaissance Fiction–Making.* Ed. John Patrick Lynch. Berkeley: U. of California P., 1988, pp. 147–85.

Rejects the "sentimental" reading of *Tmp.*, which has Prospero putting his suffering behind him and causing others in the play to suffer in order to effect a reconciliation. In this view, Prospero willingly renounces his magical powers and prepares to return to Milan. The play's chief thrust is in other directions, however. Prospero's "study" derives from a meliorist view of man consonant with that of the Florentine Neoplatonists: He is private and inward, and he wishes to use art and magic to uproot the accumulated evils of civilization and return to an ancient golden age. He is, at least for part of the play, like Raphael Hythloday in More's *Utopia*, a frustrated idealist wishing for a new world with an idyllic society engendered more or less spontaneously, not laboriously built up over the centuries. The mention of Amphion's "miraculous harp" (II.i.88) by Antonio in poking fun at Gonzalo provides an important emblem for the play. Originally, the harp raised the walls of Thebes by music. Antonio uses it to jeer at Gonzalo's somewhat shaky vision of creating a golden world on the island, but it can also be applied to Prospero's more serious attempt to do the same thing. In this connection, it stands for fantasy, for the magical power to rearrange history, for the resources of art to create things new. Through the play's Virgilian references, which suggest that civilization's "progress" is an arduous pilgrimage, never reaching a goal, never erasing the burdensome past to make possible a fresh start, we arrive at a perspective on Prospero's endeavor: His work of twelve years on the island, or of three hours, will not "finally jeopardize the good, or uproot the evil of the ancient globe we inherit and transmit." Prospero's disenchantment with this project comes near the end of act IV, when he becomes convinced that Caliban is "the real model of man." Increasingly pessimistic, he says farewell to his magic, but then proceeds to hog the stage as "actor, director, and hero." He is clearly reluctant to take leave of his harp, but at the end of the epilogue he lays it aside, "preparing to confront life with only the ordinary means of persuasion."

2546 Berger, Karol. "Prospero's Art." *ShakS*, 10 (1977), 211–39.

Discusses Prospero's art as a kind of spiritual and artistic magic deriving ultimately from the Florentine Neoplatonists, particularly Marsilio Ficino. The methods used by Prospero are Ficinian; that is, they are primarily artistic and musical. During the play, he undermines one of the proudest Renaissance myths of man, that of "the dignity of the divinely free magus," as well as the more modern myth of "the nobility of the natural savage." But Prospero's humanism permits him to maintain a delicate balance between a sense of people's limitations and their potentialities.

2546a Bond, Ronald B. "Labour, Ease and *The Tempest* as Pastoral Romance." *JEGP*, 77 (1978), 330–42.

Cites ancient writers like Horace, Virgil, and Cicero to support the proposition that *Tmp.* tempers the classical tradition of pastoral by emphasizing labor in the arduous activity that Prospero undertakes to educate himself and others for civic duty. Prospero synthesizes *otium* (leisure) and *negotium* (work), two things that are kept apart in classical pastoral. The "facile sentimentalism" of ancient pastoral is qualified with "the puritanical conviction that sloth is sinful," and the play "exults not in the pleasures accruing to *otium*, but in the satisfactions of tasks well done."

2547 Boss, Judith E. "The Golden Age, Cockaigne, and Utopia in *The Fairie Queene* and *The Tempest*." *GaR*, 26 (1972), 145–55.

Describes the three utopian traditions known in the Renaissance. The notion of a Golden Age of innocence had been described by Hesiod in his *Works and Days*, echoed by Ovid and Virgil, and fused with the Christian myth of a lost paradise. The tradition of Cockaigne derived from the idea that "fallen man's infected Will would tempt him to seek private benefits rather than public good in a paradise of sensual pleasures that explicitly contrasted with the tradition of Eden or the Golden Age." Literary antecedents for Cockaigne include Circe's isle in the *Odyssey*, the *Satyricon* of Petronius, Apuleius's *The Golden Ass*, and the poetry of Callimachus, Anacreon, and Ovid. According to Neoplatonists like Marsilio Ficino, Pietro Pomponazzi, and Giovanni Pico della Mirandola, man could follow his reason and thus be god-like; or he could follow his vegetative and sensitive nature and become brutish. Rational men would be suited for a Golden Age, while brutish men would be fitted only for Cockaigne. Since these two ways of living could not exist in the world simultaneously, the philosophers' utopia offered a way to incorporate them into a functioning society. In *Tmp.*, Sh shows the rational, god-like man (Prospero) creating a utopia by establishing a hierarchical commonwealth. Elements of the Golden Age (Gonzalo's "plantation of the isle" speech and the appearance of Juno and Ceres) and Cockaigne (the conspiracy) traditions are also woven into the play.

2548 Boughner, Daniel C. "Jonsonian Structure in *The Tempest.*" *SQ*, 21 (1970), 3–10.

Maintains that in *Tmp.*, Sh uses the neoclassical four-part structure for comedy first used by Terence in *Andria*; described by Aelius Donatus, a grammarian of the 4th c. A.D.; revived by 16th-c. Italian writers like Machiavelli; given further critical definition by J. C. Scaliger in his *Poetics* (1561); and adapted to the English stage by Ben Jonson. According to Scaliger, the four parts of a comedy are the *protasis* (in which "the principal subject of the story is narrated without disclosure of the outcome"); the *epitasis* ("the section in which the turmoil of events is either stirred or intensified"); the *catastasis* (the phase in which the plot "is thrown into confusion by the tempest to which fortune has led it"); and the *catastrophe* ("the conversion of all troubles of the plot into unexpected calm"). Sh exploits the full flexibility of this structure (which does not depend on act divisions) in *Tmp.* by developing a very long *protasis* that includes exposition and the introduction of four subactions (acts I–II); by complicating the subactions during the *epitasis*, which includes acts III and IV and the early part of V; by bringing to a climax in V.i the question of whether Prospero will take vengeance on his enemies (the *catastasis*); and by reuniting the characters in a happy ending and releasing the audience from its fear and uncertainty in the *catastrophe.*

2549 Bradbrook, M. C. "Romance, Farewell!: *The Tempest.*" *ELR*, 1 (1971), 239–49.

Maintains that *Tmp.* includes transformed elements of old romances, harmonized into a Jacobean play. Severity of control, most clearly seen in strict observance of the unities, helps Sh build up to "an abdication of the play world."

2550 Carnes, Valerie. "Mind, Imagination, and Art in Shakespeare's *The Tempest.*" *NDQ*, 35 (1967), 93–103.

Provides an overview of Aristotelian and Platonic notions of "the relationship of mind, imagination, and art" as held in the Renaissance and then explores *Tmp.* in light of these notions. Both Aristotelian and Neoplatonic thought "conceive knowledge as transmitted through a hierarchy of powers; from the outer senses to the inner senses (imagination and/or phantasy) and thence to a higher rational power (thought, will, or understanding)." The major difference is that for Neoplatonists like Ficino there is a power above the rational faculty, *mens*, "a mystic, even supernatural, illumination." In *Tmp.*, Sh uses both Aristotelian and Neoplatonic notions, though the latter predominate. Neoplatonic themes in *Tmp.* include magic, music, language, and love in all of its forms. Also, the "Platonic image of the *theatrum mundi*" becomes "fused with the Neoplatonic doctrine of illumination and thus catches up many of the play's comments on imagination and art." Prospero's renunciation of "a quasi-Platonic realm of ideas and essences" is "both practical and Platonic."

2551 Carnicelli, D. D. "The Widow and the Phoenix: Dido, Carthage, and Tunis in *The Tempest.*" *HLB*, 27 (1979), 389–433.

Proposes to explain the references to Dido, Carthage, and Tunis in the conversation between Gonzalo and the courtiers in *Tmp.* (II.i) by reference to a wide range of authorities, classical (for example, Virgil and Livy) and contemporary (for example, Leo Africanus's *Description of Africa* [1526] and Richard Hakluyt's *Voyages*). This background material shows that there were varying opinions during Sh's time about Dido: She could be admired as the chaste, responsible queen in book 1 of the *Aeneid* or scorned as the victim of passion in book 4. That Gonzalo sees her one way and the courtiers another is not a competition over who is right; rather, it suggests one of the major concerns of the play: "the untrustworthiness of human perception and the shifting nature of reality." The background material also casts light on Gonzalo's confusion of Carthage and Tunis. In ancient and recent sources, the two cities were both seen as powerful symbols of the endless process of decay and regeneration. These contradictory attitudes raise for the characters, the audience, and the reader the question of whether we can know anything, of whether "the reality of a given experience may be illusory."

2551a Clark, Sandra. *William Shakespeare: "The Tempest."* (Penguin Critical Studies.) Harmondsworth: Penguin, 1988. 95 pp.

Includes a chapter on Renaissance magic, which discusses the derivation from classical sources like Plato and Pythagoras of ideas about controlling the natural world by exercising spiritual discipline. These ideas, which influenced *Tmp.*, were developed in the Renaissance by Marsilio Ficino, Cornelius Agrippa, and the Englishman John Dee. The chapter on sources includes comment on Sh's use of Ovid's *Metamorphoses* and possibly the Hellenistic romance *Daphnis and Chloe*.

2552 Clayton, M. G. "'Tempests and such like drolleries': Jonson, Shakespeare and the Figure of Vergil." Ph.D. thesis, Cambridge University, 1986. *ITA*, 35 (1987), 1083.

Chapter 1 describes various continental Renaissance editions of and commentaries on Virgil. These "esoteric objects" made available to the 16th-c. English reader several options for representing the Roman poet. Chapter 2 analyzes Ben Jonson's works, especially *Poetaster*, to show one way of appropriating Virgil. Chapter 3 contrasts Sh's treatment of Virgil in *Tmp.* with Jonson's. Sh exposes "the limits of the Old World figure and texts," a process that for Jonson is a kind of desecration, as shown in chapter 4's discussion of *Bartholomew Fair*.

2553 Cutts, John P. "Widow Dido: A Note on *The Tempest*." *AN&Q*, 1 (1962–63), 134–35, 150–52.

Offers an explanation for Antonio's reference to "Widow Dido" in *Tmp.* (II.i.79–80) and subsequent lines relating to Dido. The travelers may perceive a parallel "between their own fortunes and those of Aeneas, and do so in a way that humorously suggests they hope such an unmarried patroness as Dido" might come to their aid. In addition, Antonio and Sebastian may have sung the first stanza of the ballad "Queene Dido" or snatches of it, demonstrating their disharmony with "the celestial music of the island."

2554 Davidson, Clifford. "Ariel and the Magic of Prospero in *The Tempest*." *SUS*, 10 (1978), 229–37.

Contends that Prospero's magic in *Tmp.* is "neither purely white nor absolutely black." Explains that in borrowing from the *Aeneid* for the banquet scene in III.iii and from Ovid's *Metamorphoses* for the catalogue of Prospero's feats of art in V.i, Sh carefully selected details that convey this ambivalence. Notes that Prospero is dependent for his skill on the knowledge passed down by generations of learned men, including Hermes Trismegistus.

2555 Davidson, Clifford. "The Masque within *The Tempest*." *Notre Dame English Journal*, 10 (1976), 12–17.

Views the masque in act IV of *Tmp.* as an iconographical key to the play's meaning. Prospero uses the machinery of myth, as interpreted by Renaissance authorities, to make available illumination from a higher realm than ordinary means can penetrate. The first goddess that appears in the masque, Iris, dwells in the air and acts both as Juno's messenger and intermediary between upper and lower regions. Juno represents the harmonizing power of love, and Ceres "is linked with the physical, psychological, and sociological factors [that] sustain life." Ceres mentions her daughter, Proserpine, whose abduction by Pluto and periodic return was interpreted in the Renaissance as "an explanation for the mystery of fertility." Sh might have been inspired to create Prospero's name by Abraham Fraunce, who derived *Proserpine* from the Latin word *prosperpo*, "which is to creep forwards, because the rootes creepe along the body of the earth." Prospero evokes through the masque a Neoplatonic cosmos of innocence, presenting "essential truths," though the magic through which he creates his vision is not blameless.

2556 Davison, Mary Carol. "The Metamorphosis of Odysseus: A Study of Romance Iconography from the *Odyssey* to *The Tempest*." Ph.D. dissertation, Stanford University, 1971. *DAI*, 32 (1971–72), 1467-A.

Surveys scholarship on the ancient and Renaissance romances in part 1 and then sets forth a method of interpreting them. Originating in the *Odyssey*, the romance developed through the *Aeneid* and Latin and Greek prose works like *Daphnis and Chloe*. Writers of the ancient romances used certain conventions closely linked to the symbols of classical art, and passages in these works that seem obscure can be explained if the iconographic symbols are known. The enduring appeal of the romance genre can be illustrated by tracing the Apollonius of Tyre legend from its beginnings in the 2nd c. to *Per*. Part 2 analyzes and interprets *Tmp*. against the background established in part 1. Following the iconographical tradition of romance, Sh composed his last plays as "speaking pictures," thus enabling romance to realize its dramatic potential. The spectacular scenes in his romances depend on symbols drawn from romance tradition and the visual arts. An understanding of these symbols enables the reader to interpret hitherto baffling lines like the quibbles on "widow Dido," as well as come to terms with the whole dramatic spectacle in *Tmp*.

2557 DiMatteo, Anthony. "'The Figure of This Harpy': Shakespeare and the Moralized Ovid." *N&Q*, 38 (1991), 70–72.

Argues that the representation of the harpy (*Tmp*., III.iii) is indebted to an allegorical commentary on the episode of Phineus and the harpies from Ovid's *Metamorphoses*. The commentary, Georg Shuler's *Metamorphosis or Poetic Fables* (1555), interprets Ovid's three harpies as three sorts of men "by whom kings and princes are made miserable": these three types are embodied, respectively, in Sebastian, Antonio, and Alonso. Sh reduces the number of Ovid's harpies from three to one but retains their allegorical significance in his characters.

2558 Drexler, R. D. "Ovid and *The Tempest*." *N&Q*, 28 (1981), 144–45.

Points out that the scene in which Stephano, Trinculo, and Caliban are driven out of Prospero's cave by "*divers Spirits, in shape of dogs and hounds*" (*Tmp*., IV.i) is indebted to Ovid's story of Actaeon. All three usual Renaissance interpretations of the Actaeon myth are relevant to this scene: Actaeon's hounds represent his uncontrolled emotions; Actaeon's fate is a warning against looking too closely into the secrets of princes; and Actaeon himself is seen as the victim of ingratitude.

2559 Ebner, Dean. "*The Tempest*: Rebellion and the Ideal State." *SQ*, 16 (1965), 161–73.

Mentions the classical background for Renaissance visions of utopia like Montaigne's, which is the basis of Gonzalo's primitivism in *Tmp*. Travel accounts by voyagers to the New World also gave the Renaissance idealized pictures of primitive life. Sh, however, would have read accounts of a shipwreck in the Bermudas that contradicted Montaigne's view of the noble savage and that may have helped him to refute that view through his dramatic structure.

2560 Flagstad, Karen. "'Making this Place Paradise': Prospero and the Problem of Caliban in *The Tempest*." *ShakS*, 18 (1986), 205-33.

Investigates *Tmp*. as an exhibit of Shakespearean contrariety, with Prospero as myth–maker god attempting to exclude his opposite, the beast Caliban, and to impose an idealism on the island that reverses the consequences of the Fall. In the masque Prospero orders for Ferdinand and Miranda (IV.i), the classical myth of the Rape of Proserpine, revisioned as the Rape of Miranda, is reversed. However, the interruption of the masque by Prospero's recognition that Caliban cannot be exorcised bears witness to the failure of his utopian project. Revision of part of item 2560a.

2560a Flagstad, Karen. "'Such Stuff As Dreams Are Made On': Shakespeare's *The Tempest* and the Utopian Imagination." Ph.D. dissertation, University of California, Los Angeles, 1978. *DAI*, 39 (1978–79), 6774-A.

Discovers "a magico-utopian analogue" for "the dream of Prospero" in the work of Giordano Bruno. Prospero's masque presents "a Brunian cosmic vision of Paradise regained in which the Rape of Proserpine, the Rape/Fall of Prosperpine/Miranda, is averted. Cupid as counterpart of the would-be Rapist Caliban, the 'beast' Caliban, is effectively expelled." Part revised as item 2560.

2561 Garber, Marjorie. "The Eye of the Storm: Structure and Myth in Shakespeare's *Tempest*." *HUSL*, 8 (1980), 13–43.

Provides a structuralist reading of *Tmp.* that recognizes in Prospero's situation, "poised between Ariel and Caliban," the pattern of Daedalus, "the greatest artisan in all of Greek mythology." Two aspects of the myth of Daedalus—Daedalus as builder of the labyrinth and Daedalus's relationship to his son, Icarus—are important for understanding the deep structure of *Tmp.*

2562 Gardiner, Judith K. "Shakespeare's *The Tempest* IV.i.76–82 (Iris and Hymen)." *Expl*, 35, no. 1 (1976–77), 25–26.

Cites Ceres's greeting to Iris in Prospero's masque, arguing that Iris's "saffron wings" (line 78), not one of her usual attributes, derive from a description of her in Thomas Phaer's translation of the *Aeneid* 4 (1584). Sh borrowed this detail from Virgil because it was commonly associated with Hymen (for example, in Golding's translation of the *Metamorphoses* and in Jonson's *Hymenaei*), and he wanted to make Juno's messenger appropriate for "an epithalamic celebration."

2562a Gillies, John. "Shakespeare's Virginian Masque." *ELH*, 53 (1986), 673–707.

Views *Tmp.* as specifically and profoundly Virginian. Notes that the play dramatizes two important ideas—temperance and fruitfulness—that were associated with "the official portrait of Virginia." These two motifs take "a distinctively Ovidian form," especially in the masque of Ceres. The emphasis on chastity, which in some ways seems excessive, is explicable only when we perceive "the Ovidian link between unchastity and sterility and the Ovidian enmity of Ceres and Venus." Sh is also ultimately indebted to Ovid for the iconography of the moral landscape that the masque presents. Maintains that the more immediate inspiration for the odd combination of temperance and chastity in *Tmp.* is the Ovidian way in which Virginia was constructed in contemporary accounts: that is, as "a temperate and virginal land whose chastity is threatened by her own 'ruder natives.'" The play reveals, however, that Sh was aware of the limitations of this classical inscription of Virginia: For all of his poetic prowess, Prospero is forced to recognize that he cannot "assimilate the nature of Caliban into his European idea of a moralised nature."

2562b Grant, Patrick. "The Magic of Charity: A Background to Prospero." *RES*, 27 (1976), 1–16.

Calls attention to the Neoplatonic background of Prospero's role as magus and masquer. The aristocratic, secretive traditions of the Florentine Neoplatonists, linked with Vitruvius in the masques of the Jacobean court and interpreted through John Dee and Inigo Jones, seem to guide Prospero in his attempt to present "a series of fixed significances" that unveil "a truth in which we participate." The Prospero of the masque, however, is educated through the drama of *Tmp.* to accept and enact the Augustinian principle of charity. Sh thus effects a delicate synthesis between "Hermetic sympathetic magic" and *caritas*.

2563 Gruber, William E. "Heroic Comedy and *The Tempest*." CML, 1 (1980–81), 189–204.

Argues that Sh's comedy, though it conforms chiefly to the features of New Comedy, does incorporate in some of the later plays important features of Old Comedy. Instead of the character types inferior to ourselves (in Aristotle's formulation) who are contained in an artistic construct, Old Comedy provides a hero who is both victim and master of circumstances and whose fantastic vision merges with the play itself. *Tmp.* is the Shakespearean play closest to Old Comedy. Prospero is the comic hero, who is at the same time both actor in the play and author of it; his heroism consists of sacrificing himself and his play so that the audience may participate in the rare vision of revelry his art has wrought.

2564 Hamilton, Donna B. "Defiguring Virgil in *The Tempest*." *Style*, 23 (1989), 352–73.

Provides background on the Renaissance theory of rhetorical imitation to demonstrate that *Tmp.* rigorously imitates the first six books of the *Aeneid*. Imitation involves mastering the parent work in detail as well as being able to conceptualize its patterns. Sh would have had intimate knowledge of Virgil's epic and familiarity with the theories of imitation, which emphasize both revelation and concealment of the parent text. The tempest with which the play begins has an obvious connection with Virgil, but Sh has adjusted the tone of the scene in the direction of comedy. More interesting is the description of Ferdinand swimming to shore (II.i), which is analogous to Virgil's account of the Trojans swimming ashore at Carthage, but the specific details of which come from the episode in which the snakes swim ashore to attack Laocoon and his son. The point is that Sh is not borrowing a plot; he is imitating, which requires that he handle Virgil's text discontinuously. Virgilian patterns that Sh translates include the love affair of Dido and Aeneas (the model for the happy love story of Miranda and Ferdinand); the plot for overthrowing Troy (the basis for a series of ultimately unsuccessful conspiracies in the play); and the character of Aeneas (the pattern for almost all of the male characters in *Tmp.*). Sh was heir to the medieval and Renaissance tradition of reading the *Aeneid* allegorically, and in *Tmp.* he follows the structure imposed on the poem by its commentators to reveal a moral progress; at the same time, he rearranges Virgil's narrative and incorporates it into this structure so that he can also tell "a public story of political commitment." Revised as the first section of part 1 of item 2565.

2565 Hamilton, Donna B. *Virgil and "The Tempest": The Politics of Imitation.* Columbus: Ohio State U. P., 1990. xvi + 185 pp.

Argues that *Tmp.* is, in a clearly recognizable Renaissance sense, a rigorous imitation of the *Aeneid*, which dismantles, reverses, and rewrites its precursor text in response to the "high politics" of 1610, when it was being composed. The introduction emphasizes that the form of writing chosen by Sh, and by most other Renaissance poets for the imitation of Virgil and of other heroic poetry, is epideictic, "a discourse of praise that involves articulation of a society's commonly held values." Though primarily concerned with celebrating virtues, epideictic writing can also be used for argument, persuasion, and criticism.

Part 1, "Imitation and Occasion," begins with a revision of item 2564, which provides a detailed discussion of the Renaissance theory of imitation as it applies to *Tmp.* The second section of part 1 describes three contemporary political issues—"the situation of the royal children, the 1610 parliamentary debates on the royal prerogative, and the colonization projects in Virginia and Ireland"—that have relevance for the play and for Sh's commitment to Virgilian imitation. Though including absolutist discourse that supports the position of King James, Sh uses Virgil to present, in decorous manner, an oppositional argument in favor of constitutionalism.

Part 2 shows how Sh constructs his argument by analysis of "the play's three scenes of spectacle—the harpy banquet scene, the betrothal masque, and the glistering apparel episode"—and of the role of Ferdinand. This rewriting of the *Aeneid* often praises cooperation as an element of the heroic, as well as "discipline, austerity, retrenchment, and limit."

Part 3 comments on "the Virgilian patterns" used by Sh in constructing the character of Prospero and on the issues and rhetoric "of the political debates of 1610, which Prospero, especially in his relations with Ariel and Caliban, replicates."

2565a Hennedy, John F. "*The Tempest* and the Counter-Renaissance." *Studies in the Humanities*, 12, no. 2 (1985), 90–105.

Discerns in *Tmp*. the dramatization of three "Counter-Renaissance" strains of thought: Montaigne's naturalism (Gonzalo), Machiavelli's materialism (Antonio and Sebastian), and magical occultism (Prospero during the first part of the play). Mentions the Neoplatonic influence on occultism. Argues that toward the end of the play the magician's esoteric and elitist perspective is replaced in Prospero by the more rational and balanced view of Renaissance humanism, which is also demonstrated to be superior to the other two philosophies. Notes the classical components of humanism.

2566 Hondo, Masao. "The Meaning of Magic and Masque in *The Tempest*." *Poetry and Drama in the Age of Shakespeare: Essays in Honour of Professor Shonsouke Ishii's Seventieth Birthday*. Eds. Peter Milward and Tetsuo Anzai. (Renaissance Monographs 9.) Tokyo: Renaissance Institute, Sophia U., 1982, pp. 167–83.

Views Prospero as a benign "white magician." The masque Prospero designs to entertain Ferdinand and Miranda includes Juno, queen of love, and Ceres, goddess of harvests, who represent to the young people the ideal of chaste and fertile love. Suggests a parallel between the action of the play and the initiation rites of the Eleusinian mysteries.

2566a Hooker, J. M. "Widow Dido." *N&Q*, 32 (1985), 56–58.

Notes that Sh is the "supreme sympathizer with betrayed women" and that he regarded Aeneas as the wronger of Dido. Analyzes the conversation during which Sebastian and Antonio mock Gonzalo with their gibes about "widow Dido" (*Tmp.*, II.i.98–105). Argues that the inability of these two cynics to sympathize with the Carthaginian queen marks them as uncivilized bores, set in opposition to the love of Ferdinand and Miranda. See item 2588a.

2567 Hulme, Peter. "Hurricanes in the Caribbees: The Constitution of the Discourse of English Colonialism." *1642: Literature and Power in the Seventeenth Century*. Eds. Francis Barker, Jay Bernstein, John Coombes, Peter Hulme, Jennifer Stone, and Jon Stratton. Proceedings of the Essex Conference on the Sociology of Literature, July 1980. Colchester: Department of Literature, U. of Essex, 1981, pp. 55–83.

Examines English texts from the first half of the 17th c., especially *Tmp*., to observe the process by which the ideological discourse of colonialism is constituted. Cites the account of Odysseus's visit to the country of the Cyclops in book 9 of the *Odyssey* and an extract from George Sandys's commentary in his translation of Ovid's *Metamorphoses* to demonstrate that Caliban has a double valence. As a part of Mediterranean discourse, he is a "wild man or classical monster" (Polyphemus, Minotaur); in terms of the newly emerging Atlantic discourse, he is a ferocious cannibal. His anomalous character, a "compromise formation" in ideological terms, is the key to the play.

2568 Ingram, William. "*The Tempest* and Plato's *Republic*." *CEA*, 28, no. 4 (1966), 11–12.

Proposes a Platonic reading of *Tmp*. In the *Republic*, the individual soul is composed of appetite, spirit, and reason, which when projected on the state, are identified with "the social activities represented by the tradesmen, the auxiliaries or soldiers, and the guardians." Caliban, Ariel, and Prospero fall, respectively, into these three categories. Prospero governs Caliban and Ariel through reason.

2569 James, D. G. *Prospero's Dream.* Oxford: Clarendon P., 1967. viii + 174 pp.

Provides a "live reading" of *Tmp.*, emphasizing its valedictory status, its relationship to Sh's tragedies, its treatment of learning, its incorporation of the New World, and its foregrounding of doctrine. Chapter 3, on Prospero as magician, surveys the history of "European thought and speculation" that lies behind him. Begins with the Neoplatonism of Plotinus in the 3rd c. A.D.; describes the compromise between Neoplatonism, Hermetism, and Christian thought attempted by the Italian humanists Marsilio Ficino and Pico della Mirandola; and explains the breakdown of this confused mixture in the work of Giordano Bruno. In *Tmp.*, we encounter "the farewell of the human imagination to magic and all its ways."

2569a Kay, Dennis C. "Gonzalo's 'Lasting Pillars': *The Tempest*, V.i.208." *SQ*, 35 (1984), 322–24.

Discusses the "lasting pillars" [*Tmp.*, V.i.210] on which Gonzalo proposes to record the miraculous pattern of events that has resulted in the union of Ferdinand and Miranda and the various discoveries involving the rest of the characters. Explains that at the time *Tmp.* was written the pillars, associated with the pillars of Hercules in the motto of Charles V, were "a standard feature of imperial iconography." Queen Elizabeth, for example, appears in a portrait beside a column "decorated with medallions telling the story of Dido and Aeneas." Gonzalo's speech could also be making an allusion to a passage in Flavius Josephus's *Jewish Antiquities* about how Seth's progeny recorded on pillars of brick and stone "truths about the operations of nature and Providence." Gonzalo's pillars, then, are "an emblem of rule, ambition, dynastic continuity, and the operation of Providence" as well as of "apocalyptic prophecy and scientific learning."

2570 King, Katherine Callen. "Go to Hell, Sycorax." *ELN*, 27, no. 4 (1990), 1–3.

Supposes that the name of Sycorax in *Tmp.* is derived from *es korakos*, "to the ravens," a frequent imprecation in Aristophanic comedy expressing the wish that the object of one's wrath will self-destruct. Such a memorable phrase could have been communicated to Sh by one of his learned or semi-learned drinking companions, like Christopher Marlowe or Ben Jonson.

2570a Kirsch, James. "Some Comments about the Masque in Shakespeare's Tempest." *The Shaman from Elko: Papers in Honor of Joseph L. Henderson on His Seventy-Fifth Birthday.* Eds. Gareth Hill, Virginia Detloff, Thomas Kirsch, William McGuire, and Louis Stewart. San Francisco: C. G. Jung Institute, 1978, pp. 81–86.

Conjectures that in the masque directed by Prospero in *Tmp.* (IV.i), Sh "used his knowledge of the Eleusinian mysteries, of the *Aeneid*, and of antique lore to describe his own initiation into the mysteries of spiritual reality."

2571 Kott, Jan. "The *Aeneid* and *The Tempest*." *Arion*, 3 (1976), 424–51.

Asserts that Sh invokes the *Aeneid* throughout *Tmp.*, most notably in "the tempest of the Prologue, the interrupted banquet and the wedding masque." The shipwreck is derived, for example, from book 1 of the *Aeneid*; and Ariel resembles Virgil's Mercury, transformed by Renaissance Neoplatonists into an agent of purification and punishment. The most obviously Virgilian scenes in *Tmp.* are also the most spectacular and depend on the iconographical tradition developed for presenting classical motifs in the court masques and the *dramma per musica*. Despite all of this, however, the Virgilian myths are ultimately rejected by the play. They are evoked, but their presentation is effected through theatrical "tricks," and they prove insubstantial.

2572 Kott, Jan. "*The Tempest*, or Repetition: I. Plantation on a Mythical Island. II. The Three Hours of Purgatory." *Mosaic*, 10, no. 3 (1976–77), 9–36.

Notes that the myths of Greece and Rome informed the thinking of Renaissance colonizers and those who wrote about exploration and colonization. In *Tmp.*, several mythical patterns are repeated—including, prominently, the journeys of Aeneas and Odysseus—and opposed by experience. A case in point is Caliban; his hybrid nature, as classical monster in the old world and slave in the new world, is expressed in a conflict between two different linguistic codes. The play is located both on a Mediterranean island and in the Bermudas. To this island, the old feudal world brings "its exiled rulers" as well as "its great myths of the Golden Age and Utopia." These myths are revived and reenacted, up to a point; but they cannot be sustained, and the hopes they raise are bitterly disappointed. Invokes the *Aeneid* to argue that in *Tmp.* "time reverts to its beginning through the recurrence and repetition of past events." During the three hours of the play's action, the past turns into the future, as it does in the Hades of the *Aeneid*, "so that history can renew itself again." Argues that *Tmp.* subjects the *Aeneid* to a "bitter reading," in which "everything is repeated," but nothing is purified. We are left with the "history of kings and usurpers."

2573 Kramer, Jerome A. "Prospero's Natural Magic." *Inscape*, 9 (1971). [12 pp.].

Approaches *Tmp.* by focusing on "certain of the popular and scholarly conceptions regarding witchcraft, spirit doctrine, magic and philosophy current in sixteenth- and seventeenth-century England." Argues that "Prospero's magic is at all times 'natural'" and suggests that the play's meaning is best explicable in terms of "Prospero's dual roles of man and theurgist." Points out that Neoplatonism, as represented in the writings of Plotinus, Porphyry, Iamblichus, Cornelius Agrippa, and others was an influence on the Elizabethan beliefs regarding magic.

2574 Langbaum, Robert, ed. *The Tempest*. (Signet Classic Shakespeare.) New York: New American Library, 1964. xxxiv + [35]–224 pp.

The introduction notes that Sh sets his island in the Mediterranean in order to bring "the European tradition to bear on the question of nature versus art." The newest ideas about the New World are assimilated to "traditional ideas of the Golden Age and the Garden of Eden." We are reminded of the career of Aeneas, whose adventures exhibit many parallels to those of the court party. The introduction, text, and note on the sources are reprinted as part of item 0123.

2575 Latham, Jacqueline E. M. "The Magic Banquet in *The Tempest*." *ShakS*, 12 (1979), 215–27.

Provides a context for a modern audience to understand the banquet scene (III.iii). Sh's immediate source might have been one of Erasmus's *Colloquies*, "The Epicurean," which places Tantalus at a table but unable to eat the bountiful feast spread before him. Although other classical writers (Homer, Ovid, Horace) mention the story of Tantalus, the tradition of placing him at a banquet table seems to derive from book 6 of the *Aeneid*.

2576 Latham, Jacqueline E. M. "*The Tempest* and *The Masque of Queenes*." *N&Q*, 23 (1976), 162–63.

Suggests that several of the disparate elements that make up *Tmp.* came together in Sh's mind under the influence of Jonson's *Masque of Queenes* (1609). Jonson's marginal notes to the masque refer to Ovid's description of the harpies depriving Phineus of food (*Fasti*, 6). This provides a link to "Ariel's appearance as Harpy." Both Gonzalo's discourse on the commonwealth, "taken from Florio's Montaigne, and Prospero's farewell to magic, based on Medea's speech from Ovid's *Metamorphoses* Book VII," are anticipated in Jonson's masque.

The Tempest

2577 Lees, F. N. "*Dido, Queen of Carthage* and *The Tempest*." *N&Q*, 11 (1964), 147–49.

Suggests that Marlowe's *Dido, Queene of Carthage*, as well as the *Aeneid*, influenced *Tmp.*, II.i, and the treatment of Ferdinand and Miranda.

2578 Lindley, David. "Music, Masque and Meaning in *The Tempest*." *The Court Masque*. Ed. David Lindley. (Revels Plays Companion Library.) Manchester: Manchester U. P., 1984, pp. 47–59.

Notes that the use of music in *Tmp.* accords with the probing of the nature of the masque to which the play devotes itself. We see the older, Neoplatonic idea of "music's correspondence with the music of the spheres" being "replaced by a rhetorical model of its affects."

2578a Lucking, David. The Artifice of Eternity: An Essay on "The Tempest." (Collana del Dipartimento di Lingue e Letterature Straniere 5.) Lecce: Adriatica Ed. Salentina, 1983. 133 pp.

Proposes to investigate the relationship of nature and art in *Tmp*. The play reveals that art is not opposed to nature but is rather implicit within it, "and with the discovery that apparent opposites are really dialectical complements the claims of nature, at first denied and then deliberately repressed, are acknowledged as possessing a real, if not sovereign, validity of their own." Cites Elizabethan commonplaces about the three parts of the soul, derived from Plato, commenting that they are relevant to the relationship between Prospero, Ariel, and Caliban. However, Sh does not present a neatly harmonized picture of the intellectual part of the soul confidently controlling the two lower parts in the configuration of these three characters; Prospero's denial of the real world and his failure in it do not allow us to view the situation in this way. He is in the process of undergoing a kind of symbolic fragmentation, analogous to the differentiation of the elements in the cosmology of Empedocles. According to the latter, the four elements of earth, water, air, and fire are at certain moments mingled together in a sphere under the influence of Love; but then Strife initiates a process of separation. When this process has gone as far as possible, Love begins to draw the elements together again, and eventually "the original homogenous mixture is restored." The cycle is then repeated. By attempting to exclude nature from his world, Prospero shows himself to be undergoing differentiation. Notes later that the connection of fertility with chastity figured in the masque of Ceres and Iris Prospero produces for Ferdinand and Miranda illustrates for the young couple "the perfect concord of body and soul." After the dissolution of his masque, Prospero undergoes a similar process of atonement, though on a different level. There is no final or complete wholeness in the play; the pull of natural chaos is too strong for that. However, the conclusion brings into momentary focus a *theatrum mundi*, "a metaphysical theater in which action is endowed with transcendent meaning."

2579 McGovern, D. S. "'Tempus' in *The Tempest*." *English* (London), 32 (1983), 201–214.

Suggests that in addition to the meanings of "violent storm" and "inward turmoil," the word *tempest* in Sh's title is connected with the Latin word *tempus* and has a range of meanings relating to "time and season." Given Sh's grammar school education, with its emphasis on Latin authors, it is likely that he would have been familiar with the noun *tempestas* ("time or season") and its adjective *tempestivus*, both of which occur in the *Metamorphoses* and the *Georgics*. Examination of other plays reveals that Sh participated in the contemporary practice of using "Latin words in English in their etymological sense." The play's concern with time can be seen in numerous ways: It observes the unity of time; it establishes "a correspondence between past and present events"; it presents time as "occasion or opportunity," as "agent of growth or decay," and as "inner rhythm"; and it calls attention to the delicate relationship between "clock time" and "a regenerative pattern of events whose motive force lies beyond time." Prospero responds appropriately to the occasion offered by time, submits to the decay of senses imposed by time, and promises finally to internalize time's rhythm.

2580   Mebane, John S. *Renaissance Magic and the Return of the Golden Age: The Occult Tradition and Marlowe, Jonson, and Shakespeare.* Lincoln: U. of Nebraska P., 1989. xviii + 309 pp.

Revision of item 2581.

2581   Mebane, John Spencer. "Art and Magic in Marlowe, Jonson, and Shakespeare: The Occult Tradition in *Dr. Faustus, The Alchemist,* and *The Tempest.*" Ph.D. dissertation, Emory University, 1974. *DAI*, 35 (1974–75), 7316-A.

Points out that Renaissance Neoplatonism provided a philosophical foundation for the humanists' optimism about man's ability to recuperate "the universal knowledge and powers [that] Adam possessed before the Fall." Neoplatonic magic became the most radical expression of this optimism. *Tmp.* corroborates much of the occultists' vision about the beneficial power of magic, but Sh also suggests that Prospero's art is limited because of certain ineradicable stains of evil in human nature. Revised as item 2580.

2582   Mowat, Barbara A. "Prospero, Agrippa, and Hocus-Pocus." *ELR*, 11 (1981), 281–303.

Asserts that Prospero's role as a magician has been too narrowly considered. Sh combines in his hero the Neoplatonic magus, the sorcerer (of Apuleian and Ovidian derivation), and the juggler or illusionist.

2583   Orgel, Stephen, ed. *The Tempest.* (Oxford Shakespeare.) London: Oxford U. P., 1987. x + 248 pp.

The introduction contains a discussion of the "points of contact" between Virgil's *Aeneid* and *Tmp.* Notes that the "notorious exchange about widow Dido" is best understood in light of a tradition about her older than that of Virgil and in which she is a model of heroic chastity. Discusses the masque of Iris, Juno, and Ceres (IV.i) as "re-enacting central concerns of the play as a whole. It invokes a myth in which the crucial act of destruction is the rape of a daughter; it finds in the preservation of virginity the promise of civilization and fecundity; and it presents as its patroness of marriage not Hymen but Juno, the goddess who symbolizes royal power as well." Appendix E comprises Medea's incantation (the source of Prospero's "Ye elves of hills" speech [V.i]) both in Ovid's Latin and in Golding's translation.

2584   Paster, Gail Kern. "Montaigne, Dido, and *The Tempest*: 'How Came that Widow in?'" *SQ*, 35 (1984), 91–94.

Proposes to interpret the dialogue in which the references to Dido appear in *Tmp.,* II.i, in light of Montaigne's essay "Of Diverting and Diversions," which serves to mediate between the *Aeneid* and the play.

2585   Pearson, D'Orsay W. "'Unless I Be Reliev'd by Prayer': *The Tempest* in Perspective." *ShakS*, 7 (1974), 253–82.

Takes issue with those who see Prospero as "a positive theurgist," or white magician. Sh was not familiar with the writings of Neoplatonists like Proclus, Plotinus, and Iamblichus, which present a positive view of theurgy. *Tmp.* presents Prospero's art as damnable and unlawful, and Sh's sources were contemporary vernacular condemnations of all magic.

2586 Peterson, Douglas L. "*The Tempest* and Ideal Comedy." *Shakespearean Comedy*. Ed. Maurice Charney. New York: New York Literary Forum, 1980, pp. 99–110.

Describes ideal comedy as "devoted to the depiction and praise of exemplary instances of virtue." It features significant dangers to life that must be overcome through virtuous action. This type of drama originated in the efforts of a group of 16th-c. humanist playwrights "to transform Roman Comedy into a mode of moral instruction." *Tmp.* is an especially significant example among Sh's works.

2587 Phillips, James E. "*The Tempest* and the Renaissance Idea of Man." *SQ*, 15, no. 2 (1964), 147–59. Reprint. *Shakespeare 400: Essays by American Scholars on the Anniversary of the Poet's Birth*. Ed. James G. McManaway. New York: Holt, Rinehart and Winston, 1964, pp. 147–59.

Observes a "striking similarity between the functions of Prospero, Ariel, and Caliban" in *Tmp.* and "the functions of the three parts of the soul—Rational, Sensitive, and Vegetative—almost universally recognized and described in Renaissance literature on the nature of man." Notes the origin of this tripartite scheme in Aristotle and Plato.

2588 Pitcher, John. "A Theatre of the Future: *The Aeneid* and *The Tempest*." *EIC*, 34 (1984), 193–215.

Discusses the connection between the harpy episode in book 3 of the *Aeneid* and III.iii of *Tmp.*, in which Ariel, behaving like a harpy, pronounces a seemingly terrifying judgment against Antonio, Sebastian, and Alonso. Because the harpy in book 3 is an absurd trickster, we might be led to view Ariel's imitation of her as a meretricious manipulation to induce submission. After all, what Ariel says is "spectacularly untrue." However, if we link III.iii with the vision in book 6 of the *Aeneid* in which the guests are punished at a banquet that is eternal and their famine is mocked by a fury like the harpy, we gain a sense of how the often-spectral presence of Virgil can be half-seen "at the back of an episode, a line, or even a single word." Virgilian resonances can have this effect even when there is another, more immediate, source. In the speech in which Prospero abjures his rough magic in act V, mostly adapted from book 7 of Ovid's *Metamorphoses*, a submerged allusion to the fate of the impostor Salmoneus (*Aeneid* 6) allows us "to glimpse that shadow of hell and personal danger which Prospero's magic exposes him to." The fate of Aeneas's helmsman Palinurus, who fell overboard and whose soul can find no rest in the underworld until his body is buried (*Aeneid* 6), haunts the characters in *Tmp.*, especially Alonso and Ferdinand, each of whom believes the other to have been drowned. Discovers a series of invitations from Virgil that Sh could hardly have declined, chief among them Aeneas's observation of the building of a theater by the Tyrians in Carthage (book 1). This account of an actual theater built before Rome existed would have impressed Sh, but more important was the idea, reinforced by Renaissance genre theory, that "the stage-to-be, the structure left uncompleted in an epic poem," is the drama, a new literary kind waiting to emerge from an epic past into the future. *Tmp.* owes to the *Aeneid* "the debt of origin"; there are many indications in the play "of a return to origins, of a longing to start again." Understanding of this relationship can help to contextualize the series of apparently trivial references to Dido, whose abandoned widowship in Virgil stands as an emblem of spoiled beginnings. The story of Ferdinand and Miranda, with the masque of the gods celebrating their wedded future, is a recoding of "the fate of Dido and Aeneas," not only "in terms of plot and theme, but as the activity of a whole new form, a form [that] transcended what the epic form could do." Virgil is present again when Prospero has to dissolve the masque in IV.i; this recalls Aeneas's experience in viewing the story of Troy's siege by the Greeks (*Aeneid* 1). Both Aeneas and Prospero are tempted to assume that a history of pain and grief can be transformed into something "new and consoling without further sacrifice and risk." Each breaks away from the spell of insubstantiality offered by the images before him, though Prospero is escaping from Virgilian images enhanced by his own will and *enargeia*, while Aeneas simply avoids being entrapped in his own story. Like the Theater, the timbers of which crossed water to become the Globe, episodes from the *Aeneid* often reconstitute themselves in *Tmp.* under new names. A striking example is the transformation at sea that saves the Trojan ships from burning (*Aeneid* 9), which not only foregrounds many elements involved in a metamorphosis that would have attracted Sh but also furnishes "the very language" of *Tmp.* See item 2588a.

2588a Pittock, Malcolm. "Widow Dido." *N&Q*, 33 (1986), 368–69.

Challenges the assumption of J. M. Hooker (item 2566a) and John Pitcher (item 2588) that Gonzalo's reference to "Widow Dido" in *Tmp.* (II.i.78) is derived directly from the *Aeneid*. Argues that Gonzalo conceives of Dido as the chaste widow of medieval tradition, found in Giovanni Boccaccio's *De Claris Mulieribus* and *De Casibus Virorum Illustrium* and John Lydgate's *The Fall of Princes*. Antonio and Sebastian mock Gonzalo "because their Dido is Virgil's and Ovid's." The two different perceptions mark Gonzalo as a good man and the others as egotistic, complacent, and ignorant.

2589 Platt, Michael. "Shakespeare's Apology for Poetic Wisdom." *Shakespeare and the Arts: A Collection of Essays from The Ohio Shakespeare Conference, 1981.* Eds. Cecile Cary Williamson and Henry S. Limouze. Washington, D. C.: U. P. of America, 1982, pp. 231–44.

Analyzes *Tmp.*, especially the opening scene of storm and shipwreck, in light of a Renaissance emblem of Fortuna blowing on the sails of a ship at the same time that she directs its course; of Marsilio Ficino's Neoplatonic commentary on such an emblem; and of a passage in Plato's *Laws* (book 4) to which the icon can be traced. The view of Plato's Athenian Stranger about how the wise ruler controls Fortuna can be used to assess Prospero's powers; Sh's magus resembles the Platonic wise ruler, but he is also different in that his art is "both more powerful and less enduring."

2590 Rhoads, Diana Akers. "Shakespeare's Defense of Poetry: *A Midsummer Night's Dream* and *The Tempest*." Ph.D. dissertation, University of Virginia, 1979. *DAI*, 40 (1979–80), 4059-A.

Examines Sh's treatment of the role of the poet in civil society. In *Tmp.*, Sh defends poetry by making Prospero a poet–philosopher–politician. Chapter 5 finds the origin of this combination in Plato's *Republic* and explains Prospero's power in "the practical world" in terms of "Neoplatonic occult philosophy."

2591 Righter, Anne, ed. *The Tempest*. (New Penguin Shakespeare.)Harmondsworth: Penguin, 1968. 187 pp.

The introduction notes the source in Ovid's *Metamorphoses* for Prospero's renunciation of magic in act V. Downplays the importance of most other sources that have been suggested for *Tmp.*, including Virgil's *Aeneid*. Finds the play's adherence to the neoclassical unities to be of great significance. Notes that, paradoxically, the unities do not make *Tmp.* more verisimilar; instead, "they make a strange tale even stranger."

2592 Rockett, William. "Labor and Virtue in *The Tempest*." *SQ*, 24(1973), 77–84.

Describes Prospero's "active spiritual vigilance" to correct "the ill husbandry of his own past." Cites Cicero's attack on Epicurean ethics in the *De Finibus* to show the nobility of Ferdinand's attitude toward the task imposed on him by Prospero: Ferdinand does not seek or expect a reward extrinsic to his labors. In terms of Aristotle's *Nicomachean Ethics*, Ferdinand enjoys true happiness because he wants nothing outside the activity in which he is engaged; in terms of the *Politics*, his willingness to labor for his own sake or for the sake of his friends demonstrates his liberality of spirit.

The Tempest

2593 Schmidgall, Gary. *Shakespeare and the Courtly Aesthetic*. Berkeley: U. of California P., 1981. xxiv + 299 pp.

Discusses *Tmp*. as the most profoundly political play Sh wrote, an exemplar of the "courtly aesthetic." Suggests that the epic is the genre most closely associated with *Tmp*. and that the *Aeneid* is especially relevant to the "'fiction' and structure" of Sh's play. Chapter 3, on the themes promoted by the courtly aesthetic, links *Tmp*. with the *Aeneid* in considering the power of civilization, the glories of a golden age, the establishment of a dynasty, and the nature of a perfect ruler, particularly in his embodiment of temperance. Chapter 5, "The Polarities of Courtly Art," contains a section on "*Furor* and *Pietas*," in which manifestations of these two qualities from the *Aeneid* are opposed to each other in a series of twelve pairs. Prospero and Aeneas resemble each other in the ways they struggle to control the forces of *furor*, which threaten civilization.

2594 Schorin, Gerald. "Approaching the Genre of *The Tempest*." *Shakespeare's Late Plays: Essays in Honor of Charles Crow*. Eds. Richard C. Tobias and Paul G. Zolbrod. Athens: Ohio U. P., 1974, pp. 166–83.

The wide range of critical responses to *Tmp*. can be accounted for by identifying certain archetypal elements that provide a key to its mixed genre. Prospero is a version of the priest–king, subject to usurpation and death, and Ferdinand suffers through an initiation that closely resembles primitive ritual. Ancient death and rebirth rites contain seeds for both tragedy and comedy, and *Tmp*., because it bears the imprint of these rites, exhibits features of both genres, though the comic predominates. Another appropriate label is romance, which involves selective intensification of certain aspects of life, a feat that Prospero's magic manages to achieve on the island. *Tmp*. may thus be considered a tragicomic romance.

2595 Sparacino, Dennis N. "Caliban: Shakespeare's Sources and Analogues." Ph.D. dissertation, New York University, 1973. *DAI*, 34 (1973–74), 5204-A-5205-A.

Examines "the sources and analogues of Sh's Caliban," finding in him a mixture of "comedians, wild men, satyrs, and so on," whose function always involves satire and buffoonery and whose genealogy can be traced back to antiquity, especially "the *fabula Atellana* of Rome and the satyr plays of ancient Greek Dionysiac fertility rites." However, Caliban is directly descended from the Arlecchino figure of the *commedia dell'arte*.

2596 Svendsen, James T. "The Fusion of Comedy and Romance: Plautus' *Rudens* and Shakespeare's *The Tempest*." *From Pen to Performance: Drama as Conceived and Performed*. Ed. Karelisa V. Hartigan. (U. of Florida Department of Classics Comparative Drama Conference Papers 3.) Lanham: U. P. of America, 1983, pp. 121–34.

Analyzes the romance elements in the *Rudens* that make it unique in the Plautine canon, discovers parallels for them in *Tmp*., and suggests that Plautus's play is a source for Sh's. The father–daughter relationship is important in both plays, and in *Tmp*. "both Miranda and Prospero are analogues to Palaestra's search for identity and recognition." Both plays have an exotic, isolated setting, associated with the sea, which is identified with the self-discovery and ultimate freedom of the protagonists. Both plots contain strong resonances of fairy tale and myth. In the *Rudens*, the blocking characters Labrax and Gripus are analogous to Caliban in *Tmp*., and in both plays there is "moral stratification" of sexuality, with the chaste and loyal lovers at the top. In each play, figurative language is patterned to reinforce the supernatural atmosphere. Provides, in a two-page appendix, a summary of scholarly opinion about the influence of the *Rudens* on Sh's plays, especially *Tmp*., and on other Elizabethan drama.

2597 Taylor, A. B. "Shakespeare and the Apes." N&Q, 16 (1969), 144–45.

Argues that Caliban's fear that the conspirators will be changed into apes (*Tmp.*, IV.i.250) was suggested to Sh by Ovid's story of the Cercopes, who were transformed into apes as punishment for their rebellion against the gods (*Metamorphoses* 14).

2598 Taylor, Anthony Brian. "'O brave new world': Abraham Fraunce and *The Tempest.*" *ELN*, 23, no.4 (1985–86), 18–23.

Suggests that Ovid's myth of the Creation was on Sh's mind as he composed *Tmp.* with its world of metamorphoses. On the evidence of Miranda's "brave new world" speech, her repeated use of the word "brave," and Prospero's account of his previous life, it appears that Sh's source for the Creation myth is Abraham Fraunce's translation of parts of the *Metamorphoses* in *Amintas Dale* (1592).

2599 Tovey, Barbara. "Shakespeare's Apology for Imitative Poetry: *The Tempest* and *The Republic.*" *Interpretation*, 11 (1983), 275–316.

Discusses Plato's comments on poetry in *The Republic* and hypothesizes that Sh responded to a hint in book 10 from Socrates, who, having concluded his case against imitative poetry, admits that there might be ways to show that poetry is beneficial. Regards *Tmp.* as a defense of poetry against the charges of Socrates and, further, and perhaps half playfully, "a dramatic and poetic imitation of *The Republic* itself." Discusses the parallels between Prospero and Sh and analyzes the play's characters to establish Platonic resonances. Views Prospero as an imitation of Plato's philosopher-king, who at the play's end possesses "a well-balanced, harmonious soul in which reason rules over the spirited and desiring elements." Even Prospero's view of punishment is identical to that of Plato. Notes that, as Prospero, Sh is "philosopher and poet in one."

2600 Traister, Barbara Howard. *Heavenly Necromancers: The Magician in English Renaissance Drama.* Columbia: U. of Missouri P., 1984. x + 196 pp.

Chapter 1, "Literary and Philosophical Background," notes the close links between magic and Neoplatonism, including a discussion of three theorists of magic (Henry Cornelius Agrippa, Giordano Bruno, and John Dee) active in England during the 16th c. who were influenced by this philosophy. Chapter 6 is devoted to Prospero in *Tmp.*, who "embodies the paradox of superhuman power that is humanly limited." Revision of item 2601.

2601 Traister, Barbara Howard. "Heavenly Necromancy: The Figure of the Magician in Tudor and Stuart Drama." Ph.D. dissertation, Yale University, 1973. *DAI*, 34 (1973–74), 3438-A.

Suggests that Neoplatonists like Ficino may have served as prototypes for the stage figure of the magician in English Renaissance drama. In *Tmp.*, as in other plays in which he has a major role, the magician illustrates man's paradoxical position in the world: "powerful, intelligent, and ambitious to fulfill his potential to raise himself to wisdom and a higher station" but "limited by his flawed humanity." Revised as item 2600.

2601a Urban, Raymond A. "Why Caliban Worships the Man in the Moon." *SQ*, 27 (1976), 203–5.

Explains Stephano's identification of himself with the man in the moon and his insistence that Caliban worship him as indications that Caliban is being "inducted into the religion of drunkards," a Bacchanalian sect invented by the vagabond clerics of the Middle Ages. In this parodic worship, "taverns became churches" and "the Bacchic drinking-songs prayers and hymns."

2602 Vanderslice, Stephen Jerome. "The *Poetics* and *The Tempest*: Prospero as *Spoudaios*, and Comedy Saved." Ph.D. dissertation, University of Dallas, 1979. *DAI*, 41 (1980–81), 4406-A-4407-A.

Develops from hints in the *Poetics* a theory of "serious comedy," a kind of poetry that gives an account of how people come to happiness as defined in the *Ethics* and the *Politics*. A paradigm of this serious comedy can be seen in *Tmp.*, whose protagonist receives an Aristotelian political education.

2603 West, Robert H. "Ariel and the Outer Mystery." *Shakespeare 1564–1964: A Collection of Modern Essays by Various Hands*. Ed. Edward A. Bloom. Providence: Brown U. P., 1964, pp. 115–23.

Treats Ariel in *Tmp.* as part of the outer mystery—the incomprehensible supernatural realm that surrounds us. Ariel derives from "the elaborate literature of Cabalistic pneumatology," which in the Renaissance was combined with Neoplatonic and Christian pneumatologies. The play "invites us to account for Ariel in pneumatological terms, but it does not permit us to be positive we have chosen the right ones." For example, he seems to be a Neoplatonic "elemental," but he does not match the idea of the elemental as described by the Neoplatonic writers Psellus and Paracelsus. Ariel leaves us with a feeling of ambiguity entirely appropriate in a play that "conveys the poignance of man's insubstantial pageant."

2604 West, Robert H. "Ceremonial Magic in *The Tempest*." *Shakespearean Essays*. Eds. Alwin Thaler and Norman Sanders. Knoxville: U. of Tennessee P., 1964, pp. 63–78.

Discusses Sh's borrowing from Medea's incantation speech in the *Metamorphoses* for Prospero's renunciation of his magic. The claim to have raised the dead, though it does not make Prospero a black magician, reinforces the impression of ambiguity in his art. Sh is quite deliberate in creating a tension between the beneficial, hopeful nature of Prospero's enterprise and its darker implications.

2605 Wiltenburg, Robert. "The *Aeneid* in *The Tempest*." *ShS*, 39 (1987), 159–68.

Sums up scholarship on specific Virgilian influences on *Tmp.* and then argues that Sh imitated, with significant modifications, the chief patterns of the *Aeneid* "in its beginning, middle, and end; that is, in its situation, development, and resolution." The Virgilian structure with which Sh begins is marked by "tempests, defiled banquets, and 'widowhood.'" Broadly viewed as the separation of men from their own fulfillment, widowhood in the *Aeneid* seems inevitable, a necessary condition for the pursuit of civilization to which Virgil's hero is committed. Sh's interest in this sense of bereavement is clear in *Tmp.*, but, unlike Virgil, he creates a hopeful world in which separations are only temporary. Both Aeneas and Prospero must resolve the action by sacrifice, but the former must relinquish part of his humanity in destructive fury, while the latter gains peace by surrendering his anger and renouncing his art. Virgil's story of the search for justice is subsumed by Sh into a search for "kindness," a richer foundation for civilization.

2606 Wood, Kamal. "Renaissance Values in *The Tempest*." *Jadavpur Journal of Comparative Literature*, 13 (1975), 42–54.

Argues that in *Tmp.* Sh stays within the Neoplatonic cosmogony that the Renaissance inherited from the Middle Ages. He enriches it, however, by a new sense of power bestowed by man's individualism and a new urgency about the need for the proper use of free will—all derived from the speculations of Renaissance Neoplatonists like Pico della Mirandola. The complex intellectual background of *Tmp.* involves Christian, Platonic, and Neoplatonic elements. Prospero is "the pious magus" of Pico, who through study and meditation brings himself into cooperation with "the powers of the higher Neoplatonic regions." Although Prospero uses his holy magic as a kind of "religious exercise" to bring about reconciliation, forgiveness, and regeneration, he does not wish to escape the order of nature. Points out the new idea of Fortune in the play; instead of being presented in her medieval capriciousness, the goddess is now seen as "bountiful."

2607 Wright, Neil H. "Reality and Illusion as a Philosophical Pattern in *The Tempest.*" *ShakS*, 10 (1977), 241–70.

Focuses on the pattern of illusion and reality in *Tmp.*, arguing that the world of illusion is normative for this play, that Prospero is an artist who works with illusion to reveal truth, and that philosophically *Tmp.* is dominated by the Renaissance notion of the poet as teacher of the highest truth, through feigning. Prospero creates three illusions to instruct Alonso and the court party. The third of these, the banquet that is brought on by strange shapes and then disappears amid lightning and thunder, is best understood by reference to the third book of Virgil's *Aeneid*. In Virgil, Aeneas and his men slaughter the Harpies' cattle but have the meat torn from their hands before they can eat it. Sh, like Virgil, is using the idea of hunger as punishment for a blood crime and as a reminder of guilt.

2608 Zimbardo, Rose Abdelnour. "Form and Disorder in *The Tempest.*" *SQ*, 14 (1963), 49–56.

Calls attention to the neo-Terentian rules that seem to govern the form of *Tmp.* and asks why Sh chose such a formal structure "in dealing with the extravagant materials of romance." The answer may be that the tension between form and content reflects the theme of the play: the conflict between order and chaos and the limited power of art to impose structure on the flux of life.

2609 Zucker, David H. "Miranda's Nature and Her Education." *Thoth*, 5 (1964), 55–61.

Discusses the theory of the *melior natura*, the idea that an earthly thing could be "perfect" in its nature, as it applies to Miranda in *Tmp.* Mentions the ultimate source of the concept in Plato and Aristotle. Miranda's nature, unlike that of Caliban, "can be nurtured by further experience, as well as by homework." From her education on the island, she has gained "a vision at once ideal and limited."

Timon of Athens

2610 Ansari, A. A. "The Protagonist's Dilemma in *Timon of Athens.*" *AJES*, 11 (1986), 142–61.

Contends that the characterization in *Tim.*, especially that of the protagonist, is subordinated to a kind of "conceptual schematism." Timon begins as a generous but uncritical benefactor of everyone; he is so weakened by his obsessive prodigality that he cannot be weaned from it, even by his honest steward. Disappointed by the hypocrisy and betrayal of those on whom he has bestowed so much largesse, Timon, with no one to turn to, isolates himself in the woods outside Athens. Claims that, in contrast to Timon, Alcibiades represents "the Aristotelian 'mean'" and Apemantus "the muted tone of sanity."

2611 Bergeron, David M. "Alchemy and *Timon of Athens.*" *CLAJ*, 13 (1969–70), 364–73.

Argues that alchemical terminology is prominent in the play and, more important, that alchemy is an informing principle for its structure. Timon is a kind of "disillusioned and perverse alchemist," and the play's tripartite structure resembles the process of transmutation in alchemy.

2612 Bergeron, David M. "*Timon of Athens* and Morality Drama." *CLAJ*, 10 (1966–67), 181–88.

Suggests thematic and structural similarities between *Tim.* and *Everyman* to show that Sh is indebted to medieval drama. The conversation between the Painter and the Poet at the beginning of *Tim.* serves much the same purpose as the Prologue to *Everyman*; the role of Flavius is similar to that of Death; and the fates of Timon and Everyman are parallel, at least until each is undeceived, after which they go in opposite directions.

2613 Berlin, Normand. "The Base String: The Underworld in Elizabethan Drama." Ph.D. dissertation, University of California, Berkeley, 1965. *DA*, 25 (1964–65), 4123.

Includes a discussion of *Tim.* Revised as item 2614.

2614 Berlin, Normand. *The Base String: The Underworld in Elizabethan Drama.* Rutherford New Jersey: Farleigh Dickinson U. P., 1968. 244 pp.

Includes in chapter 5, on Sh, a discussion of *Tim.*, a play that both condemns and uses the underworld. Timon's curses include references to whores, thieves, and brothels; and two whores and three banditti appear on stage. These characters represent direct villainy; Timon, in his misanthropy, calls on them to destroy indirect villainy, by which he means the rest of the world. Through the appearance of Alcibiades with Phrynia and Timandra, Sh seems to suggest, as he does in other plays, that contact with the underworld and its ways is necessary for anyone who wishes to rule. Revision of item 2613.

2615 Berry, Ralph. *Shakespearean Structures.* Totowa, New Jersey: Barnes & Noble, 1981. xi + 151 pp.

Chapter 7, on *Tim.*, regards this play as an especially bald instance of Sh's use of two-part structure. For the first part, the key image is the feast, which helps, through the metaphor of eating, to develop a "running commentary" on "human voracity." In part 2, the energizing impulse is the curse, focused in the word "plague," which "unites the senses of anathema and pestilent disease." Explains that gold, an important presence in the play's second part, reveals the corruption of Athenian society and of Timon through its association with sexual disease and excrement. The word "leech" used by Alcibiades near the play's end (V.iv.84) concentrates in itself both the blood-sucking that is the city's problem and the blood-letting that is its only remedy.

2616 Bizley, W. H. "Language and Currency in *Timon of Athens*." *Theoria* (Natal), 44 (1975), 21–42.

Maintains that in *Tim.* Sh achieves tragedy by dramatizing a conflict between "the language of money" and "a more primary language, the language that is in fact its source." Timon himself is presented in this primary language, which uses words like "flowing" and "currency" to create "intrinsic" value through "bounteous presence." The monetary language, on the other hand, describes everything in terms of "equity and exchange." Notes that several things in the play—the jewel, the painting, Timon himself—are presented as current in themselves, not subject to the laws of exchange to establish their value. The dualism characteristic of the mercantilist habit of mind (which distinguishes between public and private) can be seen in the senators' condemnation of Alcibiades' hotheaded friend in III.v, while Alcibiades' defense emphasizes his friend's frank, "undivided posture." Discovers in *Tim.* a contention between the medieval cyclical idea of Fortune (under whose auspices Timon seems to live) and the more abstract notion of individual competition for prosperity (which seems to guide Timon's trafficking compatriots). Further, there are two competing concepts of time: Timon's unitary, common time and the proliferating versions of individuals, each bent on seizing his own now.

2617 Bradbrook, M. C. "*The Comedy of Timon*: A Reveling Play of the Middle Temple." *RenD*, 9 (1966), 83–103.

Presents evidence that *The Comedy of Timon*, a play that survives in manuscript from Sh's time, is a law students' burlesque of *Tim.*, presented at the Middle Temple for the Christmas revels in 1611. This is suggested by the *Comedy*'s use of legal metaphors, by its references to the signs of the zodiac, and by its mockery of Timon as an earthly Jove.

2618 Bradbrook, Muriel C. *The Tragic Pattern of "Timon of Athens."* Cambridge: Cambridge U. P., 1966. 38 pp.

Views *Tim.* as an experimental work for the newly occupied indoor theater in Blackfriars, designed in collaboration with Richard Burbage, who painted the scenery with a variety of emblems. *Tim.* may be designated as a "shew" or a "pageant." It describes Timon's progress through the four seasons, the four humors and their associated elements, and the zodiac. The play also progresses through a series of dramatic forms, often parodying them as it goes. At first, Timon is the Liberality figure of the old moral interludes, but gradually he is transformed into the dupe of city comedy. There is also a masque in the performance of the Amazons. Sh's chief source, Lucian's *Dialogue of Timon*, lies behind the bitter mockery with which Apemantus approaches his world; his spirit dominates act III. In the last two acts, Timon becomes godlike in his hatred, magically discovering all-powerful gold, the common whore of mankind. The Lucianic mood returns in Timon's final two encounters with Athenians, but through his death and burial by the sea he moves toward an ultimate reconciliation with the elemental powers. The play resembles other shews of the time in several ways: Timon is a role, not a character; the structure is articulated by juxtaposition rather than by plot development; and the chief mode of dramatic utterance is paradox. *Tim.*, then, is not unfinished, as some critics have maintained; it is a different kind of work for a new theater. What we have is based on Sh's manuscript, which was performed in 1609. Revised as chapter 8 of item 0186.

2619 Brill, Lesley. "Truth and *Timon of Athens*." *MLQ*, 40 (1979), 17–36.

Uses citations from radically divergent critical opinions of *Tim.*'s characters, story, and genre, as well as analyses of key episodes, to establish that the play requires a variety of responses. The dominant pattern in *Tim.* involves the statement or presentation of a fact, then a commentary on that fact, then one or more reappraisals of the commentary. With no character achieving the status of reliable choric commentator, the tangle of competing assessments makes ethical truth impossible to discern. *Tim.* suggests that the closest man can get to truth is the feigning of art.

2620 Brownlow, F. W. *Two Shakespearean Sequences: "Henry VI" to "Richard II" and "Pericles" to "Timon of Athens."* Pittsburgh: U. of Pittsburgh P., 1977. 245 pp.

Claims that *Tim.* is Sh's last play. It is a metaphysical tragedy that shows neoclassical influence. There is much satire, ranging from Horatian urbanity to Juvenalian savagery. Timon's Athens is a consumer society, where self-interest reigns, and money and traffic are gods. Sh presents a clear analysis of certain current ideas about "the basis and purpose of life." The play is spare in form, with diagrammatic and abstract characterization, features it shares with the playwright's very late work.

2621 Bulman, James C. Jr. "The Date and Production of *Timon* Reconsidered." *ShS*, 27 (1974), 111–27.

Reopens the question of when the "old *Timon*" play was first presented. Considers it to be an Inns of Court production performed "no later than 1602." This conclusion raises the possibility that in composing *Tim.*, Sh was indebted to *Timon* and may have derived most of his Lucianic material from it (rather than directly from Lucian's dialogue of *Timon*). He may also have written *Tim.* "quite a bit earlier than the

Roman plays, perhaps even earlier than *King Lear*." Revision of the appendix of item 0222. Revised as parts of chapters 1 and 5 of item 0220.

2622   Bulman, James C. Jr. "Shakespeare's Use of the *Timon* Comedy." *ShS*, 29 (1976), 103–16.

Contends that the academic *Timon* comedy was a source for *Tim*. Much of the material that Sh is thought to have gleaned directly from *Misanthropos*, Lucian's dialogue about Timon, is more likely to have come from the academic play. As an example, Gelasimus, a character in the comedy, seems to have served as a model for Ventidius: They both "boast of the wealth they inherited when their fathers died." In Lucian, there is no equivalent character. Revised as part of chapter 6 of item 0220.

2623   Bulman, J. C., and J. M. Nosworthy, eds. *Timon*. With the assistance of G. R. Proudfoot. Oxford: Oxford U. P. for the Malone Society, 1978 [1980]. xxii + 86 pp.

Provides an edition of "the comedy of Timon" from MS. 52 in the Dyce Collection at the Victoria and Albert Museum. Notes *Timon*'s borrowings from Ben Jonson's comical satires and from three of Sh's romantic comedies. Points out that the author of *Timon* was "well versed in Greek and Latin literature" and that he used as a source Lucian's dialogue *Misanthropos*, either in the original Greek or the Latin translation by Erasmus. He also used other classical sources. The date of *Timon* (c. 1602–3), its almost certain connection with one of the Inns of Court, and a number of other factors make it likely that Sh used it as a source for *Tim*.

2624   Butler, Francelia. *The Strange Critical Fortunes of "Timon of Athens."* Ames: Iowa State U. P., 1966. xiii + 188 pp.

Surveys the criticism of *Tim*., with sections on "Structure," "Meaning," "*Timon* as a Stage Play," and "Synthesis," and appendices dealing with sources and dating. The five chapters in the first section deal with the early editors, the divided-authorship theory, the fragmentation of the play, the unfinished theory, and the defenders of *Tim*.'s structure. The second section has two chapters, on classical and romantic approaches and on imagery and thematic studies. The third and fourth sections have only one chapter apiece. Summarizes criticism on each topic chronologically, with analytic commentary. Revision of item 2625.

2625   Butler, Francelia McWilliams. "A History of the Literary Criticism of Shakespeare's *Timon of Athens*." Ph.D. dissertation, University of Virginia, 1963. *DA*, 24 (1963), 2459–2460.

Charts the changes in critical estimation of *Tim*. from the 17th c. to the mid-20th c. Revised as item 2624.

2626   Campbell, John Libby Jr. "*Timon of Athens*: An Existential and Psychological Approach." D.A. dissertation, Middle Tennessee State University, 1976. *DAI*, 37 (1976–77), 1560-A.

Uses depth psychology and existential philosophy to reevaluate *Tim*. This approach leads to a more positive assessment of the play than has yet emerged. *Tim*. is revealed as a work wholly by Sh, carefully executed as drama, and demonstrably related to other of his less problematic plays.

2627   Cartelli, Thomas. "The Unaccommodating Text: The Critical Situation of *Timon of Athens*." *Text, Interpretation, Theory*. Eds. James M. Heath and Michael Payne. (*BuR*, 29, no. 2.) Lewisburg: Bucknell U. P.,1985, pp. 81–105.

Attempts a reading of *Tim*. that is based on "performative considerations." Views the play as a "radical experiment in the psychology of theatrical experience" that evokes a tragic world but then refuses to offer the consolations that arise from conventional tragic closure. The audience is constrained "to identify and engage in a critical dialogue with a character who is at once its bane and its ideal, its representative and its accuser, the anatomizer and embodiment of its own values and assumptions." Analyzes Timon's encounters with Apemantus and Alcibiades to show how Sh guides us to identify with the misanthrope, to find his invective appealing. Revised as chapter 8 of item 0243.

2628   Charney, Maurice, ed. *The Life of Timon of Athens.* (Signet Classic Shakespeare.) New York: New American Library, 1965. xxxviii + [39]–239 pp.

The introduction acknowledges that *Tim.* is unfinished in the sense that it lacks final polishing but insists that it is "completely finished in conception." Asserts that the play is well-structured as "a dramatic fable divided into two sharply contrasted parts." Surveys the action scene by scene to demonstrate the integrity of its design. Discovers "inner consistency" in the imagery of *Tim.* and calls attention to the play's "twisted lyricism" and "epigrammatic conciseness." Notes that *Tim.* possesses many of the qualities of "satire and high comedy." Finds connections between *Tim.* and satirical plays like *MM* and *Tro. Tim.* also closely resembles *Cor.*: In neither tragedy does the protagonist have much awareness of what is happening to him. The introductory note to the sources mentions Lucian's dialogue of *Timon* as Sh's "ultimate source," though the means by which the playwright assimilated Lucian are not clear. The most obvious source is North's translation of Plutarch's *Lives*, especially the lives of Marcus Antonius and Alcibiades. Another likely source is *Timon*, an anonymous English academic play from the late 16th c. The introduction, text, and note on the sources are reprinted as part of item 0123.

2629   Chorost, Michael. "Biological Finance in Shakespeare's *Timon of Athens.*" *ELR*, 21 (1991), 349–70.

Asserts that the idea of usury in *Tim.* is derived from Aristotle's comment in the *Politics* that interest accrued in money lending is similar to biological reproduction. Aristotle condemns such interest as "unnatural." Sh based Timon's transformation from philanthrope to misanthrope on these concepts. Discusses the nearly total absence of women and the depiction of nature in the play.

2630   Cook, Ann Jennalie. "Timon's Servant Takes a Wife." *Shakespeare: Text, Subtext, and Context.* Ed. Ronald Dotterer. (Susquehanna University Studies.) Selinsgrove, Pennsylvania: Susquehanna U. P., 1989, pp. 150–56.

Challenges critics who applaud Timon's generosity toward his servant Lucilius (*Tim.*, I.i), which enables the latter to marry. Refers to social custom in Sh's day to prove that Lucilius's wooing of the old Athenian's daughter is utterly reprehensible: He has carried on a clandestine courtship, meeting her at night; he has failed to inform his master of his suit; and the girl is very young. Timon's instant promise of three talents to build Lucilius's fortunes is an early instance of his use of wealth "to overturn social conventions and to reward questionable behavior."

2631   Cook, David. "*Timon of Athens.*" *ShS*, 16 (1963), 83–94.

Suggests that *Tim.* is an examination of departures from natural order in the individual "promoted by subtle forms of pride." The protagonist can be judged according to the commonly accepted Renaissance idea that a man apart from others of his kind is either a god or a beast. Godlike in his indiscriminate generosity at the beginning, Timon sinks to the level of a beast in the play's second half. In neither role can Timon accept the fallible human condition, and in both he shows himself to be presumptuous and lacking in self-knowledge. His rapid shift from generosity to niggardliness also invites us to measure him in terms of Aristotle's distinction in the *Ethics* between liberality and prodigality. Timon's excesses make his behavior an example of the latter. Two contrasting characters help define Timon. Apemantus, a figure in the philosophical tradition of Diogenes, is the unpleasant voice of reason. He is essentially right about Timon's lack of moderation. Alcibiades, in his plea to the Senate (III.v) and his conquest of Athens at the end, recognizes human frailty in ways that Timon is unable to do. Sh shows a great deal of technical daring in constructing the second half of the play out of a series of interviews. However, the attempt to dramatize Timon's last denial of man in act V is not fully realized; the Alcibiades and Timon plots are not integrated; and the dramatic distinction between the cynicism of Timon and that of Apemantus in act IV is not entirely successful. The play is thus "no more than an advanced draft."

2632   Crawford, John W. "Asem—Goldsmith's Solution to Timon's Dilemma." *The Pendulum of Time and Arts,* 14 (September–October 1970), 4–6. Reprint. *Discourse: Essays on English and American Literature. Costerus,* N. S., 14 (1978), 77–81.

Argues, by contrasting Timon with Goldsmith's Asem, that the former's bitter intractability indicates a refusal to appreciate the complexities of life. Timon's attitude is, then, an example of how not to respond to the world.

2633   Davidson, Clifford. "*Timon of Athens:* The Iconography of False Friendship." *HLQ,* 43 (1979–80), 181–200.

Analyzes the iconography of *Tim.* and discovers visual tableaux that elucidate the classical conception of friendship in negative ways. Timon was known to the Renaissance primarily as a hater of mankind; Sh probably learned from Lucian's dialogue of *Timon* that his protagonist could be portrayed as a wealthy man who ruins himself through generosity. Sh presents Timon at the outset as engaging in heroic acts of charity. In Timon's mind, he is following one of friendship's most important precepts, as laid down by Cicero: to promote, through giving, a cohesive society of equals, whose love for each other disdains considerations of profit. As the play goes on, other pronouncements by Cicero on friendship (against covetousness and flattery, in favor of community of goods, and on the need to share misfortune) are relentlessly demonstrated in their negative applications. Timon begins as a picture of both prodigality and magnanimity; the two are inseparable in his character. Several other images help clarify what happens to him. His flattering friends are seen as mirrors and dogs, which, like Actaeon's dogs, turn on their master. In the feasting, a parody of the Last Supper can be discerned, with Timon's friends—so many Judases—devouring him. Timon is shown as prodigally pouring forth his wealth; he is referred to ironically as Plutus, the god of riches; and he is a magician whose spell is broken when he runs out of money. His Epicurean delight in the five senses is presented by the masque of the Amazons, and his fall is predicted in the Poet's "iconographic landscape" of Fortune. The iconography of Icarus probably informs Timon's fall, through which he declines from phoenix to gull. In his last phase, Timon is, on one level, Misanthropy personified, and, on another, "an icon of the bestial man," isolated from his humanity. The play's iconography thus works negatively to exhibit "the failure of an ideal through human fault."

2634   De Alvarez, Leo Paul S. "*Timon of Athens.*" *Shakespeare as Political Thinker.* Eds. John Alvis and Thomas G. West. Durham, North Carolina: Carolina Academic P., 1981, pp. 157–79.

Discusses the three chief characters of *Tim.* in terms of the political. Timon wishes for a golden Athens, filled with beautiful things and free of the harshness of politics. In this desire, he resembles (and may be modelled on) the great Athenian general Cimon, as described by Plutarch. He fails to recognize, however, that this kind of society depends on an unnatural acquisitiveness. In the second half of the play, Timon's alienation involves his recognition that civilization is based on ingratitude in all of man's relationships, what he comes to view as "the eating of men." The gods in the play seem on the one hand to be "the culminating expression of the Athenian love of beauty" and on the other hand as "independent alike of man and of nature." In both cases they are "irrelevant to human action." Apemantus imitates the gods in his self-sufficiency; he tries to teach Timon that all men are beastly, a lesson that Timon fails to learn. In his agreement with the Senate to save Athens, Alcibiades shows himself to be the only person in the entire play who is able to suit his actions to "the beastly nature of man." In creating an "everlasting image" with his grave, Timon finally discovers a way to transform "the beastliness of human existence" and to achieve self-sufficiency. By leaving Alcibiades in control of Athens at the end, Sh suggests an alternative course for Western civilization; that is, an Athens led by Alcibiades would have won the Peloponnesian War. Such an Athens, aware of the need for continual acquisition, would have survived by oscillating between periods of peace and periods of war. Thus would the city prefigure Rome and her exploits.

2635 Elton, W. R., and E. A. Rachut, comps. *A Selective Annotated Bibliography of Shakespeare's "Timon of Athens."* (Studies in Renaissance Drama 11.) Lewiston: Edwin Mellen, 1991. xii + 84 pp.

Covers "items of scholarly or critical interest through 1989." Classifies entries under nine headings, including Editions (22 items), Criticism (315 items), Commentary (119 items), and Sources (59 items). Arranges entries in each category except editions alphabetically by author. Arranges editions chronologically. Provides annotations that are brief and unnumbered.

2636 Erlich, Avi. "Neither to Give nor to Receive: Narcissism in *Timon of Athens.*" *CUNY English Forum*. Eds. Saul N. Brody and Harold Schechter. Vol. 1. New York: AMS P., 1985, pp. 215–30.

Views *Tim.* as "rigorously psychological, a mosaic of fantasies that fit precisely together to delineate a single state of mind," narcissism. Like the true narcissist, Timon evades "relatedness" by forcing everyone, including himself, to fit a stereotype from his disturbed childhood. Other characters besides the protagonist (the Poet, Apemantus, Flavius) share features of Timon's (and the play's) narcissism. Emphasizes the importance to the narcissist of the play's images of women as whores, as devouring mothers, and as dogs. Masochism also appears as another aspect of narcissism.

2637 Fly, Richard D. "The Ending of *Timon of Athens*: A Reconsideration." *Criticism*, 15 (1973), 242–52.

Proposes to account for the disjunctive ending of *Tim.*—which emphasizes both the isolated demise of the protagonist and the reintegration of Athenian society engineered by Alcibiades—by adopting two contrasting viewpoints simultaneously. On the one hand, Timon himself should be seen as a tragic figure, disillusioned with every dimension of human existence, utterly alone in his nihilistic condemnation of the universe. Alcibiades, on the other hand, does not inhabit this visionary world. He works within the boundaries of ordinary history to restore civic order. Finally, Timon's vision of "existential absurdity" throws Alcibiades' reconciliation with Athens into "a bitterly ironic perspective."

2638 Fulton, Robert C. III. "Timon, Cupid, and the Amazons." *ShakS*, 9 (1976), 283–99.

Views the masque in I.ii of *Tim.* as an integral part of the play which concentrates in itself important themes and images. In the masque, Sh skillfully exploited the doubleness that pervaded Renaissance symbolism of Cupid and the Amazons. On the one hand, Cupid could represent harmony, social grace, and festivity; on the other, his blindness might stand for the destructive power of Eros. Amazons were admired for their heroic virtue but disparaged for their ferocity, cruelty, and lack of hospitality. In *Tim.*, we may catch a glimpse of positive qualities from both Cupid and the Amazons, but their negative characteristics are more heavily stressed: They appear in a pageant celebrating sensuality, and Apemantus's bitter, subversive commentary is a continual reminder of their disruptive tendencies. The banquet scene visually presents the imagery through which the play develops Timon's relationship with his city. For example, Timon acts as both whore and bawd to Athens, and Sh later (IV.iii) has him encounter two real whores, often identified by the Elizabethans with Amazons, who will help him to eat Athens as the city has previously cannibalized him. The masque figures, then, are appropriate symbols for the "radical broken world of Timon's Athens." Revision of chapter 3 of item 0421. Revised as chapter 3 of item 0420.

2639   Goldstein, Leonard. "Alcibiades' Revolt in *Timon of Athens*." ZAA, 15 (1967), 256–78.

Argues that Alcibiades' revolt is "a revolt against the new bourgeois ethos." In his debates with the senators and particularly in his animus against usury, Alcibiades "expresses the moral and religious as well as the social resentment of wide sections of the population not only against usury but also against the activities, policies, and values of the bourgeoisie as a whole." The extirpation of usury promised at the end of the play is, from the point of view of capitalism, reactionary: It retreats from the tensions and contradictions "resulting from the growing strength of the manufacturing bourgeoisie."

2640   Hampton, Christopher. *The Ideology of the Text*. Philadelphia: Open U. P., 1990. viii + 200 pp.

Offers a Marxist view of literature as conditioned by the forces of society. Chapter 3, on Sh, includes a discussion of *Tim.* as a raw, almost unmediated presentation of conflict between the ceremonial, orderly medieval world and the aggressively individualistic new world of incipient capitalism.

2641   Handelman, Susan. "*Timon of Athens*: The Rage of Disillusion." AI, 36 (1979), 45–68.

Regards *Tim.* as the exploration of narcissism, which involves "the conflict between the drive to recapture the primal feeling of undifferentiated unity with the original object [the 'nurturant mother' and the self], and the opposing drive to assert one's own separate ego." Timon is unable to provide authentic generosity because he excludes women from his brotherhood of friends; having denied the female, he divides himself and "becomes his opposite." The world of the play is one of "mutually destructive" contrarieties; there is no acceptance of loss, no "transformative magic."

2641a   Heaney, Seamus. *Preoccupations: Selected Prose 1968–1978*. London: Faber and Faber, 1980. 226 pp.

Comments, in a chapter on Gerard Manley Hopkins entitled "'The Fire i' the Flint,'" on the passage in *Tim.* in which the Poet says that the work he is contemplating is "A thing slipp'd idly from me" (I.i.22–27). Observes that the word "slipp'd" hints at "what is accidental, energetic, and genetic in the poetic act."

2642   Hibbard, G. R., ed. *The Life of Timon of Athens*. (New Penguin Shakespeare.) New York: Penguin, 1970. 271 pp.

The introduction characterizes *Tim.* as "the bitterest and most negative of all Shakespeare's tragedies," noting that the generalized quality of the play brings it close to fable and parable. Several loose ends and the unevenness of some of the writing suggest that *Tim.* is unfinished. Discusses sources in Plutarch's lives of Alcibiades and Antony and Lucian's dialogue *Timon*. Links the protagonist's belief in "the inseparability of promise and performance" as "the foundation of human society" to the writings of Aristotle, Cicero, and the 16th-c. humanists. Elaborates on Timon's connection with the extravagance of aristocrats in Sh's day; discerns three movements in the play, in the last of which Timon gains new insight; describes Timon's tragedy as that of "innocence betrayed"; accounts for Timon's obsession with sex; and recognizes that, though Timon never really looks at himself, he does in the last part seem to come to a better understanding of nature's bounty as he shifts his attention from the ingratitude of men to the impersonal rhythms of the sea.

2643 Hinman, Charlton, ed. *The Life of Timon of Athens*. (Pelican Shakespeare.) Baltimore: Penguin, 1964. 128 pp.

The introduction argues that *Tim.* is organized into two sections (I–III and IV–V), that many of its scenes (like the first one) are fully and excellently set forth, that it is essentially complete, but that it contains a number of anomalies suggesting that Sh left it unfinished in some sense. Some of the more serious defects of the play are that the Alcibiades plot is not sufficiently developed, that Timon seems foolish and his errors trivial, and that he gains no self-awareness. Furthermore, Timon's response to his misfortune is "not only unheroic but undramatic." Still, parts of it can be favorably compared with Sh's greatest works. Revised as part of item 0496.

2644 Holbrook, David. "Cambridge Entrance: A Baffling Examination Paper." *English* (London), 35 (1986), 123–36.

Finds fault with an examination question that includes a passage from *Tim.*, IV.iii, in which Timon comments on universal thievery. Argues that this difficult play can be satisfactorily interpreted only in terms of depth psychology, something with which most candidates for university admission have no acquaintance.

2645 Holdsworth, R. V. "Biblical Allusions in *Timon of Athens* and Thomas Middleton." *N&Q*, 37 (1990), 188–92.

Identifies previously unnoticed biblical allusions in five passages of *Tim.* Since these allusions also occur in the works of Thomas Middleton, they shed light on the question of Middleton's part-authorship of *Tim.*

2646 Honigmann, E. A. J. "Timon of Athens." *SQ*, 12 (1961), 3–20.

Presents evidence that for *Tim.* Sh drew more thoroughly on Plutarch than has hitherto been suspected. Instead of using only the miniature life of Timon in Plutarch's *Life of Marcus Antonius* and the bits of information in the *Life of Alcibiades*, the play appropriates names, imagery, and plot details from elsewhere in these two lives, as well as from those of Coriolanus (like Timon, a renegade against his city) and Demetrius. Sh also seems to have borrowed, among other things, meat, tree, and animal images from Lucian's dialogue of *Timon*, probably in the French translation of Filbert Bretin (1582–83). Given the extent of *Tim.*'s dependence on Plutarch and Lucian, the theory of a lost source for Sh's play and the anonymous manuscript *Timon* can be discarded. Many of the problems critics profess to find in *Tim.*—the isolation of the hero, the episodic action, the inconclusive ending, the intellectualizing, and the protagonist's sex-disgust—can be dismissed if it is viewed, like *Tro.*, as an Inn of Court play.

2647 Hunt, John Dixon. "Shakespeare and the *Paragone*: A Reading of *Timon of Athens*." *Images of Shakespeare: Proceedings of the Third Congress of the International Shakespeare Association, 1986*. Eds. Werner Habicht, D. J. Palmer, and Roger Pringle. Newark: U. of Delaware P., 1988, pp. 47–63.

Calls attention to Sh's explicit treatment of the Renaissance concept of the *paragone*, the comparison or competition between the arts of painting and poetry, in *Tim.* Our attention is called to this idea at the very beginning of the play in the rivalry between the Painter and the Poet. Though they both claim to represent Timon, neither is given endorsement by the text; Sh seems to be showing that when the other two arts fail, theater can succeed in representing human beings, especially those difficult to comprehend like Timon. To put it another way, dramatic representation employs both verbal and pictorial art in such a way as to transcend the narrow limits of either one alone. In the later part of his career, Sh was drawn to the more complex presentations of character allowed by dramatic deployment of the *paragone*. In particular, the theme of the *paragone* was suggested to him in Plutarch's "sophisticated biographical material": hence its explicit use in *Tim.* and implicit use in *Cor.* and *Ant.*

2648 Jankowski, Andrzej. *Shakespeare's Idea of Art.* (Uniwersytet Im. Adama Mickiewicza w Poznaniu, Seria Filologia Angielska 22.) Poznan: Adam Mickiewicz U. P., 1988. ix + 156 pp.

Includes a discussion of the poet in *Tim.*, whose "social and economic status parallels Shakespeare's" but who is not Shakespeare's spokesman "as far as theory of poetry is concerned." In theory, poetry should "praise the good and extol their virtues; in practice, poets often praise the vile and show them as virtuous." The poet in *Tim.* advocates praise of the virtuous but seems ready to sacrifice his principle for money.

2649 Janzen, Henry D. "Shakespeare's *Timon of Athens*, III.vi." *Expl*, 36, no. 3 (1977–78), 3–4.

Connects the "lukewarm water" (*Tim.*, III.vi.89) with which Timon asperses his banquet guests with the Spirit of God's condemnation of the "lukewarmness" of the Laodicean Church in Revelation 3:15–16. Notes Timon's antipathy to lukewarmness throughout the play.

2650 Kahn, Coppélia. "'Magic of bounty': *Timon of Athens*, Jacobean Patronage, and Maternal Power." *SQ*, 38 (1987), 34–57.

Joins psychoanalytical and new historical approaches to interpret *Tim.* The play makes use of "the cultural forms that constituted patronage" for the Elizabethans and the Jacobeans: "gift-giving and credit finance, then known as usury." This system of patronage is given a "psychological dimension" through its "core fantasy" of "maternal bounty and maternal betrayal."

2651 Kerrigan, John. "'Knowing the Dead . . .': For Pete Laver 1947–83." *EIC*, 37 (1987), 11–42.

Notes that Sh understood that inscriptions on tombs place the dead in the domain of the god Hermes, "in a territory of interpretation," and explores the origins of this in Greece. Comments on Timon's hermetic epitaph (*Tim.*, V.iv.70–73): "it gives and conceals, names and denies," evoking Alcibiades' hermeneutic response of remembrance. Timon's inscription and what is said about it reveal Sh seeking a connection between language and loss, "and finding it in style itself."

2652 King, Rosalind. "Black Vesper's Pageants: Emblems of Tragic Stagecraft in Shakespeare." *Shakespearian Tragedy.* Eds. Malcolm Bradbury and David Palmer. (Stratford-upon-Avon Studies 20.) London: Edward Arnold, 1984, pp. 76–95.

Discusses the allegory of Fortune introduced by the Poet at the beginning of *Tim.* and the masque of Cupid and the Amazons performed during the first banquet scene of the same play as illustrations of the ways in which Sh uses emblems in his tragedies. These emblems suggest an important theme: "sensual indulgence to the exclusion of all true thought."

2653 Entry deleted.

2654 Knight, G. Wilson. "*Timon of Athens* and Buddhism." *EIC*, 30 (1980), 105–23. Reprint. *Shakespearian Dimensions.* Brighton, Sussex: Harvester P., 1984, pp. 72–91.

Notes several "points of contact" between *Tim.* and Buddhism, including asceticism, emphasis on the forest as a place of enlightenment, sympathy for animal life, vegetarianism, attraction to the symbolic power of gold and jewels, repudiation of lust, compassion, and belief in the desirability of retreating from the world of the senses into a nonperceptual transcendent state.

2655 Knight, G. Wilson. "*Timon of Athens* and Its Dramatic Descendants." *REL*, 2 (1961), 9–18. Reprint. *Stratford Papers on Shakespeare, 1963.* Ed. B. W. Jackson. Toronto: W. J. Gage, 1964, pp. 99–109. Reprint. *Shakespeare and Religion: Essays of Forty Years.* London: 1967, pp. 211–21.

Describes the themes of *Tim.*: A great-souled man, initially generous, is deeply angered by the ingratitude of his former friends; he becomes a "naked prophet of social denunciation" and after discovering gold, he is sought out by representatives of his native city and asked to save them from destruction. Later dramatists who have reworked these themes include Richard Brome (*The City Wit*), John Gay (*The Beggar's Opera*), Henry Fielding (*The Modern Husband*), Richard Cumberland (*The Fashionable Lover*), Richard Sheridan (*The School for Scandal*), M. G. Lewis (*Alfonso, King of Castile*), and W. S. Gilbert (*Dan'l Druce, Blacksmith*).

2656 Knights, L. C. "*Timon of Athens*." *The Morality of Art: Essays Presented to G. Wilson Knight by His Colleagues and Friends.* Ed. D. W. Jefferson. New York: Barnes & Noble, 1969, pp. 1–17. Reprint. *Explorations 3.* Pittsburgh: U. of Pittsburgh P., 1976, pp. 129–44.

Maintains that *Tim.* is unfinished "in the sense that it has not been finally worked over for presentation on the stage." In its use of representative character types and didactic elements, *Tim.* is close to the morality tradition. Timon himself is not admirable as some have maintained: He suffers "self-revulsion, the shattering of an unreal picture and the flight from hitherto concealed aspects of the self that are found insupportable." His "wholesale condemnation of the world" is not noble; rather, it is a means of evading "the pain of self-recognition." Much of what Timon says may be true, but more important is his lack of self-knowledge and integrity (a failing that Alcibiades and the senators share with him).

2657 Konstan, David. "A Dramatic History of Misanthropes." *CompD*, 17 (1983), 97–123.

Discusses *Tim.* as exhibiting one of three important dramatic misanthropes, each one specific to his author's time and place. Provides a survey of Timon's appearances in literature before Sh's play, including Plutarch's lives of Mark Antony and Alcibiades; the *Dialogue of Timon* by Lucian, a Greek writer of the 2nd-c. A.D.; and an anonymous English comedy contemporary with Sh. Notes that the contrast between Timon and his city "is that between a medieval ideal of a natural economy marked by gift-giving and personal ties on the one hand and the new conditions of merchant finance on the other"; each way of life has its own view of the other's besetting vice, whether prodigality or greed. Sh has a complex view of the new state of society, expressed chiefly through the Alcibiades subplot.

2657a Kurrik, Maire Jaanus. *Literature and Negation.* New York: Columbia U. P. 1979. xi + 276 pp.

Regards Timon of Athens as "the greatest figure of pure negation produced in the Renaissance." Argues that Timon negates "not only the other but also himself," recommending "universal suicide." In *Tim.*, we have "willed, subjective nothingness," a demonstration that the self, lacking relationship, has the power to annihilate itself and is willing to exercise that power.

2658 Lancashire, Anne. "*Timon of Athens*: Shakespeare's *Dr. Faustus*." *SQ*, 21 (1970), 35–44.

Contends that in *Tim.*, "Shakespeare, like Marlowe in *Faustus*, is writing his own secularized, anti-traditional morality play." Where Marlowe relies on the psychomachic drama like *Mankind* as a model, Sh "uses the tradition of such plays as *Everyman*." Both playwrights reverse the traditional ending of spiritual salvation. From the beginning of *Tim.*, "as in *Everyman*, and as in none of Shakespeare's generally recognized sources," we sense, "through the eyes of outsiders," that ruin is hovering over "a prosperous protagonist." Like Everyman, Timon loses false friends as his material wealth declines. Apemantus parallels Knowledge in *Everyman*, offering the hero self-knowledge in the secular realm and "a kind of pagan salvation." At this point, Sh turns the morality tradition against itself by having Timon reject "the classical equivalent of spiritual knowledge." Alcibiades, however, having suffered many of the same disappointments as Timon, chooses the mode of behavior appropriate for an Everyman figure when he takes a stand for reconciliation at the end. The morality of *Tim.* helps explain the play's generalized characterization, its episodic plot, and its resemblance to a moral exemplum.

2659 Levin, Harry. "Shakespeare's Misanthrope." *ShS*, 26 (1973), 89–94. Reprint. *Shakespeare and the Revolution of the Times: Perspectives and Commentaries.* Oxford: Oxford U. P., 1976, pp. 197–209.

Notes that the change from gregarious prodigal to misanthrope in the protagonist of *Tim.* is a "sudden recoil rather than a gradual disillusionment." Sh seems to have had trouble depicting stages of alienation. Comments on the presiding influence of Fortune, the absence of sexual love, the role of Apemantus in prefiguring the second half during the first, the predominance of type characters, and the dehumanization of Timon by grief. Concludes that Sh found misanthropy an uncongenial theme.

2660 Levitsky, Ruth. "*Timon*: Shakespeare's *Magnyfycence* and an Embryonic *Lear.*" *ShakS*, 11 (1978), 107–21.

Compares *Tim.* with Skelton's *Magnyfycence* and suggests that *Tim.*'s unity can be better understood if it is viewed as a secular morality in which all other virtues are subsumed in magnificence, a virtue that Skelton's Prince learns (in a Christian context) but that Timon (a pagan) lacks from beginning to end. Magnificence was often equated in Elizabethan thought with fortitude: the ability to stand firm against flattery, to be unswayed by prosperity, and to bear loss without flinching. Cynic and Stoic were often equated. Sh shows some admiration for Cynic–Stoic characters (Timon and Apemantus are two types of Cynics) but finally reveals them as inadequate. Alcibiades represents the Aristotelian ideal of action and is seen as preferable. Flavius is the only character who exhibits magnificence well, and he is too minor to matter. The play finally rejects Cynic–Stoic philosophy as a means of attaining magnificence.

2661 Lewis, Allan. "Shakespeare and the Morality of Money." *Social Research*, 36 (1969), 373–88.

Cites the soliloquy of Philip Faulconbridge (the Bastard) from *Jn.*, II.i, as evidence of a recognition on Sh's part of his society's new materialism, which was making gain into a god. In *Tim.*, the protagonist's bitterness toward gold is a further development of this same attitude.

2662 Lombardo, Agostino. "The Two Utopias of *Timon of Athens.*" *SJW*, 120 (1984), 85–89.

Proposes *Tim.* as Sh's most intense meditation on "the great social and ideological crisis [that] accompanies the birth, in England, of modern man." In *Tim.*, Sh expressed his dismay about "an England dominated by the new economy of profit through the metaphor of an Athens [that] has lost all mythical aspects to assume those of an unmovable, modern Hell." This is achieved by contrasting two utopias: In the first half of the play, Timon, blind to the reality of a mercantile society, believes in an ideal Renaissance polity with the Lord "at the center of a harmonious universe"; in the second half, he attempts to create, through his invective, a negative utopia of destruction. Timon's only weapon, however, is language, which fails to shift "the passive immobility of Gold." Timon is able to enact only "the end of a genre, the impossibilities of tragedy."

2663 Maher, Michael Kevin. "Shakespeare's *Timon of Athens* and Elizabethan Prodigal-Son Plays." Ph.D. dissertation, University of Georgia, 1974. *DAI*, 35 (1974–75), 5353-A.

Points out that *Tim.* shows significant similarity to two Elizabethan moralities, the anonymous *Contention Between Liberalitie and Prodigalitie* and Gascoigne's *The Glasse of Government*. *Tim.*'s resemblance to these two plays, especially in the commercial attitudes of the protagonist and his followers toward their relationship, suggests that it should be classified as a moral play, in which Timon's misanthropic outbursts are excesses to be deplored.

2664 Maxwell, J. C. "Desperate Debts." *N&Q*, 14 (1967), 141.

Points out that "sperate" and "desperate" were used in Sh's time to designate, respectively, debts that had some hope of being paid and those that were irrecoverable. Sh had this dichotomy in mind when he had Hortensius refer to Timon's debts as "desperate" (*Tim.*, III.iv.103–104).

2665 Miola, Robert S. "Timon in Shakespeare's Athens." *SQ*, 31 (1980), 21–30.

Insists that familiarity with popular Elizabethan notions about Athens is essential to understanding *Tim.* From Plato, Aristotle, and Plutarch, as well as other ancient and contemporary commentators, Sh's audience would have been accustomed to viewing Athens as a city whose perennial license and disorder derived inevitably from its democratic polity. Timon's first banquet symbolizes the democratic depravity of the city in its emphasis on the inhabitants' unbridled appetite for food and drink, wealth, and sexual pleasure. The notorious Athenian practice of banishing the city's best men is used by Sh to underline the confusion of democracy. Alcibiades, an honored soldier and loyal friend, is also a hotheaded rebel. His expulsion by the Senate is thus partly justified and partly unjustified. Timon, in his self-banishment, is equally ambiguous. Sh clearly associates him with "well-known Athenian soldiers—Aristides, Themistocles, Cimon—who were banished unjustly." Once out of Athens, however, Timon, unlike "his historical counterparts," behaves ignobly. The movement back to the city at the end of *Tim.* shows Sh employing the widely held idea that Athenian democracy was inherently unstable. Alcibiades' motives in assuming control are suspect, his army disorderly, and his new regime tyrannous; but the suggestion is that any central authority, no matter how seriously compromised, is better than democracy.

2666 Morsberger, Robert E. "*Timon of Athens*: Tragedy or Satire?" *Shakespeare in the Southwest: Some New Directions*. Ed. T. J. Stafford. El Paso: Texas Western P., 1969, pp. 56–70.

Claims that *Tim.* is primarily a satire, directed both at society and at the misanthrope. Three strands of imagery—gold and riches, beasts, and disease, especially venereal—convey a "feeling of universal disgust and loathing for the world." Much of what is said, especially by Timon, about the corruption of society hits home, but it is a mistake to take the misanthrope as a tragic hero. His excessive reactions to ingratitude end by debasing him and making him, even more than Athenian society, an object of scorn and loathing.

2667 Morse, Ruth. "Unfit for Human Consumption: Shakespeare's Unnatural Food." *SJH*, 1983, 125–49.

Focuses on a "large-scale hierarchy of images in Shakespeare which systematically plays on the threats" posed by man's animal nature, "especially in relation to animal-like eating habits and 'unnatural' food, to underscore and convey judgments of characters' moral status." Surveys a number of plays but highlights *Tim.* In the first half of the play, Timon is cannibalized by his guests, including Alcibiades. In the second half, Timon is himself reduced to a bestial level, as he eats roots.

2668 Neiditz, Minerva. "Primary Process Mentation and the Structure of *Timon of Athens*." *HSL*, 11 (1979), 24–35.

Recommends that *Tim.* be approached like a dream, in which we experience "the simultaneity of time, the fulfillment of erotic and aggressive wishes through diction and plot, the predominance of cannibalistic and persecutory imagery, the splitting of four major figures to represent different aspects of the divided self, and the unity [that] depends upon the dramatization of an unconscious mental state." Notes that "the structure of *Tim.* is strongly influenced by primary process mentation which ignores consideration of time, space, and logical consistency, fulfilling wishes magically; and employs symbolism in a crudely associative manner." Revision of part of item 0791.

2669 Nichols, Mariane. "Dramatic Language in Shakespeare, Jonson and Middleton." Ph.D. dissertation, New York University, 1971. *DAI*, 32 (1971–72), 5799-A-5800-A.

Argues that in certain of their works the playwrights discussed made significant use of ideas of "disjunctive art" to create tensions in their audience and that in these works language and style are employed in such an unusual way that they take precedence over all other considerations. Part 2 is a detailed examination of *Tim.*, in which language and attitudes about language are so important to meaning that they come to be "subjects of the drama." The play is a "rhetorical pageant" whose protagonist is vanquished by "the limits of his own verbal universe."

2670 Nichols, Marianna da Vinci. "*Timon of Athens* and the Rhetoric of No." *CahiersE*, 9 (1976), 29–40.

Contends that *Tim.* is about language; it is a rhetorical experiment in which the protagonist takes "his heroic stance as a rigid idealist incapable of ordinary discourse and therefore vulnerable to ordinary men." Timon's "language of absolute negation" lacks reference to "an objective reality" to which the audience can assent. Images of sterility do not convince us of Timon's suffering. Sh seems to have accepted the radical disjunction between word and dramatic meaning in this play, perhaps tiring of the project.

2671 Nuttall, A. D. "*Timon of Athens.*" (Twayne's New Critical Introductions to Shakespeare.) Boston: Twayne, 1989. xxii + 164 pp.

Argues that *Tim.* is a relentlessly intellectual play that dramatizes inhumanity and explores alienation. Analyzes "the succession of figures or postures of the drama" in eight chapters of part 1: "The *Paragone*"; "Timon Among the Suitors"; "One Playwright or Two?"; "The Suitors Press Harder"; "Timon Slighted by His Former Friends"; "Digression: Some Jacobean Attitudes"; "Timon Furibundus"; and "Timon in the Wilderness." Focuses, finally, on "the central parodic version of the eucharistic feast."

2672 Paolucci, Anne. "Marx, Money, and Shakespeare: The Hegelian Core in Marxist Shakespeare-Criticism." *Mosaic*, 10, no. 3 (1976–77), 139–56.

Notes that Marx's discussion of money derives from his contact with Hegel's *Philosophy of Right*. Cites Marx's reaction to the protagonist of *Tim.* to show how he can be distinguished from Hegel. The latter maintains that Timon's experiences need not transform him into a misanthrope, though such a result is understandable. Marx, however, suggests that money, which is to say "exchangeable capital," is itself enough to turn "*any* reasonable, sensible man" into a misanthrope. Claims that Marx might have identified with Alcibiades in his mission to destroy Athens.

2673 Pauls, Peter. "Shakespeare's *Timon of Athens* and Renaissance Diogeniana." *UC*, 3 (1980), 54–66.

Holds that Sh's portrait of Timon is based not only on Lucian, Plutarch, and possibly the anonymous Timon comedy but also on "the numerous allusions to Timon and Diogenes in Renaissance literature generally." The two cynics were associated in continental as well as English literature. There were both "low" and "high" views of Diogenes, the former focusing on his antifeminism and bitterness and the latter on his Stoicism. Sh's Timon is most like the philosophic Diogenes: Though he goes through a railing, bitter phase in acts III and IV, he is rhetorically superior to the profesional cynic Apemantus, and in act V he becomes a reclusive Stoic. Thomas Lodge's *Diogenes in His Singularitie* provides more parallels to Sh's *Tim.* than any other English Renaissance treatment of Diogenes: Like Timon, Lodge's Diogenes lives a Spartan existence, is an enemy of hypocrisy and pretense, and attacks usurers and false friends. He even suggests that one of his flatterers hang himself on "Timon's fig tree" and tells a fable of the sea and the bank that suggests Timon's location of his "ever-lasting mansion" on the shore. Timon lacks the "imperturbable calm" of the noblest Renaissance portraits of Diogenes (like Montaigne's), and he exceeds in imprudence the most extreme world-hating versions of the cynic philosopher. But his strenuous rejection of Fortune and her gifts is worthy of Diogenes at his best. Revision of part of item 2674.

2674 Pauls, Peter. "Shakespeare's *Timon of Athens*: An Examination of the Misanthrope Tradition and Shakespeare's Handling of the Sources." Ph.D. dissertation, University of Wisconsin, 1969. DA, 30 (1969–70), 1146-A-1147-A.

Acknowledges that *Tim.* is unfinished in many of its details and speculates that the task of expanding the scant sources available to Sh preoccupied him to such an extent that he was unable to revise the obviously inferior text. What finish there is in *Tim.* seems largely due to the nature of Sh's source materials. Plutarch's *Life of Alcibiades*, with its emphasis on Alcibiades as a subject of fortune and mutability, might have influenced Sh to portray Timon, by contrast, as "an example of the constant man." The Renaissance treatment of Timon by Richard Barckley, which does not stress Timon's brutishness, may also have provided hints to Sh, who makes Timon's false friends more beastly than he is. More indirect influences—such as "Renaissance treatises on friendship, gratitude, and anger"—may also help explain Sh's handling of the Timon story. In particular, Renaissance Diogeniana is helpful in understanding Sh's depiction of the Timon–Apemantus contrast. Because he lacked adequate sources for this play, Sh was forced to expand his basic materials. In such circumstances, "minor, indirect sources assume a much greater importance, and cross-pollination from plays written previously is more likely." Part revised as item 2673.

2675 Preston, Thomas R. *Not in Timon's Manner: Feeling, Misanthropy, and Satire in Eighteenth-Century England.* (Studies in the Humanities 9.) University: U. of Alabama P., 1975. 217 pp.

Traces, in the first chapter, the history of the traditional misanthrope through the great Timon figures in literature, beginning with portrayals by Plutarch and Lucian. Explains that these early versions present Timon as a malevolent satirist who is himself the object of scorn. Renaissance versions of the character, especially Sh's, continue this tradition of "the satirist satirized."

2676 Ramsey, Jarold W. "Timon's Imitation of Christ." *ShakS*, 2 (1966), 162–73.

Asserts that *Tim.* explores "confounding contraries"—"the contradictions that are *inherent* in human institutions and values." In the first part of the play, Timon's philosophy is "an essentially Christian vision of universal harmony," but it is counterpoised by the selfish preoccupations of other Athenians. This opposition of values is reinforced by two dominant images: water (natural, benign) and gold (artificial, malignant). Timon is "a severely limited man trying to follow certain Christian moral directives without moderation, in the face of a fallen human nature, for which these directives do not account." Through a series of Scriptural images and allusions (like those to the Last Supper during the first banquet), Timon becomes a pre-Christian Christ, "a painfully human caricature of the Son of God." He can live in the world neither as Christ figure nor as misanthrope: In one of Sh's most pessimistic visions, he is simply nullified.

2677   Rasmussen, Eric. "Shakespeare's Use of *Everyman* in *Timon of Athens*." *AN&Q*, 23 (1985), 131–35.

Proposes *Everyman* as a source for *Tim.* on the basis of several similarities: The prologue of *Everyman* outlines the career of the protagonist just as the Poet foretells Timon's future; like Everyman's goods, Timon's prosperity is not his own; neither character anticipates his fall, and each temporizes when faced with ruin; both turn to friends for help; both think of their destruction as a journey; and each is supported by only one faithful follower.

2678   Rauchut, Edward A. "Shakespeare's *Timon of Athens*: Problems of Attribution, Text, Sources, Chronology and Interpretation." Ph.D. dissertation, City University of New York, 1984. *DAI*, 45 (1984–85), 626-A.

Surveys criticism of *Tim.* on each of the five problems mentioned in the title.

2679   Reid, Stephen A. "'I am Misanthropos'—A Psychoanalytic Reading of Shakespeare's *Timon of Athens*." *PsyR*, 56 (1969), 442–52.

Contends that Timon at first is seen denying his persecutory anxiety about the vital things in his life by adopting a "manic defense" against the guilt he feels for destroying in fantasy the things [that] threaten him (in particular, his mother's "bad breast"). Unable to sustain the great energy needed for his manic defense, however, he works himself into bankruptcy, a situation from which he can regress to his earlier persecutory position, "spewing forth the destroyed bad breast—by projecting it on the whole outside world." See item 2688.

2680   Robinson, Christopher. *Lucian and His Influence in Europe*. Chapel Hill: U. of North Carolina P., 1979. vii + 248 pp.

Notes that although Sh based the plot of *Tim.* on Plutarch's *Lives*, certain details "ultimately derive from Lucian." Argues against Sh's direct knowledge of Lucian and concludes that *Tim.* "is Lucianic only in some secondhand and relatively insignificant way."

2681   Ross, Daniel W. "'What a Number of Men Eats Timon': Consumption in *Timon of Athens*." *Iowa State Journal of Research*, 59 (1984–85), 273–84.

Maintains that imagery of consumption—"gastronomic, sexual, and commercial"—pervades *Tim.*, providing a key to Athenian society's besetting sin of greed and to the bitterness that it provokes in Timon and others. In the first part of the play, Timon is both consumer and consumed, as the Athenians throw themselves into an orgy of sensual indulgence, most clearly signified by the masque of Cupid and the Amazons. In acts IV and V, Timon is the severest and most accurate critic of Athenian excesses, asserting that man has become bestial. He assumes the role of instructor to Apemantus, the professional cynic. Because of its consumption, the society of Athens is at the end "used up, worn." Alcibiades' new dispensation promises to halt "the cycle of consumption" and restore balance.

2682   Ruszkiewicz, John J. "Liberality, Friendship, and *Timon of Athens*." *Thoth*, 16 (1975–76), 3–17.

Considers the protagonist of *Tim.* in the light of Renaissance ideas about liberality and friendship. Calls attention to the derivation of most of these ideas from classical authors like Aristotle and Cicero and their assimilation and modification by Renaissance writers like Pierre de la Primaudaye, Sir Thomas Elyot, Thomas Wilson, and Nicholas Haward. As far as liberality is concerned, Timon seems to possess some of Aristotle's qualifications for the practice of this virtue. That is, he is wealthy, and he enjoys giving; furthermore, he is not presented as personally vicious. However, he fails in his practice of liberality by choosing unworthy beneficiaries, by giving in excess, and by refusing all reciprocation. Timon's friendships fail all tests: There is no common ground of thought and feeling, no continuity, no selectivity, no exchange of kindness, and no honesty. Timon neglects to test his friends, something insisted upon by classical and Renaissance moralists, until it is too late. His bitter experience teaches him nothing; he ends by becoming "an active enemy of friendship and liberality." Revised as part of item 2685.

2683 Ruszkiewicz, John J. *"Timon of Athens": An Annotated Bibliography.* (Garland Shakespeare Bibliographies 10.) New York: Garland, 1986. xxvii + 274 pp.

Covers materials published primarily between 1940 and 1980, with a few earlier items and some others from 1981 and 1982. Classifies entries under seven headings, including Criticism (340 items), Sources (24 items), Bibliographies (9 items), and Editions (174 items). Begins each section with the oldest entries and proceeds chronologically. Concludes with an index. Provides substantial annotations.

2684 Ruszkiewicz, John J. "'Traffic's thy god': Wealth and Rhetoric in *Timon of Athens.*" *CCTE Studies*, 51 (Sept. 1986), 20–26.

Analyzes the rhetoric of *Tim.* in terms of its dependence on mercantilism. Emphasizes the greed that pervades Athens. Notes the predominance of wealth imagery in Timon's language before and after his fall, in the refusal of Timon's friends to lend him money, and in the deal made by Alcibiades and the senators to save Athens at the end. The resolution "is achieved through slippery rhetoric" that provides "the only free commerce between untrustworthy men in a world of contingencies." Revision of part of item 2685.

2685 Ruszkiewicz, John Joseph. "Shakespeare's Moral Economics and *Timon of Athens.*" Ph.D. dissertation, Ohio State University, 1977. *DAI*, 38 (1977–78), 2816-A.

Points out that *Tim.*, more than any other Shakespearean play, is focused on the role of "economic forces and moralities" in men's lives. Surveys the treatment of moral–economic themes in Sh's other works and comments, for example, that in *Tro.* lust and riches are equated. *Tim.* sets liberality, the proper use of riches to serve humanity, between the extremes of prodigality and covetousness but avoids the obvious choices of a moral drama in favor of the "more problematic discriminations of tragedy." As a work about economic morality, one of *Tim.*'s virtues is its often faulted irresolution—its unrelenting questioning of human actions and motives "in the commercial sphere." Part is a revision of item 2682; part is revised as item 2684.

2686 Savage, James E. "Ben Jonson and Shakespeare, 1623–1626." *UMSE*, 10 (1969), 25–48.

For *Tim.*, Sh probably borrowed from Jonson's *Sejanus*: Both plays are tragedies of a state, not an individual, and each contains "a massive satirical attack on national corruption." Jonson, in turn, is likely to have borrowed elements of structure and theme from *Tim.* for *The Staple of Newes* (1626). Both plays, for example, open with a group of tradesmen waiting to prey on a prodigal; in each case the prodigal is warned against extravagance, and in both cases the prodigal pays a large sum to advance one of his followers. Jonson's condemnation of usury as cannibalism is reminiscent of *Tim.*, as is his treatment of wealth (Lady Pecunia is like Fortune in Sh's play). Ideas and phrases from *JC, Tro.*, and other plays in Sh also surface in *The Staple of Newes*.

2687 Scott, William O. "The Paradox of Timon's Self-Cursing." *SQ*, 35 (1984), 290–304.

Finds interest in "forms of language that undermine themselves, whether deliberately or not," in Sh. Focuses on "the self-exile of Timon of Athens and the curses he launches at all mankind." Singles out "the paradox of the liar" as something Sh is likely to have been exposed to as a schoolboy. Investigates the ways in which the language of Timon, of Alcibiades, and of Apemantus undermines itself.

2688 Seward, T. C., and M. D. Faber. "A Note on Stephen Reid's Essay, 'I am Misanthropos'—A Psychoanalytic Reading of Shakespeare's *Timon of Athens.*'" *PsyR*, 58 (1971), 617–23.

Summarizes and agrees with much of Reid's argument (item 2679) that Timon's misanthropy results from "his externalizing and attacking his own feelings of guilt which had originated in childhood." Supplies the efficient cause for Timon's regression (which Reid omits): Timon wants to repeat the experience of Ventidius by being forgiven for his evil by his betters. When this fails to happen, he is forced to regress to a stage in which he denies any guilt and sees himself as persecuted.

2688a Shainess, Natalie. "Shakespeare's *Timon of Athens*: The Progress from Naiveté to Cynicism." *Journal of the American Academy of Psychoanalysis*, 12 (1984), 425–40.

Argues that *Tim.* is "one of Shakespeare's greatest plays," an allegory "written with heartfelt purpose." Timon is like a child who has been forced unquestioningly to accept a parent's viewpoint about the goodness of others, and is thus incapable of distinguishing between the genuine and the spurious. When something painful or traumatic occurs that challenges his naivete, he has no defenses, and his outlook is transformed into "all-pervasive cynicism."

2689 Shaw, Catherine M. *"Some Vanity of Mine Art": The Masque in English Renaissance Drama.* 2 vols. Salzburg: Institut für Anglistik und Amerikanistik, U. of Salzburg, 1979. iii + 580 pp.

Analyzes masques and masque elements in other types of drama. Chapter 9, "The Masque in Tragedy," includes a consideration of *Tim.*, which presents a masque of Amazons in I.ii to epitomize the protagonist's "world of illusion" and a parallel banquet scene in III.vi to symbolize his "world of disillusion."

2689a Shaw, Catherine M. "The Visual and the Symbolic in Shakespeare's Masques." *Shakespeare and the Arts: A Collection of Essays from the Ohio Shakespeare Conference, 1981.* Eds. Cecile W. Cary and Henry S. Limouze. Washington, D. C.: University P. of America, 1982, pp. 21–34.

Includes a discussion of the masque in *Tim.*, which is situated so that the audience can juxtapose Timon's uncritical reaction with Apemantus's sardonic undercutting. Contends that the introduction by Cupid is followed by "a dumb show of the senses," which then gives way to the masque of Amazons. The audience is led to view the masque as "an extension of the problem inherent within the *paragone* between the Painter and the Poet in the first scene." In this competition of the arts, the masque truly depicts the characteristic features of Timon's life as "effeminate and bizarre." Notes the iconographic ambivalence of both Cupid (love/licentiousness) and the Amazons (war/prostitution). In the view of the audience, Timon is both bawd and whore.

2690 Shugg, Wallace. "Prostitution in Shakespeare's London." *ShakS*, 10 (1977), 291–313.

Provides an account of the historical conditions under which prostitution was practiced and comments that Sh shows an accurate knowledge of the trade in his plays. There is a vivid description of the symptoms of syphilis in Timon's instructions to the prostitutes (*Tim.*, IV.iii.153–166).

2691 Siegel, Paul N. "Marx, Engels, and the Historical Criticism of Shakespeare." *SJW*, 113 (1977), 124–34.

Notes that Marx and Engels anticipated modern literary scholarship in remarking on Sh's accurate portrayal of the atomized society in which he lived. Marx's perception of capitalism was influenced by his reading of the two apostrophes to gold in *Tim.* (IV.iii.26–47 and 386–397): He commented on the aptness of Sh's linking of money and prostitution.

2692 Šimko, Ján. "*King Lear* and *Timon of Athens*." *PP*, 8 (1965), 320–42.

Notes that *Tim.* addresses a number of problems that arose when the feudal order was being supplanted by the new capitalist dynamic. Discusses the unique and yet generalized nature of Timon's situation; Timon's lack of realism and need for friendship; the play's relatively unelaborated characters; the Alcibiades subplot, taken from Plutarch; the positive representation of "the working petty bourgeoisie" (Flavius); the influence of Lucian's dialogue *Timon*; and the combination of Timon's tragic fate with an optimistic conclusion brought about through the reconciliation promised by Alcibiades.

2693 Slights, William W. E. "*Genera mixta* and *Timon of Athens*." *SP*, 74 (1977), 39–62.

Holds that in *Tim.* Sh was primarily concerned with examining "the proper uses of authority in an established social order." To achieve this end, he blended and modified elements of various dramatic genres. *Tim.* is to some extent modeled on Jacobean stage satire, but its effects have been considerably broadened by the contrasting masque and antimasque movements. In addition, Timon, whose role is somewhat like that of the satirist in Marston and Webster, is given a tragic dimension. Other components come from moralities and interludes, works that share *Tim.*'s concern for community and authority in society. Sh's mix of genres allows him to go beyond the exposure of luxury and flattery that might be expected in the usual stage satire; he is thus able to "explore a tragicomic world which has been inverted and diminished by its most principled citizens."

2694 Soellner, Rolf. *"Timon of Athens": Shakespeare's Pessimistic Tragedy.* Columbus: Ohio State U. P., 1979. 245 pp.

Offers "a comprehensive critical analysis" of *Tim.* "in its dramatic and cultural contexts." Claims that the play is a pessimistic tragedy of great power, on a par with *Ant.* Attempts to contextualize *Tim.* by relating it to Pierre Boaistuau's *Theatrum Mundi* and Richard Barckley's *Discourse on the Felicity of Man* as sources for its *contemptus mundi* and decay-of-the-world rhetoric. Argues that *Tim.* follows the structural formula that the humanists derived from Roman drama and applied to vernacular comedy and tragedy. Includes chapters on Alcibiades (his impact is almost wholly negative), Timon himself (he exemplifies the upward movement characteristic of the tragic hero), and characters like Apemantus and the steward Flavius. Other chapters deal with word patterns and images, economic thought in Sh's society, the competition between painting and poetry, and Fortune as both the dominating influence on Timon and the model for his behavior. The third appendix suggests Plutarch, Lucian, the old *Timon* comedy, and Pliny's *Natural History* as sources.

2695 Steadman, John M. "Iconography and Methodology in Renaissance Dramatic Study: Some Caveats." *SRO*, 7–8, 1972/74 (1975), 39–52.

Cites the episode of Timon's carving his own epitaph and his subsequent burial by the sea in *Tim.*, pointing out how Sh both follows Plutarch's *Lives* and departs from it. This example illustrates the problems that can arise when dramatic texts are interpreted iconographically.

2696 Swigg, R. "*Timon of Athens* and the Growth of Discrimination." *MLR*, 62 (1967), 387–94.

Maintains that *Tim.* "asserts the need for discrimination, for the critical sense which can discern true value amidst the confusion of mixed motives and wrong associations; which can sift and, in its final, lucid judgment, dissociate the pure from the impure." In the early part of the play, Timon is the focus for a divorce between word and deed, promise and performance. Reality is devalued, and confusion reigns. The second half of the play features Timon in isolation, behaving even more irresponsibly in his hatred than he did earlier in his benevolence. The process of debasement is thus exposed: "The tainter is clearly discerned in the act of tainting." As "the supreme, indiscriminating figure of the play," Timon now exemplifies "the absurdity of generalization." The conclusion restores a sense of discrimination: Timon, the creature of chaos, "is contained within and neutralized by an encircling scheme of order"; and in Alcibiades "youthful compassion" is balanced with "aged authority."

2697 Tinker, Michael. "Theme in *Timon of Athens.*" *Shakespeare's Last Plays: Essays in Honor of Charles Crow.* Eds. Richard C. Tobias and Paul G. Zolbrod. Athens: Ohio U. P., 1974, pp. 76–88.

Maintains that *Tim.* is a complete play, unified principally by the imagery of eating. Timon's complete materialism, his tragic failure to rise above the level of beast, is signified by his contrast with Flavius and Alcibiades, two characters who refuse to live by bread alone.

2698 Tobin, J. J. M. "Apuleius and *Timon of Athens.*" *RRWL*, 1, no. 4 (1980), 1–5.

Asserts that Timon's apostrophe to gold (*Tim.*, IV.iii.386–397) echoes both Othello's address to the lamp before he kills Desdemona and Tyrel's description of the murder of the princes in *R3*, and returns for much of its imagery and theme to the source of the two latter passages, Apuleius's *Metamorphoses*, known to Sh in the original Latin and in William Adlington's translation, *The Golden Asse*. Specifically, Sh modeled Timon's description of the gold on the Apuleian account of the innocent, sleeping Cupid, whom Psyche attempts to kill. Revised as part of chapter 5 of item 1052.

2699 Waggoner, G. R. "*Timon of Athens* and the Jacobean Duel." *SQ*, 16 (1965), 303–11.

Examines English attitudes toward duelling in the early part of the 17th c., before King James's vigorous attempts to abolish the practice in 1613 and 1614. John Selden's book *The Duello or Single Combat* (1610) is representative of most contemporary discussion: It regards the duel as only "one form of the single combat and it traces the history of single combat back through English history to the Romans, Greeks, and Hebrews." Although there was some opposition to duelling in the first decade of the 17th c., it is clear in *Tim.* that both audience and dramatist would have agreed with Alcibiades in the defense of his friend (III.v), who has killed to protect his honor.

2700 Walker, Lewis. "Fortune and Friendship in *Timon of Athens.*" *TSLL*, 18 (1977), 577–600.

Takes the allegory of Fortune with which *Tim.* begins as warrant for analyzing the play in terms of "certain concepts of Fortune familiar to Shakespeare and his contemporaries." Sh's attempt "to demonstrate the operations of the goddess through dramatic action" results in a mingling of naturalistic and allegorical elements that perplexes the modern reader. Cites Boethius's *Consolation of Philosophy* and Cicero's *Of Friendship* as possible sources of the ideas about Fortune and friendship that influenced Sh. The favors of Fortune, given and withdrawn indiscriminately, include the friends whom Timon believes he can count on as "brothers" and whose casual desertion of him precipitates his misanthropy. Revision of part of chapter 1 of item 2703.

2701 Walker, Lewis. "Money in *Timon of Athens.*" *PQ*, 57 (1978), 269–71.

Argues that the various sums of money mentioned in *Tim.*, which have seemed absurdly inconsistent to most commentators, can be read emblematically. In having Timon request widely discrepant amounts of money (5, 50, and 1,000 talents, respectively) from his flatterers, Sh may be drawing on Cicero's *Of Friendship* (available in the translation of John Harington), which recommends trying the constancy of one's friends through money. Some men, according to Cicero, can be exposed as inconstant in a small money matter, whereas it takes a large sum to reveal the untrustworthiness of others. Revision of part of chapter 1 of item 2703.

2702 Walker, Lewis. "*Timon of Athens* and the Morality Tradition." *ShakS*, 12 (1979), 159–77.

Argues that *Tim.*, with its allegorical tendencies, is significantly indebted to the morality plays. Describes a number of important morality conventions and explains how Sh assimilated them. Timon's career, especially its first half, can be better understood if its relationship to that of Everyman, the generic protagonist of the moralities, is taken into account. Other peculiarities of *Tim.* that may have morality roots are the detailed stage directions; the unusually strong visual appeal; the masque of the five senses; and the music. Revision of chapter 2 of item 2703.

2703 Walker, John Lewis III. "Shakespeare's *Timon of Athens* and Its Background." Ph.D. dissertation, University of Virginia, 1977. *DAI*, 39 (1978–79), 4290-A.

Attempts to free *Tim.* from the strictures imposed on it by naturalistic criticism and to view it as a more finished work of art than most readers have been willing to grant. Chapter 1 interprets the play's action in terms of the workings of Fortune, attempting to provide a better understanding of its treatment of friendship and its emphasis on money, flattery, and prostitution. Chapter 2 considers the debt of *Tim.* to the morality plays by analyzing "the detailed stage directions; the visual appeal; the masque of the five senses; and the music." Chapter 3 sets *Tim.* in its theatrical context and argues that a number of elements place it near Sh's last plays in date and spirit: its exploration of the satiric persona; its emphasis on two "city" vices, lust and usury; and its syncopated tragicomic rhythm. Suggests that *Tim.* was written for "the coterie audience at the Blackfriars Playhouse." Parts of chapter 1 revised as items 2700 and 2701. Chapter 2 revised as item 2702.

2704 Wallace, John M. "*Timon of Athens* and the Three Graces: Shakespeare's Senecan Study." *MP*, 83 (1985–86), 349–63.

Contends that Seneca's *De Beneficiis*, or at least Senecan ideas about "obligations derived from gifts," are subjected to searching but inconclusive criticism in *Tim*. Notes the enormous influence of *De Beneficiis* in Sh's time, mentioning translations by Nicholas Haward (1569) and Arthur Golding (1578). Summarizes the most important ideas of the seven books of Seneca's treatise, which are "epitomized in two remarkable and closely related images, the contest of benefits and the Three Graces." For Seneca, the Graces represent in a variety of ways the virtuous competition between bestowers and recipients of benefits, a competition fueled by a sense of natural obligation. In *Tim*., the Three Graces surface as three graces said at meals, each one with different and often derisory implications. Together, these "grotesque distortions" of Seneca's image amount to a mocking dismissal of Seneca's notion that society can be held together by "gratitude and good turns." However, the conclusion of the play, in which Alcibiades gives over his fury to accept a reconciliation with Athens, acknowledges that there is an attractiveness to the Senecan ideal, unworkable though it is.

2705 Ware, Malcolm. "'Smoke and Lukewarm Water': A Note on *Timon of Athens*." *Anglia*, 82 (1964), 342–44.

Argues that Timon's insult to his guests—"Smoke and luke-warm water / Is your perfection" (III.vi.89–90)—is an effective expression of his disillusionment and misanthropy. Timon is saying that the "final and highest state" of his companions (their "perfection") amounts only to "smoke" and "water" (terms used elsewhere in Sh to mean hypocrisy and duplicity).

2706 Waters, D. Douglas. "Shakespeare's *Timon of Athens* and Catharsis." *UC*, 8 (1988), 93–105.

Defines catharsis as the audience's "intellectual, emotional, and moral clarification" of the tragic hero's experience. Intellectually, we come to understand Timon's flaw as "excessive feelings of kindness, joy, and friendship." Emotionally, we respond with pity and fear because of the falseness of Timon's friends, his limited resources, and his ultimate despair. Morally, we recognize that Timon is responsible for his own destruction. The fact that Timon does not undergo any profound moral regeneration does not disqualify him as a tragic hero or the play as a tragedy.

2707 Wilcher, Robert. "*Timon of Athens*: A Shakespearian Experiment." *CahiersE*, 34 (1988), 61–78.

Surveys many of the contradictory critical attempts to understand *Tim.* Proposes to discover the play's generic affiliations through an analysis of its structure and then to speculate about Sh's purpose. The first section of the play is comprised of acts I–III and is structurally derived from the late morality plays. It consists of episodes that accumulate to illustrate Timon's generosity, his financial ruin, and the desertion of his friends. The second section (acts IV–V) is modeled on verse satire, itself based on classical paradigms; here, a variety of characters approach Timon and are verbally abused. *Tim.* is "a play about satire," which demonstrates that although this mode does serve a purpose in a flawed world (as in the morality plays), it has a tendency to corrupt its practitioners and "to revile life rather than enhance it" (as in verse satire).

2708 Wood, K. "The Phoenix and the Gull: A Study of Shakespeare's *Timon of Athens*." *Studies in Elizabethan Literature: Festschrift to Professor G. C. Bannerjee.* Ed. P. S. Sastri. New Delhi: Chand, 1972, pp. 74–90.

Argues that the protagonist of *Tim.* is consistently ostentatious and that throughout the action he is isolated. The play is thus unified in tone.

TITUS ANDRONICUS

2709 Adams, John Cranford. "Shakespeare's Revisions in *Titus Andronicus*." *SQ*, 15, no. 2 (1964), 177–90. Reprint. *Shakespeare 400: Essays by American Scholars on the Anniversary of the Poet's Birth.* Ed. James G. McManaway. New York: Holt, Rinehart and Winston, 1964, pp. 177–90.

Argues that the original *Tit.*, not extant, was written for a stage of two units (the platform and the gallery), whereas the revised version was written for three (platform, gallery, and inner stage). Cites, among other pieces of evidence, a passage in the first quarto that indicates Titus arrived at the tomb earlier in the day and there sacrificed Tamora's eldest son. This is irreconcilable with the stage business involving the tomb and is a vestige of the earlier version, which was performed without the inner stage.

2710 Barnet, Sylvan, ed. *The Tragedy of Titus Andronicus.* (Signet Classic Shakespeare.) New York: New American Library, 1964. xxxiv + [35]–181 pp.

The introduction emphasizes that *Tit.* anticipates Sh's great tragedies in its portrait of a man whose well-intentioned deeds have consequences that lead to his destruction. Discusses the way in which the wealth of Latin quotations and mythological allusions, frequently derived from or inspired by Seneca and Ovid, helps to elevate the style and to distance the audience from the play's horrors by describing them with "elegant luxuriance." The note on the source calls attention to a mid-18th-c. booklet entitled *The History of Titus Andronicus*, which contains a ballad and a prose narrative. The latter is a reprint of a much older piece, possibly the tale that Sh used as his source. The introduction, text, and note on the source are reprinted. as part of item 0123.

2711   Bolton, Joseph S. G. "A Plea for 3 1/2 Rejected Shakespearian Lines." *SQ*, 23 (1972), 261–63.

The unique first quarto of *Tit.*, discovered only in the 20th c., contains 3 1/2 lines (beginning at I.i.35) that were previously unknown but that have not been generally accepted by modern editors because "at this day" (line 35) seems inconsistent with what happens later in the scene. If "at this day" is emended to "at this door," the difficulty is removed.

2712   Braekman, W. *Shakespeare's "Titus Andronicus."* (Seminar of English and American Literature of the University of Ghent.) Ghent, 1969. 173 pp. Originally published in two parts by *Studia Germanica Gandensia*: 9 (1967), 9–118; 10 (1968), 7–65.

Offers detailed comparisons of *Tit.* with "the two Continental plays on the same subject: the German play preserved in the 1620 collection of plays performed by wandering English companies in Germany, and the Dutch play [*Aran en Titus*] by Jan Vos." Uses these analyses to support the hypothesis that *Tit.* is a revision by Sh of an old tragedy of the school of Kyd.

2713   Breight, Curtis Charles. "Reality and Representation: Symbolic Performance and Political Power in England in the Early 1590s." Ph.D. dissertation, Yale University, 1988. *DAI*, 50 (1989–90), 3598-A.

Discusses how symbolic performance could be utilized as a means of exercising social or political power. Chapter 4 construes *Tit.* as an example of how ancient Rome settled a succession crisis and, in light of Elizabeth's successor problems, how vulnerable England could be to the influence of marginal political players.

2714   Brooke, Nicholas. "The Intrusive Fly: A Note on Act III, Scene ii of *Titus Andronicus*." *Filološki Pregled* (Beograd), 1–2 (1963–64), 99–102.

Argues that the "fly scene" in *Tit.* has no clear place in the development of the plot: It seems to revive "the indecisive lamentations with which III.i opened, as though the decisive turn to revenge had not taken place." It is excellent as a study of hysteria, but because it does not fit into the pattern of the play and because it first appeared in the Folio of 1623 (not in the earlier quartos), it must be supposed an addition, possibly but not necessarily by Sh.

2715   Brooke, Nicholas. "The Tragic Spectacle in *Titus Andronicus* and *Romeo and Juliet*." *Shakespeare: The Tragedies: A Collection of Critical Essays*. Ed. Clifford Leech. Chicago: U. of Chicago P., 1965, pp. 243–256.

Asserts that the distinctions among Sh's earliest tragedies are so definitive as to suggest that the playwright was deliberately experimenting with "different modes of tragedy": in the case of *Tit.*, Roman (Senecan and Ovidian) tragedy. Finds similarities between the emblematic qualities of *Tit.* and those of the nondramatic Ovidian poems, *Ven.* and *Luc.* Notes that the attempt to expose the audience to "extreme physical horror" on the one hand and to give us a sense of detachment on the other by alternating between savage farce and formal verse "is not uniformly successful."

2716   Broude, Ronald. "Four Forms of Vengeance in *Titus Andronicus*." *JEGP*, 78 (1979), 494–507.

Asserts that the concept of revenge, better designated as "retribution," had a variety of manifestations in the 16th c. Sh incorporated four different kinds of revenge in *Tit.*: "human sacrifice by which the ghosts of the slain are placated with the blood of their slayers; the vendetta, in which families ruthlessly avenge past injuries in order to discourage future ones; the state justice which maintains civil order by punishing those who transgress its laws; and the divine vengeance which upholds cosmic order, and, directed by Providence, turns crime and punishment alike to the uses of an inscrutable Purpose." In *Tit.*, human sacrifice and vendetta are shown to be basically futile because they perpetuate a state of strife. At the end of the play, however, Titus's vengeance, though part of a vendetta, serves the purposes of state justice and divine vengeance to set Rome back on the right course and make possible the reconciliation of the Romans and the Goths.

2717 Broude, Ronald. "Roman and Goth in *Titus Andronicus.*" *ShakS*, 6 (1970), 27–34.

Points out that the settlement at the end of *Tit.*, with the Goths being incorporated into the Roman state, has seemed unsatisfactory to modern readers and audiences because of an oversimplified perception that the Goths are barbarous and the Romans civilized. In the Elizabethan histories of Rome, however, there was at least as much emphasis on the vices of Rome as on her virtues. The Goths were often seen as noble and energetic, and their conquest of the Empire was regarded as a regeneration. Because of a confusion in terminology, 16th-c. Englishmen also thought of the Goths as their Germanic ancestors. In the 1580s and 1590s, English hostility to Rome was at its peak, and there was widespread acceptance of the tradition "by which Roman dominion was understood to have passed to the Germans with the crowning of Charlemagne as Emperor of the Holy Roman Empire." *Tit.* depicts the Romans and Goths in accord with informed English thought of Sh's time. There are some Roman virtues but many vices, among them disorder, cruelty, and tyranny. To reform Rome, the Andronici need an infusion of Gothic vitality. Sh's attitude toward the Goths is neutral, not negative. Their union with the Romans at the end is an appropriate resolution to the play's political crisis.

2718 Brucher, Richard T. "'Tragedy, Laugh On': Comic Violence in *Titus Andronicus.*" *RenD*, N. S. 10 (1979), 71–91.

Explains the comic aspects of the violence in *Tit.* Other playwrights of the Renaissance had staged atrocities so outrageous that they seemed funny, and Sh followed their practice, though with some modifications. In *Tit.*, we encounter two manifestations of comic savagery, the crude and the witty, both initially directed against sympathetic victims. The outlandish brutality of the rapists, Chiron and Demetrius, is grotesquely comic, as is the witty depravity of Aaron. The audience's involvement in the violent escapades of these characters plunges it into a morally chaotic world. Though we are disgusted by the horrors wrought by Aaron, we are perversely amused by his ingenuity. Titus, at first a victim of this kind of asthetic violence, eventually learns to play the game and proceeds, with great wit, to stage-manage his revenge. The comic exaggeration of brutality in *Tit.* marks a world too disorderly to sustain "the redemptive tragic emotions of pity and fear."

2718a Bryant, J. A. Jr. "Aaron and the Pattern of Shakespeare's Villains." *RenP*, 1984 (1985), 29–36.

Points out that Sh's handling of his source for *Tit.* makes clear that Aaron is not a purely evil villain in the mold of the vice of the morality plays. As wicked as he is, Aaron deserves some sympathy for the protective attitude he takes towards his child. He is a prototype for Sh's other villains, all of whom have a limited claim on our sympathy.

2718b Calderwood, James L. *Shakespearean Metadrama: The Argument of the Play in "Titus Andronicus," "Love's Labour's Lost," "Romeo and Juliet," "A Midsummer Night's Dream," and "Richard II."* Minneapolis: U. of Minnesota P., 1971. 192 pp.

Argues that "dramatic art itself—its materials, its media of language and theater, its generic forms and conventions, its relationship to truth and the social order—is a dominant Shakespearean theme, perhaps his most abiding subject." A chapter on *Tit.* suggests that the play "metadramatically presents us with a rape of language, with the mutilation that the poet's 'tongue' suffers when forced to submit to the rude demands of the theater." It is appropriate for Sh to rely on Ovid for Lavinia's rape and mutilation and on Seneca for the dramatic form of revenge tragedy seen in the last act: Lavinia, like Sh, is a figure of the Ovidian poet trying to find a voice within theatrical action and suffering mutilation in order to serve the needs of revenge tragedy. Other chapters treat *LLL, Rom., MND,* and *R2.*

2718c Campbell, Gordon. "Chequered Shades and Shadows in Shakespeare and Milton." *N&Q,* 28 (1981), 123.

Speculates that the "chequer'd shadow" to which Tamora refers (*Tit.,* II.iii.15) derives from Virgil's *Eclogues 7.*

2719 Carducci, Jane S. "Shakespeare's *Titus Andronicus*: An Experiment in Expression." *CahiersE,* No. 31 (1987), 1–9.

Maintains that the failure of the protagonist and other characters in *Tit.* to find adequate expression—either verbal or gestural—for their suffering reflects the incapacity of "the Roman masculine ideal" to communicate "internal states" of any kind. Sh explores this inadequacy again in "his later Roman plays." See item 1211.

2720 Champion, Larry S. "*Titus Andronicus* and Shakespeare's Tragic Perspective." *BSUF,* 12, no. 2 (1971), 14–25.

Argues that *Tit.,* though unsuccessful as a tragedy, provides guidelines to the various elements of dramatic form with which Sh was later to experiment. *Tit.* sets forth a powerful protagonist, noble but flawed by furious pride, who moves through stages of wrath, self-pity, and madness. Thus far Titus seems to be a good tragic character. However, Sh fails to endow him with any philosophical depth, and structural devices like pointer characters and soliloquies, which might have helped the audience penetrate his character, are used ineffectively. Revised as chapter 1 of item 0250.

2721 Charney, Maurice. "*Titus Andronicus.*" (Harvester New Critical Introductions to Shakespeare.) New York: Harvester Wheatsheaf, 1990. xxii + 128 pp.

Includes a prefatory section on "The Critical Reception" and provides a commentary on the major movements in *Tit.* The play is an "emblematic tragedy" of revenge and suffering. It is emphatically a Roman play, dealing with Roman values, their disintegration, and their recovery. There is abundance of classical allusion, especially to the works of Ovid and Virgil and to mythology. In addition, the style owes much to Ovid's *Metamorphoses* and to other classical works. Concludes with a discussion of two "image themes," blood and sea, and a consideration of rape, which in both *Tit.* and *Luc.* is regarded as dishonoring the innocent victim.

2721a Cowhig, Ruth. "Blacks in English Renaissance Drama and the Role of Shakespeare's Othello." *The Black Presence in English Literature.* Ed. David Dabydeen. Manchester: Manchester U. P., 1985, pp. 1–25.

Alludes to the scene (*Tit.,* IV.ii) in which Aaron evidences a fierce devotion to his child to argue that he gains a measure of sympathy as a member of his race. In the midst of the atrocities of *Tit.,* Aaron is the only character "who attains a certain vitality, and in this sense he belongs to the tradition of the villain-hero."

2722 Cross, Gustav, ed. *Titus Andronicus.* (Pelican Shakespeare.) Baltimore: Penguin, 1966. 127 pp.

The introduction catalogues the faults of *Tit.,* most of which can be attributed its lack of a "frame of moral reference." The play does have virtues, chief among which is the characterization of Aaron; and it anticipates Sh's great tragedies. Notes that the "excessively artificial diction" seems incompatible with the savagery of the events exhibited. Suggests that this decorative style betrays the play's kinship with Sh's two early narrative poems, *Ven.* and *Luc.,* and, "through them, with Ovid's

Metamorphoses." The source of *Tit.* was probably the prose *History of Titus Andronicus*, which survives in an 18th-c. chapbook reprint. Revised as part of item 0496.

2723   Cunningham, Karen. "'Scars can witness': Trials by Ordeal and Lavinia's Body in *Titus Andronicus.*" *Women and Violence in Literature: An Essay Collection.* Ed. Katherine Anne Ackley. (Garland Reference Library of the Humanities 1271.) New York: Garland, 1990, pp. 139–62.

Maintains that in *Tit.* Sh is critically examining the uncertainties involved in trying to ascertain truth by publicly subjecting the human body to violence, much in the way that "trial by ordeal," a local English practice, attempted to establish guilt or innocence. Lavinia, whose rape and mutilation are variously misinterpreted, is the central exhibit in this critique. Even the allusions to classical texts that are used as precedents possess no special privilege as guides to interpretation; Lavinia, for example, is assimilated into the "alien text" of Virginius and his daughter when she is killed by her father. At the very end of the play, there is a movement away from the corporeal test of truth and toward the rhetorical, toward something that more resembles a jury trial than a trial by ordeal.

2724   Cutts, John P. "Shadow and Substance: Structural Unity in *Titus Andronicus.*" *CompD,* 2 (1968–69), 161–72. Revised as a chapter in *The Shattered Glass: A Dramatic Pattern in Shakespeare's Early Plays.* Detroit: Wayne State U. P., 1968, pp. 59–75.

Analyzes *Tit.* in terms of a common Renaissance *topos*—mistaking shadow for substance. Throughout the play, Titus takes "false shadows for true substances" (III.ii.80). The play's unity can be demonstrated by calling attention to the pervasiveness of this *topos*.

2725   Danson, Lawrence N. "The Device of Wonder: *Titus Andronicus* and Revenge Tragedy." *TSLL,* 16 (1974–75), 27–43.

Analyzes *Tit.* to show that revenge is not the central fact of much so-called revenge tragedy. Throughout the play, there is great emphasis on devices—petitions and madspeeches, for example—that indicate the necessity for "relief through expression." Death is the central fact, and the playwright must find a way (revenge is one way) to ritualize death so that at the end there is a sense of "something attained, at once fearful and wonderful." Revision of part of item 0303. Revised as chapter 1 of item 0302.

2726   Dasgupta, Arun Kumar. "A Note on *Titus Andronicus* II.i.1–11." *SQ,* 12 (1961), 340–41.

Disagrees with Wolfgang Clemens's opinion that Aaron's comparison of Tamora to the sun (*Tit.,* II.i.5–8) is "inorganic." The simile builds on the previous lines and gives an appropriate description of Tamora's power and beauty through the eyes of her lover.

2727   Davidson, Clifford. "A Reading of *Titus Andronicus.*" *SUS,* 10 (1975–78), 93–100.

Sees *Tit.* as "a veritable Dance of Death." Calls attention to Titus's foolishness in choosing Saturninus to rule, the almost allegorical resonances of the coupling of Tamora and Aaron, Aaron's Vice-like qualities, the symbolic evil of the forest, the model of Lavinia's rape in the Philomela story from Ovid's *Metamorphoses,* the reminiscence of the rape of Lucrece in Lavinia's fate, the elements from Seneca's *Thyestes* incorporated into the account of Titus's grisly banquet, the descent of Rome into animal-like ferocity, and the return of long-absent Justice at the end.

2728 de Armas, Frederic A. "Astraea's Fall: Senecan Images in Shakespeare's *Titus Andronicus* and Calderón's *La vida es sueño*." *Parallel Lives: Spanish and English National Drama 1580–1680*. Eds. Louise and Peter Fothergill-Payne. Lewisburg Pennsylvania: Bucknell U. P., 1991, pp. 302–21.

Shows how *Tit.* elaborates the myth of Astraea as derived from Seneca's *Thyestes*. Sh's play mirrors "the sacrificial crisis, the loss of order, and the threat of chaos that are symbolized by the fall of Astraea." In IV.iv, when Titus launches a search for Astraea, we see an imitation of and commentary on the fourth chorus of *Thyestes*. *Tit.* is also patterned by other texts: Ovid's *Metamorphoses* helps the protagonist discover the truth about what happened to Lavinia and gives him the Latin words to describe Astraea's departure from the earth; the play parodies Virgil's Eclogue 4, exhibiting the tyrannical age of Saturninus instead of the age of gold; and the golden time of Roman peace hailed in the *Aeneid* is turned into a vision of violence and disorder. Titus's attempt to bring down celestial influences by shooting arrows at the gods produces a chaotic admixture of celestial, terrestrial, and infernal elements. There may be a precarious return to justice at the end, with young Lucius representing "the mysterious child" of Virgil's Eclogue, "who is to actualize the return of Astraea."

2729 Diehl, Huston. "The Iconography of Violence in English Renaissance Tragedy." *RenD*, N. S. 11 (1980), 27–44.

Hypothesizes that some episodes of stage violence in Renaissance English tragedy have an allusive, symbolic value as well as an emotional one. Examples can be found in *Tit.*, in which various acts of dismemberment are used to characterize the strife-ridden city of Rome.

2729a Edwards, Philip. "Thrusting Elysium into Hell: The Originality of *The Spanish Tragedy*." *The Elizabethan Theatre XI*. Eds. A. L. Magnusson and C. E. McGee. Port Credit, Ontario: P. D. Meany, 1990, pp. 117–32.

Presents Thomas Kyd's *The Spanish Tragedy* as a work set more or less in modern Spain that gives control of its world over to pagan deities, the infernal powers. Within the play, the characters call on a variety of gods, in this regard resembling Kyd's source, the plays of Seneca; but mostly we find Kyd's characters placing nervous faith in a sort of Christian providence in the air above. Of course, no such providence is in evidence; the play is "a denial of God's care for man." Argues that *Tit.* is similar to *The Spanish Tragedy* in its rejection of Christian providence but unlike Kyd's play in its refusal "to substitute an alternative view of the government of the cosmos." Cites a number of examples to show that *Tit.* "has no metaphysical frame of reference at all."

2729b Eland, Cynthia Graham. "The Rhetoric of Revenge: The Use of Forensic Rhetoric in *The Spanish Tragedy*, *Titus Andronicus*, and *The Jew of Malta*." Ph.D. dissertation, McMaster University, 1984. *DAI*, 45 (1984–85), 1121-A.

Maintains that the authors of the plays under consideration are "making a case for and against the protagonist as in a revenge trial, not as it would be conducted in an Elizabethan court, but as it might be constructed from the works of the Roman rhetors studied in the schools." Points out that the rhetors emphasize "the forensic oration and the dramatic quality of rhetoric"; that rhetorical precepts taught in the schools would probably have been applied in the writing of plays; that forensic rhetoric was already an influence in pre-Elizabethan drama.; and that the legal status of blood revenge as "criminal homicide may have appeared over-simplified to a generation trained in the Roman rhetors' view of revenge" as an action calling for a fair decision according to the circumstances of the case." Observes that the revenge trial seems to supply many of the "structural, persuasive and argumentative features" of *Tit.*

2730 Enck, John J. "A Chronicle of Small Latin." *SQ*, 12 (1961), 342–45.

Points out that in *Tit.*, IV.ii., Chiron pretends to understand the Latin sentence accompanying the gift of a weapon sent by Titus. This pretension to classical learning by a foolish character was a common gag in Elizabethan and Jacobean drama and may help explain the tone of Jonson's comment about Sh's small Latin.

2731 Ettin, Andrew V. "Shakespeare's First Roman Tragedy." *ELH*, 37 (1970), 325–41.

Argues that in *Tit.* Sh was testing "the nature and meaning of the Roman legacy." His allusions to Roman mythology "almost invariably stem from the darker, crueler, uncivilized reaches of the Roman mind." References to the *Aeneid* are used to emphasize the "cruelty and irreligious piety" of Titus. Senecan conventions are also strained, and violent metamorphoses are described in Ovidian rhetoric that avoids confrontation with reality. Sh seems to have been aware of the difficulties inherent in the use of Roman tradition by Renaissance writers, and in *Tit.* he tested the extent to which Roman models could be assimilated.

2731a Fawcett, Mary Laughlin. "Arms/Words/Tears: Language and the Body in *Titus Andronicus*." *ELH*, 50 (1983), 261–77.

Discusses *Tit.* as "a meditation on language and the body." Suggests that in this play, language "is caught somewhere between the possibilities represented by wounding/connection and mourning/separation; these trains of imagery stand, respectively, for the written and the spoken word." Contrasts the "heavy, culture-bound, Andronici rhetoric" with the "freer, more self-expressive form of speech" we hear from Aaron. Includes analysis of the emblematic scene (IV.i) in which Lavinia tosses Ovid's *Metamorphoses* with her stumps: She here enacts "a relationship between the body and the telling word."

2732 Forker, Charles R. "*Titus Andronicus*, *Hamlet*, and the Limits of Expressibility." *HamS*, 2, no. 2 (1980), 1–33.

Argues that in *Tit.*, Sh addresses the problems (1) of presenting suffering so great that the sufferer's verbal resources are not equal to its expression and (2) of discovering a means of manifesting in drama horrors beyond the audience's experience. Through a variety of techniques (many nonverbal or antiverbal) Sh dramatizes the frustrations of characters who cannot quite communicate the physical and psychological tortures they are enduring. The play also depends heavily on emblematic and semiallegorical devices, which show on the stage what might naturalistically be expressed in words. Classical allusions, as well as revealing the learned virtuosity of the young playwright, provide evidence of an intense search for some way to render adequately "a wilderness of tigers" (III.i.54).

2732a Gibbons, Brian. "The Human Body in *Titus Andronicus* and Other Early Shakespeare Plays." *SJH*, 1989, 209–22.

Explores the ways in which Sh endows the human body with "some significance beyond its biographical status in the dramatic fiction." Focuses on *Tit.*, explaining the complex set of signals transmitted by the bodies of Titus Andronicus and Lavinia. Sh denies both characters early release, thus ensuring that "there is no full tragic crisis until the very end of the play."

2733 Green, Douglas E. "Interpreting 'her martyr'd signs': Gender and Tragedy in *Titus Andronicus*." *SQ*, 40 (1989), 317–26.

Argues that it is "largely through and on the female characters that Titus is constructed and his tragedy inscribed." Tamora at first is an opposite to Titus, but later, when she displays villainy, lust, and greed, she serves as a yardstick by which to measure Titus's own vengeful extremes. Lavinia's mutilated and violated body articulates Titus's suffering and victimization.

2734 Hamilton, A. C. "*Titus Andronicus*: The Form of Shakespearian Tragedy." *SQ*, 14 (1963), 201–13.

Argues that Sh adapted classical materials to present a vision of fallen nature in *Tit*. In imitating *Thyestes*, Seneca's most popular play, Sh "tells the story of a father who devours his own sons." Naming the emperor Saturninus suggests awareness on Sh's part of the traditional image of Saturn devouring his child; Saturn's wife was Rhea, the earth, "and in the play Saturnine's wife eats her children," like the earth. In Ovid, Sh found the story of Tantalus serving his son Pelops to the gods next to the story of Philomel, on which he based the portrayal of Lavinia. Ovid's Philomel becomes, in Lavinia, a symbol for the fallen world projected by the tragedy. Sh also derived the pattern of *Tit.* from Ovid, beginning with the departure of Justice from the world of the play. Throughout the play, the inner chaos of human nature is reflected in a kind of inverted pastoralism: Thus *Tit.* parodies Virgil's Eclogue 4. Revised as chapter 4 of item 0484.

2735 Hansen, J. W. "Two Notes on Seneca and *Titus Andronicus*." *Anglia*, 93 (1975), 161–65.

Suggests that in IV.iii, the details of Titus's plan to search for Justice in earth, hell, sea, and heavens is probably derived from Seneca's *Hercules Furens*. The source of Tamora's "barren detested vale" (III.iii) is the description of Atreus's wood in *Thyestes*.

2736 Hibbard, G. R. "'The Forced Gait of a Shuffling Nag.'" *Shakespeare 1971: Proceedings of the World Shakespeare Congress, Vancouver, August 1971*. Eds. Clifford Leech and J. M. R. Margeson. Toronto: U. of Toronto P., 1972, pp. 76–88.

Cites Marcus's speech reacting to the rape and mutilation of Lavinia (*Tit.*, II.iv.11–57) as an early instance of incongruity between poetry and dramatic context in Sh's work. Proceeds to show how Sh was able to synchronize the two as his career progressed. Revised as chapter 2 of item 2736a.

2736a Hibbard, G. R. *The Making of Shakespeare's Dramatic Poetry*. Toronto: U. of Toronto P., 1981. vii + 194 pp.

Chapter 2, "Words, Action, and *Titus Andronicus*," analyzes Marcus's speech in response to Lavinia's violation and mutilation (*Tit.*, II.iv.11–57) to demonstrate that Sh, in emulating the virtuosity of his mentor Ovid, failed to adapt his Ovidian language sufficiently to the exigencies of stage action. Revision of item 2736.

2737 Hiles, Jane. "A Margin for Error: Rhetorical Context in *Titus Andronicus*." *Style*, 21 (1987), 62–75.

Attempts to demonstrate that the plot of *Tit.* turns on a series of rhetorical failures, which occur when a character fails to recognize that the context for his discourse has shifted. As a result, he fails to respond appropriately. This is the case with Lavinia, Titus, and Tamora. Power consists of the ability to manipulate the contexts of discourse as well as discourse itself.

2738 Hirsh, James. "Laughter at *Titus Andronicus*." *Essays in Theater*, 7 (1988–89), 59–74.

Suggests that inappropriate laughter is invited by *Tit*. to reinforce a major theme: "the impossibility of finding appropriate responses to certain situations" (like the rape and mutilation of Lavinia). Sh is dramatizing "incongruity in the human condition" by depicting characters who laugh at the horrors with which they are confronted and by inducing the audience to laugh as well.

2738a Holdsworth, R. V. "A Crux in *Titus Andronicus*." *N&Q*, 35 (1988), 44–45.

Tends to support Stanley Wells's interpretation of Aaron's comment that his new born son is "the vigour" of his youth (*Tit.*, IV.ii.110). Supplies evidence to reinforce the idea that *vigour* is a spelling for *figure*.

2739 Huffman, Clifford Chalmers. "Bassianus and the British History in *Titus Andronicus*." *ELN*, 11 (1973–74), 175–81.

Attempts to explain the discrepancy between Sh's portrayal in *Tit.* of Bassianus as the good younger brother and the cruel character ascribed to him by classical historians Dio Cassius and Herodian. Suggests that the notion of Bassianus as the emperor's second son, the formulation of the choice between Bassianus and Saturninus as one between consanguinity and primogeniture, and "the identification of the younger son" as more worthy were all derived by Sh from British chronicles, which had modified the classical accounts.

2740 Huffman, Clifford Chalmers. "*Titus Andronicus*: Metamorphosis and Renewal." *MLR*, 67 (1972), 730–41.

Follows the degeneration of Rome through her abandonment of true public justice almost immediately after *Tit.* opens. In acts II and III, the city falls into an "Iron Age of injustice," of which the mutilated Lavinia is the emblem. Sh takes the idea of justice departed from Ovid's *Metamorphoses*, and the search for justice throughout the play can be understood in terms of Pythagoras's discourse in book 15 of Ovid on how to regain the Golden Age: Pythagoras insists on the renunciation of animal killing of all kinds and a return to vegetarianism. In Virgil's fourth Eclogue, the Golden Age is set in the future, a notion that appealed to many Christian writers. This became part of a view that understood history as a "succession of four, or five, kingdoms." In some renditions, Rome is the doomed fourth kingdom; in others, it is the fifth, a "new kingdom established by God." This last version allowed for Rome, though degenerate, to be punished and cured from within. In *Tit.*, Rome's renewal is dramatized through Lucius, who is banished by the Tribunes, departs and returns, and renews the city. Lucius is suited for his mission because (1) he modifies his original purpose of revenge, (2) he is not linked with the bloody doings of Titus, (3) he is reconciled with Rome's former enemies (the Goths), and (4) he reestablishes public justice by justly condemning Tamora (in contrast to the barbarous sacrifice of Alarbus at the beginning of the play).

2741 Hulse, S. Clark. "Wresting the Alphabet: Oratory and Action in *Titus Andronicus*." *Criticism*, 21 (1979), 106–18.

Argues that *Tit.* begins (act I) with Ciceronian rhetoric that is appropriate to the public, civic nature of the action. In the middle parts of the play, as the Andronici are subjected to enormous suffering, this classical rhetoric becomes inadequate; Titus and his family must find a new language, "in which physical appearance is given formal vestments." They are metamorphosized into "dumb shows" that formalize the horrors of the plot. Out of this situation, Titus discovers the means of transforming his "rhetoric of helpless woe to a rhetoric of vengeful action." Titus's sacrifice at the end "restores Roman order and with it restores the ordinary function of language."

2742 Hunt, Maurice. "Compelling Art in *Titus Andronicus*." *SEL*, 28 (1988), 197–218.

Challenges the view of certain critics that the pervasive use of Ovidian myth in *Tit.* to order the experiences of the characters is evidence of bookish immaturity on Sh's part. Maintains instead that the characters' reliance on pagan models for their behavior, especially in the last two acts, is evidence of their own limited vision, not the playwright's. Sh embeds in the play certain hints of Christian providence, which offers, though the characters do not perceive it, a more hopeful aesthetic paradigm than Ovid's deadly formulas.

2742a Hunter, G. K. "Sources and Meanings in Titus Andronicus." *Mirror Up to Shakespeare: Essays in Honour of G. R. Hibbard*. Ed. J. C. Gray. Toronto: U. of Toronto P., 1984, pp. 171–88.

Reiterates the author's position that *Tit.* is not derived from a prose history whose earliest printed version dates from the 18th c. Suggests other sources in keeping with the play's bifurcated view of Rome. On the one hand, there is a sense of "primitive republican virtue," derived from Livy; on the other, there is a strong feeling of "decadent imperial miscegenation," indebted to Herodian's *History*. Spectacle is used in *Tit.* to indicate the "collapse of order before decadence" that for humanists was the chief lesson of Roman history, and in particular "the relationship of primitive and decadent." See items 2743, 2743a, 2760, 2760a, and 2761.

2743 Hunter, G. K. "The 'Sources' of *Titus Andronicus*—Once Again." *N&Q*, 30 (1983), 114–16.

Supports Marco Mincoff's argument (item 2761) that the chapbook *History of Titus Andronicus* was not a source for *Tit.* but was based on the ballad of *Titus Andronicus*, which was itself derived from Sh's play. Attempts to counter G. Harold Metz's attack on Mincoff (item 2760) that defends the *History* as a source.

2743a Jackson, MacD. P. "*Titus Andronicus*: Play, Ballad, and Prose History." *N&Q*, 36 (1989), 315–17.

Defends the view—held by the author and others—that *Tit.* was composed before a Titus Andronicus ballad (transcribed 1600–1603) and a prose *History of Titus Andronicus* found in an 18th-c. chapbook. Responds to an attack on this view by Harold Metz (item 2760a) by pointing out that Metz ignores two important points in the author's argument and distorts a third. There is no convincing evidence to refute the hypothesis that "the line of descent was play—ballad—history." See also items 2742a, 2743, 2760, and 2761.

2743b Jacobs, Henry E. "The Banquet of Blood and the Masque of Death: Social Ritual and Ideology in English Revenge Tragedy." *RenP*, 1985 (1986), 39–50.

Discusses four specific social rituals within revenge plays of the English Renaissance. In the context of the revenge play, each of these rituals, by itself representing the ideology of the status quo, subverts that ideology. Includes analysis of the bloody banquet scene in *Tit.*, which perverts a royal social ritual into "gustatory vengeance." Notes that Sh's most immediate sources, Ovid's *Metamorphoses* and Seneca's *Thyestes*, feature "the same radical dislocation of social ritual and symbolic order."

2744 Johnson, Robert. "*Titus Andronicus*: The First of the Roman Plays." *Essays on Shakespeare in Honour of A. A. Ansari*. Meerut, India: Shalabh Book House, 1986, pp. 80–87.

Argues that *Tit.* shares crucial thematic concerns with *JC*, *Ant.*, and *Cor*. In all of these plays, the audience feels an ambivalence toward the Roman world and toward the protagonists who represent it. At the root of this ambiguity is the conflict between the main characters' public and private roles. *Tit.*, like the later Roman plays, highlights the opposition between a need for ritual, order, and civilization, and various private desires (in Titus's case, for revenge) that tend to undermine these public values.

2745 Jones, Eldred D. "Aaron and Melancholy in *Titus Andronicus*." *SQ*, 14 (1963), 178–79.

Points out that in rejecting Tamora's advances (*Tit.*, II.ii.30–39), Aaron temporarily assumes the pose of melancholy, an appropriate disguise for a black

Moor, since this humor was supposed to be more prevalent in hot countries like Spain and Africa. Because of his wit and ebullience throughout the play, Aaron cannot be classified as a melancholy villain, but in this scene he does briefly take on that role.

2746   Karr, Judith M. "The Pleas in *Titus Andronicus*." *SQ*, 14 (1963), 278–79.

Maintains that a series of six pleas occurring throughout *Tit.* forms a pattern that gives unity to the play. The pleas often echo and mirror one another; tears and kneeling, for example, are frequent. The pleas also provide ironic contrasts when "the positions of refusing and being refused are significantly reversed." Finally, the pleas can be used to chart the rise of Gothic power, the decline of Roman power, and the restoration of Roman power. See item 2770.

2747   Kendall, Gillian Murray. "'Lend me thy hand': Metaphor and Mayhem in *Titus Andronicus*." *SQ*, 40 (1989), 299–316.

Claims that in *Tit.* violent language begets the physical violence of the play, and violence in turn is wreaked on language because it fails to bridge the gap between words and reality. Characters seem unable to control their rhetoric: The figurative can become unexpectedly and frighteningly literal. Further distortions of reality take place as a result of the characters' reference of their experiences to myth (for example, Titus's viewing of Lavinia's situation in terms of the stories of Philomela and Virginius).

2748   Kirov, Fodor T. "The First Steps of a Giant." *SJW*, 104 (1968), 109–40.

Discusses the imagery in Sh's early plays, emphasizing its notional nature. That is, images in the early works usually participate in sentences with a notion of their own and are not rooted in the dramatic context. *Tit.* exemplifies this rootlesnes: Its imagery "is either inadequate to the character [who] utters it, to the emotional trend, or to the object it is called upon to elucidate." *Tit.* is like four early comedies—*Err., Shr., TGV,* and *LLL*—in remaining "on the euphuistic plane of thought." The *H6Triad* is pervaded by notional imagery, but shows signs of moving beyond it toward Sh's mature style.

2749   Kistner, A. L., and M. K. Kistner. "The Senecan Background of Despair in *The Spanish Tragedy* and *Titus Andronicus*." *ShakS*, 7 (1974), 1–9.

Notes that scholarship has clearly established Seneca's influence on early Elizabethan tragedy "in the areas of content and external form." There is also an internal form, a governing pattern that was borrowed from the Roman playwright by Elizabethan dramatists. The pattern involves a character's discovery that he has been deprived of "whatever means most to him, his absolute." His initial response is despair, which produces one of the following: "(a) madness, (b) desire for suicide, (c) desire for revenge, or (d) any combination of these responses." *Seneca: His Tenne Tragedies* (1581) exhibits the pattern and some of its variations. In *Gorbuduc*, the king and queen follow the pattern, despairing over the death of Ferrex, then wishing for death and seeking revenge. *The Spanish Tragedy* follows the pattern closely with Hieronimo's despair at the loss of his absolute (his son), his madness, his desire for revenge, and his contemplation of suicide. In *Tit.*, the protagonist's absolutes are his surviving children, and his despair at their death or mutilation leads to madness and obsession with revenge. Titus never entertains thoughts of suicide, but omission of this element is one of the common variations of the Senecan pattern.

2750   Kolin, Philip C. "Performing Texts in *Titus Andronicus*." *BNYSS*, 7, no. 3 (1989), 5–8.

Points out that *Tit.*, especially in its self-conscious allusions to classical literature, is unusually concerned with the presentation of texts as part of the dramatic action. Analyzes the four scenes of act IV to show how the characters and the audience are compelled to read texts accurately. Beginning with Lavinia's use of the *Metamorphoses* to "inscribe herself into Ovid's tale of rape and revenge" and thus to become an Ovid for an ignoble post-empire Rome, act IV contains a series of characters, each of whom enters with a bundle, a text, that needs to be deciphered. Sh is dramatizing a number of current (late 20th-c.) ideas about "the way text is experienced."

2751 Kramer, Joseph E. "The Revengeful City: A Study of *Titus Andronicus*." Ph.D. dissertation, Princeton University, 1966. *DA*, 25 (1964–65), 6698.

Proposes to explain what Sh attempted in *Tit.* and what he accomplished. Surveys "the morality of revenge" in various dramas before Sh to provide a context for the play's treatment of this theme. Three chapters on *Tit.*, each dealing with one of the drama's major movements, use a variety of critical approaches. The third appendix considers Herodotus as a possible source for elements of *Tit.*

2752 Kramer, Joseph E. "*Titus Andronicus*: The 'Fly-killing' Incident." *ShakS*, 5 (1969), 9–19.

Maintains that the banquet scene in *Tit.* (III.ii) involving the killing of a fly, though accepted by many scholars as genuine, bears many marks of being a later addition by someone who made certain superficial efforts to patch it into the rest of the play. The episode requires, for example, that a banquet be brought on stage, which would, at midpoint in the play, "seriously undercut the effectiveness of the novel and spectacular state–Thyestean–Ovidian banquet of the final scene." In sum, III.ii is probably not by Sh because it is "bathetic in its conceits, textually remote from the rest of the play, and dramatically inept."

2753 Lacey, Stephen Wallace. "Structures for Awareness in Dante and Shakespeare." Ph.D. dissertation, State University of New York at Buffalo, 1972. *DAI*, 33 (1972–73), 4421-A.

Suggests that Sh, without the "structures of awareness" on which Dante relied, was terrifyingly vulnerable to life but that he found that artistic creation can be a channel for self-mastery. Explores Sh's ambivalence about his art in an analysis of *Tit.*

2754 Lamb, Mary Ellen. *Gender and Authorship in the Sidney Circle.* Madison: U. of Wisconsin P., 1990. 297 pp.

Notes that treatments of Philomela during the Renaissance usually ignore her rape and her role as avenger. Most emblem books of the day focus on the nightingale's song and poetry in an attempt to dismiss women's anger. *Tit.* is especially blunt in its comparison of Lavinia to Philomela, but instead of creating an avenging heroine, Sh makes Lavinia a passive sufferer. This is a typical Renaissance representation of Philomela, one in which rage is displaced by pathos.

2755 Legouis, Pierre. "*Titus Andronicus*, III.i. 298–299." *ShS*, 28 (1975), 71–75.

Holds that these lines [III.i.297–298], which speak of making Saturnine and Tamora "Beg at the gates, like Tarquin and his queen," may owe something to Dionysius of Halicarnassus, who goes into much more detail than Livy, Sh's other likely source, about the Etruscan envoys sent on behalf of Tarquin to plead for the restoration of his property after he was expelled from Rome. Neither Livy nor Dionysius mentions Tarquin's queen, the notorious Tullia, in connection with begging, so it must be assumed that Sh included her to provide a counterpart in the simile to "the hardly less hellish Tamora."

2756 MacDonald, Joyce Green. "'The Force of Imagination': The Subject of Blackness in Shakespeare, Jonson, and Ravenscroft." *RenP*, 1991 (1992), 53–74.

Provides a brief account of the part translations of classical works by Pliny, Herodotus, and others played in shaping the 16th-c. perception of Africa and its inhabitants. In

Tit., Sh creates a multivalent work, unclear about its identity as "an Elizabethan version of Roman paganism, a revenge drama, a tragedy of state, or some combination of these." Although Aaron is given great prominence, he is ultimately "unknowable except as the product of European imagination."

2757 Marcus, Jane. "Still Practice, A/Wrested Alphabet: Toward a Feminist Aesthetic." *Tulsa Studies in Women's Literature*, 3, nos. 1–2 (1984), 79–97.

Makes suggestions for the development of a "socialist feminist criticism," arguing that the Procne–Philomel story and its retelling in the rape of Lavinia in *Tit.* provide a model for learning to read "the text of the oppressed and silenced."

2758 Marshall, Cynthia. "'I can interpret all her martyr'd signs': *Titus Andronicus*, Feminism, and the Limits of Interpretation." *Sexuality and Politics in Renaissance Drama*. Eds. Carole Levin and Karen Robertson. (Studies in Renaissance Literature 10.) Lewiston, New York, 1991, pp. 193–213.

Argues that *Tit.* "enacts a male terror of female power, conceived primarily in sexual terms." Lavinia and Tamora are stereotyped as two confining and opposite images of woman that are ultimately linked. Lavinia's mutilation and rape cannot be truly told because she has been silenced; she is fixed, through her identification with a character in the Ovidian text she brings on stage and through the perceptions of male characters, as a suffering victim and sexual object. However, her sexual knowingness, indicated in her comments to Tamora shortly before her rape (II.iii), suggests that she does not entirely conform to this image of the violated virgin. Both Tamora and Lavinia are killed at the end in a display of male vengefulness toward the mother and the body and in an attempt to erase or pervert female expressions of desire and appetite. Sh's presentation of the "issues of gender, sexuality, and power" is dialectical in *Tit.* and hints that the author did not wholly accept "the projected female stereotypes."

2759 Metz, G. Harold. "The Early Staging of *Titus Andronicus*." *ShakS*, 14 (1981), 99–109.

Avers that the early staging of *Tit.*, as seen in the quartos and the First Folio, shows Sh making full use of the resources of the Elizabethan theater. The trap in the stage was used for the pit that is the focus of the action in II.iii. Extensive use was also made of the gallery, especially in the opening scene, where important segments take place "aloft." Some device, probably a double-hung stage door, was decorated as the entrance to the tomb of the Andronici; and there was abundant spectacle in Titus's triumph, the entombment of the dead, the procession of senators and judges accompanying Titus's sons to execution, and the daring presentation of Titus dressed as a cook.

2760 Metz, G. Harold. "*The History of Titus Andronicus* and Shakespeare's Play." *N&Q*, 22 (1975), 163–66.

Challenges Marco Mincoff's view that *Tit.* is the source for the ballad of Titus Andronicus, which is in turn the source of *The History of Titus Andronicus*, contained in an 18th-c. chapbook (item 2761). Points to a number of elements "common to the play and the *History*" but absent from the ballad and concludes that the ballad cannot be a link between the other two versions. Furthermore, the *History* "cannot be merely a prose version of *Tit.*" See also items 2742a, 2743, and 2743a.

2760a Metz, G. Harold. "Titus Andronicus: Three Versions of the Story." *N&Q*, 35 (1988), 451–55.

Restates the author's position that a prose *History of Titus Andronicus* is the source of *Tit.*, with a ballad on the same subject deriving from both Sh's play and the *History*. Attempts to refute a competing hypothesis—that the order of the three accounts is play—ballad—history—by recapitulating seven important elements of the story that are shared by the *History* and the play but are absent from the ballad. Responds to G. K. Hunter's arguments (item 2743) on each of these elements and reaffirms the author's original contention. See also items 2742a, 2743a, 2760, and 2761

2761   Mincoff, M. "The Source of *Titus Andronicus*." *N&Q*, 18 (1971), 131–34.

Argues that the ballad and prose "history" of Titus Andronicus in the Folger Library chapbook postdate Sh's play. The ballad is based on the play, and the history is a reexpansion of the ballad. The source of *Tit.* has not yet been found. See items 2760, 2760a, 2742a, 2743, and 2743a. .

2762   Miola, Robert S. "*Titus Andronicus* and the Mythos of Shakespeare's Rome." *ShakS*, 14 (1981), 85–98.

Suggests that *Tit.* shows more clearly than some of Sh's more mature plays about Rome how the poet's imagination assimilated and reworked materials from a variety of sources to dramatize classical themes. The rape of Lavinia and its consequences are clearly based on Ovid's story of Philomela in the *Metamorphoses*, and the contrast between Rome and the woods is related to the Ovidian tension between Athens, where Philomela lives in civilized comfort, and the wild forest where she is raped. As in Ovid, the rape is an example of the barbarism that subverts all laws. Ovid seems to resonate in Sh's mind with Virgil, whose account of the fall of Troy informs much of *Tit.* At one point, for example, Titus compares himself to the unhappy Aeneas called upon to tell again his tale of destruction (III.ii.26–28); Lucius is later asked to assume the same duty (V.iii.85–87), thus signaling the transfer of power from father to son. More important is Sh's use of the archetypal invasion by barbarian Greeks of the civilized Trojan city as a way to gain perspective on the invasion of Rome by the Goths. *Tit.* also owes much to Ovid's myth of the four ages, especially his vision of the Iron Age, which resembles the world of the play in its pervasive civil discord, injustice, deceit, violence, and impiety. Virgil's conception of this myth, found in Eclogue 4, was also an influence on Sh, as were the comments of various Renaissance mythographers. Saturninus, whose name associates him with Saturn, reigns over a city that, like the god, devours its children. It should be recognized that Sh's idea of Rome was built up over time from a variety of sources; it is a mistake to explain the various manifestations of Rome in the plays according to a single source, political philosophy, or ideology. Also, Virgilian sources should be acknowledged as making a significant contribution to the portraits of Rome that appear in the plays. Revised as chapter 3 of item 0759a.

2763   Nevo, Ruth. "Tragic Form in *Titus Andronicus*." *Scripta Hierosolymitana* (The Hebrew University Publication, Jerusalem), 25 (1973), 1–18.

Perceives in *Tit.* "a blueprint of Shakespearean tragedy," the outline of which can be seen in later plays. Notes that the structure Sh inherited for laying out the progress of a tragic figure came from the five-act Terentian play. Analyzes the movement of *Tit.* in terms what happens to its hero in each of the five acts, laying particular stress on the pathos and irony of act IV. Notes the classical origins (in Seneca and Ovid) of the rape of Lavinia and the cannibalistic banquet.

2764   Palmer, D. J. "The Unspeakable in Pursuit of the Uneatable: Language and Action in *Titus Andronicus*." *CritQ*, 14 (1972), 320–39.

Claims that in *Tit.* Sh uses formal and stylized speech to ritualize response to the horrors represented. The episodes in the story are related to "analogues in Roman literature and mythology, most notably to Ovid's tale of Tereus and Philomela." In addition, "the classical references are also designed to suggest a pattern in the events of the past as though the tragedy is a re-enactment of a primordial Roman experience." By giving the name Saturninus to the Emperor, Sh associates the action with the chaos that succeeded the overthrow of Saturn by his son Jupiter. Saturn was also associated with mutilation and cannibalism, both important in *Tit.* In Titus's enactment of his suffering, "ritual and game, the solemn and the farcical, are mingled," and we are sometimes moved to laughter in complicity with his mood. *Tit.* is an "elaborately-designed work" in which "Sh takes some extremely bold yet calculated risks with the resources of his art."

2765 Parker, Douglas H. "Shakespeare's Use of Comic Conventions in *Titus Andronicus*." *UTQ*, 56 (1987), 486–97.

Regards *Tit.* as an experiment that uses four major comic conventions parodically to intensify tragic effect. First, "the traditional comic pattern of discord" resolved is parodied at the end of the first scene; second, a comic pastoral environment is used to bring about diabolical results; third, a birth motif is used to suggest death; fourth, a banquet is the context for enacting grotesque murders.

2766 Paxton, Nancy L. "Daughters of Lucrece: Shakespeare's Response to Ovid in *Titus Andronicus*." *Proceedings of the IXth Congress of the International Comparative Literature Association/Actes du IXe Congrès de l'Association internationale de littérature comparée, Innsbruck, 1979.* Vol. 1, *Classical Models in Literature/Les Modèles classiques dans les littératures/Klassische Modelle in der Literatur.* Innsbruck: Institut für Sprachwissenschaft der U. Innsbruck, 1981, pp. 217–24.

Challenges Roy Battenhouse's view (see item 0133) that in *Luc.* Sh alters his source, Ovid's *Metamorphoses*, to register disapproval of Lucrece's lengthy justification for committing suicide. Analyzes *Tit.* to show that Sh reshapes Ovid to reveal the connection between the patriarchal power to silence women and the power to rape. In particular, the speech of Marcus upon seeing the ravished and mutilated Lavinia makes several allusions to other Ovidian tales of rape that show how Ovid can be moralized, in the manner of Arthur Golding, to call attention to the tragedy of rape. Sympathetic to Lavinia, Sh uses her plight to emphasize how "patriarchally defined language and art serves to confuse violence with sex and dishonour with rape by violently silencing the female point of view."

2767 Plasse, Marie Ann. "The Human Body in Shakespearean Representation." Ph.D. dissertation, Boston University, 1987. *DAI*, 48 (1987–88), 1778-A.

Examines four plays that "offer sustained reflections on the human body as dramatic medium." Chapter 3 explores *Tit.*, focusing on its "deliberately disjunctive exhibition of verbal and corporeal modes of representation."

2768 Price, H. T. "The Yew-Tree in *Titus Andronicus*." *N&Q*, 10 (1963), 98–99.

Cites Stephen Batman on the poisonous properties of the yew tree and John Gerarde on how he and his school fellows proved the tree harmless by eating its berries and sleeping in its shadow. Sh in *Tit.*, II.iii.107, exploited a superstition he may have known was false.

2769 Price, Hereward T. "*Titus Andronicus* and the Additions to *The Spanish Tragedy*." *N&Q*, 9 (1962), 331.

Points out that in the first quarto of *Tit.*, there is the line "I pried me through the *crevice* of a wall" (V.i.114). The second (1600) and third (1611) quartos have *crevie*, while the First Folio goes back to *crevice*. In the 1602 edition of Kyd's *Spanish Tragedy*, there are several additions to the original text, one of which is "I prie through every crevie of each wall." Clearly, the writer of this was stealing a line from *Tit.*; there is no warrant for assuming, as some do, that the author of the additions had a hand in *Tit.* or that Sh was imitating Kyd.

2770 Reese, Jack E. "The Formalization of Horror in *Titus Andronicus*." *SQ*, 21 (1970), 77–84.

Recalls that Peter Brook's 1955 production of *Tit.* was praised for formalizing the horror, but Brook was merely recognizing and translating "into modern stage practice" what Sh had already done in his text. The play succeeds because of its abstract, stylized presentation of bloody events. Its world is black and white, with no nuances. Characters are largely emblematic (for example, Lavinia is a type of Injured Innocence rather than an actual woman). The "literary" flavor of the play is enhanced by obvious parallels and oppositions among characters and groups of characters (symbolizing, for example, Roman civilization and pagan barbarism). Patterns of repetition dominate the play, most notably the pleas for mercy, which are frequently made on bended knee. (See item 2746.) These are of two types, genuine and hypocritical. That the former usually fail and the latter succeed is neatly symbolic of the chaos into which Rome has fallen. The play's tableau-like artificiality is enhanced by the detailed stage directions (for example, the exquisitely precise instructions in I.i about the arrangement of the various groups on stage and "aloft," and about their accoutrements).

2771   Schrickx, W. "*Titus Andronicus* and Thomas Nashe." *ES*, 50 (1969), 82–84.

Discusses Chiron's suggestion in *Tit.*, II.iii.129–130, that he and Demetrius ravish Lavinia, using her husband's body as a pillow. Sh seems to have gotten this image of human flesh as a bolster from Thomas Nashe's *The Unfortunate Traveller*; Nashe's priority in using the image is confirmed by a similar passage in his *Pierce Penniless*.

2772   Scuro, Daniel Ervinn. "'Victorious in Thy Mourning Weeds': A Study of William Shakespeare's *The Most Lamentable Roman Tragedy of Titus Andronicus*." Ph.D. dissertation, Ohio State University, 1974. *DAI*, 35 (1974–75), 7439-A–7440-A.

Argues that *Tit.* is informed by *romanitas*, whose essential virtue is *pietas*. Addresses Sh's classical heritage, *romanitas*, and *pietas* in the introductory chapter. Concludes that *pietas* causes the Rome of *Tit.* to "undergo a tragic metamorphosis" and enables the play to offer a political lesson to Elizabethan audiences.

2773   Shadoian, Jack. "*Titus Andronicus*." *Discourse*, 13 (1970), 152–75.

Conducts a close reading of *Tit.* to support the contention that the play is "adequate and effective on its own terms." Sees *Tit.* as "an assault on our emotions," a "mixture of the tragic and the melodramatic." It is "essentially theatrical, immediate, and visceral, more than thematically substantial or psychologically penetrating."

2774   Shaffer, Larry E. "Shakespeare's Earliest Tragedy: A Study of *Titus Andronicus*." Ph.D. dissertation, University of Illinois at Urbana-Champaign, 1979. *DAI*, 40 (1979–80), 278-A.

Considers "the literary, historical, and intellectual context of *Tit.*, and thereby assesses the importance of this tragedy in Shakespeare's canon and in the literature of the Renaissance." In *Tit.*, Sh reexamines and upsets the conventions of revenge tragedies like *The Spanish Tragedy*. He also reconsiders the nature of another Renaissance commonplace, the "providentially directed metamorphosis in this world." Character tableaux are prominent in *Tit.*, with the playwright creating scenes that are psychologically unrealistic but may reveal less about the characters' inner states than they do about the futility of pleas for mercy in Rome. The play's violence gives rise to several problems. Sh attempts to move his audience to pity with an excess of horrors, but he succeeds only in benumbing us. The instigator of most of the violence, Aaron, arouses our interest but not our sympathy. His concern for his child is not so much fatherly solicitude as a desire that his evil propensities be passed on.

2775 Slights, William W. E. "The Sacrificial Crisis in *Titus Andronicus.*" *UTQ*, 49 (1979), 18–32.

Interprets *Tit.* in terms of ideas developed by René Girard about society's employment of ritual violence. In serving justice, a society evolves certain ceremonies of sacred violence, which are enacted to purify the social fabric and prevent men from becoming engulfed in an endless cycle of private revenge. When the rite of purification goes wrong, sacred violence becomes indistinguishable from competitive violence within the community. This breakdown, the sacrificial crisis, is what is studied in *Tit.*

2775a Smidt, Kristian. "Levels and Discontinuities in *Titus Andronicus.*" *Multiple Worlds, Multiple Words: Essays in Honour of Irène Simon*. Eds. Hena Maes-Jelinek, Pierre Michel, and Paulette Michel-Michot. Liège: Department of English, 1987, pp. 283–93.

Argues that the chief difficulty in appraising *Tit.* is that it "moves uneasily between the levels of allegory and realism." Points to the play's emblematic features, especially in the first act, with its emphasis on ritual. Beyond that, there are other tendencies towards abstraction, such as the personification by several characters of qualities like piety, impiety, evil, lust, revenge, and confusion. However, the realistic aspects of the play are too strong to be blended smoothly into an allegorical framework. The characters are inconsistent, being developed on "two different levels" and being "discontinuous on the realistic level." It is in the portrayal of Titus's "troubled consience, torn between contrary impulses and muddled by madness, that Shakespeare gets closest to a sustained triumph of realism." Revised as chapter 1 of item 0986a.

2776 Stamm, Rudolf. "The Alphabet of Speechless Complaint: A Study of the Mangled Daughter in Shakespeare's *Titus Andronicus.*" *ES*, 55 (1974), 325–39. Reprint *The Triple Bond: Plays, Mainly Shakespearean, in Performance.* Ed. Joseph G. Price. University Park: Pennsylvania State U. P., 1975, pp. 255–73.

Notes that Lavinia is deprived of speech in act II of *Tit.* Analyzes the scenes in which she appears in order to study the ways in which Sh not only employs her as "a passive image of horror" but also endows her with hints of "an active life and touches of individuality." The scene in which Lavinia, mutilated and ravished, is first encountered by her uncle Marcus (II.iv), shows Sh trying to "integrate a pattern derived from epical poetry in a dramatic event." The speech in which Marcus comes to recognize what has happened to his niece is at times successful in mirroring her mutilations and the gestures by which they are communicated and at times, because of its "excessive elaboration," unsuccessful. Discusses other scenes in which Lavinia appears, focusing on the effectiveness with which the dialogue suggests actions that humanize her. These scenes include III.i (when Titus and Lucius become aware of her plight), III.ii (a banquet scene in which the increasingly deranged Titus feels confident that he can "interpret all her martyr'd signs" [line 36]), and IV.i (in which, through a series of actions, she teaches the other members of her family how to read Ovid in such a way that the identities of her ravishers are revealed). Remarks that Sh's handling of "his mute heroine" allowed him to gain experience "in the art of expressing emotion and meaning not through language alone, but through gesture and the other visual elements of the theatre as well."

2777 Taylor, Anthony Brian. "Golding's *Metamorphoses* and *Titus Andronicus.*" *N&Q*, 25 (1978), 117–20.

Discovers two debts to Golding's translation of Ovid's *Metamorphoses* in *Tit.* The first comes in Tamora's invitation to Aaron to sit down with her in the woods (II.iii.14–20). Her reference to "the babbling echo" seems to be indebted to Golding's description of Echo as a "babbling Nymph" (III.443–444). In a second instance, Aaron, explaining why he killed the Nurse who brought him his child, calls her "A long-tongu'd babbling gossip" (IV.ii.153). It is likely that Sh was thinking of Echo here because Golding had characterized her in his preface and in his translation as a bawd and a gossip.

2777a Taylor, Anthony Brian. "Shakespeare's Use of Golding's Ovid as a Source for *Titus Andronicus*." *N&Q*, 35 (1988), 449–51.

Contends that in *Tit*. Sh is indebted to Golding's translation of the *Metamorphoses* for several incidental allusions (to Echo, Phaethon, and the Pythogorean Sermon); for aspects of the rape and mutilation of Lavinia and the cannibalistic banquet; and for "the image of the tiger as an emblem for female cruelty."

2778 Taylor, Sally Thorne. "Children in Shakespeare's Dramaturgy." Ph.D. dissertation, University of Utah, 1975. *DAI*, 36 (1975–76), 2228-A-2229-A.

Uses young Lucius in *Tit*. to show that Sh endows his children with some "complexity and depth." Also in *Tit*., the protagonist is given crucial aid by children.

2779 Teller, Stephen J. "Lucius and the Babe: Structure in *Titus Andronicus*." *MQ*, 19 (1978), 343–54.

Examines the 18th-c. chapbook *The History of Titus Andronicus*, which is probably a reprint of Sh's chief source, to call attention to the playwright's addition of the sacrifice of Alarbus and the character of Lucius and his elaboration of the matter of Aaron's baby. Sh made these changes to structure his action in three parts and to provide a relatively virtuous restorer of order at the end.

2779a Tennenhouse, Leonard. "Violence Done to Women on the Renaissance Stage." *The Violence of Representation: Literature and the History of Violence*. Eds. Nancy Armstrong and Leonard Tennenhouse. London: Routledge, 1989, pp. 77–97.

Discusses, in the course of considering "the particular form of violence directed against the aristocratic female body in Jacobean drama," the case of Lavinia in *Tit*. Argues that Lavinia's rape "represents the crime of dismemberment," providing "the setting for political rivalry among the various families with competing claims to power over Rome."

2779b Tobin, J. J. M. "Nomenclature and the Dating of *Titus Andronicus*." *N&Q*, 31 (1984), 186–87

Discovers a "proximate source" for *Tit*—Thomas Nashe's *Christ's Tears over Jerusalem*—that, unlike any other source, has the names *Titus* and *Saturninus*, as well as a "banquet in which a mother eats her son." To allow for Sh's consulting the manuscript of this work, *Tit*. should be dated in late 1593.

2780 Tokson, Eliott H. *The Popular Image of the Black Man in English Drama, 1550–1688*. Boston: G. K. Hall, 1982. xii + 178 pp.

Mentions Aaron from *Tit*. several times to illustrate the ways in which white attitudes toward black men constructed a stereotyped image of the latter on the stage. Aaron is shown as relentlessly evil and is prized by Tamora only for his sexual prowess; he does, however, exhibit some positive qualities when he places his son's life ahead of his own.

2781 Toole, William B. III. "The Collision of Action and Character Patterns in *Titus Andronicus*: A Failure in Dramatic Strategy." *RenP*, 1971 (1972), 25–39.

Contends that the mounting horror evoked by the action pattern of *Tit*. comes into conflict with the character pattern through which Sh attempts to induce sympathy for his protagonist. The problem is that, although Titus is the victim of terrible violence, he is also the agent of the play's climactic horror.

2782 Tricomi, Albert H. "The Aesthetics of Mutilation in *Titus Andronicus*." *ShS*, 27 (1974), 11–19.

Maintains that *Tit.* is an experiment in which Sh wittily and obsessively literalizes figurative language to point relentlessly and precisely to the horrifying events being depicted. Apparently metaphorical references to "hands" and "head" frequently foreshadow or recall mutilations specifically involving those body parts. For example, Lavinia's request that Titus bless her "with thy victorious hand" (I.i.166) anticipates the cutting off of both of her hands and one of Titus's. Sh, in *Tit.*, subordinates everything, including metaphor, to the "single task of conveying forcefully the Senecan and Ovidian horrors that he has committed himself to portraying."

2783 Tricomi, Albert H. "The Mutilated Garden in *Titus Andronicus*." *ShakS*, 9 (1976), 89–105.

Discovers a "thematic matrix" in *Tit.* that is manifested in a contrast between "predatory animal images" and the image of the "enduring but mutilated garden." At the beginning of the play, Lavinia is associated with the idyllic pastoral setting of the forest; indeed, she seems to embody it. Once she is raped and disfigured by the beast-like sons of Tamora, the forest is transformed into a dark, hellish place: She and the forest have both been mutilated. After Lavinia's rape, all of the Andronici are portrayed as plants that have been stunted or hewn down, the victims of animal-like cruelty. Titus eventually adopts the beastly behavior of his tormentors to enact his revenge. He and Lavinia cannot survive their own foray into savagery, but Lucius, Titus's last remaining son, is, at the play's end, associated with the growth of a plant: He will restore Rome to organic wholeness.

2783a Waith, Eugene M. "The Ceremonies of Titus Andronicus." Mirror up to Shakespeare: Essays in Honour of G. R. Hibbard. Ed. J. C. Gray. Toronto: U. of Toronto P., 1984, pp. 159–70. Reprint. *Patterns and Perspectives in English Renaissance Drama*. Newark: U. of Delaware P., 1988, pp. 138–47.

Notices the unusual number of ceremonies, either visual spectacles or verbal scene paintings, in *Tit*. In the early part of the play, principally act I, the ceremonies have genuine, traditional forms and embody ideals "to which the hero subscribes," even though these ceremonies are inappropriate for the contexts in which they appear. The ceremonies of the play's middle figure forth the hero's fantasies, reflecting his "obsession with redress of some sort." Tamora's visit to Titus as Revenge, with her two sons playing the roles of Rape and Murder (V.ii), is a spectacle that "means the exact opposite of what it seems to signify." The banquet of (V.iii), with the contrast between its initial formality and "the ensuing carnage," is perfectly suited to a play "where every ceremony is in some way at odds with the situation which it solemnizes."

2784 Waith, Eugene M. "*Titus Andronicus* and the Wounds of Civil War." *Literary Theory and Criticism: Festschrift Presented to René Wellek in Honor of His Eightieth Birthday. Part I: Theory; Part II: Criticism.* Ed. Joseph P. Strelka. 2 vols. New York: Peter Lang, 1984, pp. 1351–62.

Discovers in *Tit.* considerable emphasis on conventions of rhetoric and spectacle associated with portraying "the wounds of civil war" in other plays of the time: The threat of disorder is seen in the opening scene; the hero experiences radical shifts of fortune; revenge and counter-revenge are prominent; and brutal actions, like the various dismemberments, symbolize disorder in the state.

2785 Waith, Eugene M., ed. *Titus Andronicus*. (Oxford Shakespeare.) Oxford: Clarendon P., 1984. ix + 226 pp.

The introduction, in discussing sources, gives special attention to four analogues of the Titus story. The first is the tale of Philomela in the sixth book of Ovid's *Metamorphoses*, a work that is frequently alluded to in the play and a copy of which is brought on stage in IV.i. Two of the other analogues, a prose *History of Titus Andronicus* printed in chapbook form in the 18th c. and a ballad of Titus Andronicus composed in the late 16th c. have problematic relationships to Sh's play. Rehearses the scholarly arguments of Mincoff (item 2761), Metz (item 2760), and Hunter (item 2743) and concludes that the prose history was a source for *Tit.*, which was in turn a source for the ballad. Notes that the prose history makes use of information about wars with the Goths that could have been derived from historians of the late Roman Empire like Pedro Mexia, Paulus Diaconus, and Procopius. These authors had not been translated into English in the 16th c., but they were available in Italian, from which the author of the chapbook claims to be translating. Notes the imaginative appeal of Rome to the authors of medieval romances as well as the Renaissance use of Roman history as a source for "model orations and for episodes on which to base declamations, the popular exercises in forensic oratory derived from the Roman *controversiae*, in which the student invented speeches for and against an accused person." Suggests that the chapbook author combined "controversial episodes" as adapted by Renaissance writers like Matteo Bandello and Alexandre Sylvain with material from Ovid and the Roman historians. To the chapbook history Sh added elements derived from his own reading of Ovid and Roman historians like Livy and Herodian. He also incorporated hints from Plutarch's *Lives*, the *Aeneid*, and possibly Euripides' *Hecuba* and Seneca's *Thyestes*. *The Spanish Tragedy* of Kyd may have influenced Sh to interlard his text with Latin quotations in order to "claim kinship with a respected tradition" and to attract the well-read in his audience. Important to the interpretation of *Tit.* are concerns with ceremony and spectacle, orotund political speech and Ovidian love poetry, and atrocities.

2786 Warren, Roger. "Trembling Aspen Leaves in *Titus Andronicus* and Golding's Ovid." *N&Q*, 29 (1982), 112.

Suggests that the image of aspen leaves used by Marcus Andronicus in describing the ravaged Lavinia (*Tit.*, II.iv.45) may be derived from Golding's translation of Ovid's *Metamorphoses*.

2787 West, Grace Starry. "Going by the Book: Classical Allusions in Shakespeare's *Titus Andronicus*." *SP*, 79 (1982), 62–75.

Argues that the pervasive classical allusions in *Tit.* are calculated by Sh to connect the characters with decayed Roman tradition. In particular, Sh "is exploring the relationship between Roman education—the source of all the bookish allusions—and the disintegration of the magnificent city [that] produced that education." Ovid and Horace, whose literary works are constantly pointed at, instruct the characters in the techniques of rape, mutilating, revenge, and murder, instead of exerting a beneficial influence. Everyone seems obsessed with writing, but what is written serves perverse ends. The Romans, especially Titus, are limited rather than liberated by their education, and the barbarians have learned to be even worse than they already were through their contact with Roman tradition.

2788 Willbern, David. "Rape and Revenge in *Titus Andronicus*." *ELR*, 8 (1978), 159–82.

Provides a psychoanalytical reading of *Tit.*, in which revenge is viewed as a "heroic male effort" to save "an assaulted woman (wife, daughter, mother, city)." In pursuing revenge, the male figures are spurred by fears of being "devoured or dismembered" by a malevolent female (Tamora). In his revenge plot, Titus uses oral villainy to respond to oral threats. Revision of part of item 2789.

2789 Willbern, David Pierce. "The Elizabethan Revenge Play: A Psychoanalytic Inquiry." Ph.D. dissertation, University of California, Berkeley, 1973. *DAI*, 34 (1973–74), 1261-A.

Describes "the unconscious determinants" of Aeschylus's *Oresteia* and of three Elizabethan revenge plays. Comments that "revenge repeats and imitates the original injury." Argues that *Tit.* "dramatizes a rape and revenge reciprocation, structured on a basic oral threat." Part revised as item 2788.

2789a Wynne-Davies, Marion. "'The Swallowing Womb': Consumed and Consuming Women in *Titus Andronicus.*" *The Matter of Difference: Materialist Feminist Criticism of Shakespeare.* Ed. Valerie Wayne. Ithaca: Cornell U. P., 1991, pp. 129–51.

Argues that *Tit.* highlights the difference between "the sexual constraint and sexual self-determination of women." At times, it seems to "offer women control over their own corporal identities": Further, it empowers Tamora; provides Lavinia "a means of self-expression"; privileges, through contemporary allegory, an aged queen; focuses the audience's attention upon "the symbolic centre of the 'swallowing womb'"; and holds out hope for women's redemption "through the metamorphosing power of Ovidian rhetoric." The patriarchal and patrilineal power structures of Rome are challenged and unsettled, but they finally reassert themselves by circumscribing the location of women "in relation to the dominant male body—corporal and politic."

TROILUS AND CRESSIDA

2790 Adams, Howard C. "'What Cressid is.'" *Sexuality and Politics in Renaissance Drama.* Eds. Carole Levin and Karen Robertson. (Studies in Renaissance Literature 10.) Lewiston, New York: Mellen, 1991, pp. 75–93.

Maintains that Cressida's inconstant self results from the necessity in the world of *Tro.* for her to seek her identity as it is reflected in those around her. Lacking an "adequate feminine role model," she relies first on Pandarus, then Troilus, then Diomede and the Greeks to tell her who she is. She longs to discover genuine love but also wants to use her beauty and her wit to gain security in a world of men, and she remains painfully lonely, "seldom understood" by those around her.

2791 Adamson, Jane. "Drama in the Mind: Entertaining Ideas in *Troilus and Cressida.*" *CR,* 27 (1985), 3–17.

Analyzes *Tro.* in terms of the various senses in which the characters, the audience, and the play may be said to entertain ideas or to be entertained by them. The characters are constantly delivering themselves of ideas but show themselves to be unable or unwilling to recognize the ideas that drive others. The play cultivates in the audience a "simultaneous recognition of multiple and discrepant possibilities" but at the same time surprises us, disappoints our expectation: We are disturbed by its willful lack of resolution.

2792 Adamson, Jane. *"Troilus and Cressida."* (Twayne's New Critical Introductions to Shakespeare.) Boston: Twayne, 1987. xx + 174 pp.

The preface contains a concise discussion of modern scholarship on texts and sources of *Tro.,* including comments on recent editions. An introductory section entitled "The Stage History and the Critical Reception" surveys key works of criticism from the 20th c. Works cited in these prefatory sections are included in the "Select Bibliography" at the end, which consists of three parts: (1) Texts; (2) Source Materials; and (3) Stage History and Critical Reception.

The first chapter insists on the importance of conflict, both in the play's manifest subject matter and in its exploration of the irresolvable tension between discordance and harmony: This is especially noticeable in the first half–dozen scenes.

The second chapter considers the "edgy wit" of the play itself, focusing on the humor, or near-humor, of forcing the audience to accommodate, at any given moment, "several distinct, incongruous and even incompatible ideas of what is happening." We cannot align ourselves with the point of view expressed by any of the characters, though we participate in all of them. Sh is experimenting with "a new way of discovering and knowing the multifariousness of experience." Pays special attention to the scene in which Pandarus brings the two lovers together (III.iii) and the two council scenes (I.iii and II.ii).

The third chapter examines the love affair as it is developed in the middle of the play, arguing that there is a deeper concern for the inner lives of the characters than earlier. Even in scenes that foreground civilized amity (like III.i), however, reminders of the opposing ugliness of war are present. Highlights the importance of being open to each moment in the play; that is, we should recognize momentarily the beauty and power of the love affair of Troilus and Cressida, just as we acknowledge momentarily the reductive force of Pandarus's and Thersites' comments. Notes that "the monstruosity" of love (as Troilus sees it)—its excitation of infinite desire in subjects whose capacity for performance is limited—is powerfully apprehended in the play. In a larger sense, "the nexus between desires and limits" is the focus of Tro.'s comic and tragic awareness.

The fourth chapter, covering the end of the play, uses Troilus's response to Cressida's betrayal (V.ii) to epitomize "that state of soul or mode of human being" that Tro. expresses, analyzes, and evaluates: "a way of experiencing the world as radically paradoxical and contradictory" and of remaining open to it "without the protection of any guaranteeed objective values, any certainties and comforting presuppositions on which to rely."

2793 Adelman, Janet. "'This Is and Is Not Cressida': The Characterization of Cressida." *The (M)other: Essays in Feminist Psychoanalytic Interpretation.* Eds. Shirley Nelson Garner, Claire Kahane, and Madelon Sprengnether. Ithaca: Cornell U. P., 1985, pp. 119–41.

Contends that the plot of Tro. enacts Troilus's fantasies, which involve his attempt to regain an "infantile fusion with a maternal figure" through his liaison with Cressida. The soilure of Cressida through sexuality results in a besmirching of the mother figure and a rupture of the union with this figure that Troilus hoped to achieve. Troilus's sexual guilt is transferred to Cressida, she is divided into maternal and ideal selves, and her wholeness as a character is sacrificed by Sh in an effort to keep Troilus pure.

2794 Aggeler, Geoffrey D. "Madness in Reason: A Paradoxical Kinship in *Troilus and Cressida*." WascanaR, 9, no. 1 (1974), 39–57.

Maintains that Tro. is a preliminary study for Sh's great tragedies and final tragicomedies. In it, he attacks various philosophical stances that claim to be founded in reason. Agamemnon is a Stoic because he can think of no alternative; Ulysses' Machiavellian analysis of the stalled war effort proves to be irrelevant; Hector plays at reasoning only as a game, having long since given himself over to the game of chivalry; Troilus, viewing Cressida's desertion, flees from reality by positing a Platonically ideal Cressida; and Thersites' cynicism is reductive. The play is an indictment of "rational illusion."

2795 Alexander, Peter. "*Troilus and Cressida*." TLS, Mar. 18, 1965, p. 220.

Letter to the editor disputes a number of points made by Nevill Coghill about Tro. Maintains, contrary to Coghill, that "your" in the epistle inserted in the second issue of Tro. can refer to Sh; that the evidence of the title page does not prove public performance; and that the Prologue is a parody of Jonson's "Prologue arm'd" to the *Poetaster*. Regards Tro. not as "evidence of Sh's cynicism but as his medicine for cynics." See items 2837, 2796, 2797, 2838, 2839, 2845, 2846, 2847, 2861, 2862, 2863, and 2962.

2796 Alexander, Peter. "*Troilus and Cressida.*" TLS, Feb. 16, 1967, p. 136.
Letter to the editor replies to Nevill Coghill's letter of Jan. 19, 1967 (item 2837). Explains the exuberant style of the prefatory epistle to *Tro.* as justifiable puffery, not evidence of dishonesty. In addition, the epistle provides us "with the key to the interpretation of this enigmatic drama" and helps confirm that it was composed for private performance. The armed Prologue was not simply borrowed from Jonson to intimidate the audience. Sh "imitated Jonson far enough to allow everyone to recognize the imitation"; only, however, to provide an ironic commentary on Jonson's bellicose attitude toward his audience. The Prologue and Epilogue are in keeping with the spirit of the play and were not composed years after its original performance, as Coghill maintains. See also items 2795, 2797, 2838, 2839, 2845, 2846, 2847, 2861, 2862, 2863, and 2962.

2797 Alexander, Peter. "*Troilus and Cressida.*" TLS, Apr. 20, 1967, p. 340.
Letter to the editor disputes "known facts" presented by Nevill Coghill (item 2838), among which are statements that the Epilogue to *Tro.* was not in existence by 1603; that armed Prologues by Sh and Jonson and an armed Epilogue by Marston are all intended by their authors to serve the same purpose; and that *Tro.* was performed several times in 1602–3. Cites Bertrand Evans as support for the view that Sh's treatment of his material in *Tro.* is so unusual as to suggest composition for a private audience. See also items 2795, 2796, 2837, 2839, 2845, 2846, 2847, 2861, 2862, 2863, and 2962.

2797a Annal, Charles William. "Black Humor in Selected Works of Donne, Jonson, Shakespeare, and Burton." Ph.D. dissertation, University of Connecticut, 1976. DAI, 37 (1976–77), 5840-A.
Regards *Tro.* as dominated by "a black comic perspective." The characters in the play habitually overvalue themselves, refusing to accept limitations and blaming their failures "on time and chance"; they are thus "simultaneously comic and pitiful."

2798 Ansari, A. A. "Moral Dilemma in *Troilus and Cressida.*" IJES, 10 (1970), 96–108.
Examines the ambiguity of *Tro.* The action of the play is seen from several points of view (those of Hector, Troilus, Ulysses, Achilles, and Thersites), most of them unreliable: This makes "the reader's responses rather indeterminate." Spiritual apostasy in the characters—allowing the unitive self to disintegrate and the lower self to dominate the higher—results in chaos.

2799 Ansari, A. A. "The Problem of Identity in *Troilus and Cressida.*" AJES, 3 (1978), 199–214.
Maintains that *Tro.* gives us the "sense of being in a labyrinth" and that the relationship between Troilus and Cressida, especially, is characterized in this way. Troilus suffers from self-division: On the one hand, he is idealistic, believing in subjective appraisal as a source of value; on the other hand, he cannot square his idealism with the evidence of Cressida's perfidy furnished by his own senses. Cressida also has a divided identity, but her two halves are not self-subsistent like those of Troilus; rather, they are deliberately constructed to deceive her lover.

2800 Arnold, Margaret J. "'Monsters in Love's Train': Euripides and Shakespeare's *Troilus and Cressida.*" CompD, 18 (1984), 38–53.
Calls attention to the many translations of and commentaries on the works of Euripides, especially his Trojan War plays, available to Sh and his contemporaries. Claims that "these Renaissance conceptions of Euripides" had a significant influence on *Tro.* Euripidean features of Sh's play include a chaotic world, the "anti-heroic Greeks," the vanity of Helen, the fragile idealism of Troilus and Cressida (which leads to their deflation and self-division), and an episodic structure.

2801 Asp, Carolyn. "In Defense of Cressida." *SP*, 74 (1977), 406–17.

Presents Cressida as the chief embodiment in *Tro.* of the play's central philosophical question: Does value reside in the object or does it depend on variable, subjective perceptions from outside? Although several characters attempt to fix value in the object, the play insists on an ambivalent world where observers fix worth in a fluctuating market. Cressida is one of only two characters who seem to recognize this (Ulysses is the other), but her attempts to achieve a stable identity by accommodating herself to forces beyond her control are pathetic and futile.

2802 Asp, Carolyn. "Th' Expense of Spirit in a Waste of Shame." *SQ*, 22 (1970), 345–57.

Argues that *Tro.* is a satiric attack on the conventions of courtly love, which, despite their unrealistic and immoral nature, were accepted by the courtiers of Elizabethan England. Following satiric dramatists like Jonson and poets like Donne, Sh mocks such courtly notions as the ennobling effect of love and the idealization of the lady and "demonstrates that the forms of courtly behavior are contrary to a realistic, moral, and rational view of life."

2803 Asp, Carolyn. "Transcendence Denied: The Failure of Role Assumption in *Troilus and Cressida*." *SEL*, 18 (1978), 257–74.

Depicts the world of *Tro.* as one of mutability, in which the characters continually strive to escape change by entering or remaining in the realm of art. They are caught up in a tension between the traditional roles they try to play and the impersonated selves that are called forth to encounter the realities of everyday life. Troilus and Cressida provide a clear example when, at the end of III.ii, they step forward and assume the roles to which they have been assigned by literary tradition, roles that are at odds with their behavior elsewhere in the play. Troilus attempts to reduce himself and others, especially Cressida, to "the one-dimensional proportions of the world of art," but fails and is left with no control over anything. Hector tries to cast himself in the role of the rational man in his judgment of Helen, but when Troilus, with his habitual idealizing, transforms her into "the emblem of Trojan honor," Hector relents and now sees himself as "the chivalric hero." This role, of course, also fails to sustain him. Instead of trying to escape their impersonated selves, as the Trojans do, the Greeks, who begin in their traditional roles (Ulysses as the wise statesman, Achilles as the great warrior), struggle to maintain them. The result is the same, however: They are carried away by the flux. The only characters who remain constant are the diminishers, Pandarus and Thersites.

2804 Bache, William B. "Affirmation in *Troilus and Cressida*." *Discourse*, 10 (1967), 446–55.

Argues that *Tro.* is a difficult play because "the clues to goodness are not so obvious as they are in perhaps almost every other" Sh play. Decadence is evident in the vanity of the Trojans, the pride of the Greeks, and the breakdown of the family in both societies. The Trojans have love, but no wisdom or power; the Greeks have wisdom and power, but no love. There are two significant affirmations that help counteract all this negation: We are meant to think of Ulysses' subsequent voyage home and his reunion with wife and family, and we are reminded of Aeneas's future role as "the founder of Rome (the seat of Christianity), the father of the Western World."

2805 Barfoot, C. C. "*Troilus and Cressida*: 'Praise us as we are tasted.'" *SQ*, 39 (1988), 45–57.

Maintains that Sh, in *Tro.*, is examining the nature of human transaction. Takes note of the mercantile imagery and observes that, "once we have something to sell," we tend to betray some kind of trust, either by undervaluing or overvaluing. The play makes us aware that we trade in selves, in words, and in literature. Initially, we may feel honored to be witnesses "to the greatness of the classical past," but *Tro.* soon makes us dubious about "the capability of drama or literature to enshrine and pass on."

2806 Bayley, John. "Shakespeare's Only Play." *Stratford Papers on Shakespeare 1963.* Ed. B. W. Jackson. Toronto: W. J. Gage, 1964, pp. 58–83.

Argues that *Tro.* is unique among Sh's plays because it denies time. Ordinarily, Sh uses the past to give meaning to human fate, but in *Tro.* there is neither past nor future: Everything takes place in the present. We are confronted with "the immediacy and incoherence of the moment," which rob love and war of meaning and value. Revised as item 2807.

2807 Bayley, John. "Time and the Trojans." *EIC,* 25 (1975), 55–73.

Locates the unique quality of *Tro.* in its treatment of time, that is, "in the formal impact of *Tro.* there is neither past nor future: everything takes place in, and ends in, the present." Sh here seems to dissolve history; he "appears to deny that the famous and legendary ever existed as time has reported them, or that we would ever find anything at any moment in history beyond scraps of idiotic dialogue and meaningless event." Abandoning his usual practice of developing his characters in time, Sh gives us random moments in the experience of people we do not know. The domination of Thersites is appropriate in this climate because he speaks so clearly for the present moment, to which all the characters are in bondage. Every character in the play is both victim and intriguer, betrayer and betrayed, "but it is in the heroine that this loss of stability appears most emphatically." Revision of item 2806. Revised as chapter 1 of section 3 of item 0138.

2808 Beckerman, Bernard. "Shakespeare's Industrious Scenes." *SQ,* 30 (1979), 138–50.

Explains that in constructing his scenes Sh shapes dialogue to give expression to "the natural energies of presentation on which all acting is based," organizes these energies "into a binary form," and "at his best arranges the two elements of the binary form in such a way as to create a compelling dialectic." Analyzes six scenes from the battle sequence in act V of *Tro.* as a major illustration.

2809 Benson, Morris. *Renaissance Archetypes: The Long Shadows.* London: Coleman Publishing Company, 1977. xl +180 pp.

The first chapter analyzes in detail Sh's treatment of the story he found in Chaucer's *Troilus and Criseyde.* Points out that in *Tro.* Sh condenses time in depicting the betrayal of Troilus by Cressida to "produce an emotional shock" and places Troilus in the Greek camp as witness of Cressida's seduction by (or of) Diomedes to demonstrate "the difference between belief and reality." The play subverts the myth of courtly love to expose the frailties of humanity. Sh skillfully uses the Trojan war, especially "the miasmatic atmosphere in the Greek camp," to explain how human conduct is determined by outside forces. The play exploits a series of ironic disparities to effect a masterful transformation of Chaucer's narrative.

2810 Berger, Harry Jr. "*Troilus and Cressida*: The Observer as Basilisk." *CompD,* 2 (1968-69), 122–36. Reprint. *Second World and Green World: Studies in Renaissance Fiction-Making.* Ed. John Patrick Lynch. Berkeley: U. of California P., 1988, pp. 130–46.

Contends that the armed Prologue of *Tro.*, unlike the choral speaker in *H5*, refuses to impose a point of view on the audience, thereby leaving their responses to the play to be determined by their own characters. In Ulysses' degree speech (I.iii), the optical imagery suggests that viewers or seers are subjective and influence "their objects by the way they see." Evil gazers, like basilisks, can taint an object by infecting it with "the poison of their inferior natures" (as does Thersites). The problem raised by Sh is that, in the absence of objective value, too much power to determine worth is placed under the control of observers who are not up to the task. Sh, however, suggests that this need not be the case: If Trojan idealism were more tough-minded, it might succeed.

2810a Berke, Bradley. *Tragic Thought and the Grammar of Tragic Myth.* Bloomington: Indiana U. P., 1982. vi + 119 pp.

Devises a grammar to formalize "the multitudinous possibilities for expressing and understanding the informational content of a fundamental proposition, a basic Plot sentence: 'A (mythical) self-annihilator annihilates himself with an instrument of self-annihilation.'" Chapter 4 proposes "the Central Desire Triangle" as a "primary landmark" in a tragic plot; the destruction of this configuration is "important for the tragicness of a play." Notes that *Tro.* is an interesting test case because it has several pairs of characters each of which could be part of a Central Desire Triangle. In no case, however, does such a configuration manifest itself. Thus *Tro.* can be shown to be a "nearly tragic nontragic" play.

2811 Bernhardt, W. W. "Shakespeare's *Troilus and Cressida* and Dryden's *Truth Found Too Late.*" *SQ*, 20 (1969), 129–41.

Discusses *Truth Found Too Late*, Dryden's revision of *Tro.*, to help modern readers approach one of Sh's problem plays relatively free from their own prejudices. This task is made easier by Dryden's clear statement of his aims in "The Grounds of Criticism in Tragedy," prefaced to his revision. Viewing *Tro.* as an incomplete heroic tragedy, Dryden reshaped it by (1) reducing much of its figurative language to something closer to prose discourse; (2) making the unresolved plot more coherent and more overtly tragic; and (3) purifying Sh's mixed characters, especially Troilus. The character of Troilus, which in Dryden's view does not sufficiently realize its heroic potential, is radically transformed. However, the play can be defended as Sh left it. Troilus is an adolescent hero whose extravagant language is evidence of his self-delusion. Although not unsympathetic, he is often a source of amusement, even a target of satire. He gains no tragic insight, and the unresolved ending demonstrates that his experience "is simply an interpolated chapter in the larger history of the destruction of Troy." The play is best described as a type of comedy, perhaps "dark comedy" or "problem play."

2812 Berry, Francis. "Troy's Gender." *N&Q*, 26 (1979), 125–26.

Explains the effect of having Ulysses, in his speech on degree or hierarchy, refer to Troy at first with the masculine pronoun "his" (*Tro.*, I.iii.75) and then, at the end, with the feminine pronoun "her" (I.iii.137). Suggests that "his" refers to Troy's present strength and that "her" refers to the weakness that would be evident in Troy if the Greeks were observing hierarchy, which at the time they are not.

2813 Binney, James. "Shakespeare's Heroic Warriors." *Discourse*, 11 (1968), 257–68.

Argues that the satire in *Tro.* is directed primarily "against the general tendency of men to make heroes of the wrong material." Sh's enlargement of the role Thersites has in Homer shows his interest in debunking the idea that heroism must be military. In many other plays, especially the English histories, Sh exposes the futility of war. *Tro.* is his most powerful indictment of the worship of military glory. Disillusioned as they are with heroic warriors, modern readers may be the first since Sh's time who can experience the play without feeling a need to apologize to Homer.

2814 Biswas, D. C. *Shakespeare in His Own Time.* New Delhi: Macmillan Co. of India, 1979. xix + 162 pp.

Chapter 4, "*Troilus and Cressida* and the Renaissance Concept of Value," invokes Machiavelli and Montaigne to point out that the idea of "absolute or intrinsic value" is challenged at two levels—materialistic and spiritual—in the play, as it was being challenged in Sh's society. The Greeks represent the materialistic aspect of the Renaissance, while the Trojans, with their individualism, enact, especially through Hector and Troilus, the notion that value is relative.

2815 Blissett, William. "Paradox and Ambiguity in *Troilus and Cressida.*" *WascanaR*, 9, no. 1 (1974), 5–28.

Asserts that Sh adopted the targets and the paradoxical style of the verse satirists of the 1590s to construct a play out of paradox. Several features and characters in the play contribute to an ambiguity that gives it "a conclusion of inconclusion": the Prologue, whose style is both ornate and low; Ulysses, whose speech on order seems to intensify our sense of chaos; Hector, whose reason is impaired by impulse and whose magnanimity is tainted by pettiness; Cressida, the rarefied vulgarian; Troilus, the Platonic sensualist. The rhetoric of soilure, "comparisons with dirt," is pervasive and reflects a philosophical concern with questions of order and disorder, form and formlessness, life and death. Sh is careful to maintain the ambiguity throughout. For example, the love of Troilus and Cressida and the inconsistency of the heroes never become repellent on the one hand or laughable on the other. The play comes as close as possible to giving a dramatic form to unresolved paradox.

2816 Blythe, David-Everett. "Shakespeare's 'Compass'd Window.'" *N&Q*, 31 (1984), 201.

Challenges the "received annotation" that equates the "compass'd window" in which Pandarus sees Troilus meet Cressida (*Tro.*, I.ii.112) with a "bay," which is an architectural and poetic improbability. Cites other passages in *Tro.* to support the idea that the "compass'd window is "an upright in-wall arch" or "an aperture of horseshoe outline."

2817 Boatner, Janet Williams. "Criseyde's Character in the Major Writers from Benoît through Dryden: The Changes and Their Significance." Ph.D. dissertation, University of Wisconsin, 1970. *DAI*, 31 (1970–71), 4705-A.

Argues that Sh's Cressida is of little interest in herself; she is merely a vehicle for conveying Troilus's incapacity to perceive and follow "right reason."

2818 Boitani, Piero. "Eros and Thanatos: Cressida, Troilus, and the Modern Age." *The European Tragedy of Troilus.* Ed. Piero Boitani. Oxford: Clarendon P., 1989, pp. 281–305.

Notes that "a highly critical moment in the story of Troilus is reached" around the end of the 16th c. in the works of Sh. First, in *MV*, V.i, Lorenzo describes Troilus's experience as a tragic love story. Then, in *AYL*, IV.i, Rosalind gives a burlesque, overly realistic version of his death; and, in *Ado*, Benedick sneers at him as "the first employer of pandars" (V.ii.31). In *Tro.*, Sh "deals a mortal blow to the story": He undermines the epic element while linking the love affair much more closely than before with the Trojan War; he foregrounds the romantic aspect at the same time that he betrays skepticism about it; and he divides the personalities of Troilus and Cressida into contrasting halves so that "we can no longer know them fully."

2819 Bonheim, H. "Shakespeare's 'Goose of Winchester.'" *PQ*, 51 (1972), 940–41.

Offers an explanation of Pandarus's reference to a "Goose of Winchester" in the concluding lines of *Tro.* Cites other plays to prove that the hissing of the goose refers to an expression of disapproval by a theater audience. Pandarus thus defers making his will in order to avoid boring the spectators.

2820 Bonjour, Adrien. "Hector and the 'One in Sumptuous Armour.'" *ES*, 45 (1964), 104–8.

Disputes S. L. Bethell, who questions Hector's chivalry because the hero refers to the Greek in "goodly armor" as a "beast" and says "I'll hunt thee for thy hide" (*Tro.*, V.vi.30–31). Hector's use of the hunting metaphor shows his disappointment at the cowardice of his opponent and in no way diminishes his knightly virtue.

2821 Bowen, Barbara. "Representation in Shakespeare: New Readings of Three Middle Plays." Ph.D. dissertation, Yale University, 1986. *DAI*, 48 (1987–88), 2633-A.

Studies the ways in which Sh's drama "takes representation as its constant subject." Analyzes the "competing rhetorical patterns" of *Tro.*, as well as "its alternately hostile and celebratory attitude towards representation."

2822 Bredbeck, Gregory W. "Constructing Patroclus: The High and Low of Renaissance Sodomy." *The Performance of Power: Theatrical Discourse and Politics*. Eds. Sue-Ellen Case and Janelle Reinelt. Iowa City: U. of Iowa P., 1991, pp. 77–91.

Contends that *Tro.* "exploits the bifurcated potentiality encoded in Renaissance sodomy." On the one hand, sodomy is stigmatized as an especially low and ugly form of social activity through Thersites' gibes at Patroclus. Thersites exemplifies, in a particularly pure form, the Renaissance use of satire as a base means of containing baseness. On the other hand, the attempt of the Greeks in the high discourse of their council scene (I.iii) to construct Patroclus "as an absolute base Other to the world of order" implicates them in the baseness of the satirist, and thus destabilizes the absolute distinction between high and low that they seek to maintain through the notion of degree. Unable to seal themselves off from contamination by the low, they are led from "the world of precept into the mutable world of improvised praxis." Revision of chapter 2 of item 2824. Extract from item 2823.

2823 Bredbeck, Gregory W. *Sodomy and Interpretation: Marlowe to Milton*. Ithaca: Cornell U. P., 1991. xv + 261 pp.

Chapter 2, "The Authority of Sodomy," includes a section, "Constructing Patroclus," extracted as item 2822. The book as a whole is a revision of item 2824.

2824 Bredbeck, Gregory William. "The Use of Ganymede from Marlowe to Milton: Homoeroticism in Renaissance Thought and Literature." Ph.D. dissertation, U. of Pennsylvania, 1989. *DAI*, 50 (1989–90), 2059-A.

Considers how English Renaissance literature "engaged aspects of sodomy and homoeroticism." Chapter 2 includes a discussion of how *Tro.* employs "homoerotic themes to demonstrate the internal contradictions of Tudor and early Stuart political theory." Revised as item 2823; chapter 2 revised as item 2822.

2825 Breuer, Horst. "Shakespeare's 'humble bee': A Note on *Troilus and Cressida*, 5.10.41–44." *RLV*, 43 (1977), 380–83.

Attempts to explicate Pandarus's quatrain on the bumble bee by glossing several key words: "humble-bee" is the bawd, the "honey" represents the various sweetnesses enjoyed by the lovers, "sting" has to do with the lover's sexual desire and his mistresss' erotic appeal, and "subdued in armed tail" refers to "the maid's vanquished virginity." The passage, then, means that once the lover has attained his desire (or the mistress has given up her virginity), the bawd loses his influence.

2826 Brooks, Harold. "*Troilus and Cressida*: Its Dramatic Unity and Genre." *"Fanned and Winnowed Opinions": Shakespearean Essays Presented to Harold Jenkins*. Eds. John W. Mahon and Thomas A. Pendleton. London: Methuen, 1987, pp. 6–25.

Describes how the two actions of *Tro.*, martial and romantic, are united. This is done primarily through the character of Troilus, but also through Hector, Achilles, Helen, Pandarus, and Thersites. At a deeper level, the two actions are linked by various themes of evaluation. Sh provides two definitive standards for evaluation in the Greek council scene (I.iii) and the Trojan council scene (II.ii). In the former, Ulysses provides a clear explication of order and degree, which should govern political enterprises. In the latter, Hector expounds natural law and the law of nations in such a way as to leave no doubt about what is right for the Trojans to do. The fact that neither Ulysses nor Hector is true to the principles he announces does not render the principles inapplicable to the world of the play. Concludes that *Tro.* is both a tragedy and a bitterly sardonic comedy.

2827   Bullough, G. "The Lost *Troilus and Cressida.*" *E&S*, 17 (1964), 24–40.

Analyzes, for its relevance to Sh's *Tro.*, the "plot," or prompter's and call-boy's outline, for a *Troilus and Cressida* play written by Thomas Dekker and Henry Chettle in 1599 and produced by the Admiral's Men. The Dekker and Chettle plot seems to have influenced Sh in its use of multiple sources, its interweaving of love and war themes, and its general layout of the material. Sh rehandled "his predecessors' double theme with an unromantic, unsentimental and unheroic bias," adding among other things the cynical commentator Thersites.

2828   Burns, M. M. "*Troilus and Cressida*: The Worst of Both Worlds." *ShakS*, 13 (1980), 105–30.

Argues that in *Tro.* Sh presents a picture of human beings debased by the forces of aggression. The natural process by which, on the one hand, human beings single out others as individuals and, on the other, make abstract judgments by observing groups of individuals is corrupted. Cressida attempts to individualize and to abstract, but her own character is subjected to negative stereotyping by the males in the play, including Troilus. Hector resembles Cressida in many important ways: Like her, he attempts to behave as an individual by responding to others as individuals; but, as Cressida falls victim to a sexist view of women, so Hector is pressured into confining himself to the role of the fierce soldier. In the wartime setting of *Tro.*, it is easy for all of the characters, men and women alike, to fall into familiar patterns of behavior that are destructive to their humanity.

2829   Burrill, Tom. "Ulysses on 'Degree': Shakespeare's Doctrine of Political Order?" *Parergon*, N. S. 2 (1984), 191–203.

Challenges the notion that Ulysses' speech on "degree" in *Tro.*, I.iii, is evidence for Sh's support of Tudor social orthodoxy. Cites passages from Elyot's *Governor*, the Homilies on Obedience, and Hooker's *Laws of Ecclesiastical Polity* to show that the sources of this speech, like the speech itself, are not "informed by a comfortable sense of universal harmony." Instead, their urgent rhetoric emphasizes the political danger of disorder and is intended, like Ulysses' oration, to serve the governing class. Sh, in other words, does not subscribe to the commonplaces about hierarchy voiced by Ulysses; rather, he exposes the fears and uncertainties of conservative authorities in the face of change.

2830   Byles, Joan. "*The Winter's Tale*, *Othello* and *Troilus and Cressida*: Narcissism and Sexual Betrayal." *AI*, 35 (1979), 80–93.

Maintains that in *Tro.*, Troilus, as an idealistic lover, attempts to impose on Cressida an image of moral excellence constructed by his superego. When the idealistic lover is betrayed, he reacts, as does Troilus, with aggressive hatred directed at himself and/or at others.

2831   Callahan, Robert D. "Shakespeare's *Troilus and Cressida*: Lechery as Warfare." *Paunch*, 23 (1965), 57–67.

Dissents from idealist critics of *Tro.*, who echo Ulysses in using "techniques of manipulation and coercion" to produce a conformity in their audience. Ulysses is the spokesman for an order that insists on rigid control of instinctual desire. Confronted with this repressive system, Cressida learns how to play the game of power, articulating "with her words and her body, the fantastic coup achieved by the patriarchal culture: a divorce of sex and desire, denigration of sex and encouragement of an appetite for violence."

2832 Cartelli, Thomas. "Ideology and Subversion in the Shakespearean Set Speech." *ELH*, 53 (1986), 1–25.

Includes an analysis of Ulysses' speech on degree (*Tro.*, I.iii) that construes it as an "act of self-concealment," which submerges Ulysses' subjectivity in "a language of universal signifiers." Regards set speeches of this nature in Sh, which seem to promote dominant ideology, as subversive of that ideology even while expounding it. Revised as chapter 6 of item 0243.

2833 Cary, Cecile Edith Williamson. "*Troilus and Cressida* and *All's Well That Ends Well*: Shakespeare's Ironic Plays." Ph.D. dissertation, Washington University, 1969. *DAI*, 30 (1969–70), 2961-A.

Contends that *Tro.* and *AWW* are Sh's only totally ironic plays. They both use "anticlimax, burlesque, and reductive imagery." In each play, there is "a series of anticlimaxes leading to stasis," which in *Tro.* "evokes futility and frustration." Both plays burlesque exaggerated language; in the case of *Tro.*, this includes the code of courtly love. The images of animals, disease, food, and trade operate in both plays to show "the ugly realities behind the characters' extravagant pretensions."

2834 Chapman, Antony U. "The Influence of Shakespeare's Sources on the Dramaturgy of *Troilus and Cressida*." Ph.D. dissertation, Kent State University, 1975. *DAI*, 36 (1975–76), 1502-A.

Suggests that Sh's fidelity to his two main sources for *Tro.*—Chaucer's *Troilus and Criseyde* and Caxton's *Recuyell of the Historyes of Troye*—is responsible for many of the play's problems (indeterminacy of genre, ambiguities of characterization, and disjunctiveness of plot). In the first two scenes, for example, Sh attempts to reconcile Chaucer's notions of medieval love and the very different conventions of Elizabethan romantic comedy. In the Trojan council scene, Troilus's character is derived from Caxton and bears little resemblance to the Troilus of the first act, who is taken chiefly from Chaucer.

2834a Charnes, Linda. "'So Unsecret to Ourselves': Notorious Identity and the Material Subject in Shakespeare's *Troilus and Cressida*." *SQ*, 40 (1989), 413–40.

Maintains that *Tro.* enacts the tension between the characters' "notorious identity," their "legendary citationality," and "an essentialist longing for something self-evident, something apprehendable without the publishing of rhetoric and narrative authority." Discusses "the subversive relation of the mimetic to authorized discourse," the ways in which women are used to confirm masculine identity, the homoeroticizing of war, and the failure of the masculine attempts to separate private from public existence.

2835 Choi, Young. "Reality Versus Appearance: Three Patterns in Shakespeare's *Henry IV, Part I*, *Troilus and Cressida*, and *Measure for Measure*." Ph.D. dissertation, Oklahoma State University, 1978. *DAI*, 39 (1978–79), 7353-A–7354-A.

Analyzes in Sh's plays three patterns that illustrate the discrepancy between appearance and reality. *Tro.* exemplifies the second of these patterns, in which the protagonists are victimized by "the false appearances of the manipulating characters."

2836 Clarke, Larry R. "'Mars His Heart Inflam'd with Venus': Ideology and Eros in Shakespeare's *Troilus and Cressida*." *MLQ*, 50 (1989), 209–26.

Regards *Tro.* as an allegory for the competition between the "late feudal aristocracy and the rising bourgeoisie," with the Trojans representing the English aristocracy and the Greeks the "new men." Sh intentionally veiled his social critique because he feared reprisal from the aristocracy, who may have condemned the play anyway, thus accounting for its lack of success.

2837 Coghill, Nevill. "*Troilus and Cressida*." *TLS*, Jan. 19, 1967, p. 52.

Letter to the editor responds to Peter Alexander's letter of March 18, 1965 (item 2795). Maintains that Bonian and Walley, the publishers of the first quarto of *Tro.*, were lying when they claimed in the epistle inserted in the second issue of the quarto that the play had never been performed in the public theater. Counters Alexander by asserting that the armed Prologue is intended to intimidate the audience, not to mock Jonson or the Trojan War. *Tro.* is not a comedy, but "a shocking tragedy." See also items 2796, 2797, 2838, 2839, 2845, 2846, 2847, 2861, 2862, 2863, and 2962.

2838 Coghill, Nevill. "*Troilus and Cressida*." *TLS*, Mar. 30, 1967, p. 274.

Letter to the editor sums up facts and inferences to support the position that *Tro.* was performed "at the Globe in 1602–03 and later, but without the Prologue and 'epilogue,' which were added to protect the play from a foreseeably rowdy audience, at a Christmas revel at the Inns of Court, probably in 1608." Reviews the use of armed prologues in the drama of the time. Argues that without the Prologue and Epilogue the play begins and ends in a tragic vein and that the tragedy is reinforced by the traditional identification of the Trojans with the British. See also items 2795, 2796, 2797, 2837, 2839, 2845, 2846, 2847, 2861, 2862, 2863, and 2962.

2839 Coghill, Nevill. "*Troilus and Cressida*." *TLS*, May 4, 1967, p. 384.

Letter to the editor attempts to show that the end of *Tro.* was carefully planned by Sh to emphasize the heartbreak of Troilus, the murder of Hector, and the dismissal of Pandarus as a broker–lackey. This would have been perfectly suitable for a Globe performance, but the reappearance of Pandarus with "a long, scurrilous and incongruous chat to the audience about venereal disease" is obviously an afterthought, uncharacteristic of Sh's work. It makes sense only as an addition for the special audience at an Inn of Court. See also items 2795, 2796, 2797, 2837, 2838, 2845, 2846, 2847, 2861, 2862, 2863, and 2962.

2840 Colahan, Clark. "Calderón and Shakespeare on Universal Order: Two Passages Compared." *English Studies* (Valladolid), 8 (1978), 125–55.

Includes discussion of Ulysses' speech on degree in *Tro.* Considers rhetorical patterns, imagery, and the idea of universal order. Notes that Sh juxtaposes and mixes "the figurative and the literal levels of language" and that he views pessimistically the possibility for order in the world.

2841 Cole, Douglas. "Myth and Anti-Myth: The Case of *Troilus and Cressida*." *SQ*, 31 (1980), 76–84.

Maintains that in *Tro.* Sh avoids conventional satiric debunking of heroic characters and parodic treatment of epic conventions, and offers instead a radical critique of the idealizing process of myth-making itself. Sh's technique is to maintain a constant tension between the idealized mythical notions of love and war and "their roots in baser and more absurd motivation." The audience is thus led to be skeptical about the possibility of creating myths to embody civilized values—and in particular about its own myths of "personal and social order." Crucial to this strategy is Sh's portrayal of Hector, who is endowed with an unsettling combination of Socratic perception and quixotic behavior.

2842 Collins, David. "The Story of Diomede and Criseyde: Changing Relationships in an Evolving Legend." *PAPA*, 7, no. 2 (1981), 9–30.

Includes an analysis of Cressida and Diomede in *Tro.* Regards Sh's presentation of Cressida as "sympathetic": In contrast to Chaucer's Criseyde, she is a virgin—"more innocent, more vulnerable." Sh's Diomede is more competitive and more arrogant than Chaucer's; his meanness cannot erase "the fact of Cressida's infidelity," but it does make her betrayal "less shocking."

2843 Cook, Carol. "Unbodied Figures of Desire." *ETJ*, 38 (1986), 34–52. Reprint. *Performing Feminisms: Feminist Critical Theory and Theatre*. Ed. Sue-Ellen Case. Baltimore: Johns Hopkins U. P., 1990, pp. 177–95.

Investigates the economy of masculine desire in *Tro*. The woman's body is the means through which men's desire "represents itself to itself," though it is an insufficient image, provoking violent impulses, articulated in "images of fragmentation of the woman's body." The masculine desirer goes from object to object, always seeking something beyond the woman and, faced with inevitable disappointment, views the woman as monstrous. As bodies, then, Helen and Cressida threaten "entrapment in finitude, repetition, representation"; it is only in fantasy that they can be enjoyed "as disbursed and fetishized signs, flickering images, unbodied figures of the thought." Notes that the heterosexuality sustained by the commerce in women is "a mediated homosexuality."

2844 Cook, Hardy M. "*Troilus and Cressida*: Shakespeare's World of Disorder." *SRASP*, 8 (1983), 21–28.

Accounts for the difficulty in characterizing *Tro*. by explaining that Sh, in this play, is rendering dramatically the dissolution of order in both love and the state. The breakdown of Troilus's ideal love, occasioned by Cressida's inconstancy, is paralleled by the subversion of Ulysses' vision of the ideal political state that culminates in the death of Hector.

2845 Cook, Ivor R. W. "*Troilus and Cressida*." *TLS*, Mar. 9, 1967, p. 202.

Letter to the editor points out that the arguments of Coghill (item 2837) and Alexander (items 2795 and 2796) depend on the integrity of Heminge and Condell as editors. Voices the suspicion that the Prologue to *Tro*. is not by Sh but rather was fabricated for the First Folio. See also items 2797, 2838, 2839, 2846, 2847, 2861, 2862, 2863, and 2962.

2846 Cook, Ivor R. W. "*Troilus and Cressida*." *TLS*, Apr. 6, 1967, p. 296.

Letter to the editor hypothesizes a lost quarto of *Tro*. from 1603 that was the basis for the 1609 quarto. Complains that Alexander, Coghill, and Empson have based their interpretations "upon too little solid evidence." See also items 2795, 2796, 2797, 2837, 2838, 2839, 2845, 2847, 2861, 2862, 2863, and 2962.

2847 Cook, Ivor R. W. "*Troilus and Cressida*." *TLS*, May 4, 1967, p. 384.

Letter to the editor attempts to answer the objections of William Empson (item 2863) to the idea of a lost quarto of *Tro*. published around 1603. See also items 2795, 2796, 2797, 2837, 2838, 2839, 2845, 2846, 2861, 2862, and 2962.

2848 Cox, John D. "The Error of Our Eye." *CompD*, 10 (1976), 147–71.

Considers *Tro*. in the context of other Elizabethan and Shakespearean interpretations of the Trojan War to show that in its pessimistic tone and in many other respects it is more typical than anomalous. Refers to George Peele's *Arraignment of Paris* and *Luc*. to establish that in *Tro*. Sh emphasizes the commonly used imagery and theme of failed vision. Every character in the play is tainted by some form of myopia, even Hector, who fails to follow through on his insight in the Trojan council scene. Just as the characters suffer from a partial vision of the Trojan story, so the play's structure, beginning and ending in the middle, tempts the spectator to take a distorted or limited perspective on the action.

2849 Daniels, F. Quinland. "Order and Confusion in *Troilus and Cressida* I.iii." *SQ*, 12 (1961), 285–91.

Presents a rhetorical analysis of Agamemnon's and Ulysses' speeches and argues that the former "revels in excessive abstractions," thus avoiding reality, while the latter diagnoses the disease afflicting the Greek camp by presenting specific instances. In contrasting Agamemnon's muddled euphuisms with Ulysses's directness, Sh is dramatizing the divorce between thought and action that has been paralyzing the Greek camp.

2850 Dannreuther, Daphne Davis. "Shakespeare's 'Fantastical Trick': A Reader-Response Approach to the Problem Comedies." D.A. dissertation, Middle Tennessee State University, 1986. *DAI*, 47 (1986–87), 1733-A.

Explores each of the problem comedies, including *Tro.*, as "a dynamic interaction between artist and audience." Notes that these plays produce the effects of "tension, discomfort, surprise, and frustration."

2851 de Almeida, Barbara Heliodora C. de M. F. "*Troilus and Cressida*: Romantic Love Revisited." *SQ*, 15 (1964), 327–32.

Perceives *Tro.* as "the embodiment of the conception that irresponsibility in government inevitably results in the collapse of society, and that the ultimate result of that collapse is the impossibility of the preservation of absolute values on an individual plane." Sh used the Trojan War to demonstrate negatively what he had been demonstrating positively in the second tetralogy of English histories. He also used romantic love to show how individual relationships are corrupted by the general breakdown of society. *Tro.* may be compared to *Rom.*: Both are plays that end in the destruction of romantic love. In *Rom.*, society is not so much corrupt as blind, and the lovers achieve a moral victory. In *Tro.*, however, society's decadence is so far advanced that there is nothing to be salvaged. As a vision of pervasive corruption, the play cannot be easily classified as tragedy or comedy.

2852 Dodd, Mark Robert. "The History of *Troilus and Cressida*." *UC*, 11 (1991), 39–51.

Argues that *Tro.* is a history play, noting that "the fall of Troy was regarded as the ultimate historical secular catastrophe by Renaissance England." Enumerates several features of the history play found in *Tro.*: noble, melodramatic scenes; comic scenes; battle scenes; truth to history; entertainment; and episodic structure. *Tro.* is "Shakespeare's portrait of a pagan and, thus, a doomed and damned world." As appropriate in a history play, the characters are subordinated to events; Sh is not much interested, for example, in the psychological process of Hector's decision "to agree with his brothers and not return Helen."

2853 Dollimore, Jonathan. "Marston's 'Antonio' Plays and Shakespeare's *Troilus and Cressida*: The Birth of a Radical Drama." *E&S*, 33 (1980), 48–69.

Contends that *Tro.* undermines Christian providentialism by exposing, especially in the two philosophical debates of I.iii and II.ii, the inadequacy of its pagan counterpart, natural law. Analyzes Troilus as an example of the tendency in Jacobean tragedy "to decentre man," to create a tragic hero who lacks "that explicit or quasi-spiritual self–sufficiency (Christian or stoic) which is the source of the individual's tragic potential in humanistic tragedy." Troilus survives suffering, though he is brutalized by it; and he is "defined by and dependent upon" the social conditions that "are responsible for his suffering." Revised as chapter 2 of item 0324.

2854 Donaldson, E. Talbot. "Cressid False, Criseyde Untrue: An Ambiguity Revisited." *Poetic Traditions of the English Renaissance*. Eds. Maynard Mack and George deForest Lord. New Haven: Yale U. P., 1982, pp. 67–83.

Contends that Sh's Cressida (*Tro.*), despite her manifest differences in personality from Criseyde, is nevertheless modeled on Chaucer's heroine. Notes that, in the first four books of Chaucer's *Troilus and Criseyde*, the narrator's infatuation with Criseyde prevents the resolution of several ambiguities about her status, her motivation, her attitude toward love, even her physical appearance. Assessing these ambiguities shrewdly, Sh presented the qualities of his Cressida as sometimes reflections and sometimes refractions of Criseyde's qualities. He exploited the dramatic possibilities offered by Chaucer's ambivalent presentation of her vulnerability, but he made Cressida's desire for security greater than that of Criseyde. Perhaps his most radical change was to assign Cressida a passion for Troilus before the story begins. Cressida's character is charged with ambiguity, but it is of a kind different from Criseyde's. Unfiltered by the mystifications of an adoring narrator, Cressida's speeches reveal an attractive young woman of independent mind in the process of development. That she ends by betraying her lover is used by moralistic critics (like Ulysses in the play) to pronounce anything she does or says earlier as evidence of her bad character. Points out several instances in which commentators have manufactured evidence of her bawdry or impropriety. Admits Cressida's ultimate wrongdoing but insists that up until the end (including IV.v, in which she arrives in the Greek camp and is set down by Ulysses as a daughter of the game), she cannot be morally categorized. Finally, she is "both unforgivable and understandable," giving the play a "sadder and deeper" vision than what Ulysses can perceive.

2855 Dusinberre, Juliet S. "*Troilus and Cressida* and the Definition of Beauty." *ShS*, 36 (1983), 85–95.

Uses Dio Chrysostom (a 1st-c. critic of Homer), Plato (especially the dialogue "Greater Hippias"), Plotinus, and Marsilio Ficino's *Commentary on Plato's Symposium* to show that Sh has created in *Tro.* a disjunction between beauty and goodness. The play employs Platonic terms to consider whether the fairness of Helen and Cressida, especially as perceived through the "higher" senses of sight and hearing, leads to any idea of the good. However, the absence of a religious dimension forecloses the possibility that beauty can be worshipped in anything other than its material forms. The pursuit of beauty in *Tro.* leads finally to a conviction of its worthlessness. As corollaries, rational discourse is destroyed, and all things are trivialized, even the burning of Troy.

2856 Dyer, Frederick B. Jr. "The Destruction of Pandare." *Shakespeare Encomium*. Ed. Anne Paolucci. New York: City College, 1964, pp. 123–33.

Maintains that in *Tro.* Sh reduced Chaucer's Pandare from "a warm, benevolent courtier, sincerely interested in bringing happiness to his dearest friend and beloved niece, into a coarse, obscene old lecher, who seems to derive sexual pleasure from the lovers' happiness." Sh's Pandarus has been simplified in such a way that he resembles one of Ben Jonson's humors characters.

2857 Edwards, Philip. "The Declaration of Love." *Shakespeare's Styles: Essays in Honour of Kenneth Muir*. Eds. Philip Edwards, Inga-Stina Ewbank, and G. K. Hunter. Cambridge: Cambridge U. P., 1980, pp. 39–50.

Examines Sh's treatment of the idea that in expressions of love "words may be inadequate or treacherous." Adduces examples from four plays, including several from *Tro.* Comments that Troilus inflates his feelings for Cressida with an overwhelming, self-absorbed flood of language.

2858 Eldridge, Elaine. "Moral Order in Shakespeare's *Troilus and Cressida*." *Anglia*, 104 (1986), 33–44.

Argues that the moral order of *Tro.* can be discerned by considering Cressida as a Trojan and then noting how she and two other Trojans, Hector and Troilus, are guilty of significant wrongdoings and are appropriately punished. Hector abandons rational and moral arguments in favor of honor and dies due to a lack of the fair play that he has denied the Greeks. Cressida announces her position on love, then violates the love she embraces, and is punished by falling into the hands of the unscrupulous Diomedes. Troilus suffers defeats in both love and war, having substituted pride and glory for honor, and sexual indulgence and self-regard for love. Revison of part of item 2858a.

2858a Eldridge, Elaine May. "The Admirable Genius of the Author: A Study of Shakespeare's *Troilus and Cressida*." Ph.D. dissertation, University of Washington, 1981. *DAI*, 42 (1981–82), 1644-A-1645-A.

Uses John Dryden's revision of *Tro.*, *Troilus and Cressida, Or, Truth Found Too Late*, and his *Preface to Troilus and Cressida, Containing the Grounds of Criticism in Tragedy* to analyze Sh's play. Finds that Dryden, like many later critics, concentrates on the ways in which *Tro.* is unlike Sh's other plays. Maintains, however, that "a mimetic approach," stressing Sh's "psychological realism," is helpful in illuminating the true excellencies of *Tro.* and in pointing us toward what *Tro.* shares with the other plays. Part revised as item 2858.

2859 Elton, W. R. "Shakespeare's Ulysses and the Problem of Value." *ShakS*, 2 (1966), 95–111. Reprint. *Odysseus / Ulysses*. (Major Literary Characters.) Ed. Harold Bloom. New York: Chelsea House, 1991, pp. 144–160.

Points out that terms and concepts concerned with value are "central to at least one meaning level" in *Tro.* and can be usefully studied through certain of Ulysses' speeches. The Prologue and the first two scenes establish a technique of valuing characters and events at second- and third-hand, thus allowing for subjectivity and relativity. The nature of the valuing process is also held up for scrutiny. All of this sets up the relativity of Ulysses' famous speech in I.iii, in which degree is shown to be a pragmatic last resort to preserve order in an unstable world, not the divinely sanctioned first principle some have seen in it. The comments of Ulysses on value bear a strong resemblance to those of Thomas Hobbes: Both consider value relative and quantifiable and discuss it in terms of marketplace images. All values, including honor, are validated only through ceaseless competition. There is no absolute good or evil. Hobbes and Ulysses speak for the state and patriotic pragmatism, opposing the "asocial individualism" of figures like Troilus and Achilles.

2860 Elton, W. R. "Textual Transmission and the Genre of Shakespeare's *Troilus*." *Literatur als Kritik des Lebens: Festschrift zum 65. Geburtstag von Ludwig Borinski*. Eds. Rudolf Haas, Heinz-Joachim Müllenbrock, and Claus Uhlig. Heidelberg: Quelle & Meyer, 1975, pp. 63–82.

Analyzes the printing history of *Tro.* as a key to its genre. Important points include (1) that John Marston, who was in residence at one of the Inns of Court (the Middle Temple) during the time of the play's first performance there (1601–2), provided the presentation manuscript (from the Inns) of *Tro.* to his friend Henry Walley before leaving London in 1609; (2) that Walley, having already acquired another manuscript of the play (the foul papers), made the assumption, clearly favorable for business, that the play had been performed for a popular audience; (3) that, based on this assumption, Walley included on the first title page for his 1609 quarto the misinformation that the play had been performed at the Globe; (4) that acquisition of the fair copy manuscript from one of the Inns of Court forced Walley to recognize that the play had been performed only for a private audience, thus prompting his issuance of a second, corrected title page, along with the Epistle (in which Marston may have had a hand) explaining the play's genre (a comedy of "pungent wit"). Argues that the text of the 1609 quarto, as contrasted to the version of the play printed in the First Folio, is carefully edited to remove false starts by the author and difficult or obscure passages that would be especially reminiscent of the play's original elite audience. Discusses significant omissions in the quarto that are present in the Folio, including three lines from I.iii that parody a central passage in Aristotle's *Nicomachean Ethics* on moral responsibility. Concludes that the 1609 quarto, with its corrected title page, its Epistle, and its excisions, represents an attempt to render the play more palatable to popular taste. Credits the Epistle's description of *Tro.*'s genre (comedy).

2861 Empson, William. "*Troilus and Cressida*." *TLS*, Mar. 2, 1967, p. 167.

Letter to the editor adopts a half-way position between Coghill (item 2837) and Alexander (items 2795 and 2796). Suggests that *Tro.* was composed for the Globe in 1602 or 1603, but not performed. A few years later it might have been farmed out to an Inn of Court with the Prologue added to amuse young lawyers. See also items 2797, 2838, 2839, 2845, 2846, 2847, 2862, 2863, and 2962.

2862   Empson, William. "*Troilus and Cressida.*" *TLS,* Apr. 6, 1967, p. 296.

Letter to the editor suggests that the evidence of the *Stationers' Register* and the title pages of the first quarto of *Tro.* can support the conjecture that the play was not performed before it was published in 1609. See also items 2795, 2796, 2797, 2837, 2838, 2839, 2845, 2846, 2847, 2861, 2863, and 2962.

2863   Empson, William. "*Troilus and Cressida.*" *TLS,* Apr. 20, 1967, p. 340.

Letter to the editor challenges the view of Ivor Cook (items 2845 and 2846) that a quarto of *Tro.* was printed by Sh's company in 1603 and has not survived. See also items 2795, 2796, 2797, 2837, 2838, 2839, 2847, 2861, 2862, and 2962.

2864   Enck, John J. "The Peace of the Poetomachia." *PMLA,* 77 (1962), 386–96.

Finds clues to the nature of *Tro.* in the Poetomachia that involved several dramatists at the beginning of the 17th c. Jonson was responsible for introducing four elements that Sh and other dramatists took over and developed: discontinuity of plot (Jonson's characters devote themselves to extravagant schemes that fail or fade away, and the action is interrupted by commentary on these schemes); psychological principles (Jonson revived the ancient theory of the humors and used the character sketch); decorum (Jonson liberated the drama from "ramshackle customs" by resurrecting rules "or applying the neglected ones with a new rigor"); and satire. Sh's use of these elements in *Tro.* can be seen in the inconclusive councils and the ineffectual vows and stratagems of the lovers, the emphasis on psychological portraits of eccentrics like Ajax and Thersites, the glance at rules in the Prologue, and the yoking together of intensity and lightness.

2865   Erlich, Bruce. "Patterns of the Bourgeois in the Jacobean Shakespeare." *Gulliver: German-English Yearbook,* Band 6: *Shakespeare inmitten der Revolutionen.* Berlin: Argument, 1979, pp. 121–32.

Points out, in arguing that Sh demystifies or reformulates the dominant myths of his time, that *Tro.* sets side by side "the text of ideal love and inherited tales of the Trojan expedition" and "the text of bitter empirical experience in an English world of war in Ireland and the Netherlands, of syphilis, opportunism, and moral treachery."

2866   Everett, Barbara. "The Inaction of *Troilus and Cressida.*" *EIC,* 32 (1982), 119–39.

Contends that although *Tro.* makes use of two of the greatest stories known to the author and his contemporaries (the death of Hector and the infidelity of Cressida), it is an essentially storyless play. Sh replaced the "expressive self-containment of the old stories with the alogical, non-sequential activity of a quasi-modern consciousness." We begin with an awareness of how the Cressida and Hector stories end, but the play does not lead us through these stories in conventional ways: Our expectancy about the action, subverted and teased, constitutes the narrative. A number of features contribute to this effect: (1) The play has a peculiar sense of beginning late and ending prematurely; (2) every action is "self-indicting" (*doing* is the readiest way to *undoing*); and (3) betrayal is the play's key concept (Sh has revised the stories of Hector and Cressida to purify the sense of betrayal in each and to incorporate them both into a "great system of betrayal"). Though without a story, *Tro.* does have virtues: It makes us "see and feel things both as History and as Now, as very great and very small, as far removed and detached and also as the stuff of most immediate sensation." When he focuses on the small, Sh is able to write with "an almost sociological realism," placing characters in a particular social context.

2867 Faber, Kristina. "*Troilus and Cressida*: 'The Expense of Spirit in a Waste of Shame.'" *CCTE Studies*, 52 (Sept. 1987), 61–69. Revision. "Shakespeare's *Troilus and Cressida*: Of War and Lechery." *Colby Quarterly*, 26 (1990), 133–48.

Asserts that *Tro.* is intended to be a tragedy, but that its focus on "the greatest of all human lusts," war, undermines what Aristotle sees as the nobility requisite for tragic heroes and makes catharsis impossible. The "problem" of *Tro.* is that Sh grounds "plot, theme, character, and language in an unresolvable psychological paradox: that war alternately attracts and repels men, but always dehumanizes them."

2868 Farnham, Willard. "Troilus in Shapes of Infinite Desire." *SQ*, 15, no. 2 (1964), 257–64. Reprint. *Shakespeare 400: Essays by American Scholars on the Anniversary of the Poet's Birth*. Ed. James G. McManaway. New York: Holt, Rinehart and Winston, 1964, pp. 257–64.

Argues that Troilus is "created within the frame of Renaissance infinitization of man's quest on earth." As a figure of infinite desire in love, Troilus is defeated, but as a figure of infinite desire in honor (a warrior), he succeeds.

2869 Ferguson, Arthur B. *The Chivalric Tradition in Renaissance England*. (Folger Books.) Washington, D. C.: Folger Shakespeare Library, 1986. 184 pp.

Notes that in *Tro.* Sh gives the impression of unqualified disillusionment with chivalric values. Traditional chivalric notions of martial excellence, public responsibility, honor, and courtly love are subverted by a radical individualism that is also part of the chivalric heritage.

2870 Fineman, Joel. "Fratricide and Cuckoldry: Shakespeare's Doubles." *PsyR*, 64 (1977), 409–53.

Discusses Sh's use of doubles, observing that they were for him both "a congenial form" and "a suggestive content." Observes that *Tro.* is one of three plays in which the playwright begins "to question duplicity." That is, *Tro.* lacks "an organizing myth with which to control violence between equals," and its world seems paralyzed by the chaos deriving from "sexual duplicity."

2871 Flannery, Christopher. "*Troilus and Cressida*: Poetry or Philosophy?" *Shakespeare as Political Thinker*. Eds. John Alvis and Thomas G. West. Durham, North Carolina: Carolina Academic P., 1981, pp. 145–56.

Analyzes the Greek council scene (I.iii) to demonstrate that Sh is considering the relationship between poetry and philosophy carefully in *Tro*. Points out that, according to Ulysses, the preservation of degree is dependent on the recognition in society that wisdom, an intellectual achievement, is superior to every other human ability, especially the physical prowess of Achilles. Ulysses' explanation of the reason for degree's suffocation among the Greeks is that Patroclus is doing scurrilous imitations of "the entire Greek universe for the pleasure of Achilles" and that everyone else in the Greek camp is imitating this scandalous imitation of Patroclus. In other words, Patroclus is assuming "the classic role of the dramatic poet," and the result of his poetry and others' emulation of it is to undermine "the ordering principle" among the Greeks. Sh's play exhibits the chaotic, contradictory tendencies of "the passions governing the political life of man, and of the passions associated with poetry of any form." In pursuing truth about these matters, the author is willing to risk the appearance of dramatic inconsistency. The solution to the disorder is philosophical, not poetic or political.

2872 Fly, Richard D. "Cassandra and the Language of Prophecy in *Troilus and Cressida*." *SQ*, 26 (1975), 157-71.

Examines the language of *Tro.* in an attempt to show how in almost everything that is said there is a sense of impending catastrophe. Cassandra, in her two appearances (II.ii and V.iii), gives voice to demonic prophecies that haunt the play's action. Other characters occasionally prophesy, and what they say is usually doom-ridden as if under Cassandra's influence. For the most part, the characters other than Cassandra labor under the burden of not being able to see clearly into the future; their murky vision is set in sharp contrast to Cassandra's clairvoyance. There is a general desire in *Tro.* to find a center, a solid foundation, and the imagery of centeredness, often involving the sun, teases us by momentarily identifying several characters as focuses of strength: Agamemnon, Cressida, Achilles, and Nestor. Each of these, however, turns out to be spurious. Thersites is not discredited: His "degrading commentary ... should be understood as the temporal complement to Cassandra's more radical and static version of inevitable ruin."

2873 Fly, Richard D. "'I cannot come to Cressid but by Pandar': Mediation in the Theme and Structure of *Troilus and Cressida*." *ELR*, 3 (1973), 145-65.

Discovers in *Tro.* an unusually compelling exploration of the dramatist's difficulties as a mediator. The characters' problems with achieving desired goals—and their awareness of their paralysis—are so pervasive that the critic's attention is directed beyond personalities to the world of the play, and beyond that, to the form of the play and its creator. Sh seems to be dealing with materials intractable to his artistic power. The play is crowded with images of incomplete or unsatisfactory exchange and merchandising; the scenes are discontinuous; and the language is peculiarly clogged and non-communicative. *Tro.* seems to be focused on the obstacles that lie between "the apprehension of a whole and harmonious design and its actualization." Characters who attempt mediation—Ajax, Paris, and particularly Pandar—unknowingly but inevitably pervert the schemes under their administration. Pandarus, as a "playwright-surrogate," represents Sh's awareness of his own "inability to mediate adequately between his received mythic materials and the expectations of his audience." Revised as chapter 2 of item 0393.

2874 Fly, Richard D. "'Suited in like conditions as our Argument': Imitative Form in Shakespeare's *Troilus and Cressida*." *SEL*, 15 (1975), 273-92.

Calls attention to the problematic structure of *Tro.* and asserts that its disjunctive plot, inconsistency of characterization, and other difficulties are part of an attempt by Sh to force the audience to experience the radically contingent nature of the world as seen through a variety of devices, including synecdoche (the whole depending on the part), processional or pageant-like stage action, and an obsession with being exhaustive (for example, the urge to describe every step in a sequence). Throughout, there is a sense that one defective part, one false step, can set off a reaction that will engulf the world in chaos. The troubling form of the play, then, is deliberate—an attempt to image apocalypse.

2875 Foakes, R. A. "The Ending of *Troilus and Cressida*." *KM 80: A Birthday Album for Kenneth Muir, Tuesday, 5 May 1987*. Liverpool: Liverpool U. P. for Private Circulation, [1987], pp. 51-52.

Challenges those critics who exclude Pandarus's epilogue from *Tro.* as inauthentic. Asserts that Pandarus has stepped out of character to address the audience once before, just after he acts the role of pander by pushing Troilus and Cressida into the bedchamber (III.ii); it completes the design of the play for him to step out of character again as his role generalizes into that of pander at the end.

2876 Foakes, R. A. "Stage Images in *Troilus and Cressida*." *Shakespeare and the Sense of Performance: Essays in the Tradition of Performance Criticism in Honor of Bernard Beckerman.* Eds. Marvin and Ruth Thompson. Newark: U. of Delaware P., 1989, pp. 150–61.

Disputes the view that Elizabethan plays were staged "with a minimum of scenery or properties, and with the smallest number of actors made possible by doubling the parts." Uses *Tro.* to show that Sh's company staged its plays as elaborately as its resources permitted. Emphasizes the importance to the meaning of "tents, torches, groupings, and processions."

2877 Foakes, R. A. "*Troilus and Cressida* Reconsidered." *UTQ*, 32 (1962–63), 142–54.

Notes the two endings of *Tro.*—one that has Troilus making solemn promises of revenge and one that features Pandarus's bawdy epilogue—and claims that they are "not opposed, but complementary." On the one hand, the first three acts are richly comic, exploring the gaps between pretension and reality in love and war; on the other, the tone changes in the last two acts because "the game of love and the sport of war have to be played in earnest." Another argument for the rightness of the play's double ending can be found in its twofold treatment of time, which is presented both as a destructive force that mocks human achievement and as the power that sifts deeds and values and registers finally "what is true and worthwhile." The audience senses the weakness and folly of characters like Troilus, Hector, and Achilles as they are presented on a day-to-day basis within the play; but at the same time, we recognize the greatness of these characters as established by myth outside the play. The balance or tension provided by the two endings is thus appropriate. In keeping with its double nature, the play might be best labeled a heroic farce.

2878 Foakes, R. A., ed. *Troilus and Cressida.* (New Penguin Shakespeare.) Harmondsworth: Penguin, 1987. 253 pp.

The introduction discusses the uncertainty of the play's genre, the differences between the quarto text of 1609 and the First Folio text, the deliberate introduction of conflicting perspectives on the chief characters and themes (love, chivalry, honor, order, and policy), the use of archetypes of Homeric legend, the preoccupation with time, and the remarkable range of vocabulary and style (from Cressida's witty prose repartee to the Latinate language that both elevates and renders absurd much of the debate). Summarizes, under "Further Reading," some of the most important modern criticism.

2879 Franson, J. Karl. "An Antenor–Aeneas Conspiracy in Shakespeare's *Troilus and Cressida*." *Studies in the Humanities* (Indiana, Pennsylvania), 7, no. 1 (1978), 43–47.

Finds evidence that Antenor and Aeneas are involved in a treasonous conspiracy against Troy in *Tro.* Cites several post-Homeric writers on the war who describe such collusion and suggests that Sh knew the tradition. Within the play, some sort of plot is hinted at by Agamemnon's alacrity in agreeing to the exchange of Antenor for the worthless Cressida, by Aeneas's repeated contact with the enemy camp, and by the frequency with which Aeneas and Antenor appear onstage together.

2880 Freund, Elizabeth. "'Ariachne's broken woof': The Rhetoric of Citation in *Troilus and Cressida*." *Shakespeare and the Question of Theory.* Eds. Patricia Parker and Geoffrey Hartman. New York: Methuen, 1985, pp. 19–36.

Suggests that in *Tro.* Sh refashions, decomposes, vulgarizes, and declassicizes powerful canonical texts, stripping "*both* his sources *and* his own text of their 'original' substance" with "spirited iconoclasm."

2881 Friedman, Lester D. "Shakespeare's Ambiguous Hero: A Re-examination of Hector." *Thoth*, 12, no. 2 (1971–72), 50–58.

Contradicts those critics who see Hector as virtuous: He is an ambiguous character, rational and noble on the one hand, but incapable of matching his eloquently stated wisdom with deeds on the other. His actions are motivated more by a desire for personal glory than by the principles he is so fond of articulating. More pathetic than tragic, Hector is the key to seeing *Tro.* as Sh's most pessimistic work.

2882 Gagen, Jean. "Hector's Honor." *SQ*, 19 (1968), 129–37.

Asserts that Hector's sudden acquiescence to the arguments of Troilus and Paris in the Trojan council scene of *Tro.* (II.ii) would not have been considered base or ignoble by Sh's audience, presumably a group of sophisticated young lawyers. Points out that honor, the basis for Hector's decision, was highly valued in Renaissance humanist thought. In its inner essence, honor was equated with virtue or justice, a comprehensive term including all of the moral virtues. Valor, one of these virtues, was prized so highly that it was sometimes allowed to obscure the others. In their writings on the duel, Renaissance humanists often invoked the authority of Aristotle to sanction, however reluctantly, violating the laws of the realm as well as Christian morality to "avenge insults to a gentleman's honor." Hector's situation is similar: Because he recognizes that Trojan honor (in the sense of valor) is at stake, he assents to fighting in "a cause [that] he still considers both unjust and unreasonable."

2883 Garlick, H. F. "Shakespeare Pun." *AN&Q*, 9 (1970–71), 133.

Maintains that the pun emphasizing Cressida's fickleness ("The Troyans' trumpet" [*Tro.*, IV.v.64]) is used again by Sh in *Oth.*, when he has Iago speak of Othello's arrival in Cyprus after bantering with Desdemona about women's lustfulness: "The Moor. I know his trumpet" (II.i.177).

2884 Girard, René. "The Plague in Literature and Myth." *"To double business bound": Essays on Literature, Mimesis, and Anthropology*. Baltimore: Johns Hopkins U. P., 1978, pp. 136–54.

Includes a discussion of Ulysses' evocation of "cultural crisis" in his speech on degree in *Tro.*, I.iii.

2885 Girard, René. "The Politics of Desire in *Troilus and Cressida*." *Shakespeare and the Question of Theory*. Eds. Patricia Parker and Geoffrey H. Hartman. New York: Methuen, 1985, pp. 188–209.

Explains the controlling dynamic of *Tro.* as "mimetic desire," which inspires rivals to want the same thing and to imitate an admired model or each other in order to get the desired object. This accounts for Troilus's initial need for Cressida (as Pandarus keeps insisting, she is like Helen in her desirability) and his jealousy when she is going to the Greek camp (she will be desired by the Greek youths). It also accounts for Cressida's understanding of sexual relationships and her technique of making Troilus jealous. Mimetic desire is equally powerful in the military and political realm: Ulysses' analysis of Greek weakness is based on his awareness of emulation, and he makes this the foundation of his political maneuvering with regard to Ajax and Achilles. Notes that "the politics of eroticism and the politics of power are really one and the same." The play is "a formidable indictment of mimetic desire."

2886 Glasser, Marvin. "Baroque Formal Elements in Shakespeare's *Troilus and Cressida*." *UC*, 6 (1986), 54–70.

Analyzes *Tro.* as "exemplification of the formal effects of the new perceptions arising from—or contributing to—the breakdown" of the traditional system of thought inherited by the 16th c. In the play, "dislocation of traditional modes of thought about space and time are articulated through generic shifts, the blurring of definitive frames for place and historical emblems, and the increasingly diffuse focus of conventional character types." Discusses, in light of these considerations, the Prologue, Troilus's observation of Cressida's betrayal of him with Diomedes (V.ii), the pledges of the lovers and Pandarus (III.ii), and the erratic shifts of Ulysses and Hector. Characters and events are experienced subjectively; they cannot be referred to a fixed notion of human nature or history. It is Troilus's tragedy that, as an idealist, he cannot separate himself from "these now meaningless absolutes."

2887 Gomez, Christine. *The Alienated Figure in Drama from Shakespeare to Pinter.* New Delhi: Reliance Publishing House, 1991. viii + 320 pp.

Chapter 3, "The Malcontent Outsider," discusses Thersites in *Tro.* as the interpreter of "the irrationality and meaninglessness of earthly life."

2888 Green, Lawrence D. "'We'll dress him up in voices': The Rhetoric of Disjunction in *Troilus and Cressida.*" *QJS,* 70 (1984), 23–40.

Observes that *Tro.* is relatively rare among dramas in adopting inconsistency as a basic structural principle. Ideals of love, heroic courage, and chivalry are subjected to a bewildering assault of discrepancies "between word and action, between word and word, and even between successive actions." These disjunctions call into question not only ideals but the trustworthiness of language itself. All of this makes it difficult to see the play as a comedy: What we learn is that social and personal catastrophe will result if we as humans choose to talk in this way about our world.

2889 Greene, Gayle. "Language and Value in Shakespeare's *Troilus and Cressida.*" *SEL,* 21 (1981), 271–85.

Views *Tro.* as an exploration of the chaos that results when language is divided from reality. The play reflects a loss of faith in a transcendent order to which words can reliably refer. Similitude, in the early Renaissance a means of perceiving correspondences or of illuminating a hierarchical order, is turned here into an agent of confusion. The characters struggle unsuccessfully to achieve appropriate styles for their sentiments by using language that calls attention to itself rather than clarifying meaning. Bogged down in their relativistic notions of honor, value, and identity, they are unable to express themselves with precision. Troilus provides the most glaring example of this tendency. Other evidences of the corruption of language include the pervasiveness of gossip and rumor, the failure of elaborately articulated designs to come to fruition, and an obsession with comparison and tautology.

2890 Greene, Gayle. "Shakespeare's Cressida: 'A Kind of Self.'" *The Woman's Part: Feminist Criticism of Shakespeare.* Eds. Carolyn Ruth Swift Lenz, Gayle Greene, and Carol Thomas Neely. Urbana: U. of Illinois P., 1980, pp. 133–49.

Points out that the society portrayed in *Tro.* has a "purely destructive" effect on "the individual life." In presenting Cressida "in relation to the men and society who make her what she is," Sh critiques the misogynist habit of stereotyping. Cressida fulfills expectations that "require the worst of her," and she fashions herself into an object that is valued according to its appearance.

2890a Grene, Nicholas. *Shakespeare, Jonson, Moliere: The Comic Contract.* Totowa, New Jersey: Barnes & Noble, 1980. xvii + 246 pp.

Provides, in chapter 8, a discussion of *Tro.* as an anti-history play, in which the audience sees "the incoherent reality behind the historical myth," with the characters attempting but not entirely succeeding in acting out "their historical parts with all the meaning normally attributed to them." Sh seems to be asking us "to watch a sort of ultimate human comedy, in which even the most serious concerns of life and death are set askew."

2891 Grudin, Robert. "The Soul of State: Ulyssean Irony in *Troilus and Cressida*." *Anglia*, 93 (1975), 55–69.

Maintains that Ulysses, far from being unprincipled, is a consistent moralist, who frequently finds it necessary in the chaotic world of *Tro.* to express himself ironically to achieve his purposes. In his famous speech on degree (I.ii), for example, he implies that "traditional monarchic government" is ineffective under "conditions of complex and extreme disorder." He attempts to cure "the sickness of pride and emulation" among the Greeks "by a measured encouragement of these vices themselves" (for example, in his praise of Ajax's wisdom [II.iii] and in his discussion with Achilles about fame [III.iii]). In IV.v, the scene in which the Greeks welcome Cressida to their camp, Ulysses expresses himself with rare directness, condemning the war and Cressida and praising Troilus's frankness and generosity. Revision of chapter 2 of item 2892. Revised as part of chapter 4 of item 0469.

2892 Grudin, Robert. "Wisdom and Rule in *Troilus and Cressida, Measure for Measure*, and *The Tempest*." Ph.D. dissertation, University of California, Berkeley, 1969. *DAI*, 31 (1970–71), 2877-A.

Analyzes a particular kind of government as it is presented in three of Sh's characters: Ulysses in *Tro.*, the Duke in *MM*, and Prospero in *Tmp*. These characters all claim a broad understanding of human nature and employ deceit and illusion to achieve order in society. Chapter 2, revised as item 2891, considers Ulysses and argues that his speech on degree in I.iii is not incompatible with the deceitful stratagems he later employs, but rather may be viewed as a justification for these stratagems.

2893 Guha, P. K. "The Plot Structure in *Troilus and Cressida*." *Essays on Shakespeare*. Ed. Bhabatosh Chatterjee. Bombay: Orient Longmans, 1965, pp. 1–20.

Dismisses the double-authorship and satire theories that have been advanced to explain the apparently chaotic plot of *Tro.* The play is unified: The two threads of the plot—the love story and the camp story—are carefully interwoven to produce a unity of atmosphere. The camp story is converted into a series of love stories resembling that of Troilus and Cressida in which a man is paralyzed by infatuation for a woman. The play is a comedy, and a lot of its confusion would disappear if we altered its Homeric names and called it *Much Ado About Woman*.

2894 Gupta, Kajal Sen. "From Medieval to Modern: A Study of *Troilus and Cressida*." *Calcutta Essays on Shakespeare*. Ed. Amalendu Bose. Calcutta: Calcutta U., 1966, pp. 44–62.

Argues that *Tro.* represents a deliberate attempt by Sh to contrast Renaissance values with the medieval values presented in Chaucer's *Troilus and Criseyde*. In Sh's play, the characters are active architects of their own destiny, not passively subject to higher powers as in Chaucer's poem. The numerous discussions and debates in *Tro.* "create the impression of men who are determined to think and act for themselves." Other Renaissance values are seen in the emphasis on self-reliance, the defiance of Time, the concern for honor as a public virtue, the exaltation of reason (especially in Ulysses), the conception of order as universal but not eternal, and the insistence on the subjective nature of idealism (particularly in Troilus).

2895 Habib, Imtiaz Hasan. "Shakespeare's Pluralistic Concepts of Character: A Study in Dramatic Anamorphism." Ph.D. dissertation, Indiana University, 1984. *DAI*, 45 (1984–85), 1407-A.

Uses the Elizabethan "pictorial technique of anamorphism" to help understand the notions of "paradox and contrariety" as they apply to Sh's "pluralistic concept of character." Devotes a chapter to *Tro.*

2896 Halio, Jay L. "*Perfection* and Elizabethan Ideas of Conception." *ELN*, 1 (1963–64), 179–82.

Points out that the idea of women receiving *perfection* from men was widespread in Elizabethan England and referred to the Aristotelian theory of conception and generation. According to this idea, in the act of conception the male "contributes the form and efficient cause" while the female "contributes the material cause." In the "elegant sexual courting between Troilus and Cressida" (*Tro.*, III.ii), the word *perfection* is twice used (lines 85–91), both times with a sexual double entendre. See item 0478.

2897 Hargreaves, H. A. "An Essentially Tragic *Troilus and Cressida*." *HAB*, 18, no. 2 (1967), 49–60.

Finds that the character of Troilus is central to the play and contains thematic material for several tragedies: He is an idealistic youth who plays the leading part in both the love and war plots, but is destroyed by corruption and expediency. *Tro.*, however, stops short of being a tragedy because Sh is trying to recapitulate a number of themes from earlier plays before going on to write tragedy and because Troilus "lacks insight into his own feelings."

2898 Harris, Sharon M. "Feminism and Shakespeare's Cressida: 'If I be False . . .'" *Women's Studies*, 18, no. 1 (1990), 65–82.

Reviews the history of male-dominated literary criticism of Cressida's character. If discussed at all, she has been viewed negatively. Feminist critics, however, have challenged the traditional views of Cressida as debauched, "weak and frail," or betraying the conventions of courtly love. Instead, she can be seen as a woman who understands her own value amid the turbulence of war and uses her wits and will to survive. Sh uses Cressida to parody the chivalric ideal and collapse the rhetorical conventions associated with it.

2899 Hart, Edward L. "'War and Lechery': Thematic Unity of *Troilus and Cressida*." *RMMLA Bulletin*, 27 (1973), 181–86.

Views *Tro.* as a negative image of life, "in which all values are reversed." Instead of the "golden mean" of marriage, Cressida and Helen are devoted to promiscuity. In this atmosphere, Paris is unmanned, Hector is morally disarmed, the Greek commanders are caught up in petty factionalism, and sexual inversion (in the Achilles–Patroclus relationship) is part of life. The defining language for *Tro.* comes from Thersites, who is obsessed with disease. Every hope is frustrated; every action "falls short or ends in anti-climax." To reduce love to the pursuit of sexual gratification is "to make war on life itself."

2900 Helms, Lorraine. "'Still Wars and Lechery': Shakespeare and the Last Trojan Woman." *Arms and the Woman: War, Gender, and Literary Representation*. Eds. Helen M. Cooper, Adrienne Auslander Munich, and Susan Merrill Squier. Chapel Hill: U. of North Carolina P., 1989, pp. 25–42.

Discovers the seeds for Sh's "bitter appraisal" of the Trojan War in the voices of the Trojan women as they were mediated to him through the texts of Homer, Euripides, Virgil, and Chaucer. In *Tro.*, violence is used by the patriarchy to underwrite "every cultural rite and every representation." The world of the play, where war's violence is eroticized and sexuality is militarized, forces the Trojan women, especially Cressida, to fall back on "the defensive roles the literary tradition has given them."

2901 Helton, Tinsley. "Paradox and Hypothesis in *Troilus and Cressida*." *ShakS*, 10 (1977), 115–31.

Explores Sh's use of paradox and hypothesis in *Tro.* as a way to explain (1) the nature of the experience provided for the audience, (2) the reason the play's genre is so difficult to determine, and (3) certain peculiarities in structure. The love affair of Troilus and Cressida is shot through with anti-Petrarchan paradoxes, and in their wariness the lovers often comment about their relationship with hypothetical *ifs*. The ending of *Tro.*, which one might expect to help define its genre, seems to be under the control of the paradoxical wheel of Fortune, which comes full circle without any sense of resolution. The play's structure features continual frustration of the audience's expectations (for example, in Hector's volte-face in the Trojan council scene and throughout the love action). In *Tro.* Sh seems to have been appealing to contemporary taste for paradox (the formal paradox, of classical origin, had come to England in the late 16th c. from Italy), especially among young intellectuals. Such an audience would have been able to appreciate an irreverent treatment of classical legends, sustained by the detachment of paradox and hypothesis.

2902 Hiken, Arlin J. "Texture in *Troilus and Cressida*." *ETJ*, 19 (1967), 367–69.

Contends that in *Tro.* Sh deliberately avoids unity of theme and mood. Parallel characters and situations, which should be emphasized in production, reveal the play's complexity.

2903 Hodgdon, Barbara. "He Do Cressida in Different Voices." *ELR*, 20 (1990), 254–86.

Suggests that *Tro.* calls into question absolutist constructions of gender relations. Investigates this proposition by focusing on "the issue of Cressida's authenticity." By the end of the play, Cressida's identity as a whore has been established by several males whose gazes position her in such a way that they can inscribe their values on her. In the end, she seems to be constructed as a female subject by Troilus, who suppresses her voice by tearing up her letter, assimilating her "within a male system of desire and representation." However, the final scene harbors the "transgressive suggestion" that Pandarus has been turned into "the female body confiscated by male systems of repression."

2904 Honigmann, E. A. J. "The Date and Revision of *Troilus and Cressida*." *Textual Criticism and Literary Interpretation*. Ed. Jerome J. McGann. Chicago: U. of Chicago P., 1985, pp. 38–54. Revised as "Shakespeare Suppressed: The Unfortunate History of *Troilus and Cressida*." *Myrid-Minded Shakespeare: Essays, Chiefly on the Tragedies and Problem Comedies*. New York: St. Martin's P., 1989, pp. 112–29.

Argues that *Tro.* was written in early 1601 and performed privately, perhaps at Cambridge University. Notes the parallels between the play and the story of the Earl of Essex, with the earl as a kind of Achilles: Other writers of Sh's time found connections between aspects of the Trojan War and important features of the Essex affair. Speculates that the play was not performed publicly because these unintended parallels came to the attention of Sh and his company and were thought to make the play too dangerous in the current political climate.

2905 Hooker, Deborah A. "Coming to Cressida Through Irigaray." *SAQ*, 88 (1989), 899–932.

Discovers in the modern critic Luce Irigaray an analogue for Cressida in *Tro.* and reads the play in this light. Examines the various linguistic strategies (primarily riddles) that Cressida employs to contest the homosocial masculine world in its attempts to reduce her "to commodity status."

2906 Hotine, Margaret. "*Troylus and Cressida*: Historical Arguments for a 1608 Date." *The Bard* (London), 1, no. 4 (1977), 153-61.

Argues for a 1608 date of composition for *Tro*. Notes that three factors—the use of mercantile imagery and argument, the absence of "heroic battle scenes and humorous camp scenes," and "the criticism of war"—suggest that the play was composed "in time of peace, not war, and therefore not earlier than 1604." Favors 1608 because the three main issues being deliberated in the 1608 peace negotiations between the Spanish, the Dutch, the French, and the English at the Hague have a number of similarities to matters discussed in the play. If the play is assigned to 1608, the question of the theater for which it was written can be readily cleared up: That is, it would have been intended for performance at the Blackfriars, with its more educated audience.

2907 Houser, David J. "Armor and Motive in *Troilus and Cressida*." *RenD*, N. S. 4 (1971), 121-34.

Proposes to show how, by the use of "emblematic tableaux" and a "recurring visual motif—armor and the act or arming or disarming, fighting or refusing to fight"—Sh emphasizes, compares, and defines motives in *Tro*. We are made to see that the actions of the characters are motivated by "self-feeding pride in war and self-deluding, besotted lust."

2908 Hunter, G. K. "*Troilus and Cressida*: A Tragic Satire." *ShStud*, 13 (1974-75), 1-23.

Argues that in composing *Tro.*, Sh was influenced by "Homeric" attitudes, which he encountered in George Chapman's translation of the *Iliad* and which he set beside the medieval attitudes of chivalry and courtly love. What struck Sh in Homer was the absence of order and the rule of "animal violence." In *Tro*. he politicized the world of Homer to reflect this perception. For example, in Homer the Greek legation sent to persuade Achilles to rejoin the battle is given a desperate dignity, while Sh presents the episode as an exercise in "political chicanery." In terms of style, the play gives voice to a variety of impressive languages dealing with chivalry, love, heroism, knowledge, and power but makes clear that all of these are forever detached from the ends at which they aim. At the beginning, *Tro*. resembles a comedy, with Troilus and Cressida both believing that they can, by an effort of will, achieve their desires. Before long, however, this optimism fades and is replaced by the recognition that they are subject to external forces that they can neither understand nor control. Such destruction of optimism should probably be labeled tragic, and if the play is a satire, it must be a tragic satire.

2909 Hurst, Mary L. "Shakespeare, Chaucer, and 'False Cressida': A Reinterpretation." *SRASP*, 8 (1983), 1-8.

Compares Chaucer's Criseyde with Sh's Cressida to demonstrate that the two are more similar than has been thought. Finds significant differences between the two authors' versions of Troilus, with Sh's being "more sensual and more self-centered." Concludes that Sh's Cressida is a woman of "amazing strength," an "embryonic feminist," who survives in an imperfect society.

2910 Hyland, Peter. *William Shakespeare: "Troilus and Cressida."* (Penguin Critical Studies.) London: Penguin, 1989. 96 pp.

The introduction emphasizes the refusal of *Tro*. to allow the audience "an unequivocal response." Chapter 2, "Context and Materials," attempts to locate the play in its time, to explain why Sh chose to write on Troy, and to identify his sources. Chapter 3, "The Play," concerns genre (indeterminate, but perhaps leaning in the direction of a history play) and structure (depending on the juxtaposition of conflicting perspectives and dissonant images). Chapter 4, "Character and Idea," discusses

"Greeks and Trojans," "Troilus and Truth," "Cressida and the Position of Women," "Hector: Heroism and Tragedy," "Ulysses: Order, Rhetoric and Policy," "Achilles: Pride and Desire," and "Comedy and Satire: Pandarus and Thersites." Chapter 5, "Language, Style and Rhetoric," notes the enormous variety of stylistic effects as well as the failure of all of the verbiage to get at the truth. Chapter 6, "Time and Theatre," focuses on two important themes: time as the destroyer of all that is valuable and "the theatricality of life."

2911 Ingram, R. W. "Music as Structural Element in Shakespeare." *Shakespeare 1971. Proceedings of the World Shakespeare Congress*. Eds. Clifford Leech and J. M. R. Margeson. Toronto: U. of Toronto P., 1972, pp. 174–89.

Considers *Tro.* as one of four plays, all primarily concerned with "war, politics, and public events," in which music is a crucially important structural element. In *Tro.*, music is used to indicate the conflict between appearance and reality, between chivalry and the brutality of war, and between romantic love and degraded coquetry. Examples can be seen in Pandarus's parody love-song for Helen, the chivalric challenge of Hector's trumpet in the midst of a war council (I.iii), and the triumphal march called for by Troilus at the end to camouflage the inward woe of the Trojans at the death of Hector.

2912 Jackson, R. L. P. "The Interpretation of Tragic Experience." *CR*, 30 (1990), 74–90.

Focuses on the "tragic moment" in certain works of literature. The tragic imagination accepts the connection of the tragic moment with the deeper rhythm of the whole work, whereas the puritan or romantic imagination resists such acknowledgment. In *Tro.*, Troilus is controlled by such a romantic vision; he recoils, for example, from recognizing that the Cressida who surrenders to Diomedes is the same Cressida he has known. Likewise, *Tro.* itself seems finally unable to come to terms with tragic experience. By contrast, *Ham.* does achieve a "tragic interpretation" of the tragic moment.

2913 Jagendorf, Zvi. "All against One in *Troilus and Cressida*." *English*, 31 (1982), 199–210.

Reads *Tro.* as a somewhat abstract exploration of a debate about character. On one side, there is the attempt to recognize the autonomous individual and to endow him with meaning; on the other, there is the reduction of everything specific to an undifferentiated sameness. The word "all," especially as used by the satiric voice of Thersites, subverts any heroic claim to distinction. With the lovers, Sh is somewhat less reductive, but they are ultimately assimilated into stereotypes.

2914 Jago, David M. "The Uniqueness of *Troilus and Cressida*." *SQ*, 29 (1978), 20–27.

Inventories the features that set *Tro.* apart from Sh's other plays: (1) Its differences are to a great extent due to Sh's *treatment* of source material rather than the material itself; (2) it is outside the popular traditions Sh normally worked in; (3) it is calculated to leave a theater audience unsatisfied and to intrigue a reflective reader; (4) it introduces a pair of lovers and then subordinates them to political and military concerns; (5) it treats formlessness as a theme; and (6) its realism is inimical to traditional dramatic form. Finally, it seems a failure.

2915 Jamieson, Michael. "The Problem Plays, 1920–1970: A Retrospect." *ShS*, 25 (1972), 1–10.

Surveys recent criticism of *Tro.*, which focuses on the play's preoccupation with time, its exploration and reflection of chaos, its "three endings," its sources, and its genre.

2916 Jones, David E. "'Mad Idolatry': Love in *Troilus and Cressida.*" *Drama Critique*, 7 (1964), 8–12.

Contends that in *Tro.* "Ulysses' speech on degree in the Grecian council (I.iii.75–137) and Hector's castigation of Troilus and Paris in the Trojan council (II.ii.168–89) present the standards of natural law ... from which Grecian and Trojan society have lapsed." In particular, Sh exposes the fallacy of courtly love in its attempt "to appropriate values [that] belong to religion."

2917 Jones-Davies, M. T. "Discord in Shakespeare's *Troilus and Cressida*; or, The Conflict between 'Angry Mars and Venus Queen of Love.'" *SQ*, 25 (1974), 33–41.

Analyzes the play's pervasively discordant elements in light of the myth of Mars and Venus, as interpreted by the Renaissance. Plutarch's *Moralia* provides the best summary of what was to become the standard allegorical reading of the myth: From the union of Venus ("generous and pleasing") and Mars ("fierce and contentious") was born Harmony, who represents the benevolent concordance of opposites. From several passages in *Tro.* that variously present love and war in terms of each other, it can be seen that Sh had this ideal union in mind. There is, however, no true tempering of one extreme with the other, no "marvelous consonance": At the outset of the play, Venus reigns over Mars; in the last act, Mars triumphs. The ideal combination within one person of valor and grace, nobility and sweetness, that was supposed to obtain in the Renaissance courtier cannot be found in any of the Greek or Trojan heroes.

2918 Kamachi, Mitsuru. "The Purblind Argus: A Hidden Emblem in *Troilus and Cressida.*" *SELit* (English No. 1985), 21–35.

Argues that Alexander's description of Ajax, which notes that he has "the joints of everything, but everything so out of joint that he is a gouty Briareus" and that he is a "purblind Argus, all eyes and no sight" (*Tro.*, I.ii.27–30), is emblematic of the disintegrative world of *Tro.* and, more particularly, of the degeneration of Hector and Cressida. Discusses several scenes in which Hector moves from being a sponsor of unity (which is jointed in one sense) to being a representative of fragmentation and chaos (which are jointed in another sense). He is also like purblind Argus in that his spiritual eyesight gradually fails him. Cressida's spiritual blindness is evident from the beginning, and she progressively involves others in it. Suggests that the audience members become "purblind Arguses," whose hundred eyes can never distinguish the right shape of the heroine. The play itself may be seen as "a huge purblind Argus, whose myriad glass-eyes reflect the images of the viewers back to themselves."

2919 Kaufmann, R. J. "Ceremonies for Chaos: The Status of *Troilus and Cressida.*" *ELH*, 32 (1965), 139–59.

Regards *Tro.* as a "pre-tragic dramatization of human need for ceremonial participation appropriately stressing the imagery and practice of self-consumption, and technically devised to permit complex scrutiny of suspension in multiplicity." Sh assumes a variety of critical stances toward his previous works and disposes of a large inventory of "inadequate tragic formulae." The way is thus cleared for the great tragedies to follow.

2920 Kaula, David. "'Mad Idolatry' in Shakespeare's *Troilus and Cressida.*" *TSLL*, 15 (1973–74), 25–38.

Uncovers significant religious imagery in *Tro.* that reinforces the major theme of "mad idolatry." Helen, the cause of the war, is described in terms reminiscent of the Whore of Babylon; plague imagery, chiefly applied to the Greeks, is drawn from Revelation and other books of the Bible; and Troilus is shown masquerading his profane love as divine.

2921 Kaula, David. "Will and Reason in *Troilus and Cressida.*" *SQ*, 12 (1961), 271–83.

Argues that in *Tro.* Sh provides "a complex vision of the perennial earthly city, the unregenerate community forever exposed to the errant and self-destructive tendencies of the human will." The two most important factors in the vision are "the contrary modes of thought represented in Troilus and Ulysses, the one essentially passional and idealistic, the other rational and realistic." Troilus suffers from a basic tension between two senses of "will": "strong desire, usually sexual in nature," and "the deliberate exercise of choice" or "the movement of an intelligent being toward the object it conceives as the highest good." He is frustrated because he cannot find a being that corresponds with his "yearning for the ultimate." Ulysses, who possesses superior rational powers, is severely limited in his application of them because he has no sense of a created order or of a providential will. He accurately diagnoses the moral sickness from which the Greeks suffer, but because the potential for meaningful action is so limited within the moral sphere he inhabits, "he can use his rational prowess only for the promotion of unworthy ends."

2922 Kelleher, V. M. K. "*Troilus and Cressida*: Shakespeare's Vision of Fallen Man." *UES*, 11, no. 2 (1973), 8–14.

Accepts the hypothesis that *Tro.* was written and performed for one of the Inns of Court, whose intellectual audience, with its "classical education and awareness of close historical connections with the Middle Ages," would have perceived Sh's ironic intention. The playwright's purpose is to present a vicious society, driven entirely by self-interest; and his method is to contrast this "disturbing image of modern man" with classical and Chaucerian materials that remind the audience of the admirable values of heroism and courtly love in former ages. In Sh's hands, the story, especially the fall of Cressida, is deprived of its emotional impact because the characters lack concern for what is taking place around them. Beyond this, the play depicts two contrasting philosophical outlooks, Trojan idealism and Greek realism, each of which is perverted by those who profess it, and both of which are finally reduced to nihilism. Yet the fallen world of *Tro.* "implies its own antithesis," and reminds us of the nobler times of which it is a debased image.

2923 Kermode, Frank. "'Opinion' in *Troilus and Cressida.*" *Teaching the Text.* Eds. Susanne Kappeler and Norman Bryson. London: Routledge & Kegan Paul, 1983, pp. 164–79.

Focuses on the play's critique of *opinion*, which is articulated through the characters' obsession with value. Notes that there is much talk of reflecting, of mirroring the value of people through opinion; there are also preoccupations with self-evaluation and with time. Truth is constantly discussed, but the concern with opinion tends to undermine it, as can be seen, for example, in the Trojan council scene (II.ii), when Hector states the truth but then defers to opinion.

2924 Kimbrough, Robert. "Ilium Revisited: Mixed Genre in *Troilus and Cressda.*" *AJES*, 13, no. 1 (1988), 72–78.

Contends that in *Tro.* Sh created "one of the world's most sustained, tough, and wistful presentations of the human comedy." In doing this, he consciously mixed "the three genres of his day," each with its own plot, "primary setting, and thematic concern": "the comedy of Troilus and Cressida with its emphasis on love, the tragedy of Hector and the Trojans with its focus on honour, the history of Achilles and the Greeks with its evocation of the problems of social order."

2925 Kimbrough, Robert. "The Origins of *Troilus and Cressida*: Stage, Quarto, and Folio." *PMLA*, 77 (1962), 194–99.

Sums up the "main established facts" and safest conjectures about "the origins of *Tro.* and the history of its texts." Goes on to argue that the play was performed in

1601 (it was parodied in Middleton's *Family of Love*, 1602); that the Prologue was composed at the same time as the play; that the play was probably not commissioned by one of the Inns of Court; and that the apparent confusion of the editors of the First Folio about where to put *Tro.* was due to printing-house politics rather than aesthetic uncertainty.

2926 Kimbrough, Robert. "The Problem of Thersites." MLR, 59 (1964), 173-76.

Argues that Sh would have known Thersites from Latin rhetoric books and popular traditions as a type of the railing detractor, notorious for distorting the truth. Thersites in *Tro.* has mistakenly been taken as the play's definitive voice, which has prompted two unwarranted emendations: Editors have made Patroclus Achilles' "brach" or "bitch" instead of "brooch" (as in the quarto of 1609 and the Folio) and his "male harlot" instead of "varlet." If Thersites' insults are taken less seriously, *Tro.* becomes "less bitter than it has seemed to many."

2927 Kimbrough, Robert. *Shakespeare's "Troilus and Cressida" and Iits Setting.* Cambridge: Harvard U. P., 1964. xiii + 208 pp.

Chapter 1, the introduction, proposes to examine *Tro.* aesthetically and historically in order to find a solution to the problems raised by reading it as a piece of dramatic literature.

Chapter 2, "The Theatrical Origins of the Play," discusses the theatrical scene, 1598-1603, and argues that in *Tro.* Sh attempted to write a play for the popular theater, with popular subject matter, but at the same time employed techniques borrowed from the coterie theater.

Chapter 3, "The Literary Origins: The 'Matter of Troy,'" surveys the treatments of Troy, including Sh's, in literature and theater prior to *Tro.* and points out that Sh's play "reflects in miniature the wide variety, contradictions, and stereotypes prevalent in the Trojan literature tradition."

Chapter 4, "The Plot of the Play and the Problem of Structure," identifies three chief locales, each linked to a major plot line and each with "its own thematic environment." The house of Pandarus is associated with the love plot, which focuses on love and lust; Priam's palace (Ilium) "introduces the Trojan plot-line which mainly analyzes the demands of honor and war on the individual"; and the Greek camp concentrates on "the implications of order and disorder in man and society." Analyzes the beginning, middle, and final actions of the play as a whole, and suggests that Sh deliberately weakened the play's structural effectiveness. Notes that unlike all previous treatments of the Troy legend, Sh's does not attempt to point the story with "moral or ethical observation."

Chapter 5, "The Concerns of Love and Lust," investigates the question of why Troilus and Cressida are so mismatched as lovers and concludes that Sh, influenced by the private theater, was concerned to depict their love as lethargic and debilitating.

Chapter 6, "The Demands of War and Honor," discusses the problem raised by the Trojan plot of what "the permissible demands of war and honor" are. Sh "followed his own precedent, the theatrical practice of his day, and his sources" in portraying honor as a positive value when it is "sought with due regard for ethical considerations." If pursued through an ethically questionable strife, honor becomes an unworthy goal, and this is the case in *Tro.*

Chapter 7, "The Rhetoric of Order and Disorder," considers the Greek plot and its use of an elevated rhetoric of order that is then undermined by petty actions and "the debased rhetoric of Thersites." Explains that a variety of influences lie behind this contradiction: "Positive, Shakespearean philosophy, a theatrical demand for strong speeches, and a story that emphasized debate" all "work against the negative nature of the material and its traditional significance."

Chapter 8, "Conclusion and Epilogue," views the Prologue to *Tro.* as containing both popular and coterie features. Because it combines so many disparate elements, *Tro.* is a critical problem and a dramatic failure, but it is not an artistic failure.

2928 Kimbrough, Robert. "The *Troilus* Log: Shakespeare and 'Box Office.'" *SQ*, 15 (1964), 201–9.

Argues that the unusual nature of *Tro.* is in part due to Sh's sensitivity to the competition from the private playhouses and his attempt at "a coterie approach to the writing of a public play." Coterie elements in *Tro.* can be seen in its emphasis on attitudes rather than action, on lust rather than love, and on satiric humor rather than romance. It also appears that Sh intentionally weakened the play's structural effectiveness to enhance its critical, ambivalent effects. He did, however, include traditional matter to please the public theater audience: Hector's challenge and Ulysses' plan to deal with it, both additions to the Trojan story by Sh, are presented with dignity, and in Hector's visit to the Greek camp, "the main persons of the siege story" are treated with veneration. The closest thing to an authoritative statement about the purpose of *Tro.* is the Prologue, which, like the play, sends mixed signals.

2929 Koinm, Albert J. "Tragedy and the Whole Truth: A Discussion of *Troilus and Cressida*." *CCTE Studies*, 41 (1976), 20–29.

Maintains that Sh's tragedies are problematic because each attempts to tell the whole truth. That is, Sh tries to include in each play "all the possible emotional and intellectual responses to the world of that play." Focuses on the character of Hector to show that *Tro.* validates both the relativism that must be accepted in everyday worldly pursuits and the absolute standards of moral and religious law. The result is a complex and moving tragedy.

2930 Kolb, Catherine Sutton. "Frustrated Expectation in Shakespeare's Problem Plays." Ph.D. dissertation, Indiana University, 1975. *DAI*, 36 (1975–76), 5319-A.

Suggests that Sh's four "problem plays," including *Tro.*, can be distinguished by the obvious ways in which they engage in manipulating audience expectations. Our anticipations are frustrated, and we are furnished with no means of resolving apparent contradictions. We cannot, for example, establish the true cause for Achilles' withdrawal from the war and thus become quite detached from him.

2931 Kopper, John M. "Troilus at Pluto's Gates: Subjectivity and the Duplicity of Discourse in Shakespeare's *Troilus and Cressida*." *Shakespeare and Deconstruction*. Eds. G. Douglas Atkins and David M. Bergeron. (American U. Studies Series 4: English Language and Literature 57.) New York: Peter Lang, 1988, pp. 149–71.

Essays a rhetorical analysis of *Tro.*, using the play's ambivalence toward Pluto—as both god of riches and as god of the underworld—for a point of departure. Like other ambivalent names (*Cressida, Ariachne*), *Pluto* undermines "the very possibility that language can be referential." The pervasiveness of "the language of valuation" constitutes a challenge to "the stability of language as a structure" and to the social order with which language is associated. Uses Jacques Lacan's account of the child's movement from the Imaginary stage to the Symbolic stage, from the visual to the linguistic, as a way to understand the lawlessness of *Tro.*'s plot. The play dramatizes "the uncompleted movement from Imaginary to Symbolic." Troilus goes through this transition: He learns, acquires subjectivity, through his contact with the tragic. However, his dramatic expression of Cressida's duplicity, the closest thing to a tragic moment, has "no audience in the play and therefore cannot be recognized as tragic." Discusses four characters—Achilles, Ajax, Thersites, and Pandarus—who obstruct the tragic progress of Troilus. Notes that the play "enacts the moment of transition from comedy to tragedy."

2932 Kreps, Barbara Irene. "Shakespeare's *Troilus and Cressida*: Troy and Its Meaning in the Last Years of Elizabeth's Reign." Ph.D. dissertation, University of Wisconsin-Madison, 1975. *DAI*, 36 (1975–76), 8076-A.

Argues that Sh's unheroic version of the Troy story in *Tro.* was not the inevitable result of borrowing from medieval sources like Lydgate and Caxton. Rather, the play's negative treatment of the matter of Troy was due to the playwright's rejection of the humanistic optimism of his own day.

2933 Kujawińska-Courtney, Krystyna. "Myth and Anti-Myth in *Troilus and Cressida* by William Shakespeare." *Acta Universitatis Lodziensis, Folia Litteraria* (Lódź), 24 (1988), 69–89.

Discusses the difficulty that various characters in *Tro.* have in establishing value and discovering their identity. The world of the play permits no absolute values, simplicity, or stability. We are exposed to "a world of anti-myth" from which, paradoxically, a myth has been created.

2934 LaBranche, Linda. "Visual Patterns and Linking Analogues in *Troilus and Cressida*." *SQ*, 37 (1986), 440–50.

Contends that "stage pictures" and "visual patterns" in *Tro.* cooperate with verbal effects to create a coherence that has been largely ignored. First, the handing over of Cressida to the Greeks reinforces the idea of female helplessness. Next, the "round-game," in which one person is subjected to a group assault, occurs several times, each instance less comic than the last. Finally, the "unsoldierly soldier," the most dominant visual image in the play, elicits an ambiguous response that maintains a sense of uneasiness in the audience. Visual and verbal techniques link diverse characters (for example, Cressida is analogized with Helen, Troilus with Paris and Hector, Ulysses with Pandar and Hector). This technique fosters a variety of associations that make it difficult to classify anyone as villain or hero. Revision of part of item 2935.

2935 LaBranche, Linda Berning. "The Theatrical Dimension of *Troilus and Cressida*." Ph.D. dissertation, Northwestern University, 1984. *DAI*, 45 (1984–85), 3646-A.

Argues that Sh's treatment of individual scenes, as well as of larger structure, forces the viewer to make initial judgments that he must subsequently reverse. The play's dramaturgy insists on the relativity of values. Part revised as item 2934.

2936 Langman, F. H. "*Troilus and Cressida*." *Jonson and Shakespeare*. Ed. Ian Donaldson. Atlantic Highlands, New Jersey: Humanities P., 1983, pp. 57–73.

Finds inadequate the two chief schools of *Tro.* criticism, one going back to Wilson Knight and viewing the play as a tragedy and the other originating with O. J. Campbell and seeing it as a comical satire or comedy. Proposes to make a fresh start and look at *Tro.* from within to apprehend "more clearly what it is." Distinguishes several different levels of the comic: the raw, ugly, and unfunny farce of the dispute between Ajax and Thersites; the more good-humored scene in which the Greek captains induce Ajax to boast of his humility (II.iii) that also demonstrates how "the contagion of pride" spreads to the other men (Achilles, Troilus, Paris, Diomede); the "reflexive" comedy when the Greek commanders slip into self-parody and act as an audience "to watch Ulysses play Patroclus playing themselves"; the "high-spirited gaiety" of Pandarus, which indicates both "the civilizing ritual" and the decadence of the courtly code. Maintains that Achilles' erotic longing to see Hector (III.iii) indicates the fusing of love and war in his character and is a key to the interrelation of the two occupations at every level in the play. Love and war are two manifestations of "the same passionate assertion of self, and the whole movement of the play draws them together again into undifferentiated anarchy." Calls attention to the richness of the play's "many-layered" and artful style, focusing on one "special poetic effect": the use of several "ghost languages" to suggest outside standards by which the world of the play may be judged. A series of phrases and allusions that suggest Christian values but that are "sufficiently equivocal to fit into the pagan past" is the most important of these ghost languages.

2937 Lavine, Anne Rabiner. "This Bow of Ulysses: Shakespeare's *Troilus and Cressida* and Its Imitation by Dryden." Ph.D. dissertation, Bryn Mawr College, 1961. *DA*, 22 (1961–62), 3186–3187-A.

Part 4 consists of "a detailed study of Shakespeare's and Dryden's plays." Gives special attention to similarities between Sh's practices and those of Homeric epic.

2938 Lecercle, Ann. "Words, Wards, Watches: Going-between in *Troilus and Cressida*." *Shakespeare, "Troilus et Cressida."* Actes du colloque, 9–10 novembre 1990, Université Lumière-Lyon 2. Lyon: C.E.R.A.N., Dept. d'Anglais, Université Lumière-Lyon 2, 1991., pp. 123–40.

Argues that in *Tro.* the Trojan War and the love of Troilus are both idolatrous affairs, and the idol "is at the frontiers of the semantic and the scopic, the sexual and the textual: 'words, wards and watches' (I.ii.260–66)." Hypothesizes that the play "is a global dissemination, a stringing out along the syntactic line of dramatic development, of what is paradigmatically embodied in the bifold authority of formal *abyme* and fantasmatic *abyssus*." Notes that the "strange chimaera" conceived by Troilus in "the climactic abyme" of V.ii, when he divides his beloved, is Ariachne, "a deformation of the original *weaver*, replicating in textuality the divided sexuality of the deceiver Cressid." Discusses "four admonitory miniatures" from the tale of Ariachne in the *Metamorphoses* of Ovid that "compose a configuration that subtends Sh's delineation of character in relation to name in *Troilus and Cressida*."

2939 Leonard, Nancy S. "Substitution in Shakespeare's Problem Comedies." *ELR*, 9 (1979), 281–301.

Argues that *Tro.* denies uniqueness to its characters by "reductive substitution." The attempt to view Helen as "singular" is thus countered by the "common" image of her; Ajax is substituted for Achilles to accept Hector's challenge, which denies singularity to the Greeks' greatest warrior; and Troilus, who is replaced by Diomede, substitutes one version of Cressida for another.

2940 Lessenich, Rolf P. "Shakespeare's *Troilus and Cressida*: The Vision of Decadence." *SN*, 49 (1977), 221–32.

Contends that in *Tro.* Sh used ancient classical legend to expose the decadence of his own society, which had corrupted itself by perverting its Neoplatonic/medieval ideals.

2941 Levenson, Jill. "Shakespeare's *Troilus and Cressida* and the Monumental Tradition in Tapestries and Literature." *RenD*, N. S. 7 (1976), 43–84.

Reviews the medieval and Renaissance tapestry illustrations of the Trojan War, which reflect the "narrative tradition established by Benoît de Sainte-Maure in the 12th century with his *Le Roman de Troie*." In keeping with this tradition, the tapestries depicted the Troy narrative with "immensity, opulence, and action with a philosophical dimension." Sh subjected this monumental tradition to wholesale debunking, contracting "immensity into a span" and turning "all-embracing opulence into an occasional symbol of mutability and decay." The medieval tradition adopted an ambivalent attitude toward the legend: Admiration for the nobility of the ancients existed alongside censure for their failings. In Sh, all is obloquy.

2942 Levin, Richard. *The Multiple Plot in English Renaissance Drama*. Chicago: U. of Chicago P., 1971. xiv + 277 pp.

Considers *Tro.* in chapter 5 under "Equivalence Plots," those in which the two actions of the double plot, drawn from quite different areas of life, must be given equal weight in considering the drama's form. In *Tro.*, the love and war plots are analogous, with Troilus and Diomedes contending for Cressida (love) in one, and Hector and Achilles contending for honor in the other. Their connection is confirmed by a detailed parallelism and the appropriation by one of the other's subject matter.

2943 Lindley, David. "Shakespeare's Provoking Music." *The Well Enchanting Skill: Music, Poetry, and Drama in the Culture of the Renaissance: Essays in Honour of F. W. Sternfeld.* Eds. John Caldwell, Edward Olleson, and Susan Wollenberg. Oxford: Clarendon P., 1990, pp. 79–90.

Cites the use of music in *Tro.* as an example of the ambivalence of Renaissance thinking about music. The play's bringing together of "music, love and effeminacy," in the song sung by Pandarus (III.i), in the references to music elsewhere, and even in the sounding of the martial trumpet (IV.v), exploits the contemporary opinions of detractors of music. All of this undermines the famous appeal to cosmic harmony by Ulysses in I.iii.

2944 Loggins, Vernon P. "Perspectives in *Troilus and Cressida*." *DR*, 70 (1990–91), 503–15.

Observes that, in order to present the enormously complex matter of the Trojan War in a play, Sh constructs each scene so that it is dominated by the perspective of a different character. This method of recapitulating the action is seen in its purest form during the first two scenes, devoted to the viewpoints of Troilus and Cressida, respectively. Thereafter, Sh uses variations of this strategy. Revision of part of item 2945a.

2945 Loggins, Vernon P. "Rhetoric and Action in *Troilus and Cressida*." *CLAJ*, 35 (1991–92), 93–108.

Follows the dichotomy between words and action in *Tro.* as it defines character roles, develops the relationship between lust and violence, and demonstrates how private desires determine public policy. Revison of part of item 2945a.

2945a Loggins, Vernon Porter. "Design and Tropes in *Troilus and Cressida*." Ph.D. dissertation, Purdue University, 1987. *DAI*, 49 (1988–89), 1151-A.

Provides a reading of *Tro.* by examining several strategies used in the play: (1) tropes, including the story of the Apple of Discord, "the Elizabethan fair, the brothel, the church, the bee with its honey and wax, the outside-inside trope, [and] the Trojan horse"; (2) recapitulation (a way of bringing the perspectives of several major characters to bear on the complex material); (3) an elaborate system of prologues and epilogues; and (4) "the revised or re-written scene." Parts revised as items 2944 and 2945.

2946 Lombardo, Agostino. "Fragments and Scraps: Shakespeare's *Troilus and Cressida*." *The European Tragedy of Troilus.* Ed. Piero Boitani. Oxford: Clarendon P., 1989, pp. 199–217.

Argues that *Tro.* enacts the death of the idealizing medieval values attached to love and war and the initiating of an anguished search for new ways to encounter the contingency of existence. Hector is presented as a man of the past, the prisoner of illusions, whereas Ulysses, though nostalgic for the traditional notion of "degree," recognizes that in the new world he must rely on "experience, political realism, and intellectual acumen." The play participates in deconsecrating the myths of the past and in demystifying "the forms used to construct and celebrate those myths." It also reflects an awareness of the decline of the aristocracy in Sh's own society.

2947 Longo, Joseph A. "Apropos the Love Plot in Chaucer's *Troilus and Criseyde* and Shakespeare's *Troilus and Cressida*." *CahiersE*, 11 (1977), 1–15.

Maintains that in composing *Tro.* Sh was directly influenced by Chaucer's *Troilus and Criseyde*, both in the treatment of the love story and in the presentation of the "governing issues and spirit" of the play. The narrator of Chaucer's poem adopts a philosophical stance that is similar to that of Sh's Prologue; Troilus in both works uses boat imagery (derived by Chaucer from Boethius's *Consolation of Philosophy*) to describe his emotional state; both Chaucer and Sh establish at the beginnings of their respective works the bankrupt nature of the chivalric code; Chaucer's Criseyde and Sh's Cressida are alike in their rumination about and recognition of love; and in each work the two lovers react similarly to the transfer of Cressida to the Greeks, especially in the emphasis they place on "truth."

2948 Lynch, Stephen. "Shakespeare's Cressida: 'A Woman of Quick Sense.'" *PQ*, 63 (1984), 357–68.

Contends that in *Tro.* Cressida is the only character who clearly understands herself and her world. She comments cynically and accurately on warriors and lovers, briefly adopting Troilus's idealism but discarding it when she recognizes its fraudulence. Moving from Troy, where the men speciously idealize women, to the Greek camp, where women are regarded as whores, she makes the best bargain she can by accepting the "protection" of Diomede. In some sense, she is "true" because guided by self-knowledge. Revision of chapter 5 of item 2951.

2949 Lynch, Stephen J. "Hector and the Theme of Honor in *Troilus and Cressida*." *UC*, 7 (1987), 68–79.

Analyzes "the entire range of Hector's actions" in *Tro.* to establish that "the notion of honor he pursues is flawed by a disregard for intrinsic virtue and an excessive desire for public reputation." In the eyes of the Greeks and Trojans, he is an ideal hero, but the audience perceives him as radically imperfect. Revision of chapter 2 of item 2951.

2950 Lynch, Stephen J. "The Idealism of Shakespeare's Troilus." *SAB*, 51, no. 1 (1986), 19–29.

Maintains that the quality Troilus prizes most highly in himself, his idealism, is tainted by the corrupt world within which he lives. His egotism leads him to view himself as a model lover and warrior, though his actions are more moody and erratic than constant in both roles. Our sympathies for him are heightened at several points (especially in Ulysses' tribute in IV.v and during his betrayal by Cressida in V.iii), but his suffering results in no insight. He ends by pursuing revenge against Diomede with the same irrationality that he formerly exhibited in his love for Cressida. Revision of chapter 4 of item 2951.

2951 Lynch, Stephen Joseph. "Shakespeare's *Troilus and Cressida*: A Study of the Characters, Themes, and Sources." Ph.D. dissertation, Indiana University, 1982. *DAI*, 43 (1982–83), 2681-A.

Finds that emulation—"an inordinate appetite for fame and honor—perpetuates the war." Hector, Ulysses, and Troilus manifest, respectively, three forms of destructive self-interest. Pretending to pursue ideals such as "chivalric honor, social order, or constancy in love," these characters hunger instead for "fame, victory, and sensual indulgence." Chapters 2 to 5 treat Hector, Ulysses, Troilus, and Cressida, respectively, and include a review of criticism for each character, as well as discussion of relevant episodes from the sources. Chapter 2 revised as item 2949; chapter 4 as item 2950; and chapter 5 as item 2948.

2952 Lyons, Charles. "Cressida, Achilles, and the Finite Deed." *EA*, 20 (1967), 233–42.

Contends that in *Tro.* "the sense of experience itself is held up to scrutiny." Both honor, supposedly gained from war, and the permanence with which Troilus strives to invest sexuality, "are temporal, dependent for their reality on the deed itself, and subject to the flux of time." Both Trojans and Greeks seek a constant identity, but neither is able to achieve it: Their deeds of military and amatory prowess are self-consuming and leave the audience with a sense of fragmentation and dissolution.

2953 Lyons, Clifford P. "The Hector–Achilles Encounters in Shakespeare's *Troilus and Cressida*." *All These to Teach: Essays in Honor of C. A. Robertson.* Eds. Robert A. Bryan, Alton C. Morris, A. A. Murphree, and Aubrey L. Williams. Gainesville: U. of Florida P., 1965, pp. 67–79.

Amplifies the stage directions that are found in the quarto (1609) and the First Folio for the two encounters of Hector and Achilles on the battlefield (*Tro.*, V.vi and viii). The expanded directions emphasize the prowess and magnanimity of Hector in the first encounter and the brutality of Achilles in the second.

2954 Lyons, Clifford P. "The Trysting Scenes in *Troilus and Cressida*." *Shakespearean Essays.* Eds. Alwin Thaler and Norman Sanders. Knoxville: U. of Tennessee P., 1964, pp. 105–20.

Analyzes the scene in which Pandarus brings Troilus and Cressida together (III.ii) and the scene in which Cressida acquiesces to Diomedes (V.ii) to show how much they are alike. In his anguished repudiation of what he has seen in V.ii, Troilus fails to notice that "Troilus plus Pandarus plus Cressida pretty much equals Diomedes plus Cressida."

2955 Macaraig-Profeta, Lydia. "Man's Position in the 'Chain of Being' in Shakespeare's *Troilus and Cressida*." *Far Eastern University Faculty Journal* (Manila), 12 (1967), 89–94.

Reviews the notion of the "chain of being," describing its Platonic, Aristotelian, Neoplatonic, Stoic, and Christian elements. In 16th-c. England, writers could draw on the optimistic view of man as an essential link in the chain or on views like those of Montaigne and Machiavelli, who saw man as something else. In *Tro.*, Sh uses both optimistic and skeptical conceptions: Troilus's faculties embody "the optimistic view of man created in God's image," but Cressida's infidelity finally causes his passions to overwhelm his reason. Cressida's beauty should be accompanied by virtuous qualities, but the divine in her nature "never has a chance when her will and her reason choose to let her wallow in the filth of her lusts." Ajax represents "the corruption of the ideal of what man should be," and Thersites is a man in whom the gift of reason is utterly perverted.

2956 Mackinnon, Lachlan. *Shakespeare the Aesthete: An Exploration of Literary Theory.* New York: St. Martin's P., 1988. xii + 186 pp.

Chapter 1 includes a discussion of *Tro.*, which first compares Sh's version of the story with those of Chaucer and Henryson, and then analyzes the play as presenting "a complex view of the relation between selfhood and social context." None of the characters receives support from a world in which "nothing remains settled." Sh makes "a rancorous farce" out of Homer and Chaucer, undermines heroic dignity, "questions the nature of personal identity," and "pokes fun at the stuffy classics."

2957 Main, William W. "Character Amalgams in Shakespeare's *Troilus and Cressida*." *SP*, 58 (1961), 170–78.

Argues that a survey of English drama from 1598 to 1603 yields recurrent character types and that critics have been puzzled because *Tro.* does not present any of these types in clearly defined form. Instead, Sh composed his characters out of elements from several different stereotypes. Cressida, for example, exhibits features of the modest maid, the forward maid, the shrew, and the fallen woman. Hector is a combination of hero and villain, and Thersites is both satiric critic and fool. These amalgams of standard character types evoke ambivalent responses.

2958 Mallin, Eric S. "Emulous Factions and the Collapse of Chivalry: *Troilus and Cressida.*" *Representations*, 29 (1990), 145–79.

Discovers in *Tro.* parallels to the cultural consciousness and political maneuverings of the late Elizabethan era. The threat of invasion imbued the English with something like the siege mentality of the Trojans; the factionalism of the court, with two or more camps competing for power over the queen, resembles the emulous strivings of the Greeks; the aging queen, in the context of male jockeying for position, faded into insignificance, just as the female figures in the play are reduced to whores and/or ciphers. The chivalric myth of the ideal knight in the service of his virtuous lady is thus subverted both at the Elizabethan court and in Sh's play. Revision of part of item 2959.

2959 Mallin, Eric Scott. "The End of Troy: Elizabethan Dissolution in Shakespeare's *Troilus and Cressida.*" Ph.D. dissertation, Stanford University, 1986. *DAI*, 47 (1986–87), 3435-A.

Views *Tro.* as inscribing crucial challenges to "political, social, and literary authority" at the end of Elizabeth's reign: "factionalism and false ideology in the court; the rampant disorder of epidemic disease; and the problem of interpreting the play itself." Part revised as item 2958.

2960 Mann, Jill. "Shakespeare and Chaucer: 'What is Criseyde worth?'" *The European Tragedy of Troilus.* Ed. Piero Boitani. Oxford: Clarendon P., 1989, pp. 219–42. Reprint. *CQ*, 18 (1989), 109–28.

Emphasizes the access the reader has to the inner world of Criseyde's feelings in Chaucer's *Troilus and Criseyde* and contrasts with this Sh's denial to the audience of such access in *Tro.* Speculates that the reason for Cressida's inaccessibility is that she plays a central part in clarifying the theme of value in the play. Cites Aristotle's *Nicomachean Ethics* and its medieval translations and elaborations as influential in forming Sh's notion that value is determined subjectively, by the need or demand of the consumer. Aristotle's insistence that it is through exchange that value is fixed is played out when Cressida is traded for Antenor: Her worth is determined by men, her value imposed from outside. In providing such an Aristotelian demonstration of the process of valuation, Sh was obliged to externalize his presentation of her character.

2961 Marsh, Derick R. C. "Interpretation and Misinterpretation: The Problem of *Troilus and Cressida.*" *ShakS*, 1 (1965), 182–98.

Maintains that if *Tro.* is accepted for what it is—a satire—then many of the problems associated with its interpretation disappear. The play is constructed on the principle of anticlimax and deflation, "through the technique of ironic juxtaposition." For example, Troilus's image of himself as a disprized courtly lover in the first scene is undermined by his rapid shifts to warrior and then to sensualist. No character in the play represents a standard to be consistently admired. Troilus, Hector, and Ulysses, the leading candidates for heroic stature, all fail to advance in self-awareness. This is not to say that the play presents a universal picture of cynicism and despair. Several of the characters suggest positive values, even though they are not followed.

2962 Maxwell, J. C. "*Troilus and Cressida.*" *TLS*, Apr. 6, 1967, p. 296.

Letter to the editor probes Coghill's statement (item 2838) that the epilogue to *Tro.* was not in the "original version." Acknowledges that the epilogue was an afterthought, but suggests that it might have been added as part of "the original process of composition, with Sh's first thoughts left undeleted in the manuscript [that] lies behind the Folio text of V.iii." See also items 2795, 2796, 2797, 2837, 2839, 2845, 2846, 2847, 2861, 2862, and 2863.

2963 McAlindon, T. "Language, Style, and Meaning in *Troilus and Cressida.*" *PMLA*, 84 (1969), 29–43.

Calls attention to the "several kinds of stylistic dissonance" that pervade *Tro.* and argues that the play's design is based on the Renaissance theory, derived from Quintilian and Cicero, that imperfect speech is "an omen of personal and social disorder." Both Greeks and Trojans violate the doctrine of decorum, which decrees that "word and style should suit the speaker, the person addressed, the subject, and the situation." Failure to observe this law signifies that one neither understands nor accepts his "appointed place in the ordered universe." Through his characters' use of defective style, Sh calls attention to their failures in heroism and love. In this regard, the abuse of solemn vows is especially noteworthy. In *Tro.*, two fundamental techniques of figurative language—"surplusage" and "diminishing"—are often misused, resulting in a number of clearly identifiable stylistic vices (as defined in the rhetorical treatises of the day). Sh adds to the dissonance by juxtaposing widely divergent styles.

2964 Mead, Stephen X. "Shakespeare's Concept of Chastity: A Study of the Problem Plays." Ph.D. dissertation, Indiana University, 1986. *DAI*, 47 (1986–87), 1735-A.

Regards *Tro.*, in which Sh modifies the Cressida figure to emphasize that her reputation and identity are entirely under the control of others, as a turning point in Sh's portrayal of chastity. After this, he begins to create true heroines of chastity.

2964a Medcalf, Stephen. "Epilogue: From *Troilus* to *Troilus.*" *The Later Middle Ages.* Ed. Stephen Medcalf. New York: Holmes & Meier, 1981, pp. 291–305.

Compares the ways in which Chaucer's *Troilus and Criseyde* and *Tro.* reflect the thought of their respective ages. Maintains that Chaucer, "in style and in the presentation of consciousness," is "more single in his view than Shakespeare and less disposed to develop certain contrasts, as of inner and outer, authenticity and gorgeousness." There is a gap in Chaucer's poem, however; it lies "between Troilus's betrayed and enduring love and God's." The poet seems finally to retreat to Boethianism, viewing things from the perspective of eternity. In Sh's play, there is no sense of Boethius or eternity. From the beginning, and at all levels, *Tro.* is "paradoxical, multifold and full of warring contradictions."

2965 Mehl, Dieter. "Forms and Functions of the Play within a Play." *RenD*, 8 (1965), 41–61.

Cites *Tro.* as providing examples of the technique by which "part of the play itself is observed and commented on by some characters from the play as if it were a kind of performance for them."

2966 Melchiori, Barbara Arnett. "Bawds, Panders, and Go-betweens." *L'Eros in Shakespeare.* Eds. Alessandro Serpieri and Keir Elam. Parma: Pratiche Editrice, 1988, pp. 63–76.

Notes that Pandarus, in *Tro.*, is used for a bit of "inverted prophecy"; that his temporary role as Cressida's father is given an ambiguous twist by the innuendo of the "baby-language" he deploys in teasing her about Troilus; and that, though Cressida participates in his "pattern of repartee," she despises "him and his role."

2967 Mendelsohn, Leonard Richard. "The Legends of Troy in English Renaissance Drama." Ph.D. dissertation, University of Wisconsin, 1966. *DAI*, 27 (1966–67), 1033-A.

Examines the three dozen plays written on the matter of Troy during "the century and a half following the presentation of 'Troylus and Pandor' in 1516." No matter what part of the story is dramatized in these plays and no matter what genre is used, the results are disappointing. There always seem to be "a duality of characterization, a confusion of metaphoric structure, a blurring of the dramatic," and other flaws. The conclusion seems inescapable that there is something in the Troy theme itself that inhibits adequate dramatic conception and structure. Chapters 3 and 4 treat *Tro.*, which shares the weaknesses of the other plays.

2968   Mercier, Joseph Raymond. "Shakespeare and the Function of Irony." Ph.D. dissertation, University of Connecticut, 1969. *DAI*, 30 (1969–70), 2975-A.

Finds extensive use of irony in Sh's plays, but argues that irony is seldom used for its own sake or allowed to define a play's vision. One exception may be *Tro.*, in which mankind stands self-condemned and ironic detachment is invited.

2969   Miller, J. Hillis. "Ariachne's Broken Woof." *GaR*, 32 (1977), 44–60.

Analyzes the speech in which Troilus reacts to Cressida's dalliance with Diomede as a challenge to monologic, logocentric metaphysics. In his reference to "Ariachne," Troilus conflates two myths, those of Ariadne and of Arachne, which are both congruent and not congruent. The conflation thus represents exactly what happens in the rest of Troilus's speech, which exhibits the terrible anguish involved in dividing a mind against itself, in recognizing a bifold authority, in feeling helpless before the implications of dialogue.

2970   Miskimin, Alice S. *The Renaissance Chaucer.* New Haven: Yale U. P., 1975. xii + 315 pp.

Reexamines the evidence for the transformation of medieval Chaucer into the "English Homer" of the Elizabethans. Focuses on "the changing shape and meaning" of Chaucer's works rather than their "broad impact" on later poets. Compares Chaucer with the major Elizabethans to reopen philosophical questions of "the status of the poet and of his fiction," which Chaucer was "the first English poet to raise."

Chapter 7, "The Evolution of *Troilus and Criseyde*: A History of Imitations," comments that Sh significantly increased the number of characters he found in the legend of Troilus and Cressida, compressed the action to the few days before and after the truce, and concluded with the resumption of an unfinished battle. Cressida's unfaithfulness, the focus of Robert Henryson's continuation of Chaucer's poem, is "subsumed in the deeper futility of the war." The lovers are satirized both from within the fiction and from the outside. The stage is so crowded with illustrious heroes that no one can carry the play; the chief issue becomes "the flux of time itself." From the medieval versions of Chaucer and William Caxton, deriving from Virgil and other Latin sources, Sh had absorbed a viewpoint favorable to the Trojans. However, he had also been exposed to the pro-Greek bias of Chapman's *Seven Books of the Iliad* (1598). He did not attempt to reconcile these incompatible histories. Instead, he intensified the stalemate that resulted from bringing the two together: Corruption on both sides undermines the honor of the warriors and their women. The power of *Tro.*, as distinct from all of the earlier versions of the story, comes from the removal of intermediaries like the narrator of Chaucer's poem. The audience is closer to the action, which proceeds episodically, dragging us through a meaningless, inconclusive series of experiences. Troilus's return to battle at the end, with Cressida still at large among the Greeks, shows how Sh "set free the tragic irony of the myth from its medieval Christian sublimation."

2971   Mowat, Barbara A. "Shakespearean Tragicomedy." *Renaissance Tragicomedy: Explorations in Genre and Politics.* Ed. Nancy Klein Maguire. (AMS Studies in the Renaissance 20.) New York: AMS P., 1987, pp. 80–96.

Maintains that Sh's three "problem plays," including *Tro.*, can be fruitfully examined as experiments in tragicomedy, as described by Giovanni Battista Guarini. Though Sh does not follow Guarini in all respects (especially the happy ending), he does seem in these three plays to pay close attention to the Guarinian concepts of blending and tempering tragic and comic elements. Having chosen central events for *Tro.* that are surely tragic, Sh "wrenches the tone toward the comic, toward the scurrilous, the bawdy, the rhetorically empty, the parodic."

2972   Muir, Kenneth, ed. *Troilus and Cressida.* (Oxford Shakespeare.) Oxford: Clarendon P., 1982. 205 pp.

The introduction contains a discussion of the sources, noting that Sh derived the love plot from Chaucer's *Troilus and Criseyde,* though he altered considerably the characters of Troilus, Cressida, and Pandarus. For the war plot, he used at least four sources: George Chapman's translation of *Seven Books of the Iliad,* William Caxton's *Recuyell of the Historyes of Troye,* John Lydgate's *Troye Booke,* and Ovid's *Metamorphoses.* Discusses interpretations of the play, commenting that the style, especially that of the debates, was fashioned by Sh to be appropriate for "a classical subject"; that time is a significant theme; that both the love and war plots are subjected to realistic scrutiny; the the play is more somber than cynical; and that the genre is impossible to determine.

2973   Nakayama, Randall Shige. "Divided Duty: Gender Identity and Marriage in *Much Ado About Nothing, All's Well That Ends Well, Troilus and Cressida,* and *Othello.*" Ph.D. dissertation, University of California, Berkeley, 1986. *DAI,* 48 (1987–88), 1211-A-1212-A.

Examines "the transition of the male from soldier to husband" and "the reconstruction of the male's identity." Notes that the male trafficking in women is the cause of the Trojan war in *Tro.,* while "gender identity" leads the women to believe "in their own inherent weakness."

2974   Nass, Barry. "'Yet in the Trial Much Opinion Dwells': The Combat Between Hector and Ajax in *Troilus and Cressida.*" *ES,* 65 (1984), 1–10.

Argues that the combat between Hector and Ajax (*Tro.,* IV.v) begins by seeming to confirm the impulses that have sustained the war, but ends by challenging them. Throughout the play, characters question the names and identities of people who should be well known to them, thus divorcing actions, persons, and epic conventions from "their once-heroic value and meaning." When Hector affirms that his kinship with Ajax is more important than "the contest that is a microcosm of the war," he is renouncing the pervasive tendency of others to divide things into two parts. In doing so, he stands in strong contrast to Troilus, who denies truth and logic by attempting to create two Cressidas, and Cressida, who invents another self in order to justify her infidelity.

2975   Newlin, Jeanne T. "The Modernity of *Troilus and Cressida*: The Case for Theatrical Criticism." *HLB,* 17 (1969), 353–73.

Surveys 20th-c. British and American productions of *Tro.* to show how its peculiar modernity can be brought home to critics and scholars through staging. For example, a Brattle Players production of 1948 presented the play in all its diversity, with comments on the ugly, the heroic, the romantic, and the comic elements in human nature. Arthur Colby Sprague wrote about this production that it revealed the play's coherence by the musical employment of the voices and the offstage use of sounds.

2976   Nicholson, Eric Arthur. "Stages of Travesty: The Sexual Politics of Early Modern Comedy." Ph.D. dissertation, Yale University, 1990. *DAI,* 52 (1991–92), 531-A-532-A.

Includes a chapter on *Tro.* that shows how in this play Sh subverts the patriarchal rituals by which sexual transgressors are mocked by comically exposing the mockers.

2977 Oates, J. C. "The Ambiguity of *Troilus and Cressida*." *SQ*, 17 (1966), 141–50.

Designates *Tro.* as a problem tragedy, which contains three strains that "work against final tragic elevation." First, Sh begins the love of Troilus and Cressida, the diplomatic game of the Greek generals, and the chivalric activities of Hector according to elaborate ritual patterning, which in all three cases is broken off by realistic disorder. Second, the nobility associated with tragedy is undermined by being mixed with comic motives. Third, Troilus, the only character with tragic potential, seems incongruous in an anti-tragic atmosphere (for example, the savagery of Troilus's anger is undercut by Pandarus's buffoonish final words). Unlike "ideal tragedy," the play offers "no affirmation of values."

2978 Ogden, James. "Satire and Sympathy in *Troilus and Cressida*." *Essays on Shakespeare in Honour of A. A. Ansari*. Ed. T. R. Sharma. Meerut, India: Shulabh Bookhouse, 1986, pp. 223–30.

Notes similarities between *Tro.* and Jonson's satiric plays, especially in the exhibition of "a whole series of characters with ruling passions." In *Tro.*, however, we are not so ready to pass judgment. Comments that Sh analyzes the love story against the background of the Trojan War. Focuses on the two council scenes (I.iii and II.ii), in which it is demonstrated that men do not base their actions on "abstract ideas and moral imperatives," though they may claim to do so. Yet we retain some sympathy for most of the the chief characters, especially the lovers.

2979 Okerlund, Arlene N. "In Defense of Cressida: Character as Metaphor." *Women's Studies*, 7, no. 3 (1980), 1–17.

Proposes Cressida as a central metaphor for the play; she changes for the worse, as do all other characters except Hector. To offer her as a scapegoat for society's ills is to ignore the epilogue's accusation that the members of the audience are guilty of everything they have just seen on stage. Troilus, whose character is often elevated at the expense of Cressida's, is interested only in satisfying his lust and is embarrassed at being associated with her; and Ulysses, whose negative assessment of her is often cited, is unreliable and politically motivated. Cressida develops strategies of survival that make her no better, but certainly no worse, than others in the play.

2980 Owen, Trevor. "Twenty Questions on Shakespeare's *Troilus and Cressida*." *SRASP*, 13 (1988), 9–14.

Provides brief answers to key questions about *Tro.*, drawing on the author's annotated bibliography of modern scholarship on the play. Addresses such issues as genre, protagonist, Sh's attitude to the lovers, the trustworthiness of Thersites and Ulysses as spokesmen for the playwright, the degradation of Achilles, Hector's reversal of opinion during the Trojan council scene, and theme.

2981 Owens, Roger. "The Seven Deadly Sins in the Prologue to *Troilus and Cressida*." *SJW*, 116 (1980), 85–92.

Argues that the Prologue found in the Folio text of *Tro.* (though not in the quarto of 1609) is genuine because it emphasizes the Seven Deadly Sins and thus serves as an appropriate introduction to the play. Throughout *Tro.*, the characters pursue their own selfish desires and consequently subject themselves to the destructive force of the Sins.

2982 Oyama, Toshiko. "'This is, and is not, Cressid!'—An Interpretation of *Troilus and Cressida*." *Anglica*, Apr. 1964, 72–86. Reprint. *Shakespeare's World of Words*. Tokyo: Shinozaki-Shorin, 1975, pp. 86–101.

Finds that "the level of supposition plays a very important part in *Tro.*" and that therefore the two major characters "have a very complicated quality, and they always remain as the types of ambiguity."

2983   Painter, Alice Lorraine. "*Troilus and Cressida:* Hollow Victories and Empty Defeats." *Tennessee Philological Bulletin,* 21 (1984), 24–75.

Disputes the traditional view that the Trojans represent honor and the Greeks reason; in *Tro.,* the two sides are very similar.

2984   Palmer, Barbara D. "'The Eagles Are Gone': Soliloquies in the Tragi-Comedies." *Iowa State Journal of Research,* 54 (1980), 441–48.

Explains the ambiguity of *Tro.*as partly due to a paucity of soliloquies. Instead of soliloquies, the play takes long speeches that resemble soliloquies in form and content and places them in the public sphere. Another substitute for the soliloquy is the foul-mouthed prose commentary of Thersites. These two techniques contribute to the play's unheroic effect.

2985   Palmer, Kenneth, ed. *Troilus and Cressida.* (Arden Shakespeare.) London: Methuen, 1982. xiii + 337 pp.

The introduction includes a section on sources, which discusses in some detail Chaucer's *Troilus and Criseyde* (for the love action), William Caxton's *The Recuyell of the Historyes of Troye,* John Lydgate's *Troy Book,* Ovid's *Metamorphoses,* Homer's *Iliad* (in various translations, but especially in that of George Chapman), and Robert Greene's *Euphues his Censure to Philautus* (for the Trojan council scene, II.ii). Begins critical commentary on the play by observing that Sh is primarily concerned with characters looking forward or backward from a point in the middle of the war. Notes that the war plot and the love plot are connected by analogy, but that seldom is the whole person involved in making any choice about war or love. The play is largely about inaction; its characters wait, and, while they wait, "they question, argue and play." Devotes sections to "Crucial Scenes," "Time and Time's Subjects," "Time, Treason and Prophecy," " Identity and Attributes," "Pride and Envy," and "Styles and Methods." Appendix 2 judges the theory that *Tro.* was written and first performed for an audience at one of the Inns of Court as unproven but plausible. Appendix 3 sets forth parallel passages from *Tro.* and Aristotle's *Nicomachean Ethics* as support for a suggestion that the latter work may be an influence on the former. Appendix 4 describes possible sources for Ulysses' commonplaces on degree (I.iii), placing special emphasis on Ovid. Appendix 5 consists of selections from several sources.

2986   Partridge, A. C. "The Language of Shakespeare's *Troilus and Cressida.*" *Poetica* (Tokyo), 4 (1976), 78–96.

Provides rhetorical analyses of several passages of poetry and prose from *Tro.,* including the Prologue (with its "pseudo-epical style"), the conversation between Cressida and Alexander in I.ii about Hector's impatience and Ajax's contradictory qualities (with its superabundance of rhetorical devices), Ulysses' degree speech in I.iii (with its labored, portentous verse, its excess of Latinate terminology, and its use of the ancient Greek metaphor of the planets), the Trojan debate (with its wordplay and disorderly syntax), the meditation of Achilles in III.iii on why he has declined in reputation (with its rhetorical question answered by the speaker himself and its self-centered catch words), and the admonition of Ulysses to Achilles on time in III.iii (with its resemblance to the formal oration and its "resonant polysyllables"). Notes that Sh seems not to have read Homer in the original, that he may not have read the classical rhetoricians, but that he clearly had read Ovid. *Tro.*was an experiment in which the author indulged his spleen, playing to "an audience of lawyers and intellectuals" by incorporating in one play "elements of comedy, tragedy, and pseudo-history." Satire appears in the play, though it is incidental. Certain characters are chosen to parody "the high style of English epical translation"; most of the serious verse is carefully crafted to reflect the thoughts of the major figures; there are a few lines that create atmosphere and are independent of the characters who utter them; and the comic prose in the early scenes undercuts seriousness. The play offers "a Brechtian view of a corrupt society."

2987 Patke, Rajeev S. "*Troilus* and the Divisiveness of Experience." *Shakespeare in India*. Eds. S. Nagarajan and S. Viswanathan. Delhi: Oxford U. P., 1987, pp. 1–17.

Calls attention to "the divided ancestry" of the materials Sh brought together in *Tro.*, attempting among other things "a synthesis of the classical and medieval emphases, heroism in war with chivalry in love." Surveys classical and medieval sources available to Sh and his audience, noting that the familiarity of these traditions has the effect of making the play, as well as the persons within it, "self-referential." Characters are often "at odds with themselves," and the play features "the clash of opposites" as a structural principle. Argues that honor and love in *Tro.* are valorizing objectives: That is, the value of a person or thing or activity is neither intrinsic nor fixed, but external, arbitrarily assigned by the individual will in search of self-esteem. When the valuer is shown by experience that his estimation does not square with reality, he, like Troilus, turns on himself, attacking his own ideals. The play commits itself to this kind of double-mindedness "as an irreconcilable constant to life."

2988 Potter, A. M. "*Troilus and Cressida*: Deconstructing the Middle Ages?" *Theoria*, 32 (1988), 23–35.

Regards *Tro.* as a deliberate, systematic effort to deflate the medieval "myths and attitudes central to the Elizabethan world view." Notes Sh's emphasis on demolishing the Trojans' chivalric code, and hence on questioning the value of the traditional belief that the Trojans founded Britain. Specifies ways in which all of the characters, especially the Trojans, violate the tenets of medieval chivalry. The play undermines the belief that humanity lives in "an ordered, purposeful universe," governed by immutable law.

2989 Powell, Neil. "Hero and Human: The Problem of Achilles." *CritQ*, 21, no. 2 (1979), 17–28.

Suggests that in the midst of the shifting values and changes of belief that pervade *Tro.*, Achilles is the one consistent and reliable character. Having seen through the empty honor that everyone else pursues and tries to goad him into pursuing, Achilles seeks to replace heroic values by private ones (he invites Hector to visit his tent, he honors a promise to Hecuba by refusing to let Ulysses' political maneuvering draw him back into battle, and he rearms only to avenge the death of his friend). Though Achilles' slaughter of Hector is brutal, it is consistent with his rejection of honor: Because he has renounced heroism as a sham, the only way he can use violence is unheroically. Achilles provides a standard for the play: The other characters fail to fit heroic roles, and he simply does not try to do so. In *Tro.*, Sh reinvents his characters, especially Achilles, to such an extent "that the relationship between the play and its sources is far more tentative" than "the relationship between the Roman plays and Plutarch."

2990 Powers, Kathleen Emily. "Shakespeare's Use of Lies and Deceptions in the Comedies." Ph.D. dissertation, Brown University, 1988. *DAI*, 49 (1988–89), 2233-A.

Notes that as Sh "turns away from comedy" in *Tro.*, the lies decrease in number, and "the use of them changes."

2991 Rabkin, Norman. "*Troilus and Cressida*: The Uses of the Double Plot." *ShakS*, 1 (1965), 256–82. Reprint. *Essays in Shakespearean Criticism*. Eds. James L. Calderwood and Harold E. Toliver. Englewood Cliffs, New Jersey: Prentice Hall, 1970, pp. 304–22.

Holds that ideas are given life in *Tro.* by being built into the double plot structure. The two plots concern (1) the affair of Troilus and Cressida and (2) the plan among the Greeks to bring Achilles back into battle. Sh weaves a structure like a spider web, connecting these two plots by exploring in each the question of how time determines value. This theme becomes clear at the center of the play for both the love plot and the war subplot. III.ii, which ends with the ritualistic protestations of Troilus, Cressida, and Pandarus about what they will come to represent when time has grown old, is followed immediately by the scene in which Ulysses articulates for Achilles the power of time to assign value to martial deeds. For the rest of the play, Sh varies the theme in both plots, skillfully making them intersect at numerous nodes in the web. Revised as part of chapter 2 of item 0873.

2992   Ramsey, Jarold W. "The Provenance of *Troilus and Cressida*." *SQ*, 21 (1970), 223–40.

Cites Peter Alexander's theory that *Tro.* was composed for a special festivity at one of the Inns of Court (see item 2797) and points out that this view has gained wide acceptance. For example, O. J. Campbell's estimate of the play is based on its purported appeal to "an audience of gay and dissolute benchers." Leslie Hotson has found this argument compatible with his own opinion that *Tro.* is actually *Love's Labor's Won*. "Bawdy political satire" was characteristic of the "purely intramural entertainment" at the Inns of Court, but according to surviving records, the plays presented there during the first decade of the 17th c. were mainly romantic comedies like *TN* and masques. *Tro.* would thus have been an oddity for an Inns of Court audience. J. M. Nosworthy and Nevill Coghill have argued that *Tro.* was composed for the Globe and later revised for one of the Inns. Nosworthy maintains that Sh had written about half of a tragedy on the subject when, in response to a request from one of the Inns, he changed course and completed it as a comedy in 1603. Coghill's argument is that *Tro.* was originally completed without Prologue or epilogue as a "straight tragedy" and performed at the Globe in 1603-4. Then Sh revised it "for the Christmas Revels at one of the Inns in 1608" and "self-protectively added a mocking beginning and ending calculated to disarm his audience." (See item 2838.) There are several objections to the revision theory, one of which is that Sh's company would have been too busy at Court during the Christmas seasons of 1603–4 and 1608–9 to "revise and stage a difficult play for one performance at an Inn of Court." Another point is that the Prologue and epilogue are consistent "in tone and imagery" with the rest of the play, thus invalidating the argument that they were especially composed to suit an audience different from the original one. A more likely account of the play's provenance begins with the fact that the Troy legend had become particularly prominent around 1600, possibly because its foreboding of change and disintegration symbolized for literate Elizabethans their greatest fears. Chapman had published his translation of seven books of the *Iliad* in 1598, the Admiral's Men produced Dekker and Chettle's version of the play in 1598-99, and Sh was evoking romantic elements of the Troy legend in plays like *TN*. There was an abundance of sources, including Chaucer's *Troilus and Criseyde* and Caxton's *Recuyell of the Historyes of Troye*. In this climate, Sh wrote *Tro.* for the Globe, but it did not succeed and was therefore suspended. This would explain the attempt to forestall piratical publication by having James Roberts, as agent for the Company, enter a claim in the Stationers' Register "to print when he hath gotten sufficient authority for it." In his book on *Tro.* (item 2927), Robert Kimbrough deserves credit for taking seriously the evidence that the play was written for the public theater, but his argument is vitiated by his insistence that its mixture of seemingly incongruous elements represents Sh's attempt to accommodate the tastes of both public and private theater audiences. A more likely explanation is that Sh was experimenting in *Tro.* "for his own artistic and philosophical purposes."

2993   Reid, Stephen A. "A Psychoanalytic Reading of *Troilus and Cressida* and *Measure for Measure*." *PsyR*, 57 (1970), 263–82.

Explains the uneasiness caused by *Tro.* in terms of the Freudian insight that "something in the nature of the sexual instinct is unfavorable to the achievement of absolute gratification." Because of the incest obstacle, no love object in an adult's life can equal the original one in childhood: The play is pervaded by references to inadequate love objects. Freud also observed that the sexual instinct is composed of several elements, many of which are suppressed in the adult. In the play, some of the coprophilic and sadistic components of sexuality have been assigned to Thersites; the absence of these elements in Troilus's vision of love inhibits his sexual satisfaction. Another reason for general dissatisfaction in *Tro.* is the characters' awareness of the workings of time, which causes frustration in their instinctual lives.

2994 Reinert, Otto. "The Unmended Gear: The 'Problem' in *Troilus and Cressida.*" *Essays in Honour of Kristian Smidt.* Eds. Peter Bilton, Lars Hartveit, Stig Johansson, Arthur O. Sandved, and Bjørn Tysdahl. Oslo: U. of Oslo Institute of English Studies, 1986, pp. 90–103.

Attempts to define the kind of "problem" play that *Tro.* is. It is generically indeterminate, with a structure consisting of "a collage of scenes that serve as images-in-action of the moral and psychological climate of the play." Analyzes the prologue and epilogue, the chief characters, Ulysses' famous speech on degree (I.iii), and the scene before Calchas's tent in which Troilus eavesdrops on the assignation between Diomede and Cressida and is himself overheard by Thersites (V.ii). Finds that *Tro.* is pervaded by a "ubiquitous motif of dissolution," which makes it especially appealing to moderns. Sh draws on the various sources of the Troy matter available to him, juxtaposing contradictory traditions and showing how chaos can be contained through the power of art to shape "ugly debris into design not pleasant but beautiful."

2995 Richardson, Mark Lewis. "The Legends of Troy in the English Renaissance: A Study in Decadent Literature." Ph.D. dissertation, Emory University, 1980. *DAI*, 41 (1980–81), 3121-A.

Argues that the decadence imbuing most English Renaissance depictions of the Troy legend (like *Tro.*) is in large measure due to the way in which the legend was transmitted. Redactors like Dares of Phrygia (a rationalist) and Benoît de Sainte Maure (a Christian) excised all references to pagan deities from the story. Medieval writers like Chaucer and Lydgate tried to invest the legend with the moral vision of feudal society, but Troy's destruction ensured the death of their dream. Robbed of central meaning, then, the matter of Troy could not be assimilated into a Christian aesthetic, and Renaissance writers who chose to treat it turned to the decadent style of late Roman writers like Ovid and Seneca.

2996 Rickey, Mary Ellen. "'Twixt the Dangerous Shores: *Troilus and Cressida* Again." *SQ*, 15 (1964), 3–13.

Argues that *Tro.* deals with "the single problem of corruption and its causes." The love plot and the war plot are two manifestations of "the same essential decay." Throughout the play, for example, there are strong metaphoric links between "decadent love and decadent war." Characters are greatly stylized so that parallel conditions of decadence can be explored: The relationship of Troilus and Cressida is similar to that of Paris and Helen in this regard. Disease imagery is used to characterize both Trojans and Greeks. Appetite undermines degree on both sides.

2997 Roberts, David A. "Mystery to Mathematics Flown: Time and Reality in the Renaissance." *CentR*, 19 (1975), 136–56.

Cites Ulysses' speech on degree in the Greek camp (*Tro.*, I.iii) as a key statement of the Elizabethan concept of order. In the play, the Greeks have violated the natural order in "self-destructive rebellion."

2998 Robertson, Mary Catherine. "An Iconographic Study of the Tokens in Shakespeare's Sleeveless Love Affair." Ph.D. dissertation, University of Pittsburgh, 1982. *DAI*, 44 (1983-84), 1094-A.

Analyzes the iconographic properties of the sleeve and glove tokens in *Tro.* to reveal the moral ambiguity of the two lovers.

2998a Ronan, Clifford J. "Daniel, Rainolde, Demosthenes, and the Degree Speech." *Ren&R*, 9, no. 2 (1985), 111–18.

Inventories various sources that have been suggested for Ulysses' degree speech (*Tro.*, I.iii) and adds two new ones: Samuel Daniel's "Musophilus" (for a hunting image, the phrase *universal* prey, and the tendency to consider "cosmic harmony [or its absence] in musical terminology") and Richard Rainolde's *Foundacion of Rhetorike*, a translation of Aphthonius's *Progymnasmata* (for the phrase *take away*, divided into its two halves; the words *chaos* and *follow[s]*; imagery of cutting down and uprooting; and other phrases that reinforce "tendencies and devices" that Sh was assimilating "under pressure from Platonic and other influences"). Notes that behind Richard Hooker's *The Laws of Ecclesiastical Polity*, one of the acknowledged sources for Ulysses' discourse, lies the *First Oration against Aristogiton*, often attributed in the Renaissance to Demosthenes.

2999 Rose, Mary Beth. *The Expense of Spirit: Love and Sexuality in English Renaissance Drama*. Ithaca: Cornell U. P., 1988. xi + 240 pp.

Chapter 4, "Transforming Sexuality: Jacobean Tragicomedy and the Reconfiguration of Private Life," contains a discussion of *Tro.* as a scathing critique of chivalric heroism. Sh manipulates the legendary material to expose the emptiness of Western history, and in particular the hollow values of the Elizabethan aristocracy. Chivalry defines itself in the play by connecting "military prowess and abstract idealism with narcissistic self-absorption and the rigid resistance of history," a set of qualities embodied most fully in Troilus. Love and sexuality, especially as manifested in marriage, are seen by the male heroes, even the noble Hector, as inimical to heroic action. Chivalry is seen as a dead end, no longer capable of facilitating cultural change.

3000 Rowan, Stephen Charles. "A Dancing of Attitudes: Burke's Rhetoric on Shakespeare." Ph.D. dissertation, University of British Columbia, 1985. *DAI*, 47 (1986–87), 1338-A.

Uses the rhetorical theory of Kenneth Burke to characterize the problem plays, including *Tro.*, as works that dance "toward symbols of order and toward conventional forms which would provide a clear sense of an ending." They do not, however, allow identification with such symbols.

3001 Rowe, George E. *Distinguishing Jonson: Imitation, Rivalry, and the Direction of a Dramatic Career*. Lincoln: U. of Nebraska P., 1988. xii + 220 pp.

Argues that in *Tro.* Sh offers a critique of the struggle to distinguish oneself from others that marked the War of the Theaters. Emulation, practiced by nearly all of the characters, is futile, since time ultimately undermines all achievement. The play makes this point in another way by subverting its own artistic heritage, mocking the claims of Homer and Chaucer to have treated the same materials authoritatively.

3002 Rowland, Beryl. "A Cake-Making Image in *Troilus and Cressida*." *SQ*, 21 (1979), 191–94.

Contends that the culinary imagery of the first exchange between Troilus and Pandarus in *Tro.* (I.i.14–28) is "humorlessly bawdy." Popular metaphor is used to describe the process of love, "from coition (grinding and bolting), conception (leavening), gestation (kneading, making the cake, heating the oven), to birth (the final baking)." That such images come readily to Troilus is evidence of the flawed, sensual nature of his love.

3003 Roy, Emil. "War and Manliness in Shakespeare's *Troilus and Cressida*." *CompD*, 7 (1973), 107–20.

Argues that in *Tro.* the basic conflict is between fathers and sons over mother figures. The Greeks view themselves chiefly as fathers and sons and are concerned with the aggressive and intrusive aspects of masculinity. They wish to prevent the rebellious sons of Troy from keeping "the mother-goddess Helen." The Trojans, however, see masculinity as "submission to an idealized image of woman" (Helen, Cressida, Troy itself) and attempt to possess this image. The behavior of characters on both sides is marked to an unusual degree by "the unresolved issues of earlier phases of childhood development." For example, Ulysses' desire to watch everything, to pry into the secrets of others, grows out of a child's interest in sharing forbidden experiences; and Hector's obsession with chivalry and careful deliberation mark him as an anal compulsive.

3004 Rutter, Russell Keenan. "Shakespeare's *Troilus and Cressida*: Mythical History and Renaissance Satire in a Theological Framework." Ph.D. dissertation, University of Wisconsin, 1972. *DAI*, 33 (1972–73), 2342-A.

Analyzes *Tro.* in light of the commonly held belief that Britain was founded by Trojans. Notes another important tradition: that Troy exemplified the way in which civilization could be destroyed by moral corruption. Troy, portrayed in Sh's play as the Augustinian Earthly City, would have reminded its original spectators of England and forced them to confront the question of whether their country would follow the ruinous path of Old Troy or become Troynovant, "a type of the Augustinian Heavenly City."

3005 Sacharoff, Mark. "The Orations of Agamemnon and Nestor in Shakespeare's *Troilus and Cressida*." *TSLL*, 14 (1972–73), 223–34.

Rejects the view that the speeches of Agamemnon and Nestor in *Tro.*, I.iii, are objects of scorn or ridicule. Sh's audience, with its reverence for Cicero and Quintilian, would have regarded the two speeches as "eloquent and cogent." Agamemnon begins the scene (lines 1–30) with a complete essay on the theme that the inevitable frustration of men's goals need not dismay superior beings. The structure of his discourse is simple: "There are no digressions, but rather amplifying illustrations." Moreover, Sh has Agamemnon employ imagery (for example, the tempest) that he uses with the utmost seriousness in other plays. Nestor's speech (lines 31–54), far from depicting a senile mind, is a lively attempt to stir the Greeks to action by applying what Agamemnon has said; its outstanding feature is the parable of the boat. These two orations, when taken together with the famous speech by Ulysses that follows them, constitute a passage of eloquence and power hardly consonant with the notion that the speakers are objects of satire or that the play is pervasively satiric. Revision of part of item 3009.

3006 Sacharoff, Mark. "Thersites as Crucial Figure in Shakespeare's *Troilus and Cressida*." *HAB*, 21, no. 4 (1970), 3–9.

Takes issue with critics who base their reading of *Tro.* as a satire on Thersites' scurrilous comments. Because his victims are often less culpable than he makes them, Thersites is an unreliable critic. Once this is understood, other elements in the play (for example, moments of tragic seriousness and romantic comedy) can be recognized as part of its mixed generic structure. Revision of part of item 3009.

3007 Sacharoff, Mark. "The Traditions of the Troy-Story Heroes and the Problem of Satire in *Troilus and Cressida*." *ShakS*, 6 (1970), 125–35.

Rejects the classification of *Tro.* as a satire by some modern scholars. This is developed from an erroneous belief in a "debased tradition" of the heroes in the Troy story, transmitted to Sh through the medieval versions of William Caxton and John Lydgate. The play does have strong elements of satire, but these are intermittent. A careful reading of Caxton's *Recuyell of the Historyes of Troye* and Lydgate's *Troye Booke* reveals that both authors portray the Homeric heroes, with the exception of Achilles, as admirable. References to these characters in Renaissance English literature present them largely as exemplars of virtue. A true understanding of the traditions from which Sh was working can reopen the question of the genre of *Tro.* Instead of forcing the entire play into a satiric mold, we are free to notice that its style is often that of "tragedy and high history" and that many of its scenes fit the criteria of "amorous comedy." Sh seems to have created a mixture of genres: comic, satiric, historic, and tragic materials "ultimately resolve themselves into a tragic conclusion." Revision of part of item 3009.

3008 Sacharoff, Mark. "Tragic vs. Satiric: Hector's Conduct in II. ii of Shakespeare's *Troilus and Cressida*." *SP*, 67 (1970), 517–31.

Challenges the view that Hector's volte-face in the Trojan council scene is cynical or absurd. Maintains that Hector, aware of the logical superiority of his own arguments, defers to what he senses is the greater pathos in what Troilus says. This is a grave error of judgment by a fundamentally admirable man, not the whim of a lightweight, and Sh's tone towards Hector is essentially tragic, not satiric. Revision of part of item 3009.

3009 Sacharoff, Mark Leon. "Shakespeare's *Troilus and Cressida* as a Mixture of Genres." Ph.D. dissertation, City University of New York, 1967. *DA*, 28 (1967–68), 1408-A.

Maintains that *Tro.* is "a mixture of genres, rather than pervasively a satire." The play contains a comic love plot and a historic war plot, both with tragic endings. It also includes a strong satiric emphasis, made chiefly through the agency of Thersites, but it is not decisive enough to subsume the other two strains. Several important parts of the play can be interpreted in ways that relieve them of satiric coloring. For example, in the Trojan council scene, Hector and Troilus make an erroneous but honest decision; the speeches of Nestor and Agamemnon, though "highly rhetorical," are ceremoniously correct, not foolish; and the scenes focused on the lovers are amorous comedy rather than scornful railing. Moreover, the style (which is frequently grand), the tone (which is often tolerant), and the characterization (which is two-sided) are all too complex for satire. Parts revised as items 3005, 3006, 3007, and 3008.

3010 Savage, James E. "*Troilus and Cressida* and Elizabethan Court Factions." *UMSE*, 5 (1964), 43–66.

Suggests that *Tro.* reflects contemporary events. In Hector, there is a reference to the Earl of Essex, and Sh's commentary on factions at court can be seen in other characters.

3011 Schwartz, Elias. "Tonal Equivocation and the Meaning of *Troilus and Cressida*." *SP*, 69 (1972), 304–19.

Claims that the "tonal equivocations" of *Tro.* are intentional and designed to "produce a varied but ultimately harmonized set of feelings and attitudes." The Greek council scene (I.iii) presents Agamemnon and Nestor satirically (that is, their speeches mock them). Ulysses' speech on degree is true, but only ironically for the Greek camp, where no one is worthy to rule. The overall effect of the scene is satiric. Hector's capitulation to Troilus in the Trojan council scene (II.ii) is puzzling, but Hector is acknowledging that "in the world of the play objective truth cannot exist and that all values are relative, dependent on man's will." Troilus, though continually ridiculed, is also to be taken seriously: He is foolish in aspiring to be a true lover, but this is not an unworthy goal. The play "envisions the world as a meaningless chaos, to which one may respond in various ways, none of them really adequate." Revised as chapter 3 of item 0939.

3012 Scott, William O. "Self-Difference in *Troilus and Cressida*." *Shakespeare and Deconstruction*. Eds. G. Douglas Atkins and David M. Bergeron. (American U. Studies Series 4: English Language and Literature 57.) New York: Peter Lang, 1988, pp. 129–48.

Explores "self-difference" in *Tro.* by examining dualities, inversions, self-divisions, and ironies in Troilus, Cressida, Hector, and Ulysses. The audience is also divided against itself: It is tempted to judge the characters of Troilus, Cressida, and Pandarus according to the by-words of their names (III.ii), while at the same time being presented with evidence that such judgment would be a radical oversimplification; it is required to appraise the complicated and unattractive events of the play in the light of simpler and more appealing patterns traditionally associated with the Trojan War; and it is forced to share, at least in part, the viewpoints of Thersites and Pandarus, two unsavory commentators. Calls attention to a variant of the classical story of Helen, in which Helen remains loyal to Menelaus though parted from him. Maintains that Sh's Troilus, in dividing Cressida and clinging to an ideal image of her, is creating something analogous to "the wishful story about Helen."

3013 Seltzer, Daniel, ed. *Troilus and Cressida*. (Signet Classic Shakespeare.) New York: New American Library, 1963. xl + [41]–288 pp.

The introduction summarizes the complex printing history of *Tro.* and comments on the kind of audience for which it was written. Argues that the play's experimentation with "motive and personality" results in "inconsistent characterization" and gives Hector and Cressida as especially noteworthy examples. Notes that the exploration of inconstancy as a theme undermines dramatic consistency. Points out that in *Tro.* Sh tried for the first time in his career to combine a story of love with one of public affairs. Maintains that the play, located at a sort of midpoint in Sh's career, contains all of the elements that he came to employ in his typical tragic pattern but arranges them in such a way that no tragic resolution is possible. The note on the sources comments that Sh might have known enough Greek to read Homer's *Iliad* as background for the Trojan war material. Certainly he used George Chapman's translation (1598) as well as medieval versions of the story by Lydgate and Caxton. Some details might have been derived from Ovid's *Metamorphoses*. Sh's primary source for the love story was Chaucer's *Troilus and Criseyde*. He was probably influenced by Henryson's *The Testament of Cresseid* to coarsen the character of Cressida. The introduction, text, and note on the sources are reprinted as part of item 0123.

3014 Seng, Peter J. "Pandarus's Song and Lily's Grammar." *MLJ*, 48 (1964), 212–15.

Suggests that Pandarus's song celebrating the pains and pleasures of physical love (*Tro.*, III.iii) alludes to the section on interjections in Lily.

3015 Shalvi, Alice. "'Honor' in *Troilus and Cressida*." *SEL*, 5 (1965), 283–302.

Argues that in *Tro.* Sh is examining critically a world obsessed with outward appearance rather than inward reality, with honor in the sense of reputation rather than moral integrity. There is little difference between Trojans and Greeks. On the one side, Paris is the slave of passion who merely mouths chivalric sentiments; Hector's honor is marred by pride and sensuality; and Troilus's love for Cressida is based on lust and leads to vengeance. On the other side, Ulysses appeals to pride in manipulating Ajax and Achilles. Even this base ploy is unsuccessful. It is only when the two warriors are prompted by something even more base—the personal desire for revenge—that they return to battle. Revised as a chapter in item 0955.

3016 Shaw, William P. "*Troilus and Cressida* V.iv–V.x: Giving Chaos a Name and a Local Habitation." *SRASP*, 1, no. 2 (1977), 24–48.

Describes the seven violent scenes that come at the end of *Tro.* and contends that in them Sh is skillfully imaging the descent from order into chaos that is the play's theme. Notes that through V.ii, *Tro.* follows "conventional, vertical development" but that after Troilus's recognition of Cressida's faithlessness the action becomes static, moving out "on a horizontal plane," neither rising nor falling. Separated from order and from any sense of value, the characters become trapped in a vacuum, subject to the kind of physical and metaphysical disorientation often found in 20th-c. drama of the absurd.

3017 Siddiqui, M. Naimuddin. "*Troilus and Cressida*—Treatment of the Theme by Chaucer and Shakespeare." *Osmania Journal of English Studies*, 4 (1964), 105–13.

Argues that significant differences in theme, plot, and characterization lead to the conclusion that Sh did not use Chaucer's *Troilus* as the main or direct source of *Tro.*

3018 Simmons, J. L. "Holland's Pliny and *Troilus and Cressida*." *SQ*, 27 (1976), 329–32.

Suggests that *Tro.* is indebted to Philemon Holland's translation of Pliny's *Natural History* (1601). In Pliny, Sh found a statement about the sexual insatiability of man and its unhappy consequences—particularly relevant to the love tragedy he was writing. On the same page, his attention was caught by a description of the copulation of vipers, during which the male thrusts his head into the female's mouth, whereupon she bites it off. When Sh has Pandarus refer to love as "a generation of vipers" (III.i.133), he has in mind this passage from Pliny. The copulation of vipers becomes a death image, just as sexual passion in *Tro.* results in death.

3019 Sinfield, Alan. "Kinds of Loving: Women in the Plays." *Self and Society in Shakespeare's "Troilus and Cressida" and "Measure for Measure."* Eds. J. A. Jowitt and R. K. S. Taylor. (Bradford Centre Occasional Papers 4.) Bradford: U. of Leeds Centre for Adult Education, 1983, pp. 27–44.

Forms part of a collection of essays on *Tro.* and *MM.* Provides a materialist analysis of love in *Tro.* Distinguishes two main literary ways of viewing love in Elizabethan culture, the Ovidian and the Romantic. The Ovidian lover subverts the established doctrine of love and marriage by focusing on extramarital conquest. The Romantic lover, however, idealizes the object of his affections. Both codes subordinate women to circumscribe the role of sexuality in life. For these two modes of love to survive, they must remain apart. When they are juxtaposed or mixed in a work of literature (as they are in *Tro.*), complexity and sometimes confusion result. As an example, Cressida's two goals—to hold Troilus and to return his love—are mutually exclusive because each derives from a different code, and Troilus oscillates between Romantic lover and Ovidian lover. *Tro.* is also related to the new Protestant emphasis on shared love and equality in marriage but reflects the contradictory Protestant insistence on male dominance.

3020 Slack, Robert C. "The Realms of Gold and the Dark Comedies." *"Starre of Poets": Discussions of Shakespeare.* (Carnegie Series in English 10.) Pittsburgh: Carnegie Institute of Technology, 1966, pp. 48–64.

Focuses on *Tro.* after brief discussions of *AWW* and *MM.* In treating the Trojan War, Sh developed a structure based on balanced pairs of characters, locations, and scenes. Discusses a pair of lovers (Helen and Cressida), a pair of heroes (Hector and Achilles), and a pair of choric commentators (Ulysses and Thersites). Argues that "all these corresponding pairs—the two sets of lovers, the two hero warriors, the two voices of wisdom—set up reverberations amongst themselves, each member with its correspondent, and each pair with all the others."

3021 Slights, Camille. "The Parallel Structure of *Troilus and Cressida*." *SQ*, 25 (1974), 42–51.

Argues that *Tro.* is best described as a tragic satire whose tone is effectively conveyed to the audience through an elaborate parallel structure. As an example, the Greek council scene (I.iii) begins with Ulysses' eloquent public denunciation of Achilles for violating order and degree but degenerates into the private scheming of Ulysses and Nestor to bring Achilles back to the battlefield. The Trojan council scene follows a similar pattern. By presenting the two sets of leaders in parallel councils of war, Sh allows the audience "to see distinctions in the ways people pervert moral values without obscuring the fundamental assumption that men are capable of discerning values [that] give significance to their lives." As the play proceeds, the parallelism tends to darken the tone. The parallel love scenes, for example, at first suggest only the tainting of man's reason by the costs of appetite. The largest and most obvious structural parallel is between the war story and the love story, which are thus linked in tone and theme. They intersect on the battlefield in the last act, leaving behind a scene of absurdity and frustration. The play does not permit a cynical denial of established values, but neither does it hold out much hope that human beings can live up to those values.

3022 Smith, Don. "Truth and Seeming Truth: The Language of *Measure for Measure* and *Troilus and Cressida*." *Self and Society in Shakespeare's "Troilus and Cressida" and "Measure for Measure."* Eds. J. A. Jowitt and R. K. S. Taylor. (Bradford Centre Occasional Papers 4.) Bradford: U. of Leeds Centre for Adult Education, 1982, pp. 45–60.

Highlights the quality of variance—of things being other than what they seem—in the language of *Tro.* and *MM*. One form of linguistic variance in the plays is the tautology, which offers a false sense of security by stating the obvious in a morally uncertain world. Another comes from disparity between the name and the thing, which is achieved either by exposition or "by putting forward a variety of questions, equivocations, quibbles, contrasts, and other methods of blurring names, things, and names for things." A final kind of variance is between vows (in *Tro.*, both military and romantic) and their nonfulfillment (or their fulfillment in a destructive way). Comments that Sh withholds resolutions of variance in *Tro.*

3023 Smith, J. Oates. "Essence and Existence in Shakespeare's *Troilus and Cressida*." *PQ*, 46 (1967), 167–85.

Asserts that *Tro.* is a special kind of tragedy: one that denies the possibility of conventional tragedy. Tragic elevation and devastation are undermined in this most modern of Sh's works. Sh evokes in the audience a number of tragic expectations and then demolishes them through a pervasive manifestation of infidelity—of woman to man, of body to soul, of "ideal" to real, of time to life, even of the play's structure to its apparent commitment to tell a familiar story. It is not satire, though it contains satirical elements; it is an "existential" tragedy ruthlessly subverting the "essentialist" efforts of its characters to transcend their physical limitations.

3024 Smith, Jeffrey George. "The Unified Voice of Shakespeare's *Troilus and Cressida*." Ph.D. dissertation, University of California, Irvine, 1977. *DAI*, 38 (1977–78), 5502-A–5503-A.

Studies *Tro.* from a variety of perspectives in order to disclose its complexities as well as its "fundamental unity." Chapter 1 maintains that *Tro.* has no clearly defined genre; instead, it articulates the inconclusive clash of several generic propensities. Links this argument with the theme of appetite: Appetite eats into the form of the play. Chapter 2 considers the themes of time and value, first with regard to the war plot and then with regard to the love plot. The play distinguishes between two types of value, one based on "the intrinsic worth of the individual" and one based on the "particular will" of a character. The latter form of evaluation is given special emphasis and shows that "the fallibility of the perceiving senses" is an important theme. Chapter 4 discusses the metadramatic features of the play, the most important of which is its "amount of mediation." The constant use of go-betweens in the action suggests that the play, like Pandarus, is itself a mediation between its author and his audience.

3025 Smith, Rowland J. "Personal Identity in *Troylus and Cressida*." *ESA*, 6 (1963), 7–26.

Argues that *Tro.* "deals with love and war, and with the attitudes of the two warring parties towards public and private obligation in love and war. At the same time the treatment of this theme involves a discussion on personal identity, and how the public image of a man can become his only image." On both the realistic, unscrupulous Greek side and the ineffectual, idealistic Trojan side, the play constantly stresses that "time and circumstances radically alter the way men are regarded and that the way they are regarded is often the only personality they have." This point is driven home immediately and painfully with the betrayal that accompanies Cressida's movement from one environment to another.

3026 Smith, Valerie. "The History of Cressida." *Self and Society in Shakespeare's "Troilus and Cressida" and "Measure for Measure."* Eds. J. A. Jowitt and R. K. S. Taylor. (Bradford Centre Occasional Papers 4.) Bradford: U. of Leeds Centre for Adult Education, 1982, pp. 61–79.

Recapitulates the story of Cressida as it appears in several important sources prior to *Tro*. Finds the germ of Cressida's history in the experience of Briseis and Chryseis in the *Iliad*. Chaucer's poem portrays Criseyde as caught in a trap, unable to use in the new situation at the Greek camp the feminine graces she relied on in the past. Henryson's *Testament of Cresseid* has been misinterpreted by modern critics, who are too concerned with her sexual misconduct and underplay her moral and intellectual faithlessness: They seem to view her through the eyes of Sh's Thersites. In their assessment, she is either a chaste lover or a whore; since she is not the former, she must be the latter. Until quite recently, this same oversimplification has predominated in views of Sh's Cressida. New attitudes toward women's sexuality, their economic status, and their education for social roles have brought about a recognition that Sh's Cressida, though not a noble figure, is far from being merely a daughter of the game.

3027 Snyder, Richard C. "Discovering a 'Dramaturgy of Human Relationships' in Shakespearean Metadrama: *Troilus and Cressida*." *Shakespeare and the Arts: A Collection of Essays from The Ohio Shakespeare Conference, 1981*. Eds. Cecile Cary Williamson and Henry S. Limouze. Washington, D. C.: U. P. of America, 1982, pp. 199–216.

Explores Sh's use, in *Tro.*, of "the problems in the artist/audience situation as a metaphor for the breakdown of healthy relationships in society." Takes account of the theatrical language (beginning with the Prologue's "scene" in the first line), the many metadramatic scenes (including the procession of officers directed by Ulysses "to pass by and ignore Achilles"), and the various types of artists (withdrawn, like Troilus; pandering, like Cressida) and audiences. Discusses five key metadramatic themes in the play: (1) characters become victims of dramatic circumstances; (2) characters become victims of "audience expectation or audience demand" (3) attempts are made to create a "'theatrical distance' in love from the lover"; (4) one attempts to "fulfill theatrical stereotypes to create sexual appeal"; (5) language, love, and art are seen "as acts of violence."

3028 Soellner, Rolf. "Prudence and the Price of Helen: The Debate of the Trojans in *Troilus and Cressida*." *SQ*, 20 (1969), 255–63.

Argues that Sh probably used Cicero's *De Officiis*, the standard Renaissance work on moral duty, when constructing the debate of the Trojans in *Tro.*, II.ii. In his argument, Hector uses Cicero's system of the cardinal virtues: He asserts that his attitude is not determined by fear, thus showing his fortitude. As a sign of his prudence he urges rational calculation in determining the value of Helen. His sense of justice, combined with charity, leads him to call for the return of Helen in accord with the law of nature, and his temperance prevents him from being ruled by passion. Troilus, however, opposes the world of order represented by the cardinal virtues in his appeals to passion, his skepticism, and his relativism.

3029 Southall, Raymond. "*Troilus and Cressida* and the Spirit of Capitalism." *Shakespeare in a Changing World*. Ed. Arnold Kettle. London: Lawrence and Wishart, 1964, pp. 217–32.

Argues that in *Tro*. Sh anatomizes disapprovingly "the weakening of feudal relations that had taken place during the 16th c. by bringing to bear upon a world of romance and chivalry . . . the powers of personal and social corruption inherent in the appetitive spirit of capitalism." This is achieved in great measure through "use of the language of commerce to define, amongst other things, the nature and dignity of love" and through imagery of physical appetite, which pervasively reduces life to the "demands of the belly."

3030 Spencer, Luke. "Mediation and Judgement: The Challenge of *Troilus and Cressida*." *Self and Society in Shakespeare's "Troilus and Cressida" and "Measure for Measure."* Eds. J. A. Jowitt and R. K. S. Taylor. (Bradford Centre Occasional Papers 4.) Bradford: U. of Leeds Centre for Adult Education, 1982, pp. 80–95.

Argues that in *Tro.* Sh presents a world so chaotic that the means by which the characters attempt to order their lives result only in more confusion and corruption. Designates these means as "mediation," of which there are two kinds: "(a) the communication of ideas and feelings, principally through the 'medium' of language; (b) the intervention of third parties, as messengers, interpreters or organizers, in the relations between people." Troilus and Cressida cannot mediate their love experiences to each other or to themselves; their language, full of clichés, does not provide access to their true feelings. Throughout the play, the public vehicles (like parades, war councils, sending and receiving envoys, and the ceremony of single combat) employed to mediate between competing interests and create unity prove to be useless. The efforts of the two wisest statesmen (Ulysses and Hector) are defeated because of their own self-interest. In the play's two principal mediators, Pandarus and Thersites, we see how corrupt the process can become. The most egregious example of debased mediation comes in the betrayal scene (V.ii). By denying us a central character whose judgment we trust to clarify the major issues and by presenting us with the moral consequences of defective mediation, Sh challenges us to take our own role as mediators for the play seriously.

3031 Sprigg, Douglas C. "Shakespeare's Visual Stagecraft: The Seduction of Cressida." *Shakespeare: The Theatrical Dimension.* (AMS Studies in the Renaissance 3.) Eds. Philip C. McGuire and David A. Samuelson. New York: AMS P., 1979, pp. 149–63.

Attempts to convey an idea of "the range and complexity of Shakespeare's visual stagecraft" through an analysis of the scene in *Tro.* in which Diomede, observed by Thersites, Ulysses, and Troilus, has an assignation with Cressida (V.ii). Our response to the scene is affected, among other things, by the differing degrees of awareness among the observers, certain implied and stated stage directions, and the fact that the scene takes place at night.

3032 Stafford, T. J. "Mercantile Imagery in *Troilus and Cressida*." *Shakespeare in the Southwest: Some New Directions.* Ed. T. J. Stafford. U. of Texas at El Paso: Texas Western P., 1969, pp. 36–42.

Suggests that Sh uses the imagery of commerce, especially that of sailing merchants, to communicate a debasement of love and honor in the Greek–Trojan world and to provide a thematic connection between these two attributes in their debased state.

3033 Stamm, Rudolf. "The Glass of Pandar's Praise: The Word–Scenery, Mirror Passages, and Reported Scenes in Shakespeare's *Troilus and Cressida*." *E&S*, 17 (1964), 55–77. Reprint. *The Shaping Powers at Work: Fifteen Essays on Poetic Transmutation.* Heidelberg: Carl Winter, 1967, pp. 32–51.

Suggests that Sh regulates his audience's response to *Tro.* by references in the text to place, time, atmosphere, appearance, gestures, and business. The study of such references "makes visible the inner form of the play-in-performance." As examples, the Prologue places the action in time and space; the word scenery of V.viii, evoking the image of the setting sun, establishes the atmosphere for Hector's death; and the language of several speakers mirrors the action in the complex scene (V.ii) in which Cressida gives herself to Diomedes while Ulysses, Troilus, and Thersites observe.

There are numerous spoken references to silences and sounds, and several effectively reported scenes (like Alexander's account of Hector's anger in I.ii and Ulysses' description of how Achilles spends his time while declining to fight for the Greek cause in I.iii).

3034 Stehlíková, Eva. "Thersites, a Deformed and Scurrilous Grecian." *Charles University on Shakespeare.* Eds. Zdeněk Stříbrný and Jarmila Emmerová. Universita Karlova, 1966, pp. 143–50.

Maintains that Thersites is the key to the interpretation of *Tro.* The only character in the play who has not been distorted by medieval tradition, Thersites may have come from as far back as the *Iliad.* He has a special place among Sh's clowns and fools: Although he shares some of their functions, his rightful place is among the great skeptics and pessimists, like Jaques of *AYL*, Hamlet, and Apemantus. Thersites' bitter, destructive attitude is not, however, that of Sh, whose portrayal of the Trojans reflects "understanding and sympathy for the world that is dying out, and [sounds] a note of protest at the destruction of human values."

3035 Stein, Arnold. "*Troilus and Cressida*: The Disjunctive Imagination." *ELH*, 36 (1969), 145–67.

Analyzes the ways in which the "dramatic imagination" is used in *Tro.* to stymie itself. Discusses chief characters (Troilus, Cressida, Ulysses, Hector, Pandarus) to show that Sh has relentlessly divided them against themselves. Moreover, the society depicted within the play, as well as the themes and symbols, are thoroughly infected by disunity. Between the characters and their world, however, there is little conflict: They remain passive, untouched by their surroundings and playing the roles forced on them. Generically, *Tro.* is "closer to the tragedy it is not than to any of the other forms it is not." As in tragedy, there is great evil, but it is unfocused, producing a uniformity of tone. There is no character through whom we can experience tragedy. Tragic materials abound, but they are "disordered and kept from any juncture that might produce a tragic effect."

3036 Stiller, Nikki. *The Figure of Cressida in British and American Literature: Transformation of a Literary Type.* (Studies in Comparative Literature 4.) Lewiston: Edwin Mellen P., 1990. 193 pp.

Chapter 4 makes a comparison between Sh's Cressida (in *Tro.*) and Chaucer's Criseyde (in *Troilus and Criseyde*). Whereas the latter is presented as demure and submissive, a remorseful victim, the former is portrayed as a glib and cunning whore, trading herself as a commodity. Sh's play lacks the resolution of plot found in Chaucer's poem. *Tro.* seems designed to undermine the ideal of courtly love and the cherished status it accords women. The play's misogynist views reflect the increasing influence in Sh's time of the patriarchal Puritan movement.

3037 Stiller, Nikki. "Robert Henryson's Cresseid and Sexual Backlash." *L&P*, 31 (1981), 88–95.

Sketches the history of the identification of women with an evil sexuality from classical times through the Middle Ages. Notes that the code of courtly love reversed this tendency, according women a high status. Robert Henryson's *Testament of Cresseid* rejects this code, returning to the older tradition with a savage indictment of female sexuality. Henryson may have influenced Sh in *Tro.*, which is an attempt "to debunk all the tropes, aims, and attitudes of courtly love at once."

3038 Stockholder, Katherine. "Power and Pleasure in *Troilus and Cressida*, or Rhetoric and Structure of the Anti-Tragic." *CE*, 30 (1969), 539–54.

Argues that in *Tro.* the characters, by their rhetoric, suggest the large historical concerns of tragedy, but then detach themselves from those problems to indulge merely personal whims. Prevented from realizing a tragic vision, the play also fails to work as comedy because the claims of the characters to historical significance make personal happy endings inappropriate. The characters also preclude the play's classification as a satire "because they have depleted the values upon which satire relies." The play dramatizes the process "by which values are drained of their reality and disappear from the world." Revision of part of item 1026.

3039 Stříbrný, Zdeněk. "Time in *Troilus and Cressida*." *SJW*, 112 (1976), 105–21.

Argues that a double-time structure operates in *Tro*. In both the love and war stories, the characters—and the audience—are constantly made aware of the pressures of the moment, but they are also frequently reminded of the larger historical and mythological perspectives that relate the events of the play to the past and the future. The play itself is affected by this dialectic between "short time" and "long time": Its actual events take place in four days, but Sh places it in the middle of the Trojan War, and the characters refer to both past and future. Ulysses' view of a fixed, hierarchical world order in his degree speech (I.iii) is at odds with his later vision of "envious and calumniating time" (III.iii.174). And the appeal by Troilus and Cressida to standards of permanence attempts to deny the exigencies of the moment in their love affair. The play sets forth an exciting tension "between myth and motion, illusion and reality, old order, both social and moral, and the irresistible progress of time."

3040 Suzuki, Mihoko. "Helen's Daughters: Woman as Emblem in the Matter of Troy." Ph.D. dissertation, Yale University, 1982. *DAI*, 44 (1983–84), 484-A–485-A.

Studies "Helen of Troy and her analogues as either emblems of doubleness or characters of ambiguity in the Homeric epics, Virgil's *Aeneid*, Spenser's *Fairie Queene*, and Shakespeare's *Troilus*." Part revised as item 3042; the whole revised as item 3041.

3041 Suzuki, Mihoko. *Metamorphoses of Helen: Authority, Difference, and the Epic*. Ithaca: Cornell U. P., 1989. xi + 271 pp.

Provides a comparative feminist reading of the representations of Helen of Troy in Homer's *Iliad* and *Odyssey*, Virgil's *Aeneid*, Spenser's *Fairie Queene*, and Sh's *Tro*. Revision of item 3040. The section on *Tro*. is a revision of item 3042.

3042 Suzuki, Mihoko. "'Truth tired with iteration': Myth and Fiction in Shakespeare's *Troilus and Cressida*." *PQ*, 66 (1987), 153–74.

Maintains that in *Tro*. Sh challenges the process of myth-making by treating a story whose meaning is already overdetermined by tradition. To the mystifying power of myth, which produces absolute meanings, Sh opposes a more fluid fiction of indeterminacy. Troilus, who insists on an abstract notion of truth, fails to understand Cressida's difference from himself as an individual; Ulysses' speech on degree is an attempt to assert that "an essential and orderly hierarchy prevails," but this notion is belied by the emulation that pervades the action. Cressida, however, sees herself in relation to others, recognizing the indeterminacy of identity. The many crossings between the Greek and Trojan camps, which blur the distinction between them, also make this point. Sh crowds together many sources, with the effect that ambiguity is multiplied: Troilus's phrase "Ariachne's broken woof" (V.ii.156), for example, conflates Ariadne and Arachne. The former is described by Plutarch as being betrayed by Theseus and having either an ultimately tragic or happy fate. Plutarch also records the tradition that there were two Ariadnes. In Ovid, Arachne, in a contest with Minerva, weaves a tapestry that depicts the metamorphoses of the gods. These subtexts subvert the ideas of the fixed self. In its generic indefiniteness, *Tro*. enacts a "critique of codification and classification." Revision of part of item 3040. Revised as the section on *Tro*. in item 3041.

3043 Sypher, Wylie. *The Ethic of Time: Structures of Experience in Shakespeare*. New York: Seabury P., 1976. xi + 216 pp.

Chapter 7, "Space, Time and Duty: *Troilus and Cressida*," argues that *Tro*. juxtaposes the older hierarchical view of the world, in which order is spatialized (as seen in Ulysses' discourse on degree in I.iii) with a new awareness of the disintegrating power of time (as described by Ulysses in his conversation with Achilles in III.iii). The play features a fine distinction between "lived time, which is inaccessible to reason," and "thought time," which is so conformable to reason that it leads "certain characters either to absurd idealism" (Troilus and Paris) or to facile cynicism (Ulysses). Cressida and Hector both acknowledge that they are caught up in "lived time," but the former commits herself to the moment in an act of despair, while the latter resists his predetermined fate by acting as if he had freedom in the present.

3044   Takada, Yasunai. "How to Do Things with 'Fall-Out' Systems in *Troilus and Cressida*." *ShakSt*, 20 (1981–82), 33–58.

Interprets *Tro.* as informed by the "fall-out" of "past ideological systems," including chivalric love, Petrarchism, and natural love (love subordinated to the will of God). Troilus's irrationalism is manifested in completely subjective notions of love, which come to dominate Trojan thinking despite Hector's momentary advocacy of natural law. Ulysses' speech on degree constitutes a systematic endorsement of natural law, but this is undermined by the homosexual relationship of Achilles and Patroclus, which stands for the general depravity of the Greek camp. Cressida's desertion of Troilus results in his disillusionment: He is finally confronted with the "irrelevance of his own system."

3045   Taylor, Gary. "*Troilus and Cressida*: Bibliography, Performance, and Interpretation." *ShakS*, 15 (1982), 99–136.

Attempts to establish, by detailed comparison of the quarto text of *Tro.* (1609) with the First Folio text (1623), that the manuscript for the former was Sh's foul papers, while the latter was derived from an annotated copy of the quarto, which was in turn based on a promptbook ultimately descended from Sh's fair copy. The Folio thus provides Sh's preferred text. Most of the variants between the two texts are insignificant in our overall response to the play, but the rejection of Pandarus by Troilus, transferred by the Folio from the ending of the play to V.iii, raises questions about Troilus's final judgment of Cressida and Pandarus.

3046   Taylor, Hawley C. "The Stoic Philosophy and Shakespeare's *Troilus and Cressida*." *San Jose Studies*, 4, no. 1 (1978), 82–93.

Argues that in *Tro.* Sh shows how the Stoic moral vision—with its four cardinal virtues of temperance, wisdom, courage, and justice—is used as a standard by which the conduct of the characters is judged and in nearly all cases found wanting. Each of the ethical goods honored by Cicero in his *De Officiis*, perhaps the most influential conduit of Stoic ideas to Elizabethan England and a work probably known to Sh, is deliberately violated in *Tro.*: The play seems constructed to display negative examples of Stoic virtues. Taking extraordinary pains to undermine any heroic qualities in the Troy story, Sh adds to it the Cressida theme, which further subverts it. The only positive expression of the Roman–Stoic ideal comes in Ulysses' degree speech (I.iii), but it is clear that no one acts in accord with this ideal.

3047   Thomas, Vivian. *The Moral Universe of Shakespeare's Problem Plays*. Totowa, New Jersey: Barnes & Noble, 1987. [iv] + 236 pp.

Treats *Tro.* as one of three "problem plays" by Sh. Defines a problem play as one that explores "fundamental problems relating to personal and social values within a framework which makes the audience acutely aware of the problems without providing amelioration through the provision of adequate answers or a dramatic mode which facilitates a satisfactory release of emotions." Chapter 2, "Shakespeare's Use of His Source Material," provides an outline of the sources of *Tro.* and detailed discussion of the more important ones: George Chapman's translations of Homer; John Lydgate's *The Hystorye Sege and Dystruccyon of Troye* (1513); William Caxton's *Recuyell of the Historyes of Troye* (c. 1474); and Chaucer's *Troilus and Criseyde*. Chapter 3, "The Fractured Universe: Wholeness and Division in *Troilus and Cressida*," emphasizes the tension in the play between "the human desire to believe wholly or achieve wholly and the inevitable forcing back into accepting the reality of and necessity for disintegration." Also important are frequent references to "the identity and nature of the characters in the play," which promote a constant evaluation of others and self. All of this foregrounds questions of value and worth. In both the love story and the war story, the physical is privileged over the intellectual. Important images are those of appetite, eating (food, regurgitation, leftovers), body parts, and animals. Time is also a key theme. Comments that *Tro.* is "the most brilliantly versatile of all Shakespeare's plays."

3048   Thompson, Ann. "The Characters of Oblivion: Shakespeare De-constructs Troy." *Shakespeare, "Troilus et Cressida."* Actes du colloque, 9–10 novembre 1990, Université Lumière-Lyon 2. Lyon: C.E.R.A.N., Dept. d'Anglais, Université Lumière-Lyon 2, 1991, pp. 89–104.

Notes that the word *oblivion* occurs three times in *Tro.*, more than in any other play of Sh's, and examines these three occurrences "to develop a view of the play in terms of its exploration of the notions of forgetting and being forgotten." Oblivion is seen as an agent of Time, but more indefinite and monster-like; it works with Time to "destroy by devouring"; and its effects can be counteracted through the use of characters (writing). In *Tro.*, Sh seems to be keenly aware that he is engaged in a radical alteration of Chaucerian and Homeric materials. Through the play "he is acknowledging that the power of writing to counter the effects of Oblivion is neither a straightforward nor, necessarily, a benign one."

3049   Thompson, Ann, and John O. Thompson. *Shakespeare: Meaning and Metaphor.* Iowa City: U. of Iowa P., 1987. xi + 228 pp.

Presents five studies of Sh, each taking its method from a recent "extra-literary" theory of metaphor. Chapter 1, "Time Metaphors in *Troilus and Cressida*," employs George Lakoff and Mark Johnson's *Metaphors We Live By* to understand "conceptual metaphors" of time in Sh's play. Sections are entitled "Time is a Person," "Oblivion," "Implicit Time: Creation is Birth," "Time as Space," "Temporal Ironies," and "The Heightened and the Everyday."

3049a   Thompson, Diane Paige. "Human Responsibility and the Fall of Troy." Ph.D. dissertation, City University of New York, 1981. *DAI*, 42 (1981–82), 1139-A.

Analyzes versions of the Trojan War story to consider their treatment of responsibility—human or supernatural—for "the disasters that occurred." Includes discussion of *Tro.*

3050   Thompson, Karl F. "*Troilus and Cressida*: The Incomplete Achilles." *CE*, 27 (1966), 532–36.

Finds the play unsatisfactory after Ulysses' speech to Achilles on honor (III.iii). Sh "fails to deal consistently," either seriously or satirically, "with the courtly tradition and its basic premise that honor pledged with love is the paramount motive of the noble heart." Ulysses is "neither consistently noble nor altogether cynical," and Achilles is a buffoon.

3051   Thompson, Karl F. "The Unknown Ulysses." *SQ*, 19 (1968), 125–28. Reprint. *Odysseus / Ulysses.* (Major Literary Characters.) Ed. Harold Bloom. New York: Chelsea House, 1991, pp. 48–52.

Attempts to reconcile the critics' apparently opposing views of Ulysses in *Tro*. Sees the character as a blend of the philosophical statesman, the Stoic moralist, and the sardonic humorist.

3052   Thomson, Patricia. "Rant and Cant in *Troilus and Cressida*." *E&S*, 22 (1969), 33–56.

Points out that "word power," or "passionate rhetoric," though suspect to the modern ear, was admired by Sh's audience when employed in an appropriate situation. The problem with much of the noble speech in *Tro.* is that it seems incongruous with the trite occasions on which it is employed. It would require an Inns of Court man to gauge the extent to which some of the dignified speeches by the noble characters are to be considered as comic as those of Thersites, Pandarus, and Cressida. It is clear, however, that Ajax is guilty of rant, as is Troilus in his love speeches. The other major characters can be more or less culpable depending on the spectator's assessment of the style appropriate to the context.

3053   Toole, William B. *Shakespeare's Problem Plays.* The Hague: Mouton, 1966. 242 pp.

Uses medieval religious background as the basis for interpreting four plays. In *Tro.*, Achilles and Cressida are both false to idealistic codes, Achilles to the code of war and honor and Cressida to the code of love. Hector and Troilus are both noble but imperfect beings. The play is a tragedy because the protagonist, Troilus, devotes himself passionately to ideals, but fails to recognize that these ideals are false. It is an imperfect tragedy because Troilus never comes to understand himself.

3054   Tylee, Claire M. "The Text of Cressida and Every Ticklish Reader: *Troilus and Cressida* and the Greek Camp Scene." *ShS*, 41 (1989), 63–76.

Maintains that Cressida's character, especially as it is read through Ulysses' comments in the Greek camp scene of *Tro.* (IV.v), fails to achieve authenticity. Cites the need for the reintroduction of two production techniques from Sh's time (the use of male actors for female roles and doubling) in order to demonstrate to modern audiences that "women are constructed by cultural values."

3055   Ure, Peter. "'Addition' (*Troilus and Cressida,* IV.v.141)." *N&Q*, 13 (1966), 135.

Presents evidence to suggest that "addition" [line 142] has the heraldic meaning of "mark of honor."

3056   Ure, Peter. "The Enigmatic Problem Plays." *SN*, 14 (1964), 22–23.

Examines the term "problem plays" as it has been applied by numerous critics to *AWW, MM, Tro.,* and sometimes other works of Sh. Concludes that the term is no longer useful to indicate a group of plays. *Tro.*, for example, seems to stand alone as something experimental about which there is little agreement. On the one hand, O. J. Campbell and Alice Walker see *Tro.* as a satire, whereas on the other Theodore Spencer and Brian Morris find tragic stature in Troilus.

3057   Ure, Peter. "*Troilus and Cressida* II.ii.162–193." *RES*, 17 (1966), 405–9.

Argues that in the debate among the Trojans about keeping Helen (II.ii.163–193), Hector's appeal to both natural law and the law of nations clearly puts him in the right. Having won the debate, Hector behaves inconsistently when he does an about-face. Sh found this necessary for the play to continue.

3058   Vaughan, Virginia Mason. "Daughters of the Game: *Troilus and Cressida* and the Sexual Discourse of 16th-Century England." *Women's Studies International Forum,* 13 (1990), 209–220.

Provides the historical context of the England in which *Tro.* was written, focusing on the status of women as property—desirable, valuable, and powerful only when chaste. Cressida understands that she must use her desirability to best advantage; she makes a mistake when she yields to Troilus, thus sacrificing what power she possessed. Once in the Greek camp, and without her chastity, she becomes a piece of property to be handed about.

3059 Vickers, Brian. "Rites of Passage in Shakespeare's Prose." *SJH*, 1986, 45–67.

Notes that Sh has developed for *Tro.* "two prose characters, one for the Trojan, one for the Greek camp, whose function it is to reduce the two great themes of epic, love and war, to their lowest common denominator."

3060 Viswanathan, S. "A Shakespearean Device: The Scene within the Scene." *Anglia*, 90 (1972), 456–69.

Comments on the effects of having Thersites observe and comment on the scene between Diomede and Cressida (*Tro.*, V.ii) in counterpoint to Troilus's comments on the same scene. This scene within the scene produces an ambivalence in the audience, a tension "between cynicism and faith in values."

3061 Voss, A. E. "Tragedy and History: The Case of *Troilus and Cressida*." *UCTSE*, 15 (1986), 1–11.

Argues that in *Tro.*, Sh undermines the notion that tragedy can be found within history. To achieve this, he afflicts the major candidates for tragic status (Hector, Ulysses, Troilus), as well as the two major commentators on the action (Pandarus and Thersites), with inarticulateness, a disjunction between word and deed. In plays before *Tro.*, Sh treats tragedy as action, something that happened; in plays after it, he views tragedy as a condition, something that happens.

3062 Voth, Grant L. "Ulysses and 'Particular Will' in Shakespeare's *Troilus and Cressida*." *SJW*, 113 (1977), 149–57.

Characterizes Ulysses in *Tro.* as mean-spirited and petty. His degree speech in I.iii is designed to deceive the Greek leaders about the reason for Achilles' absence from battle, which Ulysses knows is love, but which he says is emulation. He misleads his colleagues so that he can gain credit for maneuvering Achilles back into battle. His second major initiative in the play, convincing Troilus of Cressida's wantonness, is even more underhanded than the first. Ulysses is responsible for some of the most reprehensible acts of "particular will" in the entire play.

3063 Voth, Grant L., and Oliver H. Evans. "Cressida and the World of the Play." *ShakS*, 8 (1974), 231–39.

Considers Cressida much less culpable than many have argued. In the world of *Tro.*, there is no metaphysical or temporal dimension, "no possibility of a universal order reasserting its claim." The central symbol for this world is the putrefied core in sumptuous armor: Throughout the play, many characters, most particularly Troilus, attempt to paper over the corruption at the center with magnificent language. Cressida begins with a cynical and realistic view of the world in which she lives. In the early scenes, her language reveals shrewd calculation and defensive maneuvering. However, in the trysting scene (III.ii), she is seduced by Troilus into sharing his idealism. In pledging loyalty to him, she betrays herself. Among the Greeks, she again becomes a realist. The world of the play is not an attractive one, but Cressida at first reads it accurately. She has been blamed too much for returning to this view at the end.

3064 Vroonland, Jewell Kay. "Mannerism and Shakespeare's 'Problem Plays': An Argument for Revaluation." Ph.D. dissertation, Kansas State University, 1969. *DAI*, 30 (1969–70), 2502-A-2503-A.

Suggests that Sh's "problem plays" (*Tro.*, *MM*, *AWW*) are examples of mannerist art. Like the mannerist painters, he uses art to capture "the effects of frustration and disillusion." Chapter 2 analyzes *Tro.*, arguing that the irresolution of the play reflects the inability of the various characters to decide on Helen's worth. The participants in the various debates are unreliable, and the imagery of merchandising reinforces the relativity of values.

3064a Weil, Herbert S. Jr. "'I Know You All': Possible Assaults upon and Invitations to the Audience by Shakespeare's Characters." *The Elizabethan Theatre IX.* Papers Given at the Ninth International Conference on Elizabethan Theatre Held at the University of Waterloo in July 1981. Ed. G. R. Hibbard. Port Credit, Ontario: P. D. Meany, [1986], pp. 169–85.

Explores the problematic relationship between character and audience in three Shakespearean soliloquies, including the one with which Cressida concludes II.ii of *Tro.* Here Cressida juxtaposes an expression of love for Troilus with exremely cynical observations about "sex, woman, joy, and transitory values." The audience is invited to engage with or react against "the bitter perspective that is asserted."

3065 West, Thomas G. "The Two Truths of *Troilus and Cressida.*" *Shakespeare as Political Thinker.* Eds. John Alvis and Thomas G. West. Durham, North Carolina: Carolina Academic P., 1981, pp. 127–43.

Argues that the Greeks in *Tro.* seek truth in "the nature of man," basing conduct on knowledge of the cosmos and understanding of "human passions through self-knowledge." The Trojans, however, discover truth through "something whose value is established by an act of the will." These two approaches to truth are exemplified by Ulysses and Troilus, respectively. They are worked out in the Troilus and Cressida love plot and "in the war plot depicting Ulysses' scheme to draw Achilles back into the battle." Neither approach is successfully pursued by its partisans: The Greeks look outward for guidance, but the unpredictability of human passions and the uncertain workings of chance make the attainment of their kind of knowledge virtually impossible; the Trojans tend to look within, forgetting that they are attributing infinite value to things of finite worth. In the play, Sh's truth is Greek, ugly but without the bitterness of Thersites. We are given a philosophical glimpse into the "inner workings" of Western civilization, which requires "clear-headed insight into the heart of things" but rests "on a public order whose appearance belies its inner truth."

3066 Whitaker, Virgil K. "Still Another Source for *Troilus and Cressida.*" *English Renaissance Drama: Essays in Honor of Madeleine Doran and Mark Eccles.* Eds. Standish Henning, Robert Kimbrough, and Richard Knowles. Carbondale: Southern Illinois U. P., 1976, pp.100–107.

Argues for the "strong probability" that Sh used Robert Greene's Euphues His Censure to Philautus (1587) as a source for *Tro.*, especially the Trojan council scene (II.ii). Greene's work contains a series of debates or discussions among the characters involved in the Troy story about the rights and wrongs of war. In Sh, Hector's speech about "the laws of nature" seems closely related to arguments advanced in Greene by other characters, while Sh's Troilus and Paris "take over arguments given to Hector in Greene." Greene's portrayal of Hector as a somewhat unreflective "devotee of fortitude" may have something to do with the sudden turnaround of Sh's Hector in regard to continuing the war.

3067 Wilan, Richard Anthony. "The Relation of Logic and Rhetoric to Meaning in Shakespeare's *Troilus and Cressida.*" Ph.D dissertation, University of Maryland, 1970. *DAI,* 31 (1970–71), 2359-A.

Contends that *Tro.* dramatizes the inadequacy of logic and rhetoric to render a systematic account of reality. Sh is reacting against a commonly held assumption of his day that through the arts of language man can establish truth and thus make sound ethical decisions. Throughout the play—in the mock tutor-pupil relationship of Pandarus and Troilus, in the various failed attempts to define man through reason and rhetoric, in the Trojan reliance on empty Ciceronian formulae to set values—there is "overinflation and subsequent ironical undercutting of language."

3068 Wilson, Douglas B. "The Commerce of Desire: Freudian Narcissism in Chaucer's *Troilus and Criseyde* and Shakespeare's *Troilus and Cressida*." *ELN*, 21, no. 1 (1983), 11–22.

Discovers that Cressida exemplifies Freud's idea of the narcissistic woman, who deals in the commerce of masculine desire. Notes that while Chaucer's lovers escape the trap of narcissism and courtly convention as they progress toward mutuality and "respect for otherness," Sh's lovers grow apart. Sh treats the story ironically; subverting "the modes of heroism and romance, respectively, of Homer and Chaucer," he provides "an anatomy of narcissistic closure."

3069 Windham, Lauren F. "An Interpretation of Shakespeare's *Troilus and Cressida*." Ph.D. dissertation, University of Missouri, Columbia, 1966. *DA*, 27 (1966–67), 3022-A.

Argues that *Tro.* is "a satire on those types of people who elevate personal desire above public duty." Sh uses several normative Elizabethan concepts—order, honor, and courtly love—to judge the characters. A primary cause of the disorder that prevails in the play is that the major characters seek personal honor without regard for their responsibility to the state. Through the vehicle of courtly love, Sh also satirizes those people who are corrupted by lust.

3070 Wood, Robert E. "The Dignity of Mortality: Marlowe's *Dido* and Shakespeare's *Troilus*." *ShakS*, 11 (1978), 95–106.

Discovers similarities in style and dramatic technique between *Tro.* and Marlowe's *Dido, Queen of Carthage*, suggesting that Sh learned much from the earlier work. Most important is the relationship between V.ii of *Tro.* and II.i of *Dido*, in which Troilus and Aeneas, respectively, attempt to deny what they see and are eventually forced to return to reality. Cressida's interview with Diomedes in the same scene of *Tro.* resembles Dido's treatment of her discarded suitor, Iarbus: In each case, there is vacillation on the part of the lady, rejecting and then recalling the would-be lover. Marlowe's play preceded Sh's in directing satiric humor at its tragic protagonist. Sh went further than Marlowe in satirizing his chief characters, but, like his predecessor, he succeeded in subordinating the satiric to the tragic. The characters who fall in both plays do so as a result of their own guilt; they are not overcome by an evil stronger than their good. Unlike most of Sh's tragic heroes, they develop virtues for which we admire them in the course of their fall; we recognize that even in their flawed mortality there is considerable dignity. Revision of part of item 3072.

3071 Wood, Robert E. "*Troilus and Cressida*: The Tragedy of a City." *PQ*, 56 (1977), 65–81.

Views *Tro.* as a "dramatic anatomy of the fall of Troy," which avoids full depiction of individual tragic figures in order to focus on the communal guilt and the punishment of the Trojans for Helen's rape. This guilt is continually before us: In the council scene (II.ii), for example, there is a retrospective acknowledgment of the whole city's complicity in the crime, and this takes precedence over whatever personal motives emerge in the debate. Hector, the "quintessential Trojan," makes decisions without internal struggle and serves, especially in his death, as a symbol of the city. Troilus's love affair reflects the larger struggle. In losing Cressida to Diomede, for example, he reverses the pattern of the rape of Helen; and love and war are always closely connected in his mind. Though portrayed with greater psychological realism than Hector, Troilus lacks the "solitary grandeur" of the tragic hero, instead suffering in community with his people for their crime. Revision of part of item 3072.

3072 Wood, Robert Edward. "A Critical Study of Shakespeare's *Troilus and Cressida*." Ph.D. dissertation, University of Virginia, 1973. *DAI*, 34 (1973–74), 5129-A-5130-A.

Attempts to answer a number of standard criticisms of *Tro.*, in particular that its large satiric component mars its tragic effect and that the audience's interest is fragmented by the large number of characters. The satirical content of *Tro.* is consistent with its tragic effect, which depends more on "ritual and pattern" than on character. This technique, perhaps derived in part from the private theater plays of John Marston, is appropriate for depicting the corporate nature of Troy's crime. Examines the relationship between Marlowe's *Dido* and *Tro.*, showing how the focus on the suffering protagonist and some satirical elements are seen in more complex forms in Sh. Devotes a chapter to considering food, disease, and music imagery, as well as to analyzing time and Fortune and "their effect on value and honor." Comments that Troilus is sufficiently entangled in all of the play's events to be regarded as the hero, but that Hector's symbolic role subverts his brother's claim. Troilus's love affair reflects the pain of the war, and his betrayal by Cressida parallels the death of Hector: Both are analogies for the fall of Troy. Seen throughout as a second Hector, Troilus succeeds his brother as leader, "a role in which his doom merges with that of Troy." Parts revised as items 3070 and 3071.

3073 Yoder, R. A. "'Sons and Daughters of the Game': An Essay on Shakespeare's *Troilus and Cressida*." *ShS*, 25 (1972), 11–25.

Attempts to demonstrate that the "ugly realities" of the world of *Tro.* "are at cross purposes with the codes of courtly love and honor that seem to govern it." The characters, in order "to avoid seeing their world for what it is," cling desperately to "the superstructures they have erected to deny it." Their treatment of time is symptomatic: They fear the present, embedded as it is in the process of time, and prefer to appeal "to ultimate time, the process ended, as an escape." Whatever is said about differing values in the play, all of the characters agree that public order, consistency, and unity must prevail over any private concerns. The state of war encourages this public game, and the characters, especially Troilus and Cressida, play by its rules.

3074 Zulandt, George Klemm. "Shakespeare's *Troilus and Cressida* in Relation to English Drama of 1597 to 1604." Ph.D. dissertation, Ohio State University, 1968. *DAI*, 30 (1969–70), 347-A-348-A.

Surveys all extant plays written for the commercial London theater between 1597 and 1604 to challenge the argument that *Tro.* is outside the mainstream of Renaissance drama. Playwrights of this period turned away from the affirmative philosophy and coherent structure of chronicle history and looked to "continental and classical history to raise problems that did not admit of easy solutions." Experimentation with new forms accompanied the treatment of these new themes. In exploring private life, playwrights also broke new ground. Not satisfied with amusing treatments of young love, they "developed characters and plots that dealt with serious social evils and explored dangerous discrepancies between appearance and reality." *Tro.* is the natural outcome of Sh's experimentation with these problems and materials.

Twelfth Night

3075 Araki, Musazumi. "A Fantastical Perspective of A (b/d)—The Suppressed 'Incest' Theme in *Twelfth Night*." *ShStud*, 18 (1979–80), 29–56.

Sees the number "two" as a key to reading *TN*, particularly as it applies to the symbolism of the androgyne, which can be taken to represent "the unity of binary oppositions." On a subnarrative level, Orsino can be related to Olivia's dead brother, with the Viola–Sebastian pairing as its counterpart. Each couple enjoys, in some sense, "(1) a brother–sister relationship, (2) a twin relationship, and (3) an incestuous relationship." Uses Ovid's *Metamorphoses* to help establish the connection between the story of Apollo and his sister Artemis and *TN*. This story has the theme of incest and involves separation and reintegration of most characters.

3076 Baker, Herschel, ed. *Twelfth Night, or What You Will*. (Signet Classic Shakespeare.) New York: New American Library, 1965. xxxi + [32]–208 pp.

The note on the source of *TN* (Barnabe Riche's "Of Apolonius and Silla," from *Riche his Farewell to Militarie Profession*) notes the derivation of the basic plot ("the adventures and misadventures of a pair of identical twins") from Greek comedy, the Roman playwrights Plautus and Terence, Renaissance Italian Plautine imitations, and Elizabethan English adaptations. The introduction, text, and note on the source are reprinted as part of item 0123.

3077 Calkins, Roger. "The Renaissance Idea of 'Imitation' and Shakespeare's *Twelfth Night*." *Twenty-Seven to One: A Potpourri of Humanistic Material Presented to Dr. Donald Gale Stillman on the Occasion of His Retirement from Clarkson College of Technology by Members of the Liberal Studies–Humanities Department Staff, 1949–1970*. Ed. Bradford B. Broughton. Ogdensburg, New York: Ryan P., 1970, pp. 52–66.

Defines the Renaissance idea of imitation as "wading farther" or improving on materials borrowed from earlier writers. The first example of the *TN* plot, found in the anonymous *Gl'Ingannati* (1531), is "a mixture of the erudite forms from classical literature and the ribald humor of the carnival." In *TN*, Orsino's description of his love combines "the classical idea of love as a disease from Ovid's *Remedia Amoris*" with "the Puritanical view of love as base desire" and "the courtly ideal of Petrarchan love." Revision of part of item 3078.

3078 Calkins, Roger Willard. "The Social and Intellectual Background of *Twelfth Night*." Ph.D. dissertation, Yale University, 1966. *DA*, 27 (1966–67), 175-A.

Seeks to develop an interpretation of *TN* based on a study of how its basic plot—that of the disguised page—was used in various sources to suit the social and intellectual makeup of different audiences. For example, the *commedia erudita* dramatists used this plot "in a modified form from Plautus for aristocratic entertainment." Sh first used the plot in *TGV*; his modification of it in *TN* is based on a heightened awareness of social conditions. Part revised as item 3077.

3079 Carroll, William C. "The Ending of *Twelfth Night* and the Tradition of Metamorphosis." *Shakespearean Comedy*. Ed. Maurice Charney. New York: New York Literary Forum, 1980, pp. 49–61.

Points out that in *TN* Sh fused two familiar comedic motifs: The first is the Plautine device of "lost or separated twins brought to the same location, unknown to each other or anyone else, thus leading to much confusion and raising questions of identity and knowledge." The second motif, "broadly Plautine but also associated with romance, has a girl disguised as a boy (occasionally but rarely the reverse) and disguised parties of the same sex falling in love with one another." Sh increased the complication by adapting yet another theatrical tradition, that of sexual metamorphosis, and adding it to the mix. This tradition, which appears to begin with Ovid's story of Iphis and Ianthe, involves the sexual transformation of a disguised maiden and sometimes a male. Sh's most immediate contact with the drama of metamorphosis would have been through the comedies of John Lyly, especially *Gallathea* and *Loves Metamorphosis*. Though not arranging a magical sexual transformation as Lyly does, Sh offers something both comparable and incomparably richer. In the final scene of *TN*, mysterious powers turn two into one and one into two. Similarity is revealed in "twinship, the harmony of marriage, forgiveness, an unexpected commonality of interests, blood relation." But there is also emphasis on differences, on what "is not": Malvolio is still separated from the others, Viola leaves the stage as "herself and not herself," and Feste in his final song is both a clown and an actor commenting on the play we have just seen. Sh induces the audience to view these things from various perspectives and thus to adopt the metamorphic principle in responding to the play. Revised as part of chapter 3 of item 0242.

3080   Gaskill, Gayle. "The Role of Fortune in *Twelfth Night*." *Iowa English Bulletin*, 30 (Fall 1980), 20–23, 32.

Explains how, in *TN*, the noble characters, best exemplified by Viola, are able to take advantage of the blessings of fortune, or chance, while the arrogant and ignorant, best exemplified by Malvolio, misread their own schemes as the design of fortune. Fortune "reveals and rules" the play's characters.

3081   King, Walter N. "Shakespeare and Parmenides: The Metaphysics of *Twelfth Night*." *SEL*, 8 (1968), 283–306.

Views Sh's treatment of the appearance versus reality theme, especially in *TN*, as closely resembling that of Parmenides. Some of Feste's comments (for example, "that that is, is" and "nothing that is so is so") suggest that "a Parmenidean metaphysics, with its Platonic qualifications, is singularly appropriate as a foundation for a metaphysic of Shakespearian comedy." In *TN*, there is a facing up to the question of "what is permanent in a world of constant flux": "hence the iteration of characteristic questions and paradoxical answers that embrace both the sensible and the intelligible worlds."

3082   Lamb, M. E. "Ovid's *Metamorphoses* and Shakespeare's *Twelfth Night*." *Shakespearean Comedy*. Ed. Maurice Charney. New York: New York Literary Forum, 1980, pp. 63–77.

Begins by describing the two contradictory attitudes toward Ovid in the Renaissance. The first, developed in the Middle Ages, sees the tales of metamorphoses as "allegorical lessons about the human soul." The second delights in the urbane narrator of the tales as he performs "verbal gymnastics" and assumes a variety of narrative poses. Sh's adaptation of Ovidian metamorphoses and their allegorical applications can be seen in Orsino's comparison of himself to Actaeon, which indicates a state of spiritual stagnation. Orsino's name, which means "bear," also links him with Callisto, who was, like Actaeon, a hunter hunted, but, unlike Actaeon, was transformed into a star by Jove. This metamorphosis suggests Orsino's potential for either subhuman bestiality or transcendence through love. Olivia is associated with Daphne and the sisters of Phaethon, who were transformed into trees. This can indicate inner paralysis, but Olivia's name also suggests the olive, a tree of peace and fertility. Viola is connected with a variety of metamorphoses, including those of Niobe and Iphis; Sebastian is revealed by Viola's assumed name of Cesario, or "little Caesar," which refers to "the culmination of the *Metamorphoses*, Caesar's metamorphosis and Augustus' projected metamorphosis into stars." Transformation into stars, internalized "to represent a spiritual state" in *TN*, signifies happiness for the loves of Sebastian and Olivia and Orsino and Viola. In the *Metamorphoses*, Ovid's narrator repeatedly calls attention to himself, changing his perspective on the events he recounts. Ovidian interest in manipulating roles and the ambiguity it creates can be seen in a female wooer like Olivia. Even more impressive is the succession of roles Viola goes through in wooing

Olivia. Like Ovid's narrator, Viola is a good actor, which means she is adaptable, open to change. Malvolio, by contrast, is a bad actor, incapable of transformation. Feste, able to take on any role, is the most Ovidian character of all. Through him, and particularly in his final song, the distinction between actor and character, reality and play is dissolved, and the audience is made aware of the reality of role-playing in the world outside of the play.

3082a McAvoy, William C., comp. "Twelfth Night, or What You Will": A Bibliography to *Supplement the New Variorum Edition of 1901*. New York: Modern Language Association, 1984. vi + 57 pp.

Attempts to cover "everything published between 1901 and 1981 that is of genuine worth for the scholar," as well as a few earlier and later items. Comprises 1126 items, classified into eight sections, and an index of authors and editors. Includes sections on Editions, Commentary, Criticism, and Sources. Lists entries alphabetically within each section, except in the section on editions, which is arranged chronologically. Includes brief annotations in brackets to indicate specific passages being discussed in the commentary section and to convey special emphases of items in the criticism and sources sections that cannot readily be discerned from their titles.

3083 McPherson, David. "Herculean Malvolio." *N&Q*, 20 (1973), 135–36.

Argues that Malvolio's donning of yellow stockings with cross garters is an allusion to the similar footwear worn by Hercules out of love for Omphale in Seneca's *Hippolytus*. Malvolio is forced by Maria's plot "to re-enact a parody of two humiliating episodes in Hercules' career: madness on the one hand and enslavement to a woman on the other."

3083a Pafford, J. H. P. "Pigrogromitus: *Twelfth Night*, II.iii.23." *N&Q*, 33 (1986), 358.

Suggests that the nonce word *pigrogromitus* mentioned by Sir Andrew in his conversation with the Clown is a compound of late Latin *pigro* (lazy) and *gromettus* (servant).

3084 Palmer, D. J. "Art and Nature in *Twelfth Night*." *CritQ*, 9, no. 3 (1967), 201–12. Reprint. *Shakespeare: "Twelfth Night": A Casebook*. Ed. D. J. Palmer. London: Macmillan, 1972, pp. 204–21.

Observes that *TN*'s concern with "the instability and impermanence of life" is reflected in its art: The dramatic form "corresponds to the flux and changefulness represented in each situation." Cites Ovid's *Metamorphoses* as a crucial influence on Sh's conception of impermanence in the play. Notes that the Ovidian notion of metamorphosis as "a transformation to a more enduring plane of existence" was interpreted by the Elizabethans as "a symbolic change which altered the form in order to express its true nature." In the play, this idea of metamorphosis informs the use of disguise (Viola, Malvolio, Feste, the figure of Patience).

3085 Palmer, D. J. "*Twelfth Night* and the Myth of Echo and Narcissus." *ShS*, 32 (1979), 73–78.

Suggests that the myth of Echo and Narcissus, as found in the *Metamorphoses* and Elizabethan love poetry, furnishes some important motifs for *TN*. Orsino's opening speech plays on the complaint of Ovid's Narcissus that "my plentie makes me poore," and, like Narcissus, he is infatuated with an image, not in love with a real person. Malvolio, who is described as "sick of self-love" (I.v.87) and who is seen "practicing behavior to his own shadow" (II.v.17), is also presented as narcissistic, and Viola's reproaches of Olivia for scorning love and procreation recall the vanity of Narcissus. The plight of Viola herself, unable to speak with her own voice of her love for Orsino, may owe something to Echo, as may her capacity to frame her speech to any occasion. "Concealment and reciprocation," essential features of the Echo motif, are important in other ways: Viola, Olivia, and Sebastian all need, in some sense, to reveal themselves, and "requiting what is freely given" is the key to civility throughout the play.

3085a Slights, William W. E. "'Maid' and Man' in *Twelfth Night*." *JEGP*, 80 (1981), 327–48.

Summarizes the classical tradition of the androgyne myth, especially as it appears in the tale of Hermaphroditus and Salmacis in Ovid's *Metamorphoses*. Contends that this myth informs *TN*, allowing Sh "to reconcile independence and mutuality, physical passion and visionary idealism."

3086 Taylor, Anthony Brian. "Shakespeare and Golding: Viola's Interview with Olivia and Echo and Narcissus." *ELN*, 15 (1977–78), 103–6.

Discovers two echoes from Golding's translation of Ovid in the interview between Viola and Olivia in *TN*. The borrowings come from the account of Echo and Narcissus in book 3 of the *Metamorphoses* and can be seen in Olivia's reference to her lips as "indifferent red" (I.v.242) and Viola's use of the words "hallow" and "babbling" (I.v.267–268).

3087 Wood, James O. "Malvolio's Nose." *AN&Q*, 6 (1967), 38–39.

Interprets Feste's ostensibly nonsensical reasons for thrift in *TN*, II.iii.26–28, to mean (1) that the shape of Malvolvio's nose (hooked, like that of Julius Caesar) proves his potential for (mock) greatness, (2) that Olivia is ripe for marriage, and that therefore (3) Malvolio aspires to outdistance all others in winning her hand. The idea that the hooked nose presages greatness had been imported into Elizabethan school comedy from Plutarch by way of Erasmus's *Adagia*. The last part of Feste's statement, which suggests that Malvolio is one of the "Myrmidons," derives this image for upstart courtiers from book 7 of Ovid's *Metamorphoses*.

THE TWO GENTLEMEN OF VERONA

3088 Godshalk, William Leigh. "The Structural Unity of *Two Gentlemen of Verona*." *SP*, 66 (1969), 168–81.

Suggests that Sh uses recurrent structural elements to unite the play. Foremost among these are allusions to classical myth, letters, and journeys. The classical allusions, which compare Valentine and Sylvia to Hero and Leander and Proteus and Julia to Theseus and Ariadne, build a sense of impending tragedy, which is reinforced by the various recurrences of epistolary noncommunication. The journeys, however, coupled with the theme of education, lead to comic resolution. Revised as chapter 2 of item 0446.

3089 Pearson, D'Orsay W., comp. "*The Two Gentlemen of Verona*": *An Annotated Bibliography*. (Garland Shakespeare Bibliographies 16.) New York: Garland, 1988. xv + 251 pp.

Covers materials published between 1940 and 1985. Classifies entries under eight headings, including Criticism (418 items) and Sources and Influences (43 items). Begins each section with the oldest entries and proceeds chronologically. Provides substantial annotations. Concludes with an index. Includes, in the sections on criticism and sources and influences, a number of items that discuss the relationship of *TGV* to the classics.

3090 Scott, William O. "Proteus in Spenser and Shakespeare: The Lover's Identity." *ShakS*, 1 (1965), 283–93.

Explains Spenser's Proteus, who woos Florimell by assuming various shapes to tempt her in book 3 of *The Faerie Queene*, as a full elaboration of the combined Proteus and Vertumnus myths. Vertumnus, who in book 14 of the *Metamorphoses* woos Pomona by changing shapes, was interpreted by many Renaissance commentators as signifying the variability of passions in lovers and especially the loss of identity a lover suffers under the pressure of desire. In *TGV*, Proteus, like Spenser's Proteus and like Vertumnus, loses his identity to pursue his lust for Silvia in a variety of transformations. He is brought back to himself by Julia, his true love, and Valentine, his true friend. The myth of Proteus also enriches the meaning of *TGV* by suggesting that there is "an underlying reality of character which will remain after the fickleness and its resultant treacheries have been purged." Proteus is not referred to by name in Sh's other comedies with changeable heroes, but the myth is implicit in the careers of the lovers in *MND*, Orsino in *TN*, and Bertram in *AWW*.

THE TWO NOBLE KINSMEN

3090a Abrams, Richard. "Gender Confusion and Sexual Politics in *The Two Noble Kinsmen*." *Drama, Sex and Politics*. Ed. James Redmond. (Themes in Drama 7.) Cambridge: Cambridge U. P., 1985, pp. 69–76.

Explores gender confusion and contestation in TNK, noting Emilia's lesbian preferences, her flirtation with heterosexuality, the kinsmen's interlocking in each other's fantasies of love, and the conflict between the patriarchal Theseus and the female power of Emilia. Emilia's speculation that Arcite is a Ganymede and Palamon a Narcissus is as revealing as their own choices to be soldiers of Mars and Venus, respectively. Cites a passage from Plutarch's *Life of Pelopidas* about a select band of fighting men recruited for their homosexuality as background for considering the relationship between Sh's Theseus and Pirithous.

3091 Bawcutt, N. W., ed. *The Two Noble Kinsmen*. (New Penguin Shakespeare.) Harmondsworth: Penguin, 1977. 249 pp.

The introduction notes the clear relationship between the play and its primary source, *The Knight's Tale* of Chaucer. Sums up and comments on the action of *TNK*, hinting that Sh's knowledge of Plutarch and of the tragic myths connected with Thebes might have contributed to his composition of the first act. In act V, the gods are frequently referred to or called upon, but they do not reveal themselves, nor is there a clear sense of a benevolent providence, as in Sh's other later plays. The play resists allegorical or mythological interpretation.

3092 Beecher, D. A. "Antiochus and Stratonice: The Heritage of a Medico-Literary Motif in the Theatre of the English Renaissance." *The Seventeenth Century*, 5 (1990), 113–32.

Identifies a "sub-genre of love story" well-known to the Elizabethans that involves a lover (usually male) who is frustrated in achieving the object of his desire and falls into a life-threatening state of despair. Various circumstances "of propriety or propinquity" prevent the consummation of the love, which is often concealed and may be detected only "by a specialist such as a physician." Unique to this type of narrative is "the diagnostic scene," wherein the lover's secret is discovered and furtively communicated to the beloved. Notes that the "earliest prototype" of this story is the account of the beautiful Stratonice, wife of King Seleucus of Babylon, whose stepson, the Prince Antiochus, conceived an obsessive passion for her. A shrewd physician arranges to transfer her to Antiochus to save him from the condition known as "*amor hereos* or erotic melancholy." The first literary record of Stratonice is that of Valerius Maximus, but a more influential version is found in Plutarch's *Life of Demetrius*. The medical philosophy of Galen, whose influence extended into the Renaissance, "gave physiological authority to the concept of erotic melancholy." In *TNK*, Sh and Fletcher reveal a thorough familiarity with this "medico-literary phenomenon." Though their treatment of the jailer's daughter and her amorous fixation on Palamon is somewhat removed from its narrative prototype, "in formal and structural terms all the identifying features" of the Stratonice genre are present.

3093   Bradbrook, M. C. "Shakespeare and His Collaborator." *Shakespeare 1971: Proceedings of the World Shakespeare Congress: Vancouver, August 1971*. Eds. Clifford Leech and J. M. R. Margeson. Toronto: U. of Toronto P., 1972, pp. 21–36.

Supports the view that *TNK* is partly by Sh. Mentions classical materials in the Shakespearean scenes.

3094   Clements, Robert Morrison Jr. "A New Look at *The Two Noble Kinsmen*." Ph.D. dissertation, University of California, Berkeley, 1974. *DAI*, 35 (1974–75), 7251-A.

Examines *TNK* from four perspectives: (1) a survey of the history of its reputation; (2) a comparison with other tragicomedies of its time; (3) a consideration of the play as part of "the literary tradition of friendship"; and (4) a discussion of its masque elements. *TNK* departs from its source, Chaucer's *The Knight's Tale*, in making the friendship of Palamon and Arcite a major concern. Notes that the literature of friendship goes back to Cicero.

3094a   Hamlin, Will. "A Select Bibliographical Guide to *The Two Noble Kinsmen*." *Shakespeare, Fletcher and "The Two Noble Kinsmen."* Ed. Charles H. Frey. Columbia: U. of Missouri P., 1989, pp. 186–216.

Provides "a survey of major scholarship and criticism on *The Two Noble Kinsmen* from the early eighteenth century through 1987." Classifies entries into five sections: (1) Editions, (2) Studies of Authorship and Date, (3) Source Study, (4) Criticism, and (5) Accounts of Recent Performances. Arranges entries within each section chronologically. Provides substantial and detailed annotations.

3095   Heisler, Ron. "Shakespeare and the Rosicrucians." *Hermetic Journal*, 33 (1986), 16–19.

Includes, in an argument supporting the idea that *TNK* is "a Rosicrucian rallying call," the comment that this play is Sh's "most truly pagan effort," structured from first to last by pagan ritual; full of invocations to the classical gods; and perhaps consciously referring to "the Eleusinian Mysteries of ancient Greece."

3096   Leech, Clifford. *The John Fletcher Plays*. London: Chatto and Windus, 1962. ix + 180 pp.

Discusses the relationship of Fletcher and Sh in chapter 6. *TNK* has two parts that were probably written by Sh: the first scene, in which "the three Queens interrupt the wedding of Theseus with the prayer that he shall at once undertake a campaign against Thebes" and "the passages in the first scene of act V" in which Palamon, Arcite, and Emily invoke the aid, respectively, of Mars, Venus, and Diana. There is some relation between *TNK* and *Per.*, for example "in the romantic presentation of a classical setting."

3097   Leech, Clifford, ed. *The Two Noble Kinsmen.* (Signet Classic Shakespeare.) New York: New American Library, 1966. xli + [42]–268 pp.

The introduction attempts to establish a connection between *TNK* and Sh's late romances by noting its Greek setting and its invocation of the gods. It also resembles the earlier comedies, especially *MND*, which, like *TNK*, begins with the plans of the Athenian duke Theseus to marry Hippolyta. The note on the source discusses five broad ways in which *TNK* differs from *The Knight's Tale* of Chaucer. One important series of changes has to do with the influence of the gods: In Sh, a single power seems to work through the gods, whereas in his source the gods are at odds with one another. The introduction, text, and note on the source are reprinted as part of item 0123.

3098   Lief, Madelon, and Nicholas F. Radel. "Linguistic Subversion and the Artifice of Rhetoric in *The Two Noble Kinsmen*." *SQ*, 38 (1987), 405–25.

Advances the hypothesis that Sh and Fletcher undermine "idealist mimesis and decorum" in *TNK*. Notes that "at the heart of Fletcherian tragicomedy" there is an insistence on disjunction between word and action. Sh exploits this gap to suggest that "rhetoric and pageantry are impotent and fail to create order." Places particular emphasis on the rhetoric of Theseus and on the prayers of Arcite and Palamon to Mars and Venus, respectively.

3099   Metz, G. Harold, comp. *Four Plays Ascribed to Shakespeare: An Annotated Bibliography.* (Garland Shakespeare Bibliographies 2.) New York: Garland, 1982. xxiv + 193 pp.

Covers primarily works published between 1930 and 1980. Begins with a section on the plays as a group (including items on any two or more) and then devotes a separate section to each play. Includes, under each section, subsections on criticism and commentary, date, sources, and text and editions. Begins each subsection with the oldest entries and proceeds chronologically. The last section, on *TNK*, has sixty-seven entries under criticism, two entries under sources, and twelve under text and editions. Concludes with a single index. Provides substantial and detailed annotations.

3100   Proudfoot, G. R., ed. *The Two Noble Kinsmen.* (Regents Renaissance Drama Series.) Lincoln: U. of Nebraska P., 1970. xvi + 141 pp.

The introduction notes that Chaucer's *The Knight's Tale* is the chief source for the main plot. Act I also makes use of Sir Thomas North's translation of Plutarch's "Life of Theseus" for Theseus's relationship to Pirithous and for "his admiration of Hercules." It is possible, though not certain, that Sh or Fletcher knew Chaucer's source, Giovanni Boccaccio's *Teseida*, or 16th-c. prose versions of it in French and Italian. It is also probable that Sh or Fletcher had some acquaintance with "classical texts relating to Thebes, such as the *Thebais* of Statius."

3100a   Roberts, Jeanne Addison. "Crises of Male Self-Definition in *The Two Noble Kinsmen*." *Shakespeare, Fletcher and "The Two Noble Kinsmen."* Ed. Charles H. Frey. Columbia: U. of Missouri P., 1989, pp. 133–44.

Provides a brief historical account of Amazonian women in classical, medieval, and Renaissance tales. Contends that the presence of an Amazon in most contexts is "an infallible clue to an area of male anxiety, a signal of threatened erosion to a systematically constructed patriarchal world view." Notes that the two Amazons in *TNK*, Hippolyta and her sister Emilia, play a part in blurring the boundaries that ensure stable male self-definition. Theseus is confronted with two conflicts, one between Mars and Venus that is played out by Arcite and Palamon, and the other between Venus and Diana that is projected onto the women. The allegorical precision of Sh's source, *The Knight's Tale* of Chaucer, is disrupted in *TNK*. Though "male boundaries threatened by the inroads of both females and their surrogate horses" are "temporarily shored up" at play's end, there is a strong sense of uneasiness, reinforced by the unconventional generic form." Revised as part of chapter 3 of item 0901.

3100b Waith, Eugene M. "Shakespeare and Fletcher on Love and Friendship." *ShakS*, 18 (1986), 235–50. Reprint. *Patterns and Perspectives in English Renaissance Drama*. Newark: U. of Delaware P., 1988, pp. 289–303.

Surveys the conflict between love and friendship in western literature from the 12th c. A.D. through the early 17th c., noting that "the the classical ideal of friendship," based on a relationship between two virtuous and equal males, was widely known through Cicero's *De Amicitia*, its Christianized medieval versions, and Renaissance commentators like Montaigne. Maintains that Sh and John Fletcher, authors of *TNK*, adjust their sources to make the friendship of Arcite and Palamon their chief concern. The death of Arcite, as Sh depicts it, leads at play's end to bewilderment at the inexplicable loss.

3101 Waith, Eugene M., ed. *The Two Noble Kinsmen*. (Oxford Shakespeare.) Oxford: Clarendon P., 1989. ix + 233 pp.

The introduction includes a section on sources. Notes that the primary source is *The Knight's Tale* of Chaucer, which is based on Boccaccio's *Teseida*, itself an attempt to write "a vernacular epic in the tradition of Virgil's *Aeneid*" and Statius's *Thebaid*. The *Teseida* is actually more allied to medieval romance than to classical epic. Sh also made use of Plutarch's *Life of Theseus* and may have been influenced by Lydgate's *Story of Thebes*. Surveys, in the section on interpretation, the conventions of chivalric romance; comments on the importance of friendship; and emphasizes the hopelessness of the ending.

3102 Weller, Barry. "*The Two Noble Kinsmen*, the Friendship Tradition, and the Flight from Eros." *Shakespeare, Fletcher and "The Two Noble Kinsmen."* Ed. Charles H. Frey. Columbia: U. of Missouri P., 1989, pp. 93–108.

Regards *TNK* as a dramatization of "the conflict between friendship and marriage." The play's presentation of the friendship between Palamon and Arcite as inimical to marriage-based order in the state is part of a tradition that can be traced back to Aristotle's *Ethics*, and which holds that friendship distracts men from pursuing "the goal of public honor."

3103 Wickham, Glynne. "*The Two Noble Kinsmen* or *A Midsummer Night's Dream, Part II?*" *The Elizabethan Theatre VII*. Papers Given at the Seventh International Conference on Elizabethan Theatre Held at the University of Waterloo, Ontario, in July 1977. Ed. G. R. Hibbard. Hamden, Connecticut: Archon Books in Collaboration with the U. of Waterloo, 1980, pp. 167–96.

Argues that, like *MND*, *TNK* was written to mark the occasion of a wedding, in this case the marriage of Princess Elizabeth in 1613. Makes the case that the bittersweet temper of *TNK* was suited to the mood of the court, still mourning over the recent death of Prince Henry. Notes the Athenian setting and the classical gods that preside over the action.

3104 Wing, Susan Laura. "*The Two Noble Kinsmen*: Shakespeare and Fletcher's Reinterpretation of Chaucer's The *Knight's Tale*." Ph.D. dissertation, University of California, Los Angeles, 1984. *DAI*, 45 (1984–85), 2889-A.

Gives considerable attention to the changes Sh and Fletcher made in Chaucer's *Knight's Tale*. Analyzes the play's "language, style, structure," and key themes. The first four chapters examine significant characters, and chapter 5 scrutinizes "the play's ironic world ruled by inscrutable gods and capricious fate."

Venus and Adonis

3105 Adkins, Betty Jean VanNus. "A Critical Analysis of the Erotic, Mythological Narrative Poem 1589–1598." Ph.D. dissertation, University of Miami, 1974. *DAI*, 35 (1974–75), 2211-A.

Investigates the causes for "the flourishing of a minor genre of narrative poetry based on classical mythology and focused on a theme of frustrated love which concludes in tragedy." Evaluates the ways in which the authors of these poems borrowed and modified their materials, mainly from Ovid but also from other sources of classical myth. Discusses, for example, Sh's contradictions of his Ovidian source in making Adonis a reluctant lover in *Ven*.

3106 Allen, Michael J. B. "The Chase: The Development of a Renaissance Theme." *CL*, 20 (1968), 301–12.

Cites *Ven.* to illustrate the associations of the Adonis myth that make it "one of three basic strands woven into the Renaissance idea of the chase." Particularly important is Venus's fascination with the wound, derived from Ovid. It seems to stand for "the reversal of roles, in which she was the hunter instead of the hunted and the reluctant Adonis loved instead of loving."

3107 Asals, Heather. "*Venus and Adonis:* The Education of a Goddess." *SEL*, 13 (1973), 31–51.

Interprets the Venus in *Ven.* in light of "the Neoplatonic Hierarchy of the senses." At first, she seems to be moved by the basest desire, but she then proceeds to a noble appreciation of what she beholds. As Love in the Neoplatonic system, she is drawn to Adonis, who represents Beauty. The Venus and Mars myth focuses other concerns in the poem: the Renaissance confounding of *armare* and *amare*, the close connection between Love and Death, and hence the poem's association of Venus with the boar that kills Adonis. Since Love is a kind of Death, Venus resembles the boar. Finally, though, she distinguishes herself from the boar: She perceives the beauty of Adonis, to which the boar is blind; and the boar represents straightforward Lust and Death, whereas Venus as Love makes possible a "life in death," a rebirth in another.

3108 Bauer, Robert J. "Rhetoric and Picture in *Venus and Adonis.*" *EIRC*, 1 (1974), 41–56.

Probes the question of why Venus's artful rhetoric, which is so appealing to us, fails to win over Adonis. Throughout *Ven.*, Sh makes several references to the fine arts, suggesting that Venus views Adonis merely in terms of his external attractiveness. She is unable to stimulate his "speculative instincts" about what might happen if he were to assume the role of an amorous hero—something that a good painting would do well and that skillful rhetoric would do superlatively. That her oratory leaves him unmoved, or rather repels him, is testimony to her own lack of artistic double vision: She is aware of the handsome youth before her, but she does not understand his boyish diffidence. If she did understand, she would fashion her speeches to work on his imagination, to overcome his reluctance, to seduce him.

3109 Baumlin, Tita French. "The Birth of the Bard: *Venus and Adonis* and Poetic Apotheosis." *PLL*, 26 (1990), 191–211.

Suggests that Sh's language and characterization of Venus are analogous to his development as a poet. Just as Venus must grow into the role of Goddess of Love, so Sh must learn to conform to the paradigm of poet–creator. Sh's Venus, initially aggressive and thus nonseductive, must master the language necessary to fulfill her destiny. At first, she fails miserably in her pedantic use of Petrarchan love imagery and commits all the sins of a fledgling poet. Only after the death of Adonis does Venus (or the poet) attain maturity, discovering in her (his) eulogy the previously missing language of grace. Venus, through her suffering, re-creates Adonis (as the flower, the nature of love) and herself (as the potent Goddess of Love). Similarly, Sh's poem utilizes the Ovidian device of the "creation story." The poet–child manages to "out Ovid," his poetic father, thus progressing from unseasoned wordsmith to creative master.

3110 Beauregard, David N. "*Venus and Adonis*: Shakespeare's Representation of the Passions." *ShakS*, 8 (1975), 83–98.

Proposes that *Ven.* figures forth (in Sidney's terms) the concupiscible and irascible parts of the sensitive soul. In the first half of the poem, "Venus is the concupiscible power in pursuit of the good, the beautiful Adonis; Adonis is the concupiscible power attempting to avoid evil, the voracious and lustful Venus." In the second half, "Venus displays the emotions corresponding to the irascible power: fear, boldness, hope, despair, and anger." The ambivalence perceived in the poem by many readers is actually caused by a shift in rhetorical intent between the two parts: In the first half, Venus's unnatural words and deeds evoke laughter and amusement; in the second half, we are moved to some measure of pity for the grief-stricken goddess. Throughout the poem, we remain detached, as "spectators viewing the affections of love in two different situations."

3111 Berry, J. Wilkes. "Loss of Adonis and Light in *Venus and Adonis*." *Discourse*, 12 (1969), 72–76.

Suggests that in *Ven.*, Sh mirrors "the failure of Venus's sanguine plans for winning Adonis in the day's moving from dawn through sunset to black night."

3112 Bowers, A. Robin. "'Faire-fall the wit': Narrative Irony and Crux in Shakespeare's *Venus and Adonis*." *PLL*, 17 (1981), 198–203.

Argues that the hyphen in "Faire-fall" in the first edition of *Ven.* (line 472) should be retained in modern editions because it is the key to a triple pun that enriches our response to Venus's feigned swoon and Adonis's decision to revive her with a kiss. The narrator can thus be saying "may good befall" Venus's wit, or that Venus's wit is "fearful," or that Venus is a "fair fool."

3113 Bowers, A. Robin. "'Hard Armours' and 'Delicate Amours' in Shakespeare's *Venus and Adonis*." *ShakS*, 12 (1979), 1–23.

Challenges interpretations of *Ven.* that regard it as "disturbingly ambiguous" about love. Surveys literary, philosophical, and artistic traditions of two chief symbols in the poem—the boar hunt and the erotic kiss—to support the conclusion that Sh unified it both morally and structurally. Hunting in general, and particularly the boar hunt, was viewed as a proper exercise for virtue. The boar was associated with lust, and Adonis' death is the result of his succumbing to that vice, symbolized by the erotic kissing to which he consents.

3114 Bowers, R. H. "Anagnorisis, or the Shock of Recognition in Shakespeare's *Venus and Adonis*." *RenP*, 1962 (1963), 3–8.

Contends that the chief focus of *Ven.* is "the mind of Venus." As she laments Adonis's death, Venus comes to the ironic realization that the motive she is attributing to the boar (that he was trying to kiss Adonis) was also her motive. In an Aristotelian anagnorisis, she sees her own lust.

3115 Bradbrook, Muriel C. "Beasts and Gods: Greene's *Groatsworth of Witte* and the Social Purpose of *Venus and Adonis*." *ShS*, 15 (1962), 62–72.

Suggests that Sh may have ventured into Ovidian romance as a response to Robert Greene's attack on him in *Groatsworth of Witte*. In *Ven.*, he invokes "a lofty form and classic authority" to treat love with "aristocratic boldness and freedom."

3116 Brown, Huntington. "*Venus and Adonis*: The Action, the Narrator, and the Critics." *MichA*, 2, no. 2 (1969), 73–87.

Disagrees with the condescending, fault-finding commentators on *Ven.*, as well as those who admire it for the wrong reasons. An example of the latter is Hereward T. Price, who sees the poem as a didactic tragedy in narrative form. Price's reading, which emphasizes the vileness of Venus in destroying Adonis's exquisite purity, is too abstract, too black-and-white, and too moral: It fails to take into account the poem's strain of comedy, the narrator's sympathy and enthusiasm for Venus, and the dramatic interplay between two characters who are individuals, not abstractions.

3117 Butler, Christopher, and Alastair Fowler. "Time-Beguiling Sport: Number Symbolism in Shakespeare's *Venus and Adonis*." *Shakespeare 1564–1964: A Collection of Modern Essays by Various Hands*. Ed. Edward A. Bloom. Providence: Brown U. P., 1964, pp. 124–33.

Offers a numerological analysis of *Ven.* The poem uses number symbolism to express a common Renaissance understanding of the Venus and Adonis myth, whereby "Adonis was thought to symbolize the sun," and his separation from Venus "was interpreted as the entry of the sun into the lower or nocturnal hemisphere." The separation was said to contrast "summer fulfillment and winter deprivation," and "the transition from one to the other" took place at the equinox. The equinoctial state is formally represented in the second half of the poem, in which "the metrical durations of the night and the second day of the poem (stanzas 89 to 144, and 144 to the end) turn out to be equal, as are the durations of day and night at the equinox." Not only do numerical patterns in the poem's formal structure provide a counterpoint to its themes, but specific numbers mentioned in the text have a symbolic value.

3118 Buxton, John. *Elizabethan Taste*. London: MacMillan, 1963. Reprint. 1965. xiv + 370 pp.

Contains, in chapter 6 ("Literature"), a discussion of *Ven.* Notes that the poem suffers "from the defects of Sh's supreme qualities as a dramatist." That is, in Sh's hands, the story could not remain in the world of myth: He made his protagonists too human and his flowers too natural. His language is "pictorial, adjectival, static"—not suited to the process of myth-making— and his attempts to be learned (as in his treatment of the set piece of the Banquet of Sense) are perfunctory. However, Sh's audience of youthful intellectuals enjoyed *Ven.* for what they perceived as its artificiality: its rhetorical skill and metrical subtlety.

3119 Cantelupe, Eugene B. "An Iconographical Interpretation of *Venus and Adonis*, Shakespeare's Ovidian Comedy." *SQ*, 14 (1963), 141–51.

Argues that the tone of *Ven.* is predominantly comic and satiric. Throughout the poem, "Shakespeare satirizes Neoplatonic love because the relationship that it insists upon among love, beauty, procreation, and the spirit . . . is unrealistic and absurd." This theme is expressed through "comic characterization, humorous actions, and witty speeches." An accompanying motif of "propelling and repugnant lust is implicit in the images of animals and gluttonous feeding."

3120 Chand, Sunil. "'A Tale Told': Shakespeare's Exploration of the Narrative Mode in *Venus and Adonis*, *Othello*, and the Falstaff Plays." Ph.D. dissertation, Kent State University, 1982. *DAI*, 43 (1982–83), 806-A.

Describes the "particularity, energy, and purpose" gained by *Ven.* through its use of "dramatic elements": dialogue, character portrayal, and character interaction. In this way, Sh achieves a secularization of the myth with which he is dealing.

3121 Daigle, Lennet J. "*Venus and Adonis*: Some Traditional Contexts." *ShakS*, 13 (1980), 31–46.

Challenges interpretations of *Ven.* that view its action as a battle between concupiscence and virtue. Cites mythographic and allegorical traditions, deriving from medieval and Renaissance Platonism, that shed a different light on the poem. According to these traditions, Venus is the agent of generation, forming an alliance with fecund Nature to defeat death through propagation of the race. Seen from this perspective, Adonis is the representative of beauty and its fragility. He is also a source of begetting whose self-absorption prevents him from carrying out his responsibility to reproduce and thus to forestall chaos. He is rightly rebuked by Venus for delighting too much in his own beauty. Revision of part of item 3122.

3122 Daigle, Lennet Joseph. "*Venus and Adonis*: Genre and Meaning." Ph.D. dissertation, University of South Carolina, 1976. *DAI*, 38 (1977–78), 275-A-276-A.

Challenges the modern critical classification of *Ven.* as an epyllion or minor epic. Maintains that Sh's generic approach in *Ven.* depends largely on "the love complaint and elegiac traditions." In discussing the poem's meaning, we should note that Sh relies on a tradition, popularized by Lucretius, that vindicated Venus because she inspires passion to promote regeneration. The arguments of Venus are thus justified, and Adonis is seen as a culpable figure who refuses to fulfill his proper function. The episode of the courser and jennet, based in part on Virgil's third *Georgic*, reinforces the theme of propagation. Part revised as item 3121.

3123 Doebler, John. "The Many Faces of Love: Shakespeare's *Venus and Adonis*." *ShakS*, 16 (1983), 33–43.

Interprets *Ven.* as a "drama of the mind" that, by keeping its audience at a distance, explores the shifting, diverse personae of Venus as found in Renaissance mythography and philosophy.

3124 Doebler, John. "The Reluctant Adonis: Titian and Shakespeare." *SQ*, 33 (1982), 480–90.

Recapitulates scholarly discussion of the sources for *Ven.*, especially for the reluctance of Adonis and the sexual rapacity of Venus, neither of which is found in Ovid's *Metamorphoses*, commonly acknowledged as Sh's chief source. Suggests that Sh may have derived both of these features from Titian's painting *Venus and Adonis* (1554), which is known to have been in England during the latter part of the 16th c. Titian, in showing Adonis tearing himself away from Venus's embrace to pursue the hunt, revived "a motif of antique art known as the Leave-Taking of Adonis."

3125 Doebler, John. "*Venus and Adonis*: Shakespeare's Horses." *Images of Shakespeare: Proceedings of the Third Congress of the International Shakespeare Association, 1986*. Eds. Werner Habicht, D. J. Palmer, and Roger Pringle. Newark: U. of Delaware P., 1988, pp. 64–72.

Discusses the horse *topos* in authors and painters before Sh and explains that the horse, like many emblems, was commonly explained *in bono* and *in malo*. On the one hand, horses were seen as the animals "bringing nature closest to perfection, further brought toward perfection by the artist"; on the other hand, they were regarded as symbolic of irrationality. In *Ven.*, the horses provide an erotic and visual version of "the attempted seduction of Adonis by Venus." Carnality is evident in both human and beast. Maintains that "both the classical lovers and the animals are images of physical perfection inviting the attention of an artist; but the stallion and the mare do with grace and ease what Venus and Adonis make awkward and tiresome."

3126   Donaldson, Ian. "Adonis and His Horse." N&Q, 19 (1972), 123-25.

Points out that the distinction between rational man and irrational horse, which goes back as far as the Neoplatonist Porphyry of the 3rd c. A.D., might have been suggested to Sh when he was writing *Ven.* by John Astley's *The Art of Riding* (1584). In addition, Sh's description of the sexually aroused horse (*Ven.*, 271-280) is strikingly similar to a passage in Astley.

3126a   Dundas, Judith. "'To See Feelingly': The Language of the Senses and the Language of the Heart." CompD, 19 (1985), 49-57.

Shows how Sh uses the rivalry, or *paragone*, of the senses to suggest their limited capacity to convey the truth of the heart. Observes that Venus in *Ven.* exhibits unqualified faith in the power of the senses, especially those lowest on the Neoplatonic ladder, to express love.

3127   Dundas, Judith. "Wat the Hare, or Shakespearean Decorum." ShakS, 19 (1987), 1-15.

Shows that, in *Ven.*, Venus's elaborate advice to Adonis to hunt the hare, which Sh developed from a slight hint in Ovid's *Metamorphoses*, is an example of the author's use of *copia* in the service of decorum. Ovid's story of Venus and Adonis is only one of many woven together to populate a landscape dominated by metamorphosis; Sh, however, confines himself to an extended treatment of a single story. The hare and the hunting *topos* in which it is embedded are emblematic of both main characters. Concludes with a discussion of emulation in the poem: Sh announces in the dedication his intention to rival Ovid, and he later mentions the painter's competition with nature and nature's rivalry with herself.

3128   Fienberg, Nona. "Thematics of Value in *Venus and Adonis*." Criticism, 31 (1989), 21-32.

Contends that *Ven.* involves a conflict between Adonis, who is locked into "a single sense of selfhood, characterized by epistemological, social, and sexual fears," and Venus, who manifests dynamism, a great "range of self-representation." In contrast to Adonis's orderly, "natural" mode of expression, Venus uses the mutable language of negotiation characteristic of emergent capitalism. She employs the rhetorical tools of the patriarchy to undermine its fixed values.

3129   Gent, Lucy. "*Venus and Adonis*: The Triumph of Rhetoric." MLR, 49 (1974), 721-29.

Notes that the overflowing abundance of rhetorical figures in *Ven.* leads us to what is probably the poem's central issue: "the relation between hyperbole and reality." In this work, Sh is competing with Marlowe's *Hero and Leander*, and within the poem he makes Venus engage in a rhetorical contest with Adonis. Notes the importance of eloquence among the young intellectuals for whom *Ven.* was intended and analyzes several passages in terms of the rhetorical devices they deploy. Mentions that Sh redirects the pattern of the familiar myth he is treating. Maintains that neither Venus nor Adonis is psychologically consistent; rather, both use rhetoric to expound upon a variety of arguments about love. Adonis proves to be an apt pupil for Venus in artful speaking, though not in love. The poem allows a collision between Venus's world of hyperbole and the actual world, but this results in a lack of focus, an unresolvedness.

3130   Hamilton, A. C. "*Venus and Adonis*." SEL, 1 (1961), 1-15.

Proposes to examine *Ven.* in light of the opinion Sh's contemporaries had about the myth of Venus and Adonis and of the treatments of the myth by 16th-c. poets. The myth could be interpreted literally, morally, or philosophically (revealing, as Abraham Fraunce wrote in 1592, "the hidden mysteries of naturall ... philosophie"). That Sh had primarily the myth's philosophical significance in mind is suggested by the title page's Ovidian motto about shunning the enthusiasms of the masses. Sh's treatment of Venus and Adonis is based on the Platonic belief that "love is the desire for beauty." However, he plays wittily on this doctrine by having the action turn on a kiss, the means in Castiglione for rational lovers to unite their souls. Venus's dilemma is that she is Love: Both flesh and spirit, she attempts to "do and become all things" to ensure the operation of her law. Adonis also faces a dilemma: As Beauty, he will be destroyed whether he yields to Venus or not. By altering the myth so that Adonis does not yield, Sh places the action of his poetry in a prelapsarian world where Love strives to enjoy divine Beauty. Adonis's death and Venus's flight signal a fall of this world into mutability. Revised as chapter 8 of item 0484.

3131   Hart, Jonathan. "'Till forging Nature be condemned of treason': Representational Strife in *Venus and Adonis*." *CahiersE*, 36 (1989), 37–47.

Examines Sh's exploration of mimesis in *Ven.*: Reflective imagery involves the characters and the reader in interpreting and evaluating representations of nature and the self. A tension exists between "description and action on the one hand and the long speeches on lust and love on the other," which thwarts the climax of the poem; and "the laws of nature" are both appealed to and denied, especially by Venus.

3132   Harwood, Ellen Aprill. "*Venus and Adonis*: Shakespeare's Critique of Spenser." *Journal of the Rutgers University Libraries*, 39 (1977), 44–60.

Regards *Ven.* as a critique of Spenser's Ovidianism, especially as it is exhibited in the Garden of Adonis in book 3 of *The Fairie Queene*. Maintains that Spenser, in the Garden, joins the erotic and the philosophical sides of Ovid while excluding the rhetorical side. Further, Spenser attempts to impose a "Virgilian purpose and ethic" on his Ovidian materials. By contrast, Sh, in *Ven.*, combines the erotic Ovid with the rhetorical Ovid. He does borrow the episode of the stallion and the jennet from the *Georgics*, but he treats it in an Ovidian manner, "parodying Virgilian epic for erotic comedy." Spenser distinguishes clearly between benevolent, fertile sex (the Garden of Adonis) and sterile, destructive sex (the Bower of Bliss), whereas Sh insists on the double nature of erotic love.

3133   Hulse, S. Clark. "Shakespeare's Myth of Venus and Adonis." *PMLA*, 93 (1978), 95–105.

Proposes a mythographic reading of *Ven.* as a way to gain access to the experience it conveys. The poem is not so much a narrative as it is the unfolding of the characters' allegorical attributes. Adonis, for example, is Beauty, and his seemingly unmotivated death allows us to glimpse beauty's transience. Throughout the poem, the two figures, endowed with the self-sufficiency of pictorial representation, cannot interact in the traditional manner (with Adonis becoming Venus's lover). Sh, then, must achieve his "narrative unity" in another way. In portraying Venus and Adonis as antagonists, the poet transforms his action into a conflict of ideas about love, an unresolved argument held together by visual images. The debate is momentarily crystallized at several points, each time by a different paradoxical metaphor; but the paradoxical tension in each case is released by movement toward another image, another shift in structure. The "pattern of tension and release" gives the poem its unity. Revision of part of item 0573. Revised as part of chapter 4 of item 0571.

3134   Jahn, J. D. "The Lamb of Lust: The Role of Adonis in Shakespeare's *Venus and Adonis*." *ShakS*, 6 (1970), 11–25.

Rejects the interpretation of *Ven.* as a poem about the simple opposition of passion and reason. Although Venus is excessive in her desire, using the idea of breeding as an excuse for lust, Adonis is no rational defender of Platonic ideals. He is physically vain and excessive in his disdain of love, being associated with Hermaphroditus (who was too young for love) and Narcissus (who was too self-centered). During the first part of the poem, Adonis toys with Venus; he is a male coquette, arousing lust that only he has the power to control. When his horse runs off, Adonis is forced to drop his pose of disdain and flee, which renders suspect his "reasoned" argument against love. In the last third of the poem, Adonis's refusal to acknowledge that a proper outcome of courtship is propagation leads him to ignore mortality. Destroyed by the boar, he wastes his beauty.

3135 Jahn, Jerald Duane. "The Elizabethan Epyllion: Its Art and Narrative Conventions." Ph.D. dissertation, Indiana University, 1972. *DAI*, 33 (1972–73), 2331-A.

Begins by describing the characteristics of the epyllion: Its mythological subject comes almost entirely from Ovid; it presents a tale of human courtship that is often comic in many details but that always ends tragically; it lays stress on the human shortcomings of the mythological figures; its plots often seem excessively ornamental and deliquescent; and its lovers are trapped in transitory passion, which limits their understanding. In *Ven.*, the tragic theme is complicated by "the conflict of two modes of mutable love." The authors of epyllia seem to have viewed their works as "a kind of tragic–epic hybrid for which sensual, digressive writing was particularly appropriate."

3136 Johnson, Paula. *Form and Transformation in Music and Poetry of the English Renaissance.* New Haven: Yale U. P., 1972. ix + 170 pp.

Deals with music and literature as serial arts, "whose perception is sequentially fixed"; argues that "important changes were taking place in both arts toward the end of the sixteenth century"; and suggests an approach to understanding the two arts and their relationship at Sh's time through "the psychology of whole forms." Treats *Ven.* as a work governed by "climactic progression," with "carefully controlled, evenly paced rise of tension," "muted climax," and "melting away of passion in the closing stanzas." Sh arouses the expectation that Adonis might yield (exploiting an ambiguity in Ovid, his source), then allows that possibility to be carried forward in the action of the horse, then returns to Adonis's amorous potential and finally moves us to anticipate not Adonis's sexual arousal but his death.

3137 Kahn, Coppélia. "Self and Eros in *Venus and Adonis*." *CentR*, 20 (1976), 351–71.

Argues that in *Ven.* Sh is dramatizing narcissism—"self-love in the form of withdrawal from others into the self." Improvising on several tales from Ovid's *Metamorphoses*, the poet depicts "the paradox of the narcissist, whose attempt to protect himself against the threat of love actually results in his self-destruction." The character of Adonis is derived from Ovid's stories of Salmacis and Hermaphroditus and of Narcissus. As in Ovid, Sh's youth attempts to protect his identity by recoiling from sexual union but loses his fragile sense of self because he rejects the only means by which his maturity as a man can be affirmed. His transformation into a flower recalls many episodes in which Ovid shows how those who sequester themselves from love are trapped in the impersonal natural world. Venus is an ambiguous figure, whose various aspects of "mother, woman, eros itself" are conveyed through oral imagery of eating or kissing. For Adonis, she promises fulfillment as a man at the same time that she threatens to devour him. When he is finally transformed into a flower that she vows to keep in her breast, he can be seen to have regressed to an infantile state, completely dependent on her as nurturing mother. But paradoxically he has allowed her to achieve intimacy with him on the only terms that can be tolerated by a narcissist: "her total subservience to his need for constant reassurance." Revised as chapter 2 of item 0614.

3138 Keach, William. *Elizabethan Erotic Narratives: Irony and Pathos in the Ovidian Poetry of Shakespeare, Marlowe, and Their Contemporaries.* New Brunswick: Rutgers U. P., 1977. xviii + 217 pp.

Revision of item 3139.

3139   Keach, William Carroll. "Artifice, Eroticism, and Irony in the Elizabethan Epyllion." Ph.D dissertation, Yale University, 1970. *DAI*, 31 (1970–71), 2922-A.

Provides a detailed examination of several "less well known Elizabethan mythological narrative poems," or epyllia, and reexamines *Ven.* and Marlowe's *Hero and Leander* "with a view to bringing out more clearly their distinctive qualities and their similarities to other poems in the genre." A preliminary chapter on the "Elizabethan Ovid" considers late 16th-c. attitudes toward the allegorical tradition of interpreting Ovid and toward "the use of Ovid as a stylistic model in the schools." At this time, there was also a new awareness of the erotic and strictly literary qualities of Ovid's poems. Chapter 3, on *Ven.*, begins with a consideration of how Sh reinterprets his sources and proceeds to investigate the poem's "complex theme and tone." Revised as item 3138.

3140   Klause, John. "*Venus and Adonis*: Can We Forgive Them." *SP*, 85 (1988), 353–77.

Notes recent critical pluralism about *Ven.*, which finds in the poem "a multivalency of meanings" and a doubleness of tone. Seeks to move interpretation of *Ven.* beyond a sensitivity to contradiction by promoting forgiveness. Attempts to establish that forgiveness is a crucial issue by comparing *Ven.* to Marlowe's *Hero and Leander*, in which the narrator is toughminded and conspicuous, the imagery is hard and cold, and the irony preserves a distance between the flawed lovers on the one hand and the superior observer on the other. In *Ven.*, the narrator is neither as obtrusive nor as judgmental, the imagery is soft and warm, and the irony, though critical, promotes a sympathetic response to the principals. Furthermore, the poem endorses pity as a value, and we are invited to see Venus and Adonis as "part of ourselves and our world."

3141   Lake, James H. "Shakespeare's Venus: An Experiment in Tragedy." *SQ*, 25 (1974), 351–55.

Argues that *Ven.* begins in a comic–erotic mode but turns serious when Venus learns of the hunt. From this point on, her preoccupation with the sensual is qualified by a "more selfless concern for Adonis." She begins her ascent toward tragic stature with the Neoplatonic kiss she shares with Adonis (lines 545–546). In seeking Adonis during the hunt (lines 871–882), she seems more tragic victim than predator; she is subject to tragic ironies when she hopes falsely that Adonis is still alive (line 992), exonerates the boar (lines 1111–1117), and prophesies at Adonis's grave (lines 1135–1164). Also, she experiences a reversal (in that her advances have spurred Adonis to join the hunt) and a recognition (when she equates the flower with Adonis).

3142   Leech, Clifford. "Venus and Her Nun: Portraits of Women in Love by Shakespeare and Marlowe." *SEL*, 5 (1965), 247–68.

Compares the portraits of women in love in Marlowe's *Hero and Leander* and *Ven.* In *Hero and Leander*, Venus is "the figure to be dreaded"; in *Ven.*, "she is the comic aggressor and ultimately the human sufferer." Though different in many ways, Marlowe's Hero and Sh's Venus both become images of woman in love.

3143   Lever, J. W. "Venus and the Second Chance." *ShS*, 15 (1962), 81–88.

Maintains that Venus and Adonis are mythical beings, not moral abstractions. Modern commentators have often overmoralized the poem, reducing Venus, for example, to a representation of sweaty bestiality. Venus is a divinity who is never clearly visualized and has more than mortal powers. She also epitomizes the Lucretian and late-Renaissance vision of Nature in her growth and fertility; she bases her first appeal to Adonis on the doctrine of increase, then seeks to move him "at the vegetable level of mindless sentience," and finally calls up before him "animal nature in its most vigorous form." Adonis, like the youth of *Son.* and several characters in the comedies, commits the grave folly of refusing to love. Unlike the others, however, he cannot be saved. The myth of Venus and Adonis, profiting by Sh's mature conception of tragedy as a paradoxical triumph, got a second chance in *Ant.* Cleopatra and Antony are Venus and Adonis in a fallen, mortal world, but their defeat is transcended by Sh's vision "of a paradise regained in the union of love and death."

3144 Lindheim, Nancy. "The Shakespearean *Venus and Adonis.*" SQ, 37 (1986), 190–203.

Argues that in *Ven.* Sh developed a new, more complex understanding of love, which he conveyed through technical experimentation. Using the basic features of Ovidan narrative—"single action, few characters, and little extension in time"—the poet enriches his work by identifying Venus with love in all of its complexity, by stressing Adonis's adolescence, and by tying both characters to mortality (which explains the two digressions, the incident of the horses and Venus's discourse on Wat the hare). By a variety of tonal modulations, the poem achieves a "double perspective": It is "a comic poem with a tragic action." Although not a fully realized poem, *Ven.* shows Sh surpassing Ovid and Marlowe, and moving toward the plays in which his early period culminates.

3145 Merrix, Robert P. "The '*Beste Noire*': The Medieval Role of the Boar in *Venus and Adonis.*" UC, 11 (1991), 117–30.

Discusses the complex tradition from which Sh fashioned the story of Adonis and his hunt for the boar. Clearly, the direct influence of Ovid was great, but medieval moralizations of Ovid and medieval accounts of the chase were also important. Analyzes many medieval works and concludes that the boar in *Ven.* represents "militant chastity," the need to gratify one's ego by compulsively pursuing transcendence in an alien environment, a force "subversive to all social and psychological restraints."

3146 Meyer, Russell Joseph. "Tudor Laughter: A Preliminary Study for a Theory of Humor." Ph.D. dissertation, University of Minnesota, 1976. DAI, 37 (1976–77), 6504-A-6505-A.

Attempts to articulate the general principles behind humor "in Tudor prose fiction and narrative verse." Chapter 5 argues that Sh fails to distinguish sufficiently between comic and pathetic elements in *Ven.*

3147 Muir, Kenneth. "*Venus and Adonis:* Comedy or Tragedy?" *Shakespearean Essays.* Eds. Alwin Thaler and Norman Sanders. Knoxville: U. of Tennessee P., 1964, pp. 1–13. Revised as chapter 10 of *Shakespeare the Professional and Related Studies.* London: Heinemann, 1973, pp. 171–86.

Finds the poem difficult to categorize. It is not a didactic warning against lust, nor does it offer unqualified praise of sexual love. It is frequently witty but not funny. and it has a tragic ending. Sh, it may be surmised, set out to write a poem based on Ovid, and produced an ambivalent work because he accepted conflicting feelings about love and delighted in dramatizing them.

3148 Murphy, Patrick Martin. "The Perplexity of Desire: Representation and Poetic Thinking in Shakespeare's *Venus and Adonis* and *Love's Labor's Lost.*" Ph.D. dissertation, University of Illinois at Urbana-Champaign, 1989. DAI, 50 (1989–90), 2066-A.

Chapter 2 analyzes desire in *Ven.* as something forbidden/taboo. Discovers incest prohibitions in the narration and erotic action of both Sh and Ovid.

3149 Palmatier, M. A. "A Suggested New Source in Ovid's *Metamorphoses* for Shakespeare's *Venus and Adonis.*" HLQ, 24, no. 2 (1961), 163–169.

The source of Adonis's hard-heartedness and scorn can be found in the passage in the *Metamorphoses* (10.503–528) that describes his origins. His mother Myrrha was inspired by Venus with a lustful desire for her father Cinyras, tricked him into an incestuous union, and, after fleeing his anger, was turned into a tree from whose tough rind Adonis was delivered. Adonis's cruelty to Venus in Sh is derived from the harshness of his birth as described by Ovid and constitutes the first step in his revenge on her, completed when he dies, for causing his unnatural birth.

3150 Pegg, Barry Malcolm. "Optimistic and Pessimistic Attitudes to Generation and Corruption in Selected Literary and Scientific Texts, 1590–1660." Ph.D. dissertation, University of Wisconsin, Madison, 1976. *DAI*, 37 (1976–77), 6508-A- 6509-A.

Maintains that *Ven.* is informed by Aristotelian pessimism about the dichotomy between spirit and matter. Adonis's spiritual nature disdains the claims of his "reproductive nature" and thus fails to raise him above the cycle of generation and corruption from which he aspires to escape.

3151 Rabkin, Norman. "*Venus and Adonis* and the Myth of Love." *Pacific Coast Studies in Shakespeare*. Eds. Waldo F. McNeir and Thelma N. Greenfield. Eugene: U. of Oregon Books, 1966, pp. 20–32.

Argues that *Ven.* is best read in terms of the double vision that Sh brings to his treatment of love in the plays. The two protagonists of his poem embody two aspects of love that Renaissance Neoplatonism "delighted in seeing paradoxically fused." Venus wishes to disport herself on the rungs of the Neoplatonic ladder with no vision of its uppermost step. Adonis hungers for the "spiritual consummation" to which sensual love "claimed to aspire," but renounces the means to that consummation. Revised as part of chapter 4 of item 0873.

3152 Ramsey, Allen. "Pastoral as Structure in Shakespeare's *Venus and Adonis*." *PAPA*, 2, no. 3 (1976), 37–42.

Argues that the pastoral setting of *Ven.* enables Sh to link the earlier (comic) and later (tragic) parts of the poem and thus to unify it structurally. Focuses on two strands of pastoral imagery (the metaphor comparing Adonis to flowers and the recurrence of the colors red and white) that help Sh to blur the boundary between comedy and tragedy and thus to maintain an equilibrium of tone. Revision of part of item 3153.

3153 Ramsey, Allen Rodell. "*Venus and Adonis* as a Type of Ovidian Narrative Poetry." Ph.D. dissertation, Tulane University, 1972. *DAI*, 33 (1972–73), 6322-A-6323-A.

Classifies *Ven.* as the most accomplished example of "the comic persuasion to love," a distinct type of Ovidian poetry originating with Thomas Lodge's *Scillaes Metamorphosis* (1589) and characterized by a travesty of the long-established allegorical treatment of classical myth. Part revised as item 3152.

3154 Rebhorn, Wayne A. "Mother Venus: Temptation in Shakespeare's *Venus and Adonis*." *ShakS*, 11 (1978), 1–19.

Presents Venus's attempted seduction of Adonis in terms of a maternal invitation to return to childhood. Venus, the narrator, and Adonis himself all refer to him as a boy or a child. Adonis's rejection of Venus's advances stems from an understandable reluctance to regress. *Ven.* can be interpreted as a critical commentary on courtly love as it was seen by some Renaissance commentators, who believed that to surrender to a woman is to become infantile. The poem is also related to the heroic tradition established in the epics of antiquity and continued in the Renaissance. In all of these works, the hero is tempted by an enchantress to shun his duty and to serve her as lord. His realm of service—geographically extended, involving military action—comes into conflict with a limited, childish world offered by the temptress. The hero's devotion to "an elusive future goal" is replaced by his absorption into a "protective environment of pleasure and ease." He becomes passive, conquered both psychologically and physically by his lady. The model for later enchantresses is Circe in book 10 of the *Odyssey*; and Dido in the *Aeneid* follows the pattern, as do similar characters in Ariosto, Tasso, and Spenser. The Christian tradition influenced Renaissance writers to present lust in terms of gluttony: In *Ven.*, the goddess's invitation to feed on her delectable body carries with it the danger that Adonis himself will be consumed. Another Christian notion operative here is that indulgence in the pleasures of the flesh causes the effeminization of a man. The loss of manhood could also be expressed in terms of a return to childishness or infancy, which is what Adonis fears.

3155 Rothenberg, Alan B. "The Oral Rape Fantasy and Rejection of Mother in the Imagery of Shakespeare's *Venus and Adonis*." *PsyQ*, 40 (1971), 447–68.

Maintains that in *Ven.* the attempt of Venus to seduce Adonis has as its substructure "a preoedipal conflict between an overactive, too-loving mother and her resistant nursing infant." On a deeper level, "the seduction becomes the fantasy of an oral rape of a passive infant's mouth by the breast or mouth of his aggressive mother (or nurse)," with fatal consequences for the infant. Suggests that Sh's works contain other subsurface fantasies concerning "child-mother relationships."

3156 Sheidley, William E. "'Unless It Be a Boar': Love and Wisdom in Shakespeare's *Venus and Adonis*." *MLQ*, 35 (1974), 3–15.

Contends that in *Ven.* Sh is "content neither to join the crusade of the antiamatory moralists nor simply to propagate the tradition that has fallen under their attack." To some extent, Sh endorses Venus's argument; the poem, like Spenser's *Epithalamion*, is an attempt to "mediate between the claims of love and virtue, flesh and spirit." Though the proper union is denied, Sh allows glimpses of its possibilities.

3157 Smith, Gordon Ross. "Mannerist Frivolity and Shakespeare's *Venus and Adonis*." *HSL*, 3 (1971), 1–11.

Reviews criticism of *Ven.* and cites a number of 16th-c. Italian artists to argue that it is a Mannerist poem in its "dense and succulent style" and in its gentle satire of classical myth. Furthermore, it is entirely comprehensible in its historical context, "characteristic of its age, and a great success."

3158 Steinberg, Theodore L. "The Comedy of Love: The Medieval Venus and Shakespeare's *Venus and Adonis*." *The Mythographic Art: Classical Fable and the Rise of the Vernacular in Early France and England*. Ed. Jane Chance. Gainesville: U. of Florida P., 1990, pp. 235–45.

Surveys the history of Venus in the Middle Ages, when she was divided into two figures, designated by Boccaccio as Venus Magna (divine Venus) and Venus Secunda (the goddess of wantonness). Sh follows Renaissance mythographers like Natalis Comes in combining the attributes of these two figures into one. *Ven.* is thus an allegorical account, both humorous and tragic, of the first stirrings of sexuality in a young man's life. Psychologically, Adonis cannot accept sexual love, though physically he is ready for it. The result of rejecting Venus, we see, is tragic; she must be regarded as comic and accepted.

3159 Streitberger, W. R. "Ideal Conduct in *Venus and Adonis*." *SQ*, 26 (1975), 285–91.

Examines the poem's two major episodes, "the seduction attempt and the hunt," and their background. Maintains that the three episodes from Ovid's *Metamorphoses*—the stories of Venus and Adonis, Salmacis and Hermaphroditus, and Echo and Narcissus—that Sh used as his sources show an attempt to explore matters of serious consequence for a young nobleman. The courser and jennet episode is a warning against allowing passion to overthrow reason; and Venus's persuading Adonis to hunt the rabbit, the fox, and the deer is a very real temptation to neglect his duty for the easy life.

3160 Thomas, Troy. "Interart Analogy: Practice and Theory in Comparing the Arts." *JAE*, 25, no. 2 (1991), 17–36.

Attempts to show that problems of interpretation arise when the sister arts of painting and poetry are assumed to be "more interchangeable than they really are." Challenges Erwin Panofsky's claim that Titian's painting of Venus and Adonis (1553) was the source of Sh's unusual portrayal of Adonis as a reluctant lover in *Ven*. Points out several differences between the painting and the poem, maintaining that Titian is presenting a kind of "symbolic and synthetic" image of the story: His Adonis is more "anxious to hunt than reluctant to love."

3161 Tyson, Mary Hanna. "Marlowe, Shakespeare, and the Ovidian Narrative Tradition." Ph.D. dissertation, University of California, Berkeley, 1966. *DA*, 27 (1966–67), 752-A-753-A.

Contends that Sh and Marlowe are the most faithful of Ovid's disciples among Elizabethan poets because they were able to imitate not only the sensuousness and decorativeness of their master but his hyperbolic style and mocking tone as well. In order to mock Petrarchism in *Ven*., Sh exploits the disparity between Venus's description to Adonis of her beauty and divinity, and the narrator's presentation of her as "the embodiment of animal lust."

3162 Uhlmann, Dale C. "Red and White Imagery in *Venus and Adonis*." *SRASP*, 8 (1983), 15–20.

Finds that the opposition of red and white in *Ven*. "symbolizes the conflict between Venus and Adonis, or between the realistic world of love and the unrealistic world of the hunt." The combination of red and white in the description of the boar near the end suggests that a kind of union between Venus and Adonis has been consummated in death, and the anemone, which blends the two colors, symbolizes a resolution of the conflict between love and romanticism in romantic love.

3163 Watson, Donald G. "The Contrarieties of *Venus and Adonis*." *SP*, 75 (1978), 32–63.

Attempts to deal with some traditional difficulties in interpreting *Ven*. by seeing the two major figures as dispositions toward two sides of the sensible soul, concupiscence and irascibility. Sh plays ironically with Petrarchan conceits, wittily reversing the roles of male pursuer and female resister. Both Venus and Adonis use rhetorics that are clearly inappropriate for the reality that confronts them. The ironic voice of the narrator (for example, in its Petrarchan description of the courtship of two horses) reinforces the ambiance of an Ovidian world, where the natural setting is home to "elemental strife" and uncontrolled sexual activity. Of all Elizabethan poems, *Ven*. is philosophically most closely attuned to Ovid. Revision of part of item 3164.

3164 Watson, Donald Gwynn. "Transformations of Ovid: The Mythological Narrative Poem in Elizabethan England." Ph.D. dissertation, University of Virginia, 1972. *DAI*, 33 (1972–73), 3679-A-3680-A.

Suggests that the English poets of the Renaissance used myths as patterns for exploring and defining the nature of love. Explains 16th-c. shifts in the allegorical interpretation of myths. Provides a survey of "the immediate literary contexts" for the Ovidian works of the late 1580s and 1590s. Chapter 5 includes a discussion of *Ven*. and offers guidelines for interpreting its "playful seriousness and comic ironies." Part revised as item 3163.

3165 Whidden, Mary Bess. "Love's Fool: Shakespeare's Venus and the English Petrarchans." Ph.D. dissertation, University of Texas, 1965. *DA*, 26 (1965–66), 1030.

Acknowledges that *Ven*. is indebted to "the Ovidian or moralized mythological tradition" but emphasizes its close relationship to Petrarchan love poetry. Petrarchan features of Sh's poem can be seen in its exploration of Venus's psychology as a lover and in its concern with "the brevity of beauty, the threat of death and the means of immortality." Petrarchan attitudes and elements are also satirized.

3166 White, R. S. "'Now Mercy goes to Kill': Hunting in Shakespearean Comedy." *DUJ*, 69 (1976), 21–32.

Explains that the complex way in which hunting is related to love in *Ven.* helps Sh to display "a comprehensive anatomy of love's perplexity."

3167 Williams, Gordon. "The Coming of Age of Shakespeare's Adonis." *MLR*, 78 (1983), 769–76.

Argues that in *Ven.* Sh, unlike Ovid, is not interested in "sexual rapport" between Venus and Adonis. Rather, he wishes to scrutinize the painful situation of the adolescent who has to deal with sexual inexperience. Venus, at first a temptress, becomes wholly sympathetic, tragically frustrated by the consummation, denied to her, that the boar has achieved with Adonis.

3168 Wright, Ellen Faber. "Rhethoricke to Deceive: The Elizabethan Epyllia." Ph.D. dissertation, Indiana University, 1975. *DAI*, 36 (1975–76), 7450-A-7451-A.

Analyzes six major Ovidian epyllia of the Elizabethan period, including *Ven.* These poems incorporate characters who use rhetoric unreliably, deliberately distorting myths for spurious purposes. The narrators of the epyllia are guilty of the same sorts of distortions. Thus the meaning of the poems lies primarily in the witty conduct of "the relationships between the narrator and characters, narrator and reader, and poet and reader." The major epyllia seem to be "elaborately contrived *jeux d'esprit*," expressing a philosophical skepticism more common in Elizabethan England than modern commentators recognize.

3169 Yoch, James J. "The Eye of Venus: Shakespeare's Erotic Landscape." *SEL*, 20 (1980), 59–71.

Maintains that Sh develops *Ven.* by relating details of landscape to Venus, whose increasing imaginative control of the natural world organizes our response to the poem. At first, Venus merely describes the landscape in the outside world, in herself, and in Adonis. Then she proceeds to transform the landscape (the boar into a lover, Adonis into a flower), attributing to nature the kinds of affection she feels in herself. Sh has provided a sympathetic view of Venus, whose distraction over Adonis causes her to re-create nature in her own erotic image.

THE WINTER'S TALE

3170 Ansari, A. A. "The Mockery of Art in *The Winter's Tale*." *AJES*, 4 (1979), 124–41.

Shows how Perdita, connecting herself with Proserpina, becomes, in the last two acts of *WT*, a vegetation goddess, "a seminal principle, a directing and controlling power, an exemplar to which the innovations of art approximate and for which she serves as the model." She thus serves to tie together the play's two principal themes: the merging of art and nature and the regeneration of society through a myth of fertility.

3171 Asp, Carolyn. "Shakespeare's Paulina and the *Consolatio* Tradition." *ShakS*, 11 (1978), 145–58.

Points out that Paulina's role as female counselor to Leontes in *WT* makes her unique in English Renaissance literature. No such character can be found in courtesy books or other contemporary works, nor are there any models for her in the political and social context. However, she can be associated with the female *consolatio* figure found in many medieval works. One significant female adviser from this tradition is Lady Philosophy, who counsels the male protagonist in Boethius's *Consolation of Philosophy*. As Lady Philosophy does with her pupil, Paulina guides Leontes from a state of self-centered spiritual blindness to a recognition of his place in a providentially ordered world.

3172 Barkan, Leonard. "Living Sculptures: Ovid, Michelangelo, and *The Winter's Tale*." *ELH*, 48 (1981), 639–67.

Summarizes the literary genealogy of statues coming to life as part of an analysis of the scene in which Hermione's "statue" comes to life (*WT*, V.iii). Ovid's *Metamorphoses* is full of such accounts, the most important of which, and Sh's most direct source, is that of Pygmalion. In addition, the story of Deucalion and Pyrrha is relevant here. Ovid also has tales of living things turning to stones; in these cases, the statues are "signs of essential life within." Because of Ovid's interest in sculpture, and because of the general classicizing influence of Michelangelo's intellectual milieu, the artist is likely to have known the *Metamorphoses*. As a sculptor, Michelangelo is a "concrete examplar of an art" that Ovid writes of in the abstract. Though the question of Sh's knowledge of Michelangelo is highly problematic, the two can be regarded as mutually illuminating because of their similar attitudes toward art, and in particular toward sculpture, the most lifelike of the arts. Sh, in *WT*, writes an intricate and profound essay on the *paragone*, the rivalry of the arts, which finally comes down to a rivalry between art and life. In a sense, nature triumphs over art with Hermione's coming to life. But from another perspective, Hermione's essence is captured in the "four-dimensional sculpture" through which Sh creates her "dramatic statue." The history of statues coming to life, from classical times onward, combines a triumph of nature with a triumph of art. Revised as part of chapter 6 of item 0119.

3173 Bernard, John D. "The Pastoral Vision of *The Winter's Tale*." *Iowa State Journal of Research*, 53 (1979), 219–25.

Notes that in the classical versions of pastoral the poetic imagination is essential to the re-creation of a culture faced with disintegration. In 16th-c. Italy, the sophisticated notion of the imagination developed through Christian–Platonic thought made possible a more subtle pastoralism, one in which there is a temporary withdrawal from the disorder of life to "a kind of visionary space where the eyes of the mind are purged" and one is able to see again. Discovers this kind of pastoral in *WT*, which uses images of sight and speech to dramatize the loss and then restoration of a worldly paradise.

3174 Blissett, William. "The Wide Gap of Time: *The Winter's Tale*." *ELR*, 1 (1971), 52–70.

Finds a "hungry chaos at the center of *WT*," represented through the sudden appearance and sudden removal of the storm and bear (III.iii). Argues that the proper response of the audience is to look before and after this brief scene of destruction in which the storm wrecks the ship and the bear consumes Antigonus: Devouring time and tempest predominate in the first part of the play, redeeming time and calmness in the second. Cites, as a possible influence, a passage from book 15 of Ovid's *Metamorphoses* that attacks "the eating of flesh as contrary to the harmony of nature," exclaims against time as a "great devourer," and addresses nature as "the great renewer."

3175 Bryant, Jerry H. "*The Winter's Tale* and the Pastoral Tradition." *SQ*, 14 (1963), 387–98.

Sketches the classical influences (Theocritus, Virgil, and the Greek romance) on the English pastoral drama before proceeding to a fuller account of the more direct influences (Italian pastoral drama and pastoral prose romance) and a discussion of *WT* in light of these influences. To explore Leontes' inability to distinguish between appearance and reality, "Shakespeare converts the stereotyped conventions of the pastoral drama into highly original instruments."

3176 Clubb, Louise. "The Tragicomic Bear." *CLS*, 9 (1972), 17–30.

Argues that Sh's use of a man-eating bear in *WT*, III.iii, is appropriate as an element in the play's transformation from tragedy to comedy. The ambivalent nature of the bear, as established in Italian pastoral tragicomedy, and in classical sources like Aristotle, Pliny, and Apuleius, made it perfect for transitions like that effected by Sh at this point in the play.

3177 Cosgrove, Brian. "*The Winter's Tale* and the Limits of Criticism." *Studies* (Dublin), 66 (1977), 176–87.

Distinguishes two ways of interpreting *WT* based on two different attitudes toward time: the cyclical and the transcendent. Notes the compatibility of the transcendent view with Christianity and hints that the cyclical view derives, at least in part, from classical myth.

3178 Curtis, Harry Jr. "The Year Growing Ancient: Formal Ambiguity in *The Winter's Tale*." *CLAJ*, 23 (1980), 431–37.

Uses Perdita's apostrophe to Proserpina in act IV of *WT* to support the idea that there is a dark, ambiguous side to the love of Perdita and Florizel.

3179 Duncan-Jones, E. E. "Hermione in Ovid and Shakespeare." *N&Q*, 13 (1966), 138–39.

Maintains that Ovid's *Heroides* is a likely source for the name of Leontes' wife in *WT*. Ovid's Hermione is the daughter of Helen and Menelaus, and she figures in a tale that has many similarities to what happens to Sh's character.

3179a Fleissner, Robert F. "What *The Winter's Tale* Unveils: Who is 'the Best'?" *N&Q*, 36 (1989), 336–38.

Examines the question of who is meant by the person "that did betray the Best" in Polixenes' outburst (*WT*, I.ii.418). Argues in favor of a pagan reading (Brutus betraying Caesar) and against a Christian one (Judas betraying Christ).

3180 Fowler, Alastair. "Leontes' Contrition and the Repair of Nature." *E&S*, 31 (1978), 36–64.

Concentrates on the "symbolic and mythological" strands that provide thematic continuity in *WT*. Leontes' sin of jealousy causes his loss of Hermione, whose name alternates with that of Harmonia in Renaissance commentaries to indicate "the Pythagorean harmony of the moral or cosmic order." Such harmony of soul is what Leontes loses, and the last stage of his repentance and restoration is symbolized and carried out through "the allegorical romance" of the last three acts. In this sequence, the symbolic identifications of Perdita with Proserpina and with Flora play a key part. Sh draws on Neoplatonic interpretations of Ovid's myth of Flora to show Perdita engaging in a presentation of flowers that represents "the process of natural growth" as well as growth linked with grace. Comments that Autolycus, true to the mythological suggestions of his name, is "a mercurial genius presiding over the many disguises of the last two acts." Pastoral scenes, then, are used to indicate metaphorically the transformation of Leontes' character and to exhibit "the repair of nature," the power of art to civilize, "the gentling effect of time," and "integration."

3181 Frey, Charles. *Shakespeare's Vast Romance: A Study of "The Winter's Tale."* Columbia: U. of Missouri P., 1980. vii + 174 pp.

Attempts a "relatively comprehensive account" of WT. Chapter 3, "Backgrounds," includes discussion of the mythic associations of Hermione and Perdita. In Ovid's *Heroides*, which Sh may have known, Hermione is the daughter of Helen and Menelaus. Sh's character, whose daughter is lost for a time, may thus be connected with an ancient figure who, "again in the context of sexual jealousy, lost her mother for a time." From the very beginning, then, Sh may be hinting "at separation and eventual reconciliation." Perdita is linked to Proserpina, which "links Hermione with Ceres, Proserpina's mother." These mythic figures are present in the background, not so much as sources or analogues, but as hints of greater forces at work.

3182 Frye, Northrop. "Recognition in *The Winter's Tale*." *Essays on Shakespeare and Elizabethan Drama in Honor of Hardin Craig*. Ed. Richard Hosley. Columbia: U. of Missouri P., 1962, pp. 235–46. Reprint. *Fables of Identity*. New York: Harcourt, Brace & World, 1963, pp. 107–18. Reprint. *Shakespeare: "The Winter's Tale": A Casebook*. Ed. Kenneth Muir. London: Macmillan, 1968, pp. 184–97. Reprint *Shakespeare's Later Comedies*. Ed. D. J. Palmer. Harmondsworth: Penguin, 1971, pp. 332–45.

Discusses the double recognition scene at the end of WT: "the recognition of Perdita's parentage" and "the awakening of Hermione and the presenting of Perdita to her." The machinery of the former derives from New Comedy, "where the heroine is proved by birth tokens to be respectable enough for the hero to marry her." Sh combines "two traditions which descended from Menander, pastoral romance and New Comedy." The power controlling the dramatic action is identified with the will of the pagan gods, particularly Apollo: It is "a secular analogy of Christian grace."

3182a Gasper, Julia, and Carolyn Williams. "The Meaning of the Name 'Hermione.'" *N&Q*, 33 (1986), 367.

Observes that Hermione's name in WT may be derived from the English word *herm* or *herma*, which in turn came from the Greek name Hermes and was first used in North's translation of Plutarch, a source for many other Greek names in the play. In neo-Latin, *herma* came to mean any statue, not necessarily one of Hermes or even of a male figure. In 1596, the word appeared with another meaning: a volume of obituary verses. The idea that Paulina constructs a memorial from words instead of stone comes close to describing Hermione's situation in the last act. If these associations influenced Sh, Hermione's name "would mean principally a stone statue, with possible further implications of mourning, sanctity, and the working of miracles."

3183 Guj, Luisa. "*The Winter's Tale* and the Eleusinian Goddesses." *RLMC*, 36, no. 1 (1983), 5–24.

Proposes "a mythological reading" of WT, which may be "best understood by associating its narrative, and a great deal of its incidental symbolism, with the rites of Eleusis as they were known to, and understood by, cultivated persons in the sixteenth and seventeenth centuries." Cites Renaissance mythographers like Vincenzo Cartari and George Sandys to show the kind of knowledge Sh's contemporaries would have had about the Eleusinian mysteries. The mysteries were rooted in a myth of natural renewal in the vegetable world, but they also involved a renewal of the soul, aroused from its sleep in the body, dying to the world of sin, and being reborn "to the world of the spirit." There seemed to have been a final initiatory rite, "called *epopteia*, full vision," during which an aspirant "acquired the title of *epoptes* and became a seer." The movement of the play seems designed to lead Leontes through a process of spiritual death and rebirth like that experienced by the Eleusinian neophytes. The story of Ceres and Proserpine, also connected with the Eleusinian cult, underlies the Hermione–Perdita relationship. Antigonus's physical destruction by a bear, a creature linked by the mythographers to wrath, may mirror the spiritual death of Leontes. In the last act, the reunion between Leontes and Perdita is not shown to the audience or to the courtiers who report it. As in the mysteries, the uninitiated are excluded. It is only at the very end, when the action moves into the chapel, that the spectators, both onstage and in the audience, are allowed to become seers.

3184 Hardman, C. D. "Theory, Form, and Meaning in Shakespeare's *The Winter's Tale*." *RES*, 36 (1985), 228–35.

Cites established critical opinion that *WT* is a diptych composed of a tragedy and a comedy hinged in the middle. Finds the hinge in the Shepherd's remark to the Clown that "thou mett'st with things dying, I with things new-born" (III.iii.110–111), which reflects a familiar passage from the essay(s) *De Tragoedia et Comoedia* by the 4th-c. A.D. grammarians Evanthius and Donatus, often printed in "Renaissance school editions of Terence." The statement made by Evanthius compares tragedy and comedy as separate genres, but *WT* contains both forms and has each accord "in some detail with the grammarians' prescriptions" for its type. Notes that in the consciousness of theory, the appearance of the bear (an emblem for art's superiority over nature) and the figure of Time, as well as other devices, the play calls attention to the art with which it joins the two forms.

3184a Hardman, Christopher. "*The Winter's Tale*." (Penguin Critical Studies.) London: Penguin, 1988. viii + 125 pp.

The introductory chapter, on structure, explains how Sh would have learned definitions of tragedy and comedy from studying Plautus and Terence, and especially from an essay put together by the 4th-c. A.D. critics Evanthius and Donatus and used as an introduction to Terence in school editions of Sh's time. The definitions of tragedy and comedy in this essay "describe the two parts of *The Winter's Tale* quite well." The chapter on sources notes that one change Sh made in his main source, Robert Greene's *Pandosto*, was to use Greek names, possibly borrowed from North's translation of Plutarch's *Lives*, in his play. He also removed Fortune as the power controlling events, making the characters responsible for their own fates. In addition, Sh drew generally on the pastoral romance tradition, which goes back to such Greek works as *Daphnis and Chloe*. He also may have used *Daphnis and Chloe* directly. The bringing to life of Hermione's statue may owe something to Ovid's *Metamorphoses*. The chapter on "Character, Speech and Style" remarks on Sh's adoption of the classical practice of using "names with meaning" in comedy; an example is Autolycus, whose name has a classical source as well. Describes Apollo as "the presiding oracular deity of the play."

3185 Harp, Richard L. "*The Winter's Tale*: An 'Old Tale' Begetting Wonder." *DR*, 58 (1978), 295–308.

Connects *WT* with the central Western tradition concerning wonder. Canvasses classical thinkers like Plato, Aristotle, and Plutarch as well as their medieval and Renaissance descendants to show that wonder was regarded as "a truly rational movement of the mind towards fresh knowledge." Maintains that *WT*, with its series of incredible episodes, relies on this idea about wonder, taking what seems like an "old tale" and through it revealing "the true nature of experience." Discusses the link between sorrow, joy, and wonder, especially in the account of the reunions at Leontes' court (V.ii) and the scene in which Hermione's "statue" comes to life. Cites Aristotle's opinion that wonder is an important effect of imitation and applies this insight to the play. Notes that the key to understanding Leontes' tragedy in the first three acts is his "substitution of premature, egotistical knowledge for reverential wonder."

3186 Holland, Joanne Field. "The Gods of *The Winter's Tale*." *PCP*, 5 (1970), 34–38.

Argues that in *WT* Sh introduces three significant changes from his source, Robert Greene's *Pandosto*: the character of Autolycus, the emphasis on the Oracle of Apollo, and the "amazingly happy ending." Explains the connection of Autolycus with Hermes and of Hermes with Apollo. Apollo and Autolycus, "the divine and human manipulators of the action, epitomize or incarnate two categorical ways of coping with history. The association in the play between the rogue we see and the god we hear about ironically intimates the indissolubility of kindly providence and capricious bungling."

3186a Hunt, Maurice. "Leontes' 'Affection' and Renaissance 'Intention': *Winter's Tale* 135-146." *UMSE*, 4 (1983), 49-55.

Highlights Leontes' use of dense Latinate diction in his initial reasoning about Hermione's supposed infidelity. Focuses on the terms *affection* and *intention* and their technical meanings in Renaissance philosophy to argue that the king relies on "a cynical materialism" to deduce evil "from love's innocent image." Late in the play, however, in contemplating the "statue" of his wife, Leontes demonstrates that his imagination has been redeemed when he recalls her "exquisite tenderness."

3187 Hunt, Maurice. "'Standing in Rich Place': The Importance of Context in *The Winter's Tale*." *RMR*, 38 (1984), 13-33.

Presents *WT* as a "treatment of context—especially as it relates to speech—as a dramatic subject in its own right." One of the four contexts for Perdita is indicated by her identification with the goddess Flora, which relates her to classical myth and art and "invests her with a mysterious fertility."

3188 Kermode, Frank, ed. *The Winter's Tale*. (Signet Classic Shakespeare.) New York: New American Library, 1963. xxxv + [36]-223 pp.

The introduction suggests that *WT*, as one of Sh's tragicomic romances, is derived from "the Greek novel, especially perhaps from *Daphnis and Chloe*." Sh alludes to the Proserpine myth in Perdita's flower speech. He found in the romance stories the pattern he needed to write about "the destruction and renewal of life." The note on the source explains how Sh reshaped Robert Greene's romance *Pandosto*. The introduction, text, and note on the source are reprinted as part of item 0123.

3189 Lamb, Mary Ellen. "Ovid and *The Winter's Tale*: Conflicting Views Toward Art." *Shakespeare and Dramatic Tradition: Essays in Honor of S. F. Johnson*. Newark: U. of Delaware P., 1989, pp. 69-87.

Contends that in *WT* Sh presents contradictory views of art, especially the theater, in Ovidian terms. Autolycus, whose character as a thief and liar derives from moral commentaries on book 11 of the *Metamorphoses*, is an artist figure embodying many of the evils feared by those of Sh's contemporaries who railed against the theater: its untruthfulness, its encouragement of immorality, its use of disguise or impersonation. Autolycus's cynicism reduces anyone who is playing a role to a liar, a con man, and it temporarily infects both Leontes and Polixenes. The other artist figure is Paulina, whose regeneration of Hermione's "statue" recalls Ovid's myth of Pygmalion. Though the statue scene strikes us with wonder at the renewing power of art, it also reminds us that we have been tricked. Sh's art declines to settle the question of where the artist stands; instead, it suggests that the audience has a range of options in interpreting the play. We can agree for the moment to accept *WT* as an absorbing fable of providential redemption, fully aware that it can also be regarded as "a silly hoax."

3189a Laroque, François. "A New Ovidian Source for the Statue Scene in *The Winter's Tale*." *N&Q*, 31 (1984), 215-17.

Maintains that in *WT* Sh was more indebted to the myth of Deucalion in book 1 of Ovid's *Metamorphoses* than to the myth of Pygmalion in book 10.

3190 Laroque, François. "Pagan Ritual, Christian Liturgy, and Folk Customs in *The Winter's Tale*." *CahiersE*, 22 (1982), 25-33.

Finds that the bipartite structure of *WT*, like the cyclical course of the year, which it resembles, can be interpreted from pagan, Christian, and popular perspectives. In pagan terms, the oracle of Apollo sets the tragic tone for the first half of the play. In the second half, "the miraculous coming to life" of Hermione is borrowed from classical myth. Also in the second half, the pastoral scenes set up a parallel between Hermione and Perdita on the one hand and Ceres and Proserpina on the other, thus calling attention to the separation between mother and daughter and the central theme of fertility. There is a link here with the Eleusinian mysteries. Cites Christian texts that represent the moods of the first and second halves, respectively, and notes that folk customs, "relics of paganism," serve in the play to bridge the gap between pagan and Christian ways of apprehending the world.

3191   Lee, B. S. "Florimell and Galatea: Statuesque Love in the Middle Ages." *UES*, 27, no. 1 (1989), 1–8.

Traces the origin of the Pygmalion story to Ovid's *Metamorphoses* 10. This story, in which Venus answers a sculptor's prayer that his statue be brought to life as a wife for him, was interpreted in the Middle Ages as symbolic of idolatry. The early 17th c. by and large shared the medieval view of Pygmalion as an irrational, idolatrous competitor with Nature, God's vicegerent. The end of *WT* includes "a Pygmalion-like scene" that allows Sh to make an allegorical point about chastity: As a painted statue, Hermione is an idol fashioned by Leontes' jealousy; the art that Paulina uses in bringing her mistress to life is "simply the reconciling power of true love," not a usurpation of Nature's power.

3192   Lees, Francis Noel. "Plutarch and *The Winter's Tale*." *N&Q*, 23 (1976), 161–62.

Suggests that Plutarch's *Life of Dion*, set mainly in Sicily, may have given Sh the idea for changing the name of his hero in *WT* from "Pandosto" in his main source to "Leontes" and for making Leontes Sicilian rather than Bohemian. Also in the *Life of Dion*, Polyxenus is forced to flee from the disfavor of a Sicilian tryant—as does his namesake in *WT*. Finally, in the *Life*, Dion's wife, like Hermione in *WT*, is cruelly mistreated.

3193   Leimberg, Inge. "'Golden Apollo, A Poor Humble Swain . . . ' A Study of Names in *The Winter's Tale*." *SJH*, 1991, 135–58.

Follows up the author's study (item 3194) of Hermione's name in *WT*. Sees *WT* as controlled by a mythopoeic pattern, presided over by Apollo, which can be understood through close analysis of the characters' names. Polixenes, whose name in Greek means "receiving many guests," represents Hades, the god of the underworld; he has the dangerous power to draw Leontes back to the world of boyhood illusion. Paulina derives many of her characteristics from Athena Polias, patroness of town and palace; her name also can be connected with the Greek word for "grey-headed one," thus confirming her wisdom. Autolycus, whose name is the same as that of the son of Hermes, Apollo's younger brother, plays "the Lord of Misrule to Apollo's ruling deity." His introduction as a comic counterpart to his uncle "corresponds to the reversal pattern dividing the Bohemian revels from the first three acts of the play." The names of Perdita and Florizel clearly associate them with the story of Proserpina, to which Perdita refers, and make plain Sh's focus on "the idea of mythological renewal." Leontes, whose name links him with the lion, is, like that beast, both noble and savage. He is a good king, but, seeking to deal with the contradictions of experience solely through male friendship, he loses all reason and attacks his beloved like a rapacious brute. He needs to outgrow childhood. Father Time (Cronus) and Lady Fortune are also present in the play and part of its mythopoeic power.

3194   Leimberg, Inge. "'The Image of Golden Aphrodite': Some Observations on the Name Hermione.'" *SJH*, 1988, 130–39.

Attempts to explain, through "etymological, pseudo-etymological, literary and mythological data," what Hermione's name would have meant in *WT*, for a "hypothetical Elizabethan playgoer." Hermione is also called Harmonia, which means she is Helena as well as Aphrodite. Helen is a seducer as well as one who is seduced; Aphrodite is both Venus Urania and Venus Genetrix. In her *alter ego* of Harmonia, Aphrodite "personifies the happy wife and mother as well as the bereft, unhappy mother, who, however, finally is metamorphosed into the eternally happy wife." See item 3193.

3195 Mahon, John W. "Perdita's Reference to Proserpina in Act IV of *The Winter's Tale*." *N&Q*, 31 (1984), 214–15.

Summarizes previous critical opinion that there are parallels between Perdita and Proserpina and between Hermione and Ceres. In addition to these thematic similarities, there are passages in William Golding's translation of the account of Proserpina in the *Metamorphoses* that seem to be echoed in *WT*. Ceres, for example, is said to stand "as starke as stone" (line 632) when she hears that her daughter has become queen of the underworld. This could have contributed to Sh's handling of Hermione at the end. Golding's version seems indeed to have served as Sh's Ovid.

3196 Martz, Louis. "Shakespeare's Humanist Enterprise: *The Winter's Tale*." *English Renaissance Studies Presented to Dame Helen Gardner in Honour of Her Seventieth Birthday*. Ed. John Carey. Oxford: Clarendon P., 1980, pp. 114–31.

Declares that Sh atticized the material he found in Robert Greene's *Pandosto* to produce *WT*. Notes that most of the Greek or Greek-like names of the characters seem to have been recalled from Plutarch. Comments that the handling of the scene in which the oracle is revealed (III.ii) brings the episode close to the Greek tragic mode, especially when, in a touch added by Sh, Leontes commits blasphemy against Apollo by rejecting the oracle. Speculates that Sh might have become acquainted with the Greek tragic spirit by reading Aeschylus in a Latin translation. Suggests that *WT* might be seen as "a trilogy of redemption on the Aeschylean model." Insists that the play, in any case, has a three-part structure: tragedy, pastoral, miracle. We move from classical blood tragedy, through a cyclical pagan world of "great creating nature," to a time when, in accordance with humanist precepts, the world is restored to goodness through faith, "nourished by art and grace." In keeping with this progression, much language that is nearly Christian appears in the third part.

3197 Maveety, S. R. "What Shakespeare Did with *Pandosto*: An Interpretation of *The Winter's Tale*." *Pacific Coast Studies in Shakespeare*. Eds. Waldo McNeir and Thelma N. Greenfield. Eugene, Oregon: U. of Oregon Books, 1966, pp. 263–79.

Contends that Sh, in writing *WT*, altered his source, Greene's *Pandosto*, so that the first half of the story features a Senecan hero whose jealousy is a madness sent by Apollo. In the second half of the play, Sh again alters his source, this time presenting in allegorical fashion a Christian dispensation according to which Leontes attains forgiveness for his mistakes. Looking back from the conclusion to the classical tragedy of the first three acts, we can see Leontes' madness as "a symbol of man's incapacity to guarantee his own salvation."

3198 Mueller, Martin. "Hermione's Wrinkles, or Ovid Transformed: An Essay on *The Winter's Tale*." *CompD*, 5 (1971), 226–39.

Points to the changes Sh made in Greene's *Pandosto*, the primary source of *WT*: Leontes is kept alive (instead of committing suicide) and Hermione is "resurrected" (instead of dying). Argues that these alterations are part of an aesthetic strategy that manipulates the audience into a response of naive surprise at the ending. Sh conflated two classical myths here: that of Alcestis (rescued from the dead by Heracles) and that of Pygmalion (whose statue was transformed into a living woman by Venus). The first of these Sh could have known from George Buchanan's translation of Euripides' *Alcestis*; the second, from book 10 of Ovid's *Metamorphoses*. Sh's version of the Ovidian myth differs from his source in accepting a modest role for art in the scheme of things, in prizing unselfish love, and in acknowledging gracefully the power of time (as seen in Hermione's wrinkles). Thematically, the play progresses from art to nature, at the same time that the sophisticated spectator is transformed to a naive one. Sh's artful montage of classical myths paradoxically helps demonstrate the triumph of nature over art.

3199 Nelson, Thomas Allen. *Shakespeare's Comic Theory: A Study of Art and Artifice in the Last Plays.* (De Proprietatibus Litterarum, Series Practica, 57.) The Hague: Mouton, 1972. 95 pp.

Mentions, in a discussion of Sh's use of pastoral in *WT*, that the playwright inherited from Greek works like *Daphnis and Chloe* the connection between pastoral and romance.

3200 Pafford, J. H. P., ed. *The Winter's Tale.* (Arden Shakespeare.) London: Methuen, 1963. lxxxix + 225 pp.

The introduction discusses, under "Minor Influences," Sh's borrowing from Ovid's *Metamorphoses* (various details from the stories of Proserpine, Autolycus, and Pygmalion), the close parallels to the *Alcestis* of Euripides in the revealing of the statue, and the significant number of names borrowed from North's translation of Plutarch's *Lives*. Notes the possible derivation from classical comedy of the device, used in *WT* and Sh's other romances, of identifying "recovered children by clothing, jewellery, or special marks."

3201 Pogson, Beryl. *Three Plays by Shakespeare: An Esoteric Interpretation of "Romeo and Juliet," "All's Well That Ends Well," "The Winter's Tale."* London: Coole Book Service, 1963. viii + 56 pp.

Analyzes *WT* in terms of the myth of Demeter and Persephone, which in ancient times was central to the Eleusinian Mysteries. Sh weaves many threads from these rituals of antiquity into his play, bringing Leontes, like a candidate in the Mysteries, to "an inner peace through the harmonizing of his own being."

3202 Randall, Dale B. J. "A Glimpse of Leontes through an Onomastic Lens." *SJH*, 1988, 123–29.

Argues that Sh made Leontes ruler of Sicily in *WT* because of that island's association in the classical world with wrathful tyrants. The name *Leontes* probably comes from the connection of the lion with anger and with kings, and the link between lions and Sicily is reinforced by knowledge of Leontini, an early Greek colony in Sicily whose identification with lions is manifested through its name and through the images on its coins.

3203 Randall, Dale B. J. "'This is the Chase': or, The Further Pursuit of Shakespeare's Bear." *SJW*, 121 (1985), 89–95.

Argues that the bear that pursues Antigonus off the stage and eats him in *WT* (III.iii) may have been suggested to Sh by a passage in Horace's *Epistles* (II.1) in which the poet complains about ignorant theater audiences interrupting plays to call for "a bear or for boxers." The appearance of the bear on stage enables Sh to emphasize the death of Antigonus at the same time that he distances the audience from any feelings of tragic loss. In addition, the bear is set at the climax of the first half of the play, thus allowing Sh to balance the moral tone with the contrasting climax of the statue scene at the end.

3204 Ray, Bonnie MacDougall. "The Metamorphoses of Pygmalion: A Study of Treatments of the Myth from the Third Century B.C. to the Early Seventeenth Century." Ph.D. dissertation, Columbia University, 1982. *DAI*, 44 (1983–84), 3676-A.

Locates the origins of the Pygmalion story in classical antiquity and surveys the many ways the myth came to be treated. Notes especially that, in the English Renaissance, the myth is "reembodied" through "displacement" and that material associated with the myth is used independently ("defection"). Chapter 5 shows that the myth informs *WT* and that Sh "redefines it in the statue scene."

3205 Schanzer, Ernest, ed. *The Winter's Tale*. (New Penguin Shakespeare.) London: Penguin, 1969. 247 pp.

The introduction remarks that Sh's treatment in *WT* of the story he found in Robert Greene's *Pandosto*, his source, brings it closer to the world of Greek romance. Sh achieved this by giving Greek names to most of the characters, by "reviving" Hermione and by staging her "resurrection" in such a way as to provoke wonder, and by adding three motifs ("the vision of Antigonus, the shipwreck of the mariners, and the bear"). He was partly influenced by his own work a few years earlier on *Per.*, a play based on Greek romance.

3206 Smith, Hallett. "Leontes' *Affectio*." *SQ*, 14 (1963), 163–66.

Suggests that *WT*, I.ii.138-146, regarded as incoherent by most editors, can be clearly understood if the first word, *Affection*, is taken as "the equivalent of the Latin *affectio*, as Cicero used it." Instead of being glossed as "lust," then, the word should be seen as referring to "a sudden, violent perturbation of mind or body." The passage thus makes sense as Leontes' apostrophe to his own disordered mental state.

3207 Smith, Jonathan. "The Language of Leontes." *SQ*, 19 (1968), 317–27.

Analyzes the language of Leontes in *WT* as composed of recognizably pompous words used in their Latin sense and vulgar, plain, colloquial terms. In the first part of the play, Leontes' speech alternates, sometimes violently, between the pseudorationality and dignity of Latinisms and the coarse brutality of common speech. Argues that Sh was using the contrast between low and high speech to reflect the tension between Leontes' *hysterica passio* and his tenuous attempt to maintain decorum as a ruler. This hypothesis is strengthened by reference to Henry Cockeram's *The English Dictionary* (1623), which provides an alphabetical list of plain words with a "translation" of each into "the pompous dialect." Over two-thirds of the heavily Latinate words used by Leontes are found in Cockeram's list of "choicest language." Furthermore, most of these words are rare in Sh's works. Whether or not Cockeram knew the play, his concern with the levels of language and their effect seems parallel to Sh's. Once Leontes comes to himself, his language settles into a blend of ordinary speech and Latinate words (almost none of which are found in Cockeram's *Dictionary*) that represents kingly wholeness.

3208 Trousdale, Marion. "The Grace of Government in *The Winter's Tale*." *Law, Literature, and the Settlement of Regimes*. (Folger Institute Center for the History of British Political Thought: Proceedings 2.) Eds. Gordon J. Schochet, Patricia E. Tatspaugh, and Carol Brobeck. Washington, D. C.: Folger Institute, Folger Shakespeare Library, 1990, pp. 113–20.

Views *WT* as centrally concerned with the process of exchange involved in gift giving. Argues that Seneca's *De Beneficiis* is a likely influence because it explains the economy of giving as a sort of "social glue." The relationship between Leontes, Polixenes, and Hermione involves a complex giving and receiving of benefits in which certain values are "knowable as functions of one another." This is also true of Leontes' relationships with his subjects. The end of *WT* replaces the old with the new, making renewal and rebirth possible. The play as a whole is a gift to King James, before whom it was performed. It is also a response to Seneca that exemplifies the exchange between humanist and classical text: The poet makes return for a benefit received.

3209 Williams, John Anthony. *The Natural Work of Art: The Experience of Romance in Shakespeare's "Winter's Tale."* Cambridge: Harvard U. P., 1967. 47 pp.

Proposes that the setting of WT in the pre-Christian Greek world has the effect of restricting the characters' view of nature. The only divine power in this world is Apollo, and his temple is on an island "separate from the world of the play." Thus the larger view of nature, time, and art—which would enable any character to see how everything works in concord to achieve a providential end—is obscured until the final scene, in which Sh brings his characters and his audience to a recognition of "the harmony of the natural order."

3210 Wilson, Douglas B. "Euripides' *Alcestis* and the Ending of Shakespeare's *The Winter's Tale*." *Iowa State Journal of Research*, 58 (1984), 345–55.

Suggests that Sh knew Euripides' *Alcestis* in a Latin translation and that he used it as both "source and foil" for the ending of WT. In the Greek play, Admetus's deceased wife Alcestis is brought back from the dead by Heracles, Admetus having promised when she was dying that he would have a statue of her made to lie in his bed. Sh modifies this idea of imitation by having the living Hermione counterfeit her statue. In both Sh and Euripides, the husband of a "dead" woman transforms himself through suffering to become worthy of her, though Sh alone involves the younger generation in the healing of their elders. Sh could have turned to *Alcestis* to counter the forces of disintegration that predominate in his main source for WT, Robert Greene's *Pandosto*.

Index of the Names of Modern Scholars, Including Authors, Editors, and Compilers

A
Abartis, Caesarea, 1753
Able, Lionel, 1781
Abraham, Lyndall, 1159
Abrams, Richard, 3090a
Accardi, Bernard., 0001
Adams, Barry M., xx, 2461
Adams, Howard C., 2790
Adams, John Cranford, 2709
Adams, Martha Latimer, 0067
Adams, Martha Lou Latimer, 0068
Adams, Robert M., 1160
Adams, Robert P., 1939a
Adamson, Jane, 2791, 2792
Adelman, Janet, xvi, 1161, 1590, 2793
Adelman, Janet Ann, 1162
Adkins, Betty Jean VanNus, 3105
Adlard, John, 1163
Aggeler, Geoffrey D., 2794
Aggeler, Geoffrey Donovan, 0069
Agnew, Gates Kennedy, 2185
Ahern, Matthew Joseph Jr., 0070
Ahrens, Rüdiger, 1782
Aiken, Ralph, 2477
Albright, Daniel, 0070a
Aldus, P. J., 1783
Alexander, Marguerite, 0071
Alexander, Nigel, xvi, 1784
Alexander, Peter, xxi, 0072, 0073, 0074, 0725, 2795, 2796, 2797, 2845, 2846, 2861
Ali, Raza, 0075
Allen, D. C., 2390
Allen, Guy Pierce, 1591
Allen, M. J. B., 0076
Allen, Michael J. B., xv, 1531, 3106
Allman, Eileen Jorge, 0077, 0078
Altman, Joel B., 1565, 2325
Altmann, Ruth, 1164
Alvis, John, 0079, 0080, 0080a, 0081, 0599, 1165, 1592, 1940, 2515, 2634, 2871, 3065
Alvis, John Edward, 0082
Amiran, Minda Rae, 0083
Amur, G. S., 0084
Anderson, Donald K. Jr., 1166
Anderson, Frances Elizabeth, 0085
Anderson, M. J., 1127
Anderson, Peter S., 1941, 2028
Anderson, Ruth L.
Andreas, James R., 0087
Andresen, Martha, 2138
Andrew, Malcolm, 2391
Andrews, John F., xii, 0002, 2462
Andrews, Michael, xviii, 2139
Andrews, Michael Cameron, 1166a, 2202, 2268a
Ang, Gertrudes, 0088
Anikst, Alexander, 0089
Annal, Charles William, 2797a
Ansari, A. A., 1167, 1593, 1941a, 2269, 2610, 2798, 2799, 3170
Anson, John, xvii, 1942
Aoki, Kazuo, 0090
Aoyama, Seiko, 1168
Araki, Musazumi, 3075
Archer, M., 0091
Archibald, Elizabeth, xv, 0092
Ardinger, Barbara R., 1169
Ardolino, Frank A., 0093
Arieti, James A., 1035, 1899
Armstrong, John, 0095
Armstrong, Nancy, 2779a
Arnold, Margaret J., 2800
Arnold, Matthew, 0072
Aronson, Alex, 0096, 0097
Arthos, John, 0098, 0099, 0100, 0101, 0102, 1566
Asals, Heather, 3107
Ashley, Leonard R. N., 0103
Asimov, Isaac, 0104
Asp, Carolyn, 2801, 2802, 2803, 3171
Astington, John H., 0105
Aston, Margaret E., 1911
Atkins, G. Douglas, 2931, 3012
Aubrey, Brian, 1170
Auchincloss, Louis, 0106
Auden, W. H., 0787
Auffret, Jean, xvii, 1943
Axton, Marie, 2374
Aycock, Wendell M., 0440, 0936
Azar, Inés, 1594

B
Bache, William B., 1171, 2804
Bagchi, Jasodhara, 0108
Bagchi, Josodhara, 1785
Bagg, Robert, 2477a
Baines, Barbara J., 0109, 1944
Baker, Herschel, 0362, 3076
Baker, Peter, 1691
Baker, Susan, 1207
Bal, Mieke, 2392
Baldi, Sergio, 2478

Baldwin, Leonora Leet, 0110
Baldwin, T. W., xvi, 0724, 0937, 1567, 2270
Balestri, Charles Angelo, 0111
Bamber, Linda, 0111a
Bamber, Linda Vigderman, 0112
Banerjee, Ron D. K., 1171a
Bannerjee, G. C., 0177
Bannerjee, Srikumar, 2479
Barber, Benjamin R., 2279
Barber, C. L., 0061, 0114
Barber, Charles, 0113
Barber, Lester E., 2544
Barfield, Rayford Elliott Jr., 0115
Barfoot, C. C., 2805
Barish, Jonas A., 0116, 0117
Barkan, Leonard, 0118, 0119, 0120, 3172
Barker, Francis, 2567
Barker, G. A., 2354
Barnes, Arthur Dale, 0121
Barnes, Richard, 1945
Barnet, 2710
Barnet, Sylvan, 0122, 0123, 2203
Barnett, Louise, 2531
Barnwell, H. T., 2465
Barrett, D. S., 2247
Barrett, Debbie L., 2355
Barroll, J. Leeds, xv, 0002, 0003, 0004, 0005, 0006, 0124, 0125, 1172, 1173, 1174, 1175
Barroll, J. Leeds III, 0127, 0128
Barron, David B., 1595
Barton, Anne, xvi, 0129, 0130, 0131, 0362, 1176, 1596, 1597, 1880
Bashier, Kathleen Ryniker, 2440a
Basu, Kajal, 1946
Bate, A. Jonathan, 1947
Bate, Jonathan, xx, 0132, 2480
Bates, Paul A., 2481
Bath, Michael, xvi, 0132a, 1532
Battenhouse, Roy, 0061, 1917
Battenhouse, Roy W., xi, 0133, 1177, 1786, 1787
Bauer, Robert, 0134
Bauer, Robert J., 2140, 3108
Baumbach, Lydia, 0135
Baumlin, Tita, xxii
Baumlin, Tita French, 3109
Bawcutt, N. W., 3091
Bayerl, Francis James, 0136
Bayley, John, x, 0137, 0138, 1598, 2807
Bayley, john, 2806
Bean, John C., 0139
Beardsley, Theodore S. Jr., 1788
Beauregard, David N., xviii, 2248, 3110
Beck, Ervin., 0140
Beckerman, Bernard, 0002, 0141, 1178, 2808
Beckman, Margaret Boerner, 1533
Beckwith, Marc Allan, 0142
Beecher, D. A., xxii, 3092
Beecher, Donald, 0273
Bell, Arthur H., 1179, 1599
Bellringer, A. W., 1948
Belsey, Catherine, 0142a, 2204, 2205

Bender, Daniel Robert, 0143
Bennett, J. A. W., 2239
Bennett, Josephine Waters, 1155
Bennett, Robert Beale, 0144
Benoit, Raymond, 1180
Bensel-Meyers, Linda, 0145
Benson, Morris, 2809
Bentley, Gerald Eades, 0146
Bentley, Gregory Wayne, 0148
Bentley, Greg W., 0147
Bentley, Jonathan Scott, 0149
Berek, Peter, 1181
Berger, Harry Jr., xx, xxi, 2545, 2810
Berger, Karol, xx, 2546
Bergeron, David M., xiii, xv, xvi, xxi, 0150, 0792, 0988, 1156, 1754, 2612, 2931, 3012
Bergeron David M., 2611
Berggren, Paula S., 0151, 1182
Berke, Bradley, 2810a
Berkeley, David S., 1183
Berlin, Normand, 2613, 2614
Berman, Ronald, xvii, 1938, 1949
Berman, Ronald S., 0152, 1918
Bermel, Albert, 0153
Bernard, John D., 1836, 3173
Bernhardt, W. W., 2811
Bernstein, Jay, 2567
Berry, Edward I., 1919
Berry, Francis, 0154, 1600, 2812
Berry, J. Wilkes, 2393, 3111
Berry, Philippa, 2394
Berry, Ralph, 0155, 1601, 1950, 1951, 2615
Betts, John H., xvii, 1920, 1921
Bevington, David, xi, 0002, 0156, 0156a, 0157, 0158, 0159, 0576, 1069, 1184, 1590, 1900, 1951a
Bhattacherje, M. M., 0160
Bianciotto, Gabriel, 0132a
Bieman, Elizabeth, 0160a, 2141
Biggs, Murray, 0812
Billington, Sandra, 0160b
Bilton, Peter, 0161, 2994
Binney, James, 2813
Binns, J. W., 0162
Birkinshaw, Philip, xv, 1185
Birney, Alice Lotvin, 0163, 0164
Birringer, Johannes H., 1186
Bishop, Thomas Geoffrey, 2356
Biswas, D. C., 0164a, 2814
Biswas, Dinesh Chandra, 0165
Bitter, Barbara W., 0662, 1030
Bizley, W. H., 1952, 2616
Björk, Lennart, 1255
Black, James, xvii, 1912
Black, Matthew W., 0166, 0167, 0168
Blackwood, Robert J. Jr., 1602
Blake, N. F., 0169
Blakiston, J. M. G., 1187
Blamires, Harry, 0170
Blanpied, John W., 1412, 2534
Bligh, John, 1603, 1953
Bliss, Lee, 0171

Index of Modern Scholars

Blisset, W. F., 2142
Blissett, W. F., xviii
Blissett, William, 1188, 1604, 2815, 3174
Blistein, Elmer M., 0937, 1188a, 1787
Blits, Jan H., 1954, 1955
Blits, Jan Harold, 1956
Bloch, R. Howard, 2404
Bloom, Allan, 0172
Bloom, Edward A., 0296, 0395, 0522, 1010, 1191, 1791, 2603, 3117
Bloom, Harold, 1423, 1525, 2859, 3051
Bloomfield, Morton W., 1189
Bluestone, Max, 0172a
Blythe, David Everett, 2143
Blythe, David-Everett, 1534, 2816
Blythe, David-Everette, 1190
Boatner, Janet Williams, 2817
Bock, Philip K., 1605
Boitani, Piero, 1789, 2818, 2946, 2960
Bolgar, R. R., 2510
Bolger, Stephen G., 1901
Bolton, Joseph S. G., 2711
Bolton, W. F., 1606
Bonaventure, Sister Mary, O. S. F., xix, 2375
Bonazza, Blaze Odell, 1568
Bond, Ronald B., 2546a
Bonheim, H., 2819
Bonheim, Helmut, 0173
Bonjour, Adrien, 0173a, 1191, 2820
Bono, Barbara J., 1192
Bono, Barbara Jane, 1193
Boorman, S. C., 0174
Boose, Lynda E., 2326
Booth, Stephen, 1194, 2482
Borinski, Ludwig, 0175
Borthwick, E. Kerr, 1789a
Bose, Amalendu, 0176, 0177, 0948, 1195
Boss, Judith, 2547
Bosworth, Denise Mary, 0178
Boughner, Daniel, xx
Boughner, Daniel C., 2548
Boulukos, Athanasios, 1569
Bowden, William R., 1607, 1957
Bowen Barbara, 2821
Bowers, A. Robin, 0179, 2395, 3112, 3113
Bowers, Fredson, xvii, xviii, 0180, 0181, 0182, 1196, 1196a, 1790, 1791, 2144
Bowers, J. L., 0183
Bowers, John M., 1197
Bowers, R. H., 3114
Bowers, Robin, xix
Bowling, Lawrence Edward, 1198
Boyd, Heather, 0879
Boyle, Anthony Thomas, 0184
Bradbrook, M. C., xxi, 0002, 0185, 0185a, 0186, 0187, 0188, 2549, 2617, 3093
Bradbrook, Muriel C., 0189, 2618, 3115
Bradbury, Malcolm, 0076, 0814, 0844, 2258, 2652
Braden, Gordon, 0190, 0191
Bradford, Alan Taylor, xv, 1535
Bradford, William Clark Jr., 1958

Bradshaw, Graham, 0192
Braekman, W., 2712
Brand, Alice Glarden, 1199
Brandão, Nielsen da Neves, 1200
Braunmuller, A. R., xviii, 2137
Bredbeck, Gregory W., xxii, 2822, 2823
Bredbeck, Gregory William, 2824
Breight, Curtis Charles, 2713
Brennan, Anthony S., 1201
Brenner, Myra, 0193
Breuer, Horst, 0194, 1792, 2825
Brewer, D. S., 0195
Brewer, Derek, 0195a
Bridges, Phyllis, 2145
Briggs, K. M., xvi, 1570
Brill, Lesley, 2619
Brind'Amour, Pierre, 1842
Brissenden, Alan, 0196, 0197
Bristol, Michael, 1608
Brittain, Kilbee Cormack, 0198
Brittin, Norman A., 1959
Britton, Elizabeth Lindsey, 1202
Broadbent, J. B., 0199
Brobeck, Carol, 3208
Brockbank, J. P., 0200
Brockbank, J. Philip, 1793
Brockbank, Philip, 0201, 0202, 1609
Brodwin, Leonora, 1203
Brody, Saul N., 2636
Broich, Ulrich, 1782
Bromham, A. A., 0203
Bromley, John C., 1960
Bromley, Laura G., 2395a, 2396
Brook, G. L., 0204
Brooke, Nicholas, 0206, 0207, 2206, 2714, 2715
Brooks, Harold, xvi, 1571, 2271, 2826
Brooks, Harold F., xx, 2453, 2454
Broude, Ronald, xxi, 2716, 2717
Broughton, Bradford B., 3077
Broussard, Mercedes, 1204
Brower, Reuben, 0057, 1599
Brower, Reuben A., 0208, 1610
Brown, Arthur, 0209
Brown, Elynor Pettus, 0210
Brown, Huntington, 3116
Brown, James Neil, 0211
Brown, Jane K., 2272
Brown, John Russell, 0002, 0518, 0556, 0578, 0581, 0829, 1114, 1415, 1571, 1961, 2119, 2224
Browne, Marlene Consuela, 0211
Browne, Thomas, xx, 2463
Brownlow, F. W., 2620
Brucher, Richard T., 2718
Brucher, Richard Thomas, 0213
Bruckmann, Patricia, 1604
Bruster, Douglas, xiii, 0214
Bruster, Douglas S., xvi, 1794
Bruzzi, Zara, 0203
Bryan, Margaret B., 1612
Bryan, Robert A., 1032, 1309, 2953

Bryant, J. A. Jr., xviii, 0061, 0215, 1962, 2718a
Bryant, Jerry H., 3175
Bryson, Norman, 2923
Buck, William Stuart, 0216
Buechmann, Claus-Peter, 1613
Bullough, G., 2827
Bullough, Geoffrey, xii, 0008, 0009, 0010, 0011, 0012, 0165, 0217, 0218, 0219
Bulman, J. C., 2623
Bulman, James C., 0220, 0221, 1614
Bulman, James C. Jr., xxi, 2621, 2622
Bulman, James Cornelius Jr., 0222
Bunselmeyer, Josephine Elizabeth, 0223
Burckhardt, Sigurd, 0224, 1963
Burelbach, Frederick M., 1795
Burelbach, Frederick M. Jr., 0225
Burgess, Glyn S., 2199b
Burke, Kenneth, 0824, 1205, 1615
Burke, Mary Kathleen, 0226
Burke, Peter, 0227
Burnet, R. A. L., 1964
Burns, Edward, 0228
Burns, M. M., xxi, 2828
Burns, Margie, 1536
Burrill, Tom, 2829
Burt, Richard A., xvii, 1965
Burton, Dolores M., 1206, 1616
Burton, J. Anthony, 1796
Burton Dolores M., 2455
Bush, Douglas, 0229
Bushman, Mary Ann, xv, 1207
Bushnell, Rebecca, xviii
Bushnell, Rebecca W., 1966
Bushnell, Rebecca Weld, 0230, 1967, 2207
Bushrui, Suheil Badi, 1108, 1246
Butler, Christopher, 3117
Butler, F. G., xviii, 1617, 2145a, 2146
Butler, Francelia, 0231, 2624
Butler, Francelia McWilliams, 2625
Butler, Guy, 2146a
Buxton, John, 2376, 3118
Byles, Joan, 2830

C
Cahn, Victor L., 0232
Caie, Graham D., 2274
Cairncross, Andrew S., 0233, 0234, 1208, 1968
Cairns, Christopher, 0235
Calarco, N. Joseph, 2147, 2148
Calder, Alexander Charles, 0236
Calder, William M. III, 2331
Calderwood, James L., xvi, 0237, 0238, 1343, 1615, 1618, 2013, 2273, 2718b, 2991
Calderwood, James Lee, 1619
Caldwell, Ellen Cashwell, xvii, 1936
Caldwell, John, 2943
Calkins, Roger, 3077
Calkins, Roger Willard, xxii, 3078
Callahan, Robert D., 2831
Camden, Carroll, 1196, 1797

Campbell, Gordon, 2718c
Campbell, John Libby Jr., 2626
Campbell, O. J., 2936
Campbell, Oscar James, 0012a
Candido, Joseph, 1572, 1922
Canfield, J. Douglas, 0238a
Cantelupe, Eugene B., 3119
Cantor, Paul, 0057
Cantor, Paul A., 0041, 0239, 1798
Cantrell, John Bruce, 1969
Caputi, Antony, xv, 1210
Carducci, Jane, 1211, 1970
Carducci, Jane S., 1620, 2719
Carducci, Jane Shook, 0240
Carey, Anna Kirwan, 2192
Carey, Anna Kirwan Steck, 1621
Carey, John, 1780, 2376, 3196
Carlsen, Hanne, xii, 0013, 2274
Carnes, Valerie, 2550
Carnicelli, D. D., 2551
Carr, Joan, xvi, 1755
Carr, W. I., 1622
Carroll, D. Allen, 2275
Carroll, William C., xxii, 0242, 2185a, 3079
Carson, David L., 1971
Carson, Ricks, 1798a
Cartelli, Thomas, 0243, 2627, 2832
Cartwright, Kent, 1212
Cary, Cecile Edith Williamson, 2833
Cary, Cecile Williamson, 1062
Case, Sue-Ellen, 2822, 2843
Casey, John, 0243a
Cath, Stanley H., 1972
Cavell, Stanley, 0244, 1212a, 1623, 1747
Chafee, Alan Jewell, 0245
Chakravorty, Jagannath, 0246, 0247
Chambers, R. W., 0725
Champion, Larry S., xxiii, 0248, 0249, 0250, 2149, 2720
Chance, Jane, 1812, 3158
Chand, Sunil, 3120
Chang, Joseph S. M. J., xvii, 0251, 0252, 1973
Chapell, Fred, 1624
Chapman, Antony U., 2834
Chapman, Gerald W., 0687
Chappell, Fred, xvi
Charnes, Linda, 2834a
Charnes, Linda Anne, 0253
Charney, Maurice, 0062, 0254, 0255, 0256, 0272, 0515, 0798, 0810, 0899, 1003, 1213, 1799, 2072, 2150, 2586, 2628, 2721, 3082
Chatterjee, Bhabatosh, 0782, 1449, 1785, 2893
Chatterjee, Sati, 0257
Chaudhuri, Sujata, 0258
Chaudhuri, Sukanta, 0259, 0260
Cheadle, Brian, 1214
Cheetham, Mark A., 2392
Cheney, Donald, 0261
Cherry, Mary Jane, 0262
Cheuse, Alan, 1213

Index of Modern Scholars

Chew, Audrey, 0263
Chew, Samuel C., 0264
Choe, Jaisou, 0265
Choi, Young, 2835
Chorost, Michael, 2629
Christian, Lynda G., 0266
Christopher, Georgia B., 1215
Ciavolella, Massimo, 0273
Clark, John R., 0038
Clark, Sandra, 0267, 2551a
Clark, Stephen Kay, 0268
Clarke, Joseph Kelly, 0269
Clarke, Larry R., xxii, 2836
Clarke, M. L., 1974
Claro, Sílvia Mussi da Silva, 1800
Clayton, F. W., 2276
Clayton, M. G., 2552
Clayton, Thomas, 1216
Clemen, Wolfgang, 0270, 0271, 1975, 2277
Clements, Robert Morrison Jr., 3094
Clemon-Karp, Sheila, 1217
Clubb, Louise, 3176
Clubb, Louise George, 0272, 0273, 1573, 1801
Cluck, Nancy A., 1217a
Coates, John, xv, 1218
Coates, Richard, 0014
Cody, Richard, 0274
Cody, Richard John, 0275
Coggin, Bruce Wayne, 0276
Coghill, Nevill, 0277, 2837, 2838, 2839, 2845, 2846, 2861
Cohen, Brent Martin, 1219
Cohen, Eileen Z., 1802
Cohen, Marion, 2278
Colahan, Clark, 2840
Cole, Douglas, 2841
Cole, Howard C., 0278
Cole, Susan Letzler, 0278a
Coleman, Althea Mae, 0279
Coleman, William S. E., 1624a
Colie, Rosalie, 0280
Colie, Rosalie L., 0281, 2138, 2142, 2166
Collier, Gordon, 0452b
Collier, Lewis Arlen, 0282
Collins, David, 2842
Collins, Stephen L., 0282a
Collura, Jane Haney, 0282b
Colman, E. A. M., 0283, 1220, 1625, 1976
Comito, Terry, xi, 0284
Conejero, Manuel Angel, 0566a, 0743, 1113
Conrad, Peter, 0285
Conway, Daniel J., 0286
Cook, Ann Jennalie, 0002, 2630
Cook, Carol, 2843
Cook, Carol Jane, 0287
Cook, David, 2631
Cook, Elizabeth, 1221
Cook, Hardy M., 2844
Cook, Ivor R. W., 2845, 2846, 2847, 2863
Cook, W. A., 1977
Cooke, Michael G., 1221a

Cooke, Nan Cooke, 0241
Cooke, William, 1803
Cookson, Linda, 1229, 1247, 1265, 1280, 1281, 1314, 1315, 1400, 1425, 1509
Coombes, John, 2567
Cooper, David Jay, 1573a
Cooper, Helen M., 2900
Cooperman, Stanley, 1804
Cope, Jackson I., 0287
Copland, Murray, 2377
Coppedge, Walter R., xv, 1222
Coppedge, Walter Raleigh, 1223
Corballis, R. P., 1913
Cornelia, Marie, 0289
Cornelia, Sister M. Bonaventura, 0290
Cosgrove, Brian, 3177
Cosgrove, Mark Francis, O. S. B., 2249
Costa, C. D. N., 0582
Costa, Maria Gláucia de V., 1224
Costa de Beauregard, Raphaelle, 1225
Couchman, Gordon W., 1226
Council, Norman, xvii, 0291, 1902
Council, Norman Briggs, 0292
Coursen, Herbert, 0292a
Coursen, Herbert R. Jr., 1978
Cowhig, Ruth, 2721a
Cowser, Robert G., 1227
Cox, C. B., 1668
Cox, John D., 2848
Cox, Richard H., 2279
Craig, D. H., 0293
Craig, Hardin, 0294, 0295, 0296, 1626, 1979
Craik, T. W., 0630
Crane, Milton, 1371
Cranfill, Thomas, 0297
Crawford, John W., xvii, 1903, 1980, 2632
Crawley, Thomas Francis, 2186
Crewe, J. V., 1981
Crewe, Jonathan, 2397
Cribb, T. J., 2464
Crichton, Andrew B., xix, 2319
Crockett, Bryan, xix, 2280
Crookes, David Z., 1626a
Cross, Gustav, 2722
Crowley, Richard C, 1627
Crowley, Richard Charles, 1628
Crupi, Charles William, 1537
Cruttwell, Patrick, 0298
Cullum, Graham, 1228
Cunningham, John E., 1229
Cunningham, Karen, 2123
Currell, Mario, 0648, 1095
Curtis, Harry Jr., 3178
Curtis, M. H., 0299
Cutts, John P., xv, xviii, 0299a, 1230, 2151, 2208, 2281, 2357, 2553, 2724
Czerwinski, Edward J., 1766, 1844

D

Daalder, Joost, 2250
Dabydeen, David, 2721a
Dachslager, E. L., 1992

Daiches, David, 1231
Daigle, Lennet J., 3121
Daigle, Lennet Joseph, 3122
Daly, Peter, 0300
D'Amico, Jack, 0301
Daniels, F. Quinland, 2849
Dannreuther, Daphne Davis, 2850
Danson, Lawrence, 0302
Danson, Lawrence N., 1629, 2725
Danson, Lawrence Neil, 0303
D'Ardenne, S., 1983
Dasgupta, Arun K., 0304
Dasgupta, Arun Kumar, 2726
Dash, Irene G., 1232
Datta, Amaresh, 0305
Datta, Pradip Kumar, 0306
Davenport, Machael, 1007
Davidson, Clifford, xxi, 0117, 1070, 1233, 1234, 1630, 1736, 1829, 1983a, 2554, 2555, 2633, 2727
Davies, Rowena, 1756
Davies, Stevie, xi, 0307
Davis, Ethel H., 0752
Davis, Richard Beale, 1022
Davis, Timothy C., 1235
Davison, Mary Carol, 0308, 2556
Davison, Peter, xiii, 0309
Dawson, Anthony B., 0310
Dawson, R. MacG., 1235a
Deal, Kenneth Lee, 0310a
de Almeida, Barbara Heliodora C. de M. F., 2851
De Alvarez, Leo Paul S., 2634
Dean, John, xi, 0311, 0311a, 0312
Dean, Leonard F., 2093
Dean, Paul, xv, 0313, 0314, 1236, 1631
de Armas, Frederic A., 2728
deBrito, João Batista Barbosa, 1237
Debus, Allen G., 0968
Dees, Jerome S., 0014a
de Gerenday, Lynn, 1983b
De Grazia, Margreta, 0002
DeGrazia, Margreta, 1632
Denham, Robert, 1273a
Denney, Constance Dorothy Baldwin, 0315
Dent, Robert W., 0048
Der, Don W., 0317
De Rachewiltz, Siegfried Walter, 0316
Desai, S. K., 0318
Des Jardins, Gregory, 1805
Desmet, Christy, 0319
Dessen, Alan, 1632a, 1806
Dessen, Alan C., 0319a, 0319b
Devereux, James A., S. J., x, xx, 2483, 2486
Dias, Walter, 1238
Dickinson, John W., 2240
Diehl, Huston, 2729
DiGiovanni, Robert Bernard, 2398
Dillon, Andrew, 1807
Dillon, Janette, 0320, 0321
DiMatteo, Anthony, 2557
Diverres, A. H., 2465

Dodd, Mark Robert, xxi, 2852
Doebler, John, xvi, 0322, 0322a, 1538, 3123, 3124, 3125
Dollarhide, Louis E., 0323
Dollimore, Jonathan, xii, xxii, 0062, 0324, 2853
Doloff, Steven, 2152
Donaghue, Denis, 0327
Donahue, Patricia Ann, 2398a
Donaldson, E. Talbot, ix, 0325, 2309, 2854
Donaldson, Ian, xx, 2399, 2936, 3126
Donawerth, Jane, 0326, 2153
Donno, Elizabeth Story, 1632b
Donow, Herbert S., 2484
Doran, Madeleine, xv, xix, 1239, 1539, 1633, 1808, 1984, 2282, 2283, 2327
Dorey, T. A., 0491
Dorius, R. J., 1240, 1241
Dorsch, T. S., 0270, 1574
Dotterer, Ronald, 1666, 2630
Downer, Alan S., 1242
Drakakis, John, 1985
Draper, John W., 0328, 0329, 0330, 0331, 1243, 1634, 1986
Draudt, Manfred, xvi, 1809, 2187
Drexler, R. D., 2558
Driscoll, James P., 1987
Dronke, Peter, 1244, 2378
duBois, Page, 1635
Dubrow, Heather, xx, 0332, 2400, 2401
Dudley, Donald R., 0491
Duffy, Maureen, 2284
Dunbar, Florence W., 1733
Dunbar, Georgia, 1245
Duncan, Charles F. Jr., 0333
Duncan, Douglas, 0334
Duncan-Jones, E. E., 3179
Duncan-Jones, Katherine, xviii, 2241
Dundas, Judith, xix, 0335, 2402, 3126a, 3127
Dunn, Catherine M., 0336
Dunn, T. A., 1246
Durer, Christopher, 1740a
Durham, Mildred O., 1987a
Dusinberre, Juliet, 0337
Dusinberre, Juliet S., 2855
Duthie, G. I., 1648
Dutton, Richard, 0338
Dyer, Frederick B. Jr., 2856
Dyson, H. V. D., 0339, 0340, 0341

E
Eade, J. C., 2208a
Eagleton, Terence, 0342
Eagleton, Terry, 0343
Easson, Angus, 2358
Eastman, Arthur M., 0344
Eaton, Sara, 1810
Ebel, Henry, xi, 1988
Ebner, Dean, 2559
Eccles, C. M., 0345
Eckert, Charles W., xvi, 1811

Index of Modern Scholars

Economou, George D., xvi, 1812
Edelman, Edward, 1989
Eden, Kathy Hannah, 1813
Edens, Walter, 1740a
Edgar, Irving I., 0346
Edinborough, Arnold, 1990
Edmunds, John, 0347
Edwards, Philip, xiii, 0062, 0217, 0347a, 0348, 0349, 0350, 0351, 0812, 1310, 1814, 2359, 2729a, 2857
Efron, Arthur, 0352, 0492a
Eggers, Walter, 1740a
Eggers, Walter F. Jr., 0353
Elam, Keir, 0353a, 1540, 2188
Eland, Cynthia Graham, 2729b
Eldridge, Elaine, 2858
Eldridge, Elaine May, 2858a
El-Gabalwy, Saad, 2403
Ellis, Mark Spencer, 1247
Ellis-Fermor, Una, 0354, 0355
Ellrodt, Robert, xix, 2379
Else, Gerald, 0166
Else, Gerald F., 0166
Elton, W. R., xii, 0015, 0016, 0017, 0018, 0019, 0356, 1732, 2154, 2635, 2859, 2860
Elton, William R., 1632b
Emmerová, Jarmila, 1060, 1834, 3034
Emmett, V. J. Jr., 1904
Empson, William, 0357, 2846, 2847, 2861, 2862, 2863
Enck, John J., xxi, 2730, 2864
Enozawa, Kazuyoshi, 0020, 0021
Erickson, Peter, 0386, 1248
Erickson, Peter B., 1923
Eriksen, Roy T., 1991, 2380
Erlich, Avi, 2636
Erlich, Bruce, 0358, 2865
Erlich, Richard Dee, 1249
Erskine-Hill, Howard, 0359, 1250
Eskin, Stanley G., 0360
Esslin, Martin, 0652
Estrin, Barbara L., 1250a, 1251
Ettin, Andrew V., 2731
Evans, Barbara Lloyd, 0369, 0370
Evans, Bertrand, 0361
Evans, G. B., 0996
Evans, G. Blakemore, 0362, 1814a
Evans, Gareth Lloyd, 0363, 0364, 0365, 0366, 0367, 0368, 0369, 0370
Evans, Malcolm, 2189
Evans, Maurice, 0370a
Evans, Oliver H., 3063
Evans, Robert O., 2466, 2467
Evans, T. M., 0371
Everett, Barbara, 1252, 2866
Ewbank, Inga-Stina, xviii, 0217, 0372, 0372a, 0373, 0812, 1252a, 1310, 2209, 2857
Ewing, Marilyn McKee, 0374

F

Faas, Ekbert, 0375, 0376
Faber, Kristina, 2867

Faber, M. D., xvii, 0377, 1253, 1992, 2688
Fabian, Bernhard, 1362, 1472, 1743
Fabiny, Tibor, 0377a, 0377b, 0828a
Fabricius, Johannes, 0377c
Falk, Doris V., 1815
Farley-Hills, David, 0378, 2532
Farmer, Harold, 1254
Farnham, Willard, 0379, 2868
Farrell, Kirby, 0379a, 1935
Farrell, Robert T., 2239
Fawcett, Mary Laughlin, 2731a
Fawkner, H. W., 1255, 1256
Fegan, James, 1257
Feinstein, Blossom Grayer, 0380
Felperin, Howard, 0380a, 0381, 0382
Ferguson, Arthur B., 2869
Ferguson, Frances, 2404
Ferguson, Susan French, 0383
Fergusson, Francis, 0384, 0385, 1258
Ferlo, Roger A., 0385a
Fernandez, Maria Luisa Dañobeitia, 1259
Fichter, Andrew, xv, 1260
Fiedler, Leslie, 0386
Fiedler, Leslie A., 2485
Fields, Albert W., 0386a, 1636
Fienberg, Nona, 3128
Findlay, Heather, 0387
Findlay, L. M., xvi, 1816
Fineman, Joel, 2404, 2870
Finkelstein, Sidney, 1993
Finklestein, Sidney, 0388
Fisch, Harold, xv, 0389, 1261
Fischer, Sandra Kay, 0390
Fish, Stanley, xvi, 1594, 1747
Fish, Stanley E., 1637
Fisher, S. T., 2190
Fiskin, A. M. J., 1262
Fitch, Robert E., 0391, 1263
Fitz, L. T., xv, 1264
Flagstad, Karen, 2560, 2560a
Flahiff, F. T., 2138, 2142, 2166
Flannery, Christopher, 2871
Fleissner, R. F., 1816a, 1924, 1994
Fleissner, Robert F., 0392, 1995, 2155, 2156, 2328, 2441, 3179a
Flint, Kate, 1265
Fly, Richard, 0393
Fly, Richard D., xxi, 2637, 2872, 2873, 2874
Foakes, R. A., xv, 0062, 0394, 0395, 1266, 1575, 1817, 2285, 2875, 2876, 2877, 2878
Foakes, Reginald A., 0396
Ford, P. Jeffrey, 0397
Foreman, Walter C. Jr., 0398, 1267
Foreman, Walter Cyril Jr., 1268
Forker, Charles, x, xx
Forker, Charles, R., 2732
Forker, Charles R., 0398a, 1922, 2486
Forrest, James P., 1996
Fortescue, Jonathan, xvi, 1638
Fortin, René, xvi, xvii, 0399, 1818
Fortin, René E., 1541, 1997
Fortin René Ernest, 1998

Fothergill-Payne, Louise, 0639, 2728
Fothergill-Payne, Peter, 0639, 2728
Fowler, Alastair, 2487, 3117, 3180
Fox, Jan, 1269
Foy, Ted Cecil, 0400
Franson, J. Karl, 2879
Frantz, David O., 2263
Franz, David Oswin, 1270
Fraser, Russell, xiii, 0401
Fraser, Russell A., xviii, 2157
Freehafer, John, 0402, 0403
Freeman, Arthur, 2442
Freeman, James A., 1819
Fregly, Marilyn S. S., 0404
French, A. L., xv, 1271
French, Marilyn, xiii, 0405
French, Tita, 0405a, 2405
Freund, Elizabeth, 2880
Frey, Charles, 0406, 3181
Frey, Charles H., 3094a, 3100a, 3102
Friedenreich, Kenneth, 1558
Friedlander, Douglas Richard, 0407
Friedman, Lester D., 2881
Friedman, Stanley, 1272
Friesner, Donald Neil, 0408
Frost, David L., xv, 0409, 1273
Frye, Dean, 1639
Frye, Dean Carson, 0410
Frye, Northrop, 0061, 0411, 0412, 0413, 0414, 0415, 0416, 0507, 0518, 1273a, 2488, 3182
Frye, Roland M., 1640
Frye, Roland Mushat, 0417, 0418, 0419, 1274, 1820, 2406
Fujita, Minoru, 1275, 1276
Fulton, R. C., 0420
Fulton, Robert C. III, 2638
Fulton, Robert Campbell, 0421
Fuzier, Jean, 1277, 1999

G
Gagen, Jean, 2882
Gajdusek, R. E., 1641
Gajowski, Evelyn Jacqueline, 1278
Galloway, David, 1853
Gallwey, Kay, 1279
Garber, Marjorie, xvi, 0422, 0423, 0424, 1757, 2561
Garber, Marjorie B., 0425
Garber, Marjorie Beth, 0426
Gardiner, Alan, 1280
Gardiner, Judith K., 2562
Gardner, C. O., 0427, 2000
Gardner, Helen, 1137
Garlick, H. F., 2883
Garner, Bryan A., xiv, 0428, 0429, 0429a, 0430, 2532a
Garner, Shirley Nelson, 2793
Garton, Charles, xvi, 1576
Garvin, Harry R., 1082, 1233, 2432
Garvin, Katharine, 1821
Gash, Anthony, 0431

Gaskill, Gayle, 3080
Gasper, Julia, 3182a
Gatti, Hilary, 1822
Gaudet, Paul, 1642
Gaunt, D. M., xvi, 1823
Gazelles, Brigitte, 1699
Gearin-Tosh, Michael, 1281, 2360
Geller, Lila, 1758
Gellert, Bridget, 1824
Gent, Lucy, 3129
George, Kathleen, 0432
Gerson, Lloyd, 1035, 1899
Gerstung, Estella Rose Baker, 0433
Gesner, Carol, xi, xvi, 0434, 0928, 1759
Ghosh, Gauri Prasad, 0435
Ghosh, Gouri Prasad, 2209a
Ghosh, P. C., 0435a
Gianakaris, C. J., 0117, 1070, 1736, 1829, 2264
Gianetti, Robert Michael, 2488a
Gibbons, Brian, 2242, 2732a
Giese, Loreen Lee, 1643
Gilbert, A. J., 2489, 2490
Gill, Roma, 0436, 1558, 2001
Gillett, Peter J., 1905
Gillham, E. G., 1644
Gillies, John, 2562a
Gira, Catherine R., 0437
Gira, Catherine Russell, 0438
Girard, René, 0439, 0440, 0441, 0442, 1391, 1699, 2002, 2407, 2884, 2885
Givan, Christopher, 1645
Givan, Christopher Forrest, 1282
Glasser, Marvin, 2886
Gleason John B., 0443
Glendinning, Charles Henry, 0444
Gless, Darryl J., 2002a
Glickman, Susan, 0445
Godlfarb, Barry, 1646
Godshalk, W. L., 1283, 2158
Godshalk, William Leigh, xviii, xxii, 0446, 2210, 3088
Goldberg, S. L., 1284
Golden, Leon, 0446a
Goldfarb, Barry, xvi
Goldman, Michael, 0447, 0448, 1647
Goldman, Rachel Margaret, 2408
Goldsmith, Ulrich K., 2331
Goldstein, Leonard, 2639
Goldstein, Philip, 1825
Goldstien, Neal L., xviii, 2191
Gomez, Christine, 2887
Goodale, Geoffrey Chartres, 0449
Goodman, Alice, 0450
Goodwin, Sarah Webster, 1691
Gordon, D. J., 1648
Gourlay, Patricia S., 1826
Gourlay, Patricia Southard, 0452
Gouws, John, 2328a
Gowda, H. H. Anniah, 1112
Goy-Blanquet, Dominique, 2003
Grabes, Herbert, 0452a, 0452b

Index of Modern Scholars

Grace, William J., 0453
Grafton, Anthony, 0002
Graham, Kenneth John Emerson, 0454
Grant, Michael, 1285
Grant, Patrick, 2333, 2562b
Graves, Wallace, xix, 2329
Gray, Douglas, 0650a
Gray, J. C., 0547a, 0594, 1703, 2468, 2783a
Gray, J. L., 1614
Greaves, Margaret, 0455
Green, André, 2004
Green, Brian, 2381, 2382
Green, David C., xviii, 0456, 2005
Green, Douglas E., 2733
Green, J. T., 1286
Green, Lawrence D., 2888
Green, Roger Lancelyn, 2286
Green, Rosemary M., 0457
Greenberg, Robert David, 0458
Greene, Gayle, xxi, 1182, 2006, 2007, 2889, 2890
Greene, Gayle Jacoba, 2008
Greene, James, xv
Greene, James J., 0459, 1287
Greenfield, Thelma N., xix, 0460, 0593, 1626, 1709, 2361, 2472, 3151, 3197
Greenwood, John Philip Peter, 0461
Greenwood, Kathy Lynn, 1288
Greer, Germaine, 0462
Gregory, Patrick, 0442
Gregson, J. M., 0463
Grenander, M. E., 2211
Grene, David, 0464
Grene, Nicholas, 2890a
Grene, W. D., 1289
Grieve, Thomas F., 0049
Griffin, Jasper, 0464a
Griffin, Robert J., 0465
Griffith, John William, 0465a
Grivelet, Michel, xvi, 0466, 1577, 1827
Grossman, Allen, 0467
Grubb, Shirley Carr, 2455a
Gruber, William, xxi
Gruber, William E., 0468, 1290, 2563
Grudin, Robert, 0469, 2891, 2892
Grund, Gary R., 0470
Guha, P. K., 2893
Guilfoyle, Cherrell, xvii, 1828, 1829
Guilhamet, Leon, xix, 2287
Guj, Luisa, xviii, 2212, 3183
Gupta, Kajal Sen, 2894
Gura, Timothy James, 0471
Gurr, Andrew, xvi, xvii, 1649, 1925
Guthke, Karl S., 0472
Guthrie, Tyrone, 0473

H
Haas, Rudolf, 1241, 2860
Habenicht, Rudolph E., 0049
Habib, Imtiaz Hasan, 2895
Habicht, Werner, 2647, 3125
Hackett, Michael Joseph III, 0474

Haffenreffer, Karl, 1760
Hageman, Elizabeth H., 1935
Hager, Alan, xviii, 0475, 2009
Hale, D. G., xvi, 1650, 1651
Hale, David G., 1652
Hale, David George, 1653
Hale, John K., 0476
Hale, John R., 0477
Halio, Jay L., 0478, 0576, 1542, 1590, 1654, 2010, 2896
Hall, Anne Drury, 0479
Hall, Joan Lord, 1291, 1292
Hall, Marie Boas, 0480
Hall, Michael, 0481
Halle, Louis J., 1293
Hallett, Charles, 1294
Halliday, F. E., xiii, 0482, 0483
Hamer, Mary, 1295
Hamill, Monica J., 2251
Hamilton, A. C., xii, xxii, 0022, 0484, 2734, 3130
Hamilton, Donna, xv
Hamilton, Donna B., 1296, 2564, 2565
Hamlin, Will, 3094a
Hammer, Letha Ann Graves, 0485
Hammersmith, James Philip, 0486
Hammil, Carrie Esther, 0487
Hammond, Anthony, 2456
Hammond, Paul, 2213
Hampton, Christopher, 2640
Hampton, Timothy, 2011
Handelman, Susan, 2641
Handwerk, Gary, 12691
Hanifin, Michael J. F., 0103
Hankins, John E., xvi, 1543
Hankins, John Erskine, 0488
Hanna, Sara, xi, 0489
Hansen, Abby Jane Dubman, 0490, 2330
Hansen, Erik, 1007
Hansen, J. W., xxi, 2735
Hanson, John Arthur, 0491
Hapgood, Robert, 0023, 0062, 0352, 0492, 0492a, 1297, 2012, 2013
Haponski, William Charles, 0493
Harbage, Alfred, 0494, 0495, 0496
Harder, Helga Irene Kutz, 0497
Harder, Kelsie B., 0249
Harding, D. W., 0498
Harding, F. J. W., 0499
Hardison, O. B., 0500
Hardison, O. B. Jr., xviii, 0501, 0502, 0503, 0504, 2159
Hardman, C. D., xxii, 3184
Hardman, Christopher, 3184a
Hardy, Barbara, 0504a, 0505
Hargreaves, George Brooks, 1298
Hargreaves, H. A., 2897
Harley, Maria Power, 1543a
Harlow, C. G., 1906
Harner, James L., 0023a, 0023b
Harp, Richard L., 3185
Harrier, Richard C., 1299

Harris, Bernard, 0556, 0578, 0581, 0829, 1114, 1415, 1571, 2119
Harris, Duncan, 1740a
Harris, Duncan S., 1300
Harris, Sharon M., xxii, 2898
Harrison, Thomas P., 0182, 0295, 0506, 2421
Harrold, William E., xx, 2533
Hart, Edward L., 2899
Hart, Jonathan, 3131
Hart, William Joel, 0507
Hartigan, Karelisa V., 1040, 2596
Hartman, Geoffrey, 2880, 2885
Hartman, Geoffrey H., 2433
Hartmann, Geoffrey, 2340a
Hartsock, Mildred E., 1301, 2013a
Hartveit, Lars, 2994
Hartwig, Joan, 0508
Harvey, John, 0509
Harvey, Nancy Lenz, 2192
Harwood, Ellen Aprill, 3132
Haselkorn, Anne M., 1349
Hassel, Chris R. Jr., xx, 2457
Hassel, Rudolph Christopher Jr., 0510
Hathorn, Richard Y., 1830
Hatlen, Burton, 2014
Hattaway, Michael, xvii, 1934
Haupt, G. E., 0511
Hauser, Arnold, 0512
Hawkes, Terence, xviii, 0513, 1302, 1303, 2193
Hawkins, Harriett, 0514, 0515, 2015, 2016, 2409
Hawkins, Harriett Bloker, 0516
Hawkins, Peter S., 1303a
Hawkins, Sherman, xiii, 0517, 0518, 0519
Hayse, Joseph M., 0519a
Heaney, Seamus, 2641a
Heath, James M., 2627
Hebert, Catherine A., 2160
Hedayet, A. A. El. A., 1304
Hedrick, Carlyle Paff, 0520
Hedrick, Donald Keith, 1831
Heffner, Ray L. Jr., 1305
Heilman, R. B., 2139
Heilman, Robert, xvi, 2170
Heilman, Robert B., 0521, 0522, 0523, 0524, 1578
Heinemann, Margot, 1306
Heisler, Ron, 3095
Helgerson, Richard, 1832
Heller, Agnes, 0525
Helms, Lorraine, xxii, 2362, 2900
Helphinstine, Frances, 1655
Helsa, David H., 0526
Helton, Tinsley, xviii, 2194, 2901
Henderson, Archibald, 1656
Hendricks-Wenck, Aileen Alana, 1307
Heninger, S. K. Jr., xiv, 0002, 0527, 0528, 0529
Henn. T. R., 0530
Hennedy, John F., 2565a
Henning, Standish, 2288, 3066

Henry, Graeme, 1308
Henry, Karen S., 2017
Henze, Richard, 1579, 2018, 2288a
Henze, Richard Harold, 0531
Herbert, Edward T., 2019
Herbert, T. Walter, 1309, 2289
Herndl, George C., 0532
Herrick, Marvin T., 0533, 0534
Heyartz, Irene, 0535
Heyworth, P. L., 2047
Hiatt, Ann Carolyn, 2161
Hibbard, G. R., 0062, 0319a, 0536, 0537, 0538, 0539, 0807, 1310, 1657, 2195, 2642, 2736, 2736a, 3064a, 3103
Hibbard, George R., 0540
Hicks, Cora Eiland, 0541
Hieatt, A. Kent, 1761
Hieatt. A. Kent, 2491
Hieatt, Charles W., 1543b
Higdon, David Leon, 2458
Higgins, Anne, xv, 1311
Higgins, Lynn A., 2413
Hiken, Arlin J., 2902
Hiles, Jane, 2737
Hill, Archibald A., 0182, 0295, 2421
Hill, James L., 1312
Hill, R. E., 1658
Hilliard, Margret Wilson, 0542
Hillman, Richard, xx, 1313, 2410
Hinchcliffe, Judith, 0023c
Hinely, Jan Lawson, xix, 2265
Hinman, Charlton, 2643
Hirsh, James, 2738
Hirsh, James E., 0544
Hobday. C. H., xix
Hobday, C. H., 0545, 2353
Hobsbaum, Philip, 0546
Hochberg, Shifra, 0547
Hockey, Dorothy C., xx, 2443
Hodgdon, Barbara, 2903
Hoeniger, F. D., xvi, 0061, 0547a, 1762, 2363
Hoeniger, F. David, 0024
Hoey, M. P., 2021
Hogan, Patrick Colm, 0830
Holbrook, David, 0548, 2644
Holbrook, Peter James, 1659
Holderness, Graham, xv, 1314
Holdsworth, R. V., 2645, 2738a
Holland, Joanne, xxii
Holland, Joanne Field, 3186
Holland, Norman N., 0549, 1346, 1470
Holland, Peter, 0940a, 2290
Hollander, John, 0550
Holleran, James V., 2291
Hollindale, Peter, 1315
Holloway, John, 0551
Holloway, Julia B., 2331
Holmer, Joan Ozark, 2332
Holstun, James, 1660
Holt, Douglas Leigh Jr., 1661
Holt, Leigh, 1662

Index of Modern Scholars

Homan, Sidney, xviii, 0552, 1316, 1317, 1346, 1470, 2022, 2534
Homan, Sidney R., 1318
Hondo, Masao, 2566
Honigmann, E. A. J., xvi, xxi, 0553, 1318a, 1833, 2022a, 2076, 2459, 2646, 2904
Honigmann, Ernest A. J., 0553a
Hooker, Deborah A., 2905
Hooker, J. M., 2566a, 2588a
Hooks, Roberta M., 1319
Hoover, Claudette, 2161a
Hoover, Sister Mary Frederic, 0554
Hope, Alec Derwent, 1320
Horálek, Karel, 1834
Hornblower, Simon, xxiii
Horner, Winifred, xii
Horner, Winifred Bryan, 0025
Horowitz, David, 0555
Horstmann, Ulrich, 0905a
Hosley, Richard, xiii, 0494, 0556, 1011, 1370, 1763, 2535, 3182
Hotine, Margaret, 2906
Houser, David J., 2907
Housman, A. E., 0072
Houston, John Porter, 0557, 0558
Howard, Jean E., 1608, 1728
Howarth, Herbert, 0559, 0560, 0561
Howarth, R. G., 0183, 1142, 1321
Howatson, M. C., xi
Howe, Quincy Jr., 2006
Hoy, Cyrus, 0562
Hoyle, James, 0563
Hubank, Roger, 1410
Hubert, Judd D., 1834a
Hubler, Edward, 0564
Huebert, Ronald, 2266
Huffman, Clifford Chalmers, xxi, 0041, 1663, 1664, 1665, 2739, 2740
Hughes, Geoffrey, 0565, 0566
Hughes, Vivienne, 0566a
Hughes-Hallett, Lucy, 1322
Hull, Keith, 1740a
Hulme, Hilda, 0567, 0568
Hulme, Hilda M., 0026, 0569, 0570
Hulme, Peter, 2567
Hulse, Clark, xiv, 0571
Hulse, S. Clark, xix, xxii, 0572, 2741, 3133
Hulse, S. Clark III, 2411
Hulse, Shirley Clark III, 0573
Hume, Robert D., xv, 1323
Humphreys, A. R., 0062, 0574, 1914, 1926
Humphreys, Arthur, 0575, 2023, 2024
Hunningher-Schilling, Erica, 2233
Hunt, John Dixon, 0002, 0576, 2647
Hunt, Maurice, xviii, 0577, 1543c, 1666, 1667, 2252, 2742, 3186a, 3187
Hunter, G. K., xiv, xxi, 0057, 0217, 0578, 0579, 0580, 0581, 0582, 0583, 0584, 0585, 0586, 1310, 2742a, 2743, 2857, 2908
Hunter, George K., 0587
Hunter, Robert G., 1324

Hunter, William B. Jr., 2214
Hurst, Mary L., 2909
Hurstfield, Joel, 0209, 0219
Husain, Syed Sajjad, 0618, 0722
Hussey, S. S., 0588
Hutchings, W., 1668
Hutton, James, ix, xxiii
Huzar, Eleanor G., 1325
Hyland, Peter, 2910
Hyman, Stanley Edgar, 1326
Hymel, Cynthia D., 1326a

I
Ibrahim, Gamal Abdel-Nasser T., 2536
Ide, Richard S., 0589, 0590
Ide, Richard Smyth, 0591
Ingram, Angela J. C., 0592
Ingram, R. W., 0593, 0594, 0595, 2911
Ingram, W. G., 2492
Ingram, William, 2568
Irot, M. Kristina Faber, 1544
Isler, Alan D., 1915, 2025
Iwasaki, Soji, 0596, 2162
Iyengar, K. R. Srinivasa, 0597

J
Jackson, B. A. W., 1990
Jackson, B. W., 0575, 0675, 0676, 0747, 1581, 2655, 2806
Jackson, Gabriele Bernhard, 1935
Jackson, MacD. P., xix, 2364, 2743a
Jackson, MacDonald P., 0598
Jackson, R. L. P., 2912
Jackson, Russell, 1327
Jacobs, Henry E., 1764, 2743b
Jacobs, Linda Lee, 0598a
Jacobson, Howard, 0927, 2215
Jaffa, Harry V., 0172, 0599
Jagendorf, Zvi, 0600, 1669, 2913
Jago, David M., 2914
Jahn, J. D., 3134
Jahn, Jerald, xx
Jahn, Jerald D., 2493
Jahn, Jerald Duane, 3135
James, D. G., 2569
James, Max H., 1328
Jamieson, Michael, 1329, 2915
Janakiram, Alar, 0601
Janakiram, Alur, 2412
Jankowski, Andrzej, 2648
Jankowski, Theodora A., 1330
Jankowski, Theodora Ann, 1330a
Janzen, Henry D., 2649
Jardine, Lisa, 0602
Jayne, Sears, 0027
Jefferson, D. W., 0389, 2656
Jefferson,. D. W., 1845
Jeffrey, David L., 2333
Jenkins, Harold, x, xvii, 0603, 1835
Jenkins, Raymond, 0604, 2163
Jensen, Enjer J., 0605
Jensen, Paul A., 1331

Jewett, Mike, 0606
Jochum, Klaus Peter, 0607
Johansson, Stig, 2994
Johnson, Anthony L., 1332, 1333
Johnson, Paula, 3136
Johnson, Robert, 2744
Johnson, Robert C., 1670
Johnson, Vernon E., 1670a
Johnson, W. R., 1836
Johnston, Arthur, 1837
Jones, David E., 2916
Jones, David Edwards, 0608
Jones, Eldred, 0609
Jones, Eldred D., 2745
Jones, Emrys, xv, 0610, 1334, 1335, 1765
Jones, G. P., xv
Jones, Gordon P., 1336, 1438
Jones, Thora Burnley, 1410
Jones, William John, 0611
Jones, William M., 1337
Jones-Davies, M. T., 0672, 2066, 2917
Jones-Davies, Margaret, 1838
Jones-Davies, Marie-Thérèse, 0200, 1404, 1838
Jorgensen, Paul, 1907
Jorgensen, Paul A., 0612, 0613, 1338, 1580, 2216
Jose, Nicholas, 1339
Joseph, B. L., 1839
Josephs, Lois, 1340
Jowitt, J. A., 0903, 3019, 3022, 3026, 3030
Jump, John, 0062, 2026

K
Kahane, Claire, 2793
Kahn, Coppélia, xx, xxii, 0057, 0386, 0614, 1590, 2413, 2414, 2650, 3137
Kaiser, Gerhard, xiv
Kaiser, Gerhard W., 0615
Kaiser, Walter, 0616
Kallendorf, Craig, xii, 0028, 0029
Kalmey, Robert P., xv, 1341
Kamachi, Mitsuru, 2918
Kaminsky, Judith, 2415
Kantas, Alexander Anastasios, 0617
Kanzer, Mark, 2027
Kaplan, Marion, 2383
Kappeler, Susanne, 2923
Karim, Md. Enamul, 0618
Karr, Judith M., 2746
Kastan, David Scott, 0619, 1342, 1840
Kaufmann, R. J., xxi, 0620, 2028, 2919
Kaul, R. K., xvi, 1545
Kaula, David, xviii, 1343, 2029, 2494, 2920, 2921
Kavros, Harry Emanuel, 0621
Kay, Dennis, 2569a
Kayser, John R., xiii, 0622
Kazarian, Albert I., 0623
Keach, William, 3138
Keach, William Carroll, 3139
Kearney, Colbert, 2030

Kearns, Torrance Brophy, 0624
Keast, W. R., 2170
Keeton, George W., 0625
Kehler, Dorothea, 1207
Kelleher, V. M. K., 2922
Kelly, Lois, 0626
Kelly, William Joseph, 1344
Kendall, Gillian Murray, 2747
Kenevan, Phyllis B., 2331
Kennedy, George, 2031
Kennedy, Milton Boone, 0057
Kennedy, William J., 1345
Kermode, Frank, 0362, 0629, 2923, 3188
Kermode, J. F., 0627, 0628
Kernan, Alvin, 0630, 1841
Kernan, Alvin B., 0631, 1841a
Kerrigan, John, xviii, 2184, 2495, 2651
Kerrigan, William, 1346
Kettle, Arnold, 0637, 0775, 1406
Keyes, Laura Catherine, 0632
Khanna, Urmila, 0633
Kiefer, Frederick, xi, xii, 0030, 0031, 0634, 0635
Kiefer, Harry Christian, 0636
Kiernan, V. G., 0637
Kiliński, Janusz, 2468a
Kilpatrick, Ross, 1842
Kim, Kwang-Ho, 1671
Kimbrough, Robert, 0637a, 0638, 2924, 2925, 2926, 2927, 2928, 3066
Kindred, Jerome Clayton, 1348
King, Bruce, 1671a
King, Katherine Callen, 2570
King, Rosalind, 2652
King, T. J., 2164
King, Walter N., 3081
Kinney, Arthur F., 1935, 2165
Kinney, Clare, 1349
Kinney, Joseph A. Jr., 2032
Kinsley, Dominic Alfonso, 1350
Kirov, Fodor T., 2748
Kirsch, Arthur, 0002
Kirsch, James, 2570a
Kirschner, Teresa J., 0639
Kishlansky, Mark A., 1672
Kistner, A. L., 2749
Kistner, M. K., 2749
Kitto, H. D. F., 0640, 1010, 1673, 1674
Klause, John, xxii, 3140
Klein, David, 0641
Klein, H. M., 1842a
Klein, Joan Larsen, 1843
Klein, Theodore M., 0440
Klene, Mary Jean, 0642
Kliman, Bernice W., xviii, 2242a
Klink, Eileen Smith, 0643
Knapp, Peggy, xix
Knapp, Peggy A., 1330, 1345, 2292
Knapp, Peggy Ann, 2365
Knight, G. Wilson, 0061, 0644, 0645, 0646, 0647, 2654, 2655
Knight, George Wilson, 0648

Index of Modern Scholars

Knight, W. Nicholas, 2033, 2034, 2035
Knight, William Nicholas, 2036
Knight, Wilson, 2936
Knights, L. C., 2036a, 2656
Knowles, Richard, xvi, 1546, 1547, 3066
Knowles, Richard Paul, 0649
Kobayashi, Minoru, 2496
Koffler, Richard, 1213
Kohler, Richard C., 0650
Koinm, Albert J., 2929
Kolb, Catherine Sutton, 2930
Kolin, Philip C., 0032, 2750
Kollmann, Judith J., 2309
Konigsberg, Ira, 0439
Konstan, David, 2657
Kopper, John M., 2931
Koskenniemi, Inna, 0650a
Koskimies, Rafael, xx, 2497
Kossick, S. G., 0651
Kott, Jan, xvi, xx, 0652, 1766, 1844, 2292, 2571, 2572
Kowalski, Carl Francis, 1675
Kozikowski, Stanley J., 1351, 2253
Kozikowski, Stanley John, 0653
Kraemer, Don J. Jr., 2037
Kramer, Jerome A., 2415, 2573
Kramer, Joseph E., 2751, 2752
Kranz, David L., 0654, 1352
Kranz, David Lord, xiii, 0656
Krause, David Harold, 1352a
Kreiswirth, Martin, 2392
Kreps, Barbara Irene, 2932
Krohn, Janis, 1353
Kronenfeld, Judy Z., xv, 1548, 1549
Kronenfeld, Judy Zahler, 1550
Krook, Dorothea, xv, 0083, 1354
Kruegel, Sister Mary Flavia, 0657
Krueger, Robert, 0658
Kujawińska-Courtney, Krystyna, 1354a, 2933
Kujoory, Parvin, 0659
Kuriyama, Constance, xv
Kuriyama, Constance B., 1558
Kuriyama, Constance Brown, 1355
Kurland, Stuart M., 2038
Kurrik, Maire Jaanus, 2657a
Kushari, Ketaki, 0660
Kytzler, Bernhard, 1676

L
LaBelle, Jenijoy, 2217
LaBranche, Linda, 2934
LaBranche, Linda Berning, 2935
Labriola, Albert, xv, 1356
Labriola, Albert Christy, 1357
LaBriola, Joseph Charles, 0661
LaCerva, Patricia, 0662
Lacey, Stephen Wallace, 2753
Lake, James, xxii
Lake, James H., 3141
LaMar, Virginia A., 0065
Lamb, M. E., xxii, 2293, 3082
Lamb, Mary Ellen, 2754, 3189

Lampson, Robin, 1844a
Lanahan, William Francis, 0663
Lancashire, Anne, xxi, 2658
Landis, Joan Hutton, 0663a
Landman, Sidney James, 0664
Landry, Hilton, 2498, 2499, 2509, 2516
Langbaum, Robert, 2574
Langford, Larry, 2294
Langman, F. H., 1677, 1678, 2936
Lanham, Richard A., xxiii, 0665, 2416
Laroque, François, 0666, 0667, 3189a, 3190
Larson, Gale Kjelshus, 0668
Larson, Marilyn, 1358
Latham, Jacqueline E. M., xx, 2500, 2575, 2576
Latif, Eva Leoni, 0669
Laub, Martin, 1359
Lavine, Anne Rabiner, 2937
Lawlor, John, 0670
Lawrence, Harold Whitney, 2366
Lawrence, Judiana, 1767
Lawrence, Larry Lee, 0671
Leavenworth, Russell E., 1360
Lecercle, Ann, xv, 0672, 1157, 2253a, 2295, 2938
Lechay, Daniel T., 1679
Lee, B. S., 3191
Lee, Brian S., 0586
Lee, G. M., 2296
Lee, Sung-Il, 0673
Lee, Virgil Jackson Jr., 0674
Leech, Clifford, xvii, 0116, 0630, 0675, 0676, 0677, 1674, 1827, 1845, 2715, 2736, 3093, 3096, 3097, 3142
Lees, F. N., 2577
Lees, Francis Noel, xxii, 3192
Leggatt, Alexander, xiii, 0678, 0679, 1680
Legouis, Pierre, xxi, 2755
Leimberg, Inge, 3193, 3194
Leishman, J. B., 2501
Leisi, Ernst, 1561
Lenson, David, 0680
Lenz, Carolyn Ruth Swift, 1182, 2890
Leonard, Frances McNeely, 0503, 0658
Leonard, Nancy S., 2939
Lepley, Jean, 1680a
Lerner, Laurence, 0681, 1361, 1551, 2502
Lessenich, Rolf P., 2940
Lettieri, Ronald J., xiii, 0622
Levang, Lewis D., 2039
Levenson, Jill, 2941
Lever, J. W., 0033, 0682, 0683, 0684, 2243, 2417, 3143
Levi, Peter, xiii, 0685, 2503
Levin, Carole, 2758, 2790
Levin, Harry, 0362, 0686, 0687, 1362, 1581, 1582, 2659
Levin, Lawrence L., 1908
Levin, M. H., 1846
Levin, Richard, 2418, 2942
Levine, Laura Ellen, 0688
Levine, Richard A., 1846

Levith, Murray J., 0689, 0690
Levitsky, Ruth, xix, 2334, 2660
Levitsky, Ruth M. ., 1848
Lewalski, B. K., xix, 2320
Lewalski, Barbara K., 2321
Lewalski, Barbara Kiefer, 0424, 2400
Lewis, Allen, 2661
Lewis, Anthony, xviii, 2254
Lewis, Anthony J., 0691
Lewis, Anthony Joseph, 0692
Lewis, C. S., 0813
Lezberg, Amy Kirle, xv, 1363
Liebler, Naomi Conn, 2040
Lief, Madelon, 3098
Lievsay, John Leon, 1022
Lim, C. S., xix, 2335
Limouze, Henry S., 1062, 2589, 3027
Lindenbaum, Peter Alan, 0693
Lindheim, Nancy, 3144
Lindheim, Nancy R., 2166
Lindley, David, 2578, 2943
Lindsay, Jack, 1364
Lings, Martin, 0694
Linn, Robert James, 0695
Little, Nancy Glass, 0696
Littlewood, J. C. F., 1681, 1682
Livermore, Ann, 0697
Lloyd, Michael, 0698, 1163
Logan, George M., xx, 1761, 1774, 2444
Logan, Marie Rose, 1965
Logan, Robert A., 1365
Loggins, Vernon P., 2944, 2945
Loggins, Vernon Porter, 2945a
Lombardo, Agostino, xxi, 2662, 2946
Long, John, xiv
Long, John H., 0699, 0700, 1366
Long, Michael, 0701
Long, T. H., 0267
Long, Timothy, xvi, 1583
Long, William B., 1632b, 1732
Longo, Joseph A., 1367, 1683, 2297, 2947
Longo, Joseph Anthony, 0702
Loomba, Ania, 0703
Lorant, André, 1849
Lord, George deForest, 1841a, 2854
Lordi, Robert J., 0704
Loughrey, Bryan, 1229, 1247, 1265, 1280,
  1281, 1314, 1315, 1400, 1425, 1509
Low, J. F., 2041
Lowe, Lisa, 1684
Lowenthal, David, 2042
Lucking, David, 2578a
Luckyj, Christina, 1685
Ludowyk, E. F. C., 2043
Lyle, E. B., 2218
Lyman, Stanford M., 0705
Lynch, Barbara Furber, 0706
Lynch, James Joseph, 0707
Lynch, John Patrick, 2545
Lynch, Robert E., 1686
Lynch, Stephen, 2948
Lynch, Stephen J., 2949, 2950

Lynch, Stephen Joseph, 2951
Lyons, Bridget, xvii
Lyons, Bridget Gellert, 1850
Lyons, Charles, 2952
Lyons, Charles R., 0708, 1368
Lyons, Clifford, 1369, 1370
Lyons, Clifford P., 2953, 2954
Lyons, John D, 1834a
Lyons, M., 2044

M
Macaraig-Profeta, Lydia, 2955
MacCallum, M. W., 0005
MacDonald, Joyce Green, 0709, 2756
MacDonald, Michael, 0002
MacDonald, Ronald R., 1370a
Macey, Samuel L., 2336
MacIntyre, Jean, 1687, 2167
Mack, Maynard, 1371, 1841a, 2854
Mackail, J. W., 0072
MacKenzie, Clayton G., 1372, 2445
Mackinnon, Lachlan, 2956
Maclean, Norman, 2170
MacMullan, Katherine Vance, 1373
Maes-Jelinek, Hena, 2775a
Magnusson, A. Lynne, 1688
Magnusson, Augusta Lynne, 0710
Maguin, Jean-Marie, 2045, 2046
Maguire, Nancy Klein, 2971
Maher, Michael Kevin, 2663
Mahon, John W., 0529, 0711, 2826, 3195
Mahood, M. M., 2255
Main, William W., 2957
Majors, G. W., 2419
Makaryk, Irena Rima, 0712
Malagi, R. A., 1851
Mallery, Mary Aileen, 1374
Mallin, Eric S., 2958
Mallin, Eric Scott, 2959
Mandel, Oscar, 0713
Manley, Frank, 1852
Manlove, Colin N., 0714
Mann, Jill, 2960
Manzalaoui, M. A., 2047
Maquerlot, Jean-Pierre, 2253a
Marathe, Sudhakar, 1584
Marchant, Robert, 1375
Marcotte, Paul, 0715
Marcus, Jane, 2757
Marcus, Leah, 1689
Marder, Louis, 0716
Margeson, J. M. R., 0116, 0717, 1674, 1827,
  2736, 3093
Markels, Julian, 0718, 1376, 2219
Marker, Lise-Lone, 1853
Marsh, D. R. C., 1768
Marsh, Derick R. C., 0719, 1377, 2961
Marsh, George Reid Jr., xiv, 0720
Marshall, Cynthia, xix, 2048, 2367, 2758
Marshall, Roderick, 0720a
Martín, María Jesús Pérez, 1378
Martin, Randall, 2537

Index of Modern Scholars

Martin, William Franklin, 2168
Martindale, Charles, xiii, xiv, 0721, 0815, 0918, 1551, 2448, 2502
Martindale, Michelle, xiii, 0721
Martino, Alberto, 0648, 1095
Martland, T. R., 2048a
Martz, Louis, xxii, 3196
Martz, Louis L., 1085a
Marx, Steven, 1551a
Mason, H. A., 1379, 1380, 1381
Matchett, William H., xix, 1382, 2384
Matinuddin, Abu Rushd, 0722
Mattern, Evelyn Joseph, 1546
Matthews, Honor, 0723
Matthews, Roger, 1383
Maus, Katharine Eisaman, 2420
Maveety, S. R., 3197
Maxwell, J. C., 0724, 0725, 0726, 1585, 1738, 1937, 2049, 2050, 2446, 2504, 2664, 2962
Maxwell-Mahon, W. D., 1384
May, Robin, 0727
Mazzeo, Joseph A., 0229
McAlindon, T., xiii, xiv, 0728, 0729, 2963
McAlindon, Thomas, 0730, 2051
McAvoy, William C., 3082a
McCall, John, 0731
McCanles, Michael, 1690, 2220
McClelland, John, 2051a
McCombie, Frank, 1855
McConnel, Frances Hunt Ruhlen, 2052
McCown, Gary M., xx, 2469
McCown, Gary Mason, 2470
McCullen, J. T. Jr., 2169
McDonald, Charles O., 1856
McDonald, Charles Osborne, 1857
McDonald, Russ, 0732
McElroy, Bernard, 0733
McFarland, Ronald E., 0734
McFarland, Thomas, 1691
McFarlane, Brian, 1269, 1308
McGann, Jerome J., 0553a, 2904
McGee, Arthur, xviii
McGee, Arthur R., 2221
McGovern, D. S., 2579
McGrail, Mary Ann, 0735
McGrath, Michael J. Gargas, 2279
McGuire, Philip C., 1178, 3031
McIntosh, William, xix
McIntosh, William A., 2368
McIntosh, William Alexander, 0736
McKay, Margaret Rachel, 0737
McKenzie, Stanley D., 1692
McKernan, John J., 2505
McKernan, John Joseph, 2506
McLean, Susan Kay, 1858
McMahon, C. E., 0738
McMahon, Robert, 2256
McManaway, James, 0718
McManaway, James G., 0294, 0564, 1385, 1473, 1475, 1539, 1790, 1797, 2709, 2868
McMillan, Douglas, 0739
McNamara, Robert Jeremy, 0740
McNamee, Lawrence F., 0034, 0035, 0036
McNeir, Waldo, 3197
McNeir, Waldo F., 0460, 0593, 1626, 1709, 2053, 2472, 3151
McPeek, James A. S., 2298
McPherson, David, xxii, 3083
McQuain, Jeffrey Hunter, 0741
McRoberts, J. Paul, 0037
Mead, Stephen X., 2964
Mebane, John S., 2580
Mebane, John Spencer, 2581
Medcalf, Stephen, 2964a
Mehl, Dieter, 0742, 2965
Melchiori, Barbara Arnett, 2966
Melchiori, Giorgio, 0743, 2337
Mellers, Wilfrid, 0744
Melrose, Susan, 2054
Meltzer, Gary Stephen, 1386
Mendelsohn, Leonard Richard, 2967
Mendilow, A. A., 0745
Mendl, R. W. S., 0746
Merchant, W. Moelwyn, 0747, 2222, 2257
Mercier, Joseph Raymond, 2968
Meredith, Peter, 1387
Merkels, Ingrid, 0968
Merrix, Robert, xvii, 2447
Merrix, Robert P., 1927, 3145
Meserole, Harrison T., 0049
Meszaros, Patricia K., 1693
Metz, G. Harold, xxi, 2759, 2760, 2760a, 3099
Meyer, Russell Joseph, 3146
Michael, Nancy C., 2369
Michael, Nancy Carolyn, 1694
Michel, Laurence, 0748, 0749
Michel, Pierre, 2775a
Micheli, Linda McJ., 1939
Michel-Michot, Paulette, 2775a
Middleton, David Loren, 1769
Midgaard, Anne, 2055
Mikesell, Margaret Lael, 2338
Miklachki, Jody Beth, 1770
Miles, Gary B., 0750
Miles, Thomas Geoffrey, 0751
Millard, Barbara C., 1542
Miller, Anthony, 1695, 2056
Miller, Donald S., 0752
Miller, J. Hillis, 2969
Miller, Milton, 1387a
Miller, William E., 0753, 1552
Mills, Laurens J., 1388
Milward, Peter, 0754, 0755, 0756
Mincoff, M., 2761
Mincoff, Marco, xiii, xxi, 0757, 0758, 0759
Miner, Earl, 1275
Miola, Robert S., xi, xiii, xvii, xviii, xix, 0759a, 0759b, 1771, 1859, 2057, 2058, 2339, 2665, 2762
Miola, Robert Steven, 0760
Mise, Raymond S., 2059
Miskimin, Alice S., 2970

Mitchell, Bruce, 1389
Mitchell, Charles, 1696
Mitchell, Charles Edgar, 0761
Mitchell, Dennis S., 1390
Mitchell, Robin Norman, 1391
Mitra, P. K., 1697
Miyauchi, Bunshichi, 1392
Moffet, Robin, 1772
Molan, Ann, 2060
Monitto, Gary V., 1860
Monsarrat, Gilles D., 0762
Montano, Rocco, 0763
Montgomery, H. C., 2044
Montgomery, Robert L. Jr., 2421
Montrose, Louis Adrian, xviii, 2196, 2197
Mooney, Michael E., 1393, 2061
Moore, James A., 2460
Moore, John Rees, 1394
Moore, Nancy, 2062
Morgan, Margery, 1395
Morris, Alton C., 1032, 1309, 2953
Morris, Harry, 1553
Morris, Helen, 1396, 1397
Morris, Ivor, 0764
Morrison, Mary, 1398
Morsberger, Robert E., 2666
Morse, 2667
Morse, David, 0765
Morton, A. E., 0766
Mosbacher, Eric, 0512
Moseley, C. W. R. D., 0767, 1399, 1773
Moseley, Charles, 1400
Moseley, Francis Sheeran, 0768
Mossner, Ernest C., 0182, 0295, 2421
Motohashi, Edward Tetsuya, 2063
Motto, Anna Lydia, 0038
Mowat, Barbara, xi, 0769, 0770
Mowat, Barbara A., 2299, 2582, 2971
Mowat, Barbara Sue Adams, 0771
Moynihan, Robert D., 2064
Mueller, Martin, xiii, xvii, xxii, 0772, 0773, 1909, 3198
Muir, Kenneth, xx, 0061, 0062, 0354, 0355, 0356, 0586, 0683, 0774, 0775, 0776, 0777, 0778, 0779, 0780, 0781, 1074, 1401, 1402, 1403, 1817, 1861, 2422, 2507, 2508, 2972, 3147, 3182
Mukherji, A. D., 0782
Mukherji, Asoke Kumar, 2065
Müllenbrock, Heinz-Joachim, 1241, 2860
Mullin, Donald C., 0783
Mulryne, J. R., 0235, 1404, 2066, 2076
Munich, Adrienne Auslander, 2900
Munkelt, Marga, 1468
Murakami, Toshio, 0784
Murerji, Ena, 0785
Murphree, A. A., 1032, 1309, 2953
Murphy, Avon Jack, 0786
Murphy, Georgeann, 2198, 2300
Murphy, James J., 1073
Murphy, Patrick Martin, 3148
Murr, Priscilla, 1405

Murray, Gilbert, 0061
Murray, Patrick, 0787, 1698
Murty, G. Srirama, 2067

N
Nagarajan, M. S., xviii, 2170
Nagarajan, S., 2987
Naito, Kenji, 2223
Nakayama, Randall Shige, 2973
Namm, Milton, 0788
Nandy, Dipak, 1406
Nass, Barry, 2340, 2974
Nass, Barry Nathan, 0789
Nass, Verna Marlene, 0795
Nathan, Norman, 0790, 2068
Neely, Carol Thomas, 1182, 1407, 2890
Neiditz, Minerva, 2668
Neiditz, Minerva Helen, 0791
Neill, Michael, 0792
Nejgebauer, A., 0039
Nelson, C. E., 1408
Nelson, Conny Edwin, 0793
Nelson, Thomas Allen, 0794, 3199
Nemoianu, Virgil, 1699, 1700
Nesbitt, Bruce, 0049
Neumeyer, Peter F., 1701, 1702
Neuville, H. Richmond Jr., 0796
Nevo, Ruth, 0797, 0798, 0799, 1409, 2763
Newey, Vincent, 1131
Newkirk, Glen Alton, 0800
Newlin, Jeanne T., 2975
Newman, Charles, 0686
Newman, Karen, 0801
Newman, Karen Alison, 0802
Nichols, Mariane, 2669
Nichols, Marianna da Vinci, 2670
Nicholson, Eric Arthur, 2976
Nicol, Bernard de Bear, 1410
Niculescu, Luminitsa, 0802a
Niculescu, Luminitsa Irene, 0803
Nielsen, Hans Freda, 1007
Nochimson, Richard L., 1411
Norem, Lois, 1680
Norgaard, Holger, 2274
Norvell, Betty G., 0803a
Norvell, Betty Jeannine Groah, 0804
Nosworthy, J. M., 0062, 0805, 0806, 0807, 2199, 2623
Novy, Marianne, 0807a, 1412
Nowottny, Winifred, 0808, 0809, 1413, 2509
Nugent, S. Georgia, 0810
Nunes, Herta Maria F. de Queiroz, 1414
Nuttall, A. D., xvi, xx, 0811, 0812, 0812a, 0813, 0814, 0815, 1862, 2448, 2671

O
Oates, J. C., 2977
O'Connor, Marion F., 1608, 1728
O'Dea, Raymond, 0816
Ogden, James, 2978
Okerlund, Arlene N., 2979
Oliver, H. J., 0816a, 1854, 2538

Index of Modern Scholars

Olleson, Edward, 2943
Olson, David Bennett, 0817
Olson, Elder, 0818, 0819, 2170
O'Malley, Sister Judith Marie, 0820
Ong, W. J., 2510
Orgel, Stephen, 1648, 2583
Orkin, M. R., 0821
Orkin, Martin R., 2068a
Orme, Nicholas, 0821a
Ormerod, David, xix, 2301, 2322
Ornstein, Robert, 0822, 1415
Orr, David, 0823
Osborn, Neal J., 0824
Oshio, Toshiko, 2511
Ostwald, Barbara Lynne, 0825
Otten, Charlotte F., 1863
Owen, Trevor, 2980
Owen, Trevor Allen, 2069
Owens, Roger, 2981
Oyama, Toshikazu, 2171
Oyama, Toshiko, 2982
Oz, Avraham, 2070

P
Pacheco, Anita, 0826
Packert-Hall, James Michael, 0827
Pafford, J. H. P., 3083a, 3200
Paglia, Camille, 0828
Painter, Alice Lorraine, 2983
Pal, Jozsef, 0828a
Pal, R. M., 1864
Palmatier, M. A., 3149
Palmer, Barbara D., 2984
Palmer, D. J., xviii, xxii, 0062, 0829, 0829a, 0844, 1668, 2071, 2224, 2258, 2647, 2764, 3084, 3085, 3125, 3182
Palmer, David, 0076, 0814, 2258, 2652
Palmer, Kenneth, x, 2985
Pandit, Lalita, 0830
Pandurangan, Prema, 1416
Paolucci, Anne, xviii, 2225, 2672
Paris, Bernard, 0831, 1470
Paris, Bernard J., 1346, 2072
Parker, Barbara, 0832
Parker, Barbara L., 2073
Parker, Derek, 0832a
Parker, Douglas H., 2302, 2765
Parker, Patricia, xvi, 0833, 1774, 2340a, 2433, 2880, 2885
Parker, R. B., 1703
Parotti, Philip, 2172
Parr, A. N., 0834
Parten, Anne, 2266a
Partridge, A. C., 0040, 0835, 2986
Pasicki, Adam, xix, 2323
Paster, Gail Kern, 0836, 1704, 2074, 2584
Patke, Rajeev S., 2987
Patrick, J. Max, 1417
Patrides, C. A., 1705
Patterson, Annabel, 0837, 1706, 1771
Patterson, Annabel M., 2512
Patton, Jon Franklin, 2423

Pauls, Peter, xxi, 2673, 2674
Paulson, Ronald, 0838
Paxton, Nancy L., 2766
Payne, Michael, 0839, 1418, 2075, 2627
Payne, Michael D., 1082, 2432
Payne, Michael David, 0840
Payne, Robert, 0841
Pearce, T. M., 0842, 2471
Pearlman, E., 0843, 2226
Pearson, D'Orsay W., xix, xx, 2303, 2585, 3089
Pearson, Jacqueline, 0844, 0845
Pechter, Edward, 0041, 2076
Pegg, Barry Malcolm, 3150
Pek, Giselle Mary, 0846
Pellegrini, G., 0847
Pelling, C. B. R., 1419
Pendleton, Thomas A., 0529, 0848, 2826
Penninger, Frieda Elaine, 1215
Percy, LeRoy Pratt Jr., 2424
Perkin, J. R. C., 1417
Perret, Marion, 1420, 2539
Perryman, Judith, 2199b
Perryman, Judith C., 2199a
Peterson, Douglas L., 2077, 2472, 2513, 2586
Peterson, Richard S., 0848a
Petrey, Sandy, 1707
Petronella, Vincent F., xix, 2078, 2385
Phillips, Emerson, 0057
Phillips, James E., 2587
Piccolomini, Manfredi, 0849
Pickford, T. E., 2370
Pinciss, G. M., 2079
Piper, H. W., 1421
Pirkhofer, Anton M., 2514
Pitcher, John, xx, 2588, 2588a
Pitt, Angela, 0849a
Pittock, Malcolm, 2588a
Plasse, Marie Ann, 2767
Platt, Michael, 0850, 0850a, 2425, 2515, 2589
Platt, Michael David, 0851
Pocock, J. G. A., 0002
Pogson, Beryl, 3201
Pohl, Frederick J., 0852
Poisson, Rodney, 1708, 1709, 2516
Pollin, Burton R., 1865
Pollock, John, 1067a
Poole, Adrian, xiv, 0853, 1710
Pope, Maurice, 0854
Popham, Elizabeth Anne, 0855
Porter, Joseph A., xx, 2473
Potter, A. M., xxi, 2988
Potter, Simeon, 0856
Powell, Henry Wesley, xiii, 0857
Powell, Neil, 2989
Powers, Kathleen Emily, 2990
Poynter, F. N. L., 0858
Prager, Carolyn, 0859
Prater, Neal Byron, 0860
Pratt, Norman, 2173
Pratt, Norman T., 2173a

Praz, Mario, 0861
Presson, Robert K., 0862, 2174
Preston, Thomas R., 2675
Price, George R., 1928
Price, H. T., 2768
Price, Hereward T., 2769
Price, Joseph G., 1242, 2776
Priest, Dale G., 1554
Prince, F. T., 0863
Pringle, Roger, 2647, 3125
Prior, Moody, 0864
Prior, Moody E., 2080
Proser, Matthew, 1711
Proser, Matthew N., 0865, 0866, 1866
Proudfoot, G. R., 0062, 2623, 3100
Pughe, Thomas, 2081
Pujante, A. Luis, 1712
Purdom, C. B., 0867
Purdon, Noel, 0868
Putney, Rufus, 1713

Q
Qazi, Javaid, 1867
Quennell, Peter, xiii, 0869
Quinn, Edward, 0459, 1240
Quinn, Edward G., 0012a
Quinn, Michael, 1303, 1714
Quinney, Laura, 1423
Quinones, Ricardo J., 0870, 0871, 1422
Quinones, Richard Joseph, 0872
Quint, David, 1929

R
Rabkin, Norman, 0873, 0874, 1715, 2082, 2991, 3151
Race, William H., 0875
Rackin, Phyllis, 0876, 1716, 2083
Radbill, April, 0877
Radcliffe-Umstead, Douglas, 2519
Radel, Nicholas F., 3098
Rajec, Elizabeth M., 0043
Ramsay, Paul A., 0978
Ramsey, Allen, 3152
Ramsey, Allen Rodell, 3153
Ramsey, Jarold W., xxi, 2676, 2992
Ramsey, Paul A., 0654
Randall, Dale B. J., 3202, 3203
Rao, Kolar Surya Narayana, 2084, 2104
Rao, O. M. Gopala, 0878
Rappoport, Rose, 0879
Rasmussen, Eric, 2677
Rauchut, E. A., 2635
Rauchut, Edward A., 2678
Ray, Bonnie MacDougall, 3204
Ray, Robert H., 1424
Reaske, Christopher, 0880
Rebhorn, Wayne, xxii
Rebhorn, Wayne A., 2085, 3154
Redmond, James, 1214, 1387a, 3090a
Redpath, Theodore, 2492
Reed, James Kennedy, 2259
Reed, Regina Balla, 1717

Reed, Robert Rentoul Jr., 0881
Reedy, Gerard, S. J., xvi, 1868
Rees, Joan, 0882
Reese, Jack E., 2770
Reese, Max Meredith, 0883
Reid, Stephen A., 2679, 2993
Reinelt, Janelle, 2822
Reinert, Otto, 2994
Reinhard, Julia, xvii, 1869
Reinsdorf, Walter, 2085a
Relihan, Constance C., 1718
Renault, Mary, 1930
Reppen, Joseph, 2072
Rexroth, Kenneth, 2227
Reynolds, Peter, 1425
Reynolds, Robert C., 2086
Reynolds, Robert Charles, 2087
Rhinehart, Raymond Patrick, 0884
Rhoads, Diana Akers, 2590
Rhodes, Ernest L., 1426
Ribner, Irving, 0885
Rice, Julian, xvii
Rice, Julian C., 1427, 2088
Rice, Julian Carl, 1428
Richards, Bernard, 1869a
Richardson, Mark Lewis, 2995
Richmond, Hugh M., xvi, 0886, 0887, 1775
Richmond, Velma Bourgeois, 0888
Rickey, Mary Ellen, 1555, 2996
Ricks, Christopher, 0202
Rico, Barbara Roche, 0888a
Ridley, M. L., 0889
Ridlington, Sandra Schwartz, 0890
Riehle, Wolfgang, 0891
Riemer, A. P., 0891a, 1377, 1429
Riemer, Seth Daniel, 1430, 1431
Riggs, David, xiii, 0892, 0893, 0894
Righter, Anne, 0895, 2591
Rinehart, Keith, 1432
Rish, Shirley, 2088a
Rissanen, Matti, xviii, 2228
Rivers, Elias L., 1594
Rivers, Isabel, 0045
Rizzolo, Patricia, 0896
Robbins, Martin Lewis, 0897
Roberts, David A., 2997
Roberts, G. J., 0898
Roberts, Gareth, 1585a
Roberts, Jeanne Addison, xii, xix, xx, 0899, 0900, 0901, 2267, 2540, 3100a
Roberts, Josephine A., 2449
Roberts-Baytop, Adrianne, xiv, 0902
Robertson, Hugh, 0903
Robertson, Jean, 2229
Robertson, Karen, 2758, 2790
Robertson, Mary Catherine, 2998
Robertson, Patricia R., 1433
Robinson, Christopher, 0904, 2680
Robinson, James E., 2304
Robinson, Marsha Studebaker, 2089
Robinson, Randal Fink, 0905
Roche, Thomas P. Jr., 2517

Index of Modern Scholars 805

Rockett, William, 2592
Roerecke, Edith M., 1434
Rogers, Stephen, xix, 2341
Rolle, Dietrich, 0905a
Ronan, Clifford, 0906
Ronan, Clifford J., xviii, 1435, 1869b, 2028, 2090, 2091, 2998a
Rosand, David, 0907
Rose, Mark, 0908, 1178, 1415, 1870, 2091a
Rose, Mary Beth, xxi, 2999
Rose, Paul Lawrence, 1436
Rose, Remington Edward II, 2092
Rosen, Barbara, 2093, 2094
Rosen, William, 2093, 2094
Rosenheim, Judith, xviii, 2244, 2245
Ross, Daniel W., 2681
Ross, Gordon N., 1437
Ross, Lawrence J., 2342
Rossi, Sergio, 2462
Rossiter, A. P., xiii, 0909
Rossiter-Smith, H., 2175
Rossky, William, 1438
Roston, Murray, 0909a
Rothenberg, Alan B., 0910, 3155
Rothschild, Herbert B. Jr., 1439, 1719
Rouda, F. H., 1720
Rouse, W. H. D., 0046, 0910a
Rovine, Harvey, 0911
Rowan, Stephen Charles, 3000
Rowe, George E., 3001
Rowland, Beryl, 3002
Rowse, A. L., xiii, 0912, 0913, 0914, 0915, 0916
Roy, Emil, 3003
Royle, Nicholas, 1440
Rozett, Martha, 0917, 1871
Rozett, Martha Tuck, 1441
Rozsnyai, Balint, 0377a
Rudat, Wolfgang E. H., 1872
Rudd, Niall, xiv, xix, 0918, 2305, 2541
Rudnytsky, Peter L., 1965
Ruoff, James, 1873
Rusche, Harry, 2176
Ruszkiewicz, John J., 2682, 2683, 2684
Ruszkiewicz, John Joseph, 2685
Rutter, Russell Keenan, 3004
Rylands, G. H. W., 0919

S
Saagpakk, Paul F., 0920
Sabol. Andrew J., 0047
Saccio, Peter, 0002
Sacharoff, Mark, xvii, 1994, 2096, 3005, 3006, 3007, 3008
Sacharoff, Mark Leon, 3009
Sachs, Arieh, 1354, 1874
Sacks, Peter, 0921
Sahel, Pierre, 1442
Salgãdo, Gãmini, 0062, 1586
Salingar, L. G., 0922
Salingar, Leo, xiii, 0922a, 0923, 2177
Salmon, Vivian, 0924

Saltzer, Nancy Kay Clark, 0925
Salu, Mary, 2239
Salvat, Michel, 0132a
Samsey, Patricia Jane Collins, 0926
Samuelson, David A., 1178, 3031
Sanders, Frederick K., 0662, 1030
Sanders, Norman, 0506, 0861, 1543, 1937a, 2097, 2098, 2289, 2343, 2604, 2954, 3147
Sanders, Wilbur, 0927
Sandved, Arthur O., 2994
Sandy, Gerald N., 0928
Saner, Reginald, 1443
Sargent, Seymour H., 2099
Saslaw, Naomi Ruth, 0929
Sastri, P. S., 0177, 2708
Satin, Joseph, 0048
Savage, James E., 2686, 3010
Schaar, Claes, 2518
Schalkwyk, David, 2306
Schanzer, Ernest, xiii, 0845, 0930, 0931, 0932, 0933, 2371, 3205
Schechter, Harold, 2636
Schell, E. T., 1875
Scheman, Lillian, 0934
Schleiner, Louise, xvii, 1876
Schlesinger, Giselle, 0019
Schlösser, Anselm, 1721
Schmidgall, Gary, xx, 0935, 2593
Schmitz, Götz, 2426
Schochet, Gordon J., 3208
Schoenbaum, S., xiii, 0002, 0356, 0586, 0683, 0936, 0936a, 0937, 0938, 1074
Schorin, Gerald, 2594
Schork, R. J., 1776
Schrickx, W., 2771
Schrickx, Willem, 2372
Schulman, Norma M., 1444
Schwartz, Elias, 0939, 1445, 1446, 2386, 3011
Schwartz, Jerome, 2519
Schwartz, Louis, 0940
Schwartz, Murray M., 1447, 1590
Scolnicov, Hanna, 0940a
Scott, Marvin B., 0705
Scott, W. I. D., 0941
Scott, William O., xvii, xxii, 0942, 2100, 2687, 3012, 3090
Scoufos, Alice Lyle, 0943
Scoufos, Alice-Lyle, xvi, 1556
Scragg, Leah, xix, 2307
Scuro, Daniel Ervinn, 2772
Seamster, John Allan, 0944
Sears, Lloyd C., 0945
Segal, Charles P., 1877
Seidenberg, Robert, 1722
Seko, Emmanuel Vincent, 0946
Seltzer, Daniel, 2387, 3013
Selzler, Bernard John, 1723
Semon, Kenneth Jeffrey, 0947
Sen, R. K., 0948
Sen, Taraknath, 0258, 2065, 2479
Seng, Peter J., 1448, 3014

Sen Gupta, S. C., 0949, 0950, 0951, 1449
Sen Gupta, Satya Prasad, 2250
Serpieri, Alessandro, 1333, 1540
Sewall, Richard B., xiii, 0952, 0953
Seward, T. C., 2688
Shaaber, M. A., 1916
Shadoian, Jack, 2773
Shady, Raymond C., 2450
Shaffer, Larry E., 2774
Shaheen, Naseeb, 0954, 1724
Shainess, Natalie, 2688a
Shalvi, Alice, xxi, 0745, 0955, 3015
Shanker, Sidney, 0956
Shapiro, Gloria Kaufman, 0957
Shapiro, I. A., xiv, 0958
Shapiro, Michael, 1450
Shapiro, Stephen A., 1451
Shapiro, Susan C., 1452, 1453
Sharma, Ram Bilas, 0959
Sharma, T. R., 1077, 2978
Shaw, Catherine, 1587
Shaw, Catherine M., 2689, 2689a
Shaw, John, 1454, 1455
Shaw, William P., 3016
Shawcross, John T., 0960
Shaw-Smith, R., 1456
Sheidley, William E., 3156
Shenk, Robert, 0961
Shenk, Robert Edwards, 0962
Shepherd, Simon, 0963
Shewring, Margaret, 02351
Shintri, Sarojini, 0964
Shirley, Frances A., 0965, 0966
Shugg, Wallace, 2690
Shulman, Jeff, 1557, 2200
Shulman, Jeff I., 0967
Shumaker, Wayne, xiv, 0968
Sicherman, Carol M., 1725
Siddiqui, M. Naimuddin, 3017
Sider, John William, 0969
Siegel, Aaron Howard, 0970
Siegel, Paul N., xi, 0971, 0972, 0973, 2474, 2691
Siemon, James Edward, 1457
Siemon, James R., 0973a
Siemon, James Ralph, 0974
Sierz, Krystyna, 0974a
Silber, Patricia, 0975
Sillars, Stuart, 2308
Silver, Brenda R., 2413
Silver, Larry, 0976
Simard, Rodney, 1458
Šimko, Ján, 2692
Simmons, J. L., x, xi, 0002, 0041, 0057, 0977, 0978, 0979, 0980, 1459, 2101, 3018
Simmons, Joseph Larry, 0981
Simonds, Peggy Muñoz, 0982, 1726, 1777, 1778, 2521
Simone, R. Thomas, 2427
Simone, Reno Thomas Jr., 2428
Sinfield, Alan, 1878, 3019
Singh, Jyotsna, 0983, 1460

Singh, Satyanarain, 2522
Sircar, Bibhuti Bhusan, 0983a
Sisson, C. J., 0984
Sjögren, Gunnar, 1879
Skemp, J. B., 0985
Skiffington, Lloyd A., 0985a
Sklar, Elizabeth S., 2260
Skulsky, Harold, 1879a, 2178
Skura, Meredith, 0002
Slack, Robert C., 3020
Slater, Eliot, 0986
Slavutych, Yar, 0712
Sledd, James, 0182, 0295, 2421
Slights, Camille, 2102, 3021
Slights, Camille Wells, 2102a
Slights, William W. E., xxi, 2693, 2775, 3085a
Sloan, Thomas O., 2528
Smallwood, R. L., 2076
Smidt, Kristian, 0986a, 2775a
Smith, A. J., 0986b
Smith, Alan R., 2103
Smith, Bruce R., 0986c, 0987, 0988, 0989, 0990, 0991, 0992
Smith, Charles G., xiv, 0993
Smith, Don, 3022
Smith, Eric, 0054
Smith, Gerald A., 1460a
Smith, Gordon R., 2084
Smith, Gordon Ross, 1173, 1331, 1434, 1461, 1866, 2104, 2475, 3157
Smith, Grover, 2230
Smith, Hal H., xiv, 0994
Smith, Hallett, xiv, 0002, 0362, 0995, 0996, 0997, 2523, 3206
Smith, J. Oates, 1462, 3023
Smith, James C., 2475a
Smith, Jeffrey George, 3024
Smith, John B, 0049
Smith, John Hazel, 2344
Smith, Jonathan, 3207
Smith, Jonathan, Clark, 0998
Smith, Maria Selma A., 1463
Smith, Marion, 0999
Smith, Marion Bodwell, 1000
Smith, Michael Harold, 1464
Smith, Robert A. H., 2451
Smith, Rowland J., 3025
Smith, Sheila M., 1465
Smith, Stella T., 1466
Smith, Valerie, 3026
Smither, G. V., 2179
Snyder, Richard C., 3027
Snyder, Susan, 1001, 1002, 1003, 1467
Sochatoff, A. Fred, 1004
Soellner, Rolf, xiv, xxi, 1005, 1006, 2179a, 2345, 2429, 2694, 3028
Sokol, B. J., 2245a
Song, Nina, 1469
Sorelius, Gunnar, 2346, 2347
Sorensen, Knud, 1007
Sorge, Thomas, 1728

Southall, Raymond, 3029
Southwell, Michael G., 2105
Spakowski, R. E., 2106
Spann, Philip, 1008
Sparacino, Dennis N., 2595
Spawforth, Antony, xxiii
Speaight, Robert, 1009
Spencer, Janet Marie, 1931
Spencer, Luke, 2107, 3030
Spencer, T. J. B., 0055, 0057, 0062, 0373, 1010, 1011, 1012, 1013, 1880
Spevack, Marvin, 0002, 1013a, 1468, 2108
Spisak, James W., 2309
Spivack, Charlotte, 1014
Sprague, Arthur Colby, 1015
Sprengnether, Madelon, 1470, 1729, 2793
Spriet, Pierre, 2109
Sprigg, Douglas C., 3031
Sprott, S. E., 1881
Spurgeon, Caroline, 0545
Squier, Susan Merrill, 2900
Stack, Robert Douglas, 1016
Stafford, T. J., 1656, 2169, 2471, 2666, 3032
Stallings, Alden Page, 1471
Stamm, Rudolf, 2776, 3033
Stampfer, Judah, 1017
Stanford, Charles, 0025
Stanivukovic, Goran, 2524
Stanley, E. G., 0650a, 2180
Stanton, Kay, 1558
Starnes, D. T., 2430
Starr, G. A., 2110
Staton, Walter F. Jr., 2310
Steadman, John M., 1018, 2268, 2695
Steane, J. B., 1019
Stehlíková, Eva, 3034
Stein, Arnold, 3035
Steinberg, Theodore L., 3158
Stemmler, Theo, 1782
Steppat, Michael, 1468, 1472
Steppat, Michael Payne, 1019a
Sternfeld, F. W., xi, 0002, 1020, 1021
Stewart, Bain Tate, 1022
Stewart, Douglas, xix
Stewart, Douglas J., xvii, 1910, 2348
Stewart, J. I. M., 2111
Stewart, Patricia Lou, 1023
Still, Colin, 0061
Stiller, Nikki, 3036, 3037
Stimpson, Catharine R., 1024
Stirling, Brents, 1473, 2112
Stock, R. D., 1025
Stockholder, Katherine, 1730, 2181, 3038
Stockholder, Katherine Sally, 1026
Stockholder, Kay, 1474, 1474a
Stoller, Robert J., xvi, 1731
Stone, Jennifer, 2567
Story, Elizabeth, 1732
Strachan, Peter, 2525
Strathmann, Ernest A., 0496
Stratmann, Gerd, 1782
Stratton, Jon, 2567

Streitberger, W. R., 3159
Streites, Aaron, 1027
Strelka, Joseph P., 2211, 2784
Stretkowicz, Victor, 1727
Stríbrný, Zdeněk, 1028, 1060, 1834, 3034, 3039
Stroud, James Ronald, 1029
Stroup, Thomas B., 1030, 1031, 1032, 1475
Stroupe, John H., 1070, 1736, 1829
Strozier, Robert M., 1033
Stugrin, Michael, 1034
Stugrin, Michael A., 1345, 2292
Stukey, Johanna H., 1034a
Stump, Donald V., 1035, 1899
Stump, Eleonore, 1035, 1899
Sturzl, Erwin A., 1035a
Styan, John Louis, 1036
Sugnet, Charles J., 1476
Summers, Joseph H., 1477
Sutherland, James, 0209, 0219, 1037
Sutherland, Jean Murray, 1038
Suzuki, Mihoko, 1039, 3040, 3041, 3042
Svendsen, James T., 1040, 2596
Swander, Homer, 1478
Sweeney, Mary Clare, 2246
Swigg, R., 2696
Sylvester, Bickford, 2431
Syme, Ronald, 2112a
Sypher, Wylie, 3043

T
Taborski, Boleslaw, 0652, 1766, 1844
Takada, Shigeki, 2113
Takada, Yasunai, 3044
Takano, Miyo, 0020, 0021
Takei, Naoe, 1479
Talbert, Ernest W., 2452
Talbert, Ernest William, 1041
Tanaka, Susumu, 1480
Tanner, Jeri, 1481
Tanner, John S., 1482
Tanner, R. G., 1042
Tanner, Tony, 1483
Tanselle, G. Thomas, 1733
Tarlinskaja, Marina, 2113a
Tatspaugh, Patricia E., 3208
Taylor, A. B., 2597
Taylor, Anthony Brian, xix, xxi, 1042a, 1043, 1931a, 2311, 2312, 2312a, 2475c, 2475b, 2598, 2777, 2777a, 3086
Taylor, Arvilla Kerns, 1044
Taylor, Donn Ervin, 1559
Taylor, Gary, xvii, 1932, 1933, 2113c, 2113d, 2113b, 3045
Taylor, Hawley C., 3046
Taylor, Marion A., 1484, 1882
Taylor, Michael, 1734, 1734a, 1883
Taylor, Myron, 2114
Taylor, R. K. S., 0903, 3019, 3022, 3026, 3030
Taylor, Robert A., 2199b
Taylor, Sally Thorne, 2778

Teague, Frances, 1044a, 1735, 2349
Teller, Stephen J., 2779
Tennenhouse, Leonard, xvi, 1045, 1736, 2779a
Teruhira, Kimura, 1347
Teskey, Gordon, 1761, 1774
Tetel, Marcel, 1258
Thaler, Alwin, 0506, 0861, 1046, 1543, 2289, 2604, 2954, 3147
Thomas, Helen A., 1484a
Thomas, Mary Olive, 1485, 1486
Thomas, Shirley Forbes, 1487
Thomas, Troy, 3160
Thomas, Vivian, xiii, 1047, 3047
Thompson, Ann, xiv, 1048, 1049, 1131, 2476, 2542, 3048, 3049
Thompson, Diane Paige, 3049a
Thompson, John O., 3049
Thompson, Karl F., 3050, 3051
Thompson, Karl R., 1050
Thompson, Marvin, 2876
Thompson, Ruth, 2876
Thomson, Leslie, 1488
Thomson, Patricia, 2526, 3052
Thorne, Barry, 2201
Thorssen, Marilyn, 1489
Thron, Edward Michael, 1560
Tice, Terrence N., 2115
Tillyard, E. M. W., 2543
Tinker, Michael, 2697
Tobias, Richard C., 0781, 1627, 2373, 2697
Tobin, J. J. M., xiv, 1051, 1052, 1490, 1884, 1885, 1886, 2116, 2116a, 2324, 2350, 2351, 2698, 2779b
Tobin, John J. M., 1053
Tokson, Eliott H., 2780
Toliver, Harold, 1491
Toliver, Harold E., 1054, 1055, 1343, 1615, 1618, 2013, 2991
Tolmie, L. W., 1492
Tomlinson, Maggie, 1493
Toole, William B., 2117, 2118, 3053
Toole, William B. III, 2781
Torrance, Robert, xiii, 1056
Tovey, Barbara, xx, 2599
Traci, Philip J., 1494
Traci, Philip Joseph, 1495
Tracy, Robert, 1887
Traister, Barbara Howard, 2600, 2601
Traschen, Isadore, 1057
Trautvetter, Christine, 1561
Traversi, D. A., 1273
Traversi, Derek, 1058, 1495a
Travitsky, Betty S., 1349
Tribe, David H., 1059
Tricomi, Albert H., 2782, 2783
Trnka, Bohumil, 1060
Trousdale, Marion, 1061, 1737, 3208
Truax, Elizabeth, 1062, 2231, 2432
Trueman, A. W., xx, 2527
Trussler, Simon, 0056
Tucker, Kenneth, 1496

Turner, Frederick, 1063
Turner, Paul, 0042
Turner, Robert Y., 1064
Tylee, Claire M., 3054
Tylus, Jane Cecilia, 1779
Tysdahl, Bjørn, 2994
Tyson, Mary Hanna, 3161

U

Uéno, Yoshiko Y., 1497
Uhlig, Claus, 1241, 2860
Uhlmann, Dale C., 3162
Underwood, Richard Allan, xviii, 2184a, 2388, 2389
Uphaus, Robert W., 1498
Urban, Raymond A., 2601a
Ure, Peter, 1065, 1738, 2119, 3055, 3056, 3057

V

Vaish, Y. V., 1499
van den Berg, Sara, 1066
Vanderslice, Stephen Jerome, 2602
Van Dyke, Joyce, xvi, 1739, 1740
Van Laan, Thomas S., 1067
Van Norden, Linda, 1067a
Van Woensel, Maurice J. F., 1500
Vaughan, Virginia Mason, 2338, 3058
Vawter, Marvin L., xvii, xviii, 2120, 2121
Vawter, Marvin Lee, 2122
Vecchio, Monica Jean, 1068
Velz, John W., ix, xiv, xviii, 0057, 0058, 0059, 1069, 1070, 1071, 2030, 2123, 2124, 2125, 2126, 2127, 2128, 2129
Velz, Sara C., 2130
Venugopal, C. V., 2130a
Verma, Rajiv, 0059a
Verma, Rajiva, 1501
Vickers, Brian, xiv, 0002, 0059b, 1072, 1073, 1074, 1740a, 2527a, 3059
Vickers, Michael, 2231a
Vickers, Nancy, 2433
Vickers, Nancy J., 1834a, 2434
Vincent, Barbara C., 1502
Vincent, Barbara Cutts, 1503
Vincent, Jeffrey S., 1075
Viswanathan, S., xiv, 1076, 1077, 1078, 2181a, 2987, 3060
Von Rosador, K. Tetzeli, 1079
Von Rosador, Kurt Tetzeli, 1362
von Rosador, Kurt Tetzeli, 1472, 1743
Vosevich, Kathi Ann, 1080
Voss, A. E., 3061
Voth, Grant L., 3062, 3063
Vroonland, Jewell Kay, 3064
Vyvyan, John, 1081

W

Waage, Frederick O., 1082
Waddington, Raymond B., 1504, 1562, 2261, 2528
Wadsworth, Frank W., 0496

Index of Modern Scholars

Wagenknecht, Edward, 1083
Waggoner, G. R., 2699
Wain, John, xiii, 1084, 1085
Waith, Eugene M., xiv, 1085a, 1086, 1087, 2783a, 2784, 2785, 3100b, 3101
Wakeman, Carolyn Grant, 1741
Waldo, Tommy Ruth Blackmon, 1088
Walker, Alice, 1158
Walker, Ellen Louise, 1089
Walker, John Lewis III, 2703
Walker, Lewis, xxi, 2700, 2701, 2702
Wallace, John M., 2704
Wallach, Luitpold, 0533
Waller, G. F., 1090
Walley, Harold R., 2435
Walsh, Sister Mary Brian, O.S.B., 1091
Walter, J. H., 1505, 1563
Ware, Malcolm, 2705
Warren, Roger, 1092, 2786
Washington, Edward T., 1093
Waterhouse, Ruth, 1506
Waters, D. Douglas, 2706
Watson, Donald G., 3163
Watson, Donald Gwynn, 3164
Watson, Gilbert, 1507, 1508
Watson, Robert N., 1093a, 1741a
Watson, Robert Nathaniel, 1742
Watterson, William Collins, 1094
Watts, Cedric, 1095, 1509
Wayne, Don E., 1096
Wayne, Valerie, 2789a
Webb, J. Barry, 0060
Webber, Joan, 1097
Weckermann, Hans-Jurgen, 1743
Weidhorn, Manfred, 1098, 1099, 1100, 2182
Weightman, Franklin Case, 1101
Weil, Herbert S. Jr., 1102, 1510, 3064a
Weimann, Robert, 1103, 1104, 1393
Weiner, Andrew D., 2313
Weinstock, Horst, 1105
Weis, René J. A., 1511, 1512
Weisinger, Herbert, xiv, 0061, 1106
Weiss, Theodore, 1107
Weitz, Morris, 1513, 1888
Weixlmann, Joseph, 1744, 1745
Welch, Robert, xiv, 1108, 1246
Weller, Barry, 2313a, 3102
Weller, Barry Leigh, 1109
Weller, Philip James, 1110
Wells, Charles, 1111
Wells, Henry W., 0116, 1112
Wells, S. M., 0373
Wells, Stanley, 0062, 0584, 1113, 1114, 1588, 1817, 2314
Welsh, Andrew, 2373
Wendorf, Richard, 0976
Wentersdorf, Karl P., 1889, 1890
Wertime, Richard Allen, 1514
West, D. A., xvi, 1833
West, Gilian, 1891
West, Grace Starry, 2787
West, Michael, 2529

West, Robert H., 2603, 2604
West, Thomas G., 0080, 0599, 2515, 2634, 2871, 3065
Westlund, Joseph, 1892
Westney, Lizette I., xiv, 1115
Whallon, William, 1515
Wheater, K. I., 1116
Wheeler, Richard P., 0114, 1117
Wheeler, Thomas, 2262
Wheeler, Thomas P., 2232
Whidden, Mary Bess, 3165
Whitaker, Juanita Josephine, 1516
Whitaker, Virgil K., 1118, 1119, 3066
White, Beatrice, 1893
White, G. A., 0686
White, Gail Lana, 1121
White, Howard B., 0057, 1122, 1123, 2232a
White, Jeannette Smith, xiv, 1124
White, R. S., 1125, 3166
Whitney, Cynthia Kolb, 1517
Whitt, Nancy Marie, 1746
Whittier, Gayle, xiv, 1126
Wickham, Glynne, 1127, 1128, 1780, 2233, 3103
Widdicombe, Karen Elizabeth, 2436
Wigginton, Waller B., 1518
Wihl, Gary, 1747
Wilan, Richard Anthony, 3067
Wilbur, Richard, 1129
Wilcher, Robert, 2707
Wilders, John, 0062, 1130
Wilkes, G. A., 1377
Wilkinson, Andrew M., 2131
Willbern, David, xxi, 0062, 2437, 2788
Willbern, David Pierce, 2789
Willems, Michèle, 2253a
Willems, Raymond, 2253a
Williams, Aubrey, 1085a, 2953
Williams, Aubrey L., 1032, 1309
Williams, Carolyn, 3182a
Williams, Edith Whitehurst, 2234
Williams, Gary Jay, 2275
Williams, George Walton, xviii, 1131, 1519, 2132, 2183
Williams, Gordon, 3167
Williams, Gwyn, 1589
Williams, Jimmy Lee, 1132
Williams, John Anthony, 3209
Williamson, Cecile Cary, 2589, 3027
Williamson, Marilyn, 1520, 1521, 1564
Williamson, Marilyn L., 1522, 1523, 1524, 1525, 1748
Willis, Paul Jonathan, 1133
Willson, Robert F., xix, 2315
Willson, Robert F. Jr., 1134, 1135, 1136, 1526, 1527, 1893a, 2133
Wilson, C. R., 0002
Wilson, Douglas B., 3068, 3210
Wilson, E. Rawdon, 2438
Wilson, Emmett Jr., 1749
Wilson, F. P., 1137
Wilson, John Delane, 1138

Wilson, John Dover, 2530
Wilson, Luke, 1894
Wilson, Richard, 1750, 2134
Wilson, Robert Benjamin, 1139
Wilson, Robert Rawdon, 1895
Wilson, Rodney Earl, 1140
Wiltenburg, Robert, 2605
Wimsatt, James J., 1896
Windham, Lauren F., 3069
Wing, Susan Laura, 3104
Winny, James, 2439
Winter, E. O., 2021
Witt, Robert W., 1140a
Wolf, William D., 1528
Wollenberg, Susan, 2943
Womersley, D. J., xvii, 1937b
Womersley, David, 2134a
Wood, James O., 2135, 2235, 2236, 2237, 2316, 3087
Wood, K., 2708
Wood, Kamal, 2606
Wood, Robert E., 3070, 3071
Wood, Robert Edward, 3072
Woodbridge, Linda, xiv, 1141
Woodhead, M. R., 1897
Woodward, A. G., 1142
Worden, Blair, 1143
Worthen, W. B., 1528a
Wray, William R., 1898
Wright, Ellen Faber, 3168
Wright, George T., 0002
Wright, Louis B., 0065, 2478
Wright, Neil H., 2607
Wright, Neil Hutchinson, 1144
Wymer, Roland, 1145
Wynne-Davies, Marion, 2789a
Wyrick, Deborah Baker, 1146

Y

Yachnin, Paul, 1529
Yaffee, Glenn, 1146a
Yamada, Yumiko, 1147
Yates, Frances, xiv, 0958, 1148, 1149
Yates, Frances A., 1149a, 1150
Yoch, James J., 3169
Yoder, R. A., 2136, 3073
Yoshioka, Fumio, 1530
Young, David, 0002, 1151
Young, David P., 2317
Young, David Pollock, 2318

Z

Zach, Wolfgang, 0905a
Zedworna-Fjellestad, Danuta, 1255
Zeeveld, W. Gordon, xvi, 1152, 1751
Zeong, Yun-Shig, 2238
Zesmer, David M., 1153
Ziegler, Georgianna, xx, 2440
Zimbardo, Rose Abdelnour, 2608
Zitner, S. P., 1899, 2352
Zolbrod, Paul G., 0781, 1627, 1752, 2373, 2697
Zucker, David H., 2609
Zukofsky, Louis, 1154
Zulandt, George Klemm, 3074

Index of Names of Shakespeare's Works

A
All's Well That Ends Well, xv, 0062, 0067, 0096, 0140, 0326, 0353a, 0405a, 0412, 0513, 0529, 0579, 0642, 0687, 0690, 0699, 0789, 0901, 0909, 0920, 0923, 0955, 0957, 0969, 0997, 1001, 1027, 1065, 1072, 1081, 1155, 1156, 1157, 1158, 2833, 3020, 3056, 3064, 3090
Antony and Cleopatra, xi, xiii, xv, 0009, 0029, 0042, 0048, 0054, 0055, 0058, 0062, 0065, 0067, 0068, 0070a, 0071, 0073, 0075, 0076, 0079, 0080a, 0081, 0082, 0083, 0084, 0095, 0098, 0104, 0106, 0110, 0112, 0113, 0114, 0116, 0123, 0124, 0131, 0133, 0135, 0137, 0138, 0141, 0142a, 0154, 0156, 0156a, 0160b, 0161, 0166, 0170, 0171, 0173a, 0174, 0175, 0177, 0178, 0180, 0181, 0182, 0185, 0186, 0187, 0192, 0194, 0197, 0198, 0199, 0202, 0208, 0215, 0219, 0220, 0224, 0232, 0234, 0237, 0238a, 0239, 0240, 0243a, 0244, 0250, 0253, 0255, 0259, 0260, 0261, 0263, 0264, 0265, 0268, 0270, 0277, 0279, 0281, 0283, 0285, 0286, 0287, 0290, 0292a, 0293, 0305, 0306, 0310, 0313, 0319b, 0321, 0324, 0326, 0328, 0333, 0337, 0338, 0341, 0342, 0343, 0349, 0350, 0351, 0355, 0358, 0359, 0360, 0361, 0367, 0369, 0372a, 0379a, 0380, 0381, 0382, 0383, 0384, 0388, 0395, 0398, 0400, 0405, 0409, 0410, 0411, 0419, 0422, 0424, 0425, 0432, 0435, 0436, 0437, 0446, 0447, 0452, 0452a, 0456, 0461, 0463, 0464, 0464a, 0469, 0471, 0472, 0481, 0482, 0483, 0486, 0494, 0495, 0497, 0498, 0503, 0504a, 0511, 0512, 0518, 0522, 0529, 0530, 0534, 0545, 0546, 0548, 0551, 0553, 0554, 0555, 0557, 0558, 0562, 0566, 0581, 0584, 0585, 0587, 0589, 0599, 0602, 0603, 0606, 0607, 0609, 0613, 0618, 0619, 0623, 0625, 0626, 0628, 0630, 0632, 0633, 0635, 0637a, 0646, 0652, 0653, 0655, 0663a, 0677, 0679, 0681, 0685, 0687, 0688, 0690, 0694, 0697, 0700, 0701, 0702, 0703, 0705, 0707, 0708, 0710, 0712, 0713, 0714, 0716, 0717, 0721, 0723, 0728, 0729, 0733, 0734, 0742, 0744, 0745, 0746, 0749, 0751, 0756, 0759a, 0759b, 0764, 0765, 0773, 0778, 0779, 0782, 0784, 0787, 0789, 0792, 0795, 0799, 0805, 0807a, 0808, 0816a, 0821, 0821a, 0824, 0827, 0828, 0831, 0835, 0840, 0841, 0844, 0849a, 0850, 0851, 0852, 0857, 0866, 0867, 0870, 0871, 0872, 0873, 0874, 0876, 0882, 0885, 0887, 0888, 0889, 0895, 0898, 0906, 0908, 0909, 0911, 0912, 0914, 0922a, 0927, 0931, 0932, 0935, 0939, 0949, 0951, 0954, 0956, 0959, 0960, 0963, 0964, 0965, 0966, 0970, 0973, 0977, 0978, 0980, 0981, 0983, 0983a, 0985a, 0986a, 0986b, 0990, 1000, 1002, 1004, 1009, 1013, 1013a, 1015, 1017, 1019, 1019a, 1020, 1021, 1025, 1031, 1032, 1036, 1037, 1042a, 1044a, 1045, 1046, 1047, 1050, 1055, 1058, 1067, 1072, 1083, 1085, 1086, 1087, 1090, 1098, 1099, 1101, 1102, 1111, 1117, 1118, 1119, 1126, 1128, 1130, 1135, 1138, 1145, 1152, 1153, 1159, 1160, 1161, 1162, 1163, 1164, 1165, 1166, 1166a, 1167, 1168, 1169, 1170, 1171, 1171a, 1172, 1173, 1174, 1175, 1176, 1177, 1178, 1179, 1180, 1181, 1183, 1184, 1185, 1186, 1187, 1188, 1188a, 1189, 1190, 1191, 1192, 1193, 1194, 1195, 1196, 1196a, 1197, 1198, 1199, 1200, 1201, 1202, 1203, 1204, 1205, 1206, 1207, 1208, 1210, 1211, 1212, 1212a, 1213, 1214, 1215, 1216, 1217, 1217a, 1218, 1219, 1220, 1221, 1221a, 1222, 1223, 1224, 1225, 1226, 1227, 1228, 1229, 1230, 1231, 1232, 1233, 1234, 1235, 1235a, 1236, 1237, 1238, 1239, 1240, 1241, 1242, 1243, 1244, 1245, 1246, 1247, 1248, 1249, 1250, 1250a, 1251, 1252, 1252a, 1253, 1254, 1255, 1256, 1257, 1258, 1259, 1260, 1261, 1262, 1263, 1264, 1265, 1266, 1267, 1268, 1269, 1270, 1271, 1272, 1273, 1273a, 1274, 1275, 1276, 1277, 1278, 1279, 1280, 1281, 1282, 1284, 1285, 1286, 1287, 1288, 1289, 1290, 1291, 1292, 1293, 1294, 1295, 1296, 1297, 1298, 1299, 1300, 1301, 1302, 1303, 1303a, 1304, 1305, 1306, 1307, 1308, 1309, 1310, 1311, 1312, 1313, 1314, 1315, 1316, 1317, 1318, 1318a, 1319, 1320, 1321, 1322, 1323, 1324, 1325, 1326, 1326a, 1327, 1328, 1329, 1330, 1330a, 1331, 1332, 1333, 1334, 1335, 1336, 1337, 1338, 1339, 1340, 1341, 1342, 1343, 1344, 1345, 1346, 1347, 1348, 1349, 1350, 1351,

1352, 1352a, 1353, 1354, 1354a, 1355,
1356, 1357, 1358, 1359, 1360, 1361, 1362,
1363, 1364, 1365, 1366, 1367, 1368, 1369,
1370, 1370a, 1371, 1372, 1373, 1374,
1375, 1376, 1377, 1378, 1379, 1380, 1381,
1382, 1383, 1384, 1385, 1386, 1387,
1387a, 1388, 1389, 1390, 1391, 1392,
1393, 1394, 1395, 1396, 1397, 1398, 1399,
1400, 1401, 1402, 1403, 1404, 1405, 1406,
1407, 1408, 1409, 1410, 1411, 1412, 1413,
1414, 1415, 1416, 1417, 1418, 1419, 1420,
1421, 1422, 1423, 1424, 1425, 1426, 1427,
1428, 1429, 1430, 1431, 1432, 1433, 1434,
1435, 1436, 1437, 1438, 1439, 1440, 1441,
1442, 1443, 1444, 1445, 1446, 1447, 1448,
1449, 1450, 1451, 1452, 1453, 1454, 1455,
1456, 1457, 1458, 1459, 1460, 1460a,
1461, 1462, 1463, 1464, 1465, 1466, 1467,
1468, 1469, 1470, 1471, 1472, 1473, 1474,
1474a, 1475, 1476, 1477, 1478, 1479,
1480, 1481, 1482, 1483, 1484, 1484a,
1485, 1486, 1487, 1488, 1489, 1490, 1491,
1492, 1493, 1494, 1495, 1495a, 1496,
1497, 1498, 1499, 1500, 1501, 1502, 1503,
1504, 1505, 1506, 1507, 1509, 1510, 1511,
1512, 1513, 1514, 1515, 1516, 1517, 1518,
1519, 1521, 1522, 1523, 1524, 1525, 1526,
1527, 1528, 1528a, 1529, 1530, 1620, 1657,
1715, 1729, 1775, 1861, 2107, 2647, 2694,
2744, 3143
As You Like It, xv, 0055, 0062, 0090, 0091,
0108, 0132a, 0157, 0163, 0185a, 0211,
0266, 0281, 0320, 0322, 0322a, 0334,
0353a, 0375, 0377b, 0384, 0414, 0420,
0421, 0434, 0490, 0500, 0518, 0525,
0531, 0637a, 0667, 0687, 0690, 0693,
0695, 0758, 0759, 0789, 0797, 0801,
0807, 0814, 0828, 0828a, 0833, 0899,
0920, 0963, 0969, 0995, 0997, 1027,
1063, 1072, 1077, 1081, 1085a, 1094,
1151, 1531, 1532, 1533, 1534, 1535, 1536,
1537, 1538, 1539, 1540, 1541, 1542, 1543,
1543c, 1543a, 1543b, 1544, 1545, 1546,
1547, 1548, 1549, 1550, 1551, 1551a, 1552,
1553, 1554, 1555, 1556, 1557, 1558, 1559,
1560, 1561, 1562, 1563, 1564, 2166, 2818,
3034

C
Comedy of Errors, The, xi, xvi, 0062, 0072,
0073, 0074, 0084, 0092, 0099, 0100,
0102, 0119, 0153, 0154, 0165, 0168, 0170,
0187, 0209, 0225, 0235, 0272, 0285,
0331, 0353a, 0369, 0384, 0385a, 0400,
0415, 0418, 0433, 0434, 0439, 0440, 0484,
0489, 0502, 0510, 0518, 0556, 0564,
0597, 0608, 0675, 0676, 0678, 0685,
0690, 0715, 0720, 0721, 0745, 0746,
0759, 0797, 0818, 0822, 0836, 0881,
0887, 0891, 0891a, 0898, 0901, 0922,
0923, 0969, 0986c, 0989, 0991, 0995,
0997, 1000, 1006, 1009, 1015, 1031,
1032, 1041, 1064, 1079, 1103, 1109,
1114, 1135, 1137, 1146, 1565, 1566, 1567,
1568, 1569, 1570, 1571, 1572, 1573, 1573a,
1574, 1575, 1576, 1577, 1578, 1579, 1580,
1581, 1582, 1583, 1584, 1585, 1585a, 1586,
1587, 1588, 1589
Coriolanus, xi, xiii, xvi, 0009, 0040, 0042,
0055, 0058, 0062, 0065, 0071, 0073,
0075, 0076, 0077, 0078, 0079, 0081,
0082, 0085, 0102, 0104, 0105, 0106,
0112, 0113, 0114, 0116, 0120, 0123, 0125,
0129, 0131, 0133, 0135, 0137, 0138, 0141,
0142a, 0155, 0156, 0156a, 0161, 0166,
0170, 0171, 0172, 0172a, 0174, 0175,
0177, 0180, 0182, 0185, 0186, 0187, 0192,
0194, 0200, 0202, 0208, 0210, 0232,
0237, 0239, 0243a, 0244, 0250, 0255,
0256, 0259, 0260, 0263, 0265, 0279,
0282a, 0285, 0286, 0293, 0297, 0302,
0305, 0306, 0318, 0320, 0321, 0324,
0326, 0328, 0329, 0338, 0342, 0345,
0348, 0350, 0351, 0354, 0355, 0358,
0359, 0360, 0361, 0367, 0369, 0372,
0377, 0381, 0383, 0384, 0388, 0395,
0396, 0397, 0398, 0405, 0407, 0408,
0411, 0416, 0435, 0444, 0448, 0452,
0454, 0456, 0458, 0459, 0460, 0463,
0464, 0464a, 0465a, 0471, 0473, 0483,
0494, 0495, 0498, 0511, 0518, 0521,
0522, 0528, 0542, 0544, 0545, 0546,
0547, 0551, 0553, 0558, 0561, 0562,
0566, 0570, 0581, 0584, 0589, 0591,
0593, 0594, 0599, 0603, 0607, 0610,
0612, 0613, 0614, 0622, 0625, 0630, 0632,
0633, 0639, 0641, 0646, 0648, 0652,
0655, 0661, 0664, 0666, 0670, 0671,
0677, 0678, 0679, 0685, 0686, 0687,
0690, 0697, 0700, 0701, 0702, 0707,
0710, 0712, 0714, 0716, 0717, 0721, 0723,
0733, 0742, 0745, 0746, 0751, 0752,
0756, 0759a, 0761, 0765, 0775, 0776,
0778, 0779, 0782, 0784, 0791, 0792,
0795, 0799, 0804, 0805, 0811, 0817,
0826, 0831, 0836, 0840, 0841, 0844,
0846, 0849a, 0850, 0851, 0852, 0857,
0867, 0869, 0874, 0876, 0877, 0882,
0883, 0885, 0886, 0895, 0906, 0909,
0911, 0912, 0914, 0927, 0931, 0936a,
0949, 0951, 0954, 0956, 0959, 0960,
0964, 0966, 0971, 0973, 0974a, 0977,
0978, 0980, 0981, 0986a, 0987, 0999,
1000, 1004, 1009, 1012, 1013, 1017, 1026,
1031, 1036, 1044a, 1046, 1047, 1050,
1058, 1067, 1072, 1073, 1083, 1086,
1087, 1092, 1099, 1101, 1103, 1110,
1111, 1112, 1117, 1118, 1128, 1130, 1135,
1142, 1147, 1152, 1153, 1175, 1250, 1267,
1419, 1590, 1591, 1592, 1593, 1594, 1595,
1596, 1597, 1598, 1599, 1600, 1601, 1602,
1603, 1604, 1605, 1606, 1607, 1608, 1609,
1610, 1612, 1613, 1614, 1615, 1616, 1617,
1618, 1619, 1620, 1621, 1622, 1623, 1624,

Index of Names of Shakespeare's Works

1624a, 1625, 1626, 1626a, 1627, 1628, 1629, 1630, 1631, 1632, 1632a, 1632b, 1633, 1634, 1635, 1636, 1637, 1638, 1639, 1640, 1641, 1642, 1643, 1644, 1645, 1646, 1647, 1648, 1649, 1650, 1651, 1652, 1653, 1654, 1655, 1656, 1657, 1658, 1659, 1660, 1661, 1662, 1663, 1664, 1665, 1666, 1667, 1668, 1669, 1670, 1670a, 1671, 1671a, 1672, 1673, 1674, 1675, 1676, 1677, 1678, 1679, 1680, 1680a, 1681, 1682, 1683, 1684, 1685, 1686, 1687, 1688, 1689, 1690, 1691, 1692, 1693, 1694, 1695, 1696, 1697, 1698, 1699, 1700, 1701, 1702, 1703, 1704, 1705, 1706, 1707, 1708, 1709, 1710, 1711, 1712, 1713, 1714, 1715, 1716, 1717, 1718, 1719, 1720, 1721, 1722, 1723, 1724, 1725, 1726, 1727, 1728, 1729, 1730, 1731, 1732, 1733, 1734, 1734a, 1735, 1736, 1737, 1738, 1739, 1740, 1740a, 1741, 1741a, 1742, 1743, 1744, 1745, 1746, 1747, 1748, 1749, 1750, 1751, 1752, 2628, 2647, 2744

Cymbeline, xi, xiii, xvi, 0012, 0055, 0062, 0109, 0119, 0150, 0160a, 0183, 0189, 0215, 0282b, 0284, 0290, 0299a, 0311, 0311a, 0319, 0322a, 0336, 0353, 0359, 0367, 0382, 0384, 0406, 0413, 0433, 0434, 0437, 0518, 0542, 0619, 0628, 0632, 0649, 0690, 0694, 0699, 0710, 0721, 0759a, 0769, 0771, 0781, 0789, 0794, 0816a, 0843, 0850, 0873, 0891, 0907, 0922a, 0947, 0953, 0969, 0973, 0982, 0989, 0996, 0997, 1024, 1042a, 1044a, 1048, 1050, 1052, 1071, 1083, 1098, 1123, 1125, 1133, 1141, 1753, 1754, 1755, 1756, 1757, 1758, 1759, 1760, 1761, 1762, 1763, 1764, 1765, 1766, 1767, 1768, 1769, 1770, 1771, 1772, 1773, 1774, 1775, 1776, 1777, 1778, 1779, 1780

H

Hamlet, x, xvi, xvii, 0011, 0062, 0069, 0080a, 0081, 0083, 0096, 0101, 0125, 0128, 0132a, 0133, 0156, 0191, 0207, 0208, 0220, 0222, 0228, 0230, 0246, 0247, 0251, 0259, 0266, 0278, 0280, 0291, 0292, 0297, 0320, 0326, 0346, 0368, 0375, 0376, 0381, 0382, 0389, 0394, 0404, 0409, 0418, 0423, 0446a, 0457, 0460, 0462, 0464a, 0470, 0494, 0500, 0507, 0518, 0519a, 0526, 0529, 0533, 0547, 0557, 0558, 0566a, 0578, 0588, 0590, 0607, 0610, 0623, 0635, 0636, 0640, 0641, 0642, 0645, 0654, 0663, 0663a, 0665, 0674, 0685, 0690, 0700, 0713, 0717, 0721, 0728, 0729, 0733, 0745, 0748, 0749, 0759b, 0762, 0764, 0772, 0773, 0789, 0790, 0795, 0801, 0804, 0806, 0812, 0821, 0830, 0834, 0849, 0850a, 0853, 0875, 0891, 0892, 0917, 0919, 0929, 0944, 0945, 0955, 0956, 0959, 0961, 0984, 1004, 1021, 1022, 1030, 1040, 1042, 1043, 1053, 1057, 1061, 1063, 1076, 1077, 1091, 1108, 1115, 1118, 1131, 1132, 1138, 1139, 1145, 1149a, 1277, 1301, 1375, 1376, 1428, 1781, 1782, 1783, 1784, 1785, 1786, 1787, 1788, 1789, 1789a, 1790, 1791, 1792, 1793, 1794, 1795, 1796, 1797, 1798, 1798a, 1799, 1800, 1801, 1802, 1803, 1804, 1805, 1806, 1807, 1808, 1809, 1810, 1812, 1813, 1814, 1814a, 1815, 1816, 1816a, 1817, 1818, 1819, 1820, 1821, 1822, 1823, 1824, 1825, 1826, 1827, 1828, 1829, 1830, 1831, 1832, 1833, 1834, 1834a, 1835, 1836, 1837, 1838, 1839, 1840, 1841, 1841a, 1842, 1842a, 1843, 1844, 1844a, 1845, 1846, 1847, 1848, 1849, 1850, 1851, 1852, 1853, 1854, 1855, 1856, 1857, 1858, 1859, 1860, 1861, 1862, 1863, 1864, 1865, 1866, 1867, 1868, 1869, 1869a, 1869b, 1870, 1871, 1872, 1873, 1874, 1875, 1876, 1877, 1878, 1879, 1879a, 1880, 1881, 1882, 1883, 1884, 1885, 1886, 1887, 1888, 1889, 1890, 1891, 1892, 1893, 1893a, 1894, 1895, 1896, 1897, 1898, 1899, 1968, 2035, 2102, 2435, 2912

Henry IV, Part 1, xvii, 0136, 0140, 0153, 0214, 0249, 0291, 0300, 0301, 0315, 0380a, 0401, 0404, 0470, 0519, 0529, 0542, 0547, 0616, 0619, 0672, 0704, 0734, 0767, 0773, 0796, 0815, 0820, 0857, 0862, 0881, 0894, 0905, 0968, 0989, 1022, 1070, 1648, 1900, 1901, 1902, 1903, 1904, 1905, 1906, 1907, 1909, 1910

Henry IV, Part 2, xvii, 0140, 0151, 0231, 0249, 0300, 0301, 0392, 0519, 0616, 0642, 0767, 0773, 0815, 0829a, 0857, 0905, 0943, 0963, 0994, 1904, 1911, 1912, 1913, 1914, 1915, 1916

Henry IV, Parts 1 & 2, xiii, 0008, 0080a, 0259, 0387, 0431, 0450, 0519, 0563, 0720a, 0833, 0882, 1044, 1054, 1072, 1093a, 1146a, 1241, 1912

Henry V, xiii, xv, xvii, 0008, 0080a, 0185a, 0214, 0221, 0231, 0249, 0264, 0301, 0314, 0339, 0358, 0375, 0387, 0392, 0450, 0457, 0519, 0528, 0563, 0569, 0578, 0657, 0692, 0720a, 0767, 0780, 0785, 0815, 0820, 0829a, 0832, 0905, 0907, 1044, 1054, 1072, 1093a, 1140a, 1241, 1334, 1904, 1917, 1918, 1919, 1920, 1921, 1922, 1923, 1924, 1925, 1926, 1927, 1928, 1929, 1930, 1931, 1931a, 1932, 1933, 1945, 1946, 1990

Henry VI, Part 1, xvii, 0270, 0300, 0610, 0619, 0918, 1934, 1935

Henry VI, Part 2, xvii, 0152, 0221, 0322a, 0539, 0610, 0691, 0862, 0881, 0894, 1051, 1936, 1937, 2025

Henry VI, Part 3, xvii, 0152, 0191, 0368, 0466, 0533, 0610, 0691, 0804, 0821, 0821a, 0918, 0985a, 1937a, 1937b

Henry VIII, xvii, 0008, 0062, 0096, 0327,

0382, 0550, 0556, 0559, 0700, 1080,
1122, 1756, 1938, 1939
Henry VI Triad, xiii, 0152, 0216, 0368, 0517,
0663, 0789, 0894, 0915, 0968, 0998, 1094

J
Julius Caesar, xi, xiii, xvii, xviii, 0006, 0009,
0040, 0042, 0048, 0055, 0058, 0062,
0065, 0071, 0073, 0076, 0079, 0081,
0082, 0083, 0097, 0101, 0104, 0106,
0113, 0116, 0125, 0129, 0135, 0136, 0137,
0142a, 0156, 0156a, 0161, 0166, 0170,
0172, 0174, 0175, 0186, 0192, 0200, 0201,
0202, 0206, 0207, 0208, 0210, 0219,
0220, 0222, 0224, 0230, 0232, 0234,
0237, 0239, 0240, 0246, 0247, 0250,
0255, 0256, 0261, 0263, 0264, 0265,
0271, 0277, 0282a, 0285, 0291, 0292,
0293, 0294, 0297, 0302, 0305, 0313, 0314,
0318, 0319a, 0322a, 0326, 0329, 0333,
0337, 0338, 0340, 0347, 0348, 0350,
0351, 0352, 0358, 0360, 0361, 0369,
0377, 0379, 0383, 0384, 0388, 0397,
0398, 0398a, 0405, 0407, 0408, 0411,
0419, 0422, 0423, 0424, 0425, 0432,
0441, 0444, 0452, 0453, 0459, 0463,
0464, 0464a, 0473, 0475, 0482, 0483,
0486, 0492, 0492a, 0494, 0495, 0503,
0508, 0511, 0524, 0525, 0534, 0539,
0540, 0545, 0549, 0550, 0552, 0560,
0561, 0566, 0566a, 0570, 0578, 0584,
0587, 0588, 0593, 0599, 0603, 0607,
0610, 0613, 0619, 0621, 0623, 0625, 0630,
0632, 0635, 0637, 0639, 0641, 0645,
0646, 0648, 0655, 0658, 0661, 0670,
0671, 0674, 0677, 0678, 0679, 0685,
0687, 0690, 0697, 0700, 0701, 0704,
0713, 0716, 0717, 0721, 0723, 0729, 0733,
0734, 0742, 0745, 0746, 0749, 0750,
0751, 0756, 0759a, 0759b, 0761, 0762,
0764, 0765, 0778, 0779, 0782, 0787,
0789, 0792, 0795, 0799, 0808, 0811,
0812a, 0821, 0826, 0829, 0831, 0832a,
0836, 0840, 0844, 0845, 0848, 0849,
0850, 0851, 0852, 0857, 0866, 0867,
0869, 0873, 0874, 0876, 0882, 0886,
0893, 0896, 0905, 0906, 0909, 0911,
0912, 0914, 0915, 0932, 0939, 0940a,
0944, 0945, 0949, 0951, 0954, 0956,
0959, 0964, 0965, 0968, 0973, 0973a,
0974, 0978, 0979, 0980, 0981, 0983a,
0985a, 0986a, 0990, 1000, 1009, 1012,
1013, 1013a, 1015, 1017, 1019a, 1021,
1031, 1036, 1037, 1046, 1047, 1050,
1058, 1061, 1067, 1069, 1070, 1073,
1076, 1083, 1098, 1100, 1101, 1106,
1110, 1111, 1112, 1118, 1119, 1128, 1130,
1131, 1135, 1142, 1145, 1147, 1152, 1153,
1175, 1267, 1318a, 1376, 1384, 1419,
1428, 1439, 1620, 1664, 1729, 1775, 1814,
1816a, 1849, 1918, 1939a, 1940, 1941,
1941a, 1942, 1943, 1944, 1945, 1946,
1947, 1948, 1949, 1950, 1951, 1951a,
1952, 1953, 1954, 1955, 1956, 1957, 1958,
1959, 1960, 1961, 1962, 1963, 1964, 1965,
1966, 1967, 1968, 1969, 1970, 1971, 1972,
1973, 1974, 1975, 1976, 1977, 1978, 1979,
1980, 1981, 1982, 1983, 1983a, 1983b,
1984, 1985, 1986, 1987, 1987a, 1988,
1989, 1990, 1991, 1992, 1993, 1994, 1995,
1996, 1997, 1998, 1999, 2000, 2001, 2002,
2002a, 2003, 2004, 2005, 2006, 2007,
2008, 2009, 2010, 2011, 2012, 2013,
2013a, 2014, 2015, 2016, 2017, 2018,
2019, 2021, 2022, 2022a, 2023, 2024,
2025, 2026, 2027, 2028, 2029, 2030,
2031, 2032, 2033, 2034, 2035, 2036,
2036a, 2037, 2038, 2039, 2040, 2041,
2042, 2043, 2044, 2045, 2046, 2047,
2048, 2048a, 2049, 2050, 2051, 2051a,
2052, 2053, 2054, 2055, 2056, 2057,
2058, 2059, 2060, 2061, 2062, 2063,
2064, 2065, 2066, 2067, 2068, 2068a,
2069, 2070, 2071, 2072, 2073, 2074,
2075, 2076, 2077, 2078, 2079, 2080,
2081, 2082, 2083, 2084, 2085, 2085a,
2086, 2087, 2088, 2088a, 2089, 2090,
2091, 2091a, 2092, 2093, 2094, 2096,
2097, 2098, 2099, 2100, 2101, 2102,
2102a, 2103, 2104, 2105, 2106, 2107,
2108, 2109, 2110, 2111, 2112, 2112a,
2113, 2113c, 2113a, 2113b, 2114, 2115,
2116, 2116a, 2117, 2118, 2119, 2120,
2121, 2122, 2123, 2124, 2125, 2126, 2127,
2128, 2129, 2130a, 2131, 2132, 2133,
2134, 2134a, 2135, 2136, 2485, 2744

K
King John, xviii, 0008, 0088, 0120, 0296,
0326, 0610, 0905, 1122, 2137, 2661
King Lear, xviii, 0011, 0062, 0073, 0081,
0083, 0088, 0096, 0097, 0121, 0125, 0132,
0133, 0134, 0166, 0182, 0194, 0208, 0220,
0247, 0251, 0254, 0259, 0263, 0264,
0266, 0278a, 0280, 0282, 0291, 0300,
0304, 0315, 0320, 0322a, 0346, 0352,
0376, 0380a, 0385, 0400, 0404, 0460,
0506, 0509, 0513, 0518, 0519a, 0526,
0533, 0534, 0542, 0547a, 0557, 0584,
0585, 0596, 0610, 0615, 0620, 0631,
0635, 0640, 0642, 0695, 0700, 0713, 0718,
0729, 0733, 0748, 0762, 0764, 0772,
0780, 0790, 0819, 0821, 0834, 0835,
0853, 0879, 0881, 0907, 0945, 0956,
0959, 0961, 0966, 0978, 0984, 0986,
0995, 0997, 1004, 1006, 1023, 1026,
1030, 1053, 1072, 1073, 1091, 1118, 1132,
1145, 1149a, 1151, 1375, 1376, 1382,
1666, 2135, 2138, 2139, 2140, 2141, 2142,
2143, 2144, 2145, 2145a, 2146, 2146a,
2147, 2149, 2150, 2151, 2152, 2153, 2154,
2155, 2156, 2157, 2158, 2159, 2160, 2161,
2161a, 2162, 2163, 2164, 2165, 2166, 2167,
2168, 2169, 2170, 2171, 2172, 2173,

Index of Names of Shakespeare's Works   815

2173a, 2174, 2175, 2176, 2177, 2178, 2179, 2179a, 2180, 2181, 2181a, 2183, 2621, 2692

L
Lover's Complaint, A, xviii, 0002, 0052, 0357, 0863, 1761, 2184, 2184a, 2487
Love's Labor's Lost, xviii, 0062, 0084, 0090, 0099, 0102, 0162, 0188, 0211, 0235, 0238, 0274, 0275, 0309, 0326, 0331, 0334, 0353a, 0369, 0375, 0483, 0518, 0528, 0580, 0588, 0601, 0621, 0645, 0678, 0720, 0756, 0758, 0759, 0797, 0807, 0818, 0821a, 0832, 0842, 0877, 0905, 0915, 0957, 0963, 0967, 0969, 1006, 1044, 1052, 1060, 1061, 1064, 1071, 1079, 1081, 1149a, 2185, 2185a, 2187, 2188, 2189, 2190, 2191, 2192, 2193, 2194, 2195, 2196, 2197, 2198, 2199, 2199a, 2199b, 2200, 2201, 2586, 2718b

M
Macbeth, xviii, 0011, 0062, 0081, 0083, 0086, 0093, 0096, 0105, 0120, 0121, 0125, 0128, 0166, 0182, 0196, 0220, 0230, 0254, 0259, 0266, 0278, 0278a, 0280, 0292a, 0320, 0385, 0389, 0423, 0449, 0490, 0498, 0513, 0518, 0526, 0533, 0539, 0557, 0565, 0581, 0591, 0596, 0610, 0615, 0636, 0641, 0652, 0666, 0672, 0674, 0681, 0691, 0700, 0701, 0721, 0728, 0729, 0733, 0764, 0772, 0773, 0784, 0806, 0809, 0821, 0835, 0853, 0881, 0900, 0901, 0915, 0929, 0944, 0945, 0959, 0961, 0968, 0978, 0984, 0996, 1000, 1004, 1030, 1042, 1053, 1063, 1070, 1071, 1072, 1073, 1091, 1098, 1118, 1132, 1138, 1145, 1149a, 1277, 1318a, 1375, 1501, 2015, 2135, 2202, 2203, 2204, 2205, 2206, 2207, 2208, 2208a, 2209, 2209a, 2210, 2211, 2212, 2213, 2214, 2215, 2216, 2217, 2218, 2219, 2220, 2221, 2222, 2223, 2224, 2225, 2226, 2227, 2228, 2229, 2230, 2231, 2232, 2233, 2234, 2235, 2236, 2237, 2238
Measure for Measure, xviii, 0062, 0067, 0096, 0121, 0214, 0259, 0263, 0309, 0315, 0334, 0353a, 0385, 0412, 0513, 0559, 0579, 0590, 0623, 0642, 0690, 0699, 0801, 0823, 0836, 0842, 0843, 0888a, 0903, 0909, 0923, 0932, 0945, 0955, 0957, 0961, 0963, 0969, 0995, 0997, 1000, 1026, 1061, 1065, 1071, 1072, 1075, 2239, 2240, 2241, 2242, 2242a, 2243, 2244, 2245, 2245a, 2246, 2628, 3019, 3020, 3056, 3064
Merchant of Venice, The, xviii, 0062, 0109, 0168, 0201, 0211, 0214, 0266, 0326, 0335, 0336, 0353a, 0377b, 0405a, 0460, 0464a, 0476, 0500, 0542, 0550, 0556, 0599, 0608, 0641, 0653, 0721, 0759, 0770, 0773, 0780, 0789, 0797, 0835, 0836, 0843, 0893, 0923, 0957, 0963, 0968, 0969, 1005, 1028, 1043, 1070, 1072, 1149a, 2247, 2248, 2249, 2250, 2251, 2252, 2253, 2253a, 2254, 2255, 2256, 2257, 2258, 2259, 2260, 2261, 2262, 2485, 2818
Merry Wives of Windsor, The, xix, 0062, 0118, 0119, 0151, 0153, 0162, 0211, 0273, 0300, 0339, 0353a, 0401, 0483, 0518, 0529, 0667, 0699, 0797, 0806, 0818, 0821a, 0899, 0969, 1072, 1077, 2135, 2263, 2264, 2265, 2266, 2266a, 2267, 2268
Midsummer Night's Dream, A, xi, xix, 0062, 0079, 0087, 0096, 0101, 0104, 0119, 0158, 0165, 0196, 0209, 0211, 0214, 0238, 0248, 0270, 0274, 0288, 0307, 0322a, 0325, 0353a, 0371, 0375, 0379, 0380a, 0385a, 0394, 0439, 0440, 0441, 0464x, 0467, 0489, 0495, 0502, 0518, 0525, 0528, 0529, 0536, 0560, 0561, 0566a, 0588, 0601, 0608, 0630, 0667, 0676, 0687, 0690, 0692, 0721, 0727, 0729, 0756, 0758, 0759, 0785, 0797, 0802a, 0807, 0818, 0828a, 0868, 0890, 0892, 0893, 0899, 0900, 0901, 0928, 0967, 0968, 0969, 0987, 0996, 0997, 1001, 1009, 1035a, 1039, 1052, 1064, 1072, 1081, 1085a, 1098, 1107, 1108, 1123, 1134, 1146, 1149a, 1277, 2268a, 2269, 2270, 2271, 2272, 2273, 2274, 2275, 2276, 2277, 2278, 2279, 2280, 2281, 2282, 2283, 2284, 2285, 2286, 2287, 2288, 2288a, 2289, 2290, 2291, 2292, 2293, 2294, 2295, 2296, 2297, 2298, 2299, 2300, 2301, 2302, 2303, 2304, 2305, 2306, 2307, 2308, 2309, 2310, 2311, 2312, 2312a, 2313, 2313a, 2314, 2315, 2316, 2317, 2318, 2541, 2718b, 3090, 3097, 3103
Much Ado About Nothing, xix, 0062, 0067, 0088, 0091, 0096, 0151, 0188, 0211, 0353a, 0434, 0518, 0556, 0601, 0610, 0623, 0642, 0690, 0758, 0789, 0797, 0801, 0832, 0923, 0963, 0969, 0995, 0997, 1044, 1072, 1080, 2319, 2320, 2321, 2322, 2323, 2324, 2818

O
Othello, xix, 0011, 0062, 0081, 0110, 0121, 0128, 0132, 0145, 0166, 0182, 0191, 0193, 0208, 0220, 0233, 0247, 0263, 0270, 0273, 0278a, 0280, 0291, 0292, 0315, 0378, 0380a, 0385a, 0434, 0446a, 0464a, 0478, 0490, 0494, 0505, 0507, 0509, 0518, 0526, 0546, 0556, 0557, 0589, 0591, 0599, 0601, 0609, 0610, 0615, 0642, 0653, 0661, 0674, 0700, 0721, 0722, 0724, 0728, 0729, 0733, 0748, 0764, 0821, 0824, 0833, 0835, 0859, 0929, 0944, 0959, 0984, 0999, 1004, 1020, 1021, 1052, 1053, 1061, 1067a,

1071, 1072, 1073, 1076, 1091, 1118, 1132,
1145, 1277, 1373, 1375, 2325, 2326, 2327,
2328, 2328a, 2329, 2330, 2331, 2332,
2333, 2334, 2335, 2336, 2337, 2338,
2339, 2340, 2340a, 2341, 2342, 2343,
2344, 2345, 2346, 2347, 2348, 2349,
2350, 2351, 2352

P
Passionate Pilgrim, The, xix, 0357, 2353,
2485, 2541
Pericles, xi, xix, 0010, 0062, 0079, 0092,
0104, 0114, 0149, 0160a, 0183, 0214,
0284, 0299a, 0307, 0308, 0311, 0311a,
0336, 0353, 0369, 0382, 0406, 0434,
0437, 0489, 0547a, 0556, 0590, 0623,
0649, 0676, 0687, 0690, 0699, 0736,
0781, 0794, 0847, 0873, 0906, 0947,
0968, 0969, 0982, 0997, 1020, 1021,
1052, 1114, 1123, 1125, 2354, 2355, 2356,
2357, 2358, 2359, 2360, 2361, 2362,
2363, 2364, 2365, 2366, 2367, 2368,
2369, 2371, 2372, 2373, 2556
Phoenix and Turtle, The, xix, 0002, 0052,
0101, 0350, 0357, 0370a, 0462, 0601,
0628, 0726, 0863, 0939, 1129, 1489,
2374, 2375, 2376, 2377, 2378, 2379,
2380, 2381, 2382, 2383, 2384, 2385,
2386, 2387, 2388, 2389

R
Rape of Lucrece, The, xi, xix, xx, 0002, 0029,
0052, 0062, 0071, 0073, 0080a, 0102,
0104, 0105, 0119, 0123, 0133, 0154, 0156,
0160, 0172a, 0179, 0187, 0192, 0203,
0261, 0267, 0278, 0283, 0301, 0332,
0338, 0347a, 0350, 0357, 0370, 0370a,
0375, 0377c, 0394, 0398a, 0401, 0437,
0441, 0448, 0452a, 0458, 0465, 0483,
0484, 0539, 0553a, 0571, 0572, 0599,
0601, 0602, 0622, 0632, 0634, 0655,
0665, 0683, 0685, 0709, 0715, 0721,
0726, 0746, 0756, 0759a, 0759b, 0778,
0789, 0816, 0850, 0851, 0852, 0863,
0882, 0888, 0907, 0919, 0921, 0934,
0955, 0963, 0973a, 0974, 1009, 1024,
1034, 1045, 1062, 1070, 1071, 1078,
1082, 1093, 1111, 1129, 1141, 1145, 1153,
1428, 1664, 1837, 2210, 2390, 2391, 2392,
2393, 2394, 2395, 2395a, 2396, 2397,
2398, 2398a, 2399, 2400, 2401, 2402,
2403, 2404, 2405, 2406, 2407, 2408,
2409, 2410, 2411, 2412, 2413, 2414, 2415,
2416, 2417, 2418, 2419, 2420, 2421, 2422,
2423, 2424, 2425, 2426, 2427, 2428,
2429, 2430, 2431, 2432, 2433, 2434,
2435, 2436, 2437, 2438, 2439, 2440,
2541, 2715, 2722, 2766
Richard II, xx, 0080a, 0105, 0125, 0150,
0207, 0208, 0221, 0231, 0238, 0266,
0300, 0320, 0322, 0352, 0377b, 0380a,
0385, 0460, 0529, 0547a, 0550, 0557,
0563, 0610, 0635, 0663, 0720a, 0728,
0767, 0815, 0816a, 0820, 0835, 0845,
0968, 1044, 1054, 1061, 1093a, 1097,
1301, 2440a, 2441, 2442, 2443, 2444,
2445, 2446, 2447, 2448, 2449, 2450,
2451, 2452, 2718b
Richard III, xx, 0086, 0093, 0136, 0191,
0207, 0216, 0253, 0314, 0320, 0338, 0352,
0368, 0377b, 0404, 0418, 0501, 0533,
0565, 0582, 0596, 0610, 0663, 0691,
0692, 0772, 0796, 0804, 0835, 0894,
0915, 1028, 1033, 1051, 1069, 1073,
1074, 1098, 1138, 2453, 2454, 2455,
2455a, 2456, 2457, 2458, 2459, 2460
Romeo and Juliet, xx, 0062, 0067, 0068,
0083, 0110, 0181, 0196, 0207, 0238, 0261,
0263, 0270, 0273, 0325, 0352, 0376,
0379, 0385, 0434, 0464a, 0467, 0507,
0524, 0533, 0557, 0585, 0615, 0700,
0729, 0828a, 0829a, 0832, 0835, 0929,
0968, 0970, 0978, 1000, 1022, 1033,
1034, 1052, 1072, 1080, 1081, 1098,
1126, 1145, 1149a, 1219, 1277, 1373,
1441, 2015, 2461, 2462, 2463, 2464, 2465,
2466, 2467, 2468, 2468a, 2469, 2470,
2471, 2472, 2473, 2474, 2475, 2475c,
2475a, 2475b, 2476, 2718b

S
Sonnets, x, xx, 0039, 0052, 0062, 0071,
0245, 0280, 0281, 0320, 0332, 0350,
0377b, 0401, 0448, 0457, 0588, 0646,
0665, 0685, 0802a, 0835, 0863, 0871,
0987, 1006, 1052, 1063, 1108, 1153, 1257,
1761, 1785, 2477a, 2478, 2479, 2480,
2481, 2482, 2483, 2485, 2486, 2487,
2488, 2488a, 2489, 2491, 2492, 2493,
2494, 2495, 2496, 2497, 2498, 2501,
2503, 2505, 2506, 2507, 2508, 2509,
2511, 2512, 2513, 2514, 2516, 2517, 2519,
2520, 2522, 2523, 2525, 2527a, 2530,
3143
Sonnet 7, 1043, 2514
Sonnet 15, 2528
Sonnet 18, 0809
Sonnet 19, 0809
Sonnet 20, 0685, 0809, 1126
Sonnet 21, 2500
Sonnet 23, 0809
Sonnet 24, 2490
Sonnet 27, 2493
Sonnet 37, 2483
Sonnet 43, 2493
Sonnet 46, 2493
Sonnet 47, 2493
Sonnet 53, 2483, 2493, 2495, 2499
Sonnet 55, 0345, 2492, 2508, 2530
Sonnet 59, 2480
Sonnet 60, 0872, 2480, 2494, 2501, 2524,
2530
Sonnet 61, 2493
Sonnet 64, 0835, 2501, 2530

Index of Names of Shakespeare's Works 817

Sonnet 65, 2501
Sonnet 66, 2499
Sonnet 67, 2483
Sonnet 73, 2501, 2518
Sonnet 74, 2501
Sonnet 76, 2483
Sonnet 77, 0809, 2493
Sonnet 80, 0809
Sonnet 86, 0809
Sonnet 91, 0875
Sonnet 94, 0080a, 0721, 2515
Sonnet 98, 2483, 2526
Sonnet 100, 2493
Sonnet 101, 2493
Sonnet 107, 2489
Sonnet 108, 2483
Sonnet 113, 2493
Sonnet 122, 2493
Sonnet 129, 1251, 2510, 2513, 2527a
Sonnet 130, 0332, 2477, 2489, 2927
Sonnet 140, 2502
Sonnet 141, 0627
Sonnet 144, 2478
Sonnet 146, 2504, 2529
Sonnet 153, 0685, 2495, 2499, 2517, 2521
Sonnet 154, 0685, 2495, 2517, 2521

T
Taming of the Shrew, The, xx, 0062, 0073, 0121, 0140, 0328, 0331, 0335, 0353a, 0369, 0405a, 0483, 0518, 0556, 0608, 0699, 0720, 0759, 0789, 0797, 0818, 0821a, 0888a, 0907, 0923, 0963, 0969, 1035a, 1064, 1107, 2531, 2532, 2532a, 2533, 2534, 2535, 2536, 2537, 2538, 2539, 2540, 2541, 2542, 2543
Tempest, The, xx, 0012, 0029, 059b, 0062, 0080a, 0095, 0096, 0097, 0101, 0119, 0140, 0149, 0153, 0160a, 0183, 0214, 0247, 0282a, 0282b, 0283, 0288, 0290, 0299a, 0308, 0311, 0311a, 0336, 0338, 0353, 0371, 0373, 0375, 0377b, 0380, 0382, 0405a, 0406, 0419, 0420, 0421, 0434, 0449, 0462, 0474, 0483, 0490, 0495, 0500, 0518, 0529, 0531, 0536, 0546, 0566a, 0577, 0581, 0599, 0631, 0634, 0649, 0699, 0736, 0769, 0771, 0780, 0781, 0789, 0802a, 0807, 0812, 0813, 0814, 0822, 0828a, 0834, 0835, 0850, 0859, 0873, 0881, 0891, 0891a, 0892, 0899, 0900, 0902, 0922, 0936, 0947, 0951, 0953, 0956, 0968, 0969, 0982, 0997, 1000, 1020, 1021, 1025, 1027, 1044a, 1052, 1075, 1085a, 1090, 1092, 1110, 1114, 1121, 1123, 1125, 1133, 1134, 1149a, 1151, 1153, 2316, 2544, 2545, 2546, 2546a, 2547, 2548, 2549, 2550, 2551, 2551a, 2552, 2553, 2554, 2555, 2556, 2557, 2558, 2559, 2560, 2560a, 2561, 2562, 2562a, 2562b, 2563, 2564, 2565, 2565a, 2566, 2566a, 2567, 2568, 2569, 2569a, 2570, 2570a, 2571, 2572, 2573, 2574, 2575, 2576, 2577, 2578, 2578a, 2579, 2581, 2582, 2583, 2584, 2585, 2586, 2587, 2588, 2588a, 2589, 2590, 2591, 2592, 2593, 2594, 2595, 2596, 2597, 2598, 2599, 2600, 2601, 2601a, 2602, 2603, 2604, 2605, 2606, 2607, 2608, 2609
Timon of Athens, xi, xxi, 0002, 0010, 0012, 0042, 0055, 0058, 0059, 0062, 0070a, 0073, 0076, 0079, 0085, 0089, 0104, 0114, 0123, 0125, 0131, 0137, 0147, 0148, 0156, 0160b, 0161, 0163, 0166, 0174, 0178, 0186, 0192, 0194, 0197, 0201, 0220, 0222, 0232, 0233, 0237, 0243, 0250, 0260, 0264, 0282, 0283, 0304, 0308, 0320, 0321, 0327, 0328, 0330, 0334, 0338, 0342, 0343, 0347a, 0349, 0350, 0361, 0365, 0368, 0369, 0372, 0372a, 0373, 0375, 0378, 0382, 0384, 0386, 0388, 0390, 0391, 0393, 0394, 0395, 0396, 0398, 0405, 0410, 0411, 0413, 0416, 0418, 0420, 0421, 0435a, 0441, 0454, 0461, 0471, 0483, 0489, 0495, 0518, 0521, 0522, 0538, 0545, 0548, 0549, 0551, 0553a, 0562, 0569, 0576, 0581, 0607, 0610, 0613, 0625, 0627, 0630, 0634, 0635, 0646, 0648, 0664, 0666, 0675, 0676, 0678, 0685, 0687, 0690, 0696, 0700, 0711, 0712, 0714, 0723, 0729, 0742, 0744, 0745, 0746, 0749, 0752, 0775, 0779, 0782, 0784, 0791, 0792, 0806, 0817, 0825, 0835, 0836, 0843, 0846, 0848, 0849a, 0852, 0869, 0873, 0876, 0882, 0883, 0895, 0901, 0904, 0906, 0907, 0912, 0914, 0920, 0922a, 0931, 0935, 0936, 0945, 0951, 0954, 0959, 0966, 0971, 0976, 0983a, 0986, 1000, 1009, 1011, 1015, 1017, 1023, 1031, 1044a, 1046, 1065, 1072, 1082, 1083, 1085, 1111, 1112, 1117, 1123, 1133, 1147, 1152, 1153, 1267, 1419, 1615, 1630, 1657, 1677, 2610, 2611, 2612, 2613, 2614, 2615, 2616, 2617, 2618, 2619, 2620, 2621, 2622, 2623, 2624, 2625, 2626, 2627, 2628, 2629, 2630, 2631, 2632, 2633, 2634, 2635, 2636, 2637, 2638, 2639, 2640, 2641, 2641a, 2642, 2643, 2644, 2645, 2646, 2647, 2648, 2649, 2650, 2651, 2652, 2654, 2655, 2656, 2657, 2657a, 2658, 2659, 2660, 2661, 2662, 2663, 2664, 2665, 2666, 2667, 2668, 2669, 2670, 2671, 2672, 2673, 2674, 2676, 2677, 2678, 2679, 2680, 2681, 2682, 2683, 2684, 2685, 2686, 2687, 2688, 2688a, 2689, 2689a, 2690, 2691, 2692, 2693, 2694, 2695, 2696, 2697, 2698, 2699, 2700, 2701, 2702, 2703, 2704, 2705, 2706, 2707, 2708
Titus Andronicus, xi, xiii, xxi, 0010, 0029, 0054, 0058, 0059, 0062, 0072, 0073, 0074, 0076, 0080a, 0084, 0102, 0104, 0105, 0114, 0116, 0119, 0156, 0178, 0179,

818   *Shakespeare and the Classical Tradition*

0185a, 0187, 0203, 0206, 0207, 0208, 0225, 0232, 0238, 0240, 0246, 0247, 0250, 0271, 0285, 0300, 0302, 0304, 0318, 0319a, 0329, 0330, 0338, 0350, 0352, 0361, 0363, 0368, 0369, 0377c, 0384, 0397, 0398, 0398a, 0401, 0405, 0418, 0437, 0446, 0467, 0483, 0492, 0497, 0506, 0522, 0524, 0533, 0542, 0549, 0566, 0570, 0582, 0583, 0584, 0585, 0594, 0597, 0602, 0606, 0609, 0610, 0613, 0618, 0626, 0630, 0632, 0646, 0655, 0666, 0678, 0685, 0690, 0696, 0700, 0703, 0707, 0709, 711, 0716, 0717, 0721, 0722, 0729, 0745, 0752, 0759a, 0759b, 0770, 0789, 0792, 0804, 0821a, 0829, 0836, 0840, 0844, 0848, 0850, 0859, 0863, 0867, 0873, 0876, 0883, 0895, 0901, 0905, 0906, 0908, 0910, 0921, 0936, 0951, 0954, 0959, 0964, 0966, 0973, 0974a, 0979, 0985a, 0986c, 0986a, 0994, 1009, 1013, 1013a, 1017, 1024, 1031, 1033, 1039, 1041, 1043, 1044a, 1046, 1047, 1048, 1067a, 1077, 1083, 1093, 1095, 1101, 1113, 1115, 1118, 1132, 1133, 1135, 1141, 1152, 1153, 1267, 1620, 1664, 2035, 2135, 2709, 2710, 2711, 2712, 2713, 2714, 2715, 2716, 2717, 2718, 2718a, 2718b, 2719, 2720, 2721, 2721a, 2722, 2723, 2724, 2725, 2726, 2727, 2728, 2729, 2729a, 2729b, 2730, 2731, 2731a, 2732, 2732a, 2733, 2734, 2735, 2736, 2736a, 2737, 2738, 2738a, 2739, 2740, 2741, 2742, 2742a, 2743, 2743a, 2743b, 2744, 2745, 2746, 2747, 2748, 2749, 2750, 2751, 2752, 2753, 2754, 2755, 2756, 2757, 2758, 2759, 2760, 2760a, 2761, 2762, 2763, 2764, 2765, 2766, 2767, 2768, 2769, 2770, 2771, 2772, 2773, 2774, 2775, 2775a, 2776, 2777, 2777a, 2778, 2779, 2779a, 2779b, 2780, 2781, 2782, 2783, 2783a, 2784, 2785, 2786, 2787, 2788, 2789, 2789a

Troilus and Cressida, x, xi, xxi, 0002, 0010, 0040, 0054, 0058, 0059, 0062, 0065, 0071, 0073, 0075, 0077, 0078, 0079, 0084, 0096, 0097, 0098, 0104, 0106, 0113, 0121, 0123, 0125, 0131, 0137, 0138, 0147, 0148, 0155, 0156, 0156a, 0160b, 0161, 0163, 0165, 0168, 0170, 0172a, 0174, 0186, 0189, 0192, 0199, 0201, 0208, 0215, 0220, 0222, 0238a, 0243, 0253, 0259, 0263, 0265, 0277, 0281, 0282a, 0283, 0287, 0291, 0292, 0294, 0297, 0302, 0310, 0319a, 0319b, 0324, 0326, 0334, 0337, 0338, 0339, 0342, 0343, 0347, 0349, 0350, 0365, 0369, 0372a, 0376, 0378, 0379, 0380, 0382, 0384, 0386, 0388, 0390, 0391, 0393, 0396, 0398, 0400, 0405, 0410, 0411, 0412, 0414, 0415, 0418, 0422, 0424, 0432, 0433, 0435a, 0437, 0439, 0440, 0441, 0458, 0463, 0469, 0472, 0475, 0478, 0481, 0482, 0489, 0504a, 0508, 0512, 0513, 0518, 0520, 0538, 0544, 0546, 0547, 0549, 0552, 0553, 0553a, 0554, 0555, 0558, 0560, 0561, 0564, 0576, 0578, 0584, 0588, 0589, 0591, 0601, 0602, 0606, 0621, 0625, 0630, 0631, 0642, 0645, 0648, 0652, 0657, 0658, 0675, 0676, 0678, 0685, 0686, 0687, 0688, 0691, 0692, 0697, 0700, 0701, 0702, 0705, 0708, 0714, 0716, 0721, 0723, 0734, 0742, 0745, 0746, 0752, 0765, 0775, 0776, 0780, 0789, 0798, 0806, 0807a, 0813, 0817, 0825, 0826, 0827, 0829a, 0832, 0832a, 0833, 0841, 0845, 0849a, 0852, 0867, 0869, 0870, 0871, 0872, 0873, 0879, 0882, 0883, 0890, 0895, 0896, 0901, 0903, 0909, 0912, 0916, 0919, 0924, 0929, 0936a, 0939, 0945, 0954, 0955, 0956, 0959, 0964, 0966, 0971, 0983, 0986a, 0986b, 0987, 0994, 1000, 1002, 1009, 1011, 1017, 1021, 1023, 1026, 1027, 1031, 1036, 1046, 1049, 1055, 1060, 1063, 1065, 1067, 1072, 1073, 1076, 1081, 1083, 1085, 1090, 1095, 1102, 1110, 1111, 1112, 1117, 1130, 1147, 1267, 1474, 1614, 1616, 1630, 1648, 2628, 2685, 2790, 2791, 2792, 2793, 2794, 2795, 2796, 2797, 2797a, 2798, 2799, 2800, 2801, 2802, 2803, 2804, 2805, 2806, 2807, 2808, 2809, 2810, 2810a, 2811, 2812, 2813, 2814, 2815, 2816, 2817, 2818, 2819, 2820, 2821, 2822, 2824, 2825, 2826, 2827, 2828, 2829, 2830, 2831, 2832, 2833, 2834, 2834a, 2835, 2836, 2837, 2838, 2839, 2840, 2841, 2842, 2843, 2844, 2845, 2846, 2847, 2848, 2849, 2850, 2851, 2852, 2853, 2854, 2855, 2856, 2857, 2858, 2858a, 2859, 2860, 2861, 2862, 2863, 2864, 2865, 2866, 2867, 2869, 2870, 2871, 2872, 2873, 2874, 2875, 2876, 2877, 2878, 2879, 2880, 2881, 2882, 2883, 2884, 2885, 2886, 2887, 2888, 2889, 2890, 2890a, 2891, 2892, 2893, 2894, 2895, 2896, 2897, 2898, 2899, 2900, 2901, 2902, 2903, 2904, 2905, 2906, 2907, 2908, 2909, 2910, 2911, 2912, 2913, 2914, 2915, 2916, 2917, 2918, 2919, 2920, 2921, 2922, 2923, 2924, 2925, 2926, 2927, 2928, 2929, 2930, 2931, 2932, 2933, 2934, 2935, 2936, 2937, 2938, 2939, 2940, 2941, 2942, 2943, 2944, 2945, 2945a, 2946, 2947, 2948, 2949, 2950, 2951, 2952, 2953, 2954, 2955, 2956, 2957, 2958, 2959, 2960, 2961, 2962, 2963, 2964, 2964a, 2965, 2966, 2967, 2968, 2969, 2970, 2971, 2972, 2973, 2974, 2975, 2976, 2977, 2978, 2979, 2980, 2981, 2982, 2983, 2984, 2985, 2986, 2987, 2988, 2989, 2990, 2991, 2992, 2993, 2994,

Index of Names of Shakespeare's Works

2995, 2996, 2997, 2998, 2998a, 2999, 3000, 3001, 3002, 3003, 3004, 3005, 3006, 3007, 3008, 3009, 3010, 3011, 3012, 3013, 3014, 3015, 3016, 3017, 3018, 3019, 3020, 3021, 3022, 3023, 3024, 3025, 3026, 3027, 3028, 3029, 3030, 3031, 3032, 3033, 3034, 3035, 3036, 3037, 3038, 3039, 3040, 3041, 3042, 3043, 3044, 3045, 3046, 3047, 3048, 3049, 3049a, 3050, 3051, 3052, 3053, 3054, 3055, 3056, 3057, 3058, 3059, 3060, 3061, 3062, 3063, 3064, 3064a, 3065, 3066, 3067, 3068, 3069, 3070, 3071, 3072, 3073, 3074

Twelfth Night, xxii, 0062, 0091, 0092, 0157, 0168, 0211, 0235, 0272, 0273, 0278, 0307, 0353a, 0377c, 0431, 0434, 0476, 0490, 0500, 0518, 0546, 0556, 0590, 0621, 0637a, 0690, 0695, 0718, 0721, 0758, 0797, 0801, 0812, 0821a, 0843, 0881, 0892, 0920, 0923, 0969, 1000, 1027, 1040, 1063, 1072, 1077, 1109, 1114, 1945, 2135, 3075, 3076, 3077, 3078, 3079, 3080, 3081, 3082, 3082a, 3083, 3083a, 3084, 3085, 3085a, 3086, 3087, 3090

Two Gentlemen of Verona, The, 0062, 0096, 0099, 0102, 0119, 0140, 0168, 0211, 0274, 0275, 0353a, 0446, 0466, 0510, 0518, 0580, 0637a, 0690, 0693, 0720, 0721, 0745, 0758, 0759, 0797, 0969, 1052, 1064, 1067a, 1079, 1081, 3078, 3088, 3089, 3090

Two Noble Kinsmen, The, xi, xxii, 0062, 0087, 0104, 0185, 0325, 0406, 0437, 0489, 0710, 0781, 0901, 1043, 1049, 1133, 3090a, 3091, 3092, 3093, 3094, 3094a, 3095, 3096, 3097, 3098, 3099, 3100, 3100a, 3100b, 3101, 3102, 3103, 3104

V

Venus and Adonis, xi, xxii, 0002, 0045, 0052, 0062, 0065, 0071, 0073, 0102, 0104, 0119, 0123, 0154, 0160, 0173a, 0185a, 0187, 0192, 0267, 0283, 0319, 0327, 0332, 0338, 0350, 0357, 0370, 0370a, 0377c, 0379a, 0394, 0398a, 0401, 0437, 0438, 0448, 0458, 0465, 0483, 0489, 0560, 0561, 0571, 0572, 0573, 0597, 0601, 0614, 0627, 0665, 0683, 0685, 0715, 0721, 0724, 0727, 0746, 0756, 0816, 0816a, 0835, 0841, 0852, 0863, 0869, 0873, 0882, 0888, 0901, 0910, 0922a, 0934, 0935, 1009, 1025, 1034, 1052, 1062, 1129, 1153, 1428, 1785, 2406, 2485, 2541, 2715, 2722, 3105, 3106, 3107, 3108, 3109, 3110, 3111, 3112, 3113, 3114, 3115, 3116, 3117, 3118, 3119, 3120, 3121, 3122, 3123, 3124, 3125, 3126, 3126a, 3127, 3128, 3129, 3130, 3131, 3132, 3133, 3134, 3135, 3136, 3137, 3139, 3140, 3141, 3142, 3143, 3144, 3145, 3146, 3147, 3148, 3149, 3150, 3151, 3152, 3153, 3154, 3155, 3156, 3157, 3158, 3159, 3160, 3161, 3162, 3163, 3164, 3165, 3166, 3167, 3168, 3169

W

Winter's Tale, The, xi, xxii, 0012, 0062, 0095, 0096, 0104, 0108, 0114, 0119, 0149, 0151, 0160a, 0164a, 0183, 0194, 0281, 0282b, 0299a, 0300, 0307, 0311, 0311a, 0336, 0353, 0375, 0382, 0385, 0385a, 0394, 0406, 0434, 0457, 0474, 0489, 0495, 0505, 0518, 0531, 0542, 0556, 0577, 0590, 0610, 0623, 0649, 0676, 0690, 0693, 0699, 0721, 0727, 0769, 0771, 0781, 0794, 0804, 0807, 0830, 0843, 0873, 0888a, 0891, 0891a, 0892, 0898, 0901, 0907, 0922, 0922a, 0941, 0942, 0947, 0953, 0957, 0969, 0976, 0982, 0990, 0994, 0997, 1021, 1043, 1052, 1063, 1080, 1082, 1090, 1108, 1114, 1121, 1125, 1128, 1133, 1151, 2432, 3170, 3171, 3172, 3173, 3174, 3175, 3176, 3177, 3178, 3179, 3179a, 3180, 3181, 3182, 3182a, 3183, 3184, 3184a, 3185, 3186, 3186a, 3187, 3188, 3189, 3189a, 3190, 3191, 3192, 3193, 3194, 3195, 3196, 3197, 3198, 3199, 3200, 3201, 3202, 3203, 3204, 3205, 3206, 3207, 3208, 3209, 3210

INDEX OF SUBJECTS

Index of Subjects includes key concepts, descriptive terms, and names and works of dramatists, poets, writers of fiction, philosophers, artists, musicians, and others mentioned in studies of Shakespeare

A
Aaron
 in *Titus Andronicus*, 0062, 0185a, 0206, 0207, 0234, 0283, 0330, 0609, 0613, 0618, 0646, 0662, 0703, 0759b, 0895, 0985a, 0994, 1013a, 1113, 2718, 2718a, 2721a, 2722, 2726, 2727, 2731a, 2738a, 2745, 2756, 2774, 2777, 2779, 2780
Aaron's son
 in *Titus Andronicus*, 0318
Abel, 1983a
 Cain and, 1422
Abhorson
 in *Measure for Measure*, 0842
ab ovo, 0556
Abraham, 0542
absolutism, 1720
accidie, 0198
Achilles, 0019, 0208, 0589, 0680, 1610, 1614, 1627, 1628, 1680a, 1766, 2182, 2942, 3007
 in *Troilus and Cressida*, 0097, 0106, 0172a, 0265, 0294, 0396, 0481, 0576, 0692, 0987, 1029, 1103, 2803, 2826, 2859, 2871, 2872, 2877, 2885, 2891, 2899, 2904, 2910, 2924, 2926, 2930, 2931, 2936, 2939, 2953, 2980, 2986, 2989, 2991, 3015, 3020, 3021, 3027, 3033, 3043, 3044, 3050, 3053, 3062, 3065
Achilles Tatius, 0928, 1762, 2363
 Clitophon and Leucippe, 0067, 0068, 0284, 0769, 0987, 0997, 1114
Actaeon, xiv, xix, 0118, 0126, 0721, 1077, 1352, 2135, 2266a, 2267, 2268, 2270, 2284, 2352, 2558, 2633, 3082, 06678
acting, 0099, 0228, 1853
action
 thought and, 2849
 words and, 2945
action, unity of, 0534, 0779, 0822
action (as concept or element of drama), 0061, 0125, 0161, 0167, 0177, 0197, 0202, 0208, 0223, 0238, 0245, 0302, 0310, 0319, 0376, 0432, 0446, 0464, 0473, 0504, 0644, 0690, 0748, 0759a, 0891, 0969, 1031, 1032, 1034, 1035, 1038, 1047, 1048, 1072, 1084, 1126, 1181, 1241, 1242, 1258, 1309, 1326, 1370, 1467, 1474, 1498, 1521, 1961, 2141, 2144, 10051
Actium, battle of, 1169, 1388
 in *Antony and Cleopatra*, 0073, 0106, 0255, 0521, 0828, 1047, 1174, 1175, 1238, 1252, 1255, 1264, 1324, 1328, 1351, 1362, 1369, 1492, 1525
actor, 0129

Adam, 1362, 1543, 2581
 in *As You Like It*, 0322a, 1543c
Ad Herennium (Rhetorica ad Herennium), 0759a, 1920, 2242a
Adlington, William
 translation of Apuleius's *Metamorphoses* as *The Golden Asse*, 0807, 1051, 1052, 1053, 1163, 1490, 1884, 1885, 1886, 2116, 2285, 2298, 2301, 2324, 2698. *See also under* Apuleius, Lucius
Admetus, 3210
Admiral's Men, 0605
admiratio, 0947
adolescence, 2463
Adonis, xix, 0685, 1934, 2332, 2468, 2495, 2538, 2540, 3149, 3159
 in *Venus and Adonis*, xxii, 0237, 0283, 0332, 0379a, 0437, 0438, 0448, 0458, 0627, 0638, 0665, 0910, 0996, 3105, 3106, 3107, 3108, 3109, 3110, 3111, 3112, 3113, 3114, 3116, 3117, 3121, 3122, 3124, 3125, 3126, 3127, 3128, 3129, 3130, 3133, 3134, 3136, 3137, 3140, 3141, 3143, 3144, 3145, 3149, 3150, 3151, 3152, 3154, 3155, 3158, 3159, 3160, 3161, 3162, 3163, 3167, 3169
Adrian
 in *Coriolanus*, 1676
Adriana
 in *Comedy of Errors, The*, 1006, 1575, 1578, 1584, 1587
aduluscens, 0556
Aegeus, 1576
Aelian (Claudius Aelianus), 0739, 0760, 1532, 1906
Aeneas, xv, xvii, 0029, 0152, 0208, 0216, 0322a, 0421, 0436, 0533, 0610, 0647, 0759a, 0759b, 0789, 0815, 0902, 0932, 0961, 1162, 1171a, 1193, 1201, 1206, 1287, 1296, 1310, 1312, 1346, 1370a, 1371, 1512, 1543c, 1562, 1774, 1776, 1800, 1804, 1805, 1808, 1836, 1837, 1859, 1872, 1880, 1883, 1892, 1895, 2166, 2390, 2401, 2553, 2564, 2566a, 2569a, 2572, 2574, 2588, 2593, 2605, 2762
 in *Troilus and Cressida*, 0700, 2804, 2879, 3070
Aeschylus, 0007, 0152, 0468, 0597, 0615, 0788, 1098, 1673, 1793, 3196
 Agamemnon, 0355, 0574
 Oresteia, 0853, 1515, 1851, 1876, 1880, 2789
 Persians, 0725
 Persians, The, 0278a
Aesculapius, 1039

Index of Subjects

Aesop, 0916, 0936, 0938, 1146, 1650, 1652, 1706
aesthetics, 0213, 0285
Aethiopica, by Heliodorus. See under Heliodorus
aevum, 0628
Africa, 0609, 2756
Africans, 0609
Africanus, John Leo
  History and Description of Africa, The, 0609
Africanus, Leo
  Description of Africa, 2551
Agamemnon, 0610
  in *Troilus and Cressida,* 0208, 0265, 0700, 0734, 2794, 2849, 2872, 2879, 3005, 3009, 3011
age, 0095
  youth and, 0970, 0997
agedness, 1789a
ages of man, four, 0840
ages of man, seven, xv, 0377b, 0807, 1531, 1535, 1546, 2367
aggression, xvi, 0377c, 1590, 2828
agon, 0061, 0414, 1146a, 1627
Agricola, Rudolf, 1810
agriculture, 1920
Agrippa, 1522
  in *Antony and Cleopatra,* 1464
Agrippa, Cornelius, 2551a, 2573, 2600
  Of the Nobilitie and Excellencie of Womankynde, 2537
Agrippa, Henry Cornelius
  De Occulta Philosophia, 1149a
Aguecheek, Sir Andrew
  in *Twelfth Night,* 0821a, 3083a
Ajax, 0509, 0687, 1002, 1312, 1760, 1766, 2199a
  in *The Rape of Lucrece,* 0105
  in *Troilus and Cressida,* 0265, 0342, 2864, 2873, 2885, 2891, 2918, 2931, 2936, 2939, 2955, 2974, 2986, 3015, 3052
Alarbus
  in *Titus Andronicus,* 0610, 0792, 2740, 2779
alazon, 0616, 0798, 1188, 2181, 2265
Albany, Duke of
  in *King Lear,* 2172
Albee, Edward
  American Dream, The, 1102
Alberti, Leon Battista
  On Painting, 0907
Alceste
  in Molière's *Le Misanthrope,* 1752
Alcestis, xxii, 3198, 3210
alchemical imagery, 2199b
alchemy, 0160a, 0307, 0480, 0637a, 0729, 0802a, 0828, 1067a, 1159, 2118, 2381, 2473, 2611
Alciati, Andrea, 2521
Alciatus, Andrea
  Emblematum Liber, 0300
Alcibiades, 0109, 0359, 0387, 0450, 1940, 2642
  in *Timon of Athens,* 0161, 0201, 0232, 0328, 0343, 0393, 0398, 0522, 0690, 0700, 0782, 0792, 0941, 0971, 0986a, 1023, 1112, 1123, 2610, 2615, 2616, 2627, 2631, 2634, 2637, 2639, 2643, 2651, 2656, 2657, 2658, 2660, 2665, 2672, 2681, 2684, 2687, 2692, 2694, 2696, 2697, 2699, 2704
Alcmaeon, 1828
Alcyone, 0132, 2274
alethes, 0616
Alexander
  in *Troilus and Cressida,* 2918, 2986
Alexander of Pherae, 1819, 1823, 1826, 2231a
Alexander the Great, xvi, xvii, 0387, 0537, 0805, 1175, 1831, 1868, 1907, 1927, 1929, 1931, 1933, 2152, 2199a
Alexandria, 0882, 1159, 1175, 1185, 1225, 1419
  Rome and, 0927, 0935
Alexas
  in *Antony and Cleopatra,* 1525
alienation, 0284, 1057, 1593, 2671
allegories, 0370a
allegory, 0120, 0203, 0232, 0573, 0726, 0813, 0884, 0934, 1062, 1095, 1129, 1371, 1679, 2230, 2253, 2355, 2775a
Alonso
  in *Tempest, The,* 0490, 2557, 2588, 2607
amalgams, character, 2957
Amazons, 0963, 1935, 2172, 3100a
  in *Timon of Athens,* 0197, 0290, 0373, 0421, 0700, 0744, 2618, 2633, 2638, 2652, 2681, 2689, 2689a
ambiguity, 2982
ambition, 0080a, 0152, 0219, 0239, 0369, 0432, 0452, 0932, 0949, 1306, 1453, 1458, 1464, 1524, 1741a, 1927, 2010, 2021, 2042, 2046, 2216, 2452, 2569a
ambitions, 0086, 1047
amenorrhea, 2216
amibition, 2205
amimetobion, 1165
Ammon, 0132
Amphion, xx, 1539, 2251, 2545
amphitheater, 0783
Amyot, Jacques
  preface to French translation of Plutarch's *Lives,* 0345, 2477
  translation of Plutarch's *Lives* into French, 0208, 1419, 1945
anachronism, 0413, 0721, 0749, 1774, 1775, 1963
anachronisms, 0778, 0780
Anacreon, 2517, 2547
anadiplosis, 0835, 1074
anagnorisis, 0795, 0946, 1014, 1054, 1091, 1789, 2142, 3114
analogy, 2006
anamorphism, 2895
anaphora, 1072, 1074, 2323
anarchy, 0106
  order and, 2157
anatomy, 0606
Anchises, 0322a, 0759a, 1543c, 1872
ancients, 0059, 0124, 0160, 0229, 0460
ancient world, 0010, 0057, 0100, 0119, 0137, 0384, 0694, 1138, 1322
ancilla, 0556

Andrea dell' Anguillara, Giovanni
 translation of Ovid's *Metamorphoses,* 2282
androgyne, 0637a, 0828, 1217, 2519, 3075, 3085a
androgynous vision, 0598a
androgyny, xiv, 0307, 0431, 0637a, 0638, 1126, 1287, 2380
Andromache, 0610, 1070, 1819, 1826, 2454
 in *Troilus and Cressida,* 0964
Angelo, 2240
 in *Measure for Measure,* 0078, 0801, 0961, 0962, 1071, 2242, 2244, 2245a
angels, 1455
anger, 0091, 0106, 0191, 0350, 0377, 0454, 0697, 0959, 1086, 1175, 1183, 1225, 1420, 1454, 1590, 1602, 1709, 1712, 1748, 2605
anger, women's, 2754
Angus
 in *Macbeth,* 2223
animal
 man and, 0901
animal imagery, 0060
Anna, 0436, 2532
Anouilh, Jean
 Lark, The, 1385
Anselm, St., 2046
Antaeus, 1538, 1543c
antagonists, 0439
antanaclasis, 1072
Antenor
 in *Troilus and Cressida,* 2879, 2960
Anteros
 Eros and, 2521
anticlimax, 0844, 2833, 2961
antifeminism, 0057, 2673
Antigone, 0464a, 0509
Antigonus
 in *Winter's Tale, The,* 0300, 3174, 3183, 3203, 3205
antimasque, 1409
antimetabole, 2323, 2443
anti-myth, 2933
Antiochus
 in *Pericles,* 2360, 2368, 2372
Antiochus IV Epiphanes, 2372
Antiopa, 2303
anti-Petrarchism
 Petrarchism and, 2488a
Antipholus of Ephesus
 in *Comedy of Errors, The,* 1137, 1575
Antipholus of Syracuse
 in *Comedy of Errors, The,* 1570, 1575, 1576, 1589
antipophora, 0470
antiquarianism, 1770
antiquity, 0002, 0092, 0098, 0102, 0119, 0129, 0153, 0175, 0443, 0525, 0578, 0976, 1122, 1123
anti-rhetoricism, 0454
anti-theatricality, 0688
antithesis, 0332, 0835, 1129, 1237, 1250, 1633, 1658, 2513

Antium
 in *Coriolanus,* 1009, 1613
Antonio
 in *Merchant of Venice, The,* 1006, 2247, 2248, 2258
 in *Tempest, The,* 2545, 2553, 2557, 2565a, 2566a, 2588, 2588a
Antonio's Revenge. See under Marston, John.
Antony, Mark (Marcus Antonius), 0009, 0208, 0290, 0324, 0555, 0629, 0698, 0765, 0778, 0873, 1193, 1202, 1325, 1334, 1345, 1374, 1398, 1472, 1520, 1524, 2031, 2642
 in *Antony and Cleopatra,* 0070a, 0082, 0095, 0106, 0112, 0113, 0131, 0141, 0154, 0167, 0171, 0173a, 0174, 0177, 0180, 0187, 0192, 0208, 0215, 0232, 0234, 0239, 0244, 0255, 0277, 0283, 0292a, 0305, 0306, 0310, 0319b, 0321, 0329, 0330, 0333, 0344, 0351, 0359, 0372a, 0388, 0391, 0400, 0422, 0424, 0427, 0452, 0452a, 0455, 0463, 0464a, 0468, 0471, 0498, 0503, 0504a, 0521, 0530, 0546, 0551, 0553, 0554, 0581, 0599, 0602, 0607, 0609, 0613, 0633, 0646, 0663a, 0679, 0700, 0703, 0705, 0729, 0732, 0734, 0751, 0759a, 0778, 0779, 0827, 0865, 0867, 0870, 0887, 0889, 0898, 0911, 0927, 0931, 0932, 0964, 0983a, 0985a, 0986a, 1000, 1002, 1017, 1021, 1037, 1047, 1055, 1058, 1084, 1086, 1087, 1099, 1100, 1106, 1135, 1139, 1152, 1164, 1165, 1167, 1168, 1171, 1171a, 1172, 1174, 1175, 1176, 1178, 1179, 1181, 1183, 1185, 1186, 1188, 1188a, 1191, 1195, 1196, 1196a, 1198, 1200, 1201, 1205, 1206, 1210, 1211, 1212a, 1214, 1215, 1216, 1217a, 1218, 1220, 1223, 1224, 1226, 1228, 1229, 1231, 1233, 1235, 1238, 1239, 1240, 1242, 1243, 1245, 1246, 1247, 1248, 1250a, 1251, 1253, 1254, 1255, 1256, 1258, 1260, 1261, 1262, 1264, 1266, 1271, 1276, 1278, 1280, 1281, 1284, 1285, 1287, 1290, 1291, 1293, 1297, 1299, 1301, 1303a, 1305, 1307, 1309, 1310, 1312, 1313, 1315, 1318a, 1319, 1321, 1322, 1323, 1327, 1328, 1330, 1331, 1333, 1335, 1336, 1337, 1339, 1340, 1343, 1347, 1349, 1350, 1353, 1354, 1354a, 1355, 1356, 1360, 1362, 1364, 1366, 1367, 1368, 1369, 1370, 1370a, 1371, 1372, 1373, 1375, 1376, 1377, 1378, 1380, 1383, 1384, 1385, 1386, 1387, 1388, 1390, 1391, 1392, 1393, 1394, 1397, 1399, 1400, 1403, 1404, 1405, 1406, 1409, 1410, 1411, 1414, 1415, 1417, 1418, 1419, 1420, 1422, 1423, 1424, 1425, 1427, 1428, 1429, 1430, 1433, 1436, 1437, 1438, 1439, 1443, 1444, 1445, 1446, 1449, 1451, 1453, 1455, 1457, 1458, 1459, 1460a, 1461, 1462, 1463, 1465, 1466, 1474, 1474a, 1477, 1479, 1480, 1481, 1483, 1485, 1488, 1489, 1490, 1491, 1492, 1493, 1500, 1502, 1503, 1505, 1506, 1510, 1512, 1513, 1514, 1517, 1518, 1521, 1522, 1524, 1525, 1526, 1527, 1528, 1528a, 2107, 3143
 in *Julius Caesar,* 0175, 0186, 0201, 0219, 0246, 0247, 0255, 0271, 0305, 0377, 0398,

Index of Subjects

0432, 0463, 0495, 0508, 0537, 0599, 0637, 0641, 0661, 0679, 0690, 0700, 0723, 0792, 0805, 0886, 0949, 1021, 1047, 1100, 1941, 1943, 1944, 1946, 1952, 1961, 1968, 1976, 1981, 1982, 1983b, 1984, 1999, 2005, 2006, 2007, 2008, 2011, 2012, 2013a, 2014, 2016, 2018, 2022, 2022a, 2029, 2034, 2037, 2040, 2044, 2047, 2050, 2051, 2051a, 2053, 2061, 2063, 2066, 2068, 2071, 2073, 2076, 2077, 2078, 2079, 2083, 2093, 2097, 2098, 2103, 2104, 2107, 2113, 2114, 2117, 2123, 2126, 2128, 2130, 2133, 2135, 2136
anxiety, 1873
anxiety, persecutory, 2679
anxiety of influence, 2480
Apemantus
  in *Timon of Athens*, 0161, 0163, 0197, 0232, 0372a, 0373, 0393, 0545, 0690, 0825, 0920, 0986a, 2610, 2618, 2627, 2631, 2634, 2636, 2638, 2658, 2659, 2673, 2674, 2681, 2687, 2689a, 2694, 3034
aphorisms, 2138
Aphrodite, 0999, 3194
Aphthonius, 0616, 0685, 1857
  Progymnasmata, 0404, 0663, 1856, 2998a
Apocalypse, 1257, 1397
apocalypse, 2874
Apollo, xviii, 0107, 0375, 0382, 0807, 1121, 1708, 2148, 2183, 2189, 2190, 2193, 2194, 2199, 2199b, 2305, 2452, 2478, 2540, 3075, 3182, 3184a, 3193, 3196, 3197, 3209
  Pan and, 1021
  in *Winter's Tale, The*, 0649, 0942
Apollo, oracle of
  in *Winter's Tale, The*, 3186, 3190
Apollonian principle
  Dionysian principle and, 0644
Apollonius of Tyre, 0092, 0284, 0308, 0415, 1114, 1580, 2354, 2363, 2366, 2371, 2373, 2556
  version of John Gower, 0434, 1574
  version of Lawrence Twine, 0434
Apollonius of Tyre, 0814, 0997, 2370
apostrophe, 0737
appearance, 0252
  reality and, 1138, 1857, 2320, 2835, 2911, 3015, 3074, 3175
appetite, 0548, 0685, 0708, 1095, 1111, 3024, 3047
Appian, 0101, 0668, 0759a, 0932, 0973, 1009, 1345, 1468, 1524, 2031
  Bella Civilia, 2044
  Chronicle of the Romans' Wars, 2024
  Civil War, 0778
  Civil Wars, The, 1047
  Romanes Warres, The, 1468
Apuleius, Lucius, 0928, 0999, 1468, 2276, 2317, 2473, 3176
  Apologia, 1052, 2351
  Golden Ass, The (Metamorphoses, The Golden Asse), xv, 0118, 0307, 0369, 0415, 0807, 0900, 1051, 1052, 1053, 1163, 1261, 1490, 1570, 2116, 2271, 2285, 2292, 2298, 2301, 2313a, 2324, 2343, 2346, 2350, 2547

  Metamorphoses (The Golden Ass, The Golden Asse), 1884, 1885, 1886, 2698. *See also under* Adlington, William
Aquinas, St. Thomas, 0101, 0110, 0218, 0499, 0513, 0625, 0820, 0945, 0961, 2046, 2145, 2223
Arachne, 2931, 2969, 3042
Aragon, Prince of
  in *Merchant of Venice, The*, 2256
Arcadia, 0855
Archaionomia, 1995
archetype, 0096, 1405
archetypes, 0096
Arcite
  in *Two Noble Kinsmen, The*, 0406, 0901, 3090a, 3094, 3096, 3098, 3100a, 3100b, 3102
Ardea
  in *The Rape of Lucrece*, 0261
Arden
  in *As You Like It*, 1553
arete, 0446a, 0526, 0946
Aretino, Pietro, 0235, 2403
  L'Ipocrito, 0235
Argus, 2918
Ariachne, 2938, 2969, 3042
Ariadne, 2249, 2293, 2969, 3042, 3088
Ariel
  in *Tempest, The*, 0336, 0490, 0759b, 0881, 2544, 2561, 2565, 2568, 2576, 2578a, 2587, 2588, 2603
  in *The Tempest*, 0095
Ariosto, Ludovico, 0102, 0281, 2172, 3154
  Studenti, 0556
  Suppositi, 0923
  Suppositi, I, 2535, 2542
Aristides, 2665
aristocracy, 0388, 0561, 1681, 2836, 2946
aristocrat, 0355
aristocrats, 0750, 2642
  in *Coriolanus*, 1596, 1644, 1683
  in *Julius Caesar*, 0949
Aristophanes, 0468, 0788, 0890, 0923, 1146a, 2519
  Clouds, 0450
  Lysistrata, 0153
  Wasps, 1650
Aristotelians, 2170
Aristotle, xvii, xviii, xx, 0056, 0080, 0080a, 0091, 0167, 0182, 0193, 0258, 0266, 0291, 0298, 0299, 0319, 0320, 0321, 0323, 0332, 0346, 0353, 0370a, 0375, 0385, 0386a, 0394, 0401, 0408, 0472, 0485, 0488, 0499, 0500, 0501, 0504, 0511, 0513, 0517, 0519, 0526, 0529, 0557, 0566, 0601, 0611, 0614, 0625, 0640, 0657, 0674, 0728, 0729, 0748, 0760, 0785, 0787, 0812, 0818, 0835, 0846, 0893, 0903, 0905a, 0920, 0926, 0945, 0948, 0955, 0961, 0969, 0989, 1000, 1004, 1005, 1006, 1022, 1023, 1044, 1059, 1061, 1063, 1079, 1098, 1109, 1116, 1122, 1123, 1175, 1258, 1565, 1674, 1680a, 1723, 1813, 1879a, 1881, 1888, 1907, 1999, 2042, 2096, 2106, 2118, 2170, 2227, 2248, 2440a, 2490, 2498,

Aristotle *(continued)*, 2563, 2587, 2609, 2642, 2665, 2682, 2867, 2882, 3176, 3185
  Ethics, 0455, 0604, 0616, 0699, 0999, 1592, 1709, 1894, 2211, 2471, 2515, 2602, 2631, 3102
  Metaphysics, 0097, 0804a
  Nicomachean Ethics, 0174, 0359, 0886, 0962, 1175, 1354, 1842a, 2240, 2592, 2860, 2960, 2985
  Poetics, 0083, 0113, 0120, 0124, 0128, 0143, 0145, 0166, 0218, 0228, 0278, 0329, 0404, 0446a, 0476, 0484, 0572, 0575, 0604, 0664, 0788, 0804a, 0917, 0959, 1035, 1118, 1354, 1375, 1634, 1783, 1789, 1871, 1875, 1899, 2211, 2219, 2238, 2287, 2356, 2471, 2602
    hamartia and, 0133
  Politics, 0212, 0384, 0735, 0843, 0999, 1630, 1650, 1894, 2592, 2602, 2629
  Problems, 0144
  Rhetoric, 0145, 0661, 0788, 0804a, 0917, 1810, 1871, 1908, 2213, 2242a, 2499
arithmetic, 0299
Arlecchino, 2595
Armado
  in *Love's Labor's Lost,* 0455, 0905, 2187, 2190, 2199, 2199a
armies, 1036
Armin, Robert, 1638
armor, 1387a
art, 0888a, 1184, 1511, 2550, 2554, 2563, 2581, 2604, 2803, 2994, 3027, 3180, 3189, 3198, 3209
  history and, 0467
  life and, 2608
  magic and, 2545, 2546
  nature and, 0375, 0402, 0513, 0656, 0729, 0802a, 0848a, 0884, 0922a, 1514, 2185a, 2574, 2578a, 3170, 3172, 3184, 3198
  science and, 1016
  truth and, 2619
art, mannerist, 3064
art, visual, 0576
Artemidorus
  in *Julius Caesar,* 2077
Artemidorus of Daldis
  Oneirocritica, 2290
Artemis, 3075
Arthur
  in *King John,* 0296
artificiality, 1061
artisans
  in *Julius Caesar,* 2134
  in *Midsummer Night's Dream, A,* 2279
artists, 0070a
artists, Italian, 3157
arts, 1824
arts, visual, 0002, 2556
arts of the actor, 0105
Arviragus
  in *Cymbeline,* 1772
asceticism, 1139, 2654
Asclepiades, 0547a
Asclepius, 0096

Ashley, Robert
  Of Honour, 0291
asp, 1351, 1507, 1508, 1511
asps, 1175, 1176, 1316
ass, 1146
assassination, 0610, 1008
assassination of Julius Caesar
  in *Julius Caesar,* 0106, 0161, 0172, 0213, 0224, 0252, 0255, 0337, 0377, 0508, 0607, 0655, 0679, 0776, 0778, 0973, 0998, 1952, 1953, 1954, 1963, 1972, 2007, 2012, 2015, 2018, 2033, 2040, 2042, 2045, 2046, 2047, 2051, 2052, 2057, 2059, 2061, 2064, 2071, 2076, 2078, 2079, 2097, 2102a, 2109, 2112a, 2113b, 2118, 2133
assassinations, 0654
assassins, 0764
asteismus, 1072
Astley, John
  Art of Riding, The, 3126
Astraea, xvii, 0359, 0620, 1934, 2728
astrologers, 1531
astrological thought, 2475a
astrology, 0480, 0832a, 1067a, 2176, 2208a, 2473, 2526
astronomy, 0729
asyndeton, 0558, 2527a
Atalanta, 1561
Ate, 0382, 2233
Athamas, 2237
atheism, 0756
Athena, 1887, 2433
Athena Polias, 3193
Athenian drama, 0399, 0640
Athenians, 0833
Athens, 0080, 0630, 0675, 0678, 0971, 1123, 2146a, 2610, 2620, 2631, 2634, 2637, 2638, 2665, 2672, 2684, 2704, 2762
Athens, metaphor of, 2662
athlete, 1538
Atlas, 0605
Atreus, 2735
aubade, 0336
Aubrey, John, 0072
Aufidius, 0594
  in *Coriolanus,* 0106, 0120, 0129, 0171, 0172a, 0237, 0369, 0398, 0407, 0459, 0473, 0593, 0607, 0776, 0779, 0782, 0792, 0873, 0911, 0927, 1593, 1601, 1602, 1603, 1609, 1610, 1614, 1644, 1654, 1660, 1667, 1670a, 1671, 1690, 1692, 1693, 1696, 1697, 1699, 1702, 1703, 1710, 1718, 1730, 1740a, 1745, 1749
augury, 0230, 1790, 1791
Augustan idea, 0359
Augustine (Aurelius Augustinus), St. Augustine of Hippo, xi, 0101, 0124, 0191, 0218, 0385a, 0499, 0625, 0635, 0697, 0940, 0973, 0998, 1063, 1068, 1175, 1532, 1813, 2096, 2122, 2145, 2223, 2390, 2397, 2403, 2409, 2418, 2528
  City of God, The (De Civitate Dei), 0127, 0133, 1175, 2333
  Confessions, 0133

Index of Subjects

Augustus, first Roman emperor, 1765, 2056, 3082
Aurelius, Marcus, 0721, 1874, 2096
  Meditations, 1063, 1994
authority, 0648, 0765, 1377, 1474
Autolycus, 3200
  in *Winter's Tale, The*, 0577, 0690, 0807, 0891, 0942, 1009, 2199, 3180, 3184a, 3186, 3189, 3193
  in *The Winter's Tale*, 0095
avarice, 2248
avenger, 0208, 0246, 1830, 1834a
Averell
  Marvailous Combat of Contrarieties, 1609

B

Bacchus, 1184, 1222, 1301, 1312, 1313, 1366, 1455, 2280
  in *Antony and Cleopatra*, 0700, 1171
Bacon, Francis, Lord Verulam and Viscount St. Albans, 0375, 0621
Bacon, Roger, 0624
Bacon, Sir Francis, 0760, 1122
Ballet Comique, 0099
Bandello, Matteo, 2465, 2785
banditti
  in *Timon of Athens*, 2614
banishment, 0791, 0831, 0971, 1633, 1689, 1735, 1745, 2144
banishments, 0654
banquet, 0178, 0373, 0607, 0700, 0954, 1123, 1697, 2554, 2565, 2571, 2575, 2588, 2607, 2638, 2665, 2676, 2689, 2727, 2743b, 2752, 2763, 2765, 2776, 2777a, 2779b, 2783a
Banquet of Heavenly Love, 0627
banquet of sense. *See* sense, banquet of
Banquo
  in *Macbeth*, 0292a, 0610, 2214
Barabas
  in *The Jew of Malta*, by Christopher Marlowe, 0185a, 0206, 0829
barbarism, 0398a, 1135, 1539
barbarity, 0792
Barckley, Richard, 2674
  Discourse on the Felicity of Man, 2694
Bardolph
  in *Henry IV, Part 2*, 1911
Barnardine
  in *Measure for Measure*, 2244
Barnes, Joseph
  Praise of Musicke, The, 0699
Barnfield, Richard
  Affectionate Shepherd, 2481
Baroque
  Shakespeare and, 0298
baroque, 1112, 1434, 2345
Bassanio
  in *Merchant of Venice, The*, 2248, 2251, 2252, 2253, 2254, 2260, 2261
Bassianus
  in *Titus Andronicus*, 0792, 2739
Batman, Stephen, 0760, 2768
  Golden Booke of the Leaden Goddes, The, 0868

battle, 1749
battle sequence in *Troilus and Cressida*, 2808
Baucis, 2274
bawd, 1246, 2825
bawdiness, 0731
bawdry, 1395, 2854
bawdy, 0283
Beard, Thomas, 1242
Beatrice
  in Dante, 0385
  in *Much Ado About Nothing*, 0088, 0610, 0758, 0963, 2319, 2322
Beaumont, Francis, 1753
Beauty, 1185, 2386, 2512
beauty, 0075, 0097, 0335, 0347a, 0435, 0549, 0573, 0726, 0863, 0907, 1081, 1175, 1191, 1195, 1229, 1242, 1257, 1275, 1477, 1506, 1956, 2191, 2252, 2377, 2383, 2385, 2434, 2464, 2468a, 2478, 2483, 2501, 2520, 2634, 2726, 2790, 2792, 2855, 3121, 3130, 3133, 3165
beauty, epicene, 2483
Beeston, William, 0072
beginning (as element of drama), 0846
Belleforest, François de
  Histoires Tragiques, 1811
Bellerophon, 0563, 1893a
Bellona, 1163
belly, fable of the
  in *Coriolanus*, xvi, 0120, 0456, 0528, 0553, 0686, 0759a, 1609, 1629, 1630, 1638, 1649, 1651, 1652, 1653, 1660, 1669, 1704, 1710, 1716, 1728
belly, parable of the
  in *Coriolanus*, 1674, 1703
Belly and the Members, The
  in *Coriolanus*, 1706
Belmont
  in *Merchant of Venice, The*, 0550, 1028
Benedick
  in *Much Ado About Nothing*, 0088, 0610, 0758, 2319, 2818
benevolence, 0523
Benoît de Sainte Maure, 2995
  Roman de Troie, Le, 2941
Beowulf
  in *Beowulf*, 1983
Berowne
  in *Love's Labor's Lost*, 0334, 0375, 0807, 0933, 2185a, 2191, 2199
Bertram
  in *All's Well That Ends Well*, 157, 0493, 1081, 1156, 3090
betrayal, 1521, 2034, 2650, 2866
Bianca
  in *Taming of the Shrew, The*, 0923, 2532, 2537, 2540, 2543
Bible, 0162, 0689, 1068, 1468, 2418
  1 Corinthians, 0627, 2292
  Ecclesiastes, 0954
  Exodus, 1505
  Genesis, 1543c, 1547, 2253a
  Job, 0954
  Lamentations, 0954

Bible *(continued)*
  Luke, 0201
  Matthew, 0215
  New Testament, 0057, 0746
  New Testament (Rheims version), 1724
  Old Testament, 0746, 1261
  Psalms, 0215, 0954
    Psalm 41, 1532
  Revelation, 0954, 1188, 1455, 2649, 2920
  Song of Solomon, 2326
Bible, Authorized Version, 0429
Bible, Geneva, 1964, 2326
Bingham, John
  translation of *Tactics of Aelian, The*, 0477
  biography, 0228, 1524
black, 1067a
black characters of Shakespeare, 1093
Blackfriars Playhouse, 2703
Blackfriars theater, 0806, 0958, 1150, 2618, 2906
Blackfriars theater (old), 0753
blackness, 2756
blame, 0894
blasphemy, 3196
blazon, 2433, 2434
blinding, 0254
blindness, 0097, 0156a, 0208, 0719, 2051, 2056, 2070, 2087, 2164, 2225, 2918
blindness, spiritual, 3171
blood, 0255, 0368, 0569, 0792, 2029, 2074, 2091, 2092
Bloody Mary, 1436
Bloudy Murther, 1443
Blundeville, Thomas
  translation of essay from Plutarch's *Moralia*, 2507
Boaistuau, Pierre, 2465
  Theatrum Mundi, 2694
Boccaccio, Giovanni, 0102, 0434, 0868, 0997, 1417, 1520, 2172, 2179a, 3158
  Decameron, 1109, 1763
  De Casibus Virorum Illustrium, 2588a
  De Claribus Mulieribus, 1295, 2588a
  Teseida, Il, 3100, 3101
Bodin, Jean, 1973, 2056
body, 1045, 1141, 1936, 1942, 2066, 2420, 2731a, 2758
  soul and, 1006, 1838, 2578a
  state and, 1609
body, female, 2433, 2779a, 2903
body, human, xiv, 0120, 0174, 1108, 1678, 2723, 2732a, 2767
body, male, 2789a
body, woman's, 2440, 2843
body natural, 1330
body politic, xvi, 0120, 0224, 1048, 1147, 1330, 1591, 1608, 1624, 1649, 1650, 1651, 1653, 1660, 1669, 1703, 1751, 1942
Boethius, Anicius Manlius Severinus, xi, 0058, 0191, 0263, 0299, 0336, 0499, 0547a, 0566, 0595, 0635, 0699, 0721, 0736, 0780, 0897, 0982, 1021, 1139, 1468, 2145, 2179a, 2223, 2342, 2450, 2964a

Consolation of Philosophy, The (De Consolatione Philosophiae), 1000, 1896, 2333, 2700, 3171
De Consolatione Philosophiae (The Consolation of Philosophy), 0124, 1175, 2174
De Institutione Musica, 0550, 0636
Bohr, Niels, 0873
Bolingbroke, Henry (Henry IV), 0358, 1093a
  in *Henry IV, Part 1*, 0136
  in *Richard II*, 0221, 0231, 0635, 2443, 2444, 2452
bomolochos, 0798
Bonian, Richard, 2837
Booth, Barton
  Death of Dido, The, 0902
Botticelli, Sandro
  Birth of Venus, The, 0437
  Primavera, La, 0437
Bottom
  in *Midsummer Night's Dream, A*, 0118, 0515, 0807, 0890, 0899, 01119, 2271, 2279, 2285, 2287, 2290, 2292, 2293, 2295, 2298, 2301, 2302, 2308, 2310, 2312a, 2317
Boult
  in *Pericles*, 2358, 2362
boundaries, 0901, 1418, 1483, 1748
boundaries, male, 3100a
bounty, 0941
Bourbon, Duke of
  in *Henry V*, 1932
bourgeoisie, 2836
Bower of Bliss in Spenser's *Fairie Queene*, 3132
boy, 0232, 1702
boy actor, 1470
boys
  men and, 0987
Brabantio
  in *Othello*, 0263, 2348
Bradley, A. C., 0785, 0984
braggart soldier, 0153
Branden, Samuel, 1468
bravery, 1174, 1620
Breca
  in *Beowulf*, 1983
Brecht, Bertolt, 1306, 1721
Bretchgirdle, John, 0936
Bretin, Filbert
  translation of Lucian's *Timon* into French, 2646
brevity
  copiousness and, 0833
Bright, Timothy
  Treatise of Melancholy, A, 0601
Briseis, 3026
Britain, 1761, 1765, 1769, 1774, 1780
Brome, Richard
  City Wit, The, 2655
Brook, Peter, 2770
Brooke, Arthur, 0325
  Tragicall Historye of Romeus and Juliet, The, 2473
brother, 1172, 1460a
  sister and, 1114

Index of Subjects

brothers, 2029, 2075
Bruno, Giordano, 0102, 0380, 0469, 0756, 0834, 1060, 1090, 1171a, 1822, 2560a, 2569, 2600
  De gli eroici furori, 2380
brutality, 2953
Brutus
  in *Coriolanus*, 0388, 1593, 1639
Brutus, Decius
  in *Julius Caesar*, 1971, 2134a
Brutus, founder of Britain, 2146a
Brutus, Lucius Junius, 1811, 1834, 1882, 1949, 2033, 2126
  in *Rape of Lucrece, The*, 0301, 0332, 0553a, 0665, 2393, 2401, 2419
Brutus, Marcus Junius, 0009, 0208, 0302, 0508, 0656, 0668, 0776, 0778, 0849, 1070, 1131, 3179a
  in *Julius Caesar*, xvii, 0062, 0073, 0080a, 0082, 0106, 0113, 0129, 0156, 0156a, 0166, 0167, 0172, 0186, 0201, 0202, 0206, 0207, 0219, 0222, 0224, 0232, 0246, 0247, 0250, 0252, 0255, 0277, 0282a, 0294, 0297, 0318, 0319a, 0333, 0337, 0347, 0351, 0359, 0369, 0377, 0379, 0388, 0398a, 0422, 0432, 0452, 0455, 0456, 0459, 0464, 0464a, 0468, 0473, 0492, 0495, 0503, 0508, 0523, 0525, 0539, 0550, 0553, 0560, 0561, 0566a, 0578, 0587, 0588, 0593, 0603, 0607, 0610, 0613, 0619, 0622, 0635, 0637, 0638, 0641, 0646, 0655, 0661, 0679, 0685, 0700, 0701, 0704, 0713, 0723, 0729, 0745, 0754, 0759a, 0761, 0762, 0765, 0777, 0779, 0792, 0795, 0799, 0811, 0812a, 0832a, 0850, 0851, 0865, 0866, 0867, 0873, 0876, 0886, 0905, 0911, 0932, 0939, 0940a, 0944, 0945, 0949, 0978, 0981, 0983a, 0985a, 1017, 1021, 1027, 1029, 1037, 1047, 1058, 1072, 1073, 1083, 1100, 1113, 1118, 1145, 1147, 1152, 1775, 1940, 1941, 1941a, 1942, 1943, 1944, 1945, 1946, 1948, 1949, 1951a, 1952, 1953, 1954, 1956, 1957, 1958, 1959, 1960, 1962, 1963, 1970, 1971, 1973, 1974, 1975, 1976, 1980, 1981, 1982, 1983b, 1984, 1987, 1988, 1990, 1992, 1993, 1994, 1997, 1999, 2000, 2002, 2002a, 2003, 2004, 2005, 2006, 2007, 2008, 2009, 2010, 2011, 2012, 2013, 2013a, 2014, 2016, 2018, 2021, 2022, 2022a, 2023, 2024, 2028, 2029, 2030, 2033, 2035, 2037, 2040, 2042, 2046, 2047, 2048, 2049, 2051, 2053, 2059, 2060, 2062, 2063, 2064, 2065, 2066, 2068, 2068a, 2071, 2072, 2073, 2076, 2078, 2079, 2080, 2082, 2083, 2085, 2085a, 2086, 2087, 2088, 2088a, 2093, 2096, 2097, 2098, 2101, 2102, 2103, 2104, 2105, 2108, 2111, 2112, 2113, 2113a, 2114, 2117, 2118, 2119, 2120, 2121, 2126, 2128, 2130, 2130a, 2133, 2136
Buchanan, George
  translation of Euripides' *Alcestis*, 3198
Buddhism, 2654
Bullen, Anne
  in *Henry VIII*, 1938
Buonamici, Francesco, 0375
Burbage, Richard, 1814a, 2233, 2618

Burgundy, Duke of
  in *Henry V*, 1920, 1921
burlesque, 2280, 2617, 2833
burlesques, 0890
Burton, Robert
  Anatomy of Melancholy, The, 0601, 0920

C
cabala, 0968
Cabala, Christian, 1149a
cabalism, 1067a
cabbala, 0307
Cade, Jack
  in *Henry VI, Part 2*, 0766, 1051, 2025
Cadmus, 2305
Caesar, Julius. *See* Julius Caesar (Gaius Julius Caesar)
Caesar, Lucius, 2130
Caesar, Octavius. See Octavius Caesar (C. Julius Caesar Octavianus)
Caesar and Pompey, or Caesar's Revenge, 0845
Caesar Augustus, 0359
Caesarism, 1009, 1954, 2018, 2030, 2078, 2134
  in *Julius Caesar*, 0175
Caesar's Revenge, 1331, 1435, 1468, 1512
Cain, 1898, 1983a
  Abel and, 1422
Caius, 0687
Calchas
  in *Troilus and Cressida*, 2994
Caliban
  in *Tempest, The*, 0095, 0096, 0326, 0577, 0814, 0899, 2544, 2545, 2558, 2560, 2560a, 2561, 2562a, 2565, 2567, 2568, 2572, 2578a, 2587, 2595, 2597, 2601a, 2609
Callimachus, 2547
Callisto, 2310, 3082
Calpurnia
  in *Julius Caesar*, 0201, 0759a, 0964, 1961, 1972, 2012, 2045, 2055, 2066, 2091, 2115, 2130a
Calvin, John, 0191, 0635, 1878
Calvinism, 2244
Cambio (Lucentio)
  in *Taming of the Shrew, The*, 2532
Camden, William
  Remaines of a Greater Worke, Concerning Britaine, 1609
Camillo
  in *Winter's Tale, The*, 0096, 0942
cannibal, 2567
cannibalism, 0237, 0446, 0666, 1595, 1623, 2686, 2764
Canterbury, Archbishop of
  in *Henry V*, 0221, 0528, 1920, 1921, 1925, 1926
Capella, Martianus. See Martianus Capella
capitalism, 0637, 2639, 2640, 2691, 3029, 3128
Captain
  in *Macbeth*, 2208a
Capulet
  in *Romeo and Juliet*, 0995

carbuncles, 1042a
Cardano, Girolamo, 2169
Cardanus, Girolamo, 1865
caritas, 2333
Carlisle, Bishop of
  in *Richard II*, 0221, 2443, 2444
carnival, 1608, 2134
carnivalesque, 2292
Cartari, Vincenzo, 2473, 3183
  Imagini de i Dei degli Antichi, 1086
Carthage, 2166, 2551, 2564
cartography, 0480
Casca
  in *Julius Caesar*, 1943, 1953, 1971, 1974, 2046, 2063, 2065, 2086, 2112
Cassandra, 0610
  in *Troilus and Cressida*, 0319a, 2872
Cassio
  in *Othello*, 1021, 2329, 2336, 2342
Cassius
  in *Julius Caesar*, 0029, 0097, 0113, 0129, 0144
Cassius, Gaius Longinus, 0359, 0773, 0776, 1941
  in *Julius Caesar*, 0172, 0201, 0224, 0294, 0297, 0322a, 0333, 0347, 0351, 0407, 0422, 0424, 0456, 0464a, 0525, 0553, 0607, 0610, 0637, 0641, 0679, 0700, 0704, 0723, 0734, 0759b, 0777, 0832a, 0850, 0851, 0886, 0911, 0940a, 0949, 0978, 0983a, 1029, 1037, 1047, 1073, 1100, 1147, 1940, 1942, 1943, 1944, 1948, 1949, 1954, 1956, 1957, 1959, 1970, 1971, 1974, 1976, 1980, 1981, 1983, 1984, 1987, 1993, 2005, 2007, 2008, 2009, 2010, 2014, 2015, 2016, 2023, 2024, 2027, 2029, 2030, 2042, 2046, 2051, 2053, 2060, 2065, 2068a, 2071, 2072, 2073, 2077, 2078, 2085, 2086, 2088, 2088a, 2091, 2093, 2098, 2101, 2104, 2106, 2111, 2112, 2113a, 2114, 2117, 2118, 2121, 2123, 2124, 2126, 2130, 2136
Castalio, Sebastian, 0938
Castelvetro, Lodovico, 0375, 0485, 1666
Castiglione, Baldassare, 0091, 0469, 0624, 0796, 1185, 2252, 2520, 3130
  Book of the Courtier, The, 0375, 0453, 1081, 1140a, 2086, 2468a
  Courtier, The, 2255, 2320
castration, 1749
cataphora, 1007
catastasis (element of drama), 0818, 2548
catastrophe (as element of drama), 0181, 0182, 0201, 0328, 0535, 0603, 0757, 0799, 0819, 0960, 1000, 1176, 1386, 1633, 1666, 1790, 2173a, 2548
catechresis, 0557
catharsis, 0163, 0166, 0167, 0182, 0440, 0453, 0500, 0797, 1054, 1615, 1666, 2264, 2462, 2706, 2867
Cato, Marcus Porcius ("Of Utica"), 1994, 2003, 2096, 2126
Cato, Marcus Porcius ("The Elder"), 0916

Cato (Young Cato)
  in *Julius Caesar*, 2126
Catullus, Gaius Valerius, 0281, 0628
  Carmina, 2477a
  epithalamia, 2469, 2470
Caucasus, 0533
Caxton, William, 2932, 2970, 3013
  Recuyell of the Historyes of Troye, The, 1002, 2834, 2972, 2985, 2992, 3007, 3047
  translation of LeFevre's *Le Receuil des histoires de Troye* as *The Recuyell of the Historyes of Troye*, 1557
Cebes of Thebes
  Tabulae Vitae, 2181a
Cecil, Robert, 2038, 2085
Celaeno, 0759b
Celia
  in *As You Like It*, 0690
centaur, xvii, 1576
Centaurs, 2139
centaurs, 0132, 2159, 2330
Cephalus, 0132
Cerberus, 1931a
Cercopes, 2597
ceremonies in *Titus Andronicus*, 2783a
ceremony, 0373, 1135, 1704, 2091a, 2136, 2785
Ceres, xvii, 0107, 0307, 1163, 1938, 3181, 3183, 3190, 3195
  in *Tempest, The*, 0283, 0421, 0631, 0997, 1134, 2547, 2555, 2562, 2562a, 2566, 2578a, 2583
Cerimon
  in *Pericles*, 2368
Cervantes Saavedra, Miguel de, 0434
Cesariano, Cesare, 0783
Cesario (Viola)
  in *Twelfth Night*, 0307, 0690, 3082
Ceyx, 0132, 2274
chain of being, 2955
Chaldean Oracles, 0380
change, 0466, 1084, 1103, 1130, 1133
changeableness, 1224
Changeling, The. See under Middleton, Thomas, and William Rowley
chaos, 0070a, 0305, 0332, 0380, 0508, 0527, 0724, 0729, 0754, 0804, 0807, 0897, 1081, 1242, 1612, 1630, 1959, 1976, 2040, 2077, 2092, 2178, 2273, 2347, 2447, 2509, 2578a, 2696, 2728, 2754, 2770, 2798, 2815, 2870, 2874, 2889, 2915, 2918, 3011, 3016, 3121
  order and, 1877
Chapman, George, 0591, 0721, 1621
  Bussy D'Ambois, 0589
  Byron, 0589
  Caesar and Pompey, 0684, 1979
  continuation of Marlowe's *Hero and Leander*, 2321
  Ovid's Banquet of Sense, 1563, 2490
  Revenge of Bussy D'Ambois, The, 0251
  translation of Homer, 0208, 0780
  translation of Homer's *Iliad*, xvii, 0589, 0721, 1879, 2908, 2985, 3013

Index of Subjects 829

translation of Homer's *Seven Books of the Iliad*, 2970, 2972, 2992
translation of *Seven Books of the Iliads of Homer*, 1933
translations of Homer, 3047
character (as concept or element of drama), 0077, 0084, 0123, 0128, 0135, 0138, 0143, 0145, 0154, 0165, 0177, 0193, 0228, 0250, 0275, 0319, 0333, 0340, 0369, 0435, 0463, 0476, 0491, 0493, 0510, 0547, 0556, 0565, 0640, 0678, 0737, 0776, 0787, 0793, 0801, 0802, 0807, 0819, 0831, 0840, 0949, 0951, 0965, 0985a, 0986a, 1032, 1035a, 1064, 1076, 1087, 1103, 1112, 1118, 1132, 1133, 1162, 1354, 1510, 1568, 1647, 1704, 2170, 2307, 2913
characterization, 0002, 0162, 0195a, 0219, 0232, 0446, 0588, 0640, 0650a, 0661, 0891, 0896, 0966, 1191, 1494, 1528a, 1529, 1647, 1856, 2620, 2834, 2874, 3013
character (prose portrait), 1688
Chariton
  Chaereas and Callirrhoe, 0434, 1759
charity
  magic and, 2562b
Charlemagne, 2717
Charles
  in *As You Like It*, 1538, 1543c, 1547
Charles the Dauphin
  in *Henry VI, Part 1*, 1934
Charles V, 2569a
Charmian
  in *Antony and Cleopatra*, xv, 0931, 1230, 1336, 1486
Charron, Pierre
  Of Wisdom, 0601
chase, 3106
chastity, 145, 0337, 0405, 0437, 0577, 0642, 0730, 0754, 0967, 1062, 2246, 2268a, 2281, 2300, 2321, 2362, 2379, 2383, 2395, 2396, 2400, 2403, 2405, 2412, 2413, 2414, 2418, 2434, 2562a, 2583, 2964, 3058, 3145, 3191
fertility and, 2578a
Chaucer, Geoffrey, ix, 0281, 0504a, 0635, 0741, 1009, 1417, 1520, 1558, 2046, 2286, 2303, 2397, 2403, 2410, 2473, 2842, 2856, 2900, 2909, 2956, 2995, 3001, 3026
Canterbury Tales, The
  Knight's Tale, The, 0087, 0248, 0325, 0729, 1009, 1049, 2277, 2285, 2299, 2314, 3091, 3094, 3097, 3100, 3100a, 3101, 3104
  Merchant's Tale, The, 0325, 2285
  Monk's Tale, The, 1833
  Tale of Sir Thopas, The, 2311
Legend of Good Women, The, 0133, 0325, 0484, 0852, 1311, 2309, 2398, 2417
Legend of Thisbe, The, 2311
Parliament of Fowls, The, 0862
translation of Boethius's *De Consolatione Philosophiae*, 2174
Troilus and Criseyde, 0137, 0189, 0199, 0325, 1049, 2476, 2809, 2834, 2854, 2894, 2947, 2960, 2964a, 2970, 2972, 2985, 2992, 3013, 3017, 3036, 3047, 3068

Chester, Robert
  Love's Martyr (Loves Martyr), 2374, 2376, 2378
Chettle, Henry, 2992
child, 0225, 0542, 0556
  mother and, 1319
child actors, 1621
childhood, 3154
children, 0254, 0318, 0632, 0848, 1114, 2209, 2749, 2778
children's plays, 1450
Chiron, 0720a, 1910, 2159
  in *Titus Andronicus*, 0283, 0368, 0906, 2718, 2730, 2771
chivalry, xxi, 0106, 0208, 0700, 0754, 1002, 1524, 2794, 2820, 2878, 2888, 2908, 2911, 2987, 2988, 3003, 3029
Choice of Hercules, 1399, 2196
choler, 0328
choreography, 0099
Chorus
  in *Henry V*, 1334, 1917, 1920, 1933
  in *Romeo and Juliet*, 0829a
chorus, 0829a
Chorus, Senecan, 1042
chorus in Greek tragedy, 2514
Christ, xxi, 0198, 0382, 0610, 0972, 0974a, 1188, 1212a, 1230, 1252, 1421, 1556, 1623, 1757, 1765, 1769, 1775, 1793, 1852, 1983a, 2067, 2074, 2106, 2476, 2676, 3179a
Christian beliefs, 0252, 0307
Christian dispensation, 0133
Christian doctrine, 0133, 0417, 0756
Christian ideas, 0755
Christianity, 0079, 0080a, 0133, 0149, 0208, 0314, 0378, 0391, 0599, 0685, 0746, 0763, 0850, 0851, 0978, 1503, 1799, 1874, 2515, 2517, 2804, 3177
Christianization, 1123
Christian mystics, 0487
Christians, 1139
Christian thinkers, 0149
Christian thought, 0045
Christian tradition, 0133
Christian tragedies, by Shakespeare, 1017
Christina, St., 1311
chronicle play, 0768
chronicle plays, 0717
chronicles, British, 2739
chronographia, 0692
Chronos
  Kronos and, 0596
Chryseis, 3026
Church Fathers, 0528, 0739
Cicero, Marcus Tullius, xviii, 0002, 0080a, 0258, 0263, 0280, 0299, 0320, 0326, 0363, 0375, 0394, 0457, 0470, 0472, 0479, 0487, 0488, 0519, 0529, 0557, 0575, 0624, 0625, 0657, 0674, 0721, 0728, 0751, 0759a, 0809, 0835, 0841, 0905, 0907, 0936, 0938, 0955, 0956, 1005, 1011, 1021, 1023, 1061, 1064, 1078, 1468, 1548, 1554, 1565, 1834a, 1856, 1879a, 1881, 1907, 1995, 1999, 2031, 2122, 2158, 2165, 2245, 2245a, 2290, 2328a

Cicero, Marcus Tullius *(continued)*, 2440a, 2505, 2546a, 2633, 2642, 2682, 2963, 3005, 3094, 3206
  De Amicitia (Of Friendship), 1109, 1111, 1896, 2516, 3100b
  De Divinatione, 1570, 1852, 2120
  De Finibus Bonorum et Malorum, 2042, 2121, 2592
  De Inventione, 2461, 2528
  De Officiis (Of Offices), 0124, 0174, 0465a, 0938, 1000, 1175, 1869b, 2110, 3028, 3046
  De Oratore, 0270, 1853
  De Senectute, 0995, 2175
  Of Friendship (De Amicitia), 2700, 2701
  in *Julius Caesar*, 0129, 1015, 1953, 1983b, 1997, 2005, 2042, 2071, 2081
  letter to Lucceius, 1552
  Of Offices (De Officiis), 1650
  Pro Sexto Roscio Amerino, 2304
  Tusculan Disputations, 2446
Cimber, Publius, 2125
Cimon, 2634, 2665
Cinna
  in *Julius Caesar*, 0201, 0224, 1971, 2039
Cinna, a poet
  in *Julius Caesar*, 0508, 0513, 0687, 0777, 0909, 1015, 1977, 2009, 2015, 2025, 2039, 2045, 2076, 2097
Cinthio, G. B. Giraldi
  Hecatommithi, 2329
Cinthio, Giraldo, 0485, 0534, 1035, 1468
Cinyras, 3149
Circe, 0119, 1188, 1233, 2301, 2317, 2547, 3154
citation, rhetoric of, in *Troilus and Cressida*, 2889
citizens
  in *Antony and Cleopatra* and *Coriolanus*, 0977
  in *Coriolanus*, 0116, 0594, 0613, 0686, 0759a, 0775, 1047, 1605, 1639, 1649, 1728, 1735
  in *Julius Caesar*, 1952
city, 0836, 1646, 1704, 1711, 1752
City, Earthly, 0980, 3004
City, Heavenly, 3004
civility, 1152, 1539
civilization, 0238a, 0337, 0398a, 0792, 1741, 1757, 2583, 2593, 2605, 2634, 2744
civil war, 0314, 0517, 0789, 1008, 2090, 2092, 2784
civil wars, 0998
Clapham, John
  Narcissus, 0185a
Clarence, Duke of, 1022
  in *Richard III*, 0323, 0610, 2453, 2456
class, 0566, 0652, 0701, 0778, 1047, 1630, 1657, 1698, 1703, 1721
class, lower, 0428
class, upper, 0428
classes, 0766
classical allusions, 0054, 0229, 0314, 0787, 0816a, 0985a, 1536, 2536, 2537, 2538, 2732

classical authors, 0045, 0299, 0370, 0417, 0421, 0480, 0586, 0742, 0799, 0849, 2154
classical drama, 0012a, 0445, 0542, 0835, 0986c, 1028, 1032, 2161a
classical dramatists, 1010, 2144
classical handbooks, 0421
classical historians, 0883, 1175
classical histories, by Shakespeare, 0495
classical historiography, 0619
classical influences, 0159, 0160, 0375, 0496, 0583, 1764, 2149, 2338, 2449, 2460
classical learning, 0299, 0369, 0403, 0909a, 1039, 1104, 1573a, 1937a, 2257
classical plays, by Shakespeare, 0010, 0059b, 0174, 0178, 0358, 0391, 0424, 0518, 0912, 1036
classical tradition, 0028, 0057, 0058, 0080, 0249, 0316, 0535, 0765, 0798, 0848a, 1798, 2344
classical tragedies, by Shakespeare, 0156a, 0742, 1017
classicism, 0369, 0721, 0759a, 0915, 1066, 1096, 1112, 1963
Claudian (Claudius Claudianus), 0739, 0862, 2470
Claudio
  in *Measure for Measure*, 0217, 0263, 1065
  in *Much Ado About Nothing*, 0437, 0610, 2320, 2321
Claudius
  in *Hamlet*, 0358, 0500, 0961, 1139, 1784, 1791, 1792, 1795, 1796, 1803, 1804, 1806, 1807, 1812, 1819, 1822, 1830, 1834a, 1844a, 1848, 1865, 1872, 1873, 1879a, 1889, 1891, 1892, 1893a, 1896, 1898
Claudius (Tiberius Claudius Nero Germanicus), 1795
clemency, 1925, 2125
Clement, St., 0730
Cleopatra, 0019, 0668, 0713, 1169, 1202, 1277, 1285, 1297, 1345, 1374, 1417, 1472, 1520, 1524, 1833
  in *Antony and Cleopatra*, xv, 0062, 0095, 0106, 0112, 0113, 0131, 0154, 0173a, 0175, 0177, 0181, 0192, 0208, 0212, 0232, 0234, 0239, 0244, 0255, 0277, 0283, 0305, 0306, 0310, 0329, 0343, 0344, 0347, 0372a, 0379a, 0391, 0398, 0400, 0424, 0427, 0436, 0437, 0452, 0464a, 0498, 0504a, 0512, 0513, 0529, 0530, 0546, 0548, 0553, 0555, 0592, 0599, 0602, 0603, 0607, 0613, 0633, 0646, 0663a, 0679, 0681, 0685, 0690, 0703, 0721, 0722, 0729, 0734, 0751, 0759a, 0784, 0824, 0827, 0828, 0849a, 0850, 0857, 0865, 0876, 0882, 0887, 0888, 0895, 0898, 0911, 0912, 0925, 0927, 0931, 0949, 0963, 0964, 0977, 0981, 0983, 1000, 1021, 1025, 1037, 1045, 1047, 1055, 1084, 1086, 1099, 1100, 1135, 1139, 1152, 1159, 1160, 1163, 1164, 1165, 1166a, 1167, 1168, 1171, 1174, 1175, 1176, 1178, 1181, 1182, 1183, 1185, 1186, 1188, 1189, 1191, 1194, 1195, 1196, 1196a, 1198, 1200, 1201, 1204, 1205, 1206, 1207,

Index of Subjects 831

1210, 1211, 1212a, 1214, 1215, 1216, 1217, 1220, 1221a, 1222, 1223, 1224, 1225, 1227, 1228, 1229, 1230, 1233, 1234, 1238, 1240, 1241, 1242, 1244, 1245, 1247, 1248, 1250a, 1251, 1252, 1252a, 1253, 1254, 1255, 1256, 1259, 1260, 1261, 1262, 1264, 1265, 1266, 1267, 1271, 1273, 1275, 1276, 1278, 1279, 1281, 1283, 1285, 1286, 1287, 1288, 1290, 1291, 1293, 1295, 1296, 1299, 1300, 1301, 1303, 1304, 1307, 1309, 1310, 1311, 1312, 1313, 1314, 1315, 1316, 1318, 1318a, 1319, 1321, 1322, 1323, 1324, 1325, 1326a, 1327, 1328, 1329, 1330, 1330a, 1331, 1332, 1333, 1335, 1336, 1337, 1338, 1339, 1340, 1341, 1343, 1347, 1348, 1349, 1350, 1352, 1353, 1354, 1354a, 1355, 1356, 1358, 1360, 1361, 1362, 1364, 1367, 1368, 1369, 1370, 1371, 1373, 1375, 1376, 1378, 1379, 1380, 1383, 1384, 1385, 1388a, 1388, 1389, 1391, 1392, 1393, 1394, 1396, 1397, 1398, 1399, 1402, 1403, 1404, 1405, 1406, 1409, 1410, 1411, 1412, 1415, 1418, 1419, 1420, 1421, 1423, 1424, 1425, 1426, 1427, 1428, 1429, 1430, 1432, 1436, 1438, 1439, 1444, 1445, 1446, 1449, 1450, 1451, 1453, 1454, 1456, 1457, 1458, 1459, 1460, 1461, 1462, 1463, 1466, 1470, 1473, 1474, 1476, 1477, 1479, 1480, 1481, 1483, 1484, 1484a, 1485, 1486, 1488, 1489, 1490, 1491, 1492, 1493, 1500, 1502, 1504, 1505, 1507, 1510, 1511, 1512, 1513, 1514, 1518, 1521, 1522, 1524, 1525, 1527, 1528, 3143
Clifford, Young
  in *Henry VI, Part 2*, 0152
climax (as an element of drama), 0180, 0181, 0182, 1196, 2144
Clitophon and Leucippe, by Achilles Tatius. See under Achilles Tatius
Cloten
  in *Cymbeline*, 0336, 0437, 0769, 1048, 1754, 1755, 1757, 1761, 1763, 1774
clothes, 0718
clothing, 0688
Clown
  in *Antony and Cleopatra*, 0084, 1176, 1197, 1261, 1273, 1326a, 1527
  in *Othello*, 2342
  in *Titus Andronicus*, 0116, 1095
  in *Winter's Tale, The*, 3184
Clown (Feste)
  in *Twelfth Night*, 3083a
clowns, 1072
  in *Hamlet*, 1824
Clyomon and Clamydes, 0997
Clytemnestra, 0208, 0610, 2206
Cobbler
  in *Julius Caesar*, 1947, 2054, 2081, 2117
Cobham, Lady Eleanor
  in *Henry VI, Part 2*, 0862
Cockaigne, 2547
Cockeram, Henry
  English Dictionary, The, 3207
Coleridge, Samuel Taylor, 0465, 1234, 1340
Collatine, 2419

  in *Rape of Lucrece, The*, 0441, 2392, 2407, 2410, 2414, 2433, 2434, 2440
colonialism, discourse of, 2567
colonization, 2572
Colonna, 0380
Colosseum, 0443
Colossus, 1399, 1400, 1425, 2086
Colossus of Rhodes, 0734
combat, 2974
combat, single, 2699
comedies, by Shakespeare, xi, xiii, 0037, 0049, 0052, 0053, 0058, 0059a, 0062, 0080, 0090, 0097, 0112, 0115, 0123, 0139, 0143, 0162, 0165, 0174, 0176, 0208, 0214, 0218, 0226, 0248, 0262, 0272, 0350, 0353a, 0362, 0363, 0364, 0365, 0369, 0385, 0386, 0405a, 0410, 0413, 0418, 0439, 0468, 0476, 0497, 0518, 0520, 0535, 0597, 0600, 0636, 0663a, 0690, 0699, 0701, 0706, 0719, 0754, 0756, 0759, 0774, 0794, 0797, 0798, 0801, 0805, 0807a, 0818, 0822, 0836, 0880, 0891, 0891a, 0899, 0914, 0916, 0923, 0942, 0967, 0969, 0997, 1035a, 1056, 1064, 1072, 1079, 1089, 1102, 1107, 1133, 1137, 1165, 1241, 1407, 1412, 2188, 2623, 2748, 3097, 3143
comedies, Greek, 0092, 0226
comedies, Roman, 0226
comedies, romantic, 2992
comedy, amorous, 3007
comedy, Aristophanic, 2570
comedy, classical, xiii, 0209, 0235, 0385, 3200
comedy, four-part structure for, 2548
comedy, Greek, 3076
comedy, human, 2924
comedy, Italian, xiii, 0102, 0272, 0801, 0923, 1573
Comedy, New, 0123, 0140, 0195, 0273, 0309, 0386, 0412, 0413, 0414, 0415, 0468, 0797, 0798, 0814, 0891, 0923, 1056, 1114, 2348, 2349, 2544, 2563, 3182
Comedy, Old, xiii, xxi, 0309, 0414, 0468, 2563
comedy, Roman, xix, 0201, 0384, 0510, 0556, 0745, 0970, 0991, 0995, 1085a, 1581, 2304, 2341, 2542, 2586
comedy, romantic, 3006
comedy (as concept or genre), 0071, 0073, 0077, 084, 0098, 0119, 0130, 0131, 0137, 0140, 0160b, 0195, 0199, 0242, 0273, 0285, 0331, 0349, 0350, 0378, 0386, 0396, 0412, 0413, 0431, 0435a, 0465a, 0468, 0469, 0502, 0507, 0510, 0515, 0534, 0536, 0546, 0553, 0580, 0599, 0608, 0683, 0685, 0701, 0712, 0718, 0758, 0788, 0798, 0810, 0818, 0823, 0850a, 0852, 0887, 0891, 0895, 0923, 0934, 0967, 0969, 1003, 1010, 1026, 1065, 1123, 1135, 1155, 1162, 1188a, 1219, 1252, 1271, 1278, 1320, 1358, 1385, 1459, 1502, 1503, 1540, 1587, 1589, 1856, 2168, 2181, 2196, 2304, 2586, 2594, 2602, 2628, 2694, 2811, 2826, 2834, 2837, 2851, 2860, 2888, 2893, 2908, 2910, 2986, 2990, 3038, 3116, 3152, 3176, 3184, 3184a
Comedy of Timon, The, 2617. See also *Timon* (old Timon comedy)

Comes, Natalis, 0868, 3158
comic characters of Shakespeare, 0084
comic resolution, 0214
Cominius, 0759a
  in *Coriolanus,* 0297, 0546, 0873, 1603, 1701, 1708, 1710
commedia dell'arte, 0153, 2595
commedia erudita, 0556, 0802, 0923, 3078
commodity, 3036
Common Conditions, 0997
commoners, 0079, 1710
  in *Coriolanus,* 0613
  in *Julius Caesar,* 2002a
common people, 0408, 1135
  in *Coriolanus,* 0120, 1599
  in *Julius Caesar,* 0388
commonplace books, 0300, 0868
commons
  in *Coriolanus,* 1644
commonweal, 1743
commonwealth, 0120, 0299, 0709, 0897, 0981, 1020, 1021, 1152, 1612, 1630, 1693, 1751, 1925, 2547
communion, 1987a
community, 0078, 0200, 0393, 0422, 0442, 0492, 0538, 0865, 1003, 1045, 1629, 1648, 1657
competition, 2400, 2413, 2434, 2616
complaint, xviii, 0370a, 1094, 1129, 2184, 2184a, 2398, 2400, 2401, 3122
complaint poems, female, 2423, 2426
complementarity, 0873, 1362, 1667
complexions, four, 0858
conception, Aristotelian theory of, 2896
conception, metaphor of, 0478
concord, 0377a
concordia, 0587
concordia discors, 1533
concupiscence, 1270, 1437, 3121, 3163
Condell, Henry, 2845
confirmatio, 0433
conjuring, 2078
conqueror, 1338
conscience, 0520, 0983a
consolatio, 0875, 3171
consolation, 1005, 1065
conspiracies
  in *Tempest, The,* 2564
conspiracy
  in *Coriolanus,* 1654
  in *Julius Caesar,* 0129, 0172, 0252, 0379, 0607, 0700, 0729, 0850, 0851, 0911, 0949, 1009, 1131, 1941a, 1952, 1956, 1963, 1971, 1980, 2002, 2006, 2024, 2030, 2036, 2043, 2068a, 2072, 2085a, 2088a, 2098, 2105, 2116a, 2118
  in *Tempest, The,* 2547
  in *Troilus and Cressida,* 2879
conspirator, 0553
conspirators, 0668
  in *Julius Caesar,* 0106, 0113, 0167, 0201, 0237, 0271, 0539, 0545, 0607, 0679, 0690, 0779, 0873, 0949, 0954, 0986a, 1058, 1942, 1950, 1965, 1966, 1984, 1987a, 1990, 2009, 2012, 2022a, 2027, 2029, 2046, 2051, 2056, 2057, 2064, 2071, 2073, 2074, 2092, 2097, 2112, 2128, 2134
  in *Tempest, The,* 2597
Constable of France
  in *Henry V,* 0301
Constance
  in *King John,* 0610
constancy, 0252, 0405, 0721, 0729, 0751, 0759a, 0861, 0990, 1047, 1111, 1140, 1393, 1520, 1711, 1984, 2038, 2112a, 2119, 2121, 2376, 2379, 2395
consumption, 2681
contaminatio, 0272, 2242
contemptus mundi, 0191, 2488a, 2694
Contention Between Liberalitie and Prodigalitie, 2663
Conti, Natalis
  Mythologiae, 1086
contradictions, 2964a
contraries, 0729
contrariety, xiii, 0469, 0926, 1633, 2560, 2895
control, 0255
controversia, 0470
controversiae, 0601, 2785
Cooper, Thomas
  Thesaurus linguae Romanae & Britannicae, 1324, 2050, 2164
copia, 0891, 3127
copiousness, 1061
  brevity and, 0833
copulatio, 1080
Cordelia, 2147
  in *King Lear,* 0400, 2141, 2144, 2145a, 2147, 2154, 2159, 2162, 2163, 2164, 2171, 2183
Corderius, Maturinus, 0938
  Dialogues, 2155
Coriolanus, Gnaeus Marcius (Caius Martius Coriolanus), 0009, 0359
  in *Coriolanus,* 0078, 0080a, 0082, 0106, 0112, 0113, 0120, 0129, 0133, 0138, 0141, 0142a, 0144, 0171, 0172, 0172a, 0178, 0187, 0202, 0208, 0232, 0234, 0237, 0239, 0240, 0247, 0268, 0297, 0305, 0318, 0320, 0321, 0324, 0330, 0343, 0344, 0355, 0369, 0372, 0396, 0416, 0427, 0447, 0448, 0455, 0459, 0464, 0464a, 0471, 0473, 0493, 0512, 0521, 0523, 0547, 0553, 0562, 0581, 0593, 0594, 0599, 0607, 0610, 0612, 0613, 0633, 0641, 0652, 0655, 0656, 0677, 0687, 0701, 0712, 0732, 0759a, 0766, 0792, 0811, 0812a, 0817, 0831, 0838, 0840, 0848, 0850, 0866, 0873, 0880, 0909, 0911, 0927, 0949, 0980, 0981, 0999, 1008, 1009, 1029, 1047, 1073, 1086, 1087, 1092, 1100, 1136, 1250, 1291, 1590, 1591, 1592, 1593, 1594, 1595, 1596, 1598, 1600, 1601, 1602, 1603, 1604, 1605, 1607, 1608, 1609, 1610, 1612, 1613, 1614, 1617, 1618, 1620, 1622, 1623, 1624a, 1625, 1626, 1626a, 1627, 1628, 1629, 1630, 1632, 1632a, 1633, 1634, 1635, 1636, 1637, 1638, 1639, 1640, 1641, 1642, 1644, 1645,

Index of Subjects

1646, 1647, 1648, 1651, 1654, 1655, 1657, 1658, 1660, 1661, 1663, 1667, 1668, 1669, 1670, 1672, 1676, 1679, 1680a, 1681, 1682, 1683, 1684, 1688, 1690, 1691, 1694, 1695, 1696, 1697, 1699, 1701, 1702, 1703, 1704, 1707, 1708, 1709, 1710, 1712, 1714, 1715, 1716, 1718, 1719, 1720, 1721, 1722, 1724, 1725, 1726, 1730, 1731, 1734, 1734a, 1735, 1738, 1740, 1740a, 1741, 1742, 1743, 1744, 1745, 1747, 1748, 1749, 1752
Corneille, Pierre, 0191
Cinna, 1430, 1431
Horace
 Coriolanus and, 0210
Mort de Pompée
 Julius Caesar and, 0210
Cornelia (wife of Pompey the Great), 2444
corruption, 1493, 3150
cosmography, 0527
cosmology, 0002, 0107, 0480, 0487, 0496, 0528
cosmology, Boethian, xix
cosmos, 0019, 0079, 0120, 0215, 0640, 0651, 0733
costume, 0156, 0255, 0994
costume, classical, 2303
costumes, xiv, 0172a, 1687
Cotus
 in *Coriolanus*, 1676
Countess of Rossillion
 in *All's Well That Ends Well*, 1155
courage, 0208, 0240, 0255, 1023, 1111, 1218, 1907, 1915, 2888
courtesan, 1062, 1246, 1415, 1575
courtesy, 0091, 1165, 1335
courtier, 0211, 0935
courtier-gentleman, 0796
courtiers
 in *Hamlet*, 1841a
courtly love. *See* love, courtly
courtship, 0201, 1003
covetousness, 0133, 2685
Crates, 2146
creativity, 0380
Creon, 0509, 1872, 2216
Cressida, 0060, 0441, 2249, 2257, 3026
 in *Troilus and Cressida*, xxii, 0032, 0096, 0097, 0106, 0156, 0199, 0208, 0253, 0325, 0337, 0347, 0372a, 0424, 0437, 0481, 0512, 0513, 0549, 0554, 0576, 0592, 0631, 0652, 0687, 0708, 0789, 0849a, 0879, 0888, 0925, 0964, 1029, 1055, 1065, 1102, 1291, 1411, 2790, 2792, 2793, 2794, 2799, 2800, 2801, 2803, 2809, 2815, 2816, 2817, 2818, 2828, 2830, 2831, 2842, 2843, 2844, 2854, 2855, 2857, 2858, 2866, 2872, 2875, 2878, 2879, 2883, 2885, 2886, 2890, 2891, 2893, 2896, 2898, 2899, 2900, 2901, 2903, 2905, 2908, 2909, 2910, 2912, 2918, 2922, 2924, 2927, 2931, 2934, 2938, 2939, 2942, 2944, 2947, 2948, 2950, 2951, 2954, 2955, 2957, 2960, 2964, 2966, 2969, 2970, 2972, 2974, 2977, 2979, 2991, 2994, 2996, 3003, 3012, 3013, 3015, 3016, 3019, 3020, 3025, 3026, 3027, 3030, 3031, 3033, 3035, 3036, 3039, 3042, 3043, 3044, 3045, 3046, 3052, 3053, 3054, 3058, 3060, 3062, 3063, 3064a, 3065, 3068, 3070, 3071, 3072, 3073
Criseyde
 in Chaucer's *Troilus and Criseyde*, 0325, 2842, 2854, 2909, 2960, 3026
crisis, cultural, 2884
crocodile, 1172, 1235
Cromwell, Oliver, 2085
crone, 0900, 0901
cross-dressing, xv, 1336
crowd, 0639
crowds, 1036
Crucifixion, 0610, 2034
cruelty, xiv, 0152, 0368, 0369, 0384, 1108, 1188a, 1817, 2717, 2783
cruelty, female, 2777a
cuckoldry, 0118
Culman, Leonard
 Sententiae Pueriles, 0993
culture, 0701
Cumberland, Richard
 Fashionable Husband, The, 2655
Cupid, 0119, 0283, 0373, 0577, 0758, 0807, 0868, 1051, 1053, 1490, 1885, 2183, 2298, 2301, 2322, 2346, 2350, 2467, 2468a, 2469, 2472, 2476, 2495, 2517, 2521, 2560a, 2698
 in *Timon of Athens*, 0421, 0848, 1044a, 2638, 2652, 2681, 2689a
Cupid and Psyche, 1155
cupiditas, 2333
currency
 language and, 2616
Curtius, Ernst Robert, 1915
cycle plays, 0542, 0610
Cydnus River
 in *Antony and Cleopatra*, 0679, 0685, 0721, 0927, 1160, 1171, 1185, 1242, 1244, 1252, 1253, 1276, 1300, 1379, 1389, 1397, 1449, 1511
Cymbeline, 0384, 1763, 1765, 1769, 1772
 in *Cymbeline*, 0299a, 0434, 1754, 1757, 1759, 1774, 1775
Cynic, 1943, 2153
cynic, 0234, 0920, 1242
Cynicism, 2244
cynicism, 0113, 0234, 0391, 0912, 0935, 0945, 1082, 1406, 1580, 2688a, 2794, 2795, 3043, 3060
Cynics, 2146
cynics, 0222, 2795
Cynic tradition, 0201
Cytherea, 2538, 2540

D

Daedalus, xiv, 0054, 0918, 2293, 2561
Dalila, 1387a
dance, 0196, 0197, 1587
dancing, 0700, 1366, 2368
Daniel, Samuel, 1417
 Civil Wars, xx, 2444
 Cleopatra, 1173, 1360, 1450, 2504

Daniel, Samuel *(continued)*
  Letter from Octavia to Marcus Antonius, A, 1468
  Musophilus, 2113c
  "Musophilus," 2998a
  Tragedie of Cleopatra, The, 1468, 1472, 1473
  Tragedy of Cleopatra, The, 0009, 2429
  Vision of the Twelve Goddesses, The, 2357
Dante Alighieri, 0119, 0385, 0849, 1417, 1520, 2046, 2172, 2179a, 2753
  Divine Comedy
    Purgatorio, 0385
Daphne, 2305, 2538, 2540, 3082
Daphnis and Chloe. See under Longus
Da Porto, Luigi
  Giulietta, La, 2465
Dares of Phrygia, 2995
Dark Lady
  in *Sonnets,* 2481, 2487, 2497
daughter, 0452a, 0814, 1875, 2583, 2596, 2723, 3190
Daughter of Antiochus
  in *Pericles,* 2360, 2368
daughters, 0092, 0406, 0964, 2167
Davies, Sir John
  Nosce Teipsum, 2113c
  Orchestra, 0197
day, 0539
Day, Angel, 0332
  adaptation of *Daphnis and Chloe,* by Longus, 1549
Death
  Love and, 3107
  Sleep and, 1078
death, 0067, 0068, 0110, 0113, 0129, 0137, 0183, 0201, 0206, 0208, 0215, 0232, 0237, 0255, 0265, 0271, 0284, 0298, 0302, 0340, 0341, 0344, 0375, 0379a, 0392, 0398a, 0400, 0411, 0427, 0434, 0459, 0464a, 0513, 0529, 0541, 0548, 0553, 0594, 0596, 0603, 0613, 0633, 0663a, 0665, 0679, 0691, 0700, 0746, 0751, 0759a, 0784, 0799, 0829a, 0831, 0849a, 0875, 0882, 0943, 0946, 0957, 0981, 0994, 1013a, 1039, 1047, 1057, 1065, 1100, 1131, 1136, 1139, 1141, 1165, 1167, 1171a, 1175, 1178, 1184, 1188, 1200, 1201, 1211, 1214, 1215, 1216, 1218, 1222, 1231, 1240, 1245, 1246, 1252, 1256, 1260, 1271, 1275, 1277, 1287, 1293, 1299, 1300, 1304, 1306, 1307, 1308, 1315, 1316, 1319, 1323, 1339, 1342, 1343, 1355, 1361, 1362, 1363, 1369, 1370, 1373, 1375, 1385, 1388, 1392, 1393, 1399, 1404, 1405, 1406, 1414, 1415, 1418, 1440, 1446, 1453, 1459, 1461, 1463, 1465, 1469, 1476, 1477, 1487, 1489, 1493, 1502, 1507, 1511, 1516, 1524, 1525, 1527, 1553, 1609, 1625, 1668, 1669, 1689, 1696, 1704, 1710, 1721, 1809, 1844, 1849, 1850, 1862, 1865, 1866, 1868, 1875, 1876, 1941, 1954, 1970, 1973, 1976, 1987a, 2015, 2025, 2087, 2144, 2154, 2180, 2241, 2382, 2415, 2518, 2725, 2765, 3018, 3100b, 3113, 3136, 3162, 3165, 3203
  love and, 2476, 3143
  death, spiritual, 3183
  death of Falstaff
    in *Henry V,* 0610
  debate, 0076, 0350, 0683, 0721
  debates, 3066
  debunking, 2941
  decadence, 0956, 2742a, 2940, 2996
  de casibus, 0635, 0905a, 1034, 1069, 1473, 1521, 1985, 2186, 2423
  De Casibus Virorum Illustrium, 2514
  decay, 1328, 1368, 2551
  deceit, 0789
  declamation, 0470
  De Copia, 1560
  decorum, 0022, 0102, 0131, 0381, 0728, 0751, 1029, 1064, 1175, 1502, 1525, 2185a, 2214, 2455, 2512, 2864, 2963, 3098, 3127, 3207
  Dee, John, 1149a, 2551a, 2562b, 2600
  defeat, 1000
  degree, 0192, 0208, 0441, 0442, 0469, 0538, 0625, 0658, 0686, 0699, 0718, 0832a, 1004, 1019, 1021, 1095, 2812, 2822, 2826, 2829, 2832, 2840, 2859, 2871, 2884, 2891, 2892, 2916, 2946, 2985, 2986, 2994, 2996, 2997, 2998a, 3011, 3021, 3039, 3043, 3044, 3046, 3062
  Deianira, 1174, 2231
  deities, 0087, 0239, 0307, 0829, 1025, 2314, 2995
  Dekker, Thomas, 2992
  Dekker, Thomas, and Henry Chettle
    outline for *Troilus and Cressida* play, 2827
  deliberation, 0080
  Delphic Oracle, 2207
  Demeter, 0307, 1224, 3201
  Demetrius
    in *Antony and Cleopatra,* 0911, 1000, 1178, 1439, 1486, 1502
    in *Midsummer Night's Dream, A,* 2281, 2291
    in *Titus Andronicus,* 0283, 0368, 2718, 2771
  Demetrius of Phalerum, 0557
  de Meun, Jean
    Roman de la Rose, Le, 1896
  democracy, 1123, 1698, 2665
  Democritus, 0266, 1098, 1852
  demons, 0881
  Demophon, 0132, 2340
  Demosthenes, 2998a
  De Mundo, 0926
  denouement (as concept or element of drama), 0535, 0769
  dependency, 1696
  Dercetas
    in *Antony and Cleopatra,* 1370
  Derrida, J., 1354a
  Desdemona
    in *Othello,* 0097, 0132, 0167, 0437, 0490, 0610, 0824, 0999, 1278, 2328a, 2330, 2347, 2348, 2698, 2883
  Desire, 1185

Index of Subjects

desire, 0232, 0239, 0343, 0387, 0439, 0440, 0441, 0614, 0719, 0759a, 1062, 1175, 1391, 1623, 2295, 2407, 2417, 2500, 2758, 2792, 2831, 2868, 2910, 3148
desire, homosexual, 0987
desire, male system of, 2903
desire, masculine, 2843, 3068
desire, mimetic, 2885
despair, 0124, 0198, 0723, 1108, 1145, 1175
despot, 1436
Destiny, 1980
destiny, xvii, 0680, 0687, 0978, 0998, 1374, 2024, 2070
Deucalion, 3172, 3189a
devil, 1175
DeWitt, Johannes, 0443
Diaconus, Paulus, 2785
dialectic, 0076, 0280, 0359, 0381, 0389
dialogue (as concept or element of drama), 0819
dialogue (as concept or genre), 1123
Diana, 0107, 0437, 0868, 0881, 1156, 1163, 2283, 2284, 2300, 2317, 2352, 2357, 2359, 2458, 2521, 2532, 3096, 3100a
  in *All's Well That Ends Well*, 0686, 1158
  in *Pericles*, 0687, 0781, 2368, 2371
  in *Two Noble Kinsmen, The*, 0781
dianoia, 0404
Dian's Bud
  in *Midsummer Night's Dream, A*, 2278
dictator, 0641
diction, 0208, 0572, 0710, 0728, 0924, 1051
diction, Latinate, 3186a
dictionaries, classical, 0421
diction (as concept or element of drama), 0145, 0353a, 1053
Dido, xiv, xv, 0208, 0322a, 0421, 0436, 0533, 0759a, 0759b, 0789, 0815, 0902, 0932, 1162, 1171a, 1187, 1193, 1202, 1296, 1312, 1346, 1370a, 1371, 1512, 1532, 1800, 1804, 1808, 1837, 1861, 1880, 1883, 1892, 1895, 2249, 2257, 2422, 2532, 2541, 2551, 2553, 2556, 2564, 2566a, 2569a, 2583, 2584, 2588, 2588a, 3070, 3154
Digges, Leonard, 0401
Digges, Thomas
  Stratioticos, 1926
dignitas, 1059
dignity, 0828, 1145, 3070
dike, 0526
dilemma, 1633
dining, 1572
Dio Cassius (Cocceianus Cassius Dio), 0668, 1193, 1345, 1468, 1524, 1650, 2031, 2739
  Roman History (Historia Romana), 1522, 2044
Dio Chrysostom (Dio Cocceianus), 2855
Diogenes, xxi, 2631, 2673
Diogenes Laertius, 0721, 2153
Diogenes the Cynic, 1831, 2146, 2152, 2153
Diogeniana, 2674
Diomedes (Diomede), 2948
  in *Troilus and Cressida*, 0096, 0156, 0576, 0631, 0708, 1102, 2790, 2809, 2842, 2858, 2886, 2912, 2936, 2939, 2942, 2950, 2954, 2969, 2994, 3031, 3033, 3060, 3070, 3071
Diomedes (early grammarian), 1003
Dionysian principle
  Apollonian principle and, 0644
Dionysius of Halicarnassus, xxi, 0557, 1650, 2755
Dionysus, 0153, 0183, 0828, 1025, 1121, 1322, 1419, 2148
Dioscorides (Dioscurides), 0858, 2539
Diotima, 2497
disciplina, 0587
discord, 0105, 0197, 0377a, 0382, 0789, 1081, 1164, 1210, 1284
discord, comic pattern of, 2765
discordance
  harmony and, 2792
discourse, 1707, 2063, 2134, 2455, 2737, 2834a
discourse, public, 1999
discovery (as concept or element of drama), 0600, 1091
discretion, 1907
discrimination, 2696
disease, 0798, 1054, 1095, 1683, 2615, 2959
disenchantment, 0747
disguise, 0078, 0237, 0310, 0434, 0466, 0704, 0923, 3084
disintegration, 3210
dismemberment, 1039, 1045, 1048, 2729, 2779a
disorder, 0160a, 0174, 0186, 0197, 0215, 0255, 0292a, 0369, 0398, 0467, 0648, 0666, 0702, 0759a, 0895, 0903, 1045, 1147, 1335, 1348, 1610, 2012, 2036, 2064, 2172, 2665, 2717, 2784, 2891, 2977
  order and, 2927
dispensation, Christian, 3197
dispositio, 2337, 2455a
disposition (in rhetoric), 0611
disputation, 0470
dissembling, 1692
dissolution, 0475, 2952, 2994
dissonance, stylistic, 2963
disunity, 0956, 1198, 2136, 3035
divinity, 1966
divisio, 0433
division, 1390
division, motif of, 0714
Dogberry
  in *Much Ado About Nothing*, 0258, 1052, 2324
Dogstar, 2475a
Dolabella
  in *Antony and Cleopatra*, 0372a, 0679, 1000, 1037, 1164, 1174, 1175, 1221a, 1283, 1299, 1427, 1511
Dolce, Lodovico
  Marianna, 0191
Dollabella
  in *Antony and Cleopatra*, 1172
Doll Tearsheet
  in *Henry IV, Part 2*, 0963, 1911
domesticity, 1295

Donatus, Aelius, xiii, xxii, 0375, 0810, 0891, 0893, 0923, 0957, 0989, 1003, 1035, 1064, 1118, 2204, 2548, 3184, 3184a
Donne, John, 1185, 1482, 2802
Doomsday, 2029
double-mindedness, 2987
doubleness, 1983b
doubles, 1583, 2870
doubling, 1282
Dowden, Edward, 2475
drama, Italian, 0823
drama, Roman, 2694
dramatic lament, 0270
dramatist
  historiographer and, 1439
Drayton, Michael
  Mortimeriados, 1272
dream, 0187, 0208, 0288, 0344, 0425, 0426, 0499, 0610, 0663a, 0677, 0749, 0807, 0830, 1084, 1098, 1134, 1251, 1339, 1368, 1378, 1446, 1459, 1474, 1474a, 1479, 1511, 2045, 2066, 2115, 2116a, 2120, 2130a, 2453, 2456, 2560a
dreams, 0218, 0271, 0377c, 0382, 0534, 0773, 0862, 1022, 1184, 1842, 2290
dress, 1737
Dromio
  in *Comedy of Errors, The*, 0084, 0690
Dromio of Syracuse
  in *Comedy of Errors, The*, 1578
Dromios
  in *Comedy of Errors, The*, 0891
Dryden, John, 0403, 0787, 2937
  All for Love, 0713, 1320, 1326
  Preface to Troilus and Cressida, 2858a
  Troilus and Cressida, Or, Truth Found Too Late, 2811, 2858a
dualism, 147, 2616
dualities, 1000
duality, 0729, 1047, 1224, 1237, 1405, 2967
Du Bartas, Guillaume de Salluste, 0380
Du Bellay, Joachim
  Antiquez de Rome, Les, 2491
duel, 2699, 2882
Duke (of Milan)
  in *Two Gentlemen of Verona, The*, 0580
Duke Senior
  in *As You Like It*, 0490, 1543, 1551
Duke Vincentio
  in *Measure for Measure*, 0078, 0096, 0214, 0217, 2241, 2242, 2242a, 2243, 2244, 2245, 2245a, 2892
Dull
  in *Love's Labor's Lost*, 1006
Duncan
  in *Macbeth*, 0093, 0097, 0167, 0490, 2203, 2214, 2216, 2224, 2230, 2231a, 2234
du Plessis-Mornay, Philippe
  Discourse of Life and Death, A, 2241
duplicity, 2870, 2931
Dürer, Albrecht, 1397, 1455
duty, 0784, 0824, 1000, 1188, 1202, 1223, 1228, 1264, 1458, 1631, 3069

DuVair, Guillaume, 0191
  Moral Philosophie of the Stoicks, The, 0291
du Vair, Guillaume, 1139
dynamism, 3128

E
early comedies, by Shakespeare, 0099
eating, 1869b
Echo, xxii, 2777, 2777a, 3085, 3086, 3159
economics, 0390
ecphrasis, xix, 2402, 2411. See also *ekphrasis*
ecstasy, 2385
Eden, 1358, 2547
Edgar
  in *King Lear*, 0322a, 0400, 1057, 2146, 2153, 2154, 2156, 2160, 2167, 2175
Edmund
  in *King Lear*, 0134, 0323, 0662, 1057, 2140, 2154, 2172, 2176, 2183
education, xiii, 0079, 0092, 0296, 0796, 0821a, 1074, 1556, 2609
education, Christian, 0080a
education, classical, 2922
education, Roman, 2787
educational contexts
  Shakespeare and, 0019
education of Shakespeare, 00002, 0072, 0362, 0363, 0401, 0450, 0597, 0720, 0727, 0759a, 0914, 0916, 1035, 2579
Edward II, 1272
effeminacy, 1188, 1310, 2943
effeminization, 3154
Egeon
  in *Comedy of Errors, The*, 0154, 0400, 0672, 0822, 0891, 1135, 1137, 1567, 1574, 1578, 1580, 1587
Egeus
  in *Midsummer Night's Dream, A*, 1123
ego, 0096
egoism, 0949, 1175, 1463
egotism, 0662, 2950
Egypt, 0232, 0255, 0358, 0409, 0432, 0498, 0607, 0609, 0828, 0851, 0927, 0932, 1047, 1058, 1135, 1164, 1167, 1175, 1178, 1180, 1188, 1199, 1211, 1213, 1225, 1228, 1229, 1253, 1276, 1302, 1331, 1333, 1349, 1352, 1405, 1410, 1411, 1415, 1418, 1419, 1420, 1421, 1428, 1435, 1459, 1461, 1466, 1467, 1480, 1483, 1500, 1502, 1503, 1509, 1514, 1517, 1524, 1528
Egyptians, 0613, 0690, 1292, 1508
Eilzabeth, Queen
  in *Richard III*, 2454
eiron, 0222, 0616, 0798, 1188
ekphrasis, 0572, 0759b, 0907. See also *ecphrasis*
Electra, 0509, 1789
elegy, 0786, 2386
elements, four, 0107, 0480, 0729, 0858, 1000, 1167, 1333, 2578a
Eleusis, 0307
Eliot, John
  Ortho-epia: Eliots Fruits for the French, 2473

Index of Subjects

Elizabeth, Princess (daughter of James I), 3103
Elizabeth I, 0358, 0421, 0841, 0884, 0912, 1000, 1330, 1396, 1402, 1432, 1756, 1945, 2085, 2093, 2284, 2569a
elocutio, 1074, 2455a
elocution, 0611
eloquence, 0255, 0905, 1314, 1725, 2362, 2433
Elyot, Sir Thomas, 0479, 0796, 0973, 1009, 1064, 2243, 2682
  Boke named the Governour, The, 1926
  Governor, The, 0197, 1518, 2829
  Of the Knowledge Which Maketh a Wise Man: A disputation Platonike, 1904
Elysium, 0663a
emasculation, 1355, 1512
emblem, 0014a, 0109, 0142a, 0179, 0207, 0300, 0828a, 0988, 1304
emblematists, 2162
emblem book, 1777
emblem books, 0300, 0437, 0576, 0847, 0868, 1233, 1399, 1400, 1532, 1562, 1778, 2373, 2754
emblem literature, 2157
emblems, 0016, 0019, 0156, 0563, 1562, 1780, 2618, 2652
Emilia (Abbess)
  in *Comedy of Errors, The*, 0891a, 1584, 1587
Emilia (Emily)
  in *Two Noble Kinsmen, The*, 0437, 0781, 3090a, 3096, 3100a
Emmaus, 0610
emotion, 1058, 2068
emotions, 0208, 0959
Empedocles, 0380, 0729, 2578a
empire, 1152, 1193, 1399, 1482, 1524, 1774
emulation, 0872, 2085, 2885, 2951, 3001, 3062, 3127
enargeia, 0529, 2588
ending, double, of *Troilus and Cressida*, 2877
ending (as element of drama), 0846, 3101
energeia, 0674
Engels, Friedrich, 2691
English history, 0219
Enobarbus, 0306
  in *Antony and Cleopatra*, 0095, 0154, 0161, 0192, 0232, 0268, 0359, 0456, 0546, 0679, 0685, 0707, 0721, 0828, 0927, 0931, 0949, 0985a, 1000, 1013a, 1047, 1160, 1164, 1172, 1174, 1175, 1185, 1188, 1189, 1190, 1194, 1195, 1196, 1234, 1235a, 1242, 1244, 1252, 1253, 1271, 1276, 1300, 1303a, 1318a, 1323, 1327, 1336, 1347, 1348, 1350, 1379, 1388, 1389, 1392, 1393, 1406, 1414, 1416, 1419, 1430, 1437, 1438, 1449, 1456, 1465, 1477, 1492, 1496, 1502, 1511, 1514, 1521, 1522
entelechy, 0768
enumeratio, 2037
envy, 0193, 0452, 0850, 0949, 1673, 2985
Ephesus, 0675, 1567, 1570
epic, 0056, 0092, 0124, 0191, 0208, 0216, 0281, 0308, 0320, 0381, 0464a, 0485, 0505, 0517, 0519, 0572, 0589, 0983, 1018, 1087, 1175, 1193, 1310, 1503, 1627, 1628, 1862, 1883, 1919, 1933, 2230, 2588, 2593, 2937, 3059, 3101
epic, minor, xiv, 0571, 0572
epics, 0216, 3040
Epictetus, 1031, 1139, 1874, 1943, 2096
Epicureanism, 0113, 0263, 0756, 1233, 1312, 2042, 2088, 2244
Epicurus, 0834, 1067a, 1090
epideictic writing, 2565
epideixis, 0281, 1810
epigram, 0281, 0300
epilogue of *Troilus and Cressida*, 2796, 2797, 2838, 2875, 2877, 2962, 2979, 2992, 2994
epistle prefaced to *Troilus and Cressida*, 2795, 2796, 2837, 2860
epitaph, 1645, 2651, 2695
epitasis (element of drama), 2548
epithalamium, 2469, 2470
epyllia, 0332, 3168
epyllion, 0019, 0028, 0884, 0934, 3122, 3135, 3139
equality, 0525, 0850
equity, 1894, 2240, 2243
equivocation, tonal, 3011
Er, 0487
Erasistratus, 0854
Erasmus, Desiderius, 0058, 0109, 0143, 0235, 0314, 0386a, 0431, 0470, 0488, 0610, 0621, 0674, 0780, 0796, 0809, 0891, 0904, 0938, 1011, 1031, 1061, 1064, 1788, 1815, 2122, 2623
  Adages, 0450, 1158
  Adagia, 0300, 0610, 1822, 3087
  Amicitia, 2202
  Apophthegmata, 0610, 1253
  Apophthegmes, 2146
  Colloquies, 0334, 2575
  De Conscribendis Epistolis, 2505, 2506
  Dialogus Ciceronianus, 2480
  Education of a Christian Prince, 1917
  Enchiridion Militis Christiani, 2333
  Institutio principis Christiani, 1925
  Lingua, sive de linguae usu ab abusu, 0833
  Parabolae sive milia, 2524
  Praise of Folly, The (Moriae Encomium), 0090, 0274, 0280, 0334, 0450, 0616, 1554, 1855, 1917
ergon, 0310a
Eros, 1000
  Anteros and, 2521
  in *Antony and Cleopatra*, 0277, 0646, 0690, 0931, 1037, 1173, 1175, 1255, 1347, 1414, 1465, 1526
Eros (eros), 0080a, 0239, 0375, 0382, 0412, 0414, 0622, 0967, 0988, 1089, 1294, 1956, 2464
eroticism, 0701, 3139
error, 0156a, 0166, 0182, 0207, 0891, 1118, 1565, 1575, 1583, 1787, 1790, 1791, 1957, 2010, 2144
errors, 0208, 1998
Escalus
  in *Measure for Measure*, 2240
Escalus, Prince

in *Romeo and Juliet*, xx, 2461
Escanes
  in *Pericles*, xix, 2364
escapism, 1281
Essex, Earl of, 0174, 0765, 0869, 0912, 0916, 1945, 2038, 2085, 2284, 2904, 3010
estates, 1031
eternity, 0628, 1090, 1263, 2147, 2380, 2491, 2964a
ethical appeal, 2037
ethics, 0033, 0079, 0201, 0213, 0218, 0252, 0285, 0408, 0462, 0542, 0587, 0813, 1734, 2306
ethnocentrism, 0701
ethopoeia, 0663, 1856
ethos, 0002, 0208, 0236, 0336, 0404, 1071, 1856, 1857, 1999, 2455a
ethos, Roman, 0409
ethos, tragic, 1659
ethos of music, 1021
etymology, 0690
eulogy, 1378
eunuch, 1626a
eunuchs, 1205
euphuistic style, 0685
Euripides, xviii, 0376, 0468, 0534, 0597, 0615, 0624, 0640, 0748, 1035, 1040, 1673, 1829, 2800, 2900
  Alcestis, 1009, 3198, 3200, 3210
  Bacchae, 0153, 0853, 1025, 1428, 1623, 1962
  Hecuba, 0610, 1115, 1962, 2785
  Helen, 0598a
  Heracles, 1086
  Hippolytus, 1391
  Ion, 0598a, 0860
  Iphigenia, 0598a
  Iphigenia in Aulis, 0610, 1962
  Iphigenia in Tauris, 0860
  Orestes, 1876
  Phoenissae, 1962
  Troades, 1819, 1826
  Trojan Women, The, 1115
Europa, 2532
Euryalus, xvii, 1936
Eurydice, 1816, 2365
Eusebius, 1758
Evans, Sir Hugh
  in *Merry Wives of Windsor, The*, 0283, 2263
Evanthius, xxii, 0810, 0891, 1003, 3184, 3184a
Eve, 1233, 1261, 1362
Everyman, 0607, 2612, 2702
Everyman, 2612, 2658, 2677
evil, 0071, 0097, 0252, 0330, 0347a, 0368, 0374, 0395, 0396, 0434, 0435, 0478, 0582, 0613, 0666, 0674, 0683, 0721, 0759a, 0779, 0863, 0945, 0949, 0978, 0981, 1073, 1095, 1113, 1139, 1168, 1204, 1506, 1556, 1791, 1839, 1937a, 2083, 2101, 2139, 2161a, 2181, 2209, 2209a, 2223, 2250, 2365, 2396, 2435, 2581, 2688
  good and, 2174, 2545

excess, 0728, 1483
exercitatio, 0848a
exile, 0085, 0284, 0581, 0594, 0670, 0712, 1669, 1682, 1710, 1712, 1859, 2370
existentialism, 1873
exordium, 0433, 1999
exposition (as concept or element of drama), 0433
eyes, 1534

F
fable, 0232, 2642
fables, 0375, 1706
fabula Atellana, 2595
facial action in Shakespeare, 0674
factionalism, 1110, 1689, 2056, 2958, 2959
fairies
  in *Midsummer Night's Dream, A*, 0721, 2285, 2286, 2288, 2293, 2295, 2298, 2310, 2317
fairy tale, 2181
faith, 2322
fallacies, 0323
fallax servus of Roman comedy, 2341
falseness, 0170
Falstaff, Sir John, xiii, 0084, 0258, 0331, 0379, 0450, 0491, 0720a, 0788, 0798, 0815, 0899, 0943, 1052, 1054, 1056, 1072, 1093a, 1127, 1140a, 1241, 1288, 1377, 1924
  in *Henry IV, Part 1*, xvii, 0153, 0563, 0734, 1900, 1902, 1903, 1904, 1907, 1908, 1912
  in *Henry IV, Part 2*, 0151, 1911, 1915
  in *Henry IV, Parts 1 & 2*, 0078, 0616, 0833, 1146a
  in *Henry IV, Parts 1 & 2* and *Henry V*, 0387
  in *Henry V*, 0392
  in *Merry Wives of Windsor, The*, xix, 0118, 0119, 0151, 2263, 2265, 2266, 2266a, 2267, 2268
Fama, 0505, 0829a
fama (good name), 2327
fame, 0133, 0253, 0575, 0610, 0721, 0759a, 0861, 0894, 1609, 1655, 1869b, 1954, 2189, 2333
family, 0057, 0092, 0114, 0121, 0152, 0156, 0187, 0226, 0239, 0406, 0599, 0613, 0709, 0730, 0759a, 0911, 0949, 1047, 1101, 1114, 1135, 1198, 1278, 1474, 1586, 1613, 1646, 1654, 1670, 1684, 1703, 1710, 1716, 1742, 1858, 2145a, 2426, 2471
famine, 1610, 1660
Famous Victories of Henry the Fifth, The, 0450
fancy, 0499, 1228
fantasy, 0499, 1355, 1444
farce, xvi, 0153, 0283, 0564, 0822, 0891a, 1395, 1410, 1568, 1575, 1578, 1587, 2181, 2305, 2715, 2956
farces, 0153
farewells, 1463
Farmer, Richard
  Essay on the Learning of Shakespeare, 0937
fashion, 2322
fatalism, 0978, 1139

Fate, 1193, 2462
  reason and, 0729
fate, 0174, 0229, 0613, 0615, 0730, 1089,
  1476, 1567, 1985, 2036, 2114, 2225, 3104
Fates, 1641
father, 0278a, 0292, 0307, 0318, 0322a, 0377,
  0549, 0850, 0879, 0940a, 1054, 1641, 1656,
  1741a, 1749, 1844, 1859, 1862, 1872, 1910,
  1937b, 2019, 2027, 2059, 2075, 2161, 2234,
  2393, 2596
father figures, 0216
fathers, 0092, 0152, 0216, 0406, 1517, 3003
  mothers and, 1869
Faulconbridge, Philip (the Bastard)
  in *King John*, 2661
fear, 0166, 0254, 0283, 0453, 0554, 0917,
  0959, 0969, 1108, 1666, 1871, 2032, 2150,
  2706
feast, 0178, 1710, 2615, 2671
feasting, 1253, 2034, 2035
fecundity, 0115
feeding, 0696, 1501, 1704
female, 0237, 0307, 0311, 0319a, 0370a,
  0377c, 0644, 0824, 2485
  male and, 0828, 0901, 1383, 1533, 1543a
female impersonation, 1515
femaleness, 2074
feminine, 1447, 1489
femininity, 0614, 1316, 1345, 1418, 1460, 1729
feminism, 0142a
feminist criticism, 0032
Fenton
  in *Merry Wives of Windsor, The*, 2265
Fenton, Geoffrey
  Tragicall Discourses, 2430
Ferdinand
  in *Tempest, The*, 0336, 0373, 0375, 0421,
    0490, 0577, 0850, 1123, 1134, 2560, 2564,
    2565, 2566, 2566a, 2569a, 2577, 2578a,
    2588, 2592, 2594
fertility, 0373, 2555, 3143, 3170, 3187, 3190
  chastity and, 2578a
Feste
  in *Twelfth Night*, 0084, 0690, 3079, 3081,
    3082, 3084, 3087
feudalism, 0191, 0766
feudality, 0819
feudal order, 0637
Ficino, Marsilio, 0101, 0144, 0288, 0307,
  0488, 0547a, 0627, 0808, 0982, 1031, 1081,
  1149a, 1185, 1531, 2188, 2223, 2385, 2483,
  2521, 2546, 2547, 2550, 2551a, 2569, 2589,
  2601
  commentary on Plato's *Symposium (In
    Convivium Platonis De Amore
    Commentarius)*, 2464, 2495, 2516, 2519,
    2855
  *In Convivium Platonis De Amore
    Commentarius* (commentary on Plato's
    Symposium), 2537
  Platonic Theology, 1903
fickleness, 1520, 2883
fidelity, 2377
fides, 0587

Fielding, Henry, 0904
  Modern Husband, The, 2655
fierceness, 1612
figures, rhetorical, 3129. *See also* rhetoric,
  figures of
figures of rhetoric. *See* rhetoric, figures of
figures of speech. *See* speech, figures of
figures of thought. *See* thought, figures of
First Citizen
  in *Coriolanus*, 0076
First Folio, 0402, 0848a, 1066, 1347, 1370,
  1390, 1426, 1438, 1478, 1519, 1585a, 1727,
  1861, 1914, 1924, 2051a, 2110, 2112, 2125,
  2155, 2199, 2233, 2332, 2484a, 2714, 2759,
  2769, 2845, 2860, 2878, 2925, 2926, 2953,
  2962, 2981, 3045
First Oration against Aristogiton, 2998a
First Senator
  in *Timon of Athens*, 0522
fixity, 1467
flattery, 0232, 0452, 0545, 1123, 2077, 2082,
  2633, 2660, 2693, 2703
Flavius
  in *Julius Caesar*, 2018, 2054, 2097
  in *Timon of Athens*, 0161., 0232, 0522, 0610,
    0983a, 2612, 2636, 2660, 2692, 2694, 2697.
    See also steward
flaw, 1972, 2706
flaws, personal, 2471
Fleming, Abraham
  translation of *Georgics*, by Virgil, 0753
  translation of letter of Cicero to Lucceius in *A
    Panoplie of Epistles*, 1552
Fleming, John, 2137
flesh
  spirit and, 2529
Fletcher, John, 0860, 1753, 3092, 3096, 3098,
  3100, 3100b, 3104
Flora, 1850, 3180, 3187
Flora Meretrix, 1850
Florio, John, 2503
  translation of Montaigne's *Essays*, 2376
Florizel
  in *Winter's Tale, The*, 0151, 0577, 3178, 3193
Florus (Lucius Annaeus), 1695
fluctuation, 1528
Fludd, Robert, 1148
  Ars Memoriae, 0958, 1149
  Theatrum Orbi, 1426
  Utriusque Cosmi Historia, 1150
Fluellen
  in *Henry V*, 0537, 1920, 1926, 1927, 1929, 1933
flux, 1371, 1429, 1467, 3081
folklore, 0667, 0716, 1834
  myth and, 2316
  mythology and, 2318
following
  imitation and, 1255
  leaving and, 1256
folly, 0616, 0653, 0657, 1005, 1147, 2304
food, 1572, 1590, 1623, 1649, 1669, 1716
Fool
  in *King Lear*, 0695, 2141, 2147
  in *Timon of Athens*, 1015

840   *Shakespeare and the Classical Tradition*

fool, 0118, 0616, 0695, 0718, 0797, 0798, 0825, 2181
fools, 0084, 0125, 0889
foresight, 2528
forest, 1133, 1134, 2727, 2783
forgiveness, xxii, 0464a, 3140
form, imitative, 2874
formlessness as theme in *Troilus and Cressida*, 2914
forms, ideal, 0457
formulae, tragic, 2919
Forset, Edward
  Comparative Discourse of the Bodies Natural and Politique, 1649
Fortinbras
  in *Hamlet*, 1830, 1848, 1856, 1860, 1868, 1883
fortitude, 0208, 0262, 0294, 0519, 1023, 1047, 1086, 3066
Fortuna, 1848, 2179a, 2589
fortuna, 0191
Fortune
  Love and, 2253
Fortune, wheel of, 0377a, 0923, 0950, 1136, 1294, 2179a, 2450, 2901
Fortune (fortune), xi, 0076, 0102, 0125, 0164a, 0186, 0234, 0251, 0264, 0266, 0292a, 0303, 0322, 0355, 0393, 0446, 0484, 0535, 0555, 0563, 0596, 0610, 0634, 0635, 0653, 0664, 0697, 0698, 0718, 0729, 0730, 0850, 0859, 0860, 0886, 0923, 0942, 0950, 1021, 1130, 1139, 1206, 1218, 1262, 1294, 1312, 1344, 1362, 1374, 1523, 1537, 1559, 1566, 1820, 1830, 1842, 1855, 1860, 1896, 1920, 2046, 2069, 2093, 2128, 2157, 2174, 2183, 2261, 2333, 2367, 2371, 2450, 2461, 2462, 2476, 2606, 2633, 2652, 2659, 2673, 2674, 2686, 2694, 2700, 2703, 2784, 3072, 3080, 3193
  in *Timon of Athens*, 2616
four ages, Ovid's myth of, 2762
fragmentation, 1704, 2918
Francesca
  in Dante, 0385
Francis
  in *Henry IV, Part 1*, 1901
Francis, Friar
  in *Much Ado About Nothing*, 0096
Francis I, 2432
fraternity, 0525
Fraunce, Abraham, 2555, 3130
  Amintas Dale, 2598
Frederick, Duke
  in *As You Like It*, 1081
free choice, 0526
freedom, 0174, 0191, 0304, 0389, 0630, 0743, 1089, 2113, 2596
Freud, Sigmund, xvii, 0377, 0377c, 1691, 1869, 2048, 2475, 2993, 3068
  Totem and Taboo, 2019
Freytag, Gustav, 1723
friend, 1257
  in *Sonnets*, 2478, 2483, 2486, 2493, 2494, 2495

friends, 0102, 1278, 2641
friendship, xxi, 0091, 0110, 0139, 0347a, 0523, 0525, 0613, 0729, 0850, 0861, 1047, 1109, 1111, 1569, 1862, 1879a, 1896, 1954, 1955, 2010, 2042, 2136, 2258, 2479, 2516, 2633, 2674, 2682, 2692, 2700, 2703, 2706, 3094, 3100b, 3101, 3102
friendship, male, 3193
fruitfulness, 2562a
Fulbecke, William, 2056
Fulvia
  in *Antony and Cleopatra*, 1174, 1285, 1325, 1330, 1420
  in *Julius Caesar*, 1046
Fulvia (wife of Mark Antony), 1238
funeral of Julius Caesar, 2031
funerals, 0792
Furies, xviii, 2221
furies, 2231
furor
  pietas and, 2593
furores, Neoplatonic, 2385
furor poeticus, 0375
fury, 1225
future, 0691, 0759a, 1128, 1251, 1318a, 2806, 2807, 2872

G
Gager, William
  Dido Tragoedia, 0902
Gaius, 2247
Galen, 0218, 0331, 0346, 0392, 0499, 0547a, 0601, 0650a, 0752, 0854, 0920, 1147, 1243, 1508, 1924, 3092
  Theriake, 1507
Gallus, Cornelius, 0938
game-playing, 1259
Gammer Gurton's Needle, 1484a
Ganymede, 0387, 0987, 1555, 2281, 2310, 3090a
  in *As You Like It*, 0687
garden, 1130
Garden of Adonis in Spenser's *Fairie Queene*, 3132
Garden of Eden, 0045, 1543c, 2574
Garnier, Robert
  Antonie, 2429
  Antonius, 1468
  Cornelia, 2429
  Marc Antoine, 1472
garrulity, 0833
Gascoigne, George
  Glasse of Government, The, 2663
  Supposes, 0556, 0608, 0923, 2535, 2542
Gaunt, John of, Duke of Lancaster
  in *Richard II*, 0231, 2443, 2445
Gay, John
  Beggar's Opera, The, 2655
gender, xiv, 0032, 0253, 0287, 0405, 0688, 0703, 0807a, 1013a, 1407, 1460, 1470, 1748, 2413, 2733, 2758, 2812
gender boundaries, 0032
gender role, 0638

Index of Subjects

gender roles, 0637a
generation, 3150
generosity, 1087, 1174, 1218, 1335, 2641, 2707
Genet, Jean
  Balcony, The, 1102
genre, xxi, 0032, 0034, 0062, 0067, 0110,
  0147, 0160a, 0272, 0308, 0332, 0375, 0376,
  0381, 0393, 0434, 0547, 0571, 0767, 0850a,
  0875, 0884, 1013a, 1407, 1801, 2198, 2426,
  2588, 2594, 2619, 2826, 2834, 2860, 2878,
  2901, 2910, 2915, 2972, 2980, 3024
genres, 0037, 0077, 0089, 0155, 0176, 0262,
  0272, 0273, 0293, 0370a, 0464a, 0465a,
  0468, 0557, 0663a, 1018, 1782, 2693
genres, mixture of, 3007, 3009
gentleman, 0800, 0955
gentleness, 0560, 0561
Geoffrey of Monmouth
  Historia Regum Britanniae, 1769
Gerarde, John, 2768
  Herball, 2281
Germanicus, Nero Claudius, 1754, 1923, 1928
Gertrude
  in *Hamlet*, 0875, 1810, 1850, 1876, 1890,
  1898
Gervinus, G. G., 2475
gesture, 0105, 1740, 1970, 2066, 2776
gestures, 0172a, 0302, 1047, 1642, 2013, 2224
ghost, 0669, 0881
Ghost of Banquo
  in *Macbeth*, 2216, 2218
Ghost of Hamlet's father
  in *Hamlet*, 0812, 1784, 1786, 1807, 1828,
  1832, 1837, 1849, 1859, 1869a, 1872
Ghost of Julius Caesar
  in *Julius Caesar*, 0552, 0566a, 0593, 0603,
  0679, 0700, 2030, 2078
ghosts, 0377c, 0534, 0566a, 0745
ghosts of the Leonati
  in *Cymbeline*, 1772
Gilbert, W. S.
  Dan'l Druce, Blacksmith, 2655
Gildon, Charles, 0403
Giorgi, Francesco, 1149a
Giraldi, 0868
Giraldo Cinthio
  Cleopatra, 0534
Gismond of Salerne. See under Wilmot, Robert
Globe playhouse, 1814a
Globe theater, 0200, 0277, 0378, 0605, 0806,
  0930, 1034a, 1148, 1149, 1869a, 1985, 2292,
  2588, 2838, 2839, 2860, 2861
Globe theater, second, 0958, 1149, 1150
glory, 0079, 0172, 0208, 0261, 0312, 0378,
  0491, 0656, 0759a, 0929, 0971, 1081, 1233,
  1289, 1296, 1327, 1354, 1436, 1463, 2333,
  2858, 2881
Gloucester, Earl of
  in *King Lear*, 0097, 0254, 0322a, 0400, 2150,
  2154, 2168, 2169
gluttony, 3154
Gnosticism, 0637a
God, 1081, 1772
god, 0320, 1086, 1719

goddess, 0332, 0830
goddesses, 0290, 0307, 0335, 1134
gods, xviii, 0239, 0251, 0325, 0335, 0382,
  0413, 0421, 0447, 0577, 0631, 0649, 0690,
  0694, 0721, 0749, 0781, 0841, 0966, 0980,
  1021, 1047, 1095, 1123, 1796, 1956, 1962,
  2154, 3095, 3103, 3104
gods, invocation of, 3097
goety, 0449
Golden Age, 0045, 0233, 0693, 1536, 1539,
  1541, 1543, 1543c, 1547, 2447, 2545, 2572,
  2580, 2593, 2740
Golden Ages, 1538
Golden Fleece, 2260
  Jason and, 0546
golden mean, 1059
golden world, 2288a
Golding, Arthur, xvi, 2766
  Epistle prefacing his translation of Ovid's
    Metamorphoses, 1543
  "To the Reader," prefacing his translation of
    Ovid's *Metamorphoses*, 1996
  translation of Caesar's *Gallic War*, 1821
  translation of Ovid's *Metamorphoses*, xix, xxi,
    0046, 0126, 0190, 0332, 0721, 0910a,
    1042a, 1043, 1324, 1708, 1816, 2235, 2254,
    2256, 2270, 2271, 2281, 2305, 2312, 2314,
    2315, 2316, 2352, 2387, 2447, 2453, 2456,
    2468, 2475c, 2482, 2530, 2541, 2562, 2583,
    2777, 2777a, 2786, 3086, 3195. *See also
    under* Ovid (Publius Ovidius Naso)
  translation of Seneca's *De Beneficiis*, 2704
Goldsmith, Oliver, 2632
Goneril
  in *King Lear*, xviii, 2139, 2154, 2161a, 2172
Gonzalo
  in *Tempest, The*, 2545, 2547, 2551, 2559,
  2565a, 2566a, 2569a, 2576, 2588a
good, 0478
  evil and, 2174, 2545
goodness, 0075, 1506, 2855
Googe, Barnabe
  translation of *Zodiacae Vitae*, by Palingenius,
  0142
Gorgeous Gallery of Gallant Inventions, A
  "History of Pyramus and Thisbe," 2311
Gorgon, 0093, 1518, 2224
Gospel, Christian, 1108
Goths
  Romans and, 2717
  in *Titus Andronicus*, 0906, 2762
Goulart, Simon, 0359
  Life of Octavius Caesar Augustus, 1468
government, 0113, 0201, 0221, 0517, 0760,
  0855, 0897, 0916, 1649, 1665, 1990, 2042,
  2851
governor, 0563
governors, 0121, 0665
Gower, John, 1417, 1520, 2303, 2373, 2403
  Confessio Amantis, xx, 0690, 1574, 2047,
  2260, 2363, 2371, 2410
grace, 0091, 0681, 1191, 2475
grace, Christian, 3182
Graces, 0196, 1185

Graces, Three, 2704
gradatio, 2245a, 2527a
grammar, 0187, 0296
grammar of *Hamlet*, 0558
grammars, 0821a
grammar school, 0369, 0567, 0568, 0569, 1596
grammar school curriculum, 0317
grammar school curriculum of Shakespeare, 0937
grammar school of Shakespeare, 0187, 0221, 0483, 0496, 0586, 0611, 0745, 0869, 0915, 0936, 0936a, 1726
grammar schools, 0262, 0299, 0821, 1565
grandeur, 0208, 1392, 1618
gravitas, 1059, 2043
 voluptas and, 0759a
Gray's Inn, 1587
Great Chain of Being, 0107, 0706, 1104, 1110
greatness, 0098, 0208, 0564, 0578, 0685, 0909, 1000, 1047, 1087, 1372, 1455, 1506, 1681, 1984, 2098, 2103, 2106
greatness of mind *(mentis integritas)*, 0655
great-souled man, 2515
Grecian works, by Shakespeare, 0079
Greco-Roman plays, by Shakespeare, 0670
Greece, xvii, 0057, 0093, 0123, 0307, 0382, 0645, 0664, 0677, 0832a, 0869, 1419, 1827, 1912, 1934
greed, 0369, 2657, 2681, 2733
Greek, 0056, 0092, 0204, 0300, 0401, 0402, 0597, 0610, 0645, 0721, 0842, 0994, 1010, 1066, 1863, 1930
Greek and Roman plays, by Shakespeare, 0625, 0882
Greek Anthology, ix, 0401, 2501
Greek drama, 0117, 0158, 0401, 0985a
Greek dramatists, 0124, 0229, 1175
Greek plays, by Shakespeare, 0080, 0410, 0489, 0676
Greeks, 0057, 0059a, 0276, 0277, 0278a, 0299, 0342, 0489, 0517, 0534, 0646, 0652, 0742, 0757, 0833, 0966, 0983, 1011, 2588
 in *Troilus and Cressida*, 0106, 1002, 1147, 2790, 2804, 2814, 2822, 2836, 2871, 2891, 2910, 2934, 2958, 2983, 3065
Greek works, by Shakespeare, 0104
Greene, Robert, 0860, 0997, 2473
 Euphues His Censure to Philautus, 2985, 3066
 Groatsworth of Witte, A, 3115
 Pandosto, xxii, 0690, 1114, 3184a, 3186, 3188, 3196, 3197, 3198, 3205, 3210
green world, 0518
Grenewey, Richard
 translation of Tacitus's *Annales (Annals)*, 1926, 1928, 2024
Greville, Fulke
 Caelica, 1063
 Treatie of Warres, 1063
grief, 0124, 0198, 0370a, 0663, 1175
grotesque, 0379
Grumio
 in *Taming of the Shrew, The*, 2533

Guarini, Giambattista, 0282b
 Pastor Fido, Il, 0579, 1753, 1779. See also Guarini, Giovanni Battista
Guarini, Giovanni Battista, 2971. See also Guarini, Giambattista
Guiderius
 in *Cymbeline*, 1766, 1772
Guildenstern
 in *Hamlet*, 1021, 1843, 1896
guilt, 0524, 0615, 0749, 0939, 3070, 3071

H
Hades, 0890, 2190, 2453, 2572, 3193
Hadrian (Publius Aelius Hadrianus), 2328a
Hakluyt, Richard
 Voyages, 2551
Hal, Prince, 0387, 0450, 0537, 0636, 0647, 0815, 1054, 1056, 1093a, 1097, 1140a, 1241, 1734a
 in *Henry IV, Part 1*, xvii, 0153, 0519, 0563, 0734, 0894, 1901, 1902, 1903, 1904, 1905, 1909, 1910
 in *Henry IV, Part 2*, 0151, 0519, 1911, 1915
 in *Henry IV, Part 1* and *Henry V*, 0214
 in *Henry IV, Part 2* and *Henry V*, 0392
 in *Henry IV, Parts 1 & 2*, 0833, 1146a, 1377
 in *Henry IV, Parts 1 & 2* and *Henry V*, 0301
Hales, John, 0403, 0409
Hall, Edward
 Union of the Two Noble and Illustre Famelies of Lancastre and Yorke, 0864, 2457
hamartia, 0166, 0167, 0446a, 0511, 0757, 0905a, 1035, 1888, 1899, 2010
Hamlet, 1968
 in *Hamlet*, xvii, 0029, 0075, 0078, 0080a, 0166, 0167, 0182, 0201, 0208, 0246, 0294, 0301, 0375, 0381, 0396, 0446a, 0462, 0468, 0499, 0509, 0524, 0549, 0610, 0680, 0685, 0785, 0787, 0789, 0801, 0805, 0806, 0808, 0830, 0875, 0902, 0919, 0920, 0940a, 0961, 0962, 0978, 1021, 1025, 1043, 1053, 1072, 1115, 1131, 1139, 1149a, 1252a, 1782, 1784, 1787, 1791, 1792, 1794, 1796, 1799, 1800, 1802, 1803, 1804, 1805, 1806, 1808, 1809, 1811, 1812, 1816, 1817, 1818, 1819, 1820, 1821, 1822, 1823, 1824, 1825, 1828, 1830, 1832, 1833, 1834, 1834a, 1835, 1836, 1837, 1840, 1841, 1841a, 1842, 1842a, 1843, 1844, 1844a, 1845, 1848, 1853, 1855, 1856, 1859, 1860, 1862, 1866, 1867, 1868, 1869, 1869a, 1869b, 1870, 1872, 1874, 1875, 1876, 1877, 1880, 1881, 1883, 1885, 1886, 1889, 1892, 1893a, 1897, 1898, 2080, 3034
Harbert, William, 1272
Hardy, Alexandre
 Coriolan, 1602
Harington, John
 translation of Cicero's *Of Friendship*, 2701
Harmonia, 3180, 3194
Harmony, 2917
harmony, 0047, 0078, 0100, 0119, 0196, 0197, 0257, 0290, 0398, 0460, 0487, 0490, 0595,

Index of Subjects

0615, 0636, 0699, 0729, 0747, 0814, 0897, 1000, 1021, 1056, 1081, 1084, 1110, 1122, 1164, 1165, 1210, 1313, 1504, 1536, 1850, 2147, 2208, 2257, 2272, 2287, 2306, 2342, 2365, 2519, 2543, 2676, 2829
  discordance and, 2792
harmony, cosmic, 2943
harmony, Pythagoran, 3180
harpies, 2557
harpy, 0759b, 2588
  in *Tempest, The,* 1044a, 2557, 2576
Hastings
  in *Richard III,* 0093
hate, 1592
hatred, 0197, 0232, 0393, 0549, 0570, 0867, 1673, 2696
Haward, Nicholas, 2682
  translation of Seneca's *De Beneficiis,* 2704
Haywood, Jasper
  translation of Seneca's *Thyestes,* 2215
headgear, 1735
Healey, John, 0127
hearing, 0627
heart, 1292
  tongue and, 1632b
Hecate, 0096, 0307, 0536, 0881, 1163, 2171, 2233, 2317
  in *Macbeth,* 2222, 2236
Hecate, Triple, 0900, 0901
Hector, 0054, 0192, 0759a, 1002, 1070, 1310, 1614, 1627, 1628, 2199a
  in *Troilus and Cressida,* 0078, 0106, 0137, 0208, 0215, 0265, 0277, 0396, 0455, 0478, 0481, 0508, 0561, 0625, 0691, 0692, 0700, 0766, 0903, 0909, 0987, 1081, 1111, 2794, 2798, 2803, 2814, 2815, 2820, 2826, 2828, 2839, 2841, 2844, 2848, 2852, 2858, 2866, 2877, 2881, 2882, 2886, 2899, 2901, 2910, 2911, 2916, 2918, 2924, 2928, 2929, 2934, 2936, 2939, 2942, 2946, 2949, 2951, 2953, 2957, 2961, 2974, 2977, 2979, 2980, 2986, 2989, 3003, 3008, 3009, 3010, 3011, 3012, 3013, 3015, 3020, 3028, 3030, 3035, 3043, 3044, 3053, 3057, 3061, 3066, 3071, 3072
Hecuba, 0602, 0663, 0749, 0759a, 0770, 1115, 1800, 1819, 1826, 1837, 1856, 1883, 1889, 1892, 2392, 2435, 2454
  in *Troilus and Cressida,* 2989
Hegel, Georg Wilhelm Friedrich
  Philosophy of Right, 2672
hegemony, 1330
Helen, 0900, 0907, 2422, 3179, 3181
  in *All's Well That Ends Well,* 1001
  in *Midsummer Night's Dream, A,* 1001
  in *Troilus and Cressida,* 0106, 0342, 0390, 0437, 0592, 0625, 2800, 2803, 2826, 2843, 2852, 2855, 2885, 2899, 2911, 2920, 2934, 2939, 2996, 3003, 3020, 3028, 3041, 3057, 3064, 3071
Helena, 3194
  in *All's Well That Ends Well,* 0096, 0690, 0789, 1081, 1156, 1157
  in *Midsummer Night's Dream, A,* 2289, 2291, 2298, 2302, 2305

Helen of Troy, 0249, 0789, 0975, 1001, 1244, 2289, 2302, 2454, 2495, 3012, 3040
Helenus
  in *Troilus and Cressida,* 0379
Heliodorus, 0769, 0928, 1468, 1762, 2363
  Aethiopica, 0067, 0068, 0284, 0311a, 0434, 0997, 1035, 1114, 1759, 1763, 1767
Helios, 2447, 2514
Hell, 2453
Hellenism, 1122
Hellenistic romances, 0123, 0311
Heminge, John, 2845
Henriad, by Shakespeare, 1376
Henry, Earl of Richmond, later Henry VII
  in *Richard III,* 2455a, 2457, 2458
Henry, Prince (son of James I), 3103
Henry Bolingbroke, Duke of Hereford, afterwards Henry IV
  in *Richard II-Henry V* tetralogy, 2136
Henry IV, 0599, 0895
Henry IV cycle, by Shakespeare, 0789
Henry IV tetralogy, by Shakespeare, 0228
Henry of Monmouth
  in *Henry IV, Part 1, Henry IV, Part 2,* and *Henry V,* 0905
Henryson, Robert, 0789, 2473, 2956, 2970
  Testament of Cresseid, The, 3013, 3026, 3037
Henry V, 0080a, 0599, 0762, 0943, 1093a
  in *Henry IV, Part 2,* 0387
  in *Henry V,* 0078, 0214, 0294, 0383, 0455, 0517, 0537, 0569, 1140a, 1917, 1920, 1923, 1925, 1926, 1927, 1929, 1931, 1946, 2026
  in *Richard II-Henry V* tetralogy, 2136
Henry VI, 0998
  in *Henry VI, Part 1,* 1934
  in *Henry VI, Part 3,* 0918, 0985a
  in *Henry VI Triad,* 0236
Henry VIII
  in *Henry VIII,* 1938
Hephaistos, 1157
Hera, 2139
Heracles, 0509, 1850, 3198, 3210
Heraclitus, 0266, 0375, 0469, 0729, 1063
heraldry, 1067a
Hercules, xiv, xv, xvi, xix, xxii, 0107, 0605, 0627, 0721, 0759a, 0778, 0930, 0932, 0967, 0988, 1000, 1043, 1167, 1171a, 1175, 1184, 1188, 1212a, 1218, 1222, 1223, 1225, 1266, 1312, 1313, 1315, 1336, 1366, 1371, 1372, 1400, 1419, 1433, 1455, 1483, 1504, 1538, 1541, 1543c, 1547, 1557, 1562, 1792, 1807, 1812, 1814a, 1869a, 2185a, 2197, 2199a, 2200, 2231, 2254, 2262, 2268, 2319, 2322, 2339, 3083, 3100
  in *Antony and Cleopatra,* 0700
  in *Merchant of Venice, The,* 2251
Hercules, pillars of, 2569a
Hercules Furens as stage convention, 2345
hermaphrodite, 1126, 2519, 2540
Hermaphroditus, 0863, 2353, 2540, 3085a, 3134, 3137, 3159
Hermes, 0307, 2651, 3182a, 3186, 3193
Hermetica, 0380

Hermeticism, 0149, 0307, 0637a, 0803, 0968, 2473, 2569
Hermia
  in *Midsummer Night's Dream, A,* 1001, 2279, 2290, 2291, 2298
Hermione, 1082
  in *Winter's Tale, The,* xxii, 0307, 0336, 0807, 0907, 1009, 2432, 3179, 3180, 3181, 3182, 3182a, 3183, 3184a, 3185, 3186a, 3189, 3190, 3191, 3192, 3193, 3194, 3195, 3198, 3205, 3208, 3210
Hermione's "statue"
  in *Winter's Tale, The,* 0990
Hermogenes, 0557
Hermogenes of Tarsus, 2455
  Concerning Ideas, 2512
Herne the Hunter (Falstaff)
  in *Merry Wives of Windsor, The,* 2266, 2268
Hero, 2468, 3088
  in *Much Ado About Nothing,* 0437, 0690, 2320, 2321
hero, 0062, 0075, 0095, 0096, 0106, 0112, 0131, 0137, 0160a, 0161, 0166, 0167, 0172, 0182, 0191, 0192, 0208, 0210, 0220, 0222, 0229, 0230, 0231, 0232, 0237, 0239, 0250, 0252, 0271, 0282, 0283, 0305, 0306, 0310, 0320, 0321, 0342, 0347a, 0350, 0381, 0396, 0398, 0399, 0426, 0444, 0446a, 0458, 0463, 0471, 0493, 0509, 0518, 0524, 0553, 0584, 0591, 0594, 0602, 0603, 0607, 0610, 0613, 0614, 0633, 0661, 0663a, 0678, 0702, 0712, 0745, 0748, 0751, 0757, 0784, 0792, 0838, 0846, 0865, 0867, 0874, 0894, 0905, 0925, 0949, 0960, 0999, 1000, 1017, 1026, 1055, 1056, 1091, 1099, 1114, 1119, 1135, 1139, 1142, 1154, 1179, 1457, 1497, 1607, 1723, 1811, 1962, 1986, 1989, 2053, 2077, 2085a, 2130a
hero, comic, xiii
hero, Greek, 1714
hero, tragic, 1739, 2204, 2219
Herod, 1230, 1477
Herod and Marianne story, 0191
Herodian, 2739, 2785
  History, 2742a
Herodotus, 0609, 0739, 1967, 2376, 2389, 2751, 2756
  Histories, 0312
heroes, 0075, 0097, 0123, 0167, 0171, 0172, 0187, 0219, 0229, 0232, 0233, 0292a, 0306, 0311, 0320, 0321, 0329, 0330, 0381, 0395, 0398, 0521, 0551, 0581, 0604, 0615, 0630, 0646, 0655, 0657, 0729, 0730, 0733, 0805, 0880, 0909, 0961, 0980, 0981, 1067, 1072, 1081, 1103, 1106, 1130
  villains and, 2113a
heroes, Greek and Trojan
  in *Troilus and Cressida,* 2917
heroes, Homeric, 3007
Heroicall Devises of M. Claudius Paradin, The, 0847
heroic tradition, 0062, 0208, 0591

heroine, 0067, 0142a, 0305, 0325, 0350, 0434, 0437, 0518, 0599, 0687, 0778, 0784, 0849a, 0850, 0923, 1070, 1078, 1083, 1114, 1115, 1155, 1497
heroines, 0437, 0642, 0730, 1080, 1081
heroism, 0080a, 0096, 0147, 0171, 0189, 0208, 0220, 0239, 0244, 0286, 0359, 0379a, 0459, 0464a, 0578, 0589, 0602, 0646, 0647, 0678, 0700, 0754, 0811, 0870, 0886, 0890, 0959, 0988, 1002, 1056, 1058, 1086, 1090, 1193, 1225, 1260, 1300, 1372, 1433, 1483, 1614, 1715, 1798, 1818, 1868, 1870, 1912, 1915, 2011, 2102a, 2319, 2426, 2563, 2813, 2922, 2987, 2989
heroism, chivalric, 2999
hero-villain, 0368
Hesiod, 0380, 1078, 2389, 2473
  Works and Days, 2547
Hesione, 2257
heterosexuality, 2843
Heywood, Thomas, 0394
  Iron Age, The, 0378
hierarchy, 0194, 0566, 0602, 0622, 0705, 0899, 1152, 1651, 2812, 2829, 3042
Hieronimo
  in *The Spanish Tragedy,* by Thomas Kyd, 0191
Hippocrates, 0346, 0392, 0547a, 0650a, 0752, 0920, 1147, 2539
  Aphorisms, 0858
  Prognostica, 1924
Hippolyta, 1039
  in *Midsummer Night's Dream, A,* 0630, 0690, 1009, 2273, 2277, 2281, 2287, 2291, 2293, 2301, 2303, 2305, 2313, 2316
  in *Two Noble Kinsmen, The,* 3097, 3100a
Hippolytus, 1039, 1830, 2303
Historia Apollonii Regis Tyri, xv, 0092
historians, 1143, 1602
historians, Tudor, 0587
historicism, new, xii
historicity, 2108
histories, by Shakespeare. See history plays, by Shakespeare
historiographer
  dramatist and, 1439
historiography, 0980
history, xvii, 0002, 052, 0104, 0123, 0158, 0174, 0175, 0181, 0200, 0201, 0208, 0261, 0263, 0285, 0314, 0320, 0327, 0332, 0338, 0343, 0369, 0389, 0413, 0447, 0453, 0464, 0496, 0504a, 0540, 0566, 0575, 0584, 0596, 0619, 0630, 0652, 0656, 0664, 0668, 0678, 0679, 0686, 0721, 0743, 0759a, 0765, 0772, 0794, 0805, 0844, 0857, 0874, 0882, 0883, 0887, 0892, 0894, 0938, 1003, 1047, 1050, 1054, 1058, 1067, 1069, 1076, 1101, 1110, 1180, 1206, 1246, 1260, 1261, 1318a, 1370a, 1393, 1398, 1436, 1439, 1457, 1480, 1483, 1509, 1528a, 1670a, 1675, 1693, 1703, 1710, 1712, 1734, 1769, 1776, 1919, 1929, 1936, 1952, 1972, 1973, 2013a, 2014, 2022a, 2038, 2040, 2057, 2070, 2077, 2082, 2089, 2091a, 2097, 2111, 2114, 2136, 2231, 2394,

Index of Subjects 845

2401, 2439, 2545, 2572, 2637, 2740, 2807, 2852, 2866, 2886, 2999, 3007, 3061, 3186
art and, 0467
myth and, 2417
history, classical, 3074
history, Roman, xv, 2742a, 2785
History of Titus Andronicus, The (18th-c. chapbook), xxi, 2710, 2761. *See also under* Titus Andronicus, prose history of; Titus Andronicus, ballad of
history play (as concept or genre), 0464a, 1054
history plays, by Shakespeare, xiii, xvii, 0037, 0049, 0052, 0058, 0059a, 0062, 0102, 0115, 0170, 0174, 0175, 0193, 0208, 0216, 0218, 0219, 0221, 0222, 0262, 0263, 0292, 0310a, 0350, 0358, 0360, 0362, 0363, 0364, 0369, 0372a, 0383, 0384, 0410, 0418, 0424, 0464, 0517, 0574, 0575, 0588, 0599, 0606, 0619, 0624, 0636, 0644, 0652, 0657, 0663a, 0665, 0671, 0675, 0677, 0700, 0746, 0755, 0765, 0767, 0772, 0780, 0802a, 0831, 0849a, 0850a, 0864, 0871, 0883, 0894, 0895, 0906, 0915, 0916, 0950, 0951, 0981, 0985, 1013a, 1044, 1056, 1068, 1073, 1107, 1130, 1241, 1334, 1407, 2026, 2080, 2094, 2098, 2114, 2136, 2813, 2851
Hobbes, Thomas, 1098, 2859
Hoby, Sir Thomas
 translation of *The Courtier,* by Baldassare Castiglione, 1140a, 1185
Holinshed, Raphael, 0690, 0773, 0794, 2210, 2226
 Chronicles of England, Scotland, and Ireland, The, 0384, 0864, 1763, 2137
Holland, Philemon, 0120
 translation of *Lives of the Caesars (The Historie of Twelve Caesars),* by Suetonius, 1047
 translation of Livy's *Romane Historie,* 1609
 translation of *Moralia,* by Plutarch, 1163
 translation of Pliny's *Naturalis Historia (Natural History)* as *The Historie of the World,* 0546, 0685, 2332, 2343, 3018
 translation of Plutarch's *Moralia,* 0127
Holofernes
 in *Love's Labor's Lost,* 0084, 0515, 0842, 2185a
Holy Communion, 0711
homeopathy, 1666
Homer, 0100, 0208, 0216, 0230, 0789, 0833, 1009, 1078, 1098, 1468, 1534, 2233, 2473, 2575, 2813, 2855, 2900, 2956, 2986, 3001, 3068
 Iliad, 0088, 0518, 0589, 0685, 0721, 0759a, 1011, 1154, 1879, 1933, 2182, 2413, 2908, 2985, 2992, 3013, 3026, 3034, 3041
 Odyssey, 0092, 0308, 0311, 0311a, 0316, 0382, 0466, 0518, 0814, 2547, 2556, 2567, 3041, 3154
Homilies on Obedience, 2829
homocentrism, 1349
homoeroticism, 0286, 2824
homosexuality, xiv, 0106, 0387, 2027, 2131, 2495, 2843, 3090a
honesty, 0642, 1970

honor, xxi, 0069, 0079, 0080a, 0102, 0113, 0133, 0232, 0246, 0247, 0277, 0291, 0292, 0319b, 0369, 0432, 0459, 0481, 0491, 0522, 0541, 0547, 0553, 0555, 0563, 0599, 0613, 0627, 0642, 0656, 0657, 0685, 0704, 0729, 0735, 0743, 0749, 0750, 0754, 0756, 0759a, 0761, 0792, 0824, 0826, 0831, 0850, 0873, 0874, 0894, 0955, 0971, 0972, 0980, 0981, 0999, 1062, 1086, 1096, 1111, 1145, 1198, 1246, 1303, 1323, 1328, 1345, 1433, 1459, 1517, 1526, 1592, 1609, 1619, 1627, 1641, 1648, 1696, 1715, 1736, 1848, 1859, 1902, 1948, 1972, 2008, 2012, 2021, 2024, 2051a, 2084, 2403, 2405, 2412, 2414, 2415, 2699, 2858, 2868, 2869, 2878, 2882, 2889, 2894, 2924, 2942, 2949, 2952, 2970, 2987, 2989, 3015, 3032, 3050, 3053, 3055, 3069, 3072, 3073, 3102
honors, 0079, 0080a
Hooker, Richard
 Of the Laws of Ecclesiastical Polity, 0756, 2829
 Laws of Ecclesiastical Polity, The, 2998a
hope, 0377a, 0665, 0863, 1123
Hopkins, Gerard Manley, 2641a
Horace (Quintus Horatius Flaccus), 0164a, 0299, 0320, 0370a, 0394, 0472, 0485, 0610, 0668, 0685, 0780, 0804a, 0812, 0836, 0841, 0875, 0893, 0907, 0936, 0938, 0940a, 0989, 1021, 1335, 1417, 1468, 1500, 1524, 1834a, 2122, 2287, 2450, 2473, 2503, 2506, 2508, 2511, 2546a, 2575, 2787
 Ars Poetica, 0624, 0848a, 1085a, 1118
 Art of Poetry (Ars Poetica), 22133
 Epistles, 0848a, 1011, 3203
 Odes, 0721, 0848a, 0987, 1158, 1202, 1345, 1842, 2492, 2501
 Satires, 0848a
Horapollo, 0300
Horatio
 in *Hamlet,* 0263, 0464a, 0663a, 0721, 1021, 1791, 1794, 1795, 1822, 1842, 1848, 1849, 1852, 1860, 1876, 1883, 1895, 1896
Horney, Karen, 0831
horror, 0178, 0350, 1025, 1041, 1048, 1354, 2715, 2770
horrors, 1047, 2710, 2732, 2738, 2741
horse, 3126
horsemanship, 1044, 1093a
horses, 1190, 1437, 3125
Hortensio
 in *Taming of the Shrew, The,* 2543
Hortensius
 in *Timon of Athens,* 2664
Horvendile, 1968
hospitality, 0711
Hostess
 in *Henry V,* 0392, 1924. *See also* Quickly, Mistress
Hotspur, 0815
 in *Henry IV, Part 1,* xvii, 0153, 0529, 0563, 0619, 0636, 0647, 0704, 0773, 0852, 1054, 1093a, 1140a, 1902, 1904, 1908, 1909
 in *Henry IV, Parts 1 & 2,* 1912

Hubert De Burgh
  in *King John,* 0296
hubris, 1054, 1634, 1984
humanism, xiii, 0002, 0045, 0143, 0307, 0314, 0337, 0610, 0748, 0763, 0834, 0929, 0971, 1096, 1104, 1874, 1929, 2546, 2565a
humanist, 1059
humanists, 0058, 0089, 0139, 0169, 0272, 0280, 0299, 0300, 0307, 0314, 0334, 0385a, 0479, 0566, 0662, 0772, 0796, 0799, 0821, 0849, 0891, 0945, 1005, 1031, 1039, 1127, 1218, 1543c, 2037, 2642
humanitas, 1059
humanity, 0232, 0239, 0384, 0452, 0467, 0546, 0899, 0978, 1031, 1046, 1092, 2605
humility, 1617, 1923, 2253
humor, xv, 1271, 2792, 3146
humor, black, 2797a
humor, satiric, 2928
humor (as psychological tendency), 0328, 1147
humor figure, 1026
humors, 0107, 0328, 0453, 0488, 0520, 2864
humors, four, 0858, 1149a, 2618
humors character, 1730
humors characters, 0235, 2264, 2856
humors theory of psychology, 0330
hunger, xvi, 1590, 1595
Hunsdon, Lord, 2265
hunt, 1428, 3124, 3141, 3162
hunting, 3113, 3127, 3166
  love and, 0721
husband, 0225, 0850, 1070, 1157, 1575, 1641, 2393, 2440
husbandry, 1920, 1921
hydra, 0374
hyena, 1543a
Hymen, 2562, 2583
  in *As You Like It,* 0421, 1536, 1543c, 1547, 1564
"Hymn to Hermes," 2473
hypallage, 2532a
hyperbole, 0240, 0319, 0504a, 0557, 0835, 1239, 1293, 1380, 1633, 3129
Hyperion, 1807
hypermasculinity, 1722
hyperontology, 1256
hypocrisy, 0657, 0877, 1172, 1636, 2610, 2673, 2705
hypocrite, 1175
hypotaxis, 0558
hypothesis, 2901
Hyrcanian tigers, 0533
hysteria, 2714
hysterica passio (the Mother), 1505
Hystorie of Hamlet, The, 1968

I
Iachimo
  in *Cymbeline,* 0323, 0350, 0433, 0721, 0759a, 1071, 1756, 1773, 1774, 1776
Iago
  in *Othello,* xix, 0223, 0234, 0323, 0661, 0824, 0962, 1025, 1057, 1061, 1667, 2329, 2334, 2341, 2348, 2349, 2352
Iamblichus, 0160a, 2573, 2585
Ianthe, 3079
Iarbus, 3070
Ibis, 0868
Icarus, xiv, 0918, 0998, 2561, 2633
iconoclasm, 0973a, 0974, 2880
iconography, xvii, 0022, 0120, 0308, 0322, 1233, 2633, 2695
iconology, 2157
icons, 0884
ideal, 2483
ideal, chivalric, 2898
ideal, masculine, 2719
idealism, 0184, 0222, 0277, 0370a, 0382, 0452, 0584, 0589, 0754, 0761, 0779, 0870, 0939, 0940, 0945, 0949, 0980, 1009, 1111, 1394, 1461, 1603, 1825, 1949, 2022, 2098, 2112, 2560, 2799, 2800, 2810, 2894, 2922, 2948, 2950, 3043, 3063, 3085a
  materialism and, 0702
idealisms, 0508
idealist, 0232, 0886
ideals, 0071, 0075, 0192, 0657, 0759a, 0885, 1047, 1184, 1332, 1734, 2951
ideas, 2791
Iden, Alexander
  in *Henry VI, Part 2,* 0221
identities, 0225, 1136
identity, 0078, 0119, 0132, 0191, 0237, 0242, 0248, 0253, 0321, 0342, 0351, 0415, 0466, 0475, 0512, 0566, 0614, 0665, 0678, 0703, 0729, 0730, 0801, 0802, 0901, 0920, 0967, 1067, 1076, 1099, 1174, 1231, 1291, 1298, 1349, 1368, 1428, 1530, 1575, 1576, 1589, 1643, 1645, 1648, 1668, 1718, 1719, 1729, 1734a, 1737, 1741a, 1742, 1866, 1987, 2313a, 2403, 2433, 2447, 2596, 2790, 2799, 2801, 2834a, 2889, 2933, 2952, 2956, 2985, 3025, 3047, 3079, 3090
identity, gender, 2973
identity, masculine, xiv
ideology, 2832
Ides of March, 0850
idleness, 1172
idolatry, 0888a, 2920, 3191
ignominy, 0861
Ilium, 0789
illeism, 0057, 1076
illusion, 0310, 0347, 0375, 0380a, 0381, 0394, 0601, 0922a, 1016, 1144, 1273a, 1314, 1516
  reality and, 2607
illusionist, 2582
illusions, 1211
image patterns in *Julius Caesar,* 2098, 2132
image patterns in *King Lear,* 2170
imagery, 0255, 0317, 0787, 0876, 1019, 1044, 1072, 1093a, 1095
  of *Antony and Cleopatra,* 1403, 1415, 1494
  of *Coriolanus,* 1624a
  of *Julius Caesar,* 2111
  of *Macbeth,* 2216

Index of Subjects

of *Phoenix and Turtle, The*, 2384
of *Rape of Lucrece, The*, 2392, 2431
of *Romeo and Juliet*, 2475a
of *Timon of Athens*, 2628, 2633, 2646, 2666, 2667, 2668, 2676, 2697, 2698
of *Titus Andronicus*, 2731a, 2748
of *Troilus and Cressida*, 2805, 2810, 2833, 2840, 2848, 2872, 2906, 2919, 2920, 2947, 2992, 2996, 2998a, 3002, 3005, 3029, 3032, 3033, 3064, 3072
of *Venus and Adonis*, 3131, 3137, 3140, 3152
imagery, stage, 1370
images, presentational, 1745
images, stage, 2876
images, visual, 3133
imagest, 1383
imagination, 0095, 0098, 0202, 0208, 0327, 0359, 0363, 0369, 0375, 0382, 0426, 0447, 0478, 0499, 0504a, 0529, 0555, 0630, 0679, 0721, 0729, 0759a, 0773, 0785, 0807, 0811, 0815, 0828a, 0830, 0841, 0882, 0997, 1022, 1055, 1083, 1084, 1160, 1193, 1206, 1228, 1240, 1241, 1263, 1284, 1288, 1289, 1316, 1317, 1318, 1342, 1370a, 1372, 1380, 1409, 1444, 1455, 1511, 1524, 1682, 1695, 2081, 2185a, 2288a, 2296, 2298, 2300, 2306, 2313, 2437, 2498, 2550, 3173, 3186a
imitatio, 0848a
imitation, 0128, 0133, 0191, 0208, 0257, 0298, 0317, 0381, 0385, 0394, 0501, 0610, 0721, 0759a, 0788, 0848a, 0922a, 0940, 0940a, 1016, 1018, 1039, 1096, 1567, 1581, 1840, 2185a, 2219, 2288a, 2480, 2564, 2565, 2599, 2796, 3185, 3210
  following and, 1255
immortality, 0237, 0341, 0345, 0861, 1415, 2189, 2478, 2492, 2503, 2508, 2511, 2522, 3165
Imogen, 1773
  in *Cymbeline*, 0299a, 0434, 0437, 0721, 0759a, 0769, 1048, 1083, 1115, 1755, 1756, 1757, 1759, 1766, 1772, 1776, 1777
impatience, 0704
imperator, 2127
imperialism, 0113, 0191, 0703, 1335, 1435
impiety, 2762
impulse, 1436
inarticulateness, 3061
Incarnation, 1758
incest, xv, 1842, 1849, 1858, 2167, 3075, 3148
incident (as concept or element of drama), 0819
incongruity, 0788
inconsistency, 2888
inconstancy, 1047, 2844, 3013
indeterminacy, 3042
individual
  society and, 0714
individualism, 1691, 1734, 1743, 2859, 2869
individuation, 0377c, 1405, 1729
infancy, 1355
infant, 3155
infants, 2230
infidelity, 1773, 2842, 2974, 3023, 3186a
influence, Senecan, xii
Ingannati, Gl', 3077

ingratitude, 0012, 0646, 1701, 2159, 2558, 2634, 2655
initiation, 0226, 1866
injustice, 1122
Inkhorn controversy, 0479
inkhorn terms, 0588
in medias res, 0556, 0812
innocence, 0749, 1543c, 2419, 2420, 2428, 2437, 2555
Inn of Court, 0073, 2646, 2839, 2861
Inns of Court, 0147, 0277, 0463, 0685, 2621, 2623, 2838, 2860, 2922, 2925, 2985, 2992, 3052
Ino, 2237
insanity, 0920
instability, 0698, 0729, 1294, 1315, 1493, 3084
insurrection, 1686
integrity, 0252, 0523, 0562, 0588, 0655, 0656, 0679, 0701, 0723, 0765, 0779, 0804a, 0927, 0980, 1029, 1439, 1625, 1633, 1640, 1644, 1657, 1661, 2145a
intellectual context
  Shakespeare and, 0015
intellectuality, 1834a
intemperance, 0961, 0962, 1044, 1233, 2088
interludes, 0201, 2618, 2693
intermediate sources, 0059
interpretation, 0729
interrogatio, 1080
interruptio, 2037
intimacy, 0987, 1178, 1212a, 1327, 1334, 1335, 1729, 1987
intrigue, 0494, 0717, 0759, 1011, 1075, 1571
introspection, 1548
intuition, 0513
invasion, 1141
inventio, 2455a
invention, 0375, 0611, 1047, 1783
Io, 1312, 1324, 2538, 2540
Iole, 2319
Iphis, 3079, 3082
Iras
  in *Antony and Cleopatra*, 0931, 1356, 1486
irascibility, 1902, 3163
Ireland, colonization in, 2565
Iris
  in *Tempest, The*, 0421, 0997, 1134, 2555, 2562, 2578a, 2583
Iron Age, 0620
irony, 0156a, 0333, 0424, 0490, 0557, 0616, 0678, 0799, 0839, 0844, 0884, 0891, 0923, 0927, 0931, 0940, 1000, 1034, 1188, 1334, 1373, 1450, 1628, 1690, 1709, 1762, 1999, 2007, 2051a, 2052, 2124, 2225, 2309, 2461, 2763, 2891, 2968, 3139, 3140
  in *Coriolanus*, 0137
irony, tragic, 2970
irrationality, 2269, 2293, 2950, 3125
Isaac, 0542
Isabel, Queen
  in *Richard II*, 2444, 2445
Isabella
  in *Measure for Measure*, 0350, 0801, 0963, 1071, 2239, 2242a, 2244

Isabella, wife of Edward II, 1272
Isis, xv, 0966, 1163, 1184, 1188, 1223, 1224, 1261, 1266, 1312, 1324, 1355, 1362, 1490, 1504, 2301
Isis and Osiris, 0307, 0437, 0729
Isocrates, 0280, 0905, 1907
 Areopagitica, 1650
 Letter to Demonicus, 1815
 Oratio ad Demonicum, 1788
isolation, 0332, 0410, 0411, 0453, 0607, 0633, 0784, 0999, 1117, 1423, 1620, 1638, 1702, 1836
Israel, 2370
Italians
 in *Cymbeline*, 1768
Italy, 0380a, 0381, 1774
Ixion, xviii, 0126, 0132, 2139, 2157, 2159, 2162, 2216

J
Jacob, 2258
Jaggard, William
 Passionate Pilgrim, The, 2353
Jailer's Daughter
 in *Two Noble Kinsmen, The*, xxii, 3092
James I, 0464, 0765, 1128, 1649, 1736, 1765, 1780, 2565, 3208
Janssen, Gheerart
 bust of Shakespeare in Holy Trinity Church, 0937
Jaques, a lord
 in *As You Like It*, 0163, 0190, 0334, 0377b, 0414, 0807, 0814, 0880, 0920, 1531, 1535, 1546, 1548, 1551a, 1552, 1556, 1560, 3034
Jason, 0095, 0610, 0770, 2249, 2257, 2258, 2260
 Golden Fleece and, 0546
jealousy, 0557, 2349, 3180, 3197
Jephtha, 1837
Jephthah, 1875
Jessica
 in *Merchant of Venice, The*, 0119, 0335, 2257, 2258
Jesus, 0201, 0215, 0954, 2370
jingoism, 0749, 1776
Joan la Pucelle (Joan of Arc)
 in *Henry VI, Part 1*, xvii, 0975, 1934, 1935
Joan of Arc, 1385
Jocasta, 2225
Jodelle, Étienne, 1402, 1468
John, King
 in *King John*, 1122
John, Prince
 in *Henry IV, Part 2*, 1915
 in *Richard II-Henry V* tetralogy, 2136
Johnson, Mark, 3049
Johnson, Samuel, 0292a, 0640, 1010
 Preface to Shakespeare, 0515, 1016
John the Baptist, xv, 1230
Jones, Ernest, 1872
Jones, Inigo, 2562b
Jones, William

translation of Lipsius's *Sixe Bookes of Politickes*, 2165
Jonson, Ben, 0075, 0103, 0137, 0157, 0158, 0235, 0293, 0334, 0335, 0375, 0396, 0402, 0409, 0419, 0627, 0721, 0732, 0806, 1066, 1096, 1787, 1876, 1995, 2110, 2548, 2570, 2623, 2796, 2802, 2837, 2856, 2864, 2978
 Bartholomew Fair, 2552
 Hero and Leander story and, 0209
 Catiline, 0587, 0836, 2122
 Hymenaei, 2562
 Masque of Queens, The, 2233, 2576
 Poetaster, 0359, 2552, 2795
 Poetaster, The, 0482
 Sejanus, 0120, 0378, 0587, 0684, 0836, 1754, 2038, 2056, 2122, 2242, 2358, 2686
 Staple of Newes, The, 2686
 "To the Memory of Mr. William Shakespeare," 0848a
 Volpone, 0904
Joseph of Exeter, 1244
Josephus, Flavius, 0668
 Jewish Antiquities (Antiquitates Iudaicae), 2569a
Jove, 0151, 1312, 2159, 2266, 2267, 2281, 2617, 3082
 in *Cymbeline*, 1044a, 1780
Judas, 0776, 1235a, 1257, 3179a
Judas Iscariot, 2332
Judas Maccabeus, 2372
judgement, 1130
judgment, 0520, 0719, 0723, 1998, 2071
Judgment of Paris, 2196
Julia
 in *Two Gentlemen of Verona, The*, 0466, 3088, 3090
Juliet
 in *Romeo and Juliet*, xx, 2470, 2471, 2475c, 2475a, 2475b
 in *Romeo and Juliet*, 0385, 0928, 1126, 1278, 2463, 2468, 2468a, 2469
Julius Caesar (Gaius Julius Caesar), 0009, 0208, 0224, 0363, 0365, 0423, 0473, 0495, 0537, 0578, 0629, 0668, 0729, 0776, 0778, 0805, 0916, 0932, 0938, 0973, 1227, 1347, 1789a, 1803, 1833, 1849, 1868, 1958, 1984, 2031, 2069, 2091a, 2096, 2097, 2199a, 2444, 3082, 3087, 3179a
 in *Antony and Cleopatra*, 1166a
 Commentaries, 1676, 2134a
 Gallic War, 1821
 in *Julius Caesar*, 0062, 0106, 0129, 0136, 0172, 0201, 0206, 0210, 0213, 0219, 0222, 0246, 0255, 0271, 0319a, 0322a, 0329, 0337, 0347, 0358, 0359, 0377, 0379, 0422, 0424, 0432, 0452, 0492, 0545, 0553, 0607, 0637, 0655, 0679, 0685, 0700, 0723, 0734, 0759a, 0764, 0779, 0792, 0805, 0850, 0851, 0873, 0876, 0886, 0911, 0940a, 0944, 0949, 0954, 0978, 0979, 0983a, 0986a, 0990, 1047, 1058, 1100, 1131, 1135, 1147, 1152, 1940, 1941, 1942, 1943, 1944, 1945, 1949, 1950, 1951a, 1952, 1954, 1956, 1958, 1961,

Index of Subjects

1966, 1967, 1968, 1970, 1972, 1973, 1975, 1976, 1977, 1978, 1980, 1981, 1982, 1983, 1983a, 1983b, 1987, 1987a, 1988, 1990, 1995, 1997, 1999, 2001, 2002, 2005, 2006, 2007, 2008, 2009, 2010, 2011, 2012, 2013a, 2014, 2016, 2018, 2021, 2022, 2022a, 2024, 2027, 2028, 2029, 2030, 2034, 2035, 2037, 2040, 2042, 2044, 2045, 2048, 2048a, 2053, 2057, 2060, 2063, 2066, 2067, 2068, 2069, 2070, 2071, 2072, 2073, 2074, 2077, 2079, 2082, 2085, 2085a, 2087, 2092, 2093, 2094, 2098, 2101, 2102, 2103, 2106, 2109, 2112a, 2113b, 2114, 2117, 2119, 2120, 2121, 2123, 2125, 2126, 2128, 2130a, 2131, 2132, 2134a, 2135, 2136
Jung, C. J., 2463
Jung, Carl, 0160a, 0377c, 0720a, 1405, 1496
Jungian theory, 0096
Junius, Hadrianus, 1777
Juno, 0107, 1163, 1324, 1372, 1726, 2159, 2183, 2231, 2310
  in *Tempest, The*, 0421, 0631, 0997, 1134, 2547, 2555, 2562, 2566, 2583
Jupiter, 0987, 1555, 1754, 1796, 2183, 2298, 2310, 2532, 2764
  in *Cymbeline*, 0290, 0781, 1763, 1772, 1777
jus gentium, 0625
Justice, 2253, 2727, 2734, 2735
justice, 0062, 0080a, 0102, 0174, 0182, 0246, 0247, 0313, 0342, 0359, 0397, 0452, 0490, 0500, 0519, 0582, 0596, 0613, 0617, 0642, 0681, 0723, 0820, 0829, 0849, 0864, 0903, 0917, 0945, 0984, 1095, 1123, 1323, 1851, 1865, 2042, 2051, 2248, 2605, 2716, 2728, 2740, 2882, 3028
Justinian (Flavius Petrus Sabbatius Justinianus), 2247
Juvenal (Decimus Junius Juvenalis), 0806, 0836, 0938, 1468, 1944, 2276
  Satires, 1842
    Satire 6, 1893a
    Satire 10, 0995

K

Kabbala, 0637a
kairos, 1543c
Kant, Immanuel, 0788, 1255
Kate (Katharina)
  in *Taming of the Shrew, The*, 2532, 2539, 2540
Katharina (Kate)
  in *Taming of the Shrew, The*, 0328, 0331, 0963, 2531, 2537
Katharine
  in *Henry V*, 1140a
Katherine, Queen
  in *Henry VIII*, 1122
Kedalion, 0720a
Kent
  in *King Lear*, 1057
kinesis, 0701
King John
  in *King John*, 0905
King of France
  in *All's Well That Ends Well*, 1157

kingship, 0092, 0519
kinship, 0102
kiss, 3113, 3130
knighthood, 2265
knowledge, 0486, 1034, 1130, 1822, 1834a, 1997, 2102, 2169, 2306, 2320, 2550
Kronos
  Chronos and, 0596
Kronos-Saturn myth, 0245
Kyd, Thomas, 0409, 0835, 2712
  Cornelia, 2024
  Spanish Tragedy, The, 0191, 0494, 0583, 1839, 2035, 2729a, 2749, 2769, 2774, 2785

L

Laban, 2258
labyrinth, 2293, 2295, 2301, 2561, 2799
Lacan, Jacques, 2931
Lactantius, Lucius Caecilius Firmianus, 0628, 1907, 2122
ladder, Neoplatonic, 3126a
Lady Anne
  in *Richard III*, 0772, 2454, 2455, 2456
Lady Macbeth
  in *Macbeth*, 0212, 0490, 0773, 0920, 1070, 2203, 2206, 2209, 2210, 2214, 2217, 2222, 2225, 2231, 2231a, 2234, 2237
Laertes
  in *Hamlet*, 1788, 1791, 1796, 1815, 1830, 1835, 1836
Lafew
  in *All's Well That Ends Well*, 1155
Laius, 1872, 2216
Lakoff, George, 3049
Lambinus, D.
  edition of Plautus's *Menaechmi*, 1567
lament, 0985a, 2417
lamentation, 0829, 1129
Lancastrian tetralogy, by Shakespeare, 0120
Landino, Cristoforo, 2418
landscape, 3169
landscapes, 0901
language, xvi, xxi, 0002, 0040, 0076, 0099, 0102, 0129, 0156, 0169, 0172a, 0186, 0204, 0208, 0223, 0224, 0236, 0238, 0242, 0256, 0261, 0284, 0287, 0302, 0303, 0310a, 0325, 0332, 0343, 0350, 0353a, 0369, 0372a, 0375, 0385a, 0387, 0393, 0405a, 0430, 0450, 0460, 0469, 0470, 0486, 0504, 0546, 0552, 0557, 0567, 0569, 0588, 0645, 0660, 0665, 0787, 0793, 0802a, 0807, 0808, 0818, 0856, 0857, 0877, 0879, 0882, 0910, 0921, 0979, 0999, 1016, 1024, 1034, 1038, 1061, 1073, 1092, 1135, 1143, 1164, 1172, 1186, 1210, 1214, 1221, 1221a, 1223, 1252a, 1256, 1302, 1315, 1323, 1326, 1352a, 1370a, 1380, 1413, 1423, 1435, 1462, 1474, 1482, 1483, 1529, 1532, 1597, 1609, 1618, 1624a, 1629, 1632, 1637, 1646, 1648, 1668, 1669, 1670, 1671a, 1678, 1699, 1710, 1736, 1740, 1743, 1808, 1838, 1944, 1952, 1961, 1966, 1970, 2006, 2007, 2008, 2011, 2066, 2113, 2134, 2170, 2185a, 2188, 2189, 2198, 2199a, 2216, 2224, 2347, 2394, 2401, 2404

language *(continued)*, 2413, 2420, 2440, 2550,
    2588, 2596, 2651, 2662, 2669, 2670, 2718b,
    2731a, 2741, 2747, 2776, 2811, 2832, 2910,
    2931, 3022, 3027, 3030, 3063, 3104
  of *Coriolanus*, 1606
  currency and, 2616
  reality and, 2889
  of *Troilus and Cressida*, 2986
  in *Venus and Adonis*, 3109
language, arts of, 3067
language, baby, 2966
language, figurative
  in *Titus Andronicus*, 2782
  in *Troilus and Cressida*, 2963
language, legal, 1733
language, Ovidian, 2736a
language, rape of, 2718b
language, visual, 1687
languages, 1252a
languages, ghost, in *Troilus and Cressida*, 2936
languages of *Troilus and Cressida*, 2908
Laocoon, 2564
Lartius, Titus
  in *Coriolanus*, 0297, 1645, 1710, 1744
Last Judgment, 1175
last plays, by Shakespeare, 0058, 0299a, 0942
Last Supper, 0764, 0954, 1257, 1260, 1421,
    2633, 2676
Latin, 0012, 0025, 0026, 0056, 0060, 0072,
    0073, 0084, 0092, 0135, 0146, 0158, 0162,
    0169, 0190, 0204, 0283, 0286, 0350, 0369,
    0402, 0483, 0488, 0509, 0567, 0568, 0569,
    0586, 0588, 0597, 0610, 0645, 0660, 0685,
    0690, 0721, 0780, 0815, 0821a, 0841, 0842,
    0856, 0915, 0924, 0936a, 1010, 1039, 1066,
    1574, 1588, 1798a, 1803, 1863, 1930, 1932,
    1937, 2050, 2066, 2091, 2137, 2155, 2179,
    2218, 2271, 2280, 2298, 2305, 2312, 2351,
    2541, 2579, 2698, 2710, 2728, 2730
Latinate past participles, 0428
Latinate words, 0169, 0557, 0588
Latin authors, 0028, 0107, 0162, 0187, 0363,
    0401, 0852, 0936a, 0993
Latin grammar, 0299, 0363
Latini, Brunetto
  Livres dou Tresor, 2047
Latinism, 1796
Latinisms, 0482, 0645, 0879, 3207
Latinity, 0208
Latinization, 0856
Latin learning, 0074, 0401
Latin lesson
  in *Merchant of Venice, The*, 2263
  in *Merry Wives of Windsor, The*, 2266
  in *Taming of the Shrew, The*, 2532, 2540
Latin literature, 0169, 0296, 0299, 0369, 0426,
    0496, 0916
Latin plays, 1126
Latin poets, 0208, 0610
Latin-Saxon hybrids, 0429
laughter, 0788, 0899, 0923, 1064, 2738
Laurence, Friar
  in *Romeo and Juliet*, 2466, 2475a

Lavinia
  in *Titus Andronicus*, 0029, 0119, 0207, 0238,
    0283, 0319a, 0368, 0446, 0467, 0759b,
    1045, 1048, 1083, 1141, 2718b, 2723, 2727,
    2731a, 2732a, 2733, 2734, 2736a, 2737,
    2738, 2740, 2750, 2754, 2757, 2758, 2762,
    2763, 2766, 2770, 2771, 2776, 2777a,
    2779a, 2782, 2783, 2786, 2789a
Law
  nature and, 0701
law, 0080, 0106, 0672, 0708, 0961, 0962,
    1003, 1122, 1123, 1193, 1733, 1769, 1775,
    1813, 1858, 1894, 2251, 2279
law, immutable, 2988
law, natural, 0469, 0532, 2826, 2853, 2916,
    3044, 3057
law, religious, 2929
law, Roman, xix, 0526, 0843, 2247, 2327
laws, 0079
leader, 0641, 1640
leadership, 0239, 1152, 1301
Leander, 1558, 2468, 3088
Lear
  in *King Lear*, 0075, 0097, 0132, 0166, 0167,
    0208, 0292, 0400, 0464a, 0468, 0479, 0506,
    0509, 0636, 0680, 0819, 0838, 0920, 0961,
    0962, 1053, 1065, 1139, 1382, 1666, 1739,
    2080, 2139, 2141, 2143, 2145a, 2146,
    2146a, 2151, 2153, 2154, 2156, 2159, 2161,
    2162, 2163, 2168, 2169, 2170, 2171, 2182
learning, 0090, 0092, 2569a
learning, Latin, xxi
learning of Shakespeare, 0628, 0659
leaving
  following and, 1256
lechery, 1011, 2899
Leda, 2532
LeFevre, Raoul
  Receuil des histoires de Troye, Le, 1557
legend, classical, 2940
legend, Homeric, 2878
legends, classical, 2901
leno, 0556
Lent, 1608
Leonato
  in *Much Ado About Nothing*, 2320
Leontes
  in *Winter's Tale, The*, 0577, 0610, 0807,
    0941, 3171, 3175, 3179, 3180, 3183, 3185,
    3186a, 3189, 3191, 3192, 3193, 3196, 3197,
    3198, 3202, 3206, 3207, 3208
Lepidus, Marcus Aemilius
  in *Antony and Cleopatra*, 1159, 1175, 1235,
    1280, 1323, 1347, 1430, 1461, 1464, 1506
  in *Julius Caesar*, 0319b, 2116
le Roy, Louis, 1139
Leslie, John, 2236
Letter
  Spirit and, 0672
letters, 1040
Lewis, M. G.
  Alfonso, King of Castile, 2655

Index of Subjects

l'Hermite, Tristan
  Mariane, 0191
liars, 0372a
liberality, 0329, 1248, 2248, 2592, 2631, 2682, 2685
libertas, 0587
libertinism, 0260, 0814
liberty, 0237, 0525, 1143
libido, 0377
lies, 2990
life
  art and, 2608
Life of Octavius Caesar Augustus, 1754
Ligarius, Caius
  in *Julius Caesar*, 2086
light, 2469, 3111
Lilly (Lily), William, 3014
  Latin Grammar, 0727, 0914
  Shorte Introduction of Grammar, 0938
Lincke, Richard
  Fountaine of Ancient Fiction, The, 0868
lion, 1541, 1547
Lipsius, Justus, 1139, 2028
  De Amphitheatro, 0443
  De Constantia, 0721
  Sixe Bookes of Politickes or Civil Doctrine, 2165
liquefaction, 1167
literacy, 1040
literae humaniores, 0299
literalism, 1172
literary criticism, by Shakespeare, 0673
Lives, by Plutarch. See under Plutarch, *The Lives of the Noble Grecians and Romans*
Livia (wife of Augustus, first Roman emperor), 1754
Livy (Titus Livius), xvi, 0012, 0133, 0261, 0363, 0484, 0587, 0685, 0721, 0726, 0778, 0916, 0973, 1045, 1152, 1609, 1649, 1650, 1652, 1672, 1834, 2234, 2330, 2397, 2401, 2408, 2410, 2416, 2419, 2434, 2551, 2742a, 2755, 2785
  From the Founding of the City (Ab Urbe Condita Libri), 2433
  History of Rome (Ab Urbe Condita Libri), xviii, 0120, 0301, 0852, 1949, 2210, 2403, 2405, 2407, 2417
  Romane Historie, The (Ab Urbe Condita Libri), 0011
  Roman History (Ab Urbe Condita Libri), 1047, 1596, 1695, 2393
location (as concept or element of drama), 2307
Lodge, Thomas, xvi
  Diogenes in His Singularitie, 2673
  Pandosto, 0997
  Rosalynde, 0384, 0997, 1545, 2441
  Scillaes Metamorphosis, 0884, 3153
  Scilla's Metamorphosis, 0934
  translation of *Epistle LVIII* from the *Workes of Seneca*, 0127
lodging, 1572
Lodovico
  in *Othello*, 2352

logic, 0296, 0299, 0350, 0356, 0363, 0404, 0508, 3067
logorrhea, 1725
logos, 0236, 0310a, 1999, 2455a
London, as New Troy, 1128
Longinus, 0101, 0785, 0804a, 1468
  Sublime, The, 2238
Longus, 0928
  Daphnis and Chloe, 0067, 0068, 0382, 0434, 0997, 1114, 1549, 2551a, 2556, 3184a, 3188, 3199
Lope de Vega. See Vega Carpio, Lope Félix de
Lord
  in *Taming of the Shrew, The*, 2531, 2534
Lord, in Induction of *Taming of the Shrew, The*, 1107
Lord Chamberlain's Men, 0605
Lord Chief Justice, 0450
Lord of Misrule, 1056
Lorenzo
  in *Merchant of Venice, The*, 0335, 0336, 0460, 0699, 2252, 2257, 2258, 2818
  in *The Merchant of Venice*, 0119
Lorich, Reinhard
  Latin translation of Aphthonius's *Progymnasmata*, 1856
Love, 2378
  Death and, 3107
  Fortune and, 2253
  Strife and, 2578a
love, 0067, 0068, 0080a, 0098, 0110, 0113, 0118, 0119, 0139, 0147, 0155, 0160, 0174, 0178, 0185, 0199, 0208, 0218, 0232, 0239, 0242, 0261, 0269, 0277, 0278, 0281, 0283, 0305, 0311a, 0312, 0325, 0332, 0337, 0342, 0344, 0347, 0350, 0357, 0369, 0370a, 0375, 0379a, 0391, 0396, 0398a, 0435, 0441, 0459, 0463, 0464a, 0471, 0481, 0525, 0551, 0554, 0577, 0601, 0619, 0679, 0699, 0702, 0714, 0715, 0719, 0720, 0729, 0735, 0736, 0754, 0756, 0758, 0779, 0789, 0813, 0827, 0829a, 0841, 0852, 0863, 0873, 0882, 0884, 0890, 0909a, 0911, 0912, 0923, 0927, 0934, 0959, 0964, 0967, 0981, 0983a, 0986b, 0989, 1027, 1034, 1049, 1055, 1063, 1064, 1065, 1077, 1081, 1086, 1089, 1090, 1109, 1111, 1139, 1140a, 1145, 1154, 1165, 1167, 1174, 1176, 1177, 1184, 1185, 1193, 1200, 1202, 1203, 1205, 1215, 1220, 1221, 1223, 1238, 1240, 1241, 1251, 1260, 1263, 1269, 1273a, 1281, 1293, 1298, 1301, 1310, 1311, 1317, 1322, 1331, 1332, 1336, 1346, 1353, 1359, 1365, 1368, 1369, 1371, 1373, 1384, 1394, 1398, 1406, 1408, 1410, 1433, 1439, 1440, 1445, 1451, 1458, 1459, 1462, 1469, 1471, 1472, 1474, 1477, 1480, 1482, 1485, 1488, 1489, 1493, 1495, 1502, 1513, 1523, 1524, 1526, 1528, 1532, 1543b, 1545, 1556, 1558, 1592, 1603, 1627, 1630, 1631, 1740a, 1785, 1797, 1859, 1956, 2013, 2057, 2072, 2101, 2121, 2136, 2174, 2186, 2191, 2199a, 2260, 2267, 2269, 2272, 2274, 2277, 2282, 2291, 2320, 2322, 2335, 2366, 2375, 2376, 2377, 2379, 2382, 2385, 2387, 2412, 2420

love *(continued)*, 2423, 2465, 2467, 2468, 2468a, 2474, 2478, 2483, 2488, 2497, 2517, 2519, 2521, 2532, 2537, 2541, 2550, 2555, 2566, 2566a, 2790, 2792, 2804, 2806, 2841, 2844, 2851, 2854, 2858, 2865, 2868, 2877, 2878, 2888, 2897, 2911, 2924, 2927, 2928, 2942, 2943, 2946, 2947, 2972, 2985, 2987, 2996, 3013, 3014, 3019, 3025, 3027, 3032, 3039, 3047, 3050, 3053, 3059, 3062, 3064a, 3071, 3072, 3077, 3082, 3085, 3100b, 3110, 3113, 3115, 3129, 3130, 3131, 3132, 3133, 3134, 3137, 3144, 3147, 3156, 3162, 3164, 3191, 3198
  death and, 2476, 3143
  hunting and, 0721
  reason and, 0832
  war and, 2917, 2936
love, chivalric, 3044
love, courtly, 0110, 0700, 2802, 2809, 2833, 2869, 2898, 2908, 2916, 2922, 3036, 3037, 3069, 3073, 3154
love, fantasies of, 3090a
love, language of, 2857
love, mutable, 3135
love, natural, 3044
love, Neoplatonic, 3119
love, profane, 2920
love, sexual, 3158
love, two aspects of, 3151
lover, 0080, 0097, 0110, 0192, 0211, 0239, 0281, 0323, 0375, 0387, 0422, 0452, 0481, 0529, 0708, 0729, 1179, 1220, 1291, 2195
lovers, 0068, 0110, 0284, 0422, 0434, 0556, 0580, 0730, 0871, 0923, 0964, 1134, 1272, 1273, 1278, 1296, 1300, 1306, 1344, 1363, 1370, 1393, 1412, 1440, 1441, 1482, 1496, 1506, 1509, 1530, 2386, 2856, 2864, 2913, 2914, 2978, 2980, 2998, 3009, 3068
  in *All's Well That Ends Well*, 1155
  in *Antony and Cleopatra*, 0029, 0114, 0123, 0178, 0187, 0237, 0338, 0409, 0512, 0548, 0551, 0555, 0635, 0678, 0723, 0759a, 0831, 0872, 0927, 0931, 0960, 0970, 0986b, 1019, 1090
  in *Cymbeline*, 0769
  in *Midsummer Night's Dream, A*, 0439, 0721, 1081, 2273, 2281, 2293, 2301, 3090
  in *Phoenix and Turtle, The*, 0101, 1129
  in *Romeo and Juliet*, 0261, 2474
  in *Tempest, The*, 0631
  in *Troilus and Cressida*, 0208, 0817
  in *Two Gentlemen of Verona, The*, 0102
  in *Winter's Tale, The*, 0577
  in *As You Like It*, 1564
loyalty, 0068, 0152, 0322a, 0599, 0784, 0789, 0861, 1086, 1123, 1297, 1355, 1410, 1477, 1528, 1695, 1795, 1842
Lucan (Marcus Annaeus Lucanus), 0487, 0668, 1468
  Pharsalia, xviii, xx, 0517, 0610, 1019, 2024, 2090, 2091, 2444
Lucentio
  in *Taming of the Shrew, The*, 0923, 2532, 2541
Luciana
  in *Comedy of Errors, The*, 1006, 1015, 1137, 1584, 1587
Lucian (Lucianus), 0012, 0280, 0334, 0890, 0891, 0904, 2673, 2675, 2680, 2694
  Charon, 1760, 1766
  Dialogues, 1031
  Dialogues of the Dead 19, 0904
  Misanthropos, 2262, 2623. See also *Timon*
  Necromantia, 0610
  Timon, 0384., 2457, 2618, 2621, 2628, 2633, 2642, 2646, 2692. See also *Misanthropos*
Lucianus
  in *Hamlet*, 0891
Lucifer, 0723
Lucilius
  in *Timon of Athens*, 2630
Lucio
  in *Measure for Measure*, 2244
Lucius
  in *The Golden Ass (The Golden Asse)*, by Apuleius, 0900, 1051, 1056, 2116, 2298, 2301, 2324
  in *Julius Caesar*, 0318, 0550, 0848, 1021, 1974, 1975, 2046, 2101, 2111
  in *Titus Andronicus*, 0208, 0398, 0492, 2740, 2762, 2776, 2779, 2783
Lucius Pella, 1974
Lucrece, 0133, 0179, 1949, 2532, 2727
  in *Rape of Lucrece, The*, xix, 0080a, 0133, 0156, 0172a, 0187, 0203, 0208, 0261, 0278, 0283, 0332, 0370a, 0437, 0438, 0448, 0539, 0553a, 0602, 0665, 0759a, 0759b, 0850, 0852, 0919, 0955, 0963, 0973a, 1062, 1071, 1078, 1129, 1141, 1837, 2390, 2392, 2393, 2394, 2395, 2396, 2397, 2399, 2400, 2401, 2402, 2403, 2405, 2407, 2409, 2410, 2411, 2412, 2413, 2414, 2415, 2416, 2417, 2418, 2419, 2421, 2422, 2423, 2426, 2428, 2430, 2431, 2433, 2434, 2437, 2439, 2440, 2766
Lucretia, xx, 2210, 2408
Lucretius
  in *Rape of Lucrece, The*, 0452a
Lucretius (Titus Lucretius Carus), 0488, 0499, 0875, 0999, 1067a, 1090, 1156, 1428, 1468, 1943, 2511, 3122
  De Rerum Natura, 0834, 0862, 1154, 2228
  On the Nature of Things, 2279
lunatic, 0375
Lupercalia, 2040
lust, 0369, 0370a, 0481, 0484, 0534, 0577, 0602, 0697, 0754, 0852, 1044, 1045, 1071, 1081, 1345, 1451, 1837, 2159, 2263, 2268, 2274, 2330, 2412, 2415, 2416, 2417, 2421, 2422, 2437, 2468a, 2485, 2510, 2654, 2703, 2733, 2907, 2927, 2928, 2945, 2979, 3015, 3069, 3107, 3113, 3114, 3119, 3131, 3134, 3147, 3154, 3161
Luther, Martin, 0763
Luxury, 1233
luxury, 2693

Index of Subjects

Lydgate, John, 1520, 2932, 2995, 3013
  Historye Sege and Dystruccyon of Troye, The, 2588a, 3047. See also *Troye Booke, The Story of Thebes, The (The Siege of Thebes),* 3101
  Troye Booke, The, 1002, 2972, 2985, 3007. See also *Historye Sege and Dystruccyon of Troye, The*
Lyfe of Virgilius, The, 2268
Lyly, John, 0099, 0102, 0158, 0173, 0331, 0580, 0758, 0860, 0967, 2277
  Campaspe, 1331, 1338, 1831
  Endymion, 2201, 2284
  Gallathea, 2285, 2307, 3079
  Loves Metamorphosis, 3079
  Midas, 2285
  Sapho and Phao, 0580, 2285
Lysander
  in *Midsummer Night's Dream, A,* 2279, 2289, 2291, 2302
Lysimachus
  in *Pericles,* 0214, 0906

M

Macbeth
  in *Macbeth,* 0093, 0097, 0208, 0292, 0292a, 0385, 0423, 0468, 0479, 0509, 0680, 0681, 0721, 0773, 0787, 0809, 0895, 0962, 1053, 1071, 1122, 1139, 1636, 1723, 1739, 2202, 2209, 2214, 2215, 2218, 2219, 2221, 2223, 2224, 2225, 2226, 2229, 2230, 2231, 2232a
Macduff
  in *Macbeth,* 0093, 0254, 1091, 2224, 2226
Machiavelli, Niccolò, 0359, 0599, 0735, 0775, 0796, 0985a, 2397, 2548, 2565a, 2814, 2955
  Discourses, 1596
  Discourses on Livy, 0080a, 0136, 0301
  Mandragola, 0102
Machiavellian, 2085a
Machiavellianism, 0251, 0723, 1775
Macrobius, Ambrosius Theodosius, xviii, 0488, 0868, 2212, 2290
  Saturnalia, 0691
macrocosm, 0453, 1480, 1629
  microcosm and, 1332, 1516
madness, xiv, 0097, 0124, 0280, 0283, 0301, 0319a, 0519a, 0547a, 0828a, 0897, 0962, 1013a, 1072, 1115, 1122, 1175, 1811, 1850, 1863, 1866, 1887, 1890, 2033, 2164, 2170, 2339, 2720, 2749, 3083, 21161
magic, xx, 0002, 0160a, 0375, 0385a, 0449, 0536, 0631, 0742, 0881, 0922a, 1134, 1149a, 1540, 2118, 2473, 2550, 2551a, 2554, 2555, 2569, 2573, 2576, 2580, 2581, 2585, 2588, 2591, 2594, 2600, 2604, 2606
  art and, 2545, 2546
  charity and, 2562b
magician, 0153, 0834, 2601
magnanimity, 0080a, 0201, 0808, 0927, 1354, 1409, 1410, 1602, 2633, 2815, 2953
magnanimous man, 0234, 0455, 0604, 0886, 0955, 0999, 1592, 1709
magnificence, 0359, 0861, 1250, 1276, 1409
magnitude, 1086

magus, 0307, 2546, 2562b, 2582, 2589, 2606
Malcolm
  in *Macbeth,* 2226
malcontent, 0075, 0144, 0825, 0920
male, 0237, 0307, 0311, 0644, 1970
  female and, 0828, 0901, 1383, 1533, 1543a
  male bonding, 1248
maleness, 1322, 1349, 2074
males, 0987
Malone, Edmund, 0930
Malvolio
  in *Twelfth Night,* 0084, 2265, 3079, 3080, 3082, 3083, 3084, 3085, 3087
Mammon, Sir Epicure, 0732
man, 0142a, 0194, 0324, 0387, 0637a, 1238
  animal and, 0901
  woman and, 1253
manhood, 0337, 0427, 0459, 0498, 0614, 1086, 1287, 1328, 1415, 1501, 1694
Manilius, Marcus, 2475a
mankind, 0368, 0379, 1086
Mankind, 2658
manliness, 0080, 0522, 1174, 1248, 1620, 1716, 1792, 1954, 1955
mannerism, 0512
Mantuanus, Baptista Spagnuoli, 0938
Maphaeus Vegius
  Thirteenth Book of the *Aeneid,* 0216
maps, 1166, 1187
Marcade
  in *Love's Labor's Lost,* 0807
Marcellus
  in *Hamlet,* 1852
Marcus
  in *Titus Andronicus,* 0207, 0368, 0707, 1048, 2736, 2736a, 2766, 2776, 2786
Mardian
  in *Antony and Cleopatra,* 1525
Margarelon
  in *Troilus and Cressida,* 0734
Margaret, later married to Henry VI
  in Shakespeare's first tetralogy, 0975
Margaret, Queen
  in *Henry VI, Part 1,* 1934
  in *Henry VI, Part 3,* 0152
  in *Richard III,* 2454
Maria
  in *Twelfth Night,* 3083
Marina
  in *Pericles,* 0369, 0437, 0781, 0906, 2358, 2362, 2373
Marlowe, Christopher, 0074, 0206, 0243, 0259, 0829, 1365, 1489, 1558, 1621, 2216, 2473, 2570, 3144, 3161
  Dido, Queen of Carthage, 0436, 0806, 0919, 1845, 1854, 1861, 2451, 2577, 3070, 3072
  Doctor Faustus, 2266, 2658
  Hero and Leander, 0185a, 0835, 1428, 2321, 3129, 3139, 3140, 3142
  Jew of Malta, The, 0185a
  Massacre at Paris, The, 1854
  Tragedy of Dido, The, 1019
  translation of *Amores,* by Ovid, 1428

marriage, xx, 0068, 0110, 0139, 0147, 0218, 0244, 0284, 0309, 0421, 0577, 0614, 0729, 0741, 0868, 0888, 0897, 0923, 0931, 1021, 1126, 1198, 1212a, 1264, 1295, 1315, 1458, 1463, 1491, 1564, 1584, 1587, 1598, 1849, 1862, 2002a, 2029, 2291, 2351, 2413, 2414, 2470, 2505, 2537, 2540, 2583, 2899, 2999, 3019, 3079, 3087, 3102
marriages, 0226
Mars, xv, 0173a, 0332, 0729, 0759a, 0988, 0999, 1000, 1156, 1162, 1167, 1175, 1184, 1185, 1222, 1261, 1266, 1312, 1313, 1371, 1372, 1387a, 1393, 1504, 1518, 1533, 1613, 1628, 1676, 1726, 1741a, 2346, 2466, 2917, 3090a, 3096, 3098, 3100a, 3107
Marston, John, 0075, 0378, 0396, 0482, 0780, 1621, 2693, 2797, 2860, 3072
   Antonio and Mellida, 0605
   Antonio's Revenge, 0395
Marsus, Paulus, 0759a
Marsyas, 0720a, 1708
Martial (Marcus Valerius Martialis), 0281, 2276
Martianus Capella, 0868, 2473
   De Nuptiis Philologiae et Mercurii, 0296
Martius
   in *Titus Andronicus*, 0792
Marullo, 0380
Marullus
   in *Julius Caesar*, 1991, 1996, 2018, 2040, 2054, 2097
Marx, Karl, 0201, 2672, 2691
Mary, Queen of Scots, 1396, 1402, 1432
Mary (Virgin Mary), 0999
masculine, 1447, 1489
masculinity, 0459, 0549, 0614, 0703, 1418, 1460, 1729, 1730, 2226, 3003
masochism, 2636
masque, 0197, 0289, 0290, 0335, 0373, 0375, 0495, 0627, 0631, 0700, 1044a, 1121, 1134, 1564, 2320, 2555, 2560, 2560a, 2562, 2562a, 2562b, 2565, 2566, 2570a, 2571, 2578, 2578a, 2583, 2588, 2618, 2633, 2638, 2652, 2681, 2689, 2689a, 2693, 2702, 2703, 3094
masques, 0197, 0420, 0421, 2992
Mass, 2034
master, 0225, 0239
   servant and, 1105
materialism, 0201, 0277, 0834, 2114, 2565a, 2661, 2697, 3186a
   idealism and, 0702
materialism, cultural, xii
matriarchy, 1253
matricide, 1876
matrona, 0556
maze, 0371
mechanicals
   in *Midsummer Night's Dream, A*, 2305
Medea, 0095, 0152, 0208, 0536, 0610, 0770, 0900, 1071, 2206, 2249, 2257, 2258, 2316, 2576, 2583, 2604
mediation, 2873
mediation, defective, 3030
mediator, 0707

medical knowledge of Shakespeare, 0858
medicine, 0346, 0496, 0729, 0897, 0922a, 1863
medieval drama, 1175
medievalism, 2359
Medusa, 0423, 2433
Megara, 2231
meiosis, 1633
Melampus, 2352
melancholia, 1543b
melancholy, 0144, 0547a, 0920, 0921, 0927, 0941, 1006, 1149a, 1824, 1857, 2033, 2071, 2745
melancholy, erotic, 3092
melodrama, 1578
melodrama (as concept or genre), 1048
melting, 1368
Melville, Sir James, 1402, 1432
   Memoirs, 1396
memorization, 0187
memory, 0457, 0504a, 0567, 0575, 0663a, 0677, 0792, 0940a, 1148, 1149, 1150, 1784, 1832, 1869a, 1901, 2493, 2528
men, 0112, 0153, 0240, 0287, 0337, 0387, 0498, 0592, 0602, 0614, 1070, 1412
   boys and, 0987
   women and, 0708, 1013a
men, black, 2780
Menaechmi. See under Plautus, Titus Maccius
Menander, 0183, 0226, 0801, 0802, 0814, 2535, 3182
Menas
   in *Antony and Cleopatra*, 1175, 1442, 1443, 1464, 1478, 1521, 2065
Menelaus, 0610, 3012, 3179, 3181
Menenius
   in *Coriolanus*, 0120, 0306, 0359, 0369, 0456, 0528, 0553, 0707, 0759a, 0850, 0873, 1047, 1602, 1603, 1606, 1609, 1610, 1623, 1631, 1638, 1639, 1649, 1651, 1652, 1660, 1669, 1671, 1681, 1688, 1693, 1701, 1703, 1704, 1706, 1710, 1716, 1718, 1733, 1749
Mercade
   in *Love's Labor's Lost*, 2186, 2194, 2199
Mercury, xviii, xx, 0095, 0563, 0807, 0942, 1905, 2187, 2189, 2190, 2193, 2194, 2199, 2199b, 2305, 2310, 2463, 2473, 2571
Mercutio
   in *Romeo and Juliet*, xx, 0154, 0862, 1022, 2463, 2464, 2466, 2467, 2473
Mercy, 2253
mercy, 0174, 0723, 0917, 1654, 2240
mercy, pleas for, 2770, 2774
Meres, Francis, 0462, 1010
   Palladis Tamia, 0146
meretrix, 0556
Mersenne, M.
   Traité de L'Harmonie Universelle, 0699
Messala
   in *Julius Caesar*, 2023, 2112
Messenger
   in *Antony and Cleopatra*, 0239, 1175, 1188a,

Index of Subjects

1201, 1322, 1379, 1396, 1402, 1432, 1449, 1521
messengers, 1184
  in *Antony and Cleopatra*, 1178, 1305, 1370, 1419, 1420, 1423, 1444, 1451, 1486, 1527
  in *Macbeth*, 2224
metadrama, 0238
metadramatics, 0552
metamorphoses, 0095, 0132, 0151, 0316, 0466
Metamorphoses, by Ovid. *See under* Ovid (Publius Ovidius Naso)
metamorphosis, xxi, 036, 0070a, 0119, 0242, 0375, 0467, 0667, 0721, 0807, 0890, 0899, 0995, 1035a, 1236, 2185a, 2317, 2540, 2588, 3082, 3084, 3127
metamorphosis, drama of, 3079
metaphor, 1194
metaphysics, 0299, 0813
metaphysics, logocentric, 2969
metatheater, 1781
metempsychosis, 2266, 2480, 2482
meter, 0891
metonymy, 0302, 1629
Mexia, Pedro, 2785
Michelangelo, 3172
microcosm, 0120, 0453, 0528, 0622, 1135, 1475
  macrocosm and, 1332, 1516
Midas, 0119, 2301, 2317
Middleton, Thomas, 0160b, 0378, 2645
  Family of Love, The, 2925
  Ghost of Lucrece, The, 2395a
  Phoenix, The, 0598
  Witch, The, 2233
Middleton, Thomas, and William Rowley
  Changeling, The, 0395
Midlands Rising of 1607, 1706
Mignon, Jean, 2432
miles gloriosus, 0331, 0491, 0556, 0999, 1730, 1900, 2341, 2348
militarism, 1734
Milton, John, 0660, 1387a, 1652, 1945
  Aereopagitica, 0538
  Samson Agonistes, 1274
mimesis, 0195a, 0257, 0380a, 0940a, 1391, 1918, 2409, 3098
mind, 0125, 2550
Minerva, 1163, 1887, 3042
Minotaur, 2293, 2295, 2301, 2567
Minturno, Antonio, 0485, 0610, 1666, 2455
Minyades, 0119
Minyeides, 2280
miracle (as element of drama), 3196
miracle play, 0382, 2363, 2371
Miranda
  in *Tempest, The*, 0373, 0375, 0421, 0577, 0850, 0902, 1134, 2560, 2560a, 2564, 2566, 2566a, 2569a, 2577, 2578a, 2588, 2596, 2598, 2609
Mirandula, Octavius
  Illustrium Poetarum Flores, 2430
mirror, 0394, 0444, 0452a, 0452b, 0785, 0923, 0940a, 1003, 1115, 2017, 2448
Mirror for Magistrates, A, 0314, 0584, 1763, 2417, 2423

mirrors, 1940
misanthrope, 0080, 0393, 2629, 2672, 2675
misanthropy, 0012, 0416, 0607, 0613, 0749, 0849a, 0941, 0945, 2614, 2659, 2688, 2700, 2705
misconstruction, 1953, 2015, 2016, 2117
misogynist, 0943
misogyny, 0741, 1346, 1842, 1866, 2027
mob, 2073
  in *Coriolanus*, 0062, 0232, 0237, 0448, 0777, 0792, 0799, 1595
mobs, 0697, 0973
mockery, 1242, 2312, 2618
modesty, 0927
moira, 0526
Molière (Jean-Baptiste Poquelin), 0818
  Amphitryon, 1577
  Misanthrope, Le, 1752
moment, tragic, 2912
monarchy, 0517, 1949, 1951a, 1990, 2005, 2026, 2416
money, 1009, 2701, 2703
Montaigne, Michel de, 0091, 0191, 0260, 0375, 0376, 0621, 0751, 0760, 0932, 0956, 1060, 1123, 1663, 1865, 1973, 1997, 2028, 2088, 2559, 2565a, 2576, 2673, 2814, 2955, 3100b
  Apology for Raymond Sebond, 0375, 1897
  "Of Diverting and Diversions," 2584
  "Of Friendship," 2516
monument, 0792, 1186
monument of Cleopatra
  in *Antony and Cleopatra*, 0990, 1032, 1255, 1362, 1383, 1404, 1426, 1488, 1528a
Moors, 0722
  in Shakespeare, 0618
moralities, 0435a, 1127, 2253, 2663, 2693
morality, 1430
morality drama, 0985a
morality play, 0037, 0381, 0382, 0631, 0664, 1135, 1475, 2658, 2660
morality plays, xxi, 0136, 0384, 0607, 0860, 0917, 0974a, 0986c, 0992, 2702, 2703, 2707, 2718a
morality tradition, 2656
moralization, 1062
moral plays, 0319b
More, Sir Thomas, 0796, 0891, 1031
  History of King Richard III, 0610
  Richard III, 0314
  Utopia, 0334, 0538, 2545
Morgann, Maurice, 0491
Morocco, Prince of
  in *Merchant of Venice, The*, 2261
mortality, 1641, 3144
Mortimer (deposer of Edward II), 1272
Moth
  in *Love's Labor's Lost*, 2187, 2199a
mother, 0113, 0114, 0142a, 0172a, 0187, 0232, 0237, 0307, 0344, 0351, 0369, 0372, 0381, 0459, 0521, 0549, 0594, 0678, 0759a, 0811, 0831, 0850, 0852, 0861, 0878, 0900, 0910, 0911, 0927, 1008, 1009, 1047, 1083, 1091, 1092, 1134, 1136, 1517, 1591, 1593, 1602

mother *(continued),* 1603, 1605, 1631, 1633, 1635, 1656, 1657, 1661, 1691, 1695, 1696, 1703, 1711, 1715, 1729, 1730, 1731, 1738, 1872, 1876, 1889, 1893a, 2167, 2758, 2793, 3137, 3155, 3181, 3190
  child and, 1319
mother figures, 3003
motherhood, 1501
mothers, 0553, 0614, 0804, 0964, 1621
  fathers and, 1869
Mouffet, Thomas
  Of the Silkwormes and Their Flies, 2315
mourning, 0278a, 0623, 0792, 1889, 2377
multitude, 0175, 1705
munificence, 0201
murder, 0106, 0172, 0213, 0254, 0255, 0441, 0508, 0729, 0745, 0863, 0873, 0915, 0940a, 0978, 1053, 1113, 1830, 1834, 1841, 1849, 1854, 1889, 1898, 1982, 1983a, 2231a
murderer, 1892
Murder of Gonzago, The, 1841a
  in *Hamlet,* 0381, 1800, 1802, 1841
Muretus, 0724
Murray, Gilbert
  Five Stages of Greek Religion, 1793
Musaeus
  Hero and Leander, 2470
music, xiv, xix, 0002, 0047, 0070a, 0096, 0099, 0241, 0257, 0336, 0354, 0355, 0377a, 0460, 0547a, 0550, 0593, 0594, 0595, 0636, 0651, 0699, 0700, 0744, 0897, 0926, 0959, 1020, 1301, 1366, 1370, 1455, 2046, 2342, 2365, 2545, 2550, 2553, 2578, 2702, 2703, 2911, 2943, 3136
music, Dorian, 1021
music, instrumental, 1021
music, Lydian, 1021
musica humana, 0336, 0550, 0636, 0699, 0736, 1020*b*, 2342, 2368
musica instrumentalis, 0336, 0550, 0736, 1020, 2342, 2368
musica mundana, 0336, 0550, 0595, 0699, 0736, 1020, 2368
musica speculativa, 0550
music of the spheres, 0054, 0241, 0336, 0464a, 0550, 0699, 0897, 1020, 1021, 1088, 2252, 2258, 2342, 2543, 2578
Mussato, Albertino
  Ecerinis, 0191
Mussolini, Benito, 1993
mutability, 0178, 0555, 0654, 0751, 0872, 1111, 1247, 1349, 2450, 2511, 2803, 3130
  permanence and, 1564
mutilation, 1048, 2718b, 2723, 2736, 2736a, 2738, 2758, 2764, 2777a
mutuality, 0807a
myopia, 2848
Myrmidons
  in *Troilus and Cressida,* 0692
Myrrha, 0132, 2332, 3149
mysteries, Eleusinian, xi, 0183, 0307, 2566, 2570a, 3095, 3183, 3190, 3201
mystery cycles, 0860

mystery drama, 0985a
mystery play, 1446
mystery plays, 0136, 0974a
myth, xv, xvi, xix, 0001, 0012a, 0022, 0023, 0028, 0045, 0059a, 0061, 0095, 0096, 0200, 0201, 0245, 0274, 0335, 0347, 0352, 0369, 0370a, 0375, 0421, 0423, 0441, 0464a, 0466, 0467, 0492a, 0495, 0536, 0630, 0638, 0666, 0690, 0770, 0772, 0814, 0873, 0997, 1035, 1086, 1106, 1246, 1308, 1528a, 1755, 1757, 2263, 2284, 3088, 3105, 3118, 3153, 3157, 3177
  folklore and, 2317
  history and, 2417
  reality and, 2890a
myth, chivalric, 2958
myth, secularization of, 3120
myth-making, 2841, 3042
mythographers, 0118, 0423, 1758, 2159, 2762
mythographies, 0759a
mythography, 0868, 1067a, 1078, 3123
mythological allusion, 0255
mythological dictionaries, 0059
mythological handbooks, 0022
mythological scenes, 0299a
mythologizing, 1372
mythology, 0115, 0150, 0274, 0300, 0335, 0370a, 0440, 0495, 0504a, 0721, 0756, 0758, 0780, 0807, 0860, 0890, 0914, 0916, 1044a, 1304, 1776, 1933, 2721
  folklore and, 2318
mythology handbooks, 0107
mythos, 0128, 0245
myths, 0012, 0119, 0183, 0357, 0375, 0755, 1084, 2106
myths, dominant, 2865

N

name, 0130, 0672, 1076, 1099, 1609, 1618, 1648, 1663, 1702, 1710, 1829, 1898
names, 0014, 0043, 0130, 0645, 0687, 0689, 0690, 0807, 0842, 0891, 0906, 1100, 1481, 1676, 1725, 1795, 1984, 2185a
names, Greek, 3182a, 3184a, 3196, 3205
naming, 2336
narcissism, xxii, 0260, 2004, 2636, 2641, 2830, 3068, 3137
Narcissus, xx, xxii, 0863, 2256, 2448, 3085, 3086, 3090a, 3134, 3137, 3159
narratio, 0433
narrative, 0253, 0505, 1528a
narrative in Shakespeare, 2438
narrative poems, by Shakespeare, 0123
Nashe, Thomas
  Christ's Tears over Jerusalem, 2779b
  Pierce Penniless, 2771
  Terrors of the Night, The, 2116a
  Unfortunate Traveller, The, 1906, 2771
Nathaniel
  in *Love's Labor's Lost,* 1006
nationalism, 1774
Nativity, 1260, 1772

Index of Subjects

naturalism, 0102, 0380a, 1428, 1614, 2152, 2403, 2565a
naturalism, linguistic, 2188
natural philosophy, 0194
Nature, 1066, 1130, 2183, 2378, 3143, 3191
nature, 0033, 0095, 0102, 0112, 0192, 0221, 0263, 0295, 0298, 0336, 0370a, 0373, 0376, 0394, 0398a, 0411, 0457, 0484, 0625, 0630, 0633, 0654, 0683, 0693, 0706, 0728, 0729, 0785, 0805, 0828a, 0859, 0900, 1241, 1511, 1551, 1626, 1641, 1669, 1673, 1711, 1757, 1787, 1838, 1850, 1870, 1918, 2083, 2101, 2140, 2173, 2179a, 2231, 2365, 2562a, 2606, 2609, 2629, 2634, 2642, 2734, 3125, 3127, 3131, 3169, 3209
  art and, 0164a, 0375, 0402, 0513, 0656, 0729, 0802a, 0848a, 0884, 0922a, 0923, 0950, 0965, 1016, 1033, 3170, 3172, 3184, 3198
  Law and, 0701
  as law *(nomos)*
    in *King Lear*, 0134
  society and, 2304
  as vital force *(physis)*
    in *King Lear*, 0134
nature, harmony of, 3174
nature, human, 0079, 0084, 0171, 0385, 0521, 2439, 2581, 2634, 2667, 2676, 2734, 2886, 2892, 2975
nature, law of, 0263, 0625, 0723, 3028
nature, laws of, 1123, 1514, 2185a, 2574, 2578a, 3066
nature, lease of, 2228
nature, repair of, 3180
Navarre, King of (Ferdinand)
  in *Love's Labor's Lost*, 2188, 2197, 2199
necessity, 0101
negatio, 1080, 1999
negotiation, language of, 3128
negotium, 1554
  otium and, 2546a
Nell
  in *Comedy of Errors, The*, 1587
Nemean lion, 1538, 1543c, 1556, 1807
Nemesis, 0596
neoclassical forms, 0157
neoclassical French drama, 0117
neoclassicism, 1326, 1787
neoclassicists, 0111, 0822
neologisms, 0924, 0936a
neologisms, Latinate, 0429a, 0430
Neoplatonic ideas, 0353a
Neoplatonic philosophy, 0474
Neoplatonic religion of Love, 0211
Neoplatonism, xi, xiv, xviii, xix, xx, 0045, 0101, 0102, 0127, 0139, 0370a, 0375, 0431, 0460, 0513, 0756, 0803, 0909a, 1140a, 1149a, 1184, 1185, 1216, 1312, 1356, 1511, 2188, 2197, 2244, 2292, 2320, 2346, 2468a, 2569, 2573, 2581, 2600, 3151
Neoplatonists, 0059a, 0156, 0259, 0266, 0377a, 0457, 0487, 0499, 0547a, 0828a, 0999, 1021, 1031, 1086, 1548, 2545, 2546, 2562b, 2571, 2606
neo-Stoicism, 2165

Neptune, 0114, 1576, 2359, 2445
Nero, 0858, 2167, 2457
Nessus, 1174, 1188, 1218
Nestor, 2411
  in *The Rape of Lucrece*, 0105
  in *Troilus and Cressida*, 0265, 0297, 0553, 2872, 3005, 3009, 3011, 3021
Nevile, Alexander
  translation of Seneca's *Oedipus*, 1872, 2160
New Comedy. *See* Comedy, New
New Critics, 2170
new historicists, 0066
New Testament. See under Bible
Newton, Thomas
  compilation of *Seneca, His Tenne Tragedies*, 2160
  translation of Cicero's *De Senectute*, 2175
New World, 1152, 2559, 2569, 2574
Nicanor
  in *Coriolanus*, 1676
Nicolas of Cusa, 0288
Nietzsche, Friedrich, 2147
Night
  in *Rape of Lucrece, The*, 2394
night, 0465, 0539, 0691, 2469
nightingale, 2754
nihilism, 2922
Nile, 0255, 1171, 1199, 1204, 1362, 1368, 1453, 1513
Nine Worthies
  in *Love's Labor's Lost*, 0678, 2185a, 2186, 2199a
Ninus, 0928
Niobe, 0663, 3082
Nisus, xvii, 1936
nobility, 0082, 0207, 0208, 0255, 0612, 0613, 0622, 0627, 0664, 0749, 0779, 0849, 0876, 0977, 1021, 1296, 1303, 1328, 1361, 1427, 1469, 1477, 1484, 1636, 1874, 1973, 2011, 2024, 2082
noble characters, 0218
nobleness, 0192
nobles, 0079
noise, 0255
nomos, 2140
North, Sir Thomas, 0009, 0042, 0055, 0062, 0073, 0107, 0120, 0345
  "Epistle Dedicatory" to translation of Plutarch's *Lives*, 0980
  translation of Jacques Amyot's preface to French version of Plutarch's *Lives*, 2477
  translation of Plutarch's *Lives*, 0208, 0292a, 0314, 0359, 0613, 0629, 0690, 0721, 0723, 0765, 0807, 0914, 0936, 1013, 1050, 1110, 1160, 1165, 1216, 1228, 1242, 1276, 1378, 1419, 1429, 1441, 1477, 1609, 1671, 1712, 1716, 1724, 1803, 1907, 1945, 2046, 2058, 2096, 2098, 2199a, 2271, 2628, 3100, 3182a, 3184a, 3200. *See also under* Plutarch
Norton, Thomas, and Thomas Sackville
  Gorbuduc, 2749
nosce teipsum, 0386a
nosce te ipsum, 2239
nostalgia, 0805

notatio, 1879a
novel, Greek, 3188
numerology, 2487
Nurse
  in *Romeo and Juliet*, 2464, 2475c, 2476
  in *Titus Andronicus*, 2777
nurture, 0164a
Nym
  in *Henry V*, 1931a

O
oaths, 0465a, 0966, 1223
obedience, 0760
Oberon, 2279
  in *Midsummer Night's Dream, A*, 0214, 0721, 0818, 0987, 1123, 2281, 2283, 2291, 2298, 2310, 2314
oblivion, 3048
Occasio, 0950, 1559
Occasion, 0634, 0635
occasion, 2579
occultism, 0968, 2565a
occupatio, 0504a
Octavia
  in *Antony and Cleopatra*, 0729, 0828, 0898, 0964, 1047, 1175, 1188a, 1195, 1235, 1264, 1266, 1281, 1322, 1325, 1330, 1339, 1367, 1396, 1399, 1402, 1419, 1449, 1458, 1461
Octavius Caesar (C. Julius Caesar Octavianus), 0537, 0656, 0698, 1169, 1238, 1524
  in *Antony and Cleopatra*, 0113, 0141, 0171, 0232, 0292a, 0347, 0359, 0388, 0398, 0400, 0422, 0452a, 0498, 0504a, 0703, 0705, 0723, 0729, 0778, 0782, 0792, 0828, 0857, 0927, 0949, 1000, 1002, 1017, 1047b, 1058, 1106, 1152, 1163, 1164, 1166, 1174, 1175, 1178, 1181, 1183, 1184, 1187, 1188, 1191, 1196a, 1201, 1216, 1228, 1235, 1240, 1242, 1248, 1252, 1253, 1256, 1259, 1260, 1263, 1264, 1266, 1280, 1283, 1291, 1297, 1314, 1315, 1318, 1323, 1328, 1330, 1332, 1339, 1341, 1343, 1344, 1347, 1348, 1349, 1351, 1352, 1354a, 1360, 1362, 1363, 1364, 1370, 1375, 1376, 1377, 1378, 1388, 1390, 1391, 1405, 1409, 1410, 1411, 1422, 1425, 1427, 1428, 1430, 1436, 1439, 1443, 1453, 1454, 1455, 1457, 1458, 1460a, 1461, 1464, 1465, 1466, 1473, 1477, 1480, 1483, 1485, 1492, 1496, 1506, 1509, 1521, 1524, 1525, 1527, 1529, 1775
  in *Julius Caesar*, 0246, 0398, 0782, 0792, 0949, 1067, 1172, 2005, 2051, 2053, 2063, 2093, 2094, 2097, 2126, 2128, 2136
  in *Julius Caesar* and *Antony and Cleopatra*, 1019a
Odysseus, 0311, 1056, 1628, 2361, 2567, 2572
Oedipus, 0464a, 0509, 0725, 0814, 1801, 1818, 1830, 1872, 1876, 1877, 2151, 2156, 2160, 2177, 2207, 2225, 2361
Oeneus, King of Calydon, 2458
office, 0348
oikonomia, 0433
old age, 0231, 0276, 0624, 0995, 1551a, 2213

Old Athenian
  in *Timon of Athens*, 2630
Oldcastle, Sir John, 0450, 0943
Old Comedy. *See* Comedy, Old
old heroes of Shakespeare, 0297
Old Siward
  in *Macbeth*, 0721
Oldys, William, 0930
Oliver
  in *As You Like It*, 1081, 1543c
Olivia
  in *Twelfth Night*, 0307, 0515, 3075, 3082, 3085, 3086, 3087
omens, 0271, 0425, 1047, 1943, 1971, 1980, 2076, 2092
Omphale, xv, 0932, 1184, 1188, 1336, 1371, 1372, 2268, 2319, 3083
opening scenes, 0812
Ophelia, 1829
  in *Hamlet*, xvii, 0830, 0920, 1797, 1816, 1837, 1844, 1850, 1863, 1875, 1884, 1885, 1886, 1887, 1890, 1893a
opinion, 2169, 2923
Oppian, 1532
opportunism, 2112, 2865
Opportunity
  in *Rape of Lucrece, The*, 2394
opportunity, 0172a, 0832a
opposites, 1332
optimism, 2183, 2581
optimism, humanistic, 2932
oracle, 0368
oracle, Delphic, 0495
oracles, 2225
oratio, 1554, 1999
oration, 0255, 0315, 0433, 2007, 2011, 2012, 2044
oration, forensic, 2440a
oration, parts of, 2527a
orations, 2047, 3005
orator, 0129, 0432, 0905, 1073, 2184
orator, 2127
oratory, 0129, 0232, 0350, 0656, 1954, 2068, 2127
oratory, forensic, 2785
oratory, three types of, 2527a
order, 0095, 0160a, 0164a, 0174, 0191, 0206, 0208, 0224, 0229, 0238, 0255, 0265, 0282a, 0290, 0332, 0336, 0343, 0360, 0369, 0383, 0393, 0398, 0411, 0421, 0442, 0469, 0471, 0487, 0503, 0550, 0557, 0615, 0617, 0620, 0625, 0630, 0648, 0658, 0686, 0699, 0700, 0705, 0729, 0746, 0759a, 0775, 0792, 0804, 0828, 0832a, 0850, 0861, 0883, 0886, 0892, 0894, 0909, 0912, 0914, 0945, 0983a, 1012, 1027, 1029, 1039, 1046, 1055, 1057, 1058, 1083, 1084, 1175, 1242, 1253, 1370a, 1377, 1453, 1499, 1529, 1636, 1742, 1858, 1921, 1934, 1959, 2140, 2147, 2173, 2395a, 2468a, 2696, 2742a, 2744, 2815, 2826, 2831, 2844, 2878, 2910, 2997, 3016, 3021, 3069
  anarchy and, 2157

Index of Subjects

chaos and, 1877
disorder and, 2927
order, civil, 2716
order, hierarchical, 2889
order, moral, 2858
order, natural, 3209
order, public, 3073
order, social, 2693, 2924, 2931
order, symbols of, 3000
order, universal, 2840, 3063
Orestes, 0509, 0772, 1789, 1801, 1811, 1818, 1828, 1830, 1844, 1862, 1876
Orestes' Furies, 1876
organic unity, 1234
Orient, 0618
Origen of Alexandria, 1786
Orlando, 1556
  in *As You Like It*, 0322a, 0807, 0987, 1081, 1538, 1543c, 1547, 1555, 1557, 1561
Orpheus, xvi, xviii, xix, 0096, 0380, 0382, 0550, 0667, 0721, 0982, 1539, 1755, 1763, 1816, 2208, 2251, 2254, 2258, 2365, 2394
Orphism, 0307
Orsino, Duke
  in *Twelfth Night*, 0307, 0636, 0758, 0812, 3075, 3077, 3082, 3085, 3090
orthodoxy, 0324
orthography, 0188
orthopedics, 0752
Osiris, 1184, 1222, 1261, 1312. See also Isis and Osiris
Osric
  in *Hamlet*, 0790, 1057, 1796
Oswald
  in *King Lear*, 0790
Othello
  in *Othello*, xix, 0097, 0132, 0166, 0167, 0437, 0464a, 0490, 0509, 0609, 0618, 0661, 0824, 0866, 0999, 1065, 1071, 1667, 1723, 2080, 2325, 2327, 2328, 2329, 2330, 2331, 2332, 2334, 2336, 2337, 2339, 2340, 2341, 2345, 2346, 2347, 2348, 2349, 2350, 2698, 2883
Otho, 2328
otium, 1554
  negotium and, 2546a
outsider, 2887
outsiders, 0814
Ovidian elements, 0267
Ovidianism, 0119
Ovid (Publius Ovidius Naso), xiv, xvi, xvii, xviii, xx, xxi, xxii, 0012a, 0028, 0039, 0054, 0056, 0062, 0073, 0080a, 0095, 0190, 0238, 0278, 0280, 0325, 0350, 0363, 0380, 0401, 0421, 0437, 0462, 0488, 0534, 0580, 0586, 0597, 0620, 0627, 0628, 0665, 0683, 0726, 0739, 0754, 0770, 0780, 0807, 0862, 0868, 0869, 0890, 0899, 0900, 0909a, 0914, 0919, 0934, 0938, 0999, 1009, 1077, 1084, 1085, 1092, 1126, 1146, 1153, 1236, 1468, 1532, 1534, 1536, 1539, 1545, 1558, 1567, 1570, 1576, 1585a, 1623, 1779, 1785, 1858, 1887, 2185a, 2195, 2235, 2268, 2276, 2283, 2286, 2310, 2353, 2389, 2397, 2401, 2410, 2419, 2434, 2448, 2453, 2456, 2465, 2473, 2480, 2488, 2494, 2503, 2508, 2511, 2534, 2547, 2558, 2562a, 2575, 2583, 2588a, 2710, 2731a, 2734, 2736a, 2742, 2763, 2764, 2776, 2787, 2985, 2986, 2995, 3042, 3079, 3105, 3106, 3109, 3132, 3135, 3136, 3139, 3144, 3145, 3147, 3148, 3161, 3163, 3164, 3167, 3180
Amores, 0370a, 0720, 1129, 1428, 2268a, 2375, 2378, 2502
Ars Amatoria, 1518, 2335, 2531, 2532, 2540
Art of Love (Ars Amatoria), 0269, 0466, 0720
Epistulae Ex Ponto, 2506
Fasti, 0322a, 0484, 0721, 0759a, 0778, 0852, 0932, 1009, 1129, 1726, 1850, 2393, 2398, 2403, 2405, 2417, 2433, 2576, 2718b
Heroides, 0685, 0720, 0759a, 1202, 1296, 1345, 2184, 2184a, 2303, 2340, 2426, 2503, 2506, 2532, 2540, 3179, 3181
Metamorphoses, xix, 0012, 0046, 0096, 0107, 0118, 0119, 0123, 0126, 0132, 0133, 0151, 0155, 0208, 0242, 0332, 0369, 0370a, 0384, 0446, 0467, 0483, 0484, 0536, 0560, 0561, 0572, 0573, 0584, 0613, 0667, 0685, 0690, 0720, 0721, 0727, 0729, 0835, 0841, 0882, 0884, 0888a, 0910a, 0916, 0928, 0936, 0987, 0995, 1035a, 1042a, 1043, 1071, 1095, 1107, 1115, 1129, 1324, 1543, 1543a, 1708, 1776, 1816, 1838, 1934, 1996, 2024, 2135, 2200, 2208, 2229, 2237, 2254, 2256, 2258, 2270, 2271, 2274, 2277, 2280, 2281, 2282, 2284, 2285, 2287, 2288, 2299, 2303, 2305, 2307, 2311, 2312, 2313a, 2314, 2315, 2316, 2331, 2332, 2333, 2346, 2352, 2387, 2422, 2447, 2458, 2468, 2475c, 2475b, 2482, 2485, 2492, 2501, 2509, 2523, 2530, 2531, 2540, 2541, 2551a, 2554, 2557, 2562, 2567, 2576, 2579, 2588, 2591, 2597, 2598, 2604, 2721, 2722, 2727, 2728, 2740, 2743b, 2750, 2762, 2766, 2777, 2777a, 2785, 2786, 2938, 2972, 2985, 3013, 3075, 3082, 3084, 3085, 3085a, 3086, 3087, 3090, 3124, 3127, 3137, 3149, 3158, 3172, 3174, 3184a, 3189, 3189a, 3191, 3195, 3198, 3200. See also under Golding, Arthur
Remedia Amoris, 3077
Tristia, 1896, 2506
owl, 1585a
oxymoron, 2466, 2467

P
Pacuvius, Marcus, 1920
Page, 0943
Page, Anne
  in *Merry Wives of Windsor, The*, 2265
Page, William
  in *Merry Wives of Windsor, The*, 2263
pageant, xxi, 1031, 1304, 1952, 2186, 2199a, 2603, 2618, 2669
pageantry, 0150, 0186, 0700, 0965, 1275, 1276, 1409, 3098
pageants, 0107, 0988, 1128
paideia, 0079

Painter
  in *Timon of Athens*, 0076, 0264, 0372, 0545, 0613, 0912, 1082, 2612, 2647, 2689a
Painter, William
  Palace of Pleasure, 1949
  translation of Livy, 0484
painters, 0437
painting, 0187, 0264, 0926, 1070, 1082, 1129, 1518, 3108
  poetry and, 0976, 2694, 3160
Palamon
  in *Two Noble Kinsmen, The*, xxii, 0406, 0901, 3090a, 3092, 3094, 3096, 3098, 3100a, 3100b, 3102
Palatine Anthology, 0685, 2503
Palingenius
  Zodiacae Vitae, 0142
  Zodiacus Vitae, 0488, 0938
Palinurus, 0610, 2588
Pan, 0720a
  Apollo and, 1021
Pandarus
  in Chaucer's *Troilus and Criseyde*, 2476
  in *Troilus and Cressida*, 0078, 0147, 0160a, 0161, 0396, 0424, 0441, 0481, 0553, 0652, 0687, 0700, 0789, 0798, 0817, 0827, 0879, 0986a, 0994, 1021, 2790, 2792, 2803, 2816, 2819, 2825, 2826, 2839, 2856, 2873, 2875, 2877, 2885, 2886, 2903, 2910, 2911, 2927, 2931, 2934, 2936, 2943, 2954, 2966, 2972, 2977, 2991, 3002, 3012, 3014, 3018, 3024, 3030, 3035, 3045, 3052, 3061, 3067
Pandora, 1757, 2169
Pandosto, by Robert Greene. *See under* Greene, Robert
Panofsky, Erwin, 3160
parabasis
  Old Comedy and, 0468
parable, 1638
parables, 0201
Paracelsus, 0469, 0752, 1666, 2603
paradigm, 2480
paradise, 0663a, 1543, 1547, 2445, 2547, 2560a, 3173
paradiso terrestre, 1556
paradox, 0280, 0281, 0424, 0512, 0857, 1185, 1327, 1359, 1371, 1409, 1415, 1434, 1451, 1452, 1453, 1482, 1633, 1692, 1717, 1719, 2426, 2468, 2477a, 2482, 2521, 2600, 2618, 2687, 2815, 2867, 2895, 2901
paradoxical encomium, 0217
paragone, 0156, 0281, 0907, 0976, 2647, 2671, 2689a, 3172
parallelism, 0844, 1196, 1224
parallelism in *Troilus and Cressida*, 3021
parasite of Roman drama, 0331, 0556, 1146a
parasites, 0613
parent, 0225, 0542
Paris (son of Priam), 1157, 1244, 1934, 2422
  in *Troilus and Cressida*, 0106, 0215, 2873, 2882, 2899, 2916, 2934, 2936, 2996, 3015, 3043, 3066
Parmenides, 2378, 3081

parody, 0353a, 0891, 0915, 0943, 1395, 1448, 1908, 2266, 2282, 2308, 2315
Parolles
  in *All's Well That Ends Well*, 1156, 2265
paronomasia, 1072, 2185a
parricide, 0849
passion, 0167, 0180, 0208, 0283, 0350, 0370a, 0397, 0411, 0421, 0437, 0464a, 0499, 0509, 0531, 0548, 0572, 0610, 0920, 0951, 0955, 0962, 0978, 0985a, 0986b, 1000, 1022, 1039, 1071, 1077, 1112, 1124, 1229, 1286, 1322, 1340, 1373, 1388, 1398, 1403, 1428, 1434, 1440, 1480, 1715, 1943, 2071, 2101, 2258, 2339, 2345, 2398a, 2419, 2462, 2466, 2472, 2551, 3028, 3085a
passions, 0070, 0191, 0193, 0208, 0829, 0945, 0961, 1027, 1044, 1543c, 1997, 2173a, 2232a, 2301, 2439, 2871, 2955, 3065, 3090
passions, ruling, 2978
past, 0691, 1251, 1318a, 1343, 2807
  present and, 1529, 1844, 1965
past, classical, 2805
pastoral, 0108, 0320, 0384, 0386, 0647, 0666, 0693, 0807, 0814, 0837, 1094, 1121, 1151, 1543b, 1546, 1551a, 1779, 2166, 2481, 2546a, 3152, 3173, 3196, 3199
pastoral ideals, 1549, 1550
pastoralism, xv, 0274, 0275, 0531, 0667, 0794, 0807, 1537, 1540, 2734
pastoral plays, by Shakespeare, 0855
pastorals, 0211, 1544, 1564
pastoral tradition, 0233
pathetic appeal, 2037
pathos, 0236, 0404, 0608, 0721, 0799, 0907, 1034, 1856, 1857, 1999, 2007, 2455a, 2763, 3008
Patience, 3084
patience, 0263, 0400, 0546, 0804, 0997, 1023, 1140, 2361, 2371
patriarchal ideas, 0194
patriarchalism, 0406
patriarchy, 0142a, 0614, 0703, 0807a, 1253, 1307, 1684, 2362, 2900, 3128
patricians, 0080, 0113, 0239, 0255
  in *Coriolanus*, 0599, 0850, 1009, 1047, 1086, 1603, 1605, 1630, 1633, 1639, 1658, 1695, 1699, 1703, 1704, 1710, 1740a
  in *Julius Caesar*, 0388
patriot, 0865, 0866, 0949, 2013a
patriotism, 0566, 0599, 0622, 0742, 0906, 1122, 1698
Patroclus
  in *Troilus and Cressida*, 0084, 0172a, 0987, 2822, 2823, 2871, 2899, 2926, 2936, 3044
patron, 0935, 1146a
patronage, 2650
patterns, visual, 2934
Paul, St., 0191, 0627, 0742, 1011, 1793, 2122, 2292
Paulina
  in *Winter's Tale, The*, 0307, 0610, 3171, 3189, 3191, 3193
Paul of Aegina, 1507

Index of Subjects

Pausanias, 2521
Pax Augustus, 1758
pax Romana, 0359
peace, 0113, 0219, 0239, 0359, 0641, 0647, 0698, 0720a, 0729, 0760, 0804, 1141, 1233, 1260, 1339, 1408, 1477, 1596, 1765, 1769, 2035, 2056
Peacham, Henry, 2466
  Minerva Britanna or a Garden of Heroical Devises, 0847
Peacham drawing of scene in *Titus Andronicus*, 0105, 0994
peacock, 1067a
pederasty, 0387
Peele, George, 0860
  Arraignment of Paris, The, 2848
Pegasus, 1905
Peloponnesian War, 2634
Pelops, 2734
Pembroke, Countess of, 1417
  translation of Garnier's *Antonius*, 1468
  translation of Garnier's *Marc Antoine*, 1472
  translation of Plessis-Mornay's *A Discourse of Life and Death*, 2241
Penelope, 2532
Pentecost, 1448
Penthesilea, 1935
Pentheus, 1623, 1962
perambulation, 1816a
perception, 0486, 2073, 2493, 2551
Percy, Lady (Kate)
  in *Henry IV, Part 1,* 0862, 1070
Perdita
  in *Winter's Tale, The,* 0095, 0577, 0781, 0830, 3170, 3178, 3181, 3182, 3183, 3187, 3188, 3190, 3193, 3195
perfection, 3125
periaktoi, 0753
Pericles, 0268, 2371
  in *Pericles,* 0092, 0307, 0336, 0699, 0781, 0920, 0941, 2361, 2368
Peripatetics, 2042
peripeteia, 0128, 0603, 0799
peripety, 0156a, 0484
permanence, 0870
  mutability and, 1564
peroratio, 0433, 1999
Persephone, 3201
Persephone (Proserpina), 2190
Perseus, 0093, 2433
Persius (Aulus Persius Flaccus), 0938, 1943
  Satires, 1158
personification, 0124, 0369, 0868, 1175, 1189, 2775a
personifications, 1127, 2501
persuasion, 0129, 0234, 0294
Pescetti, Orlando
  Il Caesare, 0534
pessimism, 0252, 0325, 0765, 0945, 1060, 2174, 2386
Petrarchanism, 2191
Petrarch (Francesco Petrarca), 0227, 0635, 0940, 1109, 1520, 1548, 2046, 2418, 2501, 2517

Africa, 0191
De Remediis Utriusque Fortunae, 0191
Lives of Illustrious Men, 0102
Petrarchism, 0332, 3044, 3161
  anti-Petrarchism and, 2488a
Petronius Arbiter, 1034a
  Satyricon, 2547
Petruchio
  in *Taming of the Shrew, The,* 2531, 2532, 2532a, 2537, 2539, 2540
Phaer, Thomas
  translation of Virgil's *Aeneid,* 2312a, 2562
Phaethon, 0322, 0998, 1043, 1093a, 2441, 2447, 2452, 2777a, 3082
Pharisees, 0215
pharmakos, 2265
Phebe
  in *As You Like It,* 1534
philanthropy, 0523
Philemon, 2274
Philharmonus, a soothsayer
  in *Cymbeline,* 1780
Philippi, battle of
  in *Julius Caesar,* 0201, 0302, 0566a
Philo
  in *Antony and Cleopatra,* 0911, 0927, 1000, 1178, 1257, 1310, 1372, 1429, 1439, 1486, 1502
Philoctetes, 0509, 1043
Philomel, 0208, 1048, 2734
Philomela, 0119, 0179, 0283, 0467, 0721, 0770, 2727, 2747, 2754, 2757, 2762, 2764, 2785
philosopher-king, 0796, 2599
philosophers, 0321, 0336, 0437, 0625, 0864, 1067a
Philosophers Banquet, The, 2406
philosophy, 0069, 0097, 0102, 0120, 0149, 0172, 0184, 0191, 0269, 0307, 0380a, 0385, 0426, 0450, 0464a, 0488, 0496, 0526, 0542, 0652, 0938, 0971, 1000, 1005
  poetry and, 2871
philosophy, Epicurean, 0616
Philosophy, Lady, 3171
philosophy, occult, 1149a, 2590
philosophy, Stoic-Cynic, 2660
philospher-statesman, 0949
Philostratus, 0375, 2411
Philumenus, 1508
Phineus, 2557, 2576
Phoebe, 2283, 2308, 2317
Phoebus, 1042a, 2183, 2308, 2514
Phoenix, 0060, 0739, 0998, 1129, 1756, 2374, 2389
  in *Phoenix and Turtle, The,* 2375, 2377, 2378, 2379, 2383, 2385, 2387
Phrynia
  in *Timon of Athens,* 0849a
Phyllis, 0132, 2340
physiognomy, 1138
physiological terms, 0650a
Physiologus, Greek, 0739
Physiologus, Latin, 0739
physiology, 0854

Piccolomini, Alessandro, 0375
Pico della Mirandola, Giovanni, 0101, 0307, 0380, 0808, 1149a, 1185, 2188, 2287, 2547, 2569, 2606
pictura, 0179
pictures, 0070a, 1107
pictures, mythological
   in *Taming of the Shrew, The*, 2534
pietas, 0135, 0587, 0759a, 1657, 1768, 2014, 2772
   furor and, 2593
piety, 0152, 0792, 1859
pilgrimage, 0264
Pindar, 0848a, 2501
Pindarus
   in *Julius Caesar*, 2124
Pirithous, 2299
   in *Two Noble Kinsmen, The*, 3090a, 3100
Pirithous and Theseus, 0987
Pistol
   in *Henry IV, Part 2*, 1912
   in *Henry V*, 1920, 1927, 1931a, 1933
pity, 0166, 0208, 0254, 0453, 0613, 0647, 0917, 0959, 0969, 1602, 1666, 1871, 2150, 2227, 2706, 3140
place, 1213
places in Shakespeare's plays, 1032
plain style, 0240
Plato, 0080, 0120, 0124, 0125, 0127, 0149, 0184, 0257, 0266, 0280, 0320, 0336, 0375, 0380, 0450, 0457, 0469, 0478, 0487, 0488, 0499, 0517, 0519, 0528, 0566, 0601, 0621, 0657, 0665, 0699, 0728, 0729, 0785, 0804, 0813, 0903, 0920, 0949, 0955, 0959, 0968, 0982, 1006, 1031, 1063, 1068, 1081, 1098, 1122, 1123, 1126, 1175, 1437, 1468, 1603, 1785, 1881, 1888, 1907, 1967, 2042, 2049, 2096, 2153, 2195, 2198, 2223, 2279, 2478, 2551a, 2578a, 2587, 2609, 2665, 3185
   Cratylus, 0130, 2185a, 2188
   First Alcibiades, 1940
   "Greater Hippias," 2855
   Ion, 1144
   Laws, 0101, 0197, 1650, 2589
   Parmenides, 0280
   Phaedo, 0097, 0943, 2328a
   Phaedrus, 0529, 0672, 1093a, 1129, 1783, 1934, 2169, 2193, 2255, 2299, 2488a, 2520
   Philebus, 0788
   Protagoras, 0877
   Republic, xxi, 0101, 0212, 0431, 0515, 0599, 0940, 1122, 1123, 1556, 1650, 2232a, 2409, 2590, 2599
   Symposium, 0599, 0627, 0637a, 0788, 0850a, 1667, 2464, 2488a, 2495, 2497, 2516, 2519, 2520
   Timaeus, 0101, 0197, 0527
Platonic ideal, 0462
Platonic ideas, 0039
Platonic tradition, 0110
Platonism, x, xv, 0027, 0045, 0101, 0102, 0127, 0160, 0288, 0307, 0375, 0453, 0599, 0835, 0863, 0891a, 1000, 1016, 1081, 1153, 1903, 1994, 2347, 2379, 2389, 2464, 2496, 2497, 2501, 2520, 3121
Platonists, 0118, 0372a, 0487, 1786, 2394
Plautus, Titus Maccius, xiii, xvi, 013, 0062, 0072, 0092, 0099, 0123, 0140, 0153, 0165, 0170, 0209, 0226, 0248, 0350, 0363, 0369, 0401, 0415, 0418, 0472, 0491, 0494, 0535, 0556, 0597, 0600, 0608, 0695, 0746, 0754, 0759, 0774, 0801, 0802, 0814, 0829a, 0836, 0891, 0895, 0914, 0916, 0923, 0938, 0989, 1075, 1085a, 1146a, 1566, 1589, 2259, 2473, 2535, 3076, 3078, 3184a
   Amphitruo, 0073, 0439, 0556, 0887, 0891, 1567, 1569, 1571, 1574, 1575, 1577, 1580, 1586, 1587, 1588
   Amphitryon, 0283, 0415
   Menaechmi, 0073, 0100, 0102, 0283, 0439, 0546, 0556, 0678, 0685, 0721, 0822, 0887, 0986c, 1032, 1114, 1137, 1567, 1568, 1569, 1571, 1573, 1574, 1575, 1577, 1578, 1579, 1580, 1581, 1582, 1583, 1584, 1585, 1586, 1587, 1588
   Miles Gloriosus, 2164
   Mostellaria, xx, 2247, 2533
   Persa, 2137
   Poenulus, 1887
   Pseudolus, xvi, 0214, 1794
   Rudens, 0891, 1574, 2596
Plautus, Titus Maccius), 1858
play-acting, 1395, 1661, 1983b
Player
   in *Hamlet*, 0080a, 0246, 0297, 0610, 0685, 0721, 0749, 0772, 0789, 1115, 1799, 1800, 1802, 1804, 1806, 1808, 1817, 1819, 1823, 1827, 1830, 1835, 1837, 1841, 1845, 1854, 1856, 1868, 1883, 1889, 1892, 1895, 2435
Player King
   in *Hamlet*, 1896
players
   in *Hamlet*, 0381, 0462, 0801, 1782, 1787, 1841a, 1853, 1889
playhouses, private, 2928
playing of roles, 1412
plays on classical themes, by Shakespeare, 0058
play within a play in *Troilus and Cressida*, 2964
pleas, 2746
pleasure, 0464a, 1005, 1025, 1163, 1175, 1188, 1228, 1241, 1250, 1263, 1293, 1333, 2197
   politics and, 0703
   virtue and, 1218
pleasures, 1060
plebeians, 0080, 0239, 0255, 0622, 0654, 1608
   in *Coriolanus*, 0599, 0625, 0648, 0652, 0766, 0831, 0850, 1086, 1590, 1596, 1602, 1603, 1618, 1630, 1633, 1638, 1658, 1660, 1683, 1694, 1696, 1703, 1704, 1706, 1716, 1719, 1728, 1736
   in *Julius Caesar*, 0186, 0508, 0648, 0729, 2009, 2021, 2037, 2061, 2063, 2083
plebs
   in *Coriolanus*, 1009
Pleiade, 0924
plenitude, 0115

Pliny the Elder (Gaius Plinius Secundus), 0375, 0490, 0609, 0666, 0685, 0739, 0907, 0990, 1067a, 1468, 1532, 1926, 2375, 2376, 2389, 2411, 2539, 2756, 3176
  Natural History (Naturalis Historia, Naturall Historie, The Historie of the World), 0546, 0734, 1852, 1891, 2332, 2694, 3018
  Naturalis Historia (Natural History, Naturall Historie, The Historie of the World), 2343
  Naturall Historie (Naturalis Historia, Natural History, The Historie of the World), 2326
plot, double, 0556
plot (as concept or element of drama), xvii, 0127, 0145, 0165, 0166, 0215, 0232, 0275, 0319, 0339, 0355, 0368, 0425, 0426, 0460, 0473, 0476, 0484, 0663a, 0685, 0706, 0721, 0745, 0787, 0819, 0822, 0860, 0873, 0893, 0978, 0986a, 1016, 1017, 1028, 1050, 1053, 1064, 1075, 1079, 1114, 1119, 1137, 1164, 1571, 1587, 1633, 1790, 2170, 2211, 2220, 2307, 2348, 2834, 2874, 2893
Plotinus, 0101, 0499, 0699, 1031, 1063, 2223, 2287, 2296, 2569, 2573, 2585, 2855
plots, 0099, 0117, 0235, 0248, 0287, 0802, 0818
Plutarch, xvi, xvii, xxi, 0009, 0012, 0012a, 0056, 0073, 0080, 0095, 0101, 0102, 0106, 0107, 0123, 0137, 0172a, 0199, 0200, 0202, 0239, 0255, 0261, 0277, 0305, 0314, 0320, 0329, 0337, 0384, 0388, 0416, 0452, 0456, 0488, 0495, 0508, 0540, 0546, 0547a, 0551, 0602, 0603, 0633, 0641, 0652, 0668, 0684, 0685f, 0721, 0743, 0750, 0760, 0765, 0777, 0778, 0811, 0828, 0841, 0909a, 0932, 0936a, 0945, 0949, 0954, 0956, 0973, 1005, 1019a, 1021, 1076, 1083, 1105, 1123, 1130, 1152, 1156, 1164, 1168, 1172, 1175, 1179, 1193, 1200, 1212a, 1216, 1220, 1228, 1234, 1238, 1240, 1242, 1244, 1248, 1252a, 1262, 1271, 1287, 1294, 1301, 1322, 1329, 1331, 1347, 1350, 1358, 1362, 1366, 1376, 1389, 1392, 1398, 1404, 1411, 1415, 1416, 1417, 1426, 1429, 1432, 1439, 1441, 1443, 1455, 1461, 1477, 1480, 1483, 1485, 1491, 1507, 1508, 1521, 1525, 1595, 1602, 1613, 1617, 1647, 1649, 1650, 1654, 1672, 1673, 1676, 1687, 1699, 1710, 1712, 1716, 1725, 1730, 1748, 1777, 1803, 1868, 1907, 1943, 1953, 1957, 1961, 1974, 1977, 1979, 1982, 1983, 1987, 1992, 2022a, 2028, 2029, 2030, 2031, 2033, 2042, 2043, 2059, 2071, 2077, 2078, 2093, 2101, 2104, 2113a, 2116, 2122, 2124, 2145a, 2279, 2371, 2389, 2524, 2634, 2642, 2647, 2665, 2673, 2675, 2692, 2694, 3042, 3087, 3091, 3182a, 3185, 3196
  On Listening, 0375
  Lives of the Noble Grecians and Romans, The, xv, xviii, 0042, 0055, 0062, 0081, 0082, 0113, 0133, 0135, 0174, 0187, 0208, 0219, 0286, 0292a, 0321, 0338, 0359, 0369, 0398, 0464a, 0473, 0483, 0517, 0537, 0553, 0566, 0578, 0613, 0664, 0690, 0717, 0723, 0754, 0759a, 0762, 0806, 0807, 0873, 0886, 0914, 0919, 0936, 0941, 0973a, 0987, 0989, 0999, 1008, 1009, 1013, 1047, 1050, 1058, 1110, 1112, 1153, 1160, 1197, 1235a, 1269, 1276, 1283, 1307, 1313, 1334, 1336, 1338, 1351, 1378, 1419, 1450, 1520, 1523, 1604, 1657, 1671, 1680a, 1690, 1691, 1697, 1740a, 1754, 1988, 1999, 2001, 2005, 2011, 2013a, 2048a, 2055, 2056, 2058, 2082, 2088a, 2094, 2096, 2107, 2112a, 2199a, 2271, 2277, 2303, 2314, 2361, 2628, 2680, 2695, 2785, 3184a, 3200. *See also under* North, Sir Thomas
  Comparison of Demetrius with Antonius, The, 1468
  Life of Alcibiades, The, 0450, 2457, 2646, 2674
  Life of Alexander, The, 1918, 2022, 2123
  Life of Caius Martius Coriolanus, The, 1609, 1610, 1624, 1660, 1663, 1695, 1724, 2646
  Life of Cato Utican, The, xix, 2329, 2343
  Life of Demetrius, The, xxii, 2022, 2646, 3092
  Life of Dion, The, xxii, 2022, 3192
  Life of Julius Caesar, The, xviii, 1914, 1918, 2024, 2043, 2044, 2046, 2098, 2108
  Life of Marcus Antonius, The, xviii, 0208, 0700, 1021, 1164, 1165, 1173, 1175, 1183, 1184, 1222, 1243, 1252, 1254, 1277, 1335, 1345, 1419, 1468, 1486, 1524, 2024, 2043, 2044, 2046, 2098, 2130, 2646, 2657
  Life of Marcus Brutus, The, xviii, 0773, 2024, 2043, 2044, 2046, 2098, 2108
  Life of Marcus Cato, The, xvi, 1624
  Life of Octavius Augustus Caesar, The, 1347
  Life of Pelopidas, The, 1819, 1823, 1826, 2231a, 3090a
  Life of Pericles, The, 2364
  Life of Romulus, The, 2040
  Life of Scipio Africanus, The, 0690
  Life of Theseus, The, 2285, 2299, 3100, 3101
  Moralia, xvi, 0127, 0409, 1163, 1823, 2245, 2287, 2360, 2507, 2917
  "De Fortuna Romanorum," 2128
  "Of Isis and Osiris," xv, 0380, 0729, 1222, 1261, 1505
  "Of the Romans Fortune," 0698
  Roman Questions, 1570, 1850
Plutarch's *Lives*. See under Plutarch, *Lives of the Noble Grecians and Romans, The*
Pluto, 2285, 2286, 2555, 2931
Plutus, 2633
pneumatology, 2603
poems, by Shakespeare, xiv, 0053, 0058, 0059a, 0062, 0332, 0350, 0357, 0362, 0370, 0465, 0597, 0601, 1129
Poems, by Shakespeare
  Benson edition of 1640, 0402
Poet
  in *Julius Caesar*, 0777
  in *Sonnets*, 2481
  in *Timon of Athens*, 0076, 0264, 0349, 0372a, 0375, 0545, 0613, 0777, 0785, 0904, 0912, 1082, 2612, 2633, 2636, 2641a, 2647, 2648, 2652, 2677, 2689a

poeta figure
  in Plautus, 0214
  in Shakespeare, 0214
Poet (Another Poet)
  in *Julius Caesar*, 1015, 2112
poetic justice, 0640, 1016
poetics, 0462, 0802a, 0803
poetics of Shakespeare, 0375
poetic style, 0040
Poetomachia, 2864
poetry
  painting and, 0976, 2694, 3160
  philosophy and, 2871
poetry, narrative, 3105
poetry, Ovidian, 3153
poetry, Shakespeare's defense of, 2590, 2599
poets
  in *Julius Caesar*, 2081
poiesis, 1673
Poins
  in *Henry IV, Part 2*, 1911
point of view, 1998
poison, 1013a, 1440, 1508, 1624, 1754, 1842
policy, 0873, 0986a, 1179, 2878
political plays, by Shakespeare, 0857
politician, 0983a, 1047
politics, xiii, 0033, 0062, 0076, 0079, 0080, 0175, 0253, 0292a, 0360, 0369, 0388, 0462, 0503, 0540, 0551, 0584, 0599, 0625, 0658, 0679, 0686, 0760, 0793, 0815, 0867, 0874, 0883, 1009, 1033, 1045, 1101, 1110, 1175, 1200, 1294, 1352a, 1392, 1436, 1480, 1493, 1601, 1671a, 1703, 1734, 1775, 1824, 1954, 1985, 1990, 2036a, 2094, 2108, 2112a, 2565, 2634
  pleasure and, 0703
politics, sexual, 3090a
polity, 0082, 0850, 0864, 0873, 0999, 1000, 1123, 1719
Polixenes
  in *Winter's Tale, The*, 3179a, 3189, 3193, 3208
  in *The Winter's Tale*, 0164a
Polonius
  in *Hamlet*, 0850a, 0933, 1010, 1053, 1131, 1782, 1788, 1789a, 1790, 1803, 1806, 1815, 1822, 1835, 1841a, 1848, 1875, 1879, 1879a, 1885, 1898
Polybius, 2330
Polydore Virgil, 0699
Polyphemus, 2567
Polyxena, 2454
Pomfret Castle
  in *Richard II*, 0550
Pomona, 3090
Pompey (Gnaeus Pompeius Magnus, "The Great"), 0246, 0487, 0610, 1131, 1347, 1941, 1952, 1979, 1991, 2009, 2066, 2096, 2117, 2126, 2128, 2132, 2199a, 2444
Pompey (Sextus Pompeius)
  in *Antony and Cleopatra*, 0197, 0290, 0319b, 0700, 0909, 0927, 1021, 1032, 1164, 1171, 1172, 1174, 1175, 1188, 1253, 1280, 1323, 1366, 1375, 1383, 1425, 1442, 1443, 1460a, 1461, 1464, 1467, 1500, 1521, 1525, 1529, 2065
Pompey's statue, 2066, 2117, 2132
  in *Julius Caesar*, 0990
Pomponazzi, Pietro, 2547
Pomponius Mela
  De Situ Orbis, 1570
Poor Tom (Edgar)
  in *King Lear*, 2151, 2153, 2156, 2160
Pope, Alexander, 1519
Porphyry, 2573, 3126
portents, 0255, 0271, 0369, 0765, 2029, 2088, 2120
Portia
  in *Julius Caesar*, xvii, 0337, 0459, 0587, 0603, 0637, 0638, 0687, 0964, 1013a, 1070, 1954, 1974, 1984, 1987, 1992, 2002a, 2023, 2033, 2046, 2055, 2088, 2101, 2111, 2112, 2120, 2121, 2126
  in *Merchant of Venice, The*, 0687, 0773, 0963, 1070, 2247, 2248, 2251, 2253, 2254, 2257, 2258
  in *The Merchant of Venice*, 0214
Portia (wife of Marcus Brutus), 0773, 2257
Pory, John
  translation of *The History and Description of Africa*, by John Leo Africanus, 0609
Poseidon, 1576
Posthumus Leonatus, 1774
  in *Cymbeline*, 0290, 0437, 0781, 1048, 1754, 1755, 1763, 1772, 1773, 1775, 1777
Poussin, Nicolas
  Et in Arcadia Ego, 1553
power, 0079, 0086, 0095, 0160b, 0172, 0191, 0212, 0228, 0232, 0332, 0358, 0397, 0599, 0632, 0652, 0679, 0703, 0721, 0743, 0765, 0775, 0793, 0802a, 0849, 0883, 0900, 1044, 1045, 1058, 1087, 1117, 1122, 1152, 1156, 1157, 1228, 1232, 1239, 1241, 1247, 1263, 1330, 1333, 1363, 1408, 1420, 1422, 1423, 1436, 1446, 1480, 1524, 1596, 1605, 1617, 1644, 1669, 1693, 1717, 1736, 1834a, 1944, 1948, 1966, 1972, 2018, 2038, 2057, 2069, 2085a, 2093, 2097, 2127, 2131, 2159, 2232a, 2413, 2416, 2726, 2804
power, female, 2758
power, patriarchal, 2766
power, political, 2713
power, Roman, 2746
power, royal, 2583
praeceptor amoris, 0269
praenomen, 1481
praeteritio, 2037
praise, 0501, 0848a, 0894, 1810, 2565
prayer, 2183
prayers, 3098
precious stones, 0490
present, 0691, 1318a, 1343, 2806, 2807
  past and, 1529, 1844, 1965
presenter, 0353, 0373
pre-Socratics, 0134
  physis, 2140

Index of Subjects

Preston, Thomas
  Cambises, 2205
Priam, 0080a, 0208, 0297, 0721, 0789, 0919, 1805, 1806, 1808, 1817, 1830, 1835, 1837, 1841, 1845, 1854, 1868, 1880, 1883, 1889, 1892, 2216
  in *Troilus and Cressida*, 0994, 2927
priamel, 0875
Priapus, 0720a
pride, 0172a, 0206, 0239, 0255, 0329, 0334, 0369, 0458, 0493, 0553, 0664, 0779, 0876, 0909, 0927, 0986a, 1252, 1620, 1632, 1673, 1734, 1771, 1956, 2007, 2013a, 2030, 2205, 2256, 2431, 2447, 2631, 2720, 2858, 2907, 2910, 2936, 2985, 3015
Primaudaye, Peter de la
  French Academie, The, 0601
Primaudaye, Pierre de la, 2682
  French Academic, 1063
primitivism, 2559
Princess of France
  in *Love's Labor's Lost*, 0963
prisoners, 1663
private life, 0057
private man, 1101
problem comedies, by Shakespeare, 0062, 0418, 0997, 2850
problem plays, by Shakespeare, 0365, 0369, 0932, 1052, 1065, 1407, 2930, 2971, 3000, 3047, 3056, 3064
Proclus, xv, 2585
  commentary on *First Alcibiades*, by Plato, 1531
Procne, 0283, 2757
Procopius, 2785
procreation, 1044, 2494
Procris, 0132
Proculeius
  in *Antony and Cleopatra*, 1174, 1175, 1183, 1283
prodigality, 0012, 0201, 0983a, 2248, 2610, 2631, 2633, 2657, 2685
prodigal son, 0860
Prologue
  in *Troilus and Cressida*, 0829a, 2795, 2796, 2810, 2815, 2837, 2838, 2845, 2859, 2861, 2864, 2886, 2925, 2927, 2928, 2947, 2981, 2986, 2992, 2994, 3027, 3033
prologue, 0829a
prologues and epilogues in *Troilus and Cressida*, 2945a
Prometheus, 0096, 1539, 1757, 2162, 2442
promises, 0465a
pronuntiatio, 2455a
propagation, 3121, 3122, 3134
properties, 0994
Propertius, Sextus, 1417, 1524
property, women as, 3058
prophecies, 0271, 0424, 0873
prophecy, 0347, 0368, 0881, 1128, 1130, 1318a, 1717, 1777, 2070, 2225, 2569a, 2872, 2985
prophecy, inverted, 2966
propositio, 0433

propriety, 1775
prose fiction, 0023a
prose of Shakespeare, 0002, 0116, 1072
Proserpina, xvii, 0095, 0307, 0375, 0721, 0807, 0830, 1163, 1938, 2283, 2286, 2317, 2357, 3170, 3178, 3180, 3190, 3193, 3195
Proserpine, 2285, 2555, 2560, 2560a, 3183, 3188, 3200
prose style, 0040
prosody, 0710, 1245
Prospero
  in *Tempest, The*, 0078, 0080a, 0096, 0119, 0153, 0214, 0282a, 0288, 0290, 0294, 0311, 0326, 0336, 0421, 0495, 0499, 0536, 0577, 0581, 0721, 0759b, 0781, 0814, 0822, 0828a, 0850, 0892, 0899, 0900, 0933, 0936, 0951, 0997, 1044a, 1085a, 1092, 1114, 1134, 1144, 1149a, 1182, 2544, 2545, 2546, 2546a, 2547, 2548, 2550, 2554, 2558, 2560, 2560a, 2561, 2562, 2562a, 2562b, 2563, 2565a, 2566, 2568, 2569, 2570a, 2573, 2576, 2578a, 2582, 2583, 2585, 2587, 2588, 2589, 2590, 2591, 2592, 2593, 2594, 2596, 2598, 2599, 2600, 2604, 2605, 2606, 2607, 2892
Prostitute Priestess, 2362
prostitutes, 1887
  in *Timon of Athens*, 0941
prostitution, 2690, 2691, 2703
protasis (element of drama), 1079, 2548
protasis-epitasis-catastrophe structure, 2304
Protestants, 0763
Proteus, xxii, 0119, 0466, 1893a, 3090
  in *Two Gentlemen of Verona, The*, 0441, 0690, 3088, 3090
proverb, 0569, 1907, 2068a
proverbs, 0040, 0162, 0262, 0610, 0993, 1725, 1815
Providence (providence), 0081, 0215, 0252, 0400, 0589, 0596, 0635, 0664, 0730, 0973, 0978, 1130, 1139, 1567, 1757, 1791, 1796, 1839, 1847, 1848, 1851, 1860, 1878, 1943, 2077, 2154, 2157, 2178, 2245, 2261, 2359, 2367, 2458, 2462, 2474, 2569a, 2716, 2729a, 2742, 3091
providentialism, xxii, 1193, 2853
provocatio, 1080
Prudence, 2528
prudence, xx, 0091, 0172, 0262, 0782, 1399, 1400, 2461, 3028
Prudentius (Aurelius Prudentius Clemens), 0124, 1175
  Psychomachia, 2205
Psalms. *See under* Bible
Psellus, Michael, 2603
Pseudo-Aristotle
  Problemata Physica, 1149a
pseudo-classical tragedies, by Shakespeare, 0059
pseudo-Dionysius, 0101
Pseudolus
  in *Pseudolus*, by Plautus, 0214
Psyche, 1051, 1053, 1884, 1885, 1886, 2298, 2301, 2350, 2698

psychetypes, 1496
psychiatry, 0346
psychoanalysis, 0549
psychoanalytic criticism, 0063
psychology, 0002, 0033, 0091, 0124, 0218, 0328, 0331, 0386a, 0453, 0469, 0478, 0488, 0520, 0565, 0601, 0606, 0658, 0831, 0941, 0945, 0961, 1022, 1149a, 1150, 1175, 1243, 1856, 1904, 2071, 2412, 2626, 2627, 2644
psychomachia, 0799, 0868, 1475
psychomatics, 0738
psychopathology, 0346
Ptolemy (Claudius Ptolemaeus), 0480, 1535, 2208a
Tetrabiblos, 2176
public life, 0057
public sphere, 0218
Publius (son of Mark Antony's sister), 2130
Puck
  in *Midsummer Night's Dream, A*, 0087, 0119, 0190, 0881, 1085a, 2290, 2297, 2298, 2305
pudicitia, 0587
pun, 1072, 2883
punishment, 2216, 2571, 2599, 2607, 2716
punning, 0891
puns, 0195a, 1003, 1010, 1789a
purgation, 1847
purification, 2571
Puritans, 2085
purity, 2014, 2362
Puttenham, George, 0479, 0837
Pygmalion, xxii, 0721, 0888a, 3172, 3189, 3189a, 3191, 3198, 3200, 3204
pygmies, 0088
Pylades, 1876
Pyramus, 2249, 2274
  in *Midsummer Night's Dream, A*, 2311
Pyramus and Thisbe, 0325, 0685, 2331, 2465, 2468
  in *Midsummer Night's Dream, A*, xix, 0119, 0209, 0379, 0721, 0727, 0928, 0967, 1134, 1277, 2269, 2271, 2277, 2280, 2281, 2282, 2285, 2291, 2297, 2302, 2304, 2305, 2307, 2309, 2312, 2314, 2315
  in *Romeo and Juliet*, 2475c
Pyrocles, 2371
Pyrrha, 3172
Pyrrhonism, 0945, 1428, 2088
Pyrrhus, 0080a, 0246, 0721, 0806, 0835, 0919, 1800, 1802, 1804, 1805, 1806, 1830, 1832, 1840, 1845, 1854, 1868, 1880, 1883, 1889, 1892, 1897
  in *Hamlet*, 1799, 1817
Pythagoras, 0241, 0266, 0336, 0528, 0547a, 0699, 0968, 0995, 1838, 2253a, 2482, 2523, 2551a, 2740

Q
Queen
  in *Cymbeline*, 1754, 1757, 1774
Queen Mab, 0154, 0862, 1022, 2466
Quickly, Mistress
  in *Merry Wives of Windsor, The*, 2266. See *also* Hostess
Quince, Peter
  in *Midsummer Night's Dream, A*, xix, 2302, 2312
Quintilian (Marcus Fabius Quintilianus), 0270, 0326, 0353, 0470, 0479, 0529, 0557, 0610, 0611, 0643, 0674, 0695, 0728, 0759a, 0835, 0905, 0907, 0938, 1061, 1064, 1097, 1189, 1606, 1810, 1813, 1853, 1857, 1920, 1999, 2037, 2276, 2963, 3005
Institutio Oratoria (Institutes of Oratory), 0404, 0809, 1784, 1856
Quintus
  in *Titus Andronicus*, 0792

R
Rabelais, François, 0191, 1324
race, 0703
Racine, Jean Baptiste, 0793, 1827
rage, 0191, 1677, 1918, 1923
Rainolde, Richard
  Foundacion of Rhetorike, 2998a
Rainolds, Richard, 0145
Raleigh, Sir Walter, 1535, 2284
Ralph Roister Doister, by Nicholas Udall. See *under* Udall, Nicholas
rape, xix, xxi, 0029, 0133, 0179, 0238, 0283, 0319a, 0347a, 0446, 0850, 0863, 0987, 1024, 1045, 1048, 1071, 1141, 2203, 2362, 2393, 2395, 2397, 2403, 2409, 2413, 2414, 2421, 2426, 2433, 2434, 2437, 2440, 2583, 2718b, 2721, 2723, 2727, 2736, 2738, 2754, 2758, 2762, 2763, 2766, 2777a, 2779a, 2783, 2789
rape, oral, 3155
rapes, 0654
Rare Triumphs of Love and Fortune, The, 0997, 1763
rationalism, 1027, 1367, 1514, 2288a
rationality, 1414, 1427, 2101, 2398a
realism, 0089, 0102, 0369, 0370a, 0378, 0396, 0640, 0811, 0835, 1060, 1114, 1185, 1193, 1226, 1238, 1328, 1406, 1677, 2053, 2138, 2489, 2692, 2775a, 2858a, 2866, 2914, 2922, 2946, 3071
realities, 1734
reality, 0237, 0252, 0425, 0555, 0601, 0665, 0679, 0872, 0873, 0874, 0973a, 0981, 0988, 1047, 1061, 1067, 1076, 1081, 1082, 1110, 1121, 1174, 1214, 1228, 1273a, 1288, 1368, 1379, 1444, 1462, 1514, 1710, 1713, 1715, 1846, 1883, 1976, 2007, 2033, 2174, 2188, 2306, 2313, 2411, 2551, 2570a, 2731, 2747, 2849, 3067, 3129
  appearance and, 1138, 1857, 2320, 2835, 2911, 3015, 3074, 3175
  illusion and, 2607
  language and, 2889
  myth and, 2890a
Reason
  in *Phoenix and Turtle, The*, 2378, 2379, 2382, 2384, 2385

Index of Subjects

reason, 0096, 0174, 0180, 0280, 0319b, 0336, 0370a, 0375, 0384, 0513, 0601, 0622, 0625, 0630, 0655, 0656, 0662, 0903, 0905, 0945, 0961, 0962, 0981, 0982, 0983a, 1027, 1092, 1093a, 1196, 1322, 1369, 1436, 1446, 1543c, 1775, 1796, 1825, 1827, 1904, 1943, 1997, 2022a, 2068, 2071, 2083, 2088, 2120, 2122, 2144, 2243, 2244, 2252, 2289, 2306, 2334, 2383, 2395, 2412, 2547, 2568, 2631, 2794, 2815, 2817, 2894, 2921, 2955
  love and, 0832
  passion and, 0729
  will and, 2157
rebellion, 1951a, 1988, 2997
recapitulation, 2945a
recognition (as concept or element of drama), 0128, 0412, 0484, 0535, 0579, 0600, 0795, 1091, 2142, 2356, 3141
reconciliation, 0759b, 1654, 2606, 2637, 2658, 2692, 2704, 2716, 3181
redemption, 0723
refutatio, 0433
Regan
  in *King Lear*, 0879, 2139, 2154, 2161a
regeneration, 2051, 2551
Regius, Raphael
  notes to Ovid's *Metamorphoses*, 1042a
relativism, 1492, 2929
relativity, 2859
religion, 0033, 0079, 0080, 0107, 0391, 0669, 0943
Rembrandt Harmensz van Rijn, 1122, 2392
representation, 0819, 2821
republicanism, 2132
  in *Julius Caesar*, 0175
reputation, 0070a, 0113, 0133, 0249, 0642, 0955, 1174, 1248, 2008, 2351, 2405, 2949
resurrection, 0431, 0730, 1114
retribution, 2450
reunion, 1466, 3183
revelry, 0700, 1500
Revenge
  in *Titus Andronicus*, 1044a
revenge, xiv, xxi, 0069, 0102, 0106, 0123, 0133, 0191, 0238, 0246, 0247, 0329, 0368, 0369, 0381, 0409, 0442, 0534, 0547, 0549, 0566a, 0613, 0626, 0685, 0717, 0723, 0745, 0792, 0831, 0917, 0921, 0955, 0963, 1050, 1095, 1115, 1124, 1183, 1221a, 1603, 1654, 1669, 1752, 1798, 1798a, 1806, 1836, 1837, 1839, 1840, 1842, 1851, 1859, 1862, 1864, 1870, 1876, 1878, 1880, 2035, 2036, 2117, 2118, 2346, 2419, 2714, 2718, 2721, 2725, 2726, 2729b, 2740, 2744, 2749, 2751, 2775, 2784, 2788, 2789, 2877
revenger, 0222, 0368, 0789, 1291, 1832, 1845
revengers, 0607
Revenger's Tragedy, The. See under Tourneur, Cyril
reversal (as concept or element of drama), 0182, 0412, 0860
revolt, 1135
Rhea, 2734

rhetoric, xii, xiv, xviii, 0022, 0028, 0034, 0040, 0076, 0129, 0145, 0186, 0187, 0191, 0204, 0206, 0223, 0228, 0236, 0238a, 0270, 0281, 0286, 0294, 0296, 0299, 0315, 0319, 0332, 0334, 0353a, 0363, 0368, 0372a, 0376, 0404, 0408, 0418, 0470, 0501, 0508, 0588, 0599, 0611, 0621, 0661, 0665, 0685, 0721, 0759a, 0767, 0830, 0831, 0835, 0868, 0894, 0914, 0916, 0938, 0979, 0985a, 1034, 1072, 1073, 1074, 1097, 1135, 1205, 1395, 1554, 1620, 1646, 1784, 1810, 1856, 1857, 1874, 1999, 2006, 2022a, 2037, 2047, 2051a, 2052, 2061, 2062, 2075, 2089, 2173a, 2304, 2325, 2337, 2340a, 2362, 2398a, 2421, 2433, 2434, 2440a, 2443, 2455a, 2466, 2525, 2527a, 2565, 2684, 2747, 2784, 2829, 2910, 3038, 3067, 3098, 3108, 3168
rhetoric, Ciceronian, 2741
rhetoric, decay-of-the-world, 2694
rhetoric, figures of, xix, 0204, 0821, 1074, 1080, 1633, 1999, 2185a, 2323, 2421, 2466, 2482, 2512, 2527a
rhetoric, forensic, 2729b
rhetoric, handbooks of, 0107, 0801, 2513, 2926
rhetoric, Ovidian, 2731, 2789a
rhetoric, passionate, 3052
Rhetorica ad Herennium, 2245a
rhetorical theory, 1565
rhetorical training of Shakespeare, 0610
rhetorical treatises, 0059
rhetorician, 0332, 0529
rhetoricians, 0332, 0335, 0353, 0479, 0557, 0692, 0864, 0877, 1080
rhetorics, 16th-century, 0025
rhetors, Roman, 2729b
Richard, later Duke of Gloucester and then Richard III, 0998
  in *Henry VI, Part 3*, 0466, 0985a, 1937a
  in *Henry VI Triad*, 0894
  in *Richard III*, 0093, 0136, 0175, 0234, 0323, 0517, 0610, 0662, 0895, 0905, 2454, 2455, 2457, 2458
Richard II
  in *Richard II*, 0078, 0331, 0375, 0442, 0468, 0517, 0550, 0635, 1093a, 1139, 1640, 2441, 2443, 2444, 2445, 2447, 2448, 2450, 2452
  in *Richard II-Henry V* tetralogy, 2136
Riche, Barnabe
  Apollonius and Silla, 0092
  Riche his Farewell to Militarie Profession
  "Of Apolonius and Silla," 3076
Richmond
  in *Richard III*, xx, 0093
riddles, 1780
Ripa, Cesare
  Iconologia, 1086
ripeness, 1543c, 2180
ritual, 0023, 0059a, 0061, 0178, 0240, 0282, 0352, 0492, 0492a, 0551, 0585, 0711, 0865, 1047, 1811, 1987a, 2029, 2040, 2059, 2743b, 2744, 2775a, 2977, 3072
ritual, pagan, 3095
ritualism, xviii
ritualization, 0940a, 1983b

rituals, 1811, 1866
rituals, patriarchal, 2976
rivalry, 2002
Rivers, Earl (Anthony Woodville, 2nd Earl Rivers)
Dictes and Sayings of the Philosophers, 0450
Roberts, James, 2992
Robespierre, François Maximilien Joseph de, 0523
Robin Goodfellow (Puck)
in *Midsummer Night's Dream, A,* 2310
Robinson, R.
Golden Mirrour, A, 1833
Roderigo
in *Othello,* 2348
Rojas, Fernando de
Celestina, La, 1594
role-playing, 1172, 1231, 1254, 1291, 1671a, 1734a, 2136, 3082
Roman Britain, 1770
romance, 0384
romance, pastoral, 3182
romance, Roman, 0510
romance (as concept or genre), 0092, 0114, 0157, 0165, 0189, 0281, 0308, 0311, 0311a, 0326, 0382, 0386, 0415, 0435, 0465a, 0721, 0822, 0922, 0923, 1050, 1114, 1151, 1162, 1221a, 1537, 1540, 1578, 1761, 1762, 2177, 2365, 2556, 2594, 2608, 3101, 3199
romances, 0023a, 0308
romances, by Shakespeare, xi, xiv, 0002, 0024, 0037, 0049, 0052, 0053, 0059a, 0062, 0123, 0151, 0160a, 0178, 0208, 0262, 0282, 0311, 0311a, 0312, 0336, 0349, 0362, 0369, 0376, 0382, 0405, 0406, 0413, 0435, 0468, 0581, 0593, 0619, 0636, 0646, 0649, 0694, 0719, 0723, 0730, 0749, 0769, 0794, 0807a, 0814, 0871, 0891, 0922, 0945, 0966, 0990, 0997, 1052, 1072, 1094, 1125, 1133, 1162, 1241, 1342, 1407, 1498, 1654, 1754, 1938, 2428, 2556, 3097, 3188, 3200
romance(s), Greek, xiv, xvi, 0037, 0067, 0068, 0173, 0183, 0284, 0307, 0382, 0415, 0418, 0434, 0590, 0730, 0769, 0771, 0794, 0814, 0997, 1035, 1114, 1125, 1759, 2354, 2359, 2371, 3175, 3205
Roman Church, 0763
Roman drama, 0208, 0491, 0985a
Roman dramas, by Shakespeare, 0646
Romane Historie, The, by Titus Livius. See under Livy (Titus Livius)
Roman Empire, 0057, 0239, 0255, 0338, 0359, 0587, 0628, 0629, 0750, 0759a, 0805, 0850, 1909, 1943, 2003, 2056, 2717, 2785
Roman Empire, Holy, 1945, 2717
Roman heroes of Shakespeare, 0612
Roman historians, 0587, 0864, 1610
Roman histories, 0102
Roman history, 0002, 0012, 0057, 0070, 0071, 0080a, 0186, 0201, 0210, 0219, 0237, 0261, 0285, 0314, 0384, 0587, 0684, 0750, 0756, 0778, 0840, 0852, 0973, 1013, 1443, 1710,
1754, 1758, 1985, 2011, 2056, 2087, 2127, 2128
Roman History, by Livy. See under Livy (Titus Livius), *History of Rome*
Roman history plays, 0070
Roman ideals, 1655
Romanitas, xiii, 0587, 1101, 2011, 2024, 2772
Roman literature, 0114, 0610
Roman names
Ben Jonson and, 0103
Shakespeare and, 0103
Romanness, 1184
Romano, Giulio, 0891
Romano, Julio, 1082, 2432
Roman people, 0232
in *Julius Caesar,* 0142a
Roman plays, by Shakespeare, x, xiii, 0009, 0034, 0041, 0057, 0076, 0079, 0080a, 0081, 0113, 0137, 0170, 0175, 0186, 0200, 0218, 0227, 0239, 0255, 0261, 0263, 0265, 0360, 0372a, 0383, 0397, 0410, 0452, 0456, 0463, 0464, 0494, 0495, 0544, 0566, 0588, 0599, 0610, 0632, 0636, 0656, 0676, 0677, 0679, 0684, 0701, 0717, 0721, 0723, 0743, 0749, 0754, 0755, 0778, 0831, 0839, 0840, 0886, 0919, 0936, 0973, 0981, 1010, 1013, 1047, 1058, 1111, 1112, 1128, 1135, 1143, 1175, 1294, 1428, 1716, 2621, 2719, 2744
Roman Republic, 0057, 0080, 0123, 0129, 0210, 0219, 0239, 0622, 0750, 0778, 0850, 0851, 0932, 1596, 1649, 1695, 1882, 1895, 1945, 1949, 1952, 1954, 2003, 2056, 2112a, 2113, 2425
Romans, 0080a, 0081, 0113, 0186, 0208, 0239, 0299, 0332, 0381, 0489, 0517, 0607, 0612, 0613, 0690, 0742, 0759, 0833, 0927, 1291, 1292, 1309, 1462, 1492, 1600, 1660, 1753, 1768
Goths and, 2717
in *Titus Andronicus,* 1152
romanticism, 1009
Roman tragedies, by Shakespeare, 0113, 0171, 0279, 0584, 0805, 0844, 0906, 0980, 1021
Roman values, 1609
Roman works, by Shakespeare, 0104, 0654, 0655, 0759a
Roman world, 0081, 0135, 0638, 0778, 2013
Rome, xi, xiii, xvii, 0029, 0057, 0080, 0081, 0082, 0102, 0106, 0129, 0137, 0141, 0172, 0178, 0186, 0189, 0200, 0201, 0203, 0232, 0239, 0255, 0261, 0293, 0318, 0332, 0337, 0347, 0357, 0358, 0365, 0372, 0380a, 0381, 0384, 0409, 0413, 0423, 0432, 0434, 0441, 0443, 0446, 0459, 0463, 0547a, 0566, 0587, 0593, 0594, 0599, 0607, 0610, 0613, 0622, 0633, 0641, 0645, 0654, 0655, 0656, 0664, 0678, 0698, 0700, 0702, 0705, 0721, 0759a, 0765, 0831, 0832a, 0836, 0841, 0850, 0869, 0873, 0882, 0911, 0932, 0978, 0980, 0992, 0998, 1008, 1009, 1039, 1050, 1058, 1083, 1123, 1129, 1135, 1141, 1143, 1147, 1164, 1167, 1175, 1178, 1180, 1185, 1196a, 1211, 1213, 1225, 1228, 1229, 1239, 1247, 1253,

Index of Subjects

1280, 1283, 1302, 1326, 1327, 1333, 1340, 1341, 1349, 1352, 1362, 1405, 1415, 1418, 1419, 1420, 1428, 1459, 1461, 1466, 1467, 1480, 1483, 1500, 1502, 1503, 1509, 1511, 1514, 1517, 1523, 1524, 1528, 1590, 1591, 1593, 1613, 1618, 1626, 1629, 1631, 1635, 1644, 1661, 1670, 1681, 1682, 1690, 1701, 1702, 1704, 1710, 1715, 1716, 1718, 1719, 1726, 1732, 1736, 1741, 1741a, 1748, 1753, 1759, 1761, 1765, 1771, 1774, 1776, 1780, 1803, 1813, 1887, 1912, 1942, 1948, 1949, 1950, 1952, 1954, 1965, 1970, 1972, 1976, 1984, 1986, 1987a, 1988, 1990, 2002, 2007, 2014, 2024, 2040, 2042, 2061, 2074, 2088a, 2092, 2097, 2099, 2136, 2395a, 2489, 2634, 2713, 2716, 2727, 2729, 2740, 2750, 2762, 2770, 2774, 2779a, 2783, 2785, 2789a, 2804
  Alexandria and, 0927, 0935
Romeo
  in *Romeo and Juliet*, 0181, 0385, 0978, 1126, 2463, 2464, 2468, 2471, 2472, 2475a
Rosalind
  in *As You Like It*, 0687, 0828, 0833, 0963, 0987, 1081, 1085a, 1533, 1543c, 1543a, 1554, 1555, 1557, 1558, 1560, 2818
Rosencrantz
  in *Hamlet*, 1021, 1814a, 1843, 1896
Rowe, Nicholas, 0403, 0937
royalty, 1966
rule, 0239
ruler, 0796, 1330, 1330a, 1377, 1399, 1436, 1466, 1521, 2593
rulers, 1142
Rumor
  in *Henry IV, Part 2*, 0829a, 0994
rumor, 0505, 2327
Rutland, Earl of
  in *Henry VI, Part 3*, 0152

S

Sachs, Hans, 1468
Sackville, Thomas, and Thomas Norton
  Gorbuduc, 2749
sacrifice, 0255, 0302, 0307, 0352, 0442, 0475, 0492, 0492a, 0542, 0610, 0613, 0759a, 1191, 1299, 1375, 1623, 1757, 1793, 1866, 1941, 1950, 1983a, 2009, 2029, 2034, 2040, 2716
sage, 1179
Sagittarius, 2330
saint, 0080, 0208
Saint-Ravy, Jean de
  Agamemnon, 1876
Salerio
  in *Merchant of Venice, The*, 1006
Sallust (Gaius Sallustius Crispus), 0363, 0841, 0916, 0936, 0938, 2047
  Bellum Catilinae, 1869b
Salmacis, 0685, 0863, 2353, 2540, 3085a, 3137, 3159
Salmoneus, 2588
Sandys, George, 3183
  commentary on Ovid's *Metamorphoses*, 0126
  Ovid's Metamorphoses Englished,
    Mythologiz'd, and Represented in Figures, 2208
  translation of Ovid's *Metamorphoses*, xviii, 2567
Santa Claus, 0523
Sappho, 0875
Saris, Captain John, 1456
satire, 0075, 0157, 0160b, 0187, 0238a, 0258, 0320, 0378, 0657, 0742, 0756, 0821a, 0836, 0838, 0882, 0891, 0934, 1094, 1621, 1660, 1831, 1910, 2595, 2620, 2628, 2666, 2693, 2707, 2811, 2822, 2864, 2961, 2986, 2992, 3005, 3006, 3007, 3009, 3023, 3038, 3056, 3069, 3157
satire, tragic, 2908, 3021
satires, 0147, 0148
satirist, 0163, 0838, 1139, 2675
Saturn, 0596, 1531, 1535, 1547, 1824, 1911, 2526, 2734, 2764
saturnalian experience, 0160b
Saturninus
  in *Titus Andronicus*, 2727, 2728, 2734, 2739, 2755, 2762, 2764, 2779b
satyr, 0118
satyr plays, 2595
savage, 2544, 2546, 2559
savagery, 1152, 1771, 2718, 2722
Savile, Sir Henry
  translation of Tacitus's *Histories*, 1937b
Saxo Grammaticus, 1834
  Gesta Danorum, 1811
  Historia Danica, 1882
Scaliger, Julius Caesar, 0610
  Poetics (Poeticae), 0228, 2548
scapegoat, 0492, 1615, 1622
scapegoats, 2265
Scarus
  in *Antony and Cleopatra*, 1175, 1324, 1328, 1369, 1424, 1484a
scene, 1315
scenes, choric, 1746
schemes of rhetoric, 0223, 0611, 1072, 1074
scholasticism, 0532, 0948
Scholasticus, Marianus
  epigram in the Greek Anthology, 2521
schoolmaster, 0084
schoolmasters, 0821a
science, 0488, 0834
  art and, 1016
Scipio (Publius Cornelius Scipio Aemilianus), 0487
Scot, Reginald, 2236
  Discoverie of Witchcraft, The, 0119, 2288, 2299
scriptural allusions, 0215
Scripture, 0954
sculpture, 0990, 1082, 3172
Scythians, 2145a
seasons, four, 2618
Sebastian
  in *Tempest, The*, 2553, 2557, 2565a, 2566a, 2588, 2588a
  in *Twelfth Night*, 0307, 3075, 3082, 3085

Second Citizen
  in *Coriolanus*, 1606, 1651
Second Folio of Shakespeare's plays, 0402
seeming, 1757
Sejanus, 2358
Selden, John
  Duello or Single Combat, The, 2699
Seleucus
  in *Antony and Cleopatra*, 1196a, 1216, 1454, 1473
self, 0191, 1109, 1117, 2076
self-authorship, 1679
self-awareness, 0799, 2643, 2961
self-consciousness, 1450
self-control, 0903, 1086, 1093a, 1630
self-deception, 0831, 1636, 1970
self-difference, 3012
self-interest, 2951
self-knowledge, xvii, 0208, 0234, 0386a, 0521, 0553, 0559, 0607, 0719, 0751, 0880, 0961, 1029, 1057, 1081, 1174, 1657, 1940, 1992, 1997, 2100, 2162, 2189, 2239, 2448, 2531, 2656, 2658, 2948, 3065
self-love, 0497, 2256
self-mastery, 1044
self-recognition, 1730
self-sacrifice, 1602
self-sufficiency, xix, 0909, 1111, 1175, 1249, 1590, 1592, 2334, 2634, 2853
senate
  in *Coriolanus*, 1644
senators
  in *Coriolanus*, 1701
  in *Timon of Athens*, 0201, 1123, 2639, 2656, 2684
Seneca, Lucius Annaeus ("The Elder"), 2362
Seneca, Lucius Annaeus ("The Younger"), xiv, xviii, xxi, 0011, 0012, 0013, 0033, 0038, 0056, 0072, 0086, 0107, 0123, 0191, 0208, 0238, 0247, 0254, 0263, 0270, 0320, 0363, 0368, 0369, 0409, 0418, 0470, 0488, 0534, 0546, 0582, 0583, 0597, 0607, 0620, 0624, 0721, 0751, 0780, 0829, 0829a, 0835, 0863, 0881, 0909, 0909a, 0917, 0919, 0955, 0956, 0978, 0986c, 0992, 1005, 1023, 1037, 1108, 1118, 1123, 1124, 1139, 1153, 1175, 1428, 1468, 1548, 1571, 1820, 1834a, 1839, 1858, 1878, 1880, 1970, 2028, 2096, 2150, 2173, 2173a, 2177, 2179a, 2245, 2287, 2430, 2455a, 2456, 2505, 2524, 2718b, 2729a, 2749, 2763, 2995
  Agamemnon, 0610, 2203, 2206
  De Beneficiis, 2704, 3208
  De Clementia, 1925, 2125
  Epistles, xvi, 1809, 2250
  Hercules Furens, xix, 0519a, 0721, 0772, 1035, 1086, 1867, 2229, 2231, 2294, 2339, 2454, 2735
  Hercules Oetaeus, 1043, 1086, 1931a, 2218
  Hippolytus, 1039, 2271, 2294, 2303, 2454, 3083
  Medea, xviii, 0191, 0610, 2206, 2209, 2216, 2217, 2271, 2294, 2475b
  Moral Epistles, 1833
  Moral Essays, 1650
  Oedipus, 1872, 2160, 2216, 2271, 2294
  Seneca: His Tenne Tragedies, 0003, 2160, 2749
  Ten Tragedies, 2459
  Thyestes, 0073, 0191, 0322a, 0610, 0613, 0666, 1095, 2215, 2250, 2294, 2710, 2727, 2728, 2734, 2735, 2743b, 2785
  Troades, 0610, 1115, 2454
  Troas, 2216
  Workes (1620)
    Epistle LVIII, 0127
Senecan drama, 0136, 1869
Senecan elements, 0202, 0368
Senecan influence, 0028, 0031, 0218
Senecan plays, 0158
Senecan tragedy, 0191, 2161
senex, 0556, 0891, 2181
senex iratus, 0995
Senior, Duke
  in *As You Like It*, 0814
sense, banquet of, 0627, 2537, 3118
senses, five, 2633, 2702, 2703
senses, Neoplatonic hierarchy of, 3107
senses, *paragone* of, 3126a
senses, power of the, 3126a
sensuality, 0283, 0409, 0437, 0700, 0705, 0967, 1175, 1191, 1484, 1887, 2191, 2293, 2431, 2537, 2638
sententiae, 0262, 0332, 0829, 0830, 2138
Sententiae Pueriles, 0938
seriousness, tragic, 3006
serpent, 0409, 0759a, 1000, 1159, 1188, 1204, 1358, 1362, 1368, 1485, 1515, 1541, 2298
serpents, 119, 0255, 1171, 1261, 1440
Sertorius, Quintus, 1008
Servant
  in *Troilus and Cressida*, 0879
servant, 0225, 0239
  master and, 1105
servant figures, 0214
servant of Aufidius
  in *Coriolanus*, 1663
servants, 1137
Servants, in Induction of *Taming of the Shrew, The*, 1107
servingmen
  in *Coriolanus*, 1697
Servius Grammaticus (Marius Servius Honoratus), 0753
servus, 0556
Setebos
  in *The Tempest*, 0096
Seth, 2569a
setting, Athenian, 3103
setting, classical, 3096
setting, Greek, 3097
setting (as concept or element of drama), 1133, 1309, 1571, 1704, 2146a, 2283
Severus, Alexander, 2243
sex, 0160, 0237, 0377c, 1095
  war and, 1601
sexes, 0644

Index of Subjects

sexuality, xiv, 0118, 0237, 0286, 0404, 0512, 0602, 0630, 0701, 0814, 0824, 0900, 1045, 1199, 1265, 1273, 1318, 1319, 1326a, 1330, 1361, 1365, 1368, 1470, 1517, 1530, 1601, 1887, 2143, 2265, 2266a, 2284, 2400, 2596, 2758, 2793, 2952, 2993, 2999, 3019
  textuality and, 2938
sexuality, female, 3037
sexuality, women's, 3026
shadow, 0431
  substance and, 2499, 2724
Shakespeare's comedies. *See* comedies, by Shakespeare
Shakespeare's histories. *See* history plays, by Shakespeare
Shakespeare's history plays. *See* history plays, by Shakespeare
Shakespeare's poems. *See* poems, by Shakespeare
Shakespeare's prose. *See* prose of Shakespeare
Shakespeare's romances. *See* romances, by Shakespeare
Shakespeare's Roman plays. *See* Roman plays, by Shakespeare
Shakespeare's romantic comedies. *See* romantic comedies, by Shakespeare
Shakespeare's tragedies. *See* tragedies, by Shakespeare
Shallow
  in *Henry IV, Part 2*, 1912
shame, 1217a, 1233
Shaw, George Bernard, 1226, 1981
  Caesar and Cleopatra, 0668
Shepherd
  in *Winter's Tale, The*, 3184
Sheridan, Richard
  School for Scandal, The, 2655
shipwreck, 1580
Shuler, Georg
  Metamorphosis or Poetic Fables, 2557
Shylock
  in *Merchant of Venice, The*, 2247, 2248, 2250, 2258, 2259, 2265
Sicinius
  in *Coriolanus*, 0388, 1593, 1623, 1639
Sidney, Sir Philip, 0111, 0211, 0375, 0394, 0485, 0504, 0515, 0610, 0837, 0973a, 0997, 1762, 1813, 1841, 1919, 2288a, 2313, 3110
  Apology for Poetry, An, 1511, 1782
  Arcadia, 1035, 1549, 2025, 2154, 2371, 2470
  Astrophil and Stella, 0120, 2185, 2229, 2245a, 2500
  Defence of Poesie, The, 1144
sight, 0627, 2224, 2225
silence, 0240, 0632, 0911, 1685
Silenos, 0720a
Silenus, 1822
Silenus box, 0109
Silvia
  in *Two Gentlemen of Verona, The*, 3090
sin, 0723, 2391
singing, 1366
Sinon, 0347a, 0505, 1776, 2402, 2411, 2422
sins, seven capital, 2373

Sins, Seven Deadly, 2981
Sir Andrew Aguecheek
  in *Twelfth Night*, 0515
Sirens, 0316
Sir Orfeo, 2365
Sir Thomas More, 0598
Sir Toby Belch
  in *Twelfth Night*, 0515
Sir Topas (Feste)
  in *Twelfth Night*, 0490
sister, 0225, 1575, 1581
  brother and, 1114
Skelton, John
  Magnyfycence, 2660
skepticism, 0156, 0192, 0244, 0259, 0349, 0945, 1212a, 1428, 1482, 1842, 1997, 3168
skill, rhetorical, 3118
skimmington, 2266a
slander, 0505, 0829a
slavery, 0859
Sleep
  Death and, 1078
sleep, 0862, 1869b, 2229
sloth, 0961, 1869b
Sly, Christopher, 2538
  in *Taming of the Shrew, The*, 0576, 1107, 2531, 2534, 2537, 2540
Sly, Christophero
  in *Taming of the Shrew, The*, 0335
smell, 0627
snake, 1383
snakes, 1311, 1399
society, 0033, 0082, 0095, 0120, 0121, 0140, 0229, 0232, 0238a, 0282a, 0284, 0320, 0321, 0330, 0332, 0337, 0342, 0347a, 0358, 0369, 0388, 0393, 0408, 0410, 0444, 0452, 0589, 0613, 0625, 0644, 0670, 0686, 0690, 0712, 0766, 0775, 0777, 0796, 0814, 0832a, 0903, 0905, 0912, 0916, 0940a, 0973, 1009, 1011, 1029, 1047, 1058, 1089, 1103, 1123, 1137, 1141, 1143, 1152, 1203, 1249, 1475, 1549, 1579, 1591, 1668, 1669, 1683, 1691, 1698, 1703, 1707, 1715, 1779, 1866, 2008, 2009, 2029, 2040, 2119, 2189, 2394, 2416, 2471, 2657, 2666, 2851, 2871, 2890
  individual and, 0714
  nature and, 2304
  poet in, 2590
society, Athenian, 2615, 2637
society, corrupt, 2986
society, feudal, 2995
society, market, 1750
society, mercantile, 2662
society, order in, 2892
society, regeneration of, 3170
sociology, 0705
Socrates, 0386a, 0387, 0450, 0559, 0599, 0610, 0665, 0850a, 0943, 1554, 1646, 1940, 2328a, 2478, 2599
sodomy, xxii, 0387, 2822, 2823, 2824
soldier, 0106, 0211, 0297, 0355, 0589, 0591, 0633, 0679, 0927, 1101, 1211, 1233, 1246, 1502, 1736, 1738, 1740a

soldiers, 0700, 1140a, 1333, 1370, 1455, 1528
 in *Antony and Cleopatra,* 1021
soldiership, xvii, 1174, 1331, 1912
soliloquies, 1071, 2984
soliloquy, 0944, 0985a, 2204
Solinus, Duke
 in *Comedy of Errors, The,* 0672, 0891
Solinus, Julius, 0739
solitariness, 0321, 1086, 1647
solitude, 0320, 0793, 1548
Solon, 0672
somnium animale, 0862
son, 0095, 0106, 0137, 0141, 0187, 0231, 0278a, 0369, 0498, 0522, 0549, 0599, 1083, 1635, 1641, 1937b, 2075
song, 1021
sonnet, 1371
sonnet (as concept or genre), 0281
sonnets, by Shakespeare, 1165, 2433, 2489
sons, 0152, 0216, 1137, 2027, 3003
Soothsayer
 in *Antony and Cleopatra,* 1175, 1196a
 in *Julius Caesar,* 2070, 2113b
sophistry, 0306
Sophists, 0376, 0833
sophists, 1565
Sophocles, 0152, 0230, 0329, 0468, 0509, 0534, 0597, 0615, 1035, 1634, 1673, 1766, 2209a
 Ajax, 0509, 1673, 1674, 1722
 Antigone, 1650
 Oedipus Coloneus (Oedipus at Colonus), 0772, 0853
 Oedipus Rex (Oedipus Tyrannus, Oedipus the King), 1793, 1877, 2225
 Oedipus the King (Oedipus Tyrannus, Oedipus Rex), xviii, 1781, 2173, 2173a, 2207
 Oedipus Tyrannus (Oedipus Rex, Oedipus the King), 0097, 0446a, 0579, 0772, 0853, 1057, 1846
 Trachiniae, 1674
 Women of Trachis, 1086
sophrosyne, 1004
sorcerer, 0881, 2582
sorcery, 2086
Sosius
 in *Antony and Cleopatra,* 1411
soul, 0174, 0208, 0694, 1006, 1021, 1093a, 1123, 2568
 body and, 1006, 1838, 2578a
soul, sensible, 3163
soul, sensitive, 3110
soul, three parts of, 2578a, 2587, 2599
sound, 1194, 1297, 1370, 1710, 1777
sounds, 0965, 1047, 1624a
South English Legendary, 1311
space, 0111, 0156, 0512, 0554, 0652, 0889, 0951, 1171a, 1530, 2404, 2440, 2886
space, female, xx
spaciousness, 1419
Spartans, 0833

speaker
 in *Sonnets,* 2514, 2517
spectacle (as concept or element of drama), 0099, 0154, 0253, 0375, 0552, 0700, 0745, 0991, 2219, 2565, 2742a, 2784, 2785
spectatorship, 1212
speech, 1710, 2193
speech, figures of, 2037, 2443
Spenser, Edmund, 0091, 0207, 0211, 0281, 0485, 0828, 0835, 0924, 1185, 2172, 2489, 3154
 Epithalamion, 3156
 Faerie Queene, The, xvii, 0120, 0160, 1763, 1936, 2279, 2284, 3040, 3041, 3090, 3132
 Fowre Hymnes, 0160
 Hymne in Honour of Beautie, An, 1081
 Ruines of Rome: by Bellay, 2491
 Ruins of Rome, 1761
 Shepherds' Calendar, The, 2158
Sphinx, 2151
Spirit
 Letter and, 0672
spirit
 flesh and, 2529
spiritedness, 0239
spirituality, 2191
spying, 0445
St. Augustine. See Augustine (Aurelius Augustinus), St. Augustine of Hippo
stability, 1370a, 1492, 1652
stage, 0783
stage, parts of, 2709
stagecraft, visual, 3031
stage directions, 1044a, 2702, 2703, 2770
stage properties, 1044a, 1687
staging of *Titus Andronicus,* 2759
Stair of Love, 1356
stasis, 1406
state, 0079, 0120, 0152, 0200, 0221, 0255, 0320, 0503, 0566, 0588, 0599, 0612, 0636, 0656, 0678, 0679, 0709, 0775, 0800, 0844, 0873, 0903, 0986a, 1045, 1047, 1113, 1122, 1131, 1147, 1198, 1630, 1651, 1661, 1718, 1739, 1770, 1830, 1939a, 1942, 2010, 2568, 2844
 body and, 1609
state, tragedies of, 2686
Statelie Tragedie of Claudius Tiberius Nero, The, 1754
statesman, 0080a, 0668, 1047, 1220, 1341
Stationers' Register, 2862, 2992
Statius, Publius Papinius, 2470
 Silvae, 2378
 Thebaid, 3100, 3101
 Thebiad, 1828
statue, 1082, 3182a, 3200, 3203, 3204, 3210
statue of Cleopatra, 1398
statues, 0990, 1950
Steevens, George, 0930, 2446
Stephano
 in *Tempest, The,* 0336, 2558, 2601a
stereotyping, 2828, 2890

Index of Subjects 873

steward
  in *Timon of Athens.*, 0328, 1123, 2610. See also Flavius
stichomythy, 0772
Stoicism, xvii, xviii, 0045, 0056, 0057, 0124, 0191, 0251, 0252, 0263, 0292, 0452, 0632, 0701, 0721, 0756, 0762, 0811, 0812a, 0945, 0956, 0978, 1033, 1096, 1139, 1140, 1145, 1175, 1233, 1313, 1362, 1543b, 1799, 1820, 1848, 1865, 1873, 1878, 1988, 1994, 2042, 2049, 2062, 2083, 2088, 2120, 2122, 2173, 2197, 2226, 2244, 2673
stoicism, 0234, 0566, 1620, 2241
Stoics, 0059a, 0625, 0655, 1650
Stoic thought, 0125, 0217
Stow, John, 2146a
Strabo, 2145a
Stratford Grammar School, 0073
Stratford-upon-Avon, 0187, 0363, 0370
Stratonice, 3092
Strife
  Love and, 2578a
structure, double plot, 2991
structure, five-act, xiii, 0583, 0759, 0798, 0891, 1035, 1571, 2045
structure, four-part, xx
structure, three-part, of *Winter's Tale, The*, 3196
structure, two-part, 2615
Studley, John
  translation of Seneca's *Hercules Oetaeus*, 1043, 1931a
  translation of Seneca's *Medea*, 2217, 2475b
style, 0186, 0255, 0807, 1088
style, high, 0557
style, simplicity of, 2185
style of *Troilus and Cressida*, 2878, 2972
styles, 0117, 0208, 0949
styles, Attic and Asiatic, 0281
styles of literary language, 2489
subjectivity, 0142a, 0244, 0830, 1055, 1174, 1997, 2404, 2832, 2859, 2931
substance
  shadow and, 2499, 2724
substitution, 2939
Suckling, Sir John, 2406
Suetonius (Gaius Suetonius Tranquillus), 0668, 1019a, 1843, 1983, 2044, 2112a, 2167
  Historie of Twelve Caesars, Emperours of Rome, 1754
  Lives of the Caesars, 1047
    Life of Caesar, 1789a
    Life of Claudius, 0610
    Life of Tiberius, 0610
suffering, 0615, 0713, 0721, 0829, 0829a, 0945, 0952, 0978, 1006, 1057, 1086, 1260, 1354, 1622, 1874, 1892, 2166, 2178, 2363, 2405, 2545, 2721, 2732, 2733, 2764, 2853
Suffolk, William de la Pole, fourth Earl and first Duke of
  in *Henry VI, Part 1*, 1934
suicide, 0133, 0186, 0227, 0252, 0255, 0263, 0277, 0283, 0310, 0391, 0464a, 0484, 0541, 0548, 0599, 0646, 0652, 0655, 0668, 0723, 0729, 0756, 0759a, 0863, 0920, 0955, 0986a, 1013a, 1047, 1070, 1086, 1111, 1145, 1172, 1174, 1175, 1176, 1179, 1197, 1217a, 1220, 1254, 1255, 1277, 1281, 1283, 1311, 1314, 1315, 1326a, 1349, 1358, 1362, 1400, 1404, 1409, 1425, 1441, 1521, 1524, 1798, 1833, 1848, 1865, 1874, 1881, 1943, 1954, 1974, 1994, 2003, 2028, 2030, 2033, 2049, 2083, 2096, 2102a, 2225, 2327, 2332, 2362, 2395, 2396, 2408, 2410, 2411, 2412, 2414, 2416, 2422, 2426, 2429, 2431, 2440, 2657a, 2749, 2766
suicides, 0654, 0694, 1083, 1504, 1942
Sulla, Lucius Cornelius, 1008
sun, 1531, 1535
superego, 1713, 1722, 2830
supernatural, 0552, 0863, 0944, 1175, 1318a, 1846
supernaturalism, 2114
superstition, 0669, 2154
supposition, 2982
Surrey, Henry Howard, Earl of
  translation of *Aeneid*, 0208
Susenbrotus, Joannes, 0938
Swan theater, 0443
Sycorax
  in *Tempest, The*, 0096, 2570
syllepsis, 1072
Sylvain, Alexandre, 2785
Sylvia
  in *Two Gentlemen of Verona, The*, 3088
symbol, 1315, 2039
symbolism, 0057, 0226, 0349, 0375, 0711, 1067a
symbolism, musical, 0636, 0699
symbolism, number, 1237, 2051, 3117
symbolism, visual, 0372
symbols, 0847
Symphosius, 2373
synapothanumenon, 1165
syndeton, 0558
synecdoche, 2874
syneciosis, 0332, 1633
synonymy, 2185a
syntax, 0558, 0588, 0710, 1206
syphilis, 0147, 0148, 0752, 0941, 2690, 2865
Syrus, Publius
  Sententiae, 0993

T
Table of Cebes, 0125
Tablet of Thebes, The, 0377b
Tacitus, Publius Cornelius, xvii, 0008, 0012, 0575, 0587, 0610, 0739, 0894, 0973, 1009, 1923, 2056, 2165, 2167, 2358
  Annales of Cornelius Tacitus, The, 1754
  Annals, 1926, 1928, 2024
  Germania, 1570
  Histories, 1937b
Tactics of Aelian, The, 0477
Talbot, Bess, Countess of Shrewsbury, 1062
Talbot, John
  in *Henry VI, Part 1*, 0918

Talbot, Lord
  in *Henry VI, Part 1,* 0619, 0894, 1934
Tamburlaine, 0206
Taming of A Shrew, The, 2533
Tamora, 2740
  in *Titus Andronicus,* xxi, 0223, 0283, 0318, 0377c, 0437, 0592, 0703, 0759b, 0792, 0878, 0964, 1135, 2709, 2718c, 2726, 2727, 2733, 2735, 2737, 2745, 2754, 2758, 2777, 2780, 2783, 2783a, 2788, 2789a
Tantalus, 2575, 2734
Tarquin, 2408
  in *Rape of Lucrece, The,* 0133, 0208, 0261, 0283, 0332, 0347a, 0370a, 0441, 0458, 0484, 0665, 0683, 0726, 0759a, 0850, 0973a, 0996, 1071, 1078, 2203, 2391, 2395, 2396, 2402, 2407, 2410, 2412, 2413, 2414, 2415, 2416, 2417, 2419, 2420, 2421, 2422, 2427, 2428, 2431, 2433, 2434, 2435, 2436, 2440
Tarquin (Lucius Tarquinius Superbus), 1834, 1949, 2457, 2755
Tasso, Torquato, 0281, 0485, 0531, 3154
  Aminta, 0274, 0275
  Gerusalemme liberata, La, 1991
taste, 0627
Tate, Nahum, 0403
Taverner, Richard, 1815
teleology, 0356
temper, 0234
temperance, 0255, 0519, 0903, 0945, 1250, 1630, 1665, 2562a, 2593, 3028
tempest, 3174
temptress, 3154, 3167
Terence (Publius Terentius Afer), xiii, 0102, 0123, 0140, 0209, 0226, 0248, 0272, 0350, 0363, 0369, 0401, 0413, 0494, 0535, 0556, 0597, 0600, 0608, 0754, 0759, 0774, 0801, 0802, 0810, 0829a, 0841, 0891, 0895, 0914, 0916, 0938, 1003, 1035, 1075, 1118, 1146a, 1565, 1571, 1587, 2204, 2242, 2455a, 2532, 2535, 3076, 3184, 3184a, 1085a
  Andria, 0556, 0860, 0923, 2548
  Eunuch, The (Eunuchus), 2541
Terentian play, five-act, 2763
Tereus, 0119, 0283, 2764
terror, xv, 1210, 2227
Tertullian (Florens Quintus Septimus Tertullianus), 2403
tetralogies, by Shakespeare, 0485, 0517, 0679, 0700, 0975
tetralogy, by Shakespeare, 0725
text, humanist and classical, 3208
Textor, Ravisius
  Epitheta, 2510
textuality, 1834a
  sexuality and, 2938
Thaisa
  in *Pericles,* 0307, 0781, 0847, 2368
Thales, 0901
thaumaturgy, 1157
theater, coterie, 2927
theater, popular, 2927

theater, private, 1450, 2992, 3072
theater, public, 2928, 2992
Theater, The, 2588
theater in *Aeneid,* 2588
theater of Shakespeare, 0185
theatricalism, 1423
theatricality, xv, 1434, 1460, 1478, 2910
theatrum humanae vitae, 0377b
theatrum mundi, 0109, 0266, 0288, 0377b, 0516, 2111, 2550, 2578a
Thebes, 3091, 3100
Thecla, St., 0730
theme (as concept or element of drama), 0510, 0737, 0748, 1000, 1049, 1053, 1069, 1434, 1494, 1495a, 2307
Themistocles, 2665
Theobald, Lewis, 1885
Theocritus, 0281, 0531, 0855, 1121, 3175
theology, 0299, 0380a, 1758
theophanies, 0566a, 0649, 0756, 0781
theophany, 0299a, 2464
Theophrastus, 2381
Thersites, 0833, 1760, 1766
  in *Troilus and Cressida,* 0075, 0080, 0084, 0156, 0161, 0163, 0379, 0396, 0481, 0523, 0576, 0588, 0631, 0652, 0752, 0798, 0825, 0827, 0833, 0838, 0880, 1111, 2792, 2794, 2798, 2803, 2807, 2810, 2813, 2822, 2826, 2827, 2864, 2872, 2887, 2899, 2910, 2913, 2926, 2931, 2936, 2955, 2957, 2980, 2984, 2993, 2994, 3006, 3009, 3012, 3020, 3026, 3030, 3031, 3033, 3034, 3052, 3060, 3061, 3065
Theseus, 3042, 3088
  in *Midsummer Night's Dream, A,* xix, 0080, 0087, 0096, 0214, 0325, 0375, 0528, 0529, 0630, 0690, 0773, 0828a, 1009, 1039, 1123, 2270, 2271, 2273, 2277, 2279, 2281, 2285, 2286, 2287, 2288a, 2291, 2293, 2296, 2297, 2299, 2301, 2303, 2313, 2314, 2316
  in *Two Noble Kinsmen, The,* 0781, 0901, 3090a, 3096, 3097, 3098, 3100, 3100a
theurgy, 0449, 2585
Thidias
  in *Antony and Cleopatra,* 0239, 1174, 1175, 1225, 1264, 1420, 1451, 1461, 1477, 1521
thievery, 2473
Thirteenth Book of the *Aeneid,* by Maphaeus Vegius, 0216
Thisbe, 2249, 2257, 2274
Thisbe. *See* Pyramus and Thisbe
Thomas Aquinas, St. *See* Aquinas, St. Thomas
Thoth, 1159
thought
  action and, 2849
thought, figures of, 2037
thought (as concept or element of drama), 2170
Thrasileon, 1053
Thucydides, 1673, 2279
Thyestes, 0152
thymos, 0191
Tiber, 0322a

Index of Subjects

Tiberius (Tiberius Claudius Nero Caesar), 0610, 1754
Timandra
  in *Timon of Athens*, 0849a
Time, 1294, 1344, 2162, 2530
  in *Pericles*, 0933
  in *Rape of Lucrece, The*, 2394
  in *Winter's Tale, The*, 0892, 0994, 3184, 3193
time, xviii, 0111, 0117, 0155, 0172a, 0208, 0245, 0261, 0327, 0375, 0377a, 0380a, 0389, 0400, 0411, 0468, 0512, 0554, 0596, 0619, 0628, 0634, 0652, 0678, 0691, 0698, 0719, 0721, 0729, 0807, 0870, 0871, 0872, 0873, 0889, 0892, 0922, 0951, 0986b, 1003, 1028, 1055, 1063, 1068, 1090, 1110, 1111, 1121, 1130, 1172, 1179, 1213, 1241, 1252, 1261, 1263, 1343, 1419, 1420, 1440, 1457, 1477, 1501, 1530, 1543c, 1559, 1586, 1824, 1936, 1963, 2001, 2011, 2051, 2059, 2108, 2147, 2212, 2367, 2404, 2461, 2491, 2492, 2494, 2495, 2501, 2508, 2523, 2524, 2528, 2572, 2579, 2616, 2668, 2797a, 2806, 2807, 2877, 2878, 2886, 2894, 2910, 2915, 2923, 2952, 2970, 2972, 2985, 2986, 2991, 2993, 3001, 3024, 3039, 3043, 3047, 3048, 3049, 3072, 3073, 3174, 3177, 3180, 3198, 3209
  truth and, 2355
time, unity of, xiv, 0933, 2579
Timon, 0201, 2617, 2657, 2673, 2675
  in *Timon of Athens*, xxi, 0070a, 0075, 0080, 0114, 0144, 0163, 0187, 0197, 0201, 0223, 0232, 0237, 0290, 0320, 0321, 0328, 0329, 0334, 0342, 0373, 0388, 0393, 0396, 0471, 0493, 0521, 0522, 0523, 0538, 0545, 0548, 0553a, 0562, 0581, 0603, 0613, 0625, 0627, 0646, 0664, 0690, 0697, 0700, 0712, 0825, 0838, 0848, 0849a, 0920, 0941, 0954, 0972, 0986a, 1099, 1100, 1112, 1123, 2610, 2612, 2616, 2620, 2627, 2629, 2630, 2631, 2632, 2633, 2634, 2636, 2637, 2638, 2641, 2642, 2643, 2644, 2646, 2647, 2649, 2651, 2656, 2657a, 2659, 2660, 2662, 2664, 2665, 2666, 2670, 2671, 2672, 2673, 2674, 2676, 2677, 2679, 2681, 2687, 2688, 2688a, 2689a, 2690, 2693, 2694, 2695, 2696, 2698, 2702, 2705, 2706, 2707
Timon (old Timon comedy), xxi, 0904, 2621, 2622, 2623, 2628, 2646, 2657, 2673, 2694. See also *Comedy of Timon, The*
Tiresias, 2156
Titania, 0890
  in *Midsummer Night's Dream, A*, 0118, 0807, 0818, 0996, 2268a, 2277, 2279, 2281, 2283, 2286, 2291, 2298, 2300, 2310, 2314
Titian, 0994
  Sacred and Profane Love, 0437
  Venus and Adonis, 3124, 3160
Titinius
  in *Julius Caesar*, 2028
Tito and Gisippo
  in *Decameron*, by Boccaccio, 1109
Titus
  in *Titus Andronicus*, 0114, 0156, 0208, 0232, 0247, 0283, 0297, 0506, 0613, 0700, 0759b, 0792, 0841, 0905, 1095, 1135, 1152, 1291, 2709, 2716, 2718, 2720, 2724, 2727, 2728, 2730, 2731, 2732a, 2733, 2735, 2737, 2740, 2741, 2744, 2747, 2749, 2759, 2775a, 2776, 2779b, 2781, 2782, 2783, 2783a, 2787, 2788
Titus Andronicus, ballad of
  in *The History of Titus Andronicus* (18th-c. chapbook), 2710, 2743, 2743a, 2760, 2760a, 2761, 2785
Titus Andronicus, prose history of
  in *The History of Titus Andronicus* (18th-c. chapbook), 2710, 2722, 2742a, 2743, 2743a, 2760, 2760a, 2761, 2785
Tityus, 2346
tomb, 0792, 2709
tombs, 0848a, 1197
tongue, 1732
  heart and, 1632b
touch, 0627
Touchstone
  in *As You Like It*, 0695, 1554, 1558, 1560, 1563
Tourneur, Cyril
  Revenger's Tragedy, The, 0395
Tractatus Coislinianus, 0798
tradesmen
  in *Julius Caesar*, 0116, 2040
  in *Midsummer Night's Dream, A*, 1107, 1134, 2293, 2295, 2312
  in *Timon of Athens*, 2686
tragedian, 0850a
tragedians, Greek, 0270, 0597, 0881, 1010, 1789, 2179a
tragedies, 0110, 0270, 0494, 0500
tragedies, by Euripides, 0814
tragedies, by Seneca, 0123, 0191, 0978
tragedies, by Shakespeare, xiii, 0002, 0037, 0049, 0052, 0058, 0059a, 0071, 0073, 0075, 0076, 0079, 0081, 0089, 0097, 0100, 0112, 0115, 0123, 0125, 0137, 0166, 0170, 0174, 0180, 0186, 0207, 0208, 0218, 0223, 0232, 0233, 0251, 0262, 0268, 0282, 0302, 0305, 0313, 0328, 0329, 0330, 0350, 0351, 0358, 0360, 0361, 0362, 0365, 0369, 0382, 0386a, 0398, 0405a, 0407, 0410, 0411, 0418, 0426, 0435, 0447, 0453, 0463, 0464a, 0492, 0492a, 0497, 0513, 0518, 0521, 0522, 0524, 0532, 0551, 0557, 0562, 0565, 0581, 0585, 0603, 0606, 0607, 0613, 0620, 0629, 0636, 0644, 0646, 0661, 0663a, 0671, 0674, 0682, 0685, 0692, 0700, 0701, 0707, 0712, 0719, 0726, 0729, 0733, 0742, 0746, 0754, 0755, 0756, 0765, 0772, 0782, 0784, 0793, 0804a, 0805, 0807a, 0808, 0819, 0870, 0871, 0873, 0874, 0876, 0895, 0905a, 0909, 0909a, 0924, 0952, 0953, 0959, 0972, 0978, 0981, 0985, 0990, 0997, 1000, 1004, 1013a, 1034, 1042, 1052, 1053, 1063, 1072, 1073, 1105, 1117, 1118, 1119, 1132, 1133, 1136, 1147, 1152, 1175, 1182, 1234, 1238, 1241, 1334, 1407, 1408, 1412, 1447, 1465, 1469, 1479, 1480, 1497, 1625, 1654, 1657, 1661, 1678, 1737, 1963, 2010, 2080, 2102a, 2109, 2136, 2387, 2398,

tragedies, by Shakespeare *(continued)*, 2428, 2435, 2569, 2642, 2652, 2710, 2715, 2722, 2794, 2929
tragedies, by Sophocles, 0509
tragedies, Christian, 1030
tragedies, classical, 1030
tragedies, closet, 2429
tragedies, Greek, 0158
tragedies, Latin, 0534
tragedies, Senecan, 2453
tragedies about Cleopatra, 1398
tragedy, ancient, 0215
tragedy, Christian, 0133, 0215
tragedy, classical, 0992, 1791, 2227, 3197
tragedy, Greek, xiii, xvii, 0097, 0182, 0191, 0208, 0442, 0519a, 0526, 0615, 0772, 0944, 0985, 1793, 1844, 1862, 1894, 2147, 2161, 2514
tragedy, heroic, 2811
tragedy, Italian, 0534
tragedy, love, 3018
tragedy, Roman, 2715
tragedy (as concept or genre), xiv, xv, xviii, xxii, 0030, 0075, 0077, 0083, 0097, 0101, 0106, 0110, 0114, 0124, 0125, 0128, 0142a, 0160b, 0163, 0172, 0181, 0182, 0191, 0199, 0201, 0208, 0223, 0238, 0238a, 0250, 0251, 0255, 0265, 0277, 0278, 0278a, 0285, 0289, 0303, 0305, 0320, 0324, 0329, 0331, 0338, 0350, 0364, 0370a, 0376, 0377, 0378, 0381, 0382, 0396, 0398, 0399, 0401, 0411, 0418, 0435, 0435a, 0437, 0444, 0446a, 0465a, 0468, 0469, 0494, 0509, 0512, 0526, 0533, 0534, 0540, 0553, 0555, 0556, 0584, 0597, 0599, 0603, 0607, 0615, 0626, 0633, 0635, 0642, 0646, 0664, 0677, 0680, 0681, 0683, 0685, 0713, 0717, 0718, 0740, 0745, 0748, 0749, 0759a, 0764, 0768, 0788, 0792, 0793, 0795, 0819, 0830, 0831, 0845, 0850a, 0852, 0853, 0863, 0865, 0867, 0873, 0885, 0887, 0889, 0905a, 0909, 0909a, 0917, 0923, 0934, 0948, 0956, 0959, 0960, 0979, 0980, 0983, 1003, 1010, 1021, 1026, 1033, 1035, 1038, 1050, 1057, 1086, 1118, 1123, 1124, 1135, 1145, 1152, 1153, 1175, 1177, 1184, 1193, 1203, 1207, 1212, 1219, 1236, 1238, 1242, 1252, 1253, 1260, 1274, 1278, 1297, 1320, 1342, 1352a, 1354, 1358, 1375, 1380, 1386, 1428, 1446, 1457, 1476, 1496, 1500, 1502, 1503, 1513, 1589, 1613, 1615, 1623, 1626, 1627, 1660, 1668, 1674, 1675, 1723, 1781, 1813, 1827, 1864, 1871, 1962, 1963, 1976, 1985, 1989, 2002, 2016, 2035, 2045, 2098, 2147, 2168, 2177, 2181, 2238, 2325, 2348, 2349, 2514, 2594, 2620, 2662, 2685, 2694, 2706, 2718b, 2720, 2725, 2763, 2826, 2837, 2838, 2851, 2853, 2867, 2897, 2929, 2977, 2986, 3007, 3023, 3035, 3038, 3053, 3061, 3071, 3116, 3141, 3143, 3152, 3176, 3184, 3184a, 3185, 3196
Tragedy of Caesar and Pompey, 2024
tragic flaw, 0166, 0167, 0329, 0511, 0613, 0615, 0795, 0946, 0948, 0984

tragicness, 2810a
tragicomedies, 3094
tragicomedies, by Shakespeare, 0307, 0418, 0988, 2794
tragicomedy (as concept or genre), 0002, 0215, 0282b, 0285, 0289, 0364, 0472, 0579, 0788, 0860, 0982, 1016, 1048, 1207, 1753, 2971, 3098, 3176
Tranio
  in *Taming of the Shrew, The*, 2532, 2532a, 2533, 2541
transcendence, 1528, 1690
transformation, 0119, 0151, 0248, 1107, 2534
transformations, 0119, 0132, 0160a, 0208, 0577, 1513, 3090
transgressors, sexual, 2976
translation, 0208
transmigration, 1256
transvaluation, 1192
transvestism, 1185
tribunes
  in *Coriolanus*, 0106, 0177, 0180, 0369, 0388, 0607, 0641, 0927, 0974a, 1073, 1602, 1609, 1623, 1631, 1651, 1654, 1681, 1688, 1690, 1693, 1695, 1699, 1710, 1718, 1730, 1733, 1734, 1736, 1751
  in *Julius Caesar*, 0377, 0949, 1135, 1954, 2009, 2029, 2040, 2063, 2117, 2132, 2134
  in *Titus Andronicus*, 2740
trickster, 0923
Trigon, 1911
Trinculo
  in *Tempest, The*, 2558
Trismegistus, Hermes, 2554
  Emerald Table, 1159
Trissino, Giangiorgio, 0485, 0534
Triumph, Roman, 1327
triumvirate
  in *Antony and Cleopatra*, 0197
trivium, 0296
Troilus, 0441, 1558, 2249, 2818
  in *Troilus and Cressida*, 0096, 0098, 0137, 0156, 0192, 0199, 0208, 0215, 0253, 0265, 0325, 0347, 0372a, 0379, 0396, 0422, 0424, 0432, 0455, 0481, 0493, 0512, 0513, 0547, 0553a, 0554, 0576, 0652, 0687, 0708, 0789, 0817, 0867, 0870, 0872, 0903, 1055, 1065, 1081, 1411, 1474, 2178, 2790, 2792, 2793, 2794, 2798, 2799, 2800, 2803, 2809, 2811, 2814, 2815, 2816, 2817, 2818, 2826, 2828, 2830, 2834, 2839, 2844, 2853, 2854, 2857, 2858, 2859, 2868, 2875, 2877, 2882, 2885, 2886, 2889, 2891, 2893, 2894, 2896, 2897, 2901, 2903, 2908, 2909, 2910, 2911, 2912, 2916, 2921, 2924, 2927, 2931, 2934, 2938, 2939, 2942, 2944, 2947, 2948, 2950, 2951, 2954, 2955, 2961, 2966, 2969, 2970, 2972, 2974, 2977, 2979, 2987, 2991, 2993, 2994, 2996, 2999, 3002, 3008, 3009, 3011, 3012, 3015, 3016, 3019, 3027, 3028, 3030, 3031, 3033, 3035, 3039, 3042, 3043, 3044, 3045, 3052, 3053, 3056, 3058, 3060, 3061, 3062,

Index of Subjects

3063, 3065, 3066, 3067, 3070, 3071, 3072, 3073, 3964a
Trojans, 0277, 0342, 0652, 0983, 2564
  in *Troilus and Cressida*, 0106, 1002, 1147, 2804, 2814, 2836, 2838, 2910, 2958, 2983, 2988, 3065
Trojan War, xx, xxii, 0105, 0589, 0890, 0919, 1065, 2422, 2809, 2818, 2837, 2848, 2851, 2900, 2904, 2938, 2944, 2973, 2978, 3012, 3020, 3039, 3049a
Trojan War, tapestry illustrations of, 2941
tropes in *Troilus and Cressida*, 2945a
tropes of rhetoric, 0611
Troy, 0080a, 0105, 0131, 0133, 0187, 0189, 0203, 0208, 0277, 0278, 0319b, 0347a, 0370a, 0448, 0602, 0610, 0675, 0685, 0721, 0754, 0759a, 0759b, 0789, 0850, 0852, 0936a, 0998, 1070, 1082, 1115, 1129, 1543c, 1753, 1774, 1826, 1827, 1837, 1841, 1856, 1895, 1933, 2416, 2445, 2451, 2476, 2564, 2588, 2762, 2811, 2812, 2852, 2855, 2910, 2927, 2932, 2967, 2992, 2994, 2995, 3004, 3007, 3066, 3071, 3072
  in *Troilus and Cressida*, 0106, 3003
Troy, painting of, xix
  in *Rape of Lucrece, The*, 2390, 2392, 2394, 2396, 2402, 2404, 2405, 2411, 2417, 2420, 2421, 2422, 2426, 2428, 2432, 2439
True Chronicle History of King Leir, The, 2161a
trust, 2057
Truth, 2162, 2386, 2512
truth, 0098, 0125, 0156, 0170, 0224, 0238, 0288, 0372a, 0375, 0387, 0393, 0424, 0454, 0466, 0470, 0505, 0513, 0575, 0587, 0596, 0615, 0811, 0857, 0863, 0973a, 1065, 1122, 1439, 1514, 1558, 1603, 1822, 1853, 2007, 2042, 2306, 2385, 2562b, 2607, 2723, 2923, 2947
  art and, 2619
  time and, 2355
Tubal
  in *Merchant of Venice, The*, 2253a
Tullia (queen of Lucius Tarquinius Superbus), 2210, 2234, 2755
Tunis, 2551
Turnèbe, Adrien, 1876
Turner, Victor, 0156, 0422
Turnus, xvii, 0381, 0647, 0759a, 0815, 0961, 1836, 1909
Turtle
  in *Phoenix and Turtle, The*, 2376, 2377, 2378, 2379, 2383, 2385
Twine, Lawrence
  Patterne of Painefull Adventures, The, 2363, 2371
twins, 1574, 3079
twins, identical, 3076
twinship, 1569
Tybalt
  in *Romeo and Juliet*, 2464, 2475c
Tyndale, William, 2403, 2418
type characters, 0384, 0884
tyrannical man, 1122
tyrannicide, 0849, 2057

tyranny, 0106, 0123, 0517, 0735, 0850, 1141, 1665, 1795, 1939a, 1967, 2003, 2088a, 2114, 2415, 2455a, 2717
tyrant, 0136, 0796, 1458, 1931, 1951a, 1966, 1976, 2015, 2057, 2069, 2232a
tyrants, 0080a, 0123, 0587, 2125
Tyrrel, Sir James
  in *Richard III*, 1051, 2698

U
ubi sunt, 0805, 2186
Ugolino
  in Dante, 0385
Ulysses, 1627, 1879, 2335
  in *The Rape of Lucrece*, 0105
  in *Troilus and Cressida*, 0078, 0106, 0156, 0172a, 0208, 0265, 0294, 0342, 0433, 0442, 0469, 0475, 0478, 0481, 0513, 0538, 0553, 0576, 0631, 0658, 0686, 0775, 0832a, 0909, 0945, 1004, 1019, 1021, 1029, 1095, 1103, 1291, 2178, 2794, 2798, 2801, 2803, 2804, 2810, 2812, 2815, 2829, 2831, 2832, 2840, 2844, 2849, 2854, 2859, 2871, 2884, 2885, 2886, 2891, 2892, 2894, 2916, 2921, 2928, 2934, 2943, 2946, 2950, 2951, 2961, 2979, 2980, 2985, 2986, 2989, 2991, 2994, 2997, 2998a, 3003, 3005, 3011, 3012, 3015, 3020, 3021, 3027, 3030, 3031, 3033, 3035, 3039, 3042, 3043, 3044, 3046, 3050, 3051, 3054, 3061, 3062, 3065
Underdowne, Thomas, 0868
  translation of Heliodorus's *Aethiopica*, 1035
Unferth
  in *Beowulf*, 1983
unities, dramatic, 0419, 0534, 0785, 0889, 0922, 0936a, 0951, 1016, 1128, 1571, 1588, 1844, 2227, 2429, 2549, 2591
unity, 0208, 0501, 0655, 0711, 0729, 0745, 0897, 1000, 1039, 1058, 1180, 1198, 1335, 1390, 1695
universality, 1031
Upton, John, 2467
Urania, 2543
Ur-Hamlet, 0772
usuries, 0843
usurpatioin, 2157
usury, 0147, 1123, 1610, 1649, 1660, 1695, 2629, 2639, 2650, 2686, 2703
utopia, 0184, 2547, 2559, 2572
utopias, 2662

V
Valentine
  in *Two Gentlemen of Verona, The*, 0441, 0580, 3088, 3090
Valeria
  in *Coriolanus*, 0594, 0964, 0986a
Valerius Maximus, 3092
valiantness, 0778, 1716
valor, 0106, 0297, 0642, 1086, 1528, 1628, 1907, 2882
valuation, 2960

value, xxi, 0208, 0233, 0239, 0342, 0343, 0390, 0721, 0873, 2801, 2810, 2859, 2889, 2923, 2933, 2991, 3024, 3047, 3072
value, intrinsic, 2814
values, 0201, 0207, 0227, 0457, 0759a, 0879, 0945, 1047, 1376, 3021, 3060, 3073
values, chivalric, 2869
values, medieval, 2894, 2946
values, relativity of, 2935
values, Roman, 2721
values, transitory, 3064a
van Buchel, Aernout, 0443
van Gennep, Arnold, 0156, 0422
vanity, 0378, 0679, 0873
vates, 1144
Vega Carpio, Lope Félix de, 0639
vegetarianism, 2740
vengeance, 0721, 0829a, 0961, 0971, 1680a, 1790, 1828, 1892, 2548, 2743b, 3015
Venice
  in *Merchant of Venice, The*, 1028
Ventidius
  in *Antony and Cleopatra*, 1015, 1174, 1196a, 1327, 1411, 1522
  in *Timon of Athens*, 2622, 2688
Venus, xv, xix, 0095, 0107, 0139, 0173a, 0283, 0437, 0438, 0685, 0729, 0759a, 0907, 0987, 0988, 0999, 1000, 1081, 1156, 1162, 1163, 1175, 1184, 1185, 1233, 1261, 1266, 1312, 1313, 1331, 1338, 1371, 1372, 1387a, 1393, 1456, 1490, 1504, 1533, 1885, 1911, 2298, 2321, 2346, 2466, 2468, 2521, 2562a, 2917, 3090a, 3096, 3098, 3100a, 3149, 3158, 3159, 3191, 3198
  in *Two Noble Kinsmen, The*, 0781
  in *Venus and Adonis*, xxii, 0283, 0332, 0379a, 0438, 0458, 0638, 0665, 0910, 0996, 1062, 3106, 3107, 3108, 3109, 3110, 3111, 3112, 3114, 3116, 3117, 3121, 3122, 3123, 3124, 3125, 3126a, 3128, 3129, 3130, 3131, 3133, 3134, 3137, 3140, 3141, 3142, 3143, 3144, 3149, 3151, 3154, 3155, 3156, 3158, 3159, 3161, 3162, 3163, 3165, 3167, 3169
Venus and Adonis, 1155
Venus and Adonis sonnets, by Shakespeare, 2353
Venus Coelestis, 0437, 2468a
Venus Naturalis, 0437
verbosity, 2405
verisimilitude, 0375, 1016, 2282
Vernon, Sir Richard
  in *Henry IV, Part 1*, 0563, 1905
versification, 0040
Vertumnus, xxii, 3090
Vice, 2341
vice, 0359, 0653, 1147, 2231
Vice figure, 0917, 0974a
vices, xviii, 0258, 0338
victim, 0191, 0442, 0448, 0602, 0667, 0850, 1048, 1054, 2035, 2721
victims, 0234, 0717, 2718
victory, 0239, 1000, 2037

villain, 0251, 0829, 0905, 1776, 2130a
villain-hero, 2721a
villains, 0234, 0330, 0361, 0395, 0662, 0740, 0888, 1072, 1106, 2718a
  heroes and, 2113a
villainy, 2614, 2733
Vincentio, Duke
  in *Measure for Measure*, 0690, 1065
Viola, 0812
  in *Twelfth Night*, 0307, 0546, 0758, 3075, 3080, 3082, 3084, 3085, 3086
violation, 2736a
violence, 0213, 0254, 0338, 0350, 0368, 0379a, 0397, 0418, 0442, 0459, 0464a, 0467, 0593, 0610, 0614, 0626, 0630, 0632, 0701, 0717, 0792, 1013a, 1039, 1135, 1474, 1655, 1736, 1748, 1936, 2009, 2061, 2139, 2150, 2407, 2431, 2718, 2723, 2728, 2729, 2747, 2762, 2766, 2774, 2779a, 2781, 2831, 2870, 2900, 2908, 2945, 2989, 3027
violence, ritual, 2775
vipers, copulation of, 3018
Virgilia, 1612
  in *Coriolanus*, 0137, 0232, 0553, 0594, 0759a, 0911, 0927, 0964, 1598, 1671, 1710, 1730, 1740a
Virgilian allusions
  in Shakespeare, 0029
Virgil (Publius Vergilius Maro), xii, 0057, 0080, 0261, 0281, 0299, 0320, 0322a, 0359, 0363, 0436, 0464a, 0488, 0504a, 0531, 0647, 0780, 0814, 0829, 0841, 0850, 0855, 0936, 0938, 0997, 1011, 1044, 1121, 1153, 1192, 1206, 1310, 1370a, 1417, 1468, 1500, 1524, 1532, 1539, 1543b, 1834a, 1892, 1926, 2184, 2283, 2312a, 2473, 2546a, 2547, 2552, 2721, 2900, 2970, 3175
  Aeneid, xv, xvii, xx, 0029, 0208, 0216, 0308, 0338, 0381, 0421, 0505, 0518, 0533, 0610, 0685, 0759a, 0759b, 0812a, 0815, 0829a, 0902, 0961, 1193, 1202, 1287, 1296, 1345, 1567, 1774, 1805, 1832, 1836, 1859, 1861, 1862, 1872, 1897, 1909, 1936, 2166, 2172, 2184a, 2233, 2301, 2303, 2333, 2394, 2405, 2411, 2413, 2422, 2453, 2527, 2541, 2551, 2554, 2556, 2562, 2564, 2565, 2570a, 2571, 2575, 2577, 2583, 2584, 2588, 2588a, 2591, 2593, 2605, 2607, 2728, 2731, 2785, 3040, 3041, 3101, 3154
  Eclogues, 0837, 1551, 1551a, 2718c
  Eclogue 2, 2481
  Eclogue 4, 1934, 2728, 2734, 2740, 2762
  Georgics, xvii, 0221, 0753, 0759a, 1324, 1796, 1913, 1920, 1921, 1925, 2024, 2143, 2579, 3122, 3132
virgin, 0900, 0901, 1134
Virginia, colonization in, 2565
virginity, 0284, 0868, 1330, 1887, 2825
Virginius, 1045, 2723, 2747
virgo, 0556
virility, 1205, 1353, 2267, 2319
virtu, 2394

Index of Subjects

virtue, 0164a, 0172, 0239, 0252, 0263, 0283, 0322, 0357, 0369, 0382, 0397, 0446a, 0452, 0493, 0522, 0560, 0561, 0572, 0575, 0599, 0604, 0619, 0641, 0655, 0665, 0674, 0761, 0826, 0850, 0850a, 0852, 0863, 0886, 0894, 0945, 0955, 0971, 1000, 1023, 1139, 1157, 1349, 1430, 1903, 2011, 2084, 2197, 2434, 2586, 2882, 3121
  pleasure and, 1218
virtue, republican, 2742a
virtues, xviii, 0091, 0338, 0427, 0490, 0519, 0523, 0587, 0699, 0841, 0885, 1388
virtues, Stoic, 3046
virtus, 0135, 0191, 0324, 0876, 0988, 1086, 1409, 1657, 1680a, 1695, 1716, 1768, 1770, 2043
vision, 2124
vita solitaria, 1548
vita triplex, 1550
Vitruvian principles, 0650
Vitruvius Pollio, 0753, 0783, 1149, 2562b
vituperatio, 0501
Vives, Juan Luis, 0127, 0139, 0470, 0938
vocabulary, xiv, 0040, 0169, 0565, 0856, 1116, 1138, 1969
vocabulary, Neoplatonic, 2486
vocabulary, scholastic, 2387
Volpone, 0732
Volscians, 1629
  in *Coriolanus*, 0129, 0344, 0544, 1047, 1086, 1593, 1596, 1600, 1603, 1618, 1626, 1633, 1660, 1726, 1744, 1745
Volumnia
  in *Coriolanus*, xvi, 0106, 0112, 0120, 0137, 0141, 0427, 0473, 0498, 0522, 0553, 0594, 0599, 0613, 0759a, 0784, 0849a, 0850, 0873, 0878, 0911, 0927, 0964, 0986a, 1073, 1590, 1595, 1599, 1601, 1609, 1610, 1612, 1616, 1623, 1625, 1642, 1654, 1670, 1671, 1684, 1685, 1690, 1692, 1693, 1699, 1701, 1704, 1710, 1713, 1716, 1718, 1726, 1727, 1736, 1740a, 1748, 1749
Voluptas, 1312
voluptas, 1409
  gravitas and, 0759a
voluptuosity, 1174
Vos, Jan
  Aran en Titus, 2712
vows, 0465a, 0966, 1184

W

wager, 1759
Walley, Henry, 2837, 2860
war, 0076, 0080, 0113, 0155, 0185, 0201, 0208, 0219, 0232, 0239, 0277, 0337, 0396, 0434, 0441, 0459, 0477, 0522, 0592, 0642, 0647, 0652, 0679, 0701, 0721, 0759a, 0789, 0815, 0864, 0873, 0890, 0916, 0965, 1047, 1200, 1310, 1436, 1523, 1596, 1601, 1603, 1608, 1697, 1726, 1759, 1925, 2022, 2792, 2806, 2813, 2834a, 2841, 2858, 2867, 2877, 2897, 2906, 2907, 2911, 2942, 2946, 2972, 2985, 2996, 3025, 3039, 3047, 3053, 3059, 3066, 3071, 3072
  love and, 2936
  sex and, 1601
warfare, 0955, 1002
Warner, William
  translation of Plautus's *Menaechmi*, 1567, 1572, 1575
Warning for Fair Women, A, 1819
War of the Theaters, 0365, 3001
warrior, 0232, 0292a, 0383, 0388, 0427, 0521, 0865, 0866, 1086, 1135, 1291, 1331, 1601, 1628, 1647, 1695, 1698, 1711, 1719, 1734a, 2113
warriors, 0191, 0297, 0647, 0851, 1716
Wars of the Roses, 0216
  in history plays, by Shakespeare, 1028
Warwick, Earl of
  in *Henry VI, Part 2*, 0610
wealth, 0955, 2630, 2633, 2665, 2684, 2686
Webster, John, 2693
wedding, 1749, 3103
Weird Sisters
  in *Macbeth*, 2207, 2221, 2222
Welles, Orson, 1993
Whetstone, George, 1035
Whitney, Geoffrey
  Choice of Emblemes, A, 1843, 2518
whore, 0592, 0900, 0901, 1457
Whore of Babylon, 1233, 2920
whores, 0197
  in *Timon of Athens*, 2614, 2638
Widow of Florence
  in *All's Well That Ends Well*, 1001
wife, 0142a, 0225, 0599, 0642, 1070, 1099, 1134, 1137, 1405, 1415, 1574, 1575, 1581
Wilkins, George, 2372
  Painefull Adventures of Pericles, Prince of Tyre, The, 0010, 2354, 2371
will, 0125, 0191, 0208, 0319b, 0520, 0526, 0630, 0719, 0903, 0909, 0945, 1428, 1904, 1907, 1918, 2244, 2252, 2334, 2395, 2475, 2547, 2921, 3062, 3065
  reason and, 2157
Williams
  in *Henry V*, 1923
Wilmot, Robert
  Gismond of Salerne, 0270
Wilson, Robert
  Cobbler's Prophecy, The, 2199
Wilson, Thomas, 0479, 2682
  Arte of Rhetorique, The, 0809, 2079, 2506, 2513
  Rule of Reason, The, 0323
wisdom, 0519, 0616, 0879, 0880, 1005, 1122, 1123, 1163, 1399, 1400, 1907, 1915, 2145, 2197, 2243, 2804, 2871, 2881, 3156
wit, 1034
witch, 0548, 0898
witchcraft, xvi, 0375, 0566a, 0900, 1567, 1570, 2233, 2351
witches, 0196, 0745, 1149a, 2288

Wittgenstein, Ludwig, 0353a, 1214
wives, 0704, 0964
woman, 0142a, 0194, 0249, 0307, 0325, 0387, 0436, 0548, 0592, 0637a, 0901, 1081, 1089, 1232, 1238, 1257, 1561, 1636, 1729, 1829, 1862, 2394, 2399
  man and, 1253
woman, assaulted, 2788
womanhood, xx
womanliness, 1716
woman of Brainford (Falstaff), 2268
womb, 2789a
women, 0097, 0112, 0114, 0118, 0132, 0153, 0197, 0212, 0258, 0287, 0311, 0332, 0337, 0498, 0592, 0598a, 0602, 0614, 0620, 0632, 0638, 0643, 0741, 0759a, 0772, 0807a, 0821a, 0833, 0849a, 0850a, 0888, 0888a, 0963, 0964, 0975, 1001, 1010, 1024, 1071, 1123, 1207, 1241, 1248, 1322, 1330a, 1360, 1412, 1433, 1460, 1484, 1517, 1524, 1710, 1770, 2055, 2074, 2161a, 2184a, 2195, 2246, 2266a, 2293, 2298, 2303, 2331, 2537, 2566a, 2629, 2636, 2641, 2789a, 2910, 3036, 3054
  men and, 0708, 1013a
women, trafficking in, 2973
women, Trojan, xxii, 2900
women as collective protagonist
  in *Richard III*, 2455a
women's bodies, 1141
wonder, 0190, 0302, 0303, 0353, 0804a, 0922a, 0947, 0959, 1123, 1242, 1511, 1565, 2356, 3185, 3205
Woodvilles
  in *Richard III*, 2455
Worcester, Earl of
  in *Henry IV, Part 1*, 0529, 0704
word play, 0040
words
  action and, 2945
world as stage, 0895, 1031
World Soul, 1000, 1356
world-stage analogy, 1014
wounds, 1590

wrath, 0881, 1518, 1680a, 1908, 3183
wrestling, 1543c, 1547, 1557
writing, 2193, 3048
Wyatt, Sir Thomas, 0940, 1250a, 2507

X

Xenophon, 0007, 0627, 2363
  Anabasis, 1930
  Cyropaedia, xiii, 0517, 0519
  Memorabilia, 0932
Xenophon of Ephesus
  Ephesiaca, 0928

Y

York, Duchess of
  in *Richard III*, 2454
York, Edmund of Langley, Duke of
  in *Richard II*, 0231, 2443
York, Richard Plantagenet, Duke of
  in *Henry VI, Part 3*, 0152, 0610
young Clifford
  in *Henry VI, Part 2*, 0322a
young Lucius
  in *Titus Andronicus*, 0318, 0467, 0848, 2728, 2778
young man
  in *Sonnets*, 2491, 2497
young Martius
  in *Coriolanus*, 0318, 0848, 1695
Young Seyward (Young Siward)
  in *Macbeth*, 2214
Youth
  in *Sonnets*, 2481
youth, 1227, 1720
  age and, 0970, 0997
  in *Sonnets*, 2488, 2520

Z

zeal, 1337
Zeno, 0280
Zeuxis, 0907
zodiac, 2618
Zodiacae Vitae. See under Palingenius, 0142

For Product Safety Concerns and Information please contact our EU
representative GPSR@taylorandfrancis.com
Taylor & Francis Verlag GmbH, Kaufingerstraße 24, 80331 München, Germany

www.ingramcontent.com/pod-product-compliance
Lightning Source LLC
Chambersburg PA
CBHW070852300426
44113CB00008B/810